Encyclopedia of
THE NOVEL

Volume 1
A – L

Encyclopedia of
THE NOVEL

Volume 1
A – L

Editor
PAUL SCHELLINGER

Assistant Editors
CHRISTOPHER HUDSON
MARIJKE RIJSBERMAN

FITZROY DEARBORN PUBLISHERS
CHICAGO · LONDON

Copyright © 1998
FITZROY DEARBORN PUBLISHERS

FITZROY DEARBORN PUBLISHERS
919 North Michigan Avenue
Chicago, IL 60611
USA

or

FITZROY DEARBORN PUBLISHERS
310 Regent Street
London W1R 5AJ
England

British Library and Library of Congress Cataloguing in Publication Data are available.

ISBN 1-57958-015-7

First published in the USA and UK 1998

Index prepared by AEIOU Inc., Pleasantville, New York

Typeset and printed by Braun-Brumfield, Ann Arbor, Michigan

Cover design by Peter Aristedes: *The Human Condition,* by René Magritte, 1934

CONTENTS

EDITOR'S NOTE

The *Encyclopedia of the Novel* attempts an international exploration of a literary genre from its beginnings to the present day. Contained here are entries on novelists and their works, on types of novels, on technical and formal aspects of novels, on critical approaches and theoretical frameworks that critics have developed for discussing the genre, as well as entries relating to various material factors behind the rise, spread, and enormous popularity of the novel through the 20th century. The encyclopedia also contains entries (many of them quite long) tracing the origins and development of the novel in countries and regions around the world. These regional surveys discuss important practitioners alongside the cultural, aesthetic, economic, and political conditions that have shaped the novel's course within particular regional contexts.

All entries were selected with the assistance of the advisers listed on page ix of volume 1. The job of selection, always difficult, is especially so in a reference book that covers such a large topic even as it attempts to maintain a fair and balanced coverage of writers and novels in all regions of the world. Entries on novelists and novels here were chosen on the basis of their importance in the history of the novel form, and contributors of these entries were asked to discuss their subjects as such—that is, to assess their role in the development of the genre rather than offer a general overview of a writer or a work. We have tried to include separate entries for those writers and texts that may be argued to represent an important watershed—whether for reasons of formal innovation, of breaking new ground in subject matter, or other distinctions of historical significance—within the history of the novel form. In short, we have asked, Which writers and novels opened up new *possibilities* for the future of the novel? Our selection of entries reflects our answers to that question.

Still, objections can and no doubt will be raised about why some writers and novels were included while others were left out. We have purposely limited the number of writer and novel entries to make space for larger thematic entries. Thus several substantial discussions of a novelist may appear across the encyclopedia without there being a separate entry on that figure. We hope that all readers will make use of the general index, which lists several thousands of writers and is designed to help situate their various contributions to the genre. By treating writers and their works not as isolated phenomena but as participants in a vast novelistic network, and by giving substantial space to broader rubrics—whether topical or regional—under which a large number of writers, texts, and concepts may be discussed together, the editors, advisers, and contributors hope to provide the reader with a resource for the study of the novel unlike any that currently exists.

The emphasis throughout the encyclopedia is on *genre*. As an *exploration* of that genre to which more than 350 experts from around the world have contributed some 650 articles, the *Encyclopedia of the Novel* offers many views about the nature of the novel and the role individuals have had in shaping its history. Although the encyclopedia has been designed to give ample factual information about authors' lives and works, its larger purpose is to help foster an understanding of the novel as a form that has evolved over time, and to explore what critics have long pointed out: that the novel, the genre widely claimed to be best suited for representing modern life, has its roots in many sources and has assimilated an astonishing range of prose and verse forms, written and oral.

The emphasis on genre has demonstrated, among other things, that nothing like a consensus exists as to what constitutes a novel, or what kinds of texts the genre may be said to contain, or to what period we may trace its origins. Especially now in the often fruitful, often contentious climate of debate that has grown up around the novel in the last decades of the 20th century, the problem of defining the novel inevitably recurs in a collection of 650 essays calling itself an *encyclopedia* of that genre. Under a variety of headings, the encyclopedia's contributors address this vexed question of generic definition—and their answers do not always agree. In fact, it has been my hope since the earliest stages of planning the encyclopedia that the question *what is a novel?* would provoke fresh approaches to the process of compiling a reference source and ring throughout the finished product itself. My hope has been richly fulfilled.

The reader must not look here for a consistent statement about what is perhaps too easily referred to as *the novel.* Concerning the European tradition alone, several viewpoints have gained wide currency in recent decades and find expression here. One model—first put forward in 1957 by Ian Watt in his influential *The Rise of the Novel*—holds that the novel emerged in England during the early 18th century, at the hands of Daniel Defoe. The appearance at that time and in that place of the *novel,* as distinguished from earlier prose *romance* forms, is, according to this model, ascribed in part to a concern (derived from Locke and other Enlightenment philosophers) for the individual and the particularity of individual experience. Above all, the rise of the novel in this view is associated with the rise in England of an educated middle class with access to a rapidly expanding print culture, and indeed the novel has ever since been regarded by many as embodying the aspirations of primarily middle-class readers.

Since Watt, numerous critics have expanded upon, modified, and attacked this model, finding, for example, in Cervantes evidence of a novelist's concern for particular—even subjective—experience, and a productive tension in *Don Quixote* of a writer working simultaneously within and against romance conventions. Starting from the prose romances written in Greek and dating from around the 1st century, critics recently have developed a history of the novel that focuses on such elements as self-mockery and an appreciation for the *fictionality* of fiction (or as Hugh Mason puts it in his fine entry on Greek and Roman narrative, "the freedom to digress and parenthesize"), linking these ancient novelists not only to Cervantes but to the metafictional games and preoccupations that characterize much postmodernist writing. The *Encyclopedia of the Novel* has attempted to chart the long history of the novel so as to explore just these kinds of relations.

Any effort to define the novel as a genre distinct from other genres would face still further challenges when we move beyond the European traditions to regions such as Asia, where the tendency to distinguish between long and short prose forms has not been so pronounced and where often no set of words exists separating the two. (Lu Xun, for example, wrote nothing that Westerners—or Chinese scholars for that matter—would label a novel, yet his importance to modern Chinese prose fiction is such that an entry is devoted here to discussing his influence on the novel in that country.) Throughout the encyclopedia, contributors address and argue questions of genre and of generic importance, but the questions, finally, remain open, in the hope of prompting further reflection and debate.

Working on this project has been rewarding in ways I could not have expected at the outset. First and foremost, I wish to thank the advisers and contributors for bringing their knowledge and enthusiasm to bear on a project the scope of which required participants of the highest qualification and imagination. The assistant editors, Christopher Hudson and Marijke Rijsberman, gave to the book all their resources of patient, thoughtful editorial talent as well as perseverance in the face of numerous difficulties. The encyclopedia could not have been accomplished without them. Thanks also go to various of my Fitzroy Dearborn colleagues in Chicago and London whose advice or assistance I drew on, especially Daniel Kirkpatrick for his invaluable conceptual input at the initial stages, and George Walsh for sharing his store of knowledge about both reference books and novels—and for, here as elsewhere, giving me the opportunity. My last and lasting thanks go to my wife Jennifer, who supported and assisted me in ways too numerous to count.

Paul Schellinger
Chicago, October 1998

ADVISERS

Roger Allen
University of Pennsylvania

Bruce Bennett
Australian Defence Force Academy

Malcolm Bradbury
University of East Anglia

Peter Brooks
Yale University

Carlo Coppola
Oakland University

Lennard J. Davis
State University of New York, Binghamton

Ian Duncan
University of Oregon

David William Foster
Arizona State University

Richard Freeborn
University of London

Michal Peled Ginsburg
Northwestern University

James L. Hill
Michigan State University

C.T. Hsia
Columbia University

Peter Hutchinson
University of Cambridge

W.J. Keith
University of Toronto

Bernth Lindfors
University of Texas at Austin

Franco Moretti
Columbia University

Mary Poovey
Johns Hopkins University

Gerald Prince
University of Pennsylvania

Scott Simpkins
University of North Texas

Patricia Ann Meyer Spacks
University of Virginia

Mark Williams
University of Leeds

CONTRIBUTORS

Rachel Karol Ablow
Edward A. Abramson
Chris Ackerley
Edward A. Adams
Angela K. Albright
Joseph Alkana

Mathé Allain
Elizabeth Brereton Allen
Elizabeth Cheresh Allen
Alma Amell
Lise Andries
Katherine A. Armstrong

Melvin S. Arrington, Jr.
Stuart Atkins
Harold Augenbraum
Paul Baines
Aida A. Bamia
Samantha J. Barber
Maria José Somerlate Barbosa
Joseph F. Bartolomeo
Thomas O. Beebee
Neil K. Besner
Carolyn Betensky
Neil B. Bishop
Ruth M. Blair
Carolyn Bliss
Roy C. Boland
M. Keith Booker
Sara Steinert Borella
Susan Brantly
A.D.P. Briggs
Catharine Savage Brosman
Robyn Brothers
Judith Burdan
James M. Cahalan
Mark Canuel
Kenneth E. Carpenter
Joseph Carroll
Frederick Ivor Case
David J. Caudle
Helen Chambers
Ann Charters
Seymour Chatman
Henry Claridge
Cherry Clayton
William Cloonan
John D. Cloy
Anne Clune
Debra Rae Cohen
Monica F. Cohen
Tom Conley
Carlo Coppola
Marcel Cornis-Pope
Neil Cornwell
Jane Costlow
J. Randolph Cox
Linda J. Craft
Ralph J. Crane
Martine Cremers Pearson
Julian Croft
Isagani R. Cruz
Jan Čulík
Lennard J. Davis
Liselotte M. Davis
Kirk A. Denton
John S. Dixon
Paul B. Dixon
Simon Dixon
R.P. Draper
Andrew M. Drozd
J. Patrick Duffey
Ian Duncan

Edwin M. Duval
Bernard Duyfhuizen
Scott Earle
Thomas Easterling
Fraser Easton
Milton Ehre
Stanislaw Eile
Dorice Williams Elliott
Ernest N. Emenyonu
Elizabeth Deeds Ermarth
Herman Ermolaev
Graham Falconer
César Ferreira
Carole Ferrier
Brian Finney
Suzanne Fleischman
Monika Fludernik
Paul A. Fortier
Ian Foster
Keith Foulcher
Richard Freeborn
Bruce Fulton
Susanne Fusso
Hafid Gafaiti
Allan Gardiner
Colin Gardner
Christine Gaspar
Sabah Ghandour
M.R. Ghanoonparvar
James Gibbs
Simon Gikandi
Michal Peled Ginsburg
Chris GoGwilt
Howard Goldblatt
Jane Goldman
George Gömöri
David J. Gordon
Colin Graham
Sharon Green
Suzanne D. Green
David Greetham
Helena Grice
Gareth Griffiths
Kathryn M. Grossman
Edward Gunn
Marina Guntsche
Andrew Hadfield
Andrew Hagiioannu
Stirling Haig
Pierre Halen
Yael Halevi-Wise
N. John Hall
Martin Halliwell
Walid Hamarneh
Lynne Hapgood
Sherrill Harbison
John A. Hargraves
Thomas R. Hart
Carol J. Harvey
Anthony J. Hassall

Robert E. Hegel
Margaret Henderson
Nicholas Hewitt
Gregory Heyworth
James L. Hill
Philip Hobsbaum
Anne Golomb Hoffman
J. Martin Holman
Virginia Matheson Hooker
Louise K. Horowitz
Lothar Huber
Malcolm Humble
Peter Hunt
Peter Hutchinson
Theodore Huters
Ken K. Ito
William A. Johnsen
Toni Johnson-Woods
Lawrence Jones
Malcolm V. Jones
Priya Joshi
Dubravka Juraga
Andrew Kahn
Martin Kanes
Thomas M. Kavanagh
W.J. Keith
Gary Kelly
Catherine Kerrigan
R. Brandon Kershner
Martha Khoury
Brian Kiernan
Suzanne Kiernan
Douglas Killam
Adele King
Andrew L. King
Jeffrey C. Kinkley
David Kirby
Scott W. Klein
Jerome Klinkowitz
Liza Knapp
Haili Kong
Delia Caparoso Konzett
Matthias Konzett
Edward A. Kopper, Jr.
Kurt J. Krueger
Jerzy R. Krzyżanowski
John Kucich
Timothy Colin Langen
Wendy Larson
A. Robert Lee
Wai Sum Amy Lee
Susan Lever
Peter Li
Sylvia Li-Chun Lin
Naomi Lindstrom
Parvin Loloi
Olga López Cotín
Martin Löschnigg
William Luis
Mary Lydon

Deidre Lynch
Barbara Mabee
Sandra Macpherson
Deborah L. Madsen
Jean Mainil
Phillip Mallett
Edward Maloney
A.A. Mandal
James Mandrell
Bryant Mangum
Sharon Marcus
Uri Margolin
Ismael P. Márquez
Gerald Martin
Hugh J. Mason
Richard Maxwell
Gita May
Laurence W. Mazzeno
Mary McAlpin
Anne E. McCall
Ian McCormick
Philip McGowan
Arnold McMillin
Christopher McNab
Stella McNichol
Kenneth W. Meadwell
Frances Meuser
Siegfried Mews
Stefan Meyer
Thérèse Michel-Mansour
David Midgley
Vasa D. Mihailovich
Michael Minden
Yolanda Molina Gavilán
Maxine Lavon Montgomery-Crawford
Warren Motte
Harriet Murav
Anne Marie Musschoot
Harald S. Naess
Susan J. Napier
T.G.A. Nelson
Catherine Nelson-McDermott
Amanda Nettelbeck
Judie Newman
K.M. Newton
Ansgar Nünning
George O'Brien
Chidi Okonkwo
Salvador A. Oropesa
Oyekan Owomoyela
Jeffrey Oxford
Norman Page
J.T. Parnell
Richard Peace
John Peck
Rebecca Pelan
Anne Pender
Genaro J. Pérez
Janet Pérez
Massimo Mandolini Pesaresi

Sandy Petrey
James Phelan
Peter Pierce
Mark Pietralunga
Nicola Pitchford
Charles Porter
Sally-Ann Poulson
Michèle Praeger
Catherine Pratt
Daniel Punday
Moumin Quazi
Eric S. Rabkin
Dominic Rainsford
Tsila Ratner
Dwight Reynolds
John Richetti
Marijke Rijsberman
Angela Robbeson
Eamonn Rodgers
Gary Rosenshield
Susan Rowland
Nicholas Royle
Christine A. Rydel
Darlene Sadlier
Victor Sage
Lori Saint-Martin
Jeffrey L. Sammons
Heather Sanderson
Ralph Sarkonak
Richard E. Schade
William J. Scheick
George C. Schoolfield
Naomi Schor
Sydney Schultze
David Seed
Thomas Seifrid
Eric Sellin
Ben-Z. Shek
Sarah Shieff
Janet P. Sholty
Hinrich Siefken
Norman Simms
John D. Simons
Harriet Simpson
Angela Smith
John Smylie
Stephen Snyder
Bettina Soestwohner
Naomi Sokoloff
Andreas Solbach

John Allen Stevenson
Richard C. Stevenson
Joan Hinde Stewart
Mary E. Stewart
Philip Stewart
Alexander Stillmark
Erin Striff
Martin Swales
Imre Szeman
Gina L. Taglieri
Emile J. Talbot
Xiaobing Tang
Sheila Teahan
Victor Terras
John Thieme
Kathleen Smith Thomas
Janet Todd
Leona Toker
Michael Tratner
Katie Trumpener
Andrew P. Vassar
Andres Virkus
Dionisio Viscarri
Andrew Wachtel
Kathy Wagner
Dennis C. Washburn
Susan Watkins
Philip Watts
William Weaver
Edwin Weed
Jennifer Wheelock
Shane Wilcox
Mark Williams
Philip F. Williams
Raymond Leslie Williams
Judith Wilt
Susan Winnett
Tom Winnifrith
Mark A. Wollaeger
Henry B. Wonham
Tim S. Woods
Derek Wright
Yenna Wu
Richard A. Young
Leon I. Yudkin
Celia Correas Zapata
Deborah Zeraschi
Wendy Zierler
Harry Zohn

LIST OF ENTRIES

SELECT BIBLIOGRAPHY

Compiled by William Weaver, with the aid of contributors

General Sources for Research

Dictionaries, Encyclopedias, and Reference Guides

Benson, Eugene, and L.W. Conolly, editors, *Encyclopedia of Post-Colonial Literatures in English,* 2 vols., London and New York: Routledge, 1994

Brown, Susan Windisch, editor, *Contemporary Novelists,* 6th edition, Detroit: St. James Press, 1996

Chevalier, Tracy, editor, *Contemporary World Writers,* Detroit and London: St. James Press, 1993

Cornwell, Neil, editor, *Reference Guide to Russian Literature,* Chicago and London: Fitzroy Dearborn, 1998

Coyle, Martin, et al., editors, *Encyclopedia of Literature and Criticism,* London: Routledge, 1990

de Beaumarchais, Jean-Pierre and Daniel Couty, editors, *Dictionnaire des oeuvres littéraires de langue française,* Paris: Bordas, 1994

Elliott, Emory, editor, *Columbia History of the American Novel,* New York: Columbia University Press, 1991

Henderson, Lesley, editor, *Reference Guide to World Literature,* Detroit and London: St. James Press, 1995

Kirkpatrick, D.L., *Reference Guide to English Literature,* 2nd edition, Chicago and London: St. James Press, 1991

Merriam-Webster's Encyclopedia of Literature, Springfield, Massachusetts : Merriam-Webster, 1995

Modern Language Association Bibliography

Richetti, John, editor, *Columbia History of the British Novel,* New York: Columbia University Press, 1994

Shipley, Joseph, editor, *Encyclopedia of Literature,* New York: Philosophical Society, 1946

Smith, Horatio, editor, *Columbia Dictionary of Modern European Literature,* New York: Columbia University Press, 1947

Smith, Verity, editor, *Encyclopedia of Latin American Literature,* Chicago and London: Fitzroy Dearborn, 1996

Wheeler, Kathleen, *A Guide to Twentieth-Century Women Novelists,* Oxford: Blackwell, 1997

Journals

Eighteenth-Century Fiction
Modern Fiction Studies
Narrative
Nineteenth-Century Prose
Novel: A Forum on Fiction
Roman 20-50
Studies in the Novel

Historical and Genre-Based Criticism, Narratology, and Other Theoretical Approaches to the Novel

The following list contains notable recent studies of the novel and narrative encompassing a wide range of critical perspectives, as well as standard works written earlier in the 20th century. For more extensive lists of secondary sources on particular approaches to the novel (i.e., Marxist criticism, feminist criticism, postcolonial criticism), or on subgenres (i.e., adventure novel, Bildungsroman), the reader is directed to the bibliographies accompanying entries by those names.

Abel, Elizabeth, Marianne Hirsch, and Elizabeth Langland, editors, *The Voyage In: Fictions of Female Development,* Hanover, New Hampshire, and London: University Press of New England, 1983

Alter, Robert, *Partial Magic: The Novel as a Self-Conscious Genre,* Berkeley: University of California Press, 1975

Armstrong, Nancy, *Desire and Domestic Fiction: A Political History of the Novel,* New York: Oxford University Press, 1987

Ashcroft, Bill, Gareth Griffiths, and Helen Tiffin, *The Empire Writes Back: Theory and Practice in Post-Colonial Literatures*, London and New York: Routledge, 1989

Auerbach, Erich, *Mimesis: The Representation of Reality in Western Literature*, Princeton, New Jersey: Princeton University Press, 1953

Bakhtin, M.M., *The Dialogic Imagination*, translated by Caryl Emerson and Michael Holquist, edited by Holquist, Austin: University of Texas Press, 1981

Bal, Mieke, *Narratology: Introduction to the Theory of Narrative*, Toronto: University of Toronto Press, 1985

Barker, Francis, Peter Hulme, and Margaret Iversen, editors, *Colonial Discourse, Postcolonial Theory*, Manchester: Manchester University Press, and New York: St. Martin's Press, 1994

Barthes, Roland, *S/Z*, London: Cape, and New York: Noonday, 1975

Booth, Wayne C., *The Rhetoric of Fiction*, Chicago: University of Chicago Press, 1961; 2nd edition, Chicago: University of Chicago Press, and London: Penguin, 1983

Brink, André, *The Novel: Language and Narrative from Cervantes to Calvino*, New York: New York University Press, 1998

Brooks, Peter, *Reading for the Plot: Design and Intention in Narrative*, New York: Vintage, 1985

Brooks, Peter, *Body Work: Objects of Desire in Modern Narrative*, Cambridge, Massachusetts: Harvard University Press, 1993

Chambers, Ross, *Story and Situation: Narrative Seduction and the Power of Fiction*, Minneapolis: University of Minnesota Press, and Manchester: Manchester University Press, 1984

Chandler, James, *England in 1819: The Politics of Literary Culture and the Case of Romantic Historicism*, Chicago: University of Chicago Press, 1998

Chatman, Seymour, *Story and Discourse: Narrative Structure in Fiction and Film*, Ithaca, New York: Cornell University Press, 1978

Cohen, Margaret, and Christopher Prendergast, editors, *Spectacles of Realism: Body, Gender, Genre*, Minneapolis: University of Minnesota Press, 1995

Cohn, Dorrit, *Transparent Minds: Narrative Modes for Presenting Consciousness in Fiction*, Princeton, New Jersey: Princeton University Press, 1978

De Lauretis, Teresa, *Alice Doesn't: Feminism, Semiotics, Cinema*, Bloomington: Indiana University Press, and London: Macmillan, 1984

Doody, Margaret Anne, *The True Story of the Novel*, New Brunswick, New Jersey: Rutgers University Press, 1996

Fludernik, Monika, *Towards a "Natural" Narratology*, London and New York: Routledge, 1996

Forster, E.M., *Aspects of the Novel*, London: Edward Arnold, and New York: Harcourt Brace, 1927

Frye, Northrop, *Anatomy of Criticism: Four Essays*, Princeton, New Jersey: Princeton University Press, 1957

Gates, Henry Louis, *The Signifying Monkey: A Theory of African-American Literary Criticism*, New York: Oxford University Press, 1988

Genette, Gérard, *Narrative Discourse: An Essay in Method*, translated by Jane E. Lewin, Ithaca, New York: Cornell University Press, and Oxford: Blackwell, 1980

Genette, Gérard, *Narrative Discourse Revisited*, translated by Jane E. Lewin, Ithaca, New York: Cornell University Press, 1988

Gilbert, Sandra, and Susan Gubar, *The Madwoman in the Attic: The Woman Writer and the Nineteenth-Century Literary Imagination*, New Haven, Connecticut: Yale University Press, 1979; London: Yale University Press, 1980

Girard, René, *Deceit, Desire, and the Novel*, Baltimore: Johns Hopkins University Press, 1965

James, Henry, Prefaces to the New York Edition of his novels, New York: Scribner, 1907–09; published as *The Art of the Novel*, edited by R.P. Blackmur, New York: Scribner, 1934; collected in *Henry James: Literary Criticism*, 2 vols., edited by Leon Edel, New York: Library of America, 1984

Jameson, Fredric, *The Political Unconscious: Narrative as a Socially Symbolic Act*, Ithaca, New York: Cornell University Press, and London: Methuen, 1981

Johnson, Claudia, *Jane Austen: Women, Politics, and the Novel*, Chicago: University of Chicago Press, 1988

Kundera, Milan, *The Art of the Novel*, translated by Linda Asher, New York: Grove Press, and London: Faber, 1988

LaCapra, Dominick, *History, Politics, and the Novel*, Ithaca, New York: Cornell University Press, 1987

Lanser, Susan Sniader, *The Narrative Act: Point of View in Prose Fiction*, Princeton, New Jersey: Princeton University Press, 1981

Leavis, F.R., *The Great Tradition: George Eliot, Henry James, Joseph Conrad*, London: Chatto and Windus, and New York: Stewart, 1948

Lukács, Georg, *The Historical Novel*, translated by Hannah Mitchell and Stanley Mitchell, Lincoln: University of Nebraska Press, 1983

Lynch, Deidre, and William B. Warner, editors, *Cultural Institutions of the Novel*, Durham, North Carolina: Duke University Press, 1996

Martin, Wallace, *Recent Theories of Narrative*, Ithaca, New York: Cornell University Press, 1986

Miller, D.A., *Narrative and Its Discontents: Problems of Closure in the Traditional Novel*, Princeton, New Jersey: Princeton University Press, 1981

Miller, D.A., *The Novel and the Police*, Berkeley: University of California Press, 1988

Moretti, Franco, *The Way of the World: The Bildungsroman in European Culture*, London: Verso, 1987

Moretti, Franco, *Atlas of the European Novel 1800–1900*, London: Verso, 1998

Moses, Michael Valdez, *The Novel and the Globalization of Culture*, New York: Oxford University Press, 1995

Phelan, James, *Reading People, Reading Plots: Character, Progression, and the Interpretation of Narrative*, Chicago: University of Chicago Press, 1989

Phelan, James, editor, *Reading Narrative: Form, Ethics, and Ideology*, Columbus: Ohio State University Press, 1989

Prince, Gerald, *Narratology: The Form and Functioning of Narrative*, Berlin and New York: Mouton, 1982

Prince, Gerald, *A Dictionary of Narratology*, Lincoln: University of Nebraska Press, 1987; Aldershot: Scolar, 1988

Rabinowitz, Peter, *Before Reading: Narrative Convention and the Politics of Interpretation*, Ithaca: Cornell University Press, 1987

Rimmon-Kenan, Shlomith, *Narrative Fiction: Contemporary Poetics*, London and New York: Methuen, 1983

Robbe-Grillet, Alain, *For a New Novel: Essays on Fiction*, New York: Grove Press, 1965

Said, Edward W., *Beginnings: Intention and Method*, New York: Basic Books, 1975

Sedgwick, Eve Kosofky, *Between Men: English Literature and Male Homosocial Desire*, New York and Guildford: Columbia University Press, 1985

Stevick, Philip, editor, *The Theory of the Novel*, New York: Free Press, 1967

Suleiman, Susan Rubin, *Authoritarian Fictions: The Ideological Novel as a Literary Genre*, New York: Columbia University Press, 1983

Summers, Claude J., *Gay Fictions: Wilde to Stonewall: Studies in a Male Homosexual Literary Tradition*, New York: Continuum, 1990

Tatum, James, editor, *The Search for the Ancient Novel*, Baltimore: Johns Hopkins University Press, 1994

Toolan, Michael, *Narrative: A Critical Linguistic Introduction*, London and New York: Routledge, 1988

Watt, Ian, *The Rise of the Novel: Studies in Defoe, Richardson, and Fielding*, Berkeley: University of California Press, and London: Chatto and Windus, 1957

White, Hayden, *Metahistory: The Historical Imagination in Nineteenth Century Europe*, Baltimore and London: Johns Hopkins University Press, 1973

Williams, Raymond, *The Country and the City*, London: Chatto and Windus, and New York: Oxford University Press, 1973

The Novel in Its Regional Contexts

The following sections list key texts for the study of various national or regional novelistic traditions. More complete bibliographies are given at the end of each regional survey in the encyclopedia.

Europe

Austrian Novel

Daviau, Donald G., editor, *Major Figures of Turn-of-the-Century Austrian Literature*, Riverside, California: Ariadne Press, 1991

Vansant, Jacqueline, *Against the Horizon: Feminism and Postwar Austrian Women Writers*, New York and London: Greenwood Press, 1988

English Novel

Davis, Lennard J., *Factual Fictions: The Origins of the English Novel*, New York: Columbia University Press, 1983

Ermarth, Elizabeth Deeds, *Realism and Consensus in the English Novel*, Princeton, New Jersey: Princeton University Press, 1983; new edition, with subtitle *The Construction of Time in Narrative*, Edinburgh: Edinburgh University Press, 1998

Gallagher, Catherine, *Nobody's Story: The Vanishing Acts of Women Writers in the Marketplace, 1670–1820*, Berkeley: University of California Press, and Oxford: Clarendon Press, 1994

Hunter, J. Paul, *Before Novels: The Cultural Contexts of Eighteenth-Century English Fiction*, New York: Norton, 1990

Keating, Peter, *The Haunted Study: A Social History of the English Novel, 1875–1914*, London: Secker and Warburg, 1989

Kelly, Gary, *English Fiction of the Romantic Period, 1789–1830*, London and New York: Longman, 1989

Levine, George, *The Realistic Imagination: English Fiction from Frankenstein to Lady Chatterley*, Chicago: University of Chicago Press, 1981

McKeon, Michael, *The Origins of the English Novel 1600–1740*, Baltimore: Johns Hopkins University Press, 1987

Richetti, John, *Popular Fiction Before Richardson: Narrative Patterns 1700–1739*, Oxford: Clarendon Press, 1969

Scanlan, Margaret, *Traces of Another Time: History and Politics in Postwar British Fiction*, Princeton, New Jersey: Princeton University Press, 1990

Sinfield, Alan, *Literature, Politics and Culture in Postwar Britain*, Oxford: Blackwell, and Berkeley: University of California Press, 1989

Van Ghent, Dorothy, *The English Novel: Form and Function*, New York: Rinehart, 1953

French Novel

Bersani, Leo, *Balzac to Beckett: Center and Circumference in French Fiction*, New York: Oxford University Press, 1970

Brombert, Victor, *The Intellectual Hero: Studies in the French Novel, 1880–1955*, Philadelphia: Lippincott, and London: Faber, 1961

DeJean, Joan, *Tender Geographies: Women and the Origins of the Novel in France*, New York: Columbia University Press, 1991

DiPiero, Thomas, *Dangerous Truths and Criminal Passions: The Evolution of the French Novel, 1569–1791*, Stanford, California: Stanford University Press, 1992

Holier, Denis, editor, *A New History of French Literature*, Cambridge, Massachusetts: Harvard University Press, 1989

Levin, Harry, *The Gates of Horn: A Study of Five French Realists*, New York: Oxford University Press, 1963; London: Oxford University Press, 1986

Petrey, Sandy, *Realism and Revolution: Stendhal, Balzac, Zola, and the Performances of History*, Ithaca, New York: Cornell University Press, 1988

Porter, Charles A., editor, *After the Age of Suspicion: The French Novel Today*, New Haven, Connecticut: Yale University Press, 1988

Prendergast, Christopher, *The Order of Mimesis: Balzac, Stendhal, Nerval, Flaubert*, Cambridge and New York: Cambridge University Press, 1986

Schor, Naomi, *Breaking the Chain: Women, Theory, and French Realist Fiction*, New York: Columbia University Press, 1985

Showalter, English, *The Evolution of the French Novel,*

1641–1782, Princeton, New Jersey: Princeton University Press, 1972

Terdiman, Richard, *The Dialectics of Isolation: Self and Society in the French Novel from the Realists to Proust,* New Haven, Connecticut: Yale University Press, 1976

Thompson, William, editor, *The Contemporary Novel in France,* Gainesville: University Press of Florida, 1995

Turnell, Martin, *The Novel in France: Mme de Lafayette, Laclos, Constant, Stendhal, Balzac, Flaubert, Proust,* London: Hamish Hamilton, 1950; New York: New Directions, 1951

German Novel

Bullivant, Keith, editor, *The Modern German Novel,* Leamington Spa and New York: Berg, 1987

Hardin, James, editor, *Reflection and Action: Essays on the Bildungsroman,* Columbia: University of South Carolina Press, 1991

Swales, Martin, *The German Bildungsroman from Wieland to Hesse,* Princeton, New Jersey: Princeton University Press, 1978

Ziolkowski, Theodore, *Dimensions of the Modern Novel,* Princeton, New Jersey: Princeton University Press, 1969

Hungarian Novel

Czigány, Lóránt, *The Oxford History of Hungarian Literature from the Earliest Times to the Present,* Oxford: Clarendon Press, and New York: Oxford University Press, 1984

Reményi, Joseph, *Hungarian Writers and Literature: Modern Novelists, Critics, and Poets,* New Brunswick, New Jersey: Rutgers University Press, 1964

Irish Novel

Cahalan, James M., *Great Hatred, Little Room: The Irish Historical Novel,* Syracuse and New York: Syracuse University Press, and Dublin: Gill and Macmillan, 1983

Cahalan, James M., *The Irish Novel: A Critical History,* Boston: Twayne, 1988

Flanagan, Thomas, *The Irish Novelists, 1800–1850,* New York: Columbia University Press, 1959

Weekes, Ann Owens, *Irish Women Writers: An Uncharted Tradition,* Lexington: University Press of Kentucky, 1990

Italian Novel

Brand, Peter, and Lino Pertile, editors, *The Cambridge History of Italian Literature,* Cambridge and New York: Cambridge University Press, 1996

Dombroski, Robert S., *Properties of Writing: Ideological Discourse in Modern Italian Fiction,* Baltimore: Johns Hopkins University Press, 1994

Lucente, Gregory L., *Beautiful Fables: Self-consciousness in Italian Narrative from Manzoni to Calvino,* Baltimore: Johns Hopkins University Press, 1986

Netherlandish Novel

Goedegebuure, Jaap, and Anne Marie Musschoot, *Contemporary Fiction of the Low Countries,* Rekkem: Stichting Ons Erfdeel, 1991; 2nd revised edition, 1995

Meijer, Reinder P., *Literature of the Low Countries: A Short History of Dutch Literature in the Netherlands and Belgium,* Assen: Van Gorcum, and New York: Twayne, 1971; new edition, Cheltenham: Stanley Thornes, and Boston: Nijhoff, 1978

Polish Novel

Eile, Stanislaw, *Modernist Trends in Twentieth-Century Polish Fiction,* London: School of Slavonic and East European Studies, 1996

Milosz, Czeslaw, *The History of Polish Literature,* New York: Macmillan, 1969; 2nd edition, Berkeley: University of California Press, 1983

Romanian Novel

Ciopraga, Constantin, *The Personality of Romanian Literature: A Synthesis,* Iasi: Junimea, 1981

Cornis-Pope, Marcel, *The Unfinished Battles: Romanian Postmodernism Before and After 1989,* Iasi: Polirom, 1996

Russian Novel

Brown, Deming, *Soviet Russian Literature since Stalin,* Cambridge and New York: Cambridge University Press, 1978

Brown, Edward J., *Russian Literature since the Revolution,* New York: Collier, 1963; revised and enlarged edition, Cambridge, Massachusetts: Harvard University Press, 1982

Brown, William Edward, *A History of 18th Century Russian Literature,* Ann Arbor, Michigan: Ardis, 1980

Clark, Katerina, *The Soviet Novel: History as Ritual,* Chicago: University of Chicago Press, 1981; 2nd edition, 1985

Freeborn, Richard, *The Rise of the Russian Novel: Studies in the Russian Novel from "Eugene Onegin" to "War and Peace,"* Cambridge: Cambridge University Press, 1973

Karlinsky, Simon, and Alfred Appel, editors, *The Bitter Air of Exile: Russian Writers in the West, 1922–72,* Berkeley: University of California Press, 1977

Marker, Gary, *Publishing, Printing and the Origins of Intellectual Life in Russia, 1700–1800,* Princeton, New Jersey: Princeton University Press, 1985

Porter, Robert, *Russia's Alternative Prose,* Oxford and Providence, Rhode Island: Berg, 1994

Struve, Gleb, *Russian Literature under Lenin and Stalin, 1917–1953,* Norman: University of Oklahoma Press, 1971; London: Routledge and Kegan Paul, 1972

Scandinavian Novel

Various Editors, *A History of Scandinavian Literatures, Vols. 1–4,* Lincoln: University of Nebraska Press, 1988–1996

Scottish Novel

Duncan, Ian, *Modern Romance and Transformations of the Novel: The Gothic, Scott, Dickens,* Cambridge and New York: Cambridge University Press, 1992

Fielding, Penny, *Writing and Orality: Nationality and Culture in Nineteenth-Century Scottish Fiction,* Oxford and New York: Clarendon Press, 1996

Trumpener, Katie, *Bardic Nationalism: The Romantic Novel*

and the British Empire, Princeton, New Jersey: Princeton University Press, 1997

Southern Balkan Novel

Beaton, Roderick, *An Introduction to Modern Greek Literature,* Oxford: Clarendon Press, and New York: Oxford University Press, 1994

Elsie, Robert, *History of Albanian Literature,* New York: Columbia University Press, 1995

Moser, Charles A., *A History of Bulgarian Literature, 1865–1944,* The Hague: Mouton, 1972

Winnifrith, T.J., *Shattered Eagles, Balkan Fragments,* London: Duckworth, 1995

Spanish Novel

Landeira, Ricardo, *The Modern Spanish Novel, 1898–1939,* Boston: Twayne, 1985

Medina, Jeremy T., *Spanish Realism: The Theory and Practice of a Concept in the Nineteenth Century,* Potomac, Maryland: Porrúa, 1979

Rico, Francisco, *The Picaresque Novel and Point of View,* Cambridge and New York: Cambridge University Press, 1984

Swiss Novel

Flood, John L., editor, *Modern Swiss Literature: Unity and Diversity,* London: Wolff, and New York: St. Martin's Press, 1985

Yugoslavian Novel

Mihailovich, Vasa D., and Mateja Matejic, editors, *A Comprehensive Bibliography of Yugoslav Literature in English, 1593–1980,* Columbus, Ohio: Slavica, 1984; *First Supplement, 1981–1985,* 1988; *Second Supplement, 1986–1990,* 1992

Wachtel, Andrew, *Making a Nation, Breaking a Nation: Literature and Cultural Politics in Yugoslavia,* Stanford, California: Stanford University Press, 1998

Asia and Oceania

Australian Novel

Goodwin, Ken, *A History of Australian Literature,* London: Macmillan, and New York: St. Martin's Press, 1986

Green, H.M., *A History of Australian Literature: Pure and Applied,* Sydney: Angus and Robertson, 1961; revised edition, Sydney and London: Angus and Robertson, 1984

Kramer, Leonie, editor, *The Oxford History of Australian Literature,* Melbourne and New York: Oxford University Press, 1981

Chinese Novel

Gunn, Edward, *Rewriting Chinese: Style and Innovation in Twentieth-Century Chinese Prose,* Stanford, California: Stanford University Press, 1991

Hegel, Robert E., *Reading Illustrated Fiction in Late Imperial China,* Stanford, California: Stanford University Press, 1998

Hsia, C.T., *A History of Modern Chinese Fiction,* New Haven, Connecticut: Yale University Press, 1961; 2nd edition, 1971

Hsia, C.T., *The Classic Chinese Novel: A Critical Introduction,* New York: Columbia University Press, 1968

Huang, Martin W., *Literati and Self-Re/Presentation: Autobiographical Sensibility in the Eighteenth-Century Chinese Novel,* Stanford, California: Stanford University Press, 1995

Rolston, David L., editor, *How To Read the Chinese Novel,* Princeton, New Jersey: Princeton University Press, 1990

Rolston, David L., *Traditional Chinese Fiction and Fiction Commentary: Reading and Writing Between the Lines,* Stanford, California: Stanford University Press, and Cambridge: Cambridge University Press, 1997

Wang, David Der-wei, *Fictional Realism in Twentieth-Century China: Mao Dun, Lao She, Shen Congwen,* New York: Columbia University Press, 1992

Yu, Anthony C., *Rereading the Stone: Desire and the Making of Fiction in Dream of the Red Chamber,* Princeton, New Jersey: Princeton University Press, 1997

Indian Novel

Clark, T.W., editor, *The Novel in India: Its Birth and Development,* Berkeley: University of California Press, and London: Allen and Unwin, 1970

Iyengar, K.R. Srinivasa, *Indian Writing in English,* London and New York: Asia Publishing House, 1962; 6th edition, New Delhi: Sterling, 1987

Mukherjee, Meenakshi, *Realism and Reality: The Novel and Society in India,* Delhi and New York: Oxford University Press, 1985

Japanese Novel

Fowler, Edward, *The Rhetoric of Confession: Shishōsetsu in Early Twentieth Century Japanese Fiction,* Berkeley: University of California Press, 1988

Katō, Shūichi, *A History of Japanese Literature,* 3 vols., Tokyo and New York: Kodansha International, and London: Macmillan, 1979–83

Keene, Donald, *World Within Walls: Japanese Literature of the Pre-modern Era, 1600–1867,* New York: Holt, Rinehart, and Winston, and London: Secker and Warburg, 1976

Keene, Donald, *Seeds in the Heart: Japanese Literature from Earliest Times to the Late Sixteenth Century,* New York: Holt, 1993

Miyoshi, Masao, *Accomplices of Silence: The Modern Japanese Novel,* Berkeley: University of California Press, 1974

Washburn, Dennis C., *The Dilemma of the Modern in Japanese Fiction,* New Haven, Connecticut: Yale University Press, 1995

Korean Novel

Kim, Hunggyu, *Understanding Korean Literature,* translated by Robert J. Fouser, Armonk, New York: M.E. Sharpe, 1997

Skillend, W. E., *Kodae Sosŏl: A Survey of Korean Traditional Style Popular Novels,* London: School of Oriental and African Studies, University of London, 1968

New Zealand Novel

Evans, Patrick, *The Penguin History of New Zealand Literature*, Auckland and New York: Penguin, 1990

Hankin, Cherry, editor, *Critical Essays on the New Zealand Novel*, Auckland: Heinemann Educational, 1977

Stevens, Joan, *The New Zealand Novel, 1860–1960*, Wellington: Reed, 1961; 2nd revised edition, *The New Zealand Novel, 1860–1965*, 1966

Southeast Asian Novel

Banks, David J., *From Class to Culture: Social Conscience in Malay Novels since Independence*, New Haven, Connecticut: Yale University Southeast Asia Studies, 1987

Hellwig, Tineke, *In the Shadow of Change: Women in Indonesian Literature*, Berkeley: Centers for South and Southeast Asian Studies, University of California, 1994

Mojares, Resil B., *Origins and Rise of the Filipino Novel: A Generic Study of the Novel until 1940*, Quezon City: University of the Philippines Press, 1983

Quinn, George, *The Novel in Javanese: Aspects of Its Social and Literary Character*, Leiden: KITLV Press, 1992

Wahab Ali, A., *The Emergence of the Novel in Modern Indonesian and Malaysian Literature: A Comparative Study*, Kuala Lumpur: Dewan Bahasa dan Pustaka, 1991

Africa and the Middle East

African Novel

Booker, M. Keith, *The African Novel in English: An Introduction*, Portsmouth, New Hampshire: Heinemann, 1998

Gikandi, Simon, *Reading the African Novel*, London: Currey, and Portsmouth, New Hampshire: Heinemann, 1987

Gurnah, Abdulrazak, editor, *Essays on African Writing*, Portsmouth, New Hampshire, and Oxford: Heinemann, 1993

JanMohamed, Abdul R., *Manichean Aesthetics: The Politics of Literature in Colonial Africa*, Amherst: University of Massachusetts Press, 1983; London: University of Massachusetts Press, 1989

Ker, David, *The African Novel and the Modernist Tradition*, New York: Peter Lang, 1997

Msiska, Mpalive-Hangson, and Paul Hyland, editors, *Writing and Africa*, London and New York: Longman, 1997

Obiechina, Emmanuel N., *Culture, Tradition and Society in the West African Novel*, Cambridge and New York: Cambridge University Press, 1975

Priebe, Richard, *Myth, Realism, and the West African Writer*, Trenton, New Jersey: Africa World Press, 1988

Shava, Piniel Viriri, *A People's Voice: Black South African Writing in the Twentieth Century*, London: Zed, and Athens: Ohio University Press, 1989

Smith, Angela, *East African Writing in English*, London and New York: Macmillan, 1989

Stratton, Florence, *Contemporary African Literature and the Politics of Gender*, London and New York: Routledge, 1989

Trump, Martin, editor, *Rendering Things Visible: Essays on South African Literary Culture*, Johannesburg: Raven Press, and Athens: Ohio University Press, 1990

Woodhull, Winifred, *Transfigurations of the Maghreb: Feminism, Decolonization, and Literatures*, Minneapolis: University of Minnesota Press, 1993

Egyptian Novel

Badawi, Muhammad Mustafa, *Modern Arabic Literature*, Cambridge and New York: Cambridge University Press, 1992

Jad, Ali, *Form and Technique in the Egyptian Novel, 1912–1971*, London: Ithaca Press, 1983

Kilpatrick, Hilary, *The Modern Egyptian Novel*, London: Ithaca Press, 1974

Israeli Novel

Alter, Robert, *After the Tradition: Essays on Modern Jewish Writing*, New York: Dutton, 1969

Rabinovich, Isaiah, *Major Trends in Modern Hebrew Fiction*, Chicago: University of Chicago Press, 1968

Yudkin, Leon I., *Beyond Sequence: Current Israeli Fiction and Its Context*, Northwood: Symposium, 1992

Iranian Novel

Ghanoonparvar, M.R., *In a Persian Mirror: Images of the West and Westerners in Iranian Fiction*, Austin: University of Texas Press, 1993

Kamshad, Hassan, *Modern Persian Prose Literature*, Cambridge: Cambridge University Press, 1966; Bethesda, Maryland: Iranbooks, 1996

Yarshater, Ehsan, editor, *Persian Literature*, Albany, New York: Bibliotheca Persica, 1988

Levantine Arabic Novel

Allen, Roger, *The Arabic Novel: An Historical and Critical Introduction*, Syracuse, New York: Syracuse University Press, and Manchester: Manchester University Press, 1982; 2nd edition, Syracuse, New York: Syracuse University Press, 1995

Boullata, Issa J., and Roger Allen, editors, *The Arabic Novel Since 1950: Critical Essays, Interviews, and Bibliography*, Cambridge, Massachusetts: Dar Mahjar, 1992

Ghazoul, Ferial J., and Barbara Harlow, editors, *The View from Within: Writers and Critics on Contemporary Arabic Literature*, Cairo: American University in Cairo Press, 1994

Turkish Novel

Evin, Ahmet, *Origins and Development of the Turkish Novel*, Minneapolis: Bibliotheca Islamica, 1983

Ostle, Robin, editor, *Modern Literature and the Near and Middle East*, New York: Routledge, 1991

The Americas and the Caribbean

Canadian Novel

Hutcheon, Linda, *The Canadian Postmodern: A Study of Contemporary English-Canadian Fiction*, Toronto and New York: Oxford University Press, 1988

Keefer, Janice Kulyk, *Under Eastern Eyes: A Critical Reading of*

Maritime Fiction, Toronto and London: University of Toronto Press, 1987

Moss, John, *A Reader's Guide to the Canadian Novel,* Toronto: McLelland and Stewart, 1981; 2nd edition, 1987

Ricou, Laurence, *Vertical Man, Horizontal World: Man and Landscape in Canadian Prairie Fiction,* Vancouver: University of British Columbia Press, 1973

Shek, Ben, *French-Canadian and Québécois Novels,* Toronto: Oxford University Press, 1991

Smart, Patricia, *Writing in the Father's House: The Emergence of the Feminine in the Quebec Literary Tradition,* Toronto: University of Toronto Press, 1991

Toye, William E., editor, *The Oxford Companion to Canadian Literature,* Toronto and New York: Oxford University Press, 1983; 2nd edition, 1997

Caribbean and South American Novel

Anim-Addo, Joan, editor, *Framing the Word: Gender and Genre in Caribbean Women's Writing,* London: Whiting and Birch, and Concord, Massachusetts: Paul, 1996

Brushwood, John Stubbs, *The Spanish American Novel: A Twentieth-Century Survey,* Austin: University of Texas Press, 1975

Case, Frederick Ivor, *The Crisis of Identity: Studies in the Guadeloupean and Martiniquan Novel,* Sherbrooke, Quebec: Naaman, 1985

Duncan, J. Ann, *Voices, Visions, and a New Reality: Mexican Fiction since 1970,* Pittsburgh, Pennsylvania: University of Pittsburgh Press, 1986

Ellison, Fred P., *Brazil's New Novel: Four Northeastern Masters,* Berkeley: University of California Press, 1954

Foster, David William, *The Argentine Generation of 1880: Ideology and Cultural Texts,* Columbia: University of Missouri Press, 1990

Franco, Jean, *Plotting Women: Gender and Representation in Mexico,* New York: Columbia University Press, and London: Verso, 1989

González Echevarría, Roberto, *The Voice of the Masters: Writing and Authority in Modern Latin American Literature,* Austin: University of Texas Press, 1985

González Echevarría, Roberto, *Myth and Archive: A Theory of Latin American Narrative,* New York and Cambridge: Cambridge University Press, 1990

Lewis, Marvin, *Treading the Ebony Path: Ideology and Violence in Afro-Colombian Prose Fiction,* Columbia: University of Missouri Press, 1987

Luis, William, *Literary Bondage: Slavery in Cuban Narrative,* Austin: University of Texas Press, 1990

Martin, Gerald, *Journeys through the Labyrinth: Latin American Fiction in the Twentieth Century,* London and New York: Verso, 1989

Martins, Heitor, editor, *The Brazilian Novel,* Bloomington: Department of Spanish and Portuguese, Indiana University, 1976

Ormerod, Beverley, *An Introduction to the French Caribbean Novel,* London and Portsmouth, New Hampshire: Heinemann, 1985

Ramchand, Kenneth, *The West Indian Novel and Its Background,* London: Faber, and New York: Barnes and Noble, 1970; 2nd edition, London: Heinemann, 1983

Sommer, Doris, *One Master for Another: Populism as Patriarchal Rhetoric in Dominican Novels,* Lanham, Maryland: University Press of America, 1983

Williams, Raymond Leslie, *The Colombian Novel, 1844–1987,* Austin: University of Texas Press, 1991

United States Novel

Baker, Houston A., *Blues, Ideology, and Afro-American Literature: A Vernacular Theory,* Chicago: University of Chicago Press, 1984

Baym, Nina, *Woman's Fiction: A Guide to Novels by and about Women in America, 1820–1870,* Ithaca, New York: Cornell University Press, 1978; 2nd edition, Urbana: University of Illinois Press, 1993

Bold, Christine, *Selling the Wild West: Popular Western Fiction, 1860 to 1960,* Bloomington: Indiana University Press, 1987

Bradbury, Malcolm, *The Modern American Novel,* Oxford and New York: Oxford University Press, 1983; new edition, 1993

Brown, Herbert Ross, *The Sentimental Novel in America, 1789–1860,* Durham, North Carolina: Duke University Press, 1940

Carby, Hazel, *Reconstructing Womanhood: The Emergence of the Afro-American Woman Novelist,* New York: Oxford University Press, 1987; Oxford: Oxford University Press, 1989

Chénetier, Marc, *Beyond Suspicion: New American Fiction Since 1960,* Philadelphia: University of Pennsylvania Press, and Liverpool: Liverpool University Press, 1996

Cowie, Alexander, *The Rise of the American Novel,* New York: American Book, 1948

Cowley, Malcolm, *Exile's Return: A Literary Odyssey of the 1920s,* New York: Viking Press, 1951

Davidson, Cathy N., *Revolution and the Word: The Rise of the Novel in America,* New York: Oxford University Press, 1986

Fiedler, Leslie, *Love and Death in the American Novel,* New York: Dell, 1960; London: Cape, 1967

Hassan, Ihab, *Radical Innocence: The Contemporary American Novel,* Princeton, New Jersey: Princeton University Press, and New York: Harper and Row, 1961

Massa, Ann, *American Literature in Context: 1900–1930,* London and New York: Methuen, 1982

Matthiessen, F.O., *American Renaissance: Art and Expression in the Age of Emerson and Whitman,* London and New York: Oxford University Press, 1941

Rideout, Walter B., *The Radical Novel in the United States, 1900–1954: Some Interrelations of Literature and Society,* Cambridge, Massachusetts: Harvard University Press, 1956

Saldívar, José David, *The Dialectics of Our America: Genealogy, Cultural Critique, and Literary History,* Durham, North Carolina, Duke University Press, 1991

Smith, Henry Nash, *Democracy and the Novel: Popular Resistance to Classic American Writers,* New York: Oxford University Press, 1978

Tompkins, Jane, *Sensational Designs: The Cultural Work of American Fiction, 1790–1860,* New York: Oxford University Press, 1985

A

À la recherche du temps perdu. *See* In Search of Lost Time

À rebours. *See* Against Nature

Absalom, Absalom! by William Faulkner

1936

William Faulkner sowed the seed of what was to become *Absalom, Absalom!* in "Evangeline," a short story he wrote in 1931 and twice failed to get published. Even if Faulkner had not had to cope with the death of his favorite brother and financial hardship, it is conceivable that he would have needed five years to bring the complex *Absalom, Absalom!* to fruition. The novel, through incredibly complicated narrative sequences, tells one story in several different ways. Recounting the rise and fall of Thomas Sutpen, the central narrative is replete with the tensions of love, murder, and race. This story is told by four different storytellers—Rosa Coldfield, Quentin Compson, Mr. Compson, and Shreve McCannon—who take essentially the same details but present them in their own way. Each version of the story becomes more compelling and more believable; ironically, as the story progresses, fact and fiction become indistinguishable.

Absalom, Absalom! is the second novel, after *Light in August* (1932), in the Yoknapatawpha saga that addresses the issue of race in the South. Like its predecessor, *Absalom, Absalom!* makes the most of ambiguities involving the race of particular characters. In fact, only a few events in *Absalom, Absalom!* may be marked as incontrovertibly true within the scope of the narrative. Thomas Sutpen arrives in Yoknapatawpha County in 1833 with a French architect and 20 French-speaking slaves and sculpts a fabulous plantation out of the Mississippi wilderness.

Soon thereafter he acquires a respectable wife and produces the male heir who makes his plans legitimate in his own eyes. Sutpen's successes alone merit interest. His rise from rags to riches—he was born in West Virginia to poor whites and dedicated himself to the idea of owning the "big house" because, when he was a child, he was turned away from one by a black butler—is as archetypically American as that of Benjamin Franklin and Jay Gatsby. However, the most important event in *Absalom, Absalom!* involves Sutpen's fall: the murder of Charles Bon at the hands of Sutpen's heir, Henry. All the stories converge on that fact.

Faulkner employs to perfection the technique inspired by the multilayered narratives of Joseph Conrad, James Joyce, and George Eliot and practiced in his own earlier novels, *The Sound and the Fury* (1929) and *As I Lay Dying* (1930): he allows each narrator to tell one version of the tale that leads to Charles' death. The significant difference between *Absalom, Absalom!* and Faulkner's earlier novels is that the later novel demands the narrators to relate a history of other people, not primarily accounts of their own travails. The plot progresses only as quickly as the narrators can piece together the information—and the speculations—they share with each other. Perspective mediates the significance of all their stories. Rosa Coldfield portrays Sutpen as a demon. Sutpen swindles her father out of a small fortune, marries her sister and then treats her poorly, and after his wife dies, promises to marry Rosa—if she can produce for him another male heir. Insulted, and blinded by the desire to explain the failure of her relationship with this remarkable man, she decides that any cause, including the cause of her beloved South, must be tainted if it enlists Sutpen. Mr. Compson, who sees himself as doomed to inactivity by the burden of his own knowledge of the world, admires Sutpen's ability to carve his dreams into the Mississippi landscape. Instead of attributing Charles' death and the subsequent fall of the House of Sutpen to the consequences of human action, he attributes it to fate, even after concluding that Charles Bon is Henry's half brother, the son of Thomas Sutpen and his estranged Haitian wife.

Rosa's and Mr. Compson's conclusions reinforce their preconceived notions about life in the South, which are often as full of moonlight and magnolias as those in *Gone with the Wind* (published the same year as *Absalom, Absalom!*). Because Quentin Compson is so perplexed about the South and Shreve McCannon so curious about it, psychoanalytic critics argue that their explanation for Charles' death exposes the issue that Rosa and Mr. Compson ignore: race. Sutpen reveals that he left his first wife and family in Haiti because they were "unsuitable to his purpose and so put aside." Only Quentin and Shreve contemplate the tie between that claim and Charles' death. They conclude that Charles is Thomas' Haitian son, so that Charles' relationship with Judith Sutpen, Henry's sister, would have been incestuous. Shreve quickly convinces Quentin that the possibility of incest alone would not have provoked Henry to kill Charles. After all, the two are best friends at the University of Mississippi, and when he first finds out that Charles is his brother, Henry repudiates his own name rather than his friendship with Charles. The two are still constant comrades during the Civil War. To find a reason strong enough to drive Henry to kill, Quentin and Shreve analyze Charles Bon's genealogy and decide that he must have been part black. It is the sole requirement of the race-obsessed South that Charles does not fulfill. He is daring, sophisticated, and handsome, but, being part black, he cannot be allowed to marry Judith. Henry, although he no longer lays claim to Sutpen's Hundred, still clings to its racist foundation.

Absalom, Absalom!, like many Southern novels, evinces a fascination with the relationship between genealogy and power. This trait evokes the influence of 19th-century British novelists such as Jane Austen, Emily Brontë, and Charles Dickens. But Faulkner brilliantly subverts the conventions of this fascination in *Absalom, Absalom!* Sutpen's design reveals itself as faulty: the legitimacy of his family line cannot come from his ancestors, and so he looks to his heirs to legitimate himself. Genealogy, Faulkner shows, far from naturalizing power and rank, is pressed into service to justify and mask the continuing violence of social inequalities. The inadequacy of genealogy to accomplish these goals is also reflected in the fact that the narratives continually unravel. Even the narrative of Quentin and Shreve's friendship

falls apart at the end, when Quentin tells Shreve—who has just stayed up most of the night helping to reconstruct the history of Thomas Sutpen—that he cannot know the South as he was not born there. The novel's greatest tragedy is that the narrators tacitly accept the racial bias of Sutpen's design. Quentin in particular is given the opportunity to repudiate Southern racism when Shreve taunts him at the end of the book. Quentin replies that he does not "hate the South" even though he knows he is wrong. His subsequent moral confusion becomes dead weight to his soul, and he throws himself into the Charles River soon thereafter.

Absalom, Absalom! is important not only as a study of the price paid for racism by Southern whites but also as a modernist experiment in perspectivism. Building on the juxtapositions of different viewpoints in *As I Lay Dying* and *The Sound and the Fury, Absalom, Absalom!* takes the technique to a new level of complexity and expressiveness. In Faulkner's hands, point of view becomes a powerful tool of characterization and historical analysis. The multiple perspectives deny the availability of an objective understanding of history, and indeed of reality. But at the same time they underscore the irrelevance of objectivity: the refraction of Thomas Sutpen's story through the experience of others offers a rich and authoritative view of the meaning of history, even as it leaves uncertainty about fact. *Absalom, Absalom!*'s technical explorations also affirm the connection of Southern regional fiction to world literature.

THOMAS EASTERLING

See also William Faulkner

Further Reading

Brooks, Cleanth, *William Faulkner: The Yoknapatawpha Country,* New Haven, Connecticut: Yale University Press, 1963

Brooks, Peter, *Reading for the Plot: Design and Intention in Narrative,* New York: Knopf, and Oxford: Clarendon Press, 1984

Cash, W.J., *The Mind of the South,* New York: Knopf, 1941; London: Thames and Hudson, 1971

Donaldson, Susan V., "Subverting History: Women, Narrative, and Patriarchy in *Absalom, Absalom!*" *The Southern Quarterly: A Journal of Arts in the South* 26 (1988)

Faulkner, William, *Faulkner in the University: Class Conferences at the University of Virginia, 1957–58,* edited by Frederick L. Gwynn and Joseph Leo Blotner, Charlottesville: University of Virginia Press, 1959

Karl, Frederick R., "Race, History, and Technique in *Absalom, Absalom!*" in *Faulkner and Race: Faulkner and Yoknapatawpha, 1986,* edited by Doreen Fowler and Ann J. Abadie, Jackson: University of Mississippi Press, 1987

Kartiganer, Donald M., *The Fragile Thread: The Meaning of Form in Faulkner's Novels,* Amherst: University of Massachusetts Press, 1979

Chinua Achebe 1930–

Nigerian

Chinua Achebe is one of the most distinguished contemporary African writers. He has written short stories, poetry, children's fiction, and essays, but he is best known for his novels, which reflect on the colonial and postcolonial African experience. Achebe's fiction spans the period from the "European Scramble for Africa" in the 1880s to decolonization in the 1960s and the new political realities of contemporary African states.

Things Fall Apart (1958) and *Arrow of God* (1964) focus on the colonial period. Both challenge and refute the stereotypical European view of Africa and Africans and examine the consequences of the imperialist colonial mission with its professed emphasis on the need to civilize and humanize the so-called subject races. Achebe's most acclaimed work, *Things Fall Apart* is often accounted the first novel to describe the content and quality of Ibo life in eastern Nigeria from an African point of view. It portrays the cultural and religious traditions of the remote village of Umuofia, a society that prizes individual manliness and the acquisition of wealth but is held together by spiritual convictions and practices that supersede individuality. Then the European colonizers, missionaries first, begin to arrive. Even as it offers a loving embrace to Umuofia's outcasts, Christianity compromises traditional religion. A cash economy undermines traditional agricultural practices. The combined foreign presence, commercial and religious, also exerts a more positive influence, promoting change through the force of ideas. Okonkwo, the protagonist of *Things Fall Apart,* a proud and irascible man, resists the changes in his society and organizes an attack on the local mission. But the clock cannot be turned back, and Okonkwo's little band is squashed. The novel ends with a demonstration of the indisputable power of the colonial agents and with Okonkwo's suicide. His inflexibility made it impossible for him to accept change, but Ibo society as a whole is more resilient. Although the story seems plain on the surface, the novel is written in a complex and allusive style that yields fresh meaning and insight at each rereading and contributes to its international reputation.

Arrow of God, set in a period when colonial rule is already firmly established, also underscores the irreversible nature of the historical process. The novel examines the complexity of African and European relations through a conflict between the chief priest of an African religion and a British district officer, a conflict most immediately precipitated by the fact that the priest's son has become a zealous Christian. A similar dynamic unfolds in *Things Fall Apart,* in which Okonkwo's son Nwoye converts to Christianity. This scenario points up the internal reasons for the changes African societies undergo upon the imposition of colonial rule.

A second grouping of novels is concerned with the experience of contemporary Africans, focusing on the colonial legacy. Those novels also examine the role of art, expressing Achebe's faith in the power of the word to nurture civility and his conviction that, as he puts it, there is a truth in fiction that provides a "new handle on reality." *No Longer at Ease* (1960) is set in preindependence Nigeria and dramatizes the predicament of a young Nigerian caught between the traditional village world of his youth and the modern Western world of his European educa-

tion. Lacking the necessary moral courage, the young man is unable to resolve the conflict and yields to the temptation of bribery. This individual story of a tragically divided allegiance mediates an exploration of the consequences of colonial rule and the ways Nigerians have used colonial practices. *No Longer at Ease* anticipates the ambiguities that will accompany independence and throws light on the processes that lead to widespread corruption in postcolonial African society.

A Man of the People (1966) and *Anthills of the Savannah* (1987) are set in imaginary African countries that strongly resemble Nigeria. This device allows Achebe to describe the social and political problems that have beset Nigeria and other African countries trying to recover from colonialism. *A Man of the People* is narrated by a cynical young university graduate and schoolteacher, Odili Samalu, whose commentary exposes the corruption of the country's government. The novel, ending with a military coup that causes the complete collapse of the civil political system, was published only days before the coup that brought down the First Republic in Nigeria in 1966. As he has explained, Achebe's "prediction" was based on the perception that Nigeria's political machine had become so dysfunctional that a coup was inevitable.

Achebe joined the diplomatic service of the Biafran Republic upon the outbreak of the Biafran War in 1967. Although he wrote in other genres, he did not return to the novel for the next 20 years. Achebe has explained that he needed those years to assimilate the horrendous Biafran experience. The product of that period of reflection, *Anthills of the Savannah* again broaches the subject of corruption and abuse of power in contemporary African politics. A military government rules the country of Kangan with no intention of giving up power, despite promises to pave the way for a civil government. Sam, His Excellency, H.E., relies not only on military support to secure his position but on his Commissioner of Information, Chris, and on the government-owned newspaper, run by Ikem. The novel focuses on the moral dilemma that confronts Chris and Ikem as they are pressured to help manufacture information and news that hide the realities of internal dissent and resistance. Achebe also focuses attention on the function of the writer in a dangerous and deteriorating political situation, making an explicit comparison with the traditional African storyteller who functions as the moral historian of the tribe.

Achebe's development of an authoritative, modern storytelling that functions as a medium for reflection on political and historical processes from an African point of view is the single most important achievement of his oeuvre.

DOUGLAS KILLAM

See also Things Fall Apart

Biography

Born Albert Chinualumogu in Ogidi, 16 November 1930. Attended Government College, Umuahia, 1944–47; University College, Ibadan, 1948–53, B.A. (London) 1953. Employed as talks producer, Lagos, 1954–57, controller, Enugu, 1958–61, and director, Voice of Nigeria, Lagos, 1961–66, Nigerian

Broadcasting Corporation; chairman, Citadel Books Ltd., Enugu, 1967; professor of English at the University of Nigeria, 1973–81, and professor emeritus from 1984; visiting professor at various universities in the United States, 1972–76, 1984, 1987–89. Founding editor, Heinemann African Writers series, 1962–72, and from 1970 director, Heinemann Educational (Nigeria) Ltd., and Nwankwo-Ifejika Ltd. (later Nwamife), publishers, Enugu; from 1971 editor, *Okike: An African Journal of New Writing,* Nsukka; from 1983 governor, Newsconcern International Foundation, London; from 1984 founder and publisher, *Uwa Ndi Igbo: A Bilingual Journal of Igbo Life and Arts.* Served on diplomatic missions for Biafra, 1967–69, during Nigerian Civil War; deputy national president, People's Redemption Army, 1983. Seriously injured in car accident in 1990.

Novels by Achebe

Things Fall Apart, 1958
No Longer at Ease, 1960
Arrow of God, 1964
A Man of the People, 1966
Anthills of the Savannah, 1987

Other Writings: short stories, poetry, essays, stories for children.

Further Reading

Carroll, David, *Chinua Achebe,* New York: Twayne, 1970; 2nd edition, New York: St. Martin's Press, and London: Macmillan, 1980

Gikandi, Simon, *Reading Chinua Achebe: Language and Ideology in Fiction,* London: Currey, and Portsmouth, New Hampshire: Heinemann, 1991

Innes, Catherine Lynette, *Chinua Achebe,* Cambridge and New York: Cambridge University Press, 1990

Killam, G.D., *The Novels of Chinua Achebe,* London: Heinemann Educational, 1969; revised edition as *The Writings of Chinua Achebe,* 1977

Ojinmah, Umelo, *Chinua Achebe: New Perspectives,* Ibadan, Nigeria: Spectrum, 1991

Wren, Robert, *Achebe's World: The Historical and Cultural Contexts of the Novels of Chinua Achebe,* Washington, D.C.: Three Continents Press, 1980; Harlow, Essex: Longman, 1981

Adaptations. *See* **Film and the Novel; Translation**

Adolphe by Benjamin Constant

1816

Since its 1816 publication in London and Paris, *Adolphe* has excited both enthusiasm and distaste. Although broadly recognized as a masterpiece of the psychological novel, it also has repelled many readers by its amoral stance toward human relations. This rather bleak vision accounts in large measure for the novel's continued controversial status.

Idle and alienated at 22, Adolphe, residing in a small German court, sets out to seduce the rather sad and beautiful Ellénore, a woman of Polish origin ten years his senior and the avowed mistress of the Comte de P***, to whom she has borne two children. In the face of her initial resistance, Adolphe soon believes he loves her. However, once he succeeds in making her his mistress, the dynamics change: Ellénore develops a tenacious and consuming passion for her seducer, and the rest of the text recounts his ineffectual efforts to get free of her. She dies in the end, a victim of Adolphe's inability to take decisive action.

Adolphe and Ellénore are a joined figure of acrimony and misery. But whereas Ellénore has a certain pathetic grandeur, a willingness to give up everything for love—fortune, relative respectability, even her children—Adolphe is more elusive, his desire nourished by obstacles. Racked by a convulsive sense of loyalty and remorse, he nevertheless wants only what he does not have and tires rapidly of what he possesses. Tormented and tormentor, Adolphe most desires Ellénore when she becomes, in death, definitively unattainable.

Born in 1767 in Lausanne into a prominent Swiss clan, Benjamin Constant de Rebecque received an international education and led a life of continual peregrinations. An outspoken politician, his career included both election to public office and banishment, and he played an important role in French political life during the Restoration. In addition to his masterwork, *Adolphe,* he left upon his death in 1830 an unfinished novel entitled *Cécile* (a story resembling *Adolphe*); a tragedy entitled *Wallstein*; an important record of correspondence; extensive autobiographical writings; political brochures and pamphlets; and writings on history, literature, and especially religion.

From its initial publication, *Adolphe* aroused immediate biographical interest. Consistently liberal in his political ideas, Benjamin Constant was notoriously fickle in his personal life, and Adolphe was seen as a thinly disguised version of the author. Constant's love life in particular was spectacularly complicated, and his letters and journals record melodramatic and overlapping infatuations. In the fall of 1806, when he composed *Adolphe,* he had already been divorced from his first wife, Wilhelmine (Minna) von Cramm; had for a dozen years been the lover of Germaine de Staël; and had just become lover to the twice-married Charlotte de Hardenberg (whom he would secretly marry in 1808). Various women whom he loved have been discussed as the inspiration for Ellénore, including, among others, Charlotte, object of his interrupted attentions and ongoing tenderness; a beautiful Irishwoman named Anna Lindsay, who bore two children to one of her lovers (not Constant); and, chiefly, Germaine de Staël, with whom Constant's tempestuous liaison, full of harangues and betrayals, was played out in cities across France, Switzerland, and Germany (Staël was repeatedly in political exile).

Speculation about the "real" Ellénore impelled Constant to add a preface to the second edition as a protest against the "scourge" of biographical interpretations of fictional works. Modern critics incline to agree, emphasizing the novel's complicated genesis and suggesting that it likely found its inspiration in more than one figure and experience. Regardless, *Adolphe*'s importance has less to do with any aspects of autobiography than it does with the literary and psychological qualities that assure it a prominent place in the French analytical tradition.

The preface added to the second edition is only one of several framing documents that problematize the first-person singular narrative addressed to nobody in particular. Adolphe's narrative is preceded by two author's prefaces (yet another was added to the third edition), and by an *avis de l'éditeur* (a "publisher's notice" from the fictional finder of the manuscript). The story ends with Adolphe quoting at length a letter left him by Ellénore, followed by a letter to the publisher from an unidentified acquaintance of Adolphe, and, finally, by the publisher's response to the correspondent that explains his rationale behind publishing the book. Constant thus adopts the sort of framing technique commonly used in the era's fiction, and as a result Adolphe's voice reaches us through layers of textual apparatus, mediated by the moralizing pronouncements of a series of personae, both real and fictional, both within and outside the main story—all underscoring the novel's unstable and impenetrable "I."

Adolphe is a transitional work. With its classical spareness of style, its universalizing maxims, and its "publisher's notice" that presents the text as historical truth, the hero's confessions are, on the one hand, part of an 18th-century literary tradition. However, while Adolphe may profitably be compared to other transitional romantic heroes—Goethe's Werther, Chateaubriand's René—Constant's originality becomes clearer when he is contrasted with contemporaneous works that also convey the social and psychological pressures that shape the relations between passionate women and depressive, indecisive men: Staël's *Corinne* (1807), for instance, or Isabelle de Charrière's *Caliste* (1788). (Interestingly enough, the young Constant also had an intense friendship with Charrière, 29 years his senior, who died in 1805, never quite having forgiven his defection to Staël.)

If Constant's Adolphe is less palatable, because more emotionally abusive, than either Staël's Oswald or Charrière's William, his story has a more exceptional modernity. With its self-ironizing sentimentalism that bridges Rousseau and Romanticism, with its account of the rapidity with which Adolphe falls lyrically in and brutally out of love, the work's themes became essential to Stendhal and the other great French novelists of the succeeding decades: the power of words not just to reflect but to create feeling; the subjection of the individual to a particular sociohistorical moment; the paralysis of the will; and the implacability of time and change.

JOAN HINDE STEWART

See also Framing and Embedding

Further Reading

Cruickshank, John, *Benjamin Constant,* New York: Twayne, 1974

Delbouille, Paul, *Genèse, structure et destin d'Adolphe,* Paris: Les Belles Lettres, 1971

Fairlie, Alison, "The Art of Constant's *Adolphe*: Creation of Character," *Forum for Modern Language Studies* 2 (1966)

Fairlie, Alison, "The Art of Constant's *Adolphe*: Structure and Style," *French Studies* 20 (1966)

Fairlie, Alison, "The Art of Constant's *Adolphe*: The Stylization of Experience," *Modern Language Review* 62 (1967)

Russo, Elena, *Skeptical Selves: Empiricism and Modernity in the French Novel,* Stanford, California: Stanford University Press, 1996

Todorov, Tzvetan, *The Poetics of Prose,* Oxford: Blackwell, and Ithaca, New York: Cornell University Press, 1977; originally published as *Poétique de la prose,* 1971

Unwin, Timothy, *Constant, Adolphe,* London and Wolfeboro, New Hampshire: Grant and Cutler, 1986

Waller, Margaret, *The Male Malady: Fictions of Impotence in the French Romantic Novel,* New Brunswick, New Jersey: Rutgers University Press, 1993

Wood, Dennis, *Benjamin Constant: Adolphe,* Cambridge and New York: Cambridge University Press, 1987

Adventure Novel and Imperial Romance

From Old French, the term *adventure* signified at first "a thing about to happen to anyone." In much modern adventure fiction, particularly in thrillers and spy stories, that meaning is latent. "Anyone" can be the unsuspecting protagonist of an adventure novel. Ordinary lives can be precipitately put at hazard. People can be transplanted from their familiar surroundings to strange and threatening places. As the term *adventure* evolved, elements of danger, recklessness, and daring attached themselves to it. Thus we can trace a parallel movement toward a literature in which adventure is less a matter of chance than of will and desire: adventure becomes something that is sought after by intrepid characters rather than something that accidentally happens to characters. This shift is especially evident in that fecund subbranch of adventure fiction, the imperial romance.

This form of popular fiction, which was often written for serious, polemical purposes, belongs to the late 19th and early 20th centuries (although important elements of the genre may be traced back to earlier examples of prose fiction, as discussed below). The connection has been pithily hypothesized by Martin Green (1979). "Adventure," he contends, is "the energizing myth of empire"; it generates myths that inspire action, both military and mercantile. Imperial romance is itself a kind of imperial phenomenon, spreading from the centers of the European empires—notably London and Paris—in search of exotic subject matter in their colonized territories. In time, authors from those territories (notably Australia, Canada, New Zealand, South Africa, and the Caribbean) began to write adventure fiction in ways indebted to, but revisionist of, their predecessors. Their particular need was to retrieve or confect a usable past in their own countries that would validate the romance enterprise, to discover what Rolf Boldrewood called, in *Robbery Under Arms* (1888), "the domain of legend and tradition."

Adventure fiction is retrospective, a disposition that appears early and perhaps most significantly in the historical novel, which was pioneered by Sir Walter Scott and James Fenimore Cooper and their emulators around the world. In this mode, adventure fiction treats the development of nation states, revives episodes of their heroic pasts, or furnishes myths of national values and virtues as in, for example, Scott's account of Anglo-Saxon and Norman rivalry in *Ivanhoe* (1819). His novels, like Cooper's *The Last of the Mohicans* (1826), often are set in borderlands, such as that between England and Scotland. In Cooper's case it is the "bloody ground" where the French and English territorial claims clashed in North America. In the temporal settings of their fiction, outlawry is powerful, but heroic virtue still may prevail in what ultimately is the settling of national destinies. Such backward-glancing fiction is also frequently imbued with nostalgia for more adventurous times, which—if in fact lost forever—are imaginatively recoverable.

There is also an alternative, prospective mode of adventure fiction that imagines the recovery of mysterious lost worlds and lost races, the pioneering of lands new to Europeans and the exploitation of the rich domains hitherto unknown to them. The extension of the territory of imperial romance fiction was the literary counterpart of the geographical expansion of the 19th-century European empires. Ghosted by the fear that their material might be exhausted, these writers colonized darkest Africa, the dead heart of Australia (for example, in Rosa Praed's romance about a lost race, *Fugitive Anne,* 1904), and in due course the moon (to which Jules Verne led the way) and the future (notably in H.G. Wells' *The Time Machine,* 1895). Their enterprise was to refute the gloomy judgment on the possibilities for adventure that were voiced by the newspaper editor in Arthur Conan Doyle's *The Lost World* (1912): "I'm afraid the day for this sort of thing is rather past. . . . The big blank spaces in the map are all being filled in, and there's no room for romance anywhere." The author made it his business to rebut such pessimism.

Some adventure fiction was devoted to imperialist boosting, as with former war correspondent G.A. Henty, whose long and successful series of novels was intended chiefly for juvenile audiences. These books sported such formulaic titles as *Under Drake's Flag* (1882) and dealt with the heroic ages of the British Empire. War has been a prime subject of adventure fiction. Scott, for instance, wrote of the Crusades, Cooper of the Seven Years' War. C.S. Forester's series of ebullient novels of the Napoleonic War at sea had a hero, Hornblower, who was modeled on Lord Nelson. Among innumerable modern successors are Patrick O'Brian and Bernard Cornwell, who treat the same historical period as Forester with an ironic tinge but also with an almost pedantic care for detail. Both show a concern as intense and scrupulous as Scott's to ground their adventure stories plausibly in the time in which they are set. Thus, paradoxically, adventure fiction can seek a realistic validation for its imaginative license.

One of the most curious, specialized instances of this circumstance is the turn-of-the-century, pan-European adventure literature that—by imagining in detail the war to come—helped prepare Europeans for the likelihood of World War I. For instance, journalist William Le Queux's *The Invasion of 1910* (1906) was originally published in Northcliffe's *Daily Mail* with maps showing what parts of Britain the Germans would secure the next day. Erskine Childers, who was executed by British authorities in 1922 for his Irish nationalist beliefs, wrote the best of these works of prediction, *The Riddle of the Sands* (1903). The phenomenon is analyzed by I.F. Clarke in *Voices Prophesying War, 1763–1984* (1966).

The tone of imperial romance fiction has also been melancholy, cautionary, preferring to demythologize the strange lands upon which European adventurers intrude as often as it exults in their conquest. This writing sometimes becomes the vehicle for social criticism, prophecy, and satire. Jonathan Swift's *Gulliver's Travels* (1726) is a satire of European Enlightenment pretensions in the form of an adventure novel and is perhaps a proleptic satire of that form as well. H.G. Wells' *The War of the Worlds* (1898), with its famous imagining of a Martian invasion (a piece of psycho-pathology from which the world has not since been spared), castigates British imperial hubris. Yet those who were public proponents of the virtues of the empire often responded ambivalently to its possible fate. At the end of the 19th century, Rudyard Kipling's poem "The Recessional" sounded a solemn note. He believed, as did H. Rider Haggard (probably the most influential of all imperial romance authors), in the cyclical pattern of history. The "wheel of empire" (a title adopted by Alan Sandison in his fine study of the "Imperial Idea" in late 19th- and early 20th-century fiction, 1967) would continue to turn.

Thus the British Empire, just because it was near its zenith, faced imminent decline. The civilization of ancient Rome was the model for Kipling's and Haggard's gloomy prognostications. A more general scepticism about the worth, distinct from the likely fate, of civilization was explored in novels such as Haggard's *Allan Quatermain* (1887), in which civilization is seen as merely veneer over the essentially savage nature of mankind.

The imperial romance involves an outward journey into unknown, faraway lands and perils. Just as importantly, it enforces a vertiginous descent into the unconscious mind of the adventurer. That is, imperial romance is intimately concerned with regression, whether it is Haggard's unpeeling of the layers of civilization as his adventurers are jolted by the experience of "lost" African lands, or Marlow, musing in Joseph Conrad's "Heart of Darkness" (1902) on his mission up the Congo to find the charismatic Kurtz: "going up that river was like travelling back to the beginnings of the world." The "primitives" whom adventurers encounter may be more horribly fascinating for being signs of the atavism in themselves than they want to admit. The landscape of imperial romance is strikingly expressionistic; compelling and fearsome, it is studded with caves, grottoes, and underground rivers into which the adventurers are perilously drawn. This is a literature that seems to have foreknowledge of the depth psychology of Freud and Jung (the latter one of Haggard's most distinguished admirers). By contrast with their subterranean reaches, the romance landscapes are frequently mountainous, better to afford European interlopers the illusion that their proconsular sweep of vision confers command. Descending into undiscovered realms, they will be chastened as well as imperiled. The challenges they have to face are epistemological as well as physical. The derangement occasioned by what they learn (in the case of Conrad's Kurtz, for example) is as much a jeopardy to them as dangers sought out and confronted.

According to Paul Zweig in his study of "the fate of adventure in the modern world" (1974), adventure fiction is obsessed with escape and therefore harbors a corresponding fear of imprisonment. Typically this involves a flight from domestic life and its obligations and, in particular, from the social and sexual power of women. James Fenimore Cooper's Natty Bumppo, hero of the Leatherstocking Tales, is a resolute misogynist. Herman Melville's Ahab in *Moby-Dick* (1851) has turned his back on a loved wife and child. The nature of adventure in this fiction frequently involves an escape from savage or sinister imprisonment. Sometimes the imprisonment is politically based, as in Alexandre Dumas' *Le Comte de Monte-Cristo* (1844–45; *The Count of Monte-Cristo*), in which the eponymous hero escapes from the Chateau d'If to make a fortune and wreak revenge on those responsible for his incarceration. More generally, adventure fiction is escapist. It indulges the primal desire of readers, those happy, vicarious adventurers, to be someone—and somewhere—else. They are transported out of their familiar surroundings into the world of espionage, to a lost world deep in the South American jungles, or to new worlds beyond the solar system. Willingly they surrender to the pleasures and the *frissons* of an escape they know to be temporary.

Despite its recent, unrespectable reputation, adventure literature has a distinguished pedigree. Zweig sees Homer's wily and indomitable Odysseus (whose name he translates as approximately equal to "trouble") as the precursor of all adventure heroes. The adventurer's condition is "to be at one with trouble."

His destiny is solitary: he is at home everywhere and therefore nowhere. Perhaps the first adventure novel is Daniel Defoe's *Robinson Crusoe* (1719), whose eponymous hero is marooned on a desert island where he endures and triumphantly surmounts decades of mental and physical trials. Yet Crusoe is the most unadventurous of men. That is, one of the earliest protagonists of adventure fiction resists the ethos of circumstance in which unwillingly he has been placed. During the 19th century, although the literature of adventure may have been marginalized critically, it flourished in popular culture in Europe and the United States, whether in Grimm's fairy tales, the French *romans noirs* of Eugène Sue, Frédéric Soulié, and Pinson du Terrail, or Edgar Allan Poe's short fiction and his novel *The Narrative of Arthur Gordon Pym of Nantucket* (1838), in which—following Samuel Taylor Coleridge—Antarctica becomes an adventure precinct. As the century proceeded, more serious players became engaged in the deployment and transformation of adventure fiction. Among them were such canonical authors as Joseph Conrad, Rudyard Kipling, Herman Melville, Mark Twain, and Robert Louis Stevenson.

Melville's early novel *Typee* (1846) purported to be the true story of how the author had fallen among "singular and interesting people" (cannibals) on an island in the South Pacific. Part of the iconoclastic burden of the book is its assault on the harm done by European missionaries in the Pacific. A further controversy is occasioned by the issue of whether this tale of exotic racial and cultural contact is fact or fiction. This question serves to illuminate the formal similarities between imperial romance and adventure fiction and 19th- and early 20th-century travel writing. Beguiling, dangerous encounters between European explorers and travelers and the native peoples of distant lands are the substance, for example, of Charles Doughty's *Travels in Arabia Deserta* (1888), Gertrude Bell's *The Desert and the Sown* (1907), and T.E. Lawrence's *The Seven Pillars of Wisdom* (1926), among many similar so-called true stories of hazardous exploration. In an important sense, adventure fiction is always travel literature, involving as it does a journey away from the physically, morally, and culturally familiar to unknown places whence return can never be guaranteed and where the danger endured will have been as much to mind as to body.

Imperial romance and travel books typically dramatize, at some vital moment in their narratives, the penetration of mysterious and alluring lands and of alien manners that are best known by intimidating but enticing rumor. The possession of such a strange, new world—whether in fact or as a grandiose delusion—has an evident sexual intimation that many of these works may be more fully aware of than they choose to disclose. In one of the most famous imperial romances, Haggard's *King Solomon's Mines* (1885), the object of the quest is multifaceted; this is a search for a lost brother, for the fabled diamond mines of the Biblical king, and for the satisfaction of curiosity. The quest is triggered by the discovery of a map. Here Haggard acknowledged his debt to Stevenson's seminal tale *Treasure Island* (1883), in which the passing of the map from the aging pirate Bill Bones to Jim Hawkins initiates the hunt for the buried treasure of the notorious pirate Captain Flint. Haggard's novel sparked other, literal quests. The year following its publication, several British parties set off into the interior of Africa to seek Solomon's mines. They misread the text. Although Haggard was not proffering an imperialist fantasy of plunder, he, too, was susceptible: a few years later he ventured to Mexico in search of the Aztec treasure that had been plundered, and then lost, by the Spaniards. This journey furnished his romance *Montezuma's Daughter* (1893).

Having made their fortunes in *King Solomon's Mines,* Quatermain, Captain Good, and Sir Henry Curtis abandon them willingly in the sequel, *Allan Quatermain* (1887), to undertake another quest the objects of which are altogether intangible. They seek adventure for itself, particularized as the satisfaction of their curiosity regarding the existence of a fabled lost city (the mysterious Zu-Vendis), again supposed to be somewhere in the capacious heart of Africa. They are in recoil from the jaded civilization of England. As Quatermain admits, "the thirst for the wilderness was on me; I could tolerate this place no more; I would go and die as I had lived, among the wild game and the savages." If this is an atavistic dream, it is not exactly fulfilled, for Quatermain dies among a lost *white* race, whose ruler Curtis becomes, guaranteeing to preserve its state of "comparative barbarism."

There is no palpable treasure at the end of this quest. The treasure, which is the object of desire in so much imperial romance fiction, is, after all, a complex and ambiguous thing. Indeed, the adventuring impulse may run contrary to, and even impede, the desire for gain. Quatermain pockets some of Solomon's diamonds as a canny afterthought. Dead stuff that has been accumulated in past ages, a treasure is not any simple means to redeem and secure the future for those who seek to win it. There is a strange, ineradicable, antimaterialistic streak in the ethic of some of the cardinal works of imperial adventure, whether Haggard's, or Kipling's *Kim* (1901), or the scientific romances of Wells and Verne.

Zweig contends that another crucial element of the adventure tale is that it is "anti-novelistic" because it celebrates risk and privileges deracination; its energies are profoundly antisocial, altogether averse to such temperate accommodations within the bourgeois social fabric as marriage, the substance of 19th-century realist fiction in Europe. Insofar as this is the case, the abiding critical unease with adventure fiction is better understood. Imperial romances have suffered not only from their central celebration of domestic irresponsibility, but they have also, unjustly, been subject to political-cum-literary prejudice about a system of power, late 19th-century imperialism, that the best of them endorse—if at all—with the most radical reservations. Nowhere is that system more consistently called to account than in the works of Kipling, Haggard, and Wells, for the two former, at least, have suffered from accusations of jingoism.

Unfashionable, too, is the emphasis of adventure fiction on story. Airport paperback schlock, or "page-turners," have done a great deal to discredit the force of adventure narrative, the stories in its hoard that are at once unique and exemplary, whether they tell of Odysseus or Beowulf, Lancelot or Don Quixote. Such accounts of heroic loneliness as those by Stevenson, Haggard, or Conan Doyle, however imbued with pride and folly, have indelibly marked Western reckoning of the value and costs of adventures for those driven to embark upon them. Staple elements of later adventure narrative, in particular of imperial romance, have a formulaic force. They speak of collective, rather than resolutely individual, quests. They tell of assembling and equipping the party for its journey to the unknown; the thrilling relation of the rites of passage, losses, and discoveries of its members; scrutiny of their personal transformations in the course of encounters with people other than themselves; and, fi-

nally, the imagining of their return to a prosaic world unwilling to credit, but credulous about, their tales of miracles.

Certain notable 19th-century examples of adventure fiction have been subjected to an ironic reinspection. Famously, R.M. Ballantyne's *The Coral Island* (1857) was revised for supposedly cynical modern sensibilities by William Golding in *Lord of the Flies* (1954). Yet it is questionable whether Ballantyne's Jack—going berserk, regressing, as he fights with cannibals—is less terrible than the incremental cruelties practiced by Golding's stranded party of British schoolchildren. Homage has been paid to Haggard's plot lines by the best-selling thriller writer Wilbur Smith, notably to *King Solomon's Mines,* in *The Leopard Hunts in Darkness* (1981). In *Miss Smilla's Feeling for Snow* (1993), set in Greenland, a hitherto unexplored romance frontier, Peter Hoeg treats a modern treasure hunt with ambivalence and moral complexity. The medium of cinema has been adept at the parodic translation, whether intentional or not, of thousands of old and new adventure stories to the screen.

The adventure genre is the staple of many Hollywood studios and of many actors' careers. Imperial romance is the business of George Lucas' "Star Wars" trilogy. Johann David Wyss' *The Swiss Family Robinson* (1812–13) was the basis of a television series of adventures in outer space. Much before that series, Wyss' novel of a marooned family who effortlessly cope with adversity (and so advertise national virtues) had been reprovingly revised by Captain Frederick Marryat in *Masterman Ready* (1841–42), in which work is the watchword of survival.

Few of the film adaptations of adventure literature entertain the iconoclasm that so regularly marks out imperial romance, especially during that hectically creative time at the turn of the century in Britain, when Wells, Conrad, Kipling, Haggard, and a host of imitators and less imaginatively daring writers flourished. Nor, despite publicists' earnest endeavors, has cinema sent so many archetypal figures into the Western imagination as the novel of adventure. That imaginary loom of adventure includes Victor Hugo's Quasimodo and the Hunchback of Notre Dame, Alexandre Dumas' D'Artagnan and the Man in the Iron Mask, Mary Shelley's Dr. Frankenstein and his monster, Robert Louis Stevenson's Jekyll and Hyde, Long John Silver and Blind Pew, Herman Melville's Ahab and indeed the White Whale, Mark Twain's Huckleberry Finn, Haggard's She (of the 1887 novel of that name and its three sequels), Kipling's Kim, Wells' Time Traveler, Sir Arthur Conan Doyle's Sherlock Holmes, Baroness Orczy's Scarlet Pimpernel (a hero whose existence is now almost wholly metaphorical, scarcely connected to his fictional context of reactionary politics during the French Revolution), Bram Stoker's Dracula (and the whole subliterature of vampire sequels that that novel spawned), and Joseph Conrad's Nostromo and Lord Jim (the first a meretricious hero, the second a man immobilized by his heroic dreams).

In the main these monomaniacal, courageous protagonists of adventure fiction are essentially uncomplicated. Freed from the trammels of social obligation, they are shorn willfully and willingly of domestic attachments. Enamored of a heroic idea of the self, they are secretive yet narcissistic, capable of violent and precipitate action, although frequently paralyzed by its prospect. To lump them together as adventurers, or heroes, is to miss the anguish and self-doubt of the main characters of adventure fiction, especially in its manifestation as imperial romance. By extension, it is to overlook the ambivalence at the heart of the enterprise of

European imperialism. Exotic settings—whether in the Pacific Islands of Melville's novels, in Louis Becke's *By Reef and Palm* (1894), in the Africa over-frequented by literary travelers, or in South American "countries" such as Conrad's Costaguana in *Nostromo* (1904)—provide a sharp means of dissection of European manners, morals, and imperialist presumptions. The comparisons with their own societies that venturers felt compelled to make did not always tell against the "savage" races with which they came in contact. Ever afterward, a moral relativism began to infect such comparisons: they became the basis of chastening knowledge of oneself and one's culture rather than a facile means for the assertion of superiority. Above all, novels of adventure seek to be exciting. They allow and solicit readers' indulgence, at second hand, in terrifying journeys and mortal dangers. Yet the escapes that this literature encourages—in the hands of its most serious practitioners—are always conditional. Adventure fiction, especially imperial romance, has always been as much in earnest as in game.

PETER PIERCE

See also Joseph Conrad; James Fenimore Cooper; Daniel Defoe; Alexandre Dumas (père); Gulliver's Travels; His-torical Novel; Kim; Herman Melville; Postcolonial Narrative and Criticism of the Novel; Romance; Sir Walter Scott; Robert Louis Stevenson; War Novel

Further Reading

Clarke, I.F., *Voices Prophesying War, 1763–1984,* London and New York: Oxford University Press, 1966

Green, Martin, *Dreams of Adventure, Deeds of Empire,* New York: Basic Books, 1979; London: Routledge and Kegan Paul, 1980

McClure, John A., *Late Imperial Romance,* London and New York: Verso, 1994

Sandison, Alan, *The Wheel of Empire: A Study of the Imperial Idea in Some Late Nineteenth and Early Twentieth-Century Fiction,* London: Macmillan, and New York: St. Martin's Press, 1967

Street, Brian V., *The Savage in Literature: Representations of "Primitive" Society in English Fiction, 1858–1920,* London and Boston: Routledge and Kegan Paul, 1975

Zweig, Paul, *The Adventurer,* London: Dent, and New York: Basic Books, 1974

The Adventures of Huckleberry Finn by Mark Twain

1884

According to Twain's definition of a classic as a book that everybody praises and nobody talks about, *The Adventures of Huckleberry Finn* hardly qualifies for classic status, since it is a book everybody talks about and almost nobody praises, unless they do so with serious reservations. In an essay that articulates a widespread contemporary attitude toward Twain's masterpiece, Greil Marcus (1997) argues that while *Huckleberry Finn* "may be the carrier of our national soul, it is also the carrier of our national poison: the word 'nigger.'" This last part is unarguable; passages that portray the runaway slave Jim as childlike and that depict his constant humiliation, especially at the hands of the two boys he calls friends, are impossible to read without cringing. The question of the masterpiece's flaw is settled, then. What remains is to consider the extent to which it is a masterpiece—in other words, how well does Twain's novel function as "the carrier of our national soul"?

There is no denying that *Huckleberry Finn* is Twain's greatest success as a writer. By 1885, the year of its publication, Twain had written an undisputed classic of children's literature, *The Adventures of Tom Sawyer* (1876), a nostalgic tale of boyish adventure in a town much like the Hannibal, Missouri, where Twain had grown up. But most of his books were thinly veiled accounts of his travels: *The Innocents Abroad* (1869), which deals with the Mediterranean and the Holy Land; *Roughing It* (1872), an account of his time in the American West; *A Tramp Abroad* (1880), which focuses on a walking tour through Germany and Switzerland; and *Life on the Mississippi* (1883), a recreation of Twain's days as a riverboat pilot. If the so-called "matter of Hannibal" fueled Twain's best writing, the travel narrative attracted him in a way that the more static material did not. Twain's genius was to combine in *Huckleberry Finn* the stuff of childhood memories with the story of a boy and a man on a sometimes frightening, sometimes idyllic voyage down the Mississippi River. Moreover, he added a third and completely new element that propelled his new book beyond the limitations of children's literature and humor: a moral dimension that peaks in Huck's decision to let Jim go free and his famous statement, uttered as he realizes that he is defying the white, Christian, slave-holding morality of his day, "'All right, then, I'll *go* to hell.'"

Huckleberry Finn was a radical novel when published, one in which Twain attacked everything America held dear—family, religion, politics, money—through the person of an illiterate 12-year-old. Immediately, the novel was attacked because of the character of Huck, who was seen as a poor example for America's children. A typical notice appeared in the 2 March issue of the *New York World*, where it is noted that only Twain's established reputation as a humorist saves "this cheap and pernicious stuff" from complete condemnation. The story, the notice continued, is one of "a wretchedly low, vulgar, sneaking and lying

Southern country boy" who, in the company of "a runaway negro" and a pair of "impostors" (the King and the Duke), practices an "irreverence which makes parents, guardians and people who are at all good and proper ridiculous." Victor Fischer (1983) observes that negative reviews of *Huckleberry Finn* were consistent in criticizing Twain for making light of lying in a book seemingly written for children and that this was the reason given for banning the novel from a number of libraries well into the early 20th century.

In the last half of the century, of course, *Huckleberry Finn* is regularly the subject of calls for removal from classrooms and libraries, not because of its endorsement of Huck's mischief, but for its racist portrayal of Jim. Ironically, as Shelley Fisher Fishkin (1993, 1996) and others have pointed out, Twain drew on African-American source materials in composing the novel, although, to the reviewers of Twain's day, who were preoccupied with Huck, Jim seems like a forerunner of Ralph Ellison's *Invisible Man* (1952). Now, of course, it is impossible to overlook the condescension of the final chapters, in which Tom Sawyer reappears to re-enslave Jim while the morally reborn Huck reverts to his old status as Tom's passive sidekick, and Twain's epic turns into a farce. The objectionable final chapters of the novel have led scholars such as Guy Cardwell (1991) to say that Twain must now be viewed as a representative American figure rather than a heroic one, a writer who, if he "helped to make America's culture . . . was also its prisoner."

In answer to Hemingway's citation of *Huckleberry Finn* as the source for all subsequent American literature, novelist Jane Smiley (1996) has said it would have been better had that source been Harriet Beecher Stowe's *Uncle Tom's Cabin* (1852), with its "thoughtful, autonomous, and passionate black characters," which prompted Roy Blount Jr.'s response that this is like saying it would be better for people to come from heaven than from sex. There have been various retellings of the story of Huck and Jim, including John Seelye's *The True Adventures of Huckleberry Finn* (1970) and Greg Matthews' *The Further Adventures of Huckleberry Finn* (1983), although, as African-American author David Bradley points out, no one has been able to write a better ending to Twain's novel or, for that matter, to the story of blacks and whites together in America.

DAVID KIRBY

See also Mark Twain

Further Reading

Budd, Louis, "The Recomposition of *Adventures of Huckleberry Finn,*" *Missouri Review* 10 (1987)

Cardwell, Guy, *The Man Who Was Mark Twain: Images and Ideologies,* New Haven, Connecticut: Yale University Press, 1991

Fiedler, Leslie, *Love and Death in the American Novel,* New York: Criterion, 1960; 3rd edition, London: Penguin, 1982

Fischer, Victor, "Huck Finn Reviewed: The Reception of *Huckleberry Finn* in the United States, 1885–1897," *American Literary Realism* 16 (1983)

Fishkin, Shelley Fisher, *Was Huck Black? Mark Twain and African-American Voices,* Oxford and New York: Oxford University Press, 1993

Fishkin, Shelley Fisher, editor, *Lighting Out for the Territory: Reflections on Mark Twain and American Culture,* New York: Oxford University Press, 1996

Marcus, Greil, "The Real Thing," *Los Angeles Times Book Review* (26 January 1997)

Smiley, Jane, "Say It Ain't So, Huck: Second Thoughts on Mark Twain's 'Masterpiece'," *Harper's Magazine* 292 (1996)

The Adventures of Pinocchio by Carlo Collodi

Le Avventure di Pinocchio 1883

The Adventures of Pinocchio by Carlo Collodi (the pen name of Carlo Lorenzini) has elicited at least three kinds of response. First, as a children's novel it has been praised for its moral instruction and its psychological realism. Second, it has been dissected as a political or psychological allegory. Finally, it has been treated as the subject for illustrations, translations, and adaptations. Collodi's early publications included several school texts, and his interest in education continues to be unmistakable in *Pinocchio*. The moralism is, however, served up with humor and deft character development, so that while children respond to the humor and suspense, adults are attracted to the text's ethical and psychological values. *The Bookman* reviewer (1892) favored the "straightforward and aboveboard character of the morals" in the novel, while *The New York Times Book Review* (1909) recommended it as "a guide to self-control, self-government, and self-determination in children."

Although the novel includes an element of fantasy, Collodi's puppet has adventures that come from the quality of his character rather than from arbitrary invention. As a real child might be, Pinocchio is hungry or sad, happy or inquisitive. He sells his schoolbook, plays hooky, and is deceived by the Fox and the Cat, or led astray by his friend Lampwick. No magic occurs, but Pinocchio's ungoverned impulses produce the inevitable consequences. With each temptation and each disaster the puppet learns the lessons of cause and effect in the adult world. In the introduction to Walter S. Cramp's translation (1937), Carl Van Doren argues that the novel, like childhood itself, is "taken up with the work of cutting nature to society."

Pinocchio was an immediate success, perhaps with children, but certainly with adults who buy books for children. Yet in view of the range of Collodi's interests—as a soldier, revolutionary, theatre critic, and journalist—it is perhaps not surprising that the book includes a complex web of metaphor and allusion to then-present social and emotional issues. Several critics have noted the antiauthoritarian tone and working-class ethic of the novel. M.L. Rosenthal (1989) parallels Pinocchio's career with that of Julien Sorel in Stendhal's *Le Rouge et le noir* (1830; *The Red and the Black*). Rosenthal stresses Collodi's frequently brutal contrast between wealth and poverty, noting both the hardships of the poor and the callous indifference of the rich, with particular reference to Pinocchio's reaction to the citizens of *Acchiappa-citrulli* ("Foolville"). Rosenthal also sees Collodi's distaste for the hypocrisy of the judicial system as exemplified when Pinocchio is jailed for being robbed. In these and other episodes, Rosenthal finds "anger against the arbitrary and unfair order of the world," a theme directed to "an elemental and sophisticated adult audience."

The psychological studies of *Pinocchio* include Freudian analysis of the puppet's nose and a Jungian approach to "shadow" figures such as Lampwick. Lois Rostow Kuznets (1994) sees Pinocchio as a boy in the "stage of industry," as described by Erik Erikson in *Childhood and Society* (1950). Kuznets examines Pinocchio's misadventures as part of the experience through which a boy learns self-control and mastery of the tools of adult society. Describing him as one of Leslie Fiedler's "good bad boys," Kuznets sees Pinocchio as a child whose struggles to mature demonstrate "moral and ethical implications."

The third area of *Pinocchio*'s critical reception, and one that raises the question of a relation between the novel and other art forms, is that of illustration, translation, and adaptation. If, as Percy Lubbock suggests, an essential element of a novel is the reader's memory of it, then *Pinocchio* has been created as much by its adaptations as by Collodi himself.

In the 20th century, at least, one element that distinguishes children's literature from adult fare is the presence of illustrations. These visual forms both represent and interpret the characters, setting, and action of a story. The illustrations of *Pinocchio*, which fall into two general groups, have had a significant impact on the interpretation of the work. The drawings of Eugenio Mazzanti (1883) and Attillio Mussino (1911) reflect an angular European style of drawing, while Walt Disney's animated film (1940) and illustrated book (1939–40) show the softer, rounded figures that appeal to American taste.

This difference in illustration style extends also to the values and selections of translations and adaptations. Richard Wunderlich (1988) points out that many versions differ in length from the original by 50 or 60 pages, as they elaborate some episodes and shorten or eliminate others. This narrative manipulation is especially apparent in the film adaptations. The Disney film, directed by Ben Sharpsteen, minimizes the harsh poverty and the often irascible impulses of the puppet. Instead, as Wunderlich points out, Disney's puppet is a "happy toddler" who shows a "wide-eyed awe toward and joy about everything around him." In the film the puppet's troubles come not from an ungovernable temper but from a dangerously naive trust and affection.

Through visual images the Disney version also posits a Christian allegory that, although implied in the novel, is deeply submerged. The visual motifs of sacrifice, death, and resurrection in the film borrow directly from the iconography of medieval and Renaissance religious painting. Further, the connection between the Blue Fairy and the Italian representations of Maria Stella Maris, hinted at in the novel, is explicit in the film. Martha Bacon's analysis of the Blue Fairy as a religious figure seems to rely as much on Disney's drawings as on the descriptions of the character in the novel (see Bacon, 1970).

Although likely to be far less influential than the Disney animated feature, a live-action film, *The Adventures of Pinocchio*, was produced in 1996 in cooperation with the Jim Henson Creature Shop and directed by Steve Barron, featuring Martin Landau and Jonathan Taylor Thomas. By using live-action and computer-generated effects, Barron departs from the visual style of the Disney adaptation and adds several characters and a romantic interest for Gepetto. Yet the selection of episodes is very similar, and, like the earlier version, this film uses religious imagery to represent emotional growth and moral instruction.

The Italian philosopher Benedetto Croce remarked that the "wood out of which Pinocchio is carved is humanity itself." The variety of analysis, interpretation, and adaptation surrounding the novel would seem to support that view, as *Pinocchio* shows different faces to each succeeding generation of readers.

JANET P. SHOLTY

Further Reading

Bacon, Martha, "Puppet's Progress," *The Atlantic Monthly* 225:4 (April 1970)

Kuznets, Lois Rostow, *When Toys Come Alive: Narratives of Animation, Metamorphosis, and Development,* New Haven, Connecticut: Yale University Press, 1994

Rosenthal, M.L., "The Hidden *Pinocchio*: A Tale of a Subversive Puppet," in *Literature and Revolution,* edited by David Bevin, Amsterdam and Atlanta, Georgia: Rodopi, 1989

Street, Douglas, "*Pinocchio*—From Picaro to Pipsqueak," in *Children's Novels and the Movies,* edited by Douglas Street, New York: Ungar, 1983

Van Doren, Carl, introduction to *The Adventures of a Marionette,* New York: Heritage Press, 1937

Wunderlich, Richard, *The Pinocchio Catalogue: Being a Descriptive Bibliography and Printing History of English Language Translations and Other Renditions Appearing in the United States, 1892–1987,* New York: Greenwood Press, 1988; London: Greenwood Press, 1989

African-American Novel

The African-American novel, like its European-American counterpart, mirrors sociohistoric and political influences present at various moments in United States history. But because of the persistence of racism, blacks have been excluded from full participation in the social mainstream, and thus their experience is unique. Life in Africa, the middle passage, slavery, Emancipation, the urban migration, integration, and the Black Power movement of the 1960s are more than just discrete periods in time. They are major points of reference for the black experience—as for novels by blacks—and show how that experience is at the same time part of, yet distinct from, that of the larger society.

African-Americans participate in two societies, not one, and this simultaneous partnership in two separate but related worlds, or what W.E.B. DuBois refers to in *Souls of Black Folk* (1903) as double-consciousness, sets black reality and the novel tradition emerging from it apart from that of European-Americans. It is out of the sense of doubleness that novelists write, adopting an intensely ironic perspective on life in an America polarized along race, class, and gender lines. Therefore, instead of validating aspects of the American mythos, the black novelist tends not only to challenge those myths but to present a portrait of a society that offers freedom, selfhood, and dignity to a once oppressed people. Deploying the novel in the cause of sociopolitical change, black writers present a portrait of an alternate world reconfigured along new, socially just lines. The African-American novel reveals the particular realities confronting blacks in America and sheds light on the elusive quest for freedom, literacy, and a sense of self in a peculiarly American promised land.

As a hybrid narrative form, the African-American novel derives its force from distinctly black oral modes of expression as well as from Western literary genres. Indeed, when black novelists draw on texts in the Western tradition they do so, as Henry Louis Gates aptly demonstrates (1988), with a difference—a signifying black difference stemming from the vernacular tradition. An attempt to situate the emergence of the African-American novel within its proper sociocultural context requires us to consider aspects of oral tradition—religion, speech, and music—and abolitionist oratory, the slave narrative, and the Bible. These rhetorical modes have had a profound influence on the African-American novel tradition in terms of theme, style, and character.

Williams Wells Brown is considered the first African-American novelist. His *Clotel; or, The President's Daughter, a Narrative of Slave Life in the United States* (1853), first published in London, is principally about the fate of an African-American female slave, Clotel, whom Brown describes as the daughter of Thomas Jefferson. Clotel's mother, Currer, was a servant of Jefferson's before his departure to Washington, when Currer was passed on to another master. In the context of the narrative, Currer's daughters, Clotel and Althesa, are Jefferson's offspring. The young girls fall victim to the lust of Richmond's white men, who view mulatto females as a select choice for concubinage. After giving birth to a daughter, Clotel is sold down South, where she is subjected to the lechery of white men and the jealousy of their wives. Clotel escapes from slavery by disguising herself as a white man and returns to Richmond in search of her daughter, but she is caught. Rather than return to slavery, Clotel commits suicide by jumping into the Potomac River.

Clotel is a highly melodramatic novel that is heavily influenced by the tradition of the slave narrative. Its structure is episodic, and its subject matter is grounded in firsthand fugitive slave accounts. Brown quotes the Declaration of Independence and Jefferson's antislavery speeches in an attempt to point out the disparity between America's Christian ideals and the hypocrisy of public officials such as Jefferson. White ministers who pervert the gospel are objects of the novel's pointed social criticism as well. The novel suggests that slavery erodes the moral fabric of the entire nation.

Brown thus uses popular literary conventions of the antebellum era to expose the evil of slavery and appeal to a predominantly white audience. The use of the tragic mulatto as heroine, the dependence upon such texts as the Bible and the Declaration of Independence, and the adoption of the conventions of the slave narrative are key elements that later novelists would explore more fully.

Harriet Wilson was the first African-American to publish a novel in the United States rather than in England. *Our Nig; or, Sketches from the Life of a Free Black* (1859) is an autobiographical novel based on Wilson's life as an indentured servant in New England. The work synthesizes the sentimental novel with the slave narrative in an examination of the life of Frado, a mulatto who is indentured to a white Massachusetts family following the death of her black father and white mother. Frado finds that her status as an indentured servant is little better than that of a slave. She is subjected to beatings at the hands of Mrs. Bellmont and faces isolation because of her mixed race. Frado marries a fugitive slave who deserts her during pregnancy. After indenture, Frado, who becomes an invalid, finds herself in the foster care of a woman who introduces her to needlework and books. The heroine's evolving sense of self parallels her growing literacy and creativity.

The 12-chapter narrative chronicles Frado's movement from exploitation to self-reliance. Instead of focusing on male desertion, as is the case with many 19th-century women's novels, *Our Nig*'s emphasis is on race and class relations. Frado's story is not about the attempt to hold on to virtue in the face of moral assault but about race and class oppression actively supported by middle-class white women. Frado asserts herself despite this oppression, and, as with the slave narrative, her quest for literacy is symbolic of her struggle for liberation.

Martin Delany's *Blake; or, The Huts of America: A Tale of the Mississippi Valley, the Southern United States and Cuba* (1859) is the story of Corolus Henrich Blacus, alias Henry Blake, a black Cuban revolutionary and a fugitive slave who helps to organize slaves in Cuba and the southern United States in the attempt to overthrow white rule. The son of a wealthy black Cuban tobacco manufacturer, Blake runs away from home at the age of 17, serves as an apprentice on a slave ship, is sold to Colonel Franks, marries Franks' mulatto daughter, and fathers a son. The first part of the novel traces Blake's search for his wife and his work organizing slaves in the American South. The second part focuses on the nature of slavery in Cuba during the 1840s. The Bible is a distinct presence in *Blake,* and biblical passages introduce each of the two major sections of the novel, foreshadowing the protagonist's messianic role. At the same time, the novel points out that white Christianity is a tool of the oppressor used to keep blacks in place with the argument that freedom will occur in the next life.

Delany endows his protagonist with a profound awareness of the function of cultural, economic, and political power in bringing about sociopolitical change. The Cuban section of the novel indicates Delany's concern with international liberation. Slavery, the reader learns, is as brutal in Cuba as it is in the American South. But unlike enslaved African-Americans, Afro-Cubans are ready to rebel against Spain and the United States. Blake and Placido, director of the civil government, are the principal leaders in a successful revolt. The realization of black nationalism occasions an era of peace and prosperity, a kind of golden age reminiscent of life in precolonial Africa.

Blake is the most radical black novel of the 19th century. Delany's use of a pure black as protagonist signals a departure from the tragic mulatto theme. With its suggestion of the revolutionary potential of oppressed blacks in overthrowing white rule, the novel foreshadows much of the fiction of the 1960s and 1970s.

Frances Harper's *Iola Leroy; or, Shadows Uplifted* (1892) develops the story of a brother and sister—both mulattoes—who reject the urge to pass for white and dedicate themselves instead to racial uplift. During the Civil War, the heroine Iola serves as a nurse in a field hospital. Her brother Harry enlists in a black regiment. After the war ends, both of them become active in assisting the freedmen. Robert Johnson, Iola and Harry's uncle, serves as a lieutenant in a black company and works on behalf of the temperance movement.

The novel reflects Harper's deep involvement in the abolitionist, women's rights, and temperance movements. Social reform is the primary aim among the novel's mixed race characters. Thus, after a series of marriages, Iola rejects a white suitor in order to marry a mulatto doctor who has dedicated himself to the race cause. Harry eventually weds a black woman who founds a school for freedmen. With its antislavery emphasis, *Iola Leroy* continues the pattern of the abolitionist novel but offers a more complex rendering of mulattoes, the black family, and the role of blacks in furthering the race cause.

Set in the postbellum South, Sutton Griggs' *Imperium in Imperio* (1899) is a comparative account of the lives of a black and a mulatto boy. Belton Piedmont, the black protagonist, rises above discrimination, racial prejudice, and abject poverty to become president of a black college. He is able to achieve his goals largely through industry, scholarship, and the support of a white benefactor. By contrast, Bernard Belgrave's light complexion and family influence are responsible for his rise to the position of Virginia legislator and Supreme Court lawyer. Because Belton subordinates race consciousness to patriotism, he is destined for martyrdom, while Bernard's vanity, bitterness toward whites, and separatist ideals lead him to a revolutionary alliance with foreign powers.

Griggs stresses the need for a black political organization, and the last part of the novel outlines the formation of an exclusively black secret nation. Belton recruits Bernard into the nation, but the two move through its ranks by different paths. Bernard endorses a plan involving open revolt against racial oppression. Belton's repudiation of this plan, however, is more in tune with the author's more moderate solution to the race problem. With its nationalist thrust, *Imperium in Imperio*, like Delany's *Blake,* is a radical novel that glorifies black character and challenges the myth of white supremacy. The novel represents another step toward social realism, even as it extends the boundaries of melodrama and romance.

Charles Waddell Chesnutt has the distinction of being the first major African-American fiction writer. His second novel, *The Marrow of Tradition* (1901), is a historical work based on the lynchings that occurred during the 1898 elections in Wilmington, North Carolina. At the center of the novel is the conflict between the reactionary white aristocratic Carterets and the liberalism of the mulatto Millers. That conflict is made even more dramatic by the revelation that Janet Miller and Olivia Carteret are half-sisters. Sam Merkel, their white father, had an affair with Julia, who is black, and bequeaths a portion of his estate to Julia and her daughter Janet. When Olivia learns of her father's will, she destroys it, thereby depriving Janet of her rightful inheritance.

The family scenario involving the Millers and Carterets dramatizes the blood and cultural ties uniting the races. Chesnutt intends Janet Miller to symbolize the black middle-class, wrongfully deprived of its place in the larger society. Despite opposition, however, Janet and her husband William rise to prominence in Wellington (Chesnutt's fictional name for Wilmington). William Miller, a medical doctor, is the epitome of black middle-class success; he is cultured, well educated, and refined. Miller establishes a hospital and training center for black nurses. In a series of confrontations between the two families, their children's lives hang in the balance. Major Carteret writes a series of race-baiting editorials in the *Morning Chronicle,* the local paper, and a race riot ensues. The Millers lose their only child. Forgoing vengeance, Janet Miller nevertheless persuades her husband to save the life of the Carterets' only child. Although the novel closes with the fate of the Carteret child unresolved, Chesnutt's message is clear: love, forgiveness, and acceptance are the pathways to harmony in the New South. As long as individuals persist in nursing grievances about past racial injustices, the future will be characterized by the kind of racial violence erupting in Wellington. With his use of black oral tradition, his treatment of the color line, his unmasking of racial prejudice, and his exploration of the influence of color and caste on black character, Chesnutt further moves the African-American novel toward social realism.

James Weldon Johnson's *The Autobiography of an Ex-Colored Man* (1912) chronicles the experiences of an anonymous protagonist as he discovers his blackness and later decides to "pass" as white. The protagonist and narrator is a musician and composer, the son of a black woman and a rich white father. He is well read, has good manners, and is cultured. Reared by his mother, who withholds the truth of his race from him, the narrator finds that his moment of racial awareness is traumatic. After witnessing a lynching in the rural South, he chooses to pass for white. He would rather deny his racial identity than experience the hardships associated with being black in America. Although the narrator achieves a measure of social success, his self-respect is compromised by the fact that he is afraid to live as a black man. The narrator's decision to "pass" constitutes a moral failure on his part. Because the novel was published anonymously, readers and critics suspected that the work might in some ways be autobiographical. The novel was a major achievement that furthered the groundwork Chesnutt and others had laid and heralded Johnson's championship of such black cultural forms as ragtime, the sermon, and spirituals.

Recognized widely as the major literary achievement of the Harlem Renaissance, Jean Toomer's *Cane* (1923) emerged from the author's experiences as the temporary head of a Georgia industrial and agricultural school for blacks. The work is a montage comprised of 15 poems, six prose vignettes, seven stories, and a play—all about black life in the 1920s. *Cane* is divided into three parts, the first and third set in rural Georgia, the narratives of the second part set in Chicago and Washington, D.C. Recurring image-symbols of sawdust, smoke, pine, cane, ripeness and fertility, and singing unify the work. The novel's dominant theme, the importance of the soil in the lives of African-Americans, further reinforces this unity. Through story and song, prose and poetry, Toomer recuperated black cultural forms at a time when African-Americans were torn between maintaining fidelity to their folk past and moving toward assimilation into the American mainstream. Linguistically, thematically, and formally, Toomer's novel is as experimental as the work of such modernist writers as T.S. Eliot, Ernest Hemingway, Gertrude Stein, and Ezra Pound. *Cane* thus represents an important moment in the African-American novel in its move beyond realism to animate novelists in ways that would become increasingly important throughout the 20th century.

Nella Larsen's *Quicksand* (1928) deals with the experiences of Helga Crane, a mulatto in her 20s, half Danish, half black, who is light enough to pass for white. Helga is poised, cultured, and refined—a member of DuBois' talented tenth. The novel's title is richly suggestive of the various agents that entrap the beautiful heroine. "Quicksand" refers to Helga's inner turmoil—her sense of doubleness—as well as society's failure to accommodate itself to her complex identity. Because Helga is unable to fit in anywhere, she is doomed to frustration. Perhaps more than any earlier novelist dealing with the theme of the tragic mulatto, Larsen explores fully the psychological struggles of the heroine, her literal and metaphoric journey through various segments of American and European societies. Ultimately, Helga's failure to find acceptance is a commentary on American race and gender politics.

Zora Neale Hurston's *Their Eyes Were Watching God* (1937), set in rural Florida during the 1920s, deals with the search for fulfillment on the part of its mixed-race heroine, Janie Crawford. Regarded as a forgotten classic of the Harlem Renaissance, *Their Eyes Were Watching God* marks a departure from earlier novels dealing with the mulatto theme. Although the heroine experiences a series of trials owing to her mixed-race heritage, she is able to find a sense of fulfillment among the folk. Contentment is to be found, the novel implies, not by moving up the socioeconomic ladder in pursuit of material success, but by moving down toward the essence of self. The closer Janie moves toward the folk and their rich culture, the more satisfied she becomes. With its affirmation of black culture and its fidelity to the vernacular tradition—incorporating aspects of religion, speech, and music—the novel is grounded in a black aesthetic.

The publication of Richard Wright's *Native Son* (1940) constituted a watershed in the tradition of the African-American novel, signaling the triumph of naturalism as novelists began to turn their attention to the myriad ways in which the harsh urban environment stifles black achievement. The novel's protagonist, Bigger Thomas, along with his mother, his younger sister Vera, and his brother Buddy, are displaced southerners residing in a one-room tenement on Chicago's south side. Bigger, who is about 20 years old, is frustrated by the lack of opportunities available to young blacks, especially men. The novel's tripartite structure—"Fear," "Flight," and "Fate"—reveals the psychosocial influences prompting Bigger to commit murder. He is motivated by an intense fear of those around him, and that fear erupts into the murder of Mary, the daughter of a wealthy philanthropist who has taken Bigger into his employ. Wright suggests that the urban black community is powerless to change its situation, being too passive and fragmented.

In "Fate," Bigger's communist attorney Boris Max makes clear that America is responsible for Bigger's crimes. Bigger is a type or symbol, and there are countless others—black and white—like him. Max's polemical, melodramatic courtroom address is aimed at conveying one major theme: Bigger is the product of American society, and if the nation does not accept responsibility for Bigger's existence, then there will be widespread violence resulting in America's day of doom. Even though Max's protestations to the white judge and jury who wish to execute Bigger fall on deaf ears, Wright's message regarding violence as a means to creative selfhood for the oppressed was a powerful counterbalance to the myth of the American dream.

Ralph Ellison's *Invisible Man* (1952) is a novel that tells of the experiences of a nameless, anonymous protagonist—a kind of picaresque hero—who assumes a number of different roles as he journeys through various segments of modern America. Ellison directs attention to the ways in which life in fast-paced, industrialized, technological America fosters invisibility. In the first segment of the novel, narrative action is set in the rural South. The narrator is first a high school student, then a college student at a black industrial school. In the novel's second segment, which is set in the urban North, he is a factory worker and then a spokesperson for the Brotherhood, a group whose anticapitalist ideology recalls that of the Communist Party. In all of these roles, the protagonist is exploited, duped, antagonized, and kept running in futile pursuit of acceptance until he finally acknowledges his racial identity. After donning a hat and glasses and being mistaken for Rinehart, a Harlem confidence man, the protagonist encounters Ras the Exhorter, a comic portrait of Marcus Garvey. A race riot erupts in Harlem as a result of the actions of various political groups vying for dominance among the dispossessed masses. In an effort to escape Ras the Exhorter, who becomes Ras the Destroyer, the narrator retreats to an underground coal cellar where he recounts his story and insists that one day he will reenter society.

Instead of focusing attention on the environmental elements in the urban North that hinder black achievement, Ellison emphasizes the bicultural heritage of African-Americans. He is indebted not only to literary genres in the Western tradition but to black oral modes as well. In the creation of the narrator's grandfather, for instance, a wise ex-slave adept at manipulating whites, Ellison owes as much to the trickster tradition of which Herman Melville's confidence man is a part as to black folklore. Much of the novel's action involves the protagonist's attempt to reconcile his American self and his black identity. With his representation of black life in all its rich complexity, Ellison helped to move the novel away from the naturalistic mode that Wright popularized and toward a celebration of myth, ritual, and legend.

James Baldwin's *Go Tell It on the Mountain* (1953) explores the complex family relations surrounding the youngster John

Grimes, whom everyone expects to become saved and enter the ministry. Narrative action is set for the most part in 1920s Harlem, where John lives with his mother Elizabeth, stepfather Gabriel, younger brother Roy, and younger sisters Sarah and Ruth. John's passage into manhood is complicated as a result of his stepfather's tyrannical rule, his perceived unattractiveness, and his uncertain sexual identity. The youth is torn between pursuing his secular goals—which include becoming a writer—and joining the church.

A major theme in this highly autobiographical novel is the influence of history—personal and collective—on individual action. The novel's tripartite structure suggests this concern. Parts One and Three are narrated from John Grimes' point of view, while Florence, Gabriel, and Elizabeth Grimes function as narrators in the second part. Their narratives, thinly disguised as "prayers," tell of the journey north during the Great Migration. Each has come north in search of fulfillment, only to find a greater set of limitations. For each, the urban promised land is a hell of deferred dreams. Their main emotional outlet is the church, and this is the central irony Baldwin explores: although the church offers shelter in the urban storm, it reinforces the characters' sense of alienation. Baldwin was a Pentecostal preacher, and his novel is heavily influenced by the Bible and the rituals of the holiness church. Eschewing the protest tradition, he creates a variety of complex characters and allows them to tell their own stories. Ultimately, the novel tells of the power of the oppressed to transcend life's difficulties, if not through a belief in God then by finding an alternative means to fulfillment.

In the second half of the 20th century, the African-American novel has received enormous impetus from women writers, notably Alice Walker and Toni Morrison. Walker's *The Color Purple* (1982) is an epistolary novel revealing the author's attempt to rescue the long-suppressed voices of women from silence and oblivion. The novel also celebrates the black vernacular and oral tradition with a first-person narrator who tells her story in her own words. With her frank examination of taboo topics such as sexual abuse and lesbianism, her exploration of secular humanism as an alternative to orthodox Christianity, and her experimental use of language, Walker expands the possibilities of black feminism in the African-American novel.

Toni Morrison's *Beloved* (1987) focuses on the experience of Sethe, an ex-slave from Sweet Home Plantation in Kentucky, who, along with her four children, Howard, Buglar, Beloved, and Denver, escape to Cincinnati, Ohio, in search of freedom. Morrison's use of multiple narrative perspectives and numerous flashbacks results in a narrative reflecting the importance of memory. She tries to give voice to the "Sixty Million and More" who died during the slave trade and whose stories are missing from extant historical accounts. Much of the slavery experience is preserved through oral tradition, present in *Beloved* in stories, songs, and sermons that suggest the persistence of black oral forms among ex-slaves. *Beloved,* a neo-slave narrative, reflects Morrison's concern with the past. Its creative use of language, its dependence upon the supernatural, and its reliance on history and memory are a culmination of the blend of history and romance in the African-American novel tradition.

In its rendering of life in a society divided because of racism, sexism, and classism, the African-American novel is thus not a closed system. Rather, it mirrors America's changing sociopolitical realities even as it seeks to reconfigure those realities along more equitable lines. Novelists read and revise one another, thereby establishing a close intertextual relationship among works; but the issues that novelists explore and the narrative strategies they employ reflect the attempt to create an authentic fictional voice. Trends in the development of the novel tradition in its 20th-century manifestation suggest the willingness on the part of African-American novelists to experiment with a range of styles, techniques, and forms. As already suggested, novelists since the 1940s have moved beyond the naturalism of *Native Son,* which, while representing vividly race relations in the turbulent postwar era, fails to capture the black experience in all its diversity. Many African-American novelists have abandoned a treatment of themes involving the individual struggling against society, environment, or the forces of nature and have turned their attention to an exploration of the complex bicultural identity that is the heritage of African-Americans. In this pursuit, novelists have relied increasingly on myth, fable, and legend. Characters, narrative strategies, and themes hark back to the past—to slavery and life in ancient Africa. Toni Morrison attempts to transcend a chaotic America and recover a mythic realm existing outside the context of Western linear history. Whether the journey through time is a literal one, as is the case with Solomon the Flying African in *Song of Solomon* (1977), or symbolic, as with Son, whose trip back to a Caribbean island on one level reunites him with a prelapsarian island community in *Tar Baby* (1981), or is couched in ambiguity, as with the mysterious ghost-child in *Beloved,* Morrison's characters are united by the need to reclaim their cultural heritage.

It is possible here to mention only a few of the many other contemporary novelists whose work reflects this concern with maintaining contact with an African heritage in an American context. Ntozake Shange's *Sassafrass, Cypress, and Indigo* (1982) chronicles the experience of three sisters from Charleston, South Carolina. Their movement into adulthood parallels their search for a medium through which to express their creativity. Dance, weaving, and doll-making not only allow these women to make a lasting artistic contribution, these mediums suggest the women's collective need to reestablish a connection with Africa. The novel itself, consisting of letters, recipes, and magic potions as well as prose, thereby forming an innovative fictional work that challenges traditional notions of textuality, also reflects the cultured and gendered space African-American women occupy.

Paule Marshall's *Praisesong for the Widow* (1983) examines the pitfalls associated with the black pursuit of the American Dream: the loss, primarily, of history, culture, and identity. Avey Johnson represents the contemporary African-American woman who has sacrificed her sense of self in attempting to embrace middle-class values. The novel traces her search to recover her lost identity, which occurs as she abandons middle-class trappings of success and recovers the rituals of her family and the other people of the African diaspora. Marshall's use of myth, the heroic quest, and ritual is especially effective and represents an innovation in the novel of social realism.

Other recent novels treating issues of African-American female identity include Gloria Naylor's *The Women of Brewster Place* (1982). Although the novel offers a realistic portrayal of the black woman's condition in America, the blues-like, poetic quality of Naylor's prose results in a naturalism at odds with that of Richard Wright's *Native Son* or Ann Petry's *The Street*

(1946). Gayl Jones' *Corregidora* (1975), which incorporates into the novel form the techniques, rhythms, and motifs of American blues, exposes the racial and sexual politics involved in male-female relations, rendered largely through the collective stories of the Corregidora women. With its innovative approach to narrative and language and its adaptation of a quintessential black musical form, *Corregidora* is a striking work of fiction that again finds in a past rooted in racial violence the material to move the African-American novel forward.

Whether African-American novelists will continue to look to the past for inspiration or begin to find in their own era more substantial material to give form and essence to their works remains to be seen. In either case, the 20th-century African-American novel, no less than the tradition out of which it evolves, reveals the creative ways in which blacks adjust to the strictures of life in America and demands a thorough exploration.

MAXINE LAVON MONTGOMERY-CRAWFORD

See also James Baldwin; Invisible Man; Toni Morrison; Native Son; Their Eyes Were Watching God

Further Reading

Baker, Houston A., *The Journey Back: Issues in Black Literature and Criticism,* Chicago: University of Chicago Press, 1980

Baker, Houston A., *Blues, Ideology, and Afro-American Literature: A Vernacular Theory,* Chicago: University of Chicago Press, 1984

Bell, Bernard, *The Afro-American Novel and Its Tradition,* Amherst: University of Massachusetts Press, 1987

Bone, Robert, *The Negro Novel in America,* New Haven, Connecticut: Yale University Press, 1958; revised edition, 1965

Bone, Robert, *Down Home: A History of Afro-American Short Fiction from Its Beginning to the End of the Harlem Renaissance,* New York: Putnam, 1975

Carby, Hazel, *Reconstructing Womanhood: The Emergence of the Afro-American Woman Novelist,* New York: Oxford University Press, 1987; Oxford: Oxford University Press, 1989

Christian, Barbara, *Black Women Novelists: The Development of a Tradition, 1892–1976,* Westport, Connecticut: Greenwood Press, 1980

Cooke, Michael G., *Afro-American Literature in the Twentieth Century: The Achievement of Intimacy,* New Haven, Connecticut: Yale University Press, 1984; London: Yale University Press, 1986

Gates, Henry Louis, *The Signifying Monkey: A Theory of African-American Literary Criticism,* New York: Oxford University Press, 1988

Gayle, Addison, *The Way of the New World: The Black Novel in America,* Garden City, New York: Anchor Press, 1975

Hughes, Carl Milton, *The Negro Novelist: A Discussion of the Writings of American Negro Novelists, 1940–1950,* New York: Citadel Press, 1953

Margolies, Edward, *Native Sons: A Critical Study of Twentieth Century Negro American Authors,* Philadelphia: Lippincott, 1968

Montgomery, Maxine Lavon, *The Apocalypse in African-American Fiction,* Gainesville: University Press of Florida, 1996

Ostendorf, Berndt, *Black Literature in White America,* Brighton, Sussex: Harvester Press, and Totowa, New Jersey: Barnes and Noble, 1982

Rosenblatt, Roger, *Black Fiction,* Cambridge, Massachusetts: Harvard University Press, 1974; London: Harvard University Press, 1976

Stepto, Robert, *From Behind the Veil: A Study of Afro-American Narrative,* Urbana: University of Illinois Press, 1979; 2nd edition, 1991

Williams, Sherley Anne, *Give Birth to Brightness: A Thematic Study in Neo-Black Literature,* New York: Dial Press, 1972

African Novel

Western Africa

The exact beginnings of the Western African novel are very difficult to determine with any authority since much of the prose writing from the region calls into question exactly what we mean when we speak of the novel. A further difficulty lies in the fact that new claimants to the title of earliest fiction or earliest novel continue to be put forward as fresh texts are discovered. To take anglophone writing as an example, until recently it was generally accepted that the first full-length prose fiction was *Ethiopia Unbound* (1911) by the well-known Ghanaian nationalist, lawyer, and educator J.E. Caseley-Hayford. This strongly polemical account of Gold Coast (modern Ghana) "creole" soci-

ety, based largely on Caseley-Hayford's own life in law and politics, is cast in a fictional form. A much earlier contender for the title is Sierra Leonean J.J. Walters' *Guanya Pau: The Story of an African Princess,* published while he was attending Oberlin College in Ohio in 1891. An attack on the mistreatment of women in traditional Vai society, this powerful short fiction was published by Walters to raise money for the education of young Sierra Leonean women. Although it reflects the missionary objections to practices such as polygamy, it also registers a strong note of local pride in the richness and diversity of the African landscape and, unlike the conventional mission texts of the period, it affirms many aspects of African (Vai) culture. *Guanya Pau* vies for the title of earliest African novel also in formal terms, since it exhibits such classic features of the genre as character development, plot, and realistic description. Another early fictional narrative is also from the Gold Coast: R.E. Obeng's *Eighteenpence* was published in Britain in 1941, although at fewer than 150 pages it might be more fairly described as a novella.

Alongside the development of the novel written by Africans in English, French, and Portuguese in the late 19th and early 20th centuries, prose fiction was written in the local languages. A strong tradition of local language fiction developed in some parts of Western Africa, for example among the Yoruba, beginning with missionary patronage but rapidly leading to publications in locally owned and sponsored secular journals and newspapers (see Barber, 1997). In 1929 and 1930, J.B. Thomas, the founder of the Yoruba language journal *Akede Eko,* published in serial form what is regarded as the first Yoruba novel, *Itan Igbesi Aiye Emi Segilola* (The Life Story of Me, Segilola). The colonial powers, meanwhile, promulgated the novel for their own purposes. For example, in the 1930s figures such as Rupert East, the Director of the Colonial Literature Bureau set up in Northern Nigeria, actively encouraged young Hausas to write fiction. His efforts were part of a colonial policy of modernization that included support for local newspapers that published short prose and poetry, as well as political articles and news reports acceptable to the colonial authorities. The encouragement of prose fiction by figures like East was part of a conscious policy of control, and it illustrates how the development of the short story and the novel was part of the hegemonic practices of colonization. However, like so many other aspects of the colonial period, the development of the novel was an ambiguous, two-edged process, on the one hand, serving to control the indigenous world and, on the other, offering the tools by which that world could articulate itself and its concerns. As the Ibo novelist Chinua Achebe was to put it much later in a memorable phrase, colonial languages and literary forms "took away our songs but gave us a voice to sing with." It may be more accurate to say that they gave Africans songs and a voice that could be heard by Europeans and Americans.

Many local languages already had a long tradition of writing using Arabic script to produce the so-called *ajami* literatures, but these did not usually involve the production of long prose fictions. Writing in languages such as Hausa, Wolof, Ibo, Yoruba, and many others continued to flourish alongside the new forms in the colonial languages. The development of long fiction in all these languages bent the novel form to new uses, even as traditional narrative techniques were adapted to the demands of the new genre. Powerful new synergies emerged both in African languages and in the colonial languages. The writing in all these languages remained mutually influential even after the colonial period came to an end (see Barber, 1997). For example, D.O. Fagunwa wrote the famous and often reprinted Yoruba novel *Ogboju ode ninu Igbo Irunmale* (1938; The Expert Hunter in the Forest of the Spirits), which combines elements from traditional narratives with references to European sources from Homer to Bunyan. The fact that Fagunwa's work was subsequently translated into English by Nobel prize-winning author Wole Soyinka as *The Forest of a Thousand Daemons* (1968) suggests how difficult it is to separate writing in Western Africa into discrete language regimes or to draw a simple line between the novel and

other hybridized prose forms that emerged in the region. More recent Yoruba novels such as Femi Jeboda's *Olowolaiyemo* (1963) illustrate the continuing strength of the novel form in Yoruba. *Olowolaiyemo* is especially significant because its realist mode, its urban slum setting, and its antiheroic protagonist show that modern Yoruba fiction is not restricted to traditional material. However, traditional material has been a mainstay of Western African fiction, including Fagunwa's work and the novels of Amos Tutuola. Tutuola's *The Palm-Wine Drinkard* (1952) and *My Life in the Bush of Ghosts* (1954), using Yoruba oral material, were hailed by critics as the first Western African novels. However, in retrospect it is clear how much they resemble the forms already developed in local languages, of which European and American critics remained ignorant for a very long time.

Transpositions of forms from local to colonial languages were less in evidence in francophone writing, although some writers have used both French and indigenous languages to express themselves in the modern period. For example, the Senegalese novelist and filmmaker Ousmane Sembène has written in both French and Wolof, beginning with francophone novels such as *Le Docker noir* (1956; *Black Docker*) and *Les Bouts de bois de Dieu* (1960; *God's Bits of Wood*) and later using Wolof in the development of film scripts such as *Taw* (1970) and *Ceddo* (1976) or in mixtures of the two such as *Le Mandat* (1968; The Mandate) and *Xala* (1974). The greater distance between indigenous and French writing is the result, perhaps, of the French colonial educational policy that insisted on the use of French in the schools from the earliest years. (Portuguese colonies followed a similar policy, although in English colonies education was conducted in local languages until upper-secondary and tertiary levels.) In addition, intellectuals from the French and Portuguese colonies studied in Paris and Lisbon rather than at local universities such as those that had been established in the anglophone colonial world. These policies may have discouraged the use of local languages at least in the production of long prose fictions.

Portuguese prose writing in Western Africa appears to have been limited to a few Cape Verdean novels such as Baltasar Lopes da Silva *Chiquinho* (1947) and Manuel Lopez' *Chupa Braba* (1956). On the whole, lusophone writing from Western Africa does not seem to have been as extensive as that from Angola and Mozambique, but Portuguese has been the most critically neglected of the colonial languages, and relatively little published criticism exists on which to base an assessment. Similarly, there is little or no published evidence of writing in local languages from former Portuguese colonies in Western Africa. The mulatto composition of Cape Verdean society suggests that little precolonial local language literature could emerge there. As for Guinea-Bissau, no significant local language texts appear to have been recorded.

Perhaps because of the different educational policies of the colonial powers, the first generation of novelists to emerge in Western Africa using French were more obviously influenced by modern French novel forms and by postwar Parisian intellectual fashions. However, in novels such as Guinean writer Camara Laye's *L'Enfant noir* (1953; *The Dark Child*) and *Le Regard du Roi* (1954; *The Radiance of the King*), the influence of movements such as symbolism and expressionism or of specific contemporary French writers like Camus are often profoundly modified and overlaid by concerns and forms rooted in the local Mande culture (see Miller, 1990). A similar recognition of the importance of Akan culture as a crucial determinant of narrative choices and stylistic concerns has also been recognized in the work of the anglophone Ghanaian writer Ayi Kwei Armah, whose work was also influenced by European movements and writers (see Wright, 1989). This widespread acknowledgment of the local influences on the form and content of the early Western African novel is one of the most important critical revaluations to have emerged in recent times.

The francophone *négritude* movement also was an important influence on many of the novelists who emerged in the 1950s and 1960s. This movement of Caribbean and African francophone intellectuals like Leopold Sédar Senghor and Aimé Césaire who lived in Paris in the 1940s attempted to define the character of negro (black) cultures, stressing the specific and distinctive nature of black experience and seeking to define the essential features of black expression. Although it probably made a less direct contribution to the novel than to poetry, the movement represented a new mood of confident assertiveness in black culture that sparked an upsurge of cultural production by all Africans after World War II. The war itself, having exposed Africans to experience abroad as soldiers, was also a factor in the shifting mood in the colonies. Perhaps because of the influence of the largely French *négritude* movement, the francophone novel showed a steady growth through the 1950s, with novels such as Cameroonian Mongo Beti's *Ville cruelle* (1950), *Le Pauvre Christ de Bomba* (1956; *The Poor Christ of Bomba*), *Mission terminée* (1957; *Mission to Kala*), and *Le Roi miraculé* (1958; *King Lazarus*); his compatriot Ferdinand Oyono's *Une vie de boy* (1956; *Houseboy*), *Le Vieux nègre et la médaille* (1956; *The Old Man and the Medal*), and *Chemin d'Europe* (1960; *Road to Europe*); as well as the work by Laye and Sembène already mentioned.

In anglophone writing, the real upsurge of the novel occurs a little later, with Nigerians Amos Tutuola and Cyprian Ekwensi working in relative isolation in the early 1950s. Ekwensi embraced popular forms, writing social novels of city life such as *Jagua Nana* (1961), the story of the struggle of a part-time whore and "high life" girl to survive in modern Lagos. He also wrote children's stories and a novel set in the cattlelands of the north entitled *Burning Grass: A Story of the Fulani of Northern Nigeria* (1962), which clearly shows the influence of the American Western. Ekwensi also produced a number of folklore collections, including his earliest text, *Ikolo the Wrestler and Other Ibo Tales* (1947). In this respect Ekwensi's work, although heavily influenced by Euro-American genres, reflects indigenous oral narrative forms.

Nigerian writer Chinua Achebe's *Things Fall Apart* (1958) reflects the desire to supplant the biased accounts of African societies and the African past that predominated in the curricula of the colonial institutions of higher education with a new and recuperative local form. This novel and others that followed set out to celebrate and recover the African past in its own terms and from the perspective of those societies themselves. The writers of this generation perceived themselves as having been cut off from the culture they sought to celebrate and record and engaged strenuously and self-consciously in a process of recovering local knowledge from a wide variety of sources. The novels they produced were transcultural forms too, then, despite their realist

surface and their more obvious similarity to European examples of the genre. Like their francophone counterparts, these anglophone writers integrated aspects of the European novel with elements of their own traditions. Many novels strove to dramatize the colonial "moment of contact" and its consequences for the generations that followed. *Things Fall Apart* remains one of the earliest and best of such contact narratives. Achebe's later novels followed the stages of development of Nigerian society, *No Longer at Ease* (1960) telling the story of Obi and the social problems facing the new generation of "been-to's" (overseas-educated Africans) as their country is on the brink of independence. Achebe's third novel, *Arrow of God* (1964), deals with the 1920s and the British colonial administration's attempt to introduce forms of government that clashed with local Ibo social practices. In the satirical novel *A Man of the People* (1966), Achebe castigates the Nigerian politicians running the newly independent country. Twenty years later, in *Anthills of the Savannah* (1987), Achebe made an even stronger and more focused attack on the corruption and violence of contemporary Nigerian regimes. His novels, often deceptively simple in language and form, offer direct and always deeply moral analyses of personal and social pressures in the Western African world. He comes closest perhaps of all Western African writers to the 19th-century European social novel, yet at the same time his novels are quintessentially African, embedded inextricably in the perspective and values of his own culture and people.

Fellow Nigerian Elechi Amadi's *The Concubine* (1966) and *The Great Ponds* (1969) offer a slightly different perspective on the precolonial period. They focus even less on the invader's influence, seeking rather to picture and recover the precolonial world as complete in itself and as generating its own conflicts, tragedies, and joys. Amadi's principal aim is to construct a narrative that is referentially self-contained.

Although best known as a playwright and poet, Africa's first Nobel prize winner, the Nigerian writer Wole Soyinka, also has contributed powerfully to the development of the Western African English novel. His two novels, *The Interpreters* (1970) and *Season of Anomy* (1973), focus on the role of the intellectual in a society threatened with corruption or catastrophe. *Season of Anomy* is perhaps more politically focused, anatomizing the power of an international cartel and its neocolonialist role in contemporary Nigerian politics. Both are written in a fairly dense, symbolic language that renders their message obscure in places. Soyinka's long prose writing continues with the autobiographical works *Aké: The Years of Childhood* (1981) and *Isara: A Voyage Around "Essay"* (1989), which contain more effective accounts of the places and events that shaped Soyinka's generation than the fictional works. More recently in *Ibadan: The Penkelmes Years: A Memoir 1946–1965* (1994) Soyinka has dealt with his early manhood and the years in which he began his still-continuing work as an activist for democracy and change in the new Nigeria. He has called this latest work a "faction," which places his autobiographical texts in some relationship to the long fiction of the novel. These are, perhaps, more effective vehicles to express how the individual and his choices mesh with the community to form the values of a society.

The autobiography generally has been an influential form for Western African prose writing. Soyinka's texts follow in the tradition of earlier African autobiographical "factions" such as the classic *Ethiopia Unbound* already mentioned and more recently the Nigerian poet and playwright John Pepper Clark's *America, Their America* (1964). Critics have speculated that the autobiography allows the writer to fold in his own story with the historical representation of the culture and people he is seeking to celebrate, or to critique it in a direct and unpretentious way. Similarly important in the Western African tradition are childhood narratives, which may be used metonymically to represent the process of development from a colonialist hegemony in which the native is perceived as "half savage and half child," to a full and independent postcolonial adulthood.

Soyinka's two mainstream novels form part of a wider tradition of symbolist writing in Western Africa that contrasts with the more realist tradition of Achebe, Amadi, and their followers. Like oral performance, the symbolist tradition makes no distinction between poetry and prose. For example, there is a strong prose-poetry element in Ghanaian Kofi Awoonor's first novel, *This Earth, My Brother: An Allegorical Tale of Africa* (1971). Even more strongly, *Our Sister Killjoy: or, Reflections from a Black-Eyed Squint* (1977) by Ama Ata Aidoo of Ghana blends prose and verse to tell the story of Sissie, a Ghanaian volunteer working in Europe, and her return to Africa. The text is structured as a series of separate episodes and includes both poetry and prose broken up by experimental typography in a conscious fracturing of traditional European genre expectations. Fellow Ghanaian Ayi Kwei Armah's work—*The Beautyful Ones Are Not Yet Born* (1969), *Fragments* (1970), and *Why Are We So Blest?* (1972)—blends symbolism with satirical portraiture. His later work integrates mythical and legendary elements with historical narrative, as in *Two Thousand Seasons* (1973) and *The Healers* (1978). Although the results resemble European symbolist, modernist, and postmodernist forms, these novels are rooted in Western African cultural traditions.

Recently, feminist criticism has sought to draw critical attention away from these male novels to reevaluate writing by women such as Ama Ata Aidoo and Flora Nwapa. Critics argue that the early male writers employed a biased and inaccurate, gendered view of the "traditional" world, which helped to construct the myth of African woman as dutiful and subservient. Early novels neglected or criticized by male critics, including Flora Nwapa's *Efuru* (1966), which is generally cited as the first novel by a Nigerian woman writer, have recently been reread to contest these biased representations of women.

The emergence and recognition of women writers is one of the most marked features of recent Western African writing in both French and English. Buchi Emecheta, Mariama Bâ, and Beyala Calixthe are receiving increasing attention. For example, Bâ's two novels, *Une si longue lettre* (1980; *So Long a Letter*) and *Un Chant écarlate* (1981; *Scarlet Song*), completed just before her untimely death, present powerful insights into the pressures on married women in Senegalese societies. The novels register a strong resistance to traditional features of the Muslim society in which they are set, particularly those features related to the subjugation of women. The plight of the French heroine of *Un Chant écarlate*, who marries a Senegalese, shows that change cannot be effected by individuals until social institutions such as polygamy and the extended family are radically reformed.

Ama Ata Aidoo's second novel, *Changes* (1991), eschews the technical experimentation of *Our Sister Killjoy* for a more conventional narrative of personal relationships, bringing it closer to the work of francophone women writers like Bâ and Calixthe.

Buchi Emecheta's novels, such as *The Bride Price* (1976), *The Slave Girl* (1977), *The Joys of Motherhood* (1979), *The Rape of Shavi* (1983), and *Gwendolen* (1989), all address the issue of women's roles both in traditional societies, which are far less idealized than in male novels, and in modern society, where the defense of traditional values works to oppress women. Emecheta's own refusal to classify her work as feminist may be the result of her concerns, shared with Aidoo and other women writers, that Western feminism may be prejudicial when applied to non-Euro-American societies. They argue that it is necessary to acknowledge the legitimate differences of African social practices. Despite these concerns, a text like *The Joys of Motherhood* presents a strong and vigorous attack on the masculinist bias of traditional and contemporary Western Africa. Its biting ironies expose the hypocrisy and negativity of traditional attitudes as they operate to control women in the modern, urbanized Nigerian world.

More recently, a new generation of writers led by figures such as the Nigerian Ben Okri, Ghanaian Kojo Laing, and Sierra Leonean Syl Cheney-Coker have used local forms and the style and themes of oral culture in fiction that has been characterized as magic realism. Although they may well have been influenced by the success of other writers who have blended the modern novel form with elements from oral cultures, including Gabriel García Márquez or Salman Rushdie, they are returning to an earlier strain of Western African writing and the symbolically rich texts of such writers as Camara Laye or Amos Tutuola. Ben Okri's work, which has received a great deal of international notice, includes *The Landscapes Within* (1981), *Flowers and Shadows* (1980), *Incidents at the Shrine* (1986), *The Famished Road* (1991), *Songs of Enchantment* (1993), and *Dangerous Love* (1996). His Booker Prize-winning novel *The Famished Road* deals with the ubiquitous Western African idea of the spirit-child or *abiku* (as it is known in Yoruba), the endlessly reborn child who is caught between the worlds of mortals and spirits, inhabiting one of those liminalities that are so crucial to Western African cosmologies. Clearly this exploration of the special and unique worldview of a particular African culture also reflects the works of Tutuola and Laye, in which European rationalism is subject to a revision at the hand of African systems of belief and thought. Kojo Laing's novels, including *Search Sweet Country* (1986), *Woman of the Aeroplanes* (1988), *Godhorse* (1989), and *Major Gentl and the Achimota Wars* (1992), and Syl Cheney-Coker's *The Last Harmattan of Alusine Dunbar* (1990) also express the alternative worldviews and themes of Western African cultures.

All these novels return to an earlier fictional style that was temporarily supplanted by more realist modes of fiction. Some commentators have speculated that the realist interlude was stimulated by the new demand for texts suitable for the newly developed local educational market that emerged in the 1960s and 1970s. The international market and overseas publishers continue to exercise an undue influence on Western African writing. The work of Okri, Emecheta, and Bâ has received a great deal of attention abroad, and as a result their work has sometimes been evaluated less favorably at home. Western African writers are confronted with the choice of writing for the local or international market. Publishing houses that refuse the right to retain local publishing rights in contracts for international publication exacerbate this division, making it difficult for local audiences to access the work of writers who choose to publish mainly abroad. On the other hand, Isidore Okpewho's powerful study of polygamy, *Victims* (1970), and his civil war novel, *The Last Duty* (1976), or Festus Iyayi's studies of domestic violence and of corruption in business and the army in his novels *Violence* (1979), *The Contract* (1982), and *Heroes* (1986) have received far less international critical attention than novels published by writers resident abroad or whose work has been published in international imprints. The relative neglect outside Western Africa itself of the tradition of writing in local languages is also very marked, with only a few critics drawing attention to the existence of a flourishing body of writing in local languages. Choosing an audience and language is therefore a difficult, complex, and politically charged process for Western African novelists.

Interestingly, novels in English and French show an increasing experimentation with style and form, for example in the use of creole and pidgin to structure both dialogue and narration. Nigerian Gabriel Okara's *The Voice* (1964), which sought to wed English words to the syntax of Ijaw, has been followed by more recent experiments like late Nigerian writer Ken Saro-Wiwa's novel *Sozaboy* (1985), written in what Saro-Wiwa calls "rotten English" on the title page. This powerful account of the recruitment of a young man to the army on the eve of the Nigerian civil war employs a simplified form of Nigerian pidgin, sufficiently modified to be comprehensible to a nonpidgin speaker but still deliberately and ubiquitously marked with the distinctive features of modern Nigerian English usage. It seems likely that this kind of experimentation will continue and will increase if a strong enough local market for Nigerian texts can be maintained. Perhaps as a result, the call for a return to the exclusive use of local languages has been much weaker in Western Africa than in Eastern Africa.

The novel genre has now been adopted so widely in Western Africa that it is a feature of writing in many of the major regional African languages as well as in the ex-colonial languages, which continue to flourish. Additionally, popular forms such as the crime novel, the children's novel, and the romance novel have found a significant readership. It seems unlikely that the novel will disappear from the scene, despite occasional calls for cultural decolonization.

GARETH GRIFFITHS

See also Chinua Achebe; Ayi Kwei Armah; Cyprian Ekwensi; Interpreters; Mission to Kala; Flora Nwapa; Postcolonial Narrative and Criticism of the Novel; Ousmane Sembène; Radiance of the King; Amos Tutuola

Further Reading

Barber, Karin, "Time, Space and Writing in Three Colonial Yoruba Novels," *Year's Work in English Studies* 27 (1997)

Brown, Stewart, editor, *The Pressures of the Text: Orality, Texts and the Telling of Tales,* Edgbaston, Birmingham: Centre of West African Studies, University of Birmingham, 1995

Burness, Donald, editor, *Critical Perspectives on Lusophone Literature from Africa,* Washington, D.C.: Three Continents Press, 1981

Gikandi, Simon, *Reading the African Novel,* London: Currey, and Portsmouth, New Hampshire: Heinemann, 1987

JanMohamed, Abdul R., *Manichean Aesthetics: The Politics of Literature in Colonial Africa,* Amherst: University of Massachusetts Press, 1983

Maja-Pearce, Adewale, *A Mask Dancing: Nigerian Novelists of the Eighties,* London and New York: Hans Zell, 1992

Mezu, Rose Ure, *Women in Chains: Abandonment in Love Relationships in the Fiction of Selected West African Writers,* Randallstown, Maryland: Black Academy Press, 1994

Miller, Christopher L., *Theories of Africans: Francophone Literature and Anthropology in Africa,* Chicago: University of Chicago Press, 1990

Obiechina, Emmanuel N., *Culture, Tradition and Society in the West African Novel,* Cambridge and New York: Cambridge University Press, 1975

Priebe, Richard, *Myth, Realism, and the West African Writer,* Trenton, New Jersey: Africa World Press, 1988

Sanon, J. Bernardin, *Images socio-politiques dans le roman négro-africain,* Sherbrooke, Quebec: Editions Naaman, 1983

Stratton, Florence, *Contemporary African Literature and the Politics of Gender,* London and New York: Routledge, 1994

Wright, Derek, *Ayi Kwei Armah's Africa: The Sources of His Fiction,* London and New York: Hans Zell, 1989

Zabus, Chantal J., *The African Palimpsest: Indigenization of Language in the West African Europhone Novel,* Amsterdam and Atlanta, Georgia: Rodopi, 1991

African Novel

Northern Africa

The Role of Language

Literary production in the countries of the Maghrib, with the exception of Libya, is still bilingual, in Arabic and French, even more than 30 years after the last of the Maghribī countries, Algeria, won its independence. In fact, the last decade or so has seen an increase in the number of writers writing in French. English vocabulary is incorporated into their texts with growing frequency. The Tunisian Mustapha Tlili, to cite only one example, uses English terms and expressions in his texts. Other novelists, in addition to borrowing syntax, morphology, and style from Arabic, use words and expressions written in Arabic script.

It must be stressed that the works written in French most often use French as a mere linguistic channel for their ideas. Francophone Maghrib literature is increasingly international in outlook, probably because novelists seek to free themselves from the hegemony of French culture. The Moroccan Abdelkébir Khatibi's *Un été à Stockholm* (1990; A Summer in Stockholm), for example, is set in New York and Sweden. The fact that the protagonist is an interpreter reflects on the novel's own position between linguistic worlds. Khatibi's thoughts about "plurilangue" find their full expression in *Amour Bilingue* (1983; Love in Two Languages). Nabile Fares' bilingual poems, *Chants d'histoire et de vie pour des roses de sable* (1978; History and Life Songs for Sand Roses), use Spanish. Laila Abou Zaid uses English rather than French to connect her to Western culture, in a conscious anticolonial choice. Those who live in English-speaking countries, particularly in North America, have naturally developed a connection with the culture of the region. Writers like Hédi Bouraoui in Canada and Réda Bensmaïa in the United States exhibit Anglo-Saxon cultural traits in their creative works. As a matter of fact, Bensmaïa's *The Year of Passages* (1995) was written in French, she claims, only in her subconscious.

The novelists writing in Arabic, on the other hand, have had limited contact with Western literature. The flourishing literary circles of the Mashriq in the eastern Mediterranean were out of reach for the majority of Algerian writers, especially in the first half of the 20th century. Arabic literature in Algeria thus experienced a literary flowering much later. The Maghrib continues to develop independently of the Mashriq, asserting its separateness from a region that, it is felt, long ignored the Maghrib. This trend is particularly noticeable in Morocco.

However, there were some ties with the Mashriq in Algeria, even during the French colonial period. The most obvious influence is visible in the work of Aḥmad Riḍā Ḥūhū, whose choice of the title *Maᶜ Ḥimār al-Ḥakīm* (1953; With Al-Ḥakim's Donkey) testifies to his familiarity with the Egyptian writer Tawfīq al-Ḥakīm's works. Yet only when college students went to the Mashriq en masse to study did the Arabic language in Algeria undergo great rejuvenation. Writers such as Wasīnī Laᶜraj, Mirzāq Baqtāsh, Zaynab al-Aᶜwaj, and others received their higher education in Syria. Wasīnī was among the first Algerian novelists to experiment with both style and form, taking the Algerian novel in a new direction. Tunisia and Morocco have a longer history, since their cultural and literary heritage was enriched by their famous centers of learning, Al-Zaytūnah and Al-Qarawiyyīn. Tunisia's added advantage was its geographical proximity to the Mashriq, with which it maintained strong cultural ties. This is true also of Libya, whose writers were greatly involved in their neighbors' literary and cultural activities.

In their common endurance of French colonialism, Maghribī writers share a similar reaction to occupation that is portrayed in their novels. They experienced a traumatic culture shock that led them to revolt against their own culture in order to be assimilated into Western culture. This theme was championed in Morocco by Driss Chraibi, whose *Le Passé Simple* (1954; The Simple Past) and *Succession ouverte* (1962; Heirs to the Past)

remain the most powerful works on the subject. In Algeria the same theme was tackled by Mouloud Mammeri's *Le Sommeil du juste* (1955; The Sleep of the Just), Mohammed Dib's *Un été Africain* (1959; An African Summer), and Assia Djébar's *Les Impatients* (1958; The Impatient Ones), while the Tunisian Albert Memmi presents the double conflict of the colonized and the Jew in *La Statue de sel* (1953; The Pillar of Salt).

The Maghribī novels written in French are quite distinct from the novels of their compatriots written in Arabic. Both the vision and the preoccupation of the two groups move on different tangents. Nowhere is the gap greater than in Algeria, where French-educated intellectuals immersed themselves in the illusion of belonging to a culture that did not claim them. A certain mistrust between francophone and "Arabophone" writers kept the channels of communication long closed. The linguistic divide acted as a barrier that led to two separate realms of literary production that evolved with little contact.

Even translations failed to create a real rapprochement among writers, although they certainly benefited readers. Al-Ṭāhir Waṭṭār's *Al-Zilzāl* (1974; The Earthquake), translated into French as *Le Seisme*, was received with great enthusiasm by the inhabitants of Constantine, the setting of the novel. But the translation of French fiction into Arabic, in Algeria in particular, is rare. Translations from Arabic into French are more common, particularly the work of Rashīd Abū Jadrah, whose books, first published in Arabic, are almost simultaneously translated into French. However, on the whole, translation efforts are rather sporadic and aimed primarily at the most popular novels. Such was the case with Muḥammad Barādah's *Luᶜbat al-Nisyān* (1987; The Game of Forgetfulness), which was translated into French as *Le Jeu de l'oubli* soon after its choice as a literary text in the secondary school curriculum in Morocco.

At the height of the Arabization movement in Algeria, following independence, some writers announced their decision to write in Arabic, if not on a regular basis, at least occasionally. While Assia Djébar's intentions have never been realized, Rashīd Abū Jadrah began the process with his novel *Al-Tafakkuk* (1981; The Dismantling). Mālik Ḥaddād, frustrated by his inability to write in Arabic, ended his writing career voluntarily. More recent years have witnessed the return of the Maghribī soul to the novel written in French, and the interaction of bilingualism and multiculturalism has resulted in a fascinating hybridity.

Narrative Forms and Themes

The Maghribī novel—the novel being a genre comparatively new to the Arab world—has matured slowly. Writers lacked guidance and models in their early efforts. The short story, in Arabic and French, initially proved a more congenial form. Maghribī writers frequently have worked with autobiographical or semi-autobiographical forms. Abdelkébir Khatibi's *La Mémoire tatouée* (1971; The Tattooed Memory) set the tone for a postmodernist approach to this form. Three writers have followed in his footsteps: the Algerian Nabile Fares, like Khatibi a sociologist by training; Tahar Ben Jelloun, whose novel *Harrouda* (1973; Harrouda) is believed to have been inspired by *La Mémoire tatouée*; and the Tunisian Abdelwahab Meddeb, whose postmodernist *Talismano* (1979) and *Phantasia* (1986; Fantasy) focus on his Arab-Islamic heritage. In Algeria, Kateb Yacine blurred the lines delineating literary genres, mixing plays, poems, historical essays, fiction, and personal memories in *Nedjma*

(1956; *Nedjma*) and *Le Polygone étoilé* (1966; The Stellated Polygon).

History, whether political or social, has become central to many novels. One of the techniques used by Maghribī writers in both languages is the amalgam of personal, historical, and fictional narratives, many works falling under none of the traditional, existing forms of the novel, whether autobiographical or historical. The resulting collage of genres symbolizes the Maghribīs' search for identity and their effort to define themselves in a fast-changing world. Change often created new trauma before the old ones were resolved. For the Algerians, who form the largest group of Maghribīs writing in French, the homeland was hardly regained when it was lost again. The poem-like text at the end of Djébar's *Vaste est la prison* (1995; Wide Is the Prison) summarizes the feeling of renewed exile as a result of the turmoil that has gripped the country since the late 1980s.

Some writers have been overwhelmed by history. Eager to remain faithful to reality, they write novels that read more like journalistic reportage. This trend marked the post-independence period in Algeria in particular, when writers were eager to report on the events of the war of independence. But a younger generation of writers has been able to sift through the pivotal events of the war of independence and shed the emotional baggage attached to it. This is the case with Aḥlām Mustaghānmī's first novel, *Dhākirat al-Jasad* (1993; The Body's Memory) and Wasīnī Laʿraj in *Mā Tabaqqā Min Sīrat Lakhḍar Hamrūsh* (1980; Whatever Is Left of the Biography of Lakhḍar Hamrūsh).

Two writers who dominate the field of Arabic fiction in Algeria, ʿAbd al-hamīd ibn Hadūqah and Al-Ṭāhir Waṭṭār, began their careers with work in a social realist mode. Hadūqah touched his readers through the human situations in which he placed his characters, particularly the father in *Rīḥ al-Janūb* (1971; The Southern Wind) and the teacher in *Nihāyat al-Ams* (1975; The End of Yesterday). Waṭṭār relied heavily on political history and promoted socialist ideology, while writing according to the realist trend. This tendency is quite obvious in *L'Āz* (1974; The Ace) and *Al-ʿIshq wa-al-Mawt fī al-Zaman al-Harāshī* (1980; Passion and Death in the Harāshī Era) and *Al-Zilzāl* (The Earthquake). Both writers developed a different approach in their later novels, as the needs and direction of the country changed. Symbolism became the technique of choice, often dictated by a need for a more subtle criticism of their government's shortcomings and mistakes. They found suitable allegories in folklore. Waṭṭār constructed his entire novel *Al-Ḥawwāt wa-al-Qaṣr* (1984; The Fisherman and the Palace) on a folktale. Hadūqah portrayed the folk character of the Jāziyah in *Al-Jāziyah wa-al-Darāwīsh* (1983; The Jāziyah and the Dervishes).

The depiction of the national struggle was also a preoccupation of a number of Moroccan and Tunisian writers. The Moroccan ʿAbd al-Karīm Ghallāb was openly nationalistic and didactic in his efforts to rid his country of the "Francophone" spirit. His novels served often as a mere fictional frame for his anticolonial ideology, which was closely related to his own experience. *Sabʿat Abwāb* (1965; Seven Gates) tells the story of his imprisonment during the colonial period, and *Al-Muʿallim ʿAlī* (1981; Master Ali) conveys a patriotic message.

In Tunisia, the early fiction writers were not concerned with the burning national issues debated in their country. A group of excellent writers known as *Jamāʿat Taḥt al-Sūr* lived bohemian

lives, were motivated by a love of literature for its own sake, and had little interest in financial gain. Their works reveal great talent. Among them was ʿAli al-Duʿājī, who achieved fame through his *Jawlah bayna Ḥānāt al-Baḥr al-Mutawassiṭ* (1935–36; A Trip around the Bars of the Mediterranean Sea), a collection of shorter pieces that combine the travel vignette and the short story. An accomplished fiction writer, Duʿājī's ability to balance fact and fiction is visible in his collection of short stories, *Saḥirtu minhu al-Layālī* (1969; Sleepless Nights). Its realism is attenuated by a subtle sense of humor and of the ridiculous. Another member of the group, Al-Bashīr Khurayyif, launched the use of colloquial Tunisian in the dialogue of *Iflās, Aw Ḥubbak Ḍarbānī* (1958; Penniless, or Your Love Got Me) and later in his collection of short stories, *Mashmūm al-Full* (1971; The Arabian Jasmin). Khurayyif is considered the pioneer of the realistic school in Tunisia because of his concern for the people, whose suffering he depicted in *Al-Diglah ʿArājīnihā* (1969; The Date Bunch). Maḥmūd al-Masʿadī took a very different direction in his writings. Perfectly bilingual, he wrote in Arabic, concentrating on philosophical themes. His novel *Ḥaddatha Abū Hurayrah Qāla . . .* (1973; *Abū Hurayrah Said . . .*) combines modern technique with the traditional style and form of the Ḥadīth. Muṣṭafā Fārisī's novel *Al-Munʿaraj* (1965; The Turn) also raises philosophical issues. Its author was preoccupied with the role of the intellectual in society. ʿAbd al-Qādir ibn Shaykh, on the other hand, turned his attention to the plight of the Tunisian peasants in his novel *Wa Nasībī min al-Ufuq* (1970; My Share of the Horizon).

The generation of writers who followed the *Jamāʿat Taḥt al-Sūr* group showed great interest in the political life of the country. Some of the major works in this vein were Rashād al-Ḥamzāwī's *Būdūdah Māt* (1961; Boudouda Died), ʿAbd al-majīd ʿAṭiyyah's *Al-Manbat* (1967; The Fountainhead), and Muḥammad Ṣāliḥ al-Jābirī's *Yawm Min Ayyām Zamrah* (1968; A Day in Zamrah), to cite only a few. The novels evoke the national struggle in Tunisia and reveal their authors' concern for social justice. Although the action is set in the colonial period, the colonial power is not, at least not directly, blamed for the country's economic hardships. Quite often, traditions and a changing social structure are held responsible for social inequalities, as shown in Muḥammad al-ʿĀbid Al-Jābirī's *Al-Baḥr Yanshur Alwāḥah* (1975; The Sea Spreads Its Boards). Among the novelists motivated by nationalism we must mention Muḥammad al-Mukhtār Jannāt, whose ambitious project to write the history of the Tunisian people under the general title *Urjuwān* bogged down over difficulties in publication. Only two volumes were published, *Tarīq al-Rushd* (1970; The Road of Wisdom) and *Khuyūṭ al-Shakk* (1972; Threads of Doubt). His second novel, *Nawāfidh al-Zaman* (1974; Windows of Time), revolves around the evacuation of the French army of occupation from Bizert. It is in his short stories, however, that he becomes artistically innovative, moving from realism to symbolism. In what appears to be a nostalgic look back at the national history of his country, Hédi Bouraoui tackles the subject of national resistance in his most recent novel, *Retour à Thyna* (1996; Return to Thyna). The book is a far cry from the author's abstract novel *L'Icônaison* (1985) with its extremely symbolic and experimental language. Nevertheless, the novel won its author the adulation and recognition of his compatriots as he was awarded Le Grand Prix littéraire de la Ville de Sfax in 1995. It is rather surprising to watch this writer, who exploded the limitations of literary genres, return to a great simplicity in form.

The 1980s witnessed a decisive break away from the old forms, which had remained close to the traditional shape of the novel. A modernist trend, fed by decades of hybridity, shaped the style and the language of the Maghribī writers writing in French. The major characteristic of these novels was the weaving of French texts with Arabic expressions, as in Meddeb's *Phantasia*. Their French exhibits a strong Arabic influence in constructions and figures of speech. The phenomenon is best illustrated in Assia Djébar's *Vaste est la prison,* in these words: "L'œil qui, dans la langue de nos femmes, est fontaine" (The eye that, in the language of our women, is a fountain), a reference to the Arabic word *ᶜayn,* meaning both an eye and a spring. The Arab Islamic heritage became a source of inspiration for novelists looking for symbolism and allegories. Ḥabīb Tengour's evocation of Omar al-Khayyām and Hassan Al-Ṣabbāh in *Le Vieux de la Montagne* (1983; The Old Man of the Mountain) is an impressive commentary on the relationship between the writer and political power.

Leila Sebbar infuses her writings with folk culture. She has created a protagonist, Shérazade, who, through a slight variation in spelling, is both connected with and differentiated from Shéhérazade of *The Arabian Nights.* In this way, the writer connects her French fiction with her Arabic culture. Sebbar's series of novels portraying Shérazade, *Les Carnets de Shérazade* (1985; Sherazade's Notes), *Shérazade, 17 ans, brune, frisée, les yeux verts* (1982; *Sherazade: Missing, age 17, dark curly hair, green eyes*) and *Le Fou de Shérazade* (1991; Crazy About Sherazade), is primarily concerned with the fate of second-generation Mahgribīs in Europe, known as the Beurs.

Assia Djébar's *Ombre Sultane* (1987; *A Sister to Scheherazade*) tackles the character of Shéhérazade from a feminist angle, focusing on relationships between men and women and their difficulties in communicating. Laᶜraj Wasīnī's *Raml al-Māyah: Fājiᶜat al-Laylah al-Sābiᶜah baᶜda al-Alf* (1993; Raml al-Māyah: The Tragedy of the One Thousand and Seventh Night), on the other hand, presents this legendary storyteller in a modern setting. Shéhérazade, like the narrator of a Maqāmah, reveals bitter truths about a country that the reader guesses to be Algeria.

Some writers who had sought greater freedom of expression in foreign lands returned to their native countries to live under the rule of governments they came to criticize bitterly, such as the Algerians Kateb Yacine and Rashīd Abū Jadrah and the Moroccan Mohammed Khair-Eddine. Others failed in their endeavor to resettle in their countries of origin. This situation gave rise to a literature of exile. The most prominent though not necessarily the most sophisticated work is produced by the Beurs. Theirs is a literature in the making, since few have so far published regularly. Their writings are diatribes against their countries of origin, their host countries, and the older generation of immigrants. Their anger is provoked by their lack of affiliation and the rejectionist policy of the host country, primarily France. Some of the most promising novelists, such as Farīda Belghoul, Leila Houari, Sakinna Boukhedenna, and Ferrudja Kessas, have published only one novel, *Georgette* (1986), *Zeida de nulle part* (1985; Zeida of Nowhere), *Journal, "Nationalité: immigré(e)"* (1987; Journal, Nationality: Immigrant), and *Beur's Story* (1990), respectively. They have not fully revealed their talents yet. Sebbar

is the least affected by the difficulties surrounding the majority of the Beurs and portrays best the tragic side of exile, death, and moral solitude in *Le Silence des rives* (1993; The Silence of the Shores). The tragic events of the early 1990s in Algeria, which claimed a number of writers among their victims, have not yet given rise to works that successfully convey the extent of the horror, but Rachid Mimouni's *La Malédiction* (1993; The Malediction), or Djébar's récit, *Le Blanc de l'Algérie* (1995; The Whiteness of Algeria), do attempt to tackle the subject.

The mood of protest that swept Algeria beginning in the late 1980s and that led to the multi-party system, giving minorities a political voice, caused the recalcitrant but so far quiet Berber population to voice its opinion. The early Berber writers had expressed themselves through the evocation of their traditions. Prominent among them is the Amrouche family—the mother Fadhma, the son and poet Jean, and the daughter, novelist, and singer Marguerite [Marie-Louise] Taos Amrouche. Taos Amrouche's *Jacinthe noire* (1947; Black Hyacinth), *Rue des Tambourins* (1960; Tambourins Street), and *L'amant imaginaire* (1975; The Imaginary Lover) are semi-autobiographical novels. Equally subtle was the voice of Tahar Djaout in *Les Chercheurs d'Os* (1984; The Bone Seekers), in which he rejoined other non-Berber novelists in their opposition to the exploitation of the memory of the martyrs. Al-Ṭāhir Waṭṭār had voiced a similar concern in his well-known short story *Al-Shuhadā' yaᶜūdūn Hādhā al-Usbūᶜ* (n.d.; The Martyrs Are Coming Back This Week), as had Mohammed Dib in *La Danse du roi* (1968; The King's Dance) and Rachid Mimouni in his sarcastic novel *Le Fleuve détourné* (1982; The Redirected River) and *L'Honneur de la tribu* (1989; *The Honor of the Tribe*).

Mouloud Mammeri was more aggressive in his militant promotion of Berber culture in his writings. While using Berber life as a background in his early novels, *La Colline oubliée* (1952; The Forgotten Hill) and *The Sleep of the Just,* his focus shifted in *La Traversée* (1982; The Crossing). His play *Le Banquet* (1973; The Banquet), on the annihilation of the Aztecs in Mexico, hints at a similar fate for the Berbers. Another champion of the Berber cause, Nabile Fares, vented his bitterness on the situation of the Berbers in Algeria in a trilogy, *Découverte du nouveau monde* (The Discovery of the New World). The trilogy consists of *Un Passager de l'Occident* (1971; *A Passenger of the West*), *Mémoire de l'absent* (1974; *The Memory of the Absent*), and *L'Exil et le désarroi* (1976; Exile and Disarray). In Morocco, the Berber flame is carried by Driss Chraibi, particularly in his latest novels. In the semi-historical novel *La Mère du printemps* (1982; *Mother Spring*), the author tries to reconcile Berberity and Islam, while rejecting Arabism, which arrived with Islam. His ensuing novels, *L'Inspecteur Ali* (1991; *Inspector Ali*), *Enquête au pays* (1981; *Flutes of Death*), and *Naissance à l'aube* (1986; *Birth at Dawn*), evoke the Kabyle traditions which shield the Berbers against assimilation in Arabized society. The three last novels rely heavily on symbolism and allegory to convey the author's message and display a certain hostility toward the non-Berber component of Moroccan society.

Literary Trends and Currents

It is not always possible to speak of a literary trend for Maghribī novels, as writers were guided by a thematic approach rather than by a desire to experiment with the form and style of fiction, particularly in the early stages of their literary careers. Books were, generally, written in reaction to certain policies and conditions, whether in the colonial period or in the post-independence years. The Moroccan Muḥammad Shukrī stands alone in his pursuit of naturalism in his novels portraying the extreme poverty and deprivation of the social underclass. His first novel, *Al-Khubz al-Ḥāfī* (n.d; *For Bread Alone*), published in a French translation before it finally appeared in the Arabic version, is still shocking to this day. *Al-Shuṭṭār* (1992; *Streetwise*), a sequel to *For Bread Alone*, reveals the same realism, providing a revealing sketch of Moroccan life as experienced by a specific group.

In Algeria, the writings of Albert Camus and Emmanuel Roblès launched Mouloud Feraoun's career as a writer. His approach was both ethnographic and didactic in *Le Fils du pauvre* (1950; Poverty's Son) and *La Terre et le sang* (1953; Land and Blood). His third novel, *Les Chemins qui montent* (1957; The Ascending Roads), reveals a sophistication that he did not have time to develop further (Feraoun was assassinated by the OAS in 1962). The same pattern is discernible in the work of Mouloud Mammeri and Mohammed Dib's trilogy *L'Algérie*, consisting of *La Grande maison* (1952; The Main House), *L'incendie* (1954; The Fire), and *Le Métier à tisser* (1957; The Weaving Machine). In Morocco, Ahmed Sefrioui concerned himself with the folk heritage of his people. Most of his novels, *Le Chapelet d'ambre* (1949; The Amber Rosary), *La Boîte à merveilles* (1954; The Magic Box), and *La Maison de servitude* (1973; The House of Servitude), are ethnographic in nature, revealing the customs and traditions of his country.

The colonial period was dominated by the concept of politically engaged literature. This trend, particularly strong in Algeria, continued in the post-independence years for the majority of novelists. A few, however, managed to break away and focus on other topics. Mohammed Dib was one of the first writers to declare the end of commitment, after 1962. His novel describing the Algerian war of independence, *Qui se souvient de la mer* (1962; *Who Remembers the Sea*), one of the most original books on the war, advances into the realm of the fantastic. He then turned his attention to one of his favorite themes, the relation between men and women. Both his style and imagery changed drastically as a result, becoming more abstract and symbolic. The complex symbolism made the interpretation of some themes quite difficult. Such is the case in *Habel* (1977), where the biblical references seem to apply to the political and socioeconomic realities of Maghribī emigrants. Similarly perplexing is *Les Terrasses d'Orsol* (1985; The Terraces of Orsol), also concerned with Maghribī emigration to Europe. Dib's hermetic prose compounds the difficulty. In both *Neiges de marbre* (1990; Marble Snows) and its sequel, *L'Infante maure* (1994; The Moorish Infanta), he delved into the cultural differences and communicative difficulties between mixed couples. Communication difficulties, whether due to generational, cultural, or linguistic differences, have preoccupied most Maghribī writers. Leila Sebbar, in the fiction-essay *Parle mon fils, parle à ta mère* (1984; Speak My Son, Speak to Your Mother), views such difficulties in terms of the widening gap between younger and older generations of Maghribī immigrants in France. She revisited that theme in *Le Silence des rives*, revealing a lingering regret for the lost maternal language, both in its figurative and real sense.

Writers with an educational background in the social sciences or humanities have been more open to innovations and originality. A historian, Djébar found in her studies the substance for her later novels, *L'Amour, la fantasia* (1985; *Fantasia, An Algerian Cavalcade*), *Loin de Médine* (1991; *Far From Madina*), as well as her feminist documentary films, *La Nouba des femmes du Mont Chenoua* (1977; The Nuba of the Women of Mount Chenoua) and *La Zerda ou les chants de l'oubli* (1982; The Zerda or the Songs of Forgetfulness).

Maghribī writers, generally, have felt a sense of responsibility toward their people. With firsthand experience of the oppression they have described, they have acted as the voice of the silent majority in their countries. Their political urgency long deterred them from experimentation. However, a new trend reveals itself in the spiritual and temporal labyrinths of Tahar Ben Jelloun's *L'Enfant de sable* (1985; *The Sand Child*). This novelist, who received the Prix Goncourt in 1987, figures among Morocco's postmodernist writers. Moroccan novelists writing in Arabic are leading the way in the Maghrib as far as experimental fiction is concerned. Their work displays a particular interest in multiple points of view, as in Barādah's *The Game of Forgetfulness*. Another Moroccan, al-Milūdī Shaghmūm, pushes the point of view in the direction of the old Arabic tradition of *isnād* (ascription) in his novel, *Al-Ablah wa-al-Mansiyyah wa-Yāsamīn* (1982; The Idiot, the Forgotten and Jasmin). The same approach can be found in ʿAbd al-Qādir Al-Shāwī's *Dalīl Al-ʿUnfuwān* (1989; The Evidence of Vigor). Edmond Amran El-Maleh is equally concerned with the nature of narrative. In *Mille ans, un jour* (1986; A Thousand Years and a Day) and *Le Retour d'Abou El-Haki* (1990; The Return of Abou El-Haki), he abandons the traditional linear approach, relying on an intricate combination of images, flashbacks, and snatches of dialogue interjected in the narrative.

Maghribī Women Writers

Women writers in both Arabic and French are few and far between in the Maghrib. For a long time, the only name was that of Assia Djébar. From *La Soif* (1957; *The Mischief*) to the recent *Le Blanc de l'Algérie*, her work has evolved from early romantic themes to a political engagement motivated by her country's struggle for liberation and an interest in women's causes.

New women writers have made their appearance in the last two decades, but most remain authors of a single book. Among this group of writers is Nina Bouraoui, who made a triumphal entrance onto the literary scene with her perceptive novel *La Voyeuse interdite* (1991; *Forbidden Vision*). This young Algerian writer, like her protagonist, returned to her country of origin with the hope of going home, only to face unacceptable restrictions. She remains one of the rare novelists who look at Algerian society with a foreign eye. Myriam Ben, a journalist, teacher, painter, and musician, is also the author of a novel, *Sabrina ils t'ont volé ta vie* (1986; Sabrina, They Stole Your Life). She is one of a small group of Jewish writers who still reside in the Maghrib. She is concerned with relationships between men and women, an interest she shares with another Algerian writer, Hawa Djabali. Djabali's single novel, *Agave* (1983), is her only published fiction work. Yamina Mechakra, hailed as a brilliant writer by Kateb Yacine and much influenced by his style, also has only a single novel to her name, *La Grotte éclatée* (1979; The Exploding Cave). Mechakra's novel is a narration of the events of the war and a poetic tribute to her Berber origins. Aicha Lemsine is the author of two novels, *La Chrysalide* (1976; *The Chrysalis*) and *Ciel de porphyre* (1978; *Beneath a Sky of*

Porphyry), but she attracted critical attention with a series of interviews with women in different Arab countries in *Ordalie des voix* (1983; The Chastisement of Voices). This book revealed a sophistication of thought and a poetic style far superior to that of her novels. In Arabic, the situation is no brighter. There are very few women writers. The first to publish a significant amount of fiction was Zuhūr Wanīsī. She failed, however, to produce a major work of fiction. Her most significant book is *Min Yawmiyyāt Mudarrisah ḥurrah* (1979; Memoirs of a Free Teacher), an autobiography. A poet, Aḥlām Mustaghānmī, is taking the lead as a fiction writer in Algeria. Her first work, a novel entitled *Dhākirat al-Jasad* (1993), revolves around childhood memories of the war of liberation, part of a new trend of accountability from the young generation of Algerians toward their elders.

The contribution of women writers in Arabic is more significant in Tunisia. The work of an original and lively group of male writers served as models for their fiction, particularly the short story. Yet the fact that some women used pseudonyms reveals the tenuousness of women's literary activities, a situation bitterly criticized by the Moroccan Laylā Abū Zayd. The bulk of women's literary production is in the genre of the short story. There is a conservative trend, represented by Najiyyay Thāmir and Hind ʿAzzūz, and a liberal one, associated with Ḥayāt ibn Shaykh and Faḍīlah al-Shābbī, writers who do not hesitate to portray reality as it is or to describe their own vision of it. Conservative and realist writers share similar concerns for their personal and civic rights, and their choice of language, French or Arabic, does not reflect any political position. The most notable of the women writers, Al-Shābbī, a poet, recently published a novel, *Al-Ism wa-al-Ḥadīd* (1992; The Name and Lowliness), in which she places herself at the center of the book, even the world. With this self-confidence has come a greater freedom to experiment with the language and the form of the novel, as more recent writers move away from a transparent realism to more abstract and symbolic narrative forms. What distinguishes Al-Shābbī and other young women writers is the use of a new language to assert their individuality. Naflah Dahab's *Al-Ṣamt* (1993; Silence) creates dramatic effects through the choice of the language, sentence construction, and figures of speech. Ḥayāt ibn Shaykh moved women's concerns to topics considered traditionally masculine, such as politics. Her novel *Wa-Kāna ʿUrs al-Hazīmah* (1991; And Then Was the Celebration of Defeat) portrays a Nasserite protagonist who marries the daughter of a Jewish mother and a Tunisian father, symbolizing the peace agreement between Egypt and Israel. ʿAliyyah al-Ṭibāʿī followed suit in *Zahrat al-Sabbār* (1991; The Cactus Flower), which relies extensively on dialogue and reflects on mixed marriages and Tunisian politics, highlighting the bread riots of January 1978. Fāṭimah Salīm denounces the moral degradation of the country in *Nidā' al-Mustaqbal* (1972; The Call of the Future) and *Al-Tajdīf fi al-Nīl* (1974; Rowing in the Nile). Tunisian fiction written by women, however, is characterized by a lack of perseverance. A whole decade sometimes separates one work from the next. This inconsistency is due in large part to social and family pressures, which makes it difficult to predict the future of the Tunisian Arabic novel written by women. Moroccan women writers are slowly emerging as players in the cultural circles of their country. One of the pioneers in the field is Khannātha Bannūnah. Like most writers of her generation, such as Rafīqat al-

Tabīʿah's (Zainab Fahmī), Laylā Abū Zayd, Laylā al-Shāfiʿī, and Nuzhā ibn Sulaymān, she launched her career as a short-story writer. While her major concern is with the social ills of her country, she shows a great interest in the Palestinian problem and devotes an important number of her short stories to this subject. Laylā al-Shāfiʿī, in her collection *Al-Wahm wa-al-Ramād* (1994; Delusion and Ashes), reveals herself as a mature writer and a militant thinker. Laylā Abū Zayd's novel *ʿAm al-Fīl* (1983; Year of the Elephant) examines the emotional state of a Moroccan women as she waits for her divorce papers to arrive. A flashback focuses on the political struggle of women in her country. A strong anticolonial spirit animates the novel.

The Libyan Novel

Libya occupies a marginal place both geographically and culturally between the Mashriq and the Maghrib. Sandwiched between those two regions, it is a little uncertain of its identity. Culturally, however, the Libyan novel is closer to the Mashriqī novel in both form and style. Yet it is distinguished by a special spirituality and symbolism. The style, on the other hand, is in line with the semi-sufi language launched by the Egyptian Jamāl al-Ghīṭānī in *Kitab al-Tajalliyāt* (1983, 1985, 1987; The Revelations). Aḥmad al-Faqīh, one of Libya's prominent writers, acknowledges the influence of Egyptian writers on his work. These similarities are not surprising, given the close contacts existing between Libya and the Arab countries of the Mashriq.

Early Libyan novels were concerned with the urbanization resulting from the oil boom. This change created an imbalance in the social structure, shaking up traditions without supplying other structures to meet the challenges of modern urban society and its different values. This confrontation between the old and the new is reflected in the fiction of the past 50 years. Most writers seemed torn between three worlds—the world they lived in, which was undergoing profound change, the Western, modern, industrialized world, and the world they dreamed of. This vision is particularly clear in Aḥmad al-Faqīh's *Ḥādā' iq al-Layl* (1991; Gardens of the Night), which relies heavily on symbolism and allegories. While al-Faqīh's main intention is to describe the breakdown of human relationships, Ibrahim al-Kūnī appears bent on a mission to revive Libya's ancient Berber roots. His novels abound in Berber expressions and symbols. Both his *Al-Mājūs* (1992; The Magi) and *Kharīf al-Darwīsh* (1994; The Dervish's Autumn) rely heavily on Berber traditions and culture as well as allusions to Old Testament figures, the historical and religious references serving as a symbolic portrait of the present. He joins al-Faqīh in his general preoccupation with social change and a nostalgic yearning for the past. The desert is a powerful presence in al-Kūnī's novels as well as in his collection of short stories, *Al-Khurūj al-Awwal* (1992; The First Departure), and so are animals. The transformation of women as seductresses into snakes in *Kharīf al-Darwīsh* recalls the story of creation and Adam and Eve's fall from grace. This trait in al-Kūnī's fiction links him to other Maghribī writers. The personality of the dervish as the one who voices truth is central to much of their work.

The short story dominates the field of Libyan fiction. Writers such as ʿAlī Muṣṭafā al-Miṣrātī, ʿAbd Allah al-Quwayrī, Al-Sadiq al-Nahūm, and Zaʿīmah al-Bārūnī have all published collections of short stories and few novels. While some of the Maghribī novelists may be compared to Western novelists in their quest for innovative techniques, most are more interested in a return to their roots and to indigenous traditions. The post–World War II period has revealed to the novelists the true value of their cultures, which they have embraced without being bound by them. For those living in exile, whether voluntary or imposed, the return to their cultural heritage seems to bring particular solace.

AIDA A. BAMIA

See also Egyptian Novel; Levantine Arabic Novel; Nedjma; Postcolonial Narrative and Criticism of the Novel; Sand Child and Sacred Night

Further Reading

Allen, Roger, editor, *Modern Arabic Literature*, New York: Ungar, 1987

Baccar, Taoufik, and Salah Garmadi, *Ecrivains de Tunisie*, Paris: Sindbad, 1981

Bamia, Aida, "Algerian Literature," in *Encyclopedia of World Literature in the Twentieth Century*, revised edition, edited by Steven Serafin, New York: Continuum, 1993

Bonn, Charles, editor, *Anthologie de la littérature algérienne: 1950–1987*, Paris: Librairie Generale Française, 1990

Déjeux, Jean, *La Littérature Maghrébine de langue française*, Sherbrooke, Quebec: Naaman, 1973

Fontaine, Jean, *La Littérature Tunisienne Contemporaine*, Paris: Editions du Centre National de la Recherche Scientifique, 1991

Hargreaves, Alec, *Voices from the North African Immigrant Community in France: Immigration and Identity in Beur Fiction*, New York: Berg, 1991

Mortimer, Mildred, *Journeys through the French African Novel*, Portsmouth, New Hampshire: Heinemann, and London: Currey, 1990

Tankul, Abd al-Rahman, *Littérature Marocaine d'ecriture française: Essais d'analyse sémiotique*, Casablanca: Afrique Orient, 1985

Woodhull, Winifred, *Transfigurations of the Maghreb: Feminism, Decolonization, and Literatures*, Minneapolis: University of Minnesota Press, 1993

African Novel

East and Central Africa

When the Kenyan writer Ngugi wa Thiong'o returned to his village from his boarding school in Nairobi after his first term, during what the British government termed the Emergency, he found, as he describes in *Detained* (1981), that not "only my home, but the old village with its culture, its memories and its warmth had been razed to the ground." His sense of violation and incredulity suggests how the experience of East and Central African writers differs from those in West Africa, with a legacy that lasts into the present. The British Imperial Land Act of 1915 transferred official ownership of all land to the British Crown, and in the East African protectorate the governor was empowered to sell land to white settlers. Africans became laborers on land they and their ancestors had farmed; as the struggle intensified between the white settlers in Kenya, who claimed that Winston Churchill had sold them the land in perpetuity, and local people fighting to retrieve their traditional territory, villages were removed and reconstructed under surveillance conditions. During the Federation of Rhodesia and Nyasaland (Southern Rhodesia is now Zimbabwe and Nyasaland is Malawi) the most productive estates, for coffee, tea, and tobacco, were owned by whites, resulting in major labor migration to the gold and diamond mines of southern Africa, and in disrupted communities.

As a consequence of this disruption in East African communities, the confident assertion of a Yoruba community that is expressed in Wole Soyinka's autobiography *Ake: The Years of Childhood* (1981), for instance, or the Ibo village life recreated in Chinua Achebe's *Things Fall Apart* (1958), have no equivalent in East African writing, where physical boundaries and the limits of sanity are habitually depicted as being under threat. In the process the formal boundaries of fiction are pushed back, as writers remodel the Western form that most of them encountered during a Eurocentric educational process and make it carry the culturally specific burden of their experience. The irrelevance of much of that education is comically evoked in Tsitsi Dangarembga's *Nervous Conditions* (1988), when Tambu has to recite a poem to visiting American nuns: "'Hamelintown'sin-BrunswickbyfamousHanoverCity,' I began, raising a gasp of admiration from my class, who knew I was bright but not quite that bright."

Mission education initiated the possibility of African novels in European languages. Many of the writers, like Ngugi, went to mission schools and entered their writings in competitions; Ngugi's *The River Between* (1965) was entered in 1961 for a competition organized by the East African Literature Bureau. Ngugi now sees the apparent flexibility of the missionary-owned presses and government-controlled publishing bureaus as sinister; texts in English that questioned or attacked Christian values and practices could win prizes, but language "held the soul prisoner. . . . Language was the means of spiritual subjugation" (*Decolonising the Mind*, 1986). This is arguable, of course; the first major publication from an East African writer was the Ugandan Okot p'Bitek's dramatic monologue *Song of Lawino* (1966), a vigorous and witty attack on the cultural destructiveness of colonialism. His first novel had been published in Luo in 1953 by the East African Literature Bureau. *Song of Lawino* may be seen as a crucial text in empowering East and Central African writers to appropriate and transform in English both traditional and Western genres, or it may be interpreted as a crucial severance between writers and a local public for their work.

Local publishing outlets, for writing in whatever languages were favored by writers and editors, increased the opportunity for writers. As universities opened in the region, literary magazines were established: *Penpoint* at Makerere, *Nexus* at Nairobi, *Darlite* at Dar-es-Salaam, *Odi* in Malawi, and *The Jewel of Africa* in Zambia. Similarly, publishing houses such as The Tanzanian Publishing House; Neczam in Zambia; Mambo Press, the Zimbabwean Publishing House, and Baobab Books in Zimbabwe; and Montfort Press in Malawi were established after independence to promote the work of local writers. Multinational companies, notably Heinemann, Longman, and Macmillan, also began to publish the work of African writers, although their interest obviously privileged writing in English. The Heinemann African Writers Series introduced the work of new writers from all over Africa to a new public, creating a world market for African writing in English and so, arguably, constituting an elite local audience—those whose education enabled them to read English without difficulty.

It would be misleading to suggest that cultural and linguistic circumstances—as these relate to the novel—are comparable in all the countries of East and Central Africa. Kiswahili is spoken and understood by the majority of Tanzanians, so writing in English is much less developed there because it is not needed. The political situation in Uganda prevented free expression in any language for long stretches of time after independence; censorship under Idi Amin was terminal. Although Kiswahili is the indigenous lingua franca in Kenya, the country has produced more writing in English than other parts of East or Central Africa, perhaps partly because, long after independence, Kenyan government-owned theatres and television channels offered British or American drama and culture, and because East Africans had earlier access to university education than people from Central Africa. In Central Africa English is the lingua franca; local publishers, in Malawi for instance, produce short novels in local languages, and a market literature exists in both local languages and English, based on romance and thriller genres. The issue of a writer's choice of language in this region is as contentious as her/his choice of form and theme, and is part of what is perhaps optimistically referred to as postcolonialism. Many writers—those under discussion here, for example—are using a form that has no equivalent in their indigenous cultures, in a language that is not their mother tongue. One argument is that, in reworking the form and the language to bear the pressure of their experience, they are making positive use of the hybridity that becomes an inevitable part of the colonial process, for the colonizers as well as for the colonized; this is Chinua Achebe's view. The opposing position is that language colonizes the mind with its own system of values, and so a truly postcolonial writer, in order to break from the hold of colonization, must use his or her mother tongue. Since his detention in 1977, Ngugi has written in Gikuyu; his works are translated into English only after they have appeared in Gikuyu. Somalian Nuruddin Farah, who fits into none of the categories suggested so far, uses English as his fourth language, his first three being Somali, Arabic, and Italian. The colonial history of the Somali people leads to thematic links between Farah's novels and those of other writers in the region, although aesthetically his work is distinctive.

A common experience for the first generations of African students to go to new universities, Ibadan or Makerere for example, was that they were offered versions of themselves and their people that seemed to them unrecognizable. The Africans of Joseph Conrad's "Heart of Darkness" (1902) are either silent, dehumanized shadows or twirling savages, parts of bodies: "a burst of yells, a whirl of black limbs, a mass of hands clapping, of feet stamping, of bodies swaying, of eyes rolling. . . . They howled and leaped, and spun, and made horrid faces." They either make noises or speak a crude pidgin English. Only Kurtz's "wild and gorgeous apparition of a woman" is impressive; "She must have had the value of several elephant tusks upon her. She was savage and superb, wild-eyed, and magnificent." Although Ngugi responded to Conrad's ability to pose questions for his reader rather than supplying answers, he was appalled by the constructions of blackness he found in European writing, from Shakespeare through Daniel Defoe to Conrad. The howling savage and the sexually predatory and challenging black woman are replicated in European writing about Kenya in the first part of the 20th century, in Richard Meinertzhagen's *Kenya Diary, 1902–1906* (1957) and *Diary of a Black Sheep* (1964), and in Karen Blixen's (Isak Dinesen's) *Out of Africa* (1937) although she focuses more on the Kenyan as childlike or animal-like; her cook would sometimes offer her a local delicacy "even as a civilised dog, that has lived for a long time with people, will place a bone on the floor before you, as a present." These stereotypes are deployed in the media coverage of the Emergency (1952–60), where the Mau Mau are constructed as barbaric; although the treatment by the British of internees in the Hola camp, for instance, could not be called civilized, it was presented as the necessary containment of savages. Elspeth Huxley uses similar images in her *A Thing to Love* (1954) where she links Gikuyu pleasure in killing with pleasure in sex; Gitau looks at his hands and thinks they are "strong and cunning, they could bring death to a man as easily as pleasure to a woman." A description of an oathing ceremony in the same novel combines bestiality, cannibalism, and necromancy as "the people in the circle came forward and stood before Raphaelo stark naked, the firelight playing on their dark skins." The first generations of Kenyans who went to university discovered what Frantz Fanon articulates in *Les damnés de la terre* (1961; *The Wretched of the Earth*), that colonialism "turns to the past of the oppressed people, and distorts, disfigures and destroys it."

Ngugi argues in *Writers in Politics* (1981) that what was called Kenyan writing at that time was not East African but "*Afro-Saxon literature,* part of that body of literature produced by African writers in foreign languages"—what V.S. Naipaul might call the mimic man syndrome. Certainly the first East African novelists accept the agenda implicitly defined by Conrad and Huxley; they write in a critical realist mode and engage with the politics of colonialism. The two major novelists of the immediate post-independence period, Ngugi and Nuruddin Farah, both wrote a sequence of novels that could be seen as a response to those colonial versions of East African history in which the "native" is constructed as child-like, naive, cunning, animalistic, barbaric, or intuitive and irrational: noble savage or violent Caliban. Ngugi's *The River Between* is set at the beginning of the colonial period in Kenya; *Weep Not, Child* (1964) takes place before and during the independence struggle, and *A Grain of Wheat* (1967) happens during the days leading up to *uhuru*, independence, but moves back to the past through the memories of the group involved in the narrative. Farah's trilogy *Variations on the Theme of an African Dictatorship* includes *Sweet and Sour Milk* (1979), *Sardines* (1981), and *Close Sesame* (1983).

The history that is being rewritten in these and other fictions focuses on the peculiarly painful internecine wars that often accompany the colonial process. In Kenya, the Emergency was the focus of a range of novelistic treatments, from the popular fiction, cynical in tone, of Charles Mangua's *A Tail in the Mouth* (1972) through Meja Mwangi's focus on pursuer and pursued in *Carcase for Hounds* (1974) to the psychological complexity of Ngugi's *A Grain of Wheat*. It is difficult to see Ngugi's novel as Afro-Saxon, harder still to apply the term to Farah's *Maps* (1986), which also concerns civil war. With Chenjerai Hove's *Bones* (1988) the reader encounters a treatment of the war for Zimbabwean independence that, in form and content, is distinctively not in a European tradition of writing.

Both *A Carcase for Hounds* and *A Grain of Wheat* take their titles from canonical Western texts; Ngugi's use of the biblical phrase is ironic, but in *A Carcase for Hounds* Mwangi uses Shakespeare's *Julius Caesar* as an implicit counterpoint to his story of civil war, precipitated by the colonial situation. The action of the novel covers only a few days and focuses on the battle of wills that occurs between Haraka, the Mau Mau general, and his pursuer, Captain Kingsley. Mwangi, here as in his other novels, is conspicuous by comparison with other East African writers for his ability to evoke place, whether it is the muddy mountains of this novel or the back alleys of Nairobi; in this respect he resembles Karen Blixen.

Ngugi's use of the Bible is much more ambivalent and ironic than Mwangi's respectful treatment of Shakespeare; the epigraph to *A Grain of Wheat* warns that "thou sowest not that body that shall be, but bare grain, it may chance of wheat, or of some other grain." This seems a reflexive comment about the novel itself; when the missions introduced their pupils to subversive texts such as the Bible, they did not know what they were planting. The text of the novel is punctuated by underlined passages from the freedom fighter Kihika's Bible; it was he who identified himself with Moses and the British with the Egyptians. Instead of framing the action, the narrator of *A Grain of Wheat* takes the reader straight into the mind of the obsessive Mugo, who is on the verge of a breakdown, although there is apparent rejoicing as the country is about to celebrate independence. As the flexible narrative moves between different interior monologues, the reader becomes aware that everyone, Kenyan and British, is haunted by the past, and by moments of betrayal and being betrayed. The insistent movement between past and present indicates that all sorts of weeds, which were planted in the past, germinate and grow into a present that people want to believe is a new heaven and a new earth, with nothing of the old colonial past to hamper it. It becomes clear that postcoloniality is a state to be worked for and aspired to, but not something that automatically arrives with independence; the war has created mistrust between people who were on the same side, between husband and wife, between elders and their community.

Two later treatments of war use forms that cannot be called Afro-Saxon, Farah's *Maps* and Hove's *Bones*. Askar, the boy born at the beginning of *Maps,* is the allegoric representative of the Ogaden; his surreal story offers a reading of the history of a territory that is mapped by different colonial cartographers—British, Ethiopian, Italian, and Somali. His adoptive mother, Misra, represents the practice, used in many cultures, of gendering the nation-state as female, which the novel suggests is absurd within the brutal patriarchies of the Horn of Africa: Misra is abused and sexually exploited by a series of men of different ethnicities, and is eventually murdered. All the boundaries in the novel are problematic: the limits of the body, of nationality, and of gender are questioned and disturbed. *Bones* is disturbing in a different way; it gives a voice to an oral tradition, and specifically to an illiterate peasant woman, Marita, who will not be silenced by the authorities in her search for her son, who has disappeared in the civil war for Zimbabwean independence. The narrative is constructed of a series of monologues not from her but from people who knew her and quote her, principally her son's girlfriend, Janifa; but the spirits of the ancestors speak in one section, recalling the bones that were spread across the land when Cecil Rhodes first irrupted into their country. The language is textured with Shona proverbs: "I tell you with this mouth of mine, there are no new stories, only new ears for old stories." Reading becomes an experience of hearing the wisdom of a series of tough women who will not allow themselves to be marginalized by white patriarchy; although Marita dies and Janifa goes mad, they are still heard, with the text shifting fictional boundaries to incorporate orality without the rather clumsy device of transliteration, used for example in Gabriel Okara's *The Voice* (1964). A story similar to the narrative in *Bones* is told through a series of interviews in *Mothers of the Revolution* (1990) edited by Irene Staunton, in which Zimbabwean women tell of their part in the struggle for independence.

Many of the issues raised in *Maps* relate as much to nationality as to war; most of the national boundaries in East and Central Africa were created at the end of the 19th century in the European "scramble for Africa," and have little relation to linguistic, clan, or geographic boundaries. While some parts of the world feel they can transcend national boundaries and move into a global culture of communications systems and the Internet, the difficulty of attaining an enlightened sense of nationality that recognizes hybridity in religion, ideology, ethnicity, and language is the theme of much East and Central African fiction. Ngugi's *Petals of Blood* (1977) is set in "independent" Kenya, which the novel shows to be colonized by multinational capitalism. The form of the novel, a detective story in which four suspects are interrogated about the deaths of three entrepreneurs, fragments and moves backward and forward in time, entering the consciousnesses of the four central characters and showing that all four had a reason for killing each of the three victims. The suspects are a fanatically Christian schoolmaster, a crippled Muslim veteran of the Emergency, a prostitute, and a left-wing political activist. All at some point in their lives were idealists, but the coincidences in the plot reveal to the reader that the characters are caught in a delusion when they think they are free, and they become disillusioned and disabused. Any local initiative, such as the brewing of Theng-eta, which has a spiritual role in local religious practice, is appropriated by a neocolonial conspiracy to control and disempower the people who had fought for "freedom." For much of the novel the reader struggles to piece together the mystifying narrative, and New Kenyans are having to decode state rhetoric to find out what is really going on; the question of what is the New Kenya resonates throughout the novel. Similarly Farah's *Sardines* questions who controls the Somali republic. The title is never overtly referred to in the novel, but its narrative method suggests its meaning: the text shifts from one interior monologue to another, mostly of female characters. They are trapped by the other sardines around them in the can, and cannot see the whole can, let alone the canning factory. The complex mosaic of Somali nationality is explored: the novel asks whether orthodox Muslims can coexist with Western-educated feminists, and particularly what role women can play within a repressive regime that colludes with foreign powers to silence its own people, and authorizes rape and female circumcision.

Sardines is preoccupied by censorship, a dominant theme in East and Central African writing; in many places what one writes has been or still is literally a matter of life and death. The Ugandan dramatist Byron Kawadwa was killed for producing plays that the regime did not like, and members of the audience were killed for attending performances; although this situation has not obtained in Uganda for some years, Okot p'Bitek, the poet, was in exile from 1967 until 1979. Nuruddin Farah left Somalia in 1974, part of an exodus of a Westernized urban elite who were being harassed by the security service. He was about to return in 1976 when he discovered by chance that a 30-year prison sentence awaited him if he did so. Throughout his subsequent nomadic existence, in Europe, the United States, and various parts of Africa, he has insisted that it is the dictators of Africa that are in exile and not he, although he is physically absent from his country. The Malawian poet Jack Mapanje, who was head of the English Department of the University of Malawi, was abruptly taken into detention in September 1987; when he was eventually released in May 1991, he was not reinstated in his academic post and now lives in Britain, although the regime in Malawi has changed to a multiparty democracy. The choice between silence or enforced exile for writers is a brutal one.

This choice is exemplified particularly clearly in the case of Ngugi, in whose person and in whose work issues relating to censorship and language intersect. In 1977, when he was head of the Literature Department at the University of Nairobi, Ngugi wrote a play in Gikuyu, with a collaborator, for a literacy project at a community education center. Local people involved in the production improvised alterations to the script; the community built an open-air theatre with seating for 2,000, and huge audiences arrived on weekends to see the local actors and musicians perform the play. The performances were officially stopped by the government after a month, and on the last day of the year Ngugi was arrested. The assumption was that he was detained because *Petals of Blood* was published that year, but he believed that the government only saw him as a threat when he used an indigenous Kenyan language as he and his collaborators had done in the play. Ngugi was released from detention but not reinstated in his post when President Jomo Kenyatta died in December 1978. When the same community group wrote a musical, they applied to perform it at the Kenya National Theatre in Nairobi in 1981. The application was refused, and heavily armed police demolished the open-air theatre the community had built for itself. By a curious irony, a British television adaptation of Elspeth Huxley's *The Flame Trees of Thika* (1959) was being screened on Kenyan television at that time. Ten thousand people attended "rehearsals" of the musical at the University of Nairobi during the week when the group was unable to stage the play officially at the National Theatre, but Ngugi had defied a

new president; in 1982 he had to go into exile in the country that had colonized his own, and he has not been able to return to Kenya. What probably precipitated this was the success of his novel *Caitaani Mutharaba-ini* (1980; *Devil on the Cross*). The novel was published by Heinemann in Gikuyu before Ngugi translated it into English, and it had a huge popular success in Kenya; it was read aloud to illiterate audiences in bars, and 15,000 copies were printed in less than a year. The novel itself is about censorship, as *Petals of Blood* is, but here the form is allegorical, and the language more direct, with the assertiveness of parables and proverbs. There is no moral ambivalence or tentativeness about the novel.

Two younger novelists from Zimbabwe, Tsitsi Dangarembga and Yvonne Vera, provide a new perspective on issues of gender, although Rebeka Njau, a Kenyan contemporary of Ngugi, begins this process in *Ripples in the Pool* (1975). The epigraph to Dangarembga's *Nervous Conditions* (1988) is taken from Sartre's introduction to Fanon's *The Wretched of the Earth*: "The condition of native is a nervous condition." The novel's nervous conditions are those of a group of Shona women and girls in colonial Rhodesia; the focus is refreshingly not on sexual relationships but on the pressures of being doubly colonized, by Shona patriarchy as well as by white supremacism. The narrator, Tambudzai, has an aggressive and feisty tone from the beginning, as she contests her father's "idea of what was natural" and of "the real tasks of feminine living." What she reveals is that she and the women she loves are governed by a series of images. The insistence on mirrors and images, on constructions of the self, leads to a recognition of the difficulty for the women in this society of doing more than conforming to patriarchal images.

Yvonne Vera's three novels, *Nehanda* (1993), *Without a Name* (1994), and *Under the Tongue* (1996), have some thematic resemblance to *Nervous Conditions* in that Mazvita in *Without a Name* is looking for a new self, but because she is part of a land at war she only knows about departures: "she had mistaken them for beginnings." The narrative method in these three books is quite different from the briskly witty irony of *Nervous Conditions*; all of them have female protagonists but are highly allegorical and surreal, full of mythic motifs and images. There is close visual attention to landscape, as in *Nehanda*: "The bees wander uncertainly into the bushes, hovering with outstretched forelegs in ritual dances over the fertile ground." The prose is poetical, though rather opaque for a non-Zimbabwean reader. The fact that these books are all published by a Zimbabwean press (Baobab Books) may suggest that a local audience can access the mythic aspects of the texts in a way that remains, partially at least, closed to other readers.

Nehanda, Mazvita, and Zhizha, the protagonists of Vera's novels, are all in extreme nervous conditions, like Tambu's mother and cousin in Dangarembga's novel. Most major East and Central African novelists depict people on the edge of sanity, and they often precipitate the reader into the character's state of mind, as Ngugi does at the beginning of *A Grain of Wheat* with the near-mad Mugo, and as Farah does at the opening of *A Naked Needle* (1976) when an unidentified voice asks: "My marital status. I mean, am I married? The frank, honest-to-God answer to this is: I don't know." Koschin is part of a society that he wants to believe in but increasingly does not trust; betrayal and mistrust dominate his experience. Unlike Mugo, he is Western-educated; it is often the difficulty of reconciling a Western education with a wish to belong to an African society that tests mental stability in these fictions. Dambudzo Marechera's *The House of Hunger* (1978), *Black Sunlight* (1980), and *The Black Insider* (1990) express the obverse position from Ngugi's in that it is the indigenous culture that makes their characters feel alienated.

Publication itself is a problem in many parts of East and Central Africa; hopes that African publishing houses would flourish and be able to translate novels from one African language to another have not materialized, and such marketing as is done happens through organizations such as the African Book Collective in Oxford, which disseminates information and copies from one part of Africa to another. Book shops and libraries, in Malawi and Kenya for instance, are closing or reducing their stock. The vitality that was so evident in the immediate post-independence period in Kenya seems to have subsided, although Meja Mwangi published a comic novel in 1990, *Striving for the Wind*. Ngugi remains in exile, cut off from hearing the changes in the only language he wants to write in, Gikuyu, and the Mogadiscio that Farah evokes in his novels no longer exists, although Farah addresses a new question, foreign aid, in his most recent novel, *Gifts* (1992). The focus for innovative writing in English seems to have shifted, following independence, to Zimbabwe, but the short history of the novel in English in East and Central Africa demonstrates a distinctive quality that is not concerned with replying to the former metropolitan center. It analyzes with subtlety and psychological insight that elusive boundary between decolonization, neocolonialism, and the promised land of postcoloniality.

ANGELA SMITH

See also Ngugi wa Thiong'o; Postcolonial Narrative and Criticism of the Novel

Further Reading

Amuta, Chidi, *The Theory of African Literature: Implications for Practical Criticism,* London and Atlantic Highlands, New Jersey: Zed Books, 1989
Cook, David, and Michael Okenimkpe, *Ngugi wa Thiong'o: An Exploration of His Writings,* London: Heinemann, 1983; 2nd edition, Oxford: Currey, and Portsmouth, New Hampshire: Heinemann, 1997
Davies, Carole Boyce, and Anne Adams Graves, editors, *Ngambika: Studies of Women in African Literature,* Trenton, New Jersey: Africa World Press, 1986
Gakwandi, Shatto, *The Novel and Contemporary Experience in Africa,* London: Heinemann, and New York: Africana, 1977
Gikandi, Simon, *Reading the African Novel,* London: Currey, and Portsmouth, New Hampshire: Heinemann, 1987
Gurnah, Abdulrazak, editor, *Essays on African Writing,* Portsmouth, New Hampshire, and Oxford: Heinemann, 1993
Harrow, Kenneth, editor, *Thresholds of Change in African Literature: The Emergence of a Tradition,* London: Currey, and Portsmouth, New Hampshire: Heinemann, 1994
Ikonne, Chidi, editor, *African Literature and African Historical Experiences,* Ibadan, Nigeria: Heinemann, 1991
Julien, Eileen, *African Novels and the Question of Orality,* Bloomington: Indiana University Press, 1992
Killam, G.D., editor, *The Writing of East and Central Africa,* London and Exeter, New Hampshire: Heinemann, 1984
Maughan-Brown, David, *Land, Freedom, and Fiction: History and Ideology in Kenya,* London: Zed Books, 1985
Msiska, Mpalive-Hangson, and Paul Hyland, editors, *Writing and Africa,* London and New York: Longman, 1997
Nasta, Susheila, editor, *Motherlands: Black Women's Writing from Africa, the Caribbean, and South Asia,* London: Women's Press, 1991; New Brunswick, New Jersey: Rutgers University Press, 1992
Ngugi wa Thiong'o, *Homecoming: Essays on African and Caribbean Literature, Culture and Politics,* London: Heinemann, and New York: Lawrence Hill, 1972
Ngugi wa Thiong'o, *Writers in Politics,* London and Exeter, New Hampshire: Heinemann, 1981
Ngugi wa Thiong'o, *Decolonising the Mind: The Politics of Language in African Literature,* London: Currey, and Portsmouth, New Hampshire: Heinemann, 1986
Ngugi wa Thiong'o, *Moving the Centre: The Struggle for Cultural Freedoms,* London: Currey, and Portsmouth, New Hampshire: Heinemann, 1993
Smith, Angela, *East African Writing in English,* London and New York: Macmillan, 1989
Stratton, Florence, *Contemporary African Literature and the Politics of Gender,* London and New York: Routledge, 1989
Wright, Derek, *The Novels of Nuruddin Farah,* Bayreuth: Bayreuth University Press, 1994

African Novel

South Africa

The rise of the African novel has become one of the most important phenomena in world culture in the second half of the 20th century, largely because of the obvious importance of the African novel in the construction of new cultural identities for postcolonial African nations. The special political relevance that is characteristic of the African novel in general has in some ways been especially intense in the Republic of South Africa. The literature of South Africa as a whole is a special case in the history of African culture because the history of South Africa, as the postcolonial African nation to have the most substantial white population descended from European settlers, differs from that of other African nations in important ways, especially given that South African history has been blighted by the phenomenon of apartheid, through which the white minority population sought to maintain economic and political control of the country through brutal repression of the black majority. Apartheid, based on a strict separation of races and on an assumption of the absolute superiority of whites over nonwhites, was part of a long legacy of racism in South Africa, becoming the official policy of the South African government from 1948 to 1990, when apartheid began to be dismantled, leading to the election in 1994 of Nelson Mandela as the first president of post-apartheid South Africa in the first genuinely free elections in the country's history.

The fact of apartheid dominates the history of post–World War II South African literature, which consists almost entirely of works that are critical of the policy and of the ruthless manner in which it was generally carried out. The novel was an important venue of political protest during the apartheid years, although it was less prominent as a genre in apartheid South Africa than it has long been in the West. This is owing in part to censorship and other strict forms of control that left many writers opposed to apartheid unable to publish anything so extensive as a novel in South Africa. This was especially the case for black South African writers who, faced with limited access to publication, found poetry and drama more amenable to their immediate expressive needs. These essentially oral genres also responded better to the needs of black audiences in South Africa, where inequities in the educational system assured that literacy rates among blacks remained low by Western standards. Numerous important anti-apartheid novels did appear during these years, however, although many of them had to be published abroad and were available in South Africa only through illegal, underground modes of distribution.

Despite this legacy of repression, the South African novel has a proud history dating to the early years of the 20th century, during which a surprising number of works were published in indigenous languages, especially Sotho and Zulu. Most of these early works were produced by presses controlled by missionaries working in the area and are little more than religious tracts. However, at least one, Thomas Mofolo's Sotho-language novel *Chaka* (submitted for publication as early as 1910, but first published in 1925) has claim to considerable literary merit and continues to be read and to receive extensive critical attention even today. Indeed, since the publication of Daniel Kunene's new English translation of the book in the Heinemann African Writers Series in 1981, *Chaka* has achieved a new prominence in critical discussions of South African literature. Mofolo's book, based on the story of an early 19th-century Zulu king, may be taken in part to be an early attempt to recover elements of the African past that have been suppressed in colonialist histories, thus initiating what would become one of the major projects of later African literature. South African literature has in fact long been marked by a special intensity in its engagement with history, perhaps out of a sense of the urgency in speaking out against apartheid.

One of the important founding figures of black South African

literature in English was Peter Abrahams, who became politically aware in the 1930s and then went into exile in 1939 better to pursue his ambition to be a writer. After two years at sea, Abrahams settled in London, where he married an Englishwoman and became an editor of the Communist Party organ *Daily Worker*. Abrahams' first two novels, *Song of the City* (1945) and *Mine Boy* (1946), address overtly Marxist themes of opposition to class-based oppression under industrial capitalism (which, in South Africa as in the United States, is inseparable from racial oppression). Abrahams' third novel, *The Path of Thunder* (1948), is optimistic in its treatment of the possibility of love across racial barriers. Taken together, his first three novels are informed by a powerful hope that conditions in South Africa will be greatly improved if white South Africans put aside their racial hatred. With the publication of *Wild Conquest* (1950), Abrahams turned his attention to more historical themes in an attempt to locate the roots of apartheid in the early history of encounters with the indigenous Matabele people of Afrikaner settlers during their "Great Trek" into the interior of South Africa in the 1830s and 1840s. One of Abrahams' most important works is his 1954 autobiography, *Tell Freedom,* the first published autobiography by a black South African. The 1956 novel *A Wreath for Udomo* is also especially important in the way its indictment of colonialism and its understanding of the dangers of neocolonialism anticipate the works of later writers such as Chinua Achebe, Ayi Kwei Armah, and Ngugi wa Thiong'o. Abrahams extends this theme in *This Island Now* (1966), a critique of neocolonialism in an island nation modeled on Haiti and Jamaica. Other important novels by Abrahams include *A Night of Their Own* (1965) and *The View from Coyaba* (1985), which employ South African and Jamaican settings, respectively, to explore the role of the writer in the liberation of the black race.

Abrahams has been an important inspiration for a number of other black South African writers, although many of these writers draw upon indigenous oral traditions to go beyond Abrahams' relatively conventional adherence to a Western aesthetic. Es'kia Mphahlele is another important early figure in the development of a black South African literature. Perhaps his most important single work is his autobiography *Down Second Avenue* (1959), which joins Abrahams' *Tell Freedom* as perhaps the two most important South African works in that genre. Mphahlele is also the author of two novels, *The Wanderers* (1971) and *Chirundu* (1979). But Mphahlele's most important contributions to South African fiction may be in the genre of the short story, both for his own work in the genre and for his work with the important literary magazine *Drum,* which became one of the major forces in the development of South African literature. Mphahlele's short-story collections include *The Living and Dead* (1961), *In Corner B* (1967), *The Unbroken Song* (1981), and *Renewal Time* (1988). Mphahlele is also an important critic, known for volumes of commentary such as *The African Image* (1962) and *Voices in the Whirlwind* (1972) and for his sometimes controversial stands, as in his vigorous opposition to the ideology of the *négritude* movement and for his scepticism about the ultimate ability of literature in English to contribute to the development of a genuinely African cultural identity.

Beginning in the 1950s, the short story has been a particularly important genre among black writers in modern South African literature, largely because magazines such as *Drum* and *Classic* offered publication venues for black writers of short stories that were not available to novelists. In addition to Mphahlele, important short-story writers have included Richard Rive, James Matthews, Njabulo Ndebele, Mbulelo Mzamane, and Alex La Guma. Rive's 1964 novel, *Emergency,* which deals with events surrounding the 1960 police massacre of dozens of peaceful demonstrators at Sharpeville, near Johannesburg, although banned in South Africa, was also an important contribution to the development of the novel in South Africa. Rive's engagement with political developments in South Africa continued in his other novels, including *"Buckingham Palace," District Six* (1986) and *Emergency Continued* (1990). The politically engaged novels of La Guma, meanwhile, have made him perhaps the most important of all nonwhite South African novelists. As Abdul JanMohamed notes, "The life and fiction of Alex La Guma perfectly illustrate the predicament of nonwhites in South Africa and the effects of apartheid on their lives" (see JanMohamed, 1983).

Born and raised in the notorious District Six, the "colored" ghetto of Capetown, La Guma experienced firsthand the tribulations of South Africa's poor and oppressed. His communist parents also exposed him to leftist politics at an early age, and by 1948 (at the age of 23) he had joined South Africa's Communist Party, which would be outlawed two years later, forcing La Guma into a particularly marginal position in South African society. In the 1950s his active involvement in trade union politics led to his harassment and detention by the authorities on several occasions, eventually forcing him to leave the country for England in 1966. By this time he had established a considerable international reputation as a writer, both for his short stories and for the novels *A Walk in the Night* (1962) and *And a Threefold Cord* (1964). *The Stone Country* (1967) was also written while he was still in South Africa. These novels combine an uncompromising description of the squalor of life in South Africa's urban slums with a strong commitment to the possibility of radical political change. La Guma's novels written in exile, *In the Fog of the Seasons' End* (1972) and *Time of the Butcherbird* (1979), continue this passionate political commitment and concern for the plight of those whom Frantz Fanon called "the wretched of the earth."

La Guma's novels are all informed by a sophisticated Marxist understanding of the problems of South African society and of the steps necessary for the ultimate solution to those problems. They are also distinctive in their journalistic style, which is reminiscent of the works of American naturalist writers such as Frank Norris and Theodor Dreiser, but for which the closest American analog is probably the 1930s proletarian fiction produced by writers such as Mike Gold, Jack Conroy, and James T. Farrell. La Guma himself characterized his work as socialist realism, thus indicating the crucial influence of Soviet writers such as Maksim Gor'kii, Fedor Gladkov, and Mikhail Sholokhov on his work. La Guma's dialogical relationship with a number of international literary movements parallels his extensive international reputation, although it is typical of conditions in the South Africa of the apartheid years that his works, banned in that country, were virtually unknown there until the end of apartheid.

While La Guma's journalistic realism is typical of the dominant mode of black South African fiction, poets such as Sipho Sepamla and Mongane Serote also have written novels the styles of which show the clear influence of their poetic backgrounds. Serote, writing in a street-smart mode influenced by Amiri Baraka and other African-American activist writers of the 1960s, became perhaps the best-known poet in South Africa by the early 1970s. This poetry is marked by the same intense political commitment that distinguishes his only novel, the 1981 *To Every Birth Its Blood.* The first part of this novel presents a vivid evocation of township life as background to the personal angst of its protagonist, Tsi. But the second part expands its scope into the public sphere by suggesting the possibility for change through collective resistance to oppression and to the madness of apartheid. Sepamla's novel *A Ride on the Whirlwind* (1981) focuses on the experiences of its protagonist, Mzi, who returns to South Africa to work for the violent overthrow of the government after training abroad in revolutionary techniques. Its focus on both interracial violence and violence among blacks (especially as perpetrated by blacks working in collusion with the South African regime) anticipates the specific incidents of violence that would mark life in South Africa during the 1980s. This novel thus echoes Sepamla's earlier *The Root Is One* (1979) in its concern with the possibility of change through violent political action. But Sepamla's real subject, reminiscent of that of the Nigerian Iyayi, is the everyday violence, both psychic and physical, that the phenomenon of apartheid wrought on the lives of ordinary black people in South Africa. His later novels, *Third Generation* (1986) and *A Scattered Survival* (1989), focus particularly on the breakdown of personal relationships under the squalid conditions of life in the ghettos of South Africa's black townships.

Also of note among recent South African novels is Lewis Nkosi's *Mating Birds* (1983), which shows a large degree of sophistication. Nkosi is also the author of numerous works of literary criticism, including the important *Tasks and Masks: Themes and Styles of African Literature* (1981). His novel is a blistering indictment of the crippling effects of apartheid on personal relationships in South Africa. In its focus on an aspiring writer who is in a South African prison awaiting execution, *Mating Birds* participates in a tradition of prison novels that has, not surprisingly, been a prominent aspect of South African literature. Important earlier examples of the prison genre include D.M. Zwelonke's *Robben Island* (1973) and Moses Dlamini's *Robben Island, Hell-Hole* (1984); prison and jail experiences also figure prominently in many of La Guma's works.

Black South African women writers have been more active in the short-story genre than in the novel, although at least one nonwhite woman from South Africa, Bessie Head, became, in a career cut short by her premature death in 1986, one of Africa's leading women novelists. It is indicative of conditions in South Africa that all of Head's novels were written while in exile, in Botswana, where most of her fiction is also set. Her first novel, *When Rain Clouds Gather* (1968) is, like so many African novels, a story of conflict between modern and traditional societies. The book takes on special political force, however, by the fact that modern ideas are brought to the rural Botswanan village of Golema Mmidi not by white colonizers but by political exiles fleeing from the apartheid regime in South Africa. Indeed, the book's major English character, Gilbert Balfour, is a positive figure, an agricultural expert who tries to help the poor villagers modernize their farming methods and thus decrease their poverty.

In *Maru* (1971) Head continues her focus on Botswanan village life but considerably increases the complexity of her fictional technique. The novel is a complex, multilayered narrative that employs a basic love-story plot (revolving around the competition of two men, Maru and Moleka, for the affections of the same woman, Margaret) to explore the psychic consequences of African social phenomenon such as tribalism, racism (among different groups of blacks), and the oppression of women. The major characters all have a rather allegorical quality, standing as representatives of social, racial, and gender positions in the book's exploration of traditional African prejudices in relation to these positions. In its final affirmation of the individual will as opposed to the demands of social conventions, Head's vision in the novel appears to be more in line with European individualism than with African socialistic traditions, but the work nevertheless makes some important points about Botswanan village society.

Head's best-known novel is the 1973 A Question of Power, a frighteningly intense and at least partially autobiographical exploration of psychological instability in the context of a Botswanan village. The protagonist, Elizabeth (who seems directly modeled on Head), is a colored South African woman in exile in Botswana who must battle to find a stable sense of identity in the midst of a mental breakdown, a battle that is complicated by her social position as an exile and by her situation as a woman in a strongly male-dominated society. Head's style powerfully evokes Elizabeth's simultaneous experience of mental illness and social marginalization, and it is clear that Elizabeth's nightmarish psychic pain and fragmentation represent both Head's own personal experiences and the larger social damage wrought in South Africa by the insane policy of apartheid. The novel ends, however, on a positive (if somewhat unconvincing) note, with a suggestion of the healing power of individual love, although it also indicates the positive potential of communal activities such as cooperative gardening for the production of food.

In Serowe: Village of the Rain Wind (1981) Head turns to a more historical focus, telling the story of the development of Botswana from 1880 to 1970 through a compilation of oral accounts supplied to her in interviews with the real inhabitants of the village of Serowe. The book is one of the more interesting among numerous African experiments in the blending of written and oral narrative. Head's last novel, A Bewitched Crossroad: An African Saga (1984), also focuses on themes in Botswanan history, mingling fact and fiction in an ambitious attempt to tell the story of Botswana from a human perspective. Head's short stories, many of which are collected in the volumes The Collector of Treasures, and Other Botswana Tales (1977) and Tales of Tenderness and Power (1989), are also important.

If the novel has not been an especially rich genre for black South African women, it is also the case that South Africa's best-known novelist on an international scale is a white woman, Nadine Gordimer, who won the Nobel prize for literature in 1991. Indeed, the tradition of novels by white South African women dates back to the late 19th century in the work of Olive Schreiner, whose The Story of an African Farm, first published in 1883, is still widely read today. Although Schreiner's work may be criticized for its focus on white settlers almost to the exclusion of South Africa's indigenous black population, it has been inspirational for a number of later women novelists. For example, the British novelist Doris Lessing, who grew up in colonial Rhodesia (where much of her early fiction is set) credits Schreiner with having taught her that it was possible to write seriously about Africa.

Gordimer is unquestionably the most important white South African woman novelist working today, and her combination of deft literary technique and an uncompromising sense of social responsibility stands as a model for novelists worldwide. Her first novel, The Lying Days, was published in 1953. A somewhat autobiographical Bildungsroman, it traces the development of its female protagonist, Helen Shaw, from her early childhood in a mining town to bohemian young adulthood in a Johannesburg caught up in the turmoil of the early years of apartheid. The novel, like most of Gordimer's early work, focuses on the damaging and dehumanizing impact of racism on the lives of white South Africans. However, The Lying Days, like A World of Strangers (1958) and Occasion for Loving (1963), treats conditions in South Africa in a mode of relatively light satire. These early novels have been described by Abdul JanMohamed (1983) as works of Gordimer's "bourgeois phase." He sees novels such as The Late Bourgeois World (1966), A Guest of Honour (1970), and The Conservationist (1974) as examples of a "postbourgeois" phase in which Gordimer's growing outrage at social and political conditions in South Africa brings her to a more and more urgent criticism of those conditions. These novels criticize social conditions in South Africa in increasingly strong terms, although they continue to concentrate on the damaging effects of apartheid on South Africa's white population. For example, The Conservationist (winner of the 1974 Booker Prize, the first novel by an African writer to win that prestigious award) is a probing examination of the psychological alienation of its protagonist, the white businessman Mehring, who seeks, amid his emotional estrangement from friends, family, and lovers, to regain a sense of his humanity through contact with nature on a farm he purchases outside Johannesburg. However, political conditions in South Africa make this project impossible.

In Burger's Daughter (1979) Gordimer begins to take a more radical political stance in her positive treatment of the anti-apartheid activities of South African communists, initiating what JanMohamed considers the beginning of the "revolutionary" phase in Gordimer's writing. Burger's Daughter is a large-scale work that follows in the tradition of the 19th-century European novel, reflecting among other things the influence on Gordimer's work of Georg Lukács' readings of the realistic novel, while at the same time including strategies typical of both postmodernist and postcolonial novels. Meanwhile, both Burger's Daughter and The Conservationist are informed by an atmosphere of impending upheaval. This sense of historical crisis becomes the central motif of July's People (1981), an imaginative study of a future South African society in which a black revolution has toppled white rule and in which the formerly prosperous white Smales family fears that they may be the targets of racial violence amid the postrevolutionary chaos that reigns in the country. Their loyal black servant, Mwawate (whom they call July), leads them to his village for safety. There, they find themselves in the midst of an alien culture they do not understand, and their subsequent sense of inferiority and confusion serves as a defamiliarizing commentary on the situation in which July and other blacks had long found themselves in the white-dominated urban regions of South Africa. Gordimer also comments on the power of white propaganda by showing the village chief in terror of the revolution, which he assumes (after years of official anticommunist hysteria) to have been the work of Cuban and Russian agitators. Accepting white technological superiority, the chief begs Bam Smales to use his gun to protect the tribe from the communists, whom he believes will soon come to take control of the village. A strong sense of political commitment and engagement with South African history continues to inform novels such as *A Sport of Nature* (1987) and *My Son's Story* (1990), while Gordimer in these works also begins to meditate on the potential for a post-apartheid cultural identity for South Africa and for post-apartheid personal identities for South Africans.

The tradition of white men's writing in South Africa goes back for some time as well, with a particularly rich growth in this tradition in the early years after the official establishment of apartheid in 1948. Works in English such as Alan Paton's *Cry, the Beloved Country* (1948), Dan Jacobson's *The Evidence of Love* (1960), and Jack Cope's *The Dawn Comes Twice* (1969) typically mix a commitment to liberal values with a critique of apartheid, although there is generally a growing sense of pessimism in such works. By far the most important white male novelist writing in English in South Africa today is J.M. Coetzee, who has combined a self-consciously postmodern and experimental literary style with an intense concern with the evils of apartheid to produce an impressive body of novels marked both by technical sophistication and by powerful and disturbing content (showing the impact of South African political and social reality). Coetzee's novels begin with the 1974 *Dusklands*, a parody of colonialist discourse reminiscent of the work of postmodern European writers such as Samuel Beckett and Vladimir Nabokov, and *In the Heart of the Country* (1977), a stream-of-consciousness exploration of the master-slave mentality of South African society.

Coetzee's best-known novel is probably the 1980 *Waiting for the Barbarians,* which combines starkly realistic descriptions of violence with almost surrealistic scenes of symbolic imagery to comment upon the phenomenon of imperialism in general and apartheid in particular. He became the second African writer to win the Booker Prize with the 1983 novel *Life & Times of Michael K,* which marks an increasing turn toward metafictional explorations of the nature of fiction and its role in the world. This Kafkaesque novel employs experimental modes of writing reminiscent of much 20th-century European literature to explore themes of official oppression versus individual freedom that have distinctly South African (anticolonial, anti-apartheid) resonances. *Foe* (1986) is even more self-consciously literary, drawing upon the plots of Daniel Defoe's 18th-century novels *Robinson Crusoe* (1719) and *Roxana* (1724) to construct a profound philosophical fiction that explores both the nature of artistic creation and the impact on such creation of political oppression. *Age of Iron* (1990) similarly explores the impact of social marginalization on the writer.

Coetzee is also the editor, with André Brink, of the anthology *A Land Apart* (1986), which includes fiction, poetry, and autobiography from a number of South African writers in both English and Afrikans. Brink, like Coetzee a professor of English at the University of Cape Town, is the only South African writer working in the Afrikans language who has any significant critical reputation. Since he translates his own work into English, he may well also be considered an English-language novelist. It is certainly in English that his work is best known and most widely read. Novels such as *Kennis van die aand* (1973; *Looking on*

Darkness), *A Dry White Season* (1979), *A Chain of Voices* (1982), and *An Act of Terror* (1991) draw directly upon South African history to produce powerful anti-apartheid statements that make Brink, along with Gordimer and Coetzee, one of the leading figures in South African literature today.

With the end of apartheid, the South African novel (along with South Africa itself) entered an entirely new phase, featuring, among other things, the new availability in South Africa of previously banned works by important authors such as La Guma. Meanwhile, many of the major novelists of the apartheid era continued to be active. Coetzee's first post-apartheid novel, *The Master of Petersburg* (1994), shows the clear effect of this historical change by veering away from his earlier engagement with South African history. At the same time, the novel, a fictional recreation of the life of the 19th-century Russian novelist Fedor Dostoevskii, continues Coetzee's long postmodernist dialogue with the European literary tradition. Gordimer's first post-apartheid novel, *None to Accompany Me*, was also published in 1994. However, this novel continues her engagement with South African history by tracing the attempts of several South Africans (both black and white) to contribute to the development of a new post-apartheid national identity while at the same time seeking to revise their own personal identities, which had long been shaped by apartheid and their resistance to it. Brink's 1996 novel *Imaginings of Sand* also deals directly with events surrounding the end of apartheid, while at the same time including materials that reach far into the South African past.

Several important new black novelists have become prominent in the post-apartheid era, most of them continuing the political commitment and engagement of the novels of the apartheid era. Zakes Mda, already well known as a dramatist, has emerged as a particularly important novelistic voice with such works as *She Plays with the Darkness* (1995), which examines the cultural contrasts between urban South Africa and a Lesotho mountain village, and *Ways of Dying* (1995), which contrasts life in the slums of a Cape Town township with the images of splendor promulgated in Western popular culture. Another recent novel of black township life is Isaac Mogotsi's *The Alexandra Tales* (1994), which considers the growing political awareness of a young boy growing up in the township and coming to understand the injustices of the society around him. Among new white novelists in the post-apartheid era is Mark Behr, whose first novel, *The Smell of Apples* (1995), similarly deals with the growing awareness of a young boy, this time of the son of an Afrikaner general during the era of apartheid. *The Year of the Tapeworm,* by Chris Van Wyk, who had earlier coauthored a biography of Oliver Tambo, was published in 1996. The period since the end of apartheid has not been an especially rich one for the production of South African novelists, probably owing to the dramatic changes underway in South African society. But the future looks especially bright as novelists begin to find their voice in the new post-apartheid society and to solidify their relationship with the novels of the apartheid past.

M. KEITH BOOKER

See also André Brink; J.M. Coetzee; Cry, the Beloved Country; Nadine Gordimer; Alex La Guma; Postcolonial Narrative and Criticism of the Novel; Story of an African Farm

Further Reading

Barnett, Ursula, *A Vision of Order: A Study of Black South African Literature in English (1914–1980)*, Amherst: University of Massachusetts Press, and London: Browne, 1983

Booker, M. Keith, *The African Novel in English: An Introduction*, Portsmouth, New Hampshire: Heinemann, 1998

Chapman, Michael, Colin Gardner, and Es'kia Mphahlele, editors, *Perspectives on South African English Literature*, Parklands, South Africa: Donker, 1992

Davidson, Basil, Joe Slovo, and A.R. Wilkinson, *Southern Africa: The New Politics of Revolution*, Harmondsworth, Middlesex: Penguin, 1976

Gray, Stephen, *Southern African Literatures: An Introduction*, New York: Barnes and Noble, and London: Collings, 1979

JanMohamed, Abdul R., *Manichean Aesthetics: The Politics of Literature in Colonial Africa*, Amherst: University of Massachusetts Press, 1983

Jolly, Rosemary Jane, *Colonization, Violence, and Narration in White South African Writing: André Brink, Breyten Breytenbach, and J.M. Coetzee*, Athens: Ohio University Press, 1996

Ngara, Emmanuel, editor, *New Writing from Southern Africa: Authors Who Have Become Prominent since 1980*, London: Currey, and Portsmouth, New Hampshire: Heinemann, 1996

Nkosi, Lewis, *Tasks and Masks: Themes and Styles of African Literature*, Harlow, Essex: Longman, 1981

Povey, John, "English-Language Fiction from South Africa," in *A History of Twentieth-Century African Literatures*, edited by Oyekan Owomoyela, Lincoln: University of Nebraska Press, 1993

Shava, Piniel Viriri, *A People's Voice: Black South African Writing in the Twentieth Century*, London: Zed, and Athens: Ohio University Press, 1989

Thompson, Leonard, *A History of South Africa*, New Haven, Connecticut: Yale University Press, 1990; revised edition, 1992

Trump, Martin, editor, *Rendering Things Visible: Essays on South African Literary Culture*, Johannesburg: Raven Press, and Athens: University of Ohio Press, 1990

Van Wyk Smith, Malvern, *Grounds of Contest: A Survey of South African English Literature*, Kenwyn, South Africa: Jutalit, 1990

Afterword. *See* Framing and Embedding in Narrative

Against Nature by Joris-Karl Huysmans

À rebours 1884

*A*gainst Nature was published in 1884, exactly ten years after Huysmans' first work, *Le Drageoir à épices* (*A Dish of Spices*), a collection of prose poems, was printed at his own expense. *Against Nature,* Huysmans' fifth novel, signaled a movement away from his naturalistic phase under the tutelage of Émile Zola, toward decadence and the late nightmarish works, such as *En Rade* (1887; *Becalmed*), and especially *Là-bas* (1891; *Down There*), which deals with Satanism. *Against Nature* became infamous as the "incendiary device, that would not only light the course of all his later work, but all the prose of the Decadent period" (see Banks, 1990). It is the "poisonous" yellow book to which Oscar Wilde's Dorian Gray refers, and whose protagonist Dorian imitates. *Against Nature* may justly be claimed as the central book of the decadent movement.

The protagonist of *Against Nature,* the Duc des Esseintes, is certainly an agglomeration of different characters, not the least

Huysmans himself. Other models for Des Esseintes have been posited as Jean Folantin from his earlier novel *A vau-l'eau* (1882; *Downstream*); Edmond de Goncourt; the dandy critic Jules Barbey d'Aurevilly; most usually, the outrageous Comte Robert de Montesquiou has been cited; as well as a number of Poe's characters, most notably Roderick Usher. Aside from possible ancestors, Des Esseintes personifies various currents that had been developing in French literature and culture during the previous three decades, principally in the works of Charles Baudelaire and Théophile Gautier. By the 1880s the French literary scene was dominated by the school of naturalism, with its refusal to idealize experience and its focus on human life as governed by natural laws. The most noteworthy pioneers of naturalism were Émile Zola (with *Thérèse Raquin,* 1867, for example) and the Goncourt brothers (especially with *Germinie Lacerteux,* 1865). Huysmans began writing against the backdrop of Zola's 20-novel series influenced by theories of heredity and scientific empiricism, beginning in 1871 with *Les Rougon-Macquart* and concluding in 1893. French naturalism was echoed in broader terms across Europe, especially in Britain, with the movement away from the "high" realism of George Eliot, Charles Dickens, and Elizabeth Gaskell, toward a more deterministic concept of writing governed by the establishment of evolutionary theory as an accepted, if not sanctioned, theory. Important fiction from the period of the late 1870s to mid-1880s includes Thomas Hardy's mature novels, Anthony Trollope's last works, and Henry James' protomodernist writing. There was a growing movement away from the depiction of life for a didactic purpose, toward an attempt to document the conditions of daily existence devoid of moral judgment, and within this niche *Against Nature* may be placed.

Early in 1877 Huysmans first met Zola, who had admired the former's review of his *L'Assommoir* (*The Gin Palace*) in the same year. While these reviews may be read ostensibly as an apology for naturalism, they are, in essence, an articulation of Huysmans' own aesthetic theory. Huysmans never believed that Zola's pseudo-scientism was a valid, creative framework for the novelist, and if he ever employed naturalistic motifs it was for very antinaturalistic reasons—to access their symbolic resonances. While Huysmans certainly courted Zola and shared many of his beliefs (for example, that writers should be very much of their time and that they should depict the world around them), for Huysmans this was no theory of writing, but personal belief. *Against Nature,* with its naturalistic detailing of an unreal world, displays Huysmans' concept that style, not social commentary, is tantamount. Unlike Zola, who reveled in portraying real life, Huysmans wrote about it because it had alienated him.

A closer acquaintance of Huysmans was Gustave Flaubert, whom Huysmans also met in 1877. While their communications revealed Flaubert's condescension toward the younger man, there are fundamental Flaubertian echoes within *Against Nature* that cannot be ignored. Like Huysmans, Flaubert believed that the only way to write successful fiction was to write about "Beauty," something that they both equated with "truth." This possibility, however, is denied to the novelist because truth requires a retrospective gaze—to look back from the end to the beginning, in order to see the whole—and only God has this privilege. In novels such as *Bouvard et Pécuchet* (1881; *Bouvard et Pécuchet*) and *La Tentation de Saint Antoine* (1874; *The Temptation of St. Anthony*), Flaubert's protagonists are repeatedly faced with the impossibility of making sense of their worlds, and finish only with an awareness of their own insignificance and powerlessness. The modern author is the victim of fragmentation and, like Des Esseintes, can only mediate the world in terms of these fragments—memories, hallucinations, and fantasies—without ever perceiving the whole.

Fundamental to Flaubert's texts is the notion of mediocrity: the condition of being caught in the mid-point between beginning and end, in a middling world of the middling classes, in which the ontological absolutes are denied to humanity. This condition of mediocrity is a modern one: the 19th-century writer is condemned to nostalgically sentimentalize an indecipherable past, or renounce past forms for scientific ones (much as Zola's naturalism does) that thrive on the lack of style. Flaubert's concept is essentially a reconstituting of the term "decadence," and like Flaubert, Des Esseintes finds himself trapped between two worlds—the past world, vaguely remembered and impossible to recapture, and the future world, uncertain and sterile. Nowhere are the parallels between Flaubert's *weltanschauung* and Des Esseintes' malaise more noteworthy than in utterances made by both figures. At the end of *Against Nature*, Des Esseintes is left to feebly conclude, "Like a tide-race, the waves of human mediocrity are rising to the heavens and will engulf this refuge," while, in a letter to a friend, Flaubert complains that "mediocrity is invading everything, even the stones are becoming stupid. . . . Should we perish by it (and we shall perish, though it matters little) we must by all means stem the flood of dung that is invading us." It is, of course, significant that neither could Huysmans have read Flaubert's private correspondence, nor Flaubert *Against Nature* (having died four years before its publication), yet both came to almost identical conclusions about this central decadent subject.

"To be at the centre of the world, and yet to remain hidden from the world" (Baudelaire, 1846) encapsulates Des Esseintes' philosophy. Disgusted by the mercantilism of society, he finds comfort in "the idea of hiding away far from human society, of shutting himself up in some snug retreat," and moves to the outskirts of Paris. One of the major tropes of decadent literature is manifest in the novel's preoccupation with the artificial, and Des Esseintes surrounds himself with "useless" manmade creations, signifying his hatred for the cause-and-effect utilitarianism of the bourgeoisie, whose "idiotic sentimentality combined with commercialism clearly represented the dominant spirit of the age." Another characteristic decadent symptom is Des Esseintes' ennui, and as a victim of such he indulges in inventive, unnatural stimulations to relieve his tedium: he decorates his bedroom to resemble a monk's cell with the most luxurious furnishings; he purchases exotic flowers simply because they appear manmade; and he has a fake ship's cabin in his dining room, complete with seawater and mechanical fish. Such actions make him feel that "by transferring this ingenious trickery, this clever simulation to the intellectual plane, one can enjoy, just as easily as on the material plane, imaginary pleasures, similar in all respects to the pleasures of reality." This encapsulates a third aspect of fin-de-siècle literature: the *intellectual* locus of the decadent's perversions. Everything, whether sexual, sensuous, or aesthetic, is merely a reflection of the decadent obsession with the mind and the exercise of willpower over one's environment.

The decadent's obsession with mental states is what essentially differentiates him from the romantic hero. While characters such as Johann Wolfgang von Goethe's Werther and François René de Chateaubriand's René are disgusted by the world and move into retirement in search of supreme emotions to satisfy enormous desires, the decadent—while sharing such recoil—is paralyzed with satiety, searching instead for the newest sensations at their most intense. Nowhere is this more obvious than when Des Esseintes is administered an enema by his doctor during a bout of illness; instead of feeling aversion, he is ecstatic over the very artificiality of the thing: "No one, he thought, would ever go any further; taking nourishment in this way was undoubtedly the ultimate deviation from the norm."

Des Esseintes' obsession with satisfying his appetites leads to an acute neurosis, and he suffers from a variety of afflictions that become characteristic of many decadent protagonists. Des Esseintes flees to the suburbs to escape a lifestyle he thinks is destroying him, yet finds himself plagued by hallucinations and recurring nightmares that he cannot evade, leading him to conclude that the source of his malady is *himself*. R.K.R. Thornton (1983) notes that *Against Nature* "is not only the Bible of Decadence, but also one of its severest criticisms. . . ." Typifying decadence as a whole, Des Esseintes attempts to escape into artifice, and fails: his plants die and leave him nauseated, his enema is actually a medicinal expedient to combat his neurotic symptoms; finally, he is compelled to return to detested society for the sake of his physical health. Taken to its logical conclusion, artificiality becomes impossible for the human being, who must face "the difference between a good recovery on the one hand and insanity speedily followed by tuberculosis on the other." As the quintessential decadent, Des Esseintes withdraws himself for ostensibly good principles—honesty, love of intelligence and art, and abstinence—but his essential failure lies in the withdrawal from society's other mechanisms, especially its commercialism, upon which his luxurious tastes are dependent.

The decadent hero, as typified in such a pivotal work as *Against Nature,* is disillusioned with his society and turns solely to art—a gesture unacceptable to that society—and the novel closes with the triumph of nature over art. Of course this triumph is itself decadent, because it is an illness, an aberration against the natural process, that forces him to relinquish his artificiality in any case. Des Esseintes, like decadence itself, is forced to go out with a whimper rather than a bang, and has nothing left to say but the feeble "crumble then, society! perish, old world!" Betrayed by artificiality, Des Esseintes turns to another decadent penchant, Roman Catholicism, a faith he can hardly believe in; and his last words signify that final, fundamental decadent malaise—impuissance, a spiritual impotence brought on by boredom and satiety: "Well, it is all over now. Like a tiderace, the waves of human mediocrity are rising to the heavens and will engulf this refuge, for I am opening up the flood-gates myself, against my will."

By the 1880s, the absolutes that had sustained much of 19th-century culture had been irrevocably eroded away. The universe was no longer a quantifiable arena based on observable rules; it was a world of flux and indeterminism. From the feelings of impuissance in which the Western world lingered arose the short-lived movement of the decadents. At a time when novelists like Hardy and James were shifting the bases of writing from the authentic depiction of life to a more philosophically based study of heredity and environment, Huysmans' personal vision of the dark night of the soul managed to affect distinctly the literature that followed it. According to Brian R. Banks (1990), *Against Nature* "changed the course of literature, both French and European, both for its style and influence on artists and writers." A.E. Carter (1958) notes that the novel articulated completely the whole impetus behind decadence, and after 1884 there was nothing new to be written: all other decadent writing was merely a reiteration of Huysmans' principal novel. Such was its significance that, within this short-lived movement, *Against Nature*

had such an enduring effect that toward the end of the decadent period Oscar Wilde chose to include it as the central book within his own novel of decadence, *The Picture of Dorian Gray* (1891).

Arthur Symons (1893), another decadent writer, called Des Esseintes "the effeminate, over-civilized, deliberately abnormal creature who is *the last product* of our society. . . ." The novel demonstrates that the decadent who perceives himself to be *à rebours,* against society, is actually its logical conclusion. While spurning the proliferation of the bourgeoisie and identifying himself with a dying aristocracy, the decadent is utterly dependent on, and would not have materialized but for, the mercantilism of the former despite shamming a veneer of the latter. *Against Nature* is, in typically decadent fashion, both the celebration and condemnation of the movement. Des Esseintes' resistance to society is an attempt to repress his actual dependence on the market forces that constitute it; his very rebellion necessitates a return to this world, and aesthetic subversion becomes impotent dissent. In *Against Nature,* while aestheticism has replaced the mechanisms of morality, it is critiqued, and provides no intrinsic alternative to the moral order. This is, perhaps, the very essence of *Against Nature*: it represents a movement that used its own criteria to criticize and subvert itself; a movement ultimately responsible itself for destroying the creative impulse that had initiated it some 30 years previously.

A.A. MANDAL

See also Decadent Novel

Further Reading

Baldick, Robert, *The Life of J.-K. Huysmans,* Oxford: Clarendon Press, 1955
Banks, Brian R., *The Image of Huysmans,* New York: AMS Press, 1990
Baudelaire, Charles, "The Painter of Modern Life" (1846), in *The Painter of Modern Life and Other Essays,* translated by Jonathan Mayne, London: Phaidon Press, 1964; 2nd edition, 1995
Carter, A.E., *The Idea of Decadence in French Literature, 1830–1900,* Toronto: University of Toronto Press, 1958
Donato, Eugenio, *The Script of Decadence,* New York: Oxford University Press, 1992; Oxford: Oxford University Press, 1993
Lane, Christopher, "The Drama of the Impostor: Dandyism and Its Double," *Cultural Critique* 28 (Fall 1994)
Ridge, George Ross, *The Hero in French Decadent Literature,* Atlanta: University of Georgia Press, 1961
Symons, Arthur, "The Decadent Movement in Literature," *Harper's New Monthly Magazine* 87 (November 1893)
Thornton, R.K.R., *The Decadent Dilemma,* London: Arnold, 1983

The Age of Innocence by Edith Wharton

1922

The best-selling novel that won Edith Wharton the Pulitzer Prize, *The Age of Innocence* builds upon themes found in several of Wharton's earlier novels: negotiating happiness from life's limitations; assessing honestly the qualities and failures of both traditional society and the often volatile modern world; and the economical and intellectual limitations imposed upon women by society. The theme of the unlived life, found in *Ethan Frome* (1911), is resolved in *The Age of Innocence* with greater balance and less extreme tragedy. Whereas Lily Bart's miserable economic circumstances and gender restrictions are described by the narrator with pathos in *The House of Mirth* (1905), Wharton renders these circumstances in *The Age of Innocence* by having several characters comment upon them, often compassionately.

"The nineteenth century," Edith Wharton wrote to a friend immediately after the end of World War I, "is such a blessed refuge from the turmoil and mediocrity of today—like taking sanctuary in a mighty temple" (see Lewis, 1975). Having witnessed the savagery of the war when she lived and performed volunteer work in France, Wharton relates in her novel an appreciation for the more stable, restrained period of her life among old New York society. The novel is sumptuous with physical details of New York City between 1872 and 1899, focusing exclusively on the behavior and ethics found in society's most elevated stratum. Nonetheless, Wharton's novel never sentimentalizes the past's conventions and limitations; the repressive and intellectually torpid social circle of her youth is satirized sharply throughout the novel by the ironic and perceptive narrator, who clearly speaks from Wharton's personal perspective.

Similar to Jane Austen, who drew the material for her novels of manners from her experience in well-bred sitting rooms, Wharton illustrates both the refined aesthetic of her characters' existence as well as the absurdity and pretentiousness of New York's elite. Often, stunning descriptions of personal ornamentation and interior design are juxtaposed with the character's shallowness, acquisitiveness, and relentless jockeying for social prominence.

Wharton's comparative experience of her adopted country, France, with that of her birth country convinced her that America should maintain the virtues of continuity, community obligation, and tradition seen in older European societies, while attempting to infuse its culture with more liberal ideals, especially concerning women. Chiefly, Wharton's novel denounces society's limited uses for talented, intelligent women, protesting against the idea that a well-educated and cultivated woman had no purpose beyond that of bearing children and entertaining guests.

The novel itself is a Bildungsroman concerned with the development of its principal character, Newland Archer. Newland, whose name combines Wharton's middle name, Newbold, with the last name of Henry James' famous innocent, Isabel Archer (heroine of *The Portrait of a Lady,* 1881), finds himself in a love triangle with the exotic cousin of his naive and utterly American fiancée, May. As the novel charts Newland's growing love for the Europeanized Ellen, the reader sees each of the key figures as representative symbols, often in conflict with one another. Although May represents the apotheosis of 19th-century upper-crust domestic virtue, her behavior often reveals her as subtly canny and calculating, ensnaring Newland by the very societal conventions that he simultaneously upholds and despises. While Ellen strongly resembles the worldly and droll Wharton, she longs to feel shielded by a predictable, family-oriented American environment. At the same time, however, the stability Ellen seeks is suffocating, denying her freedom much as it did Wharton's in her earlier years.

Using Newland as the central figure and locus of conflict (both romantic and ideological), Wharton demonstrates the value of individual sacrifice performed for the fortification and advancement of important societal institutions, such as family. Newland's personal sacrifice promotes his family's growth and enhances society's progress, underlining the novel's point that individual happiness is secondary to the strength of the culture.

Although written at the height of the modernist period, *The Age of Innocence* has little in common with the experimental fiction of James Joyce, Virginia Woolf, Gertrude Stein, and other modernist writers. Rather, the novel demonstrates the rich characterizations, sense of place, and detailed descriptions that mark the classic novel of manners, exemplifying Wharton's admiration for the traditional even as her novel derides certain aspects of tradition. During her lifetime, Wharton's enduring friendship with Henry James often led to comparisons between the two writers' work—rarely to Wharton's advantage. While both authors produced novels focusing on the journey from inexperience to experience and both examined "the unlived life," James' aesthetic and methods, especially in his final novels, focus intensely on specific characters' inner psychological development. Wharton, on the other hand, gives an equal emphasis to place and atmosphere, on a character's physical and social environment as these relate to the character's growth. She uses a fairly conventional romantic plot to reflect upon the weaknesses of the surrounding culture and the hypocrisy of that culture's leading figures.

Novelist Sinclair Lewis' masterwork, *Babbitt* (1922), published the same year as *The Age of Innocence,* also portrays the negative results of America's striver culture. Although *Babbitt*'s milieu is decidedly middle class, Lewis and Wharton both regarded the country's shallow materialism as a threat to deeper, nonmaterial values that the authors saw disappearing in modern life. Another admirer of Wharton, F. Scott Fitzgerald, whose writing defined for the United States the decade in which *The Age of Innocence* was published, further demonstrates the seductive dangers of wealth and materialism in virtually all his novels, most notably in his *The Great Gatsby* (1925).

In diagnosing the ills of American society at the turn of the century, Wharton's novel takes a backward glance that reflects her interest in archaeology and underscores her sense of old New York as antiquated. Descriptions of society's "tribal" behavior and archaic customs abound in the novel. Symbols such as archaeological museum fragments and "ancient" houses call to mind the burden that time and tradition place on the individual, while also emphasizing the individual's significance as a linkage from past to present and future.

This concept is elaborated in the novel's final chapter, where the middle-aged main character, now widowed, reflects on his life's modest achievements and contributions, sometimes wistful at their meagerness but proud nevertheless. Such coming to terms with one's place in society's future is the key concept in Wharton's novel; its universality makes this arguably Wharton's greatest work in terms of thematic resonance.

GINA L. TAGLIERI

See also Edith Wharton

Further Reading

Ammons, Elizabeth, *Edith Wharton's Argument with America,* Athens: University of Georgia Press, 1980
Auchincloss, Louis, *Edith Wharton: A Woman in Her Time,* New York: Viking Press, 1971
Goodman, Susan, *Edith Wharton's Women: Friends and Rivals,* Hanover, New Hampshire: University Press of New England, 1990
Lewis, R.W.B., *Edith Wharton: A Biography,* New York: Harper and Row, and London: Constable, 1975
Wershoven, Carol, *The Female Intruder in the Novels of Edith Wharton,* Rutherford, New Jersey: Farleigh Dickinson University Press, and London: Associated University Presses, 1982
Wolff, Cynthia Griffin, *A Feast of Words: The Triumph of Edith Wharton,* New York: Oxford University Press, 1977; Oxford: Oxford University Press, 1978; 2nd edition, Reading, Massachusetts: Addison-Wesley, 1995

S.Y. Agnon 1888–1970

Israeli

Israel's Nobel laureate Shmuel Yosef Agnon was born in Eastern Europe in 1888 and died in Jerusalem in 1970. In its geographic and temporal span, his life touches on some major points in the history of the 20th century, a history felt not only in his literary production but also in his sense of himself as a modern Jewish writer. Ranking with the major modernist writers of this century, Agnon differs from his European peers in his intense engagement in a universe of sacred language. Resisting easy classification, Agnon has been read by some as a pious storyteller, by others as a modern ironist. He is both and more, a writer whose work ranges from the psychological to the grotesque, from the romantic to the surrealist and experimental. From an Eastern European background that placed the study and commentary of Scripture at the center of communal life, Agnon acquired a grounding in traditional Jewish sources that he later drew upon in an ongoing intertextual relationship that was quite often parodic or subversive of the sources themselves. (Gershon Shaked [1989] refers to Agnon's "pseudo-midrash," a kind of pseudo-exegesis that invents more than it interprets.) In this, Agnon was very much a modernist, a "revolutionary traditionalist" in Shaked's phrase, who sought ways of renewing an experience of the world through artistic experimentation.

The very name *Agnon* is a fabrication, a central instance of the interpretive play that identifies Agnon's art. Using the title of *Agunot,* the first story he published in Palestine in 1908, Agnon adapted the Hebrew noun *agunah,* a term in Jewish law that designates a woman who is not free to marry because her husband has disappeared or left without divorcing her. The *agunah* is thus an indeterminate figure, at once connected to the community and separate from it; Agnon's appropriation of the term gives insight into his creation of himself as a modern Jewish writer, blurring the boundaries of sacred and secular, enlarging the domain of the literary, and implying a claim for writing that goes beyond the aesthetic to the collective.

Widely read in European and Scandinavian literatures, Agnon's choice of Hebrew, after early experiments in both Yiddish and Hebrew, links him with others of his generation who turned to Hebrew as a potent resource in the enterprise of national renewal. But while Agnon's writing makes us feel keenly the centrality of Hebrew to a worldview centered on Scripture, sharply modern disjunctions within self, social world, and tradition are all the more startling for their interaction with a deeply rooted mystique of the wholeness inherent in sacred language. The precipitous pace of events of the last century, including not only the rise of Jewish nationalism but also the Nazi effort at genocide, has made of modern Jewish identity less a stable set of concepts than an ongoing field of forces. Agnon's work is inscribed within that cultural-political upheaval; while retaining a detachment from the urgency of events, his writing explores the ways in which cultural constructions and ideologies derive from deeper levels of subjective and collective experience.

In 1931 the first four volumes of Agnon's *Kol sipurav shel Sh. Y. Agnon* (The Collected Works) appeared, inaugurating the Schocken Publishing House in Berlin. A second, much enlarged edition appeared in 1966. Agnon's major novels offer striking stylistic variations within the genre. Dan Miron (1987) argues that Agnon was never really at home with the European genre of the novel and that issues of larger cohesion and closure reflect his uneasy transactions with the conventions of the form, particularly in the two novels set in the land of Israel, *Hakhnasath kallah* (1931, revised and amplified 1953; *The Bridal Canopy*) and *Temol shilshom* (1945; The Day before Yesterday). As a novelist, Agnon exploited those discomforts in particularly productive ways, engaging the tensions between Yiddish modes of storytelling and larger epic structures associated with the novel form.

The Bridal Canopy, Agnon's first major novel, chronicles the travels of an the early 19th-century Eastern European Hasid, something of a Jewish Don Quixote, as he seeks a dowry for his eldest daughter. *Sipur pashut* (1935; *A Simple Story*), whose title resonates with echoes of Gustave Flaubert's *Un Coeur simple,* is set in the small town of Szybucz, Agnon's fictional name for his hometown of Buczacz. *A Simple Story* traces the decline of a self-enclosed community, focusing on a crisis in the maturation of its protagonist, who is among the first of Agnon's recurring portrayals of male passivity and ambivalence.

Playing with the relationship of the writer to the larger Jewish community, *Ore'ah nata lalun* (1938–39; *A Guest for the Night*) invokes the social tapestry of Eastern Europe between the wars and conveys a foreboding about the future of Jewish life in Europe. Dissecting the various impulses that enter into the very act of telling, this first-person narrative produces an ironic tension between its writer-protagonist's yearning for restoration of an imagined past, on the one hand, and the actualities of communal disintegration and his own ambivalence, on the other.

Temol shilshom is Agnon's novel of the period of the second *aliyah*, the wave of Jewish emigration to Palestine between 1907 and 1913. The novel intertwines two plots—a vivid social history in the story of Yitzhak Kummer, would-be pioneer, and the comic-grotesque account of the wanderings of the dog Balak, on whose back Yitzhak has painted the words *mad dog*. *Shirah* (1971; *Shira*) is an unfinished masterpiece (Agnon wrote an ending that he later rejected) that is an antimonumental work, a novel set in the German-Jewish academic community of Jerusalem during the historical moment at which the destruction of German Jewry became clear. In its anatomy of culture, *Shira* challenges distinctions between self and other, male and female, flesh and spirit, taking the perspective of the German Jew who is the product of the very culture that rejects him. The final destruction of Agnon's Eastern European hometown in the Holocaust became the occasion for its re-creation in art, in a work of epic proportions, *'Ir umelo'ah* (1973; *A City and Its Fullness*), a compendium of narratives that includes legends, tales, family sagas, and grotesque renditions of folk culture.

ANNE GOLOMB HOFFMAN

See also Bridal Canopy

Biography
Born Shmuel Yosef Halesi Czaczkes in Buczacz, Galicia, Austro-Hungarian Empire (now in Poland), 17 July 1888. Attended private schools; Baron Hirsch School. Lived in Palestine, 1907–13, serving as first secretary of Jewish Court in Jaffa, and secretary of the National Jewish Council; lecturer and tutor in Germany, 1913–24; returned to Palestine and lived there from 1924. Fellow, Bar Ilan University. Awarded Nobel prize for literature, 1966. Died 17 February 1970.

Novels by Agnon
Hakhnasath kallah, 1931; revised and amplified 1953; as *The Bridal Canopy*, translated by I.M. Lask, 1937
Sipur pashut, 1935; as *A Simple Story*, translated by Hillel Halkin, 1985
Ore'ah nata lalun, 1938–39; as *A Guest for the Night*, translated by Misha Louvish, 1968
Temol shilshom [The Day before Yesterday], 1945
Shirah, 1971; as *Shira*, translated by Zeva Shapiro, 1989

Other Writings: *Kol sipurav shel Sh. Y. Agnon* (8 vols., 1952–62; The Collected Works), which includes novels, novellas, short stories; topically and thematically organized anthologies, culled from Jewish sources; a selection of short stories in *A Book That Was Lost and Other Stories*, edited by Alan Mintz and Anne Golomb Hoffman, 1995.

Further Reading
Alter, Robert, *The Invention of Hebrew Prose: Modern Fiction and the Language of Realism*, Seattle: University of Washington Press, 1988
Band, Arnold, *Nostalgia and Nightmare: A Study in the Fiction of S.Y. Agnon*, Berkeley: University of California Press, 1968
Ben-Dov, Nitza, *Agnon's Art of Indirection: Uncovering Latent Content in the Fiction of S.Y. Agnon*, Leiden and New York: Brill, 1993
Hoffman, Anne Golomb, "Agnon for All Seasons: Recent Trends in the Criticism," *Prooftexts* 11 (1991)
Hoffman, Anne Golomb, *Between Exile and Return: S.Y. Agnon and the Drama of Writing*, Albany: State University of New York Press, 1991
Mintz, Alan, "Agnon in Jaffa: The Myth of the Artist as a Young Man," *Prooftexts* 1 (1981)
Miron, Dan, "Domesticating a Foreign Genre: Agnon's Transactions with the Novel," *Prooftexts* 7 (1987)
Patterson, David, and Glenda Abramson, editors, *Tradition and Trauma: Studies in the Fiction of S.J. Agnon*, Boulder, Colorado: Westview Press, 1994
Shaked, Gershon, *Shmuel Yosef Agnon: A Revolutionary Traditionalist*, New York: New York University Press, 1989
Yudkin, Leon, editor, *Agnon: Texts and Contexts in English Translation*, New York: Wiener, 1988

Alas, Leopoldo. *See* Clarín

Alice's Adventures in Wonderland; Through the Looking-Glass, and What Alice Found There by Lewis Carroll [Charles Lutwidge Dodgson]

1865 and 1871

Perhaps more than any other 19th-century literary works in English, the *Alice* books defy classification and make a turtle mockery of every encyclopaedism. Published under the pseudonym "Lewis Carroll" in 1865 and 1871, they were an instant commercial success, much to the surprise of their author, the stammering don at Christ Church, Oxford, and author of mathematical treatises.

To classify these works as "children's literature" is absurd. Virginia Woolf remarked, "the two *Alices* are not books for children; they are the only books in which we become children" (see Phillips, 1971). This is elegant, but perhaps too neat: the pleasures and anxieties provoked by these works entail an uncertainty about everything, not least about the distinctions between child and adult. To be a child, according to Woolf, is "to find everything so strange that nothing is surprising," which might also be said of dreams. Indeed, the distinctions between dream and waking are not secure in the context of the *Alice* books: the return to "dull reality" at the end of *Alice's Adventures in Wonderland*—the conventional topos of "it was all a dream"—gives way at the end of *Through the Looking-Glass* to the more troubling logic that casts life itself as dream.

The *Alice* books have no obvious precursors. Of course, links can be made with earlier literature: in vigor and concision of characterization they compare with Chaucer; in ferocity and relentlessness of wordplay they resemble Shakespeare; in their constant inventiveness and absurdity they recall Laurence Sterne; and their poetry in particular has parallels with Edward Lear's and is parasitical upon English (especially Wordsworthian) romanticism. Carroll's work may also be related to the emergence and popularization of fairy tales in English (Hans Christian Andersen's tales were first published in English in 1846) and of so-called children's literature as such. And in their focus on the development of a child (however inept that phrase must be in trying to describe Carroll's texts), the *Alice* books reflect the same focus as that in so-called adult Victorian fiction, such as Dickens' or George Eliot's. But all of these links are of limited value or interest and tend to efface the nature and specificity of Carroll's extraordinary texts: the *Alice* books are, as Jean-Jacques Lecercle suggests, "a Victorian creation, an event in the field of literature" (see Lecercle, 1994). In a similar fashion, the *Alice* books really have no successors—if one excepts the numerous explicit reworkings, such as Jeff Noon's *Automated Alice*. And yet, like the smile of the Cheshire Cat, they may be said to haunt everywhere—from the work of G.K. Chesterton to surrealism, from Franz Kafka to Walt Disney, from James Joyce's *Finnegans Wake* to everyday conversation, for instance in the figure of the Cheshire Cat itself or Tweedledum and Tweedledee.

Alice's Adventures in Wonderland and *Through the Looking-Glass* foreground the basic questions of literary writing. Can literature be merely entertainment? But what *is* entertainment, and who is being entertained? How or what does "literature" *mean* if, as Humpty Dumpty suggests, a word means anything that one chooses it to mean? And where does this unhinging of meaning leave literary criticism?

"'Oh, you can't help that,' said the Cat: 'we're all mad here. I'm mad. You're mad.' 'How do you know I'm mad?' said Alice. 'You must be,' said the Cat, 'or you wouldn't have come here'." The *Alice* books engulf the reader in a kind of madness. Of course it is possible and even necessary to take a critical distance, to draw up typologies, impose classifications, inventory the kinds of "non-sense" they embody. This includes, of course, trying to think critically about the fact that, for all their reductiveness, the *Alice* books continue to be categorized as books "for children." Jacqueline Rose phrases the difficulties as follows: "*Alice* has been saved as a classic for children, and the question of what we mean by that '*for*'—the question of its more difficult implications—remains unasked" (see Rose, 1984).

Generally, however, psychoanalytical (and especially psychobiographical) attempts to write about the *Alice* books tend to flounder: Carroll's works seem at once too knowing and too strange. Other valuable efforts to deal with the "madness" of the *Alice* books would include those of Susan Stewart (1979), Gilles Deleuze (1979), and Francis Huxley (1976). Stewart seeks to situate Carroll's work within an interdisciplinary analysis of the relations between common sense and nonsense. She considers the extent to which the strangeness of the thinking in the *Alice* books is generated through effects of reversal, inversion, discontinuity, the catachresis of taking the metaphorical literally, and other forms of wordplay. She is especially good on dialogue, noting for example that "The nonsense conversations are continually halted by gaps in any common stock of knowledge, by a clash between members' biographical situations, and by a systematic use of randomness rather than a purpose at hand" (see Stewart, 1979).

Gilles Deleuze's celebrated essay, "The Schizophrenic and Language," pits Lewis Carroll against Antonin Artaud in order to argue that the *Alice* books are all about surface, not depth: it is a question of "discovering surface entities and their games of meaning and non-sense, of expressing these games in portmanteau words, and of resisting the vertigo of the bodies' depths and their alimentary, poisonous mixtures." Humpty Dumpty becomes, for Deleuze, the archetypal "body without organs," while Carroll is "the master or the surveyor of surfaces we thought we knew so well that we never explored them" (see Deleuze, 1979). One of the critical accounts that most fully engages with the dream-like inventiveness of the *Alice* books is Francis Huxley's *The Raven and the Writing Desk*, which mimes the playfulness and superficiality, in Deleuze's terms, of Carroll's writing. "Why is a raven like a writing-desk?" The mad Hatter's question is still with us and leaves all literary criticism in a flap. Perhaps the closest Huxley comes in suggesting an answer to this question is in quoting from Charles Lutwidge Dodgson's own *Symbolic Logic* (1896): "My writing-desk is full of live scorpions."

NICHOLAS ROYLE

Further Reading

Blake, Kathleen, *Play, Games and Sport: The Literary Works of Lewis Carroll,* Ithaca, New York: Cornell University Press, 1984

Deleuze, Gilles, "The Schizophrenic and Language: Surface and Depth in Lewis Carroll and Antonin Artaud," in *Textual Strategies: Perspectives in Post-Structuralist Criticism,* edited by Josue V. Harari, Ithaca, New York: Cornell University Press, 1979; London: Methuen, 1980

Guiliano, Edward, editor, *Lewis Carroll: A Celebration,* New York: Potter, 1982

Huxley, Francis, *The Raven and the Writing Desk,* New York: Harper and Row, and London: Thames and Hudson, 1976

Lecercle, Jean-Jacques, *Philosophy of Nonsense: The Intuitions of Victorian Nonsense Literature,* London and New York: Routledge, 1994

Noon, Jeff, *Automated Alice,* New York: Crown, and London: Doubleday, 1996

Phillips, Robert, editor, *Aspects of Alice: Lewis Carroll's Dreamchild as Seen Through the Critics' Looking-Glasses, 1865–1971,* New York: Vanguard Press, 1971; London: Gollancz, 1972

Rose, Jacqueline, *The Case of Peter Pan; or, The Impossibility of Children's Fiction,* London: Macmillan, 1984; revised edition, 1994

Stewart, Susan, *Nonsense: Aspects of Intertextuality in Folklore and Literature,* Baltimore: Johns Hopkins University Press, 1979

Isabel Allende 1942–

Chilean

Isabel Allende is perhaps the most widely read Hispanic author in the world. Although known principally for her novels and short stories, Allende has also written plays, essays, and film scripts. Her first novel, *La casa de los espíritus* (1982; *The House of the Spirits*), brought her immediate recognition.

Allende was born in Lima, Peru, in 1942, the daughter of a Chilean diplomat and niece of Salvador Allende, Chile's first Socialist president. She did not begin writing novels until after the 1973 military coup that led to Salvador Allende's death. Her novels reflect the social and political upheaval of her Chilean homeland wrought by dictator Augusto Pinochet's regime, which lasted until 1990.

Allende initially gained fame in 1968 in Santiago as a journalist, and she wrote a regular column for the magazine *Paula*. She also was a popular talk show host on Chile's first television network. Following the coup, Allende moved with her family to Venezuela, where the seeds of *The House of the Spirits* began to germinate.

Allende's emergence as a novelist came at a time when the Latin American literary movement known as the Boom had already been passed to the next generation. The Boom of literary innovation (1940–70) began a new era of modern Hispanic letters that brought international acclaim for Latin American writers such as Jorge Luis Borges, Alejo Carpentier, and Gabriel García Márquez. Post-Boom writers were defined by their desire to attack oppressive social and political structures with a mix of myth and history. The success of *The House of the Spirits* immediately marked Allende as a member of this new generation, which included Argentina's Luisa Valenzuela and Mempo Giardinelli and Chile's Antonio Skármeta. Allende herself shuns literary trends and resists classification.

Allende's signature work, *The House of the Spirits* began as a letter to her dying grandfather on his 100th birthday. Born of nostalgia, rage, and desperation at having reached the age of 40 without, as the author states, "a major accomplishment in my life," the novel bears witness to a family's 50-year saga, moving through recent Chilean history as it chronicles the political maelstroms that culminate in Chile's bloody 1973 coup. *The House of the Spirits* recounts the story of the Trueba family, whose patriarch, Esteban Trueba, ruthless and respectable, personifies the ruling class in a society of steep hierarchies. Trueba is the archetypal Latin American landowner, and Allende sets him alongside a new breed of Latin American female embodied in young Alba, a political activist. The women of *The House of the Spirits,* whose names denote light—Clara, Blanca, Alba, and Nivea—combat a dark legacy of oppression with passion and compassion. Allende's characters are fashioned out of the real, the eccentric, and the mythical, as well as a touch of magical realism (Clara is chided for her telekinetic tendencies; Férula returns from the dead to say good-bye to Clara). Magical realism, a literary style developed by the authors of the Latin American Boom, combines objective reality with fantasy. Allende's first novel has brought comparisons to Gabriel García Márquez's landmark Boom novel *Cien años de soledad* (1967; *One Hundred Years of Solitude*). Indeed, both novels are family sagas with recognizable historical settings in unnamed Latin American countries, and both are brilliant examples of magical realism at its best.

Allende's subsequent novel, *De amor y de sombra* (1984; *Of Love and Shadows*), like *The House of the Spirits,* relies on real life events, and in this case the discovery of the remains of 15 corpses secretly buried in the Lonquen region near Santiago, Chile. The novel's protagonist, Irene Beltrán, a journalist, sets out to cover a story behind the bodies, and in the process exposes a clandestine war of brutality and torture during Pinochet's military rule in Chile.

Eva Luna (1987; *Eva Luna*) departs from Allende's historical focus and enters into fantasy and adventure in the city and jungle. The author suppresses real life names and places but hints that the novel's events take place in Venezuela, where she lived in exile. Eva Luna is an orphan, offspring of the brief union of a servant woman and a dying Indian man. Subsisting as a servant at the beginning and holding a number of odd jobs as she moves from place to place, Eva eventually involves herself in guerrilla warfare in the jungle. She survives this lifestyle as a modern Scheherezade, telling stories that not only save her life but carry her from obscurity to fame when she becomes a successful soap opera writer. Allende, who identifies with Eva Luna more than any of her other characters, plays with this theme of soap operas and storytelling, inviting the reader to interpret the text on three distinct levels with several possible endings: Eva is telling her true story; she made up a story about her life; or she is writing a soap opera. Eva Luna the soap opera writer or protagonist is a picaresque heroine in what could be called a feminist novel. *Los cuentos de Eva Luna* (1990; *The Stories of Eva Luna*) is a collection of 23 short stories unified by the theme of love. Allende employs the Balzacian device of recurring characters in this work, which is set, like *Eva Luna,* in the tropical region of Agua Santa. Allende's stories address the talismanic power of language, and her compelling characters are intensified with strong strokes of color and humor.

Unlike Allende's other works, *El plan infinito* (1991; *The Infinite Plan*) is an American story set in California and Vietnam during the 1950s and 1960s. It fictionalizes the life and times of Gregory Reeves, a white American raised in a Los Angeles barrio, who becomes a successful lawyer. (The real-life model for Reeves is Allende's husband, William Gordan.) The novel addresses American attitudes toward religion and focuses on the racial-social tensions of the times.

Paula (1994; *Paula*), Allende's most widely read work after *The House of the Spirits,* begins as an intimate letter to her daughter Paula, who lay in a coma in a Madrid hospital. Allende's letter begins "Listen, Paula, . . ." and with her mother's voice, Allende speaks to her sleeping Paula, distracting anguish in a family memoir that unfolds into a dialogue of love between mother and daughter. This book is the biography of Paula, the autobiography of Isabel Allende, and the history of her family. It is the present tense account of a mother losing the fight for her child's life. Structurally more complex than Allende's previous works, as it intertwines past and present, blending the two at its conclusion, *Paula* has been called a "fictionalized memoir": it is the true life recollection lit, at times, by the creations of memory and imagination. Allende credits no formal plan for the development of the narrative, only "inspirational forces of the beloved family spirits standing behind me."

Afrodita (Allende's latest work, 1997), is a collection of essays on aphrodisiacs, erotic recipes, and adventure full of illuminating illustrations. Allende's writings have been translated into more than 30 languages and made into films. She continues to draw both scholarly attention as well as international public affection.

CELIA CORREAS ZAPATA

See also House of the Spirits

Biography
Born in Lima, Peru, 2 August 1942; niece of former Chilean President Salvador Allende who died in the course of the military takeover of September 1973. Attended a private high school in Santiago de Chile, graduated 1959. Secretary, United Nations Food and Agricultural Organization, Santiago, 1959–65. Worked as a journalist, editor, and advice columnist for *Paula* magazine, Santiago, 1967–74; interviewer for Canal 13/Canal 7 television station, 1970–75; worked on movie newsreels, 1973–75; administrator, Colegio Marroco, Caracas, 1979–82; guest teacher, Montclair State College, New Jersey, 1985, and University of Virginia, Charlottesville, 1988; taught creative writing at the University of California, Berkeley, 1989.

Novels by Allende
La casa de los espíritus, 1982; as *The House of the Spirits,* translated by Magda Bogin, 1985
De amor y de sombra, 1984; as *Of Love and Shadows,* translated by Margaret Sayers Peden, 1987
Eva Luna, 1987; as *Eva Luna,* translated by Margaret Sayers Peden, 1988
Los cuentos de Eva Luna, 1990; as *The Stories of Eva Luna,* translated by Margaret Sayers Peden, 1991
El plan infinito, 1991; as *The Infinite Plan,* translated by Margaret Sayers Peden, 1993

Other Writings: short stories, journalism, essays, plays, film scripts, and an informal family history (*Paula,* 1994).

Further Reading
Crystall, Elyse, Jill Kunheim, and Mary Lahoun, "An Interview with Isabel Allende," *Contemporary Literature* 33:4 (Winter 1992)
Foreman, Gabrielle P., "Past-On Stories: History and the Magically Real, Morrison and Allende on Call," *Feminist Studies* 18:2 (Summer 1992)
Gould Levine, Linda, "Isabel Allende," in *Spanish American Women Writers: A Bio-Bibliographical Source Book,* edited by Diane E. Marting, New York: Greenwood Press, 1990
Hart, Patricia, *Narrative Magic in the Fiction of Isabel Allende,* Rutherford, New Jersey: Fairleigh Dickinson University Press, and London: Associated University Presses, 1989
Meyer, Doris, "Exile and the Female Condition in Isabel Allende's *De amor y de sombra,*" *International Fiction Review* 15:2 (1988)
Zapata, Celia Correas, *Isabel Allende: Vida y espíritus: Una biografía literaria,* Madrid: Plaza & Janes, 1998

Jorge Amado 1912–

Brazilian

Jorge Amado is Brazil's most widely read and most widely translated novelist. In the course of a career now spanning seven decades, he has written numerous novels, as well as memoirs, travel writing, biography, drama, and books for children. His work has been translated into at least 38 languages. Some observers argue that Amado's prominence has become a mixed blessing and that he has become a victim of his own successes. Since the publication of *Gabriela, cravo e canela* (1959; *Gabriela, Clove and Cinnamon*), they charge, Amado has abandoned his earlier, more explicit and hard-edged political and ideological fiction to sentimentalize, popularize, and simplify his characters and his vision, presenting a more naive and uncritical view of Brazilian culture.

Amado's earlier novels—*Cacau* (1933), *Jubiabá* (1935), *Capitães da areia* (1937; *Captains of the Sands*), *Mar morto* (1936; *Sea of Death*), and *Terras do sem fim* (1943; *The Violent Land*)—may be read as relatively straightforward critiques of the brutal socioeconomic conditions of his home region, the state of Bahia on Brazil's central east coast, beginning in the early 20th century. These novels were hailed as Marxist denunciations of the region's endemic poverty and the exploitation of workers, including women and children, both on the feudally organized cocoa plantations and in the coastal cities of Ilheus and Salvador. Even though he draws on his own experience as the child of plantation owners who were driven from the land by natural and social forces, Amado's sympathies in these earlier fictions are clear.

It is simplistic, however, to see in Amado's early fiction an unvarnished social realism or in his later fiction a retreat into sentimentality. First, his earlier fiction is not without its own kind of sentimentality and its own limitations, and Amado has never been simply a social realist. For example, his portraits of the street children at the center of *Captains of the Sands* are at once naturalist, literary, and warmly sentimental, indebted to depictions of children in earlier literature and representing the stark lives of the real children of the era in Bahia. In addition, the mystical, magical, and spiritual elements of Afro-Brazilian culture illuminate many of Amado's fictions in improbable ways to make them distinctive amalgams, early and late, of complementary styles, modes, and intentions. Amado's longstanding familiarity with (and participation in) the rituals and traditions of *candomblé*, for example, animate much of his fiction. Amado's home state of Bahia is the center of the widespread Brazilian practice of African spiritual traditions brought to Brazil originally by African slaves, and these elements surface powerfully in many of Amado's novels. The Afro-Brazilian goddess of the sea, Iemanjá, for example, figures prominently in *Sea of Death*, and Afro-Brazilian gods and goddesses converge to magical effect at the end of Amado's later novel, *Dona Flor e seus dois maridos* (1966; *Dona Flor and Her Two Husbands*).

The division into socialist and sentimental periods is also undermined by the parodic or satirical intention in much of Amado's fiction, particularly his later novels, which makes his plots, characters, and social vision more richly ambiguous than is sometimes allowed. Amado is a master caricaturist: his charac-

ters can function at once on realist, symbolic, comic, and allegorical levels, all explicitly alluded to as his many-layered texts unfold. This is the case with the two husbands (Vadinho and Teodoro) alluded to in the title of *Dona Flor and Her Two Husbands,* and, on another level, with the character of Dona Flor herself. It is also the case with Gabriela, the protagonist of the novel of the same title. And Amado frequently employs a supple and many-voiced point of view that reflects on its own powers, mocks and apes earlier literary styles for parodic purposes, and adopts extravagant poses.

Amado's love of Brazilian Portuguese in all its registers (a love faithfully served by most of Amado's translators into English) typically extends to an exuberant display of its own capacity for excess. For example, Amado is fond of comic amplification, both in description and development of character and scene. While not in the service of the kind of Latin American magic realism more closely associated with Colombian novelist Gabriel García Márquez, his play with language moves his fictional mode well beyond a social realist frame.

It remains true, however, that Amado's fiction, including his work after *Gabriela, Clove and Cinnamon,* has functioned both as popular entertainment and as a moral instrument to expose the complex restrictions and hypocrisies of Brazilian culture. In fact, it is the wide popularity of Amado's later novels that has created the critical reservations alluded to above. In *Gabriela* and in *Dona Flor,* Amado's critics find his clearest failings, reading his portraits of his female characters as shallow, patronizing, and condescending depictions that do as much to imprison them in their constrained roles as to liberate them.

Regardless of one's position in the continuing debate over Amado's importance in Brazilian letters, his unique contribution has been as impressive for its qualities as its quantity. Amado's fiction has successfully bridged the gap between popular and highbrow art. In his later novels, his many-faceted interrogation of 19th-century codes of honor and conduct and of the conventions governing marriage and a woman's proper comportment is set within a deep and wide understanding of Brazilian mores. In turn, these fictions rest on the broad shoulders of an array of novels that celebrate, as they lament, many of Brazilian culture's most complex paradoxes, including the riches of its language and traditions, the profuse beauties and harshness of its land and climate, the abiding strengths of its many faiths, and the continuing despair of large segments of its people.

Neil K. Besner

See also Dona Flor and Her Two Husbands

Biography

Born in Ferradas, Itabuna, Bahia, Brazil, 10 August 1912. Attended the Jesuit Colégio Antônio Vieira, Salvador, 1923–26; entered the Ginásio Ipiranga, Salvador, 1926; studied law at the Federal University, Rio de Janeiro from 1931 to 1935 and received a diploma in law. Reporter with *Diário da Bahia,* 1927, and contributor to *A Luva, Samba, Meridiano, A Semana, O Momento, O Jornal, Diário de Notícias, A Gazeta* de *Notícias,* and *O Correio do Povo,* 1927–30. Moved to Rio de Janeiro in 1930. Editor for *Revista Rio,* 1933; worked for the publishing company José Olympio from 1934; editor for *A Manhã,* the publication of the oppostion Aliança Nacional Libertadora [National Freedom Alliance]; coeditor, Centro de Cultura Moderna's *Movimento,* 1934–35; imprisoned for suspected involvement in coup attempt, 1935, and his books banned, 1938–43. Traveled to Mexico and the United States in 1937. Editor, *Dom Casmurro,* 1938–39, and contributor to *Diretrizes,* 1939. Lived mainly in Argentina, 1941–42; returned to Brazil, 1942, and was rearrested and confined to the Bahia region; contributor to "Diário da Guerra" column for *O Imparcial,* from 1943; delegate at the first Brazilian Writers' Congress, 1945; editor, *Hoje,* São Paulo, 1945. After the fall of Getúlio Vargas's regime (1930–45) elected Communist deputy for the São Paulo region, 1945, until the Party was again declared illegal in 1947. Went into exile in Paris, 1947–49, in Scandinavia and Eastern Europe, 1949–50, and in Prague, 1950–51. Traveled to China and Mongolia in 1952. Vice President of the Brazilian union, 1954. Founder, *Para Todos,* Rio de Janeiro, and its editor from 1956 to 1958. Co-organizer, first Festival of Brazilian Writing, 1960. Traveled to Cuba and Mexico in 1962; settled in Salvador in 1963. Writer-in-Residence at Pennsylvania State University, 1971.

Novels by Amado

O país do carnaval, 1931

Cacau, 1933

Suor, 1934

Jubiabá, 1935; as *Jubiabá,* translated by Margaret Neves, 1984

Mar morto, 1936; as *Sea of Death,* translated by Gregory Rabassa, 1984

Capitães da areia, 1937; as *Captains of the Sands,* translated by Gregory Rabassa, 1988

Terras do sem fim, 1943; as *The Violent Land,* translated by Samuel Putnam, 1945

Seara vermelha, 1946

Gabriela, cravo e canela, 1959; as *Gabriela, Clove and Cinnamon,* tranlated by James L. Taylor and William Grossman, 1962

Os velhos marinheiros: Duas histórias do cais da bahia, 1961; as *Home Is the Sailor,* translated by Harriet de Onís, 1964

Os pastores da noite, 1964; as *Shepherds of the Night,* translated by Harriet de Onís, 1966

Dona Flor e seus dois maridos, 1966; as *Dona Flor and Her Two Husbands,* translated by Harriet de Onís, 1969

Tenda dos milagres, 1969; as *Tent of Miracles,* translated by Barbara Shelby, 1971

Tereza Batista, cansada de Guerra, 1972 as *Tereza Batista, Home from the Wars,* translated by Barbara Shelby, 1975

Tieta do agreste, pastora de cabras, 1977; as *Tieta, the Goat Girl,* translated by Barbara Shelby Merello, 1979

Farda, fardão, camisola de dormir, 1979; as *Pen, Sword, Camisole: A Fable to Kindle a Hope,* translated by Helen Lane, 1985

Tocaia grande: A face obscura, 1984; as *Showdown,* translated by Gregory Rabassa, 1988

O sumiço da santa, 1988; as *The War of the Saints,* translated by Gregory Rabassa, 1993

Other Writings: a play (*O amor de Castro Alves,* 1947), a book of poems (*A estrada do mar,* 1938), biography, travel writings, political essays, memoirs.

Further Reading

Brookshaw, David, *Race and Color in Brazilian Literature,* Metuchen, New Jersey: Scarecrow Press, 1986

Chamberlain, Bobby J., *Jorge Amado,* Boston: Twayne, 1990

Ellison, Fred P., *Brazil's New Novel: Four Northeastern Masters,* Berkeley: University of California Press, 1954

Hamilton, Russell G., "Afro-Brazilian Cults in the Novels of Jorge Amado," *Hispania* 50 (1967)

Martin, Gerald, *Journeys Through the Labyrinth: Latin American Fiction in the Twentieth Century,* London and New York: Verso, 1989

Pescatello, Ann, "The Brazileira: Images and Realities in Writings of Machado de Assis and Jorge Amado," in *Female and Male in Latin America: Essays,* edited by Ann Pescatello, Pittsburgh, Pennsylvania: University of Pittsburgh Press, 1973

The Ambassadors by Henry James

1903

Inspired by a remark made to a mutual friend by the novelist William Dean Howells, *The Ambassadors* was described by Henry James himself as the best of his novels. Influenced, too, by his experiments in writing drama and his growing sense that the novel offered the possibility for exploring the depths of human consciousness in ways not available to other literary forms, James gave exceptional attention to structuring a work that would reveal not only the details of reality but the influence of the apprehension of those details in shaping the thoughts, opinions, and actions of a single character affected by what he sees and hears.

As Frederick Crews (1957) observed, James in his later novels achieves "depth" in his work by restricting the "width" of his vision; these novels "record no historical crises, show us a minimum of background scenery, and contain no philosophical reflections irrelevant to the scene at hand." *The Ambassadors* is complex not in its plotting but in its depth of characterization and exploration of social and moral situations. The story seems simple enough on the surface. Lambert Strether, a 55-year-old New Englander, is dispatched by his fiancée Mrs. Newsome, a widow and matron of one of the region's leading business and social families, to rescue her son Chad who has been, in the view of his mother, beguiled by the evils of Parisian society. Strether arrives in Paris to find the son much improved, thanks to the tutelage of Marie de Vionnet, an older woman who is already married. As a consequence Strether does little to bring the son home; Mrs. Newsome, annoyed with Strether, dispatches her daughter and son-in-law to rescue both Chad and her finacé. Convinced of the virtuousness of the attachment between Chad and Marie, Strether defends the relationship against the protests of the family, only to learn by accident that the affair is adulterous, and that Chad is tiring of the liaison. Realizing he can do nothing more for Chad, Strether reluctantly decides to return to New England.

This bare outline hardly does justice to the novel. Using a story that seems to have little action and only modest social consequence, James constructs a work of immense insight and sensibility. As he does in so many of his novels, especially those written late in his career, James displays how the slightest phrase or gesture, or even the arrangement of a room, can reveal worlds of information to the discerning consciousness. Not surprisingly, this refinement of perception taken to extremes has not met the taste of a large reading public. One of the first reviewers of the novel criticized James for having "fallen deplorably below the accepted standards" for clarity of expression and for engaging in psychological explorations that become "absolutely wearisome" (*San Francisco Chronicle*, 6 December 1903). Subsequent generations of readers have proven the validity of the observation of the *Literary World* reviewer who felt that, although the book "could never be popular," a "very small class—the knowing" would always find *The Ambassadors* "a perpetual and high delight" (December 1903).

In the celebrated preface to the novel composed for the New York edition of his works, James observes that "one's work should have composition, for composition alone is positive beauty." The elements of composition James stresses are the tightly constructed series of dramatic scenes in which he reveals character and plot, the limitation of point of view to the consciousness of his principal character, and the use of the *ficelle*/confidante (in the person of Maria Gostrey, Strether's and Marie de Vionnet's friend) to provide plot details and background that could not otherwise be known to Strether.

The limitation of point of view often creates in the novel a situation that is ripe for irony, and James has proven himself a master of that technique. He exploits Strether's naive high-mindedness from the very first moments after his arrival in Europe. Enamored with what he perceives as his heightened powers of consciousness, Strether comes to learn near the end of the tale that he has been deceived all along about Chad's and Marie's relationship, not only by the principals in the love affair, but by others (Americans and Europeans alike) who have been complicit in condoning the illicit liaison. There is irony, too, in the fact that Strether comes to save Chad, only to be lost himself to the wonders of Paris, while Chad finally succumbs to the arguments of the American ambassadorial corps that his mother has sent to fetch him from the corruption of European civilization.

While James has always had a small coterie of staunch admirers for his later novels, *The Ambassadors* (and its companion pieces *The Wings of the Dove* [1902] and *The Golden Bowl* [1904]) are open to charges of obfuscation. James devotes entire paragraphs to examining the simplest remark or gesture. His insistence on using dramatic techniques to convey important information coupled with a penchant for indirection—which he gives to virtually all of his principal characters—sometimes make it difficult to discern not only motive but also details of plot. The history of the novel's publication ironically attests to the problem: in the first American edition of *The Ambassadors*, published shortly after the work appeared in serial format in the *North American Review,* chapters 29 and 30 were reversed; the error was repeated in subsequent editions and went unnoticed until 1950.

Nevertheless, the importance of *The Ambassadors* cannot be overstressed. In the fifth volume of his biography of the writer, Leon Edel (1972) describes the work as a "Stendhalian mirror in the roadway" toward modernist fiction. James' techniques of composition influenced such diverse writers as Marcel Proust, Gertrude Stein, and William Faulkner. The novel remains one of the most studied in the James canon and justifies James' own high estimate of his achievement in what he calls in the preface "the most independent, most elastic, most prodigious of literary forms."

LAURENCE W. MAZZENO

See also Henry James

Further Reading

Anderson, Charles R., *Person, Place, and Thing in Henry James's Novels*, Durham, North Carolina: Duke University Press, 1977

Berland, Alwyn, *Culture and Conduct in the Novels of Henry James,* Cambridge and New York: Cambridge University Press, 1981

Bloom, Harold, editor, *Henry James's "The Ambassadors": Modern Critical Interpretations,* New York: Chelsea House, 1988

Crews, Frederick C., *The Tragedy of Manners: Moral Drama in the Later Novels of Henry James,* New Haven, Connecticut: Yale University Press, 1957

Edel, Leon, *The Life of Henry James: The Master (1901–1916),* Philadelphia: J.B. Lippincott, 1972

Gargano, James W., editor, *Critical Essays on Henry James: The Late Novels,* Boston: G.K. Hall, 1987

Kaston, Carren, *Imagination and Desire in the Novels of Henry James,* New Brunswick, New Jersey: Rutgers University Press, 1984

Macnaughton, William R., *Henry James: The Later Novels,* Boston: Twayne, 1987

American Western Novel

The American Western novel, commonly known as "the Western," is a popular, male-dominated genre of fiction that uses clear, melodramatic formula plots to relate the sensational and often violent adventures of frontier men and women, scouts, Indian fighters, marshals, saloon girls, prostitutes, outlaws, ranchers, and cowboys in the late 19th-century American West.

The popular Western operates under clear and specific rules. The first of these is locale; the Western is named after its geographical setting, the American West at the precise historical moment of the frontier's passing, about 1860 to 1890–93, when the frontier was declared closed by both the US Census Bureau and historian Frederick Jackson Turner. Thus for John Cawelti, whose definitions of the genre in his *The Six-Gun Mystique* (1971) are an accepted standard, the Western is historically set between savagery and civilization, a transition represented by the genre's major character types: townspeople, savages, and heroes. The (mostly female) townspeople are agents of civilization divided into pioneers or common folk—Eastern escapees—or banker-villains. This first group is threatened either by bloodthirsty Indians or by outlaws who represent the violence, brutality, and ignorance of the frontier, which civilized society seeks to control and eliminate. The hero is an archetypal character torn between his loyalty to civilization and his wilderness past. Women in Westerns are characterized by a similar duality: they are either blonde, whereby they represent pure, genteel femininity; or brunette, in which they are more passionate and spontaneous, often slightly tainted by a mixture of race or a sinister past.

Another rule of Westerns is that their stories follow certain patterns arising from the Western environment they depict. Because there are so few basic narrative types of Westerns, many critics consider the genre simply a "horse opera" of formula novels. A useful outline by Western pulp writer Frank Gruber explains these limited plots and their variations: one, the Union Pacific or Epic Construction story (often of a railroad, stagecoach, wagon train, or telegraph line) in which various obstacles arise, from Indian attacks to outlaw holdups; two, the Ranch story (often ranchers against rustlers or ranchers against each other over water rights, with a cowboy hero emerging from the ranch hands); three, the Empire or Range War story (often like the Ranch story but larger in that cattle barons of the West duke it out over grazing, fencing, or water rights, with the hero wandering in from nowhere, taking up for the homesteaders, and winning the war for them); four, the Avenger or Revenge tale (the hero makes a quest for the person responsible for his or others' misfortunes; sometimes the heroine is the character benefited, and the story may conclude with a plot or identity twist); five, the Cavalry and Indians story (variations on the theme of Custer's last stand told from a cavalryman's point of view but perhaps through a renegade sympathetic to the Indians); six, the Outlaw story (the hero is presented sympathetically as a "good boy turned bad man" by unfortunate circumstance or being wronged, and he eventually dies in a suicidal gunfight because he cannot settle down owing to danger and reputation); a similar tale is the "Good But Not Worthy" story (the hero is or was a gunfighter trying to quit but falls in love with a homesteader's daughter in the course of a range war or similar conflict—after defeating the opponent's gunslingers, he realizes he is a killer unworthy of a good woman and rides away, usually into the sunset); lastly there is the Marshal or Dedicated Lawman story (an honest peace officer stands alone against evil elements of the town and either wins, whereby he is often shunned as a killer, or dies, whereby the townspeople rise to clean up the town so his death is not in vain).

A third rule for Westerns is that, like their stark landscapes, their conflict must be clear and unambiguous with an absolute resolution. Western writer Henry Wilson Allen (pen name Clay Fisher) explains that the genre "presents a precut slice of homespun life which is a gallant trial of good against evil in a perilous place and time where bravery and clean intent will not be matched by cowardice and dishonor." For Cawelti (1971), the Western operates like a medieval morality play, with a clear resolution toward "justice," nothing more. Additionally, the Western tolerates strong man-woman relationships without overt sex. Love must participate in the motivation of the characters and the action of the story so that while sexual relationships may occur if the plot demands it, the Western remains traditionally conservative on sexuality (although not on violence).

The Western may be traced back to the Leatherstocking Tales of James Fenimore Cooper, such as the popular *The Last of the Mohicans* (1826) and *The Prairie* (1827). Set in the Eastern forest frontier of the 18th century, these books portray the first Western hero, Natty Bumppo, as a noble forest hunter, scout, and warrior. Cooper introduced several elements that became a part of the formula Western: the kidnapped heroine(s); the single-handed duel; the treacherous Indian villain; and the plot of chase, capture, escape, chase, and rescue from captivity narratives and popular melodrama. However influential Cooper was, most of his devices were elements of the historical romance of Sir Walter Scott transplanted to the American frontier.

The appearance of cheaply produced dime novels for the mass market during the latter half of the 19th century helped shape the modern popular Western. Publishers Beadles and Adams produced their first dime-novel Western, *Seth Jones* by Edward Ellis, in 1860. The plot was straight Cooper: a settler's daughter is kidnapped by Mohawk Indians, and a cultured Easterner disguised as a rugged frontiersman helps save her after chases, escapes, and rescues. Ellis' story was a paradigm for other dime novels, which were churned out weekly by non-Westerners at 30,000 words apiece in an assembly-line method. Most of the heroes were based upon an Eastern backwoodsman or plainsman Daniel Boone-Natty Bumppo figure, like an 1869 dime novel by the popular writer Ann Stephens. As the nation expanded westward, the distinction between invented Eastern characters such as Deadwood Dick and historical Western personas such as Kit Carson became slighter. Then, in the late 1880s, the cowboy stepped in as the hero of the yellow-backed dime novels, but more as a gunman fighting outlaws and Indians like his hunter and scout predecessors—perhaps revealing how the dime-novel Western had also grown more violent as readers tired of its formula, although it remained incredibly popular as a genre.

The same plots, settings, and characters of the dime novels would be influential in what is usually considered the first Western novel proper, Owen Wister's *The Virginian* (1902). Yet the popular Western novel expanded upon the dime novel. New was the slowly progressing courtship-romance between the (Southern) gentlemanly Western cowboy and an Eastern schoolmarm and also the walkdown duel, the climax in which two gunmen approach each other on an empty street until one draws. Although *The Virginian* contains all the elements that make it the first Western, it also has been called a mere character sketch owing to its extended plot containing whole chapters of Western tall tales of a masculine hen and frog ranch, an emphasis on the dialect of the cowboy folk hero, and the narrative intrusions of the tenderfoot Eastern narrator more interested in the courtship than the background of the 1892 Johnson County War.

The Virginian's commercial success prompted a torrent of popular Western novels and pulp magazines in the early part of the 20th century. Emerson Hough wrote several novels in the early 1910s in the Wister Western formula, then entrenched his later novels, such as *The Covered Wagon* (1922), with historical context by having his characters participate in historical events. The ex-cowboy Eugene Manlove Rhodes was yet another formula writer of Westerns in the early 20th century. One of his best books, *Paso por Aqui* (1925), takes the typical cowboy hero into a nostalgic escape novel with Pat Garrett. William McLeod Raine wrote novels about the rancher-sheepman conflict, averaging two books a year. Clarence Mulford's ubiquitous Hopalong Cassidy was a tough, resourceful, and humorous ranch hand with a limp who first appeared in *Bar-20* in 1907. B.M. Bower (Bertha Sinclair) created *Chip of the Flying U* (1906), one of the better known cowboy-gentleman novels of the period before World War I. Another female Western author was Caroline Lockhart, who produced strong heroines that showed women could find freedom in the Old West, such as in her last novel, *The Fighting Sheperdess* (1919).

With the filming of Edward S. Porter's "The Great Train Robbery" (1903), silent film Westerns began to rival literary Westerns, eventually causing the extinction of the dime novels by the late 1920s. But the pulps' decline also was brought on by the rise of "the slicks": variety magazines targeted for middlebrow audiences that sold for the price of the pulps. It was in these magazines that Zane Grey, one of the two most popular Western writers of all time, began his amazing career. From 1917 to 1926 at least one Grey book appeared on every best-seller list, and every book he wrote netted at least a half a million dollars in sales. Grey harnessed all of the elements of Cooper, the dime-novel Western, and Wister to create the prototypical Western novel. He had action. He used almost all the formulaic conflicts Gruber describes, although it was joked that the substance of any two of his books could be written on the back of a postage stamp. He had violence—in fact, he was the first writer of popular Westerns to really seize upon the image of the gunfighter and the climactic shoot-out, which was then picked up by other Western novels and movies. He had historical settings, such as the building of the transcontinental railroad in *The U.P. Trail* (1918). His stereotyped female characters were either bad girls exuding sensuality or good girls who were either wild but pure, or sophisticated yet passionate; his heroes were bland and upper-class stereotypes from the popular novel. His original semioutlaw heroes were his most influential creation: outcast older men with a dark past and special costume, like Lassiter, the doomed gunman in Grey's most famous book, *Riders of the Purple Sage* (1912), or Buck Duane, the agonized killer of *Lone Star Ranger* (1915).

Also original was the way Grey's novels described the Western landscape almost religiously; hence in *Riders of the Purple Sage,* a massive rock slide creates an Edenic valley in which there can be no Fall.

Two other prewar writers, Frederick Faust (Max Brand) and Ernest Haycox, stand out. The former turned out 196 novels and 226 novelettes under 20 different pseudonyms. A poet by profession, Faust ashamedly turned out novels (many as sequels and series) merely for profit, repeatedly using his formula: the tale of an Easterner gone West who undergoes a transforming trial under violent experiences. The date or place of Faust's novels is often left blank—like the town of Wham in his most famous *Destry Rides Again* (1930)—and his brisk style leaves off any commentary. Haycox's career worked conversely. He participated freely in the commercialism of the pulps, slicks, and paperbacks but tried to free himself artistically upon graduating from each stage. By the time he wrote his novel *Bugles in the Afternoon* (1944), he was able to place the rituals and formulas of the Western inside the naturalistic method that made (in this case) Custer's men brutes in a meaningless universe. Haycox continued to write naturalistic fiction after it was well out of style. One female writer of the era to note is Vingie Roe, who introduced masculine superwomen in many of her more than 30 novels. In *Black Belle Rides the Uplands* (1935), Roe creates a woman who outperforms men in traditionally masculine practices while maintaining her femininity.

In looking at more recent Westerns, one should consider that since the 1940s Western writers have confronted the dilemma of writing in an overwritten genre (see Bold, 1987). Such a dilemma surely affected Jack Schaefer, whose *Shane* (1949) features the classic hero-with-a-shady-past arriving from nowhere to save nesters from a big rancher. Schaefer's succeeding works became less patterned and plotted, but by 1961 he declared the genre dead, which his later novels affirm by their lack of self-regeneration. Alan Le May faced the same over-saturation of the Western; his answer was to take the genre's stock devices and make them the subject, not the tools, of his fiction. Thus in *The Searchers* (1954), characters must read linguistic and visual codes to track down an Indian captive. Unlike Le May and Schaefer, other recent writers have continued to churn out Westerns in the same formulaic style as before. Henry Wilson Allen's "Will Henry" Westerns followed Haycox's historical style of combining romance with historical realism, which Luke Short (Frederick Glidden) has also done in his work.

The most significant writer of Westerns since the 1950s has been Louis L'Amour, whose publishing numbers surpass Faust, while his popularity rivals Grey. Hailed on one book cover as the "World's Greatest Writer," L'Amour has sold over 225 million of his well over 100 novels, making him the third top-seller in the world according to *Saturday Review*. Just as he claims to be a storyteller in the oral tradition, he is often accused of total conventionalism; even the casual reader remarks that each of his books is just like the next. L'Amour's early works were entertaining in the unbridled violence and directness of morality, with sprinklings of Western trivia and lore, and a middle phase (1958–74) saw him rely on this standard pattern of violence with historical trivia while leading up to his later work based on a family mythology. Perhaps owing to his overwhelming popularity and a large new contract with Bantam Books, L'Amour became his own historian and apologist for Western settlement in his later phase, which began in the early 1970s; in time for bicentennial fever, he began writing interlocking family histories, such as *The Sacketts,* which reached back to 1599, when the first Sackett sailed from Wales. As Christine Bold (1987) asserts, with his family sagas cutting across history with myriad historical allusions, "L'Amour threatens to plot out every possible combination of time, place, and character in the West." Eventually, even L'Amour ran low on Western material; his book *The Last of the Breed* (1986) follows the escape of a part-Indian pilot shot down over Siberia.

Perhaps in response to the genre being overcrowded (as well as a general changing of the times), a group of Westerns written completely opposite the Western formula began to appear in the late 1950s and continued through the 1970s: the anti-Western Western, novels in which the entire Western formula was written in converse. The idea was not wholly new: in the late 1890s, Stephen Crane showed how such Western elements as walkdown duels and town hangings could be thwarted by the presence of domesticating women in "The Bride Comes to Yellow Sky" and "Moonlight on the Snow." Walter Van Tilburg Clark's *The Ox-Bow Incident* (1940) begins as a conventional Western in a saloon but ends with the lynching of three innocent men by a justice-hungry posse. Without a hero, Clark's book surely qualifies as an anti-Western Western novel. The first of the more recent anti-Westerns may have been Edward Abbey's *The Brave Cowboy* (1956), which closes with its behind-the-times cowboy hero run over by a truck carrying, appropriately, toilet fixtures. Larry McMurtry's *Horseman, Pass By* (1961) describes how Hud, the young antihero, deposes his stepfather, virtually a deity of the Old West, by killing him. Perhaps the wildest anti-Western of the era is Ishmael Reed's *Yellow Back Radio Broke-Down* (1969), which according to its author means "the dismantling of a genre done in an oral way like radio." Writing an African-American postmodern Western, Reed pokes fun at racial stereotypes of the Western in a conventional package, with the black hero, the Loop Garoo Kid, fighting against an evil rancher for children; the final juxtaposition of modern and Old West society (seen years later in *Blazing Saddles*) completes the postmodern effect. What is remarkable about these anti-Westerns is not that they parody the formula Western but that in exploiting its devices they represent extensions of the genre as much as departures, proving the formula is still very much alive.

While novels by L'Amour and Grey remain popular today, the successes of the adult Western, such as those of George Gilman's pornographic and violent Edge series, Jake Logan's unoriginal Slocum series and Tabor Evans' Longarm series, make it difficult to gauge where the Western is headed. Perhaps the other rival vying for L'Amour's position is Larry McMurtry, whose 1985 *Lonesome Dove* broke many sales records; prequels and sequels such as *Streets of Laredo* (1993) have continued to sell well because of McMurtry's combination of metaphysical questioning, scenes of sex and violence, and realistic, sustained narrative that make his novels satisfying to the modern reader. But perhaps the latest Western writer to emerge both popularly and critically is Cormac McCarthy, whose *All the Pretty Horses* (1992), volume 1 of his "Border Trilogy," tells of the adventures of young Texans in a mythical Mexico. Volume 2, *The Crossing* (1994), describes a ruinous quest for a dubious grail. With these inventive Westerns, McCarthy proves there is still space in the genre—in Mexico, at least.

The Western is inherently connected to American expansionism, the late 19th- and early 20th-century policy of the United States to expand American-owned territories, in that the genre reflects on the country's drive to settle the land and conquer the people of the West. If we historicize even the appearance of the earliest Westerns, we see expansionism at work. The Leatherstocking series was immensely popular, perhaps because of high interest in the frontier and in expanding Jacksonian America, an interest generated in part by biographies that worshiped Cooper's real-life models, Daniel Boone of Kentucky and Davy Crockett of Tennessee, both of whom had fought against Indians to secure territory for the fledgling republic. Interest in the frontier grew around the time the frontier was declared closed late in the 19th century. As Americans became uncertain about the class polarization, industrialization, urbanization, and economic monopolization around them, they longed for an escape to the pastoral West, away from the harsh realities of everyday modern life. Thus the Western became inherently escapist, considered a "brain fag" by one dime novelist. The resulting Western may best be seen in Zane Grey's novels' combination of sexuality, romance, and traditional middle-class social values with the violence, lawlessness, and immorality that characterize the West, giving Americans of the roaring twenties (and afterward) the thrill of thinking about the past without suffering that past's harsh effects.

ANDREW P. VASSAR

See also Adventure Novel and Imperial Romance; James Fenimore Cooper; Dime Novels and Penny Dreadfuls

Further Reading

Bold, Christine, *Selling the Wild West: Popular Western Fiction, 1860 to 1960,* Bloomington: Indiana University Press, 1987

Cawelti, John G., *The Six-Gun Mystique,* Bowling Green, Ohio: Bowling Green University Popular Press, 1971; 2nd edition, 1984

Cawelti, John G., "The Western: A Look at the Evolution of a Formula," in *Adventure, Mystery, and Romance: Formula Stories as Art and Popular Culture,* by Cawelti, Chicago: University of Chicago Press, 1976

Davis, Robert Murray, *Playing Cowboys: Low Art and High Culture in the Western,* Norman: University of Oklahoma Press, 1991

Dinan, John A., *The Pulp Western: A Popular History of the Western Fiction Magazine in America,* San Bernadino, California: Borgo Press, 1983

Etulain, Richard W., and Michael T. Marsden, editors, *The Popular Western: Essays Toward a Definition,* Bowling Green, Ohio: Bowling Green University Popular Press, 1974

Folsom, James K., *The American Western Novel,* New Haven, Connecticut: College and University Press, 1966

Folsom, James K., editor, *The Western: A Collection of Critical Essays,* Englewood Cliffs, New Jersey: Prentice-Hall, 1979

Jones, Daryl, *The Dime Novel Western,* Bowling Green, Ohio: Bowling Green University Popular Press, 1978

Marsden, Michael T., and Jack Nachbar, "The Modern Popular Western: Radio, Television, Film and Print," in *A Literary History of the American West,* edited by the Western Literature Association, Fort Worth: Texas Christian University Press, 1987

Milton, John R., "The Popular or Formula Western," in *The Novel of the American West,* by Milton, Lincoln: University of Nebraska Press, 1980

Nye, Russel Blaine, "Sixshooter Country," in *The Unembarrassed Muse: The Popular Arts in America,* by Nye, New York: Dial, 1970

Pilkington, William T., editor, *Critical Essays on the Western American Novel,* Boston: G.K. Hall, 1980

Smith, Henry Nash, *Virgin Land: The American West as Symbol and Myth,* Cambridge, Massachusetts: Harvard University Press, 1950

Tompkins, Jane, *West of Everything: The Inner Life of Westerns,* New York: Oxford University Press, 1992

Yates, Norris, *Gender and Genre: An Introduction to Women Writers of Formula Westerns, 1900–1950,* Albuquerque: University of New Mexico Press, 1995

Amor en los tiempos del cólera. *See* Love in the Time of Cholera

---

Analytical Novel. *See* Psychological Novel

Mulk Raj Anand 1905–

Indian

Mulk Raj Anand is usually identified (along with R.K. Narayan and Raja Rao) as one of the three leading Indian novelists writing in English prior to the 1980s, when Salman Rushdie spearheaded a veritable explosion in the production of English-language novels by Indian writers. Anand also precedes Rushdie as a cosmopolitan writer whose works enact important dialogues between the cultural traditions of East and West. Anand himself has characterized his writing as bearing the double burden of "the Alps of European tradition and the Himalaya of my Indian past." Anand's work is intensely political, and this combination of Eastern and Western influences goes beyond language and style to include a dedication to Indian social and political reform that is strongly informed by Western socialism.

Anand's first novel, *Untouchable,* was published in Britain in 1935 and remains one of his best known works. It narrates a day in the life of Bakha, a young Indian "Untouchable." Fated by his low birth to work as a latrine sweeper—and thus to be regarded as an unclean outcaste by Hindus born into higher castes—Bakha suffers a number of undeserved abuses and humiliations in the course of his day. Through its depiction of these humiliations and Bakha's painful emotional reaction to them, *Untouch-*

able presents a powerful critique of the Indian caste system. At the same time, the book's treatment of the caste system may also be read as a more general critique of the inequities of class society, including that which prevails in the presumably more modern and democratic Britain. Finally, Anand supplements his critique of Hindu tradition with suggestions of the ways in which British colonial domination of India, while bringing a certain amount of modernization, has actually exacerbated, rather than ameliorated, the suffering of outcastes such as Bakha.

Anand's second novel, *Coolie* (1936), grows out of Anand's extensive involvement with the Left in England in the 1930s and remains popular in England, India, and elsewhere. Saros Cowasjee, who believes that *Coolie* is probably Anand's best novel, argues in his *Studies in Indian and Anglo-Indian Fiction* (1993) that "no Indian writer of fiction in English comes anywhere near Mulk Raj Anand in providing a social and political portrait of India from the time of the Delhi Durbar of 1911 to the demise of the Indian princes following Indian Independence in 1947." In this vein, R.K. Dhawan (1985), in a discussion of *Coolie,* notes that Anand often has been characterized by detractors as more a propagandist than a novelist. But Dhawan concludes that Anand has effectively integrated his political message into his fictional framework to produce "an intensely realised and credible narrative that is both political thesis and absorbing fiction."

Coolie, which focuses on the experiences of a lowly worker, Munoo, shares much with the proletarian novels published in Britain and the United States during the 1930s. Munoo, the child of impoverished parents in a rural village, is orphaned early in life and forced to support himself. At age 14 he travels to the town of Shampur to work as a much-abused household servant. As the book proceeds, he moves to the small city of Daulatpur, where he works in a pickle factory and then as a coolie seeking odd jobs in the city's market. Eventually he travels to Bombay, where he works in a large British-owned textile mill. In the end, Munoo moves from Bombay to Simla to become the servant of Mrs. Mainwaring, a somewhat disreputable, although socially ambitious, Anglo-Indian woman. Munoo's movements thus present the reader with a broad cross-section of Indian society in the period between World War I and World War II. They also make *Coolie* a historical novel that follows Munoo from his childhood in a remote rural area through a variety of experiences that bring him into increasingly modern and urban environments, thus to an extent tracing the arc of world history of the last several centuries. In so doing, the book also suggests that an element of exploitation and inequity has been central to the historical process of modernization, presenting Munoo as an emblem of the poor and oppressed whose labor has fueled the growth of global modernization but who have themselves largely been excluded from the benefits of that process.

Two Leaves and a Bud (1937) continues in a somewhat similar vein, relating the story of Gangu, a poor Punjabi peasant who, in search of economic opportunity, is lured to work in a tea plantation in Assam. In Assam, however, he is brutally exploited by his new bosses and killed by a British official who tries to rape Gangu's daughter. Similarly, the trilogy of novels that includes *The Village* (1939), *Across the Black Waters* (1940), and *The Sword and the Sickle* (1942) deals with the unsuccessful attempts of a Punjabi peasant, Lal Singh, to achieve justice in an inhospitable world. After World War II, Anand's work turned in a different direction. *Seven Summers* (1951) and the much respected *The Private Life of an Indian Prince* (1953) are highly autobiographical and focus more on interior personal struggles than on public political ones. Anand continued to write in this autobiographical vein in such novels as *Morning Face* (1968), *Confession of a Lover* (1976), and *The Bubble* (1984), although he occasionally returned, as in *The Road* (1961), to the mode of earlier works such as *Untouchable.* Anand has also published numerous volumes of short stories, social commentary, and art criticism.

DUBRAVKA JURAGA

See also Untouchable

Biography
Born in Peshawar, 12 December 1905. Attended Khalsa College, Amritsar; Punjab University, 1921–24, B.A. (honors) 1924; University College, University of London, 1926–29, Ph.D.; Cambridge University, 1929–30; League of Nations School of Intellectual Cooperation, Geneva, 1930–32. Lecturer, School of Intellectual Cooperation, summer 1930, and Workers Educational Association, London, on and off between 1932 and 1945; taught at Indian universities, 1948–66; Tagore Professor of Literature and Fine Art, University of Punjab, 1963–66; visiting professor, Institute of Advanced Studies, Simla, 1967–68. Fine art chairman, Lalit Kala Akademi (National Academy of Art), New Delhi, 1965–70; from 1946 editor, *Marg* magazine, and director, Kutub Publishers, both Bombay; from 1970 president of Lokayata Trust, for creating a community and cultural center in the village of Hauz Khas, New Delhi.

Novels by Anand
Untouchable, 1935
Coolie, 1936
Two Leaves and a Bud, 1937
The Village, 1939
Across the Black Waters, 1940
The Sword and the Sickle, 1942
The Big Heart, 1945
Seven Summers: The Story of an Indian Childhood, 1951
The Private Life of an Indian Prince, 1953; revised edition, 1970
The Old Woman and the Cow, 1960; as *Gauri,* 1976
The Road, 1961
Death of a Hero, 1963
Morning Face, 1968
Confession of a Lover, 1976
The Bubble, 1984

Other Writings: short stories, a play, an autobiography, children's stories, and essays on a wide variety of topics.

Further Reading
Cowasjee, Saros, *Studies in Indian and Anglo-Indian Fiction,* New Delhi: HarperCollins, 1993
Dhawan, R.K., "Mulk Raj Anand: *Coolie,*" in *Major Indian Novels: An Evaluation,* edited by Narindar S. Pradhan, New Delhi: Arnold-Heinemann, 1985; Atlantic Highlands, New Jersey: Humanities Press, 1986
Dhawan, R.K., editor, *The Novels of Mulk Raj Anand,* New Delhi: Prestige, 1992
Kaushik, Asha, *Politics, Aesthetics, and Culture: A Study of the Indo-Anglian Political Novel,* New Delhi: Manohar, 1988
Rajan, P.K., *Mulk Raj Anand: A Revaluation,* New Delhi: Arnold, 1994
Sharma, Kaushal Kishore, editor, *Perspectives on Mulk Raj Anand,* Ghaziabad: Vimal, 1978; Atlantic Highlands, New Jersey: Humanities Press, 1982

Ivo Andrić 1892–1975

Bosnian

In his 1961 Nobel prize acceptance speech, Ivo Andrić placed his work in the context of the eternal concerns of the simple storyteller: "In a thousand different languages, in the most varied conditions of life, from century to century . . . the tale of human destiny unfolds, told endlessly and uninterruptedly by man to man." Andrić's emphasis on traditional storytelling rather than on the philosophical and linguistic problems that were of primary interest to many of his contemporaries was justified by the combination of an unusual talent of tale-telling with a well-developed modernist literary sensibility.

Andrić produced work in many genres in a literary career that spanned some 60 years. Before World War II, he was known primarily for exquisitely wrought short stories set in his native Bosnia, and for more modernist lyric poetry and prose poems. He spent the war years in occupied Belgrade, and it was there that Andrić completed his first novels, *Na Drini ćuprija* (1945; *The Bridge on the Drina*), *Travnička hronika* (1945; *Bosnian Chronicle*), and *Gospodjica* (1945; *The Woman from Sarajevo*). Published practically simultaneously, in 1945, these quite varied works made Andrić's reputation as a novelist.

The Woman from Sarajevo, generally and justifiably seen as the weakest of the three, is a psychological novel set mostly in the inter-war period. It concentrates on a single individual, the miser Rajka Radaković. Powerful at times, this novel nevertheless does not display any great originality in terms of its structure or content. Rajka remains an isolated individual, and although Andrić's description of her inner life displays subtlety, he fails to make her story broadly meaningful. In *Bosnian Chronicle* and *The Bridge on the Drina,* however, Andrić succeeds brilliantly at balancing skillful storytelling with broad historical and philosophical concerns.

Bosnian Chronicle is set in the town of Trávnik during the period 1806–13 and consists of an intricately interlinked series of stories including those of Travnik insiders (drawn from the Muslim, Orthodox, Roman Catholic, and Jewish populations), as well as outsiders like the Ottoman viziers and the newly arrived European consular officials and their families. All are filtered through the consciousness of a narrator who is distanced in space and time from the events. The result is a cross-sectional portrait of Bosnian life at one moment in history. In Bakhtinian terms, *Bosnian Chronicle* employs the standard chronotopic assumptions of the historical novel, which tends to focus on historical moments rather than historical processes. If a novelist wishes not only to capture a single period but the *longue durée* of historical experience, however, this approach is problematic, for it would take a gigantic number of horizontal slices to provide a comprehensive national portrait. Walter Scott did this in the Waverly novels, but few novelists possess his graphomanic energy. Andrić, on the other hand, invented an entirely new way to overcome the chronotopic limitations imposed by the historical novel in his most famous work, *The Bridge on the Drina.*

Andrić's great innovation in *The Bridge* was to focus not on human characters, with their inevitably limited life span, but on an object—the beautiful 16th-century stone bridge over the Drina at the town of Višegrad. The novel is structured as a series of vignettes—practically separate short stories, in fact—each one presenting some aspect of life in the town from the time of the bridge's construction to the outbreak of World War I. The characters, drawn from the town's typically Bosnian mixed population of Muslims, Christians, and Jews, live out their lives in the shadow of the bridge, which remains an ambiguous presence throughout. While in some ways the bridge symbolizes the connection of East and West (and in this respect stands metonymically for Andrić's novelistic project of uniting Eastern storytelling with Western novelistic form), in other ways it fails to form a link. Most importantly, it does not connect the local people. Christians, Muslims, and Jews all use the bridge, to be sure, but each community has its own legends, customs, and attitudes toward it. They recognize only the differences, ignoring potential similarities. Nevertheless, there is an overarching synthetic truth in the text, provided by the narrator. He can and does reconcile the various stories he presents, and it is through his selection and presentation of material that the reader comes to see the repetitions and links that the townspeople fail to notice. The novel, then, dramatizes the central tension of Bosnian (and, by extension, Yugoslav) history: the coexistence of similarity and difference that can lead either to synthesis or violence.

Andrić's final completed novel, *Prokleta avlija* (*Devil's Yard*), appeared in 1954. Structured as a complex series of frame stories many of which are told by inmates of a Turkish prison, this work foregrounds the author's interest in pure storytelling. While the earlier novels could be seen as attempts to make sense of Bosnian and Yugoslav history as a whole, in *Devil's Yard* we recognize that for Andrić it is the process of storytelling itself that matters. Like modern-day Scheherazades, the prisoners (whose extreme situations are quantitatively rather than qualitatively different from ours) tell stories as the only way to remain alive in a chaotic world: storytelling provides rational order in an otherwise meaningless world. In this sense, the novel is a brilliant illustration of what Andrić meant when, in his Nobel speech, he said: "frequently we learn what we have done and what we have left undone, what to do what not to do, from the words of a good story-teller. Perhaps it is in those tales . . . that the true history of mankind is contained."

ANDREW WACHTEL

See also Bridge on the Drina

Biography

Born in Trávnik, Bosnia (then in the Austro-Hungarian Empire), 9 October 1892. Educated at schools in Višegrad and Sarajevo, 1898–1912; University of Zagreb, 1912; Vienna University, 1913; Jagiellonian University, Cracow, 1914; received Ph.D., Graz University, 1923. Member of Mlada Bosna [Young Bosnia] and interned for three years during World War I; served in the army, 1917, and in the Yugoslav diplomatic service, 1920–41 (his posts included the Vatican [Rome], Geneva, Madrid, Bucharest, Trieste, Graz, Belgrade, Marseilles, Paris, Brussels, and, as ambassador to Germany, Berlin); full-time writer, 1941–49; Bosnian representative, Yugoslav parliament, 1949–55. Cofounder and member of the editorial board, *Knjiž̌evni jug* [The Literary South], 1918–19. President, Federation of Writers of Yugoslavia, 1946–51. Awarded Nobel prize for literature, 1961. Died 13 March 1975.

Novels by Andrić

Gospodjica, 1945; as *The Woman from Sarajevo*, translated by Joseph Hitrec, 1965

Na Drini ćuprija, 1945; as *The Bridge on the Drina*, translated by Lovett Edwards, 1959

Travnička hronika, 1945; as *Bosnian Story*, translated by Kenneth Johnstone, 1958; as *Bosnian Chronicle*, translated by Joseph Hitrec, 1963; as *The Days of the Consuls*, translated by Celia Hawkesworth with Bogdan Rakić, 1996

Prokleta avlija, 1954; as *Devil's Yard*, translated by Kenneth Johnstone, 1962; as *The Damned Yard*, translated by Celia Hawkesworth in *The Damned Yard and Other Stories*, 1992

Other Writings: short stories, poetry, letters, and diplomatic papers.

Further Reading

Hawkesworth, Celia, *Ivo Andrić: Bridge Between East and West*, London and Dover, New Hampshire: Athlone Press, 1984

Hawkesworth, Celia, editor, *Ivo Andrić: Proceedings of a Symposium Held at the School of Slavonic and East European Studies, 10–12 July, 1984*, London: School of Slavonic Studies, 1985

Singh Mukerji, Vanita, *Ivo Andrić: A Critical Biography*, Jefferson, North Carolina: McFarland, 1990

Vucinich, Wayne, editor, *Ivo Andrić Revisited: The Bridge Still Stands*, Berkeley: International and Area Studies, University of California, 1995

Wachtel, Andrew, *The Failure of Multiculturalism: Literature, Cultural Politics, and the Rise and Fall of Yugoslavia*, Stanford, California: Stanford University Press, 1998

Anna Karenina by Lev Tolstoi

1875–77

After the publication of his sprawling masterpiece *Voina i mir* (1863–69; *War and Peace*), Lev Tolstoi turned in the 1870s to a novel of smaller scope, *Anna Karenina*. Influenced by his recent study of Greek and by his rereading of Aleksandr Pushkin, Tolstoi created in *Anna Karenina* a much tighter, more elegant novel with fewer settings and characters, simpler language, and without the philosophical and historical digressions that characterize its predecessor. *Anna Karenina* represents a pinnacle in world literature, one of the half-dozen best novels in the great 19th-century realist tradition.

Early reaction to the novel was mixed. The public was exceptionally enthusiastic about it from its earliest installments in the journal *Russian Herald*, while professional critics tended to respond to it on the basis of their politics: conservatives liked it, and radical critics did not. Tolstoi was attacked for writing about a tedious upper-class love affair rather than the pressing social problems of the day. That Tolstoi explored issues such as the role of women and of peasants, agriculture, and education, as well as the eternal problems of existence, was overshadowed for critics who felt that the central plot concerned "merely" an affair. Many early critics considered the character of Anna herself uninteresting and the plot structure confusing.

Tolstoi originally conceived the story of Anna to illustrate the pathetic plight of a woman who engages in adultery and comes to a bad end. For contrast, Tolstoi developed the Levin story, in which Levin learns that the path to tranquillity and joy lies in living correctly, rather than through selfishly satisfying one's own needs, as Anna does. In the finished novel, Tolstoi interweaves the two stories, concentrating first on one character, then the other. Anna and Levin are distantly linked (Anna's brother Stiva is married to Dolly, sister of Levin's wife Kitty), but they meet only once, in a minor scene toward the end of the novel. After an elaborate introduction in which all the major characters are introduced in successive scenes, the alternation of Anna and Levin plots proceeds regularly throughout the novel, both characters facing similar situations in parallel scenes. The elaborate introduction and the prominence of secondary characters like Stiva and Dolly obscured the plan enough for the editor of the *Russian Herald* (who was angry at Tolstoi's comments on war in the Balkans expressed in the last installment of the novel) to claim that the final section was superfluous and to refuse to publish it. True, Anna is already dead, but it is in this section that Levin finds the key to life. Omitting this section left the plan for the novel incomplete.

Anna Karenina has been criticized on the grounds that it is really two novels, only loosely linked. An argument can be made that the plots are strongly linked by theme and that the link is further strengthened by the movement of the major secondary characters between the two stories. Although Levin carries the positive message in the novel, his story pales before that of Anna. Early critics found her uninteresting, but subsequent generations of readers certainly have not, debating endlessly whether Anna should have stayed with her husband and child or left a humdrum marriage for Vronsky. Early readers may have applauded or condemned the fact that Anna's defection from her marriage leads to disaster, but recent scholars ask whether

Tolstoi might actually be a feminist at heart, sensitively exploring the very real problems that face all women.

There is some question as to whether Anna's character and situation are developed sufficiently at the beginning of the novel to provide motivation for her failure to resist temptation. Tolstoi uses very short chapters to advance the plot through representative mini-scenes and shows action rather than describes it. In many cases, he allows a single instance to stand for what might be a whole constellation of similar events. As a consequence, the reader does not see the characters slowly and carefully built up through long descriptive passages, but sees them whole each time they appear. We see the changes in the characters, but we do not always have descriptions of the process of change. Tolstoi's abandonment of "biography" and extended description thus marks a departure from earlier realistic writers.

Tolstoi used symbols and dreams and foreshadowing to good effect, developing a complex set of imagery (train, French, red, peasant, telegram, death, light, heat, falling, devil, drowning) that creates a resonance among key scenes in the novel. Yet Tolstoi is hardly a "symbolist." Despite the artistry of the novel's unusual architecture and its imagery, the novel sits firmly within, although near the end of, the realist tradition. Its elegantly simple language remains a model to this day, and its characters live on in the Russian imagination. But aside from Chekhov, who learned much of his craft from Tolstoi, the great age of realism in Russia was nearly over; Chekhov, in any case, specialized in forms shorter than the novel.

In the Russian tradition, Tolstoi owes much to Pushkin's sparklingly clear language, memorable characters, and deceptively simple storytelling techniques. He also learned from his slightly older contemporary Turgenev, who, like Tolstoi, wrote novels mixing love with contemporary issues in supple, beautiful Russian. As to Tolstoi's influence in the 20th century, novels like Vladimir Nabokov's *Ada* (1969) or Boris Pasternak's *Doktor Zhivago* (1957; *Doctor Zhivago*), or Andrei Belyi's *Peterburg* (1916; *St. Petersburg*), owe a debt to *Anna Karenina*. Indeed, throughout the West, many serious works exploring the themes of women and love were written in the knowledge that Anna had been there before. In fact, the novel still makes its presence felt in such recent fiction as Cathryn Alpert's *Rocket City* (1995), a half-serious, half-mocking tribute to *Anna Karenina* that follows the structure of the earlier novel closely to explore the nature and demands of love from a different perspective.

SYDNEY SCHULTZE

See also Lev Tolstoi

Further Reading

Armstrong, Judith, *The Unsaid Anna Karenina*, London: Macmillan, and New York: St. Martin's Press, 1988

Eikhenbaum, Boris, *Tolstoi in the Seventies*, Ann Arbor, Michigan: Ardis, 1982

Mandelker, Amy, *Framing "Anna Karenina": Tolstoy, the Woman Question, and the Victorian Novel*, Columbus: Ohio State University, 1993

Schultze, Sydney, *The Structure of "Anna Karenina,"* Ann Arbor, Michigan: Ardis, 1982

Stenbock-Fermor, Elisabeth, *The Architecture of "Anna Karenina": A History of Its Writing, Structure, and Message*, Lisse: Peter de Ridder, 1975

Turner, C.J.G., *A Karenina Companion*, Waterloo, Ontario: Wilfrid Laurier University Press, 1993

Antihero. *See* Character

Antiroman. *See* Nouveau Roman

Aharon Appelfeld 1932–

Israeli

Holocaust survivor Aharon Appelfeld was the first Israeli writer to confront the Holocaust and make it a legitimate subject for serious Hebrew prose fiction. For several years after World War II, until the Eichmann trial in 1961, Israeli writers and readers, committed to the Zionist rejection of the Diaspora and to nationalist regeneration, repressed the memory of the Shoah, focusing on the partisans and ghetto uprisings rather than on the 6 million. Given this climate, it is not surprising that it took Appelfeld several years (from 1956 to 1962) to find a publisher for his first collection of stories, *Ashan* (1962; Smoke), which the author himself has described as a book "about lost people." Despite the initial opposition to his subject matter, the publication of *Ashan* was a watershed event in Israeli literary history. Since then, Appelfeld has published more than 20 books in Hebrew and has become one of Israel's foremost novelists.

Appelfeld's success in breaking the taboo in Israel against writing about the Shoah derives in part from his own refusal to write directly about the camps. Paradoxically, there are virtually no Nazis in Appelfeld's Holocaust fiction and almost no concentration camp scenes. Most of his novels deal with events before or after World War II, with the areas surrounding memory rather than with memory itself. Appelfeld is keenly aware of the moral risks of representing the brutality of the death camps. "It is clear to me," he has said, "that it is almost impossible to write anything about the Holocaust, that is, the concentration camps. In Jewish tradition there are holy, spiritual places where one cannot enter lest one go out of one's mind; for me the concentration camp is one of those places."

In much of his fiction, then, Appelfeld practices what Robert Alter has called an "art of intimation," relying on the retrospective knowledge of the reader, familiar with the details and recurrent images of the Holocaust, to supply a historical context and ironic meaning for his stories. When combined with a reader's knowledge, these images and motifs—the cattle cars, the barbed wire, the comparisons between Jews and vermin—evoke the Holocaust, but they also have universal application. Appelfeld favors shorter narrative forms, which he situates in an abstract place, at a slight remove from precise details of historical or biographical event. Even in *Tzili: The Story of a Life* (1983), a novel that draws heavily from his own experiences as a child hiding away in the forests from the Nazis, Appelfeld transforms the protagonist into a simple, naive girl so as to be able to treat his autobiography as fiction rather than testimony. Appelfeld's style is always spare, brief, precise, yet unrealistic, reminiscent of S.Y. Agnon, Bruno Schulz, and, most importantly, Franz Kafka. Often Appelfeld's novels verge on the fantastic, evincing a dreamlike or nightmarish quality, portraying people whose lives are permeated by voices, spirits, and evil rumors, steeped in mystery and dark secrets.

Appelfeld's approach to the representation of the Holocaust—his tendency to intimate but not reveal the horror and his use of a Kafkaesque blend of simple style and fantastic incident—is apparent even in the earliest stories from *Ashan*. For example, in "Bertha," Appelfeld dramatizes the strange relationship of two survivors living together in Israel—a man named Max and a dwarflike, mentally disabled girl/woman named Bertha who never seems to grow or change and whose identity, disability, and relationship to Max are never made explicit. As in most of Appelfeld's novels, the open-ended, enigmatic quality of this story gives rise to multiple interpretations, among them an allegorical reading in which Bertha becomes a figure for the Holocaust experience itself, a memory that Max desperately wants to forget but that remains an ineradicable part of his being. Impervious to changes in Israeli life and forever caught in the emotional grip of the Holocaust, Max prefigures Bartfuss, the title character of the novel *Bartfus ben ha'almavet* (1988; *The Immortal Bartfuss*), which tells of an emotionally scarred Holocaust survivor living in Jaffa.

In contrast to works like *The Immortal Bartfuss* and *Ha'or vehakutonet* (1971; The Skin and the Gown), which deal with the experiences of survivors in Israel, Appelfeld's best known translated novels portray uprooted, assimilated Austrian Jews living in prewar Vienna. Their cultural pretensions and self-hatred blind them almost fantastically to the dangers around them. In *Badenheim, ir nofesh* (1979; *Badenheim 1939*), *Tor hapela'ot* (1978; *The Age of Wonders*), *To the Land of the Cattails* (1986; *El eretz ha'gomeh*), and *Ba'et uve'onah achat* (1985; *The Healer*), Appelfeld's characters develop an ironic urge just before the outbreak of the war to return to their origins—their Jewish parents, their hometowns in the Carpathians, their religion. In *Badenheim 1939*, his most celebrated and controversial novel, a group of secular Jews assemble on the eve of the Holocaust at an Austrian resort town, which, through a series of bureaucratic measures by the euphemistically named "Sanitation Department," is gradually transformed into a Nazi transit camp. As their liberties are stripped away and their contact with the outside word is severed, Appelfeld's Badenheimers are beset by dark thoughts and fears, but still they cling to their petit-bourgeois ways—their disdain for the vulgar East European Jew (the Ostjude), their love of music, mineral baths, and pastry. Throughout the novel, a character named Samitsky speaks wistfully of his yearning to return to his native Poland, a desire which is chillingly gratified at the end of the novel, when an "engine coupled to four filthy freight cars, emerged from the hills and stopped at the station." Many critics have praised this novel for its reticence and indirection in representing the terror of the Holocaust. Others have criticized Appelfeld's writing, particularly *Badenheim 1939*, for its historically inaccurate scenarios and impossibly naive characters and for the retrospective blame it places on the victims of the Holocaust for their own demise (see Bernstein, 1994; Wisse, 1983).

Appelfeld's fiction is hardly forgiving, however, of European anti-Semitism. Jew hatred emerges repeatedly in his writing as a kind of bestial genetic trait among the gentile population of Austria and Appelfeld's native Bukovina. The self-hating Jewish characters in such novels as *Badenheim 1939*, *The Retreat* (1984), and *The Age of Wonders* err in that they integrate this hatred into their own psyche. In a more recent work called *Katerinah* (1989; *Katerina*), Appelfeld seems to make up for his harsh criticism of his fellow Jews by writing a novelistic elegy for European Jewish life. *Katerina* tells the life story of a gentile housekeeper who comes to love and identify with her Jewish employers so strongly that she becomes, in the words of Gershon Shaked, "an honor guard" for the memory of a Jewish way of life that was wiped out by the Holocaust (see Shaked, 1990).

Significantly, *Katerina* does not focus specifically on the Holocaust period. In his other recent novels, *Mesilat barzel* (1991; The Railway), *Timyon* (1993; *Conversion: A Novel*), *Ad nefesh* (1994; *Unto the Soul*), *Layish* (1994), and *Ad she'ya'aleh amud ha'shahar* (1995), Appelfeld writes about Jewish life in the 19th and early 20th centuries, focusing on the broader problems of assimilation, Jewish identity, and memory. In this sense, Appelfeld is not strictly speaking a Holocaust writer but a chronicler of modern Jewish life. As Appelfeld himself has said, "for me the Holocaust is a subject through which I try to understand the Jew in the modern world, sociologically, psychologically, religiously. Essentially, my project is to write a saga about the modern Jew over the last 200 years." As part of a saga, Appelfeld's novels, both early and recent, share many interconnecting motifs: train rides, homeward voyages, cigarette and alcohol addictions, religious conversions and longings, and tragic separations. Appelfeld's work remains preoccupied with Diaspora Jewry, and thus outside the major trends of modern Israeli fiction. There are no native-born Israelis in his novels, and no attention is granted to current Israeli life or politics. In his concern with questions of Jewish identity, religion, and memory, however, Appelfeld may be considered the most Jewish novelist writing in Israel today.

WENDY ZIERLER

See also Badenheim 1939

Biography

Born in Czernowitz, Bukovina, in 1932. Imprisoned in Transnistria concentration camp in Romania during World War II; escaped to the Ukrainian countryside, hiding there for some time and then joining the Russian army; arrived in Palestine, 1947; served in Israeli army. Educated at Hebrew University, Jerusalem; Visiting Fellowship for Israeli Writers, St. Cross College, Oxford University, 1967–68. Visiting Lecturer, School of Oriental and African Studies, University of London, Oxford University, and Cambridge University, 1984. Currently professor of Hebrew literature at Ben Gurion University in the Negev.

Novels by Appelfeld

Ha'or vehakutonet [The Skin and the Gown], 1971
Ke'ishon ha'ayin [Like the Pupil of an Eye], 1972
Tor hapela'ot, 1978; as *The Age of Wonders*, translated by Dalya Bilu, 1981

Badenheim, ir nofesh, 1979; as *Badenheim 1939*, 1980
Michvat ha'or [A Burn on the Skin], 1980
Tzili: The Story of a Life, 1983
Hakutonet vehapasim [The Shirt and the Stripes], 1983
The Retreat, translated by Dalya Bilu, 1984
Ba'et uve'onah achat, 1985; as *The Healer*, translated by Jeffrey M. Green, 1990
To the Land of the Cattails, translated by Jeffrey M. Green, 1986; published in Hebrew as *El eretz ha'gomeh*
Bartfus ben ha'almavet, as *The Immortal Bartfuss*, 1988
Ritspat esh [Tongue of Fire], 1988
Al kol hapesha'im, as *For Every Sin*, translated by Jeffrey M. Green, 1989
Katerinah, 1989; as *Katerina*, translated by Jeffrey M. Green, 1992
Mesilat barzel [The Railway], 1991
Timyon, 1993; as *Conversion: A Novel*, translated by Jeffrey M. Green, 1998
Ad nefesh, translated as *Unto the Soul*, 1994
Layish, 1994
Ad she'ya'aleh amud ha'shahar, 1995

Other Writings: short stories and essays.

Further Reading
Appelfeld, Aharon, *Beyond Despair: Three Lectures and a Conversation with Philip Roth*, New York: Fromm International, 1994
Bernstein, Michael Andre, *Foregone Conclusions: Against Apocalyptic History*, Berkeley: University of California Press, 1994
Ezrahi, Sidra DeKoven, *By Words Alone: The Holocaust in Literature*, Chicago: University of Chicago Press, 1980
Mintz, Alan, *Hurban: Responses to Catastrophe in Hebrew Literature*, New York: Columbia University Press, 1984
Ramraz-Raukh, Gilah, *Aharon Appelfeld: The Holocaust and Beyond*, Bloomington: Indiana University Press, 1994
Rattok, Lily, *Bayit al belimah: Omanut ha'sipur shel A. Appelfeld*, Tel Aviv: Hekker, 1989
Shaked, Gershon, "Now There Are No More Victims in the World, Only Murderers," *Modern Hebrew Literature* 5 (Fall/Winter 1990)
Shvarts, Yig'al, *Kinat ha-yahid ve-netsah ha-shevet: Aharon Appelfeld, temunat olam*, Jerusalem: Keter, Hotsa'ot Magnes, 1996
Sokoloff, Naomi, *Imagining the Child in Modern Jewish Fiction*, Baltimore: Johns Hopkins University Press, 1992
Wisse, Ruth, "Aharon Appelfeld, Survivor," *Commentary* 76:2 (August 1983)

The Apprenticeship of Duddy Kravitz by Mordecai Richler

1959

For a novel that has become an undoubted classic of Canadian fiction, critical reception of Mordecai Richler's *The Apprenticeship of Duddy Kravitz* has been surprisingly mixed. While the novel has been almost universally acknowledged as Richler's best and most assured, critics also have suggested repeatedly that its real artistic accomplishment is slight. Richler has been criticized for creating caricatures rather than fully realized characters, for treating Montreal's Jewish community with insufficient complexity and too little sympathy, and for writing a novel that is either outrightly amoral or, on the contrary, far too moralistic in its intentions. It is not entirely surprising that the novel should invite such opposing opinions. A blend of social realism and broad social satire, *The Apprenticeship of Duddy Kravitz* is both more complicated and more ambiguous than either its explicit form or its content might suggest.

Even without having to compare *The Apprenticeship of Duddy Kravitz* to the other landmark Canadian novel that appeared in 1959, Sheila Watson's *The Double Hook* (the first truly experimental novel in Canadian literary history), it is clear that the originality of Richler's novel does not lie in its form. With the exception of one flashback, the narrative of the novel is linear, uncomplicated, and fairly traditional. Duddy's apprenticeship is the familiar story of a young man's transition into independent adulthood within the constrictive social setting of Montreal's Jewish ghetto, from which he yearns to break free. Unlike Stephen Dedalus in James Joyce's *A Portrait of the Artist as a Young Man* (1916), Duddy's success in becoming his own man is at the same time a failure to become anything more than a shallow, materialistic person. Duddy's transformation from mischievous schoolboy into ruthless entrepreneur is driven by a blinding desire to purchase a piece of land that he hopes will secure his position in the community. In the end, Duddy achieves his dream, only to find that he has alienated those whose love and recognition he sought. The attainment of an adult maturity suggested by the apprenticeship of the title never does occur, although in part this is because Duddy retains a remarkable naïveté even as he mercilessly destroys the lives of Mr. and Mrs. MacPherson, and cruelly takes advantage of his epileptic friend, Virgil, and his girlfriend, Yvette.

This familiar, essentially moralistic narrative about the passage from adolescence to manhood and the heavy price paid for worldly and material success is made considerably more complicated and interesting through Richler's imaginative use of humor, exaggeration, and farce. It is for its use of black humor that *The Apprenticeship of Duddy Kravitz* has become most well known. At its most basic level, the humorous situations are established by an initial incongruity that runs throughout the novel. Simcha Kravitz, Duddy's grandfather, tells him that "A man without land is nobody." What is for the old man an expression of pastoral longing is transformed by Duddy into a materialist maxim that comes to define all of his actions and hopes. The plot of the novel follows Duddy through a series of humorously exaggerated schemes to make money, all of which are pushed dangerously to the brink of collapse in his haste to achieve his goal. The most famous of these comic schemes involves the production of a terrible avant-garde bar mitzvah film for Mr. Cohen, one of Jewish Montreal's leading citizens.

If Duddy so desperately wants to be "somebody" it is because he comes from such a harsh social and economic background. Richler balances Duddy's obsessive and exaggerated pursuit of property with a realistic depiction of what was the author's own milieu—Montreal's lower-class Jewish community. The novel's social realism lends Duddy's quest an authenticity that tempers and balances his extremes. It also provides Richler with ample opportunity for a satirical exploration of Montreal's Jewish community and of North American society in general. Duddy is motherless; his father moonlights as a pimp; his role model of a successful Jew, Jerry (the Boy Wonder) Dingelman, turns out to be a petty thief; and his family's attentions are all turned toward his brother, Lenny, who is planning to make his way out of the ghetto by studying medicine. Although Duddy is ridiculed as a *pusherke*, a "pushy Jew," for his blatant, consuming desire to prove his worth through material success, the hypocrisy of the community is exposed in its own obsession with social climbing and status. Duddy's quest, if perhaps in a more extreme and exaggerated fashion, is his community's quest as well. His error lies in undertaking this quest so sincerely and naively, as he is unable to play the complicated social games that would make his materialism more acceptable to his community and so establish him as a person of means.

In the character of Duddy, Richler creates an appealing anti-hero for whom it is alternately possible to feel both sympathy and hate. Duddy is often cruel to those around him, but at the same time he abandons his money-making schemes at the point at which they are most in jeopardy of failing in order to help out the same family members who have treated him indifferently. His conscienceless pursuit of his objectives is fueled by his love of his grandfather and his own naïveté about the world. Although he is ruthless and unthinking, Duddy can also feel gripped by remorse when his actions inflict pain on others. The contradictions in Duddy's character, which Richler has managed to portray convincingly, remain unresolved at the conclusion of the novel. Duddy has "made it," as he now has the authority to sign for a bill he has incurred; but his dream is also a nightmare since he has lost the respect of Yvette and, most importantly, of his grandfather Simcha.

The lasting influence of *The Apprenticeship of Duddy Kravitz* is found in its broadening of both the language and subject matter of Canadian fiction. The novel's loose, colloquial dialogue, comprised of obscene jokes, insults, and straightforward and unpretentious language, opened the way for increasingly more realistic language in Canadian fiction that genuinely reflected contemporary vernacular. Although it is not the first Canadian novel to explore urban spaces, for a younger generation of Canadian writers *The Apprenticeship of Duddy Kravitz* has also been an important model of the realistic treatment of an urban community in a literature that has been dominated by rural and regional novels.

IMRE SZEMAN

See also Mordecai Richler

Further Reading
Darling, Michael, editor, *Perspectives on Mordecai Richler,* Toronto: ECW Press, 1986
Davidson, Arnold, *Mordecai Richler,* New York: Ungar, 1983
Gibson, Graeme, "Mordecai Richler," in *Eleven Canadian Novelists Interviewed by Graeme Gibson,* Toronto: Anansi, 1973

McSweeney, Kerry, "Mordecai Richler," in *Canadian Writers and Their Works,* Fiction Series, edited by Robert Lecker et al., Downsview, Ontario: ECW Press, 1983
Ramraj, Victor, *Mordecai Richler,* Boston: Twayne, 1983
Sheps, G. David, editor, *Mordecai Richler,* Toronto and New York: Ryerson Press, 1971
Woodcock, George, *Introducing Mordecai Richler's "The Apprenticeship of Duddy Kravitz,"* Toronto: ECW Press, 1990

Hubert Aquin 1929–77

Canadian

Unique in his complex plot construction and enigmatic character depiction, original in the creation of an esoteric and captivating style, Hubert Aquin had a profound effect on the evolution of the modern Quebec novel. From the 1940s to the mid-1960s, the Quebec novel, greatly influenced by the tenets of social realism, mirrored Quebec's new urban society. The isolated and conservative rural world—dominated by the Roman Catholic church and by the ideology espousing the importance of cultivating the land, raising a family, and preserving traditional mores—garnered less novelistic attention as the industrialization and urbanization of Quebec society became evident. With this modernization came attempts to liberate fiction from its traditional form and content. For Aquin, firmly committed to the secession of Quebec from Canada, the novel became an instrument of protest in the service of aesthetic and political freedom. Despite publishing only four novels in nine years, Aquin has come to be known as one of Quebec's most original writers. His work has similarities to the self-reflexive style of the *nouveau roman,* which requires active participation from the reader. His novels are carefully crafted puzzles that continually shift between reality and illusion, clarity and subterfuge.

Published in 1965, *Prochain épisode* (*Prochain Episode*) resembles a spy thriller in its general plot construction and offers an innovation to the Quebec novel through the use of "I" as both narrator/novelist and principal character. Aquin's omniscient character leads the reader not only into the mysteries of espionage, but also into the intricacies associated with the act of writing. In this way, *Prochain épisode* introduced French Canadian literature to the self-reflexive novel, to the notion that writing can be an ongoing interaction between character, narrator, and reader, challenging conventional expectations that an omniscient narrator will act as a guide to the reader.

The unnamed narrator and main character of *Prochain épisode* perceives reality through his fatalistic view of his inadequacies as a writer and as a revolutionary. While incarcerated in a Montreal psychiatric prison, he is writing a novel—entitled *Prochain épisode*—in which he recounts the circumstances that led to his imprisonment. Complete with espionage, counterespionage, and international intrigue in Geneva, Lausanne, and Montreal, *Prochain épisode* paints a psychological portrait of the main character as an individual who is committed to the liberation of Quebec but who has failed in his mission to track down and assassinate the mysterious H. de Heutz, a counterspy. Beyond the unmistakable traits of the spy thriller, *Prochain épisode* offers a profound psychological analysis of the narrator's impotence as an assassin, a writer, and a lover. The psychological landscape, although bleak, is spellbinding.

Trou de mémoire (1968; *Blackout*) offers another eloquent example of Aquin's penchant for the exotic, the unpredictable, and the mysterious in plot construction. It is a much more complex work than *Prochain épisode,* for it reveals itself through a set of documents—journal entries and editor's notes—that lead the reader to the realization that none of the various versions of "truth" presented in the work can be trusted. Clarity emerges from the complexity, however, in the two pairs of doubles—two English sisters, each involved with one of two revolutionary pharmacists, one from Quebec and the other from Africa—who serve as parallels of each other. England's influence over its Canadian and African colonies is mirrored in both pairs, symbolizing Aquin's unfinished search for personal, aesthetic, and political liberation.

L'Antiphonaire (1969; *The Antiphonary*) elaborates on Aquin's conception of reality as existing only in the perception of the observer. This novel bears a striking resemblance to Aquin's earlier works in that it, too, contains complex character partnerings and focuses on the realization of failure in life. In the novel, Christine Forestier, writing a thesis on 16th-century medicine, escapes from the violence of her epileptic husband by committing suicide. Endeavoring to take control of life through biographical writing leads Forestier, paradoxically, to seek peace in death, foreshadowing perhaps Aquin's own eventual suicide.

Aquin's last finished novel, *Neige noire* (1974; *Hamlet's Twin*) is another innovative work. It is clearly more direct than his other novels in that it recounts the television production of *Hamlet,* a familiar work that provides the reader with a stable point of reference. The novel's engagement with the play replaces the intertextuality of fictive manuscripts, journal entries, and editor's notes present in the earlier works and informs another profoundly psychological plot. *Hamlet's Twin* is the culmination of Aquin's vision of the novel as a liberating experiment with language, as an investigation of psychological realities, and as a meditation on the unpredictable and complicitous relationships between text, reader, and author.

Hubert Aquin is heralded as one of the finest and most innovative novelists of French Canada, and, indeed, of modern literature. His conception of the novel as a self-reflexive artifact that creates binding relationships between text, reader, and author is exemplified in each of his works, and carries with it a perception that the novel is also a means of asserting autonomy, be it personal, collective, aesthetic, or ideological.

KENNETH W. MEADWELL

Biography

Born in Montreal's east end, 1929. Attended l'École Olier; l'Externat Saint-Croix; Collège Sainte-Marie; completed a licentiate in philosophy at the Université de Montréal, 1951; studied at the Institut d'Études politiques in Paris, 1951–54. Producer, Radio-Canada, 1955–59; script-writer and film director, 1959–63. Joined the Rassemblement pour l'Indépendance nationale (RIN), 1960; in 1964 announced in a press release that he was joining an underground terrorist movement; in July of that year was arrested for illegally possessing a firearm and driving a stolen car; transferred from Montreal Prison to Albert Prevost psychiatric institute while awaiting trial; acquitted in December 1965. Left RIN in 1968 when it merged with another group to form the Parti québécois. Served on the editorial board of *Liberté* and as literary director of *Éditions La Presse*. Died (suicide) 15 March 1977.

Novels by Aquin

Prochain épisode, 1965; as *Prochain Episode,* translated by Penny Williams, 1967
Trou de mémoire, 1968; as *Blackout,* translated by Alan Brown, 1974
L'Antiphonaire, 1969; as *The Antiphonary,* translated by Alan Brown, 1973
Neige noire, 1974; as *Hamlet's Twin,* translated by Sheila Fischman, 1979

Other Writings: political writings, television plays, film scripts.

Further Reading

Cagnon, Maurice, "Palimpsest in the Writings of Hubert Aquin," *Modern Language Studies* 8:2 (1977)
Iqbal, Françoise Maccabee, *Hubert Aquin, romancier,* Montreal: Presses de l'Université Laval, 1978
Jameson, Fredric, "Euphorias of Substitution: Hubert Aquin and the Political Novel in Québec," *Yale French Studies* 65 (1983)
Merivale, Patricia, "Hubert Aquin," in *Profiles in Canadian Literature,* volume 4, edited by Jeffrey M. Heath, Toronto: Dundurn Press, 1980
Moorhead, Andrea, "Double Life: An Analysis of Hubert Aquin's *Prochain épisode,*" *L'Esprit créateur* 23:3 (Fall 1983)
Sherry, Simon, "Hubert Aquin: Hamlet in Quebec," *Canadian Forum* 59 (February 1989)
Smart, Patricia, *Hubert Aquin, agent double,* Montreal: Presses de l'Université de Montréal, 1973
Stratford, Philip, "The Uses of Ambiguity: Margaret Atwood and Hubert Aquin," in *All the Polarities: Comparative Studies in Contemporary Canadian Novels in French and English,* Toronto: ECW Press, 1986

Argentine Novel. *See* Latin American Novel: Argentina

Ayi Kwei Armah 1938–

Ghanaian

Ayi Kwei Armah is a controversial figure in the younger generation of postwar African novelists, partly because of the polemical vigor of his writing and partly because of a visionary symbolism and audacious use of metaphor that place his work outside the mainstream realism of African fiction.

Armah's childhood and adolescence coincided with his

country's growth, under the charismatic leadership of Kwame Nkrumah, into Africa's first independent state. His subsequent disillusionment with the betrayed ideals of Ghanaian nationalism and Nkrumahist socialism colored Armah's early novels, stories, and essays. These tell of Africa's continuing oppression under the "mystification" of independence and entrapment in a cycle of neocolonial dependency, and the destruction of human values in the lives of modern urban Africans by manipulative and exploitative systems of relationships. The West is seen to maintain a posthumous existence in Africa through the indirect controls of political influence, cultural exports, and educational programs, and through financial strangleholds that force the continent to remain a subordinate partner in what is still an essentially colonial economy.

Armah's first two novels, *The Beautyful Ones Are Not Yet Born* (1968) and *Fragments* (1970), paint an excoriating picture of an indolent, parasitical African ruling bourgeoisie whose hankerings after Western luxury and privilege result in wholesale embezzlement, bribery, and fraud and lead to the slavish aping of European manners at all levels of society. In *The Beautyful Ones* an anonymous railway office clerk wages a futile struggle to retain his integrity against pressure from his acquisitive family and an onslaught of temptation from bribe-proffering traders, venal fellow clerks, and corrupt influential relations in the government. In *Fragments*, contemporary Ghanaians are compared to cargo cult worshipers who ascribe to the white world godlike powers of invention that they are unwilling to develop themselves. Starving their traditionally honored ancestors of libations, they regard with superstitious awe the returning "been-tos" from abroad, the foreign-educated "reborn spirits" who act as transmission lines for the trinkets of Western technology. Traditional ritual practices and folk myths, perverted almost beyond recognition, are kept alive solely for expedience and profit. Even the group economics of the extended family system has been undermined by individual greed and locked into the service of a vicious selfish materialism. In Armah's third novel, *Why Are We So Blest?* (1972), Western-inspired aspirations to bourgeois comforts, class hierarchies, and American mistresses have even infiltrated African revolution, which is perpetually subverted by an induction into the leadership of Westernized intellectuals from American educational exchange programs.

Armah's is an extreme and one-sided vision, prone to exaggerated pessimism, conspiracy theory, and oversimplification. His political portrait of Nkrumah's Ghana records the unfinished public utilities and waste but leaves out the industrial development. Though the blame in the first two books falls on the Ghanaians who collaborate with the alien values destroying their culture, there is a growing tendency in his later work to lay all of Africa's woes at the door of the West. Armah's sometimes troubling political analysis is combined with a tremendous poetic energy. The power of his language, his haunting metaphoric resonances, and his complexly orchestrated poetic structures draw the reader in regardless of political allegiance. For instance, the lurid rescue scene in the highly stylized finale of *The Beautyful Ones* is based on the motif of an indigenous purification rite in which the detritus of the dying year is ceremonially borne to sea. In this surreal episode, set during Ghana's 1966 coup, the corrupt politician Koomson is imaged as the nation's collected excrement—and, by implication, the accumulated unpurged ills of Nkrumah's moribund regime—which has to be

evacuated through the public latrine hole and carried off by the novel's unnamed hero before a new era can be born. Armah pushes the imagery of consumer waste and excreta to extremity, lavishing orgies of description on the mountains of undisposed-of filth that a decade of unproductive consumption has heaped in streets and latrines. In his inventive, exuberant hyperbole, which owes something to the graphic scatology of African oral tradition, everything is endowed with excremental characteristics: breath is flatulent, voices constipated, and fraud and collusion are metaphorically transformed into urinary and excretory functions. The imagery is orchestrated by an intricate and formidably symmetrical network of correspondences between the human ingestion-evacuation cycle, the body politic, and the Ghanaian environment.

The poetic intensity and metaphoric richness is equally strong in the multilayered *Fragments,* in which a mythic scheme of figurative death and rebirth conflates images of resurrected cargo-spirits, reincarnated ancestors, repatriated "been-tos," and visionary Mermen from local coastal folklore. Once again, the narrative resonates with an allusive ritualistic subtext, drawing in this case upon arcane areas of Akan custom and theology to rehabilitate a dead order of traditional moral value as a living presence in a rootless and sterile contemporary world. Less successfully, Armah pushes metaphor to bizarre limits in the ambitious politico-sexual allegory of *Why Are We So Blest?* In this novel interracial sexual relationships are made to serve as a microcosm of Africa's historical encounter with the West. The colonial plunder of Africa's people and material resources is unconvincingly transposed into a corresponding depletion of black sexual potency by white women.

In his next books, Armah experimented with new literary forms, moving from historical realism to myth and racial epic, and from naturalism to simulated oral narrative. *Two Thousand Seasons* (1973) presents a thousand years in the migratory history of a fictitious pan-African, intertribal brotherhood, in which the continent's vanished precolonial cultures are represented as all closely connected to an essentially African way of life. A pluralized communal voice speaks through this novel for the whole social body, repudiating the alienated individualistic perspectives of the first three novels. Characterization is concerned only with the representation of the group experience and collective states and feelings.

Armah attempted to put the abstract communalist rhetoric and cultural polemics of *Two Thousand Seasons* onto a more concrete footing in the historical novel *The Healers* (1978), which focuses on the Second Ashanti War. After a 17-year silence, Armah published another novel, *Osiris Rising* (1995), about a radical educational reform group, which reinstates ancient Egypt at the center of its curriculum. Envisioning the decolonization of African history, *Osiris Rising* has the broader aims of liberating African intelligence from Eurocentric ideologies and seeding a long-term social revolution.

The visionary mythologies of these last three books are clearly designed to cure an errant modern Africa of its distrust in its own indigenous forms and values, but Armah's search for a more overtly African focus and democratic base in his later fiction is necessarily marked by a corresponding loss of subtlety both in his symbolism, which has become disappointingly diagrammatic, and in his characterization, which tends to polarize into principles, substituting type for complex consciousness. In these didactic, ideologically weighted works Armah fails to recover the rich poetic textures and dramatic tensions that arise from the imaginative engagement between myth, ritual subtext, and historical realism in the first two novels.

Nevertheless, Armah's novels and career constitute watersheds in post-independence African writing. Most particularly, they were important touchstones during the decolonization debates of the 1970s, when a number of writers and critics attempted to recover from the complex matrix of African literature an authentic African worldview or cultural essence and to unshackle these from Western ideological and aesthetic influences. In keeping with these trends, Armah's fiction (especially after *Why Are We So Blest?*) revealed a deepening suspicion of all conceptual systems derived from European traditions; Armah sought to shed the foreign literary styles and techniques that were plainly discernible in the modernist poetics, intricate leitmotifs, and descriptive tableaux of his first three novels. The ensuing epic and historical works were clearly are turning points in African writing, marking major shifts in narrative style and consciousness in their use of indigenous oral devices and storytelling techniques. These works did not, finally, prove to be enduring models either for Ghanaian or for African fiction, which, over the next 20 years, moved away from a narrow cultural homogeneity and from exclusivist models of African identity toward a greater diversification and cosmopolitan hybridization of form. Even so, a later generation of West African novelists has picked up on selected elements of Armah's work, notably Ben Okri on the mythology of the African "way" in his *Songs of Enchantment* (1993). The Ghanaian writer's polemical ideas continue to be an important reference point in contemporary African writing and criticism.

DEREK WRIGHT

Biography

Born in Takoradi in 1938. Attended Achimota College, Accra; Groton School, Massachusetts; Harvard University, Cambridge, Massachusetts, A.B. in social studies; Columbia University, New York. Translator, *Révolution Africaine* magazine, Algiers; scriptwriter for Ghana Television; English teacher, Navrongo School, Ghana, 1966; editor, *Jeune Afrique* magazine, Paris, 1967–68; has taught at Teacher's College (Dar-es-Salaam), University of Masssachusetts, Amherst, University of Lesotho, and University of Wisconsin, Madison.

Novels by Armah
The Beautyful Ones Are Not Yet Born, 1968
Fragments, 1970
Why Are We So Blest?, 1972
Two Thousand Seasons, 1973
The Healers, 1978
Osiris Rising, 1995

Other Writings: short stories, including "The Offal Kind" (1969) and "Doctor Kamikaze" (1989).

Further Reading
Damodar Rao, K., *The Novels of Ayi Kwei Armah*, New Delhi: Prestige Books, 1993
Fraser, Robert, *The Novels of Ayi Kwei Armah: A Study in Polemical Fiction*, London: Heinemann, 1980
Gikandi, Simon, *Reading the African Novel*, London: James Currey, and Portsmouth, New Hampshire: Heinemann, 1987
Lazarus, Neil, *Resistance in Postcolonial African Fiction*, New Haven, Connecticut: Yale University Press, 1990
Wright, Derek, *Ayi Kwei Armah's Africa: The Sources of His Fiction*, London and New York: Hans Zell, 1989
Wright, Derek, "Ayi Kwei Armah," in *Dictionary of Literary Biography No. 117: Twentieth Century Caribbean and Black African Writers,* first series, edited by Bernth Lindfors and Reinhard Sander, Detroit, Michigan: Gale Research, 1992
Wright, Derek, editor, *Critical Perspectives on Ayi Kwei Armah*, Washington, D.C.: Three Continents Press, 1992

L'Astrée by Honoré d'Urfé

1607–27

By the time Balthazar Baro, Honoré d'Urfé's longtime secretary, published posthumously in 1627 the fourth volume of the pastoral novel *L'Astrée*, the French cultivated reading public had already had two decades of exposure to d'Urfé's opus. In the 20 years separating the 1607 publication of Part I from the posthumous edition of Part IV, two years after d'Urfé's death in 1625, the French nobility had become enthralled by the work. While waiting for d'Urfé to complete and publish new sections of *L'Astrée*, they dressed up in the costumes of the novel's shepherds and shepherdesses, mimicking their interminable comedies of love and seeking to experience vicariously the passions of d'Urfé's fictional world. These same aristocrats also circulated "keys" to *L'Astrée*, in an attempt to determine exactly which contemporary figures d'Urfé had intended to represent.

Such efforts must have been no small matter, for d'Urfé's novel is massive in length, breadth, and scope. Each of the volumes runs to many hundred pages and is divided into several books. *L'Astrée* scarcely offers the type of experience most familiar to contemporary readers. Nonetheless, in the early and middle years of the 17th century, extraordinarily long, multivolume fictional works formed a major part of the literary scene in France and in other European nations. Such monumental works were particularly dominant in Spain; in fact, it was largely from late 16th-century Spanish novelists that Honoré d'Urfé sought inspiration. France's production of the pastoral novel prior to d'Urfé was relatively slight; and it was, therefore, upon the *Diana* (1559) of Jorge de Montemayor and the *Galatea* (1585) of Miguel de Cervantes that the author of *L'Astrée* patterned his work. However, while building his novel on a foundation inherited from the Spanish pastoral novelists, d'Urfé also incorporated themes and forms culled from medieval chivalric romances, from the adventure romances of ancient Greece, and from the much shorter Renaissance fictional genre of the *nouvelle*.

Moreover, d'Urfé altered significantly the essential structure of the pastoral genre that forms the heart of his work. He provided far greater historical and geographical accuracy than did earlier pastoral fiction, which had been located traditionally in vaguely delineated Arcadias. D'Urfé, situating *L'Astrée* in fifth-century Forez (his native region, near Lyon) offered a double perspective: while idealizing Forez and endowing it with the qualities of an Edenic paradise, he simultaneously created a more realistic and geographically accurate area, which was in keeping with the tastes of a sophisticated reading public accustomed to the specifically French atmosphere that prevailed in nonpastoral fiction of the time.

Likewise, while preserving the fundamental conventions of 16th-century Spanish pastoral fiction, d'Urfé strove to develop the complexity and subtlety both of his characters and of his writing. Traditional elements of pastoral fiction—the typically prolonged love stories of shepherds and shepherdesses (whose bucolic ancestors were never rustic workers but disaffected aristocrats grown weary of court life); the sexual suspense dictated by the convention of delayed consummation; the many exterior obstacles to satisfaction and fulfillment in love; the veiled eroticism of tightly knit, clanlike groups whose members live in intensely close, communal fashion; the interminable discussions concerning matters of the heart; the variety of magical and supernatural phenomena; and the seemingly endless production of secondary and tertiary characters, whose own stories frequently sever and interrupt the primary ones—all readily commingle in d'Urfé's massive work. The primary love stories of the shepherd Céladon and the shepherdess Astrée, and of their friends Silvandre and Diane, also adhere fundamentally to the pastoral format. Nonetheless, d'Urfé, in composing their stories, creates highly original passages of textual/sexual play. By taking advantage of the convention of disguise (predominant in both Renaissance pastoral and nonpastoral literature), he quickly transcends the limitations of both travesty and transvestism. For much of the novel, Céladon is disguised as a woman and referred to by his female name, Alexis, in order to woo Astrée who, out of misplaced jealousy, has banished him. Through the many prolonged and complicated travesty episodes, where the ambiguity of pronouns eventually doubles that of costume and name, the reader finds increasingly difficult the task of sustaining a clear picture of maleness and femaleness, as d'Urfé artfully fabricates a writing experiment that moves beyond the traditional constrictions of gender.

L'Astrée is above all a fantasy romance. The doctrinal side of the novel, based loosely on the precepts of Renaissance Platonism, which postulates an abstract, metaphysical view of love as the source for a spiritually purifying transformation of true lovers' souls, fades quickly when matched against the erotically charged narratives. The codes of *courtoisie*, inherited from me-

dieval literature, also are undercut as Céladon, dressed and living as a woman, finds his status as "perfect lover" in shambles. Yet it is precisely in these passages that d'Urfé, cognizant of the projections of fantasy and imagination and working to endow the pastoral format with its truest and freest spirit, moves to liberate his world from the more limiting binds of cultural definition and prescription.

D'Urfé's novel, however, is a *summa* that offers, both thematically and structurally, a host of compelling elements. *L'Astrée* contains richly imaginative fantasy episodes that coexist with doctrinal, metaphysical passages; historical sections on the role of Forez at the dawn of European civilization; religious commentary on the shepherds' Druidism, which bears a striking resemblance to Catholicism; and "action" passages depicting battles and knightly activities that are modeled on earlier European fiction. *L'Astrée* offers a panoply of literary forms as well. While the individual story is its basic unit, many of the most developed tales continue for whole books and volumes, as d'Urfé carefully controls the intercalated structure inherited from the Spanish novels, whereby stories ceaselessly interrupt stories, fragmenting the novel and, above all, avoiding a conclusion. He also employs debates, judgments, letters, and poetry that create a compendium not only of Western literary themes but also of forms. Indeed, parts of *L'Astrée* may be read almost as a self-contained epistolary novel. If this extensive reliance on missives may be viewed in hindsight as a harbinger of later epistolary works, such as Jean-Jacques Rousseau's *Julie; ou, La Nouvelle Héloïse* (1761; *Julie; or, The New Eloise*) or Pierre Choderlos de Laclos' *Les Liaisons dangereuses* (1782; *Dangerous Acquaintances*), d'Urfé's use of verse moves readers backward in literary history. Poetry within the prose format of the novel disappears shortly after *L'Astrée*, in which d'Urfé displays openly the lyrical premise at its base. The novel's dominant prose becomes an extension of earlier lyrical, poetic writing in Western literature. In so doing, d'Urfé presents within the boundaries of his work the very genesis of the French novel.

Yet both pastoral fiction, as inherited and practiced by d'Urfé, and the long, multivolume novel soon were to disappear from the French literary scene, replaced during the second half of the 17th century by historically based, highly concise works. Today, it is Madame de Lafayette's tightly conceived novel of the 16th-century French court, *La Princesse de Clèves* (1678; *The Princess of Cleves*), that is most familiar to readers and scholars. Except for the brief period between World Wars I and II, the novel in France would never again offer such long and continuous narratives. *L'Astrée* represents *that* work written at *that* historical juncture when, in the words of Gérard Genette (1966), "all the old was poured into all the new."

LOUISE K. HOROWITZ

See also Pastoralism in the Novel

Further Reading

Ehrmann, Jacques, *Un Paradis désespéré: L'amour et l'illusion dans "L'Astrée,"* New Haven, Connecticut: Yale University Press, and Paris: Presses Universitaires de France, 1963

Gaume, Maxime, *Les Inspirations et les sources de l'oeuvre d'Honoré d'Urfé,* Saint-Etienne: Centre d'études foréziennes, 1977

Genette, Gérard, "Le Serpent dans la bergerie," in *Figures,* Paris: Seuil, 1966; reprinted from introduction to *L'Astrée,* Paris: Union générale d'éditions, 1964

Gregorio, Laurence, *The Pastoral Masquerade: Disguise and Identity in "L'Astrée,"* Saratoga, California: Anma Libri, 1992

Henein, Eglal, *Protée romancier: Les Déguisements dans "L'Astrée" d'Honoré d'Urfé,* Paris and Fasano: Schena-Nizet, 1996

Horowitz, Louise K., *Honoré d'Urfé,* Boston: Twayne, 1984

Jehenson, Myriam Yvonne, *The Golden World of the Pastoral: A Comparative Study of Sidney's "New Arcadia" and d'Urfé's "L'Astrée,"* Ravenna: Longo, 1981

Kevorkian, Servais, *Thématique de "L'Astrée" d'Honoré d'Urfé,* Paris: Honoré Champion, 1991

Miguel Ángel Asturias 1899–1974

Guatemalan

Miguel Ángel Asturias is the leading Central American novelist of the 20th century. A sojourn in Paris in the 1920s gave him an important insight into Europe and European ways of seeing and writing, but it also gave him the determination to resist European hegemonies and find specifically Latin American narrative languages and forms. He became a Third World and a postcolonial writer before those concepts existed, and his work has as much in common with that of the Martiniquais poet Aimé Césaire or the Senegalese writer Léopold Sédar Senghor as with his Latin American fiction-writing contemporaries. He was also among the first of the great Spanish American magic realists, effectively turning Surrealism against the Europeans who invented it. His stories *Leyendas de Guatemala* (1930; Legends of Guatemala) were some of the earliest examples of this literary mode.

Asturias' first major novel was *El Señor Presidente* (1946; *The President*). It is a hallucinatory account of the regime of the dictator Estrada Cabrera, in power in Guatemala during the whole of Asturias' childhood and adolescence. Asturias began the book in Guatemala in 1922 but wrote most of it in Paris between 1924 and 1933. The novel draws on the whole gamut of French avant-garde resources to produce a literary experience of extraordinary energy and intensity. Nevertheless, the book has suffered a strange displacement in Latin American literary history because political circumstances prevented its publication until 1946, and its effect on subsequent novels was therefore postponed until after World War II. *The President* was the first major novel in Latin America to unite the demand for a revolution in politics and society with the call for a revolution in language and literature and to challenge patriarchy and authoritarianism at the level of consciousness by exploring myths from within. Thus it questions the very basis of Latin American social and psychic existence. It remains the single most famous dictator novel in Latin American literary history.

Hombres de maíz (1949; *Men of Maize*) was similarly radical in its sophisticated use of myth and language but even more challenging to the reader since its basic reference system was the civilization of the ancient Maya and its prolongations in contemporary Guatemalan Indian culture. Its place as the first great magic realist novel in Latin America is secure.

Both *The President* and *Men of Maize* were works conceived on a large scale, and both had taken more than a decade to write. By the time *Men of Maize* was completed, Asturias was a diplomatic representative of the 1944 Guatemalan revolution and, in an age of Sartrean *engagement,* he turned to faster production techniques and a still more overtly political discourse with his controversial *Trilogía bananera* (1949–60; *Banana Trilogy*). The three novels are *Viento fuerte* (1949; *Strong Wind*), *El papa verde* (1954; *The Green Pope*), and *Los ojos de los enterrados* (1960; *The Eyes of the Interred*). They chart the impact of North American imperialism in Guatemala from the turn of the 20th century until the 1960s, concentrating in particular on the notorious United Fruit Company's banana plantations on the tropical coastlands of the small Central American republic. Asturias is undoubtedly the most distinguished Latin American writer to have lent his pen to overtly anti-imperialist fiction, and few critics were impressed with the results. Nevertheless, the attempt to fuse a tropical form of magic realism with the more familiar narrative modes of socialist realism is an intriguing literary experiment. These novels undoubtedly repay study.

In 1963 *Mulata de tal* (*Mulatta*) appeared, an extraordinarily dynamic, almost Rabelaisian experiment concerning a Guatemalan Indian's journey into the national underworld of folklore, legend, and myth. Here Asturias forges Latin American Spanish into a dazzlingly flexible instrument, which produces linguistic miscegenations as disconcerting as the cultural and biological syncretisms that are at the heart of the novel's subject matter.

After 1967, when Asturias won the Nobel prize at the age of 68, he wrote two more novels and a work that is impossible to categorize. The first of the novels, *Maladrón* (1969; The Bad Thief), looks back at the Spanish conquest of Central America in the 1520s and juxtaposes the collectivist, pantheist worldview of the native inhabitants with the individualistic, positivistic philosophy and religion of the European invaders. *Viernes de Dolores* (1978; Black Good Friday), published posthumously, is an autobiographical novel about the Guatemalan student movement of the 1920s. Neither novel is as dazzling as the more characteristic *Tres de cuatro soles* (1977; Three of Four Suns), a kind of Maya-based science-fiction narrative about the role of language and the human voice itself in the cosmos. It is a fitting postscript to a career of great dedication and audacity.

GERALD MARTIN

See also Magic Realism; Men of Maize

Biography

Born in Guatemala City, Guatemala, 19 October 1899. Family moved to Salamá fearing government persecution, 1903; returned to Guatemala City in 1908. Attended schools in Guatemala City; gave up studying medicine in 1917 and studied law at San Carlos University, Guatemala City, 1917–23; helped found the People's University [Universidad Popular] of Guatemala, 1922, and the Association of University Students; studied anthropology under Georges Raymond at the Sorbonne, Paris, 1923–28. Founder of *Tiempos Nuevos,* 1923; traveled to England in the same year and was based in Paris, 1923–32; traveled through Europe and the Middle East in the 1920s. Returned to Guatemala in 1933, and worked as radio broadcaster (co-creator, "Diario del arie" series, 1937) and journalist, 1933–42; served as a deputy at the Guatemalan National Congress, 1942; held a number of diplomatic posts, 1945–54: cultural attaché, Mexico City, 1945–47, and Buenos Aires, 1947–53, minister-counselor, Buenos Aires, 1951–52, Guatemalan ambassador, Paris, 1952–53, and San Salvador (El Salvador), 1953–54; exiled for his support of the left-wing leader Jacobo Àrbenz Guzmán, 1954, and moved to Argentina; journalist for *El Nacional* (Venezuela), 1954–62; cultural exchange program member, Columanum, Italy, 1962; Guatemalan ambassador in Paris, 1966–70; spent his final years in Madrid. Awarded Nobel prize for literature, 1967. Died 9 June 1974.

Novels by Asturias

El Señor Presidente, 1946; as *The President,* translated by Frances Partridge, 1963
Hombres de maíz, 1949; as *Men of Maize,* translated by Gerald Martin, 1974; critical edition, translated by Martin, 1993
Viento fuerte, 1949; as *The Cyclone,* translated by Darwin Flakoll and Claribel Alegría, 1967; as *Strong Wind,* translated by Gregory Rabassa, 1969
El papa verde, 1954; as *The Green Pope,* translated by Gregory Rabassa, 1971
Los ojos de los enterrados, 1960; as *The Eyes of the Interred,* translated by Gregory Rabassa, 1973
El alhajadito, 1961; as *The Bejeweled Boy,* translated by Martin Shuttleworth, 1971
Mulata de tal, 1963; as *Mulatta,* translated by Gregory Rabassa, 1967
Maladrón [The Bad Thief], 1969
Viernes de Delores [Black Good Friday], 1978

Other Writings: short fiction, poetry, plays, and essays.

Further Reading

Brotherston, Gordon, *The Emergence of the Latin American Novel,* Cambridge and New York: Cambridge University Press, 1977
Callan, Richard J., *Miguel Angel Asturias,* New York: Twayne, 1970
Harss, Luis, and Barbara Dohmann, *Into the Mainstream: Conversations with Latin American Writers,* New York: Harper and Row, 1967
Martin, Gerald, *Journeys Through the Labyrinth: Latin American Fiction in the Twentieth Century,* London and New York: Verso, 1989
Prieto, René, *Miguel Angel Asturias's Archeology of Return,* Cambridge and New York: Cambridge University Press, 1993

At Swim-Two-Birds by Flann O'Brien

1939

Six months after the initial publication of *At Swim-Two-Birds,* only 244 copies had been sold, and for the next 20 years, despite a 1951 US edition, the book was known only to a few people. It was not until its republication in England in 1960 that it became widely read, and even then it met critical responses ranging from the adulatory to the frankly dismissive. On the adulatory side, the novel was praised—either upon its original publication or after its reappearance—by James Joyce, Dylan Thomas, and Graham Greene. Other readers were, however, repelled by the book, finding it boring and derivative, or were deterred by the unfamil-iarity of much of the Irish source material. An anonymous reviewer in the Washington *Port Angeles News,* for example, lamented that "A background of the Irish literature O'Brien mimics would help the reader to understand what he's about. It would help, probably, if the reader were a bit unhinged too." The word most often used in connection with the book was "indescribable," and many reviewers contented themselves with giving a synopsis of the intricacies of the "plot" and confessing themselves "flummoxed" by a novel about a novelist writing a novel about the writing of a novel.

The idea, in itself, was not new—Flann O'Brien himself pointed to the influence of Aldous Huxley and of James Branch Cabell—but, typically, O'Brien took their experiments to even greater lengths and had the characters of the novel within a novel assume some sort of "reality," turn on their creator, and set out to punish him for his "despotic" treatment of them by writing a story about him in which he is subjected to torments that are a pastiche of those meted out to an earlier character in Irish literature. Added to this is the stylistic confusion caused by the fact that the narrator, and his novelist Dermot Trellis, do not believe in creating their own characters when they can borrow from others—and they do: from Cowboy stories, popular romances, old Irish legend, middle Irish Romance, encyclopedias, folklore, school books, and the popular press, creating a bewildering mélange of styles and often relating the same episode in a different style and from another point of view. All this confusion is justified by the narrator, who proposes, in a parody of Joyce's Stephen Dedalus, his own theory of the novel:

> A satisfactory novel should be a self-evident sham to which the reader could regulate at will the degree of his credulity. . . . Characters should be interchangeable as between one book and another. The entire corpus of existing literature should be regarded as a limbo from which discerning authors could draw their characters as required, creating only when they failed to find a suitable existing puppet. The modern novel should be largely a work of reference. Most authors spend their time saying what has been said before—usually said much better. A wealth of reference to existing works would acquaint the readers instantaneously with the nature of each character, would obviate tiresome explanations and would effectively preclude mountebanks, upstarts, thimbleriggers and persons of inferior education from an understanding of contemporary literature.

Although Brinsley, to whom the narrator proffers this "aesthetic," considers that it is "all my bum," the novel actually follows these prescriptions. Characters are borrowed from old and contemporary stories and complain bitterly about the uses to which they are put. Finn Mac Cool, Suibhne Geilt, the Pooka, the Good Fairy, a trio of cowboys, various Indians, St. Ronan Finn, and an 18th-century melancholic are all incorporated into the story, and each plays a role quite out of keeping with his or her character and previous literary incarnation. An unprincipled villain (who chooses not to play the role of villain) is created, and a peerless heroine. The novelist, overcome by the heroine's beauty, ravishes her and, when she dies of shame giving birth to a quasi-literary, quasi-real son, there is much debate as to how to represent the half-reality of this literary character—only his upper, or lower, body? The demands of realism being so imperative, both these options are discarded and the son uses his inherited literary powers (although borrowing freely from existing models) to subject the father to a series of excruciating punishments from which he is saved only by the accidental burning of the papers on which the reality of the characters had been inscribed.

At one level, this technique allows for the creation of a comic masterpiece that is, as Graham Greene said in recommending it, a serious "attempt to present, simultaneously as it were, all the literary traditions of Ireland . . . ." *At Swim-Two-Bird's* relationship to the work of Laurence Sterne, Joyce, as well as to the Italian playwright Luigi Pirandello, is clear. At another level, the ostensible theme of the book, embedded in all its interacting levels, may be said to be sin and the punishment thereof, and this marks it as one of those "Catholic novels" of which Graham Greene was himself such a notable practitioner. There were, however, others who recognized that the true importance of *At Swim-Two-Birds* was its interrogation of the claims and practices of realism itself. One of the first of these was Jorge Luis Borges in an article "Cuando la ficción vive en la ficción" (*El Hogar*, June 1939). Michael Wharton, writing in 1951, pointed out that *At Swim-Two-Birds* "anticipated, 20 years ago, quite a lot that has now attained the status of high literary fashion." In fact, the book is now treated, even if a bit controversially, as one of the more important forerunners of postmodern, self-interrogating metafictions. While it is arguable whether Flann O'Brien was influenced more by medieval Irish literature than by European modernism, it is true that the book's exposure of the process of "character creation" and fictional strategies, its juxtaposing of many styles and points of view, its carefree admixture of fantasy and reality, and its allusive and referential format anticipated and provided a model for the more consciously directed experiments with, and interrogations of, the mimetic claims of the novel form itself.

ANNE CLUNE

See also Metafiction; Flann O'Brien

Further Reading

Asbee, Sue, *Flann O'Brien,* Boston: Twayne, 1991

Booker, M. Keith, *Flann O'Brien, Bakhtin, and Menippean Satire,* Syracuse, New York: Syracuse University Press, 1995

Clissmann, Anne, *Flann O'Brien: A Critical Introduction to His Writings,* Dublin: Gill and Macmillan, and New York: Barnes and Noble, 1975

Clune, Anne, and Tess Hurson, editors, *Conjuring Complexities: Essays on Flann O'Brien,* Belfast: Institute of Irish Studies, The Queen's University of Belfast, 1997 (contains comprehensive bibliography)

Cronin, Anthony, *No Laughing Matter: The Life and Times of Flann O'Brien,* London and Toronto: Grafton, 1989

Hopper, Keith, *Flann O'Brien: A Portrait of the Artist as a Young Post-modernist,* Cork: Cork University Press, 1995

Imhof, Rüdiger, editor, *Alive, Alive, O! Flann O'Brien's "At Swim-Two-Birds,"* Dublin: Wolfhound, 1985

Shea, Thomas F., *Flann O'Brien's Exorbitant Novels,* Lewisburg, Pennsylvania: Bucknell University Press, and London: Associated University Presses, 1992

Wäppling, Eva, *Four Irish Legendary Figures in "At Swim-Two-Birds": A Study of Flann O'Brien's Use of Finn, Suibhne, the Pooka, and the Good Fairy,* Stockholm: Almqvist and Wiksell, 1984

Margaret Atwood 1939–

Canadian

Margaret Atwood's novels reflect her concern for the artist within society. Her writing anatomizes social and political forces and at the same time explores the depths of the protagonist's psyche through such devices as myth and fairy tale. Unsurprisingly, this double vision and Atwood's examination of a tendency to polarity in thought and perception grants the writer a dual role. She herself is both a Canadian author consciously mapping her culture and a femininst novelist of international renown.

Atwood's texts diverge from the traditional realist novel in that they provide female, often first-person narrator-protagonists who are neither heroic nor even highly individualized. Rather, they are victims, and the ways in which they deal with their assumed status as victims have profound implications for Atwood's art and her contribution to the genre. In 1972 Atwood published *Survival: A Thematic Guide to Canadian Literature,* which proposes that Canadian fiction is deeply marked by a myth of survival, with characters often falling into four basic victim positions. These positions consist of denying victim status, claiming victimhood as inescapable fate, combatting the role of the victim, and, finally, becoming a nonvictim. Clearly influenced by Northrop Frye's structuralist myth criticism which it cites, *Survival* proved controversial but does illuminate Atwood's own work. At one point she suggests that the typical Canadian hero is not the individualist of Anglo-American literary tradition, but a collective or representative being for his or her social group. Her own female heroes, victimized by gender and politics, do function at one level as representative, almost "everywoman" characters, although they are always located in a specific culture. Indeed, Atwood's protagonists embody the twin directions of her art: consideration of an individual psyche and social diagnosis. Their collective nature allows the reader a personal identification with both fantasy and political expression. This does not mean that the narrators are reliable guides. Atwood's readers are required to be detectives at some level, since active participation in constructing the story is part of the political aims of her fiction. Traditional novels, Atwood seems to suggest, package the reader as a passive consumer, a victim rather than an active agent in the art.

Although Atwood's novels are rooted in traditional realism, they trouble its borders by employing fantasy, myth, fairy tale, history, and even science fiction. Atwood's departures from realism are not evasions of social concern, but a means to further political aims more completely. *Surfacing* (1972) uses myth to explore a woman's psyche fractured through gender and social pressures and to represent anxieties about the environment and Canadian identity. *The Handmaid's Tale* (1985), usually defined as science fiction, is a chilling critique of totalitarian strategies made all the more immediate to the reader by the narrator's realistic evocation of her experience. The recent *Alias Grace* (1996) uses a genuine 19th-century criminal case to weave a fictional exploration of the class, psychological, and gender politics surrounding an alleged female murderer. Again the reader is invited into the detective role, but the novel offers no unequivocal answers to historical puzzles.

Atwood also employs postmodernist devices to unsettle the certainties of traditional realism. There is more than a hint of postmodern consciousness in *Alias Grace*'s argument about the fictional and erotic drives within historical texts. Similarly, *The Handmaid's Tale* contains a marvellous coda detailing the reconstruction of the text by future male academics in an account that casts considerable doubt on their "authenticity." As a result, the fiction situates itself somewhere between "fake" and "history."

Throughout her oeuvre, Atwood has employed both parody and poetry to debunk the ideological codes of literary genres while drawing on the psychic resources of art to reenchant or to "commit" the reader. *Lady Oracle* (1976) is both a witty satire that parodies Gothic romance and a profound exploration of the perils of fantasy in a society hostile to women's self-development. Significantly, it contains "genuine" occult art when its heroine, a commercial romance author, produces a poem through automatic writing. Atwood's novels value the creative powers of the unconscious while never losing sight of society's oppressive codification of their products. Similarly, fairy tales pinion female characters in victim roles they need to overcome, but they are also a means to represent unconscious powers of renewal. Deploring the tendency to divide experience into good and evil, conscious and unconscious, and even Canadian and American, Atwood suggests that this binarism is a habit of mind that allows her female protagonists to see themselves as pure victims, without recognizing the ways in which they oppress others. Atwood's examinations of female bullying in *Cat's Eye* (1988) and of suffocating mothers (in both senses) in *The Robber Bride* (1993) underscore the point that women participate in oppression themselves.

Similarly, Atwood's use of the novel form constructs polarities of fantasy and social realism, myth and parody, poetry and pastiche. *The Robber Bride,* for instance, is a seamless spanning of the genres of fairy tale and social realism. Its central focus, the irredeemable Zenia, operates simultaneously as a fantasy of the characters' inner lives and as a social agent in a recognizable contemporary world of war and politics. Such a text presents psychological healing as a route to social and political engagement.

Atwood's novels show how the weaker members of society, particularly but not exclusively women, are victimized, but then they trace a route from suffering through self-awareness to resistance. To this purpose, Atwood draws on all the resources of the novel in the 20th century—on realism, modernist experimentation, and postmodern bricolage. At the same time, she relies on a poetic faith in the unconscious. To the Canadian novel, she contributes a polemical self-consciousness. To the development of the art, she offers a poetic mapping of psychic realities onto acute social and political criticism. Such a union is itself an evolution of the novel form.

Susan Rowland

See also Handmaid's Tale

Biography

Born in Ottawa, Ontario, 18 November 1939. Received B.A. from Victoria College, University of Toronto, 1961; A.M.,

Radcliffe College, Cambridge, Massachusetts, 1962; attended Harvard University, Cambridge, Massachusetts 1962–63, 1965–67. Has taught widely at colleges and universities in Canada, the United States, and elsewhere.

Novels by Atwood

The Edible Woman, 1969
Surfacing, 1972
Lady Oracle, 1976
Life Before Man, 1979
Bodily Harm, 1981
The Handmaid's Tale, 1985
Cat's Eye, 1988
The Robber Bride, 1993
Alias Grace, 1996

Other Writings: poetry, short stories, essays, criticism (including *Survival: A Thematic Guide to Canadian Literature,* 1972, and *Second Words,* 1983).

Further Reading

Auerbach, Nina, *Romantic Imprisonment: Women and Other Glorified Outcasts,* New York: Columbia University Press, 1985

Christ, Carol P., *Diving Deep and Surfacing: Women Writers on Spiritual Quest,* Boston: Beacon Press, 1980

Davey, Frank, *Margaret Atwood: A Feminist Poetics,* Vancouver: Talonbooks, 1984

Nicholson, Colin, editor, *Margaret Atwood: Writing and Subjectivity,* New York: St. Martin's Press, 1994

Rao, Eleonora, *Strategies for Identity: The Fiction of Margaret Atwood,* New York: Peter Lang, 1993

Rigney, Barbara Hill, *Margaret Atwood,* London: Macmillan, and Totowa, New Jersey: Barnes and Noble, 1987

Rosenberg, Jerome H., *Margaret Atwood,* Boston: Twayne, 1984

Rubenstein, Roberta, "*Surfacing:* Margaret Atwood's Journey to the Interior," *Modern Fiction Studies* 22 (Autumn 1976)

Aufzeichnungen des Malte Laurids Brigge. *See* Notebooks of Malte Laurids Brigge

---

Jane Austen 1775–1817

English

Nowadays Jane Austen's novels are established as "classics" of the genre, yet they also enjoy a large readership around the world, have provided the model for the popular 20th-century "regency romance," and, through film and television adaptations, have stimulated the "heritage" and tourism industries in Britain. To readers of Austen's own time, this complex achievement would have seemed unlikely. These readers considered her novels well-made but unambitious reworkings of the novel of manners, sentiment, and emulation as developed by Frances Burney. Paradoxically, this assessment forms the basis of Austen's contribution to the novel form. Austen reduced and concentrated novel elements familiar to her readers, so as to engage those readers, and generations of their successors, in novel reading as a serious intellectual and artistic task having moral and ethical implications.

Austen knew the novel form well. The members of her family were avid and unashamed novel readers who discussed what they read. The young Austen amused them with brief burlesques of the leading novel forms of the day, from sentimental tale to Gothic romance. Austen began writing serious novels in the 1790s, including early versions of *Sense and Sensibility, Pride and Prejudice,* and *Northanger Abbey.* By the time she revised these works a decade later, she had decided on her formal method and central themes and, like Burney, reworked these throughout her published work with little variation.

Austen uses third-person omniscient narration with free indirect discourse, or reported inward thought of characters. Unlike Burney, she restricts the use of free indirect discourse almost entirely to the protagonist, thereby focusing attention on the heroine's subjectivity as she attempts to understand herself and her social world in making the most important choice in life for women of her class—a husband. Austen employs just two types of heroine—the active and the passive—and she alternates between them. Her first published novel, *Sense and Sensibility* (1811), contains both types, although the passive (Elinor) dominates. *Pride and Prejudice* (1813) has an active heroine, its successor *Mansfield Park* (1814) a passive one, *Emma* (1815) again an active one, and the unfinished *Persuasion* and the early

Northanger Abbey, posthumously published (1818), return to the passive type. The narrator, at times intrusive and judgmental, at times unobtrusive and sympathetic, and intermittently ironic, guides reader response to each heroine as she attempts to read the often deceptive and misleading social world around her, as well as her own often self-deceptive feelings, opinions, prejudices, and desires.

The conventional courtship plot signifies more than may appear, enacting what for Austen, as a committed Christian, is the ethical task of every human individual: directing the passions, guided by knowledge and reason, to the good rather than to evil. Yet the heroine's judgment is shown to be insufficient for this task. As a Christian, Austen believed that all humans are fallible. To show her heroine reasoning her way unerringly through the world would be to admit the rationalist optimism of revolutionary philosophers and novelists of her day, as expressed in the English Jacobin novels of the 1790s. Austen also was a committed Anglican, and her plots embody the Anglican belief that faith and works alone are insufficient for salvation, either earthly or eternal. Grace, or an instance of divine intervention in the individual life, is also necessary. Such moments of grace, as important turning points in Austen's plots, may seem like mere coincidence, as with Darcy's unexpected appearance at Pemberley in *Pride and Prejudice*. Coincidence is conventionally considered a defect in plotting, and thus in artistic technique, but Austen can plausibly be supposed to resort to it from religious conviction and resistance to the rationalist optimism of certain contemporaneous novelists. At the same time, use of free indirect discourse tempts the reader to identify closely with the heroine and to share her judgments, which often turn out to be wrong. In this way, both heroine and reader are made aware of their human fallibility and chastened accordingly. To this extent Austen is a didactic novelist.

As the appropriate setting for representing the human condition according to Anglican Christianity, Austen chooses contemporary life. She reduces the range of settings deployed by Burney, thereby concentrating attention on the protagonist's moral discernment and ethical choices in everyday life. Austen rejects the extreme situations and exotic settings depicted in the Gothic romances and overtly political novels of her day. Home life, countryhouse visits, rare trips to town or touring farther afield, dinners, balls, and outings in local society—these are where the gentry and the professional middle class live, meet, and form mutually beneficial relations, including marriages. The few exceptions, such as the Price household in *Mansfield Park*, are represented as undesirable. Additionally, Austen's settings are accessible to women of the upper and professional middle classes. Implicitly, these comprise the feminized world of "civil society"—strikingly so in *Persuasion*, where many of the characters are home from the otherwise uncivil (that is, martial) society of the navy.

With regard to character and characterization, Austen again reduces the range found in Burney's novels in order to concentrate on particular social groups. Almost all of Austen's characters come from the lesser gentry and the professional middle class, who together constituted the reading public at that time. This social group also constituted the "political nation," or those involved in the political system, with their immediate assistants and state officials. Austen rejected the idea promoted by some sensationalist or political novelists that the "real" nation is the peasantry, or the victimized, or the aristocratic, courtly, and

fashionable, or the excessively vicious or virtuous (consider Henry Tilney's rebuke to Catherine and her Gothic imaginings in *Northanger Abbey*). Austen's "characterology," or selection and stationing of characters by comparison and contrast, again accentuates the central moral and ethical task of the individual, as member of a fallen humanity in a fallen and conflicted world. Characters are graded on a moral and intellectual scale in relation to the narrator, who is a textual construction, setting a standard of informedness and rightness, sympathy and ironic detachment, for the reader to assimilate.

Language and dialogue in Austen's novels serve characterization. Her narrator uses standard written English, a social dialect standardized by the late 18th century as the dialect of the professional middle class. The narrator's syntax does exhibit traits of the essay style of Samuel Johnson, Austen's favorite moral writer, especially in her earlier novels; similarities include the use of parallelism, balance, and also triple units in sentence structure, enacting through syntax the mind in the act of discriminating and judging, rather than merely gushing with feeling or political passion. Austen's protagonist "thinks" and speaks in standard written English, as do other "serious" characters, thereby being associated with the narrator's character and values. Comic and vicious characters use sociolects larded with fashionable slang—a sign in Austen's novels of incorrect and improper values. Again, Austen reduces the range of dialogue to social dialogue, or "conversation" as an aspect of manners, and to intimate dialogue, which consists of an exchange between two characters interpreting a certain social occasion or character, as in the dialogues between Elizabeth and Jane in *Pride and Prejudice*. Letters supplement dialogue, as in Darcy's explanatory letter to Elizabeth after his first proposal and her changing subjective response to it.

Unlike many contemporaries, Austen refused to "dignify" her chosen genre by devices such as frequent quotation and allusion, incorporation of more prestigious discourses such as poetry and historiography, the claim to be writing something other than a novel, or criticism of novel writing itself. At a time when the novel was widely regarded as subliterary, Austen defiantly advertised her genre on her title pages and defended the moral and artistic seriousness of the novel, as in the passage in *Northanger Abbey* beginning "only a novel . . ." Her contribution was to rework the elements of what may seem "only a novel" in order to produce not disposable formula fiction but fiction that is re-readable—the criterion for at least the past two centuries of what is deemed a literary "classic."

GARY KELLY

See also Emma; Persuasion; Pride and Prejudice

Biography
Born in Steventon, near Basingstoke, Hampshire, 16 December 1775. Attended Mrs. Cawley's school, Oxford and Southampton, 1783–84; Abbey School, Reading, Berkshire, 1785–87. Lived with her family in Steventon, 1775–1800, Bath, 1801–06, Southampton, 1806–09, and Chawton, Hampshire, 1809–17. Died 18 July 1817.

Novels by Austen
Sense and Sensibility, 1811
Pride and Prejudice, 1813

Mansfield Park, 1814
Emma, 1815
Northanger Abbey, 1818
Persuasion, 1818

Other Writings: correspondence, collected in *Letters,* edited by R.W. Chapman (2 vols., 1932; revised edition, 1952); a play entitled *Sir Charles Grandison* (edited by B.C. Southam, 1981), from the novel by Samuel Richardson.

Further Reading

Babb, Howard S., *Jane Austen's Novels: The Fabric of Dialogue,* Columbus: Ohio State University Press, 1962

Butler, Marilyn, *Jane Austen and the War of Ideas,* Oxford: Clarendon Press, and New York: Oxford University Press, 1975

Duckworth, A.M., *The Improvement of the Estate: A Study of Jane Austen's Novels,* Baltimore: Johns Hopkins University Press, 1971

Gard, Roger, *Jane Austen's Novels: The Art of Clarity,* New Haven, Connecticut: Yale University Press, 1992

Gilson, David, *A Bibliography of Jane Austen,* Oxford: Clarendon Press, and New York: Oxford University Press, 1982

Kirkham, Margaret, *Jane Austen, Feminism and Fiction,* Brighton, Sussex: Harvester Press, and Totowa, New Jersey: Barnes and Noble, 1983

Johnson, Claudia L., *Jane Austen: Women, Politics, and the Novel,* Chicago: University of Chicago Press, 1988

Lascelles, Mary, *Jane Austen and Her Art,* Oxford: Clarendon Press, 1939

Litz, A. Walton, *Jane Austen: A Study of Her Artistic Development,* New York: Oxford University Press, and London: Chatto and Windus, 1965

MacDonagh, Oliver, *Jane Austen: Real and Imagined Worlds,* New Haven, Connecticut: Yale University Press, 1991

Moler, Kenneth L., *Jane Austen's Art of Allusion,* Lincoln: University of Nebraska Press, 1968

Page, Norman, *The Language of Jane Austen,* Oxford: Blackwell, and New York: Barnes and Noble, 1972

Roberts, Warren, *Jane Austen and the French Revolution,* London and New York: Macmillan, 1979

Sulloway, Alison G., *Jane Austen and the Province of Womanhood,* Philadelphia: University of Pennsylvania Press, 1989

Wallace, Tara Ghoshal, *Jane Austen and Narrative Authority,* London: Macmillan, and New York: St. Martin's Press, 1995

Australian Novel

Nearly 70 years after the establishment of a British penal colony at Botany Bay, the first European settlement on the continent, Frederick Sinnett surveyed "The Fiction Fields of Australia," as he titled his essay in the *Journal of Australasia* (1856). His judgment was that the few Australian novels that had appeared were "*too* Australian," because they were "too apt to be books of travels in disguise . . . at best, works of simple instruction as to facts, rather than works of art."

There were good reasons why this was so. Although Sinnett was writing his survey after the establishment of free, self-governing colonies across the continent and after the mid-century goldrushes, most books about Australia, including those that could loosely be considered novels, were published in London and Edinburgh (as they continued to be throughout the 19th century) for English readers curious about their exotic antipodean colonies or intending to emigrate to them. Among "emigrant handbooks" Sinnett mentions, which variously blended the picaresque and the picturesque with the documentary, are Charles Rowcroft's *Tales of the Colonies* (1843), Alexander Harris' *Settlers and Convicts* (1847) and *The Emigrant Family* (1849), and William Howitt's sketches of pastoral life, which he subsequently incorporated into *Tallangetta, the Squatter's Home* (1857). With his preference for novels "as works of art" (and he was writing in the year that "realism" passed into literary parlance), Sinnett singled out for praise Catherine Helen Spence's *Clara Morison: A Tale of South Australia During the Gold Fever* (1854) for not being yet another book of travels in disguise but a study of relationships that happened to be set in Australia.

His survey omits what today are understood to be the first novels published in Australia, Henry Savery's autobiographical and self-justifying account of convictism, *Quintus Servinton* (1830), as well as the first novel by an Australian-born writer, John Lang's *The Forger's Wife* (1855), and the first novel by an Australian-born woman, Louisa Atkinson's *Cowanda: The Veteran's Grant* (1859). Twentieth-century scholarship has unearthed other examples of early colonial fiction, the best known being James Tucker's *Ralph Rashleigh,* written in the 1840s but not published, in an abbreviated version, until 1929 (when it was assumed to be an autobiography) and not in its entirety until 1952. However, although Sinnett was not bibliographically comprehensive, he astutely identified issues relating to the "Australianness" of local fiction and tensions between realism and romance that continued to engage writers and commentators for more than a century.

The first "classic" Anglo-Australian novel was Henry Kingsley's often-reprinted *The Recollections of Geoffrey Hamlyn* (1859). Its author—the brother of Charles Kingsley, who wrote *The Water Babies* (1863)—had spent five years in Australia. His romance, about the dispossessed remnants of the English feudal order who make their fortunes in New South Wales and eventually reinstate themselves in the Old World, exploits the colonial "local color" that Sinnett had disparaged in early fictions:

descriptions of discovering, settling, and developing the land, of encounters with Aborigines and escaped convicts turned bushrangers, of the alien, indifferent bush in which, poignantly, children became lost, and of the native-born Australians.

Later Anglo-Australian novels that also became popular and accepted as classics throughout the English-speaking world included Marcus Clarke's *For the Term of His Natural Life* (1874), which powerfully combines melodrama with an extensively researched study of the convict system, and *Robbery Under Arms* (1888) by "Rolf Boldrewood" (T.A. Browne). The latter is a conventional "ripping yarn" about bushranging but, in being narrated in the vernacular by a Currency Lad, or native-born Australian (as opposed to "Sterling," or English-born), it anticipated by only a few years the "antiliterary" idioms adopted by a generation of native-born realists, most notably Henry Lawson, Joseph Furphy, and Miles Franklin.

The closest Lawson came to fulfilling his intention of writing a novel was the set of interrelated Joe Wilson stories published in London in 1901. Nevertheless, the humor and pathos of his austerely realistic sketches and stories of bush life, especially those published in the nationalistic Sydney *Bulletin* and collected in *While the Billy Boils* (1896), had by the turn of the century established his reputation as the most popular and representative Australian writer. Lawson assisted the publication of Miles Franklin's *My Brilliant Career* (1901), an exuberant, if uncertainly ironic, autobiographical Bildungsroman. Written when Franklin was 19, *My Brilliant Career* is set in contrasting literary versions of the bush, one realistic and Lawsonian, the other romantic and Kingsleyan. Influential on subsequent generations of younger readers were Ethel Turner's *Seven Little Australians* (1894) and the Billabong series of novels by Mary Grant Bruce, which began with *A Little Bush Maid* (1910).

In 1903, the *Bulletin*, which had established its own publishing house, issued *Such Is Life* by Tom Collins, pseudonym of Joseph Furphy. Completed and extensively revised before the turn of the century, *Such Is Life* is the most relentlessly realist and explicitly antiromantic representation of life in a particular Australian region (the Riverina on the New South Wales-Victoria border) and simultaneously a parody of romance and realism. Furphy's narrator, Tom Collins, sets out to expand from his diary entries the random events of a single week, so avoiding plot and other contrivances of romance, but the alert reader can detect multiple plots and a vernacular version of romance unsuspected by the polymathic and pedantic Tom. The doubleness of the narrative is perhaps best illustrated by the appearance of a character from Henry Kingsley's *Recollections of Geoffrey Hamlyn*, in greatly reduced circumstances. Unaware of the literary artifice of his "own" narrative, Tom remains ignorant of the character's provenance. Assumed to be a set of reminiscences when it first appeared, *Such Is Life* is now widely regarded as the most imaginative, as well as the most distinctively Australian, novel written in the 19th century.

The use of local color and dialect humor by the turn-of-the-century "nationalists" gave them much in common with contemporary Americans writing about the West Coast. Mark Twain's influence, for instance, is apparent in the early Lawson and in Furphy's *The Buln-Buln and the Brolga* (1948), a section excised from the original manuscript of *Such Is Life*. The "nationalists" subsequently acquired a reputation as forgers of a distinctively Australian strain of realist fiction, which has obscured the work of women writers of romance prominent in the same period. In recent decades, feminist critics have attempted to reappraise romance, particularly the novels of Catherine Martin, Mrs. Rosa Campbell Praed, and "Tasma" (Mrs. Jessie Couvreur). Until after the first half of the 20th century, however, the most prominent novelists were women who extended realist traditions in various directions.

Chief among them was Henry Handel Richardson, pseudonym of Ethel Florence Lindesay Robertson. Although she left Australia in 1888 at the age of 18 and returned only for a brief visit, Richardson was long considered the author of the "Great Australian Novel" after her trilogy, *The Fortunes of Richard Mahony*, was published in its entirety in 1930. Richardson's first novel was *Maurice Guest* (1908), a study of the psychopathology of love set in Leipzig, where Richardson had studied music (as well as the European naturalists). It was followed by *The Getting of Wisdom* (1910), a novel of education with strong autobiographical elements. *Australia Felix* (1917), the first book of the *Richard Mahony* trilogy, commenced with the mid-19th-century goldrushes to Victoria. *The Way Home* (1925) and *Ultima Thule* (1929) continued the story, based on family history, of Irish-born Mahony's restless search for belonging told in tandem with the history of the colony's development. The appearance of the trilogy in Britain and the United States as a single volume, under the title *The Fortunes of Richard Mahony*, coincided with a vogue for "epic" historical novels that represent the travails of nation-building through the fortunes of a family. Significant examples include *A House Is Built* (1929) by "M. Barnard Eldershaw" (Marjorie Barnard and Flora Eldershaw), Brian Penton's *Landtakers* (1934) and *Inheritors* (1936), and *The Montforts* (1928) by Richardson's fellow expatriate "Martin Mills," pseudonym of Martin Boyd. Under his real name and drawing on family history, Boyd was eventually to develop his major theme of the dual allegiances of Anglo-Australians in his Langton tetralogy: *The Cardboard Crown* (1952), *A Difficult Young Man* (1955), *Outbreak of Love* (1957), and *When Blackbirds Sing* (1962).

While Richardson, living in England, wrote about Australia in the style of European naturalism, her near contemporary Katharine Susannah Prichard in Western Australia was imaginatively extending the tradition of regional realism of Henry Lawson and Joseph Furphy. As its title suggests, her first novel, *The Pioneers* (1915), was in the historical mold that would soon become prevalent. The novels that followed were intended to counter prevailing literary stereotypes by presenting life in various Australian communities, each with its own relationship to a distinct environment: the opal fields in *Black Opal* (1921), the karri forests in *Working Bullocks* (1926), the cattle stations of the far northwest in *Coonardoo* (1929), and the goldfields in a later trilogy. Incidentally, *Coonardoo* was the first novel to provide a sustained examination of relationships between whites and Aborigines.

Prichard became a founding member of the Communist Party of Australia in 1920 and, with other prominent writers, a promoter of social realism (or the Lawson-Furphy tradition) as *the* national tradition. Others broadly identified with the left during the build-up to World War II and for 20 years after included Christina Stead and Eleanor Dark. Stead was little known in Australia for most of her writing life because she lived in, and wrote about, the United States and Europe. Only *Seven Poor*

Men of Sydney (1934) and *For Love Alone* (1944) are set in Australia, while the novel which is now regarded as her masterpiece, *The Man Who Loved Children* (1940), imaginatively transposes much of her own early experiences to Washington, D.C. In theory, social realism was inimical to modernism, but Stead's social realist novels revealed the influence of earlier European experimenters with stream-of-consciousness techniques. So also did the early novels of Eleanor Dark, most notably *Prelude to Christopher* (1934) with its complex timeshifts. However, Dark is better remembered for her historical "nation-building" trilogy *The Timeless Land* (1941), *Storm of Time* (1948), and *No Barrier* (1953).

Xavier Herbert employed historical and regional frames of epic proportions for *Capricornia* (1937). The title refers to the Northern Territory, and Herbert savagely satirizes its white-supremacist history for the havoc it has wreaked on a natural paradise and its indigenous people. Yet his exuberance and inventiveness transcend the generic classifications of the prevailing nation-building epics and social and regional realism. Long standing apart in the Australian tradition, his work has been joined by other parodic historiographic fiction in recent decades. (Another stylistically exuberant work from the same period is Eve Langley's *The Pea Pickers* [1942], narrated by a cross-dressing *picara*. Unfortunately, apart from the sequel *White Topee* [1954], Langley published no further work.) Xavier Herbert's *magnum opus, Poor Fellow My Country* (1975), the longest Australian novel ever published, returns to *Capricornia*'s major settings and themes, particularly the destruction of traditional Aboriginal society, but it is marred by the author's too apparent identification with his didactic hero.

At the end of the 19th century, some critics observed that, on the evidence of its fiction, Australia had no cities. This remained true through World War II, although significant exceptions included Stead's two novels set in her native Sydney, Louis Stone's pioneering *Jonah* (1911), and Kylie Tennant's *Foveaux* (1939). The most common locales for exploring "distinctive" Australian life were country towns and settled districts, as in Norman Lindsay's *Redheap* (1928), Vance Palmer's *The Passage* (1930), Tennant's *Tiburon* (1935), and Leonard Mann's *Mountain Flat* (1939), which appeared the same year as Patrick White's first published novel, *Happy Valley,* itself a modernist version of life in a rural community. After the war, the contemporary city became a more familiar setting through Barnard Eldershaw's *Tomorrow and Tomorrow* (1947), Ruth Park's *The Harp in the South* (1948), and, most notoriously, Frank Hardy's *Power Without Glory* (1950), a muckraking exposé of a Melbourne criminal that provoked a much-publicized libel suit. Other novels of city life included Judah Waten's *The Unbending* (1954), David Martin's *The Young Wife* (1962), and George Johnston's nostalgic evocation of prewar Melbourne, *My Brother Jack* (1964).

Social realism remained the predominant mode, although it increasingly came to accommodate a wide variety of individual styles and experiments with narrative technique. The effects of Patrick White's attack on social realism as "the dreary, dun-colored off-spring of journalistic realism" in 1958 can only fully be appreciated in relation to the institutionalization of Australian literature within universities around the time that White was winning international recognition for *The Tree of Man* (1955) and *Voss* (1957). Ironically, these were high modernist retellings of some of the staples of earlier Australian fiction, pioneering, and exploration. Both novels are filled with realistic detail, but they are also highly self-conscious of their European literariness, which, during the heyday of the New Criticism, made them eminently teachable alongside English and American texts.

White's mid-20th-century version of Sinnett's charge that most Australian novels were "books of travels in disguise," combined with his examples showing that Australian novels could be both local and universal (or marketed nationally and internationally) and with the recently developed academic interest in Australian writing, created a receptive climate for a new kind of novel. Randolph Stow's *To the Islands* (1958) and *Tourmaline* (1963) invited comparison with the mythopoeic aspects of White's work. Thea Astley's *Girl with a Monkey* (1958), *A Descant for Gossips* (1960), and *The Slow Natives* (1965) approach White's satiric social comedy. Thomas Keneally, who had already published two autobiographical novels, temporarily became the "White hope" with his novel of the convict system *Bring Larks and Heroes* (1967), which implied a correspondence between the moral dilemmas posed for individuals in the original penal settlement and in the Australia of the present involved in the Vietnam War. Peter Mathers with his anarchic satires *Trap* (1966) and *The Wort Papers* (1972) and David Ireland with *The Unknown Industrial Prisoner* (1971), a blackly comic evocation of the alienating effects of multinational capitalism, pioneered what would later be recognized as postmodernist modes.

The country's divisive involvement in the Vietnam War, which coincided with the maturation of the unprecedentedly well-educated and affluent generation born after World War II, profoundly affected Australian culture. The younger generation of writers and readers were, like their contemporaries elsewhere, influenced more by the American counterculture than by the English, or even Australian, models that had prevailed previously. The now classic expression of this shift, and the uncertainties that accompanied it, was Frank Moorhouse's *The Americans, Baby* (1972), which rejected the "Sydney or the Bush" stereotypes of earlier fiction to engage simultaneously with the political activism and the personal, sexual politics of the time. Announcing itself to be "a discontinuous collection of stories and fragments," *The Americans, Baby* proved to be more cohesive than a collection of discrete stories, yet calculatedly less unified than a novel.

Although Moorhouse would not describe any of his fictional works as a novel until *Grand Days* in 1993, for most readers and reviewers by then the once-clear distinction between discontinuous narrative and novel had long broken down. Other experimenters with new short fictional forms who emerged in the early 1970s and explicitly rejected local social realism and responded to such contemporary international influences as Jorge Luis Borges, Italo Calvino, Gabriel García Márquez, and Thomas Pynchon soon turned to longer "fabulations" and "metafictions." Michael Wilding, closely associated with Moorhouse in the practice and promotion of new short fiction during the early 1970s, played with traditional generic distinctions as well as social conventions in his episodic comedies of countercultural life: *Living Together* (1974), *The Short Story Embassy* (1975), *Scenic Drive* (1976), and *Pacific Highway* (1982). Following his first novel, *The Pure Land* (1974), a relatively conventional variation on the family saga, David Foster published nine novels that are inventive comic pastiches of a formidable array of forms, styles, settings, and subjects. Whereas Foster continues to be prolific, Murray Bail's first novel, *Homesickness* (1980) has, to date, been followed only by *Holden's Performance* (1987); both are droll, episodic satires, the first of modern tourism, the second of "typical" Australian masculinity. Gerald Murnane's first novel, *Tamarisk Row* (1974), with its elaborately, even obsessively, patterned repetitions within a claustrophobic compass, established him as a most individual stylist, in the sense that influences on his work are not readily apparent.

Peter Carey was the most "magic" of the realists who emerged through short fiction in the early 1970s. His first published novel, *Bliss*, did not appear until 1981; since then he has won international recognition for *Illywhacker* (1985), *Oscar and Lucinda* (1988), *The Tax Inspector* (1991), *The Unusual Life of Tristan Smith* (1994), and *Jack Maggs* (1997), while continuing to engage, freshly and subversively, with Australian themes. Even more prominent internationally is David Malouf. His relatively conventional first novel, the semi-autobiographical *Johnno* (1974), was followed by a lyrical re-creation of Ovid's last days in exile, *An Imaginary Life* (1978). Continuing, like White before him, to display a mastery of various modes, Malouf came to seem his illustrious predecessor's long-awaited heir with *Harland's Half Acre* (1984), which invites comparison with White's *The Vivisector* (1970) and *The Great World* (1990), the title of which indicates its epic ambitions. For some other writers, however, success overseas does not necessarily lead to critical esteem at home. Morris West (*The Shoes of the Fisherman*, 1963), Colleen McCullough (*The Thorn Birds*, 1977), and Thomas Keneally (*Schindler's List*, 1982) are examples of internationally best-selling novelists who are considered more popular than literary within Australia.

Across the country, the counterculture of the 1970s spawned alternative small presses committed to new, experimental writing, among them McPhee Gribble, Wild and Woolley, Fremantle Arts Centre Press, Outback Press, and the University of Queensland Press with its Paperback Prose series. Early in the 1980s, Penguin Books Australia embarked on a program to attract the new writers, and their readers, to its imprint. Other mainstream publishers also realized that there was a new and diversified readership for postmodernist fiction. Unhelpful as this term might be in the abstract, it was employed to identify not only works that foregrounded their structures and styles but also those that directly engaged with (or at least impinged upon) the contemporary concerns of a now postcolonial society. New novels by long-established and new novelists continue to be received by critical commentators and educators in terms of their relationship to the (often overlapping) categories of women's writing, gay and lesbian writing, Aboriginal writing, migrant or ethnic writing, and postcolonial writing.

While initially the most prominent practitioners of new fiction were male, they were soon joined by women, most conspicuously Helen Garner and Elizabeth Jolley, whose first books were published by alternative presses. Garner's first book, *Monkey Grip* (1977), is a realistic, but also lyrical, account of life in inner-city alternative households and of a doomed love affair with a heroin addict. Garner continued to explore conflicts between the satisfactions of stable relationships and the excitement of sexual attractions in *The Children's Bach* (1984) and *Cosmo Cosmolino* (1992).

Elizabeth Jolley, considerably older than the new generation of women novelists that included Garner, began her prolific and immensely popular publishing career in the early 1980s after years of having her manuscripts rejected—indicating how far mainstream publishers lagged behind the tastes of their potential readerships. Jolley's *Miss Peabody's Inheritance* (1983) is a postmodern play on the theme of the death of the author that could equally be described as a parody of postmodernism, filled with quirky and sexually transgressive characters. It was quickly followed by *Mr. Scobie's Riddle* (1983), *Milk and Honey* (1984), *Foxybaby* (1985), *The Well* (1986), *The Sugar Mother* (1988), and the autobiographical Vera trilogy, *My Father's Moon* (1989), *Cabin Fever* (1990), and *The Georges' Wife* (1993).

Women's writing continues to constitute so large a part of the mainstream—in terms of the number of women novelists and the diversity of their subjects and styles—that attempts to separate it from the "malestream" seem artificial. Kate Grenville's novels—*Lilian's Story* (1985), a study of the effects of patriarchal repression, loosely based on the life of a famous Sydney eccentric; *Joan Makes History* (1988), a feminist revision of the mythic past to mark the country's bicentenary; and *Dark Places* (1994), a sequel to *Lilian's Story* but narrated from the patriarch's point of view—offer examples of women's writing overtly influenced by modern feminism. But works by long-established women writers such as Jessica Anderson's *Tirra Lirra by the River* (1978), which hauntingly records the outwardly unfulfilled life of a "typical" woman of an earlier generation, are also read as implicitly feminist. Neither Grenville nor Anderson is ostensibly experimental in terms of style and structure, in comparison, for example, with Janette Turner Hospital (*Borderline*, 1985) or, even more markedly, Marion Campbell (*Lines of Flight*, 1985).

Attempts to identify gay and lesbian traditions have brought the recognition that much previous writing has been "queer" and part of the mainstream. Patrick White's last major novel, *The Twyborn Affair* (1979), an exploration of the indeterminacy of gender, assisted this realization. Similarly, while multicultural, migrant, or ethnic novels may be isolated for separate consideration, interest in crosscultural interactions has been so pervasive, especially in recent fiction, that once again the category seems artificial.

This would not seem to be the case with Aboriginal or "black" writing. As distinct from the numerous representations of Aborigines by white novelists since colonial days, novels attributed to Aborigines are relatively recent and few. The first is commonly held to be *Wild Cat Falling* (1965) by Colin Johnson, who subsequently published *Long Live Sandawara* (1979), *Doctor Wooreddy's Prescription for Enduring the End of the World* (1983), and *Master of the Ghost Dreaming* (1991) under his tribal name Mudrooroo (also Mudrooroo Nyoongah, or Narogin). The first "Aboriginal" novelist to become well known internationally is B. (sometimes Banubir, or Birimbir) Wongar, whose *The Trackers* (1975) was followed by his "nuclear" trilogy, *Walg* (1983), *Karan* (1985), and *Gabo Djara* (1987). Wongar, however, was found to be the pseudonym of Serbian immigrant Streten Bozic, who claimed to have been initiated into a native tribe in the Northern Territory. In 1996 it was disclosed that the rest of Mudrooroo's family claimed descent not from Aborigines but from an American black who had come to Australia after the Civil War. Archie Weller (*The Day of the Dog*, 1981) then announced that he could not prove his claimed Aboriginality. These revelations suggest that commentators who categorize novels according to their authors' perceived subcultural affiliations still want "books of travels in disguise," with the travels now being multicultural tourism.

Over the past two decades, which have seen an expansion of publishing opportunities for Australian novelists at home and abroad, there has been a general break from social realism, with respect to both technique and assumptions of distinctive national norms. Numerous novels have employed historiographic pastiche (the term implying structural and stylistic self-consciousness) to reexamine aspects of the past in the light of contemporary, and postcolonial, concerns. Robert Drewe's *The Savage Crows* (1976) juxtaposes the present with the past through the figure of G. A. Robinson, Protector of the Tasmanian Aboriginals (a figure who appears also in Mudrooroo's *Doctor Wooreddy's Prescription for Enduring the End of the World* and *Master of the Ghost Dreaming*). Drewe's *Our Sunshine* (1991) reworks a recurrent subject in Australian writing generally, that of the outlaw Ned Kelly's defiance of British colonial authority. Jean Bedford explores the same subject from a feminist perspective in *Sister Kate* (1982). Hong Kong-born Brian Castro's first novel *Birds of Passage* (1983) juxtaposes a Chinese immigrant's experiences on the mid-19th-century goldfields with those of his descendent in the present, an anticipation of Castro's even more unmistakably postmodern experiments with narrative technique in his subsequent novels. Alex Miller's *The Ancestor Game* (1992) also engages with Chinese experience—on the goldfields, in China itself, and in present-day Australia—but employs more traditional narrative techniques. David Foster's farcically comic satire of historical novels, *Moonlite* (1981), shows his picaro's "progress" from the Outer Hebrides to colonial Australia. Michael Wilding's *The Paraguayan Experiment* (1984) draws on unpublished documents to tell, playfully, the "inside" story of one of the most fabled incidents in Australian political history—the late-19th-century attempt to found a socialist utopia in South America. More conventionally narrated, but concerned with the European colonizers' construction of Australia as a signifier, Rodney Hall's widely translated trilogy spans the first century of settlement in New South Wales: *Captivity Captive* (1988), *The Second Bridegroom* (1991), and *The Grisly Wife* (1993). Among novels defamiliarizing the stereotypes of Australian history and exploring cultural exchanges are David Malouf's *Remembering Babylon* (1993) and *Conversations at Curlow Creek* (1996), and Frank Moorhouse's *Grand Days,* which takes its heroine to Geneva and the League of Nations between the world wars. Also historiographic, but looking back from the future, Peter Carey's *The Unusual Life of Tristan Smith* (1995) is a speculative fantasy that satirizes Australia's subservience to American cultural imperialism.

Another tendency—and a further manifestation of postcolonial consciousness—is the widening of settings to include the entire region in which Australia is situated. An early example is Christopher Koch's *The Year of Living Dangerously* (1978), in which the protagonist is an Australian journalist in Sukarno's Indonesia. Koch later followed this with *Highways to a War* (1995), set against the background of American and Australian incursions into Indochina in the 1960s. Blanche d'Alpuget's *Monkeys in the Dark* (1980), also set in Indonesia during the same period, has a journalist as its heroine, as has her *Turtle Beach* (1981), set in Malaysia. Robert Drewe's *A Cry in the Jun-*

gle Bar (1979) is set in Manila and elsewhere in Southeast Asia and shows a "typical" Australian, an agricultural expert, fumblingly attempting to understand an alien culture. Cultural understanding and misunderstanding are very much at the center of Nicholas Jose's two novels with Asian settings: the realist *Avenue of Eternal Peace* (1989) takes an Australian to present-day China, and the action of the fabulistic *The Rose Crossing* (1994) takes place well before the settlement of Australia. Other novelists have imagined settings or disguised actual ones for their fables of colonialization: Randolph Stow in *Visitants* (1979), Thea Astley in *Beachmasters* (1985), and Matthew Condon in *The Ancient Guild of Tycoons* (1994).

To identify these broad tendencies, to deconstruct the stereotypes of the past and extend the range of cultural reference beyond Australia itself, is not to claim that all the works by the novelists mentioned above exhibit them, nor that only novelists who do are of interest today. Tim Winton's critical and popular success parallels, almost exactly over the same period, that of Elizabeth Jolley. Since the manuscript of *An Open Swimmer* (1982) won a young writer's award, Winton has published prolifically, setting his novels most often within family life on his native West coast—a latterday, individual return to regional realism and traditional concerns. Emerging reputations include (among many others) those of Peter Goldsworthy and Sue Woolfe. Goldsworthy's *Maestro* (1989), about the influence of a refugee from postwar Europe and the Holocaust on a youth growing up in Darwin, and *Honk If You Are Jesus* (1992), a playful satire of genetic engineering, have been followed by the much more impressive *Wish* (1995), "a biologically engineered love story" that crosses the presumed borderline between humans and other higher primates. Sue Woolfe's second novel, *Leaning Towards Infinity* (1996), wittily combines the seemingly incongruous themes of motherhood and mathematics.

The range of subjects, structures, and styles of Australian novelists today is much wider than at any previous time. Rather than seeming too Australian, as they did to Sinnett nearly a century and a half ago, Australian novelists have long confirmed Sinnett's observation that the country "offers fresh scenery, fresh costumes, and fresh machinery . . . and, for the rest, presents a field neither better nor worse than most others, in which people love, and hate, and hope, and fear . . . and obey the good and evil impulses of their infinitely various natures."

BRIAN KIERNAN

See also Peter Carey; Fortunes of Richard Mahoney; His Natural Life; Thomas Keneally; David Malouf; Postcolonial Narrative and Criticism of the Novel; Christina Stead; Such Is Life; Patrick White

Further Reading

Argyle, Barry, *An Introduction to the Australian Novel, 1830–1930,* Oxford: Clarendon Press, 1972

Burns, David Robert, *The Directions of Australian Fiction, 1920–1974,* Melbourne: Cassell Australia, 1975

Clancy, Laurie, *A Reader's Guide to Australian Fiction,* New York and Melbourne: Oxford University Press, 1992

Daniel, Helen, *Liars: Australian New Novelists,* Ringwood, Victoria, and New York: Penguin, 1988

Gelder, Ken, and Paul Salzman, editors, *The New Diversity:*

Australian Fiction, 1970–88, Melbourne: McPhee Gribble, 1989

Goodwin, Ken, *A History of Australian Literature,* London: Macmillan, and New York: St. Martin's Press, 1986

Green, H.M., *A History of Australian Literature: Pure and Applied,* Sydney: Angus and Robertson, 1961; revised edition, Sydney and London: Angus and Robertson, 1984

Healy, J.J., *Literature and the Aborigine in Australia, 1770–1975,* St. Lucia: University of Queensland Press, 1978; 2nd edition, St. Lucia and London: University of Queensland Press, 1988

Hergenhan, Laurie, *Unnatural Lives: Studies in Australian Fiction about the Convicts, from James Tucker to Patrick White,* St. Lucia and London: University of Queensland Press, 1983; New York: University of Queensland Press, 1984

Hergenhan, Laurie, editor, *The Penguin New Literary History of Australia,* Ringwood, Victoria, and New York: Penguin, 1988

Huggan, Graham, *Territorial Disputes: Maps and Mapping Strategies in Contemporary Canadian and Australian Fiction,* Toronto and Buffalo, New York: University of Toronto Press, 1994

Keesing, Nancy, editor, *Australian Postwar Novelists: Selected Critical Essays,* Milton, Queensland: Jacaranda Press, 1975

Kiernan, Brian, *Images of Society and Nature: Seven Essays on Australian Novels,* Melbourne and New York: Oxford University Press, 1971

Kramer, Leonie, editor, *The Oxford History of Australian Literature,* Melbourne and New York: Oxford University Press, 1981

Wilding, Michael, *Studies in Classic Australian Fiction,* Sydney: Sydney Studies in Society and Culture, and Nottingham: Shoestring Press, 1997

Wilkes, G.A., *Australian Literature: A Conspectus,* Sydney: Angus and Robertson, 1969

Austrian Novel

The definition of a national canon of literature, as recent criticism has shown, is, if not entirely questionable, subject to various doubts concerning the imputed characteristics of a nation, the typification of its representative voices, and the often arbitrary delimitation of cultural geographies. Austrian literature offers a perfect example of the ambivalence that surrounds the definition of national literatures. As a multilingual and supranational monarchy, the Austro-Hungarian empire could not secure a single national identity except through elevating the language of its privileged Austro-German ethnic population to the status of the official and print language of the empire. Not surprisingly, Austria's first prominent German prose writers (Franz Grillparzer, Adalbert Stifter) rose from the ranks of the empire's administrative and clerical professions. Ever since the break-up of the empire, Austrian literature has been defined in terms of its Austro-German tradition, thereby obscuring both the cross-cultural sources in the former empire and the cross-cultural definition of the Austro-German tradition, which had come into being in an exchange with its acculturated minorities, particularly its diverse Jewish communities.

Austrian literature, evolving from medieval poetry and a long-standing tradition of court and religious drama, came to prose only in the middle of the 19th century, reflecting the ascent of a liberal bourgeois culture. The consolidation of this culture is amply illustrated in the works of Austria's first prominent novelist, Adalbert Stifter. Unlike earlier writings rooted in religious dogma or court decorum, Stifter's prose foregrounds the self-legitimating male bourgeois subject taking charge of his profession and accounting for himself (to himself) in writing and narration. In *Die Mappe meines Urgrossvaters* (1842, 1847, 1870; The Journal of My Great-Grandfather), a work that Stifter continually revised in order to soften its initial romantic elements, the protagonist, a young medical doctor, learns to detach himself from his emotional shocks by keeping a journal. His initial rejection by his beloved inspires suicidal thoughts, which the protagonist all but cures through writing. The journal instills productive contemplative habits that lead to careful attention to his daily work and a consideration of the demands of his community over his own needs. Stifter's ethical idealization of bourgeois virtues contrasts with the more pessimistic vision of Franz Grillparzer. Grillparzer's prose narration *Der arme Spielmann* (1848; *The Poor Musician*), published in the aftermath of Austria's failed revolution, is a tale of bourgeois decline and self-withdrawal. The son of a high administrative official, Grillparzer's hero cannot cope with the demands of social reality and adopts instead an amateurish artistic lifestyle as a second-rate violin player, ruining his career, his marriage prospects, and ultimately his life. As a pathetic and tragically altruistic hero, he reflects the shattering of bourgeois hopes for self-realization in the post-1848 empire and the desire for an aesthetic retreat from political reality.

While Stifter's characters are similarly removed from political reality, they have significantly more agency, albeit in the confined realm of reflection and in response to the unremarkable events of everyday rural life. Stifter's *Der Nachsommer* (1857; *Indian Summer*) depicts Heinrich Drendorf, son of a wealthy Viennese merchant, who is educating himself as a geologist during his travels through the Alps. His ensuing encounter with von Risach and his visit to the latter's meticulously maintained estate introduces Heinrich not only to efficient and careful conservation of nature's resources but also to art, patience, and moderation—Stifter's ideal "gentle law" of humanity. With regard to his *Biedermeier* (restoration) vision, Stifter has been rightfully criticized for his political conservatism. Aesthetically, however, Stifter's in-

tensified concentration on the mundane thoughts of his protagonists provides an early model for modern narrative techniques
evolving entirely from within the consciousness of a character.
More recently, Stifter's ecological, regionalized, and nationally
decentered perspective has been acknowledged as an unsuspected progressive element in his otherwise conservative political
ideology.

Marie von Ebner-Eschenbach, the first prominent Austrian female novelist, shows the influence of the European tradition of
realism, focusing on the social conditions of impoverished rural
workers. However, her novel *Das Gemeindekind* (1887; *Their
Pavel*), while shedding light on social inequality, still upholds the
bourgeois values of individual self-determination and moral responsibility as sufficient means to overcome social disadvantages. Indebted to the Bildungsroman, the novel challenges the
determinism of character by social milieu as given in the naturalist novels of Émile Zola and holds forth an ideal vision of morality and education. Pavel, the son of parents sentenced for murder, becomes a welfare child and initially answers the criminal
stereotypes that are projected onto him. Under the influence of
his sister and his local schoolteacher, however, he undergoes a
radical social reeducation, freeing himself from his background.
In her socially critical perspective, von Ebner-Eschenbach anticipates the modern *kritische Heimatsroman* (critical regional novel), which shatters the romantic idyll of rural life and reveals its
modern conditions of alienation and poverty.

Bourgeois liberal culture and its various public spheres (salons, literary circles, newspapers, and theaters) constituted the
main reading audience during the late imperial era of the Habsburg monarchy. At the turn of the century, this public sphere
flourished especially in the modern urban environment of Vienna, where an assimilated and largely secular Jewish population
had become the most ardent producers and consumers of art.
Between 1860 and 1910, Vienna's Jewish population had
grown, primarily through migration from Bohemia, Moravia,
and Galicia, from 1 percent (6,000) to almost 10 percent
(175,000) of the city's population. Drawing on the experience of
cultural diaspora and a critical double perspective as formerly
excluded members of society, Viennese Jewish writers shaped a
transnational and cosmopolitan culture that had heretofore remained within the narrow confines of a supranational nobility.
Formal usage, social status symbols, and so-called Austrian cultural sensibilities, such as a critical irony toward nationalism,
were substantially shaped by the multicultural Jewish influence.
Prominent Jewish writers and thinkers such as Hugo von Hofmannsthal, Arthur Schnitzler, Sigmund Freud, Ludwig Wittgenstein, Otto Bauer, Alfred Adler, Rudolf Hilferding, Karl Kraus,
Stefan Zweig, Joseph Roth, and Hermann Broch also helped
spread the significance of Austrian intellectual culture beyond its
immediate geographic boundaries.

Hugo von Hofmannsthal, although known primarily as a
poet, dramatist, and librettist for Richard Strauss' operas, inaugurated the new sceptical century with his seminal prose text
"Ein Brief" (1905; The Chandos Letter). In a fictive letter to
Lord Francis Bacon, Lord Chandos confesses a major crisis of
language, in which subsequently all social and cultural constructs are called into doubt. The letter is purposely dated before
the publication of Bacon's scientific and rational philosophy in
The Advancement of Learning (1605), thereby questioning the
project of the Enlightenment at its very inception. The letter's in-

tent—to raise the crisis suffered by Lord Chandos to a reflective
level "of proper awareness of my inner condition"—sets the
tone for much that is to follow in modern Austrian writing. For
example, a novel like *Die Aufzeichnungen des Malte Laurids
Brigge* (1910; *The Notebooks of Malte Laurids Brigge*) by Rainer Maria Rilke, one of the great modernist European poets, similarly relies on this crisis format. In a journal depicting the corro-
sive impact of Paris metropolitan life and its modern anonymous
mass culture upon its protagonist-narrator, the once securely
held conceptions of self, family, and tradition are suspended and
challenged by a new mass experience.

Arthur Schnitzler, recognized by Sigmund Freud as his literary
double, is often said to point to the inherent contradictions between society's public codes of respectability and honor and its
repressed desires. However, Schnitzler links a phenomenon like
the imputed hysterical nature of women much more critically to
the stringent patriarchal codes than Freud ever did. The novella
Fräulein Else (1924), for instance, depicts the desperate attempt
of its heroine to save her father from recurrent financial ruin by
accepting the dubious proposal to bare herself to her father's
friend von Dorsday, in exchange for the much needed money.
After prolonged consideration and critique of the tiresome expectations placed upon women, she eventually does so in a hotel
lobby and provokes a public scandal. What is interpreted by by-
standers as a hysteric fit is in fact an assertive act that cannot be
comprehended by society and must end in suicide. Schnitzler
was highly sensitive to the plight of the oppressed, including
women, as is evident in *Therese: Chronik eines Frauenlebens*
(1928; *Theresa: The Chronicle of a Woman's Life*), and Jews,
apparent in *Der Weg ins Freie* (1908; *The Road to the Open*), as
well as the play *Professor Bernhardi* (1912).

Schnitzler was also an acute social analyst of privileged groups.
Leutnant Gustl (1901; *None But the Brave*), an early novella, depicts its hero in a moment of crisis that is partially real and partially promoted by a socially paranoid imagination. Airing his
narrow-minded anti-Semitic and anti-socialist views during a
concert performance, a lieutenant, already lined up for a duel the
next day, manages to draw yet another insult after the concert.
Unable to defend his honor owing to the lower social rank of the
man who insulted him, he contemplates suicide while remembering his uneventful life of military routine and meaningless love affairs. In the end, he is miraculously spared from having to go
through with the duel because of the challenger's accidental
death. Regaining his arrogant composure, he brags that he will
prevail in the upcoming fencing duel against a weaker opponent.
In its satirical insight into the lieutenant's mind, the novella characterizes the military code of honor not so much as an ethical
mode of conduct but as a social grammar allowing for a pretense
of respectability. Written entirely as an interior monologue (introduced here for the first time into the German language), the narration exposes a sociopathological obsession with power and social rank, as well as the exclusionary political unconscious of the
emerging petty bourgeois. The story anticipates what Hannah
Arendt was to call the banality of bureaucratic evil in Nazi Germany, with its institutionalized prejudice and resentment. This
administered racism already had begun to install itself in turn-of-
the-century Vienna led by its anti-Semitic mayor Karl Lueger.

Schnitzler's later work, particularly *The Road to the Open*,
heightens the impression of a Vienna plagued by prejudice, imperial decline, and the disintegration of liberal society. The

younger generation of its Jewish characters have little choice but to abandon traditional bourgeois expectations and pursue the new unstable paths of art, socialism, and Zionism. The novel's main character, Georg von Wergenthin, artist and aristocrat, likewise can no longer sustain the aesthetic pretense of his existence and succumbs to indecision and paralysis. His life endlessly drifts between his private and public affairs. As a frequent guest at the Ehrenberg salon, he gains a special insight into Viennese Jewish culture, which is disintegrating into political factionalism, generational divides, and immobility. With its multiple plots and its conversational style, the novel suggests unsuspected overlappings and interrelations of contradictory ideologies, thus evoking a shared cross-cultural space before the oncoming collapse and fragmentation.

The demise of bourgeois culture and the emergence of the intolerant petty bourgeois mass subject is a theme that also preoccupied Schnitzler's contemporaries Karl Kraus and Joseph Roth. Kraus, known for his satirical magazine *Die Fackel* (The Torch), almost single-handedly took it upon himself to document the Viennese cultural decline by means of an acute analysis of clichés, slips, and euphemisms that exposed Viennese society's prejudices and lack of integrity. Kraus' momentous play *Die letzten Tage der Menschheit* (1923; *The Last Days of Mankind*) reflects the influence of the novel in Mikhail Bakhtin's definition of it, as a heteroglot construct of competing social discourses. The play, episodically structured and plurivocal in style, begins at the dawn of World War I and parodies the blind fervor, misguided patriotism, and pervasive opportunism of its major participants and professional orientations such as the military, the clergy, the industrialists, the press, and the nobility. One of Kraus' last critical pieces includes a haunting textual montage entitled "Protective Custody" (1933), describing the political atrocities directed against Jews and communists and their euphemistic distortion in the media (which was controlled by the new Nazi regime in Germany).

Joseph Roth, along with Franz Kafka and Robert Musil, offers a postimperial perspective on Austrian culture, dissecting the internal malaise that had led to its logical collapse. Roth's novel *Radetzkymarsch* (1932; *The Radetzky March*) retells the historical transformation of the Habsburg empire from the perspective of a single family history. The story begins with the Battle of Solferino, when lieutenant Trotta accidentally saves the young emperor from a flying bullet. He is awarded the title of nobility, allowing him to leave behind his Slovenian rural origins and become a legitimate member of the privileged Austro-German society. The novel analyzes the complex relationship of domestic and national myth, which sustain the empire and the prosperity of its subjects. Trotta's grandson, Carl Joseph, standing at the end of this family genealogy, however, proves incapable of preserving this heroic legacy and succumbs to gambling and alcoholism on the Russian border. He dies in World War I and is survived by his father, the district captain and Austrian bureaucrat who dies on the day of the emperor's funeral, thus bringing full circle a genealogy that built its meaning around a sentimental feudal patriotism embodied by the emperor. Roth's novel, which empathizes with its weak hero, also shifts the focus from a more colorful bourgeoisie to the petty and pathetically powerless clerk as the expression of a new mass subject. Hermann Broch similarly captures, although less nostalgically than Roth, the decline of Wilhelminian Germany, particularly the re-

placement of its feudal order by the institutions and values of a modern capitalist economy in his novel *Die Schlafwandler* (1932; *The Sleepwalkers*).

Unlike its German counterpart, the postimperial and interwar Austrian novel does not develop the extensive insight into mass and proletarian culture as given, for example, in Alfred Döblin's *Berlin Alexanderplatz* (1929), the dramas of Bertolt Brecht, or the sociological analyses of Georg Simmel, Walter Benjamin, and Siegfried Kracauer. This absence of social realism has given Austrian literature a conservative bourgeois appearance that contrasts with the avant-garde advances of the Weimar Republic. Recently, however, the more open ideological perspective adopted by many German writers itself has been found too conventional, and renewed interest has been paid to the intricate evasions of meaning in the literary heritage of fin-de-siècle Vienna. According to Jacques Le Rider, turn-of-the-century Vienna already reflects the absence and loss of credibility of "grand narratives" that Jean-François Lyotard views as one of the defining characteristics of postmodernism. Thus Austrian literature from the first half of the 20th century is, at the very end of that century, experiencing a revival and a revaluation as an anticipation of the postmodern epistemic crisis and the radical decontextualization of Western culture. The Habsburg decline is no longer seen solely in terms of a bourgeois nostalgia for a fading imperial order but as a deeper crisis in which the entirety of Enlightenment culture is called into doubt.

This postmodern aspect of Austria's post-Habsburg legacy is best reflected in the writings of Franz Kafka and Robert Musil. In their influential work *Kafka: Toward a Minor Literature* (1986), Gilles Deleuze and Felix Guattari have shown how a literature such as Kafka's undermines and subverts the grand narratives of family, economy, race, and nation that define Western culture. As a Czechoslovakian Jew living in the outer domain of the Habsburg empire, Kafka, they claim, is the paradigmatic "minor" writer unable to feel at home in any of Prague's languages—Yiddish, Czech, and the dominant language of German. Kafka responds to this condition of cultural and linguistic displacement strategically with what he calls a "gypsy literature that has stolen the German child out of its cradle." This literature consciously employs a deformed and twisted "Prague German" in order to challenge the standardized officialese of the empire and its myths of enlightenment. According to Deleuze and Guattari, Kafka's writings inaugurate a wholesale "deterritorialization" or decolonization of cultural geographies and their concomitant master narratives.

The stylistic strategies of Kafka's work would seem to substantiate the deflationary style of writing attributed to Kafka by Deleuze and Guattari. Depersonalization (the anonymous K.), atavistic regression to the animal level (*Die Verwandlung* [1915; *The Metamorphosis*]), labyrinthine settings of an endless bureaucratic machinery, and a tragicomic sense of human banality have become stereotypical Kafkaesque effects that convey the seemingly absolute impasse of modern culture. However, Kafka's literary style must also be understood historically as a complex evasion of monolithic identities that had shaped the diasporic, multicultural, and cosmopolitan tradition of Austrian literature. Kafka's writings, then, reflect not solely the overdetermination of a cultural landscape by means of reductive language policies and growing standardization. Rather, in their strangely affirmative sense, they also reveal the tensions of multiple and contradictory definitions that lay claim upon the identity of individuals and society.

In his novel *Das Schloss* (1926; *The Castle*), for example, the protagonist K. is not merely at the mercy of an endlessly receding bureaucracy but enters his futile quest for a work permit as part of his imagined or real work assignment. As a limited and forever truncated project of meaning, his quest nevertheless guarantees a sense of autonomy no matter how absurd. This remaining sense of volition in a world of eroding certainties has left a deep impact upon existential novelists such as Albert Camus and Jean-Paul Sartre, who view existence as an act of self-projected meaning. This hallucinatory sense of reality is also evident in Kafka's novel *Der Prozess* (1925; *The Trial*), in which the relationship between the law and the individual is reduced to a masochistic sense of guilt. The protagonist Joseph K., in his constant need for self-legitimation, paradoxically projects the institutional order to which he eventually succumbs, reflecting the intertwined construction and internalization of an oppressive state apparatus. Kafka's work has thus also been read as a critique of institutional power and administrative coercion in an anonymous modern mass culture that goes far beyond his more immediate context of a literature critical of patriarchal and imperial traditions.

In opposition to Kafka's method of deflation, Robert Musil's *Der Mann ohne Eigenschaften* (3 vols., 1930–43; *The Man Without Qualities*) carries the pretension of Habsburg power and culture to its inherent absurdity by means of comical and baroque stylistic inflation. In Musil's parodistic assessment, Austrian power and sovereignty become a contradiction in terms:

> One spent tremendous sums on the army; but only just enough to assure one of remaining the second weakest among the great powers. . . . There was a parliament which made such vigorous use of its liberty that it was usually kept shut . . . when everyone was just beginning to rejoice in absolutism, the Crown decreed that there must now again be a return to parliamentary government.

The inherent absence of clearly defined national interests is mirrored in the novel's major protagonist Ulrich, a modern-day aristocratic "dropout." While Ulrich's critical self-consciousness reduces him to the role of spectator in Viennese society, he also becomes the hidden reflective center of the many ironies that escape the all-too-eager participants in Vienna's public and social life. The farcical pretense for the novel's action with its many social gatherings is a secretly planned parallel event (*Parallelaktion*) honoring the 70th year of reign by the Austrian emperor competing with a similar event honoring the 30th year by the German emperor. This parallel event comically foregrounds an inherent lack of originality in Austrian society, where imitation and tiresome repetition prevail. It also defines a cultural space not yet totally overcome by the rising pan-Germanic tendencies of the declining Habsburg era. Musil, whose views eventually forced him into exile, is clearly attempting to depict—in the face of emerging militant nationalisms—a defunct but ultimately more benign and openly defined empire. Offering a critique of essentialisms that defines social and cultural identity in a supranational setting, Musil's *The Man Without Qualities* constitutes in this sense an early work of resistance to rising fascist ideologies.

Ödön von Horváth gives an even more powerful illustration of the growing annihilation of values in his *Jugend ohne Gott* (1938). The novel consists of the journal entries of a high school teacher, which portray a disturbing younger generation of school children growing up devoid of morality and tolerance in their cynical fascination with violence and power. Horváth's novel was published as part of an Austrian exile literature also including Joseph Roth's work and Hermann Broch's that unfortunately found its audience mostly in the postwar era. Thus, Horváth's ominous premonition of fascist terror could only be appreciated retrospectively. However, exile writers like Jean Améry, Elias Canetti, and the poet Paul Celan, who confront the traumas of violence, language, and memory that have affected their exposed and threatened existence as Jews in the Nazi era, have had a more direct impact in postwar Europe. Their diasporic work further complicates the definition of Austrian literature in that it is situated multinationally and therefore cannot be reduced to one cultural and geographic setting.

The reconstruction of a separate national and cultural identity after Austria's era of German nationalism appears as both a necessary and contradictory enterprise. With regard to the supranational heritage of the empire, the peaceful coexistence of diverse cultures had become a matter of nostalgia since those cultures were no longer co-present to any significant degree. The attempt to revive Austria's national identity in the postwar era was a revival ex nihilo based on no applicable prior model in Austrian history. And as critics have pointed out, the revival of a national identity was inspired not so much by a critique of fascism as by the desire to emphasize Austria's difference from and noncomplicity with Nazi Germany. Austria could thereby regain its sovereignty as a state without having to account fully for its role in the Jewish genocide. Particularly, the benign Habsburg world as revived in the novels of Heimito von Doderer, particularly *Die Strudlhofstiege* (1951), initially provided a welcome distraction from embarrassing truths that were already being voiced in the works of survivors, such as Ilse Aichinger's *Die grössere Hoffnung* (1948; The Greater Hope).

To a generation of younger writers and thinkers, Austria's regained national identity and its accompanying economic reconstruction appeared as an insidious ideological device covering up its problematic past rather than projecting a positive set of national and constitutional tenets shared by its citizens. This critique begins in the early 1950s with the Wiener Gruppe (Vienna Group), which consisted of H.C. Artmann, Konrad Bayer, Gerhard Rühm, Oswald Wiener, and others. This group of young artists and poets scorned Austria's restorative cultural ideology in their avant-garde and neo-Dadaist works. Influenced by Wittgenstein's critique of language and Gertrude Stein's experimental prose, they challenged in particular the literary mystifications that shaped the propaganda narratives of fascism and nationalist discourse in general. While they left no memorable works as such—with the exception of Oswald Wiener's experimental novel *Die Verbesserung von Mitteleuropas* (1969; *The Correction of Central Europe*)—neo-avant-garde movements like the Wiener Gruppe and the Grazer Literaturforum nevertheless had a profound impact on postwar Austrian novelists. They encouraged a strong iconoclastic stance and drew renewed attention to experimentation and the medium of literary language itself. In this respect, the Austrian postwar novel differs strongly from its German counterpart, which remained rooted in traditional realist form.

The attention given to language in much Austrian postwar writing is not, however, purely poetic and formal in nature. Rather, language is understood in the Wittgensteinian sense of a structural paradigm shaping cultural perspective and experience. In its critical examination of authoritarian discourse, Austrian prose turns in particular to subjective styles of narration in which a single subject is situated within coercive institutional and linguistic structures. Peter Handke's early play *Kaspar* (1967) exposed the mechanism of linguistic and social indoctrination, the oppressive regime of meaning (*Sprachfolter*), and has been emulated by many prose attempts that seek to capture the structural confinement of individuals in social, cultural, and political paradigms. Critical regional novelists such as Franz Innerhofer, or more recently Josef Winkler, have focused strongly on the authoritarian structures of feudalism that survive virtually unchallenged in Austria's rural communities. Emancipation from authoritarian structures also figures as a major theme in Austria's emerging women's literature. Barbara Frischmuth's *Die Klosterschule* (1968; *The Convent School*), for example, examines the subjective voice of its protagonist-narrator under the influence of a patriarchal Catholic religion, reflecting critically the internalization of authoritarian discourse.

Standing apart from the highly diversified and regional Austrian literatures, Ingeborg Bachmann, Thomas Bernhard, Peter Handke, and Elfriede Jelinek have taken not only the German literary market by storm but have gained international recognition. Bachmann, who first achieved recognition as a poet, eventually shifted toward prose and became one of the foremost German writers. Her story collection *Simultan* (1972; *Three Paths to the Lake*) shows her female characters unconsciously caught in and perpetuating patriarchal paradigms in banal everyday preoccupations. Women's marginalization becomes a struggle with language and with an overpowering and inflated male discourse that silences the female characters' attempts at self-comprehension. Bachmann's novel *Malina* (1971) similarly evokes a crisis of self-definition on the part of its female protagonist whose identity is erased by her two lovers Malina and Ivan as well as by an imagined "third man" who mirrors the protagonist's own torment and anxieties. The novel's intense subjective focus contributed largely to the literary trend of the new subjectivity that influenced major East and West German and Austrian writers, including Christa Wolf, Nicholas Born, Botho Strauss, and Peter Handke.

With Bachmann's premature death in 1973, Peter Handke became the heir to her subjective lyrical approach to the novel. Formerly known for his experimental approach, Handke's style radically changed with his novel *Wunschloses Unglück* (1972; *A Sorrow Beyond Dreams*) documenting the life and eventual suicide of his mother. As with Bachmann, the novel portrays Handke's mother unsuccessfully struggling with her tenuous identity in an ideological climate coded socially and culturally to suppress female individuality. The search for an "unoccupied" language has since become the defining goal in Handke's own narrative quest for identity. Handke's prose texts are mostly devoid of any concrete actions but reflect, in the manner of Adalbert Stifter, a conscientious meditative attention to the unremarkable details of the everyday and to the task of writing, as in *Nachmittag eines Schriftstellers* (1987; *The Afternoon of a Writer*). Apart from this contemplative emphasis, Handke's novels are rich travelogues that take in such various settings as Alaska, Slovenia, Andalusia, and the remote suburbs of Paris in a conscious peripheral shift away from cultural centers into "nowhere" lands. Prominent examples are *Langsame Heimkehr* (1979; *Slow Homecoming*), *Versuch über die Jukebox* (1990; *The Jukebox and Other Essays on Storytelling*), and *Mein Jahr in der Niemandsbucht* (1994; *In the Bay of Nowhere*). Examining the ethnic cleansing in the former Yugoslavia as an issue of media distortion in his recent *Gerechtigkeit für Serbien* (1996; Justice for Serbia), Handke has rightly drawn criticism for turning violence into a literary rather than a political occasion. This absence of a self-critical perspective toward the limits of literature has helped to bring about a recent critical shift away from Handke toward the more iconoclastic work of Thomas Bernhard and Elfriede Jelinek.

Thomas Bernhard, who had been temporarily in the shadow of the impressively prolific and innovative Handke, now figures as the towering writer in German and Austrian postwar literature. Not only does Bernhard's relentlessly critical prose (a mixture of Nietzsche and Samuel Beckett) challenge the ideological complacencies of Heinrich Böll and Günter Grass, but it also maintains a critical scrutiny against becoming its own mystification. Following in the self-critical spirit of Karl Kraus and Theodor Adorno, Bernhard distrusts any pose, including that of the writer. His provocative style has reached beyond the immediate sphere of literature into the cultural public sphere at large, where his works have triggered a wholesale critique of Austria's narcissistic self-infatuation with its cultural status. This critical demolition of Austria's endemic Eurocentric conception of culture is expressed, for example, in Bernhard's *Alte Meister* (1985; *Old Masters*), with its scathing criticism of Western cultural accomplishment. The influence of Bernhard's cultural satire upon the subsequent generation of writers has been profound in not only encouraging a persistent iconoclasm but also in creating a space for Austria's cultural minorities whose viewpoints have been silenced by the postwar myth of a homogeneously styled Austrian nationality. Bernhard's thematic recoveries of forgotten Austrian Jewish and Jewish exile legacies have helped to bring into focus a younger generation of Jewish writers such as Elfriede Jelinek, Robert Schindel, Robert Menasse, and Doron Rabinovici.

Elfriede Jelinek has rightfully been considered Bernhard's heir in her own unsparing criticism of Austrian culture, its historical amnesia, its recent neofascist specters, and its enduring climate of bureaucratic mediocrity and enforced social consensus. Jelinek's early works such as *Die Liebhaberinnen* (1975; *Women as Lovers*) and *Die Klavierspielerin* (1983; *The Piano Teacher*) focus on the stereotypical roles that are not only imposed upon women but are actively adopted and perpetuated by them. Her work thus contributes to a type of feminism critical of its own presumptively innocent viewpoint and extends its critique to the thorough commodification of all social roles in a consumer society. A pathological voyeurism in *The Piano Teacher,* for example, reveals both the heroine's inability to achieve an identity and the desire to redirect the violence of the male/consumer gaze onto others. Jelinek, who also translates into German the work of American novelist Thomas Pynchon, has developed a thoroughly postmodern style in her many textual collages and genre parodies.

More recently, Jelinek's work, like that of her contemporaries Gerhard Roth and Robert Schindel, has turned to Austria's fascist legacy. All three writers pay particular attention to the continuities of fascism in the discourse of *Heimat* (fatherland) and nativism. Jelinek sees nativist discourses reemerging in the marketing of an indigenous Alpine tourist sanctuary, in the exclusionary politics toward immigrants, and in dubious cultural hygienics of ecological, health, and fitness concerns. Gerhard Roth's work offers an unusual documentary focus on forgotten legacies and crimes in Austria's seemingly normalized political climate. His prose cycle *Archive des Schweigens* (1991; Archives of Silence) constitutes a critical ethnography of a people capable of genocide and hiding behind codes of civic behavior allowing for institutionalized violence. Robert Schindel's bestselling novel *Gebürtig* (1992; *Born Where*) takes a more conciliatory approach, exploring the productive boundaries in the interaction between Jewish and non-Jewish characters trying to come to terms with their legacies. Schindel also revives the turn-of-the-century coffeehouse ambience as a reminder of a potential public sphere informed by cross-cultural encounters.

The recent Austrian novel continues to have a vital output and reception beyond its national boundaries, as is evident in Christoph Ransmayr's *Die letzte Welt* (1988; *The Last World*), Robert Menasse's *Selige Zeiten, brüchige Welt* (1991; Blessed Times, Broken World), and Marlene Streeruwitz's *Verführungen* (1996; Seductions). Ransmayr's surrealist work explores Ovid's exile in what is today Romania, moving between prehistoric and modern times. Menasse reconnects Austria with its Jewish exile community in Brazil, and Streeruwitz provides a feminist parody of a woman incapable of living up to the high standards of emancipation. While modern Austrian literature has enjoyed a long-standing popularity on the German and the European reading markets, its reception in the United States is often obscured by an excessive focus on turn-of-the-century Vienna and on Germany's realist tradition (as exemplified by Thomas Mann, Heinrich Böll, and Günter Grass). This tentative and often typified reception of Austrian literature is especially deplorable since it neglects a rich diasporic and continuing cross-cultural heritage. Austrian literature in large part defines itself outside and beyond its national boundaries in a productive blend of regionalism and cosmopolitanism.

MATTHIAS KONZETT

See also Ingeborg Bachmann; Thomas Bernhard; Hermann Broch; German Novel; Franz Kafka; Robert Musil; Joseph Roth; Adalbert Stifter

Further Reading

Bartsch, Kurt, Dietmar Goltschnigg, and Gerhard Melzer, editors, *Für und wider eine österreichische Literatur*, Königstein: Athenäum, 1982

Beller, Steven, *Vienna and the Jews 1867–1938: A Cultural History*, Cambridge and New York: Cambridge University Press, 1989

Broch, Hermann, *Hugo von Hofmannsthal and His Time: The European Imagination, 1860–1920*, Chicago: University of Chicago Press, 1984

Daviau, Donald G., editor, *Major Figures of Contemporary Austrian Literature*, New York: Peter Lang, 1987

Daviau, Donald G., editor, *Major Figures of Turn-of-the-Century Austrian Literature*, Riverside, California: Ariadne Press, 1991

Daviau, Donald G., editor, *Austrian Writers and the Anschluss: Understanding the Past—Overcoming the Past*, Riverside, California: Ariadne Press, 1991

Daviau, Donald G., editor, *Major Figures of Austrian Literature: The Interwar Years 1918–1938*, Riverside, California: Ariadne Press, 1995

Deleuze, Gilles, and Felix Guattari, *Kafka: Toward a Minor Literature*, Minneapolis: University of Minnesota Press, 1986

Demetz, Peter, *After the Fires: Recent Writings in the Germanies, Austria, and Switzerland*, San Diego, California: Harcourt Brace, 1986

Doppler, Alfred, *Wirklichkeit im Spiegel der Sprache: Aufsätze zur Literatur des 20 Jahrhunderts in Osterreich*, Vienna: Europa, 1975

Greiner, Ulrich, *Der Tod des Nachsommers: Aufsätze, Porträts, Kritiken zur österreichischen Gegenwartsliteratur*, Munich and Vienna: Hanser, 1979

Janik, Allan, and Stephen Edelston Toulmin, *Wittgenstein's Vienna*, New York: Simon and Schuster, and London: Weidenfeld and Nicolson, 1973

Johnston, William M., *The Austrian Mind: An Intellectual History 1848–1938*, Berkeley: University of California Press, 1972

Le Rider, Jacques, "Between Modernism and Postmodernism: The Viennese Identity Crisis," in *Vienna 1900: From Altenberg to Wittgenstein*, edited by Edward Timms and Ritchie Robertson, Edinburgh: Edinburgh University Press, 1990

Luft, David S., *Robert Musil and the Crisis of European Culture, 1880–1942*, Berkeley: University of California Press, 1980

McGowan, Moray, and Ricarda Schmidt, editors, *From High Priests to Desecrators: Contemporary Austrian Writers*, Sheffield: Sheffield Academic Press, 1993

Menasse, Robert, *Die sozialpartnerschaftliche Ästhetik: Essays zum österreichsichen Geist*, Vienna: Sonderzahl, 1990

Schmidt-Dengler, Wendelin, "Borderlines: Von der Schwierigkeit, über die österreichische Indentität einiger Autoren zu reden," in *Literaturgeschichte: Österreich: Prolegomena und Fallstudien*, edited by Wendelin Schmidt-Dengler, Johann Sonnleitner, and Klaus Zeyringer, Berlin: Erich Schmidt, 1995

Schorske, Carl E., *Fin-de-Siècle Vienna: Politics and Culture*, New York: Knopf, and London: Weidenfeld and Nicolson, 1979

Sebald, Winfried Georg, *Unheimliche Heimat: Essays zur österreichischen Literatur*, Salzburg: Residenz, 1991

Timms, Edward, and Ritchie Robertson, editors, *Vienna 1900: From Altenberg to Wittgenstein*, Edinburgh: Edinburgh University Press, 1990

Ungar, Frederick, editor, *Handbook of Austrian Literature*, New York: Ungar, 1973

Vansant, Jacqueline, *Against the Horizon: Feminism and Postwar Austrian Women Writers*, New York and London: Greenwood Press, 1988

Von Bormann, Alexander, *Sehnsuchtsangst: Zur österreichischen Literatur der Gegenwart*, Amsterdam: Rodopi, 1987

Ward, Mark G., *From Vormärz to Fin-de-siècle: Essays in Nineteenth Century Austrian Literature*, Blairgowrie, Scotland: Lochee, 1986

Zeyringer, Klaus, *Innerlichkeit und Öffentlichkeit: Österreichische Literatur der achtziger Jahre*, Tübingen: A. Francke, 1992

Autobiographical Novel

The autobiographical novel is an interesting hybrid form, since its two components—the autobiography and the novel—are at first sight mutually exclusive. It is therefore not surprising that there is no consensus about the definition of this literary category or about the novels that belong to it. However, a general concept can be construed from the association of the two genres.

In principle, every novel is to some extent autobiographical. No matter what a novel is about, it always contains certain autobiographical elements, for naturally one can only write about things that one knows, whether from firsthand experience or from reading or communicating with others. Jane Austen's work may be called autobiographical in this sense, as it focuses almost exclusively on Austen's relatively narrow circle of experience. While there may be some usefulness in applying the term to Austen's novels, it would be manifestly absurd to call every novel autobiographical. However, it is impossible to draw a clear line between autobiographical and nonautobiographical fiction. How much of the author's life should be present in a novel to qualify it as autobiographical? This essay will take a highly pragmatic approach to the term, applying it to novels that exhibit a significant and generally uncontested autobiographical presence.

The distinction between autobiographical fiction and fictional autobiography is more straightforward. An autobiographical novel follows novelistic conventions but contains some material taken from the life of the author. A fictional autobiography, such as Daniel Defoe's *Moll Flanders* (1722), is entirely fictional but observes the conventions of autobiography in its account of the life of the narrator. As this distinction suggests, autobiography is a more narrowly circumscribed genre than the novel. The novel can accommodate autobiographical conventions, but the opposite is not generally understood to be the case. Autobiography is governed by an understanding between writer and reader—the autobiographical pact, to use Philippe Lejeune's phrase—that the life story is told as truthfully as possible. As Elizabeth Bruss has shown (1976), to assure the reader of their veracity autobiographies tend to follow very specific rhetorical procedures.

Fidelity to fact has no relevance to autobiographical fiction, but, interestingly, autobiographical novels are frequently judged in terms of their authenticity as a representation of the experience of the author. Charles Dickens' *David Copperfield* (1850), for instance, is commonly felt to be a more "authentic" account of Dickens' life than his autobiography. Similarly, Mary McCarthy asserted that her fictional characters express her true self better than her autobiographical writings do. Ironically, the occasionally greater "authenticity" of autobiographical fiction is often explained with reference to its release from the strict truthfulness required of autobiographies proper.

Another generally valid distinction between autobiography and autobiographical fiction lies in the focus on the autobiographical subject. Autobiographies tend to focus on the author exclusively, while autobiographical fiction usually develops a full cast of characters. The autobiographical burden may in fact even be carried by minor characters.

Autobiography, of course, is a much older form than the novel. Augustine of Hippo's *Confessions* (A.D. 397–98) is often considered the first autobiography. Augustine focuses the story of his life on his religious conversion, laying the foundation for what later came to be called spiritual autobiography, a form of writing particularly popular with the introspective Puritans. John Bunyan's *Grace Abounding to the Chief of Sinners* (1666) is one of the better known examples of spiritual autobiography. Jean-Jacques Rousseau's *Les Confessions* (1782–89; *The Confessions*) is the first romantic autobiography. Serving as an illustration of Rousseau's conviction that humans are inherently good, it contains a minute exploration of his childhood as the key to understanding the mature individual. Romantic autobiography is structurally similar to the Bildungsroman, which is essentially an identity quest that follows the protagonist from innocence to maturity. Johann Wolfgang von Goethe's *Wilhelm Meisters Lehrjahre* (1795–96; *Wilhelm Meister's Apprenticeship*) is often identified as the first Bildungsroman. James Joyce's *A Portrait of the Artist as a Young Man* (1916) is an important 20th-century example. The Bildungsroman tends to have a very strong autobiographical slant. A third subtype of autobiography is the philosophical autobiography, an early example of which is Benjamin Franklin's *Autobiography* (1868). In this type of autobiography, the story of the developing self is used to illustrate a philosophical point. In Franklin's case, his own success story and the revelation of his genius underwrite a social philosophy of individualism and self-reliance.

The rising popularity of the novel in the 18th century did not immediately bring the development of autobiographical fiction. Among the first novels with a strong autobiographical slant is Jean-Jacques Rousseau's *Julie; ou, La Nouvelle Héloïse* (1761; *Julie; or, The New Eloise*). Elements of this novel were inspired by Rousseau's love affair with Sophie d'Houdetot, a fact to which he drew attention in his autobiography. Another important early example is Johann Wolfgang von Goethe's *Die Leiden des jungen Werthers* (1774; *The Sufferings of Young Werther*). This epistolary novel tells a story very similar to Goethe's frustrated love for Charlotte Buff. The protagonist ends by committing suicide, and Goethe claimed that he wrote the novel so as to avoid doing the same. Autobiographical novels have served different purposes to different authors, but—if the testimonies of the novelists themselves may be taken at face value—the potential therapeutic effects of writing autobiographical fiction has lent a powerful motivating force to the genre.

One of the first novels in English with an autobiographical impulse takes the form of the Gothic romance. Mary Shelley's *Frankenstein; or, The Modern Prometheus* (1818) originated in a dream Shelley had. The novel has frequently been read as a key to Shelley's personality and has aroused the particular interest of Freudian critics. Charlotte Brontë's *Jane Eyre* (1847) is usually taken to be autobiographical in a similar way: the novel is thought to reproduce not only the social conditions of mid-19th-century England, but also the psychological realities of Brontë's life. Although the plot of *Villette* (1853) is informed by actual events from Brontë's life in ways that *Jane Eyre* is not, the latter is often taken to be more authentically autobiographical.

Oscar Wilde's *The Picture of Dorian Gray* (1891) broke new ground with its carefully cultivated self-absorption, which makes the subject into a work of art. Wilde flaunted his self-preoccupation and simultaneously maintained a certain ironic distance by claiming that all the characters in the novel were images of himself—as others saw him, as he saw himself, and as he would like to be in another life. Such a self-conscious assertion of the link between the fictional text and the real subject was not general practice even among decadent novelists, but it found many followers in the 20th century. André Gide and Jean Genet in France, Henry Miller, James Baldwin, and Edmund White in America, and the dramatist Joe Orton in Britain are among the more noteworthy 20th-century writers who made themselves into their own central subject. *The Picture of Dorian Gray* is significant in the present context also because of the role it played in Wilde's trial and conviction for homosexuality. The novel was read by the court as a literal autobiography and served as evidence of Wilde's alleged degeneracy, thus contributing to his conviction.

The late 19th century saw an outburst of autobiographical fiction not only in England but all over Europe. August Strindberg, the Swedish playwright and novelist, wrote several intensely autobiographical novels, *Röda rummet* (1879; *The Red Room*), *Tjänstekvinnans son* (4 vols., 1886–87; *The Son of a Servant*), *Le Plaidoyer d'un fou* (1895; *The Confession of a Fool*), and *Inferno* (1897). Born into the working class, Strindberg displays an almost obsessive preoccupation with his social position. His sexual experiences and his intense ambivalence toward women, not to say misogyny, play a similarly prominent role in virtually everything he wrote. The Russian novelist Fedor Dostoevskii also wrote extensively about his own emotional struggles and religious doubts, most prominently in the novellas *Zapiski iz podpol'ia* (1864; *Notes from Underground*) and *Igrok* (1866; *The Gambler*).

Modernism brought new departures in autobiographical fiction. Virginia Woolf—in her criticism as much as in her fiction—foregrounded the "political" dimensions of women's personal experience. *A Room of One's Own* (1929) is particularly significant in this respect. The book laid the intellectual groundwork for the feminist battle cry "the personal is political," which has inspired a great deal of autobiographical fiction by women in the 20th century. Woolf's *Orlando* (1928) is an experiment of a different sort, portraying a central character with peculiarly metamorphic proclivities, frequently shifting roles and even genders in the course of the narrative. The novel has raised persistent questions about the possibility that the fluid sexual identity of the protagonist reflects Woolf's own experience. Her known association with Vita Sackville-West and Violet Trefusis, who were alleged to be lovers, has fueled these speculations. As in Oscar Wilde's case, then, Virginia Woolf's work has become an image of herself, to be scrutinized for possible clues to the author's actual experience and personality.

To most critics, Franz Kafka has been coterminous with his work in a similar manner. His novels *Der Prozess* (1925; *The Trial*), *Das Schloss* (1926; *The Castle*), and *Amerika* (1927; *America*), as well as the short stories in *Das Urteil* (1916; *The Verdict*), all portray tragically isolated and alienated characters desperately wishing they were at home in the world of action and normalcy. Their plight bears a resemblance to Kafka's own emotional predicaments, as he described them in his letters and autobiographical writings. Kafka's work resists any simple autobiographical interpretation, but his own preoccupation with his family situation, particularly his relationship with his father, has invited intense Freudian speculation, both in relation to the fiction and to Kafka himself. These psychoanalytical readings tend to understand Kafka's life and work as an autobiographical expression of a specific pathology. The cosmic dimension of the alienation experienced by Kafka's characters, on the other hand, continues to provoke metaphysical interpretations of personal and societal damnation that take Kafka's work as a searing description of the modern condition. Such interpretations see no evidence of pathology and also carry a very different sense of what is autobiographical in Kafka's fiction.

Another modernist experiment with autobiography is Marcel Proust's monumental *À la recherche du temps perdu* (1913–27; translated as *Remembrance of Things Past* and more recently as *In Search of Lost Time*), which is specifically concerned with the function of art and memory in recreating a life. Proust, however, declined the autobiographical label, insisting that the Marcel in the text was not the same person as the author. A terminological ambiguity of a rather different kind is involved in Gertrude Stein's *The Autobiography of Alice B. Toklas* (1933). Although professedly an autobiography, it was not written by its ostensible subject, Alice B. Toklas. In fact, it is not even clearly a biography of Toklas, since it focuses as much on Stein and on the circle of French artists and expatriate Americans she cultivated. Although it is often read as a historical document conveying information about important artists, Stein used the form to undermine the strict distinction between fact and fiction that itself underlies the distinction between autobiography and novel. Playing with traditional forms, *The Autobiography of Alice B. Toklas* may in fact be read as an autobiographical *novel* that understands "identity" as a fictional construct. In this sense, Stein's work forms an interesting counterpoint to the "identity novels" of the second half of the 20th century.

The autobiographical novel has become the preferred literary form of oppressed social groups in the course of the 20th century. What started as a trickle has become a flood by century's end. Women, members of racial minorities, gays, victims of incest or domestic violence—all have used the autobiographical novel to describe and legitimate their experience outside the mainstream. Such novels are marked by an intense preoccupation with identity and qualify as latter-day descendants of the Bildungsroman. There is perhaps a particular kinship with the Künstlerroman and its tendency to focus on the misunderstood artist who does not fit in with the rest of society. James Joyce's Stephen Dedalus and D.H. Lawrence's Paul Morell are possible precursors of the protagonists of identity novels in the English-language tradition.

One of the earliest instances of the identity novel is Radclyffe Hall's *The Well of Loneliness* (1928), an autobiographical fiction that recounts the author's experiences in coming to terms with her sexual identity. The French author Jean Genet may also be placed in this lineage, although Genet consciously cultivated an outcast status on the basis not only of his homosexuality but also as a thief and artist. His *Notre Dame des Fleurs* (1944; *The Lady of the Flowers*), *Miracle de la rose* (1946; *Miracle of the Rose*), *Querelle de Brest* (1947; *Querelle of Brest*), and *Journal de voleur* (1949; *The Thief's Journal*) are all strongly autobiographical.

The last decades of the 20th century have seen many novels, increasingly explicit and graphic in their approach, that give more or less fictional records of "coming-out" experiences. A whole new generation of gay and lesbian writers emerged, during the 1980s particularly, who were especially interested in representing their experience of social marginality and in fighting for recognition. Edmund White, Adam Mars-Jones, Rita Mae

Brown, and Kathy Acker are among the more important representatives of this type of fiction.

Autobiographical fiction also has served an important function in the feminist movement. One of the central texts in this tradition is Sylvia Plath's *The Bell Jar* (1963). Recounting several suicide attempts by the protagonist, this novel has proved particularly tantalizing to critics because it was published just before Plath's own suicide. The fiction of Marguerite Duras, particularly *L'Amant* (1984; *The Lover*), gives a more complex account of sexual oppression and the way it affects identity. Galvanized by the notion that "the personal is political," feminist autobiographical fiction has tended to undermine the distinction between the public and private, and in so doing it has played an important role in the redefinition of what is appropriate subject matter for the novel.

Cultural and racial identity constitute another major focus of the late 20th-century identity novel, which has flourished particularly in the United States. African-American writers like Alice Walker, Toni Morrison, John Edgar Wideman, and Toni Cade Bambara follow in the footsteps of the popular author Alex Haley, whose *Roots* (1976) first attempted to integrate an awareness of an African heritage into a sense of identity hedged about by the experience of racism in 20th-century America. The work of Walker and Morrison, for instance, is not autobiographical in the sense of recording the personal experience of the authors. However, in such novels as Walker's *The Color Purple* (1982) and Morrison's *Beloved* (1987), they create an experiential lineage stretching back to the days of slavery that functions as a sustaining force in a contemporary sense of identity. The "self" put forward in such fiction is not an individual but a collective identity, an entire tradition, of which the individual is a vital member. American-Chinese writers such as Amy Tan (*The Joy Luck Club*, 1989; *The Kitchen God's Wife*, 1991; *The Hundred Secret Senses*, 1995) and Maxine Hong Kingston (*The Woman Warrior*, 1976; *China Men*, 1980) have embarked on a similar quest for an integrated cultural identity that embraces both the Chinese heritage bequeathed to them by their parents and the American culture they are surrounded by.

An interesting development in autobiographical fiction has taken place in 20th-century China. Traditional Chinese culture did not encourage the kind of individualism required for the autobiographical novel, but the influx of Western thought and literature at the beginning of the 20th century laid the foundations for the outpouring of autobiographical fiction that followed the communist revolution. The formation of the People's Republic of China in 1949 and the subsequent Cultural Revolution (1967–76) brought about a high point of autobiographical consciousness in Chinese literature. A new genre called "scar literature" emerged after the Cultural Revolution, recounting individual experiences during this period of turmoil that tend to be shaped specifically by the threat of being engulfed by the social collective. Jung Chang's *Wild Swans* (1991), Steven Mosher's *A Mother's Ordeal* (1993), and Anchee Min's *Red Azalea* (1993) are examples of scar literature. As the example of China shows, the progressive foregrounding of the subject that marks the history of the Western novel is also making itself felt in non-Western literatures.

WAI SUM AMY LEE AND MARIJKE RIJSBERMAN

See also Bildungsroman

Further Reading

Bruss, Elizabeth, *Autobiographical Acts: The Changing Situation of a Literary Genre,* Baltimore: Johns Hopkins University Press, 1976

Marcus, Laura, *Auto/Biographical Discourses: Theory, Criticism, Practice,* Manchester and New York: Manchester University Press, 1994

Rothfield, Lawrence, "Autobiography and Perspective in the *Confessions* of St. Augustine," *Comparative Literature* 33:3 (Summer 1981)

Spengemann, William C., *The Forms of Autobiography: Episodes in the History of a Literary Genre,* New Haven, Connecticut: Yale University Press, 1980

Steedman, Carolyn, *Past Tenses: Essays on Writing Autobiography and History,* London: Rivers Oram Press, and Concord, Massachusetts: Paul, 1992

Stull, Heidi I., *The Evolution of the Autobiography from 1770–1850: A Comparative Study and Analysis,* New York: Peter Lang, 1985

Tracy, Robert, "Stranger than Truth: Fictional Autobiography and Autobiographical Fiction," *Dickens Studies Annual: Essays on Victorian Fiction* 15 (1986)

Weinstein, Arnold, *Fictions of the Self: 1550–1800,* Princeton, New Jersey: Princeton University Press, 1981

Wilson, Elizabeth, "Tell It Like It Is," in *Sweet Dreams: Sexuality, Gender, and Popular Fiction,* edited by Susannah Radstone, London: Lawrence and Wishart, 1988

Avalée des avalés. *See* Swallower Swallowed

Avventure di Pinocchio. *See* Adventures of Pinocchio

The Awakening by Kate Chopin

1899

The Awakening represents Kate Chopin's crowning achievement as a writer. A prolific producer of short stories and essays, Chopin also wrote poetry and song lyrics. In addition to *The Awakening,* Chopin wrote two other novels, *At Fault* (1890), which still survives, and *Young Dr. Gosse,* which she destroyed after her attempts to place the novel with a publisher failed. While Chopin's contemporaries relegated much of her short fiction to the realm of "local color," *The Awakening* transcends the regionalist label because of its universal themes as well as its poetic prose style.

The Awakening burst onto the literary scene amid controversial reviews and rumors of bannings and burnings. The story of a 19th-century woman who rejects the role of wife and mother in favor of seeking a fulfilling life for herself, Chopin's novel presented a threat to the contemporary social order that prescribed appropriate roles for men and women in marriage and in the community. Chopin's novel suggested that women should pursue alternative avenues of self-satisfaction if the traditional path did not offer them emotional fulfillment and a means to satisfy their inner selves. *The Awakening*'s protagonist, Edna Pontellier, gradually rejects her role: rather than spending time with her children, she engages in an affair with a young, unmarried man with whom she falls in love; rather than doting on her husband, who provides her with a materially comfortable daily life, she moves out of his luxurious home and into a cottage, disregarding the social impropriety of such a move. Her actions illustrate her attempts to escape from the inexplicable feelings of restlessness and malaise that separate her from the majority of the women of her community. Edna realizes that she cannot give up her emerging sense of self, even for her children, and ultimately chooses freedom in death rather than a lifetime of servitude to people who cannot, or will not, fulfill her needs and desires.

Because of its unconventional suggestions about the rights of women, the critical reception that *The Awakening* met with upon its appearance on the literary scene was mixed, with many reviewers criticizing it harshly for its immorality and its overt dismissal of mores surrounding sexual propriety. Published in 1899 by H.S. Stone, the book fell from public favor rapidly and was out of print from 1906 until 1961, when H.S. Stone reissued a version of the 1906 edition. Since its reissue, *The Awakening* has been the focus of a resurgence of interest among feminist critics, literary scholars, and recreational readers alike. Some critics have argued that the novel deserves recognition as a cornerstone of the feminist movement.

While reviews of *The Awakening* served to bring national scrutiny to Chopin's text, and caused some readers to question her categorization as a local colorist, these reviews also served effectively to end her publishing career. Chopin's contract for *A Vocation and a Voice,* a third collection of short stories that was to follow *Bayou Folk* (1894) and *A Night in Acadie* (1897), was canceled after *The Awakening*'s largely unpopular public reception. The *St. Louis Globe-Democrat* remarked that

[*The Awakening* is] not a healthy book, if it points any particular moral or teaches any lesson the fact is not apparent. But there is no denying the fact that it deals with existent conditions, and without attempting a solution handles a problem that obtrudes itself only too frequently. Though the characters are deftly drawn, it is a morbid book.

Other city dailies offered similar scathing critiques. The *Chicago Times-Herald* gave Chopin credit for writing a "strong" book, but criticized her, saying:

It was not necessary for a writer of so great refinement and poetic grace to enter the over-worked field of sex fiction. This is not a pleasant story, but the contrast between the heroine and another character who is utterly devoted to her husband and family saves it from utter gloom.

Perhaps the most pithy summation of contemporary reception of *The Awakening* came from *Public Opinion,* whose reviewer remarked not only that readers "doubt . . . the possibility of a woman of solid old Presbyterian Kentucky stock ever being at all like the heroine" but that "we are well satisfied when she drowns herself."

National sources were kinder to *The Awakening. Book News Monthly* called it a "remarkable novel, and likely to cause a sensation. The style is curiously analytical and feminine, and yet of such force as to make the final scene very effective." *New York Times Saturday Review* praised Chopin's writing, remarking that "the author has a clever way of managing a difficult subject, and wisely tempers the emotional elements found in the situation."

Because of the protagonist's refusal to submit to the traditional values that are stifling her, *The Awakening* has been compared to Gustave Flaubert's *Madame Bovary,* an earlier novel that refused to be limited by either social mores or the restrictions of the regionalist genre.

SUZANNE D. GREEN

Further Reading

Boren, Lynda S., and Sara deSaussure Davis, editors, *Kate Chopin Reconsidered: Beyond the Bayou,* Baton Rouge: Louisiana State University Press, 1992

Elfenbein, Anna Shannon, *Women on the Color Line: Evolving Stereotypes and the Writings of George Washington Cable, Grace King, Kate Chopin,* Charlottesville: University Press of Virginia, 1989

Gilbert, Sandra M., and Susan Gubar, *No Man's Land: The Place of the Woman Writer in the Twentieth Century,* volume 2: *Sexchanges,* New Haven, Connecticut, and London: Yale University Press, 1989

Inge, Tonette Bond, "Kate Chopin," in *Dictionary of Literary Biography: American Short Story Writers, 1880–1910,* edited by Bobby Ellen Kimbel, Detroit, Michigan: Gale Research, 1989

Martin, Wendy, editor, *New Essays on "The Awakening,"* Cambridge and New York: Cambridge University Press, 1988

Petry, Alice Hall, editor, *Critical Essays on Kate Chopin,* New

York: G.K. Hall, and London: Prentice-Hall International, 1996

Showalter, Elaine, *Sister's Choice: Tradition and Change in American Women's Writing,* Oxford: Clarendon Press, and New York: Oxford University Press, 1991

Showalter, Elaine, Lea Baechler, and A. Walton Litz, editors, *Modern American Women Writers,* New York: Scribner, 1991

Taylor, Helen, *Gender, Race, and Region in the Writings of Grace King, Ruth McEnery Stuart, and Kate Chopin,* Baton Rouge: Louisiana State University Press, 1989

Toth, Emily, *Kate Chopin: A Life of the Author of "The Awakening,"* New York: Morrow, 1990

Toth, Emily, editor, *Kate Chopin's Private Papers,* Bloomington: Indiana University Press, 1998

B

Ba Jin 1904–

Chinese

Ba Jin is probably the most popular Chinese novelist of his time. His heyday spanned the years 1929 to 1947, during which he published more than ten novels and numerous short stories. He also won fame as a leading literary journal editor, a literary translator, and an advocate of anarchism and Esperanto before 1949. Ba Jin was also a staunch defender of humanism, particularly after the Cultural Revolution (1966–76).

Ba Jin's almost exclusive focus on family obligations and on the young intellectual's search for truth in a turbulent era deeply touched the hearts of thousands of young readers and stirred a sensational response in the 1930s and 1940s. Drastic social changes during these two decades are reflected in a change in Ba Jin's narrative style and tone from passionate romanticism to meticulous realism. His protagonists change from rebellious heroes to vulnerable mediocrities. He often used the trilogy to present a panoramic view of contemporary life in novels that demonstrate his literary debt not only to the Chinese traditional domestic novel but also to Western writers, such as Émile Zola, Honoré de Balzac, Stendhal, and Lev Tolstoi.

Ba Jin was born to a wealthy family in Sichuan in 1904. He received a traditional Confucian education at home but was greatly influenced by the May Fourth Movement (1919) and called himself "a product of May Fourth." In 1927 he went to France, where he studied European literature and accepted Western humanism. His literary debut, the passionate *Mie wang* (1929; *Destruction*) was a revolutionary romance, touching issues that concerned most young intellectuals, particularly the urgent need for social change and the conflict between ideas and reality. After returning to China in 1929, he settled on a writing career in Shanghai. His first trilogy, *Aiqing de san bu chu* (1931–33; Love: A Trilogy), continued the pattern of his first novel but was less successful.

However, his next novel, *Jia* (1931; *Family*), the first volume of the *Jiliu* (1931–40; Turbulent Stream) trilogy, was a sensational success that immediately gained Ba Jin international recognition. A scathing condemnation of the patriarchal family system, this autobiographical trilogy, which also includes *Chun* (1938; Spring) and *Qiu* (1940; Autumn), reveals the ugliness and immorality in the declining feudal Gao family. Almost without exception, all the younger members of the Gao family seek to break with the patriarchal tradition, particularly in their romantic relationships, but no matter how they try to escape, they are unable to make a life of their own. In *Family*, Juexin, the eldest son of the Gaos, is portrayed as both a model son and the victim of an arranged marriage. He witnesses the deaths of two women he loved because of the prejudiced decisions of the family elders. The intense conflict between pursuing personal happiness and fulfilling family obligations also dominates the lives of the rebellious second son, Juemin, and the radical third son, Juehui. As for the female characters, their lives are completely controlled by the patriarch of the family, whether they are servants or mistresses. *Chun* continues the family tragedy, but, although the fruitless love relationships among cousins are worthy of sympathy, it is more sentimental and less powerful than *Family*. However, *Qiu* is a more mature novel than the previous two, offering a more sophisticated portrayal of characters and a better understanding of social and domestic issues. The division between good and evil is no longer simply decided by age, wealth, or social status, and it doesn't simply map onto the division between tradition and modernity. The less passionate, more pessimistic tone of the novel casts an air of gloom and uncertainty over the ending, even though the patriarchal family system has finally collapsed. The family in the trilogy functions as a microcosm of society, reflecting prevalent social problems and the May Fourth generation's profound anxiety, as well as its naive wish for immediate social change.

Ba Jin's next three novels, *Qi yuan* (1944; Garden of Rest), *Disi bingshi* (1946; Ward Number Four), and *Han ye* (1947; *Cold Nights*), represent a new style and direction. Ba Jin started focusing on "little people and little events" rather than grand revolutionary themes. Characterization becomes more subtle and the characters undergo a more profound development. *Qi yuan*, in a sense, is an extension of the *Jiliu* trilogy, because family matters remain central. However, the main concern of the novel is about the corrupting power of money. The decadent father, Yang, loses his property, the Garden of Rest, and is driven out of his home by his own son. On the other hand, the new owner of the Garden of Rest spoils and finally loses his son. *Disi bingshi* gives a realistic description of a badly run wartime hospital, vividly presented through the experience of the first-person narrator. The daily rounds of the ward, the impatience of doctors, nurses, and workers, the nonsensical chatting among patients, and their endless fear and anxiety—all these seemingly tedious aspects of hospital life reveal how humanity can be twisted or depressed in a life-and-death situation. *Cold Nights* is Ba Jin's last and perhaps best novel. The protagonist, Wenxuan, unbearably poor, is caught in the endless antagonism between his mother and his wife, who both love him dearly. Although all three characters are basically good people, the hatred and jealousy between mother and wife create intense suffering and finally bring an inevitable tragedy to the family. Ba Jin's characterization is masterful, while his questioning of the voluntarily organized modern family balances the fierce protests against patriarchal families of his earlier work.

Between 1949 and 1966, Ba Jin continued writing short stories. He was sent to Korea in the early 1950s for almost one year for both observation and ideological reformation. Although he tried hard to adapt to the new society, he became the target of persecution during several political movements, especially the Cultural Revolution, during which he lost his wife.

In the post-Mao era, he has become, in a sense, a spokesman for liberal intellectuals in China. His proposal for establishing a Virtual Museum of the Cultural Revolution, his deep regret for his "lies" in the past and advocacy of "telling truth" have significantly boosted his extraordinary reputation. He has received literary honors and awards from Italy (1982), France (1983), and the United States (1985). He was granted an honorary doctoral degree in literature from the Chinese University of Hong Kong in 1984.

Ba Jin has said, "I am not a literary writer, nor do I understand art. The fact that I write does not indicate that I have talent, but that I have passion." In his early novels, the author is too obtrusive and the rhetoric too plain. However, most critics agree that Ba Jin's fictional world truthfully reflects the mentality and development of Chinese intellectuals, from passionate idealism to pessimistic disillusionment, during the 1930s and 1940s. His passionate pursuit of truth, keen observation of life, and great psychological acumen are unlikely to stop attracting readers, both at home and abroad.

HAILI KONG

See also Cold Nights

Biography
Ba Jin is the pseudonym for Li Feikan and Li Yaotang. Born in Chengdu, Sichuan, 25 November 1904 (some sources say 1905). Attended Foreign Language School, Chengdu; Southeastern University, Nanjing, graduated 1925; graduate work in France, 1927–28. Editor, *Ban Yue*, 1928; editor-in-chief, Wenhua shenghuo [Cultural Life Publishing House], Shanghai, 1935–38, 1946; member of editorial board, *Fenghuo* [Beacon], 1937–38, *Na han* [Outcry], from 1937, *Jing chun* [Warning the People], and *Pingmin zhisheng* [Voice of the Proletariat]; chief editor, People's Literature Publishing House, Beijing, 1957–58, and Shanghai Literature, 1961; purged during Cultural Revolution, 1966–76; vice chair, 5th Municipal Congress, 1977–83, member of Presidium, 6th National Congress, 1983–88, and vice chair, 7th National Congress, from 1988, all Chinese Communist Party. Founder, Chinese Writers Anti-Aggression Association, 1938; committee member, China Association of Literary Workers, 1949, and Cultural and Educational Commission, 1949–54; vice chair, All-China Federation of Literary and Art Circles, 1953; vice chair, from 1953, and chair, 1958–68, China People's Union of Chinese Writers, Shanghai; deputy chief, Afro-Asian Writers' Congress, 1958; vice president, Sino-Soviet Friendship Association, 1959–68; member of executive council, China Welfare Institute, and vice chair, China Federation of Literary and Art Circles, from 1978; president, China PEN, 1980–91, and National Literary Foundation, 1986–89.

Selected Fiction by Ba Jin
Mie wang, 1929; as *Destruction*, 1995
Aiqing de san bu chu [Love: A Trilogy], 1939
   Wu [Fog], 1931
   Yu [Rain], 1932
   Dian [Thunder], 1933
Jiliu [Turbulent Stream] trilogy
   Jia, 1931; as *The Family*, 1958; as *Family*, 1972
   Chun [Spring], 1938
   Qiu [Autumn], 1940
Qi yuan [Garden of Rest], 1944
Disi bingshi [Ward Number Four], 1946
Han ye, 1947; as *Cold Nights*, 1978

Other Writings: short stories, essays, travel notebooks, autobiographical works.

Further Reading
Hsia, C.T., *A History of Modern Chinese Fiction,* New Haven, Connecticut: Yale University Press, 1961; 2nd edition, 1971
Lang, Olga, *Pa Chin and His Writings: Chinese Youth between the Two Revolutions,* Cambridge, Massachusetts: Harvard University Press, 1967
Mao, Nathan K., *Pa Chin,* Boston: Twayne, 1978

Ingeborg Bachmann 1926–1973

Austrian

Along with Christa Wolf, Ingeborg Bachmann is often considered the woman author with the greatest impact on literary discourse in German-speaking countries in the 20th century. During her short life she was lauded as one of the greatest German poets, although the political underpinnings of her texts remained largely unrecognized until after her untimely death. She was the first writer to deliver the now legendary Frankfurt Lectures on Poetics in 1959–60, a turning point in her writing career. Soon after, she switched from poetry to other genres. In the third of her five Frankfurt lectures, she affirmed the literary ego as an "I without guarantees," when tracing the disintegration of the narrating "I" from Céline to Beckett. Her radicalism in deconstructing the novel, in questioning prevailing norms, and expanding the borders of language and reality link her to literary modernism and its greatest writers, among them Virginia Wolf, Samuel Beckett, James Joyce, Robert Musil, and Franz Kafka. Interest in Bachmann's work in the 1980s grew amid growing discontent with the autobiographical realism that had resulted from the rise of the women's movement in the 1970s. She is an author who understood literature as utopia and whose late prose, misinterpreted and disregarded at the time of its publication, examines the contradictions within female experience and authorship.

The novels or fragments in the *Todesarten* (Death Styles) cycle traverse various myths, ideas, and the deeply rooted violation of the female "I." For Bachmann, female subjectivity has no real historical locus because of Western emphasis on logical thinking and hierarchical structures. Her texts, highly encoded with intertextual allusions to works in music, philosophy, and world literature, are countercompositions to a rationally and patriarchally defined culture and society. Reasons for her characteristic absence of plot and lack of narrative realism may be found in her preface to the posthumously published fragment *Der Fall Franza* (1979; The Franza Case) of the *Todesarten* cycle, where she suggests that the real setting of her stories and novels is in thought processes and the interior; the external loci simply provide a physical space in which to demonstrate or perform the work of the mind.

Struggling to find her female voice in a latently fascist postwar Austria and Germany, Bachmann in her poetry and prose focuses on a coming to terms with various forms of fascism in a post-Holocaust world, including interpersonal fascism and the constant state of war throughout civilization. The oppressive nature of the relationship between the sexes, power structures in the public and private spheres, alienation, and the eradication of "otherness" throughout history are central topics that occupied her with increasing intensity during the last decade of her writing career. In the *Todesarten* cycle, originally conceived as several prose volumes before her premature death, she intended to undertake an investigation into what she saw as "the ways of dying" and destruction in contemporary society. The female characters in this cycle, driven to the brink of madness and destruction by the callous men in their lives, are depicted as accomplices in their own destruction by accommodating themselves to these structures and conventions in family units and relations between the sexes. This may also be seen in the five women in Bachmann's thematically related collection of stories, *Simultan* (1972; *Three Paths to the Lake*).

In her creation of the literary double or doppelgänger in *Malina* (1971), Bachmann was the first 20th-century female author in German-speaking countries to connect explicitly the literary double with female authorship and patriarchy. The female protagonist, an unnamed writer vacillating between her desire to submit and to achieve autonomy, cannot bring herself to imitate the rationality and superiority of her male alter ego, the shadowy figure Malina, an employee of the Austrian Military Museum and her apartment mate. Neither can she find a voice of her own to complete the novel *Exsultante Jubilate* (a Mozartian title), an inspiration and brainchild of her Hungarian lover Ivan. Wishing to please Ivan (she "lives in him"), who wanted her to write a "happy book" upon discovery of notes among her papers for a book entitled *Death Styles,* she had simply complied. Ivan invigorates her female imagination during their short, hopeless love affair in their private *Ungargasseland,* a place where they do not "mutilate or torture" themselves but find "shelter" and "protect what is [their] own." Neglected by her emotionally cold lover, the narrator hides herself in fairy tales and in a utopian legend of a woman who never existed. Frequently she also projects Malina into various fairy tale settings so that he exists more in song and legend and in the narrator's mind than in real life.

Haunted in a series of nightmares by the memory of acts of violence and torture committed by her father in her childhood, the narrator agrees to confront pain and incest at the urging of Malina. As Malina patronizingly interprets her dreams for her, the narrator loses more and more linguistic control and space in the text until she disappears in the end into a crack in the wall. The two male characters, Malina and Ivan, may be read both as distinct characters and as fragments of the narrator's own mind as she struggles to find her female voice as a writer. Some critics have seen Malina as the narrator of the entire novel, which begins only after the female murder (Bartsch, 1988), and the female split subject as representative of the process of disintegration of the narrative "I" in literary modernism (Achberger, 1995). Explicit and implicit allusions throughout the novel to musical, literary, and critical works create a modern montage novel, in which the themes of murder, crime, and war are repeated and varied and readers are asked to decode meanings.

In both *Malina* and *Der Fall Franza*, the female's destruction is recounted in memories and against the backdrop of National Socialism. In *Der Fall Franza*, set in Vienna and Egypt, new and old civilizations display similar crimes. The Viennese psychiatrist Jordan makes his wife into an object by connecting her with his book on female concentration camp inmates who had to endure experiments by Nazi physicians. She is reduced to a psychiatric "case" and "murdered" by her husband "in the cage of his notes." When traveling with her brother, a geologist, to Egypt to recuperate from a nervous breakdown, she is able to link her own exploitation to that of victims of racial violence and various forms of misogyny: a brutally slaughtered camel, a bound woman believed to be insane, a cretin, Jews, the Papuas, and an Egyptian queen mistreated by her son. With the awareness that a retreat from violence is impossible in any civilization, she dies after being raped at a pyramid and protesting by banging her head against a stone wall. In *Requiem für Fanny Goldmann* (1979), the title character, an actress, is depicted as the muse and killed (she dies of alcoholism and a lung infection) while the male text is written about her by an opportunistic playwright. Fanny's death, like Franza's, is preceded by psychological destruction.

At the heart of Bachmann's prose texts in the *Todesarten* cycle is her concern to uncover "truths" about fascist residues in contemporary cultures and to explore the unchartered territory of female authorship and communication between the sexes. Informed by the study of Ludwig Wittgenstein's philosophical writings, Bachmann reaches beyond the limits of language to create encounters with the unspeakable and "the impossible." In her first Frankfurt lecture she expressed her search for a new, nonviolent poetic language: "If we had the word, if we had language, we would not need the weapons."

BARBARA MABEE

Biography

Born in Klagenfurt, Austria, 25 June 1926. Lived in Carinthia as a child. Attended coeducational high school until 1938, girls' school, 1938–44; studied philosophy at Graz, Innsbruck, and Vienna universities, Ph.D. in philosophy, 1950. Employed as scriptwriter and editor, Rot-Weiss-Rot radio station, Vienna, 1951–53; freelance writer in Ischia, Naples, Rome, and Munich, 1953–57; traveled to the United States in 1955; lived in Rome and Zurich, 1958–62, West Berlin, 1963–65, and Rome from 1965; visiting lecturer, Frankfurt University, 1959–60. Died 17 October 1973.

Novels by Bachmann

Malina, 1971; as *Malina*, translated by Philip Boehm, 1989
Der Fall Franza, 1979
Requiem für Fanny Goldmann, 1979

Other Writings: poetry collections, radio plays, short stories, philosophical essays; delivered the inaugural lectures (1959–60) for a newly created chair of contemporary poetry at the University of Frankfurt (Frankfurt Lectures on Poetics); collaborated with Hans Werner Henze on libretti for two operas and a ballet.

Further Reading

Achberger, Karen, *Understanding Ingeborg Bachmann*, Columbia: University of South Carolina Press, 1995

Bartsch, Kurt, *Ingeborg Bachmann*, Stuttgart: Metzler, 1988
Beicken, Peter, *Ingeborg Bachmann*, Munich: Beck, 1988; 2nd edition, 1992
Gürtler, Christa, *Schreiben Frauen anders: Untersuchungen zu Ingeborg Bachmann und Barbara Frischmuth*, Stuttgart: Heinz, 1983; 2nd edition, 1985
Hapkemeyer, Andreas, *Ingeborg Bachmann: Entwicklungslinien in Werk und Leben*, Vienna: Österreichischen Akademie der Wissenschaften, 1990
Höller, Hans, editor, *Der dunkle Schatten, dem ich schon seit Anfang folge: Ingeborg Bachmann, Vorschläge zu einer neuen Lektüre des Werks*, Vienna: Locker, 1982
Lennox, Sara, "In the Semitary of the Murdered Daughters: Ingeborg Bachmann's *Malina*," *Studies in Twentieth Century Literature* 5:1 (1980)
Lennox, Sara, "The Feminist Reception of Ingeborg Bachmann," in *Women in German Yearbook 8*, Lincoln: University of Nebraska Press, 1993
Mahrdt, Helgard, "'Society Is the Biggest Murder Scene of All': On the Private and Public Spheres in Ingeborg Bachmann's Prose," in *Women in German Yearbook 12*, Lincoln: University of Nebraska Press, 1996
Weigel, Sigrid, "'Ein Ende mit der Schrift. Ein andrer Anfang': Zur Entwicklung von Ingeborg Bachmanns Schreibweise," in *text + kritik Sonderband Ingeborg Bachmann*, edited by Sigrid Weigel, Munich: text + kritik Sonderband, 1984

Badenheim 1939 by Aharon Appelfeld

Badenheim, ir nofesh 1979

Badenheim, ir nofesh (literally translated as Badenheim, Resort Town) was the first novel by the Romanian-born Israeli storyteller Aharon Appelfeld to be translated into English, and, despite the success of several succeeding novels published in the United States, it remains his best-known and most characteristic work. It was originally one of two stories included in a volume entitled *Shanim vesha'ot* (Years and Hours) and published in Tel Aviv by Hakibbutz Hameuchat in 1975. The same publisher issued the author's expanded version in 1980, the year in which Dalya Bilu's translation appeared in the United States. The English title, *Badenheim, 1939*, places Appelfeld's narrative in the context of world history.

The very name of Appelfeld's fictional spa indicates a homey watering place, and as such it is prized by a whole typology of central European Jews. Ostensibly located somewhere in Austria, a scant 200 kilometers from Vienna, the spa is noted for its Spring Festival, arranged by the impresario Dr. Pappenheim. However, as spring turns into summer and autumn, the community increasingly "lives its life inside itself," and the town seems to be quarantined because of a "Jewish epidemic." A strange malaise takes hold of this microcosm of largely assimilated and acculturated European Jews, and a nameless force appears to guide the destiny of those people, most of them lapsed Jews who regard themselves as "Austrian citizens of Jewish origin," although they are allowed to dance on a volcano for a while to their accustomed light music, the prelude to the Holocaust.

In a new form of storytelling, Appelfeld, himself a survivor of the Holocaust, keeps his authorial voice muted. He seems to feel that the events of the 1930s and 1940s must not and cannot be described or explained in rational terms. Appelfeld achieves his effects—the building up of an almost unbearable tension in a repressive, doom-laden atmosphere, a sense of foreboding, the feeling that a masquerade is coming to an end and a society and way of life are being unraveled—by indirection. In this way he tempts readers, who have the benefit of hindsight, to fill in the gaps, as it were, to empathize with those undergoing a spiritual and physical displacement, and mentally to warn all those self-deluding innocents who accept greater and greater restrictions as they allow themselves to be sucked into the vortex of extinction. The novelist challenges all claims of order, reason, and civility by holding Badenheim and its denizens in suspended animation and letting the many signs of impending catastrophe go unnoticed.

Masking the bitter irony that is at the core of this novel's structure, Appelfeld lets his slow pace and cool, matter-of-fact, almost childlike style contrast with the outrageous transformation that is taking place by using such innocent and euphemistic terms as "order," "transfer," and "emigration procedures." The Department of Sanitation, with which the vacationers have to register, apparently promotes only a "nice train journey" to Poland, where the air is purer, but it assumes more and more power. Its slogan "Labor is our life" is reminiscent of the cynical inscription *Arbeit macht frei* (Work makes you free) atop the entrance to a notorious Nazi extermination camp.

Princess Milbaum resents "those clowns, the *Ostjuden* [Eastern Jews] who had taken over Badenheim and were dragging every bit of true culture through the dust." The striking thing, however, is the reversal of the old trend toward assimilation and the movement from the East to the West as the author appears to "take back" a hundred years or more of acculturation. Poland, where the roots of some of those Jews may be found, is the only part of the outside world that is discussed, and it is presented as the cherished motherland that exerts a strangely atavistic attraction.

The reader's hindsight is not afflicted with the characters' studied blindness. Seemingly innocent situations and statements are endowed with an ominous significance. Among the many reflections or foreshadowings of the impending catastrophe that provide a glimpse of the true situation are the beer-swilling, predatory musicians; the peculiar goings-on in an aquarium; the return of an old Yiddish-speaking rabbi; the twins from Vienna who intone a "morbid melody" as they recite the poetry of Rainer Maria Rilke; a waiter who studies Yiddish and a child prodigy who sings in that language; the elusive maestro Mandelbaum who arrives unexpectedly and promises to head a "band of Jewish minstrels"; and Professor Fussholdt, who rejects such Jewish activists and thinkers as Theodor Herzl and Martin Buber but

praises Karl Kraus, who "had revived satire . . . the only art form appropriate to our lives."

In his brilliant evocation of a doomed community in our "age of anxiety," Aharon Appelfeld creates a hermetically sealed place that is reminiscent of Thomas Mann's "magic mountain" and also calls to mind the Romanian-born poet Paul Celan's breathtaking line, "Death is a master from Germany." If the author does not want to write from a perspective of the future, he presumably wants to express his solidarity with his characters, for whom there is no future. At the end of the novel a train with filthy carriages pulls into the Badenheim station. The rest is silence.

HARRY ZOHN

See also Aharon Appelfeld

Further Reading

Govrin, Nurit, "To Express the Inexpressible: The Holocaust Literature of Aharon Appelfeld," in *Remembering for the Future: Theme II,* compiled by Elisabeth Maxwell and Roman Halter, Oxford and New York: Pergamon, 1988

Gunn, Daniel, "Appelfeld the Immortal," *Jewish Quarterly* (Winter 1989–90)

Langer, Lawrence, "Aharon Appelfeld and the Uses of Language and Silence," in *Remembering for the Future: Theme II,* compiled by Elisabeth Maxwell and Roman Halter, Oxford and New York: Pergamon, 1988

Ramraz-Raukh, Gilah, *Aharon Appelfeld: The Holocaust and Beyond,* Bloomington: Indiana University Press, 1994

Stone, Les, "Aharon Appelfeld," in *Contemporary Authors,* volume 33, Detroit, Michigan: Gale Research, 1991 (includes a list of book reviews and other biographical-critical sources)

Wisse, Ruth E., "Aharon Appelfeld, Survivor," *Commentary* 76:2 (August 1983)

James Baldwin 1924–87

United States

The balance of judgment has long favored Baldwin the essayist over Baldwin the novelist. He won great acclaim with *Go Tell It on the Mountain* (1953), his novel of the rite of passage of John Grimes in 1930s Harlem told through three framing acts of memory. Baldwin had conceived a powerful fable about the tension between flesh and spirit in a world of family and pentecostal religiosity. But more than that, a decade of revising and polishing drafts gave his story design, focus, and a clear narrative unity. Thereafter, it seemed to many, his novels either ran to formula or to ever looser and baggier shapelessness.

The view became widespread that Baldwin wrote too much or too quickly, and that his life lacked the repose to allow for a reprise of the quality of his first novel. His itinerant habits, European exile, rising celebrity status, unabridged sexual adventuring, drinking, and even the cigarettes that led to his death of can-

cer at Saint-Paul-de-Vence on the Riviera, all seemed to militate against the imaginative good order of his work.

In addition, his novels had to compete with his other writing, most of all the Bible-driven and yet streetwise essays that began so passionately and with so formidable a command of voice in his three landmark collections—*Notes of a Native Son* (1955), *Nobody Knows My Name* (1961), and *The Fire Next Time* (1963). Who in an America just entering the era of civil rights and Black Power had written better, more exhilaratingly, of white and black and of all the fraught circlings and love-hates of race? Yet the later essays impart a sense of repetition and overinsistence. *No Name in the Street* (1972), his backward glance at the 1960s of Black Power, Malcolm X, and Martin Luther King; *The Devil Finds Work: An Essay* (1976), his account of race stereotypes and iconographies within the American cinematic tradition; and *Evidence of Things Not Seen* (1985), his investigations of a spate of black child murders in Atlanta—for all their competence, these essays do not recapture the spirit of Baldwin's earlier work.

Baldwin sought his mentors across the board: Richard Wright and Henry James, the painter Beauford Delaney and the film maker Ingmar Bergman. His novels, likewise, drew on both black and white worlds, with settings in Harlem but also the Village and beyond, Afro-America but also Europe. Despite Baldwin's frequent virtuosity as a stylist, his work is in the neorealist tradition, with timeline, plot, character, and place all conceived in the single sweep of cause and effect. Not for Baldwin the reflexivity of, say, Ralph Ellison's *Invisible Man* (1952), or the postmodern turns and riffs of an Ishmael Reed.

Go Tell It on the Mountain is a black "Remembrance of Things Past" that reworks the Old Testament story of Abraham, Sarah, Hagar, and Ishmael into an episode in the Great Migration, focusing on a family with roots in Dixie carried north to Harlem in the wake of World War II. John Grimes' story bears on his unresolved sexuality, his feeling for Elisha, a church member, and the search for a workable identity within family, street, and church. Prayers serve as epigraphs and framing devices, the voices John must heed before choosing a voice of his own.

In Gabriel Grimes, a preacher and John's stepfather, Baldwin portrays a black Southerner whose relationships first with the abused Deborah, then the wayward Esther, and finally, John's mother, Elizabeth, are warped by a bitter tension between physical need and spiritual duty. The histories of his own two sons ("Royal" and "Roy") bear witness to his failings as a parent. In Florence Grimes, Gabriel's sister, lovelessness strikes in a different way. She knows Gabriel's errors and is protective of John, yet she is consumed by cancer and resentments in equal measure. And in Elizabeth Grimes, whose first husband killed himself after a false police accusation, Baldwin offers a "saintly" enduring mother. The balance of each contributing part and the economy of the narration deservedly won *Go Tell It on the Mountain* its immediate fame.

Baldwin's fiction, however, was never again to win unalloyed praise. *Giovanni's Room* (1956) is an austere, deeply Gidean tale of doomed androgyny that explores the triangle of David, a young, bisexual American, Giovanni, his Italian lover, and Helga, his would-be wife. Many critics charged the novel with being formulaic. *Another Country* (1962) came under censure for shapelessness. Ringing the changes on sexual identity, the novel inventories the legacy of Rufus Brown, a jazz drummer who kills himself in despair, across different permutations of love and sex. *Tell Me How Long the Train's Been Gone* (1968), again a novel with an artist figure at its center, depicts the actor Leo Proudhammer's return to personal and political health through his love for the Malcolm X-like figure of Black Christopher. Detractors again pointed to a lack of structure.

If Beale Street Could Talk (1974) fared no better, for all its relative brevity. A tale of two cities as it were, New York and Puerto Rico, this stylized black love story of a young sculptor, Fonny, imprisoned on a false charge of theft, and his pregnant lover, Tish, is sentimental and contrived. It would have been gratifying had Baldwin's last novel, *Just above My Head* (1979), made amends. Unhappily, its multisexual story—of Arthur Montana, gospel singer, and his lover Jimmy and sister Julia, as told by his brother Hall—for all Baldwin's invocations of black musical life

and genius, fails to cohere. Although he was an evident and richly endowed writer, it may well be that after *Go Tell It on the Mountain* Baldwin's true calling lay outside the novel.

A. ROBERT LEE

Biography

Born in New York City, 2 August 1924. Attended Public School 139, Harlem, New York, and DeWitt Clinton High School, Bronx, New York, graduated 1942. Worked as handyman, dishwasher, waiter, and office assistant in New York, and in defense work, Belle Meade, New Jersey, in early 1940s; began writing full-time in 1943; lived in Europe, mainly in Paris, 1948–56. Member, Actors Studio, New York, National Advisory Board of CORE (Congress on Racial Equality), and National Committee for a Sane Nuclear Policy. Died 1 December 1987.

Novels by Baldwin

Go Tell It on the Mountain, 1953
Giovanni's Room, 1956
Another Country, 1962
Tell Me How Long the Train's Been Gone, 1968
If Beale Street Could Talk, 1974
Just above My Head, 1979

Other Writings: poetry, short stories, plays, a screenplay (*The Inheritance*, 1973), and essays.

Further Reading

Campbell, James, *Talking at the Gates: A Life of James Baldwin,* London: Faber, and New York: Viking, 1991

Chametzky, Jules, editor, *Black Writers Redefine the Struggle: A Tribute to James Baldwin,* Amherst and London: University of Massachusetts Press, 1989

Eckman, Fern Marja, *The Furious Passage of James Baldwin,* New York: Evans, and London: Joseph, 1966

Gibson, Donald B., *Five Black Writers: Essays on Wright, Ellison, Baldwin, and Le Roi Jones,* New York: New York University Press, 1970

Inge, M. Thomas, Maurice Duke, and Jackson R. Bryer, editors, *Black American Writers, Bibliographical Essays,* volume 2: *Richard Wright, Ralph Ellison, James Baldwin, and Amiri Baraka,* New York: St. Martin's Press, and London: Macmillan, 1978

Kinnamon, Keneth, editor, *James Baldwin: A Collection of Critical Essays,* Englewood Cliffs, New Jersey: Prentice-Hall, 1974

Macebuh, Stanley, *James Baldwin: A Critical Study,* New York: Third Press, 1973; London: Joseph, 1975

O'Daniel, Therman, editor, *James Baldwin: A Critical Evaluation,* Washington, D.C.: Howard University Press, 1975

Porter, Horace A., *Stealing the Fire: The Art and Protest of James Baldwin,* Middletown, Connecticut: Wesleyan University Press, 1989

Standley, Fred L., *James Baldwin, a Reference Guide,* Boston: G.K. Hall, 1979

Troupe, Quincy, editor, *James Baldwin: The Legacy,* New York: Simon and Schuster, 1989

Weatherby, William J., *James Baldwin: Artist on Fire,* New York: Dell, 1989; London: Joseph, 1990

Balzac, Honoré de. *See* Human Comedy; Père Goriot

Barchester Towers. *See* Barsetshire Novels

The Barsetshire Novels by Anthony Trollope

1855–67

Trollope readers are fond of saying that they do not absolutely insist that the six Barsetshire titles—*The Warden* (1855), *Barchester Towers* (1857), *Doctor Thorne* (1858), *Framley Parsonage* (1861), *The Small House at Allington* (1864), and *The Last Chronicle of Barset* (1867)—form the most distinguished series of English-language novels with recurring characters; they are willing to concede one close competitor, Trollope's series of six Palliser novels. Victorians credited (or blamed) Trollope for the device of reintroducing characters and locations in loosely connected novels, but this was an exaggeration. Sequels and recurring characters had been used, in a small way, by Daniel Defoe, Samuel Richardson, Sir Walter Scott, William Makepeace Thackeray, and others less well known to posterity. Trollope, however, with his two series of six novels, did so on a new scale. After Trollope's success, series and sequels proliferated, beginning with his direct imitator, Mrs. Oliphant, and continuing through such diverse novelists as Arthur Conan Doyle, Arnold Bennett, Paul Scott, and John Updike (who even borrowed from a Trollope title, in *Rabbit Redux*). Trollope wrote only one true sequel—*Barchester Towers,* following directly from the plot of *The Warden.* (The two Phineas Finn novels, Trollope asserted, were actually two parts of *one* novel.)

When Trollope began writing *The Warden,* he was 38 years old and had written three novels, two set in Ireland, and one set in Revolutionary France. None had sold. Trollope had all the while been working as a post office surveyor's assistant in Ireland. Then in 1851 he was sent "on loan" to expand the rural post in western England. His writing had come to a standstill. But in late May 1852, at Salisbury, "whilst wandering there on a midsummer evening through the purlieus of the cathedral I conceived the story of *The Warden*—from whence came that series of novels of which Barchester, with its bishops, deans, and archdeacon, was the central site." Post office demands were great, and *The Warden* was not published until January 1855.

In *The Warden* Trollope chose to deal with two evils—the misuse of charitable endowments by bishops and clergy of the Church of England and the "undeserved severity" with which the press treated those clergymen who had been paid large sums from such endowments. Drawing upon scandals recently un-earthed by *The Times,* Trollope presented a case morally more interesting, because he did not make his central figure, Mr. Harding, a lazy pluralist doing nothing for the elderly men in his care; rather, Mr. Harding is a good, almost a saintly, man, who unwittingly finds himself in the bad position of receiving high pay for little work. Trollope said his attempt to treat both evils was "altogether wrong," a view eventually repudiated by later readers who would appreciate the novel's delicate balance. Reviewers, while objecting to the "ambiguity" of the novel, found the story on the whole "clever"; and while the book was not a financial success, it had fair critical success. The *Leader* innocently said that *The Warden* "certainly promises well for the author's future, if he gives us more books." Trollope himself said, "The novel-reading world did not go mad about *The Warden;* but I soon felt that it had not failed as the others had failed . . . and I could discover that people around me knew that I had written a book."

In writing *Barchester Towers,* Trollope adopted two strategies for increased efficiency. First, he began his practice of writing while traveling and soon found that he could compose as quickly in a railway carriage as at his desk. Second, he devised ledger-like columned records of his writing, marking off the days in weekly sections, entering daily the number of pages written each session and noting the week's total. He set a goal of 40 manuscript pages per week. Some weeks he would write only a few pages; at full throttle he could manage 12 pages a day, or 84 pages per week; and on some extraordinary occasions, he pushed himself to as many as 112 pages a week. This diary-regulated writing led to startling results, and with *Barchester Towers* Trollope's famous (or infamous) productivity took hold, and for good. He eventually wrote some 70 books, including 47 novels.

In *Barchester Towers,* Trollope took to heart some of the strictures voiced in reviews of *The Warden.* The sequel contained nothing like the parodies of Charles Dickens and Thomas Carlyle in the earlier work. On the other hand, Trollope paid no attention to the cautions about facetious names, and until the very end he used names such as Slow and Bidawhile for lawyers, Fillgrave and Rearchild for physicians (Henry James would say of the name Quiverful for a man with 14 children: "We can believe in the name and we can believe in the children; but we cannot manage the combination"). However, Trollope did heed the most persistent criticism of *The Warden,* its ambiguity of purpose: reviewers had wanted to know where he stood on ecclesiastical reform. For Trollope the answer was to get away from the novel of "purpose." In *Barchester Towers* the wardenship is eventually given to Mr. Quiverful (who, with 14 children to support, dearly needs the appointment), but the old scandal and the rights and wrongs of the case no longer matter; the issue of reform has been lost to the personalities of the protagonists. Although *Barchester Towers,* like the *The Warden,* was again about clergymen, Trollope dealt with his clerics in their social and economic rather than religious lives. As a review in *The Times* put it, "the ideas are ecclesiastical, the dresses are canonical, and the conversations have a rubrical tinge. Yet the subject is so fresh and the representation so vivid that the contracted limits of the story are forgotten." Trollope saw the Church as a sort of privileged division of the civil service.

When *Barchester Towers* appeared in May 1857, it met almost unanimous praise from critics, and again the label "clever" was used to describe the work. George Meredith in *The Westminster Review* wrote that *Barchester Towers* was "decidedly the cleverest novel of the season" and recommended that any novel reader who had not done so get the book and its "dashing predecessor" immediately. Trollope himself could afford years later in *An Autobiography* (1883) to be more modest, saying only that *Barchester Towers,* like *The Warden,* "achieved no great reputation, but it was one of the novels which novel readers were called upon to read . . . one of those novels which do not die quite at once, which live and are read for perhaps a quarter of a century." In fact, *Barchester Towers* has come down to posterity as the quintessential Trollope novel. To be sure, it is still "early" Trollope—although written when he was 41—and it lacks some of the control that developed with greater maturity. On the other hand, it abounds in Trollopian "personages"— the engaging characters that Trollope regarded as the sine qua non of a successful novel. Some were carried over from *The Warden*: Septimus Harding, although less the focus of attention than in the earlier novel, is nonetheless still Trollope's unlikely hero, a timid old man with a conscience who wins his distinctions by declining advancement; Archdeacon Grantly becomes a more sympathetic, indeed lovable, character, with a worldliness that itself makes him, although a churchman, more attractive. The newcomers, the henpecked Bishop Proudie, the formidable Mrs. Proudie, their hypocritical chaplain Mr. Slope, and the unsettling family of Dr. Vesey Stanhope, the absentee vicar who has spent long years collecting butterflies on Lake Como, raise the novel considerably above *The Warden.* The most memorable character has proved to be the combative Mrs. Proudie, more than a match for her husband and Mr. Slope combined, and a worthy adversary for Archdeacon Grantly; in her militant Sabbatarianism, she is the classic killjoy of comedy; yet, in a characteristic Trollopian turn, she is capable of evoking the reader's sympathy when she champions Mrs. Quiverful and her 14 children.

The plot of the next Barchester novel, *Doctor Thorne,* more sensational than those of his other novels, had been suggested to Trollope by his brother, Thomas Adolphus Trollope. Trollope, by placing the story in Barsetshire, used it as a vehicle for looking closely at rural England. The opening describes the West Country county of Barsetshire as

> very dear to those who know it well. Its green pastures, its waving wheat, its deep and shady and—let us add—dirty lanes, its paths and stiles, its tawny-coloured, well-built rural churches, its avenues of beeches, and frequent Tudor mansions, its constant county hunt, its social graces, and the general air of clanship which pervades it, have made it to its own inhabitants a favoured land of Goshen. It is purely agricultural; agricultural in its produce, agricultural in its poor, and agricultural in its pleasures.

Doctor Thorne introduces the famous Duke of Omnium; he is unmarried, and said to be a "great debauchee" and indifferent to everything but his own pleasure. He remains a constant and important background presence in the subsequent Barsetshire novels and gains still more prominence in the first three Palliser novels. Toward the Duke, the author's attitude is one of disapproval mixed with grudging admiration; toward the other great Whig family of the novel, the De Courcys, Trollope's attitude is altogether critical. The entire De Courcy clan returns as leading figures in the series' fifth book, *The Small House at Allington.*

Framley Parsonage, the fourth Barsetshire novel, brought Trollope enormous popularity. In late 1859, when a new magazine, the *Cornhill,* edited by W.M. Thackeray and published by George Smith, was about to be launched, Trollope was engaged to write the lead novel. He offered Smith a half-finished Irish novel, but the publisher made it clear that he wanted "an English tale, on English life, with a clerical flavour"—a Barsetshire novel. Trollope quickly complied, and produced "on these orders . . . the morsel of the biography of an English clergyman" that was *Framley Parsonage.* It was Trollope's first effort at serial publication, a form that he used almost exclusively thereafter. The first issue of the *Cornhill Magazine* appeared at Christmas 1859 and was a stupendous success, selling an unheard of 120,000 copies. Much of the magazine's success was owing to Trollope's novel. Elizabeth Gaskell wrote to George Smith, "I wish Mr. Trollope would go on writing *Framley Parsonage* for ever. I don't see any reason why it should ever come to an end, and every one I know is always dreading the *last* number."

The reviews of the book issue of *Framley Parsonage,* even those that were grudging in their praise, testified to the novel's extraordinary popularity. The *Saturday Review* reported:

> At the beginning of every month the new number of his book has ranked almost as one of the delicacies of the season; and no London belle dared to pretend to consider herself literary who did not know the very latest intelligence about the state of Lucy Robarts' heart, and of Griselda Grantly's flounces. It is a difficult thing to estimate the exact position and merit of a book with which we are all so familiar, and which has diverted us so long. It seems a kind of breach of hospitality to criticise *Framley Parsonage* at all. It has been an intimate of the drawing-room—it has travelled with us in the train—it has lain on the breakfast-table. We feel as if we had met Lady Lufton at a country house, admired Lord Dumbello at a ball, and seen Mrs. Proudie at an episcopal evening party.

Trollope observed in 1879 that *Framley Parsonage* "was received with greater favour than any [book] I had written before or have written since." In *An Autobiography,* Trollope discussed, with his usual self-deprecation, how he had added Lucy Robarts and Lord Lufton to the story of the embarrassed young clergyman "because there must be love in a novel." He judged his heroine "perhaps the most natural English girl that I ever drew . . . of those who have been good girls." In writing the book so quickly to order, Trollope explained that, not having much time to think about his characters, he had placed the novel in Barchester so as to be able "to fall back upon my old friends Mrs. Proudie and the Archdeacon":

> As I wrote it I became more closely acquainted than ever with the new shire which I had added to the English counties. I had it all in my mind,—its roads and railroads, its towns and parishes, its members of Parliament, and the different hunts which rode over it. I knew all the great lords and their castles, the squires and their parks, the rectors and their churches. This was the fourth novel of which I had placed the scene in Barsetshire, and as I wrote it I made a map of the dear county. Throughout these stories there has been no name given to a fictitious site which does not represent to me a spot of which I know all the accessories, as though I had lived and wandered there.

The penultimate Barsetshire novel, *The Small House at Allington,* featured Lily Dale (a "female prig," Trollope characterized her in *An Autobiography*) and her unsuccessful suitor, Johnny Eames, a partial self-portrait. This story also introduces Plantagenet Palliser and forms a bridge between the Barsetshire and the Palliser novels. *The Small House at Allington* was another huge success. The *Athenaeum* said that during serialization the question of whether Johnny Eames would marry Lily Dale was as much speculated upon as any " 'marriage on the tapis' . . . in any town or village in Great Britain," and demanded emphatically that Trollope reopen the story of the leading characters; similarly the *Illustrated London News* insisted that the "unsatisfactory conclusion" of the novel be righted in another tale: "Flesh and blood cannot endure that [Lily Dale] should be sentenced to lead the life of a 'widowed maid'." Only the *Saturday Review*—which had earlier objected that *Framley Parsonage* was a mere "*réchauffé*" of *Barchester Towers* and that this "borrowing from himself" was "a lazy and seductive artifice" wherein the novelist lost much in freshness and vigor—persisted in its view that characters should not be carried over from one novel to another, protesting against the reappearance of Mr. Harding, Archdeacon Grantly, and Lady Dumbello, stating that "This is all very good fun for [Mr. Trollope], but it is very poor fun for his readers."

In 1866 Trollope decided to have one final go with his Archdeacon, with the Proudies, and indeed with almost all the inhabitants of his "beloved county." This return to Barchester, eventually entitled *The Last Chronicle of Barset,* worthily crowns the series in adding to it a new dimension. The novel's distinctive quality lies in the dominating presence of the Reverend Mr. Crawley, a character from *Framley Parsonage.* Here, although his story is allowed to end happily, Crawley is essentially a tragic figure. In him Trollope combined what he had learned from his father's unhappy years of poverty and near madness with his now expert knowledge of the conditions to which many poor clergy were reduced.

In the course of writing this novel, Trollope overheard two clergymen at the Athenaeum Club abusing his practice of introducing reappearing characters, including Mrs. Proudie. Trollope recounts, "I got up, and standing between them, I acknowledged myself to be the culprit. 'As to Mrs. Proudie,' I said, 'I will go home and kill her before the week is over.' And so I did." He occasionally would lament having burned his bridges to Barsetshire and claimed he sometimes regretted having killed Mrs. Proudie—"so great was my delight in writing about Mrs. Proudie, so thorough was my knowledge of all the little shades of her character." Reviewers lamented that the series had come to an end: R.H. Hutton, arguably the most acute of Victorian critics, professed "loneliness very oppressive" at the prospect of never again meeting "the best known and most typical of his fellow-countrymen." Mrs. Oliphant in *Blackwood's Magazine* wrote, "We did not ask that this chronicle should be the last. We were in no hurry to be done with our old friends. And there are certain things which [Trollope] has done without consulting us against which we greatly demur. To kill Mrs. Proudie was murder, or manslaughter at the least. We do not believe she had any disease of the heart. She died not by natural causes, but by [Trollope's] hand in a fit of weariness or passion." The reviews singled out the novel as Trollope's best so far, and Mr. Crawley as Trollope's highest achievement. Hutton concluded, "Of its own kind, there has been no better novel ever written than *The Last Chronicle of Barset.*" Trollope himself thought *The Last Chronicle* his best novel.

In March 1878 Chapman and Hall issued a collected edition, *The Chronicles of Barsetshire.* The same project had come to grief in 1867 when George Smith had declined to buy the copyrights. When the uniform set finally appeared, Trollope wrote a brief introduction, explaining how the books, except for *The Warden* and *Barchester Towers,* were not intended to form a sequence, although one did exist "in the Author's mind": "I . . . had formed for myself so complete a picture of the cathedral town and the county in which I had placed the scene, and had become by a long-continued mental dwelling in it, so intimate with sundry of its inhabitants, that to go back to it and write about it again and again have been one of the delights of my life."

Henry James wrote of Trollope that he "did not write for posterity; he wrote for the day, for the moment; but these are just the writers that posterity is apt to put into its pocket." That is precisely what has happened.

N. JOHN HALL

See also Anthony Trollope

Further Reading

Epperly, Elizabeth R., *Patterns of Repetition in Trollope,* Washington, D.C.: Catholic University of America Press, 1989

Hall, N. John, *Trollope: A Biography,* Oxford: Clarendon Press, and New York: Oxford University Press, 1991

Hall, N. John, editor, *The Trollope Critics,* London: Macmillan, and Totowa, New Jersey: Barnes and Noble, 1981

Hall, N. John, editor, *The Letters of Anthony Trollope,* 2 vols., Stanford, California: Stanford University Press, 1983

Herbert, Christopher, *Trollope and Comic Pleasure,* Chicago: University of Chicago Press, 1987

Kendrick, Walter M., *The Novel-Machine: The Theory and Fiction of Anthony Trollope,* Baltimore: Johns Hopkins University Press, 1980

Kincaid, James R., *The Novels of Anthony Trollope,* Oxford: Clarendon Press, 1977

Page, Frederick, editor, *An Autobiography,* by Anthony Trollope (originally published, 1883), London and New York: Oxford University Press, 1950

Smalley, Donald, editor, *Trollope: The Critical Heritage,* London: Routledge and Kegan Paul, and New York: Barnes and Noble, 1969

Wall, Stephen, *Trollope: Living with Character,* New York: Henry Holt, 1989

Samuel Beckett 1906–89

Irish

Samuel Beckett is better known for his plays than for his fiction. Yet he has had as radical an effect on the development of fiction in the second half of the 20th century as on modern drama. It may be argued that he and Jorge Luis Borges laid the foundations of postmodern fiction. Where modernists had experimented with new forms that better lent themselves to what T.S. Eliot called "the immense panorama of futility and anarchy which is contemporary history," postmodernists attempted to subvert all varieties of artistic form in order to render the reality of the abyss, the nullity of postwar life. If, as Beckett believed, life constitutes an "issueless predicament" and amounts to a meaningless "void," then how is the postmodern writer to respond to this meaninglessness with words, those signs that cannot help but proliferate meaning? Beckett was obsessed by a desire to create what he called "a literature of the unword." He waged a lifelong war on words, which led him to startling innovations in form and language. His fictions offer a record of his struggle to force words to yield to the silence that underlies them and that, for him, represents the only true reality.

Beckett withheld from publication his first novel, *Dream of Fair to Middling Women,* written in 1932, until 1992. But he drew on it and used the same protagonist, Belacqua, for his first published work of fiction, *More Pricks Than Kicks* (1934), a collection of ten connected short stories. In both texts Belacqua, like his namesake in Dante's *Purgatorio,* aspires to silence and stasis. A failed artist, Belacqua defies the modernist obsession with (unconscious) motive, refusing for instance to reveal any reason for his decision to commit suicide. Beckett manipulates plot with the same capricious abandon. Major events such as marriage and death are mentioned in asides, while several pages are devoted to Belacqua's preparation of a sandwich. In both narratives the narrator intervenes metafictionally to stress the purely fictional nature of his antihero and to comment that "the only unity in this story [*Dream*] is, please God, an involuntary unity." *More Kicks* dismisses the language of *Dream* as "torrents of meiosis." This is a fair description of Beckett's early Baroque style in both narratives.

Beckett's next novel, *Murphy* (1938), shows him exercising greater control over language. He employs pun, paradox, allusion, repetition, and inversion in an attempt to disrupt the semantic function of language. He cultivates self-negating patterns of dialogue that parallel the protagonist's efforts to achieve physical stasis and mental communication with what he calls "the dark of absolute freedom." Beckett followed this, his most accessible novel, with *Watt* (1953), his most inaccessible one, written between 1942 and 1945. Even less eventful than his previous works, it contains familiar Beckett motifs that are not satisfactorily embedded in the fictional text. Watt's is an inner journey of the mind made up of ordered enquiries that only demonstrate the futility of human rationality. Watt (or What?), the wordy protagonist, is negated by another character, Knott (or Not), whose wordlessness turns What? into Whatnot, that which cannot be named.

In 1946 Beckett determined to investigate the darkness within him that he "had struggled to keep under." At about the same time he began writing in French because, he said, when using an alien language "it is easier to write without style." He delayed publishing his first French novel, *Mercier et Camier* (*Mercier and Camier*), until 1970, because he drew on it for *Waiting for Godot* (1952), the play that first established his international reputation. Next he wrote four novellas, which anticipate in form and theme the trilogy of novels that would establish him as a novelist of major stature. Between 1947 and 1949 he wrote *Molloy* (1951), *Malone meurt* (1951; *Malone Dies*), and *L'Innommable* (1953; *The Unnamable*). In each book the protagonist is progressively immobilized, finally reduced in the third novel to a disembodied voice. Using interior monologue, Beckett portrays human consciousness telling itself fictions about itself, each one aspiring to be the last. Simultaneously, Beckett portrays the predicament of the modern artist, which is "to fail, as no other dare fail." Each successive narrator pursues a more reductive excavation of the self, and each fails. Failure, it is implied, is inevitable for those using language as the means of reaching silence and death.

In *The Unnamable,* Beckett claimed, "there is complete disintegration." His next book, *Nouvelles et Textes pour rien* (1955; *Stories and Texts for Nothing*), a series of 13 short linked texts, "was an attempt," Beckett said, "to get out of the attitude of disintegration, but it failed." Yet its strategy of countering the linearity of language by a circularity of structure and repetition of motifs is put to brilliant use in Beckett's last full-length novel, *Comment c'est* (1961; *How It Is*). Searching for a postmodern form "that admits the chaos," Beckett offers a protagonist whose existence consists of crawling across the mud dragging a sack of canned food behind him. The novel, reminiscent of Canto 7 of Dante's *Inferno,* is divided into three sections in which the crawler remembers his old "life in the light," overtakes another crawler whom he tortures into speech, and is left alone waiting to be overtaken himself by another crawler who will torture him in turn. The circular form is accompanied by a radically pared down use of language that depends for its near-poetic effect on the blank spaces between each of the unpunctuated versets that constitute the text. The murmurings in the mud are so many stains on the silence to which the speaker and narrator aspire, a silence given visual and aural presence by the blank spaces in the text.

After *How It Is,* Beckett's fiction took the form of what he called "residua" or "têtes mortes" (death's-heads). These are not short stories but minimalist works of fiction. During the 1960s he wrote eight brief "Fizzles" and six more substantial texts: *All Strange Away* (1976; written 1963–64), *Imagination morte imaginez* (*Imagination Dead Imagine,* 1965), *Assez* (1966; *Enough*), *Le Dépeupleur* (1971; *The Lost Ones*), *Bing* (1966; *Ping*), and *Sans* (1969; *Lessness*). Except for *Enough,* the remaining five texts evolve from each other. In these "skullscapes," Beckett abandons the first person for an impersonality and reliance on mathematical calculations that still fail to fully represent the futility of human existence.

In the late 1970s, Beckett produced a second trilogy of novella-length texts. *Company* (1980), first written in English, is divided between a third-person description of one who lies on his back in the dark and a second-person voice that remembers scenes from the past that come close to autobiography. The subject is hopelessly split between these pronominal stand-ins that offer it delusive company. The last paragraph returns the "you" to where "you always were. Alone." *Mal vu mal dit* (1981; *Ill Seen Ill Said*) takes the postmodern penchant for self-referentiality to extreme lengths. Its subject is the process of composition itself. The imagination summons up a minimal scenario, an ill-seen image that is then consumed by the ill-said narrative that aspires to narrate it out of existence. In *Worstward Ho* (1983), Beckett starts by conjuring up images of a woman, an old man, a child, and a skull and progressively pares them down until he is left with "Three pins. One pinhole." He has effectually deconstructed realist narrative by prioritizing the marginalized act of narration and reinscribing plot and character within this new hierarchy. Simultaneously he strips language to its essentials in one final attempt to force it to express the inexpressible reality of nothingness. Of course he fails. But he fails magnificently. "On. Say on. Be said on. Somehow on. Till nohow on. Said nohow on." Beckett has many imitators, but no successors. As Joyce took modernism to its ultimate conclusion in *Finnegans Wake,* so Beckett not only helped initiate postmodernist fiction, but pursued it ruthlessly to a point that might prove to be its final expression.

BRIAN FINNEY

See also Molloy, Malone Dies, The Unnamable; Murphy

Biography
Born in Foxrock, near Dublin, Ireland, 13 April 1906. Attended Ida Elsner's Academy, Stillorgan; Earlsfort House preparatory school; Portora Royal School, County Fermanagh; Trinity College, Dublin (foundation scholar), B.A. in French and Italian 1927, M.A. 1931. French teacher, Campbell College, Belfast, 1928; lecturer in English, École Normale Supérieure, Paris, 1928–30; lecturer in French, Trinity College, Dublin, 1930–31; translator and writer in Paris in the 1920s and 1930s, and closely associated with James Joyce's circle; lived in Dublin and London, 1933–37; returned to Paris, 1937; joined French Resistance, 1940; fled to Roussillon in unoccupied France, where he lived, 1942–45; worked at the Irish Red Cross Hospital, St. Lô, France, 1945; resumed literary career in Paris after World War II, usually publishing his work both in French and English versions. Awarded Nobel prize for literature, 1969. Died 22 December 1989.

Novels and Major Works of Fiction by Beckett
(All translations from French to English by Beckett)
More Pricks Than Kicks, 1934
Murphy, 1938
Molloy, 1951; as *Molloy,* translated with Patrick Bowles, 1955
Malone meurt, 1951; as *Malone Dies,* 1956
L'Innommable, 1953; as *The Unnamable,* 1958
Watt, 1953
Nouvelles et Textes pour rien, 1955; as *Stories and Texts for Nothing,* translated with Richard Seaver, 1967
Comment c'est, 1961; as *How It Is,* 1964
Imagination morte imaginez, 1965; as *Imagination Dead Imagine,* 1965
Assez, 1966; as *Enough,* in *No's Knife,* 1967
Bing, 1966; as *Ping,* in *No's Knife,* 1967
Sans, 1969; as *Lessness,* 1971
Le Dépeupleur, 1971; as *The Lost Ones,* 1972
All Strange Away, 1976
Company, 1980
Mal vu mal dit, 1981; as *Ill Seen Ill Said,* 1982
Worstward Ho, 1983
Dream of Fair to Middling Women, 1992

Other Writings: plays for the stage (including *En attendant Godot* [1952; *Waiting for Godot*]), screenplays, and radio plays; theatrical notebooks, poems, and essays (including studies of Joyce's "Work in Progress" and Proust); also translator of poetry by Arthur Rimbaud, Guillaume Apollinaire, and others.

Further Reading
Abbott, H. Porter, *The Fiction of Samuel Beckett: Form and Effect,* Berkeley: University of California Press, 1973
Brienza, Susan, *Samuel Beckett's New Worlds: Style in Metafiction,* Norman and London: University of Oklahoma Press, 1987

Federman, Raymond, and John Fletcher, *Samuel Beckett: His Works and His Critics: An Essay in Bibliography*, Berkeley: University of California Press, 1970; London: University of California Press, 1971

Fletcher, John, *The Novels of Samuel Beckett*, New York: Barnes and Noble, and London: Chatto and Windus, 1964; 2nd edition, 1970

Kenner, Hugh, *A Reader's Guide to Samuel Beckett*, New York: Farrar Straus and Giroux, and London: Thames and Hudson, 1973

Knowlson, James, *Damned to Fame: The Life of Samuel Beckett*, New York: Simon and Schuster, and London: Bloomsbury, 1996

Knowlson, James, and John Pilling, *Frescoes of the Skull: The Later Prose and Drama of Samuel Beckett*, London: Calder, 1979; New York: Grove, 1980

Levy, Eric, *Beckett and the Voice of Species: A Study of the Prose Fiction*, Dublin: Gill and Macmillan, and Totowa, New Jersey: Barnes and Noble, 1980

Murphy, P.J., *Reconstructing Beckett: Language for Being in Samuel Beckett's Fiction*, Toronto: University of Toronto Press, 1990

Rabinovitz, Rubin, *Innovation in Samuel Beckett's Fiction*, Urbana: University of Illinois Press, 1992

Toyama, Jean Yamasaki, *Beckett's Game: Self and Language in the Trilogy*, New York: Peter Lang, 1991

Beginnings and Endings

Theories and Typologies of How Novels Open and Close

An author ought to consider himself, not as a Gentleman who gives a private or eleemosynary Treat, but rather as one who keeps a public Ordinary at which all persons are welcome for their money.
—Henry Fielding, The History of Tom Jones, A Foundling (1749)

Emma Woodhouse, handsome, clever, and rich, with a comfortable home and a happy disposition, seemed to unite some of the best blessings of existence; and had lived nearly twenty-one years in the world with very little to distress or vex her.
—Jane Austen, Emma (1815)

"*What's your name?*"
"*Fletch.*"
"*What's your full name?*"
"*Fletcher.*"
"*What's your first name?*"
"*Irwin.*"
"*What?*"
"*Irwin. Irwin Fletcher. People call me Fletch.*"
"*Irwin Fletcher, I have a proposition to make to you. I will give you a thousand dollars for just listening to it. If you decide to reject the proposition, you take the thousand dollars, go away, and never tell anyone we talked. Fair enough?*"
"*Is it criminal? I mean, what you want me to do.*"
"*Of course.*"
"*Fair enough. For a thousand bucks I can listen. What do you want me to do?*"
"*I want you to murder me.*"
—Gregory Mcdonald, Fletch (1979)

You are about to begin reading Italo Calvino's new novel, If on a winter's night a traveler.
—Italo Calvino, Se una notte d'inverno un viaggiatore (1979; If on a winter's night a traveler)

I lingered round them [the gravestones], under that benign sky; watched the moths fluttering among the heath and hare-bells; listened to the soft wind breathing through the grass; and wondered how any one could ever imagine unquiet slumbers for the sleepers in that quiet earth.
—Emily Brontë, Wuthering Heights (1847)

But the effect of her being [i.e., Dorothea Brooke's] on those around her was incalculably diffusive: for the growing good of the world is partly dependent on unhistoric acts; and that things are not so ill with you and me as they might have been, is half owing to the number who have lived faithfully a hidden life, and rest in unvisited tombs.
—George Eliot, Middlemarch (1872)

After a while I went out and left the hospital and walked back to the hotel in the rain.
—Ernest Hemingway, A Farewell to Arms (1929)

Beloved.
—Toni Morrison, Beloved (1987)

*   *   *

Although no set of four opening and four concluding gestures will adequately represent the range of beginnings and endings novelists have employed over time, these two groupings of first and last sentences should provide some concrete reminder of that variety. Indeed, generalizations about how novels began and ended in a single period are hard to maintain. Modernist novels, unlike their predecessors, it might be said, typically begin by plunging the audience inside the consciousness of a single protagonist. But exceptions abound: on the one hand, Jane Austen's *Persuasion* (1818), hardly a modernist novel, quickly takes us into Sir Walter Elliot's consciousness, while E.M. Forster's *A Passage to India* (1924) opens with the heterodiegetic narrator's description of the city of Chandrapore. As for endings, one might say that 18th-century novels typically have clear and firm closure while postmodern novels typically resist closure. But then we could point to Laurence Sterne's *Tristram Shandy* (1759–67), which arguably stops rather than ends, or to *If on a winter's night a traveler,* which winds up with an echo of its beginning that also strongly signals closure: the novel's "you" says to his companion, "just a moment, I've almost finished Italo Calvino's *If on a winter's night a traveler.*" Perhaps the wisest generalization about beginnings and endings is that they are what Peter J. Rabinowitz (1987) calls "privileged positions," places of special emphasis for both novelists and readers.

Beginnings have received less attention from theorists than endings, perhaps because novelistic beginnings seem less determinative of what happens next than endings do for what has happened before. (To take one notable dissenting view, Marcel Proust insisted that the key to everything in his massive *A la recherche du temps perdu* [1913–27; *In Search of Lost Time*] was to be found in the novel's beginning.) Although beginnings set novels in motion, there are multiple routes a novel may take after any beginning. An ending, on the other hand, provides a destination for the previous motion of the plot, a destination that may seem, in retrospect, to have been determining the beginning and the middle.

Although beginnings have not been discussed extensively by literary theorists, they have been considered both philosophically and formally. Edward Said's *Beginnings: Intention and Method* (1975) is an intriguing philosophical meditation on the concept of narrative beginning. Aristotle states in his wonderfully logical (although sometimes infuriating) way that a beginning is that which is not itself necessarily after anything else and has naturally something else after it. A.D. Nuttall (1992) resists the notion that a beginning is "not itself necessarily after anything else," maintaining instead that although everything except the origin of the universe may be seen as depending on some prior event, some natural events (such as births) and some formal events (such as the openings of narrative texts) deserve to be regarded as beginnings. Nuttall accompanies his philosophical argument with detailed practical criticism of a range of narratives from Virgil's *Aeneid* to Dickens' *Great Expectations* (1861).

Turning to more formal treatments, structuralist theorists, following Vladimir Propp (1968), who analyzed the basic functions underlying all Russian folktales, identify the beginning with the introduction of a lack. Psychoanalytic theorists such as Peter Brooks (1984) define the beginning as the initiation of narrative desire. In Phelan's work on narrative progression (1989), the beginning is identified as that which generates the progression of the narrative by introducing unstable relationships between characters (instabilities) or between implied author and reader or narrator and reader (tensions). These different perspectives obviously have much in common and suggest that beginnings not only set the narrative in motion but give it similar incentives and a particular direction.

Beginnings, however, involve more than igniting the engine that drives the plot. They provide exposition about character and setting, they invite readers to move from the world outside the novel to the world of the novel, and they establish relationships among authors, narrators, and audiences. In order to recognize the multiple functions of novelistic openings, four different aspects of beginning may be identified. The first two focus on the "aboutness" of the narrative and on the textual dynamics, while the second two focus on the reader's activity.

1. *Exposition*: This includes everything—even the front matter illustrations and epigraphs—that provides information about the story world, the characters (traits, past history, and so on), the setting (time and place), and events of the narrative. Exposition is the inclusive term that also covers background and orientation

2. *Initiation*: This is the revelation of the first set of global instabilities or tensions into the narrative. This moment in the narrative marks the boundary between the beginning and the middle. The initiation may come early or it may come late, but once it arrives the novel establishes its direction

3. *Introduction*: This includes the initial rhetorical transactions among implied author and narrator, on the one hand, and the flesh and blood and authorial audience on the other

4. *Entrance*: This involves the flesh and blood reader's multi-leveled—cognitive, emotive, ethical—movement from outside the text to a specific location in the authorial audience at the end of the initiation. One chief feature of the cognitive dimension of an entrance is the hypothesis, implicit or explicit, about the general direction of the novel formed by its audience

This conception of a beginning means that it is a unit whose length will vary considerably from narrative to narrative, since some beginnings will include more exposition than others and some will take longer to establish the first set of global instabilities or tensions. Thus, the initial sentences from *Tom Jones, Emma, Fletch,* and *If on a winter's night a traveler* quoted above are not complete beginnings, but they do indicate how the great variety of beginnings results in part from different initial emphases on different aspects of beginning. The first sentence of *Tom Jones* offers no exposition and initiation; instead, its function is to introduce the implied author to the audience and, with its explicit, metaphorical comment on the role of the author, to facilitate real readers' entrance into Fielding's fictional world. The first sentence of *Emma* is a classic example of exposition, efficiently conveying information about Emma's age, material circumstances, and character and preparing us for the initiation. The directness of the narrator's commentary contributes to the introduction and to the assumptions underlying that commentary—namely, that Emma's world is much like the reader's; it also smooths the audience's entrance into the novel.

The first sentences of *Fletch* combine exposition and initiation as they introduce the protagonist by name, give some sense of his attitudes toward crime, and establish the first major instability.

This dramatic scene also provides an effective introduction to Mcdonald's style even as the proposition itself reinforces an entrance for which the conventions of the detective novel are appropriate. The first sentence of *If on a winter's night a traveler* performs all four functions and develops a nice interplay between the exposition and the initiation. The exposition makes it clear that the "narratee" is about to begin reading the novel, but the initiation arises out of the tension between the actions of "you" and the authorial audience, which *has already begun* reading Calvino's not necessarily new novel. The sentence functions as an introduction to Calvino's playfulness and also as an entrance to a self-reflexive world in which the activity of reading will be foregrounded.

Theorists as distinguished as Walter Benjamin (1968) and Peter Brooks (1984) have advanced the claim that endings are the ultimate determiners of plot. This view is both logical and somewhat misleading. The logic resides in the fact that narratives are told retrospectively, which means that their narrators and ultimately their authors know how they end (although authors may not know the ending when they begin to compose, they certainly know it as they do final revisions). It is both natural and appropriate to assume that this knowledge of the end affects everything else: where and how to start, what to include or exclude, what to emphasize or de-emphasize from the beginning and the middle. But the claim about the power of endings is also misleading because it fails to recognize that endings are themselves constrained by beginnings and middles, and that all three parts of a plot are part of some overall design (whether successfully or unsuccessfully executed). In other words, while the ending of, say, *Persuasion* exerts an influence on how Austen begins the novel and manages the plot through the middle sections, that ending itself occurs within parameters that are established by the overall design of the plot as it is revealed from the beginning and the middle. If Anne Elliot were to become engaged to William Elliot rather than Frederick Wentworth, something would have gone radically wrong not with the beginning and the middle but rather with the ending of Austen's novel. At the same time, the authorial audience's emotional response to the ending is deeply influenced by the beginning and the middle, which have not only touched on Anne's earlier, missed opportunity to have become engaged to Wentworth but also emphasized the largely unhappy consequences of that missed opportunity. Anne's engagement to Wentworth could have come after many possible sequences, but because it comes after eight years of avoidable suffering, it has a very different emotional quality than, say, Elizabeth Bennet's engagement to Darcy in Austen's *Pride and Prejudice* (1813), and this different quality is very much a part of Austen's different design for this novel.

One reason Peter Brooks places so much emphasis on endings is that his psychoanalytic approach leads him to analogize the end of narrative to the end of life, the desire to reach the end with the death drive. Frank Kermode (1967) offers a highly engaging account about the relation between the formal endings of narrative and such natural endings as death and apocalypse; Kermode's book also discusses the relation between endings in narrative and endings in other realms of activity. David Richter (1974) presents an insightful analysis of formal devices of ending in "thesis novels," such as Samuel Johnson's *Rasselas* (1759) and Joseph Heller's *Catch-22* (1961). Marianna Torgovnick (1981) develops a helpful categorization of endings, suggesting that

novelistic endings need to be thought of along four different axes: their relation to beginnings and middles (circular, parallel, tangential, linking); the perspective they offer (overview or close-up); the relation between author and reader (complementary, incongruent, confrontational); and the author's awareness of the effects of the ending (self-aware, self-deceiving). D.A. Miller (1981) advances the deconstructive argument that endings never succeed in providing adequate closure because that which gives rise to narrative (the narratable) can never fully be contained or exhausted.

Phelan, influenced more by Richter than by Torgovnick or Miller, posits two related ways by which novelists signal endings: through signs of closure and through signs of completeness. In addition, novelists will sometimes seek to alter the audience's understanding of the action through the use of a coda. Signs of closure signal the end of the conditions of a novel's action or of its occasion of narration. Picaresque novels, for example, will signal closure by returning the *picaro* to the place from which his adventures began. Novels that employ a temporal or a numerical structure (Virginia Woolf's *Mrs. Dalloway,* 1925; Agatha Christie's *Ten Little Indians,* 1939) signal closure as they reach the end of that structure. Ring Lardner's "Haircut" signals closure by the barber-narrator's question to the customer-narratee, "Comb it wet or dry?" Signs of completeness are stronger signals of ending because they resolve the instabilities or tensions of a plot. In Austen's novels and others that involve the marriage plot, the engagement of the heroine is typically the signal of completeness. In the detective novel, the identification of the murderer is typically the signal of completeness. In thesis novels, completeness arises either from an accumulation of incidents all pointing to the same conclusion or from an especially telling example of the thesis. In modernist novels, completeness often entails some internal change in the protagonist rather than some significant external change of fortune.

A small sample of text will not provide a complete ending, but the four examples with which this essay begins do provide some sense of the variety of endings. In *Wuthering Heights,* completeness has occurred with the resolution of the instabilities surrounding Heathcliff's revenge on the Lintons through his apparently willed death and through the engagement of Cathy and Hareton. The final paragraph provides closure because Lockwood's visit to the graves as he leaves the Heights completes the sequence begun with his initial visit to Heathcliff on Lockwood's own taking up residence at Thrushcross Grange the previous year. His comment on the appearance of the graves also functions as a coda. Because Brontë has so firmly established Lockwood as an unreliable narrator, she effectively uses the coda to influence the audience's understanding of the resolution: if Lockwood is convinced that Heathcliff and Catherine rest quietly in their graves, we can be confident that their ghosts do, in fact, walk the moors. In *Middlemarch,* Eliot's final paragraph is an example of a more straightforward coda. The resolutions of the four main plots have already occurred and the "finale" is filled with signs of closure, including the narrator's remark that "every limit is a beginning as well as an ending." The last paragraph doesn't contain any new information about Dorothea's fate, but it does strongly establish Eliot's estimation of that fate: Dorothea is to be admired for what she is able to accomplish through her unhistoric acts. The coda, we should note, is persuasive not only because of Eliot's eloquent rhetoric but because Eliot has shown

Dorothea, particularly in her efforts to help Lydgate, capable of unselfish but effective action.

In *A Farewell to Arms,* the final sentence is a rare example of the coincidence of closure, completeness, and the very end of narrative. The closure occurs in the reported action: after trying to say good-bye to Catherine Barkley, who has just died giving birth to his child, Frederic Henry leaves the hospital to begin a new chapter of his life. The completeness occurs in the attitude conveyed through Frederic's style. The paratactic structure and the pace of the sentence reflect Frederic's slow, deliberate, measured departure, one that acknowledges his awareness of what he has lost in Catherine's death and his ability to carry on, despite the enormity of that loss. In *Beloved,* the final word comes at the end of a two-page coda that also adds to the completeness of the novel. Before this coda, many of the instabilities have been resolved: the community in Cincinnati chases Beloved away, and Paul D returns to Sethe and tells her that she is her own "best thing." But the final section develops the tension in the relationship between Morrison as implied author and her authorial audience of contemporary readers. What will you do with this story of slavery and its aftermath? she asks, and she goes on to insist that this is more than a story, that it is a legacy to be confronted. By ending with the single word *Beloved* she completes the challenge of both the final section and the novel as a whole because by this point *Beloved* represents the individual character whose story we have read as well as all who have come to America on the middle passage. The word is also an address to the audience, a final appeal: my beloved readers, what difference does this story make? Morrison's final section does not resolve the tension it establishes, but it provides a highly effective ending to her novel.

Of course, not all beginnings or endings will be as effective as the ones discussed here. The assessment of any beginning's or ending's effectiveness will require an examination not only of the specific details of the opening or closing pages but also of the larger context of the plot. However privileged and however exquisite or flawed, beginnings and endings are always already implicated in the larger structure of plots. In that sense, discussing them is itself only a beginning.

JAMES PHELAN

See also Framing and Embedding; Plot

Further Reading

Aristotle, *The Rhetoric and the Poetics of Aristotle,* New York: Modern Library, 1984

Benjamin, Walter, *Illuminations,* New York: Harcourt Brace, 1968; London: Cape, 1970

Blau DuPlessis, Rachel, *Writing Beyond the Ending: Narrative Strategies of Twentieth-Century Women Writers,* Bloomington: Indiana University Press, 1985

Brooks, Peter, *Reading for the Plot: Design and Intention in Narrative,* New York: Knopf, and Oxford: Clarendon Press, 1984

Kermode, Frank, *The Sense of an Ending: Studies in the Theory of Fiction,* New York: Oxford University Press, 1967

Miller, D.A., *Narrative and Its Discontents: Problems of Closure in the Traditional Novel,* Princeton, New Jersey: Princeton University Press, 1981

Nuttall, A.D., *Openings: Narrative Beginnings from the Epic to the Novel,* Oxford: Clarendon Press, and New York: Oxford University Press, 1992

Phelan, James, *Reading People, Reading Plots: Character, Progression, and the Interpretation of Narrative,* Chicago: University of Chicago Press, 1989

Propp, Vladimir, *Morphologie du conte,* Paris: Seuil, 1970; as *Morphology of the Folktale,* revised edition, Austin: University of Texas Press, 1968

Rabinowitz, Peter J., *Before Reading: Narrative Conventions and the Politics of Interpretation,* Ithaca, New York: Cornell University Press, 1987

Richter, David H., *Fable's End: Completeness and Closure in Rhetorical Fiction,* Chicago: University of Chicago Press, 1974

Said, Edward W., *Beginnings: Intention and Method,* New York: Basic Books, 1975

Sternberg, Meir, *Ekspozitsyah ve-seder mesirah bi-yetsirah ha-sipurit,* Jerusalem: Hebrew University of Jerusalem, 1971; as *Expositional Modes and Temporal Ordering in Fiction,* Baltimore: Johns Hopkins University Press, 1978

Torgovnick, Marianna, *Closure in the Novel,* Princeton, New Jersey: Princeton University Press, 1981

Aphra Behn 1640–89

English

Aphra Behn, known in her time primarily as the author of at least 19 staged plays, was always a reader of romances and novels. Her first written plays, dating from the late 1660s and early 1670s, take their plots or motifs from these sources, especially from the French romanticist La Calprenède and from the Spanish writer Miguel de Cervantes. In 1682 the two patent theatre companies set up by Charles II during the Restoration merged together, and far fewer new plays were required. Thus, playwrights moved to other forms of writing to make a living. In particular, they turned to fiction and translation. Behn began her novel career with the roman à clef *Love Letters Between a Nobleman and His Sister,* a long work that appeared anonymously in three parts between 1683 and 1687. It was based on a sensational aristocratic scandal of the time, the seduction of the young and virginal lady Henrietta Berkeley by her brother-in-law, Ford Lord Grey, a famous dissident and intimate of Charles II's wayward illegitimate son, the Duke of Monmouth. The book clearly was propaganda for the royalist government that Behn notably supported and, in its portrayal both of Monmouth and of Grey as inept or duplicitous rebels, it fulfilled this role. Nonetheless, during the writing, Behn became more and more fascinated with the possible fate of Henrietta Berkeley, rewritten as Silvia, a woman abandoned on the continent with only her wit and beauty with which to make a living. Although there is much about the Monmouth Rebellion of 1685 and its failure, and much of the interest in the displaying of fact as fiction, it is the extraordinary transformation of this woman, from an aristocratic daughter into a wandering whore, that is the main attraction of the book. There is nothing quite like *Love Letters* in English before Behn, although it has some resemblance to Lady Mary Wroth's withdrawn fiction, *Urania,* and to some scandalous chronicles of the French, especially Brémond's *Hattigem,* which details the affair of Charles II and Barbara Lady Castlemaine. However, these books have none of the heady eroticism of Behn's long work.

Her next foray into fiction was in story form. Toward the end of her life, when her much admired James II seemed to be tottering on his throne, Behn wrote a series of stories that seem to have had direct bearing on his political predicament. These stories called on her early years as a visitor to Surinam and as a spy in Antwerp. *The Fair Jilt* (1688), *Oroonoko* (1688), and *The History of the Nun* (1689) are spare stories that hint at extraordinary psychologies and manage to make a series of covert political points that could serve to warn the king of his danger and alert the nation to what was happening in high places. Like *Love Letters Between a Nobleman and His Sister, The Fair Jilt* was based on real events, part of which Behn took from English newspapers and part of which she probably learned from eyewitnesses in Antwerp. In the story, a manipulating woman uses her predatory sexuality to triumph over men, much as the heroine of *Love Letters* had done, but the hero who claims to be a prince is brought to the scaffold and nearly executed. A similar execution of James II following his father Charles I was fearfully anticipated if he did not tone down his pro-Catholic policies. In *Oroonoko,* set in Surinam, the parallels to James II are even closer, since a mixture of sincerity and gullibility brings down the black hero, prince in his land but slave in the English colony, much as was happening to James II. *The History of the Nun,* set in Flanders and drawing on the convent life Behn seems to have observed there, has a curious disjunction between the overt moral, the danger of failing to keep vows—England was planning to break its vow to the King—and the psychological dynamics that reveal a woman culturally constrained by impossible beliefs.

Most of the other novels ascribed to Behn were published posthumously and may well be hers. Then again, they may be, in part, clever forgeries produced by several young men, Charles Gildonk, Tom Brown, and Samuel Briscoe, in an attempt to capitalize on her name after she earned new fame following Thomas Southerne's 1696 dramatization of *Oroonoko.* Much may be genuine, however, and there are touches in the novels that remind the reader of Behn in other modes, especially in the Scarronesque "The Court of the King of Bantam," which describes the kind of Christmas feasting that Behn enjoyed, as well as alluding to some theatre performances that she may have attended. A similar story, "The Adventures of the Black Lady," also has some touches of Behn in its robust but scatterbrained heroine who comes close to the self-reliant and resilient heroines of her earlier plays. Other stories occasionally move away from Behn's known political and religious ideas. "The Unfortunate Happy Lady," for example, allows a rake to reform and provides unusual praise for a chapel-going councilor. It is possible that the story was written by Behn and later revised by her friend Brown, whose Protestantism was more in line with the view of this tale.

Behn's fictional works play with genre. For example, *Oroonoko* begins in the romantic world of La Calprenède, of wondrous warriors and chaste and fair brides in an African scene that has much in common with exotic oriental romance settings. It then moves to the realistic site of Surinam, with its mercenary settlers and brutal struggles. In the three novels, *The Fair Jilt, Oroonoko,* and *The History of the Nun,* as well as in *Love Letters,* Behn creates a narrator—a gossipy older person, more often than not a woman—who is as morally at sea as the reader. She is by no means omniscient: sometimes she plays a direct part in the plot, as in *Oroonoko;* at others, as in *The Fair Jilt* and *Love Letters,* she is an interested bystander who tends to feel commonplace emotions at the events and swings from side to side as actions and interpretations unfold. This creation of a narrative voice gives considerable complexity to Behn's work, and the reader is not given any firm ground on which to stand. That is because none of these stories has a single appropriate interpretation, and none has quite given up its political and psychological secrets.

In recent years, because of the burgeoning interest in gender, class, and especially race, *Oroonoko* has been the object of much study, particularly in the United States. The views occasionally expressed during the 18th and 19th centuries—that it is an abolitionist text—have been reiterated, while other critics have found Behn wanting in political correctness in her portrayal of Oroonoko, with his European features, his slave-owning habits, and his ambiguous relationship with the narrator.

JANET TODD

See also Oroonoko

Biography

Born c. 1640. May have lived in the British colony Surinam, c. 1663–64; served as an English spy in Antwerp during second Dutch war, 1666; imprisoned for debt in the late 1660s; arrested for opposing the Duke of Monmouth in her writings, 1682. Died 16 April 1689.

Fiction by Behn

Love Letters Between a Nobleman and His Sister, 3 vols., 1683–87
The Fair Jilt; or, The History of Prince Tarquin and Miranda, 1688
Oroonoko; or, The Royal Slave, 1688
The History of the Nun; or, The Fair Vow-Breaker, 1689
The Lucky Mistake, 1689
Histories and Novels, 1696; revised edition, 1697, 1700

Other Writings: plays (including *The Town Fop*, 1677; *The Rover*, 1677; *The Emperor of the Moon*, 1687), poetry, and translations.

Further Reading

Ballaster, Ros, *Seductive Forms: Women's Amatory Fiction from 1684 to 1740*, Oxford: Clarendon Press, and New York: Oxford University Press, 1992

Ferguson, Margaret, "Juggling the Categories of Race, Class and Gender: Aphra Behn's *Oroonoko*," *Women's Studies* (1991)

Hutner, Heidi, editor, *Rereading Aphra Behn: History, Theory, and Criticism*, Charlottesville: University Press of Virginia, 1993

Pearson, Jacqueline, "Gender and Narrative in the Fiction of Aphra Behn," *Review of English Studies* 42 (1991)

Todd, Janet, *The Secret Life of Aphra Behn*, London: André Deutsch, 1996; New Brunswick, New Jersey: Rutgers University Press, 1997

Todd, Janet, editor, *Aphra Behn Studies*, Cambridge and New York: Cambridge University Press, 1996

Belgian and Luxembourgeois Novel

Francophone

Belgium and Luxembourg are small countries fragmented by language divisions. Neither has a French-speaking population large enough to support an entirely autonomous literary market. Strongly oriented toward Paris as a consequence, Belgian and Luxembourgeois literature in French is nevertheless often treated as a poor cousin by the Parisian book industry. While Belgium and Luxembourg may share an uncomfortable position, similarities end there. This survey will discuss the two traditions separately.

Belgium

From the medieval period, the southern region of Belgium had been closely linked, culturally and economically, with the northern areas of France. Modern borders cut across a once cohesive area made up of Artois and Picardia (France), Flanders and Hainaut (Belgium). People spoke the *langue d'oïl* (early northern French) throughout that region and seem to have shared much the same oral tradition. The area is the birthplace of the *fabliaux*, comic tales in verse that first appeared in the 12th century. It is also associated with *Le Roman de Renart* (late 12th century; *Renard the Fox*), a collection of beast fables that parodies the heroic *chansons de geste*. The famous *chroniqueurs* (chroniclers) of the 14th and 15th centuries, retained by the dukes of Burgundy who dominated the region at the time, were, properly speaking, Belgian. Other early works include *Gillion de Trazegnies* (c. 1450), a tale influenced by the chivalric ideal that held sway at the Burgundian court, and the *Cent nouvelles nouvelles* (c. 1456–61), a collection of novellas chiefly notable with respect to the novel for their pursuit of narrative verisimilitude.

Although it is clear that these texts bear some relationship to Belgian literature, it would be inappropriate to see in them the beginnings of a national tradition—a difficulty nicely illustrated by the fact that they are all claimed by the French. In fact, Belgium was a possession of Spain from the 16th century until 1713, when it passed into Austrian hands. It was annexed by France in 1794 and by the Netherlands in 1815, upon the collapse of the Napoleonic empire. Independence was achieved in 1830, but as a result of divisions between speakers of French (or Walloon) and Flemish its cultural identity remained highly contested.

The period of the French and Dutch occupation saw the tentative beginnings of an independent intellectual life and a debate about national identity. The romantic movement stimulated discussions of national history and speculations about "l'esprit du Nord" (the northern spirit), which still continue today. Belgian printers, meanwhile, were engaged in piracy on a massive scale, distributing unauthorized editions of contemporary French works to various countries and infuriating their authors and authorized publishers. The phenomenon had two contrary effects. On the one hand, inexpensive pirated editions made French literature more accessible to the public, fostering the intellectual awakening of the country. At the same time, it encouraged the notion that all genuine literature emanated from Paris.

Broadly speaking, the first century of independence was marked by the effort to create a climate of autonomous cultural production and by a focus on national themes. Most literary production was in French, but cultural, historical, and geographical themes and motifs were predominantly Flemish. It is not surprising that Belgian writers should have turned to the historical novel. Henri Moke, for instance, wrote *Gueux de mer* (1827; The Sea Beggars), about the struggles against the Spanish in the 16th century. Such novelists as Jules de Saint-Genois and Jean-Baptiste Coomans, now almost entirely forgotten, wrote about the same period, helping to construct a national past that has had an enduring claim on the collective imagination. The novel of manners also found several practitioners in the early years of independence, but such works were highly derivative, and nothing of lasting value was produced.

Around mid-century, a fierce debate about realism with reference to painting and literature dominated Belgian literary circles.

A "populist" interpretation that focused, rather condescendingly, on the lives of the "little people" of the countryside and provincial towns was espoused by the majority of Belgian novelists at the time. The association between realism and regionalism marks the work of Emile Greyson and Joseph Demoulin, as well as a group of women writers who have recently been rediscovered—Marie Nizet, Henriette Langlet, Caroline Gravière, and the very young Marguerite Van de Wiele. The most notable novels of the realist era include *Dom Placide* (1875; Dom Placide), the only work of Eugène Van Bemmel. A historical novel, *Dom Placide* evokes, through a narrative of thwarted love, the final years of the Abbey of Villers-la-Ville until its destruction by French revolutionary troops. Xavier de Reul's *Roman d'un géologue* (1874; Novel of a Geologist) was also elevated to classic status immediately upon its publication. Another significant work of the time, Octave Pirmez's *Jours de solitude* (1869; Days of Solitude), consciously stands apart from the concerns of the realists. A meditative, even lyrical, autobiographical "portrait of the artist," it is primarily concerned with the nature of writing and the evocation of psychological reality.

Paul Heusy is the first of the Belgian naturalists. His *Un coin de la vie de misère* (1878; A Slice of Misery) signals the arrival of a new aesthetic for which the groundwork had been laid in the literary magazine *Uylenspiegel,* run by Félicien Rops. In different ways, Charles De Coster and Camille Lemonnier, both contributors to *Uylenspiegel,* led the "generation of 1880." De Coster had published *La Légende d'Ulenspiegel* (The Legend of Ulenspiegel) in 1867, a novel that broke with established convention and initially attracted little attention (so little, in fact, that De Coster died in abject poverty in 1879). Based on an ancient German legend, De Coster's characters—Thyl Ulenspiegel and Lamme Goedzak—are transplanted to the 16th century. The embodiment of freedom, reason, and resistance to oppression through humor, obscenity, and poetry, they have held an important place in the national imagination ever since the generation of 1880 adopted *Ulenspiegel* as its founding text.

The so-called Spring of 1880, generally associated with the magazine *La Jeune Belgique* (1881–97; Young Belgium), made itself felt primarily in poetry. Invoking De Coster and Octave Pirmez against middle-class values and conformism, the poets Emile Verhaeren and Georges Rodenbach, the playwright Maurice Maeterlinck, and the novelists Camille Lemonnier and Georges Eekhoud privileged art as the supreme value. However, social and political interests did not disappear altogether, reasserting themselves particularly in the novel.

Lemonnier, a Fleming writing in French, is one of the foremost members of the generation of 1880. One of his first publications, *Sedan* (1881; Sedan) was well received by the French naturalists. The novel that secured his reputation, *Un mâle* (1880; A Male) created a scandal in Brussels. He was accused of using an overwrought style and of displaying a bestial conception of humanity. Lemonnier had to defend himself in court three times on charges of endangering public morality, an experience he wrote about in *Les Deux Consciences* (1902; Double Consciousness). In *L'Hystérique* (1885; The Hysteric), he adopted a scientific naturalism, while in *Happe-chair* (1886) he wrote about the industrial proletariat and in *La Fin des bourgeois* (1892; The End of the Middle Class) about the capitalist class. In spite of an unmistakable orientation toward naturalism, Lemonnier's work has a lyrical quality that is based on an understanding of human ties to nature and finds particularly clear expression in *Au coeur frais de la forêt* (1900; In the Heart of the Forest).

A giant like Lemonnier, who easily survives comparison with Émile Zola, should not erase the memory of other novelists. Georges Eekhoud, for instance, mined a regional vein, first in *Kermesses* (1884; Carnivals) and later in *La Nouvelle Carthage* (1884; The New Carthage), a true novel of a city (Antwerp). Other regionalists included Eugène Demolder, Georges Virrès, Maurice des Ombiaux, Léopold Courouble, as well as, later on, Neel Doff and Jean Tousseul. A number of Walloon storytellers—Hubert Krains, Edmond Glesener, Louis Delattre, and Hubert Stiernet—may be grouped with the practitioners of the more conventional regional novel. Hubert Krains' tragic novel *Le Pain noir* (1904; Black Bread) and his collection of stories *Mes amis* (1921; My Friends) are among the most engaging works of the regional sensibility, which is sometimes wrongly accused of nostalgia for an idealized life on the land.

The novel that achieved the greatest international recognition was Georges Rodenbach's *Bruges-la-morte* (1892; *Bruges-la-morte*), often described as the only successful symbolist novel. A poet of the fin de siècle, Rodenbach constructed an imaginary Flanders, lost in the fogs of the north and resonating to perpetual funeral chimes. The novel first appeared with photographic illustrations of the actual city of Bruges, in a crossover with the genre of travel literature.

World War I, during which almost all of Belgium was occupied by German forces, created an intense break in Belgian literary production. In the wake of the war, the need for a profound revision of literary aesthetics was clear to all. André Baillon, identifiable as a symbolist before the war, was instrumental in establishing new forms of expression. He went to live in the countryside others had merely written about and wrote a series of autobiographical works preoccupied with modes of literary expression—*Moi quelque part* (1920; Me, Somewhere), *Un homme si simple* (1925; A Simple Man), and *Histoire d'une Marie* (1928; History of a Wife). The most radical in this series are *Délires* (1927; Delirium), which questions language itself and the identity of the speaking subject, and *Le Perce-oreille de Luxembourg* (1928; The Earwig of Luxembourg), which displays the same scepticism. Embracing a radical modernity and questioning the accepted definition of reason, Baillon, who was institutionalized several times, cultivated an intimate acquaintance with madness. His work establishes a strange connection, through the forms and conventions of regionalism, between a Baudelairean aesthetic of extremity and contemporary anxieties.

Franz Hellens underwent a similar development. His early work—stories with Flemish motifs and fantastical elements—shows the varied influence of Georges Rodenbach, Edgar Allan Poe, and Georges Eekhoud. After the war he tried his hand at several modernist projects, among them *Mélusine* (1920; Melusine), the first surrealist novel in Belgium; *Bass-Bassina-Boulou* (1922), a novel in the style of the *négritude* movement; and *Oeil-de-Dieu* (1925; The Eye of God), a parody of a police thriller. As leader of the important magazine *Le Disque Vert,* he devoted special issues to Freud and Chaplin. Following this experimental phase, Hellens began to develop a classical plain style in which he wrote the autobiographical trilogy *Frédéric* (1935) and *Les Nouvelles réalités fantastiques* (1931; New Fantastical Realities). One of his strongest works is *Mémoires d'Elseneur* (1954; Memories of Elseneur), in which his gift for the fantastical is given free rein to operate on his personal myths. He eventually developed a theory of "le fantastique réel," or fantastic realism, that relies on apparitions, talismans, and other forms of magic to create an atmosphere of "inquiétante étrangeté" (disturbing strangeness).

Hellens was one of the motive forces behind the *Manifeste du Groupe du Lundi* (1937; Manifesto of the Monday Group), which called for a move away from the accustomed preoccupation with nationalism and its associated Flemish themes. Instead, it proclaimed the universality of French and oriented itself strongly toward Paris. The most prominent of the Lundi writers was Charles Plisnier, who almost received the prestigious Prix Goncourt in 1936 for his collection of short stories *Faux-Passeports* (1936; False Passports). He was finally turned down because the judges could not decide whether it was appropriate to award the prize to someone not French. (He did receive the prize the following year, for *Faux-Passeports* and *Mariages* [1937; Marriages].) Plisnier's romans-fleuves *Mariages, Meurtres* (1939–41; Murders), and *Mères* (1946–49; Mothers) overturn accepted genre conventions through the admixture of surrealist motifs. Odilon-Jean Périer's *Le Passage des anges* (1926; The Passage of Angels), Eric de Haulleville's *Le Voyage aux îles Galapagos* (1934; Voyage to the Galapagos Islands), and Fernand Dumont's *La Région du coeur* (1939; Region of the Heart) evince a similar poetic.

The most widely read novelist of the 1930s was Marie Gevers, a francophone writer from Flanders. Closely linked to Antwerp, several of her works are in the regionalist tradition: *La Ligne de vie* (1937; Lifeline) and *Paix sur les champs* (1941; Peace over the Fields). Others, such as *La Comtesse des digues* (1931; The Countess of Dikes) concern themselves primarily with the status of women. Her masterpiece, *Madame Orpha* (1933), shows a highly original handling of point of view and register, which is also apparent later in the cyclical representation of time and the use of subjective viewpoints in *Plaisir des météores* (1938; The Pleasure of Meteors) and *Vie et mort d'un étang* (1961; Life and Death of a Pond).

Hellens' interest in paranormal phenomena also appears in the work of Gevers and other contemporary novelists. Robert Poulet's *Hanji* (1931) and *Les Ténèbres* (1934; Dusk) must be counted as examples of magic realism, and Marcel Thiry's work—*Échec au temps* (1945; Failure in Time) and *Juste ou la quête d'Hélène* (1953; Just, or the Search for Helen)—similarly shows a persistent preoccupation with the irrational and mythological. Michel de Ghelderode's *Sortilèges* (1941; Spells) shows a closer relationship with the tales of E.T.A. Hoffmann and is an example of a kind of national specialty also practiced by Jean Ray, Gérard Prévot, Jean Muno, and Thomas Owen. The fantastical novel *Malpertuis* (1943) by Jean Ray, which imagines the end of the Olympian gods, is a masterpiece of the genre.

Other writers of note emerging between the wars include Georges Simenon, who wrote serious realist fiction besides his famous Maigret detective series; Madeleine Ley, whose *Olivia* (1936) is an extraordinary love story that rewrites romance novel stereotypes; and Madeleine Bourdouxhe, who also transforms banal romance materials into serious fiction in *La Femme de Gilles* (1937; Gilles' Wife). The most innovative novel published on the eve of World War II may be the cyclical *Le Denier du rêve* (1936; A Coin in Nine Hands) by Marguerite Yourcenar, pseudonym of Marguerite de Crayencour.

After the war, women writers became more prominent. Susanne Lilar, with *Confession anonyme* (1960; Anonymous Confession), and Lilar's daughter Françoise Mallet-Joris, with *Rempart des béguines* (1951; Beguine Rampart), which created a scandal with its lesbian subject matter, led a group of distinguished female authors including Nicole Malinconi, Jacqueline Harpman, Amélie Nothomb, Françoise Lalande, Chantal Myttenaere, Véra Feyder, Anna Geramys, and many others.

Alexis Curvers, with *Tempo di Roma* (1957; The Time of Rome), and Charles Bertin, with *Journal d'un crime* (1961; Journal of a Crime) and *Les Jardins du désert* (1981; Gardens of the Desert) have published novels of a neoclassical sensibility that place themselves in the French tradition. Paul Dresse, with *Chronique de la tradition perdue* (1956–65; Chronicle of a Lost Tradition), and above all Daniel Gillès, with *Le Cinquième commandement* (1974–81; The Fifth Commandment) have continued the tradition of the roman-fleuve and its broad historical reach. A more complex relationship to history and language obtains in the work of Gaston Compère, including *Portrait d'un roi dépossédé* (1978; Portrait of a Dispossessed King), *L'Office des ténèbres* (1979; The Function of Dusk), and *Robinson 86* (1986; Robinson 1986), which are dedicated to complete freedom of expression to the point of abuse. The universe of Henry Bauchau, open to the voice of the unconscious, approaches uncertainty with more circumspection and hopefulness. His *La Déchirure* (1966; The Dismemberment), *Le Régiment noir* (1972; Black Regiment), and the unforgettable *Oedipe sur la route* (1990; Oedipus on the Way) have all made their mark.

The recent work of Jean Muno is marked by a questioning of convention sparked by a personal crisis recorded in *Ripple-Marks* (1976). His subsequent work includes the remarkable autobiographical *Histoire exécrable d'un héros brabançon* (1982; Adventures of an Execrable Hero from Brabant), as well as his best fantastical tales in the collection *Histoires singulières* (1983; Peculiar Histories).

Although Belgium has not produced any true adherents of the nouveau roman, several novelists are frequently accused of espousing that aesthetic. Dominique Rolin disdains conventional plotting in her *L'Infini chez soi* (1980; The Infinite at Home). Jacques-Gérard Linze had achieved a similar discourse in *La Conquête de Prague* (1965; The Conquest of Prague), in which the conquest is that of identity, an undertaking devoted to failure. His *L'Étang Coeur* (1967; Pond Heart) and *La Fabulation* (1968; Fabulation) insist on the existential incomprehension of being and the world that may also be found in the work of Guy Vaes, particularly *Octobre long dimanche* (1956; October Long Sunday). Nicole Malinconi has written the moving *Hôpital silence* (1985; Hospital Silence) and *L'Attente* (1989; The Waiting), which evince a kinship with the work of Marguerite Duras. Although these four novelists show the strongest influence of the "nouveau romanciers," all Belgian fiction published after 1970 registers their presence to some degree. The work of Paul Emond in particular testifies to their influence with novels such as *La Danse du fumiste* (1979; Dance of the Smoker), an astonishing soliloquy written in a single sentence. Pierre Mertens, a brilliant stylist who has received recognition in Paris, has, for that reason, achieved greater visibility for his quests of identity, *L'Inde ou l'Amérique* (1969; India or America), *Les Bons offices* (1974; Good Offices), and *Les Éblouissements* (1987; Shadowlight). The decade of the 1990s has been dominated by a host of young novelists, whose numbers ensure a rich future for the Belgian novel.

Luxembourg

The Grand Duchy of Luxembourg has shared in many of the annexations that lie in Belgium's past, but this tiny country nevertheless achieved a sense of national identity much earlier in its history as a consequence of its early prominence in the European political landscape. A fief of the Holy Roman Empire in the late Middle Ages, Luxembourg's ruling family supplied such important monarchs as Henry VII of Germany (later Holy Roman emperor) in the 14th century. Henry's son John of Luxemburg became the ruler of Bohemia only a few years after Henry assumed the German throne, while Henry's great-grandson was the Holy Roman emperor Charles IV. However, Luxembourg lost its independence to the Burgundians in the mid–15th century, and it was passed from Burgundy to Spain to Austria and finally to France in subsequent centuries. With the reorganization of Europe after the collapse of the Napoleonic empire, Luxembourg became nominally independent, but in effect the grand duchy fell under Dutch influence, while part of Luxembourg was subsequently incorporated into Belgium. Independence was further formalized in 1867, but Luxembourg did not pass out of the control of the Dutch royal family until 1890.

Luxembourgeois, French, and German are the country's officially recognized languages, and many inhabitants speak all three. Indeed, many Luxembourgeois writers have adopted different languages in different works. French, however, has long been the language of the middle class and of government functions.

As Georges Rodenbach "invented" Flanders when he lived in Paris, so Félix Thyes wrote the first francophone Luxembourgeois novel at Brussels. Occasionally guilty of cosmetic touch-up, his portrait of Luxembourg rather tends toward the nostalgic. *Marc Bruno, profil d'un artiste* (1855; Marc Bruno, Profile of an Artist), the history of a workingman's love for an aristocratic lady, is suffused with the revolutionary spirit of 1848.

In the 20th century, the regional inspiration of *Marc Bruno* found expression in Nicolas Ries *Le Diable aux champs* (1936; The Devil in the Fields), which he called a "simple history." This novel of the land is marked by a concern for tradition and a sense of fatalism that, in this genre, is often associated with rural society. Firmly identified with realist conventions, the tragic romantic novel *Folle jeunesse* (1938; Mad Youth) by Nicolas Konert is also set in the Luxembourgeois vineyards and attempts a psychological portrait of the people of the Mosel Valley.

World War II served to reinforce the nationalism of the Luxembourgeois, but sparked modes of expression that were less popular in nature. The novelist Willy Gilson, for instance, started out with *Le Chevalier aux fleurs* (1933; Knight with Flowers), which evinces a clear affinity with the fairy tale, but in the wake of the war, in *Je maintiendrai* (1947; I Will Endure), he adopted a very different tone that reflects the bitter experiences of the occupation. Albert Borschette catches the same tone in his *Continuez à mourir* (1959; Continue to Die).

Joseph Leydenbach, himself a banker as well as a novelist, is the premier chronicler of the middle class in modern industrialized Luxembourg. *Les Désirs de Jean Bachelin* (1948; The Desires of Jean Bachelin) evokes the conflict between the protagonist's wish for beauty and happiness and the necessities of life, a theme that returns in the later *Jeu d'échecs* (1976; Chess Game). Leydenbach favors linear plotting and classical form. Tracing the socioeconomic evolution of his country since 1945, his work also probes the most private aspects of human existence.

The most visible woman writer in Luxembourg is Rosemarie Kieffer. However, she has written several *feuilletons* (serial novels) and many shorter fictions, but no true novel.

Luxembourg's first women's novel appeared very late: Noëlle Noli published *Il neigeait à Val Fex* (It Snowed in Fex Valley) in 1975 and Maria C. Haller came out with *Le Chemin de Cannobio* (The Road of Cannobio) in 1995. Both novelists situate their characters in medical environments, a plotting device also adopted by Albert Mambourg, a physician, in *Approches* (1973; Approaches) and *Le Crime parfait* (1975; The Perfect Crime), which register the influence of the nouveau roman. Another physician, Georges Erasme, initially wrote a novel about the theatre and the two-volume family chronicle *Histoire d'une famille luxembourgeoise* (1991–92; History of a Luxembourgeois Family). But he finally turned to his own profession for setting and theme in *Armand et les chimères hippocratiques* (1996; Armand and the Hippocratic Chimaeras).

The most recent wave of Luxembourgeois fiction is full of promise. Jean Portante debuted with *Projets pour un naufrage prémédité* (1987; Projects for a Premeditated Shipwreck), which renounces consistent psychological analysis to develop a deeper understanding of uncertainty. *Un deux cha-cha-cha* (1990; One Two Cha-Cha-Cha) is a novel of successive emigrations that finally take the narrator to Cuba in search of himself. Put forward as the best novel ever written in Luxembourg, *Mrs. Haroy, ou, La Mémoire de la baleine* (1993; Mrs. Haroy, or, the Memory of Whaling), a Bildungsroman and a chronicle of immigration, simultaneously offers an amused portrait of contemporary Luxembourgeois society from the perspective of an outsider. Another major novelist who has appeared in recent years is Jean Sorrente, whose first work, *La Visitation* (1990; The Visitation), is perhaps better classified as a text than a novel. As *La Visitation* progresses, the story crumbles and finally disappears altogether. Whereas Portante has relied on his story-telling ability, Sorrente concentrates on the discontinuities of identity crisis. The characters from his first novel reappear in *Nuits* (1994; Nights), which renews earlier questions about the reality and validity of experience in different states of consciousness. Sorrente opens up a painful past in *Le Vol de l'aube* (1995; Dawn Flight), about the voluntary collaboration of German-speaking Belgians with the Nazis during World War II. Indirectly, the novel also speaks to Luxembourg's own history of collaboration.

Lambert Slechter also questions the assumptions of the traditional novel. His first, *Angle mort* (1988; Blind Angle), is a kind of diary in which style is subordinated to plot. The first two volumes of *Pieds de mouche* (1990–91; Fly Feet) are subtitled "little prose pieces" and continue Slechter's project of self-analysis and the simultaneous disassembly of the plot. However, the third volume of *Pieds de mouche*, although it has much the same character as the first two, is subtitled "novel"—underscoring the fact that Slechter, with other young writers, means to reinvent the Luxembourgeois novel.

PIERRE HALEN
(Translated by Marijke Rijsberman)

See also Netherlandish Novel

Further Reading

Aron, Paul, editor, *Charles Plisnier: Entre l'Evangile et la Révolution,* Brussels: Labor, 1988

Aron, Paul, editor, *La Belgique artistique et littéraire: Une anthologie de langue française (1848–1914),* Brussels: Complexe, 1997

Block, Jane, editor, *Belgium: The Golden Decades, 1880–1914,* New York: Peter Lang, 1997

Charlier, Gustave, and Joseph Hanse, editors, *Histoire illustrée des lettres françaises de Belgique,* Brussels: Renaissance du Livre, 1958

Durand, Pascal, and Yves Winkin, *Marché éditorial et démarches d'écrivains: Un état des lieux et des forces de l'édition littéraire en Communauté française de Belgique,* Brussels: Communauté française de Belgique, 1996

Gérard, Marcel, *Le roman français chez nous,* Luxembourg: St. Paul, 1968

Hanse, Joseph, *Charles De Coster,* Brussels: Palais des Académies, 1928

Kieffer, Rosemarie, editor, *Littérature luxembourgeoise de langue française,* Sherbrooke, Quebec: Naaman, 1980

Klinkenberg, Jean-Marie, "La production littéraire en Belgique francophone: Esquisse d'une sociologie historique," *Littérature* 44 (December 1981)

Linkhorn, Renée, editor, *La Belgique telle qu'elle s'écrit: Perspectives sur les lettres belges de langue française,* New York: Peter Lang, 1995

Pope, Frederick Russell, *Nature in the Work of Camille Lemonnier,* New York: Institute of French Studies, Columbia University, 1933

Quaghebeur, Marc, "Balises pour l'histoire de nos lettres," in *Alphabet critique des lettres belges de langue française,* Brussels: Association pour la Promotion des Lettres belges, 1982

Schroeder, Muriel, "Le Statut de la femme dans quelques romans luxembourgeois de langue française," Dissertation littéraire, Luxembourg, 1994

Thyes, Félix, *Marc Bruno, profil d'artiste,* Luxembourg: Centre d'études de la littérature luxembourgeoise, 1990

Trousson, Raymond, and Robert Frickx, editors, *Lettres françaises de Belgique: Dictionnaire des oeuvres,* Paris: Duculot, 1988–94

Turquet-Milnes, Gladys Rosaleen, *Some Modern Belgian Writers: A Critical Study,* London: Muirhead, 1916; New York: McBride, 1917

Van Welkenhuyzen, Gustave, *L'Influence du naturalisme français en Belgique de 1875 à 1900,* Brussels: Renaissance du Livre, 1930

Weisgerber, Jean, editor, *Les Avant-gardes littéraires en Belgique: Au confluent des arts et des langues, 1880–1950,* Brussels: Labor, 1991

Wilhelm, Frank, "Études sur la littérature luxembourgeoise de langue française," Thèse de doctorat, Paris IV-Sorbonne, 1992

Saul Bellow 1915–

United States

Saul Bellow's first published novel, *Dangling Man* (1944), opened with a manifesto that declared his formal rejection of Ernest Hemingway's "tough guy" model of American fiction and openly espoused the powers of feeling and intelligence. For Bellow's narrator, who transgresses the prevailing code by keeping a personal diary of his alienation, the 1940s were an era of "hardboileddom," dominated by the tough guy and athlete. The narrator sums up that attitude in a series of questions: "Do you have feelings? There are correct and incorrect ways of indicating them. Do you have an inner life? It is nobody's business but your own. Do you have emotions? Strangle them."

With the introspective, self-questioning, urban heroes of *Dangling Man* and *The Victim* (1947), Bellow charted a new course for the American novel away from its pastoral, romance form and atemporal engagement with American dreams and toward a renewed engagement with ideas and an organic connection with Europe. Strongly influenced at the beginning of his career by Trotskyism and the *Partisan Review* group of intellectuals, Bellow continued to demonstrate as his distinctive qualities a thorough awareness of the intellectual currents of the day, a persistent engagement with the movement of history, and an eclectic gathering of a wide range of cultural fields and traditions (see Hyland, 1992). This eclecticism is reflected in the variety of responses to his work. John J. Clayton takes a strongly psychoanalytic view, discovering within the works a psychic pattern based on Oedipal conflicts and the fear of deserved death (see Clayton, 1979). Judie Newman, on the other hand, reads Bellow as deeply engaged with Nietzsche's "sixth sense," the sense of history (see Newman, 1984). Ellen Pifer's essential thesis is that each of Bellow's protagonists is polarized between the alternative claims of reason (which ultimately failed) and faith (which finally triumphs); that Bellow's development reflects a deepening commitment to articulating the reality of the soul; and that his opposition to the ruling orthodoxies of secularism makes him a radical writer (see Pifer, 1990). Psyche, History, and Soul continue to be identified as central to Bellow's fiction, although they are variously weighted in different critical readings. Opinion also divides over the question of Bellow's affirmative qualities, some critics seeing an Emersonian denial of evil, while others find a darker side in his work.

Voice (and particularly monologue) was identified almost immediately as the unifying characteristic of Bellow's fiction, from the first published story ("Two Morning Monologues") to the rhetorical, declamatory protagonists of such later works as *Herzog* (1964), *Humboldt's Gift* (1975), *The Dean's December* (1982), and *More Die of Heartbreak* (1987), who are often mistaken for mere mouthpieces of their creator. Sharp, ironic effects are fostered by the problematic relation of author-character-narrator, while Bellow's characteristically rich mixture of high seriousness, low comedy, esoteric reference, street slang, lyrical power, and savage wit speed the reader through a thickly textured realist world, densely populated with memorable characters. Drawing upon his Russian-Jewish heritage and his American immigrant upbringing, Bellow uniquely brings together the worlds of high and popular culture, employing his early training in social anthropology to present his vision of society, in the manner of a participant-observer, simultaneously engaged and critically detached. Motifs from social anthropology provide structural pivots in the plots of *Seize the Day* (the trickster figure), *Henderson the Rain King* (East African cattle cultures), *Humboldt's Gift* (gift exchange), "Mosby's Memoirs" (death customs), and "Cousins" (shamanism), among others. Bellow's associated reading in psychoanalytic theory is also mined for comic effect with debts to Otto Rank's account of the double (*The Victim*), biting attacks on naive Freudianism in his play *The Last Analysis* (1965) and *Herzog*, and a final phase (*The Dean's December, More Die of Heartbreak, A Theft*) of deepening debate and engagement with the writings of Jung. Bellow's intertextuality is creative, complex, and something of a challenge to most of his readers.

Although a remarkably unified achievement, Bellow's oeuvre falls into several phases of development, beginning with an initial period of "victim literature" and featuring tightly controlled, short, and spatially ordered forms, of which *Seize the Day* (1956) is a good example. A major change in style occurred with the publication of *The Adventures of Augie March* (1953), a loose and baggy monster of a novel—exuberant, unapologetic, picaresque, and ebullient—which made in its title explicit homage to Mark Twain and declared itself as defiantly American. *Augie March* prepared readers for the comic invention of its equally picaresque successor, *Henderson the Rain King* (1959).

It was *Herzog*, however, that established Bellow's reputation and initiated his great theme—memory. Mr. Sammler, Willis Mosby, Dean Corde, the unnamed narrator, the founder of the Mnemosyne Institute, *The Bellarosa Connection* (1989), and the central figures of "Cousins" (1984) and "A Silver Dish" (1984) are all memory-driven characters, deeply and imaginatively engaged in coming to terms with the past. Even Bellow's nonfiction, *To Jerusalem and Back* (1976), a personal account of a visit to Israel (from a decidedly pro-Israeli perspective) is conceived as a journey back into his own past. "It is my childhood revisited," he declares in the opening paragraph, contemplating a group of Hasidim.

Unlike many American novelists, Bellow is less concerned with "making it new," than with revisiting the old. The orientation toward the past, especially when combined with unreliable narrator/mouthpieces, has not always enhanced Bellow's reputation. Critics have been particularly harsh regarding Bellow's portrayal of women, chastising his tendency to create images of sadistic brutes, compliant slaves, sex goddesses, or pseudointellectuals. Bellow's treatment of race in *Henderson the Rain King*, *Mr. Sammler's Planet* (1970), and *A Theft* (1989) also has generated complaints of racial "othering" on the author's part, although later criticism has defended Bellow's exposure of the violent specular machinery of racial optics and his challenge to binarized tropes of blackness. Robustly independent of current critical and cultural fashions, Bellow remains a deeply thought-provoking novelist for whom answers to such problems as race never come easily.

JUDIE NEWMAN

See also Herzog

Biography
Born in Lachine, Quebec, Canada, 10 June 1915; as a child lived in Montreal; family moved to Chicago, 1924. Attended Tuley High School, Chicago, graduated 1933; University of Chicago, 1933–35; Northwestern University, Evanston, Illinois, 1935–37, B.S. (honors) in sociology and anthropology 1937; graduate study in anthropology at University of Wisconsin, Madison, 1937. Served in the US Merchant Marine, 1944–45. Teacher, Pestalozzi-Froebel Teachers College, Chicago, 1938–42; member of the editorial department, "Great Books" project, *Encyclopaedia Britannica*, Chicago, 1943–44; freelance editor and reviewer, New York, 1945–46; has taught at several universities in the United States, including the University of Minnesota and the University of Chicago. Coeditor, *Noble Savage*, New York, then Cleveland, 1960–62. Awarded Nobel prize for literature, 1976.

Novels by Bellow
Dangling Man, 1944
The Victim, 1947
The Adventures of Augie March, 1953
Seize the Day, 1956
Henderson the Rain King, 1959
Herzog, 1964
Mr. Sammler's Planet, 1970
Humboldt's Gift, 1975
The Dean's December, 1982
More Die of Heartbreak, 1987
A Theft, 1989
The Bellarosa Connection, 1989

Other Writings: essays, short stories, and plays (including *The Last Analysis*, 1965).

Further Reading
Bach, Gerhard, editor, *Saul Bellow at Seventy-Five: A Collection of Critical Essays*, Tübingen: Gunter Narr, 1991
Clayton, John J., *Saul Bellow: In Defense of Man*, Bloomington: Indiana University Press, 1968; 2nd edition, 1979

Cronin, Gloria, and L.H. Goldman, editors, *Saul Bellow in the 1980s,* East Lansing: Michigan State University Press, 1989

Fuchs, Daniel, *Saul Bellow: Vision and Revision,* Durham, North Carolina: Duke University Press, 1984

Hyland, Peter, *Saul Bellow,* London: Macmillan, and New York: St. Martin's Press, 1992

Newman, Judie, *Saul Bellow and History,* London: Macmillan, and New York: St. Martin's Press, 1984

Pifer, Ellen, *Saul Bellow: Against the Grain,* Philadelphia: University of Pennsylvania Press, 1990

Saul Bellow Journal, special issue on *More Die of Heartbreak* 11:1 (1992)

Beloved by Toni Morrison

1987

When *Beloved* received the Pulitzer Prize, the event simultaneously marked Toni Morrison's prominence within contemporary American letters and a turning point in her fiction. In an interview shortly after the publication of the novel, Morrison remarked,

> We live in a land where the past is always erased and America is the innocent future in which immigrants can come and start over, where the slate is clean. The past is absent or it's romanticized. This culture doesn't encourage dwelling on, let alone coming to terms with, the truth about the past. That memory is much more in danger now than it was 30 years ago.

In *Beloved,* Morrison sets out to discover the truth about the racial past of the United States. She bases the novel on a historical incident: the story of Margaret Garner, an escaped slave who kills her children rather than have them return with her to slavery. In Morrison's novel, the heroine, Sethe, is haunted by the ghost of her murdered baby girl. The arrival of Paul D, who had been enslaved with Sethe before emancipation, drives away the specter, but she returns in corporeal form as "Beloved"—the only name on her tombstone—to continue her vengeance.

Beyond the importance of the subject matter, the significance of the novel lies in its fusion of oral folk tradition with modern techniques of magic realism and postmodern ontological ambiguity. Morrison's formal innovation lies in the role of the narrator, who gives an oral-aural dimension to the fiction. In a 1988 interview, Morrison comments on this quality of her work:

> Even though I don't speak it when I'm writing it, I have this interior piece, I guess, in my head that reads, so that the way I hear it is the way I write it and I guess that's the way I would read it aloud. The point is not to need the adverbs to say how it sounds but to have the sound of it in the sentence, and if it needs a lot of footnotes or editorial remarks or description in order to say how it sounded, then there's something wrong with it.

In *Beloved,* Morrison creates an oral-aural narrative tone to explore the meaning of American slavery. The past that is so unspeakably horrific and painful is recalled through the characters' "rememory" as fragments are brought with difficulty to consciousness, where they can be exorcised. Only by confronting the demons of the past can the characters find peace and healing. The narrator determines the pace of the release of memories by Sethe and Paul D, interposing the stories of Grandmother "Baby" Suggs, Sixo, the Cherokee people, Ella, and Stamp Paid. Suffering, deprivation, loneliness, despair, and injustice form recurring motifs in the stories of black people's lives, countering that other thematic motif, the power of white ideology, which takes shape in the stories of the Kentucky plantation Sweet Home and the owners, the Garners; the story of Amy, the servant girl who has escaped her indenture and is heading for Boston; and the story of the abolitionist brother and sister, the Bodwins.

All the characters are destroyed by their confrontation with white power. Sethe sees Beloved's return as an opportunity to explain why she had killed her rather than allow her to be taken back into slavery: worse than death was "what Baby Suggs died of, what Ella knew, what Stamp saw, and what made Paul D tremble. That anybody white could take your whole self for anything that came to mind." After her redemption by her son Halle, Baby Suggs starts preaching to raise black consciousness, urging people to claim their freedom by claiming pride in their bodies and themselves, to counter the poison of institutionalized racism. But she is defeated, first by the Fugitive Slave Law and then by the spectacle of her daughter-in-law killing her own children. Though Baby Suggs is legally free, the slave-catchers still enter her house to claim Sethe and the children. Morrison suggests that in this world, all blacks are forced to see themselves from a racist perspective, which Baby Suggs names "the Misery." "The Misery" is the reason Sethe kills.

At first, Sethe is amused by her owner, "Schoolteacher," who measures the slaves, counts their teeth, and asks questions, until she understands that this behavior is an expression of his inability to recognize the slaves as human beings. Sethe refuses to submit to Schoolteacher's racial vision and escapes. But this assertion of self alienates the black community and compromises the success of her escape. Without the support of the community, which has been corrupted by the perverted values of white racism, Sethe is isolated and the slave-catchers discover her. Her subsequent attempt to murder her children rather than return them to slavery is also an act of self-definition, of agency, in the only way available to her.

A significant condition of white supremacy is that blacks can direct their anger, rage, and aggression only inwardly, in acts of self-destruction. Of all the members of the outraged black community, only Stamp Paid realizes, finally, the significance of Sethe's action and how it demonstrates the extent of white power over black lives. This realization makes him understand that the ghost haunting 124 Bluestone Road is not singular but plural, that the voices are not personal but political, and that the people who speak are all those who have been tortured, lynched, and murdered.

Realization, when it comes in this narrative, is the result of a reluctant and painful piecing together of the torn fragments of history. The narrative is characterized by twin movements of fragmentation and repetition. This duality may be seen in Morrison's handling of time: the narrative opens in medias res. Only gradually do readers learn that 1873 is the present; that 1855 is the year of Sethe's escape; and that she enjoys only 28 days of freedom. Time before the escape is generalized and imaged by the slave plantation, Sweet Home; time since her escape is measured against the loss of her baby and the onset of the haunting. Slave time is fractured, repetitious, and obsessive. The impulse to fragmentation reaches a pitch in the section that begins, "I am Beloved and she is mine." In this section, an accumulation of nightmarish images presents the full horrors of slavery: conditions on board the slave ship, the suffocation, the stench of rotting flesh, the rats, the deafening noise of human suffering; and then the soul-destroying indignities of manacles and neck halters, loss, and pain. The near incoherence of the narrative in places is counterbalanced by the obsessive repetition of narrative units, words, phrases, and images. Elements that keep returning include Schoolteacher's view of blacks as animals, Paul D's accusation that Sethe has behaved like an animal, and Stamp's unanswered questioning of the humanity of the lynchers. Biblical references permeate the text as does imagery associated with food, particularly the theft of Sethe's baby milk and the blackberry feast that is interrupted by the arrival of the slave-catchers. Snippets of story are repeated, gathering significance and clarity with each repetition, until gradually the fragments come together in a ritual of accelerating repetition and assume the stature of myth. So, too, is Sethe's trauma repeated in her mind until, at the end of the novel, she attacks Mr. Bodwin, mistaking him for Schoolteacher. In this way—by directing her fury at a legitimate target (a white man)—Sethe is able to exorcise the ghost of her past, and Beloved disappears.

The fragmented narrative mirrors the fragmented subjectivity of the slave. Paul D, for instance, advises against loving things that are too big or loving too much. The suggestion is that slaves deal in pieces, not wholes; that they do not see the grand picture because they are pawns rather than agents in the history that affects them. In *Beloved,* Morrison creates that grand picture as a corrective to the history of slavery and Reconstruction seen through the eyes of whites. First, she focuses upon the experience of slavery for women, emphasizing the ways in which the experience of marriage, childbirth, and motherhood is unique for enslaved black women. In a sense she is writing against a masculine view of slavery. Second, she presents this history as a legacy to the 20th century, particularly in the failure of the black family. For instance, Baby Suggs has no way to trace her husband or children who have been sold; Sethe has no effective model of motherhood to follow, as Baby Suggs lost all her children except Halle, and Sethe's mother (whose offspring were almost exclusively the result of rape) remains a shadowy figure in her recollection. Thus, racial, personal, and national history coincide—reluctantly but necessarily—as the future that must be claimed by blacks who take possession of their own selves in order to become truly free.

DEBORAH L. MADSEN

See also Toni Morrison

Further Reading

Bloom, Harold, editor, *Toni Morrison,* New York: Chelsea House, 1990

Carmean, Karen, *Toni Morrison's World of Fiction,* Troy, New York: Whitston, 1993

Harris, Trudier, *Fiction and Folklore: The Novels of Toni Morrison,* Knoxville: University of Tennessee Press, 1991

Heinze, Denise, *The Dilemma of "Double-Consciousness": Toni Morrison's Novels,* Athens: University of Georgia Press, 1993

Mbalia, Doreatha D., *Toni Morrison's Developing Class Consciousness,* Selinsgrove, Pennsylvania: Susquehanna University Press, and London: Associated University Presses, 1991

Rigney, Barbara Hill, *The Voices of Toni Morrison,* Columbus: Ohio State University Press, 1991

A Bend in the River by V.S. Naipaul

1979

V.S. Naipaul's seventh full-length novel, *A Bend in the River* belongs to the small group of novels written by non-Europeans in the tradition known, since M.J.C. Echeruo's *Joyce Cary and the Novel of Africa* (1973), as "the European novel of Africa," a genre that exploits the African setting and "various [European] myths of Africa" to explore a supposedly universal human condition. The novel's subject matter is the violent cycle of false starts at self-renewal in newly independent African states following the withdrawal of colonial regimes, and the intertwined fates of expatriate communities, particularly Indians, enmeshed in such apocalyptic upheavals. Predictably, its publication intensified the controversy generated by Naipaul's earlier writing. Highly acclaimed by Western critics, *A Bend in the River* equally reinforced African critics' views of Naipaul as, in Chinua Achebe's memorable phrase, "a smart restorer of the comforting myths of the white race" (see Neill, 1982).

Set between the mid-1960s and mid-1970s in Zaire (now Democratic Republic of Congo) under President Mobutu, the novel reworks Joseph Conrad's "Heart of Darkness" (1902). Through subtle allusions to European and Indian literature, parodies of Third World decolonization literature ranging from the liberation theories of Frantz Fanon (*Les damnés de la terre*, 1961; *The Wretched of the Earth*) and Walter Rodney (*How Europe Underdeveloped Africa*, 1972) to contemporary African literature, Naipaul places his themes at the center of contemporary controversies about the role of imperialism and neocolonialism in former colonial states. The allusions to European literature and 19th-century anthropology serve to transform Africa into a pre-cosmos, a kind of hell temporarily made habitable by Indo-Arab and then European colonizers.

Like African writers Chinua Achebe, Wole Soyinka, Ayi Kwei Armah, and Ngugi wa Thiong'o, Naipaul portrays post-independence Africa as plagued with technological backwardness, corrupt leadership, and ethnic rivalries (or class conflicts in Ngugi's Marxist model). But whereas Africans view these problems as temporary, reversible phenomena historically rooted in a conjunction of internal moral or institutional failures and former colonial rulers' aggression, Naipaul interprets them in racial ontological terms, as demonstrations of what he terms in his short story, "In a Free State" (1973), "the pre-man side of Africa." Critics such as Bruce King (1993) have defended this thesis in terms of Naipaul's personal memories of bitter rivalry between Africans and Indians in Trinidad following the end of colonial rule and the nationalization of Indian businesses in some African countries in the early 1970s. The outbreak of a rebellion soon after the state's neonatal civil war provides a context for parodying Fanon's theory of the role of violence both in decolonization and in restructuring the new society to cast out the legacy of colonialism. Apocalypse, as Frank Kermode has written (*The Sense of an Ending*, 1967), ends either in "a great New Year" or a "Final Sabbath," and, given Naipaul's Hobbesian view of Africa, it is the Final Sabbath that is ushered in by this rebellion.

The vista of chaos is painted from within the fast-crumbling security of the retreating imperial order by the first-person narrator Salim, an Indian Muslim whose family long ago settled on the East African coast. As the novelist's *raissoneur,* Salim articulates Naipaul's anxieties over the decline of the Indian civilization as a result of the "mingling of races" and the predicament of the Indian diaspora in various parts of the former British empire. Historically, such Indians have controlled the secondary levels of commercial activity available to non-Europeans and provoked resentment among the indigenes by their rejection of "the mingling of races"; hence, withdrawal of the European power often led to nationalization of the Indians' businesses. Salim and his compatriots Mahesh and Nazruddin also sabotage the economy by smuggling ivory and currency. The interdependence between these events does not emerge from the narrative, for Salim makes no attempt to impose order on the events. His primary role seems to be that of a medium for bringing together the numerous strands of narrative comprising his experiences, readings and speculations, as well as other characters' stories, family histories, and ancestral memories. The ultimate effect is one of flux, ambiguity, frequent self-contradiction, and inconclusiveness.

Naipaul's personal attitude toward "the mingling of races" is a familiar one from his West Indian novels, which lament multiculturalism as a debasement of Indian cultures through creolization. That this theme is now preached by a settler in a foreign land points to a fundamental flaw in Naipaul's sense of history. In a 1971 interview with Ian Hamilton (in Hamner, 1977), Naipaul confessed to "immense astonishment" at his own indifference to momentous contemporary events, such as the 1952 Kenyan rebellion against British colonialism, the Suez crisis, and the Vietnam War. The fact is that the natural tendency of his imagination is toward mythology with its simple, immutable, eternal patterns rather than secular history, which is governed by complex laws of cause and effect. This largely explains the appeal of *A Bend in the River* to critics for whom the inscrutable cyclicism of myth provides paradigms for an imaginary modern malaise that Bruce King vaguely terms "the modern condition of living in a free state." The flaws in the treatment of the Congo's history become more glaring when placed against the admission by Herman Cohen, former American Assistant Secretary of State for Africa, on a BBC Television interview (1 May 1997) that successive American governments kept the corrupt President Mobutu in power for over three decades, suppressing with military force all attempts by his people to remove him, because he served Western interests in the ideological struggle with the Soviet Union.

This antihistorical tendency, combined with its interpretation of the history of colonialism through 19th-century European anthropological perspectives, places *A Bend in the River* outside the mainstream of West Indian literature. Nevertheless, the novel represents a significant contribution to the development of the West Indian novel by virtue of its literary achievement, from which aspiring writers may derive some inspiration.

CHIDI OKONKWO

See also V.S. Naipaul

Further Reading

Cudjoe, Selwyn Reginald, *V.S. Naipaul: A Materialist Reading,* Amherst: University of Massachusetts Press, 1988

Dabydeen, David, and Brinsley Samaroo, editors, *India in the Caribbean*, London: Hansib/University of Warwick, 1987

Hamner, Robert, editor, *Critical Perspectives on V.S. Naipaul,* Washington, D.C.: Three Continents Press, 1977; London: Heinemann, 1979

Hassan, Dolly Zulakha, *V.S. Naipaul and the West Indies,* New York: Peter Lang, 1989

King, Bruce Alvin, *V.S. Naipaul,* London: Macmillan, and New York: St. Martin's Press, 1993

Neill, Michael, "Guerrillas and Gangs: Frantz Fanon and V.S. Naipaul," *Ariel: A Review of International English Literature* 13:4 (October 1982)

Nightingale, Peggy, *Journey through Darkness: The Writing of V.S. Naipaul,* St. Lucia, Queensland: University of Queensland Press, 1987

Nixon, Rob, *London Calling: V.S. Naipaul, Postcolonial Mandarin,* New York: Oxford University Press, 1992

Thieme, John, *The Web of Tradition: Uses of Allusion in V.S Naipaul's Fiction,* London: Dangaroo Press, 1987

Walder, Dennis, "V.S. Naipaul and the Postcolonial Order:

Reading *In a Free State,*" in *Recasting the Word: Writing After Colonialism,* edited by Jonathon White, Bristol: Bristol Press, 1992; Baltimore: Johns Hopkins University Press, 1993

Berlin Alexanderplatz by Alfred Döblin

1929

Alfred Döblin's *Berlin Alexanderplatz: Die Geschichte vom Franz Biberkopf* (1929; *Berlin Alexanderplatz: The Story of Franz Biberkopf*) had considerable impact on its initial publication. It was quickly followed by radio and film adaptations and has remained the best known of its author's many contributions to the genre, which include panoramic historical novels, dystopian fantasies, and fictions close to religious allegory, some marked by the same formal and thematic adventurousness that characterizes *Berlin Alexanderplatz*. By applying to the presentation of urban phenomena the techniques that were being devised and developed in the other arts and the new media during the 1920s, Döblin gave a new dimension to the metropolitan novel, which had already developed to a high degree of sophistication throughout Western Europe and the United States.

The rudimentary plot traces the life of Franz Biberkopf, a man of strong physique and limited intelligence, after his release from the prison where he has served a term for the manslaughter of his mistress Ida. Although determined to go straight, he is drawn into the criminal underworld of Berlin and takes part as a member of a gang in various robberies. During one of these he suffers a serious injury that requires the amputation of an arm. He also falls under the influence of a sinister figure, Reinhold, who eventually murders the prostitute Mieze, thanks to whom Franz had achieved a measure of stability. After this event Franz undergoes a mental and physical crisis in a psychiatric hospital, from which he emerges transformed. He appears at the end of the novel resigned to his new position as a factory porter and (perhaps) better able to cope with the forces within and outside himself that had been his undoing. This skeletal narrative line is fleshed out by a montage of elements that can be divided into various categories. Similar techniques were being developed in the work of the American John Dos Passos (*Manhattan Transfer,* 1925) and of James Joyce (*Ulysses,* 1922), but despite much speculation concerning Döblin's debt to these writers, one can say that *Berlin Alexanderplatz* is without precedent either in Germany or elsewhere in the range and complexity of its montage.

Döblin does not aim to provide a complete picture of Berlin by means of physical description. The action is confined to a small area centered on Alexanderplatz (which in function and appearance may be compared to Piccadilly Circus in London and Times Square in New York) and Rosenthaler Platz nearby. The episode most memorable for topographical density is a nat-

uralistic account of the procedures in the slaughterhouse, which serves the entire city but is situated on its edge. Although the activity of Berlin is encapsulated in recurring references to work on a new underground railway line beneath Alexanderplatz, the modernity of Döblin's representation of the metropolitan environment lies in its mediated nature, the variety and indirection of the semiotic system that conditions urban experience in general and that of Franz in particular. Döblin's manuscript is instructive, for it contains inserted cuttings from various sources, usually news items and advertisements from newspapers, but the montage material also includes soldiers' songs, salvation army songs, and popular songs; extracts from telephone directories, sex manuals, and Alfred Edmund Brehm's *Tierleben* (a well-known natural history); nursery rhymes, didactic poems, letters from convicts, weather forecasts, election speeches, prison regulations, court files, market reports, population statistics, tram timetables, and so on. At the beginning of Book 2 Döblin even goes beyond the limits set by the printed word and reproduces the logos of the various departments of the Berlin local government services. More often than not, the montage elements seem not to be filtered through the consciousness of a character but consist rather of forms of collective utterance or consumption, as in a letterhead from an official document, an extract from a kitsch novel, and the song "Vom guten Kameraden." Sound effects appear from time to time, the *rumm rumm* of the steam hammer thrusting girders into the ground, the *wumm* of the hammer in the slaughterhouse, the wind in the trees at the site of Mieze's murder, and the *wumm* and *rumm* accompanying the appearance of Death as an allegorical figure. While many of the montage elements merely form urban background noise, the more substantial ones have some bearing on the main story and its principal characters; examples include the tales told by the Jews whom Franz encounters after his release, which are offered as a warning or inspiration to him in his state of disorientation.

The voice of a traditional narrator makes itself heard in the prologue to each book and in the book and chapter titles. Their tone recalls the Moritat or Bänkelsang (broadside ballad), popular poetic genres defined by a mixture of naive moralizing and sensationalism and associated with fairground entertainment, in which the singer or speaker illustrates his or her recitation by pointing to what may best be described as a large comic strip. The many Biblical references that form chapter titles and are scattered through the text give the novel a didactic dimension. The narrator presents Franz as an exemplary figure and provides a commentary that raises the story to the level of a parable. However, Döblin widens the frame of reference by adding material from Greek mythology and other sources that have a different impact and are conveyed by other voices, increasing the number of narrators. While in the montage drawn from contemporary sources the city appears to narrate itself, there are episodes in which anonymous voices interpolate remarks, distinguished by square brackets, or address Franz (or Job, for example) directly. Some of these voices may be attributed to the allegorical figures that are more evident toward the end: indeed, this orchestra of voices culminates in the song of death in Book 9 and in the presentation of persons (as ghosts?) whom Franz has known. The confusion of his mind as he lies in a catatonic stupor is further reflected in the cacophony produced by two angels, "die Gewaltigen des Sturms" (violent storm spirits) and the Whore of Babylon.

The complexity of the narrative technique results not only from Döblin's attempt to convey the multiple impressions to which any individual is exposed in a metropolitan environment; it arises also from the uncertainty of Döblin's ideological position at the time he wrote. Throughout his career he accompanied his fiction with theoretical writings that consist of a fluid amalgam of scientific, philosophical, and theological speculation touching on the individual's relationship to the collective in society and to his fellow creatures in the cosmos. Although the critical response to *Berlin Alexanderplatz* on its first appearance was on the whole positive, critics on the left noted at once that Franz, although clearly a proletarian protagonist, totally lacked the features of a positive hero even after his "conversion." Indeed, the ending has since been viewed as problematic by other critics. Despite the religious overtones present in the mythological elements of the montage and Döblin's attraction to oriental fatalism, Franz's transformation may be defined in the language of the behavioral sciences as a conscious decision to surrender personal will and false egoism in favor of solidarity. However, such an interpretation hinges on whether he takes responsibility for his actions instead of attributing his troubles to fate. Unfortunately, the novel's final words, a marching motif, is highly ambiguous. It appears to convey solidarity, thereby reinforcing the behavioral interpretation. However, it had previously accompanied episodes in which Franz (or others) were blind and unthinking. At novel's end, the motif may be taken to imply that fate is unpredictable and arbitrary and that survival cannot be guaranteed, thus suggesting that the security achieved by Franz is weak. Moreover, Franz's psychological limitations make him an unlikely vehicle for the author's thoughts on social philosophy, politics, religion, and so on. On the other hand, it may be argued that by extending the awareness of the reader to take in "the incessant dynamism of earthly existence" (see Midgley, 1993), Döblin has broken the paradigm within which these features—the lack of narrative authority to guide the reader's perceptions and the implausibility of radical montage as a reflection of certain characters' consciousness—may be regarded as faults.

Berlin Alexanderplatz has been influential in two respects: in its development of montage and its extraordinary narrative verve. While montage is only one answer to the situation that has prompted novelists of the 20th century to abandon the linear plot and the plausible interaction of a psychologically consistent protagonist with a realistically portrayed environment, it has since been carried to extremes that even Döblin would never have envisaged, in particular by Arno Schmidt and a number of German and Austrian experimental writers who have followed in his wake. The narrative élan, associated with the urge to introduce material in an episodic, cumulative manner, is present in the work of Günter Grass (who has acknowledged a debt to Döblin) and the international trend represented especially by Salman Rushdie and postwar Latin American fiction.

MALCOLM HUMBLE

See also Alfred Döblin

Further Reading

Bance, A.F., "Alfred Döblin's *Berlin Alexanderplatz* and Literary Modernism," in *Weimar Germany: Writers and Politics,* edited by A.F. Bance, Edinburgh: Scottish Academic Press, 1982

Bayerdörfer, Hans-Peter, "*Berlin Alexanderplatz,*" in *Deutsche Romane des 20. Jahrhunderts,* edited by Paul Michael Lützeler, Königstein: Athenäum, 1983

Durrani, Osman, *Fictions of Germany: Images of the German Nation in the Modern Novel,* Edinburgh: Edinburgh University Press, 1994

Klotz, Volker, *Die erzählte Stadt: Ein Sujet als Herausforderung des Romans von Lesage bis Döblin,* Munich: Carl Hanser, 1969

Midgley, David, "The Dynamics of Consciousness: Alfred Döblin, *Berlin Alexanderplatz,*" in *The German Novel in the Twentieth Century: Beyond Realism,* edited by David Midgley, Edinburgh: Edinburgh University Press, and New York: St. Martin's Press, 1993

Mitchell, Breon, *James Joyce and the German Novel, 1922–1933,* Athens: Ohio University Press, 1976

Prangel, Matthias, editor, *Materialien zu Alfred Döblin "Berlin Alexanderplatz,"* Frankfurt: Suhrkamp, 1975; 3rd edition, 1981

Scherer, Herbert, "Individual and Collective in Alfred Döblin's *Berlin Alexanderplatz,*" in *Culture and Society in the Weimar Republic,* edited by Keith Bullivant, Manchester: Manchester University Press, and Totowa, New Jersey: Rowman and Littlefield, 1977

Ziolkowski, Theodore, *Dimensions of the Modern Novel,* Princeton, New Jersey: Princeton University Press, 1969

Thomas Bernhard 1931–89

Austrian

Thomas Bernhard emerged in the 1960s as one of Austria's major novelists alongside Ingeborg Bachmann and Peter Handke, challenging the popularity of such established writers as Heinrich Böll and Günther Grass on the German literary scene. Bernhard's abstract prose style as well as his extreme subject matter—which combined themes such as suicide, madness, and isolation with highly satirical and histrionic invective against culture, tradition, and society—stood in stark contrast to the enlightenment ethos of Germany's liberal writers (most notably represented by the *Gruppe 47*) and attracted an audience that had grown tired of ideological instruction.

Along with novels and plays that contributed quickly to Bernhard's public notoriety, the author also made himself a name as a skillful impresario of public scandals. His histrionic verbal assaults upon the institutional complicity of state and culture have earned him the epithets of *Übertreibungskünstler* (artist of exaggeration) and *Nestbeschmutzer* (one who befouls the nest). Bernhard's public provocations, however, are not a mere byproduct of his literary work but in fact provide the key to his novelistic and literary endeavors. As a relentless critic in the manner of Karl Kraus and Theodor Adorno, Bernhard consciously stages his provocations in the public sphere in order to explode the safe confines of liberal ideology, its consensus mentality, and its seemingly enlightened cultural perspectives.

The early novels of Bernhard offer a dissonant mixture of pathologically estranged expressionist prose and a dark parody of the idyllic *Heimatroman* (folkloric novel). *Frost* (1963), for example, depicts the fate of a painter whose discourses on death and the failure of art are not only existentially intriguing but also indicate a growing descent toward madness and suicide in a rural setting that is hostile to any form of artistic creativity. *Verstörung* (1967; *Gargoyles*) similarly offers a case study of cultural decline and ensuing madness in the character of Prince Sarau who has succumbed to the weight of his heritage and fortune, which he believes his son will systematically destroy. By the 1970s, Bernhard's prose had obsessively recast these stock scenarios of cultural despair in such novels as *Das Kalkwerk* (1970; *The Lime Works*) and *Korrektur* (1975; *Correction*). Alongside its Gothic thematics Bernhard's work developed complex epistemic patterns of second- and third-hand narration, casting even more doubt on the narrator's reliability and the possibility of unmediated experience. The portrayal of schizoid characters from the vantage point of a sceptical epistemology of refracted and fragmented realities lends Bernhard's early novels a haunting atmosphere of radical ambivalence. Thus, a socially oppressive climate is heightened by the persistent failure of metaphysical foundations.

In his subsequent autobiographical childhood narratives (*Die Ursache, Der Keller, Der Atem, Die Kälte,* and *Ein Kind,* together translated as *Gathering Evidence*) published between 1975 and 1982, Bernhard's misanthropic prose finally begins to relax and show more openly its human and social concerns. The increased comical stance adopted by the author in his late works of the 1980s allowed him to develop more consistently the posture of a critic aware that he himself is guilty of all the charges he makes. *Wittgensteins Neffe* (1982; *Wittgenstein's Nephew*) begins a series of late novels in which Bernhard explores art and its relation to the public sphere, subjecting them both comically and tragically to the scrutiny of a sobered criticism that harbors little illusion about the redemptive potential of art. The tragic nephew of Wittgenstein, for example, is the last embodiment of a bourgeois cultural heritage that is increasingly out of touch with the contemporary culture industry, represented in the prolific and self-promoting music and marketing genius of Herbert von Karajan. The novel revisits classic sites of the traditional bourgeois public sphere, including the opera and the Viennese coffeehouses, only to make way for the present consumer culture. In *Holzfällen* (1984; *Woodcutters*) the ideology of the autonomy of art and artistic genius is further parodied in the portrayal of an avant-garde that has turned into a petty clique indulging in calculated scandals and pseudo-rebellions and entertaining a tacit reverence for established art as represented by the *Burgschauspieler* (actor from Austria's national theatre) who is their honorary guest.

Alte Meister (1985; *Old Masters*) may be read as Bernhard's adaptation of Theodor Adorno's dictum that "Kitsch lurks beneath every work of art." Canonical art, whether it is music, painting, or literature, is exposed by the novel's spokesperson, the critic Reger, as complicit with national self-aggrandizement, intellectual arrogance, and domestic pettiness. For example, Martin Heidegger, the revered 20th-century philosopher, is ridiculed in Bernhardian fashion as a provincial "Denkspiesser" (petty bourgeois thinker) taking pride in the "authentically" knit socks and undergarments provided by his wife in their wholesome rural residence. In a similar fashion, the revival of the Austrian novelist Adalbert Stifter is seen as a reactionary eco-nostalgia. The entire novel, offering humorous tirades against established cultural icons, is nevertheless a serious attempt to point to the social contradictions that surround art as a vehicle for dubious mainstream ideologies. *Auslöschung* (1986; *Extinction*), Bernhard's last and posthumously published novel, makes these ideologies more explicit by focusing on the insidious Nazi past that haunts Austrian history. In an unorthodox move, Bernhard's hero donates the entire estate and inheritance of his Nazi family to the Jewish community in Vienna, as a belated gesture of remittance and acknowledgment of guilt.

It is not surprising that Bernhard's theatrical writing style culminated in a play entitled *Heldenplatz* (1988; Heroes Square, where Hitler's annexation speech was cheered by the Viennese), which, upon its premiere, turned the entire country of Austria into a Bernhardesque *Staatstheater,* as one critic put it. The play's reception in the media and on the political stage triggered an embarrassing display of falsely wounded national pride, in which both left- and right-wing politicians objected to the negative representation of Austria by the two Jewish characters in the play. As part of Bernhard's literary strategy, Austria was thus left with an unmanageable legacy, forcing it to confront once again its too readily forgotten past.

MATTHIAS KONZETT

Biography

Born in Heerlen, near Maastricht, The Netherlands, 10 February 1931. Lived in Austria from 1932. Attended Salzburg Gymnasium, 1943–47; studied singing, directing, and theatrical technique, 1952–55; attended the Salzburg Mozarteum, 1955–57. Commercial apprenticeship, Viennese Academy of Music and Drama, Salzburg, 1947–51; contracted tuberculosis and spent two years in convalescence, 1951–52; journalist for the socialist *Demokratisches Volksblatt*, from 1952, and contributor to the newspaper *Die Furche*, 1953–55; traveled intermittently to Italy and Yugoslavia, 1953–57, to London, 1960, and to Poland, 1962–63; lived on a farm in Ohlsdorf, Upper Austria, from 1965. Died 12 February 1989.

Novels by Bernhard

Frost, 1963
Amras, 1964
Verstörung, 1967; as *Gargoyles*, translated by Richard and Clara Winston, 1970
Prosa, 1967
Watten: Ein Nachlass, 1969
An der Baumgrenze, 1969
Das Kalkwerk, 1970; as *The Lime Works*, translated by Sophie Wilkins, 1973
Gehen, 1971
Der Kulterer, 1974
Korrektur, 1975; as *Correction*, translated by Sophie Wilkins, 1979
Der Wetterfleck, 1976
Der Stimmenimitator, 1978
Ja, 1978; as *Yes*, translated by Ewald Osers, 1991
Die Billigesser, 1980; as *The Cheap-Eaters*, translated by Ewald Osers, 1990

Beton, 1982; as *Concrete*, translated by David McLintock, 1984
Wittgensteins Neffe, 1982; as *Wittgenstein's Nephew*, translated by David McLintock, 1989
Der Untergeher, 1983; as *The Loser*, translated by Jack Dawson, 1991
Holzfällen: Eine Erregung, 1984; as *Woodcutters*, translated by David McLintock, 1987; as *Cutting Timber: An Imitation*, translated by Ewald Osers, 1988
Alte Meister: Komödie, 1985; as *Old Masters*, translated by Ewald Osers, 1989
Auslöschung: Ein Zerfall, 1986; as *Extinction*, translated by David McLintock, 1995

Other Writings: poetry, plays, a screenplay, autobiographical works.

Further Reading

Daviau, Donald, "Thomas Bernhard's *Heldenplatz*," *Monatshefte* 83:1 (1991)
Demetz, Peter, *After the Fires: Recent Writing in the Germanies, Austria and Switzerland*, San Diego, California: Harcourt Brace Jovanovich, 1986
Dowden, Stephen D., *Understanding Thomas Bernhard*, Columbia: University of South Carolina Press, 1991
Hoesterey, Ingeborg, "Postmoderner Blick auf die österreichische Literatur," *Modern Austrian Literature* 23:3 and 23:4 (1990)
Konzett, Matthias, "*Publikumsbeschimpfung*: Thomas Bernhard's Provocations of the Austrian Public Sphere," *The German Quarterly* 68:3 (Summer 1995)
Schmidt-Dengler, Wendelin, *Der Übertreibungskünstler: Studien zu Thomas Bernhard*, Vienna: Sonderzahl, 1986; 3rd edition, 1997

Besy. *See* Devils

The Betrothed by Alessandro Manzoni

I promessi sposi 1827, 1840

Alessandro Manzoni's *The Betrothed*, the best-known Italian historical novel, was the only fictional work of its author. Manzoni, a grandson of Cesare Beccaria, whose treatise *Of Crimes and Punishments* (1767) helped shape modern penal reform, was born in 1785; he wrote the first version of *The Betrothed* between 1821 and 1827, when it was published to great acclaim. He then rewrote it in the Tuscan dialect that many were advocating as a national language; this second version, which ap-

peared in 1840, has become a foundational work for both the literary tradition and the linguistic practice of modern Italy.

The structuring story of *The Betrothed* is simple. Renzo and Lucia are peasants living in the Duchy of Milan, at that time (1628) under Spanish control. Their wish to marry is blocked by a local nobleman, Don Rodrigo, who wishes to suborn Lucia's sexual virtue. Fra Cristoforo, a spiritual protector for both Renzo and Lucia, helps the couple escape Rodrigo's grasp. They must part for a time, and each separately faces danger: Renzo stumbles into Milanese bread riots and is arrested; Lucia is kidnapped by a ruthless outlaw and vows to Heaven to renounce marriage, should she be spared. Nonetheless, after human and perhaps divine intervention, as well as a bit of casuistry, the two of them are happily wed.

Startling narratives of lovers separated and reunited may be traced back to ancient Greek romance (e.g., Longus' *Daphnis and Chloe*), as well as to a source chronologically nearer. In Renaissance drama the double plot is a much-loved device for exploring a particular theme on different sociological and moral levels. *The Betrothed* fully explores the possibilities of this structure; it draws on the pan-European revival of interest in Shakespeare and his contemporaries, adapting the powerful play with perspective of a work like *Henry IV, Part 1*, for the purposes of fiction.

However, compared with Renaissance predecessors, as with most earlier novels, Manzoni's approach to his subject matter is unusual. The crucial contrast in *The Betrothed* is between two *peasant* protagonists. Perhaps it is for this strong emphasis on popular life that Marxist critics have so often admired the novel. Thus, Georg Lukács (1937) finds in Manzoni's treatment of Renzo's and Lucia's contrasting fortunes an evocation of "a general tragedy of the Italian people," and Fredric Jameson (1981) describes the integration of the two separate stories as "a symbolic act," which reconciles social and psychological narrative—Renzo's picaresque wanderings and Lucia's inward crises of conscience. A comparison may be drawn with Sir Walter Scott's *The Heart of Mid-lothian* (1818), for Jeanie Deans' journey to London in that novel is the most obvious fictional precedent to Renzo's wanderings; Scott—who, as Lukács notes, was an admirer of Manzoni—seems to have understood fully that he had been bested.

The double plot of *The Betrothed* is enriched by the interpolated tale, another age-old device revived and reconceived, of which Manzoni was perhaps the greatest master in the 19th century. Manzoni has a way of stopping his two main stories to give a picture of a subordinate character, and several of these pictures turn out to be biographies. The most famous one is of Gertrude, an unfortunate woman who is forced to become a nun and who later betrays Lucia when she attempts to take refuge from Rodrigo in a convent. This section of *The Betrothed* (considerably longer in the earlier version of the novel) owes much to a real-life case (see Mazzuchelli's *The Nun of Monza*) and just as much to Denis Diderot's *La Religieuse* (1796; *The Nun*), to which it provides an extraordinarily subtle and qualified riposte. Manzoni's interpolated tales (of Gertrude, Fra Cristoforo, Federigo Borromeo, and the Unnamed) are not only all biographical in form; they are all, at least implicitly, stories of failed or successful religious conversions among members of the upper classes. The peasant or "popular" framework of *The Betrothed* is thus counterbalanced by a succession of micronarratives that expand the novel's sociological range while opening up a new range of ideological questions about moral conviction in a time of quick and disorienting historical change. Such change, Manzoni believes, can be transcended; morality triumphs over relativism. This use of the interpolated tale stands in striking contrast to that of such Gothicists as Jan Potocki (*The Saragossa Manuscript*, 1805–14) and Charles Maturin (*Melmoth the Wanderer*, 1820), who exploit a very different potentiality of their chosen device: its capability to create a *mise-en-abîme*, where all moral certainty seems to be destroyed.

Manzoni's novel should be read in connection with (at least) two other prose works by its author: *Storia della colonna infame* (*The Column of Infamy*), published as an appendix or sequel to the 1842 edition of his novel, and his treatise *Del romanzo storico* (*On the Historical Novel*), written over many years (including those when he was engaged in revising *The Betrothed*) but not published until 1850. *The Column of Infamy* is an interpolated tale that took on a life of its own. It is an analysis of the trial of the *untori*, those who had been accused of magically causing the plague of Milan, which provides *The Betrothed*'s final historical set piece. Neither a part of the novel nor entirely separate from it, this work shows once again how difficult it was for Manzoni to reconcile historical and contextual thinking with his need for moral absolutes. His study of the historical novel considers the related problem of how and why one should mix history with fiction and offers a defense of this mixture, despite its deceptive potentialities.

Considered in light of 19th-century fiction as a whole, Manzoni's novel has incalculable significance. Whether directly or indirectly, the great canonical novels written later in the 19th century may be traced to it. Dickens' *Bleak House* (1853), George Eliot's *Middlemarch* (1872), and Tolstoi's *Anna Karenina* (1875–77) owe much to *The Betrothed* in their presentation of related but distinct actions through intricately woven back-and-forth narratives. Such contrapuntal structures create the impression of a society miraculously represented in its completeness— seen from every side. Decades earlier than these other books, Manzoni showed how this feat could be accomplished. Paradoxically, then, *The Betrothed* is a romance that made possible the major works of realist fiction.

RICHARD MAXWELL

See also Historical Novel; Alessandro Manzoni

Further Reading

Baldi, Guido, *"I promessi sposi": Progetto di società e mito*, Milan: Mursia, 1985

Barricelli, Gian Piero, *Alessandro Manzoni*, Boston: Twayne, 1976

Colquhoun, Archibald, *Manzoni and His Times*, London: Dent, and New York: Dutton, 1954

Dombroski, Robert S., *L'apologia del vero: Lettura ed interpretazione dei "Promessi Sposi,"* Padua: Liviana, 1984

Ginzburg, Natalia, *The Manzoni Family*, New York: Seaver Books, and Manchester: Carcanet, 1987; originally published as *La famiglia Manzoni*

Jameson, Fredric, *The Political Unconscious: Narrative as a Socially Symbolic Act*, Ithaca, New York: Cornell University Press, and London: Methuen, 1981

Lucente, Gregory L., *Beautiful Fables: Self-consciousness in Italian Narrative from Manzoni to Calvino*, Baltimore: Johns Hopkins University Press, 1986

Lukács, Georg, *A történelmi regény*, Budapest: Hungaria, 1937; as *The Historical Novel*, London: Merlin Press, 1962; New York: Humanities Press, 1965

Manzoni, Alessandro, *On the Historical Novel*, Lincoln: University of Nebraska Press, 1984; originally published as *Del romanzo storico*, 1850

Mazzuchelli, Mario, *The Nun of Monza*, London: Hamish Hamilton, and New York: Simon and Schuster, 1963

Biblical Narrative and the Novel

While there are certainly novels based on characters and events in the Bible, ranging from Thomas Mann's massive Old Testament trilogy *Joseph und seine Brüder* (1933–43; *Joseph and His Brothers*) to pietistic retellings of Gospel stories, a deeper relationship exists between the Bible and the genre of the novel. First, the Bible may be examined in terms of how its constituent books and key episodes, characters, and thematic discussions qualify as novelistic. Second, one may consider how European novelists since the 17th century have drawn typical scenes, characters, narrative techniques, and psychological insights from the Bible in order to explore aspects of their stories.

The Bible refers to a double collection of Christian writings known as the Old and New Testaments. For Protestants a section of works has been separated as noncanonical and yet spiritually useful to read, called the Apocrypha. Many of these texts derive from the intertestamental period and show a marked influence of Hellenistic romance, lyric, and satire. They distinguish themselves by their development of character, their grounding of imaginary situations within historical events, and their emotional thematization. All of these techniques provide authoritative protonovelistic paradigms.

What Christians call the Old Testament is for Jews not a preliminary, incomplete, and dependent set of textual promises but a three-part collection known by its acronym of *Tanakh*, representing *Torah* (the Pentateuch), most sacred of the sections; *Neviim* (Prophets), next in order of precedence and usually read as a supplementary accompaniment to the first; and a miscellany of lyrical, proverbial, and homiletic books known as *Ketuvim* (Hagiography). Each of these three sections contains narrative, lyrical, and homiletic models that have proven significant for future novel writers.

Similarly, the New Testament is divided into a narrative section made up of the four Gospels and the second half of Luke called the Acts of the Apostles; letters from Paul and other apostles containing personal news, directives on church organization, *responsa* on theological problems and ecclesiastical practice, and sermons; and a single apocalypse, the Book of Revelation. Like the Old Testament, the New Testament has proved an encyclopedic source of characters, situations, images, and themes for novelists because of the pervasive influence of Christianity even into the secularizing centuries of the post-Renaissance Western world. So-called "gospel speech" and the value attached to *sermo humilis* (demotic and "low style" prose) signal the New Testament's inversions of classical stylistics and generic decorum. These inversions provide paradigms for developing "serious" narratives in a matrix of ordinary, marginalized, and illicit versions of textual reality. Such aspects are more important to the development of the novel than the inversions of formal generic categories drawn from classical and medieval experiences that play such an important role in Mikhail Bakhtin's account of the origins of the novel in *The Dialogic Imagination* (1981).

Although many writers have attempted to retell episodes from the Bible in a novelistic form that, while motivated by religious conviction, contain little or no allegorical or symbolic distortions, few serious novelists have sought to recreate the events and characters of the Scriptures within the commonly accepted parameters of the novel, with its focus on psychological motiva-

tion and social relationships. Among the few examples, Gustave Flaubert's *Hérodias* (1877) and the more recent *Mariamne* (1967) of Pär Lagerkvist creatively fill out allusive episodes and minor characters of the New Testament.

More often, writers have alluded to characters, events, and thematic complexes in their titles; have given quick summaries of particular stories to provide resonance for their own fictional plots; or have woven in familiar phrases, rhythms, and conceptions of biblical thought to add depth and resonance to their own discourses. Sometimes, as with Romanian Liviu Rebreanu's *Adam şi Eva* (1936; Adam and Eve), which weaves together the stories of different "original" couples in different historical periods, biblical allusions do not point to actual characters or events in the novel, but only establish a general interpretive framework. The American William Faulkner's *Absalom, Absalom!* (1936) asks of the reader, not a recognition of details in Scriptural narrative, but a general identification of the ambiguous relationship between father and son, with a hint at the tragic conclusion of the beautiful prince's rebellion against King David.

In making these general intertextual connections, the secular writers in English lean toward two processes characteristic of both Jewish and Christian exegetes—*midrash* and *targum,* both processes inherent to the novelistic elaboration of biblical narrative. By *midrash* is meant a way of illuminating, enhancing, and filling out the "gaps" in biblical narrative, these gaps being the very essence of biblical narrative and the primary difference from the kind of storytelling we call novelistic (see Sternberg, 1985). The gaps are not just textual lacunae created by a shorthand that reduces a story to salient characters, images, events, and themes; they are also deliberate logical and chronological deletions precisely at moments when psychological, spiritual, or historical motive is called for, which makes the reading of the Bible necessarily an active engagement with the situations recounted. Every textual encounter confronts the questions of why and how persons acted as they did, why and how events turned out in the fashion reported, and why connections between episodes in a historical event are established. In terms of generic definition, the novel emerges when these points are made the center of attention and when deep emotional, moral, and long-term historical patterns are created, invented, or discovered. *Midrash* tends to provide new scenes, characters, and psychological and emotional aspects of personality to fill in such gaps and may therefore be considered to be impelled by a novelistic drive. Many noncanonical gospels, saints' lives, and narrative commentaries on the Old and New Testament serve similar functions of filling out these gaps and hence may themselves be accounted as part of a protonovelistic tradition within Christian tradition.

The *targum* in the strict sense is a translation of the Hebrew Scriptures into an Aramaic version, but it is usually more than a translation of the words. It is an attempt to accommodate biblical narrative to another language, culture, and cultural milieu. Key words and concepts are expanded into lengthy paraphrases, complete with additional examples of some character trait, ethical point, or motivational decision.

In some novels, such as Daniel Defoe's *Robinson Crusoe* (1719), the discovery, reading, and meditation on the Bible provides one of the key or pivotal actions in the narrative. Others, such as John Bunyan's *Pilgrim's Progress* (1678–84), while echoing the rhythms and vocabulary of the Bible in its English translations, also largely reconfigures a Christian hermeneutic into an allegorical narrative dotted with allusions, citations, and abstracted lessons. Allusions to names of persons, places, or events may give a clue to the character or action of the novel or may be ironically subversive of surface meaning. For instance, aside from its deep exploration of the imagery and themes associated with the leviathan in the Book of Job and in Psalms, Herman Melville's *Moby-Dick* (1851) opens with the declaration, "Call me Ishmael," a designation that resonates with all the power and complexity of the ancient legends and sagas in the Book of Genesis. Biblical allusions may be indirect, as when Marcel Proust compares the figure of Odette in *Du côté de chez Swann* (*Swann's Way*), the first volume of *A la recherche du temps perdu* (1913–27; translated as *Remembrance of Things Past* and also as *In Search of Lost Time*), via works of art to "Zipporah, Jethro's Daughter" (as told in the Book of Judges). Each allusion to a different painting or fresco increases the reader's sense of the similarities between Odette and this biblical daughter sacrificed to a father's hasty and ill-conceived vow.

Some narratives in the Bible, if not short novels, may be considered novelistic. As Thomas Mann realized, the saga of Joseph in Genesis, for example, presents a complex biography of a hero whose rise in status involves sibling rivalries, dislocation to a foreign land, cultural misunderstandings and jealousies, and eventually the assumption of power, the clarification of earlier domestic relations, and the temporary resolution of a larger national difficulty. But smaller episodes, such as the confrontation between Joseph and Potiphar's wife, provide a key type of scene and plot complication in many novels. For example, Henry Fielding's *Joseph Andrews* (1742), depicting the young Joseph almost caught in the snares of Lady Booby's sexual wiles, is a modern version of the episode from Genesis.

Another complete narrative in the Hagiography, the Book of Esther presents a condensed novelistic account of a woman's heroism and guile. Esther compromises her integrity as a Jew by marrying and living as a pagan wife to Ahasuerus in Persia to save her people. She cautiously overcomes the problems faced by her predecessor Vashti and spreads her influence in the royal household beyond the bounds allowable to her uncle Mordechai. By setting up the villain Haman to be caught in the posture of a rapist, Esther thwarts the genocidal pogrom against the Jews and turns the political event into a triumph for her people. Samuel Richardson alludes to this story in the first volume of *Pamela* (1740), when the eponymous heroine records her influence over her would-be rapist Mr. B. as her moral resistance begins to change his posture to her: "Thus poor Hester, to her royal husband, ventured her life, to break in upon him unbidden. But that eastern monarch, great as he was, extended to the fainting suppliant the golden sceptre." As in all good allusions, however, the effect is not only to establish a biblical precedent to an action in a novel. Richardson here places a mantle of moral and spiritual authority on his female protagonist and points to her eventual triumph over seduction and violation.

In the early modern period, when knowledge of the Bible was more widespread, the use of the allusion could be subtle and ironic. Novelists could depend not only on recognition of the names of persons, places, and events, but on an understanding of the social, moral, and spiritual values associated with them. For instance, in Samuel Richardson's *Clarissa* (1747–48), Anne Howe writes in response to the already evident ambiguities and tensions in the feelings of Clarissa to her would-be seducer Mr. Lovelace, "Your Israelitish hankerings after the Egyptian onions (testified still more in your letter to your aunt), your often repeated regrets for meeting him, for being betrayed away by him—these he cannot bear." For readers familiar with the Israelites' complaints to Moses and their yearnings for the onions and leeks of Egypt in the early stages of Exodus, this remark signifies an incomplete release from moral and psychological bondage. The allusion signals Anne Howe's insight into Clarissa's mixed feelings of attraction and repulsion to Lovelace. Yet Anne does not recognize the full implications of her own remarks, since she can neither know the real dangers Clarissa is in nor imagine the obduracy of her friend's resistance to Lovelace's seductive ploys. Readers of Richardson's novel would nonetheless later recall these words and their place in the Bible, and the way they signal a determination to pass into the promised land despite a few weak moments of nostalgic forgetfulness.

Allusions may be more complex where the author assumes an informed response by readers. In his third novel, *Sir Charles Grandison* (1753–54), Richardson juxtaposes two allusions. One is to the key passage in the Book of Esther referring to the moment when the heroine's predecessor precipitately aroused her husband's wrath and so lost her status: "Some wives would have played the queen Vashti on their tyrant, and refused to go. But I, all obedience (my vow, so recently made, in my head) obeyed." This allusion has ironic overtones since the speaker, Miss Byron, both claims to be and not to be an obedient wife in the style of the Jewish heroine. The second allusion places her husband's wrathful behavior in a biblical context, comparing him unfavorably to a Hebrew King, thus endowing her obedience and suffering with a moral quality: "I go to my harpsichord; melody enrages him. He is worse than Saul; for Saul could be gloomily pleased with the music even of the man he hated."

With the declining biblical literacy and growing pluralism of more modern times, novelistic use of the Bible has become more complicated. While Chaim Potok, for example, can write whole books that turn on the protagonist's study of the Scriptures, Potok needs to instruct his American readers in how to understand the debates on biblical matters that motivate the Jewish characters in *In the Beginning* (1975):

> I opened my *Mikraot Gedolot* and reread the Rashi commentary on the first word of the Hebrew Bible, *bereshit*, "in the beginning." Then I reread the Ramban, another commentary. "Listen to how they talk to one another, David," Mr. Bader had said to me the week before in his study. "Look at how the different parts of the page are arranged and you'll understand how Jews have been talking to each other for two thousand years about the Bible. . .".

This teaching directed at the hero is also a way of bringing the reader's own sensibility into an understanding of the character being developed and the tensions at work in the social milieu depicted. Even if each text, commentator, and debating point are not fully explained, Potok's general drift becomes clear, and the novel is shown to involve not just a young Jewish boy's growing to moral and psychological maturity in New York but a larger and longer-lasting community absorbing a new son into its matrix of intellectual discourses. These Jewish discourses, as the protagonist comes to comprehend their meanings and implications, are keyed to the historical circumstances of World War II and the Holocaust, but at the same time they are distanced by an American perspective.

Finally, it is important to note that biblical characters, themes, and imagery may pervade a novel at a deeper level, while only a few matching points break through the surface of the text. Jonathan Lamb's excellent study *The Rhetoric of Suffering: Reading the Book of Job in the Eighteenth Century* (1995) shows how the Book of Job pervades many 18th-century novels, ranging from Oliver Goldsmith's *The Vicar of Wakefield* (1766) through Laurence Sterne's *Tristram Shandy* (1759–67) to Samuel Johnson's *Rasselas* (1759), each author finding in the complaints of Job and his rage at the injustices of the world a correlative to the modern, secularizing insight into the breakdown of more traditional and rhetorical schemes of narrative. What afflicts Job cannot be generalized into moral patterns or articulated in symbolic actions but only expressed in the very cries of a painful experience. If we take the Book of Job, then, as a central paradigm of this inward, anti-rhetorical drive of narrative, we may conclude that the Bible stands behind the development of the novel in a long-term generic sense and behind each great work's unique existence.

NORMAN SIMMS

Further Reading

Alter, Robert, *The Art of Biblical Narrative,* London: Allen and Unwin, and New York: Basic Books, 1981

Alter, Robert, and Frank Kermode, editors, *The Literary Guide to the Bible,* London: Collins, and Cambridge, Massachusetts: Harvard University Press, 1987

Faur, José, *Golden Doves with Silver Dots: Semiotics and Textuality in Rabbinic Tradition,* Bloomington: Indiana University Press, 1986

Frye, Northrop, *The Great Code: The Bible and Literature,* London: Routledge and Kegan Paul, and New York: Harcourt Brace, 1982

Lamb, Jonathan, *The Rhetoric of Suffering: Reading the Book of Job in the Eighteenth Century,* Oxford: Clarendon Press, and New York: Oxford University Press, 1995

Mustaph-Andriesse, Rosetta C., *From Torah to Kabbalah: A Basic Introduction to the Writings of Judaism,* London: SCM Press, 1981; New York: Oxford University Press, 1982

Norton, David, *A History of the Bible as Literature,* 2 vols., Cambridge and New York: Cambridge University Press, 1993

Simms, Norman, *The Humming Tree: A Study in the History of Mentalities,* Urbana: University of Illinois Press, 1992

Spencer, Richard, editor, *Orientation by Disorientation: Studies in Literary Criticism and Biblical Literary Criticism,* Pittsburgh, Pennsylvania: Pickwick Press, 1980

Sternberg, Meir, *The Poetics of Biblical Narrative: Ideological Literature and the Drama of Reading,* Bloomington: Indiana University Press, 1985

Weiss, Meir, *The Bible from Within: The Method of Total Interpretation,* Jerusalem: Magnes Press, Hebrew University, 1984

Bibliothèque bleue

The *Bibliothèque bleue,* a collection of small books produced to be sold by itinerant peddlars, first began to appear in France during the second half of the 17th century. The earliest publishers, the Oudots of Troyes, took the name from the blue paper that they used as wrappers. Early volumes in the collection were printed in northern centers such as Troyes, Lyon, and Rouen, but by the end of the 18th century volumes were also being issued in southern towns such as Limoges and Avignon.

The *Bibliothèque bleue* may be said to be the earliest form of literature produced in France specifically for a mass readership. While exact statistics concerning print runs have not survived, we know that in the 18th century the Oudots alone produced several hundreds of thousands of volumes annually. Badly printed on low-quality paper, the books were sold cheaply but in sufficient numbers to make their publishers a great deal of money. Born in the 17th century, the *Bibliothèque bleue* disappeared at the end of the 19th century as other types of popular publication, such as newspapers and serial novels, first rivaled and finally replaced it.

Such a literature intended for mass circulation was not, of course, a purely French phenomenon. Throughout Europe, peddlars sold books similar to those in the *Bibliothèque bleue,* including the English "chapbooks" (which first appeared about 50 years earlier), the *pliegos* in Spain, and the *Volksbücher* in Germany. Traditions differed, however, from country to country, both in terms of form—English and Spanish readers seemed to prefer ballad-style stories in verse—and in methods of distribution: the *pliegos,* for example, were sold exclusively by blind peddlars.

The catalogue of titles in the *Bibliothèque bleue,* as it was built up over the two and a half centuries of its existence, comprises approximately 500 works. While literature, and more specifically fiction, accounts for the largest number of titles, cookbooks, collections of cures, saints' lives, hymnals, spelling books, and books of magic also figure prominently. The reason for this variety was the desire to reach the largest public possible and give readers practical guides to living, similar to that provided by almanachs, as well as books of religious instruction and others to stimulate the imagination. The exact social makeup of *Bibliothèque bleue* readers is a matter of conjecture, since detailed records have not survived; but the best modern authorities agree that, as the 18th century progressed, they were drawn increasingly from the lower classes and from people living in the country. In his *Tableau de Paris* (1781) Louis-Sébastien Mercier notes that the habit of reading had spread to all classes of urban society: "It is quite common these days to see chambermaids in their bedrooms, or lackeys in the anteroom busy reading a brochure. People of every class can read, and a good thing too: the more they read the better!" No doubt Paris was a special case, but we may be sure that the spread of literacy fostered by the growing number of charity schools gave the lower classes access to the books available in the *Bibliothèque bleue.*

Novels formed the largest portion of the collection, comprising one-quarter of the published titles. Within the category of fiction, however, there were distinct shifts in taste over the *Bibliothèque's* long history. In the earliest years, novels of chivalry taken from medieval manuscripts and first printed during the Renaissance formed the basis of the collection; the emphasis was on battles and crusades rather than the love stories associated with the Knights of the Round Table. Typically, the novels in the *Bibliothèque bleue* relate the heroic exploits of Charlemagne, introducing readers to characters like Robert le Diable, Richard sans peur, and Huon de Bordeaux, on the borderline between history and fiction. In such novels, feelings play a minimal role: what is presented is a warlike, strictly masculine version of the Middle Ages.

As far as the general public was concerned, the stories in the *Bibliothèque bleue,* which continued to be republished well into the 19th century, probably constituted the principal source of knowledge about French medieval history and the age of chivalry. At the same time, the prominence given to magic and to geographically and socially remote settings meant that such stories also functioned as escapist literature, taking readers to countries as far away as China, peopled by princes and supernatural beings like Mélusine, Bayard (the horse of the four sons of Aymon "who talked like a man, and was wise"), or Orson, the savage who was raised by a bear. Clearly, there are numerous affinities between such tales and the oral tradition: the story of Mélusine, for example, relating the union of a mortal man and supernatural woman, half serpent or siren, may also be found in folklore.

Despite these links with the oral literature, it must be stressed that the texts printed in the *Bibliothèque bleue* are invariably derived from written sources, i.e., medieval manuscripts. Their connection to popular oral culture lies in the fact that they themselves influenced the production of new versions of old tales.

From the second half of the 18th century onward, the types of novels offered to *Bibliothèque bleue* readers began to change. Alongside the old novels of chivalry, there appeared love stories (such as *Histoire de Jean de Calais* [1731], by Madame de Gomez), moral tales, and, above all, fairy tales, which became increasingly popular in the 19th century: most of these new forms were short narratives rather than novels proper. Of the fairy tales, those by Madame d'Aulnoy and of Madame de Murat outnumber those of Charles Perrault, despite the latter's closer ties with folklore. *L'Oiseau bleu, Jeune et belle, La Chatte blanche, La Belle et la bête* became bestsellers that inspired oral versions that folklore specialists would eventually collect. Originally meant for an adult public, the *Bibliothèque bleue,* in its final years, seems to have appealed increasingly to younger readers, as witnessed by the publication of a large number of moralizing or simplified versions of traditional tales. Already in the early years of the 19th century, new forms of popular fiction were emerging, with a strong emphasis on love and adventure: among them, the cheap editions of Madame Cottin, of Ducray-Duminil, and of Pigault-Lebrun, to which Emma Bovary, heroine of Gustave Flaubert's *Madame Bovary* (1857), will fall victim because she cannot tell the difference between fiction and reality.

LISE ANDRIES
(Translated by Graham Falconer)

See also entries under the heading Libraries

Further Reading

Andries, Lise, *La Bibliothèque bleue au dix-huitième Siècle: Une tradition éditoriale,* Oxford: Voltaire Foundation, 1989

Andries, Lise, and Geneviève Bollème, editors, *Les Contes bleus,* Paris: Montalba, 1983

Chartier, Roger, *Lectures et lecteurs dans la France d'Ancien Régime,* Paris: Editions du Seuil, 1987

Big Money. *See* U.S.A. Trilogy

Bildungsroman

German Origins

The word *Bildungsroman* has been translated variously as apprenticeship novel, novel of formation, novel of individual development, novel of self-cultivation, novel of initiation, novel of socialization, novel of education, pedagogical novel, philosophical novel, psychological novel, novel of youth, and life novel. Historically, the term refers to a fairly well-defined group of German novels of the late 18th, 19th, and 20th centuries. The model for these novels is Johann Wolfgang von Goethe's *Wilhelm Meisters Lehrjahre* (1795–1821; *Wilhelm Meister's Apprenticeship*). In this context, the word *Bildung* (formation) has a specific historical and cultural meaning. It contains vestiges of both religious and secular notions of formation as an inner process. Through the work of J.G. Herder it became established as one of the key words of the new German culture, along with *Geist* (mind, spirit), *Kultur,* and *Humanität,* all betokening aspects of a neohumanist worldview. Through the work of Wilhelm von Humboldt, *Bildung* entered the educational theory and practice of post-Enlightenment Germany. In Goethe's novel the focus is upon the fictional representation of the development of personality as a complex expression of humanist and idealist optimism, rooted in the politically backward but intellectually vigorous Germany of the period. An unspoken but significant factor is Goethe's rejection of the violence of the French Revolution.

The historical origin of the term *Bildungsroman* (as distinct from the novels that gave rise to it) also identifies it as referring to a consciously German genre. The word itself, although first documented in 1803, did not enter the critical lexicon until Wilhelm Dilthey used it to describe the *Lehrjahre* and its cognates, among which he included works by Jean Paul, Friedrich Hölderlin, and others. Dilthey's famous and influential book, *Das Erlebnis und die Dichtung* (1906; *Experience and Poetry*), contains the classical definition of the German Bildungsroman: a type of novel that deals with a young man "entering into life in a happy dream, seeking kindred spirits, finding friendship and love, but now also encountering the struggles of hard reality and thus maturing amidst the many experiences of life, to find himself, and to ascertain his true task in the world." Because Dilthey had defined a specifically German contribution to the European novel, and one with the theme of a successful journey toward maturity, the term was enthusiastically taken up in the newly unified Germany, even though Dilthey himself had viewed the type as characteristic of a bygone era.

In fact, the emphasis upon development toward a goal of social integration, which has become a constitutive part of what is normally understood by the term *Bildungsroman,* is less important in the novels that gave rise to the term historically than a sense of the abrasive cooperation between inner and outer forces in the maturation process of a representative young man. This is because implicit in the term *Bildung* itself is the post-Enlightenment ambition to harmonize the modern rational state with the autonomy of the individual. What is at stake is a process, within which inner and outer combine fruitfully, without one being subordinated to the other. Since this is a utopian notion, it is not surprising that no individual novel has ever been able to live up to it completely: all have had to make unsatisfactory compromises of one kind or another.

The specific literary-historical circumstances in which the German Bildungsroman came about may be seen by examining the novel that is agreed to have been the precursor to Goethe's seminal text, Christoph Martin Wieland's *Die Geschichte des Agathon* (1766–67; *The History of Agathon*). The title alludes to Henry Fielding's *The History of Tom Jones* (1749), and Wieland makes it clear that he wishes his protagonist to be psychologically and morally realistic in the manner of Fielding rather than morally exemplary in the manner of Samuel Richardson. Yet where Fielding in England had a socially and morally distinct

and developed modern world within which to set his psychologically realistic hero, and a capital city to which to send him, Wieland in Germany had none of these things and was obliged to set his narrative in a playfully artificial ancient Greek setting. This setting is handled with pleasant irony, but Wieland was left with the problem of finding a suitable physical destination and moral telos for his hero, whose rich and problematic inner life is the main topic of the novel. So unsatisfied was Wieland with his first solution to the problem—the utopian state of Tarent, ruled over by the sage Archytas—that he felt obliged in a third version of the novel (1794) to add a lengthy account of the philosophy of Archytas, to the detriment of the novel's artistic composition.

The German Bildungsroman is thus preformed as a mixture of, on the one hand, English social realism, and on the other, the need to fill the gaps left by contemporary German historical reality by recourse to speculation. The German Bildungsroman is a philosophical kind of novel. It deals with possibilities as well as actualities. The philosophical seriousness of Wieland's novel was perpetuated in the first German novel theory, C.F. von Blanckenburg's *Versuch über den Roman* (1774; *Essay on the Novel*), which held up *The History of Agathon* as an example of what a novel should be and proposed the depiction of the inner life and development of an individual toward moral maturity as the desirable theme for the novel genre in general.

The discourse of moral self-examination that distinguishes *The History of Agathon* as a serious psychological novel owes much to the introspective spirituality of pietism, to which both Wieland and Goethe were exposed when young. The secular inflection of this inward-looking religious discourse is particularly apparent in Goethe's use of it in "Die Bekenntnisse einer schönen Seele" ("The Confessions of a Beautiful Soul"), book six of his novel, to represent a profound and authentic, yet problematic, inwardness.

Like *The History of Agathon, Wilhelm Meister's Apprenticeship* grew around a Fieldingesque core: an early version now known as the *Theatralische Sendung* (*Wilhelm Meister's Theatrical Mission*), written between 1777 and 1786. Since the version remained a fragment, it is not certain where it was leading, but the most likely assumption is that the establishment of a national theatre would have been the external telos of the moral development depicted in it. What had been a living aspiration during the 1770s was no longer so during the 1790s when Goethe returned to the manuscript. It is Goethe's *revision* of his early draft that really inaugurates the model to which the concept of the Bildungsroman may credibly be traced.

The key to this revision was to enclose a realistic narrative, largely identical with the earlier Fieldingesque fragment, within a larger symbolic organization in which it became transparent upon a belief in the human potential for development, or *Bildung.* By incorporating aspects of the *Geheimbund* (secret society) novel and other ironized borrowings from the popular novel, as well as inserting the pietistic autobiography mentioned previously at a structural turning point, Goethe shows that the vicissitudes of the hero's life are at once a series of mistakes and the necessary manifestations of a process of becoming. The theatrical vocation ceases to be the central theme, to become instead the most important single mistake Wilhelm makes about himself. This shift in the thematic function of the theatre is particularly felicitous for Goethe's view of *Bildung* in its application to individual personality. The theatre is an illuminating metaphor for the need to be oneself, that is, to develop a social persona commensurate with one's inner life. Wilhelm learns that he is mistaken to believe that he has a future in the theatre. At the same time he learns that he *must act* himself, but on the stage of social and moral life rather than upon the boards of the contemporary theatre.

The fusion of social realism with idealism by means of ironic elements from the popular novel is perhaps most neatly exemplified in the novel's ending. Wilhelm stands on the threshold of marriage to Natalie, a figure who is both an idealized female and his social superior. Real social types are put into realistically impossible relations to make a symbolic point about the need for a new fusion of inner and outer realities. However, there is no facile harmony about the ending. Until the last pages, Wilhelm is confused about the meaning of his life, and the marriage is deferred until after the end of the fiction. Like most other examples of the genre in German, this Bildungsroman is much more open-ended than the Dilthey-inspired official definition encourages one to expect. The notion of *Bildung* is not merely one of conscious self-development (although Wilhelm himself does consciously want to form—*ausbilden*—himself as fully as possible) but of a development of the whole personality, within which the conscious mind, being but a part of this whole, will always lag behind.

The inevitability of less-than-perfect compromise in any accommodation between individual and society is most prominently represented by the famous figure of Mignon. This character, who in the *Theatrical Mission* is mysteriously androgynous, stands for the unbounded yearnings of the soul that must be renounced in the process of socialization. Thus neither of the two agencies that embody, facilitate, and explain Wilhelm's true predestined form of development, Natalie and the Society of the Tower, is able to find a place in their dispositions for Mignon. Although much beloved of and protected by Wilhelm, she must fade and die, even while evidently representing the deepest impulses of human nature toward fulfillment and perfection.

The influence of Goethe's novel, the profundity and complexity of which is only hinted at here, extends to all the successive generations of the German novel, at least until Thomas Mann's *Der Zauberberg* (1924; *The Magic Mountain*), and some say even further. The German romantics—and their counterparts elsewhere in Europe—took the *Lehrjahre* extremely seriously, seeing in it a paradigm for all literature but disturbing its subtle equilibrium by stressing—for instance in Novalis' *Heinrich von Ofterdingen* (1802), which was conceived as an answer to the *Lehrjahre*—the potential within subjectivity for unbounded poetic creativity, at the cost of the need for social accommodation. The generation of the 1830s produced, in Karl Immermann's *Die Epigonen* (1836; The Epigones), a conscious travesty of the *Lehrjahre,* in which prevailing historical and social circumstances make a mockery of the ideal of development associated with Goethe's text.

Adalbert Stifter's *Der Nachsommer* (1857; *Indian Summer*) takes the antirealist potential of the Bildungsroman to the limit. Wishing to defend Goethe's neohumanist optimism in an historical period marked by rapid and unsettling social, economic, and political developments, Stifter consciously wrote against the prevailing taste of the time for realism. Whereas the realist potential of the *Lehrjahre* lay in the narration of the protagonist's mistakes, through which an organic and meaningful process was to be discerned by means of the consciously artificial, symbolic

components of the text, Stifter presents the reader with the organic and meaningful process on its own. Here, the gradual unfolding of a subject's proper relationship with the world, through natural science, love, and the appreciation of art, is recounted with the greatest clarity. In this sense, the novel qualifies as the quintessential German Bildungsroman. However, the high degree of stylization required in the plot as in the prose makes this unique book more the nostalgic expression of a desirable impossibility than the lived literary representation of a hope.

Gottfried Keller's novel *Der grüne Heinrich* (1853–55, 1880; *Green Henry*), on the other hand, demonstrates that the German Bildungsroman is compatible with novelistic realism. Like Wilhelm Meister, Keller's hero Heinrich Lee mistakes his vocation, thinking he is called to be an artist. The socially and psychologically realistic narrative of this mistake makes up the bulk of the novel. Where Stifter's hero completed a flawless development, but at some evident distance from reality, reality proves a very unforgiving educator in Keller, whose hero is nearly destroyed by it. Yet there are unmistakable (if at times parodistic) structural allusions to the *Lehrjahre*: Heinrich Lee's development proceeds by way of different kinds of erotic attachment, as was the case with Wilhelm Meister, and there is a noble educator figure—noble in rank as well as in moral persona—who perceives continuity in Heinrich's artistic and personal development even where Heinrich himself has seen none. Heinrich Lee's personality sustains lasting damage from his overestimation of the potential of his own imaginative powers to secure social identity and position as an artist, and this distinguishes the novel from the organic *Bildung* of the *Lehrjahre*. Yet more importantly, *Green Henry* explores the *relation between* inner and outer realities, even if it is not a happy one, and this orientation authenticates the novel as a genuine Bildungsroman in the German sense.

Thomas Mann's revisiting of the Bildungsroman in *The Magic Mountain* extends the group of recognized *Lehrjahre* novels into the 20th century. It is at once a parody of the genre—the hero effectively takes a seven-year holiday to look into his inner life—and a renewal of it, since Thomas Mann wished to reaffirm humanist values in the changed circumstances of post–World War I Germany. Within the framework of a young man's educational and formative experience, Mann's representatively mediocre but suggestive protagonist Hans Castorp is exposed to a range of intellectual and emotional experiences and an array of educators. While his original inauthentic social persona is completely scattered by this comprehensive learning experience, his fundamental integrity as a human individual emerges from it strengthened. At the end of the novel he leaves the Swiss sanatorium in which he has spent the previous seven years ostensibly receiving treatment for tuberculosis but in fact enabling the development of his character. His departure to fight in World War I has been seen by some as an arbitrary curtailment of his development. Yet his formation, like all the formation processes represented in these novels, gains a meaning only in interaction with external reality, in this case the reality of World War I. Neither Thomas Mann nor anybody else can guarantee the survival of the humanist aspirations embodied in *Bildung* in the face of that catastrophe.

Generic Problems

The generic definition of the term *Bildungsroman* is necessarily more diffuse than the preceding historical account of it. The problem may be approached in three stages. First, two attempts from the German idealist tradition to articulate a theory of the novel provide a broad conceptual framework. Second, cognate and contrasting novel types suggest contours of the genre, without the need for inevitably contentious substantive definitions. Finally, contemporary revaluations and appropriations demonstrate how the term continues to be employed creatively in criticism and fiction.

Both G.W.F. Hegel and Georg Lukács offer generic definitions of the Bildungsroman without using the word. Hegel sees the novel in general as the heir to epic poetry but in degenerate form, now under the sign of the historical split between subject and object. The modern novel accordingly takes as its preferred theme the collision between "the poetry of the heart and the opposing prose of prevailing conditions and the contingencies of external circumstances." This conflict may be resolved in various ways, but in a certain type of novel—and it is probable that he had the *Lehrjahre* in mind—it is characterized by a mutual influence of the heart and external reality such that both the youthful protagonist and the effect of his activity in the world are enriched by the encounter. In another place in the *Aesthetics* (1835) Hegel famously dismisses the novel in terms that seem to refer to the Bildungsroman. He characterizes it as representing the encounter between an excessively subjective individual who, having had his fling, settles down to an ordinary philistine bourgeois existence with wife and job, capitulating inevitably to the force of prosaic circumstance. Whether or not Hegel had the *Lehrjahre* in mind in writing this oft-quoted passage is by no means clear, yet the intellectual kinship between the subject-object problematic proper to the classical Bildungsroman and to Hegel's overall project is clear enough. The *Phänomenologie des Geistes* (1807; *Phenomenology of Spirit*) itself has been called a sort of philosophical Bildungsroman concerning the process of "becoming" of historical consciousness. Both models of development have a common ancestor in Johann Gottfried von Herder. Both teleological processes entail uncertainty about exactly what the telos involved is, and both suffer from the twin dangers of, on the one hand, premature acquiescence in the status quo, and, on the other, a utopian projection bearing little relationship to existing possibilities.

A more positive and differentiated generic definition in the same tradition is provided by Lukács in his early work *Die Theorie des Romans* (1920; *The Theory of the Novel*). For Lukács the inner form of the modern novel is the journey of the "problematic individual" to himself in the context of the "transcendental homelessness" that is the condition of the modern world, following the "lost totality" of the Hellenic past. Two types of novel may be discerned, the novel of abstract idealism, in which the idealistic protagonist misrecognizes the world (for example, Miguel de Cervantes' *Don Quixote*, 1605–15), and the novel of romantic disillusion (for example, Gustave Flaubert's *L'Éducation sentimentale*, 1869; *Sentimental Education*), in which the defeated hero withdraws into himself, presaging such modernist texts as Rainer Maria Rilke's *Die Aufzeichnungen des Malte Laurids Brigge* (1910; *The Notebooks of Malte Laurids Brigge*). Between these two possibilities, *Wilhelm Meister's Apprenticeship* is an attempted synthesis, in which a reconciliation between the interiority of the human subject and the existing possibilities of society is "problematic, but possible."

Lukács writes of the *Erziehungsroman* (novel of education) rather than of the Bildungsroman. The term *Erziehungsroman* has often in the past been used interchangeably with *Bildungsroman* but currently tends to be reserved for novels that deal specifically with theories or practices of education, such as Fénelon's *Télémaque* (1699), Jean-Jacques Rousseau's *Émile* (1762), or Johann Heinrich Pestalozzi's *Lienhard und Gertrud* (1781). The distinctions cannot be watertight, however, especially in view of the association of the Bildungsroman since 1820 with the idea not only of the protagonist's education but also the reader's. This is an inheritance from the didacticism of Enlightenment novels and specifically from novels—such as *Télémaque*—that were both successful, popular works and written as instruction manuals for noblemen or princes. The *Lehrjahre* itself may be described as an *Erziehungsroman* with some justice, since Natalie and the Society of the Tower are dedicated educators, and Wilhelm's years of apprenticeship are said to be over at the point when he has to learn to be an educator to his own son, Felix.

The term *Entwicklungsroman*, novel of development, also has been used interchangeably with *Bildungsroman*. The consensus now is that it is a useful umbrella term to cover all novels treating the formative years of young people, while Bildungsroman might be restricted to those novels that deal with the specific ideal of formation embodied in the *Lehrjahre*. Boundaries between these types will of necessity be fluid, since much will depend upon the individual critical reading of a given text. *Green Henry*, for instance, is a borderline case, since so much of its importance has to do with disillusion, yet it relies upon the generic expectation of the Bildungsroman to articulate its complex meaning.

The fact is that the word *Bildungsroman* has been accepted widely in criticism and journalism without any consensus as to what it means beyond its German genesis. Indeed, even there the uncertainty persists, since within the canon itself, defined as narrowly as possible, there is no novel, not even excepting the *Lehrjahre* and *The Magic Mountain*, of which it has not vigorously been denied that it is a Bildungsroman at all. On the other hand, the currency of the term in English is authoritatively established by its presence in the second edition of the Oxford English Dictionary, in which it is defined in connection with the most unlikely names, such as Grimmelshausen, Kafka, and Musil.

One final cognate novel type is the *Künstlerroman*, or artist novel. Novels that recount the development of an artist (for instance *Heinrich von Ofterdingen* or James Joyce's *Portrait of the Artist as a Young Man*, 1916) are recognizably novels of development, with an obvious family relationship to the Bildungsroman (the Bildungsroman is often semiautobiographical and its hero often wrongly imagines he is called as an artist) but disqualify themselves from the aspiration of the Bildungsroman—to deal with representative human beings—by being about a particular and unusual sort of human being. One structural advantage enjoyed by the *Künstlerroman*, on the other hand, is that the problem of resolving the collision between the poetry of the heart and the prose of the world is solved when the telos of development becomes the vocation of the artist, and thus at once a social identity and a rejection of philistine conformity.

The Bildungsroman genre is widely understood to be distinct from other genres or types in which there is one central character, such as the picaresque and the confessional or autobiographical novel. Here, too, while there are certainly gray areas, the contrast can contribute to useful distinctions. The picaresque novel, for instance, employs heroes who, in a series of episodes, are knocked about by experience but are not formed, although they might well be damaged, by it. The anonymous *Lazarillo de Tormes* (1554), Francisco de Quevedo's *El Buscón* (1626; *The Swindler*), Hans Jakob Christoffel von Grimmelshausen's *Simplicissimus* (1669), and Günter Grass's *Die Blechtrommel* (1959; *The Tin Drum*) are examples that are predictably rooted in less anthropocentric worldviews than that of German idealism. *The History of Tom Jones* is a borderline case, episodic and knockabout, yet imbued with the social and moral values of the historical middle class.

Autobiographical or confessional novels (for instance Goethe's *Werther*, 1774; Chateaubriand's *René*, 1802; Benjamin Constant's *Adolphe*, 1816; Rilke's *The Notebooks of Malte Laurids Brigge*), on the other hand, may be described as works of self-revelation rather than works about the development of a self. This contrast allows for an important distinction, since the Bildungsroman is necessarily not narrated from the point of view of the self whose development it recounts. There is a distance—usually ironic—between narrator and protagonist. As with Hegel's *Phenomenology of Spirit*, there is a developing consciousness and another consciousness that oversees the development. While necessarily distinct, they belong inseparably together. The Bildungsroman is about subjectivity but is not itself subjective.

The greatest difficulty with definitions arises when one tries to distinguish between the Bildungsroman, with its emphasis upon one person, and the broad social novel, with its emphasis upon many and upon the dynamics of social interaction. The Bildungsroman may be recognized as a philosophical novel in the sense that it adds an ideal dimension to the representation of social reality. In this view, there is a clear distance between it and the bustle of an Honoré de Balzac or a Charles Dickens. It may, however, also be defined, as it often is in non-German literary critical contexts, with heavy emphasis upon the social circumstances with which the protagonist has to integrate himself. To inflect the definition in this way is to make of it the *quintessence* of the social novel, defined as a novel of necessary disillusionment, a novel of reality. One can then make a distinction between a somewhat utopian German variety and a somewhat less utopian French and English one (examples of the latter include Stendhal's *Le Rouge et le noir* [1830; *The Red and the Black*], Balzac's *Illusions perdues* [1843; *Lost Illusions*] or Dickens' *David Copperfield* [1850]). Even a distinction based upon the opposition between one and many characters falls into a sea of nuances if one considers that few great social realist novels have lacked a character with whom readers are meant to identify, and no Bildungsroman may be described as such unless there are other characters (e.g. "society") for the protagonist to come up against. (George Eliot's *The Mill on the Floss* [1860], with its *two* protagonists, is sometimes cited as a double Bildungsroman.) Furthermore, the preoccupation with youth, as Franco Moretti (1987) points out, is a characteristic of modernity as a whole, not just of the European Bildungsroman, which makes the presence of maturing or developing characters with whom the reader is meant to identify more likely than not.

The terms suggested by Hegel and Lukács perhaps clarify the matter by providing an overall framework in which the modern realistic novel as a whole is seen as a genre relating the alienation of the human subject from the objective world. Where it tends toward the objective part of the equation, the Bildungsroman genre will incline toward the realism of lost illusions or even the sarcasm of a sentimental education, while where it tends toward the subjective part, the Bildungsroman genre will define itself as a secular humanist moment of precarious balance between both elements. Retrospectively, the genre then becomes interpretable as the historical precursor of the extreme fragmentary subjectivism of some forms of modernist prose.

The classical Bildungsroman is a predominantly masculine affair in which women characters traditionally play the part of extensions, reflections, or victims of the developing male personality. This high-definition patriarchalism has made the genre interesting to feminist critics. On one hand, they point out how gendered the genre actually was. This has been fruitful in the identification of contrasting types of novels—by both male and female authors—the shape of which is defined by aspects of women's historical experience. Female *Bildung* may be seen as a development toward inevitable exclusion and death—the inheritance of Mignon and the beautiful soul—as in *The Mill on the Floss* or Theodor Fontane's *Effi Briest* (1895). Flaubert's *Madame Bovary* (1857), Kate Chopin's *The Awakening* (1899), and Eliot's *Middlemarch* (1872) may be identified as novels of awakening, in which a woman's development consists of an insight into her actual disempowerment and often leads to her death. But whereas the women in Bildungsromane, symbolically speaking, often die so that the male hero may live, these literary deaths are rather a coming to consciousness in literature of the position and the lack of social possibilities of women.

The other use that feminism and other historically marginalized constituencies can make of the Bildungsroman is a positive one. The very idealism of the genre in its classical form offers a model of how to think and write about unacknowledged, suffering subjectivity while at the same time entering a productive, if by no means unproblematic, relationship with existing social and moral conditions. The genre has been appropriated explicitly (as in Doris Lessing's autobiographical novels *Children of Violence* [1952–69]), or implicitly (as in Ralph Ellison's *Invisible Man* [1952] or Christa Wolf's *Kindheitsmuster* [1976; *A Model Childhood*]) for new fictions as equipped to navigate the perilous channel between the Scylla of resignation and the Charybdis of utopianism as the neohumanist Bildungsroman had done before them.

MICHAEL MINDEN

See also Autobiographical Novel; German Novel; Romantic Novel

Further Reading

Abel, Elizabeth, Marianne Hirsch, and Elizabeth Langland, editors, *The Voyage In: Fictions of Female Development*, Hanover, New Hampshire, and London: University Press of New England, 1983

Beddow, Michael, *The Fiction of Humanity: Studies in the Bildungsroman from Wieland to Thomas Mann*, Cambridge and New York: Cambridge University Press, 1982

Buckley, Jerome Hamilton, *Season of Youth: The Bildungsroman from Dickens to Golding*, Cambridge, Massachusetts: Harvard University Press, 1974

Fraiman, Susan, *Unbecoming Women: British Women Writers and the Novel of Development*, New York: Columbia University Press, 1993

Hardin, James N., editor, *Reflection and Action: Essays on the Bildungsroman,* Columbia: University of South Carolina Press, 1991

Hirsch, Marianne, "The Novel of Formation as Genre: Between *Great Expectations* and *Lost Illusions,*" *Genre* 12 (1979)

Howe, Susanne, *Wilhelm Meister and His Kinsmen, Apprentices to Life,* New York: Columbia University Press, 1930

Jacobs, Jürgen, and Markus Krause, editors, *Der deutsche Bildungsroman: Gattungsgeschichte vom 18. bis zum 20. Jahrhundert,* Munich: Beck, 1989

Kester, Gunilla Theander, *Writing the Subject: Bildung and the African American Text,* New York: Peter Lang, 1995

Kontje, Todd, *The German Bildungsroman: History of a National Genre,* Columbia, South Carolina: Camden House, 1993

Lukács, Georg, *Die Theorie des Romans: Ein geschichtphilosophischer Versuch über die Formen der grossen Epik,* Berlin: Cassiver, 1920; as *The Theory of the Novel: A Historico-Philosophical Essay on the Form of Great Epic Literature,* Cambridge, Massachusetts: MIT Press, 1971; London: Merlin Press, 1978

Mayer, Gerhart, *Der deutsche Bildungsroman: Von der Aufklärung bis zur Gegenwart,* Stuttgart: Metzler, 1992

Miles, David H., "The Picaro's Journey to the Confessional: The Changing Image of the Hero in the German Bildungsroman," *PMLA* 89 (1974)

Minden, Michael, *The German Bildungsroman: Incest and Inheritance,* Cambridge and New York, Cambridge University Press, 1997

Moretti, Franco, *The Way of the World: The Bildungsroman in European Culture,* London: Verso, 1987

Roberts, David, *The Indirections of Desire: Hamlet in Goethe's "Wilhelm Meister,"* Heidelberg: Winter, 1980

Selbmann, Rolf, *Der deutsche Bildungsroman,* Stuttgart: Metzler, 1984; 2nd edition, 1994

Swales, Martin, *The German Bildungsroman from Wieland to Hesse,* Princeton, New Jersey: Princeton University Press, 1978

Biography. *See* Autobiographical Novel; Prose Novelistic Forms

---

Black Rain by Ibuse Masuji

Kuroi ame 1965

Among the various developments in postwar Japanese fiction, atomic bomb literature (*hibakusha bungaku*) is perhaps the most morally and critically challenging. Atrocity, as John Treat (1995) argues, has the power to undermine literature itself, making it seem "hopelessly ironic, useless, or worse, complicitous, when compared to the issues raised by the destruction of Hiroshima and Nagasaki." Yet the bombings have been narrated with great regularity and persistence. The most important examples of bomb fiction were, initially, by survivors themselves, notably the works of Ōta Yōko and Hara Tamiki. These writers created raw, politicized fiction that insisted on the horror of their experience and, often, on the impossibility of adequately representing it, despite almost compulsive attempts.

The great irony of bomb fiction is that the first work in the genre to be labeled a success, and the work that has since come to represent the genre as a whole both in Japan and abroad, was not written until 20 years after the bombings, by a writer who was not himself a victim. Ibuse Masuji (1898–1993) began seri-alizing *Black Rain* in the magazine *Shinchō* in January 1965, when he was already an elder statesman in the Japanese literary establishment and, it was generally thought, on the verge of retirement. The appearance, so relatively late in Ibuse's career, of the work now universally considered his masterpiece astonished critics and released a flood of praise and critical examination that, in many ways, continues 30 years later.

Black Rain has been called a "documentary novel" in that it is based on historical records painstakingly collected and assembled by Ibuse in the novel form. In effect, the work partakes of two genres that have been central to the development of modern Japanese fiction: the so-called "I novel"—the personal, confessional mode that has dominated 20th-century fictional discourse in Japan—and the historical novel. Ibuse had written a number of important historical fictions prior to *Black Rain,* among them *Sazanami gunki* (1930; *Waves*), an account of Japan's 12th-century civil wars, and *Hyōmin Usaburō* (1954; Castaway Us-aburō), a fictionalized rendering of the experiences of an Edo-period sailor. These works served as models for the technique that Ibuse perfected in *Black Rain*: the narration of the historical through the lens of the personal.

Black Rain is, at least on the surface, a hybrid work that juxtaposes accounts of the devastation caused by the atomic bombing of Hiroshima with a realist tale of bourgeois manners centering on the attempts of the protagonist, Shizuma Shigematsu, to find a husband for his dependent niece, Yasuko. Ibuse employs dual settings and time frames, alternating his narrative between Kobatake, a rural hamlet some distance from Hiroshima, at a time several years after the end of the war, and Hiroshima itself in the days immediately after the bombing. Kobatake is described in idealized terms familiar from Ibuse's previous fiction, with agrarian festivals and natural cycles marking a peaceful, measured existence that seems to have left the effects of the war behind. The memories of Hiroshima are evoked almost exclusively through extended quoted sections of the journals that Shigematsu, his wife Shigeko, and Yasuko are recopying as evidence to reassure prospective husbands that Yasuko, who was some ten kilometers from the hypocenter, was not affected by the radiation (despite having been struck by the literal black rain that fell on Hiroshima after the bombing). The interweaving of these two narratives, representing on the one hand the familiar, Jane Austen-like world of realist fiction and on the other an utterly unimaginable atomic hell, constitutes a generic innovation that has earned the novel a reputation as one of the most significant Japanese literary achievements of the postwar period. Conservative critics such as Etō Jun immediately hailed *Black Rain* as the first work to "aestheticize" the bomb, to view it through the mediation of time and distance and thus to render it a work of art. This very praise, however, is the basis for criticism of the work by Hiroshima writers and their political sympathizers, among them Nobel laureate Ōe Kenzaburō (1967), who see Ibuse's fiction as an attempt to humanize the inhuman, to normalize and naturalize one of the greatest atrocities of the century. Survivors of Hiroshima and Nagasaki have insisted on the uniqueness of their experience, on the "difference" conferred on them by suffering. In Shigematsu, Ibuse creates an Everyman whose calm, objective process of remembering serves to recuperate the unthinkable into the realm of narrative, that is, the representable and recognizable.

This criticism, however, ignores the ways in which Ibuse willfully erodes and ultimately destroys the division between his two narratives, as the world of the past and of memory, of the Hiroshima journals being copied out by Shigematsu and his family, begins to infect the pastoral present of Kobatake. The Hiroshima escapees who inhabit the peaceful countryside grow increasingly debilitated, and the burgeoning nature around them serves less as a comfort than as a reminder of their own unnatural dilemma. Despite Shigematsu's good intentions, the journals fail to reassure prospective partners for Yasuko, instead calling attention to the very fact that Shigematsu had hoped to minimize: her status as a bomb victim. Finally, having given up all hope of marrying, Yasuko falls ill with radiation sickness. *Black Rain* ends on an ominous, if ambiguous, note with Shigematsu bargaining with nature for Yasuko's unlikely recovery.

> "If a rainbow appears over those hills now, a miracle will happen," he prophesied to himself. "Let a rainbow appear . . . and Yasuko will be cured."
>
> So he told himself, with his eyes on the nearby hills, though he knew all the while it could never come true.

Debate over the politics of Ibuse's novel continues: is it a radical criticism of war in general and nuclear weapons in particular? Or is it a complicitous attempt to distance, dull, and normalize? In any case, readers have conferred on *Black Rain* the status of classic, with Ibuse's complex, innovative representation of Hiroshima having become the shared imagined experience of an immensely significant historical reality.

STEPHEN SNYDER

Further Reading

Lifton, Robert Jay, *Death in Life: The Survivors of Hiroshima*, New York: Simon and Schuster, 1967

Liman, Anthony, *A Critical Study of the Literary Style of Ibuse Masuji: As Sensitive as Waters*, Lewiston: Mellen Press, 1992

Ōe Kenzaburō, "Kuroi ame to Nihon bundan" (*Black Rain* and Japan's literary establishment), in *Gendai Nihon bungakkan*, volume 29, *fuzoku*, 6–7, Tokyo: Bungei Shunjū, 1967

Ōe Kenzaburō, editor, *The Crazy Iris and Other Stories of the Atomic Aftermath*, New York: Grove Press, 1985

Treat, John, *Pools of Water, Pillars of Fire: The Literature of Ibuse Masuji*, Seattle: University of Washington Press, 1988

Treat, John, *Writing Ground Zero*, Chicago: University of Chicago Press, 1995

Bleak House by Charles Dickens

1853

Charles Dickens' earlier novels, which developed the legacies of Henry Fielding and Tobias Smollett, typically emphasized a central male hero. In *Bleak House* Dickens disrupts this focus of interest by making the most obvious candidate for the role, Richard Carstone, a peripheral failure. For *Bleak House* is not a novel that is much concerned with conventional heroes; its orientation is toward the collective experience of London, and of England. It presents a panoramic view of England and a powerful critique of leading institutions. Most obviously, it exposes the Court of Chancery, the moribund center of a corrupt and wretchedly slow legal system. But abuses of religion, unscrupulous politics, disruptive industrialization, and the antagonistic relations between classes are all presented with great satirical force. Beyond its ambitions as an entertainment—and it is as funny as any of Dickens' novels—*Bleak House* is the work of Dickens the would-be reformer.

But *Bleak House* does not preach to its readers. At times, it may be read as a great, early work of sensational fiction, for example, in the scenes concerning the French murderess, Hortense. Dickens disrupts and eventually destroys the superficially romantic love plot that looms at the beginning of *Bleak House,* but in other respects emphasizes strong romantic elements. The Gothic, for example, is clearly an influence: a celebrated scene involves the quasi-supernatural occurrence of spontaneous combustion, which Dickens invests with all the portentousness that it can take. But he ties the sensationalism to social concerns. The character who goes up in smoke is the grotesque rag-and-bottle shop proprietor, Krook, popularly known as the "Lord Chancellor." Readers may view this event as a wishful image of Chancery and all its horrors disappearing in a final conflagration.

In describing the chambers of the evil lawyer, Tulkinghorn, Dickens notes their "painted ceilings, where Allegory . . . sprawls among balustrades . . . and big-legged boys, and makes the head ache—as would seem to be Allegory's object always, more or less." Dickens' narrator appears to hate portentous systems of all kinds (in this way, allegory is like Chancery) and is particularly antagonistic toward the trappings of the powerful. However, against this privileged world of obfuscation, Dickens mobilizes his own array of metaphors and analogies. Tulkinghorn himself is "[a]n Oyster of the old school, whom nobody can open." In other words, Dickens attacks the system with something equivalent to its own rhetorical devices, seen on a larger scale in the theme of disease. A major plot element in *Bleak House* traces the passage of smallpox from one person to another. This narrative of infection functions in a way that could be called "allegorical" (but that is utterly remote from the pointed figures on Tulkinghorn's ceiling) to present society as a network of desires and sufferings, moral failures and their consequences, where belonging to any particular class is no more a barrier to moral ruin than it is a protection against physical decay. Dickens' presentation of disease may also be taken literally; by showing the sickness spawned in the dwellings of London's poorest, he draws his readers' attention to the specific negligences of the state.

Crime is another multivalent focus of the novel: it is both a real evil and a metaphor for patterns of malign causality between social groups. Scholars regard *Bleak House* as a pioneering work of crime fiction, with descendants from Wilkie Collins to P.D. James, but Dickens' Inspector Bucket may be interpreted as a type of antidisease: someone of sinister but extraordinary skills, who, like smallpox, climbs rapidly from one class to the next, except that, instead of bringing death to the innocent, he momentarily picks the locks of a corrupt society, assisting a few good people. Bucket is benign, but the manic mysteriousness through which he operates again confirms the pollution and intractability of his society as a whole.

The focus of Dickens' sympathetic interest in *Bleak House* remains on isolated communities, pockets of real human activity within a framework that is irredeemably dehumanized. This is equally the case with the Deadlocks' ancestral seat in Lincolnshire, the slum, Tom-all-Alone's, or the shooting gallery, which paradoxically represents peace for Trooper George. Dickens seems to imply that these compact environments give readers a chance to see life as it is. Looking beyond local detail leads one to the meaninglessness of "allegory" or the "telescopic philanthropy" of Mrs. Jellyby, who works tirelessly for "Borrioboola-Gha," but overlooks the chaos in her own family and, by implication, the dire condition of her immediate, English environment. One might suspect Dickens of parochialism in this context, but his real interest in other nations is obvious from his essays; what he is mocking, rather, is the society of one nation, many of whose members are foreign to one another.

Bleak House is also concerned with people who are foreign to themselves. Above all, much of the story revolves around the orphan, Esther Summerson, a character Dickens developed, partially, from Charlotte Brontë's heroine Jane Eyre. Like Jane, Esther feels profoundly confused about her place in a world containing so much disorder and hostility. She explores this confusion through the space given her by Dickens' greatest formal innovation in *Bleak House,* the double narrative. The novel's chapters are shared between an impersonal voice, similar in many respects to the narrative point of view of Dickens' previous works, and the first-person retrospective account of Esther. Dickens infuses the latter narrative with a loving spirit that befits Esther's surname, "summer-sun," but also constantly evokes the insecurities of an unhappy childhood. Many readers have seen Esther as too good to be true and irritatingly coy in her partial self-disclosures. But this interpretation misses the point: her quirks and pretensions make sense as part of the general absurdity that the world of this novel daily inflicts upon itself. Esther's defects of character, and the greater flaw that Dickens introduces to the novel by scattering its events between two idiosyncratic voices, seem entirely fitting in a text in which the nearest thing to a figure of sanity and wisdom is Jarndyce, Esther's patron. This character seems split in an almost Jekyll-and-Hyde way between his philanthropic actions within the world and his brooding home life.

The complexity of *Bleak House* and its concern with secrets and duality have encouraged deconstructive readings. J. Hillis Miller, for example, has argued that the fictional house that gives the novel its title may be read as an image of the unreadability of the fiction *Bleak House:* a meandering structure in which the reader becomes irretrievably lost, so that to embark on this novel is almost like taking a lawsuit to Chancery. One has to wonder whether Dickens, the implied author, is ultimately less insidiously manipulative than the institutions he so vigorously satirizes. On the other hand, Bleak House is held up as a place of peace and forgiveness: the prototype for a happier society. In the end, this is a text suspended between platitude and mystery, in which obvious social concern is inextricable from a sense of the excitement of living in such a complex and dangerous world.

The "legacy" of *Bleak House* and Dickens' other late, complicated novels is immeasurable. For example, Franz Kafka's *Trial* is often compared with *Bleak House,* as both works plunge the reader into the nightmare of judicial bureaucracy beyond control. The term *Dickensian* often denotes a quaint kind of old-fashioned ricketyness of physical and social structures, whereas

Kafkaesque is always sinister. However, Dickens' Chancery has a real horror that challenges this distinction. The writer who comes nearest to producing the equivalent of a *Bleak House* in the 20th century is probably James Joyce. *Ulysses* (1922), in its large picture of modern urban society, moral turbulence, black humor, linguistic inventiveness, and, above all, the considerable demands that Joyce places on the novel's readers, owes a debt to Dickens.

DOMINIC RAINSFORD

See also Charles Dickens

Further Reading

Andrews, Malcolm, *Dickens and the Grown-Up Child,* London: Macmillan, and Iowa City: University of Iowa Press, 1994

Bloom, Harold, editor, *Charles Dickens's "Bleak House,"* New York: Chelsea House, 1987

Collins, Philip, "Some Narrative Devices in *Bleak House,*" *Dickens Studies Annual* 19 (1990)

Hawthorn, Jeremy, editor, *"Bleak House,"* London: Macmillan, and Atlantic Highlands, New Jersey: Humanities Press International, 1987

Lucas, John, "Past and Present: *Bleak House* and *A Child's History of England,*" in *Dickens Refigured: Bodies, Desires and Other Histories,* edited by John Schad, Manchester: Manchester University Press, 1996

Miller, Karl, *Doubles: Studies in Literary History,* Oxford and New York: Oxford University Press, 1985

Page, Norman, *"Bleak House": A Novel of Connections,* Boston: Twayne, 1990

Sadrin, Anny, *Parentage and Inheritance in the Novels of Charles Dickens,* Cambridge and New York: Cambridge University Press, 1994

Shatto, Susan, *The Companion to "Bleak House,"* London: Allen and Unwin, 1988

Storey, Graham, *Charles Dickens, "Bleak House,"* Cambridge and New York: Cambridge University Press, 1987

Blechtrommel. *See* Danzig Trilogy

Heinrich Böll 1917–85

German

Nobel prize laureate Heinrich Böll is widely perceived as one of the chief luminaries of postwar German literature. After his death, critics lamented the lack of a successor capable of carrying on his public mission as "conscience of the nation," as moral authority, as compassionate literary spokesperson for the disadvantaged. Böll's prewar existence had been shaped by the Rhine, Cologne (the city of his birth), and Catholicism. His experience as a soldier in a catastrophic and ruinous war provided further constitutive elements of his fiction.

Böll's first stories, published in 1947, are usually told by first-person narrator-protagonists of low military rank who take a "worm's-eye" view of World War II. The laconic yet symbolic style of the American short story prevails. The war's senselessness and the inevitability of death are also key themes of narratives that blur generic boundaries. Examples are *Der Zug war pünktlich* (1949; *The Train Was on Time*) and *Wo warst du, Adam?* (1951; *And Where Were You, Adam?*).

In a 1952 essay, Böll accepted the label "rubble literature" as a designation of his generation's literary orientation, which was thematically defined by war, coming home, and ubiquitous ruin.

Rejecting an "escape into some idyll," Böll strove, as he put it in 1964, for an "aesthetics of the humane" expressed in home (*Heimat*) and family. Böll's emphasis on home implied a potential conflict for the individual between his family on the one hand and society on the other—a theme that Böll developed in his novels of the 1950s.

Böll's first commercially and critically successful novel, *Und sagte kein einziges Wort* (1953; *And Never Said a Word*), innovatively alternates the first-person narratives of a man and a woman whose marriage is in crisis because of their poverty and the husband's loss of faith. Like Böll's posthumously published first novel *Der Engel schwieg* (1992; *The Silent Angel*), the novel bears the hallmarks of "rubble literature" by virtue of its setting in the destroyed city of Cologne. Böll's criticism of the Catholic church, whose officials are portrayed as publicity seekers oblivious to genuine suffering and deprivation, is counterbalanced by his suggestion that individual acts of faith and Christian charity, which do not require the mediation of the church, may serve as a remedy for social ills.

In *Billard um halb zehn* (1959; *Billiards at Half-Past Nine*),

Böll temporarily abandoned the protagonist who is a maladjusted outsider on the fringes of society. Instead he developed an intricate structural dialectic of a narrated present—the occurrences of one day in 1958—and the characters' memories of the past. The time frame extends from imperial Germany to the Federal Republic under Chancellor Konrad Adenauer. In the manner of a family chronicle, Böll introduces three generations of a prominent architect's family whose members were successively involved with the building of an abbey at the beginning of the 20th century, its destruction during World War II, and its rebuilding after 1945. The abbey serves Böll both as an objective correlative for the baleful continuities of German history and as a vehicle for expressing his profound concern with the Catholic church's influence on society and politics. The dualistic pattern of the "sacrament of the beasts" (perpetrators) versus that of the "lambs" (victims) to which the characters adhere proved perhaps insufficient as an explanation of the reasons for Germany's calamitous history.

Ansichten eines Clowns (1963; *The Clown*) is overtly a novel about the failure of the nonlegal marriage of "clown" Hans Schnier and his resulting existential and professional crisis. But it entails a severe indictment of the social and political practices of the Catholic church, a church that is seen as an ideological supporter of the establishment. The protagonist's highly subjective perspective, which both results from and reinforces his status as an outsider, did not diminish the novel's appeal as oppositional literature.

In his two following novels, Böll employed a quasi-documentary approach. In *Gruppenbild mit Dame* (1971; *Group Portrait with Lady*), in many respects Böll's crowning achievement, the narrator, a journalist, seeks to reconstruct the life of the simultaneously saintly and sensuous heroine through interviews with those who have known her. The large number of characters enabled Böll to present a panorama of Cologne society and the changes it has undergone throughout the course of history. When the unworldly heroine falls upon hard times, all the good people rally around her and form a community in which relationships are based on love and trust rather than on power and money—perhaps an overly optimistic vision of a future society. In the novella *Die verlorene Ehre der Katharina Blum* (1974; *The Lost Honor of Katharina Blum*), Böll again featured a heroine with saintly features. He became embroiled in a raging controversy because the novella, in attacking the practices of yellow journalism, was construed to convey sympathy for terrorists such as Ulrike Meinhof.

Fürsorgliche Belagerung (1979; *The Safety Net*) satirizes the pervasive fear of terrorism in the Federal Republic of the 1970s, which threatened to lead to the creation of a police state. The novel depicts from a number of shifting perspectives three days in the life of a prominent newspaper magnate who, as a potential target of terrorists, is caught in a tight security network that destroys any semblance of privacy and freedom. In the newspaper magnate's children, Böll invested his hope for a humane society, for they have embraced an alternative lifestyle that renounces the profit motive, fights the destruction of the environment, and rejects violence as a means of changing the prevailing socioeconomic order.

Frauen vor Flusslandschaft (1985; *Women in a River Landscape*), a posthumously published "novel in dialogues and soliloquies," takes place among the power elite in Bonn, then shifts to the capital of the Federal Republic. The women mentioned in the title remain rather shadowy figures. The pervasive atmosphere of suspicion, intrigue, and hidden guilt is indicative of the lost chances and opportunities for social and political reform after the "zero hour" of 1945—one of Böll's abiding preoccupations.

Although Böll did not systematically explore his views on the novel, his emphasis on humanity and social compassion, his attention to common people and everyday occurrences, his appreciation of society's outsiders and outcasts, and his concern for the use and function of language in public discourse may be identified as characteristic of his fiction, which chronicles—generally in a traditional realistic mode—the development of the Federal Republic and therefore constitutes one of the major novelistic oeuvres of postwar German literature.

SIEGFRIED MEWS

Biography

Born in Cologne, Germany, 21 December 1917. Educated at Gymnasium, Cologne, and the University of Cologne. Served in the German army, 1939–45; wounded four times, and taken prisoner, 1945. Joiner in his father's shop, then apprentice as a bookseller before the war; began writing full-time in 1947; coedited *Labyrinth*, 1960–61, and *L*, from 1976; president, PEN International, 1971–74. Awarded Nobel prize for literature, 1972. Died 16 July 1985.

Novels by Böll

Der Zug war pünktlich, 1949; as *The Train Was on Time*, translated by Richard Graves, 1956
Wo warst du, Adam?, 1951; as *Adam, Where Art Thou?*, translated by Mervyn Savill, 1955; as *And Where Were You, Adam?*, translated by Leila Vennewitz, 1973
Und sagte kein einziges Wort, 1953; as *Acquainted with the Night*, translated by Richard Graves, 1954; as *And Never Said a Word*, translated by Leila Vennewitz, 1978
Haus ohne Hüter, 1954; as *The Unguarded House*, translated by Mervyn Savill, 1957; as *Tomorrow and Yesterday*, translated by Savill, 1957
Das Brot der frühen Jahre, 1955; as *The Bread of Our Early Years*, translated by Mervyn Savill, 1957; as *The Bread of Those Early Years*, translated by Leila Vennewitz, 1976
Billard um halb zehn, 1959; as *Billiards at Half-Past Nine*, translated by Patrick Bowles, 1961
Ansichten eines Clowns, 1963; as *The Clown*, translated by Leila Vennewitz, 1965
Gruppenbild mit Dame, 1971; as *Group Portrait with Lady*, translated by Leila Vennewitz, 1973
Die verlorene Ehre der Katharina Blum, 1974; as *The Lost Honor of Katharina Blum*, translated by Leila Vennewitz, 1975
Fürsorgliche Belagerung, 1979; as *The Safety Net*, translated by Leila Vennewitz, 1982
Frauen vor Flusslandschaft: Roman in Dialogen und Selbstgesprächen, 1985; as *Women in a River Landscape: A Novel in Dialogues and Soliloquies*, translated by David McLintock, 1988
Der Engel schwieg, 1992; as *The Silent Angel*, translated by Breon Mitchell, 1994

Other Writings: short stories, plays, a book of verse (*Gedichte*, 1972), essays, autobiographical works, and translations (with Annemarie Böll).

Further Reading

Conard, Robert C., *Understanding Heinrich Böll*, Columbia: University of South Carolina Press, 1992

Prodaniuk, Ihor, *The Imagery in Heinrich Böll's Novels*, Bonn: Bouvier, 1979

Reid, James Henderson, *Heinrich Böll: A German for His Time*, Oxford: Berg, 1988

Sowinski, Bernhard, *Heinrich Böll*, Stuttgart: Metzler, 1993

Vogt, Jochen, *Heinrich Böll*, Munich: Beck, 1978; 2nd edition, 1987

Zachau, Reinhard K., *Heinrich Böll: Forty Years of Criticism*, Columbia, South Carolina: Camden House, 1994

The Bone People by Keri Hulme

1983

Keri Hulme was almost unknown when *The Bone People* burst on the New Zealand literary scene. Her first novel, *The Bone People* had taken 12 years to write, and was offered to three commercial publishers before being taken up by Spiral, a feminist publishing collective. Spiral's faith in the novel was quickly vindicated. In 1984 *The Bone People* won the New Zealand Book Award for Fiction, the Mobil Pegasus Award for Maori Literature, and, the following year, the Booker McConnell Prize. International success fanned an enthusiastic local response to the novel, while the book's popularity was further buoyed by the newly elected Labour government's empowerment of the Waitangi Tribunal to investigate Maori grievances dating back to 1840. At the time the book was published, *The Bone People* seemed to satisfy a desire for a myth of origin among Pakeha (an elastic term usually referring to New Zealanders of European descent) while allegorizing a utopian bicultural future for New Zealand predicated on the magical healing of past wounds.

The Bone People is narrated mostly in the third person but includes passages of interior monologue. This mixture finds parallels in the novel's blending of poetry and prose and also in the sudden shifts between florid and vernacular language. Although the novel has three main characters, the dominant fictional presence belongs to Kerewin Holmes, who, somewhat like her creator, lives as a recluse in a remote part of the South Island of New Zealand. Kerewin identifies herself as a Maori, even though she has only one Maori great-grandparent. Estrangement from her family has blighted Kerewin's artistic talent, and she has built for herself a Yeatsian tower on a promontory in a lagoon; its protecting walls repel visitors and permit the narcissistic enjoyment of her isolation, her intellect, and her collections of books, shells, weapons, and Maori artifacts.

Simon Peter, a Pakeha child with no history, manages to infiltrate Kerewin's sanctuary. The only survivor of a mysterious shipwreck, the mute and occasionally vandalous Simon has been fostered by Joseph Gillayley, a local Maori laborer who has lost his wife and son to influenza. Simon's relationship with his foster father is complex: Joe and Simon love each other tenderly, but Joe vents his grief and frustration on the boy in brutal violence.

Simon sees how his foster father's pain might be healed through a union with Kerewin; in turn Kerewin finds their company congenial and reluctantly allows herself to be drawn into their lives. While her professed "neuter gender" undermines Joe's hope of a happy ending, Kerewin's insularity contributes indirectly to the narrative's utopian resolution: out of self-centeredness, she fails to protect Simon from a horrific assault. This act of violence becomes the story's pivotal event.

Until this point, the novel's mode is best described as expressive realism; thereafter, the quest narrative begins, and the mode becomes rather more mythic and allegorical. Joe serves three months in jail for child abuse; after his release, he attempts suicide on an isolated beach and is rescued by the ancient Maori *kaumatua* (elder) who has been awaiting his arrival. The *kaumatua* has been guarding a sacred site that contains a *mauri*, or life-force, the waning soul of the country embodied in a luminous pierced stone. The *kaumatua* aids Joe's return to health and passes on to him the responsibility for the *mauri* before dying. In the meantime, Kerewin has undertaken a journey of her own. She realizes that she possessed the power to prevent the assault on Simon, and she believes her sudden abdominal pain stems from a cancer brought on by spiritual unease. Kerewin's solution is to dismantle her tower, burn its remains, and journey into the wilderness of Central Otago, where she expects to die. While in this state she is convinced that her life is meaningless without family and community. This realization is the turning point in her illness; purified by suffering and newly aware of her responsibility as a leader, her recovery is assured by the ministrations of a mysterious, sticklike creature.

Simon, too, makes his own journey toward recovery. Deafened by the assault and made a ward of the state, he absconds from care in search of his beloved foster father. When he arrives home, however, he finds the tower burned and Kerewin and Joe gone. Although Simon is returned to welfare custody, Kerewin's new-found sense of responsibility means she can eventually offer Simon the security he needs. After rebuilding the *marae* (community center) at her tribal home of Moerangi, she returns to the lagoon at Whangaroa and starts to rebuild her home—this time, a spiral structure over the ruins of the destroyed tower. Joe, Simon, and Kerewin are finally united in "commensalism"; reconciled with her own family, she offers Joe and Simon the shelter of her name. The *mauri* Joe has brought with him is absorbed like a talisman into the earth.

Although Hulme at times uses the conventions of romance fiction, she refuses the expected closure of the romance plot. If Kerewin, Joe, and Simon are to be "the bone people"—the beginning people, the founders of a new way of living in Aotearoa/New Zealand—their relationship and their community must also be new. Hence, *The Bone People* consistently attempts to destabilize the binaries and hierarchies structuring Western society: Maori/Pakeha, man/woman, husband/wife. Similarly, the book's circular structure (its first section is entitled "The End at the Beginning") reflects the values and symbolism of community embodied in the spiral, rather than the values of hierarchy represented by the tower.

The novel itself is a magpie compilation of literary allusion. Its most obvious intertexts include Daniel Defoe's *Robinson Crusoe*, William Shakespeare's *The Tempest*, and the New Testament; other sources include the works of James Joyce, Mervyn Peake, C.S. Lewis, and J.R.R. Tolkien. Hulme also weaves in Maori mythology and esoteric Eastern philosophies. The novel is equally eclectic in form: part mystery novel (Kerewin indulges in some amateur sleuthing in her efforts to ascertain Simon's origins), part romance, and part quest narrative. Hulme invokes these generic elements in order to expose the myths they perpetuate—the triumph of the intellect, the fulfillment of heterosexual love, and the artist's need for isolation—while true value is associated with Maori spirituality and community.

The nature of the novel's conclusion has been the subject of much discussion locally. Is it a sentimental new-age vision or does it heal the wounds of history? Does it galvanize present possibilities or offer readers the comforting illusion of an achieved biculturalism? While *The Bone People* continues to generate important debate, the work of Maori writers such as Witi Ihimaera, Patricia Grace, and Hone Kouka issue equally profound challenges to a Pakeha population perhaps too quick to congratulate themselves on the speed with which the inequities of colonialism are currently being redressed.

SARAH SHIEFF

Further Reading
Alley, Elizabeth, "Keri Hulme" (Interview), in *In the Same Room: Conversations with New Zealand Writers*, edited by Elizabeth Alley and Mark Williams, Auckland: Auckland University Press, 1992

Brown, Ruth, "Contextualising Maori Writing," *New Zealand Books* 6 (June 1996)

Dale, Judith, "*the bone people*: (Not) Having It Both Ways," *Landfall* 39:4 (December 1985)

During, Simon, "Postmodernism or Postcolonialism?" *Landfall* 39:3 (September 1985)

Edmond, Rod, "No Country for Towers: Reconsidering *the bone people*," *Landfall* (new series) 1:2 (November 1993)

Fee, Margery, "Why C.K. Stead didn't like Keri Hulme's *the bone people*: Who can write as Other?" *Australian and New Zealand Studies in Canada* 1 (Spring 1989)

Fee, Margery, "Keri Hulme: Inventing New Ancestors for Aotearoa," in *International Literature in English: Essays on the Major Writers*, edited by Robert L. Ross, Chicago and London: St. James Press, 1991

Jones, Lawrence, "*the bone people* and *All Visitors Ashore*," in *Barbed Wire and Mirrors: Essays on New Zealand Prose*, Dunedin: University of Otago Press, 1987; 2nd edition, 1990

Stead, C.K., "Keri Hulme's *The Bone People*, and the Pegasus Award for Maori Literature," *Ariel* 16 (1985)

Williams, Mark, "Keri Hulme and Negative Capability," in *Leaving the Highway: Six Contemporary New Zealand Novelists*, Auckland: Auckland University Press, 1990

Bonheur d'occasion. *See* Tin Flute

Boom. *See entries under* Latin America

Elizabeth Bowen 1899–1973

Irish

During the 1940s and 1950s, Elizabeth Bowen was frequently regarded as Ireland's leading novelist. Soon afterward her reputation began to slip, and it was not substantially revived by the rise of feminist criticism. She is seldom now included in surveys of the 20th-century novel. Yet there are those who argue, like her biographer Victoria Glendinning (1977), that "she is what happened after Bloomsbury" and stands as the link connecting Virginia Woolf with Iris Murdoch and Muriel Spark. Still others have praised her in entirely different terms. Andrew Bennett and Nicholas Royle (1994) see her as a fundamentally postmodern writer, aggressively destabilizing the novel form, while Renée Hoogland (1994) finds in her books a subversive lesbian subtext.

More conventional readings present Bowen as an heir to Henry James—an influence against which Woolf cautioned her. She characteristically deals with English (and less frequently Irish) characters anywhere from the lower to the upper reaches of the amorphous British middle class. Her novels have been characterized as presenting "life with the lid on." The phrase, accurate enough as far as it goes, does not take account of her sense of the depth of life's tragedies or of her forays into the Gothic and into a kind of melodrama, especially in some of her stories and in her later work. Some of her best writing deals with young protagonists who are displaced, perhaps reflecting her childhood displacements from apartment to apartment with her mother after her father's mental breakdown. Most of her novels involve disillusionment, a theme she is especially capable of dramatizing because her sensibility—rather unusually—combines a powerful romantic strain with a coldly realistic eye. By the same token, the emotional impact of Bowen's works is ambiguous because she sees disillusionment, however painful, as an inevitable accompaniment to personal growth.

Allan Austin (1989) has suggested that Bowen's novels divide themselves fairly neatly into three groups. *The Hotel* (1927), *The Last September* (1929), and *To the North* (1932) all concern a young woman either experiencing or anticipating her first serious love, and unprepared to face the consequences; the young women at the end of the first two novels are unattached but transformed, while the protagonist of *To the North* dies. The most successful of these, *The Last September*, is set in one of Ireland's Anglo-Irish "big houses" in 1920, during the time of the "Troubles." Lois' courtship by a young English army officer brings the menacing political situation to bear on the romantic and social dance of the characters, and the occasional eruptions of violence into the ceremonious world of the Irish ascendancy give an ironic feel to the elaborate social machinations. Bowen introduces one of the more successful of her older female figures in Marda, a snobbish woman of conservative convictions who is nevertheless acute and personally powerful.

In three novels from mid-career—*Friends and Relations* (1931), *The House in Paris* (1935), and *The Death of the Heart* (1938)—Bowen explores the consequences of apparently disastrous early romances, and she structures all three novels by contrasting the periods before and after the disappointment of romantic hopes. While *The Death of the Heart* is Bowen's generally acknowledged masterpiece (*see separate entry*, Death of the Heart), *The House in Paris* is also an impressive achievement. Cast in a more Gothic mode, much of the novel's power is based on the feeling that the characters are trapped in a "dreaming wood": indeed, like several of her novels, this one builds upon the scaffolding of a fairy tale, in this case Hansel and Gretel. In the novel's present time, two children meet in Madame Fisher's foreboding house in Paris, while in its past readers learn the story of the boy's parents. His father, Max Ebhart, has committed suicide to escape Madame Fisher's baleful influence. Karen Michaelis, the boy's rebellious mother, is planning on coming to claim him for the first time, but at the end is replaced by her husband, Ray Forrestier.

Bowen's last four novels are substantially different from their predecessors and from one another. *The Heat of the Day* (1949), set in wartime, shows a woman's relationship with her lover, who is revealed to be a spy, and with an odd counterspy who pursues him. A strong and unusual novel, it has been successfully dramatized. Both *A World of Love* (1955) and *The Little Girls* (1964) are intellectually complex novels; the former is also highly stylized. The latter concerns three women in their 50s who come together to explore their childhood relationship, and shows most vividly Bowen's fascination with the meaning of childhood experience. Bowen's last novel, *Eva Trout* (1968)—easily her strangest—features a severely ill-adjusted woman whose illusions, coupled with her great wealth and her lack of intelligent concern for others, lead to disaster. In some ways she is a parody of Bowen's gallery of dangerous innocents. Critics have conventionally seen a falling-off in Bowen's powers from their heights in the 1940s, but more recently some have argued that her later work, with its diminished role for the commenting narrator and its movement toward grotesquerie, is a powerful anticipation of the postmodern mode.

As a whole, Bowen's work probably stands or falls with her narrators; her preference is for the omniscient narrator who is licensed to comment occasionally in rather poetic, impressionistic miniature essays and who may "hover above" several consciousnesses in a novel. While this old-fashioned narrative technique is susceptible to abuse, Bowen usually maintains a modernist ambiguity by means of the obliquity and density of the narrator's comments. The structures and patterns of her novels reward investigation, and the best ones are rich with unexpected mirrorings of character and situation, motif and symbol. She is technically resourceful and surprisingly inventive, if never as radical as James Joyce or Woolf in her novelistic practice. There is certainly a conservative element in her literary attitude: in her short book on *English Novelists* (1942) she ends the record with Woolf and E. M. Forster, avoiding the issue of Joyce and D. H. Lawrence entirely, and even lavishes some praise on Woolf's *bêtes-noirs*, H. G. Wells, Arnold Bennett, and John Galsworthy. But whatever the eventual fate of her reputation as a novelist, she may have a better guarantee of lasting fame through her remarkable short stories. Harold Bloom (1987) has argued that after Joyce and Lawrence, Bowen may be the most distinguished writer of short stories of our time, and particularly singles out for praise the wartime volume *Ivy Gripped the Steps* (1946).

Certainly her *Collected Stories* (1981) is also a remarkable achievement.

R. BRANDON KERSHNER

See also Death of the Heart

Biography

Born in Dublin, 7 June 1899. Attended a day school in Folkestone, Kent; Harpenden Hall, Hertfordshire; Downe House School, Kent, 1914–17; London County Council School of Art, 1918–19. Hospital worker in Dublin, 1918; worked for the Ministry of Information, London, during World War II. Reviewer, the *Tatler,* London, beginning in the mid-1930s; associate editor, *London Magazine,* 1954–61. Died 22 February 1973.

Novels by Bowen

The Hotel, 1927
The Last September, 1929
Friends and Relations, 1931
To the North, 1932
The House in Paris, 1935
The Death of the Heart, 1938
The Heat of the Day, 1949
A World of Love, 1955
The Little Girls, 1964
Eva Trout; or, Changing Scenes, 1968

Other Writings: short stories, autobiographical fragments, essays, prefaces, book reviews, and travel pieces.

Further Reading

Austin, Allan E., *Elizabeth Bowen,* New York: Twayne, 1971; revised edition, Boston: Twayne, 1989
Bennett, Andrew, and Nicholas Royle, *Elizabeth Bowen and the Dissolution of the Novel,* London: Macmillan, and New York: St. Martin's Press, 1994
Bloom, Harold, editor, *Elizabeth Bowen,* New York: Chelsea House, 1987
Glendinning, Victoria, *Elizabeth Bowen: A Biography,* London: Weidenfeld and Nicolson, 1977; New York: Knopf, 1978
Heath, William, *Elizabeth Bowen: An Introduction to Her Novels,* Madison: University of Wisconsin Press, 1961
Hildebidle, John, *Five Irish Writers: The Errand of Keeping Alive,* Cambridge, Massachusetts: Harvard University Press, 1989
Hoogland, Renée C., *Elizabeth Bowen: A Reputation in Writing,* New York: New York University Press, 1994
Kenney, Edwin J., *Elizabeth Bowen,* Lewisburg, Pennsylvania: Bucknell University Press, 1975
Kershner, R.B., "Bowen's Oneiric *House in Paris,*" *Texas Studies in Literature and Language* 28 (Winter 1986)
Lee, Hermione, *Elizabeth Bowen: An Estimation,* London: Vision Press, and Totowa, New Jersey: Barnes and Noble, 1981
Wyatt-Brown, Anne M., "The Liberation of Mourning in Elizabeth Bowen's *The Little Girls* and *Eva Trout,*" in *Aging and Gender in Literature: Studies in Creativity,* edited by Anne M. Wyatt-Brown and Janice Rossen, Charlottesville: University Press of Virginia, 1993

Brat'ia Karamazovy. *See* Brothers Karamazov

Brazilian Novel. *See* Latin American Novel: Brazil

The Bridal Canopy by S.Y. Agnon

Hakhnasath kallah 1931

The Bridal Canopy is the first full-length novel by the 20th-century Hebrew writer and Nobel prize winner S.Y. Agnon (1888–1970). Published in 1931, it holds a distinguished place in the history of modern Hebrew literature, both because of its style and its content. Written in a pietistic mode that was to become Agnon's trademark, *The Bridal Canopy* weaves together scores of traditional Jewish textual references to create a kind of tapestry of biblical, rabbinic, and Hasidic lore within the framework of a simple plot.

The narrative, set in the early 19th century, concentrates on the adventures of Reb Yudel Hasid, a poverty-stricken but pious Jew from the town of Brody in Galicia. In picaresque style reminiscent of Miguel de Cervantes' *Don Quixote*, the plot follows the travels of Reb Yudel, who embarks on a journey through the towns and hamlets of Galicia for the sake of collecting dowries for his three unmarried daughters. The quixotic Reb Yudel is accompanied by his own Sancho Panza, a hard-headed wagon-driver named Nuta. Reb Yudel's journey, however, does not allow him to see the world in the conventional sense, since most of his adventures are experienced secondhand via the pious and often wondrous tales related to him by the various characters he encounters along the way. Reb Yudel finally returns home after he unwittingly manages to find a groom for his eldest daughter, in a farcical scene involving a mistaken identity. The novel ends even more "miraculously," with the discovery of a buried treasure in the vicinity of Reb Yudel's own home. This treasure not only provides the needed dowries, but it also makes Reb Yudel into a wealthy man, allowing him to marry off all his daughters and eventually to make his way to Israel.

At the time Agnon composed *The Bridal Canopy*, most Hebrew writers who wrote about Jewish religious life generally continued to follow the Enlightenment tradition of viewing religion from a highly critical perspective. Apart from a few earlier writers, such as I.L. Peretz and Micha Yosef Berdichevsky, who went to the opposite extreme of creating romanticized portraits of the life of the Hasidim, most of Agnon's contemporaries still portrayed the Jewish religion as stultifying and untenable for modern Jews. Agnon's work was revolutionary in that he appeared to be stemming the tide and embracing the very religious life that had been rejected so vehemently by most of his fellow Hebrew writers. In fact, when *The Bridal Canopy* was first published, it was viewed by critics as an homage to the traditional religious world of Eastern European Jewry, in all its simple piety and naive faith.

In subsequent years, however, critics such as Dov Sadan (1959) began to unearth the deeply ironic underpinnings of the novel, with the result that *The Bridal Canopy* is now regarded as much more complex than it originally seemed. Although the novel appears on the surface to be devoted to portraying the transcendent beauty of Reb Yudel's simple faith in God, a closer reading captures something else at work—the utter passivity engendered by that faith. From the very beginning of the novel, the reader sees that Reb Yudel has done nothing to relieve the grinding poverty and suffering of his own family until he is summoned to do so by a rabbi (and only after Reb Yudel's wife begs for the rabbi's intercession). Even Reb Yudel's journey to collect the dowries is spent in a more or less passive mode—eating, drinking, praying, listening to tales, and waiting for the Almighty to send good fortune his way.

Agnon scholars such as Arnold Band (1968) and Gershon Shaked (1989) have pointed out that despite Reb Yudel's contin-

uous stream of pious statements, his actions show that he is consummately self-absorbed. Indeed, he has little desire to return home to his starving family because he is having too good a time on the road. Significantly, it is the less pious wagon driver, Nuta, who seems to possess a more acute sense of right and wrong, for he berates Reb Yudel for his lack of compassion for his family. Even the match that is made for Reb Yudel's daughter is based on a deception in which Reb Yudel knowingly participates, but which he rationalizes, as he does most other things, as part of the divine will.

The question that remains for most scholars is whether the deep irony discovered within *The Bridal Canopy* actually reveals the novel as the opposite of what it appears to be on the surface, a parody of religious life rather than an ode to it. Although the debate about this novel is hardly resolved, most critics agree that one of the main innovations of *The Bridal Canopy* is that Agnon was tacitly able to do two things at once—praise and condemn—because, as the scholar Gershom Scholem (1976) has so acutely perceived, Agnon had mastered the "dialectics of simplicity." By adopting a pious writing style that appears to emanate from the very world he describes, Agnon casts his portrait in such a way that allows the reader to see the virtues *and* the vices of traditional religious Judaism in Eastern Europe.

Perhaps more than anything else, it is Agnon's highly controlled irony that keeps the plot from descending into burlesque, an irony whose subtlety has rarely been matched in Hebrew fiction. It is the utter delicacy of Agnon's ironic technique that allows *The Bridal Canopy* to hang in the balance between pious fable and comedic farce and that ultimately gives this unconventional work a singular place in the history of the modern novel.

SHARON GREEN

See also S.Y. Agnon

Further Reading

Band, Arnold, *Nostalgia and Nightmare: A Study in the Fiction of S.Y. Agnon,* Berkeley: University of California Press, 1968

Hochman, Baruch, *The Fiction of S.Y. Agnon,* Ithaca, New York: Cornell University Press, 1970

Holtz, Avraham, *Mar'ot u-mekorot: Mahadurah mu'eret u-me'uyeret shel Hakhnasat kalah le-Shai 'Agnon,* Jerusalem and Tel Aviv: Schocken, 1995

Kurzweil, Baruch, *Masot 'al sipure Shai 'Agnon,* Jerusalem: Schocken, 1962

Sadan, Dov, *'Al Shai 'Agnon: Masah, 'iyun, ve-heqer,* Tel Aviv: Ha-kibbutz ha-meuhad, 1959

Scholem, Gershom, "S.Y. Agnon—The Last Hebrew Classic?" in *On Jews and Judaism in Crisis,* New York: Schocken, 1976

Shaked, Gershon, *Schmuel Yosef Agnon: A Revolutionary Traditionalist,* New York: New York University Press, 1989

The Bridge on the Drina by Ivo Andrić

Na Drini ćuprija 1945

The leading Yugoslav writer of the 20th century and the only Nobel prize winner among the Southern Slav writers, Ivo Andrić was always interested in his native Bosnia, as manifested in many of his works. *The Bridge on the Drina* is the best example. The story of this famous bridge at Višegrad in eastern Bosnia, on the border with Serbia, offers a novelistic overview of Bosnian history between 1516 and 1914.

A diplomat, Andrić was also a historian, and he often studied historical facts and documents before writing his novels. His doctoral thesis, "The Development of the Spiritual Life of Bosnia under the Influence of Turkish Sovereignty" (1924), reveals an early interest in Turkish rule over the Balkans, which found expression later in *The Bridge on the Drina*. The novel's historical sweep encompasses the beginning and end of the Ottoman occupation of Bosnia. It focuses on the cultural changes brought about by the Turkish presence and the cultural and religious fermentation resulting from it. Although not a substitute for scholarly history, the novel is a reliable source of information about the period it focuses on.

Several symbolic readings of the novel are possible. The actual bridge of the title is closely associated with the author's personal history. As a little boy, Andrić was brought to Višegrad after the death of his father and was left there by his mother to live with relatives. Andrić's personal story is mirrored in the story of Mehmed Pasha Sokolli, who was taken from his Serbian mother by the Turks when he was a little boy and eventually became a famous Turkish vizier. Mehmed ordered the bridge built in memory of his origins. Thus, the bridge symbolizes a return to one's roots and serves as a monument to childhood.

The long history of the bridge, spanning three and a half centuries of change and upheaval, offers another symbolic connotation. Built in 1516 and 1517, the bridge survived many difficult times and was partially destroyed in 1914. Yet it still stands. Andrić concludes half of the chapters in *The Bridge on the Drina* with a short paragraph extolling the structure as a symbol of permanence, comforting and life-affirming in the midst of endless change. Andrić also finds it a thing of beauty, symbolizing the human desire to enrich life with art.

The bridge spans the River Drina, connecting two worlds, East and West, linking the different nationalities, religions, and cultures of Bosnia. Through the metaphor of the bridge, Andrić urges his Bosnian readers to try to overcome their differences and live in harmony. Fully aware of the complexity and the turbulent history of his native region, the author predicted a calamity if his pleas, as well as those of others, went unheeded. In view of the tragic events of Bosnia in the 1990s, *The Bridge on the Drina* has an eerily prophetic quality.

Andrić's narrative is characterized by a measured realistic style, reflecting the stoic firmness and beauty of the bridge. As his translator, Lovett F. Edwards, notes in the introduction to the translation, Andrić's style has "the sweep and surge of the sea, slow and yet profound, with occasional flashes of wit and irony." Yet beneath that calm exterior life pulsates in many forms, and events are never static. However, the historic range of the novel makes it difficult to concentrate on character or plot development. The episodic nature of the narrative produces individual pieces and stories that could stand by themselves. When put together, they create a colorful mosaic rather than an organic unity.

The publication of *The Bridge on the Drina* in 1945, at the end of an enormously destructive war, meant more than just the appearance of an important novel. Because of Andrić's prewar reputation as one of the best Serbian fiction writers, this novel augured a Phoenix-like rebirth of Serbian literature. Yet, because of its straightforward, realistic style, the novel has failed to inspire other writers to follow in the same vein. As it is, *The Bridge on the Drina* stands alone in its beauty, just like the bridge it immortalizes.

VASA D. MIHAILOVICH

See also Ivo Andrić

Further Reading

Bergman, Gun, *Turkisms in Ivo Andrić's "Na Drini ćuprija," Examined from the Points of View of Literary Style and Cultural History,* Uppsala: Almqvist and Wiksell, 1969

Goy, E.D., "The Work of Ivo Andrić," *Slavonic and East European Review* 41 (1963)

Hawkesworth, Celia, *Ivo Andrić: Bridge Between East and West,* London and Dover, New Hampshire: Athlone Press, 1984

Hawkesworth, Celia, editor, *Ivo Andrić: Proceedings of a Symposium Held at the School of Slavonic and East European Studies,* London: School of Slavonic Studies, 1985

Juričić, Želimir B., *The Man and the Artist: Essays on Ivo Andrić,* Lanham, Maryland, and London: University Press of America, 1986

Kadić, Ante, "The French in *The Chronicle of Travnik,*" *California Slavic Studies* 1 (1960)

Loud, John, "Between Two Worlds: Andrić the Storyteller," *Review of National Literatures* 5:1 (1974)

Mihailovich, Vasa D., "The Reception of the Works of Ivo Andrić in the English-Speaking World," *Southeastern Europe* 9 (1982)

Singh Mukerji, Vanita, *Ivo Andrić: A Critical Biography,* Jefferson, North Carolina: McFarland, 1990

Vucinich, Wayne, editor, *Ivo Andrić Revisited: The Bridge Still Stands,* Berkeley: International and Area Studies, University of California, 1995

André Brink 1935–

South African

Claiming to have been "born again" in Paris during the 1960s while studying comparative literature at the Sorbonne, André Brink's politicization led him to repudiate all the inherited values that he had absorbed from South Africa's system of white exclusionary apartheid politics. Associated with the Sestigers, a group of new young Afrikaans writers in the 1960s, Brink has constantly urged the interrogation and subversion of the ideology of Afrikanerdom in South Africa. From his early apolitical novel, *Die ambassadeur* (1963; translated as *The Ambassador* and also as *File on a Diplomat*), Brink sought to break with the romantic-colonist tradition of Afrikaans literature, which, in the realm of poetry, had been dubbed the "Veld and Vlei" movement, with its nostalgic appropriation of native landscape to lyrical, romanticized, and Eurocentric traditions. In opposition to the rigidly Calvinistic doctrines of the Afrikaner, he desired a new Afrikaans voice: a right to choose one's own subject matter, to question cultural taboos and social repressions (particularly with regard to sex as a literary subject), to criticize and challenge social structures, and to produce technical and aesthetic experiments in writing. Brink passionately argues many of these issues in his literary essays on South African cultural politics in *Mapmakers: Writing in a State of Siege* (1983), especially in "The Position of the Afrikaans Writer." For Brink, fiction "can expand an awareness of the human condition. What the writer does essentially implies that his work, if it is worthwhile, acts as a conscience in the world."

Brink was able to subvert the traditional forms of Afrikaans literature and develop his growing sense of a writer's responsibility within a repressive regime through his perception of writing as an act of revolution and political duty. His novel *Kennis van die aand* (1973; *Looking on Darkness*) became the first Afrikaans novel to be banned by the South African government, due to its explicit treatment of sex, racism, persecution, and the torture of political prisoners in South African jails. One of the first Afrikaans novels to openly confront the apartheid system, *Looking on Darkness* is an account of an illicit love affair between a "Cape Coloured" and a white woman, which results in her murder in a mutual pact. After the novel was banned, Brink translated most of his work into English to avoid being silenced by the government censors. Brink's political struggle with his native language was central to his development as a writer, as he sought to create a counterhegemonic Afrikaans literature in which Afrikaans as a language is not identified with apartheid as an ideology. Brian Macaskill has suggested that in *Rumours of Rain* (1978) Brink develops a "double-voiced discourse," as the novel explores interruption as a mode of attacking Afrikaans hegemony (see Macaskill, 1990). In *An Instant in the Wind* (1976), Brink uses the same illicit relationship between a black man and a white woman as in *Looking on Darkness*, this time set in an 18th-century context, in order to probe the origins of contemporary racial tension. *Die Eerste lewe van Adamaster* (1988; *The First Life of Adamastor*), a rewriting of a European myth, also explores the tensions of interracial sexual relationships, while in *A Chain of Voices* (1982), set in a slave revolt in the Cape colony in 1825, Brink uses the voices of 30 different narrators to explore the relationships of a society shaped by the forces of oppression. His fiction has always sought to open consciousness to the multiplicity of the human existence by challenging closure: "A literature which does not constantly and insistently confront, affront, offend—and thereby explore and test and challenge—the reader and the world, is moribund" (*Mapmakers*, 1983).

Brink's interest in the innovative forms of narrative and aesthetic experiment is manifest in what some have considered his postmodern narrative techniques, which he uses to investigate the politics of racism. Brink has assserted that "the study of history" is an abiding interest in his fiction, and some of his novels display what has been termed "historiographic metafiction." Rewritten in a "knowing" retrospective voice, history is shown always to be dependent on its narrative form rather than on "objective" facts. A good example is *On the Contrary* (1993), which is set in the early colonial exploration of the Cape colony in the 1730s. The novel shows explicit concerns with authorship, control of "truth," and power, and it employs intertextuality to engage with the lies of history and the search for "truth." At one point the narrator remarks, "This fascinates me: how each story displaces others, yet without denying or ever entirely effacing them." Elsewhere, Brink's fiction self-consciously foregrounds the act of writing and narrating, as if to draw attention to the instabilities of stories as "truth." *States of Emergency* (1988) is a persistently self-referential, discontinuous, and intertextual love story. With constant use of borders, demarcations, boundaries, and divisions, the novel gradually places itself at the border of fiction and criticism through the inclusion of allusions and footnotes to Jacques Derrida's deconstructive work, to semiotics, and to structuralism. These metafictional techniques compel the reader to reassess his or her practices of interpretation and evaluation, as the novel simultaneously inscribes and subverts the oppositions through which the love story is traditionally narrated—self/other, love/politics, inside text/outside world. Through such narrative strategies, Brink urges the reader to consider the extent to which the love story is a naively humanist attempt to wish apartheid away; whether it displaces or domesticates the implications of political struggle by the familiarity of the genre; and whether a love story can effectively oppose apartheid and act as an effective transformative narrative structure for a future South Africa.

Brink asserts, often in unabashed polemics, the necessity of thinking through the complex relationships among history, fiction, and politics. In a recent book of essays, he states: "Since we experience our own lives as a compilation of narrative texts . . . and *because* the text is not offered as definitive, final, absolute, but as the exploration of a possibility among others, it invites the reader to keep her or his critical faculties alive by pursuing the processes of imagination in order to arrive at whatever proves more relevant, more meaningful, or simply more useful in any given context" (*Reinventing a Continent*, 1996). André Brink maintains in his novels that pragmatic yet political sense of aesthetic experience as a guiding principle.

TIM S. WOODS

Biography

Born in Vrede, Orange Free State, 29 May 1935. Educated at Lydenburg High School; Potchefstroom University, Transvaal, B.A. 1955, M.A. in English 1958, M.A. in Afrikaans and Dutch 1959; the Sorbonne, Paris, 1959–61. Lecturer, 1963–73, Senior Lecturer, 1974–75, Associate Professor, 1976–79, and Professor, 1980–90, Department of Afrikaans and Dutch Literature, Rhodes University, Grahamstown. From 1991 Professor of English, University of Cape Town. Editor, *Sestiger* magazine, Pretoria, 1963–65. From 1986 editor, *Standpunte* magazine, Cape Town. President, Afrikaans Writers Guild, 1978–80.

Novels by Brink

(All translations into English by Brink)

Die gebondenes, 1959
Die eindelose weë, 1960
Lobola vir die lewe [Dowry for Life], 1962
Die ambassadeur, 1963; as *The Ambassador,* 1964; as *File on a Diplomat,* 1967
Orgie [Orgy], 1965
Miskien nooit: 'n Somerspel, 1967
Kennis van die aand, 1973; as *Looking on Darkness,* 1974
An Instant in the Wind, 1976
Rumours of Rain, 1978
A Dry White Season, 1979
A Chain of Voices, 1982
The Wall of the Plague, 1984
States of Emergency, 1988
Die Eerste lewe van Adamaster, 1988; as *The First Life of Adamastor,* 1993
An Act of Terror, 1991
On the Contrary: Being the Life of a Famous Rebel, Soldier, Traveller, Explorer, Reader, Builder, Scribe, Latinist, Lover and Liar, 1993
Imaginings of Sand, 1996

Other Writings: short stories, plays, children's stories, travel writing, and critical works, including *Mapmakers: Writing in a State of Siege* (1983), *Reinventing a Continent: Writing and Politics in South Africa 1982–95* (1996), *Reinventions: Old Literature—New Climates* (1996), and *The Novel: Language and Narrative from Cervantes to Calvino* (1998).

Further Reading

Andon-Milligan, Lillian Hilja, "André Brink's South Africa: A Quality of Light," *Critique: Studies in Contemporary Fiction* 34:1 (1992)

Cope, Jack, "A Driving Ferment," in *The Adversary Within: Dissident Writers in Afrikaans,* Cape Town: David Philip, and Atlantic Highlands, New Jersey: Humanities Press, 1982

Jacobs, Alan, "The Nightmare of History Revisited: André Brink's *An Instant in the Wind,*" in *Postcolonial Literature and the Biblical Call for Justice,* edited by Susan V. Gallagher, Jackson: University Press of Mississippi, 1994

Jacobs, J.U., "The Colonial Mind in a State of Fear: The Psychosis of Terror in the Contemporary South African Novel," *North Dakota Quarterly* 57:3 (1989)

Jolly, Rosemary, *Colonization, Violence, and Narration in White South African Writing: André Brink, Breyten Breytenbach and J.M. Coetzee,* Johannesburg: Witwatersrand University Press, and Athens: Ohio University Press, 1996

Kossew, Sue, *Pen and Power: A Post-Colonial Reading of J.M. Coetzee and André Brink,* Amsterdam and Atlanta, Georgia: Rodopi, 1996

Macaskill, Brian, "Interrupting the Hegemonic: Textual Critique and Mythological Recuperation from the White Margins of South African Writing," *Novel* 23:2 (1990)

Sorapure, Madeleine, "A Story in Love's Default: André Brink's *States of Emergency,*" *Modern Fiction Studies* 37:4 (1991)

Viola, Andre, "André Brink and the Writer 'in State and Siege'," *Commonwealth Essays and Studies* 7:2 (1985)

Voss, Tony, "Emerging Literature: The Literature of Emergency," in *Emerging Literatures,* edited by Reingard Nethersole, Bern and New York: Peter Lang, 1990

Hermann Broch 1886–1951

Austrian

Hermann Broch, who is ranked with Thomas Mann, Franz Kafka, and Hermann Hesse as one of the greatest writers of German in this century, was an Austrian novelist, poet, and philosopher of the modernist period. Like Robert Musil, with whom he is often compared, he came to literature after first pursuing a technical and commercial career. Broch oversaw his family's interests in the weaving industry until 1927, when he sold the family business and devoted himself solely to writing. Although Broch did not have a university degree (which denied him the security of an academic appointment during his American exile), he had attended lectures at the University of Vienna in mathematics, physics, and philosophy while working in the family business.

Broch's interest in philosophy and epistemology lies at the heart of his literary output. Broch saw it as the unique task of literature to grapple with certain problems whose solutions elude the "hard" sciences, either because they do not admit of rational answers, or because their solution is still beyond the current state of scientific progress. Literature straddles this gap between the twin poles of what Broch called "nicht mehr" and "noch nicht" ("no more" and "not yet"). This is, for the moment, the irrational, which intrudes on reality in an increasingly less obvious manner as a culture runs its natural course toward annihilation and eventual renewal. This process Broch dubs the disintegration of values (*Wertzerfall*), most apparent in his first work, the trilogy *Die Schlafwandler* (1932; *The Sleepwalkers*), a large-scale study of the decline of late modernist European culture at three different phases of disintegration: *Pasenow; oder, Die Romantik—1888* (1931), *Esch; oder, Die Anarchie—1903* (1931), and *Hugenau; oder, Die Sachlichkeit—1918* (1932). The eponymous protagonists exhibit their society's normative attitudes toward religion, sex, and the spectrum of aesthetics and ethics. Pasenow, a Prussian aristocrat, is caught up in the dominant romantic fictions of his time. Esch is a transitional figure, living uneasily between the old and new value systems, between romanticism and realism. For him, religion has become sterilized and diluted into sectarian radicalism, while its mysticism has eroded into a deluded eroticism. Hugenau, a deserter, epitomizes a social system devoid of traditional values, which brings forth a revaluation of the tradition and political revolution. Symbolic throughout is the shadow character Bertrand, who appears in all three novels. His outward life as an international financier ends in suicide, while his inner life and ambivalent sexuality represent the irrational and dreamlike elements of the three parts of the novel.

Hugenau has a polyhistoric structure. Its 88 chapters alternate narrative sequences of the Hugenau plot with poems, epigrams, and narrative sequences belonging to a different, outwardly unrelated narrative about a Salvation Army zealot in Berlin. The novel also offers ten philosophical digressions on the disintegration of values.

Broch felt that *The Sleepwalkers*, although his first work, ranked with the great works of world literature. His high opinion seemed justified by the trilogy's reception: reviews in Europe and America remarked on the astounding depth and sureness of its little-known author. James Joyce and other influential writers were so impressed by the trilogy that they helped him escape Nazi Austria in 1938, first to Scotland and then to America.

Another major, although shorter, work is *Die Verzauberung* (written in 1934, first published in English translation in 1987 as *The Spell*), an unfinished novel in various versions that have different names, including *Der Bergroman* (*The Mountain Novel*) and *Demeter*. It is a powerful psychological portrait of the effect of a fanatic fundamentalist named Marius Ratti on a small Tyrolean village. Its plot is a prophetic vision of how a society can be brought to commit atrocities by manipulating the levers of mass psychosis. At the same time, its landscape depictions in the manner of Adalbert Stifter are reminiscent of the traditional *Heimat* novel, which focuses on traditional rural Austrian life.

As was the case with Elias Canetti and other writers of the period, Broch's interest in mass psychosis went beyond expression in fictional forms. His scientific and epistemological inclinations as well as his horror at what had overtaken Europe in the 1930s and 1940s led him to attempt a massive study written with the aid of several American foundations during and after the war, *Massenwahntheorie* (1979; The Theory of Mass Psychosis).

In 1945 Broch published the work for which he is best remembered, *Der Tod des Vergil* (*The Death of Virgil*). A long monologue, the entire novel is narrated by the Roman poet Virgil as he lies on his deathbed. In despair over the failure of his political hopes and over the inability of art to influence the political process, he wishes to burn the Aeneid. A mystical experience of hope persuades him to save the work for posterity. Broch establishes a parallel between Roman history and the 20th century, so that Virgil's vision of hope is equally applicable to our situation. (*See separate entry*, The Death of Virgil.)

Die Schuldlosen (1950; *The Guiltless*) is a collection of novellas loosely connected by certain thematics and a central character, Andreas, or A. The novellas were written at various times between 1913 and 1950. Although radically different in style from the earlier work, *The Guiltless* bears certain structural similarities to *The Sleepwalkers*. It is divided into three sections, each headed by a significant date: 1913, 1923, 1933. Each contains verses at the head, called "Voices." Andreas and several other characters are highly symbolic: Andreas' role is a combination of the roles of Bertrand and Hugenau in the earlier trilogy. As the first trilogy sets out the inner history of certain German characters in the historical process culminating in World War I, so does *The Guiltless* probe the false consciousness of certain "types" in the German milieu during the period leading to the catastrophe of the Third Reich. With one notable exception, characters are not drawn in realistic detail, even the central character of Andreas. However, the housekeeper-narrator of *Die Erzählung der Magd Zerline* (1967; *Zerline's Tale*) is unforgettably well drawn. The many characters are united partly through the thematics of the Don Juan legend that connects several stories, and partly through their "guilty guiltlessness," their political indifference and philistine values, or lack of values, which Broch sees as leading Germany and the world to the disasters of the mid-century.

Broch considered his discursive prose to be as important as his fiction. He wrote many essays on literature, art, and philosophy, both of a critical and a theoretical nature. One of the most important is a book-length essay, *Hofmansthal und seine Zeit* (1984; *Hugo von Hofmansthal and His Time: The European Imagination 1860–1920*), in which Broch discusses the arts in the context of the normative values during the decline of the Hapsburg empire. Other important essays include an outline of the historical position of the novel in the 20th century, several essays on kitsch and literature, poetry and myth, the philosophy of translation, and the epistemology of music, to name just a few.

JOHN A. HARGRAVES

See also Death of Virgil

Biography

Born in Vienna, 1 November 1886. Educated privately, 1892–96; Imperial and Royal State Secondary School, Vienna, 1897–1904; Technical College for Textile Manufacture, Vienna, 1904–06; Spinning and Weaving College, Mülhausen, 1906–07. Administrator for Austrian Red Cross during World War I. Administered family's factory in Teesdorf, 1907–27; reviewer, *Moderne Welt,* Vienna, 1919; studied mathematics, philosophy, and psychology at Vienna University, 1926–30; arrested by the Nazis and detained briefly, 1938; moved to London, 1938, and then to the United States, where he lived thereafter; involved in refugee work from 1940; became American citizen, 1944;

fellow, Saybrook College, Yale University, New Haven, Connecticut, 1949. Died 30 May 1951.

Fiction by Broch

Die Schlafwandler: Ein Romantrilogie, 1952; as *The Sleepwalkers: A Trilogy,* translated by Edwin and Willa Muir, 1932
   Pasenow; oder, Die Romantik—1888, 1931
   Esch; oder, Die Anarchie—1903, 1931
   Hugenau; oder, Die Sachlichkeit—1918, 1932
Die unbekannte Grösse, 1933; as *The Unknown Quantity,* translated by Edwin and Willa Muir, 1935
Der Tod des Vergil, 1945; as *The Death of Virgil,* translated by Jean Starr Untermeyer, 1945
Die Schuldlosen, 1950; as *The Guiltless,* translated by Ralph Manheim, 1974
Der Versucher, edited by Felix Stössinger, in *Gesammelte Werke* 4, 1953
Der Bergroman, edited by Frank Kress and Hans Albert Maier, 4 vols., 1969
Barbara und andere Novellen, edited by Paul Michael Lützeler, 1973
Die Verzauberung, edited by Paul Michael Lützeler, 1976; as *The Spell,* translated by H.F. Broch de Rothermann, 1987

Other Writings: plays and essays (the latter including *Hofmansthal und seine Zeit* [1984; *Hugo von Hofmansthal and His Time: The European Imagination 1860–1920*]).

Further Reading

Brude-Firnau, Gisela, editor, *Materialien zu Hermann Brochs "Die Schlafwandler,"* Frankfurt: Suhrkamp, 1972
Dowden, Stephen D., editor, *Hermann Broch: Literature, Philosophy, and Politics: The Yale Broch Symposium, 1986,* Columbia, South Carolina: Camden House, 1988
Kahler, Erich, editor, *Dichter wider Willen: Einführung in das Werk Hermann Brochs,* Zurich: Rhein-Verlag, 1958
Kessler, Michael, and Paul Michael Lützeler, editors, *Hermann Broch: Das dichterische Werk, neue Interpretationen,* Tübingen: Stauffenburg, 1987
Lützeler, Paul Michael, *Hermann Broch: Eine Biographie,* Frankfurt: Suhrkamp, 1985
Lützeler, Paul Michael, editor, *Brochs "Verzauberung,"* Frankfurt: Suhrkamp, 1983
Lützeler, Paul Michael, editor, *Hermann Broch: Materialien,* Frankfurt: Suhrkamp, 1986
Lützeler, Paul Michael, and Michael Kessler, editors, *Brochs theoretisches Werk,* Frankfurt: Suhrkamp, 1988
Schlant, Ernestine, *Hermann Broch,* Boston: Twayne, 1978

Charlotte Brontë 1816–55

English

It is both unavoidable and undesirable that we link Charlotte Brontë's novels with her life. She writes about schools and governesses and Yorkshire and Belgium, after working as a governess and teacher in Yorkshire and Belgium. She fell in love with a married Belgian teacher: her heroes are married men, or Belgians, or teachers. And so the novels have been seen as autobiographical and often not considered for their literary merit. Indeed, her reputation as a novelist has suffered from much tedious biographical speculation. Brontë herself said that reality should suggest rather than dictate, and she paid tribute to the importance of imagination. Unlike Thackeray, whom she much admired, she cannot be accused of writing only one novel, nor is there really much resemblance between her drab and lonely life and the varied and exciting adventures of her heroines.

Nevertheless, it is true that Charlotte Brontë was popular in the 19th century and unpopular during the first half of the 20th. This would suggest that she was writing a novel for her times and not for all time (the reverse may be said of her sister Emily). Charlotte's brave, outspoken heroines with their strange mixture of unconventionality and pious morality struck a chord with Victorian readers. Originally *Jane Eyre* (1847) was thought to be rather shocking, but the greater emphasis Brönte placed on duty in *Shirley* (1849) and *Villette* (1853), combined with the public's knowledge of Brontë's sad life, tended to reverse this impression among Victorian readers. In the 20th century critics have been less concerned with moral imperatives and more with aesthetic and formal issues surrounding her novelistic technique. Within this new critical framework, Brontë's unrealistic coincidences and sudden shifts of emphasis have attracted unfavorable attention. It is odd, for example, that in *Jane Eyre, Shirley,* and *Villette* the heroine falls into a timely swoon and awakes to find she has met a long lost relative. Odd, too, that in *Jane Eyre, Villette,* and *The Professor* (1857) we begin the novel in one place with one set of characters, and then almost lose sight of this setting altogether. This is not quite true of *Shirley,* but this, Brontë's one novel with a third-person narrator and a wide range of characters, does suffer badly from a lack of unity. In *Villette* the Brettons and Humes return to haunt the heroine, as does Mrs. Reed in *Jane Eyre,* while Hunsden reemerges in *The Professor,* but these reappearances seem almost as unrealistic as the coincidences.

Twentieth-century critics of Charlotte Brönte's novels also have registered a shift in moral values; Jane Eyre now seemed foolish rather than virtuous in running away from Rochester on discovering that he had a wife. With his guilt and bravado Rochester appeared rather a preposterous character. The discovery of Charlotte's juvenile writings, filled with even wilder coincidences and more preposterous characters, further eroded her standing. Her reputation for having written such strongly autobiographical novels did little to gain the favor of the formalist-minded New Critics of the 1930s, 1940s, and 1950s, who as a group tended to regard authors' biographies as irrelevant to their works and therefore unimportant for critics. The New Criticism's most influential voice about the genre of the novel, F.R. Leavis, therefore excluded Charlotte Brontë from the Great Tradition of English novelists. After World War II, except among Brontë enthusiasts, there was little interest in any novel, although *Jane Eyre* was still seen either as the kind of book people read in youth and discarded thereafter or, alternatively, as an escapist romance.

In the past 40 years Charlotte Brontë's reputation has risen rapidly, to the extent that both *Villette* and *Jane Eyre* have received almost as much critical attention as her sister Emily's one novel, *Wuthering Heights* (1847). *Shirley* and *The Professor,* although generally regarded as inferior to the other two novels, have been dragged along in their train. Two factors have contributed to this change. Critics like David Lodge have pointed out that although *Jane Eyre* may be somewhat crudely episodic, the episodes are linked by symbols such as fire and water, representing passion and duty (see Lodge, *The Language of Fiction: Essays in Criticism and Verbal Analysis of the English Novel,* 1966; new edition, 1984). Seen in this light, the novel's lapses in realistic integrity seem unimportant. Similarly in *Villette,* symbol plays an important part in representing Lucy Snowe's inner struggle and is more important than the petty realistic details of life at Madame Beck's school.

Feminist criticism has done much to show that Brontë was not writing a mere tract for her times but was speaking up for oppressed women of every age. Thus Sandra Gilbert and Susan Gubar in their appropriately named *The Madwoman in the Attic* (1979) revealed a web of imagery involving imprisonment and bondage linking Jane Eyre and the first Mrs. Rochester as victims of patriarchal oppression. They and their successors were able to extend the same method to *Shirley* and *Villette,* linking women and the working class as joint victims in the former novel, Paul Emanuel and Graham Bretton as joint villains in the latter. Perhaps they went too far; Brontë is not all that enthusiastic about Bertha Mason or the working class, and had a soft spot for Belgian teachers like Louis Moore and Paul Emanuel, whose superiority rather tamely Shirley Keeldar and Lucy Snowe seem to acknowledge.

At the time of their writing, Charlotte Brontë's novels, together with those of her sisters Emily and Anne, were attacked for being coarse. This rather vague term encompassed religious and social unconventionality but was really a euphemism for sexual immorality. By allowing her heroines to have sexual feelings, Brontë appeared to be rebelling against an accepted Victorian norm, and contemporary reviewers worried by the events of 1848, a year of revolutions in Europe, saw *Jane Eyre* and even *Shirley* and *Villette* as dangerous, licentious books. With her own brand of sincere religion and gentle political conservatism, Brontë is an unlikely revolutionary, but she did believe in the power of passion, even though by modern standards her heroines behave most demurely. Jane Eyre flees Rochester, and Caroline Helstone accepts the apparent loss of Robert Moore without protest. But there are obvious sexual symbols in all the novels—even *The Professor,* where Charlotte confuses the issue by making her central character a man, although one with very feminine sensibilities. Feminist criticism has done much to show the rich variety of interpretations to which Brontë's novels are open.

It is still possible to see why Leavis could find no place for Brontë in the Great Tradition of the English novel, because she does not fit into any tradition. The Brontës were too poor to buy or borrow contemporary novels, and thus it is hard to fit them into a historical period; indeed, contemporary reviewers were dismayed by their work because they seemed to hark back to the morality and manners of a previous generation. George Eliot, whom Leavis placed firmly in the Great Tradition, admired Brontë's work, but Eliot saw that Charlotte had inspired a host of inferior imitators, with whom it is equally wrong to link her. Daphne du Maurier's *Rebecca* (1938) is probably the last and most famous of these imitations, but as we can see from Jean Rhys' *Wide Sargasso Sea* (1966), a reworking of the story of *Jane Eyre* from the point of view of the first Mrs. Rochester, the 20th century has been unable to catch the blend of simplicity and complexity that make Charlotte Brontë's novels unique.

TOM WINNIFRITH

See also Jane Eyre

Biography
Born in Thornton, Yorkshire, 21 April 1816; sister of the writers Anne Brontë and Emily Brontë; moved with her family to Haworth, Yorkshire, 1820. Attended Clergy Daughters' School, Cowan Bridge, Lancashire, 1824–25; at home, 1825–31; Roe Head School, Yorkshire, 1831–32; Pensionnat Heger, Brussels, 1842. Assistant teacher, Roe Head School, Roe Head and Dewsbury Moor, Yorkshire, 1835–38; governess to the Sidgwick family, Stonegappe, Yorkshire, 1839, and the White family, Rawdon, Yorkshire, 1841; teacher, Pensionnat Heger, 1843. Died 31 March 1855.

Novels by Brontë
Jane Eyre, 1847
Shirley, 1849
Villette, 1853
The Professor, 1857

Other Writings: short stories, tales, poetry.

Further Reading
Barker, Juliet, *The Brontës,* London: Weidenfeld and Nicolson, and New York: St. Martin's Press, 1994
Eagleton, Terry, *Myths of Power: A Marxist Study of the Brontës,* London: Macmillan, and New York: Barnes and Noble, 1975; 2nd edition, 1988
Ewbank, Inga-Stina, *Their Proper Sphere: A Study of the Brontë Sisters as Early-Victorian Female Novelists,* London: Arnold, and Cambridge, Massachusetts: Harvard University Press, 1966
Gaskell, Elizabeth, *The Life of Charlotte Brontë,* London: Smith Elder, and New York: Appleton, 1857
Gerin, Winifred, *Charlotte Brontë: The Evolution of Genius,* Oxford: Clarendon Press, 1967; New York: Oxford University Press, 1991
Gilbert, Sandra, and Susan Gubar, *The Madwoman in the Attic,* New Haven, Connecticut: Yale University Press, 1979
Martin, Robert, *The Accents of Persuasion: Charlotte Brontë's Novels,* London: Faber, and New York: Norton, 1966
Winnifrith, Tom, *The Brontës and Their Background: Romance and Reality,* London: Macmillan, and New York: Barnes and Noble, 1973; 2nd edition, 1988

The Brothers Karamazov by Fedor Dostoevskii

Brat'ia Karamazovy 1880

When *The Brothers Karamazov,* Fedor Dostoevskii's final and longest novel, appeared serially in 1879 and 1880, it was greeted by the Russian public as a national event. Since then, countless critics and readers, Einstein and Freud among them, have considered *The Brothers Karamazov* to be Dostoevskii's masterpiece—even, some say, the greatest novel ever written. *The Brothers Karamazov* has been found very modern, both in its "polyphonic" form and its thematic concern with questions such as the nature of evil, the relationship between science and faith, and why God allows the suffering of innocent children.

The Brothers Karamazov combines elements of the murder mystery, the family saga, conceivably also the saint's *vita.* Like *Prestuplenie i nakazanie* (1867; *Crime and Punishment*), *The Brothers Karamazov* focuses on the psychological and philosophical conditions for, and aftermath of, a murder. But as critics have noted, Dostoevskii adapts the murder mystery in various ways: while *Crime and Punishment* alters the traditional form by removing the "whodunit," *The Brothers Karamazov* maintains narrative suspense about the identity of the murderer of Fedor Karamazov for much of the novel but subverts the traditional murder mystery by presenting three and possibly all four sons as partly responsible for the murder. This subversion adds a psychological layer that shows considerable affinity with Freudian theory. (Referring to the Oedipus complex, Freud commented that "it is a matter of indifference who actually committed the crime; psychology is only concerned to know who desired it emotionally and who welcomed it when it was done.") The brothers' shared guilt also adds a religious layer, illustrating the Dostoevskian precept that "all are guilty for all," or that a brother *is* his brother's keeper.

As a family saga, *The Brothers Karamazov* follows in the Russian tradition of the novel of the family, Sergei Aksakov's *Semeinaia Khronika* (1956; *Family Chronicle*) and Lev Tolstoi's *Voina i mir* (1863–69; *War and Peace*) being, respectively, the founding and the most famous Russian representatives. Whereas these novels celebrate the happy feudal life of the Russian aristocratic family on the estate and in the capital cities, Dostoevskii's chronicle of the provincial Karamazov family presents a portrait of dabauchery, instability, and resentment. Parricide is but the culmination of a long series of family crimes. The family is composed of Fedor Karamazov, a poor excuse for a father, and the four sons he has fathered by three different women—two of whom were his wives, while the third was a "holy fool" figure—also common in Russian literature—whom he raped. When the action of the novel begins, all the mothers are dead, and father and sons confront each other. By the time the novel ends, however, this singularly unhappy Russian family, through the miracle of brotherly love, has been reborn. And weddings loom in the future: Grusha will follow Mitia to Siberia; Alesha will, as ordered by Zosima, leave the monastery and eventually marry Lise Khokhlakova; even Ivan may pair off with Katerina Ivanovna. The new brotherhood of the Karamazovs is extended by Alesha to the troop of boys who, in a funeral feast, prepare to mourn and remember the death of their friend Ilyusha. Thus, the novel ends celebrating earthly biological life and continuity.

As Dostoevskii's writings on the family and on its chroniclers reveal, he felt that the Russian family was in a state of crisis. The "accidental" family, which he tended to depict in his own fiction, had replaced the "genetic" family chronicled by Tolstoi. Consequently, a new poetics and new forms were called for. In *The Brothers Karamazov,* he perfected this new poetics, which he had been working out in his earlier novels, especially *Podrostok* (1875; *A Raw Youth*). A key to the new poetics of *The Brothers Karamazov* may be found in its epigraph from the Gospel of John: "Verily, verily, I say unto you, except a corn of wheat fall into the ground and die, it abideth alone: but if it die, it bringeth forth much fruit." Robin Feuer Miller argues that the epigraph reflects the novel's cyclical narrative structure (see Miller, 1992). Situational and compositional "rhymes" of various sorts have been identified in the novel. Multiple narrative voices ("polyphony" in Bakhtin's terminology, 1984) take the place of the monologic voice of the classical novel of the "genetic" family.

Another important structural element is the inserted narratives. The most famous of these is the "legend" of the Grand Inquisitor (the opus of Ivan Karamazov), often read out of context. In the context of the novel, it is paired with the "Life of Zosima" (as recorded by Alesha Karamazov). Together the pair presents conflicting ideologies, with the Grand Inquisitor promoting control, suggesting the inefficacy of Christ and the weakness of man, and the "Life of Zosima" (as well as the "Onion Story" told by Grushenka) depicting a Russian Orthodox vision and aesthetic that may constitute the most important innovation of Dostoevskii's novels. Also central to *The Brothers Karamazov* is the theme of memory, which functions as a religious idea (the anamnesis of the dead) and also as a compositional device, whereby the text remembers and recalls itself.

Critics have shown that Dostoevskii, from novel to novel, experimented with different formulas and techniques. That experimentation came to its fullest fruition in *The Brothers Karamazov,* where fitter and more perfect forms emerged. In particular, the narrator-chronicler of *The Brothers Karamazov* has been seen as the perfection of Dostoevskii's previous experimentation with various types of first- and third-person narrators. And the positive heroes, Alesha Karamazov and Zosima, are often seen as improvements on Dostoevskii's previous attempts at embodying virtue, including Sonia Marmeladov in *Crime and Punishment* and Myshkin in *Idiot* (1869; *The Idiot*).

LIZA KNAPP

See also Fedor Dostoevskii

Further Reading

Bakhtin, M.M., *Problemy tvorchestva Dostoevskogo,* Leningrad: Priboi, 1929; 2nd edition, revised, as *Problemy poetiki Dostoevskogo,* Moscow: Sov. Pisatel, 1963; as *Problems of Dostoevsky's Poetics,* Ann Arbor, Michigan: Ardis, 1973; new edition and translation, Minneapolis: University of Minnesota Press, and Manchester: Manchester University Press, 1984
Belknap, Robert, *The Genesis of "The Brothers Karamazov":*

The Aesthetics, Ideology, and Psychology of Text Making, Evanston, Illinois: Northwestern University Press, 1990

Jackson, Robert Louis, *The Art of Dostoevsky: Deliriums and Nocturnes,* Princeton, New Jersery: Princeton University Press, 1981

Jackson, Robert Louis, editor, *Dostoevsky: New Perspectives,* Englewood Cliffs, New Jersey: Prentice-Hall, 1984

Knapp, Liza, *The Annihilation of Inertia: Dostoevsky and Metaphysics,* Evanston, Illinois: Northwestern University Press, 1996

Miller, Robin Feuer, *"The Brothers Karamazov": Worlds of the Novel,* New York: Twayne, 1992

Terras, Victor, *A Karamazov Companion: Commentary on the Genesis, Language, and Style of Dostoevsky's Novel,* Madison: University of Wisconsin Press, 1981

Thompson, Diane, *"The Brothers Karamazov" and the Poetics of Memory,* Cambridge and New York: Cambridge University Press, 1991

Wellek, René, editor, *Dostoevsky: A Collection of Critical Essays,* Englewood Cliffs, New Jersey: Prentice-Hall, 1962

Buddenbrooks by Thomas Mann

1901

A landmark of German and European fiction, Thomas Mann's *Buddenbrooks* significantly expanded the realist tradition. On the one hand, it brought together the epic sweep of the great 19th-century European novels and drew on traditional German forms such as the Bildungsroman, but it also started questioning the limits of realism. The novel shows that new literary forms would be necessary to reflect the fragile, individualistic, self-searching spirit that arose in the new century with the degeneration of the older, solid merchant class. Despite Mann's doubts about the length and nature of his novel, *Buddenbrooks* immediately became popular. He began writing it during a one-year stay in Italy with his brother Heinrich, also a writer, and completed it in about two and a half years. For years afterward, in spite of such outstanding later works as *Tonio Kröger* (1903), *Der Tod in Venedig* (1912; *Death in Venice*), and *Der Zauberberg* (1924; *The Magic Mountain*), Mann was lauded everywhere as the author of *Buddenbrooks,* which had achieved 159 printings by 1925.

Two camps emerged among the critical responses to the novel. One group perceived *Buddenbrooks* as a text about the historically verifiable world of 19th-century German society and the saga of the rise and decline of a well-to-do Lübeck family over a period of four generations. Outraged citizens of Lübeck at the time of the novel's publication in 1901 were among this group, for they saw the novel as only a thinly disguised account of local residents and real incidents. They claimed that Mann had drawn extensively on physical, psychological, and sociological details of his own family and his hometown. Since then, Georg Lukács (1964) and other critics have reinforced this focus on the novel's realistic and naturalistic elements in their arguments that *Buddenbrooks* accurately illuminates the period and the problems of the merchant class.

The opposing camp has focused on the artistry of the novel's structure and on its unique narrative techniques. Critics point to the intricate patterns of leitmotivs, the recurrence of contrasting and parallel structures, the use of free indirect discourse to reveal the characters' consciousness, and the novel's manifold associations with music, particularly the music of Richard Wagner.

Increasingly, critics have come to believe that both positions are valid. Many modern critics agree that Mann uses artistic, stylistic, and symbolic organization; philosophical references to Friedrich Nietzsche and Arthur Schopenhauer; and musical motivs as vehicles to represent a carefully observed, historically accurate social world.

Through the novel's subtitle "Verfall einer Familie" ("Decline of a Family"), Mann alerts his readers to the surface movement of the novel, namely the disturbance of order. The first two Buddenbrook generations—sturdy, aggressive, and practical-minded businessmen—create the family's capital; the last two in quick succession develop physical and mental weaknesses that cause the decline of the business and the family. Basic in Mann's work is the tension in his attitude toward *Bürger* (citizen) and *Künstler* (artist). He wavers between admiration for the healthy, diligent, shrewd businessperson and worshiper of strength, decency, and property on the one hand, and, on the other, an admiration for the artist and his work, for the sufferer, the vulnerable person with an inner wound and tortured spirit. In *Buddenbrooks,* he develops these distinct polarities as a constant circling in life. Johann Buddenbrook, born in 1765, a farsighted, progressive, and vigorous man, and his son, the consul Johann, who marries into one of the wealthiest Lübeck families, are both healthy and vibrant people. Consul Johann's three children, Thomas, Tony, and Christian, represent the nervous, deteriorating third generation. The last Buddenbrook, the young son Hanno, is an artist in the modern decadent way. With his precocious intelligence and emotional sensitivity, and an affinity for Wagner's world of music and Schopenhauer's somber view of human experience, he is not suited to be a man of action. In fact, he dies in his youth of typhoid. As in much of Mann's work, great vitality often means a lack of spirituality, while the leaning toward the artistic is often destructive or deathly.

When Mann began to write *Buddenbrooks,* he was interested only in the story of the sensitive, delicate Hanno and the conflict between Hanno and his ambitious father. As this father-son antagonism took shape, Mann's insights into the interrelationship between art, literature, philosophy, and music—all things of the spirit—compelled him to connect his view of the artist with Nietzsche, Schopenhauer, Max Weber, and a plethora of works in literature and music. Art, disease, physical and spiritual suffering, dreams, and refinement are intricately related for Mann and form a counterforce to health, normality, and vigorous life. The consistency of values that give the novel unity reflect Mann's study of Nietzsche. These values pervade Mann's early stories and novellas, such as "Der kleine Herr Friedmann" (written 1897, published 1898) and "Tobias Mindernickel" (1898), and develop further in *Tonio Kröger, Death in Venice,* and *The Magic Mountain.*

In a more theoretical text, *Betrach eines Unpolitischen* (1918; *Reflections of a Non-Political Man*), Mann further explores the tension between artist and burgher, between art and politics, by separating the cultural Germany of music, poetry, and philosophy from the political Germany. Ironically, Mann emerges from this work as a defender of the bourgeois age, even though his novels after *Buddenbrooks* address the decay of the old burgher patricians and the conflict between the bourgeois and the artist. The outcome of World War I, coupled with Mann's acceptance of his social responsibility as an artist and an intellectual during a time when a world of order and commerce changed into a world of political disorder and conflict, is reflected in his *Magic Mountain,* in which his reflections on time and history propelled his narrative style beyond the 19th-century epic style of *Buddenbrooks.*

BARBARA MABEE

See also Thomas Mann

Further Reading

Goldman, Harvey, *Politics, Death, and the Devil: Self and Power in Max Weber and Thomas Mann,* Berkeley: University of California Press, 1992
Harpprecht, Klaus, *Thomas Mann: Eine Biographie,* Reinbek: Rowohlt, 1995
Hayman, Ronald, *Thomas Mann: A Biography,* New York: Scribner, 1995; London: Bloomsbury, 1996
Koopmann, Helmut, *Thomas Mann: Konstanten seines literarischen Werks,* Göttingen: Vandenhoeck and Ruprecht, 1975
Lukács, Georg, "Thomas Mann: Auf der Suche nach dem Bürger," in his *Werke,* volume 7, Neuwied: Luchterhand, 1964
Nichols, R.A., *Nietzsche in the Early Work of Thomas Mann,* Berkeley: University of California Press, 1955
Prater, Donald, *Thomas Mann: A Life,* Oxford and New York: Oxford University Press, 1995
Ridley, Hugh, *Thomas Mann: "Buddenbrooks,"* Cambridge and New York: Cambridge University Press, 1987
Rothenberg, Klaus-Jürgen, *Das Problem des Realismus bei Thomas Mann,* Cologne: Böhlau, 1969
Swales, Martin, *"Buddenbrooks": Family Life as the Mirror of Social Change,* Boston: Twayne, 1991
Vogt, Jochen, *Thomas Mann: Buddenbrooks,* Munich: Fink, 1983; 2nd edition, 1995

Mikhail Bulgakov 1891–1940

Russian

Playwright, biographer, novelist, and short-story writer, Mikhail Bulgakov was above all a satirist whose talent lay in translating the events of his turbulent era into humorous, classical works of literature. Bulgakov's satire, which bears witness to the influence of Nikolai Gogol's *Mertvye dushi* (1842; *Dead Souls*), offers a general portrait of urban tensions in Soviet times. Despite its satirical thrust, his work has a highly personal quality, relying extensively on autobiographical material. His story "Molière," for example, is as much about himself writing under Stalin as it is about Molière writing under Louis XIV. Similarly, the novel *Dni Turbinykh* (1927–29; *The White Guard*) and its stage adaptation *The Days of the Turbins* (1926) reflect Bulgakov's civil war experience.

Bulgakov's first career was in medicine. He graduated from medical school in 1916 and was practicing in Kiev at the time of the Bolshevik Revolution. As a member of the intelligentsia, he had espoused radical ideas but quickly became disenchanted with them in the face of the bloody realities of the struggle between revolutionaries and loyalists. He served as a field doctor during the war, witnessing much of its cruelty and barbarism at first hand. After spending two years in the Caucasus with his seriously wounded patients, Bulgakov decided to abandon the medical profession in favor of a career as a writer. However, his medical training, particularly his knowledge of the world under the microscope, informed all of his writing and is most evident in such works as "Notes on the Cuff," "The Fatal Eggs," and *Sobach'e Serdtse* (published posthumously in 1969; *The Heart of a Dog*).

Bulgakov moved to Moscow in 1921 and began work on *The White Guard,* an account of the civil war that draws heavily on his own experience in the field. Introducing a theme that was to recur throughout his work, the novel emphasizes the moral demands upon the witness of evil, condemning passivity as cowardice. *The White Guard* was well received by critics, who compared it to the debut of such giants as Fedor Dostoevskii and Lev Tolstoi. The novel stands out among other work published at the time for its relatively sympathetic portrayal of the enemies of the Bolsheviks. When Bulgakov finally managed to get the stage adaptation performed, it became, paradoxically, one of Joseph Stalin's favorite plays.

Bulgakov's experience of Moscow formed the basis of his subsequent satirical work. When he arrived in 1921, the city was experiencing runaway inflation, fuel shortages, and extraordinary snowfalls. Famine along the Volga propelled people from the provinces into the city, exacerbating an already difficult housing situation. Communal apartment living—cramped, noisy, cold, and devoid of all opportunities for privacy—as well as bungling bureaucrats came to function as allegories of the failings of Soviet communism in Bulgakov's later work.

Bulgakov's second novel, *Zapiski pokoinika* (1966; *Black Snow,* also known as *A Theatrical Novel*), was begun in the 1930s but remained unfinished at his death. It is primarily about the world of the theatre and his attempts, fruitless for many years, to bring *The Days of the Turbins* and other plays to the stage. A satiric portrait of life in Moscow forms the backdrop to the narrative. At the same time that he was working on *A Theatrical Novel,* Bulgakov wrote *Master i Margarita* (1966–67; *The Master and Margarita*). Although he was still making changes to it on his death bed, this novel was completed. Generally considered Bulgakov's greatest work, *The Master and Margarita* combines biting satire with an exuberant magic realism and a Kafkaesque sense of absurdity. Bulgakov displays a talent for making the absurd and magical seem ordinary. Working an extreme suspension of disbelief, he makes the reader accept that men can change into pigs and fly and that women can ride them or that a small flat suddenly accommodates a grand ball worthy of a palace. It seems logical that Margarita converses with the devil and that a cat carries a machine gun. The ludicrous accounts of renters and their apartments and the Muscovite's penchant for quick-fix schemes and con men make for entertaining and disturbing reading. Breaking all narrative conventions, *The Master and Margarita* juxtaposes chapters on Old Jerusalem and the encounter between Christ and Pontius Pilate with the most pedestrian details of Muscovite living. It is at once paradoxical and logical that Satan should show up in Moscow to see if he can do some good.

At the heart of the novel lies the idea of honor, sadly lost in the world of bureaucratic indifference and individual scheming. The novel also makes an eloquent plea for artistic integrity. The high value Bulgakov attached to integrity is also evident in the publishing history of his later work. *The Master and Margarita* was suppressed because Bulgakov refused to make the changes required by the authorities. A first Soviet edition, seriously bowdlerized, appeared in 1966–67, while an unexpurgated edition first appeared in the West in 1973. It became an instant literary sensation in the Soviet union, where it fetched high prices on the black market.

KATHLEEN SMITH THOMAS

See also Master and Margarita

Biography
Born in Kiev, Ukraine, 3 May 1891. Attended First Kiev High School, 1900–09; Medical Faculty, Kiev University, 1909–16, doctor's degree 1916. Served as doctor in front-line and district hospitals during World War I. Doctor in Kiev, 1918–19, but gave up medicine in 1920; organized a "sub-department of the arts," Vladikavkaz, 1920–21; lived in Moscow from 1921, working as a journalist for various groups and publications; assistant producer for the Moscow Art Theatre, 1930–36; librettist and consultant for the Bolshoi Theatre, Moscow, 1936–40. Much of his work was published after his death. Died 10 March 1940.

Novels by Bulgakov
Dni Turbinykh (Belaia gvardiia), 2 vols., 1927–29; as *The White Guard,* translated by Michael Glenny, 1971
Zapiski pokoinika (Teatralnyi roman), in *Izbrannaia proza,* 1966; as *Black Snow: A Theatrical Novel,* translated by Michael Glenny, 1967
Master i Margarita, 1966–67; uncut version, 1969; complete version, 1973; as *The Master and Margarita,* translated by Mirra Ginsburg, 1967; uncut version, translated by Michael Glenny, 1967; complete version translated by Diana Burgin and Katherine Tiernan O'Connor, 1995; also translated by Richard Pevear and Larissa Volkhonsky, 1997

Other Writings: short stories, plays, letters, diary entries.

Further Reading
Chudakova, M., "*The Master and Margarita*: The Development of a Novel," *Russian Literature Triquarterly* 15 (1978)
Curtis, J.A.E., *Manuscripts Don't Burn: Mikhail Bulgakov, A Life in Diaries and Letters,* London: Bloomsbury, 1991; Woodstock, New York: Overlook Press, 1992
Haber, Edythe, "The Mythic Structure of Bulgakov's *The Master and Margarita,*" *Russian Review* 34 (October 1975)
Proffer, Ellendea, *Bulgakov: Life and Work,* Ann Arbor, Michigan: Ardis, 1984
Vozkvizhenskii, V.G., *Mikhail Bulgakov and His Times: Memoirs, Letters,* Moscow: Progress, 1990
Wright, Anthony Colin, *Mikhail Bulgakov: Life and Interpretations,* Toronto and Buffalo, New York: University of Toronto Press, 1978

C

Cabinets de lecture. *See* Libraries: France

Caleb Williams by William Godwin

1794

William Godwin's *Caleb Williams* was originally published as *Things as They Are; or, The Adventures of Caleb Williams*. William Hazlitt judged it to be "unquestionably the best modern novel." He hailed it as a "startling event in literary history" because Godwin, celebrated among his peers as a "metaphysician," had written a "romance." Although critics of the novel seldom singled it out for its formal perfection, it was one of the most popular novels of its day: it had been through three editions by 1797, and James Mackintosh declared in 1815 that it was the book most commonly in need of replacement in circulating libraries. Critics of the late 20th century increasingly have valued it for its rigorous philosophical speculations and its densely layered generic resonances, that is to say, for its connections to late 18th-century radical thought and for its importance in literary history.

Caleb Williams frequently has been understood as one of a variety of "jacobin" social protest novels of the 1780s and 90s, including the works of Thomas Holcroft (*Anna St. Ives* [1792] and *Hugh Trevor* [1794]) and Robert Bage (*Man as He Is* [1792] and *Hermsprong; or, Man as He Is Not* [1796]). The writings of Holcroft and Bage, and other novelists such as Elizabeth Inchbald and Charlotte Smith, were influenced by the Godwinian opposition to hereditary rule and established religion. Godwin was in turn influenced by the works of these contemporaries. He was not new to novel writing when he wrote *Caleb Williams,* and he wrote several more after it, including *St. Leon* (1799), *Fleetwood* (1805), and *Mandeville* (1817)—all of which have had their admirers. Recognized as Godwin's best, however, *Caleb Williams* has been widely recognized as one of the most successful literary ventures from the circle of Jacobin novelists.

Published a year after Godwin's *An Enquiry Concerning Political Justice* (2 vols., 1793), *Caleb Williams* is an example of the author's radical political leanings, yet it is also remarkable for its importance in the development of the novel. Godwin's novel is praised particularly for its plot of "flight and pursuit," as Godwin described it, for its vigorous first-person narration, and for its brilliant and complex characterization. The novel exhibits formal techniques and thematic interests reminiscent of the work of such writers as Daniel Defoe, Samuel Richardson, and Tobias Smollet, all authors whom Godwin mentions in his journal while writing his novel. *Caleb Williams,* moreover, anticipates important later innovations in the genre. Only Mary Shelley (Godwin's daughter), the American Charles Brockden Brown, and Edward Bulwer-Lytton openly acknowledged Godwin's influence, yet the importance of this novel and his other writings is visible in the works of authors as diverse as Jane Austen, Charles Dickens, Herman Melville, Joseph Conrad, and Franz Kafka.

In the 1831 edition of the novel, Godwin changed the title to *Caleb Williams,* which has often been considered evidence of his desire to heighten the emphasis on individual psychology. The novel's vivid representation of emotion and internal states of mind has suggested a relationship between Godwin's work and "sentimental" novels of Richardson, Frances Burney, and Mackenzie. Inchbald praised it for its "minute" and "concise" depiction of human sensations. It also has suggested a connection with Gothic fiction, which thrilled readers with narratives of innocent victims terrorized by such villains as Ann Radcliffe's Schedoni, Matthew Lewis' Ambrosio (from *The Monk,* 1796) or Mary Shelley's monster in *Frankenstein* (1818). Godwin's novel is indeed an unrelenting tale of terror, in which young Caleb finds himself at the mercy of the aristocratic Count Ferdinando Falkland, who has employed Caleb as his personal secretary.

Falkland, guilty of murder, shares his secret with Caleb, yet vows to hate him forever. Caleb is falsely accused of theft and pursued not only by his master but by an entire nation that has turned against him.

Although it bears recognizable Gothic traces, *Caleb Williams* is also a narrative of detection, anticipating the works of writers like Dickens, Wilkie Collins, Edgar Allan Poe, and Arthur Conan Doyle. It is occupied with the drama of secret crime and its discovery: Caleb's curiosity about the obscure torments of his employer leads him to set himself up as a "watch" on his patron. When he discovers Falkland's secret, however, Caleb is transformed from pursuer into pursued. He becomes the object rather than the agent of detection, continually devising disguises and escape routes to avoid Falkland's persecution. The activity of detection goes beyond one character's pursuit of another, for the novel also represents an emerging institutionalized practice of detection that colludes with systems of policing and criminal prosecution. Falkland's agents pursuing Caleb appear to multiply throughout the novel, a characteristic that bears some resemblance to the increasingly sophisticated representations of detection and policing in Dickens' *Oliver Twist* (1838) or Collins' *The Moonstone* (1868). Also significant is Godwin's interest in false accusations of criminality, an early example of the detective story's productive fascination with conflicting confessions and character misidentifications.

This narrative of crime, detection, pursuit, and eventual punishment forms the basis of an extended speculation on the relationship between individual and society, revealing *Caleb Williams'* affinities with the domestic novels of Austen and Maria Edgeworth, in which women are continually reminded that their fate in the marriage market is dependent upon the management of their "character," or reputation. In ways more specific to Godwin's political philosophy, *Caleb Williams* represents a conflict in character formation between merited and inherited marks of character. As some critics have observed, Godwin's opposition to Edmund Burke's traditionalist defense of the ancient constitution is visible in Falkland, a character who is publicly perceived as good, not because of his actions, but because of his aristocratic family and established reputation for benevolence.

Caleb Williams has a strong political thrust, and readers have correctly pointed to the novel's reformist agenda. As the title *Things as They Are* intimated, Godwin's political aim is to represent society and all of its abuses as they are. The author himself emphasized the political directions of his work in his response to an early critic of the novel, observing that it was "designed to expose the evils which arise out of the present system of civilized society; and, having exposed them, to lead the enquiring reader to examine whether they are, or are not . . . irremediable." Indeed, the novel comments on the conditions of Britain's criminal justice and penal systems, following the lead of novelists like Defoe, Henry Fielding, and Oliver Goldsmith, in its critical perspectives on criminal law and penal conditions in the 18th century. Critics have often pointed out that the treason trials of 1794 were in Godwin's mind as he represented the plight of his hero. From the novel's very first page, Caleb, the son of peasant parents, is deserted and friendless, a "victim" of the "persecution" by his "enemy" Falkland. The system of criminal justice is at the service of a rigid class system that protects the crimes of the wealthy and unjustly punishes the poor. In this world turned upside-down, officers of the law are barely distinguishable from criminals, and criminals easily adapt themselves to the rhetoric and practical functioning of the law.

Two endings exist for *Caleb Williams,* the first in manuscript, the second published. Caleb returns to the town of Falkland's residence and persuades the magistrate to summon his employer for trial. In the manuscript version, Caleb's accusations carry no weight compared to Falkland's unimpeachable reputation, which is the ground for his acquittal. The search for justice, in this version, ends only with the mystification of truth through the application of power. In the ending that Godwin eventually chose for the published version—an ending that is sometimes described as optimistic but that is also disturbing and complex—Caleb is successful and forces Falkland's public confession of guilt, which clears Caleb's own name. The victory, however, is a hollow one. While Falkland accepts responsibility and is punished for the murder he committed, Caleb miserably reproaches himself for Falkland's death. The triumph of empirical truth yields a more profound defeat, suggesting that the novel's political messages are as subtle and complicated as its formal strategies.

MARK CANUEL

Further Reading

Balfour, Ian, "Promises, Promises: Social and Other Contracts in the English Jacobins (Godwin/Inchbald)," in *New Romanticisms: Theory and Critical Practice*, edited by David L. Clark and Donald C. Goellnicht, Toronto and Buffalo, New York: University of Toronto Press, 1994

Bender, John, "Impersonal Violence: The Penetrating Gaze and the Field of Narration in *Caleb Williams*," in *Critical Reconstructions: The Relationship of Fiction and Life*, edited by Robert Polhemus and Roger B. Henkle, Stanford, California: Stanford University Press, 1994

Butler, Marilyn, "Godwin, Burke, and *Caleb Williams*," *Essays in Criticism* 30 (July 1982)

Clemit, Pamela, *The Godwinian Novel: The Rational Fictions of Godwin, Brockden Brown, Mary Shelley*, Oxford: Clarendon Press, and New York: Oxford University Press, 1993

Dumas, D. Gilbert, "Things as They Were: The Original Ending of *Caleb Williams*," *Studies in English Literature* 6 (1966)

Ferguson, Frances, *Solitude and the Sublime: Romanticism and the Aesthetics of Individuation*, New York: Routledge, 1992

Handwerk, Gary, "Of Caleb's Guilt and Godwin's Truth: Ideology and Ethics in *Caleb Williams*," *English Literary History* 60 (1993)

Hazlitt, William, "Review of *Cloudesley: A Tale*," *Edinburgh Review* 51 (1830)

Kelly, Gary, *The English Jacobin Novel 1780–1805*, Oxford and New York: Clarendon Press, 1976

Myers, Mitzi, "Godwin's Changing Conception of *Caleb Williams*," *Studies in English Literature* 9 (1974)

Rajan, Tilottama, *The Supplement of Reading: Figures of Understanding in Romantic Theory and Practice*, Ithaca, New York: Cornell University Press, 1990

Rothstein, Eric, *Systems of Order and Inquiry in Later Eighteenth-Century Fiction*, Berkeley: University of California Press, 1975

Sedgwick, Eve Kosofsky, *Between Men: English Literature and Homosocial Desire*, New York: Columbia University Press, 1985

Call It Sleep by Henry Roth

1934

Literary works produced during the 1930s frequently succumbed to the tenor of the times in stressing political instead of artistic concerns. Some novelists managed to write successfully of class struggle and the plight of the unemployed, such as Michael Gold in *Jews without Money* (1930), but most attempts disappeared into polemic and are no longer read. Henry Roth never managed to cope successfully with this problem, despite having joined the Communist party in 1933. Although he had never been terribly active, he said, he did try to write a novel based upon a character he had met through the party. He received an advance from Scribner's but was unable to complete the work because he could not write about class struggle; he could not, he said, keep to the party's requirements that members who were writers devote themselves to proletarian themes. *Call It Sleep* succeeded precisely because Roth had failed as a social critic. The novel is concerned first and foremost with subtleties of character and its development, with linguistic and psychological considerations. It is not a proletarian novel, and because of this it was dismissed by the leftist *New Masses* as "introspective and febrile." The novel's success as a work of art, however, has been assured.

Critical reactions to *Call It Sleep* were otherwise very positive, sometimes ecstatic. However, as a result of the Depression, Roth's publisher went bankrupt and the novel disappeared from view. Roth found it impossible to publish another novel for 60 years, probably suffering the longest writer's block in literary history. He has stated in interviews that he suffered from both the political pressures on his writing and from his early life with Eda Lou Walton, a much older university professor with whom he lived, who supported him during the Depression so that he did not have to cope with the difficulties of the times. She gave him literary as well as emotional and financial support; and he dedicated *Call It Sleep* to her. Roth believes that because of this experience he could never get beyond the level of the child in his writing, that he became fixed at that level, never having grown up himself.

Call It Sleep concerns the psychological and emotional development of David Shearl, a six- to eight-year-old boy living on the Lower East Side of New York. The novel stands out for its application of Freudian psychology in analyzing an Oedipus complex; its use of interior monologue, in which it is more impressive than any American novel before or since; and the subtleties of dialect, in which it is comparable to Mark Twain's *The Adventures of Huckleberry Finn* (1884) in its range.

Roth stated that he had never formally studied Freud's ideas but that they were in the air, and any alert person could achieve a basic understanding of them. His situation was similar to that of Sherwood Anderson in *Winesburg, Ohio* (1919), in which the problems of the "grotesques" are seen through a Freudian lens. David is subconsciously aware of the competitive situation in which he exists in relation to his father for the attention of his mother. Indeed, Roth presents scenes between David and Genya in which the dialogue is closer to that between lovers than between son and mother. Albert's belief that David is not his son and his maladjustment resulting from his having been accused of standing motionless while his own father was gored by a bull complicate the situation.

Call It Sleep brings Joycean interior monologue into American literature. The reader is brought into David's mind throughout the novel and thus is forced to perceive the alien world of the immigrants' Lower East Side through the eyes of a fearful, sensitive child. Precocious and impressionable, David experiences a series of shocks to his psyche because of the unpredictable violence of his father, the terror caused by neighborhood gangs of non-Jewish youths, and an early introduction to sex, which he sees as dirty and terrifying. The free association that Roth presents as an essential part of David's thoughts, with misspellings and faulty syntax, gives this character a stunning reality. It is the all-pervasiveness of this technique in the novel that sets it apart from other American works.

The novel shows an extremely impressive use of dialect, which immerses the reader in the immigrant world. The first-generation Jewish immigrants speak only in Yiddish when talking to other Jews, and Roth presents Yiddish dialogue, as does Abraham Cahan in "Yekl: A Tale of the New York Ghetto," through using perfect English. But when a Jewish adult immigrant tries to communicate in English, or when both Genya and Albert must when they attempt to speak to policemen, or when their neighbor does when trying to communicate with a doctor, Roth presents their words in broken, misspelled English. The Jewish boys on the street, who have had the advantage of going to an American school, speak English with a mixture of Yiddish inflections and street slang. The non-Jewish street boys have inflections all their own, laced with slang and mispronounced words. The Irish policeman and Italian street sweeper, too, have dialects of their own. Finally, there is the dialect of David's mind, the choppy, free-associative interior monologue with its non sequiturs and childish references. The novel has set a standard of sophistication in the use of dialect unmatched in American literature. *Call It Sleep* is among that small group of American novels that reaches the standard of world literature.

EDWARD A. ABRAMSON

Further Reading

Adams, Stephen, "'The Noisiest Novel Ever Written': The Soundscape of Henry Roth's *Call It Sleep*," *Twentieth Century Literature* 35 (1989)

Altenbernd, Lynn, "An American Messiah: Myth in Henry Roth's *Call It Sleep*," *Modern Fiction Studies* 35 (1989)

Diamant, Naomi, "Linguistic Universes in Henry Roth's *Call It Sleep*," *Contemporary Literature* 27 (1986)

Ferguson, James, "Symbolic Patterns in *Call It Sleep*," *Twentieth Century Literature* 14 (1969)

Knowles, Sydney, Jr., "The Fiction of Henry Roth," *Modern Fiction Studies* 11 (1965–66)

Lyons, Bonnie, *Henry Roth: The Man and His Work*, New York: Cooper Square, 1976

"On Being Blocked and Other Literary Matters: An Interview," *Commentary* 64 (1977)

Roth, Henry, *Shifting Landscape*, Philadelphia: Jewish Publication Society, 1987

Studies in American Jewish Literature 5 (1979), special issue on Henry Roth

Italo Calvino 1923–85

Italian

Italo Calvino was a master of allegorical fantasy, a writer attracted to folktales, tales of knights and chivalry, social allegories, and fables for our time. His characters challenged and questioned the problems of daily life in the modern world. In addition to his fiction, Calvino wrote a number of essays, prefaces, and critical articles.

His first novel, *Il sentiero dei nidi di ragno* (1947; *The Path to the Nest of Spiders*), is an unorthodox account of the antifascist armed resistance in Italy. Calvino presents the partisan struggle through the adventures of a young street urchin, Pin, with the fabulous qualities that were to typify all his writings. The interrelation between fantastic and realistic elements distinguishes Calvino's early novel from the documentary style of other novels of the period and helped establish Calvino's reputation as a writer of neorealism in postwar Italy.

By the early 1950s, Calvino, growing dissatisfied with the common themes connected with the experience of war, began to steer away from the neorealist current. In response to this creative impasse, Calvino wrote a novel that had no apparent link to his previous artistic production. *Il visconte dimezzato* (1952; *The Cloven Viscount*) narrates the fantastic story of a man cut in half by a cannonball during the Turkish-Christian war. The publication of the novel provoked a debate on realism by the Italian Communist party. *The Cloven Viscount* was followed by *Il barone rampante* (1957; *The Baron in the Trees*) and *Il cavaliere inesistente* (1959; *The Nonexistent Knight*), completing the trilogy *I nostri antenati* (1960; *Our Ancestors*). Drawing from the fairy-tale and adventure-story tradition, the trilogy represents a variety of contemporary and social issues. Calvino noted that as many interpretations could be applied to these stories as readers wished.

With *La nuvola di smog* (1965; *Smog*), Calvino returned to the social-realistic mode to satirize the political, economic, and environmental abuses associated with an ever-growing industrial society. The novel appeared also to be a polemical reaction to the Italian avant-garde group known as the Gruppo 63, which had been deeply critical of the canons of naturalism.

Marcovaldo; ovvero, le stagioni in città (1963; *Marcovaldo; or, The Seasons in the City*) is composed of 20 vignettes depicting the events surrounding the protagonist, a naïve, unskilled laborer from the country who is frustrated by the realities of the big city and of consumer society. Calvino explained that the first ten stories, or fables, were written in the early 1950s and "thus are set in a very poor Italy of neorealistic movies," and the last ten "date from the mid-60s, when the illusions of the economic boom flourished."

In 1964 Calvino moved to Paris and strengthened his ties with the latest innovative literary trends—from the narrative formulas of the *nouveau roman*, structuralism, semiotics, and narratology to those discussed by the Ouvroir de Littérature Potentielle (Oulipo), a Parisian literary group led by the writer Raymond Queneau. This experimental environment combined with Calvino's long-standing interest in astronomy, geology, and biology to inspire the science-fiction narratives of *Le cosmicomiche* (1965; *Cosmicomics*) and *Ti con zero* (1967; *T Zero*). These two texts express Calvino's speculative, yet rationalistic, interpretations of the origins of the universe.

In *Le città invisibili* (1972; *Invisible Cities*), Calvino creates an imaginary dialogue between Marco Polo and Kublai Khan. The Great Khan's labyrinthine empire becomes a metaphor of the universe itself. Like the fairy tale as Calvino interprets it, *Invisible Cities* is constructed on the basis of an imaginary narrative idea, which is in turn rationalized; consequently, each invisible city functions as an allegory.

In *Il Castello dei destini incrociati* (1973; *Castle of Crossed Destinies*), Calvino finds his source of inspiration in two ancient packs of tarot cards. The author is intrigued by the infinite number of interpretations that may be found in the signs and symbols of the playing cards. The novel represents a type of open text that allows for a similar variety of possible readings.

Se una notte d'inverno un viaggiatore (1979; *If on a winter's night a traveler*) comprises ten beginnings of ten different novels, each in its fragmentary way treating the difficulty of communication. The novel explores the dynamics of reading and establishes the supremacy of reading over writing. It is a semiotic text in which all the functions, pleasures, and inventions of telling a story are exhibited, discussed, and ironically treated.

Palomar (1983; *Mr. Palomar*), the last book published during Calvino's lifetime, consists of a number of meditations on different subjects by its title character. Palomar, named after the famous observatory in California, is keenly intent on defining the phenomena surrounding him. In a 1985 interview, Calvino spoke of the book's objective: "My aim was to dream of achieving a minute knowledge of the nature of things to the point that their very substance dissolved at the moment of being grasped."

From the immediate postwar years to his death in 1985, Calvino's writings spanned nearly four decades and gained him a reputation as one of the great writers of the 20th century. His work, more than that of any other contemporary Italian writer, is characterized by technical innovation and a spirit of constant thematic, narrative, and linguistic renewal as it engages in a creative dialogue with contemporary aesthetic, philosophical, and scientific thought. His investigation of fictional possibilities reflects a sensitivity and response to the newest literary movements and theories. Although distinctly breaking away from accepted literary paradigms, Calvino does not alienate the reader; rather, he engages the reader in a continuous experimentation that embraces the universe.

Mark Pietralunga

See also Invisible Cities

Biography

Born in Santiago de las Vegas, Cuba, 15 October 1923. Moved with his family to San Remo, Italy, 1925. Attended Ginnasio-liceo Cassini, San Remo; University of Turin, 1941–47; Royal University, Florence, 1943. Conscripted into the Young Fascists, 1940; escaped to the Alps with his brother, and joined the Communist Resistance, 1943–45. Contributor to *La Nostra*

Lotta, Il Garibaldino, Voce Della Democrazia, and other periodicals beginning in 1945; first contributed to L'Unità in 1945; member of editorial staff at Einaudi, publishers, Turin, 1948–84; contributor to Contemporaneo and Città Aperta from 1954; coedited Il Menabò with Elio Vittorini, Milan, 1959–67; visited the Soviet Union, 1952, and the United States, 1959–60; settled in Paris, 1967, and continued to work for Einaudi; contributor to La Repubblica from 1979; moved to Rome, 1980; member of editorial board, Garzanti, publishers, 1984. Died 19 September 1985.

Novels by Calvino

Il sentiero dei nidi di ragno, 1947; as The Path to the Nest of Spiders, translated by Archibald Colquhoun, 1956

Il visconte dimezzato, 1952; as The Cloven Viscount, translated by Archibald Colquhoun, published with The Nonexistent Knight, 1962

Il barone rampante, 1957; as The Baron in the Trees, translated by Archibald Colquhoun, 1959

Il cavaliere inesistente, 1959; as The Nonexistent Knight, translated by Archibald Colquhoun, published with The Cloven Viscount, 1962

Marcovaldo; ovvero, le stagioni in città, 1963; as Marcovaldo; or, The Seasons in the City, translated by William Weaver, 1983

La nuvola di smog, 1965; as Smog, published in Difficult Loves; Smog; A Plunge into Real Estate, translated by William Weaver, Archibald Colquhoun, and Peggy Wright, 1983

Le città invisibili, 1972; as Invisible Cities, translated by William Weaver, 1974

Il Castello dei destini incrociati, 1973; as Castle of Crossed Destinies, translated by William Weaver, 1976

Se una notte d'inverno un viaggiatore, 1979; as If on a winter's night a traveler, translated by William Weaver, 1981

Palomar, 1983; as Mr. Palomar, translated by William Weaver, 1985

Other Writings: short stories, essays, opera libretti, articles; commissioned by his publisher Einaudi to collect and translate folktales from the various regions in Italy (Fiabe italiane, 1956; as Italian Folktales, 1980) into standard Italian.

Further Reading

Adler, Sara Maria, Calvino: The Writer as Fablemaker, Madrid and Potamac, Maryland: Porrua Turanzas, 1979

Benussi, Cristina, Introduzione a Calvino, Rome: Laterza, 1989; 2nd edition, 1991

Bonura, Giuseppe, Invito alla lettura di Italo Calvino, Milan: Mursia, 1972; 10th edition, 1992

Cannon, JoAnn, Italo Calvino: Writer and Critic, Ravenna: Longo, 1981

Carter, Albert Howard, III, Italo Calvino: Metamorphoses of Fantasy, Ann Arbor, Michigan: UMI Research Press, 1987

Olken, Ilene T., With Pleated Eye and Garnet Wing: Symmetries of Italo Calvino, Ann Arbor: University of Michigan Press, 1984

Re, Lucia, Calvino and the Age of Neorealism: Fables of Estrangement, Stanford, California: Stanford University Press, 1990

Weiss, Beno, Understanding Italo Calvino, Columbia: University of South Carolina Press, 1993

Camel Xiangzi by Lao She

Luotuo Xiangzi 1937

When first serialized in the journal Yuzhou feng (Wind of the Universe) during 1936 and 1937, Camel Xiangzi struck Lao She, pen name of Shu Qingchun, as the most accomplished novel of the several he had written since the early 1920s. Critics and literary historians have generally concurred with his view, not only consistently ranking Camel Xiangzi as Lao She's finest achievement but also among the top half-dozen Chinese novels of the 20th century. A proletarian novel focusing upon the yearnings and travails of rickshaw pullers and other manual laborers in the old northern capital of Peking, Camel Xiangzi is so unflinchingly honest about the social conditions weakening manual laborers as a class that the pessimistic final chapter of the novel eventually had to be excised before the novel could be published in the People's Republic of China (PRC). It was not until the cultural thaw following the death of Mao Zedong in 1976 that some scholarly editions of Lao She's masterpiece once again included

the final chapter; however, as late as 1982, the PRC cinematic version of the novel reverted to a defensive political posture and cut the entirety of this chapter's depiction of the protagonist's final degradation as a shiftless vagrant and unscrupulous police informer.

Within the context of Lao She's career, Camel Xiangzi (also translated as Rickshaw and Rickshaw Boy) marks the transition from an emphasis upon a robustly conceived individual will to a preoccupation with the individual as largely a representative of a social stratum or class. Independent-minded characters from earlier novels, such as Lao Lee of Lihun (1933; The Quest for Love of Lao Lee) are able to persevere in solitary defiance of corrupting influences from the societal environment, but collective endeavor becomes the only possible deliverance from calamity in later novels such as Camel Xiangzi and Huozang (1944; Cremation). In Camel Xiangzi Lao She embodies this shift in perspective, from the robust individual to the all-embracing collective, partly through a curious framing device that brings the urban backdrop to center stage during much of the first and last chapters of the novel; the character does not even enter chapter one until Lao She has described the hierarchy of Peking rickshaw pullers in some detail, and there is a far more elaborate description of crowds in Peking than of Xiangzi himself in chapter 24 at the novel's conclusion. The author's often intimate and sympathetic portrayal of Xiangzi commences only after providing a detached and sweeping panorama of Peking rickshaw pullers at the outset, and this authorial sympathy dissolves in the final chapter as the author again rises to Olympian heights from which to contemplate the urban society that has played such a key role in the downfall of his pathetic, and now even despicable, protagonist.

Other signs of the shift from individual to collective are more direct. Most prominently, the narrator's final comments about Xiangzi at the novel's end include the term *individualism* in the cluster of negative attributes to which the disreputable protagonist is finally assigned; Lao She's use of *individualism* lacks the positive connotations of the term, instead implying a sense of "everybody out for himself," or an irresponsible and petty selfishness. And in the next to last chapter, the futility of a rickshaw puller's individual effort comes across vividly in a somber dialogue between Xiangzi and an aged rickshaw puller called Xiao Ma's grandfather, who is too poor to afford medicine to administer to his sick grandson. The boy subsequently dies, and before long his grandfather's treasured rickshaw has to be sold off when the old man becomes too infirm to pull it anymore. The old man, whom Xiangzi had formerly admired as a rickshaw owner who pulled his own vehicle instead of renting one from an agency, is reduced to eking out a living as a lonely and ragged street peddler. Likening the existence of a rickshaw puller to that of a grasshopper, the old man quips that however strong a grasshopper might imagine itself to be when leaping through the air, it can be easily immobilized by a little boy who decides to tie it up with a bit of thread. Yet, if a swarm of grasshoppers were to advance as a group and devour entire fields of crops, there would be no force strong enough that could stop them from having their way. However, involvement in unionizing rickshaw pullers or some other type of constructive collective action never really enters Xiangzi's mind as a viable alternative to purely individual endeavor; his final encounter with Xiao Ma's grandfather merely leads him to dwell on the futility of any and all striving for individual advancement. Once Xiangzi's long-term resolve to save enough money to buy a rickshaw crumbles, the news of his fiancée's death sends Xiangzi over the edge into a repulsive existence of vagrancy and parasitism.

The bulk of the novel relates how this "camel" is one whose back is not easily broken by major setbacks. Xiangzi is originally the very picture of self-reliance, diligence, and resilience. Even though the first rickshaw he buys after years of scrimping and saving is stolen by marauding soldiers who force Xiangzi to work as their unpaid porter, Xiangzi has enough presence of mind to escape from the military encampment and lead a small team of army camels back to the outskirts of Peking. There he sells the camels and recoups at least a part of his hard-earned savings that had been tied up in his former rickshaw.

The story of Xiangzi's shrewd escape from the army and commandeering of a few of its camels spreads rapidly among his fellow rickshawmen, who give the country boy the simultaneously admiring and mocking nickname of Camel. In this novelistic inversion of the Bildungsroman, Xiangzi keeps scrambling back onto his feet after blundering into one mishap after another, yet he does not seem to learn anything constructive about avoiding the kind of unreflective and impulsive behavior that has contributed so greatly to his problems. Time after time he ignores warnings, such as the sound advice to stay off the streets when marauding soldiers are in the vicinity. Instead of portraying the education of a youthful protagonist, Lao She suggests that the gradual disillusionment resulting from so many setbacks can lead even the most determined and promising migrant rural laborer to moral exhaustion and irredeemable depravity. Lao She's personal experience of poverty as a youth in Peking infuses this story of Xiangzi's plunge to the city's lower depths with a cogency and vividness rarely found in modern Chinese proletarian novels.

PHILIP F. WILLIAMS

See also Lao She

Further Reading

Dolezelová-Velingerová, Milena, editor, *A Selective Guide to Chinese Literature, 1900–1949*, volume 1: *The Novel*, Leiden: Brill, 1988

Hsia, C.T., *A History of Modern Chinese Fiction*, New Haven, Connecticut: Yale University Press, 1961; 2nd edition, 1971

Hu Jinquan, *Lao She he tade zuopin* (Lao She and His Works), Hong Kong: Wenhua shenghuo chubanshe, 1977

Kao, George, editor, *Two Writers and the Cultural Revolution: Lao She and Chen Jo-hsi*, Hong Kong: Chinese University Press, and Seattle: University of Washington Press, 1980

Shi Chengjun, "Shilun jiefanghou Lao She dui *Luotuo Xiang Tzu* de xiugai" (Lao She's Revision of *Camel Hsiang-tzu* after the Liberation), *Zhongguo xiandai wenxue yanjiu congkan* (Compendium of Research on Modern Chinese Literature) 4 (1980)

Vohra, Ranbir, *Lao She and the Chinese Revolution*, Cambridge, Massachusetts: Harvard University Press, 1974

Wang, David Der-wei, *Fictional Realism in Twentieth-Century China: Mao Dun, Lao She, Shen Congwen*, New York: Columbia University Press, 1992

Canadian Novel

Anglophone

In 1763, Frances (Moore) Brooke, an Englishwoman, sailed to Quebec and spent the next six years there with her husband, John Brooke, chaplain to the English garrison. Her epistolary novel, *The History of Emily Montague*—the first novel written in North America—was published in 1766. Brooke's circumstances, along with the novel's form and content, are apt reflections of fiction's cultural provenance in Canada. In early Canadian history *English* simply meant British (commentators on Canadian literature over the last 40 years, too, have had to wrestle with the increasingly charged implications of the term). Coming before one beginning of Canada's "foreshortened history" (the phrase is Northrop Frye's), Brooke's novel predates confederation by roughly a century; the Dominion of Canada was established by an act of parliament (the British North America Act) in 1867. The letters that comprise *The History of Emily Montague* make up a rich catalogue of British perspectives on its exotic northern New World colony, with its Edenic natural expanses waiting to be cultivated, its *habitants* providing local color, its Indians a frisson of excitement and an opportunity for allegedly objective description, and all of this a likely setting for gallantry and romance. Although under Brooke's pen her letter-writers' imperialist perspectives are both asserted and subverted, *The History of Emily Montague* shows how strongly the British presence in early Canada engaged a readership whose interest in the colony, ten years after General Wolfe's decisive victory over General Montcalm at the battle of the Plains of Abraham (1759), is essentially proprietary.

In England Brooke had edited and contributed to several periodicals, including *The Old Maid* (1755–56). Her contributions, explains William New (1989), were informed by a "feminist argument running through the journal, which asserted the rights of independence but at the same time conservatively acknowledged the claims of social order." That constellation of views informed much of her work, and the epistolary form, so closely associated with the development of the novel after Samuel Richardson's *Pamela* (1740), was familiar to her, Brooke having written one of her own, the successful *The History of Julia Mandeville* (1763).

Complementing this gaze both ways across the Atlantic was early Canada's other equally complex set of relations with the definitive New World culture immediately to the south. Canada's perennially ambivalent relations with the United States find one of their earliest fictional incarnations in Thomas Chandler Haliburton's sketches featuring Sam Slick, which first appeared in 1835 in *The Novascotian*, a Halifax newspaper, and were first collected in *The Clockmaker; or, The Sayings and Doings of Samuel Slick of Slickville* (1836–40). Haliburton, a lifelong Tory in Nova Scotia, admired American enterprise, cleaved to British conservative values (he retired to England in 1856 and died there in 1865), and lamented his countrymen's inertia. The irony and self-deprecation of this perspective would inform the writing of a long line of Canadian humorists beginning with Haliburton (called by some the father of North American humor and widely admired in the United States during his time).

Canadian immigration included an influx of Americans with Tory sympathies who left the United States for Canada in the late 17th and early 18th centuries, forming the nucleus of the United Empire Loyalists. One of their most eloquent literary spokesmen was William Kirby. Born in England, Kirby emigrated with his family to the United States in 1832 and to Niagara in 1839, where he lived the rest of his life. Set in 1748, Kirby's historical romance, *The Golden Dog* (1877), mixes Gothic convention with Québecois history and legend to present a vision of the collapse of New France owing to internecine corruption and intrigue.

Like many 17th- and 18th-century Canadian works, *The Golden Dog* has a tortured publishing history. Kirby was unable to secure copyright from his original American publisher, and the novel appeared in various pirated and abridged versions, with Kirby lamenting that the eventual "authorized" version (Boston, 1897) was a "poor mutilated thing." Although the current of translation in Canada historically has run more powerfully from French to English, Kirby's novel, with its renditions of French Canadian life and history, appeared in a French version by Léon-Pamphile Le May as *Le Chien d'Or: Légende canadienne* in 1884.

In the work of two of the Strickland sisters, Susanna Moodie and Catharine Par Traill, it is tempting, if not entirely accurate, to read a metaphor for two visions of Canada that have reappeared in various forms throughout Canada's literary history. The first finds one of its most powerful expressions in Moodie's *Roughing It in the Bush* (1852), a book part novel, part journal, part settler's narrative, in which Moodie documents and imagines her Canadian sojourn (she and her husband, J. Dunbar Moodie, settled in the bush near Peterborough, Ontario). One of Moodie's explicit purposes is to tell a cautionary tale warning away prospective emigrants; yet the book is such an amalgam of modes and intentions that the warning is submerged beneath flights of Gothic description of Moodie's new surroundings, vivid sketches of uncouth fellow immigrants and impudent Yankee neighbors, and tales of imperfect adaptation to life in the bush. If Moodie's work reveals an imagination at once unsettled and inspired by Canadian experience, her sister's works align themselves for the most part with the documentary tradition that in its various forms has also animated Canadian fiction. In books such as *The Backwoods of Canada* (1836), *The Canadian Settler's Guide* (1854), or *Canadian Wild Flowers* (1868), Traill's work names, catalogs, and directs, dispensing brisk and cheerful instructions to the prospective settler.

The European origins and dispositions of early Canadian writers of fiction reveal themselves not only in their chosen forms but also in their stance before two abiding Canadian subjects: nature and the aboriginal presence. Major John Richardson's *Wacousta; or, The Prophecy: A Tale of the Canadas* (1832) is the most vividly Gothic but also one of the most popular treatments of the latter subject. In Richardson's heated imagination, the historical setting—Chief Pontiac's 1763 siege of Forts Detroit and Michilimackinac—recedes as Richardson conceives a blood-soaked tale of Wacousta's revenge upon the British commander, Colonel de Haldimar, who has betrayed Wacousta (formerly a fellow soldier and friend) by marrying his fiancée. Wacousta, an archetypal Rousseauian noble savage endowed with supernatural strength, stands as the most memorable of attempts by an early Canadian writer to reinvent Indian character and material to entertain American and British audiences.

Turn of the century Canada still held to its twinned dispositions to cleave to Empire and to look to the United States with both fear and longing in its attempts to define itself—an inclination, aptly reflected in Canada's fiction, that was an early version of Canadian culture's longstanding anxiety with defining a national identity. This calling, much remarked upon by Canadian critics until the 1960s, resonates in one of its clearest fictional forms in Sara Jeannette Duncan's best-known novel, *The Imperialist* (1904). Duncan set *The Imperialist* in Elgin, an Ontario town modeled on her native Brantford, where the novel's plot twins politics and romance. In one of the plot's prophetic resolutions, the imperialist of the title, Lorne Murchison, an admirably idealistic if naive young lawyer, loses both love and political clout as his vision of a Canada that cleaves to the mother country is defeated.

As Canada entered the 20th century, its expansion westward meant that cultural visions from the center like that of *The Imperialist* began to be accompanied by regional perspectives from both east and west. The pull of regional claims on Canadian fiction has always exerted an influence running alongside the claims of a national (often equated with an Ontario) vision, in part because of the pattern of Canada's settlement, spread out as it has been along a relatively narrow east-west line that, after Newfoundland joined Canada in 1949, extends some 4,500 miles. It has been remarked that communications theory (in the work, for example, of Harold Innis or later of Marshal McLuhan)—a field in which Canadians have been prominent in the 20th century—has been an appropriate area for Canadian culture to excel in, just as its signal act of nation building, the east-west railroad that was its first prime minister's dream, underlines the importance for Canada of literal connection across the continent.

The regional vocation of Canadian fiction made its presence more strongly felt as the generalized proto-European apprehensions of Canadian landscape faded. Canada was no longer, in Voltaire's famous phrase, simply *quelques arpents de neige* ("several acres of snow"—he was said to have described Quebec in this way), and its notorious "garrison mentality" in the face of a hostile or indifferent nature (a mainstay of Northrop Frye's influential theory of Canadian culture), eminently noticeable, say, in the quasi-pathologically conceived setting of a novel such as *Wacousta*, began to modulate into differentiated regional apprehensions of local space and setting. Regional Canada is made up, east to west, of five entities: the Maritimes, Canada's most impoverished area and its least understood in the national arena (Nova Scotia, New Brunswick, Prince Edward Island, and Newfoundland); Quebec, with its French component and, until the mid–20th century, the powerful presence of the Catholic Church; the most populous and politically powerful "center," Ontario; and the west (Manitoba, Saskatchewan, Alberta, and British Columbia), which may be subdivided into the prairie provinces (the first three) and the far west (British Columbia). The prairie provinces are divided from the rest of the country by two formidable natural barriers: the rock formations of the Great Canadian Shield on the east and the Rockies to the west.

It is impossible in this short space to adequately survey the history and significance of fiction in Canada's far eastern or western regions, beyond noting that each has contributed, early and late, important novels that have imagined important facets of their respective territories: in the Maritimes, Lucy Maud Montgomery's famous novel of childhood, *Anne of Green Gables* (1908), Ernest Buckler's lyrical novel of initiation, *The Mountain and the Valley* (1952), and David Adams Richards' gritty naturalist novel *Lives of Short Duration* (1981), among many others; in British Columbia, the novels of Ethel Wilson, most notably *The Swamp Angel* (1954) with its evocation of a woman's escape from a bad marriage into the British Columbia interior; Howard O'Hagan's *Tay John* (1960), in which a messianic Indian leads his people across the Rockies to the coast of British Columbia; Sheila Watson's *The Double Hook* (1959), often called one of Canada's first modernist fictions; and poet and novelist George Bowering's *Burning Water* (1980), a prize-winning reinvention of Captain George Vancouver's voyage of discovery. The surge of fiction in the 1960s was produced by a proliferation of important writers east and west; in the far west, three residents of Vancouver Island and the Gulf Islands off the coast number among the many significant novelists from British Columbia: Jane Rule draws on her experience as a lesbian artist in the essays of *A Hot-Eyed Moderate* and *Lesbian Images* (1985) and novels such as *Contract with the World* (1980) and *Memory Board* (1987); the novels and short stories of Audrey Thomas—including *Songs My Mother Taught Me* (1973), *Intertidal Life* (1985), and *The Wild Blue Yonder* (1990)—draw on her experience on the west coast and her sojourn in Africa, and depict strongly developed female characters; and Jack Hodgins, the west coast novelist with the strongest myth-making imagination, draws on local and literary sources to shape story collections such as *Spit Delaney's Island* (1976) and novels such as *The Invention of the World* (1977), *The Barclay Family Theatre* (1981), and *The Honorary Patron* (1987).

One model for the development of regional writing in Canada is the case of the prairies. Until the 1940s, prairie fiction was dominated by taut realist accounts of struggles with the land, and depictions of this conflict sometimes extended into evocations of tensions within the farming family that threatened its integrity. These are the dynamics of Martha Ostenso's *Wild Geese* (1925). Ostenso emigrated from Norway to the United States and then to Canada; she went to high school in Winnipeg and taught briefly in rural Manitoba before returning to the United States in 1921. The prize-winning *Wild Geese* charts a man's obsessive and destructive control over his land and family—a pattern repeated with variations by another immigrant writer on the prairies, Frederick Philip Grove. Grove fled his native Germany in 1909, adopting his new name in place of his real one, Felix Paul Greve, and came to Manitoba in 1913. His collection *Over Prairie Trails* (1922) documents his travels through the province as a schoolteacher and a keen observer of landscape and weather, while his prairie novels—*Settlers of the Marsh* (1925), *Our Daily Bread* (1928), *The Yoke of Life* (1930), and *Fruits of the Earth* (1933)—affirm the rise of realism in prairie fiction and further develop the pattern of settlers paying dearly for their misapprehensions of the land and of the limits of their own human nature.

The most important novel to come from the prairies before mid-century, however, was Sinclair Ross' *As for Me and My*

House (1941). Set in the prototypical false-fronted prairie town of Horizon, Saskatchewan during the infamous drought years, the novel is narrated as the journal kept by Mrs. Bentley as she chafes in her strained marriage to her preacher husband, Philip, a failed artist. Ross is the subject of a recent biography, novelist Keath Fraser's *As for Me and My Body* (1997), which traces Ross' reclusive life, his conflicted sexuality, and his presence in his most important book; *As for Me and My House,* interestingly, is one of the novels most written about by several generations of Canadian critics, as documented in David Stouck's edited collection, Sinclair Ross' *As for Me and My House: Five Decades of Criticism* (1991).

Lines of influence in a relatively new literature are sometimes difficult to trace, but as the novelist Margaret Laurence has explained, without Ross' work she would not have been able to write her Manawaka novels. Laurence's Manawaka (based on her home town, Neepawa; Manawaka is to Canadian fiction what Faulkner's Yoknapatawpha or Hardy's Wessex are to their national literatures) is the setting for five of Laurence's best-known fictions; of these, *The Stone Angel* (1964) and her last novel, *The Diviners* (1974), are the strongest. Laurence's fiction is among the most important Canadian literature for establishing modern female consciousness, character, imagination, and voice in all their complexity: her principal Manawaka characters, figures such as old Hagar Shipley, "rampant with memory" (*The Stone Angel*), young Rachel Cameron, the repressed daughter and schoolteacher of *A Jest of God* (1966), or Morag Gunn, the novelist, wife, and mother at the center of *The Diviners,* show how Laurence took Ross' fictionalized prairie to heart and then opened it out into the setting for her more fully realized prairie women. The prairie also has figured as one ground for Mennonite author Rudy Wiebe's fiction, with its portraits of the substantial Mennonite presence in western Canada, but also, more recently, representing some of the first serious attempts to depict aboriginal and Métis history, in novels such as *The Temptations of Big Bear* (1973) or *The Scorched-Wood People* (1977).

While the prairies have inspired a fiction of taut social and psychological realism, they have more recently been the ground for some of the most experimental and theoretically sophisticated writing in Canada. The major figure in this antitradition has been Robert Kroetsch, whose fiction, like his poetry and his criticism, has melded myth, legend, a serious delight in linguistic play, and a postmodernist's stance into a series of novels that reenvision western Canada in unabashedly comic and mythological terms, debunking archetypal male heroic quests, for example (*The Studhorse Man,* 1969), or playing fast and loose with myth and the archaeology of the prairie landscape (*Badlands,* 1975).

Ross' and Laurence's legacies have been extended by writers such as Guy Vanderhaeghe in his story collection *Man Descending* (1982) and in novels such as *My Present Age* (1984), *Homesick* (1989), and his most ambitious novel to date, *The Englishman's Boy* (1996), and Sandra Birdsell in her books of short fiction *Night Travellers* (1982) and *Ladies of the House* (1984) and in novels such as *The Missing Child* (1989), which evokes the contours of the prehistoric Lake Agassiz, or the more autobiographically inspired *The Chrome Suite* (1992). Fiction set in the city on the prairies includes John Marlyn's novel of the immigrant Hungarian experience, *Under the Ribs of Death* (1957), and, more recently, the fiction of Carol Shields, particu-

larly the Winnipeg novel *The Republic of Love* (1992) and *The Stone Diaries* (1993), which merges biography and fiction to explore a woman's attenuated interior life. Kroetsch's experiments, meanwhile, have been followed by writers such as poet Kristjana Gunnars in her novel *Prowler* (1989) and Alberta's Aritha Van Herk, whose fictions include more traditional novels of initiation such as *Judith* (1978) as well as more experimental work such as her meditation on the far north, *Places far from Ellesmere: a geografictione* (1990), or her *in visible ink: crypto-fictions* (1991).

The path of fiction's development on the prairies and elsewhere in Canada's regions did not, of course, subsume Canadian fiction's national and international vocations. Toronto-based Morley Callaghan, for example, author of some 25 novels and collections of stories (one of the finest is *Such Is My Beloved* [1934], the story of a guilt-ridden priest who attempts to save two prostitutes), was a colleague of the famous expatriates gathered in Paris that included F. Scott Fitzgerald and Ernest Hemingway. Callaghan wrote about this sojourn in *That Summer in Paris: Memories of Tangled Friendships with Hemingway, Fitzgerald, and Some Others* (1963). And in the career of Hugh MacLennan, readers may witness the best example in Canadian fiction of a steady preoccupation with the national identity in many incarnations; MacLennan's readers looked to his fiction for just those articulations of a national vision, as well as a national vision lost. *Barometer Rising* (1941), set in Halifax, shows MacLennan's talents for drawing on historical material (here, the explosion of a munitions ship in the harbor that devastated the city) to shape his fictions, as does his use of Quebec political realities in *Return of the Sphinx* (1967); but in *Two Solitudes* (1945), in some ways MacLennan's most famous novel and in others his most awkwardly constructed, lies an instructive lesson in the disposition of his Canadian readership. MacLennan took his title from a Rilke love poem in which two solitudes "protect, and touch, and greet each other." He intended the title as a watchword for the eventual, hoped-for meeting of French and English cultures in Canada. Set mainly in Quebec, the novel charts the social, political, and religious life of a Quebec town alongside the English cultural realities of Ontario as these are manifest in Montreal; the entrance of Canada into World War II—often conceived of in Canadian history as Canada's entrance onto the world stage—is imagined as the moment when French and English might meet to make common cause. MacLennan's fictional intentions, however, have been consistently read in a different way in the Canadian media and the national imagination: "Two Solitudes" has become Canada's most famous phrase for the rift between French and English, the widening separation that has been developing as one of Canada's most serious problems since mid-century.

While regional and national visions informed Canadian fiction's thematic development, and realism (until the 1960s) was Canada's dominant mode, the inflections of irony, parody, and satire that began with Haliburton's *Clockmaker* series in Nova Scotia were also carried forward. The careers of Stephen Leacock, Robertson Davies, and Mordecai Richler have traced three different pathways in this general development. Leacock, who taught political science at McGill in Montreal, is the representative Canadian humorist in a tradition that survives to this day: the affectionate but also critical vision of small-town life that celebrates its virtues as it strips away its hypocrisies. His best-known book, *Sunshine Sketches of a Little Town* (1912), transforms Leacock's Orillia, Ontario into Mariposa, home to a gallery of small-town characters who play out Leacock's disarming but incisive cultural critiques. Leacock's lasting influence may be traced in the institution of the Leacock Society, based in Orillia, and more particularly in the annual awarding of the Leacock Medal, a cherished prize for the best work of humor in Canada.

Robertson Davies was an admirer of Leacock, edited a collection of his work, and had successful careers as an actor, playwright, newspaperman, and essayist—including his widely popular columns written under the pseudonym Samuel Marchbanks, first collected in *The Diary of Samuel Marchbanks* (1947). But his fiction gained him the widest readership and marks the continuation, in Davies' first of three trilogies, of the comic tradition established with Haliburton and extended by Leacock and others. As Davies' biographer Judith Skelton Grant (in Toye, 1983) has observed, his Salterton novels (*Tempest-Tost*, 1951; *Leaven of Malice*, 1954; and *A Mixture of Frailties*, 1958) "have been called satiric romances and there is some truth in the term, for their plots are romantic and their omniscient narrator observes the foibles of small-town Ontario sharply." Davies' fiction took a celebrated turn toward the psychoanalytical (he was an avowed Jungian) and mythological in the Deptford trilogy; its first novel and Davies' finest, *Fifth Business* (1970), departs from a similar small-town Ontario ground to chart the spiritual and psychological journey toward the self-realization of schoolmaster and hagiographer Dunstan Ramsay. Davies' fiction, particularly the later Cornish trilogy, imports his considerable erudition in art and mythology, sometimes to the detriment of conciseness and engagement, and Davies' eminent figure as magus-professor (he was the head of the University of Toronto's Massey College), a learned master of many masks, beguiled his Canadian and international audience.

Mordecai Richler's career is the most important exemplar of the strengths of Canadian fiction with Jewish themes (including, among others, Henry Kreisel's novel *The Rich Man* [1948], tracing an immigrant's ironic return from Canada to Europe on the verge of war; Adele Wiseman's powerful Winnipeg novels, *The Sacrifice* [1956] and *Crackpot* [1974]; and Montreal poet A.M. Klein's agonized poetic novel of the diaspora, *The Second Scroll* [1951]). Richler's humor has a sharp moral edge that emerges in all his work; he has written pungent social criticism in essays and books—most recently in *Oh Canada, Oh Quebec* (1992), which attracted national and international attention for its indictment of Quebec's language laws and its attention to the history of anti-Semitism in Quebec. Like many Canadian writers early and late, Richler has lived for long periods outside of Canada (in London in his case), and in novels such as *A Choice of Enemies* (1957) he documents the chilled European postwar moral climate of expatriate allegiances and disaffections. But in his most important novels set in Canada, including *The Apprenticeship of Duddy Kravitz* (1959), *St. Urbain's Horseman* (1971), *Joshua Then and Now* (1980), and his most recent, most daring *Solomon Gursky Was Here* (1989), Richler has made good on his early vow to get his first world of Saint Urbain Street in Montreal right, and moved beyond that local material to explore the wider Jewish presence in recent history. His fiction's alloy of satire, gritty realism, and—most importantly in *Gursky*—mythology exuberantly deployed and reshaped for his own comic uses, has gained him a wide readership in Canada and abroad.

Canadian fiction's ambivalence toward American and British antecedents and connections and the related founding of a Canadian humor; its search for forms to depict land, nature, and aboriginal presence; the rise of regionalism and realism; the call on Canadian literature to define a national identity—from these origins Canadian fiction during the 1960s, like Canadian culture more generally, grew into forms that have become so remarkably variegated, speaking to an audience so much more diverse, that it is difficult to do more than mark the bare outlines of this proliferation.

The late 1950s saw the Canadian government and the national publishing industry promote and market Canadian writing in a more direct and concerted way. The Canada Council, charged with fostering Canadian culture, was founded in 1957, and the first and most important of several paperback reprint series, the New Canadian Library, was founded in 1958. In 1937 the Governor-General's Awards had been established—the first of a lengthening series of awards for Canadian writing—and until the deficit-obsessed 1990s, when funding began to be cut, grants for the small Canadian literary presses that published significant work across the country were awarded by provincial and federal government agencies. Fiction during the 1960s was marked by predictable shifts in theme that accompanied the sexual revolution, the rise of feminist visions, the birth of the ecological movement, and the reflection of a more ethnically diverse readership and of many more writers—of Italian, East Indian, Ukrainian, Japanese, and Caribbean origin, among others—who were not simply "English." In broader cultural terms, the 1960s may also be seen, from the vantage point of the 1990s, to have incorporated at once the latest surge of Canada's recurring waves of national self-consciousness and to have witnessed the rise, accompanying Empire's continuing decline, of the postcolonial stance—cultural, political, ideological—reflected and created in all of the arts.

Canadian fiction of the 1960s developed formally in striking ways: away from the dominance of realism and the calls for a national vision toward a formally and stylistically more sophisticated inquiry into an increasingly ambivalent understanding of Canadian and Western history (Canada has always, notes Frye among others, been a culture fixated on its past), and also toward incorporation of more politicized and ideological concerns. In the related, at times indistinguishable fictional form, the short story (as well as the novella), in which a significant number of Canadians have excelled in the last 30 years, two writers, Mavis Gallant and Alice Munro, have gained wide readerships in Canada and beyond. Their respective ranges (Gallant's, surveying the fractured postwar history of the West with a cool and ironic eye; Munro's, departing from her rich evocations of small-town and rural southwestern Ontario) are exemplified in Munro's and Gallant's 1996 collections, *Selected Stories* and *The Selected Stories of Mavis Gallant*.

Obasan (1981) by Joy Kogawa exemplifies the many Canadian fictions that bear witness—here, to the history of the internment of Japanese-Canadians during World War II—in an attempt to come to personal and collective terms with the past. The postmodernist fiction of Timothy Findley interrogates World War I from a Canadian perspective (*The Wars*, 1977), recasts recent European history (*Famous Last Words*, 1981), and reincarnates a host of literary antecedents (from Conrad to Susanna Moodie) to forge a dark vision of contemporary Toronto (*Headhunter*, 1993).

At the head of the host of women writers who have constituted a major force in Canadian fiction since the 1960s stands Margaret Atwood, whose 1972 survey of Canadian literature, *Survival*, subscribes to Frye's view of a hostile or indifferent nature and argues that Canadian culture is beset by a victim mentality in various guises. Atwood deserves to be better known for her poetry, but it is her fiction that has gained more attention: in deadpan and ironic, at times comic narrative voices, her novels, beginning with *The Edible Woman* (1969) and *Surfacing* (1972) and including, recently, the dystopian *The Handmaid's Tale* (1985), *The Robber Bride* (1993), and *Alias Grace* (1996), evoke the labyrinthine course of women's lives among contemporary as well as historical, political, cultural, and sexual minefields. Among the many other women currently establishing major careers, perhaps the most accomplished is Jane Urquhart; her third novel, *Away* (1993), traces an Irish family's generations and struggles in Ireland and then in Canada.

As Canadian fiction became more variegated in form and subject, Canadian poets increasingly turned to the novel to explore the widening possibilities of the form. Poet and songwriter Leonard Cohen's *Beautiful Losers* (1966) anticipates many of these fictions; among the most prominent of these writers has been Michael Ondaatje, originally from Sri Lanka, who moved toward fiction with novels such as *Coming Through Slaughter* (1976), an evocation of jazz great Buddy Bolden's madness, *In the Skin of a Lion* (1987), a re-creation of parts of Toronto's architectural history, the autobiographical fiction *Running in the Family* (1982), or *The English Patient* (1992), a many-faceted inquiry into postwar history set in a crumbling Italian villa.

The first- and second-generation immigrant writers who settled in Canada from the Caribbean, from modern India, from Italy and elsewhere brought memories and imaginations inflected with themes of displacement, oppression, and exile. Among the most important of these writers are Caribbean novelists such as Austin Clarke and, a generation later, Neil Bissoondath, with story collections such as *Digging Up the Mountains* (1985) and novels such as *A Casual Brutality* (1988). Bissoondath's *Selling Illusions: The Cult of Multiculturalism in Canada*, an indictment of Canada's official multicultural policy, stirred passions across the country. Dionne Brand published her collection of stories *Sans Souci* in 1988, invoking both her Caribbean childhood and the daily oppression of living as a black woman in Toronto and Montreal. Nino Ricci, an Italian-Canadian writer, published his powerfully imagined tale of growing up in an Italian village, *Lives of the Saints*, in 1990, following it with a sequel, *In A Glass House*, in 1993. Rohinton Mistry is the most prominent of the many contemporary Canadian writers with East Indian origins; his *Such a Long Journey* (1991), a rich account of an East Indian family's intertwined generations in their home culture, won the Governor-General's Award for fiction that year, as did Ricci's first novel in 1990.

Among writers exiled, voluntarily or not, in Canada, Malcolm Lowry is one of the best known; Lowry completed *Under the Volcano* (1947) while living just outside of Vancouver, British Columbia. The most important contemporary novelist in this group is the former Czechoslovakia's Josef Škvorecký; his best-known fiction remains *The Engineer of Human Souls* (1984).

Recent Canadian fiction continues to move outward, away from the old nation-building strictures, to include new forms through which to imagine the North, the land, the regions, and to evoke the contemporary and prehistoric aboriginal presence; to include the continuing pursuit of encyclopedic fictional projects (the best-known and most ambitious of these is Montreal writer Hugh Hood's projected series, "The New Age," now in its ninth volume); and to engage an increasingly cosmopolitan and international audience alongside the traditional, still growing strengths of a local and diverse Canadian readership. Two examples among many must suffice as illustrations: in 1993, Thomas King, a writer of Cherokee and Greek-German descent, published *Green Grass, Running Water*, the finest and most ambitious novel to date to intertwine North American native myth with Christian traditions, playing seriously with a host of literary and legendary sources from both popular and high culture to explore contemporary aboriginal and white relations. Recently, Anne Michaels' poetic novel of an imagined and historical holocaust, *Fugitive Pieces* (1996), already much celebrated in Canada, was declared the winner of Britain's coveted Orange Prize, awarded annually to a woman writer. Neither book may be said to satisfactorily represent or even to do more than faintly refer to current Canadian fiction's protean presence, or to its many-layered history. But both novels reflect the impressive vitality and the growing promise of the form in Canada and elsewhere.

NEIL K. BESNER

See also Margaret Atwood; Robertson Davies; Margaret Laurence; Hugh MacLennan; Alice Munro; Mordecai Richler

Further Reading

Atwood, Margaret, *Survival: A Thematic Guide to Canadian Literature*, Toronto: Anansi, 1972

Dahlie, Hallvard, *Varieties of Exile: The Canadian Experience*, Vancouver: University of British Columbia Press, 1986

Daymond, Douglas, and Leslie Monkman, editors, *Canadian Novelists and the Novel*, Ottawa: Borealis Press, 1981

Dooley, D.J., *Moral Vision in the Canadian Novel*, Toronto: Clarke, Irwin, 1978

Frye, Northrop, *The Bush Garden: Essays on the Canadian Imagination*, Toronto: Anansi, 1971

Harrison, Dick, *Unnamed Country: The Struggle for a Canadian Prairie Fiction*, Edmonton: University of Alberta Press, 1977

Hutcheon, Linda, *The Canadian Postmodern: A Study of Contemporary English-Canadian Fiction*, Toronto and New York: Oxford University Press, 1988

Keefer, Janice Kulyk, *Under Eastern Eyes: A Critical Reading of Maritime Fiction*, Toronto and London: University of Toronto Press, 1987

McGregor, Gaile, *The Wacousta Syndrome: Explorations in the Canadian Langscape*, Toronto and Buffalo, New York: University of Toronto Press, 1985

MacLulich, T.D., *Between Europe and America: The Canadian Tradition in Fiction*, Downsview, Ontario: ECW Press, 1988

Moss, John, *Patterns of Isolation in English-Canadian Fiction*, Toronto: McLelland and Stewart, 1974

Moss, John, *Sex and Violence in the Canadian Novel: The Ancestral Present*, Toronto: McLelland and Stewart, 1977

Moss, John, *A Reader's Guide to the Canadian Novel*, Toronto: McLelland and Stewart, 1981; 2nd Edition, 1987

New, William H., *A History of Canadian Literature*, London: Macmillan, and New York: New Amsterdam, 1989

Northey, Margot, *The Haunted Wilderness: The Gothic and Grotesque in Canadian Fiction*, Toronto and Buffalo, New York: University of Toronto Press, 1976

Ricou, Laurence, *Vertical Man, Horizontal World: Man and Landscape in Canadian Prairie Fiction*, Vancouver: University of British Columbia Press, 1973

Steele, Charles, editor, *Taking Stock: The Calgary Conference on the Canadian Novel*, Downsview, Ontario: ECW Press, 1982

Sutherland, Ronald, *The New Hero: Essays in Comparative Quebec/Canadian Literature*, Toronto: Macmillan, 1977

Toye, William E., editor, *The Oxford Companion to Canadian Literature*, Toronto and New York: Oxford University Press, 1983; 2nd edition, 1997

Canadian Novel

Francophone

In spite of sluggish beginnings and a submission to rigid ideological constraints for about 100 years, the French-language novel in Quebec rapidly entered the modern era by the end of World War II and is now one of the most dynamic literary genres in the francophone world.

The first Quebec novel, *Le Chercheur de trésors* (1837; The Treasure Seeker) by Philippe Aubert de Gaspé *fils,* a most primitive text, combines a main plot (the search by a poor alchemist, Saint-Amand, for the philosopher's stone) with two subplots (a hideous murder, and the romance between a medical student and Saint-Amand's daughter) interrupted by the insertion of various folk legends and songs. The author ambiguously both condemns and is attracted to emergent capitalism. This book was among the first to suffer from censorship, its second edition (1864) having been expurgated of any hint of eroticism and epigraphs of authors condemned by the papal Index of forbidden books.

The imitative Gothic constituted the first phase of the novel genre among Canadian francophone writers. By the mid-1840s, it was overtaken by the *roman de la fidélité,* a mode that was to be dominant for about 100 years. It espoused faithfulness to the French language, traditional (rural) folkways, and Catholicism. It was rooted in the movement of *survivance,* or defensive survival, that shaped the dominant ideological discourse until about 1960, but particularly after the defeat of the uprisings for independence (1837–38). The mode had two currents: the *roman du terroir* (or novel of the land) and the historical novel. The *roman du terroir* was launched by Patrice Lacombe's novella *La Terre paternelle* (1846; The Family Farm), which promoted the ideology of *agriculturisme,* the mythified, compensatory worldview that held rural life to be the essence of French-Canadian civilization. P.-J.-O. Chauveau's more developed *Charles Guérin: Roman de moeurs canadiennes* (1853) deals with a similar retrieval of a threatened patrimony. Both works were among the first to render popular speech and to present genre scenes that would become the landmark of the novel of the land.

In the two-volume *Jean Rivard* (1862, 1864), by Antoine Gérin-Lajoie, the author's stated purpose was to stop mass emigration southward by promoting settlement of sparsely populated regions of Quebec through the creation of a network of agricultural centers coupled with farm-related industries. His work, reprinted numerous times over a century, describes the pioneer hero's founding of a nearly perfect utopian microsociety, "Rivardville." A recent close rereading by Robert Major (1996) has proposed a (largely) convincing revaluation of the work, stressing the "Americanism" of the self-made hero and his forward-looking values.

Philippe Aubert de Gaspé *père*'s *Les Anciens Canadiens* (1863; *Canadians of Old*) is a "retrospective" novel, the action beginning in 1757, three years before the fall of New France. The author responded to the call of the literary ideologue H.-R. Casgrain for the exploitation of legends and historical subjects, but shunned his simultaneous warning against treating political themes. De Gaspé's seigneurial roots led him to idealize New France's landholding system, focused here on the d'Haberville manor. Jules, the family scion, and the Scot, Archibald de Locheill, find themselves on opposite sides in the Seven Years' War. Against his will, Arché takes part in the sacking of the d'Haberville property, something Blanche, Jules' sister, will never forgive, thus preventing the union to which each aspires. The author vacillates between a strong desire for reconciliation of the two peoples and nationalist discourse. Thus, beneath the intermingling of supernatural elements, legends, sorcerers, songs, and humor (much of it centered on popular speech, which is set off in italics), there is a serious thread of ethnic conflict.

Angéline de Montbrun (1884) by Laure Conan (Félicité Anger), French Canada's first psychological novel, was praised for its promotion of Christian resignation, but during the past 35 years critics have found a strong intimation of an incestuous attraction between daughter and father. The novel is divided into three parts. The fact that Angéline does not speak in her own name until the final section (except for two letters in part one) has been interpreted by Patricia Smart and others as reflecting her subordinate position as an "object," possession of whom is being negotiated between her father and her (future) fiancé (see Smart, 1991). Her taking pen in hand in the final section is seen as a parallel for the author's composition of the work, the first novel by a female francophone writer in Canada and the most important Canadian francophone novel of the 19th century.

Laure Conan's psychological approach stood out from other French Canadian novels of the time. Although Quebec's population was nearly evenly divided between rural and urban areas as early as 1911, the novel of the land continued to dominate literary production until about the middle of the 20th century, when Quebec had become overwhelmingly urban and industrialized. French-born Louis Hémon wrote *Maria Chapdelaine* (1916), his all-time best-seller and a model for all subsequent novels of the land. Although *Maria Chapdelaine* has many touches of realism in its depiction of the harsh climate and stubborn physical labor of pioneer farmers, its tone shifts toward the end when mystical voices urge the heroine to forget her US-exiled suitor and remain in her birthplace. Her true love, lumberjack François Paradis, had already died halfway through the novel, thus eliminating a potential agent of instability and assuring the *agriculturiste*-nationalist apotheosis.

The priest-novelist F.-A. Savard's *Menaud maître-draveur* (1937; *Master of the River*), the last major example of the *roman de la fidélité*, also employs Hémon's supernatural "voix du Québec," which echoes throughout the novel, inspiring the old log-driver hero of the title to try to rally his ilk against the encroachments of the *étrangers*. This work, too, has perceptive touches of realism, regional speech, and striking poetry. It signals economic and cultural alienation but eventually cedes to a narrow nationalist vocabulary ("race," "destiny," "blood") and an ancestor cult.

Against the tide of static rural idylls in the first quarter of the 20th century stood two quasi-clandestine novels, Rodolphe Girard's Rabelaisian *Marie Calumet* (1904) and the starkly naturalistic *La Scouine* (1918; *Bitter Bread*), by Albert Laberge. Both flayed the rural idyll, mocked the clergy, and demythified the traditional family.

In 1938, Ringuet's classic *Trente arpent* (*Thirty Acres*) dealt the death blow to the novel of the land. Ringuet painted a broad canvas in poetico-realistic (and even mythological) terms of the fissures that were threatening the very survival of *agriculturisme*. *Thirty Acres* brought the novel genre in Quebec to formal maturity. Paradoxically, it is the supreme *roman du terroir* at the same time that it dismantles the myths on which the *roman du terroir* was based and fatally undermines the rural mystique.

The novel traces some 40 years in the life of a Laurentian farmer, Euchariste Moisan, from the end of the 19th century until the late 1930s, marking his decline and prostration as he is transformed from independent landowner to nightwatchman at the municipal garage in White Falls, Massachusetts. It is dominated by a somber fatalism, lyricism being reserved for the mythified Earth, which imperturbably watches its creatures crushed. While the author leans toward the traditional critique of the city, with its stereotyped temptresses, he also displays a protofeminism in his treatment of Moisan's wife, Alphonsine, whose lack of power over her life and her children is treated with sensitivity.

In *Thirty Acres,* the French pacifist farmhand Albert, a *survenant* (unannounced stranger), brings his nonconformist habits and sensitivity to the closed rural parish, buttressing the author's critical gaze on an enshrined way of life. Seven years later, Germaine Guèvremont turned the episodic outlander into the central figure of her *Le Survenant* (1945). Similar to Ringuet but with more overt empathy, her work—together with its sequel, *Marie-Didace* (1947)—traces the collapse of the Beauchemin dynasty after six generations on the same soil. Their disintegration is brought on by the physical and moral weaknesses of Amable, son of the patriarch, Didace, and the son's insecure wife, Alphonsine. Dominating the story is the mysterious, anonymous red-headed stranger who brings the ideas of the outside world to the Beauchemins' closed community.

Until World War II, urban working-class characters, if they appeared at all in the Francophone Canadian novel, played bit parts. The situation changed with Roger Lemelin's *Au Pied de la pente douce* (1944; *The Town Below*) and especially Gabrielle Roy's *Bonheur d'occasion* (1945; *The Tin Flute*), which placed working-class characters front and center of the action. Lemelin's work was part of a quasi-trilogy—with *Les Plouffe* (1948; *The Plouffe Family*) and *Pierre le Magnifique* (1952; *In Quest of Splendour*)—centered on the inability of Lower Town Quebec City youth to rise, literally and figuratively, and find prosperity in a secular career. The first novel, the author's most spontaneous and vibrant, has two parts, counterbalancing two "cities," two Lower Town clans: the crushed "mulots" (field-mice) and the pretentious petty bourgeois "soyeux" (silky ones). Each of the clans is represented by an adolescent hero (Denis Boucher and Jean Colin, respectively). Denis Boucher functions as the author's alter ego and also makes an appearance in the other novels—as sidekick to the protagonist, Ovide Plouffe, in the second and as a deformed version of his early self in the third. In *Les Plouffe,* attention is focused on the family of the title. The Church seems in disarray, as strikers picket the hierarchy's daily and Americanism (in the form of baseball, films, and pop tunes) becomes more and more dominant in the culture. Sexuality and Catholicism's sexual prohibitions become more explicit themes. In *In Quest of Splendour,* the hero, a Lower Town seminarian spurred on by Denis, makes an unsuccessful attempt to avenge the poor. Lemelin's novels suffer from melodrama and caricature, but they display the verve, humor, and satire (particularly of the clergy) of a keen observer of Quebec society.

Gabrielle Roy created a classic of social realism with *The Tin Flute.* While just as specific as Lemelin's in its setting, this novel has had a much more universal appeal and has been translated into nine languages. Roy created unforgettable characters, played with flashbacks and chronological leaps, rhythmic devices, cinematic close-ups, symbolic description, and a cast of main characters and anonymous figures similar to those of Zola and Steinbeck to give her novel a richness beyond bare realism. Her ironic treatment of war as "salvation" for the destitute struck a chord with thousands of readers. The core of the story is formed by the loves of the young waitress, Florentine, for her romanticized Jean, father of her unwanted child, and for Emmanuel, her more humdrum soldier-admirer who eventually becomes her husband and unconscious savior.

Roy's only other Montreal-centered novel was *Alexandre Chenevert* (1954; *The Cashier*), in which she again shaped her realistic aesthetic into a tool of social criticism (directed especially at the other-worldliness of the Catholic Church, seven years before Vatican II). This novel also reflects the existentialist current that pervaded the literary scene in 1950s France, where Roy wrote the novel. Roy's hero, a bank-teller and a kind of Everyman of the metropolis, in his groping attempts to understand the confused, impersonal, mechanized world around him, probes (and inverts) the humanity's relationship to God, weighs the urban-rural dichotomy, and sounds the meaning of sickness and death.

While urban social realism was coming to the fore, Catholic intellectuals around the journal *La Relève,* influenced by François Mauriac and Georges Bernanos, began to create a sub-genre centered on internal spiritual yearning and a personalist philosophy. The work of writers like Robert Charbonneau, Robert Elie, and André Giroux reflected the malaise of the chilly social and moral climate of religiosity and corruption during the reign of Premier Maurice Duplessis (1944–59). Their novels contain vague elements of social criticism but are usually arid and schematic. Their introspection and fluid treatment of time, however, influenced the development of narrative technique in the French Canadian novel.

André Langevin is the most important in this group of novelists focusing on psychological analysis and moral conflict. Unlike the above authors, however, he was influenced by the secular existentialist current of Albert Camus and Jean-Paul Sartre. He became a towering figure of Quebec fiction with the publication of *Poussière sur la ville* (1953; *Dust over the City*). Narrated in the first person, it reads like the oral diary of Dr. Alain Dubois, a young physician of petty bourgeois origins who lives with his working-class wife, Madeleine, in "Macklin," in Quebec's asbestos region. Dubois lives through his wife's adultery—a failed affair with a strapping truck driver—and her subsequent suicide, as well as his own alcoholism, finding the strength to remain in the town. His anger gradually turns to pity as he witnesses his marriage break down. He yearns to become Madeleine's "ally against absurd cruelty," isolating himself from the elite and earning condemnation from the priest.

Another important novelist, Yves Thériault, Quebec's most prolific, began as a short-story writer, turning to the novel with *La Fille laide* (1950; The Ugly Girl), in which the writer's "primitivism"—a celebration of instinctive, untrammeled acts—is manifest. In *Aaron* (1954), tradition and revolt are weighed in the balance in the dingy workshop in central Montreal of the Orthodox Jewish immigrant tailor, Moishe, and his grandson Aaron. The young man changes his name and enters the world of finance to his grandfather's chagrin. Thériault habitually sides with the rebel, but the portrait of the patriarch in *Aaron* is so compelling that it tips the scales in the other direction.

Historical conflicts are sparsely represented in the pre-1960 French Canadian novel. The most important historical novel of the period is Léo-Paul Desrosiers' *Les Engagés du Grand Portage* (1938; *The Making of Nicolas Montour*), tracing the meteoric career of Nicolas Montour to the heights of power in a Northwest fur company at the turn of the century, crushing all who stood in his way. It is striking in the sweep of its social canvas, breathtaking pace, and immediacy of narration.

Refus global (1948; Global Refusal), a manifesto written by the automatist painter Paul-Emile Borduas and signed by other artists in various fields, was to be a milestone in the struggle against religious obscurantism, self-satisfied ignorance, and repression. It celebrated aesthetic experimentation and eroticism. From the end of the 1940s to the end of the 1950s, the broad alliance of forces seeking change (trade unionists, intellectuals, progressive clergy) grew and was strengthened by the death of autocratic Premier Duplessis in 1959. With the victory of the Liberals in the 1960 provincial elections, a new period, dubbed the Quiet Revolution, began in earnest. There were rapid re-

forms in education, health care, and trade union rights; the creative arts, including literature, were catalysts of these changes and their by-products. The omnipresent Catholic Church lost much of its power as secularization spread to all spheres of activity. The term "Québécois" quickly replaced the vaguer coast-to-coast term of "French Canadians" to refer to the majority in the precise confines of Quebec. The novel began to flower in an unprecedented variety of forms. First-person narration became predominant, and a new frankness emerged, including an explosion of eroticism and expressions of anger and violence.

Each of the three decades since 1960 has begun with a pivotal moment in Quebec's evolution. During the October Crisis of 1970, a provincial minister, Pierre Laporte, was strangled. In 1980 the *Parti québécois* government lost its referendum on sovereignty-association. The failure of the Meech Lake constitutional accord and the Mohawk crisis at Oka in 1990 both affected Quebec deeply. These events left their mark on the novel in complex ways.

The 1960s saw the first appearance or the maturation of first-class writers like Gérard Bessette, Claire Martin, Marie-Claire Blais, Jacques Ferron, Jacques Godbout, Hubert Aquin, and Réjean Ducharme. A shock wave of young naturalistic/realistic writers was associated with the review *Parti pris* (1963–68). Meanwhile, Gabrielle Roy and Yves Thériault continued to publish important work.

With *Le Libraire* (1960; *Not for Every Eye*) and *L'Incubation* (1965; *Incubation*), Gérard Bessette became a novelist of stature. The first is the journal of a jaded antihero, the provincial bookseller Hervé Jodoin, who outsmarts his hypocritical boss and the clerical censors who try to stop his under-the-counter sale of books on the Index and removes the stock to a warehouse in Montreal. This self-reflexive work deals with writing, language, book distribution, and censorship and is full of references to writers—Voltaire, Rousseau, Flaubert. *Incubation* was the first of Bessette's fictionalized forays into Freudianism. The entire novel is constituted by the stream of consciousness of the narrator, the library aide Lagarde, who tries to fathom the reasons for a female colleague's suicide. There is an uninterrupted flow of memories, imagined projections, dreams and nightmares, disjointed strands of speech, and an explosion of neologisms.

Jacques Godbout coined the term *texte national* to describe neonationalist works that were mainly concerned with Quebec's place in Canada and the world. Most of his own novels belong to this category, and he, together with Hubert Aquin, is one of the prime representatives of that approach. His *Le Couteau sur la table* (1965; *Knife on the Table*), in the style of the nouveau roman, brought together a French-Canadian army deserter and a wealthy anglophone woman in a troubling relationship that, under the impact of the 1970 October Crisis, threatened to end in bloodshed. In *Salut Galarneau!* (1967; *Hail Galarneau!*), the action is concentrated in Quebec itself. Unlike the tension-filled *Knife on the Table*, *Galarneau* is a work of positive self-affirmation. The novel's simpler, more direct yet imaginative form, differentiates it from the complex nouveau roman techniques of *Knife on the Table*. Unfortunately, its sequel, *Le Temps des Galarneau* (1993; *The Golden Galarneaus*), signals the return to a certain xenophobic vision of present-day Quebec.

Hubert Aquin is a tragic figure who took his life in 1977 after a failed attempt at a new novel. His best and most popular work is his brilliant first novel, *Prochain épisode* (1965; *Prochain*

Episode). It is marked by multiple narrative voices, a plot that hinges on the heroes' Hamlet-like procrastination in carrying through a revolutionary act (a double failure, as it is mirrored in the novel-within-the-novel), lyrical eroticism, and mock-epic humor. *Trou de mémoire* (1968; *Blackout*) is a symbolic treatment of the anglophone-francophone conflict focusing on the rape and murder of his English-Canadian mistress by the revolutionary druggist and would-be novelist Pierre-X. Magnant. These violent acts are reflections of the love-hate relationship already delineated in *Prochain épisode* and represent a compensatory inversion of the historical process in what has been called a baroque exercise.

The search for identity also preoccupied the young writers of *Parti pris*. Influenced by Marxism, existentialism, and anticolonialist thought, this group favored an independent, secular, and socialist Quebec. Most of its editors and contributors were in their 20s, divided between those of educated middle-class and self-taught working-class origins. *Parti pris'* influence went far beyond its small readership, for it helped change the self-image of the francophone majority of Quebec from that of *Canadiens français* to *Québécois*. In a special issue entitled "Pour une littérature québécoise" (January 1965), the group outlined its literary theories, including the controversial call for the use of *joual*—the highly anglicized speech of the uneducated masses—as a prime literary tool. The most emblematic work of the *Parti pris* group is Jacques Renaud's novella *Le Cassé* (1964; *Broke City*). Its use of *joual* in narration broke with the realistic tradition of rendering popular speech solely in dialogue.

Directly related to the political violence of the period is Claude Jasmin's *Ethel et le terroriste* (1964; *Ethel and the Terrorist*), one of that prolific author's most successful works. The journal of Paul, a fleeing revolutionary, it transposes a 1963 incident that claimed the first fatal casualty caused by an F.L.Q. (*Front de libération québécois*) bomb. The work is filled with Paul's erotic effusions over Ethel, a Jewish survivor of the Holocaust, which made *Ethel and the Terrorist* one of the first fictional works to sound interethnic tensions in Montreal.

Jacques Ferron weds social and nationalist themes, which linked him ideologically to *Parti pris*. But where the *Parti pris* writers take a naturalist/realist approach, Ferron's writing is shaped by fantasy, myths, legends; he has been called a magic realist. His work displays a certain nostalgia for Quebec's traditional past, for which the journal had contempt. Best known for his brilliant collections of *contes* (tales), his most successful novels are *Cotnoir* (1962; *Dr. Cotnoir*) and *L'Amélanchier* (1970; *The Juneberry Tree*), both of which imaginatively probe "deviant" mental behavior and were inspired by Ferron's work as a physician in a Montreal mental hospital.

Marie-Claire Blais, the wunderkind of Quebec letters, came into prominence with her somber first novel, *La Belle Bête* (1959; *Mad Shadows*), when she was not yet 20. But the real revelation of her immense talent came with *Une saison dans la vie d'Emmanuel* (1965; *A Season in the Life of Emmanuel*), set in a vaguely defined countryside at an unspecified time—clearly a microcosm of Quebec, circa 1940. The baby Emmanuel is born into a crowded, abjectly poor household. Grand-mère Antoinette confuses the children, living or dead, except for her favorite, the poet of the ruins, Jean-Le Maigre. Jean dies of tuberculosis, but leaves behind his "autobiography." A parody of the idealized family and the church, *Emmanuel* takes part in

the movement of revolt and renewal, but it does so in an unusual way, reviving a rare carnivalesque register. Sociological readings have given way to an emphasis on the novel's fanciful and surrealistic elements.

The term "carnivalesque" has also been applied to Roch Carrier, especially to his best-known novel, *La Guerre, yes sir!* (1968). The grotesque is certainly present in that work, as is the nationalist theme, in the presence of six anglophone soldiers who bring back the casket of a local resident for burial. The wake covers most of this satirical novel, which ends in a symbolic brawl between the two language groups. But Carrier's "caricatural realism" has none of the profuse tenderness of Blais' *Une saison dans la vie d'Emmanuel*.

A more ambivalent attitude to nationalism is also seen in the writing of that other wunderkind, Réjean Ducharme, who illuminated the literary landscape in the 1960s with his verbal fireworks, highly imaginative plot structures, and bizarre characters. His major theme is the refusal of adulthood by his child-heroes. The narrator of his dazzling first published novel, *L'Avalée des avalés* (1966; *The Swallower Swallowed*), Bérénice Einberg, creates her own "language," "le bérénicien," and chooses to "swallow" everything she encounters rather than be swallowed. Like other Ducharme protagonists, she is attracted to her brother, but prefers "tenderness" to sexuality.

In *L'Hiver de force* (1973; *Wild to Mild*), another brother-sister couple attempts to live by doing nothing and denouncing everything and everyone. While appalled at what "biligualism" is doing to the French language through advertising, they also reject the pretentious new elite of the *Parti québécois*. Yet they are obliged to work as proofreaders for the nationalists against their will, and thus, in the middle of summer, they enter the metaphoric winter of the title. They find solace by reading *La Flore laurentienne*, a compendium of Quebec plants.

Ducharme's flirtation with nationalism continues in *Le Nez qui voque* (1967; *Equivocation*), in which the narrator Mille Milles, lashes out at immigrant restaurateurs who refuse to speak French. In a later work, *Les Enfantômes* (1976; *The Phantom Children*), Ducharme creates an unhappy symbolic couple, Vincent Falardeau and Alberta Turnstiff. Vincent is drawn to his sister, Fériée, in a triangle that, in addition to the habitual incestuous attractions, has ethnopolitical overtones.

Certain major authors in the 1960s were writing works outside the main thrust of "le texte national." Although they do not possess the incandescence of her semiautobiographic writing, starting with *Rue Deschambault* (1955; *Street of Riches*), Gabrielle Roy produced two important novels in 1961 and 1970: *La Montagne secrète* (*The Hidden Mountain*) and *La Rivière sans repos* (*Windflower*), both set in the northern reaches of Canada. The first, about a painter, treats the artist's impossible quest for the perfect work. *Windflower* consists of short stories and a novel, all set in the tundra of the Inuit. Perhaps to be read as an allegory, the work probes some of Roy's key concerns: cultures in contact and in conflict, "primitive" carefreeness versus "civilization," and the search for identity. The heroine, Elsa, is torn between her attraction to white ways and fidelity to her own heritage after she is raped by a US soldier and gives birth to a blond, blue-eyed son, Jimmy. He becomes a bomber pilot in Vietnam, the faces of whose people, seared by napalm, remind her of her own folk.

Thériault also turned to the Inuit for subject matter in his preoccupation with "primitivism." In 1958, he published *Agaguk*, which was followed by two sequels of lesser quality. *Agaguk,* one of his best writing achievements, was one of the first postwar novels to deal explicitly with sex. In it, the author opposes the corrupt "chief," Ramook, with his eponymous son, who quits the Ungava village to settle on the tundra alone with his bride. The novel skillfully develops tensions between the two microsocieties, sustains highly dramatic incidents, and creates an epic atmosphere. But the allegedly amoral "nature" of the Inuit rings false. Thériault wrote more convincingly in his short novel *Ashini* (1960), a "lyrical meditation" by a Montagnais chief who ends his life because of a failure to stop white encroachment.

Claire Martin and Louise Maheux-Forcier showed particular sensitivity to women characters before feminism became a movement. They opened up taboo subjects such as extramarital sex and lesbianism. Claire Martin excelled in treating psychological aspects of love and diagnosing the Quebec bourgeois family and its institutional props. A pioneer in the use of first-person narrative and shifting point of view, her two novels, *Doux-amer* (1960; *Best Man*) and *Quand j'aurai payé ton visage* (1962; *The Legacy*), are more concerned with the individual subject than with the contextual society. Her outstanding autobiography, *Dans un gant de fer* (1965; *In an Iron Glove*), implicitly yet powerfully links the particular with the general. Although evidently nonfiction memoirs (no generic label is indicated), it reads like a novel, especially in the portrait of the monstrous father and anguished mother. Martin is admired for flaying the xenophobia of her upper-class milieu.

In Maheux-Forcier's beautifully crafted *Une forêt pour Zoé* (1969; *A Forest for Zoe*) and other novels, the female characters strive to create socially proscribed relationships with each other, usually closely linked to epiphanous childhood memories and in reaction to vulgar and insensitive men. Together with *Amadou* (1963; *Amadou*) and *L'Île joyeuse* (1964; *Isle of Joy*), she composed three variations on a theme. Martin and Maheux-Forcier might be considered protofeminists in that their charges against men are not systematized, as will often be the case in the feminist works to be considered next.

It is widely held that the most notable development in Québécois literature in the 1970s was the emergence of feminist writing. France Théoret (in "Le déplacement du symbolique," in her *Entre raison et déraison: Essais,* 1987) defined feminist fiction as writing that consciously aims to create a feminine "subject" and challenges patriarchal language structures and traditional genres. She and others began to create their own institutional infrastructures and treated the feminine condition frankly. While influenced by writers in the United States and France, Quebec feminist authors also reflected the evolution of their own society and the place of women within it. They left a sure mark on both the form and content of the novel. Their rise to prominence paralleled the founding of militant women's groups and feminist journals, the creation of women's theatre companies, and the founding of two publishing companies run exclusively by women.

Nicole Brossard, a prominent poet, turned to the novel form in 1970 and produced three books within four years, all of them treating a novel-in-the-making. Her self-conscious writing has usually earned her—and several other feminist writers—the label "postmodernist." In *French kiss: Etreinte/Exploration* (1974), the space represented is clearly Montreal, but there is a nearly complete break with psychology and character development. The first word of the subtitle is echoed in Brossard's treatment of

lesbian and incestuous relationships; the second, in the book's probing of the creative process through a form of automatic writing. More concretely feminist is Brossard's *L'Amèr; ou, Le chapitre effrité* (1977; *These Our Mothers; or, The Disintegrating Chapter*), in which she attacks the delimiting reproductive role of women, skilfully weaving variations on the title which combines "la mère" (mother), the adjective "amer, amère" (bitter), "la mer" (sea) and "l'amer" (seamark). In the later *Le Désert mauve* (1987; *Mauve Desert*), Brossard focuses the story on the murder of a woman geometer by a shadowy engineer and on a network of lesbian relationships, but the novel seems more concerned with formal and aesthetic questions. There is a novel-within-the-novel, which bears the same title (but has a different author and publisher), plus a "translation" of the latter under a slightly different title.

Less postmodernist in its structure, more varied in its depiction of sexual orientation, and hilariously satirical of male pretention and exploitation is Louky Bersianik's *L'Euguélionne* (1976; *The Euguelionne*), from the Greek for "the [intergalactic] woman who brings the good news." The book defies genre boundaries by combining elements of the novel, essay, science fiction, manifesto, academic thesis, feminized dictionary, code of ethics, collection of maxims, and manual of (especially) female sexuality. It mixes humor (mainly puns and the transformation of clichés) with serious commentary on war and colonialism. As in many other contemporary novels, especially feminist ones, the intertext contains a plethora of literary, artistic, and musical references. Sigmund Freud and Jacques Lacan come in for a drubbing, as does the Catholic Church, and the novel contains pastiches of Genesis and the Sermon on the Mount. The play with language and spelling is often brilliant.

Of a more autobiographical nature are the novels of Madeleine Gagnon (*Lueur, Roman archéologique* [1979; Glimmer: An Archaeological Novel]) and France Théoret (*Nous parlerons comme on écrit* [1982; We'll Talk the Way People Write]). Both are poets, and their prose sparkles with imagination and self-reflexivity. At the heart of *Lueur* is a rehabilitation of the female lineage of the narrator-author, particularly the mother and Gaspé grandmother, "slaves with invisible chains." Gagnon creates neologisms and feminizes the gender of some nouns that are masculine in French. Théoret's book is also concerned with language, expression, communication (as the title suggests), and the narrator names herself "a woman born without a tongue, destined for silence and obedience." Théoret alternates between traditional narrative and fragmented and syncopated techniques, and varies narrative voice.

Jovette Marchessault's *La Mère des herbes* (1980; *Mother of the Grass*), part of a trilogy begun in 1975, excoriates male (especially clerical) dominance and celebrates the matriarchal heritage by evoking the ancestral goddesses of her Amerindian heritage. The author draws on a wartime working-class childhood, but the realistic passages are tempered by the overall structure of the work. Divided into seven "chants," the novel is a lyrical blending of autobiography, myth, and symbolism.

Madeleine Ouellette-Michalska has given us another variant of the feminist text in her fascinating *La Maison Trestler; ou, Le 8e jour d'Amérique* (1984; *The House of Trestler; or, America's Eighth Day*). The author probes the relations between history and fiction through the narrator's fascination with an 18th-century house of a German mercenary near Montreal and especially the fate of his younger daughter, Catherine, who becomes the focus of a novel the narrator is writing. The nearly total absence of women in approved historiography leads the narrator to declare that the discipline is akin to fiction. Yet her work is full of references to contemporary and past historical events, and she shows interest not only in the demeaned position of Catherine and her sister but also in Trestler's exploitation of peasants and Amerindians. The narration alternates between the recounting of the gestation of "le roman Trestler" and Catherine's telling of her own story.

Finally, feminism is just one component in Yolande Villemaire's *La Vie en prose* (1980; Life in Prose), a book applauded for its exuberance and formal experimentation. It interweaves a novel-in-the-making, a journal, letters, conversation fragments, reflections on writing, literature, and other arts, and a heterogeneity of places and people. Villemaire's concerns are more countercultural than feminist. Typically postmodern, its anecdotal component is tenuous, confused, and confusing. Humor is created by the use of hyper-*joual* and eccentric juxtapositions (e.g., Marilyn Monroe and Rosa Luxembourg). More serious references to Québécois and world literature and to feminist theoreticians and creators abound. The feminist writers discussed here have, in the main, shaken institutionalized patriarchy in Quebec and helped reshape the literary and cultural landscape. They also have broken literary conventions by the inventiveness and expressiveness of their experimentation.

From the 1960s on, significantly, the novel replaced poetry as the dominant literary mode. From 1970 to 1990, the number of novels published annually quadrupled, and there is a wider variety of formal and thematic approaches than ever before. A marked change also took place in the greater place given to Québécois literature in college and university curricula.

Several major established novelists were very active in the 1970s. Anne Hébert, a poet, turned to short stories, culminating in her striking collection *Le Torrent* (1950; *The Torrent*). In 1958 her first novel, the poetic *Les Chambres de bois* (*The Silent Rooms*), appeared. In what may be an allegory, the heroine, Catherine, breaks out of the dark and dementia-inducing rooms of the title and moves toward the light and shared love. Hébert would reach the pinnacle of her art with *Kamouraska* (1970), her prize-winning, best-known work.

Hébert continued to bring out other fine novels in the 1970s and 1980s. In *Les Enfants du sabbat* (1975; *Children of the Black Sabbath*), she establishes two antipodal environments—the shackling one of a Quebec City convent in the late 1930s and the wild and unfettered life among a family of sorcerers—between which the heroine moves. In *Les Fous de Bassan* (1982; *In the Shadow of the Wind*), six narratives relate from different angles the rape and murder of two cousins, Nora and Olivia, by their cousin Stevens. The characters belong to a fundamentalist anglophone community strongly resembling the "Jansenist" environment of French Canada.

Gérard Bessette developed his psychoanalytic approach to the novel in *Le Cycle* (1971; *The Cycle*), in which seven members of a family (widow, children, grandchild) reflect on their relations with a deceased man. Bessette invented a punctuation system to render different levels of awareness and physiological states. Perhaps his most imaginative work is *Les Anthropoïdes* (1977; The Anthropoids), a "prehistoric" novel set 500 millenia ago in the area of the Nile delta. It is an action-filled work recounting the epic struggle for survival of a primitive people, the "Kalahoumes." But the novel is also highly self-reflexive, focused on the telling of this tale, which is assigned to the budding *paroleur,* an adolescent boy training to become the official oral guardian of their saga. Bessette's last novel was *Le Semestre* (1979), a work clearly marked by autobiography, relating through indirect internal monologue the last teaching stint of an aging professor, novelist, and critic. (It contains a *psychocritique* by the hero of an excellent novel, *Serge d'entre les morts* [1976], by Gilbert La Rocque).

Nationalism is central to André Langevin's nouveau roman *L'Élan d'Amérique* (1972; The North American Moose). Focused on two indirect internal monologues interweaving in complex fashion, it is an ironic and profoundly pessimistic look at the survival of the francophone world in the face of the massive US technological assault on traditional ways of making a living in the North. His *Une chaîne dans le parc* (1974; *Orphan Street*) saw Langevin returning to the traumatic orphan theme that haunted his first novels (and his own early years).

The preoccupation with American economic and technological hegemony is also uppermost in Jacques Godbout's *L'Isle au dragon* (1976; *Dragon Island*), but in its witty style and fabulous structure it is different from Langevin's in tonality. One of Godbout's most ingenious works is *Les Têtes à Papineau* (1981; Papineau's Heads). The narrator is the two-headed monster Charles-François Papineau, with his anglophile and Gallic split, clearly an allegorical construct of Canada itself. In the form of a journal, it comes to an abrupt stop when the "heads" undergo surgery to unify them. François is subsumed by his other half, and a unilingual English being, Charles F. Papineau, survives. It is worth noting that the novel was published a year after the defeat of the *Parti québécois*' 1980 referendum.

Another "endangered species," the francophone Acadians of Atlantic Canada, long confined to an oral tradition, had a cultural revival in the late 1960s and 1970s. Its most illustrious representative is Antonine Maillet, who came into prominence in 1971 with the publication and staging of her series of brilliant dramatic monologues, *La Sagouine* (*La Sagouine*) centered on the slattern of the title. *Mariaagélas* (1973; *Mariaagélas; Maria, Daughter of Gélas*) followed, again presenting a strong heroine, this time in the setting of the illicit rum smuggling of the Prohibition era. In 1979, Maillet won the prestigious Prix Goncourt for her *Pélagie-la-charrette* (*Pélagie: The Return to a Homeland*), a novel that uses a more stylized dialect than *La Sagouine* and relies on legends and folktales to recount the 1755 expulsion of the Acadians, their scattering throughout the American colonies, and their epic return (1770–80). This saga is narrated by a lineage of chroniclers. In the midst of tragedy, Maillet also offers an earthy, Rabelaisian, and hyperbolic humor.

While all three had published earlier, André Major, Jacques Poulin, and Victor-Lévy Beaulieu came to prominence in the 1970s. Major's most praised work is his trilogy, *Histoires de déserteurs: L'Épouvantail* (1974; *The Scarecrows of Saint-Emmanuel*), *L'Épidémie* (1975; *Inspector Therrien: Tales of Deserters*), and *Les Rescapés* (1976; *Man on the Run*), set in the paradoxically named fictional village of Saint-Emmanuel-de-l'Epouvante. All three novels are fast-paced and suspenseful stories of crime and political intrigue, in a rural setting, with colorful dialogue and a motley host of secondary characters.

There are some parallels between Major's trilogy and Victor-

Lévy Beaulieu's multi-volume "saga" of the Beauchemin family. But Beaulieu's novels are more naturalistic and full of degradation and sexual aberration. In some, the line between dream and reality is blurred by the phantasms of the narrator or main character. *Race de monde!* (1969; What a Gang of People), the first, tells the story of a rural family's move to Montreal. *Les Grands-pères* (1973; *The Grandfathers*) recounts the last day of Milien, the maternal grandfather. The plural title and other devices emphasize a resemblance between named and unnamed characters. Real or imagined sexual violence against women occurs here as elsewhere in Beaulieu's work. In *Don Quichotte de la démanche* (1974; *Don Quixote in Nighttown*)—the title is a play on Cervantes' work, but also contains the idea of de/armed and dementia—Abel, the author's alter ego, reflects on the writer's status, his creativity, and the problems he faces combining writing with earning a living. The novel begins and ends with Abel's hospitalization for depression.

Reflections on writing, the writer, and the reader are also constants in the work of Jacques Poulin. But the subtle, muted tonality of his fiction, its avoidance of *joual* and naturalistic settings, and its sexual reticence set his novels apart from Beaulieu's. Poulin relies on a limpid style that disguises the complexity of his work. Writers of one sort or another (or characters concerned with language or book distribution) play an important role in Poulin's novels, which move between first- and third-person narration. Poulin's most substantial book in every sense is *Volkswagen Blues* (1984). It is emblematic of the Quebec novel of the 1980s, which opened up to the wider world and especially to *américanité*, or America-consciousness. The hero sets out in a Volkswagen minibus in search of his brother Théo (with whom he has lost contact), picks up a Métis hitchhiker named Pitsémine, a woman car mechanic, and the two traverse the continent from Gaspé to San Francisco. When they finally find Théo, he is in a pitiful physical and mental state, speaks no French, and does not recognize Jack. Throughout their long journey, the two "read" history differently; she is ever conscious of the slaughter and robbery of her Native ancestors, while he is absorbed by the French penetration of the continent. Pierre L'Hérault has seen in this novel "the exploration of a culture and an identity . . . now necessarily become hybrid . . ." ("*Volkswagen Blues*: Traverser les identités," *Voix et images: Littérature québécoise* 43:15 [Autumn 1989]). But it is also possible to read the novel as an expression of the fear of the loss of francophone culture in the continental melting pot. In most of Poulin's novels, there is a *ménage à trois*, a preference for friendship over physical love, and a search for an androgynous ideal. In *La Tournée d'automne* (1993; The Autumn Tour), however, sensuality and pleasurable physical congress finally triumph.

In Jacques Godbout's *Une histoire américaine* (1986; *An American Story*), the hero and sometime narrator is the mixed-stock Gregory Francoeur, a professor doing research on what makes people happy in California. He concludes that neither he nor his sometime Ethiopian mistress will ever belong to "the troops of the richest nation in the world." Nor do they want any part of a state where military laboratories are preparing "the end of the world . . . inexorably." But such a critical view of California as an ironic microcosm of the American dream is not shared by other Quebec writers. Yolande Villemaire's *La Vie en prose* and other novels focus on the attraction for its countercultural underground. And Gabrielle Roy drew on the climatic and human magnetism of coastal California in her last work of fiction, *De quoi t'ennuies-tu Eveline?* (1982). The title character, the mother in several of Roy's semiautobiographical works, goes to California by bus from Manitoba to visit her brother Majorique. He dies before she gets there, but Roy's utopian vision of interethnic harmony is reflected in Majorique's multiethnic family.

Marie-Claire Blais has used the American South in her work. In her novel *Soifs* (1995; *These Festive Nights*), the (mostly psychological) action takes place during a three-day period in which a group of individuals on an island resembling Key West are loosely linked together. The group includes a woman lawyer recovering from surgery for cancer, her militant feminist niece, a black pastor, a professor dying of AIDS, and several others. The entire novel, using techniques first developed in the equally acclaimed *Le Sourd dans la ville* (1979; *Deaf to the City*), consists of a single paragraph. Long, winding sentences reproduce the inner thoughts of the characters, fragments of dialogue, and descriptions of natural beauty. But death is everywhere, and the characters are obsessed by nightmarish events—the execution of relatives by the Nazis, the resurgence of the Ku Klux Klan, the electrocution of black prisoners, the bombing of Baghdad in the Gulf War.

Michel Tremblay recreates the gay colony in Key West in his highly autobiographical *Le Coeur éclaté* (1993; Heartburst), the sequel of *Le Coeur découvert: Roman d'amours* (1986; *The Heart Laid Bare*). Haunted by the ravages of AIDS, both deal with the breakup of a long-lasting homosexual relationship and its aftermath. Tremblay is a celebrated playwright who also has been a best-selling prose writer. His "Chroniques du Plateau Mont-Royal," centered on the universe of the author's childhood in east-end Montreal and combining a tenderly realistic recreation of the crowded quarter in wartime with the fantasy world of Marcel, an avatar of the creative personality, have been very successful. However, his "autobiographical" adult works lack the social sweep of the childhood autobiography and fetishize *joual*.

There is a substantial group of writers in Quebec who, born abroad, have brought distant and "exotic" milieus into the contours of the Quebec novel. They reflect the growing diversity of Montreal's population, even within the dominant French-speaking group. Among them are Monique Bosco (born in Austria), Naim Kattan (Iraq), Jacques Folch-Ribas (Catalonia), Dany Laferrière and Emile Ollivier (Haiti), Régine Robin (France), Sergio Kokis (Brazil), and Ying Chen (China). All have produced interesting and significant works of fiction. We shall discuss briefly here by way of example two works that juxtapose the abandoned birthplace and the new home and deal with the painful quest for identity of transplanted individuals—Régine Robin's *La Québécoite* (1983; *The Wanderer*), and Sergio Kokis' prize-winning *Le Pavillon des miroirs* (1994; The Pavilion of Mirrors).

Robin's novel traces the difficult move in the 1970s from Europe to neonationalist Quebec of a left-wing academic/writer of French nationality and Jewish ancestry. Steeped in Yiddish culture and literature, depressed by the destruction of European Jewry and its *shtetl* life, haunted by the massive roundup of French Jews for deportation in July 1942, the narrator no longer feels at home in Paris. Yet she is equally uncomfortable with certain narrow nationalist symbols and historical references in her new milieu. *The Wanderer* is postmodernist in that the narrator is attempting to write a novel and imagines two possible scenarios, each of which, in the conditional mode, also reflects the harrying search for an integrated self. But her novel remains incomplete, like the narrator herself.

Kokis' narrator is a Brazilian-born painter of partly Latvian origin, who is also perplexed as to his identity. He, too, is insecure culturally and emotionally in Quebec. The text is comprised mainly of memories of childhood, adolescence, and youth in the steamy lumpen-proletarian ambience of Rio de Janeiro. The cityscapes are full of putrescence, degeneracy, and poverty, yet they have a beguiling pace and color. Shorter alternating passages are set in the narrator's present in Montreal, but the past clearly dominates. The novel's strength lies in its passionate descriptions of Rio street life. Its weakness is a misogyny that stands in contrast with Robin's feminism.

Monique Bosco, mentioned above, and Gilles Archambault, are important novelists outside the dominant modes. An existentialist angst looms large in their work, and, in their own way, they are successors of the psychological novelists of the 1940s and 1950s, but without the torturing guilt of rigoristic Catholicism. Bosco's novels have been called "lamentations," shaped by her Jewish roots and by the literature of antiquity. Sardonic and self-deprecating, the equally inward-turned novels of Gilles Archambault are usually narrated in the first person. His heroes are weak petty bourgeois men who drift aimlessly through life from one emotional or occupational crisis to another, which sometimes ends in violence.

Several notable novels reached a mass market in the 1980s and 1990s, among them Louis Caron's trilogy *Les Fils de la liberté* (1981–90; *The Sons of Liberty*), which paints a broad canvas from the 1837 Rebellion to the October Crisis of 1970, and especially Yves Beauchemin's runaway hit, *Le Matou* (1981; *The Alleycat*). With nearly a million copies sold on both sides of the Atlantic, *The Alleycat*'s huge success has been attributed to its blending of traits from several popular subgenres (the detective story, the novel of manners, the picaresque work, the fantastic tale, and the serial), to its focus on the life of an average couple, and to its specific naming of streets and familiar buildings in Montreal. The novel pits a young and amoral French Canadian against a diabolical and mysterious European, Ratablavasky. Fast-paced and replete with dramatic incident, the novel traces the economic success of the protagonist, Florent Boissoneau. Its anti-Semitic (and generally xenophobic) subtext caused a public controversy, leading to the elimination of some contested expressions in the 1984 English translation.

Recent analyses of the orientation of the contemporary Quebec novel have stressed its diversity, distinctness, maturity, and autonomy. One may also note that the novel of political commitment and that of the counterculture have declined; feminist writing is the only major trend to survive from the 1970s. In his study *Le Roman mauve*, critic Jacques Allard designates a dominant type of novel in the recent period, characterized by the painful quest for identity, a focus on agony and death, a search for lost origins, and the lies of love (see Allard, 1997). Among the authors he cites are new novelists of the late 1980s or early 1990s, such as the highly imaginative Monique Proulx (*Homme invisible à la fenêtre* [1993; *Invisible Man at the Window*]) and the incisive journalist turned deft creative writer Lise Bissonnette (*Choses crues* [1995; *Affairs of Art*] and *Marie suivait l'été* [1992; *Following the Summer*]), as well as established writers (Poulin, Ducharme, Beauchemin). In any case, whatever the thematic or formal approach, it is clear that, with twice as many novels published in Quebec proportionally than in France, the vitality of the Canadian francophone novel is incontestable.

BEN-Z. SHEK

See also Hubert Aquin; Anne Hébert; Gabrielle Roy; Swallower Swallowed; Tin Flute

Further Reading

Allard, Jacques, *Le Roman mauve: Microlectures de la fiction récente au Québec*, Montreal: Québec/Amérique, 1997

Babby, Ellen, *The Play of Language and Spectacle: A Structural Reading of Selected Texts by Gabrielle Roy*, Toronto: ECW Press, 1985

Gould, Karen, *Writing in the Feminine: Feminism and Experimental Writing in Quebec*, Carbondale: Southern Illinois University Press, 1990

Heidenreich, Rosmarin, *The Postwar Novel in Canada: Narrative Patterns and Reader Response*, Waterloo, Ontario: Wilfrid Laurier University Press, 1989

Kandiuk, Mary, *French-Canadian Authors: A Bibliography of Their Works and of English-Language Criticism*, Metuchen, New Jersey: Scarecrow Press, 1990; London: Scarecrow, 1991

Major, Robert, *The American Dream in Nineteenth-Century Quebec: Ideologies and Utopia in Antoine Gérin-Lajoie's "Jean Rivard,"* Toronto and Buffalo, New York: University of Toronto Press, 1996

Mezei, Kathy, *Bibliography of Criticism on English and French Literary Translations in Canada: 1950–1986, Annotated*, Ottawa: University of Ottawa Press, 1988

New, William H., editor, *Canadian Writers Since 1960*, volume 53, *Dictionary of Literary Biography*, first series, Detroit, Michigan: Gale Research, 1986

New, William H., editor, *Canadian Writers, 1920–1959*, volume 68, *Dictionary of Literary Biography*, first series, Detroit, Michigan: Gale Research, 1988

Purdy, Anthony, *A Certain Difficulty of Being: Essays on the Quebec Novel*, Montreal and Buffalo, New York: McGill-Queen's University Press, 1990

Shek, Ben-Zion, *Social Realism in the French-Canadian Novel*, Montreal: Harvest House, 1976

Shek, Ben-Zion, *French-Canadian and Québécois Novels*, Toronto: Oxford University Press, 1991

Smart, Patricia, *Writing in the Father's House: The Emergence of the Feminine in the Quebec Literary Tradition*, New York and Toronto: Oxford University Press, 1991

Socken, Paul, *Myth and Morality in "Alexandre Chenevert" by Gabrielle Roy*, Frankfurt am Main and New York: Peter Lang, 1987

Socken, Paul, *The Myth of the Lost Paradise in the Novels of Jacques Poulin*, Rutherford, New Jersey: Farleigh Dickinson University Press, and London: Associated University Presses, 1993

Toye, William E., editor, *The Oxford Companion to Canadian Literature*, Toronto and New York: Oxford University Press, 1983; 2nd edition, 1997

Warwick, Jack, *The Long Journey: Literary Themes of French Canada*, Toronto: University of Toronto Press, 1968

Yale French Studies 65 (1983), issue entitled "The Language of Difference: Writing in QUEBEC(ois)"

Candide; or, Optimism by Voltaire

Candide; ou, l'Optimisme 1759

Voltaire developed the *conte philosophique*, or philosophical tale, a genre that he brought to such perfection that it was never successfully imitated. His *contes*, and in particular *Candide*, have aptly been called *contes cruels*, or cruel tales, doubtless because they stand out as exceptionally and relentlessly ferocious, satirical, and ironical in their onslaught on evil, both natural and man-made, and on such common human failings as ignorance, stupidity, and prejudice.

Candide was written and published in 1759, after Voltaire had undergone several traumatic personal experiences, notably the premature death of his patron and friend Madame du Châtelet, which deprived him of intellectual and emotional companionship as well as of a luxuriously comfortable refuge at her chateau of Cirey. He also was bitterly disappointed at the Potsdam court of Frederic II, who, after offering his hospitality to the bereaved *philosophe*, took a malicious pleasure in repeatedly humiliating him. Catastrophic events of a less personal nature, notably the terrible 1755 Lisbon earthquake and the murderous and protracted conflict between England and France during the Seven Years' War (1756–63), also had a powerful impact on Voltaire's emotional and moral outlook. He felt compelled to acknowledge evil in all its horrific immediacy, specificity, and random arbitrariness and could therefore no longer reconcile evil with the Leibnitzian notion that it was a necessary component in this "best of all possible worlds." By 1759 Voltaire clearly had renounced the moderate and rational philosophical optimism he had so cheerfully advocated in his *Lettres philosophiques* (1734; *Letters on England*) and had become a man overwhelmed with the distressing spectacle of suffering humanity.

Of Voltaire's prodigious literary output, *Candide* continues to be his best-known and best-selling work. It has no parallel as a fast-moving, rollicking tale of the travails and travels of a naive young man. Candide believes that this is the best of all possible worlds, a belief imparted to him by his obtuse and pedantic mentor, Pangloss. This idea is sorely tested from the day Candide is roughly expelled from his earthly paradise in the castle of the baron of Thunder-ten-Tronckh for kissing the comely and very receptive Cunégonde. Candide encounters innumerable catastrophes and various forms of natural cataclysm and human cruelty in his globe-trotting adventures, notably the havoc brought about by war, disease, earthquake, religious fanaticism, and greed. He enjoys a brief idyllic interlude during the El Dorado episode, the utopian paradise that our restless hero decides to leave in his stubborn pursuit of his beloved Cunégonde. At the end, a chastened Candide, having barely survived his transcontinental trials and ordeals and having at last been reunited with the now ugly and shrewish Cunégonde, responds to Pangloss' self-satisfied speeches with the direct, down-to-earth, yet somewhat mystifying statement: "That is well said, but we must cultivate our garden." By that frequently quoted and widely discussed affirmation, Voltaire perhaps quite simply meant that the best remedy against human affliction and injustice is work—the perennial effort to give meaning and order to one's life and the most reliable source of comfort and satisfaction in an otherwise bewilderingly chaotic world.

Candide is a persistently fierce recital, full of malicious verve, of the countless tribulations that befall an innocent young man propelled through a terrifyingly incomprehensible and cruelly indifferent world. It skillfully mingles purely fictive sequences with references to actual contemporaneous events. Almost every one of the 30 swift-moving chapters introduces new places and events and a gallery of sharply silhouetted characters, or rather caricatures, with comically suggestive names such as the Baron of Thunder-ten-Tronckh, Cunégonde, Pangloss, Cacambo, Vanderdendur, Pococurante, or Fernando d'Ibarra y Figueroa. The hero himself bears a name that clearly proclaims his initially naive and good-natured disposition. Candide's common sense and down-to-earth wisdom, however, ultimately prevail over the darkly pessimistic views and dire predictions of universal gloom of his Manichaean friend Martin and over the pedantic, extravagant verbiage and metaphysics of his blithely optimistic mentor Pangloss. It is the latter's perpetually repeated psuedophilosophical discourse justifying the cause and effect of every encountered disaster that constitutes the main comical leitmotiv of the novel.

Candide also is a picaresque tale that in many ways parodies not only the narrative conventions of the sentimental novel of adventure then in vogue but also what would later become known as the *roman d'apprentissage, roman de formation,* or Bildungsroman, a genre that deals with a young man's experience of the hard lessons of life. That the novel is meant to be read at two levels, the narratological and the ideological, or didactic, is made clear by its title, *Candide; ou, l'Optimisme.* The accumulation of natural and human disasters and catastrophes that are related in a most light-hearted, elegantly pithy style by a seemingly detached narrator, or by the characters themselves, creates a uniquely compelling and jarring tableau of a world gone mad. But, even though Candide holds a central place in Western culture, it stands apart from the main developments in the history of the novel.

GITA MAY

See also Conte Philosophique; Voltaire

Further Reading

Besterman, Theodore, *Voltaire,* London: Longman, and New York: Harcourt Brace, 1969; 3rd edition, Oxford: Blackwell, and Chicago: University of Chicago Press, 1976

Bottiglia, William F., *Voltaire's "Candide": Analysis of a Classic,* Geneva: Institut et Musée Voltaire, 1959; 2nd edition, 1964

Mason, Hadyn, *Voltaire,* New York: St. Martin's Press, and London: Hutchinson, 1975

McGhee, Dorothy, *Voltairian Narrative Devices,* Menasha, Wisconsin: George Banta, 1933

Mylne, Vivienne, "Literary Techniques and Methods in Voltaire's *contes philosophiques," Studies on Voltaire and the Eighteenth Century* 57 (1967)

Propp, Vladimir, *Morfologiia skazki,* Leningrad: Academia, 1928; as *Morphology of the Folktale,* Bloomington: Research

Center, Indiana University, 1958; 2nd edition, Austin: University of Texas Press, 1968

Sareil, Jean, *Essai sur "Candide,"* Geneva: Droz, 1967

Sherman, Carol, *Reading Voltaire's "Contes": A Semiotics of Philosophical Narration,* Chapel Hill: Department of Romance Languages, University of North Carolina Press, 1985

Starobinski, Jean, "Sur le style philosophique de *Candide,"* *Comparative Literature* (Summer 1976)

Stewart, Philip, "Holding Up the Mirror to Fiction: Generic Parody in *Candide,"* *French Studies* 33 (1979)

Torrey, Norman, *The Spirit of Voltaire,* New York: Columbia University Press, 1938

Voltaire, *Voltaire par lui-même,* edited by René Pomeau, Paris: Editions du Seuil, 1959

Waldinger, Renée, editor, *Approaches to Teaching Voltaire's "Candide,"* New York: Modern Language Association of America, 1987

Canon

In the history of its usage, the word *canon* has developed at least two significantly different and yet interrelated meanings. Deriving from the Greek *kanon,* meaning "measure" or "rule," the word has always implied the notion of a standard: a yardstick for measuring objects. It also has referred to a body of objects that adheres to such a standard. While the latter definition suggests that a canon is simply a collection of objects, the former definition further suggests that such a collection also involves a particular judgment about them: a set of principles that governs inclusion and exclusion. To use the word *canon,* then, is to refer to a fact—that some works are included in a collection and others are not. But it is also used to refer to a more or less explicit set of values; these values presumably inform the sum total of judgments or selection processes that yield the set of objects called a canon.

Although *canon* has referred to laws or rules—to "canon law" or ecclesiastical law, for example—the word has been used historically to describe the actual written sources of laws or rules. One of the oldest uses of the term in relation to written texts refers to a biblical or scriptural canon on which the authority of a religious orthodoxy is based. Scholars have located the secular reference to a literary canon only as late as the 18th century; the earliest connection between literary works and the scriptural canon has been traced to David Ruhnken in 1768. By the early 19th century, Samuel Taylor Coleridge was writing of "canons of criticism respecting poetry" and a "canon of general taste." In literary studies, however, the term has not been universally accepted and has continued to exist alongside other related expressions. Charles-Augustin Sainte-Beuve's favored word was *classic,* which referred to a work by an author who "has enriched the human mind, who has actually added to its treasures and carried it a step forward." F.R. Leavis (1948) understood certain authors to be part of a Great Tradition: authors who "not only change the possibility of the art for practitioners and readers, but . . . are significant in terms of the human awareness they promote; awareness of the possibilities of life." Critics tend to view these separate terms as ways of talking about the same thing: however variable and arbitrary, terms such as *classic* are concerned with defining—and finding examples of—literary greatness. As Richard Ohmann (in Von Hallberg, 1984) writes,

the sense of canon in a literary context, along with associated synonyms for canon, signifies "a shared understanding of what literature is worth preserving."

Although today's readers tend readily to accept the literary genre of the novel into their notions of the canon, such acceptance is actually rather recent. The novel frequently was considered by critics to be a form of writing unworthy of consideration alongside great works of poetry. Scholars working in the field of 18th-century British literature, for example, frequently point to the ways in which Alexander Pope's *Dunciad* (1728) and Jonathan Swift's *Battle of the Books* (1704) resisted the movement of literary culture toward the increasingly popular genre of realist prose fiction. The Augustan resistance to social and political "novelty," J. Paul Hunter (1990) explains, was paired with a hostility to the novel and its frequently derided Grub Street practitioners.

For later generations of critics, however, the understanding of a literary canon has proved general enough to include novels; the question of canonicity for such critics has simply involved recognizing the greatness of certain novelists who may be grouped with certain great poets. For Harold Bloom (1994), for example, authors worthy of being considered canonical have a "tang of originality" or a "strangeness" capable of being ascribed to either poetry or novels; hence Bloom's inclusion, in *The Western Canon,* of writers such as Charles Dickens, Fedor Dostoevskii, George Eliot, and Franz Kafka, along with John Milton and William Shakespeare.

For other critics, however, modes of measurement and evaluation pertaining to novels in particular have given shape to a novelistic canon. As with the criteria used to define a canon of literature in general, the criteria defining a canon of novels in particular are highly variable. These criteria, it is important to note, are related to issues of literary history and literary genre. It might be said, in fact, that the history of the novel as a genre distinguishable from other genres implicitly informs discussions of the novelistic canons. Any evaluation of the qualities of novels must have determined how far back in time a process of selection may legitimately begin and what kinds of texts are suitable for consideration as great examples of the genre.

Traditionally, however, issues of literary history and literary genre are not necessarily connected to issues of canonicity. The question of what a canon is and how works get to be canonical tends to involve applying diverse sets of criteria that determine particular works as great or valuable examples within a historical framework or genre. The question of which novels are of literary value, in other words, often presupposes their inclusion as legitimate contestants within the genre. The determination of value, as F.R. Leavis claimed, does not necessarily involve a speculation on the novel's origins: "To be important historically is not . . . to be necessarily one of the significant few." The determination of value, moreover, is also not necessarily a question of genre. What makes a novel a "typical" or "peripheral" example of a genre, according to Northrop Frye (1957), doesn't necessarily involve a question regarding its "merit." As in the more general notion of a literary canon, a critic's particular determinations of value both recommend a set of criteria for judgment of those works and recommend examples of works that adhere to those criteria. Although no single list can itself be called a canon, such lists are best regarded as possible candidates for a set of works that are to be more widely recognized as great. Examples of evaluative criteria and their application range from Henry James' regard for Gustave Flaubert as a "novelist's novelist" in "The Art of Fiction" (1885) to Dale Peck's denunciations, in the *London Review of Books,* of late 20th-century "voyeuristic" realists (such as Terry McMillan) and "silly" postmodernists (such as David Foster Wallace) who do not live up to the "stylistic and formal innovation" of Henry James and James Joyce.

Such evaluations of the novel, literary historians observe, are relatively recent. Although 18th- and early 19th-century writers discussed the merits of individual works, the earliest conception and evaluation of the novel as a distinct art form is often traced to the theoretical writing of Henry James. It would be impossible to summarize the history of novelistic canon formation here, but it may be said that James would be significant in any account of that history for having considered the value of fiction according to the mastery of technique—a notion that influenced generations of later critics. It was James who, as both a practitioner and critic of the genre, established his own position in a tradition of novelists that were great because of the centrality of character and point-of-view. James thus prefaced his *The Portrait of a Lady* (1881) with a ranking of Dickens, Sir Walter Scott, and Robert Louis Stevenson below George Eliot; throughout the prefaces and in essays on European writers, he set Ivan Turgenev and Flaubert (specifically *Madame Bovary*) above others— authors of realist fiction, or what James called "loose baggy monsters"—such as George Sand, Alexandre Dumas, Lev Tolstoi, Honoré de Balzac, and Émile Zola. James' preferences were also strenuously argued by William Dean Howells, and his criteria for evaluation found later defenders in the work of Joseph Arren Beatch, Percy Lubbock, and Mark Schorer. The last of these critics, often said to represent the judgments of the New Criticism, identified the greatness of James, Joseph Conrad, and Joyce with "technique"; they rose above writers, such as H.G. Wells and D.H. Lawrence, who were impatient with or contemptuous of "style" or "technical resources." In a similar way, F.O. Matthiessen's *American Renaissance* (1941) defined the American canon according to the standards of formal integration, praising Nathaniel Hawthorne and Herman Melville. Although Mark Twain was frequently added to American critics' lists of

great American authors, social realists such as Harriet Beecher Stowe or Howells frequently were excluded.

Important as the mastery of technique may have been in defining greatness in novels, precisely what kind of technique contributed to this greatness has been a matter of some debate. Critics such as George Saintsbury, Edmund Gosse, J.A. Symonds, Andrew Lang, Arthur Symons, and W.E. Henley led a counterattack against Howells and James by championing Scott and Stevenson, both masters of romance. Saintsbury, in *The English Novel* (1913), declared Henry Fielding, Jane Austen, Sir Walter Scott, and William Makepeace Thackeray to be the greatest English novelists; elsewhere he championed Harrison Ainsworth and Bulwer-Lytton (*The Historical Novel,* 1895). For Virginia Woolf, great novelists were masters of psychological realism, which justified her preferences for Tolstoi, Dostoevskii, Charlotte Brontë, Thomas Hardy, and Conrad; E.M. Forster took a similar view in order to denounce James and Joyce for the way that perspectivalism deprived their works of "round" characters. For analogous reasons, D.H. Lawrence opposed himself to the self-consciousness of Joyce as well as Marcel Proust in his essay "The Novel." Yet another set of criteria, explicitly opposed to the apparent fetishism of technique, has been employed by Marxist critics such as Granville Hicks (*The Great Tradition,* 1933) and Ralph Fox (*The Novel and the People,* 1937), champions of social realism who faulted certain writers for their lack of attention to the social conditions and particularities of material life of their time.

Perhaps the most influential work in the history of canon formation in the 20th century is F.R. Leavis' *The Great Tradition* (1948). Leavis represents a modified version of formalism that attempts to fuse technical mastery with human concerns: great poets and novelists alike are significant for changing the "possibilities of the art for practitioners" and for promoting a "human awareness . . . of the possibilities of life." Great novelists are not merely concerned with aesthetic principles, Leavis claims; they have an interest in "life," "human potentialities," or "human nature." In *The Great Tradition,* Leavis counts Austen, Eliot, and Conrad among these great novelists; he ultimately broadened his list to include Hawthorne, Dickens, James, Melville, Twain, and Lawrence.

It would be a mistake, however, to see the canon of novels—or the canon of literature generally—as the product of critics alone. It is best understood as the product of numerous cultural forces. The growth and increasing sophistication of print culture, for example, has continually provided the means through which the literary form of the novel is not only published but also defined as an art form. Collections such as the *Bibliothèque Universelles des Romans* in 18th-century France, the publisher R. Bentley's "standard novel" series and James Ballantyne and Sir Walter Scott's *Ballantyne's Novelist's Library* (8 vols., 1821) in 19th-century England, and the *Norton Critical Editions* in 20th-century North America have suggested how editorial selection and publication act as implicit or explicit recommendation for particular works in these published collections. To notice how canons of literature are structured and mobilized by institutions and social processes, however, is often the starting point for contemporary critics to notice the instrumental value of canons and the means through which canons are constructed.

Since the 1970s critical attention has been drawn to the subject of canon formation in order to assess the boundaries of canons, to seek out their social origins and purposes, and to advocate alternatives to the conventional shapes of canons. Virtually every theoretical perspective has been applied to these tasks. Deconstruction, feminism, race theory, queer theory, and other modes of analysis have thus organized the criteria for inclusion and exclusion through which works do or do not become part of the canon. Discovering those criteria leads critics, as Paul Lauter (1991) suggests, to discover the "means by which culture validates social power." Such critics have given more attention to the specific political interests that are at stake in the evaluation of literary greatness or Leavis' "significant few." Even more than this, however, critics have suggested that the apparent distinction between literary history or genre and literary canons is in fact spurious. The study of literary history and literary genre—and the critical works and institutional structures (college courses and examinations, for example) that sponsor this study—are supported by (politically motivated) criteria that canonize particular works of literature. It has been pointed out, for example, that the Puritan legacy in American literature, as opposed to other organizing structures such as urban culture or colonization, underwrites a literary history that nominates particular novels for canonicity and leaves out others—often works by women and writers of color. Or, to cite another example, critics of the 18th-century novel recently have suggested how definitive readings of the novel's history have excluded certain works from the list of paradigmatic examples of the genre. Literature programs in universities, moreover (such as the University of Chicago's "Great Books" program), come under the same scrutiny for the way they canonize certain works in the process of outlining a history of literature or assembling representative works in a genre. In these ways, discussions of history and discussions of genre have dovetailed with discussions of the canon: to discuss a genre and its history is to recommend candidates for a canon, usually with specific political motivations that critics of canon-formation scrutinize.

Although many critics agree that canons are the products of social forces, they do not agree on the response to this predicament. Some critics suggest that canons should be opened to include larger and more diverse sets of works. Occasionally this requires reconfiguring the criteria for inclusion. Toni Morrison calls for a revaluation of the literary canon to acknowledge the long-denied presence of African-American authors; she seeks to reconfigure the canon by including those works that thematize race relations. Jonathan Arac (1992) suggests that the American canon should include works, such as the novels of James Fenimore Cooper, that are cognizant of and engaged in national politics. Other critics of the canon have suggested that new, alternative canons be constructed. In contrast to Morrison, Henry Louis Gates (1992) calls not for a different set of criteria for canonical inclusion but for a new canon of African-American writers. In a similar response from a feminist perspective, Elaine Showalter ("Towards a Feminist Poetics," in *Women's Writing and Writing about Women*, edited by Mary Jacobus, 1979) seeks a canon of women's writing that explores the cause of women's liberation from patriarchal norms. In yet another form of re-

sponse, some critics, among them Robert Von Hallberg (1984), recommend that perhaps the notion of a canon ought to be eliminated altogether.

MARK CANUEL

See also Censorship; Epic and Novel; Genre Criticism; Ideology and the Novel; Politics and the Novel

Further Reading

Arac, Jonathan, "Nationalism, Hypercanonization, and *Huckleberry Finn*," *boundary* 2:19 (1992)

Baker, Houston A., Jr., and Leslie Fiedler, editors, *English Literature: Opening Up the Canon,* Baltimore: Johns Hopkins University Press, 1981

Baldick, Chris, *Criticism and Literary Theory 1890 to the Present,* London and New York: Longman, 1996

Bloom, Harold, *The Western Canon,* New York: Harcourt Brace, and London: Macmillan, 1994

Brown, Homer Obed, *Institutions of the English Novel from Defoe to Scott,* Philadelphia: University of Pennsylvania Press, 1997

Frye, Northrop, *Anatomy of Criticism: Four Essays,* Princeton, New Jersey: Princeton University Press, 1957

Gates, Henry Louis, Jr., *Loose Canons: Notes on the Culture Wars,* New York: Oxford University Press, 1992

Guillory, John, *Cultural Capital: The Problem of Literary Canon Formation,* Chicago: University of Chicago Press, 1993

Hunter, J. Paul, *Before Novels: The Cultural Contexts of Eighteenth-Century English Fiction,* New York: Norton, 1990

Lauter, Paul, *Canons and Contexts,* New York: Oxford University Press, 1991

Leavis, F.R., *The Great Tradition: George Eliot, Henry James, Joseph Conrad,* London: Chatto and Windus, and New York: New York University Press, 1948

Lynch, Deirdre, and William B. Warner, editors, *Cultural Institutions of the Novel,* Durham, North Carolina: Duke University Press, 1996

Pease, Donald, "New Americanists: Revisionist Interventions into the Canon," in *The New Historicism Reader,* edited by H. Aram Veeser, New York: Routledge, 1994

Schorer, Mark, "Technique as Discovery," in *The Novel: Modern Essays in Criticism,* edited by Robert Murray Davis, Englewood Cliffs, New Jersey: Prentice-Hall, 1968

Sinfield, Alan, *Cultural Politics, Queer Reading,* Philadelphia: University of Pennsylvania Press, and London: Routledge, 1994

Von Hallberg, Robert, editor, *Canons,* Chicago and London: University of Chicago Press, 1984

Wonham, Henry B., editor, *Criticism and the Color Line: Desegregating American Literary Studies,* New Brunswick, New Jersey: Rutgers University Press, 1996

Peter Carey 1943–

Australian

To date, there have been surprisingly few sustained critical responses to the astonishing fiction of Australian novelist and short-story writer Peter Carey. The books about him number only four (slim volumes ranging from 50 to about 150 pages), most expressing puzzlement in equal measure with appreciation despite the fact that Carey has published two collections of short stories, a handful of uncollected stories, several autobiographical statements, a children's book, a number of screenplays (on which he collaborated with others), and six novels. In the process, he has won the New South Wales Premier, National Book Council, *Age* Book of the Year, NBC Australian Literature, and Miles Franklin awards, and eventually the prestigious Booker Prize. The relative silence of critics in the face of such achievement is difficult to explain given the fact that Carey's work is immensely readable and, as a result, immensely popular with both academic and nonacademic readers. Although reviews of his work have been mixed and occasionally nasty, they have become steadily more enthusiastic, if still often bewildered, as Carey's career has progressed.

Perhaps the explanation for critical reticence lies in Carey's stylistic slipperiness. He is an adept practitioner of 19th-century realism, late 20th-century postmodernism, and everything in between, including allegory, parable, fabulism, symbolism, psychologized modernism, and even naturalism. Franz Kafka, Jorge Luis Borges, and Gabriel García Márquez are obvious influences, but so are William Faulkner and Charles Dickens. Carey has been seen as simultaneously a realist, postmodernist, and postcolonialist, with Marxist leanings. Thus his work invites a wide range of critical response; as Graham Huggan (1996) states, "Carey's fictions are eclectic, excuse enough for my own [critical] eclecticism."

Unfortunately, Carey's pronouncements on his work are not much help. He told an interviewer in 1991, "There's a way in which my work is pushing towards realism, but at the same time I'm happiest talking about myself as somebody who invents worlds" (*Sydney Morning Herald,* 27 July 1991). If not inventing worlds, he at least displaces them. In the 1989 video *Beautiful Lies,* Carey told producer and director Don Featherstone of his desire to "turn the world around to odd angles, to transform reality to make it clearer, like looking at the world from between your legs. Everything becomes dislocated and the relations of things to each other become more apparent." This description of praxis also seems to apply to his genre sleight of hand as well as to his characters and plots.

Carey's first published fictions, a series of often disturbing short stories, were certainly exercises in looking at the world from odd angles. Often set in an uncertain and unspecified future, the stories mix science fiction with treatments of existential absurdity, and South-American-style magic realism with postcolonial political commentary. Carey's short fiction imagines often nightmarish future worlds whose outlines are implicit in the present. Some of these are recognizably Australian, but most might be anywhere. It was not until he started publishing novels that his urge to invent worlds began to manifest itself as a compulsion to invent Australia.

Carey had written but failed to publish some four novels before his short fiction was released to critical acclaim. Shortly thereafter, he began to write *Bliss.* Published in 1981, the novel is the story of Harry Joy, an advertising executive who undergoes a near-death experience only to discover that he has been dead already, relegated to a hell of his own design. On one level a parodic rewriting of Dante's *Divine Comedy* and on another a meditation on Katherine Mansfield's story "Bliss," the text also announces a continuing theme in Carey's fiction: the role of stories and the storyteller in the mythmaking that passes for life. The particular inflection here, as in his subsequent fiction, is the myth of Australia and the function of stories in constituting that myth.

This theme is explicitly treated in Carey's next two novels, both of which deal with the "beautiful lies," as Mark Twain called them, of which Australia's sense of its history and identity are woven. *Illywhacker* (1985) takes its title from an Australian colloquialism for *con artist* and is narrated by Herbert Badgery, who announces himself at the novel's beginning as an incorrigible liar. As Anthony Hassall (1994) points out, Badgery is probably lying even about that. Badgery tells all kinds of lies—personal, cultural, and historical—that Carey manages to make transparent to his vision of the truth. In proper postmodernist fashion, no transcendental signified—no stable "reality"—is posited; history is seen as story, always told by someone with a point of view and an investment in it. Yet each view is also seen to carry a certain moral cargo, some decidedly more savory than others.

The same process of moral interrogation is applied to Australia's colonial legacy in *Oscar and Lucinda* (1988), the novel many readers believe to be Carey's best to date and the work that won him the Booker Prize. This tale of improbable lovers in impossible predicaments set in 19th-century Australia resembles its predecessor in offering what Graham Huggan calls "allegorisations of national history," but in deploying allegory as a means of displacing and critiquing versions/visions of the colonial past. This is done, as Ruth Brown (1995) has shown, not so much to jettison the past as to sort through it for what is valuable. That value remains is suggested by the loving accumulation of accurate detail about the period that makes this novel so rich and engrossing.

Carey's next novel, *The Tax Inspector* (1991), leaves Australia's multifaceted past for what seems to be an increasingly bleak present. Carey trades the layers of Victorian realism and postmodern play, from which *Oscar and Lucinda* was constructed, for a sort of stripped down surrealism. This dark tale of a dysfunctional family in an equally dysfunctional urban world pushes realism toward the endpoint of hallucination yet also structures the terrible plot so symmetrically as to gesture toward the meaning-laden genre of parable. Again, as always in Carey, the reader is sent searching for a moral center, and although Carey never allows the reader to be comfortably ensconced there, he does seem to authorize, even insist upon, the quest.

Moral centers are even harder to find in the novel that follows *The Tax Inspector. The Unusual Life of Tristan Smith* (1994), although it returns to the allegorical mode to explore Australian-American relations and mutual perceptions and misperceptions, yet resolutely resists allegory's drive toward moral absolutism. The moral uncertainties derive in large measure from the fact that Carey sets out to investigate the paradox of the postcolonial enterprise as undertaken by settler colonies; that is, those colonies—like Australia and America—whose settlers colonized indigenous peoples either prior to or while beginning their own struggles to free themselves politically, culturally, and psychologically from their colonizers. Thematically, the novel both recapitulates old themes and advances into new territory, territory that perhaps opened up for Carey as a result of his 1989 relocation from Australia to New York City, where he began teaching writing at New York University. The move seems to have forced a confrontation with American culture and its neoimperialism, as well as awareness of what Australians have both to admire in and fear from its hegemony. Stylistically, too, the novel looks both backward and forward, employing grotesquerie, surrealism, and fabulism, but in the service of morally conscious (if somewhat murky) allegory.

Carey's most recent novel, *Jack Maggs* (1997), joins his others in examining stories for the way they construct past, present, and future. In this work the story under scrutiny is the one Dickens told in *Great Expectations*, but as always in Carey, with the angle of vision adjusted. The reader looks through the eyes of the illegally returned convict Maggs (Dickens' Magwitch), their vision clouded by his reluctance to remember his painful exile in Australia and by Carey's reluctance to tease out his complicated secrets too soon. The effect of this removal from Maggs' consciousness forces the reader's complicity in reworking the character's definitions of self, home, and identity, a complicity into which Carey readers have always been invited and have often been coerced.

If Patrick White and Christina Stead show the highwater mark of modernism in Australian literature, surely Peter Carey and David Malouf may be nominated as Australia's premiere postmodernists. Carey's work displays many of the hallmarks of postmodernism: the divorce of signifier from signified (which means there is no "natural" relation between the name for something and the thing named); the recognition that fiction represents not reality but discourses about a problematical, bracketed "reality" that is always under construction and negotiation; the parodic deployment of the past and its genres; the metafictional awareness of and reflection upon art as artifice; the game playing into which readers are bullied or seduced; and the interrogation, blurring, or overturning of traditional value systems. In this latter feature, of course, postmodernism may meld with postcolonialism, whose concerns with contesting and undermining colonial understandings of value Carey also emphatically, but never simplistically, shares. Carey's technical repertoire extends beyond postmodernism, however, to include Victorian realism, naturalism, modernism, and the skillful use of allegory, fable, parable, and the fantastic. He is worth reading just for the sake of experiencing someone that juggles so may literary devices simultaneously and successfully.

More important to an explanation of Carey's popularity and a defense of his central role in contemporary fiction is the fact that his technical virtuosity is married to moral vision, not so as to make the novels preachy but to place moral questions always at their hearts. Such questions are close to Carey's heart, as evidenced by his confessional autobiographical statements, in which he rehearses what he sees as moral lapses and speculates

on the transformative power of love to redeem them. Not all his readers or critics would agree, but most do seem to identify moral growth and metamorphosis as possibilities Carey cannot leave alone. He warns as well against the traps that can be set by the siren song of change, and he frequently pushes his characters into them. But Carey nonetheless stands by the proposition that growth and even renewal are possible.

CAROLYN BLISS

Biography
Born in Bacchus Marsh, Victoria, 7 May 1943. Attended Geelong Grammar School; Monash University, Clayton, Victoria, 1961. Worked in advertising in Australia, 1962–68, and after 1970, and in London, 1968–70; partner, McSpedden Carey Advertising Consultants, Chippendale, New South Wales, until 1988. Began writing full-time in 1988.

Novels by Carey
Bliss, 1981
Illywhacker, 1985
Oscar and Lucinda, 1988
The Tax Inspector, 1991
The Unusual Life of Tristan Smith, 1994
Jack Maggs, 1997

Other Writings: short story collections, screenplays, autobiography ("A Letter to Our Son," *Granta* 24 [1988]; "From an Alien to His Second Son," *HQ Magazine* [Autumn 1993]; "A Small Memorial," *The New Yorker* [25 September 1995]), and a children's book (*The Big Bazoohley*, 1995).

Further Reading
Bliss, Carolyn, "The Revisionary Lover; Misprision of the Past in Peter Carey," *Australian and New Zealand Studies in Canada* 6 (Fall 1991)
Brown, Ruth, "English Heritage and Australian Culture: The Church and Literature of England in *Oscar and Lucinda*," *Australian Literary Studies* 17:2 (October 1995)
Daniel, Helen, *Liars: Australian New Novelists*, Ringwood, Victoria, and New York: Penguin, 1988
Dovey, Teresa, "An Infinite Onion: Narrative Structure in Peter Carey's Fiction," *Australian Literary Studies* 11 (1983)
Hassall, Anthony, *Dancing on Hot Macadam: Peter Carey's Fiction*, St. Lucia and Portland, Oregon: University of Queensland Press, 1994
Huggan, Graham, *Peter Carey*, Melbourne and New York: Oxford University Press, 1996
Kane, Paul, "Postcolonial/Postmodern: Australian Literature and Peter Carey," *World Literature Today* 67:3 (Summer 1993)
Krassnitzer, Hermine, *Aspects of Narration in Peter Carey's Novels: Deconstructing Colonialism*, Lewiston: Edwin Mellen Press, 1995
Lamb, Karen, *Peter Carey: The Genesis of Fame*, Sydney: Collins/Angus and Robertson, 1992
Tausky, Thomas, "'Getting the Corner Right': An Interview with Peter Carey," *Australian and New Zealand Studies in Canada* 4 (1990)
Willbanks, Ray, *Australian Voices: Writers and Their Work*, Austin: University of Texas Press, 1991

Caribbean Novel

Anglophone

The anglophone Caribbean novel is generally considered to have come of age in the 1950s, when writers such as George Lamming, Sam Selvon, V.S. Naipaul, and Andrew Salkey, all of whom had migrated to London, published their work in the metropolis to considerable critical acclaim. They had been preceded by V.S. Reid, whose *New Day*, a novel often seen as the seminal work in ushering in the renaissance of the 1950s, had also been published outside the Caribbean region, in New York, in 1949. However, before the 1950s there had been important instances of fiction writing, largely but not entirely directed toward expressing local concerns for a local audience. In fact, the first significant Caribbean novels actually date from the beginning of the 20th century.

In 1903 the Jamaican nationalist Tom Redcam (Thomas Mac-Dermot) published his *Becka's Buckra Baby* as the inaugural volume of the "All Jamaica Library," a project designed to provide "a literary embodiment of Jamaican subjects" for a local readership at an affordable price. The library was no great success: as Kenneth Ramchand (1970) points out, "Only five volumes seem to have been issued, and there were only two supporting authors." Nevertheless, Redcam's "Library" signaled an attempt to shift the emphasis of Caribbean creative writing away from the concerns of the white plantocracy, which had dominated publishing in the region prior to the 20th century.

Redcam is also considered a forerunner of H.G. de Lisser, whose fiction commanded a considerable following in Jamaica during the first third of the 20th century. De Lisser's novels fulfilled Redcam's ideal of providing fiction for a local readership. Most were originally published in Jamaica, with some subsequently achieving wider circulation through publication in the United Kingdom. Whether they genuinely offered "a literary embodiment of Jamaican subjects" is questionable. His best-known novel, *The White Witch of Rosehall* (1929), is a sensational tale of obeah and intrigue based on the life of a 19th-century plantation owner. It is notable for employing an expatriate perspective to frame its account of a struggle between black and white obeah practitioners: events are seen through the eyes of a newly arrived Englishman who has come to Jamaica to learn the arts of planting and estate management. Other de Lisser novels, such as *Revenge* (1919) and *Morgan's Daughter* (1953), offer a similarly exotic view of the Caribbean past, but de Lisser also wrote about contemporary subjects in a vein of social comedy in such novels as *Jane: A Story of Jamaica* (1913; reprinted in Britain as *Jane's Career*, 1914), *Triumphant Squalitone* (1916), and *Under the Sun* (1937). *Jane: A Story of Jamaica* has been seen as a notable first among anglophone Caribbean novels because it takes a black proletarian character as its central protagonist. Jane herself, a 15-year-old who goes to Kingston to work in the home of a mixed-race, lower-middle-class mistress, has been seen as a forerunner of independent black female heroines in Caribbean fiction. However, de Lisser's social perspective is informed by his own social distance from the real-life Janes of Jamaican society, and he frequently treats his heroine with condescending irony. Her ultimate "career" goal is a middle-class marriage, which she attains by much the same means as those employed by the eponymous heroine of Samuel Richardson's *Pamela* (1740). Jane's story is finally, like Pamela's, one of bourgeois success, achieved through having "walked strictly in the paths of righteousness" by using her chastity as her most precious asset.

Other Caribbean novels in English from the first part the 20th century engage in an attempt to bridge the gap between the middle-class worlds of the author and his readership and the hitherto extra-literary world of the Caribbean populace. A.R.F. Webber's *Those That Be in Bondage* (1917), a historical romance set in Guyana, Tobago, and Trinidad around the turn of the century, focuses on psychological and physical bondage, drawing parallels between the inner malaise of the society's ruling elite and the living conditions of the indentured Indo-Caribbean plantation workers with whom their lives are entwined. The prolific Guyanese novelist Edgar Mittelholzer followed this formula in a number of his novels, beginning with *Corentyne Thunder* (1941), a tale that intersperses an account of the social conditions under which the Hindu peasantry were living on Guyana's Corentyne coast with the psychological dilemmas of a fair-skinned middle-class protagonist. Like Webber's *Those That Be in Bondage,* and most of Mittelholzer's own subsequent fiction (of which the lurid "Kaywana" trilogy [1952–58], a plantation epic spanning more than three centuries of Guyanese history, is generally considered the outstanding example), *Corentyne Thunder* alternates between romanticism and realism. Mittelholzer saw himself as a serious, philosophical novelist, but his work moves uneasily between attempts to probe the specifics of particular psychological and social predicaments and, especially prior to being influenced by the demands of the English pulp fiction market of the 1950s and 1960s, the increasing use of Gothic and lurid melodrama. He commited suicide in 1965, an event prefigured by numerous references to suicide in his fiction. Various explanations can, of course, be advanced to explain his suicide, but one aspect of his tragedy seems to typify that of Caribbean writers of his generation: brought up in a colonial environment that isolated them from the grassroots realities of the societies about which they wrote, and caught between the conflicting imperatives of metropolitan publishing and local cultural registers and needs, writers as different from one another as de Lisser, Webber, and Mittelholzer all seem to become trapped between discourses, victims of a hybrid social situation that, unlike later postcolonial writers such as Wilson Harris, Salman Rushdie, and Derek Walcott, they were unable to draw on as a source of strength.

Arguably the most successful—and it is only partially so—attempt to resolve these tensions is found in the work of a small group of writers who came to the fore in Trinidad in the late 1920s and published novels in the 1930s. Known as the "Beacon Group," from the title of a little magazine to which they all contributed, this group numbered among its members C.L.R. James, who was to become internationally known as a black radical, literary critic, cricket journalist, and Marxist commentator; Portuguese-Trinidadian writers Alfred Mendes and Albert Gomes (editor of *The Beacon*); and French Creole novelist Ralph de Boissiere. Once again, their fiction broached the subject of the relationship between the middle-class world to which the writers and their reading public belonged and the grassroots West Indian world. De Boissiere, who emigrated to Australia, provided a wide-ranging canvass in two later novels dealing with social unrest and change in Trinidad in the late 1930s and early 1940s, *Crown Jewel* (1952) and *Rum and Coca-Cola* (1956). Mendes went to live in a Trinidadian yard and drew on this experience for his novel *Black Fauns* (1935). And in Mendes' *Pitch Lake* (1934) and James' *Minty Alley* (1936), the finest novel produced by a member of the group, the writers' attempts to come to grips with local realities are acted out as middle-class protagonists come into contact with the ordinary Trinidadian world of which they have hitherto been largely ignorant. Thus in *Minty Alley* the 20-year-old, middle-class Mr. Haynes has his world turned upside down when his mother dies and he finds himself financially unable to go to England to study medicine. In order to make ends meet he gives up the family house and moves into a room at No. 2 Minty Alley, where he is initiated into the way "ordinary people" live, quickly learning that there are more things in Trinidadian society than he has dreamed of in his philosophy. Haynes is not only initiated into a different social world, he also discovers a world of human passions that he has not known existed. Throughout the novel James skillfully uses Haynes' limited (sometimes almost voyeuristic) point of view as a correlative for what the novel is doing, opening up a window on ordinary Caribbean urban life.

At the same time as the Beacon Group was attempting to forge the link between literature and lived experience in Trinidad, expatriate Jamaican writer Claude Mackay, who had migrated to the United States where he came to play a significant part in the Harlem Renaissance of the 1930s, was engaging in a similar endeavor in his novel *Banana Bottom* (1933). The novel deals with the return of a black Jamaican woman who has been sent abroad for her education by a missionary couple who have raised her as an experiment. Like his Trinidadian contemporaries, Mackay's main concern is the initiation of the middle-class Caribbean character into the ways of the ordinary West Indian world. The main difference is that he places more emphasis on race and, in particular, on the way negative middle-class socialization threatens the emotional development of the protagonist. Gradually, his heroine Bita Plant rejects the European side of her upbringing and chooses the Caribbean natural world and the emotional values of black Jamaicans. In this respect *Banana Bottom* anticipates major later novels such as George Lamming's *Season of Adventure* (1960) and Erna Brodber's *Jane and Louisa Will Soon Come Home* (1980), which depict a similar process of female awakening. Before he left Jamaica in 1912, Mackay had pioneered the use of dialect in Caribbean poetry. But his fiction, most of which is set in American locations, is less innovative; the most noteworthy influence on *Banana Bottom,* which becomes a manifesto for the unrepressed emotional life, is D.H. Lawrence.

Caribbean fiction from the first half of the 20th century tends to alternate between historical romance and novels that attempt to engage with the local world, which attempt realist modes. In neither case is there any significant attempt to evolve a form that departs significantly from European novelistic practice, and Creole language forms are used only occasionally in dialogue. V.S. Reid's *New Day* is generally seen as the first anglophone Caribbean novel that attempts to find a form organic to the grassroots Jamaican experience. Written in a modified form of Jamaican Creole, it is the story of an 87-year-old man who relives the events of his life through memory, dwelling particularly on a period during his boyhood when he was involved in the Morant Bay rebellion, a key episode in 19th-century Jamaican history. The language of *New Day* has been criticized as inauthentic, but it remains a major landmark in Caribbean fiction as the first novel to attempt to find a voice appropriate for the expression of a people's concerns and, in particular, to write history from the other side of the colonial divide—to refashion the past from oral testimony rather than from the historical records of colonial society. As Louis James (1968) puts it, history in *New Day* is "not simply a matter of General Eyre's [the colonial governor's] soldiers, but of herbs, of scents, the mountain slopes, a total human experience rooted in the cycle of nature." Reid's novel is notable not simply as revisionist history and for its use of a Creole language register as the narrative medium of the novel, but also for its commitment to realizing the minutiae of Jamaican rural life on the printed page and for its employment of a boy's angle of vision to do so. The elderly narrator effectively becomes the eight-year-old boy he was nearly eight decades before, as he relives the events of the Morant Bay rebellion in memory. And the Jamaican world in which these memories are set comes alive with a freshness of vision appropriate to the act of literary discovery in which Reid is engaging as he creates a Jamaica unparalleled in earlier writing about the island.

Reid's literary nationalism is sometimes related to his association with the sculptress Edna Manley, the leading figure in an artistic circle known as the Focus Group. Manley's husband, Norman, subsequently became prime minister of Jamaica, and *New Day* offers a thinly disguised fictional portrait of him in the character of Garth, who provides a resolution of the island's political dilemmas by synthesizing the values of capital and labor in the latter stages of the novel. Like De Boissiere's *Crown Jewel* as well as Jamaican Alice Durie's *One Jamaica Gal* (1940), in which the heroine (a cognate figure to de Lisser's Jane, but a character who is treated in an altogether less sentimentalized manner) is killed by a ricocheting bullet in the Kingston riot of 1938, Reid treats the social and political unrest that swept through the Caribbean in the late 1930s, but he does so from a gradualist position that has disappointed some Caribbean critics, who have consequently tended to underestimate Reid's importance as a literary innovator.

The novels of writers who migrated to Britain in the post–World War II period, and who helped to establish the international reputation of Caribbean fiction in the 1950s and 1960s, deal with a number of recurrent themes, and despite their diversity they share a concern with exploring issues of personal, national, and regional self-definition. Although sometimes seen as formally traditional, they exhibit a range of narrative techniques, frequently employing a polyphonic form.

Novels such as Lamming's *The Emigrants* (1954), Sam Selvon's *The Lonely Londoners* (1956), Andrew Salkey's *Escape to an Autumn Pavement* (1959), and V.S. Naipaul's *The Mimic Men* (1967) take the encounter with the metropolis as their central subject, and this encounter frequently—Naipaul's fiction is a significant exception—proves to be an experience that is at once alienating *and* unifying, as Caribbean men from different countries feel a sense of exile in Britain but begin to bond together as West Indians. Consciously or unconsciously they come to realize the extent to which racism in their own countries is shaping the way they are perceived in Britain and, consequently, is limiting the opportunities available to them in their new environment. The beginning of *The Lonely Londoners* illustrates this duality and thus establishes the mood for the whole of Selvon's episodic novel: the protagonist Moses Aloetta sets out to meet a fellow Trinidadian arriving from a boat-train on a London evening, "with a fog sleeping restlessly over the city and the lights showing in the blur as if not London at all but some strange place on another planet." Moses is a reluctant host to the new arrival and resents the extent to which he seems more generally to be acting as an unofficial welfare officer for other West Indians. Yet he fulfills this role and becomes the focal point for a male community, which provides mutual support systems amid the loneliness engendered by living in a "strange place." Meanwhile the style of the novel reflects a similar duality, as it moves between rich humor rooted in Caribbean oral storytelling and a somber and philosophic tone, which surfaces in the text's more reflective passages.

Other Caribbean novels of the period, such as Reid's *The Leopard* (1958) and O.R. Dathorne's *The Scholar-Man* (1964), look back to Africa as a matrix for self-definition. The finest novel to treat this subject, Denis Williams' *Other Leopards* (1963), focuses on a Guyanese archaeological draughtsman working in the Sudanic belt of Africa who finds himself caught between a range of competing ancestral claims: Arab and sub-Saharan Africa, Islam and Christianity, rationalism and sensuality, European and Afro-Caribbean models of womanhood, and also European and African strains in his own inheritance. The novel, which stands alongside Edward Kamau Brathwaite's poetic trilogy *The Arrivants* (1967–69) as one of the most probing explorations of the Caribbean relationship to Africa to have appeared to date, anticipates the work of many subsequent postcolonial writers and cultural theorists in preferring a Foucauldian archaeological model of investigation to a historiographical approach, and ends, appropriately, with its protagonist up a tree, seemingly as far away from resolving his complex dilemmas as he was at the outset.

Like *New Day*, a number of novels of the 1950s and 1960s provided vivid accounts of Caribbean boyhood, and in so doing found an ideal vehicle for bringing hitherto unchronicled Caribbean milieux and experiences to fiction. While Lamming's *In the Castle of My Skin* (1953) is the finest of these novels, Trinidadian Michael Anthony is the writer who returned most frequently to the subjects of boyhood, adolescence, and initiation. His novels *The Games Were Coming* (1963), *The Year in San Fernando* (1965), and *Green Days by the River* (1967) all use a boy-protagonist in a deceptively simple manner. The finest of this triptych, *The Year in San Fernando*, is particularly noteworthy for the subtlety with which it uses the boy's ingenuous angle of vision to throw light on adult mores, while also describing his rite of passage into adolescence and the natural and seasonal rhythms of the society in a sensitive and generally understated way. Like Lamming, Geoffrey Drayton in *Christopher* (1959) and Austin Clarke, who would later migrate to Canada and write a number of penetrating accounts of immigrant experience in Toronto, in *Among Thistles and Thorns* (1965) produced accounts of Barbadian boyhood. In Drayton's case, the eponymous hero is a white boy who seems isolated from the world around him, partly as a result of his particular family circumstances, but also, one feels, as a consequence of his ethnic

makeup. The Trinidadian Ian McDonald explored similar territory in *The Humming-Bird Tree* (1969), in which the adolescent love between a white boy and an Indian girl runs counter to society's expectations.

Other novelists were more successful than their prewar precursors in bringing the Caribbean folk experience, rural and urban, onto the printed page. Selvon wrote about the lives of Trinidad's East Indian peasantry in such novels as *A Brighter Sun* (1952) and its sequel *Turn Again Tiger* (1958). Naipaul provided an exhaustive tragicomic account of Indian life in rural Trinidad and Port of Spain in *A House for Mr. Biswas* (1961). Salkey's first novel, *A Quality of Violence* (1959), focused on Pocomania cult practices in rural Jamaica at the turn of the century. Roger Mais, who was associated with Reid in the Focus Group, wrote about both country peasantry and impoverished city dwellers in his novels *The Hills Were Joyful Together* (1953), *Brother Man* (1954), and *Black Lightning* (1955). *Brother Man* was particularly significant as the first novel to deal with the Rastafarian community of West Kingston: its hero is a Christlike leader figure whose social attitudes are as far from those of the middle-class norms of late colonial society as Mais' fragmentary and jazz-based narrative structure is from European naturalism. At the opposite end of the social spectrum, Mais' friend John Hearne produced a group of novels, "the Cayuna Quartet" (*Stranger at the Gate*, 1956; *The Faces of Love*, 1957; *The Autumn Equinox*, 1959; and *Land of the Living*, 1961), that focuses on the problems encountered by middle-class West Indians relating to the Caribbean mainstream. However, Hearne's best novel, *The Sure Salvation* (1981), did not appear until two decades later. Like Lamming's *Natives of My Person* (1972), it is a historical novel, dealing with a slave ship's illicit Atlantic crossing, which can be read allegorically as a comment on tensions persisting in the Caribbean present.

In trying to bring a range of Caribbean and Caribbean-diaspora experiences into literature, the novelists *might* have been expected to employ primarily realistic or naturalistic modes: one *might*, for example, expect a writer like Mais to turn to a form of gritty naturalism to document the squalid aspects of the poverty that provides a backdrop to the action of *Brother Man*; one *might* expect a writer like Naipaul to use social realism as the mode for his 500-plus-page biography of Mr. Biswas. Naipaul's technique *is* closer to the European novel than that of most of his contemporaries, and some commentators have tended to make the mistake of seeing a novel such as *A House for Mr. Biswas* as cloning Dickensian characteristics. Yet even here there is a marked difference from the Dickens-Wells tradition of the novel that provides Naipaul with a departure point, since the narrative framework and structure never suggest that a fundamentally benevolent Providence underlies events, as is generally the case in the fiction of his English precursors.

The need to depart from or rework European models is more pronounced among other Caribbean novelists of the period, and attempts at evolving new forms and techniques are to be found everywhere, although the degree of innovation varies. In Lamming's novels the action moves between different groups of characters, and the form often complements this by employing a polyphonic approach. Thus in *In the Castle of My Skin*, the narrative voice shifts between first person, third person, a range of dramatic dialogues that draw on oral storytelling traditions, and a diary. Selvon follows Reid in using a modified form of

Caribbean Creole as the main narrative medium of his London novels and draws heavily on oral storytelling to produce a form of episodic narration that has affinities with calypso, the most significant popular narrative genre in Trinidad. The Dominican-born Jean Rhys' *Wide Sargasso Sea* (1966), a counter-discursive response to Charlotte Brontë's *Jane Eyre* that tells the story of "the madwoman in the attic," Rochester's first wife, Bertha, now renamed Antoinette, is similarly polyphonic in approach. Instead of simply reversing the negative representation of Bertha—and by extension the Caribbean—which one finds in *Jane Eyre,* Rhys essays a relativistic approach, using Rochester as well as Antoinette as a narrator for major sections of the novel, and also briefly employing minor characters' perspectives as a further challenge to the univocal nature of the 19th-century English novel. The effect is to unsettle the sense of stability that underlies Charlotte Brontë's novel. Rhys' world seems altogether more provisional, dialogic, unsettled; and she evolves a fictional technique that brilliantly expresses these qualities.

In fact everywhere one turns in post–World War II Caribbean fiction, one finds forms that, overtly or implicitly, challenge the notion of cultural identity as something settled. Where polyphony is not to the fore, there is a challenge to generic conventions, and one finds this even in the work of those novelists who at first sight seem to work closest to European models. Thus Mittelholzer, in his novel *A Morning at the Office* (1950), sets out to produce an "objective" naturalistic account of a single morning in a Trinidadian office, but allows disturbing Gothic elements to infiltrate his text; and in later works by Naipaul there is an increasing reliance on mixed-mode narratives that conflate what would normally be separated out as "fact" and "fiction": a spare, ironic novella, comic short stories, and travel journal fragments in *In a Free State* (1971); fiction and autobiography in *The Enigma of Arrival* (1987); and fiction, historiography, and autobiography in *A Way in the World* (1994).

The anglophone Caribbean novelist whose technique frequently offers the most radical challenge to European practice is the Guyanese writer Wilson Harris, all of whose work beginning with his first novel, *Palace of the Peacock* (1960), has been concerned with the breakdown of perceived oppositions in human behavior and society and the resolution of conflicts in an ideal of psychic wholeness, which draws its inspiration from sources as diverse as medieval alchemical theory and Amerindian myth. Harris' work dispenses with many of the staple conventions of the novel form, such as linear progression and consistent characterization, and blurs distinctions between life and death and dream and reality as part of an attempt to force his readers to perceive experiences in new, visionary ways. His work has sometimes been compared to that of the Latin American magic realists, but is finally uniquely his own.

Until the 1980s Caribbean fiction was largely dominated by male writers, but in the last two decades there has been an upsurge of important work by women novelists and short-story writers. Prior to this only a handful of novels by women writers had been published. These include, in addition to Rhys' *Wide Sargasso Sea, The Orchid House* (1953) by Rhys' fellow white Dominican Phyllis Shand Allfrey, Jamaican Sylvia Wynter's *The Hills of Hebron* (1962), and Trinidadian Merle Hodge's *Crick Crack, Monkey* (1970). Since 1980, the earlier dearth has been remedied with the appearance of outstanding short-story collections from Jamaican Olive Senior (*Summer Lightning,* 1986; and

Arrival of the Snake-Woman, 1989) and the publication of major novels by Senior's fellow Jamaican Erna Brodber, Grenadian Merle Collins, and the American-based Antiguan Jamaica Kincaid.

Brodber's *Jane and Louisa Will Soon Come Home* (1980) is a complex, poetic exploration of the negative effects that colonial brainwashing has had on Jamaican women's psyches. Although supposedly intended as a case study of an aberrant mentality, Brodber's protagonist, Nellie, is in one sense *any* Jamaican woman. A woman who gradually learns to oppose the negative view of black sexuality inculcated in her by turning to local folk traditions as an alternative source of cultural sustenance, Nellie grapples with the cultural schizophrenia that has plagued a region taught to repress its primarily African origins in favor of its imposed colonial legacy. Formally Brodber's fiction vies with Harris' in complexity, and *Jane and Louisa Will Soon Come Home* employs a fragmentary but cyclic form as a correlative of its subject matter, which is concerned with replacing the broken heritage foisted upon the Caribbean by Europe with a more integrated, folk-based culture, symbolized by the name of the children's ring game that gives the novel its title. Brodber has also published the novels *Myal* (1988), which uses the Afro-Caribbean religious cult of myalism as a central metaphor for the reclamation of submerged African-based identities, while also proposing the model of a transracial Jamaican community, and *Louisiana* (1994), where the focus shifts to an African American anthropologist with Caribbean family connections who is researching folk life in Louisiana, where hoodoo and conjure are celebrated alongside myal and obeah.

Merle Collins' *Angel* (1987) is one of a group of 1980s novels that trace the gradual growth to maturity of a young female protagonist against a background of social change within her society. In some ways these works complement the novels of boyhood that appeared in the 1950s and 1960s, when there was no equivalent outcrop of novels about girlhood, and they represent a similar coming of age for Caribbean women's fiction. Other novels of girlhood published in the 1980s include two works by British-based Guyanese writers, both set in the country's turbulent late-colonial period: Janice Shinebourne's *Timepiece* (1986) and Grace Nichols' *Whole of a Morning Sky* (1986). Zee Edgell's *Beka Lamb* (1982), the first Belizean novel to be published internationally, is a similar study of girlhood in late colonial Belize; it has been followed by Edgell's *In Times Like These* (1991), in which the protagonist strives to reconcile personal and professional aspects of her life at a moment when her country, with independence approaching, is engaged in a similar struggle to find a new identity. Jamaica Kincaid's *Annie John* (1983) takes as its subject a girl's socialization in Antigua, placing particular importance on a complex mother-daughter relationship; Kincaid's *Lucy* (1990), which follows the fortunes of a Caribbean au pair coming to terms with her identity—and in particular her sexuality—in North America, also places particular stress on an ambivalent mother-daughter relationship.

Writers such as Kincaid, Collins, Shinebourne, and Nichols who live in Britain or the United States have repeatedly returned to their Caribbean origins and so may reasonably be classified as primarily Caribbean writers. Other Caribbean-born writers who have lived most of their lives in Britain are more difficult to categorize in this way. The Guyanese-born writers David Dabydeen, whose *Disappearance* (1993) is a contemporary Condition-of-

England novel and whose *The Counting House* (1996) is a historical novel about East Indian indentureship, and Fred D'Aguiar, whose powerful first novel *The Longest Memory* (1994) is set on a 19th-century Virginian plantation, fall into this group. Others belonging to the group include Jamaican-born Joan Riley, whose novels, which include *The Unbelonging* (1985) and *Waiting in the Twilight* (1987), are mainly concerned with the problems faced by Caribbean women who have migrated to Britain, and American-based Michael Thelwell, best known for his novel *The Harder They Come* (1980), which was inspired by the popular 1972 reggae film of the same name. The finest writer in this group is Caryl Phillips, whose first novel, *The Final Passage* (1985), moves from the Caribbean to Britain, but whose subsequent novels, such as *Higher Ground* (1989) and *Crossing the River* (1991), offer a larger panorama of the experience of the black diaspora. Despite its very different ideological orientation, *Crossing the River* has affinities with Naipaul's recent work in its employment of a number of narratives (in this case four stories framed by a short prologue and epilogue) that complement one another as accounts of the African diaspora. Phillips' novel *Cambridge* (1991) is set on a Caribbean plantation in the last days of the slave era and, like *The Longest Memory,* offers a powerful indictment of the brutalities of a system that had received comparatively little attention in Caribbean fiction until the 1990s.

Within the Caribbean the most significant anglophone novelist—with the possible exception of Erna Brodber—to have emerged since the early 1960s is Trinidadian Earl Lovelace, whose novels *The Dragon Can't Dance* (1979), *The Wine of Astonishment* (1982), and *Salt* (1996) are searching explorations of aspects of Trinidadian popular culture and the force it exerts on individual psychologies. *The Dragon Can't Dance* investigates whether the island's annual Carnival contains genuine revolutionary potential or is only a vehicle for hedonistic escapism. *The Wine of Astonishment,* which is centered on two forms of folk expression in the colonial period, the Spiritual Baptist Church and stickfighting, is narrated by a countrywoman and is one of the finest Caribbean novels yet to have been written in Creole. *Salt* returns to the same terrain as the two earlier novels

but with a broader sense of historical context, which locates the struggle contemporary Trinidadians undergo in their attempt to achieve "personhood" to the country's traumatic slavery-dominated past. Like Erna Brodber, Olive Senior, and Caryl Phillips, Lovelace moves away from the individualism that characterized the writing of some of the "Independence" generation of Caribbean novelists to produce fiction that succeeds, both formally and thematically, in articulating the concerns of a community.

JOHN THIEME

See also Wilson Harris; George Lamming; V.S. Naipaul; Postcolonial Narrative and Criticism of the Novel

Further Reading

Baugh, Edward, editor, *Critics on Caribbean Literature,* London and Boston: Allen and Unwin, 1978

Cudjoe, Selwyn Reginald, *Resistance and Caribbean Literature,* Athens: Ohio University Press, 1980

Dance, Daryl Cumber, editor, *Fifty Caribbean Writers: A Bio-Bibliographical Critical Sourcebook,* New York: Greenwood Press, 1986

Davies, Carole Boyce, and Elaine Savory, editors, *Out of the Kumbla: Caribbean Women and Literature,* Trenton, New Jersey: Africa World Press, 1990

Gilkes, Michael, *Wilson Harris and the Caribbean Novel,* Trinidad: Longman Caribbean, 1975

Gilkes, Michael, *The West Indian Novel,* Boston: Twayne, 1981

James, Louis, editor, *The Islands in Between: Essays on West Indian Literature,* London: Oxford University Press, 1968

King, Bruce, editor, *West Indian Literature,* London: Macmillan, and Hamden, Connecticut: Archon, 1979; 2nd edition, London: Macmillan, 1995

Ramchand, Kenneth, *The West Indian Novel and Its Background,* London: Faber, and New York: Barnes and Noble, 1970; 2nd edition, London: Heinemann, 1983

Ramchand, Kenneth, *An Introduction to the Study of West Indian Literature,* Sunbury-on-Thames, Middlesex: Nelson Caribbean, 1976

Caribbean Novel

Francophone

Caribbean literature, that is, literature written in the Caribbean that acknowledges the topology of the region, has existed since the period of the conquest and slavery. Many early works were characterized by a psychological distance from the local landscape and culture and by a patronizing view of the colonies. Caribbean people tended to be judged in relation to their distance—geographical and cultural—from France. These works—primarily travelogues, diaries, essays, and poetry—give life and substance to the social relationships of the region and to the per-

sonal hopes and fears of the plantocracy, and they complement the historical studies of the 17th and 18th centuries. But more often than not, early Caribbean writers to varying degrees excluded the region from their work. For instance, Nicolas-Germain Léonard, a Frenchman born in 1744 in Guadeloupe, wrote poetry, essays, and sentimental novels that hardly recognize the island of his birth. This denial long remained an important aspect of the Caribbean literary experience.

In Haiti, black and white writers produced poetry, plays, and essays that are primarily Eurocentric in all aspects of their discourse. Even the great 19th-century Haitian writer Démesvar Delorme wrote novels in which the action was situated in Europe, such as *Francesca: Les jeux du sort* (1872; Francesca: The Games of Fate) and *Le damné* (1877; The Damned). The first novelistic dramatization of Caribbean history, Éméric Bergeaud's posthumously published allegory *Stella* (1859) provided the impetus for the development of a major genre that remains a significant social factor to this day. Recreating history in much the same way that oral culture might, the genre does not aim at verisimilitude or objective reality but emphasizes the hidden psychic realities of narrative as a powerful force of change. Bergeaud's ideological, social, and racial understanding of history may well be questioned, but his elitist anthropological discourse marked the Haitian novel for several generations.

Haiti was the first Caribbean nation to free itself of the double yoke of slavery and colonialism. The upheavals of its revolution led to a fundamental reordering of society and a desire to produce institutions that recalled those of the former colonial masters. The majority of the population remained illiterate in French and the Haitian language. Literature was primarily oral and expressed in the language of the people. Those who wrote and read novels were of the relatively wealthy and well-educated classes who had been nurtured on the appreciation of Greek, Latin, and French authors. Little has changed. Haitian novelists are, with a few outstanding exceptions, university graduates, and their readership in the Caribbean and abroad consists of highly sophisticated intellectuals. Foreign models of writing and mythology may be clearly seen in the work of several 19th-century writers who turned their backs on their African cultural heritage. Writing in French was, and remains to this day, associated with political and economic power and with a hierarchy of discourse that positions oral expression in an inferior social and psychological space. Tensions between oral and written forms of literature very gradually led to a versatility of form, a richness of style, and a density of mythological expression that results in a profound philosophical reconsideration of long accepted literary concepts. Similarly, the tensions inherent in diglossia (French and Creole) were eventually transformed into sophisticated literary devices.

The first major rupture with the conventional Eurocentric novel is perhaps Justin Lhérisson's *La famille des Pitite-Caille* (1905; The Pitite Caille Family) and *Zoune chez sa ninnaine* (1906; Zoune with Her Godmother). Lhérisson's use of irony, his frequent manipulation of different language registers, and the significance of onomastics in his work announce the major literary contributions of Caribbean novelists of the 20th century such as the Cuban Alejo Carpentier and the Jamaican Alvin Bennett. The theme of *Zoune chez sa ninnaine* is the exploitation of the labor of an adolescent from a destitute family. She is physically abused, and her godmother's male friend attempts to rape her. The delicate sexual politics of the novel is interwoven with its ideological message and the implicit criticism of the abuse of power. The would-be rapist is a military man whose name, Cadet Jacques, has entered the Haitian language as a verb synonymous with rape. The text employs some of the techniques of orality to convey its very clear messages. There is no religious moralizing, but a profound examination of ethical considerations that are revealed through stark contrasts: powerlessness is opposed to the power of the state and the church; abject poverty to commercial prosperity; moral integrity to arbitrary abuse.

It would be another 60 years or more before a frank exposition of sexuality appeared in the Haitian novel. René Depestre's *Alléluia pour une femme-jardin* (1981; Hallelujah for a Woman-Garden) was the first of several erotic novels by the same author that seem to have released the inhibitions of other francophone Caribbean writers. However, it is in *Saison des abattis* (1996; The Killing Season) by the Guyanese Lyne-Marie Stanley, a full 90 years after Lhérisson's novel, that there is unambiguous and intelligent treatment of a sexual relationship between an adult male and a female minor. Stanley renders the sexuality of the couple without sensationalism or moralizing and in a fully developed social and cultural context. The novel is set in Cayenne and, although French colonialism forms an essential backdrop, the central focus on the couple and the sociopsychological configuration of gender is never lost in the interests of the geopolitical realities.

Published between 1933 and 1945, J.B. Cinéas' novels deepen the implicit political criticism of *Zoune chez sa ninnaine*, demonstrating the profound ideological influence of Jean Price-Mars' essay *Ainsi parla l'Oncle* (1928; Thus Spoke Uncle). This spirited intellectual response to the United States occupation of Haiti served to commit an entire generation of young intellectuals to the culture, language, and religion of the people. Price-Mars' ethnographical text is correctly associated with the literary movement of *indigénisme* (indigenism), which advocated the value and authenticity of a national peasant culture that included the overwhelming majority of the population. Since novelists were primarily urban-based intellectuals, they had to make a transition in class and in culture to come to terms with the expression of the people.

Price-Mars' insistence on local language and religion led to a significant process of literary transformation resulting in the general abandonment of French models, particularly the classical French style Caribbean authors had cultivated so assiduously. This new aesthetic resulted in such significant novels as Jacques Roumain's internationally acclaimed *Gouverneurs de la Rosée* (1940; *Masters of the Dew*) and René Depestre's *Le mât de cocagne* (1979; *The Festival of the Greasy Pole*). Both convey a profound respect for the Haitian people and their history, a scepticism, even scorn, of government, and a more than passing acknowledgement of the social and psychological force of *vaudou* (voodoo). The spiritual ethos of *vaudou* provides the semiotic basis of the aesthetic of both novels. In this respect, they may be compared to Wole Soyinka's use of Yoruba religion in *The Interpreters* (1965). The novels of Roumain, Depestre, and Jacques Stephen Alexis, like many other literary works of the region, were generally untouched by the *négritude* movement, despite the attempts of certain critics to reduce all francophone Caribbean writing to this common denominator. The ideological implications of the fight against black fascism in the case of the Haitians and against colonialist hegemonic thought in Guadeloupe, Guyane, and Martinique were far more important.

Much of Depestre's work was written and published in political exile outside of Haiti, which significantly has been the fate of an entire generation of novelists from the 1950s to the 1980s. Of those who remained in Haiti, Franké-tienne made a highly significant contribution to the novel form with a full-length work in the Haitian language, *Dézafi* (1975; Anguish). Although it is not the first work written in the Haitian language, *Dézafi* came at a particularly opportune moment, renewing the language when it faced the challenges of English and French, and of television and radio. *Dézafi* is itself a challenge in its versatility of literary form, stylistic expression, and exploitation of oral forms. There are parallels between Frankétienne's work and that of the Egyptian Nagīb Mahfūz. Frankétienne's bold affirmation of Haitian culture has had its effects on the novel throughout those parts of the Caribbean where French is the official language and Creole the usual language of oral communication. Writers from Guadeloupe, Guyane, and Martinique in particular have made significant use of these tensions—semantic and semiotic—inherent in the diglossia that constitutes the lives of these writers and their readers.

Guyane had led the way with fiction in Creole with Alfred Parépou's *Atipa, roman guyanais* (1885; Atipa, a Guyanese Novel), the first complete work to appear in its original form in Creole. However, its use of Creole and its anticlericalism, combined with the effects of colonial domination, meant that *Atipa* remained almost entirely unknown by the reading public until Auguste Horth mentioned it in his *Patois guyanais* (1949; Guyanese Patois). Parépou's novel is particularly valuable for its attempt at linguistic consistency, for its vision of Guyanese society of the 19th century, and for the foundations of a cultural identity established by the text. Even though *Atipa* may appear to use Caribbean linguistic vehicles to promote French republican and socialist causes, this work is firmly rooted in an artistic tradition of nonconformity. In form and in content, *Atipa* sets the tone for the most audacious literary experiments of the 20th century.

Through their exclusion from anthologies and from study in schools and universities, certain novelists have been excluded from the Caribbean cultural consciousness because of their ideological positions, because they did not claim a Caribbean identity, or simply because of their long absence from the Caribbean. For instance, René Maran's literary identity is often seriously questioned. Born in the Caribbean, Maran grew up in France and later served as a colonial administrator in the French colonies in Africa. He wrote numerous novels that have little or nothing to do with the Caribbean experience. His audience, at the time of publication, consisted primarily of Europeans, and the interlocutor in the novels is invariably European. Maran's style and form fit into the classical mode of introspective French writing of the earlier part of the 20th century and may be compared with those of his contemporaries André Gide and François Mauriac. Nevertheless, there is little doubt that his work is shaping—and will continue to do so—the themes and forms of fiction published by authors of Caribbean origin living in France. His themes of alienation, racism, interracial relationships, and colonial power assure him a place in Caribbean literary history. Maran was immortalized by the acerbic criticism of Frantz Fanon in *Peau noire, masques blancs* (1952; *Black Skin, White Masks*), which raised questions of identity and racial and racist ambiguities to a level of reflexion that thus far had been associated primarily with the works of African-American writers such as Chester Himes and Nella Larsen. Fanon criticizes Maran for failing to provide a coherent sociopolitical understanding of the workings of colonialism and racism and for the naivete of the introspective emotional struggles of his characters. But this kind of criticism tends to emphasize ideological and social affirmation to the detriment of psychological insight and aesthetic accomplishment. Critical emphasis on explicitly anti-imperialist works has

overshadowed the personal, sociopsychological themes of significant authors who have contributed to the evolution of the francophone Caribbean novel.

Claude and Marie-Magdalene Carbet from Martinique provide the first example of the close collaboration that has become a common feature of cultural life in the region. Their several collaborative works as well as their individual publications reveal a deep love of Martinique and a devotion to the region and its people. Their style is carefully polished, aiming at aesthetic perfection, and their work is thematically attentive to the problems of racism and power at a time in their teaching careers when such preoccupations could have led to sanctions against them. Although they wrote during the period marked by the *négritude* movement, they do not in any way submit their writing to its principles. The Carbets helped create the climate that allowed the writing of Aimé Césaire's long poem *Cahier d'un retour au pays natal* (1947; *Return to My Native Land*), the pivotal work of 20th-century Caribbean literature. Their Guadeloupean friend and collaborator Gilbert de Chambertrand, who produced literary work in several genres between 1917 and 1965, also made an important contribution to that literary foundation.

The novels of the Martiniquan historian Léonard Sainville and his compatriot Joseph Zobel, a literary critic as well as a novelist, may be generally classed as social realism. Little distinguishes them in form, but they are quite significant in the literary history of the Caribbean. Zobel's *La Rue Cases-Nègres* (1950; *Black Shack Alley*), undoubtedly one of the best known Caribbean novels, presents the world through the eyes of an adolescent and offers a profound, explicit social analysis of plantation and colonial society. The film version of Zobel's novel emphasizes the literary dimensions of orality and the importance of transmission of culture from one generation to another. The relationship between the boy José and the aging Médouze is comparable to that of Mathieu and Longoué in Edouard Glissant's *Le Quatrième siècle* (1964; The Fourth Century), even though *Black Shack Alley* lacks the philosophical depth and the literary experimentation of the later work: Zobel's socialist realism leaves little room for ontological musings and debates.

Similarly, the Guadeloupean Ernest Moutoussamy's novels, particularly *Il pleure dans mon pays* (1979; My Country Weeps) and *Aurore* (1987; Dawn), are examples of Marxist realism with significant ideological perspectives on questions of race and power. Thematically, Moutoussamy's work, limpid and unpretentious in its discursive structure, is similar to the work of Trinidadian Samuel Selvon without the latter's stylistic experimentation, linguistic innovation, and humor. Like Alejo Carpentier, Edouard Glissant, and the Barbadian George Lamming, Moutoussamy gives life and voice to the countless thousands of unnamed and unsung slaves and indentured laborers who fought for their dignity. In his novels, there is a place for subjective hope and optimism concerning humanity.

French philosophical and literary currents have played a significant role in Caribbean francophone literature at different times. Existentialist pessimism may clearly be seen as a factor in the works of the Guadeloupean Michèle Lacrosil and the Guyanese Bertène Juminer. Lacrosil's three novels use the sociopolitical realities of her native Guadeloupe as the foundation of the characters' psychology, but *Cajou* (1961), which has a Guadeloupean protagonist, is set entirely in France. Cajou's morbid introspection is based on her own understanding of sexism and racism. Unable to resolve her philosophical dilemmas, she drowns herself in the Seine. In the Caribbean, Lacrosil's most well-known and appreciated novel is perhaps *Sapotille et le serin d'argile* (1960; Sapotille and the Clay Canary), in which the female protagonist struggles through several levels of racism and colonial power in an attempt to secure her own identity. The concentric circles of oppression are embodied by a convent school, a house, her room, a ship, her cabin, and her skin. Like George Lamming's *In the Castle of My Skin* (1953), *Sapotille* creates a semiotic structure that implicitly compares educational oppression to the oppression of the master/slave relationship and presents exile as the only escape from the limitations of island life. Lacrosil's style is marked by a careful precision and a high level of control while her sensitive treatment of brutal emotional relationships recalls the finest achievements of Chester Himes. Her work presents a significant perspective on feminism and racism but is characterized by a pervasive pessimism concerning human existence.

In the case of Juminer's *Les bâtards* (1961; The Bastards), existentialist angst is taken as far as it will go in the Caribbean context of exile. Novels from Guyane are different from works from the Caribbean islands: rather than the limited horizons of water and the continuous reminders of the slave ships, Juminer's protagonists have as their psychological backdrop the vast Amazonian hinterland. In spite of the fact that the topological dimensions are different, the psychological introspection and the ideological search for identity are nevertheless comparable to those of the writers from the islands, because the relationships and discourse of power and domination are comparable. Juminer's most important contribution to the genre is undoubtedly his least esteemed novel, *La revanche de Bozambo* (1968; Bozambo's Revenge), which may be classified as sociopolitical fiction. Its inverted vision of conquest and domination leads to a reexamination and redefinition of imperialist and revolutionary concepts of power and the dynamics of oppression.

The most recent phase of novelistic production has been marked by the novels and essays on culture by Edouard Glissant, whose ideas now permeate most novels from the region. *Le Quatrième siècle* has completely redefined the concept of the novel through its consistent experimentation with form. Its long paragraphs without punctuation recall Jean-Paul Sartre's *La Nausée* (1938; Nausea) and at the same time echo literary representations of orality. The reader is invited to evaluate the style as a factor of philosophical expression. The frequent use of italics, parentheses, and poetic prose serves to illustrate and to deepen the ontological questions raised. The major emphasis appears to be on the subject of temporality because Glissant revalorizes concepts of history, historicity, and notions of the self. He also has redefined notions of the real and realism within the Caribbean context, honoring their psychic and spiritual dimensions. His subsequent novels have taken these ideas to greater depths, demonstrating the extent to which the semantics of diglossia, the intersemiotics of race and ethnicity, and the versatility of form may be combined to elucidate the ethos of Caribbean artistic expression. In this way, Glissant has created a truly Caribbean philosophical framework that helps us to understand Caribbean literature written in French, English, and Spanish.

Glissant's literary and philosophical works have produced an intellectual climate in which others have been able to carry his experimentation even further. Patrick Chamoiseau and Raphaël Confiant, also Martiniquan, have collaborated with Jean Bernabé on the theory of *créolité*. At the same time, they have each developed their own distinctive notion of the novel. Confiant's works have established him as an innovative novelist whose understanding of history is as subjectively Caribbean as Glissant's. His major departure from convention is the series of shorter novels consisting of *Bassin des ouragans* (1994; Hurricane Basin), *La Savane des pétrifications* (1995; The Savannah of Petrifications), and *La Baignoire de Joséphine* (1997; Josephine's Bathtub). These works are satirical, outrageously irreverent, and deeply cynical in their rejection of Euro-American cultural hegemony and values. In his epic wanderings, the hero of the three novels transforms all incidents, social phenomena, and political events into laughter. The satire is turned even against the author, a move that makes the irreverence of the texts acceptable. Although he treads carefully at times, Confiant lays out the contradictions of life in the French overseas departments of Guadeloupe, Martinique, and Guyane more clearly than any sociological treatise does. The alienating policy of assimilation is shown at its most psychologically damaging in the minds and behavior of the characters. The entirely artificial economy, the surfeit of consumer goods, the very use of the French language and French symbols of power, and foreign popular culture—associated particularly with the United States and CNN, Japan and its cartoon industry, and Brazil and its soap operas—are all factors in the rapid transformation of the Martiniquan mode of life and way of thinking. Technological sophistication now coexists with belief in *soucougnans, diablesses, dorlis,* and other *vaudou* phenomena, creating a dislocation of sociopsychic associations that is reflected in the diverse semantic registers of these short works. The irony is relentless, and there is a constant shift of focus from Martinique to other parts of the Caribbean and the world. Confiant's novels undoubtedly have set a different tone with their reliance on humor and their reconstitution of the recent past through a narrative form that skillfully exploits and even invents several language registers.

But in many ways the Guadeloupean Simone Schwarz-Bart had already made the first steps toward the renewal of the novel form with the publication of *Ti Jean l'Horizon* (1979; Between Two Worlds), in which myth and geopolitical realities are freely associated. Although Ti Jean's quest has little of the biting irony of Confiant's works, Schwarz-Bart succeeds in shifting historical focus from Guadeloupe to Africa and Europe in a mythical voyage that has all the conceptual qualities of an apocalyptic time machine. Schwarz-Bart's most well-known work is *Pluie et vent sur Télumée Miracle* (1972; The Bridge of Beyond), which has become a classic of Caribbean writing for its perfection of structure, the psychological development of its characters, its very lucid analyses of male-female power relationships, and its optimism concerning female interdependence. The novel underlines the psychic dimensions of Caribbean reality through narrative voice as well as the women characters' preoccupations.

Some of the poetic processes of the Guadeloupean Ernest Pépin's *L'homme au bâton* (1992; The Man with the Stick) recall those of Depestre's *Alléluia pour une femme-jardin*. However, Pépin consistently has demonstrated his literary independence from his Martiniquan contemporaries, even though he knows them well and has collaborated with them. Pépin's work is un-pretentious, and he is capable of considerable humor. His use of irony may best be compared with that of the Jamaican Alvin Bennett since it demands an intimate knowledge of Caribbean mythology. Pépin has brought the characters of Caribbean oral literature and spiritual belief to the novel in the same way that Depestre has peopled his novels with the divinities and spirits of *vaudou*. But if *L'homme au bâton* provokes laughter, it also demands deep reflexion on culture, power, and sexuality. In these ways, his work is thematically and structurally comparable to that of Schwarz-Bart.

Gisèle Pineau's contribution to the novel is undoubtedly sig-nificant in its detailed, sensitive exploration of the sociopsycho-logical aspects of sexuality. Pineau's treatment of sexuality is not necessarily characterized by male-female oppositions of power, sometimes exploring the dynamics of female relationships. *Un papillon dans la cité* (1992; A Butterfly in the Housing Project), a novel for young adults, is a work unique in its execution and theme. The action is divided between an urban setting in France and a rural setting in Guadeloupe. A preadolescent couple—the girl from Guadeloupe, the boy from North Africa—are the pro-tagonists, and their uninhibited reaching across diversity of lan-guage, religion, and culture announces the new construction of social and psychological realities of the generation of those Caribbean and African people who were born in Europe or have spent most of their young lives there. The protagonists are unit-ed in their sociopsychological needs and specifically in the grandmothers they share. There is no doubt that Pineau has made a significant contribution to the literature for a sector of the reading public that is often neglected.

Maryse Condé's *Moi, Tituba, sorcière Noire de Salem* (1986; *I, Tituba, Black Witch of Salem*) takes a historical figure at the center of a macabre and barbaric drama and completely reval-orizes her. Diversity of language, religion, and culture also char-acterize this novel, but there are some glimmers of harmony in this work, which explores the most brutal and tortured recesses of the mind. Condé combines the themes of sexuality, spirituali-ty, and power within the specific contexts of master-slave and male-female relationships. The conceptual, social, and psycho-logical characteristics of sexism and racism are clearly explored in a variety of settings, including a ship at sea, a plantation in Barbados, a Christian home in a small New England Puritan community, and a Jewish home in Boston. Condé does not draw her social images in simple oppositions between black and white. There are as many convergences as divergences, and the unpredictable nature of human relationships guides her novel to its psychic conclusion in African-Jewish synthesis. Condé's nov-els cover a diversity of subjects in Africa, Europe, and the Caribbean. While *Segou* (1984, 1985; *Segu* and *The Children of Segu*) is a significant historical work, *Hérémakhonon* (1976) re-calls the introspection of the novels of Maran and the cultural questions raised by intercultural sexuality in Africa as developed in Ayi Kwei Armah's *Why Are We So Blest?* (1972).

Although many francophone Caribbean works have been cat-egorized as magic realist, on close examination such a classifica-tion proves to be superficial and quite beside the point. The fact that several authors have recourse to indigenous religious beliefs and structures is simply an acknowledgement of the social reali-ty of Caribbean life and literature. Oral culture has always made abundant use of the psychic world as a point of reference and

has developed its own dynamic and highly sophisticated narra-tive processes to transmit and translate the mythical into the realm of the social community. Depestre, Schwarz-Bart, Pépin, Glissant, Condé, and others write in a context in which psychic discourse is often an integral aspect of the social realism of the novel. It is never far from the psychological factors surrounding the characters. Together with this integration of indigenous spir-ituality, the importance of onomastics, the reconstruction and reliving of history, the recontextualization of temporality, and the recasting of language are the major common characteristics of the Francophone Caribbean novel.

FREDERICK IVOR CASE

See also Maryse Condé; Postcolonial Narrative and Criti-cism of the Novel

Further Reading

Antoine, Régis, *Les écrivains français et les Antilles: Des premiers Pères blancs aux surréalistes noirs*, Paris: Maisonneuve et Larose, 1978

Antoine, Régis, *La Littérature franco-antillaise*, Paris: Karthala, 1992; 2nd edition, 1995

Arnold, A. James, editor, *A History of Literature in the Caribbean*, volume 1, Amsterdam and Philadelphia: Benjamins, 1994

Bernabé, Jean, Patrick Chamoiseau, and Raphaël Confiant, *Eloge de la Créolité*, Paris: Gallimard, 1989

Case, Frederick Ivor, *The Crisis of Identity: Studies in the Guadeloupean and Martiniquan Novel*, Sherbrooke, Quebec: Naaman, 1985

Corzani, Jack, *La littérature des Antilles-Guyane françaises*, 6 vols., Fort-de-France: Désormeaux, 1978

Crosta, Suzanne, *Le Marronnage créateur: Dynamique textuelle chez Edouard Glissant*, Sainte-Foy, Quebec: GRELCA, 1991

Dash, J. Michael, *Literature and Ideology in Haiti, 1915–1961*, London: Macmillan, and Totowa, New Jersey: Barnes and Noble, 1981

Dorsinville, Max, *Le pays natal: Essais sur les littératures du Tiers-Monde et du Québec*, Dakar: Nouvelles Editions Africaines, 1983

Fanon, Frantz, *Peau noire, masques blancs*, Paris: Editions du Seuil, 1952; as *Black Skin, White Masks*, New York: Grove Press, 1967; London: MacGibbon and Kee, 1968

Fauquenoy, Marguerite, editor, *Atipa revisité; ou, Les itinéraires de Parépou*, Fort-de-France: Presses Universitaires Créoles, and Paris: L'Harmattan, 1989

Glissant, Edouard, *Le Discours antillais*, Paris: Editions du Seuil, 1981; as *Caribbean Discourse*, Charlottesville: University Press of Virginia, 1989

Gouraige, Ghislain, *La Diaspora d'Haïti et l'Afrique*, Sherbrooke, Quebec: Naaman, 1974

Herdeck, Donald E., editor, *Caribbean Writers: A Bio-Bibliographical-Critical Encyclopedia*, Washington, D.C.: Three Continents Press, 1979

Laroche, Maximilien, *L'Haïtien*, Montreal: Editions de Sainte-Marie, 1968

Laroche, Maximilien, *La Littérature haïtienne: Identité, Langue, Réalité*, Montreal: Leméac, 1981

Laroche, Maximilien, *Contribution à l'étude du réalisme merveilleux*, Sainte-Foy, Quebec: GRELCA, 1987

Laroche, Maximilien, editor, *Tradition et Modernité dans les littératures francophones d'Afrique et d'Amérique,* Sainte-Foy, Quebec: GRELCA, 1988

Ojo-Ade, Femi, *René Maran, the Black Frenchman: A Bio-Critical Study,* Washington, D.C.: Three Continents Press, 1984

Ormerod, Beverley, *An Introduction to the French Caribbean Novel,* London and Portsmouth, New Hampshire: Heinemann, 1985

Viatte, Auguste, *Histoire littéraire de l'Amérique française des origines à 1950,* Quebec: Presses Universitaires Laval, and Paris: Presses Universitaires de France, 1954

Caribbean Novel: Hispanic. *See* Latin American Novel: Hispanic Caribbean

---

Caricature. *See* Parody and Pastiche

Alejo Carpentier 1904–1980

Cuban

Alejo Carpentier wrote *¡Ecué-Yamba-Ó!* (Lord, Praised Be Thou!), the first of his eight novels, in 1927 while imprisoned in Cuba for his suspected communist sympathies. Although the novel was a product of Afro-Cubanism and the aesthetics of the European avant-garde of the 1920s, it was written when fiction in Latin America was still dominated by the naturalist/realist tendencies of 19th-century Europe. As a work intended to convey the worldview of black Cubans, it would join a new wave of fiction seeking to describe Latin America from a more autochthonous perspective. It also began Carpentier's long quest for a more "authentic" representation of Latin America.

The subsequent development of Carpentier's aesthetics occurred as a result of his closer association with the avant-garde and with surrealism during his period of exile in France (1928–39), his extensive reading about the history of Latin America, and his visit to Haiti in 1943. These elements coalesced in *El reino de este mundo* (1949; *The Kingdom of This World*), a novel about Haiti's slave rebellions, its fight for independence from France, and the establishment of a republic. The novel is a landmark in Latin America for its introduction of the concept of "lo real maravilloso" (marvelous reality), which Carpentier described in his prologue and applied in the novel, and with which he distanced himself from the "artificial" marvels of surrealism in favor of a sense of the marvelous that he considered occurred more "naturally" in Latin America as a result of

its history, the preservation of a belief in myth, and the juxtaposition of disparate cultural phenomena within the same social context.

"Lo real maravilloso" was also a significant factor in *Los pasos perdidos* (1953; *The Lost Steps*) and *El siglo de las luces* (1962; *Explosion in a Cathedral*). The former is about a composer's encounter with an unspoiled primeval world during his search for primitive musical instruments in the Amazon jungle. The latter examines the effect of the French Revolution in the Caribbean, a further foray into some of the thematic material of *The Kingdom of This World*. In both novels, the character of human society and detailed descriptions of the natural world are significant elements in the evocation of the marvelous, but in the broader context of Latin American fiction "lo real maravilloso" has tended to be subsumed by the concept of magic realism, regardless of fundamental differences between them. While authors like Gabriel García Márquez elaborated a fictional world through the mythification of history, Carpentier relied heavily on recorded history in order to reveal the myths underlying it. His fidelity to the details of history is a fundamental characteristic of all his fiction.

Carpentier's prologue to *The Kingdom of This World* was extended and reedited in a book of essays entitled *Tientos y diferencias* (1964; Themes and Variations) and has remained an essential point of reference even for the novels he published in the 1970s. However, the same volume also contained another essay, "Problemática de la actual novela latinoamericana" (Problems of the Latin American Novel Today), in which the issues facing a novelist intent on writing about Latin America are addressed through reference to particular Latin American "contexts"—racial, economic, political, cultural, culinary, and ideological, among others.

His next two novels, both published in 1974, *Concierto barroco* (*Baroque Concerto*) and *El recurso del método* (*Reasons of State*) may be read profitably against his 1964 essay. Both demonstrate the hybrid nature of Latin American culture as a product of the diverse elements combined and transformed in the context of Latin American society. *Reasons of State,* for example, with the play in its Spanish title on Descartes' philosophical treatise *Discours de la méthode* (1637), is the story of an archetypical Latin American country under the rule of a political *supremo* whose political practice is a parody of European rationalism and whose life is essentially a composite biography of many post-independence rulers of Latin American countries.

Carpentier's two final novels did not introduce any new dimensions. *La consagración de la primavera* (1978; The Rite of Spring), as the title suggests, is a return to the period of the avant-garde. However, it also addresses the revolutionary movements that affected the Hispanic world during the 20th century, especially the Cuban Revolution (1959), which has been a constant subtext of Carpentier's writing since the 1960s. By contrast, *El arpa y la sombra* (1979; *The Harp and the Shadow*) returns to a more remote historical past: this narrative of Christopher Columbus' self-vindication during his deathbed confession is framed by the 19th-century attempt to have the explorer canonized. History and the interpretation of the past therefore remain at the core of Carpentier's concerns, and his last novel is also written with the same degree of irony and picaresque humor that had surfaced in earlier work, most notably in his representation of the archetypical Latin American country and the figure of its president in *Reasons of State.*

As a writer whose work matured in the 1950s and 1960s, Carpentier contributed to the internationalization of Latin American fiction during the 20th century, helping to bring it into the mainstream of the Western tradition. Although deeply influenced by the cultural traditions of Europe, Carpentier also wrote against them in order to offer his own definition of the specificity of Latin America, and he did so on a grand scale. Carpentier was an intensely erudite writer. His evocation of Latin America is richly intertextual; his vocabulary is vast and unapologetically obscure at times; and his narratives trace the cyclical trends and revolutionary patterns of modern history through stories that are often structured by the movement of his characters across land and between continents over long periods of time. Carpentier's work played an important role in the development of a Latin American perspective on history and literature that went beyond its European roots.

RICHARD A. YOUNG

See also Lost Steps

Biography
Born in Havana, Cuba, 26 December 1904. Educated at the University of Havana. Journalist, Havana, 1921–24; editor, *Carteles* magazine, Havana, 1924–28; director, Foniric Sudios, Paris, 1928–39; writer and producer, CMZ radio station, Havana, 1939–41; professor of music history, Conservatorio Nacional, Havana, 1941–43; lived in Haiti, Europe, the United States, and South America, 1943–59; director, Cuban Publishing House, Havana, 1960–67; cultural attaché, Cuban Embassy, Paris, from 1967. Columnist, *El Nacional*, Caracas; editor, *Imam*, Paris. Died 24 April 1980.

Novels by Carpentier
¡Ecué-Yamba-Ó! [Lord Praised Be Thou!], 1933
El reino de este mundo, 1949; as *The Kingdom of This World,* translated by Harriet de Onís, 1957
Los pasos perdidos, 1953; as *The Lost Steps,* translated by Harriet de Onís, 1956
El siglo de las luces, 1962; as *Explosion in a Cathedral,* translated by John Sturrock, 1963
El recurso del método, 1974; as *Reasons of State,* translated by Frances Partridge, 1976
Concierto barroco, 1974; as *Baroque Concerto,* translated by Asa Zatz, 1991
La consagración de la primavera [The Rite of Spring], 1978
El arpa y la sombra, 1979; as *The Harp and the Shadow,* translated by Thomas Christensen and Carol Christensen, 1990

Other Writings: poetry, plays, short stories (including those in *Guerra del tiempo* [1958; *War of Time*]), a novella (*El acoso* [1956; *The Chase*]), essays, a history of music in Cuba (*La música en Cuba*, 1946), and a prodigious number of newspaper articles.

Further Reading
Giacoman, Helmy F., editor, *Homenaje a Alejo Carpentier: Variaciones interpretativas en torno a su obra*, New York: Las Americas, 1970
González Echevarría, Roberto, *Alejo Carpentier: The Pilgrim at Home*, Ithaca, New York: Cornell University Press, 1977
González Echevarría, Roberto, and Klaus Müller-Bergh, *Alejo Carpentier: Bibliographical Guide*, Westport, Connecticut, and London: Greenwood Press, 1983
Harss, Luis, and Barbara Dohmann, *Into the Mainstream: Conversations with Latin-American Writers*, New York: Harper and Row, 1966
Márquez Rodríguez, Alexis, *El barroco y lo real maravilloso en la obra de Alejo Carpentier*, Mexico City: Siglo XXI, 1982
Müller-Bergh, Klaus, editor, *Asedios a Carpentier: Once ensayos criticos sobre el novelista cubano*, Santiago de Chile: Editorial Universitaria, 1972
Rubio de Lertora, Patricia, and Richard A. Young, *Carpentier ante la crítica: Bibliografía comentada*, Xalapa: Universidad Veracruzana, 1985
Shaw, Donald Leslie, *Alejo Carpentier*, Boston: Twayne, 1985

Angela Carter 1940–92

English

Over a period of approximately 26 years, Angela Carter wrote numerous and diverse texts, ranging from novels and short fiction to film scripts, polemic, and journalism. Carter is often seen as a central figure in recent British writing, especially women's writing, and her work represents a successful intersection between postmodern literary devices and feminist politics. In her afterword to *Fireworks,* her first collection of short stories, published in 1974, Carter stated that "we live in Gothic times." This diagnosis is repeated throughout her work, where the bizarre, the grotesque, and the fantastic are presented as the everyday, and the commonplace is seen as menacing. By subverting literary, sexual, and ideological codes and conventions, Carter attempts to demythologize Western culture, to expose Western patriarchy's strangeness masquerading as the "natural" or the "real."

Her early novels—*Shadow Dance* (1966), *Several Perceptions* (1968), and *Love* (1971)—could be described as generally realist in approach. However, these accounts of failed love affairs and sexual passions in the emerging youth subculture of 1960s Britain do contain undercurrents of menace, darkness, the fantastic, and the Gothic, which surface fully in her later works and with which Carter is most commonly associated. These early novels also mark her typical concerns and stylistics: the underside of human desire, captured in an elegant and seductive prose that plays at the borders between poetry and parody. Although Carter identifies herself as a feminist writer—"because I'm a feminist in everything else and one can't compartmentalise these things in one's life"—these early novels show little concern with questions of feminism or sexual politics.

Carter's second novel, *The Magic Toyshop* (1967), differs from her other early novels in that it shifted from realist representational strategies to a style that later became her signature. *The Magic Toyshop* reveals Carter's fascination with fairy tales, the Freudian unconscious, and the tensions between appearance and reality, and it combines these elements into an eerie fairy or folk tale of family taboos and repressions. This combination of simple, fantastic, and highly symbolic codes of fairy tales, legends, and myths that construct our civilization is prominent in her fiction from *Heroes and Villains* (1969) and *The Infernal Desire Machines of Dr. Hoffman* (1972) onward.

Carter explained her growing political consciousness and her interest in alternative modes of representation by noting that

> we were truly asking ourselves questions about the nature of reality. . . . I can date to that time and to that sense of heightened awareness of the society around me in the summer of 1968, my own questioning of the nature of my reality as a *woman*. How that social fiction of my "femininity" was created, by means outside my control, and palmed off on me as the real thing. This investigation of the social fictions that regulate our lives—what Blake called the "mind-forg'd manacles"—is what I've concerned myself with consciously since that time.

Throughout her career, she experimented with genre, appropriating and blending techniques and styles from horror, science fiction, fairy tales, fantasy, and family sagas to rewrite Western sexual metanarratives from a feminist and magic realist perspective.

Carter's usage of diverse antirealist modes and genres leads to an unorthodox and sometimes quite disturbing exploration of sexuality and cruelty, particularly in her short fiction. Her socialist-feminist politics mean that her rewritings of Western sexuality are firmly located in a historical context and avoid simplistic moralism, yet at times the seductive prose verges on voyeurism. Both *Heroes and Villains* and *The Infernal Desire Machines of Dr. Hoffman* are ambitious parodies that render the Freudo-Marxism of Herbert Marcuse and Wilhelm Reich into picaresque fantasies. These novels explore what chaos and order mean to the male and female, privileged and powerless subjects that constitute the cultural paradigm of the West. Carter satirizes the Western obsession with rationality and order and depicts a connection between psychic and social forces, although her attitude to the anarchic potential of sexuality is quite ambivalent.

The Passion of New Eve (1977) is Carter's first novel to link gender to explorations of sexuality. Carter employs a dystopian science-fiction mode to write an allegory of the social construction of the feminine. Set in the not-too-distant future in the deserts of the United States, *The Passion of New Eve* is a gloomy satire of a social order at the breaking point but still clinging to its mythologies of femininity. The characters of Tristessa, an aging drag queen, and Evelyn/Eve, a male chauvinist who is surgically reconstructed into the perfect woman, function as devices to show the illusory and farcical nature of current gender ideology and social conditioning. History and myth are locked in struggle in Carter's tale of civil war and the New Woman.

Carter's next novel, *Nights at the Circus* (1984) continues her interest in iconic representations of women and femininity and their role in maintaining a particular social order. *Nights at the Circus* was shortlisted for the Booker Prize, won the James Tait Black Memorial Prize, and is regarded as her finest novel. The dystopia of *The Passion of New Eve* is replaced by the optimism, humor, and parodic re-creation of the 19th-century novel. In its organizational structure, *Nights at the Circus* resembles the triple decker Victorian novel. Carter parodies the bourgeois novel as proponent of naturalism and realism with her carnivalesque humor, intertextual allusions, larger-than-life characters, sprawling plot, and lucky coincidences. Again, Carter's central protagonist is a freak: Fevvers the bird woman and circus star, who deconstructs the hoax of femininity through the laughter of this melodramatic feminist bodice ripper.

Carter's final novel, *Wise Children* (1991), is also marked by bawdy humor, optimism, feisty and unlikely heroines, and a feminist revisioning of aspects of Western culture—this time targeting Shakespeare and show business. Carter creates three generations of a theatrical family, focusing on the female members, to narrate the changing fortunes and forms of theatrical popular culture throughout the 20th century. *Wise Children* shares the scope and playfulness of *Nights at the Circus* and may serve as evidence that Carter died at the peak of her creative powers.

Lorna Sage's description of Carter's work as a "savage sideshow" is appropriate for a writer who regarded nothing as sacred and delighted in exploring the bizarre and in upsetting reader expectations. She employed postmodern aesthetic techniques to their fullest potential in all her forms of writing. She subverted genres and created glittering word pictures, energetic and colorful narratives, and hyperbolic characters. She parodied and pastiched Western culture—a realm of savagery, but also of magic and wonder. In so doing, Carter re-energized the novel form.

MARGARET HENDERSON

Biography

Born in Eastbourne, Sussex, 7 May 1940. Attended the University of Bristol, 1962–65, B.A. in English 1965. Journalist, Croydon, Surrey, 1958–61; lived in Japan, 1969–70; Arts Council Fellow in Creative Writing, University of Sheffield, 1976–78; Visiting Professor of Creative Writing, Brown University, Providence, Rhode Island, 1980–81; writer-in-residence, University of Adelaide, Australia, 1984. Died in 1992.

Novels by Carter

Shadow Dance, 1966
The Magic Toyshop, 1967
Several Perceptions, 1968
Heroes and Villains, 1969
Love, 1971
The Infernal Desire Machines of Dr. Hoffman, 1972; as *The War of Dreams*, 1974
The Passion of New Eve, 1977
Nights at the Circus, 1984
Wise Children, 1991

Other Writings: film scripts, a translation of children's fairy tales; journalism, collected in *Nothing Sacred* (1982) and *Expletives Deleted* (1992); a radio play; collections of short fiction, for example, *Black Venus* (1985) and *The Bloody Chamber* (1979); an essay on pornography, *The Sadeian Woman* (1979).

Further Reading

Hallab, Mary Y., "'Human Diversity' in the Novels of Angela Carter: Which Ones Are the Freaks?" *Studies in Contemporary Satire: A Creative and Critical Journal* 19 (1995)
Jordan, Elaine, "Enthrallment: Angela Carter's Speculative Fiction," in *Plotting Change: Contemporary Women's Fiction*, edited by Linda Anderson, London: Edward Arnold, and New York: Routledge, Chapman and Hall, 1990
Kendrick, William, "The Real Magic of Angela Carter," in *Contemporary British Women Writers: Narrative Strategies*, edited by Robert E. Hosmer, New York: St. Martin's Press, 1993
Palmer, Paulina, "From 'Coded Mannequin' to Bird Woman: Angela Carter's Magic Flight," in *Women Reading Women's Writing*, edited by Sue Roe, Brighton: Harvester, and New York: St. Martin's Press, 1987
The Review of Contemporary Fiction 14:3 (1994), special issue on Angela Carter
Wilson, Robert Rawdon, "SLIP PAGE: Angela Carter, In/Out/In the Post-Modern Nexus," in *Past the Last Post: Theorizing Post-Colonialism and Post-Modernism*, edited by Ian Adam and Helen Tiffin, Calgary, Alberta: University of Calgary Press, 1990; London and New York: Harvester Wheatsheaf, 1991

Casa de los espíritus. *See* House of the Spirits

Castle Rackrent by Maria Edgeworth

1800

Published in 1800, Maria Edgeworth's *Castle Rackrent* is very careful to situate itself at its particular historical moment. The preface to the novel, which is crucial to understanding how the text functions, places its writing and completion in 1800 and shows itself fully aware of the impending Act of Union, joining Ireland and Britain constitutionally. *Castle Rackrent*, set in Ire-land and narrated by an Irish servant, looks forward, in both senses, to this momentous event. *Castle Rackrent* is aware that by the time the book will be read a new political situation in Ireland will have arisen and that the society described by the novel (which is rapidly altering anyway) will have gone through a major legal as well as social change.

Castle Rackrent is the story of the Rackrents, a family of Irish landowners. Through the course of the novel, three generations of Rackrents are served by the almost impossibly long-lived Thady, who is the novel's narrator. The Rackrents' decline is told with a subtle and complex irony and humor; their final humiliation comes when Thady's son takes over the house and title from the Rackrent family. This plot summary, however, does not provide an adequate impression of a novel that has played a central role in the development of Anglo-Irish writing. Its analysis of the "Big House" decline, for example, is an element of many subsequent novels, while its rendition of the Irish "voice" and its delight in the often cutting and unsettling humor of Irish speech was revolutionary.

Critics, in their praise of *Castle Rackrent,* have mentioned Edgeworth as an inheritor of Laurence Sterne and precursor of James Joyce in that her use of language, irony, and mildly fantastical narrative lift the novel out of any realist pretensions. To Walter Scott, on the other hand, *Castle Rackrent* was primarily proof that a regional (nonmetropolitan) novel was possible within the British tradition. That *Castle Rackrent* is so apparently "open" a text is a testament to the novel's construction and Edgeworth's ability to weave the picaresque into a more serious generic format.

The novel is littered with notes in the form of a glossary that accompanies the text and explains words, phrases, and idioms that would otherwise "not be intelligible to the English reader." In this way, Edgeworth makes an important political point: the Union between Britain and Ireland will not lead smoothly to a neatly unified new polity. Edgeworth implies that some act of translation is still needed between the two cultures and that their differences should not be underestimated.

The most remarkable feature of *Castle Rackrent* is its narrator, Thady. Although openly and proudly servile, Thady is a mildly ironically portrayed character whose sincerity is called into question on occasion. Thady's very deliberate and heavy penchant for pointing out both his loyalty to the family Rackrent and his noninterference at crucial moments in their affairs is meant, superficially, to suggest the singularity of his affection for the Rackrents and his knowledge that he cannot have an influence over their behavior. Yet at other times Thady's often repeated phrase "Yet I said nothing" can seem mocking, belligerent, and deliberately dull, yet always humorous. Thady's condescension toward the Rackrents is, in narrative terms, a reversal of their relationship in social terms. Such reversals are the staple of *Castle Rackrent*: while Thady is finding his own ways to subvert (but continue) his servile status within the Rackrent household,

his son, Jason, is undertaking the same project in a much more direct and public way. Gradually buying up Rackrent land as the family self-destructs, Jason eventually effects a complete reversal of the situation in which his father found himself. This, from a novel so consciously set at a particular historical moment, is a profound commentary on a coming political upheaval.

The difficulty of reading *Castle Rackrent* as a political parable is that it tends to obscure the many other possible ways to experience and enjoy the novel. *Castle Rackrent* has, for example, much to say on the nature of marriage, since the Rackrents are beset by marital difficulties that lead to breakdown. (The marital crisis also serves as an indirect commentary on the Act of Union, itself a kind of marriage.) Another important aspect is Edgeworth's humor, at times farcical (as when Sir Condy Rackrent stages his own funeral in order to see how his friends regard him), and at times a mixture of situation comedy and linguistic jokes (as when Sir Kit's Jewish wife, to Sir Kit's embarrassment and Thady's horror, describes the beloved bog of Allballycarrick-o'shaughlin as "that black swamp out yonder").

Castle Rackrent has earned an important place in the Irish novel and in the British regional novel. Its mixing of genres and style, its ability to handle a "difficult" narrator, and its gentle self-mocking humor make it an extraordinary novel, both in its own time and today.

COLIN GRAHAM

See also Maria Edgeworth

Further Reading

Butler, Marilyn, *Maria Edgeworth: A Literary Biography,* Oxford: Clarendon Press, 1972

Dunne, Tom, *Maria Edgeworth and the Colonial Mind,* Dublin: National University of Ireland, 1984

Kirkpatrick, Kathryn, "Putting Down the Rebellion: Notes and Glosses on Maria Edgeworth's *Castle Rackrent,*" *Éire-Ireland* 30 (1995)

McCormack, W.J., *Ascendancy and Tradition in Anglo-Irish Literary History from 1789 to 1939,* Oxford: Clarendon Press, and New York: Oxford University Press, 1985; revised edition, as *From Burke to Beckett: Ascendancy, Tradition, and Betrayal in Literary History,* Cork: Cork University Press, 1994

Mortimer, Anthony, "*Castle Rackrent* and Its Historical Contexts," *Études Irlandaises* 9 (1984)

Newcomer, James, *Maria Edgeworth,* Lewisburg, Pennsylvania: Bucknell University Press, 1973

Cat and Mouse. *See* Danzig Trilogy

Catch-22 by Joseph Heller

1961

Since its publication in 1961 to mixed reviews regarding its incoherent structure, length, exaggeration, grotesque characters, and black humor, Joseph Heller's *Catch-22* has come to be viewed as a masterpiece that articulates the absurdity of war and life in a standardized mass society governed by a ruthless corporate capitalism and the irrational logic of "Catch-22." A World War II novel set on the fictitious island of Pianosa off the coast of Italy, *Catch-22* captures the sense of confusion of a postwar generation that had experienced the massive destructiveness of American atomic bombings and German mass murder as well as the creeping fallout of the Cold War, the Korean War, and the McCarthy-era witch hunts. *Catch-22* also expresses the emerging dissatisfaction and rebelliousness of the Vietnam generation, with its suspicion and provocation of all authority.

Artistically, Heller's work marks a dramatic break from the established tradition of realism in American novels (as given in Stephen Crane, Theodore Dreiser, Frank Norris, Ernest Hemingway, Norman Mailer, Bernard Malamud), reinventing the picaresque novel with its hilarious plots and characters in a modern manner. The novel also departs from the subgenre of the war novel, which relied heavily on realistic technique to portray war and its physical and psychological effects. Crane's *The Red Badge of Courage* (1895), generally considered to be the first modern war novel, provided the basic model with its exacting depiction of combat scenes, informing traditional World War II novels such as Mailer's *The Naked and the Dead* (1948), Irwin Shaw's *The Young Lions* (1948), and James Jones' *From Here to Eternity* (1951). The publication of *Catch-22* in 1961 signaled a more experimental approach to the war novel, being among the first of its type to use satire, exaggeration, and discontinuity to depict the internalized logic of war rather than its apparent brutalities. Through its use of black humor and absurdist and surrealist techniques, *Catch-22* also anticipated and influenced such novels as Thomas Pynchon's *V.* (1963) and Kurt Vonnegut's *Slaughterhouse-Five* (1969), which likewise use unconventional portrayals of war to depict the dysfunctional nature of contemporary society.

With the legal loophole of "Catch-22" and its self-defeating rationality, Heller has not only added a permanent term to the English lexicon but articulated a pervasive sense of frustration with an overgrown and ubiquitous civil system. Used to justify the many contradictions within the system, "Catch-22" functions legally to revoke legal rights. Thus the novel's protagonist, Captain John Yossarian, lead bombardier of the 256th squadron, has no recourse within the system when his commanding officer requires that he fly double the 40 missions required by the Air Force. "Catch-22" says he must follow all orders given by his commanding officer even if this order directly disobeys an Air Force ruling. Similarly, when Yossarian attempts to have himself grounded by acting mad, he is informed of "Catch-22," which states that "anyone who wants to get out of combat duty isn't really crazy." Indeed, "Catch-22" forces Yossarian to counter with equally insane responses, revealing an upside-down world in which madness is the only sane response.

This irrational logic is depicted in the novel's rambling and episodic structure, which seems to defy any sort of progression or cohesion. Indeed, the only chronological thread is given in Colonel Cathcart's continual raising of the number of required flying missions, structuring the action of the novel in the manner of an escalating sense of public and administrative insanity. Interspersed between these numbers are a variety of absurd and shifting subplots, surreal flashbacks, fantastic jokes, and an even more fantastic cast of characters. Among them are Chief White Halfoat, an American Indian, whose family is constantly chased and evicted by oil companies from any place they settle, because oil is discovered wherever they settle; Colonel Cathcart, Yossarian's commanding officer, who eagerly volunteers his men for dangerous tasks in order to secure a promotion to general and get his picture on the cover of the *Saturday Evening Post*; and the peerless Milo Minderbinder, company mess officer, who forms the syndicate M&M Enterprises, an international black-market cartel that makes huge profits from buying up available foodstuffs from around the world and reselling it to his mess hall.

Milo, in Heller's satirical depiction, represents the essence of the American businessman who believes mightily in the credo of democracy and spreads its values of industriousness, resourcefulness, and, above all, free enterprise and profit around the world with missionary zeal. He has been designated mayor of Palermo (where his pictures line the streets because he brought Scotch to Sicily), Carini, Monreale, Bagheria, Termini Imerese, Cefali, Mistretta, and Nicosia; he also holds the titles Vice-Shah of Oran, Caliph of Baghdad, Imam of Damascus, and the Sheik of Araby. However, to keep a contract with German outfits, Milo is neither above bombing his own squadron nor reselling much-needed medical supplies. When Yossarian attempts to treat the fatally wounded Snowden, he finds in place of the morphine a message bearing Milo's motto "What's good for the syndicate is good for the country!" The innocent and likeable Milo, who is nevertheless able to commit atrocities in the spirit of free enterprise, is perhaps Heller's most shrewdly drawn character in the novel, pointing to the basic amorality of capitalism.

In a 1986 appraisal that celebrates the 25th birthday of *Catch-22* and traces its passage from modest success through "massive best-sellerdom and early canonization as a youth-cult sacred text" to "monumental artifact of contemporary American literature," John Aldridge aptly remarks that readers had "to learn how to read this curious book," linking the history of the work's reception to that of an evolving literary criticism. *Catch-22* was in many ways ahead of its time, challenging its readers whose expectations lay firmly within the realistic tradition of American fiction and who had yet to learn the necessary critical skills to comprehend its unconventionality and subversive humor.

DELIA CAPAROSO KONZETT

Further Reading

Brustein, Robert, "The Logic of Survival in a Lunatic World," *New Republic* 145 (13 November 1961); reprinted in *Critical Essays on Joseph Heller,* edited by James Nagel, Boston: G.K. Hall, 1984

Harris, Charles B., *Contemporary American Novelists of the Absurd,* New Haven, Connecticut: College and University Press, 1971

Hassan, Ihab, "Laughter in the Dark: The New Voice in American Fiction," *American Scholar* 33 (Autumn 1964)

Karl, Frederick R., "Joseph Heller's *Catch-22:* Only Fools Walk in Darkness," in *Contemporary American Novelists,* edited by Harry T. Moore, Carbondale: Southern Illinois University Press, 1964

Merrill, Robert, *Joseph Heller,* Boston: Twayne, 1987

Nagel, James, editor, *Critical Essays on Joseph Heller,* Boston: G.K. Hall, 1984

Pinsker, Sanford, *Understanding Joseph Heller,* Columbia: University of South Carolina Press, 1991

Ruderman, Judith, *Joseph Heller,* New York: Continuum, 1991

Seed, David, *The Fiction of Joseph Heller: Against the Grain,* London: Macmillan, and New York: St. Martin's Press, 1989

Sorkin, Adam J., editor, *Conversations with Joseph Heller,* Jackson: University Press of Mississippi, 1993

Tanner, Tony, *City of Words: American Fiction 1950–1970,* London: Cape, and New York: Harper and Row, 1971

The Catcher in the Rye by J.D. Salinger

1951

Since its publication in 1951, J.D. Salinger's *The Catcher in the Rye* has become one of the most widely read and controversial post–World War II American novels. Attempts—sometimes successful—to ban the novel have done little to diminish its popularity. Considering the continuing disparity between supporters and critics of the book, the novel's initial reception was surprisingly lukewarm. Apart from a few critics—mostly in New York—who had become familiar with Salinger's earlier short fiction and felt that he successfully reflected life in the city, responses to the novel were often less than ecstatic, although many still found much in it to admire, and others found much to disparage. While some praised its humor, style, and insights into the life of a teenage boy growing up in an unfriendly society full of "phonies," others found the novel simplistic, lacking focus, morally bankrupt, or even obscene. Despite this initial mixed critical reaction, the novel sold fairly well and over time has made deep inroads into the literary consciousness of American culture.

Salinger's narrator and main character, Holden Caulfield, has his origin in a number of Salinger's earlier short stories. A character with the same name first appears in print in 1944 in "The Last Day of the Furlough," although it appears that Salinger had been toying with a character of that name for a number of years prior to that. It isn't until the story "I'm Crazy" (1945) that readers first see a Holden who has many of the same experiences as the Holden Caulfield in the final novel. In 1946, a slightly shorter, novella-length version of *The Catcher in the Rye* was accepted for publication by *The New Yorker,* but the book was subsequently withdrawn by Salinger. Although some of Holden's experiences in the earlier works are similar to those in the final version, by 1951 the sensitivities of the character had changed significantly. As Warren French (1988) notes in *J.D. Salinger, Revisited,* Holden is no longer the apologetic misfit doomed to the undistinguished life of "I'm Crazy"; in *The Catcher in the Rye* he has "learned to transcend the morons and show his compassion for them by generous gestures."

Often read as a quest narrative, as a religious metaphor, or as a scathing critique of American capitalism, *The Catcher in the Rye* fits in most clearly with the tradition of the novel of development, the Bildungsroman. Like Charles Dickens' *David Copperfield* (1850), Mark Twain's *The Adventures of Huckleberry Finn* (1884), and James Joyce's *A Portrait of the Artist as a Young Man* (1916), Salinger's novel depicts a boy coming of age in a society that he finds more and more alienating. In each of these stories, the reader watches a young man's attempts to understand and respond to the world around him. (It should be noted that *Catcher,* unlike the novels just cited and unlike the traditional Bildungsroman, restricts its timeframe of narrated events to just a few days in the life of the protagonist.) Holden's story is both a personal reflection and a larger cultural critique, and the combination of the two has helped secure its place in the development of the 20th-century American novel.

The story of the three days after Holden leaves Pencey Prep, a boarding school from which he has been expelled, is told with honesty and irreverence. Salinger shows Holden's frustration with himself and the world through a series of interactions with people he meets during his trip to New York. His interactions with these people are sometimes compassionate and other times cruel, and his immediate reflections on his behavior help to foreground his concerns about himself and the world around him. However, unlike many other Bildungsromane, his introspections and experiences do not lead to dramatic changes in his behavior, and this is often as frustrating for him as it is for the reader. Holden wants to be the catcher of all the kids in the world—to keep them from harm—and yet he feels impotent toward his own inability to change things. Holden, like Joyce's Stephen Dedalus or even William Faulkner's Quentin Compson, questions his own physical, emotional, and psychological abilities, and is disturbed by what he finds. Like the struggles of these other characters, Holden's internal conflicts represent a broader, more general criticism of the lack of honesty and compassion Salinger sees in the conservative, class-conscious world of 1950s American culture.

Many parallels have been made between Twain's use of an impudent and naive Huck Finn to criticize 19th-century America and Holden's reflections on the realities behind the perceived ease, comfort, and prosperity of post–World War II America. Like Huck's thoughts, Holden's reflections on his life are uncensored by an adult perspective, and part of the complexity of the novel is watching him, a year after the events of the story, try to come to terms with the experiences he is narrating—although it is not clear that he ever does. But unlike *The Adventures of Huckleberry Finn*, there is no voice behind *The Catcher in the Rye* warning readers not to find a motive, moral, or plot; Salinger does not guide his readers toward a specific critical satire as Twain does. When Huck chooses to help Jim, thereby breaking the moral laws (or lack thereof) of the culture that has enslaved him, he makes what readers know is the right decision; in part, Twain uses Huck to make a larger cultural critique. Similarly, novels in the Bildungsroman tradition often have engaged in broader cultural critiques by having the innocent main character reflect, often naively, on the problems around him. This is true, to an extent, with Holden as well, but unlike a character such as Stephen Dedalus, it is not clear that Holden has grown or developed much by the end of the novel—and in many respects this might be the point of the book. His perspective on the events of the previous December has changed little if any. Salinger's resistance to creating a clear moral direction for Holden—and ultimately for the novel—is aided by the use of retrospective, first-person narrative. Every so often the reader is reminded that Holden is telling these events from a hospital one year after the events of the story. The reason for his hospital stay is unclear, but the narrative perspective creates an expectation in the reader of some evaluative reflection on the events of the novel, or even of some clear account of how Holden ends up in the hospital. But this reflection is never revealed, and in the end the reader is left wondering, like Holden, what to think about it all.

The Catcher in the Rye's influence on the novel form may be seen in many of the novels that come after it. The frustration—found in numerous postmodern novels—with our inability finally to define foundations and truths for our culture may be felt in its earliest stages in Salinger's book. Its choices of technique, and its representation of the anxiety and anger of growing up, may also be seen in the work of novelists as varied as Jamaica Kincaid, Dorothy Allison, and Kaye Gibbons. Finally, *The Catcher in the Rye*'s most enduring influence owes to its accessibility and its voice, and to the strength of its observations on the life of a young man in post–World War II America.

EDWARD MALONEY

Further Reading

Bloom, Harold, editor, *J.D. Salinger,* New York: Chelsea House, 1987

French, Warren, *J.D. Salinger, Revisited,* Boston: Twayne, 1988

Gwynn, Frederick L., and Joseph L. Blotner, *The Fiction of J.D. Salinger,* Pittsburgh, Pennsylvania: University of Pittsburgh Press, 1958

Laser, Marvin, and Norman Fruman, editors, *Studies in J.D. Salinger,* New York: Odyssey Press, 1963

McSweeney, Kerry, "Salinger Revisited," *Critical Inquiry* 20:1 (Spring 1978)

Miller, James, *J.D. Salinger,* Minneapolis: University of Minnesota Press, 1965

Modern Fiction Studies 12:3 (Autumn 1966), J.D. Salinger special issue

Nadel, Alan, "Rhetoric, Sanity, and the Cold War: The Significance of Holden Caulfield's Testimony," *The Centennial Review* 32:4 (Fall 1988)

Ohmann, Carol, and Robert Ohmann, "Reviewers, Critics, and *The Catcher in the Rye*," *Critical Inquiry* 3 (Autumn 1976)

Pinsker, Sanford, *"The Catcher in the Rye": Innocence Under Pressure,* New York: Twayne, 1993

Salzberg, Joel, editor, *Critical Essays on Salinger's "The Catcher in the Rye,"* Boston: G.K. Hall, 1990

Salzman, Jack, editor, *New Essays on "The Catcher in the Rye,"* Cambridge and New York: Cambridge University Press, 1991

Willa Cather 1873–1947

United States

Willa Cather's literary career has been the subject of scholarly debate since she began publishing in 1903. Cather authored 12 novels, the most popular of which include *My Ántonia* (1918), *O Pioneers!* (1913), *The Song of the Lark* (1915), and *Death Comes for the Archbishop* (1927). Various critics have placed Cather among feminist writers, antifeminist writers, and even lesbian writers. Although much scholarly attention has focused on Cather's sexuality, and its latent or overt presence in her narratives, this criticism has tended to focus on what lies beneath the texts rather than on the texts themselves. Coupled with this politicized interpretation of Cather's texts is the difficulty critics have encountered in placing her work in the context of the literary canon; her work defies easy categorization as realism, modernism, or naturalism. Because Cather is not easily classified, she is often left out of discussions of 20th-century literature.

Traditionally, critics have considered Cather a regionalist whose primary contribution to the novel form, and to American letters in general, was her record of life during frontier development in the Midwest. Cather, who was known as the great muse of the Midwest, was strongly influenced and advised by Sarah Orne Jewett, one of a number of "marginal" late 19th-century women writers that also included Kate Chopin and Mary E. Wilkins Freeman. Much of Cather's fiction is drawn from her experiences in Nebraska, where her family moved when she was nine. This perspective allowed Cather to explore the "smooth, unreal conventions about little girls" and the roles they were expected to fulfill when they reached adulthood. Some of Cather's fiction shows women fulfilling their expected roles, as in the case of Ántonia Shimerda (in *My Ántonia*), who ultimately finds contentment as a wife and mother. Yet as Sharon O'Brien has argued, Cather herself rejected the traditional female role prescribed by her own mother, by popular women's fiction, and by the society in which she was raised (see O'Brien, 1987). Accordingly, Alexandra Bergson (in *O Pioneers!*), as head of her family, runs the family farm against the wishes of her brothers, who demand that it either be sold or that they be allowed to manage it themselves. Alexandra refuses, choosing instead to assume the "unwomanly" roles of administrator, planner, and farmer.

Cather's contemporaries were divided in their opinions of Cather's accomplishments. Ernest Hemingway, in a letter to critic Edmund Wilson, expressed disdain at Cather's having received the Pulitzer Prize for fiction for *One of Ours* (1922), remarking that Cather must have drawn the battlefield scene from the film *Birth of a Nation.* However, F. Scott Fitzgerald admired Cather to the point of what Joan Acocella (1995) calls "self-admitted plagiarism," and William Faulkner praised Cather as "one of the foremost American novelists." While literary critics, during and after Cather's career, have tried to define her writings as calls-to-arms for critics with politicized agendas, the beauty and value of Cather's writing come from her recognition of the "enduring qualities of the land and the value of human union with it" (see Magill, 1994).

When looking beyond these politicized examinations of Cather's writing, her contribution to the novel form becomes clear. Cather repeatedly returns to three issues: the struggle of immigrants, as James Woodress (1981) has argued, to "come to terms with the land," which serves as a metaphor for the "American westering experience"; the conflict between land and civilization, and the destructive nature of materialism; and the "tug-of-war between the East and the western prairie" (see Magill, 1994). Cather's novels, such as *My Ántonia* and *O Pioneers!,* which take place in Nebraska, as well as *Death Comes for the Archbishop,* set in the New Mexico Territory, illustrate her efforts to reconcile "the central urges toward land and toward art, or civilization" (see Magill, 1994). Cather was torn between her love for the Nebraska plains, which constantly beckoned to her, and, according to critic Deborah Carlin (1991), finding these same plains "unequivocally antithetical to art and . . . to the sensibilities of the artist."

Another of Cather's major contributions to the novel lies in the simplicity of her prose. Although not clearly aligned with either the realist or modernist novel, Cather's fiction has been universally acknowledged for its clarity and simplicity, yet her writing is simultaneously subtle and filled with allusion. Joan Acocella (1995) argues that Cather uses direct language to illustrate that human beings are "permanently exiled from some realm of happiness which they nevertheless remembered and kept in view," and that "the dream [of this happiness] is still there; we just can't have it." Cather does not wrap up the world in pretty little packages, nor does she present women as one-dimensional subjects. Instead, Cather addresses a broad range of issues from the point of view of a woman pioneer in a literary world of male writers.

Suzanne D. Green

Biography

Born in Back Creek Valley, near Winchester, Virginia, 7 December 1873; moved with her family to a farm near Red Cloud, Nebraska, 1883. Attended Red Cloud High School, graduated 1890; Latin School, Lincoln, Nebraska, 1890–91; University of Nebraska, Lincoln, 1891–95, A.B. 1895. Wrote column for the Lincoln *State Journal,* 1893–95; editorial staff member, *Home Monthly,* Pittsburgh, Pennsylvania, 1896–97; telegraph editor and theatre critic, Pittsburgh *Daily Leader,* 1897–1901; Latin and English teacher, Central High School, Pittsburgh, 1901–03; English teacher, Allegheny High School, Pittsburgh, 1903–06; editor, *McClure's* magazine, New York, 1906–11; began writing full-time in 1912. Died 24 April 1947.

Novels by Cather

Alexander's Bridge, 1912; as *Alexander's Bridges,* 1912
O Pioneers!, 1913
The Song of the Lark, 1915
My Ántonia, 1918
One of Ours, 1922
A Lost Lady, 1923
The Professor's House, 1925
My Mortal Enemy, 1926
Death Comes for the Archbishop, 1927
Shadows on the Rock, 1931
Lucy Gayheart, 1935
Novels and Stories, 13 vols., 1937–41
Sapphira and the Slave Girl, 1940

Other Writings: journalism, short stories, poetry, essays on writing.

Further Reading

Acocella, Joan, "Cather and the Academy," *New Yorker* 27 (November 1995)
Carlin, Deborah, "Willa Cather," in *Modern American Women Writers,* edited by Elaine Showalter, Lea Baechler, and A. Walton Litz, New York: Scribner, 1991
Donovan, Josephine, *After the Fall: The Demeter-Persephone Myth in Wharton, Cather, and Glasgow,* University Park: Pennsylvania State University Press, 1989
Gerber, Philip, *Willa Cather,* Boston: Twayne, 1975; revised edition, New York: Twayne, and London: Prentice-Hall, 1995
Lee, Hermione, *Willa Cather: A Life Saved Up,* London: Virago, 1989
Magill, Frank N., editor, *Great Women Writers,* New York: Holt, and London: Hale, 1994

Nettels, Elsa, *Language and Gender in American Fiction: Howells, James, Wharton, and Cather,* Charlottesville: University Press of Virginia, and London: Macmillan, 1997

O'Brien, Sharon, *Willa Cather: The Emerging Voice,* New York: Oxford University Press, 1987

Reynolds, Guy, *Willa Cather in Context: Progress, Race,* *Empire,* New York: St. Martin's Press, and London: Macmillan 1996

Rosowski, Susan J., *The Voyage Perilous: Willa Cather's Romanticism,* Lincoln: University of Nebraska Press, 1986

Woodress, James, "Willa Cather," in *Dictionary of Literary Biography: American Novelists, 1910–1945,* edited by James J. Martine, Detroit, Michigan: Gale Research, 1981

Camilo José Cela 1916–

Spanish

Camilo José Cela has frequently emphasized his experimentalism and constant variation of novelistic form. While his half-dozen controversial early novels brought him fame, Cela also authored scores of essays, short-story collections, poetry, some theatrical pieces, criticism, memoirs, philology, and many unclassifiable works. Often the latter seem to be spin-offs of his narratives, amplifying settings or further developing characters only glimpsed in prior fictional appearances. Significant examples are the seven volumes of *Nuevas escenas matritenses* (1965–66; New Scenes of Madrid), *costumbrista* sketches of manners, and several other series, including *Apuntes carpetovetónicos* (1965; Mountain Sketches), *Los viejos amigos* (1960–61; Old Friends), and *Historia de España: Los ciegos, Los tontos* (1958; Spanish History: The Blind, The Idiots). Other miscellaneous works expand his fiction's prominent erotic vein, including the three-volume *Enciclopedia del erotismo* (1982–86) and the two volumes of the truncated *Diccionario secreto* (1968–72)—esoteric investigations of the truculent or erudite origins of the obscenities liberally integrated into his literary language.

Cela achieved instant notoriety with *La familia de Pascual Duarte* (1942; The Family of Pascual Duarte), his most famous and popular work and the one most translated and critically favored. Although often compared with Albert Camus' *L'Étranger* (1942; The Stranger), the only similarity is that both novels are the purported "confession" of a condemned prisoner awaiting execution. Pascual, an ignorant, impoverished Extremaduran peasant (a symbolic scapegoat and victim of social determinism), recites his crimes—violent murders and atrocities—in matter-of-fact understatement. The style spawned a flood of novelistic imitations in the postwar movement know as *tremendismo.*

Pascual is Cela's only fully developed character, based on the 16th-century picaresque novel, an autobiographical recounting of the loss of innocence that serves as a vehicle of social satire. He returns to the picaresque tradition in *Nuevas andanzas y desventuras de Lazarillo de Tormes* (1944; New Wanderings and Misadventures of Lazarillo de Tormes). This novel resuscitates the rogue whose sly misdeeds launched the genre and sends him out on Spain's roads in the 20th century. The result is reminiscent not only of the picaresque but of Cadalso's *Cartas marruecas* (c. 1774) or Montesquieu's *Lettres persanes* (1721). A hybrid form close to Cela's many travel books, this third novel is his least successful.

Pabellón de reposo (1943; Rest Home) employs multiple autobiographical narrative perspectives, being ostensibly the diaries of several patients terminally ill with tuberculosis, a disease for which Cela himself was twice confined to a sanatorium. Identifying the diarists only by room number, this novel offers a clear example of Cela's "dehumanization" of his characters and emphasizes the indifference of the strong and healthy—including doctors and nurses—who callously laugh at suffering and quickly consign the dead to oblivion. Psychologically violent, *Rest Home* disconcerted readers of *The Family of Pascual Duarte* and achieved limited success, as was also the case with *Mrs. Caldwell habla con su hijo* (1953; Mrs. Caldwell Speaks to Her Son), Cela's personal favorite, also set in a sanatorium. Employing a pseudo-autobiographical perspective, the text features a one-way dialogue in the second person as the protagonist addresses her son. The radically experimental format comprises some 200 brief "chapters," including poems, lyric prose, and surrealistic fragments, slowly revealing that Mrs. Caldwell is totally unbalanced and her son long since dead.

La colmena (1951; The Hive), considered Cela's masterpiece, took more than five years to write, in contrast to the rapidity with which he produced his previous novels. Experiments here include the use of collage and simultaneity (instead of plot) and a collective protagonist made up of some 250 to 360 characters (the count is bedeviled by the fact that some have several names). Most of the characters are sketchy, shadowy caricatures. The five parts of the novel portray postwar Madrid from five focal points during a three-day period in the winter of 1943.

Nobel prize citations (1989) stressed *The Hive* and *The Family of Pascual Duarte* to the virtual exclusion of Cela's remaining works, as do most critics. They are, however, of considerable interest. *La catira* (1955), set in Venezuela and incorporating Cela's observations of local dialect, purports to be a biography of the female protagonist (who recalls Rómulo Gallegos' *Doña Bárbara*) but shocks with its catalog of horrible deaths, sexual aberrations, and deviant crimes. Rather dull by contrast is *Tobogán de hambrientos* (1962; Bobsled of the Starving), consisting entirely of character description and subterranean connections between characters, without action or sequentiality. These minor novels end Cela's "first period"; a new and still more experimental phase began in 1969.

San Camilo, 1936 (1969) and Oficio de tinieblas, 5 (1973; Office of Darkness) are written largely in the second person, as was Mrs. Caldwell Speaks to Her Son. San Camilo, 1936, an interminable monologue by the protagonist-narrator, re-creates events in Madrid during the week preceding the outbreak of the Spanish Civil War, using techniques found in John dos Passos' Manhattan Transfer (newspaper clippings, radio commercials, signs from businesses) to convey the capital's confusion, demoralization, and near chaos. Oficio de tinieblas, 5, comprising almost 1,200 "monads" ranging from a few words to three pages in length, is an atemporal anti-novel without protagonist, plot, character delineation or development, identifiable setting, or sustained action or sequentiality. It is unified only by the reiterated motifs of boredom, absurdity, death, sexuality, bestiality, violence, fear, betrayal, defeat, pain, and excrement, which are interrupted by unexpected lyric sequences. Upon publishing Oficio, Cela publicly "abdicated" his novelist status and did not return to the genre for nearly a decade. Mazurca para dos muertos (1983; Mazurka for Two Dead Men) employs lyric interludes as counterpoint to a pseudomythic re-creation of the civil war in rural Galicia through the portrayal of the conflict and death of two emblematic antagonists.

Cela's last three novels (Cristo versus Arizona, 1988; El asesinato del perdedor [1994; The Murder of the Loser]; La cruz de San Andrés [1994; St. Andrew's Cross]) all intensify and exaggerate the Eros and Thanatos themes characterizing his earlier works, all dredge the depths of human depravity, and all are fully postmodern, using unreliable, limited narrators who unwrite and rewrite the text. Lacking plot or sequential, sustained action, all three novels reiterate certain key episodes with minor variations—as did Mazurka—blurring outlines, confusing "facts," and confounding motivations. His somewhat tongue-in-cheek definition of the genre—"Novel is everything that says 'novel' underneath the title"—appears well exemplified by the corpus of his 13 long novels.

JANET PÉREZ

See also Hive

Biography
Born in Iria Flavia, la Coruña, 11 May 1916. Attended the University of Madrid, 1933–36, 1939–43. Served in Franco's forces, 1936–39: Corporal. Worked as freelance writer in Madrid until 1954, then in Mallorca; founder, Papeles de Son Armadans, 1956–79. Awarded Nobel prize for literature, 1989.

Novels by Cela
La familia de Pascual Duarte, 1942; as Pascual Duarte's Family, translated by John Marks, 1946; as The Family of Pascual Duarte, translated by Anthony Kerrigan, 1964
Pabellón de reposo, 1943; as Rest Home, translated by Herma Briffault, 1961
Nuevas andanzas y desventuras de Lazarillo de Tormes [New Wanderings and Misadventures of Lazarillo de Tormes], 1944
La colmena, 1951; as The Hive, translated by J.M. Cohen, 1953
Mrs. Caldwell habla con su hijo, 1953; as Mrs. Caldwell Speaks to Her Son, translated by J.S. Bernstein, 1968
La catira, 1955
Tobogán de hambrientos [Bobsled of the Starving], 1962
San Camilo, 1936: Vísperas, festividad y octava de San Camilo del año 1936 en Madrid, 1969; as San Camilo, 1936: The Eve, Feast and Octave of St. Camillus of the Year 1936 in Madrid, translated by J.H.R. Holt, 1992
Oficio de tinieblas, 5 [Office of Darkness], 1973
Mazurca para dos muertos, 1983; as Mazurka for Two Dead Men, translated by Patricia Haugaard, 1993
Cristo versus Arizona, 1988
El asesinato del perdedor [The Murder of the Loser], 1994
La cruz de San Andrés [St. Andrew's Cross], 1994

Other Writings: nearly 100 in all, including novelettes, short stories, poetry and ballads, memoirs, travel books, essays, criticism, philology, journalism, modern renderings of Old Spanish classics, vignettes and sketches, texts for art books and volumes of photographs, an oratorio, and numerous works beyond classification.

Further Reading
Foster, David W., Forms of the Novel in the Work of Camilo José Cela, Columbia: University of Missouri Press, 1967
Ilie, Paul, La novelística de Camilo José Cela, Madrid: Gredos, 1963; 3rd edition, 1978
Insula 45:518–19 (1990), special issue on Cela
Kirsner, Robert, The Novels and Travels of Camilo José Cela, Chapel Hill: University of North Carolina Press, 1963
McPheeters, D.W., Camilo José Cela, New York: Twayne, 1969
Review of Contemporary Fiction 4:3 (Fall 1984), special issue on Cela
Roy, Joaquín, editor, Camilo José Cela: Homage to a Nobel Prize, Coral Gables, Florida: University of Miami Press, 1991
Suárez Solis, Sara, El léxico de Camilo José Cela, Madrid: Alfaguara, 1969
Zamora Vicente, Alonso, Camilo José Cela: Acercamiento a un escritor, Madrid: Gredos, 1962

La Celestina by Fernando de Rojas

1499/1502

La Celestina is a curious work. Although it is more properly classified as a drama, it has been nominated as the first European novel and, in fact, has had a significant influence on prose fiction.

La Celestina first appeared in print with the title *Comedia de Calisto y Melibea* (Comedy of Calisto and Melibea) in Burgos, probably in 1499 (there is uncertainty about the date, place of publication, and even the existence of some of the early editions). An acrostic formed by the first letters of the first lines of an introductory poem identified the author as Fernando de Rojas, a native of Puebla de Montalbán in the province of Toledo. A second version, perhaps of 1502, inserted five new acts near the end, bringing the total number to 21, and changed the title from *Comedia* to *Tragicomedia*. The young lovers Calisto and Melibea were overshadowed by the go-between Celestina, whose name eventually became the title of the work. *La Celestina* was immensely popular; it was reprinted often and translated into the major European languages. Rojas spent the rest of his life practicing law in Talavera de la Reina, where he died in 1541, apparently without having written anything else.

In the letter to a friend that serves as a prologue, Rojas claims that he found an anonymous manuscript copy of the first act and decided to take a little time off from his legal studies in order to complete it. Most scholars have accepted Rojas' statement that he was not the author of the first act, which is much longer than any of the others and differs not only in language and style but also in the authors cited or alluded to.

The plot structure of *La Celestina*, already foreshadowed in the first act by the anonymous author, is essentially that of Roman comedy, which Northrop Frye calls "less a form than a formula" (*Anatomy of Criticism,* 1957). It may be summed up as "boy meets girl; boy loses girl; boy gets girl." To this nucleus Rojas adds a sobering postscript: everyone dies. Calisto is killed by falling from a ladder as he leaves Melibea's garden, and she, overcome by grief, jumps to her death from a tower. The old procuress Celestina who brings Calisto and Melibea together is eventually murdered by Calisto's servants Sempronio and Pármeno for refusing to share her gains. The killers are promptly captured and executed as her murderers.

Although it was clearly never meant for performance, *La Celestina* is nevertheless indubitably a dramatic work. Its ultimate sources are Roman comedy, in particular the plays of Terence, and medieval Latin elegiac comedy, with perhaps a special debt to the *Pamphilus,* which gives a dramatic form to the teachings of Ovid's *Ars amatoria* (*The Art of Love*). The more immediate source is humanistic comedy, long prose works in dramatic form that are not intended for the stage. The genre was cultivated both in Latin and in such vernacular masterpieces as the Italian, or rather Venetian, *La Venexiana,* which bears a striking resemblance to *La Celestina.*

Both Rojas and the anonymous author of the first act use their pseudo-dramatic form with enormous ingenuity, establishing the physical setting of the action and the movements of the actors by incorporating stage directions in the dialogue. As María Rosa Lida de Malkiel points out, "the action projected in *The Celestina* is not the uninterrupted flow of reality," but a selection of incidents separated by intervals that allow the characters time to change (see Lida de Malkiel, 1961).

Rojas and the first author use a variety of devices to expose the distance between the characters' thoughts and their words. Celestina displays both enormous psychological insight and a mastery of the rhetorical techniques of persuasion that may owe something to Rojas' training as a lawyer, for example in her successful attempt to gain Pármeno's help by playing upon her friendship with his dead mother. Here, and in many other references to her own past, she becomes a fully rounded character whose experiences are not confined to the limited time-span of the action. An additional complexity derives from the fact that it is often impossible to decide whether she is remembering something that actually happened or inventing a story that will persuade her listener to do what she wants. Another important feature of the text is Rojas' serious presentation of Calisto's servants and in particular of the prostitutes Elicia and Areúsa, rare in a period when lower-class characters were usually considered only as comic types and not as individuals.

Such realistic elements as its social inclusiveness and psychological depth are counterbalanced by other features that demonstrate indifference to verisimilitude. The authors make elaborate use of asides, which are half-overheard and must then be rephrased in a way that will both protect the speaker and satisfy the listener. As in Roman comedy, all the characters address each other with the familiar pronoun *tú,* in defiance of the rigidly hierarchical society of 15th-century Spain. The characters display an erudition that is not always in keeping with their social station and education. Their fondness for citing moralizing maxims, largely drawn from the Latin works of Petrarch, often highlights a disparity between their words and their actions.

La Celestina primarily left a mark on Spanish Renaissance theatre. Juan del Encina, Lope de Vega, and other playwrights imitated its realistic representations of everyday life and freely borrowed plot elements and characters from the earlier work. More significantly for our purposes, *La Celestina* also exerted an important influence on the novel, making an immediate contribution to the development of the picaresque. The vivid and psychologically realistic representations of lower-class, even disreputable, characters, which is new in *La Celestina,* will later emerge as one of the distinguishing features of the picaresque tradition. Celestina's ironic running commentary—which undercuts social pieties as well as the tragic worldview implied by the book's fatalistic ending—is translated into the *pícaro*'s disillusionment with humanity and the often biting social satire it gives rise to. *La Celestina*'s contributions to the realistic novel, if not sufficient to qualify it for the label of "first European novel," are nevertheless substantial enough to make it one of the more important precursor texts.

THOMAS R. HART

Further Reading

Bataillon, Marcel, *"La Célestine" selon Fernando de Rojas,* Paris: Didier, 1961

Dunn, Peter N., *Fernando de Rojas,* Boston: Twayne, 1975

Gilman, Stephen, *The Spain of Fernando de Rojas: The Intellectual and Social Landscape of "La Celestina,"* Princeton, New Jersey: Princeton University Press, 1972

Lida de Malkiel, María Rosa, *La originalidad artística de "La Celestina,"* Buenos Aires: Editorial Universitaria de Buenos Aires, 1962; 2nd edition, 1970

Lida de Malkiel, María Rosa, *Two Spanish Masterpieces: The "Book of Good Love" and "The Celestina,"* Urbana: University of Illinois Press, 1961

Russell, P.E., *Temas de "La Celestina" y otros estudios: Del "Cid" al "Quijote,"* Barcelona: Ariel, 1978

Louis-Ferdinand Céline 1894–1961

French

Louis-Ferdinand Céline was a literary maverick who opened radically new directions for the novel. Considered at first an heir of Zola's naturalism, Céline invented new forms of writing, in particular through his use of a colloquial, fragmented, and non-literary language. Like Marcel Proust, Céline wrote autobiographical novels, but his voice is that of a disgruntled, resentful, and angry grouser. A medical doctor by training, Céline often portrayed the life, and death, of the Parisian working class. His novels reject all forms of polite or academic literature and remain anti-establishment and anarchistic to the core. Céline was a satirist who mocked the institutions of contemporary society, who engaged in some of the most hateful politics of our century, and who continually pushed the limits of what literature can do.

Céline's first novel, *Voyage au bout de la nuit* (1932; *Journey to the End of the Night*), remains one of the 20th century's seminal works of fiction. Narrated in the first person, the novel recounts the picaresque adventures of a young innocent, Ferdinand Bardamu, as he confronts the horror, the misery, and the despair of the world. Through Bardamu's addled vision the text denounces war, nationalism, colonialism, capitalism, and the terrible monotony of everyday life. *Journey to the End of the Night* is the work of a moralist who draws upon a number of sources: from Voltaire's *Candide* (1759) to Conrad's "Heart of Darkness" (1902), from Sigmund Freud to the French writers of the populist movement. But Céline is also a profoundly original author who combines despair, black humor, and moments of sublime lyricism to create what he called an "emotive symphony."

Four years after the publication of his first novel, Céline released *Mort à crédit* (1936; *Death on the Installment Plan*), a novel that represents a quantum leap forward in Céline's writing. Set during the author's childhood in Paris, *Death on the Installment Plan* is a tale of failure: a family's economic failure, a scientist's failure to create a utopian society in turn-of-the-century France, the young narrator's failure at every enterprise he undertakes. The novel is also a major stylistic achievement. With *Death on the Installment Plan*, Céline created a polyphonic text by commingling argot with academic French, archaic linguistic forms with a medical vocabulary. Céline matched his work on the French language with a fragmentation of the syntax. In this second novel, he began to use his trademark three-dot style to break apart the traditional sentence. This stylistic transformation marked the creation of a new, self-conscious, and irremediably modern writing practice.

In the years preceding World War II, Céline interrupted his literary output to write some of the most vitriolic and hateful anti-Semitic tracts ever published in the French language. Trading his stylistic verve for racist slander, Céline first published *Mea Culpa* (1936), a short anti-Communist pamphlet, and then *Bagatelles pour un massacre* (1937; Trifles for a Massacre), *L'École des cadavres* (1938; The School of Cadavers), and *Les Beaux Draps* (1941; A Fine Mess). Céline's anti-Semitism as it appeared in the *Bagatelles pour un massacre* and *L'École des cadavres*, in particular, relied on vulgar racist stereotypes, falsified statistics, and an intense emotional commitment on the part of both writer and reader. Céline's present-day readers sometimes distinguish between the novelist and the ignominious anti-Semite. Indeed during the war, Céline published a novel, *Guignol's Band* (1944; *Guignol's Band*) that is set in London in 1914 and has little relation to the events in war-torn Europe. Still, while Céline's novels of this period never give way to racist diatribes, the style, the voice, the emotion, and the authorial persona in the novels are remarkably similar to what one finds in the pamphlets. Céline's reputation as well as his postwar fiction remain tainted by these texts.

After World War II, Céline wrote a series of novels in which he recounts his last days in Paris at the end of the war, his flight through Germany, his imprisonment in Denmark in the immediate postwar years, his trial for crimes of collaboration, and his return to France from 1952 until his death in 1961. The novels reactivate the autobiographical vein that Céline never really left but also constitute another major stylistic innovation. Céline felt that he could save his reputation by abandoning politics and devoting himself to what he called "pure style." The first of his postwar texts, *Féerie pour une autre fois* (1952; Fairy Tale for Another Time), is a stylistically complex novel in which Céline all but abandons realist modes of representation. As always with Céline, however, political considerations are never far removed, and the author's pure style reveals an attempt to rewrite the history of World War II and justify the positions he had taken in the 1930s.

Céline's final three novels, *D'un château à l'autre* (1957; *Castle to Castle*), *Nord* (1960; *North*), and *Rigodon* (1969; *Rigodon*), marked a literary comeback of sorts. Borrowing from the form of the medieval chronicle, Céline gives a personal and biting account of the final months of the war in Europe, while at the same time writing one of the great satires of postwar France. The text unhinges time and space as it moves quickly back and forth from war-torn Germany to the Deux Magots café in Paris, from Marshal Pétain to Richard Nixon's kitchen debate with Khrushchev. Céline's final novels, sometimes referred to as the German Trilogy, are written with a verve, an intimacy, and a musicality that place them among the strongest novels of postwar France. Weary of politics and of Parisian literary schools, Céline created works that reestablished his reputation as a master of the modern novel.

Céline's influence on other writers is immeasurable. In France, he directly inspired Jean-Paul Sartre, and one cannot imagine *La Nausée* (1938; *Nausea*) having been written without *Journey to the End of the Night*. In the 1960s, the writers at *Tel Quel* revived Céline as a model for postmodern textuality. Spanish writer Camilo José Cela and Uruguayan Juan Carlos Onetti have both spoken of Céline's importance to their writing. In the United States, Céline's influence has been acknowledged by several generations of writers, from Henry Miller and Kenneth Rexroth to William Burroughs, Allen Ginsberg, Jack Kerouac, Joseph Heller, Thomas Pynchon, Philip Roth, Maxine Hong Kingston, and Kurt Vonnegut.

It is perhaps one of the lasting paradoxes of modern times that a writer so thoroughly committed to stylistic innovation should also have been so closely involved in the horrors of our century. For all of his contradictions and paradoxes, Céline remains an inescapable presence in modern literature.

PHILIP WATTS

See also Journey to the End of the Night

Biography

Born Louise-Ferdinand Destouches in Courbevoie, France, 27 May 1894. Adopted the pseudonym Céline. Attended a school in Paris; Diepholz Volksschule in Germany, 1908; a school in Rochester, Kent, 1909; employed as a clerk in a silk shop, an errand boy in Paris and Nice, and an assistant to a goldsmith while studying for his baccalauréat; Rennes Medical School, 1919–24, qualified as a doctor 1924. Served in the French cavalry, 1912–15: sergeant; military medal; worked in French passport office, London, 1915; employed as a ship's doctor, 1939–40; trader for a French forestry company, West Africa, 1917; practicing doctor: in Rennes, then with League of Nations, 1925–28; in Clichy, 1928–38; in Bezons, 1940–44, Germany, 1944–45, and Denmark, 1945; imprisoned in Denmark, 1945–47; returned to France in 1950; found guilty of collaboration with Germany during World War II, and sentenced to one year in prison: pardoned in 1951; then lived in Meudon, near Paris. Died 1 July 1961.

Novels by Céline

Voyage au bout de la nuit, 1932; revised edition, 1952; as *Journey to the End of the Night*, translated by John H.P. Marks, 1934, revised edition, 1983; also translated by Ralph Manheim, 1988

Mort à crédit, 1936; as *Death on the Installment Plan*, translated by John H.P. Marks, 1938; also translated by Ralph Manheim, 1966; as *Death on Credit*, translated by Manheim, 1989

Guignol's Band, 1944; as *Guignol's Band*, translated by Bernard Frechtman and Jack T. Nile, 1954

Féerie pour une autre fois, 1952

D'un château à l'autre, 1957; as *Castle to Castle*, translated by Ralph Manheim, 1968

Nord, 1960; as *North*, translated by Ralph Manheim, 1972

Rigodon, 1969; as *Rigodon*, translated by Ralph Manheim, 1974

Other Writings: plays, pamphlets, letters.

Further Reading

Bellosta, Marie-Christine, *Céline, ou, L'art de la contradiction: Lecture de "Voyage au bout de la nuit,"* Paris: Presses Universitaires de France, 1990

Bonnefis, Philippe, *Céline: The Recall of the Birds*, Minneapolis: University of Minnesota Press, 1997

Dauphin, Jean-Pierre, and Pascal Fouché, *Bibliographie des écrits de Louis-Ferdinand Céline: 1918–1984*, Paris: Bibliothèque de Littérature Française Contemporaine de L'Université Paris 7, 1985

Godard, Henri, *Poétique de Céline*, Paris: Gallimard, 1985

Kaplan, Alice, *Reproductions of Banality: Fascism, Literature, and French Intellectual Life*, Minneapolis: University of Minnesota Press, 1986

Kristeva, Julia, *Powers of Horror: An Essay on Abjection*, New York: Columbia University Press, 1982

Murray, Jack, *The Landscapes of Alienation: Ideological Subversion in Kafka, Céline, and Onetti*, Stanford, California: Stanford University Press, 1991

Ostrovsky, Erika, *Céline and His Vision*, London: University of London Press, and New York: New York University Press, 1967

Richard, Jean-Pierre, *Nausée de Céline*, Montpellier: Fata Morgana, 1973

Scullion, Rosemarie, Philip H. Solomon, and Thomas C. Spear, editors, *Céline and the Politics of Difference*, Hanover, New Hampshire: University Press of New England, 1995

South Atlantic Quarterly 93:2 (Spring 1994), edited by Alice Kaplan and Philippe Roussin, special issue entitled *Céline, USA*

Watts, Philip, "Postmodern Céline," in *Céline and the Politics of Difference*, edited by Rosemarie Scullion, Philip H. Solomon, and Thomas C. Spear, Hanover, New Hampshire: University Press of New England, 1995

Censorship and the Novel

Keeping in mind Freud's observation that "The history of man is the history of his repression," one should note that censorship as a social function has always existed. In fact, it is as old as humanity. What have changed are its forms throughout history and its exercise in relation to various social organizations. In other words, it is not a question of society tolerating a state of absolute freedom (noncensorship) versus a state of absolute repression (censorship), as we tend to put it in modern terms, but rather the ways censorship operates in a sociocultural context. In this sense, the commonly shared view that censorship is a detestable practice that contradicts the bases of a democratic society no longer has the utility and worthy contribution to society it was considered to have in many past civilizations. In this perspective, ancient China is the most remarkable example, with a system of rules and customs that justified the nearly total authority of the government over the individual. Structured by Confucianism, the Chinese form of regulation of culture stressed the absolute necessity of submission to a social order based on hierarchy (cult of ancestors, observation of traditional rites, and respect of property) and control of expression (modesty in speech and respect of established teachings regulating education).

In the Western tradition, the notion of censorship as we know it originally refers to the role of the censor in Rome in the 5th century B.C. This highly esteemed officer's duty was to secure the harmony between the people and the state by regulating the values and morals of the community in accordance with the nature and interests of the government. However, a radical shift took place when philosophers and citizens began to question the function of the government. This shift corresponds to the new notions of the individual versus the community, private sphere versus public sphere (issues, it is worth noting, that would take center stage in the genre of the novel). It became increasingly clear that the consensus between the citizens and the central power was going to be substituted for individual affirmation of freedom. In the Anglo-American context, in the middle of the 17th century, the issue of censorship took the form of a decisive controversy between those who were in favor of the direct intervention of the state exercising what was called "previous restraints," that is to say, the review of manuscripts before their publication, and those who opposed such control. At the center of this debate, *Areopagitica* (1644), John Milton's famous essay, is still considered the exemplary argument against censorship.

Deeply rooted in the Christian tradition and its prevailing belief in the human being's ultimate redemption, Milton's view was centered on the idea that truth always overcomes error and that the condition for its triumph is the necessary confrontation between good and evil. Briefly, it is only on the basis of the exercise of freedom of expression and publication that truth and good can prevail:

> As therefore the state of man now is, what wisdom can there be to choose, what continence to forbear without the knowledge of evil? He that apprehend and consider vice with all her baits and seeming pleasures, and yet abstain, and yet distinguish, and yet prefer that which is truly better, he is the true wayfaring Christian. I cannot praise a fugitive and cloistered virtue, unexercised and unbreathed, that never sallies out and sees her adversary, but slinks out of the race where that immortal garland is to be run for, not without dust and heat. Assuredly we bring not innocence into the world, we bring impurity much rather; that which purifies is trial and trial is by what is contrary.

Leo Strauss (1952) summed up this evolution by suggesting that "the quarrel between the ancients and the moderns concerns eventually, and perhaps even from the beginning, the status of 'individuality'." On the other hand, the emergence of the novel as a dominant literary genre corresponds to the development of capitalism and the Industrial Revolution, and to the correlative status of the individual as well as to the new notion of the author in modern civilizations and their reshaping of cultural productions and roles. As a consequence, the social function of censorship has been related to the social function of the writer and the status of literature in a given society. Thus, it is not surprising that in the 19th century a work of art was appreciated on the basis of the effect it would have on ordinary citizens, and on the youth in particular. In this respect, it is important to note that throughout history the issue of censorship has been intrinsically linked not only to the question of freedom of expression but also to the question of obscenity and decency. In France the 1857 trial of Gustave Flaubert for the publication of *Madame Bovary* (1857) was paradigmatic of many famous cases worldwide that illustrate the contradiction between the necessity to protect simultaneously the values of the community and the free creation of the artist.

The case against Flaubert was that his novel attacked religious and moral values by directly exposing the predicament of an adulterous woman. Moreover, according to his prosecutors, his fundamental fault was to confront the reader with a text in which religious figures and sexual content were intertwined, a reproach very similar to the one on the basis of which, in a contemporary situation, Ayatollah Khomeini condemned Salman Rushdie to death for the writing of *The Satanic Verses* (1988). Flaubert's defense against the accusations of prosecutor Pinard was that the intention of the novelist prevails on the content alone because the exposition of Emma Bovary's sins was meant to educate rather than to debauch. Furthermore, the argument was made that realism constituted a new aesthetic and that a novel should be judged first for its artistic quality. In this perspective, it was argued that first, a work of art should not be evaluated on the basis of short passages but as an organically aesthetic and ethical whole, and second, a distinction should be made between strictly pornographic writings and genuine literary productions. Flaubert won the case on the basis of this distinction. In the United States, the 1933 trial of James Joyce's *Ulysses* (1922) was conducted along the same lines, thus reflecting the evolution of the definition of obscenity. In the ruling on whether *Ulysses* could enter the United States, the argument was based on the idea that Joyce's intent was not pornographic but rather to "show exactly how the minds of his characters operate." As Ellen S. Burt has argued in an article published in *Writing between the Lines: Censored* (a special issue of *Diacritics* 27:2 [1997]):

The case of *Ulysses* supports the contention that the censoring of obscenity operates according to a different logic than that of the censorship of philosophical texts. In the literary text, where knowledge of language is at stake, the representation of obscenity can be seen as necessary. The judge, representative censor, lifts the quarantine on *Ulysses* because he finds it to be good for linguistic hygiene: it purifies and reclaims the language for use where it can by quoting, and purges dirt where it cannot.

The cultural liberalization that took place during the 20th century—at least in democratic Western countries—would result in a revaluation of numerous works of art that were originally censored because they were considered obscene or subversive. However, because censorship exists and functions in a context, which is also the condition of existence of the text itself, both the censors and their victims are stuck in what Michael Holquist (1994) perceptively calls a "negotiation." A good example of this fluctuation may be seen in the way in which Charles Baudelaire's *Les fleurs du mal* (1861; *The Flowers of Evil*) was treated by two different French tribunals at two periods of time (initial condemnation was reversed in 1949) or in the various treatments of Henry Miller's novels in the United States (in 1973 a California court abandoned a 1966 ruling and stated that works "which portray sexual conduct in a patently offensive way, and which, taken as a whole, do not have serious literary, artistic, political or scientific value" could be banned).

In the context of communist regimes, until recently censorship was a matter of state intervention. Indeed, since the Soviet government has had the monopoly on import, sale, and distribution, locally it has exercised nearly complete control of the consumption of this literature inside the former USSR. This led to nearly total censorship of literary production. Under the Marxist regime, writers were confronted with a new series of dilemmas. First, they would be asked to complete the task initiated by the October 1917 revolution, in other words to generate a discourse that furthered the goal of creating a national identity that was anti-imperialist, and the project of creating a communist society. They were summoned to comply with the official ideology embodied by the Bolshevik Party. This compliance involved being requested to write for and address the masses' needs, and, consequently, to allow content to prevail over form, and to embrace the aesthetics of socialist-realism. As explained by Miklos Haraszti (1987):

> Society is the state's property. Art is the product of society. That part of Marxist tradition which emphasizes art's social aspects and political enthusiasms has led to the nationalization of art. Every artist is a state employee. All art is directed art. The economy has reached the peak of the development of monopolism in one heroic leap. Under socialism, the state is sole owner of aggregate capital and sole employer of the total workforce. It is also the guardian of knowledge and the supervisor of sensibility.

Therefore, in most communist regimes the attempt to exercise total control over the literary production led the party to create a Writers' Union. The aim of this body was to organize the activities of writers and to put them at the service of the community, that is to say, to illustrate the principles and to praise the actions of the government. This situation divided writers into two categories. On the one hand, there were those who generally had no talent, who would use any means to benefit from the privileges offered by the regime and who, therefore, gladly joined the party and the Writers' Union. They became the censors of the others or they wrote superficial and mediocre texts that followed the party line. On the other hand, the more authentic and socially critical writers were condemned either to silence, hard labor in concentration camps, or exile.

In the Middle East, until recent years, censorship has generally been exercised indirectly without the need for banning and imprisonment of those publishing abroad. As a writer, one was free to write and publish whatever one wanted; however, by means of its financial and commercial monopoly, the state could exert control by not buying one's books. As a result, one had no readers and one's books, for all purposes, did not exist in one's homeland. The way censorship is handled in Egypt is similar to the way it is dealt with in many Third World countries. Feminist writer and psychoanalyst Nawāl al-Saʿdāwī eloquently describes the Egyptian policy of censorship by introducing the idea of a "gray list." According to her perspective, the gray list is an indirect form of repression that combines the mechanisms that an Arab-Muslim authoritarian regime uses to maintain itself and the machinations needed to create a positive image of an aspiring democratic state for Western consumption. In this context, the artist or the thinker is neither totally free nor totally prisoner, even though he or she is more often repressed than free; he or she is not on a black list as is usually the case, but on the gray one.

Because of the structural dependence of censorship on its context, the obligation of the censor to comply with the rules of "negotiation" can easily be seen in what may be called selective censorship. Within the framework of selective censorship producers are treated differently in accordance with their fame, their national and international status, and the existence of relatively strong or weak support for their work within the government and society. An artist or writer may thus have his work censored or seized, and he can himself be arrested, imprisoned, or, in the present context, tortured or murdered. For example, in the last five years in Cairo, Muslim fundamentalists burned numerous copies of *The One Thousand and One Nights,* assassinated the novelist Farag Fuda, and attempted to kill Nobel prize winner Nagīb Mahfūz. The fluctuation of the repression process can also be seen in the different treatment given to writers by the Western media depending on whether they are Westerners or not. Being herself in a situation comparable to that of Salman Rushdie, Nawāl al-Saʿdāwī addressed the question of repression very eloquently in a 1993 interview:

> This is how the Rushdie affair is presented. On June 9, 1992, Farag Fouda [or Fuda], an Egyptian writer who believed in the separation of state and religion, was murdered. What does the West say about that? Nothing. Writers in Egypt are being threatened. . . . The West is indifferent to all of this, as if our lives are worth less. And I am angry and I speak to this question wherever I go. Our lives are as valuable as Salman Rushdie's, our writing is as good, sometimes better than Rushdie's. So why this?

In the tragic case of Algeria, the secular government in the past attacked the work, not the writer. Since the rise of Muslim fundamentalists in the late 1980s, a deadly shift has taken place. Muslim fundamentalists do not target the product but the producer. Their declared aim is the total eradication of art. In his article "Khomeini Shoots Writers," (in *Index on Censorship* 13:5 [1984]), Esmail Kho'i describes the fate of Iranian writers in the following terms: "The rule was that the Shah's regime was against the work, not against the author, against the book, not the writer. (. . .) But things are very different now. In its look-backward-move-backward attitude, Khomeinism goes back from effects to causes. Now we are faced with a regime that concerns itself essentially not with the work but with the author." The exercise of censorship and extreme repression in Algeria is similar to what has been happening in Iran since 1979.

In the opening essay of *Persecution and the Art of Writing* (1952), Leo Strauss bases his description of the process linking thought and its repression on two fundamental propositions. He claims that free speech and censorship are inseparable and that the existence of one conditions the existence of the other. Having established that they constitute a dyad, he explains that their relationship in the public sphere relies on how writers develop systems of interpretation to convey certain ideas. Strauss points to modern literary theory's privileging of the relationship between the writer and the reader. Indeed, articulating the postulates of reception theory, he argues that since censorship and free expression are inseparable, one of the central dimensions of literature is the art of publicly exposing that which is forbidden, a process he calls "writing between the lines." On this basis, using the examples of the Parmenides and of Gulliver's Houyhnhnms, he writes: "Persecution is therefore the indispensable condition for the highest efficiency of what may be called *logica equina*." The conclusion of this dialectical relationship between art and power is that censorship cannot eradicate free expression; however, because power cannot tolerate free expression, it must call for its repression. In this sense, following the Aesopian tradition, writers must use oblique language in order to resist and fight censorship.

Censorship has been understood for the most part as the state's control over cultural production. However, many critics in the postwar period have argued that other forms of censorship, such as market censorship, are comparable to the actions of the state. The Christian right's attacks on art in the United States in the 1980s and early 1990s, together with the Congressional moves to disempower and dismantle the National Endowment for the Arts, have generated a new set of debates about censorship in that country. What is understood is that the extreme right sought to repress cultural productions carrying a message of ethnic and sexual difference, targeting, for example, works by rappers, the photographer Robert Mapplethorpe, and Madonna's music videos. The right provided rhetoric to support the privatization of public space, the control of language and public images, and the promotion of "safe" art.

While many critics referred to this as new censorship, structurally it is exactly the same as the old censorship, that is, state control intervening in the liberal subject's absolute right to free expression. It appears that the dichotomy between the left's claim of the absolute freedom of the artist and the right's attempt to repress it is usually conceived in moral terms and is paradigmatic of the Western liberal oppositional categories used to describe censorship. This position views the relationship between art and censorship as either a bourgeois romantic oppo-

sition to political order or a corrupt collaboration by opportunistic *apparatchicks*. It leaves no room for what Michael Holquist (1994) calls "negotiation" in this process. Moreover, it does not take into account the fact that in Third World or socialist contexts, for example, the way certain intellectuals view their role vis-à-vis the state, society, and/or the people, determines their degree of cooperation with censorship mechanisms.

The problem with this Manichean vision is that it implies a notion of censorship that is ahistorical, that it posits that there is an essential distinction between the censor and the creator, or free mind. As Richard Burt (1994) rightly suggests:

> What counts as censorship is not always clear. Indeed, it is hard to see how one could call many contemporary cases censorship without either seriously distorting the traditional understanding of the term or redefining it to include so many practices—ranging from institutional regulation of free expression, market censorship, cutbacks in government funding for controversial art, boycotts, lawsuits, and marginalization and exclusion of artists based on their gender or race to "political correctness" in the university and the media—that the term is overwhelmed, even trivialized, its usefulness as a tool of cultural criticism called into question.

Recent events, not only in the United States but also in other parts of the world, show that one cannot seriously conceive the question of censorship along the lines of closed, distinct, conceptual categories expressing absolute oppositions. In other words, it is necessary to take the concept of censorship out of the realm of morality and put it into the world of history, and to displace it from the framework of philosophy to the context of culture.

HAFID GAFAITI

See also Copyright; Pornographic Novel

Further Reading

Abdallah, Anuar, editor, *For Rushdie: Essays by Arab and Muslim Writers in Defense of Free Speech*, New York: Braziller, 1994

Bourdieu, Pierre, "Censorship and the Imposition of Form," in *Language and Symbolic Power*, edited by John B. Thompson, Cambridge, Massachusetts: Harvard University Press, 1991

Burt, Richard, editor, *The Administration of Aesthetics: Censorship, Political Criticism, and the Public Sphere*, Minneapolis: University of Minnesota Press, 1994

Derrida, Jacques, "Declarations of Independence," *New Political Science* 15 (Summer 1986)

Diacritics 27:2 (1997), issue entitled *Writing between the Lines: Censored*, edited by George Van Den Abbeele

Ernst, Morris, and Alan Schwartz, *Censorship: The Search for the Obscene*, New York: Macmillan, 1964

Haraszti, Miklos, *The Velvet Prison: Artists Under State Socialism*, New York: Basic Books, 1987; London: Tauris, 1988

Holquist, Michael, editor, *Publications of the Modern Language Association of America* 109:1 (1994), issue entitled *Literature and Censorship*

Index on Censorship 13:5 (1984)

Jansen, Sue Curry, *Censorship: The Knot That Binds Power and Knowledge,* New York: Oxford University Press, 1988

Kant, Immanuel, *The Conflict of the Faculties,* translated by Mary J. Gregor, New York: Abaris Books, 1979

Levine, Michael G., *Writing through Repression: Literature, Censorship, Psychoanalysis,* Baltimore: Johns Hopkins University Press, 1994

Lewis, Felice, *Literature, Obscenity, and Law,* Carbondale: Southern Illinois University Press, 1976

Milton, John, *Areopagitica* and *Of Education,* in *Complete English Poems,* edited by Gordon Campbell, London: Dent, 1990

Post, Robert C., editor, *Censorship and Silencing: Practices of Cultural Regulation,* Los Angeles: Getty Research Institute, 1998

Strauss, Leo, *Persecution and the Art of Writing,* Glencoe, Illinois: Free Press, 1952

Zeisel, William, editor, *Censorship: 500 Years of Conflict,* New York: Oxford University Press, 1984

Central American Novel. *See* Latin American Novel: Central America

---

Miguel de Cervantes 1547–1616

Spanish

In the prologue to Part I of *Don Quixote*, Miguel de Cervantes records some good advice on writing fiction:

> Make sure that you express yourself in clear language, in simple, honest, and well-measured words, and make it sound good and cheerful, depicting your ideas as well as you possibly can and stating your thoughts in a straightforward and understandable manner. See to it also that, by reading your story, the sad be made to laugh, the cheerful even more so, the simple-minded not be puzzled, the intelligent admire your ideas, the serious not despise them and the wise praise them.

This statement reveals the basis of the tremendous success that *Don Quixote* (1605–15) and the *Novelas ejemplares* (1613; *Exemplary Novels*) enjoyed immediately after their publication. This success continued over the years as novelists adapted the unique formal and thematic concerns of these works to their own writing.

Clarity of language was not a common literary ideal in Cervantes' time. For most of Cervantes' contemporaries, the desire to show off their erudition was stronger than the desire to reach a large reading public. Cervantes' close acquaintance with many types of people, acquired through his work as a tax collector and his several stays in prison, enabled him to re-create speech habits very accurately and across an enormous social range. The intrusion of "common speech" into a literary context proved to be enormously popular with the contemporary reading public while also setting an important precedent for subsequent novelists. A text's literary qualities could now be founded on its realistic character rather than its stylistic complexity. Both English novelists of the 18th century and French novelists of the 19th century would pick up on this aspect of Cervantes' works in devising their own conceptions of the realist or naturalistic novel.

Cervantes' novels also significantly departed from contemporary literary genres by pitting the genres against each other within a single narrative framework. Both the picaresques and traditional romances of the time may be characterized as monologic, in that they operated within well-defined generic constraints and characterized a single point of view, either that of the cynical *pícaro* or the romantic idealist. The picaresque genre itself offers an implicit critique of the naiveté of traditional romantic views of Spanish society, but the object of the critique remains entirely outside of the picaresque narrative. Cervantes brought these two jarringly different views of Spanish society into close contact in *Don Quixote* and *Exemplary Novels*; by doing so he established the novel as a generically indeterminate form, one that could contain all genres.

This clash between literary genres was also perceived in thematic terms, as a clash between opposing views of the world. The German romantics in particular responded to the opposition between the picaresque and traditional romance narrative embodied by Sancho Panza and Don Quixote in *Don Quixote* as a universal clash between an idealist and a realist approach to life. Freidrich von Schelling felt that, on this basis, *Don Quixote* was the archetype of the modern novel. Goethe's conception of the

Bildungsroman may be seen as arising from the same interpretation of Cervantes' works. Goethe particularly praised *Exemplary Novels* as "a veritable treasury of delights and teachings" that were "composed according to the same principles which we employ . . . in the kind of writing with which we ourselves are engaged."

Novelists were similarly intrigued by the thematic possibilities offered by dramatizing the adventures of quixotic figures whose essential naiveté was tested upon exposure to harsh reality. In the novels of Henry Fielding and Daniel Defoe, for example, the quixotic figure offers a way to explore the relationship between the individual character and society as a whole. Fielding uses Parson Adams' essential naiveté in *Joseph Andrews* (1742) to reveal the essential depravity of English society, while Defoe concentrates in *Moll Flanders* (1722) on how a depraved society shapes individual character itself.

Cervantes was also influential because he made literature itself the subject of his novels' thematic concerns. In Part II of *Don Quixote,* Don Quixote and Sancho Panzo are made aware of the fact that someone has written an account of their adventures, and the characters are forced repeatedly to assert the difference between their "real" existence and their literary representations. In one of his *Exemplary Novels,* the Colloquy of the Dogs, Cervantes presents us with one character telling his life story to another, who comments upon and criticizes it. Furthermore, the Colloquy is nested within another story, The Deceitful Marriage, where it is actually a novel being read by one character while another character sleeps. By using these metafictional conceits, Cervantes demonstrates a sophisticated awareness of the artificiality of literary representation while also demonstrating how easy it is to confuse the boundaries between representation and reality. Similar concerns arise in Henry Fielding's self-conscious reflections on writing in *Joseph Andrews* and *Tom Jones* (1749), while Laurence Sterne's *Tristram Shandy* (1759–67) is itself a novel about someone unsuccessfully attempting to write a novel. The metafictional conceit may also be seen at the heart of much modernist and postmodernist fiction.

Cervantes' influence on the novel has been widely acknowledged by legions of subsequent writers and critics. No writer has left so great an impact and caused such unqualified universal admiration among his fellow writers. It is quite remarkable that, in spite of continual changes in literary taste, Cervantes' works have always remained popular. Perhaps the most important reason for this success is that Cervantes' deeply human portrayal of his characters reveals a universal, perpetual truth: regardless of developments in society, history, culture, and technology, the human psyche remains as vulnerable, unpredictable, and incomprehensible as that of the very first man on earth.

ALMA AMELL AND ANDRES VIRKUS

See also Don Quixote

Biography

Born in Alcalá de Henares, October 1547. As a child lived in Córdoba, Cabra, and Seville. Educated at the Estudio de la Villa, Madrid, 1567–68, and studied under the Erasmian humanist López de Hoyos. Went to Rome, 1569; chamberlain to Cardinal Giulio Acquaviva, 1570; enlisted as soldier by 1571, when he fought with the Spanish fleet and was injured at the battle of Lepanto; expeditions to Corfu and Navarino, 1572, and to Tunis, 1573, then stationed at military posts in Palermo, Sardinia, and Naples; was captured by pirates and imprisoned by Turks in Algiers, 1575–80 (ransomed, 1580); served on diplomatic mission to Oran, North Africa, 1581; returned to Spain and worked as tax inspector and purchasing agent (excommunicated for a short time in 1587 for financial zeal); suffered bankruptcy and two short prison terms in 1597 and 1602 for financial irregularities; denied administrative post in America; lived primarily in Seville, 1596–1600, and Madrid from c. 1606. Died 23 April 1616.

Novels by Cervantes

El ingenioso hidalgo Don Quijote de la Mancha, 2 vols., 1605–15; edited by Francisco Rodríguez Marín, 8 vols., 1911, and by Vicente Gaos, 3 vols., 1987; as *The History of Don Quixote of the Mancha,* translated by Thomas Shelton, 1612; numerous subsequent translations including by Tobias Smollett, 1755, Charles Jarvis, 1883, Samuel Putnam, 1949, J.M. Cohen, 1950, Walter Starkie, 1957, and P.A. Motteux, 1991
Novelas ejemplares, 1613; edited by F. Rodríguez Marín, 2 vols., 1969, and by Juan Bautista Avalle-Arce, 3 vols., 1987; as *Exemplary Novels,* translated in part by James Mabbe, 1640; B.W. Ife and others, 4 vols., 1992; as *Six Exemplary Novels,* translated by Harriet de Onís, 1961; as *Exemplary Stories,* translated by C.A. Jones, 1972

Other Writings: plays and verse.

Further Reading

Canavaggio, Jean, *Cervantes,* Paris: Mazarine, 1986; translated as *Cervantes,* New York: Norton, 1990
Close, Anthony J., *The Romantic Approach to Don Quixote: A Critical History of the Romantic Tradition in Quixote Criticism,* Cambridge and New York: Cambridge University Press, 1978
Duran, Manuel, *Cervantes,* New York: Twayne, 1974
El Saffar, Ruth S., *Novel to Romance: A Study of Cervantes' "Novelas ejemplares,"* Baltimore: Johns Hopkins University Press, 1974
El Saffar, Ruth S., editor, *Critical Essays on Cervantes,* Boston: G.K. Hall, 1986
Flores, Angel, and M.J. Benardete, editors, *Cervantes across the Centuries,* New York: Gordian Press, 1969
Forcione, Alban, *Cervantes and the Humanist Vision: A Study of Four "Exemplary Novels,"* Princeton, New Jersey: Princeton University Press, 1982
Gerli, E. Michael, *Refiguring Authority: Reading, Writing, and Rewriting in Cervantes,* Lexington: University Press of Kentucky, 1995
Gilman, Stephen, *The Novel According to Cervantes,* Berkeley: University of California Press, 1989
Martinez-Bonati, Felix, *Don Quixote and the Poetics of the Novel,* Ithaca, New York: Cornell University Press, 1992
Murillo, L.A., *A Critical Introduction to Don Quixote,* New York: Peter Lang, 1988
Nelson, Lowry, Jr., editor, *Cervantes: A Collection of Critical Essays,* Englewood Cliffs, New Jersey: Prentice-Hall, 1969
Riley, E.C., *Cervantes' Theory of the Novel,* Oxford: Clarendon Press, 1962
Riley, E.C., *Don Quixote,* London and Boston: Allen and Unwin, 1986

Eileen Chang 1920–95

Chinese

Eileen Chang (the Anglicized name for Zhang Ailing) generally is recognized as one of the superb stylists of modern Chinese fiction. Her novel *Jin suo ji* (1943; The Golden Cangue), which revolves around the emotional torment experienced by a poor woman who marries into a wealthy family, becomes addicted to opium, and eventually torments and destroys everyone around her, possesses the characteristic trademarks of Chang's style: a boudoir mood, somber lyricism, symbolic use of the moon and mirrors, and striking visual imagery. Chang also wrote serious scholarship on Cao Xueqin's classical novel, *Dream of the Red Chamber*, and her fiction is indebted to this novel in both content and style. Although *Dream of the Red Chamber* (also translated as *Story of the Stone*) has neither precedent nor successor within the tradition, the commentaries it has spawned, its popular links to drama and storytelling, its privileging of a feminized artistic consciousness, and its identification by 20th-century critics as something uniquely Chinese allows some of Chang's work to be viewed as a splice between classical chapter novels and modern fiction. In both *Dream of the Red Chamber* and the novels of Eileen Chang there are traces of a secluded, sad, and lamenting feminine voice typical of classical poetry, and both focus on familial or kin groups and the human relations within them.

Claiming that those who enjoy classical texts feel uncomfortable when they read her fiction and that those who want modern stories experience a vague dissatisfaction with her work, Chang places herself in the in-between time that by rights should have occurred at the end of the last dynasty, 40 years before she became well known as a writer. By 1942 Mao Zedong had delivered his *Talks on Art and Literature at the Yan'an Forum* and outlined the ideological basis that would define Chinese literature for the next 30 years. Writing far away in Shanghai, Chang refused to work with the overarching trope of revolution that was mandatory for writers who had committed themselves to the anti-Japanese or communist struggles. In her article "Ziji de wenzhang" (1944; "My Writing") she wrote: "Things are even to the point where I only write about trivial things between men and women. There are no wars or revolution in my work. I believe people are more free and unadorned in love than in war or revolution."

Eileen Chang started publishing fiction at the age of 12. In addition to *Jin suo ji*, her other well-known novels, novellas, or long stories include *Qingcheng zhi lian* (1985; Love in a Fallen City), *The Rice Sprout Song* (written in English and translated by the author as *Yang ko*, 1955), *Jidi zhi lian* (1954; *Naked Earth*), and *The Rouge of the North* (written in English and translated by the author as *Yuan nü*, 1967). A prolific writer, Chang also wrote stories, translations, and scholarly works; her complete work was published in 15 volumes in Taiwan in 1994. Focusing on ordinary human relationships, Chang's fiction depicts people who are far from heroic but who, under difficult circumstances, make reasonable if sometimes flawed decisions. While she does not shirk from showing her characters' deficiencies, Chang's perspective is often mildly sympathetic. Even the vindictive Qiqiao, the main character of *Jin suo ji*, appears as someone driven to cruelty not by an innately defective personality but by circumstances that are largely out of her control.

Although Chang's writing evokes a sense of traditional language and sensibility, her subtle metaphorical comparison of the family and the nation positions her directly within a modern context where creative writing invariably is a kind of cultural critique. The attack on the past that was essential to writing in China during the 1920s emerges in Chang's fiction as the persistent implication that as goes the family, so goes China. The moribund sense of ritual, hierarchy, and place that deadens human relations within Qiqiao's new family, Chang suggests, is so pervasive that it may be thought of as a national characteristic. The household furniture and the house itself, starkly present in weighty, dark, wooden forms, are analogous to a traditional China that is now under censure as stagnating, becoming corrupt from within.

Women's fiction in China gained increased critical attention during the early 20th century, when readers saw in it a level of sensitivity unmatched by male writers. The emphasis on social engagement that leftist literary ideology promoted during the late 1920s, however, meant that women's writing once again was seen as overly cautious, narrow in scope, and romanticized—criticisms that originally had appeared much earlier. While Chang's ability to bring female characters to life links her with an earlier generation of women writers, it also has opened her work to feminist analysis. In *Qingcheng zhi lian*, the divorced woman Liusu refuses an offer to become a dandy's mistress; with the Japanese invasion of Hong Kong forming a tumultuous background, Liusu carefully negotiates her own marriage. Chang writes, "Liusu escapes from a corrupt family, yet the baptism by war in Hongkong does not change her into a revolutionary woman" ("My Writing"). Chang's emphasis on personal relationships at the expense of larger social issues may be read as her attempt to ground women's actual experience and to reject a masculinist insistence on the grandiose. In other words, Chang constructs a sphere of interaction wherein the small and seemingly insignificant are not trivialized but probed and forced to yield important meanings at the personal and national level.

Always a well-liked writer in Taiwan, Chang's distance from the prevailing interest in socialist realism and its ideological basis made her a target of attack in Maoist China. That situation has changed. With another critique of the past well underway in the post-Mao era, Chang's writing has been reprinted and studied anew. In an introduction to a series devoted to women writers, former Minister of Culture Wang Meng posits a tradition of Chinese women writers dating from the early 1920s: "Women and literature seem to have a natural link" (*Hidden Natures Lost Affairs*, Qianxing yishi, 1995). Wang praises these women writers and their relatively unpoliticized work for providing an alternative to revolutionary discourse. Interest in Eileen Chang's work, therefore, is part of a larger attempt to redefine and discredit the revolutionary zeal that brought the country to grief during the Cultural Revolution. In view of the widespread corruption perpetrated by a male-dominated power structure, which was exposed after the death of Mao, the small scope of human relations and emotional angst in Chang's fictional world becomes a space that houses a smaller, more manageable universe consisting of personal emotions and the inner world's relation to a limited outer reality. Chang's rejection of war and revolution thus becomes a resistance to totalizing state narratives of domination and control.

WENDY LARSON

See also Rice Sprout Song

Biography
Born in Shanghai, 30 September 1920 (some sources say 1921). As a child lived in Beijing and nearby Tianjin; returned to Shanghai in 1929. Educated at the University of Hong Kong, 1939–42; returned to Shanghai in 1942 because of war. Worked for *The Times* and *Twentieth Century,* Shanghai; moved to Hong Kong in 1952; worked for *The World Today*; moved to the United States in 1955; associated with Chinese Study Center, University of California, Berkeley, from 1955; visiting writer, Cambridge University, 1967, and Miami University, Oxford, Ohio; associate scholar, Radcliffe Institute for Independent Study, Cambridge, Massachusetts. Died 8 September 1995.

Fiction by Chang
Chenxiangxie [Bits of Incense Ashes], 1943
Moli xiangpian [Jasmine Tea], 1943
Xinjing [Heart Sutra], 1943
Qingcheng zhi lian [Love in a Fallen City], 1943
Fengsuo [Sealed Off], 1943
Liuli pian [Glazed Tiles], 1943
Jin suo ji [The Golden Cangue], 1943
Deng [Waiting], 1943
Hongyingxi [Happiness], 1943
Hua diao [Withered Flowers], 1943
A Xiao bei qiu [A Xiao's Sad Autumn], 1943
Lianhuan tao [Chain of Rings], 1944
Nianqing de shihou [Time of Youth], 1944
Hong meigui bai meigui, 1944; as *Red Rose and White Rose*, 1978
Chuanqi xiaoshuo ji [Selected Romances], 1944
Yinbao yan song hualouhui, 1944
Sanwen ji [Selected Prose], 1945
Liu qing [Mercy], 1945

Chuang shiji [Genesis], 1945
Chuanqi [Romances], 1947
Jidi zhi lian, 1954; as *Naked Earth*, 1956
Zhang Ailing Xiaoshuoji [Selected Short Stories by Zhang Ailing], 1954
The Rice Sprout Song, 1955; translated by the author as *Yang ko*
Wu si yi shi [Remnants from May 4th Movement], 1958
The Rouge of the North, 1967; translated by the author as *Yuan nü*
Wang ran ji [Disappointment], 1968
Liu yan [Gossip], 1969
Zhang kan [Zhang's View], 1976
Xia tuanyuan [Reunion], 1976
Se jie [Threshold of Eroticism], 1979
Haishanghua liezhuan [Biography of Prostitutes], 1981
Zhang Ailing juan [Zhang Ailing], 1982
Lian zhi bei ge, 1983
Yin Bao Yan kan Hualouhui, 1983
Sheng ming de yue zhang [Music of Life], with Lin Haiyin, 1983
Qingcheng zhi lian: Zhang Ailing duanpian xiashuo xuan [Love in a Fallen City: Zhang Ailing's Short Stories], 1985
Chuanqi [Romance], 1986
Si yu [Whispers], 1990

Other Writings: a translation, *Fool in the Reeds,* by Chen Chi-ying, 1959, as well as essays on Chinese literature.

Further Reading
Chen Bingliang, *Zhang Ailing duanpian xioashuo lunji* (On the Stories of Eileen Chang), Taipei: Yuanjing chubanshe, 1983
Cheng, Stephen, "Theme and Technique in Eileen Chang's Stories," *Tamkang Review* 8:2 (1977)
Hsia, C.T., *A History of Modern Chinese Fiction,* New Haven, Connecticut: Yale University Press, 1961; 2nd edition, 1971
Renditions: A Chinese-English Translation Magazine 45 (Spring 1995), special issue on Eileen Chang
Shui Jing, *Zhang Ailing de xiao shuo yi shu* (The Art of Eileen Chang's Fiction), Taipei: Da Di, 1974
Yu Qing, editor, *Zhang Ailing: Tiancai qinü* (Eileen Chang: Woman of Genius), Beijing: Zhongguo qingnian chubanshe, 1994

Character

Types of Characters and Theories about Characters in Novels

In the widest, minimal sense, *character* designates any human or humanoid (such as a robot or a talking animal) entity, individual or collective, that occurs in a story world and plays a role, no matter how minor, in one or more of its states, events, or actions.

In this sense, the term does not necessarily include any psychological aspects or features and may refer to an entity whose only characterization is in terms of, say, a physical feature: "a tall man was standing at the street corner." In the narrower, more specific sense, *character* designates any individual or group as above who possess one or more physical, interactional (behavioral, social), locutionary, or—especially—psychological (mental) properties or features. The psychological dimension may be further divided into cognitive, emotive, volitional (ethical), and perceptual traits, attitudes, and dispositions. The kinds of properties any individual or group possesses, and the number and diversity of features within each kind may vary enormously, depending, among other factors, on the individual's role in the story world (central or merely auxiliary), the type of story world portrayed within its corresponding novelistic genre (science fiction, the detective novel, autobiographical or psychological novel), and the school or movement within which a novelist may be said to belong (realist, modernist, postmodernist, etc.).

Two concepts related closely to character are those of subject (self, mind, interiority, inner life) and of the "image of man." The first refers to the operation of the mind on all levels of consciousness and self-consciousness, and the other to global views on the nature of human beings as governed by emotion or reason, as able or unable to comprehend their situation, communicate with others and act accordingly, and the like.

Although instances of complex, psychologically nuanced individuals may be found in earlier novels—Madame de La Fayette's *La princesse de Clèves* (1678), for example—it is by and large true to say that the development of the European novel from the 17th century to the 20th century reveals an ever increasing interest in psychologically complex, unique, and changing individuals or small groups. However, recent novelistic schools such as the *nouveau roman* and postmodernism reject this individual psychologizing tendency as artistically exhausted and philosophically untenable. Both the growth and the rejection of psychological realism in the novel are closely correlated with changes in philosophical and aesthetic trends.

Literary characters may be classified according to different criteria, both substantive ("what") and formal ("how"). All taxonomies in this area are based on the same constitutive fact: characters in a novel, whether historically based or purely fictional, are semiotic or conceptual constructs, hypothetical entities analogous to human beings, not independently existing individuals. They are artistic products, assembled by authors according to their aesthetic, cognitive, or ideological goals, drawing on the repertoire of literary and general cultural codes available to them, and on the corresponding inventory of artistic means and procedures.

Whenever a model exists in the culture according to which the various properties (physical, mental, etc.) of an individual in a story world may be interrelated to form an intelligible whole of some kind, the character is semiotically motivated or naturalized. Such models derive from a variety of discourses, not all of which are realistic, such as radical science fiction and fairy tales for adults. A character in a novel is verisimilar (like a real person) if it is motivated and if, in addition, the model that renders it intelligible is thought to reflect reality in the given culture. In other words, the character is now considered not only intelligible but also possible in the actual world. A character is realistic in the strict sense if the model that renders it verisimilar belongs to the dominant scientific (including social science) worldview of the late 18th to early 20th centuries. Characters are often termed *realistic* by their authors because they conform to these authors' own view of what is possible or probable in the actual world,

but without further specification this usage of *realistic* is uninformative. A radically new type of character occurs in a novel when its initial readers cannot render it either verisimilar or even just semiotically motivated. One should note that the preceding typology takes into account a character's cultural status, defining a relation between something that is in the text (the character) and something that is outside it (the model). As codes and cultures change, the same character can shift from verisimilar to purely semiotically motivated or even unintelligible, or vice versa. The same is also true from a cross-cultural perspective.

Characters in a novel may also be counterparts of actual people because of extensive similarity in properties (for example, in a roman à clef), because of identity of proper name, or because of both, as in the traditional historical novel. But the historical originals are inevitably fictionalized because they coexist and interact with purely fictional individuals, because unconditional claims are made about their mental life, and because some of their historically documented properties are changed, sometimes radically, to fit artistic needs. A standard example is provided by the historical French and Russian leaders as portrayed in Lev Tolstoi's *Voina i mir* (1863–69; *War and Peace*). Much more extreme examples are provided by the historical metafictions of postmodernism.

Characters may be categorized according to their relation to abstraction or general classes, yielding a scale of personification, type, and individual. A personification character (allegorical character) is an anthropomorphization of a conceptual entity, such as an idea, a faculty of mind, a vice, or a virtue. The abstract term is turned into the proper name, such as Mr. Legality or Mr. Worldly-Wiseman in Bunyan's *Pilgrim's Progress* (1678, 1684), of a character whose properties and mode of behavior serve as a concrete manifestation of the corresponding concept. A "type" is a character that instantiates a limited, fixed set of properties, a cliché or stereotype predefined in the cultural "encyclopedia," one supposed to have some general human validity and often associated with a social class, age, role, or nationality. The provenance of the stereotype may be a sociohistorical category (ruthless capitalist, degenerate aristocrat, social climber), a pseudopsychological type (introvert, hysterical woman), or a literary model (picaro, suffering artist, femme fatale). In the latter case, the character embodying the model is referred to as a stock character. The boundary between cultural and literary models is permeable in both directions, and the range of models available to the novelist varies historically. Furthermore, what begins as a unique, individual literary creation may over time become generalized into a recurrent literary type or even a cultural model (Don Quixote, Don Juan). An individual is understood as a character who is unique, possessing a nonrecurrent pattern of traits and dispositions, whether physical, social, or mental. To ensure uniqueness, individual characters are usually highly specified in terms of numerous dimensions and richness of details. Closely related to the type/individual distinction is the one between *flat* and *round* characters (a term first used by E.M. Forster), or *schematic* and *full* characters, based on the amount and variety of information that the text provides about them, explicitly or implicitly. But the two dimensions (specificity and number of features) are logically independent. A recurrent type such as the struggling artist may be rich and nuanced in terms of number of features, while a striking, unique individual may be constructed by means of a few unusual or extreme features.

Limiting the discussion to the psychological dimension, an array of binary oppositions has been proposed, with each specific character to be placed somewhere between the two poles of each. The two most common ones are simple versus complex and static versus dynamic. A simple character normally possesses few features that form a stable pattern and is therefore easy to fathom and predict. A complex character possesses not only more features but features belonging to different mental faculties (emotion, reason, will). The relation between these features is full of stresses and tensions, leading to inner conflicts and contradictions, to unexpected shifts and low predictability. The labels *dynamic* and *static* refer to major changes (or the lack thereof) in a character's central traits and dispositions or their hierarchy in the course of the novel's actions. One should note that, contrary to popular belief, the majority of characters in the novel's history are static, and that a character can be complex and yet static, as is the case with the hero of Fedor Dostoevskii's *Zapiski iz podpol'ia* (1864; *Notes from Underground*).

Individuals in story worlds do not exist in isolation. They are intimately connected with and in part also defined and determined by their relations to other aspects of narrative—primarily action, theme, and the structure of narrative transmission. With respect to action, characters are viewed as essentially narrative agents, that is, as independent entities potentially able to carry out actions and activities in the story world (see Suvin, 1988). The hero of the classical novel is someone with a clear set of values, goals, and intentions, an individual capable of undertaking and sustaining a series of actions against opposition and adversity and who keeps on striving even though he may not succeed in the end. Beginning in the 19th century and increasingly throughout the 20th, the main novelistic character is often an antihero, an individual whose role is primarily passive and whose situation is one of resigned defeat. This reverse of the classical hero lacks the capacity for action and is occupied instead with interminable analysis. The character's paralysis is often accompanied by social isolation, a disillusioned view of life, and a lack of faith in the power of language to serve as the basis for interpersonal understanding.

The narrative agent who is the main subject of the narrative sequence or the chief focus of readerly interest and attention is usually termed the protagonist (from the Greek for first actor). Much of the action revolves around the protagonist, who of all characters in the novel receives the sharpest delineation. The protagonist is also intimately linked with the main thematics of the work. Although usually a single individual, the protagonist can sometimes be a group, such as the Cossacks in Nikolai Gogol's *Taras Bulba* (1835, 1842). In a narrative articulated in terms of interpersonal conflict, the protagonist is opposed by the antagonist, another major or central figure with opposite values or goals, such as a rival or enemy. The conflict between Myshkin and Rogozhin in Dostoevskii's *Idiot* (1869; *The Idiot*) may serve as an example. Although hero, protagonist, and sympathetic character (see below) often converge in the same narrative agent, the three are logically distinct, being defined respectively by power of action, centrality to the plot, and positive evaluation according to a moral or ideological norm.

Since characters as narrative agents are by definition involved in interactions with one another, numerous attempts have been made to define a minimal quasi-universal set of basic narrative and thematic roles, of actors and actants. The goal was to identify specific narrative agents as different surface specifications or concretizations of the same basic action or plot functions. All such typologies treat narrative agents in terms of a purely formal narrative syntax, according to the kind of slot they occupy in the action sequence. On the most abstract or deep level, A.J. Greimas and Joseph Courtes (1979), for example, have defined six basic actants: subject, object, sender, receiver, helper, and opponent. As a second step, actants undergo some qualitative semantic investment, which gives them a social role or station (father, rich merchant, impoverished laborer), with its standard class features. At this point, such stereotyped, codified attributes, together with norms of action and appropriateness, expectations, and values associated with the social role, become the defining features of the character. The coupling of social role and standardized expectations, which the individual narrative agent may or may not fulfill, can then serve as a clue to the novel's ideology, system of values, and worldview.

A good example of role norms fulfilled by a narrative agent is provided by Squire Allworthy in Henry Fielding's *Tom Jones* (1749). Allworthy is a perfect embodiment of the conservative, morally upright social and ethical position associated with a country gentleman. Conversely, hypocrite figures serve as narrative agents who deliberately subvert the standard expectations associated with their station while outwardly pretending to uphold them faithfully. The most famous example in the English novel is probably Uriah Heep, the scheming clerk in Dickens' *David Copperfield* (1850). His ultimate exposure and punishment serve to reassert the role expectations he has transgressed. One should note in this context that social roles are by and large associated with gender (which some argue is itself a social construct) and that an extra dimension of characterization occurs whenever a female figure assumes a traditionally male role or mode of behavior, and vice versa.

In terms of the purely formal architectonics or design of the narrative, characters may be classified according to their role in the plot: central and peripheral (major and minor) characters, agents and foils, cards and ficelles. In this context, characters may also be regarded as devices for fulfilling an organizational function (retarding the action, imparting information, setting the stage for further action), creating a tone or effect (suspense, comic relief, horror), or embodying general architectonic patterns (parallelism, contrast, gradation, analogy).

A novel in its totality projects a certain worldview, ideology, system of norms and values, and illustrates a number of general themes or human concerns. Characters contribute to such overarching concerns in numerous ways. Most obviously, they can explicitly voice an ideological position. Their dispositions and destinies may embody the novel's underlying abstract themes and views. A *sympathetic character*, for example, is one who evokes in the reader an emotional attitude of liking, care, or even identification, because that character's attributes and attitudes are presented as positive or desirable according to the novel's system of values. In extreme cases, as in the roman à thèse, characters may be little more than the anthropomorphization of an abstract view or idea.

Characters in a novel occur within a system of narrative transmission and may be defined with respect to their position in it. Any textually identified individual must occupy one or more of the four basic positions of narrator, narratee, focalizer, and narrative agent. Narrative agents can possess any kind of attributes, while focalizers as such are limited to acts of perception and cognition, and narrators and narratees to locutionary ones.

So far, we have treated characters as finished products, images of individuals projected by textual means. In conclusion we should define the basic differences between textually projected individuals and actual individuals, the minimal constitutive conditions for their occurrence in story worlds, and the major means and stages of their psychological characterization.

Fictional individuals are created and sustained exclusively by verbal means. All the information about them is contained, explicitly or implicitly, in the text that evokes them. Their set of features is limited and closed, and they are always incomplete or schematic to some degree. They are presented as a series of discontinuous stages, which may exclude some phases of their lives. They need not conform to any pattern of coherence, possibility, or even consistency formulated for the actual world, as one can see from the novels of magic realism. In some kinds of novels, it is possible to have full knowledge of their inner states and features and to observe their minds in action. The features ascribed to literary characters are governed by criteria of selectivity and relevance. The individuals in narrative always form a configuration of interrelations, so that much information about each character can be gleaned from his or her confrontation with others. Finally, as we have seen, many characters are relatable to specific literary traditions or codes, not to actuality, as the source of their intelligibility.

An individual character may be said to be fully represented or representational in a given novel if five constitutive conditions are fulfilled.

1. The character's existence in the story world is not open to doubt; the narrator is not just playing with names and descriptive phrases, but is actually referring to such an individual
2. It is possible to determine with certainty some of the properties of this character
3. The character in question is qualitatively unique, different in some respect(s) from all other characters in this story world
4. The character's properties at each phase of the action form an intelligible pattern of some kind
5. The changes, especially psychological, that the character undergoes over time themselves form an overall coherent pattern (development, disintegration, etc.)

Characters, at least main characters, in the realistic novel generally fulfill all five conditions, while in modernist novels often only the first three are met. Postmodernism undermines all five, bringing about the "death of the character" as a basic representational unit (see Docherty, 1983).

Direct, explicit information about a character's mental features may be provided by the narrator, by other characters, or by the character in question. But in the last two cases, the information may be unreliable owing to ignorance, misconception, or deliberate deception. Most information in this area is, however, implicit, to be inferred by the reader from three sources:

1. The character's physical, verbal, and mental actions and interactions—their substance, manner, and relation to the context in which they occur
2. Features of the character's physique and of his environment—appearance, gestures, manners, natural setting, and man-made milieu (the literary convention here is that proximity or contiguity implies similarity or parallelism between external and internal features, that the physical can act as a signifier whose signifieds are the invisible, internal mental features)
3. Formal textual patterns—the character's name, groupings of characters and the analogies and parallels engendered by them, parallel and embedded stories, repetition and gradation, and the use of epithets, formulas and schemas familiar from earlier works (intertextuality)

The inference by the reader of a character's mental features from the foregoing "database" may be governed by rules explicitly formulated by a reliable omniscient narrating voice, or, in their absence, by culturally established but historically variable maxims, norms, and rules that may stem from literary models or from world knowledge. Such inferences are never logically binding. They are, rather, probabilistic or merely plausible, like most informal inferences in the social sphere. They are often gender specific, and always context dependent.

Having identified and accumulated a list of features for a given character, the reader might then construct an overall psychological portrait of the character. This construction involves a set of operations: sorting the features into categories (emotive, cognitive, etc.); inferring second-order features such as consistency; separating the features into permanent versus temporary and strong versus weak; noting the absence of features possessed by related characters; rank ordering the features within each category into central and marginal; networking the relevant categories themselves. The abiding and dominant features of the central category may then be regarded as the essential mental properties of the character, the sense of her proper name, so to speak. Finally, the whole set of categories may be identified in terms of a global personality type, borrowed from cultural models or from the literary codes of a period. Innovative authors may deliberately project characters that are not amenable to recuperation or naturalization in terms of any existing model or who cannot logically cohere into any global configuration, as in many postmodern novels.

URI MARGOLIN

See also Discourse Representation; Narrator; Person in Narrative; Plot

Further Reading

Bal, Mieke, editor, *Mensen van Papier: Over Personages in de Literatuur*, Assen: Van Gorcum, 1979

Docherty, Thomas, *Reading (Absent) Character: Towards a Theory of Characterization in Fiction*, Oxford: Clarendon Press, and New York: Oxford University Press, 1983

Garvey, James, "Characterization in Narrative," *Poetics* 7 (1978)

Grabes, Herbert, "Wie aus Saetzen Personen werden," *Poetica* 10 (1978)

Greimas, A.J., and Joseph Courtes, *Sémiotique: Dictionnaire raissonné de la théorie du langage*, Paris: Hachette, 1979; as

Semiotics and Language: An Analytical Dictionary, Bloomington: Indiana University Press, 1982

Hamon, Philippe, "Pour un statut sémiologique du personnage," in *Poétique du recit,* edited by Roland Barthes, Paris: Seuil, 1977

Hamon, Philippe, *Le Personnel du roman: Le system des personnages dan "Les Rougon-Macquart" d'Émile Zola,* Geneva: Droz, 1983

Harvey, W.J., *Character and the Novel,* Ithaca, New York: Cornell University Press, and London: Chatto and Windus, 1965

Hochman, Baruch, *Character in Literature,* Ithaca, New York: Cornell University Press, 1985

Kahler, Erich, *The Inward Turn of Narrative,* Princeton, New Jersey: Princeton University Press, 1973

Knapp, John V., editor, *Literary Character,* Lanham, Maryland: University Press of America, 1993

Lavergne, Gerard, editor, *Le Personnage romanesque: Colloque international,* Paris: Klinksieck, 1995

Phelan, James, *Reading People, Reading Plots: Character, Progression, and the Interpretation of Narrative,* Chicago: University of Chicago Press, 1989

Suvin, Darko, "Can People be (Re)Presented in Fiction?" in *Marxism and the Interpretation of Culture,* edited by Cary Nelson and Lawrence Grossberg, Urbana: University of Illinois Press, and London: Macmillan, 1988

Zeraffa, Michel, *Personne et personnage,* Paris: Klincksieck, 1969

Children's Novel

Children's literature is of immense cultural, literary, and commercial importance, although, like women's writing and colonial writing, it has until recently been critically marginalized. It is now widely appreciated that rather than being inferior to its adult counterpart, the children's novel is different: it is written for a different audience and has different requirements. This difference, as many writers have observed, requires different skills and forms. In comparison to the adult novel, as the British novelist Jill Paton Walsh has noted (see Meek, et al, 1977): "The children's book presents a technically more difficult, technically more interesting problem—that of making a fully serious adult statement, as a good novel of any kind does, and making it utterly simple and transparent. . . . The need for comprehensibility imposes an emotional obliqueness, an indirectness of approach, which like elision and partial statement in poetry is often a source of aesthetic power."

With an estimated 8,000 children's novels published annually in the English language alone, and a 200-year history, generalizations have to be made cautiously. However, we may say that as the nature of childhood has changed over time, so children's novels have searched for a different voice and a different subject matter. Children's books tend to portray society, on the surface, as it wishes to be or to be seen. They reflect what society thinks is culturally and educationally suitable for its children, from protective (often self-protective), idealistic, or educational motives. One consequence is that the classic realist mode dominates. This may be because of the power-relationship between adult author and child reader, or it may be because adult writers underestimate the ability of children to adapt to complex forms; again, it may be because, for cultural and commercial reasons, children's novels have longer "shelf-lives" than their adult equivalents.

There is a paradox here, for the picture-book, generally designed for younger readers than those who read novels, has become a "super-genre," the area where modernism and postmodern experimentation has been most evident. Equally, as

John Stephens has pointed out in "Modernism to Postmodernism" (1992): "some of the key characteristic features [of postmodernism] are endemically present in anti-modernist children's literature, albeit put to the service of premodern conceptions of morality and society." He cites the tendency "to collapse the boundaries between high and popular culture" and argues that one of the dominant modes of the children's novel, fantasy, "displays a pervasive affinity with postmodernist fiction."

Similarly, the episodic structure of the majority of early extended texts for children may be seen as providing a different fictional experience rather than a fragmented form of the novel. Examples of such episodic narrative include Sarah Fielding's *The Governess; or, The Little Female Academy* (1749), E. Nesbit's *The Wouldbegoods* (1901), and Rudyard Kipling's *Stalky and Co.* (1899). William Mayne's Australian novel *Salt River Times* (1980) provides a recent example of the same structure. Where children's novels have followed the forms of the popular adult novel, these have been adapted and transformed. The "series," for example, frequently has been developed into a meta-novel, with its own distinctive literary and narrative dynamics, as for example Enid Blyton's "Famous Five" series (1949 on) or C.S. Lewis' "Narnia" novels (1950–56). However, despite the conservatism of international publishing, there are some startling examples of postmodern experimentation, a recognition that the child-reader is a complex phenomenon, not to be lightly constructed by author, critic, or historian.

In gender terms, children's novels have been the site of a sustained and subtle conflict: the majority of writers, readers, publishers, and mediators of children's books have been female, and yet the surface modes—fantasy, myth, folktale, adventure—have been male. The "landmark" texts, such as Mark Twain's *The Adventures of Tom Sawyer* (1876), A.A. Milne's *Winnie-the-Pooh* (1926), or J.R.R. Tolkien's *The Hobbit* (1937) have been male-oriented, or, in the case of Astrid Lindgren's *Pippi Langstrump* (1945; *Pippi Longstocking*), Lewis Carroll's *Alice's*

Adventures in Wonderland (1865), or Patricia Wrightson's *The Ice Is Coming* (1977), female with male characteristics. But if we characterize the "male" as confrontational, individualistic, nostalgic, and concerned with power, and the "female" as relating to negotiation, involvement, the present, and caring, then we see that the children's novel, for a far longer period than the adult novel, has remained subversive—undercutting dominant stereotypes.

The general pattern for the children's novel has been to move away from the controlling storyteller and the dominating narrator at the same time that it moved away from educational and religious motivations. English has dominated the development of the children's novel, which has also been particularly strong in France, Germany, and Scandinavia. It is perhaps simpler to say that the children's novel has *not* developed so rapidly in Africa, South America, China, and the Arab world, for different cultural and political reasons. The traffic in translation is very much a one-way avenue; very few novels are translated *into* English—although those that are tend to have an influence disproportionate to their number. Examples are Erich Kästner's *Emil und die Detektive* (1928; translated into English in 1930 as *Emil and the Detectives*) and Felix Salten's *Bambi* (1923; English 1928).

There is no simple correspondence between adults' and children's novels, nor between the children's novel and its culture. For example, World War II was treated seriously in children's novels only when children who experienced it grew up. Children's novels about World War II include Hans Peter Richter's view of Nazism, *Wir waren dabei* (1962; *I Was There*), Judith Kerr's semi-autobiographical trilogy of displaced German Jews, beginning with *When Hitler Stole Pink Rabbit* (1971), Jill Paton Walsh's account of the Dunkirk evacuation, *The Dolphin Crossing* (1967), and Bette Greene's novel of a German prisoner of war in the United States, *Summer of My German Soldier* (1973).

A condition of a recognizable children's literature is a recognizable childhood, and although childhood is one of the least documented of social phenomena, it seems that the conditions for the creation of the children's novel came about in the West in the early 19th century. Very few countries, in fact, have any substantial tradition of literature written especially for children before the 19th century. Previously, in Britain, texts for children had been part of the chapbook trade, which were established in the 1740s on a serious commercial footing by booksellers such as John Newbery and Mary Cooper. But, while the novel was rapidly becoming the dominant adult popular literary form, few books for children resembled adult novels. Brief exemplars for conduct and education were the commonest publications, and even the extended prose narrative fictions expressly intended for children, such as Sarah Fielding's *The Governess*, were really loose collections of independent tales held together largely by didactic intent. Adaptations of adult novels come closest to following patterns established for adult readers. Early examples include *The Paths of Virtue Delineated or the History in Miniature of the Celebrated Pamela, Clarissa Harlowe and Sir Charles Grandison, Familiarised and Adapted to the Capacities of Youth*, which Samuel Richardson authorized in 1756, and the abridged version of the complete *Robinson Crusoe* (1719), which appeared in 1722.

The first novels in English for children, then, were extended tracts, with little character development other than that required to point a moral and engineer a pious death. Much the same is true of French and German children's literature. This didactic tradition survived well into the 19th century. The classic example is Mary Martha Sherwood's *The History of the Fairchild Family* (1818), in which only slightly recalcitrant children are shown the most gruesome consequences of, for example, quarreling (a behavior that leads to being left to rot in a gallows-cage) or playing with matches (which results in being burned to death). This book was immensely popular, but by 1847, when its third volume was published, it presented a more child-friendly atmosphere.

The didactic children's novel blended easily into the domestic novel of sentiment, which became a dominant form in the United States. In Britain, because of the influx of folktales and fairy tales from Europe, which were soon adapted for children, the 19th century became a battleground between evangelical and popular tendencies, the popular variety increasingly taking the form of the fantastic. Ironically for the educators, the children's novel came to resemble the lower forms of the popular adult novel, and, just as the popular adult novel had done, children's novels divided along gender lines.

Boys were provided with sea stories and empire-building stories derived from such 18th-century authors as Defoe and Smollett, while in the United States, the "dime novel" was developed into outdoor and frontier adventure stories. Johann David Wyss' *Der schweizerische Robinson* (1812; *The Swiss Family Robinson*) is one of the most influential of adventure stories. It also is a classic example of another feature of children's literature, the "unstable" text. Because of their low literary status but large cultural influence, books such as this—and Carlo Collodi's *Le avventure di Pinocchio* (1883; *The Adventures of Pinocchio*), Johanna Spyri's *Heidi* (1881), and J.M. Barrie's *Peter Pan* (1904)—have been adapted and modified at will. *The Swiss Family Robinson* was edited from Wyss' notes by his son. The French translation (1814) added material, and the English translation from the German used some material from the French. The book provoked Captain Frederick Marryat, already a successful popular novelist for adults, into writing *Masterman Ready* (3 vols., 1841–42), a more plausible (if ineffably pious) "Robinsonnade," which in turn influenced much 19th-century writing for boys. R.M. Ballantyne's *The Coral Island* (1858) was similarly influential and, as the century passed, these "manly" adventures became increasingly influenced by British imperialism. There is no question that these books reveal Victorianism in its rawest state—sexist, racist, patronizing, and brutal. The large popular output of such writers as G.A. Henty (1832–1902) influenced children's novels well into the 20th century, another demonstration of the inertia characteristic of publishing for children.

Books for girls, on the other hand, echoed both the sentimentalism of the Victorian adult domestic novel and a charitable religiosity which, perhaps ironically, led it to a muted form of Dickensian social realism. Charlotte Yonge, who herself wrote 150 books, summed up the situation in 1886: "girls are indiscriminate devourers of fiction . . . the semi-religious novel or novelette is to them moralizing put into action, and the most likely way of reaching them." Just as boys' novels were a potent cultural weapon, inculcating manliness and dominance, so women and girls were portrayed as domestic angels, ministering to the deserving poor—an image which, of course, kept both females and the poor in their appointed places. As ever, the inertia principle operated; one of the most popular American books of the period, Martha Finley's *Elsie Dinsmore* (1867) was published when evangelical sentimental novels were no longer a staple of the adult market. Finley nevertheless produced 27 sequels. But just as boys' books moved away from the influence of the schoolroom, so the grip of evangelism was slowly loosened in fiction for girls. Catherine Sinclair's *Holiday House* (1839) is one of the earliest books to portray children and adults in collusion against established adult authority.

Precious little rebelliousness is to be found in a new genre—almost exclusively for children and largely British—the school story. In its setting and its tireless insistence upon codes of conduct, relationships with authority, and initiation, it encapsulates both the characteristics of children's novels and the culture's attitude toward children. Key examples were Harriet Martineau's novella *The Crofton Boys* (1841), Thomas Hughes' *Tom Brown's Schooldays* (1856), and Frederick William Farrar's now somewhat risible *Eric, or Little by Little* (1858). Such was their influence that some of the earliest Canadian children's novels, such as James de Mille's *Fire in the Woods* (1871) took the form of school stories. Books in the former British colonies followed a similar pattern, although in Australia there was some attempt to reflect local conditions, as in Ethel Sybil Turner's *Seven Little Australians* (1894).

While the United States were still in the grip of the utilitarian educationalists, in Britain children's novels were increasingly influenced by fairy tales. The most famous survivors that made direct use of these tales are Frances Browne's *Granny's Wonderful Chair and Its Tales of Fairy Time* (1857) and W.M. Thackeray's pastiche *The Rose and the Ring* (1855). Thackeray's book, which owes something to burlesque and pantomime, demonstrates once again how closely linked children's literature was (and is) to the popular mind. Fantasy—a low form of literary life as far as the mainstream novel was concerned—was also being absorbed into children's novels by writers like Juliana Horatia Ewing and Mary Louisa Molesworth. The blending of realism and fantasy in Molesworth's novels, such as *The Cuckoo Clock* (1877), was particularly influential.

Toward the end of the 19th century, changes in cultural patterns and health care brought a different attitude to childhood among the middle classes. It was now seen as a separate and valuable stage of life, and children's books began to reflect this new vision of childhood.

Louisa May Alcott's *Little Women* (1868) marks the beginning of a remarkable period in which a group of landmark novels transformed the materials of the previous century and changed the tone and content of the children's novel. *Little Women*, although it has a moral and religious framework, established in the children's novel a fashion for domestic realism, intimate, undidactic, and (comparatively) unsentimental. The book was highly popular in Britain, where the independence of Jo and her sisters was greatly envied. The foregrounding of the independent child as hero became a trend, which, mixed with a romantic view of childhood, produced Frances Hodgson Burnett's fashionable *Little Lord Fauntleroy* (1886), Eleanor Porter's *Pollyanna* (1913) and the Canadian L.M. Montgomery's *Anne of Green Gables* (1908).

Mark Twain's thoroughly ambivalent *The Adventures of Tom Sawyer* changed the boys' novel in the United States from a pious to an iconoclastic genre. Richard Jefferies' *Bevis, the Story of a Boy* (3 vols., 1882) had a similar effect in Britain. Although a typical three-decker of its day (Victorian publishers often imposed the same three-volume structure on children's novels as they did on the adult novel), complete with subplots, it nevertheless portrayed the anarchy and amorality of the "real," rather than the socially constructed, child. The novel's curious mixture of freedom and "manly" discipline, of literary fantasy and cool practicality, of mystic appreciation of nature coupled with attitudes of empire and dominance, resonated through children's novels for nearly 100 years.

Fantasy finally became respectable through the elaborate allegories of Charles Kingsley (*The Water-Babies*, 1863) and George MacDonald (*The Princess and the Goblin*, 1871), and through Lewis Carroll's *Alice* books (1864, 1871). All these books demonstrate that the children's novel is often profoundly different in structure and form from the adult novel. Relying on a complex mixture of folk- and fairy-tale structures, they are (especially in the case of Carroll) still yielding the secrets of their social and political satire and linguistic-philosophic explorations. Faced with a book such as *Alice's Adventures in Wonderland,* which seems at its most obvious level to be exploring Victorian adult-child relationships and states of desire, but which has virtually no character development, and whose original illustrations are an integral part of the satiric purpose, critics of the novel need, perhaps, a new vocabulary.

In other genres, Robert Louis Stevenson, in the apotheosis of the adventure story, *Treasure Island* (1883), brought moral ambiguities to what had become a mere vehicle for imperialism or an easy subject for "penny dreadful" writers and "dime novelists." Frances Hodgson Burnett melded the romantic Gothic tradition of the Brontës to the Cinderella story and explored the limits of the empowerment of women in *The Secret Garden* (1911). L. Frank Baum reinvented the fantasy for a utilitarian society with *The Wonderful Wizard of Oz* (1900). Rudyard Kipling brought a jolt of raw realism to the stylized and increasingly fantastic school story. But the most fundamental shift in this period was one of tone. Adult authors such as Kipling and Edith Nesbit, instead of addressing the adult over the head of the child or addressing the child as an inferior, powerless being, developed a new narrative stance that implied mutual respect between narrator and reader. (It is important to note that one of the most famous books of this period, Kenneth Grahame's *The Wind in the Willows* [1908], is only superficially a children's book. Thematically and stylistically anomalous, it is far more profitably regarded as a politically conservative male fantasy for adults, a protest about the death of Victorian England and the demise of empire.)

There is no obvious equivalent to modernism in children's literature. Indeed, after 1918, children's books in general became quietist, a trend epitomized by Milne's *Winnie-the-Pooh*. But there were many subtly experimental works. John Masefield's *The Box of Delights* (1935) is a novel without chapters. Tolkien's *The Hobbit* introduces sophisticated linguistic and mythic allusions. P.L. Travers' *Mary Poppins* (1934) is a far more mystic, complex, and acid book than the famous Disney version would have us believe. And Geoffrey Trease's *Bows Against the Barons* (1934) features a socialist Robin Hood.

The classic realist tradition was maintained by highly influential writers such as Arthur Ransome in Britain. His 12 *Swallows and Amazons* novels (1930–47) use the structures of the fairy tale and show a steady development away from "closed" narratives. Ransome incorporated traditional themes of skills, child-independence, and initiation, but combined these with concepts of family, negotiation, and security and an awareness of the child characters' (and readers') literary heritage. It was a potent mixture, reminiscent of Richard Jefferies, and Ransome's influence has been pervasive.

Ransome, who reported the Russian Revolution for English newspapers, was a man in retreat: his books do not mention the world outside their boundaries. A similar retreatism was seen in the United States, where small-town "middle America" became a symbol of security, exemplified by domestic novels such as Maud Hart Lovelace's *Betsy-Tacy* (1940) and Eleanor Estes' *The Moffats* (1941). Very similar values are found in Laura Ingalls Wilder's "Little House" novels (from *Little House in the Big Woods*, 1932), which portray pioneering life in the late 19th century and reassert the importance of individuality and individual strength, especially in the context of Roosevelt's "New Deal."

The 30 years after World War II are commonly regarded as the children's novel's second "golden age." Children's literature became one of the most successful publishing phenomena, and several major publishers survived only because of their children's books departments. Mainstream writers such as Jill Paton Walsh, Nina Bawden, Scott O'Dell, Ivan Southall, and Katherine Paterson established a high, thoughtful conventional standard, which differed in little more than subject matter from its adult counterparts. Broadly speaking, British writers—as in 1918—turned to fantasy. Americans moved toward social realism, which became a dominant genre, probably deriving from the first-person demotic narration of J.D. Salinger's *Catcher in the Rye* (1951), although it may be traced back to Dorothy Canfield Fisher's *Understood Betsy* (1917).

As the "teenager" was constructed by society following the war, so the "teenage" or "young adult" novel developed, allowing a broadening of subject matter but increasing the problems of authors. The children's book has always been susceptible to control and censorship, and consequently books that broke taboos became the center of extensive debate.

In fantasy, the children's novel set a fashion that ultimately legitimized the genre in adult literature. Texts with ambiguous status, such as Tolkien's *The Lord of the Rings* (1954), were followed by several novels originally published for children now republished in adult imprints, notably Susan Cooper's *The Dark Is Rising* sequence (1965–77), loosely based on Arthurian legend; Ursula Le Guin's *Earthsea* quartet (1968–90), an "otherworld" quest fantasy; Richard Adams' *Watership Down* (1972), a contemporary animal fable that broke several publishing records; and, from the German, Michael Ende's *Die Unendliche Geschichte* (1979; *The Neverending Story*). Of these, Le Guin is perhaps the most interesting case, as the fourth novel in the quartet, *Tehanu* (1990), is a feminist "revisioning" of the epic hero-tale, which the author had come to see as unacceptably male-oriented. It represents the way in which critical and cultural theory is being absorbed much more rapidly into the children's novel than it was in the past.

The influence of the United States on Britain and the rest of the world continued to increase, especially in the area of realism. As childhood was reconceptualized, notably under the influence of television, so the realistic children's novel reflected a bleaker world, where, for example, parents were as likely to be weak as not, the family was an unstable unit, and adult preoccupations eroded childhood. Judy Blume's *Forever* (1975) was the first to describe teenage sexual intercourse explicitly; Robert Cormier's novels included sexual perversion, terrorist murder, and, in *The Chocolate War* (1974), a school story in which the "hero" is finally defeated by the schoolboy "mafia" and corrupt teachers. Books featuring drug abuse, violence, death, the holocaust, and other previously taboo subject areas have become commonplace, although their form has tended to be conventional. The difficulty lies in mediating such material to children without falsifying the fiction. Ursula Le Guin has summed up the problem (see Haviland, 1980): "But what, then, is the naturalistic writer for children to do? Can he present the child with evil as an insoluble problem . . . and say, 'Well, baby, this is how it is, what are you going to make of it'—that is surely unethical. If you suggest that there is a 'solution' to . . . monstrous facts, you are lying to the child." Realistic novels for children continually confront this question.

Since the 1970s, the twin pressures of competition from other media and the exigencies of mass publishing have limited the possibilities of experimentation in the children's novel. There are, however, some notable examples of postmodernism and metafiction. Aidan Chambers' remarkable group of novels, *Breaktime* (1978), *Dance on My Grave* (1982), *Now I Know* (1987), and *The Toll Bridge* (1992) have been seen as redefining children's literature in terms of postmodernism, portraying an intelligent adolescent consciousness seeking to make new sense of the world. Peter Hunt has explored multiple unreliable narratives in *A Step Off the Path* (1985) and *Backtrack* (1986). Australia has produced some outstanding examples, such as Gary Crew's *Strange Objects* (1990), and Scandinavia has maintained its reputation for high-quality novels with the Norwegian Tormod Haugen's *Zeppelin* (1976) and the Swedish Peter Pohl's *Janne, min vän* (1985; *Johnny My Friend*).

The novel for children has come a long way, in both form and content, from its highly controlled beginnings, reflecting very clearly the condition of society. The children's novel has been seriously neglected by serious critics, but it could be argued that the most important writers are not necessarily those who are most experimental. Writers like Margaret Mahy (New Zealand), Astrid Lindgren (Sweden), William Mayne and Alan Garner (Britain), and Patricia Wrightson (Australia), who have blended experiment with convention, have had a widespread and subtle influence. Their work has extended the range not only of the children's novel, but of the novel in general. That they are so little known outside the bounds of children's literature is a serious loss to the literary world.

PETER HUNT

See also Adventure Novel and Imperial Romance; Adventures of Pinocchio; Alice's Adventures in Wonderland; Dime Novels and Penny Dreadfuls; Illustrations and Engravings; Little Women

Further Reading

Avery, Gillian, *Behold the Child*: *American Children and Their Books, 1621–1922*, London: Bodley Head, and Baltimore: Johns Hopkins University Press, 1994
Carpenter, Humphrey, and Mari Prichard, *The Oxford*

Companion to Children's Literature, Oxford and New York: Oxford University Press, 1984

Griswold, Jerry, *Audacious Kids: Coming of Age in America's Classic Children's Books,* New York: Oxford University Press, 1992

Haviland, Virginia, editor, *The Openhearted Audience: Ten Authors Talk About Writing for Children,* Washington, D.C.: Library of Congress, 1980

Hunt, Peter, *An Introduction to Children's Literature,* Oxford and New York: Oxford University Press, 1994

Hunt, Peter, editor, *Children's Literature: An Illustrated History,* Oxford and New York: Oxford University Press, 1996

Hunt, Peter, editor, *International Companion Encyclopedia of Children's Literature,* London and New York: Routledge, 1996

Meek, Margaret, Aidan Warlow, and Griselda Barton, *The Cool Web: The Pattern of Children's Reading,* London: Bodley Head, 1977; New York: Athenaum, 1978

Stephens, John, *Language and Ideology in Children's Fiction,* London and New York: Longman, 1992

Stephens, John, "Modernism to Postmodernism, or the Line from Insk to Onsk: William Mayne's *Tiger's Railway,*" *Papers in Children's Literature* 3:2 (1992)

Chilean Novel. *See* Latin American Novel: Chile

Chinese Novel

Beginnings to the 20th Century

During the final century or so of Chinese imperial history, the indigenous novel was lumped together with other forms of prose and dramatic narratives in the bibliographic category known as *xiaoshuo.* Two thousand years earlier this term, meaning "lesser discourses," had designated minor philosophical and other informal writings. By the eighth century it was applied, with similar connotations, to imaginative narratives in the classical language. During the 13th century, vernacular prose narratives appeared, again under this classification, and by the end of the 19th century the *xiaoshuo* category of writing included long narrative plays as well. Modern critics generally have interpreted the term as indicating Confucian disregard for, or even dismissal of, fiction as serious writing. But this was not always the case, as the historical record clearly indicates.

The vernacular novel was a particularly productive form in China, even though only the six "classic novels" are commonly known now among general readers (*see separate entry,* Six Classic Chinese Novels, and also C.T. Hsia, 1968). A recent bibliographic guide lists 1,160 titles, of which around 900 are still extant. Of those, nearly 600 appeared during the final century of imperial rule, which ended in 1911. Scholarly study of this class of writings really began only in the 1920s with Lu Xun's pioneering study that took part in the revaluation of tradition by a generation of youthful, reform-minded intellectuals (see Lu Xun, 1924). Virtually all detailed studies of individual works, genres, and periods are the product of the past few decades.

The earliest extant antecedents for the Chinese novel are collectively known as *pinghua,* or "plain[ly-told] tales," because of the common element in the titles of a group of texts printed by a Fujian bookseller between 1321 and 1323. All are historical narratives, and all appeared in uniform small-sized editions with intricate illustrations across the top of each page. Although they had been lost in China, a partial set was discovered in a Japanese library. Several other titles having similar structure and characteristics, dating from about the same time, were later discovered in China. Extant *pinghua* narrate exciting periods of Chinese history or the remarkable careers of specific individuals. They include the founding of the Zhou dynasty in the 11th century B.C., the unification of the feudal states by the First Emperor of the Qin, the Three Kingdoms era of the second century, when the great Han dynasty collapsed to begin hundreds of years of political chaos, and the exploits of the sixth-century general Xue Rengui during his campaigns in Korea and Manchuria. Although the extant corpus is incomplete, one can infer that by 1400 there were *pinghua* versions of the entire sweep of China's known history. One in particular is structurally different from the others. Termed a *shihua* or "poetic tale," it is the discontinuous account of the pilgrimage of the seventh-century monk Xuanzang from China to India, accompanied by a supernatural monkey, to obtain Buddhist scriptures. It may well be that there were a number of other nonhistorical "proto-novels" that no longer exist.

The Chinese novel is a product of the Ming period (1368–1644). Modern scholars generally suggest that the earliest works in this form came to be written soon after the *pinghua* appeared, around 1400, starting with the work of one or two individuals. However, proprietorial authorship is a later concept, appearing first around 1600, and attempts to link shadowy figures such as the 14th-century dramatist Luo Guanzhong with the creation of the novel form rest on very shaky evidence. The oldest extant novel is the printed edition of *Sanguo zhi yanyi* (commonly referred to as *The Three Kingdoms* or *Romance of the Three Kingdoms*) with prefaces dated 1494 and 1522. With deliberate slowness, it narrates the individual acts that led inexorably to the demise of the Han empire and the bloody civil wars that ensued, pitting virtuous but flawed individuals against vicious but brilliant enemies in endless games of strategy that seemingly hold the empire as prize for the victor. However, all contenders ultimately fail in this remarkable exploration of complex human motivations and abilities. The narrative focuses on Liu Bei, who, because he is the descendant of an emperor, believes he is the rightful heir to the throne. His loyal followers include the military commanders Zhang Fei, Guan Yu, and Liu Bei's divinely insightful advisor Zhuge Liang, all paragons of fidelity who fall through their own blind adherence to loyalty, either to their cause or to each other. Many copies of this work exist; clearly it was respected, even prized, and carefully preserved. For several decades it had no competitors. The next novel, also historical, was published only after the middle of the century.

The second half of the 16th century witnessed the appearance of numerous works of historical fiction, the genre that has had the most enduring appeal for Chinese readers. Early examples are stylistic hybrids of uneven quality combining formal historical sources with legends and entertainers' tales of individual heroes. As the form became ever more popular, booksellers sought unemployed scholars to rewrite earlier versions. For each dynastic period there was produced, over the next 300 years, a series of historical novels, each of which freely quoted from and modified its predecessor(s). These story materials were seen to be in the public domain, and the authorship—much less the degree of originality—of any individual title is frequently difficult to determine. With a few noteworthy exceptions, early examples were produced in relatively inexpensive, poorly printed editions.

This interest in historical fiction prompted the production of the second of China's recognized "classics," *Shuihu zhuan* (c. 1550), an adventure novel known in English primarily as *Water Margin* or *All Men Are Brothers* but now best represented by the translation *Outlaws of the Marsh*. Like the early historical novels, this draws heavily on tales that circulated among theatrical troupes and storytellers. In fact, several competing versions of this novel were in print during the last few centuries of imperial rule. *Outlaws of the Marsh* describes the interwoven adventures of a number of individual heroes on the fringes of polite society: they include guards, butchers, vagabonds, soothsayers, and thieves. One by one they are forced to flee by their own mistakes and, more commonly, by official abuse of power. They join together in mountain strongholds to become bandit gangs that ultimately constitute a rebel force of considerable proportions. Although much is made up, the band is factual. The name of its leader and several of its commanders do occur in the historical records of the time of its setting, the 12th century. The individual exploits for which the novel is much beloved are purely fictional, however. Each of its 108 heroes has a special nickname, special martial skills or insights, and usually a special weapon. In addition to their close ties of sworn brotherhood, these men are knights-errant who right wrongs, especially acts of exploitation of the defenseless by local authorities. Such chivalrous action is usually identified as the reason for their socially marginal status. But in the novel they are not rebels against imperial authority; rather, their purpose is to rid the court of its corrupt ministers. To this end the bandits form the kind of alternative society that has always appealed to readers, despite its problematic premises.

This outlaw band is misogynistic and self-righteous. It punishes with death all who dare to oppose it, and it justifies acts of cruelty against individual members (or their families) for the sake of the greater common good. Undoubtedly, the novel's enduring appeal is a function of its fundamentally subversive nature. Explicitly or by implication, the novel challenges virtually every tenet of conventional Confucian family values. Its individual male heroes delight in violence in the name of order. The novel glorifies gluttony rather than moderation.

The most widely read version of the novel was edited by Jin Shengtan in the middle of the 17th century. Jin truncated the work just after the 108 heroes have constituted a single band to conclude the novel with a dream of their mass extermination by Heaven. His purpose, Jin explained, was to demonstrate the fate that awaited all rebels against the throne. (Jin himself was later executed for leading a protest against abuses by Suzhou tax officials.)

A new genre appeared toward the end of the 16th century, the often fantastic adventures of religious figures. Drawn from both the Buddhist and Taoist religious traditions, these novels took on the air of moral seriousness by presenting inspiring, model behavior. Several were produced by the same individual, a publisher. The earliest and most outstanding example is *Xiyou ji* (c. 1580; *The Journey to the West*), the third of the classics still widely read today.

The Journey to the West develops what was by then a large and growing group of stories and plays about the Tang period pilgrim Xuanzang and his supernatural companions into a narrative that is best known for its far-ranging humor and verbal complexity. It also explores religious and philosophical themes with such subtlety that some readers still revere the work as virtual scripture. Here the Monkey King, along with the Pig, the Sand Monk, and a dragon who has been turned into a horse, guard the spiritually pure but timid Tang priest as he wends his allegorical way from China through Central Asia—which is populated by demons who seek personal immortality by eating a morsel of his flesh or obtaining a drop of his semen. These adventures are widely loved and frequently appear in later entertainment forms, most recently cartoon movies and a television series. On the allegorical level, it is the Monkey who makes the pilgrimage, however. Nominally already enlightened in a Buddhist sense, the Monkey must transcend all attachments to egotistic conceptions of self to become fully emancipated. *The Journey to the West* is generally, and probably accurately, attributed to a literatus named Wu Cheng'en, a compiler of literary anecdotes whose life spanned virtually the entire 16th century and who especially admired tales of the supernatural. It would appear that *Journey* inspired other novels of fantastic adventure (including contests of magic and trips to exotic places), but none had the enduring appeal of its artistic complexity and multifaceted humor.

The fourth "classic" also belongs to the Ming period and was nearly contemporaneous with *The Journey to the West*, although its career took a decidedly different path. Unlike *Journey*, which was reprinted frequently and widely read, manuscripts of *Jin Ping Mei* (which has been translated as *The Golden Lotus* and, more recently, *The Plum in the Golden Vase*) circulated for decades from about 1580 among only a handful of the most talented intellectuals of the day. The reasons for its exclusiveness are many. First, it includes erotic descriptions (most frequently presented in euphemistic terms) that have generally been condemned as pornographic. For that reason, it was probably circulated quietly to protect the identity of its author, perhaps a member of that select circle. In addition, it appears to have been written for the few readers who might appreciate its references to contemporary figures and events and, particularly, to contemporary culture. Recent scholarship has highlighted the work's extremely complex structure, demonstrating it to be a virtual pastiche of popular stories and plays with quotations from—and parodies of—contemporary jokes, gossip, and songs. Some of the juxtapositions of this borrowed material are howlingly funny, but for the most part the effect is horrifying. The novel focuses its central didactic concern on the disastrous effects of self-indulgence, and few characters are bound by any degree of human affection. *The Plum in the Golden Vase* is set in a sprawling merchant household, where the master's numerous wives, concubines, and maids are in constant competition for his attention, which means their power over the others. The protagonist, Ximen Qing, will go to any lengths to attain new partners to indulge his insatiable sexual appetite. His fifth wife, Pan Jinlian, is equally willing to do anything that will attract him to her. These pursuits reach startling degrees of moral degradation in this powerful exposé of human greed and its devastating consequences. The novel has been banned repeatedly since its first printing in 1617, and even today most editions are bowdlerized.

The Chinese novel had come of age by the 17th century. Literati had taken up the form as a vehicle for intense literary experimentation and for the most serious intellectual concerns (see Hegel, 1981). Novels such as *Sui Yangdi yanshi* (1631; The Merry Adventures of Emperor Yang) used historical figures as a vehicle for castigating contemporary politics. *Xiyou bu* (1641; A Supplement to Journey to the West, or *The Tower of Myriad Mirrors*) borrowed the central characters from the earlier *Journey* to explore the world of dreams and delusions. In a daring reversal of gender roles, *Xingshi yinyuan zhuan* (Marriage Destinies to Awaken the World) gave women dominant and domineering, even malicious, control over their husbands. While irony had been a common element of the Ming period masterpieces, parody became a mainstay of certain novels of the 17th and subsequent centuries. *Sui shi yiwen* (1633; Forgotten Tales of the Sui) reduces its martial hero to a bumbling fool for most of its chapters. The wildly bawdy *Rou putuan* (1658?; *The Carnal Prayer Mat*), attributed to the playwright Li Yu (1611–80), makes outrageous fun of both the courtship in popular romances and the quests in religious novels of the time. The 17th century was also the time when detailed novel criticism came of age in China (see Rolston, 1990, 1997).

Besides these novels written primarily for discerning elite readers, the bulk of novel production from around 1650 to early in the 18th century was in the form of romances. Presumably the earliest and still the best known was *Haoqiu zhuan* (c. 1650; *The Fortunate Union*) by an anonymous author. It was followed by dozens of similar works associated with very few individual writers, perhaps only two. The protagonists of these works were talented young men who wooed virtuous young ladies through poetry and music. After numerous trials and tribulations, customarily instigated by a dastardly and powerful rival, the young man and one or more young women are formally married to live happily ever after. The conventions of the form were simple and easily parodied, as in *The Carnal Prayer Mat*, which appeared within a few years of *The Fortunate Union*. But the romances became popular soon after the Manchu conquest of China, a time of devastating natural disasters as well as great loss of life through fighting—a time when predictable, optimistic fiction found a ready audience as a means of escape from the horrors of reality. Not surprisingly, *The Fortunate Union* was the first Chinese novel to be translated into a European language, by James Wilkinson and Bishop Thomas Percy, as *Hau Kiou Choaan; or, The Pleasing History* (1761).

The Manchu Qing dynasty (1644–1911) enforced conventional Confucian morality with considerable strictness. Few novels were produced and few were printed during the first century of Manchu rule, but by the 18th century the form was taken to new heights by a small number of excellent literati novelists. Justifiably the most famous is *Honglou meng* (known primarily to English readers under the title *Dream of the Red Chamber*, although the best translation uses the novel's first title, *Shitou ji*, or *Story of the Stone*). Its author, Cao Xueqin (1715?–c. 1764), was an obscure member of what had been China's wealthiest commoner family. Cao was an unimposing little man who supported himself, reportedly badly, by selling his poems and his art (he specialized in the painting of rocks). During his early childhood, he had lived on his family's enormous estate, complete with imposing halls and a labyrinthine garden, but then in 1728 the emperor appropriated all the property of his predecessor's closest retainers, including the Caos. For the rest of his life, Cao Xueqin lived modestly, drank frequently, and apparently worked on *Story of the Stone*. He wrote and rewrote through several decades, sharing his drafts with family members, whose extensive commentaries to extant manuscripts reveal the collaborative process of rendering memory and feeling into fiction. He died with the text incomplete, and various versions circulated for several decades. Then in 1791, a publisher hired a writer to piece together the various fragments to produce a "complete" edition. His movable-type editions of 1791 and 1792 are the basis for the standard version today, although a number of the manuscripts have been reprinted during the 20th century.

To a remarkable degree, the novel revolves around indeterminacy. It seemingly begins several times—with the story of a celestial stone imbued with divine intelligence that cares for a frail celestial flower; with the same romantic and religious misadventures experienced by a young man in a wealthy household; with these stories carved on a rock that attracts the attention of a passing monk. The monk reads the tale and, through the emotional attachments generated by his reading, becomes further enlightened and goes off to get the story published. But even the act of reading is compromised further on in the novel, as it warns the reader, "Truth becomes fiction when the fiction's true; Real becomes unreal where the unreal's real."

Story of the Stone is most often read either as a great and tragic love story of a young couple or as an exposé of the moral decay and the exploitative nature of old China's privileged class. It is both. The stone and its flower from the supernatural realm in the introduction are reborn as cousins who are desperately attached to each other with bonds that they never fully comprehend and that drive them both to distraction (see Li, 1993). Their relationship is complicated by the appearance of several equally attractive but constitutionally quite different female cousins with whom they pursue poetry and the other arts. Moreover, they are manipulated by their elders, particularly the matriarch of the family—whose well-being and that of her family takes precedence over all concerns of the individuals under her authority. The bulk of its narrative is devoted to minute descriptions of the mansion and its garden, the clothing and accoutrements of its inhabitants, and the constant conversations between its several hundred characters. The novel is also a poetic evocation, often through intertextual references to earlier stories and plays, of the difficulties of communication, of the expression of true feelings, and of the attainment of genuine spiritual detachment in this complicated, mundane world. So vivid are its descriptions of the opulence of the protagonists' extended residence that re-creations have been constructed in public parks across China and for an ever increasing number of film and television adaptations. But the theme of spiritual quest underlies and winds explicitly through the narrative to keep the wary reader always informed of its philosophical dimension, whether in chaste tea tasting, in poetic competition, or during childish sensual play.

Cao Xueqin's contemporaries were to create other, quite different masterpieces of the form. After *Story of the Stone*, the most widely recognized Qing period classic is *Rulin waishi* (c. 1750; An Unofficial History of the Scholars, or, more simply, *The Scholars*). Its vivid presentations of speech, behavior, and complex social relationships suggest autobiography, and indeed many of the characters are reminiscent of the author's contemporaries. The novel is created from interwoven tales of individuals or small groups (rather like *Outlaws of the Marsh* structurally), virtually all of whom are looking for ways to press their personal advantage in business, in the civil service examinations, or in currying favor with the powerful and wealthy. Gentle humor pervades the first half of the novel, but by the crucial central episode—a community sacrifice in honor of an ancient paragon of self-denial—the novel's tone becomes more serious. Characters in its second half are treated with a degree of scorn reminiscent of the later chapters in Jonathan Swift's *Gulliver's Travels*. In *The Scholars*, novelist Wu Jingzi (1701–54) created a scathing exposure, despite its humor, of the foibles of his contemporaries that can still make uncomfortable reading today. Its perennial relevance may explain why *The Scholars* is the least widely read of the "six classics" despite its rich language and powerful use of irony.

Other noteworthy 18th-century literati novels reflect on the lives of the literati. *Lüye xianzong* (1771?; Tracks of an Immortal in the Mundane World) by Li Baichuan (c. 1719–71) is firmly based on the author's own experiences, according to the preface. It chronicles his frustrations in life, his fondness for ghost stories, and his romantic encounters. *Qilu deng* (Lamp at the Crossroads), written by Li Lüyuan (1707–90), provides a detailed narrative of a student's life as he proceeds through the civil service examinations to success as an official. *Yesou puyan* (The Humble Words of an Old Rustic) by Xia Jingqu (1705–87) is an immodest attempt to demonstrate the author's worth as a participant in the Confucian intellectual tradition and appeals to someone of appropriately high position to appreciate his true moral stature.

One Qing period novel reflects the fashion for collecting that occupied many of the elite. *Jinghua yuan* (1821; Flowers in the Mirror) by Li Ruzhen, a "novel of erudition," in C.T. Hsia's apt phrase (see Hsia, 1977), accumulates an impressive amount of pure cultural data seemingly intended to display just how much its author knew. This work also takes up social causes of the time, most particularly the status of women and the painful process of footbinding.

Especially in these outstanding Qing period works, the role of the cultural elite is unmistakable. Philosophical trends starting late in the Ming focused first on the moral nature of the individual and then on the proper social role of the intellectual. By the middle of the Qing, the dominant thinkers had come to focus on the capacity of the individual to effect social change instead of the universal social harmony projected as the goal of the individual thinker in classical Confucianism. Thus the movement toward increasing self-awareness in writing was paralleled by a new sense of autonomy among China's cultural elite (see Huang, 1995).

In the novel, these developments were exemplified in *The Scholars*, where the individual protagonist becomes the only standard of morality—even though he often falls far short of exemplary behavior—while members of the Confucian establishment are caricatured as ignorant and egotistical. In other novels, *Story of the Stone* prime among them, the action moves into the private sphere of life. Quotidian detail is supplied for all aspects of life, including personal tastes and sexuality. But in contrast to the fiction of the Ming, these later novels generally limit their purview to the elite themselves, as literati novels become clearly distinguished from the action fiction seemingly intended for more general reading audiences.

Many of the central characters in these literati novels are female, but they often serve as metaphors for men subordinated by failure in the civil service examinations and for others displaced from the position of social dominance they had been raised to expect. What has been termed the "feminization" of literati novelists came to its most sophisticated level in the androgynous protagonist Baoyu in *Story of the Stone*. But later novels call into question both the viability of the Confucian state and the morality it professed to embody. This was reflected in the innumerable shrews, lechers, and other antisocial characters in many Qing novels who are impervious to Confucian blandishments. This tendency came to its fullest expression in the flood of novels that appeared during the last century of imperial rule.

Many of the better known late Qing novels are highly critical of their milieu. Building on the satirical attacks in *The Scholars*, some expose the ineptitude of Confucian teachers and administrators; others take up a variety of social problems. *Ershinian mudu zhi guai xianzhuang* (Vignettes from the Late Ch'ing) by Wu Woyao (also known as Wu Jianren, 1867–1910) castigates official malfeasance and stupidity, as did others of the time. Cultural exoticism plays a central role: the lengthy *Pinhua baojian* (1849; Precious Mirror for the Evaluation of "Flowers"), by Chen Sen (c. 1791–1848), narrates the lives of opera performers and male prostitutes, while *Haishang hua liezhuan* (1892; Lives of "Flowers on the Sea"), by Han Ziyun (c. 1855–94), explores the female sex trade of the time. Several novels written after the turn of the century are even more virulent in their condemnation of social ills. Unusual crime cases are the focus of *Jiuwei gui* (1906–10; The Nine-Tailed Tortoise), by Zhang Chunfan, and the role of love and sex in personal life found an airing in two 1906 romantic novels also by Wu Woyao. But by then, the influence of European fiction was visible in the themes and structure of these novels (see Dolezelová-Velingerová, 1980).

Novels in China generally are considered vernacular writings even though the style of language varies considerably within the more complex examples of the form. *The Three Kingdoms* is written in a relatively easily read version of the classical literary language, the style most familiar to anyone who had any formal education in preparation for the civil service examinations. Other of the middle Ming historical novels were written in a similar style. However, by the time of the late Ming masterpieces *The Plum in the Golden Vase* and *The Journey to the West*, the vehicle for extended prose narrative was clearly the "vernacular" language, a term that needs some clarification.

Generally, the linguistic medium of premodern Chinese novels was the lingua franca of administration throughout the linguistically diverse Chinese empire—the style known to foreigners as Mandarin. Yet most novels also incorporate colloquialisms from the lower Yangtze region, home to many of China's novelists—and bookstores—and a major cultural center. Many novels are punctuated with classical verse and documents written in a formal style. Speech for socially marginal characters is often constructed from dialectical expressions and slang. The masterpieces of the form are generally known for their linguistic richness.

The original edition of *Three Kingdoms* had been divided into 240 sections. Later, when the novel was edited slightly in the 17th century by Mao Lun (born 1605) and his son Mao Zonggang (born 1632) to form the standard version, these were grouped into 120 chapters, which by then had become the conventional structural division. Chapters in novels from the late 16th century onward were usually given titles in couplet form, each line of which refers to a major event within the chapter. Chapters end on a note of mild suspense, and many conclude with variations on the line, "If you wish to know what happened next, then read the following chapter." The mystery is always resolved in the first page or two of the next chapter, but by then the reader is considered to have been "hooked."

Many of China's premodern novels are long, having more than 60 chapters. Novelists often used chapter divisions in larger structural schemes. The clearest example is *The Plum in the Golden Vase,* the chapters of which, as Andrew Plaks has effectively demonstrated, are arranged in groups of ten (see Plaks, 1987). The two halves of the narrative are likewise symmetrically arranged, with, for example, disaster matching disaster in equal distance from the center point of the work. (More than any other work, *The Plum in the Golden Vase* also balances events: "hot" episodes are followed by "cold" episodes, cruelty by seduction, and the like.) Likewise, most novelists regularly employed what Patrick Hanan has termed the "storyteller's manner," a collection of rhetorical tags that ostensibly recreate the circumstances of oral narration, complete with conspiratorial fictive dialogue between the narrator and the reader, explanatory asides, and moral advice and admonitions to the reader,

who, by convention, is more insightful and better informed than any character in the narrative (see Hanan, 1981).

In complex ways, Chinese novels are all firmly embedded in their tradition. Many take up matters of social, political, or ethical import for exploration and explicit evaluation. Clarifying the date and provenance of a novel generally allows identification of the "cause" that the moralistic Confucian novelist had in mind as he wrote. Even though not all novelists were equally engaged with their times, virtually all made free use of their common literary heritage. There was only one education system during the Ming and Qing: all schools, regardless of sponsorship, had as their first priority training young men for administration, and the state set the curriculum for the civil service examinations. In addition, all educated people, men and women alike, had memorized large sections of the Confucian canon. This large fund of common knowledge and the widespread practice of close reading allowed the novelist to employ allusion and verbal play to an extraordinary degree. Elite readers would appreciate even the most subtle reference to earlier writings. And, of course, the corpus to draw from was enormous. Printing had spread widely at about the same time that the novel developed (see Hegel, 1998), making large private collections of poetry, prose, and even plays and other informal writings relatively commonplace among the wealthy. Literati novelists generally wrote for an audience who knew traditional literature very well and who saw the novel as a complex artistic form. Like the virtuoso performer who lends his own personal artistic variations to a role already familiar to theatre audiences, the novelist, even when substantially rewriting an earlier narrative, could be confident that his discerning readers would appreciate his own contribution to the growing tradition. Readers were helped along in this process of close reading by fiction critics, who contributed introductory critical essays and interlineal commentary to most editions (see Rolston, 1990, 1997).

Given the great diversity of expression within the novel format, exceptions may easily be found for virtually any generalization about the content of premodern Chinese novels. Even so, certain themes recur with considerable frequency, whether or not they are dominant within any individual work. Perhaps the most obvious theme is that of the general ineptitude and moral weakness of central leaders, emperors in particular. Virtually all are subject to the same human foibles as any other character. Some delude themselves that they are true "sons of Heaven" in moral terms, while others are merely self-indulgent. Often they are the helpless pawns of those who provide information about and access to the empire. These negative views of the imperial institution are generally balanced by appeals to basic Confucian ideals of the perfectability of the individual and the possibility of human harmony throughout society. This optimism, most frequently offered without irony, prevents the novel from being a politically subversive form, but surely the negative images of the throne—and positive images of rebels—entered into justifications for censorship that recurred at local and regional administrative levels for the last three centuries of imperial rule.

In a similar vein, many novels record the perversity of humanity in ignoring that basic Confucian goodness of which all are capable. Personal moral reform and a return to uprightness appear far less commonly in these works than does the punishment that self-indulgent, socially exploitative, or criminal activity rightly deserves. Didactic messages appear in virtually all works, and most are explicit. Even *Carnal Prayer Mat,* which parodies the homilies about sexual indulgence common to other works, ends with the spiritual progress of the central character.

Perhaps more than any other, *Carnal Prayer Mat* points to another theme that runs through the literati novels that were written for more sophisticated readers: the difficulty of true spiritual emancipation. The Chinese poetic tradition is commonly known in the West by its few outstanding poets, such as Wang Wei (c. 699–761), who express a sense of transcendence in their poetry, and yet other poets equally well known to Chinese readers, such as Tao Qian (365–427) and Su Shi (1037–1101), wrote numerous poems that complain of their failed attempts to find true solace. In the great novels, *Story of the Stone* and *The Scholars* among them, emancipation from human entanglements, the achievement of a general feeling of contentment, is rare, if not illusory. In sum, the novelistic tradition is Confucian in its concern for the individual in society; Buddhist or Taoist enlightenment does not appear in these works as a realistic goal.

With few exceptions, until approximately 1900 all Chinese novels appeared in blockprinted editions that facilitated the incorporation of pictures into the text. The Yuan period *pinghua* had been printed in small format with poorly proofread texts but with relatively fine illustrations: they compare favorably in quality with illustrated books in other categories of that time. They were produced in Fujian in southeast China, a major publishing area throughout the Ming. The early historical novels were produced as the quality of Fujian publishing was declining, and they tend to be illustrated at a significantly lower level of artistry than these precursors. *Three Kingdoms* appeared as text only, but virtually all subsequent novels were produced with illustrations. The 1522 *Three Kingdoms,* a large format edition (with pages measuring 6 x 9 inches), set the standard for later novels, the best editions of which were produced in the lower Yangtze cultural centers Nanjing, Suzhou, and Hangzhou. In pure physical size, many novels compared favorably with other, culturally more privileged publications during the Ming. Several novels from the early Qing have been identified as exceptionally fine examples of the printer's art. But by the middle of the Qing period, novels were increasingly produced in smaller size editions on poor paper with simple, even unattractive illustrations. By 1800, the social stature of the novel clearly had changed.

From the quality of the books as physical objects, one can deduce some characteristics of the intended audiences. The original readers must have been relatively affluent, for many novels appeared in editions that could only have been expensive. By 1800, however, masterpieces and more popular fiction alike were produced in smaller formats on pages crowded with type and introduced by a limited number of crudely drawn portraits of the central characters. Books were everywhere by then, and China's literate population was growing rapidly. In addition to the few large and relatively fine editions that easily accommodated leisure reading by candlelight, these small editions assumed a readership with the daytime leisure to allow sustained reading of these lengthy texts. Lithographic printing technology was introduced from Europe late in the 19th century, and Shanghai publishers began to produce small editions with tiny print, some so small that a magnifying lens was required to make it legible. The new novels of the time clearly were intended for readers unfamiliar with the workings of government, not the privileged literati of an earlier age. Thus in physical form as in content, the transition from premodern novels to the modern form can be observed to occur around 1900.

One final note on readership: *The Plum in the Golden Vase* had circulated in manuscript for decades before it was printed, although most late Ming novels were probably printed very soon after compilation. In contrast to the anguished condemnation of venality in *The Plum in the Golden Vase,* most novels were less serious, and many were produced for commercial gain throughout the 16th and 17th centuries. However, the masterpieces of the 18th century generally circulated only in manuscript form during their authors' lifetimes. Their message, it would appear, was too personal to make public. Likewise, none of the 18th-century literati novelists had the connections with publishers or financiers who would support the initial cost of publication. These most complex examples of the novel form thus were initially meant to be read exclusively by small circles of selected friends for their personal message and to be appreciated by the discriminating for their painstaking art.

ROBERT E. HEGEL

See also Six Classic Chinese Novels

Further Reading

Dolezelová-Velingerová, Milena, editor, *The Chinese Novel at the Turn of the Century,* Toronto and Buffalo, New York: University of Toronto Press, 1980

Hanan, Patrick, *The Chinese Vernacular Story,* Cambridge, Massachusetts: Harvard University Press, 1981

Hegel, Robert E., *The Novel in Seventeenth-Century China,* New York: Columbia University Press, 1981

Hegel, Robert E., *Reading Illustrated Fiction in Late Imperial China,* Stanford, California: Stanford University Press, 1998

Hsia, C.T., *The Classic Chinese Novel: A Critical Introduction,* New York: Columbia University Press, 1968

Hsia, C.T., "The Scholar-Novelist and Chinese Culture: A Reappraisal of *Ching-hua yuan,*" in *Chinese Narrative: Critical and Theoretical Essays,* edited by Andrew H. Plaks, Princeton, New Jersey: Princeton University Press, 1977

Huang, Martin W., *Literati and Self-Re/Presentation: Autobiographical Sensibility in the Eighteenth-Century Chinese Novel,* Stanford, California: Stanford University Press, 1995

Li, Wai-yee, *Enchantment and Disenchantment: Love and Illusion in Chinese Literature,* Princeton, New Jersey: Princeton University Press, 1993

Liu Ts'un-yan, *Buddhist and Taoist Influences on Chinese Novels,* Wiesbaden: Harrassowitz, 1962

Lu Xun, *Zhongguo xiaoshuo shilüe,* Beijing, 1924; as *A Brief History of Chinese Fiction,* Beijing: Foreign Languages Press, 1959; 3rd edition, 1976

Ma, Y.W., "The Chinese Historical Novel: An Outline of Themes and Contexts," *Journal of Asian Studies* 34:2 (February 1975)

McMahon, Keith, *Misers, Shrews, and Polygamists: Sexuality and Male-Female Relations in Eighteenth-Century Chinese Fiction,* Durham, North Carolina: Duke University Press, 1995

Nienhauser, William H., editor, *Indiana Companion to Traditional Chinese Literature,* Bloomington: Indiana University Press, 1986

Plaks, Andrew H., *Archetype and Allegory in the "Dream of the Red Chamber,"* Princeton, New Jersey: Princeton University Press, 1976

Plaks, Andrew H., "Full-length *Hsiao-shuo* [*xiaoshuo*] and the Western Novel," *New Asia Academic Bulletin* 1 (1978); reprinted in *China and the West: Comparative Literature Studies,* edited by William Tay et al., Hong Kong: Chinese University Press, and Seattle: University of Washington Press, 1980

Plaks, Andrew H., *Four Masterworks of the Ming Novel: Ssu ta ch'i-shu,* Princeton, New Jersey: Princeton University Press, 1987

Rolston, David L., editor, *How to Read the Chinese Novel,* Princeton, New Jersey: Princeton University Press, 1990

Rolston, David L., *Traditional Chinese Fiction and Fiction Commentary: Reading and Writing Between the Lines,* Stanford, California: Stanford University Press, and Cambridge: Cambridge University Press, 1997

Ropp, Paul S., *Dissent in Early Modern China: "Ju-lin wai-shih"* [Rulin waishi] *and Ch'ing Social Criticism,* Ann Arbor: University of Michigan Press, 1981

Widmer, Ellen, *The Margins of Utopia: Shui-hu hou-chuan and the Literature of Ming Loyalism,* Cambridge, Massachusetts: Council on East Asian Studies, Harvard University, 1987

Wu, Yenna, *The Chinese Virago: A Literary Theme,* Cambridge, Massachusetts: Council on East Asian Studies, Harvard University, 1995

Yu, Anthony C., *Rereading the Stone: Desire and the Making of Fiction in Dream of the Red Chamber,* Princeton, New Jersey: Princeton University Press, 1997

Chinese Novel

20th Century

Mainland China

In 1900 the final efforts of the Chinese Empress Dowager to expel foreign powers, liquidate their Chinese associates, and forestall modernization failed, and the ensuing decade was given over to wide-ranging reforms toward modernization under the imperial Qing dynasty government. The reforms greatly stimulated the publication of newspapers and periodicals, which in turn promoted both Chinese and foreign fiction. Between 1901 and 1911 the topic of reform inspired several notable Chinese novels of social criticism and satire devoted to representing the tribulations of common Chinese subjects and the failures of Chinese officials and the cultural elite either to adopt effective reforms or to live up to their own Confucian code of leadership through moral example and benevolence. Prominent among these novels are Li Boyuan's *Wenming xiaoshi* (1903–05; A Brief History of Civilization) and *Guanchang xianxing ji* (1903–05; The Bureaucrats), Wu Woyao's *Ershi nian mudu zhi guai xianzhuang* (1903–10; *Bizarre Happenings Eyewitnessed Over Two Decades*) and *Hen hai* (1905; Sea of Woe), Zeng Pu's roman à clef *Nie hai hua* (1905–07; Flower on an Ocean of Sin), and Liu E's *Lao Can youji* (1904–07; *Travels of Lao Can*). Of these, *Travels of Lao Can* exemplifies the striking social criticism and formal innovations among novels of this decade. While maintaining the traditional, vernacular, storyteller style of most previous Chinese novels, the new novels introduced such innovations as first-person and unreliable narrators. Such a hybrid form is found in *Travels of Lao Can,* where lyrical passages in prose, previously distinctive of poetry, are incorporated into the narrative as internal monologues of the narrator, with an effect close to stream of consciousness. As an author, Liu E viewed himself as a Confucian intellectual promoting reforms in an ef-

fort to forestall the threat of republican revolution. His protagonist, Lao Can, a Chinese physician, is episodically drawn into several situations that evoke his sympathies for ordinary subjects of the empire and indignant reflections on the harshness and irresponsibility of officials, all of which could lead to revolution.

The link between the cultural capital of a Confucian education and sociopolitical status was loosened but not entirely broken by the termination of the Confucian Civil Service Examination in 1905. The collapse of the last imperial dynasty in 1912 was followed directly by the formation of a republic with a constitution that provided a place for Confucian principles as "the basis for the cultivation of personal character in national education." Confucian discourse had resisted giving fiction the same status as poetry and essays, and the classic Chinese novel had developed as an institution outside the academy. However, the reform movements at the close of the Qing, the last imperial dynasty, brought translations of foreign novels and a revaluation of the status of fiction in light of Hegelian aesthetics and a concern with national spirit. Fiction came to be discussed by writers with very respectable credentials as Chinese scholars.

The bulk of Chinese novels had developed vernacular styles and a form imitative of storytellers' conventions. However, many of the most popular foreign novels of the late Qing dynasty were translated into the classical, literary styles that were the mark of status culture and avoided the idioms of storytelling. The fiction that attracted the most widespread attention among the youth of the cultural elite immediately following the Republican Revolution followed this trend. The most famous of a popular series of romance novels were Xu Zhenya's *Yu li hun* (1911–12; The Soul of Jade Pear Flowers) and Su Manshu's

Duan hong ling yan ji (1912; *The Lone Swan*). Eventually, Xu Zhenya's *Yu li hun* reportedly so impressed the daughter of the prestigious Chinese scholar who, prior to the revolution, had placed first in the final Confucian civil service exam ever administered, that he felt compelled to acknowledge Xu's literary talent and arrange for his daughter to marry the author. Until the success of *Yu li hun,* Xu's career had been confined to tutoring and composing textbooks for a commercial publishing house while composing his romance fiction. In the novel, a young male Confucian tutor admires and arouses the affections of a young widow, who nevertheless holds to the ideal of chastity expected of virtuous widows. She initiates an arrangement for the tutor to marry her sister-in-law, instead. Although the sister-in-law has developed an active distaste for elite Chinese customs through a foreign-style education, she agrees to marry the tutor out of a sense of filial piety. She eventually gains so much admiration for her sister-in-law's virtuous suicide in defense of her chastity that she follows her example. The unhappy tutor then hastens to sacrifice himself to the cause of the Republican Revolution and dies on the barricades, politically radical, culturally conservative. In *The Lone Swan,* a young monk accepts money from the girl to whom he was formerly betrothed in order to find his Japanese mother. Once in Japan, he is introduced to a Japanese girl with a view to marriage. However, he returns to his monastery in China, where he learns that his former Chinese fiancée has committed suicide to avoid an arranged marriage. These novels introduced formal innovations and a concern for psychology to Chinese fiction, and they flirt with the culturally exotic and socially radical. Nevertheless, these narratives assimilated the new elements to culturally conservative values, which threatened to vitiate the novel's culturally radical role that reformers and revolutionaries had envisioned.

The failure of the new republic to fully affirm the dominance of foreign cultures, as exemplified in *Yu li hun* and *The Lone Swan,* galvanized groups of younger members of the educated elite, whose status depended heavily on the cultural capital of the foreign education they received. In 1915 and 1916, Chen Duxiu, editor of the radical *Xin qingnian* (New Youth) magazine and an overseas student contributor, Hu Shi, inaugurated a critical movement that denounced the maudlin sentiments and elaborate style of the romance novels, associating them with a weak and archaic aristocratic society. They argued for a literature of authentic emotion, vernacular language, and fidelity to the real. On the one hand, they were inspired by 19th-century Western realism. On the other hand, elements of their platform—particularly their preference for vernacular Mandarin Chinese—were also consistent with features of the classic Chinese novel and its vernacular tradition. Hu Shi was joined by other scholars in the project of evaluating and elevating the status of certain classic novels as a voice of the people groping in rebellion against traditional status culture and as a contribution to the development of values appropriate to a modern nation. At the same time, the critic-reformers introduced translations of realist and romantic literature in vernacular Mandarin with a distinctively Europeanized style, and they searched for a novelist to write the ideal modern Chinese novel. The group and its activities were greatly expanded in 1919 when feelings of humiliation over the Treaty of Versailles led to a student demonstration in Beijing on May 4, from which the literature of the May Fourth movement took its name.

The large numbers of students and teachers of the movement wrote to promote a new culture of modernity elevating the role of Mandarin vernacular style. During the first ten years, they produced short stories, essays, poetry, and a few novels that were semi-autobiographical accounts of maturation. The most sustained narrative of the era to win acclaim was a novella, "A Q zhengzhuan" (1921; "The True Story of Ah Q"), by the acknowledged literary lion of the times, Lu Xun (Lu Hsün, penname of Chou Shu-jen). This sardonic narrative focuses on the life of a casual village laborer, known only as Ah Q, who is caught up in the Republican Revolution and executed. Through his mentality and that of his fellow citizens, as well as the metafiction concerning the author's research of the character's life story, the novella satirizes national culture. It was inspired in part by Nietzsche and by foreign cultural critics of China. The story is famous for savaging the concept of a national essence valued by cultural conservatives, which Lu Xun depicts as akin to a Nietzschean "slave mentality" unchanged by the revolution. Writers for the newly formed Communist Party of China reread the story as a study of class conflict in which Ah Q's mentality is that of the proletariat in ferment prior to the enlightened leadership of communism.

By the late 1920s, short fiction had introduced a full range of themes, including sexuality and gender, ethnicity, and new urban lifestyles, and it had expanded the scope of regional, peasant, and proletarian literature. However, it was political upheaval, resulting from the rise of political parties vying with one another and with regional warlords for control of the republic, that fostered the realist novel. Young students and teachers developed the maturation, or *Bildung,* themes of existing works into reflections on dramatic national events. With few exceptions, the writers and the majority of their readers came from the families of merchants, landed gentry, scholars, civil officials, or military officers and were provided early on with some degree of classical education, followed by Westernized schooling. Some were sent to study in Japan, Europe, or the United States.

Whether distressed by the impoverishment of their families or by guilt over their enrichment during the constant political turmoil, the novelists of realism now assumed the classic stance of the educated elite as the voice of social conscience and reflection. In *Ni Huan-chih* (1928–29; *Ni Huanzhi*), by Ye Shengtao (Yeh Sheng-t'ao, Yeh Shao-chün), the eponymous protagonist is a young schoolteacher whose attempt to put the principles of John Dewey's philosophy into practice is frustrated by special interests of his local community. Realizing that only revolution can introduce the social changes to implement educational reforms, Ni Huanzhi discovers that—like Goethe's young Werther, a popular figure of the early 1920s—he is too sensitive for the times and dies of typhoid fever. Meanwhile, his colleagues, representing the Communist Party, are slaughtered as the Nationalist Party comes to power in 1927. The landmark maturation novels of the gentle anarchist Ba Jin (Pa Chin; Li Feikan) endowed their sensitive protagonists with more resolve, either to sacrifice themselves in acts of desperate violence against authoritarian politicians, as in *Mie wang* (1929; *Destruction*), or at least to renounce their elite families, ruled as they are by authoritarian patriarchs, as in *Jia* (1931; *Family*).

The genre of the maturation novel set against public events of epic scope reached its climax through the depiction of a landlord household declining amid the disorder of banditry, peasant rebellion, and Japanese colonial aggression during the early 1930s in *Keerqinqi caoyuan* (1933, 1939; *The Korchin Banner Plains*) by Duanmu Hongliang (Tuan-mu Hung-liang). In addition to civil war and Japanese military aggression in China, the onset of worldwide economic depression in 1929 inspired a series of novels that abandoned the maturation themes in favor of stories of people who are undone by their adherence to capitalist ideology, whether as captains of industry, as in *Ziye* (1933; *Midnight*), by Mao Dun, or as independent workers, such as the rickshaw puller of *Luotuo Xiangzi* (1937; translated as *Rickshaw, Rickshaw Boy,* and *Camel Xiangzi*), by Lao She (Shu Ch'ing-ch'un). Both of these novels involved an unprecedented amount of meticulous background research by their authors.

The principal alternatives to this growing stream of social realism were the novels employing structures of fantasy to mount topical social satire, as in *Alisi you Zhongguo ji* (1926; *Alice in China*), by Shen Congwen (Shen Ts'ung-wen), *Guitu riji* (1931; *Ghostland Diaries*) and other titles by Zhang Tianyi (Chang T'ien-i), and *Mao cheng ji* (1932–33; *Cat Country*), by Lao She, and the commercial fiction of the popular romance writers of the Mandarin Duck and Butterfly School, led by Zhang Henshui (Chang Hen-shui). Zhang Henshui's *Tixiao yinyuan* (1930; Fate in Tears and Laughter), an account of a young man's involvement with a female street entertainer, a Europeanized girl of the social elite, and the young daughter of a martial arts expert, outsold virtually all of the novels of social realism of the era.

When full-scale war with Japan on Chinese soil broke out in 1937, writers committed to the war effort saw it as an opportunity to mobilize the large numbers of Chinese to whom the novel of social realism was still unknown. This effort in mass propaganda favored other genres, so that novels treating the activities of the War of Resistance to Japan (1937–45) were not as popular as other works. Many of them have received little critical attention. With respect to novels, the period is best remembered for writing about noncombatants largely removed from the fighting. Frequently, plot is neglected in favor of lyrical, psychological, and even existential reflection. Shen Congwen solidified his reputation as a pastoral mythmaker of the remote western Hunan province in his novel *Chang he* (1943; The Long River), depicting the families of boatmen and orange growers encountering the exploitation of modern political officials. In Ba Jin's *Han ye* (1947; *Cold Nights*), an unemployed teacher's wife leaves him for her career as he slowly succumbs to tuberculosis, dying as China celebrates victory over Japan. Personality studies dominated other works, such as the celebrated novella by Eileen Chang (Zhang Ailing), *Jin suo ji* (1943; The Golden Cangue), in which a humiliated and frustrated widow in an extended family avenges herself on her children. The novels of Shi Tuo (Shih T'o; Wang Ch'ang-chien), whose schoolteacher characters engage in disastrous adventures in social climbing, in *Jiehun* (1947; Marriage), or futile engagements with love and politics, in *Ma Lan* (1948; Ma Lan), also belong to this category. Perhaps the best selling of these novels at the end of the war period was *Wei cheng* (1947; *Fortress Besieged*) by the scholar-author Qian Zhongshu (Ch'ien Chung-shu), a protean text of social satire, caricature, and comedy of manners set among the educated elite. It concludes with an extended passage on the marital clash of a Shanghai couple that approaches existential dimensions.

These novels, for all their social criticism, assert an aesthetic of the writer as a member of an autonomous cultural elite. While boundaries to these aspirations had been set by the various governments claiming authority over China, the rise of the successfully defended communist base of Yan'an in northwest China signified the beginning of the end for such pretensions. Dissatisfied with criticisms of life in Yan'an by various writers migrating from the urban cultural citadels to the rural base, Mao Zedong (Mao Tse-tung), as chairman of the Communist Party of China, disciplined, purged, or executed critics. He also issued a set of prescriptive guidelines that in effect were an apologia for Soviet socialist realism in his "Talks at the Yan'an Forum on Literature and Art" in 1942. The result was first to enhance the status of oral and performing literature employing features of folk literature. As a consequence, a new set of authors gained prominence, including He Jingzhi (Ho Ching-chih) and Zhao Shuli (Chao Shu-li). Like Mao, they had a peasant background, in contrast to the writers of the May Fourth generation. By the mid-1940s Yan'an authors also had produced a number of novels on communist-led peasant resistance to the Japanese invasion featuring folk narrative techniques. After the war, the most prestigious projects for the novel were the depictions of communist land reform activities in north China, which served both to engage and to inform urban white-collar readers and to create an international place for communist Chinese literature, at least among those works awarded Stalin prizes in the Soviet Union. The land reform novels were meant to compete as realist novels rather than as folk art, and they were to enhance the image of the Communist Party. They gave a place in cultural circles to peasant writers such as Zhao Shuli, author of *Lijiazhuang de bianqian* (1946; *The Changes in Li Village*) and to former writers of social criticism in the urban press, such as Zhou Libo (Chou Li-po), author of *Baofeng zouyu* (1948; *The Hurricane*) and Ding Ling, the most prominent woman author on the political left, whose novel *Taiyang zhaozai Sangganhe shang* (1949; *The Sun Shines over the Sanggan River*) may be the most complex treatment of village social relationships in the land reform genre.

Following the civil war that established the People's Republic of China in 1949, the Yan'an-based novelists dominated the field through much of the 1950s. Their novels of land reform were followed by novels on agricultural collectivization, the central theme of art at that time. However, the formulas laid down by socialist realism generated dissatisfaction in critical circles, and the initial failures of communization during the Great Leap Forward of 1958 and 1959 also made such novels controversial. Following the disasters of the Great Leap Forward, a new series of novels on communization appeared by authors with peasant backgrounds, most notably *Chuang ye shi* (1960; *The Builders*), by Liu Qing (Liu Ch'ing), and *Yanyang tian* (1964; Bright, Sunny Skies), by Hao Ran (Hao Jan; Liang Jinguang), which argued the need for communization in order to avoid a return to private property and, with it, economic exploitation. However, the reading public was more drawn to a wave of historical novels celebrating the history of the communist revolution, particularly *Hong yan* (1962; *Red Crag*), by Luo Guangbin (Lo Kuang-pin) and Yang Yiyan (Yang I-yen), a tale of wartime espionage recounting the lives of communist agents imprisoned by their Nationalist Party adversaries, and *Qingchun zhi ge* (1960; *The Song of Youth*), also a quasi-autobiographical story of a girl among the educated elite during the Nationalist Republican era awakening to the perfidy of her acquaintances and the justice of socialism.

Nevertheless, virtually none of the new novels of socialist realism, let alone the works of previous generations, proved sufficiently politically correct to survive censorship during the massive power struggles of the Great Proletarian Cultural Revolution, instigated by Mao Zedong to purge his rivals in the party for their disagreements with him over economic development, an event that stretched from 1966 to Mao's death in 1976. Except for the works of the deceased Lu Xun, all modern works were banned, and it was not until 1972 that a new novel was commissioned, *Jinguang dadao* (1972; The Golden Highway) by Hao Ran, an account of agricultural collectivization in the early 1950s in which local peasants appear more enthusiastic and assertive in initiating this process than in novels prior to the Cultural Revolution.

The death of Mao Zedong in 1976 was followed within a year by officially published criticisms of the art and literature of the Cultural Revolution, as national political leadership, eventually favoring Deng Xiaoping, sought a new constituency in a coalition of educated elite, youth, and party cadres who had suffered during the Maoist era. The swiftly shifting political scene again favored the production of short stories over novels, and the most celebrated piece of the late 1970s that approached novel length was the novella "Bodong" (1979; "Waves") by the underground writer Bei Dao (Zhao Zhenkai/Chao Chen-k'ai), appearing in one of the "unofficial" magazines produced by young people outside the state publishing system but allowed to circulate briefly in the late 1970s. "Waves" alludes both to the Maoist rhetoric of revolution as a sea and to the characters in the story as uprooted, displaced, and stripped of faith in a revolutionary historical telos by the turmoil of the Cultural Revolution. Among the prominent motifs of this work, which would be echoed in other works throughout the following decade, were its demotion of party officials to undistinguished or problematic roles; its protagonist's abandonment of conformity to expectations of the public world in favor of a search for fulfillment in private and intimate relationships, in illicit affairs and illegal activities; and its reflection on a series of topics that displace class struggle from its previously privileged position, among them existential, religious, and nationalistic themes. "Waves" also reintroduced the use of multiple narrative voices, nonlinear time schemes, and associative interior monologues.

The bureaucratic attack on unofficially published works such as "Waves" commenced once Deng Xiaoping's leadership position was secure, only to be followed by attempts to reintroduce aspects of modernism to Chinese literature through translations of foreign works. These were done in the name of supporting the broad plan for modernization announced by the new regime, and a number of writers sought to reconcile modernism with modernization, as in Wang Meng's novella "Hudie" (1980; Butterfly). However, a series of associative interior monologues of a young mother and proof-editor in the novella "Wo'men zhege nianji de meng" (1982; "The Dreams of Our Generation"), by Zhang Xinxin, exceeded the boundaries of an appropriate socialist construction of contemporary life. An assertion of liberal humanism over the vision of class struggle that dominated the Maoist era marks the novel of social exposure *Ren ah, ren!* (1981; Ah, Humanity!), by Dai Houying. The early 1980s saw the unprecedented growth in the number and status of women writers, including Zhang and Dai, as the realm of the private and intimate was opened to fiction and welcomed by readers. However, the works of both Zhang and Dai were attacked or banned during the campaign against "spiritual pollution" led by the Central Propaganda Department of the Communist Party in 1983.

Following the "spiritual pollution" campaign, political circumstances again favored shorter works, this time emphasizing a protagonist's mental reconciliation of cultural and spiritual conflicts with contemporary socialist policies. But even works dedicated to these themes, notably the novellas of Zhang Xianliang (Chang Hsien-liang), introduced such controversial material as sexuality. Official censorship under the Communist Party, having already demonstrated its power, was inclined to accede to liberalizations that did not openly confront its authority. There followed, from 1984, an increasingly ambitious production of fiction implying rejection of or alternatives to heretofore fundamental Maoist views of Chinese culture, history, and modernity. At first this movement took the form of alternative historical visions, promoting the role of transgressive sexuality and blurring the role of the party and the relationship of the rational to the sublime in historical reconstructions of culture and modernization. Some of the most widely read novels in this vein took the form of family histories. The most prominent of these family histories are novels by the female author Wang Anyi (Wang An-i), from *Xiaobaozhuang* (1985; Baotown), an example of the enthusiastic response to Gabriel García Márquez's *One Hundred Years of Solitude*, to *Jishi he xugou* (1993; Fact and Fiction), a partially researched, partially fantasized reconstruction of her mother's maternal line back to a tribe of 14th-century nomads. The Nietzschean *Hong gaoliang jiazu* (1985; Red Sorghum) by Mo Yan (Mo Yen; Kuan Mo-yeh) also introduced a trend toward the grotesque.

The grotesque became a hallmark of a wide range of Chinese works by the late 1980s. Where social and socialist realism had placed transgression and violence in the light of an ideal of progress toward modernity and beauty, novels by the late 1980s stripped transgression of these attributes and developed the illicit and the violent in terms of an unredeemed exploration of the irrational and the grotesque. The grisly is combined with magic realism in the contemporary portrait of impoverished schoolteachers and corrupt party officials in Mo Yan's *Shisan bu* (1990; Thirteen Steps). The same combination marks the more conventional account of a peasant disturbance over economic exploitation in *Tiantang suantai zhi ge* (1988; The Garlic Ballads). Short stories and novellas by an avant-garde often noted for metafictional writing culminated in such novels as Ge Fei's *Diren* (1991; Enemy) and Su Tong's *Mi* (1992; Rice), both historical novels. The former depicts the patriarch of an extended family household whose identity is gradually destroyed by a series of murders and disappearances that decimate his household. The latter follows the rise and fall of a ruthless peasant boy who comes to dominate a rice merchant's household and eventually the local underworld. The grotesque also plays a prominent role in *Meigui men* (1988; The Rose Gate), by Tie Ning (T'ieh Ning), a novel of female maturation set largely in Beijing during the Cultural Revolution, and in the fantastic, parodic mimicry of masculinist discourse in *Tuwei biaoyan* (1990; Breakthrough Performance) by another female author, Can Xue (Ts'an Hsüeh; Teng Hsiao-hua). Can Xue is one of a handful of avowed feminist writers whose project of disordering conventions of narrative and identity had begun in the mid-1980s with short fiction as disturbing in its psychological and sensual details as the similar defamiliarizing of transgression and violence pursued by the male avant-gardists.

These trends in the novel were obviously dominated by a desire to respond to Western culture and be recognized in the West on the part of writers who collectively shared some position, however unsettled, among the state-sponsored cultural elite as the proprietors of high culture. The late 1980s, however, saw the rise of a market system, reductions in state subsidies to cultural organizations and publications, and the stifling of political reforms, together with an uneven access to advancement through status culture from overseas. Students and the youthful white-collar workforce welcomed the streetwise satirical fiction of Wang Shuo, which at once boosted the sales of the state-supported periodicals publishing his work and ridiculed the pretensions of the educated elite to cultural leadership. Wang's work condemns the elite for self-aggrandizement and complicity in a state project offering fantasy to a public that finds its reality too unbearable to recognize. The irreverent or cynical attitudes of his less than reputable characters and his satire of official nationalism are evident in *Qianwan bie ba wo dang ren* (1989; Never Take Me for Human) and *Wande jiushi xintiao* (1988; Playing for Thrills). His novels of youth during the Cultural Revolution fed into a nostalgia among those entering middle age who valued the period not for its Maoism but for their personal experiences of that turmoil, also famously represented in *Xuese huanghun* (1987; Blood Red Sunset), by Lao Gui (Ma Bo; Ma Po). Finally, Wang Shuo represented the only significant commercial competition with the fiction of popular culture entering China from Taiwan and Hong Kong during the late 1980s and 1990s.

Hong Kong and Taiwan

While conditions in Hong Kong never favored the sustained production of high culture locally, following the Liberation of 1949 a number of émigré writers published significant titles there. *Yang ko* (1955; The Rice Sprout Song) by Eileen Chang offered perhaps the most trenchant cultural critique of the socialist realist representation of China in its time. Together with her short stories written in the 1940s, the novel established her as one of the few serious writers to gain wide popularity. Another émigré, Liu Yichang (Liu I-ch'ang), published the most sustained experiments in modernism in Chinese during the 1960s, notably *Jiutu* (1963; The Drunkard). Like Hong Kong, Taiwan always had been on the periphery of the mainstreams of high culture. For a decade after the retreat of the Nationalist Party to this island province in 1949, novels were dominated by state-sponsored anticommunist propaganda, such as *Lan yu hei* (1958; The Blue and the Black), by Wang Lan, and *Huocun zhuan* (1951; Fool in the Reeds), by Chen Jiying. By the early 1960s a group of students and professors, followed by small publishing houses, sought to initiate autonomous literary production. The effort eventually resulted in important novels by Bai Xianyong (Pai Hsien-yung) and Wang Wenxing (Wang Wen-hsing). Wang Wenxing's novels, *Jia bian* (1972; Family Catastrophe) and *Beihai de ren* (1981; Backed Against the Sea), accomplished the most radical and thoughtful innovations in style, narrative voice, and form in their time. Bai Xianyong's *Niezi* (1979; Crystal Boys) was bold in introducing the gay subculture of Taipei. At the same time, these modernists (*xiandai pai*) were attacked by a dissident "Homeland Literature" movement, in part socialist

and in part representative of a subversive movement for a Taiwan identity separate from Chinese nationality. As legal sanctions were reduced, the theme of Taiwan identity eventually inspired several novels, among them *Lang tao sha* (1988–90; Wave-Washed Sands), by Dongfang Bai, both a roman-à-clef and a roman-fleuve recounting the tribulations that shaped the identity of the Taiwan educated elite from the Japanese occupation (1895–1945) to the contemporary era. Another novel reconstructing history, *Miyuan* (1991; The Labyrinth), by Li Ang (Shih Shu-tuan), treated the theme of Taiwan identity from a feminist position developed in Li Ang's earlier fiction. Her celebrated novel *Shafu* (1983; The Butcher's Wife) is a graphic depiction of spousal abuse in its social context. An engagement with postmodernist narrative reached novel length in *Da shuohuangjia* (1989; Big Liar), by Zhang Dachun (Chang Ta-ch'un), originally published as entertaining daily installments in a Taipei newspaper, adapting a front-page story as material for fantastic elaboration in each fictive chapter.

The political implications or the open discussion of sexuality in many of these novels made them unacceptable for publication in the People's Republic of China, and their readership for the most part remained socially limited. However, a substantial number of commercially successful action and romance novels that defined aspects of the popular cultures of Taiwan and Hong Kong also became bestsellers in China from the mid-1980s into the 1990s. The novels of the Hong Kong writer and publisher Jin Yong (Chin Yung; Cha Liang-yung; Louis Cha) dominated the field of martial arts fiction. A student of history turned newspaper publisher, Jin Yong established the circulation of his principal newspaper, *Ming Pao*, in the late 1950s by using it to serialize his own novels of knight errantry, such as *Xueshan feihu* (Fox Volant of the Snowy Mountain) and *Shujian enchiu lu* (Romance of Book and Sword). Turning away from the trends among other modern Chinese intellectuals, Jin Yong wrote narratives in archaic language that raised popular fiction to a new cultural status. He championed the knight errant figures derided by modernizing intellectuals and censored by governments in China, recontextualized old moral and aesthetic issues, and provided a platform for reconstructing Chinese history through heroes and activities marginalized by both the Nationalist Party and the Communist Party.

Melodramatic romance novels were the other form of bestseller, particularly the dozens of novels published by Qiong Yao (Ch'iung Yao; Ch'en Che), first in Taiwan beginning in the early 1960s and again in China in the 1980s and 1990s. Qiong Yao's first novel, *Chuang wai* (1963; Outside the Window), caused a sensation that also intrigued the educated elite. The novel is a semiautobiographical account of the destructive intervention of domestic and public authorities in the budding romance between a high-school girl and her teacher. However, her subsequent novels were increasingly dismissed by critics as commercial, stereotyped, sentimental fantasies. Nevertheless, her novels have insisted on the significance of the private and intimate at a time of intellectual preoccupation with the public realm. Her work proposes an "emotional realism" focused on reconciling conflicts between longings for parental love and recognition on the one hand and inescapable needs and demands to make intimate decisions independently on the other; on coping with expectations and injuries; and on the legitimacy of efforts on the part of public authority and social milieu to set and enforce standards and ideals.

By the mid-1990s, much of the force of imported popular culture novels had been spent; the state had banned a series of locally written novels by serious authors on charges of obscenity; and the popular writer Wang Shuo had joined many other writers in going overseas, either for extended stays or to acquire permanent residence. As the final years of the century approached, the appeal of the novel in China appeared to have waned.

EDWARD GUNN

See also Ba Jin; Eileen Chang; Fortress Besieged; Lao She; Lu Xun; Mao Dun; Mo Yan; Pai Hsien-yung; Shen Congwen; Travels of Lao Can; Wang Anyi; Xiao Hong; Zhang Xianliang

Further Reading

Anderson, Marston, *The Limits of Realism: Chinese Fiction in the Revolutionary Period*, Berkeley: University of California Press, 1990

Chang, Sung-sheng Yvonne, *Modernism and the Nativist Resistance: Contemporary Chinese Fiction from Taiwan*, Durham, North Carolina: Duke University Press, 1993

Dolezelová-Velingerová, Milena, editor, *A Selective Guide to Chinese Literature, 1900–1949*, volume 1: *The Novel*, Leiden and New York: Brill, 1988

Gunn, Edward, *Rewriting Chinese: Style and Innovation in Twentieth-Century Chinese Prose*, Stanford, California: Stanford University Press, 1991

Hsia, C.T., *A History of Modern Chinese Fiction*, New Haven, Connecticut: Yale University Press, 1961; 2nd edition, 1971

Huang, Joe C., *Heroes and Villains in Communist China: The Contemporary Chinese Novel as a Reflection of Life*, New York: Pica Press, and London: Hurst, 1973

Lee, Leo Ou-fan, *The Romantic Generation of Chinese Writers*, Cambridge, Massachusetts: Harvard University Press, 1973

Lin, Fang-mei, "Social Change and Romantic Ideology: The Impact of the Publishing Industry, Family Organization, and Gender Roles on the Reception and Interpretation of Romance Fiction in Taiwan, 1960–90," Ph.D. diss., University of Pennsylvania, 1992

Link, E. Perry, *Mandarin Ducks and Butterflies: Popular Fiction in Early Twentieth-Century Chinese Cities*, Berkeley: University of California Press, 1981

Lu Tonglin, editor, *Gender and Sexuality in Twentieth-Century Chinese Literature and Society*, Albany: State University of New York Press, 1993

Wang, David Der-wei, *Fictional Realism in Twentieth-Century China: Mao Dun, Lao She, Shen Congwen*, New York: Columbia University Press, 1992

Wang, Jing, *High Culture Fever: Politics, Aesthetics, and Ideology in Deng's China*, Berkeley: University of California Press, 1996

Yang, Winston L.Y., and Nathan K. Mao, editors, *Modern Chinese Fiction: A Guide to Its Study and Appreciation*, Boston: G.K. Hall, 1981

Zhang, Xudong, *Chinese Modernism in the Era of Reforms: Cultural Fever, Avant-Garde Fiction, and the New Chinese Cinema*, Durham, North Carolina: Duke University Press, 1997

Chinmoku. *See* Silence

Chronicles of Barsetshire. *See* Barsetshire Novels

Chto delat'? *See* What Is To Be Done?

Cien años de soledad. *See* One Hundred Years of Solitude

Circulating Libraries. *See* Libraries

Cities of Salt by ᶜAbd al-Raḥmān Munīf

Mudun al-milḥ 1984–89

ᶜAbd al-Raḥmān Munīf's *Cities of Salt* is the crowning achievement of his career and the beginning of a new Arabic literature. The work consists of five volumes, *Al-tīh* (1984; *Cities of Salt*), *Al-ukhdūd* (1985; *The Trench*), *Taqāsīm al-layl wa-al-nahār* (1989; *Variations on Night and Day*), *Al-munbatt* (1989; The Uprooted), and *Bādiyat al-ẓulumāt* (1989; The Desert of Darkness). A historical novel, *Cities of Salt* portrays the social, economic, and technological changes in traditional desert society that followed upon the discovery of oil.

Desert life had played an important role in Munīf's earlier fiction, but it is only in *Cities of Salt*—and for the first time in the Arab novel—that the desert peoples, represented by the inhabitants of Wādī al-ᶜUyūn, come to function as a kind of collective protagonist. Its broad historical focus and sweeping social perspective explain why the novel has been called an epic work, although strictly speaking the label is inappropriate.

The overarching theme of *Cities of Salt* is the clash between traditional Arab and technological Western culture brought about by modernization. The novel has been read as a chronicle of the bewilderment and dislocations associated with the sudden transformation of traditional society. But in fact *Cities of Salt* goes far beyond the mere description of social upheaval and individual alienation. A critique of the West and of current Westernized regimes, the novel is also an ethnological study of the behavior of the Western "other." Using the Western genre of the novel to make Western culture an object of study, Munīf reverses the usual patterns of dominance and subordination in the encounter between Western and indigenous cultures.

Cities of Salt constitutes a turning point in the history of Arabic literature. It has virtually no reference to the Arabic literary past, but dramatizes the genesis of the Arab novel as a product of the modernization and Western influence that operates on the whole of desert culture. In the first volume, the inhabitants of Wādī are described as a collective, a society with very little individualism or even individual differentiation. As a consequence, there is very little social contradiction. The people are deeply embedded in an oral tradition and their temporal experience is thoroughly ahistorical. They have no expectation of significant social change and therefore make no projections of the future.

The collective orientation of the group and their mythical experience of time adds up to a kind of prehistory that, in generic terms, may be associated with the epic.

Wādī's fall into history comes with World War I, the discovery of oil, the appearance of the state as the overarching form of social organization, and the advent of writing as the central form of cultural transmission. These changes are associated with tremendous conflict. The knowledge and experience of the group does not prepare the individual inhabitants of Wādī to deal with the new problems and choices they are confronted with. In consequence, contact with modernity can only destabilize and dismantle their traditional way of life.

The Trench, the second volume of *Cities of Salt,* is set in the 1950s and offers a different perspective on Arab traditionalism. Al-Maḥmaljī, the protagonist of *The Trench*, is an Arab intellectual typical of his time in that he keeps aloof from social reality. Instead, he is preoccupied with traditional Arab discourse, which, in its central focus on eloquence and its pursuit of rhyme and rhythm even in prose, supports his apolitical stance. In *Variations on Night and Day*, Munīf raises the question of the writing of history, showing how a historical consciousness has penetrated a society that until recently lived in mythical time. An oral history project of sorts, *Variations* offers a critique of written culture and the official histories it produces by telling the (unofficial) stories of actual people who lived through that history. This resistance to official versions of history and their tendency to ignore individual experience also appears in Munīf's other work.

Not only *Variations*, but the whole of *Cities of Salt* brings together many voices and styles drawn from the literary and popular traditions, including such forms as proverbs and maxims, poetry, fables, and event protest songs of the day. Through these different forms, Munīf stages the voices of traditional and modern Arab culture. Bridging traditions, the novel becomes a repository of collective memory.

Cities of Salt does not depict the passage from mythical to historical time, from epic to novel, from oral to written culture as a linear process. As pockets of tradition survive into modern urbanized Arab society, so does epic atemporality coexist with novelistic historicity. This coexistence holds the key to the way Munīf situates himself with respect to the cultures he depicts. Although he is highly critical of Western intervention in Arab politics, Munīf does not simply adopt the values of traditional Arab culture. By the choice of his medium alone—the thoroughly Western genre of the novel—Munīf ranges himself with other Arab writers who seek to reconcile Western modernity and the Arab cultural heritage. *Cities of Salt* succeeds in mediating modernization and historical time, while it also allows writing to interrogate history. Rooting his work in the epic national past of Arab society and mixing genres in new ways, Munīf opens a future for the Arab novel that is truly its own.

Cities of Salt is a significant presence in the work of other Arab novelists. For instance, the Syrian novelist Nabīl Sulaymān's tetralogy *Madārāt al-Sharq* (1994; Orbits of the Orient) and the Jordanian novelist Ziyād Qāsim's *Al-Zawbaᶜah: al-Jīl al-Awwal* (1994; The Storm: The First Generation) are both historical novels that trace the political and economic origins of modernity in their respective countries. Although Munīf's work has found an avid readership, his criticisms of current Arab regimes has made him anything but popular with the authorities, most notably in the Gulf countries, where his work is banned.

MARTHA KHOURY

See also ᶜAbd al-Raḥmān Munīf

Further Reading

Allen, Roger, *The Arabic Novel: An Historical and Critical Introduction,* Syracuse, New York: Syracuse University Press, and Manchester: Manchester University Press, 1982; 2nd edition, Syracuse, New York: Syracuse University Press, 1995

Boullata, Issa, and Roger Allen, editors, *The Arabic Novel since 1950: Critical Essays, Interviews, and Bibliography,* Cambridge, Massachusetts: Dar Mahjar, 1992

El-Enany, Rasheed, "*Cities of Salt*: A Literary View of the Theme of Oil and Change in the Gulf," in *Arabia and the Gulf: From Traditional Society to Modern States,* London: Croom Helm, and Totowa, New Jersey: Barnes and Noble, 1986

Siddiq, Muhammad, "The Contemporary Arabic Novel in Perspective," *World Literature Today* 60 (1986)

Siddiq, Muhammad, "The Making of a Counter-Narrative: Two Examples from Contemporary Arabic and Hebrew Fiction," *Glimmer, Train, Stories* (Summer 1994)

Upchurch, Michael, "Abdelrahman Munif: Mixing It Up with Oil, Politics, and Fiction," *Glimmer, Train, Stories* (Summer 1994)

The City and the Novel

The novel as a literary form came into being during a period when the modern city was taking shape. It is appropriate that one of the founding practitioners of the modern novel, Daniel Defoe, should be a Londoner and that the capital should be the privileged site of action in such novels as *Moll Flanders* and *Colonel Jack* (both 1722). The pregnant Moll uses the city as a refuge where landladies ask no questions provided they are paid promptly. Similarly Colonel Jack rises from poverty to "live like a gentleman" by stealing, that is, by exploiting money's capacity to cut through the barriers of class and inheritance. Both Moll and Colonel Jack gloss their thefts euphemistically as "adventures," but essentially they engage in a process of social learning that is topographical insofar as both characters learn the layout of the city streets that might serve as escape routes. London is a "capital centre of trades and distribution" (see Williams, 1973), and thieving and other criminal behaviors function as trades in that urban environment. Moll learns "trades" (just as, more than a century later, Charles Dickens' Oliver Twist is "tutored" by the Artful Dodger to pick pockets), but even more importantly she learns the fluidity of social guises. At the peak of her success she declares, "I had several shapes to appear in."

This concept of metropolitan duplicity feeds into other novels of the 18th century. In *Fanny Hill* (originally published as *Memoirs of a Woman of Pleasure,* 1748–49), John Cleland's eponymous character arrives in town and is promptly taken to a brothel where she assumes she is going to serve as a linen maid. In Henry Fielding's *Tom Jones* (1749), the untrustworthy nature of appearances is elaborated into a whole social system of elegant masquerade. Masking in that novel is a style of speech and behavior within which, as in Samuel Richardson's *Clarissa* (1747–48), conspiracies can be formed. London offers possibilities of anonymity inconceivable in the country. William Godwin's Caleb Williams (in the novel of that name, 1794) heads to London because it is a "place in which, on account of the magnitude of its dimensions, it might well be supposed that an individual could remain hidden and unknown." One of the most articulate comic commentators on urban change in this period is Tobias Smollett, whose character Matthew Bramble in *Humphrey Clinker* (1771) fumes at the social consequences of the sprawl he has noticed taking place within only a few years. "The capital is become an overgrown monster," he exclaims, thereby helping to establish a trope that will run right through 19th-century urban discourse. Bramble's fear of the city mob grows out of his reaction to the constrictions of urban space, where figures from all walks of life and all class levels jostle each other in an alarmingly democratic anarchy.

The transition into a Victorian vision of the city may be seen in *Vanity Fair* (1848), which William Makepeace Thackeray originally planned as a series of sketches of London society. The novel preserves a Fieldingesque sense of social life as theatre but further elaborates this vision as a world held together by the intangible and fragile bond of credit, both social and financial. Although Thackeray links his scenes within a larger sequence of rising and declining fortunes, the isolated episode he employed remains a stock ingredient of urban fiction, from the fleeting encounters in James Joyce's *Ulysses* (1922) and John Dos Passos' *Manhattan Transfer* (1925) right up to Donald Barthelme's *City Life* (1970) and Armistead Maupin's *Tales of the City* (1978).

Charles Dickens added new sophistication and complexity to the depiction of the city. In his fiction the hearthside becomes a privileged domestic space, idealized as an actual substitute for the transcendental security of religious belief and contrasted with the street, which is a public space of alienation where city-dwellers are constantly hurrying to and fro. The comforting clarity of this opposition is undermined by the processes of industrial change, as in the descriptions of railway excavations in Dickens' *Dombey and Son* (1848), producing surreal shapes "unintelligible as any dream."

A constantly recurring issue in urban fiction is the degree to which the city can be a knowable community. In early novels such as *Oliver Twist* (1838), Dickens evokes such discrete, separate areas within the metropolis that they scarcely can be conceived as part of the same society. In his later works a darker vision produces a more complex continuity between these distinct urban settings. *Our Mutual Friend* (1865), for example, explores the money nexus that binds together the different characters and in the process establishes a series of close associations between waste, money, and death. The novel opens with an act of "salvage" in describing a man securing a precarious livelihood by searching the pockets of drowned corpses for money. Living or dead, whole bodies or parts, human figures are reified into commodities with a market value. As the novel unfolds, it keeps adding to its cast of characters glimpsed in pursuit of wealth. Money emerges from the primeval slime of the River Thames (a river of death, not life), and the nouveau riche Boffins attract to their household "all manner of crawling, creeping, fluttering, and buzzing creatures." Dickens forcibly reminds us that the city is an environment that assaults the senses. The famous fogs of *Bleak House* (1853) and *Our Mutual Friend* at once confuse sight and hearing and also suggest the covert activities—from swindling to murder—of those pursuing money. The city's dimension of secrecy, an elaboration of the urban irony that thousands of inhabitants live in close proximity without ever knowing each other, is addressed by novels later in the 19th century, including Robert Louis Stevenson's *Strange Case of Dr. Jekyll and Mr. Hyde* (1886), which inscribes concealment into the narrative through Jekyll's windowless and apparently neglected house.

The sheer speed with which fortunes can be made or lost in the city corresponds with the transient nature of urban accommodation. In *Vanity Fair,* Becky Sharp constantly changes her address; Honoré de Balzac chose a lodging house in *Le père goriot* (1835; *Le Père Goriot*) to locate the representatives of a social microcosm. In Balzac's novel, the tenants of the Pension Vauquer have been drawn there by chance, all in pursuit of cheap accommodation; they represent an atomization of the community that is conceptualized by the cynical "philosopher" Vautrin, to whom life is merely a struggle for survival. Balzac anticipates by almost a century the perception formulated in E.M. Forster's *Howards End* (1910) that the metropolis represents a "nomadic

civilization which is altering human nature so profoundly." While Balzac preserves a distinction of types among his characters, the mobility of the urban populace can erase their identifiable features, as seen in several contemporaneous novels of industrialization. The notion of the "mass" emerges in such novels to denote the disappearance of individuality within a depersonalized collective.

By the middle of the 19th century, English novelists had turned to a new kind of city that had sprung up in the industrial north and was characterized by a single or very limited number of manufacturing outlets. Dickens' *Hard Times* (1854) strikes an explicit keynote for its narrative through the depiction of Coketown, which is based on Preston. In implicit contrast to the endlessly varied neighborhoods of London, Dickens presents Coketown's houses and inhabitants as the very embodiment of uniformity, presided over by a machine-god. Elizabeth Gaskell's *North and South* (1855) pursues a different but related tack by having its characters approach Milton Northern gradually so that they perceive first a "lead-coloured cloud," then a smoky taste to the air, and finally the streets themselves: "long, straight, hopeless streets of regularly-built houses, all small and of brick." The visual impact of the place, powerful as it is, only tells part of the story, however, for Gaskell presents the city as a different region with its own dialect and its own power struggle. The relationship between workers and mill-owners is tense, shifting from implicit to actual strife when a strike is mounted. Even more importantly, Gaskell explicitly represents the city in dialogue with the country in a series of debate scenes running through her novel.

Throughout the 19th century authors portrayed the city as containing particular districts defined by class, occupation, or race. At the end of the century, George Gissing's *The Nether World* (1889) describes a hell-like city-within-a-city in Clerkenwell (at the "heart" of London), whose inhabitants live within an enclosed environment dominated by work and totally separated from the natural cycles of day and season. Gissing, like Rudyard Kipling, follows a tradition established at least as early as the 1840s in guiding his readers into darkest London, the locale all the more shocking for being so near. During this period, the realist novel established itself as a powerful vehicle for exposing social conditions whether of urban poverty or, for example, the Chicago stockyards in Upton Sinclair's *The Jungle* (1906).

From the very beginning the problem of knowability has hung over novelistic depictions of the city. Burton Pike explains this as follows: "the city as a spatial form presents both the image of a map and the image of a labyrinth" (see Pike, 1981). In other words, the city promises clarity and entrapment, especially when, for instance, a subterranean layer emerges, as occurs in Victor Hugo's *Les Misérables* (1862). In this work, the famous pursuit through the sewers introduces the reader to a bizarre reflection of the street layout with its own highways and side passages. The underground city carries repeated connotations of refuge or social rejection as in Fedor Dostoevskii's *Zapiski iz podpol'ia* (1864; *Notes from Underground*) or in Graham Greene's *The Third Man* (1950), where the Vienna sewers offer a means of moving between the different zones of allied occupation. In all these cases, the city functions as a microcosm of society, reflecting its tensions or fissures. This tendency may be seen clearly in the last two volumes of Émile Zola's *Les Trois Villes*

("Three Cities") trilogy (*Lourdes*, 1894; *Rome*, 1896; *Paris*, 1898). When the protagonist Abbé Pierre Froment first reaches Rome from Lourdes, he has a sublime vision of that city's historical permanence: "the city of the Caesars, the city of the Popes, the Eternal City." Like Henry James, he highlights Rome's historical accretions, but another Rome quickly forces itself on his attention—the "City of Misery," the districts of great poverty. Following a dialectical sequence, Froment imagines a new Rome, a Rome as it might be. Here again, however, Zola denies the reader any great optimism, since the concluding volume *Paris* opens with a morning mist that creates a "Paris of mystery, shrouded by clouds, buried as it were beneath the ashes of some disaster." These suggestions of death and destruction are realized in the action of the novel, which shows overt political struggle through anarchist bombings. Like Joseph Conrad's *The Secret Agent* (1907), the capital city in both cases is the heart of power and contains within its murk covert machinations to destroy that power, which Zola renders symbolically through the guillotine erected in the poorest quarter of the city.

In urban fiction, the city often takes on symbolic meaning. For Thomas Mann, Venice suggested decadent eroticism. Paris, for Henry Miller, was a sexual playground. James Joyce breaks apart the city in a series of symbolic episodes, each one presided over by a respective building or monument. Joyce's "groundplan" for *Ulysses* gives us some clues to the elaborate procedures he used to describe Dublin. Homeric wanderings are compressed into an urban space which it was still possible to traverse on foot. Joyce's scrupulous efforts to get the details of place exactly right were devoted primarily to the common street experiences of his Dubliners, and key buildings and monuments unobtrusively remind the reader that Dublin is a city steeped in history. The characteristic experience of Joyce's Dubliners is therefore to experience chance meetings in the jostle of the streets, encounters that raise questions about the nature of the city as a community. It is no coincidence that Joyce "datelines" *Ulysses* with the three multiethnic cities where the novel was composed: "Trieste-Zürich-Paris, 1914–21." Both of his protagonists live in Dublin as exiles in some way cut off from the centers of the city's social life. Joyce was extremely alert to the discourses of the Irish metropolis. He shuns a single-perspective naturalist precision, turning more and more as the novel progresses to different modes of representation relative to the local subject: a visit to a newspaper office is rendered through an imitation of the newspage format, a romantic "encounter" on the beach by Bloom is described in a novelettish style, and so on.

Ulysses represents the ultimate in urban documentation, and Joyce was probably responding to a tendency to sprawl in his method by using so many structural patterns. Virginia Woolf similarly used the layout of the West End of London and the time sequence of an individual day to contain *Mrs. Dalloway* (1925). Again, as in *Ulysses* and other city novels, characters' paths intersect, juxtaposing the fortunes of an outsider (a war casualty experiencing mental collapse) and an insider (Clarissa Dalloway is the wife of a Member of Parliament). The contrast collapses as we begin to perceive Clarissa's own sense of marginality. Susan Squier has argued cogently that there is a progression in Woolf's fiction and that of other women novelists from female characters' sense of being on the margin of city life to a realization of their own centrality. Squier finds a "doubled gaze" in works such as Woolf's *Orlando* (1928), which uses its London setting to celebrate human connectedness (see Squier, 1985).

The move toward the city as both setting and subject occurred slightly later in the United States than in Britain, and it was only after the Civil War that American novels began to explore the narrative possibilities of the new urban environment. William Dean Howells' *The Rise of Silas Lapham* (1885) describes the opportunities presented by the filling in of Boston's Back Bay. Parcels of land (the "lots" that recur in American fiction right up to the work of Thomas Pynchon) became commodities that could be bought on speculation as the new rich competed socially with Boston's increasingly embattled gentry. By the turn of the century, city development was reaching fever pitch, and Theodore Dreiser introduced his protagonist in *Sister Carrie* (1900) to a Chicago enjoying a boom in anticipation of doubling its population. As streetcar lines and residential plans extend outward, the city appears to have a strangely autonomous organic life of its own. The impact on a newcomer is intimidating all the more because of the sheer speed of urban activity. Dreiser depicts his city as a vast and dynamic environment where the individual is swept along by the forces playing within it. The city reflects a composite image that, like brightly lit Manhattan for example, exerts a pull on its visitors, focusing their desires on wealth. The city center of Chicago is thus described as self-consciously grand in order to emphasize the "gulf between poverty and success." From the turn of the century and after, Edith Wharton's New York fiction similarly presented the city as a spectacle, a social performance gradually emptied of significance in the perspectives of Wharton's disillusioned protagonists.

Blanche Gelfant has argued that in American city fiction, especially John Dos Passos' work, the city itself functions as an antagonist to human desire and that it emerges as itself a protagonist (see Gelfant, 1954). However, Adrienne Siegel has concluded from a survey of works published between 1820 and 1870 that popular fiction presented a much more optimistic and positive image of the city than had been expressed in high-brow novels, in which fortunes were made by pure luck (see Siegel, 1980). Dos Passos' *Manhattan Transfer* (1925) also mystifies the process of achieving prosperity by presenting characters in a never-ending process of rising and falling, where fortunes are made by chance opportunities and lost in stock market fluctuations. Gelfant takes Dos Passos to task for doing damage to characters by absorbing them into the city as "discontinuous states of mind and feeling," but this is an inevitable result of the urban experience. Dos Passos' New York is literally a city of signs, an environment packed with advertisements that promise success in return for conformity to projected general images of beauty or ideal behavior. To call the city a protagonist is at once to recognize the novelists' reliance on personifications and to underline the perception of the city as a dynamic environment, constantly transforming itself. Dos Passos' descriptions of New York bring out the material dimensions of the city, stressing the use of glass and asphalt. His chapter "Metropolis" puts the American city within the larger historical sequence of such vanished cities as Nineveh and Babylon. On every level, then, transience becomes a determinant of city life, from the constant motion of its inhabitants (hence Dos Passos' title, *Manhatten Transfer,* taken from a railroad station) to the lack of permanence in the city fabric itself. Dos Passos invites us to read across characters' destinies rather than to follow linear narratives, since by definition no city-dweller's experience is unique.

For Dos Passos, Manhattan functions like a vortex sucking its inhabitants into a never-ending and futile pursuit of a "center of things" that does not exist. For Richard Wright, however, in his novel *Native Son* (1940), Chicago does not possess a center so much as discrete areas marked off racially by the city authorities. The promise of success makes a fraudulent offer to African Americans who can never realize it.

Postwar American fiction moved from realism into a range of surreal techniques in an attempt to capture the frenetic and fantastic pace of urban life. Thus in Ralph Ellison's *Invisible Man* (1952), New York is packed with the imagery of national prosperity, but these signs are constantly deconstructed as arbitrary and meaningless, or as a screen of the most blatant exploitation. "Learn to look beneath the surface," the protagonist is told, but the novel narrates his repeated failure to do so. He experiences an increasingly surreal series of shocks that reduce his experience of the city to a flickering phantasmagoria of bizarre images. More recently, J.G. Ballard demonstrated a sensitivity as acute as Dos Passos' to the signs of the city. His London trilogy, *Crash* (1973), *Concrete Island* (1974), and *High-Rise* (1975), approaches the constructs of the city as desires literally made concrete, where character cannot be perceived in isolation from the urban environment.

Many modern novels represent the city in dystopian terms as an unknowable Kafkaesque terrain or as an extension of the factory system into all areas of social life. Thea von Harbou's *Metropolis* (1926), Aldous Huxley's *Brave New World* (1932), and some of H.G. Wells' science fiction show environments in which the city possesses a machine-life of its own that extends beyond identifiable boundaries. The cyberpunk novelist William Gibson depicts just such an urbanized environment, which flattens the notional distinctions between, say, Tokyo or New York, in *Neuromancer* (1984). In works by Italo Calvino and Alain Robbe-Grillet, the city remains a problematic and ambiguous concept, scarcely possessing an existence beyond the narrating consciousness. Urban fiction has characteristically investigated the tempo of social and environmental change, and over the last 100 years novels have speculated about an imminent future when cities are destroyed and human life is almost wiped out. Disasters of different kinds, whether natural or manmade, have been used by writers like George Stewart, Philip Wylie, and Samuel Delany to evoke a posturban world where surviving remnants of differing sizes wander around the ruins of what were once thriving cultural centers.

DAVID SEED

See also Class and the Novel; Journalism and the Novel; Modernism; Pastoralism in the Novel; Social Criticism; Space

Further Reading

Bradbury, Malcolm, and James McFarlane, editors, *Modernism: 1890–1930,* London and New York: Penguin, 1976
Byrd, Max, *London Transformed: Images of the City in the Eighteenth Century,* New Haven, Connecticut: Yale University Press, 1978
Caws, Mary Ann, editor, *City Images: Perspectives from Literature, Philosophy, and Film,* New York: Gordon and Breach, 1991
Clarke, Graham, editor, *The American City: Literary and Cultural Perspectives,* London: Vision, and New York: St. Martin's Press, 1988
Conrad, Peter, *The Art of the City: Views and Versions of New York,* New York: Oxford University Press, 1984
Cope, Jackson I., *Joyce's Cities: Archaeologies of the Soul,* Baltimore: Johns Hopkins University Press, 1981
Gelfant, Blanche H., *The American City Novel,* Norman: University of Oklahoma Press, 1954; 2nd edition, 1989
Gelfant, Blanche H., "Residence Underground: Recent Fictions of the Subterranean City," *Sewanee Review* 83 (1975)
Howe, Irving, "The City in Literature," *Commentary* 51:5 (1971)
Hulin, Jean Paul, and Pierre Coustillas, editors, *Victorian Writers and the City,* Villeneuve-d'Ascq: University of Lille III, 1979
LeGates, Richard T., and Frederic Stout, editors, *The City Reader,* London and New York: Routledge, 1996
Modern Fiction Studies 24:1 (1978), special issue: "The Modern Novel and the City"
Mumford, Lewis, *The Culture of Cities,* London: Secker and Warburg, and New York: Harcourt Brace, 1938
Olsen, Donald J., *The City as Work of Art: London, Paris, Vienna,* New Haven, Connecticut: Yale University Press, 1986; London: Yale University Press, 1988
Pierce, David, *James Joyce's Ireland,* New Haven, Connecticut: Yale University Press, 1992
Pike, Burton, *The Image of the City in Modern Literature,* Princeton, New Jersey: Princeton University Press, 1981
Prendergast, Christopher, *Paris and the Nineteenth Century,* Oxford and Cambridge, Massachusetts: Blackwell, 1992
Schwarzbach, F.S., *Dickens and the City,* London: Athlone Press, 1979
Sheckley, Robert, *Futuropolis,* New York: A. and W. Visual Library, 1978; London: Bergström and Boyle, 1979
Siegel, Adrienne, *The Image of the American City in Popular Literature, 1820–1870,* Port Washington, New York: Kennikat Press, 1980
Squier, Susan Merrill, editor, *Women Writers and the City: Essays in Feminist Literary Criticism,* Knoxville: University of Tennessee Press, 1984
Squier, Susan Merrill, *Virginia Woolf and London: The Sexual Politics of the City,* Chapel Hill: University of North Carolina Press, 1985
Weimer, David R., *The City as Metaphor,* New York: Random House, 1966
Welsh, Alexander, *The City of Dickens,* Oxford: Clarendon Press, 1971; Cambridge, Massachusetts: Harvard University Press, 1986
Williams, Raymond, *The Country and the City,* London: Chatto and Windus, and New York: Oxford University Press, 1973

Clarín [Leopoldo Alas] 1852–1901

Spanish

The novelistic trajectory of Leopoldo Alas, popularly known by the pseudonym Clarín, is intimately connected with a historicist and critical approach to reality. The social content of his writings reflects a disappointment with the shortcomings of the September Revolution of 1868, which had resulted in a mere realignment of political and social forces, empowering the bourgeoisie and frustrating the expectations of the working class. Clarín denounced the social injustices that prevailed in Restoration Spain. The plight and oppression of the weaker segments of society, the political corruption of an ineffective system, the exclusivist policies carried out by the groups in power, and the unfounded and superficial optimism prevalent in prosperous social circles were in Clarín's view representative of the spiritual and moral decay of the nation.

With the introduction of naturalism in Spain during the early 1880s Clarín found a suitable approach to the concept of the novel and to the depiction of the challenges of modernity. He was at the forefront of the Spanish naturalist movement, defending its aesthetic program in newspaper articles and in critical treatises. In his prologue to Emilia Pardo Bazán's series of essays *La cuestión palpitante* (1883; The Burning Question) and in his own *Del Naturalismo* (1882; On Naturalism), Clarín welcomes the scientific qualities of the empirical observation of reality, and the freedom from the prejudices of constant narratorial intervention. His adherence to the movement was not unconditional, for he rejected the exclusion of all spiritual factors from the positivistic model presented by Émile Zola. Clarín's acceptance of naturalism is driven by a desire to adapt its techniques and form to the particularities of Spanish social reality.

His first novel, *La Regenta* (1884; La Regenta), exemplifies his conception and interpretation of naturalism. Widely considered to be Spain's best novel of the 19th century, along with Benito Pérez Galdós' *Fortunata y Jacinta* (1886–87; Fortunata and Jacinta), it is a lengthy and highly detailed exposition of a triangular adulterous relationship in a provincial town. The female protagonist's spiritual and physical longings are intricately connected with the moral decrepitude of the townspeople's reactionary value system and with the perverse laxity of the clergy. Although the influence of the environment is omnipresent, Clarín is equally interested in the psychology of his characters. The fate of the protagonist is not only a product of her oppressive surroundings but also of her personal inauthenticity. *La Regenta* initially caused a stir in Asturian society, which saw itself reflected in the story, but the novel was soon relegated to secondary status. Today, it has been fully rehabilitated by scholars to its rightful place.

Clarín's commitment to the multifaceted characterization drove him to employ many narrative devices that were being used only sporadically by his contemporaries, with the exception of Pérez Galdós. His frequent use of interior monologue and his use of free indirect discourse are examples of his attempts to grant full autonomy to his characters while exploring their inner depths. Clarín's extensive exposure to other European writers such as Lev Tolstoi and Charles Dickens and especially to the French (Victor Hugo, Zola, Gustave Flaubert) gave him a highly sophisticated grasp of narrative techniques.

Su único hijo (1890; His Only Son) lacks the descriptive intensity and the diverse presentation of personality types of *La Regenta*. The characters of this novel are all unattractive and frequently deformed through caricature, satire, or parody. It is the tale of a delusional adulterer whose life is guided by an anachronistic romanticism. He interrupts his relationship with an opera singer when he discovers that his wife is pregnant, at which point his romantic idealism is refocused at the prospect of becoming a father, disregarding the fact that his ex-lover scornfully tells him that it is someone else's child. The satiric nature of the novel and its condemnation of romantic ideology is representative of the author's dissatisfaction with a way of life that was incongruent with the progressive ideas he upheld. Equally important in this work are some of his innovations, including impressionistic descriptions and the flexible use of time and space. The naturalist element does not disappear, at least in its most concrete aspects, but the paternal idealism that the protagonist experiences at the conclusion of the story signals the gradual attraction that Clarín experienced toward a more spiritual content. Part of an unfinished sequel to *His Only Son*, entitled *Una medianía* (A Mediocrity), which was to form part of a sequence of four novels that never materialized, was published in a popular journal in 1889.

Cuesta abajo (1890–91; Down Hill) is Clarín's least-known and least-studied novel. Published in installments, it is a pseudoautobiographical tale narrated in the first person by a university professor who finds himself attracted to two sisters. The strong philosophical content mirrors the writer's own lifelong internal struggles between reason and faith and between idealism and realism.

Along with his novelistic production, Clarín enjoyed a prolific career as a critic. Through his many articles that appeared in the most important newspapers and journals of the time, he established himself as a feared and respected evaluator of Spanish literary activity. Some of his commentaries were replete with acute observations about the novelist's responsibility to the reading public, while many of his attacks were directed against artistic mediocrity, including that motivated by commercial interests. He considered the novel to be the most complete and representative of literary forms, proclaiming it to be the modern version of the epic and identifying society as its collective protagonist. Although initially a proponent of the ideologically committed novel, his position gradually evolved into a more flexible concept in which aesthetic value shared importance with utilitarian criteria. Contemporary critics agree in considering Clarín a significant voice in establishing the novel at the center of Spanish letters.

Dionisio Viscarri

See also Regenta

Biography

Born in Zamora, 25 April 1852. Moved with his family to Oviedo, 1869. Studied law at the University of Oviedo beginning in 1870; after receiving degree, appointed professor of law and political economy at the university, remaining in the post for the rest of his life. Died 13 June 1901.

Novels by Clarín

La Regenta, 1884; as *La Regenta,* translated by John
  Rutherford, 1984
Su único hijo, 1890; as *His Only Son,* translated by Julie Jones,
  1981
Cuesta abajo [Down Hill], 1890–91

Other Writings: short stories and literary criticism.

Further Reading

Beser, Sergio, *Leopoldo Alas, crítico literario,* Madrid: Gredos,
  1968
Brent, Albert, *Leopoldo Alas and "La Regenta": A Study in
  Nineteenth Century Spanish Prose Fiction,* Columbia:
  Curators of the University of Missouri, 1951
Eoff, Sherman Hinkle, "In Quest of a God of Love," in *The
  Modern Spanish Novel; Comparative Essays Examining the
  Philosophical Impact of Science on Fiction,* New York: New
  York University Press, 1961

García Sarriá, Francisco, *Clarín o la herejía amorosa,* Madrid:
  Gredos, 1975
Martínez Cachero, José Maria, editor, *Leopoldo Alas "Clarín,"*
  Madrid: Taurus, 1978
Rutherford, John, *Leopoldo Alas—La Regenta,* London: Grant
  and Cutler, 1974
Sieburth, Stephanie Anne, *Reading "La Regenta": Duplicitous
  Discourse and the Entropy of Structure,* Amsterdam and
  Philadelphia: Benjamins, 1990
Sobejano, Gonzalo, *Clarín en su obra ejemplar,* Madrid:
  Castalia, 1985
Valis, Noel M., *The Decadent Vision in Leopoldo Alas: A Study
  of "La Regenta" and "Su único hijo,"* Baton Rouge:
  Louisiana State University Press, 1981
Valis, Noel M., *"Malevolent Insemination" and Other Essays
  on Clarín,* Ann Arbor: Department of Romance Languages,
  University of Michigan, 1990

Clarissa; or, The History of a Young Lady by Samuel Richardson

1747–48

Clarissa was originally published in three parts in 1747 and
1748. Richardson, one of the most prominent printers in London, had enjoyed an initial sensational success as a novelist with
the publication of *Pamela* in 1740, and he spent much of the decade that followed planning and composing and revising his
next, vastly more ambitious, tale of virtue in peril. While intended for moral uplift, *Pamela* was basically comedic in its design,
and the ultimate marriage of the rakish Mr. B. to his resolutely
chaste serving girl fulfilled a wide audience's fondest wish.
Richardson saw *Clarissa,* however, as a tragic narrative, and the
threat of sexual violence that was averted in his first novel is here
realized in a grim and unforgettable way.

The novel is one of the longest ever written, but its story may
be summarized briefly. Clarissa Harlowe, a young woman of
great beauty, wealth, intelligence, and virtue, finds herself besieged by both her family, who wish to marry her to "rich
Solmes" (a loathsome neighbor, who promises to so enrich them
that they can gain a peerage), and by a notorious but charming
rake, Robert Lovelace. Lovelace's motives for his pursuit are
complex, as he wavers between desire for a seduction that will
prove his name in what he calls "rakish annals" and hope for a
marriage that will reform him. Clarissa ultimately seeks protection from her family by running off with Lovelace, although she
does so reluctantly and with more than a suspicion that he has
manipulated circumstances to force this step. A long, uneasy period of mutual testing and occasional courtship follows. Marriage surfaces as a possibility, but Lovelace also obsessively tests
the firmness of her virtue. The rake persuades her to go to Lon-

don, where he imprisons her in what she does not realize is a
brothel. He finally drugs and rapes her. In the concluding sections of the novel, Clarissa is able, with difficulty, to escape from
Lovelace and to regain a sense of her integrity and moral worth,
but she also dies, apparently as a result of a conviction that she
has no place in a world where such grief as she has experienced
is possible. Both Lovelace and her own heartless family are left
with a profound burden of remorse, and at the close of the novel Lovelace dies in a duel with Clarissa's cousin.

No summary can do justice to the actual experience of reading
the novel, for plot alone can give no sense of either *Clarissa*'s formal intricacy or of its psychological depth and emotional intensity. Like *Pamela,* *Clarissa* is an epistolary novel, but it
represents a stunning leap in sophistication over its predecessor.
Richardson's first book was essentially monologic, and its story
unfolds almost exclusively as a series of letters from the heroine
to her parents. *Clarissa,* on the other hand, is multivocal. Much
of the narrative is structured by (as Richardson calls it) "a double
yet separate correspondence" between Clarissa and her friend,
Anna Howe, and between Lovelace and his fellow rake, John
Belford. Each event is thus recounted and considered from multiple viewpoints. We also hear the voices of Clarissa's family and
her suitor, and Lovelace's shady servants, and we see documents
such as wills and marriage licenses. Richardson uses this form
both to build suspense (a technique he called "writing to the moment," as characters describe situations still in doubt) and to represent the inevitable ambiguity of human affairs, since readers are
forced to weigh different accounts of the same events.

Epistolary form also gave Richardson an unprecedented manner of representing the hearts and minds of his characters: they detail their inmost thoughts in a way that creates a powerful sense of authenticity and emotional immediacy. In so doing, Richardson was appealing to the taste of his own time for art that provoked a strong emotional reaction, the movement known as "sensibility." But Richardson's high regard among his contemporaries rested not only on his power to provoke an emotional response, but also on his reputation as a psychologist. Many at the time praised him as "the Shakespeare of the Heart," an epithet meant specifically to suggest his psychological acumen. Certainly, any history of the novel would have to acknowledge his status as a pioneer of psychological realism, and his examination of the intricacies of the inner life have always constituted a large part of his appeal.

Despite its daunting length and slow plotting, *Clarissa* continues to attract readers. Some respond to its apparent early feminism, revealing as it does the ways in which patriarchal society can victimize women. Others find appealing the novel's sophisticated representation of the complex dynamics of reading, writing, and interpretation. *Clarissa* also stands out for many as a revealing moment in the development of the modern self with its emphasis on human experience as essentially private and inward.

The editorial history of *Clarissa* is unusually contentious and complex. Many of the novel's first readers, licensed partly by its initial serial publication (which left the conclusion in doubt) and encouraged by the interpretive openness of the epistolary form, hoped for another *Pamela* and urged the author to find a way to marry his heroine to her tormentor. In the wake of these pleas, a frustrated Richardson began a long process of further revision, one designed to clarify his belief that Lovelace was irredeemable and that Clarissa was beyond fault. As a result *Clarissa* exists in several different forms, and the modern reader is faced with a choice of texts: the first edition of 1747–48 (reprinted by Penguin, 1985), the third edition of 1751 (published by the Clarissa Project, 1990), an incomplete version of the third edition (Everyman, 1962), and several abridgments. Recent scholars have vigorously debated the merits of the various versions; no consensus on the issue is likely.

JOHN ALLEN STEVENSON

See also Samuel Richardson

Further Reading

Castle, Terry, *Clarissa's Ciphers: Meaning and Disruption in Richardson's "Clarissa,"* Ithaca, New York: Cornell University Press, 1982

Doody, Margaret, *A Natural Passion: A Study of the Novels of Samuel Richardson,* Oxford: Clarendon Press, 1974

Doody, Margaret, and Peter Sabor, editors, *Samuel Richardson: Tercentenary Essays,* Cambridge and New York: Cambridge University Press, 1989

Eagleton, Terry, *The Rape of Clarissa: Writing, Sexuality, and Class Struggle in Richardson,* Oxford: Blackwell, and Minneapolis: University of Minnesota Press, 1982

Eaves, T.C. Duncan, and Ben D. Kimpel, *Samuel Richardson: A Biography,* Oxford: Clarendon Press, 1971

Warner, William Beatty, *Reading "Clarissa": The Struggles of Interpretation,* New Haven, Connecticut: Yale University Press, 1979

Class and the Novel

The novel has been identified with the middle class ever since its appearance as a new literary form in the 18th century, mostly because the middle class itself gained identity and became the dominant group in European society at about the same time. Since the conjunction of a new literary form and a new social group seemed too fortuitous to be accidental, historians and critics have identified features of the novel that seem to make it particularly appropriate as the expression of middle-class mentality and interests. These theories—from the definition of the "novel" as a genre that "rose" during the 18th century in England, to the claim that it is the literary form proper to the middle class—have become very well known, but they are by no means universally accepted. Indeed, important critics have flatly disagreed, arguing a wide range of alternatives, such as that the novel is the form that mixes the "voices" of all classes and hence presses for the breakdown of class barriers; that some types of novels are elitist and others proletarian; and that the novel has a very different relationship to social groupings in non-European countries that have not had the same economic history and hence do not have the same kinds of classes. We cannot, therefore, authoritatively answer the question of whether the novel is in fact a middle-class literary form, but we *can* say that the belief that the novel is a middle-class literary form has played an important role in history and criticism. We can document the various ways that such a belief has been justified, and we can consider its limitations.

As early as 1725, one of the authors credited with originating the form of the novel, Daniel Defoe, commented that "Writing . . . is become a very considerable Branch of the English Commerce. The Booksellers are the Master Manufacturers or Employers. The several Writers, Authors, Copyers, Sub-writers, and all the other Operators with Pen and Ink are the workmen employed by said Master Manufacturers." To call oneself an employee or a tradesman is to take on the language of economic self-definition, the language of class. While Defoe might identify writers as workers, writing itself seemed, to practitioners and readers alike, a white-collar or middle-class trade.

In the generations preceding Defoe, writers usually conceived of themselves in quite different terms. Oliver Goldsmith, another

18th-century author, commented that earlier writers did not have to deal with booksellers because they had "patrons" who came from "great" families. Literature then was a part of a social order directed by an aristocratic elite that justified its prominence on the basis of family bloodlines and divine right, not wealth. Individuals did not earn status, they had it bestowed on them by transcendent sources, ultimately God. Writing was a process of drawing on and glorifying such sources—for example, tracing religious themes, narrating epic events involving great persons, or presenting the lower classes as a source of low comedy.

When writers began to think of themselves as employed by booksellers rather than great families, they conceived of their money as coming from sales to a vast audience rather than from the pleasure of a few individuals. This shift affected writers of all genres, and so critics talk, for example, about 19th-century middle-class poetry. The novel, however, often has been singled out as the genre most in tune with the middle class, in part because it had no history of association with any other group. Early in the 19th century, for example, the French critic de Bonald theorized that the novel had none of the nobility of other literary genres and so fit the lack of nobility of the new commercial classes.

Recent critics have developed rather more complex ways of understanding the relationship of the novel to the middle class. Ian Watt (1957) argues that the novel reflects the philosophical underpinnings of the capitalist order. The new readers who fueled the market for novels worked in businesses and factories and so did not consider their income as deriving from the largesse of great persons or divine bounty but rather from their own individual labor. Their interest in reading reflected this new valuing of labor: they wanted to know how to tap resources around them and how to develop their own potential, so they wanted to read about people like themselves and to learn the newest ways of doing things. Hence, the expansion of readers fueled a tremendous increase in the publishing of newspapers and journals. The novel emerged as, in effect, a literary or fictional version of the newspaper: just as the newspaper reveals what is "new," the novel reveals what is "novel," and both find this newness within the real world. Even when what happened in an early novel was quite remarkable, it was generally presented as if it were just an odd part of the world everyone knew. Watt argues that realism is the most important feature of the novel and the feature that identifies the genre as middle class.

A corollary of the novel's and the newspaper's interest in realism was a new conception of the role of the writer: journalists and novelists did not represent themselves as divinely inspired geniuses; rather they claimed to tell their readers what is observably true, what their readers might see themselves. One of the first English novelists, Samuel Richardson, initially made his living by teaching women how to write letters, and his early novels consist of imaginary letters written by women. His works imply that he is doing the very same kind of writing that his readers could be doing if they were well trained. So the novel at this stage contributed to a sense that education could create a common mentality. The historian Benedict Anderson (1983) argues that novels and newspapers, by presenting what appears to be a common point of view, created the "solidarity" of the middle class, the sense that all in that class can identify with and understand each other.

The common point of view does not, however, mean that all people are alike; indeed, novels are also credited with promoting the philosophy of individualism, the view that every person has a distinctive character worth developing. As part of the new capitalist idea that individuals create wealth through their own labor, it became important to discover all the resources within the individual. A common form of the early novel, the Bildungsroman, traces the education of a young person—the acquisition of a character's skills and knowledge—until that character can survive without depending on anyone of greater income or status.

The typical happy ending of a novel consisted of an individual's acquiring a house, a job, and a family. These goals reflect a change in the relative importance of various parts of the social and political order. In the old aristocratic order, individuals supposedly labored to add to the glory of the kingdom and its ruling families, not to build their own houses. As kings were replaced by presidents and prime ministers, the state was redefined as something created by independent individuals in order to preserve their property and freedom. To create the best kind of private life for individuals became the goal of the state. The novel reflects this new valorization of private life.

These four features—realism, individualism, ostensible universality of point of view, and the valuing of private life—are what recent critics (such as Watt and Anderson) point to as defining the novel's middle-class form. While these features are evident in many novels, some critics have argued that to consider them as defining is to slight the complexity of the literary form. Some texts look very much like novels yet are quite unrealistic; others imply, as much as any religious allegory, that the individual should be subservient to God. To account for some of this variety, Michael McKeon (1987) developed a somewhat more complex version of Watt's theory by adding in the tenet that no genre, no literary form, is ever a pure expression of one group or one moment in history. McKeon argues that the novel emerged as a mixture of previous forms and continues to change as the social order changes.

The features Watt points out may reflect the novel's ties to the middle class, but other elements in the novel reflect the mentality of the earlier, aristocratic social order. To give one example, many early novels end with a person discovering a previously unknown inheritance. Dickens' Oliver Twist seems a poor boy in the beginning of the novel named after him and undergoes an educational process that would seem capable of teaching him how to escape poverty, but the key element that allows him to rise out of the lower classes is that he is revealed to be descended from a wealthy family. That revelation seems quite magical and would appear to support a belief that ultimately bloodlines matter more than individual qualities (or that bloodlines are the source of individual qualities). This plot twist thus supports the older, aristocratic view, even if the style of most of the novel and its general plot of education support the newer, middle-class view that one must make one's way by learning about and utilizing elements of the real world rather than hoping for divine help. McKeon argues that all novels contain within them such tensions between the attitudes of different social groups; furthermore, the form of the novel has continually shifted as those social tensions have shifted.

The process McKeon describes was particularly evident in the early 20th century, when modernist novels broke away from the realism that, according to Watt, defined the novel itself. Finnegans Wake (1939) has such obscure sentences that readers cannot tell what scene is being described or who is speaking, much less whether anything is presented realistically or not. In a peculiar way, however, criticism of modernist novels has supported Watt's theory because critics have argued that as these novels veer away from the traditional form of the novel they also veer away from the middle class. Modernist texts have been seen as reactionary attempts to restore a pre-capitalist social order (Bersani, 1990) and as revolutionary breaks toward socialism or anarchy (Kristeva, 1980; MacCabe, 1979; Marcus, 1977). We might conclude, then, that the class affiliations of these works are inscrutable, or we might note that critics generally agree that modernism emerges from dissatisfaction with the middle class. Modernist authors themselves wrote numerous essays condemning middle-class conformity. One might then summarize the views of quite a range of critics by saying that modernist writers observed the connection between the traditional form of the novel and the middle class and altered the novel to break out of the middle class, some heading to the right and some to the left (a conclusion argued by Berman, 1989, and Tratner, 1995).

A similar conclusion could be drawn from critical debates about the later attack on realism found in magic realist novels: some critics view magic realism as a continuation of the elitism of modernism, others as a reaction against the whole of European literature, a postcolonial break with the dominant literary form of European capitalism/realism.

While new forms of unrealistic novels continue to be developed, the vast majority of published novels remain traditional, realistic works. The dominance of realistic novels has led to the unusual new forms being labeled "experimental," and somehow they continue to seem experimental decades after they are written. The field of novel forms has in effect arranged itself into a central domain of realistic, middle-class novels, with various experimental forms of varying class affiliations on the margins. For many critics, then, it still seems true that the dominant form of the novel is tied to the middle class.

Several schools of criticism, however, have proposed quite different interpretations of the dominance of realist novels. Some Marxist critics have argued that the realist novel's conjunction with the middle class was simply an accident of history, not an essential part of the form. Georg Lukács (1958), for example, claims that the realism and individualism of the novel are not a reflection of middle-class ideology but rather function in the novel to reveal the insoluble tension between the individual and the surrounding social reality. By revealing such tensions, the novel serves the progressive development of society toward individual freedom. In the 18th and 19th centuries, this progressive tendency favored the middle class in its efforts to break up the older feudal order. In the 20th century, however, the middle class has become dominant and repressive in its own ways, so that the realist novel now becomes a tool for criticizing the middle class and for furthering a socialist revolution.

A wide range of feminist and cultural-studies critics (e.g., Gilbert and Gubar, 1979; Gallagher, 1985; Gates, 1988; Sáldivar, 1990) have argued that the novel form has always been more flexible than Watt would have it: women, minorities, and colonial writers have used the form throughout its history to challenge dominant social groups and hence to undermine the middle class. To do so, however, has required authors to struggle against the market and against certain dominant features of the novel. Feminist and cultural-studies critics end up describing the novel as a form embodying contradictions within it. One critic,

Mikhail Bakhtin (1981), has argued that the defining feature of the novel is precisely that it combines contradictory forms of expression derived from different social classes. Bakhtin disagrees as well with Watt's dating of the origins of the novel, tracing the form back to the 14th century at least, to the wild fantasies of François Rabelais. The unrealistic novels of the 20th century would appear in Bakhtin's theory to be continuations of quite old novel forms, not challenges to a single dominant form.

Probably the strongest challenge to the theory that the novel is middle class derives from novels written in non-European countries that do not have developed capitalist class systems. Considering now the different kinds of social orders in which novels are written and the varied forms novels take, it becomes less and less plausible to draw any conclusions at all about the relationship of the novel to any class. However, the association of the novel and the middle class continues to haunt critical commentary. For example, discussions of non-European novelists sometimes revolve around the question of whether or not such writers are consciously or inadvertently fostering the creation of European-style middle-class cultures within their countries. Such critical debates demonstrate that theories about the novel that have gained prominence become part of the context in which novels are written and read, regardless of whether those theories are true or not. The belief that the novel is a middle-class form, although unprovable, has become, in a sense, a social fact and continues to exert influence even as the grounds that support that belief disappear.

MICHAEL TRATNER

See also Critics and Criticism (18th Century); Genre Criticism; Ideology and the Novel; Journalism and the Novel; Marxist Criticism of the Novel; Picaresque; Politics and the Novel; Proletarian Novel; Realism; Reviewers and the Popular Press; Social Criticism; Socialist Realism

Further Reading

Anderson, Benedict, *Imagined Communities: Reflections on the Origin and Spread of Nationalism,* London: Verso, 1983; revised edition, London and New York: Verso, 1991

Bakhtin, M.M., *The Dialogic Imagination: Four Essays,* translated by Caryl Emerson and Michael Holquist, edited by Holquist, Austin: University of Texas Press, 1981

Berman, Russell, *Modern Culture and Critical Theory: Art, Politics, and the Legacy of the Frankfurt School,* Madison: University of Wisconsin Press, 1989

Bersani, Leo, *The Culture of Redemption,* Cambridge, Massachusetts: Harvard University Press, 1990

Gallagher, Catherine, *The Industrial Reformation of English Fiction: Social Discourse and Narrative Form, 1832–1867,* Chicago: University of Chicago Press, 1985

Gallagher, Catherine, *Nobody's Story: The Vanishing Acts of Women Writers in the Marketplace, 1670–1820,* Berkeley: University of California Press, and Oxford: Clarendon Press, 1994

Gates, Henry Louis, Jr., *The Signifying Monkey: A Theory of Afro-American Literary Criticism,* New York: Oxford University Press, 1988

Gilbert, Sandra, and Susan Gubar, *The Madwoman in the Attic: The Woman Writer and the Nineteenth-Century Literary*

Imagination, New Haven, Connecticut: Yale University Press, 1979; London: Yale University Press, 1980

Harrison, John R., *The Reactionaries,* London: Gollancz, 1966; New York: Schocken, 1967

Kristeva, Julia, "Oscillation Between Power and Denial," in *New French Feminisms: An Anthology,* edited by Elaine Marks and Isabelle de Courtrivron, Amherst: University of Massachusetts Press, 1980; Brighton: Harvester Press, 1981

Lukács, Georg, *Wider den missverstandenen Realismus,* Hamburg: Claasen, 1958; as *The Meaning of Contemporary Realism,* London: Merlin Press, 1963; as *Realism in Our Time: Literature and the Class Struggle,* New York: Harper, 1964

MacCabe, Colin, *James Joyce and the Revolution of the Word,* London: Macmillan, and New York: Barnes and Noble, 1979

Marcus, Jane, "No More Horses: Woolf on Art and Propaganda," *Women's Studies* 4 (1977)

McKeon, Michael, *The Origins of the English Novel, 1600–1740,* Baltimore: Johns Hopkins University Press, 1987; London: Raduis, 1988

Moretti, Franco, *The Way of the World: The Bildungsroman in European Culture,* London: Verso, 1987

Sáldivar, Ramon, *Chicano Narrative: The Dialectics of Difference,* Madison: University of Wisconsin Press, 1990

Tratner, Michael, *Modernism and Mass Politics: Joyce, Woolf, Eliot, Yeats,* Stanford, California: Stanford University Press, 1995

Watt, Ian, *The Rise of the Novel: Studies in Defoe, Richardson, and Fielding,* Berkeley: University of California Press, and London: Chatto and Windus, 1957

Closure. *See* Beginnings and Endings

J.M. Coetzee 1940–

South African

J.M. Coetzee's novels mark the convergence of postmodernist and postcolonial modes of discourse in South African fiction. They are a milestone in a body of English-language writing that traditionally has been oriented toward mainstream narrative realism and liberal humanist values. Trained as a linguist, Coetzee has been influenced by ideas from poststructuralist linguistics and critical theory. His affiliation with the European literary heritage is openly declared in both his creative and critical writings. Nevertheless, his seven novels, their diverse locales and period settings notwithstanding, are oblique fictional extrapolations from his country's moral and political crisis in the second half of the 20th century. The polemics of his books engage with Afrikaner society's embattled national myths and authoritarian modes of literary discourse, and they grapple with the hermeneutical dilemmas forced upon the white South African writer by the language of apartheid and the displaced, marginal position from which he writes. In the course of these investigations, Coetzee challenges traditional assumptions about authority and agency in fiction and targets some of its key ingredients—myth, ideology, historical vision—as principal sources of hostility to human values in the colonial context.

Many of the preoccupying themes of Coetzee's work—the paranoia of imperial power structures, the complicity of the colonial writer, and the moral dubiety of art—are present in his first novel. *Dusklands* (1974) suggestively couples the megalomaniacal narratives of an American media propagandist researching modes of psychological warfare against Vietnam with an 18th-century frontier account of a brutal punitive expedition against a tribe of African Bushmen. To the imperial power of the gun is added, in the modern context, the displaced aggression and camera-eye sadism of television in its dehumanizing coverage of war. But the twin narrative also implicates in the colonization process the agency of the printed word, through which the new explorers—academics, media-men, and writers—impose their own mental fictions upon their subjects, locking the colonial Other into the imperial self's foreign code of consciousness. Significantly, Coetzee gives his own surname to the author and translator of the expeditionary narrative. The so-called settler narrative is specifically singled out as one of the privileged modes of literary discourse institutionally endorsed by colonialism. As the novel demonstrates, it is not only through violent military conquest that colonialism is achieved, but also through language and, most particularly, through the conventional sign systems of "realism" that pass themselves off as "natural" and "universal" when they are really only the products of one limited kind of language code. To the extent that historical realism is the favored mode of the settler narrative, its deconstruction in Coetzee's novel is an imaginative act of decolonization.

In *In the Heart of the Country* (1977), Coetzee responds to Afrikaner myths of national identity as expressed in the South African *plaasroman*, or farm novel. Coetzee's antipastoral takes aim at the patriarchal fantasy of paternal landowner, supportive wife and mother, and grateful Africans, all bound together by a mystique of earth. Rather than the conventional mother-martyr and sustainer of racial purity, Magda is a spinster, and in her neurotic fantasies she constantly kills and buries her Afrikaner father and the regime he represents. She treats her black servants as familiars, but she is nevertheless trapped within the racist discourse she is subverting, trapped within inherited patterns of dominance and subservience. Undermining the narratives that shore up apartheid and Afrikaner authority through Magda, Coetzee also disallows the possibility of assimilating her to the alternative tradition that casts whites as champions of the antiapartheid cause. Improbably, Magda uses ideas drawn from modern psychoanalysis and sociolinguistics. The multiple voices and indeterminate outcomes of her narrative contest the monologic, omniscient authority and closure not only of Afrikaner patriarchal discourse but also of conventional realism's approaches to language.

Waiting for the Barbarians (1980) is a timeless fable of empire set on the frontier of an anonymous imperial power that routinely tortures and massacres the local nomadic peoples. It is clear that, in its paranoid need for an enemy to define itself against, the empire merely imagines that the local people are a threat. The novel focuses on the moral crisis of a compassionate, liberal-minded Magistrate who is jailed and tortured for his kindness to a crippled barbarian woman, a kindness that amounts to treason under imperial law. By taking the side of the oppressed, the Magistrate effectively becomes one of them and is finally left stranded in the muddled minority position of the reluctant colonizer. He is, for instance, nostalgic for luxuries bought by the exploitations of imperial conquest and oppression, which, nevertheless, causes him to live in shame and self-hatred. The novel's graphic torture scenes warn the reader, with Coetzee's customary reflexiveness, of the dangers of such fictional depictions. In his voyeuristic fascination with the forbidden, the reader may be guilty of an insidious complicity with the oppressor.

Life & Times of Michael K (1983) is set in a future Cape Town and Karoo that are ravaged by war. The baffled attempts of an internment camp medical officer to understand an inarticulate black vagrant serve as a paradigm for the dilemma of the white literary interpreter who, in his craving for meaning, tries to compose stories for a silenced and ultimately unknowable black majority. This dilemma became acutely relevant to Coetzee's personal situation in 1985, following the novel's Booker Prize success. Coetzee came increasingly to be regarded by the international community as a literary spokesman for a country the Afrikaner regime's State of Emergency had immersed in silence. His quandary was given dramatic expression in *Foe* (1986), which is simultaneously a revision of the Robinson Crusoe settler fable, an allegory of South Africa's racial dilemmas, and a meditation on the art of fiction. Here the author, since he cannot challenge a white power structure that he himself is part of and cannot speak for the oppressed without becoming a party to their oppression, renounces his right to speak through his characters. In *Foe* Coetzee keeps Friday, the "savage" in Defoe's *Robinson Crusoe*, tongueless and mute for the entire novel. In fact, all attempts at communication with him through music, speech, and writing, by both his creator (Defoe) and his fellow characters, are fruitless since they are founded on erroneous European cultural and political assumptions. Abandoning the token psychological realism of *Michael K, Foe* employs a metafictional strategy and a renunciatory aesthetic that allow the text to subvert its own ethnocentricity.

After the rigorous postmodernism of *Foe*, narrative realism became a heavily qualified, provisional component of Coetzee's fiction. *Age of Iron* (1990) guardedly allegorizes the imminent apocalyptic death of white minority rule in South Africa through the terminal cancer of a Cape Town academic. *The Master of Petersburg* (1994) is a convoluted analysis of the insidious, incestuous symbiosis of the novelist's personal life and his fiction, in which a reinvented Dostoevskii, unraveling the political murder of his backsliding revolutionary stepson, confronts both characters from his own earlier novels and the real-life anarchist Nechaev. He then revenges himself upon Nechaev by transforming him into the demonic Verkhovenskii, a character in *Besy* (1872; *The Devils*). Both books are parables of contemporary world politics, pitting ineffectual redemptive theologies against ruthless terrorism in a context of historical tyranny. They pose Coetzee's crucial familiar questions about the responsibilities of the artist and about who has the right to speak for "the nation" and "the people" in the periods preceding revolutionary crisis: rebellious children or perfidious parents? the makers of revolutions or of statements? the oppressed or those who get rich writing about them? In its disturbing revision of the literary and political discourses through which it is itself written, Coetzee's fiction is a profoundly historical exercise of the moral imagination.

DEREK WRIGHT

Biography
Born in Cape Town, 9 February 1940. Attended the University of Cape Town, B.A. 1960, M.A. 1963; University of Texas, Austin, Ph.D. 1969. Applications programmer, IBM, London, 1962–63; systems programmer, International Computers, Bracknell, Berkshire, 1964–65; Assistant Professor, 1968–71, and Butler Professor of English, 1984, State University of New York, Buffalo. Lecturer, 1972–83, and Professor of General Literature, University of Cape Town, from 1984.

Novels by Coetzee
Dusklands, 1974
In the Heart of the Country, 1977; as *From the Heart of the Country*, 1977
Waiting for the Barbarians, 1980
Life & Times of Michael K, 1983
Foe, 1986
Age of Iron, 1990
The Master of Petersburg, 1994

Other Writings: essays on literature, including *White Writing: On the Culture of Letters in South Africa* (1988) and *Giving Offense: Essays on Censorship* (1996).

Further Reading
Attwell, David, *J.M.Coetzee: South Africa and the Politics of Writing*, Berkeley: University of California Press, and Cape Town: David Philip, 1993
Coetzee, J.M., *White Writing: On the Culture of Letters in*

South Africa, New Haven, Connecticut, and London: Yale University Press, 1988

Coetzee, J.M., *Doubling the Point: Essays and Interviews,* edited by David Attwell, Cambridge, Massachusetts: Harvard University Press, 1992

Dovey, Teresa, *The Novels of J.M.Coetzee: Lacanian Allegories,* Johannesburg: Ad Donker, 1988

Gallagher, Susan VanZanten, *A Story of South Africa: J.M.Coetzee's Fiction in Context,* Cambridge, Massachusetts: Harvard University Press, 1991

Penner, Allen Richard, *Countries of the Mind: The Fiction of J.M.Coetzee,* Westport, Connecticut: Greenwood Press, 1989

Cold Nights by Ba Jin

Han ye 1947

It is not incidental to the despairing tone of Ba Jin's last novel *Cold Nights* that its composition spanned three bitter winters, from late 1944 to the very last day of 1946. The opening scene of the novel, in which the protagonist is introduced as lost in thought while an air-raid siren empties the streets around him, was reportedly written hours after Ba Jin witnessed such an eerie moment during the winter of 1944, when Japanese bombers were systematically strafing Chongqing, the war-time capital of China. After this seminal beginning, however, Ba Jin did not resume writing until the winter of 1945, when the Japanese had already surrendered and the Chinese nationalist government had claimed a grand victory. The greater part of the novel was finished toward the end of 1946 in Shanghai, where postwar euphoria had quickly dissipated in the face of the grim reality of poverty, social disorder, and civil war.

Although 5,000 copies were sold within a year of its publication in 1947, *Cold Nights* was never as popular as Ba Jin's earlier writings, such as the Turbulent Stream (1931–40) and Love (1931–33) trilogies. Nor was it meant to arouse the same enthusiastic response. As Olga Lang observes in her pioneering study, during the 1930s a compassionate and ebullient Ba Jin "helped to create among the intellectuals an emotional climate that induced them to accept the Chinese revolution" (see Lang, 1967). The heroes Ba Jin created in his early fiction are mostly rebels and idealists who excited the imagination of the eager and romantic May Fourth generation of educated urban youth.

By the mid-1940s, however, a sense of helplessness entered into Ba Jin's narratives. This change certainly owed much to the wartime condition under which the writer was first forced to flee Shanghai and then move around in the southwest hinterland. In his 1944 novel *Qi yuan* (Garden of Rest), for example, a writer-narrator finds himself caught in the widening gap between the fictional world he wishes to construct and a murky reality that unfolds, uncontrollably, before his eyes. In the same novel, the inescapable bond between father and son becomes an organizing theme. A later collection of short stories, aptly entitled *Xiao ren xiao shi* (1947; Little People, Little Things), best describes the writer's concerns during this period. An apparent insulation of ordinary characters from larger historical movements (specifically the war of resistance as a national cause) led Ba Jin to take a

hard look at unheroic lives and mundane situations. The passionate outcry of *"J'accuse"* that underlies his most popular novel *Jia* (1931; *Family*) grew into a subdued and mournful groan, and the focus of his literary representation became less idealistic. The previous faith in resolute action gave way to a sobering recognition that life was an encompassing and complicitous mass of attachments that defies rationalization.

The significance of *Cold Nights*, therefore, lies in the "inward turn" it marks in Ba Jin's development as a novelist. A third-person narrative, it centers on the tragic fate and consciousness of its antihero Wang Wenxuan, a professional proofreader. By patiently exploring Wenxuan's inner life and examining the intricate relationship between him and the people around him, Ba Jin establishes himself, in the words of C.T. Hsia, as a "psychological realist of great distinction" (see Hsia, 1961). The central narrative device that enables the psychological analysis is the tuberculosis that inflicts intense pain on Wenxuan and eventually causes his voiceless death. Close and clinically accurate descriptions of his sick body accompany a relentless dissection of Wenxuan's psyche, hopelessly incapacitated by indecision, anguish, and fear. In the process, his predilection for endless inner musings registers feeble social protest and, more poignantly, indexes the failures of his social and personal life. The use of tuberculosis as a metaphor for a sensitized and embattled interiority readily reminds us of a similar tradition in modern European literature and culture. It also culminates a long fascination with the social and psychic meanings of the consumptive body that is found in prominent modern Chinese writers such as Lu Xun, Yu Dafu, and Ding Ling.

Yet tuberculosis is just a symptom of the general malaise that plagues Wenxuan, who soon realizes that his disease actually helps him relate to the two women in his life: his doting but possessive mother and his independent and vivacious common-law wife. Unable to bring together these two strong-willed women and yet unwilling to choose one over the other, Wenxuan seeks solace in masochistic pain in a desperate effort to postpone and eventually avoid decision and responsibility. The impossible choice between mother and wife faced by Wenxuan underscores two conflicting conceptions of and claims against the individual: the traditional notion of filial duty versus the modern discourse of self-realization. Indeed, Wenxuan may well be the most agonized masochist ever represented in modern Chinese literature. The two mother figures who define his private world can be momentarily reconciled only when he resorts to self-infantilization and physical pain. The war as a crisis situation only further exposes his inadequacy as son and husband, and his failure is complete when his own son and mirror image, Xiaoxuan, finds him a stranger. Eventually, his wife Shusheng, having left for another city to seek happiness and a passionate life, asks to be freed of their modern-style marriage. Wenxuan stays behind with his mother and son in Chongqing and expires on the evening when the city pours out to celebrate the victory over the Japanese.

Wenxuan's death is not the only place in the novel where irony becomes irresistible; Shusheng's pursuit of freedom also is fraught with ambiguous consequences. Yet the greatest irony lies in the fate of the novel itself. Certainly the most mature and sophisticated novel by Ba Jin, *Cold Nights* may also be one of the few truly modern Chinese narratives from the first half of the 20th century. Its maddening ambivalence and its undaunted look into the individual psyche mark a sharp divergence from the aesthetics of exteriority endorsed by socialist realism, which became the dominant mode of writing with the founding of the People's Republic in 1949. The impact of Ba Jin's last novel, therefore, could not be fully measured until the late 1980s when, once again, there was a literary interest in psychological depth and in such themes as illness.

Xiaobing Tang

See also Ba Jin

Further Reading

Anderson, Marston, *The Limits of Realism: Chinese Fiction in the Revolutionary Period,* Berkeley: University of California Press, 1990

Hsia, C.T., *A History of Modern Chinese Fiction,* New Haven, Connecticut: Yale University Press, 1961; 2nd edition, 1971

Lang, Olga, *Pa Chin and His Writings: Chinese Youth between the Two Revolutions,* Cambridge, Massachusetts: Harvard University Press, 1967

Mao, Nathan K., and Liu Ts'un-yan, editors, *Cold Nights, A Novel by Pa Chin,* Hong Kong: Chinese University Press, and Seattle: University of Washington Press, 1978

Prusek, Jaroslav, "Subjectivism and Individualism in Modern Chinese Literature," in his *The Lyrical and the Epic: Studies of Modern Chinese Literature,* edited by Leo Ou-fan Lee, Bloomington: Indiana University Press, 1980

Colmena. *See* Hive

Colombian Novel. *See* Latin American Novel: Colombia

Colonial Romance. *See* Adventure Novel and Imperial Romance

Comédie humaine. *See* Human Comedy

Comedy and Humor in the Novel

The novel, unlike tragic drama or epic poetry, has always been hospitable to comedy and laughter. The earliest (some would say prenovelistic) manifestations of the form demonstrate narrative's propensity for humor. The *Satyricon* of Petronius (Roman, first century) is famous for the ludicrous vulgarity of the feast at the home of the wealthy freedman Trimalchio; *Daphnis and Chloe* by Longus (Greek, c. second century) draws comedy from the touching naïveté of two rustic lovers; there is humor as well as pathos in the sufferings of the protagonist of *The Golden Ass* by Apuleius (Greek, third century) where a man is magically transformed into a donkey.

While in any literary mode "pure comedy" is more a concept than a phenomenon, this is particularly true of the novel, for although many of the best-known novels are comic masterpieces, few are solely, consistently, or determinedly comic. (It is difficult, for example, to draw a clear division between the comic novel and the satiric novel.) François Rabelais alternates chapters full of sexual and scatological humor with others that contain sober advice for rulers. Miguel de Cervantes' humor in *Don Quixote* (1605–15) is tinged with melancholy. Jonathan Swift's *Gulliver's Travels* (1726), described as a "merry work" by the author's friend and contemporary Dr. Arbuthnot, has more often been read since their time as pessimistic and misanthropic. Laurence Sterne's *Tristram Shandy* (1759–67) notoriously mingles comedy with sentiment, a project that some writers on laughter, such as Henri Bergson (1900), have seen as self-contradictory or self-defeating. Mark Twain's *The Adventures of Huckleberry Finn* (1884), which boasts some of the funniest scenes in literature, also ventures serious treatments of issues as profound as slavery, human friendship, internecine family feuds, and the tensions between nature and culture. Even in a children's novel such as Kenneth Grahame's *The Wind in the Willows* (1908), the comedy is mixed with thrills and melodrama, notably in the imprisonment, escape, and pursuit of the odious yet lovable Toad of Toad Hall. The ability to mix modes and leave open the possibility of diverse responses is one that the novel possesses to a greater extent than other literary genres.

It would be perverse to argue that there exists some pure form called the tragic or serious novel from which humor should be excluded. Even the English novelist D.H. Lawrence, often accused of lacking a sense of humor, deploys it triumphantly at times, most notably in his best and most serious work. In *The Rainbow* (1915) the toddler Anna Lensky, terrified of the geese at the Marsh Farm where she has recently come to live, is told by her stepfather Tom Brangwen, "They don't know you. . . . You should tell 'em what your name is. . . . They think you don't live here." Later Brangwen finds Anna at the gate calling "shrilly and imperiously" to the geese: "My name is Anna, Anna Lensky, and I live here, because Mr. Brangwen's my father now. He *is*, yes he *is*. And I live here." This is a touching scene, but also finely comical.

In the 20th century, when the novel may seem to have taken a more somber turn than ever before, humor and comedy are still so pervasive as to seem organic rather than casual or accidental. Absurdist, existentialist, and magic realist texts all arouse laughter, although often of a grotesque, weird, or trollish kind. In *Murphy* (1938) the Irish novelist and playwright Samuel Beckett

makes comedy (compassionate but never sentimental) from the antics of the disabled and the mentally disturbed. In *La Noia* (1960; *The Empty Canvas*) the Italian Alberto Moravia constructs comic scenes around the dilemma of a man who can only love, and escape being bored by, his mistress when he is made to realize that he can never possess her. He engages in sexual congress with her while she stands in a passage talking on the telephone to another lover; later he covers her naked, living body with banknotes as she lies on a bed belonging to his wealthy mother, who is downstairs giving a party for society people. Neither action brings him closer to his goal of total possession of his mistress. The Colombian Gabriel García Márquez in *El amor en los tiempos del cólera* (1985; *Love in the Time of Cholera*) endows the elderly and respectable Dr. Juvenal Urbino with a parrot who "knew only the blasphemies of sailors but said them in a voice so human that he was well worth the extravagant price of twelve centavos." The purchase costs the doctor his life, as he dies trying to catch the bird after it has escaped: "The ladder slipped from under his feet and for an instant he was suspended in air and then he realised that he had died without Communion, without time to repent of anything or to say goodbye to anyone." To a believer such a thought will be shocking, but the comic element in the manner of the doctor's death is inescapable.

One reason for the deep affinity between comedy and the novel is that the novel generally focuses on the middle and lower levels of society, which are also the traditional domain of comedy. Comic novels produce a host of master-servant pairings: Cervantes' Don Quixote and Sancho Panza, Denis Diderot's Jacques and his master, Henry Fielding's Tom Jones and Partridge, Charles Dickens' Mr. Pickwick and Sam Weller, Mark Twain's Huck and Jim. Invariably the servant and the master are made to exemplify different kinds of wisdom and different kinds of folly.

The patronizing element sometimes present in the novel's treatment of the servant should not lead us to conclude that the comic novel belongs uniquely to the bourgeoisie. The obvious counter-example is the picaresque narrative, where society is viewed from below. The true picaro is by definition a wanderer and a petty criminal—living on the margins of society, practicing the comic wiles of the knave and trickster, and passing clear-eyed judgments on those richer or more eminent than himself. (Examples of the picara, or female rogue, are rare: Daniel Defoe's *Moll Flanders* [1722] is perhaps the most obvious.) *Lazarillo de Tormes* (1554), probably the best-known picaresque novel, has a markedly comic and unheroic finale in which the protagonist ends his wanderings and settles down to marriage, but in an arrangement that an aristocrat or bourgeois would find humiliating: his newfound security is achieved at the price of sharing his wife's favors with his new master. While the picaresque focuses on low-life characters, the middle- and upper-class stereotypes from the bourgeois novel reappear, seen now from a different perspective. By the same token the knave or trickster who takes a central role in the picaresque novel also features, although less prominently, in novels such as *Don Quixote* and *The Pickwick Papers* (1837), which offer a less plebeian view of the world. *Huckleberry Finn,* which has picaresque elements, largely avoids class categories by taking a child narrator as protagonist.

The diversity of readers' responses to humor is notorious.

What makes one reader laugh may make another weep. While this may partly be explained by extraneous factors such as cultural conditioning or personal psychology, there are cases in which it may be traced to the semiotic system of the novel itself. A novel such as Oliver Goldsmith's *The Vicar of Wakefield* (1766) appears on first reading as a near-tragedy, a catalogue of disasters analogous to the biblical Book of Job. To many readers a second or subsequent reading reveals a pervasive humor, arising chiefly from the complacent vanity and unintended self-revelations of the narrator.

In traditional criticism the word *comedy* has often been used as if it referred only to plays: *comédie* in French and *commedia* in Italian can both be used to mean "a play." Yet many of the archetypal elements of comedy—the trickster figure, the carnival mood, the wise fool, disguises and mistaken identities, ridicule of authority figures, the turning of the world upside down, grotesque realism, mockery of hypocrisy and pretense—are just as pervasive in novels as in drama. In early 18th-century Britain, often considered the birthplace of the modern novel, the favorite type-figures—the rake, the fop, the chaste young woman and not so chaste young man, the seduced woman, the learned lady, the booby squire—are inherited from the stage comedy of the immediately preceding era (Restoration Comedy). Even in the two great tragic novels of the English 18th century, Defoe's *Roxana* (1724) and Samuel Richardson's *Clarissa* (1747–48), one notices the influence of comic forms and characters, and the same may be said of *Clarissa*'s French counterpart, Choderlos de Laclos' *Les Liaisons dangereuses* (1782; *Dangerous Acquaintances*).

In the Middle Ages and Renaissance, before the novel achieved prominence among literary genres, comedy was defined less by its humor than by the movement of its plot toward a happy ending. The modern theorist Northrop Frye (1957), an enthusiast for comedy in all its forms, suggests that the typical comic ending heralds the advent of a new society, and other critics, such as M.D. Bristol and Victor Turner, have seen comedy and humor as subversive to the point of encouraging revolution. But these are exaggerations. The marriages that end many comic novels—Fielding's *Tom Jones* (1749), for example, or Jane Austen's *Pride and Prejudice* (1813)—herald a rejuvenation of the old society rather than the birth of a new one. The same is true of more bizarre comic endings like that of Graham Greene's *Our Man in Havana* (1958), where Wormold, the part-time spy who is found to have faked photographs of Cuban missile sites using mock-ups consisting of vacuum-cleaner parts, is rewarded for his deceit with a full-time job in counter-intelligence: "On our training staff. Lecturing. How to run a station abroad. That kind of thing." This is his superiors' way of masking their own incompetence: to punish Wormold would be to acknowledge that he has tricked them. However, the comic ending leaves the British defense establishment embarrassed but not destroyed: it represents an assimilation to established society rather than any real subversion of it.

Many of the novels that have aroused most laughter end on an ambiguous or sober note. In Joseph Heller's *Catch-22* (1961) the mentally and physically resourceful Orr manages to make himself look stupid so as to distract attention from his plan for escaping from the horrors of war: at the end of the book he is reported to be paddling doggedly toward neutral Sweden in a rubber dinghy. To many readers Orr's escape has seemed like a beacon of hope, but, as Heller himself suggested in an interview,

a doubt remains as to whether Orr will reach his destination. For that matter, Wormold in Greene's *Our Man in Havana* does not expect his new job to last. In the 20th-century novel, at least, there is an implicit or explicit recognition that the conventional comic ending is a fantasy.

The language of comedy in the novel is strikingly varied. Mikhail Bakhtin in *Tvorchestvo Fransua Rable i Narodnaja Kul'tura Srednevekovija i Renessansa* (1965; *Rabelais and His World*) emphasized the importance of grotesque realism—the language of the "bodily lower stratum," of uninhibited eating, drinking, urinating, defecating, and sexuality. He has found it triumphantly in Rabelais, more ambiguously elsewhere. The French novelist Raymond Queneau fills his *Zazie dans le métro* (1959; *Zazie*) with puns and vivid colloquial language to match the wide-ranging plot that encompasses gangsters, transvestites, and a very difficult little girl. But other comic novelists systematically avoid pungent demotic language. Jane Austen creates comedy in an idiom devoid of pun, slang, technical jargon, or explicit mention of bodily functions. Austen can derive as much humor from understatement—an elderly valetudinarian advising that "an egg boiled very soft is not unwholesome," and offering guests "a *very* small slice" of cake—as Rabelais can from scatological terms and comic hyperbole. More surprisingly John Cleland, in his pornographic novel *Fanny Hill* (1748–49), achieves comic effects by avoiding vernacular words for the male and female sexual organs, describing them instead through a series of elegant circumlocutions reminiscent of those used in the landscape poetry of the time.

Another time-honored source of humor in language is the fictional character who loves shapely but shop-soiled proverbs. Still more popular is the use of comic names for institutions or persons. Institutions: Balzac's Pension pour les Deux Sexes et Autres (Boarding-House for Both Sexes and Others); Dickens' Circumlocution Office, United Grand Junction Ebenezer Temperance Society, and Hot Muffin and Crumpet Baking and Punctual Delivery Company; David Lodge's Euphoric State University; Thomas Pynchon's Yoyodine Aerospace Corp. Characters: Laurence Sterne's Slawkenbergius, a ponderous scholar; Dickens' Mr. Pecksniff, a fastidious hypocrite; Rose Macaulay's Father Chantry-Pigg (a High Anglican clergyman who improbably goes searching for converts in Muslim countries); Thomas Pynchon's Moriturus (Latin for "about to die"), a name given to a Japanese who, in the middle of World War II, only wants to get back to his peaceful native city of Hiroshima (an unusually somber joke even by modern standards); Heller's Dori Duz (some girls do, some girls don't . . .), and Lieutenant Scheisskopf (shithead).

There is no clear line of development in the history of comic fiction. Swift and Sterne may owe much to Rabelais, and Fielding to Cervantes; but there is no continuous tradition such as that which, in comic drama, runs from Menander and Plautus through the Italian and English Renaissance dramatists to Molière, Carlo Goldoni, and Oscar Wilde. This is partly because so many countries have contributed to the development of the novel, and primacy has shifted with great rapidity, especially in recent times. Many of the humorous and comic masterpieces with which the history of the novel is studded are isolated ones. While Aristophanes, William Shakespeare, and Molière each wrote several memorable dramatic comedies, the novelists Petronius, Rabelais, Swift, Fielding, Jaroslav Hašek, and Heller have left only one or two memorable comic novels. Even Dickens, whose comic genius glows intermittently in many novels, wrote only one, *The Pickwick Papers,* where humor truly predominates.

T.G.A. NELSON

See also New Humor Novel; Parody and Pastiche; Picaresque; Satirical Novel

Further Reading

Bakhtin, M.M., *Tvorchestvo Fransua Rable i Narodnaja Kul'tura Srednevekovija i Renessansa,* Moscow: Khudozh, 1965; as *Rabelais and His World,* Cambridge, Massachusetts: MIT Press, 1968

Bakhtin, M.M., *The Dialogic Imagination: Four Essays,* translated by Caryl Emerson and Michael Holquist, edited by Holquist, Austin: University of Texas Press, 1981

Bergson, Henri, *Le rire: Essai sur la signification du comique,* Paris: Alcan, 1900; as *Laughter: An Essay on the Meaning of the Comic,* London and New York: Macmillan, 1911

Calvino, Italo, *The Literature Machine: Essays,* translated by Patrick Creagh, London: Secker and Warburg, 1987

Frye, Northrop, *Anatomy of Criticism: Four Essays,* Princeton, New Jersey: Princeton University Press, 1957

Gurewitch, Morton, *Comedy: The Irrational Vision,* Ithaca, New York: Cornell University Press, 1975

Meredith, George, "An Essay on Comedy," in *Comedy,* edited by Wylie Sypher, Garden City, New York: Doubleday, 1956

Nelson, T.G.A., *Comedy: An Introduction to Comedy in Literature, Drama, and Cinema,* Oxford and New York: Oxford University Press, 1990

Pirandello, Luigi, *On Humor,* Chapel Hill: University of North Carolina Press, 1960; originally published as *L'Umorismo*

Comic Books. *See* Graphic Novel

Comic Novel. *See* Comedy and Humor in the Novel

Comte de Monte-Cristo. *See* Count of Monte-Cristo

Maryse Condé 1934–

Guadeloupean

Maryse Condé's novels are set at cultural intersections, exploring the intrusion of European imperialism into Africa and the resulting diaspora cultures, particularly that of the West Indies. Her novels create a compelling Caribbean presence, their language filled with allusions to the turns and inflections of Creole. Condé has expressed the hope that her work helps restore a voice that will allow the people to imagine a tomorrow (see Pfaff, 1993). She seeks to invent the future by preserving and interrogating the past. Concerned with the devastating effects of political, cultural, and economic domination, her novels question existing versions of history as well as stereotypical images of women, to replace them with more truthful narratives.

Condé believes that wandering, not rootedness, leads to creativity, and this wandering makes her into a perpetual stranger.

She adopts this stance as a textual strategy to resist domination. For Condé, the gaze of the stranger is the gaze of discovery, arguing that too much familiarity with a place does not allow an author to write about it more truthfully but only to "mythify" it. Far from seeing it as a deplorable condition, Condé embraces her position as an outsider at the margin, commenting that "writing is largely enjoying the pleasure of displeasing."

While Condé is at all times interested in the Caribbean and in creating a Caribbean identity, she constantly resituates this project. Her early novels take issue with the myth that the rediscovery of African ancestry can solve the Caribbean question. Her first novel, *Hérémakhonon* (1976), for instance, tells the story of a young woman from Guadeloupe who, feeling alienated at home, travels to Africa to sort out her troubles and "to try to see what there was before." *Une Saison à Rihata* (1981; *A Season in Rihata*) continues the theme of an identity search in Africa, with characters of African as well as Caribbean origin seemingly lost where the circumstances of life have led them. But being in Africa does not solve any problems. Condé's refusal to idealize Africa also animates the highly acclaimed two-volume *Ségou*, consisting of *Les murailles de terre* (1984; *Segu*) and *La terre en miettes* (1985; *The Children of Segu*). Emphasizing political and religious conflict, the saga tells the story of a family in Mali over several generations from the time of the Bambara empire until the colonization by the French.

With *Moi, Tituba, sorcière noire de Salem* (1986; *I, Tituba, Black Witch of Salem*), Condé's work moves back to the Americas. *Tituba* is the story of the forgotten witch of Salem, who was tried for her healing powers. Written as an autobiographical transcription of the heroine's life, this novel is an epic "remembering" of the forgotten story of the displaced Black mother slaves. Tituba eventually returns to Barbados, her homeland in the Caribbean. Her healing powers metaphorically give a collective memory to the Caribbean and by the same token stage the entrance of the West Indies into literature and history. The validation of orality in *Tituba* is further elaborated in Condé's next two novels. *La Vie scélérate* (1987; *The Tree of Life*) follows the rise of a Guadeloupean middle-class family. Based on semi-autobiographical material, a young female narrator constructs a viable family history out of a jungle of fragmented and competing versions of her family's history. The search for a literary form for this story is embedded in the problems facing West Indian women living within patriarchal structures, which govern even oral traditions and memories. *Traversée de la mangrove* (1988; *Crossing the Mangrove*) also focuses on the search for a narrative voice that does not perpetuate oppression. Here the "missing piece" of the story is the enigmatic death of a half-stranger, which incites an entire community into telling its stories.

Les Derniers Rois Mages (1992; The Last of the Wise Men) follows the meandering of Spéro, a French West Indian man who lives on a small island off the shores of South Carolina. Against a colorful background of imaginary temptations (including visions of African royal ancestry) and Spéro's dispossession in exile, Condé leads the story toward a reconciliation with his multiple heritage. *La Colonie du Nouveau Monde* (1993; The Colony of the New World) presents a mock version of the colonial enterprise. Trying to overcome their alienation, a couple from Guadeloupe—who met in a psychiatric institution in France—stage a return to the place "before things went wrong," i.e., Egypt. Their journey ends in Columbia, where the followers

get entangled in a deadly net of past myths, contemporary corruption, and disillusionment about the possibility to erase a colonial past of dispossession.

Condé's most recent novel, *La Migration des coeurs* (1995; Migration of Hearts) is an experiment in intertextuality. Following Jean Rhys' rewriting of Charlotte Brontë's *Jane Eyre* in *Wide Sargasso Sea*, *La Migration des coeurs* transposes Emily Brontë's *Wuthering Heights* to a Caribbean context. The wild love affair, set at the end of the 19th century against the background of a reincarnation cult, negates age-old family rivalries as well as race and class conflicts. *La Migration des coeurs* is Condé's finest achievement to date.

BETTINA SOESTWOHNER

Biography

Born in Pointe-à-Pitre, 11 February 1934. Attended the Sorbonne, Paris, M.A., Ph.D. in comparative literature 1976. Instructor, École Normale Supérieure, Conakry, Guinea, 1960–64, Ghana Institute of Languages, Accra, 1966–68, and Lycée Charles de Gaulle, Saint Louis, Senegal, 1966–68; program producer for the French Services of the BBC, London, 1968–70; assistant at Jussieau, 1970–72, lecturer at Nanterre, 1972–80, and course director at the Sorbonne, 1980–85, all University of Paris; editor for the publishing house Présence Africaine, Paris, 1972; program producer, Radio France Internationale, from 1980. Since 1990, Professor, University of California, Berkeley.

Novels by Condé

Hérémakhonon, 1976; as *Hérémakhonon*, translated by Richard Philcox, 1982
Une Saison à Rihata, 1981; as *A Season in Rihata*, translated by Richard Philcox, 1988
Ségou: Les murailles de terre (first volume), 1984; as *Segu*, translated by Barbara Bray, 1987
Ségou: La terre en miettes (second volume), 1985; as *The Children of Segu*, translated by Linda Coverdale, 1989
Moi, Tituba, sorcière noire de Salem, 1986; as *I, Tituba, Black Witch of Salem*, translated by Richard Philcox, 1992
La Vie scélérate, 1987; as *The Tree of Life*, translated by Victoria Reiter, 1992
Traversée de la mangrove, 1989; as *Crossing the Mangrove*, translated by Richard Philcox, 1995
Les Derniers Rois Mages [The Last of the Wise Men], 1992
La Colonie du Nouveau Monde [The Colony of the New World], 1993
La Migration des coeurs [Migration of Hearts], 1995

Other Writings: plays; novellas; children's books; a booklet about Guadeloupe; book-length essays about francophone women writers and oral literatures in Martinique and Guadeloupe; critical booklets about Aimé Césaire's *Cahier d'un retour au pays natal*, Antillean poetry, and the Antillean novel; numerous articles mainly about Caribbean literature and cultural studies.

Further Reading

Callaloo 18:3 (1995), special issue on Maryse Condé
Hewitt, Leah Dianne, *Autobiographical Tightropes: Simone de Beauvoir, Nathalie Sarraute, Marguerite Duras, Monique*

Wittig, and Maryse Condé, Lincoln: University of Nebraska Press, 1990

Pfaff, Françoise, *Entretiens avec Maryse Condé,* Paris: Karthala, 1993; as *Conversations with Maryse Condé,* Lincoln: University of Nebraska Press, 1996

Taleb-Khyar, Mohamed B., "An Interview with Maryse Conde and Rita Dove," *Callaloo* 14:2 (Spring 1991)

Williams, John, "Return of a Native Daughter: An Interview with Paule Marshall and Maryse Condé," *SAGE: A Scholarly Journal on Black Women* 3:2 (Fall 1986)

World Literature Today 67:4 (Autumn 1993), issue focusing on Maryse Condé

Condition humaine. *See* Man's Fate

Condition of England Novel. *See* Politics and the Novel; Proletarian Novel; Social Criticism

Confessions of a Justified Sinner. *See* Private Memoirs and Confessions of a Justified Sinner

The Confessions of Zeno by Italo Svevo

La coscienza di Zeno 1923

The Confessions of Zeno is one of the definitive examples of European experimental modernist writing. The novel follows the remembered experiences of Zeno Cosini, who is persuaded to write his autobiography by his psychoanalyst, Doctor S., as a form of therapy. The psychoanalytic preface accredited to Doctor S. and the thinly disguised oedipal conflict that Zeno describes in his reminiscences combine to encourage a Freudian reading of the novel. Appropriately, the book pursues familiar modernist themes that include health, sickness, memory, intellect, abnormality, isolation, and desire. However, *The Confessions of Zeno* succeeds in inverting the traditional autobiographical narrative with its loose sequence of remembered episodes, and also mocks the psychoanalytic case study that Svevo incorporates into its form. For example, in the preface Doctor S. claims that, despite being thoroughly derided by Zeno, his analysis would have had positive results had not his patient "suddenly thrown up his cure just at the most interesting point" in the therapy. This kind of comment parodies the most famous of Sigmund Freud's case studies, *Bruchstück einer Hysterie-Analyse* (1905; *Dora: Fragment of an Analysis of a Case of Hysteria*), in which the Viennese analyst's patient broke off therapy before her sessions were due to end. Moreover, the common failure of psychoanalysis to do justice to the idiosyncratic mental life of the individual is reflected in the knowing voice of Zeno, who claims that Doctor S. is no good at interpreting his dreams. For these reasons, *The Confessions of Zeno* may be distinguished from the psychological realism of Marcel Proust and Virginia Woolf and reflects closely the ironic fiction of James Joyce (a friend of Svevo's) and Robert Musil.

One of the most interesting aspects of the novel is Svevo's dual association of clear vision with self-knowledge and of blindness with the psychological secrets of the mind (what Freud might have termed the unconscious). Although Zeno's narrative is characterized by a quickness of thought, the very first sentence of the introduction—"See my childhood? Now that I am separated from it by over fifty years, my presbyopic eyes might perhaps reach to it if the light were not obscured by so many obstacles"—reflects the fraught modernist quest to capture the essence of selfhood. Like Svevo's other two major novels, published some 25 years earlier, *Una vita* (1892; *A Life*) and *Senilità* (1898; *As Man Grows Older*), *The Confessions of Zeno* concerns itself with the vicissitudes of age and the fragility of identity. Svevo's choice of name for his protagonist evokes the early Greek philosopher Zeno of Elea, whose conundrums on space and time imply the impossibility of motion (a theory later refuted by Aristotle in the *Physics*). Reflecting both the concerns of his ancient namesake and the philosophical ruminations of James Joyce's major character Stephen Dedalus, Zeno Cosini contemplates the "bewilderment" of motion: "when one is walking rapidly each step takes no more than half a second, and in that half a second no fewer than fifty-four muscles are set in motion. . . . I could not of course distinguish all its fifty-four parts, but I discovered something terribly complicated which seemed to lose its order as soon as I began paying attention to it . . . . [E]ven today, if anyone watches me walking, the fifty-four movements get tied up in a knot, and I feel like falling." This kind of introspective analysis is indicative of the confessional form of the novel (and provides an example of its comedy), but also suggests the other meaning of *coscienza*, which the critic Massimo Verdicchio calls the "precariousness of self-understanding" that repeatedly slips from the cognitive grasp of the aging protagonist.

The major theme of the novel is that of illness, which takes on many different guises: Zeno's inability to relinquish smoking; his unfulfilled sexual desire; a preoccupation with his body; the frailty of his memory; and his increasing fear of death. In the course of his confessions Zeno begins to understand that "health cannot analyze itself even if it looks at itself in the glass. It is only we invalids who can know anything about ourselves." Appropriately, the major intellectual figure informing the novel is the German philosopher Friedrich Nietzsche who, in *Menschliches, Allzumenschliches* (1878; *Human, All Too Human*), describes health and sickness as being in constant tension with each other. In Zeno's case, only by being aware of his illness can he begin to conceive of the possibility of health. But this bourgeois understanding of self-reliance casts doubt over whether Zeno can ever be cured of his ailments by psychoanalytic means: "after practising it assiduously for six whole months I find I am worse than before." In a perverse way, Zeno actually regains a degree of sanity after he has given up on psychoanalysis; toward the end of the novel, when the doctor requests his notebooks, Zeno claims that "he is no doubt expecting to receive more confessions of weakness and ill-health, and will receive instead an account of

my perfect health. . . . For some time past I have realized that being well is a matter of conviction." However, this understanding is further undermined by Zeno's aloof separation from European "life today" in the shadow of World War I and his condemnation of the rest of humanity, both of which he repudiates for being "poisoned to the root."

The open-ended structure of the novel is complicated by two extant drafts from the unfinished sequel to *The Confessions of Zeno* that Svevo was working on in the last two years of his life: "The Old Old Man" (1929) and "An Old Man's Confessions" (1949). These fragments develop the theme of old age but also indicate possible avenues of regeneration for humanity, which Zeno rules out in the apocalyptic and disturbing last sentence of the completed novel: "There will be a tremendous explosion, but no one will hear it and the earth will return to its nebulous state and go wandering through the sky, free at last from parasites and disease."

MARTIN HALLIWELL

Further Reading

Breslin, Carol-Ann, "Odyssean Echoes in *The Confessions of Zeno*," *Nemla Italian Studies* 11–12 (1987–88)

Furbank, P.N., *Italo Svevo: The Man and the Writer*, London: Secker and Warburg, and Berkeley: University of California Press, 1966

Gatt-Rutter, John, *Italo Svevo: A Double Life*, Oxford: Clarendon Press, and New York: Oxford University Press, 1988

Lebowitz, Naomi, *Italo Svevo*, New Brunswick, New Jersey: Rutgers University Press, 1978

Minghelli, Giuliana, "In the Shadow of the Mammoth: Narratives of Symbiosis in *La coscienza di Zeno*," *Modern Language Notes* 109:1 (January 1994)

Moloney, Brian, *Italo Svevo: A Critical Introduction*, Edinburgh: Edinburgh University Press, 1974

Rabkin, Leslie, "Beyond Health and Disease: Psychoanalysis and Italo Svevo's *The Confessions of Zeno*," *Literature and Psychology* 37:1–2 (1991)

Roditi, Édouard, "A Note on Svevo," in *The Confessions of Zeno*, by Italo Svevo, translated by Beryl de Zoete, Harmondsworth: Penguin, 1964

Russell, Charles, *Italo Svevo, the Writer from Trieste: Reflections on His Background and His Work*, Ravenna: Longo, 1978

Russell, Daniel, "Zeno's Therapeutic Text," *Italian Culture* 6 (1985)

Svevo, Italo, *Further Confessions of Zeno*, translated by Ben Johnson and P.N. Furbank, London: Secker and Warburg, and Berkeley: University of California Press, 1969

Verdicchio, Massimo, "Svevo and the Ironic Conscience of the Novel," *Quaderni d'Italianistica* 11:1 (Spring 1990)

Joseph Conrad 1857–1924

English

Henry James gave the most prescient valuation of Conrad's contribution to the novel when he said that no one had ever had such first-hand experience available for intellectual use. Joseph Conrad was born in Poland to parents who suffered exile and death for their patriotism. He first served as a French merchant sailor but changed his affiliation to the English merchant service and the English language. All Europe thus went into the making of Conrad's English. His sea voyages as a merchant sailor made him the cartographer of what Edward Said has called the culture of imperialism: the Near and Far East, Africa, Latin America. Although Conrad has been criticized as a racist and an imperialist (notably by Chinua Achebe), this view misunderstands his special role in the history of colonial fiction: Conrad often fictionalized the historical moment of the liberation of the oppressed, but he focused on the colonists, especially those not already committed to liberation.

Said has properly emphasized the influence of the grand narratives of liberation in what he terms the Culture of Imperialism, but one cannot properly historicize the emergence of postcolonialism solely by articulating the point of view of those seeking liberation. Their motives were sufficient, necessary, and timely during any moment of the long history of imperialism. To understand the moment of their liberation, however, we must also recover the consciousness of those who were not already convinced by liberation, but who were no longer convinced by imperialism, either. How else can one explain the breaking away of the colonies unless one considers as well the metropolis' growing disinclination to hang on? In a novelistic style that represents a significant turning point for the English novel—notably its extremely sophisticated use of narrative irony—Conrad's fiction engages these problems and participates in what may be called an early phase of liberation.

Conrad had already published *Almayer's Folly* (1895) and *An Outcast of the Islands* (1896), two narratives of the disintegration of colonists, before he wrote the book he felt made him a writer: *The Nigger of the Narcissus* (1897). The most offensive title in modern fiction was deliberate. James Wait, the ship's "nigger," openly complains about the term early in the novel. In his 1912 preface to the American edition, Conrad thanked his publishers for returning his own title and retiring the earlier American attempt ("The Children of the Sea") to moderate his offensiveness.

In *The Nigger of the Narcissus,* Conrad shows Wait as a victim of scapegoating, a man made responsible for everything that goes wrong for the ship, even the weather. (Conrad shared this interest in modern scapegoat practices with contemporaneous authors Stephen Crane and Henry James, well before they all became friends.) If the novel exists uncertainly between reflecting and revealing persecution (as René Girard uses these terms in *Le bouc émissaire* [1982; *The Scapegoat*]), the famous Preface that Conrad wrote after he wrote the novel identifies itself unqualifiedly with all the voiceless and unremembered multitudes. Conrad's subsequent fictional representations of the culture of imperialism are to be measured by this preface, which argues for solidarity without exclusions. Conrad's subsequent fiction represents the historically limited solidarities of race and class, which unwind before the suspicion so reluctantly entertained by any "one of us" that all others are kin.

In the person of Marlow, both "Heart of Darkness" (1902) and *Lord Jim* (1900) exacerbate the "decadence" of sympathy for those unlike us, which Conrad first noted in *The Nigger of the Narcissus.* "Heart of Darkness" is the precise center of Conrad's special work of representing imperialism. When Marlow listens to his fellows enfold all English adventurers into a grand narrative or "gigantic tale," he responds first with a reflection that England too was once a place of darkness. He then finds himself elaborating a distinction between bad and good colonialism, which depends on a fidelity to efficiency. When, however, he hears his quasi-religious belief in good colonialism rhyme with Kurtz's more problematic definition ("something you can bow down before, and offer a sacrifice to"), Marlowe breaks off and tells another kind of story, against himself and good colonialism.

Nostromo (1904) is a wickedly prescient book that accurately catches the modern turbulence of Latin American politics and the American inflection of English influence, in the voice of Mr. Holroyd, an investment banker from San Francisco:

> Now what is Costaguana? It is the bottomless pit of ten per cent loans and other fool investments. European capital has been flung into it with both hands for years. Not ours, though. We in this country know just about enough to keep in-doors when it rains. We can sit and watch. We are bound to. But there's no hurry. Time itself has got to wait on the greatest country in the whole of God's universe. We shall be giving the word for everything—industry, trade, law, journalism, art, politics, and religion, from Cape Horn clear over to Smith's Sound, and beyond, too, if anything worth taking hold of turns up at the North Pole. And then we shall have the leisure to take in hand the outlying islands and continents of the earth. We shall run the world's business whether the world likes it or not. The world can't help it—and neither can we, I guess.

Conrad's beautiful transliteration of American bullishness sets an ideal English ear wondering what changes English as a linguistic and intellectual medium will endure in the world where anyone can appropriate its forms. Conrad's prose here also contrasts usefully with the value of Kipling's more complacent interest in Babuisms as comical deformations of an accepted "Englishness."

The Secret Agent (1907) extends Conrad's depiction of the uneasy coexistence of all these "other" speakers of English by considering the "foreign" population of London, which many suspected was a breeding area for anarchists and dynamitards. Well before William Burroughs and the dark spy novels of the postmodern period, Conrad shows various agents and reagents sharing a single common culture, a no man's land of uncertain state support and rewards.

After *The Secret Agent*, Conrad published *A Personal Record* (1912), *Under Western Eyes* (1911), *Chance* (1913), *Victory* (1915), *The Shadow-Line* (1917), *The Arrow of Gold* (1919), *The Rescue* (1920), and *The Rover* (1923). No work of Conrad's is without interest, but "The Secret Sharer" (1912) is a condensed fictional moment that embodies an important thread running through Conrad's fiction: it proposes a luminous radical union of "us" and "them," in which a narrating one of us can decide to identify with, but also protect, one of them.

WILLIAM A. JOHNSEN

See also Lord Jim; Nostromo

Biography

Born Józef Teodor Konrad Korzeniowski in Berdyczów (now Berdichev), Podolia, Ukrainian Province of Poland, 3 December 1857; became British citizen, 1886. Attended schools in Cracow, 1868–73. Moved to Marseilles, 1874; merchant seaman from 1874; sailed on several French merchant ships to the West Indies, 1874–76; after qualifying as an able seaman in England in 1878, sailed on British commercial ships to the Orient; received Master's Certificate in the British Merchant Service, 1886; received first command, 1888; first mate on the *Torrens*, 1892–93; retired from the Merchant Service and moved to England, 1894; lived in Ashford, Kent, from 1896. Died 3 August 1924.

Novels by Conrad

Almayer's Folly: A Story of the Eastern River, 1895
An Outcast of the Islands, 1896
The Children of the Sea, 1897; as *The Nigger of the Narcissus: A Tale of the Sea,* 1898
Lord Jim, 1900
The Inheritors: An Extravagant Story, with Ford Madox Ford, 1901
Youth: A Narrative, with Two Other Stories (includes "Heart of Darkness" and "The End of the Tether"), 1902
Typhoon, 1902
Romance, with Ford Madox Ford, 1903
Nostromo: A Tale of the Seaboard, 1904
The Secret Agent: A Simple Tale, 1907
Under Western Eyes, 1911
Chance, 1913
Victory: An Island Tale, 1915
The Shadow-Line: A Confession, 1917
The Arrow of Gold: A Story Between Two Notes, 1919
The Tale, 1919
Prince Roman, 1920
The Warrior's Soul, 1920
The Rescue: A Romance of the Shallows, 1920
The Black Mate: A Story, 1922
The Rover, 1923
The Nature of a Crime, with Ford Madox Ford, 1924
Suspense: A Napoleonic Novel, 1925
The Sisters (unfinished), 1928

Other Writings: stories and novellas (including "Heart of Darkness" [1902]), plays, essays, autobiographical writings, letters.

Further Reading

Ambrosini, Richard, *Conrad's Fiction as Critical Discourse,* Cambridge and New York: Cambridge University Press, 1991

Berthoud, Jacques A., *Joseph Conrad: The Major Phase,* Cambridge and New York: Cambridge University Press, 1978

Conroy, Mark, *Modernism and Authority: Strategies of Legitimation in Flaubert and Conrad,* Baltimore: Johns Hopkins University Press, 1985

GoGwilt, Christopher Lloyd, *The Invention of the West: Joseph Conrad and the Double-Mapping of Europe and Empire,* Stanford, California: Stanford University Press, 1995

Griffith, John W., *Joseph Conrad and the Anthropological Dilemma: "Bewildered Traveller,"* Oxford: Clarendon Press, and New York: Oxford University Press, 1995

Hamner, Robert D., compiler and editor, *Joseph Conrad: Third World Perspectives,* Washington, D.C.: Three Continents Press, 1990

Harpham, Geoffrey Galt, *One of Us: The Mastery of Joseph Conrad,* Chicago: University of Chicago Press, 1996

Henricksen, Bruce, *Nomadic Voices: Conrad and the Subject of Narrative,* Urbana: University of Illinois Press, 1992

McClure, John A., *Kipling & Conrad: The Colonial Fiction,* Cambridge, Massachusetts: Harvard University Press, 1981

Moses, Michael Valdez, *The Novel and the Globalization of Culture,* New York: Oxford University Press, 1995

Najder, Zdzislaw., *Joseph Conrad, a Chronicle,* Cambridge and New York: Cambridge University Press, 1983

Parry, Benita, *Conrad and Imperialism: Ideological Boundaries and Visionary Frontiers,* London: Macmillan, 1983

Said, Edward W., *Joseph Conrad and the Fiction of Autobiography,* Cambridge, Massachusetts: Harvard University Press, 1966

Stape, J.H., editor, *The Cambridge Companion to Joseph Conrad,* Cambridge and New York: Cambridge University Press, 1996

Watt, Ian P., *Conrad in the Nineteenth Century,* Berkeley: University of California Press, 1979; London: Chatto and Windus, 1980

Watts, Cedric Thomas, *The Deceptive Text: An Introduction to Covert Plots,* Brighton, Sussex: Harvester, and Totowa, New Jersey: Barnes and Noble, 1984

White, Andrea, *Joseph Conrad and the Adventure Tradition: Constructing and Deconstructing the Imperial Subject,* Cambridge and New York: Cambridge University Press, 1993

Wollaeger, Mark A., *Joseph Conrad and the Fictions of Skepticism,* Stanford, California: Stanford University Press, 1990

The Conservationist by Nadine Gordimer

1974

While Nadine Gordimer's novels display a steady politicization, their reception has undergone shifts of focus. Heralded at first for their acute, almost lyrical sensitivity and for their richness of style and detail, her early novels also attracted adverse comment for their lack of narrative muscle and coolness of tone. As detachment fell away, attention focused on Gordimer's ability to sustain a tense dialectic between the personal and the political. It was with *The Conservationist,* winner of the Booker Prize in 1974, that Gordimer established herself as a novelist of major international importance.

Gordimer's early fiction had concerned itself primarily with the failure of liberalism in South Africa (*The Lying Days,* 1953; *A World of Strangers,* 1958; *Occasion For Loving,* 1963), turning thereafter to the possibilities for revolution (*The Late Bourgeois World,* 1966; *A Guest of Honour,* 1970). *The Conservationist* brought the two strands together. Nadine Gordimer's story of an African farm, *The Conservationist* exposes both the colonialist biases of her predecessors, Olive Schreiner and Karen Blixen, and the liberal pastoralism of Alan Paton's *Cry, the Beloved Country* (1948), through the self-incriminating interior monologue of its central character, Mehring. Mehring is an industrialist whose international entrepreneurial activities contrast with his weekend pose as farmer and conservationist. Despite his origins in Namibia, Mehring is a thoroughly representative South African type, his story offering a classic example of the "complicity plot," as Lars Engle has called it (see Engle, 1989). In this masterplot of recent South African fiction, individual whites seek lives of relative harmlessness, separation, and privacy, only to find themselves unable to maintain any such separate peace. In *The Conservationist* the return of the politically repressed is symbolized by the slow rising to the surface of an imperfectly buried black body, accompanied by the symbolic repossession of the land by blacks. The resurfacing of the buried body, which has implications for both African and gender politics, also indicates Gordimer's understanding of the role of physicality as fundamental to resistance against oppression.

Influenced by the Black Consciousness movement, which emphasized a return to black cultural roots and traditions, Gordimer employs myth to create a buried logic of fictional events, a subtext running alongside the text of public culture and race privilege articulated by Mehring. The major events on the farm are specifically related to patterns of Zulu myth, as represented in the novel by the interpolated quotations from Henry Callaway's *The Religious System of the Amazulu* (1868–70). Rainmaking practices, mediumship, and spirit possession articulate a set of values different from those of white society. In addition, the feminine empowerment of these black cultural practices contrasts with the masculine colonialism and latent sexual fascism of Mehring's world. The African women shape the life of the surrounding community, whereas the white female characters are almost without exception sexually exploited and repressed. The point is dramatized in Mehring's airborne molestation of his flight neighbor, a young girl. Mehring's identification of women with Africa in this scene points to the parallel between colonialism and sexual predation.

Although Gordimer anchors the novel in a subtext of Zulu cultural and religious practices, she endows the religious symbols with a political significance that suits her own purposes. Thus, when floods follow the activities of the rainmakers, the weather comes from the Mozambique channel, near the Portuguese territory that was about to claim its independence. The regeneration of the land by fire and flood, a mock-apocalypse, offers a vision of Africa without the white man, as Mehring's laborers take over the farm in his absence. When the black body is reburied, the reader learns that "he had come back," a phrase that invokes the African National Congress rallying cry "Afrika! Mayibue!" ("Africa! May it come back!"). In this way, Gordimer constructs a narrative—across Mehring's ahistorical musings, which are ignorant of the possibility of political change—that foreshadows the reversion of power to South African blacks.

Mehring's colonialism colors his perception of all reality. His interior monologue creates the impression of consciousness functioning in a void, dissociated from the world about him. Just as his midflight sexual encounter with the young girl involves surreptitious contact beneath a pretense of physical separation, so his society is presented as a set of circumscribed codes and worlds that communicate only crudely, underhandedly, or with violence. Mehring's willful refusal to recognize his place in history, his botched attempts to communicate across race and class lines, and his solipsistic blindness to events in the black community culminate (in a highly ambiguous ending) in a mock death and final abandonment of his claims. As a result, *The Conservationist* offers a prophetic image of a different South African future, in the best tradition of the visionary political novel.

In formal terms, the novel throws into sharp relief the intrinsic connections between the conventional representations of realism and the imposition of colonial structures on the land of Africa. Mehring, with his conviction that he is on the side of unassailable common sense and historical truth, is also the voice of conventional realism. By undermining Mehring's monologue and pointing up the falseness of his perceptions, *The Conservationist* also mounts an attack on realism, showing how it may operate on the side of the colonizer. The novel also voices a critique of modernism and its assumption that truth is subjective, residing in the internal reality constructed by individual consciousness. In Mehring's case, that internal reality is shown to be flawed, divorced from reality.

Imaging the ascendancy of Africans at the level of politics, *The Conservationist* also represents the ascendancy of a politicized aesthetic over modernism.

JUDIE NEWMAN

See also Nadine Gordimer

Further Reading

Clingman, Stephen, *The Novels of Nadine Gordimer: History from the Inside,* London and Boston: Allen and Unwin, 1986; 2nd edition, Amherst: University of Massachusetts Press, 1992; London: Bloomsbury, 1993

Cooke, John, *The Novels of Nadine Gordimer: Private Lives/Public Landscapes,* Baton Rouge: Louisiana State University Press, 1985

Driver, Dorothy, editor, *Nadine Gordimer: A Bibliography of Primary and Secondary Sources, 1937–1992,* London: Hans Zell, 1994

Engle, Lars, "The Political Uncanny: The Novels of Nadine Gordimer," *Yale Journal of Criticism* 2:2 (1989)

Ettin, Andrew Vogel, *Betrayals of the Body Politic: The Literary Commitments of Nadine Gordimer,* Charlottesville: University Press of Virginia, 1993

Gordimer, Nadine, *Conversations with Nadine Gordimer,* edited by Nancy Topping Bazin and Marilyn Dallman Seymour, Jackson: University Press of Mississippi, 1990

Newman, Judie, *Nadine Gordimer,* London and New York: Routledge, 1988

Pettersson, Rose, *Nadine Gordimer's One Story of a State Apart,* Uppsala and Stockholm: Uppsala University, 1995

Smith, Rowland, editor, *Critical Essays on Nadine Gordimer,* Boston: G.K. Hall, 1990

Conte Philosophique

The *conte philosophique* (philosophical tale) is a short, usually satiric narrative whose characters and story illustrate a philosophical proposition. A synthesis of fiction and philosophy, the conte philosophique avoids the abstraction of logical argument by relying on allegorical characters and a fast-moving narrative freed from any concern with realism and psychology. Through a sustained practice of irony, it solicits from the reader an intellectual rather than an emotional response to its depiction of human shortcomings and social evils.

This combination of fiction and philosophy may be traced back to a tradition including Thomas More's *Utopia* (1516), François Rabelais' *Pantagruel* (1532) and *Gargantua* (1534), Tommaso Campanella's *Civitas Solis* (1623; *The City of the Sun*), and Francis Bacon's *New Atlantis* (1626). As the term itself indicates, however, its major practitioners were figures from the French Enlightenment. Montesquieu's *Les Lettres persanes* (1721; *The Persian Letters*), with its tongue-in-cheek descriptions by two foreign travelers of the foibles of Regency society and its use of tales like that of the troglodytes to illustrate the political implications of unfettered egotism, is often identified as the first example of the genre. Denis Diderot's *Les Bijoux indiscrets* (1748; *The Indiscreet Jewels*), with its satires of scholasticism and Cartesianism, and his *Jacques le fataliste* (1773; *Jacques the Fatalist*), with its comic juxtaposing of the liberties of storytelling with the rigorous determinism of fatalism, are also included in the genre. As many of the above examples indicate, the conte philosophique has not been associated exclusively with narratives that are relatively brief.

Critics generally agree that the conte philosophique reached its highest development with the short prose fiction of Voltaire. There is a real irony in the fact that Voltaire, convinced that his tragedies, epics, and formal poetry would assure his reputation, is now read primarily as the creator and paramount practitioner of the conte philosophique. He himself dismissed his short narratives, along with most other prose fiction, as little more than "bagatelles" undertaken as a diversion from his labors in more serious genres. It was in 1739, at the age of 45, that Voltaire wrote his first conte philosophique: the now lost *Voyage du Baron de Gagnan,* which became, 13 years later, *Micromégas*

(1752), the comic dialogue between giants from another planet and a shipload of French scientists on the relativity of all human knowledge. The best known of the more than 25 contes philosophiques Voltaire wrote between 1747 and 1774 are *Zadig; ou, La Destinée* (1748; *Zadig; or, The Book of Fate*), *Candide; ou, l'Optimisme* (1759; *Candide; or, Optimism*), and *l'Ingénu* (1767; translated as *The Huron* and *The Pupil of Nature*). In England, the closest equivalents to the genre are Jonathan Swift's *Gulliver's Travels* (1726) and Samuel Johnson's "didactic romance" *Rasselas, Prince of Abyssinia* (1759), whose eponymic hero, along with his philosopher companion Imlac, undergoes a series of adventures illustrating the universal fragility of human happiness.

As a genre, the conte philosophique exemplifies the French Enlightenment and its subversion of established beliefs and institutions. Its mordant satire relies not on careful logic or rhetorical eloquence but on a fast-moving, witty, and always ironic tone adapted in large part from the conversational style of the Parisian literary salons of the period. Responding to the monarchy's tight censorship, the conte philosophique relies on a practice of allusion, caricature, exaggeration, and insinuation that assumes laughter to be the most potent weapon against the abuse of power and all forms of intolerance. The most frequent structural device of the conte philosophique is an extended voyage or quest for a lost beloved by a central character and his companion in a world given over to every form of human stupidity, avarice, and suffering. The hero encounters an endless succession of brutality, abuse, and evil immediately recognizable to the reader, but portrayed in such a way that they are stripped of all the justifying reasons normally given for their existence. In a letter of 28 January 1764 to his friend Jean-François Marmontel suggesting that he try his hand at the form, Voltaire offered what is the most succinct definition of the genre: "You really should write some contes philosophiques for us where you can heap ridicule on certain fools and certain foolishness, certain evils and certain evil-doers; the whole thing quite discreetly and in your own way, nibbling at the nails of the beast when you find it dozing." Eschewing cynicism, Voltaire goes on to point out that the author of the conte philosophique must be motivated by a desire to "make men become the least unreasonable they can be . . . by casting some light even on those owls who love the darkness."

As an artifact of the Enlightenment, the conte philosophique embodies that period's abiding faith in the power of reason. It is this higher mission that explains how it was that Voltaire, even as he consistently ridiculed the novel and all imaginative fiction soliciting the reader's identification, all but singlehandedly invented this prose form. In fact, the conte philosophique assumes a posture of readership distinctly different from that associated with the then emerging novel of realism. To read a conte philosophique was never to fall under the illusion that the events portrayed in the story represented real life and might be taken by the reader as a supplement to actual experience. Reading the conte philosophique involved instead the preservation of a critical, amused, and subversive interpretive distance from the characters portrayed and the story being told. To read a conte philosophique was to laugh at and see through power's subterfuges. The ironic comprehension of life's comic tragedies that came with the conte philosophique consolidated the reader's identification not with the fiction itself, but with an elite community of enlightened citizens making up the then emerging Republic of Letters. As Amaside, the heroine of Voltaire's satire of the Old Testament entitled *Le Taureau blanc* (1774; *The White Bull*), put it: "It is especially important that, under the veil of the fable, the story reveal to practiced eyes a more refined truth that eludes the vulgar." The seduction and pleasure of the conte philosophique lay in its invitation to a solidarity of enlightenment cosubstantial with the acts of reading, laughing, and understanding.

As concerns the history of narrative forms, the conte philosophique's assumption of a value system shared by author and readers underlines its debt to similar genres. As in the religious allegories of earlier periods, an idea is translated into a series of narrative events and the story as a whole sets out to teach a lesson. Unlike allegory, however, the conte philosophique's characters are designated not by abstract terms (charity, lust, avarice, and so on) but by exotic and often ironic names evoking either a distant place or an attitude toward life. Usbek and Zadig connote the Orient; Candide and Pangloss are exactly what their names tell us they will be. The importance of extended conversations between the characters as a way of making explicit the philosophical implications of the kaleidoscopic episodes underscores the form's debt to the genre of the philosophical dialogue as popularized by such late 17th-century figures as Fontenelle. In Diderot's *Encyclopédie* (17 vols., 1751–65; *Pictorial History of Trades and Industry*), the entry for the broader category of "tale" defines that form by contrasting it to the explicitly allegorical genre of the fable. While the fable observes the unities of place, time, and action to illustrate a "moral axiom," the tale is a free-flowing form that foresakes not only the three unities but any concern with teaching a lesson. The goal of the tale is to amuse rather than to instruct. This traditional opposition between tale and fable shows how, for the period, the specificity of the conte philosophique lay in its status as a synthesis of the freedom associated with the tale and the didacticism associated with the fable. The lesson taught by the conte philosophique was, however, distinctly different from that of the allegory or fable. In the *Encyclopédie*'s entry under *philosophe*, the point is made that for the true philosopher it is reason that motivates his every

action in the same way that, for the true Christian, it is grace that motivates everything he does. The conte philosophique was, in a very real sense, both a secular allegory and a civic fable. In relation to the other major prose form of the 18th century, the novel, the tale was defined as shorter, as placing a greater emphasis on style, and as relying on a chaotic accumulation of episodes. In contrast, the novel paid greater attention to carefully integrated composition, to the development of more psychologically complex characters, and to creating an overall illusion of realism. The progressive triumph of the novel during the 19th and 20th centuries, as well as the marginalization of the tale in all its variants, obscures the fact that, during the Enlightenment, and in large part because of the success of the conte philosophique, the tale competed strongly with the novel for dominance as the most important prose genre. For many authors and readers, in fact, the psychological realism of the novel was denounced as an illusory and manipulative abuse of readers' identification that jeopardized their independent judgment. The coolly ironic didacticism of the conte philosophique, because it asked its readers to think rather than to feel, was seen as respecting its audience's intellectual autonomy and responsibility.

The self-assured militancy of the conte philosophique makes it a genre that in many ways is at odds with the aesthetic and ideological assumptions of the late 20th century. The complicity it assumes between author and readers depends on an acceptance of shared values seen as universal in scope and application. The globe-trotting heroes of the conte philosophique may encounter endless and exotic examples of folly, stupidity, and tragedy; but the constant contrast of those evils to their own innocence and reasonableness sets its heroes up as exemplars of an enlightened ideal applicable to all times and all places. A given character may be a Westphalian, a Huron, a Babylonian, a giant from another planet, or a Brahman, yet underneath that variety of appearances he will always be the spokesperson for the same enlightened understanding, pointing out the absurdity of practices by which the true philosopher must never be duped. This proliferation of reason's voice across a multiplicity of different times and places reduces human history to an unchanging scenario of greed, violence, and intolerance repeating itself only as an absurd accumulation. The textures of any specific time or place give way to the deployment of one universal paradigm. Behind the superficial variations in geography and period, author and readers share the vision of a single, unchanging human nature. For a contemporary critic like Roland Barthes (1964), the supposed universality of human nature assumed by the conte philosophique reveals the genre as a vehicle for the worldview of a soon to be triumphant bourgeoisie at its most imperial. As Barthes sees it, the universal reason assumed by the conte philosophique amounts to nothing less than "an ablation of history and an immobilisation of the world."

Tracing the evolution and influence of the conte philosophique during the 19th and 20th centuries depends largely on how one defines the genre. If, like Barthes, we emphasize the genre's cultural context and its status as the didactic universalizing of the values espoused by an emerging elite, the conte philosophique becomes a genre coterminous with the ideologies of the Enlightenment. If, on the other hand, we adopt a more formal approach, such as Yvon Belaval's definition (1967) of the conte philosophique as "a narrative where example replaces argument," the genre's stories of exemplary heroes may be seen as having had an important influence on the development of the *roman de formation* and Bildungsroman of the 19th and 20th centuries. If we emphasize instead the genre's narrativizing of philosophical premises, it may be seen as leading to a long and varied tradition that includes Guy de Maupassant's tales, the prose parables of Arthur Schopenhauer and Franz Kafka, such narrative illustrations of existential philosophy as Jean-Paul Sartre's *La Nausée* (1938; *Nausea*) and Albert Camus' *L'Étranger* (1942; *The Stranger*), Jorge Luis Borges' and Leonardo Sciascia's narrative meditations on the paradoxes of representation, and even Salmon Rushdie's distinctly Voltairean parodies of religious intolerance. Again from a strictly formal viewpoint, science fiction may be seen as a variation on the conte philosophique, as it narrativizes the implications of science as the central philosophy of a technological age.

THOMAS M. KAVANAGH

See also Candide; Voltaire

Further Reading

Barthes, Roland, "Le Dernier des Ecrivains heureux," postface to *Voltaire, Romans et contes,* Paris: Gallimard, Collection Folio, 1964

Belaval, Yvon, "Le Conte philosophique," in *The Age of the Enlightenment,* edited by W.H. Barber, Edinburgh and London: Oliver and Boyd, 1967

Bongie, L.L., "Crisis and Birth of the Voltarian Conte," *Modern Language Quarterly* 23 (1962)

Bonneville, Douglas A., "Voltaire and the Form of the Novel," *Studies on Voltaire and the Eighteenth Century* 158 (1976)

Carr, Thomas M., "Voltaire's Fables of Discretion: The Conte philosophique in 'Le Taureau blanc'," *Studies in Eighteenth-Century Culture* 15 (1986)

Keener, Frederick M., *The Chain of Becoming: The Philosophical Tale, the Novel, and a Neglected Realism of the Enlightenment,* New York: Columbia University Press, 1983

Leo, V., "Phenomenological and Experimental Styles in the French Enlightenment," *Romanische Forschungen* 62 (1950)

Mason, Haydn, "Voltaire's Contes: An Etat Présent," *Modern Language Review* 65:1 (1970)

McGhee, Dorothy Madeleine, *Fortunes of a Tale: The Philosophic Tale in France, Bridging the Eighteenth and Nineteenth Centuries,* Menasha, Wisconsin: George Banta, 1954

Mylne, Vivienne, "Literary Techniques and Methods in Voltaire's *contes philosophiques*," *Studies on Voltaire and the Eighteenth Century* 57 (1967)

Sacks, Sheldon, *Fiction and the Shape of Belief,* Berkeley: University of California Press, 1964

Schick, Ursula, *Zur Erzähltechnik in Voltaires "Contes,"* Munich: Fink, 1968

James Fenimore Cooper 1789–1851

United States

James Fenimore Cooper was America's first widely esteemed novelist and the first to achieve both commercial success from his writing and an international reputation. Cooper produced a heterogeneous body of work, including novels of manners, dystopian satire, and the sea novel. But his reputation has rested chiefly, then and even more so now, on his five novels comprising the Leatherstocking tales, *The Pioneers* (1823), *The Last of the Mohicans* (1826), *The Prairie* (1827), *The Pathfinder* (1840), and *The Deerslayer* (1841), which gave world literature one of its most important figures, the 18th-century frontiersman and wilderness dweller Natty Bumppo. A character in Cooper's 1838 novel *Home As Found,* an old acquaintance of Natty's, remarks that "I set down Washington and Natty Bumppo as the two only really great men of my time"; the comment illustrates Cooper's claim to an audacious achievement: to have created through his novels a founding national legend that thereafter would permeate the United States' cultural memory. The claim has merit. Although the character of Natty drew upon folk traditions of historical pioneers such as Daniel Boone, it was the Leatherstocking tales that crystallized and bequeathed to the national consciousness, and to the enduring international conception of the United States, the image of a distinctive "American type" as a stark, isolated male figure at home only in the outdoor spaces of a vast continent. The genre of the American Western—both novel and film—is but the most obvious example of this continuing cultural presence.

Despite Natty Bumppo's fame as a solitary in the midst of nature, however, the focus of the Leatherstocking tales, and of all of Cooper's novels, is intensely, although problematically, social and historicist. He readily adopted the genre of the historical romance pioneered by Sir Walter Scott in *Waverly* (1814), and Scott's fictional reflections on vast historical transitions, such as the demise of patriarchal societies in the Highlands of his native Scotland, proved immensely suggestive to Cooper writing in a United States barely one generation removed from its revolutionary birth and engaged upon what was considered an epic westward progress. The Leatherstocking tales took that progress, and the displacement of America's native peoples by it, as its high historical theme, tracing that process through various stages in Natty's career. The novels richly exploit Natty's paradoxical historical position, in that his flights deeper into the forest to escape the encroaching settlements also blaze the trail for the westward movement of which he is the vanguard, not least through his prowess at making war on the American Indians who resist this advance. But Natty's friendship with the Delaware chief Chingachgook and his familiarity with and partial adoption of native practices establish him as a mediating figure between the supposedly vanishing American Indians and the white settlers who succeed them on the newly cleared American soil. That mediation claims to grant to the nation a symbolic native ancestry to rival the continuity with immemorial origins in British antiquity reconstructed by the historical romances of Scott.

Seizing upon the historical romance genre in his first acknowledged novel, the Revolutionary War tale *The Spy* (1821), Cooper enlarged his canvas from the didactic domestic fiction of his first novel *Precaution* (1820), which he published anonymously. The seven years that followed marked the period of his greatest popularity, as he rapidly produced three of the Leatherstocking tales and two of his first sea novels, the widely admired *The Pilot* (1823) and *The Red Rover* (1827). Beginning with his seven-year residence in Europe dating from the late 1820s, however, Cooper increasingly carried on an intermittently quarrelsome, vexed relationship with the reading public, an embattled position brought on, ironically, by his heightened sense during his European sojourn of his representative status as "the American novelist." The didacticism of his apprentice novel *Precaution* remained a crucial, indigestible element in Cooper's fiction, originating from the political and moral discourse of republicanism that was suspicious of the novel itself as a seductive inducement to corruption. The historical romance was widely approved in America in part because it offered to redeem the novel from its disreputability by rooting it in historical actuality, and Cooper's fiction typically insisted aggressively on this actuality. But frequently he also insisted on employing the novel form as a blunt instrument for the inculcation of political and moral truth, stating in *A Letter to His Countrymen* (1834) that he had written a recent novel "to illustrate and enforce the peculiar principles of his own country, by the agency of polite literature." Those republican principles, which informed Cooper's conservatism, set him at odds with the dominant literary opinion of the European nations whose aristocratic rule he condemned in *The Bravo* (1831); but those principles, and Cooper's mode of conveying them through the novel, were increasingly unfashionable as well in the liberal, restlessly enterprising, majoritarian America he satirized in *Home As Found* (1838).

These concerns also permeate the Leatherstocking tales, as *The Last of the Mohicans* is suffused with the classical republican thematization of history as the downfall of empires, and *The Prairie*'s bleak, blasted, and far-western setting severely warns against the sacrifice of the nation's virtue to the avidity excited by the continent stretching before it. But the development of the Leatherstocking tales also arguably reveals Cooper writing his own increasing estrangement from majority public opinion in America into the framework of his most enduring legend. The trajectory from *The Pioneers* in 1823 toward *The Deerslayer* in 1841 is one that places Natty Bumppo, the pioneer marginalized by history, in an ever increasing central and idealized role, and *The Deerslayer*'s return to a pristine Lake Otsego (the location of Cooper's own childhood) in a tale of Natty's youth culminates the overwhelmingly elegiac tone accompanying the elevation of the Leatherstocking tales into the national mythology. Cooper's novels answered the call of "literary nationalism" in the most presti-

gious American journals of his day for the creation of a literature that would imbue the national scene with the historical associations, so abundant in Great Britain but felt to be so lacking in America, that would enmesh citizens of the United States in a culturally binding force more traditionally immediate than that of its nascent, fragile, and unprecedented political compact. Cooper's novels indeed gave America one of its most common shared legends, and from the initial reception of the first Leatherstocking tales it seemed remarkably, and ironically, appropriate that at the center of that legend stood an isolated figure in the wilderness.

EDWIN WEED

See also Last of the Mohicans

Biography
Born in Burlington, New Jersey, 15 September 1789; moved with his family to Cooperstown, New York, 1790. Educated in the village school at Cooperstown; in the household of the rector of St. Peter's, Albany, New York, 1800–02; Yale University, New Haven, Connecticut, 1803–05: dismissed for misconduct; thereafter prepared for a naval career: served on the Sterling, 1806–07; commissioned midshipman in the US Navy, 1808; served on the Vesuvius, 1808, and on the Wasp in the Atlantic, 1809; resigned commission, 1811. Lived in Mamaroneck, New York, 1811–14, Cooperstown, 1814–17, and Scarsdale, New York, 1817–21; began writing in 1820; lived in New York, 1821–26, and Europe, 1826–33; returned to New York, 1833, and lived in Cooperstown from 1834. Died 14 September 1851.

Novels by Cooper
Precaution, 1820
The Spy: A Tale of the Neutral Ground, 1821
The Pioneers; or, The Sources of the Susquehanna: A Descriptive Tale, 1823
The Pilot: A Tale of the Sea, 1823
Lionel Lincoln; or, The Leaguer of Boston, 1825
The Last of the Mohicans: A Narrative of 1757, 1826
The Prairie: A Tale, 1827
The Red Rover: A Tale, 1827
The Borderers; a Tale, 1829; as *The Wept of Wish Ton-Wish,* 1829; as *The Heathcotes,* 1854
The Water Witch; or, The Skimmer of the Seas: A Tale, 1830
The Bravo: A Venetian Story, 1831
The Heidenmauer; or, The Benedictines, 1832
The Headsman; or, The Abbaye des Vignerons: A Tale, 1833
The Monikins: A Tale, 1835
Homeward Bound; or, The Chase: A Tale of the Sea, 1838
Home As Found, 1838; as *Eve Effingham; or, Home,* 1838
The Pathfinder; or, The Inland Sea, 1840
Mercedes of Castile; or, The Voyage to Cathay, 1840
The Deerslayer; or, The First War-Path: A Tale, 1841
The Two Admirals: A Tale of the Sea, 1842
The Jack O'Lantern (Le Feu-Follet); or, The Privateer, 1842; as *The Wing-and-Wing; or, Le Feu-Follet,* 1842
Wyandotté; or, The Hutted Knoll, 1843
Ned Myers; or, A Life Before the Mast, 1843
Afloat and Ashore; or, The Adventures of Miles Wallingford, 1844

Satanstoe; or, The Family of Littlepage: A Tale of the Colony,
    1845; as *Satanstoe; or, The Littlepage Manuscripts,* 1845
The Chainbearer; or, The Littlepage Manuscripts, 1845
Ravensnest; or The Redskins, 1846; as *The Redskins; or, Indian
    and Injin, Being the Conclusion of the Littlepage
    Manuscripts,* 1846
Mark's Reef; or, The Crater: A Tale of the Pacific, 1847; as *The
    Crater; or Vulcan's Peak,* 1847
Captain Spike; or, The Islets of the Gulf, 1848; as *Jack Tier; or,
    The Florida Reef,* 1848
The Bee-Hunter; or, The Oak Openings, 1848; as *The Oak
    Openings,* 1848
The Sea Lions; or, The Lost Sealers, 1849
The Ways of the Hour: A Tale, 1850

Other Writings: essays, travel writings, historical works.

Further Reading

Clark, Robert, *History, Ideology, and Myth in American
    Fiction, 1823–1852,* London: Macmillan, and New York: St.
    Martin's Press, 1984
Dekker, George, *The American Historical Romance,* Cambridge
    and New York: Cambridge University Press, 1987
House, Kay Seymour, *Cooper's Americans,* Columbus: Ohio
    State University Press, 1965
Kelly, William P., *Plotting America's Past: Fenimore Cooper
    and the Leatherstocking Tales,* Carbondale: Southern Illinois
    University Press, 1983
McWilliams, John P., *Political Justice in a Republic: James
    Fenimore Cooper's America,* Berkeley: University of
    California Press, 1972
Peck, H. Daniel, *A World By Itself: The Pastoral Moment in
    Cooper's Fiction,* New Haven, Connecticut: Yale University
    Press, 1977
Ringe, Donald A., *James Fenimore Cooper,* New York: Twayne,
    1962; updated edition, Boston: Twayne, 1988
Slotkin, Richard, *Regeneration Through Violence: The
    Mythology of the American Frontier, 1600–1860,*
    Middletown, Connecticut: Wesleyan University Press, 1973
Sundquist, Eric J., *Home As Found: Authority and Genealogy
    in Nineteenth-Century American Literature,* Baltimore: Johns
    Hopkins University Press, 1979
Wallace, James D., *Early Cooper and His Audience,* New York:
    Columbia University Press, 1986

Copyright

The novel as a genre and copyright as a legal concept are coterminous and culturally interwoven. Novelists were often the early supporters of authors' intellectual rights; the composition,
marketing, and distribution of novels have reflected the changing
assumptions and practices about literary property; and novels
have frequently been test cases for the jurisdiction of copyright
and for such related legal issues as censorship, international
trade agreements, and plagiarism. For example, under the influence of what has usually been seen as John Locke's "bourgeois"
theory of property and ownership, Daniel Defoe was one of the
prime movers in beginning to secure an author's financial interest in his work (see Rose, 1993). Henry Fielding gave up writing
for the theatre and turned to the novel in part because it was easier to secure rights (and profit) in fiction than in stage works.
The careers of several of the most successful 19th-century novelists (George Eliot, Anthony Trollope, William Thackeray) record
the shift from an author's selling the work outright to a publisher to the modern system of retaining a financial interest in subsequent editions through the payment of royalties. Recent new
editions of novels of the earlier 20th century (the Cambridge
D.H. Lawrence, particularly *Sons and Lovers;* the Hans Walter
Gabler edition of James Joyce's *Ulysses*) have become test cases
for the extension of copyright beyond the time when a literary
work would otherwise fall into public domain. Recently, the
electronic publication of interactive works of prose fiction has
called into question the very concepts of authoriality, proprietorship, and control in our postmodernist culture.

That there should be a historical and cultural congruence between copyright and the novel is hardly surprising if it is acknowledged that the novel (unlike, for example, epic, classical
drama, romance, or lyric) was the first literary genre created by
the mercantile middle classes for a predominantly middle-class
readership. In the Middle Ages and the early Renaissance, a
work might be dedicated to a noble patron in the hopes of securing a pension, but Geoffrey Chaucer is quite typical of his times
in having earned his living from a diplomatic, administrative,
and governmental career, not from his highly successful literary
production. In the 16th century, Erasmus was greatly offended
when it was suggested that he had actually written a work for
money. And in the late 17th century, John Milton gave up all
rights to *Paradise Lost* (1667) "in consideration of five pounds
to him paid by [his publisher] Samuel Symons." But by the early
18th century, Defoe could assert that "'Twould be unaccount-
ably severe, to make a Man answerable for the Miscarriages of a
thing which he shall not reap the benefit of if well perform'd"
(*Essay on the Regulation of the Press,* 1704) and could then petition for an act of parliament to protect an author's work, asking "Why have we Laws against House-breakers, High-way
Robbers, Pick-Pockets, Ravishers of Women, and all Kinds of
open Violence? When [an author] has his Goods stollen, his
Pocket pick'd, his Estate ruin'd, his Prospect of Advantage rav-
ish'd from him, after infinite Labour, Study, and Expence" (*Review,* 6 December 1709). By the later 18th century, Samuel
Johnson could take it as an axiom that "no man but a blockhead

ever wrote, except for money" (James Boswell, *The Life of Samuel Johnson,* 2 vols., 1791); in the 19th century, novel-writing had become so intertwined with the profit motive that Sir Walter Scott undertook the composition of the Waverly novels for specifically financial reasons. Trollope, like Joyce Carol Oates in our own time, tried, without permanent success, to produce a different series of fictional works under a pseudonym in order to increase the return on his "product," and when Mudie's lending library, which had been one of the major outlets (and thus sources of profit) for fiction, stopped circulating the traditional three-decker Victorian novel, the very shape, size, and narrative mode of the Anglo-American novel changed. In recent commercial history, the acquisition and consolidation of publishing firms by multinational conglomerates and the subsequent concentration on blockbuster popular novels in trade publishing (often with attendant film rights negotiated by a related branch of the conglomerate) has militated against the publication of first novels by unknown experimental writers.

The novel has, for the greater part of its history, been the promoter and beneficiary of the idea of literature as commodity and thus of literature as needing the same protection against piracy, unauthorized copying, and profit-making by unlicensed producers as any other sort of proprietary product. No other genre has its origins in a capitalist theory of investment and return, and no other genre has consistently mirrored the varying cultural attitudes to copyright and the protection of authorial rights. While William Wordsworth (obviously no novelist) had an influential hand in the drafting of the British 1842 Copyright Act, which promoted the author to the status of a "national treasure" in whom the country had made an "investment" (see Vanden Bossche, 1994); and while copyright cases since then still reflect a concern with a romantic "organicism" and "unity" derived from a Wordsworthian theory of poetics rather than from the sprawling, less cohesive structure of the novel, the practical, social, and financial decisions on infringement of copyright have affected the novel more often than any other genre. Of course, this is partly because the novel has in any case become the dominant mode of literature in the last two centuries, but it is also because the novel arises within a protocapitalist culture and then becomes the most profitable (and thus the most worthy of financial investment) of all literary genres. Again, it was Defoe who first expressed the property argument most directly, arguing that a writer's "Work is his Property, and he cannot be divested of that Property at the Will and Pleasure of any Man; no, not his Prince; to suppress his Labour, is to divest him of his Property" (*Review,* 3 December 1709). Copyright makes the difference. Houghton Mifflin, copyright holders for Willa Cather's *My Ántonia* (1918), sold 1.5 million copies of the novel during the 75 years it was in copyright. Since the work moved to public domain, the original publisher's sales have dropped by more than half and will probably continue to decline as cheaper reprints of the text become available. The last quarter of the 20th century has seen many of the major modernist novels fall into public domain, and there have therefore been several attempts to prevent this occurring by publishers and literary estates wanting to hold onto the lucrative copyright. By claiming that the publication of Lawrence's *Sons and Lovers* in 1992 was a "new" work (because it included sections from Lawrence's original manuscript not printed in the original 1913 or subsequent editions), Cambridge University Press tried to start the copyright clock ticking all over again.

How did this situation occur and what are its ramifications for the novel? The history of copyright as it affects the novel is the story of a change in concepts of proprietorship and reward. From the early Renaissance until the mid–17th century, a publisher-printer (the two were often synonymous) could be granted a "privilege" to print all copies of a given work. The author had no such rights: Four hundred editions of Martin Luther's translation of the Bible were published in his lifetime, and 66 pirated editions appeared within two years of its completion. Luther received no reward for any of these editions, pirated or authorized. Such "privileges" could obviously be very profitable if they were attached to such blockbusters (including the Bible). In 1549 Edward Whitchurch and Richard Grafton were given the "privilege" to print all copies of Edward VI's *Book of Common Prayer* so that there would be enough for every church congregation in the country. The author, Thomas Cranmer, received no payments.

By the mid–17th century this situation began to change, and during the 18th century the author gradually replaced the "bookseller" (i.e., the publisher) as the chief proprietor of the work. Sometimes this could be effected by a strong-minded and successful author taking over the publication of his work: Alexander Pope oversaw the production of much of his output, down to the specific details of typesetting, format, and print run, and made appropriately larger profits (his translation of Homer's *Iliad* in 1720 made him £5,320, a far cry from Milton's £5 for *Paradise Lost*). But Pope was an anomaly, and authors of the period typically based their claims for remuneration not on owning the entire vertical system of production, from composition to distribution, but on the capitalist principle that the "sweat of the brow" established an absolute right of property, a freehold "grounded on labour and invention" (Blackstone, 1766) just as Defoe had wanted. This relation between labor (investment) and return (profit) was gradually recognized as a legal entity by several important lawsuits and acts of parliament. In England, these effectively begin with a parliamentary edict of 29 January 1642, whereby the Stationers' Company (which had been responsible for the "registering" and "licensing" of books since the early days of printing) had to secure "the Name and Consent of the Author" before licensing a work for publication. The movement from "privilege" to genuine copyright continues in the Anne statute of 1710, which was the first *copyright* rather than *licensing* act and, while it hedged on authors' rather than booksellers' rights, "marked the divorce of copyright from censorship and the reestablishment of copyright under the rubric of property rather than regulation" (Rose, 1993). And, in such cases as *Burnet v. Chetwood* (1720), *Pope v. Curll* (1741), *Millar v. Kinkaid* (1743, appeal 1747), *Tonson v. Collins* (1761), and *Donaldson v. Becket* (1774), arguments on perpetual versus limited copyright, authors' versus booksellers' rights, and the needs of society versus the encouragement of individual ownership and production were debated back and forth, culminating in the Copyright Act of 1842 (in which a distinction was drawn between the unprotectable "useful knowledge" of science and the protectable "original work" of the author of imaginative literature, and protection extended 42 years after publication or 7 years after the author's death), the Copyright Act of 1911 (which substituted life plus 50 years for the date of first publication), and the Copyright Act of 1956 (which made some adjustments to bring British copyright in line with the Universal

Copyright Convention of 1952). In the United States, the Copyright Acts of 1909 and 1976 dealt with these same issues and came to virtually the same conclusions: an original work that did not simply present already known facts should be protected from unauthorized use for a *limited* period of time. The 1976 act changed the beginning of the copyright clock from the moment of publication (defined as "the distribution of copies . . . of a work to the public by sale or other transfer of ownership, or by rental, lease, or lending") to the act of creation itself: "Copyright is secured *automatically* when the work is created, and a work is 'created' when it is fixed in a copy for the first time" (US Copyright Office). For works created after the new act went into effect (1 January 1978), the term of copyright protection is normally the life of the author plus 50 years.

Continental traditions of copyright cover the same concerns but have one major difference: a *droit d'auteur* (or author's moral rights) is also recognized, whereas in Anglo-American jurisprudence the capitalist theory of ownership is consistently applied, so that under the principle of the commodification of the product, the work can be alienated from its original producer (i.e., sold) and the rights then pass to the current holder. This was the principle under which Ted Turner defended his decision to "colorize" his purchased collection of black and white "classic" films: "When I last looked, they belonged to me" (Kernan, 1990). It was also the principle under which the sculptor Richard Serra lost his suit over his site-specific *Tilted Arc,* when the US government, the "purchaser" of the work, decided to relocate it and thus, according to its creator, to "destroy" it. Under Anglo-American law of property, it would be theoretically possible for someone to purchase the *Mona Lisa* and then burn it! Continental intellectual property law accepts that even after the lapse of formal copyright in a work, the author and his estate may bring suit if a subsequent misuse of the property would sully the creative standing of the original author.

This connection between the public persona of the author and the nature of the work is found in Anglo-American law, but under different circumstances. As Defoe asserted, it was simply wrong that an author could be punished for any socially undesirable effects of his work while receiving no reward for its successes. (Defoe knew about this problem from his own experience: he had been sentenced to the stocks for having written the satirical *The Shortest Way with the Dissenters* [1702], even though he claimed that the work was parodic and that he had no intentions of promoting the draconian measures supposedly endorsed in the pamphlet.) Similarly, the defense mounted by a group of printers accused of sedition during the English Civil War that they had not written the "seditious" works (in fact, they even claimed that they had not read them, only produced them) was unsuccessful, and they were found liable. Defoe's experience is testimony to Michel Foucault's thesis that the acknowledgment of an author's "property" in a work occurs only as an aspect of the penal code: when an author can be found legally "responsible" for his writings, he can then make claims that they "belong" to him and fix his "name" on them. That 1642 parliamentary decree about securing the "Name and Consent" of the author was not, as it might at first appear, a straightforward recognition of authors' rights. It occurred only after the lapse of Star Chamber (the supreme "court of prerogative" through which the discretionary powers, privileges, and legal immunities reserved to the sovereign were exercised in England

from the 15th century until 1641) and the consequent proliferation of anonymous books and pamphlets; the government wanted a "name" on the work so that responsibility could be traced, and if an author could not be found, the printer would be regarded as author and thus be subject to the penal code. One right (that of government to censor and control) begets another (that of an author to reap the rewards of "sweat of the brow," according to bourgeois capitalist principles of investment and profit), just as the US Copyright Act of 1976 tries to arrive at a balance between society's access to free and open information and the need to protect an author's investment under the general rubric of the US Constitution's provision that "[t]he Congress shall have power . . . to promote the Progress of Science and useful Arts, by securing for limited Times to Authors and Inventors the exclusive Right to their respective Writings and Discoveries" (Article I, ¶ 8, cl. 8).

Some recent shifts in both legal and technological arenas, however, are beginning to throw copyright into question. Copyright is not a law of nature; it is a cultural construction of a particular period. One change of potential major (but so far untested) effect on literature, including the novel and the scholarly editing of novels, is the US Supreme Court's decision in the *Feist v. Rural Telephone* case (1991), in which a publisher of a telephone directory sued another publisher for "unauthorized" reproduction of the information contained therein. In its ruling, the court overturned the traditional "sweat of the brow" claim for protectability and instead asserted that only "original" works, not mere compilations of "historical fact," were covered by copyright law. No amount of hard work could justify proprietorship if the resulting work were not original, and thus the court undercut the basic Lockean premise of labor equals ownership. The effects of this decision were modified by *CCC Information v. MacLean Hunter* (1994), in which a circuit court found that because a guide to automobile prices contained not just fact but critical speculation and interpretation, it was protectable under copyright. *Feist* itself was used by another court in deciding that only the introductions and interpretive notes but not the text of West Publishing's series of Supreme Court decisions were protectable (1997). The text, because it was simply a reporting of fact, could be reproduced by anyone, even when it included West's own corrections of errors in the original text.

Since clear-text scholarly editions of novels traditionally aim at precisely this silent correction of textual error, it may very well be that the cumulative effect of *Feist* and *West* will be that the texts of recent scholarly editions of otherwise public-domain novels will be freely available to all. Only the annotations and critical apparatus are protectable in the United States. The effects of these rulings on clear-text editions of the works of Herman Melville, William Dean Howells, Mark Twain, D.H. Lawrence—virtually the entire pantheon of British and American novelists of the 19th and early 20th centuries—cannot yet be discerned, but it is clear that the removal of the "sweat of the brow" argument will have a major impact on the presentation and marketability of expensively produced "definitive" scholarly editions of Anglo-American novelists. About all one can say at the moment is that editions with an inclusive text (i.e., with editorial critical interventions prominently marked on the textual page rather than buried in the back of the book, as they are in clear-text editions) will be less easily copyable and therefore, as a matter of practicality, less susceptible to repackaging and resale.

But with the advent of high quality and inexpensive optical scanners, the unprotectable text of even inclusive-text editions can be quite simply separated from editorial markings and apparatus and remarketed.

Similarly, the advent of electronic publication has brought traditional concepts of copyright to a crisis. While the 1996 Diplomatic Conference of the World Intellectual Property Organization tried to update the Berne Convention (1885, with subsequent revisions, up to Paris, 1971) in order to deal with electronic media and therefore included a special article on computer programs (which "are protected as literary works . . . whatever may be the mode or form of their expression" [Article 4]), the conferees did not fully address the fundamental changes in composition and transmission brought about by an electronic environment. In general, the agreement simply transferred concepts from the print era into the digital, for example, in stipulating that "[t]he reproduction right, as set out in . . . the Berne Convention . . . fully applies in the digital environment, in particular to the use of works in digital form" (*Agreed Statements,* Article 1 [4]). The conference came to pretty much the same conclusions as *Feist* and *MacLean Hunter* on the use of electronic databases: "Compilations of data or other material, in any form, which by reason of the selection or arrangement of their contents *constitute intellectual creations* [emphasis added], are protected as such. This protection does not extend to the data or the material itself" (Article 5). But, unlike the US Copyright Act of 1976 or the British Copyright Act of 1842, both of which addressed fundamental changes in the concept of the ontology of work and author, the 1996 conference rather meekly allowed that "Contracting Parties shall provide adequate legal protection and effective legal remedies against the circumvention of effective technological measures that are used by authors in connection with their rights under this Treaty" (Article 11).

In throwing responsibility for the policing of the electronic publication environment back onto the signatories, the conference was, in effect, acknowledging that, as the US Copyright Office puts it, "[t]here is no such thing as an 'international copyright' that will automatically protect an author's writings throughout the entire world." Indeed, for many years, the United States itself was the chief offender against international copyright and signed on to the Berne Convention only in 1989. For most of the 19th century, until the 1891 Chace Act, American publishers had carte blanche over non-American works. The history of the American publication of major British novels (by Dickens, Thackeray, Trollope, and so on) is often the record of a transatlantic race to get a copy of the work from Britain to the United States as quickly as possible. It really was "first come, first served." Even after Chace, it was still necessary that two copies of the work be deposited with the Library of Congress from type set within the territorial limits of the United States. Many of the textual differences between British and American editions of British 19th-century novels can doubtless be traced to the premium put on speed of travel and typesetting.

Within a digital environment, where "location" and thus national origin become a much more problematic issue (a current Internet URL for an electronic work is not necessarily a guide to either its place or time of "creation" or "publication"), such traditional problems of fixing copyright are compounded. The 1996 WIPO Treaty, while it did establish a Working Group on Information Technologies for Intellectual Properties, with meet-ings to be held in 1997, nonetheless acknowledged that in online textual production, there was currently no way to police the *international* proliferation of texts: the signatories sent back to national jurisdictions a type of transmission that no longer recognized national frontiers in the way that 19th-century steamboats had to. Furthermore, a canny digital "pirate" can easily introduce sufficient changes (in typography, layout, and text) as to make electronic piracy difficult to demonstrate, and in such fields as music, the practice of "digital sampling" (whereby various segments of otherwise protectable scores can be morphed and conflated to produce works composed out of, but not identical with, any single precedent score) is already so familiar a cultural artifact that it would seem to be swimming upstream to try to chart and control such new methods of reproduction. Some publishers (Oxford, Cambridge, Michigan) have tried to meet the electronic revolution halfway, by embracing the most "book-like" electronic medium, the CD-ROM (which, like a printed book, is a concrete artifact, is marketable by traditional methods of distribution, is self-contained, and can be encoded to strictly control those clusters of data that can be downloaded). Others (Chadwyck-Healey, Eastgate Systems, Lawrence Erlbaum) have been more hospitable to direct internet or web publication, where the possibilities for controlled access are more ambiguous and still unresolved.

Copyright, even copyright of old-fashioned printed books, is now in a state of crisis. Born out of the capitalist profit motive and later allied to the romantic ideology of the solitary genius and the unified, originary work, copyright is a quite recent invention in the history of creative writing, although it is intimately bound up with the genre of the novel. Whether copyright will survive new definitions of authoriality, compositional unity, and proprietorship in our changing and unpredictable technological and legal climate will certainly be a matter of great concern (pro and con) to writers, publishers, and readers in the next few decades.

DAVID GREETHAM

Further Reading

Blackstone, William, *Commentaries on the Laws of England,* Oxford: Clarendon Press, 1766; reprint, Chicago: University of Chicago Press, 1979

CCC Information Services, Inc. v MacLean Hunter Market Reports, Inc., 1312, Docket 83–7687 (2d Cir 1994)

Copyright Act of 1976, United States Congress

Defoe, Daniel, *An Essay on the Regulation of the Press,* London: s.n., 1704; reprint, Oxford: Blackwell, 1948

Diplomatic Conference on Certain Copyright and Neighboring Rights Questions, World Intellectual Property Organization, Geneva, 1996; available from http://www.wipo.org/eng/doc

Feist Publications, Inc. v Rural Telephone Co., Inc., US Supreme Court, 499 US 340 (1991)

Foucault, Michel, "What Is an Author?" in *The Foucault Reader,* edited by Paul Rabinow, New York: Pantheon, 1984; London: Penguin, 1991

Ginsburg, Jane, "Putting Cars on the 'Information Superhighway': Authors, Exploiters, and Copyright in Cyberspace," *Columbia Law Review* 1466 (1995)

Greetham, David, "The Telephone Directory and Dr. Seuss: Scholarly Editing After 'Feist versus Rural Telephone'," *Studies in the Literary Imagination* 29 (1996)

Greetham, David, "Rights to Copy," in *Textual Transgressions: Essays Toward the Construction of a Biobibliography*, by Greetham, New York: Garland, 1998

"Intellectual Property and the Construction of Authorship," *Cardozo Arts and Entertainment Law Journal* 10:2 (1992)

Kernan, Alvin B., *The Death of Literature*, New Haven, Connecticut, and London: Yale University Press, 1990

Rose, Mark, *Authors and Owners: The Invention of Copyright*, Cambridge, Massachusetts: Harvard University Press, 1993

Sherman, Brad, and Alain Strowel, *Of Authors and Origins: Essays on Copyright Law*, Oxford: Clarendon Press, and New York: Oxford University Press, 1994

Simmons, A. John, *The Lockean Theory of Rights*, Princeton, New Jersey: Princeton University Press, 1992

US Copyright Office, http://lcweb.loc.gov/copyright/circs

Vanden Bossche, Chris R., "The Value of Literature: Representations of Print Culture in the Copyright Debate of 1837–1842," *Victorian Studies* 23 (1994)

Corinne; or Italy by Germaine de Staël

Corinne; ou L'Italie 1807

With nearly two decades of literary activity behind her and several volumes of published writing to her credit, Germaine de Staël could reasonably surmise in 1807 that her second novel, *Corinne; or Italy,* would receive close critical scrutiny from readers already aware of her interest in politics, aesthetics, and the place of women in postrevolutionary society. However, neither her short stories, nor her essays, nor even *Delphine* (1802), a novel that had earned her exile from Napoléon's Paris, could completely have prepared readers for what was to become a founding text of 19th-century French literature. Published initially in Paris and Leipzig, translated into English in the year of its original publication, *Corinne* became an immediate and immediately controversial success. Napoléon's purportedly personal condemnation of it in *Le Moniteur* did nothing to decrease its appeal, and *Corinne* went through several dozen editions in France alone before losing literary prominence toward the end of the 19th century. After several decades during which the novel was largely neglected, contemporary scholars have come to recognize the strategic position that *Corinne* occupies in the history of the novel. Delineating and crossing essential literary, geographic, and conceptual frontiers, *Corinne* stands as a monument to neoclassical aesthetics while giving expression to early romantic sensibilities and ambitions. Above all, this novel takes into account the vexed politics of gender, genres, genealogy, and space to create a founding myth of the modern writing subject.

The title alone, *Corinne; or Italy,* brings together in a tantalizing nexus questions concerning feminine destiny, national identity, and social exile. While Staël's treatment of these issues is original, she grounds them in a plot that recycles popular elements from 18th-century novels and draws on prestigious classical figures. The entire story of ill-fated love, which begins with an Ossian-like Scotsman, Oswald Lord Nelvil who, while traveling through France and Italy after his father's death, meets Corinne and continues with Corinne giving him a guided tour of her homeland, has a familiar ring. Staël's innovation lies not in flaunting but in "aggravating" what Nancy Miller has termed "the heroine's text," the conventional plot that charts the heroine's ability or failure to maintain her virtue and adhere to the imperatives of patriarchal authority (see Miller, 1988). Thus, Corinne is destined for abandonment and death because she has broken away from socially prescribed gender roles, having chosen self-fulfillment over virtue and duty, as she has chosen maternal Italy over her father's native Scotland. Indeed, as Naomi Schor explains, Corinne is symbolically dead before the novel even begins (see Schor, 1994). In similar fashion, Corinne stands alone among female protagonists as an artistic genius of mythic proportion, worthy heir to the Roman poet whose names she bears. Once again, rather than contradict the value of neoclassical sources in which the empire was finding myths of nationhood and an increasingly harsh separation of gender spheres, Staël legitimizes Corinne's transgression—trespassing as a performing artist into the public space of modern men—through her own references to other traditions in classical antiquity. The examples of Corinne's classical namesake (who defeated Pindar in public competition), the sibyl, and the politically subversive and powerfully eloquent Sappho differentiate the heroine from contemporaneous female exiles, making her an original embodiment of feminine verbal creativity and moral superiority.

From this perspective, the choice of Italy as a travel destination is doubly significant. Corinne's peregrinations link her novelistic destiny to an itinerary known through a rich literary corpus, for the various stops on her quest for identity and authorization are part of the "grand tour," familiar to readers through the writings of travelers such as Joseph Addison, Johann Wolfgang von Goethe, Dupaty, Bonstetten, and François-René Chateaubriand. The novel's most dramatic (and at first glance unrealistic) moments incorporate stock elements from this tradition, including Corinne's lover Nelvil's autobiographical confession at the edge of Mount Vesuvius in the presence of a hermit. Long descriptions of cities, monuments, aesthetic traditions, and social customs also recall the travel narratives of the grand tour. However, Staël's text estranges her readers from this well-traveled narrative territory by establishing an enigmatic and unstable relationship between the tragic destiny of a woman's name and the exploration of the ailing geographic source of classical French culture (see Vallois, 1987). It also links the heroine with a classical tradition that early enthusiasts of romanticism like Oswald were trying to leave behind.

This central symbolic ambiguity continues to fuel critical debate, all the more so because Corinne is an allegorical figure for the political ideals France had rejected (see Kadish, 1991). A literary equivalent to the goddesses of Reason and Liberty, Corinne repeats the static poses of statues that froze women into silent signification before yielding to the Cult of the Supreme Being under the Terror and, under Napoléon, to his identification with Roman emperors. *Corinne* unveils the mutilating underpinnings of French postrevolutionary culture, delineating with great acuity the enormous social price that both fictive and real women would pay for assuaging "the male malady" (see Waller, 1993), a gendered illness from which not just Oswald but male protagonists from Chateaubriand's René to Alfred de Musset's "child of the century" claimed to suffer. In spite of her ultimate failure to survive or sustain her creative powers, Corinne remains a legendary and dazzling figure of feminine accomplishment. Her hyperbolic characterization inspired George Sand in writing the first of her *Lettres d'un voyageur* (1837), the second version of *Lélia* (1833; revised 1839), and *Consuelo* (1843). She also influenced Walter Scott, George Eliot, Elizabeth Barrett Browning, and Margaret Fuller among others. A rare and incomplete representation of feminine talent, knowledge, and prestige, *Corinne* stands out as both an exception and a key to the novels of a century devoted in large part to the narrative mastery of the feminine body.

ANNE E. MCCALL

Further Reading

Balayé, Simone, *Madame de Staël: Lumières et liberté*, Paris: Klincksieck, 1979

Balayé, Simone, "Corinne et la ville italienne ou l'espace extérieur et l'impasse intérieur," in *France et Italie dans la culture européenne: Mélanges à la Mémoire de Franco Simone*, volume 3, *XIXe et XX siècles*, Geneva: Slatkine, 1980

Besser, Gretchen Rous, *Germaine de Staël Revisited*, New York: Twayne, 1994

Dejean, Jean, "Portrait of the Artist as Sappho: The Example of *Corinne*," in *Germaine de Staël: Crossing the Borders*, edited by Madelyn Gutwirth, Auriel Goldberger, and Karyna Szmurlo, New Brunswick, New Jersey: Rutgers University Press, 1991

Gutwirth, Madelyn, *Madame de Staël, Novelist: The Emergence of the Artist as Woman*, Urbana: University of Illinois Press, 1978

Kadish, Doris, "Narrating the French Revolution," in *Germaine de Staël: Crossing the Borders*, edited by Madelyn Gutwirth, Auriel Goldberger, and Karyna Szmurlo, New Brunswick, New Jersey: Rutgers University Press, 1991

Miller, Nancy, "Performances of the Gaze: Staël's *Corinne; or Italy*," in *Subject to Change: Reading Feminist Writing*, New York: Columbia University Press, 1988

Naginski, Isabelle, "Germaine de Staël Among the Romantics," in *Germaine de Staël: Crossing the Borders*, edited by Madelyn Gutwirth, Auriel Goldberger, and Karyna Szmurlo, New Brunswick, New Jersey: Rutgers University Press, 1991

Schor, Naomi, "*Corinne*: The Third Woman," *Esprit Créateur* 34:3 (1994)

Vallois, Marie-Claire, *Fictions féminines: Mme de Staël et les voix de la Sibylle*, Saratoga, California: Anma Libri, 1987

Waller, Margaret, *The Male Malady: Fictions of Impotence in the French Romantic Novel*, New Brunswick, New Jersey: Rutgers University Press, 1993

Julio Cortázar 1914–84

Argentine

Julio Cortázar's reputation as one of Latin America's most innovative writers of the 20th century remains undiminished as the century draws to a close. The earliest of his six relatively short novels were written before 1951, the year in which he left Argentina and made Paris his permanent place of residence. However, neither *El examen* (The Test), written in 1949, nor *Divertimento*, written in 1950, were published until 1986, two years after his death. The delay was undoubtedly partially owing to his interest in distancing himself from Peronist Argentina and in developing the individuality of his style before committing himself to print. Yet, with Cortázar's diminished emphasis on plot, and with the intrusion of the surreal or the fantastic into his representation of the social and political realities of the day, both novels defy conventions while also introducing directions pursued in later works.

For its length and complexity, *Los premios* (1960; *The Winners*) was Cortázar's first major novel. The story centers on a group of people brought together when they win a mystery cruise in a lottery. The cruise-ship and its passengers represent a microcosm of Buenos Aires society, thereby sustaining the focus on Argentina evident in Cortázar's two earlier novels. *The Winners* is the only one of his major novels that approaches having a conventionally realist plot. But the mystery voyage is more a voyage of self-encounter in which no mysteries are solved and the passengers return to their point of departure to resume their daily lives. Moreover, the periodic insertion of the metaphysical musings of an astrologer and his comments, in the form of disconnected monologues, on other characters and their actions breaks the continuity of the story and diminishes a traditional sense of plot.

In a taxonomy of fiction based on content, *The Winners* could be classified among the "psychological" novels, where it would keep company with the writing of some of Cortázar's contemporaries such as Juan Carlos Onetti (Uruguay, 1909–1994) and Ernesto Sábato (Argentina, 1911–), although it lacks their more doggedly existential inclination. His later novels might also be considered psychological, since they too have a greater focus on character than on story and are concerned in a broad sense with questions of identity, authenticity, and self-understanding. But Cortázar also was one of a group of writers, including Gabriel García Márquez (1928–) and Carlos Fuentes (1928–), whose fiction contributed to the boom in Latin American writing during the 1960s and 1970s. Like them, Cortázar endeavoured to reinterpret Latin American society and culture in the context of a technically renovated novel; in Cortázar's case, however, technical innovation became even more radical.

This first became apparent in *Rayuela* (1963; *Hopscotch*), which caused a sensation when it first appeared and has since become established as one of the most important works of 20th-century Latin American fiction. In a vein similar to that of the French New Novel, *Hopscotch* is an antinovel, a revolt against literary convention, that dismantles the traditionally linear narrative. The reader is advised in a preliminary note that the book may be many books, but is at least two. After reading the first 56 chapters sequentially, the reader may dispense with the 99 that follow and consider the book completed, or may turn to chapter 73 and begin reading the book again in an entirely new sequence of chapters, among which the 99 expendable ones are also included. Thus, the reader, whose role is also a subject of the novel, is made to participate actively in its elaboration by engaging in the game suggested by the title. Moreover, the fragmentation of the text produced by reading has a counterpart in the fragmentation of its content: the quest of the protagonist, Horacio Oliveira, for authenticity and self-knowledge is represented through a series of diverse encounters with acquaintances and doubles, first in Paris and later in Buenos Aires.

What Cortázar began in *Hopscotch*, he continued, so to speak, in *62: Modelo para armar* (1968; *62: A Model Kit*), in the sense that the idea for a book based on disconnected notes and observations was presented in chapter 62 of the earlier novel. Accordingly, in *62: A Model Kit*, the reader must engage the text still more actively than in *Hopscotch*, where, for all its complexity, the structure retained some transparency and the steps to be followed were traced for the reader. Here the parts of a kit—the places, the people, and their words and actions—are provided, but the reader must discover how to assemble them in order to participate in the psychological quest of the characters.

Although *62: A Model Kit* continues to attract considerable academic criticism, it has not obtained the same readership as *Hopscotch*, perhaps because it is a denser, more complex and, therefore, less accessible text, but perhaps also because of the very task Cortázar has given to the reader. His last novel, *Libro de Manuel* (1973; *A Manual for Manuel*), had a similar reception, and a number of critics have considered it an inferior work in which the styles and structures of earlier novels are repeated somewhat mechanically. It, too, requires the reader to work with a text constructed from a collage of materials, but its more overtly political themes, focused on a group of left-wing Argentine revolutionaries in exile, make its content significantly different from that of Cortázar's other novels. *Manual for Manuel*'s content inevitably sharpened the attention given to its form by drawing it into discussions on the relation between ideology and literature and on the place of aesthetic creativity in a political struggle, a subject that owed its topicality to the political condition of Latin America in the early 1970s.

The political content of *Libro de Manuel* was not a new element for Cortázar. It is present in much of his writing, just as the focus on Latin America and particularly Argentina are constants of his work, notwithstanding that he is one of Latin America's most cosmopolitan writers who lived the most significant part of his creative career outside of the continent. However, just as he was not prepared to sacrifice the sense of aesthetic adventure he considered proper to the artist's expression of the world, he did not write within a narrow Latin American tradition but within the international contexts in which he believed the modern culture of Latin America also belonged. On both counts he has not only drawn high praise but also significant criticism.

RICHARD A. YOUNG

See also Hopscotch

Biography

Born in Brussels, 26 August 1914. Family returned to Argentina, 1918. Attended the Escuela Normal de Profesores Mariano Acosta (teachers training college), Buenos Aires, degree as primary-level teacher, 1932, degree as secondary-level teacher, 1935; University of Buenos Aires, 1936–37. Taught in secondary schools in Bolívar, Chivilcoy, and Mendoza, 1937–44; professor of French literature, University of Cuyo, Mendoza, 1944–45, and imprisoned briefly for involvement in anti-Peronist demonstrations at the university, 1945. Manager, Cámara Argentina del Libro [Publishing Association of Argentina], 1946–48; passed examinations in law and languages, and worked as translator, Buenos Aires, 1948–51. Traveled to Paris on a scholarship, 1951, and took up permanent residence there. Writer and freelance translator for UNESCO, from 1952; visited Cuba, 1961, Argentina, Peru, Ecuador, and Chile, all 1973, Nicaragua and (after the lifting of a seven-year ban on his entry into the country) Argentina, 1983. Visiting lecturer, University of Oklahoma, Norman, 1975, and Gildersleeve lecturer, Barnard College, New York, 1980. Acquired French citizenship (in addition to existing Argentine citizenship), 1981. Member, Second Russell Tribunal for investigation of human rights abuses in Latin America, 1975. Died 12 February 1984.

Novels by Cortázar

Los premios, 1960; as *The Winners*, translated by Elaine Kerrigan, 1965

Rayuela, 1963; as *Hopscotch*, translated by Gregory Rabassa, 1966

62: Modelo para armar, 1968; as *62: A Model Kit*, translated by Gregory Rabassa, 1972

Libro de Manuel, 1973; as *A Manual for Manuel*, translated by Gregory Rabassa, 1978

El examen [The Test], 1986 (written in 1949)

Divertimento, 1986 (written in 1950)

Other Writings: some drama and poetry, translations (including a translation of Poe into Spanish), criticism, essays, political writings, speeches and cultural presentations, and occasional writings; above all, a dozen highly successful volumes of short stories that contributed to a renovation of the tradition of the fantastic in Latin America.

Further Reading

Alazraki, Jaime, Ivar Ivask, and Joaquín Marco editors, *The Final Island: The Fiction of Julio Cortázar,* Norman: University of Oklahoma Press, 1978

Boldy, Steven, *The Novels of Julio Cortázar,* Cambridge and New York: Cambridge University Press, 1980

Carter, E.D., Jr., "Bibliografía de y sobre la obra de Julio Cortázar," *Explicación de Textos Literarios* 17:1–2

(1988–89), special issue entitled *Otro round: Estudios sobre la obra de Julio Cortázar*

Harss, Luis, and Barbara Dohmann, *Into the Mainstream: Conversations with Latin American Writers,* New York: Harper and Row, 1966

Hernández del Castillo, Ana, *Keats, Poe, and the Shaping of Cortázar's Mythopoesis,* Amsterdam: Benjamins, 1981

Prego, Omar, *La fascinación de las palabras: Conversaciones con Julio Cortázar,* Barcelona: Muchnik, 1985

Yovanovich, Gordana, *Julio Cortázar's Character Mosaic: Reading the Longer Fiction,* Toronto: University of Toronto Press, 1991

Coscienza di Zeno. *See* Confessions of Zeno

The Count of Monte-Cristo by Alexandre Dumas (père)

Le Comte de Monte-Cristo 1844–45

In his essay "État civil de *Monte-Cristo,*" Alexandre Dumas gives his own account of the origin of his most famous novel. During 1841–42, Dumas had been in Florence, where he often visited the Villa Quarto. This was the home of Jérôme Bonaparte, Napoléon Bonaparte's brother. Occasionally, Dumas took his host's younger son on short educational journeys; one of these was to Elba, site of the great Napoléon's pre-Waterloo exile (and, by official declaration, a sovereign principality, over which the former emperor was to rule). Returning from Elba, Dumas and his charge spotted another island, the deserted Monte-Carlo, about which Dumas determined to write a novel in remembrance of the trip. In 1843 (continues the *causerie*), the Parisian publishers Béthune et Plon commissioned Dumas to write an eight-volume work about Paris. However, Eugène Sue's *Mysteries of Paris* (which appeared in the *Journal des Débats* during 1842–43) was then creating a sensation—and making a fortune. Béthune et Plon changed their minds. Would Dumas write for them not a travel book but a romance in the Sue style with Paris as a background? Using as his main inspiration an anecdote set in the year 1807 and taken from Jacques Peuchet's *Historical Memoirs of the Archives of the Police of Paris,* Dumas and his collaborator Auguste Maquet worked out the narrative of *Monte-Cristo.* It was at Maquet's suggestion, Dumas notes, that he decided to tell the story from the beginning (i.e., from Edmund Dantès' arrest in Marseilles) rather than through flash-backs—a choice for which readers have been deeply grateful, since the account of Dantès' imprisonment and escape is one of the great suspense stories in the history of fiction.

It could be added that Dumas had already written one notable revenge novel (*Georges,* 1843), also an important source of *Monte-Cristo,* and that the character of the Abbé Faria is not, as he once claimed, fictional, but his basic account seems to be accurate. As the "État civil" implies, *The Count of Monte-Cristo* is a tale of revenge written under the double spell of Napoleonic glamour and Parisian mysteries. As such, it unites a distinctive kind of romantic hero with those dreams of conclusive urban knowledge that pervades 19th-century fiction.

The Napoleonic and romantic side of the book is established at an early moment in the story. Dantès, Dumas' protagonist, is framed by three enemies as a Napoleonic conspirator, shortly *before* Napoléon's dramatic return from Elba in 1815. He is then imprisoned in the Chateau d'If, a sort of French Alcatraz off the coast of Marseilles, by the politician Villefort who is anxious to conceal his own father's machinations on behalf of Bonaparte. (Old Villefort, paralyzed and capable of communicating only through a wink, remains a significant presence through the later, Parisian half of the novel—the embodiment of a repressed Napoleonic heritage amid the corruption of Louis-Philippe's monarchy, with its notorious slogan *Enrichissez-vous* [enrich yourselves].) Because young Villefort has thoroughly buried the whole incident, no one frees Dantès when Napoléon briefly returns to power. Educated by the Abbé Faria, the ultimate Enlightenment philosopher, Dantès remains in the Chateau d'If for 14 years. He finally escapes and locates a fabulous treasure, hidden since the time of the Renaissance (although known to Faria), and transforms himself into the Count of Monte-Cristo. Monte-Cristo is a perfect dandy, vampiristic and Byronic. He destroys his three enemies, Villefort, Danglars, and de Morcerf, in fiendishly clever and indirect ways. There is no place, Dumas indicates, in this bloated bourgeois world for the heroism of Napoléon's era, but Dantès' return will last more than the hundred days of Napoléon's return, and his vengeance will take an appropriate form for this world of financial speculation, telegraph systems, unending displays of corruptly accumulated wealth, and correspondingly rotten family structures. A revenant from a lost historical moment, Dantès is the mirror that shows the present world—in exact and devastating detail—what it has so horribly become.

However, if *Monte-Cristo* embodies the revenge of Napoleonic romanticism upon the restored royal house of Orléans, and on all the conservative backtrackings that followed Waterloo, its greatest claim to significance in the history of the novel is a rather different one. Not only is Monte-Cristo a dandy; he is also the greatest of those novelistic characters who act out the fantasy of omniscience and omnipotence that the city called forth in the middle of the 19th century. Sue's Prince Rodolphe, the most obvious analogue to Monte-Cristo, moves through Paris as a universal vigilante, aware of wrongs at every level of society and thus able to right them. But it is the subtler and more equivocal versions of this type—Charles Dickens' Shadow and his detectives, Honoré de Balzac's Vautrin, Victor Hugo's Jean Valjean, Arthur Conan Doyle's Moriarty and Holmes, or Louis Feuillade's Judex—that might more fittingly be compared with Dumas' hero. The modern city is a social formation that seems basically unknowable; such figures answer to a general need for reassurance under difficult and disorienting conditions. They are, in effect, replacements for God or Providence (a point with

which Dumas plays at many crucial moments). The aesthetics and sociology of fantasized omniscience are discussed in Arac (1979) and Maxwell (1992). Peter Brooks (1976) discusses the tendency of melodrama to try to make up for God's absence. Critiques of this sort go some way toward providing a theoretical frame of reference for understanding Monte-Cristo. The Count enacts a return of romanticism that produces—paradoxically—one of the fullest and most sweeping realist panoramas ever completed. Not surprisingly, the book is the object of countless allusions (e.g., in Eugene O'Neill's *The Iceman Cometh*). In its ubiquity, it has largely overshadowed Dumas' *second* great effort to work in the format of the Parisian mysteries novel: his gargantuan *Les Mohicans de Paris* (1854–59; *The Mohicans of Paris*), running some 850,000 words and representing an even more inclusive effort than its predecessor to encompass French society after Waterloo.

RICHARD MAXWELL

See also Alexandre Dumas

Further Reading

Arac, Jonathan, *Commissioned Spirits: The Shaping of Social Motion in Dickens, Carlyle, Melville, and Hawthorne*, New Brunswick, New Jersey: Rutgers University Press, 1979

Bassan, Fernande, and Claude Schopp, *Les Trois Mousquetaires, Le Comte de Monte Cristo: Cent Cinquante Ans Après*, Marly-le-Roi: Éditions Champflour, 1995

Bell, A. Craig, *Alexandre Dumas: A Biography and Study*, London: Cassell, 1950

Brooks, Peter, *The Melodramatic Imagination: Balzac, Henry James, Melodrama, and the Mode of Excess*, New Haven, Connecticut: Yale University Press, 1976

Maxwell, Richard, *The Mysteries of Paris and London*, Charlottesville: University Press of Virginia, 1992

Simon, Gustave, *Histoire d'une Collaboration: Alexandre Dumas et Auguste Maquet*, Paris: Éditions George Crès et Cie, 1919

The Counterfeiters by André Gide

Les Faux-monnayeurs 1926

When Gide called *The Counterfeiters* "my first novel," he indicated a deliberate departure from his previous narratives and implied a concern with the formal aspects of the novel and with the problematic nature of mimetic writing. In contradistinction to his *récits*, or short, personal narratives, and the *sotie*, his own variety of literary and social farce, he saw the novel as a privileged genre. In Gide's definition, the novel involves numerous characters and plots, has considerable thematic and social scope, aspires to a comprehensive view of experience, and thus requires a complex structure. His goal was to capture a *vertical* slice of

life instead of the horizontal, or linear, slice characteristic of psychological and social realism. Expanding on devices and structures used in his *soties Paludes* (1895; *Marshlands*) and *Les Caves du Vatican* (1914; *The Vatican Cellars*), he also drew on the work of Henry Fielding, Laurence Sterne, and Denis Diderot in the 18th century and Stendhal in the 19th, who had used such techniques as authorial intervention and correction, which destroy the realistic illusion. As early as 1891, Gide had played with specularity, or *mise-en-abyme* (the internal mirroring of the work itself), including more than one level of narration.

In *The Counterfeiters,* Edouard, a Gidean self-projection, plans to write a novel entitled "The Counterfeiters" ("Les Faux-monnayeurs"), which will include, as one would foresee, a novelist struggling to write *his* book. Edouard records in a journal—reproduced at length—his ideas about fictional aesthetics, along with observations, reflections, accounts of his activities, and conversations. Some of these are to be transposed into his future novel, of which the reader is allowed glimpses and an occasional draft. There is also another internal author—the "pseudo-author," an intervening first-person voice who comments on the action and coyly limits his own authority and omniscience. The novel is thus partly about writing a novel; it is an early illustration of metafiction and thus a predecessor of the French *nouveau roman* (new novel) of the 1950s and 1960s.

There are also two outside reflections of the novel, one a special diary Gide published as *Journal des faux-monnayeurs* (1926; *Logbook of the Coiners*), the other his regular journal. In both he discusses characters and plots, plays with fictional possibilities, and does essentially what Edouard does in *his* notebooks. While the *Logbook of the Coiners* does not fully unveil Gide's creative process—even though Edouard imagines that a novelist's notebooks should do just that—it is a curious ancillary text. Episodes in which characters bear different names from their final ones and engage in dialogues not reproduced later constitute a sort of rival fiction.

Any reader embarking upon *The Counterfeiters* thus confronts an elaborate textual complex. The novel's structure is symmetrical with 18 chapters in part one, 18 in part three, both set in Paris, surrounding a shorter middle part, set in Switzerland. Other symmetries are also to be found. However, the multiple, sometimes unfinished plots, the competing versions of material, and the various types of discourse (letter, conversation, notebook, omniscient narration) suggest how resistant reality is to human comprehension and to efforts to capture it in forms and categories, including linguistic and literary ones.

Gide also set himself the task of creating characters that were not chiefly self-projections, so as to extend the book's social scope. He drew on contemporary material, especially juvenile criminal cases, and years of observation and reflection. Nevertheless, he put a great deal of himself into the characters, not only the novelist Edouard but also the youths who play prominent roles, especially the neurotic Boris. He also chose to give homosexuality a major place in his fiction for the first time. Previously, he had treated the topic explicitly only in his autobiography and a tract. The example of Edouard, who falls in love with his nephew Olivier, illustrates what Gide saw as a constructive homosexual relationship. The novelist Passavant, Edouard's unscrupulous literary rival, ready to exploit young men, is a counterexample. Gide's decision to depict a homosexual affair in a favorable light—unlike Marcel Proust, for instance—in a society where pederasty was still prosecuted demonstrates his determination to raise the issue more widely, with the aim of contributing to its decriminalization.

Other social issues that arise in *The Counterfeiters* include juvenile delinquency, illegitimacy, education, and economic inequality. Numerous additional themes are woven into the complex structure, many of them connected to the theme of counterfeiting: false appearances, corrupt institutions, fraudu-lent (pretentious, bad) literature, false or derivative feelings, and hypocritical words and actions of all sorts, including sexual and religious hypocrisy. Gide is particularly critical of the family as a social unit. Peeling away facades and pretenses, he depicts it as oppressive and tending toward moral corruption. His young heroes all rebel against family authority, although Bernard, perhaps the most endearing character, with whom the novel begins, returns finally to his putative father. Underlying all these themes is the question of value and thus of ethics. A dialogue between Bernard and his friend Laura, placed at the novel's structural center, expresses its deep moral concerns: how should one act and according to what criteria? Bernard's position, although relativistic and individualistic, is demanding, requiring integrity and effort toward self-improvement and self-realization. The novel concludes with the suicide of Boris, and to many readers—particularly early ones—its depiction of life has seemed unduly cruel and despairing. But the moral freedom and responsibility that it illustrates act as a counterweight and foreshadow Sartre's existentialist fiction.

Given its subject matter, it is no surprise that *The Counterfeiters* evoked a hostile response. But to many critics, the work was a successful synthesis of formal experimentation and wide-ranging subject matter and marked a major departure from 19th-century formulas. Together with the *Journal,* the novel encompasses the fullest range of Gide's ideas, techniques, and stylistic mastery. Discerning readers continue to appreciate its wit, subtlety, ingenuity, and fictional vitality. While the bourgeois world it depicts and its peculiar aestheticism may seem outdated, it remains modern in its ethical considerations, its critique of social institutions, and its ingenious form.

CATHARINE SAVAGE BROSMAN

See also André Gide

Further Reading
Babcock, Arthur E., *Portraits of Artists: Reflexivity in Gidean Fiction, 1902–1946,* York, South Carolina: French Literature Publications, 1982
Brée, Germaine, *André Gide,* Paris: Belles-Lettres, 1953; 2nd edition, revised and corrected, 1970; as *Gide,* New Brunswick, New Jersey: Rutgers University Press, 1963
Goulet, Alain, *Fiction et vie sociale dans l'oeuvre d'André Gide,* 2 vols., Paris: Lettres Modernes/Minard, 1985
Goulet, Alain, *André Gide, "Les Faux-monnayeurs": Mode d'emploi,* Paris: SEDES, 1991
Holdheim, W. Wolfgang, *Theory and Practice of the Novel: A Study of André Gide,* Geneva: Droz, 1968
Ireland, G.W., *André Gide: A Study of His Creative Writings,* Oxford: Clarendon Press, 1970
Keypour, N. David, *André Gide, écriture et réversibilité dans "Les Faux-Monnayeurs,"* Paris: Didier/Erudition, and Montreal: Presses de l'Université de Montréal, 1980
Masson, Pierre, *Lire "Les Faux-Monnayeurs,"* Lyon: Presses Universitaires de Lyon, 1990
Moutote, Daniel, *Réflexions sur "Les Faux-Monnayeurs,"* Geneva: Slatkine, 1990
Tilby, Michael, *Gide, "Les Faux-Monnayeurs,"* London: Grant and Cutler, 1981

Cozy. *See* Crime, Detective, and Mystery Novel

Crime and Punishment by Fedor Dostoevskii

Prestuplenie i nakazanie 1867

Crime and Punishment, the first of Dostoevskii's great novels, is psychologically his most intense and arguably his most aesthetically satisfying work. Although elaborately plotted and brimming with philosophical, religious, social, and political issues, it is largely free of the narrative excrescences of *Idiot* (1869; *The Idiot*) and *Besy* (1872; translated as *The Possessed* and as *The Devils*), and of the lengthy—although fascinating—interpolations of *Brat'ia Karamazovy* (1880; *The Brothers Karamazov*). *Crime and Punishment*, however, did not start out propitiously. Dostoevskii experimented with several diffuse first-person diaries and confessions narrated from the point of view of an imprisoned young man (Raskolnikov) looking back at his murder of an old pawnbroker. Only when he decided to incorporate into his "psychological story about a crime" a novel about drunkards (the Marmeladov subplot)—and to abandon first- for third-person narration—did the work begin to take on its final form.

The first two parts of the novel, which appeared in the January and February issues of *The Russian Messenger,* elicited a good deal of criticism. Russian radical journals tended to condemn the novel as a tendentious vilification of the country's politically progressive youth. Less politically oriented critics, on the other hand, praised Dostoevskii for the depth and subtlety of his psychological portrayal of a murderer. This division between social and psychological interpretations also characterized much criticism of the novel after its completion. The great radical critic, Dmitrii Pisarev, dismissed as a complete absurdity the supposition that Raskolnikov's ideas of justifiable murder were representative of the younger generation; he further asserted that Raskolnikov was no ideological killer: he killed primarily because he was impoverished and hungry. Dostoevskii's close friend, the critic Nikolai Strakhov, took a middle position, arguing that *Crime and Punishment* was not a vilification of Russian youth but a penetrating study, through the character of the novel's hero, of the younger generation's tragic drift toward nihilism. However, on the whole, Dostoevskii's contemporaries were decidedly less impressed by the originality of *Crime and Punishment* than most 20th-century novelists, critics, and scholars have been.

In the last 100 years, scholars have published voluminously not only on the political aspects of *Crime and Punishment* but also on its social, cultural, literary, religious, and philosophical contexts, most admirably reflected in Joseph Frank's monumental biography (1995). But it is perhaps Leonid Grossman who most aptly pointed out Dostoevskii's aesthetic originality in dealing with such enormously heterogeneous content (see his *Poetika*

Dostoevskogo, 1925). Dostoevskii, he argued, makes this diverse material dramatically viable by harnessing it to the most common, often melodramatic, plot devices of earlier low-brow French and Russian literature. Indeed, this combination of the low and the high, the grotesquely prosaic and the tragically serious, accounts for much of the peculiar Dostoevskian character of *Crime and Punishment.*

Judging by the critical literature, the psychological side of the novel engages readers and critics no less today than it did more than a century ago. By eschewing the conventions of the murder mystery (the reader knows who the murderer is almost from the very beginning), Dostoevskii can focus attention on the hero's psychology, especially on his motivation and suffering. The notebooks show that Dostoevskii was uncertain himself about the exact motivation of the crime, and he thought it important to clarify it. Fortunately, he did not. Although much of the story is given over to the search for the murderer, as Philip Rahv points out, what is so new and original in *Crime and Punishment* is Raskolnikov's novel-long search—largely unsuccessful—for the motive of his crime, which the criminal must know in order to take responsibility and properly atone for his actions (see Rahv's "Dostoevsky in *Crime and Punishment*," *Partisan Review* 27:3 [1960]). Perhaps no novel either before or since has so skillfully presented the multifariousness and indefiniteness of psychological motivation. *Crime and Punishment* also makes an important contribution to the novelistic representation of psychological time. By confining much of the work to the consciousness of his hero, Dostoevskii expands psychological time against chronological time, so that few readers realize that the actual action of the novel takes place over the course of just one week. In general, Dostoevskii relegates larger time periods to the interstices between novelistic sections; however, in *Crime and Punishment,* this amounts to but three days when Raskolnikov is unconscious with brain fever.

For its time, *Crime and Punishment* is perhaps most distinguished by its genial handling of narration and point of view. Mikhail Bakhtin (1984), the famous 20th-century Russian critic, maintained that by radically applying narrative polyphony to novelistic point of view, Dostoevskii transformed prose narrative of his time, in effect creating the modern, or polyphonic, novel. For Bakhtin, the apogee of the novel was reached by Dostoevskii and never really approached again. In contrast to the monologic Lev Tolstoi, whose characters figure essentially as extensions or mouthpieces of their author, Bakhtin asserts that Dostoevskii's major characters (Raskolnikov, Sonia, Katerina Ivanovna, Marmeladov, Svidrigailov, Porfirii Petrovich) are autonomous, independent voices who are not subordinated to the higher point of view of the author, but rather are engaged in an equal—polyphonic—dialogue with each other as well as with the author himself. Dostoevskii's characters are not walking ideas but dynamic points of view fully capable at any moment of challenging and even subverting the point of view of the author/narrator—if not the implied author himself. Although Bakhtin's claims are considerably overstated—Raskolnikov's point of view is not on the same plane as the implied author's—polyphony does account for the strength and seeming independent reality of many of Dostoevskii's characters and occasionally their ability almost to wrench themselves from the author's control. When Svidrigailov, the novel's most famous villain, threatened in the last part to eclipse Raskolnikov as the main character, Dostoevskii probably had, as it were, little choice but to kill him off.

Henry James referred to the novels of Tolstoi and Dostoevskii as "loose baggy monsters." But the tremendous amount of heterogeneous matter characteristic of these masterpieces obscures the sophistication of their structure. *Crime and Punishment* is the best case in point. A work that began as a first-person confession—and as a short story—surprisingly developed into perhaps the most subtle and brilliant example of third-person narration in the history of the 19th-century novel. Dostoevskii resorted to third-person narration when he realized that he had to present crucial events at which Raskolnikov was not present, and to explore at times the consciousness of other major characters like Svidrigailov. Although the novel contains personal narrative commentary, the events are, for the most part, filtered through the consciousness of its hero, so much so that many readers, including Vladimir Lenin, found the narrative confinement almost unbearable. In order to give an objective representation of the events while simultaneously presenting Raskolnikov's point of view, Dostoevskii employs a highly intricate system in which he alternates between narrated consciousness, *erlebte Rede* (or free indirect discourse), and interior monologue, seamlessly going in and out of Raskolnikov's consciousness to record events and even to inject his own commentary, all the time using Raskolnikov's own words. The following passage from the first page of the novel is indicative of the technique.

Actually, he was not at all afraid of any landlady, whatever plots she might be hatching against him. But to have to stop on the stairs and listen to all kinds of nonsense about the most common trivialities, none of which had anything to do with him, all her badgering, complaints, threats about payment, and added to all this, to have to extricate himself, lie and make excuses—no, better to dart downstairs like a cat and slip out unnoticed.

Dostoevskii's other novels show equal mastery of point of view, in particular the mixture of first- and third-person narration, but nowhere is Dostoevskii's brilliant handling of point of view shown off to better effect than in the transcription of Raskolnikov's and Svidrigailov's consciousnesses.

Although we can trace Dostoevskii's techniques of transcribing consciousness in the works of Andrei Belyi (*Peterburg* [1916; *Petersburg*]) and Fedor Sologub (*Melkii bes* [1907; *The Petty Demon*]), the psychological novel in Russia declined after the death of Dostoevskii. Ivan Turgenev died in 1883, and by 1881 Tolstoi had rejected all his earlier novels as useless and immoral. In the early Soviet period, novelists such as Leonid Leonov were seen as following in the psychological tradition of Dostoevskii. But Dostoevskii became a writer non grata under Stalin, and his works were considered suspect both ideologically and artistically. Certainly many German, French, and American writers admired and were profoundly influenced by Dostoevskii, who became especially popular in the disillusionment with Western civilization that set in after World War I, although it is difficult to attribute this influence exclusively to *Crime and Punishment*. Although the ideas and characters of *The Devils* and *The Brothers Karamazov* may have proved more attractive to readers, *Crime and Punishment*, because of its narratological innovativeness, probably has had a more profound influence on the history of the novel. Wherever one finds an emphasis on the transcription of consciousness; the compression of chronological time and the expansion of psychological time; and the attempt to incorporate heterogeneous materials of a philosophical, political, religious, and cultural nature into a riveting plot, one may easily detect the fingerprints of *Crime and Punishment*.

GARY ROSENSHIELD

See also Fedor Dostoevskii

Further Reading

Bakhtin, M.M., *Problemy tvorchestva Dostoevskogo*, Leningrad: Priboi, 1929; 2nd edition, revised, as *Problemy poetiki Dostoevskogo*, Moscow: Sov. Pisatel, 1963; as *Problems of Dostoevsky's Poetics*, Ann Arbor, Michigan: Ardis, 1973; new edition and translation, Minneapolis: University of Minnesota Press, and Manchester: Manchester University Press, 1984

Carr, E.H., *Dostoevsky (1821–1881): A New Biography*, London: Allen and Unwin, and Boston: Houghton Mifflin, 1931

Cox, Gary, *"Crime and Punishment": A Mind to Murder*, Boston: Twayne, 1990

Frank, Joseph, *Dostoevsky: The Miraculous Years, 1865–1871*, Princeton, New Jersey: Princeton University Press, 1995

Ivanov, Vyacheslav, *Freedom and the Tragic Life: A Study in Dostoevsky*, New York: Noonday, and London: Harvill, 1952

Johnson, Leslie A., *The Experience of Time in "Crime and Punishment,"* Columbus, Ohio: Slavica, 1984

Mochulskii, Konstantin, *Dostoevsky: His Life and Work*, Princeton, New Jersey: Princeton University Press, 1967

Peace, Richard, *Dostoevsky: An Examination of the Major Novels*, Cambridge: Cambridge University Press, 1971

Rosenshield, Gary, *"Crime and Punishment": The Techniques of the Omniscient Author*, Lisse: Peter de Ridder Press, 1978

Wasiolek, Edward, editor, *"Crime and Punishment" and the Critics*, San Francisco: Wadsworth, 1961

Crime, Detective, and Mystery Novel

At least since Genesis 4, when God asks Cain where his brother is and the suspect gives an evasive answer, narrative has taken as one of its central subjects the problem of criminality and the process by which crimes are investigated and rectified. In particular, the tale of a violent and mysterious death, a death that somehow demands a reconstruction of its circumstances and the exposure of a concealed perpetrator, has exercised a persistent hold on the human imagination. The three elements under consideration here—crime, detective, mystery—are not always found together in these narratives, and even this loose category has affinities with others, such as the Gothic novel, the thriller, and the spy novel. Nonetheless, the story of a mysterious crime that is solved by a figure of uncommon resourcefulness has proven itself one of the most popular forms that a novel can take. The dominant strain here is Anglo-American, but the form and the impulses behind it have proven attractive in other cultures as well.

The history of detective fiction conventionally begins with a small group of related tales written by Edgar Allan Poe, but crime, mystery, and even rudimentary detection are clearly visible in much 18th-century writing. The period had a huge appetite for sensational and often subliterary accounts of criminals, both in the kind of ballad broadsheets sold to accompany public executions, and in a variety of "biographies" of such famous criminals as the thief and extraordinary jailbreaker, Jack Sheppard.

The Gothic novel almost by definition involves a mystery, typically a concealed crime. So, in the work generally considered the first of that kind, Horace Walpole's *The Castle of Otranto* (1764), the plot turns on the murder of the rightful monarch by the grandfather of the present ruler. The archaeology of the past that such a hidden crime demands points up another similarity between Gothic novels such as *Otranto* and their more purely detective progeny. Both kinds of novels revolve around an essentially retrospective plot: what drives the reader's interest forward through the story is the reconstruction of a criminal event in the past. While 18th-century Gothic novels lack a true detective figure, a character like Vivaldi, hero of Ann Radcliffe's *The Italian* (1797) is often shown exercising his powers of reason to explore mentally (if not truly to investigate) the crimes of the villainous Schedoni. Moreover, Radcliffe's characteristic note—an apparently supernatural occurrence that is later revealed to be explicable in rational terms—becomes a standard feature of much of the later literature of mystery and detection.

William Godwin's *Caleb Williams* (1794) is also important as an early instance of a novel that concerns a secret crime brought to light by persistent investigation. Godwin is significant, too, for the way he explores the symbiotic and guilt-ridden relationship between his protodetective and criminal, a motif in crime narrative as old as Oedipus, and one that recurs time and again in the history of the genre. Crime, indeed, is one of the dominant subjects of the 18th-century novel generally: Moll Flanders is a thief (in a novel that often reads like an instructional manual for petty crime), Samuel Richardson's Lovelace is a rapist, and Henry Fielding, himself a magistrate, frequently in his novels is concerned with crime, most centrally in *Amelia* (1751), partly set in Newgate prison and intended to inspire reforms in the criminal justice system; but also in the early *Jonathan Wild* (1743), with its depiction of thieftakers and the London underworld; and even in *Tom Jones* (1749), where the trial pattern is pervasive and where the plot turns on a mysterious birth and an attempt to cheat the hero of his inheritance.

What is missing in the early novel, and what Poe is credited with inventing, is a detective who serves as our focal point for the solution of a mystery. Even before Poe, however, there had been the autobiography of Eugène Vidocq, which appeared in the late 1820s and which relates the adventures of the author, who was early a thief and later a policeman. The account is interesting and influential as an early instance of detective-centered writing, and Vidocq's ambiguous status as a criminal-policeman looks back to Jonathan Wild and Caleb Williams and ahead to a legion of detectives who solve crimes by somehow knowing it from the inside. He also was the model for Honoré de Balzac's Vautrin.

But Poe's Dupin, the hero of tales such as "The Murders in the Rue Morgue" (1841) and "The Purloined Letter" (1844), does represent something new, and we can see in this character the clear outline of much that has dominated detective writing ever since. Dupin is presented as a man of uncommon intelligence and reason with powers of mind that enable him to solve crimes that baffle the authorities. For the first time, we have an analytical detective, and Poe creates for him a template of features that many have since imitated: Dupin is eccentric and a loner, his triumph is narrated by an intellectually inferior companion, the authorities are dimwitted, the body (in "Rue Morgue") is found in a locked room, the clues are difficult to read, and the eventual solution is an intellectual tour de force. Poe also slyly invites the reader to match wits with Dupin, and that implicit challenge—*can you solve the crime before the detective reveals the solution?*—has become a staple of the detective novel's formula.

The appearance of this kind of detective in the 1840s may be linked to various historical developments. The emphasis on ratiocination seems to be related to the triumph of the Enlightenment virtue of reason. If the Gothic novel was in one respect a reaction against reason (as Goya put it, "the sleep of reason breeds monsters"), detective fiction is often described as a sign of its triumph. The early 19th century also saw the development of modern police forces, such as the formation of Sir Robert Peel's "bobbies" in England in the 1830s. The creation of these new police was predicated on a more scientific and rational approach to the gathering of evidence and the prosecution of criminals.

Such considerations are important to an understanding of the development of detective fiction, but they can be overstated. As a tale like "The Murders in the Rue Morgue" demonstrates, there is an irreducible mystery at the heart of violence that no reason can dissolve; indeed, the interest in murder that is central to the genre seems to argue for its preoccupation, like that of the Gothic novel, with the dark and irrational. And the attitude toward the police, from the beginning of the detective genre, seems at best ambivalent. Especially in the Anglo-American tradition, detectives (at least until after World War II) are most often not state bureaucrats but—like Dupin—amateurs, a sign perhaps of resistance among authors and readers alike to the emerging apparatus of professional investigation.

The tale of detection in Poe becomes the detective novel proper with Wilkie Collins' *The Moonstone* (1868). Much Victorian fiction, especially that of Charles Dickens, concerns mysterious crimes, and the new professional police appear frequently, as with Inspector Bucket in *Bleak House* (1853). But Collins, tentatively with *The Woman in White* (1860) and then more definitively with *The Moonstone,* is considered the first to make a crime and its detection the central interest of a full-length novel. Sergeant Cuff is more attractive than many Victorian policemen, and his disarming alertness provided a model for the detective somewhat different from the one developed by Poe. The scope of the novel also allowed Collins to imitate at length the presentation of evidence as it might occur at a trial, as different witnesses offer testimony from their own perspective. Dickens, too, tried his hand at a purer kind of mystery novel with *The Mystery of Edwin Drood* (1870), but inadvertently left the world what some consider its most perfect mystery by dying with the novel unfinished and the secret of its solution locked firmly in his mind.

At this time, too, Fedor Dostoevskii published *Prestuplenie i nakazanie* (1867; *Crime and Punishment*), the most salient reminder possible that the exploration of the theme announced by its title is consistent with the highest reach of art. The focus is on the criminal, Raskolnikov—although the detective, Porfiry, is in his own way equally memorable—and the puzzle, at least in the typical sense, is completely missing. But Dostoevskii reminds us of what W.H. Auden will argue in his classic discussion of detective fiction (1962): in the literature of crime, however ignoble, the religious themes of sin and redemption are always at hand.

For the most part, the formal demands of Victorian serial fiction militated against the kind of tight plotting that we associate with detective fiction. Later in the century, however, the new vogue for magazine short stories helped produce the figure who remains, at least in the popular mind, the very quintessence of the fictional detective, Sir Arthur Conan Doyle's Sherlock Holmes, the hero of several short novels and a host of tales published between 1888 (*A Study in Scarlet*) and 1927. The character of Holmes is clearly indebted to Dupin: his stories are told by an intellectual inferior, the equally famous Dr. Watson; like his ancestor, Holmes is eccentric, remote, and the amateur-master of a certain kind of intellectual effort. That effort is most often called "deduction," as Holmes appears to draw revealing conclusions from apparently trivial pieces of physical evidence, such as shreds of tobacco or scuff marks on a gentleman's shoes. A better word, however, would be "interpretation": Holmes' conclusions are not always (as we are led to believe) inevitable, but they do turn out to be right, and what those solutions verify is less Holmes' method than his power to interpret. The great detectives, Holmes perhaps above all, are not so much masters of empirical method as they are supreme readers, figures who are able to take the scattered fragments of a crime scene and assemble a coherent and convincing picture. That dialectic of reason and the irrational that so often dominates detective fiction is fully on display in Holmes; his ability to solve a mystery, while presented as the triumph of scientific reason, is experienced by readers as a kind of magical power.

The lure that the irrational holds for detective fiction could also be seen in another, more obvious direction. The Gothic novel found renewed popularity toward the end of the 19th century,

and we continue to see there a deep affinity between the Gothic imagination and detective fiction broadly understood. A work like Robert Louis Stevenson's *The Strange Case of Dr. Jekyll and Mr. Hyde* (1886) confounds easy categorization, combining as it does the monstrosity of Gothic with the kind of laboratory reengineering of human nature we associate with science fiction. Those generic markers are so strong that we can forget that the plot turns on the mysterious murder of Sir Danvers Carew and on the investigation of what is, after all, called a "case" by another amateur detective, the lawyer Utterson. The climatic discovery of Hyde's body where Jekyll's should be marks Stevenson's work as among the most interesting of locked room mysteries. That association—crime, horror, the pursuit of an evildoer—turns up as well in Bram Stoker's *Dracula* (1897), where again there is a mysterious death and where the vampire must first be identified as the culprit and then tracked, not by one man but by a band of men who become a kind of collective detective, pooling individual resources of intelligence and bravery into a corporate force of good that remains staunchly amateur. The police here exist only at the margins of the novel, and in keeping with the emerging stereotype, they are ineffectual.

Holmes remained unsurpassed as the paradigmatic great detective, but the early decades of the 20th century saw a host of imitators, including the character known as the "Thinking Machine" of Jacques Futrelle and R. Austin Freeman's Dr. Thorndyke. G.K. Chesterton's Father Brown (who appears mostly in stories and in only one novel) fits the mold, yet he also demonstrates its flexibility: as a priest (he, too, is another amateur detective), he desires to save souls as well as solve crimes.

The years between the two world wars are often called the "Golden Age" of detective fiction, although the phrase has come to be applied both to the period and to a certain type of novel that was perfected at that time. That type, sometimes also called a "cozy," follows a fairly predictable form: the setting is rural (a village, a country house party), the cast of suspects is limited, everyone falls under suspicion, and the solution to the puzzle-like set of clues is provided by a detective who often (but not always) is an amateur. From one point of view, the Golden Age cozy, as its name implies, is another version of pastoral: rural life is swathed in a nostalgic glow of familiar and comforting conventions, yet death lurks in this Arcadia as well. The great popular master of this form was Agatha Christie, who wrote more than 80 books, and who was once said to be second in sales only to the Bible. She invented two great detectives, Poirot—the fussy Belgian outsider who relies upon his "little grey cells"—and Miss Marple, another kind of outsider, since she is an elderly spinster. Many of these novels were written and set in England, but the form also was attractive to such American mystery writers as Ellery Queen (a pseudonym for two collaborators). The cozy has proved to be remarkably resilient, and a significant percentage of the mystery novels published late in the 20th century are still in this mode.

Dominant as Christie was, however, even in the Golden Age, other writers found wider possibilities in the detective novel. Dorothy Sayers wrote novels that at times rely on cozy-like conventions, and some of her puzzles and solutions rival the best of Christie's. Beyond that, however, the reader of Sayers finds a much greater depth of character, and her romantic hero and heroine, Harriet Vane and Lord Peter Wimsey (who first meet in *Strong Poison* [1930] when she is a murder suspect and his detections must save her), are surely the most memorable lovers in all detective fiction. Wimsey, the foppish aristocrat, defines a certain kind of amateur *sprezzatura*; nothing, it seems, is beyond the power of his cleverness and charm.

Already, however, even in the midst of the Golden Age, a reaction against amateurism and coziness was setting in. A magazine called *The Black Mask* (the definite article was later dropped) began publishing in America in the 1920s, and it marked the beginnings of the enormously popular and influential "hardboiled" style. Indebted to American literary traditions of naturalism, and reflecting some of the grim realities of life, especially urban life, in the United States after World War I, writers such as Carroll John Terry and Dashiell Hammett dispensed with the light tone and warm village life of their Golden Age contemporaries. These detectives were professional (although normally "private eyes"; the police were still a lesser breed), cynical, and willing to kill (although usually in a good cause); the criminals, too, were professionals. The hard-boiled school was also notable for its style, relying on language as lean and tough as the world it describes.

The great practitioner in this mode was Raymond Chandler, whose Philip Marlowe was sent by his creator down, not the village lane or the path to the vicarage, but what he called "mean streets." In novels such as *The Big Sleep* (1939) and *Farewell, My Lovely* (1940), Marlowe is presented to us as a tarnished knight, a man of honor forced not just to fight evil, but to fight it in what is obviously a fallen world. Chandler and those writing like him still typically rely on a mystery, but the problem is usually not a classic puzzle, and the crime is solved not so much by a feat of intellectual magic as by experience, persistence, and luck. These detectives are less like scientists or professors and more like hunters, and the progress of the plot may resemble a stalking or a chase more than it does the reading of a set of baffling clues. Later work in this vein, notably that of Mickey Spillane, dispenses with the residual nobility of the detective and allows the full brutality of the environment to infect protagonist and antagonist alike. Spillane's world is a fully Hobbesian one.

The split described here between cozy and hard-boiled is a deep one, encompassing the city and the country, the amateur and the professional, murder as a game and murder as serious business, but the breach between these two branches begins to be bridged by the development of a new category, with a focus on the work of a group long ignored or denigrated in much detective fiction. The "police procedural," as its name implies, places its attention squarely on the work of the police, which is to say on the specifically public apparatus of crime detection, as opposed to either the amateur sleuth or the private eye, neither of whom works at the taxpayer's expense. The police procedural, as developed in the 1950s by writers such as John Creasy in England or Ed McBain in the United States, takes from the hardboiled school a generally gritty urban setting and resolutely eschews the light and nostalgic mood of the classic Golden Age puzzler. The sense of collective labor is often strong. McBain's books are identified as "the 87th Precinct novels" rather than by the name of a particular detective, and part of the appeal of these books is the way they portray the solution to a crime as the product of a set of painstaking procedures undertaken by a group of role-bound individuals—the medical examiner, the forensics expert, the street cop, and so on.

And yet elements from the Golden Age novels, appropriately transformed, are incorporated here: for instance, the suspects may all come from a closed group (a workplace, say, rather than a village), and some of the policemen do find ways, in the midst of their place in a bureaucracy, to satisfy our hunger for a detective who is brighter or more resourceful or simply more original than the standard-issue. Georges Simenon's Inspector Maigret does not, properly speaking, belong in this part of the discussion, for he is a solitary and the sense of an institutional or bureaucratic connection is not strong; but the unforgettable personality that Simenon gives his policeman in many novels written from the 1930s onward do look ahead to the sharply characterized police detectives of the postwar era. Inspector Dalgliesh, the invention of P.D. James (herself, like Fielding, a novelist-magistrate), has a Holmesian distance and is a brilliant poet, while Colin Dexter's Inspector Morse has an alcohol habit to match his ancestor's addiction to cocaine and a cleverness that marks him as an Oxford man, not only by his city of employment but also by his wits. In a marvelous bit of self-referential fun about the history of detective fiction, Dexter makes Morse a champion solver of puzzles: he can finish the *Times* crossword in only a few minutes.

Novels of detection, crime, and mystery certainly form a dominant feature of the novelistic landscape as the 20th century ends. And their variety is astonishing. Not only are cozies still being written long after their Golden Age, but even meaner streets are patrolled by even harder boiled private eyes. Amateur detectives represent every profession: we have anthropologist-detectives, writer-detectives, teacher-detectives, psychiatrist-detectives, pathologist-detectives, rabbi-detectives, and lawyer-detectives by the score. And the police are everywhere. One very successful generic marriage has been the union of detective and historical fiction, and there are immensely popular series set in Victorian London, in the Middle Ages, and in ancient Rome, to name only three.

Particularly noteworthy in the last few decades has been the proliferation of female detectives. Women made their mark writing mysteries as early as Mary Elizabeth Braddon's *Lady Audley's Secret* (1862) and Anna Katherine Green's *The Leavenworth Case* (1878), but these novels employed male detectives. Female sleuths do make a few appearances as early as the late 19th century, and the Golden Age has (among others) Christie's Miss Marple and Sayers' Harriet Vane (who takes over detecting from Wimsey in *Gaudy Night,* 1935). But the last few decades have seen a proliferation of women solving mysteries. Even that most apparently masculine of all detective preserves, the hard-boiled private eye, has been appropriated with great popularity by writers like Sue Grafton and Sara Paretsky.

The reasons for the enduring popularity of novels of mystery, crime, and detection has inspired much speculation. These fictions have been explained by psychoanalysts as a reflection of the primal scene, by Marxists as an expression of bourgeois self-satisfaction, by formalists as a set of rules, and so forth. All these perspectives are illuminating, if too narrow for a literature of such remarkable range and variety. What does seem clear is that these kinds of novels satisfy a desire for the representation of what is worst in human behavior and, at the same time, a faith in our ability to penetrate and name those very traits. Such a dialectical relationship between what is irrational and what is reasonable never comes to rest, but the apparently boundless appetite of readers for these kinds of narratives suggests perhaps that we take some satisfaction in seeing that tension made visible.

JOHN ALLEN STEVENSON

See also Gothic Novel; Horror Novel

Further Reading

Allen, Dick, and David Chacko, editors, *Detective Fiction: Crime and Compromise*, New York: Harcourt Brace, 1974

Auden, W.H., "The Guilty Vicarage," in *The Dyer's Hand and Other Essays*, New York: Random House, 1962; London: Faber, 1963

Barzun, Jacques, and Wendell H. Taylor, editors, *A Catalogue of Crime*, New York: Harper and Row, 1971; revised edition, 1989

Burns, Rex, and Mary Rose Sullivan, editors, *Crime Classics:*

The Mystery Story from Poe to the Present, New York: Viking, 1990

Chandler, Raymond, *The Simple Art of Murder*, Boston: Houghton Mifflin, and London: Hamish Hamilton, 1950

Most, Glenn W., and William W. Stowe, editors, *The Poetics of Murder: Detective Fiction and Literary Theory*, San Diego, California: Harcourt Brace, 1983

Ousby, Ian, *Bloodhounds of Heaven: The Detective in English Fiction from Godwin to Doyle*, Cambridge, Massachusetts: Harvard University Press, 1976

Sayers, Dorothy, *The Omnibus of Crime*, New York: Payson and Clarke, 1929

Symons, Julian, *Mortal Consequences: A History from the Detective Story to the Crime Novel*, New York: Harper and Row, 1972; as *Bloody Murder: From the Detective Story to the Crime Novel*, London: Faber, 1972

Winks, Robin, editor, *Detective Fiction: A Collection of Critical Essays*, Englewood Cliffs, New Jersey: Prentice-Hall, 1980

Critics and Criticism

18th Century

Although there has been considerable recent debate over when or even whether the novel "rose" in the 18th century (as the title of Ian Watt's 1957 book suggests it did), critics generally agree that it was during this period that a significant critical discourse regarding the novel emerged—that 18th-century novelists and critics alike distinguished this "new species of writing" (as Samuel Richardson called it in a letter of 1741) from the prose fiction and nonfiction that preceded it. The two most extensive and important sources for this criticism were the novelists themselves, who spoke through prefaces, dedications, letters, etc., and—especially from the middle of the century on—the critics who worked in another new genre, the book-review periodical. Like 20th-century discourse on upstart genres of uncertain status, such as the feature film or the television series, early commentary on the novel often included opportunistic self-promotion or disingenuous modesty on the part of the novelists, and condescending tolerance or vituperative ridicule on the part of the reviewers. Yet it also raised, in an eclectic, undogmatic way, concerns that continue to engage readers of the novel and consumers of culture in general.

In the earlier decades of the 18th century, novelists' prefatory statements about their works were often cloaked under—and limited by—an insistence that they were not writing fiction at all, but telling true stories. Nevertheless, these authors initiated the two perspectives that would dominate the ensuing critical discourse: a formalist, aesthetic approach to the novel that focused on its constituent elements, and a moralistic view that concentrated on the effects of reading novels on a young, impressionable audience.

Among the formalist statements, one of the most enduring is William Congreve's preface to *Incognita* (1692), in which he distinguishes between the elevated characters, "lofty" language, and improbable incidents in romances, and the more familiar characters and events in novels, concluding that "romances give more of wonder, novels more delight." Although writers and critics continued to use the words "novel" and "romance" interchangeably throughout the century, Congreve's contrast, with its emphasis on the reader's response, was echoed often, perhaps most notably in the opening of *Rambler* no. 4 (1750), in which Samuel Johnson favors works of fiction that "exhibit life in its true state" over heroic romances and the "wild strain of imagination" that they represent. Congreve concludes the preface by borrowing from the criticism of drama an Aristotelian emphasis on the importance of a unified plot, ignoring character and the moral considerations with which character is associated. Similar concerns underlie Delarivier Manley's preface to her scandal chronicle *The Secret History of Queen Zarah* (1705). The preface—actually a translation of a 17th-century French treatise—focuses on unity of design, plainness of diction, probability, and consistency in characterization, and it pointedly rejects intrusive moralizing.

In the commentary of such novelists as Jane Barker, Elizabeth Rowe, and Penelope Aubin, all of whom were popular in the 1720s, moral utility is the primary goal of and justification for fiction: novels are valuable insofar as they lure unsuspecting readers into an apprehension of moral or religious truth. Aubin, the most prolific commentator of the three, discusses probability—as Johnson and Samuel Richardson did after her—in terms of creating virtuous characters who remain human enough to serve as plausible models for readers. Like many of her contemporaries, Aubin also appropriates from drama criticism the doctrine of poetic justice, whereby virtue is rewarded and vice punished. Eliza Haywood, author of both erotic and domestic fiction and now considered the most important woman novelist of her generation, never directly refers to poetic justice but relies on its premises to approach moral instruction from a decidedly different angle. She frequently offers her "fallen" or "ruined" heroines as negative examples, as warnings against conduct that readers should avoid. Such an argument attempts to legitimate a vivid—and potentially enticing—portrayal of vice.

Daniel Defoe's critical discourse incorporates all of these approaches, thereby proving more complex and more elusive. In the prefaces to *Robinson Crusoe* (1719) and its two sequels, Defoe—in the persona of an editor and eventually of Crusoe himself—claims that the texts are entertaining, moral, and true. The assertion of literal truth is increasingly qualified, however, by the use of terms like "parable" and "allegory," and Defoe seldom specifies how readers looking for diversion would be instructed, and vice versa. In *Moll Flanders* (1722) and *Roxana* (1724), the author of the preface is even more obscure about the truth of the stories and about his proximity to their sources: he refers to revisions of both first-person accounts, but Defoe no longer identifies himself as editor. Both prefaces vindicate narratives of disreputable lives by offering them as warnings and by stressing the penitence or punishment of the heroines. Defoe also shifts moral responsibility to the reader, arguing that only a viscious mind will subordinate the sound moral to the salacious detail. As interesting as Defoe's logical and rhetorical twists may be, his refusal to acknowledge authorship and to treat his fiction as fiction limits his importance as a commentator on a genre in which he is rightly regarded as a pioneer.

Far more than their predecessors, Samuel Richardson and Henry Fielding were responsible for establishing the novel as a "respectable" genre, both through their creative achievement in the genre itself and their critical commentary about it. Each author projected, albeit in different ways, a new level of authority in discussing his craft, but neither could ultimately mask divisions and contradictions in his thinking. Richardson's criticism is immediately complicated by the three voices in which he delivered it. First, he posed as an editor in order to lend his epistolary novels an air of verisimilitude and to sustain the reader's suspension of disbelief, but then Richardson abandoned this facade in the postscripts to *Clarissa* (1748, 1751) in order to advance a single, "correct" interpretation of his work in the person of, and with the authority of, the creator of the text. Finally, he used his own letters to defend his novels and to convince individual readers to embrace his perspective on them. In all three personas, Richardson consistently and adamantly stresses the moral efficacy of his novels and offers his virtuous characters as exemplary models, but he has difficulty accounting for the seductive power of a villain like Lovelace in *Clarissa* or of some of the erotically charged scenes he created. Moreover, although he admits that his heroes and heroines need to have faults in order to serve as imitable models, he argues against every flaw imputed to them by his readers. Richardson's more directly aesthetic comments derive from his other major critical preoccupation: his originality. While he acknowledges a debt to the more established genre of drama for his method of characterization through dialogue

and unmediated letters, he frequently emphasizes both the novelty and superiority of his genre. Most significantly, he defends the unhappy ending of *Clarissa* first by belittling the doctrine of poetic justice and then by maintaining that he has observed a higher form of poetic justice by giving his heroine a heavenly reward. Similarly, he exalts the epistolary mode—in which he never acknowledges any predecessors—over linear narrative, on the grounds that the epistolary structure offers a greater variety of styles, that it more strongly engages the reader's empathy toward the characters, and that it is more probable since his letter writers presumably record events immediately after they occur. Although the final rationale is open to question (the proclivity of Richardson's characters to write so much, even after devastating events, hardly seems probable), the others help account for the popularity of epistolary fiction in the 18th century and its revival in such contemporary works as Alice Walker's *The Color Purple* (1982) and Nick Bantock's *Griffin and Sabine* (1991).

Fielding elevated his own novels as well as the genre by a different method: describing his narratives in language that associated them with older, more established literary forms. In the preface to *Joseph Andrews* (1742), he characterizes his text as a "comic epic-poem in prose" and identifies as the only precursor Homer's lost comic epic, *Margites,* thereby establishing both a classical heritage and a claim for uniqueness. In a similar vein, he frequently refers to his works as "histories," thus associating them with historical truth, but Fielding also argues that they are superior to conventional historical writing because they eschew minute circumstantial detail and describe "not men, but manners; not an individual, but a species" (*Joseph Andrews*). As clever a rhetorician as he may have been, however, Fielding never reconciled this prescription for generality, which he followed in his own novels, with his admiration for the psychological depth in fiction by others, including Richardson. Several other tensions also are left unresolved in Fielding's criticism. His advocacy of probability, for instance, extends only to characters acting consistently with their personalities and situations, and not to connections between actions, allowing Fielding to construct plots sustained by a series of coincidences. Although his conception of character is fundamentally static, Fielding not only allows for but praises a mixed character like Tom Jones, a good character who nevertheless sometimes behaves in flawed ways. Finally, in *Tom Jones* (1749) Fielding baldly attacks the doctrine of poetic justice but then follows it to the letter.

Samuel Johnson, the preeminent literary critic of the latter half of the 18th century, not only drew an early and significant comparison of Richardson and Fielding as novelists, but articulated, in *Rambler* no. 4, one of the most remembered 18th-century statements about the attractions and dangers of novels. Given the power of fictional characters "to take possession of the memory by a kind of violence, and produce effects almost without the intervention of the will," Johnson insists on selective imitation of nature, in which characters proposed as models exhibit "the most perfect idea of virtue" that humans can hope to reach, and faults novelists for mitigating characters' vices by giving them attractive qualities as well. In Johnson's other literary criticism, particularly his criticism of drama, he seldom reflected such absolutism and approved of mixed characters. But the *Rambler* was primarily a work of moral instruction in which Johnson was concerned about the effects of fiction on its principal audience, which he characterized as "the young, the ignorant, and the idle." In a more openly aesthetic context, Johnson compares Fielding's "characters of manners" unfavorably to Richardson's "characters of nature" (as recorded in James Boswell, *Life of Johnson*, 1791), voicing a preference for psychologically complex characters who reveal themselves through letters and dialogue over more superficial characters who are subordinated to an overarching narrative voice—as Johnson's own characters were in his only extended work of fiction, *Rasselas* (1759).

In the second half of the century, the enhanced status won for the novel as a genre by Richardson, Fielding, and others was continually threatened by the vast amount of inferior fiction published each year. Consequently, novelists frequently used their commentary to attract both a large popular audience and a positive response from the increasingly institutionalized critical establishment, represented most prominently in the two leading book-review journals, the *Monthly Review* and the *Critical Review*. The reviewers for these journals, eager to carve out a respectable position for their own profession, acknowledged the potential of the genre and some individual successes, but more commonly they disparaged most novels as beneath the notice of their presumably more sophisticated audience—which, they implied, did not include habitual readers of novels. These diverging goals help account for the different approaches that novelists and critics took to the common issues they discussed, which include gender, morality, and originality.

Women novelists, not to mention some "female impersonators," frequently begged critical indulgence on the grounds of poverty, widowhood, or the intellectual deficiencies of their gender, even though the reviewers frequently became impatient with this practice. For the novelists, pleading for "candour" may have been a way to attract sympathy from an audience ignorant of or unmoved by the critics; for the reviewers, focusing on the pleading allowed them to dismiss the novels in question without any additional analysis. The more talented women writers, however, seldom sought such preferential—and condescending—treatment, instead devoting their prefaces to issues more likely to engage the critics, or, like Ann Radcliffe, omitting prefaces altogether. Whatever pleading does occur in works by novelists like Frances Burney, Elizabeth Inchbald, and Charlotte Smith is often self-consciously complex or ironic. In turn, the reviewers often accorded more extended and serious treatment to these novelists, concentrating on plot design, characterization, probability, and other formal issues. Even these writers, however, were judged in relative terms and expected to maintain a "feminine," "delicate," and presumably inferior style.

A nearly universal preoccupation with morality by the novelists and critics reflects a similar mix of sincerity and opportunism. Writing in an environment in which fiction was still regularly attacked for its immorality, novelists were virtually compelled to foreground their didactic intentions, whether or not they were genuine. Many went further, arguing that good intentions should compensate for mediocre (or even bad) results. In the 1790s, radical Jacobin novelists like Robert Bage and Thomas Holcroft used the conventional, "conservative" didactic stance explicitly to announce the unconventional, politically charged messages of their novels. Reviewers took their role as censors quite seriously, often attacking even sophisticated novels like Laurence Sterne's *Tristram Shandy* (1759–67) for indecency. They commonly argued that virtue should be rewarded, and that vice, even when punished, should not be portrayed too vividly.

An aggressive moralistic stance also permitted the reviewers to peremptorily dismiss inferior novels by condemning them for impropriety. Moral rectitude, however, could not overshadow artistic deficiencies for most critics, who had little patience for works that claimed merely the negative merit of an absence of immorality. Reviewers recognized that fiction could instruct only if it entertained: even *Rasselas* was criticized by both the *Monthly Review* and the *Critical Review* for its overt and intrusive didactic reflections.

In the context of reviewers' rampant complaints about the similarity, predictability, and dullness of so many novels, as well as a general sense that the "golden age" of novel writing had already passed, novelists frequently trumpeted their innovations in style and subject matter. When the performance matched the promise, they won praise from critics, who rejected the numerous mindless sequels to and imitations of works by Richardson, Fielding, Sterne, and Radcliffe, and valued only those imitations that attempted to capture the spirit of the original and to improve upon it. Yet reviewers were, like some novelists, intolerant of the popular appetite for novelty at any cost: they usually rejected works that forsook fidelity to nature and probability in a quest for the new. Even Gothic novelists respected this balance. Horace Walpole's preface to what is generally regarded as the first Gothic novel, *The Castle of Otranto* (1764), advocates a portrayal of characters in extraordinary situations behaving in ordinary ways. Much to Walpole's consternation, Clara Reeve prefaced *The Old English Baron* (1778) with both an acknowledgment of her debt to *Otranto* and a promise to improve upon it by keeping "within the utmost *verge* of probability." Most prominently, all of Radcliffe's novels offer rational—if strained—explanations for apparently supernatural phenomena.

Classifying and evaluating subgenres like the Gothic fell less naturally to the novelists than to the review journals, given the journals' engagement with a variety of texts over a long period of time. The inductive nature of reviewing, differences among individual critics, changes over time, and the lack of absolute criteria for judgment combined to produce a remarkably balanced assessment of each subgenre. Gothic fiction was initially praised for its fertility of invention and for its appeal to the reader's imagination. With repetition, however, invention proved difficult to sustain in the eyes of the critics, who also objected when excessive and gruesome horror was added to the Gothic formula.

Historical fiction, initiated by such novels as Thomas Leland's *Longsword, Earl of Salisbury* (1762) and Sophia Lee's *The Recess* (1783–85), also was greeted with some enthusiasm at first, largely because it could communicate some historical information to otherwise uninformed and uninterested readers. This benefit was often compromised in reviewers' minds, however, by the frequent inaccuracies in historical novels and by the potential for entertaining fiction to dissuade a credulous audience from reading less appealing but more accurate historical writing. The success of novels of sensibility, like Laurence Sterne's *A Sentimental Journey* (1768) and Henry Mackenzie's *The Man of Feeling* (1771), led reviewers to an increased appreciation of pathos as a mark of value for fiction. On the other hand, critics became exasperated with the tendency toward excessive or affected sentiment and with the lack of an interesting plot—or of any plot at all—in many sentimental novels. They also expressed frustration with the haziness of the words "sentiment" and "sensibility" and with the way in which these terms were used to justify inept or immoral novels. Yet the reviewers themselves refrained from defining the terms, and disagreement over the meaning, origins, and limitations of sensibility persist to the present day.

Concerning the more local formal elements of narrative, reviewers tended to concur on the importance of a unified plot, but they divided on the relative merits of simplicity and clarity on the one hand and difficulty and complexity on the other. Some joined novelists like Sterne in defending digressions. Character received more sustained attention, largely because reviewers found a ready source of entertainment in descriptions of amusing or eccentric characters, which they often quoted at length. From drama criticism they adopted the criteria of variety, contrast, and discrimination for evaluating characterization, but reviewers mirrored the novelists themselves by debating the relative merit of exemplary and mixed characters and the desirability of portraying "low life." With regard to language, reviewers reached probably their strongest consensus by attacking the extremes of overly embellished and overly common or monotonous prose, and by advocating a middle style that combines "artlessness" with sophistication.

In this critical discourse as a whole, the contradictions, disagreements, and absence of dogmatic precepts allowed for and may well have encouraged the variety and experimentation that were characteristic of 18th-century fiction. And while some of the specific preoccupations of the novelists and critics may strike the contemporary reader as quaintly irrelevant, the underlying general issues that they examined still resonate in discussions of fiction and other genres that combine broad popular appeal and claims to serious artistic merit. Debates about the existence of a uniquely feminine mode of writing, about the suitability of mixing fact and fiction in films like *JFK* or in the "new journalism," about the necessity and effectiveness of ratings systems for movies, television series, music videos, and song lyrics, and about the dangers that a derivative and tasteless popular culture poses to young people, all have their origins in the commentary about the first literary genre that was available to and appreciated by a mass audience. While two centuries of subsequent criticism have led to more refined and sophisticated approaches to the novel, the fundamental questions raised by the earliest critics remain relevant and contested.

JOSEPH F. BARTOLOMEO

See also English Novel (18th Century); Epic and Novel; Epistolary Novel; French Novel (18th Century); Genre

Criticism; Gothic Novel; Historical Novel; Historical Writing and the Novel; Journalism and the Novel; Mimesis; Novel and Romance: Etymologies; Prose Novelistic Forms; Realism; Reviewers and the Popular Press; Romance; Sentimental Novel

Further Reading

Bartolomeo, Joseph F., *A New Species of Criticism: Eighteenth-Century Discourse on the Novel,* Newark: University of Delaware Press, and London: Associated University Presses, 1994

Davis, Lennard J., *Factual Fictions: The Origins of the English Novel,* New York: Columbia University Press, 1983

Donoghue, Frank, *The Fame Machine: Book Reviewing and Eighteenth-Century Literary Careers,* Stanford, California: Stanford University Press, 1996

Hunter, J. Paul, *Before Novels: The Cultural Contexts of Eighteenth-Century English Fiction,* New York: Norton, 1990

Mayo, Robert D., *The English Novel in the Magazines, 1740–1815,* Evanston, Illinois: Northwestern University Press, 1962

McKeon, Michael, *The Origins of the English Novel, 1600–1740,* Baltimore: Johns Hopkins University Press, 1987; London: Raduis, 1988

Richetti, John J., *Popular Fiction before Richardson: Narrative Patterns, 1700–1739,* Oxford: Clarendon Press, 1969; New York: Oxford University Press, 1992

Spencer, Jane, *The Rise of the Woman Novelist: From Aphra Behn to Jane Austen,* Oxford and New York: Blackwell, 1986

Tompkins, J.M.S., *The Popular Novel in England, 1770–1800,* London: Constable, 1932; Lincoln: University of Nebraska Press, 1961

Uphaus, Robert W., editor, *The Idea of the Novel in the Eighteenth Century,* East Lansing, Michigan: Colleagues Press, 1988

Watt, Ian, *The Rise of the Novel: Studies in Defoe, Richardson, and Fielding,* Berkeley: University of California Press, and London: Chatto and Windus, 1957

Williams, Ioan M., editor, *Novel and Romance, 1700–1800: A Documentary Record,* London: Routledge and Kegan Paul, and New York: Barnes and Noble, 1970

Critics and Criticism

19th Century

The 19th century was so much the age of the novel that one is not surprised to find that it was also one of the great ages of novel criticism. Since, however, there was virtually no academic criticism, the practical and theoretical consideration of the genre

was in the hands of the critics, the reviewers, and, above all, the practitioners themselves. The 19th century began, notably in England and France, with an inheritance bequeathed by the achievements of the 18th century. It was, however, a complex inheritance. On the one hand, the novel, like other forms of art, was an instrument of moral utility, helping readers to both understand and judge experience, so that they may be the better for reading novels. On the other hand, the novel was increasingly an instrument for depicting reality—and reality may not have been quite as amenable to the moralist's prescriptions as he would have liked and, indeed, might be at odds with them (one thinks immediately of characters such as Lovelace in Samuel Richardson's *Clarissa* [1747–48] and the eponymous hero of Henry Fielding's *Tom Jones* [1749]).

In France the novel grew in a climate of revolution and in a reaction to classicism; the reaction was as much one of subject matter as of style, but it would be misleading to think that ideas about the novel changed dramatically in the early years of the 19th century. In novels such as Chateaubriand's *Atala* (1801) and Benjamin Constant's *Adolphe* (1816) the preoccupations with romantic settings in the former and the life of the passions in the latter mark the emergence of romanticism in French fiction. Romanticism brought with it an emphasis on the personal experience of the author as a basis for art and a new kind of psychological realism, and it is in the light of these developments that individual experience came to be seen as the final arbiter of reality. Romanticism, of course, flirts with the marvelous, and in England one notices in novels such as Mary Shelley's *Frankenstein* (1818) the persistence to the attraction of the uncommon or the extraordinary coupled with a desire to find ways in which such material, belonging essentially to the tradition of the Gothic, may be rendered in a prose that is factual and objective.

In descriptive criticism of the novel, the distinctions between epic, romance, and novel remained matters of debate. In 1810, writing "On the Origin and Progress of Novel-Writing," Anna Laetitia Barbauld defined a "good novel" as "an epic in prose, with more of character and less (indeed in modern novels nothing) of the supernatural machinery." Sir Walter Scott was among the earliest 19th-century writers to try to draw clear boundaries between these forms and, thus, if only by implication, to establish a workable formal definition of the novel. In his "Essay on Romance" (1824), challenging the definition offered by Samuel Johnson, Scott writes that "we would be rather inclined to describe a *Romance* as a 'fictitious narrative in prose or verse; the interest of which turns upon marvellous or uncommon incidents'; thus being opposed to the kindred term *Novel,* which Johnson has described as 'a smooth tale, generally of love'; but which we would define as 'a fictitious narrative,' differing from the Romance, because the events are accommodated to the ordinary train of human events, and the modern state of society." Reviewing Madame Cottin's *Amélie Mansfield* (1803; *Amelie Mansfield*) in the *Quarterly Review,* Scott remarked that it was "real life" that is "the very thing which *novels* affect to imitate," although what beyond a commonsense conception of "real life" might be meant by such a phrase he does not indicate. Similar assumptions about the relationship between the novel and real life surface again in Scott's important essay on Jane Austen's *Emma* (1815) in, again, the *Quarterly Review* (1815). Here Scott considers the new type of fiction that works such as that of Austen represent, one that neither alarms our credulity nor amuses our imagination "by wild variety of incident, or by those pictures of romantic affection and sensibility, which were formerly as certain attributes of fictitious characters as they are of rare occurrence among those who actually live

and die." In their place is "the art of copying from nature as she really exists in the common walks of life, and presenting to the reader, instead of the splendid scenes of an imaginary world, a correct and striking representation of that which is daily taking place around him." This amounts, more or less, to a theory of realism, although it is unencumbered by any technical considerations of how the representation of reality is to be effected. A similar conception of the novel as an instrument (perhaps, ultimately, *the* instrument) of mimesis is to be found in Stendhal's *Le Rouge et le noir* (1830; *The Red and the Black*). Stendhal speaks of the novel as a "mirror of life," one that reflects "the blue of the skies and the mire in the road below"; such an analogy describes both the spaciousness of the novelist's concerns and the air of studied neutrality that his style seeks to effect, although Stendhal is by no means as "silent" in his novels as are some of his French descendents.

Thus there was during the opening decades of the 19th century a kind of uneasy accommodation between a romantic affection for the Gothic, with its associations of the uncommon and the fairy tale, and the beginnings of a sustained theory of the novel as an instrument of realism. The romantic poets themselves showed little interest in the kind of realism described by Scott, despite the extent to which reviewers adverted to the superiority of this new kind of fiction over Gothic romance—one thinks, for example, of Percy Bysshe Shelley's *Zastrozzi: A Romance* (1810) or William Godwin's *Mandeville* (1817). Stendhal himself articulates both positions, for his characters often embody a romantic unreality that conflicts with the demands and expectations of contemporary society. Characters who embody sensitivity or frustrated genius are not uncommon in French fiction in the early decades of the century, although they are infrequent actors in the English novels of the same period. The desire to bring fiction down to earth was a desire to rid it, perhaps once and for all, of the residues of the conventionally heroic, the sentimental, and the romantic, and to create in its place a fiction that goes even farther along the road of "copying from nature" than Scott would have anticipated. The French critic Gustave Planche is often seen as an early spokesman for fictional realism, but, although Planche was a committed "anti-romantic," realism for him sometimes meant little more than the attention to detail that we describe as local color.

Something closer to the concept of realism as it is understood by the middle of the 19th century is found in the opening pages of Honoré de Balzac's *Le père goriot* (1835; *Le Père Goriot*). Balzac insists that his drama is "neither fiction or romance," since "*All is true,* so that everyone can recognize the elements of the tragedy in his own household, in his own heart perhaps." The French critic Hippolyte Taine, who was drawn toward a sociological and scientific theory of literature, saw Balzac's triumph as a "matter of depicting base existences" since he is "armed with brutality and calculation" and in "this capacity he copies the real, he likes the monstrous on a large scale; he depicts baseness and force better than other things" ("Balzac," in *Le Journal des Debats,* 1858).

Taine's view partakes of the same kind of theory of the antiheroic subject that we associate, above all, with Gustave Flaubert's *Madame Bovary* (1857). By the middle of the century most critical debate about the novel centered on the claims of realism and, with it, the liberation of subject matter and style that had been effected. The Goncourt brothers, Edmond and

Jules de Goncourt, despite their aristocratic background and their commitment to *écriture artiste*, prefaced their novel *Germinie Lacerteux* (1865) with an assertion of the new authority brought to the novel form by the development of realism, seeing it as "the great serious, impassioned, living form of literary study and social examination, when by means of analysis and psychological research it is becoming contemporary Moral History." They suggest that since "the Novel has undertaken the studies and obligations of science, it can demand the liberties and freedom of science." In France especially, critics such as Champfleury (whose *Le Réalisme* appeared the same year as Flaubert's great novel), Edmond Duranty, and Fernand Desnoyers gave a critical endorsement to these statements on behalf of the novel's importance and, moreover, articulated a theoretical model for the kind of fiction they had found in Balzac, Flaubert, and, to a lesser extent, Stendhal: the novelist should give an accurate and truthful account of the real world, the real world to be understood as something more or less coextensive with the contemporary, and the techniques of observation should be as detached and objective as is reasonably possible. Duranty, somewhat surprisingly, was ungenerous in his review of *Madame Bovary,* finding in it "only the great force of an arithmetician who has calculated and assembled what there can be in the way of gestures, steps, and inequalities of terrain in *given* characters, events, and landscapes." Charles-Augustin Sainte-Beuve, however, a critic who had been unsympathetic to the advances of realism, recognized the unique neutrality of tone Flaubert had achieved and by so doing gave a kind of theoretical character to authorial silence: "The author has completely abstained; he is only there to see everything, but in no corner of the novel do you get even a glimpse of his profile. The work is completely impersonal."

Where 18th-century criticism of the novel may be said to have sought to give the novel respectability, it was this notion of "impersonality" that added to the novel an almost scientific authority, although there were many critics, and novelists as well, who warned against the exaggerated claims that were being made on behalf of something that was, in the final analysis, a creative act. In a letter to Nikolai Strakhov, Fedor Dostoevskii, a novelist who was drawn to the fantastic and the uncommon, concluded that the "arid observation of everyday trivialities" was not to be regarded as realism and was, indeed, "quite the reverse," while Robert Louis Stevenson in his "A Note on Realism" (1883) argued that realism was more a method than a route to truth: "The question of realism . . . regards not in the least degree the fundamental truth, but only the technical method, of a work of art." And even acknowledged realists such as Flaubert himself, Guy de Maupassant, and Lev Tolstoi were eager to point to the necessary limitations of a method of fiction valued entirely for its fidelity to observed reality.

Despite these caveats, discussion of the novel for much of the period between 1840 and 1880 turned on the question of realism, for it was realism in fiction that, above all, reflected the spirit of the age and provided, in an era in which the social sciences were still in their infancy, the most compelling and intelligent accounts of the complex relationship between the individual and society. This is not to say, however, that novelists and critics of the novel had entirely abandoned the claims of the romance. The American novel of the mid–19th century was particularly resistant to the encroachments of realism, partly because of the relative infancy of the novel form in the United States, but also because of a deeply ingrained puritanical distaste of the realistic treatment of the coarser aspects of human life. The fiction of Edgar Allan Poe, Nathaniel Hawthorne, and Herman Melville evinces a surprising degree of ignorance of the great debates about the representation of reality that preoccupied French criticism of the novel in the 1840s and 1850s. In his preface to *The House of the Seven Gables* (1851) Hawthorne draws an intelligent distinction between the claims of the novel and the romance:

> When an author calls his work a Romance, it need hardly be observed that he wishes to claim a certain latitude, both as to its fashion and material, which he would not have felt himself entitled to assume had he professed to be writing a Novel. The latter form of composition is presumed to aim at a very minute fidelity, not merely to the possible, but to the probable and ordinary course of man's experience. The former—while, as a work of art, it must rigidly subject itself to laws, and while it sins unpardonably so far as it may swerve aside from the truth of the human heart—has fairly a right to present that truth under circumstances, to a great extent, of the writer's own choosing or creation. If he thinks fit, also, he may so manage his atmospherical medium as to bring out or mellow the lights and deepen and enrich the shadows of the picture. He will be wise, no doubt, to make a very moderate use of the privileges here stated, and, especially, to mingle the Marvellous rather as a slight, delicate, and evanescent flavour, than as any portion of the actual substance of the dish offered to the public. He can hardly be said, however, to commit a literary crime even if he disregard this caution.

Hawthorne's claims for a latitude in respect of both "fashion and material" and a freedom to mingle the marvelous with the realistic were echoed elsewhere in other novels written in English, notably in Charles Dickens' defense of "fanciful treatment," Anthony Trollope's belief that it is perfectly possible for the novelist "to be at the same time realistic and sensational," and Robert Louis Stevenson's assertion that much of the pleasure that fiction provides is akin to the imaginative play of the child, the reader being transported from quotidian reality to a world where the workings of our "fancy" plunge us into "fresh experience." What I have called the American novelists ignorance of the debates about realism is largely a matter of the stage at which the American novel had found itself, whereas the reactions of Dickens, Trollope, and Stevenson may be imputed to a strain of English empiricism in matters of literary and critical theory, a distrust of systems and formulae that manifests itself in concreteness, specificity of detail, and the exercise of the poetic imagination, as against the disinterested objectivity of the French novel.

But in Europe, especially in France, the relentless pressure to push the novel more and more toward a model of scientific objectivity and neutrality in its treatment of reality was unyielding. In the critical writings of Émile Zola, particularly those on behalf of literary naturalism, we find what is, arguably, one of the most sustained and comprehensive theoretical accounts of the novel form ever written by a major practitioner of the form itself. Only the criticism of Henry James matches it in amplitude and importance in the 19th century, although James was to offer a subtlety and sophistication in his theorizing about the novel that Zola, both intellectually and temperamentally, was unable to achieve. In his preface to *La Fortune des Rougon* (1871; *The Fortune of the Rougons*), the first novel in the Rougon-Macquart series, Zola describes the methods that he brings to the novel, presenting them in terms that owe much to Taine's emphasis on *moment* and *milieu*:

> The Rougon-Macquart—the group, the family, whom I propose to study—has as its prime characteristic the overflow of appetite, the broad upthrust of our age, which flings itself into enjoyments. Physiologically the members of this family are the slow working-out of accidents to the blood and nervous system which occur in a race after a first organic lesion, according to the environment determining in each of the individuals of this race sentiments, desires, passions, all the natural and instinctive human manifestations whose products take on the conventional names of virtues and vices. Historically they originate in the lower classes, spread out through all of contemporary society, climb to every eminence under that essentially modern impulsion which the lower classes receive on their way through the whole social body; by means of their individual dramas they thus constitute a narrative of the Second Empire from the ambuscade of the coup d'État to the betrayal at Sedan.

Zola's project is Balzacian in its historical panorama of contemporary French life, but it is now grounded in a quasi-scientific account of society and the individual temperament that derives much of its authority from evolutionary theory, especially that shaped under the influence of Charles Darwin's *The Origin of Species* (1859; published in a French translation in 1860). In *Le Roman experimental* (1880; *The Experimental Novel*) Zola elaborates his approach to the novel into a broad theoretical essay in which he asserts that "the naturalistic evolution, which is the main current of our age, is gradually drawing all manifestations of human intelligence into a single scientific course" and, following the example set by Claude Bernard's *Introduction à l'étude de la médecine experimentale* (1865), he insists on the capacity of "the experimental method" to provide a knowledge both of physical life and of "passional and intellectual life," construing the novel as the final stage of a journey that leads "from chemistry to physiology, and then from physiology to anthropology and sociology."

Zola's theory of the novel is vitiated by the obvious limitations placed on fiction by an appeal to models drawn from the biological and physical sciences, as well as by his innocence (although it may be disingenuousness on his part) as to the ontological differences between science and art. But the influence of his theory of the naturalistic novel was so pervasive that very little criticism of the realistic novel in the late 19th century is untainted by his "discoveries." Indeed, insofar as Zola lends powerful support to the view that works of literature might have a social utility, many critics may be said to have adopted the naturalist manifesto, despite our reluctance to admit them as true defenders of the faith. The Russian critic Vissarion Belinskii, for example, wrote on behalf of an almost puritanical commitment to the place of truth in art and saw the novelist's duty as one in-

eluctably bound up with the denunciation of falsehood and insincerity. In France itself the critical writings of Edmond de Goncourt and Guy de Maupassant seek to defend naturalism against its detractors, and in Germany Heinrich and Julius Hart did much to promote Zola's methods for the nationalistic naturalism that was to emerge in the writings of Gerhard Hauptmann and Arno Holz (for example, in their "Für und gegen Zola" ["For and Against Zola"], in *Kritische Waffengange* [1882]). While the English novel remained relatively unperturbed by the debates about naturalism (one of the few important essays by a contemporary English critic on naturalism is Edmond Gosse's "The Limits of Realism in Fiction" [*Forum* 9 (June 1890)], which contains much cogent commentary on the necessary selectiveness of the novel and on the fallacy of considering fictional representation to be analagous to photography), the novel in the United States and the criticism it engendered was more receptive to Zola's theories. The critical writings of novelists such as William Dean Howells, Jack London, Frank Norris, and Theodore Dreiser place great emphasis on the unsentimental and scientific treatments of everyday life, even though they give a characteristically "American" register to them. But American naturalism was, in essence, more a movement in the history of ideas than a literary movement, and little significant criticism of the novel emerged from it.

In his review of Zola's *Nana* (1880; *Nana*) Henry James trenchantly comments that the "only business of nauturalism is to be—natural, and therefore, instead of saying of *Nana* that it contains a great deal of filth, we should simply say of it that it contains a great deal of nature." James' rejection of the model offered by Zola is one moment among many in his criticism of the novel in which he seeks a compromise between the demands for realism and the limitations of naturalistic reductiveness. James saw the novel as an instrument for depicting real life, and he commended *Madame Bovary* for its "revelation of what the imagination may accomplish under a powerful impulse to mirror the unmitigated realities of life." His model of the novel was more that of Flaubert and Ivan Turgenev than that of Zola, and in his extensive criticism of both individual novelists and the novel form in general (notably in his prefaces to his own works) he raises consideration of the novel as an art form to a new level of theoretical sophistication. James felt that it was from Flaubert that he could learn the most about fiction, for Flaubert was, above all, committed to the position that fiction was an art and, therefore, like any other art it involved techniques and principles that could be described, in effect, abstractly and that when described could be consulted as a kind of manual from which others might learn. It was in this way, as Stephen Hazell (1978) points out, that James was to win for the novel "the seriousness of attention which had previously been largely reserved for the long-standing literary forms, poetry and drama."

In his influential essay "The Art of Fiction" (1948) James speaks of the novel as "in its broadest definition a personal, a direct impression of life; that, to begin with, constitutes its value, which is greater or less according to the intensity of the impression." This is a statement of realism, but James' realism is more psychological than material, more a matter of perception and understanding than a matter of external detail or local color. For James the novel is a "living thing," something organic. Distinctions between novels are entirely matters of evaluation, for "there are bad novels and good novels . . . that is the only distinction in which I see any meaning." Whereas the 19th century began with much agitated debate about the distinctions to be drawn between epic, novel, and romance, James ends it with a dismissal of such discriminations: "The novel and romance, the novel of incident and that of character—these clumsy separations appear to me to have been made by critics and readers for their own convenience, and to help them out of some of their occasional queer predicaments, but to have little reality or interest for the producer, from whose point of view it is of course that we are attempting to consider the art of fiction." Subject matter, moreover, is something that should little exercise us, for "We must grant the artist his subject, his idea, his *donnée*: our criticism is applied only to what he makes of it." The matter of selection, James asserts, "will be sure to take care of itself, for it has a constant motive behind it. That motive is simply experience. As people feel life, so they will feel the art that is most closely related to it. This closeness of relation is what we should never forget in talking of the effort of the novel." James now sees the mirroring of "the unmitigated realities of life" as a matter of moral purpose, for the morality of fiction lies not in some didactic strain of realism whereby the novelist's evaluation of what he depicts is imposed, as if from above, on the reader (James resisting the moralizing and sentimentalizing tone of Victorian fiction) but in the reader's own moral apprehension of the entire world that the novel enacts. The consequence of this organic sense of how the novel depicts reality, and, indeed, the very much larger sense of what goes into reality that James' criticism invites, led to what F.R. Leavis saw as a "disproportionate interest in technique" (*The Great Tradition*, 1948) and with it a preoccupation with "a technique the subtleties and elaborations of which are not sufficiently controlled by a feeling for value and significance in living."

In his prefaces written for the New York edition of his novels (1907–09; collected in *The Art of the Novel*, 1934) James comments exhaustively on the technical matters that must necessarily exercise any novelist. These comments, along with those in his critical essays and reviews, presented a major development in both the criticism and theory of the novel. James considers genesis, plot, story, point of view, control of distance, characterization, middles, endings, and so on not in an inert or scientific sense but as indispensable tools that enable the novelist to capture life. Before James, the novelist convinced him- or herself that the novel was a transparent window on life; after James, theoretical innocence of this kind became more and more unsustainable, for while the novel does, indeed, tell a story (a sentiment strongly echoed in E.M. Forster's *Aspects of the Novel*, 1927), there is hidden behind it another story, the story of its creation, as James writes: "There is the story of one's hero, and then, thanks to the intimate connexion of things, the story of one's story itself. I blush to confess it, but if one's a dramatist one's a dramatist, and the later imbroglio is liable on occasion to strike me as really the more objective of the two." It is this emphasis on the creative act itself, as much as the technical commentary on how the act realizes itself as art, that makes James' criticism important for other practitioners, in particular those associated with the era of high modernism. James marks the watershed between the certitudes of 19th-century realism and its offshoot, naturalism, and the modern novel. It is a Jamesean perspective that sustains the conception of fiction Joseph Conrad articulates in the opening lines of his preface to *The Nigger of the Narcissus* (1897): "A work that aspires, however humbly, to

the condition of art should carry its justification in every line. And art itself may be defined as the single-minded attempt to render the highest kind of justice to the visible universe, by bringing to light the truth, manifold and one, underlying its every aspect." For Conrad the novelist's task, "which I am trying to achieve is, by the power of the written word to make you hear, to make you feel—it is, before all, to make you *see*. That—and no more, and it is everything!" These are sentiments James would endorse, as would those modernists such as Ford Madox Ford, Virginia Woolf, F. Scott Fitzgerald, and William Faulkner who, among others, learned so much from the James-Conrad "axis" that determined much of the fictional innovation of the period between 1890 and 1930. In his review of Conrad's *Chance* (1913) James noted how Conrad's "first care . . . is expressly to posit or set up a reciter, a definite responsible intervening first person singular, possessed of infinite sources of reference, who immediately proceeds to set up another, to the end that this other may conform again to the practice, and that even at that point the bridge over to the creature, or in other words to the situation or the subject, the thin 'produced,' shall, if the fancy takes it, once more and yet once more glory in a gap." Despite James' syntactical complexities we recognize the description of the modernist novel—narrators folded inside other narrators, narratives that thrive on incompleteness, that "glory in a gap." It is with James, therefore, and perhaps also the brief pieces collected in Marcel Proust's *Contre Sainte-Beuve* (1954; *Against Sainte-Beuve*), that criticism of the novel looks forward to the 20th century.

HENRY CLARIDGE

See also English Novel (19th-century sections); Epic and Novel; French Novel (19th-century sections); Henry James; Mimesis; Naturalism; Novel and Romance: Etymologies; Genre Criticism; Historical Novel; Historical Writing and the Novel; Realism; Reviewers and the Popular Press; Romance; Romantic Novel; Science and the Novel; Sir Walter Scott; Verse Narrative

Further Reading

Allott, Miriam, editor, *Novelists on the Novel*, London: Routledge and Kegan Paul, and New York: Columbia University Press, 1959

Becker, George J., editor, *Documents of Modern Literary Realism*, Princeton, New Jersey: Princeton University Press, 1963

Furst, Lilian R., and Peter N. Skrine, *Naturalism*, London: Methuen, 1971

Graham, George Kenneth, *English Criticism of the Novel, 1865–1900*, Oxford: Clarendon Press, 1965

Grant, Damian, *Realism*, London: Methuen, 1970; New York: Methuen, 1981

Hazell, Stephen, editor, *The English Novel: Developments in Criticism since Henry James*, London: Macmillan, 1978

Howells, William Dean, *Criticism and Fiction*, New York: Harper, and London: Osgood, McIlvaine, 1891

James, Henry, *The Art of the Novel*, New York and London: Scribner, 1934

James, Henry, *The Future of the Novel: Essays on the Art of Fiction*, New York: Vintage, 1956

Levin, Harry, *The Gates of Horn: A Study of Five French Realists,* New York: Oxford University Press, 1963

Mayo, Robert D., *The English Novel in the Magazines, 1740–1815,* Evanston, Illinois: Northwestern University Press, 1962

Proust, Marcel, *Against Sainte-Beuve and Other Essays,* edited by John Sturrock, London and New York: Penguin, 1988

Sage, Victor, editor, *The Gothic Novel: A Casebook,* London: Macmillan, 1990

Stang, Richard, *The Theory of the Novel in England, 1850–1870,* London: Routledge and Kegan Paul, and New York: Columbia University Press, 1959

Vogue, E.-M. de, *Le Roman russe,* Paris: Plon-Nourrit, 1886

Weinberg, Bernard, *French Realism: The Critical Reaction, 1830–1870,* New York and London: Modern Language Association of America, 1937

Zola, Émile, *Le Roman experimental,* Paris: Charpentier, 1880; as *The Experimental Novel,* New York: Cassell, 1893

Critics and Criticism

20th Century

As the century closes, the gulf seems wider than ever between two critical camps. The first consists of a dominant minority of cutting-edge academics who practice a rigorous, occasionally esoteric, often politicized, and undeniably jargonistic mix of critical approaches that developed largely in Europe and are referred to generally as "theory." The other camp consists of the academic majority, who are content to teach literature much as they were taught it by their own professors, offering an eclectic mix of biography, close reading, impressionism, and borrowings from critics with marquee names (including, of course, many theorists). Most students, literary journalists and reviewers, trade editors, and lay readers belong to this second group as well.

Thanks to its activism, the theory group gets most of the attention these days, with the result that, to observers both inside and outside the academy, the terms "criticism" and "theory" have become identical. But criticism has always consisted of both theory, which concerns itself with the function of literature, and poetics, which deals with craft. Plato offers a theory of art in *The Republic,* where philosophers rule as arbiters of truth and beauty and from which the less rational poets are exiled; Aristotle's *Poetics,* on the other hand, deals with the necessary ingredients of a successful play. More recently, Ralph Waldo Emerson's essay "The Poet" (1844) is a classic example of theory in its call for literary nationalism, whereas Edgar Allan Poe offers a poetics in "The Philosophy of Composition" (1846), a kind of recipe for effective poem construction.

Twentieth-century critics continue to work this same venerable field that is marked off by theory at one boundary and poetics at the other. Many of the most influential critics practice both types of criticism, as is the case with Henry James, the last great critic of the 19th century, the first great one of the 20th, and the source of ideas and techniques that will continue to shape both fiction and criticism in the years to come. James was also the first truly international American critic, as much at home with the works of Anthony Trollope, Gustave Flaubert, and Ivan Turgenev as those of Nathaniel Hawthorne. In the 18 prefaces to the New York Edition of his collected fiction (1907–09), James approaches fiction with a craftsman's rigor in his discussions of time, place, narration, and other technical matters. Clearly, however, James' poetics grow out of his theory of the novel, described earliest in "The Art of Fiction" (1884) as an elastic form capable of conveying a sense of deeply felt life as long as both writer and reader bring great force of mind to bear on it. For most of the 20th century, the most important criticism of the novel included both theory and poetics in varying proportion, with critics not only describing the nature and role of the novel but also suggesting—sometimes subtly, sometimes strongly—how the novelist should write.

In calling for a more formalistic attitude toward the novel, James was reacting against the late-Victorian moralism that often valued a work of fiction more for its piety than its aesthetics. Naturally, the next generation included critics disturbed by what they saw as too much formalism, an art-for-art's-sake standard unchecked by a proper concern with ethics. The so-called New Humanism, a conservative movement in American philosophy and literary criticism in the 1920s, turned away from naturalism to stress the moral qualities of literature; in turn, it would give way to the New Criticism and to Marxist and Freudian approaches to literature. Prominent New Humanists include Irving Babbitt, whose early work *The New Laokoön* (1910) called for classical restraint in American writing and who later attacked Theodore Dreiser and Sinclair Lewis for surrendering to modern chaos, and Paul Elmer More, author of *The Demon of the Absolute* (1928) and other works, who labeled John Dos Passos' *Manhattan Transfer* (1925) "an explosion in a cesspool."

Like many critics working from a conservative viewpoint, the New Humanists failed to appreciate the experimental work of their day, work that has since become part of the canon. This was left to such critics as Edmund Wilson, a literary polymath who took a number of critical stances during his long career, never aligning himself closely with any one school. His first major book, *Axel's Castle* (1931), treats modernism as a mating of naturalism and symbolism, as seen in the writing of James Joyce, Marcel Proust, and Gertrude Stein; a later volume, *The Shores of Light* (1952), studies the work of F. Scott Fitzgerald and his contemporaries. A novelist himself, Wilson responded to fiction on the aesthetic, psychological, and political levels, thus embodying the major trends of the next several decades of literary criticism.

The most important aesthetic approach to literature in this century is formalism, whether of the Russian kind or the Anglo-American New Critical variety. Both Russian formalists and New Critics emphasized detailed, logical examinations of a work's literary devices, but whereas the New Critics tended to distill their findings into humanistic aphorisms, the Russian formalists focused entirely on form, excluding the work's moral and cultural significance. As with every critical school, Russian formalism evolved into different camps. The Bakhtin school, so called after Mikhail Bakhtin, its most influential practitioner, viewed language as a social phenomenon. In his *Problemy tvorchestva Dostoevskogo* (1929; *Problems of Dostoevsky's Poetics*), Bakhtin observes that, whereas Tolstoi wrote a "monologic" type of novel in which the various voices are subordinated to the author's, Dostoevskii wrote a "polyphonic" or "dialogic" type in which the voices of different characters are not merged with or subordinated to the author's but maintain their own integrity.

The New Criticism is a method of close reading whose sources include the French tradition of *explication de texte*, the essays of T.S. Eliot, I.A. Richards' *Principles of Literary Criticism* (1924), and William Empson's *Seven Types of Ambiguity* (1930). Facetiously yet with some accuracy called "the lemon-squeezing school" of literary criticism, the New Criticism examines the text as an object in itself, excluding authorial biography and historical context and looking at the work's images, symbols, diction, and use of irony and other devices in its presentation of a single, complex, and well-wrought point. Influenced by Jules Laforgue and other French symbolists, Eliot and Ezra Pound were, in fact, writing a kind of poem that called for a new type of criticism; in the United States, John Crowe Ransom, Allen Tate, and other members of the so-called Fugitive group furthered the notion that a work of literature reflected neither the author's life nor grand moral themes but was instead an experience in itself.

As the New Criticism expanded, its focus shifted from the lyric poem to all genres, including the novel, just as the practice of it changed thanks to critics as different as R.P. Blackmur, who examined the European novel and those of Henry James in such works as *The Double Agent* (1935), and Yvor Winters, whose *Maule's Curse* (1938) looks at the writings of Hawthorne and Poe.

The two great popularizers of the New Criticism, Cleanth Brooks and Robert Penn Warren, first encountered each other as undergraduates at Vanderbilt University, then as Rhodes Scholars at Oxford, and then as faculty at Louisiana State University, where they founded *The Southern Review* and, as one observer noted, moved the center of literary criticism in the West "from the left bank of the Seine to the left bank of the Mississippi." Both ended up at Yale, Brooks continuing to produce important theoretical work and Warren extending the Jamesian tradition of composing both literature and commentary on it. Their joint efforts include two widely used textbooks, *Understanding Poetry* (1938) and *Understanding Fiction* (1943), and although their work has been challenged by other critical approaches, the New Criticism continues to be highly influential because the close reading method not only serves as the basis for many of the sub-

sequent approaches but also, as an examination of best-selling textbooks shows, is the one still preferred by the majority of classroom teachers.

In its purest form, the New Criticism prospered between the 1930s and 1950s, along with Freudian criticism, a sort of cousin to it, as well as a wholly unrelated Marxist criticism. Joseph Wood Krutch's *Edgar Allen Poe: A Study in Genius* (1926) is an early work of the Freudian school that uses psychoanalytic techniques to examine Poe's neuroses. In *The Triple Thinkers* (1938) and *The Wound and the Bow* (1941), Edmund Wilson looks at James, Edith Wharton, and Ernest Hemingway from a Freudian angle, emphasizing in the latter work the idea that the mature artist is compensating for a trauma received earlier in life. Other influential Freudian commentaries include Kenneth Burke's *The Philosophy of Literary Form* (1941), which sees literature as an expression of the writer's conflicts, and Leslie Fiedler's *Love and Death in the American Novel* (1960). A novelist himself, Fiedler offers here the provocative yet persuasive idea that the classic image in American culture is of two men, one light-skinned and one dark, fleeing civilization (and women) and clinging to their ideal of boyish togetherness, a paradigm that may be seen in the fiction of James Fenimore Cooper, Poe, Mark Twain, Truman Capote, and Ken Kesey as well as in today's "buddy movies." Frederick Crews used Freudian methods in *The Sins of the Fathers: Hawthorne's Psychological Themes* (1966) but later repudiated the Viennese master in *The Memory Wars: Freud's Legacy in Dispute* (1995). The Freud that Crews embraces and then spurns is a kind of mental mechanic familiar to American readers. In France, however, the criticism of Jacques Lacan and his followers adumbrates the vision of Freud the humanist, a more tentative, artistic thinker.

Just as the terms "New Critical" and "Freudian" changed in meaning as these movements spread, so, too, does "Marxist criticism" take on a variety of hues over time. A precursor of the Marxist approach may be found in Vernon Parrington's three-volume *Main Currents in American Thought* (1927–30), a historical examination of progressive American ideas and their expression in literature. Granville Hicks' *The Great Tradition* (1933), on the other hand, is a forthright measurement of American literature since the Civil War according to the standards of orthodox Marxism. Predictably, Marxist attacks and counterattacks flourished heatedly in journal essays, from the crude fulminations of Mike Gold in *The New Masses* to the subtle offerings in Philip Rahv's *Partisan Review*. Edmund Wilson incorporated less strident versions of Marxist views in his books and essays while pointing out that politics were no substitute for aesthetics. Critics as different as F.O. Matthiessen, Lionel Trilling, Irving Howe, Mary McCarthy, and Alfred Kazin, all of whom had at least one foot in the socialist or liberal camp, were flexible in blending sociopolitical commentary with humanistic literary judgments.

But "humanism," with its implications of classical order, rationalism, and morality, is a term that has largely disappeared from the vocabulary of the most visible critics of the last half of the 20th century—namely, those practitioners of the various reading strategies that fall under the heading "theory." These strategies had their origin in 1916 with the publication of Ferdinand de Saussure's *Cours de linguistique générale* (*Course in General Linguistics*). Saussure argued that words are arbitrary, that "horse" has no innate connection with the animal to which it refers. Saussureans make this point by listing the radically different nouns used in various languages to describe the same creature: English "horse," for example, but German "Pferd" and French "cheval." Here are three words which do not come close to resembling each other, yet a three-year-old would know instantly what a speaker meant were he to use one, providing the speaker and the child were conversing in the same language. To a German child, then, "horse" and "cheval" would mean nothing, which is Saussure's larger point: words mean nothing.

In the absence of meaning, what particular groups of humans share is an agreement to recognize a common code of signifiers ("horse") that apply to the signified (an equine quadruped). This agreement allows people to have conversations and read the newspaper, but all conversations and texts are coded. Thus there is no right or wrong language, no language better or worse for describing reality. Instead, all language is code and thus separate from reality. Therefore one might say that language is the only reality or at least the only one that counts. If there is no objective external reality (how can there be if there are all those different languages?), then there is only half-conscious linguistic interplay between perceiver and perceived. We humans, our world: everything is made of language and language only. Everything is a text.

From Saussure's arcane linguistic assumptions comes one universal idea that has been adapted by virtually every intellectual discipline, namely, that there is no self, that we and our institutions are inhabited by hidden, impersonal structures. The anthropologist Claude Lévi-Strauss was the first to apply Saussure's ideas outside of the field of linguistics. Structuralism, as Lévi-Strauss called his analytical method, assumed that tribal groups were governed by systems of relations of which they were unaware; unconscious but consistent laws determined the tribe's actions.

And if that is true for the South American Indians whom Lévi-Strauss studied, then it must be true for other communities as well. From structuralism, then, the ideas and methodology of Lévi-Strauss led to the present proliferation of theoretical strategies known collectively as poststructuralism, beginning with semiotics or the science of signs. Semioticians study, not just tribes and texts, but everything: Robert Scholes' *Semiotics and Interpretation* (1982) discusses not only poems, stories, and a scene from a play but also movies, bumper stickers, and, as he says delicately in his preface, "a portion of the human anatomy." This latter turns out to be the clitoris, which, as signifiers go, is uncommonly tricky. For one thing, its pronunciation is unsettled, with some dictionaries accenting the second syllable and others the first. The *Oxford English Dictionary* defines it as "a homologue of the male penis," thus defining the clitoris in terms of something other than itself, and so on.

In addition to the structuralists (Lévi-Strauss) and the semioticians (Roland Barthes), the theory group also includes philosophically-, psychoanalytically-, and economically-grounded thinkers: Heideggerians (Jacques Derrida), Nietzscheans (Michel Foucault), Freudians (Jacques Lacan), and Marxists (Lucien Goldmann). As different as these poststructuralist thinkers are, each is telling us that there is no us: that cultural structures or the media or corrupt Western thought or the will to power or the unconscious mind or bogus economic systems make us what we are. Or what we seem to be, since, in fact, we are not.

To the general reader, David Lodge's novel *Nice Work* (1988) offers a useful introduction to deconstruction, the most famous (or infamous) of the various poststructural strategies. Lodge's novel tells the story of an unlikely affair between two very different characters, the businessman Vic Wilcox and an *au courant* academic, Robyn Penrose. Robyn is so up-to-date that she believes the whole idea of character to be "a bourgeois myth, an illusion created to reinforce the ideology of capitalism." It is no accident that the idea of the literary character developed simultaneously with the rise of capitalism, since "both are expressions of a secularised Protestant ethic, both dependent on the idea of an autonomous individual self who is responsible for and in control of his/her own destiny, seeking happiness and fortune in competition with other autonomous selves." But Robyn knows that "there is no such thing as the 'self' on which capitalism and the classic novel are founded—that is to say, a finite, unique soul or essence that constitutes a person's identity; there is only a subject position in an infinite web of discourses—the discourses of power, sex, family, science, religion, poetry, etc."

These Derridean principles work well for Robyn Penrose in the academy, but they are put to the test when she meets Vic Wilcox and they begin their affair. Vic is intelligent if uninitiated; his problem is that he is an essentialist, one who believes each of us is an essence that exists independent of language, whereas Robyn believes in language alone. The lovers never do fully understand each other—or at least Vic never fully understands Robyn. When they are in bed together and he puts his hand between her legs, Robyn tells Vic that "'the discourse of romantic love pretends that your finger and my clitoris are extensions of two unique individual selves who need each other and only each other and cannot be happy without each other for ever and ever'." "'That's right'," says Vic. "'I love your silk cunt with my whole self, for ever and ever.'" Fictional businessman Vic Wilcox is not as ambiguous about the female anatomy as real-life theorist Robert Scholes, and even Robyn Penrose is described as "not unmoved by this declaration."

But of course the affair is doomed, although not before author Lodge dramatizes some important ideas in a manner that is comical yet sympathetic to both old-fashioned thinking and newer approaches such as deconstruction—or he would have had such a creature as "author Lodge" ever existed. In the earlier discussion of capitalism and its relation to the delusional concept of character (which, to a deconstructionist, does not exist), Lodge's narrator observes that "by the same token, there is no such thing as an author" and that, instead, "every text is a product of intertextuality, a tissue of allusions to and citations of other texts; and, in the famous words of Jacques Derrida (famous to people like Robyn, anyway), *'il n'y a pas de hors-texte,'* there is nothing outside the text."

Derrida was one of a group of thinkers representing the various schools of theory who appeared at a 1966 Johns Hopkins University symposium called "The Language of Criticism and the Sciences of Man." This symposium was the historical event that, in the course of a few days, changed permanently the reading, teaching, and writing of literature in the United States. In that instance, the Hopkins campus became the Plymouth Rock for the arrival in America of "theory," most of whose founding fathers were there: Goldmann, Barthes, Lacan, Tzvetan Todorov, and, chiefly, Derrida, who gave a talk entitled "Structure, Sign, and Play in the Discourse of the Human Sciences" (see Macksay and Donato, 1970).

His pronouncement that "there is nothing outside of the text" encapsulates one of deconstruction's most controversial doctrines. After all, how announce to an ambitious novelist or poet "The Death of the Author," to use the title of Roland Barthes' 1977 essay that serves as a lightning rod for so much antideconstructionist sentiment? How tell a writer, especially one who has already received recognition of some kind and is beginning to think of making a career of authorship, "You do not exist"? To answer that question requires a look at the Barthes essay as well as one by Michel Foucault that is perhaps less well-known yet more applicable, at least from the practicing novelist's viewpoint.

Barthes begins with a sentence from Honoré de Balzac's short story "Sarrasine" in which a narrator comments on the thoughts of a castrato disguised as a woman. Barthes then wonders who is speaking: the hero? The Balzac who is thinking of his own experience with women? The authorial Balzac who is compelled to say something literary? A universal voice? The voice of romantic psychology? "We shall never know," says Barthes, "for the good reason that writing is the destruction of every voice, of every point of origin."

From this promising and pointedly analytical beginning Barthes descends into an impressionistic dismissiveness, referring to a creature called "the scriptor" who succeeds the author and who has neither "passions, humors, feelings, impressions," but rather an "immense dictionary from which he draws a writing that can know no halt; life never does more than imitate the book, and the book itself is only a tissue of signs. . . ." Or, as Derrida says, *il n'y a pas de hors-texte*. It would be possible, of course, to think that, if there is indeed nothing outside the text, then at least writers are free to write the text themselves. But as Robert Scholes says, an author is not "a fully unified individuality [sic] freely making esthetic choices."

Foucault extends the best of Barthes' argument in an essay entitled "What Is an Author?" (1969). It will not do to "repeat the empty affirmation that the author has disappeared," says Foucault; "instead, we must locate the space left empty by the author's disappearance, follow the distribution of gaps and breaches, and watch for the openings that this disappearance uncovers." After all, "Everyone knows that, in a novel narrated in the first person, neither the first person pronoun, nor the present indicative refer exactly either to the writer or to the moment in which he writes, but rather to an alter ego whose distance from the author varies, often changing in the course of the work." Coining the phrase "author-function," Foucault offers a somewhat inelegant yet useful substitute for Barthes' "scriptor": "It would be just as wrong to equate the author with the real writer as to equate him with the fictitious speaker; the author-function is carried out and operates in the scission itself, in this division and distance." Somewhere between author Herman Melville and his narrator Ishmael is the author-function that wrote *Moby-Dick,* then.

An important corollary to deconstruction's assertion that writing is more intertextual pastiche than authorial creation is the belief that all writing, especially realism, is inherently repressive and supportive of established power. In *Tristes Tropiques* (1955), for example, Claude Lévi-Strauss argues that "the primary function of written communication is to facilitate slavery." Louis Althusser identifies "good books," in his essay "Ideology and Ideological State Apparatuses" (1970), as similar in function to the family, the army, and the church, all mechanisms that assist the state in self-replication. The realistic novel is an especially repressive tool, as Catherine Belsey says in *Critical Practice* (1980), because it reproduces reality without questioning it. And in *The Novel and the Police* (1988), D.A. Miller calls Anthony Trollope, usually considered the most genteel of novelists, "terroristic" in his implicit approval of Victorian behavior. Clearly there is a sharp distinction between the attitudes of these critics and those who still find reading a liberating activity.

In recent years, many critics dissatisfied with what they see as the closed and private world of deconstructive readings have taken up the New Historicism, which, in opposition to traditional historiography, tends to look beyond the names of politicians and dates of battles to discover the "true," hidden, and often subversive history that gives shape to literature. A New Historical reading of Henry James' *The Portrait of a Lady* (1881), for example, might focus on the ways in which 19th-century economic trends shaped the novel. Although the Civil War had settled the question of overt ownership of human beings, the rise of monopoly capitalism made the buying and selling of labor power, of men and women, more prevalent; thinkers as diverse as Henry David Thoreau and Karl Marx argued against the suppression of the individual under industrial capitalism. In his prefaces to *The Portrait of a Lady,* James allies himself with capitalism by depicting the writer as a businessman trafficking in the products he creates. James is the owner, then, of his character and speaks in his preface of the joy of "possession." Yet, a New Historical reader might point out, he also negates his self-presentation of the writer as capitalist. James is too much the partisan of Isabel Archer and the enemy of her controlling husband, Gilbert Osmond, to be comfortable with his own image as owner and manipulator of others, and this authorial ambivalence shows in the novel's inconclusive finish.

Another important 20th-century school of criticism, reader-response criticism, focuses on neither the author nor the text but the reader. Reader-response can be so subjective that it is sometimes called the anti-theory of literary theories; for that reason, many critics inclined in this direction prefer what they call reader-reception theory, which goes beyond one person's response to examine how an ideal reader should respond to a given text. For example, in *Der Akt des Lesens: Theorie ästhetischer Wirkung* (1976; *The Act of Reading*), Wolfgang Iser argues that a novel is "constituted" by a reader who fills in "blanks" left by the novelist; seeking neither to bore nor to distress the reader, the novelist leaves gaps for the reader to account for, thus insuring the reader's full and pleasurable participation.

The erasure of the author, one of deconstruction's central tenets, has been received with varying degrees of cordiality in the United States. Paul de Man's *Blindness and Insight* (1971) supports the idea that fiction is total artifice, cut off from any moral or even representational value. But de Man was a Belgian émigré who turned out to have an unsavory past with Nazi connections, as David Lehman points out in *Sign of the Times: Deconstruction and the Fall of Paul de Man* (1991). Harold Bloom, a Yale colleague of de Man and a critic with ties to deconstruction, is too various in his interpretive approaches to be comfortable in any single niche. Bloom's influential *The Anxiety of Influence* (1973) argues that each writer is a Freudian mis-reader of his literary ancestors, making new books from his misunderstandings of previous ones.

Predictably, many American feminist critics, so-called "queer theory" specialists, African-American critics, and others concerned with gender, sexual orientation, race, and ethnicity are resistant to the idea that there is no such thing as a self. Kate Millet's *Sexual Politics* (1970) is a visceral response to the sexism of such male novelists as Henry Miller and Norman Mailer, a line of argument furthered by Sandra Gilbert and Susan Gubar in *The Madwoman in the Attic* (1979), whose dominant image is of woman marginalized, as Mrs. Rochester is by her controlling husband in Charlotte Brontë's *Jane Eyre* (1847). In France, Julia Kristeva and Hélène Cixous have built on Lacan's reading of Freud to develop a feminist criticism that promotes the linking of female sexuality with creative openness.

Of course, just as "masculinist" readings have generated feminist readings, so too has an anti-feminist approach evolved, most notably in the writings of Camille Paglia, whose scholarly *Sexual Personae: Art and Decadence from Nefertiti to Emily Dickinson* (1990) is now probably less well known than the popularly oriented *Vamps and Tramps: New Essays* (1994). A diehard Madonna fan, Paglia presents herself as a pro-pornography lesbian who nonetheless recommends Jane Austen novels over the current crop of what she describes as "crappy lesbian movies." Prominent African-American critics include Darwin T. Turner, Houston A. Baker, Toni Morrison (known best for her novels but also the author of *Playing in the Dark: Whiteness and the Literary Imagination,* 1992), and Henry Louis Gates, Jr., author of the groundbreaking *The Signifying Monkey: A Theory of Afro-American Literary Criticism* (1988) and the critic largely responsible for repopularizing Zora Neale Hurston's *Their Eyes Were Watching God* (1937). There is even a return to, if not the hidebound conservatism of the New Humanists, at least a concern with values in books like novelist John Gardner's *On Moral Fiction* (1978).

Thus criticism is too diverse in the last years of the 20th century to be restricted only to "theory," with its narrow French poststructuralist implications, even though manuscripts are turned down by university presses every day and job candidates rejected for being insufficiently "theoretical." There is an air of religious fundamentalism about much theory, an all-or-nothing attitude that separates the diehards from those who want to take from theory what is useful and retain a healthy scepticism toward the rest.

For better or worse, history may favor the more moderate critics in a world where education is universal, information cheap, and consumers prone to eclecticism. At present, the committed reader is likely to be something of a *bricoleur* (sometimes translated not quite accurately as "handyman"), to borrow a term from Derrida. The verb *bricoler* actually means to tinker or putter about, with the implication of assembling disparate objects for one's own pleasure. Not surprisingly, criticism is becoming eclectic as well. Indeed, there is already a so-called *moi* criticism, taken up by such works as Frank Lentricchia's *The Edge of Night* (1994) and Eve Kosofsky Sedgwick's *Tendencies* (1994), which combine literary criticism with the self-advertisement condemned (even if often practiced) by old-school deconstruction-

ists. These two authors, like others of this only somewhat facetiously titled school, are serious and self-indulgent at the same time. Mainly, though, they dramatize the vital role of the living, breathing reader in any literary transaction, a role too often overlooked in the proliferation of arcane systems.

DAVID KIRBY

See also Dialogism; Feminist Criticism of Narrative; Formalism; Genre Criticism; Ideology and the Novel; Marxist Criticism of the Novel; Mimesis; Narrative Theory; Narratology; Politics and the Novel; Postmodernism; Postcolonial Narrative and Criticism of the Novel; Psychoanalytical Models of Narrative and Criticism of the Novel; Realism; Reviewers and the Popular Press; Structuralism, Semiotics, and the Novel

Further Reading

Adams, Hazard, and Leroy Searle, editors, *Critical Theory Since 1965,* Tallahassee: Florida State University Press, 1986

Baldick, Chris, *Criticism and Literary Theory 1890 to the Present,* London and New York: Longman, 1996

Castronovo, David, "American Literary Criticism 1914 to Present," in *Encyclopedia of American Literary Criticism,* edited by Steven Serafin, New York: Continuum, 1997

Davis, Robert Con, and Ronald Schleifer, editors, *Contemporary Literary Criticism: Literary and Cultural Studies,* New York and London: Longman, 1986; 3rd edition, 1994

Gilmore, Michael T., "The Commodity World of *The Portrait of a Lady,*" *New England Quarterly* 59 (1986)

Kirby, David, "The New Candide, or What I Learned in the Theory Wars," *Virginia Quarterly Review* 69 (1993)

Lodge, David, editor, *20th Century Literary Criticism: A Reader,* London: Longman, 1972

Lodge, David, editor, *Modern Criticism and Theory: A Reader,* London and New York: Longman, 1988

Lynn, Steven, *Texts and Contexts: Writing About Literature with Critical Theory,* New York: HarperCollins, 1994

Macksey, Richard, and Eugenio Donato, editors, *The Languages of Criticism and the Sciences of Man: The Structuralist Controversy,* Baltimore: Johns Hopkins University Press, 1970

Righter, William, *The Myth of Theory,* Cambridge and New York: Cambridge University Press, 1994

Scanlan, Margaret, "Terrorism and the Realistic Novel: Henry James and *The Princess Casamassima,*" *Texas Studies in Literature and Language* 34 (Fall 1992)

Selden, Raman, *A Reader's Guide to Contemporary Literary Theory,* Lexington: University Press of Kentucky, and Brighton: Harvester, 1985; 4th edition, London: Prentice-Hall, and New York: Harvester Wheatsheaf, 1997

Winchell, Mark Royden, *Cleanth Brooks and the Rise of Modern Criticism,* Charlottesville: University Press of Virginia, 1996

Cry, the Beloved Country by Alan Paton

1948

As the emergence of magic realism in South America clearly suggests, literary developments in the 20th century often have been closely bound up with sociopolitical realities. This general proposition has been especially true of South Africa, described half-jokingly by Roy Campbell in 1928 as "renowned both far and wide / For politics and little else beside."

To most South African writers, especially novelists and dramatists, the publication of *Cry, the Beloved Country* was a watershed. Its combination of aesthetic craftsmanship and sociomoral seriousness and commitment established a standard that demanded respect. It was of course mainly because of the nature of the apartheid regime, but also to some extent because of the example Paton set in this novel, that for more than 40 years almost all South African writing was politically engaged.

Cry, the Beloved Country made a considerable impact in the United States (where it was first published) and in South Africa, but it was also fairly widely read in Britain and other countries (it was translated into nine languages). What is most distinctive about the novel is the way in which it succeeds in combining an essentially simple but moving central story with a broad consideration of South Africa's main racial and social issues as seen by an alert liberal in the late 1940s.

Two men from different parts of South Africa's racially divided society—rural neighbors who have never met—are brought together and later begin to work together as a result of a tragedy that strikes them both: James Jarvis' only son Arthur is murdered in Johannesburg by the Rev. Stephen Kumalo's only son Absalom. The story is told realistically, but it also has archetypal, parable-like features that are emphasized by Paton's style, which is often stark and direct, with some biblical resonances. The main narrative is interspersed with passages of social comment, with vivid evocations of the reactions of ordinary South Africans to contemporary events and to the events of the story, and with authorial meditations on the implications of the realities that the book describes. The title of the book indicates the degree to which a fictional tale has been merged with an immediate, local reality.

Novels had sometimes been written in this way in the past; perhaps the most obvious example is Harriet Beecher Stowe's *Uncle Tom's Cabin* (1852), which has been thought of by some as occupying within American social and literary life a position similar to that held by *Cry, the Beloved Country* within South Africa. But in 1948 Paton's first novel, which was also something of a national epic, was perhaps particularly timely. A Western reading public that had responded enthusiastically to John Steinbeck's *The Grapes of Wrath* (1939)—which Paton had read shortly before starting this work—and to George Orwell's *Animal Farm* (1945) was clearly ready for literature that mingled fiction and fact. At the same time, while the excitements of World War II were receding, racial and social justice began emerging as significant issues, both in the United States and in South Africa. Paton and this novel have always been more widely appreciated in the United States than in any other country except South Africa. It seems safe to assert that *Cry, the Beloved Country* is one of the influences lying in the background of many of the socially conscious novels written, particularly in the United States, in the last 50 years—although no writer of any significance has attempted to imitate or develop Paton's distinctive style.

As Paton's novel has one foot in the realm of political discourse and action, its reception has to some extent varied parallel to, and in response to, the unfolding political situation. When the book was first published, its picture of the breaking down of barriers and the growth of understanding and cooperation between people of different races was regarded by many white South Africans (including those within the white nationalist government that came to power a few months after the book's publication) as either sentimental or almost revolutionary. (Paton himself became both a founding and a leading member of the Liberal Party, which the government rendered illegal in 1968.) More discriminating white readers, however, were inspired by the book, and as time went on it became acceptable to greater numbers of whites. It certainly played an important part in articulating and reinforcing a tradition of liberal tolerance, the strength of which was perhaps shown by the comparative ease with which most white South Africans accepted majority rule in 1994.

But what of black South African readers? These did not form a large constituency in 1948. Most of those who read the book when it first came out were pleased that it placed Africans at the center of the stage, but were uneasy at what seemed to be the suggestion that Stephen Kumalo's Christian forebearance was a typical African response. As the political situation became more intense in the late 1950s and the 1960s (the African National Congress was banned, Nelson Mandela and many others were imprisoned), black attitudes became more determined, and a gentle Christian-liberal solution to the country's problems—which is what the novel was often thought of as proposing—came to seem hopelessly inadequate. And in the decade and a half of open militancy, from 1975 onward, Paton's novel would have seemed laughable as reading material for those actively involved in the political struggle.

In 1990, however, when the negotiations that led to majority rule were initiated, the militant opposition had not won a simple victory. It found itself, rather to its surprise, working sincerely with its erstwhile opponents to construct a viable future for the country. In *Cry, the Beloved Country* Msimangu, a respected commentator, says, "I see only one hope for this country, and that is when white men and black men, desiring neither power nor money, but desiring only the good of their country, come together to work for it." A wheel has perhaps come full circle: although aspects of the novel seem rather dated today, *Cry, the Beloved Country* nevertheless expresses an important facet of the mood of the 1990s in South Africa.

The novel's history, then, has been much bound up with that of South Africa, and perhaps of the United States and other countries, too. But what will the novel's future be? Will it continue to sell well, as it has for nearly 50 years? Will it be read mainly as an adjunct to recent South African history? Or will it come to seem more "purely" a novel, about two families and about the haves coming to understand and work with the have-nots? If one may quote the final words of the novel, "why, that is a secret."

COLIN GARDNER

Further Reading
Alexander, Peter F., *Alan Paton: A Biography,* Oxford and New York: Oxford University Press, 1994
Baker, Sheridan, *Paton's "Cry, the Beloved Country": The Novel, the Critics, the Setting,* New York: Scribner, 1968
Callan, Edward, *Alan Paton,* New York: Twayne, 1968; revised edition, 1982
Callan, Edward, *"Cry, the Beloved Country": A Novel of South Africa,* Boston: Twayne, 1991
Daniels, Eddie, "Salute to the Memory," *Reality* 20 (July 1988)
Davies, Horton, *A Mirror for the Ministry in Modern Novels,* New York: Oxford University Press, 1959
Gardner, Colin, "Paton's Literary Achievement," *Reality* 20 (July 1988)

Cuban Novel. *See* Latin American Novel: Hispanic Caribbean; Latino-American Novel

---

Cyberpunk. *See* Science Fiction Novel

Czech Novel

Czech literature in general and the Czech novel in particular developed relatively late. In 1620, the Protestant Czechs were defeated by the Catholic Hapsburgs at the Battle of White Mountain near Prague. Bohemia, as the area was then called, was seriously ravaged by war, forcibly catholicized, and subjected to economic exploitation. The Czech language lost its official status and, with few exceptions, ceased being used as a medium of intellectual and creative discourse for almost two centuries.

At the beginning of the 19th century, a Czech nationalist movement came into being, known as the Czech National Revival. By mid-century, Czech writers had created a new literary tradition, in which poetry and later the short story were the leading genres. The first serious modern Czech fiction was written by Božena Němcová, who also wrote descriptive nonfiction pieces known as "images of national life"—folkloric descriptions of rural Czech society, which, according to the nationalists, held the essence of the national character. Němcová's fiction serves as a vehicle for her social criticism. The novels are sharply realistic in their representations of contemporary conditions, while their endings, somewhat contrived, are predicated on her social utopianism. Němcová's most important work is *Babička* (1855; *The Grandmother*), which stands halfway between the "images of

national life" and the novels. Drawing on the author's childhood memories, *Babička* paints the portrait of an archetypal rural grandmother, the absolute center of her family, who is represented as a repository of Czech virtue. The seasons function as the work's basic structural device.

Influenced by George Sand, Němcová may be called a protofeminist. Karolina Světlá similarly displayed an interest in strong women characters. Her novels of the 1860s and 1870s, set in rural northern Bohemia, are marked by gripping plots and compelling psychological analysis. *Vesnický Román* (1867; A Village Novel) explores the conflict between self and community in a general perspectivist framework that recognizes the relative nature of moral truth. Implicitly commenting on the political struggles of the time, Světlá's later work has libertarian, anti-Catholic, and nationalist overtones.

Jakub Arbes, a journalist, adopted Émile Zola's theories of scientific naturalism and wrote sprawling novels analyzing the plight of the Czech urban working class. In the 1860s and 1870s, Arbes also wrote shorter works that anticipate the modern detective novel, usually presenting a Gothic mystery that is resolved through rational analysis of clues. Introducing the use of technical knowledge and scientific reasoning into Czech literature, these works also explore Arbes' fascination with the simultaneously liberating and destructive potential of extraordinary intellectual ability. His *Svatý Xaverius* (1873; St. Xavier) is noteworthy for its refusal to provide closure for the stories it tells, anticipating some of the central concerns of literary modernism.

The work of Julius Zeyer heralds the neoromanticism of the Czech novel of the 1880s and 1890s. Dissatisfied with the banality of Bohemian life, Zeyer cultivated an interest in Czech history, Russian heroic folk poetry, the French *chanson de geste*, late medieval Christianity, and the cultural traditions of India, China, and Japan. His *Román o věrném přátelství Amise a Amila* (1880; The Romance of the Faithful Friendship of Amis and Amil), set in medieval France, is an example of what he called "restored paintings"—ancient narratives that he recast with an emphasis on stylistic embellishment and psychological analysis. Zeyer's most mature work has an autobiographical basis and grapples with the individual's duty to the nation. *Jan Maria Plojhar* (1891), set mostly in Italy, depicts the erotic and political frustrations of a middle-class dreamer who yearns for action but is immobilized by his vain search for the Absolute. The expatriate Slovak hero of *Dům u tonoucí hvězdy* (1895; The House of the Drowning Star) similarly agonizes over the predicament of his subjugated nation without being able to persuade himself to action.

Zeyer's neoromanticism reappears in the work of several historical novelists who had far less ambivalence about nationalism. The somewhat tendentious, idealized image of the Czech past of Alois Jirásek's many novels made an appeal to the sentimental patriotism of the middle class. (Ironically, his novels were later used for propaganda purposes by the Czechoslovak communists of the 1950s.) A practiced story-teller, Jirásek emulated Lev Tolstoi in his striving to combine historical accuracy and artistic integrity. The principal focus of his historical fiction is on the early 15th century and the Hussite Revolution, led by the religious reformer Jan Hus and adopted by the nationalists as an emblem of Czech heroism and drive for independence. The trilogies *Mezi proudy* (1887–90; Between the Currents), *Proti všem* (1893; Against Everyone), and *Bratrstvo* (1898–1908; The Brethren) are all set in Hussite times. But Jirásek also wrote about more recent periods, with one novel, *Temno* (1913–15; Darkness), set in the 17th century, and another, the five-volume *F.L. Věk* (1888–1906), tracing the early history of the Czech National Revival through the story of a patriotic small-town merchant.

Zikmund Winter worked on a more modest scale, focusing on individual characters. A gripping study of an individual's response to authoritarian pressure, *Mistr Kampanus* (1909; Master Kampanus) deals with life at Prague University in the cataclysmic year 1620.

A group of realists followed close on the heels of the historical novelists. Josef Holeček, Jan Herben, Karel Václav Rais, Teréza Nováková, and Karel Klostermann all wrote in the regionalist vein. The most monumental work to emerge from the realist group is Holeček's *Naši* (1898–1930; Our People), in 12 volumes. Combining both the historical and regional predilections of the Czech nationalists, it traces the rise of the Czech peasant class in the mid–19th century through its chronicle of life in a south Bohemian village. A massive tribute to the peasantry, the novel also bears witness to the gradual resurrection of the country after centuries of oppression and dependency. The other realists espouse a less sanguine vision of rural life. Nováková's work depicts country visionaries whose struggles to realize their religious and political ideals end largely in failure. Rais' short stories highlight conflicts between older and younger members of rural families, telling stories of the mistreatment of the old by their greedy younger relatives. Rais moved away from his regionalist focus in *Kalibův zločin* (1892; *Kaliba's Crime*), which has an urban setting and is marked by an incipient naturalism.

A reaction against nationalism set in before the end of the 19th century, resulting in the *Manifesto of the Czech Modern Movement* of 1895. Signed by young writers and poets, the manifesto proclaimed their right to criticize, to choose themes and style, and to focus on the expression of emotion—all without regard for the nationalist agenda. The manifesto served its intended purpose: although older writers continued to write nationalist works, the younger generation was freed from the requirement to serve the nation in their fiction.

The first decades of the 20th century saw a variety of impressionist novels, the most important of which were written by the poet Fráňa Šrámek. His *Stříbrný vítr* (1910; The Silver Wind) tells the story of an idealistic young student confronted by small-town brutality, narrow-mindedness, and hypocrisy. Šrámek's sensual novel *Tělo* (1919; Body) is a protest against the war. Traces of naturalism as well as impressionism are to be found in Vilém Mrštík's autobiographical *Pohádka máje* (1892; A May Fairy Tale), an idyllic love story, and *Santa Lucia* (1893), a tragic tale of a student lost in an indifferent, alien environment.

Karel Matěj Čapek-Chod was the most important Czech proponent of naturalism, but his work is marked by expressionist and modernist elements as well. A strong narrative talent and an extensive knowledge of different social environments produced vivid, often ironic, evocations of Bohemian life. *Turbina* (1916; The Turbine), perhaps Čapek-Chod's most successful work, is a compassionate and amusing chronicle of the gradual disintegration of an upper-middle-class Prague family.

The independent democratic Czechoslovak Republic was founded in 1918, when the Austrian empire disintegrated. During World War I, Czech deserters and prisoners of war from the Austrian army had formed a Czechoslovak legion in Russia that became known for its spectacular military achievements and paved the way for the international recognition of the young republic at the end of the war. The novelists Rudolf Medek and Josef Kopta wrote novels celebrating the exploits of the Czech legion.

A very different perspective on the war emerges from Jaroslav Hašek's *Osudy dobrého vojáka Švejka za světové války* (1921–23; The Good Soldier Švejk). In this picaresque novel, Hašek analyzed the predicament of individuals caught up in a senseless war. Švejk negates the destructive reality that surrounds him by drowning it in incessant talk. Authorities of the newly formed Czechoslovak Republic were afraid the novel would undermine morale among the armed forces and tried to suppress it. But *The Good Soldier Švejk* became popular among ordinary people and reached a world audience through a German translation.

Hašek understood World War I as an attack on European civilization itself, and this sense of doom was shared by other postwar writers, including the expressionists Richard Weiner, Jan Weiss, Jaroslav Durych, and Ladislav Klíma. Weiner, perhaps the most important representative of Czech expressionism, wrote complex stories that present human existence as an incomprehensible mystery. His later work shares traits with surrealism. Weiss, one of the founders of Czech science fiction, also wrote expressionist novels with surrealist overtones. For instance, *Dům o 1000 patrech* (1929; The 1000-Story Building) is a fantastic narrative set in a nightmarish skyscraper that symbolizes the structure of society. The story ends in the building's collapse. A Catholic, Durych used expressionism to convey his extreme religious feeling, in such works as *Bloudění* (1929; Wandering), a trilogy set in the 17th century.

Regarded by contemporary Czech critics as an important contributor to the development of modern European fiction, Klíma, who considered himself a philosopher, was inspired by the work of Bishop Berkeley, Arthur Schopenhauer, and Friedrich Nietzsche. He considered the independent will as the only reality and created absurd, horrifying visions of life to negate the outside world. Much of his work was written before World War I but subsequently lost. His most important surviving novel is *Utrpení knížete Sternenhocha* (1928; The Suffering of Prince Sternenhoch), which depicts the world as a repulsive prison full of sadomasochistic, bestial people. The text is punctuated with philosophical reflections on death, immortality, and eternity.

Between 1918 and 1939, Czech novelists experimented with the genre in many ways. The fantastic fiction of the expressionists and others was an attempt to gain a better understanding of contemporary social issues. In the 1920s, new forms were created that made use of journalistic and documentary techniques and analyzed mass social movements.

Karel Čapek, perhaps the most important writer of the interwar period and a journalist, essayist, and playwright, first introduced the experiments with nonfiction forms. Čapek was a political moderate, and most of his novels comment on national and global politics. Stylistically, the most salient feature of his work is his mixing of distinct rhetorical forms. Not only did he often use science-fiction themes as a point of departure for the analysis of moral and philosophical problems, but he also relied extensively on documentary material—some of it fictitious—to structure his novels. *Továrna na absolutno* (1922; The Absolute at Large), for instance, is a caustic commentary on religious intolerance and Czech politics that incorporates a series of fictitious newspaper articles. *Válka s mloky* (1936; War with the Newts), a satire on the immorality and self-serving short-sightedness of international diplomacy and big business, uses newspaper articles, political declarations, scholarly treatises, and news agency reports to make its point. Although it reacted to issues of Čapek's day, the novel is still surprisingly relevant. Čapek's *Krakatit* (1924; Krakatit) highlights a different aspect of international politics, foreshadowing the invention of the nuclear bomb. The invention is stolen from the inventor, who tries to recover it in a nightmarish journey.

Whereas *The Absolute at Large, War with the Newts,* and *Krakatit* are modernist in form, other novels by Čapek display the high modernist philosophical concern with the nature of truth. His trilogy consisting of *Hordubal* (1933; Hordubal), *Povětroň* (1934; Meteor), and *Obyčejný život* (1934; An Ordinary Life) experiments with point of view, illuminating the same facts from different perspectives. *Hordubal* describes the investigation of a murder that, rather than solve the crime, manages only to show how irrecoverable the past is. In *Meteor*, three different witnesses speculate about the life and identity of a pilot who has been found unconscious in an airplane wreck. *An Ordinary Life* suggests that authentic knowledge is the result of combining different subjective views and interpretations of the same events. The novel is the memoir of an ordinary clerk, who, in the act of writing about his life, discovers his own unrealized potential, which enables him to begin to understand the experience of others. Čapek's unfinished *Život a dílo skladatele Foltýna* (1939; The Cheat) again contrasts different views of reality, this time to create the portrait of a fraudulent composer. This novel also insists on the serious moral responsibilities of the creative artist.

The development of Čapek's fiction in the 1930s reflects the atmosphere of the time: writers enjoyed creative freedom and were in direct contact with international literary developments. Nevertheless, Czech fiction retained a unique character, nowhere more dramatically evident than in the work of Vladislav Vančura. Bold experiments with language, style, and form, Vančura's fiction shows the influence of biblical narrative, medieval literary traditions, Renaissance fiction, and the 18th-century novel, all of which he melded into an idiosyncratic narrative form with a prominent narrator. Told in fragments, *Pole orná a válečná* (1925; Ploughed Field and Battlefield) is a simultaneously lyrical and bitter evocation of the destruction of the traditional world by the apocalyptic brutality of World War I. His next, the playful *Rozmarné léto* (1926; Capricious Summer), shows the influence of the Czech avant-garde. The novel records the conversations of three middle-aged men who are all trying, unsuccessfully, to win the favors of a young woman whose beauty makes her seem the epitome of poetry. In spite of their failures, their talk is characterized by a Rabelaisian zest for life, which also speaks from *Hrdelní pře anebo Přísloví* (1930; Trial for Murder or Proverbs). Marked by a variety of linguistic experiments, the novel shows several protagonists who initially try to explain a mysterious death but then realize the futility of their endeavor and give themselves up to the enjoyment of life. The lyrical *Markéta Lazarová* (1931) celebrates the "strong passions" of the Middle Ages through a story of the strong erotic bond that forms between a woman and a man who belong to hostile families of highway robbers. It attempts to apply cinematic technique (Vančura was also a filmmaker), particularly the close-up, to verbal narrative.

Speaking of all the grand themes of love, death, treason, courage, and cowardice, *Markéta Lazarová* is a polemic against the overrefinement of 20th-century literature. A similar polemic marks *Poslední soud* (1929; The Last Judgment), which contrasts the life of the backward Ruthenians from the easternmost part of prewar Czechoslovakia with life in contemporary Prague. Vančura returned to the same conservative ideology in his *Rodina Horvathova* (1938; The Horvath Family), the first volume of an unfinished trilogy that was to analyze the social changes that had taken place in Czech society since the turn of the century. Although it is often considered his most mature work, *Rodina Horvathova* incontrovertibly idealizes tradition. Vančura's novelistic experiments formed an important point of departure for the work of Milan Kundera in the 1960s.

Less well-known novelists of the interwar years include the Jewish writer Karel Poláček and Ivan Olbracht. Poláček's tetralogy beginning with *Okresní město* (1936; A Provincial Town), a powerful criticism of the idealizations of nationalist regionalism, is a study of the stagnation, parochialism, narrow-mindedness, and immorality of small-town life, which is precipitated into further degradations by World War I. While he awaited deportation to a Nazi concentration camp, Poláček wrote an entertaining and penetrating memoir of his childhood, *Bylo nás pět* (1946; There Were Five of Us), which parodies the stilted style of primary school essays. Olbracht is chiefly notable for his use of Freudian psychology in the context of mythology and legend. *Nikola Šuhaj Loupežník* (1933; Nikola Šuhaj, Highwayman), based on a real-life Robin Hood story from Ruthenia, is a sophisticated modern myth with folklore elements.

During World War II, Czechoslovakia was occupied by Germany, and many Czech writers returned to the task of bolstering Czech national consciousness. The communist takeover in 1948 had an even more momentous effect on Czech literature: noncommunist authors were banned and sometimes imprisoned, and socialist realism became the only acceptable literary form. Václav Řezáč, who had written accomplished psychological fiction during the war, wrote two clichéd "novels of socialist construction," *Nástup* (1951; The Line-up) and *Bitva* (1954; The Battle), that were widely read in Czechoslovakia at the time. The best work of the postwar years managed to escape this straightjacket. Jiří Weil's *Život s hvězdou* (1949; Life with a Star) is about the everyday functioning of Nazi totalitarianism. The émigré Egon Hostovský wrote several novels bearing witness to the predicament of victims of political upheavals, lost in an alien, hostile world.

The 1964 republication of Josef Škvorecký's *Zbabělci* (The Cowards), which was originally published in 1958 and immediately banned, heralded the gradual return to more normal conditions. *The Cowards* is a casual, ironic, antiheroic account of the end of World War II, as seen through the eyes of a teenager. Stylistically, the work is influenced by Ernest Hemingway and jazz music. Quickly becoming a watershed, it played a liberating, demystifying role and helped to destroy the monopoly of the official communist worldview in Czech literature.

The 1960s are marked by a concerted effort on the part of Czech authors to subvert communist ideology through antiheroic, anti-ideological novels. Known as novels of disillusionment, they emphasized authenticity, pluralism, and the unpredictability of human experience, even under conditions of totalitarian oppression. The most important of these were *Sekyra* (1966; The Axe) by Ludvík Vaculík, which explores a moment of crisis in the narrator's life, and *Žert* (1967; The Joke) by Milan Kundera, which represents life under communism as a cruel joke played on humanity by an unknown Creator. Vladimír Páral examined some of the typical features of modern Western consumerism as it manifested itself in communist Czechoslovakia in such novels as *Veletrh splněných přání* (1964; The Trade Fair of Fulfilled Wishes).

These novels and their authors made a significant contribution to the achievements of the Prague Spring, a six-month period in 1968 of complete freedom of speech. After the Soviet invasion, Czechoslovakia was thrown back into a rigid totalitarianism that lasted until the fall of communism in 1989. Some 400 Czech authors who refused to cooperate with the authorities were banned. Many of them published their work in "samizdat," typewritten, clandestinely circulated copies. Others left the country. Paradoxically, the Czech novel achieved international recognition during this period.

Milan Kundera, who has lived in France since 1975, uses his Central European experience to create novels that contrast the shortcomings of life under communism with the shortcomings of life in a Western consumerist society. Perhaps the most well known is *Nesnesitelná lehkost bytí* (1985; The Unbearable Lightness of Being).

Josef Škvorecký emigrated to Canada in the early 1970s. Bittersweet tales with absurd overtones, his work bears witness to the cataclysmic events of the 20th century. *Mirákl* (1972; The Miracle Game) describes life in Czechoslovakia during the first two decades of communism. *Příběh inženýra lidských duší* (1977; The Engineer of Human Souls), an exercise in cultural misunderstanding, contrasts the traumatic experiences of Central Europeans to the often superficial lives of North Americans. Both novels are made up of skillfully interwoven multiple narrative strands.

Remaining in Czechoslovakia, Ludvík Vaculík wrote *Český snář* (1980; The Czech Dreambook). The novel, the diary of a Czech dissident harassed by the police, is precariously balanced between fact and fiction and exploits the tension between the two.

Bohumil Hrabal, cultivating a form of automatic writing, synthesized psychoanalysis, surrealism, slapstick comedy, abstract expressionism, and pub talk in his work. His novels include *Obsluhoval jsem anglického krále* (1971; I Served the King of England), *Příliš hlučná samota* (1976; Too Loud a Solitude), *Městečko ve Kterém se zastavil čas* (1978; The Little Town Where Time Stood Still). He has also written a three-volume autobiography, *Svatby v Domě* (1984; Weddings in the House), *Vita nuova* (1987; Vita nuova), and *Proluky* (1986; Vacant Sites). Most of Hrabal's work was suppressed by the communist censors when it was first written.

Toward the end of the 1980s, postmodernism made itself felt in Czech fiction. By this time, authors were writing under the influence of the harsh, pathological reality of a decomposing "post-totalitarian" communist system. Apocalyptic images of decay, cruelty, loneliness, alcoholic intoxication, drug addiction, and sexual promiscuity began to appear in the work of the younger novelists.

A typical example is furnished by Jáchym Topol's *Sestra* (1994; Sister). Taking Hrabal's "spontaneous" writing to an extreme, this long novel consists of an uncontrolled, gushing stream of lyrical passages. *Sestra* deals with the adventurous life of a group of young outsiders and their transition to the "grab-what-you-can" attitude after communism.

Another postmodernist, Jiří Kratochvil created his own idiosyncratic style, based on the local dialect of the Moravian city of Brno. His novels, *Medvědí román* (1990; The Bear Novel) and *Uprostřed nocí zpěv* (1992; Singing in the Night), subvert all novelistic conventions. Gripping narrative is often interrupted midstream, parodied, and debunked. Meaning is deliberately obscured by ambiguity. Concrete facts and locations are juxtaposed with fantastic, grotesque, and brutal scenes. The novels of Daniela Hodrová—*Podobojí* (1991; In Both Kinds), *Kukly* (1991; Masks), and *Théta* (1992)—also build complex and fantastic literary structures full of erudite allusions.

The Czech novel has always played an important role in Czech national life as an instrument of self-examination and of political commentary. However, since the fall of communism in 1989 the importance of the novel, and of literature in general, seems to have diminished. Although more titles are published in the Czech Republic than ever before, their print runs have fallen dramatically. Having lost its social function as an instrument of protest and national self-expression, the Czech novel seems also to have lost a significant section of its readership.

JAN ČULÍK

See also Good Soldier Švejk; Bohumil Hrabal; Franz Kafka; Milan Kundera

Further Reading

Cross Currents: A Yearbook of Central European Culture, Ann Arbor: Department of Slavic Languages and Literatures, University of Michigan, 1982–90

Čulík, Jan, *Knihy za ohradou: Česká literatura v exilových nakladatelstvích, 1971–1989* (Books behind the Fence: Czech Literature in Emigré Publishing Houses), Prague: Trizonia, 1991

Dokoupil, Blahoslav, and Miroslav Zelinský, editors, *Slovník českého románu, 1945–1991: 150 děl poválečné české prózy* (The Dictionary of the Czech Novel, 1945–1991: 150 Works of Postwar Czech Fiction), Ostrava: Sfinga, 1992

Dokoupil, Blahoslav, and Miroslav Zelinský, editors, *Slovník české prózy 1945–1994* (A Dictionary of Czech Prose 1945–1994), Ostrava: Sfinga, 1994

Doležel, Lubomír, *Narrative Modes in Czech Literature,* Toronto: University of Toronto Press, 1973

French, Alfred, *Czech Writers and Politics, 1945–1969,* New York: Columbia University Press, 1982

Galik, Josef, Lubomír Machala, and Eduard Petrů, editors, *Panorama české literatury* (An Outline of Czech Literature), Olomouc: Rubico, 1994

Harkins, William E., and Paul I. Trensky, editors, *Czech Literature since 1956: A Symposium,* New York: Bohemica, 1980

Holý, Jiří, *Česká literatura: Od roku 1945 do současnosti* (Czech Literature: From 1945 to the Present), Prague: Český spisovatel, 1996

Janousek, Pavel, editor, *Slovník českých spisovatelů od roku 1945, Díl I., A–L* (A Dictionary of Czech Writers from 1945, vol. 1, A–L), Prague: Brána, 1995

Kunstmann, Heinrich, *Tschechische Erzählkunst im 20. Jahrhundert,* Cologne: Böhlau, 1974

Makin, Michael, and Jindřich Toman, editors, *On Karel Čapek: A Michigan Slavic Colloquium,* Ann Arbor: Michigan Slavic Publications, 1992

Měšt'an, Antonín, *Geschichte der tschechischen Literatur im 19. und 20. Jahrhundert,* Cologne: Böhlau, 1984

Mukařovský, Jan, editor, *Dějiny české literatury I–III* (An [academic] History of Czech Literature I–III [from the beginnings to the end of the 19th century]), Prague: Nakl. československé akademie věd, 1959–61

Mukařovský, Jan, editor, *Dějiny české literatury IV: Od konce 19. století do roku 1945* (An [academic] History of Czech Literature IV [from the end of the 19th century until 1945]), completed in 1969, Prague: Viktoria, 1995

Novák, Arne, *Czech Literature,* translated from the Czech by Peter Kussi, edited with a supplement by William E. Harkins, Ann Arbor: Michigan Slavic Publications, 1976; revised edition, 1986

Rechcígl, Miroslav, editor, *Czechoslovakia Past and Present,* The Hague: Mouton, 1968

Sacher, Peter, *Tschechische Erzähler des 19. und 20. Jahrhunderts,* Zurich: Manesse, 1991

Schamschula, Walter, *Geschichte der tschechischen Literatur,* vols. 1–3, Cologne: Böhlau, 1990–97

Součková, Milada, *A Literature in Crisis: Czech literature, 1938–1950,* New York: Mid-European Studies Center, 1954

Součková, Milada, *The Czech Romantics,* S-Gravenhage: Mouton, 1958

Součková, Milada, *A Literary Satellite: Czechoslovak-Russian Literary Relations,* Chicago: University of Chicago Press, 1970

Thomas, Alfred, *The Labyrinth of the Word: Truth and Representation in Czech Literature,* Munich: Oldenbourg, 1995

Wellek, René, *Essays on Czech Literature,* The Hague: Mouton, 1963

D

Dangerous Acquaintances. *See* Liaisons Dangereuses

Daniel Deronda by George Eliot

1876

Daniel Deronda, George Eliot's final novel, was in many respects her most ambitious. Unlike her previous novels, all set in the past, *Daniel Deronda* takes place fairly close to Eliot's own time in the 1860s. Thus it comments more directly on contemporary Victorian society and 19th-century culture generally. Although she uses the double plot structure found in all her novels from *Silas Marner* (1861) on, here she explores areas of English life not considered in her earlier works. In the "Deronda half" of the novel, she makes a radical break with her previous fiction by focusing on various aspects of Jewish life. She also makes a formal departure, undermining conventional temporal structure by starting in medias res and leaving the ending open. Eliot also makes a modest move away from the realist paradigm normally associated with her work, as in certain respects she draws on the romance tradition and on the sensation novel. For example, figures such as Deronda's mother or Lapidoth seem to belong to the kind of fictional world created by Nathaniel Hawthorne or Herman Melville, and the Deronda plot revolves around an enigma, namely Deronda's origins. Most interestingly, *Daniel Deronda*'s fundamental concerns make it perhaps the most European of Victorian novels.

In the opening chapter of *The Rainbow* (1915), D.H. Lawrence describes how the aspirations of women introduce instability and change into the modern world: "It was enough for the men, that the earth heaved and opened its furrows to them. . . . But the woman wanted another form of life than this . . .". Lawrence's sense of women as a dynamic force for change in the modern world was anticipated by 19th-century fiction, particularly in certain key European novels in which female characters play the dominant role, notably Gustave Flaubert's *Madame Bovary* (1857), Lev Tolstoi's *Anna Karenina* (1875–77), and

Theodor Fontane's *Effi Briest* (1895). Although numerous English novels also have dominant female figures, Gwendolen Harleth, the heroine of *Daniel Deronda*, is arguably the only 19th-century English female character equal in power and scope to Emma Bovary or Anna Karenina.

Daniel Deronda, *Madame Bovary*, and *Anna Karenina* share a strong concern with the problem of modernity, a problem best dramatized by focusing on women rather than men. To oversimplify drastically, the modern world emerged from the combination of two cultural forces: the Enlightenment, which applied rationalist categories to the world, breaking with older forms of thought, and romanticism, which emphasized the power of the subjective in the relation between subject and object or mind and world, liberating human desire and aspiration from traditional constraints. One could argue that men had always enjoyed a considerable degree of freedom, so that Enlightenment and romanticist ideas merely accentuated their sense of freedom. Women, however, primarily because of their role in childbirth and their greater identification with nature and the domestic sphere, had both more to gain and more to lose from the impact of modernity.

Emma Bovary, Anna Karenina, and Gwendolen Harleth each long for self-realization, a desire viewed critically by their creators: Emma and Anna commit suicide, and it is feared that Gwendolen may do so. All three woman experience tensions and conflicts that prove almost irresolvable. Self-realization and the conflict it creates are strongly related to sexuality in the 19th-century European novels that focus on women. Emma Bovary, Anna Karenina, and Effi Briest, for example, are all guilty of adultery. Gwendolen Harleth is not technically an adulteress, but her relationship with Daniel Deronda may be viewed as a kind of symbolic adultery, since she wants Deronda and not her husband to know her at the deepest level.

However, for Gwendolen Harleth, the romantic impulse does not so much find expression in the longing for sexual fulfillment as in a desire for power. She possesses "the inborn energy of egoistic desire" and feels "the hunger of the inner self for supremacy." In Eliot's previous novel, *Middlemarch* (1872), the heroine, Dorothea Brooke, had combined Enlightenment idealism—an optimistic belief that the world can be changed for the better—with a romantic ardor and enthusiasm that one would link in particular with Percy Bysshe Shelley. Gwendolen, however, comes out of a darker, Byronic romantic tradition, the character having been partly based on Lord Byron's grandniece whom Eliot saw gambling at Bad Homburg. Unlike Emma Bovary and Anna Karenina, Gwendolen Harleth fears sexuality. Whereas Bovary and Karenina are destroyed by the irresolvable tensions created by abandoning marriage and motherhood in favor of personal fulfillment, Harleth is nearly destroyed when her imperiousness and sexual innocence lead to her relationship with the sadistic Grandcourt, a man who can achieve gratification only by subjugating others to his will. The novel strongly suggests that in the Gwendolen-Grandcourt relationship, Grandcourt's desire to subjugate takes a sexual form. This creates a murderous impulse in Gwendolen, and although she is not directly to blame for his death by drowning she feels guilty because she wanted him dead and felt capable of killing him. In some respects, the impulse to self-realization is treated more darkly in *Daniel Deronda* than in *Madame Bovary* or *Anna Karenina*, although the open ending to *Daniel Deronda* suggests some hope that Gwendolen may learn from her experience and be able to change.

Eliot and Tolstoi, perhaps in contrast to Flaubert, present a more positive philosophy through the representation of their male protagonists, Deronda and Levin. Both men look for some meaning in life and both reject romantic self-realization. All three novels, however, portray the social world in extremely negative terms. Society is very much to blame for Gwendolen's situation. Unlike Deronda's mother, who rejects her Jewish heritage in order to fulfill herself through art, the low artistic standards of both the upper and middle classes in England condemn Gwendolen to mediocrity. England offers no outlet for her energies, so she must marry a man rich enough to support her abroad.

Grandcourt exemplifies the degeneration of the English upper class. Although Deronda's guardian, Sir Hugo Mallinger, is an honorable man who is devoted to him and provides him with the best English education at Eton and Cambridge, he can offer him no larger social or moral vision. Middle-class materialism and dead upper-class tradition hold no attraction for Deronda. Even before he discovers his Jewish heritage, he has begun looking beyond England for meaning and vision. Although Eliot was greatly interested in proto-Zionist ideas, she was also suggesting parallels between the Jews and the English. In her last work, *Impressions of Theophrastus Such* (1879), she had emphasized the "affinities between our own race and the Jewish." The novel suggests that the English need to achieve a sense of vision with a communitarian purpose similar to that of Jews like Mordecai. Without such vision—and again one might see a parallel with *Anna Karenina*, particularly the last section in which Levin has a spiritual vision of hope that contrasts with Anna's final despair—a culture will inevitably become decadent, with no constraint on the desire for self-realization or self-gratification.

K.M. NEWTON

See also George Eliot

Further Reading

Beer, Gillian, *Darwin's Plots: Evolutionary Narrative in Darwin, George Eliot, and Nineteenth-Century Fiction,* London and Boston: Routledge and Kegan Paul, 1983

Carroll, David, *George Eliot and the Conflict of Interpretations: A Reading of the Novels,* Cambridge and New York: Cambridge University Press, 1992

David, Deirdre, *Fictions of Resolution in Three Victorian Novels: "North and South," "Our Mutual Friend," "Daniel Deronda,"* London: Macmillan, and New York: Columbia University Press, 1981

Irwin, Jane, editor, *George Eliot's "Daniel Deronda" Notebooks,* New York: Cambridge University Press, 1996

Leavis, F.R., *The Great Tradition: George Eliot, Henry James, Joseph Conrad,* London: Chatto and Windus, and New York: New York University Press, 1948

Newton, K.M., *George Eliot, Romantic Humanist: A Study of the Philosophical Structure of Her Novels,* London: Macmillan, and Totowa, New Jersey: Barnes and Noble, 1981

Rose, Jacqueline, *Sexuality in the Field of Vision,* London: Verso, 1986; New York: Verso, 1996

Shuttleworth, Sally, *George Eliot and Nineteenth-Century Science: The Make-Believe of a Beginning,* Cambridge and New York: Cambridge University Press, 1984

Welsh, Alexander, *George Eliot and Blackmail,* Cambridge, Massachusetts: Harvard University Press, 1985

Danish Novel. *See* Scandinavian Novel

Danzig Trilogy by Günter Grass

1959–63

Although some critics, and indeed the author himself, pointed out the close relationship among *Die Blechtrommel* (1959; *The Tin Drum*), *Katz und Maus* (1961; *Cat and Mouse*), and *Hundejahre* (1963; *Dog Years*), the name *Danziger Trilogie* (*Danzig Trilogy*) was not used until 1974 when Luchterhand, Günter Grass' German publisher, reissued the three works in separate volumes. In 1980 a special edition of the trilogy in one volume appeared; an English translation in one volume was published in 1987. As the name *Danzig Trilogy* suggests, the city of Danzig provides the location for major parts of all three narratives; in fact, although Danzig has receded into the background in some more recent works, it has essentially remained the unchallenged center of Grass' fictional universe. Hence, Grass' apparent preoccupation with Danzig, hardly of a parochial or exclusive nature, may be compared, for example, to James Joyce's focus on Dublin or William Faulkner's on Yoknapatawpha County.

When Grass was born on 16 October 1927, the city of Danzig—which until the end of World War I had been a part of the German Empire—was a free state. In 1939, at the outbreak of World War II, Danzig was annexed by the Third Reich, and after World War II Danzig became part of Poland and was renamed Gdansk. This turbulent history forms the backdrop of the trilogy, but the novels take place chiefly in the social milieu of the lower middle class in which Grass grew up. Furthermore, ethnic differences—Grass' father was a German and his mother was of Slavic origin—provide important ingredients. Because the Danzig of Grass' youth was irretrievably lost, his act of narration in the *Danzig Trilogy* is an evocation of the past. Grass resurrects Danzig from oblivion in order to keep alive in the collective memory the reasons for which the city was lost.

The Tin Drum, Grass' first novel and the first part of the *Danzig Trilogy,* begins in startling fashion with the confession of the first-person narrator/protagonist Oskar Matzerath that he is an inmate in an insane asylum in postwar West Germany, a confession that tends to disorient the reader and forces her to approach Oskar's tale with caution. During the two years of his confinement, from 1952 until his 30th birthday in September 1954, Oskar writes his fictitious memoirs, using the Matzerath family photo album as his chief source. He evokes the past by drumming on the instrument that gives the novel its name. Writing the memoirs constitutes one narrative level that is distinguishable from—albeit often parallel to—the two-year writing process itself. In his memoirs, Oskar proceeds chronologically, beginning his family's story in 1899, the year in which his mother was conceived in a potato field near Danzig. Private family affairs take place in a public context. Oskar's intertwining of the private and the public spheres is evident from the fact that the three books of the novel use important historical caesuras as structuring devices: they depict the prewar period, World War II, and the postwar period through 1954, respectively.

The Tin Drum is realistic in the sense that it provides exact details relating to the history and topography of Danzig, recreates the speech patterns of its inhabitants, and evokes the social milieu of its lower middle class. However, Oskar's evocative, spell-binding drumming and his ability to shatter glass with his voice pertain to the realm of the fantastic and the supernatural. In the final analysis, Oskar's role in the events he recounts remains enigmatic. For example, his professed complicity in the deaths of his two putative fathers appears less calculatingly cruel when these deaths are viewed as the inevitable consequences of the fathers' blind opportunism in joining political movements. Grass then poses the question of the individual's responsibility—a question from which Oskar cannot be exempted. His belated decision to abandon his self-imposed stunted growth symbolizes his readiness to accept political responsibility. However, he does not attain the stature of a physically normal adult. He has failed in his endeavor to start afresh and to assume responsibility, and his failure is shared by a society eager to ignore the past and to engage in the consumerism of the "economic miracle." Although Oskar atones for his transgressions by keeping alive the past in his memoirs, he cannot escape his feelings of guilt that result from his indifference in the face of evil.

Cat and Mouse, the centerpiece of the trilogy, originally was intended only as an episode of *Dog Years* and conforms to the generic requirements of the novella in that it lacks the epic breadth of the two other parts of the trilogy, concentrating exclusively on World War II. *Cat and Mouse* is told from the postwar perspective of the first-person narrator Pilenz, who is motivated by feelings of guilt because of his responsibility for the protagonist Mahlke's death. Young Mahlke, a devout Catholic, is an outsider among his juvenile peers who grudgingly admire him. Eventually, he becomes a war hero when he destroys large numbers of enemy tanks. This feat is attributable to his desire to compensate for his obtrusively large and constantly agitated Adam's apple, symbol of man's fall from grace, which is mistaken for the "mouse" of the title by a young cat. Mahlke's hopes to deflect attention from his Adam's apple and become fully accepted after being awarded the Knight's Cross come to naught when he is not allowed to give a speech at his old school. He goes AWOL and perishes in his old hideaway (a half-sunken minesweeper), a hero whose blindness for the injustice of the cause he served is indicative of the blindness of society as a whole.

The novel *Dog Years* derives its title from the dog that the city of Danzig presented to Adolf Hitler. Similar to *The Tin Drum, Dog Years* is divided into three books that are told by three different narrators under the guidance of Eduard Amsel. As in *The Tin Drum,* private affairs tend to be in the foreground, but they reveal the historical forces by which they are being shaped. For example, the love-hate relationship between the half-Jew Amsel, a sensitive and visionary artist who creates frightening scarecrows that symbolize evil, and his blood brother and fellow narrator Matern, who brutally victimizes Amsel and then, after the war, turns from SA thug to antifascist in order to atone for his transgressions, emphasizes the torturous history of Germans and Jews during the Third Reich. Grass' exuberant imagination is evident in the mixture of realistic, fantastic, mythical, and fairytale elements and in his linguistic ingenuity, which ranges from the imitation of biblical language to a parody of the philosopher

Martin Heidegger. Despite its difficulty, *Dog Years* attracted critical acclaim as the culmination of the two preceding works and achieved best-seller status in Europe.

Without doubt, *The Tin Drum*, which in 1958 received the prize of the influential Gruppe 47—an association of writers, critics, and publishers—has best stood the test of time and is now generally acknowledged as the most important German postwar novel. Lauded upon its publication as an irreverent, fresh voice but also severely censured as allegedly obscene and blasphemous, the novel has lost none of its appeal as attested by its impressive sales. The acclaimed 1979 film version directed by Volker Schlöndorff also enhanced its appeal. Grass, who had set out to break with "timeless and placeless parables" as the predominant mode of (West) German fiction of the 1950s, was credited with initiating the "rebirth of German letters" after the rupture caused by the end of World War II. Novelist John Irving, whose *A Prayer for Owen Meany* (1989) is indebted to *The Tin Drum* in various respects, stated in 1982 that Grass' novel "has not been surpassed; it is the greatest novel by a living author."

Grass has revisited Danzig in fiction several times: *Aus dem Tagebuch einer Schnecke* (1972; *From the Diary of a Snail*), a report of his participation in an election campaign with reminiscences of the persecution of the Jews in Danzig; *Der Butt* (1977; *The Flounder*), which vastly expands the time frame of the *Danzig Trilogy* into the distant past and attributes paradigmatic importance to Danzig; *Die Rättin* (1986; *The Rat*), which resurrects Oskar Matzerath and employs a futuristic time dimension; and *Unkenrufe* (1992; *The Call of the Toad*), a postunification novel that appears to hold out hope for Polish/German reconciliation. Despite these revisitations, Grass was not able to match the critical and commercial success of *The Tin Drum*, which remains unchallenged as his major achievement.

SIEGFRIED MEWS

See also Günter Grass

Further Reading

Cunliffe, William Gordon, *Günter Grass*, New York: Twayne, 1969

Hayman, Ronald, *Günter Grass*, London and New York: Methuen, 1985

Hollington, Michael, *Günter Grass: The Writer in a Pluralist Society*, London and Boston: Marion Boyars, 1980

Lawson, Richard H., *Günter Grass*, New York: Ungar, 1985

Mason, Ann L., *The Skeptical Muse: A Study of Günter Grass' Conception of the Artist*, Bern: Lang, 1974

Miles, Keith, *Günter Grass*, New York: Barnes and Noble, and London: Vision Press, 1975

Neuhaus, Volker, *Günter Grass*, Stuttgart: Metzler, 1979; 2nd edition, 1993

Neuhaus, Volker, and Daniela Hermes, editors, *Die "Danziger Trilogie" von Günter Grass: Texte, Daten, Bilder*, Frankfurt-am-Main: Luchterhand, 1991

Reddick, John, *The "Danzig Trilogy" of Günter Grass*, London: Secker and Warburg, and New York: Harcourt Brace, 1975

David Copperfield by Charles Dickens

1850

Boz [Dickens' pseudonym], and the men like Boz, are the true humanizers, and therefore the true pacificators, of the world. They sweep away the prejudices of class and caste, and disclose the common ground of humanity which lies beneath factitious, social, and national systems.
(Unsigned review, "Charles Dickens and *David Copperfield*," 1850)

In this pronouncement the anonymous writer summarizes what was—and what has largely continued to be—a common understanding of the value of Charles Dickens' novels. In representing the thoughts and feelings of characters from a variety of classes and situations, Dickens has seemed to encourage sympathetic connections among his readers. This skill was considered particularly important in the middle of the 19th century when social, political, and economic changes were leading many commentators to fear that rich and poor were becoming hopelessly estranged from one another. Within this context, Dickens' novels were believed to play an important social role: that of extending the understanding each class of persons could have of another.

Perhaps in no Dickens novel since *The Old Curiosity Shop* (1841) was sympathy believed to play such an important role as it did in *David Copperfield*. Partly as a result of the intimacy generated between readers and the narrator by the novel's autobiographical form, and partly because of the similarities between Dickens and his eponymous protagonist, readers consistently claimed to feel closer to David Copperfield than they had to any of the writer's other characters. In sympathizing with the character, many readers felt they were, in effect, entering into the thoughts and feelings of the writer—an understanding only reinforced by John Forster's claim in his *Life of Dickens* (1872) that *David Copperfield* had originally been undertaken as Dickens' autobiography. Whether readers regarded David Copperfield as a screen for Dickens or not, at the time they tended to laud the novel for the accuracy and intimacy with which it described the thoughts and feelings of a child as he grows into adulthood and the extent to which the reader is asked to enter into those feelings.

The form of *David Copperfield* has most often been described as a Bildungsroman—a novel that describes the development of a child, ignorant of the ways of the world, into an adult capable of recognizing and filling his appropriate role in society. In the opening scenes of the novel, the difference between the consciousness of the narrator—the mature David—and that of the character—David as a child—defines the novel's trajectory. By means of a series of life experiences, challenges, and traumas, David acquires the values and perceptions that enable him to assume the perspective of the narrator—a perspective that allows him to accept the responsibilities associated with adult manhood. David's early loss of his mother, his life at boarding school, and the hardships he endures working in a factory, appear to teach him self-reliance, perseverance, and compassion for all those who suffer. During his idyllic years with his aunt, Betsey Trotwood, he is reintegrated into the middle class—a reintegration that culminates in his pursuit of and marriage to the charming daughter of his employer. His youthful infatuation with Dora teaches him to identify and pursue a goal, even as it later teaches him the importance of forbearance and gentleness toward one weaker than himself. By the end of the novel, David has been formed by his experiences into one who can be trusted to put others before himself, to perform his duty, and to suppress his wayward desires and impulses.

This somewhat predictable Victorian narrative, which equates development with an education in self-suppression and the acceptance of responsibility, is complicated somewhat by the appearance in the later chapters of a more typically romantic narrative of the development of the artist, or the *Künstlerroman*. While the project of the Bildungsroman tends most often to be that of defining an identity in relation to a social structure, in the *Künstlerroman* the child tends to define herself or himself in a way described as prior to or autonomous from the social world. David's recognition of himself as an artist takes place almost entirely during his travels in Switzerland. While seeking consolation in the natural beauty of the Alps for his first wife's death, David receives a letter from his childhood friend Agnes in which she encourages him to use his suffering for the good of others. This letter leads David to recognize both his vocation—that of a novelist—and his true love—the woman able to bring him to this self-understanding.

This moment in the Alps is clearly reminiscent of a Wordsworthean moment of self-illumination, in that a moment of self-recognition appears to culminate and confirm an organic process of maturation. For David, however, the engagement that produces self-knowledge takes a relatively social form: he defines himself in relation to the woman he later makes his wife. For Wordsworth, by contrast, the dialogue that leads to a revelation of this kind almost invariably takes place with the natural world. Furthermore, the vocation David identifies is not that of a poet—one traditionally in the business of making larger truths available to others—but that of a novelist, a role more commonly understood to describe the outward forms of social intercourse. It is thus possible to see Dickens, in *David Copperfield*, making certain claims about the value of the novel as a significant social and ethical institution. The transcendence of which the novelist is capable is rewarded and confirmed by David's marriage with Agnes and the apparent melding of identities that results from it.

While David's story clearly ends happily—with his economic, romantic, and reproductive success—*David Copperfield* has been criticized often for the high price the other characters in the novel seem to pay for this happiness. Although to many 19th-century readers Dickens' novel seemed to generate sympathetic understandings between different classes and kinds of people, 20th-century readers have tended to call attention to how, at the end of the novel, all those characters substantially dissimilar to David are killed, exiled, or imprisoned. Ham, the Micawbers, and Emily as members of the lower class, and Steerforth as the representative of the upper class, all threaten to disrupt the homogeneity of the middle-class world David inhabits. Emily and Steerforth, and perhaps even Dora, introduce potentially transgressive sexual charges that interrupt the conclusion's valorization of accepted heterosexual monogamy. All these characters disappear by the conclusion. Even Agnes, the apparent agent of David's self-recognition, seems to be erased in the melding of their persons that takes place at the end of the novel. In becoming David's wife, her autonomous subjectivity seems wholly to be erased.

Dickens' novel has been both extremely popular and extraordinarily influential since its publication. So important has the novel been that it becomes somewhat difficult to differentiate those novels that have explicitly referred to it from those that have tacitly drawn on its assumptions. To a large extent, the notion of depth psychology it represents—a psychology that grows and changes over time—came in the late 19th and early 20th centuries to seem less like a particularly appealing, or even useful, way of understanding interiority than simply a record of the way persons "really" are.

RACHEL KAROL ABLOW

See also Charles Dickens

Further Reading

Hardy, Barbara, *The Moral Art of Dickens,* New York: Oxford University Press, and London: Athlone Press, 1970

Kucich, John, *Repression in Victorian Fiction: Charlotte Brontë, George Eliot and Charles Dickens*, Berkeley: University of California Press, 1987

McGowan, John P., "*David Copperfield*: The Trial of Realism," *Nineteenth-Century Fiction* 34:1 (June 1979)

Miller, D.A., "Secret Subjects, Open Secrets," in *The Novel and the Police*, Berkeley: University of California Press, 1988

Needham, Gwendolyn B., "The Undisciplined Heart of David Copperfield," *Nineteenth-Century Fiction* 9:2 (September 1954)

Poovey, Mary, "The Man-of-Letters Hero: *David Copperfield* and the Professional Writer," in *Uneven Developments: The Ideological Work of Gender in Mid-Victorian England*, Chicago: University of Chicago Press, 1988

Welsh, Alexander, *From Copyright to Copperfield: The Identity of Dickens*, Cambridge, Massachusetts: Harvard University Press, 1987

Robertson Davies 1913–95

Canadian

Robertson Davies had a long and varied career as a newspaper editor and columnist, a playwright, a reviewer and essayist, the first Master of Massey College in Toronto, and a novelist. He is best known for his novels, but the breadth of Davies' career is fundamental to his achievements as a fiction writer. The variety of his interests and the prose style that he developed over 20 years as a journalist and playwright, along with his two decades spent in academic circles, left their mark on his fiction, particularly in the wide range of knowledge, often arcane, that he displays in a style at once erudite, witty, dramatic, and polished. Although he had been publishing books, such as the collections of newspaper columns written under the name of Samuel Marchbanks, since the 1940s, he only turned to novels in the 1950s. He made this transition partly because he had grown frustrated with the limited success of his plays, although they had achieved critical acclaim within Canada, and with the limited resources of the Canadian theatre at that time; his success as a novelist made him a key part of the phenomenal upsurge in Canadian writing in the second half of the 20th century.

Davies' main concern as a writer is to show the process by which the individual becomes a balanced, integrated personality, acting out of self-knowledge and an understanding of the past, in terms of family history and formative influences, and of the present, in terms of recognizing the elements of the psyche that constitute the personality. His characters often face a crisis in their lives, which initiates this evaluation, and are guided by various teachers who each contribute to the total insight the character achieves. This process is frequently presented as autobiography, as in Dunstan Ramsay's explanatory memoir to his former headmaster at the college where he taught, which constitutes the narrative of *Fifth Business* (1970), and Dr. Jonathan Hullah's private case book of his life story in *The Cunning Man* (1994); or biography, as in Simon Darcourt's efforts to uncover the missing pieces of Francis Cornish's life in *What's Bred in the Bone* (1985) and again in *The Lyre of Orpheus* (1988). Part of the dramatic unfolding of these life histories is derived from the disparity between the degree of self-knowledge achieved by the central characters and the externally based, limited perspective held by other characters, even those closest to them.

These narratives reveal Davies' interest in the psychoanalytic theories of first Sigmund Freud, and then Carl Jung. The need to recognize and integrate the complementary aspects of the conscious and unconscious for a strong and balanced psyche is most explicitly presented in *The Manticore* (1972), in which David Staunton, distressed by his father's mysterious death and his own irrational reaction to it, enters into analysis with a Jungian therapist; his course of treatment occupies the core of the narrative. However, the growth of the self is explored in all of Davies' novels, and is a reflection of the extent to which Davies feels himself a Canadian writer speaking to Canadians. He began satirizing Canadian self-satisfied limitations as Samuel Marchbanks, and continued to assert the need to develop and balance the spiritual side with the rational in his plays, which now seem overly didactic and explicit. His novels are also at times didactic, but after the early *Salterton Trilogy* (1951–58, published together in 1986), which reads like a hybrid—part comedy of manners, part psychological exploration of the development of the artist—Davies has been more content to let his characters speak for themselves. The same focus on the requirements for a healthy cultural life in Canada is apparent throughout, and a similar pattern is explored: a small-town, talented Canadian attracts the attention and guidance of powerful, wise teachers, usually from Europe, and develops into a creative artist in his or her own field, choosing to return to or remain in Canada in the end. This pattern, to some extent, mirrored Davies' own life, and he felt strongly, as he said in a 1971 interview with Donald Cameron, that he was "trying to record the bizarre and passionate life of the Canadian people."

Davies is not the most technically experimental Canadian writer; the narrative devices he uses are largely tools to increase the psychological depth of his novels. The trilogy form is significant; for example, each novel in the *Deptford Trilogy* (1970–75, published together in 1983) examines the central incident—the stone in the snowball thrown by Boy Staunton at Dunstan Ramsay but hitting Mrs. Dempster, who then prematurely gives birth to Paul—and its consequences for one of the three key players. The separate books of the trilogy thus work together to disclose a story that is only completed in the last pages of the third novel, *World of Wonders* (1975). The turn inward may also be seen in the movement from an intrusive, often satiric, and omniscient narrator in the *Salterton Trilogy* to variations on first-person narration or third-person narration in which the narrator is largely unobtrusive. *The Rebel Angels* (1981), for instance, is divided chapter by chapter between two narrators, Maria Theotoky, the exceptional graduate student writing a dissertation on François Rabelais, and Simon Darcourt, the Anglican priest and professor who loves Maria as Sophia, the feminine principle of divine wisdom from the Gnostic Gospels. The novel thus embodies its debates on learning, wisdom, love, and obsession in its narrative structure. In *What's Bred in the Bone*, the narrative is framed by the Recording Angel and Daimon, who replay the life of Francis Cornish in detail that remains unavailable to his human biographer, dramatizing the internal quest for the integrated self, a process also conveyed in the allegorical emblem of Cornish's painting, the Marriage at Cana, which uses alchemical symbolism to tell the story of his life in the style of an earlier age. Cornish's masterpiece is so successful that it is misinterpreted, taken for an authentic historical piece of art by an unknown master. In *The Lyre of Orpheus*, the spirit of E.T.A. Hoffmann, whose unfinished opera is being reconstructed and completed as the doctoral dissertation of Hulda Schnakenburg, provides a contrapuntal commentary on the action at the end of each narrative section. Similarly, *Murther and Walking Spirits* (1991) is narrated by the ghost of a man murdered on the first page, who comes to understand his life through watching movies of his ancestors that only he can see.

The thematic and structural functions of Davies' narrative schema have been analyzed by a wide range of critics, some of whom have also faulted Davies for didacticism and elitism. His characters often do not sound sufficiently distinct from each other (in terms of qualities such as age and sex) to be convincing, and the narrative pattern of the education of the protagonist favors a monologic structure, revealing a one-way hierarchy of knowledge in the teacher-pupil relationship. Furthermore, some critics have pointed to an elitist conception of cultural and intellectual life in Davies' fiction, one that is dependent on education and material wealth as well as on spiritual and artistic talent; accompanying this attitude is humor, often employing class stereotypes, at the expense of the characters who are not members of this clearly defined elite.

Davies has been most influential for the scope of his fiction, which draws upon the history and techniques of literature, painting, music, theatre, and opera. He also explores unusual sources of information, such as psychoanalysis, magic, the tarot, alchemy, and hagiography, as repositories of mythic and spiritual ways of understanding the world. His novels have been compared to those of the 19th century and novels of ideas because of the wealth of knowledge they contain. His characters discourse learnedly about abstract ideas, and the narrative parallels invite the reader to explore these ideas as they are suggested by the characters and events portrayed. But Davies always provides a strong, dramatic plot as well, complete with unusual twists and turns and conveyed with a sureness of comic touch and humor that is grounded in a physical, even scatological, awareness of human frailty. Throughout his long career, Davies contributed greatly to and helped define the development of the Canadian novel.

HEATHER SANDERSON

See also Deptford Trilogy

Biography
Born in Thamesville, Ontario, 28 August 1913. Attended Upper Canada College, Toronto; Queen's University, Kingston, Ontario; Balliol College, Oxford, 1936–38, B.Litt. 1938. Teacher and actor, Old Vic Theatre School and Repertory Company, London, 1938–40; literary editor, *Saturday Night*, Toronto, 1940–42; editor and publisher, Peterborough *Examiner*, Ontario, 1942–63. From 1960 Professor of English, from 1962 Master of Massey College, and from 1981 Founding Master, University of Toronto. Governor, Stratford Shakespeare Festival, Ontario, 1953–71; member, Board of Trustees, National Arts Centre. Died 2 December 1995.

Novels by Davies
The Salterton Trilogy, 1986
  Tempest-Tost, 1951
  Leaven of Malice, 1954
  A Mixture of Frailties, 1958
The Deptford Trilogy, 1983
  Fifth Business, 1970
  The Manticore, 1972
  World of Wonders, 1975
The Cornish Trilogy
  The Rebel Angels, 1981
  What's Bred in the Bone, 1985
  The Lyre of Orpheus, 1988
Murther and Walking Spirits, 1991
The Cunning Man, 1994

Other Writings: plays, including *Overlaid* (1949), *Eros at Breakfast* (1949), and *Question Time* (1975); journalism and humor, including *The Diary of Samuel Marchbanks* (1947) and *The Table Talk of Samuel Marchbanks* (1949); criticism and essays, including *Shakespeare's Boy Actors* (1939), *Renown at Stratford: A Record of the Stratford Shakespearian Festival in Canada 1953* (1954), *A Voice from the Attic* (1960), and *One Half of Davies: Provocative Pronouncements on a Wide Range of Topics* (1977).

Further Reading
Cameron, Elspeth, editor, *Robertson Davies: An Appreciation,* Peterborough, Ontario: Broadview Press, 1991

Davies, J. Madison, editor, *Conversations with Robertson Davies,* Jackson and London: University Press of Mississippi, 1989

Grant, Judith Skelton, *Robertson Davies: Man of Myth,* Toronto: Viking, 1994

Lawrence, Robert G., and Samuel L. Macy, editors, *Studies in Robertson Davies' Deptford Trilogy,* Victoria, British Columbia: University of Victoria Press, 1980

Little, Dave, *Catching the Wind in a Net: The Religious Vision of Robertson Davies,* Toronto: ECW Press, 1996

Mills, John, "Robertson Davies," in *Canadian Writers and Their Work,* fiction series 6, edited by Robert Lecker, Jack David, and Ellen Quigley, Toronto: ECW Press, 1985

Monk, Patricia, *The Smaller Infinity: The Jungian Self in the Novels of Robertson Davies,* Toronto: University of Toronto Press, 1982

Peterman, Michael, *Robertson Davies,* Boston: Twayne, 1986

Stone-Blackburn, Susan, *Robertson Davies, Playwright: A Search for the Self on the Canadian Stage,* Vancouver: University of British Columbia Press, 1985

Dead Souls by Nikolai Gogol'

Mertvye dushi 1842

Nothing quite like Nikolai Gogol's *Dead Souls* had appeared in Russian literature before its publication, and nothing quite like it has appeared since. Yet the novel has continued to exert a powerful hold on the imaginations of Russian writers and readers because of its magnificent humor, its narrator's lyrical gestures toward explaining the enigma of Russia, and its status as an unparalleled tour de force of the Russian language.

Gogol' already had made a name for himself as a short-story

writer and playwright by the time his only novel appeared. *Dead Souls* follows the adventures of Pavel Ivanovich Chichikov, a smooth-talking rogue who makes the rounds of a strange assortment of landowners, offering to buy all of their serfs who have died since the last census was taken. According to government records, the peasants are still alive until the next census is taken. Chichikov's plan as rightful owner of those "dead souls" is to mortgage them to acquire real estate. At the climax of the novel, Chichikov's scheme, which until this point has been kept secret by those who know about it, is made public and causes a riot of speculation and suspicion in the provincial town. Chichikov is forced to flee, and as he dozes in his getaway troika we learn of his childhood and previous life, particularly the series of outlandish, ultimately failed swindles that has culminated in the dead souls scheme. The novel ends with Chichikov fleeing as the narrator apostrophizes the flying troika, now identified with the fate of Russia.

Dead Souls does not much resemble the two most important Russian novels that preceded it, Aleksandr Pushkin's novel in verse *Evgenii Onegin* (1833; *Eugene Onegin*) and Mikhail Lermontov's intricately linked set of stories *Geroi nashego vremeni* (1840; *A Hero of Our Time*). Pushkin's Onegin and Lermontov's Pechorin are world-weary Byronic heroes who move through a high-society world that is recognizable to the educated public (even if Pechorin's society is transplanted from Moscow to the Caucasian frontier); Gogol''s Chichikov is a plump, ludicrous con man who encounters a gallery of monstrous caricatures in the Russian provincial backwoods. The style in which his story is told is one of baroque excrescence and rich linguistic invention, very unlike the polished elegance of Pushkin's language and the stoical restraint of Lermontov's. The humor of *Dead Souls* is earthy and folksy (evoking accusations of obscenity from conservative critics), in contrast to the dry gallic wit of Pushkin and Lermontov.

The closest literary model for *Dead Souls* is the picaresque novel, in both its Western and Russianized versions (see LeBlanc, 1986). Gogol' himself complicated our perception of the novel's genre by labeling it a *poema* (epic poem); on the cover, designed by Gogol' himself, the word *poema* is set in much larger type than the novel's title or the name of its author. Most critics consider the most accurate definition of *poema* in Gogol's usage to have been given in his own unfinished "Textbook on Literature for Russian Youth" (c. 1844–45), under the heading "Lesser Forms of the Epic":

In modern times there has arisen a type of narrative work that constitutes a kind of middle way between the novel and the epic, the hero of which, although he is a private and not an eminent person, is nevertheless significant in many respects for the observer of the human soul. The author leads him through a chain of adventures and vicissitudes, in order to present at the same time a vivid, true picture of everything significant in the features and mores of the time he has chosen; that earthly, almost statistically captured picture of deficiencies, abuses, vices, and everything . . . that is worthy of the attention of any observant contemporary who is seeking in the past living lessons for the present. . . . Many of these works are written in prose, but may nevertheless be considered poetic works.

Gogol' mentions Ariosto and Cervantes as exponents of this genre. The invocation of "poetic works" is important for *Dead Souls* (and truer to the novel's strange vision than the label "statistically captured picture"). The decision to make "dead souls" the mysterious core of the novel does not arise in a vacuum but bears a complex relation to the aesthetics of early Russian romanticism, especially the poetical works of Gogol's friend and mentor V.A. Zhukovskii. Zhukovskii's poetry, which is preoccupied with the otherworldly and with the "soul" as a metaphysical concept, is an undeniable presence in and inspiration for *Dead Souls*, but by the end of the novel, Zhukovskii's poetic language, with its cult of the ineffable and inexpressible, has been rejected as a vehicle for Russian self-expression. In *Dead Souls* the language of the Russian peasant, maximally precise, straightforward, and expressive, achieves ascendancy over the high-society ladies' language of vagueness and indirection, inspired by the "inexpressible" ideal of early romanticism.

In the years immediately following the novel's publication, it was read mainly as a savagely satirical excoriation of the evils of 19th-century Russian society, despite the fact that Gogol's own politics were highly conservative and monarchist. The most influential 19th-century reader of Gogol', the radical critic Vissarion Belinskii, saw *Dead Souls* as a work of unflinching realism and social criticism "that mercilessly rips the coverings from reality." (This reading was revived by the Marxist-Leninist critics of the 1930s to the 1980s.) But at the beginning of the 20th century, a new generation of readers created a new Gogol' for itself, reading *Dead Souls* not as realistic social protest but as a brilliant phantasmagoria. This reading stresses the incorporeality of the novel's "souls"—Gogol's creation of a world whose existence is purely linguistic, purely artistic. As realism lost its preeminence in Russian literature, Gogol's qualifications to be a realist writer were called into question: he had spent very little time in the milieu described in *Dead Souls,* and the novel was written mostly in Rome, where Russia appeared to him as part dream, part memory, part mirage. In retrospect, Russian formalist critics and writers of a nonrealistic bent such as Vladimir Nabokov or the symbolist Andrei Belyi saw *Dead Souls* as a verbal performance, a delirious, nearly surrealistic fantasy that anticipates 20th-century experimental prose.

Gogol' spent the last ten years of his life trying to write a sequel to *Dead Souls*, sometimes envisioned as a purgatory and paradise to redeem the provincial inferno depicted in the first part. The drafts that remain show Gogol' struggling in vain to be the realist writer his critics claimed he was—trying, in Simon Karlinsky's words, "to make himself over into a second-rate Turgenev or Goncharov" (see Karlinsky, 1976). Gogol's intention to add something essential to *Dead Souls,* which is mentioned several times in the text, continues to haunt the novel, a specter that, like Chichikov's "dead souls," is insubstantial although powerfully disturbing. But when read in the context of Gogol's other works, many of which are intentional fragments whose ends look like beginnings, *Dead Souls* may be seen to be a finished work by the laws of Gogolian form. The unfulfilled promise of completion guards the text against neat solutions and fixed interpretations. Not only Chichikov escapes at the end of *Dead Souls*; the novel itself escapes its readers' (and author's) desire for the last word.

Dead Souls has few heirs in Russian literature. The 20th-century novels that come closest to reproducing its prosaic grotesquerie, its lyrical flights, and its idiosyncratic vision of Russia are

Fedor Sologub's *Melkii bes* (1907; *The Petty Demon*) and Mikhail Bulgakov's *Master i Margarita* (written 1934–40; *The Master and Margarita*).

SUSANNE FUSSO

See also Nikolai Gogol'

Further Reading

Erlich, Victor, *Gogol,* New Haven, Connecticut: Yale University Press, 1969

Fanger, Donald, *The Creation of Nikolai Gogol,* Cambridge, Massachusetts: Belknap Press of Harvard University Press, 1979

Fusso, Susanne, and Priscilla Meyer, editors, *Essays on Gogol: Logos and the Russian Word,* Evanston, Illinois: Northwestern University Press, 1992

Fusso, Susanne, *Designing Dead Souls: An Anatomy of Disorder in Gogol,* Stanford, California: Stanford University Press, 1993

Karlinsky, Simon, *The Sexual Labyrinth of Nikolai Gogol,* Cambridge, Massachusetts: Harvard University Press, 1976

LeBlanc, Ronald Denis, *The Russianization of Gil Blas: A Study in Literary Appropriation,* Columbus, Ohio: Slavica, 1986

Maguire, Robert A., *Exploring Gogol,* Stanford, California: Stanford University Press, 1994

Rabinowitz, Stanley J., *Novel Epics: Gogol, Dostoevsky, and National Narrative,* Evanston, Illinois: Northwestern University Press, 1990

Shapiro, Gavriel, *Nikolai Gogol and the Baroque Cultural Heritage,* University Park: Pennsylvania State University Press, 1993

Todd, William Mills, *Fiction and Society in the Age of Pushkin: Ideology, Institutions, and Narrative,* Cambridge, Massachusetts: Harvard University Press, 1986

The Death of Artemio Cruz by Carlos Fuentes

La muerte de Artemio Cruz 1962

When Carlos Fuentes' *The Death of Artemio Cruz* was published in 1962, it received instant acclaim and was promptly translated into many languages. The novel compares with James Joyce's *Ulysses* (1922), Gabriel García Márquez's *Cien años de Soledad* (1967; *One Hundred Years of Solitude*), Thomas Mann's *Doktor Faustus* (1947; *Doctor Faustus*), and Herman Hesse's *Magister Ludi* (1943). Its basic theme is the idea that "power founded on injustice must perish at the hands of injustice." Critics have noted that this novel constitutes the first successful literary portrait of the geography, history, ethnic configuration, and social makeup of Mexico. The novel examines the new power players, the rivalries among *caudillos* (military dictators), the opportunists, the pacts with foreign investors, and the role of capitalist, imperialist United States. To achieve his desired narrative effects, Fuentes employs flashback, stream of consciousness, interior monologue, temporal jumps, and multiple points of view to produce a vast panorama of the Aztec nation.

Artemio Cruz, the protagonist, appears during the "present" of the narrative in old age, dying of stomach cancer. He evokes, in his remaining 12 hours, 12 significant events of his life, from his humble origins as son of a mulatto woman and an impoverished landowner through the Mexican Revolution to his present position as an international tycoon and power broker. His wife, Catalina, and daughter, Teresa, linger at his deathbed, trying desperately to learn the location of his will, but, sadistically, he refuses to tell them. Having married the daughter of a wealthy landowner to become master of a great estate, Artemio does not love his wife. His beloved son, Lorenzo, died in the Spanish civil war and the only woman he truly loved, Regina, died in the Mexican Revolution.

Three voices narrate the novel, in the first, second, and third person. The first voice is that of Artemio himself as he lies dying. Events related to his final illness occur in the narrative present, and the first-person narrative deals mainly with the physical experiences and excruciating pain Artemio undergoes while his family attends him. The second-person passages are a projection of the agonizing, moribund Artemio and embark upon a voyage into Artemio's unconscious. Stream of consciousness is used extensively in these segments. Artemio reflects, recalls, and wonders about what might have been, creating a subjective reality mainly concerned with the meaning of life and with life after death. The third-person narrative is the most objective and the most distant from the dying protagonist, providing a balanced historical perspective of Artemio's life, the revolution, his marriage, and the seemingly endless series of corrupt incidents with which he was associated. These three disparate yet complementary narrative voices and points of view are amalgamated at the end of the novel. In the final segment of the text, the three voices become one.

Fuentes incorporates a tapestry of intertexts that complement and underscore the themes and motifs of the story of Artemio's life and death. Commentators have identified allusions to films (*Citizen Kane*) and plays (Pedro Calderón de la Barca's *La vida es sueño* [1636; *Life Is a Dream*]) and to numerous canonical literary texts: Stephen Crane's *The Red Badge of Courage* (1895), Ernest Hemingway's *For Whom the Bell Tolls* (1940), Joyce's *Ulysses,* Octavio Paz's *El laberinto de la soledad* (1950; *The Labyrinth of Solitude*), Jean-Paul Sartre's writings ("Man is condemned to choose"), Latin fragments from the Catholic liturgy; popular songs ("Poor People of Paris," "Las Golondrinas"); and nursery songs, to give but a brief sampling of the variety and scope. Furthermore, epigraphs from Michel de Montaigne, Calderón, Stendhal, Gorostiza, and a Mexican popular song underscore the numerous intersecting, overlapping themes of the novel as well as its experimental narrative structure. The quote from Gorostiza (". . . of myself and of Him and of we three, always three!") suggests a precedent for the multiple points of view, while at the same time alluding to the concept of the Trinity and other mythical and magic connotations of the number three. Fuentes, who employs numerical symbology and structures in much of his fiction, here alludes to numerology at the same time that more direct intertextual allusions are recast, reworked, and melded into a new, multivocal discourse representing the many peoples and languages that make up modern Mexico.

The title in Spanish is a source of different anagrams that allude to the novel's themes and motifs. The name of the protagonist also involves several anagrams. For example, *Arte, mío,* and *Cruz* can be translated into English as *art, my* or *mine,* and *cross*; thus, several possible interpretations of the protagonist's name become visible.

The Death of Artemio Cruz had an immediate influence upon younger writers in the rest of Latin America as well as in Spain. Its experimental structure influenced the nascent movement that would eventually be called the Boom in Latin American literature and the "New Novel" in the Iberian Peninsula. *The Death of Artemio Cruz,* arguably one of the first truly postmodernist novels in the Hispanic world, will remain in the canon for generations to come.

GENARO J. PÉREZ

See also Carlos Fuentes

Further Reading

Fiddian, Robin, "Carlos Fuentes: *La muerte de Artemio Cruz,*" in *Landmarks in Modern Latin American Literature,* edited by Philip Swanson, London and New York: Routledge, 1990

Girgen, Cynthia, "The Magic World in Carlos Fuentes' *The Death of Artemio Cruz,*" *Hispanic Journal* 16:1 (1995)

Schiller, Britt-Marie, "Memory and Time in *The Death of Artemio Cruz,*" *Latin American Literary Review* 15:29 (1987)

Solomon, Irvin D., "A Feminist Perspective of the Latin American Novel: Carlos Fuentes' *The Death of Artemio Cruz,*" *Hispanófila* 33:1 (September 1989)

Thompson, Currie K., "The House and the Garden: The Architecture of Knowledge and *La muerte de Artemio Cruz,*" *Hispania* 77:2 (May 1994)

Williams, Raymond Leslie, *The Writings of Carlos Fuentes,* Austin: University of Texas Press, 1996

The Death of the Heart by Elizabeth Bowen

1938

Elizabeth Bowen's place among modern novelists is ambiguous. During the 1940s many critics regarded her as Britain's leading novelist and short-story writer, yet over the past 30 years she seldom has been included in courses of 20th-century British literature, which usually cover her peers, E.M. Forster, Evelyn Waugh, Graham Greene, and Virginia Woolf. Bowen's defenders, such as the critic Hermione Lee, feel that for a writer of her accomplishment she is "peculiarly neglected" (see Lee, 1981). Most critics feel that *The Death of the Heart* is her most successful work, although there is also enthusiasm for her Irish novel *The Last September* (1929), her spy novel set during wartime *The Heat of the Day* (1949), and her brooding psychological romance *The House in Paris* (1935). Some have argued persuasively that her art reaches its peak in her story collections, such as *The Demon Lover* (1945).

In *The Death of the Heart,* Bowen explores two of her characteristic themes, the loss of a young girl's innocence and the failures of the British upper-middle class. The book's three main sections are entitled "The World," "The Flesh," and "The Devil," after the three temptations from which petitioners ask to be delivered in the Anglican *Book of Common Prayer.* In the first section the reader is introduced to Thomas and Anna Quayne, a couple much concerned with appearances—he is a partner in an advertising agency, and she is an amateur interior decorator. Their highly ordered, passionless marriage in Windsor Terrace is disturbed by the arrival of Thomas' 16-year-old half sister Portia, the daughter of Thomas' weak father and a woman named Irene, who was first his adulterous lover and then, at the insistence of the first Mrs. Quayne, his second wife. The three (Mr. Quayne, Irene, and Portia) have led a hand-to-mouth existence in a variety of hotels, much to the embarrassment of Thomas. When, following the deathbed request of Mr. Quayne, Portia is sent to Windsor Terrace for some indefinite time to experience family stability, Thomas and Anna have little idea what to do with her. Anna, who is witty, sophisticated, and cold, cedes any maternal role to Matchett, a gruff but sympathetic servant who "came with the furniture" from Mrs. Quayne's house. As the novel opens, Anna has just secretly read Portia's diary and she is confiding to her novelist friend St. Quentin how upset she is at the way Portia has portrayed her. At the end of the section, after Anna reads several passages from the diary, the irony of Anna's reaction becomes clear, since Portia seldom comments or interprets, but simply and flatly records each day's events.

Aside from St. Quentin and Matchett, Bowen introduces two

other onlookers and potential advisors for Portia. The first is Eddie, a gifted young man of 23 from a lower-class background with an Oxbridge education. He has been "taken up" by Anna, who convinces Thomas to employ him. Eddie plays a sort of mock-lover's role with Anna, although she has no interest in physical entanglements. Eddie also forms an emotional relationship with Portia, who sees him as, like her, a victim of the manipulative adult world. The most complex of Bowen's "cad" figures, Eddie is painfully self-conscious, somewhat hysterical, and ironically defensive. He resents the way he feels the upper bourgeoisie makes him perform monkey tricks, dislikes his own collusion in the process, and has little strength to spare for Portia's demands. The second important outside figure is Major Brutt, an outmoded veteran of World War I, who has just returned from an unsuccessful career in India and, taking literally a social invitation from Anna to "drop by sometime," inappropriately does just that. He mistakes the Quaynes' rather cold cordiality for welcome. Perhaps recognizing another orphaned innocent, Major Brutt also becomes fond of Portia and sends her puzzles.

In the second section of the novel, while Thomas and Anna take a vacation trip, Portia is bundled off to the seaside home of Anna's old governess, Mrs. Heccomb. Her house, named Waikiki, clearly represents a far more physical, noisy, and frank existence than the "edited" life of Windsor Terrace, where Thomas and Anna usually communicate with room-to-room telephones. In Waikiki everyone can hear everything all the time. Mrs. Heccomb's son Dickie and daughter Daphne lead strenuously social, unexamined lives, and the far more sensitive and intelligent Portia is swept into their orbit. A crisis occurs when Eddie comes to visit and, although he is rather dubiously regarded by all as Portia's "date," he is discovered holding hands with Daphne in a movie theatre. When Portia confronts Eddie with this betrayal, he insists that she is a "sweet kid" but has no right to make demands of him; when Portia confronts Daphne, the older girl is appalled at her attempt to drag embarrassing subjects into the light. Clearly, life at Waikiki may be crude and unedited, but it is hardly frank or innocent.

In the third section, several matters come to a head. St. Quentin, perhaps in his role as "devil," tells Portia that Anna has been reading her diary. Portia confides in Eddie, who in turn tells Anna; this is the final straw for Portia, who leaves Windsor Terrace determined that Eddie must take her in. When Eddie proves reluctant, Portia goes to Major Brutt at the Karachi Hotel and rather innocently but desperately offers herself to him. Brutt of course does the decent thing and insists on calling Thomas and Anna, even though Portia rather cruelly explains to him that Thomas and Anna have been laughing at him just as they have at her. At Windsor Terrace, Portia's assertion that she will return only if Anna and Thomas do the right thing—without specifying what that thing should be—leaves the couple and the visiting St. Quentin disturbed and baffled. Thomas finally lashes out at Anna for her encouragement of Eddie, her choice of Mrs. Heccomb as a caregiver for Portia, and her general heartlessness. Behind his anger is also his resentment that while his passion for Anna has remained and even grown stronger, she seems only to tolerate him as a husband. All the adults seem to realize they have failed in the role of parents, and perhaps as human beings as well. As St. Quentin puts it, "This evening the pure in heart have simply got us on toast." St. Quentin also suggests that Portia's "goofy" actions spring from a natural romanticism that deserves respect: "I swear that each of us keeps, battened down inside himself, a sort of lunatic giant—impossible socially, but full-scale—and that it's the knockings and batterings we sometimes hear in each other that keeps our intercourse from utter banality." The Quaynes decide to send Matchett for Portia, so as to minimize the drama of the occasion and because Portia has been closest to the servant. The novel ends with an extended stream-of-consciousness passage from Matchett as she is driven in a cab to the hotel.

Victoria Glendinning has called Bowen "the link that connects Virginia Woolf with Iris Murdoch and Muriel Spark" (see Glendinning, 1977). Although less experimental than Woolf, Bowen clearly shares much of her sensibility. Bowen is also a direct heir to the late 19th-century novelists of serious domestic comedy, such as Henry James and Edith Wharton. Similar to Woolf, Bowen writes a dense, textured prose that sometimes veers toward the essay and always has considerable symbolic power. In *Death of the Heart,* the various houses in their atmosphere and physical layout offer keys to the lives lived within them; a number of image complexes, such as those surrounding mirrors, puzzles, and birds, give a remarkable richness to the narration as they resonate with the novel's themes. The names of characters in Bowen's novels are often significant, and Portia is no exception: in her disguise as a lawyer in William Shakespeare's *The Merchant of Venice,* Portia memorably pleads with the judge for mercy. A remarkable number of reflections and doublings are contained in *Death of the Heart*—for instance, a lascivious older man speaks to Portia, using phrases once spoken by Eddie—that tend to bear out Anna's contention that experience is not really experience until it has repeated itself. As in her other novels, Bowen here shows that the loss of innocence can indeed be cruel, although she also implies that it is inevitable and may carry with it the promise of some redemption.

R. BRANDON KERSHNER

See also Elizabeth Bowen

Further Reading

Austin, Allan E., *Elizabeth Bowen,* New York: Twayne, 1971; revised edition, Boston: Twayne, 1989

Bennett, Andrew, and Nicholas Royle, *Elizabeth Bowen and the Dissolution of the Novel,* London: Macmillan, and New York: St. Martin's Press, 1994

Glendinning, Victoria, *Elizabeth Bowen,* London: Weidenfeld and Nicolson, 1977; New York: Knopf, 1978

Hoogland, Renée C., *Elizabeth Bowen: A Reputation in Writing,* New York: New York University Press, 1994

Kenney, Edwin J., *Elizabeth Bowen,* Lewisburg, Pennsylvania: Bucknell University Press, 1975

Lee, Hermione, *Elizabeth Bowen: An Estimation,* London: Vision Press, and Totowa, New Jersey: Barnes and Noble, 1981

The Death of Virgil by Hermann Broch

Der Tod des Vergil 1945

The Death of Virgil is generally considered Hermann Broch's masterpiece, even more than his epoch-making trilogy *The Sleepwalkers* (1931–32). Broch specifically compared *The Death of Virgil* with James Joyce's *Ulysses* (1922), to which, indeed, it bears some resemblance: it narrates the events of one day—the last—in the life of the poet Virgil, and it employs an interior monologue technique. But *The Death of Virgil* is unique among novels. On the surface, the events described are the last hours in the life of the despondent dying poet, who wants to destroy his life work in the conviction that society is doomed and poetry is useless. The day culminates in a long conversation with the Emperor Augustus Caesar, in which the poet's intention to destroy his *Aeneid* is thwarted. The novel is also a daring attempt to represent the transition from life to death through a musical and poetic technique.

The work is divided into four sections—"Water: The Arrival," "Fire: The Descent," "Earth: The Expectation," and "Air: The Homecoming"—that have been likened to the movements of a symphony. But analogies to musical structures, including the technique of verbal leitmotifs also present in the work, do not constitute the whole of the novel's musicality. Rather, Broch's *The Death of Virgil* programmatically and dramatically attempts to use musical techniques, employing language semantically but also organizing it in the way music organizes sound, simulating an effect of simultaneity or the annulment of time.

Broch gave musical cognition a privileged position among the arts. In an earlier essay on musical cognition dedicated to Arnold Schönberg, Broch distinguished between rational and irrational activity, viewing music as an attempt to master the world by seeking stasis, turning time into space, halting the onrush of time leading to death. Musical experience, in Broch's view, is characterized by the annulment of time, which forms music's cognitive center. To Broch, both music and literature have to solve the problem of attaining simultaneity. In literature, simultaneity is achieved through employing language paratactically, rather than in syntactic arrangements. Broch's own commentary to the work tries to explain his unique style: its aim is at all moments to bring unity to the contradictions of the human soul; it tries unceasingly to keep the musical motives in motion and to maintain throughout an impression of simultaneity of events. The method, oversimplified, is this: one thought, one moment, one sentence. A sentence cannot be complete until the cognitive unit which it is trying to express is complete. So, like Molly Bloom's final monologue in Joyce's *Ulysses,* which Broch insisted lasted only an instant in real time, some of Broch's sentences reach inordinate length to convey the complexity and emotional and aesthetic content of a single thought. The musicality, the repeated words and phrases, and the leitmotivic nature of the writing all serve to create a semblance of simultaneity in the work.

The Death of Virgil found its origin in Broch's reading of Theodor Haecker's *Vergil: Vater des Abendlandes* (1931; *Virgil: Father of the West*), one of the numerous works on the poet Virgil written in the early 1930s, on the occasion of the 2,000th anniversary of the poet's birth. Broch came to identify himself with

Virgil, also a poet standing at the end of one age and the beginning of another. Broch's theory of history, seen in his *The Sleepwalkers,* classifies the current period as one in which a collapse of values leads to a stage of anarchy that will give rise to a new age. He saw these views echoed in Haecker's description of Virgil's age and also in Oswald Spengler's *Untergang des Abendlandes* (1919; *The Decline of the West*).

In 1937 Broch read a portion of *Die Heimkehr des Vergil* (*Virgil's Homecoming*) on Austrian radio; this manuscript was the germ of the later novel. In this version, Broch predicts what becomes of a civilization that gives in to barbarity such as that of the Third Reich: as Virgil is carried through the streets from his boat to the palace, he witnesses scenes of disarray and violence while making apocalyptic predictions regarding the coming age. The political content of the several versions of Broch's novel was certainly influenced by the analogy between Roman imperial ambitions and Hitler's Germany. The conversations with Caesar deal partly with the nature of totalitarianism and the relationship of religion and the state. The emphasis in the novel is an overriding scepticism about the efficacy of art in a time of social and political collapse. This scepticism is based on the realities of Broch's own experience. Arrested on the day of the German annexation of Austria in March 1938, the novelist worked on the third version of the novel while in jail. He placed Virgil's motto from the Aeneid, *"fato profugus"* (exiled by fate), as the epigraph to the work—prophetically, it would seem, as he himself went into exile later that year, never to return to Europe. The importance of the motif of fate becomes apparent in the *Schicksalselegien* (elegies of fate), which are embedded throughout the text, and provide the raw material for much of the musical and poetical sections of the prose.

Hannah Arendt dubbed Broch the *Dichter wider Willen* (poet against his will), and *The Death of Virgil* in similar fashion is turned against itself. Virgil's fevered fantasies are informed by his conviction that, as one moves closer to the apocalypse, poetry becomes increasingly pointless. Virgil's obsession with destroying his life work is partly motivated by his wish to make sure that it will not be used to glorify Caesar. But Caesar's glorification was the original object of the *Aeneid,* and since Caesar holds power, Virgil's wish is frustrated. The laureate of empire despairingly sees himself as a failure.

The four sections of *The Death of Virgil* are very different from one another. The first, "Arrival," is a memorable description of the arrival of the imperial triremes bearing the dying poet into Brundisium, his passage through the noisy, filthy night streets of the port, and the beginning of the interior monologue. The second, "Descent," probably the most difficult, is predominantly a fevered dream. The third, although long, consists mostly of more or less conventional dialogue and explores the themes already mentioned. The last chapter is a tour de force intertwining reality and imagination, night and day, and life and death in a fantastic cavalcade that reverses the creation of the universe as the poet's consciousness gradually merges with the natural world. *The Death of Virgil* is a unique literary work, exhaustive in the treatment of its theme and exhausting to read. Its long sentences and recursive language make it a difficult read that requires time and effort, with the result that it is probably mostly known by name.

The book's reception in Europe was complicated by the aftereffects of Germany's defeat, not being readily available in German outside Switzerland until 1949. The work's American reception was initially more significant and has remained strong, although it was greeted with a mixture of admiration and bafflement. It was on the basis of *The Death of Virgil* that Broch was twice nominated (unsuccessfully), in 1950 and 1951, for the Nobel prize.

JOHN A. HARGRAVES

See also Hermann Broch

Further Reading

Boyer, Jean Paul, "Bemerkungen zum Problem der Musik bei Hermann Broch," in *Hermann Broch und seine Zeit: Akten des Internationalen Broch-Symposiums Nice 1979,* edited by Richard Thieberger, Bern and Las Vegas, Nevada: Peter Lang, 1980

Kessler, Michael, and Paul Michael Lützeler, editors, *Hermann Broch: Das dichterische Werk,* Tübingen: Stauffenburg, 1987

Lützeler, Paul Michael, editor, *Brochs "Tod des Vergil,"* Frankfurt am Main: Suhrkamp, 1988

Weigand, Hermann J., "Broch's *Death of Virgil*: Program Notes," *Publications of the Modern Language Association of America* 62:2 (1947)

Ziolkowski, Theodore, "Broch's Image of Virgil and Its Context," *Modern Austrian Literature* 13:4 (1980)

Decadent Novel

The decadent movement of the late 19th century occupies a significant, yet ambiguous, position in the development of modern Western literature. Decadence voiced the predicament of modern cosmopolitans who found themselves dependent on a lifestyle that they inherently despised. As A.E. Carter (1958) notes, "Civilized man, though at times so proud of his civilization, has never been able to rid himself of the sneaking fear that it is all somehow unnatural, artificial and corrupt." The term *decadence* itself is one fraught with difficulties: it is more than a synonym for *decay* or *immorality,* and the popularity of the word arose from a particular cultural application. R.K.R. Thornton (1983) comments that "its immediate currency again suggests that the phenomenon it describes was well-known before the word was found to name it." Clearly, decadence represents a more dynamic complex than its superficial associations with perversity and hedonism would imply.

The writers of the early 18th century never experienced that characteristic uneasiness with the city and civilization that became part of the romantic inheritance. It was not until Jean-Jacques Rousseau's *Discours sur les Sciences et des arts* (1750; *A Discourse on the Arts and Sciences*) that writers began seriously considering the elaborate culture of modern Europe not as an achievement, but a degeneracy. Rousseau's thesis was developed to its extreme in the romantic revulsion from the city, and the celebration of nature—the antithesis of civilization—as the source of imaginative power. The result of the romantic *Weltanschauung* was that humanity could no longer view the achievements of civilization without an awareness of its unnatural, corrupting aspects. By the mid–19th century, however, Western culture was as far removed from nature as it could be, steeped in the bourgeois world of consumerism and industrialization. It was this troubled legacy that the decadents inherited. Dependent upon the capitalistic society of the middle class, they loathed it; disinherited from the alien world of nature, they despised the city while wallowing in its seductions: from this arises the decadent's penchant for the abnormal.

The city, having become the central symbol of decadent literature, overshadows the protagonists in decadent plots, and many novels from this period seem more a collection of sketches about different aspects of city life than the biography of a particular hero. The city emerges as the "megalopolis," evil because it divorces men from nature and conditions them to the artificialities of urban life, causing them to lose their *élan vital* (spiritual energy). The central image of decadent fiction is that of the city as Babylon, the great whore. Urban existence is a machine that destroys men through its capitalistic supply-and-demand society, and the luxuries such a culture engenders are fatally, irresistibly tempting to the romantics' descendants—the decadents. The Goncourt brothers, Edmond and Jules, for instance, in novels such as *Germinie Lacerteux* (1865), show the hideous depravities of the modern city corrupting and then destroying healthy peasants, whose *élan vital* is poisoned by its seductions. Unable to restrain himself from indulging in its perversions, the decadent is often ambivalent toward civilization, despising it yet inextricably dependent on it. The city has become a highly addictive, debilitating drug.

Through the loss of *élan vital,* modern man ceases to be active, his existence attuned to the mental, rather than physical, processes of life. Hence, the decadent hero becomes an aesthete, a decadent pervert, who lustfully seeks immediate gratification in the artificial allurements of the urban world. Mental stimulation becomes the important goal of the decadent, and the need for novelty—arising from the ennui of modern life—leads toward perversion. This loss of physicality emasculates the decadent man, who begins assuming feminine characteristics, while the decadent woman assumes masculine aspects. A typical instance of this redeployment of gender roles occurs in J.-K.Huysmans' *À rebours* (1884; *Against Nature*), whose protagonist,

Des Esseintes, enters into a perverse, and eventually self-defeating, relationship with an American acrobat, Miss Urania, solely because of her manlike appearance. Furthermore, the decadent woman falls into one of two categories. Woman is often represented as the black widow, a vampire that sucks the soul of the decadent male: the archetypal example is the sadistic Englishwoman, Clara, in Octave Mirbeau's *Le Jardin des supplices* (1903; *Torture Garden*). Woman is no longer man's companion in life's struggles, but his adversary, using him for her own perverse desires. Alternatively, the decadent woman is a neurotic, who loses her self-control while remaining deadly to men, and her neuroses are realized in a number of ways: in, for example, lesbianism, nymphomania, perversion. Numerous neurotic women recur in decadent fiction: Paule Riazan in Joséphin Péladan's *Curieuse!* (1886), Emma Bovary in Gustave Flaubert's *Madame Bovary* (1857), and Honorine d'Arlement in Catulle Mendès' *La Première maîtresse* (1887; The First Mistress).

The transference of gender roles assumes its ultimate realization in the androgyne, who is less a homosexual figure than one whose natural sexual characteristics have dissipated. G.R. Ridge (1959) has pointed out that the androgyne may be seen as nature's revenge on the decadent society: s/he is usually sterile, sexless, and perverse, unable to reproduce, and so lacking the capacity to perpetuate a corrupt and dying civilization. This inherent self-abortiveness goes beyond a merely biological phenomenon: it becomes part of the decadent's worldview. Civilized man eventually tires of urban excitement, and impotence combines with ennui, inculcating a desire for death. Death becomes the aesthetic conclusion to life, necessary because life has no further artistic interest. Oscar Wilde's Dorian Gray, for example, has an obsessive interest with the murders committed by Renaissance nobles and ends his own life in an act of aesthetic recoil.

Although decadence was a broadly Western phenomenon, its literary influence was nowhere more profound than in France. As early as the Marquis de Sade in the 1790s, French writers had been aware, yet perversely proud, of the pernicious and addictive effects of city living. Charles Baudelaire, writing in the middle of the 19th century, initiated the decadent obsession with the artificial and the perverse. In *Le Peintre de la vie moderne* (1863; *The Painter of Modern Life and Other Essays*), Baudelaire argued in favor of artificiality, stating that vice is natural in that it is selfish, while virtue is artificial because we must *restrain* our natural impulses in order to be good. He extends his eulogy to artificiality to include things like make-up and costume, and argues that "Fashion should thus be considered as a symptom of the taste for the ideal which floats on the surface of all the crude, terrestrial and loathsome bric-à-brac that the natural life accumulates in the human brain." Furthermore, he argues that it is not the aim of cosmetics (nor of literature and all art) to imitate nature, but to negate it, to emphasize the artificiality of the act itself. Baudelaire was the first writer to equate *modern, artificial,* and *decadent,* most notably in *Les Fleurs du mal* (1861; *The Flowers of Evil*), in which the modern condition is shown to consist of mental games and perverse pleasures set against a squalid urban backdrop. Baudelaire's translation of Poe's works also codified the links between modern life and mental degeneration. By the late 19th century, writers such as Théophile Gautier (*Mademoiselle de Maupin* [1835]) and later Barbey d'Aurevilly (*Les Diaboliques* [1874; *The She-Devils*]), the Goncourts (*Soeur Philomène* [1861; *Sister Philomene*]), J.-K.

Huysmans (*Against Nature*), Remy de Gourmont (*Une Nuit au Luxembourg* [1906; *A Night in the Luxembourg*]), symbolist poets such as Paul Verlaine and Stéphane Mallarmé, even naturalists such as Émile Zola (*La Curée* [1872; *The Kill*]), as well as the minor decadents, began looking at modern civilization in such terms as Baudelaire had conceived, elaborating upon his vision of the artificial world and reconstructing it in the nightmarish terms of psychopathology.

Across the channel, writers in England began to share the decadent philosophy, albeit nearly two decades later, in the movements that flourished in the Victorian fin de siècle. The English decadence was not as defined a phenomenon as the French because of the absence of any coherent group of authors who accepted and fought for the title "decadent." Furthermore, censorship was much more extreme than in France, and the scandal caused by Oscar Wilde's *The Picture of Dorian Gray* (1891)—a novel that, in terms of any offense against accepted moral standards, is mild by comparison with Huysmans' *Against Nature*—testifies to the conservative climate in Britain. Wilde, perhaps the central figure of English decadence, was influenced profoundly by Huysmans and Walter Pater, whose *Renaissance* (1873) codified certain ideas about aesthetics, especially those of "that subtle and delicate sweetness which belongs to a fine and comely decadence." Wilde's only novel, *The Picture of Dorian Gray* even plays with the concept of decadence itself by explicitly alluding to *Against Nature* in its narrative, with Dorian musing that his own life mirrors exactly that of Des Esseintes.

With the exception of Wilde, English decadents, focusing more on the linguistic than the cultural implications of decadence, never expressed as resolute a philosophy as did the French writers. Although not as famous as Wilde, Arthur Symons has been identified as a central decadent writer, and his "The Decadent Movement in Literature" (1893) had possibly the most far-reaching effect on subsequent studies of English decadence. Symons was the first writer to view the movement not simply as a French incident, but as a wholly European phenomenon. Yet by 1899 he had repudiated the term *decadence* in favor of the notion that it was merely a small part of the grander movement called "symbolism." Aubrey Beardsley, the great decadent artist, had died too young to make an impact beyond the generation of the 1890s, and by the new century—marked by the death of Oscar Wilde—decadence in Britain had died a silent death. English decadents—excluding Wilde perhaps, who himself repudiated his decadent lifestyle at the 11th hour—were neither fully satisfied nor comfortable with the moral overtones of a term such as *decadence,* and were more than happy to distance themselves from the title. They adopted, almost eagerly, other appellations: most notably that of "symbolist," which was soon to take a vital role in English modernism, especially in the hands of a young decadent named W.B. Yeats.

Although the term *decadent style* is misleading, because decadence describes more than the single school that briefly took its name, several aspects may be seen as common to decadent writers. Innovations are found in both prose rhythm and vocabulary, which are convoluted and overripe, even tainted. Ridge notes that "The rich decadent style glows like a diseased person flushed with fever. Indeed, the disease accounts for the beauty." James M. Smith (1948) points out that literary culture undergoes three phases: the formative, in which various forms of expression compete for dominance; the formal, in which there is a generally agreed impetus and style; and the decadent, when the established formal (classical) style exhausts itself, and artists attempt to move beyond the staid and trite into the new. Decadent style expresses a breakdown of existing forms, distorting the healthy elements into the moribund. The decadent concern with the part over the whole, both in content and form, is the principal manifestation of decadent style, and it also emphasizes the reasons that modern decadents identified so much with the decadence of the crumbling Roman Empire. Havelock Ellis (1932) describes decadent style as one in which the unity of a text breaks down, from book to page, page to phrase, and, finally, phrase to word—resulting in an "anarchistic" style in which the whole is sacrificed to its parts. The individual unit becomes elaborated upon to its extreme, and perverse pleasures are painted in purple prose. Huysmans' passages again are representative, with descriptions running into pages of turgid language, in an attempt to depict every sensory aspect of an object to the point of surfeit. The decadent is interested exclusively in style, and therefore decadent texts attempt to contain no didactic or ethical purpose: decadent style ultimately ceases to have subject matter altogether, and as a result the decadent writer will have no identifiable view of the world to express in his work. Finally, the highly organized, limited systems of classical writing (Augustan, Victorian-realist, even romantic) give way to an ostentatious literary vocabulary, which has distorted syntax, meaning, and structure.

There is a strong concentration in decadent novels on various states of neurosis, and in some cases psychosis. It is, therefore, unsurprising that many critics have taken a psychoanalytical approach to decadent texts. As well as the accepted id/ego/super-ego division, Freud identified another trinary mental system of specific application to decadent fiction. The "reality principle," which governs perceptions of the external world, modifies the "pleasure principle," which encourages personal fulfillment; against these two is set the "death instinct," which explains the human impulse toward self-destruction. It is a perversion of the pleasure principle, occurring when the libido is unfulfilled, and it can easily be transferred aggressively onto external objects. According to the decadent philosophy, neither the id nor the pleasure principle should be checked, and because the reality principle is virtually nonexistent for decadent protagonists like Dorian and Des Esseintes, pleasure per se becomes trite and is caught up with the death instinct, leading consequently to death and perversion, characteristic aspects of decadent fiction. Dorian Gray feels that "There were moments when he looked on evil simply as a mode through which he could realize his conception of the beautiful." This leads to a psychopathology of the decadent hero, characterized by a deteriorating identity—something that forms the very basis of the decadent narrative. The decadent's sense of self-coherence begins to collapse: Des Esseintes hallucinates and must return to society or face insanity; Dorian confuses himself with his portrait and exhibits extreme paranoia, culminating in the murder of the creator of the portrait, Basil Hallward. In the absence of any controls, the instinct for self-preservation degenerates into a fear about death: haunted by James Vane—as symbol of his guilt—Dorian feels "sick with a wild terror of dying, yet indifferent to life itself."

Post-Freudian psychoanalytic criticism also shares a lexical connection with decadent fiction, most especially in the writings of the French critic Jacques Lacan (1949). According to Pater's aesthetic model, the subject is only a locus of impressions that are experienced, rather than a center of consciousness. As Christopher Lane (1994) has pointed out, the careful self-representation of the decadent possibly encouraged an ontology of deception leading away from emotion and toward materialism. Further, any continuity of consciousness is interrupted by the focus on surface. In Lacan's dynamic, Dorian Gray's portrait may be seen as the vehicle for a dramatic shift from the Imaginative (the mental world before language and sign impose upon thought) to the Symbolic (the mental world where language and sign predicate thought). The Imaginative is Dorian's conception of himself, but the Symbolic, represented by the picture, is what actually occupies the center of the novel. Wilde attempts to return to the Imaginative by not explicitly telling the reader what Dorian's "sin" is, relying on the surface of the word. Dorian's whole identity is negated by the fact that his coming into being is premised on a picture, which is another man's creation. That man, Basil Hallward, fears that he has put too much of himself into it, and Lord Henry Wotton eulogizes it as the "finest portrait of modern times." Henry is as much the creator of Dorian Gray as Basil, and it is he who provides Dorian with the "poisonous" yellow book (*Against Nature*) which becomes the latter's Bible. Dorian feels that "the whole book seemed to him to contain the story of his own life, written before he had lived it," again emphasizing the prioritization of the Symbolic (surface). In Lacanian terms, the Imaginative—the decadent's last line of defense, representing the individual identity confronting the faceless tide of "mediocrity," dissipates into Symbolic archetypicality. Dorian is no longer a person, but is the agglomeration of Basil, Henry, and Des Esseintes. In losing his uniqueness, Dorian does indeed become the "finest portrait of modern times," and, like the decadent himself, he becomes the avatar of a bourgeois society characterized by its materialism and conspicuous consumption—the very things the decadent is in recoil from.

Late 19th-century Europe suffered possibly the greatest trauma of Judaeo-Christian history: what Friedrich Nietzsche termed the "Death of God." Charles Darwin's *The Origin of Species* (1859) challenged the very basis of biblical teleology as well as the concept of a benevolent universe. A second rupture occurred with theories of relativity, and even the assured determinism of Darwinian evolution was displaced. Everything depended on mere chance: the world was in a state of flux. As empiricism became the crutch of epistemology, some novelists turned to the accurate replication of the perceived world—leading to what has generally been called "realism." This term has been applied to the works of authors such as George Eliot, Gustave Flaubert, Elizabeth Gaskell, and Fedor Dostoevskii. In France, this led to the development of "naturalism," inclined toward scientific accuracy and social documentation, and championed by Zola, the Goncourts, and Guy de Maupassant, as well as the early Huysmans. The decadent project arose both as a result and in spite of these developments toward the precise rendition of the experienced world. In "The Critic as Artist" (1891), Wilde commented that "nowadays we have so few mysteries left to us that we cannot afford to part from them. . . . It is through its very incompleteness that art becomes complete in Beauty." In the bleakness of social Darwinism, where "success was given to the strong, failure thrust upon the weak" (*Dorian Gray*), art became more reassuring than a supposed truth. Rachel Bowlby (1993) discusses Wilde's antagonism to "truth": "Wilde's novel demonstrates the untenability as well as the banality of any supposition of a fixed identity for things or people once they have been situated within any order of representation." The center of the novel—Dorian's picture—thus represents different things to the three men who view it: for Basil, it is a sign of his love for Dorian; for Harry, it is the portrait of modern times; and, for Dorian, a reminder of the ephemerality of his beauty and youth, and later a reminder of his corruption.

While the decadents problematized the canons of 19th-century culture, it is difficult to ascertain to what extent they developed the narrative form. Decadence was not a momentary irruption in a relatively stable literary atmosphere: there is a definite evolution to be traced, beginning with the romantics and filtered through mid-century realism. With such a heritage, it would be difficult to dismiss decadence as an aberration in the evolution of narrative. Rather, the obfuscation surrounding its significance arises from the discrete ways in which the phenomenon was channeled into new literary movements. By the 1890s, the term *decadence* had acquired so much moral baggage that writers began to search for alternative names to describe themselves, and many in France settled on *symbolism*, which had become a powerful movement from 1880 onward. Writers such as Mallarmé, Verlaine, Arthur Rimbaud, Villiers de L'Isle-Adam, Maurice Maeterlinck, even Huysmans himself, are associated with this school; Symons, once a champion of decadent aesthetics, signaled the move away from decadence in his refutation of the ascription in favor of symbolism, in *The Symbolist Movement in Literature* (1899). Like the decadents, the symbolists were profoundly antirealist and antinaturalist, distilling the decadent obsession with surface and exhaustive imagery with their focus on the symbol, a device able to unite the material and spiritual worlds.

Decadence, especially through the medium of symbolism, had its most profound legacy in early 20th-century modernism. Both the aesthetics and the linguistic excesses that governed decadence may be perceived as operating in the writings of many modernists. The decadent focus on ephemerality, something treated anxiously by Pater and ironically by Baudelaire, becomes a phenomenon celebrated in many modernist works. In their polyvalent texts, James Joyce (*Ulysses*, 1922; *Finnegans Wake*, 1939) and T.S. Eliot (*The Waste Land*, 1922; *The Four Quartets*, 1935–42) focus on the chaos of perception and the impossibility of giving existence any form of representational quality. For Virginia Woolf, the fleeting connection between memory and perception creates "the moment," whereby the universe may be apprehended; this belief forms the cornerstone of her theories, in essays such as "Cinema" (1926), and novels like *To the Lighthouse* (1927). W.B. Yeats evokes decadent themes perhaps most vividly of all the modernists, having involved himself with the decadents and symbolists in the 1890s. His interest in the displacement of modern humankind, the inadequacy of meaning, and the inaccessibility of a hypostatic "truth" give him the bifurcation of perspective perceivable in Huysmans and Flaubert, whose protagonists search for things that they cannot even perceive are missing. The qualities of life that haunted the decadents assume a far more millenarian aspect in Yeats' apocalyptic later works, such as "The Second Coming" (1921), and "The Gyres" (1938), whose complex symbology gives a mystical aspect to modernist aesthetics. Decadence both claimed a literary heritage stretching back into romanticism and bequeathed a legacy to the writings of modernism, a fact that precludes the argument—

despite the movement's relatively brief life span and lack of cohesion—that it had claim on neither past nor future. Indeed, decadence was not only a movement that articulated the impotent malaise of a 19th century whose very grounds of belief had been irrevocably destroyed. Decadence may also be seen as an epoch of transition wherein this very act of destruction created a dynamism that would allow the literary movement to flourish vibrantly under the auspices of the 20th-century modernism that followed it.

Decadence was less a school than a view on life: many of the movements of the late 19th century may be perceived as decadent, whether they are individually called parnassianism, naturalism, realism, or aestheticism. It is less a common style than a common view and shared focus on the qualities of modern living. The decadent is descended from the dandy, of whom he is the logical extension and conclusion, but unlike the decadent, the dandy had his own code of behavior to which he adhered. Moreover, unlike the pathological hero of romantic literature, the decadent is content with his perversities, deliberately choosing perversion, while his forebears have perversity forced upon them by conflict, external or internal. Dorian Gray remains the ultimate exemplum of this philosophy, a man who truly succeeds in replacing life with art, depth with surface. Struggling to transcend nature, the decadent hero attempts to become antinature, something *à rebours*; of course, he also completes the decadent paradigm in finally being responsible for his own destruction. The idea of "art for art's sake" transcends notions of form and style and arises out of the philosophy that life offers nothing—either in this world or the next—and only the artificial creations of humanity can sustain existence in any meaningful way. While the romantic believed that appearance was a delusion that veiled the true reality of things, the decadent believes that appearance *is* reality.

A.A. MANDAL

See also Against Nature; French Novel (1850–1914)

Further Reading

Baudelaire, Charles, "The Painter of Modern Life," in *The Painter of Modern Life and Other Essays,* translated by Jonathan Mayne, London: Phaidon Press, 1964; 2nd edition, 1995; originally published as *Le Peintre de la vie moderne,* 1863

Bowlby, Rachel, *Shopping with Freud,* London and New York: Routledge, 1993

Carter, Alfred Edward, *The Idea of Decadence in French Literature, 1830–1900,* Toronto: University of Toronto Press, 1958

Chasseguet-Smirgel, Janine, *Creativity and Perversion,* New York: Norton, 1984; London: Free Association Press, 1985

Donato, Eugenio, *The Script of Decadence: Essays on the Fictions of Flaubert and the Poetics of Romanticism,* New York: Oxford University Press, 1992; Oxford: Oxford University Press, 1993

Dowling, Linda, "The Decadent and the New Woman," *Nineteenth-Century Fiction* 33 (1979)

Ellis, Havelock, *Views and Reviews,* First Series, Boston: Houghton Mifflin, and London: Harmsworth, 1932

Ellmann, Richard, *Yeats: The Man and the Masks,* New York: Macmillan, 1948; London: Macmillan, 1949

Lacan, Jacques, "The Mirror Stage as Formative of the I as Revealed in the Psychoanalytic Experience" (1949), in *Modern Literary Theory: A Reader,* edited by Philip Rice and Patricia Waugh, London: Arnold, 1989; 3rd edition, 1996

Lane, Christopher, "The Drama of the Impostor: Dandyism and Its Double," *Cultural Critique* 28 (Fall 1994)

Lester, Richard, *Journey Through Despair, 1880–1914: Transformations in British Literary Culture,* Princeton, New Jersey: Princeton University Press, 1968

Ridge, G.R., *The Hero in French Decadent Literature,* Atlanta: University of Georgia Press, 1959

Smith, James Monroe, "Elements of Decadence and Their Convergence in the French Literature of the Late Nineteenth Century," Ph.D. diss., University of North Carolina, 1948

Symons, Arthur, "The Decadent Movement in Literature," *Harper's New Monthly Magazine* 87 (November 1893)

Thornton, R.K.R., *The Decadent Dilemma,* London: Arnold, 1983

Deconstruction. *See* Critics and Criticism: 20th Century

Daniel Defoe 1660–1731

English

Daniel Defoe's place in the canon of English novelists was not assured until the 19th century; by contemporaries he was most often thought of as a journalist, historian, or author of the topical and polemical poem *The True-Born Englishman* (1701). His claim to be considered alongside Samuel Richardson and Henry Fielding as one of the founders of the English novel was defended with increasing conviction by 19th-century commentators, and in the 20th century Defoe's status as a pioneer was firmly established by Ian Watt (1957) among others. More recently, critics have stressed Defoe's indebtedness to early novelistic forms such as the criminal biography, the prose romance, and the travel narrative.

Several factors contributed to Defoe's long neglect. First, Defoe was anxious to pass off most of his prose works as authentic histories and therefore avoided any explicit or implicit suggestion that his texts were fictional at all. This probably explains why he failed to participate in the 18th century's energetic debate about the newly emerging novel and its relationship with the romance. Second, Defoe was so successful in concealing his authorship of several of his major works that his contribution to the history of the novel was almost bound to be obscured. Even now, any select bibliography of his novels is likely to be regarded as contentious: his canon is still undergoing scholarly revision, and many of his authenticated works deliberately evade conventional distinctions between fact and fiction.

Nonetheless, Defoe is now recognized as an early novelist of major importance, and even if some critics would question the modern assumption that *Robinson Crusoe* (1719) was the first English novel, most are conscious that his particular kind of realism represents a departure in the history of the genre. Some also have suggested that the apparent artlessness of his many and varied narrators masks a subtle and sophisticated irony on the part of their creator, and few have failed to admire the sheer range of his concerns, from social issues such as crime, to political issues such as Jacobitism, to economic affairs, especially the benefits of colonization and overseas trade. Indeed, economic themes have been seen to underpin almost all his writings, and he has been regarded as exemplifying the close relationship many perceive between the rise of industrial capitalism and the rise of the novel.

Although Defoe's absence from contemporaneous debates about the nature of prose fiction has already been noted, the various prefaces to his novels bear out his reputation for indifference to aesthetic and formal matters, and conversely his concern for the rhetorical uses of his fictions. Most of Defoe's narratives are offered as the memoirs of real people, newly discovered and edited for the purposes of moral instruction or social enlightenment. *Colonel Jack* (1722), for instance, is presented as a kind of allegory, perhaps akin to John Bunyan's *Pilgrim's Progress* (1678–84), but the "editor" also hopes this text will persuade the public of the urgent need for state intervention in the care and education of orphaned children and young offenders.

Since the novels for which Defoe is now remembered were written and published during the course of a few years toward the end of his career, it is misleading to impose upon them a teleology of artistic development. (Even so, the slightly later *Roxana* [1724], by virtue of its psychologically and morally complex heroine, does perhaps belong in a class of its own.) Defoe was less interested in narratological experimentation for its own sake than in convincing readers of his historical fidelity, and many of his novels adopt the same solutions to this problem. Most notably, they display an intense preoccupation with the material realities of everyday life, epitomized by the protagonists' determination to record every fluctuation in their financial affairs, down to shillings and pence. Defoe's emphasis on material circumstances contributes in no small measure to the verisimilitude of his fiction; this preoccupation also enhances his stories' imaginative appeal by precisely and vividly evoking the world in which his protagonists lived.

Equally crucial to the authenticity of Defoe's novels was his use of the first-person narrator. One of his earliest and best known first-person narrators was Robinson Crusoe. Like Moll Flanders, Bob Singleton, and Colonel Jack (although not, perhaps, Roxana), Crusoe is notable for his ordinariness and hence his credibility. In keeping with his unremarkable background as the youngest son of a merchant in the "upper station of low life" (i.e., the middle class), Crusoe's style as a narrator is plain and matter-of-fact, and although the adventures he describes are often highly romantic, and sometimes prompt him to spiritual self-examination, he is primarily concerned with the practicalities of his existence.

Defoe's subsequent narrators would share Crusoe's ability to mimic the accents of "real" life, while manifesting a resourcefulness and vitality that explained their distinctive careers as criminals, adventurers, or travelers. Defoe's narrators are characterized as well by their engaging frankness and self-knowledge, readily if sometimes regretfully acknowledging their moral limitations; typically they mitigate their guilt by inviting the reader to admit his or her own vulnerability to temptation. Thus Moll Flanders punctuates her history of bigamy, deception, and theft with references to the bleak alternative to crime—destitution—that awaits her. First-person narration allows Defoe to achieve two mutually opposed effects: on the one hand, his protagonists are strongly individualized; on the other hand, as their rather generic names suggest, they are representative. Moll Flanders, for instance, whose name evokes such mythic figures of the London underworld as Moll Cutpurse and Callico Sarah, is typical of her class in her pragmatic attitude toward women's sexual inequality and financial insecurity. She exploits her physical charms as long as she can and steals when she grows too old to entice a man to support her.

Another means favored by Defoe for creating the illusion of historical truthfulness was the linear and (at times) digressive plot. Although his novels are not without structure—critics have offered convincing and detailed analyses of recurrent motifs and parallels—they make little use of formal divisions such as chapters and tend to be repetitive and to conclude perfunctorily. Just as his eye for detail springs less from a conscious desire for fictional innovation than from an anxiety to make his narratives credible, and hence polemically effective, so the formlessness of Defoe's narratives is likely to have resulted from pragmatic considerations. A loose structure gave him frequent opportunities to reiterate the morals to be drawn from his protagonists' experiences. (Readers see the same mistakes and infer the same lessons repeatedly in the course of the narrator's life, with cumulative rhetorical effect.) Defoe, under acute financial pressure himself through much of his life, was also often obliged to eke out his material. Although undoubtedly possessed of exceptional indus-

try and creativity, he was also very much the commercial hack, and his prolific output resulted from necessity rather than choice.

Given the particularity of so many of Defoe's novels, it is ironic that perhaps his greatest impact on the genre, nationally and internationally, has been in promulgating the mythic scenario of the desert-island castaway. *Robinson Crusoe* often was classed by contemporaries with another travel fiction of extraordinary imaginative power, Jonathan Swift's *Gulliver's Travels* (1726), and from its first publication it inspired numerous imitations and sequels. Although there are some thematic echoes of *Moll Flanders* in later novels in the sentimental tradition of Richardson's *Pamela* (1740), and although *A Journal of the Plague Year* (1722) helped to stimulate the genre's perennial interest in the ethics and politics of pandemics, Defoe has been remembered by other novelists chiefly for his account of a shipwrecked sailor whose heroic self-sufficiency is a comment both on the human need for society and the equally powerful impulse for solitude. Rightly or wrongly, Defoe has been credited with inaugurating the enduring fascination with the inner life of the individual that would be fundamental to even the most epic and socially inclusive of novels from the 18th century to the present day.

KATHERINE A. ARMSTRONG

See also Moll Flanders; Robinson Crusoe

Biography

Born Daniel Foe in London in 1660; used name Defoe from around 1703. Attended Charles Morton's Academy, London. Hosiery maker and commission merchant in the early 1680s; participated in Duke of Monmouth's rebellion against James II, 1685; involved with a tile works in Tilbury, a business that failed in 1703; accountant to the commissioners of the glass duty, 1695–99; exposed to public contempt, jailed, and fined for *The Shortest Way with the Dissenters*, 1703; political writer for Robert Harley, later Earl of Oxford, 1704–11; editor, *A Review of the Affairs of Finance, and of All Europe*, 1704–13; lived in Stoke Newington, London, from 1709; worked on government commissions and wrote pro-government pamphlets, 1710s; wrote for periodicals published by Nathaniel Mist from 1715; editor, *Mercurius Politicus*, 1716–20, the *Manufacturer*, 1720, and the *Director*, 1720–21. Died 26 April 1731.

Novels by Defoe

The Life and Strange Surprising Adventures of Robinson Crusoe, 1719
The Farther Adventures of Robinson Crusoe, 1719
Memoirs of a Cavalier, 1720
The Life, Adventures, and Piracies of the Famous Captain Singleton, 1720
The Fortunes and Misfortunes of the Famous Moll Flanders, 1722
A Journal of the Plague Year, 1722
The History and Remarkable Life of the Truly Honourable Colonel Jacque, Commonly Called Colonel Jack, 1722
The Fortunate Mistress; or, A History of the Life and Vast Variety of Fortunes of Mademoiselle de Beleau, The Lady Roxana, in the Time of King Charles II, 1724
The Memoirs of an English Officer Who Served in the Dutch

War in 1672 to the Peace of Utrecht in 1713, by Captain George Carleton, 1728; as *Memoirs of Cap. George Carleton*, 1743

Other Writings: poems, essays, journalism (especially for the periodical *The Review*, 1704–13), travel writings (including *A New Voyage round the World*, 1724, and *A Tour Thro' the Whole Island of Great Britain*, 1724–27), economic treatises, familiar letters, handbooks.

Further Reading

Armstrong, Katherine A., *Defoe: Writer as Agent*, Victoria, British Columbia: English Literary Studies, University of Victoria, 1996

Backscheider, Paula R., *Daniel Defoe: Ambition and Innovation*, Lexington: University Press of Kentucky, 1986

Brown, Homer, "The Institution of the English Novel: Defoe's Contribution," *Novel: A Forum on Fiction* 29 (1996)

Davis, Lennard J., *Factual Fictions: The Origins of the English Novel*, New York: Columbia University Press, 1983

Furbank, P.N., and W.R. Owens, *The Canonisation of Defoe*, New Haven, Connecticut: Yale University Press, 1988

Hunter, J. Paul, *Before Novels: The Cultural Contexts of Eighteenth-Century English Fiction*, New York: Norton, 1990

McKeon, Michael, *The Origins of the English Novel 1600–1740*, Baltimore: Johns Hopkins University Press, 1987; London: Raduis, 1988

Novak, Maximillian E., *Realism, Myth, and History in Defoe's Fiction*, Lincoln: University of Nebraska Press, 1983

Richetti, John, *Popular Fiction Before Richardson: Narrative Patterns 1700–1739*, Oxford: Clarendon Press, 1969

Watt, Ian, *The Rise of the Novel: Studies in Defoe, Richardson, and Fielding*, Berkeley: University of California Press, and London: Chatto and Windus, 1957

The Deptford Trilogy by Robertson Davies

1970–75

The publication in 1970 of *Fifth Business*, destined to become the opening volume of *The Deptford Trilogy*, which also includes *The Manticore* (1972) and *World of Wonders* (1975), represents a turning-point in Robertson Davies' artistic reputation. Up to that time he had been known, within the small Canadian literary community, as a witty dramatist and journalist and as the author of three light novels in the comedy of manners tradition (*Tempest-Tost*, 1951; *Leaven of Malice*, 1954; and the more ambitious *A Mixture of Frailties*, 1958) set in an Ontario cathedral city called Salterton. These had deftly satirized pomposity, social snobbery, and the stuffiness of provincial Canadian culture. In *A Voice from the Attic*, however, a collection of writings about books and reading published in 1960, Davies argued that humorists must tap deeper sources of comedy if they are to develop creatively in later middle age. With the publication of *Fifth Business*, it became clear that Davies had followed his own advice.

Fifth Business was planned as the first volume of a trilogy. It is a retrospective of the life of Dunstan Ramsay, in his own voice. An inquiry into the nature of revenge, Ramsay's story takes off from an ostensibly insignificant event: during the Christmas season of 1910, in the small Ontario town of Deptford (based on Davies' native Thamesville), a boy throws a snowball containing a stone at his friend, Dunstan (then still known as Dunstable) Ramsay. Dunstan takes evasive action, and the stone hits a pregnant woman, who gives premature birth as a result of shock, an eventuality that leaves an indelible mark on Dunstan's life. The relationships that flow from the incident—Dunstan's love-hate relationship with Boy(d) Staunton, the thrower of the stone, and his well-intentioned concern for Paul Dempster, the prematurely born baby—are the focus of the novel.

At a time when "kitchen-sink" realism and explicitly detailed sex scenes were in vogue, Davies wrote from the viewpoint of a 70-year-old bachelor-schoolmaster with an interest in the relation between history and myth, in Jungian psychology, and in the lives of the saints. To the surprise of many, Davies tapped a neglected vein of wonder, magic, imagination, and polished eloquence that proved refreshing for readers of independent taste in a literary climate where inarticulate heroes, sordid settings, and bleak social relevance were the order of the day. In fact, *Fifth Business* made such an impression on some of its readers that they requested more information about the novel's minor characters. Davies realized that the story of the snowball could form the basis for a number of independent yet intimately related narratives. These eventually took the shape of *The Manticore*, which focuses on Boy Staunton, and *World of Wonders*, which traces the strange and varied story of Paul Dempster.

Although Davies has acknowledged a structural debt to Joyce Cary's well-known trilogy (*Herself Surprised*, 1941; *To Be a Pilgrim*, 1942; *The Horse's Mouth*, 1944) and the repeated re-tellings of an original story in Robert Browning's long poem *The Ring and the Book*, the Deptford novels owe little to earlier fictional traditions. "Fifth business" is itself a theatrical term referring to a supernumerary who plays a small but essential part in working out the dénouement in a drama or opera. Ramsay, although central to his own story, plays such a role in the lives of Boy Staunton, Paul Dempster, and others. Davies then realized that this process could be illustrated in a series of interlocking fictions. The resultant trilogy develops into a profound study of the extent to which individual lives are partly determined by external circumstances and partly controlled by individual effort.

Above all, Davies succeeded in extending the boundaries of traditional fiction by challenging the dominant realistic convention and introducing unusual subject matter, bizarre incidents, and idiosyncratic perspectives. Whereas the Salterton novels had employed standard omniscient narration and a conspicuous authorial voice, *The Deptford Trilogy,* by contrast, draws upon a variety of speakers and narrative methods, which are handled with both poise and originality. Even the conventions of storytelling itself are parodied. Thus Ramsay's first-person narrative in *Fifth Business* takes the whimsical form of a 200-page letter to the headmaster of the school at which he has taught for a lifetime, protesting the inadequacy of the biography printed in the school magazine at the time of his retirement. This device draws attention to its own artifice, but also slyly suggests a confessional account addressed to the headmaster of the universe. It is an appropriate vehicle for a story that reveals a richly bizarre and intellectually challenging life conducted behind a facade of middle-class respectability and humdrum occupations.

The Manticore examines the career of Boy Staunton, the thrower of the snowball, who grows up to become a commercially successful but personally dull financier, politician, and public figure. Davies decided to examine Staunton's life via its effects upon his son, a prominent defense lawyer who seeks help from Jungian psychoanalysis in an endeavor to control his incipient alcoholism. The novel consists of transcripts of his interviews (and arguments) with his psychologist and the diary of reminiscences that he prepares at her urging. It is at one and the same time a serious account of Jungian procedures and a witty presentation of what Davies calls "the Comedy Company of the Psyche."

Davis fully exploits the potential of the perspective shifts between the novels by retelling the same incident from different viewpoints. For example, Davies provides a second rendition of a scene from *Fifth Business* in which Boy Staunton's wife attempts suicide after Ramsay rejects her sexual advances. In the first novel, this scene is recounted from Ramsay's viewpoint. In *The Manticore* we learn what Ramsay had not known in the earlier account: that the incident had also been observed by the young David Staunton and his sister. The implications of the scene are thus considerably extended. Davies rings similar changes on previously recounted scenes throughout the trilogy. The result is a constantly shifting series of insights into situations that may be examined in ever-expanding complexity but never understood completely.

World of Wonders turns to the story of the prematurely born Paul Dempster, who is kidnapped by a grubby traveling circus when he is still a child. He gradually develops into the central figure in a sophisticated magic show under the name of Magnus Eisengrim. Also an actor in a film about the 19th-century illusionist Robert-Houdin, Dempster tells his own story to the movie directory and his associates (including Ramsay as historical adviser) in order to supply a "subtext" to the story of the film. This narrative setup provides a suitably theatrical backdrop for an inquiry into the nature of dramatic illusion. The novel not only recounts Dempster's own story but casts new light on events we have already witnessed in the lives of Ramsay and Boy Staunton. The phrase "world of wonders" begins as the name of the traveling circus but develops into a way of describing the extraordinary nature of the world we all inhabit.

Davies' narrators are invariably intelligent and articulate people of diverse interest and manifold experience. While external historical events—including World War I, the Depression, and the abdication of Edward VIII of England—play their part in the trilogy, Davies' main interest is focused on the adventures of the mind. He writes for informed and thoughtful people interested in a wide range of intellectual subjects and prepared to follow him into areas of obscure erudition. His interests in religion and Jungian psychology combine to create a spiritual dimension that accentuates but never detracts from his primarily comic vision.

For Davies, life is a fascinating, unfathomable mystery that should be explored to the full. His novels are elegantly constructed, opinionated, full of bizarre situations and wise counsel, always open to the pursuit of new ideas and the exposure of trendy excess. The imagery of conjuring and magic is central to his whole endeavor. As a novelist, Davies shows a remarkable dexterity in juggling a varied array of subjects, themes, and eccentricities. Magic, on the other hand, also suggests "magus," a figure combining the qualities of sorcerer and wise counselor. Such figures recur in Davies' books, and as spellbinding purveyor of wisdom he qualifies for the title himself.

W.J. KEITH

See also Robertson Davies

Further Reading

Cameron, Elspeth, editor, *Robertson Davies: An Appreciation,* Peterborough, Ontario: Broadview Press, 1991

Davis, J. Madison, editor, *Conversations with Robertson Davies,* Jackson and London: University Press of Mississippi, 1989

Grant, Judith Skelton, *Robertson Davies: Man of Myth,* Toronto: Viking, 1994

Keith, W.J., "Robertson Davis," in his *A Sense of Style: Studies in the Art of Fiction in English-Speaking Canada,* Toronto: ECW Press, 1989

Lawrence, Robert G., and Samuel L. Macey, editors, *Studies in Robertson Davies' Deptford Trilogy,* Victoria, British Columbia: University of Victoria Press, 1980

Little, Dave, *Catching the Wind in a Net: The Religious Vision of Robertson Davies,* Toronto: ECW Press, 1996

Monk, Patricia, *The Smaller Infinity: The Jungian Self in the Novels of Robertson Davies,* Toronto: University of Toronto Press, 1982

Peterman, Michael, *Robertson Davies,* Boston: Twayne, 1986

Anita Desai 1937–

Indian

Unlike an earlier generation of anglophone Indian novelists influenced by colonialism and nationalist politics, Anita Desai is not a polemical or didactic writer. In her ten novels (not including two juvenile books) she generally has eschewed public and political themes to focus on changes in the intensely private lives of individuals since independence, illuminating interior psychological landscapes through a highly charged impressionistic style that achieves a finely nuanced alignment of image and experience.

A product of the Bengali patrician intellectual elite on her father's side and of the high literary culture of Weimar Germany on her mother's side, Desai has been exceptionally well placed to interpret India to the West and to chart the postindependence crises of the anglicized Indian bourgeoisie—a privileged, overindulged class that has fallen on hard times since the days of colonial rule. In the early novels Desai focused on women of this class, the disaffected wives and mothers who—although they enjoy privacy, leisure, and career and marriage choices denied the majority of their countrywomen—nevertheless lead unsatisfied, wastefully enervated, and illusion-ridden lives. Desai's India, as presented through the eyes of the average middle-class wife, has neither the romantic exoticism nor the squalid horror of Western stereotypes but is a commonplace, dull actuality, and the attempts by her heroines to escape its confining grayness and mediocrity seldom have any creative outcome or issue in genuine assertions of identity; rather, these attempts are futile gestures that lead Desai's female protagonists deeper into compromise and defeat, illusion and neurosis.

The psychologically disturbed wives of the first two novels, *Cry, the Peacock* (1963) and *Voices in the City* (1965), break out of their servile, anxiety-ridden marriages only by murder and suicide. In *Where Shall We Go This Summer?* (1975), Sita, pregnant with her fifth child, becomes neurotically obsessed with the violence of the world around her. To escape her surroundings Sita retreats into a fantasy in which the fetus is kept miraculously unborn in the safety of her womb and takes refuge from her marriage on the magical island homestead of her deceased father (a messianic political leader turned guru), where she can keep the fantasy intact. Sita's negation of husband and home open up no other life to her, however: she has none of her father's religious mysticism or her daughter's creative talent, only a romantic sensibility and a sterile aestheticism, which are finally no great advance upon her husband's unimaginative rationalism. In *Fire on the Mountain* (1977), the aging Nanda Kaul withdraws into a private world of self-willed inertia and isolation in revenge for a life of duty and obligation as a university vice-chancellor's wife. Into her seclusion intrudes her great granddaughter Raka, whose attention the old woman tries to capture by recreating, in bursts of nostalgic fantasy, the lost exotic India of her own childhood (including an explorer father who brought back leopards and bears from Tibet). The inward narrative vision of these novels is kept kinetic, however, by unexpected reversals and shifts of perspective that destabilize the reader's bearings on the protagonist's viewpoint. At the end of *Where Shall We Go This Summer?* the choric, commonsense voice of the islanders breaks into Sita's visionary neurosis and dismisses her as simply mad, reinvoking a continuing external reality that transcends private obsessions. Similarly, in *Fire on the Mountain,* the harrowingly real event of the rape and murder of Nanda's old schoolfriend, the grotesque Ila Das, jolts both character and reader out of a reverie that is suddenly revealed to be wholly illusory: her father never went to Tibet, her husband was a lifelong adulterer, and her present state is not one of willed solitude but abandonment.

Desai's later fiction ventures into more public territory, touching upon sociohistorical themes and turning its focus from the private worlds of isolated individuals to relationships and responsibility at family and communal levels. *Clear Light of Day* (1980) explores the disintegration of postindependence India through the fragmentation of an old Delhi family. The otherwise unexciting lives of the members of the Das family coincide with the momentous events of partition, assassination, and relocated populations, and a belated family reunion alerts family members to their distorted visions of past events. The family represents an older, resilient India, a more tolerant, all-accommodating, supraethnic world abandoned after partition and factionalized by the new Hindu-dominated nation state: a brother defects to the Muslim north, a sister to Europe, while Bim, playing the matriarchal Mother India role, stays on to take care of her retarded younger brother, an image of petrified progress and arrested time.

In Custody (1984) is a poignant satiric comedy about a humble college lecturer's misguided attempts to escape professional obscurity by interviewing the country's most famous living Urdu poet, for which privilege he is made to endure the latter's drunken garrulity and loutish companions, his demands for money, and the near loss of his own job and marriage. The lecturer learns, at his own expense, that to take his idol's poetry into protective custody is to surrender himself into the *poet's* custody, and to acquiesce to his manipulative and exploitative behavior. He also learns that art cannot be sifted and distilled from life but—as his symbolic cleaning up of the poet's vomit with his poems indicates—is sunk in the fury and the mire of the human body. In this novel and in *Baumgartner's Bombay* (1988), Desai graphically evokes the material squalor and poverty of India (from which the bourgeois wives of the early books are safely insulated) while her style is infused with a hard-grained social realism. The Mirpore of *In Custody* is a city of dust and debris, while the Calcutta and Bombay of *Baumgartner's Bombay* are cities of mud and filth in which the eponymous protagonist is a degraded and putrescent presence, unwashed, eating leftover food, and stinking of the city cats he harbors (when he is stabbed to death by a drug-crazed German youth whom he has sheltered, his body oozes "a diarrhea of blood"). Baumgartner, himself a German exile, is the archetypal marginal man who constantly renegotiates his exiled condition: first, as a German Jew who narrowly avoids the Nazi death camps; next, as an enemy alien interned in a wartime camp in British India; then as a Bombay furniture salesman dispossessed, in turn, by Muslim and Hindu business partners; and, finally, as a drifter in a seedy expatriate community of aging, alcoholic ex-showgirls and prisoners of war, speaking no indigenous language and consequently cut off from comprehending the Indian world. He is "a man without a family or a country," and the victories and defeats of the global, colonial, and religious wars in which he finds himself trapped are never his. Baumgartner sleepwalks through these moments in history, an innocent buffoon in the tradition of the Jewish schlemiel, cushioning himself against the horrors of his German past by filtering it through infantile nursery rhymes and idyllic nostalgias ("Ignorance was, after all, his element," comments the narrator as he is murdered in his bed). His fantasy world finds its dark mirror image—and his infantilism its perverse alter ego—in the demented, drug-induced deliriums that his psycho-pathic killer conjures from travelers' tall tales, Gothic fairy stories, and Tantric myth-lore.

Journey to Ithaca (1995) maintains the expatriate perspective of journeyers to the East, although in less travestied forms. In this novel a German woman of the hippie generation loses her callow Italian husband to a Himalayan ashram and embarks on detective work to uncover the cloudy origins of its enigmatic Holy Mother. It transpires from her travels and research that the Mother was originally Laila, a Franco-Egyptian who deserted her Parisian university studies in the 1920s to join a touring Indian dance troupe and came with them, via Venice and America, to Bombay where, the troupe leader Krishna assured her, "her soul was born" and was "waiting for her." But the truth does not tell us very much. Exactly what it was about India that cast a spell over Laila and, 50 years on, her own hapless husband is never made comprehensible to the wife's rationalist Western worldview, and Laila's recovered diary, which raves unintelligibly about love, truth, and beauty, does not explain how she became the Mother. As is often the case in Desai's fiction, the mystic impulse and craving for spiritual enlightenment are vividly presented but appear to originate in the mind of the quester rather than in the site of the quest. Moreover, since even Krishna, the ascetic guru of sacred dance, beds his dancers and sells out to a tawdry commercialism on the American tour, the quest is attended in the narrative by a shrewd, sceptical irony.

In these last two works, the second of which was written in Italy, Desai maintains an unapologetically European perspective on India and seems to be trying, through the characters of Baumgartner and Sophie, to come to grips with the German half of her parental heritage. Not surprisingly, her novels have been regarded within her own country as essentially works of a Europeanized sensibility (there are echoes of George Eliot, Virginia Woolf, Albert Camus, and Fedor Dostoevskii), and some Indian critics have detected in them an outsider's view of the subcontinent that expresses a Western disdain for its social customs and reveals a lack of compassion for the Indian people. Certainly, Desai's fiction is closer to that of the expatriate writer Ruth Prawer Jhabvala, with whom she has expressed an affinity, than to more thoroughly indigenized writers, whether of the vernacular or brahmin traditions of, respectively, Mulk Raj Anand and R.K. Narayan, or the domestic tradition of women writers such as Kamala Markandaya or Kamala Das. Unlike these writers and a later generation of postmodern experimenters—Salman Rushdie, Vikram Seth—Desai has no recourse to native story-telling traditions or oral narrative forms and makes sparing use of Indian mythology. Although she has branched out into history and social satire in her last four books, the bulk of her fiction is conservatively limited in range and low on formal innovation, seldom straying from European modernist narrative modes. Its tight traditional focus and intellectual intensity do, however, make for penetrating psychological portraits, a rarefied lyrical impressionism, and a comprehensiveness in the presentation of the female family—of woman as grandmother, mother, sister, daughter, and granddaughter—that are perhaps unequaled in Indian anglophone fiction.

DEREK WRIGHT

Biography

Born in Mussoorie, 24 June 1937. Attended Queen Mary's Higher Secondary School, New Delhi; Miranda House, University of Delhi, B.A. (honors) in English literature, 1957. Has taught at Girton College (Cambridge, England), Smith College, and Mount Holyoke College; currently teaches creative writing at Massachusetts Institute of Technology.

Novels by Desai

Cry, the Peacock, 1963
Voices in the City, 1965
Bye-Bye, Blackbird, 1971
Where Shall We Go This Summer?, 1975
Fire on the Mountain, 1977
Clear Light of Day, 1980
In Custody, 1984
Baumgartner's Bombay, 1988
Journey to Ithaca, 1995

Other Writings: novels for children, including *The Peacock Garden* (1974), *Cat on a Houseboat* (1976), and *The Village by the Sea* (1982), and a collection of short stories entitled *Games at Twilight* (1978).

Further Reading

Bande, Usha, *The Novels of Anita Desai: A Study in Character and Conflict,* New Delhi: Prestige, 1988
Dhawan, R.K., editor, *The Fiction of Anita Desai,* New Delhi: Bahri, 1989
Goel, Kunj Bala, *Language and Theme in Anita Desai's Fiction,* Jaipur: Classic, 1989
Jain, Jasbir, *Stairs to the Attic: The Novels of Anita Desai,* Jaipur: Printwell, 1986
Sharma, R.S., *Anita Desai,* New Delhi: Arnold/Heinemann, 1981
Tripathi, J.P., *The Mind and Art of Anita Desai,* Bareilly: Prakash, 1986

Description

The English verb *to describe* derives from the 16th-century translation of the Latin *describere*, meaning "to write down, copy off, or delineate." According to *The Shorter Oxford English Dictionary* the noun *description* refers to "the action of setting forth in words by mentioning characteristics; verbal representations or portraiture; a graphic or detailed account." As such, description is a central term in Western thought, denoting one of the most basic modes of writing used to represent nonlinguistic reality. Since the 17th century, a central opposition has been established between scientific description and literary description: most branches of science attempt to describe the physical world objectively, whereas literary writers tend to be more explicitly evaluative by making particular choices in terms of form (the shape or structure of sentences and paragraphs), style (the choice of writing technique), and genre (tragedy, comedy, epic, or romance, for example). The Canadian critic Northrop Frye (1957) draws another distinction between assertive description, which "is valued in terms of the accuracy with which it represents" and communicates reality, and literary description, which has a "hypothetical or assumed relation to the external world." In other words, because all literature is fictional to some degree, literary description does not normally entail the same "controlling aim of descriptive accuracy" as science or philosophy.

All literary description has two main features: the first feature is the quality and register of language used in a particular descriptive case, and the second refers to the subject-matter being described, in terms of location, action, character, or dialogue. Description is essential to all literary forms, but different descriptive techniques may be distinguished to characterize prose, poetry, and drama. For example, in lyric poems description tends to take the form of a spatial construction of interconnected images, whereas narrative description is normally associated closely with plot, which serves to propel spatial scenes or portraits through a prospective (or forward looking) temporal dimension. The critic George Watson (1979) states that description is "usually of persons or place, where the true sequence of narrative is abandoned in favour of analysis," whereas Robert Liddell (1947) claims that "pictorial" description is a distraction from plot and can retard the pace of a novel. For these reasons, narrative is often seen as active and dynamic, involving the careful selection of material, whereas description refers to the passive representation of a mass of extranarrative detail.

However, the relationship between description and plot depends wholly on the type of description deployed in particular cases and by particular writers. For example, the opening of Jack London's novel *White Fang* (1906) describes the following scene as a still and paralyzed landscape: "Dark spruce forest on either side the frozen waterway. The trees had been stripped by a recent wind of their white covering of frost, and they seemed to lean toward each other, black and ominous, in the fading light. A vast silence reigned over the land." Even though the narrator describes a static scene (epitomized by the bare opening sentence), the passage of time is denoted by the verb *fading* and the changes in the landscape are emphasized by the effects of the "recent wind." By way of contrast, the French writer Alain Robbe-Grillet describes the following scene at the beginning of *Dans le labyrinthe* (1959; *In the Labyrinth*): "Outside it is raining, outside in the rain one has to walk with head bent, hand shielding eyes that peer ahead nevertheless, a few yards ahead, a few yards of wet asphalt." The action in this scene is conveyed not only by the effects of the inclement weather and the difficulties that the character experiences in walking (it is notable that the scene in *White Fang* has no characters in it), but also by the rhythm and pace of the sentence that emphasizes driving rain and the passing of time.

Description of action is often more closely woven into the unfolding of plot than description of location; but again this depends not only on what is being described but also the pace of sentences and the quality of the language chosen to describe the action. Two further examples make this point clear. The first quotation is from the West Indian writer V.S. Naipaul's novel *The Mimic Men* (1967): "I stood up and she glided down to the floor. She sat on the chair and cried, her big fingers beating softly on the padded arms of the chair." Here, the verbs *glided* and *beating* convey movement but also evoke a sense of mystery that is emphasized further by the "padded arms of the chair," a phrase that carries the connotation of muffled sound and subdued movement. The following passage from Mark Twain's *The Adventures of Huckleberry Finn* (1884) is much more closely tied to plot and suggests more deliberate action than that described in the Naipaul passage: "I went along up the bank . . . all at once, here comes a canoe; just a beauty, too, about thirteen or fourteen foot long, riding high like a duck. I shot head first off the bank, like a frog, clothes and all on, and struck out for the canoe." The difference between the pace of the two passages is conveyed primarily by the choice of verbs, but the type of activity in the Twain passage is emphasized further by the use of two similes: by comparing the boat to a duck and Huck Finn to a frog the narrator provides both a sense of place (the riverbank) and of narrative action.

Description of character, like that of location, sometimes represents an incidental diversion from narrative action, but it can also develop a deeper layering of narrative that prevents it being driven purely by plot. The beginning of George Eliot's *Middlemarch* (1872) provides a good example. On one level, it presents a static description of the protagonist Dorothea Brooke's appearance, but on another level the opening provides a series of contrasts that help explain the psychological motivation of the character's later actions: "Miss Brooke had that kind of beauty which seems to be thrown into relief by poor dress, her hand and wrist were so finely formed that she could wear sleeves not less bare of style than those in which the Blessed Virgin appeared to Italian painters." Such a description conveys to the reader not only a sense of Dorothea's physical features but also her psychological complexity, class background, and cultural expectations. This point may be clarified with reference to another description of character voiced by Salman Rushdie's protagonist Saleem in *Midnight's Children* (1981): "My grandfather's nose: nostrils flaring, curvaceous as dancers. Between them swells the nose's triumphal arch, first up and out, then down and under, sweeping in to his upper lip with a superb and at present red-tipped flick." In this description of his grandfather's nose, the narrator not only reveals his grasp of language and comic vision but also describes indirectly his own physical, psychological, and cultural birthright. Both these examples show that character description is rarely just a diversion from plot, but aids in the development of a complex and nuanced narrative.

Finally, the description of dialogue often serves to develop psychological motivation as well as to generate interpersonal activity on verbal and behavioral levels. What an author chooses to omit in dialogic description may be as revealing about characters or plot as that which is included in a character's speech. For example, the sparse dialogue of Ernest Hemingway's *The Sun Also Rises* (1926) creates a tense and brooding atmosphere despite little, if any, description of character or location: "'Come in,' I called. Montaya walked in. 'How are you?' he said. 'Fine,' I said. 'No bulls today.' 'No,' I said, 'nothing but rain.'" While Hemingway often uses impoverished dialogue, this type of description is most often reserved for theatrical modes of writing in which narrators are rarely used. Narrative description usually provides more details by interspersing dialogue with description of place, action, and character, as does this example from James Joyce's "The Dead" (1914): "— Is it snowing again, Mr Conroy? asked Lily. She has preceded him into the pantry to help him off with his overcoat. Gabriel smiled at the three syllables she had given his surname and glanced at her. She was a slim, growing girl, pale in complexion and with hay-coloured hair. The gas in the pantry made her look still paler. Gabriel had known her when she was a child and used to sit on the lowest step nursing a rag doll. — Yes, Lily, he answered and I think we're in for a night of it." Although Joyce is unusual in avoiding inverted commas to denote spoken phrases, this passage clearly establishes the scene and develops character by interweaving different types of narrative description.

In summary, narrative description may be used in at least four different ways—to describe location, action, character, or dialogue—but it often combines different elements to develop the quality and texture of the narrative: for example, the choice of a first- or third-person narrator provides the writer with varying degrees of subjectivity, and the technique of pathetic fallacy enables a writer to furnish landscapes with human characteristics and emotions. These and other types of narrative layering are often called collectively *diegesis,* which refers to the whole narrative event and not merely the plot. In some cases narrative description is used to support plot, but more often it provides psychological motivation, builds suspense, or establishes a realistic sense of the fictional world presented to the reader.

Because description is such a broad term, it is important to take into account the changing attitudes of writers and critics to its various manifestations in the history of the novel. Moreover, because the novel did not exist as such until the late 17th century (although this temporal demarcation is not universally accepted), it is equally important to study the prehistory of the novel to understand how narrative description developed from broader ideas concerning literary and poetic description.

The major parameters of literary description were formulated in the Classical Greek thought of Plato and Aristotle. In *The Republic,* Plato's philosopher Socrates distinguishes between false and true language. Although he warns against the harmful effect of telling false tales to children, he claims that because poetic (or literary) language imitates, or mimics, reality it necessarily involves a degree of falsehood. In the second and third books of

The Republic, Socrates proposes that the best forms of poetry are those that make falsehood resemble truth as closely as possible; he then goes on to describe the term *mimesis,* or imitative description. He compares narrative (in which the poet writes in his own voice) with imitation (when he pretends to be someone else in character and expression) and distinguishes tragedy and comedy, which consist entirely of imitation (the drama is told by the characters, not the narrator), from epic writing, which combines imitation and narration. In book ten, Socrates compares imitative description with painting and claims that, because both are "far removed from truth," all forms of art are illusory and lack real wisdom. Socrates goes beyond merely criticizing writers who practice slavish imitation when he proposes to banish poetry from his ideal republic in favor of the wisdom and truth of philosophy.

Aristotle did not share Plato's distrust in the falsifying dimension of art, but he agreed that literature is fundamentally representational; paradoxically, literary description provides a copy of the world but also offers the reader a counterfeit reality to the world of experience. In the first chapter of his *Poetics,* Aristotle calls the poet a creator, or "verse-maker," who deploys his art for particular ends. He develops the term *mimesis* beyond Plato's conception by claiming that the poet can learn from the art of imitation rather than simply copy nature unthinkingly, but he also maintains that character description and narrative action should correspond to the "necessary or probable" qualities of real life. Aristotle asserts that mimetic description should be judged not by the categories of truth and falsehood, but in terms of the pleasurable response "its technical finish" and stylistic qualities generate in the reader. Moreover, he asserts that in the tragic genre of writing, because the writer deals with "people better than are found in the world," characters are often "more beautiful" than they actually are, whereas in comedy they tend to be worse "than are found in the world." Thus, for Aristotle, the description of character is essentially mimetic but deployed by the writer for particular aesthetic and moral ends: for example, tragedy attempts to arouse the reader's pathos and sympathy for heroic characters, whereas comedy invites ridicule and laughter.

The Renaissance interest in translating and appropriating classical thought revived the debates about description in 16th-century Europe. This is especially evident in the work of the Elizabethan writer Sir Philip Sidney. In *The Defence of Poesy* (1595) Sidney criticizes Plato for neglecting the sensuality of description, which may entice the reader to an understanding that is often inaccessible to the reader of dry philosophical prose: "the philosopher, setting down with thorny arguments the bare rule, is so hard of utterance and so misty to be conceived, that one that hath no other guide but him shall wade in him till he be old." Sidney argues that writers should attempt both to teach and to delight. In this respect, literary description can transform a "brazen" world into a "golden" one without the writer being necessarily deceptive or duplicitous: "Nature never set forth the earth in so rich tapestry as divers poets have done; neither with so pleasant rivers, fruitful trees, sweet-smelling flowers, nor whatsoever else may make the too much loved earth more lovely." Indeed, because description makes use of images, similes, and metaphors to illustrate ideas, the writer can steer a middle course between the philosopher who is tied to general rules and the historian who must remain faithful to "the particular truth of things." In conclusion, Sidney recommends that poetry can be saved from Plato's charges for two reasons: first, because it can entice and "move" the reader to acquire knowledge, and second, because it can inspire the reader to become himself a poet or "maker."

The emergence of the novel in 17th- and 18th-century Europe saw the rise of a certain type of prose description that reached its mature development in the 19th-century realistic novel. In an early essay on "The New Realistic Novel" (1750) Samuel Johnson states that realistic description exhibits "life in its true state" drawn from "accurate observation of the living world." The challenge of the realistic writer is to make his work resemble life as closely as possible, using language as a transparent window onto "the living world"; such writers "are engaged in portraits of which every one knows the original, and can detect any deviation from exactness of resemblance." Johnson is critical of the realistic novel (which he claims to be written for "the young, the ignorant, and the idle") and, echoing Sidney's recommendations, prefers the more established romance form in which the descriptions of characters and events are selected carefully from "the mass of mankind" in order to present "a diamond," which "though it cannot be made, may be polished by art, and placed in such a situation as to display that lustre which before was buried among common stones." Johnson adheres to a neoclassical formula by arguing that the writer should imitate only the most worthy aspects of life in order to instruct the reader and further his or her moral edification: "to give the power of counteracting fraud without the temptation to practice it; to initiate youth by mock encounters in the art of necessary defence, and to increase prudence without impairing virtue."

In *Mimesis* (1946), the German critic Eric Auerbach traces the development of mimetic realism from ancient Greece to early 20th-century Europe. He detects two strains of realism: the first characterizes the "fully externalized description" and "uniform illumination" of Homeric realism, and the second, in which "certain parts [are] brought into high relief [and] others left obscure," is common to Old Testament description. According to Auerbach, these two strands—the classical and the biblical—have become deeply interwoven through the course of Western literature, developing "in increasingly rich forms, in keeping with the constantly changing and expanding reality of modern life." Modern realism reached its fullest expression in the 19th century when writers such as Honoré de Balzac, Lev Tolstoi, George Eliot, and William Dean Howells deployed narrative description to accurately represent and document their respective social and cultural worlds. Nineteenth-century realism is characterized by detailed physical description and sociological accuracy in order to present the reader with a realistic and inclusive world. As such, realism eradicates the mysterious aspects of biblical description and neutralizes the classical rule of the "distinct level of styles" by focusing on everyday life and common people's experiences.

By the early 20th century in Europe and America, realism had developed from outward documentation of social life to an aesthetic preoccupation with the inward psychology of individuals. In the words of Auerbach, this presents the reader with "an extremely subjective, individualistic, and often eccentrically aberrant impression of reality." Writers such as Marcel Proust, Virginia Woolf, and William Faulkner developed a psychological realism in which the description of the individual's private and unspoken thoughts is deemed more important than the description of external or public events. Marcel Proust describes the modernist project as an attempt to "lend a voice to the crowd, to solitude, to the old clergyman, to the sculptor, to the child, to the horse, to our own soul" and focus upon elements of subjective reality that were marginalized or ignored in 19th-century realism. Consequently, modernist writing often is fragmentary and much more suggestive in its description than 19th-century realism; often it fuses philosophical prose with narrative description (as in the work of Proust and Thomas Mann) or approaches the status of poetic description as in Virginia Woolf's *The Waves* (1931) and Hermann Broch's *Der Tod des Vergil* (1945; *The Death of Virgil*).

But not all critics deemed modernist psychological description to be a positive development of realism. For example, the Marxist critic Georg Lukács was critical of modernism for its abandonment of the "full process of life" (1971). Lukács argues that a certain type of narrative order (which he calls "epic" narrative) duplicates the inner structure of reality: in other words, when deployed in a proper manner mimetic description and the temporal projection of story replicate historical reality in uncomplicated ways. Lukács was unhappy with modernist art because he believed its experimental and disruptive strategies resisted narrative integration; he claims that for modernist writers description "becomes the dominant mode in composition in a period in which, for social reasons, the sense of what is primary in epic construction has been lost. Description is the writer's substitute for the epic significance that has been lost." For this reason, Lukács asserts that the modernist move away from realism involves a "distortion," or misrepresentation, of the economic and cultural forces that shape individuals and social activity in favor of the idiosyncratic and often pathological world of the individual.

Nevertheless, by the mid–20th century, narrative description had begun to proliferate in many competing directions. In 1971 the English critic David Lodge claimed that the contemporary novelist stands at the "crossroads" between the possibilities of fiction and the demands of the empirical world. Lodge concludes that the hesitation the novelist experiences in choosing between these two poles is often built into the descriptive techniques of postmodern novels. Postmodern narratives are characterized by a pastiche of different descriptive styles (often called the "mixedmode") and a loosening of the parameters of realism. Furthermore, as the philosopher Richard Rorty (1989) claims, the decline in the 20th century of "truth" that exists "independently of the human mind" has coincided with the erasure of the sharp distinctions between literary and scientific descriptions. The traditional sense of mimetic description has consequently been challenged by postmodern writers, whereas empirical description becomes, in Rorty's words, just "one more redescription of things to be filed alongside all the others, one more vocabulary, one more set of metaphors." In this way, narrative description has become an open field for exploring the borderlines between different types of knowledge (of place, self, action, or human exchange) without the need for it to be defended against Plato's charges of duplicity and falsehood.

MARTIN HALLIWELL

See also Beginnings and Endings; Diegesis and Diegetic Levels of Narration; Discourse Representation; Mimesis; Narrator; Plot; Realism; Space

Further Reading

Auerbach, Erich, *Mimesis: Dargestellte Wirklichkeit in der abendländischen Literatur,* Bern: Francke, 1946; as *Mimesis: The Representation of Reality in Western Literature,* Princeton, New Jersey: Princeton University Press, 1953

Frye, Northrop, *Anatomy of Criticism: Four Essays,* Princeton, New Jersey: Princeton University Press, 1957

Jameson, Fredric, "Beyond the Cave: Modernism and Modes of Production," in *The Horizon of Literature,* edited by Paul Hernadi, Lincoln: University of Nebraska Press, 1982

Johnson, Samuel, "The New Realistic Novel," in *Samuel Johnson,* edited by Donald Greene, Oxford and New York: Oxford University Press, 1984 (originally published in *Rambler,* no. 4, 1750)

Liddell, Robert, *A Treatise on the Novel,* London: Cape, 1947

Lodge, David, *The Novelist at the Crossroads and Other Essays on Fiction and Criticism,* London: Routledge and Kegan Paul, and Ithaca, New York: Cornell University Press, 1971

Lukács, Georg, *Wider den missverstandenen Realismus,* Hamburg: Claasen, 1958; as *The Meaning of Contemporary Realism,* London: Merlin Press, 1963; as *Realism in Our Time: Literature and the Class Struggle,* New York: Harper, 1964

Lukács, Georg, "Narrate or Describe?," in *Writer and Critic and Other Essays,* edited and translated by Arthur Kahn, New York: Grosset and Dunlap, 1971; London: Merlin Press, 1978

Proust, Marcel, *Contre Sainte-Beuve,* Paris: Gallimard, 1954; as *Against Sainte-Beuve and Other Essays,* London and New York: Penguin, 1988

Rorty, Richard, *Contingency, Irony and Solidarity,* Cambridge and New York: Cambridge University Press, 1989

Russell, D.A., and Michael Winterbottom, editors, *Classical Literary Criticism,* Oxford and New York: Oxford University Press, 1989

Sidney, Philip, Sir, *The Defence of Poesy* (1595), edited by Jan van Dorsten, Oxford: Oxford University Press, 1966

Varsava, Jerry A., *Contingent Meanings: Postmodern Fiction, Mimesis, and the Reader,* Tallahassee: Florida State University Press, 1990

Watson, George, *The Story of the Novel,* London: Macmillan, and New York: Barnes and Noble, 1979

Detective Novel. *See* Crime, Detective, and Mystery Novel

The Devil to Pay in the Backlands by João Guimarães Rosa

Grande sertão: veredas 1956

The Brazilian João Guimarães Rosa enjoys an almost legendary reputation as a novelist on the basis of a single novel, *Grande sertão: veredas,* which has been translated as *The Devil to Pay in the Backlands.*

Guimarães Rosa follows in the footsteps of James Joyce. Although none of his experiments with fictional language is as radical as Joyce's *Finnegans Wake* (1939), his verbal procedures follow along the same lines. His prose explores popular deviations from standard Portuguese, intensifying them to such a degree that his work cannot simply be called an imitation of folk expression. At the same time, he exploits the resources of poetry, especially alliteration, assonance, rhyme, repetition of rhythmic elements, metaphor, and neologism.

Since the beginnings of Brazilian modernism in the 1920s, its dominant modality has been the exploration of national identity.

The Devil to Pay exhibits the same tendency. It centers on a well-known region in Brazilian geography—the *sertão,* the semi-arid interior plain that includes a good part of the northeast and extends down into northern Minas Gerais, where Guimarães Rosa was born. Most of the characters are *jagunços,* a widely recognized folk type, much like the members of horse-riding vigilante bands on America's western frontier. Some of the sources of the novel are to be found in Brazil's *literatura de cordel,* pulp literature on sensational themes.

The Devil to Pay is not merely an exploration of national identity. It outgrows the realistic regionalist mold of later modernism, creating a sense of the *sertão* as a mythical space. Critics have noted the text's connection with the Faust legend and with the tradition of chivalric romance and epic. The work is emphatically allegorical, equating the *sertão* with the world, and the dangerous crossing of its *veredas* (network of bifurcating paths) with living.

With no chapters or other divisions, the book is an uninterrupted monologue, or perhaps more accurately, one side of a dialogue. Riobaldo, the narrator, speaks to an unnamed interlocutor, who, the reader gradually comes to learn, is not from the *sertão* and is considered a learned man. The narrator himself has been a *jagunço,* but he has now retired to enjoy a more pacific existence. Still troubled by his earlier experiences, he asks what consequences his previous actions may have upon the welfare of his soul.

Riobaldo often refers to the dangers of living and to a continual disjunction between life's superficial evidence and its hidden, more profound dimensions. He fears he may have made a pact with the devil, not that he saw him or exchanged words with him, but rather because he intended to do so and had a peculiar feeling when he waited for him to appear at the crossroads. He narrates the troubling relationship he had with Diadorim, a companion *jagunço,* who in spite of outward appearances made him feel the kinds of emotions and desires he had only experienced with women.

The narration abounds with moral quandaries. May a pact with the devil be justified as a counterweapon if the leader of the opposing band has already made such a pact? Can one continue to believe in God, but believe that the devil does not exist? Can lies and betrayal be justified if they are at the service of honorable goals? These and other questions keep rising to the surface in Riobaldo's interview with the unnamed learned outsider.

The novel has many thematic directions (or "veredas"), but its poetic play tends to conflate these diverse elements. For example, "sertão" and "Satanás" (Satan) are unified with the neologism "Satanão." The invented word "diá" builds a bridge between "diabo" (devil) and "Diadorim." The term "caosmos" has been applied by critics to this fictional world that seems to go in every direction but in the end achieves a coherent unity.

Because of its complexity, its exuberant formal virtuosity, its strong rootedness in topical culture, its serious philosophical questioning, and its sheer mass, *The Devil to Pay* qualifies as what Adolfo Casais Monteiro has called a "literary roadblock," a monument of the Latin American neobaroque, imposing and difficult to read but impossible to ignore.

PAUL B. DIXON

Further Reading

Coutinho, Eduardo de Faria, *The Synthesis Novel in Latin America: A Study of João Guimarães Rosa's "Grande sertão: veredas,"* Chapel Hill: Department of Romance Languages and Literatures, University of North Carolina, 1991

Daniel, Mary L., "Word Formation and Deformation in *Grande sertão: veredas,*" *Luso-Brazilian Review* 2 (1965)

Dixon, Paul B., *Reversible Readings: Ambiguity in Four Modern Latin American Novels,* University: University of Alabama Press, 1985

Frizzi, Adria, "The Demonic Texture: Deferral and Plurality in *Grande sertão: veredas,*" *Chasqui* 17:1 (1988)

Lowe, Elizabeth, "Dialogues of *Grande sertão: veredas,*" *Luso-Brazilian Review* 13 (1976)

Merrim, Stephanie, "In the Wake of the Word: Translating Guimarães Rosa," *Dispositio* 7:19–21 (1982)

Merrim, Stephanie, "*Grande sertão: veredas*: A Mighty Maze but Not without a Plan," *Chasqui* 13:1 (1983)

Valente, Luiz Fernando, "Affective Response in *Grande sertão: veredas,*" *Luso-Brazilian Review* 23:1 (1986)

Vincent, Jon S., *João Guimarães Rosa,* Boston: Twayne, 1978

The Devils by Fedor Dostoevskii

Besy 1872

In the late 1860s, after completing work on *Idiot* (1869; *The Idiot*), Dostoevskii returned to an earlier project entitled in his notebooks "The Life of a Great Sinner." Living in Europe, Dostoevskii followed events at home with intense interest, especially the notorious Nechaev affair of 1869. A student group, "The People's Justice," led by S.G. Nechaev, murdered one of their own members. Whether Nechaev ordered the murder as a means of cementing the group by a bond of blood was never definitively established. Dostoevskii saw in the crime a confirmation of his own earlier novelistic projections in *Prestuplenie i nakazanie* (1867; *Crime and Punishment*) about the pernicious influence of radical thought on the shaky moral groundwork of the younger generation of Russians. He described his wish to write a "novel-pamphlet," in which he would express his ideas without restraint, even if it meant that he would gain the reputation of a retrograde. In *The Devils* (also translated as *The Possessed*), unlike *Crime and Punishment* and *The Idiot*, Dostoevskii's central concern is not the single individual but the individual's relation to the history of the nation. The Nechaev affair, and the revolutionary ideology formulated by Nechaev and Mikhail Bakunin in their *Catechism of a Revolutionary,* are the targets of Dostoevskii's attack in *The Devils*. In this respect, the novel belongs to what has been called the subgenre of the anti-nihilist novel, which included such works as Nikolai Leskov's *At Daggers Drawn* and Vs. Krestovskii's *Panurge's Herd*. This subgenre, and *The Devils* itself, may be compared to Joseph Conrad's anti-anarchist works, *The Secret Agent* (1907) and *Under Western Eyes* (1911). In *The Boundaries of Genre* (1981) Gary Saul Morson reads *The Devils* as an anti-utopian novel, thus placing it in a novelistic tradition that includes such works as Dostoevskii's own *Zapiski iz podpol'ia* (1864; *Notes from Underground*), Evgenii Zamiatin's *My* (1924; *We*), and George Orwell's *1984* (1949).

But the novel became much more than a "pamphlet." Like Ivan Turgenev's *Ottsy i deti* (1862; *Fathers and Sons*), to which it is often compared, and whose author it parodies, *The Devils* tells the story of generational conflict between the so-called "men of the forties," that is, figures such as Aleksandr Herzen, Nikolai Ogarev, and Timofei Granovskii, writers grounded in a philosophy of idealism and a literature of romanticism, and the "men of the sixties," politically radical writers such as Nikolai Chernyshevskii and Nikolai Dobroliubov, grounded in positivism, for whom, to use the language of the novel, "boots are more important than Pushkin." The twist on the generational conflict is that Dostoevskii lays the blame for the nihilism of the 1860s on the liberalism of the 1840s. The Granovskii figure in *The Devils*, Stepan Trofimovich Verkhovenskii, is father to the ringleader of the town's nihilist circle; the Nechaev figure, Petr Verkhovenskii, was additionally, in the novel's pre-history, tutor and father-figure to Nikolai Stavrogin. Dostoevskii's picture of Russian society is far bleaker than Turgenev's, revealing a world dominated by crime, scandal, suicide, moral depravity, self-delusion, and insanity. The Nechaev episode is but one of a string of disasters depicted in Dostoevskii's apocalyptic novel.

In considering the history of the novel's creation, most critics see a tension between Dostoevskii's attack on the younger generation of political radicals and a larger philosophical and religious problematic, signaled in one of the epigraphs, the exorcism of the Gadarene swine in the gospel of Luke. To a certain extent the religious and apocalyptic themes of *The Devils* may be traced to Raskolnikov's dream at the end of *Crime and Punishment*, in which the whole world is infected by a form of insanity that masquerades as wisdom. As Irving Howe has pointed out (1962), the heart of the metaphysical chaos of *The Devils* is Stavrogin, who functions as a kind of moral black hole in the novel. All of the major characters revolve around the mysterious Stavrogin, seeking in him the fulfillment of their own projections and desires: his mother wants reassurance that her son's prior Lermontovian escapades were mere youthful frivolity, Verkhovenskii junior wants Stavrogin to play a political role in his revolutionary plans, offering him before the gullible Russian people as a pretender to the throne, and Liza wants him to be the romantic figure of her dreams. Stavrogin is the source both of Shatov's fervent Slavophilism and Kirillov's philosophy of suicide. Kirillov suffers from epileptic attacks during which he experiences the cessation of time. He proposes that by his own suicide human beings will overcome their fear of God and in so doing become gods themselves.

Stavrogin has generated considerable critical controversy, adding to the mythology surrounding Dostoevskii himself. One of the controversies has to do with the identity of Stavrogin's real-life prototype. Many agree that N.G. Speshnev, whom Dostoevskii reportedly called his "Mephistopheles," is the most likely candidate. Another controversy concerns Stavrogin's confession to the monk Tikhon, which was to have been the ninth chapter of the second part of the novel. But the editorial board of *The Russian Messenger,* in which the novel first appeared in serial form during 1871–72, refused the chapter, and in the subsequent separate publication of the novel in 1873 Dostoevskii made no effort to include the expunged material. In the chapter, Tikhon reads Stavrogin's written account of what seems to be his rape of a young girl and her subsequent suicide. Speculation as to Dostoevskii's own possible involvement in a similar crime arose during his lifetime.

The leading theorist of Dostoevskii, M.M. Bakhtin, sees in Stavrogin's confession a particularly clear example of the author's dialogic discourse, that is, speech radically oriented toward another. Stavrogin desperately needs another's ear, but even as he demands forgiveness he refuses it, because with forgiveness comes the interlocutor's finalizing definition of and possible superiority over the confessing speaker. Bakhtin's concept of *carnival* is another theoretical issue important to critical discussions of the novel. Scandal, buffoonery, practical jokes, and public humiliations dominate the world of *The Devils*. As Bakhtin observes in *Problems of Dostoevsky's Poetics* (1984), the single episode of the gathering in Mrs. Stavrogin's drawing room contains multiple scandals, including Lebiadkin's poem, Peter Verkhovenskii's revelations about his father, the slap Stavrogin receives from Shatov, and Liza's fainting fit. However, Bakhtin's overly optimistic interpretation of carnival in the novel—as a means of clarifying relations between individuals—seems out of place in the dark chaos of *The Devils*. The disastrous fête for the poor governesses leads to mayhem and death, and not the joyous renewal that Bakhtin finds central to carnival.

Upon publication, *The Devils* received harsh reviews from critics sympathetic to the political movements of the young, claiming that Dostoevskii had painted a whole generation as crazed fanatics. The novel, in this view, marked a watershed in the author's career: he had abandoned his earlier political commitments, evidenced not only in his actions but in his writings, especially *Zapiski iz mertvogo doma* (1861–62; *Memoirs from the House of the Dead*). Dostoevskii defended himself in a column he published in 1873, arguing that he himself was an "old Nechaevite." The controversy about Dostoevskii's political inclinations cannot be resolved so easily. To read *The Devils* simply as the political pamphlet its author said it would be is to diminish the complexity of its artistry and the conflicting ideologies of its author.

The Devils undeniably plays a significant role in the development of European realism in the 19th century. For many 20th-century critics, *The Devils* signals the end of the 19th-century realist tradition. As Edward Said remarks in *Beginnings: Intention and Method* (1975), text, time, and understanding fall out of sync in *The Devils*. Normal genealogy is suspended, the family is shattered, and the events of the novel seem to overtake the control of their creator. The novel's narrative structure contributes to this sense of disorder. The narrator also plays a role as a character in the novel, which leads to inconsistencies in his narrative report. For example, he provides detailed accounts of scenes at which he had not been present, yet he emphasizes the gaps in his knowledge and his lack of skill as a narrator. Michael Holquist (1977) argues that the parceling out of Stavrogin's persona among all the other characters—for example, Shatov and Kirillov—signals the disruption of the coherent individual self upon which the realist novel usually depends. Rather than the formation of a personality and the development of character, *The Devils* reveals the disintegration of personality. The characters in the novel serve as screens upon which one another's fantasies may be projected. René Girard (1965) sees a stark illustration of mimetic desire in the intense mixture of love and hate that characterizes Stavrogin's relations to others. Dostoevskii's refusal to provide a totalizing narrative account, his deconstruction of the image of the family, and his deliberate deformation of the integral personality—in a word, his own unique form of fantastic realism—signals a break with the history of the 19th-century realist novel, the best examples of which in Russia would be the work of Turgenev and Lev Tolstoi. *The Devils* provides an important transition to new novelistic approaches in the 20th century.

HARRIET MURAV

See also Fedor Dostoevskii

Further Reading

Bakhtin, M.M., *Problemy tvorchestva Dostoevskogo,* Leningrad: Priboi, 1929; 2nd edition, revised, as *Problemy poetiki Dostoevskogo,* Moscow: Sov. Pisatel, 1963; as *Problems of Dostoevsky's Poetics,* Ann Arbor, Michigan: Ardis, 1973; new edition and translation, Minneapolis: University of Minnesota Press, and Manchester: Manchester University Press, 1984

Frank, Joseph, *Dostoevsky: The Miraculous Years, 1865–1871,* Princeton, New Jersey: Princeton University Press, 1995

Girard, René, *Deceit, Desire, and the Novel: Self and Other in Literary Structure,* Baltimore: Johns Hopkins University Press, 1965

Holquist, Michael, *Dostoevsky and the Novel,* Princeton, New Jersey: Princeton University Press, 1977

Howe, Irving, "Dostoevsky and the Politics of Salvation," in *Dostoevsky: A Collection of Critical Essays,* edited by René Wellek, Englewood Cliffs, New Jersey: Prentice-Hall, 1962

Jones, Malcolm, *Dostoevsky: The Novel of Discord,* New York: Barnes and Noble, and London: Elek, 1976

Murav, Harriet, *Holy Foolishness: Dostoevsky's Novels and the Poetics of Cultural Critique,* Stanford, California: Stanford University Press, 1992

Saraskina, L.I., *Fedor Dostoevskii: Odolenie demonov,* Moscow: Soglasie, 1996

Wasiolek, Edward, *Dostoevsky: The Major Fiction,* Cambridge, Massachusetts: MIT Press, 1964

Dialogism

The Russian philosopher and literary theoretician M.M. Bakhtin (1895–1975), in a series of essays and books primarily written between the 1920s and the 1940s (although many remained unpublished at the time), developed a series of interrelated ideas that have been very influential to the study of the novel over the past 25 years. Among these, his concept of *dialogism* may be the broadest in its implications. Bakhtin sees spoken and written discourse as made up of a host of competing "languages." For Bakhtin, a language may be constituted by the specialized vocabulary of a literary or popular literary genre, by that of one of the trades or professions, by the characteristic locutions of a given social class or level, and even by the ideology articulated by a particular social group. Each speaker finds, already present in the social world, different levels and genres of speech that no individual speaker can claim to own. Further, virtually all speech is *directed toward* other competing languages. More than simply stating a speaker's position, his language is always anticipating a response, attempting to foreclose one, or simply trying to win approval from someone with a different ideological stance. Language with this mixed function Bakhtin calls "double-voiced," and he analyzes different kinds of double-voicedness at some length. Dialogism, then, is the principle that declares that all speech must be in some measure *polyphonic*—another favorite term of Bakhtin's—however it may strive for the absolute authority of uncontested monologue. Bakhtin's term for the condition of existence in a dialogic world is *heteroglossia*, the chaotic but energizing mixture of languages in the midst of which every speaker finds herself and every work of literature must locate itself.

These truths are best demonstrated in the novel; in fact, "novelness" (*romannost'*)—what Bakhtin sees as the most characteristic feature of novels—best demonstrates dialogism at work. Bakhtin reacts against the inheritance of classical aesthetics, which put a premium on the genres of lyric poetry and of drama, if only because those genres existed in roughly the same form in the classical period. Instead, he finds the newer form of the novel the superior genre because, whereas poetry and drama both tend to lapse into monologism (marked by the dominance of the author's single, authoritative, unopposed voice that we can see most clearly in romantic poetry), the novel is characterized throughout by the play and competition among many voices. Actually, the novel could be described as a "super-genre," since it is capable of infecting or colonizing other genres: plays and even poems can be "novelized," and for Bakhtin this is all to the good. On the other hand, some novels do not display sufficient "novelness": Tolstoi, for instance, has an authorial voice that Bakhtin feels too often dominates the voices of his characters. By contrast, in the works of Bakhtin's hero Fedor Dostoevskii no voice is allowed to dominate; a multitude of characters are given strong voices that remain in perpetual battle or negotiation with one another and with Dostoevskii's authorial voice. Although Bakhtin sometimes speaks of an overall aesthetic unity in novels, practically speaking he stresses multiplicity, dynamics, and an "unfinalized" quality in novels that he sees as parallel to the same qualities in human selves.

The novel's dialogism is not only a function of the interacting languages of its characters and author, but also of the variety of other written genres with which the novel itself is in a perpetual process of negotiation. A given novel may borrow from romances, from true crime stories, from law court reports or other journalistic genres, as well as from ideologically powerful languages such as that of the Orthodox church; or its language at different points may be negatively or positively "oriented toward" these languages. As Bakhtin says in his essay "Discourse in the Novel" (collected in *The Dialogic Imagination*, 1981), the novelist "does not purge words of intentions and tones that are alien to him, he does not destroy the seeds of social heteroglossia embedded in words." This characteristic has been discussed by other contemporary literary critics as *intertextuality*, and for poststructuralist critics it is a fundamental property of modern texts. But Bakhtin's understanding of the intertextual phenomenon differs from that of deconstructive critics. He stresses the social context that grounds the different languages rather than the purely linguistic "free play" of "signifiers" detached from any human context.

Bakhtin's other great hero of the novel is François Rabelais, whose novels he discusses under the rubric of *carnivalism*. Like dialogism, carnivalism is a way of displaying (indeed, reveling in) otherness, difference, what Bakhtinians sometimes call *alterity*. Where in dialogism the medium of display is language, in carnival, which Bakhtin calls a "theater without footlights," it is the body. Bakhtin's concept is based on the early Modern European celebration called carnival or Mardi Gras, in which a licensed inversion of ordinary rank and values was allowed—a fool is crowned, the Church is mocked and parodied, the mighty are brought low, and the lowest are exalted. In carnivalized writing such as Rabelais' *Gargantua and Pantagruel* (c. 1532–34), the author flaunts what Bakhtin calls "the grotesque body," with an emphasis on "lower bodily" processes—eating, drinking, defecating, copulating, giving birth, dismemberment, and so forth. In Bakhtin's view all of these contribute to a celebration of the ongoing physical life of humanity, rather than any individual human. On the level of language, the carnivalized work emphasizes the forms of parody and pastiche, profanity, ritual insult, and various sorts of linguistic play. All of these language forms originally opposed the Church's monologue.

On the whole, Bakhtin's influence has been in his emphasis on an "alternative tradition" of the novel, one distinct from and in some ways opposed to the model of the Victorian realist novel with its emphasis on omniscient narrators. Bakhtin's central canon would include Miguel de Cervantes' *Don Quixote* (1605–15), Rabelais' *Gargantua and Pantagruel*, Laurence Sterne's *Tristram Shandy* (1759–67), Henry Fielding's *Tom Jones* (1749), Lord Byron's *Don Juan* (1826), various novels by Dostoevskii, and (perhaps) 20th-century works such James Joyce's *Ulysses* (1922), at the expense of works by George Eliot, Wil-

liam Makepeace Thackeray, or Henry James, which for Bakhtin are less essentially novelistic because in his view they are both less dialogical and less carnivalized. Clearly, this is a list of "exceptional" novels, but then Bakhtin's point is that the novel is a genre of exceptions. It is polyphonic, self-parodying and self-mocking, and involved in a perpetual verbal intercourse with the rich variety of languages surrounding it. At its best it is seriously comic, bawdy, verbally inventive, and engaged in dialogue with everything around it; the very existence of dialogical narratives is a challenge to any totalitarian discourse.

R. BRANDON KERSHNER

See also Epic and Novel; Parody and Pastiche

Further Reading

Bakhtin, M.M., *The Dialogic Imagination*, translated by Caryl Emerson and Michael Holquist, edited by Holquist, Austin: University of Texas Press, 1981

Bakhtin, M.M., *Tvorchestvo Fransua Rable i Narodnaja Kul'tura Srednevekovija i Renessansa*, Moscow: Khudozh, 1965; as *Rabelais and His World*, Cambridge, Massachusetts: MIT Press, 1968

Bakhtin, M.M., *Problemy tvorchestva Dostoevskogo*, Leningrad: Priboi, 1929; 2nd edition, revised, as *Problemy poetiki Dostoevskogo*, Moscow: Sov. Pisatel, 1963; as *Problems of Dostoevsky's Poetics*, Ann Arbor, Michigan: Ardis, 1973; new edition and translation, Minneapolis: University of Minnesota Press, and Manchester: Manchester University Press, 1984

Holquist, Michael, *Dialogism: Bakhtin and His World*, London and New York: Routledge, 1990

Kershner, R. Brandon, *Joyce, Bakhtin, and Popular Literature: Chronicles of Disorder*, Chapel Hill: University of North Carolina Press, 1989

Lodge, David, *After Bakhtin: Essays on Fiction and Criticism*, London and New York: Routledge, 1990

Morson, Gary Saul, editor, *Bakhtin: Essays and Dialogues on His Work*, Chicago: University of Chicago Press, 1986

Morson, Gary Saul, and Caryl Emerson, *Mikhail Bakhtin: Creation of a Prosaics*, Stanford, California: Stanford University Press, 1990

Todorov, Tzvetan, *Mikhail Bakhtin: The Dialogical Principle*, Manchester: Manchester University Press, and Minneapolis: University of Minnesota Press, 1984

Yaeger, Patricia, *Honey-Mad Women: Emancipatory Strategies in Women's Writing*, New York: Columbia University Press, 1988

Dialogue. *See* Discourse Representation

La Diana by Jorge de Montemayor

1559

Born in Montenôr-o-Velho, Portugal, Jorge de Montemayor left for Spain at an early age and adopted the Castillian version of his birthplace instead of his family name, which is unknown. He served in the households of Philip II of Spain and other members of the Hapsburg family as a professional musician until 1561 or 1562, when he was killed by a jealous rival, the result of a love triangle. Although Portuguese was his first language, Montemayor wrote almost exclusively in Spanish. He was well known and respected among his contemporaries in Spain and Portugal and was read throughout Europe.

Sometimes called the "first of the Spanish Dianas," Montemayor's *Los siete libros de la Diana,* often shortened to simply *La Diana,* is important because it is the first and best-known Spanish pastoral novel. Published in 1559, it was applauded as highly entertaining and enjoyed immediate popular success. In Spain, only *La Celestina* (1499/1502) and *Amadís de Gaula* (1508) rivaled *La Diana*'s popularity in the second half of the 16th century, and in the first part of the 17th century the novel went through nearly 50 editions and 35 translations. The critical fortunes of *La Diana* have since waxed and waned, and while it was regarded by some in the early 20th century as insignificant, artificial, and extravagant, by the 1950s the novel enjoyed a renaissance and is now generally regarded as seminal in the development of narrative fiction in Spain and elsewhere. Moreover, there are those who consider *La Diana* the forerunner of the modern psychological novel.

Nourished by the neoplatonic influence of the Italian Renaissance, *La Diana* shares with its Italian forerunner, Jacopo Sannazaro's *Arcadia* (1502), the same sources: Giovanni Boccacio, Petrarch, Dante Alighieri, Virgil, and Homer, to name only a few. On the Iberian Peninsula it was influenced by pastoral elements in the poetry and drama of the Middle Ages, including the Galician-Portuguese *pastorelas* of the 12th and 13th centuries, the Castillian *serranillas* of the 14th and 15th centuries, and the pastoral themes found in the early 16th-century chivalry novels. Introduced by the summary of a previous fictional work, which sets the scene for the novel, *La Diana* alternates between eclogues (pastoral poems usually composed of alternating stanzas of dialogue between two shepherds) and prose narrative. The dilemma is love; the resolution is marriage. In Books I–III, love triangles are revealed and the lovers set out on a journey (vaguely reminiscent of Boccaccio and Geoffrey Chaucer) to the Temple of Diana to find relief from their maladies of the heart; the stories they tell along the way are their own. In Book IV Felicia, priestess of Diana, speaks of love in neoplatonic terms and introduces a supernatural element in the form of her magic water. This is the pivotal book in that Felicia offers solutions to problems that will work themselves out in Books V–VII. In those last books, not only do the complications of Books I–III begin to be resolved, but other characters appear to weave their own stories through those already in motion. Although her story is told and retold in earlier books, Diana of the title does not appear until Book V. Her story and those of two new lover-beloved pairs are not resolved, laying the framework for a promised sequel, but like the fictional introductory work of which *La Diana* is sup-

posed to be the sequel, the promise appears to be a device to write *in media res.*

Apart from the obvious reference to Diana, the Roman goddess of nature and the hunt, the novel engages in a delightful play on names. Whether recalling the catlike qualities of the Latin *felis* or the illusive happiness of the Spanish *feliz*, the Felis/Felicia/Felismena triad is a prime example. Felicia and Felis share many qualities, she the priestess of Diana and he the gentleman; Felismena is a female only a little less (from the Spanish *menos*) than either of them, that is, a little less than priestess and a little less than male. Selvagia and Silvano invoke the magic and mystery of the forest, and Belisa the lure of beauty. Irony also has its play: Sireno, the name of one of the shepherds, is the masculine form of *siren*—usually feminine in Spanish.

The cast of characters has been called a veritable parade of shepherds and shepherdesses, some of whom do actually tend sheep. Others are knights and ladies who have left the intrigues of the court to find love in a *locus ameonus* setting. Still others are musicians and poets. In two stories the man is aided by the girl's maid who serves as go-between, hinting at the influence of Juan Ruiz' colorful character Trotaconventos and Fernando de Rojas' Celestina. Giving his novel a pastoral setting allowed Montemayor to avoid the rigid dicta of Spanish society while studying love in its many and varied dimensions. This is not the world of the Don Juan, nor is it the coquetry of the court; it is a more innocent preoccupation in which marriage, and not dalliance, is the goal, and once the lovers have committed they should not cast their attentions elsewhere. Against the backdrop of nature at its purest, pairs of lovers meet and alternately extol and lament love's vagaries.

The scene, then, is beautiful and peaceful, save for a band of savages who are introduced, perhaps, to offer a counterpoint against which the beautiful becomes truly indescribable. In this world where external beauty was considered a sign of internal virtue and where, at the sight of beauty, love blossomed, physiological differences did not always matter. With incidents involving disguise and mistaken identity, Montemayor suggests rather than explores homosexuality. It is generally considered that women in *La Diana* fared better than women in other Renaissance literature, since the female characters are better drawn and have a much larger part than their male counterparts and seem to voice a woman's perspective on courtship, love, and marriage.

There is evidence that *La Diana* was read and highly regarded by John Donne, Miguel de Cervantes, James I of England, San Juan de la Cruz, William Shakespeare, Lope de Vega, and Gracián. Subsequent Spanish pastoral writers followed Montemayor's model, rather than Sannazaro's *Arcadia*, although the mark of the Italian as stimulus and paradigm is unmistakable. Cervantes criticized the escapism of pastoral novels in his *Don Quixote* (1605–15), but echoed it in his *La Galatea* (1585). Internationally Montemayor's influence may be seen in many works, among them plot elements of Shakespeare's *The Two Gentlemen of Verona* (produced 1594?) and Sir Philip Sidney's *Arcadia* (1590). The novel has not passed through time unscathed; Baron Hans Ludwig von Kuffstein's translation of *La*

Diana significantly altered the pastoral setting and eliminated the erotic subject matter. Instead, he inserted moral observations on the conduct of his shepherds, giving the "translation" a more courtly view of love. The lack of the promised sequel, perhaps due to Montemayor's untimely death, prompted Gaspar Gil Polo's *La Diana enamorada* (1564) and Alonso Pérez' *La "Diana" de Jorge de Montemayor, Segunda parte* (1580).

FRANCES MEUSER

See also Pastoralism in the Novel

Further Reading

Avalle-Arce, Juan Bautista, *La novela pastoril española*, Madrid: Revista de Occidente, 1959; 2nd edition, Madrid: Istmo, 1974

Chevalier, Maxime, "*La Diana* de Montemayor y su público en la España del siglo XVI," in *Creación y público en la literatura española*, edited by Jean-Francois Botrel, Serge Salaun, and Andres Amoros, Madrid: Castalia, 1974

Cirurgião, Antonio A., "O papel da palavra na *Diana* de Jorge de Montemor," *Ocidente* (Lisbon) 360 (1968)

Damiani, Bruno M., *"La Diana" of Montemayor as Social and Religious Teaching*, Lexington: University Press of Kentucky, 1983

de Armas, Frederick A., "Caves of Fame and Wisdom in the Spanish Pastoral Novel," *Studies in Philology* 82:3 (1985)

El Saffar, Ruth, "Structural and Thematic Discontinuity in Montemayor's *Diana*," *Modern Language Notes* 86 (1971)

Fosalba, Eugenia, *La Diana en Europa: Ediciones, traducciones e influencias*, Barcelona: Seminari de Filologia i d'Informatica, Departament de Filologia Espanyola, Universitat Autonoma de Barcelona, 1994

Hoffmeister, Gerhart, *Die spanische "Diana" in Deutschland*, Berlin: Erich Schmidt, 1972

Johnson, Carroll B., "Montemayor's *Diana*: A Novel Pastoral," *Bulletin of Hispanic Studies* 48 (1971)

Johnson, Carroll B., "Amor-Aliqua Vincit: Erotismo y amor en la *Diana*," in *Erotismo en las letras hispánicas: Aspectos, modos y fronteras*, edited by Luce Lopez-Baralt and Francisco Marquez Villanueva, Mexico City: Centro de Estudios Linguisticos y Literarios, Colegio de México, 1995

Knightly, R.G., "Narrative Perspectives in Spanish Pastoral Fiction," *AUMLA* 44 (1975)

Mueller, RoseAnna M., "Some Considerations in Translating the *Diana*," *Centerpoint: A Journal of Interdisciplinary Studies* 2:2 (1977)

Perry, T. Anthony, "Ideal Love and Human Reality in Montemayor's *La Diana*," *Publications of the Modern Language Association* 84 (1969)

Reyes Cano, Rogelio, "*La Arcadia*" de Sannazaro en España, Seville: Universidad de Sevilla, 1973

Rhodes, Elizabeth, "Skirting the Men: Gender Roles in Sixteenth-Century Pastoral Books," *Journal of Hispanic Philology* 11:2 (1987)

Ricciardelli, Michele, *Notas sobre "La Diana" de Montemayor y "La Arcadia" de Sannazaro*, Montevideo: Garcia Morales-Mercant, 1965

Silva, J. de Oliveira e, "Structures and Restructures in Montemayor's *Diana*, Books I–III," *Bulletin of Hispanic Studies* 72:2 (1995)

Solé-Leris, Amadeu, *The Spanish Pastoral Novel*, Boston: Twayne, 1980

Stagg, Geoffrey, "Felicia's Palace and *Don Quixote*," in *Essays on Narrative Fiction in the Iberian Peninsula in Honour of Frank Pierce*, edited by R.B. Tate, Oxford: Dolphin, 1982

Wardropper, Bruce, "The *Diana* of Montemayor: Reevaluation and Interpretation," *Studies in Philology* 48 (1951)

Diary. *See* Prose Novelistic Forms

Charles Dickens 1812–70

English

Charles Dickens is one of the most important figures—some would say *the* most important figure—in the development of the 19th-century British novel. His first novel, *The Pickwick Papers* (1837), was an unprecedented blockbuster, giving Dickens a luminous national celebrity that he maintained for the rest of his life. In all, he published 14 novels and the uncompleted *Mystery of Edwin Drood* (1870), along with many short stories and novellas. Styled "the Shakespeare of the novel" by the Cambridge critics F.R. and Q.D. Leavis, Dickens dominated the literary landscape during his time, and he remained an inescapable reference point for novelists who followed him, whether they imitated or resisted his aesthetic principles and his conception of the novel's place in society.

Dickens' unsurpassed popularity over his 35-year career is the key to a number of his novelistic innovations. More than any "serious" novelist before him, Dickens drew substantially on popular literary forms and integrated them both stylistically and thematically into his fiction. He tapped early Victorian melodrama for many of his plots, for instance, and his techniques of characterization adopted melodrama's stark and histrionic delineation of moral types. Dickens also drew subjects and themes from popular novelists of the early 19th century, such as Pierce Egan and Theodore Hook, and his novels are laced with allusions to popular 18th-century "classics" by Fielding, Defoe, Goldsmith, and Smollett, as well as to Cervantes and to Scott. These allusions establish thematic parallels with earlier novels and did a great deal to consolidate in the popular imagination a sense of the historical unity of the novelistic canon, with Dickens often presenting himself as the direct inheritor and culmination of that canon.

One of the specific features Dickens associated with the novel as a genre was fantasy, and his work did much to promote the idea that the novel had its aesthetic foundations in a special mixture of fantasy and realism. Followers of Dickens have often emphasized only one half of this dualism, celebrating his powers of psychological or social realism, on the one hand, or his imaginative skills, on the other. Ultimately, however, it is the special combination of realism and fantasy—often explicitly thematized in the novels as a productive tension—that defines Dickens' aesthetic. As he puts it in his preface to *Bleak House* (1853), "I have purposely dwelt upon the romantic side of familiar things." A great many of Dickens' aesthetic pronouncements highlight this dualism. In *Household Words*, for instance, he said of his work that while it was intended to capture the "social wonders, good and evil" of "the stirring world round us," it should adopt "no mere utilitarian spirit, no iron binding of the mind to grim realities," but rather should "cherish the light of Fancy which is inherent in the human breast." This dualism is the source of the heightened idiosyncrasies of Dickens' characters, of the novels' often surreal settings, and of their sometimes manic linguistic play, as well as a number of other characteristic features of Dickens' work, from the psychological extremism of his more obsessional characters to the fairy-tale romantic conclusions of the novels' plots.

Formally, Dickens also set standards for clarity, originality, and intensity of physical description that later novelists labored to match—especially his ability to evoke a moral atmosphere through his depiction of objects, which often seem animated with intentionality. In addition, he captured colloquial speech in unprecedented ways. While he has sometimes been faulted for the apparent moral simplicity of his novels, his moral allegories often are complicated by an extensive use of subplots and character doublings that parallel and enrich the simple thematic lines of the main plot—devices that proved highly influential among later novelists.

But perhaps Dickens' greatest originality as a novelist lies in his explosive range and creativity in characterization. His career began with the publication of *Sketches by Boz* (1836), a collection of character sketches that explored human psychology through a striking array of caricatures. Dickens' skills with characterization are marked in a variety of ways by his experience with popular theatre (which he claimed to have attended every evening for two or three years running, early in his career). Dickens' characters reveal their psychological essences performatively, and their exaggerated patterns of speech and behavior, as well as the descriptive "tag lines" associated with them, imitate methods of caricature Dickens derived from the stage. An accomplished actor himself, Dickens often conceived his characters by acting them out before a mirror and then describing in prose his own appearance.

Although often disparaged for his psychological oversimplifications, Dickens pioneered a kind of psychological expressiveness that ran counter to the subtle depth-models of psychology associated with George Eliot, Henry James, Joseph Conrad, and other novelists who later came to represent the mainstream tradition of the novel. Dickens' psychologism, in contrast to that of the modern novel, revolves around his tendency to see subjectivity as a staged phenomenon and to represent psychic states, therefore, as a set of discontinuous, performative, and socially-conditioned roles. Dickens' attention to the performative nature of the psyche led him to focus on psychological mechanisms as they are presented to others in a kind of public theatre of the mind. This aspect of his work diminished Dickens' influence in some ways during the modern period, although it has made possible a postmodern revival, as his methods of characterization have influenced writers such as Charles Palliser, Thomas Pynchon, and Joseph Heller.

Dickens' importance to the history of the novel lies in several material and ideological dimensions as well. He pioneered the serialization of the novel, issuing cheap weekly or monthly installments of his novels before publishing them in book form. Cheap serialization, which was adopted by most Victorian novelists who followed him, expanded the audience for fiction dramatically. It also created new aesthetic pressures for compression, unity, and suspense within and between serial issues. Dickens also was active in exploring new methods of printing and advertising, and he was a leading figure in the campaign for copyright laws, both domestic and international.

Ideologically, Dickens was remarkable for his ability to cut across the social boundaries of his readership. This ability was predicated on the universal humanist values, molded around New Testament pieties, that he helped introduce into 19th-century literature generally. It also required him to address the ideological values of very different constituencies, at the same time that he had to suppress conflicts between them. For instance, Dickens pioneered an affirmative incorporation of lower-class culture into the novel—celebrating popular entertainments such as the circus, the pantomime, and the Punch and Judy show—while at the same time merging popular idealism about fellow-feeling with middle-class values of benevolence and patronage. Another instance of this ideological synthesis is the extreme sentimentality that characterizes his work—known most familiarly through his Christmas stories, especially *A Christmas Carol* (1843). This sentimentality has often hindered Dickens' influence on later writers (Oscar Wilde once quipped, referring to *The Old Curiosity Shop* [1841], "A man would have to have a heart of stone to read the death of Little Nell without laughing"). But in Dickens' own day, that sentimentality was able to bridge popular and elite literary sympathies. In general, Dickens combined an affirmation of charitable virtues with an acute moral intelligence to create a populism that affirmed human nature while also recognizing its worst potentials, thus making his work palatable to a very wide audience.

The social and political values of Dickens' novels are diverse. Dickens' populism manifests itself formally in a variety of ways, including his narrative persona, which borrowed the satiric tone of Fielding and Smollett but added to it a new bite. His consistent facetiousness of tone, his comic hyperbole, his mixture of caustic satire and cheerfulness, and his grudging attitude toward snobbishness of any kind—all give Dickens' narrative voice an impish character that expresses the social cockiness of his broad class base. At the same time, however, Dickens' love of Bildungsroman plots, often featuring orphans who rise to success and security, caught the general spirit of social optimism among the newly enfranchised middle class in the 1830s, when Dickens began writing. His affirmation of upward social ambitions was also careful to confine individualism within strict moral limits, making it acceptable to the Victorian middle class. Indeed, his exceptional emphasis on the nonmercenary motives of his heroes introduced a new note of moral purity into British fiction. His extraordinary separation of public and private spheres and his celebration of the "feminine" values of hearth and home also derive from Victorian middle-class culture. His adulation of the virtues of domesticity contributed to the Victorian cult of the domestic angel and allowed him to introduce childhood as a serious subject into the British novel. It also gave a vehicle for the incorporation of religious values into secular settings.

Dickens was the first great "social novelist," in the sense that his novels took on topical issues and established the novelist as a voice of social authority. In particular, Dickens tended to present himself as a spokesperson for the "common man" and concentrated his fictional satires on the harm public institutions did to the poor. *Oliver Twist* (1830), for example, is in large measure an attack on contemporary attitudes toward poverty (including workhouse legislation), and *Nicholas Nickleby* (1839) begins with a satire on the Yorkshire schools. Dickens also used his newspaper, the *Daily News,* and his magazines *Household Words* and *All the Year Round,* to speak out against social injustice—which to him largely meant the unfeeling nature of bureaucracies. His social criticism and his advocacy of certain causes, like the legalization of Sunday amusements or reform of the workhouse, contributed to political and social change.

Through the social authority he brought to the novel and the sheer brilliance of his talent, Dickens did a great deal to endow the figure of the novelist with a new kind of public visibility and dignity. He helped develop a new professional consciousness among writers—delineated in the career of David Copperfield—uniting in the figure of the writer the qualities of both the genius and the entrepreneur. But his influence on later writers is manifold, extending from Gogol', Tolstoi, and Dostoevskii in the area of characterization and plotting and to Gissing and Shaw when it comes to social mission. In this century, we can discern Dickens' work behind the linguistic self-reflexiveness of Joyce and the surreal allegories of Kafka. His importance to English fiction is captured in eloquent understatement by an obituary in the *Daily News,* which called him, quite simply, "the one writer everybody read and everybody liked."

JOHN KUCICH

See also Bleak House; David Copperfield; Great Expectations; Pickwick Papers

Biography

Born 7 February 1812 in Portsmouth, Hampshire. Studied at Wellington House Academy, London, 1824–27, and Mr. Dawson's school, Brunswick Square, London, 1827. Clerk in a law office, London, 1827–28; shorthand reporter, Doctors' Commons, 1828–30, and in Parliament for *True Son,* 1830–32, *Mirror of Parliament,* 1832–34, and *Morning Chronicle,* 1834–36; contributor, *Monthly Magazine,* 1833–34 (as Boz, 1834), and *Evening Chronicle,* 1835–36; editor, *Bentley's Miscellany,* 1837–39; visited the United States, 1842; lived in Italy, 1844–45; appeared in amateur theatricals from 1845, and managed an amateur theatrical tour of England, 1847; editor, London *Daily News,* 1846; lived in Switzerland and Paris, 1846; founding editor, *Household Words,* London, 1850–59, and its successor, *All the Year Round,* 1859–70; gave reading tours of Britain, 1858–59, 1861–63, 1866–67, and 1868–70, and in the United States, 1867–68. Died 9 June 1870.

Novels by Dickens

Sketches by Boz Illustrative of Every-Day Life and Every-Day People, 1836; second series, 1836
The Posthumous Papers of the Pickwick Club, 1837
Oliver Twist; or, The Parish Boy's Progress, 1838
The Life and Adventures of Nicholas Nickleby, 1839
Master Humphrey's Clock: The Old Curiosity Shop, Barnaby Rudge, 3 vols., 1840–41; *The Old Curiosity Shop* and *Barnaby Rudge* each published separately, 1841
A Christmas Carol, in Prose, Being a Ghost Story of Christmas, 1843
The Life and Adventures of Martin Chuzzlewit, 1844
The Chimes: A Goblin Story, 1844
The Battle of Life: A Love Story, 1846
The Haunted Man and the Ghost's Bargain: A Fancy for Christmas Time, 1848
Dealings with the Firm of Dombey and Son, Wholesale, Retail, and for Exportation, 1848
The Personal History of David Copperfield, 1850
Bleak House, 1853
Hard Times, for These Times, 1854
Little Dorritt, 1857
A Tale of Two Cities, 1859
Great Expectations, 1861
Our Mutual Friend, 1865
The Mystery of Edwin Drood, 1870

Other Writings: short stories, sketches, plays, essays, travel books; speeches and social journalism.

Further Reading

Arac, Jonathan, *Commissioned Spirits: The Shaping of Social Motion in Dickens, Carlyle, Melville, and Hawthorne,* New Brunswick, New Jersey: Rutgers University Press, 1979
Andrews, Malcolm, *Dickens and the Grown-Up Child,* London: Macmillan, and Iowa City: University of Iowa Press, 1994
Collins, Philip, "Dickens and His Readers," in *Victorian Values: Perspectives and Personalities in Nineteenth-Century Society,* edited by Gordon Marsden, London and New York: Longman, 1990
Cottom, Daniel, *Text and Culture: The Politics of Interpretation,* Minneapolis: University of Minnesota Press, 1989
Daldry, Graham, *Charles Dickens and the Form of the Novel,* Totowa, New Jersey: Barnes and Noble, 1986; London: Croom Helm, 1987

Ford, George, *Dickens and His Readers: Aspects of Novel Criticism since 1836,* Princeton, New Jersey: Princeton University Press, 1955

House, Humphry, *The Dickens World,* London and New York: Oxford University Press, 1941; 2nd edition, 1942

Jaffe, Audrey, *Vanishing Points: Dickens, Narrative, and the Subject of Omniscience,* Berkeley: University of California Press, 1991

Kucich, John, *Repression in Victorian Fiction: Charlotte Brontë, George Eliot, and Charles Dickens,* Berkeley: University of California Press, 1987

Langbauer, Laurie, *Women and Romance: The Consolations of Gender in the English Novel,* Ithaca, New York: Cornell University Press, 1990

Leavis, F.R., and Q.D. Leavis, *Dickens the Novelist,* London: Chatto and Windus, 1970; New York: Pantheon, 1971

Levine, George, *The Realistic Imagination: English Fiction from Frankenstein to Lady Chatterley,* Chicago: University of Chicago Press, 1981

Litvak, Joseph, *Caught in the Act: Theatricality in the Nineteenth-Century English Novel,* Berkeley: University of California Press, 1992

Miller, D.A., *The Novel and the Police,* Berkeley: University of California Press, 1988

Miller, J. Hillis, *Charles Dickens: The World of His Novels,* Cambridge, Massachusetts: Harvard University Press, and London: Oxford University Press, 1958

Poovey, Mary, "The Man-of-Letters Hero: *David Copperfield* and the Professional Writer," in her *Uneven Developments: The Ideological Work of Gender in Mid-Victorian England,* Chicago: University of Chicago Press, 1988; London: Virago, 1989

Sadoff, Dianne F., *Monsters of Affection: Dickens, Eliot, and Brontë on Fatherhood,* Baltimore: Johns Hopkins University Press, 1982

Schad, John, editor, *Dickens Refigured: Bodies, Desires and Other Histories,* Manchester: Manchester University Press, 1996

Welsh, Alexander, *The City of Dickens,* Oxford: Clarendon Press, 1971; Cambridge, Massachusetts: Harvard University Press, 1986

Wilson, Edmund, "Dickens: The Two Scrooges," in *The Wound and the Bow,* Oxford and New York: Oxford University Press, 1941

Dictionary of the Khazars by Milorad Pavić

Hazarski rečnik 1984

Milorad Pavić started out as a poet and excelled as a short-story writer and literary historian, but he achieved the pinnacle of success as a novelist. His first novel, *Dictionary of the Khazars: A Lexicon Novel in 100,000 Words,* one of the central works of postmodernist fiction, is made to order for speculative interpretation. The author himself invites multiple interpretation, making the truth more elusive by deliberate mystifications.

The novel rests on a false premise: the existence of a Khazar dictionary, allegedly printed in 1691 by Daubmannus, an obscure printer in 17th-century Prussia. While there was a man by that name, Pavić hastens to add that it was not that Daubmannus who printed the dictionary but someone else by the same name. Historically, there was no such dictionary at all, and the author's claim that his novel is an attempt to reconstruct the original dictionary serves only as a pretext for a revelry of myths, legends, stories, and quasi-historical documents. Reality constantly gives way to fantasy, and their borderlines are deliberately blurred. Characters change their appearance and reappear as someone else. These transformations suggest that reality and fantasy are of equal validity and that one does not exist without the other. In fact, Pavić refuses to distinguish between fantasy and realism as literary modes. Dreams also play an important role in the novel as many events take place either in dreams or dream-like hallucinations, prompting the American novelist Robert Coover to say in the *New York Times Book Review* that Pavić "thinks the way we dream," and Paul Grey to remark in *Time* that our "impression of frustration fades before the enchantment of the quest."

Pavić stresses our apparent inability to know historical truth. In the *Dictionary of the Khazars,* fact and legend are intertwined and of equal validity. Hence the abundant mixture of historical and fictional characters. The historical uncertainty about the actual fate of the Khazars is the best argument for Pavić's contention that historical fact often eludes us, and that this is probably just as well. The lines between the past, present, and future also are blurred. Characters move from one century and geographical region to another, not only in imagination or in dreams, but in waking reality as well. Without the reader's suspension of disbelief, this novel can neither be read properly nor enjoyed.

Pervasive relativity is another important aspect of the *Dictionary of the Khazars.* Few things are as they seem to be. The fact that the story is presented in three versions—the Christian in the Red book, the Islamic in the Green, and the Hebrew in the Yellow—speaks not only to the three possible points of view on the Khazar question, but to the fact that there is no single correct point of view with respect to any question, historical, philosophical, or ethical. Relativity is manifested in the fusing of historical periods, in the mixture of races and cultures in Khazar history, including the involvement of the Serbs, for example, and in the seemingly incongruous reappearance of characters at unexpected times and places. The author's possibly tongue-in-cheek suggestion that the novel may be read any way the reader pleases—horizontally (reading the same entries in all three books); vertically (following the events through history), from the beginning or from the end; or anyhow, even diagonally—also indicates relativity's function as a basic condition of Pavić's world. Mixing philosophical, historical, and cultural issues with a tale of suspense (including several murders) and using lively, modernist and postmodernist narrative techniques (which, ironically, go back to his favorite literary period, the baroque), Pavić has created what Philippe Tretiak calls in *Paris Match,* "the first novel of the twenty-first century."

Pavić has commented that literature should have no boundaries; the more it is accepted all over the world, the higher its value. He holds that an ideologically oriented literature loses its value if it lacks artistic excellence. He has also argued that we don't need a new way of writing, but rather a new way of reading. To be sure, none of these ideas is revolutionary, but each has reinforced Pavić's reputation as a consummate craftsman. His work, particularly his studied playfulness, shows similarities with the work of Jorge Luis Borges, Julio Cortázar, and Umber-

to Eco. But Pavić is a master in his own right, especially for his linguistic virtuosity and lyrical prose.

VASA D. MIHAILOVICH

Further Reading

Delić, Jovan, *Hazarska prizma: Tumacenje proze Milorada Pavića,* Belgrade: Prosveta, 1991

Gorak, Irene, "*Dictionary of the Khazars*: A Lexicon Novel in 100,000 Words," *Denver Quarterly* 24:3 (1990)

Jevtić, Miloš, *Razgovori sa Pavičem,* Belgrade: Naučna knjiga, 1990

Mihailovich, Vasa D., "Parable of Nationhood," *The World and I* 3:11 (1988)

Mihajlović, Jasmina, *Priča o duši i telu: Slojevi i značenja u prozi Milorada Pavića,* Belgrade: Prosveta, 1992

Mihajlović, Jasmina, "Elements of Milorad Pavic's Postmodern Poetics," *Serbian Studies* 7:1 (1993)

Palavestra, Predrag, "Abracadabra, a la Khazar!" *The World and I* 3:11 (1988)

Simic, Charles, "Balkan Bizarre," *The World and I* 3:11 (1988)

Šomlo, Ana, *Hazari ili Obnova vizantijskog romana,* Belgrade: BIGZ, 1990; 2nd edition, 1991

Denis Diderot 1713–84

French

Denis Diderot's first novelistic venture, *Les Bijoux indiscrets* (1748; *The Indiscreet Jewels*), was a pornographic pseudo-Oriental tale with strong philosophical and political overtones. Long dismissed as a youthful, licentious indiscretion, it has more recently been regarded not only as a work that prefigures some of the major themes of Diderot's later, more mature fictional writings but also as a significant contribution to the corpus of clandestine, subversive literature of Ancien Régime France.

In 1760, Diderot turned once more to the novel after his largely disappointing experience as a dramatist. His great esteem for the novels of Samuel Richardson had in the meantime prompted his revaluation of the novel as an officially despised, though immensely popular, genre. As Diderot proclaimed in his *Éloge de Richardson* (*Eulogy of Richardson*), first published in the *Journal étranger* of January 1762, fiction could be much more than a frivolous, inconsequential pastime for idle women, for it could achieve a high degree of verisimilitude, seriousness, emotional intensity, and morality.

La Religieuse (*The Nun*), written in 1760 and first published in 1796, is generally viewed as having been directly inspired by Diderot's admiration for Richardson. From Richardson, Diderot learned a great deal about the way a novelist can make extensive use of the small details of everyday life, as well as the importance of drawing characters from the middle class in order to create the illusion of reality and appeal to the interest and sympathy of

the reader. But *The Nun* also departs from Richardson in that it drastically reduces the number of characters, events, and incidents in order to focus almost exclusively on the heroine as a victim of cruelly overwhelming and repressive social and religious rules and conventions.

The first-person narrative of *The Nun* tells the tale of Suzanne Simonin, an unwilling yet chaste and reproachless nun. Every incident in the sad recital of Suzanne's misfortunes is meant to enhance the reader's sympathy and to underscore her innocence and vulnerability. That she does not question Christianity at any time in the story makes her case all the more pathetic and persuasive. She is a good Catholic but lacks the kind of religious vocation necessary for a contented cloistered existence. Above all, she wants the freedom of choice that has been denied her because she is the offspring of an adulterous relationship. The novel is certainly a powerful indictment of forced vows. Whether its message is ultimately antireligious and anti-Christian has been heatedly debated by commentators. This ambiguity was undoubtedly part of Diderot's strategy.

In 1761, Diderot wrote the initial draft of the dialogue *Le Neveu de Rameau* (*Rameau's Nephew*), which he periodically revised and expanded for nearly 20 years. Because of the subversive nature of the work and its many ferociously satirical references to influential contemporaries, Diderot refrained from publishing it. After his death in 1784, a copy of the manuscript reached Friedrich von Schiller, who immediately recognized its exceptional significance and hastened to show it to Johann Wolfgang von Goethe. The latter immediately set out to translate it. In fact, the first French edition, published in 1821, was merely a retranslation of Goethe's German version. In 1890, a holograph copy of the manuscript was discovered among the bookstalls of the Quai Voltaire. This fortuitous incident would undoubtedly have appealed to Diderot's sense of the bizarre and his novelist's appreciation of the unexpected and unpredictable in human affairs.

Rameau's Nephew is cast entirely in the form of a dialogue between two historically based characters—Diderot himself and Jean-François Rameau, the parasitic, ne'er-do-well nephew of the famous composer, Jean-Philippe Rameau. However, the Moi (or me) figure, supposedly referring to Diderot, is a slyly caricatured portrait of a somewhat smug, self-satisfied philosophe who has achieved a fragile measure of respectability. Lui (him), referring to Rameau, is endowed with far greater imaginative powers and self-awareness than the historical character. One of the most effectively dramatic features of *Rameau's Nephew* derives from the unruffled smugness of Moi and the volatility of mood and thought of the cynically outspoken Lui. Bitter resentment and jealousy, hatred and vindictiveness, frustration and self-mockery, yearning for success and wealth, a genuine enthusiasm for the arts, especially music, comical and evocative pantomimes, provocative insights into the nature of talent and genius are expressed in rapid succession by a posturing, provocative Moi.

In an even more experimental vein is *Jacques le fataliste* (*Jacques the Fatalist*), written from 1765 to 1784. It is a highly personal adaptation of the picaresque genre, written when Diderot was under the strong influence of Laurence Sterne's *Tristram Shandy* (1759–67). *Jacques the Fatalist* quite deliberately parodies fictional conventions and techniques. Loosely based on the device of the master-servant relationship that dates back to *Don Quixote* (1605–15), the multilayered narrative revolves around Jacques, the loquacious servant, and his taciturn, passive, and nameless master.

Because of its complex, interlocking structures, its temporal dislocations, its numerous and frequently provocative authorial asides to the reader, and its implied satire of the conventional stereotypes of storytelling, *Jacques the Fatalist* is an uncannily modern work of fiction with a special appeal for 20th-century novelists, critics, and theorists. André Gide singled it out for generous praise, and Milan Kundera wrote a brilliant dramatic variation of Diderot's text in 1968, which had a long run in Paris and was successfully staged in several other European capitals as well as at the American Repertory Theatre.

Some of the most famous interpolated stories in *Jacques the Fatalist* feature forceful, unconventional characters like the libertine Père Hudson, who adroitly undoes the plots hatched against him by envious monks, or the passionate and fiercely proud Madame de La Pommeraye, whose love for the marquis de Arcis turns to bitter hatred and vengefulness when she realizes that he no longer cares for her. The episode of Madame de La Pommeraye may indeed be read as a self-contained *conte* or novella. In its masterful handling of narrative techniques and superb characterization, it ranks among Diderot's finest achievements as a novelist and storyteller. The episode is also rich in irony, since Madame de La Pommeraye's elaborate plan to hu-

miliate her fickle lover unexpectedly works to her intended victim's advantage.

Diderot also wrote several *contes* that exemplify his artistic mastery of the short story as a means of developing a single central theme (usually of a morally problematic nature) through the behavior and actions of single-minded, willful characters who find themselves in conflict with accepted moral codes. The most notable include *Les Deux amis de Bourbonne* (*The Two Friends from Bourbonne*), written in 1770 and first published in 1773; *Ceci n'est pas un conte* (*This Is No Yarn*), written in 1772 and published in 1798; and *Madame de La Carlière,* also known as *Sur l'Inconséquence du jugement public de nos actions particulières* (*On the Inconsistency of the Public Judgment of Our Private Conduct*), written in 1772 and published in 1798. Diderot's choice of topics testifies to his preoccupation with the ambiguities and contradictions of sexual love and with the misunderstandings, ironies, and cruelties that so often attend relationships between men and women, especially when their passions are aroused.

As a storyteller, Diderot knew how to extract from his own experience and from closely observed real-life situations completely convincing, indeed memorable, characters, who were familiar and easily recognizable, yet exceptional in the intensity of their emotional involvement or moral and psychological predicament. With a keen eye for the telling, visually arresting detail and for the utterly convincing, yet revealing, dialogue, he excelled at creating scenes of stark dramatic power within a framework of unimpeachable verisimilitude.

Diderot's own theory of the *conte* is brilliantly expounded in a postscript to *The Two Friends from Bourbonne*. The *conte* as a genre, he points out, has so far dwelled in the realm of the imaginary and fanciful. It is high time to bring it down to earth, within the purview of daily human experience, a task reserved for the *conte historique,* by which Diderot means a narrative that observes the requirements of verisimilitude, rather than a historical novel or tale. But mere verisimilitude was not Diderot's sole aim, for he was keenly aware that the strictly factual representation of reality inevitably ran the risk of being flat and boring. Diderot held that the author of a historical tale must walk a tightrope between poetic exaggeration and scrupulous truthfulness, for, in addition to remaining totally credible, he has to succeed in involving and moving the reader to the extent that his skin "turn to gooseflesh and tears flow from his eyes." To combine successfully the two contradictory requirements of verisimilitude and poetic license, this new kind of fiction writer will, like a magician, strive to create and maintain the illusion of reality while retaining the creative artist's prerogative to select and set into sharp relief uncommon human idiosyncrasies and moral and psychological deviancies. Diderot's theoretical reflections take a central place in the development of realism, even as his best-known novels poke fun at mimetic conventions.

GITA MAY

Biography

Born in Langres, France, 5 October 1713. Attended Jesuit school Langres, 1723–28, became an abbé in 1726. Lived in Paris from 1728; received master of arts from the University of Paris in 1732; studied theology at the university and read law for a brief period, 1732–35. Worked as tutor, freelance writer, and translator from 1734; imprisoned for a short time in 1749 for writing *Lettre sur les aveugles*; commissioned by the publisher Le Breton to edit the *Encyclopédie*, which appeared from 1751 to 1772; contributed to F.M. Grimm's private periodical *Correspondance Littéraire* beginning in 1759; patronized by Catherine the Great from 1765, and traveled to Russia, 1773–74. Died 31 July 1784.

Novels by Diderot

Les Bijoux indiscrets, 1748; as *The Indiscreet Jewels*, 1749
Jacques le fataliste et son maître, 1796; as *Jacques the Fataliste*, edited by Martin Hall and translated by M. Henry, 1986; as *James the Fatalist and His Master*, translated anonymously, 1797; as *Jacques the Fatalist*, translated by J. Robert Loy, 1962
La Religieuse, 1796; as *The Nun*, translated by Brett Smith, 1797; also translated by Marianne Sinclair, 1966, and Leonard Tancock, 1972; as *Memoirs of a Nun*, translated by Francis Birrell, 1928
Le Neveu de Rameau, 1821; as *Rameau's Nephew*, translated by Sylvia M. Hill, 1897; also translated by Mrs. Wilfrid Jackson, 1926, Jacques Barzun and Ralph H. Bowen, 1956, and Leonard Tancock, 1966

Other Writings: plays; essays on a wide array of subjects.

Further Reading

Blum, Carol, *Diderot: The Virtue of a Philosopher*, New York: Viking Press, 1974
Caplan, Jay, *Framed Narratives, Diderot's Genealogy of the Beholder*, Minneapolis: University of Minnesota Press, 1985; Manchester: Manchester University Press, 1986
Chouillet, Jacques, *Diderot*, Paris: Société d'Édition d'Enseignement Supérieur, 1977
Fellows, Otis, *Diderot*, Boston: Twayne, 1977; updated edition, 1989
Fried, Michael, *Absorption and Theatricality: Painting and Beholder in the Age of Diderot*, Berkeley: University of California Press, 1980
Furbank, P.N., *Diderot*, New York: Knopf, and London: Secker and Warburg, 1992
Josephs, Herbert, *Diderot's Dialogue of Gesture and Language*, Columbus: Ohio State University Press, 1969
May, Gita, "Diderot," in *The Age of Reason and the Enlightenment*, edited by George Stade, New York: Scribner, 1984
Sherman, Carol, *Diderot and the Art of Dialogue*, Geneva: Droz, 1976
Undank, Jack, *Diderot, Inside, Outside, and In-Between*, Madison, Wisconsin: Coda Press, 1979
Wilson, Arthur M., *Diderot*, New York: Oxford University Press, 1972

Diegesis and Diegetic Levels of Narration

Diegesis is the Greek word for narration, the component of telling in narrative representation. In the third book of *The Republic*, Plato distinguishes between diegesis (narration) and mimesis (imitation) in literary representation. For Plato, diegesis was the more effective mode of representation because it eschewed the false illusion of reality produced by mimesis. Nevertheless, in the epics of Homer, from which the genre of the novel in part evolved, Plato observed a mixing of the diegetic with the mimetic whenever the epic singer shifts from simple narration to imitate the direct speech of a character. Aristotle, in his analysis of Greek tragic drama, *The Poetics*, concentrated critical attention on issues of imitation, on the matter of showing rather than telling. It has only been with the rise of the novel, and more specifically the rise of narratology as a critical activity, that critics have rigorously examined diegesis in narrative texts, concentrating on the conditions of narration: who narrates, when the narration occurs in relation to the events narrated, what the narrator's involvement is in the events narrated, how the narration is transmitted to the narratee, and what the relationship is among multiple narrations occurring in the same text.

Although in many texts narration appears straightforward, even the simple representation of a character's speech makes manifest a gap between story and discourse. This gap between diegesis and mimesis, however, is paradoxical since the narrative transmission of any mimetic speech act is by necessity contained within a diegesis—even in an epistolary novel, in which the reader only infers the diegesis of arranging and presenting the letters as a collection.

Critical study of diegesis has focused on the question of diegetic levels. If the initial level (the entry level or the level closest to the reader) comprises the act of narration, then the story (the events narrated) comprises a subsequent level (even though temporally the events narrated typically precede the act of narration). This distinction of level is most immediately obvious in the structural relationships of such narrative features as dialogue, temporal deformations of plotting (flashbacks, anticipations, temporal jumps), and significant description. Many narratives foreground the initial level by characterizing the narrator, who in turn may comment upon both the events narrated and the act of narrating. The question of diegetic levels becomes compounded when techniques of framing, embedding, or intercalating are used to place additional acts of narrating and additional stories within the initial (or a subsequent) diegetic level, or when a "fictional editorial transmission" frames what might be commonsensically referred to as the primary act of narration.

In *Discours du récit*, Gérard Genette offers a narratological system for distinguishing diegetic levels (see Genette, 1972). He calls the initial diegetic level "extradiegetic" narrating of an "intradiegetic narrative." That intradiegetic narrative commonly contains additional narrating acts (i.e., embedded recounting by a character of an earlier event or an intercalated moral apologue). Thus a character in the intradiegetic narrative can become an "intradiegetic" narrator, narrating a third-level narrative of events—what Genette calls a "metadiegetic narrative." Within the metadiegetic narrative further levels may arise by the same techniques of embedding or intercalating. Indeed, as some of the elaborately embedded tales in *The Thousand and One Nights* demonstrate, there conceivably could be no limit to the number of levels activated. Genette terms the next level "meta-metadiegetic," and with each additional level another "meta" prefix would be added. However, such terminology, although precise, becomes cumbersome. Mieke Bal in *De theorie van vertellen en verhalen* (1978; *Narratology*) extends consideration of diegetic levels to the microtextual level when she considers complex acts of embedded focalization within narrative sentences. Duyfhuizen (1992), considering the macrotextual narrative function of authorial prefaces, proposes a "historiodiegetic" level to refer to "nonfictional" prefaces that seek to influence how the reader will interpret the narrative. The historiodiegetic level sometimes marks a paradoxical attempt to deter readers from interpreting a text too closely as "autobiography," as is the case with Benjamin Constant's prefaces to the 2nd and 3rd editions of *Adolphe* (1816; 1824), which may have precisely the opposite effect.

Genette expands his system of diegetic levels to show how different narrators or acts of narration combine with a second system, which distinguishes the differential relationship between the narrator and the events narrated. Genette recognized that the terms "third-person narration" and "first-person narration" do not adequately describe the narrator as much as they indicate the pronoun case used when referring to the protagonist. To remedy the situation, Genette proposed three categories of diegetic relationship to the events narrated: "heterodiegetic," in which the narrator has no direct involvement in any of the narrated events; "homodiegetic," in which the narrator is witness to and occasional participant in the narrated events but is not the protagonist; and "autodiegetic," in which the narrator tells his or her own story. As Susan Lanser observes, these three categories may be artificially restrictive. A spectrum of relationships would allow for more precise comparison among different texts and for examination of variations in a narrator's relationship to the events narrated, taking into account that a narrator's degree of proximity to the narrated events may change during the course of the narrative (see Lanser, 1981). Significantly, Genette's two systems combine to identify a narrator's relationship both to other narrators and narrations and to the narrated events recounted in those narrations.

For instance, in Emily Brontë's *Wuthering Heights* (1847) Lockwood begins the narration in his journal at an extra-au-todiegetic level, telling the story of his initial two visits to Wuthering Heights. When he asks Nelly Dean to tell him the history of the novel's two families, he shifts to an extra-heterodiegetic narrating position, transcribing Nelly's intra-homodiegetic narration of Catherine and Heathcliff's experiences. Within Nelly's narration Catherine, Heathcliff, and Isabella all narrate scenes Nelly did not witness. As such, these narrators operate on a meta-autodiegetic level, as Nelly, in accordance with Lanser's spectrum, would shift toward an intra-heterodiegetic relationship during the time in her narration when she quotes their oral narrations.

Lockwood's and Nelly's shifts of narrator relationship reveal that the diegetic levels referring to acts of narrating can as well be applied to narratees—those to whom a narration is addressed. While the extra-heterodiegetic narratee may be only inferred from the fact of narration, characterized narratees such as Lockwood and Nelly can play key roles in the progression of events or in the presentation of the narration depending on whether they are "intended" or "unintended" narratees (known listeners or unknown eavesdroppers) and on whether they act to influence future events based on the narrative they have been told. Moreover, since narratees can become narrators and vice versa, the shifting of diegetic levels complicates narrative transmission, effectively revealing or withholding narrative information.

BERNARD DUYFHUIZEN

See also Discourse Representation; Framing and Embedding; Mimesis; Narratology; Narrator; Point of View

Further Reading

Bal, Mieke, *De theorie van vertellen en verhalen,* Mulderberg: Coutinho, 1978; as *Narratology: An Introduction to the Theory of Narrative,* Toronto and Buffalo, New York: University of Toronto Press, 1985

Chatman, Seymour, *Story and Discourse: Narrative Structure in Fiction and Film,* Ithaca, New York: Cornell University Press, 1978

Duyfhuizen, Bernard, *Narratives of Transmission,* Rutherford, New Jersey: Fairleigh Dickinson University Press, and London: Associated University Presses, 1992

Genette, Gérard, *Discours du récit,* in *Figures III,* Paris: Seuil, 1972; as *Narrative Discourse,* Ithaca, New York: Cornell University Press, 1980

Genette, Gérard, *Nouveau discours du récit,* Paris: Seuil, 1983; as *Narrative Discourse Revisited,* Ithaca, New York: Cornell University Press, 1988

Lanser, Susan Sniader, *The Narrative Act: Point of View in Prose Fiction,* Princeton, New Jersey: Princeton University Press, 1981

Prince, Gerald, *A Dictionary of Narratology,* Lincoln: University of Nebraska Press, 1987; Aldershot: Scolar, 1988

Rimmon-Kenan, Shlomith, *Narrative Fiction: Contemporary Poetics,* London and New York: Methuen, 1983

Dime Novels and Penny Dreadfuls

Dime novels and penny dreadfuls are generic terms for paper-bound publications with a sensational content. The terms originated in the United States and Great Britain, respectively, in the 19th century, although the British form preceded the American. *Dime novel* is derived from a specific series of publications, *Beadle's Dime Novels*, which began publication in the United States in 1860; *penny dreadful* (which designation first appeared in print in John Camden Hotten's *Slang Dictionary* in 1874) is a pejorative term applied broadly, and often inaccurately, to several classes of publications dating to the 1830s. The term *penny dreadful* is often applied not only to the Gothic or outlaw-hero penny-a-part novels of the 1830s and 1840s but also to the subsequent stories published for the juvenile market in the 1850s, as well as to the penny magazines and weekly boys' papers of the 1860s. It also includes the published plagiarisms of the novels of Charles Dickens.

Chronologically, the British penny dreadful preceded the American dime novel by about 30 years, although the two forms shared certain traits. The most obvious similarities were the content (lurid, sensational stories that have come to represent national myths) and the manner of publication. The early penny dreadful was often one long episodic story presented in many parts, each part costing only one penny. Each part was eight pages of double-column print, in which the story might break off in mid-sentence at the bottom of page eight only to resume on the first page of the next part (which would be available at the newsdealer the following week). No attempt was made to account for what had come before. The dime novel was a unit in a sequence of many stories, issued on a regular basis, that revolved around a single character or consistent theme, each story costing as little as ten cents.

The earliest penny dreadfuls were published by Edward Lloyd of London, and the form took recognizable shape with his *Lives of the Most Notorious Highwaymen, Footpads, etc.*, published in 60 parts in 1836. The outlaw as hero was a major figure in these early stories and was often loosely based on an 18th-century historic figure such as Dick Turpin, Jack Sheppard, or Claude Duval. The long series of Robin Hood stories begun by Pierce Egan Jr. belong to this category as well.

The honor of being the most infamous of penny dreadfuls is shared by two stories, *Varney the Vampyre; or, The Feast of Blood* (1847), which influenced Bram Stoker in his writing of *Dracula* (1897), and the legendary story of Sweeney Todd the Demon Barber, which may be found in different versions beginning in 1846. The author of the first is generally thought to be James Malcolm Rymer, while the second may be the work of Thomas Peckett Prest.

Edward Lloyd was only one of many publishers of penny dreadfuls. His colleagues and rivals in this enterprise included G.W.M. Reynolds, John Dicks, George Vickers, George Purkiss, and W.M. Clarke. In the 1860s the field was joined by Edward J. Brett, publisher of *Boys of England*, which contained Bracebridge Hemyng's early stories of Jack Harkaway. Brett's publications, advertised as antidotes to the previous generation of lurid stories, borrowed many of the same themes. The effective campaign waged against the penny dreadful by the Religious Tract Society and the *The Boys' Own Paper* (1879) was followed by the "half-penny papers" of Harmsworth Publications, such as the *Union Jack*. By the 1890s the detective stories of Sexton Blake outsold the old dreadfuls and soon were joined in popularity by the school stories written by Charles Hamilton under such pen names as Martin Clifford and Frank Richards.

The original dime novel was *Malaeska, the Indian Wife of the White Hunter*, by Mrs. Ann S. Stephens. Published by Irwin P. Beadle of New York in June 1860, it was the first of a long series of stories about the American frontier. It was followed by other stories based on American history that some critics feel molded the popular notion of the American Revolution and promoted the American belief in rugged individualism.

By the 1880s the frontier hero, modeled on James Fenimore Cooper's Leatherstocking tales or on historic figures such as Kit Carson, Davy Crockett, Daniel Boone, and Buffalo Bill, was in competition with the urban heroes, detectives like Old Sleuth, Old King Brady, Old Cap. Collier, and Nick Carter. Stories of bandits such as Jesse James were as popular in the United States as the stories of highwaymen had been in England. Other genres had their followers: science fiction with Frank Reade or school and sports stories featuring Frank Merriwell. As had happened in England with the penny dreadfuls, the United States audience for dime novels grew beyond adults. As in England, the writers were less well known than their heroes and their imaginary worlds.

After 1915, new forms of mass entertainment, the motion picture and the pulp magazine, replaced the dime novel. Of the five major publishers, Beadle and Adams, George Munro, Norman L. Munro, Frank Tousey, and Street and Smith, only the latter survived by adapting to new tastes.

The way in which the dime novel and the penny dreadful contribute to an understanding of the development of the novel lies not in any literary merit but in the development of marketing, in popular concepts about the Wild West or the urban sleath, that each kept before the reader, and in the response that each made to public demand. A number of factors came together at the right time to make the dime novel and penny dreadful successful business ventures for their publishers: the growing literacy in each nation; the invention of the rotary steam printing press; the development of paper-making methods that replaced rag-content paper with paper made from wood pulp; and, finally, the creation of new means of large-scale distribution. In the United States this was achieved via the American News Company, in Great Britain by the Newsagents' Publishing Company.

J. RANDOLPH COX

See also American Western Novel

Further Reading

Anglo, Michael, *Penny Dreadfuls and Other Victorian Horrors*, London: Jupiter, 1977

Bleiler, E.F., editor, *Eight Dime Novels*, New York: Dover, 1974

Carpenter, Kevin, *Penny Dreadfuls and Comics: English Periodicals for Children from Victorian Times to the Present Day*, London: Victoria and Albert Museum, 1983

Denning, Michael, *Mechanic Accents: Dime Novels and Working-Class Culture in America*, London and New York: Verso, 1987

Haining, Peter, editor, *The Penny Dreadful; or, Strange, Horrid & Sensational Tales!* London: Gollancz, 1975

James, Louis, *Fiction for the Working Man, 1830-50: A Study of the Literature Produced for the Working Classes in Early Victorian Urban England,* London and New York: Oxford University Press, 1963

Johannsen, Albert, *The House of Beadle and Adams and Its Dime and Nickel Novels: The Story of a Vanished Literature,* 3 vols., Norman: University of Oklahoma Press, 1950, 1962

Jones, Daryl, *The Dime Novel Western,* Bowling Green, Ohio: Bowling Green State University Popular Press, 1978

Lofts, W.O.G., and Derek Adley, "A History of 'Penny Bloods'," *Book and Magazine Collector* 32 (1986)

Noel, Mary, *Villains Galore: The Heyday of the Popular Story Weekly,* New York: Macmillan, 1954

Pearson, Edmund, *Dime Novels; or, Following an Old Trail in Popular Literature,* Boston: Little Brown, 1929

Quinn, Laura, *Popular Fiction: Penny Dreadfuls, Boys' Weeklies, and Half Penny Parts,* Minneapolis: University of Minnesota Libraries, 1974

Reynolds, Quentin, *The Fiction Factory; or, From Pulp Row to Quality Street,* New York: Random House, 1955

Smith, Henry Nash, *Virgin Land: The American West as Symbol and Myth,* Cambridge, Massachusetts: Harvard University Press, 1950

Springhall, John, "'A Life Story for the People'? Edwin J. Brett and the London 'Low-Life' Penny Dreadfuls of the 1860s," *Victorian Studies* 33 (Winter 1990)

Stern, Madeleine B., *Publishers for Mass Entertainment in Nineteenth Century America,* Boston: G.K. Hall, 1980

Sullivan, Larry E., and Lydia Cushman Schurman, editors, *Pioneers, Passionate Ladies, and Private Eyes: Dime Novels, Series Books, and Paperbacks,* New York: Haworth Press, 1996

Turner, E.S., *Boys Will Be Boys: The Story of Sweeney Todd, Deadwood Dick, Sexton Blake, Billy Bunter, Dick Barton, et al.,* London: M. Joseph, 1948; 3rd edition, 1975

Discourse Representation

A central issue for any novel is the representation of the characters' discourse—speech, thought, even feeling—by a narrator. In novels and other fictional as well as nonfictional writing, the voice of the current speaker—the first-level "I" of the text, or the impersonal source of the narrative discourse—frequently reports, paraphrases, cites, or reshapes utterances of third parties, whether utterances of actual people in newspaper coverage or those allegedly produced by fictional characters. In fictional(ized) texts, such discourse representations may additionally be employed to designate nonlinguistic data, particularly states of consciousness, thought processes, perceptions, even gestures, facial expressions, or a viewer/narrator's anthropomorphized impression of objects. The detailed representation of characters' thought processes, feelings, and perceptions has even been proposed as a criterion for the establishment of fictionality (see Hamburger, 1973, and Fludernik, 1996).

Apart from the medieval and Renaissance tradition of the soliloquy, thought representation did not become widespread until the later 18th century and culminated in the consciousness novel of the late 19th and early 20th centuries. Important texts in this regard include Gustave Flaubert's *Madame Bovary* (1857), Thomas Hardy's *Tess of the d'Urbervilles* (1891), Kate Chopin's *The Awakening* (1899), all of Henry James' novels, the short fiction of Katherine Mansfield, the novels of James Joyce, Virginia Woolf, and D.H. Lawrence. In the wake of the often radical breaks from traditional mimetic accounts of direct speech these and other writers accomplished, narratologists have begun to identify and analyze a wide range of types of discourse in novels.

Typically, narrators report or paraphrase words more or less explicitly attributed to characters and even verbalize their (nonlinguistic) thoughts and emotions. The different modes of representing discourse have traditionally been divided into direct and indirect discourse, a distinction that derives largely from grammatical analysis. (This analysis also proposes rules, familiar to all of us from primary school, that transform one type of discourse into the other. However, recent studies complicate the situation somewhat, indicating that direct discourse cannot be retrieved from indirect discourse.) Developments in the 19th-century novel have led to the addition of a third category, free indirect discourse, and, more recently, a fourth, variously referred to as psycho-narration (see Cohn, 1978), narrative representation of speech or thought acts (NRSA or NRTA, for short), and speech or thought report (see Stanzel, 1984).

Direct Discourse

Direct discourse (DD) has traditionally been considered a reliable mirror image of a prior utterance. However, recent linguistic analyses have demonstrated the existence of patently nonverbatim, invented DD and of fictionalized thought attributions in conversational narrative, noting also the prominence of manipulated DD and free indirect discourse in newspaper reports. It would be more accurate to say, then, that the function of direct discourse is to make believe that there was a prior utterance of the very shape indicated. In fiction, this function is obviously paramount at all times.

Direct discourse is characterized by a shift of the deictic center—that is to say, a shift in the person in relation to whom deictic words like "this" and "that" are defined—from the reporter to the person whose words are reported. In English, DD is framed by quotation marks and often accompanied by tags that identify the person reported and the nature of the utterance (saying, thinking, shouting, and so on). For example,

I woke up in the bathtub, full of water, and this woman
. . . she was saying, "Who the fuck are you?" (Amanda
Cross, *Death in a Tenured Position*, 1981)

Janet, the speaker, quotes the words of an unnamed woman to
Kate. The "you" in "Who the fuck are you?" refers to Janet, not
to Kate, even though it is Janet who addresses these words to
Kate.

Indirect Discourse

Indirect discourse (ID) integrates the reported utterance into the
reporter's discourse, and it does so without performing the deictic shift. For example,

Mellish said that there was a Medical "Ring" at Simla,
headed by the Surgeon-General, who was in league, apparently, with all the Hospital Assistants in the Empire.
(Rudyard Kipling, *Plain Tales from the Hills*, 1888)

The reported words are typically in the past tense ("there was a
Medical 'Ring'"), even though we deduce that Mellish used the
present tense ("there is a Medical 'Ring'") when he, allegedly,
spoke.

Free Indirect Discourse

Free indirect discourse (FID; frequently cited in French as *style
indirect libre* or *discours indirect libre*, or in German as *erlebte
Rede*) combines features of DD (exclamatory syntax and deictic
expressions centered in the reported speaker) and ID (the alignment of pronouns, deictic words, and tense with the reporter of
the discourse). FID is often signaled by the presence of speech
habits that are different from the narrator's and peculiar to the
character whose discourse is reported. Dialect forms, indications
of the reported speaker's nonstandard pronunciation, and expressive syntax mark the following example as FID:

He sho was what Miz Harris would call bad, cause every
time he was with her he tried to take her back of a palmet-
to clump or some'n. (Lillian Smith, *Strange Fruit*, 1944)

Other typical FID markers include deictic expressions centered
in the reported speaker, exclamations, interjections, sentence
modifiers, and derogatory expressions, many of which are present in the following example:

[speech report:] Arun had begun to hold forth with his
usual savoir-faire and charm on various subjects: recent
plays in London, books that had just appeared and were
considered to be significant, the Persian oil crisis, the Korean conflict. [FID:] *The Reds were being pushed back,
and not a moment too soon, in Arun's opinion, though of
course the Americans, idiots that they were, would probably not make use of their tactical advantage. But then
again, with this as with other matters, what could one do?*
(Vikram Seth, *A Suitable Boy*, 1993)

FID was first discovered at the end of the 19th century by German scholars in Romance literatures. Traditionally, FID has
been described as a "dual voice" (see Pascal, 1977), in which the
voices of the narrator and character are blended. More recently,

Ann Banfield has argued that this model is inadequate for interi-
or monologue (see Banfield, 1982). Fludernik has proposed that
an important distinction obtains between ironic and empathetic
uses of FID (see Fludernik, 1993).

It is frequently argued that FID may be defined (and therefore
distinguished from other types of reported discourse) in purely
linguistic terms. However, a broader view of the representation
of speech and thought suggests that DD, ID, and FID should be
treated as prototypes only. Actual instances of speech and
thought representation may display a great range of idiosyncratic combinations and formal devices. Literary scholars have
pointed out numerous contextual features that prompt the reader to decide whether a passage is rendered in the speech of a
character or is the neutral report of a narrator.

Recent studies have established that FID occurs not only in
third-person texts, but also in first- and second-person narratives; that it can be found in present-tense as well as past-tense
discourse; and that it occurs in spoken as well as written language. A recent San Francisco Bay Area radio commercial affords a good example of the kinds of shifts that are possible:

When you call Aunt Gloria for a ride to the airport . . .
she'd love to but she's not feeling too well and she doesn't
even know whether she'll make it to Bingo tonight, so she
thinks she'd better just stay home for now; and why don't
you call more often?

Many of the available options are to be found in experimental
fiction.

Free indirect discourse is of great importance in the novel primarily for its flexibility. Dispensing with the laborious inquit
tags (*he said that, she thought that*), FID allows narrative discourse to run more smoothly. It tends to make texts more vibrant and diversified by permitting the selective incorporation
of the characters' colloquial styles without committing the narrator to extended verbatim quotations of dialogue. It can mediate the expression of subtle ironies or reinforce the reader's
empathetic identification with a character. It facilitates surreptitious movements in and out of a character's speech or thought
acts and engineers a degree of ambiguity in the attribution of
discourse (is the narrator or a character responsible for a given
passage?) that plays an important role particularly in the modern novel.

Extensive passages of FID made their first appearance in the
novel late in the 18th century. However, numerous brief passages
of FID for the representation of consciousness may be found in
the work of Aphra Behn in the 17th century. Free indirect discourse for the representation of speech acts has in fact been
around since the 13th century.

Speech and Thought Report (Psycho-Narration)

In contrast to the three prototypical reporting devices (DD, ID,
and FID), speech and thought report cannot claim any specific
formal criteria. It tends to convey the general drift of a character's speech or thought, rather than the words used. For example, Hippolito

[psycho-narration:] *had like to have told her, That he was
the Man, but by good Chance reflecting upon his Friend's
Adventure, who had taken his name,* [ID:] he made An-

swer, that he believed Don Hippolito not far off. (William Congreve, *Incognita*, 1692)

Minimally, speech and thought representation can consist of such brief reportative phrases as "He turned this over in his mind," but it can also be far more elaborate, detailing arguments, circumstances of delivery, and idiosyncratic features of the reported discourse:

Mr. Wegg then goes on to enlarge upon what throughout has been uppermost in his mind. . . . He expatiates on Mr. Venus's patient habits and delicate manipulations; . . . Mr. Wegg next modestly remarks on the want of adapation. . . . Lastly, he returns to the cause of the right, gloomily foreshadowing the possibility of something being unearthed to criminate Mr. Boffin (of whom he once more candidly admits it cannot be denied that he profits by a murder), and anticipating his denunciation by the friendly movers to avenging justice. (Charles Dickens, *Our Mutual Friend*, 1865)

Speech and thought report merges smoothly with the surrounding discourse; it also manipulates reportees' utterances:

Marie St. Clare declared that . . . her nervous system was entirely inadequate to any trial of that nature; one snuff of anything disagreeable being, according to her account, quite sufficient to close the scene, and put an end to all her earthly trials at once. (Harriet Beecher Stowe, *Uncle Tom's Cabin*, 1852)

Whereas instances of speech report have had little historical significance, thought report (or, as Cohn [1978] calls it, psycho-narration) has been crucial to the development of the novel, mediating the representation of consciousness that increasingly has come to inform characterization. Consonant psycho-narration—the representation of a character's thoughts and sentiments in the narrator's words but from the character's perspective—may be traced back to the 14th century in the works of Geoffrey Chaucer and becomes quite prominent in Sir Philip Sidney's *Arcadia*, particularly the *New Arcadia* of 1590. Deploying lengthy passages of psycho-narration, Aphra Behn's texts frequently shift the narrative point of view to her characters in such a way as to create an impression of their conscious experience. Psycho-narration is also a prominent part of the stream-of-consciousness technique and is particularly important in the prose of Virginia Woolf.

Interior Monologue and Stream of Consciousness

Direct discourse's illusion of verbatim report is particularly problematic in the representation of thought processes. Consciousness clearly stretches beyond the verbal into regions of feeling and perception, involving all the senses. Even insofar as it is verbal, consciousness cannot be rendered verbatim because no records of internal speech exist. Literary representations of characters' private discourse have traditionally tended to transform quotations from the mind into set speeches, whether in the form of formal soliloquies or such speeches as Molly Bloom's at the end of James Joyce's *Ulysses* (1922). Linguistically, such speeches are all instances of pseudo-orality.

By contrast, interior monologue "proper," such as Joyce deployed for the private thoughts of Stephen Dedalus and Leopold Bloom, does not invoke colloquiality but, on the contrary, a telegram style of clipped sentences and unfinished lines of thought, visual images and associative chains of related items. Such interior monologue may be recognized by the use of first-person pronouns to refer to the consciousness portrayed and the use of present tense for finite verbs. (However, the more convincing renderings of consciousness tend to have few finite verbs and few complete sentences with full subjects.) The term stream of consciousness, including all forms of thought representation that imitate the flux of actual thought processes, is therefore an apt label for the interior monologue. The illusion is not of Bloom uttering Joyce's written words verbatim, but of his mute cravings, roving eye, and calculating mind. The language refers, or seems to refer, to nonlinguistic or only half-linguistic strata of consciousness. Close analysis of Joyce's oeuvre demonstrates that interior monologue proper is only one of the techniques he uses to create a stream of consciousness.

Narrated Perception

Narrated perception traditionally has been defined as the rendering of a character's perceptions in the shape of free indirect discourse, attributing a near-verbal state of consciousness to the character's emotional responses. For example,

Turning round upon his stool behind the counter, Mr. Gills looked out among the instruments in the window, to see if his nephew might be crossing the road. No. He was not among the bobbing umbrellas, and he certainly was not the newspaper boy in the oilskin cap who was slowly working his way along the piece of brass outside, writing his name over Mr. Gill's name with his forefinger. (Charles Dickens, *Dombey and Son*, 1848)

Banfield includes narrated perception in her category of nonreflective consciousness alongside psycho-narration, and it clearly is one of those forms of speech and thought representation that attempts to render the murky area between the verbal and the merely sensate. What comes across in many cases of narrated perception as the most true to the nature of human experience is that which is furthest from verbatim report.

Powerful as the mimetic effects of speech and thought report may be, it is an illusion that evokes a nonexistent verbal reality. In fact, the representation of consciousness in its various guises reveals the artifice of mimesis in all kinds of narrative and helps us to see that fiction does not imitate reality, but rather creates it.

Monika Fludernik

See also Diegesis and Diegetic Levels of Narration; Mimesis; Narratology; Narrator; Person in Narrative; Point of View; Stream of Consciousness and Interior Monologue; Tense in Narrative

Further Reading
Bally, Charles, "Le style indirect libre en français moderne," *Germanisch-Romanische Monatsschrift* 4 (1912)
Banfield, Ann, *Unspeakable Sentences: Narration and Representation in the Language of Fiction*, Boston: Routledge and Kegan Paul, 1982

Brinton, Laurel, "'Represented Perception': A Study in Narrative Style," *Poetics* 9 (1980)

Cohn, Dorrit, *Transparent Minds: Narrative Modes for Presenting Consciousness in Fiction,* Princeton, New Jersey: Princeton University Press, 1978

Duchan, Judith F., et al., *Deixis in Narrative: A Cognitive Science Perspective,* Hillsdale, New Jersey: Erlbaum, 1995

Fludernik, Monika, *The Fictions of Language and the Languages of Fiction: The Linguistic Representation of Speech and Consciousness,* London and New York: Routledge, 1993

Fludernik, Monika, *Towards a "Natural" Narratology,* London and New York: Routledge, 1996

Hamburger, Käte, *Die Logik der Dichtung,* Stuttgart: Klett, 1957; as *The Logic of Literature,* Bloomington: Indiana University Press, 1973

Leech, Geoffrey N., and Michael H. Short, *Style in Fiction: A Linguistic Introduction to English Fictional Prose,* London and New York: Longman, 1981

McHale, Brian, "Free Indirect Discourse: A Survey of Recent Accounts," *Poetics and Theory of Literature* 3 (1978)

Pascal, Roy, *The Dual Voice: Free Indirect Speech and Its Functioning in the Nineteenth-Century European Novel,* Manchester: Manchester University Press, and Totowa, New Jersey: Rowman and Littlefield, 1977

Stanzel, Franz Karl, *Theorie des Erzählens,* Göttingen: Vandenhoeck and Ruprecht, 1979; as *A Theory of Narrative,* Cambridge and New York: Cambridge University Press, 1984

Steinberg, Erwin R., *The Stream of Consciousness and Beyond in "Ulysses,"* Pittsburgh, Pennsylvania: University of Pittsburgh Press, 1958

Steinberg, Günter, *Erlebte Rede: Ihre Eigenart und ihre Formen in neuerer deutscher, französischer und englischer Erzählliteratur,* Göppingen: Alfred Kümmerle, 1971

Alfred Döblin 1878–1957

German

It would be no exaggeration to say that Alfred Döblin is most commonly remembered only for *Berlin Alexanderplatz* (1929), with its vibrant evocations of city life and its radical use of montage technique. He had a long and prolific writing career, however, that shows him to have been an extraordinarily protean, sometimes willful, but often strikingly inventive contributor to the culture of literary modernism. He was an intellectually restless and combative figure who took upon himself the contradictions inherent in a fervent pursuit of radicalism and innovation.

Part of the explanation for that restlessness may be found in his personality and social origins. He came from an impoverished middle-class background and a broken family, and he retained a strong commitment to the socially disadvantaged while also recognizing that his own position lay between the classes. During the period of the Weimar Republic, he was a robust defender of the liberties of the citizen against party bureaucracies and an impassioned proponent of the social responsibility of literary writers against a tradition of aesthetic detachment. His writings reflect both the heritage of scientific specialization, in which he had been trained as a medical doctor and psychiatrist, and the influence of a romantic philosophical tradition, which aimed to overcome the opposition between spirit and matter and articulate a sense of the ultimate oneness of being. Döblin was actively involved in the literary avant-garde of Berlin from approximately 1908, and was always looking for ways to advance critically beyond the programmatic positions of Italian futurism and German expressionism as these became established in public perception. In controversies with the leader of Italian futurism, Filippo Tommaso Marinetti, and with the German novelist Otto Flake, Döblin insisted that the writer should aim to communicate empirical experience of the world in ways that were immediate to the senses, rather than sustaining the rationalizing psychology and conceptual abstraction that he found to be characteristic of the novel as it had developed by the early 20th century. It was in this sense that Döblin championed the notion of epic writing as something distinctive from the customary practice of the novel. Throughout his life he often presented himself as the champion of a radical anti-subjectivism, calling upon his fellow writers to resort to whatever expressive means seemed appropriate to enable the external world to speak through the written text. On the other hand, by the late 1920s he was also finding it necessary to emphasize the creative power of the author and the need for the individual to exercise authoritative judgment over that which is given in the natural world.

The fullest articulation of Döblin's views on the potential of narrative writing, and of the tensions within his intellectual position, is to be found in the lecture "Der Bau des epischen Werks" (The Structure of the Epic Work), which he gave at Berlin University in 1928. Here he speaks not only of the imperative of faithful representation of reality but also of the author's obligation to "penetrate" that reality. He affirms the productive power of linguistic formulation in itself, of its "triumph" even over the subjectivity of the author, but Döblin also acknowledges that within the creative process a phase of self-critical reflection follows that of unconscious "incubation." He looks to ancient examples of the power of epic poetry to evoke elemental human situations (Homer, Dante) but also reflects that the disparate nature of modern society makes any notion of a collective "singing" of the world a forlorn anachronism. He pleads for a lifting of the "iron curtain" between storyteller and reader that is embodied in 19th-century conventions of retrospective and imperfect-tense narration, and he speaks of the arbitrary parameters that are imposed on epic writing by the exigencies of the book trade rather than by anything inherent in the activity of evocation itself. By contrast with Georg Lukács' notion (in *Die Theorie des Romans* [1920; *The Theory of the Novel*]) of the novel as striving to achieve completeness even while displaying the consciousness of its incompleteness, Döblin argues that any one portion of a text should be viable independently of the rest, as well as insisting on the legitimacy of lyric, dramatic, or reflexive elements within the epic text.

The vividness of which Döblin is capable is apparent from his first major novel, *Die drei Sprünge des Wang-lun* (1915; *The Three Leaps of Wang-Lun*), which combines a depiction of political upheaval in 18th-century China with some commonplace dichotomies of German intellectual culture: Wang-Lun is a devotee of nonviolent protest who becomes involved in a bloody uprising driven by a popular will that is presented as a force of nature. Döblin's use of rhythmic and assonant language in the sensuous evocation of collective tension and violent acts is equally apparent in *Berge, Meere und Giganten* (1924; Mountains, Oceans and Giants), where he imagines a future world in which the gigantomaniac projects of the technocrats lead to ever more cataclysmic confrontations between man and nature, and in *Das Land ohne Tod* (1937–38; *Amazonas*), where he works with legendary and fantastic material in an evocation of the human capacity for destruction in the context of the conflicting cultures of South America. In *Manas* (1927), he even attempts a verse epic on the theme of destruction and renewal wrought out of the imagery of Hindu myth. But Döblin was equally capable of restrained realist narration, whether in his satire of the bourgeois ethos of profit and conquest, *Wadzeks Kampf mit der Dampfturbine* (1918; Wadzek's Struggle with the Steam Turbine), in his autobiographical account of the intellectual idealist caught between political factions, *Pardon wird nicht gegeben* (1935; *Men Without Mercy*), or in a historically exact account of Germany's failed revolution, *November 1918* (1949; selections from volumes 1 and 2 as *A People Betrayed*). Döblin may be seen at his most subtle in his final novel, *Hamlet; oder, Die lange Nacht nimmt ein Ende* (1956; Hamlet: or, The Long Night Comes to an End), which combines a tensely destructive 20th-century family history with some reworkings of well-known themes from European literature, and which reflects Döblin's growing mood of renunciation in exile and his ultimate adoption of the Catholic faith. His visionary presentation of the absurdity of historical processes in *Wallenstein* (1920), on the other hand, which is set during the Thirty Years' War and contains some extraordinarily stark depictions of human excess and brutality, has been acknowledged by Günter Grass (1980) as an inspiration for his own novels.

Döblin's legacy, then, may be said to lie in the examples he sets with his pioneering attempts to extend the expressive means of the novel beyond its inherited conventional boundaries. His contribution to the development of narrative fiction lies not in the establishment of stable models for others to emulate but in his willingness to experiment with the capacity of the printed text to convey extremes of human experience.

DAVID MIDGLEY

See also Berlin Alexanderplatz

Biography

Born in Stettin, Germany, 10 August 1878. Educated at the Gymnasium, Stettin, 1888, 1891–1900; studied medicine at Berlin University, 1900–04; Freiburg University, 1904–05, medical degree 1905. Served as a medical officer in the German army during World War I. Worked in a psychiatric hospital, Regensburg; general practitioner, Berlin, 1911–14; member, Schutzverband deutscher Schriftsteller [Association of German Writers], 1920, and president, 1924; theatre reviewer for *Prager Tageblatt*, 1921–24; traveled to Poland, 1924; member of Group 1925 (a discussion group) with Bertolt Brecht; fled to France to escape the Nazi regime, 1933: became French citizen, 1936, and emigrated to the United States, 1940; script writer, Metro Goldwyn Mayer, 1940–41; converted to Roman Catholicism, 1941; returned to Germany, 1945; served as education officer, Baden-Baden, 1945; editor, *Das Goldene Tor*, 1946–51; cofounder, 1949, and vice-president of literature section, 1949–51, Academy for Science and Literature, Mainz; moved to Paris, 1951; entered sanatorium at Freiburg in Breisgau, 1956. Died 26 June 1957.

Novels by Döblin

Das Stiftsfräulein und der Tod, 1913
Die drei Sprünge des Wang-lun, 1915; as *The Three Leaps of Wang-Lun*, 1991
Wadzeks Kampf mit der Dampfturbine, 1918
Der schwarze Vorhang: Roman von den Worten und Zufällen, 1919
Wallenstein, 1920
Blaubart und Miss Ilsebill, 1923
Berge, Meere und Giganten, 1924; revised edition as *Giganten*, 1932
Die beiden Freundinnen und ihr Giftmord, 1925
Feldzeugmeister Cratz. Der Kaplan. Zwei Erzählungen, 1926
Berlin Alexanderplatz. Die Geschichte vom Franz Biberkopf, 1929; as *Alexanderplatz, Berlin: The Story of Franz Biberkopf*, translated by Eugene Jolas, 1931; as *Berlin Alexanderplatz: The Story of Franz Biberkopf*, 1978
Babylonische Wandrung; oder, Hochmut kommt vor dem Fall, 1934
Pardon wird nicht gegeben, 1935; as *Men Without Mercy*, translated by Trevor and Phyllis Blewitt, 1937
Das Land ohne Tod, 1937–38; as *Amazonas*, edited by Walter Muschg, 1963
Die Fahrt ins Lans ohne Tod, 1937
Der blaue Tiger, 1938
Der neue Urwald, 1948
November 1918: Eine deutsche Revolution, 1949; selections from volumes 1 and 2 as *A People Betrayed*, translated by John E. Woods, 1983
　Bürger und Soldaten 1918, 1939; revised edition as *Verratenes Volk*, 1948
　Heimkehr der Fronttruppen, 1949
　Karl und Rosa, 1950; as *Karl and Rosa*, translated by John E. Woods, 1983
Der Oberst und der Dichter; oder, Das menschliche Herz, 1946
Heitere Magie, zwei Erzählungen, 1948
Sinn und Form, 1954
Hamlet; oder, Die lange Nacht nimmt ein Ende, 1956

Other Writings: plays, poems, essays, autobiography, political commentaries.

Further Reading

Grass, Günter, "Uber meinen Lehrer Döblin," in *Aufsätze zur Literatur*, Darmstadt: Luchterhand, 1980

Huguet, Louis, *Bibliographie Alfred Döblin*, Berlin and Weimar: Aufbau, 1972

Keller, Otto, *Döblins Montageroman als Epos der Moderne*, Munich: Fink, 1980

Kiesel, Helmuth, *Literarische Trauerarbeit: Das Exil- und Spätwerk Alfred Döblins*, Tübingen: Niemeyer, 1986

Kobel, Erwin, *Alfred Döblin: Erzählkunst im Umbruch*, Berlin and New York: de Gruyter, 1985

Kort, Wolfgang, *Alfred Döblin*, New York: Twayne, 1974

Kreutzer, Leo, *Alfred Döblin: Sein Werk bis 1933*, Stuttgart: Kohlhammer, 1970

Links, Roland, *Alfred Döblin*, Munich: Beck, 1981

Müller-Salget, Klaus, *Alfred Döblin: Werk und Entwicklung*, Bonn: Bouvier, 1972; 2nd edition, 1988

Prangel, Matthias, *Alfred Döblin*, Stuttgart: Metzler, 1973; 2nd edition, 1987

Zmegac, Viktor, "Alfred Döblins Poetik des Romans," in *Deutsche Romantheorien: Beitrage zu einer historischen Poetik des Romans in Deutschland*, volume 2, edited by Reinhold Grimm, Frankfurt am Main: Athenäum, 1968

Doctor Faustus by Thomas Mann

Doktor Faustus 1947

One of the many possibilities for interpreting Thomas Mann's late novel *Doctor Faustus* is to read it as a roman à clef. While, in 1954, the author apologized to Hans Reisiger—one of the perhaps two dozen actual figures he had included from the intellectual scene in Munich before and after World War I—for having used traits of Reisiger's personality in the portrait of Rüdiger Schildknapp, he was very specific in his own interpretation, calling the book "the novel of Germany's ride to hell." The novel is, in part, Mann's summation of his country's tragic fall into the hands of fascism.

While writing the book Thomas Mann was a resident of the United States, living in Pacific Palisades, California. He believed himself to be the most important outpost of German culture in exile. "Where I am," he said, "there is Germany." In January 1943 he had finished the last volume of the Joseph tetralogy, and after only a few months of research he let his character Serenus Zeitblom begin his fictive biography of Adrian Leverkühn, the avant-garde and demonic German composer. He wrote *finis* on 27 January 1947, and this time frame gave Mann the opportunity to have Zeitblom reflect on the last stages of World War II, enabling Mann to use his composer's Faustian "ride to hell" as a parallel to Germany's ride to hell in the last throes of Hitler's demonic dictatorship.

Since Thomas Mann had predicted earlier that he would die in his 70th year (1945), he reckoned, in May 1943, that he would have two years to finish the task of composing the novel. He not only termed it his "last novel" at the time of writing but continued to call it that even though he lived until 1955, composing several more lengthy works. For him, *Doctor Faustus*, the work of his old age, was his "last" novel because he considered it the companion piece to *Buddenbrooks* (1901), the work of his youth; it is interesting to speculate why this is so. Generally, one could argue that the novel of the "decline of the House of Buddenbrook" has become, in *Doctor Faustus*, the decline of the whole of German civilization. Artistically, instead of letting the musically gifted lit-

tle Hanno die as a last link in the chain of progressive decadence, Mann allows the musically gifted Adrian Leverkühn to achieve unusual heights of modern composition. From a biographical standpoint one might argue that the description of the Mann family until the turn of the century in the earlier work is continued in *Doctor Faustus* by bringing the developments in the family up to date, incorporating the fate of his mother after her move from Lübeck to Munich, as well as that of his sisters. Mann further employs this mode of self-portraiture by assigning his own personal traits to both protagonists in *Doctor Faustus*, Leverkühn as well as Zeitblom. Having been aware of the Goethean "two souls in his breast" all his life, the pedantic bourgeois as well as the demonic artist, Mann uses his "last" novel to show his own split personality as two separate people, who nevertheless, at least in Zeitblom's case, feel a symbiotic relationship with each other. Thus, *Doctor Faustus* is a novel of confession; the significance of *Doctor Faustus* for its author is described in Mann's postscript in *Die Entstehung des Doktor Faustus* (1949; *The Genesis of Doctor Faustus*). The writing of a second novel about the writing of the first one indicates the significance Mann attached to the work. In the "novel about the novel" he calls *Doctor Faustus* "a legacy on the making public of which I can make no allowances," "a radical confession," and, finally, "a moral feat."

While teaching at Princeton University (1938–39), Thomas Mann prefaced a lecture on "The Art of the Novel" thus: "The epic work . . . is a miracle of an enterprise, in which are invested much of life, patience, ardent artful industry, a persevering diligence by which inspiration is renewed daily, with its gigantic miniaturism which seems obsessed by the particular, as though that were the one and only thing, and yet unswervingly keeps an eye on the whole." With this description, the author gives a reason for the employment of certain techniques he had used in his earlier narratives and that he later perfected in *Doctor Faustus*, the novel he called his "montage novel." From many disciplines of knowledge—linguistics, oceanography, geography, politics, sociology, theology, medicine, biology, history, musicology, and so on—Mann had gathered information that he reassembled in *Doctor Faustus,* the idea of which went back as far as 1901. This rich material, of course, engendered the vast and diverse receptions and interpretations of the novel, customarily focused on only one aspect of the work; from the time of the book's appearance, the reception has ranged from total condemnation to highest admiration. For the montage of *Doctor Faustus,* as in his other novels, Thomas Mann "keeps an eye on the whole" by using the leitmotiv technique to hold the main thematics together; however, in *Doctor Faustus* the leitmotiv undergoes an amazing change. Whereas its main purpose previously had been to keep the author, and his reader, at a contemplative ironic distance from plot and protagonists, the leitmotiv in *Doctor Faustus* ensures that no part of the novel remains unconnected to the whole. Thus the structure of the novel is a linguistic mirror of what its protagonist, the composer Adrian Leverkühn, endeavors to follow in his musical compositions, the *strenger Satz* (strict structure), which Thomas Mann based on the 12-tone technique invented by Arnold Schönberg.

Since the leitmotiv is no longer a means of ironic distancing, Mann had to find a new means to keep from pulling the reader into the tragic maelstrom of the novel. To this end, he deploys the fictive biographer Zeitblom, as he says in *The Genesis of Doctor Faustus, zur Durchheiterung* (for a brightening) of the tragic atmosphere. Because Zeitblom recalls the events of Leverkühn's life (1885–1940, with the last 12 years spent in the darkness of madness) and interweaves them with events from the time of writing, the novel is given an additional polyphonic dimension, yet another facet of its "musical structure." However, Zeitblom—aware of Leverkühn's hubris, as well as the composer's feelings of contrition for that character flaw—is shown to exhibit hubris as well, particularly in his tendency to be a know-it-all and a super-psychologist. When Zeitblom begins to write, he has in hand a letter from Leverkühn and Leverkühn's written record of his "conversation" with the devil, which is the content of chapter 25. Then, in the first 24 chapters, Zeitblom culls from his superior memory of their shared past life only those occurrences that have a bearing on the psychological explanation of the content of Leverkühn's "Teufelgespräch." Not only does Zeitblom want to prove that wherever Leverkühn is, there is Kaisersaschern, the medieval town of his youth, but that "hell" with its extremes of "heat" and "coldness" lies within Leverkühn, that the composer is projecting its symbolism into his own alienated psyche. Toward the end of the book the reader even loses sight of Leverkühn, the ostensible subject of Zeitblom's writing, while Zeitblom talks about his own importance in the social circles of Munich.

Just as the composer Leverkühn cancels out (Mann uses the term *zurücknehmen*) the optimism of Beethoven's *Ninth Symphony,* so Thomas Mann cancels out the optimism of the Goethean *Faust,* including the certainty of God's grace. The former goal is attained by reverting to musical "barbarism," that is, to the primitive means of the music of Monteverdi, the latter by going back to the *Faust Volksbuch* of 1587: there Faust goes straight to hell at the end of the 24 years of exceptional time granted him.

With his "last" novel, Thomas Mann means to take leave. As he has Beethoven take leave of the sonata form by composing Opus 111, the piano sonata with only two movements, and as he has Leverkühn take leave of his conscious artistic life through his last composition, *Doktor Fausti Weheklag,* so Thomas Mann means to take leave with *Doctor Faustus,* the *Roman meiner Epoche* (novel of my epoch), take leave from that epoch, and from the form of the novel as well.

LISELOTTE M. DAVIS

See also Thomas Mann

Further Reading

Ball, David, *Thomas Mann's Recantation of Faust: "Doktor Faustus" in the Context of Mann's Relationship to Goethe,* Stuttgart: Heinz-Dieter, 1986

Bergsten, Gunilla, *Thomas Manns "Doktor Faustus": Untersuchungen zu den Quellen und zur Struktur des Romans,* Stockholm: Svenska bokforlaget, 1963; as *Thomas Mann's "Doktor Faustus,"* Chicago: University of Chicago Press, 1969

Boerner, Peter, and Sidney Johnson, editors, *Faust through Four Centuries: Retrospect and Analysis,* Tübingen: Niemeyer, 1989

Carnegy, Patrick, *Faust as Musician: A Study of Thomas Mann's Novel "Doctor Faustus,"* London: Chatto and Windus, 1973

Fetzer, John F., *Changing Perceptions of Thomas Mann's "Doktor Faustus": Criticism 1947–1992,* Columbia, South Carolina: Camden House, 1996

Hoelzel, Alfred, *The Paradoxical Quest: A Study of Faustian Vicissitudes,* New York: Peter Lang, 1988

Jonas, Klaus W., and Ilsedore B. Jonas, *Thomas Mann Studies: A Bibliography of Criticism,* volume 2, Philadelphia: University of Pennsylvania Press, 1967

Kahler, Erich von, *The Orbit of Thomas Mann,* Princeton, New Jersey: Princeton University Press, 1969

Lehnert, Herbert, and Peter C. Pfeiffer, editors, *Thomas Mann's "Doctor Faustus": A Novel at the Margin of Modernism,* Columbia, South Carolina: Camden House, 1991

Doctor Thorne. *See* **Barsetshire Novels**

Doctor Zhivago by Boris Pasternak

Doktor Zhivago 1957

Until the appearance of *Doctor Zhivago*, Boris Pasternak had been famous as a poet and translator but had no reputation as a novelist. He had published short stories in an experimental vein in the 1920s, and this legacy was not wholly absent from his novel, despite the grandeur and scope of the work in its final form.

In the oppressive atmosphere of the Soviet Union after World War II, Pasternak was out of favor. When he submitted his novel to the leading Soviet journal, *Novyi mir*, in 1956, it was rejected on the grounds of its antisocialist, antidemocratic, and antihistorical bias. The manuscript was then taken abroad. In 1957, the novel appeared in Italian, published by Feltrinelli in Milan, and a year later in English. Awarded the Nobel prize for literature shortly afterward, Pasternak was pilloried in the Soviet Union and expelled from the Union of Writers. His novel was banned for three decades until it finally appeared, in Russian, in the very journal that had originally rejected it. On publication in English, *Doctor Zhivago* immediately became a best-seller despite critical reservations about its structure, its genre, and its hero. In 1965, its reputation was deservedly enhanced by a highly successful film version starring Omar Sharif and Julie Christie, with a screenplay by Robert Bolt and direction by David Lean.

Doctor Zhivago, difficult to assess at first reading, is a love story of acknowledged depth and poignancy set against a background of revolution and civil war. Partly an autobiography, partly an epic, partly a traditional 19th-century Russian novel, partly a poet's novel about the making of poetry and of revolution, it was essentially a private work about cataclysmic public events. The account of the doctor-poet Iuryi Zhivago's experience is an incipient example of latter-day Christian hagiography that claims, through the 25 poems by Zhivago in the novel's conclusion, an ultimate symbolic victory of life over death.

The novel cannot be properly understood without some awareness of the historical background. Its total chronological span extends over half a century of momentous Russian history, from 1903 to 1953, from the year Zhivago is orphaned on the eve of the first Russian revolution to the year of Stalin's death, almost a quarter of a century after his own, when his friends first feel free to discuss his poetry. It is in his poetry that he truly lives (his name derives from *zhivoi*, "living") and through his poetry he outlives the cataclysm of revolution and civil war that splits his life in half.

The revolution of 1905 first brings the young Zhivago in contact with Lara Guishar, who is to become the love of his life, but they do not fall in love until they meet by chance during World War I, shortly before the 1917 revolution. Zhivago, meanwhile, has qualified as a doctor and is already married. Lara has married her childhood sweetheart, Pasha Antipov. Improbabilities of coincidence certainly abound in what Pasternak himself called the "moving entireness" of his novel, mostly in the relationship between the lovers. Their meeting in the town of Iuratin in the Urals, after Zhivago and his family have moved to the nearby estate of Varykino to escape the ravages of the civil war, has a fairytale quality. Zhivago's life is protected by some kind of providence, whether by the timely interventions of a miracle-working half-brother or a transfiguring Christian ideal received from an uncle in boyhood. Equally paranormal, it seems, is

Zhivago's capture by partisans who force him to be their doctor. The situation obliges him to realize the ambiguities of his own loyalties in the civil war and takes him away from his settled life. He is not able to go back to what he had been, for his family, supposing him dead, have returned to Moscow and are to be deported. Once he escapes from the partisans, only Lara remains to him and the solace of his poetry in snow-bound Varykino. Even here, Lara's former lover, the lawyer who had also ruined Zhivago's father, acts as a Nemesis and spirits her away, just as her husband, Antipov, renowned as the partisan leader Strelnikov, ends his own life in disillusionment and suicide after an ironic last encounter. Zhivago's past, in short, has virtually been obliterated. Although he returns to Moscow and resumes his career when the civil war is over, he lives increasingly for his poetry. He dies of a weak heart during a protracted tram journey in August 1929.

Superficially anything but heroic and perhaps in the end a failure, Zhivago's life is a spiritual Calvary. It encapsulates the problem confronting the Russian intelligentsia of his time, as summarized in the first of his poems in the image of Hamlet forced to play the role of Christ. He had to live out a parable in his own life, to endure his own Gethsemane (as his last poem makes clear) and epitomize through his poetry a life-renewing principle.

Doctor Zhivago may now be seen to have many claims to greatness. The steely, poetic exactitude of the nature descriptions, the deeply pondered dialogues, the poetry so closely entwined with the narrative, the impact of the love story—all enhance the novel's central theme, which is the tragedy of a nation divided by revolution and civil war. Despite its initial suppression and notoriety, it may now be regarded as among the finest Russian novels to appear since 1917, standing directly in the tradition of the great 19th-century Russian novels devoted to the portrayal of the intelligentsia.

RICHARD FREEBORN

Further Reading

Bakhnov, L.V., and L.B. Voronin, *"Doktor Zhivago" Borisa Pasternaka*, Moscow: Sov. Pisatel, 1990

Barnes, Christopher J., *Boris Pasternak: A Literary Biography*, volume 1, *1890–1928*, Cambridge and New York: Cambridge University Press, 1989

Cornwell, Neil, *Pasternak's Novel: Perspectives on "Doctor Zhivago,"* Keele: Essays in Poetics, 1986

Dyck, J.W., *Boris Pasternak*, New York: Twayne, 1972

Fleishman, Lazar, *Boris Pasternak: The Poet and His Politics*, Cambridge, Massachusetts: Harvard University Press, 1990

Gifford, Henry, *Pasternak: A Critical Study*, Cambridge and New York: Cambridge University Press, 1977

Levi, Peter, *Boris Pasternak*, London: Hutchinson, 1990

Livingstone, Angela, *Boris Pasternak: Doctor Zhivago*, Cambridge and New York: Cambridge University Press, 1989

Sendich, Munir, and Erika Greber, *Pasternak's "Doctor Zhivago": An International Bibliography of Criticism (1957–85)*, East Lansing, Michigan: Russian Language Journal, 1990

Dog Years. *See* Danzig Trilogy

Doktor Faustus. *See* Doctor Faustus

Doktor Zhivago. *See* Doctor Zhivago

Dom Casmurro by Joaquim Maria Machado de Assis

1899

The seventh of nine novels published by Machado de Assis, *Dom Casmurro* is for many the culmination of the Brazilian master's novelistic output. Although his early novels are characterized, with some qualifications, as romantic, *Dom Casmurro* might more appropriately be classified as psychological realism, even though it is devoid of the accumulated detail and the sure-footed moralism typically associated with that movement. While realism usually focuses on external reality, Machado de Assis was more committed to exploring the subjectivity of his characters. *Dom Casmurro* continues the trend established with its two predecessors, *Memórias póstumas de Brás Cubas* (1881; *Epitaph of a Small Winner*) and *Quincas Borba* (1891; *Philosopher or Dog?*), by adopting a digressive style, densely charged with metaphoric associations and philosophical questioning. Machado de Assis himself acknowledges the sources for his playfully self-conscious, freely associative narrators: Laurence Sterne (England), Xavier de Maistre (France), and Almeida Garrett (Portugal).

Although translations of *Dom Casmurro* typically have preserved the original title, a reasonable English version would be "Lord Taciturn." On its most basic level, the novel is a love story with an unhappy ending. Narrating as an old man, Bento Santiago reveals his reasons for concluding that Capitu, his wife and childhood sweetheart, betrayed him with his best friend Escobar, making the latter the father of her son.

Adultery was of course one of the obsessions of the 19th-century novel. Machado de Assis' depiction of the problem, however, takes the novel to a new level of sophistication. While Nathaniel Hawthorne's *The Scarlet Letter* (1850), Gustave Flaubert's *Madame Bovary* (1857), Lev Tolstoi's *Anna Karenina* (1875–77), and other well-known novels present sexual infideli-

ty as an unquestioned fact, the act has an ambiguous status in *Dom Casmurro*. Thus, while the work explores all the usual cultural aspects of a challenged marriage, it also operates on a different level as a novel about interpretation itself. Consequently it has proved especially attractive to contemporary critics with its hermeneutic orientation and has enjoyed an expanding international reputation.

Bento Santiago's active imagination, his insecurity in his own manhood, and the manner in which he compensates for this insecurity with a controlling and jealous temperament make him an extremely problematic narrator. Although he is a lawyer and appears to construct an argument against his wife based on considerable evidence, the reader may find him an unreliable narrator and thus conclude that Capitu was merely the victim of her husband's psychological inadequacies and imaginative projections.

The novel's ambiguity, however, goes beyond the question of the narrator's reliability. The facts as represented by Bento are equivocal. A case in point is the crucial issue of the son Ezequiel's resemblance to Escobar. While even Capitu acknowledges the similarity between the two, the resemblance is made dubious by the fact that Ezequiel is skilled in mimicry and enjoys reproducing the gestures and mannerisms of others. The reader is left to wonder if the perception of resemblance might be based on nonphysical factors. Even granting a physical similarity, however, there is evidence to cast doubt on its relevance when the narrator discovers a remarkable likeness between Capitu and a photograph of an unrelated friend's mother.

Bento is more than just an unreliable narrator. A strong self-referential tendency on his part compounds the complexity of the work and confounds the reader's efforts to assign validity or irony to his statements. At one point Bento extols the virtues of books containing empty spaces, stating that he enjoys imagining all those things that were left unsaid. By indirect self-reference, he seems to be describing his own narration; however, he then concludes by saying, "That is how I fill in the lacunae of other authors; and that is also how you may fill in mine." By instructing his audience to declare its independence from the explicit text, he essentially is inviting readers to consider Capitu's innocence instead of the guilt he asserts.

In a country whose fiction is dominated by the project of national self-definition, Machado de Assis chose to move in a more universal direction. Landscapes, local tastes and sounds, and the examination of specifically Brazilian problems are not his usual business. That is not to say his works are not profoundly Brazilian. Bento's mother's bargain with God to make her son a priest and the improvised detour around that promise in *Dom Casmurro*, for example, represent often discussed aspects of a particularly Brazilian psychology. Moreover, Machado de Assis' fiction contains the seeds of the 20th-century Brazilian avant-garde. Many nontraditional narratives abounding in fragmentation, loosely linked associations, complex logical predicaments, playful "cannibalization" of other texts or formal virtuosity seem to echo or expand on techniques found in *Memórias póstumas* or *Dom Casmurro*. Even the concrete poetry movement has roots in Machado de Assis. A highly significant group of women writers may be said to have followed him in probing the intimate subjectivity of their characters. The most famous of these, Clarice Lispector, made subtle allusions to Machado de Assis in her fiction.

Until recently, few Spanish-speaking Latin Americans read Brazilian literature, so it is too early to speak of Machado de Assis' impact in that context. In spite of the general lack of attention given to Brazilian literature outside that country, however, some important contemporary North American writers have acknowledged a debt to Machado, including Maya Angelou, John Barth, and Susan Sontag.

PAUL B. DIXON

See also Joaquim Maria Machado de Assis

Further Reading

Barbosa, Maria José Somerlate, "Life as an Opera: *Dom Casmurro* and *The Floating Opera*," *Comparative Literature Studies* 29:3 (1992)

Brackel, Arthur, "Ambiguity and Enigma in Art: The Case of Henry James and Machado de Assis," *Comparative Literature Studies* 19:4 (1982)

Dixon, Paul B., *Retired Dreams: "Dom Casmurro," Myth and Modernity*, West Lafayette, Indiana: Purdue University Press, 1989

Ellis, Keith, "Technique and Ambiguity in *Dom Casmurro*," *Hispania* 45 (1965)

Fitz, Earl E., *Machado de Assis*, Boston: Twayne, 1989

Fitz, Earl E., *Rediscovering the New World: Inter-American Literature in a Comparative Context*, Iowa City: University of Iowa Press, 1991

Nunes, Maria Luisa, *The Craft of an Absolute Winner: Characterization and Narratology in the Novels of Machado de Assis*, Westport, Connecticut: Greenwood, 1983

Rego, Enylton de Sá, "The Epic, the Comic and the Tragic: Tradition and Innovation in Three Late Novels of Machado de Assis," *Latin American Literary Review* 14:27 (1986)

Shimura, Masao, "Faulkner, de Assis, Barth: Resemblances and Differences," in *Faulkner Studies in Japan*, edited by Thomas L. McHaney, Athens: University of Georgia Press, 1985

Dominican American Novel. *See* Latino-American Novel

Dominican Republican Novel. *See* Latin American Novel: Hispanic Caribbean; Latino-American Novel

Don Quixote by Miguel de Cervantes

Part I, 1605; Part II, 1615

One of the most enduringly popular stories of world literature, *Don Quixote* is often called the first modern novel. This judgment implies a sharp division between romance and the novel as two opposing types of fiction—one idealizing, the other presenting "a slice of life." The English novelist Clara Reeve, writing in 1785, formulates the distinction as follows: "The Romance is an heroic fable, which treats of fabulous persons and things.—The Novel is a picture of real life and manners, and of the time in which it is written. The Romance in lofty and elevated language describes what never happens nor is likely to happen.—The Novel gives a familiar relation of such things as pass every day before our eyes, such as may happen to our friend, or to ourselves."

On the basis of this definition, there would indeed seem to be ample grounds for labeling *Don Quixote* a novel. An unprecedented degree of psychological realism marks the characterization of major and minor figures alike. Don Quixote and Sancho in particular are widely admired for their "humanity," their similarity to "you and me," in large measure because of their lifelike complexity and capacity for change in response to their experience. The impression of realism is reinforced by the dialogue, which has struck many a reader as a faithful mirror of the everyday speech of real people in all stations of life. Moreover, many of *Don Quixote*'s scenes ring a note of historical fidelity, presenting a convincing evocation of the circumstances of life in rural Spain in the early years of the 17th century. Cervantes' rejection of the chivalric romances that turn Quixote's head further seems to confirm the idea that *Don Quixote* makes a decisive break with the idealizing romance.

However, to call *Don Quixote* a novel pure and simple is to ignore the persistence of romance forms alongside its more realistic elements. In fact, Cervantes freely mixed what only to later centuries appeared to be inimical. While it is true that *Don Quixote* gives "a picture of real life and manners," it is also full of fabulous things and lofty language. For instance, the central plot focusing on Don Quixote, his bizarre lunacy and even more outlandish adventures, is hardly what "may happen to our friend, or to ourselves." Cervantes is careful to naturalize the plot, presenting it as something that could very well happen to "you and me," but that is part of a tongue-in-cheek argument about the pernicious influence of chivalric romances. Surely, the mad knight's delusions and their origin in the romances of which he has read too many are a matter of fable rather than verisimilitude.

Interpretations of *Don Quixote* prevalent in the 19th century—inspired by the metaphysics of romanticism—emphasized the book's fabulous elements. They cast the central theme of the book as a battle between idealism (symbolized by the mad Quixote) and materialism (symbolized by Sancho Panza, ever apt to remember his stomach). Quixote's madness presented itself to 19th-century romantic readers as a sanity of a higher order, while his quest struck them as symbolic of all that was good in humankind. Although such interpretations are clearly one-sided, they have the virtue of foregrounding the idealizing elements buried in the realistic narrative. The Spanish critic Menéndez y Pelayo observed that, whatever his original inten-

tions, Cervantes did not destroy the chivalric ideal of the romances he rejected—he transfigured it.

Admittedly, *Don Quixote* contains a great deal of everyday speech, but it also takes tremendous pleasure in the lofty language of romance that it puts in Quixote's mouth. As Erich Auerbach remarks in *Mimesis,* Cervantes is "a master in the field" of the "rhythmically and pictorially rich, [the] beautifully articulated and musical bravura pieces of chivalric rhetoric." While on the one hand he represents the speech of thieves and rascals in realistic dialogue, on the other he is, to quote Auerbach again, "not merely a destructive critic but a continuer and consummator of the great epico-rhetorical tradition" (see Auerbach, 1953).

It must also be noted that, despite his attack on chivalric romances, Cervantes did not reject romance in general. His first published work, *La Galatea* (1585), was a pastoral romance. His last, *Los trabajos de Persiles y Sigismunda* (*The Trials of Persiles and Sigismunda*), published posthumously in 1617, was another. Part I of *Don Quixote* itself incorporates a number of interpolated tales in a traditional romance mode. As E.C. Riley notes, "Cervantes never moved definitively from one kind of narrative to the other, but was liable to write one kind or the other in some combination of the two to the end of his days" (see Riley, 1986).

Heedless of the customary generic constraints of later centuries, *Don Quixote* in fact predates the modern novel. It remains true, however, that the realism of its characterization, dialogue, and settings has exerted a significant influence on the development of the genre. If *Don Quixote* is not the first modern novel, it nevertheless represents a tremendous advance in its direction. Qualifying as one of "the great myths of Western civilization," to use Ian Watt's phrase, *Don Quixote*'s influence is so pervasive as to be difficult to isolate. A few examples should give an impression of its presence in the fiction of successive centuries. Henry Fielding proclaimed himself a disciple of Cervantes, and his *Tom Jones* (1749) displays the same ironic combination of heroic idealism and everyday reality as *Don Quixote.* Flaubert's Emma Bovary, her mind corrupted by the reading of cheap novels, displays a similarity to Don Quixote that is too close to be accidental. And *Ulysses'* Leopold Bloom, in his efforts to rise above his drab environment, is often likened to our hero as well. The self-reflexive features that mark Cervantes' narrative technique are commonly thought to have served as one of the seminal examples of the modern novel's tendency to reflect on itself and its formal accomplishments.

Although *Don Quixote* has enjoyed a steady popularity since its first publication, the history of its reception has been marked by major shifts in interpretation. Some of these shifts have been mentioned already. The 18th century became blind to the book's nonrealistic elements, while the 19th read its own idealism back into the story. Over the centuries, Don Quixote has also been reevaluated as a character, moving from the merely ridiculous to the sublime in the estimation of those readers who have testified to their experience of the book. During the century and a half that followed its publication, *Don Quixote* was unanimously considered a comic work. None of Cervantes' contemporaries seems to have noticed the serious and even tragic undertones modern readers find in the book, and it is clear that they laughed at many things that no longer seem funny to most of us. The humiliations and physical injuries that Don Quixote and Sancho repeatedly suffer inspire the modern reader with sympathy, whereas Cervantes' earliest readers tended to identify with the pranksters who have fun at Quixote's expense.

Cervantes' combination of sympathy for Don Quixote and Sancho and awareness that many of their actions are absurd enabled him to create two of the greatest comic figures in European literature. Neither Don Quixote nor Sancho invariably acts foolishly. Cervantes endows Don Quixote with a seriousness not found in other comic victims of deception such as Boccaccio's simpleton Calandrino. Always motivated by noble ideals, Don Quixote reveals in his lucid intervals that he is not merely good but wise. Sancho's increasing self-confidence and sophistication keep him from being simply a buffoon. Both the knight and his squire are transformed by their experiences and most of all by their contact with each other.

We can laugh at the "fabulous" exploits of Don Quixote and Sancho without ceasing, in Clara Reeve's words, to be "affected by the joys or distresses of the persons in the story, as if they were our own." One reason for the enduring appeal of *Don Quixote* is that it is both novel and romance, neither wholly tragedy nor wholly comedy.

THOMAS R. HART AND MARIJKE RIJSBERMAN

See also Miguel de Cervantes

Further Reading
Auerbach, Erich, "The Enchanted Dulcinea," in his *Mimesis: The Representation of Reality in Western Literature,* Princeton, New Jersey: Princeton University Press, 1953
Close, A.J., *Miguel de Cervantes: "Don Quixote,"* Cambridge and New York: Cambridge University Press, 1990
Forcione, Alban K., *Cervantes, Aristotle and the "Persiles,"* Princeton, New Jersey: Princeton University Press, 1970
Hart, Thomas R., *Cervantes and Ariosto: Renewing Fiction,* Princeton, New Jersey: Princeton University Press, 1989
Predmore, Richard L., *The World of Don Quixote,* Cambridge, Massachusetts: Harvard University Press, 1967
Riley, E.C., *Don Quixote,* London and Boston: Allen and Unwin, 1986
Robert, Marthe, *The Old and the New: From "Don Quixote" to Kafka,* Berkeley: University of California Press, 1977
Russell, P.E., *Cervantes,* Oxford and New York: Oxford University Press, 1985
Spitzer, Leo, "Linguistic Perspectivisim in the *Don Quijote,*" in his *Representative Essays,* edited by Alban K. Forcione, Herbert Lindenberger, and Madeline Sutherland, Stanford, California: Stanford University Press, 1988

Dona Flor and Her Two Husbands by Jorge Amado

Dona Flor e seus dois maridos 1966

With *Gabriela, cravo e canela* (1959; *Gabriela, Clove and Cinnamon*), Jorge Amado departed from the practice of his earlier, more explicitly political novels to write fiction that inquired into broader issues of contemporary Brazilian life. In this novel, set in one of his favorite territories, his home state of Bahia, Amado questions the time-honored code of conduct that sanctions a husband killing an adulterous wife. *Dona Flor and Her Two Husbands,* which is addressed to the same broad audience as *Gabriela, Clove and Cinnamon,* further develops his sympathetic portraits of Brazilian women and extends his reach as a social critic.

The novel's distensions of social realism might seem to place its mode within the magical realist tradition, whose best-known Latin American practitioner is Gabriel García Márquez. But the fabulous concatenations of time, for example, that inform García Márquez's fiction do not function in Amado's work as significantly; Amado is more interested in appealing to the widest possible audience, and his later novels, *Dona Flor and Her Two Husbands* included, are more conventional in structure and form than are most other contemporary Latin American fabulist fictions.

The point of view from which the narrator tells the story of *Dona Flor and Her Two Husbands* merges several longstanding narrative conventions to serve Amado's several purposes. On one level, the narrator is identified with Jorge Amado himself, in keeping with his populist desire to embed the fiction as seamlessly as possible within his lived reality in the city of Bahia, the major city in the state of the same name, roughly in the middle of Brazil's eastern coast. This intention is supported by occasional addresses directly to Amado from characters in the novel, as well as by the numerous references to actual local personalities (musicians, artists, and politicians), to the layout of the city of Bahia and its environs, and to local customs and traditions, including, centrally, the recording of the recipes that Dona Flor perfects in her cooking school. This point of view hews closely to the broad tradition of social realism in which Amado works, allowing him the kinds of authorial asides that have familiar antecedents for English readers, such as Henry Fielding's narrators (in *Tom Jones,* for example).

At another level, the narration merges the apparent ventriloquism of Amado's own voice with an omniscient and flexible purview that enlarges and distends the realist frame to allow for major plot elements such as the ghostly reappearance of Vadinho, the first of Dona Flor's husbands, after his death. The intent here, as signaled in the novel's title, is to create a device through which Amado can explore, often comically, the conflicting social, sexual, and moral codes that beset Dona Flor as she lives with her two husbands, one a fictional apparition, one fictional flesh and blood, after her marriage to her second husband, Teodoro. Amado intends his readers at once to see through this device—to understand that Vadinho's haunting of Dona Flor in her marriage bed and during her waking hours is an illusion—and to accept that the haunting represents something real in Dona Flor's psyche and, by extension, in the lives of Brazilian women, who are expected to live by repressive Latin American patriarchal codes that are more rigid than their Western European and North American counterparts. At the same time, the comic interplay of these two points of view, exemplified, for example, through the omniscient, often mocking commentary on Bahian mores, demonstrates that the constraints imposed upon Dona Flor run counter to the strongly permissive and expressive elements in Brazilian culture generally, and specifically in this region, the area of Brazil most heavily influenced by African culture. One aspect of this culture is *candomblé*, an Afro-Brazilian spiritual tradition (with which Amado has long been familiar) with an elaborate liturgy and a host of spiritual and demonic forces, many of which are invoked in the novel.

Another contribution of *Dona Flor and Her Two Husbands* to the novel form lies in its handling of character via the novel's comic and systematic attribution of contrasting sets of traits to the two husbands vying for Dona Flor. The characters of Vadinho and Teodoro are neither entirely realist nor entirely fabular; they are not allegorical or metaphorical. They come closest to richly detailed caricatures, but both are also assemblies of representative elements in the male Brazilian makeup. They function on two planes: one, as quasi-realist depictions of Brazilian men of their time, class, position, and temperament, and two, as forces that exert different powers over Dona Flor, who must answer to her own desires and to their fulfillments and frustrations as these are incarnated in Vadinho and Teodoro. Character in this novel is formed within a system of relations: the dance of Dona Flor's desire, played out in her relations with her nasty hidebound mother, with the Church, with her neighbors, with her pupils in the cooking school, and with her two husbands, forms the structure and progress of the novel's plot as she discovers herself and the Bahian society that envelops her.

Amado's style, here as elsewhere, tends toward the ample, the florid, and the sentimental, but it is a mistake for several reasons to underestimate or dismiss his prose on these counts. First, Portuguese translated into English—perhaps even more explicit the more faithful the translator is to the rhythms and structures typically set up in Amado's lushly cumulative extended sentences—can seem fulsome, overblown to anglophone ears and sensibilities. But to be faithful to the rhythms of Amado's own culture, the best translations attempt to imitate in English the more sonorous and melodious structures of Brazilian Portuguese. Second, Amado's style is often self-parodying, amused at its own excesses, almost lampooning itself, and this inflection is in keeping with Amado's wider intentions both to represent and to critique his culture.

Dona Flor and Her Two Husbands follows the distinctive Amado technique of melding popular and serious, lowbrow and highbrow, and romantic and realist elements to form a hybrid novel with a working- and middle-class pedigree that appeals to a middle- and upper-class readership.

NEIL K. BESNER

See also Jorge Amado

Further Reading

Chamberlain, Bobby J., "Gastronomic Interludes in Jorge Amado's *Dona Flor e seus dois maridos*," *Tropos* 6:1 (Spring 1977)

Chamberlain, Bobby J., *Jorge Amado*, Boston: G.K. Hall, 1990

Hamilton, Russell G., "Afro-Brazilian Cults in the Novels of Jorge Amado," *Hispania* 50 (1967)

Martin, Gerald, *Journeys Through the Labyrinth: Latin American Fiction in the Twentieth Century*, London and New York: Verso, 1989

Pescatello, Ann, "The Brazileira: Images and Realities in Writings of Machado de Assis and Jorge Amado," in *Female and Male in Latin America: Essays*, edited by Ann Pescatello, Pittsburgh, Pennsylvania: University of Pittsburgh Press, 1973

Silverman, Malcolm, "Moral Dilemma in Jorge Amado's *Dona Flor e seus dois maridos*," *Romance Notes* 13:2 (Winter 1971)

Dos Passos, John. *See* U.S.A. Trilogy

Fedor Dostoevskii 1821–81

Russian

As a young man, Fedor Mikhailovich Dostoevskii was an enthusiastic reader of the prose of Aleksandr Pushkin, Mikhail Lermontov, and Nikolai Gogol'. There he found the whole spectrum of burgeoning Russian realism, with its wealth of stylistic and structural experimentation, portraits of contemporary social and psychological types, studies of inner psychological and interpersonal conflict, and an obsession with the interface between the fantastic and the real. Through the works of these three major writers, active during Dostoevskii's childhood, Russian prose was finding its own distinctive voice. But Dostoevskii was no less enthusiastic in his reading of European writers. Among his favorites were Sir Walter Scott, Ann Radcliffe, Honoré de Balzac, Charles Dickens, Friedrich von Schiller, E.T.A. Hoffmann, Victor Hugo, Eugène Sue, and George Sand, all of whom contributed to the tradition that Donald Fanger, in his *Dostoevsky and Romantic Realism: A Study of Dostoevsky in Relation to Balzac, Dickens, and Gogol* (1965) has called "romantic realism." Unsurprisingly, Dostoevskii's first venture into print was a translation of Balzac's *Eugénie Grandet*. This tendency toward romantic realism in Dostoevskii's work was reinforced by the critical writing and personal enthusiasm of the critic Vissarion Belinskii, the founder of Russia's Natural School, whose aim it was to establish a genuinely Russian literature, rooted in contemporary social reality. Belinskii was ecstatic about Dostoevskii's first epistolary novel *Bednye liudi* (1846; *Poor Folk*) but less enthusiastic about *Dvoinik* (1846; *The Double*) and some of the short stories that followed because of their lapse into the fantastic. But in these works Dostoevskii was experimenting with narrative point of view and psychology in ways that anticipate his major works. This experimentation continued through the 1840s. In all of these works the voices of Dostoevskii's precursors in the European and Russian novel may be identified (see Terras, 1969).

Dostoevskii's experience of being condemned to death, led to the place of execution, and then having his sentence commuted to four years of penal servitude in the fortress of Omsk, followed by four years as a private soldier in Semipalatinsk, undoubtedly left deep marks on his psyche, already scarred by a number of dramatic childhood events, including the murder of his father. Scholars have speculated that these experiences either caused or greatly aggravated Dostoevskii's epilepsy, to say nothing of how they influenced the themes and structure of his work. Undoubtedly these events not only provided subject matter but also motivated the fiction of extreme passions and situations for which his novels are famed. Robert L. Jackson (1981) argues that *Zapiski iz mertvogo doma* (1861–62; *Memoirs from the House of the Dead*) anticipates the preoccupations of his major novels of the 1860s and 1870s. This fictional account of the penal fortress, almost documentary in tone, echoes the circles of Dante's hell. *Unizhennye i oskorblennye* (1861; *The Insulted and Injured*), Dostoevskii's longest novel at the time, has also been said to prefigure the major novels in significant ways.

But there is little doubt that the major turning point in Dostoevskii's career was marked by the publication of *Zapiski iz podpol'ia* (1864; *Notes from Underground*). That this was a watershed in Dostoevskii's spiritual and artistic development has been nowhere more eloquently argued than by Leo Shestov in his essay *Dostoevskii i Nitshe* (1903; *Dostoevsky and Nietzsche*). *Notes from Underground*, divided into two parts, begins with an anguished polemic by a mentally ill protagonist against the prevailing utilitarian philosophy of the 1860s, of which he is an unwilling prisoner. It is presented in the form of a confession by a narrator who perversely gains masochistic enjoyment from his sense of helplessness in the face of the iron laws of nature, and sadistic pleasure from the sense that he can inflict trivial injuries on other people. Much of *Notes from Underground* echoes throughout Dostoevskii's major work: the melodramatic survivals of the Gothic novel; the ideological rebel, psychologically deeply divided; the Dostoevskian scandal scene; the promise of spiritual rebirth through a relationship with a saintly companion; the foreshadowing of a Christian answer to the anguish of the divided soul; and, once again, experimentation with genre and narrative point of view in which the (real and supposed) reader is drawn into dialogue. As with the earlier *The Double*, *Notes from Underground* in some sense anticipates postmodernist preoccupations: both protagonists are confused by their vain attempts to find truth beyond the endless plurality of interrelated texts that make up the totality of their experience; and both novels lure the reader into similar vain attempts to make what Bakhtin (*Problems of Dostoevsky's Poetics*, 1984) calls "monologic" sense of the narrative. The term commonly used to describe Dostoevskii's work is "fantastic realism." Dostoevskii appears to have used these terms himself to describe his work: "I have completely different ideas about reality and realism from our realists and critics. My idealism is more real than theirs." And again: "I have my own view of reality in art and what in the view of most people verges on the fantastic and the exceptional is sometimes the very essence of the real for me."

Dostoevskii had originally planned his first major novel, *Prestuplenie i nakazanie* (1867; *Crime and Punishment*), as a first-person narrative, but instead chose an impersonal third-person form in which the field of vision almost coincides with that of the protagonist. Here again the relationship between ideas and psychology is explored, this time in relation to an ideological murder, committed by the protagonist in the early pages of the novel. The rest of the novel becomes a quest by the protagonist (and the reader) to discover his true motives as he struggles to sustain his belief that he is above good and evil while fending off thoughts that in murdering he has killed the essentially human in himself. At the close a spiritual rebirth through Christian values is foreshadowed, allowing the reader to recognize in the myth of death and resurrection the narrative's underlying structure. Here Dostoevskii emerges as a master not only of individual psychology but also of interpersonal relations.

Igrok (1866; *The Gambler*), a shorter work, was less innovative. A first-person confession, it combines Dostoevskii's gambling obsession with a highly neurotic love relationship based on his personal experience with Polina Suslova. However, *Idiot* (1869; *The Idiot*) followed shortly thereafter. Written abroad while Dostoevskii was suffering a debilitating series of epileptic fits, *The Idiot*'s structure has been said to exemplify the epileptic consciousness. At all events its Christlike, epileptic protagonist experiences in his fits both a sublime synthesis of beauty and prayer and an experience of utter desolation and darkness. Structurally the narrative seems at times to mirror the psychology of the protagonist, to teeter precariously on the knife-edge between coherence and a collapse into chaos, thus demonstrating the idea that the essential is incommunicable. Robin Feuer Miller (1981) argues that the novel draws on various genre traditions and, with them, different traditions of narrative, moving from one to the other in a bewildering, mutually subversive way so that the narrator seems to lose his grip on the narrated material as the characters lose their grip on life. *Besy* (1872; translated as *The Devils* and also as *The Possessed*) is told by a first-person narrator who plays a role on the margins of the action and allows the narrative to take on the appearance of a chronicle of current events. Dostoevskii depicts an entire town on the verge of spiritual and social collapse, focusing on the chaos surrounding an abortive public festivity, followed by riots, arson, multiple murder, and suicide. At the center of the human drama is a charismatic protagonist, Stavrogin, who is spiritually empty, a state reflected in the narrative structure of the novel. *Podrostok* (1875; *A Raw Youth*) is a lesser work, but was followed by Dostoevskii's last great novel, *Brat'ia Karamazovy* (1880; *The Brothers Karamazov*), which culminated his lifelong obsession with parricide. It traces the responsibility for and reaction to the murder of a father by his four sons and raises discussion of parricide to a metaphysical level in "The Legend of the Grand Inquisitor" that, standing at the epicenter of the novel's thematic structure, debates the existence of God. The narrator is again a minor, unnamed participant on the margins of the drama, who unsettlingly slips in and out of a state of omniscience.

Dostoevskii found admirers among a great variety of leading novelists in Russia, Europe, Asia, and the Americas. For many, such as Franz Kafka, Hermann Hesse, and Albert Camus, it was Dostoevskii's depiction of existential alienation (the "Underground type") and the modern ideological rebel that made him so important as a novelist. However, some critics hold that the most revolutionary aspect of Dostoevskii's art was his technique of presenting dynamically interacting characters with contrasting views (or ideas), any of which may be used as a key to reading the text as a whole. Mikhail Bakhtin believed Dostoevskii to be the father of the "polyphonic novel." His novels are ultimately dialogic, constructed not as the whole of a single consciousness but as a whole formed by the interaction of several consciousnesses, none of which entirely becomes an object for the other.

MALCOLM V. JONES

See also Brothers Karamazov; Crime and Punishment; Devils; Dialogism; Idiot

Biography

Born in Moscow, Russia, 30 October 1821. Educated at home to age 12; attended Chermak's School, Moscow; Army Chief Engineering Academy, St. Petersburg, 1838–43; commissioned as ensign, 1839, as 2nd lieutenant, 1842, graduated 1843 as War Ministry draftsman; resigned 1844. Political involvement led to his arrest, 1849: death sentence was reduced at the last moment to penal servitude, in Omsk, Siberia, 1850–54; exiled

as soldier at Semipalatinsk, 1854; corporal, 1855, ensign, 1856, resigned as 2nd lieutenant owing to poor health, and exile ended, 1859; served as editor of *Vremia* [Time], 1861–63; took over *Epokha* [Epoch] upon his brother's death, 1864–65; lived in Western Europe, 1867–71; editor, *Grazhdanin* [Citizen], 1873–74. Died 28 January 1881.

Novels by Dostoevskii

Bednye liudi, 1846; as *Poor Folk*, 1887; also translated by C.J. Hogarth, with *The Gambler*, 1916; Constance Garnett, in *The Novels*, 1917; Robert Dessaix, 1982; David McDuff, in *Poor Folk and Other Stories*, 1988

Dvoinik, 1846; as *The Double*, translated by Constance Garnett, in *The Novels*, 1917; also translated by Jessie Coulson, 1972; as *The Double: Two Versions*, translated by Evelyn Harden, 1985

Netochka Nezvanova, 1849; as *Netochka Nezvanova*, translated by Constance Garnett, in *The Novels*, 1920; also translated by Jane Kentish, 1985

Selo Stepanchikovo i ego obitateli, 1859; as *The Village of Stepanchikovo and Its Inhabitants*, translated by Ignat Avsey, 1983 (revised edition, 1995)

Unizhennye i oskorblennye, 1861; as *The Insulted and the Injured*, translated by Constance Garnett, in *The Novels*, 1915; also translated by Olga Shartse, 1977

Zapiski iz mertvogo doma, 1861; as *The House of the Dead*, translated by Constance Garnett, in *The Novels*, 1915; also translated by David McDuff, 1985; as *Memoirs from the House of the Dead*, translated by Jessie Coulson, 1965

Zimmie zametki na letnikh vpechatleniiakh, 1863; as *Summer Impressions*, translated by Kyril FitzLyon, 1954; retitled *Winter Notes on Summer Impressions*, 1985; also translated by Richard Lee Renfield, 1955; David Patterson, 1988

Zapiski iz podpol'ia, 1864; as *Notes from Underground*, translated by Constance Garnett, in *The Novels*, 1918; also translated by Jessie Coulson, in *Notes from Underground, The Double*, 1972; Michael R. Katz, 1989; Jane Kentish, in *Notes from the Underground and The Gambler*, 1991; Richard Pevear and Larissa Volokhonsky, 1993

Igrok, 1866; as *The Gambler*, with *Poor Folk*, translated by C.J. Hogarth, 1916 (revised edition, 1994); also translated by Jessie Coulson, in *The Gambler; Bobok; A Nasty Story*, 1966; Victor Terras, with *Diary*, by Polina Suslova, 1973; Jane Kentish, in *Notes from the Underground and The Gambler*, 1991

Prestuplenie i nakazanie, 1867; as *Crime and Punishment*, 1886; translated by Constance Garnett, in *The Novels*, 1912–20; also translated by David Magarshack, 1951; Jessie Coulson, 1953; David McDuff, 1991; Richard Pevear and Larissa Volokhonsky, 1993

Idiot, 1869; as *The Idiot*, translated by Constance Garnett, in *The Novels*, 1913; also translated by David Magarshack, 1954; Alan Myers, 1992; Richard Pevear and Larissa Volokhonsky, 1993

Besy, 1872; as *The Possessed*, translated by Constance Garnett, in *The Novels*, 1913; as *The Devils*, translated by David Magarshack, 1954; as *Devils*, translated by Michael R. Katz, 1992; as *The Possessed*, translated by Richard Pevear and Larissa Volokhonsky, 1994

Podrostok, 1875; as *A Raw Youth*, translated by Constance

Garnett, in *The Novels*, 1916; as *An Accidental Family,*
translated by Richard Freeborn, 1994

Brat'ia Karamazovy, 1880; as *The Brothers Karamazov,*
translated by Constance Garnett, in *The Novels*, 1912; also
translated by David Magarshack, 1958; Richard Pevear and
Larissa Volokhonsky, 1990; David McDuff, 1993; as *The
Karamazov Brothers*, translated by Ignat Avsey, 1994

Other Writings: notebooks, journals, letters.

Further Reading

Bakhtin, M.M., *Problemy tvorchestva Dostoevskogo,*
Leningrad: Priboi, 1929; 2nd edition, revised, as *Problemy
poetiki Dostoevskogo,* Moscow: Sov. Pisatel, 1963; as
Problems of Dostoevsky's Poetics, Ann Arbor, Michigan:
Ardis, 1973; new edition and translation, Minneapolis:
University of Minnesota Press, and Manchester: Manchester
University Press, 1984

Catteau, Jacques, *La création littéraire chez Dostoevsky,* Paris:
Institut d'études slaves, 1978; as *Dostoyevsky and the
Process of Literary Creation,* Cambridge and New York:
Cambridge University Press, 1989

Fanger, Donald, *Dostoevsky and Romantic Realism: A Study of
Dostoevsky in Relation to Balzac, Dickens, and Gogol,*
Cambridge, Massachusetts: Harvard University Press, 1965

Frank, Joseph, *Dostoevsky: The Miraculous Years, 1865–1871,*
Princeton, New Jersey: Princeton University Press, 1995

Ivanov, Vyacheslav, *Freedom and the Tragic Life: A Study in
Dostoevsky,* New York: Noonday, and London: Harvill,
1952

Jackson, Robert Louis, *The Art of Dostoevsky, Deliriums and
Nocturnes,* Princeton, New Jersey: Princeton University Press,
1981

Jackson, Robert Louis, editor, *Dostoevsky: New Perspectives,*
Englewood Cliffs, New Jersey: Prentice-Hall, 1984

Jones, Malcolm V., *Dostoyevsky: The Novel of Discord,* New
York: Barnes and Noble, and London: Elek, 1976

Jones, Malcolm V., *Dostoyevsky after Bakhtin,* Cambridge and
New York: Cambridge University Press, 1990

Knapp, Liza, *The Annihilation of Inertia: Dostoevsky and
Metaphysics,* Evanston, Illinois: Northwestern University
Press, 1996

Miller, Robin Feuer, *Dostoevsky and "The Idiot": Author,
Narrator, and Reader,* Cambridge, Massachusetts: Harvard
University Press, 1981

Murav, Harriet, *Holy Foolishness: Dostoevsky's Novels and the
Poetics of Cultural Critique,* Stanford, California: Stanford
University Press, 1992

Peace, Richard, *Dostoyevsky: An Examination of the Major
Novels,* Cambridge: Cambridge University Press, 1971; New
York: Cambridge University Press, 1975

Terras, Victor, *The Young Dostoevsky (1846–1849): A Critical
Study,* The Hague: Mouton, 1969

Wellek, René, editor, *Dostoevsky: A Collection of Critical
Essays,* Englewood Cliffs, New Jersey: Prentice-Hall, 1962

Dracula by Bram Stoker

1897

Bram Stoker's *Dracula* has become one of the most reworked, if
not reread, novels of the 19th century, spawning a Dracula/vam-
pire industry in virtually every cultural commodity from cinema
to children's cartoons. While popular enough at the time it was
published, it was nowhere near achieving its current iconographic status until being disseminated through cinema from the early
20th century onward. The popularity of the Dracula myth lies
perhaps in the fact that it has proven to be a vehicle for concerns
that, while submerged in Stoker's novel, have since been more
openly addressed in its various interpretations. Sexuality, fear of
women, the transmission of diseases (both sexual and otherwise), the threat of invasion from outside cultures—all these
themes are found "buried" in the text of *Dracula*.

Dracula is all the more remarkable when compared to the rest
of Bram Stoker's writing, which is an awkward mixture of romance, horror, and heroism (often all are pressed into service in
the same novel). *Dracula,* on the other hand, is a skillfully told
narrative, made terrifying by the uncertainty of who or what exactly its villain is, by the excruciating suspense created by these
uncertainties, and by scenes in which the terror straddles the
boundaries between the natural and the supernatural with astonishing effect. For example, Dracula's journey to England on the
Demeter, resulting in the gradual depletion and madness of the
crew and culminating in the final glimpse of a large dog jumping
off the ship, is wonderfully constructed, especially since Stoker
reveals the story through newspaper reports, which, of course,
show no inkling of the existence of Count Dracula.

While *Dracula* is in a sense the beginning point of its own
genre, it also taps into and extends the Gothic and terror genres
of late 18th and early 19th-century romanticism. Mary Shelley's
Frankenstein (1818), and John Polidori's "The Vampyre," for
example, are obvious points of connection, while the Victorian
predilection for ghost stories, especially those associated with
the "mystery" of other cultures (for example, Wilkie Collins'
The Moonstone, 1868), makes *Dracula* appear in many ways
typical of its time. One other possible way to place *Dracula* in a
tradition of novel and fiction writing is to take into account that,
because Stoker was born and lived his early life in Dublin, his
cultural environment and personal acquaintances gave him access to what was a strongly established Anglo-Irish Gothic tradition, with its particular focus on the "dark" superstitions of
Catholicism and its wariness of, yet attraction to, the peasantry.
Both Charles Maturin's *Melmoth the Wanderer* (1820) and
Sheridan Le Fanu's stories and novels provide an important con-

text for understanding the literary inheritance of *Dracula*. Le Fanu's story "Carmilla" involves a lesbian vampire, a mixing of vampirism and sexual desire repeated in *Dracula*. Stoker was closely acquainted with Oscar Wilde's family (and with Wilde himself; Stoker married Wilde's "fiancée"), and the Wildes traced a direct family line back to Maturin. *Dracula*'s obvious fear of cultural inversion (Dracula coming from the East to England) and its placing of the castle at the center of power (an equivalent, perhaps, of the Irish Ascendancy "Big House") are two ways in which the "Irishness" of *Dracula* may be made concrete. Although *Dracula* should never be understood solely as an Irish text, its connections, both literary and thematic, with Anglo-Irish culture remain largely unexplored.

In novelistic terms, the Gothic has always been a fascinating mixture of startlingly new techniques and repetitions of established formats, tropes, and character types. *Dracula* is undoubtedly one of the innovative moments of the Gothic as a genre. Its narrative technique, owing to the epistolary novel and perhaps more than a little to Emily Brontë's *Wuthering Heights* (1847), is an extraordinary feat, patching together its fiction through a variety of formats. Diaries, letters, newspapers, stenograph recordings, and telegrams are all used to allow the story to unfold. Traditionally, and originally, the novel employed this technique as a form of poor disguise for its fictionality. Stoker may have opted for the format of a supposed collection of manuscripts and sources to give the story of *Dracula* a sense of documented reality, and certainly this technique works against the supernatural narrative in interesting ways. What is perhaps most disturbing about reading a novel written in this way and on such a subject is that the action has no central, presiding character who is entirely in possession of the knowledge necessary to understand what unfolds. The technique of piecing together the novel from these fragments thus becomes part of the narrative's own intention to frighten and unsettle. When the characters write their experiences, they do so in the hope of understanding better what is happening to them. And yet when they have done so, another piece of knowledge comes the way of the reader that makes it clear that individual characters will never, until the final denouement at least, be able to use their knowledge to assert control over their destinies.

The novel's focus on the assertion of order and knowledge as the only way of defeating Dracula is most apparent in the use of technologies of knowledge. These can be as simple as a train timetable or as complex and modern as the stenograph, which records the spoken voice. Stoker's *Dracula* has a distinctly contemporary feel through the technologies it mentions, as well as through its focus on psychology. This contemporaneity is pitted against the old traditions and superstitions that Dracula himself represents. In the end, *Dracula* may wish to tell us about the defeat of the old by the new, but, as the enduring nature of its eponymous antihero attests, any such desire is thoroughly, and probably deliberately, unconvincing.

COLIN GRAHAM

See also Gothic Novel

Further Reading

Belford, Barbara, *Bram Stoker: A Biography of the Author of "Dracula,"* London: Weidenfeld and Nicolson, and New York: Knopf, 1996

Carter, Margaret L., editor, *"Dracula": The Vampire and the Critics,* Ann Arbor, Michigan: UMI Research Press, 1991

Gelder, Ken, *Reading the Vampire,* London and New York: Routledge, 1994

Leatherdale, Clive, *"Dracula": The Novel and the Legend,* Wellingborough, Northamptonshire: Aquarian Press, 1985; revised edition, Brighton, Sussex: Desert Island, 1993

Ludlam, Harry, *A Biography of Dracula: The Life Story of Bram Stoker,* London and New York: Foulsham, 1962

Roth, Phyllis A., *Bram Stoker,* Boston: Twayne, 1982

Dr. Jekyll and Mr. Hyde. *See* Strange Case of Dr. Jekyll and Mr. Hyde

Dream of the Red Chamber. *See* Six Classic Chinese Novels

Theodore Dreiser 1871–1945

United States

Theodore Dreiser's most obvious affinities in the novel form are with Honoré de Balzac, Émile Zola, and, in his own country, William Dean Howells. To say this is not to point to his detailed familiarity with their works, for few novelists of his stature have been so little exercised by questions of form, method, or theory, or what they might learn from the writings of others. Dreiser is, in other words, a realist, but his comments on the art of the novel rarely rise above the banal, the self-evident, or, indeed, the unhelpful. His realism is largely a matter of instinct, an instinct dominated above all by an acute eye for circumstantial detail and an ability to render with concreteness and vividness every aspect of daily life that impinges on the lives of his characters. Although not an intellectual, Dreiser's understanding of human experience was shaped by intellectual thought and intellectual movements, above all by Darwinian ideas of natural selection and the struggle for existence and their application by the social Darwinists, notably Herbert Spencer, to human society.

It may be hard for the modern reader to understand the reasons for the controversy that surrounded the publication of his first novel, *Sister Carrie*, in 1900. Dreiser's publishers, Doubleday, Page and Company, withheld the novel from publication, fearing that its amoral treatment of Carrie Meeber's story might give offense to a readership unfamiliar with the neutral ethical register of life that had become almost de rigueur in European realist fiction. Dreiser scorned the optimistic realism of Howells and the genteel treatment of small town life in contemporaries such as Booth Tarkington. Carrie's story is one of rags to riches. In many ways it satirizes the classical conventions of this characteristically American myth, for Carrie's good looks and her physical charms, those qualities to which her lovers Charles Drouet and, more centrally, George Hurstwood are attracted, are matters of biological accident; but they, above all, are responsible for her rise from rural poverty to a life of affluence and, finally, stardom in the musical theatre. Like Gustave Flaubert's Emma Bovary, Carrie is an adulteress and, for the time she lives with Hurstwood in New York, a kept woman, but Dreiser attaches no blame to her. Neither does he allow any other character to provide moral commentary on her life or circumstances. Instead the novel dramatizes a conflict between instinct and will, one that has more in common with Lev Tolstoi's treatment of the same in *Anna Karenina* (1875–77) than it does with the crude, mechanical naturalism of Frank Norris in *McTeague* (1899), a novel that saw publication a year before *Sister Carrie*. (It should be noted that Norris, a reader at Doubleday, Page and Company, did much to promote this first novel by his younger contemporary.) Dreiser's own commentary places a good deal of emphasis on what we might now deem pseudo-scientific analysis of human action: Carrie is drawn magnetically to the city; her attraction to clothes and jewelry bespeaks a material compulsion that is not easily checked or resisted by reason or moral judgment; like all humankind, in Dreiser's Darwinian vocabulary, she occupies an intermediate stage of civilization between beast and human, balanced on what Dreiser clumsily calls "the jangle of free will and instinct." In Dreiser's view no blame can attach to the victim of these forces, since action and moral choice are not, finally, matters of exclusively rational consideration. It is one of the ironies of Dreiser's achievement that the reader is moved much more by Hurstwood's decline and death than by the loneliness of his eponymous heroine at the end of the novel.

Dreiser was not to publish a novel again for another 11 years. It was with his next novel, *Jennie Gerhardt* in 1911, that the most active period of his novelistic career began. Between this and the last of his great novels, *An American Tragedy* (1925), he wrote three novels (*The Financier*, 1912; *The Titan*, 1914; and *The "Genius,"* 1915), an autobiography, a volume of short stories, a collection of "portrait sketches," and several "Plays of the Natural and the Supernatural." *Jennie Gerhardt* presents a more sympathetic heroine than does *Sister Carrie*, a woman of almost exaggerated goodness who gives love without its being returned and whose humble origins have ill-prepared her for life's injustices.

The novels written immediately after *Jennie Gerhardt—The Financier* and *The Titan*—form the first two volumes of a projected Trilogy of Desire that was not completed until *The Stoic* (published posthumously in 1947), by which time Dreiser's ability to keep his material in focus, particularly his central character, had waned. Frank Algernon Cowperwood, drawn carefully from Dreiser's study of the railway magnate Charles E. Yerkes, is a successful capitalist and entrepreneur whose life is tainted by bribery, violence, and vulgarity, as well as his remorseless philandering. Consistent with Dreiser's social Darwinism, Cowperwood is an economic predator; the world in which he operates is a jungle of competing forces each bent on survival. But he, too, is a victim (like Hurstwood and Jennie) of the inexorable laws of social and economic organization. *The Financier* and *The Titan* are Dreiser at his most Balzacian, and the novels are best read now as historical fiction. However, they remain the most detailed and knowing account of unregulated capitalism of the United States during the years of its emergence as a great industrial power.

It is on *An American Tragedy* that Dreiser's claim to a preeminent place in the history of American realism must rest. Dreiser was no experimentalist in the novel, and *An American Tragedy*, published in the same year as F. Scott Fitzgerald's *The Great Gatsby*, is a curiously Victorian work, entirely void of any of the narrative strategies one might associate with fictional modernism. The story of Clyde Griffiths, the son of missionary parents whose early life is marked by a dreary itinerary from one midwestern city to another, is presented in massive detail; the detail itself is the very source of both the novel's compelling power and its tragic inevitability. Like so many of Dreiser's characters, Clyde wants a better life than that into which he is born, but he is not blessed with Cowperwood's talents and energies or, indeed, Carrie's instincts for survival. Instead his progress is to be purchased through women, notably Sondra Finchley, the daughter of a prosperous family for whose love he murders Roberta Alden, a farm girl whom he has made pregnant. Clyde is quickly arraigned for Roberta's murder, and much of the last third of the novel is occupied by an intimate account of the workings of the American criminal justice system, a system that finds him guilty and, ultimately, executes him. Dreiser works on an almost Tolstoiesque canvas in *An American Tragedy* and, despite his creator's sense that he is caught in a mechanical trap, Clyde retains our sympathy and understanding, if never soliciting our admiration.

Dreiser's detractors charge him with clumsiness and prolixity, charges against which he is not easily defended. Others, notably Stuart P. Sherman, in an influential essay "The Barbaric Naturalism of Mr. Dreiser," have attacked the very foundations on which his fiction is constructed, dismissing his naturalism as naive, crude, simplistic, and intellectually uninformed. Certainly Dreiser's generalizations about human experience have none of the intelligence of Balzac's. Nor, despite the Tolstoiesque scale on which he frequently works, does he offer anything remotely close to the lucidity and penetration of the great Russian novelist's understanding of character and action. But it is entirely legitimate to talk of Dreiser in their company, for he sought to understand the relationship between the individual and the increasingly complex realities of society in exactly the terms in which they had understood it, and he knew that the novel was the literary medium in which a mature and expansive reflection on this relationship could properly take place.

HENRY CLARIDGE

Biography
Born in Terre Haute, Indiana, 27 August 1871. Attended public schools in Warsaw, Terre Haute, Sullivan, and Evansville, all Indiana; Indiana University, Bloomington, 1889–90. Worked in a restaurant and for a hardware company in Chicago, 1887–89; real estate clerk and collection agent, 1890–92; reporter for the Chicago *Globe,* 1892; dramatic editor for the St. Louis *Globe-Democrat,* 1892–93; reporter for the St. Louis *Republic,* 1893; wrote column for the Pittsburgh *Dispatch,* 1894; moved to New York, 1894; editor of *Ev'ry Month,* New York, 1895–97; freelance magazine writer, 1897–99; no steady employment or home, 1900–03; editor of *Smith's Magazine,* 1905–06, and *Broadway Magazine,* 1906–07, both New York; managing editor of Butterick Publications, New York, and editor of Butterick's *Delineator,* 1907–10; editor of *Bohemian* magazine, 1909–10; began writing full-time in 1911; lived in Los Angeles, 1919–23 and after 1938; coeditor of *American Spectator,* 1932–34; sought membership in the Communist Party, 1945. Chairman of National Committee for the Defense of Political Prisoners, 1931. Died 28 December 1945.

Novels by Dreiser
Sister Carrie, 1900
Jennie Gerhardt, 1911
The Financier, 1912
The Titan, 1914
The "Genius," 1915
An American Tragedy, 1925
The Bulwark, 1946
The Stoic, 1947

Other Writings: essays, letters, short stories, plays, poetry, autobiography.

Further Reading
Bell, Michael Davitt, *The Problem of American Realism: Studies in the Cultural History of a Literary Idea,* Chicago: University of Chicago Press, 1993

Elias, Robert H., *Theodore Dreiser, Apostle of Nature,* New York: Knopf, 1949; revised edition, Ithaca, New York: Cornell University Press, 1970

Frohock, W.M., *Theodore Dreiser,* Minneapolis: University of Minnesota Press, 1972

Kazin, Alfred, and Charles Shapiro, editors, *The Stature of Theodore Dreiser: A Critical Study of the Man and His Works,* Bloomington: Indiana University Press, 1955

Lehan, Richard, *Theodore Dreiser: His World and His Novels,* Carbondale: Southern Illinois University Press, 1969

Matthiessen, F.O., *Theodore Dreiser,* New York: William Sloane, and London: Methuen, 1951

Mencken, H.L., *Theodore Dreiser,* New York: Doubleday, 1943

Moers, Ellen, *Two Dreisers,* New York: Viking Press, 1969; London: Thames and Hudson, 1970

Pizer, Donald, *The Novels of Theodore Dreiser: A Critical Study,* Minneapolis: University of Minnesota Press, 1976

Pizer, Donald, editor, *New Essays on "Sister Carrie,"* Cambridge and New York: Cambridge University Press, 1991

Swanberg, W.A., *Dreiser,* New York: Scribner, 1965

Walcutt, Charles C., *American Literary Naturalism: A Divided Stream,* Minneapolis: University of Minnesota Press, 1956

Warren, Robert Penn, *Homage to Theodore Dreiser,* New York: Random House, 1971

Zanine, Louis J., *Mechanism and Mysticism: The Influence of Science on the Thought and Work of Theodore Dreiser,* Philadelphia: University of Pennsylvania Press, 1993

Alexandre Dumas (père) 1802–70

French

Although his enduring popularity is undeniable, Alexandre Dumas' abilities as a novelist have been disputed from the beginning. He is now credited with revitalizing the historical novel in France and with producing some of the best-known and best-loved examples of the genre. On the whole, critical appreciation of Dumas has increased since his death, yet the lasting appeal of his novels is still explained with reference to both their positive and negative traits. On the one hand, his works are riveting, fast-paced adventure tales that blend history and fiction in a unique manner; on the other, they are too long, melodramatic, and they distort and grossly oversimplify the historical record in the name of diverting the reader.

Dumas' role in the development of the historical novel owes much to an accident of history. The lifting of press censorship in France in the 1830s gave rise to a proliferation of newspapers. In order to increase subscriptions, editors began to solicit serial novels (romans-feuilletons) from well-known writers of the day. At this point, in his late thirties, Dumas had been first and foremost a playwright; his dramatic works include *Henri III et sa cour* (1829), considered the first genuine expression of romantic theatre (one year before Victor Hugo's *Hernani* [1830]). Dumas' great period of novelistic productivity roughly corresponds to the heyday of the serial novel (indeed, he claimed to have created this subgenre; see Bassan, 1993–94). Dumas' first true serial novel was *Le Capitaine Paul* (1838; *Captain Paul*). This work, a quick rewrite of a play, was an instant success. It also earned an impressive sum of money. Dumas had long collaborated on dramatic works and now began to employ a number of assistants as he contracted to produce more novels for various popular newspapers. His favorite collaborator was a scholar and playwright named Auguste Maquet, who proposed subjects and wrote first drafts for some of Dumas' most famous serial novels, including *Les Trois Mousquetaires* (1844; *The Three Musketeers*) and *Le Comte de Monte-Cristo* (1844–45; *The Count of Monte-Cristo*).

The rate at which Dumas produced novels raised considerable suspicion as to the true role of his collaborators. Dumas won a libel suit against one such detractor, Eugène de Mirecourt, following the publication of Mirecourt's "Fabrique de Romans: Maison Alexandre Dumas et Cie" (1845). Charles-Augustin Sainte-Beuve accused Dumas of creating "industrial literature"; Honoré de Balzac considered these accusations harsh, but well founded. Today, Maquet's role is generally downplayed. It is believed that Dumas considerably expanded Maquet's drafts, developing character traits and story lines and composing the all-important chapter endings. These teaser scenes ensured that readers would eagerly await the next installment. Dumas, along with Eugène Sue, was considered a master at creating such suspense. Dumas also was a master dialogist, keeping narrative descriptions at a minimum in his novels. His talent for creating dialogue and keeping the action moving is often linked to his theatrical instincts. It is certainly true that his experience in the theatre was well suited to the unique requirements of the serial novel. In the case of his fast-paced dialogue, it is also to be noted that the serial novelist was paid by the line.

Dumas' greatest innovation as a novelist was his unique use of history. He much admired Sir Walter Scott, his famous predecessor in the genre. Yet, unlike Scott, Dumas used historical events as an integral part of the story line, rather than as a picturesque backdrop. The critic Richard Stowe defends Dumas' factual lapses, noting that the best-known figures and events depicted in the novels conform to historical accounts (see Stowe, 1976). Dumas did change history to allow his main characters different, usually greater, roles than they actually played. These roles correspond to their assigned personalities; each of the musketeers, for example, personifies a different character type. Dumas' true genius lay in characterization; he had little interest in stylistic perfection and rarely revised. It is said that he laughed and cried when writing, in reaction to his own considerable melodramatic

power (*La Tour de Nesle* [1832; *The Tower of Nesle*], perhaps his most famous play, is considered the greatest masterpiece of French melodrama).

Dumas' success as a novelist made him, in Michel Fabre's words, a "cultural beacon" for African Americans before emancipation (see Fabre, 1994). Dumas' paternal grandmother, Marie-Cessette, had been a black slave in the French colony of Santo Domingo (now part of Haiti). Frederick Douglass regretted that Dumas did not generally define himself as a black man, but he greatly admired *The Count of Monte-Cristo*. Fabre conjectures that this work was so popular among 19th-century African Americans because the escape of the falsely imprisoned Edmond Dantès may be read as a parable of emancipation. A shorter work, *Georges* (1843; *George*), published a year before *The Count of Monte-Cristo*, was and remains obscure. However, it is important in this context, as it specifically examines the question of race and colonialism. The main character, a half-French mulatto, leaves Mauritius to be educated in France, then returns to avenge himself for the affronts he had suffered as a boy.

Dumas' novelistic production must be understood as part of a greater artistic enterprise, the aim of which was to bring French history to life for the French people. His serial publications quickly appeared as whole works; these novels were then usually transformed into plays and often staged at the Théâtre Historique, a theatre founded by Dumas specifically for the production of historical plays. Conversely, as with his first serial novel, *Captain Paul*, Dumas often transformed his plays into novel form. Although considered an important playwright in his day, Dumas is now known primarily as a novelist and is judged on that basis. His fame rests on his ability to sweep the reader up into the world of the past—a wholly unrealistic world, perhaps, but one peopled by characters that impress the reader as real individuals, while they simultaneously embody universal types.

MARY MCALPIN

See also Count of Monte-Cristo

Biography
Born in Villers-Cotterêts, France, 24 July 1802. Attended local school. Father of the writer Alexandre Dumas I. Articled at age 14 to a solicitor in Villers-Cotterêts, and one in Crépy, until 1822; worked in the secretariat of the Duc d'Orléans, 1822–29, and joined Charles Nodier's *salon*, the first of the Romantic *cénacles*; librarian at the Palais Royal, 1829; highly successful playwright, then historical novelist (he often revised and refined works first written by others); cofounder, Théâtre Historique, Paris, 1847–50; editor as well as contributor, *La Liberté*, 1848–50; moved to Brussels, 1852, after suffering financial failure; returned to Paris in 1853; founding editor, *Le Mousquetaire*, 1853–57, and the weekly *Le Monte-Cristo*, 1857–60; aided Garibaldi's invasion of Sicily, 1860–61; director of excavations and museums, Naples, 1860–61; editor, *Journal de Jeudi*, 1860, and *L'indipendente*, Naples, 1860–64; returned to France, 1864; revived *Le Mousquetaire*, 1866–67; editor, *Le D'Artagnan*, 1868, and *Théâtre Journal*, 1868–69. Died 5 December 1870.

Principal Novels by Dumas père
Le Capitaine Paul, with Adrien Dauzats, 2 vols., 1838; as *Captain Paul*, translated by Thomas Williams, 1846; as *Paul*

Jones, translated by William Berger, 1839; as *Paul Jones, the Son of the Sea,* translated 1849; as *Paul Jones: A Nautical Romance,* translated by Henry Llewellyn Williams, 1889; as *Paul Jones, the Bold Privateer,* n.d.

Le Chevalier d'Harmental, with Auguste Maquet, 1843; as *The Chevalier d'Harmental,* translated by P.F. Christin and Eugene Lies, 1846; as *The Chateau d'Harmental,* 1856; as *The Orange Plume,* translated by Henry L. Williams, Jr., 1860; as *The Conspirators,* 1910

Georges, 1843; as *George,* translated by G.J. Knox, 1846; also translated by Samuel Spring, 1847; as *Georges,* translated by Alfred Allinson, 1904

Le Comte de Monte-Cristo, with Auguste Maquet, 1844–45; as *The Count of Monte-Cristo,* 1846; also translated by Henry Llewellyn Williams, 1892; William Thiese, 1892; Steven Grant, 1990; as *The Chateau d'If: A Romance,* translated by Emma Hardy, 1846

Les Trois Mousquetaires, with Auguste Maquet, 1844; as *The Three Guardsmen,* translated by Park Benjamin, 1846; as *The Three Musketeers,* translated by William Barrow, 1846; also translated by William Robson, 1860; Henry Llewellyn Williams, 1892; A. Curtis Bond, 1894; Alfred Allinson, 1903; Philip Schuyler Allen, 1923; J. Walker McSpadden, 1926; Jacques Le Clercq, 1950; Isabel Ely Lord, 1952; Lord Sudley, 1952; Marcus Clapham and Clive Reynard, 1992

La Reine Margot, with Auguste Maquet, 1845; as *Margaret de Navarre,* 1845; as *Marguerite de Valois,* 1846; also translated by S. Fowler Wright, 1947; as *Queen Margot,* translated 1885

Vingt ans après, with Auguste Maquet, 1845; as *Cardinal Mazarin; or, Twenty Years After,* n.d.; as *Twenty Years After,* translated by "E.P.," 1846; also translated by William Barrow, 1846; Henry Llewellyn Williams, 1899; Alfred Allinson, 1904; as *Cromwell and Mazarin,* 1847

Le Chevalier de Maison-Rouge, with Auguste Maquet, 1845; translated as *Marie Antoinette,* 1846; as *Genevieve,* translated by Henry William Herbert, 1846; as *Chateau-Rouge,* 1859; as *The Knight of Redcastle,* translated by Henry Llewellyn Williams, 1893; as *The Chevalier de Maison-Rouge,* 1877

La Dame de Monsoreau, with Auguste Maquet, 1846; as *Diana of Meridor,* 1846; as *Chicot the Jester,* 1857; as *La Dame de Monsoreau,* 1889; also translated by J. Walker McSpadden, 1926; as *Diane,* 1901

Mémoires d'un médecin: Joseph Balsamo, with Auguste Maquet, 1846–48; parts translated under the following titles: *Memoirs of a Physician,* 1847; *Andrée de Taverney; or, The Downfall of French Monarchy,* translated by Henry L. Williams, Jr., 2 vols., 1862; *The Chevalier,* 1864; *Balsamo; or, Memoirs of a Physician,* 1878; *Joseph Balsamo,* 1878; *The Mesmerist's Victim,* translated by Henry Llewellyn Williams, 1893

Les Quarante-cinq, with Auguste Maquet, 1848; as *The Forty-Five Guardsmen,* 1847; also translated by J. Walker McSpadden, 1926; as *The Forty-Five,* 1889

Le Vicomte de Bragelonne; ou, Dix ans plus tard, with Auguste Maquet, 1848–50; as *The Vicomte de Bragelonne,* translated by Thomas Williams, 1848, as *Bragelonne, the Son of Athos; or, Ten Years Later,* translated by Williams, 1848, as *The Iron Mask,* 1850; as *Louise La Vallière,* 1851; also translated by Alfred Allinson, 1904; as *The Man in the Iron Mask,* translated by Henry Llewellyn Williams, 1889, this translation also published as *The Vicomte de Bragelonne,* 1892, and *Louise de la Vallière,* 1892; as *Louise de la Vallière,* translated by J. Walker McSpadden, 1901

Le Collier de la Reine, with Auguste Maquet, 1849; as *The Queen's Necklace,* translated by Thomas Williams, 1850; also translated by Henry Llewellyn Williams, 1892

Ange Pitou, with Auguste Maquet, 1849; as *Taking the Bastille,* n.d.; as *Six Years Later,* translated by Thomas Williams, 1851; as *The Royal Life-Guard,* translated by Henry Llewellyn Williams, 1893; as *Ange Pitou,* 1907

La Comtesse de Charny, 1852–55; as *The Countess de Charny,* translated 1853; as *La Comtesse de Charny,* 1890; as *The Countess of Charny,* translated by Henry Llewellyn Williams, 1892

Other Writings: some 40 novels in all, of which many were collaborations, and some of disputed authorship; more than 60 plays, including *Henri III et sa cour* (1829), *Antony* (1831), *La Tour de Nesle* (1832; *The Tower of Nesle*); *Mes Mémoires* (22 vols., 1852–54); journalism; poetry. The complete works of Dumas père runs to 301 volumes.

Further Reading
Bassan, Fernande, "Le Roman-feuilleton et Alexandre Dumas père (1802–1870)," *Nineteenth-Century French Studies* 22:1–2 (Fall–Winter 1993–94)

Fabre, Michel, "International Beacons of African-American Memory: Alexandre Dumas père, Henry O. Tanner, and Josephine Baker as Examples of Recognition," in *History and Memory in African-American Culture,* edited by Geneviève Fabre and Robert O'Meally, New York: Oxford University Press, 1994

Hemmings, F.W.J., *Alexandre Dumas: The King of Romance,* New York: Scribner, 1979

Maurois, André, *Les Trois Dumas,* Paris: Hachette, 1957; as *The Titans: A Three-Generation Biography of the Dumas,* New York: Harper, 1957

Parigot, Hippolyte, *Alexandre Dumas père,* Paris: Hachette, 1902

Stowe, Richard S., *Alexandre Dumas (père),* Boston: Twayne, 1976

Marguerite Duras 1914–96

French

Marguerite Duras was undoubtedly one of the most influential, diverse, productive, and recognizable French novelists of the 20th century. She was born Marguerite Donnadieu in colonial French Indochina to parents who were employed as teachers by the government. Even after immigrating to France in her late teens, Duras repeatedly claimed that specific experiences and encounters arising from the colonial context framing her youth contributed to her desire to write.

The extensive collection of works by Duras spans several genres including novels, cinema (film scripts, production, and direction), novellas, theatre, essays, and journalism. Based on her exploration and experimentation with regard to the form and structure of the novel (at the levels of character, plot, and chronology), critics often place Duras among the writers associated with the *nouveau roman* (new novel), generally defined by the works of Alain Robbe-Grillet, Michel Butor, Claude Simon, and Nathalie Sarraute. However, if Duras shares in the creative practices of some of these writers, it is perhaps most strongly evident in her folding of autobiographical elements into the act of writing narrative fiction, a strategy that acknowledges the close links between life and writing.

In a broad sense, the major developments within Duras' novelistic production may be grouped chronologically. She drew largely from her own crossings of geographic, class, and cultural lines by addressing matters of alienation, desire, passion, death, love, inexpressible emotions, time and duration, absence, sexuality, and gender. Many of these themes remain permanent throughout Duras' literary career, but they modulate from one novel to the next. Indeed, in one of her last essays, *Écrire* (1993; *Writing*), Duras noted that the act of writing is akin to inhabiting a house in which a solitary individual may wander from room to room, rearranging personal objects and pieces of furniture in order to better contemplate one's relationships through space and time. For Duras, writing is born of numerous, fluid forms of the self that change with physical and mental displacement, imagination, and remembering.

The period ranging from approximately 1943 to 1962 encompasses Duras' more conventional, realist works. The important novels from this period include *Un Barrage contre le Pacifique* (1950; *The Sea Wall*) and *Moderato cantabile* (1958; *Moderato Cantabile*), both of which were adapted to film. Even as these novels displayed an easily identifiable plot and lyrical description, others from this same period, such as *Le Marin de Gibraltar* (1952; *The Sailor from Gibraltar*) and *Dix heures et demi du soir en été* (1960; *Ten-Thirty on a Summer Night*), tended increasingly toward dialogue, character and story fragmentation, and complex narrative techniques.

During the 1960s and 1970s, Duras experimented more fully with narrative structure. Her writing displayed a heightened sensitivity to temporality, rhythm, and narrative perspective. With the appearance of *Le Ravissement de Lol V. Stein* (1964: *The Ravishing of Lol V. Stein*), she ventured into the realms of the feminine psyche in her intricate staging of madness, loss, alienation, desire, and repression. From 1964 to 1979 Duras actively participated in writing, producing, and directing works in theatre and especially cinema. She crafted a unique writing style by blending together sparse dialogue with weighted silence, vibrant imagery, and varying perspectives (focalization, point of view), all direct influences of her work in other media and her interrogation of meaning as communicated through images and language. Moreover, her writing took on slow, repetitive, sometimes incantatory and breathless qualities that later evolved into distinctively Durassian traits.

Duras skillfully adopted a strategy of staging and restaging narrative sequences that resulted in the reappearance of numerous characters and plots. This endeavor—namely, stretching the prevailing limits of different genres to chart, in Duras' words, "new narrative regions"—led one critic to describe such techniques and forms as "hybrids," referring, for example, to the triple entity *India Song* (1973), identified by Duras at once as "text theatre film." Similarly, many of these recombined, multiple narratives are described as belonging to Durassian "cycles," since they may be united thematically and structurally, such as the "Lol V. Stein cycle," which groups *The Ravishing of Lol V. Stein, Le Vice-consul* (1966; *The Vice-Consul*), and *L'Amour* (1971; *Love*).

Although Duras earned critical acclaim early in her literary career, she gained world renown when France's top literary prize, the Prix Goncourt, was awarded to *L'Amant* (1984; *The Lover*). For critics and general reading public alike, the novel's appeal was enhanced by the author's disclosure that the story was based on events from her own life. As it turned out, many of the autobiographical elements contained in *The Lover* had surfaced previously in Duras' earlier works—most notably *The Sea Wall*—only to be taken up once again in her final reworking of the story as seen in *L'Amant de la Chine du Nord* (1991; *The North China Lover*). The recurrence of the same material uncovered a need by Duras to revisit in order to better formulate, amplify, and document the metamorphosis of memories and emotions over time, resulting in a formula whereby the act of writing is a means of reading and rereading oneself.

Her writing turned increasingly minimalist in style, to the point where characters make an appearance simply to utter a few words, to observe and be observed, and often to give way to silences and gaps in the narration, such as in *Emily L.* (1987; *Emily L.*). Similarly, Duras refined the technique of repetition in order to convey continuity, trance-inspired monotony, and the banality of daily experiences. At the same time, she devoted growing attention to the rhythmic qualities of phrases and the sounds of language, employing alliteration to enhance the musical, sonorous qualities of dialogue. Other procedures included an absence of novelistic controls traditionally provided by narrators and the proliferation of pronominal ambiguities. More precisely, Duras lamented the lack of "space" allowed readers, hence her conscious interpolation of readers by calling upon their capacity for imagination in order to create meaning and coherence from encounters with texts. Finally, by returning to events from both the past and the present, she set about "translating" her own life, inexhaustibly seeking out "the unknown inside of oneself, in one's head, one's body" (see Vircondelet, 1991).

CHRISTINE GASPAR

Biography

Born Marguerite Donnadieu in Gia Dinh, near Saigon, Indo-China (now Vietnam), 4 April 1914. Attended Lycée de Saigon, baccalaureate 1931; the Sorbonne, Paris, 1933–34, degree in law and political science 1935. Moved to France, 1932. Secretary, Ministry of Colonies, Paris, 1935–41; then freelance writer; journalist for *Observateur*; also worked as script writer and film director. Member of the French Communist Party (expelled 1950). Died 3 March 1996.

Novels by Duras

Les Impudents, 1943
La Vie tranquille, 1944
Un Barrage contre le Pacifique, 1950; as *The Sea Wall*, translated by Herma Briffault, 1952; as *A Sea of Troubles*, translated by Antonia White, 1953; as *A Dam Against an Ocean*, translated by Sofka Skipworth, 1966
Le Marin de Gibraltar, 1952; as *The Sailor from Gibraltar*, translated by Barbara Bray, 1966
Les Petits chevaux de Tarquinia, 1953; as *The Little Horses of Tarquinia*, translated by Peter DuBerg, 1960
Le Square, 1955; as *The Square*, translated by Sonia Pitt-Rivers and Irina Morduch, also in *Four Novels*, 1965, and in *Three Novels*, 1977
Moderato cantabile, 1958; as *Moderato Cantabile*, translated by Richard Seaver, 1960; also in *Four Novels*, 1965
Dix heures et demi du soir en été, 1960; as *Ten-Thirty on a Summer Night*, translated by Anne Borchardt, also in *Four Novels*, 1965, and in *Three Novels*, 1977
L'Après-midi de Monsieur Andesmas, 1962; as *The Afternoon of Monsieur Andesmas*, translated by Anne Borchardt, with *The Rivers and Forests*, 1964, also in *Four Novels*, 1965; published separately, 1968
Le Ravissement de Lol V. Stein, 1964; as *The Ravishing of Lol V. Stein*, translated by Richard Seaver, 1966; as *The Rapture of Lol V. Stein*, translated by Eileen Ellenbogen, 1967
Le Vice-consul, 1966; as *The Vice-Consul*, translated by Eileen Ellenbogen, 1968
L'Amante anglaise, 1967; as *L'Amante Anglaise*, translated by Barbara Bray, 1968

Détruire, dit-elle, 1969; as *Destroy, She Said*, translated by Barbara Bray, 1970; as *Destroy . . .*, translated by Bray, 1970
Abahn Sabana David, 1970
L'Amour, 1971
La Maladie de la mort, 1983; as *The Malady of Death*, translated by Barbara Bray, 1986
L'Amant, 1984; as *The Lover*, translated by Barbara Bray, 1985
Les Yeux bleus cheveux noirs, 1986; as *Blue Eyes, Black Hair*, translated by Barbara Bray, 1989
Emily L., 1987; as *Emily L.*, translated by Barbara Bray, 1989
La Pluie d'été, 1990; as *Summer Rain*, translated by Barbara Bray, 1992
L'Amant de la Chine du Nord, 1991; as *The North China Lover*, translated by Leigh Hafrey, 1992

Other Writings: plays, screenplays, essays, autobiography (*Écrire* [1993; Writing]).

Further Reading

Bajomée, Danielle, and Ralph Heyndels, editors, *Écrire, dit-elle: Imaginaires de Marguerite Duras*, Brussels: Éditions de l'Université de Bruxelles, 1985
Duras, Marguerite, with Xavière Gauthier, *Les Parleuses*, Paris: Éditions de Minuit, 1974; as *Woman to Woman*, Lincoln: University of Nebraska Press, 1987
Marini, Marcelle, *Territoires du féminin avec Marguerite Duras*, Paris: Éditions de Minuit, 1977
Murphy, Carol, *Alienation and Absence in the Novels of Marguerite Duras*, Lexington, Kentucky: French Forum, 1982
Pierrot, Jean, *Marguerite Duras*, Paris: Corti, 1986
Ramsay, Raylene, *The French New Autobiographies: Sarraute, Duras, and Robbe-Grillet*, Gainesville: University Press of Florida, 1996
Schuster, Marilyn, *Marguerite Duras Revisited*, New York: Twayne, 1993
Tison-Braun, Micheline, *Marguerite Duras*, Amsterdam: Rodopi, and Atlantic Highlands, New Jersey: Humanities Press (distributor), 1984
Vircondelet, Alain, *Duras: Biographie*, Paris: Bourin, 1991; as *Duras: A Biography*, Normal, Illinois: Dalkey Archive Press, 1994
Willis, Sharon, *Marguerite Duras: Writing on the Body*, Urbana: University of Illinois Press, 1987

Dystopian Novel. *See* Utopian and Dystopian Novel; Science Fiction Novel

---

E

Maria Edgeworth 1768–1849

Irish/English

Maria Edgeworth has a significant place in the history of the novel for two reasons. The first is that she gave a decisive impetus to the development of regional fiction. The second is her membership in the so-called "silver fork" school of novelists, whose work depicted the manners and morals of Regency England.

Both these dimensions of her fiction developed during a complex transitional period in English society and Irish history. Edgeworth's fiction ambitiously formulates two distinct perspectives of two different countries. Through her awareness of the shared need for principled action, Edgeworth also suggests interconnections between the metropolitan world of fashion and life on the land, between center and periphery, and between leaders and led. This awareness emerges most directly in her two series of *Tales of Fashionable Life,* both of which include important works about Ireland—*Ennui* (1809) and *The Absentee* (1812)—placed alongside depictions of London society.

Edgeworth is best known as a writer on Irish themes. It might even be argued that in her first novel, *Castle Rackrent* (1800), Edgeworth invented Irish society as a fictional subject. She accomplished this by concentrating on the history of her class in its Irish context, by using her innovative voice, tone, and vocabulary, and by presenting the work "as a specimen of manners and characters, which are, perhaps, unknown in England." Indeed, the motif of discovering the Irish social world is the narrative pretext of both *Ennui* and *The Absentee*. In each of these novels, young noblemen, tiring of the oppressive exhibitionism of metropolitan life, retire to Ireland, where they have property. Their travels through the country restore in them a sense of duty and purpose that culminates in their acknowledging that they have now found a place in the world for themselves. They accept their responsibilities, marry locally, and live seriously ever after. The triviality and vexatiousness of salon existence is a necessary pretext for the role of improving landlord, while that role is in effect a critique of the way of life that predated it.

In all three works there is a strong documentary component—the subtitle of *Castle Rackrent* says the novel is "taken from facts"—an aspect of Edgeworth's approach that indicates her commitment to the novel as a form of social discourse and ostensibly empirical representation. That the protagonists of both *Ennui* and *The Absentee* see the light of duty only after they have been exposed to conditions on their Irish property is a further expression of this commitment. So seriously did Edgeworth take the novel form that she wished her works of fiction to be understood as something more than novels in the usual sense. In the advertisement for *Belinda* (1801; revised edition, 1810), she states: "The following work is offered to the public as a Moral Tale—the author not wishing to acknowledge a Novel. . . . So much folly, error and vice are disseminated in books classed under this denomination, that it is hoped the wish to assume another title will be attributed to feelings that are laudable. . . ."

Belinda is the first of Edgeworth's works in the silver fork genre. More didactic and schematic than her Irish works, it nevertheless revisits their treatment of social ills. Its sense of the theatricality of fashionable life looks forward to the more cogent treatment of the same idea in *The Absentee*. And, as in the Irish novels, the protagonist makes her way through unfamiliar terrain with a mentor and guide. This figure in *Belinda* is Lady Delacour, an impressive portrait of resilience and independence, although her belief that she is suffering from breast cancer as a symbol of society's corruption is unnecessary and uncharacteristically explicit.

Although more loosely structured, *Patronage* (1814; revised edition, 1825) maintains the same focus on the inevitable duplicities and intense interpersonal politics of the drawing room. However, this elaborate novel makes clear that, brilliant as Edgeworth's witty touch could be when she drew on her experience of town life, she felt more comfortable delineating life closer to home. In addition, the follies of the town persisted, and the sense of responsibility she urged was as far from widespread realization as ever. The two novels that effectively bring her fictional output to a close, *Harrington* and *Ormond* (both 1817), represent something of a departure. (The society novel, *Helen* [1834], although a good example of its kind, has the status of an afterthought.) Both are significant works. *Harrington* takes a more direct look at issues of identity politics latent in earlier works. Of particular note is the treatment of Jewishness, a subject of thematic and ideological relevance in *The Absentee*.

Ormond is Edgeworth's last Irish novel. Here the protagonist arrives at a realization of his obligations within a spectrum of Irish contexts. The differentiation between these contexts—

landed, native, and emigré—is one of the novel's most instructive insights. Harry Ormond, the protagonist, is modeled on Henry Fielding's Tom Jones. As a result, he is a more spirited, less stagey, and less socialized protagonist than many of Edgeworth's other protagonists. On the other hand, Harry's literary origins suggest an author who is looking to the distant past for a medium in which to represent the present. After *Ormond*, Edgeworth fell into a silence typified by her 1834 comment: "It is impossible to draw Ireland as she now is in a book of fiction—realities are too strong, party passions too violent to bear to see, or care to look at their faces in the looking-glass."

By 1834 Edgeworth's work as a novelist was done. The guidance of her father, Richard Lovell Edgeworth, and his Enlightenment outlook, and her own work as an educational theorist, had served their purpose. It may be tempting to think of that purpose as excessively utilitarian. Yet, as modern scholarship has shown, her debt to French authors of her day, notably Marmontel, conveys her awareness that "moral" does not necessarily mean "moralistic." In addition, her conception of the novel as a significant cultural agent, her gifts of satire and comedy, and her sympathetic representation of Irish conditions assure her of a unique place in the development of fiction written in English.

GEORGE O'BRIEN

See also Castle Rackrent

Biography

Born in Black Bourton, Oxfordshire, 1 January 1768; daughter of the educationist Richard Lovell Edgeworth. Attended Mrs. Lattuffiere's school, Derby, 1775–80, and Mrs. Devis' school, London, 1781–82. Lived with her family in Edgeworthstown, Longford, from 1782, and assisted her father, and later her brother, in managing the family estates; resided in England, 1791–93; collaborated with her father on educational works, 1798–1802; traveled in England, France, and Scotland, 1802–03, and in France and Switzerland, 1820–21; frequently traveled to London and occasionally toured Britain. Died 22 May 1849.

Novels by Edgeworth

Castle Rackrent, 1800
Belinda, 1801; revised edition, 1810
The Modern Griselda, 1805
Leonora, 1806
Ennui (in *Tales of Fashionable Life*, first series), 1809
The Absentee (in *Tales of Fashionable Life*, second series), 1812

Patronage, 1814; revised edition, in *Tales and Miscellaneous Pieces*, 1825
Harrington, 1817
Ormond, 1817
Helen, 1834

Other Writings: children's fiction, works on education, and a study of language, *Essay on Irish Bulls* (1802)—all of these written in collaboration with her father, Richard Lovell Edgeworth; a prolific and inimitable correspondent, her letters are partially collected in *Maria Edgeworth: Letters from England 1813–1814* (1971), *Maria Edgeworth in France and Switzerland: Selections from the Edgeworth Family Letters* (1979), and *The Education of the Heart: The Correspondence of Rachel Mordecai Lazarus and Maria Edgeworth* (1977).

Further Reading

Butler, Marilyn, *Maria Edgeworth: A Literary Biography*, Oxford: Clarendon Press, 1972

Butler, Marilyn, *Jane Austen and the War of Ideas*, Oxford: Clarendon Press, 1975

Flanagan, Thomas, *The Irish Novelists 1800–1850*, New York: Columbia University Press, 1959

Gallagher, Catherine, *Nobody's Story: The Vanishing Acts of Women Writers in the Marketplace, 1670–1820*, Berkeley: University of California Press, and Oxford: Clarendon Press, 1994

Harden, O. Elizabeth McWhorter, *Maria Edgeworth*, Boston: Twayne, 1984

Hurst, Michael, *Maria Edgeworth and the Public Scene: Intellect, Fine Feeling and Landlordism in the Age of Reform*, London: Macmillan, and Coral Gables, Florida: University of Miami Press, 1969

Kowaleski-Wallace, Elizabeth, *Their Fathers' Daughters: Hannah More, Maria Edgeworth, and Patriarchal Complicity*, New York: Oxford University Press, 1991

McCormack, W.J., *Ascendancy and Tradition in Anglo-Irish Literary History from 1789 to 1939*, Oxford: Clarendon Press, and New York: Oxford University Press, 1985; revised edition, as *From Burke to Beckett: Ascendancy, Tradition, and Betrayal in Literary History*, Cork: Cork University Press, 1994

Newcomer, James, *Maria Edgeworth the Novelist, 1767–1849: A Bicentennial Study*, Fort Worth: Texas Christian University Press, 1967

Slade, Bertha Coolidge, *Maria Edgeworth 1767–1849: A Bibliographical Tribute*, London: Constable, 1937

Éducation sentimentale. *See* Sentimental Education

Effi Briest by Theodor Fontane

1895

Fontane's international reputation rests on the novel *Effi Briest,* with which the German novel of the 19th century for the first time equaled the great European novels of the age. Fontane was almost 75 years old, an experienced novelist, looking back on many years as a travel writer, journalist, war correspondent, and theatre critic, when *Effi Briest* was first serialized in the *Deutsche Rundschau* between October 1894 and March 1895 and then published as a book in October 1895. Although the novel was widely acclaimed at the time, another 70 years were to pass before Fontane's stature became widely acknowledged. The slight plot of the novel draws on a well-publicized society scandal. Fontane, known for his skill in using the conversational mode of the social novel, in *Effi Briest* portrays the changing society of the Prussian Empire in the age of Bismarck, who is continually present in the background.

The loveless marriage of Effi Briest, a young girl of 18, to Baron von Instetten, who had once courted her mother, provides the story line. The location is the Prussian northeastern part of Germany, with Berlin at its social center. The time is recognizably that of the last two decades of the 19th century. Using the literary and narrative conventions of the social novel, Fontane substantially widened the significance of the story beyond that of a young society woman who naively accepted the wrong suitor and later had to pay the unreasonable price society demanded for a temporary indiscretion. He presents the social and moral standards and conventions of his time, the conflict between human need and the requirements of social acceptability, by reflecting them humorously in the polite conversations of well-mannered characters of German aristocratic society and individuals from other social groups they interact with. In this way the story of love and marriage, passion, jealousy, punishment, and death loses much of its directly emotional nature. What dominates Fontane's fiction is not passion but concern for respectability and social standing and the price paid for them. The narrative foregrounds the entertaining facade of polite behavior, exquisite etiquette, and good taste while playing on the wider social issue of personal moral integrity in times of change.

As a social novel, however, *Effi Briest* portrays the sociable occasions of family life and the social "season," with its games, parties, theatrical performances, concerts, fashionable outings, visits to spas, shopping expeditions, celebrations, and weddings. Yet such events are rarely presented as scenes. They provide the topics for the entertaining conversation of articulate speakers who eagerly discuss the preparation of these events and keenly reflect on them afterward in small groups of intimate friends enjoying and fearing the tranquillity of ordinary life. Fontane controls these conversational exchanges with consummate skill.

The events themselves may disappear behind the conversations about them, as the wedding of Effi Briest itself does. Details of the affair between Effi and Crampas are almost completely excluded from the narrative. Rather, the social controls and the demands of good taste ensure that key events are refracted in conversations that would be merely gossip were it not for the amusing tension between the topic and the delicately controlled mode of presenting it. Only a reader fully alert to the tone and allusive code of the speakers will grasp the complexity of Fontane's multifaceted text, which invites conclusions but does not offer them. The light touch, the humorous formulation, the fitting quotation, the entertaining riposte, the evasive generalization, the elegant use of unusual words—these are some of the delightful conversational devices with which Fontane's characters handle their situations. Their understated elegance and respect for the privacy of personal concerns are characteristic of Fontane's style of narration, which prefers subtle hint to direct statement.

With *Effi Briest* Fontane has given the German novel rather late a superb example of modern fiction of truly European standing. The inward-looking tendencies of the German tradition with its emphasis on the development of one main character have given way here to a novel in which the tension between society and individual choice is projected across a wide range of characters. Fontane's brilliant mastery of the subtle shades of socially controlled conversation, and of the humor and irony conveyed by them, enable him to turn even the apparent trivia of dialogue, typical of the social novel, into a powerful instrument of light-hearted but searching characterization. Although with the wisdom of sceptical modesty the author carefully avoids any direct intrusion into the narrative, the reader, invited to respond to the great variety of character and tone, cannot miss the wider human implications of historic social change, reflected both in the implied criticism, and the uneasy insistence on the charm, of an aristocratic world losing its social dominance.

HINRICH SIEFKEN

See also Theodor Fontane

Further Reading

Bance, Alan, *Theodor Fontane: The Major Novels,* Cambridge and New York: Cambridge University Press, 1982

Brinkmann, Richard, *Theodor Fontane: Über die Verbindlichkeit des Unverbindlichen,* Munich: Piper, 1967

Chambers, Helen, *The Changing Image of Theodor Fontane,* Columbia, South Carolina: Camden House, 1997

Demetz, Peter, *Formen des Realismus: Theodor Fontane; Kritische Untersuchungen,* Munich: Carl Hanser, 1964; 2nd edition, 1966

Müller-Seidel, Walter, *Theodor Fontane: Soziale Romankunst in Deutschland,* Stuttgart: Metzler, 1975; 3rd edition, 1994

Rowley, Brian A., "Theodor Fontane: A German Novelist in the European Tradition?" *German Life and Letters* 15 (1961–62)

Schafarschik, Walter, editor, *Theodor Fontane, "Effi Briest,"* Stuttgart: Reclam, 1972

Stern, J.P., *Re-interpretations: Seven Studies in Nineteenth-Century German Literature,* London: Thames and Hudson, and New York: Basic Books, 1964

Egyptian Novel

As a part of the Arabic-speaking world, Egypt fell under the general stagnation of Arab culture in the Levant following the 13th century. Poetry and prose lost most of their luster and gradually became instruments for linguistic clownery and rhetorical and conventional self-indulgence. Learning, education, and literacy among the upper classes reached a nadir, and literary activities virtually disappeared from courts and palaces and were restricted to the few religious schools that taught Arabic language and literature in a very rudimentary form.

Within high culture, traditional prose forms like the *maqāmah,* the *risālah,* and the *ikhwāniyāt* survived but turned into calcified and rigid literary forms characterized by verbosity, stock images, and an emphasis on showing mastery of the rhetorical devices, especially *saj^c* (rhymed prose). There was a lively narrative tradition in low culture and literature that flourished during this period, but it was never capable of exercising much influence on high literature and culture as it lacked the social and institutional bearers who could perform this function.

The short-lived Napoleonic occupation of Egypt (1798–1801) brought with it a shock as Egyptians realized that, contrary to their received beliefs as belonging to the greatest state in the world (the Ottoman Empire) and being a part of the land of Islam, they were inferior to the West. This was quickly acknowledged in fields like science, technology, economy, and the military, but it was not acknowledged in such areas as religion and literature. The tumultuous period extending from the beginning of the 19th century until World War II witnessed the continuation of this confrontation of the Egyptians with European modernity—a confrontation that took many forms. There was the economic and cultural penetration of Egypt by the European economic powers facilitated by the policies of many Egyptian rulers who became virtually independent from the Ottoman State. The integration of Egypt within the world capitalist economy was further strengthened by the opening of the Suez Canal (1869), which became one of the vital lines of trade in the world. There was also the direct contact with the West of increasing numbers of Egyptians who were sent to Europe to study. But there was also the British occupation of Egypt in 1882, which brought a more confrontational relationship with the West and provided an ideological weapon for all opponents of modernization in Egypt.

It should not then be a surprise that Rifāʿah al-Ṭahṭāwī, who spent a few years in Paris as the accompanying sheikh of the first group of students sent there by the then ruler of Egypt, Muḥammad ʿAlī, wrote a description of France emphasizing those aspects in French life that he thought useful to Egyptians. He also translated Fénélon's *Télémaque* and supervised a school for translation. Although he was mainly a traditionalist in matters of language and style, his work shows that he gave priority to the referential aspects of language over traditional conventions of prose. Whenever necessary, he avoided rhyming prose when it made the subject matter less communicable.

Following the many troubles in Greater Syria (which was a part of the Ottoman Empire) around the middle of the 19th century, many "Syrians," especially Christians, fled to Egypt. As it were, quite a few of these were educated, entrepreneurial, and knew one or more of the European languages (especially French and English). These "Syrians" played an important role in the cultural life of Egypt from the latter decades of the 19th century as they became central in the writing, translation, and publication of fictional and nonfictional works and in the press. Although many of these translations of Western works of fiction were not faithful to the original (and many were not intended to be so but were directed toward a growing market and an increasing demand for stories), their impact on the language of culture was soon noticeable. These translations avoided the old, strange, and arcane words that characterized traditional modes of Egyptian writing. Traditionalists described these translations as being linguistically and, above all, morally inferior. Yet the increasing demand for these stories could not be neglected, and soon many "serious" writers began writing narratives.

Around the turn of the 20th century, many periodicals began publishing short fiction regularly while others serialized longer narratives. More than 30 such periodicals emerged in the period 1884–1914; of these, 10 specialized in publishing fiction. Farāḥ Antūn, Zaynab Fawwāz, and Labībah Hāshim wrote novels. Yaʿqūb Ṣarrūf, the editor of *al-Muqtaṭaf* who earlier had attacked novels and novel writing and refused to publish them in his magazine, had a change of heart and not only published but also wrote novels.

By the beginning of the 20th century, three basic trends in narrative writing began to emerge. The most successful novels during these decades were the popular novels of the rising urban middle class, produced in large quantities during the last third of the 19th century and written mostly by Westernized Syrian Christian immigrants. These writers were the first intellectuals in Egypt to turn to the novel form as the genre through which the ideals of individualism and subjectivity could be expressed in a manner reminiscent of the European novel. But the novels they produced were imitations or translations of Western works, the structures of which were changed to become essentially those of the folk tale. This is why they appealed to the new middle class, still anchored to its traditional roots but living under the new conditions of pseudo-modernization. Such a genre could not become a part of the high literature still dominated by poetry.

The second trend comprised writers who utilized traditional narrative forms like the *maqāmah* to write stories. The most prominent and successful example is Muḥammad al-Muwayliḥī, whose *Ḥadīth ʿIsā ibn Hishām* (1903; The Discourse of ʿIsa ibn Hishām) initially was written according to the *maqāmah* form but gradually assumed the structure of a serialized novel. Although its language remained eloquent, it acquired a simpler syntax, a greater fluidity, and a more common diction.

The third trend is associated with writers (mostly "Syrians") who wrote novels that sought to combine fine style and language with an attractive plot. The most successful of these attempts was that of the Lebanese immigrant to Egypt and founder of *al-Hilāl* Jurjī Zaydān, who wrote narratives that were considered respectable and achieved great success with readers. Between 1891 and 1914 Zaydān wrote 21 historical novels, all of which were serialized in *al-Hilāl* before being published in book form. These novels—which remain among the most popular in the Arab world—generally combine a fictional love story with events taken from the history of Islam (thus the name given to his historical novels is *Riwāyat tārīkh al-Islām,* or novels of the history of Islam), subordinating the narrative to the historical structure. In other words, the basic theme in Zaydān's novels—lovers separated and then reunited—is manipulated so as to fit into his understanding of the historical process. Zaydān's understanding of history was based on two governing principles: chronology (temporality) and causality. In the process of subordinating the narrative to this historical structure, the results vary, but generally the structures of history crack the closedness of the narrative, giving us a narrative that is sometimes structured along the lines of what the Russian formalists called a *fabula,* or the bare chronological sequence of events in the story, while in others it is nearer to a *syuzhet,* or the plotting of the story within a narrative framework. In Zaydān, therefore, we get the first step toward the shift from story to plot, from mere chronology to causal structuration.

The tradition of the historical novel was taken up by other writers after Zaydān, the most prominent of whom were ʿAlī al-Jārim, Muhammad Farīd Abū Ḥadīd, ʿAlī Aḥmad Bākathīr, ʿAbd al-Ḥamīd Jūdah al-Saḥḥār, and the early Nagīb Maḥfūẓ. Although the first two writers paid more attention to plot structuring, their historical novels were limited by their teleological understanding of the historical development in their novels. This closed structure, together with their emphasis on a rhetorical style, inhibited the narrative from developing its own dynamics, so that the story became subordinated to the ideas of the author. Abū Ḥadīd, who was the better novelist, tried to utilize the older Arabic story traditions and to rehabilitate some popular ones, but his success was rather limited from the technical literary standpoint. The historical novel provided a continuous tradition of novel writing and, by linking fiction with history, an important transitional step toward the development of formal realism, as seen in the cases of Maḥfūẓ and al-Saḥḥār.

During this period there also developed among Egyptian writers a better understanding of the novel as a genre in Western literatures, as a result of their reading novels and novel criticism. A good example is the introduction that Muḥammad Lutfī Jumʿah wrote to his novel *Fī Wādī al-Humūm* (1905; In the Valley of Sorrows), an interesting realist manifesto. However, the novel that followed fell short of the critical and theoretical pronouncements stated in its introduction.

It was against this backdrop that the more interesting prose fiction works such as Maḥmūd Ṭāhir Ḥaqqī's *ʿAdhrāʾ Dinshway* (1906; The Virgin of Dinshway), Aḥmad Fatḥī's *Jināyat Urūbā ʿalā Nafsihā wa-al-ʿĀlam* (1906; Europe's Crime against Itself and the World), and Muhammad Ḥusayn Haykal's *Zaynab* (1912; *Zaynab*) were written. The first was generally forgotten by critics until many years later, while the last was quickly hailed as an important work and for many years was called the first Arabic novel. *Zaynab* is generally derivative (the influence of French literature, especially Pierre Loti, is clear), the language inferior, and the theme and plot well known. New in this work is the construction of characters as individuals rather than types and the emphasis on psychology, especially in the case of the narrator/character.

During the interwar years the novel became more respectable as a literary genre. Outstanding examples from the period include Ṭāhā Ḥusayn's *al-Ayyām* (1929; *The Days*), *Duʿāʾ al-Karawān* (1934; *The Call of the Curlew*), and *Adīb* (1935; A Literati); Tawfīq al-Ḥakīm's *ʿAwdat al-Rūḥ* (1933; *Return of the*

Spirit), *Yawmiyāt Nāʾib fī al-Aryāf* (1937; *Maze of Justice*), and *ʿUsfūr min al-Sharq* (1938; *Bird from the East*); Ibrāhīm al-Māzinī's *Ibrāhīm al-Kātib* (1931; *Ibrahim the Writer*); Maḥmūd Ṭāhir Lāshīn's *Ḥawwāʾ bilā Ādam* (1934; Eve without Adam); Maḥmūd Taymūr's *al-Aṭlāl* (1934), *Nidāʾ al-Majhūl* (1939; The Call of the Unknown), and his many short stories; al-ʿAqqād's *Sārah* (1938; Sara); and Yaḥyā Ḥaqqī's *Qindīl Umm Hāshim* (1939; *The Saint's Lamp*). The adoption of a novelistic model that was Western oriented and not a direct development from indigenous writing was the result of such extraliterary factors as journalism, the literary market, the rise of the educated and semi-educated urban strata as the largest section of the reading public, and the shifts in literary and cultural language that was the concentrated expression of these and other socio-economic and cultural phenomena. Attempts to develop a narrative form derived from or congruent with the rich Arabic narrative traditions did not materialize into a novelistic tradition until much later. It was the trend that adopted the models of the Western novel with its concepts of the individual, the social, and the ideological that laid the foundation for the further development and popularity of the novel in Egypt. The explanation for this may be sought outside the literary system, wherein extraliterary moments shaped the ways in which literary forms and genres are selected and become dominant.

The first and most important issue relating to the development of the novel among these different trends was the state of language. Literary language was modeled according to that of classical texts. Despite the presence of a livelier language much nearer to that spoken by people and exemplified by the late historical texts, this model was not adopted. The issue of language was framed in the following manner: those who insisted on preserving the classical literary language were generally opposed to the kind of language that was used to translate European novels. This language used in translation was that of the educated, rising middle class who had little knowledge of the literature in the language but wanted to read stories. Market mechanisms determined the results. Popular novels sold well and became within three or four decades the educational material for the urban literate and semiliterate. But the struggle for readership was not a matter to be determined on the narrative front as much as in journalism. Newspapers and weekly and monthly cultural periodicals struggled not only for sales but also for the political attitudes of the urban middle class and "intellectuals" who became a force to reckon with in political life. The development of feuilleton language, which was soon adopted as the universal mode of expression in journalism (although there remained some differences), quickly transformed the language of the literary essay.

The literary essay was an important genre in Arabic literature. Its language and some aspects of its form changed during the period under discussion, and the impact of the language of the essay on the development of literature in general, and the novel in particular, cannot be exaggerated. The essay constituted not only the bulk of the literary production of most novelists of the period (Zaydān and al-Muwayliḥī from the older generation, and Haykal, Maḥmūd Taymūr, Ṭāhā Ḥusayn, al-ʿAqqād, al-Māzinī, al-Ḥakīm, and Yaḥyā Ḥaqqī from the younger generation), but it soon became the medium of liberal and secular education of the public in general and of intellectuals in particular. Monthly journals that were both political and cultural/literary surpassed the book as educational materials, and fame was achieved through writing essays. Many important books by some of the intellectuals mentioned above and others, such as Aḥmad Luṭfī al-Sayyid and Salāmah Mūsā, for example, were collections of previously published essays.

The most important characteristics of this new literary language were not only its liveliness and its closeness to colloquial speech but also the inclusion of those tacit assumptions upon which the understanding of language is based. Arabic was always associated with both a religious text and an idealized literary (mostly poetic) tradition. It was thought that the Arabic tongue possessed a special genius that surpasses not only other languages but also human reality. In other words, Arabic was conceived of as a means for representing, not so much the world of ideas or thought, but a source, if not *the* source, of ideas and thought. The new language, on the other hand, was based on the principle of language as something pragmatic that people use in order to express themselves. Such an understanding of language as a means of representation disengaged Arabic not only from its literary tradition and genres but also from its sources of inspiration, namely the religious and the poetic. Literary language became that which expresses or reflects naturally, whereas it was traditionally considered more elevated and removed from the daily and the mundane, springing as it did from the wells of the inimitable and is humanity's access to God. The new conception of language probably aided the dominance of realism in the novel, as it certainly did in the case of its best representative, Maḥfūẓ.

These changes found their expression in the literary and cultural products of the 1920s and 1930s, which, although merely transitional from an historical standpoint, helped lay the foundation for one tradition, the realistic, while nipping in the bud the other possible alternatives. While this may seem a rather harsh and one-sided interpretation, it is meant to be an historical assessment rather than a literary evaluation of these works. In more than one way they were, despite their individual merits, pavers of the road that culminated with Maḥfūẓ.

One of the most important characteristics of this rather long period that began during the last decade of the 19th century and ended around the time of World War II was the more critical attitude toward inherited literary production and conventions. This critique of traditionalism was launched from many different perspectives and positions, all of which, despite their differences in sensibility and approach, were united by their shared emphasis on the referential function of literary language. This shift in perspective also points up one of the central problematics in the Arabic novel in general and the novel in Egypt in particular, from the moment of its birth. The novel as it developed in the West was the modern genre per se, and one of its fundamental constructive principles was a concept of the individual as a sovereign entity capable of both thinking and agency. Such an individual generally is associated with the rise of the entrepreneurial class in Europe and its ensuing philosophical, political, economic, and cultural conceptions. Modern Arabic prose fiction was championed by intellectuals and writers educated in or through the modern West and assumed at their hands the function of mediating (representing as well as containing) the clash between the ideologies of modernity as derived from the West and the unrealized project of modernization plagued by a rising indigenous middle class incapable of leading any kind of radical political or ideological transformation of society. This gave prose fiction a prominent role in the development of the mod-

ernizing aesthetic of these intellectuals and helped transform the literary institution to better accommodate fiction, especially the novel.

It is not surprising, then, that the novel and the short story shifted toward formal realism in the period following World War II. This was the period of political independence, the Palestinian *nakbah* (catastrophe) in 1948, the Suez war (1956), the rise of radical nationalisms, and the June defeat of 1967. In literature and culture it was a period of the rise of the political aesthetic that in turn gave a central place to realistic and naturalistic narrative at the expense of other literary trends and genres, especially poetry. Nagīb Maḥfūẓ dominates this period, yet other realistic writers of prose fiction excelled, including ʿAbd al-Raḥmān al-Sharqāwī, Laṭīfah al-Zayyāt, and the short-story writer and novelist Yūsuf Idrīs. Novelists such as Muḥammad ʿAbd al-Ḥalīm ʿAbd Allāh, Yūsuf al-Sibāʿī, and Iḥsān ʿAbd al-Quddūs adopted some of the basic tenets of realism, combining them with the traditions of idealized and/or popular romanticism. A few novelists attempted to chart other paths, including Idwār al-Kharrāṭ and Badr al-Dīb, and thus remained relatively unknown until they were "discovered" in the 1970s and 1980s.

The two underlying premises of realism during this period (of which Maḥfūẓ is paradigmatic) were the knowability of reality (which is founded upon the idea of the existence of reality outside of and independent from our consciousness) and the representability of this reality (which in turn is based on the idea of the transparency of language). The shifts that took place during the 1960s, most prominently in the works of Maḥfūẓ beginning with *Awlād Ḥāritnā* (1967; *Children of Gebelawi*), did not in any way problematize realism as much as a specific conception of reality. Reality now (although still knowable and representable) is more complex and necessitates, therefore, more complex forms in order to be properly represented. Problematizing the knowability and representability of reality had to wait until the 1970s. Although formal realism was abandoned by many novelists, realism as a general literary attitude was still alive and well into the 1990s. One of the most interesting works that adhered in many ways to realism but combined it with a dense language of great poetic power was *Mawsim al-hijrah ilā al-shamāl* (1966; *Season of Migration to the North*) by the Sudanese al-Ṭayyib Ṣāliḥ. He followed this novel with a number of novellas and short stories that utilized folklore and popular culture and combined them with a powerful language heavily laden with semantic possibilities.

After 1967 many novelists still adopted a realistic stance, yet they found formal realism too restrictive and started experimenting with form. A number of terms were given to describe this change, such as postrealism, modernism (*ḥadāthah*), and the new sensibility (*al-ḥasāsiyah al-jadīdah*). However, since the literary phenomena resulting from this transitional moment were so diverse, none of these terms seems capable of denoting the changes that started around the late 1960s and whose earliest manifestation was the short-lived journal *Gallery 68* founded by Ibrāhīm Manṣūr, Ghālib Halasā, Jamīl ʿAṭiyah Ibrāhīm, Idwār al-Kharrāṭ, and Ṣunʿallāh Ibrāhīm and whose editor was Aḥmad Mursī. The names of the founders and the authors whose works were published in that journal is a list of the most important writers in Egypt since the 1970s. Although these writers (some of whom belonged to the older generation, while others were still very young) were united in their dissatisfaction with the old and their continuous search for something new, they differed greatly in their choices of that "new." For the most part, one may divide them into two general trends. The first resorted to the fund of narrative traditions from the West, especially the different modernisms (and postmodernisms), the boom writers of Latin America, and recent theories of narrative and text. The results varied widely, but the most prominent and interesting within this trend are writers like Idwār al-Kharrāṭ whose trilogy *Rāma wa-al-tinnīn* (1985; Rama and the Dragon), *al-Zaman al-ākhar* (1985; The Other Time), and *Yaqīn al-ᶜaṭash* (1996; The Certainty of Thirst) uses a dialogic form that subverts the narrativity of the novel but heightens its poetic force. His other works continue this move through texts that are unclassifiable by genre. Another novelist who experimented with form and adopted diverse fictional modes and strategies was Ghālib Halasā, a Jordanian who spent most of his adult life in Egypt and became a part of the Egyptian literary scene. Ṣunᶜallāh Ibrāhīm, whose novella *Tilka al-rā'iḥah* (*The Smell of It*) was banned in Egypt because of its explicit handling of sexuality, also belongs to this group. In his other works he used multiple discursive forms (especially journalism and accounts of the most recent history of Egypt), juxtaposing them against one another. The problems of history and politics are central to his fictional worlds (*Najmat Aghustus* [The Star of August] and *Dhāt*).

The second general trend was to resort to traditional narrative forms and use them as constructional elements in the novels. Again the results differ. Jamāl al-Ghīṭānī used in his first novel *al-Zaynī Barakāt* (1974; *Zayni Barakat*) the mode of late medieval historical writings combined with the realistic mode and that of the *sufi* writers in medieval Arab culture. In his later novels he emphasized the *sufi* mode, which became the constructive principle for most of his output since the late 1970s. ᶜAbd al-Ḥakīm Qāsim was at his best in utilizing folklore and popular narrative traditions not only as materials for his novels but also as a structuring device that gave the novels their rhythm and movement. The novelist and short-story writer Yaḥyā al-Ṭāhir ᶜAbd Allāh shared these qualities with Qāsim, but his novella *al-Ṭawq wa-al-iswarah* (1975; The Necklace and the Armband) and his short stories tend to be more dense and more poetic. Other novelists of this generation are Ibrāhīm Aṣlān, Muḥammad Yūsuf al-Quᶜayyid, Muḥammad Mustajāb, and Bahā' Ṭāhir.

The late 20th century also has witnessed the increasing impor-

tance of women writers. Although women were very active in journalism, poetry, and prose since the latter decades of the 19th century, their participation in cultural life declined during the interwar period. With the 1960s, however, women novelists and short-story writers started to assume a central position in the field of prose writing. The most prominent of these are Laṭīfah al-Zayyāt and Nawāl al-Saᶜdāwī. Both were leftists and feminists, although al-Zayyāt differed from Saᶜdāwī in her emphasis on the social construction of gender differences and inequality, while Saᶜdāwī emphasized a feminist vision that is grounded in gender differences. Of the younger generation of women writers, Salwā Bakr is probably the most gifted.

The richness of the mature Arabic novel in Egypt (especially since Maḥfūẓ), which manifests itself in the presence and competition of diverse traditions, coupled with the rising importance of women writers, has resulted in an explosion of fiction writing since the 1960s. Such a situation makes it no longer possible for a specific trend to assume a paradigmatic status, as was the case during the 1950s and 1960s. The Arabic novel in Egypt is now coming of age and moving into more interesting areas, taking more ambitious paths than ever before.

WALID HAMARNEH

See also African Novel: Northern Africa; Iranian Novel; Levantine Arabic Novel; Nagīb Maḥfūẓ; Nawāl al-Saᶜdāwī

Further Reading

Allen, Roger, *The Arabic Novel: An Historical and Critical Introduction*, Syracuse, New York: Syracuse University Press, and Manchester: University of Manchester Press, 1982; 2nd edition, Syracuse, New York: Syracuse University Press, 1995
Badawi, Muhammad Mustafa, *Modern Arabic Literature*, Cambridge and New York: Cambridge University Press, 1992
Badr, Abd al-Muhsin Taha, *Tatawwur al-riwayah al-Arabiya al-haditha fi Misr, 1870–1938*, Cairo: Dar al-Maarif, 1963
Jad, Ali, *Form and Technique in the Egyptian Novel, 1912–1971*, London: Ithaca Press, 1983
Kilpatrick, Hilary, *The Modern Egyptian Novel*, London: Ithaca Press, 1974
Nassaj, Sayyid Hamid, *Banurama al-riwayah al-Arabiyah al-hadithah*, Cairo: Dar al-Maarif, 1980

Cyprian Ekwensi 1921–

Nigerian

The Nigerian novelist Cyprian Ekwensi, variously referred to as the Grandfather of the Nigerian novel, the doyen of Nigerian literature, the Nigerian Defoe, and the enigma of modern African writing, is a very important figure in the historical development of modern West African fiction in English. An avid and

versatile experimentalist, Ekwensi pioneered different literary trends. His first novel, *People of the City* (1954), for instance, was the first internationally published West African novel in modern style.

Ekwensi is, at the time of this writing, the author of nine adult novels, 18 novels for young readers, and five collections of short stories. One of the most prolific writers in Africa today, he refers to himself as a populist writer who aims to appeal to all classes of readers with his story-telling and characterization. His works also form a comprehensive portrait of Nigerian society, bearing witness to the fact that Ekwensi, himself of Igbo ancestry, was born and raised in the Hausa-Fulani north and educated in the Yoruba-speaking west. Indeed, Ekwensi's fiction has probably touched on more aspects of Nigerian life than has any other contemporary Nigerian writer.

Ekwensi has earned himself the reputation of being a sensational writer, a reveler in topicality, a novelist perpetually engrossed in the city (especially Lagos, the capital) and its morality. Some critics have objected to his handling of female sexuality, which is invariably at the center of the action in his adult novels, and some have gone so far as to dismiss his work as pornography. Ekwensi defends himself by arguing that the primary function of the novelist is to hold the mirror up to nature, regardless of the sensitivities of his public. He insists that he accurately depicts his life and the lives of others, and that he is incapable of reporting falsely. Ekwensi's penchant for unorthodox experimentation has not helped his case with unsympathetic critics.

The debate surrounding the value of Ekwensi's work began when he published People of the City in 1954. He came upon the idea for the novel from stories he had written for his weekly radio program, "Your Favorite Story Teller," on Radio Nigeria. Each weekly story had its own unique setting, theme, characters, and message. During a trip to England, Ekwensi integrated 13 of these stories into People of the City. One of the first African novels to draw attention to the moral decay in Africa's emerging urban environments following World War II, it received the praise of some critics, who described it as "a vivid picture of life in a West African city" and opined that it "tells more about West Africa than fifty government reports." But other critics quarreled with its experimental style, particularly the episodic plot, saying that the story wobbled like a nervous cricket. The novel also was criticized for its melodramatic tone and unconvincing denouement.

In the end, the historical significance of People of the City as a reflection of Western Africa was diminished by its stylistic shortcomings, a problem that has plagued Ekwensi throughout his literary career. In the main, Ekwensi's subsequent adult novels have suffered from judgments formed by People of the City. But this situation has not deterred Ekwensi from continuing what he started in his first novel: depicting the sensual and political immorality that corrodes the fabric of the new African urban centers. With the exception of Burning Grass (1962), all his other novels—Jagua Nana (1961), Beautiful Feathers (1963), Iska (1966), Survive the Peace (1976), Divided We Stand (1980), Jagua Nana's Daughter (1986), and For a Roll of Parchment (1987)—have focused on city life, portraying its problems with eloquence and compassion, even while they avoided the general defects of People of the City.

The publication of the highly accomplished Jagua Nana, which displays total control of subject matter, impeccable characterization, and charming literary innovations, confirmed Ekwensi's international reputation. Jagua, the protagonist, is an aging prostitute famed for her superlative elegance, and her experiences provide a window on the moral corruption of life in modern Nigeria. Jagua Nana registers the fact of Nigeria's newly won independence in various ways. For example, many characters speak in pidgin English as a matter of course, asserting with confidence their everyday speech habits, unconcerned with foreign standards. Ekwensi's bold use of pidgin has been emulated by many later Nigerian writers. The Africanness of the novel is also confirmed by the fact that it has no domineering white characters and that Jagua does not entertain European customers, in spite of the fact that she is a fashionable prostitute.

In spite of its accomplishments, Jagua Nana also met with controversy. Whereas the problems described in People of the City were part of the colonial era, Jagua Nana pointed out that the same problems persisted after independence. Praised by readers and critics outside Nigeria, Ekwensi was attacked by Nigerians for washing Nigeria's dirty linen in public. Women's organizations, church leaders, and politicians condemned the novel for its explicit eroticism and unfavorable portrayal of politicians. In fact, the novel was debated in Nigerian parliament, where the Minister of Information declared:

> The book of course, reflects African womanhood unfavorably and therefore would portray the country in an unfavorable light and give the impression that African womenfolk were immoral and that their lives were sordid and mercenary. . . . In my considered opinion, therefore, the outside world should not get the impression that Nigeria is a country of loose women and unscrupulous politicians like those portrayed in the imaginary world wherein Jagua Nana is set (from a press release, 16 April 1963).

At the end of the parliamentary debate, a proposed filming of the novel by an Italian company was stopped. Although they have provoked less public commotion, Ekwensi's later novels have been greeted with considerable debate.

Ekwensi is also noteworthy for his short stories, which are among the best in Africa. His contributions to African children's literature—primarily thrillers for teenage readers—surpass those of any other writer. Few African writers have matched Ekwensi's artistic versatility and inventiveness.

ERNEST N. EMENYONU

See also People of the City

Biography

Born in Minna, Niger State, 26 September 1921. Attended Government School, Jos, 1931–36; Government College, Ibadan, 1936–41; Higher College, Yaba, 1947–49; Chelsea School of Pharmacy, University of London, 1951–56; University of Iowa, Iowa City, 1974. Teacher, Igbobi College, Yaba, 1947–49; lecturer, School of Pharmacy, Lagos, 1949–51; pharmacist superintendent, Nigerian Medical Services, 1956–57; head of features, Nigerian Broadcasting Corporation, 1957–61; director, Federal Information Services, 1961–67; director-general, Broadcasting Corporation of Biafra, 1967–70, at the time of the Nigerian Civil War; proprietor, East Niger Chemists and East Niger Trading Company from 1970; chairman, East Central State Library Board, 1972–75; managing director, Star Printing and Publishing Company, 1975–79; consultant, Weekly Trumpet and Daily News, both Anambra State, and Weekly Eagle, Imo State, 1980–81;

commissioner for information, Anambra State, 1983. Member of the Board of Governors, Federal Radio Corporation, Lagos, 1985; chairman, Anambra State Hospitals Board, 1986–88.

Novels by Ekwensi

People of the City, 1954; revised edition, 1963
Jagua Nana, 1961
Burning Grass: A Story of the Fulani of Northern Nigeria, 1962
Beautiful Feathers, 1963
Iska, 1966
Survive the Peace, 1976
Divided We Stand, 1980
Jagua Nana's Daughter, 1986
For a Roll of Parchment, 1987

Other Writings: short stories and children's fiction.

Further Reading

Emenyonu, Ernest, *Cyprian Ekwensi,* London: Evans, 1974
Emenyonu, Ernest, editor, *The Essential Ekwensi: A Literary Celebration of Cyprian Ekwensi's Sixty-fifth Birthday,* Ibadan: Heinemann, 1986
Killam, Douglas, "Cyprian Ekwensi," in *Introduction to Nigerian Literature,* edited by Bruce King, Lagos: University of Lagos, London: Evans Brothers, and New York: Africana, 1971
Palmer, Eustace, "Cyprian Ekwensi," in *The Growth of the African Novel,* by Palmer, London and Exeter, New Hampshire: Heinemann, 1979
Povey, John, "Cyprian Ekwensi and *Beautiful Feathers,*" *Critique* 8:1 (Autumn 1965)
Povey, John, "Cyprian Ekwensi: The Novelist and the Pressure of the City," in *The Critical Evaluation of African Literature,* edited by Edgar Wright, London: Heinemann, 1973; Washington, D.C.: INSCAPE, 1976

The Elective Affinities by Johann Wolfgang von Goethe

Die Wahlverwandtschaften 1809

As we know from (among other indicators) a diary entry of April 1808, Goethe initially conceived of *The Elective Affinities* as a short prose tale—a "Novelle"—rather than a novel. Certainly he was aware of the European tradition of the novella that came down from Boccaccio and Cervantes, among other writers. He was attracted to the genre, it seems, for its brevity, its ability to mediate between the requirements of plausibility on the one hand and the appeal of exceptional and unheard-of events on the other, and above all because the novella frequently is a gregarious genre (existing, as it were, in sociable cycles) whereby the challenging novelty of its subject matter interacts with the implicitly communal dimension of the circle of hearers. Indeed, the narrative that subsequently became *The Elective Affinities* acknowledges its own generic pedigree; it invokes the tradition from which it derives by creating in one scene a situation in which a visitor to an estate tells a novella of passion, little aware of how greatly he will thereby disturb his hearers.

The Elective Affinities is as remarkable as it is difficult to situate generically. At one level, one can see it as a social novel. It is set in the world of the minor aristocracy. Eduard and Charlotte are happily (and recently) married. They busy themselves with various activities associated with the running of their estate—gardening, landscaping, care of buildings. The tone of their discussions is decorous, even a shade stilted. They invite two people to join them, the Hauptmann (Captain) and Ottilie, Charlotte's shy, withdrawn niece. Rapidly, the calm life on the estate gives way to emotional turmoil when Eduard and Ottilie fall passionately in love. Charlotte and the Hauptmann, while more reserved in their feelings, also fall in love. When Ottilie confronts

the chaos of which she has been the largely unwitting cause, she withdraws from human contact altogether, refusing to speak and to eat. After her death, Eduard is a broken man; he dies not long after her.

The Elective Affinities is concerned to examine human behavior in a number of contexts. One is, as we have seen, the social. The sterility of the aristocratic way of life, once it is challenged by experiences of any existential depth, shatters, leaving few psychological or moral defenses against the inroads of passion. Yet the social reading makes only partial headway with Goethe's remarkable text. The novel also inquires into the complex links between human beings and nature. The title itself refers to a concept within late 18th-century science that involves forms of chemical bonding. At one point three of the characters (before the arrival of Ottilie) discuss the applicability of scientific-material laws to human affairs. In this sense, the novel contextualizes human behavior in a materialist framework. But there are, in addition, notions of supernatural motivation; time and time again we seem to be in a world that is shaped by some inscrutable destiny or fate, whether malignant or transcendental. The novel abounds in patterns, similarities, mirrorings. The characters seem mysteriously destined for each other, as is suggested by their names. (The Hauptmann is called Otto, Eduard's real name is Otto; and the women are called Charlotte and Ottilie. Otto is a palindrome. Moreover, the initials of the four characters spell ECHO.) We find ourselves wondering what the claustrophobic density of pattern means. When is a pattern a cause—a law of nature or of psychology—and when is it merely a human construct, a playing with analogies? Ultimately, we cannot answer unequivocally, not least because the narrative voice is withdrawn and oblique. We are offered possible readings, not certainties; and this is nowhere more apparent than in the case of Ottilie. Is her abstention from material and social nourishment a moment of superhuman moral decision? A mysterious intimation of a sublime, perhaps even saintly destiny? Or is it neurosis—a form of anorexic self-obliteration?

The Elective Affinities is perhaps best seen as an experimental novel, in the literal sense that it records an experiment and creates a conjectural model of human behavior. It begins: "Eduard, so we shall call a rich baron in the prime of his life . . .". The initial gesture, then, is not one of social or psychological specificity, but rather of establishing a test case. When, in one of the most scandalously profound scenes in the whole of the 19th-century European novel, Eduard and Charlotte, husband and wife, in spite of the emotional distance opening up between them, come together for an evening and have intercourse, the text reflects on the illicitness of this seemingly licit act (each of the participants is thinking of the absent beloved—Charlotte of the Hauptmann, Eduard of Ottilie). Goethe's exploration of the complexity of being and motivation, of the interplay of social, moral, ontological, and religious values at work within human sexuality, is breathtaking. What *The Elective Affinities* may sometimes lack in terms of specificity of character it amply makes up for in the sheer range of its questioning. In the context of the (broadly speaking) realistic novel tradition of the European 19th century, *The Elective Affinities* may seem forbiddingly abstract, cerebral even. To the experimental company of 20th-century writing, however, and particularly to the highly self-reflexive climate of recent fiction, Goethe's novel appears to have its own affinities.

MARTIN SWALES

See also Johann Wolfgang von Goethe

Further Reading

Adler, Jeremy, *"Eine fast magische Anziehungskraft": Goethes "Wahlverwandtschaften" und die Chemie seiner Zeit,* Munich: Beck, 1987

Barnes, Harry George, *Goethe's "Die Wahlverwandtschaften": A Literary Interpretation,* Oxford: Clarendon Press, 1967

Blackall, Eric A., *Goethe and the Novel,* Ithaca, New York: Cornell University Press, 1976

Blessin, Stefan, *Erzählstruktur und Leserhandlung: Zur Theorie der literarischen Kommunikation am Beispiel von Goethes "Wahlverwandtschen,"* Heidelberg: Winter, 1974

Bolz, Norbert W., editor, *Goethes "Die Wahlverwandtschaften,"* Hildesheim: Gerstenberg, 1981

Rösch, Ewald, editor, *Goethes Roman "Die Wahlverwandtschaften,"* Darmstadt: Wissenschaftliche Buchgesellschaft, 1975

Schwan, Werner, *Goethes "Wahlverwandtschaften": Das nicht erreichte Soziale,* Munich: Fink, 1983

Winkelman, John, *Goethe's "Elective Affinities": An Interpretation,* New York: Peter Lang, 1987

Winnett, Susan, *Terrible Sociability: The Text of Manners in Laclos, Goethe, and James,* Stanford, California: Stanford University Press, 1993

George Eliot 1819–80

English

Henry James discerned in George Eliot's fiction a "constant presence of thought, of generalizing instinct," and he declared that in her "broad reach of vision" she seems "among English romancers to stand alone." Virginia Woolf described *Middlemarch* (1872) as "one of the few English novels written for grown-up people." Many later readers have concurred with such judgments and have accorded Eliot a singular status as the most intelligent, the most mature, and hence the wisest of the English novelists.

Eliot's central contribution to the development of the novel is to have broadened the scope of subjects available for fictional representation. She takes seriously the inner life of common people in rural areas and provincial towns, and she also depicts the life of the mind among cultivated people who are engaged in religious struggles, scholarship, scientific research, painting, musical composition, and political reform. Eliot's early novels take their subjects largely from the lower and middle classes of English provincial society. In her later novels, she depicts characters who are of a higher social class, who are occupied with spiritual and intellectual issues on her own level of education, and who function symbolically to represent the largest movements of cultural life in her time. (The only novel not set in England is *Romola* [1863], a historical novel of 15th-century Florence.)

More than any other novelist, Eliot made the subject of vocation a topic for fiction. Previous novelists seldom depicted people at work, and when they did it was usually as an adjunct to some other motive that the novelist invested with primary dramatic interest. Work is sometimes included as an aspect of adventure, as in Daniel Defoe's *Robinson Crusoe* and *Moll Flanders,* but more often it lies in the background as a source of income or as a factor in social position. In Eliot's depictions of both the lower and higher socio-cultural levels, the disciplined pursuit of constructive activity becomes an integral part of individual identity and a subject of primary dramatic interest. Adam

Bede, in the novel of that name, is a carpenter who loves his work and who educates himself as an architect. In his later incarnation as Caleb Garth in *Middlemarch,* the provincial workman serves as a medium through which Eliot evokes the "sublime" imaginative power of "that myriad-headed, myriad-handed labour by which the social body is fed, clothed, and housed." In *Romola,* Romola's father is a devoted scholar, and Lydgate, the young doctor and medical researcher in *Middlemarch,* is inspired with a passion "to make a link in the chain of discovery." Eliot sharply distinguishes between this passion, as a primary motive, and the conventional attitude of Lydgate's wife, who sees professional engagement only as the means to recognition and higher social rank. Eliot's elaborate, extended evocation of Lydgate's intellectual passion is one of the few such evocations in the fiction of any language, and it creates a new generic range—that of the intellectual sublime.

As with characters in the conventional comedy of manners, many of Eliot's characters are motivated only by the values of romantic desire and social positioning, but in Eliot's novels these commonplace values are framed within the perspective of a satirically charged moral and social idealism. Her protagonists are themselves idealists, and their struggle with the world of commonplace motives and conventional values is a central issue in their lives. The conventional comedy of manners is thus thematically embedded within a larger generic framework—a framing that corresponds to the critical perspective Eliot adopts in her review essay of fashionable women's fiction, "Silly Novels by Lady Novelists."

Eliot radically revises patriarchal conceptions of gender by investing women with the capacity for aspirations beyond the domestic sphere. Maggie Tulliver in *The Mill on the Floss* (1860) and Dorothea Brooke in *Middlemarch* are not only brave and capable young women like the protagonists of Jane Austen and the Brontës; they are women struggling consciously against the artificial constraints of the social roles accorded to women. Modern feminist critics have often been unhappy with Eliot because she depicts no women who succeed (as did Eliot herself) in rising above conventional gender roles. Maggie is trapped in an inextricable tangle of personal obligations from which she is freed only by accidental death, and Dorothea, after all her struggles, settles into a conventional domestic romance. Dinah Morris in *Adam Bede* (1859), Maggie Tulliver, Romola, and Dorothea exercise a moral authority that crucially influences the quality of life in their communities, but they accomplish little else.

Despite her realistic depiction of the difficulties encountered by her female protagonists, Eliot succeeded in undermining the belief, common in her time, that the scope of women's minds and characters was severely circumscribed. Here again Henry James takes the right measure of her achievement. He declares that those for whom "the 'development' of woman is the hope of the future ought to erect a monument to George Eliot. . . . There is much talk to-day about things being 'open to women'; but George Eliot showed that there is nothing that is closed."

Eliot's imaginative life is animated by two distinct and often opposing forces: transcendental spiritual aspiration and a proto-Darwinian naturalism. As a young woman, after an intensely pietistic youth, Eliot underwent a typically Victorian crisis of religious disillusionment. Her first contributions to the intellectual world include translating two works of German biblical scholarship that adopt an anthropological perspective on Christian belief. From among her literary reviews, the one essay that most illuminates her early novels is "The Natural History of German Life." Eliot sought to accomplish in fiction what Wilhelm Heinrich von Riehl had accomplished in naturalistic cultural history—to overcome sentimental stereotypes and to envision people as biologically constrained organisms rooted in a natural environment. Hence Henry James' complaint that *Middlemarch* "is too often an echo of Messrs. Darwin and Huxley."

Eliot's naturalism contributed immensely to the sense of vividly perceived life in her work—of experience that is concretely localized, densely circumscribed in a particular time and place. Yet the deepest shaping force in the thematic construction of her works is the need for a religious vision of life. She requires both a passionate reverence for human attachment and a sublime spiritual exaltation. Her first published fiction, *Scenes of Clerical Life* (1858), consists of three novellas that deal sympathetically with the clergy and that translate religious passion into secular terms of fellowship and moral regeneration. Dinah Morris in *Adam Bede* is a profoundly religious woman who ministers among the poor. In a depiction that draws heavily on Eliot's own girlhood experience, Maggie Tulliver's personal development in *The Mill on the Floss* leads her through a long phase of spiritual meditation. Silas Marner in the novel of that name (1861) becomes disillusioned with supernatural religion but then is brought back to reverential faith through the love of a child. Romola achieves sanctity through self-renouncing compassion, and Dorothea Brooke in *Middlemarch* virtually personifies the drive toward a spiritual nobility combined with a quasi-Christian moral vocation.

In two of her novels, *Felix Holt* (1866) and *Daniel Deronda* (1876), Eliot's idealistic protagonists are male, and their aspirations are more political than spiritual. Even so, both characters evince the extraordinary capacity for human sympathy that characterizes Eliot's female idealists. Felix is depicted symbolically as a Christ figure, and the beautiful, worldly young woman who loves him is figured as Mary Magdalene, with "her precious spikenard" and "her long tresses too, that were let ready to soothe the wearied feet." Daniel Deronda discovers that he is a Jew and devotes himself to Zionism, but he conceives of Zionism (paradoxically but sincerely) as a synecdoche for a utopian brotherhood of all humanity.

Eliot's depictions of rural life are crucial antecedents for Thomas Hardy's Wessex novels, and her depiction of high-minded, spirited young women is a primary source for James' heroines, especially for Isabel Archer in *The Portrait of a Lady* (1881). Through Elizabeth-Jane, the female protagonist of *The Mayor of Casterbridge* (1886), Hardy evokes the female cultural quest, and in *Jude the Obscure* (1895) he follows Eliot in using his characters to symbolize the largest movements of the modern cultural imagination. Eliot's cultural symbolism enters also into the thematic structures of D.H. Lawrence's novels, and her work is an essential antecedent for the moral and political meditations of Joseph Conrad. Beyond such large and obvious instances, her influence, like that of Dorothea Brooke, is "incalculably diffusive."

JOSEPH CARROLL

See also Daniel Deronda; Middlemarch; Mill on the Floss

Biography

George Eliot is the pseudonym for Mary Ann (later Marian) Evans. Born in Arbury, Warwickshire, 22 November 1819. Attended Miss Lathom's school, Attleborough; Miss Wallington's school, Nuneaton, 1828–32; Misses Franklins' school, Coventry, 1832–35. Took care of family after her mother died, 1836; lived with her father in Foleshill, near Coventry, 1841–49; lived in Geneva, 1849–50; moved to London, 1851; contributor, 1851 and 1855–57, and assistant editor, 1852–54, *Westminster Review*; lived in Germany, 1854–55, and London from 1855. Died 22 December 1880.

Novels by Eliot

Adam Bede, 1859
The Mill on the Floss, 1860
Silas Marner, The Weaver of Raveloe, 1861
Romola, 1863
Felix Holt, the Radical, 1866
Middlemarch: A Study of Provincial Life, 1872
Daniel Deronda, 1876

Other Writings: essays, stories, poems, notebooks.

Further Reading

Austen, Zelda, "Why Feminist Critics Are Angry with George Eliot," *College English* 37 (1976)

Beer, Gillian, *Darwin's Plots: Evolutionary Narrative in Darwin, George Eliot, and Nineteenth-Century Fiction,* London and Boston: Routledge and Kegan Paul, 1983

Bloom, Harold, editor, *George Eliot,* New York: Chelsea House, 1986

Carroll, David, editor, *George Eliot: The Critical Heritage,* London: Routledge, and New York: Barnes and Noble, 1971

Carroll, David, *George Eliot and the Conflict of Interpretations: A Reading of the Novels,* Cambridge and New York: Cambridge University Press, 1992

Carroll, Joseph, *Evolution and Literary Theory,* Columbia: University of Missouri Press, 1995

Chase, Karen, *Eros & Psyche: The Representation of Personality in Charlotte Brontë, Charles Dickens, and George Eliot,* New York: Methuen, 1984

Creeger, George R., editor, *George Eliot: A Collection of Critical Essays,* Englewood Cliffs, New Jersey: Prentice Hall, 1970

Haight, Gordon Sherman, *George Eliot: A Biography,* Oxford and New York: Oxford University Press, 1968

Haight, Gordon Sherman, and VanArsdel, Rosemary T., editors, *George Eliot: A Centenary Tribute,* London: Macmillan, and Totowa, New Jersey: Barnes and Noble, 1982

James, Henry, *Literary Criticism: Essays on Literature, American Writers, English Writers,* edited by Leon Edel and Mark Wilson, New York: Library of America, 1984

Kucich, John, *Repression in Victorian Fiction: Charlotte Brontë, George Eliot, and Charles Dickens,* Berkeley: University of California Press, 1987

Levine, George Lewis, with the assistance of Patricia O'Hara, *An Annotated Critical Bibliography of George Eliot,* Brighton, Sussex: Harvester Press, and New York: St. Martin's Press, 1988

Newton, K.M., editor, *George Eliot,* London and New York: Longman, 1991

Reilly, Jim, *Shadowtime: History and Representation in Hardy, Conrad, and George Eliot,* London and New York: Routledge, 1993

Stephen, Leslie, *George Eliot,* London and New York: Macmillan, 1902

Woolf, Virginia, "George Eliot," in *The Common Reader: First Series,* New York: Harcourt Brace, and London: Hogarth Press, 1925

Embedded Narrative. *See* Framing and Embedding in Narrative

Emma by Jane Austen

1815

Emma stands at the center of Jane Austen's achievement as a novelist, and at the fulcrum of the development of narrative technique within the English novel as it changed to meet the complex demands of an English society whose center of power was shifting away from the landed gentry. The only novel by Austen to take its name not from a place or a set of allegorized moral qualities, *Emma* is both modern in its brilliant, enigmatic focus on a single female character and Augustan in its insistence on the relationship between morality and an accepted social hierarchy.

One of the key themes of earlier novelists' portrayals of women's lives had been the dangers of economic dependence and class subservience, the vulnerability of women in positions of servitude, and the strategies women developed to escape into marriage with their honor intact and their fortunes improved. Samuel Richardson's *Pamela* (1740) had developed a complex epistolary narrative to enact this movement toward a reconciliation of class mobility, sexuality, and marriage, but the process remained at the level of sexual pursuit and an economic contract: the exchange of a beset virginity for the prosperity of marriage. It was Austen's achievement to develop the fictional portrayal of women's social subordination by exploring the situation of intelligent, morally strong women who seek not just marriage but also love, companionship, and intelligent equivalence. In *Sense and Sensibility* (1811) the dangers of excessive sentiment or detachment are revealed in characters who are closer to didactic illustrations than complex living beings. In *Northanger Abbey* (1818) the action is set up to show the seductions of Gothic fiction and demonstrate how misleading fantasies can exacerbate both fear and romance and impede any progress toward rationality and a marriage based on love.

In *Pride and Prejudice* (1813) Austen begins to shift her focus to the dangers of being an assured part of a ruling class (Darcy's pride and Bingley's persuadability) and the dangers for women of being simultaneously ousted from the patterns of accepted lineage and economic inheritance while being trapped within the genteel connivance of the marriage market. In *Pride and Prejudice,* too, the difficulty of any real communication between men and women amid the confinements of social convention becomes a major theme as it is shown to impede understanding of significant others in the vicinity of the heroine. The novel is partly about the complex transmission of social and moral information, and Austen develops her skillful plot management to that end. The subplot of Lydia's elopement into ruin and danger begins to uncover the illicit subtexts concealed by respectability; social secrecy about sexuality and illegitimacy is shown to be dangerous. Had the attempted seduction of Darcy's sister not been so thoroughly concealed, Lydia would have been safer. The dangers for women are shown to lie in the difficulty of distinguishing virtuous from vicious men when sexuality itself was concealed. Austen's critique of her society sharpens: it is not just weak or selfish characters who are at fault, or that the kindness, decency, honesty, and integrity that should inform a ruling class are lacking, but that the world of respectability is intertwined with a secrecy about the springs of human conduct that makes women susceptible to danger and betrayal.

In *Emma* Austen takes the critique of her society's materialistic norms to a new level, mainly by developing a sinuous narrative method that colors the narrative with Emma's consciousness and makes the reader privy to her class-blind view of the world. The reader is drawn into an intimate, uneasy bond with the heroine that renders any easy judgment on events difficult and that makes us conscious of her blunders; we become her secret mentor and guardian. The omniscient authorial method of the earlier fiction, which made the moral values undergirding Austen's social vision seem so certain, is partly sacrificed to a free indirect discourse that enters the heroine's consciousness so fluently that she becomes part of the reader's unconscious, and the reader is delivered, at the end, along with the heroine. Both narrative and morality are shown to be in process, to be socially constructed, and Austen surrenders some of her narrative detachment to open up the

springs of suffering that also release knowledge of the heart. *Emma* questions a society so focused on rank and material wealth that it eventually threatens the happiness of three women's interrelated lives: Jane Fairfax, Harriet Smith, and Emma herself. Emma is the first modern heroine, and *Emma* the first novel by a woman to make the act of imagining a woman's passage from family to marriage a narrative pact that makes the reader an integral part of the process and the story a commentary on the distortion of women's lives by false social norms.

Emma's story, that of a young woman who has enjoyed all the privileges of her rank and wealth, turns on a blindness to love and sexual desire both in herself and others; and this blindness, when coupled with a materialism that forbids unequal or premature alliances, begins to damage the lives of all the main actors. Frank Churchill's secret engagement is similarly tied up with his dependence on financial inheritance, and the damaging effects of his secret engagement to Jane becomes a metaphor for the damage done by the social concealment of love and desire. Harriet's near loss of a decent, compatible marriage is an extension and result of Emma's blindness to her own desires, and all are intertwined in a corrupting system of class patronage and financial subservience. The eruption of cruelty at the Box Hill picnic, when Emma is unkind to an older woman and social subordinate, and in the game of charades in which Emma and Frank goad Jane Fairfax with an illicit relationship that they have invented for her, while she is unable to declare publicly her real affections, arises from a confluence of a hardened class structure with a selfish, rampant materialism. Mr. Woodhouse is the feeble insignia of this system. Mrs. Elton is unforgivably vulgar because she apes the values of a bankrupt class. The intertwining of Emma's story—a love affair concealed from herself—with Jane's story—a love affair concealed by both actors—sets up a complex tension between a socially favored woman and a socially dependent woman and shows how their fates are interrelated. Jane Fairfax's difficulties are mostly economic; Emma's are mostly psychological and moral. But both suffer on their way to love and fulfillment. The novel is modern, too, in its revelation of the psychology of women under patriarchy. Emma's preference for surrogate marriage through matchmaking is a subtle index to self-protective mechanisms, self-projection, and fear. The triple release of Emma, Harriet, and Jane into the partnerships that they really desired all along functions as a psychological fulcrum of women's divided social identity: mistress of the house, illegitimate child, educated but impoverished orphan. The social conventions that worked against one worked against all, and Emma's awakening releases everyone.

In *Emma* the subtle control of narrative distance, irony, and point of view impels a profound understanding of the close relationship between the female psyche and the social construction of womanhood. The novel is a social comedy that nevertheless radically questions Austen's society by showing how very closely its protagonists avoided tragedy. In Austen's next novel, *Persuasion* (1818), the effects of vanity and social snobbery on individual happiness are even more severe. Austen's narrative achievement in the exposure of individual female consciousness in *Emma* made possible the later achievements of George Eliot and Henry James, located women's fate within a unique woman's suffering consciousness, and revealed the interrelatedness of women's lives under patriarchy. The female psyche is shown as culturally constructed but also therapeutically released through a complex storytelling that makes the reader an accomplice in a narrative pact. *Emma* and *Persuasion* reveal that Austen is not a novelist who shored up the values of the landed gentry but a profound critic of the price women paid for being extensions of male property, with their own intelligence, autonomy, and, thus, often their deepest desires driven into hiding.

CHERRY CLAYTON

See also Jane Austen

Further Reading

Butler, Marilyn, *Jane Austen and the War of Ideas,* Oxford: Clarendon Press, 1975

Hardy, Barbara, *A Reading of Jane Austen,* London: Owen, 1975; New York: New York University Press, 1979

Kaplan, Deborah, *Jane Austen among Women,* Baltimore: Johns Hopkins University Press, 1992

Kirkham, Margaret, *Jane Austen: Feminism and Fiction,* Brighton, Sussex: Harvester, and Totowa, New Jersey: Barnes and Noble, 1983

Lodge, David, *Emma: A Casebook,* London: Macmillan, 1968; Nashville, Tennessee: Aurora, 1970; revised edition, London: Macmillan, 1991

Tanner, Tony, *Jane Austen,* London: Macmillan, and Cambridge, Massachusetts: Harvard University Press, 1986

Emra'ah ᶜinda nuqṭat al-ṣifr. *See* Woman at Point Zero

Endō Shūsaku 1923–96

Japanese

Following the international acclaim accorded his novel *Chinmoku* (1966; *Silence*), the depiction of Endō Shūsaku as the "Japanese Graham Greene" gained rapid currency. The epithet was certainly convenient. Endō's own accounts had been broadly disseminated: his reluctant conversion to Christianity as a child, his subsequent struggle to come to terms with "the great flow of European culture" he experienced during the two and a half years he spent in France studying the novels of the French Catholics in the early 1950s, and his consequent determination to address in his literature the issues raised by his affiliation to the faith. Equally well documented was his desire to seek, in his literature, a reconciliation between his perceived duty as Christian to seek within humanity the potential for salvation and the necessity as a writer to remain clear-eyed in his observations of human nature.

As with so many convenient labels, however, this depiction fails to do justice to the unique quality of Endō's art. Moreover, as Endō himself was the first to acknowledge, the tension between his roles as Christian and writer was further exacerbated by the need to operate within a cultural and spiritual framework that provides less encouragement for the development of literary themes dealing with the spiritual drama of the relationship between God and humanity. Endō portrayed the ensuing trichotomy in the following terms:

As a Christian, Japanese and an author, I am constantly concerned with the relationship and conflict created by these three tensions. . . . Unfortunately, these three tensions continue to appear as contradictory in my mind.

The challenge for Endō was to make of his adopted faith, frequently depicted as an "ill-fitting Western-style suit," something better suited to his identity as Japanese—to "find God on the streets of Shinjuku and Shibuya, districts which seem so far removed from Him"—and to express this discovery in literary as opposed to theological terms. It is in this regard, as a novelist steeped in a unique literary heritage yet well versed in the Western prose narrative tradition, that Endō's literary legacy is best considered.

The predominant narrative form during Endō's formative years was the *shishōsetsu*, a Japanese variant of the "I-novel" in which textual boundaries are constantly challenged as the real world of the author's life and its fictional reenactment emerge as an unbroken continuum. Endō and fellow members of the *daisan no shinjin* (third generation of new writers) who rose to prominence in the aftermath of defeat in the Pacific War could not ignore this legacy, and it is to this, rather than to any determination to emulate the various Western narratives he had studied, that Endō's concerted examination of his spiritual journey in his literature is best attributed. To be sure, Endō's novels are far removed from the "unmediated reality" on offer in so many of the prewar *shishōsetsu*. His desire to transcribe lived experience and his concomitant attempt to plumb the depths of the self are nevertheless pronounced, resulting, particularly in the case of Endō's later novels, in some of the most concerted considerations of individual psychology available on the recent Japanese literary scene.

Endō's novels reveal an image of the individual as a complex being, an image that accords closely with the Jungian model of the human composite to which Endō had long been drawn. His literary corpus increasingly mirrors his own conviction that "to describe man's inner self, we must probe to the third dimension [within the unconscious] . . . to the territory of demons. One cannot describe man's inner being completely unless one closes in on this demonic part."

Endō's focus on the unconscious—a realm he portrays as one in which "our desire for Good conflicts with our penchant for Evil, where our appreciation of Beauty conflicts with our attachment to the Ugly"—may be cited as a defining aspect of his art. In literary terms, this focus gradually fuses two qualities that initially were established as opposing each other. Several texts, including *Silence* and *Samurai* (1980; *The Samurai*), establish a central dichotomy between East and West, with the distance between the two, initially depicted as unfathomable (for example, the Western missionaries in *Silence* are unable to penetrate what Endō calls the "mudswamp" of Japan), steadily eroding during the course of the novels as a result of the author's increasing focus not on external distinctions but on internal similarities that allow for meaningful communication across national, religious, and cultural divides. Similarly, in *The Samurai* the distance between the Western missionary, Velasco, and the lower-ranking samurai, symbol of Eastern values, at first appears to be insuperable. As the novel progresses, however, Endō's narrator breaks down the obstacles to reconciliation; Velasco acknowledges this at the personal level in his eventual recognition that "it was as if a firm bond of solidarity had formed between the envoys and myself."

Through fusing these and other oppositions in his novels, Endō emphasizes a steady growth in self-awareness. The trait is particularly pronounced in *Sukyandaru* (1986; *Scandal*), a novel that, in its depiction of Suguro, a successful Catholic author, overtly parodies the self-referential tenor of the earlier *shishōsetsu*. With Suguro disturbed at the outset of the novel by a man he attempts to dismiss as either a deliberate impostor or chance look-alike, the central narrative focuses on the protagonist's emerging conviction that the look-alike represents none other than his own doppelgänger—that "he could no longer conceal that part of himself, no longer deny its existence."

In an article written at the time of *Scandal*'s publication, Endō argued that "it is not possible to consider literature and religion without resort to the concept of the unconscious." Endō may be seen examining the ramifications of this conviction in his final novel, *Fukai kawa* (1993; *Deep River*), which portrays various Japanese tourists on journeys of self-discovery in India. Each of the tourists travels to India in response to promptings of the unconscious born of intensely personal experience. At the end of the novel, however, as they stand together on the banks of the "deep river," the Ganges at Vāranāsi, each shows signs of recognizing a spiritual dimension to his or her being.

This image, appearing at the conclusion of Endō's final novel, stands as an entirely appropriate epitaph, a fitting encapsulation of the author's lifelong quest for a literary portrayal of reconciliation.

MARK WILLIAMS

See also Silence

Biography

Born in Tokyo, Japan, 27 March 1923. Attended Keio University, Tokyo, B.A. in French literature 1949; University of Lyons, 1950–53. Contracted tuberculosis, 1959. Served as editor of the literary journal *Mita Bungaku*, chair of the *Bungeika Kyōkai* (Literary Artists' Association), and manager of the Kiza amateur theatrical troupe. Died 29 September 1996.

Novels by Endō

Umi to dokuyaku, 1957; as *The Sea and Poison*, translated by Michael Gallagher, 1972
Obakasan, 1959; as *Wonderful Fool*, translated by Francis Mathy, 1974
Kazan, 1959; as *Volcano*, translated by Richard Schuchert, 1978
Watashi ga suteta onna, 1964; as *The Girl I Left Behind*, translated by Mark Williams, 1994
Ryūgaku, 1965; as *Foreign Studies*, translated by Mark Williams, 1989
Chinmoku, 1966; as *Silence*, translated by William Johnston, 1969
Shikai no hotori [Around the Dead Sea], 1973
Iesu no shōgai, 1973; as *A Life of Jesus*, translated by Richard Schuchert, 1978
Kuchibue o fuku toki, 1974; as *When I Whistle*, translated by Van C. Gessel, 1979
Samurai, 1980; as *The Samurai*, translated by Van C. Gessel, 1982
Sukyandaru, 1986; as *Scandal*, translated by Van C. Gessel, 1988
Fukai kawa, 1993; as *Deep River*, translated by Van C. Gessel, 1994

Other Writings: short stories, essays (many on Christianity), autobiography.

Further Reading

Boscaro, Adriana, "The Meaning of Christianity in the Works of Endō Shūsaku," in *Tradition and Modern Japan*, edited by P.G. O'Neill, Tenterden, Kent: Paul Norbury, and Vancouver: University of British Columbia Press, 1981
Breuer, Hans-Peter, "The Roots of Guilt and Responsibility in Shūsaku Endō's *The Sea and the Poison*," *Literature and Medicine* 7 (1988)
Durfee, Richard E., "Portrait of an Unknowingly Ordinary Man: Endō Shūsaku, Christianity, and Japanese Historical Consciousness," *Japanese Journal of Religious Studies* 16:1 (1989)
Gessel, Van C., "Voices in the Wilderness: Japanese Christian Authors," *Monumenta Nipponica* 37 (1982)
Gessel, Van C., *The Sting of Life: Four Contemporary Japanese Novelists*, New York: Columbia University Press, 1989
Howard, Yoshiko, "The Warp and the Woof of Endō Shūsaku's

Deep River," *The Review of Studies in Christianity and Literature* (Japan) 13 (1996)

Mathy, Francis, "Shūsaku Endō: The Second Period," *Japan Christian Quarterly* 40:4 (Fall 1974)

Mathy, Francis, "Shūsaku Endō: Japanese Catholic Novelist," *Month* (May 1987)

Williams, Mark, "In Search of the Chaotic Unconscious: A Study of *Scandal*," *Japan Forum* 7:2 (Autumn 1995)

Williams, Mark, "Inner Horizons: Towards Reconcilation in Endō Shūsaku's *The Samurai*," *Japan Christian Review* (1996)

Enfant du Sable. *See* Sand Child and Sacred Night

English Novel

18th Century

Prose narrative in Britain took many and varied forms during the late 17th and early 18th centuries. After the Restoration of the Stuart monarchy in 1660, Britain began to emerge from its crippling internal conflicts and to rival France and Holland as a world power. London became Europe's largest city, a commercial and financial center. Literacy increased at a faster rate than ever in Britain, with twice as many literate adults at the beginning of the 18th century than at the start of the 17th, and an emerging and enlarging urban professional and middle class acquired more leisure and a greater appetite and disposable income for consumer goods. Consequently, a growing audience developed, mainly in London but also in some of the larger provincial cities and especially in Edinburgh and Dublin, for a wide range of books on secular and contemporary subjects. The publishing revolution of the early and mid–18th century met this demand by producing a great mass of political pamphlets, cookbooks, travel narratives, self-help and conduct books, medical manuals, criminal biographies, almanacs, periodicals, and prose narratives frequently called "novels" but sometimes "histories" or "true histories." And in these years, the issue of fictionality remains unresolved, with some of the books we now recognize as novels (like Daniel Defoe's) passing for factual. Some of these narratives were translations of French and Spanish fiction, picaresque and romantic, but many more were produced in England to serve this expanding market.

Such fiction aimed at both popular and elite audiences. It encompassed, at the high end, translations of the aristocratic heroic romances popular in the France of Louis XIV such as Madeleine de Scudéry's *Artamène; ou, Le Grand Cyrus* (1649–53; *Artamenes; or, The Grand Cyrus*) and *Clélie* (1654–61; *Clelia*), or the very popular French epistolary novel by Gabriel de Lavergne

Guilleragues, *Lettres Portugaises* (1669), five long letters in which a seduced and abandoned nun evokes her passionate affair with a cavalier, translated into English in 1677 as *Five Love-Letters from a Nun to a Cavalier*. At the low end, popular fiction of the time includes pamphlets describing the last hours of notorious criminals such as *The Ordinary of Newgate: His Account of the Behaviour, Confessions, and Dying-Words of Captain William Kidd, and Other Pirates, That Were Executed at the Execution-Dock in Wapping, on Friday May 23, 1701* or of sensational contemporary criminal cases such as *The Whole Life and Conversation, Birth, Parentage and Education of Deborah Churchill; Condemn'd Some Time since for the Barbarous Murder of Mr. William Ware in Drury Lane* (1708), or elaborate criminal autobiographies such as Defoe's *Moll Flanders* (1722). Collections of criminal lives were also popular. Captain Alexander Smith's *History of the Lives and Robberies of the Most Noted Highway-Men, Foot-Pads, House-Breakers, Shop-Lifts and Cheats of Both Sexes in and about London and Westminster* (1713) ran to many editions, and Captain Charles Johnson (thought to be one of Defoe's pseudonyms) published in 1724 the enormously popular *History of the Pirates* in two volumes. Transgressive behavior among the powerful and the wealthy was the sensationally popular subject of Delarivier Manley's *The New Atalantis* (1709) and Eliza Haywood's imitation of Manley, *Memoirs of a Certain Island Adjacent to the Kingdom of Utopia* (1725), which presented in narrative format melodramatically exaggerated scandals about prominent politicians and aristocrats.

During the first three decades of the century, readers could choose from a steady stream of amatory tales by women writers, some fairly salacious and sensational such as the novels of the prolific Eliza Haywood (for example, *Love in Excess*, 1719–20;

Idalia; or, The Unfortunate Mistress, 1723; *Lasselia; or, The Self-Abandon'd*, 1723; *The Injur'd Husband; or, The Mistaken Resentment*, 1723). Haywood's novels harked back in their amatory intensity and notoriety to the works of Aphra Behn, whose novellas such as *History of the Nun; or, The Fair Vow-Breaker* (1689) and her long novel *Love Letters Between a Nobleman and His Sister* (1683–87) continued to be read and reissued into the early decades of the 18th century. Thanks to the works of Behn, Manley, and Haywood, as well as others, the female amatory novel had a dubious moral reputation. But some other women novelists in these decades produced edifying and strictly moral as well as romantic tales, such as Jane Barker's *Love Intrigues; or, The History of the Amours of Bosvil and Galesia* (1713) and *Exilius; or, The Banish'd Roman: A New Romance* (1715). Penelope Aubin's novels like *The Life of Madam de Beaumont* (1721), or *The Strange Adventures of the Count de Vinevil* (1721), or *The Life and Adventures of the Lady Lucy* (1726) added travel to exotic places and conflict with murderous foreigners to the thrills and intensities of romantic love. Still other women novelists from these years, like Mary Davys in *The Reform'd Coquet* (1724) and *The Accomplish'd Rake; or, Modern Fine Gentleman* (1727), mixed wit and comedy with amorous intrigue.

A separate and important strand of this market is travel narrative, some of which was factual, a genre that had been popular since Elizabethan times and the opening up of new worlds for conquest and exploration in the East Indies and the Americas. But the two most famous examples of this mode are completely fictional, Defoe's *Robinson Crusoe* (1719) and Jonathan Swift's *Gulliver's Travels* (1726). These two books, the most widely read prose narratives of the first half of the 18th century, illustrate in their significantly distinct approaches to character and meaning the emerging nature of what we now understand as the novel. Swift's book is a satire, and Gulliver the narrator is more of a device for conveying ideas than for dramatizing personality. Swift's book implies a knowing reader who can see through his narrator's inconsistencies and foolish pride in his own moral superiority, and ultimately *Gulliver's Travels* is a profound critique of the modern adventuring and inquiring spirit that stands behind the popularity of travel literature and the emergence of the novel. Based on the story of a marooned sailor, Alexander Selkirk, *Robinson Crusoe* is an exploration of a new kind of specifically modern heroism, and Defoe's hero is a narrator with whom readers are invited to identify rather than to criticize, a traveler who learns from his mistakes, who matures into a forceful character, a powerful and self-aware individual by the end of his 28-year stay on his island. *Robinson Crusoe* is a remarkable amalgam of two popular narrative patterns: the travel diary and the spiritual autobiography. Robinson the resourceful survivor is an embodiment of the expansive and assertive individualism Defoe celebrated in his nonfictional works, but he is also the descendant of John Bunyan's allegorical Christian in *Pilgrim's Progress* (1678, 1684), a guilty seeker after moral and religious certainty. However, in addition to representing guilty humanity, Crusoe is a psychologically particularized and historically specific individual, representative precisely by virtue of his uniqueness. Defoe's fictional narratives, a small part of his lifelong work as a writer, are a remarkable anticipation of the insights of the mature novel. In part, Defoe was exploiting popular narrative subjects likely to sell in the flourishing new publishing industry, and his

various narratives all pretend, like *Robinson Crusoe*, to be true, first-person accounts of the lives of racy characters designed to interest the new audience. *Captain Singleton* (1720) is a pirate's autobiography, and *Colonel Jack* (1722) as well as *Moll Flanders* are the memoirs of criminals that also feature travel to America and adventures in various parts of the world. So, too, *Roxana* (1724) is in part an imitation of contemporary scandalous romans à clef as it claims to trace the life of an actual courtesan during the reign of Charles II. Defoe's most successful characters, Crusoe, Moll Flanders, Roxana, are rooted in these popular themes, but each possesses an intense awareness of how identity is constructed and manipulated for profit and pleasure in social interactions. This awareness marks them as proto-novelistic.

If Defoe's narratives originate in his exploitation of the formulas of popular fiction, Samuel Richardson's pathbreaking *Pamela* (1740) derives its powerful originality from a moralizing revision of amatory patterns. Unlike the professional writers who produced the bulk of prose narrative in the first decades of the 18th century, Richardson was a prosperous printer who turned to writing fiction as an avocation to which he brought high moral purpose. *Pamela* is written in letters from the servant-girl heroine to her parents as she struggles to avoid the seductive arts of her master, Mr B.; its innovation is to make this correspondence not simply the expression of Pamela's moral determination to resist her master's advances but also the dramatization of the heroine's complex psychosexual self-assertion within a specifically evoked sociohistorical scene. Pamela the servant girl converts her would-be seducer and rapist into an adoring husband and graduates into the ruling gentry class. In the process of telling her story, Richardson rejects and refines the compulsive and melodramatic sexuality of the amatory tradition of Behn, Manley, and Haywood. Richardson's epistolary format fosters an illusion of immediacy and personal authenticity, although Pamela's letters also hold out the possibility that the heroine is an artful self-constructor who manipulates others by her talent for self-dramatization.

Most readers were charmed, and *Pamela* was an enormous success, but some rivals found the book's moral and artistic premises spurious. Eliza Haywood's *Anti-Pamela; or, Feign'd Innocence Detected* (1741) treats the heroine as a vicious hypocrite, a designing and predatory prostitute. Henry Fielding's *Shamela Andrews* (1741) is a brilliant parody that goes beyond merely exposing the artful hypocrisy and sexual voracity of the heroine and ridicules the immediacy of Richardson's novel and its vulgar conception of character. England's most successful comic playwright in the 1730s, Fielding was a professional writer with a classical education and a patrician if impecunious background. Forced to find other means of literary production when his theatre was closed by the Licensing Act of 1737 (enacted in response to his satirical attacks on the powerful prime minister Sir Robert Walpole), Fielding turned to writing fiction. *Joseph Andrews* (1742) continues the parody of *Pamela*, telling the story of her brother, Joseph, who struggles to avoid the sexual advances of his mistress, Lady Booby, and of his guide and companion, the eccentric but courageous and learned Parson Abraham Adams. In this novel and in its great successor, *Tom Jones* (1749), Fielding offers a comic panorama of mid-century English society. Both novels look back to Miguel de Cervantes' *Don Quixote* (1605–15) and to the picaresque tradition; both take their heroes on the roads of southern England, introduce a large cast of characters, and satirically encompass all levels of society. But in place of the intense individuality Richardson strove to evoke, Fielding prefers satiric generality in which his characters illustrate forms of comically recurrent behavior and act out universal human types. For the dramatic ventriloquizing and individualizing immediacy of *Pamela*, he substitutes an authoritative narrative voice that manipulates and arranges characters and incidents and engages in an implicit conversation with his readers about the meanings of his fiction. Fielding's first two novels are a mixture of satire and comic romance, with happy endings and marriages contrived by traditional plots in which villainy is defeated and order restored.

The new novel of the 1740s is mainly the creation of Fielding and Richardson, and their influence may be seen very clearly in the imitations of their manner produced by the indefatigable Eliza Haywood, who turned in these years from her short and intense amatory fictions to more elaborate and dilated picaresque fictions such as *The Fortunate Foundlings* (1744) and *Life's Progress Through the Passions; or, The Adventures of Natura* (1748), and the comic and domestic narratives of upper-middle-class life, such as *The History of Miss Betsy Thoughtless* (1751) and *The History of Jemmy and Jenny Jessamy* (1753). But Fielding's chief contemporary rival was the Scotsman Tobias Smollett, whose first two picaresque novels, *Roderick Random* (1748) and *Peregrine Pickle* (1751), are closer imitations of the violently brutal comedy of continental models like Paul Scarron's *Le Roman comique* (1651–57; *The Comic Romance*) and Alain René Le Sage's *Gil Blas* (1715–35). Episodic, unreflective, and featuring self-serving, brutal protagonists, Smollett's novels lack Fielding's rhetorical elegance and complex structure, but they are satirically powerful, expressing in vigorous prose their author's deep dissatisfaction with social inequities and moral corruption and punishing various villains in violent and sometimes scatological scenes. Like Fielding, Smollett's characters hark back to an older tradition of moral and social generality, but his early novels are populated with a collection of satiric grotesques and caricatures. His last and posthumously published novel, *The Expedition of Humphry Clinker* (1771), marks a distinct advance in plot and characterization, as the deforming energies of picaresque satire are exchanged for novelistic and historical complexity. Matt Bramble, a Welsh squire taking a revealing tour of Great Britain with his extended family, passes from eloquent outrage and disgust over modern life as he observes it in Bath and London to self-discovery and personal fulfillment in a plot that, like Fielding's, is derived from comic romance.

The single most important novel in the mid–18th century is Richardson's *Clarissa* (1747–48), a book that contemporaries (including Fielding) in England and in Europe almost immediately recognized with awe as an unprecedented masterpiece. Epistolary in format like *Pamela*, *Clarissa* features a large cast of correspondents and characters and pits the beautiful and forceful heroine, Clarissa Harlowe, against her aristocratic, rakish antagonist, Robert Lovelace. Designed by Richardson once again as a serious alternative to frivolous popular novels, *Clarissa* may be regarded as a Christian tragedy in which the heroine struggles with the moral dilemma of obeying her father while resisting his and her family's insistence that she marry an unwanted and unappealing suitor. At the same time, she is courted by the dashing Lovelace, who tricks her into running away from home with him

and attempts by various nefarious plots to seduce her. The result is an enormous novel (more than 1 million words) of unparalleled rhetorical richness, sociohistorical complexity, and psychosexual depth. Lovelace and Clarissa represent opposing classes, the aristocracy and the upper commercial bourgeoisie, but in their antagonism they also express opposing conceptions of personality and language, with Clarissa attempting to uphold the power of moral agency and integral selfhood against Lovelace's playful amorality and self-expressive linguistic and sexual freedom. Richardson's novel is more than realistic; it examines the nature of opposing forms of self-consciousness and dramatizes powerfully how individuals construct their identities out of available cultural and moral materials.

Isolated, persecuted, and suffering female virtue and resourceful and intelligent female resistance to patriarchal tyranny and sexual oppression such as *Clarissa* puts on view are the great themes of the English novel after mid-century. Fielding's final novel, *Amelia* (1751), shows the influence of Richardson and marks in its narrative form a drastic shift from the comic style and moral control of his earlier work to a darkly melodramatic domestic realism. *Amelia* is the history of a family caught up in a dangerously unjust world, as the heroine finds herself and her feckless husband, Captain Billy Booth, threatened on all sides by financial and sexual ruin at the hands of an aristocratic villain. In a corrupt world, Amelia is pure and steadfast in her loyalty and virtue, and Fielding's novel is centered on that image of specifically female heroism in a world of viciously possessive individualism. Less fortunate than the Booths, who in the end are rescued and restored to prosperity thanks to a lucky twist of fate, is the heroine of Frances Sheridan's *Memoirs of Miss Sidney Bidulph* (1761). In long letters by the main characters, Sheridan's novel traces the heroine's disastrously unhappy marriage and the complicated circumstances of her thwarted love for the deserving Orlando Faulkland. Sidney is an icon of patient and heroically passive female suffering, and Sheridan's novel, in the unrelenting string of calamities it arranges for her, assumes an audience for whom this spectacle is edifying and instructive.

The other side of the coin of female heroism in the 18th-century novel is active resistance to patriarchal domination. Arabella, the heroine of Charlotte Lennox's *The Female Quixote* (1752), has been raised in bookish isolation and leisure-class privilege, and she is literally convinced that the heroic amatory world of French 17th-century romances is identical to her mid-18th-century domestic reality. Lennox's book looks both ways: her heroine is both satiric target and feminist champion, resisting in the name of heroic romance the demands of her world that she enter the normal world of female submission to marriage and domesticity. This double view of female cultural and moral identity dominates the work of the best of the women novelists of the 18th century, Frances Burney. Her first novel, *Evelina; or, The History of a Young Lady's Entrance into the World* (1778), features a heroine who, in her long letters to her guardian, observes the London social scene with hilarious comic accuracy but who in her participation in that scene is timid and passive until she is rescued by her aristocratic lover, Lord Orville. Burney's second novel, *Cecilia; or, The Memoirs of an Heiress* (1782), anticipates the Victorian novel in its complex plot and its exploration of the weight of financial and social pressures on the individual. Both of Burney's heroines are caught in the dilemma of reconciling their own moral agency and intelligence with the requirements of female passivity and delicacy.

Women writers achieved prominence and even dominance in the production of novels after the mid-century and, as recent critics and historians have pointed out, in the new commercial capitalist and consumerist order the male personality, traditionally bent on crude and egocentric sensual pleasures, was softened and refined, partly by widely available "luxury" goods experienced in a domestic context, and partly by the "civilizing" effects of the new financial world in which traditional ideals of masculine aggression and self-assertion were replaced by passions, fantasies, and anxieties regarded as feminine. In addition, the novel is affected by the shift in ethical understanding that makes moral action and knowledge essentially emotional rather than rational. In the 1760s, a new kind of "sentimental" hero emerges who embodies this new, feminized masculinity and intense moral feeling. A particularly lachrymose example is the hero of Sarah Fielding's *David Simple* (1744–53), whose benevolent efforts bring him and his friends and family to an affectingly disastrous end. Henry Mackenzie's *The Man of Feeling* (1771) is the century's best known example of the sentimental mode. Mackenzie's Harley is a tearful observer of human misery whose character is defined by his intense sympathy for others. Sympathy like Harley's is supplemented by heroic philanthropy in some sentimental novels, notably Richardson's third novel, *Sir Charles Grandison* (1753–54), whose hero is a prodigy of feeling and of reforming moral action.

The great master of sentimental narrative is Laurence Sterne, whose *Tristram Shandy* (1759–67) and *A Sentimental Journey* (1768) are at once celebrations of sentimental values and sharply satirical of the self-indulgent privilege they depend upon. *Tristram Shandy* is much more, however, than a sentimental novel, and the hero's comic exploration of his past experiences, beginning with his conception, is a satire with continuing resonance on the aspirations of the novel as a form to understand the nature of personality and to express individuality. Tristram, his father, Walter, and his uncle Toby are caught up in their solipsistic pursuits, and their humanity as Sterne renders it is defined by eccentricity and an isolation interrupted only by sympathetic fellow feeling. The sentimental novel, even in Sterne's satiric rendering of it, marks a retreat from the social and historical realism and moral complexity of the mid–18th century, a retreat that would find its logical extreme in the Gothic novels of Horace Walpole (*The Castle of Otranto*, 1764), Clara Reeve (*The Old English Baron*, 1777), Charlotte Smith (*Emmeline; or, The Orphan of the Castle*, 1788), Matthew G. Lewis (*The Monk*, 1796), and Ann Radcliffe (*The Mysteries of Udolpho*, 1794), where the atmosphere is dreamlike and where supernatural or temporarily mysterious events dominate a universe of pathological characters in exotic or foreign settings. In the course of the 18th century, the social-historical and moral ambitions of the novels of Richardson and Fielding give way to the Gothic novel's exploration of the mysteries of aberrant individuality and extreme psychological states.

JOHN RICHETTI

See also Aphra Behn; Critics and Criticism (18th Century); Daniel Defoe; Epistolary Novel; Evelina; Henry Fielding; Gothic Novel; Gulliver's Travels; Journalism and the Novel; Libraries; Mysteries of Udolpho; Novel of Manners; Picaresque; Pilgrim's Progress; Prose Novelistic Forms; Samuel Richardson; Romance; Sentimental Novel; Laurence Sterne; Vicar of Wakefield

Further Reading

Ballaster, Ros, *Seductive Forms: Women's Amatory Fiction from 1684 to 1740*, Oxford: Clarendon Press, and New York: Oxford University Press, 1992

Bender, John, *Imagining the Penitentiary: Fiction and the Architecture of Mind in Eighteenth-Century England*, Chicago: University of Chicago Press, 1987

Davis, Lennard, *Factual Fictions: The Origins of the English Novel*, New York: Columbia University Press, 1983

Haggerty, George, *Gothic Fiction/Gothic Form*, University Park: Pennsylvania State University Press, 1989

Hunter, J. Paul, *Before Novels: The Cultural Contexts of Eighteenth-Century English Fiction*, New York: Norton, 1990

McKeon, Michael, *The Origins of the English Novel, 1600–1740*, Baltimore: Johns Hopkins University Press, 1987; London: Raduis, 1988

Mullan, John, *Sentiment and Sociability: The Language of Feeling in the Eighteenth Century*, Oxford: Clarendon Press, and New York: Oxford University Press, 1988

Paulson, Ronald, *Satire and the Novel in Eighteenth-Century England*, New Haven, Connecticut: Yale University Press, 1967

Probyn, Clive T., *English Fiction of the Eighteenth Century, 1700–1789*, London and New York: Longman, 1987

Richetti, John J., *Popular Fiction Before Richardson: Narrative Patterns, 1700–1739*, Oxford: Clarendon Press, 1969; New York: Oxford University Press, 1992

Richetti, John, editor, *The Cambridge Companion to the Eighteenth-Century Novel*, Cambridge and New York: Cambridge University Press, 1996

Spacks, Patricia Ann Meyer, *Desire and Truth: Functions of Plot in Eighteenth-Century English Novels*, Chicago: University of Chicago Press, 1990

Spencer, Jane, *The Rise of the Woman Novelist: From Aphra Behn to Jane Austen*, Oxford and New York: Blackwell, 1986

Todd, Janet, *The Sign of Angellica: Women, Writing, and Fiction, 1660–1800*, London: Virago, and New York: Columbia University Press, 1989

Tompkins, J.M.S., *The Popular Novel in England, 1770–1800*, London: Methuen, 1932; reprinted, Lincoln: University of Nebraska Press, 1961

Watt, Ian, *The Rise of the Novel: Studies in Defoe, Richardson, and Fielding*, Berkeley: University of California Press, and London: Chatto and Windus, 1957

English Novel

1800–1840

Although long regarded as a relatively barren period for the novel, the years from 1800 to 1840 saw major developments in the novel and its place in literature, culture, and society in England. Readers and writers turned against the overtly political use of the novel in the 1790s following the French Revolution. Most critics continued to express concern for the moral, intellectual, and social effects of novel reading even as the efforts of many novelists began to raise the artistic, moral, and intellectual status of the novel as a genre. Many commentators still associated the novel with women as writers and readers, and undervalued it accordingly; yet women continued to pioneer in the thematic and formal development of the novel. Novelists continued to rework old forms while developing new ones, and the readership for the novel, and consequently its ideological, social, cultural, and political influence, continued to increase and broaden. Publishers were increasingly adventurous in exploiting the vogue for novel reading and its association with fashionable upper-class life. Finally, a wide range of moral, religious, and social reformers turned increasingly, if warily, to the novel in order to disseminate their views.

In 1800, novels were the most widely read form of print after newspapers. This was because they provided readers with cultural and social capital, or knowledge of the contemporary social and cultural scene that was useful in forming business, professional, and personal relationships. The readership for novels was dominated by the professional middle class, and although it was claimed that women comprised a large proportion of this readership, men read novels as much as or more than women did. New novels were usually called "modern novels" or "novels of the day" to distinguish them from earlier forms of prose fiction simply called novels, which were usually shorter and dealt with amorous intrigue.

Publishers developed various physical formats and pricing levels to exploit every level of the market for modern novels. The dominant format continued to be the "circulating-library novel," bought mainly by commercial circulating libraries for rental to subscribers at a certain fee per volume per night. This form of distribution encouraged issuing novels in several volumes, usually three (the "triple-decker"), so that the circulating library could maximize the return on an individual work. Otherwise, "novels of the day" were expensive to purchase, a triple-decker costing about two weeks' wages for an unskilled worker. Sometimes novels were bought and circulated among a small group who formed a local reading club to spread the cost. In either case, most "novels of the day" were not considered suitable, on grounds of both cost and content, to be owned and reread. After the ending of perpetual copyright in the 1770s, however, publishers marketed reprint series, first of established "literary" forms such as poetry, essays, and drama, and finally of novels. A reprint novel was about one-fourth the price of a triple-decker "novel of the day" and was designed for a genteel personal library and for rereading, as a literary classic or "standard" work. To reduce the unit price even further, some publishers issued reprint novels in ever less expensive serial parts or in magazine form, tending to include more of the sensational kinds of novel,

such as the Gothic. Like the other reprint genres, reprint novels marketed as "classics" were also linked to the emergent institution of "national" literature, with series titles such as *The British Novelists* (1805).

Despite—or because of—its popularity, the novel continued to be widely regarded as mere entertainment, or worse. Many considered the novel dangerously unrealistic and stimulating to the imagination, appealing to the undereducated, including children, women, and the lower classes, and a potential distraction from the "solid" and "useful" reading necessary to equip a young man for professional life and a young woman for professionalized domesticity. The popularity of the novel made many consider it ephemeral and rarely of enduring literary value, conveying information about the fashion system and thus encouraging the commercialization of culture and dangerous social emulation. Many critics portrayed novel reading as an addiction like drinking or gambling, and some blamed it for encouraging errors and vices ranging from romantic fantasies to adultery and prostitution. Nevertheless, the novel's popularity resulted in considerable experiment and innovation as publishers and writers sought new ways to catch the reading public's interest, and some writers resisted commercialization of the novel for political and artistic reasons. The most successful subgenres of the novel, however, were developed from established forms.

Several varieties were based on the dominant form of the late 18th century—the novel of manners, sentiment, and emulation. Such novels represented manners as conduct in contemporary life among the upper class and those in the middle classes who emulated them, thereby serving the aspiration for upward social mobility in the relatively open society of England. Such novels necessarily represented sentiment because a particular culture of the subjective self, or sensibility, was a sign of refinement and thus implied membership in the dominant class. It was also a sign of nobility of soul rather than nobility of birth or rank, thereby challenging historic categories of social identity and status.

One variety of the novel of manners comprised "tales of fashionable life" and "silver-fork novels," so called because of their preoccupation with upper-class society and the fashion system. Such novels also had a critical purpose. Thomas Surr's *A Winter in London; or, Sketches of Fashion* (1806) contrasts the self-indulgent upper class with professionalized men and women; it went through six editions during its year of publication. Maria Edgeworth's *Tales of Fashionable Life* (6 vols., 1809–12) criticizes the irresponsibility of English and Irish upper classes during a period of internal social conflict and external military threat. Fashionable antisocial Byronism was added to the novel of manners in the 1820s, producing works such as Benjamin Disraeli's *Vivian Grey* (5 vols., 1826–27) and Edward Bulwer-Lytton's *Pelham* (1828). Women writers placed the female protagonist at the center in further adaptations, including Maria Edgeworth's *Helen* (1834) and the novels of Catherine Gore and Margaret Power, Countess Blessington.

Although seemingly dissimilar to the novel of manners, the Gothic novel resembled it in key respects. The Gothic novel, which developed during the later 18th century, was usually classified as romance rather than novel because it often was written in an elevated style and because it represented exotic times, places, or cultures, employing extravagant characters in improbable or even supernatural events. These differences form the focus of critiques of the Gothic such as Jane Austen's *Northanger Abbey* (1818). In fact, the Gothic romance is the novel of manners in historical dress, and it, too, fictionalized actual social tensions and conflicts between the middle classes and both the decadent aristocracy and politicized lower classes from the 1790s to the 1820s. Significantly, the Gothic romance enjoyed its major vogue during this same period.

After Ann Radcliffe's pioneering romances of the early 1790s, M.G. "Monk" Lewis turned the form in a more erotic and extravagant direction with *The Monk* (1796)—hence his nickname. The Gothic novel after 1800 also appropriated elements of the political romances of the 1790s, for the reading public turned from overtly propagandistic political fiction after the intense French Revolution debate of the 1790s. Foremost among these elements was the politicized picaresque plot of "adventures of flight and pursuit," enacting the harassment and persecution of a social transgressor against the unjust system of "things as they are" (the original title of the prototype politicized Gothic, William Godwin's *Caleb Williams,* 1794). Other elements include the mysterious and menacing persecutor, representing established power; social isolation of the protagonist; settings in buildings, including prisons, that symbolize the oppressive social and political order; scenes of trials or tribunals, often involving oppressive institutions such as the Inquisition; and the intrusion of the public and political sphere in the idealized domestic sphere. These elements were used not only in Gothic romances after 1800 but also in related forms of the novel. At the same time, various burlesque and comic novels offered spirited resistance to this kind of Gothic.

The task of both the politicized Gothic and its parodies, however, was to sustain reformist social critique without inciting revolution. For example, Charlotte Dacre's Gothic extravaganza, *Zofloya; or, The Moor* (1806), opens by invoking Godwin's political principles and goes on to critique aristocratic arrogance and decadence. This novel was imitated in Percy Shelley's even more extravagant Gothic romance, *Zastrozzi* (1810). E.S. Barrett tried to stem the tide of politicized Gothic with his burlesque novel *The Heroine* (1813), an adaptation of the quixote tradition that had informed counter-revolutionary novels in the 1790s. Thomas Love Peacock's *Nightmare Abbey* (1818) moved the object of burlesque from revolutionary to romantic idealism, hypocrisy, and bombast. Frances Burney, the leading novelist of manners before 1800, incorporated Gothic elements of flight and pursuit in her last novel, *The Wanderer* (1814), which also draws in events of the French Revolution embodied in a Gothic villain. Godwin himself returned to the politicized Gothic with *Mandeville* (1817). His daughter Mary Shelley's *Frankenstein* (1818) turned the politicized Gothic into myth and a critical reflection on revolutionary idealism and postrevolutionary and romantic individualism. C.R. Maturin's *Melmoth the Wanderer* (1820) is the culmination of extravagant Gothic novel form; it is also a critique of oppressive ideology and institutions. James Hogg's *Private Memoirs and Confessions of a Justified Sinner* (1824) uses the Gothic supernatural in a critique of Walter's Scott's conservative Tory historical novels.

By the early 1820s, however, the need to be ever more sensa-tional was yielding diminishing returns. In the late 1820s and the 1830s, elements of the Gothic were incorporated in related kinds of fiction, such as the silver-fork novel and the "Newgate novel." The Newgate novel, named after a large prison in London, deals with the criminal underworld as a scene of Gothic mystery and conspiracy, exemplified in Edward Bulwer-Lytton's *Paul Clifford* (1830), Charles Dickens' *Oliver Twist* (1838), and W.H. Ainsworth's *Jack Sheppard* (1839). At about the same time, the Gothic romance as such descended the fiction market in the form of cheap sensational "shilling shockers" and "Salisbury Square fiction" (after a center of their publication in London).

The Gothic romance, Byronic silver-fork novel, and Newgate novel were related to an early 19th-century development of the long tradition of the picaresque novel, or novel of adventure. Earlier forms emphasized action and incident; early 19th-century forms also developed representation of the protagonist's subjective self. This form was also related to the earlier novel of education, sometimes called by the German term Bildungsroman. The prorevolutionary novelists of the 1790s, led by Godwin and his friend Thomas Holcroft, adapted the picaresque novel and novel of education to expose the corruption of "things as they are" and to show the protagonist's education to include an understanding of oppression. Counterrevolutionary novelists used the same form to expose revolutionary idealism and hypocrisy and to show the protagonist's education to "real life." Novelists after 1800 were less overtly political but continued to use the picaresque Bildungsroman to promote professional middle-class ideology and values and to attack both upper-class decadence and lower-class improvidence. Such novels include Godwin's *Fleetwood* (1805) and his later novels; Edgeworth's "Ennui" (from *Tales of Fashionable Life,* 1809) and *Harrington and Ormond* (1817); Pierce Egan's popular picaresque novel, *Life in London* (1821); Scott's historical novels; Byronic silver-fork and Newgate novels; and novels by Frederick Marryat, W.H. Ainsworth, G.P.R. James, and Charles Dickens.

In contrast to all subgenres of the novel described so far were the many domestic tales and novels of common life published after 1800. These were adaptations of the late 18th-century novels of sensibility, which emphasize subjective experience in domestic and common life, represent class conflict as the oppression of the "simple" and "natural" by the sophisticated and courtly, and use techniques considered simple and natural in relatively short texts, in contrast to the sophistication, complexity, elaboration, and greater length of novels of manners. The success of Harriet and Sophia Lee's *Canterbury Tales* (1798–1803) led to many imitations. In her early national tale, *Castle Rackrent* (1800), Maria Edgeworth uses the first-person narration and idiosyncratic style of the 18th-century French *conte,* as well as elements of the oral folk narrative. Amelia Opie's melodramatic and sensational one-volume domestic tale, *The Father and Daughter* (1801), was highly popular and launched Opie's career as a fiction writer; such collections as *Simple Tales* (1806), *Tales of Real Life* (1813), and *Tales of the Heart* (1820) followed. A different form of the tale or novella was the collection *Sayings and Doings* (9 vols., 1824–28) by the humorist Theodore Hook. A major appropriator of this line of the novel was Charles Dickens, from *The Pickwick Papers* (1837) on.

The domestic tale was related to other subgenres in its emphasis on domestic and local common life and its techniques of psychological and familiar realism. One of these subgenres was the national tale or regional novel, discussed later in relation to the historical novel. Another was the tale for youth, developed by writers such as Mary Sherwood and Barbara Hofland in scores of tales and novels. Another highly influential form of the domestic tale was based on the anecdote or sketch. Elizabeth Le Noir's little known *Village Anecdotes* (1804) represents the kind of class struggle that many thought led to the French Revolution, but in terms of the self-reform of the lower middle class in an English village. Hannah More attempted the domestic tale in two-volume novel form in her evangelical counter to the novel of manners, *Cœlebs in Search of a Wife* (1808). The novels of Jane Austen and Susan Ferrier participate to some degree in this subgenre. The form's most influential example, however, was Mary Mitford's *Our Village* (1824–32), which has gone into many editions to the present day and which influenced the modern idea of rural England as idyllic, harmonious, and pervaded by middle-class culture. This body of fiction provided the basis for such didactic tales as Harriet Martineau's series, *Illustrations of Political Economy* (9 vols., 1832–34), and for Victorian novels of rural, domestic, and provincial life by Elizabeth Gaskell, George Eliot, Thomas Hardy, and many others.

The most widely influential and respected form of prose fiction in this period, however, was the historical novel. Novels and plays with loosely historical settings had been produced since at least the 17th century. They addressed the increasingly widespread view that real life occurred not in the public political sphere but in subjective and domestic experience, which historiography conventionally ignored but which the novel emphasized. The historical novel also borrowed elements of the Gothic romance, such as settings remote in time or place, contrast of characters, romance plots, and liberal use of description. The Gothic supernatural is dropped and more care is taken with historical accuracy, including prefaces, footnotes, and appendices. Typically, historical novels use historical characters and events as background for the adventures of fictitious characters. This practice was controversial at the time, some claiming that it debased history and others claiming that it made history more attractive to readers.

Women writers such as Jane Porter and Sydney Owenson (later Lady Morgan) first developed the historical novel and a variety called the "biographical romance." Walter Scott then devised its most influential form. His first novel, *Waverley; or, 'Tis Sixty Years Since* (1814), uses the Jacobite rebellion of 1745 as an analogy for the regional, social, political, and religious divisions in the United Kingdom of Great Britain and Ireland, revealed by the tensions and conflicts of the long revolutionary and Napoleonic struggle. In the novels and tales that followed, known collectively as the Waverley novels, Scott explored other historical analogies to the present. He first concentrated on Scottish history, with novels such as *The Antiquary* (1816), *Rob Roy* (1817), and *The Heart of Mid-Lothian* (1818). He then moved beyond Scotland and its history, with *Ivanhoe* (1819), set in medieval England. He then explored a series of medieval, Renaissance, and near contemporaneous settings in England, Scotland, and continental Europe (*The Monastery*, 1820; *Redgauntlet*, 1824; *Anne of Geierstein*, 1829), and even Palestine (*The Talisman*, 1825) and Byzantium (*Count Robert of Paris*, 1832). There was resistance to Scott's version of history and the historical novel,

especially from James Hogg in such novels as *The Brownie of Bodsbeck* (1818) and *Private Memoirs and Confessions of a Justified Sinner*, and Mary Shelley in such novels as *Valperga* (1823) and *The Adventures of Perkin Warbeck* (1830).

Nevertheless, Scott's form of the historical novel became the dominant one, not only in England and Britain but throughout Europe and beyond. This was partly owing to the way Scott steadily shaped the Waverley novels into a modern literary monument, marketing successive editions and sets at different prices, culminating in the revised, annotated, and elegantly illustrated Magnum Opus edition, sold serially at five shillings per monthly volume. The feat was widely imitated, and almost single-handedly Scott raised the modern novel to literary status. More important, Scott's form of the historical novel was imitated in many countries by writers eager to invent their own nations' identity, history, and destiny, led by a coalition of upper and professional middle classes.

Related to the historical novel was the regional novel, often called the national tale. This subgenre was one of Scott's sources for the Waverley novels, especially the work of Maria Edgeworth in her Irish tales, including *Castle Rackrent*, *The Absentee* (from *Tales of Fashionable Life*), and *Ormond*. Lady Morgan also promoted Irish culture in novels such as *The Wild Irish Girl* (1806), *O'Donnel* (1814), *Florence Macarthy* (1818), and *The O'Briens and the O'Flahertys* (1827). Morgan extended her representation of national identity beyond Ireland to Greece (*Ida of Athens*, 1809) and India (*The Missionary*, 1811). Even before Scott's *Waverley* was published, Elizabeth Hamilton produced a highly popular and highly moralistic representation of Scottish provincial life in her *Cottagers of Glenburnie* (1808). John Galt represented Scottish provincial society and culture under the impact of modernization and thus, like Scott, appealed to a readership beyond Scotland, with novels such as *Annals of the Parish* (1821), *The Provost* (1822), and *The Entail* (1822). The growing interest in what was later called folklore was appropriated by Edgeworth, Morgan, and Scott, and by William Carleton in *Tales and Stories of the Irish Peasantry* (1830; second series, 1833) and Samuel Lover in *Legends and Stories of Ireland* (2 vols., 1831–34) and *Rory O'More* (1837). Although much of this material deals with the outer regions of the new United Kingdom, the intended readership was English because the English controlled the destinies of the periphery of this composite nation state.

This periphery was in a sense the bridge to the wider empire, and the national tale and novel of local and provincial life had an important variant, addressing the reading public's interest in foreign lands and cultures of concern to Britain's international and imperial situation. Britain's interests in the Middle and Far East were represented in such novels as Lady Morgan's *The Missionary: An Indian Tale* (1811), Thomas Hope's *Anastasius; or, Memoirs of a Greek* (1819), Scott's crusader novels, Lady Caroline Lamb's Orientalist extravaganza *Ada Reis* (1823), and James Morier's novels, beginning with *Adventures of Hajjī Baba* (1823) and extending into the 1840s. The New World was also represented, mainly through the historical novels of the American James Fenimore Cooper, from *The Spy* (1821) to *The Deerslayer* (1841), which were popular in England and almost regarded as English novels.

Perhaps the final frontier of the novel during the first half of the 19th century was its boundary with other genres. Because of the novel's popularity, several writers used the novel as a frame to set for subject matters, themes, and discourses that in fact dominated the frame. In John Thelwall's *The Peripatetic* (1793), for example, a variety of essays and poems are included in a philosophical picaresque form designed to popularize reformist philosophy for politicized artisan and lower middle-class readers. Elizabeth Hamilton presented women's history in lightly novelized form in her *Memoirs of the Life of Agrippina, the Wife of Germanicus* (1804). The antiquarian Thomas Frognall Dibdin constructed an extravaganza of scholarship in *Bibliomania; or, Book Madness: A Bibliographical Romance* (1809; expanded in 1811 and again in 1842). The poet Thomas Moore published a series of Orientalist poems in the framework of a novel in his *Lalla Rookh: An Oriental Romance* (1817). John Wilson's series of humorous sketches, often in dialogue form, presents a wide range of literary and cultural criticism in novel form as "Noctes Ambrosianae" in *Blackwood's Magazine* from 1822 to 1835. Some of these works achieved a wide readership; others did not, and were not meant to; but all show the activity and inventiveness of the novel in England (or of the novel destined to reach an English readership) and its relation with other discourses in the first four decades of the 19th century.

GARY KELLY

See also Adventure Novel and Imperial Romance; Jane Austen; Caleb Williams; Charles Dickens; Maria Edgeworth; Frankenstein; Gothic Novel; Historical Novel; Historical Writing and the Novel; Irish Novel; Libraries; National Tale; Novel of Manners; Periodicals and the Serialization of Novels; Picaresque; Private Memoirs and Confessions of a Justified Sinner; Regional Novel; Romance; Romantic Novel; Sir Walter Scott; Scottish Novel

Further Reading

Adams, Percy G., *Travel Literature and the Evolution of the Novel,* Lexington: University Press of Kentucky, 1983

Darton, F.J. Harvey, *Children's Books in England: Five Centuries of Social Life,* Cambridge: Cambridge University Press, 1932; 3rd edition, revised by Brian Alderson, Cambridge and New York: Cambridge University Press, 1982

Duncan, Ian, *Modern Romance and Transformations of the Novel: The Gothic, Scott, Dickens,* Cambridge and New York: Cambridge University Press, 1992

Hollingsworth, Keith, *The Newgate Novel 1830–1847,* Detroit, Michigan: Wayne State University Press, 1963

Kelly, Gary, *The English Jacobin Novel, 1780–1805,* Oxford and New York: Clarendon Press, 1976

Kelly, Gary, *English Fiction of the Romantic Period, 1789–1830,* London and New York: Longman, 1989

Kiely, Robert, *The Romantic Novel in England,* Cambridge, Massachusetts: Harvard University Press, 1972

Klancher, Jon P., *The Making of English Reading Audiences, 1790–1832,* Madison: University of Wisconsin Press, 1987

Lukács, Georg, *A történelmi regény,* Budapest: Hungaria, 1937; as *The Historical Novel,* London: Merlin Press, 1962; New York: Humanities Press, 1965

Mayo, Robert Donald, *The English Novel in the Magazines, 1740–1815,* Evanston: Northwestern University Press, 1962

Punter, David, *The Literature of Terror: A History of Gothic Fictions from 1765 to the Present Day,* London and New York: Longman, 1980; 2nd edition, 1996

Trumpener, Katie, *Bardic Nationalism: The Romantic Novel and the British Empire,* Princeton, New Jersey: Princeton University Press, 1997

Varma, Devendra P., *The Evergreen Tree of Diabolical Knowledge* (on circulating libraries), Washington, D.C.: Consortium Press, 1972

Wilt, Judith, *Secret Leaves: The Novels of Walter Scott,* Chicago: University of Chicago Press, 1985

English Novel

1840–1880

British novels published between 1840 and 1880 often are grouped together under the title "Victorian," as if some essential identity derived from having been published during the long reign of the person George Eliot called "our little humbug of a queen." The durability of such groupings probably is equal to their arbitrariness. And to be accurate, "Victorian novel" properly should refer to everything written between 1837 and 1901, a period beginning before the development of railways and ending after the invention of radio and the airplane. The identification of the period with an individual establishes the importance of individuals as cultural points of reference, but it says little about narrative.

The novels of the period 1840–80 belong to at least two distinct cultural epochs with a watershed somewhere in mid-century. Through the 1840s, second-rank novelists like Edward George Bulwer-Lytton and major writers like Charles Dickens maintain the episodic, picaresque character of 18th-century narrative forms like satire and the epistolary novel. Those forms made no effort whatever to provide the transparent omniscient narration that emulates the voice of the objective historian that later novelists almost unanimously favor. Dickens' major novels of the 1840s—*The Old Curiosity Shop* (1840–41), *Martin Chuzzlewit* (1844), and *Dombey and Son* (1848)—all employ with increasing sophistication the episodic and picaresque forms he had used so brilliantly a decade earlier in *The Pickwick Papers* (1837). Dickens did not essentially modify his approach until *David Copperfield* (1850). With the exception of *The History of Henry Esmond* (1852), William Makepeace Thackeray relied on the traditions of satire throughout his career.

The *annus mirabilis* of the decade was 1847, the year that saw publication of Dickens' *Dombey and Son* (serially), *Vanity Fair* (serially), and, in an achievement that still seems larger than life, three masterpieces by the Brontës, Anne coming out with *Agnes Grey*, Charlotte with *Jane Eyre*, and Emily with *Wuthering Heights*. In spite of their differences, all these books rely on narrative strategies informed by long-standing religious traditions and narrative forms. They link the workings of providence with the definitions of nature and of human motivation, and their episodic forms have a moral thrust. Behind two of the most continuingly successful books of the entire century, *Vanity Fair* and *Jane Eyre*, lies John Bunyan's *Pilgrim's Progress* (1678, 1684).

Although novelists continued to resort to the older forms, the ideas upon which these forms were predicated were undergoing radical change. Across Europe, 19th-century writers were engaged in redefining fundamental ideas of identity and social order and in giving positive value and currency to terms like "self" and "society," which, even as late as the mid–19th century, came trailing values from a not too distant feudal order. Whereas traditionally the term "society" indicated a set of positions in a hierarchy that presented itself as a natural phenomenon, by the 19th century it had come to indicate a self-contained and self-determining system, in which social difference has no stable hierarchical function and has to be entirely renegotiated. Something similar happens to the term "human": once spelled "humane" and distinguishing the fallen or mundane world from the divine and redeemed one, by the 19th century "human" had become primarily a label of the species and an inscription of belief in the principle that positively includes all individuals in a social group.

So, when interpreting novels like *Vanity Fair* or Charlotte Brontë's *Villette* (1853), it is dangerous to use terms like "self" and "society" and "human" as if current usage corresponds to that of the mid–19th century when novelists, among others, were beginning to experiment in their books with such new discursive configurations. Charlotte Brontë treats "self" in *Jane Eyre* as a threatening evil, much as Jane Austen does in *Emma* (1815) and Defoe did a century earlier in *Robinson Crusoe* (1719). Jane Eyre's lack of a specifically "social" identity, far from being the disadvantage it would be for a young woman in Anthony Trollope or George Eliot, actually signals her moral strength and her capacity for salvation. Blanche Ingram's "social" investment in *Jane Eyre* is a symptom of her sinfulness in a moral universe where "society" is a term describing a particular niche in a hierarchy; the term carried none of the inclusive value that it has developed since the republican revolutions of the late 18th century—revolutions that in any case were not carried out in England.

Something changed abruptly at mid-century. The great novels of the 1850s by Charles Dickens (*David Copperfield*, begun in 1849; *Bleak House*, 1853; and *Little Dorrit*, 1857), Elizabeth Gaskell (*North and South*, 1855), Anthony Trollope (*Barchester Towers*, 1857; *Doctor Thorne* and *The Three Clerks*, both 1858), and George Eliot (*Adam Bede*, 1859) rely on assumptions that move away from the episodic moral survey and toward historical and social causalities. These novels of the 1850s differ strikingly in their narrative strategy and cultural assumptions from the traditions still widely disseminated only ten years before. Among the masterpieces of the 1850s only Charlotte Brontë's *Villette* stands as a reminder of an older tradition.

To fathom what accounts for this change must be, again, to fathom a complex set of discursive arrangements evident across culture from economics to novels, and from political philosophy to railways. Although the radiating influences of revolution (or fear of it) across the board—in banking, demography, industrialization, politics—all belong to a common historical moment or what might be called a cultural ecosystem, it would be impossible to summarize in a single explanation how those influences work. Without lapsing into merely "literary" causalities and mindful of the political history of Europe in the 1840s, we can say with some license that one major impetus behind the changes was the publication of Walter Scott's first novel, *Waverley; or, 'Tis Sixty Years Since*, in 1814. Scott provided for revolutionary Europe a new narrative model for new social conditions. His astonishing achievement was celebrated internationally during his lifetime, but his inheritance didn't really "take" in England until after 1850, when his immediate heirs, especially Anthony Trollope and George Eliot, began to publish their novels. While Scott may not be said to have changed the novel single-handedly, he had a primary role—none more so—in shaping the terms by which general cultural reformations taking place in his time were conceived and understood in narrative fiction.

Waverley deals with the problems of establishing a common culture out of social units that no longer have their traditional hierarchical function. What Scott provided, in a word, was history, a presumptively objective common experience of past events that has become a convention of thinking about identity and sequence that is so fundamental to humanist and empiricist culture that it presents itself as a condition of "normal" sight and consciousness. Yet in 1814 it was far from "normal," and it took a long time to be broadly disseminated. That dissemination was aided by other 19th-century developments of historical thinking such as Charles Lyell's *Principles of Geology* (1830–33); Charles Darwin's *The Origin of Species* (1859); the Higher Criticism in theology that emphasized the historical Jesus over the miracle worker; the many published personal "histories" of conversion; and the endless anxious publications about the drift away from traditional practices that required people more continuously to mind the gaps between present and past.

By putting the historical convention foremost, Scott may be said to have revolutionized the tools of narrative explanation. The construction of history as a social common denominator remains the most characteristic and powerful achievement of 19th-century novels across Europe, although each national tradition developed the convention at different times. In France, Stendhal had already published his masterpieces, *Le Rouge et le noir* (1830; *The Red and the Black*) while George III was still on the English throne and *La Chartreuse de Parme* (1839; *The Charterhouse of Parma*) before Victoria married Prince Albert. It took another decade in England for the values and strategies of the historical convention to become broadly disseminated. In Russia it was another decade later still that Lev Tolstoi took a leaf from George Eliot's notebook.

The historical novel, in England as elsewhere, includes not just books with antiquarian content (content defines little), but books written according to certain principles. Chief among them is the principle that identity is not given and absolute, but emerges serially. This principle appears in various forms in other arts, in sciences, in mathematics during the era of humanist enterprise begun at the Renaissance. But by the 19th century the principle has entered the arena of personal and social redefinition. "In" history all sorts of social problems—problems of corporate order and personal identity—appear in a new light because they appear serially. "In" history, social problems that might once have appeared immutable, god-given, now appear susceptible to recuperation, restoration, revision, repair. "In" history, personal identity always is growing and capable of new definitions.

While the cultural and intellectual tools for this achievement had been available for several centuries, since the era of Renaissance humanism, they were long occupied in other media and at other tasks. The tradition of humanist representation, whether in art or in politics or even in mathematics, already had flourished for more than 400 years when, in the early 19th century, realist, historical narratives explore the *social* implications of that tradition.

Historical thinking remains a convention so much at the heart of cultural narrative in European societies that we tend to miss its extraordinary artificiality: an artifice that claims to have no artifice, but to be "simply" a window on the world. Such narratives acted for 19th-century England almost like experimental laboratories for defining and exploring a new construction of corporate order. English culture was newly intent upon—if not necessarily committed to—the political and social forms of democracy and on their relation to structures of obligation inherited from an older religious tradition and translated especially into economic terms by Adam Smith and his early 19th-century followers, David Ricardo and Thomas Malthus. The new values circulating through novels between 1840 and 1880 belong to a cultural problematic with many facets and expressed very broadly in domestic, gender, political, economic, technological, artistic arrangements.

Historical conventions accomplish a transformation of the most fundamental perceptions and definitions, and the major 19th-century novelists all call attention primarily to that potentiality conceived, not as Aristotle conceived the potentiality of acorns to become oaks, but as Lyell and Darwin conceived the potentiality of forms to mutate out of recognition into something new. (In narrative forms, readers of historical novels are asked to recognize what characters seek at the level of plot: the basis in historical—neutral—time for connecting what remains unconnected; the common denominators that support the gradual but inexorable linkages that emerge to patient observers among apparently dissimilar lives.) The historical medium holds out, above all, the promise that change will be positive: that whatever things may be, they could always be otherwise and better. That is to say, one can have more wealth, more wisdom, more satisfaction, more social relevance; and their pursuit will transform one's life.

Narrative makes a virtue of the sustaining mediation of history: this obtains in the later novels of Dickens, such as *Bleak* *House* (1853), *Little Dorrit* (1857), *Great Expectations* (1861), and *Our Mutual Friend* (1865); in all George Eliot's novels, most enjoyably *The Mill on the Floss* (1860), *Felix Holt* (1866), *Middlemarch* (1872), and *Daniel Deronda* (1876); and in all Trollope's novels, especially the 12 most successful ones belonging to the Barchester and the Palliser series and including such masterpieces as *Barchester Towers, Last Chronicle of Barset* (1867), *Phineas Finn* (1869), *The Prime Minister* (1876), and *The Duke's Children* (1880). Readers of these books must characteristically shift their attention repeatedly from one center to another, one point of view to another, one plot to another as the varying conditions unfold their potentialities. Sometimes, as in George Eliot, the writer emphasizes the potentiality of individual consciousness at moments of choice, where it is at once powerfully circumscribed by particular conditions and diffusively (as opposed to heroically) powerful. A case in point is Dorothea's dark night of the soul in *Middlemarch,* or Esther Lyon's intuitive grasp in *Felix Holt* of the warning Mrs. Transome's life presents to her. Sometimes, as in later Dickens, the writer emphasizes the individual realization (or failure to realize) as a moment of collective responsibility (or failure) and defiance of the deathly effects of class division, always in a world where events have upon them a glimmer of heavenly light. In Dickens such moments usually turn on the heavy costs of life for the poor, most famously in passages from *The Old Curiosity Shop, Dombey and Son,* or *Bleak House* concerning the deaths of children. Sometimes, as in all of Trollope, the writer focuses attention on the long-term changes of which individual character is capable, as particular characters keep renewing or redefining themselves through a series of novels and become like an extended group of friends and acquaintances. Such changes are particularly common in characters in the Barchester and Palliser novels.

But whatever the individual circumstance, the chief representation of the text is neither plot nor character but the mediating element itself: history, or the amalgam of consciousness and time that is not specific to anyone but belongs to everyone. Characters and events are merely its carriers, or ways of specifying the system in which time and telling literally produce a common, shared world.

But all this is metaphysics. Reading the novels is much more fun, as they range constantly between the quietly amusing and the hilarious. In them, the narrative voice maintains, by means of its continuous double perspective, a kind of chronic wittiness concerning the parochialisms of the perceived world. This continuing double perspective creates continuous trouble for settled opinion, both in characters and readers, but it does so for the sake of a wider horizon in which the mediations of history apply and in which this common-denominator time can reasonably underwrite the other human links that mutually implicate widely separated lives.

The problems of history and mediation among individuals and classes always remains a tense business in English narrative, and even great exemplars like Eliot and Trollope use the convention ironically and with poetic license. A number of major writers experiment with those departures, notably Elizabeth Gaskell and the later novelists George Meredith and Thomas Hardy. Gaskell's histories, especially her earlier ones, typically mediate moral issues between classes and individuals as representative members of classes in the manner of her mentor, Charles Dickens, who makes his historical mediations serve a distinct if generalized morality. Gaskell's *North and South* (1855), for example, tends toward the mode of the pilgrim's progress, even if the pilgrimage leads through industrial Britain. Her histories become more contested in *Sylvia's Lovers* (1863) and in the expansive, meandering *Wives and Daughters* (1866).

About a decade later, George Meredith's narrative experiments often focus on the threats posed, especially by English class investments, to the human continuities of what he often associates with a "natural" world, especially in *The Ordeal of Richard Feverel* (1859), *Beauchamp's Career* (1875), and *The Egoist* (1879). And a decade beyond Meredith, Thomas Hardy reduces to almost vestigial function the once-wide promises of historical mediation and presents in novels like *The Return of the Native* (1878), *The Mayor of Casterbridge* (1886), and *Tess of the d'Urbervilles* (1891), a social world riven by gender inequity and consequently reverting to the tribal.

As historical conventions become primary in narrative they transform foundational values. Where history holds, so does the value of neutrality, and the presence of neutrality virtually erases the value of hierarchy. Traditional "natural" and tribal social arrangements give way, at least in novels, to more inclusively social ones. Central among those traditional hierarchies are the gender inequalities that become so important in the implicitly democratic horizons of history. It could be argued, as John Stuart Mill implicitly does in *The Subjection of Women* (1869), that democracy in fact rises or falls on the issue, as it affects every subject who aspires to be a citizen. Where gender arrangements remain hierarchical, tribal, and inequitable, there democracy has no opportunity to flourish. Developing from the discussion of similar issues in Mary Wollstonecraft's *A Vindication of the Rights of Women* (1792), Mill's essay links the fate of democratic institutions with the progress of women's rights. The same argument emerges from novels of George Meredith, Anthony Trollope, and George Eliot. Differences based on class, nationality, ethnicity and, most universally of all, gender must be renegotiated; differences once justified hierarchically have lost their naturalized status and must compete in the inclusive horizon and neutral time of historical narrative.

ELIZABETH DEEDS ERMARTH

See also Charlotte Brontë; Critics and Criticism (19th Century); Charles Dickens; George Eliot; Elizabeth Gaskell; Thomas Hardy; Historical Novel; Historical Writing and the Novel; George Meredith; Realism; Science and the Novel; Sir Walter Scott; Social Criticism; William Makepeace Thackeray; Time in the Novel; Anthony Trollope; Wuthering Heights

Further Reading

Alter, Robert, *Partial Magic: The Novel as a Self-Conscious Genre*, Berkeley: University of California Press, 1975

Armstrong, Nancy, *Desire and Domestic Fiction: A Political History of the Novel*, New York: Oxford University Press, 1987

Beer, Gillian, *Darwin's Plots: Evolutionary Narrative in Darwin, George Eliot, and Nineteenth-Century Fiction*, London and Boston: Routledge and Kegan Paul, 1983

Beer, Gillian, *Open Fields: Science in Cultural Encounter*, Oxford: Clarendon Press, and New York: Oxford University Press, 1996

Butterfield, Herbert, *The Whig Interpretation of History*, London: Bell, 1931; New York: Scribner, 1951

Calvert, Peter, *The Concept of Class: An Historical Introduction*, London: Hutchinson, and New York: St. Martin's Press, 1982

Cosslett, Tess, *The "Scientific Movement" in Victorian Literature*, Brighton, Sussex: Harvester, and New York: St. Martin's Press, 1982

Cosslett, Tess, *Woman to Woman: Female Friendship in Victorian Fiction*, Brighton, Sussex: Harvester, and Atlantic Highlands, New Jersey: Humanities Press, 1988

Dennis, Barbara, and David Skilton, editors, *Reform and Intellectual Debate in Victorian England*, New York: Croom Helm, 1982

Ermarth, Elizabeth Deeds, *Realism and Consensus in the English Novel*, Princeton, New Jersey: Princeton University Press, 1983; new edition, with subtitle *The Construction of Time in Narrative*, Edinburgh: Edinburgh University Press, 1998

Ermarth, Elizabeth Deeds, *The English Novel in History, 1840–1895*, London and New York: Routledge, 1997

Gallagher, Catherine, *The Industrial Reformation of English Fiction: Social Discourse and Narrative Form, 1832–1867*, Chicago: University of Chicago Press, 1985

Mill, John Stuart, *Three Essays: On Liberty (1859), Representative Government (1861), The Subjection of Women (1869)*, London and New York: Oxford University Press, 1975

Miller, J. Hillis, *The Form of Victorian Fiction: Thackeray, Dickens, Trollope, George Eliot, Meredith, and Hardy*, Notre Dame, Indiana: Notre Dame University Press, 1968

Vargish, Thomas, *The Providential Aesthetic in Victorian Fiction*, Charlottesville: University Press of Virginia, 1985

Williams, Raymond, *The Long Revolution*, London: Chatto and Windus, and New York: Columbia University Press, 1961

English Novel

1880–1920

Significant changes in the structure of English culture and society as well as in the material conditions of publishing made the period 1880–1920 an important hinge in the history of the English novel. By the turn of the century the changing status of women demanded new forms of novelistic expression in order to accommodate new social realities, and increased literacy in the wake of the 1870 Education Act, along with growth in disposable income, created new demands for popular fiction from an increasingly diverse readership. Along with a dramatically expanded market for fiction, the period saw the demise of the long-dominant Victorian triple-decker and the emergence of the modern one-volume best seller, the proliferation of distinct new subgenres (the New Woman novel, slum fiction, spy novels, detective fiction, science fiction, invasion novels, sex novels, and many others), and the gradual institutionalization of a split between popular and elite fiction. While elite novels increasingly embraced a cosmopolitan perspective on English culture and an aesthetic of experimentation, popular permutations of romance and realism were more likely to assert forms of traditional Englishness (in effect often inventing them) in response to the new cross-cultural perspectives brought home by anthropology and imperial travel.

George Gissing, who together with Thomas Hardy and George Meredith dominated serious fiction from 1880 to 1900, provides an important index to the major social and literary issues of the fin de siècle. Contributing to the consolidation of a realist aesthetic in the 1880s, Gissing explored both lower-class life in London (*Workers in the Dawn,* 1880; *The Unclassed,* 1884; *Thyrza,* 1887; *The Nether World,* 1889) and the life of the English middle classes, most notably in *Demos* (1886), a grimly realistic third-generation "condition of England" novel written under the influence of Émile Zola's naturalism. Gissing's critical esteem was not matched by popular success, in part because the reading public was not yet ready for the sexual and social candor that would become almost commonplace in the decadent fiction and New Woman novels of the 1890s. Publishers were not ready either: even in 1894, *Esther Waters,* George Moore's brilliant synthesis of French naturalism and Walter Pater's aestheticized inwardness (e.g., *Marius the Epicurean,* 1885), was refused by the circulating libraries and taken up only by an obscure house, Walter Scott.

The struggles of Moore, who fought against the stifling moral and economic stranglehold of the circulating libraries, and Gissing, who decried the falling artistic standards he associated with the new commercialization of fiction, epitomize the late century's growing tension between the claims of art and commerce. When Mudie's banned Moore's novels in response to the sexual frankness of *A Mummer's Wife* (1884), he responded with a polemic, *Literature at Nurse; or, Circulating Morals* (1885). Gissing responded to the mass commodification of literature with an anatomy of the growing split between serious and popular writing in his dourly compendious masterpiece, *New Grub Street* (1891). Ironically, *New Grub Street* firmly established Gissing as an important writer, although he would not write a widely popular work until *The Private Papers of Henry Ryecroft* (1903).

Gissing's later fiction joins Hardy, Meredith, and the more popular New Woman novelists by taking up intensely debated issues about marriage and proper sexual ethics for women. Deploring women's general lack of education, Gissing looked forward in 1893 to a period of "sexual anarchy" necessary for the achievement of social equality, and the term serves well to describe the crises of gender identity generated by battles between the sexes at century's end. Gissing responded to growing demands for female emancipation sympathetically yet ambivalently (*The Odd Women,* 1893; *In the Year of the Jubilee,* 1894; *Whirlpool,* 1897): while skillfully creating a range of emancipated female characters, he also tended to stigmatize intellectually advanced women as representatives of the growing superficiality and vulgarity of modern life, a tendency that would become more pronounced among the male modernists. Meredith also began to focus on the woman question, beginning with his greatest novel, *The Egoist* (1879), which anticipates the more radical critiques of marital relations in his later novels (e.g., *Diana of the Crossways,* 1885; *Lord Ormont and His Aminta,* 1894). Like Gissing, Meredith advocated education as the key to female emancipation, yet his residual investment in traditional notions of femininity ultimately subvert on the level of narrative the overtly feminist harangues of his narrators. Despite his cultivated stylistic obscurity, Meredith was far more widely read in his own day than he is now, in part because women with independent views welcomed his frank critique of marriage as a form of erotic death and imprisonment (see Cunningham, 1978).

In "Candour in English Fiction" (1890) Hardy denounced the unofficial censorship of popular morals that placed an "insuperable bar" on the honest representation of sexual relations, yet times were changing fast. Long established as a famous novelist since the publication of *Far from the Madding Crowd* (1874), Hardy reached the pinnacle of his fame with his stark tragedy *The Mayor of Casterbridge* (1886) and the less severe *The Woodlanders* (1887) only to strike out willfully against public mores with the frankly erotic *Tess of the D'Urbervilles* (1891), to which he appended the tendentious subtitle, "A Pure Woman." *The Woodlanders* had attacked restrictive and unfair marriage laws, but with *Tess of the D'Urbervilles* Hardy outraged the public with his assertion that "pure" should refer to moral rather than sexual innocence. By the time Hardy achieved his final novelistic notoriety with *Jude the Obscure* (1895), the vogue for Ibsen had been going strong for at least five years, and Hardy soon found himself an honorary member, along with Grant Allen and other influential New Woman novelists, of Mrs. Oliphant's infamous "Anti-Marriage League" (1896). The fierce critical outcry in response to *Jude the Obscure*'s sustained disparagement of marriage and grotesquely pessimistic infanticide/suicide contributed to Hardy's decision to give up fiction for what he considered the higher art of poetry.

The sexually candid novels of Gissing, Hardy, and Meredith both anticipate and respond to the hugely popular New Woman novelists of the 1890s. Soon written by men as well as women, the New Woman novels first gained notoriety in 1893 with Sarah Grand's *The Heavenly Twins* and George Egerton's (Mary

Chavelita Bright) *Keynotes*. Initially published at the author's expense and later picked up by Heinemann, *The Heavenly Twins* owed much of its *succès de scandale* to the frank depiction of syphilis passed on from a degenerate husband to his pure wife. *Keynotes*, a highly mannered collection of stories about female sexuality, contributed significantly to the establishing of a late-century feminist voice in fiction and lent its name to a single-volume series published by Bodley Head, also the publishers of *The Yellow Book*. Most notorious, however, was Grant Allen's *The Woman Who Did* (1895), the story of a woman who refuses to marry her lover on the grounds that marriage itself is immoral. Published in the Keynote series, this enjoyably bad novel reads now like a briskly conservative cautionary tale, but at the time it elicited (along with general opprobrium) Victoria Crosse's (Vivian Cory) *The Woman Who Didn't* (1906). Mona Caird's artful *The Daughters of Danaus* (1894) deserves mention as the only New Woman novel to target motherhood as women's chief obstacle to emancipation.

The popular phenomenon of the New Woman novelists highlights the curious fact that between the death of George Eliot in 1880 and the emergence of Dorothy Richardson and Virginia Woolf in 1915, the dominant canon of English fiction recognizes very few women among the first rank of serious novelists. The best-selling spiritualized sensation novels of Marie Corelli (e.g., *The Sorrows of Satan,* 1895, in which a society woman literally goes to the devil by reading New Woman fiction) dominated popular fiction through the turn of the century. Meanwhile, the lingering efforts of the prolific Mrs. Oliphant faded away, and the later novels of Mrs. Humphrey Ward failed to match the artistic achievement and phenomenal success of her novel of religious crisis, *Robert Elsmere* (1888); Ward's *Helbeck of Bannisdale* (1898), however, is notable for its treatment of Catholic life, and Ward herself deserves credit for helping to abolish the three-volume novel in 1894. The perceived decline of fiction by women during this period has been understood variously: increasingly diversified economic opportunities drew talented women into journalism and other socially engaged activities; the professionalization of authorship late in the century entailed a masculinization of literary value that gradually "edged women out" of the field of the high-culture novel (see Tuchman and Fortin, 1989); and the rapidly growing female readership for popular fiction made such writing a viable means of support for middle-class women without independent incomes.

Yet the decline may too easily be exaggerated. Until recently the formation of the modernist canon contributed to the neglect of such novelists as Mary Cholmondeley, whose *Red Pottage* (1899) powerfully thematizes, in the destruction of the heroine's novel manuscript, the marginalization of women's fiction in literary history. The enduring cultural prestige of the high-art novel championed so effectively by Henry James, moreover, has helped to obscure the contributions and innovations of the popular fiction against which the art of the novel was defined. New Woman novels, for instance, greatly enriched the range of female characterization in late Victorian fiction while challenging the dominant convention that marriage was fiction's necessary ground. Individual novels also compare favorably with their more well known modernist successors. Olive Schreiner, herself a New Woman *avant la lettre*, became one of the most prominent intellectuals of her time (and the first widely acclaimed colonial writer in England) with the publication of *The Story of an African Farm* (1883), an astonishingly modern maturation story of agnosticism and feminist awakening that unfolds enigmatically through elliptical, shifting narrative modes.

After the mid-1890s, the success enjoyed by Bodley Head and other publishing houses with New Woman novels and decadent fiction (e.g., Arthur Machen, Ella D'Arcy, M.P. Shiel) began to fade, but not before George du Maurier cashed in with his best-selling *Trilby* (1894), a bohemian story set in the Latin Quarter whose legacy includes the ubiquitous Svengali and a vogue for the felt hat named after the heroine. The eclipse of these subgenres derived in part from a general reaction against the perceived "degeneration" of realism, a cultural anxiety crystallized in the widely read 1895 translation of Max Nordau's *Degeneration*, which saw the decline plots of slum fiction (e.g., Israel Zangwill, the so-called Dickens of the Ghetto) and naturalistic fiction more generally as signs of cultural collapse. With the tremendous notoriety surrounding the trial of Oscar Wilde that same year, Ernest Dowson's decadent novel *A Comedy of Masks* (1893) and Egerton's *Keynotes* could henceforth be linked as homologous symptoms of the racial and moral decay exemplified in the degenerate modernity of the author of *The Picture of Dorian Gray* (1891). Modernist innovation early in the next century was thus also an effort of recovery.

The reaction against realism, while closing down certain challenges to the dominant moralism of English domestic fiction, also helped fuel the popularity of adventure fiction and other forms of romance, the loose contemporary term for nonrealism of any stripe. (Hence H.G. Wells' name—scientific romances— for his groundbreaking science fiction: *The Time Machine*, 1895; *The War of the Worlds,* 1898; *The First Men in the Moon,* 1901.) Buoyed by the new imperialism and a growing hunger for the exotic in a world increasingly domesticated by global capitalism, novels of adventure moved by the end of the century from a niche market for young boys into a much broader market share, although still largely male. Robert Louis Stevenson's *Treasure Island* (1883) was first serialized in *Young Folks* (1881–82); in 1893, however, *The Beach of Falesá* was distributed in the *Illustrated London News*, and by the turn of the century Rudyard Kipling's *Kim* (1901) was serialized for adults in *McClure's* and *Cassell's*. In the meantime H. Rider Haggard, hoping to match Stevenson's success with *Treasure Island*, had consolidated the market for adult adventure with the hugely popular *King Solomon's Mines* (1885), followed by *She* (1886) and *Allan Quartermain* (1887). Stevenson, perhaps the most versatile English novelist, also momentarily revitalized historical fiction with *Kidnapped* (1886) and *The Master of Ballantrae* (1889), only to see his reputation suffer for writing in so many subgenres at a time when subgenres, spurred by the expanding periodical market, were proliferating rapidly.

The resurgence of romance adventures, long a strand within the dominant tradition, further eroded the cultural hegemony of the domestic novel by making imperialism a central concern of mainstream fiction. Turning away from realistic treatments of decay at home, romance adventures often took up anxieties about the decline of empire by fashioning regenerative narratives of the imperial frontier. In the typical regenerative adventure (e.g., Arthur Conan Doyle's *Tragedy of the Korosko*, 1898; John Buchan's *The Half-Hearted*, 1900), a complacent Englishman awakens to the need to shore up Empire against increasingly powerful imperial rivals, usually Germany, and his sudden imperial immersion revitalizes hero and nation alike (see Trotter, 1993). More sceptical adventure stories displaced degeneration from the metropolitan center to the exotic periphery in their analyses of the corruption of Englishness when isolated at the lawless boundaries of Empire. In 1899 the Boer War shook English confidence in the strength and values of Empire, but cynical treatments of imperial adventure were already on the scene. Although much of Rudyard Kipling's fiction seems designed to inculcate the values underpinning colonial rule, "The Man Who Would Be King" (1888) gives the lie to the myth of the uncomplicated and nonironic laureate of Empire. In this context, Stevenson's brilliantly chilling portrait of the gentleman trader Attwater in his unjustly neglected masterpiece *The Ebb-Tide* (1894) is even more powerful than Joseph Conrad's Kurtz (in "Heart of Darkness," 1902). Common to all these fictions is a blurring of the boundaries between the civilized and the uncivilized that prepared the ground for modernism's valuing of "primitive" energies over bourgeois rationality.

Conrad's "Heart of Darkness" and *Lord Jim* (1900) uneasily combine the Victorian tradition of imperial adventure with the Flaubertian artistry advocated by James; both novels pursue the sceptical social analysis characteristic of Arnold Bennett and John Galsworthy, yet they do so within the highly aestheticized, subjective mode characteristic of D.H. Lawrence, Dorothy Richardson, Katharine Mansfield, and Virginia Woolf. *Lord Jim*'s fragmentary narration and shifting generic modes evoke Marlow's flickering movement of mind as he tries to understand the meaning of Jim's failed adventures, yet Marlow's investment in codes of conduct remains profoundly social.

A Pole who joined the French and British Merchant Marines before becoming a novelist, Conrad achieved early critical success with his Malayan novels (*Almayer's Folly*, 1895; *An Outcast of the Islands*, 1896) and would return to similarly exotic semi-autobiographical materials as his powers declined (*The Arrow of Gold*, 1919; *The Rescue*, 1920; *The Rover*, 1923); yet even with the financial opportunities opened up by new international copyright agreements in 1886 and 1891 and the consequent rise of the literary agent, Conrad never sold well until *Chance* (1913), which was marketed specifically for women. The best of his novels (*Lord Jim*; *The Nigger of the Narcissus*, 1897; *Nostromo*, 1904; *The Secret Agent*, 1907; and *Under Western Eyes*, 1911) fell into the widening gap between elite and popular fiction, with fellow novelists imitating his innovative narrative forms and the common reader rejecting his disjunct chronologies, shifting points of view, and stylistic virtuosity. The restlessly inventive quality of Conrad's narrative techniques derived equally from efforts to evoke the mental flux of James' central reflective consciousness and to come to terms with incommensurable meanings generated by stories of cross-cultural contact. The primacy of the individual impression and the importance of cross-cultural analogies (misleadingly called "the mythical method" by T.S. Eliot) would henceforth become hallmarks of the various experimental fictions we now term modernist.

Conrad's radical scepticism also struck a characteristic note for the Edwardian period (see Wollaeger, 1990). Although Samuel Butler's semi-autobiographical dissection of the stultifying effects of the Victorian family, *The Way of All Flesh*, published posthumously to great acclaim in 1903, was begun in the 1870s, the death of Queen Victoria in 1901 signaled the onset of a new era of doubt about the past along with a growing sense that society re-

quired radical reform. The new eagerness for change soon found outlet in the movement for women's suffrage and a renewed interest in socialism—the Labour Representation Committee, aided by the Fabian Society, was founded in 1900 and renamed the Labour Party in 1906. In the wake of the Liberal landslide that same year, prominent Edwardian novelists extended the legacy of naturalism by turning increasingly to the condition of England as their main subject. In *Nostromo* Conrad had located his critique of unchecked capitalism in the mythical South American country of Costaguana; John Galsworthy brought the subject home again in his satiric treatment of the Forsyte family in *The Man of Property* (1906), later republished as part of *The Forsyte Saga* (1922). In 1909 Wells turned from social comedies (*Love and Mr. Lewisham*, 1900; *Kipps*, 1905) and the allegorical sociology of his futuristic fantasies (*In the Days of the Comet*, 1906; *The War in the Air*, 1908) to produce his most impressive contribution to the critique of English mercantile values, the quirkily brilliant *Tono-Bungay* (1908), a rambling, panoramic treatment of English dissolution as reflected in the corrupting effects of modern advertising and the dubious promise of technology. Serialized by Ford Madox Ford (then Hueffer) in *The English Review*, *Tono-Bungay* was praised by writers as diverse as the young D.H. Lawrence and Arnold Bennett.

The triumph of modernism partially accounts for the historical success of Virginia Woolf's famous critiques in "Modern Novels" (1919) and "Mr. Bennett and Mrs. Brown" (1924)—written partly in response to the advent of James Joyce (*Portrait of the Artist as a Young Man*, 1916; *Ulysses*, serialized in *The Little Review* from 1918)—of the supposed materialism of Bennett, Wells, and Galsworthy compared with the new inwardness and spirituality of Joyce and Henry James. (Constance Garnett's influential translations of Ivan Turgenev, Lev Tolstoi, and Fedor Dostoevskii had made the Russian spirit a touchstone for what the English were thought to lack.) Once the most famous novelist of his day, Bennett has been eclipsed to such a degree that few outside England (where modernism, after all, was ultimately rejected) still read his naturalistic fiction of provincial life—the Five Towns novels (*Anna of the Five Towns*, 1902; *The Old Wives' Tale*, 1908) and the Clayhanger series (*Clayhanger*, 1910; *Hilda Lessways*, 1911; *These Twain*, 1915; *The Roll-Call*, 1918)—or even his late modernist-inflected gem, *Riceyman Steps* (1923). Yet much of Bennett's searching investigation of the social construction of Edwardian selfhood retains interest, and his chronicling of the five towns, inspired by Moore's treatment of the Potteries district in *A Mummer's Wife*, remains important as a bridge between the regionalisms of Hardy and E.M. Forster.

At the same time, Woolf's complaint that Bennett's unrelenting documentation of social minutiae threatens to become complicit with the very materialism he anatomizes holds some truth, and Bennett understandably became a steady target for novelists who, like Dorothy Richardson and others writing in the wake of Freud, made consciousness itself the subject of fiction. In 1918 May Sinclair's application of William James' philosophical term "stream of consciousness" to the first three volumes of Richardson's virtually plotless 13-volume *Pilgrimage* (1915–67) marked the first literary use of the term. Antedating Woolf's explorations of female consciousness by several years, the first volume of *Pilgrimage* coincides with the emergence of Ford's modernism in *The Good Soldier* (1915) and the dazzling brilliance of

Mansfield's short stories (*In a German Pension*, 1911; *Bliss*, 1920; *The Garden Party*, 1922), the first in English to reflect the influence of Anton Chekhov.

Well before Woolf's critique of the Edwardians, influential caricatures of Henry James as mandarin connoisseur of consciousness and Wells as didactic journalist propagated by their well-known debate in 1914 had already polarized possibilities for fiction. Some novels contributed to the distinction. The spate of invasion novels written in response to Germany's growing imperial power (e.g., Erskine Childers, *The Riddle of the Sands*, 1903; William Le Queux, *The Invasion of 1910*, 1906) openly argued for increased military readiness, as did spy fiction by Le Queux (*Secrets of the Foreign Office*, 1903) and the prolific E. Phillips Oppenheim (e.g., *The Great Impersonation*, 1920). Anticipating Lawrence's explicitness in *The Rainbow* (1915) and *Lady Chatterley's Lover* (1928 in Italy; full text in England, 1960), novels of sexual maturation (e.g., Elinor Glyn, *Three Weeks*, 1907; H. de Vere Stacpoole, *The Blue Lagoon*, 1908; H.G. Wells, *Ann Veronica*, 1909) pushed beyond New Woman novels in the name of the "racial health" necessary to resist English decline at a time when parallels with the Roman Empire had become very popular. At the other extreme from "novels with a purpose" is Ford's *The Good Soldier*, a version of which first appeared as "The Saddest Story" in the inaugural volume of Wyndham Lewis' and Ezra Pound's *Blast*, one of the many "little magazines" that arose early in the century as alternative outlets for avant-garde literature and the main organ for Vorticism, England's version of Italian Futurism. Called by a contemporary the finest French novel ever written in English, *The Good Soldier* brilliantly fulfills every formal criterion for the English high modernist novel, with its intricately self-reflexive, cross-referencing immersion in the narrator's bewildering array of impressions, resistance (following the philosopher Henri Bergson) to "clock time," attenuation of plot, and ambiguous closure. The urgently hard-edged eloquence of Lewis' *Tarr* (1918; revised edition 1928) introduced an important dissenting strand within English modernism by championing the spatial over the temporal and the sharply defined surface over the inward flux of consciousness. *Tarr* and *The Good Soldier* share, however, the impulse to fold in on themselves, preferring their aesthetic patterns to those of society.

Yet neat distinctions between the hermetic and the engaged rarely hold: Ford's ambiguous treatment of "the good soldier" (the source of patriotic resentment at the time) relativizes England's Tory values on the brink of Word War I; Conrad's *The Secret Agent*, seemingly a spy novel, subverts the ideological project of such fiction through its savagely double-edged ironies. E.M. Forster also confounds emerging distinctions between social critique and the art of the novel. Forster's distaste for English cultural pretensions motivates the corrective vitalism of his Italy in *Where Angels Fear to Tread* (1905) and *A Room with a View* (1908) while the suffering of the semi-autobiographical writer figure in *The Longest Journey* (1907) measures the claims of unpopular art against the oppression of conventional domesticity and the redemptive power of nature. Forster's social criticism culminates in 1910 in *Howards End*'s attempt to reconcile the opposed values of the mercantile Wilcoxes and the artistic Schlegels within a pastoral utopia only the Schlegels could have imagined, a characteristically aesthetic solution to a social problem (and one with no room for the lower-middle classes, repre-

sented by Leonard Bast). Increasingly weary of the compulsory heterosexuality that precluded publication of his gay novel *Maurice* (finished 1914; published posthumously 1971), Forster wrote only one more novel over the next 50 years of his long life, *A Passage to India* (1924), which takes up India as a metaphor for all the English mind could not encompass and posits the "not yet" possible friendship of two men, colonizer and colonized, as another utopian space of reconciliation.

The outbreak of World War I in 1914 accelerated the social upheaval already transforming English fiction, yet the war's full effects were not felt until the 1920s. Some very fine novels ignored the war altogether: Moore's *The Brook Kerith* (1916) extends his late experiments with musical style, and Frank Swinnerton's *Nocturne* (1917), one of the most popular wartime novels, plays with the kind of strictly delimited time scheme Joyce would use in *Ulysses* (1922). Other novels hinted at the conflagration to come through portraits of a society run violently amuck (e.g., Conrad's *Victory*, 1915; Lewis' *Tarr*, 1918). Few novels took on the war directly, although in *Mr. Britling Sees It Through* (1916) Wells captures the new texture of everyday life on the homefront, and May Sinclair's imagistic *The Tree of Heaven* (1917) shows the war effort gathering even dissident suffragettes and Vorticist poets into its capacious breast. No English novelist ever matched the powerful representation of trench warfare produced by Henri Barbusse's *Le feu: Journal d'une escouade* (1916; *Under Fire: The Story of a Squad*)—to which Sinclair specifically responds—or the stark antiwar effect of Erich Maria Remarque's *Im Westen Nichts Neues* (1929; *All Quiet on the Western Front*). The early careers of Lawrence and Woolf, however, suggest how the war gradually contributed to England's emerging modernist aesthetic.

After the still underappreciated imperial romance of *The Voyage Out* (1915) and the relatively dull realistic retreat of *Night and Day* (1919), Woolf's mature aesthetic of lyrical fragmentation emerged in the brief postwar elegy *Jacob's Room* (1922) and the more developed *Mrs. Dalloway* (1925), which presents the titular society woman and a shell-shocked war veteran as enigmatic doubles. (Leonard and Virginia Woolf's founding of the Hogarth Press in 1917 and the examples of Mansfield and Joyce also made possible her new experimentalism.) Two years later the more radically disjunctive tripartite structure of *To the Lighthouse* (1927) gave fictional form to the experience of historical discontinuity by interrupting country house life with "Time Passes," the most successful stretch of experimental writing in Woolf's oeuvre. (England's greatest war novel, Ford's *Parade's End* [1924–28], extends the same interruptive structure over a tetralogy.) D.H. Lawrence published his first major novel with *Sons and Lovers* (1913), an autobiographical Bildungsroman, before producing a long manuscript, "The Sisters," later split into two novels, *The Rainbow* (1915) and *Women in Love* (finished in 1916; published in London, 1920), that exemplify the war's effects on modernist fiction. *The Rainbow*, for all its sexual frankness and notable efforts to capture characters' unconscious substrata, retains a relatively traditional structure grounded in the family saga. *Women in Love*, by contrast, was rewritten during the war, and its chapters emerge as almost autonomous episodes within a discontinuous narrative that aims to shatter, in Lawrence's words, "the old stable ego" he associated with Bennett. Following the war, Lawrence's profound loathing for the asceticism and regimentation of English modernity issued in increasingly apocalyptic visions of social transformation that ultimately took him and his fiction outside the confines of England into the primitivism of Australia (*Kangaroo,* 1923) and Mexico (*The Plumed Serpent,* 1926). Lawrence finished his last novel, the passional manifesto *Lady Chatterley's Lover,* in Italy, where he moved after his failed utopian experiment in communal living in New Mexico.

The cosmopolitan cast of modernism highlights the degree to which the idea of English literature has always been formed in relation to the competing perspectives of those outside the traditional cultural center of London-Oxbridge: Hardy's Wessex regionalism; the gendered resistance of New Woman novels; the non-normative sexualities articulated by Wilde, Forster, and Radclyffe Hall (*The Well of Loneliness,* 1928); and the racial and cultural differences explored not only by popular adventure fiction but also by influential foreigners (James, Conrad, T.S. Eliot, Ezra Pound, W.B. Yeats, and James Joyce). The key innovators in the English novel in the first decades of the century were largely (in Terry Eagleton's phrase) exiles and émigrés: of the major modernists, only Woolf and Lawrence were English by birth (Ford was half German); moreover, Woolf, like Richardson, asserted an outsider status as a feminist, and Lawrence, even before seeking more passionate climes, was an outsider by class. Insofar as modernist cosmopolitanism emerged as a critique of English insularity and an assertion of greater cultural sophistication by the outsider, modernism itself may be considered an essentially provincial phenomenon (see Crawford, 1992). Of course as Bennett remarked in defense of his own brand of regional fiction, "all the greatest novels in the world are provincial."

MARK A. WOLLAEGER

See also Adventure Novel and Imperial Romance; Joseph Conrad; Decadent Novel; E.M. Forster; Good Soldier; Thomas Hardy; Irish Novel; Henry James; D.H. Lawrence; Wyndham Lewis; George Meredith; Modernism; George Moore; Naturalism; New Humor Novel; Romance; Science Fiction Novel; Robert Louis Stevenson; Stream of Consciousness; War Novel; H.G. Wells; Virginia Woolf

Further Reading

Ardis, Ann L., *New Women, New Novels: Feminism and Early Modernism,* New Brunswick, New Jersey: Rutgers University Press, 1990

Brantlinger, Patrick, *Rule of Darkness: British Literature and Imperialism, 1830–1914,* Ithaca, New York: Cornell University Press, 1988

Crawford, Robert, *Devolving English Literature,* Oxford: Clarendon Press, and New York: Oxford University Press, 1992

Cross, Nigel, *The Common Writer: Life in Nineteenth-Century Grub Street,* Cambridge and New York: Cambridge University Press, 1985

Cunningham, Gail, *The New Woman and the Victorian Novel,* London: Macmillan, and New York: Barnes and Noble, 1978

Eagleton, Terry, *Exiles and Émigrés: Studies in Modern Literature,* New York: Schocken Books, and London: Chatto and Windus, 1970

Felski, Rita, *The Gender of Modernity,* Cambridge, Massachusetts: Harvard University Press, 1995

Frierson, William C., *The English Novel in Transition, 1885–1940,* Norman: University of Oklahoma Press, 1942

Green, Martin, *The English Novel in the Twentieth Century,* London: Routledge and Kegan Paul, 1984; University Park: Pennsylvania State University Press, 1987

Hunter, Jefferson, *Edwardian Fiction,* Cambridge, Massachusetts: Harvard University Press, 1982

Hynes, Samuel, *The Edwardian Turn of Mind,* Princeton, New Jersey: Princeton University Press, 1968; London: Pimlico, 1991

Keating, P.J., *The Haunted Study: A Social History of the English Novel, 1875–1914,* London: Secker and Warburg, 1989

Showalter, Elaine, *Sexual Anarchy: Gender and Culture at the Fin de Siècle,* New York: Viking, 1990; London: Bloomsbury, 1991

Stevenson, R.W., *Modernist Fiction: An Introduction,* New York and London: Harvester Wheatsheaf, 1992

Trilling, Lionel, "On the Teaching of Modern Literature," in his *Beyond Culture: Essays on Literature and Learning,* New York: Viking, 1965; London: Secker and Warburg, 1966

Trotter, David, *The English Novel in History, 1895–1920,* London and New York: Routledge, 1993

Tuchman, Gaye, and Nina E. Fortin, *Edging Women Out: Victorian Novelists, Publishers, and Social Change,* New Haven, Connecticut: Yale University Press, and London: Routledge, 1989

Wollaeger, Mark A., *Joseph Conrad and the Fictions of Skepticism,* Stanford, California: Stanford University Press, 1990

English Novel

1920–1950

If the advent of World War I accelerated the development of high modernism in England, its aftermath created the conditions for that movement's eventual fragmentation. While the postwar decades saw an expansion in reading audiences owing to increasing opportunities for secondary education and the rise of the redbrick universities, a growing commercialism in the publishing industry catered to an increasingly specialized and stratified readership. The gap between the intelligentsia and the educated classes as a whole, the product of the simultaneous burst into prominence of mass culture and retreat into opacity and "difficulty" of modernist practitioners, codified the category of the "middlebrow" even as high modernism produced its last masterpieces. In response, novelists who emphasized a high degree of external engagement absorbed many of the techniques of modernism and those of the newly pervasive mass media, blurring distinctions between genres in order to produce a variety of new forms of realism.

The peculiar postwar atmosphere of dizzy enervation, heady consumption, and sociological ferment found its most characteristic expression in the novels of Aldous Huxley, in which, as Malcolm Bradbury (1971) has pointed out, the expression of a fragmented history is thematized rather than given formal expression. Foregoing the traditional consolations of developed characters and involving plot as well as formal experimentation, Huxley (emulating the country-house novels of Thomas Love Peacock) pared his early novels down to conversation. In *Crome Yellow* (1921), *Antic Hay* (1923), *Those Barren Leaves* (1925) and, more portentously, *Point Counter Point* (1928), the mutually uncomprehending voices of a gallery of eccentric characters play against one another with a wit and verve that verges on the feverish, never allowed to coalesce into resolution. Huxley paints an ironic picture of postwar society as obsessively frenetic and morally bankrupt; in his later movement from diagnostic satire (e.g., *Brave New World*, 1932) to millenialist mysticism (in his writings of the 1940s and after), he exemplifies the movement in fiction during this period from self-absorption to engagement to idealistic (or nostalgic) escapism. A similar pattern may be discerned in the works of Evelyn Waugh, whose glittering, mordant early satires (*Decline and Fall*, 1928; *Vile Bodies*, 1930; *A Handful of Dust*, 1934) gave way to the sentimental Catholicism of *Brideshead Revisited* (1945). And in the work of Rose Macaulay, topical satire like *Potterism* (1920) is gradually replaced by searching investigations of the possibilities of middle-class women's lives (such as *Dangerous Ages*, 1921, and *Crewe Train*, 1926) and finally by conversion as well.

Although Huxley's emphasis on conversation set an important precedent for other "second generation," post–high modernist experiments in the 1930s, the flood of World War I novel/memoirs in the late 1920s provided the pattern for the concatenation of literary genres characteristic of the 1930s. Robert Graves' *Goodbye to All That* (1929), Richard Aldington's *Death of a Hero* (1929), Frederic Manning's *Her Privates We* (1930), and Siegfried Sassoon's trilogy, *The Memoirs of George Sherston* (1928–36) all combine combatants' claims to verisimilitude and the increasingly familiar postwar plot of gradual disillusionment, making them difficult to classify unproblematically as either fiction or fact. As subjective "literary" documents that nonetheless attempt to grapple with the social reality of the war, these works straddle the modernist preoccupation with individually observed experience and the focus on documentary realism that often characterized the writing of the 1930s.

The canonical emphasis on highbrow writing has led to the representation of the 1930s as the "Red Decade," its upscale "Auden Generation" writers (catalyzed by the General Strike of 1926 and moved by the economic slump and the rise of fascism) marked by the collision of literary values and political commitment. Within this framework, the 1930s valorization of the documentary is often taken to be an index of that commitment. Even Virginia Woolf, following the modernist apotheosis of *The Waves* (1931), in which objective externality is suppressed altogether, spent the rest of her life in overt engagement with the "fact." She first conceived *The Years* (1937) as *The Pargiters*, an "essay-novel" in which fictional narrative would have alternated with chapters of didactic commentary to give the sense of a family's history *within* history and to debunk the myth of progress (many of these concerns surfaced instead in the long essay *Three Guineas*, 1938). In her last book, *Between the Acts* (1941), Woolf superimposes historical crises—the onset of World War II and the production of a village pageant—in a direct and despairing response to contemporary events.

In fact, the documentary urge is only one pole of the historical self-consciousness that dominated 1930s writing, a self-consciousness confined neither to the highbrow nor to the left wing. Certainly, toward the end of the decade Storm Jameson's essay "Documents" in the journal *Fact* advanced the need for a deaestheticized, documentary literature in the service of socialism (a stance that paradoxically reasserts the primacy of the intellectual as the preeminent observer), echoing the call of the Mass-Observation movement for "an acceptance of the reality principle." Yet works such as George Orwell's *Down and Out in Paris and London* (1933) and *The Road to Wigan Pier* (1937), celebrated by mainstream reviewers for their fidelity to the real, are characteristic 1930s genre-bending melanges of travel writing, journalism, memoir, and fiction. A constructed "rhetoric of authenticity" (as Montefiore [1996] puts it), a self-legitimizing appeal to fact, often obscures the self-mythologizing nature of these works.

Still, as Andy Croft (1990) points out, by the mid-1930s the valorization of the documentary was widespread enough to serve as a bridge between working-class novelists and their potential middle-class readers. Evading the strictures of socialist realism and the looming spectre of D.H. Lawrence, proletarian writers in a variety of styles were helped into print throughout the period by Edgell Rickword (*Left Review*), John Lehmann (*New Writing*), and the publisher Victor Gollancz (founder in 1936 of the Left Book Club), while often aiming for a general rather than an explicitly Left readership. Novels like those of miners Harry Heslop (*Last Cage Down*, 1935; *The Gate of a Strange Field*, 1929) and Lewis Jones (*Cwmardy*, 1937; *We Live*, 1939) combined vital detail with a panoramic view of the effects of unemployment, avoiding, for many critics, the impression of propaganda. It was the unemphatic documentary "feel"—a clear euphemism for nondidacticism—of works such as Walter Greenwood's *Love on the Dole* (1933) and Walter Brierley's *Means Test Man* (1935) that allowed these "proletarian fictions" to be praised by mainstream reviewers and purchased by middle-class readers.

Such documentary dispassion was in sharp contradistinction to the lugubrious naturalism of much contemporary writing about the rural poor. The cult of the rural during this period, reflected in such best-selling novels as Mary Webb's *Precious Bane* (published in 1924 and reprinted 27 times before 1950) and Hugh Walpole's *The Herries Chronicle* (1930–43), and the eccentric, often brutally bleak works of T.F. Powys (*Mr. Tasker's Gods,* 1925; *Mr. Weston's Good Wine,* 1927), was well established enough to spawn its own parody in Stella Gibbons' brilliant *Cold Comfort Farm* (1932), which skewered mercilessly the excesses of this "dripping eaves" school of writing.

Both proletarian documentary and rural romance contributed to an overall drive during this period to reconstitute, through the novel, a middlebrow consensus, an awareness of what it meant to be English in the wake of the war and in the midst of social crisis. Novelists of all political stripes borrowed from the travelogue, the documentary, and the cinema to deliver sometimes panoramic, sometimes picaresque evocations of the variety of Englishness, emphasizing difference and often even factionalism in order to valorize community. In *South Riding* (1936) Winifred Holtby made quotidian struggles in a Yorkshire community a model for national interconnectedness, stressing the interwoven nature of the concerns of town and country, of class and class, of the personal and the political. The popular writer J.B. Priestley parleyed the success of *The Good Companions* (1929), a meandering romp including protagonists of different social backgrounds, into a career as a commentator—in fiction and otherwise—on the life of the "little man." Priestley's *Angel Pavement* (1930), a London tapestry, *Wonder Hero* (1933), a farcical, *Tom Jones*-like exposé of the effects of the Slump, and his travel book, *English Journey* (1934), all emphasize the need for national collectivity—leading directly into the image of English decency and pluck that was to buoy the home front during the German bombing of England. (Graham Greene said of Priestley, whose populist, vaguely leftish views were widely disseminated through his wartime BBC broadcasts, "he gave us what our other leaders have always failed to give us—an ideology.") And during the same period a similar, although more conservative notion of the English as "a nice, decent, essentially private people" was promulgated in the detective fiction of Agatha Christie (see Light, 1991).

In fact, genre fiction, especially crime novels and thrillers, which made up a large portion of the books borrowed from the circulating libraries, serves as a useful barometer for conflicting impulses in the years leading up to World War II. Even as the works of Christie, Dorothy Sayers, and others (like the soothing aristocratic farces of P.G. Wodehouse and the witty neo-Trollopian romances of Angela Thirkell) fed bourgeois desires for stability and reassurance, the thriller form was exploited for political capital in light of the fascist threat. Eric Ambler changed the focus of genre villains from "old-fashioned professional devils" (see Croft, 1990) to European fascists in novels such as *Epitaph for a Spy* (1938) and *The Mask of Dimitrios* (1939); the poet C.

Day Lewis (writing as Nicholas Blake) turned the attention of his series detectives from crime to political conspiracy in *The Smiler with the Knife* (1939).

Perhaps better than anyone else, Graham Greene exploited the potential of the thriller form, blurring the lines between "serious" and genre fiction even as he marked off his early experiments in the form with the tongue-in-cheek label "entertainments." In *Stamboul Train* (1932; as *Orient Express,* 1933), *A Gun for Sale* (1936), and *The Confidential Agent* (1939) Greene's characters inhabit a seedy, dimly lit world of random betrayal and ominous incoherence that also marks his 1934 "condition of England" novel *It's a Battlefield.* By the end of the 1930s Greene's "serious" fiction came increasingly to reflect the influence of the Catholicism to which he had converted in 1926. His most important novels, *Brighton Rock* (1938), *The Power and the Glory* (1940), and *The Heart of the Matter* (1948), reflect his obsession with the presence of evil in a corrupted world, charting knife-edge moral dilemmas and situational compromise—themes he also continued to explore in the thriller form, as in his examination of moral bankruptcy in postwar Vienna, *The Third Man* (1950).

Along with the thriller, writers attempting to catalyze antifascist sentiment rehabilitated and combined elements of a variety of other genres. The historical novels of Jack Lindsay (*1649,* 1938; *Lost Birthright,* 1939; and *Men of Forty-Eight,* 1948) recovered the lessons of the English radical tradition; Naomi Mitchison's *The Blood of the Martyrs* (1939) paralleled the persecution of Christians under Rome with that of socialists under fascism. More successfully, in *The Corn King and the Spring Queen* (1931), Mitchison exploited elements of the historical bodice-ripper for political capital, using ancient Greece to anchor a socialist-feminist fantasy. The distinctive mixture of allegory and fantasy (what Samuel Hynes [1976], following W.H. Auden, has dubbed "parable-art") common to late-1930s antifascist works such as Rex Warner's *The Wild Goose Chase* (1937) and *The Professor* (1938) and Edward Upward's hallucinatory *Journey to the Border* (1938) had already, in fact, been exploited to great effect throughout this period in the works of women writers. Perhaps in response to the post–World War I antifeminist backlash and the reinstitutionalization of domestic ideology, writers such as Rebecca West (in *Harriet Hume,* 1929) had used fantasy elements to explore received notions about gender. Most wide-ranging of the female "parable-artists" was Sylvia Townsend Warner, whose experiments ranged from feminist fantasy in *Lolly Willowes* (1926) and the stories of *The Cat's Cradle-Book* (1940) to the interweaving of revolutionary and romantic motifs in her novel set in the revolutionary year 1848, *Summer Will Show* (1936) and the allegorical/historical parable of the Spanish Civil War, *After the Death of Don Juan* (1938).

As conflict loomed, such feminist experiments tended to stress the gendered aspects of militarism. Stevie Smith's "next war" novel *Over the Frontier* (1938) led Pompey Casmilus, the wisecracking, associative, self-diagnostic narrator of Smith's first book, *Novel on Yellow Paper* (1936), on a dream-like, genre-bending journey into the midst of a European war. While Smith focused on the question of complicity—English anti-Semitism and its silent link to fascism, female complicity with masculine official language—Katharine Burdekin's dystopian *Swastika Night* (1937) exposed the masculinist basis of the Nazi threat.

With the onset of war, the novel suffered more than did other artistic genres from the exigencies of rationing and relocation. With publishers' paper allocations set at only 60 percent of their former usage, and further reduced throughout the war (at a time when, ironically, the demand for books was unprecedentedly high) long novels, new novels, novels by unproven names, and novels liable to be banned became economic risks. As writers were gradually siphoned into the bureaucratic machinery of war, few had the leisure or the optimism to undertake extended projects; and the potential of London's bohemian "Fitzrovia" remained largely unrealized. Energies that at other times would have been focused into a novel tended now to emerge in the form of short stories; although Elizabeth Bowen, for example, did not publish a novel during the war, her stories of the period capture the frenzied, highly charged otherworldliness of London during the Blitz.

Although established writers such as Waugh, Greene, and Priestley did manage to continue producing, the war years saw the emergence of only one new important writer. Joyce Cary's novels of the 1930s had comically juxtaposed the mores of Africa and Empire, catering to the same inquisitive audience that fueled the 1930s travel-writing boom; his wartime trilogy *Herself Surprised* (1941), *To Be a Pilgrim* (1942), and *The Horse's Mouth* (1944) established him as a major novelist. Cary's exuberant ventriloquist's prose wedded modernist technique to historical sweep, recounting the previous 50 years of English history through the eyes of a series of boldly comic characters. Cary's project, Robert Hewison has argued, rejected a broader retrospective, and often autobiographical, impulse that overtook writers during the war years, an attempt to locate where things had "gone wrong" (see Hewison, 1981).

The end of the war did not immediately signal the resurgence of the novel. Not only did paper rationing continue until 1948, but insecurity seemed to beset the entire novelistic enterprise: modernism had played itself out as a possibility (despite the anomolous appearance of Malcolm Lowry's masterpiece *Under the Volcano* in 1947); the political engagement of the 1930s had been widely and publicly jettisoned, and its history rewritten, in the wake of the Hitler-Stalin pact. If the demands and contradictions of wartime bureaucracy had provoked new doubts about the proper public role for an intellectual, the official culture of postwar austerity did little to dispel those concerns. Much writing in the years immediately following the war seemed steeped in dismay—however differently articulated—at the increasing bureaucratization of British society. Even those works that looked back at the war itself, like Elizabeth Bowen's *The Heat of the Day* (1949), did so from a perspective that foregrounded the presence of official language, of secrets and lies, as part of the moral structure of the conflict. George Orwell projected the outcome of such state control in his dystopian *Nineteen Eighty-Four* (1949), in which official language becomes the mechanism for the totalitarian control of history, and thus of thought. And Mervyn Peake transformed bureaucratic paradox into the obscurantism of outworn ritual in the claustrophobic fantasy works *Titus Groan* (1946), *Gormenghast* (1950), and *Titus Alone* (1959).

By contrast, the Oxford dons C.S. Lewis and J.R.R. Tolkien used fantasy to articulate contemporary myth as an alternative to what they saw as the modern debasement of culture and belief; as in Waugh's *Brideshead Revisited*, their antimodern nostalgia took Christian form. In Lewis' *The Space Trilogy* (*Out of the Silent Planet*, 1938; *Perelandra*, 1943; *That Hideous Strength*, 1945) technology and bureaucrats despoiling natural balance are represented as demonic forces. Similarly, the villains of Tolkien's Middle-Earth (in *The Hobbit*, 1937, and *The Lord of the Rings*, 1954–55, but written largely during the 1940s) shatter the ancient balances of rural community.

But even as the dons mourned mythic times past, higher education was becoming the next cultural (and novelistic) battleground. The postwar flood of former servicemen and servicewomen into the universities was only to intensify tensions relating to the preservation of cultural "traditions." If most of these postwar works—no matter how different their social agendas—may be read as reactions against official stultification and moral relativism, it stands as a peculiarly piquant postwar irony that the same stifling bureaucratic culture was later to produce the group known as the Angry Young Men.

DEBRA RAE COHEN

See also E.M. Forster; Graham Greene; D.H. Lawrence; Proletarian Novel; Under the Volcano; Virginia Woolf

Further Reading

Baxendale, John, and Christopher Pawling, *Narrating the Thirties*, London: Macmillan, and New York: St. Martin's Press, 1996

Bradbury, Malcolm, *The Social Context of Modern English Literature*, Oxford: Blackwell, and New York: Schocken, 1971

Croft, Andy, *Red Letter Days: British Fiction in the 1930s*, London: Lawrence and Wishart, 1990

Cunningham, Valentine, *British Writers of the Thirties*, Oxford and New York: Oxford University Press, 1988

Gloversmith, Frank, editor, *Class, Culture, and Social Change: A New View of the 1930s*, Brighton, Sussex: Harvester, and Atlantic Highlands, New Jersey: Humanities Press, 1980

Hewison, Robert, *Under Siege: Literary Life in London, 1939–45*, London: Weidenfeld and Nicolson, and New York: Oxford University Press, 1977; revised edition, London: Methuen, 1988

Hewison, Robert, *In Anger: British Writing in the Cold War, 1945–60*, New York: Oxford University Press, 1981

Hynes, Samuel, *The Auden Generation: Literature and Politics in England in the 1930s*, London: Bodley Head, and New York: Viking, 1976

Light, Alison, *Forever England: Femininity, Literature, and Conservatism between the Wars*, London and New York: Routledge, 1991

Montefiore, Janet, *Men and Women Writers of the 1930s: The Dangerous Flood of History*, London and New York: Routledge, 1996

Zwerdling, Alex, *Virginia Woolf and the Real World*, Berkeley: University of California Press, 1986

English Novel

1950–

The very question of whether "The English Novel"—or, more broadly, an identifiably English culture—may still be said to exist in the second half of the 20th century has been the topic of much debate. Novelist Allan Massie, among others, has stated flatly that such a category ceased to make sense some 35 years ago. It might be argued that the idea of "Englishness" had long ago been rendered blurry by England's incorporation into the larger entity, Great Britain, and further by the existence of millions of colonized people worldwide who were regarded—at least nominally—as "overseas Britons." However, after 1947, with virtually all of the former Empire now independent and with the emergence of the United States as the new Western superpower, it became apparent that England had in fact depended on its status as imperial center for self-definition. English culture was precisely *not* what the colonies produced; it was whatever made England and the English different. That cultural difference is no longer so clear. Public debates over the direction of English literature have made this very apparent.

By 1950, the years of scarcity immediately following World War II were coming to an end, and a period of economic growth and relative political stability had begun that was to last until the worldwide recession of the mid-1970s. However, much literature from the 1950s fails to reflect the optimism one might expect under such circumstances. While newspapers and politicians announced the advent of a class-free society with sufficient resources for all, English novelists tapped into a darker vein of disillusionment, disorientation, and, in some cases, nostalgia for the days when the English knew where they stood—both in a domestic class system and in international relations.

The emergence, in the 1950s, of several young playwrights and novelists who became known collectively as the Angry Young Men might be read as a sign of a new class mobility, an openness to new voices, but much of their work serves paradoxically to reaffirm class divisions and discontentment, despite the new affluence. These writers, including John Osborne, Alan Sillitoe, and, initially, Kingsley Amis, came from working-class or lower-middle-class backgrounds, but unlike most such writers to achieve prominence in the past they did not embrace the aesthetics of the existing (middle- and upper-class) literary establishment. Sillitoe's first novel, *Saturday Night and Sunday Morning* (1958), for example, uses grittily realistic Northampton working-class speech to tell the story of a disillusioned ex-soldier and factory worker, Arthur Seaton, who at the age of 21 owes loyalty to no one and no cause and who resolves that only the pursuit of drinking and women will give his life purpose. Amis, whose comic novel *Lucky Jim* (1954) satirizes the pretensions of provincial university life, gained a reputation as a philistine for this and subsequent attacks on English cultural aspirations.

Sillitoe, along with Colin MacInnes (*Absolute Beginners*, 1959), helped to create a presence in the reading public's imagination for a new socioeconomic group: youth. With the rise in real wages after about 1950 and high employment rates, the income of those under 21 rose at twice the rate of any other age group's. Young people who had experienced a childhood of war and rationing now had ready money for leisure spending, creating a youth culture the likes of which had never previously existed. However, novels of the time tend to evoke not so much the pleasures of increased consumption and television-fueled dreams as a sense of disenfranchisement and alienation among the young, of new desires with nothing of substance to fix upon.

This image of youths with no direction reaches its apogee in Anthony Burgess' violent dystopia, *A Clockwork Orange* (1962). Burgess' primary textual innovation was to create for his sinister juvenile narrator a hybrid language, rife with insider slang that sounds like Russianized English. The language evokes a familiar world rendered menacingly alien, an effect reinforced by Cold War era hints that the novel's England has become a crumbling totalitarian state.

Such negative visions of England's place in the new world of affluence were not confined to young or textually innovative writers. A similar pessimism and sense of decline may be seen in the postwar work of Graham Greene, a novelist already well established by mid-century. His acclaimed *Brighton Rock* of 1938 had featured a nihilistic and violent, young working-class protagonist but had held out a belief in his potential salvation. His controversial *The Quiet American* (1955) has lost that belief, exploring alienation on a national level, addressing Britain's eclipse as an international power. Narrated by a cynical English journalist in Saigon during the early years of covert United States involvement in Vietnam, the novel was perceived by many as anti-American for its depiction of an idealistic but fatally naive young CIA operative. While not necessarily nostalgic for British imperialism, *The Quiet American* portrays a new world order with little to recommend it over the old.

Lord of the Flies (1954), by Greene's slightly younger contemporary William Golding, while also stylistically distant from the gritty realism of Sillitoe and company, articulates a similar sense of social pessimism. Critics have often seen Golding's work, from this now classic first novel to his Booker Prize-winning *Rites of Passage* (1980), as falling outside prevailing literary movements and categories—as neither "realistic" nor "experimental"; its characteristic, almost allegorical evocation of universal patterns of human tragedy apparently owes more to Aeschylus than to the post-war boom. However, Golding's major novels enact the rejection of welfare-state humanist optimism and a sense of the persistence of class-based division and violently irreconcilable perspectives common to the influential novels of mid-to-late century.

Such bleak visions may have contributed to the feeling on the part of many readers and writers alike that, by 1960, English fiction suffered from a profound lack of vitality. Widespread uncertainty about where England was going may have translated into uncertainty about the direction of the English novel, and a certain scepticism toward the new applied not only to content but also to form. While late-modernist experimentation, from Nabokov to Beckett to Burroughs, received critical acclaim in the United States and France, experimental novelists in England, such as B.S. Johnson and Christine Brooke-Rose, tended to be ignored or denounced. Realism has had a deeper and longer-lasting—although by no means total—hold on the English novel, despite the central role played by English novelists such as Virginia Woolf and Dorothy Richardson in developing modernist techniques. That hold may be attributed in part to the English novel's tradition of representing class and social issues; and while many critics, myself included, would argue that Woolf and Joyce, for instance, are profoundly social novelists, others see the formal innovations of modernism as too individualistic and psychologically oriented to represent the public realm.

Many of the novelists who rose to prominence during the 1960s—Iris Murdoch, John Fowles, Margaret Drabble, Doris Lessing—combine realism with some degree of psychological experimentation, often in the service of social criticism. Murdoch, although originally Irish (and in some ways indicative of the blurred line between Irish and English literature), has been one of the most prolific and visible of novelists and critics in England since the mid-1950s. Her work has been short-listed for the prestigious Booker Prize—which she won with *The Sea, the Sea* in 1978—a record four times. Murdoch's novels, a mixture of realism and symbolism, have been praised for their dissection of complex human relationships, a dissection that is often drily analytical.

Both Drabble in *The Waterfall* (1969) and Lessing in *The Golden Notebook* (1962) address the interior lives of middle-class women going mad in their restricted worlds. Lessing is the more experimental of the two. Her epic *The Golden Notebook,* a work that now seems prescient, predating as it did the rise of second-wave feminism in Britain, employs a complex interwoven form operating on several fictional levels, combining novels-within-the-novel, first-person diaries, and third-person narration. This form allows Lessing to address both sociopolitical and personal-psychological aspects of her protagonist, Anna, who struggles with political isolation and threatened mental breakdown. Anna, an ex-communist, is a figure disillusioned with political engagement and with the forms of private life available in postwar England—but Lessing, like Drabble in her own style, adds a distinctly feminist angle to the familiar themes.

In the late 1960s, two enlivening shifts took place in English fiction: one was a significant movement toward postmodernism; the other, the establishment of the Booker Prize.

Fredric Jameson and others have argued that postmodernism responds to a historical moment in which images play an increasingly crucial role in structuring power relations (see Jameson, 1991). The peculiarly English form of postmodernism seems to be shaped, as were the countercultures of the 1960s, by some combination of the rich sense of possibilities accompanying a now prolonged period of affluence with a growing dissatisfaction with the range of available social and political visions. The sources of this dissatisfaction included antiwar sentiment, the recognition by many women that they were not sharing equally in affluence or opportunities, growing anti-immigrant sentiment and resistance against it, and disillusionment with former radical alternatives, prompted by the left's revulsion both at Stalinism and the crushing of the "Prague Spring" and, at home, at the compromises of the once-socialist Labour Party government with private business.

If these developments saddled writers' imaginations with the need to envision society anew, several of them took up the challenge, producing novels explicitly concerned with aestheticism, with art as a system allied with magic and infinite possibility as well as with the concrete social world. While some of John

Fowles' novels are more formally conventional, *The French Lieutenant's Woman* (1969), with its multiple possible endings and its self-reflexive questioning of historical inevitability, set the stage for later work, such as Graham Swift's *Waterland* (1983), D.M. Thomas' *The White Hotel* (1981), Jeanette Winterson's *Sexing the Cherry* (1989), and Fowles' own *A Maggot* (1985), all novels that critic Linda Hutcheon might categorize as "historiographic metafiction," a term she identifies with postmodernism (see Hutcheon, 1989). Such novels tend to view history as something that can be used toward numerous ends and to view the self as a fluid creation rather than an inherent given—particularly appealing ideas, perhaps, to a nation leaving its "great" imperial history and entering an unfamiliar postindustrial world order.

Angela Carter's novels, from the mid-1960s to the late 1980s, mingle the fantastic with the insistently political, in a richly artificial language filled with echoes of previous literature. Her sources tend more to popular forms such as the Gothic and fairy tales and to French philosophy and literature, from the Marquis de Sade to symbolism, surrealism, and poststructuralist theory, than to the mainstream canon of English novels. Both *The Infernal Desire Machines of Doctor Hoffman* (1972) and *The Passion of New Eve* (1977) are part dystopian fantasy, part picaresque, following predictably cynical narrators on journeys that are at once geographical adventures and explorations of our existing range of images and fantasies, many of them attended by dark and violent consequences, especially for women. The narrator of *New Eve,* meditating on classic Hollywood movies, makes explicit the connection between art or imagination and politics:

> I think it was Rilke who so lamented the inadequacy of our symbolism—regretted so bitterly that we cannot, unlike the (was it?) Ancient Greeks find adequate external symbols for the life within us—yes, that's the quotation. But, no. He was wrong. Our external symbols must always express the life within us with absolute precision; . . . the nature of our life alone has determined their forms. A critique of these symbols is a critique of our lives.

Carter's novels both critique and expand the existing range of social imagery.

Other writers have continued into the 1990s Carter's postmodernist strategy of recontextualizing existing language and texts, and thereby both opening them to critical examination and reinvigorating them for further uses. While Winterson's aestheticism has grown increasingly ponderous in recent years, her first four novels, from *Oranges Are Not the Only Fruit* (1985) to *Sexing the Cherry,* adapt, retell, and combine a variety of stories, from European history to fairy tales, to create a fantastical and sometimes subversive pastiche.

Martin Amis takes a different turn on postmodernist pastiche, not so much borrowing existing texts as reproducing the specialized dialects and discourses of contemporary English and American society, in novels striking for their stingingly accurate mimicry and reminiscent of Amis' father, Kingsley Amis, in their scathing humor. In *Money* (1984) and *London Fields* (1989), Amis satirizes the get-rich-quick ethos of life under the Thatcher government, creating in a later decade another version of the scepticism and dystopian visions of the "classless society" heralded in the late 1950s. A crucial difference, however, between Martin Amis' novels and those of that previous era is that Amis presents a world that is at once highly artificial—in the quoted reproduced quality of both its language and its rather cartoonish characters—and utterly without an outside or escape. His work can be vulnerable to Jameson's critique of postmodernism as a closed system of reproduced, shallow surfaces, and as parody without alternatives.

Amis is, in fact, one of the writers whose novels have caused controversy (accused of a "lack of sympathy") when nominated for the annual Booker Prize. The Booker, established in 1969 by multinational corporation Booker-McConnell Ltd (now Booker PLC), has served admirably its stated aim of generating renewed interest in "quality" fiction in Britain (at a time when it seemed moribund), and also its less explicit goal of helping publishers sell books. The interest generated has not always been positive, but the controversies around the prize offer intriguing insights into vastly divergent opinions on the state of the English novel and into how elusive—or embattled, according to more conservative, nationalist commentators—that adjective "English" has become.

The Booker, worth £20,000 to the winner, is open to any novel published in English, and published first in England, by a citizen of Britain, the Commonwealth, or other former British colonies (excluding the United States). Despite these broad criteria, the awarding of the prize itself is a very British affair, with a changing panel of British judges, an awards ceremony televised by the BBC, and major newspaper coverage and publisher-bookstore publicity campaigns. British bookmakers, commissioned by the prize sponsors, even take bets on the finalists and the winner.

Even more, the Booker is a question of Englishness and English high culture for many observers. There has been loud dissent in years when the list of six finalists has appeared "too un-English," or when the winning novel has been considered inaccessible. The issue of accessibility reflects concern that the Prize cannot both sustain elite culture (or serious art) and encourage popular reading. In 1994, for instance, the selection of Scottish nationalist James Kelman's somewhat experimental *How Late It Was, How Late* was criticized on both counts, with some commentators complaining that no white, heterosexual Englishman had even made the short list. These latter objections suggest that trends in literary novel writing—and practical questions about which novels will be celebrated and promoted—are still very much tied up with larger discomfort over England's loss of the centrality and preeminence it once assumed, culturally and politically, among English-speaking nations.

This discomfort also reflects on the fact that, like many former colonial powers, England has increasingly become a multiethnic society in recent decades. The 1950s and 1960s saw massive waves of labor migration from, particularly, the Anglophone Caribbean and the Indian subcontinent. When long-existing conditions in the Commonwealth of unequal land distribution and economies drained by export combined with acute labor shortages in Britain, many Commonwealth Britons took advantage of their lingering semicolonial status to immigrate to the mother country in search of work.

Likewise, the old imperial custom of sending the most promising sons of colonial families to be educated in England lingered, but now without the concomitant understanding that these Anglicized colonials would subsequently return to their native countries as civil servants, doctors, and the like. Thus, such prominent novelists as the Booker winners Salman Rushdie (born in India) and V.S. Naipaul (born in Trinidad) have come to England to study and stayed to write and live as naturalized British citizens. The differences between the two reflect the paradoxes of postimperial England. Naipaul, in largely modernist novels such as the Conrad-influenced *A Bend in the River* (1979), tends to offer grim contrasts between the inefficiency and corruption of the former colonies and the order and aesthetic vision of England; while Rushdie's postmodernist novels also depict postcolonial chaos, but simultaneously critique the racism and arrogance of the English.

Rushdie, a fascinating figure in whom to examine the paradoxes of the contemporary English novel, is probably (to his discomfort) its best-known practitioner. The death sentence issued against him for blasphemy in *The Satanic Verses* (1988) has not only made him a household name; it has also highlighted cultural tensions between England and the Commonwealth and among British Muslims (many of whom denounced Rushdie as an English traitor). Arguably, Rushdie's novels, most notably his brilliant *Midnight's Children* (1981; winner of a special "Booker of Bookers"), are indeed blasphemous, for they borrow cheerfully from history, the English literary canon, Bombay movies, and Indian sacred literature and folk traditions, regarding all with equal irreverence and subjecting all to biting satire. Nothing is sacred to them. In this, the "spicy chutney" of Rushdie's textual practice may be as English as any current aesthetic approach, reflecting profound changes in both nation and literature in the latter half of the 20th century. In 1922, when T.S. Eliot turned to sacred Indian texts for the conclusion of his epoch-defining tale of moral malaise, *The Waste Land,* those texts were being subsumed into, placed at the service of, a Western voice that bemoaned its lost cultural greatness. Six decades later, it is the Western voice that is assimilated into Rushdie's verbal cooking-pot, to emerge with its great tradition looking distinctly different—subject to sceptical revision and playful renewal.

NICOLA PITCHFORD

See also Angela Carter; Critics and Criticism (20th Century); Graham Greene; Doris Lessing; Lucky Jim; Iris Murdoch; V.S. Naipaul; Postmodernism; Salman Rushdie

Further Reading

Allsop, Kenneth, *The Angry Decade: A Survey of the Cultural Revolt of the Nineteen-Fifties*, London: Owen, and New York: British Book Centre, 1958

Anderson, Linda, editor, *Plotting Change: Contemporary Women's Fiction*, London: Edward Arnold, and New York: Routledge, Chapman and Hall, 1990

Bradbury, Malcolm, *The Novel Today: Contemporary Writers on Modern Fiction*, Manchester: Manchester University Press, and Totowa, New Jersey: Rowman and Littlefield, 1977; revised edition, London: Fontana, 1990

Higdon, David Leon, *Shadows of the Past in Contemporary British Fiction*, London: Macmillan, 1984; Athens: University of Georgia Press, 1985

Hutcheon, Linda, *The Politics of Postmodernism*, London and New York: Routledge, 1989

Jameson, Fredric, *Postmodernism, or, The Cultural Logic of Late Capitalism,* London: Verso, and Durham, North Carolina: Duke University Press, 1991

Lee, Alison, *Realism and Power: Postmodern British Fiction,* London and New York: Routledge, 1990

Massie, Allan, *The Novel Today: A Critical Guide to the British Novel, 1970–1989,* London and New York: Longman (in association with The British Council), 1990

Sage, Lorna, *Women in the House of Fiction: Post-War Women Novelists,* London: Macmillan, and New York: Routledge, 1992

Scanlan, Margaret, *Traces of Another Time: History and Politics in Postwar British Fiction,* Princeton, New Jersey: Princeton University Press, 1990

Sinfield, Alan, *Literature, Politics and Culture in Postwar Britain,* Oxford: Blackwell, and Berkeley: University of California Press, 1989

Engravings. *See* Illustrations and Engravings

Entwicklungsroman. *See* Bildungsroman

Environmental Novel

In 1962 Rachel Carson's *Silent Spring,* the book that declared the dangers of DDT, acted as a starting gun for the modern environmental movement. Like feminism, which also has its contemporary roots in the 1960s, environmentalism has produced substantial paradigm shifts in Western societies. Two grounding ideas of the modern environmental movement may be seen to have had an effect on the novel: the idea of environmental crisis produced by human beings' unchecked or unthinking exploitation of the nonhuman world, and the idea of "ecology"—of the importance of studying phenomena in relationship to one another. As "the origins of environmental crisis lie deep in human cultural traditions" (Meeker, 1972), it is clear that the kinds of stories we tell both reflect and help to produce attitudes that are related to environmental practice.

Like the feminist novel, the environmental novel is both an entity and a perception or way of reading. Environmentalists may now be considered stock characters, appearing, for example, in G.M. Ford's detective stories set in the US Pacific Northwest. Edward Abbey's *The Monkey Wrench Gang* (1975) has a plot that involves environmental activism. Dealing with a group undertaking ecologically motivated sabotage in and around Utah, it is a didactic work that demonstrates, in serio-comic mode, a clear awareness of the imperatives of the environmental movement. It was written at that moment in early environmentalism when the sense of impending disaster (of "ecocatastrophe") was the chief motivation for action. It contributed the term *monkey-wrench-*ing to the language of environmental sabotage and has served as a gleefully inspiring text for environmental activists. More recently, the plot of New Zealander Rachel McAlpine's *The Limits of Green* (1985) involves environmental activism.

The influence of environmental thinking on the novel may be seen not only in environmentally motivated plots but in less direct ways. Some novels produced in the last 20 years, like Australian Rodney Hall's *Just Relations* (1982) and Australian Beverly Farmer's *The Seal Woman* (1992), while expressing concern about environmental destruction, are much more diffusely related to the shift in ideas about nature and human responsibility for the environment that the modern environmental movement has helped to bring about. Formally and thematically, they reflect an ecological awareness and contribute to a rethinking of the idea of nature and of the human being's place in it. In Beverly Farmer's *The Seal Woman* and in Canadian Marian Engel's *Bear* (1976) there is a focus on thinking through the body and a new perspective on relationships with animals. Both novels reflect the conjunction of environmentalism and feminism that has produced the concept of "ecofeminism."

Like the environmental movement itself, novels with environmental themes are found in a variety of national literatures. Postcolonial experience has encouraged an interest in the writings of indigenous peoples, and environmentalists have turned to indigenous populations to find ways of remaking the relationship between the human and the nonhuman world. Native

American writer Leslie Marmon Silko's *Ceremony* (1977) has become a key text in environmental fiction formally as well as thematically. Marrying oral tradition to the structure of the Western quest story, it shows the power of alternative forms to break through old ways of seeing the world.

As with feminism, environmentalism can become a way of reading—a kind of attention pointing out attitudes that might not have been otherwise as readily defined. Through the lens of environmentalism, Daniel Defoe's *Robinson Crusoe* (1719), for example, seems even more clearly a text that demonstrates developing Enlightenment attitudes toward the exploitation of the nonhuman world. Crusoe as colonist is also Crusoe lord of the natural world, taming it to his needs. On the other hand, Herman Melville's *Moby-Dick* (1851) may be considered a great environmental novel not just because of its attention to the nonhuman world (animals again, and the sea) but because of its questioning, through its presentation of Ahab's monomania, of what is now called "anthropocentric" behavior. James Fenimore Cooper's Leatherstocking Tales (1823–41) contain passages not only appreciative of landscape but demonstrating a consciousness of loss brought by human exploitation. Near the beginning of *The Prairie* (1823) there is a striking description of the wanton cutting down of a tree. Richard Jefferies' neglected *After London* (1885) is also a novel about the loss of an environment, movingly depicting an English countryside after the destruction of London. W.H. Hudson's *The Purple Land That England Lost* (1885) and *Green Mansions: A Romance of the Tropical Forest* (1904) take a naturalist's eye to South America and anticipate ways in which the natural environment, rather than being an adjunct to a human story, looms as a genuine participant. Many of Thomas Hardy's novels and the more recent *Waterland* (1983) by Graham Swift may be read in this way. Indeed, the very movement of literary naturalism may be seen as in some ways prefiguring the new naturalism entailed by an environmental consciousness.

A broad category of futuristic fiction has readily accommodated environmental themes. Science-fiction themes such as the colonization of other worlds and the aftermath of disaster have been attractive vehicles for writers drawn to thinking about the possibility of environmental crisis. Occasional early novels such as Jefferies' *After London* and Hudson's *A Crystal Age* (1887), while not as "scientific" as the fantasies of H.G. Wells, anticipate the marrying of environmental ideas and futuristic, sometimes dystopic, sometimes catastrophic, fiction. Ursula Le Guin has been influential in recent years in uniting environmental concerns with science fiction, producing a major work of environmental fantasy, *Always Coming Home* (1985). Brian W. Aldiss' *The Long Afternoon of Earth* (1962) and his *Helliconia* trilogy (1982–85) are informed by ecological principles. Ecocatastrophe stories go back to Jefferies and are found intermittently throughout 20th-century fiction. Problems deriving from overexploitation of the earth are found in A.G. Street's *Already Walks To-morrow* (1938), Ward Moore's *Greener Than You Think* (1947), and John Christopher's *The Death of Grass* (1956), and more recently in Hal Clement's *The Nitrogen Fix* (1980), George Turner's *The Sea and Summer* (1987; also entitled *Drowning Towers*), David Brin's *Earth* (1990), and Gabrielle Lord's *Salt* (1990).

RUTH M. BLAIR

Further Reading

Dillard, Annie, *Living By Fiction*, New York: Harper and Row, 1982

Glotfelty, Cheryll, and Harold Fromm, editors, *The Ecocriticism Reader: Landmarks in Literary Ecology*, Athens: University of Georgia Press, 1996

Meeker, Joseph, *The Comedy of Survival: Studies in Literary Ecology*, New York: Scribner, 1972; 3rd edition, Tucson: University of Arizona Press, 1997

Murphy, Patrick D., editor, *Literature of Nature: An International Sourcebook*, Chicago and London: Fitzroy Dearborn, 1998

Robinson, Kim Stanley, editor, *Future Primitive: The New Ecotopias*, New York: Tom Doherty Associates, 1994

Epic and Novel

The debate on the relationship of the novel to epic says at least as much about the rhetoric and the history of criticism as it does about literary history and generic form. In the contrast between Samuel Johnson's 18th-century epic criticism and Guy de Maupassant's 19th-century novel criticism, we can begin to isolate its essentials:

> By the general consent of critics the first praise of genius is due to the writer of an epic poem. . . . Epic poetry undertakes to teach the most important truths by the most pleasing precepts. . . . Bossu is of opinion that the poet's first work is to find a *moral*, which his fable is afterwards to illustrate and establish. This seems to have been the process only of Milton. (*The Life of Milton*)

> If *Don Quixote* is a novel, is *The Red and the Black* another? *The Count of Monte-Cristo* . . . *L'Assommoir* . . . *Elective Affinities* . . . *Madame Bovary* . . . *M. de Camours*? Which of these works is a novel? What are these famous rules? Where do they come from? Who established them? In virtue of what principle, from what sort of authority, and with what reasons? . . . In sum, the

public is composed of various groups, each crying out: "console me, amuse me, make me sad, be sentimental, make me dream, make me laugh, make me tremble, make me cry, make me think." ("Le Roman" from *Pierre et Jean*)

The analytical Johnson, in his reasoning and his style, exhibits the definitional, rule-bound, and deductive emphases of epic criticism, whereas de Maupassant, although coming from the more classicizing and regulated French tradition, dramatically throws up his hands before the task of deducing the rules of the novel, and his impassioned criticism points out the dominance of the individual case over the formal system. One presupposes the assured authority of the high cultural critics ("general consent," "Bossu is of opinion"), while the other democratically demands to know on what grounds such authority has been assumed and, in the absence of any answer, turns to the insistent and various desires of the public. Indeed Johnson's criticism reveals just how rule-bound the epic could be in discovering that Milton's epic, although it comes toward the end of the epic tradition, was nonetheless the first such poem fully to conform to a venerable rule ("process only of Milton"). For de Maupassant, the final point seems to be that each new novel of any real interest is so not because it more perfectly fulfills a traditional expectation, but because it eludes one. And, when de Maupassant does turn to high culture, the emphasis upon the novel's freedom from a regulated paradigm only increases: "A few elite spirits make this demand of the artist: 'Create something beautiful for me, something in a form that best conforms to your imagination, that follows your unique temperament'." In short, Johnson presents the epic as the crafted product of patronage and of a guild tradition, where the long-established artisanal rules of the group take precedence over the innovations of the individual artist or the wishes of the buyer. De Maupassant points to the novel as a consumer item either mass produced to fulfill the manifold demands of an anonymous public or tastefully fashioned to appeal to a connoisseur's desire for a choice novelty—in any case a product bound by no other rule than that it be pleasing and, of course, that it sell.

This old chestnut of literary history—the novel-epic debate—still retains its interest for us, in part because it continues to be used as an objective explanatory device and as an ideology. The novel has asserted and still asserts its vitality and modernity against the supposed sterility of the antiquated epic. More generally, the debate exemplifies the ongoing popularization of literary and artistic standards, the progressive opening up of the exclusive and high cultural canon. As Margaret Anne Doody argues in *The True Story of the Novel* (1996), in its preoccupation with the elitist epic, high cultural criticism long slighted the distant antecedents of the novel in the popular ancient romance. By the same token, the contemporary critical dominance of popular cultural valuations and novelistic notions of the canon, which view the canon as best regulated by public demand subject to revolutionary change and the whims of fashion, has in turn grounded its efforts to overturn the remaining authority of the established canon on the same relative evaluation of epic and novel. In other words, the current dominance of the novel is associated with an ideology of democratic, even subversive, openness that entails a rejection of epic's artistic authority and cultural pretension, an insistence on that form's sterility, and a

rigid association of its values with those of a dead or dying past. (In contrast, one can note how the conservative F.R. Leavis in his *The Great Tradition* [1948] sought to establish a more exclusive notion of a novelistic canon precisely after the model of epic's paternal canonicity.)

The era most often associated with the rise of the novel—that is, the late 17th century and the 18th century, especially in commercial England—was also an age marked by the strenuous failures of its leading poets, above all Alexander Pope, to compose martial epics. These failures are counterbalanced by the equally remarkable successes (by the same poets) in mock-epic, a form distinguished, in Pope's *The Rape of the Lock* (1714) and William Cowper's *The Task* (1785) for example, by a contrast between a past heroic world of significant male action and a present unheroic world of circumscribed female domesticity and comfort, between male slaughter and roasted meat and female games and afternoon tea, between wearied warriors reclining on rocks and bored ladies lounging on sofas. Such a contrast, with all its subtle implications regarding the opportunities for literacy and the occasion for reading, is one that Ian Watt's still important *Rise of the Novel* (1957) places at the center of its analysis. Watt directly associates the novel's rise with the growth of the middle class, an increasing female readership, and the dominance of values associated with that class and that gender. Important works of the late 1980s by Nancy Armstrong (*Desire and Domestic Fiction*, 1987) and Michael McKeon (*The Origins of the English Novel*, 1987) only supplement the fundamental theses of Watt with Foucauldian insights and Marxist rigor. More particularly for our question, Watt, along with Armstrong and McKeon, argues for the victory of Samuel Richardson over Henry Fielding: a distinctly female and aggressively middle-class derivation of the novel won out over Fielding's efforts to claim a male and aristocratic heritage for the new form as a species of epic, a "comic epic in prose," in Fielding's own words. Rejecting Fielding's claim for an epic heritage, these critics find far more relevance for the novel's origins in conduct books, romances, letter writing, and popular ephemera than in the high tradition of Vergilian grandeur and seriousness or even Popean detail and mockery. The point to be made here is that these scholars rely upon the assumption that epic *did* fail, that it *was* the sterile form of a declining old order, and that the novel represented the positive alternative to both the epic's failure and the mock-epic's negative success.

However, as the classical scholar Brooks Otis well demonstrates, failure is one of the basic conditions of the epic tradition (see Otis, 1968). The very ambitiousness and finality posited by epic—especially in its stricter post-Homeric, Vergilian, or neoclassical, form—has from the beginning been characterized more by failure than success. Thus it is by no means obvious that the 18th century's inability to produce a canonical epic should be taken as a sign of the failure or sterility of the form. What is obvious is that since the 18th century, middle-class popular culture and its democratic and market-place canons of criticism have become increasingly dominant—to the point that a mode of literature, the epic, that makes extensive cultural knowledge of a peculiar and erudite sort explicitly necessary for the reading of its texts has emerged as the symbol of all that popular, novelistic, and middle-class culture seeks most to delegitimize. And so the Soviet critic Mikhail Bakhtin, the leading theoretician of the novel-epic question in the 20th century, can assert that epic was an essentially sterile and ossified form from its inception: "tradition isolates the world of epic from personal experience, from any new insights, from any personal initiative in understanding and interpreting. . . . The epic world is an utterly finished thing." His progressive and Darwinian rhetoric clearly renders epic both an historical and evolutionary dead end. (Tennyson anticipated such views in his poem *The Epic* [1842], by referring to that form as a "mastodon" in contrast to the novel, "the newest fashion of the day.") For Bakhtin, epic and novel define themselves in a series of rigid contrasts: absolute past versus developing present, completed genre versus evolving genre, national and authoritarian versus individual and free, antirealistic versus realistic, official versus unofficial, dead versus living. Most famously, he characterizes epic as monoglossic, that is, as a form that privileges one centralizing construction of the world, a construction determined by official authority and the dead weight of the past. By contrast, he sees the novel as heteroglossic, a form open to various voices of a developing present—voices of, presumably, different genders, races, and, above all, classes.

Although Bakhtin's model is now taken for the definitive statement on this question, critics have been too uncritical of its manifest difficulties: are we really to believe that epic has been an essentially dead form since Homer? More to the point, critics have overlooked Bakhtin's deep indebtedness to Victor Hugo, whose *Notre-Dame de Paris* (1831) implicitly sets forth the political and literary reading of the revolutionary and anti-epic carnivalesque found in Bakhtin's study of Rabelais. Hugo's "Preface" to *Cromwell* (1827) explicitly asserts most of the major antinomies found in Bakhtin's "Epic and Novel." What in Bakhtin has been accepted as objective scholarship and careful description appears in Hugo for what it mainly is—a middle-class, progressive, and liberal rhetoric that posits the novel, in opposition to the epic, as the literary equivalent of the French Revolution, the Glorious Revolution of 1688, or, more generally, the death of the aristocratic and feudal old order at the hands of economic progress and democratic freedom. All these claims may be true; the model is compelling. But they undeniably serve an ideological purpose—and to see this purpose as not incidental but primary warns us against too readily identifying epic with a dead past and too easily ceding to the novel all claims of novelty.

Epic cannot be tied wholly to the fortunes of aristocracy and feudalism. And, in fact, aspects of the epic tradition remain vital for the novel. An example will clarify the point: *Beauchamp's Career* (1875), a fine historical novel by the Victorian George Meredith, veers subtly, as historical novels are wont to do, between identifying itself with the epic (and political and military history) and the novel (and social and biographical history). In so doing, it reveals something essential about both forms and about the question of their competing notions of canonicity. Thus, on the one hand, *Beauchamp's Career* openly, in the manner of neoclassical epic, sets forth its indebtedness to epic antecedents—in this case Thomas Carlyle's *French Revolution* (3 vols., 1837), a text itself thoroughly imbued with Vergilian themes, references, and ambitions. Meredith's text propounds the stylistic and formal importance of Carlyle for its own language and structure no less than it narrates, in the history of its hero Beauchamp, a military and political career of a distinctly Carlylean stamp. On the other hand, the text hints at but disguises another and deeper debt, this time to the domestic epic of

George Eliot's great *Middlemarch* (1872), published just three years before Meredith's novel.

In the famous preface to *Middlemarch,* Eliot rehearses the typical Cervantean novelistic theme of the impossibility of epic heroism in the modern world and laments that her heroine cannot repeat St. Theresa's achievement. Her Dorothea Brooke is unable to find an "epic life wherein there was a constant unfolding of far-resonant action" and unmemorably dissipates her energies among the small circle of a domestic and female world so typical of the novel. Finding "no sacred poet," she sinks "unwept into oblivion." Meredith's characterization of Beauchamp's fate closely recalls Eliot's statement of the problem:

> The simple truth has to be told: how he loved his country, and for another and broader love, growing out of his first passion, fought it; and being small by comparison, and finding no giant of the Philistines disposed to receive a stone in his fore-skull, pummelled the obmutescent mass, to the confusion of a conceivable epic. His indifferent England refused him. That is all I can say. The greater power of the two, she seems, with a quiet derision that does not belie her amiable passivity, to have reduced in Beauchamp's career the boldest readiness for public action, and some good stout efforts besides, to the flat result of an optically discernible influence of our hero's character in the domestic circle; perhaps a faintly-outlined circle or two beyond it.

The novel refuses epic recognition to its hero even as it refuses textual recognition to *Middlemarch.* Resonant action by men or canonical permanence for texts is not a possibility in the modern world. The text openly aligns its main character with Carlylean hero-worship, but, more subtly yet silently, it plots his life through the anti-epic feminization and domesticization articulated by Eliot. Eliot's novel far more than Carlyle's epic controls the meaning of *Beauchamp's Career,* which makes it a novel instead of an epic, a social instead of a high political text. Nevertheless, Carlyle is called upon loudly and the reader is asked to take heed of his ringing words, while Eliot's subtle qualifications and generic strategies are left to be discovered by the reader who may just happen to notice and know.

The debate finally comes down to precisely the question of self-conscious memory. In the epic mode texts thematize the possibility of far-reaching glory for hero and author alike. Epics assert their recollection of previous epics and previous heroes and aspire to permanent national monuments. This call to history is not a dead weight as Bakhtin would have it; rather, it is the centerpiece of a violent drama and a vital effort by hero and poet alike. In the novelistic mode such debts to past heroes and past novels tend to be denied, covered up, or invoked dubiously or comically—as, for example, Jane Austen's *Northanger Abbey* (1818) mockingly invokes Ann Radcliffe's *The Mysteries of Udolpho* (1794). Generalization always has its exceptions, but *Beauchamp's Career* may be taken as representative—in its open acknowledgment of Carlylean epic heroism and its secretive reliance upon Eliotic novelistic heroism—of the way epic makes memory central to its heroic narrative and its authorial ambition, and the way the novel thematizes precisely the opposite, focusing on characters who accomplish only forgettable actions and on a canonical tradition unable or unwilling to assert any possibility of enduring monumentality. The popularity and readability of the novel rests to no small degree on its refusal to make its readers aware of any expectations of canonical knowledge on their part. The great modern charge against the "ossified" and "overburdened" epic rises precisely out of its repeated demands upon the reader to know Homer, Vergil, Lucan, Statius, Dante, Tasso, Spenser, and Milton. However, the fact remains that many of our finest novels do gain from such readerly mastery—they just pretend that they do not. Bakhtin's (and Hugo's and de Maupassant's) great claim for the novel rests on its status as a freely developing form, one representing a living and open-ended present, in contrast to the completed and static epic with its closed-off and absolute version of the past. But that freedom comes at the price of suppressing and deliberately forgetting the past that is nonetheless there, at the price of belittling the importance of individual acts and individual texts and denying the weight of corporate history and literary tradition.

Popular culture is no doubt popular because it refuses to make the explicit demands upon the reader that high culture does, but that refusal cannot hide the fact that, just as the *Aeneid* articulates its meaning in relation to the *Iliad*, so does *Madame Bovary* to *Don Quixote*, *Beloved* to *The House of the Seven Gables,* and *Star Wars* to *The Hidden Fortress.* No doubt, by remaining silent regarding such paternity, these texts effectively reduce the interpretive significance of their debt, magnify the thematic function of their originality, lessen the grip of an exclusive tradition, and thereby increase overall sales in the marketplace, which, after all, generated them and to which they therefore pay homage as their true canonical father.

EDWARD A. ADAMS

See also Canon; Critics and Criticism (18th Century); Dialogism; Genre Criticism; Medieval Narrative; Myth and Novel; Parody and Pastiche; Renaissance Narrative; Saga; Verse Narrative

Further Reading

Armstrong, Nancy, *Desire and Domestic Fiction: A Political History of the Novel,* New York: Oxford University Press, 1987

Bakhtin, Mikhail, "Epic and Novel," in *The Dialogic Imagination: Four Essays,* translated by Caryl Emerson and Michael Holquist, edited by Holquist, Austin: University of Texas Press, 1981

Doody, Margaret Anne, *The True Story of the Novel,* New Brunswick, New Jersey: Rutgers University Press, 1996; London: HarperCollins, 1997

Duncan, Ian, *Modern Romance and Transformations of the Novel: The Gothic, Scott, Dickens,* Cambridge and New York: Cambridge University Press, 1992

Griffiths, Frederick T., and Stanley J. Rabinowitz, *Novel Epics: Gogol, Dostoevsky, and National Narrative,* Evanston, Illinois: Northwestern University Press, 1990

Jameson, Fredric, *The Political Unconscious: Narrative as a Socially Symbolic Act,* Ithaca, New York: Cornell University Press, and London: Methuen, 1981

McKeon, Michael, *The Origins of the English Novel, 1600–1740,* Baltimore: Johns Hopkins University Press, 1987

McWilliams, John P., Jr., *The American Epic: Transforming a Genre, 1770–1860,* Cambridge and New York: Cambridge University Press, 1989

Murrin, Michael, *History and Warfare in Renaissance Epic,* Chicago: University of Chicago Press, 1994

Otis, Brooks, *Virgil: A Study in Civilized Poetry,* New York: Oxford University Press, and Oxford: Clarendon Press, 1968

Quint, David, *Epic and Empire: Politics and Generic Form from Virgil to Milton,* Princeton, New Jersey: Princeton University Press, 1993

Tillyard, E.M.W., *The English Epic and Its Background,* London: Chatto and Windus, and New York: Oxford University Press, 1954

Watt, Ian, *The Rise of the Novel: Studies in Defoe, Richardson, and Fielding,* Berkeley: University of California Press, and London: Chatto and Windus, 1957

Epilogue. *See* Framing and Embedding in Narrative

Epistolary Novel

Epistolary novels (also called "letter novels") are novels narrated wholly or in large part through letters written by the characters. Epistolary fiction can be traced back as far as the Roman author Ovid (43 B.C.–17 A.D.) and the late Hellenic author Alciphron (2nd or 3rd century A.D.). The form is still used by contemporary novelists. Epistolary fiction saw its heyday in the late 17th, 18th, and early 19th centuries, as it became fundamental to the production of the modern novel. Many landmark fictions of this period are told in letters, including Madame de Graffigny's *Lettres d'une Péruvienne* (1747; *Letters from a Peruvian*

Woman); Samuel Richardson's *Clarissa* (7 vols., 1747–48); Jean-Jacques Rousseau's *Julie; ou, La Nouvelle Héloïse* (1761; *Julie; or, The New Eloise*); J.W. Goethe's *Die Leiden des jungen Werthers* (1774; *The Sufferings of Young Werther*); Choderlos de Laclos' *Les Liaisons dangereuses* (1782; *Dangerous Acquaintances*); and Ugo Foscolo's *Ultime lettere di Jacopo Ortis* (1802; *Letters of Ortis*). These novels all enjoyed extraordinary success when first published and continue to be read and admired by scholars and educated readers. Many of the great 19th-century novelists, from Jane Austen to Fedor Dostoevskii, used the form for juvenilia or other experiments before settling on their preferred form of omniscient narration. In the late 20th century the form found particular favor among feminist authors, who expanded its base from Europe and America to Africa and Asia. Portuguese writers Maria Isabel Barreno, Maria Teresa Horta, and Maria Velho da Costa wrote their *Novas cartas portuguesas* (1972; *New Portuguese Letters*) in response to the early *Lettres portugaises* of Marianna Alcoforado and Noel Bouton Chamlly (1669); Italian writer Dacia Maraini published *Lettere a Marina* (1981; *Letters to Marina*), and Americans Anna Castillo and Alice Walker produced *The Mixquiahuala Letters* (1986) and *The Color Purple* (1982), respectively. They were joined by the Senegalese writer Miriama Bâ with *Une si longue lettre* (1981; *So Long a Letter*) and the Taiwanese Li Ang with *I feng wei chi ti ching shu* (1986; *An Unsent Love Letter*).

The straightforward definition of the epistolary novel belies the fact that it is sometimes difficult to decide whether a particular work belongs to the form. For example, early and important epistolary fictions are not novels but *Decameron*-like frame-tale collections in which miscellaneous letters are read to an assembled group and commented upon. Oddly enough, even the self-named "first" epistolary novel, the Abbé d'Aubignac's *Roman des lettres* (1667; *Novel of Letters*), falls into this category of epistolary fiction. Perhaps the two most notorious difficulties of classifying a work as an epistolary novel are deciding what proportion of letters is necessary for qualification as such and distinguishing between a letter novel and a memoir or diary novel.

Robert Adams Day (1966) describes the other genres that surround and nuance the epistolary novel: the drama, the autobiography, the diary, "real" letters, and newspapers. Elizabeth MacArthur (1990) has recuperated this manifold epistolary form into a single idea by suggesting that the early modern period preferred the epistolary form because its preoccupation with creating meaning and with questioning the received order was best conveyed in pluralistic, fragmented textual forms, such as encyclopedias, dialogues, and letters. A number of fictions use a mixed mode, in which letters carry much but not all of the narrative. Amos Oz's *Kufsah shekhorah* (1986; *Black Box*) contains—in addition to letters—telegrams, the report of a private investigator, selected notecards by a political scientist on the subject of religious fanaticism, and reviews of the resultant book. The first part of Aphra Behn's *Love-Letters Between a Nobleman and His Sister* (3 vols., 1683–87), perhaps the first epistolary novel in English, is told entirely in letters, whereas the second part contains many letters inserted into the third-person narrative, and the third part contains virtually no letters. Many Renaissance fictions, such as Diego de San Pedro's *Cárcel de amor* (1492; *Prison of Love*), include letters on nearly every page but embed them within a third-person narrative. The letters are illustrative and take the place of dialogue between characters but do not serve to propel the narrative. An inverse problem occurs when an entire narrative begins as a letter (for example, with a salutation, "Dear So-And-So") but is not subdivided into individual letters and shows no further signs of epistolarity. Such is the case with the Spanish picaresque novel *Lazarillo de Tormes* (1554), which is a *relato* (deposition) addressed to a magistrate. Lazarillo's story thus constitutes a legal brief, a form that began as an actual letter to a judge. However, since the novel is written more in spoken language than in written language, and because it is usually familiar or personal rather than comprising the sort of official letters that constitute an epistolary novel, *Lazarillo* is usually not considered epistolary.

The epistolary novel shares with the memoir or diary novel a focus on subjectivity and self-expression through language, and a concern with placing narrative within a concrete social context. Both letter collections and diaries frequently are shown as collected, exchanged, edited, and published. In other words, they account for their own origins. The epistolary novel, however, tends to emphasize these themes in dialogic fashion, through an exchange of letters, views, and perspectives, whereas the diary novel remains focused upon the interiority of a single character-narrator. However, individual works frequently mix the two modes. Mary Hays' *Memoirs of Emma Courtney* (1796) is written as a memoir of the heroine's life, but the whole of it is sent as a letter to her son Augustus Hartley in order to reveal the mystery of his true parentage. A more famous example is Goethe's *The Sufferings of Young Werther*, in which Werther writes long letters to his friend Wilhelm, but the latter's responses are never directly shown (although they may be inferred from some of Werther's language). As Werther becomes ever more deeply obsessed with his love for Charlotte and with his own death, his letters progressively lose their dialogic orientation toward their reader, and in fact are not sent. What began as an epistolary novel becomes a diary novel.

Another crucial "neighboring" genre of the epistolary novel is the letter-writing manual. Since their beginnings in the Middle Ages, these textbooks had used model and fictional letters in order to illustrate the proper form and content for writing letters. The title of the very first English manual, *The Enemie of Idlenesse* by William Fulwood (1582), indicates that such manuals frequently depicted correspondence within the broader contexts of social position and duty, which were depicted through expanded fictional description and narration in the letters themselves. This nexus of concerns may be seen in the full title of Samuel Richardson's *Letters Written To and For Particular Friends, on the most Important Occasions. Directing not only the Requisite Style and Forms To be Observed in Writing Familiar Letters; But How to Think and Act Justly and Prudently, in the Common Concerns of Human Life* (1741). By expanding the 138th and 139th letters of this manual ("A Father to a Daughter in Service on Hearing her Master's Attempting her Virtue" together with "The Daughter's Answer") into a series of letters, Richardson created the epistolary novel *Pamela* (1740), which itself was read as a kind of conduct book for the English middle classes. Richardson continued to use the epistolary form in his next two novels, *Clarissa* and *Sir Charles Grandison* (1753–54), whose characters also became focal points for the discussion of social mores and were translated, parodied, adapted, and refuted through the rest of the century. Out of the letter-writing manual Richardson had created the "novel of manners."

If we turn to the other side of the definition, the "novel," we find another constellation of neighboring genres. The earliest epistolary fictions seem to be by the Greek author Alciphron, but these are short, unconnected prose efforts that pretend to be the authentic letters of Athenian farmers, fishers, *hetairai,* and others. Ovid composed the *Heroides* circa 15 B.C. as a collection of poetic epistles written by mythical or historical women to their absent lovers (e.g., Penelope to Ulysses, Dido to Aeneas). Ovid's texts are, like Alciphron's, unrelated to each other and, in addition, are written in verse rather than prose. However, his texts exerted an enormous influence on the epistolary novels of the late 17th and early 18th centuries. Gabriel de Lavergne Guilleragues' *Lettres portugaises* (1669; *Letters from a Portuguese Nun*), for example, is often (and erroneously) seen as the first example of the modern epistolary novel. The work is a collection of five letters from a Portuguese nun to her former lover, a French officer, that relate, in impassioned language reminiscent of Ovid's heroines, her feelings of love, hatred, and betrayal, and which simultaneously represent a "talking cure" for the nun's tragic dependence. Since its anonymous publication, the work frequently has been treated as authentic, although scholarly opinion now tends to regard it as fiction.

Alciphron's avatars, on the other hand, are satires that frame miscellaneous letters within a reading context. Ferrante Pallavicino's *Il corriero svaligiato* (1641; The Postman Robbed) appears to have been the first of this genre, which produced many imitations throughout the following century. In Ferrante's text an Italian prince intercepts a rival's courier in order to obtain political information. He leaves four of his courtiers to examine the "nonpolitical" contents of the mailbag. The letters reveal a world of opportunism and immorality, which the courtiers caustically comment upon.

What today may be identified as the epistolary novel often revolves around a love between individuated, realistic characters whose relationship is consequently less than perfect, and, indeed, in many instances tragic. This certainly holds for the landmark fictions of the 17th, 18th, and 19th centuries listed earlier. Within these parameters, Juan de Segura's *Processo de Cartas de amores* (1548; *Process of Love Letters*) may rightly be called the "first epistolary novel." Segura's prose text is the first attempt in Spanish literature at a fully realistic representation of the moods and psychology of love. The story of *Process of Love Letters* is simple enough: a man attracts an unmarried woman by writing to her (virtually the only possibility for their verbal communication in 16th-century Spain), seeing her in church, and serenading her. Her brothers, apparently finding the suitor neither wealthy nor well-born enough, place their sister in a nunnery, from which she continues to write to her lover. The novel not only has the distinction of effecting a new narrative structure, but also of breaking with the eclipsed world of the *romance sentimental,* which was still linked to the system of courtly love and with other decadent characteristics. Segura places the scene of his story in an urban, middle-class setting.

In North America, epistolary fiction was a driving force in the rise of the novel because it lent a moral context to fiction that the novel per se was said to lack. Samuel Richardson's fiction was undoubtedly an important factor in this perception. Early American fictions employed the letter form to present negative images of the disasters awaiting anyone straying from the path of propriety. These works deliberately decenter their plots into various loci of moral instruction. An example is Enos Hitchcock's *Memoirs of the Bloomsgrove Family* (1790), one of the many fictional works to which critics have denied the status of novel because it lacks a central plotline. The work follows Rosella as she is educated and enters her teens. Its 93 impersonal, essay-like letters turn the reader's attention away from the plot and toward the principle by which the characters operate. One fiction frequently cited as the first American novel, William Hill Brown's *The Power of Sympathy* (1789), is also epistolary. Its main plot turns upon Harrington's courtship of Harriot, who turns out to be his sister; Harrington's father had seduced a poor young woman, who gave birth to Harriot and then died. When the two lovers discover their true origins, Harriot dies of grief, Harrington shoots himself through the head, and Harrington, Sr. narrates his debauched life. Eliza Whitman, later to be the subject of Hannah Foster's epistolary fiction, *The Coquette* (1797), appears in the footnotes. Her error, like Harrington, Sr.'s, was to believe what she read in novels and to allow herself to be seduced by them as much as by the dashing young man who impregnated and abandoned her.

Critical studies of epistolary fiction fall roughly into three categories: bibliographical-historical, formalist, and sociopolitical. Godfrey Frank Singer (1933) and Robert Adams Day (1966) take a similar approach to the form, which may be called "evolutionary." Day speaks, for example, of a "transitional form" of epistolary novel in which letters make up 5 percent to 30 percent of the work. Supposedly this structure is preparatory to the greater narrative competence of the purely epistolary novel, which in turn prepares the more competent narrative techniques of Jane Austen, Charles Dickens, and Honoré de Balzac. Bernard Bray (1967) tells a story of how the letter novel was created in the 17th century when authors raised on letter-writing manuals linked several of the instructional genre's letters together in order to create the mimesis of a letter-writing subject. According to these accounts, the epistolary novel was created almost by accident, and once the technology of narrating through letters had been achieved, it began to develop from the monologic (one letter-writer) to the polyphonic. Laurent Versini (1979), in his treatment of English, French, German, and Italian texts, uses this thesis of historical development, best summarized in the title of one of his chapters, "From Monody to Polyphony" ("De la Monodie à la Polyphonie"). According to Versini the epistolary novel gradually emerges as a subgenre when a single psychologized writing subject is provided for the French letter-writing manuals, and then moves in the direction of polyphony and a kaleidoscopic view of reality. Choderlos de Laclos, in *Les Liaisons dangereuses,* takes polyphony and empties it of content. Laclos negates the letter's mediating or revelatory function, since in his work the letter neither tells anything about the world nor reveals the desires of the sender—unless he or she is a clumsy writer. In Goethe's *The Sufferings of Young Werther,* the letter disappears into solipsistic diary form. In general, Singer, Day, Bray, and Versini do not delve into the social contexts of epistolary fiction. Epistolary literature has its own formal laws, which its own best products exhaust, causing it to metamorphose into new narrative forms.

Literary historians attribute the general abandonment of the epistolary novel in the 19th century to the development of superior techniques of narrative that avoided the clumsiness, redundancy, and occasional absurdities of epistolary narration. For example, critics have always noted with amusement the curious situations in which letters are written in epistolary novels: Valmont of *Les Liaisons dangereuses* derives ironic satisfaction from using one of his paramours as a writing table. Richardson's Clarissa, locked in an almost barren room by her irate family, somehow succeeds in smuggling in and concealing pen and paper so that she may continue to write to Anna Howe. Several of Mme. Riccoboni's heroines have the annoying habit of writing while visitors are present or when they should be speaking or listening.

It is assumed without question that such aberrances are signs of the drawbacks of epistolary technique rather than attempts to show the cloistered writer at work, to contrast the power of writing with the weakness of conversation, to show and perhaps ridicule the period's fascination with a new *techné*. One could critique in the same manner, however, the 19th century's fascination with the omniscient narrator, a character who pretends not to be a character and who knows things that no human can know. If the characters of epistolary fiction write in superhuman fashion, their knowledge is still limited to the perspectival blindness of an ordinary human being. Like our own lives, epistolary novels may have no narrator at all, since the letters written simultaneously comprise elements of the plot, and only become narrations when "overheard" by the reader of the novel. It is important, as Elizabeth MacArthur has so aptly stated, that "rather than criticizing the epistolary form for its failure to correspond to accepted definitions of narrative, [we] put into question these definitions."

Formal analyses of epistolary fiction, on the other hand, by Janet Altman (1982), Jan Herman (1989), Ronald Rosbottom (1977), and others are generally unconcerned with persistent formal features reappearing in any epoch, with a comprehensive view of a single period, or with the social contexts of letter writing. They note the formal features peculiar to using letters as a narrative device, including temporal complexity (the time in which a letter is written never corresponds to the time at which it is read) and self-reflexiveness (letters often talk about other letters).

Gender has served as a prominent topic in sociopolitical investigations of the epistolary form. Books by Kauffman (1986) and Jensen (1995), Ruth Perry's (1980) study, and the collection edited by Elizabeth C. Goldsmith (1989) all explore the complex gender relations involved in epistolary production. All of them begin from the historical record, traceable to Ovid, that the familiar letter gradually became a literary genre at which women were conceded to excel as long as they restricted themselves to certain literary and cultural stereotypes, such as that of the abandoned lover. The epistolary novel became an important cultural vehicle for giving women a voice, both as characters and as authors. Arguably, Western literature had never produced an array of female characters at once realistic and eloquent as it did starting with Mariana (the Portuguese nun) and continuing through Richardson's Pamela and Clarissa, Graffigny's Peruvian princess, Rousseau's Julie, and Laclos' Madame de Merteuil.

However, the sociopolitical dimensions of letter fiction are not restricted to gender issues. Much of epistolary fiction's power derived from the letter's instrumentality in legal, economic, and political institutions, and its use as a source of news. Much work remains to be done in recovering the carryover from these realms into that of the letter novel. Favret (1993) and Watson (1994) have made interesting contributions to constructing a political history of the letter, noting the changing fortunes of letters in En-

gland during and after the French Revolution, and the concomitant effects of such changes on letter fiction.

THOMAS O. BEEBEE

See also Critics and Criticism (18th Century); English Novel (18th Century); Framing and Embedding; French Novel (18th Century); Novel of Manners; Prose Novelistic Forms; Samuel Richardson

Further Reading

Altman, Janet Gurkin, *Epistolarity: Approaches to a Form,* Columbus: Ohio State University Press, 1982

Beebee, Thomas O., "The Rifled Mailbag: Robber as Reader in Early Epistolary Fiction," *Revue de Littérature Comparée* (January-March 1996)

Bossis, Mireille, and Charles A. Porter, editors, *L'Épistolarité à travers les siècles: Geste de communication et/ou d'écriture,* Stuttgart: Steiner, 1990

Bray, Bernard, *L'Art de la lettre amoureuse des manuels aux romans (1550–1700),* The Hague: Mouton, 1967

Brown, Homer O., "The Errant Letter and the Whispering Gallery," *Genre* 10 (1977)

Brownlee, Marina Scordilis, *The Severed Word: Ovid's "Heroides" and the Novela Sentimental,* Princeton, New Jersey: Princeton University Press, 1990

Conroy, Peter, "Real Fiction: Authenticity in the French Epistolary Novel," *Romanic Review* 72:3 (1981)

Day, Robert Adams, *Told in Letters: Epistolary Fiction Before Richardson,* Ann Arbor: University of Michigan Press, 1966

Derrida, Jacques, *The Postal Card,* Chicago: University of Chicago Press, 1984

Favret, Mary A., *Romantic Correspondence: Women, Politics, and the Fiction of Letters,* Cambridge and New York: Cambridge University Press, 1993

Goldsmith, Elizabeth C., editor, *Writing the Female Voice: Essays on Epistolary Literature,* Boston: Northeastern University Press, and London: Pinter, 1989

Herman, Jan, *Le mensonge romanesque: Paramètres pour l'étude du roman épistolaire en France,* Leuven: Leuven University Press, 1989

Jensen, Katharine Ann, *Writing Love: Letters, Women, and the Novel in France, 1605–1776,* Carbondale: Southern Illinois University Press, 1995

Kany, Charles Emil, *The Beginnings of the Epistolary Novel in France, Italy, and Spain,* Berkeley: University of California Press, 1937

Kauffman, Linda, *Discourses of Desire: Gender, Genre, and Epistolary Fictions,* Ithaca, New York: Cornell University Press, 1986

Kauffman, Linda, *Special Delivery: Epistolary Modes in Modern Fiction,* Chicago: University of Chicago Press, 1992

Koepke, Wulf, "The Epistolary Novel: From Self-Assertion to Alienation," *Studies on Voltaire and the Eighteenth Century* 192 (1980)

MacArthur, Elizabeth, *Extravagant Narratives: Closure and Dynamics in the Epistolary Form,* Princeton, New Jersey: Princeton Unversity Press, 1990

Perry, Ruth, *Women, Letters, and the Novel,* New York: AMS Press, 1980

Porter, Charles A., editor, *Men/Women of Letters,* New Haven, Connecticut, and London: Yale University Press, 1986

Rosbottom, Ronald E., "Motifs in Epistolary Fiction: Analysis of a Narrative Sub-Genre," *L'Esprit créateur* 17 (1977)

Rousset, Jean, "Une Forme littéraire: Le roman par lettres," in *Forme et signification: essais sur les structures littéraires de Corneille à Claudel,* Paris: Corti, 1962

Singer, Godfrey Frank, *The Epistolary Novel: Its Origin, Development, Decline, and Residuary Influence,* Philadelphia: University of Pennsylvania Press, 1933

Stackelberg, Jürgen von, "Der Briefroman und seine Epoche: Briefroman und Empfindsamkeit," *Cahiers d'histoire des littératures romanes* 1 (1977)

Thelander, Dorothy R., *Laclos and the Epistolary Novel,* Geneva: Droz, 1963

Versini, Laurent, *Le roman épistolaire,* Paris: Presses Universitaires de France, 1979

Watson, Nicola J., *Revolution and the Form of the English Novel, 1790–1825: Intercepted Letters, Interrupted Seductions,* New York: Oxford University Press, and Oxford: Clarendon Press, 1994

Würzbach, Natascha, *The Novel in Letters: Epistolary Fiction in the Early English Novel, 1678–1740,* London: Routledge and Kegan Paul, and Coral Gables, Florida: University of Miami Press, 1969

Erlebte Rede. *See* Discourse Representation

Erotic Novel. *See* Libertine Novel; Pornographic Novel; Sex, Gender, and the Novel

---

Erziehungsroman. *See* Bildungsroman

Péter Esterházy 1950–

Hungarian

Although Péter Esterházy is undoubtedly a master of modern Hungarian prose, it is perhaps debatable whether he is first of all a novelist. Esterházy is an outsider in various ways. He comes from a very illustrious aristocratic family (one of his ancestors was Franz Joseph Haydn's chief patron) that lost all its wealth and status in communist-ruled Hungary. Instead of literature or modern languages, he studied mathematics and has always been out of step with the Hungarian literary establishment. Working

in isolation from other Hungarian writers, Esterházy evolved a unique form of postmodernism that reflects East European concerns. More specifically, he is a satirical writer in whose prose intertextuality borders on pastiche.

His first publications were collections of short stories that already indicated his interest in word play and stylistic distortion. His first novel, *Termelési-regény (kissregény)* (1979; Production-Novel [Little Novel]), is a brave departure from the traditional novel form, a book brimming with humor and energy that uses a multitude of stylistic devices. The novel is a pastiche of socialist realist fiction—the so-called "production novel"—telling the story of a young computer technician's struggles with red tape. That narrative is followed by notes on the everyday life and travels of the author, written by a certain E. (which stands for J.P. Eckermann, Goethe's secretary and faithful chronicler), appended by way of footnotes to the "production novel." In fact, the second half of the book bears little relationship to the previous narrative. The first sentence of the novel, "We cannot find words," is a playful introduction to its central aim of finding as many amusing phrases, puns, and new word combinations as possible.

Play is the underlying feature of *Termelési-regény* but, as critics immediately noticed, in a high-stakes game. Through its sometimes distorted, sometimes real quotations, it tries to discredit self-glorifying nationalist rhetoric, whether socialist or not, as well as the traditional literary rhetoric of Hungarian and foreign classics. According to the critic Ernő Kulcsár Szabó, this is "a novel of the liberation of [different] languages" in which Esterházy effectively emancipates all possible informal and group-specific linguistic registers (including the language of football fans) and thus takes a stand against "the illusion of one authoritative speech" (see Kulcsár Szabó, 1996). *Termelési-regény* also uses a number of modern technical devices (different typefaces, arrows, drawings within the text, etc.) to indicate its distance from the traditional Hungarian realistic or psychological novel. The handwritten genealogy illustrating the author's distant but real relationship to Elizabeth II of England is a particularly delightful example of this playfulness.

Esterházy's next novel, *Függő* (1981; Appendix), is one long sentence that opens with a quotation from Robert Musil's *Der Mann ohne Eigenschaften* (1930–43; *The Man Without Qualities*). In some respects, it follows the narrative strategies of Musil and the Hungarian modernist Géza Ottlik. Reminiscing about adolescence, *Függő* introduces various time frames, and the narrator freely quotes from another narrative on the same theme, thus creating a rather eclectic narrative continuum. Esterházy's syntax and technique are postmodernist, but many of the long passages that he builds into his text as relevant quotations point to his debt to modernism.

In 1986, Esterházy published a massive collection called *Bevezetés a szépirodalomba* (Introduction to Belles Lettres), which includes *Függő* and other fiction from the 1980s, namely *Ki szavatol a lady biztonságáért?* (1982; Who Can Guarantee the Lady's Safety?), *Fuvarosok* (1983; *The Transporters*), *Kis Magyar pornográfia* (1984; *A Little Hungarian Pornography*), *Daisy* (1984), *A szív segédigéi* (1985; *Helping Verbs of the Heart*), and many other shorter pieces. Of these, *A Little Hungarian Pornography* and *Helping Verbs of the Heart* proved the most accessible and, consequently, the most popular. *A Little Hungarian Pornography* cannot be described as a conventional novel for it has no plot or coherent narrative: it is a witty and often mordantly ironic collection of odd stories, anecdotes, and linguistic jokes about Hungarian history and post-war Central European society that continues the style of *Termelési-regény*. *Helping Verbs of the Heart* is a short novel about the death of the author's mother. In Richard Aczél's view, "there are few more powerful expressions of the experience of human loss in modern fiction" than this book, in which Esterházy also makes

use of postmodern techniques and odd typographical solutions, but which nevertheless speaks about a commonly shared human experience and as such is vastly more interesting and relevant than, for example, the transvestite play-acting of *Daisy*. The entire collection concludes with an extremely long list containing more than 500 names of all those authors from whose works Esterházy has borrowed passages for quotation or alteration. Such an extraordinary degree of promiscuous intertextuality is quite unprecedented in modern Hungarian literature.

Apart from some Hungarian masters (such as Kosztolányi or Ottlik) Esterházy seems to be most impressed by such well-known contemporary German and Austrian authors as Robert Musil, Peter Handke, and Thomas Bernhard. He also has a soft spot for the Czech writer Bohumil Hrabal, to an imaginary version of whom he devoted his short novel *Hrabal könyve* (1990; *The Book of Hrabal*). Its tripartite construction consists of "The Chapter of Faithfulness," "The Chapter of Unfaithfulness," and a final chapter in which the Lord eventually converses (in Czech!) with Hrabal. The main character of the entire novel is Anna, the author's wife, who is first jealous of Hrabal and then falls in love with him. She is also tormented by the dilemma whether to continue or terminate her fourth pregnancy. Esterházy introduces two hilarious otherwordly characters—guardian angels sent by the Lord to keep an eye on the author and on the unborn baby. They drive a Soviet-made car and have a license plate usually associated with the communist secret policy, so they are truly "heavenly agents." As usual, the plot does not amount to much, but Esterházy writes with much verve and ingenuity, captivating the reader with the "peculiar and inimitable rhythm of his sentences" (see Birnbaum, 1990) and with his warm sense of humor. The book also marks a return to a less postmodernist, more "readable" type of fiction.

Esterházy's last novel to date is *Hahn-Hahn grófnő pillantása* (1991; *The Glance of Countess Hahn-Hahn*), a kind of subjective travelogue along the river Danube, from its source in the Black Forest to its delta on the Black Sea. While the structure of the novel is complex and various modes of speech and dialogue alternate in its flow, the subject matter imposes a kind of linearity and cohesiveness on the narrative, since the narrator has to follow the river whatever associative detours may occur on the way. The book is postmodernist in its extensive and eclectic quotation from other work, but its references to local beliefs and ideas evoke a far more concrete reality than Esterházy's earlier fiction—even if many of those references are ironic.

Since 1991, Esterházy has published several collections of essays and sketches. Earlier he had been responsible for a curious pastiche written under a female pseudonym, Lili Csokonai: *Tizenkét hattyúk* (1987; 17 Swans), which uses a strange mixture of archaic (18th century) language and modern expressions. This capacity for metamorphosis often produces bizarre results: the collection of short prose pieces *Egy nő* (1995; A Woman) tries to fathom the depths of the eternally complex and difficult relationship between women and men, although rather from the point of view of men and including frankly male chauvinist approaches.

Whatever the vagaries of his varied oeuvre, Esterházy is now regarded as an influential representative of postmodernist prose whose stylistic innovations have had a great impact on the development of contemporary Hungarian literature.

GEORGE GÖMÖRI

Biography
Born in Hungary, 15 April 1950. Attended the University of Budapest; Eötvös Loránd University, degree in mathematics 1974. Former staff member, Ministry of Foundries and Machine Tools. Began writing full-time in 1978.

Novels by Esterházy
Termelési-regény (kissregény) [Production-Novel (Little Novel)], 1979
Függő [Appendix], 1981
Ki szavatol a lady biztonságáért? [Who Can Guarantee the Lady's Safety?], 1982
Fuvarosok, 1983; as *The Transporters*, in *A Hungarian Quartet*, 1991
Kis Magyar pornográfia, 1984; as *A Little Hungarian Pornography*, 1995
A sziv segédigéi, 1985; as *Helping Verbs of the Heart*, 1991
Tizenkét hattyúk [17 Swans] (as Lili Csokonai), 1987

Hrabal könyve, 1990; as *The Book of Hrabal*, 1994
Hahn-Hahn grófnő pillantása, 1991; as *The Glance of Countess Hahn-Hahn*, 1994

Other Writings: short stories, essays, and sketches.

Further Reading
Aczél, Richard, introduction to *Helping Verbs of the Heart*, Budapest: Corvina, 1992
Birnbaum, Marianna D., "*Hrabal könyve*," *World Literature Today* 64:4 (Autumn 1990)
Birnbaum, Marianna D., *Esterházy-Kalauz*, Budapest: Magvető, 1991
Györguey, Clara, "A Little Hungarian Pornography," *World Literature Today* 70:2 (Spring 1996)
Kulcsár Szabó, Ernő, *Esterházy Péter*, Pozsony: Kalligram, 1996
Takács, Ferenc, "*Termelési-regeny*," *World Literature Today* 54:2 (Spring 1980)

Étranger. *See* Stranger

Eugene Onegin by Aleksandr Pushkin

Evgenii Onegin 1833

On the surface a deceptively simple, sentimental novel full of stock characters, Aleksandr Pushkin's novel in verse has nevertheless generated an enormous body of criticism that has investigated in depth every aspect of its form and content, most often resulting in contradictory conclusions. Yet critics almost universally agree that *Eugene Onegin* is one of the most influential novels in the history of Russian fiction.

Aware of Western literary tradition, Pushkin found inspiration for his novel in sources as disparate as Lord Byron, Laurence Sterne, Samuel Richardson, Jean-Jacques Rousseau, Benjamin Constant, Voltaire, Lodovico Ariosto, picaresque novels, comic epics, and various other French and Italian sources. One critic even sees in Pushkin a certain affinity with Jane Austen, another writer poised between two centuries. Yet *Eugene Onegin* is a quintessentially Russian work, so much so that Pushkin's contemporary, the civic critic Vissarion Belinskii, called it an "encyclopedia of Russian life," mainly because of its convincingly true character types seen against realistic Russian settings, both urban and rural.

The novel's hero, Eugene, a world-weary, callous youth of By-ronic cast, leaves St. Petersburg for his country estate, where he relieves his boredom by befriending a young Romantic poet, Lensky, whom he eventually kills in a senseless duel over Olga, a stylized beauty. However, Olga's sister, Tatiana, initially a dark, pensive, Clarissa-like heroine, evolves as the most complex and developed character in the novel. She sends a charming and innocent love letter to Eugene, who rejects her. Following Onegin's departure necessitated by the duel, Tatiana visits Onegin's house and peruses his library, only to realize that he is merely the parody of a hero. When the two next meet, she is a sophisticated St. Petersburg hostess married to an old friend of Eugene, who now falls in love with the inaccessible beauty. Although she still loves him, Tatiana rejects his declaration of love, telling him that she will remain faithful to her husband. This simple story with its seemingly stereotyped characters has given rise to myriad interpretations of the novel and its characters, whom Pushkin deftly portrays with lyrical suggestion and atmosphere.

Although essentially a sentimental novel with comic epic overtones, *Eugene Onegin* also exhibits romantic traits, especially in its mixing of genres. Not content with conventional forms,

Pushkin set out to write "not a novel, but a novel in verse—the devil of a difference!" The novel consists of eight cantos, which Pushkin called chapters. Of its 5,541 lines, all but 18 are written in iambic tetrameter; the remaining trochaic trimeter lines reproduce a song that peasant girls sing as they pick berries. Each chapter is comprised of 40–54 stanzas of 14 lines each, with a rhyme scheme new to Russian literature: *ababeecciddiff* (vowels designate feminine rhymes). Neither a pure sonnet nor a pure *ottava rima*, this rhyme scheme in iambic tetrameter has come to be known as the "Onegin stanza." Variety and virtuosity of rhymes, skillful use of enjambment between lines and stanzas, and two freely rhymed letters help prevent monotony in such a set pattern.

The tightly structured form of *Eugene Onegin* achieves near classical balance and symmetry. The novel begins in St. Petersburg, moves to the country, and returns to the capital. The themes of chapter eight echo those of chapter one. A Moscow theme emerges, although briefly, in chapters two and seven, forming a concentric circle within the larger one. And while the novel may be divided into two parts, with Tatiana's rejection speech to Onegin in the last chapter paralleling his refusal of her love in chapter four, Pushkin relieves this rigidity of structure with "near balance": the Lensky theme of the doomed young poet appears in chapters two and six, while Tatiana sends a letter to Onegin in chapter three and he sends one to her in chapter eight. Pushkin further undercuts classical regularity of proportion by using structural themes as natural transitions between chapters.

However, the main deterrent to classical biases lies in the novel's intrusive narrator, who is variously garrulous, chatty, digressive, nostalgic, and expository. As one critic has noted, the narrator adds a second reality to the novel, the reality of the creative process. The main unifying element of the novel, the narrator is also the source of the work's all-pervasive romantic irony. Yet he manages to stay poised between his objectivity as storyteller and loquacity as confidante. The narrator remains as conscious of his style as he is of the events he relates. His descriptions of nature and the seasons reveal his eye for beauty and allow him to exercise his poetic gifts.

Eugene Onegin has served as a rich source of characters for Russian writers after Pushkin, especially in the perpetuation of the "superfluous man"/strong woman dichotomy. The superfluous man is a product of a society from which he is alienated. Usually quite intelligent, he devises plans that he never executes, caught in a Hamlet-like paralysis. He usually falls in love with a woman, a superior being who sees the futility of a future with the suitor and so rejects him. Tatiana is the prototype of women in Russian literature doomed to what Barbara Heldt (1987) calls "terrible perfection." Ivan Turgenev perfected the paradigm in his own series of novels, and others looked to *Eugene Onegin* for models of literary language, character types, and endings.

Perhaps Pushkin's greatest achievement—not only in *Eugene Onegin* but in all his prose and poetry—lies in his extraordinary use of language. Most often described as pure, light, and spontaneous, his prose and poetry seem almost effortless. He evokes images and scenes without resorting to many tropes and figures of speech. Instead, the beauty of his verses resides in his poetic craftsmanship in manipulating sound, rhythm, meter, and rhyme. While each existing English translation of Eugene Onegin has features to recommend it (those by Vladimir Nabokov, Charles Johnston, and Walter Arndt stand out), certainly none approaches the original; however, over the years Walter Arndt's version remains the most consistently readable.

CHRISTINE A. RYDEL

See also Aleksandr Pushkin

Further Reading

Bayley, John, *Pushkin: A Comparative Commentary,* Cambridge: Cambridge University Press, 1971

Clayton, J. Douglas, *Ice and Flame: Aleksandr Pushkin's "Eugene Onegin,"* Toronto and Buffalo, New York: University of Toronto Press, 1985

Fennell, John, "Pushkin," in his *Nineteenth-Century Russian Literature: Studies of Ten Russian Writers,* Berkeley: University of California Press, and London: Faber, 1973

Gregg, Richard, "Rhetoric in Tat'jana's Last Speech: The Camouflage That Reveals," *Slavic and East European Journal* 25 (1981)

Gustafon, R.F., "The Metaphor of the Seasons in *Eugene Onegin,*" *Slavic and East European Journal* (1962)

Heldt, Barbara, *Terrible Perfection: Women and Russian Literature,* Bloomington: Indiana University Press, 1987

Hoisington, Sona Stephen, "*Eugene Onegin*: An Inverted Byronic Poem," *Comparative Literature* 27 (1975)

Hoisington, Sona Stephan, editor, *Russian Views of Pushkin's "Eugene Onegin,"* Bloomington: Indiana University Press, 1988

Katz, Michael R., "Love and Marriage in Pushkin's *Eugene Onegin,*" *Oxford Slavonic Papers* (1984)

Nesaule, Valda, "Tatiana's Dream in Pushkin's *Eugene Onegin,*" *Indiana Slavic Studies* 3 (1963)

Shaw, J. Thomas, "The Problem of Unity of Author-Narrator's Stance in Pushkin's *Eugene Onegin,*" *Russian Language Journal* 120 (1981)

Todd, W.M. III, "*Eugene Onegin*: Life's Novel," in *Literature and Society in Imperial Russia, 1800–1914,* edited by W.M. Todd III, Stanford, California: Stanford University Press, 1978

Evelina by Frances Burney

1778

Evelina, subtitled "The History of a Young Lady's Entrance into the World," is an epistolary novel that took conscious inspiration from, among others, the novels of Henry Fielding, Samuel Richardson, and Tobias Smollett. In addition, critics have noted similarities with Eliza Haywood's *History of Miss Betsy Thoughtless* (1751). Like Haywood's novel, *Evelina* is both an account of social and sexual maturation and a satire of contemporary manners. Uniting rambunctious comedy, penetrating social observation, and restrained sentimentalism, *Evelina* was an immediate publishing sensation, praised by reviewers, popular with readers, and successful in making large profits for its canny publisher, Thomas Lowndes (who notoriously paid Burney only 20 guineas for her manuscript). Successive editions followed within the year, and the work had been translated into several European languages by the end of the next decade.

Despite, or perhaps because of, her upbringing in a prominent literary and musical London family, Frances Burney wrote *Evelina* in secret and submitted it to Lowndes anonymously. Her natural reticence is suggested by the fact that for many years she had kept private notes and journals addressed to "No-body," and at first she was mortified when her authorship of *Evelina* was discovered. This concern for her privacy should not, however, deceive readers into presuming a direct autobiographical relationship between Burney and her timorous, blushing heroine. Where Evelina was a gauche and inexperienced 17-year-old, Burney was 26 when her first novel appeared, and she had grown up in a privileged and formidable circle of writers and other public figures, including her own father, the musicologist Charles Burney, Edmund Burke, Elizabeth Carter, Hester Chapone, David Garrick, Samuel Johnson, Elizabeth Montagu, Hester Piozzi, and Joshua Reynolds. The self-deprecating tone of her preface to *Evelina,* her opening statement to "The Authors of the Monthly and Critical Reviews," and her refusal to name either herself as author or her father as the addressee of her dedicatory poem were initially seen as evidence of feminine modesty and artistic self-doubt. But in recent years, critics have proposed that these are in fact strategies for the subversively ironic undercutting of male-dominated literary tradition through, in part, the parodying of the female novelist's conventional apologies and self-erasures. *Evelina* is as much a riposte to the fathers of the English novel as an attempt to emulate them, for in her preface Burney defends her claim to an artistic inheritance from such illustrious male predecessors as Rousseau, Johnson, Marivaux, Fielding, Richardson, and Smollett, while at the same time asserting the distinctiveness of her own achievement with the novel form: "though they may have cleared the weeds, they have also culled the flowers, and though they have rendered the path plain, they have left it barren."

The problem of establishing an independent authorial reputation without challenging or compromising her father's are now recognized as central concerns for Burney in *Evelina.* The problem also parallels the preoccupations of the main narrative. Issues of selfhood, self-representation, and identity are raised by the framing story of Evelina's birth, her biological father's rejection of her, and her ambiguous status as an adoptive daughter and dependent whose very name is in question. Far from accepting and endorsing the power of the father's name, *Evelina* may be seen to constitute a radical if oblique critique of patriarchy and patrilinearity, both of which are presented in the novel through the problems Evelina faces in securing her rightful patronym. Her sense of identity, her social status, her moral reputation, and her financial security all depend on her regaining her name.

Eighteenth-century readers rejoiced in the gallery of familiar social types represented in the novel, and among its most popular episodes were those involving the grotesque Madame Duval, the designing rake Sir Clement Willoughby, and the boorish Captain Mirvan. Yet 20th-century critics increasingly have been inclined to emphasize the implicit feminism of Burney's social satire. Her heroine is repeatedly slighted, bullied, and manhandled by the men she meets at balls, assemblies, plays, and concerts, and her letters chart her struggle to negotiate a competitive and bewildering marriage market without compromising her reputation or appearing, even to herself, to be in search of a husband. While Joyce Hemlow noted the novel's similarities to the courtesy books, contemporary advice manuals aimed at young middle-class women (see Hemlow, 1950), Jane Spencer has pointed out that Burney's novel is less about Evelina's blunders and misjudgments (although we do see some of these) than about her mistreatment and misinterpretation by others, particularly the selfish and unscrupulous men who pursue her (see Spencer, 1986). Women in general are represented in *Evelina* as vulnerable to abuse and neglect. At her very first ball, where she is overwhelmed with shyness, Evelina chafes at the attitude of the gentlemen who "looked as if they thought we were quite at their disposal, and only waiting for the honour of their commands."

One of the difficulties in the novel is the conflict between Evelina's supposed artlessness and the acerbic tone of some of her letters. She seems conscious herself of the problem at times, and hedges her criticisms with apologies or avowals of her determination to be submissive and polite. But if the epistolary mode presented Burney with challenges in maintaining the consistency of her first-person narrator, it also proved a flexible tool that allowed her to exploit the narratological techniques of earlier novelists such as Richardson. Her heroine, like Richardson's Pamela, writes "to the moment," that is, in the immediate wake of events that befall her. Burney also made formal innovations of her own. Unlike Pamela's letters, Evelina's are often realistically short and hurried, so that the novel avoids the prolixity that has exasperated some of Richardson's readers. The comedy stemming from the juxtapositions of Evelina's letters, whether ingenuous and eager or fastidiously disdainful, with those of her sober, moralizing guardian, the Reverend Mr. Villars, is much more pervasive than the relatively rare comic moments that punctuate *Pamela* (1740). Further, Burney makes the dramatic ironies of her heroine's self-representation much more obvious than Richardson had done: the reader is aware of Evelina's sexual interest in Lord Orville much sooner than she herself is, for example. Lastly, Burney combines the conventional emphasis of the epistolary novel on the private thoughts and feelings of its fictional correspondents with the picaresque novel's social range and episodic plot. Where Richardson's heroine is physically confined and largely deprived of company, Evelina writes of her travels, of large social gatherings, and of the perils and pleasures of making new acquaintances. Sensitive and compassionate, her letters are nevertheless not only a record of her feelings but of her social life and her opinions of other people.

Burney also wrote comedies and tragedies, and after *Evelina* she published three more novels. Two of these, *Cecilia* (1782) and *Camilla* (1796), earned her a considerable fortune; the last, *The Wanderer* (1814), was much less successful. She was admired by Jane Austen, who paid tribute to her in *Northanger Abbey* (1818), and she influenced Maria Edgeworth's novels of contemporary life. She is among the first in a long, still-flourishing tradition of English women novelists whose characteristic tone is irony; current practitioners include Iris Murdoch, Anita Brookner, and Margaret Drabble.

KATHERINE A. ARMSTRONG

Further Reading

Bloom, Lillian D., and Edward A. Bloom, "Fanny Burney's Novels: The Retreat from Wonder," *Novel: A Forum on Fiction* 12 (1978–79)

Doody, Margaret Anne, *Frances Burney: The Life in the Works,* New Brunswick, New Jersey: Rutgers University Press, and Cambridge: Cambridge University Press, 1988

Epstein, Julia, *The Iron Pen: Frances Burney and the Politics of Women's Writing,* Bristol: Bristol Classical Press, and Madison: University of Wisconsin Press, 1989

Gallagher, Catherine, *Nobody's Story: The Vanishing Acts of Women Writers in the Marketplace 1670–1820,* Oxford: Clarendon Press, and Berkeley: University of California Press, 1994

Hemlow, Joyce, "Fanny Burney and the Courtesy Books," *Papers of the Modern Language Association* 65 (1950)

McMaster, Juliet, "How to Read Like a Gentleman: Burney's Instructions to Her Critics in *Evelina,*" *English Literary History* 57 (1990)

Simons, Judy, *Fanny Burney,* London: Macmillan, and Totowa, New Jersey: Barnes and Noble, 1987

Spacks, Patricia Meyer, "'Ev'ry Woman is at Heart a Rake'," *Eighteenth-Century Studies* 8 (1974–75)

Spencer, Jane, *The Rise of the Woman Novelist: From Aphra Behn to Jane Austen,* Oxford: Blackwell, 1986

Staves, Susan, "*Evelina*: or, Female Difficulties," *Modern Philology* 73 (1975–76)

Evgenii Onegin. *See* Eugene Onegin

Experimental Novel. *See* Graphic Novel; Metafiction; Nouveau Roman

F

Fable

The fable is a distinctive narrative genre with clearly circum-scribed formal characteristics. A relatively closed form, the fable has maintained a separate identity, not showing any modification as a result of its coexistence with the novel form. However, the novel—a more open, even protean genre—has at times adopted the forms of the fable, bending them to new purposes. The most famous example of such borrowing is George Orwell's *Animal Farm* (1945). However, historical points of contact between the two narrative forms appear to be limited, no doubt because the novel's emphasis on psychological realism is foreign to the fable.

Fable as a Literary Genre Term

The fable belongs to those short or "simple" narrative genres that claim an oral origin, and indeed fables exist in the oral traditions of almost all the ancient cultures of the world. In the strictest sense, a fable is a brief narrative in verse or prose. Its characters are animals (or sometimes inanimate objects) who display human characteristics or represent human types. Whether its tone is sharply satirical or only mildly ironic, the fable has a strong didactic purpose, concentrating on the correction of human vice and folly as expressed in the anthropomorphized animal realm. For good measure, the lesson to be learned is often expressed in a formal "moral" that closes the narrative.

Narratologically, fables consist of a prototypical narrative structure that closely resembles William Labov's and Joshua Waletzky's episodic schema of the conversational storytelling mode (see Labov and Waletzky, 1967). There may not be an initial framing abstract, but the story is regularly introduced by a brief orientation section, locating the *dramatis personae* (such as the fox and the wolf) in a setting (the wood, for example) and introducing the onset of the storyline in formulaic terms—"One day . . .". Then follows a crucial dialogic exchange or, in some tales, a series of short episodes. The fable, usually focused on a contest of strength and wit, is concluded with a final result and resolution section that clearly indicates a winner. In the fable, the moral functions as an evaluation section, which, in conversational storytelling, is devoted to remarks about the events' experiential significance for the narrator.

The word *fable* has been used as a denigrating epithet to criticize the fictitiousness of a tale, a usage that derives from the link of *fable* to *fabulous* and frequently occurs in relation to novels of magic realism.

Historical Development

The Western tradition of the literary fable stems from the Aesopian fables, of the sixth century B.C. They were first versified by Phaedrus in the first century A.D. into Latin. Phaedrus also added many fables of his own, making reference to contemporary life and politics. A century later Babrius, rendering the fables into Greek verse in his *Muthiamboi Aisopeioi,* expanded the genre by directing it toward satire and the pastoral. In the fourth century, Avianus still further enriched the Babrian fables by inserting Ovidian and Virgilian phraseology in his Latin paraphrases, thus giving them a mock-heroic effect. Romulus' poetical version, which included both Phaedrus' and Babrius' fables, endured well into the 17th century.

Apart from the Latin and Greek versions of Aesop's fables, the medieval fabulists also had access to the most famous Eastern collection of animal tales, the *Pañcatantra,* also known as the *Fables of Bidpai* (or Bilpai). Unlike the simple self-contained stories of Aesop, each of the five books of the *Pañcatantra* contains a main frame-story embedding fables within fables that serve to illuminate various facets of the same situation. Moreover, the book begins with a short introduction that frames the whole work and describes its intention to be "A Mirror for Princes," putting the didactic emphasis on the practical aspects of life and politics. The original Sanskrit (100 B.C.–500 A.D.) was translated into the middle Iranian language of Pahlavi in the sixth century. Both these versions are lost, but a nearly contemporary and close translation of the Pahlavi into Old Syriac has survived. The version that found its way to Europe was a somewhat later translation of the Pahlavi into Arabic (c. 750), entitled *Kalila and Dimna.* These names are the corrupt versions of the Sanskrit names of the jackals Karataka and Damanaka of the first book of the *Pañcatantra.* The Arabic version was translated under different titles into various European languages—sometimes by way of a Hebrew translation—including Greek, Latin, Italian, Old Slavonic, Old Spanish, German, and finally into English in the late 16th century.

The versatility of the form has been exploited by writers of all ages. In the Middle Ages, the literary fable was employed for social criticism and satire, as in Marie de France's criticism of French feudal society, particularly of women's role within it. The Jewish fabulist Berechiah Ben Natronai was a great supporter of the poor and the oppressed, and his fables are very much influenced by the language of the Torah and the Bible. Another medieval fabulist, Odo of Cheriton, a preacher by profession, employed the fable in his *Sermons* and wrote a collection to criticize unpleasant aspects of ecclesiastical life as well as ignorant priests. The 15th-century Scotsman Robert Henryson's small collection of fables is explicit in its social criticism. A master rhetorician, Henryson expanded the subject matter of the fable to include otherworldly and mystical subjects. The best-known Middle English fable is perhaps Chaucer's tale of Chauntecleer, Pertelote, and the Fox in "The Nun's Priest's Tale" from *The Canterbury Tales* (c. 1387).

The Aesopean fable was diversified and developed still further by the most famous of European fabulists, the 17th-century Frenchman Jean de La Fontaine. His elegant yet simple verse fables draw not only on the traditional Latin and Greek sources but also on the *Pañcatantra*. La Fontaine's fables are informed by his love of rural life and illuminate his epicurean beliefs. They were widely translated and imitated during the 17th and 18th centuries all over Europe, and beyond. In America, the tradition of the verse fable continued in Joel Chandler Harris' *Uncle Remus: His Songs and His Sayings* (published in periodicals and collected in 1880).

Didactic fables have been used throughout the ages to instruct children. In the Middle Ages as well as in the early part of the 17th century, simple Aesopean stories were employed to teach Latin. The use of the fable in education flourished with particular vigor in the 18th century. When the fable largely lost its political and satirical power, it retained its role as children's literature.

Fable (Fabula) as a Narratological Term

The term *fable* took on a new—and entirely independent—life in the 20th century, when it emerged as a narratological term in the work of the Russian formalists. Viktor Shklovskii first used the term in his two early works "Svyaz priyomov syuzhetoslozheniya S obschimi priyomami stilya" (1919; The Relation of Devices of Plot Construction to General Devices of Style) and "*Tristram Shendi* Sterna i teoriia romana" (1921; Sterne's *Tristram Shandy* and Theory of the Novel), in which he distinguished between *fabula*, roughly equivalent to "story" in contemporary narratology, and its textural surface structure, the *syuzhet*, roughly equivalent to *plot* or *discourse*. Shklovskii noted that "The idea of *plot* (*syuzhet*) is too often confused with the description of events—with what I propose provisionally to call the story (*fabula*). The story is, in fact, only material for plot formulation. The plot of *Evgenii Onegin* [1831; *Eugene Onegin*] is, therefore, not the romance of the hero with Tatiana, but the fashioning of the subject of this story as produced by the introduction of interrupting digressions." Boris Tomashevsky, in 1925, expanded this distinction further by clarifying that the plot is an artful arrangement of the story elements. The Russian formalists' understanding of *fabula* already includes the notion of causality, as is implicit in Tomashevsky's argument that "a story requires not only indication of time, but also indication of cause."

The distinction was first introduced to a Western audience by René Wellek and Austin Warren in their *Theory of Literature* (1949), and since then it has found its way into the narratological theories of Gérard Genette and Seymour Chatman. Genette in particular maps out all the many deviations from the chrono-logical arrangement in the syuzhet/discourse, subsuming these rearrangements under the category of temporal features of the narrative.

The *fabula/syuzhet* distinction has not been applied to the analysis of the genre of the fable because most short traditional tales narrate their story in a chronological order and therefore do not require this terminological refinement. Shklovskii himself needed the distinction only when he turned from the folk tale to the novel, and he demonstrated its usefulness on the example of Laurence Sterne's *Tristram Shandy* (1759–67), which features one of the most complicated temporal structures in the history of the novel.

MONIKA FLUDERNIK AND PARVIN LOLOI

See also Formalism; Narrative Theory; Narratology; Plot; Saga

Further Reading

Blackham, H.P., *The Fable as Literature,* London and Dover, New Hampshire: Athlone Press, 1985

Bremond, Claude, Jacques Le Goff, and Jean-Claude Schmitt, *L'"Exemplum,"* Turnhout, Belgium: Brepols, 1982; 2nd edition, 1996

Daniel, Stephen H., "Political and Philosophical Uses of Fables in 18th-Century England," *The Eighteenth Century: Theory and Interpretation* 23 (1982)

Euler, Bettina, *Strukturen mündlichen Erzählens: Parasyntaktische und sentenielle Analysen am Beispiel des englischen Witzes,* Tübingen: Narr, 1991

Fiedler, Leslie A., "The Death and Rebirth of the Novel: The View from '82," in *INNOVATION/RENOVATION: New Perspectives on the Humanities,* edited by Ihab Hassan and Sally Hassan, Madison: University of Wisconsin Press, 1983

Fineman, Joel, "The History of the Anecdote: Fiction and Fiction," in his *The Subjectivity Effect in Western Literary Tradition: Essays Toward the Release of Shakespeare's Will,* Cambridge, Massachusetts: MIT Press, 1991

Fludernik, Monika, *Towards a "Natural" Narratology,* London and New York: Routledge, 1996

Henderson, Arnold Clayton, "Animal Fables as Vehicles of Social Protest and Satire: Twelfth Century to Henryson," in *Third International Beast Epic, Fable and Fabliau Colloquium,* edited by Jan Goossens and Timothy Sodmann, Cologne: Böhlau, 1981

Jolles, André, *Einfache Formen: Legende, Sage, Mythe, Rätsel, Spruch, Kasus, Memorabile, Märchen, Witz,* Halle: Niemeyer, 1930; 6th edition, Tübingen: Niemeyer, 1982

Kalila and Dimna: Selected Fables of Bidpai, retold by Ramsay Wood, with an introduction by Doris Lessing, New York: Knopf, 1980; London: Granada, 1982

Koch, Walter A., editor, *Simple Forms: An Encyclopedia of Simple Text-Types in Lore and Literature,* Bochum: Brockmeyer, 1994

Labov, William, *Language in the Inner City: Studies in the Black English Vernacular,* Philadelphia: University of Pennsylvania Press, 1972; Oxford: Blackwell, 1977

Labov, William, and Joshua Waletzky, "Narrative Analysis: Oral Versions of Personal Experience," in *Essays on the Verbal and Visual Arts,* edited by June Helm, Seattle: University of Washington Press, 1967

Lewis, Jayne Elizabeth, *The English Fable: Aesop and Literary Culture, 1651–1740*, Cambridge and New York: Cambridge University Press, 1996

The Pañcatantra, translated from the Sanskrit by Franklin Edgerton, London: Allen and Unwin, 1965 (the introduction is particularly useful)

Rubin, David Lee, and A. Lytton Sells, "Fable," in *The New Princeton Encyclopedia of Poetry and Poetics,* edited by Alex Preminger and T.V.F. Brogan, Princeton: New Jersey: Princeton University Press, 1993

Smith, M. Ellwood, "The Fable as Poetry in English Criticism," *Modern Language Notes* 32 (1917)

Faction. *See* New Journalism and the Nonfiction Novel

Fanny Hill by John Cleland

1748–49

Originally published in two volumes as the anonymous *Memoirs of a Woman of Pleasure,* the success of John Cleland's scandalous first novel secured his release both from London's Fleet prison and from habitual debt. Together with the novel's popularity came official action, which resulted in the arrest of both publisher and author for indecency, and the novel's disappearance underground. In retrospect, the government's response seems lukewarm, for no case was brought to trial, and an expurgated version appeared in 1750 renamed with the now popular title: *Memoirs of Fanny Hill.* Despite church protest over a passage depicting male sodomy, it is doubtful whether the government ever considered the novel a serious danger to public morals. Cleland's reputation, however, was ruined by his display of libertinism clearly at odds with the new respectability of the mid–18th century.

Following its controversial republication in 1963, *Fanny Hill*'s role in the development of English literature has been reassessed. Despite its recognition as a key text in the history of popular culture, critical opinion has differed fiercely over the novel's generic status, for, on the surface, *Fanny Hill* belongs to the same tradition of continental erotic literature as Michel Millot's *L'Ecole des Filles* (1655; *A School for Girls*) and Jean Barrin's *Vénus dans le Cloître* (1683; *Venus in the Cloister*). Beneath *Fanny Hill*'s libertine exterior, however, it is possible to identify a more significant relationship with the realistic novels of the 1740s, which portrayed the new sentimental union of feeling and virtue. Perhaps Cleland's most controversial achievement, therefore, was the creation of an erotic parody of the mainstream novel in a literary crossover that satirically reveals the veiled connections between sentimental and erotic feeling.

Much of the novel focuses on the necessary transition from innocence to experience that accompanies individual development. More importantly, as she journeys from Liverpool to London Fanny Hill progresses from rural naïveté to urban maturity—a trajectory of female Bildung shared by many sentimental heroines. Fanny's introduction to city life at Mrs. Brown's brothel mirrors Mrs. Sinclair's treatment of Samuel Richardson's heroine, Clarissa; and the topos of a city like London as a "learning experience" forms a common theme within narratives of sentimental female development. This trajectory is also a standard pornographic feature, and one satirized in William Hogarth's famous etching, *The Harlot's Progress.* Here, far from providing a valuable lesson in male profligacy, libertine London drives the innocent young woman to prostitution. Following this second pattern, Fanny's urban experience rapidly translates into a comprehensive sexual education, for the instructive episodes of the sentimental novel are reduced to a repetitive chain of casual sexual encounters. Cleland's pornographic desire to construct scene after scene of unvaried sensual activity subsumes the novel's character development and formal unity.

A number of popular realist motifs frame the narrative. The mature Fanny writes her first-person "memoirs" as two supposedly genuine letters to a curious "Madame," in a transparent blending of the authentic history of Daniel Defoe's *Moll Flanders* (1722) with the epistolary novels of Richardson. This device also shapes the libertine convention of the "whore's dialogue," in which an experienced prostitute narrates her history to an uninitiated pupil. A striking feature of Fanny's narration, however, is its masculine bias. As a pornographic text directed at a male readership, it is surprising that the narrative gaze focuses predominantly on the male rather than the female body. In her essay "'I's' in Drag: The Sex of Recollection" (1981) Nancy K. Miller explains this gender reversal by unmasking "Fanny" as the heterosexual cover for Cleland in drag. The manipulation of a female narrator allows the author to establish a homoerotic relationship with the male reader—a strategy that casts the adoption of a feminine narrative perspective by both Defoe and Richardson in a new light.

This complex layering of novel and pornography appears most prominently in Fanny's discourse. Renowned for its coded but pure description of wanton acts, *Fanny Hill* exploits the florid excesses of sentiment, translating, through euphemism and metaphor, the poetic language of the pastoral sublime to the sexual terrain of the body. Here, the emotional intensity of sensibility becomes the unmistakable language of sensuality, for the trembling and blushing of the erotic body locate the novel firmly within the sexually charged world of libertinism.

Cleland directs a final sally at the ideology of sentiment in the conclusion of the novel, where a semblance of bourgeois morality is belatedly tagged to Fanny's exuberant tale of vice when she avoids the dissolute end of Hogarth's Moll Hackabout by marrying her first and only true love, Charles. This late embrace of romantic monogamy binds *Fanny Hill* to the conservative morals of the sentimental tradition and distances the text from the socially subversive doctrines of libertinism. Following the novel's joyful celebration of sexual freedom, however, the mocking irony of Fanny's moral platitudes stand out sharply. Here, *Fanny Hill* occupies a central position alongside Henry Fielding's *Shamela* (1741) in the anti-Pamelist controversy of the 1740s, for Cleland demonstrates the fragility of female virtue when faced with the "manly beauty" of Charles, rather than the fumbling of Pamela's Mr. B. Therefore, despite the punning addition of "a tail-piece of morality," the philosophy of the novel remains resoundingly libertine in translating the Lockean precepts of "natural morality" into the realm of erotic pleasure. Accordingly, sexual desire is perceived to be a powerful natural force for both sexes, far removed from the prudery of Richardson or the politicized sadism of French libertinism. Richardsonian virtue is transformed into libertine sexuality by Cleland's humorous unmasking of the sentimental novel, which he achieves with only a slight angling of the perspective glass.

Fanny Hill's ironic crossing of the formal and thematic features of libertinism and sensibility reappear later in the century to influence both the sentimental excesses of Laurence Sterne's *A Sentimental Journey* (1768) and the political libertinism of Choderlos de Laclos and the Marquis de Sade. In the modern period, it is possible to view Cleland's early novel as the precursor for experimental texts like D.H. Lawrence's *Lady Chatterley's Lover* (1928) and William Burroughs' *The Naked Lunch* (1959), both of which, in similarly controversial fashion, attempt to introduce a frank sexual discourse within the bounds of the novel.

HARRIET SIMPSON

See also Pornographic Novel

Further Reading

Epstein, William H., *John Cleland: Images of a Life*, New York: Columbia University Press, 1974; London: Columbia University Press, 1975

Foxon, David, *Libertine Literature in England, 1660–1745*, London: Book Collector, 1964; New Hyde, New York: University Books, 1965

Kibbie, Ann Louise, "Sentimental Properties: *Pamela* and *Memoirs of a Woman of Pleasure*," *English Literary History* 58 (1991)

Miller, Nancy K., "'I's' in Drag: The Sex of Recollection," *The Eighteenth Century* 22 (1981)

Simmons, Philip E., "John Cleland's *Memoirs of a Woman of Pleasure*: Literary Voyeurism and the Techniques of Novelistic Transgression," *Eighteenth-Century Fiction* 3 (1990)

Todd, Janet, *Women's Friendship in Literature*, New York: Columbia University Press, 1980

Wagner, Peter, *Eros Revived: Erotica of the Enlightenment in England and America*, London: Secker and Warburg, 1988

Fantasy Novel. *See* Science Fiction Novel

A Farewell to Arms by Ernest Hemingway

1929

By 1929, the 30-year-old Ernest Hemingway had already developed a considerable following on the basis of his two short-story collections, *In Our Time* (1925) and *Men without Women* (1927), and his first novel, *The Sun Also Rises* (1926). But it was *A Farewell to Arms* that finally brought him the critical and popular acclaim that he had deeply desired since deciding to become a writer in 1918—and that has continued ever since. The novel, as Paul Smith has shown (in Donaldson, 1990), develops themes and techniques with which Hemingway had been experimenting for at least a decade: the interactions of love and war as registered in the consciousness of a male character. A more linear narrative than *The Sun Also Rises,* the novel presents Frederic Henry narrating his experiences as an ambulance driver in the Italian army during World War I: his being wounded, his falling in love with his nurse, Catherine Barkley, his defection from the Italian army, his flight into Switzerland with Catherine, and the death during childbirth first of their baby and then of Catherine. The novel is also an imaginative reworking of incidents in Hemingway's life; he had been an ambulance driver in Italy during World War I, had been hospitalized after being wounded, and had fallen in love with his nurse Agnes von Kurowsky—although Agnes broke up with him shortly after he returned to the United States.

Frederic Henry possesses the famous spare Hemingway style, one marked by simple, informal diction, coordinating rather than subordinating conjunctions and clauses, and descriptions of the external world rather than of emotional states or responses. This style requires readers to be active participants in the novel, filling in many details about Frederic's and the other characters' understanding, values, and emotional states. Our inferential activity uncovers a narrative line that follows the pattern of a Bildungsroman. Frederic Henry begins as a callow youth who regards the war as "no more real" to him "than war in the movies" and Catherine as simply a better alternative to the whores at the front. He ends as a mature adult who understands that "if people bring so much courage to this world, the world has to kill them to break them so of course it kills them" and that in losing Catherine he has lost the better part of himself. The key formal innovations of the novel involve Hemingway's use of Frederic Henry as a new type of protagonist-narrator and his merging of the pattern of the Bildungsroman with that of narrative tragedy.

Before and after *A Farewell to Arms,* the most common kinds of protagonist-narrators are those, such as Charles Dickens' Pip (in *Great Expectations,* 1861), who move back and forth between the immature perspective of the character and the mature perspective of the narrator and those, such as Mark Twain's Huck Finn (in *The Adventures of Huckleberry Finn,* 1884), who remain naive throughout the telling. Hemingway had himself experimented in "My Old Man," a story in the collection *In Our Time,* with a protagonist-narrator who is initially naive but then is suddenly enlightened at story's end. In *The Sun Also Rises,* Jake Barnes' war wound has eliminated all his naïveté. The narration of *A Farewell to Arms* departs from these patterns. Although Frederic's narration is clearly retrospective, his telling is neither consistently naive nor consistently informed with the knowledge he achieves by the end of the novel. Instead, with just a few exceptions, it is only as Frederic the character gains knowledge that Frederic the narrator reflects that understanding in his telling. Thus Hemingway initially establishes Frederic as an unreliable narrator whose beliefs about the war and about Catherine are naive and egocentric. Hemingway then gradually closes the distance between Frederic's beliefs and his own so that by the end of the novel their views of the world are virtually identical. In adopting this technique, Hemingway rejected a standard of realism that says a retrospective narrator must operate with the knowledge acquired by his experiences as a character, favoring instead the principle that a good novelist will use the most efficient strategy for achieving the desired intensity of effect.

The second innovation, one very important for both the modern and the postmodern novel, involves creating a sense of tragedy in an absurd universe. Frederic Henry's doom, unlike the doom of Shakespeare's—or even Thomas Hardy's—protagonists, is a condition of existence, not something that arises from his own choices. Yet Frederic's final state is tragic rather than pathetic because Hemingway merges the Bildungsroman pattern with that of the tragedy. Frederic's growth in knowledge and his response to that knowledge constitute a significant achievement—not one that mitigates the enormity of his loss but one that allows him to go on living in the wake of Catherine's death.

Critics have generally agreed about the novel's main themes: the trauma of war, the value of love, and the inevitability of destruction in an indifferent, if not malevolent, universe. Furthermore, as with most of Hemingway's work, the novel has received considerable biographical criticism. Especially noteworthy is Michael Reynolds' very careful and extensive study of the significant changes Hemingway made to the manuscript as he transformed his experiences into Frederic's (see Reynolds, 1976). Within the general agreement about themes and the importance of Hemingway's own experiences, there is considerable diversity of critical opinion—a consequence, in part, of Hemingway's strategy of relying on the inferential activity of his readers. Some critics infer a Frederic who never grows up, whose narration is a failed attempt at self-justification. But perhaps the greatest debate surrounds Catherine. Judith Fetterley (1978) has advanced an influential feminist argument that Hemingway's portrait of Catherine is not only a male fantasy but also a sign of his hostility toward women. Other critics, male and female, feminist and not, have maintained that in Catherine Hemingway has created a figure of strength, courage, and dignity. The more unusual aspects of Frederic and Catherine's relationship, including her desire to merge so completely with Frederic that the two of them would be identical in nearly every way, link up with unorthodox ideas about love and sexuality that Hemingway explores more fully in *The Garden of Eden* (published posthumously, 1986) and that have drawn the attention of critics influenced by developments in queer theory.

In conjunction with Hemingway's other works in the 1920s, *A Farewell to Arms* brought a new style and sensibility to American literature. The sensibility involved both an awareness of the world's destructiveness and a belief in the importance of grace under the pressure of such awareness. The style involved clarity, objectivity, and indirection. The effects of both the style and the sensibility may be seen in modern writers as different as Ross McDonald, Norman Mailer, Raymond Carver, and Ann Beattie.

JAMES PHELAN

See also Ernest Hemingway

Further Reading

Baker, Carlos, *Hemingway: The Writer as Artist,* Princeton, New Jersey: Princeton University Press, 1952; 4th edition, 1972

Brenner, Gerry, *Concealments in Hemingway's Works,* Columbus: Ohio State University Press, 1983

Donaldson, Scott, editor, *New Essays on Hemingway's "A Farewell to Arms,"* Cambridge and New York: Cambridge University Press, 1990

Fetterley, Judith, *The Resisting Reader: A Feminist Approach to American Fiction,* Bloomington: Indiana University Press, 1978

Oldsey, Bernard, *Hemingway's Hidden Craft: The Writing of "A Farewell to Arms,"* University Park: Pennsylvania State University Press, 1979

Phelan, James, "Voice, Distance, Temporal Perspective, and the Dynamics of *A Farewell to Arms,*" in his *Narrative as Rhetoric: Technique, Audiences, Ethics, Ideology,* Columbus: Ohio State University Press, 1996

Reynolds, Michael, *Hemingway's First War: The Making of "A Farewell to Arms,"* Princeton, New Jersey: Princeton University Press, 1976, Oxford: Blackwell, 1987

Scholes, Robert, and Nancy Comley, *Hemingway's Genders: Rereading the Hemingway Text,* New Haven, Connecticut: Yale University Press, 1994

Von Kurowsky, Agnes, *Hemingway in Love and War: The Lost Diary of Agnes von Kurowsky, Her Letters, and Correspondence of Ernest Hemingway,* edited by Henry Serrano Villard and James Nagel, Boston: Northeastern University Press, 1989

Young, Philip, *Ernest Hemingway: A Reconsideration,* University Park: Pennsylvania State University Press, 1966

Fathers and Sons by Ivan Turgenev

Ottsy i deti 1862

Fathers and Sons occupies a critical position within Turgenev's oeuvre and, indeed, within the Russian tradition of the novel. By the time of the novel's publication, Turgenev had established himself in public life as the author of exquisite, compact narratives that addressed the central questions of pre-emancipation Russian society. Contemporary critics and readers viewed Turgenev as a novelist with European values whose acute eye registered the subtle permutations of character and ideology in Russia on the eve of reform. A social realist whose own career had begun as a poet, Turgenev was viewed as a "man of the '40s" whose novels traced Russia's evolution away from the idealism of his own youth.

The very form of Turgenev's classic novels—and of *Fathers and Sons*—bespeaks the author's complex engagement with the world he represents. Alienated intellectuals enter the world of the rural gentry, whose estates are islands of culture in a world of striking natural beauty and great economic inequity; the intellectual is associated with an ideology that is tested through his encounter with a woman; the symbolic potential promised by their meeting goes unfulfilled as male will succumbs to doubt and disease; the life of Russia continues, an organic entity that both charms and devours its greatest talents.

Fathers and Sons repeats much of the narrative structure already limned in Turgenev's earlier works. Bazarov, the great nihilist, does ideological battle with remnants of an earlier generation; he is idolized by a coterie of younger progressives whose enthusiasms are alternately sincere and silly; he encounters, finally, forces that his scientific mind and colossal will cannot subdue—passionate love and human frailty. While Turgenev structures the novel as a narrative of ideological and generational conflict (Bazarov the nihilist first debates, then duels with, Pavel Kirsanov; Arkadii Kirsanov sets out in gentler fashion to "reform" his sentimental father), his narrative gives to that conflict a context as much lyrical and philosophical as sociohistorical. Here as in his earlier novels Turgenev sees the world not merely as a chronicler but as a lyricist. His handling of space and topography in the novel suggests a vision of how human beings contend with and structure what is "wild," both in nature and themselves. Turgenev's Bazarov is a ferocious nihilist who winds up quoting Pascal, passing through a rationalist's "dark night of the soul" in a Russian hay barn. The values of contemporary science and reason must submit, in Turgenev's telling, to a vision of human insignificance and of forces deeper than rationality within the human psyche that overwhelm conscious intention. It is in this final context that Dostoevskii's great enthusiasm for the novel (in a letter that has been lost; we have only Turgenev's response) makes most sense: the kinship between works as diverse as *Zapiski iz podpol'ia* (1864; *Notes from Underground*) and *Fathers and Sons* is that both profoundly critique the hubris of rationality and will; both allude to visions of humanity in which humility and self-knowledge are the well-springs of human culture, a culture daily threatened by the excesses of the modern world.

The form of Turgenev's novel could not be more different from Dostoevskii's, however, and it is the form of this novel that represents Turgenev's unique contribution to Russian thinking about will, destruction, and culture. The very form and language of *Fathers and Sons,* like those that preceded it, affirms Turgenev's commitment to the compassionate elaboration of measured oppositions. *Fathers and Sons* suggests in the Kirsanov estate a world of culture and nature in creative tension, a world in which the values of moderation and civility are seen as making possible whatever progress might be made in the human project. The chill aristocrats of the novel, Pavel Kirsanov and Anna Odintsova, are repressive and authoritarian because they fear the destructive forces of eros—forces whose political and emotional consequences Bazarov comes to embody. The gentler, "pastoral" figures of the novel—Arkadii, his father, Katia—suggest a medial path of accommodation and humanity, a way of living with the darker forces. Turgenev's novel is an exquisite philosophical and lyrical statement; it is also a profound political statement—one later acknowledged wistfully by Dmitrii Merezhkovskii, the symbolist writer and cultural critic: "Didn't our revolution fail because there was too much in it of Russian extremity, too little of European measure; too much of L. Tolstoy and Dostoevsky, too little Turgenev?" From the vantage point of post-1905, after Russia's first revolution, Merezhkovskii pointed back to one of the signal features of Turgenev's novelistic oeuvre, one that significantly *failed* after the publication of *Fathers and Sons*: the novel was met with virulent hostility by critics on both sides of Russia's political spectrum, whose view of the exigencies of Russian society would admit of no persuasions to moderation and order. The result of this aggressively negative reception was devastating for Turgenev as a novelist of proportional vision; the novelist essentially retreated from both Russia and the novel, moving instead toward shorter forms and experiments in fantastic, quasi-symbolic narrative. The two novels written after *Fathers and Sons, Dym* (1867; *Smoke*) and *Nov'* (1877; *Virgin Soil*), veer toward opposing extremes: *Smoke* expends its energies in shrill, vituperative satire; *Virgin Soil* does obsequious duty toward the forces of radical change in Russia. One novel displays petulant dismay at uprooted aristocratic Russia; the other verges on socialist realism in its pathetic efforts to regain a lost acclaim. In both novels the writer has lost his nerve and his vision, and in both cases the loss of narrative balance is connected to a loss within Russia of the possibility of compromise, of what Merezhkovskii called "European measure."

What is striking about this loss is how it seems to signal larger shifts within the history of the Russian novel and its representation of radical political figures. The subtle, complex vision of radical impulse and nurturing tradition that *Fathers and Sons* articulates gives way to narratives of apocalypse and violence, particularly evident in novels that depict Russian reality as a drama of "fathers and sons": Dostoevskii's *Besy* (1872; *Devils*) imagines a world of murder and psychic chaos, wrought by Bazarov's ideological confreres, aided and abetted by the generation of which Turgenev was a part (Turgenev is in fact wildly lampooned in the novel). *Brat'ia Karamazovy* (1880; *The Brothers Karamazov*) envisions a world lurching toward ultimate crimes, in which the sins of the father are to be revenged by the sons themselves. Andrei Belyi's great modernist novel *Peterburg* (1916; *Petersburg*) brings this apocalyptic tradition to a point of fulfillment, if not conclusion: where Merezhkovskii laments Russia's lack of measure, Belyi sees culture itself as bankrupt, a structure of repression that is impotent against the whirlwind of forces (from the lower classes, from the East) that will destroy it. These novels trace chaos not only in their themes but in their forms, which suggest a world of traditional values in the process of rapid disintegration. Turgenev's novel in this company might seem either hopelessly old-fashioned or blessedly curative; his response to the energies of destruction already present in his society was not to represent chaos, but to treasure form—and to imagine an order (narrative, social, psychic) that is not repressive but gentle, and ultimately creative. *Fathers and Sons* functions, in this sense, not as a cathartic drama of struggle and expulsion, but as a meditative recollection, honoring the energies of change but suggesting the need for compassion, love, beauty. The form of his novel will seem necessary or not in precise relation to our need for such qualities.

JANE COSTLOW

See also Ivan Turgenev

Further Reading

Allen, Elizabeth Cheresh, *Beyond Realism: Turgenev's Poetics of Secular Salvation,* Stanford, California: Stanford University Press, 1992

Costlow, Jane T., *Worlds within Worlds: The Novels of Ivan Turgenev,* Princeton, New Jersey: Princeton University Press, 1990

Freeborn, Richard, *Turgenev: The Novelist's Novelist, a Study,* London: Oxford University Press, 1960

Jackson, Robert L., "The Root and the Flower, Dostoevsky and Turgenev: A Comparative Esthetic," *Yale Review* (1974)

Merezhkovskii, Dmitrii, "Turgenev," in *Polnoe sobranie sochinenii,* volume 17, Moscow: Sytina, 1914

Ripp, Victor, *Turgenev's Russia: From "Notes of a Hunter" to "Fathers and Sons,"* Ithaca, New York: Cornell University Press, 1980

William Faulkner 1897–1962

United States

In signing himself "Sole Owner & Proprietor" of Yoknapataw-pha, the mythical county of his best-known fiction based on the actual Lafayette County in upstate Mississippi, Faulkner showed a typically wry touch. His 19 novels and more than 70 stories do not all turn on Yoknapatawpha, nor are they all marked by his dark and often startling social satire. Nevertheless, Yoknapatawpha is a *comédie humaine* of the American South, a massive, composite, genealogical vision of Dixie as the world, spanning the long decades of economic decline from the Civil War through the Depression. "His by-path, Mississippi, was no by-path, but a universe," observed Robert Lowell.

The best known of Faulkner's novels offer stories of "ageless eternal struggles," in his own phrase. Many of them are drawn from biblical and classical Greek sources, such as the Bundren family's mock-epic journey "through fire and flood" with Addie Bundren's body to bury her with her own people in *As I Lay Dying* (1930). At the same time, Faulkner's work draws upon the heritage of the South. Shaped by slavery and racism, the defeat of the Civil War, and a Bible-thumping Christianity, the people and the landscape Faulkner portrays always have a recognizable specificity, despite his Gothic and satirical distortions.

The novels revolve not only around recurring characters and places but around recurring themes. Racism, and all the personal and family deformity that comes trailing in its wake, makes an appearance in virtually every novel as the central organizing factor in Yoknapatawpha society, most gruesomely in *Light in August* (1932). Class divisions between "aristocracy" and "white trash" animate many other novels. Thomas Sutpen's grotesque dynastic dreams in *Absalom, Absalom!* (1936), for instance, are motivated by his dirt-poor origins. The Snopeses display a social *ressentiment* at once savagely mean-spirited and comical in the Snopes trilogy, consisting of *The Hamlet* (1940), *The Town* (1957), and *The Mansion* (1959). Other central themes include a focus on family as both life force and curse, as in *The Sound and the Fury* (1929) and *Absalom, Absalom!*; the misspent heroism of the Civil War, as in *The Unvanquished* (1938); and the wilderness as an embodiment of both stasis and change, particularly in the stories of *Go Down, Moses* (1942).

Despite his regional focus, Faulkner is commonly included with James Joyce, Marcel Proust, Thomas Mann, André Gide, and Virginia Woolf as a leading novelist in the modernist pantheon, mainly on the strength of his experimentation with shifts in point of view, temporal discontinuity, and interior monologue. His technical experimentation is driven by a shared modernist emphasis on the primacy of individual subjective experience. More specific to Faulkner is the added insistence that the meaning of history is realized in memory, whether shared through storytelling and collaborative reconstruction or guarded as a private obsession. As a result, telling becomes a drama in its own right in Faulkner's work, and the reader becomes a privileged partner in the construction of meaning—privileged because, unlike the characters, the reader has access to all the different versions of history Faulkner offers. Asked about "thirteen ways of looking at a blackbird with none of them right," Faulkner responded by saying, "The reader has his own four-teenth image of that blackbird, which I would like to think is the truth."

Faulkner's works have all helped extend the novel's repertoire of narrative forms, a principal reason that his reputation has become increasingly secure. *The Sound and the Fury,* for instance, consists of four sections, told by the three Compson brothers and a family servant, each reflecting on the fate of the once prominent, but now disintegrating, Compson family. Each section competes with the others to be taken as the most authoritative account, yet it is only in their complementarity that the Compson saga takes shape for the reader. The "idiot" Benjy's discontinuous sense data play against Quentin's rhetorical hyperconsciousness, Jason's sardonic realism against Dilsey's redemptive black Christianity. The effect is of collage, from which the "story" can indeed only be completed by the reader, who comes to grasp even the unsaid and unmentionable—such as the fact that Candace Compson, the sister, has become a prostitute.

In *As I Lay Dying,* narrative in a conventional sense is entirely absent. The novel consists of a series of snippets of consciousness, almost like snapshots, taken during the days of Addie Bundren's death and burial. They are focused not on Addie but on the experiences, feelings, and memories of the participant-witnesses in her death: Anse, Addie's resentful, manipulative husband, and her children, Cash, Darl, Jewel, Dewey Dell, and Vardaman. From the interplay of the highly individual narrative snippets, the reader is able to piece together the story of the Bundrens' blackly comic journey with Addie's coffin, as well as a composite portrait of Addie herself.

Light in August, the one major novel that most closely observes the traditional storytelling of cause and effect, launches two parallel and contrasting plot lines. On the one hand, there is the pregnant Lena Grove's circular journey in search of her missing husband, on the other, the iron "corridor" of Joe Christmas' life and eventual lynching. Around those barely intersecting plot lines, Faulkner weaves a web of subsidiary action, including Joanna Burden's descent into sexual-religious frenzy, the Reverend Hightower's thwarted withdrawal from life, Byron Bunch's comically defeated sexual chivalry, Lucas Burch's marital flight, Percy Grimm's fascism, and Doc Hines' rabid Calvinism. The result, to invoke Mikhail Bakhtin, is a carnivalesque narrative of missed connections.

Absalom, Absalom!, generally considered Faulkner's masterpiece, again operates through a range of voices, all trying to unravel the mysteries of Thomas Sutpen's violent life. Rosa Coldfield, Thomas' sister-in-law, opens the novel with her version of the Sutpen story as Gothic mystery, a seemingly inexplicable family riddle of curse and hatred. Easing the melodrama, Mr. Compson portrays Sutpen as both an interloper and a friend, a countryboy figure out of real time and place. Faulkner's best compositional stroke, however, is to have Quentin Compson and his Canadian roommate at Harvard relive the Sutpen story from start to finish, echoing the fraternal voices of Thomas Sutpen's sons, the acknowledged, white Henry and the unacknowledged, mixed Charles Bon. A narrative inquest not only on the rise and fall of Sutpen's Hundred but on the South itself, the boys' narrative reconstruction unearths a specific family history and at the same time opens up a privileged view of the tragic legacies and comic byways of a South haunted by slavery, racial mixing, and the humiliations of the Civil War.

Faulkner did not meet with immediate success, and by the late 1930s virtually all his books were out of print. Malcolm Cowley's *The Portable Faulkner* (1946) rescued him from near-oblivion. Arguing that Yoknapatawpha was "one connected story," a "living pattern," nothing less than "a permanent state of consciousness," Cowley correctly saw Faulkner's entire oeuvre as unified in theme and vision and recognized his gift for storytelling. Despite attacks on his admittedly often overworked imagery and congested syntax, Faulkner's reputation has been secure since then. The work of subsequent novelists, both conventionally realist and postmodernist, bears his stamp, particularly in the handling of point of view and the representation of experience through memory.

A. ROBERT LEE

See also Absalom, Absalom!; Sound and the Fury

Biography

Born William Cuthbert Falkner in New Albany, Mississippi, 25 September 1897; family moved to Oxford, Mississippi, 1902. Attended local schools in Oxford, and the University of Mississippi, Oxford, 1919–20. Served in the Royal Canadian Air Force, 1918. Bookkeeper in bank, 1916–18; worked in Doubleday Bookshop, New York, 1921; postmaster, University of Mississippi Post Office, 1921–24; lived in New Orleans and contributed to New Orleans *Times-Picayune,* 1925; traveled in Europe, 1925–26; returned to Oxford, 1927; a full-time writer from 1927; screenwriter for Metro-Goldwyn-Mayer, 1932–33, 20th Century-Fox, 1935–37, and Warner Brothers, 1942–45; Writer-in-Residence, University of Virginia, Charlottesville, 1957, and part of each year, 1958–62. Awarded Nobel prize for literature, 1950. Died 6 July 1962.

Novels by Faulkner

Soldiers' Pay, 1926
Mosquitoes, 1927
Sartoris, 1929
The Sound and the Fury, 1929
As I Lay Dying, 1930
Sanctuary, 1931
Light in August, 1932
Pylon, 1935
Absalom, Absalom!, 1936
The Unvanquished, 1938
The Wild Palms, 1939
The Hamlet, 1940
Intruder in the Dust, 1948
Requiem for a Nun, 1951
A Fable, 1954
The Town, 1957
The Mansion, 1959
The Reivers: A Reminiscence, 1962

Other Writings: poems, stories, sketches, essays, speeches, and letters.

Further Reading

Bassett, John E., *Faulkner: An Annotated Checklist of Recent Criticism,* Kent, Ohio: Kent State University Press, 1983

Blotner, Joseph Leo, *Faulkner: A Biography,* 2 vols., New York: Random House, and London: Chatto and Windus, 1974

Brodhead, Richard, editor, *Faulkner: New Perspectives,* Englewood Cliffs, New Jersey: Prentice-Hall, 1983

Brooks, Cleanth, *William Faulkner: The Yoknapatawpha Country,* New Haven, Connecticut: Yale University Press, 1963

Brooks, Cleanth, *William Faulkner: Towards Yoknapatawpha and Beyond,* New Haven, Connecticut: Yale University Press, 1978; London: Yale University Press, 1979

Hoffman, Frederick John, and Olga Vickery, editors, *William Faulkner: Three Decades of Criticism,* East Lansing: Michigan State University Press, 1960

Kinney, Arthur F., *Faulkner's Narrative Poetics: Style as Vision,* Amherst: University of Massachusetts Press, 1978

Lee, A. Robert, editor, *William Faulkner: The Yoknapatawpha Fiction,* Totowa, New Jersey: Barnes and Noble, 1987; London: Vision Press, 1990

McHaney, Thomas L., *William Faulkner: A Reference Guide,* Boston: G.K. Hall, 1976

Meriwether, James B., *The Literary Career of William Faulkner: A Bibliographical Study,* Princeton, New Jersey: Princeton University Press, 1961

Minter, David, *William Faulkner: His Life and Work,* Baltimore: Johns Hopkins University Press, 1980

Thompson, Lawrance R., *William Faulkner: An Introduction and Interpretation,* New York: Barnes and Noble, 1963; 2nd edition, 1967

Wagner-Martin, Linda, editor, *William Faulkner: Four Decades of Criticism,* East Lansing: Michigan State University Press, 1973

Warren, Robert Penn, editor, *Faulkner: A Collection of Critical Essays,* Englewood Cliffs, New Jersey: Prentice-Hall, 1966

Faux-monnayeurs. *See* Counterfeiters

Feminist Criticism of Narrative

The novel as a form has often been associated with women, whether as authors or characters, almost from its beginning. Not surprisingly, then, criticism focusing on gender began to appear almost as soon as the novel itself did. Women critics such as Madeleine de Scudéry, Aphra Behn, Sarah Fielding, Isabelle de Charrière, Clara Reeve, Anna Barbauld, Fanny Burney, Mary Wollstonecraft, Germaine de Staël, Maria Edgeworth, and Jane Austen frequently focused on women authors and the relation of gender to the novel. In the 19th century, women became even more prominent as novelists and critics, and a number of them, from the sensation-novel writer Mrs. Henry Wood (Eliza Lynn Linton) to the intellectual George Eliot (Marian Evans), with her famous "Silly Novels by Lady Novelists," addressed the issue of women writing fiction. Perhaps the first instance of what could genuinely be called "feminist criticism," however, was the critical writing of Virginia Woolf in the early 20th century. Woolf, an acknowledged feminist, explicitly analyzed literature and specific literary works in terms of their relation to gender and gender constructions.

In her newspaper reviews (many of which are collected in *The Common Reader*, 1925), her lecture "Professions for Women" (1942), and, especially, her famous essay *A Room of One's Own* (1929), Virginia Woolf specifically addressed both writing by women and the condition of women as professional writers. Herself an innovative novelist, Woolf also experimented with the traditional form of literary criticism, casting *A Room of One's Own*, for instance, as a lyrical personal narrative by a woman ("call me Mary Beton, Mary Seton, Mary Carmichael or by any name you please—it is not a matter of any importance") attempting to write *as a woman*. For a woman to successfully make writing her profession, Woolf concluded, she must have both an income of her own and intellectual space free from interruptions—the famous £500 inheritance and a room of one's own—so that she will be freed from the constraints imposed by women's traditional role as "the angel in the house." Woolf attempted to trace a female literary history, addressed the issue of whether there is anything unique about women's writing as opposed to men's, speculated on the viability of a "woman's sentence," and specifically critiqued the novels of various women writers, assessing not only their feminist impact but also the points at which their overt feminism, in her view, undermined their artistic integrity as novelists. Perhaps Woolf's most notable criticism of a woman novelist was her critique of Charlotte Brontë's *Jane Eyre* (1847), in which she claimed that Brontë's novel reveals an artist "at war with her lot. . . . She puts her finger exactly not only on her own defects as a novelist but upon those of her sex at the time." Woolf also examined women novelists' relation to literary realism. She notes that, like those of male authors, women's novels have "a correspondence to real life," but that even in the realm of the supposedly real, "masculine values" tend to prevail: "This is an important book, the critic assumes, because it deals with war. This is an insignificant book because it deals with the feelings of women in a drawing-room." Such attitudes, according to Woolf, not only hampered the reception of novels by women authors, but also affected women's ability to write truly and artistically.

Although a gradually increasing number of women scholars and professional writers published scholarly studies and reviews of women writers or women characters in fiction through the middle of the century, it was not until the 1970s, with the advent of the "second wave" of feminism, that serious feminist criticism of the novel began to appear with some frequency. Simone de Beauvoir's *Le Deuxième Sex* (1949; *The Second Sex*) recognized literature's place in creating and maintaining male domination, but literary criticism was not de Beauvoir's major emphasis. Kate Millett's *Sexual Politics* (1970), however, explicitly billed itself as an act of feminist literary criticism. While Millett commented briefly on a few feminist novelists, notably the Brontë sisters, the book was primarily a feminist reading of male literary texts, which she called "literary reflections" of the politics of sexuality. Her revolutionary analysis of the ideological implications of sex considers the work of four 20th-century male authors—D.H. Lawrence, Henry Miller, Norman Mailer, and Jean Genet—in the framework of her historical, sociological, psychological, and political theory of the politics of sexuality. She argues that their detailed descriptions of sexual acts represent a political stand that reinforces male domination of women in modern society. Like Millett's, much feminist criticism of narrative in the late 1960s and early 1970s focused on male writers' misogynistic representations of women characters and on women writers' exclusion from the literary tradition.

Other feminist critics in the 1970s, however, devoted their attention to recreating a canon or tradition of female writers. Along with a number of studies that sought to resurrect the reputations of individual women authors, Ellen Moers' *Literary Women* (1976) and Elaine Showalter's *A Literature of Their Own: British Women Novelists from Brontë to Lessing* (1977) identified a well-established tradition of female-authored novels that included both already well-known authors like Austen, the Brontës, Eliot, and Woolf and dozens of lesser-known novelists who were also widely read in their own time. Both Moers and Showalter endeavored not only to prove the existence and importance of such a tradition, but also to promote the study of women novelists as *women*. Jane P. Tompkins' influential essay about American literature, "Sentimental Power: *Uncle Tom's Cabin* and the Politics of Literary History" (1978), showed how even very important novels by women were effaced in traditional literary histories because they followed different literary conventions that scholars labeled "sentimental" and "didactic," which automatically disqualified them as great literature. Nina Baym's *Woman's Fiction* (1978) was another important work that addressed the questions of form and ideology in women's fiction.

Among the numerous new works of explicitly feminist criticism of narrative that emerged in the late 1970s, however, perhaps the most influential was Sandra Gilbert and Susan Gubar's *The Madwoman in the Attic: The Woman Writer and the Nineteenth-Century Literary Imagination* (1979). Gilbert and Gubar, whose joint authorship was itself a self-consciously feminist gesture, explicitly took on Harold Bloom's Freudian model of literary history, including what he called the writer's "anxiety of influence," and explored its implications for women writing in the 19th century. The woman writer's battle, Gilbert and Gubar claimed, is not "against her (male) precursor's reading of the world but against his reading of *her*." Women authors, in other words, had to struggle not only against literary precursors, but also against the proscription against women asserting themselves by writing at all; theirs was "the anxiety of *authorship*." Gilbert and Gubar's voluminous and groundbreaking study posited not only a female literary tradition, but also specific strategies used by women writers to subtly contradict, subvert, or evade dominant prescriptions for women that cast them either as angels or monsters. Drawing on psychoanalysis, deconstruction, and anthropology, as well as literary analysis, for its theoretical apparatus, *The Madwoman in the Attic* identified feminist paradigms in narratives as varied as "Snow White and the Seven Dwarves," Mary Shelley's *Frankenstein* (1818), and the poems of Emily Dickinson. However, by far the bulk of their analysis focused on well-known 19th-century novels, including an important chapter on Brontë's *Jane Eyre* (from which their title is taken) that situates Edward Rochester's mad wife Bertha Mason as the rational Jane Eyre's rebellious feminist double.

The strategy of finding an encoded feminist message within an apparently conforming text was further elaborated in an important article by Nancy K. Miller entitled "Emphasis Added: Plots and Plausibilities in Women's Fiction" (1981). Miller's essay, which focused on French women's fiction, explained how Freudian theories of artistic motives have often led to misreadings of women's novels. Miller suggested that moments in women's narratives that seemed implausible or excessive be read as expressions of resistance against prescriptive and limiting definitions of women and their roles. Another school of feminist critics, commonly termed "the French feminists," also resisted—while at the same time appropriating—the terms of psychoanalysis applied to women's literature. While radical French feminist theorists like Luce Irigaray, Hélène Cixous, Julia Kristeva, and Monique Wittig did not often address themselves specifically to works of narrative fiction, their work fundamentally influenced subsequent feminist criticism on both sides of the Atlantic. French feminism advocated an alternative model of writing and language called *écriture féminine*, which challenged the most basic conventions of Western narrative and called for a kind of writing that grew from the sexual pleasure (*jouissance*) and the rhythms of the female body.

While the late 1970s and early 1980s saw the publication of many important works of feminist criticism of narrative, only a representative few of which are mentioned here, the later 1980s and 1990s witnessed an explosion of books, articles, essays, and collections on feminist themes, using a variety of critical methodologies and approaches. Taking issue with critics who based their readings of female narratives in primarily psychological terms, materialist or socialist feminist critics called for a feminist criticism that looked at the specific material conditions of women and women writers and challenged the basic assumptions of bourgeois capitalism, including the notion of the romantic individual subject. Rather than merely including women in the literary tradition, critics such as those represented in the anthology *Feminist Criticism and Social Change* (1985), edited by Newton and Rosenfelt, began calling attention to the political and ideological effects of literature—both its content and its form—on our understanding of gender, race, class, and sexuality. The category of woman, such critics pointed out, is far more complicated and conflicted than earlier feminist critics assumed. In her book *Sea Changes* (1986), Cora Kaplan, for instance,

maintains that "however mimetic or realistic the aspirations of fiction," it always reveals "the powerful symbolic force of class and gender in ordering our social and political imagination." Drawing on the narrative theory of the Russian critic M.M. Bakhtin, Kaplan explained that even though the novel often foregrounds the consciousness of an individual, the heterogeneous nature of fiction—its ability to voice the languages of class, gender, and race simultaneously—itself undermines the notion of a unified, stable subject.

Like the materialist or socialist feminist critics, Teresa de Lauretis' *Alice Doesn't* (1984) raised questions about the symbolic force of gender constructions. Considering film and other forms of narrative, including the novel, de Lauretis focused on the "representation of woman as image (spectacle, object to be looked at, vision of beauty—and the concurrent representation of the female body as the *locus* of sexuality, site of visual pleasure or lure of the gaze)." De Lauretis hoped, as she explained in the preface to *Technologies of Gender* (1987), to "theorize gender beyond the limits of 'sexual difference'," noting, along with Kaplan, that the female subject of feminist inquiry is "constructed across a multiplicity of discourses, positions, and meanings, which are often in conflict with one another." De Lauretis' work called attention to the ways in which narratives, both films and novels, structure particular representations of women through images at which viewers or readers "gaze" and therefore desire, and theorized about what it means for women to participate in this gaze by themselves looking at women being looked at.

The construction of female subjectivity was also the focus of Nancy Armstrong's *Desire and Domestic Fiction* (1987), which raised a controversial and important challenge to standard histories of the novel such as Ian Watt's *The Rise of the Novel* (1957), as well as to other feminist works such as Jane Spencer's *The Rise of the Woman Novelist* (1986). Spencer's study had sought to account for the parallel rise of both novels and professional women writers in the 18th century, demonstrating not only that a women's tradition developed for the novel, but that this tradition fundamentally influenced the formation of what had previously been considered the mainstream novelistic tradition. Going a step beyond Spencer, Armstrong claimed that the domestic novel, which came to such popularity in the 18th century, played a crucial role in constructing the middle-class notion of the psychological subject and in combating the ideology of the aristocracy. "It is my contention," writes Armstrong, "that narratives which seemed to be concerned solely with matters of courtship and marriage in fact seized the authority to say what was female, and that they did so in order to contest the reigning notion of kinship relations that attached most power and privilege to certain family lines." Heavily influenced by French theorist Michel Foucault, Armstrong claimed that the "struggle to represent sexuality" was essential to the consolidation of middle-class power because it attached "psychological motives to what had been the openly political behavior of contending groups." In Armstrong's reading of history, the novel thus played a major role in the rise of the middle classes, which ruled by regulating individual desire, motive, and behavior rather than by displaying aristocratic wealth and power. Other historical feminist critics, such as Catherine Gallagher (*The Industrial Reformation of English Fiction*, 1985) and Mary Poovey (*Uneven Developments*, 1988), also explored ways in which representations of gender in narrative fiction were crucial to the ideological work that established, regulated, and perpetuated capitalism in England, America, and other industrialized nations.

While earlier feminist histories of the novel assumed women writers' exclusion from the literary marketplace, as well as the literary canon, other recent histories have interrogated that assumption. Gallagher's *Nobody's Story* (1994), for instance, contended that, far from being excluded from the writing of novels by their gender, women writers actively used their gender to manipulate and succeed in the literary marketplace. Women novelists, claimed Gallagher, capitalized on the textuality and fictionality of novels, using tropes of femininity to define authorship and incorporating a changing notion of womanhood into their authorial personae. Gallagher's "nobody" refers not to the invisibility or exclusion of actual women writers, but rather to their use of "disembodiment" in the abstraction of fictional characters, exchange value, authorship copyright, and credit. Women novelists were not in fact especially disadvantaged, but rather used their feminine authorial personae and the "explicit fictionality" of their works to render them "wholesome" and make them sell. Thus Gallagher's history of women novelists "concentrate[s] on the elusiveness of these authors" instead of trying to reclaim a positive identity for them. Woman, author, marketplace, and fiction, says Gallagher, were mutually constituting ideas, not discrete, stable categories.

In keeping with recent feminist critics' focus on the multiplicity of the female subject, as distinguished from earlier, more essentialist notions about women as a unified category, American feminists of the 1980s and 1990s have devoted a great deal of attention to the intersections of gender and race in the novel. Critics have retrieved works by little-known women writers of color and theorized about the effects of race on the social construction of subjectivity in and by all kinds of narrative fiction. Barbara Christian's *Black Women Novelists: The Development of a Tradition,* for instance, was published as early as 1980, while groundbreaking essays by Barbara Smith ("Toward a Black Feminist Criticism," 1977) and Deborah E. McDowell ("New Directions for Black Feminist Criticism," 1980) were widely read and reprinted. Several important African-American women novelists—especially Zora Neale Hurston, Toni Cade Bambara, Toni Morrison, and Alice Walker—quickly became part of the established literary canon partly as a result of the efforts of feminist critics to revivify their reputations.

In 1981, Cherríe Moraga and Gloria Anzaldúa published their revolutionary collection, *This Bridge Called My Back: Writings by Radical Women of Color.* When the first edition, published by a white women's press, went out of print in 1983, the editors published a second edition "conceived of and produced entirely by women of color." This collection features both poetry and experimental fiction that focuses on relationships between women, contesting the notion that "heterosexism and sexism are . . . the normal course of events."

By the mid-1980s, important works of criticism of the fiction of women of color began appearing with regularity, including works like Gloria Jean Wade-Gayles' *No Crystal Stair* (1984), Marjorie Pryse and Hortense J. Spillers' *Conjuring* (1985) and Hazel Carby's *Reconstructing Womanhood* (1987). Women novelists themselves played a key role in the feminist criticism of fiction by women of color. Like Virginia Woolf, Alice Walker, Toni Cade Bambara, Toni Morrison, and Maxine Hong Kingston wrote important works of criticism along with their novels, helping to create a climate for the reception of their own and others' work and generating new ways of reading, thinking, and writing. In the 1990s, critics of the fiction of women of color actively took on many of the newer methodologies of feminist criticism in general, in works like Claudia Tate's *Domestic Allegories of Political Desire* (1992) and Madhu Dubey's *Black Women Novelists and the Nationalist Aesthetic* (1994). In addition, fiction by and about women of many different races, ethnicities, and nationalities began to attract more critical attention, as, for instance, in Annie O. Eysturoy's *Daughters of Self-Creation* (1996), one of an increasing number of critical works on Chicana novels, and Myriam J.A. Chancy's *Framing Silence* (1997), the first book-length study devoted exclusively to Haitian women's literature.

Along with their emphasis on race and gender, American feminists in the late 1980s and the 1990s have turned their attention to narratives by and about women in colonial and postcolonial nations. From feminist analyses of standard male imperialist narratives such as Joseph Conrad's "Heart of Darkness" (1902) to works that both examine the impact of colonialism and expand notions of what constitutes a literary narrative (such as Inderpal Grewal's *Home and Harem: Nation, Gender, Empire, and the Cultures of Travel,* 1996), feminist critics found rich connections between narrative forms and imperialist ideologies. Probably the most important of the postcolonial feminist critics of narrative was Gayatri Chakravorty Spivak, who used postcolonial theory to change our understanding of classic Western texts and introduced fiction by women writers from the developing world, which challenged some of the most sophisticated modern assumptions about how to read literature. As Colin MacCabe explains in the foreword to Spivak's *In Other Worlds* (1987), her political project was to let "the subaltern speak—allowing his or her consciousness to find an expression which will then inflect and produce the forms of political liberation which might bypass completely the European form of the nation." Thus Spivak's writings about women's postcolonial narratives both used and exposed the methodologies and critical apparatus of the Western literary tradition—revealing the complicity of literary criticism in the imperialist project.

As should be obvious by this point, feminist criticism of narrative has, almost from the beginning, participated in, challenged, and revised the assumptions and conventions of literary criticism and of society in general. Feminist criticism also has played an important role in questioning traditional ways of thinking and reading regarding heterosexuality. Eve Kosofky Sedgwick's *Between Men* (1985), for instance, took a feminist approach toward a number of canonical literary texts and revealed the ways that male desire for other males, routed through their supposed desire for women, structured these texts. The work of Lillian Faderman (1981), by contrast, focused on romantic friendships between women in literary narratives. By the early 1990s, following a decade of gradually increasing interest in and legitimation of criticism related to lesbian writers and novels, lesbian-feminist critics were explicitly addressing issues of lesbian fiction. Bonnie Zimmerman's *The Safe Sea of Women* (1990), for instance, begins with a chapter entitled "'It Makes a Great Story': Lesbian Culture and the Lesbian Novel." Although Elizabeth Meese, another important lesbian-feminist critic, wrote *about* lesbian writing in two earlier books, *Crossing the Double-Cross* (1986) and *(Ex)Tensions* (1990), it was not until her 1992 *(Sem) Erotics: Theorizing Lesbian: Writing* that she could self-consciously write *as* a lesbian feminist. In her book, Meese explored "textual erotics beyond content," examining "how one takes one's 'place' in language." The early 1990s also saw the publication of two key anthologies of lesbian-feminist criticism of narrative, Sally Munt's *New Lesbian Criticism* (1992) and Susan J. Wolfe and Julia Penelope's *Sexual Practice/Textual Theory* (1993). Besides drawing renewed attention to acknowledged lesbian fiction, such as the works of Virginia Woolf, Djuna Barnes, and Gertrude Stein, lesbian-feminist critics also have attempted to define lesbian literature in a way that could include much earlier novels, such as Sarah Scott's *Millenium Hall* (1762), whose plot depends almost entirely on relationships between women but avoids touching on their sexuality in any explicit way. Most of all, however, lesbian-feminist critics have contested the notion that women—as characters or as writers—could be defined or understood solely in their relation to men and marriage, and they have exposed the ways in which traditional narrative plot mechanisms worked to enforce heterosexual relations.

Another important contribution of feminist criticism to the study of narrative is the focus of recent feminist cultural critics on various narrative forms not usually considered by the literary establishment. Janice A. Radway's *Reading the Romance* (1984) carefully examines Harlequin romance novels and, even more importantly, the significance for women of the act of reading these novels. Radway not only looked at the language and narrative discourse of the novels but also interviewed their writers and readers and researched the publishing and marketing strategies used to promote and sell romances. Laurie Langbauer's *Women and Romance* (1990) queried the stereotypical connection of women and romance from a much earlier period, looking at novels written in the 18th and 19th centuries. She concluded that the structure of romances, not only the content or subject matter, offers a particular, confining economy of desire to women. Other feminist cultural critics have examined a variety of popular genres of fiction for their appeal to and impact on women and their role in the culture's understanding of gender. Such criticism has focused on fantasy novels, best-sellers, formula westerns, speculative fiction, science fiction, crime novels, detective fiction, utopian novels, and magazine fiction. Some critics have analyzed the links between forms of fictional narrative and other cultural discourses, ranging from photography to philanthropy.

While the majority of feminist critics of narrative have directed their attention to women novelists, to the formation or existence of a female literary tradition, or to the ideological impact of various kinds of novels or novelistic structures on women and on society's understanding of women, gender, and sexuality, another group of critics has focused specifically on narrative *as narrative*. Feminist narratology takes its origin from structural criticism that attempts to isolate and identify the specific elements of narrative fiction. Feminist critic Susan Sniader Lanser gave narratology a feminist slant in a 1986 article in *Style* entitled "Toward a Feminist Narratology," which resulted in an exchange of views on the subject with Nilli Diengott (*Style*, 1988). Lanser's book-length study *Fictions of Authority* (1992) was a major contribution to feminist narratology that interrogated both feminists' and narratologists' use of the term "voice": feminists, Lanser claimed, use it as a "trope of identity and power," a way to represent a multitude of interventions into patriarchal culture and practice, while narratologists use "voice" as a technical term to describe specific formal (nongendered) practices

within novels and other narrative forms. Lanser's book combines the two senses of the word to examine the ways that the narratologist's female voice—a narrator's voice that is grammatically female—operates to disrupt or expose the ideologies inherent in textual practices. Specifically, she looks at how female voice in the novel both creates fictions of *authority* for women and exposes the *fictions* of authority generated by narrative voice. Dale M. Bauer's *Feminist Dialogics* (1988) applies feminist theories to Bakhtin's notion of dialogics, while Alison Booth's 1993 collection *Famous Last Words* provides feminist narratological studies of closure. The essays she includes, on a variety of English, American, and Caribbean novels mostly by women or focusing on female characters, consider the traditionally limited possibilities for narrative endings for women in novels (and in life) and trace the ways in which these novels escape from or in some way subvert the prescribed plots. This is an important study in the ideology of genre, based on the premise that "narrative form and gender ideology interact in historical context." Kathy Mezei edited another important collection of essays on feminist narratology entitled *Ambiguous Discourse* (1996), which included essays by several well-known feminist narratologists including Robyn Warhol, Susan Stanford Friedman, and Rachel Blau Du-Plessis, on subjects ranging from gossip to metanarrative.

DORICE WILLIAMS ELLIOTT

See also African American Novel; Class and the Novel; Sex, Gender, and the Novel; Virginia Woolf

Further Reading

Armstrong, Nancy, *Desire and Domestic Fiction: A Political History of the Novel*, New York: Oxford University Press, 1987

Bauer, Dale M., *Feminist Dialogics: A Theory of Failed Community*, Albany: State University of New York Press, 1988

Baym, Nina, *Woman's Fiction: A Guide to Novels by and about Women in America, 1820–1870*, Ithaca, New York: Cornell University Press, 1978

Booth, Alison, editor, *Famous Last Words: Changes in Gender and Narrative Closure*, Charlottesville: University Press of Virginia, 1993

Carby, Hazel V., *Reconstructing Womanhood: The Emergence of the Afro-American Woman Novelist*, New York: Oxford University Press, 1987; Oxford: Oxford University Press, 1989

Chancy, Myriam J.A., *Framing Silence: Revolutionary Novels by Haitian Women*, New Brunswick, New Jersey: Rutgers University Press, 1997

Christian, Barbara, *Black Women Novelists: The Development of a Tradition, 1892–1976*, Westport, Connecticut: Greenwood Press, 1980

De Lauretis, Teresa, *Alice Doesn't: Feminism, Semiotics, Cinema*, Bloomington: Indiana University Press, and London: Macmillan, 1984

De Lauretis, Teresa, *Technologies of Gender: Essays on Theory, Film, and Fiction*, Bloomington: Indiana University Press, 1987; London: Macmillan, 1989

Dubey, Madhu, *Black Women Novelists and the Nationalist Aesthetic*, Bloomington: Indiana University Press, 1994

Eysturoy, Annie O., *Daughters of Self-Creation: The Contemporary Chicana Novel*, Albuquerque: University of New Mexico Press, 1996

Faderman, Lillian, *Surpassing the Love of Men: Romantic Friendship and Love Between Women from the Renaissance to the Present*, New York: Morrow, and London: Junction Books, 1981

Folger Collective on Early Women Critics, *Women Critics 1660–1820: An Anthology*, Bloomington: Indiana University Press, 1995

Gallagher, Catherine, *The Industrial Reformation of English Fiction: Social Discourse and Narrative Form, 1832–1867*, Chicago: University of Chicago Press, 1985

Gallagher, Catherine, *Nobody's Story: The Vanishing Acts of Women Writers in the Marketplace, 1670–1820*, Berkeley: University of California Press, and Oxford: Clarendon Press, 1994

Gilbert, Sandra M., and Susan Gubar, *The Madwoman in the Attic: The Woman Writer and the Nineteenth-Century Literary Imagination*, New Haven, Connecticut: Yale University Press, 1979; London: Yale University Press, 1980

Grewal, Inderpal, *Home and Harem: Nation, Gender, Empire, and the Cultures of Travel*, Durham, North Carolina: Duke University Press, and London: Leicester University Press, 1996

Kaplan, Cora, *Sea Changes: Essays on Culture and Feminism*, London: Verso, 1986

Langbauer, Laurie, *Women and Romance: The Consolations of Gender in the English Novel*, Ithaca, New York: Cornell University Press, 1990

Lanser, Susan Sniader, "Toward a Feminist Narratology," *Style* 20 (1986) (see also Lanser's exchange with Nilli Diengott in *Style* 22 [1988])

Lanser, Susan Sniader, *Fictions of Authority: Women Writers and Narrative Voice*, Ithaca, New York: Cornell University Press, 1992

McDowell, Deborah E., "New Directions for Black Feminist Criticism," *Black American Literature Forum* 14 (1980)

Meese, Elizabeth A., *(Sem) Erotics: Theorizing Lesbian: Writing*, New York: New York University Press, 1992

Mezei, Kathy, editor, *Ambiguous Discourse: Feminist Narratology and British Women Writers*, Chapel Hill: University of North Carolina Press, 1996

Miller, Nancy K., "Emphasis Added: Plots and Plausibilities in Women's Fiction," *PMLA* 96 (1981)

Millett, Kate, *Sexual Politics*, New York: Doubleday, 1970; London: Hart-Davies, 1972

Moers, Ellen, *Literary Women*, Garden City, New York: Doubleday, 1976; London: W.H. Allen, 1977

Moraga, Cherríe, and Gloria Anzaldúa, editors, *This Bridge Called My Back: Writings by Radical Women of Color*, Watertown, Massachusetts: Persephone Press, 1981; 2nd edition, New York: Kitchen Table, Women of Color Press, 1983

Munt, Sally, editor, *New Lesbian Criticism: Literary and Cultural Readings*, New York: Columbia University Press, and London: Harvester Wheatsheaf, 1992

Newton, Judith, and Deborah Rosenfelt, editors, *Feminist Criticism and Social Change: Sex, Class, and Race in Literature and Culture*, New York: Methuen, 1985

Poovey, Mary, *Uneven Developments: The Ideological Work of Gender in Mid-Victorian England*, Chicago: University of Chicago Press, 1988; London: Virago, 1989

Pryse, Marjorie, and Hortense J. Spillers, editors, *Conjuring: Black Women, Fiction, and Literary Tradition*, Bloomington: Indiana University Press, 1985

Radway, Janice A., *Reading the Romance: Women, Patriarchy, and Popular Literature*, Chapel Hill: University of North Carolina Press, 1984; London: Verso, 1987

Sedgwick, Eve Kosofky, *Between Men: English Literature and Male Homosocial Desire*, New York: Columbia University Press, 1985

Showalter, Elaine, *A Literature of Their Own: British Women Novelists from Brontë to Lessing*, Princeton, New Jersey: Princeton University Press, and London: Virago, 1977

Showalter, Elaine, editor, *The New Feminist Criticism: Essays on Women, Literature, and Theory*, New York: Pantheon, 1985; London: Virago, 1986

Smith, Barbara, "Toward a Black Feminist Criticism," *Conditions: Two* 1:2 (October 1977)

Spencer, Jane, *The Rise of the Woman Novelist: From Aphra Behn to Jane Austen*, Oxford and New York: Blackwell, 1986

Spivak, Gayatri Chakravorty, *In Other Worlds: Essays in Cultural Politics*, New York and London: Methuen, 1987

Tate, Claudia, *Domestic Allegories of Political Desire: The Black Heroine's Text at the Turn of the Century*, New York: Oxford University Press, 1992

Tompkins, Jane P., "Sentimental Power: *Uncle Tom's Cabin* and the Politics of Literary History," *Glyph* 2 (1978); reprinted in *The New Feminist Criticism: Essays on Women, Literature, and Theory*, edited by Elaine Showalter, New York: Pantheon, 1985; London: Virago, 1986

Wade-Gayles, Gloria Jean, *No Crystal Stair: Visions of Race and Sex in Black Women's Fiction*, New York: Pilgrim, 1984

Wolfe, Susan J., and Julia Penelope, editors, *Sexual Practice/Textual Theory: Lesbian Cultural Criticism*, Cambridge, Massachusetts: Blackwell, 1993

Woolf, Virginia, *A Room of One's Own*, London: Hogarth Press, and New York: Fountain Press, 1929

Zimmerman, Bonnie, *The Safe Sea of Women: Lesbian Fiction 1969–1989*, Boston: Beacon Press, 1990; London: Only Women Press, 1992

Ferdydurke by Witold Gombrowicz

1937

Witold Gombrowicz's *Ferdydurke* has played a pioneering role in the development of the Polish novel. Defying classification, *Ferdydurke* is simultaneously a brilliant social satire, a parody of the conventional Bildungsroman, and a grotesque novel of adventure that takes picaresque convention to an absurd extreme. Gombrowicz brings to bear a broad range of ideas about philosophy, psychology, perception, reality, society, and art, leading John Updike to call him the last of the great moderns. At the same time, *Ferdydurke*'s irrepressible parodic drive anticipates postmodernist fiction.

The word Ferdydurke of the title does not appear in the text and does not exist in the Polish language. Ewa Thompson suggests a connection with Dostoevskii's immature hero Ferdyschenko (see Thompson, 1979), and Gombrowicz himself on one occasion claimed to have borrowed it from a story by H.G. Wells that features a character named Ferdy Durke. In its disjunction from the body of the novel, the title reflects the continuous violation of established novelistic convention as well as the reader's expectations.

Revolving around Gombrowicz's lifelong fascination with form and immaturity as two opposing forces, *Ferdydurke* consists of the absurd and fantastic narrative of Johnnie (Józio), a 30-year-old writer who is visited by Mr. Pimko, his former schoolmaster. By the sheer force of his schoolmasterly authority, Pimko transforms Johnnie into an adolescent. As in a bad dream, Johnnie is thrown back into a pit of fermenting immaturity—secondary school and its struggles for power among the boys as well as the continuing battles between teachers and students. The competition among the boys serves as a parody of philosophy, particularly in the hilarious duel of grimaces between the idealist Syphon and the materialist Mientus. Education is revealed as a mishmash of lofty truisms and meaningless formulas, while the teacher of Polish literature bores his students to tears with his pompous praise of uplifting poetry. The educational experience concludes with the utter triumph of immaturity when the classroom descends into complete chaos.

The next stage of the narrative places Johnnie as a boarder with the family Youthful, who believe in hygiene, sport, and modern technology and raise their daughter Zuta in a rational and permissive spirit. However, the Youthfuls' mental cleanliness is not equal to the immaturity Johnnie introduces into their enlightened household. Having caused another breakdown of order, Johnnie goes off to his uncle's country house to find authenticity through fraternization with the stable boys. The attempt ends in fiasco (and a very disorderly one at that) because the divide between master and servant turns out to be even greater than that between teacher and student.

Gombrowicz establishes a careful symmetry between the three parts of the narrative of Johnnie's immature adventures. For instance, each section ends in an attempted escape and the complete breakdown of behavioral codes as the entire cast of characters is reduced to a wriggling heap of bodies in violent confrontation. The symmetry is also reinforced by the fact that each section is associated, quite irrationally, with a part of the body—backside, calf, and face, respectively. The striving for symmetry, and the emptiness of it, is made explicit in the two interpolated tales that are set between the narrative parts, each accompanied by its own introduction. As the narrator remarks,

> It is my duty to provide a preface, for the law of symmetry here demands the insertion of *Philimor Honeycombed with Childishness* as balance and counterweight to *Philifor Honeycombed with Childishness*; and similarly the introduction to *Philifor Honeycombed with Childishness* must be balanced by an introduction to *Philimor Honeycombed with Childishness*.

The two tales are parodies of philosophical argument and debate, one relating the absurd battle between philosophers representing synthesis and analysis, the other explaining the causation of absurd events by detailing an equally absurd causative chain. Both tales, appropriately, end with the triumph of childishness, violence, and disorder.

Critics, by and large, offer three different models of interpretation for *Ferdydurke*. One interpretation regards the novel as a biting satire of pre–World War II Polish society. Arthur Sandauer, a leading Polish critic of the 1960s, emphasized Gombrowicz's ridicule of the values most cherished by the generation that had created independent Poland: education in a spirit of national self-sacrifice; the cult of technological progress; and the belief that through education the lower classes would be elevated and class barriers eroded. Another view, expressed perhaps most forcefully by the writer Bruno Schulz, is that *Ferdydurke* points to the "embryology of form"—the existence of a secret world in each individual, a subculture of "inferior myths" and vulgar, immature desires. This subculture is repressed by the rational mind and covered with forms (even if they are empty). Schulz's interpretation is closer to the (now more fashionable) approach to the novel that stresses form and chaos: each human being is engaged in a constant struggle against his immature self, and forms (ideals and theories, customs and conventions, as well as elaborate phrases) are necessary to control chaos. As the complete triumph of form has a petrifying effect, the artist (Johnnie) must destroy form through the chaos of immaturity, even if each act of destruction ultimately only leads to an encounter with another form.

Gombrowicz's later plays and novels tackle the same issues, sometimes in greater depth. Nevertheless, *Ferdydurke* remains the key to Gombrowicz's fiction, a genuine structural achievement and a satirical masterpiece.

GEORGE GÖMÖRI

See also Witold Gombrowicz

Further Reading

Boyers, Robert, "Gombrowicz and *Ferdydurke*: The Tyranny of Form," *Centennial Review* 14 (1970)

Fletcher, John, "Witold Gombrowicz," in his *New Directions in Literature: Critical Approaches to a Contemporary Phenomenon,* London: Calder and Boyars, 1968

Gombrowicz, Witold, *A Kind of Testament,* Philadelphia:

Temple University Press, and London: Calder and Boyars, 1973 (a translation of his statements contained in *Entretiens avec Gombrowicz*, edited by Dominique de Roux, Paris: Belfond, 1968)

Gömöri, George, "The Antinomies of Gombrowicz," *Modern Language Review* 73:1 (January 1978)

Milosz, Czeslaw, *The History of Polish Literature*, New York:

Macmillan, 1969; 2nd edition, Berkeley: University of California Press, 1983

Schulz, Bruno, "Ferdydurke," in *Proza*, Kracow: Wydawn. Literackie, 1964; 2nd edition, 1973

Thompson, Ewa M., *Witold Gombrowicz*, Boston: Twayne, 1979

Fiction. *See* Genre Criticism; Historical Writing and the Novel; Journalism and the Novel; Mimesis; Narratology; New Journalism and the Nonfiction Novel

---

Henry Fielding 1707-54

English

Henry Fielding was one of the most popular and important novelists in 18th-century England. He believed that he had created a new "species of writing" with his novels, and there can be no doubt that he was an early and influential force in the genre's development. Fielding's originality reveals itself in large part in a narrative voice that is comic, confiding, and engaging, and in his ability to introduce into his fiction a degree of self-consciousness about the novel form itself.

Fielding's social and educational background set him apart from other early novelists in England, although he resembles writers like Daniel Defoe and his great rival Samuel Richardson in that he came to novel writing relatively late in his career. Fielding was not, strictly speaking, upper class, but he had family connections to the aristocracy (his grandfather was an earl), and he was able to attend Eton, where he absorbed that deep knowledge of the classics that would inform all his work. But Fielding was forced to work for his living and in his early 20s he turned to the stage, where he reigned for almost a decade as the most successful dramatist in London. His plays, domestic comedies and political satires, eventually provoked the government (led by the formidable Prime Minister Robert Walpole, a frequent target of Fielding's) to pass the Licensing Act of 1737, which effectively ended Fielding's theatrical career.

Fielding then turned to the study of law and to political journalism and other miscellaneous writing in order to support himself and his family, and this work, along with his earlier labor as a playwright, played a significant role in his development as a novelist. From his work for the stage, Fielding developed a sharp sense of scene and dialogue. In his political essays, he began to find the voice that would later emerge as the distinctive narrative presence of his first two novels. In his legal studies and career, he

discovered themes and issues—crime, punishment, justice, and trials—that informed much of his fiction. During these years Fielding also produced his first extended work of fictional prose, *Jonathan Wild* (1743). *Jonathan Wild* is hardly a novel, but rather a mock retelling of the life of a notorious criminal that satirizes the career of Fielding's old adversary, Walpole. Characters and situations emerge in this narrative—especially the naive but virtuous hero, Heartfree—that adumbrate elements of his mature work.

Fielding would perhaps have become a novelist without the work of Samuel Richardson, but there can be no doubt that the publication of Richardson's *Pamela; or, Virtue Rewarded* in late 1740 galvanized him. An immediate popular and critical success, *Pamela* is the breathless first-person account of a serving girl who resists the sexual advances of her master and then wins his hand in marriage. Most thought her a model of virtue, but Fielding found the morality meretricious and promptly satirized it with his anonymously published *Shamela* (1741), which rewrote Richardson's story so as to make the heroine's motive shrewd self-interest and her protestations of virtue hypocritical. This devastatingly funny satire, while not a novel, led directly to Fielding's first work that could be characterized as such, *Joseph Andrews*, published in 1742.

Fielding's first novel purports to be the story of Pamela's equally chaste brother, Joseph, but the parodic elements are quickly subordinated to an attempt to create a new kind of novel, which acknowledges its debts to earlier fiction (especially Miguel de Cervantes' *Don Quixote*) but also tries to establish for the English novel a model very different from that of Richardson. Fielding's conception of the novel was that of a "comic epic poem in prose"; that is, his fiction looks back to the classical epic for a sense of variety in the plot and broad social representation, but it is also comic, exposing the human tendencies toward affectation and hypocrisy through solvent laughter.

In *Joseph Andrews*, Fielding achieves much of what has come to be seen as characteristic of his genius: good-hearted characters (such as Parson Adams) who inspire both our affection and our laughter, a journey through the English countryside full of comic misadventures, hypocritical villains whose real powers are nugatory, and a wisely ironic narrator to guide us through it all. Successful as this first novel was, however, it pales by comparison with his next work, his masterpiece, *Tom Jones*.

Published in 1749, *Tom Jones* was an immediate favorite with both critics and readers, earning widespread adulation and selling 10,000 copies, a huge number for the time. This novel returns to many of the themes and techniques of Fielding's earlier work but with a remarkable broadening of narrative sweep and comic power. *Tom Jones* merits comparison with the classical epic in its variety of character, setting, and situation: we see in detail life on a country estate, on the road, and in London. Much of the action unfolds against the backdrop of the 1745 Jacobite rebellion, and Fielding succeeds in presenting what seems like a full picture of life in mid-Georgian England. Yet for many readers, *Tom Jones*' famously intricate plot and epic sweep, impressive as they are, are overshadowed by the narrative voice. Indeed, the narrator has been called by many the most important character in the novel, and he is always before us, shaping the action, sharing a joke, and constantly reminding us that this world we have entered is his own edifice of words.

Tom Jones appeared almost simultaneously with Fielding's appointment as a magistrate, the culmination of his legal career. In the years that followed, the novelist labored to fight crime and reform the criminal justice system, and he addressed these issues in his last novel, *Amelia*, published in 1751. *Amelia* represents a turn away from much of what was distinctive in Fielding's earlier work, and it has disappointed many readers, perhaps because their expectations were raised by what he had done previously. While Fielding retains the figure of the erring but likable hero and delivers a happy ending, the tone is undeniably darker, the effect much less comic. Through *Amelia* Fielding intended to expose the corruptions of the legal system in a way that looks ahead to Charles Dickens, but the attempt at a new artistic direction was, despite scenes of undeniable power, not fully successful.

JOHN ALLEN STEVENSON

See also Tom Jones

Biography

Born 22 April 1707 at Sharpham Park, near Glastonbury, Somerset; older brother of the writer Sarah Fielding. Attended Eton College, Berkshire, 1719–24; University of Leyden, 1728–29; Middle Temple, London, 1737–40, called to the bar, 1740. Lived mainly in East Stour, Dorset, until 1739, when he moved to London; successful playwright, 1728–37; contributor, the *Craftsman*, 1734–38; writer and manager, Little Theatre, Haymarket, 1736–37 (theatre shut down by Theatrical Licensing Act); editor, with James Ralph, the *Champion*, 1739–40; editor, the *True Patriot*, 1745–46, the *Jacobite's Journal*, 1747–48, and the *Covent Garden Journal*, 1752; appointed high steward of the New Forest, Hampshire, 1746; managed a puppet theatre, 1748; principal magistrate, City of Westminster, 1748, and County of Middlesex, 1749; devised a plan for reorganizing the constabulary and aided in establishing London's first organized police force; chairman, Westminster Quarter Sessions, 1749–52; traveled to Portugal to restore his health, 1754. Died 8 October 1754.

Fiction by Fielding

An Apology for the Life of Mrs. Shamela Andrews, 1741
The History of the Adventures of Joseph Andrews and of His Friend Mr. Abraham Adams, 1742
The Life of Mr. Jonathan Wild the Great, in *Miscellanies 3*, 1743
A Journey from This World to the Next, in *Miscellanies 2*, 1743
The History of Tom Jones, A Foundling, 1749
Amelia, 1751

Other Writings: poetry, plays, political journalism, and other miscellaneous writings.

Further Reading

Alter, Robert, *Fielding and the Nature of the Novel*, Cambridge, Massachusetts: Harvard University Press, 1968
Battestin, Martin C., with Ruthe R. Battestin, *Henry Fielding: A Life*, London and New York: Routledge, 1989
Bender, John, *Imagining the Penitentiary: Fiction and the Architecture of Mind in Eighteenth-Century England*, Chicago: University of Chicago Press, 1987
Campbell, Jill, *Natural Masques: Gender and Identity in Fielding's Plays and Novels*, Stanford, California: Stanford University Press, 1995
Hunter, J. Paul, *Occasional Form: Henry Fielding and the Chains of Circumstance*, Baltimore: Johns Hopkins University Press, 1975
Paulson, Ronald, editor, *Fielding: A Collection of Critical Essays*, Englewood Cliffs, New Jersey: Prentice-Hall, 1962

Fifth Business. *See* Deptford Trilogy

Filippino Novel. *See* Southeast Asian Novel: Philippines

Film and the Novel

The advent of motion pictures at the close of the 19th century coincided with, and was to some extent anticipated by, a change in the novel. Ever since, the relationship between film and the novel has been one of reciprocal exchange, the novel both inspiring film and borrowing its aesthetic and narrative modes. Some scholars have considered film an extension of the social function of the novel as a storytelling form, while others, noting the novel's pictorial pretensions and the film's capacity to tell stories, have found common concerns in film and novel that neither shares with the theatre.

Beginning with D.W. Griffith, the classic Hollywood film that has dominated world movie screens for decades took the English Victorian novel as its narrative basis and as a source of cultural legitimacy. Prior to that, during the era of high modernism, which coincided with the spread of primitive film, the flow of influence had been reversed, as the novel also took up the then silent film's visual scope, its directness, and its treatment of time. In the 1920s and 1930s many American novelists developed a cinematic literary style, while some, including William Faulkner and Ernest Hemingway, turned to Hollywood to work as screenwriters. Still others, including F. Scott Fitzgerald and Nathanael West, set novels in Hollywood's filmmaking community.

Post–World War II Italy and France witnessed the emergence of a "New Wave" of films that were made with the philosophical and formalist ambitions of the modernist novel, and these have continued to be treated with an intellectual seriousness traditionally reserved for literary works. In the postmodern era, while film producers have continued to adapt classic and popular novels for the screen, the formerly clear divisions between novel and film have been blurred by structuralist theories of narrative and signification—notably in the fields of narratology and semiotics—and by poststructuralist theories of language. Among many points of intersection, scholars have identified several issues—authorship, point of view, and adaptation—as fundamental.

The intersection of novel and film is often said to begin with Charles Dickens and D.W. Griffith, a pairing made famous by Sergei Eisenstein's essay of 1944, "Dickens, Griffith, and the Film Today." Eisenstein detects in Griffith's inventive story construction the influence of Dickens' "parallel action," also noting in Dickens' novels a concern with the visual and the optical that seems to anticipate the advent of film. Eisenstein reveals in Dickens' *Oliver Twist* (1838) the roots of Griffith's organization of story, establishing both the filmmaker's innovative style and his debts to the English novelist. After Griffith, the Victorian novel's influence remained pervasive in Hollywood, determining the editing style eventually considered the "classical" mode. With the advent of synchronized sound to record dialogue, and anticipating Eisenstein's essay, Dickens' *David Copperfield* was adapted by George Cukor in 1935, and mainstream studios in Hollywood and England soon adapted such classic novels as Emily Brontë's *Wuthering Heights* (1939), Jane Austen's *Pride and Prejudice* (1940), Charlotte Brontë's *Jane Eyre* (1944), and Dickens' *Great Expectations* (1947).

While many critics have generally accepted Eisenstein's account of the importance of Dickens as an English literary model for Hollywood film, others have found in those works of Gustave Flaubert, Joseph Conrad, Henry James, and Émile Zola that were published *prior* to the arrival of cinema in 1895 an increasing concern with the outward appearance of things, resulting in an assiduously descriptive prose. The literary traditions of realism and naturalism have been seen as important precursors to early film aesthetics, especially in France and the United States. Both traditions shared a concern with visual experience, and literary naturalism in particular attempted to account for the increasingly urban and dynamic experience of modern life—of which film, essentially an industrial and mechanical art, has been seen, along with the railroad, as a symptom.

An intense awareness of the visual has also linked James Joyce to film. Critics have noted in his novel *Ulysses* (1922) a narrative corollary to the apparently indiscriminate representation of reality provided by the movie camera. Moving from surface to depth, the modern novel's attempt to account for inner experience, as in Virginia Woolf's *To the Lighthouse* (1927), which seemed to embody William James' theory of a "stream of consciousness," has struck some critics as a literary equivalent of film, especially film as conceived by such scenographic directors as Eisenstein, whose theories of montage seemed comparable to modernist literary methods. (Woolf, however, treated film as a predatory rival to the modern novel, not its sibling.) Critics also have noted the "cinematographic" character of much American novel writing in the modern era, citing Hemingway's concern with "perceptual facts," and his "fixed camera" viewpoint. John Dos Passos' three-part novel *U.S.A.* (1930–36), with its interchapters titled "Newsreel" and "The Camera Eye," has been seen as reflecting the modern American experience, one increasingly mediated by motion pictures. In its turn, *U.S.A.* has been cited as a source for Orson Welles' breakthrough film *Citizen Kane* (1941).

Auteur Theory

The different forms and functions of novel and film have been discussed at the level of style and cultural geography, opposing at the extremes the Hollywood studio system, with its use of classic novels for their box office promise, and the lone visionary European artist. This distinction between the motion picture, supposedly a mass medium product created on an assembly line for a "lowbrow" audience, and the novel, supposedly a bourgeois, "highbrow" minority concern, has long kept the two narrative forms apart. However, in post–World War II France, as Hollywood films were once again available in Europe, and as European directors like Fritz Lang and Alfred Hitchcock moved to Hollywood, new ideas about the possibilities of film and the individual vision were developed. Now, even in the context of a studio system, directors formerly considered contract employees could be recognized as authors of their work. In France, Alexandre Astruc's influential essay "Naissance d'une nouvelle avant-garde: La caméra-stylo" (1948; The Birth of a New Avant-Garde: The Camera-pen) argued for the literary possibilities of the film camera and signaled a borrowing by film of the novel's seriousness and authorial stamp. Henceforth, the "art" film in Europe forced the issue of literary and philosophical seriousness, establishing a new type of film characterized by a philosophical and aesthetic ambition formerly reserved for "high art."

Astruc's claim anticipated François Truffaut's landmark essay "A Certain Tendency of the French Cinema" (1954), in which he criticized the French "tradition of quality" in films of the time—many of them, as he saw it, maladroit adaptations of novels—and argued for a new role for the director as, like the novelist, the controlling source of artistic vision. In such circumstances the greatness of a film would depend not on its literary pedigree but on the creative power of the director, the *auteur*. Although many New Wave films spawned by Truffaut's *politique des auteurs* were conceived and scripted from the outset as films, Truffaut himself successfully adapted novels and shorter fiction on numerous occasions, taking on Henri-Pierre Roché for *Jules et Jim* (1962), Ray Bradbury for *Fahrenheit 451* (1966), and Henry James for *La chambre verte* (1978). The *auteur* theory enabled film viewers to identify either stylistic or thematic elements in a film that bore a clear authorial stamp, and it also enabled literary critics—and film critics with literary leanings—to treat films as they had treated novels: as works of a single artistic will.

While Truffaut, Jean-Luc Godard, Eric Rohmer, and others in the New Wave made films that would become strongly identified with their auteurs, other directors experimented, as modern novelists had done before them, with a poetics of their narrative art. Alain Resnais worked with novelist-filmmaker Marguerite Duras on *Hiroshima Mon Amour* (1959) and with so-called cinema novelist Alain Robbe-Grillet on *L'année dernière à Marienbad* (1961; *Last Year at Marienbad*), films that deliberately undermined the transparency of the film image by introducing a narrative indeterminacy that seemed rooted in experimental fiction. At the same time, Robbe-Grillet's own self-styled "new novels" such as *La Jalousie* (1957; *Jealousy*) took to an extreme limit the modern novel's accounting for visual experience, removing a central consciousness except insofar as it registered—in the fashion of a film emulsion—the visual phenomena it came across. Robbe-Grillet's appropriation of film as a model for the novel was echoed by William Burroughs' and Brion Gysin's "cut up" writing method in such works as *The Soft Machine* (1961) and *The Ticket That Exploded* (1962), which appropriated the randomness and disjunction of montage to propose a new novelistic form.

Point of View

The question of point of view, first raised by novelist Henry James, has been seen by scholars as especially crucial to the intersection of the novel and film, as both novelists and filmmakers have tested the uneasy equation of the narrator's eye with the camera's lens. James' establishment of a narrative "center of consciousness" also seemed to anticipate the film's directness by removing the ironic distance between author and novel. Many of James' own novels have been adapted for the screen, including *Daisy Miller* (1974), *The Europeans* (1979), *The Bostonians* (1984), *The Portrait of a Lady* (1996), and *The Wings of the Dove* (1997).

The novel's flexible mix of subjectivity and objectivity have proven difficult to replicate with the camera, whose directness tends to erase narrative distance and whose strength in dealing with surfaces has not matched the novel's treatment of psychological interiority. The third-person restricted narrator has been compared to the implicit position of the camera, and many mainstream or "classic" Hollywood films adhere to this narrative stance through rigid restrictions on camera movement and positioning. However, filmmakers have attempted, with varying degrees of success, to render other narrative stances—third-person omniscient, impersonal (watching as at a play, with limited knowledge), and even first-person. The issue of point of view has been the specific concern of several important films: Alain Resnais continued his exploration of the links between film and the novel with *Providence* (1977), about the mercurial workings of the novelist's mind; while Karel Reisz's *The French Lieutenant's Woman* (1981), in which John Fowles' reflexive novel is turned into a reflexive film, uses a location shoot to render into film the historical indeterminacy of the novel's prose.

Adaptation

The arguments over adaptation have been long and complex, with scholars identifying numerous approaches to the process of turning a novel into a film. There has been little consensus, however, on the benefits for either literature or film, and some critics have found only disappointment on both sides. Much popular film criticism has focused on the issue of fidelity to the original text, but critics acknowledging the limitations on such comparisons have identified a variety of approaches to adaptation, either to the letter or to the spirit of the original. Such adaptative practices include the transformation of the novel to film terms, the direct transposition of its own world, or the construction of analogous, yet distant, narratives by filmmakers more concerned with film texts than with their literary sources. Thus Conrad's novella "Heart of Darkness" (1902), adapted for the screen as *Apocalypse Now* (1979), is set during the Vietnam War, while Jane Austen's classic novel *Emma* (1815), adapted on several occasions as a period piece, has also been identified as the distant source for Amy Heckerling's *Clueless* (1995), now set in contemporary Los Angeles.

Scholars have observed that while great novels have sometimes produced indifferent films, some of the greatest films have been made from undistinguished works of literature. Many film adaptations have given literary classics a popular appeal, introducing film viewers to the source novel ("the book of the film") and to other works by the same author. In Hollywood, the Academy Award for best picture has frequently gone to an adaptation, indicating to some critics both the box office attraction and the enduring cultural capital of literary adaptation.

"Faithful" adaptation has raised the issue of film equivalents for those poetic figures—trope, metaphor, synecdoche, simile—available to the novelist but difficult to translate to film. However, after Griffith, film developed its own enunciative devices—the wipe, the dissolve, the fade, the iris shot, the close-up—which led to arguments for the fundamental autonomy of film from both the novel and the stage. At a theoretical level, some scholars have argued for the fundamentally different natures of written and cinematic signs, while claims for the novel's superiority as a form have been questioned by those arguing that both novel and film are ultimately subject to connotation. The semiotic approach to film, applying linguistic models to film signification—reading films as systemic and codified—has tended to narrow again the divergent paths that "autonomy" advocates had laid out. In the field of semiotics and narratology the novel and film are not separate but intersect at the level of sign and structure.

Extending a tradition of adaptation that includes Jean Renoir's *Madame Bovary* (1933), John Ford's *The Grapes of Wrath* (1940), and Tony Richardson's *Tom Jones* (1963), the screen adaptation of classic novels continues to attract major directors. Notable adaptations have included James Ivory's *A Room with a View* (1986) and *Howards End* (1992), both from novels by E.M. Forster; Bernardo Bertolucci's *The Sheltering Sky* (1990), which featured the novel's author, Paul Bowles, in a cameo role; and Ang Lee's version of Jane Austen's *Sense and Sensibility* (1995). Directors not generally known for tackling the novel have also done so with notable critical success: Thomas Keneally's *Schindler's List* (1982), a documentary novel in which its author attempted to "avoid all fiction," was adapted for the screen by Steven Spielberg, while Martin Scorsese turned his attention to Edith Wharton's 1921 novel *The Age of Innocence* (1993).

SIMON DIXON

See also Horror Novel; Point of View

Further Reading

Andrew, Dudley, "The Well-Worn Muse: Adaptation in Film History and Theory," in *Narrative Strategies: Original Essays in Film and Prose Fiction,* edited by Syndy Conger and Janice R. Welsch, Macomb: Western Illinois University Press, 1980

Beja, Morris, *Film and Literature: An Introduction,* New York and London: Longman, 1979

Bluestone, George, *Novels into Film,* Baltimore: Johns Hopkins University Press, 1957

Bordwell, David, *Narration in the Fiction Film,* Madison: University of Wisconsin Press, and London: Methuen, 1985

Boyum, Joy Gould, *Double Exposure: Fiction into Film,* New York: Universe Books, 1985

Branigan, Edward, *Narrative Comprehension and Film,* London and New York: Routledge, 1992

Chatman, Seymour, *Story and Discourse: Narrative Structure in Fiction and Film,* Ithaca, New York: Cornell University Press, 1978

Chatman, Seymour, *Coming to Terms: The Rhetoric of Narrative in Fiction and Film,* Ithaca, New York: Cornell University Press, 1990

Cohen, Keith, *Film and Fiction: The Dynamics of Exchange,* New Haven, Connecticut: Yale University Press, 1979

Cohen, Keith, editor, *Writing in a Film Age: Essays by Contemporary Novelists,* Boulder: University Press of Colorado, 1991

Eisenstein, Sergei, "Dickens, Griffith, and the Film Today," in his *Film Form: Essays in Film Theory,* New York: Harcourt Brace, and London: Dobson, 1949

Fell, John L., *Film and the Narrative Tradition,* Norman: University of Oklahoma Press, 1974

Klein, Michael, and Gillian Parker, editors, *The English Novel and the Movies,* New York: Ungar, 1981

Mayne, Judith, *Private Novels, Public Films,* Athens: University of Georgia Press, 1988

McDougal, Stuart Y., *Made into Movies: From Literature to Film,* New York: Holt, Rinehart, and Winston, 1985

McFarlane, Brian, *Novel to Film: An Introduction to the Theory of Adaptation,* Oxford: Clarendon Press, and New York: Oxford University Press 1996

Metz, Christian, *Film Language: A Semiotics of the Cinema,* New York: Oxford University Press, 1974

Morrissette, Bruce, *Novel and Film: Essays in Two Genres,* Chicago: University of Chicago Press, 1985

Murray, Edward, *The Cinematic Imagination: Writers and the Motion Pictures,* New York: Ungar, 1972

Peary, Gerald, and Roger Shatzkin, editors, *The Classic American Novel and the Movies,* New York: Ungar, 1977

Ropars-Wuilleumier, Marie-Claire, *De la littérature au cinéma,* Paris: Colin, 1970

Spiegel, Alan, *Fiction and the Camera Eye: Visual Consciousness in Film and the Modern Novel,* Charlottesville: University Press of Virginia, 1976

Finnegans Wake by James Joyce

1939

Joyce began *Finnegans Wake* in March 1923, and the first segment of the novel appeared in Ford Madox Ford's *transatlantic review* in April 1924, as part of what Joyce called *Work in Progress*. The final version of the *Wake* was completed late in 1938, and a copy of the novel was present at Joyce's birthday celebration on 2 February 1939, the year that marked the start of World War II and consigned *Finnegans Wake* to temporary oblivion.

The obvious difficulties of the multi-layered work cost Joyce many of his previous supporters (and provided ammunition to his previous detractors), as Richard Ellmann documents in his *James Joyce* (1959). James' brother Stanislaus, never an ardent admirer of his sibling's works, spoke of *Work in Progress* as "drivelling rigmarole," viewing the pages he received from James as "the witless wandering of literature before its final extinction," and wondering whether his brother was not suffering from softening of the brain. Harriet Shaw Weaver, Joyce's lifelong friend and patron, felt that Joyce was squandering his genius in his new work and never quite came around to appreciating the *Wake*. Ezra Pound—and several others, including Arnold Bennett, another former supporter—thought that Joyce was orchestrating a prank, a legpull, or a stunt. By 1927 Joyce had become so discouraged by the reception of *Work in Progress* that he briefly considered turning over the fragments to his fellow Irish writer James Stephens for completion. However, Joyce was heartened in May of 1929 by a collection of 12 essays (including an especially perceptive one written by Samuel Beckett), most previously published, that formed the first defense of *Finnegans Wake*. The title, *Our Exagmination round His Factification for Incamination of Work in Progress,* suggested by Joyce, reflects the punning technique of the *Wake*.

Joyce's *Finnegans Wake* is not a novel with a traditional line of plot—although it does incorporate many previous novel techniques, ranging from the portmanteau words of Lewis Carroll to the many-tiered structuring of (as Joyce himself points out) Laurence Sterne. As Joyce stated in 1926, "One great part of every human existence is passed in a state which cannot be rendered sensible by the use of wideawake language, cutand dry grammar, and goahead plot." Thus *Finnegans Wake* does not have merely one plot; it has a multitude of plots, all intricately interwoven to form a vast palimpsest that encompasses all of human history. Its form has been compared to a rosary's, without beginning or end. The last word in *Finnegans Wake* is "the," which leads, by Joyce's ever recurrent (Viconian) cycles, to the first word in the book, the eternal "riverrun." Thus the *Wake* expands themes and techniques employed in Joyce's previous two novels, *A Portrait of the Artist as a Young Man* (1916) and *Ulysses* (1922). Each novel ends with a mixture of hope and trepidation, whether it be the complex emotion of Stephen's departure for Europe or the tenuous possibility of resumed marital relations between Bloom and Molly. And devices such as flashbacks were also used to great advantage in the second half of *Ulysses,* especially in the Circe episode.

Although the *Wake* is "experimental" to the highest degree, it perfects writing techniques and themes employed in mainstream 20th-century novels: shifting points of view, compression and expansion of time, appearance and reality motifs, and merging of characters, to name a few. Above all, *Finnegans Wake* takes to its zenith the "symbolic" novel. The central characters in the work are a married couple commonly called by Joyceans HCE and ALP. The former represents on one level a Dublin tavern keeper named Humphrey Chimpden Earwicker, although in this work in which all things "reamalgamerge," HCE also stands for High Church of England. Earwicker, now in late middle age, feels guilty over a misdemeanor, apparently sexual in nature,

that he committed in Phoenix Park involving two females and three soldiers. His wife, generally seen as Anna Livia Plurabelle, represents "all beauty," the Liffey River, which bisects Dublin, the ALPs, etc. The couple have two sons, Shem and Shaun, and a daughter, Isabelle. Shem, or James, the iconoclast, is Joyce's self-parody; Shaun, the conformist, is a satirical portrait of Stanislaus. However, indicative of the difficulty of the novel, some critics believe that the central characters are named "Porter," not Earwicker at all.

The greatest innovation is that the entire novel is cast as a dream, the dreamer being Earwicker/Porter or, as has been suggested by some critics, even Leopold Bloom. Joyce, who denied any influence of Jung or Freud on his work, chose the dream setting because, he felt, dreams are realized through puns. In sleep, too, the moral censor is turned off while the physical and temporal limitations of waking life are suspended, and *Finnegans Wake,* benefiting from this freedom, ranges over an almost unimaginable scope of human experience. Only in the *Wake* can one find a "commodius vicus of recirculation," which combines a Roman emperor with a Neapolitan philosopher, with a toilet flushing at "Howth Castle and Environs."

EDWARD A. KOPPER, JR.

See also James Joyce

Further Reading

Atherton, James S., *The Books at the Wake: A Study of Literary Allusions in James Joyce's "Finnegans Wake,"* New York: Viking, and London: Faber, 1959

Begnal, Michael H., and Fritz Senn, editors, *A Conceptual Guide to "Finnegans Wake,"* University Park: Pennsylvania State University Press, 1974

Bishop, John, *Joyce's Book of the Dark: "Finnegans Wake,"* Madison and London: University of Wisconsin Press, 1986

Campbell, Joseph, and Henry Morton Robinson, *A Skeleton Key to "Finnegans Wake,"* New York: Harcourt Brace, 1944

Ellmann, Richard, *James Joyce,* New York: Oxford University Press, 1959; revised edition, 1983

Glasheen, Adaline, *Third Census of "Finnegans Wake": An Index of the Characters and Their Roles,* Berkeley: University of California Press, 1977

Hart, Clive, *Structure and Motif in "Finnegans Wake,"* Evanston, Illinois: Northwestern University Press, and London: Faber, 1962

McCarthy, Patrick A., editor, *Critical Essays on James Joyce's "Finnegans Wake,"* New York: G.K. Hall, and Toronto: Macmillan, 1992

McHugh, Roland, *The Sigla of "Finnegans Wake,"* Austin: University of Texas Press, and London: Arnold, 1976

Finnish Novel. *See* Scandinavian Novel

F. Scott Fitzgerald 1896–1940

United States

The importance of F. Scott Fitzgerald's major contributions to the development of the novel were blurred during his lifetime by contemporary images of him as historian of the Jazz Age, as creator of the American flapper, and as popular author of more than 150 short stories, many of which were written for the *Saturday Evening Post*—the mouthpiece of middle America during the 1920s and 1930s. While it would be a mistake to discount Fitzgerald's role as social historian, it has become increasingly clear to critics and literary historians in the half century since Fitzgerald's death, as it was indeed clear to a few serious artists and literary critics such as T.S. Eliot and H.L. Mencken during his lifetime, that his artistic contributions to American letters, particularly to the novel form, place him alongside such other immortals as Nathaniel Hawthorne and Henry James.

Fitzgerald's reputation as a novelist, as one observer has noted, results from "the hard core of morality" in his work and from his offering "a fiction that is hard to imitate but from which much can be learned." Fitzgerald's experiments with form led him from the novel of saturation in the case of his first novel, *This Side of Paradise* (1920), to the Jamesian and Conradian novel of selected incident in his later work, as he attempted to create believable heroes who embody the best of the genteel chivalric tradition and yet who, as inhabitants of the modern age when gods are dead and faiths are shaken, also embrace the existential quest.

Amory Blaine, the main character in *This Side of Paradise*, resembles the heroes of what he refers to as biographical "quest" books and is, in fact, a thinly disguised Fitzgerald persona. He is sent from Minneapolis (Fitzgerald's hometown) to an eastern boarding school, St. Regis (Fitzgerald's was the Newman School); he then goes to Princeton (the university that Fitzgerald attended) and goes out into the world ill prepared to earn a living but with some definite, if impractical, notions about how life should be lived. In its adherence to the conventions of the Bildungsroman, *This Side of Paradise* is not on its surface a particularly innovative novel, although it was considered experimental in its time because Fitzgerald included in it poetry and a play. Its importance in Fitzgerald's development as a novelist results from the novel's fusion of two kinds of quest. Amory Blaine is a genteel, chivalric hero, entitled by birth and surrounded everywhere by affluence and grace. By the end of the novel, however, the romantic qualities of his quest are tempered by an existential conclusion: "I know myself . . . but that is all," Amory cries in the novel's final sentence. In addition, Fitzgerald objectifies Amory's quest by associating his personal dilemma with that of an entire generation: his was a new generation, "grown up to find all Gods dead, all wars fought, all faiths in man shaken." This asso-

ciation made *This Side of Paradise* a cult novel to members of the generation that was coming of age at the beginning of the Roaring Twenties, and it prompted contemporary critics to see Fitzgerald as a novelist with promise.

In the two years separating the publication of his first novel and his second, *The Beautiful and Damned* (1922), Fitzgerald's goals as an artist were undermined by the literary marketplace of the early 1920s, and his second novel represents, at best, minor progress toward the creation of his masterpiece, *The Great Gatsby* (1925). In an attempt to align himself with what he considered serious literary theory, as opposed to the popular taste that dictated high prices for his frothy stories about flappers and young love, Fitzgerald experimented during the time of composition of *The Beautiful and Damned* with literary naturalism. Although his flirtation with naturalism led to a distinguished novelette, *May Day*, his attempts to communicate what Mencken called "the meaninglessness of life" philosophy through Anthony Patch and his wife Gloria, whose obsessive pursuit of money leads her husband to the breaking point, is not convincing. In spite of the novel's weakness, Fitzgerald advances toward what would become his trademark themes in *The Beautiful and Damned*, focusing especially on the destructive effects of materialism evident in the fate of Anthony Patch. He was also experimenting in his second novel with aesthetic distance, drawing as he does on his premonition of disaster, both in his own life and in his marriage to Zelda, and attempting to objectify it through a heavily plotted, imagined story. Contemporary reviewers were characteristically unimpressed, criticizing the novel's deterministic message and lamenting the fact that it was not a sequel to *This Side of Paradise*.

Much discussion has centered on the means by which Fitzgerald, in the span of three years, made the artistic leap necessary for the creation of his finest novel, *The Great Gatsby* (1925). Fitzgerald himself partially credited his technical experimentation with point of view to his having read Joseph Conrad's preface to *The Nigger of the Narcissus* (1898) and the evolution in his thinking about Western civilization to his exposure to Oswald Spengler's *The Decline of the West* (1926). Whatever the case, Fitzgerald brought his search for a believable hero for the 20th century and his technical mastery of the craft of fiction to a new plateau with *The Great Gatsby*. In a relatively short novel of nine chapters, Fitzgerald tells the magical story of Jay Gatsby's quest for the rich and shallow Daisy Buchanan in such a way that it also becomes a credible story, not only of the emptiness of the materialistic American Dream, but also of the ideal quest for truth and beauty. Through the first-person narrator, Nick Carraway, who can both participate in Gatsby's dream of having Daisy's love and criticize it, Fitzgerald establishes distance from material about which he felt passionately, based loosely as it was on his own rejection by the wealthy Chicago debutante, Ginevra King. Although it is Gatsby who is at least superficially the hero of *The Great Gatsby,* ultimately it is Nick who absorbs the truth of Gatsby's story: that the ability to dream is perhaps the highest end of man, but that "the foul dust that floats in the wake" of the dream, the compromise required by materialism, threatens to destroy the romantic vision.

If *The Great Gatsby* is Fitzgerald's masterpiece, his fourth and final complete novel, *Tender Is the Night* (1934), is his most ambitious. The major asset of Dick Diver, the novel's main character, is his ability to solve complex problems using psychoanalytic theory, his modern legacy. His flaw, and as it turns out his legacy from the genteel tradition, is an excess of charm, which leaves him vulnerable to anyone who would use him and ultimately leads him to moral and emotional bankruptcy. For Fitzgerald, a major challenge in handling Dick Diver's story is the technical one of making his character flaw credible and his tragic fall inevitable. With bold experiments in point of view and inversion of chronological sequence, Fitzgerald tells Dick's story, first from the vantage point of Rosemary Hoyt, a young movie star who observes him at the pinnacle of his career and at the height of his charm. Ultimately, the novel employs numerous viewpoints as Fitzgerald carefully constructs the intersecting stories of Dick's wife Nicole's triumph over mental illness and of Dick's dying fall, which Fitzgerald eloquently explains with allusions to Conrad in a 1934 letter to H.L. Mencken. Although some contemporary reviewers saw *Tender Is the Night* as a success, the majority found its chronological inversions and viewpoint shifts confusing.

It was Fitzgerald's plan with *The Last Tycoon* (1941; published posthumously as a fragment with the author's notes) to return to a story that more closely resembled *The Great Gatsby* than it did *Tender Is the Night.* It can never be known how fully Fitzgerald would have realized his conception of the last tycoon, Monroe Stahr, a sensitive, creative Hollywood producer who, like Jay Gatsby, was a poor boy who had become financially successful and who, like Dick Diver, possessed extraordinary charm. Much of Fitzgerald's success would have rested on his development of Celia's point of view, which was to have allowed his narrator, in Fitzgerald's words, "as Conrad did," to imagine the characters' actions and would have enabled Fitzgerald "to get the verisimilitude of a first person narrative, combined with a God-like knowledge of all events that happen to my characters." What can be known with some certainty, however, is that from the beginning of his career as a novelist through his last notes on *The Last Tycoon* fragment, Fitzgerald fully explored the novel form and freely experimented with its conventions. He used the novel as the primary vehicle through which he attempted to reconcile the legacy of the genteel American past with the promises and the dangers for the human spirit of an era that had just begun.

BRYANT MANGUM

See also Great Gatsby

Biography
Born in St. Paul, Minnesota, 24 September 1896. Attended the St. Paul Academy, 1908–11; Newman School, Hackensack,

New Jersey, 1911–13; Princeton University, New Jersey, 1913–17. Served in the US Army, 1917–19: 2nd Lieutenant. Married Zelda Sayre in 1920. Advertising copywriter, Barron Collier Agency, New York, 1919–20; began writing full-time in 1920; lived in Europe, 1924–26, 1929–31; screenwriter for Metro-Goldwyn-Mayer, Hollywood, 1937–38. Died 21 December 1940.

Novels by Fitzgerald
This Side of Paradise, 1920
The Beautiful and Damned, 1922
The Great Gatsby, 1925
Tender Is the Night, 1934
The Last Tycoon, 1941; published as an unfinished novel with the author's notes

Other Writings: over 150 short stories; one play, *The Vegetable*; articles and essays; prose parody, humor, and verse; book reviews; volumes of letters, his ledger, and his notebooks were published posthumously.

Further Reading
Bloom, Harold, *F. Scott Fitzgerald,* New York: Chelsea House, 1985
Bruccoli, Matthew J., *F. Scott Fitzgerald: A Descriptive Bibliography,* Pittsburgh, Pennsylvania: University of Pittsburgh Press, 1972; revised edition, 1987
Bruccoli, Matthew J., *Some Sort of Epic Grandeur: The Life of F. Scott Fitzgerald,* London: Hodder and Stoughton, and New York: Harcourt Brace, 1981; revised edition, New York: Carroll and Graf, 1993
Bryer, Jackson R., *The Critical Reputation of F. Scott Fitzgerald,* Hamden, Connecticut: Archon, 1967
Eble, Kenneth, *F. Scott Fitzgerald,* New York: Twayne, 1963; revised edition, Boston: Twayne, 1977
Fryer, Sarah Beebe, *Fitzgerald's New Women: Harbingers of Change,* Ann Arbor, Michigan: UMI Research Press, 1988
Lehan, Richard D., *F. Scott Fitzgerald and the Craft of Fiction,* Carbondale: Southern Illinois University Press, 1966; London: Feffer and Simons, 1969
Miller, James E., Jr., *F. Scott Fitzgerald: His Art and Technique,* New York: New York University Press, 1964; London: Owen, 1965
Mizener, Arthur, *The Far Side of Paradise,* Boston: Houghton Mifflin, and London: Eyre and Spottiswoode, 1951; 2nd edition, Boston: Houghton Mifflin, 1965
Mizener, Arthur, editor, *F. Scott Fitzgerald: A Collection of Critical Essays,* Englewood Cliffs, New Jersey: Prentice-Hall, 1963
Roulston, Robert, and Helen H. Roulston, *The Winding Road to West Egg: The Artistic Development of F. Scott Fitzgerald,* Lewisburg, Pennsylvania: Bucknell University Press, and London: Associated University Presses, 1994
Sklar, Robert, *F. Scott Fitzgerald: The Last Laocoon,* New York: Oxford University Press, 1967; London: Oxford University Press, 1969
Stern, Milton R., *Tender Is the Night: The Broken Universe,* New York: Twayne, and Toronto: Macmillan, 1994

Gustave Flaubert 1821-80

French

Although Flaubert detested labels and crossly objected to being categorized, his name was forever linked to French literary realism with the publication of *Madame Bovary* in 1857. The novel provoked outrage—Flaubert was even tried (and acquitted) on charges of immorality for it—because it does not flinch from the most pedestrian, even sordid aspects of life. In fact, the novel thrust the school of "sordid realism" (as it was termed) into the forefront of literary debates. *Madame Bovary* represents a reaction against the traditional emphasis on the ideal and the exceptional. While writers like Balzac and Stendhal had exploited the trivialities of everyday existence, their characters were still superior beings who triumphed or failed in spectacular fashion. Not Emma Bovary, to whom the very possibility of the unusual or dramatic seems denied. She cannot escape her stifling provincial existence. Her desire for luxury will be limited to a single night spent at a ball in an elegant country château. She will never visit Paris and can only buy maps of it on which to trace imaginary itineraries. On the eve of their elopement to some marvelous Mediterranean land, her lover Rodolphe abandons her. After a second love affair and in the face of mounting debts, Emma ends her life by taking arsenic.

Aside from a few extended voyages and a stormy liaison with his "Muse," the poetess Louise Colet, the life of *Gustavus Flaubertus Bourgeoisophobus* (as he once signed a letter) was rather uneventful. Despite his literary precocity, Flaubert seemed destined for a law career until he was stricken in 1843 with an epileptic seizure. Thenceforth, with the exception of occasional visits to Paris and travels in the Near East and North Africa, he studied and wrote at Croisset, a family property near Rouen. There he began the composition of *Madame Bovary* in September 1851, completing the manuscript five difficult years later, in April 1856. He frequently described in his correspondence, particularly to Colet, his artistic struggles and aspirations.

> Il y a en moi, littérairement parlant, deux bonshommes distincts: un qui est épris de gueulades, de lyrisme, de grands vols d'aigle, de toutes les sonorités de la phrase et des sommets de l'idée; un autre qui fouille et creuse le vrai tant qu'il peut, qui aime à accuser le petit fait aussi puissamment que le grand, qui voudrait vous faire sentir presque *matériellement* les choses qu'il reproduit . . . .

> There are inside me, literarily speaking, two distinct fellows: one who is smitten by shouts, by lyricism, by great eagle flights, by all the sonorities of the sentence and the loftiness of ideas; another who probes and digs into the true as best he can, who loves to underscore the little fact as powerfully as the big one, who would wish to make you feel almost *physically* the things he is reproducing.

Flaubert's penchant for realism is paradoxically yoked to a lyrical impulse, and heavy doses of reality revolted him. He protested that the whole "Bovary business" was inimical to his temperament: "je suis tenté parfois de foutre tout là, et la *Bovary* d'abord" ("I'm sometimes tempted to say screw it all, beginning with the Bovary woman"). But at the same time, he wrote,

"J'aime mon travail d'un amour frénétique et perverti, comme un ascète le cilice qui lui gratte le ventre" ("I love my work with a frantic and perverted love, as the ascetic loves the hair shirt that scratches his belly").

The torments of artistic composition yielded a masterpiece that confounded the moralizing critics of the day, baffled by the author's successful melding of elegant phrasing with an "immoral" subject: adultery. For Flaubert, however, there were no intrinsically beautiful or ugly subjects; all was in the style. In fact, his fondest and most famous ambition was to write "un livre sur rien, un livre sans attache extérieure, qui se tiendrait de lui-même par la force interne de son style" ("a book about nothing, a book without external attachment, which would hold up by itself through the internal force of its style").

Madame Bovary was innovative not only for its "sordid realism," but also for its narrative techniques. Flaubert was adamant that the novelist should remain neutral, withholding his opinions. Although Flaubert drew on his own temperament in creating his characters—most famously he is supposed to have said, "Madame Bovary, c'est moi" ("*I* am Madame Bovary")—but he did so in an impersonal way: as he write to Colet, "L'auteur, dans son oeuvre, doit être comme Dieu dans l'univers, présent partout, et visible nulle part" ("The author in his work must be like God in the universe, everywhere present but nowhere visible"). As a consequence, the reader must remain alert to a variety of signifying devices. Repetition of symbolic detail is one, juxtaposition another. Flaubert frequently resorts to ironic counterpoint, as in the famous scenes at the agricultural fair. He also relies heavily on *style indirect libre,* or free indirect style, a technique—largely perfected by Flaubert—that makes it impossible to attribute a thought or perception either to the narrator or a character and thus further obscures the directing hand of the narrator.

Flaubert's next novel, *Salammbô* (1862), seemed an aberration to readers who had tagged Flaubert the pontiff of realism. This historical novel of the revolt of mercenary armies against Carthage after its defeat in the first Punic War is a gory epic that foreshadows the killing fields of European wars to come and deconstructs the opposition of "civilized" and "barbarian." Its eponymous heroine is even more dream-fixated than Emma.

With *L'Éducation sentimentale* (1869; *A Sentimental Education*), Flaubert revisited and perfected the realist ideal. The deeply ironic title traces the failure of Flaubert's generation to achieve its ideals, a point made obvious through the novel's yoking of fiction (with its repeated allusions to prostitution) and history (specifically, the failure of the Revolution of 1848 and its betrayal into dictatorship). The apparent randomness of events and the focus on the characters' failed ambitions qualify this deeply personal work as another exemplar of the kind of realism Flaubert first explored in *Madame Bovary.*

Unlike the rather cold reception accorded his *Sentimental Education*, today recognized as a masterpiece the equal of *Madame Bovary*, Flaubert's next work, *La Tentation de Saint Antoine* (1874; *The Temptation of Saint Anthony*), was rather well received. Its fantastic mode and setting were inspired by a

Breughel painting, and Flaubert parades a bewildering multiplicity of religions and temptations before his saint. In the end, Anthony aspires to absorption into pure matter. *Trois Contes* (1877; *Three Tales*) is a collection of masterful short stories with three very different settings: Biblical times, the Middles Ages, and modern France. All the protagonists—John the Baptist and Salome, Saint Julian the Hospitaler, and the touching servant maid Félicité—are martyrs, all seeking a transcendence that is the innermost impulse of all Flaubertian characters. Félicité's tale, "Un Coeur simple" ("A Simple Heart"), is an excellent introduction to Flaubert's art. His final work, the posthumous *Bouvard et Pécuchet* (1881; *Bouvard and Pécuchet*), satirizes the ambitions of science and knowledge and adumbrates the self-reflexivity of the contemporary novel. Flaubert also left minor theatrical pieces, a satirical *Dictionnaire des idées reçues* (1913; *Dictionary of Received Ideas*), travel writings, and his superb correspondence, in which Flaubert expresses his love of beauty and antiquity and unleashes an Olympian wrath against the *bêtise* (stupidity) of his age.

Flaubert's insistence on achieving detachment in artistic endeavors made him a paragon of the objective approach to fiction. His relentless pursuit of formal perfection is unsurpassed in the history of the novel. In addition to advances in technique, Flaubert is admired for his meticulous planning and refusal to settle for less than *le mot juste*. Flaubert stages the dilemmas of the modern writer: the crisis of representation, the permanence of frustrated desire, the stoic awareness of man's entanglement in words.

STIRLING HAIG

See also Madame Bovary; Sentimental Education

Biography
Born 12 December 1821 in Rouen, France. Attended Collège Royal, 1831–39 (expelled); baccalauréat, 1840; law student at École de Droit, Paris, 1841–45. In poor health after suffering a seizure in 1844; lived with his family at Croisset, near Rouen, after 1845; spent winters in Paris beginning in 1856; traveled to Egypt and the Near East, 1849–51; prosecuted (unsuccessfully) for indecency for publishing *Madame Bovary*, 1857; returned to North Africa, 1858. State pension, 1879. Died 8 May 1880.

Fiction by Flaubert
Madame Bovary, 1857; as *Madame Bovary*, translated by Eleanor Marx-Aveling, 1886; numerous subsequent translations, including by Gerard Hopkins, 1949; Alan Russell, 1950; J.L. May, 1953; Francis Steegmuller, 1957; Lowell Bair, 1959; Mildred Marmur, 1964; Paul de Man, 1965; Geoffrey Wall, 1992

Salammbô, 1862; as *Salammbô*, translated by J.S. Chartres, 1886; numerous subsequent translations, including by E. Powys Mathers, 1950; A.J. Krailsheimer, 1977

L'Éducation sentimentale, 1869; as *Sentimental Education*, translated by D.F. Hannigan, 1896; numerous subsequent

translations, including by A. Goldsmith, 1941; Robert Baldick, 1964; Douglas Parmée, 1989

La Tentation de Saint Antoine, 1874; as *The Temptation of Saint Anthony*, translated by D.F. Hannigan, 1895; numerous subsequent translations, including by Lafcadio Hearn, 1932; Kitty Mrosovsky, 1980

Trois Contes (includes "Un coeur simple," "La Légende de Saint Julien l'hospitalier," "Hérodias"), 1877; as *Three Tales*, translated by George Burnham Ives, 1903; also translated by Mervyn Savill, 1950; Robert Baldick, 1961; A.J. Krailsheimer, 1991

Bouvard et Pécuchet, 1881; as *Bouvard and Pécuchet*, translated by D.F. Hannigan, 1896; also translated by A.J. Krailsheimer, 1976

La première Éducation sentimentale, 1963; as *The First Sentimental Education*, 1972

Other Writings: plays, travel writing, and correspondence (notably with George Sand, Louise Colet, and Ivan Turgenev).

Further Reading
Brombert, Victor, *The Novels of Flaubert: A Study of Themes and Techniques,* Princeton, New Jersey: Princeton University Press, 1966

Colwell, D.J., *Bibliographie des études sur G. Flaubert,* 4 vols., Egham, Surrey: Runnymede, 1988–90

Culler, Jonathan, *Flaubert: The Uses of Uncertainty,* London: Elek, and Ithaca, New York: Cornell University Press, 1974; revised edition, Ithaca, New York: Cornell University Press, 1985

Ginsburg, Michal Peled, *Flaubert Writing: A Study in Narrative Strategies,* Stanford, California: Stanford University Press, 1986

Gothot-Mersch, Claudine, *La Genèse de "Madame Bovary,"* Paris: Corti, 1966

Green, Anne, *Flaubert and the Historical Novel: "Salammbô" Reassessed,* Cambridge and New York: Cambridge University Press, 1982

Haig, Stirling, "History and Illusion in Flaubert's 'Un Coeur simple'," in his *The Madame Bovary Blues: The Pursuit of Illusion in Nineteenth-Century French Fiction*, Baton Rouge: Louisiana State University Press, 1987

Hemmings, F.W.J., editor, *The Age of Realism,* London and Baltimore: Penguin, 1974

LaCapra, Dominick, *"Madame Bovary" on Trial,* Ithaca, New York: Cornell University Press, 1982

Sartre, Jean-Paul, *L'idiot de la famille,* 3 vols., Paris: Gallimard, 1988; as *The Family Idiot: Gustave Flaubert, 1821–57,* 4 vols., Chicago: University of Chicago Press, 1981–91

Thibaudet, Albert, *Gustave Flaubert: Sa vie, ses romans, son style,* Paris: Plon, 1922; revised edition, Paris: Gallimard, 1935

Thorlby, Anthony, *Gustave Flaubert and the Art of Realism,* London: Bowes, 1956; New Haven, Connecticut: Yale University Press, 1957

Flemish Novel. *See* Netherlandish Novel

Theodor Fontane 1819–98

German

Theodor Fontane is the greatest German realist novelist, although his accomplishment is largely unrecognized outside the German-speaking world. A latecomer to fiction, Fontane spent his early years writing ballads, journalism, travelogues, and accounts of Bismarck's wars. For him, the novelist's art involved a transfiguration of reality to show the individual's fate as part of a pattern determined by inflexible social conventions. In striving to capture the essence of the individual's *Gesinnung* (attitude, mentality), Fontane deliberately pares down his meticulously crafted texts, often focusing on apparently minor matters in characters' lives as more telling than the issues more commonly thought of as important. The scepticism with regard to human endeavor inherent in this subtly subversive narrative stance is coupled with a humane tolerance and curiosity about human weakness. His finely nuanced portrayals of women locked in the rigid conventions of Prussian society not only probe gender-specific questions but expose the problematic relationship between private and public morality, nature and civilization.

Fontane's first novel, *Vor dem Sturm* (1878; *Before the Storm*), completed when he was 58, is an idiosyncratic historical narrative set in a rural community in 1812 and 1813, as Napoléon retreats offstage. Fontane often looked north for literary stimulus, and was more in sympathy with Shakespeare, Sir Walter Scott, British ballads, and William Makepeace Thackeray than with Romance literature. Not surprisingly, then, *Before the Storm* uses a multiple perspective narrative and rejects the traditional focus on a central hero and a striking event. Instead, Fontane seeks to mediate a sense of the times through the exchange of views among a wide range of characters. The evocation of a historical period serves the underlying exploration of human values, here of loyalty in particular. Fontane's preference for a close-up human focus, his sophisticated handling of conversation, his technique of symbolic prefiguration, and his ironic tone are already clearly present in this first novel. However, *Before the Storm* lacks the structural tautness of the 16 social and psychological novels that followed. It is most often compared with his final work, *Der Stechlin* (1899; *The Stechlin*), in which contemporary political developments are presented obliquely, through the multiple refractions of leisurely conversation in the remote home of a serenely aging Prussian Junker. This last novel, often read as a distillation of the author's wisdom on life, has been seen increasingly as a subtly differentiated account of the contemporary historical period and, with its apparently diffuse, self-reflexive technique, as an innovative step in the direction of modernism in the novel. Among his minor works are four crime stories, focusing on psychological motivation and the effects of the consciousness of guilt. Two late autobiographical works, *Meine Kinderjahre* (1894; My Childhood Years) and *Von Zwanzig bis Dreissig* (1898; From Twenty to Thirty), afford a limited view of his formative years.

The main body of Fontane's narrative work has traditionally been seen as bringing the German novel back into the European mainstream, bringing the social novel to a high level of accomplishment. This oversimplified view neglects the affinities of Fontane's novels with the predominant narrative genre of German realism, the novella. His novels of Berlin society put the Prussian capital on the literary map in the aftermath of German unification in 1871. The first, *L'Adultera* (1882; *A Woman Taken in Adultery*), is the story of a misalliance, a theme to which Fontane often returned. In this case, the heroine divorces and remarries happily, an unusual outcome in 19th-century literature. This work, together with the posthumously completed *Mathilde Möhring* (1906; revised version, 1969), in which the heroine is widowed and builds an independent life for herself, has attracted recent attention, especially in feminist analyses, as a radical departure from the fictional and social norms of the period. More typically in his major novels of the late 1880s and 1890s, Fontane presents the problem of marital incompatibility as symptomatic of the health of society as a whole. *Cecile* (1887; *Cecile*), *Unwiederbringlich* (1891; *Beyond Recall*), and *Effi Briest* (1895; *Effi Briest*) all have fatal outcomes, while in *Irrungen, Wirrungen* (1888; *Delusions, Confusions*) and *Frau Jenny Treibel* (1892; *Jenny Treibel*) the ostensibly more conventional approach of showing courtship leading to marriage is crucially adjusted to reveal the negative impact of social pressures on the pursuit of individual happiness. In *Delusions, Confusions*, the lower-class heroine, Lene, loses her aristocratic lover, Botho, to a marriage of convenience, and she in turn marries appropriately to her station. The novel ends, not with tragedy, but with painful resignation on both sides. *Jenny Treibel* is a richly comic, minimally plotted, conversational tour de force, in which the parvenu mentality of Frau Jenny is exposed but nevertheless prevails to force the intelligent, witty Corinna into a dull but worthy marriage to her cousin. In Fontane, marriage is never the happy end but a problematic albeit necessary social construct.

Fontane's novels enjoyed some success during his lifetime in Germany, the publication of *Effi Briest* marking the breakthrough to a wider market. The scholarly reception of his work has gathered momentum since the 1950s, and he is now an established classic with a wide general readership. Late translation has impeded his reception abroad, despite the fact that his understated, urbane style and fine sense of social distinctions—in part the product of early years as a journalist in London—should guarantee his appeal for readers of English literature. He modified and developed the German novel form, shifting it away from the Bildungsroman in the tradition of Goethe, the novel of ideas, and the historical novel. The suggestive ambiguity of his narratives brings a modern openendedness to the novel. The small events and sensitively reconstituted discourses of everyday life are the discreet signifiers of wider truths about culture, society, and humanity. Fontane's authorial voice is tolerant, avoiding the polarization of issues and pardoning everything except hypocrisy and rigidity. Fontane's seminal role in establishing an ironic tradition in the German novel is acknowledged by Thomas Mann, Heinrich Böll, and Günter Grass, among others. That critics have failed to agree whether the narratives are ultimately progressive or conservative, either formally or with regard to their content, underlines his key position at the transition from realism to modernism.

HELEN CHAMBERS

See also Effi Briest

Biography
Born Henri Théodore Fontane in Neuruppin, Germany, 30 December 1819. Attended Gymnasium, Neuruppin, 1832–33; Gewerbeschule K.F. Klödens, Berlin, 1833–36. Served in the military, 1844. Apprenticed to an apothecary, Berlin, 1836–40, and worked in Burg, Leipzig, Dresden, and Berlin, 1841–49; employed at Prussian government press bureau, 1851–55; correspondent for Berlin papers, London, 1855–59; editor for London affairs, *Kreuzzeitung*, 1860–70; theatre reviewer, *Vossische Zeitung*, 1870–89; secretary, Berlin Academy of Arts, 1876 (resigned the same year). Died 20 September 1898.

Novels by Fontane
Vor dem Sturm, 1878; as *Before the Storm*, translated by R.J. Hollingdale, 1985
Grete Minde, 1880
Ellernklipp, 1881
L'Adultera, 1882; as *A Woman Taken in Adultery*, translated by Gabriele Annan, with *The Poggenpuhl Family*, 1979
Schach von Wuthenow, 1883; as *A Man of Honor*, translated by E.M. Valk, 1975
Graf Petöfy, 1884
Unterm Birnbaum, 1885
Cecile, 1887; as *Cecile*, translated by Stanley Radcliffe, 1992
Irrungen, Wirrungen, 1888; as *Trials and Tribulations*, 1917; as

A Suitable Match, translated by Sandra Morris, 1968; as *Entanglements: An Everyday Berlin Story*, translated by Derek Bowman 1986; as *Delusions, Confusions*, translated by William Zwiebel, 1989
Stine, 1890; translated as *Stine*, 1977
Quitt, 1890
Unwiederbringlich, 1891; as *Beyond Recall*, translated by Douglas Parmée, 1964
Frau Jenny Treibel, 1892; as *Jenny Treibel*, translated by Ulf Zimmermann, 1976
Effi Briest, 1895; as *Effi Briest*, translated by Douglas Parmée, 1967; also translated by Hugh Rorrison and Helen Chambers, 1995
Die Poggenpuhls, 1896; as *The Poggenpuhl Family*, translated by Gabriele Annan, with *A Woman Taken in Adultery*, 1979; also published with *Delusions, Confusions*, 1989
Der Stechlin, 1899; as *The Stechlin*, translated by William Zwiebel, 1995
Mathilde Möhring, 1906; revised version, 1969

Other Writings: verse, travel writings, memoirs, autobiography, letters.

Further Reading
Bance, Alan, *Theodor Fontane: The Major Novels*, Cambridge and New York: Cambridge University Press, 1982
Chambers, Helen, *The Changing Image of Theodor Fontane*, Columbia, South Carolina: Camden House, 1997
Demetz, Peter, *Formen des Realismus: Theodor Fontane; Kritische Untersuchungen*, Munich: Carl Hanser, 1964; 2nd edition, 1966
Grawe, Christian, editor, *Fontanes Novellen und Romane*, Stuttgart: Reclam, 1991
Jolles, Charlotte, *Theodor Fontane* (bibliography), Stuttgart: Metzler, 1972; 4th edition, 1993
Müller, Karla, *Schlossgeschichten: Eine Studie zum Romanwerk Theodor Fontanes*, Munich: Fink, 1986
Müller-Seidel, Walter, *Theodor Fontane: Soziale Romankunst in Deutschland*, Stuttgart: Metzler, 1975; 3rd edition, 1994
Nürnberger, Helmuth, and Christian Grawe, editors, *Theodor-Fontane-Handbuch*, Stuttgart: Kröner, 1998
Swales, Martin, *Studies of German Prose Fiction in the Age of European Realism*, Lewiston, New York: Edwin Mellen Press, 1995

For the Term of His Natural Life. *See* His Natural Life

Formalism

Russian Formalists

Russian formalism emerged in the second decade of the 20th century as a school that espoused a purely aesthetic approach to literature, one that saw art as a craft and viewed literature purely as literature. However, this "first active school of literary criticism in the twentieth century" (see Bristol, 1989) must be distinguished from the long-accepted formalist method of literary analysis, which dates back to Aristotle and Plotinus. A concentrated emphasis on formalist methodology grew out of a Central European turn-of-the-century *zeitgeist* characterized by renewed interest in the form of literature. Most often mentioned in connection with a European formalist bias are the Austrian literary historian Oskar Walzel (1864–1944) and Swiss art historian Heinrich Wölfflin (1864–1945). The former postulated that all literary works have a pattern, an inner form that corresponds to their artistic purpose; the latter contrasted neoclassical and romantic painting to demonstrate his theory that artistic change in general proceeds from changes of form in art.

These ideas find their immediate source in European romanticism, especially in the theories of August Wilhelm Schlegel and Samuel Taylor Coleridge, both of whom theorized the function of inner or innate form in literature. Ewa Thompson concludes that "such ideas go back to Plotinus" (third century A.D.), whose neoplatonic concept of beauty equates form and idea, which art introduces into a medium to create ideal form (see Thompson, 1971). This tendency of formalist criticism to see form and content as inseparable—a hypostasis, to use Plotinus' term—contrasts sharply with a more prescriptive formalist approach, such as that of the 17th-century French neoclassicist Nicolas Boileau, whose *L'Art poètique* (1674; *The Art of Poetry*), for example, set out rules governing style and genre. Perfection of form in poetry also became the main focus of the French Parnassians of the 1830s, whose chief poet and theoretician was Théophile Gautier.

Such ideas also appeared in Russia, where in the 18th century Mikhail Lomonosov formulated stylistic norms for Russian literary language in various genres and in the 19th century romantic poets and theoreticians fell under the spell of the German aesthetic philosophy of the Schlegels (August Wilhelm and his brother Friedrich). After concentrating on a sociopolitical, utilitarian critical bias for about 50 years, Russian writers, especially the symbolists, again took up a more aesthetic stance in relation to literary questions. Andrei Belyi especially concerned himself with matters of form, specifically in his painstaking and detailed statistical analyses of Russian poetry. However, he used his results for purposes more metaphysical than those of the Russian formalists who would partially follow his lead.

In an ironic twist, the Russian formalists, in many ways the most radical of early 20th-century critics, reacted against an earlier radical movement of the 1840s started by Vissarion Belinskii, followed by his disciples Nikolai Chernyshevskii and Nikolai Dobroliubov, and continued through the 1860s and beyond by the Russian intelligentsia. This movement propagated a decidedly anti-aesthetic approach to art, although Belinskii himself recognized good literature based on artistic merit. This type of criticism held that content imparted value to literature, which first and foremost should function for the common good. Ideal literature should be didactic in orientation, especially in its social and political motives.

The movement known as the Formal School in Russia and Russian Formalism in the West shared traits—and members—with futurism, whose avant-garde poets were more interested in language than in reality as such. The two groups agreed that artifice and/or the literary process itself was the most essential aspect of literature. Believing that manipulation of language formed the true basis of literature, these writers and critics exalted words above all else. They sought to understand literature as literature "on its own terms." They probed deeply to uncover the essence of what Roman Jakobson called *literaturnost'* or the "literariness" of literature. While the formalists did not totally eschew content in literature, they relegated it to a lesser place and turned their attention instead to other matters, namely poetry and poetic theory; they later extended their investigations to include prose, drama, and film. The study of rhetoric and linguistic theory spurred them to develop their own theories of and approaches to literature.

Russian formalism grew out of two groups of young scholars at Moscow and Petersburg universities: the Moscow Linguistic Circle, founded by Jakobson in 1915, and *Opoiaz*, an acronym for *Obshchestvo izucheniia poeticheskogo iazyka* (Society for the Study of Poetic Language), founded by students, the most prominent of whom were Viktor Shklovskii, Osip Brik, and Boris Eikhenbaum. Others connected with this group include Iurii Tynianov, Viktor Vinogradov, and Boris Tomashevskii. *Opoiaz* published only three small collections of essays (*Sborniki po teorii poeticheskogo iazyka, I and II* [1916; Collections on the Theory of Poetic Language I and II], and *Poetika* [1919; Poetics], the third of the *sborniki*); nevertheless, they exerted a lasting influence on Russian literary criticism. The two groups merged. After *Opoiaz* was dissolved in 1923, several of the members joined *LEF* (*Levyi front iskusstva*, the Left Front of Art, 1923–25), a more organized, politically oriented organization; others with a more academic bent taught at the State Institute of Art History in Petrograd. Despite the fact that as a group the formalists never published a journal as a forum for their own ideas, they soon established themselves as the leading critics of the day.

Russian formalism as a school lasted until 27 January 1930, when one of its founders and leading spokesmen, Viktor Shklovskii, recanted in an article published that day in *Literaturnaia gazeta* (Literary Gazette) entitled *Pamiatnik nauchnoi oshibke* (Monument to a Scientific Error). Nevertheless, Shklovskii later (after Stalin's death in 1953) resumed his work and published more studies using formalist methodology. During its heyday Russian formalism counted the following among its members: the "leaders" Viktor Shklovskii, Iurii Tynianov, Roman Jakobson, and Boris Eikhenbaum; the "lesser" figures Boris Tomashevskii, Vladimir Propp, Viktor Zhirmunskii, Osip Brik, Lev Iakubinskii, Boris Engel'gardt, Viktor Vinogradov, and Aleksandr Skaftymov.

These young scholars found common ground in their complaints about the stagnant state of Russian literary criticism.

They believed the older professors and critics to be trapped in an outmoded, stale, "nonscientific" study of literature based on historical and philosophic inquiry rather than literary analysis. The formalists wanted to define a new methodology based on the techniques of the natural sciences. They wanted literary criticism to exist as an independent discipline. Reacting against the "social" literary criticism of the intelligentsia and the idealist philosophy of the symbolists, they gravitated toward theories of language, literature, and culture reaching them from Western and Eastern Europe (and even from Russia through the writings of Aleksandr Potebnia and Aleksei Veselovskii). The formalists were also influenced by the work of Jan Baudoin de Courtenay of Poland.

The formalists also fell prey to the atmosphere of revolution in the air; Tynianov especially advocated a dialectic method in his study of literary history and leaned toward Hegelian and Marxist theories. At the same time, the formalists found merit in earlier Kantian and romantic theories of language and literature, filtered through Andrei Belyi, who anticipated, and perhaps served as a model for, the more Aristotelian work of Shklovskii and Tomashevskii (who counted and classified literary devices). The formalists believed that art, through these very devices, leads people to see reality with new eyes. However, they themselves appeared less concerned about reality than about the ways literature revealed it to readers.

In general, the formalists tried to systematize literature while studying individual works in and for themselves. Various critics attempted to create specific systems to discover the secret of *literaturnost'*. Viktor Shklovskii, in his article, "Iskusstvo kak priëm" (1917; Art as Device), posited that only literary devices transformed mere words into verbal art. For the formalist, the writer was a "skilled craftsman who needed no inspiration, epiphany or inner vision" (see Terras, 1991). Boris Tomashevskii saw literature as a collection of themes and motifs and tried to systematize all genres (*Teoriia literatury: Poetika* [1925; Theory of Literature: Poetics]), while Vladimir Propp listed the various functions that elements of a specific folk tale—hero, situation, plot—perform to create a paradigm for all tales, an approach that anticipated semiotic studies (*Morfologiia skazki* [1928; Morphology of the Folktale]). Other formalists went on to apply Propp's techniques to their analyses of prose fiction, e.g. Shklovskii's *O teorii prozy* (1929; On Prose Theory), Eikhenbaum's "Kak sdelana *Shinel'* Gogolia" (1919; How Gogol's "Overcoat" Was Made) and Tynianov's *Dostoevskii i Gogol': K teorii parodii* (1921; Dostoevskii and Gogol': Toward a Theory of Parody). But perhaps the most arresting of the studies remains "*Tristram Shendi* Sterna i teoriia romana" (1921; Sterne's *Tristram Shandy* and Theory of the Novel) by Shklovskii, the most whimsical, extravagant, and controversial of the formalists. He claimed that *Tristram Shandy* was the most typical of novels because it constantly "lays bare its devices," thus revealing its artificiality (*literaturnost'*) by allowing readers to see how the novel works. In a related study he claimed that the character Don Quixote came into being only "as a result of stringing together (*nanizyvanie*) anecdotes, proverbs, stories and monologues for which the author wanted to find room in a single work of literature" (see Thompson, 1971); in effect, Shklovskii characterizes *Don Quixote* as a literary accident.

The formalists extended such arguments to include the "self-creation" of writers as well. For example, Eikhenbaum, who de-

voted much of his academic life to the study of Lev Tolstoi, saw each of the great writer's personal crises as results of frustrated attempts to provide characters with motivation and to find new modes of expression in his works. Instead of writing a typical biography of a life, Eikhenbaum produced a study of Tolstoi's literary evolution. For the formalists, ultimately, literature itself took precedence over the author.

This attitude was most apparent in the immensely valuable formalist studies of versification. Osip Brik in "Zvukovye povtory" (1917; Sound Repetitions) and Lev Iakubinskii in "O zvukakh poeticheskogo iazyka" (1916; About the Sounds of Poetic Language) located sound patterns in poetry that went far beyond alliteration and assonance. Zhirmunskii and Eikhenbaum studied in depth the semantic and prosodic features of individual poems and solved questions of prosody and the relations among various schools of Russian poetry. Tomashevskii in his *Teoriia literatury: Poetika* attempted to systematize all genres by identifying general features of each verse form and genre. Obliquely related to the formalist method were Tomashevskii's and Zhirmunskii's excellent historical studies of Russian poets and poetry.

Shklovskii and Tynianov turned their attention more widely to the history of all literature. It was here that the most revolutionary aspects of formalism manifested themselves, especially in Tynianov's "O literaturnom fakte" (1924; On Literary Fact) and "O literaturnoi evoliutsii" (1927; On Literary Evolution) in which he explained his views of the history of literature in terms of Hegelian dialectics. Tynianov viewed literature with a historicist bias. Thompson (1971) notes that Tynianov saw literature not as a collection of works "but rather as one colossal process of change. The struggle between literary forms is for Tynianov the essence of the history of literature." His dynamic view of literature also insists that each literary period must break with its immediate past. Shklovskii eloquently expressed a similar view in his *Khod konia* (1923; Knight's Move), where he noted that "literary inheritance" does not proceed directly from father to son but passes "from uncle to nephew," not unlike the moves of a knight on a chess board.

Shklovskii also coined most of the terminology associated with the formalist school, each term designating a literary device or strategy. These devices mainly direct the reader to pay attention to the text itself, to its structure, patterns, and tricks. They all fall under the general heading of *ostranenie* (making it strange), by which the narrator takes something out of context and forces the reader to see it through new eyes, usually from the point of view of a child, a foreigner, or an animal. One of the most famous examples of *ostranenie* occurs in Tolstoi's *Voina i mir* (1863–64; War and Peace) where the young Natasha Rostova attends an opera for the first time and perceives the stage set in terms of the actual component parts of the set (for example, painted boards made to look like trees) rather than what they are intended to represent. Natasha essentially "lays bare the device" (*obnazhenie priëma*) of the set painter; an author can use the same device to let the reader catch a behind-the-scenes glimpse at how the narrator constructs the text to manipulate the reader (for example, *Tristram Shandy*).

Other devices that bring the text itself to the foreground include *zatrudnënnaia forma* (defacilitation), any device that makes the text more difficult to read, and *zamedlenie* (retardation), any device that deliberately slows the reader down, whether semantically, syntactically, or rhetorically. Both of these devices force the reader to examine the text more closely in order to recognize the gestalt of the work as well as to decipher its meaning. *Stupenchatoe postroenie* (staircase-like structure) implies a layering of text with repeated episodes to demonstrate parallels among characters, themes, or ideas. Eikhenbaum and Tynianov also contributed to the formalist vocabulary with terms such as *dominanta* (the dominant, defining quality in a system) and *motivirovka* (motivation), the explicit or implicit reason for a change in the plot.

Formalist terminology has survived all the vicissitudes of the movement's short history and remains its most concrete legacy. However, Russian formalism was much more than a collection of terms and devices, more than a simple *vade mecum* to literature and literary study. The theories behind Russian formalism were more varied and subtle. In fact, it was the theories rather than the terminology that produced its more intangible legacy: numerous modern/postmodern schools of literary criticism. Victor Erlich sees a convergence, for example, with the Anglo-American New Critics, especially Cleanth Brooks, I.A. Richards, and William Empson. Although formalism as an organized movement was mainly a Russian phenomenon (as Erlich says, "a native response to a native challenge"), literary critics in Europe and America were asking the same questions about literature. Russian formalism, either directly or obliquely (perhaps in a knight's move), gave rise to, or facilitated, the emergence of semiotics and structuralism, especially through the works of Roman Jakobson and Iurii Tynianov. Ultimately, Russian formalism's greatest contribution to the study of literature was the strengthening of the independent position of literary scholarship in the humanities.

CHRISTINE A. RYDEL

See also Critics and Criticism (20th Century); Fable; Narrative Theory; Narratology; Parody and Pastiche; Plot; Russian Novel (1900–45); Structuralism, Semiotics, and the Novel

Further Reading

Any, Carol, "Introduction: Russian Formalism, 1915–1930," *Soviet Studies in Literature* 21 (1984–85), special issue entitled *The Russian Formalist Tradition: Retrospective Views*

Bann, Stephen, and John E. Bowlt, editors, *Russian Formalism: A Collection of Articles and Texts in Translation,* Edinburgh: Scottish Academic Press, and New York: Barnes and Noble, 1973

Bennett, Tony, *Formalism and Marxism,* London: Methuen, 1979; New York: Routledge, 1989

Bristol, Evelyn, "Turn of a Century: Modernism, 1895–1925," in *The Cambridge History of Russian Literature,* Cambridge and New York: Cambridge University Press, 1989; revised edition, 1992

Eagle, Herbert, editor, *Russian Formalist Film Theory,* Ann Arbor: Department of Slavic Languages and Literatures, University of Michigan, 1981

Erlich, Victor, *Russian Formalism: History-Doctrine,* The Hague and New York: Mouton, 1955; 4th edition, 1980

Erlich, Victor, editor, *Twentieth-Century Russian Literary Criticism,* New Haven, Connecticut: Yale University Press, 1975

Gorman, David, "A Bibliography of Russian Formalism in English," *Style* 26 (Winter 1992)

Hawkes, Terence, *Structuralism and Semiotics,* Berkeley: University of California Press, and London: Methuen, 1977

Jackson, Robert Louis, and Stephen Rudy, editors, *Russian Formalism: A Retrospective Glance: A Festschrift in Honor of Victor Erlich,* New Haven, Connecticut: Yale Center for International and Area Studies, 1985

Jameson, Fredric, *The Prison-House of Language: A Critical Account of Structuralism and Russian Formalism,* Princeton, New Jersey: Princeton University Press, 1972

Lemon, Lee T., and Marion J. Reis, editors, *Russian Formalist Criticism: Four Essays,* Lincoln: University of Nebraska Press, 1965

Matejka, Ladislav, and Krystyna Pomorska, editors, *Readings in Russian Poetics: Formalist and Structuralist Views,* Cambridge, Massachusetts: MIT Press, 1971

O'Toole, L.M., and Ann Shukman, editors, *Formalist Theory,* Oxford: Holdan, 1977

O'Toole, L.M., and Ann Shukman, editors, *Formalism: History, Comparison, Genre,* Oxford: Holdan, 1978

Pomorska, Krystyna, *Russian Formalist Theory and Its Poetic Ambiance,* The Hague: Mouton, 1968

Propp, Vladimir, *Theory and History of Folklore,* Minneapolis: University of Minnesota Press, and Manchester: Manchester University Press, 1984

Stacy, R.H., *Russian Literary Criticism: A Short History,* Syracuse, New York: Syracuse University Press, 1974

Stacy, R.H., *Defamiliarization in Language and Literature,* Syracuse, New York: Syracuse University Press, 1977

Steiner, Peter, *Russian Formalism: A Metapoetics,* Ithaca, New York: Cornell University Press, 1984

Streidter, Jurij, *Literary Structure, Evolution, and Value: Russian Formalism and Czech Structuralism Reconsidered,* Cambridge, Massachusetts: Harvard University Press, 1989

Terras, Victor, *A History of Russian Literature,* New Haven, Connecticut: Yale University Press, 1991

Thompson, Ewa M., *Russian Formalism and Anglo-American New Criticism: A Comparative Study,* The Hague: Mouton, 1971

Wellek, René, *German, Russian, and Eastern European Criticism, 1900–1950,* volume 7, *A History of Modern Criticism, 1750–1950,* New Haven, Connecticut: Yale University Press, 1991

E.M. Forster 1879–1970

English

Edward Morgan Forster's contributions to the novel form are various, and hardly possible to integrate into a single program. As a reviewer and critic, he was surprisingly deft at presenting his views as an ordinary reader, although one would have thought that Virginia Woolf had outmaneuvered him for the public role of exemplary common reader. In the 1927 Clark Lectures, which he gave at Cambridge (an honor Woolf refused in 1932), and which were published as *Aspects of the Novel* in 1927, Forster elegantly divides the novel's aspects into story, people, plot, fantasy, prophecy, pattern, and rhythm.

There is reason to read the late place Forster reserved for prophecy, and the limited number of four examples admitted by him (Fedor Dostoevskii, Herman Melville, D.H. Lawrence, and Emily Brontë), as his estimate of prophecy as the most exacting aspect of the novel, against which he measured his own writings. When prophecy does not "reach back," as he luminously argues, into another dimension, it degenerates into hectoring. Forster claims that Lawrence's writing exemplifies this uneven mixture of prophecy and sermonizing. According to Forster, readers raised up by the former are brought down and irritated by the latter. Yet the first person (or second—one imagines Lawrence figuring most things out in argument with his wife Frieda) to whom this observation occurred was undoubtedly Lawrence himself: in his novel *Women in Love* (1920), Ursula unerringly calls it Birkin's "Salvator Mundi touch." Virginia Woolf often served as Forster's Ursula, complaining that "Morgan" would write so much better if he stopped trying to save the world.

Aspects of the Novel, despite its modest title, keeps its distance from mere craft and from Percy Lubbock's *The Craft of Fiction* (1921), and it hardly mentions Henry James (the presiding genius of Lubbock's book) at all. (In their private correspondence, Forster and Woolf frankly dismissed Lubbock's book.) By contrast, Forster claims that novels should increase native perception (he addresses his readers familiarly as English) and nourish the capacity to meditate on places that might be sacred. Forster's design for the novel, measured in the terms of *Aspects of the Novel,* is thus to uplift the society of author and readers from second-rate cultural missionary work embodied in guidebooks to the potential of novelistic prophecy. Prophecy, somehow, will make new human relations possible.

How, then, did Forster end up in 1928, a world-famous novelist with 42 years to live and no more novels to write? There are many good answers to this inevitable question, all addressed over time in some form by Forster himself, focusing on the problems associated with his modernity, his homosexual identity, and his class.

Forster's early novels treat what Lawrence called "spirit of place." *Where Angels Fear to Tread* (1905) depicts the English veneration of Italy (promoted by guidebooks) as more passionate and immediate than England. But Gino, the Other as Italian, has "got a country behind him that's upset people from the beginning of the world." The English get more passion than they care for. *The Longest Journey* (1907), written in three sections, provokes a lyric Forster to bad infinitudinizing of a tripartite (little) England: Cambridge, Sawston, Wiltshire. *Howards End* (1910) perhaps anticipates in its title the failure of the town planner Ebenezer Howard's Garden Cities vision of a marriage between the country and the city. The novel depicts a rootless middle class, whether artistic or managerial, that cannot inherit its own land.

Forster did not publish another novel for 14 years, during the time that Joyce and Lawrence were publishing their greatest fiction. *Maurice*, Forster's sole novel about homosexual love, written in 1913–14 but not published until 1971, bears many signs that he could write only what he believed would never be read in public.

By 1924, when *A Passage to India* finally appeared, Forster could not imagine prophecy, only the forms of its failure. In a telling first paragraph, the narrator of *A Passage to India* warns the enquiring reader that the "temples happen not to be effective here." The narrator does not mean that worship is frustrated by faulty architecture, but that the advertised secular prospect one expects from guidebook culture cannot materialize in India.

In Forster's last novel, the sun and the earth no longer offer any sympathy to human need. We have come to the end of the relation of literature and myth embodied efficiently in solar myths, the long narrative of marriages and death begun in Hesiod, with Helios marrying Gaia. The end for Forster's hope of future novels is near when entire chapters are devoted to nonhuman "protagonists": the sky that settles everything in the first chapter of the "Mosque" section, and the primeval dirt never touched by light and water, much less by "nature," in the first chapter of the novel's "Cave" section.

In *A Passage to India,* systems of belief are tested until they expire: Mrs. Moore's failure of transcendence ("poor little Christianity") is the end as well of the efficacy of the dolorous mother who oversees so much of the action in Forster's fiction (earlier examples of this figure include Mrs. Herriton, Maurice's mother, and Mrs. Wilcox in *Howards End*). But there is no need to blame the end of the novel on women in general, or Forster's mother in particular. In *A Passage to India,* the theological speculation of both the missionaries and Professor Godbole cannot comprehend these alien and primary forms. India, especially to Fielding's Mediterranean aesthetics, is a muddle.

If Forster's settings aspire to be lyric, pastoral, and contemplative, rather than muddle, terrible surprises also jolt Forster's narratives and throw off easy readers; deaths and dismemberments change and terminate his plots. Such abrupt acts include child murder in *Where Angels Fear to Tread* and deaths by field sport and double amputation in *The Longest Journey.* Even *A Room with a View* (1908), which serenely solves all trouble in marriage, begins with a street knifing in picturesque Florence. In *Howards End,* Leonard Bast is attacked with a sword by Charles Wilcox, who is convicted of manslaughter even though Bast dies of heart failure. This papier-maché violence perhaps marks a larger muddle in Forster's prospects for novel writing.

By the time of *A Passage to India,* Forster no longer pains the sinews of his reader's attention. We no longer hurt for what Fredric Jameson calls history, that inexorable form of events: the misfortunes that surround Adela Quested, the death of Mrs.

Moore, and the misunderstanding between Fielding and Aziz all wear away any expectations. At the critical moment, we cannot grieve, for the earth will not permit these troubles righted.

Forster stands for the native English novel, hypnotized neither by ideas or craft alone as ends in themselves. Yet his unwillingness to publish more novels after 1924 offers more than a minor historical role as the excluded middle of the H.G. Wells-Henry James controversy. Fellow moderns like Pound and Eliot chose silence in the end for what they could not solve, "symbols perfected in death." The future of Forster's silence is oddly borne out by Samuel Beckett, who could imagine further fictions grounded in the unpromising matter of dirt and sky.

WILLIAM A. JOHNSEN

See also Passage to India

Biography
Born in London, 1 January 1879. Attended Kent House, Eastbourne, Sussex, 1890–93; Tonbridge School, Kent, 1893–97; King's College, Cambridge (exhibitioner), 1897–1901, B.A. 1901, M.A. 1910. Toured Italy, 1901–02, and Greece and Italy, 1903; lecturer, Working Men's College, London, 1902–07; contributor, and a founder, *Independent Review*, London, 1903; tutored children of Countess von Arnim (the writer Elizabeth), Nassenheide, Germany, 1905; lived in India, 1912–13; cataloguer, National Gallery, London, 1914–15; Red Cross volunteer, Alexandria, Egypt, 1915–18; literary editor, *Daily Herald*, London, 1920; private secretary to the Maharajah of Dewas, India, 1921. Fellow of King's College, Cambridge, and Clark lecturer, Trinity College, Cambridge, 1927; honorary fellow, King's College, 1946–70. President, National Council for Civil Liberties, 1934–35, 1944; vice-president, London Library; member, BBC General Advisory Council; president, Cambridge Humanists. Died 7 June 1970.

Novels by Forster
Where Angels Fear to Tread, 1905
The Longest Journey, 1907
A Room with a View, 1908
Howards End, 1910
A Passage to India, 1924
Maurice, 1971

Other Writings: short stories, plays, essays, travelogues, biographies, and letters.

Further Reading
Borrello, Alfred, *An E.M. Forster Glossary,* Metuchen, New Jersey: Scarecrow Press, 1972

Dowling, David, *Bloomsbury Aesthetics and the Novels of Forster and Woolf,* London: Macmillan, and New York: St. Martin's Press, 1985

Furbank, P.N., *E.M. Forster: A Life,* New York: Harcourt, 1977; London: Secker and Warburg, 1978

May, Brian, *The Modernist as Pragmatist: E.M. Forster and the Fate of Liberalism,* Columbia: University of Missouri Press, 1997

McDowell, Frederick P.W., compiler and editor, *E.M. Forster: An Annotated Bibliography of Writings About Him,* DeKalb: Northern Illinois University Press, 1976

Rapport, Nigel, *The Prose and the Passion: Anthropology, Literature, and the Writing of E.M. Forster,* Manchester: Manchester University Press, and New York: St. Martin's Press, 1994

Stallybrass, Oliver, editor, *Aspects of E.M. Forster,* London: Arnold, 1969; New York: Harcourt Brace, 1970

Stallybrass, Oliver, editor, *The Manuscripts of "A Passage to India,"* London: Arnold, 1978; New York: Holmes and Meier, 1979

Stone, Wilfred Healey, *The Cave and the Mountain: A Study of E.M. Forster,* Stanford, California: Stanford University Press, 1966

Trilling, Lionel, *E.M. Forster,* Norfolk, Connecticut: New Directions, 1943; London: Hogarth Press, 1944

Widdowson, Peter, *E.M. Forster's Howards End: Fiction as History,* London: Chatto and Windus, 1977

Fortress Besieged by Qian Zhongshu

Wei cheng 1947

Written in Shanghai during the bleakest days of the Japanese occupation in the early 1940s, Qian Zhongshu's *Fortress Besieged* provides a mordant portrait of the newly coalesced bourgeoisie that had come to dominate the port city in the years after 1920. Significantly, Shanghai and its urbane elites had also come to symbolize Chinese modernity in those years. Initially published in serial form in 1946–47, the novel sold quite well once it was published as a single volume in 1947. While many contemporary critics recognized the high quality of the work, others saw it as representative of lives and situations irrelevant to the burgeoning revolution, which eventually achieved success in 1949, the year of the novel's third Shanghai printing. The harsh criticism from the left presaged the reception of the work over the next 30 years, as the novel was all but forgotten in China. Mao's notions of literature's immediate social utility were contested only at great risk during those years, and *Fortress Besieged* was sublimely unconcerned with the narrative of revolutionary progress to which the new government was committed. Ironically, Qian's work was also banned in Taiwan, as he had elected to stay in Beijing when the communists came to the city in early 1949. Within a few years of Mao's death in 1976, however, the novel enjoyed a major revival, when it was widely reprinted and rediscovered by a new generation of Chinese readers. It even became the subject of an extremely popular and meticulously produced 1990 television mini-series that remained astonishingly faithful to the original text.

Qian's father was a professor and scholar of Chinese literature, and the young Qian received an impeccable Chinese education at home, eventually leaving to study foreign literature at Tsinghua University in 1929. Qian and his wife, the playwright and short-story writer Yang Jiang, departed for Oxford in 1935, where he received the B. Litt. degree in 1937. The couple returned in 1938 to a China that had already been at war for a year. In the years between 1938 and 1941, Qian went twice to teach in the Chinese interior but was trapped in Shanghai in December 1941 by the outbreak of the Pacific War. In the years following 1945, he held a variety of teaching posts in Shanghai, eventually returning to Tsinghua in 1949 as professor in the foreign languages department. He elected to remain in China that same year in spite of having received an offer to teach Chinese at Oxford. He was one of the founding members in 1952 of the Institute of Chinese Literature at the new Chinese Academy of Social Sciences, where he has remained since. Although he has apparently written no fiction since 1949, he has produced landmark works of sinological scholarship, examining classical Chinese literature in the context of European literature and literary theory. Qian's entire fictional oeuvre as we know it consists only of *Fortress Besieged* and four short stories that were written during the same period. His fictional work is marked by the same conspicuous erudition as his scholarship, and in this sense *Fortress Besieged* is a continuation of the Chinese tradition of the "man of letters" (*wenren*) novel of the late imperial period.

Set during the years 1937–41, *Fortress Besieged* draws heavily on Qian's own experiences of the time, particularly his two journeys to the Chinese interior. The novel opens on board a French ship carrying a large number of young Chinese returning from their studies in Europe. The narrative is focalized through Fang Hongjian, a young man who had been sent abroad to study with funds generously provided by his deceased fiancée's parents. Failing to have made any progress toward the doctoral degree his putative in-laws expected of him, Fang purchased a fraudulent diploma from a mail-order house strictly to placate them. On his return to Shanghai, however, Fang discovers, much to his dismay, that his in-laws have sent notice of his new Ph.D. to the newspapers, where the awarding of the degree has been prominently announced. The event sounds a key theme of the novel: a questioning of what constitutes authenticity in the new China, where the frantic onrush to Westernization has allowed all sorts of impromptu formations of identity, often self-serving and removed from fact.

The narrative first follows Fang during a social whirl through Shanghai, then on a trip to a teaching job in the rural hinterland. There is a picaresque quality to Fang's various encounters, with his rational and cynical perspective supplying ironic contrast to the wide variety of social affectations he meets as he works his way through both city and countryside. In this respect the novel resembles the contemporary British satirical novels of Aldous Huxley, Evelyn Waugh, and Kingsley Amis (there is an episode in *Fortress Besieged* almost identical to one in *Lucky Jim*). Qian has denied any direct interest in the English novels of the period, but his experience and education at Oxford, both formal and informal, may in some measure account for the resemblance.

The highly conspicuous mode of narration, in which the author flamboyantly plays with language and seems always at pains to demonstrate his erudition, is not a style with any real precedent in Chinese narrative. Satire of social pretension, however, had been a staple of Chinese fiction since the mid–18th century and reached a crescendo in the waning years of the Qing dynasty between 1900 and 1910. One of the interesting technical features of *Fortress Besieged* is the frequent virtual fusion of the narratorial voice and that of Fang Hongjian, the focalizer. The lack of any inflection to Chinese words actually makes the constant alternation of narrative voice, and narrated monologue in particular, something very easy to create, and Qian employs this technique to great effect. The conflation of voice lulls the reader into an easy identification of Fang and the narrator, even as it imparts a sense of durable playfulness in both voices.

As the novel draws to a close, both the reader and Fang realize, quite suddenly, that the apparently random progress through China will be brought to an unhappy end: Fang's ill-considered acts have actually been creating their own consequences all along. The casual encounters that Fang had handled with so little concern now return with importance, something Fang realizes only when it is too late to act. In other words, the narrator turns out to have been the voice of a notably hard fate all along, and Fang's inclination to go along for the ride, combined with a complete incapacity to imagine the future, renders him a suitably pathetic emblem of his epoch as the novel draws to its wintry conclusion. This irony of knowledge gained too late, if gained at all, is something that *Fortress Besieged* shares with a number of the novels of the late Qing, as well as much fiction of the 1920s and 1930s, such as Lu Xun's "The True Story of Ah Q" and many of the stories and novels of Shi Tuo. However, as popular as *Fortress Besieged* has been in the past 20 years, it seems to have had little direct influence on the narrative forms produced in China during this period.

THEODORE HUTERS

Further Reading

Gunn, Edward M., *Unwelcome Muse: Chinese Literature in Shanghai and Peking, 1937–1945*, New York: Columbia University Press, 1980

Hsia, C.T., *A History of Modern Chinese Fiction, 1917–57*, New Haven, Connecticut: Yale University Press, 1961; 2nd edition, 1971

Huters, Theodore, *Qian Zhongshu*, Boston: Twayne, 1982

Fortunata and Jacinta by Benito Pérez Galdós

Fortunata y Jacinta 1886–87

The indisputed masterpiece of Spanish realism, *Fortunata and Jacinta* was written when Benito Pérez Galdós was in his 40s and already a famous writer. The novel was well received by the public, and most critics also praised it and included it among Galdós' best. Marcelino Menéndez y Pelayo and Leopoldo Alas ("Clarín"), the two most influential literary critics of 19th-century Spain, reviewed the novel favorably. However, *Fortunata* was not immediately recognized as the crowning achievement of the realist period in Spain.

Fortunata was first published serially in *La Guirnalda*, self-described as a "bimonthly newspaper dedicated to the fair sex." The 1887 book edition had 1,750 pages, reflecting Galdós' desire to capture in detail the history of Madrid between 1869 and 1876, a span of years that witnessed the dissolution of the last remnants of the Old Regime and the consolidation of the middle class. Known as the Restoration, the period represents the fulfillment of a civil society dominated by the urban industrial and commercial elites, even though the agrarian sector still represented the majority of the nation's population.

If European realism is defined as a cultural movement based on the connections between institutions and the individual, *Fortunata* is its perfect example. The novel rejects the the repetitive, anachronistic language of the romantic serials (for example, the romantic serials of Alexandre Dumas [père]), the excessive sensitivity of Frédéric Soulié, and what Galdós called the "bloody pages" of Victor Hugo. Instead, Galdós sought to create a Spanish serial based on indigenous models, such as those of Miguel de Cervantes and the Baroque painter Diego de Velázquez. In their different media, Cervantes and Velázquez had developed techniques that simultaneously capture the complexity of human reality and exploit its comic potential. They also had underlined the need to represent all social classes.

Another model was provided by Charles Dickens. Galdós translated *The Pickwick Papers* (1837) into Spanish in 1863. Some critics suppose Fortunata was modeled after Nancy of *Oliver Twist* (1838). Although Dickens' influence is clear, what distinguishes Fortunata is Galdós' masterful use of ordinary language to explain everyday life. All characters use the sociolects that correspond to their class, profession, or leisure activity. Galdós' motto was less imagination and more observation.

As many as 1,500 characters populate the pages of *Fortunata*. They include 314 fictional characters with name and surname; 221 actual historical figures, mainly contemporaneous politicians, military people, and businessmen; 48 characters derived from literary tradition and/or folklore; 53 characters taken from the Bible or saints of the Catholic Church; and 10 from mythology. The rest are identified only by occupation or other group label: nuns, prisoners, workers, and so on. Thirty-seven of them, such as Torquemada and José Ido del Sagrario, had appeared in previous works by Galdós; others, such as Ramón Villaamil, who becomes the protagonist of *Miau* (1888), are developed in later novels. *Fortunata*'s three protagonists, Fortunata, Jacinta, and Juanito Santa Cruz, do not appear in other novels, however. A clever device to support the structure of a lengthy novel is that all of the main characters have parallels and antagonists. But the real

protagonist is Madrid. All the main buildings and the institutions they house are represented: the Royal Palace; Congress; the Ministries of the Interior, Colonies, Taxes, War, and Justice; several courts, including the Supreme Court; Town Hall; the Stock Market; banks; different colleges of the university; the Prado Museum; the Academy of History; seven newspapers; the Casino; the Rastro (Madrid's gigantic flea market); the Hospice; orphanages; several shelters for the elderly; 4 different prisons, including one for women and another for the military; the Leganés madhouse; Retiro park; government warehouses; 4 real convents and a fictive one; 14 churches; 5 theaters; all of Madrid's railway stations; 3 markets; 20 cafes; the slaughterhouse; and almost all of Madrid's cemeteries. It also includes 97 streets, 20 plazas, 8 avenues, and 9 roads.

Fortunata and Jacinta documents and criticizes the difficult role assigned to women in Victorian society. The novel focuses on adultery but in an unconventional way. There are two couples and different triangles, but Fortunata's desire is open and Jacinta's is repressed. The function of the bastard is to violate established societal norms so that a new social order can triumph: the illegitimate son inherits the commercial enterprise and lineage of the Santa Cruz family. A writer of humor and irony, Galdós avoids tragic determinism. He dares to introduce shocking scenes, considering the conventions of realism, including Doña Lupe's mastectomy, Jacinta's orgasm while listening to a Wagner opera, and the description of Mauricia's delirium tremens. Nevertheless, the novel avoids naturalist causality. The omniscient narrator is prominent, giving a summary of what happens as the scene itself unfolds and revealing confidences given to him by certain characters. In general *Fortunata*'s narrative technique is less sophisticated than that of other European writers at the time. Exceptions are the long mental soliloquy of Moreno Isla, which amounts to a stream of consciousness, and the "double stream of narrative" deployed several times.

Fortunata makes her case that she is the "real" wife of Juanito Santa Cruz. There is no doubt that the relationship between Fortunata and Juanito is more legitimate than the marriage of Juanito and Jacinta. Feminist critics have demonstrated that *Fortunata* is one more in the list of novels written by Gustave Flaubert, Anton Chekhov, Lev Tolstoi, José María Eça de Queiroz, Clarín, and Juan Valera in which the *solution* to the tedium of women's lives is adultery. But *Fortunata* takes a far more radical position, deconstructing the institution of marriage and its class implications. Fortunata's death, unlike Anna Karenina's, redeems her. Jacinta's inability to consummate her adulterous relationship on account of her suitor's death makes it possible for her to construct a feminine space of voluntary solitude that serves as an example to contemporary feminism. Jacinta tells her husband that their sexual relationship is over and that he will no longer be allowed entrance to her bedroom. The most important legacy of *Fortunata* is that it gave modern feminine and feminist Spanish literature a model to portray real women of different social classes. The novel depicts for the first time professional, middle-class, and urban women: store owners, loan sharks, peddlers, fund raisers. It also gives a nonstereotypical portrayal of working-class women. Galdós' influence can be traced in Federico García Lorca's heroines, Andrea in Carmen Laforet's *Nada* (1945), and many other complex female characters in the Spanish novel.

SALVADOR A. OROPESA

See also Benito Pérez Galdós

Further Reading

Gilman, Stephen, *Galdós and the Art of the European Novel: 1867–1887,* Princeton, New Jersey: Princeton University Press, 1981

Jagoe, Catherine, *Ambiguous Angels: Gender in the Novels of Galdós,* Berkeley: University of California Press, 1994

Ortiz Armengol, Pedro, introduction to *Fortunata y Jacinta,* Madrid: Hernando, 1979

Pattison, Walter T., *Benito Pérez Galdós,* Boston: Twayne, 1975

Ribbans, Geoffrey, *History and Fiction in Galdós's Narratives,* Oxford: Clarendon Press, and New York: Oxford University Press, 1993

Stern, J.P., "*Fortunata y Jacinta* in the Context of European Realism," in *Textos y Contextos de Galdós,* edited by John W. Kronik and Harriet S. Turner, Madrid: Castalia, 1994

The Fortunes of Richard Mahony by Henry Handel Richardson

1917–29

In January 1929, Henry Handel Richardson published *Ultima Thule,* the third volume of the trilogy *The Fortunes of Richard Mahony.* The first two volumes, *Australia Felix* (first published under the title *The Fortunes of Richard Mahony,* 1917) and *The Way Home* (1925), had enjoyed modest critical success but excited little public interest and were out of print at the time the third volume was ready for publication. Heinemann, Richardson's publishers, consequently declined to publish *Ultima Thule,* and Richardson's husband was forced to pay for the printing of the book. Against all expectations, it sold out immediately, eventually running to several editions and prompting reprints of Richardson's earlier books. In 1930, the three volumes were published together as *The Fortunes of Richard Mahony.* While Richardson went on to publish one more novel in her lifetime (*The Young Cosima,* 1939) as well as some short stories, her reputation, particularly in Australia, rests largely on her achievements in the trilogy.

Henry Handel Richardson (born Ethel Florence Lindesay Richardson in 1870) left Australia at the age of 18 and returned only once, in 1912, to research the historical background for the trilogy. She spent several years in Germany before moving to England, and her reading in late 19th-century European literature influenced her first novel, *Maurice Guest* (1908), which is set in Leipzig. By contrast, *The Getting of Wisdom* (1910) depicts girlhood in a Melbourne boarding school. *The Fortunes of Richard Mahony* operates on a broader scale, depicting Australian colonial life through the experiences of the Anglo-Irish immigrant Richard Mahony.

The trilogy spans more than 20 years during the mid–19th century. It traces the career of Dr. Richard Mahony from the goldfields of Ballarat to his resumption of medical practice, the sudden acquisition and loss of his fortune in mining shares, and his decline into ignominious poverty, madness, and death. Its panoramic scale recalls earlier Australian novels such as *For the Term of His Natural Life* by Marcus Clarke and *Robbery Under Arms* by Rolf Boldrewood, but it presents a much less glorious portrait of Australian life. Richardson later commented that, by contrast to the familiar tales of adventure and success, she was interested in the misfits and failures who could not adapt to colonial life. Richardson contrasts Richard Mahony's alienation with the experiences of his wife, and the story of their marriage frames the narrative, giving the trilogy a significant and unusual domestic interest.

An expatriate herself, Richardson enjoyed a modest reputation in England after the publication of *Maurice Guest,* but her work was little known in Australia until the mid-1920s. The historical subject matter and scale of the trilogy appealed to critics, and it was declared the most important Australian novel of the period. Its critical success, however, disguises the difficulty that early Australian readers had in relating the novel to familiar Australian paradigms. Although it shared descriptions of bush life with contemporary novels, Richardson's work had little in common with their values and attitudes.

Readers of *The Fortunes* should bear in mind that it was written some 50 years after the period it depicts (being, in fact, based largely on the life of Richardson's father). *Australia Felix* mimics the conventions of Victorian fiction, combining a painstaking accumulation of detail with an interest in social relations, although it largely eschews the omniscient narrative voice. The result is a smooth realist narrative in the early parts of the trilogy. But the style changes as the story moves through the 19th century and its protagonist succumbs to mental illness. Mahony's point of view dominates in the early parts of the narrative, but Richardson gradually introduces other perspectives, particularly that of his wife, Mary. This arrangement associates realism with the dominant, masculine point of view. In *Ultima Thule,* Richardson employs modernist techniques to evoke Mahony's madness, a choice that contributes to a sense of thematic and structural fragmentation. Because of its emphasis on Mahony's physical decline, *The Fortunes* may be read as a naturalist work, but the novels' psychological insights and their representation of madness align them with their modernist contemporaries, at the same time that Mahony's belief in spiritual transcendence lends the trilogy a potentially tragic aspect.

While most critics agree that the novels' dominant mode is naturalism, the narrative shifts have caused some to regard *The Fortunes* as flawed and inconsistent. The trilogy's interest in the great intellectual questions of the Victorian period frames these shifts, however, suggesting that they represent a conscious and controlled experimentation with the explanatory capacities of different narrative forms. Richardson introduces the topics of evolutionary theory, medical ethics, the Higher Criticism, and Spiritualism through Richard Mahony's reading and through his anxieties about the origins and purposes of human life. As a doctor, Mahony applauds the scientific developments of his era, in particular evolutionary theory's challenge to creationism. But the materialist, deterministic cast of evolutionary theory fails, in his view, to provide adequate meaning for individual life and for the individual's spiritual needs. Throughout the novels, for example, Mahony tries to reconcile the claims of science with his yearning for a metaphysical scheme in which science and God can coexist. His deliberations on these matters reveal that the choice for him, and for the trilogy as a whole, is not between error and truth, but between different narratives about human experience.

His reflections draw the period's competing epistemologies into debate, allowing other discourses to frame and contest the predominance and authority of naturalism. The novel's intertextuality and allusiveness is central to this strategy. For example, there are several allusions to tragedies such as *King Lear, Hamlet,* and *Oedipus Rex,* as well as to the story of Christ's agony in the Garden. The redemptive aspect of these narratives complicates any reading of the novels as transparently naturalistic and challenges the deterministic implications of naturalist discourse.

Essentially, *The Fortunes of Richard Mahony* offers the reader several narrative patterns for the story it tells, and these possibilities converge upon the problem of Richard Mahony's madness. His madness is presented as a problem of interpretation, and the novels refuse to offer an overarching narrative framework that would give meaning to Mahony's suffering and death. On the one hand, the emphasis on his physical trials and deterioration suggests that his condition has a purely physiological origin. But the self-reflexive context of the trilogy warns that this may be an insufficient explanation, which does not take account of the way Mahony experiences his predicament in spiritual terms. Unsuited to Australia in many ways, Mahony may be understood as suffering the fate of the classic romantic outsider. It is possible that his decline results from his constitutional inability to adapt to the materialism of Australian conditions, or to the conditions of late 19th-century life altogether. *Ultima Thule* balances its descriptions of Mahony's physical condition with moments when he transcends his suffering and reaches a mystical understanding of it. The novel's end is equally ambivalent: Mahony envisages his flight into eternity, but his faith is challenged by Mary's rejection of traditional spiritual consolations. From this conflict, the authorial voice remains absent. The novel succeeds in presenting a choice between different narrative forms, reproducing the philosophical impasse of the mid– to late 19th century. The trilogy's ambivalence invites the reader to take on Mahony's struggle to find a meaningful pattern to explain human life.

The Fortunes of Richard Mahony attends closely not only to the intellectual conditions of the Victorian period but also to its social conditions, and the trilogy is remarkable for its examination of 19th-century domestic ideology. Richardson manipulates point of view so that it becomes both apparent and ironic that Mahony's male perspective dominates the novels' naturalist surface. The novels juxtapose his dominant view with the gradual unfolding of Mary's character. Initially, she seems to be little more than a feminine ideal, but the novels' strategy exposes the way in which stable Victorian masculinity depends on stereotypes of women. At the same time, the novels debunk those stereotypes. In the end Mary offers an alternative way of understanding experience, one that values human relationships over the individualism characterizing Mahony's struggles.

Although it was celebrated in England, *The Fortunes of Richard Mahony* had little, if any, influence on the novel form there. In matters both of style and content it was, perhaps, too anachronistic among its modernist contemporaries. In Australia, it was one of the first novels to approach historical fiction as more than documentary, and its exploration of the colonial experience both as cultural history and as metaphor for personal alienation finds echoes in the historical fiction of Martin Boyd, Patrick White, David Malouf, and others. Once viewed as stylistically conservative, *The Fortunes of Richard Mahony* continues to reveal itself as a sophisticated meditation on the means by which experience is made meaningful through narrative.

CATHERINE PRATT

Further Reading

Ackland, Michael, *Henry Handel Richardson,* Melbourne and New York: Oxford University Press, 1996

Arkin, Marian, "A Reading Strategy for Henry Handel Richardson's Fiction," *World Literature Written in English* 30:2 (1990)

Clark, Axel, *Henry Handel Richardson: Fiction in the Making,* Brookvale, New South Wales: Simon and Schuster Australia, 1990

Green, Dorothy, *Henry Handel Richardson and Her Fiction,* Sydney and Boston: Allen and Unwin, 1986

McLeod, Karen, *Henry Handel Richardson: A Critical Study,* Cambridge and New York: Cambridge University Press, 1985

Mead, Philip, "Death and Home-work: The Origins of Narrative in *The Fortunes of Richard Mahony,*" *Australian Literary Studies* 17:2 (1995)

Robertson, J.G., "The Art of Henry Handel Richardson: An Essay in Appreciative Criticism," published with *Myself When Young,* by Henry Handel Richardson, London and Melbourne: Heinemann, and New York: Norton, 1948

Forty-Second Parallel. *See* U.S.A. Trilogy

Janet Frame 1924–

New Zealander

The New Zealand writer Janet Frame has been publishing fiction since the early 1950s, but her work has received substantial critical attention only recently. One of the striking features of Frame's literary practice is her highly self-conscious and self-reflexive use of language to produce a continual defamiliarization of everyday reality. She represents the self as continually constructed through language, over which the individual has no control. The poetic imagination, however, offers a degree of alternative power over the ways language is used to discipline and punish dissidents or outsiders. Frame herself spent time in psychiatric hospitals, and her writing—at the encouragement of her doctors and the writer Frank Sargeson—began as a form of resistance against institutional pressure to conform to some notion of normalcy. Society's intolerance of those who are different is expressed in *Intensive Care* (1970) by means of the fascist Human Delineation Act, under which people are categorized and labeled for survival or extermination. In Frame's writing, the relatively powerless are shown as deprived of speech; they live on "the edge of the alphabet where words crumble and all forms of communication between the living are useless" (*The Edge of the Alphabet,* 1962). In her novel *The Carpathians* (1988) the inhabitants of a whole street in a small country town find, in the middle of the night, that they "had each suffered a loss of all the words they had ever known, all the concepts that supported and charged the words, all the processes of thinking and feeling that once lived within the now shattered world of their words." Letters from every alphabet fall like rain, settling "now with a scab of dung, now with a cluster of jewels."

Often read as illustrating the poverty of spirit and the exploitation and oppression of life under capitalism, Frame's work has been approached from different angles. Some find a critique of patriarchy and capitalism even in her first published novel, *Owls Do Cry* (1957); others consider that there has been a development toward a more explicitly conscious politics in relation to class, gender, and race. This latter position finds some support in statements made by Frame herself. She said in an interview that she had been converted by feminism: "I myself have become more conscious of the problems of women, and this is through writing my autobiography and writing about my mother." About writers in general, she has recently said, "They sort of ignored such a lot of brutality, that they are now eyeing. There is so much to expose in New Zealand that for some reason wasn't there before." Frame has described the writing of her books as part of her own political evolution.

The Adaptable Man (1965) focuses on the social role of the outcast "witch-novelist" whose outsider's vision is uncannily intense: "Life on a heath with thunder and lightning, mixing a cauldron of uneatables for others to observe, admire, shrink from, is not much fun. But who wants fun?" The vision has to be rendered into words that make some kind of sense, "that bind with their spell" or, as Gina Mercer has it, give us "a spell from the spell(ing) of convention, which might induce dizzy spells in the reader but ultimately prove spell-binding" (see Mercer, 1994). Such a mastery of language is a crucial component of the persisting power of Frame's texts. Their radicalism lies in their treatment of an extreme experience of the everyday, but their radicalizing effects—the degree to which they can unsettle the reader—is owing as much or more to the way they are written.

To argue, as a number of critics do, that Frame's distinctive narrative style has close affinities with postmodernism is not necessarily to say that she should be read as a postmodernist thinker. A debate has emerged in recent years whether Frame reproduces the ideology of postmodernism or whether she remains closer to modernism. Janet Wilson reads Frame's orientation as essentially modernist, although she also finds, in *The Carpathians,* "a post-modernist fictive strategy in which narrative authority is continuously deferred" (see Wilson, 1993). Frame's texts embody a great complexity of ideas and language, but they choose sides rather than profess neutrality. The distinctive features of Frame's work are a profound anger about the complicity of language in exploitation and oppression and a writing back against such domination in texts of great richness and power.

CAROLE FERRIER

See also Owls Do Cry

Biography
Born 28 August 1924 in Dunedin, the daughter of an impoverished railway engineer. Attended Oamaru North School; Waitaki Girls' High School; University of Otago Teachers Training College, Dunedin.

Novels by Frame
Owls Do Cry, 1957
Faces in the Water, 1961
The Edge of the Alphabet, 1962
Scented Gardens for the Blind, 1963
The Adaptable Man, 1965
A State of Siege, 1966
The Rainbirds, 1968; as *Yellow Flowers in the Antipodean Room,* 1969
Intensive Care, 1970
Daughter Buffalo, 1972

Living in the Maniototo, 1979
The Carpathians, 1988

Other Writings: short stories, a book of poems (*The Pocket Mirror,* 1967), a children's book (*Mona Minim and the Smell of the Sun,* 1969), and a three-volume autobiography (*To the Is-Land,* 1982; *An Angel at My Table,* 1984; *The Envoy from Mirror City,* 1985).

Further Reading

Alley, Elizabeth, editor, *The Inward Sun: Celebrating the Life and Work of Janet Frame,* Sydney: Allen and Unwin, 1994
Chenery, Susan, "The Final Word," *Australian Magazine* (6–7 August 1994)
Delbaere-Garant, Jeanne, editor, *Bird, Hawk, Bogie: Essays on Janet Frame,* Aarhus, Denmark: Dangaroo Press, 1978; revised edition, as *A Ring of Fire: Essays on Janet Frame,* Sydney: Dangaroo Press, 1992
Ferrier, Carole, editor, *The Janet Frame Reader,* London: Women's Press, 1994
Frizell, Helen, "Janet Frame: NZ's Shy Genius," *Sydney Morning Herald* (19 December 1977)
Mercer, Gina, *Janet Frame: Subversive Fictions,* St. Lucia: University of Queensland Press, 1994
Munro, Alice, "Strong Mood," *Listener* (29 August 1987)
Panny, Judith Dell, *I Have What I Gave: The Fiction of Janet Frame,* Wellington: Daphne Brasell Associates, 1992; New York: Braziller, 1993
Wilson, Janet, "Postmodernism or Postcolonialism? Fictive Strategies in *Living in the Maniototo* and *The Carpathians,*" *Journal of New Zealand Literature* 11 (1993)

Framing and Embedding in Narrative

Narrative framing is the device of inserting one narrative within another. At its most basic level, framing occurs in any narrative situation when events from an earlier time are narrated by a character who is not the main narrator or when a character tells a tale that, although unrelated to the main story, contains a moral message for the listener in the text. The metaphor of the term *frame* likens its textual effect to the aesthetic effect of the frame surrounding a painting. However, a narrative frame almost always stands in a complex relationship to the framed story. Critical analysis of narrative framing also extends to the descriptive function of framing associated with windows, doors, and mirrors as devices to focus the reader's attention at a particular moment and on a particular scene in the narrative. However, the spatial description of narrative framing fails to fully capture the rich complexity of the dynamic narrative transaction that often characterizes framing.

The most common framing occurrences in narrative obtain with simple "embedding" or "intercalating" of one narrative within another. Embedding refers to the narrative situation in which a part of the main narrative or a significant detail of the plot is displaced atemporally to another location in the narration. Thus, flashbacks and other analeptic (retrospective) narratives may be said to be framed by the current moment of the narrative in which they are embedded. For example, in books 9–12 of *The Odyssey,* Odysseus tells the story of his long, adventure-filled journey to Ithaca. This crucial narrative, which takes the listener back before *The Odyssey*'s opening to Telemachus' decision to seek word of his father, is embedded at the center of the epic. Odysseus' telling is represented mimetically as reported speech, but not all embedded narratives are transmitted in that fashion. In book 8 of *The Odyssey,* the epic singer presents a summary of Demodokos' singing of other events from the Trojan War, which essentially inserts *The Iliad* within *The Odyssey.*

Intercalation occurs when the inset narrative is not directly related to the main narrative. Although intercalated narratives need to bear some thematic or contextual relevance to the main narrative, these digressions draw the reader away from the main plot movement and, therefore, function as a deferral device. Most of the tales told by Scheherazade in *The Thousand and One Nights* are intercalations within the main narrative of her survival by the act of storytelling. Other examples of intercalation are "The Tale of Foolish Curiosity" in Miguel de Cervantes' *Don Quixote* (1605–15) and "The Town Ho's Story" in Herman Melville's *Moby-Dick* (1851). In these novels the intercalated tales are told by characters that Don Quixote or Ishmael meet during their travels, but the main narrative line is hardly affected by these engagements. A special case obtains with what Sheldon Sacks calls "digressive apologues" (see Sacks, 1964). Digressive apologues are intercalated narratives that are told by a character to provide the protagonist, usually, with a moral tale that will establish the context for a change in behavior. The man of Mazzard Hill's tale in Henry Fielding's *Tom Jones* (1749) may serve as an example.

Although narrative framing often involves textual framing, the examples given so far underscore the function of "quoted speech" in the conditions of narrative framing. As Mikhail Bakhtin observes in his essay "Discourse in the Novel," any time one discourse quotes the speech of another, an act of mediation and recontextualization has occurred (see Bakhtin, 1981). Since speech is always oriented toward a specific listener or group of listeners, its contextual and ideological force is initially defined and limited to the particular discourse situation in which it occurred. Once that speech is quoted, or the entire discourse situation is represented in an embedded narrative containing dialogue, the quoting or framing discourse situation alters the conceptual horizon in which the quoted speech will be received by a new listener. The more layered the narrative framing is, the more complex the activity of reconceptualization must be. To interpret texts using framing of quoted speech requires a close analysis and reconstruction of each discourse situation or frame that the speech passes through. For Bakhtin, this analysis includes the outermost frame of the author, whose dialogic relation to the narrative discourse makes all discourse, whether quoted speech or simple narration, multivocal. Along similar lines, Wayne Booth's construct of the "implied author" (see Booth, 1961) marks an additional theoretical narrative frame for reconceptualizing the "reliability" of both narrations and quoted speech. For Booth, reliability is determined by the degree to which the values and ethics inferred from the text align with those of the author. Hence, the issue of reliability frames all narratives.

The questions raised by Bakhtin and Booth may be extended to textual framing and especially the framing act of transcription. Transcription of an oral narration for the purpose of textual transmission theoretically fixes the frame and stops the proliferation of telling. However, despite elaborate narrator promises of accuracy and faithfulness to the original, the necessary gap between the oral narration and its transcription by a framing narrative opens interpretive space for the reader to construct alternative readings, to ask what has been left out of the transcription, to ask what has been changed. Although textual framing raises fewer questions about accuracy of transmission, the "editor" or any character involved with the transmission of the framed text may engage in reconceptualizing the framed text. Since most framed texts are not written for the specific narratee identified by the framing narrative of transmission, the function of recontextualization must be considered for an overall aesthetic understanding of any novel deploying framing as a device.

Narrative framing clearly relates to the concept of diegetic levels. As each act of narration is contained within another act of narration, the text shifts its diegetic level from the initial extradiegetic level to an intradiegetic level of narration, to a metadiegetic level of narration, and beyond. (*See separate entry,* Diegesis and Diegetic Levels of Narrative.) The limit of diegetic narrative framing is set by the conditions of containment obtaining among the different narrations. For instance, in Mary Shelley's *Frankenstein* (1818) Robert Walton narrates at an extradiegetic level in his journal, in which he transcribes the intradiegetic oral narration of Victor Frankenstein, who in telling his tale quotes the metadiegetic oral narration of the Creature he created, who, in turn, had told Victor the story of his existence since the creation. The Creature's narration frames yet another narrative level when he tells the history of the De Lacey family, which he overheard while he lived in a hovel adjoining the De Lacey cottage. Spatially, these different narrations and narratives may be related as a series of embedded boxes:

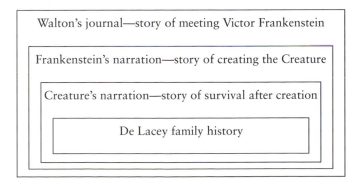

Walton's journal—story of meeting Victor Frankenstein

Frankenstein's narration—story of creating the Creature

Creature's narration—story of survival after creation

De Lacey family history

Although such a spatial representation identifies the essential framing relationship of the different narrations and narratives, it cannot account either for the finer details of embedding or for frame violations such as the Creature's meeting with Walton over Frankenstein's dead body. Moreover, a simplified spatial representation cannot account adequately for temporal issues that accompany the narrating situations or the embedded narratives. Lastly, frame narration often provides an opportunity to explore the motivations for narrating: why would Walton, Frankenstein, and the Creature tell their stories in the first place? Why tell them to the particular narratees they chose?

In *Frankenstein* and other classic frame novels—Emily Brontë's *Wuthering Heights* (1847), Abbé Prévost's *Manon Lescaut* (1731), George Sand's *Leone Leoni* (1835), Eugène Fromentin's *Dominique* (1863), Joseph Conrad's novella "Heart of Darkness" (1902), Henry James' *The Turn of the Screw* (1898), and Honoré de Balzac's "Sarrasine" (1830)—the framing device usually indicates a narrative contract between the teller and the listener. Stories are told in exchange for something else: a promise of revenge in *Frankenstein,* a promise of a night of love in "Sarrasine." This logic of exchange further connects the frame novel to the narrative of desire, which, Peter Brooks argues, is the dynamic motor of narrative fiction (see Brooks, 1984). The frame structure is particularly suited for the narrative of desire because of its similarity to the psychoanalytic scene of the "talking cure." The extradiegetic narrator is cast in the role of the analyst, listening to the intradiegetic narrator's life story, a telling that forces the "patient" to reexamine his or her life, to reveal the repressed trauma that can only be "cured" by the patient confronting the traumatic event and finally acknowledging that it is past. In *Leone Leoni,* for instance, Bustamente implores Juliette to tell the repressed story of her obsessive love for Leone; once she has done so, they believe, she will be cured of her extreme melancholy and their love can finally blossom. As in *Frankenstein,* a violation of the narrating cure's frame, which is supposed to contain the disruptive Leone in a narrative detailing his asocial behavior, is violated when he appears in the outer level, regaining Juliette's love.

Frame novels of the sort described require a fully characterized extradiegetic narrator. Although he or she may be associated with only a minimal personal narrative, such a character's role as a listener/transcriber or a reader of the internal narrative is critical. In many cases this extradiegetic narrator participates essentially in a narrative of transmission that plays with the convention of suspended belief accompanying novels that claim some prior condition of textuality or narrativity. From *Don Quixote* onward, the extradiegetic narrator has, in some cases, been cast as an editor presenting a "found manuscript" that now must be brought before the public. Manuscripts are found in trunks, as in Benjamin Constant's *Adolphe* (1816), found while hunting, as in Henry Mackenzie's *The Man of Feeling* (1771), found in a cabinet, as in Aphra Behn's *Love Letters Between a Nobleman and His Sister* (3 vols., 1683–87), or are given away, as in Mikhail Lermontov's *Geroi nashego vremeni* (1840; *A Hero of Our Time*). The fiction of the manuscript is a thinly veiled authenticating device, hardly effective in any sense other than an aesthetic one today. It usually requires the editor to provide a variety of framing devices such as prefaces, notes, and afterwords designed to tell the story of discovery and to proclaim the authenticity of the text. Epistolary, diary, and memoir novels, which always provide instances of framing the "experiencing self" by a "narrating self" who recasts the experience into a narration after the fact, inevitably require an editor for the logic of narrative transmission to make sense. The private nature of letters, diaries, and some memoirs necessitates an intermediary in the process of publication. However, this editor, even when he or she embodies the full ideological beliefs of the author (as is the case in Samuel Richardson's novels), must be interpreted as a part of the overall fiction of the text.

In *Seuils*, Gérard Genette considers the various "paratexts," as he terms them, surrounding the fictional narrative, concerning himself not only with prefaces, afterwords, and notes in the structuration of narrative textuality, but also with the effects produced by such textual features as title pages, epigraphs, tables of contents, dedications, and even the name of the author. Moreover, there are extratextual paratexts such as belated prefaces, interviews with the author, and biographical materials either provided by the author or uncovered by scholarship that also function to "frame" the horizon of interpretive expectation. Paratexts such as title pages and epigraphs are more pervasive than others, since all readers will encounter these devices, whereas an interview or biographical fact (i.e., a comment about the novel in a letter) may or may not be known by the reader at the time of reading. Duyfhuizen has argued that the most significant paratextual frame in narrative discourse occurs when an author appends an extrafictional preface to a later edition of a novel, as Lermontov did to the 2nd edition of *A Hero of Our Time* (see Duyfhuizen, 1992). "Historiodiegetic" frames of this sort often insist that the novel is not thinly veiled autobiography but only a work of the imagination. Paradoxically, historiodiegetic prefaces that emphasize a text's fictionality undermine the various and often elaborate modes of narrative framing that have been included to authenticate the framed narrative.

Frame violations and other methods of undermining narrative framing lay bare the device of framing to a self-deconstructing play with the "fiction of authenticity." For instance, in Pierre Choderlos de Laclos' epistolary *Les Liaisons dangereuses* (1782; *Dangerous Acquaintances*) an editor proclaims the letters' authenticity in his references to their uneven style, which he was not permitted to touch, and in his claim that he had to withhold certain letters. Laclos' novel also contains a "Publisher's Note" that precedes the editor's preface and prestructures its reading by claiming that the text to follow appears to be merely a novel, since the behavior and immorality represented in the letters could find no corollary in the current enlightened age. By setting these two extradiegetic texts against each other, Laclos is able to underscore the ironic intent of his novel and to suggest to readers the clever interplay between probability and fiction in the text. In a final deconstructive move, Laclos gives the "publisher" the last word in a note proclaiming the impossibility of continuing the story of the further adventures of Cécile Volanges; but a cache of additional letters exists, and someday they may be brought to the public's attention.

Using narrative framing both to authenticate and to call into question narrative transmission has been a novelistic feature since at least *Don Quixote*. This double play is often most effective in "hybrid" narratives. Novels such as Anne Brontë's *The Tenant of Wildfell Hall* (1848), Wilkie Collins' *The Woman in White* (1860), Bram Stoker's *Dracula* (1897), Doris Lessing's *The Golden Notebook* (1962), and Jeremy Leven's *Creator* (1980) are all constructed of multiple documents—letters, diaries, transcribed testimony, memoirs, and, in *The Golden Notebook* and *Creator*, an inset novel. An extradiegetic narrator must piece these together to frame a coherent narrative. Such texts raise significant questions as to access to the various documents, the shifting context from composition to transmission, and the motives of the final arranger, questions that provide a commentary on the function and status of fiction in our culture.

BERNARD DUYFHUIZEN

See also Beginnings and Endings; Diegesis and Diegetic Levels of Narration; Discourse Representation; Epistolary Novel; Implied Author; Metafiction; Narrator; Plot; Space; Unreliable Narrator

Further Reading

Bakhtin, M.M., *The Dialogic Imagination: Four Essays*, edited by Michael Holquist, translated by Caryl Emerson and Michael Holquist, Austin: University of Texas Press, 1981

Booth, Wayne C., *The Rhetoric of Fiction*, Chicago: University of Chicago Press, 1961

Brooks, Peter, *Reading for the Plot: Design and Intention in Narrative*, New York: Knopf, and Oxford: Clarendon Press, 1984

Caws, Mary Ann, *Reading Frames in Modern Fiction*, Princeton, New Jersey: Princeton University Press, 1985

Chatman, Seymour, *Story and Discourse: Narrative Structure in Fiction and Film*, Ithaca, New York: Cornell University Press, 1978

Duyfhuizen, Bernard, *Narratives of Transmission*, Rutherford, New Jersey: Fairleigh Dickinson University Press, and London: Associated University Presses, 1992

Genette, Gérard, *Discours du récit*, in *Figures III*, Paris: Seuil, 1972; as *Narrative Discourse*, Ithaca, New York: Cornell University Press, 1980

Genette, Gérard, *Nouveau discours du récit*, Paris: Seuil, 1983; as *Narrative Discourse Revisited*, Ithaca, New York: Cornell University Press, 1988

Genette, Gérard, *Seuils*, Paris: Seuil, 1987

Kestner, Joseph A., *The Spatiality of the Novel*, Detroit, Michigan: Wayne State University Press, 1978

Lanser, Susan Sniader, *The Narrative Act: Point of View in Prose Fiction*, Princeton, New Jersey: Princeton University Press, 1981

Matthews, John T., "Framing in *Wuthering Heights*," *Texas Studies in Literature* 27 (1985)

Newman, Beth, "Narratives of Seduction and the Seductions of Narrative: The Frame Structure in *Frankenstein*," *English Literary History* 53 (1986)

Sacks, Sheldon, *Fiction and the Shape of Belief*, Berkeley: University of California Press, 1964

Weisenburger, Steven, "Hyper-Embedded Narration in *Gravity's Rainbow*," *Pynchon Notes* 34–35 (Spring-Fall 1994)

Framley Parsonage. *See* Barsetshire Novels

Frankenstein by Mary Shelley

1818

Mary Wollstonecraft Shelley was the daughter of two radical thinkers, feminist Mary Wollstonecraft and philosopher William Godwin, who believed in the freedom and perfectibility of every man and woman. Shelley herself, while attempting to live up to these ideals, seems less certain about them. Her adult life began in a whirlwind of defiance—particularly her elopement with the already married Percy Bysshe Shelley—but ended in a long period of proper, conservative behavior. Shelley's lifelong ambivalence about liberty and conformity can be read in her fiction as well.

Frankenstein; or, The Modern Prometheus, the first of Mary Shelley's six novels, had its genesis at a "ghost-telling party" and in a nightmare about a doomed student of science, and it has generally been viewed either as early science fiction or late Gothic fiction. But the novel also shares characteristics with a variety of genres popular at the end of the 18th and the beginning of the 19th centuries: the romantic novel, the sentimental novel, the feminist novel, and the political novel. In fact, *Frankenstein,* which was dedicated to Godwin, was widely recognized by contemporary audiences as being Godwinian, or radically political. Shelley's novel does not, however, simply espouse those beliefs shared by her father and husband. Writing in a social context of disappointment and suspicion (the French Revolution, for instance, had collapsed into bloody chaos, and the Industrial Revolution had brought with it poverty and unrest), Shelley critiques these political, intellectual, and moral ideologies by graphically depicting their consequences. Her deployment of a shifting first-person narration reveals her ambivalence about Godwinian optimism, romantic idealism, and scientific egoism, and keeps the reader's sympathies and judgments shifting as well.

The novel is constructed within an epistolary framework, a common 18th-century form for first-person narratives. Robert Walton, a young, energetic, and visionary explorer, writes letters back to his sister in England as he journeys to the North Pole. But he soon encounters Frankenstein, and the novel disconnects from the letter-writing structure and slips into two confessionary narratives, Frankenstein's and his monster's. As a whole, then, the novel is a nested series of first-person narratives, each one leading to the next, commenting on it, questioning it. Each narrator is passionate, eloquent, and compelling. Each speaks with the voice of authority, but each is also unreliable to the extent that his perspective is clouded by ambition and self-interest. More importantly, each one depends on the sympathies of his listener.

Shelley has thus created a highly unstable narrative in which the reader's own position becomes difficult to define and maintain. First, the reader is in the position of Walton's sister, stationary and safe; then he occupies the place of Walton himself, cut off from civilization and human sympathy, listening to and iden-

tifying with Frankenstein's tale. Finally, the reader is in the position of Frankenstein himself, pursued, persuaded, and tortured by his horrible creation. The novel subtly leads the reader away from the stability of civilized, domestic culture and out into the wasteland of adventure and human striving.

Shelley uses Walton's letters to establish the primary issues of the novel: the importance of education, the power of sympathy in human relationships, and the lure of exploration and discovery versus the stability of domesticity. These themes are then played out again in Frankenstein's and his monster's narratives so that the reader is given three different accounts of human exploration: its initiation, its culmination, and its consequences. In these accounts, the novel oscillates between the revolutionary and conservative, the idealistic and disappointed. On the one hand, it celebrates the individual intellect and the individual will. Frankenstein is a Godwinian figure, a noble Prometheus who is motivated by a desire to create a better race; he is also a supremely romantic figure whose imagination leads him into realms hitherto unexplored. On the other hand, it is through his scientific pursuits that Frankenstein violates nature and creates a being who destroys the social fabric of his life.

Shelley's characterization of the monster, Frankenstein's shadowy doppelgänger, is equally fraught. The novel gives the monster a voice and a degree of humanity, depicting him as a version of Rousseau's natural man and making him a pitiable figure. But it also graphically represents his murderous rage. So, while the novel appears sympathetic toward the monster, it also seems glad for the monster's promised death. He is a figure symbolic of revolutionary potential untended, uneducated, and unsympathized with.

Ultimately, Shelley's novel enacts her ambivalence about her father's and husband's idealizing philosophies. The novel's tensions are not so much resolved as suspended in the end. Frankenstein dies, both noble and profoundly wrong. The creature honorably promises to destroy himself, but that promise remains unsubstantiated. Even Walton, who agrees to turn back for his crew's sake, believes that he is wrong to do so. The reader enters the novel with the journey already begun, and leaves with the journey incomplete. Over and over, the text itself defers judgment, leaving the reader's judgment and sympathies muddled.

The impact of *Frankenstein* was powerful and immediate. While many readers initially recoiled from the horrors of the novel, its themes and metaphors quickly worked their way into 19th-century literary, social, and political discourse. The novel's two emblematic figures—the overreaching scientist and his horrific creation—locked in mortal (and moral) combat provided subsequent generations with a powerful myth of transgression and obsession. A long list of British and American works, including Herman Melville's *Moby-Dick* (1851), Elizabeth Gaskell's *Mary Barton* (1848), Charles Dickens' *Great Expectations* (1861), Robert Louis Stevenson's *Strange Case of Dr. Jekyll and Mr. Hyde* (1886), Bram Stoker's *Dracula* (1897), Oscar Wilde's *The Picture of Dorian Gray* (1891), and Joseph Conrad's "Heart of Darkness" (1902), all bear the imprint of Shelley's novel. The 20th century has further claimed the novel, attractive to both high and low culture, for children's literature, film, and television.

While the legacy of *Frankenstein* has been largely thematic, its deployment of three unreliable but compelling narrators is also noteworthy. Through these three voices, Shelley explores the development, distortion, and destruction of human potential, allowing them to speak without explicitly judging them. Their stories stand as haunting invitations to explore these same dangerous realms. This same sort of seductive narration would emerge again with the modernists, who invite the reader into intricate, often bewildering tales and leave him there to seek the truth.

JUDITH BURDAN

See also Framing and Embedding

Further Reading

Baldick, Chris, *In Frankenstein's Shadow: Myth, Monstrosity, and Nineteenth-Century Writing,* Oxford: Clarendon Press, and New York: Oxford University Press, 1987

Bloom, Harold, editor, *Mary Shelley's "Frankenstein,"* New York: Chelsea House, 1987

Blumberg, Jane, *Mary Shelley's Early Novels: "This Child of Imagination and Misery,"* Iowa City: University of Iowa Press, and London: Macmillan, 1993

Clemit, Pamela, *The Godwinian Novel: The Rational Fictions of Godwin, Brockden Brown, Mary Shelley,* Oxford: Clarendon Press, and New York: Oxford University Press, 1993

Levine, George Lewis, and U.C. Knoepflmacher, editors, *The Endurance of "Frankenstein": Essays on Mary Shelley's Novel,* Berkeley: University of California Press, 1974

Mellor, Anne Kostelanetz, *Mary Shelley: Her Life, Her Fiction, Her Monsters,* New York and London: Routledge, 1988

Newman, Beth, "Narratives of Seduction and the Seductions of Narrative: The Frame Structure of *Frankenstein,*" *English Literary History* 53:1 (1986)

O'Flinn, Paul, "Production and Reproduction: The Case of *Frankenstein,*" *Literature and History* 9:2 (1983)

Poovey, Mary, *The Proper Lady and the Woman Writer: Ideology as Style in the Works of Mary Wollstonecraft, Mary Shelley, and Jane Austen,* Chicago: University of Chicago Press, 1984

Sunstein, Emily W., *Mary Shelley: Romance and Reality,* Boston: Little Brown, 1989; London: Johns Hopkins University Press, 1991

Free Indirect Discourse. *See* Discourse Representation

French Novel

16th and 17th Centuries

The novel as readers of French have known it in the heritage of Honoré de Balzac, Gustave Flaubert, and Marcel Proust did not exist as such in the 16th and 17th centuries. Until the end of the 17th century the early modern novel survives as a heterogeneous and sometimes monstrous form. At once built from allegories and complex aesthetic designs, and pocked with letters, poems, songs, and maps, the novel of that time bears little analogy with that of the 19th and 20th centuries. The novel owes its initial shape to the innovations of print culture. It developed from the new mobilities offered by standardized writing in the experimental years of the printing press. As a result it bears traces of reference to the materiality of its paper, as opposed to parchment and vellum; of ink and metal puncheons that produce characters and typographical pictures; and of movable type, which endowed the book with unforeseen possibilities of conveying identical impressions over a vastly extended geographical area.

Writers who undertook the novel in the wake of the invention of the printing press suddenly faced dilemmas that called into question the existence of the writer and the reader. Authors no longer knew quite for whom their works were destined. The public became an enigma, or even an illusion, whose only pertinent trait was that it harbored the unknown. Literacy, far reduced and with scattered geographical concentrations in comparison to the 20th century, caused writers to wonder about the identity of those who received or read their novels. As late as 1549 the narrator of Rabelais' fourth book of *Pantagruel* asks his audience if it can "hear" him. Hence the reader became an increasingly virtual entity, even if novels were dedicated to princely beings or bore the seal of *privilège* in a major city or the device of a reputable printer.

From its beginnings the novel was aimed at a literate public. Yet its authors could never gauge exactly *how* it would be read. Given the overriding presence of oral culture, the novel was more likely to have been read aloud among a group of listeners of varying degrees of literacy by a learned and gifted performer. Like those hearing the text, he or she was familiar with a variety of languages, dialects, slang, and jargons pertaining to crafts and trades. In its use of these idioms the printed novel reflected recent and crucial developments in the sociology of individual and collective experience. The emerging model of the fiction was no doubt in active dialogue with the feelings and senses of the reader. Although many novels were meant to be heard or read in installments, in a manner perhaps not unlike the performance of Chrétien de Troyes' great courtly novels of the early Gothic age (1170–90), the advent of the printed novel signaled the spread of silent and individual reading. Not that silent reading is tantamount to distraction or ways of passing time during idle hours or while a reader is in transit: printed narrative read in solitude remained a subject of secular mediation parallel to the reading of books of catechism or the Bible. It also betrays an increasingly erotic dimension that goes hand-in-hand with the seclusion of the reader living alone with his or her text. Thus what we know of subjectivity—the growth of singular experience and of encounters with the world—had its finest initial reflections in the way the novel offered a variety of types of mediation and meditation with respect to ambient reality.

Sixteenth Century

In 16th-century France the novel was fraught with accrued evidence of social contradiction. Included are the first indications of a centralized state in rivalry with subterranean movements of democratization and religious reform. The civil wars that riddled the economy from 1562 to 1598 led to a unified consciousness of nationhood that eventually secularized everyday life. Given that religion informed all human activity in the early modern era, it is difficult to reconstruct reading practices without stressing the propensity for the novel to be read as a reflection of metaphysical issues in the form of social conflicts. A secular meditation with theological innuendo, the novel of the 16th and 17th centuries did not resemble Stendhal's famous figure of the novel as a mirror held aloft by writers walking along the pathway of their time.

Two salient traits mark the early modern novel from its beginnings. First, many works were written in tandem with images, usually woodcuts or xylographies, that subject the written material (often translated from Latin or adapted from chivalric novels that had been set in prose in the incunabular era) to new tensions. A relation of identity and difference inhabits the most popular works composed with illustrations, such as the first French editions of the arcane allegory of self-realization, Francesco Colonna's *Le songe de Poliphile* (Dream of Poliphile) at the beginning of the 16th century; the images that interrupt

the graceful meanders of Herberay des Essarts' French translation of *Amadis de Gaule* in the early 1540s; and the sumptuous illustrations, executed by talented mannerist engravers, that exceed the billowing prose of *Le roman d'Euphrates* by mid-century. Second, the novel grew concurrently and was closely affiliated with innovations in the spatialization of knowledge. In this sense, the early French novel may be related to developments in cartographic practice. Prior to the 16th century, maps were rare forms in encyclopedias or vellum charts used for navigation about the Mediterranean Sea. With oceanic travel east and west, and with the dissemination of new editions of Ptolemy's *Geographia,* a new experience of language and space was inaugurated. As narrative extended its horizons to Cathay (China) and to the Americas, it began to bear the features either of "world-pictures" that assimilate pullulating masses of information or it included maps as spatial gazetteers to accompany or direct the otherwise chaotic impression of endless verbal flow. Novels became "topographic fictions" of a locale, such as the Chinonais (dear to François Rabelais in *Gargantua*) or the Sarthe (the region about the city of Le Mans in Paul Scarron's *Romant comique*). These areas are microcosms but also signatory places by which the writing mimes an umbilical relation with a motherland. They are also "toponymic tales" constructed from concatenations of place-names that yield the effects of verbal analogues to route-enhancing maps and *itineraria.* Spatial configurations such as maps, notes Christian Jacob, "uphold with narrative a privileged place . . . in which they invite the reader to follow both the development of the story according to a drawing, just as they can contribute to the genesis of writing" (see Jacob, 1992). Local areas and their stories are conjugated with a world that is expanding at exponential speeds in urban centers and along trade routes.

However much print culture and travel affected the novel and the uses to which it was put, one may identify six lines of development that define the genre in its embryonic moments. First, the tendency to encyclopedism in which all styles and levels of mimetic expression are mixed is seen and heard in the polyphony of Rabelais' four books of *Gargantua* and *Pantagruel* (1532–34). Rabelais plots a total creation that sums up medieval and classical avatars of fiction and lays a foundation for the entire future of the French novel. His work is an unfinished venture that gigantically devours and exceeds the best intentions and worst fears of its creator and its readers. Book II (*Pantagruel*), written before Book I (*Gargantua*), plots out its own future by telling of a gentle giant's education before it retells a similar—but more humanistically invested—tale of the father's formation. Both are narrated by Alcofribas Nasier, an "abstractor of quintessence," whose name is an anagram of the author, a medical doctor affiliated with Erasmian reform. Rabelais creates characters whose actions—more than their psychology—constitute fields of narrative and ideological tension. The princely Pantagruel is exceeded by his cunning and streetwise companion, Panurge, who is both a trickster and a wordsmith. Gargantua becomes a sage leader through a series of formative advances and setbacks. His adventures go to the limits both of credibility and of the French language, in ways that reflect a self-conscious rivalry with Latin in one of the most ebullient moments in the development of the vernacular. Book III, published in 1546, a convivium and a quest for meaning in and about the Touraine, records the wizening of the giants. The book sheds creative doubt over the condition of a surrounding world believed to be in decline. Book IV, a travel narrative, takes to the high seas to explore the unknown and to satirize ferociously the denaturing of the world at the hands of unsavory adepts of religious causes.

Second, the confessional genre inherited from Giovanni Boccaccio's *Elegia di Madonna Fiammetta* (*The Elegy of Lady Fiammetta*) led writers to sow the seeds of the autobiographical and first-person novel, which uses the newly born self to engage and reflect personal experience with the world. Herein, too, is the beginning of the feminist novel, primarily in Hélisenne de Crenne's *Les Angoysses douloureuses qui procèdent d'amours* (1538; *The Torments of Love*) and her concurrent *Lettres familières et invectives* (translated in part in *A Renaissance Woman: Hélisenne's Personal and Invective Letters*). An inner mental space becomes the subject of the novel, which is developed through the conventions of Italian and Latin sources translated and pasted into a fiction that acquires a resonance of its own. The beginnings of the novel of incarceration and of mutilation are seen in a prismatic structure that shifts between distinctly first-person and third-person narration. The letters that can be related to events in *The Torments of Love* mark an important moment in the beginnings of the epistolary novel in France.

Loosely affiliated with psychological material in *The Torments of Love*, third, is Marguerite de Navarre's mosaic of tales, *L'Heptaméron* (1558–59; *The Heptameron*). Based on an open-ended structure juxtaposed with the self-enclosing symmetry of its model, Boccaccio's *Decameron*, the book of 72 stories accumulates a mass of experience that fragments and unifies affective space and conventions of gender. It uses parataxis and juxtaposition to construct a mobile architecture of narrative in which certain stories are crafted to fit at once inside and outside the sum. The cornice-frame of Boccaccio's ten-by-ten foundation (ten days of ten stories by ten tellers told to pass the time while the plague abates in Florence) is replaced in *The Heptameron* by increased interstitial commentary and discussion exchanged among participants whose ideologies anticipate proto-Jamesian "reflectors" or limited fields of perception with respect to the fictions being told. As in Rabelais, the beginnings of the dialogic novel are felt here in conflicting voices mixed with a gamut of persons and personalities who venture stories of varying length. Some are vignettes, while others (such as the tragic story of Floride and Amadour told at the end of the first day) are miniature novels.

Fourth, and vital to the future of the 17th-century novel, is Herberay des Essarts' translation of *Amadis de Gaule* in 1544. A pastoral *roman fleuve* that many consider impossible to read in our age, the novel took hold during the year King Francis I spent incarcerated in Madrid in 1525 following the defeat of his army at Pavia. He listened to the innumerable adventures of shepherds and damsels that would later provide a pattern for the fiction that became cultivated in the French salons. *Amadis de Gaule* indeed gave rise to variants and counterparts, and, aside from its celebrated influence on Cervantes, it also set in place the tradition of the novel of sentimental education, civility, and courtly mannerisms that would be the substance of pastoral fiction in the next century. It was the site for the expression of refinement and the development of mixed creations of pictures and images. *Amadis de Gaule* bore exquisite woodcut illustrations that rivaled the prose, signaling the oncoming rift of image and text, or language from iconic forms, in the years ahead.

In this light, fifth, modern readers can finally appreciate the quasi-Freudian and cinematic novel, Barthélémy Aneau's *Alector; ou, Le coq* (1551; *Alector; or, The Cock*), known more to humanists than to a broad public, but which influenced the tradition of the first-person novel and occupies a significant place in the history of Menippean satire. "These parcels set forward in the first book of this fragment are certain pieces of sheets either whole or broken to bits. Which, by being mutilated, lacking, and inconsequential, have not been adapted to any place or chapter of the work." Thus begins *Alector*, a text built from emblematic pictures, cartographic remainders, heraldic devices, and mythographic illustrations that tell of the birth of an "anyreader" (*alector*) or subject of French identity from the egg of a Gallic volatile. A divided creation, it ranks as an important manifestation of the type of Menippean satire that would later appear in Laurence Sterne's *Tristram Shandy* (1759–67).

If images exercise the reader's memory in works of this genre, it is important to recall that their mobilization was crucial, sixth, to the structure of one of the most ideological creations of the time, the *histoire tragique*. It witnessed unequaled development from 1559 into the 1640s. Originally affiliated with an early draft of the *Heptaméron* in a prepackaged shape that Pierre Boaistuau had designed, the genre is initiated in the same author's translation and emendations of Bandello's tragic stories, recently cultivated in the French court, that figured in aesthetic programs inspired by a taste for Italian objects. Boaistuau goes a step further by scripting tales as if they were part of a tragic "theatre" or world spectacle focusing on tragic error or misconduct, the bloody outcome of which is exploited to implant corrective images in the minds of readers. A new machinery is invented: an architectural and cartographic mode that locates and humiliates both its personages and its public through appeal to pictures of unimaginable cruelty. Vital to the Counter Reformation, the genre not only contained sources for Shakespearean tragedy but also inspired variations that underscored a French style and national signature. Jacques Yver's *Le printemps* (1572; *Spring*) juxtaposes bloodcurdling tales to a delightful story of comic misrecognition on which is based William Shakespeare's *Two Gentlemen of Verona*. Bénigne Poissenot's *Nouvelles histoires tragiques* (1586) carries a preface that remains a poetics for the genre.

A crucial background to the travel novel is the first-person account of voyage and discovery. What Claude Lévi-Strauss has likened to the "ethnographer's breviary," André Thevet's *Les Singularités de la France antarctique* (1557) and Jean de Léry's *Histoire d'un voyage fait en la terre du Brésil* (1578 and 1580; *History of a Voyage to the Land of Brazil, Otherwise Called America*) also qualify as germinal novels of experience and observation. They are structured around the linear pattern of an itinerary composed of departures, obstacles, discoveries, commentary, turning points, and returns. They are also specular narratives employing mirroring effects in which the European author is compared to the indigenous other. Thevet's account is part of an ambitious and proto-Balzacian project of a universal cosmography in which all peoples and nations are enclosed in a single book (*La Cosmographie universelle* [2 vols., 1575; translated in part in *André Thevet's North America: A Sixteenth-Century View*]), but also of a universal singularization through which the world and its myths are scattered in the form of archipelagoes of isolated observations. Léry's account may be read as a Bildungsroman and a novel of Proustian reflection in its erotic representation of the Americas. His travel novel displays individuation as well as any of the narrative types of the century. A future field of research should include natural history as narrative (e.g., Pierre Belon du Mans and Antoine du Pinet) and other travelers (Charles Estienne and Nicolas de Nicolaï) as novels of experience and exile.

Seventeenth Century

The novel of the 17th century witnessed a gradual evolution from the rich and variegated forms of the emergent genre of the previous century into four distinct types: pastoral, comic, historic, and satiric. The novel also divides along a demarcation between Baroque and classical phases that, respectively, separate the creations of the first 40 years from those of the rest of the 17th century. Novels reflect profound upheavals in the political and social spheres. In addition to increased oceanic commerce, by 1620 the scientific revolution changed the means of measurement and observation of the empirical world. If allegory and analogy had melded language and reality in the Renaissance, language now was becoming increasingly distant from what it represented, effectively detaching itself from the things and actions it designated. No wonder that the triumph of monocular perspective and Euclidean geometry that René Descartes internalized in his autobiographical jewel *Le discours de la méthode* (1637; *A Discourse on Method*) led to the disappearance of tangible signs of God in the physical world. The positioning of sacred origins at vanishing points in pictural perspective, or the "lexical cleansing" of French that had mediated Latin and thousands of patois spoken over the surface of the French kingdom, showed that centrally defined systems of language and representation were taking charge in creative domains. Novelists were becoming technicians assembling fictional world-pictures.

In the same vein, experiments with new forms eventually decreased as French grammar became codified and aligned with authority: speakers and writers of the vernacular were to conform to its patron shapes. In a first phase (1590–1630) French was poeticized and "latinized" so as to fulfill the mission of being equivalent to the classical idiom. In a second phase (1640–90) French tended toward a purity, preciosity, and elegance that announced dignity and a naturally, and seemingly God-given, tenor of austere elegance. The range of French vocabulary reduced as the century advanced. Readers and writers made their careers by obeying and bending—but not breaking—rules imposed by authorities such as the French Academy (1635). The first phase is marked by the accession of the protestant Henry IV to the monarchy in 1594, his decreeing the Edict of Nantes in 1598, and the new plans for national defense. In the years from the end of the Wars of Religion up to 1640, the novel was an accurate barometer of turmoil and conflict: hence a period of innovation that fits the term *Baroque* to describe the new literature built upon and often concealing its debt to the inherited models adumbrated above. The second or *classical* phase witnessed the calming of experiment and establishment of codification that dominated the rest of the century. By the 1680s the labor of the novel led writers and readers into inner spaces, particularly in feminist writings, that yielded new and unknown psychological insight.

The Baroque phase is marked by the works of Béroalde de Verville, Charles Sorel, François de Rosset, and Honoré d'Urfé.

Béroalde's *Le Moyen de parvenir* (c. 1610; *Fantastic Tales*) and its precedent, *Le voyage des princes fortunés* (1594 and 1610; *The Voyage of Fortunate Princes*), sum up the novel of the 16th century and anticipate the birth of new forms. *Fantastic Tales*, a convivium in which almost 100 speakers banter at a dinner table (and thus are part of a subgenre Bakhtin [1968] calls "licentious table-talk"), offers a rich cacophony of anecdotes and germinal tales that run from traits raucous and Rabelaisian to others both searing and psychologically sublime. A work built according to anamorphotic perspective and mixing all registers of expression, it gives new temper and manner to the vernacular. Written as an alchemical creation, *Le Voyage des princes fortunés* is a cartographic pastoral novel based on an island-map of amorous adventure. Both books fit within a picture of universal history that collects anecdotes from local spaces and times of the Wars of Religion, from Geneva to Tours, and that shows how the novel can make chivalry and Menippean satire coexist.

Some of these same traits mark Charles Sorel's *L'Histoire comique de Francion* (first edition 1623; *The Comical History of Francion*), an account of a bumbling youth romping through a society of refined decorum, as the title suggests, which tells of the formation of a French citizen. Taking up the themes of individuation as Rabelais and his inheritors had developed it, Sorel's novel both resembles and also takes leave of recent French taste for translations of the picaresque novel and Cervantes' fiction, including *Don Quixote* (French version, 1614) and the *Novelas ejemplares* (French version, 1613). It is not a confession or a work whose narration seeks redemption but rather a young subject's entry into the turbulent world of France, like the very temper of Sorel's language, that seeks order in the midst of buffoonery.

In a different fashion, such also are the effects of the *histoire tragique* from 1613 to well into the 17th century. A best-seller, François de Rosset's (and also Jean-Pierre Camus') variations on the model of Bandello provide the theatrical stage of eros and horror so extravagant that fear and terror are mixed with delight and amusement. Narrative and peroration are mixed, as are perspective and language, building from stray news items—"cruel spectacles" destined to shatter readers into consciousness of their place in a French nation under a stern Catholic deity. The tales' obsession with fortune and change that lead to tragic destiny connotes the presence of a ruling order absent in a period of French history, marked by two *Frondes*, when nobility and centralized authority are at war.

The Baroque novel par excellence that determined taste and style for much of the century is Honoré d'Urfé's pastoral labyrinth *L'Astrée* (1607–27). Conceived during the Wars of Religion, it takes leave of contemporary political conflict by mapping out what has been called a "desperate utopia" in which the loves of Astrée and Céladon are forever deferred. They amble and cross dress in the thick of interwoven subplots, events recurring to seemingly mechanical schemes of alternation and reiteration, or that forever concatenate and invert one another. The protagonists move about the River Lignon, which seems to flow between the spectacle of Rome in decadence, oblivion, and the eastern France of contemporary time. A courtly style defines the shepherds' lives in a no-man's land in which time is tortuously bent along meanders of narrative that fray and knot their many verbal strands. A vast space of intrigue and a descriptive itinerary of sentimental movement are inverse to the increasing precision brought to the plotting of French territory by the king's engineers under Henry IV and Louis XIII. The novel offers places in which characters and readers alike get lost. All the while the seduction of d'Urfé's language and intrigue serves to anticipate the ideology of a centralizing state. In *L'Astrée* affectivity organizes an extensive and magnetically charged space that, today, few adepts of the novel would dare to enter. But in its time the novel was a manual of civility, of the art of intricate design, reversion, erotic titillation, and of sentimental and psychological intensity. So influential was *L'Astrée* that it led Sorel, possessed of Gallic wit, to write an anti-novel, *Le Berger extravagant* (1627; *The Extravagant Shepherd*), that pulls d'Urfé's innovations in the direction of comedy and satire.

The second, classical, tendency is seen in the works of Paul Scarron, Antoine Furetière, Mademoiselle de Scudéry, and Madame de Lafayette. The elegant and parodic styles prevailed in a calmer form after the mid-century in two comparatively compact novels with classical innuendo, Paul Scarron's *Le Romant comique* (1651) and Antoine Furetière's *Le Roman bourgeois* (1666). The former inaugurates a burlesque genre with a style gentler than Sorel's. Scarron depicts the life of a theatrical that moves about a locale close to the author's native Le Mans. A nodal point, the site reflects more intensely the alterity of inserted tales that come from Italy, Spain, and North Africa. The novel is larded with caricatures of contemporary figures that almost resemble Balzacian physiognomies, but it also includes sketches of voyage and adventure that had been the stuff of travel literature. It revives the unreliable narrator who, beginning with Rabelais, is a hallmark of subjectivity that dominates the French novel in general. Furetière, author of a first great dictionary and baptized as a member of the French Academy in 1662, writes a novel that patterns later fiction with its emphasis on "good people of mediocre condition." Although a realistic tendency is evinced, the eye of the observer implies that noble feelings and actions ought to constitute prevailing social norms. Shifts of mimetic level are obtained when a learned narrator offers a redemptive ethnography of old and new societies in mid-century France: old, in that local traditions coexist, as also in Molière's theatre, with the new, typified by overaffected preciosity and pretentious banter. A "novel without a hero," it might indeed be seen as a first precursor of the realist tradition of the next two centuries.

The classical novel in its historical form is embodied in two contrastive styles and authors. Mademoiselle de Scudéry's *Clélie, histoire romaine* (1654–61; *Clelia*) spins off the pastoral model of d'Urfé to impose an order that brings dignity and classical sentiment to intrigues of impressive girth. Its advocates seek to please and to put forward codes of civility in human exchange and to produce "tender geographies" in which a woman's perspective edulcorates a world of masculine arms and letters. The novel and its commentaries cement in place a complex culture of the *salon* that affords a social space where the male eros, reason, war, and statecraft are jettisoned in favor of the study of human conduct and affectivity. Scudéry's "Carte du Tendre," an allegorical map of adventure over the topography of the *salon,* further emphasizes an inversion of the military and administrative ethos that had figured in centralizing technology.

The compact historical fiction of Madame de Lafayette entirely changed the face of the classical novel. Her sources are located in accounts of the French court during civil and religious turmoil (1552–98). She transposes the imbroglios of contemporary time onto the polymorphous realm of Catherine de Medici, Charles IX, and Henry III. Her first story, "La Princesse de Montpensier" (1662), turns the tradition of fictional names taken from the pastoral novel into real historical personages, creates a claustrophobic space of ardor that knows no issue in the view of public honor, and elaborates a dispassionate style using third-person narrative to relate scenarios inaccessible to historiography. Reminders of memorial writing and histories of the Renaissance are woven into the fabric, but nowhere else does the background of the *histoire tragique* meet that of an inner theatre of personal psychomachia and, ultimately, of *noirish* death drives that send protagonists and antagonists to their demise.

La Princesse de Clèves (1678; *The Princess of Cleves*) refines a similar story but develops it with an amplitude in which the tragic destiny of love chosen to remain unfulfilled is the measure of a jewel-like narrative. If the heroine holds at bay her passion for the gallant Duke of Nemours, her renunciation of his gallant appeals replicates the refusal to yield to mannered and, by then, overly "literary" expression of sentiments of force at odds with sociality. The heroine's world is one of inner drives approached by intimations of free indirect discourse. The descriptive register is of sobriety and searing understatement. The novel rehearses scenarios of the heart in battle with reason but also invests in the prose the illusions of desire belonging to both male and female temperaments. The novel paradoxically signals some major narrative components of the 18th-century novel, in which love shared among protagonists wins over socially sanctioned marriages. In Madame de Lafayette, point of view is taken not as relativity but as a reflection of the limits of consciousness and desire that cannot utter in language what is felt in the depths of the body. Public space avers to be an intolerable world of dissimulation that requires the protagonist to take refuge in solitude of mediation, but the latter area is marked by a total void of communication. The novel expresses pathos and tragedy in the very substance of the vocables that betray an unconscious that the grammar, cast in a classical pose, cannot entirely control.

La Princesse de Clèves also offers an inspiring and crushing evocation of male desire, in which possession and destruction of the female amounts to love and honor. Madame de Lafayette's work is especially accessible to our age in its dazzling treatment of subjectivity and alterity. What is it to be in love where no social space allows for reciprocity, or where the object of female affection is unworthy of its gift? How does language overtake pathos so as to become an object that exceeds its own narrative? The first question is approached by novels and novelists in later centuries. The second had been addressed by Rabelais, whose work performs in language what all of the novels of the 16th and 17th centuries—whether sentimental or realistic, Baroque or classical, pastoral or historical, comic, satiric, burlesque or tragic—variously succeed in attaining. Two seemingly opposite and unrelated figures, Rabelais and Madame de Lafayette, may be seen as strangely complementary and indicative of the breadth and wealth of two centuries of unparalleled work forever in need of closer and more extensive analysis.

TOM CONLEY

See also Astrée; Epistolary Novel; Pastoralism in the Novel; Princesse de Clèves; Prose Novelistic Forms; François Rabelais; Renaissance Narrative; Space

Further Reading

Adam, Antoine, *Histoire de la littérature française au XVIIe siècle*, 5 vols., Paris: Del Daca, 1948–57

Bakhtin, M.M., *Tvorchestvo Fransua Rable i Narodnaja Kul'tura Srednevekovija i Renessansa*, Moscow: Khudozh, 1965; as *Rabelais and His World*, Cambridge, Massachusetts: MIT Press, 1968

Baldner, R.W., *Bibliography of Seventeenth-Century French Prose Fiction*, New York: Columbia University Press and the Modern Language Association, 1967

Cave, Terence, *The Cornucopian Text: Problems in Writing in the French Renaissance*, Oxford: Clarendon Press, and New York: Oxford University Press, 1979

Conley, Tom, *The Graphic Unconscious in Early Modern French Writing*, Cambridge and New York: Cambridge University Press, 1992

Conley, Tom, *The Self-Made Map: Cartographic Writing in Early Modern France*, Minneapolis: University of Minnesota Press, 1996

Coulet, Henri, *Le Roman jusqu'à la Révolution*, Paris: Armand Colin, 1967

Debaisieux, Martine, *Le Procès du roman: Écriture et contrefaçon chez Charles Sorel*, Saratoga, California: Anma Libri, 1989

DeJean, Joan, *Tender Geographies: Women and the Origins of the Novel in France*, New York: Columbia University Press, 1991

De Jongh, William, *Bibliography of the Novel and Short Story in French from the Beginning of Printing till 1600*, Albuquerque: University of New Mexico Press, 1944

DiPiero, Thomas, *Dangerous Truths and Criminal Passions: The Evolution of the French Novel, 1569–1791*, Stanford, California: Stanford University Press, 1992

Ehrmann, Jacques, *Un paradis désespéré: L'amour et l'illusion dans "L'Astrée,"* Paris: Presses Universitaires de France, and New Haven, Connecticut: Yale University Press, 1963

Jacob, Christian, *L'Empire des cartes: Approche théorique de la cartographie à travers l'histoire*, Paris: Michel, 1992

Jeanneret, Michel, *A Feast of Words: Banquets and Table Talk in the Renaissance*, Cambridge: Polity Press, and Chicago: University of Chicago Press, 1991

Kamuf, Peggy, *Fictions of Feminine Desire: Disclosures of Héloïse*, Lincoln: University of Nebraska Press, 1982

Kenny, Neil, *The Palace of Secrets: Béroalde de Verville and Renaissance Conceptions of Knowledge*, Oxford: Clarendon Press, and New York: Oxford University Press, 1991

Lestringant, Frank, *Écrire le monde à la Renaissance: Quinze études sur Rabelais, Postel, Bodin et littérature géographique*, Caen: Paradigme, 1993

Lever, Maurice, *Le Roman français au XVIIe siècle*, Paris: Presses Universitaires de France, 1981

Martin, Henri-Jean, *The History and Power of Writing*, Chicago: University of Chicago Press, 1994

Reynier, Gustave, *Le Roman sentimental avant "L'Astrée,"* Paris: Armand Colin, 1908

French Novel

18th Century

French literary history, unlike its English counterpart, has never viewed the novel as a creation of the 18th century. On the contrary, the genre *roman* was considered much older and was often seen as an heir of the epic. Nor did it undergo a name change (as in the English transition from "romance" to "novel"). There was nonetheless a long debate about how important a place the novel could claim in the hierarchy of literary genres.

Broadly speaking, a gradual transition took place in the 18th century from lengthy, heroic forms (what in English are called "romances") to more concise ones, these being largely first-person narratives. Of these, fictional memoirs gradually gave way to epistolary novels, which were dominant during the middle of the century. By the time of the French Revolution, this vogue had pretty much run its course. Meanwhile, the progressive convergence of the "high style" heroic novel or aristocratic novella and the "low style" comic novel brought about considerable movement of the novel's social world in the direction of the middle classes, with the exception of the horrific *roman noir* and pornography.

The late 17th and early 18th centuries saw a great increase in shorter narrative forms that were published in just one or two volumes. The historical story, in the manner of Madame de Lafayette, for a while styled *nouvelle historique*, and the autobiographical story, similar to memoirs but often in its more compact versions labeled *histoire*, were particularly popular with French novelists. These relatively new types of narrative by no means superseded the long traditional novel. In fact, the older and newer forms influenced each other. For instance, Alain René Lesage's *Histoire de Gil Blas de Santillane* (3 vols., 1715–35), in length and structure similar to Miguel de Cervantes' *Don Quixote* (2 vols., 1605–15), is an *histoire* in that it is a first-person narrative. Robert Challes' *Les Illustres Françaises* (1713; The Great Women of France) is also fairly lengthy, but it is divided into seven separate stories, each related by one of its protagonists and bearing a separate subtitle beginning with the word *histoire*. The most famous component of L'abbé Prévost's rambling, seven-volume *Mémoires d'un homme de qualité qui s'est retiré du monde* (1728–31; *Memoirs of a Man of Quality*) is its final volume, the compact *Manon Lescaut*. While the *Mémoires* were reprinted some 25 times during Prévost's lifetime, *Manon*—the full title of which is *Histoire du chevalier des Grieux et de Manon Lescaut* (1731)—was reprinted far more often as a separate work. Prévost wrote two other comparably lengthy memoir-novels in the 1730s, *Le Philosophe anglais* (7 vols., 1731–39; *The Life and Adventures of Mr. Cleveland* [better known as *Cleveland*]) and *Le Doyen de Killerine* (6 vols., 1735–40; *The Dean of Coleraine*). Pierre Carlet de Marivaux's two major novels, *La Vie de Marianne* (11 vols., 1731–41; *The Life of Marianne*) and *Le Paysan parvenu* (5 vols., 1735–36; *The Fortunate Villager*), are also multivolume serials. Nevertheless, these were the last major novelists to produce such lengthy works, with the single exception of Jean-Jacques Rousseau, whose only novel, *Julie; ou, La Nouvelle Héloïse* (1761; *Julie or, The New Eloise*), filled six volumes.

Lesage's *Le Diable boiteux* (1707; *The Devil upon Two Sticks*) and his *Gil Blas* mark the twilight in France of the venerable comic novel tradition, which had spawned so many grand satires and mock epics throughout Europe. It was not completely forgotten and would still inform works like Denis Diderot's *Jacques le fataliste et son maître* (1796; *Jacques the Fatalist*) half a century later. Nonetheless, the dominant tone shifted toward the more serious registers, many novels focusing in particular on conflicts of human passions against social restraints. An interest in the individual's perceptions and needs may have determined the great preponderance of stories related in the first person, and their proliferation has given rise to the notion that the novel is the typical voice of the rising individualistic bourgeoisie. In this sense, *Gil Blas* breaks radically with the Spanish picaresque tradition that it partially imitates, inasmuch as its protagonist does not merely rise from his humble origins to independence and prosperity but attains a heady proximity to political power as first secretary to the Spanish prime minister. However, French literary history has never been tempted to consider the novel a form emanating from a lower-class perspective. There had long been, and continued to be, many thoroughly aristocratic novels in French, and this high tradition enlarged and, over time, took in characters and situations that earlier had been found in comic fiction. Lesage, who also wrote comedies, some specifically for performance during local fairs (*théâtre de la foire*), himself helped to bring these strains together.

Challes' *Les Illustres Françaises* typifies the essentially aristocratic perspective. Its original structure as a composite of individual stories derives in part from collections such as those of Giovanni Boccaccio and Marguerite de Navarre but differs from them in that its several stories are integrated into a coherent narrative ensemble. Its protagonists are anything but historical figures, but they do harbor convictions of their individual worth as they struggle, often against their families, to realize their ambitions—most of which relate to love. This powerful novel, which was largely forgotten until Frédéric Deloffre rescued it from oblivion in 1959, set the tone for the subsequent generation of novels and was in many ways the critical model for the work of Prévost, in particular *Manon Lescaut*.

The personal story that furnishes the essence of so many novels is often a frame story, as are those of *Les Illustres Françaises* and *Manon Lescaut*; in other words, the narrator is him- or herself also a character who relates the story to someone else (who in some cases sets it down on paper). These novels, then, reflect

an age when reading was not the principal way in which people absorbed narrative. Many memoirs of the period, among them Rousseau's *Les Confessions* (2 vols., 1782–89; *The Confessions*), document the practice of two or more persons reading a book together. Marivaux's earlier novels, *La Voiture embourbée* (1714; The Carriage Stuck in the Mud) and *Les Effets surprenants de la sympathie* (5 vols., 1713–14; The Surprising Effects of Sympathy), also picture narrative situations in which whole groups of people assist in the telling of a story. In the 1730s, Marivaux modified this approach to the degree that his singular narrators, Marianne in *La Vie de Marianne* and Jacob in *Le Paysan parvenu*, are depicted in the process of *writing* their life stories for the benefit of a friend who stands in for the reading public.

A wave of eagerly consumed novels in the 1730s established the genre definitively, not only in the eyes of the cultural elite (some of whom had been reluctant to rank it alongside the higher genres like tragedy and epic) but with a much broader reading public. Besides the major novels of Prévost and Marivaux, there came in quick succession two novels by Claude Crébillon, *Lettres de la marquise de M*** au comte de R**** (1732; Letters from the marchioness of M*** to the Count of R***) and *Les Égarements du cœur et de l'esprit* (1736–38; Extravagances of the Head and Heart); two by Claudine de Tencin, *Mémoires du comte de Comminge* (1735; *Memoirs of the Count of Comminge*) and *Le Siège de Calais* (1739; *The Siege of Calais*); and many others by less prominent authors, particularly Charles de Mouhy.

Most of the information about the growing readership that made this surge possible has been indirect or anecdotal. Inventories of book sales, for instance, tend to overvalue categories of books that aristocrats were proud to exhibit on their shelves (such as sermons and histories) and underrepresent novels. But the reconstructed history of publication corroborates earlier speculations with new types of data. Much has been learned about the operations of booksellers themselves, almost all of whom were also publishers. Concentrated in the major cities and above all in Paris, they constituted a highly organized guild that worked closely with the royal book police to control production and circulation of books. In addition, some books were published clandestinely in France, while others were printed without royal permission in Holland, Germany, and England and sold in France. The popularity of subscription libraries (*cabinets de lecture*), which made it possible for many readers in the middle classes to read more books than they could afford to purchase, also gives an indication of the rapid expansion of a reading public with an appetite for novels.

A sizable readership was a necessary precondition for the rise of the novel, for only substantial sales emboldened publishers to advance money for manuscripts, which were always bought outright. Throughout the 17th century and well into the 18th, novelists were typically men and women of independent means or else men who, like Charles Sorel and Lesage, derived most of their income from their plays. Probably no novelist before Prévost was able to live on his income as a novelist, and even he moved more and more toward historical works in the 1740s.

The novelistic path was even more difficult for a woman; not until the 1760s was Marie Jeanne Riccoboni, who had begun her career as an actress, able really to make a living as a novelist. However, many of the early readers of novels were women. Indeed, some contemporaries thought novel audiences were comprised mainly of women, assuming that women were more receptive to the sentiments cultivated in the novel, but such an assertion cannot be maintained with any assurance. It is certain, however, that novels make a very large place for women characters. But until the middle of the 18th century, women novelists always published pseudonymously (which men did as well), often under cover of a male name.

Although autobiography was not yet a recognized literary category, many novels took the form of autobiographies. There was usually no objective way they could be identified as fictive, and "true" stories were considered to have greater moral and aesthetic value. Whether called *histoire* or *mémoires*, a very large proportion of the novels published between 1700 and 1760 were written in the first person, and many begin with a claim to veracity, sometimes perfunctory but sometimes quite elaborate. The protagonist ostensibly speaks about his or her own experiences, and the author disappears from sight. Such a procedure has its constraints, inasmuch as it prohibits the kind of complementary outside information that an "omniscient" narrator can supply at will. However, one individual's story could be made to accommodate those of other characters encountered along the way, as happens, for example in *Gil Blas* and *La Vie de Marianne*. Indeed, such subordinate narratives sometimes account for a very large portion of the text.

These popular first-person narratives typically focus on the age at which a young person emerges into the adult world—upon exit from the convent, for instance, in the case of a girl from a well-to-do family, or from a *collège,* tutorship, or academy for a young man in the same circumstances. Almost no attention was paid to the first 15 years of life, and frequently the story bogged down in the initial stages or—since novels were very often published serially—never even made it past the first few phases. *Les Égarements du cœur et de l'esprit* by Crébillon never completes the action announced at the inception. The same is true of Marivaux's *La Vie de Marianne, Cleveland,* and many other works. This fact seems to correspond to an intense interest in the formative period in the young person's life, and, from the standpoint of authorial imagination, to the huge gap separating the conception of a novel's framework and the ability to work out its entire trajectory. When the book police tried to suppress the genre of the novel, the official reason given was the abuse of the public perpetrated by writers and printers who brought out the initial installments of novels not yet—nor perhaps ever to be—completed. The proposed remedy was to authorize only completed manuscripts for publication.

Much of the activity in works treating high society was erotic. Such novels, often styled "libertine," mainly string out the successive love affairs—and they may be very numerous—of a young man "establishing" himself in the world, or, rather, being established by a woman a bit older than he, who acts as sponsor and sexual tutor. Whether sex is understood in this context as society's principal (or perhaps sole) activity, or as a focus and pretext for a wide range of other concerns, one cannot help but notice the insistence of the pattern. In addition to Crébillon's novels, Charles Pinot Duclos' *Les Confessions du comte de * * ** (1742) and many more egregiously erotic novels may serve as evidence of the trend. At the very least, this shared focus indicates a kind of fictional/social norm at a certain level of society. It has long been recognized that this genre remained popular for some

50 years. Although *Les Liaisons dangereuses* (1782; *Dangerous Acquaintances*) by Choderlos de Laclos is in many ways its epitome, a remarkable number of that work's most salient characteristics are already clearly delineated in *Les Égarements du cœur et de l'esprit.*

In the background, the epistolary novel was developing—another first-person form but potentially polyphonic—and it was to assert itself strongly in the second half of the century. Usually an exchange between two or more characters, the epistolary novel occasionally had a single narrator/letter writer, as in the case of the enormously popular *Lettres persanes* (1721; *Persian Letters*) by Montesquieu. The author later recounted with delight that booksellers would grab passing writers by the lapel, begging them to "write me some *Persian Letters.*" Montesquieu's novel is not very intimate; indeed, it is mostly social satire. But the impetus was important, and the form gathered steam, slowly at first, with Crébillon's *Lettres de la marquise de M*** au comte de R**** in 1732 and *Lettres d'une Péruvienne* (*Letters from a Peruvian Woman*) by Françoise de Graffigny in 1747. The tremendous success of Samuel Richardson, whose *Pamela* (1740) and *Clarissa* (1747–48) were quickly translated into French (the latter by Prévost in 1751) further contributed to the popularity of the epistolary novel.

The most important epistolary novels are Jean-Jacques Rousseau's *Julie; ou, La Nouvelle Héloïse* and Laclos' *Les Liaisons dangereuses.* Both were highly controversial and international best-sellers. Although Laclos' novel is more widely known today (having been adapted several times for the cinema), Rousseau's had a much greater impact at the time. For one thing, rather than continuing the Crébillon tradition as Laclos was to do, Rousseau prominently announced a reaction against it: *Julie* is much more about virtue than about vice, and its protagonists deliberately live far from the corrupt capital. To Rousseau, worldliness was precisely the problem, and the best models of a genuinely moral alternative were to be found in the countryside. *Julie* was devoured by thousands, dozens of pirate editions were published, and it was immediately translated into English by William Kenrick. Of all 18th-century novels, *Julie* was the most prominent in France, to be rivaled only by Johann Wolfgang von Goethe's *Die Leiden des jungen Werthers* (1774; *The Sufferings of Young Werther*) and then Benjamin de Saint-Pierre's *Paul et Virginie* (1788; *Paul and Mary*). These were the first novels to provoke an enormous production of imagery ranging from engraved prints to china and tapestries, as well as many print imitations of one sort or another, not to mention counterfeit editions.

Another popular epistolary novelist was Marie Jeanne Riccoboni, who established herself very quickly in the late 1750s with *Lettres de Mistriss Fanni Butlerd* (1759; Letters of Mistress Fanni Butlerd), *Histoire du marquis de Cressy* (1759; *The History of the Marquis of Cressy*), and *Lettres de Milady Juliette Catesby* (1759; *Letters from Juliet Lady Catesby, to her Friend Lady Henrietta Campley*). She alternated between the *histoire* and the epistolary novel, and indeed all of her novels—the last in 1777—have titles beginning with either *Lettres* or *Histoire.* Other prominent women novelists include Françoise Benoist, Anne Elie de Beaumont, and Jeanne Le Prince de Beaumont. Their audience appreciated their more open, but also often delectably subtle, expression of sentiment, which was often combined with elements taken from domestic drama such as Baculard d'Arnaud's *Les*

Époux malheureux (1746; The Unhappy Spouses), the art of Jean-Baptiste Greuze and Jean Chardin, and the theatrical drama of the 1760s.

Meanwhile, historical tales were still around and had been given renewed popularity by the work of Claudine de Tencin. Other women authors also contributed to the form, some of whom have drawn renewed attention—and for good reason—in recent years, particularly Fanny de Beauharnais, Marie (Sophie) Cottin, Isabelle de Montolieu, and Félicité de Genlis. It is no exaggeration to say that the French novel in the 1760s and 1770s was very largely dominated by women authors. The ensuing two decades saw the publication of the work of the most gifted of them all, Isabelle de Charrière. Born in Holland but married to a Swiss, Charrière wrote *Lettres neuchâteloises* (1784; Letters from Neuchâtel), *Lettres de Mistriss Henley* (1784; Letters of Mistress Henley), *Lettres écrites de Lausanne* (1788; Letters from Lausanne), and *Honorine d'Userche* (1798), as well as several plays, which, because she was a woman, she was unable to have performed.

From mid-century on, there was a rise in intense, sometimes morbid, human dramas called *romans noirs*. Their most successful promulgator, little read today, is Baculard d'Arnaud. The tempestuous Restif de la Bretonne wrote two major novels in this vein, *Le Paysan perverti* (1775; The Perverted Peasant) and *La Paysanne pervertie* (1777; The Perverted Peasant Girl), both in epistolary form. They chronicle the slow and sad demise of a brother and sister who leave the tranquil and honorable countryside to begin a new, and ultimately fatally corrupt, life in the big city. In spite of a great deal of emotion and violence, there is also an insistent, if somewhat perverse, moral preoccupation. The novels contain events from Restif's own life story and purposefully carry on Rousseau's withering criticism of modern urban life. So did the novels of the Marquis de Sade, all of which were published only after censorship ended during the revolutionary period. These include the counterparts *Justine; ou, Les Malheurs de la vertu* (2 vols., 1791; *Justine; or, The Misfortunes of Virtue*) and *Juliette; ou, Les prospérités du vice* (1797; *Juliette*). But in Sade's work violence (especially sexual violence) is methodical and is coupled with a maniacal will to rationalize the ecstasies it procures. This combination of a kind of libertinism with a rationalism gone beserk gave sadism its name.

Apart from Sade, who was intensely active through the 1790s, the revolutionary era was not particularly propitious for the novel. A number of important earlier works did come to light during this period, however, thanks to the unprecedented freedom accorded to publishers. Diderot's *La Religieuse* (1796; The Nun) and *Jacques le fataliste,* for example, are thought to have been written in the 1760s, but neither was published until 1796. Until then, only a handful of people who had access to manuscript copies knew anything about them; today they are universally considered among Diderot's most important works.

Extreme as he seems, Sade symbolizes the ambiguities of the late 18th century. His protagonists' unfettered individualism makes a break with the solidarity of the existing social fabric and gives them an egomaniacal will to dominate those less powerful than they. Paradoxically, Sade's work seems at the same time to represent the last gasp of aristocratic arrogance, tied to implicit privileges of class (and Sade did come from a prestigious family). The gist of the Revolution was to destroy the past and usher in the future, but aspects of the past came back. Like everything else, the novel had to make its accommodations with the old before it found its way to the new in the 19th century.

PHILIP STEWART

See also Bibliothèque Bleue; Comedy and Humor in the Novel; Conte Philosophique; Denis Diderot; Epic and Novel; Epistolary Novel; Genre Criticism; Julie, or, The New Eloise; Justine; Liaisons dangereuses; Libertine Novel; Libraries; Manon Lescaut; Novel and Romance: Etymologies; Novel of Manners; Romance; Sentimental Novel; Sex, Gender, and the Novel; Voltaire

Further Reading

Chartier, Roger, *Lectures et lecteurs dans la France d'Ancien régime,* Paris: Seuil, 1987

Coulet, Henri, *Le Roman jusqu'à la Révolution,* Paris: Armand Colin, 1967

Démoris, René, *Le Roman à la première personne: Du classicisme aux Lumières,* Paris: Armand Colin, 1975

DiPiero, Thomas, *Dangerous Truths and Criminal Passions: The Evolution of the French Novel, 1569–1791,* Stanford, California: Stanford University Press, 1992

Goodden, Angelica, *The Complete Lover: Eros, Nature, and Artifice in the Eighteenth-Century French Novel,* Oxford: Clarendon Press, and New York: Oxford University Press, 1989

Martin, Angus, Vivienne G. Mylne, and Richard Frautschi, *Bibliographie du genre romanesque français, 1751–1800,* London: Mansell, 1977

May, Georges, *Le dilemme du roman au XVIII siècle: Étude sur les rapports du roman et de la critique, 1715–1761,* New Haven, Connecticut: Yale University Press, and Paris: Presses Universitaires de France, 1962

Mylne, Vivienne, *The Eighteenth-Century French Novel: Techniques of Illusion,* Manchester: Manchester University Press, and New York: Barnes and Noble, 1965

Robert, Marthe, *Roman des origines et origines du roman,* Paris: Grasset, 1972; as *Origins of the Novel,* Bloomington: Indiana University Press, 1980

Rousset, Jean, *Narcisse romancier: Essai sur la première personne dans le roman,* Paris: Corti, 1972

Showalter, English, *The Evolution of the French Novel, 1641–1782,* Princeton, New Jersey: Princeton University Press, 1972

Stewart, Joan Hinde, *Gynographs: French Novels by Women of the Late Eighteenth Century,* Lincoln: University of Nebraska Press, 1993

Stewart, Philip, *Imitation and Illusion in the French Memoir-Novel, 1700–1750,* New Haven, Connecticut: Yale University Press, 1969

Versini, Laurent, *Laclos et la tradition, essai sur les sources et la technique des "Liaisons dangereuses,"* Paris: Klincksieck, 1968

French Novel

1800–1850

The 19th century in France opened with the rise of the romantic novel following the success of François-René de Chateaubriand's *René* (1802). The culmination of a long-standing French tradition of first-person narratives, the romantic novel displays an intense interest in the psychology of its protagonists. The dominant form was that of a life story related face to face, in letters written to a privileged correspondent, or in diaries and notes intended for the writer alone. All enhance the reader's feeling of direct engagement with the narrator's problems.

The problems saturating romantic first-person psychological fiction were dominated by a syndrome called the *mal du siècle,* or "world-weariness"—a deep melancholy that sapped the characters' energy, spoiled their pleasure, and cast a dishonorable light on their actions. *René,* which codified the *mal du siècle* as a French literary motif, was quickly followed by Etienne Pivert de Senancour's *Obermann* (1804), while other influential works kept the motif prominent as the century progressed. Benjamin Constant's *Adolphe* (1816), Charles-Augustin de Sainte-Beuve's *Volupté* (1834; Pleasure), Alfred de Musset's *La confession d'un enfant du siècle* (1836; *Confessions of a Child of the Century*), and other novels regularly applied the first-person form to a life filled with first-magnitude miseries. The protagonists of France's first-person novels were by no means the only characters who suffered. The men in torment had ghastly effects on those who loved them, especially their women. Betrayal and cruelty were salient in relations between the sexes in the lives of successors to René, who repeatedly took sadistic pleasure in the varieties of pain they inflicted on their lovers.

The period also produced a number of women authors whose works took a radically different view of the sexual contact zone. Near the beginning of the century, for example, Germaine de Staël wrote two novels that challenged women's standard place in romantic fiction. *Delphine* (4 vols., 1802) and *Corinne; ou, L'Italie* (3 vols., 1807), which set female title characters against the male title characters of *René, Adolphe, Obermann,* and other works by Staël's contemporaries, widened the horizons of the French novel by taking women's accomplishments as seriously as their tears. Staël's critical and philosophical writings, for which she is better known, added force to her novelistic representation of women.

A development of capital importance in the history of the French novel took place in the second quarter of the 19th century with Stendhal's and Honoré de Balzac's elevation of realist fiction to hitherto unknown levels. The forms those two authors adopted had a huge impact on subsequent novelistic developments, not only in Europe and the Americas but in Asia and Africa as well. Although many schools have mounted vigorous challenges to realism since Balzac and Stendhal wrote their major works, alternative forms are invariably presented and understood as just that—alternatives to realism. Dominance provokes dissent as well as imitation, and for almost two centuries novelists who do not follow realist conventions have felt obliged to explain why. Opponents as well as partisans certify realism as the closest thing to a standard form the novel has yet known. This status owes largely to the fact that French realism incor-

porated a social vision far sharper than its predecessors, as two scenes from before and after the turning point of 1830 illustrate. The first comes from a romantic novel, Chateaubriand's *René,* the second from Balzac's *Le père goriot* (1835; translated as *Le Père Goriot* and as *Old Goriot*). René, Chateaubriand's protagonist and narrator, is a tormented young man who movingly communicates his feelings through description and imagery. During a visit to Mount Etna, at the crater's lip, René peers into the inferno below and compares it to his own emotions. He too is a churning, molten mass threatening to explode. The symbol—apposite, memorable, and communicated in well-wrought prose—is superbly suited to René's psychology. But the episode leaves extrapsychological questions unanswered. How did René travel during the tour that took him to Etna? What were his lodging arrangements? Who packed his bags? How did he deal with money while away from France? More immediately, how did he get to the top of the active volcano that showed him the state of his soul? The text's goal is only to represent its protagonist's inner state, and it comfortably ignores the outer world.

Balzac's *Le Père Goriot* concludes by setting its protagonist, Eugène de Rastignac, in an elevated place that is also charged with intense symbolic meaning. But the similarities end there. Rastignac's elevation signals not volcanic feelings but prosaic participation in a funeral ceremony. If *René* is silent on the concrete arrangements surrounding its protagonist's ascent of Mount Etna, *Le Père Goriot* goes to the opposite extreme. The narrative specifies what means of transportation took Rastignac from what church to what cemetery and answers a wealth of other questions as to who conducted the funeral ceremony, how much they were paid for it, who carried the coffin, and who tipped the grave diggers. In the romantic novel, psychological delineation is so compelling that nothing else matters. In the realist novel, material conditions have a textual presence of their own.

Yet the most important difference between the romantic and the realist novel is not in how the protagonists reach their high places but in what they see when they look down. René finds a symbol for his soul, a perfect image of his character and condition. Rastignac finds not an image of himself but a city that is supremely indifferent to his existence. He resolves to become prominent and powerful in that city, but he does so with the awareness that the only way to succeed is to play by the city's rules, which decree that he must abandon all the personal qualities that made him think he deserved success in the first place. The romantic hero comes down from the heights with a confirmed sense of identity. The realist hero gains a deflating awareness that he is becoming a person he never has been nor ever wanted to be. In the one case, the world reflects the protagonist. In the other, it transforms him.

The achievement of Balzac and Stendhal was to create this powerful method for conveying the way the external world transforms individual lives, which is largely responsible for French realism's status as a fictional model. Realist characters have to make their way through a solid universe, a resistant physical environment that reflects an interest in the impact of social and economic conditions. Realist narratives unfold in precisely defined circumstances shaped by historical forces that exercise intense pressure on the characters' lives.

Balzac took the word *milieu* to describe the social and economic environment of his novels from zoological writings. To him, looking at a person without examining society was as foolish as looking at a fish without considering water. Balzac's most explicit statement of the importance of milieu is to be found in his 1842 preface to *La Comédie humaine* (*The Human Comedy*), the collective title for the immense series of novels and tales he wrote in the 20 years before his death in 1850. Besides their common concern for the determining influence of social and economic factors on biography and personality, the works in *The Human Comedy* are linked through the many characters that appear in more than one of them. The confines of a single novel were inadequate to Balzac's vision of the human condition and the complexities of milieu. He widened the scope of his novels by linking them through the reappearance of characters in different novels. As Balzac's preface put it, *The Human Comedy* set itself the task of "copying all of society, grasping it in the immensity of its upheavals." Each individual tale was to be a chapter in that overarching design.

The project was grand, the execution admirable. *The Human Comedy* includes several novels that have mattered most in the history of prose fiction. *Eugénie Grandet* (1833), *Les Illusions perdues* (1837–43; *Lost Illusions*), *La Cousine Bette* (1846), and *Le Cousin Pons* (1847) have joined *Le Père Goriot* in stimulating the ambition of writers and satisfying readers.

Perhaps because of Balzac's importance in the Marxist critical tradition, his representation of the economic constituents of social interaction has pride of place in standard definitions of Balzacian realism. Friedrich Engels claimed that he and Karl Marx had learned more from Balzac than from all the economists, historians, and social theorists who ever lived, and critics have abundantly shown the extent to which *The Human Comedy* prefigures Marx's historical materialism. But Balzac's reputation has survived intact in an age that has dealt crushing blows to Marx's, and it would be a mistake to restrict Balzac's concern with collective social forces to his prophetic insights into economic organization.

That error would even more seriously distort the novels of French realism's other founder, Stendhal, whose fascination with society never focused primarily on economics. Stendhal's pluralist vision of social practices has special weight in the history of realism because he was writing a masterpiece while Balzac was still feeling his way. Stendhal's *Le Rouge et le noir* (*The Red and the Black*) appeared in 1830, before any of the monuments of *The Human Comedy*. In it as in Stendhal's other major works, *La Chartreuse de Parme* (1839; *The Charterhouse of Parma*) and *Lucien Leuwen* (written 1834–35, posthumously published), the realist drama that pits the self against the world is in no sense limited to financial conflict. Stendhal's characters, similar to Balzac's in their awareness that money is essential to survival, differ in their strong feeling that money is only one of many requisites of a life worth living. They differ even more in the extent to which they overcome obstacles imposed by their milieu and are able to experience—always intensely, almost always briefly—the kind of life they want. Those whom Stendhal called the "happy few" learn to think original thoughts and feel powerful emotions despite their existence in a world that rewards nothing

but stale clichés and affectless conformity. Some of Stendhal's characters too are crushed by the drab world around them, but they have a lot more fun than Balzac's before they succumb. Both Balzac and Stendhal relied on omniscient narrators who have access to the thoughts of all principal characters.

Roughly contemporaneous with Balzac, George Sand wrote novels that continued Staël's achievements in subverting gender stereotypes. *Indiana*, the first work Sand signed with the name she would make famous, appeared in 1832. Its defiance of received ideas on woman's place was spirited and explicit, and a series of novels of comparably subversive purport immediately followed. One, *Lélia* (1833), joined repudiation of standard novelistic structures to a denunciation of standard models for female behavior. Other social concerns also acquired a prominent place in Sand's writing. Her fiction has striking affinities with that of Flora Tristan (*Méphis*, 1838) and Claire de Duras (*Ourika*, 1824), whose novels also integrate feminist issues with inquiry into other social problems. At the same time, Sand's ongoing interest in new models for heterosexual relationships resonated strongly with works like *Nélida* (1846), written by Daniel Stern, a woman who, like Sand, published under a man's name.

In the late 1840s, Sand wrote a series of pastoral novels including *La Petite Fadette* (1849; *Little Fadette*) and *François le champi* (1848; *Francis the Waif*). The great popularity of her pastoral fiction has sometimes prevented Sand's other work from receiving the critical respect and popular interest it deserves. Yet her novels, like Balzac's, cross generic frontiers with fully justified confidence. The volume of work she produced is only slightly more breathtaking than its variety.

Again like Balzac, Sand was quite receptive to a new publication format opened to French novelists in the 1830s: serial appearance in newspapers. But readers of novels published in short segments demanded a highly suspenseful plot, which the authors who have become classics did not always take as their primary compositional goal. Partly in consequence, the period when novels began to appear serially is also the period in which "serious" and "popular" fiction began to diverge from one another. Popular novels were those that made readers eager to learn what happened next, and in the 1840s Alexandre Dumas and Eugène Sue proved adept at instilling such eagerness with steady regularity and unfailing ingenuity. Dumas' *Les Trois Mousquetaires* (1844; *The Three Musketeers*) and *Le Comte de Monte-Cristo* (1845; *The Count of Monte-Cristo*), which continue to provide narrative delight in our own day, were only two of the many page-turners with which he made newspaper readers and newspaper publishers happy. Eugène Sue's tales have aged less gracefully, but his best-known works—*Les Mystères de Paris* (1843–44; *The Mysteries of Paris*) and *Le Juif errant* (1844–45; *The Wandering Jew*)—were extremely successful in their day. Serial publication in newspapers gave novelists access to a vastly increased reading public, and Sue satisfied its desires as well as anyone ever has.

Dumas' *Three Musketeers*, set in the 17th century, demonstrates that newspaper serials were open to historical fiction as well as to the focus on contemporary life of Sue's *Mysteries of Paris*. This interest in the past also sustained an important tradition of historical fiction that went back to the first part of the 19th century and French enthusiasm for the novels of Sir Walter Scott. Scott's influence across the channel was so great that Balzac wrote of France's need for less "walterscotted" fiction, works that did something more than apply Scott's method to French chronicles.

Several historical novels did succeed in following Scott's lead without walking in his footsteps. Victor Hugo's *Notre Dame de Paris* (1831; *The Hunchback of Notre Dame*) was set in the Middle Ages, Alfred de Vigny's *Cinq-Mars* (1825) in the 17th century, Prosper Mérimée's *Chronique du règne de Charles IX* (1829; *A Chronicle of the Reign of Charles IX*) in the 16th. Each helped to form a particularly French tradition of historical fiction, and each continues to find readers in France and elsewhere. With its large number of cinematic adaptations, *The Hunchback of Notre Dame* is finding viewers as well.

Development of historical fiction with a thoroughly French cast coincided with a renewal of French historiography, principally in reaction to the Revolution. That cataclysm was the first of a series of events that was to mark French novels as well as French life in the 19th century. Between 1800 and 1850, France's endless political upheavals were the wonder of Europe. In 50 years, the nation changed its constituent principles no fewer than six times, moving from an empire through two distinct monarchies headed by two different dynasties before becoming a republic. Moreover, shifts from one political system to another were marked by revolutions and abdications generally considered impossible right up to the moment that they became actual. The omnipresence of politics in French life led some novelists to resolve that nothing in fiction should recall it—Théophile Gautier's *Mademoiselle de Maupin* (2 vols., 1835) is a foundational document for the aesthetic creed of art for art's sake—but the more common response was to bring the same sociohistorical passions into the novel. That response, which characterized historical fiction as well as realist novels focusing on contemporary life, makes the first half of the 19th century in France a time of remarkable interaction between the real and the fictional. Scholars have often seen the French Revolution as the beginning of the modern world. It was during the national effort to comprehend and live with that beginning that authors developed the forms of the modern novel.

SANDY PETREY

See also Adolphe; City and the Novel; Corinne; Alexandre Dumas; Historical Novel; Victor Hugo; Human Comedy; Mimesis; Mysteries of Paris; Père Goriot; Realism; René; Romantic Novel; George Sand; Stendhal

Further Reading

Auerbach, Erich, *Mimesis: Dargestellte Wirklichkeit in der abendländischen Literatur,* Bern: Francke, 1946; as *Mimesis: The Representation of Reality in Western Literature,* Princeton, New Jersey: Princeton University Press, 1953

Barthes, Roland, *S/Z,* Paris: Editions du Seuil, 1970, as *S/Z,* London: Cape, and New York: Hill and Wang, 1975

Kelly, Dorothy, *Fictional Genders: Role and Representation in Nineteenth-Century French Narrative,* Lincoln: University of Nebraska Press, 1989

Levin, Harry, *The Gates of Horn: A Study of Five French Realists,* New York: Oxford University Press, 1963; London: Oxford University Press, 1986

Lukács, Georg, *Essays über Realismus,* Berlin: Aufbau, 1948; as *Studies in European Realism: A Sociological Survey of the Writings of Balzac, Stendhal, Zola, Tolstoy, Gorki, and Others,* London: Hillway, 1950; New York: Fertig, 1996

Petrey, Sandy, *Realism and Revolution: Stendhal, Balzac, Zola, and the Performances of History,* Ithaca, New York: Cornell University Press, 1988

Praz, Mario, *The Romantic Agony,* London: Oxford University Press, 1933; 2nd edition, London and New York: Oxford University Press, 1951

Prendergast, Christopher, *The Order of Mimesis: Balzac, Stendhal, Nerval, Flaubert,* Cambridge and New York: Cambridge University Press, 1986

Schor, Naomi, *Breaking the Chain: Women, Theory, and French Realist Fiction,* New York: Columbia University Press, 1985

Turnell, Martin, *The Novel in France: Mme de Lafayette, Laclos, Constant, Stendhal, Balzac, Flaubert, Proust,* London: Hamish Hamilton, 1950; New York: New Directions, 1951

Waller, Margaret Ann, *The Male Malady: Fictions of Impotence in the French Romantic Novel,* New Brunswick, New Jersey: Rutgers University Press, 1993

French Novel

1850–1914

Eighteen Forty-Eight, the year the workers rose up and toppled the July Monarchy, has long been held to be the great turning point in 19th-century French history and literature. In 1842, Stendhal was struck down in the street by a fatal stroke, and in 1850 Balzac died prematurely of a heart attack; when, following the Coup d'État of 2 December 1851, his arch-enemy "Napoléon le Petit" was installed as Emperor, Victor Hugo went into a 19-year self-imposed exile on the island of Guernsey, and George Sand, who had been an active participant in the Revolution of 1848, retired in disillusionment to her country manor in the Berry to write her autobiography. Events in the year 1848 produced a split between art and society and deeply marked the generation that lived through it, the reigning bourgeois class and its sons and daughters that eventually gave birth to the avant-garde movements of the dawning modernist age.

There was, however, no violent aesthetic rupture at

mid-century; romanticism did not die out—and neither, of course, did realism—with the coming of the Second Empire; their legacies were long lasting and have continued to pervade the novel throughout the decades, well into the 20th century. Realism, which initially was pitted against classical idealism, triumphed at mid-century and became the dominant aesthetic movement and representational mode, drawing much of its power from such realist painters as Courbet and Manet and such apologists of realism as Duranty and Champfleury. The relationship between narrative mimetic realism and realist painting does not, however, begin to exhaust a far more complex play between the two media, or rather between writing and visual culture in the 19th century. The study of the relationship between pictorial and literary representation, a Platonic inquiry still at work in recent structuralist poetics, is based on the assumption that the only proper relationship is that between two forms of high art. But realism participates in, is informed and indeed transformed by a culture increasingly more visual, consisting in alternative, "spectacular" forms of realism, such popular art forms as panoramas, wax museums, and other spectacles that fulfill a nearly insatiable desire for the real in a society increasingly invaded by a technology of seeing.

Both Flaubert and Zola, the two preeminent novelists of the latter half of the 19th century, labored in the giant shadow cast by Balzac. Their prime concern was to distinguish themselves from their great predecessor, and they did so in vastly different ways. Flaubert's case is particularly complex as he steadfastly refused the tag *realist* that contemporary critics had affixed to his work. Moreover, several of his works lie beyond the pale of realism, not to say the novel. Neither *La Tentation de Saint Antoine* (1874; *The Temptation of Saint Anthony*) nor *Salammbô* (1862; *Salammbô*) deals with contemporary life that is the stuff and substance of 19th-century French realism. And yet in some of his masterworks, *Madame Bovary* (1857), *L'Éducation sentimentale* (1869; *A Sentimental Education*), and "Un Coeur simple" (1877; "A Simple Heart"), Flaubert adhered in exemplary fashion to the realist emphasis on the detailed description of bourgeois spaces, objects, and commodities and of the lives of ordinary people.

In the place of such energetic Balzacian heroes as Eugène de Rastignac, Flaubert substituted such "unheroic heroes" as Frédéric Moreau in *A Sentimental Education*. Rastignac's focused, ruthless, and successful ambition is replaced by Frédéric's passivity, indecisiveness, and ultimate failure. But what really distinguishes Flaubert from Balzac are Flaubert's formal innovations, notably his use of "free indirect discourse" to provide the reader with unimpeded access to the characters' interiority. Whereas the typical realist novel features an omniscient, interventionist, and solicitous narrator, Flaubert's stated ideal was a god-like narrator, a *deus absconditus*, everywhere present, nowhere visible.

In the preliminary notes he wrote for himself before undertaking his 20-volume Rougon-Macquart cycle, Zola outlined the "differences" between Balzac and himself, notably his focus on the family as the prime social unit in lieu of Balzac's creation of a micro-society of recurrent characters. But the disengagement of Zola from Balzac, that is of naturalism from realism, is a more complex move than Zola recognizes, so much so that one can begin by asking whether the difference between the two is quantitative (in which case naturalism is merely a heightened form of realism) or qualitative (in which naturalism is an autonomous

movement that breaks with realism and paves the way for symbolism). Although the answer to this question remains ultimately indeterminate, one can point to certain significant differences, such as Zola's use of the laws of heredity, social Darwinism, and the Second Law of Thermodynamics. The enlisting of scientific models and paradigms was not in itself an innovation, for already Balzac had invoked the methods of the paleontologists Cuvier and Geoffroy Saint-Hilaire as models for undertaking the detailed description of contemporary society. What distinguishes naturalism from realism—an elusive difference at best—are the scientific paradigms that undergird them. Basing himself on the work of Claude Barnard, Zola theorized a new "experimental novel," and in his hands realism became a determinism.

A famous telegram by a Henri Céard, a member of the so-called "School of Médan," declared in the late 1880s, "Naturalism not dead. Letter follows." Although Zola survived into the 20th century, naturalism as a literary movement did die, marking the end of the dominance of realism in the 19th century or, more precisely, of 19th-century realism. In Zola's wake the family, situated midway between the individual and the collective, became the pivotal mediating social unit, and the Rougon-Macquart inspired later family cycles such as Roger Martin du Gard's *Les Thibaults* (1922–40; *The Thibaults*). But the main legacy of naturalism was its break with the French avatar of Victorian prudery, and as such naturalism opened the way to psychoanalysis—Zola was a favorite author of Freud's—and the exposure of the body, with its functions and pathologies: defecation, childbirth, and delerium tremens among others. In Zola's late novel, *Fécondité* (1899; *Fruitfulness*) Paris is a city drowning in wasted sperm and aborted fetuses. Whereas realism in its heyday focused on the individual bourgeois, naturalism redrew the social hierarchy and for the first time workers such as miners, maids, conductors, roofers, and fishmongers were admitted onto the scene of representation, even as the crowd replaced the solitary, solipsistic hero or heroine. Hugo's *Les Misérables* (1862; *Les Misérables*), the Goncourts' *Germinie Lacerteux* (1865), and Jules Vallès' Jacques Vingtras trilogy, *L'Enfant* (1879; The Child), *Le bachelier* (1881; The Bachelor), and *L'insurgé* (1886; *The Insurrectionist*), are among the novels that represent this extension of the novel to include the class of the disenfranchised and the language of the uneducated.

Between the fall of the Second Empire and the Commune and the outbreak of World War I in 1914, the French novel, freed of the constraints and conventions of realism and naturalism, entered a fascinating period of experimentation and innovation that paved the way for future developments. Traditionally, *fin-de-siècle* fiction is categorized as *decadent*, the literary production of a society bereft of ideals and suffering from an aesthetic hangover. J.-K. Huysmans, who had been a member of the School of Médan, wrote the book that came to epitomize decadence, *À rebours* (1884; *Against Nature*), where the main protagonist, the aesthete Des Esseintes, retires from the social world into a world of his own making, dedicated to realizing his fantasies and enjoying exquisite sensual pleasures. In this ultimate travel novel, Des Esseintes never leaves home.

The fear and mobility of castration are a salient feature of decadent fiction, and gender bending is rampant. The most celebrated of these sexually perverse novels, *Monsieur Vénus* (1884; *Mister Venus*) by the prolific woman novelist who wrote under the pen name Rachilde, represents an astonishing instance of role reversal. But by far the most striking example of late 19th-century fiction is a remarkable novel written at the point of intersection between decadence and symbolism, Villiers de l'Isle Adam's *L'Eve future* (1886; *Eve of the Future Eden*). A rich mix between the most precious symbolist prose and a conventional 19th-century plot (just as Proust incorporates a traditional French psychological novel, *Un Amour de Swann* [*Swann's Love*] in the innovative *Du Côté de chez Swann* [1913; *Swann's Way*] Villiers grounds his science fiction in an eminently readable love story), *Eve of the Future Eden* rings the changes on a century of misogyny and inaugurates a century of technology, not that the two are mutually incompatible. On the contrary. Realism had a pronounced affinity for the representation of woman; thus the superseding of realism by symbolism entails the replacement of "real" women by replicants: the future Eve is an android.

The major historical event of the fin de siècle was the Dreyfus affair, which inspired various novels, including Marcel Proust's *Jean Santeuil* (written 1895–99, published 1952; *Jean Santeuil*), Roger Martin du Gard's *Jean Barois* (1913; *Jean Barois*), and Zola's *Vérité* (1903; *Truth*). As French nationalism grew anti-Semitic, nationalist fiction became popular, producing a subgenre of realist fiction, the *roman à thèse* (ideological novel)—notably Maurice Barrès' *Les Déracinés* (1897; *The Rootless*), Paul Bourget's *L'Étape* (1902; The Stage), Octave Mirbeau's *Journal d'une femme de chambre* (1900; Diary of a Chambermaid), and Zola's post–Rougon-Macquart city trilogy (*Lourdes, Rome,* and *Paris,* 1894–98) and his unfinished evangelical quartet (*Fécondité, Travail,* and *Vérité*).

Decadence was, ultimately, a short-lived movement, and the turn of the century may be viewed in another perspective as *la belle époque,* which is generally said to begin in 1885, the date of Victor Hugo's extraordinary state funeral, and to extend to 1914. Viewed from this angle, the turn of the century appears as a fertile period that saw the emergence of those writers—Colette, André Gide, and Marcel Proust—who were to become the major figures of what we might call French modernism, although modernism is strictly speaking a foreign, especially British, movement with no French homologue; it is not part of French periodization.

Both Colette's and Gide's early works testify to a veritable explosion of new sexualities, exploring realms of the senses that heretofore had been largely occulted: female sexuality, including lesbianism, as lived by a female subject, as in Colette's *La Vagabonde* (1911; *The Vagabond*), and male homosexuality, as in Gide's *L'Immoraliste* (1902; *The Immoralist*). Interestingly, both texts revert to the pre-realist first-person narrative form, the traditional French psychological novel form adequate to the exploration and constitution of subjectivity. However, these texts renew the genre by artfully combining fiction and autobiography, when they do not call into question the seemingly clear-cut opposition between the two. Moreover, whereas there had been many women writers in earlier periods, Colette's writing broke new ground, earning Hélène Cixous' designation of Colette as one of the rare practitioners of what Cixous has called *écriture féminine* (*feminine writing*), a writing out of the female body.

Curiously, French writers of the modernist period share a common trait, a certain marginality in relation to dominant French bourgeois social norms. Femininity, homosexuality, Protestantism, and Jewishness—these are the lived conditions out of which, variously, Colette, Gide, and Proust emerged, of-ten with great difficulty. Whereas Colette's early works seem to spring like Minerva full blown from Jupiter's brow, Gide's early fiction emerges slowly from a heterogeneous corpus of early works steeped in symbolist neo-classicism and metafictional parody, notably *Paludes* (1895; *Marshlands*). Gide's prewar fiction consists in the curious trilogy: *La Porte étroite* (1909; *Straight Is the Gate*), *The Immoralist,* and *Les Caves du Vatican* (1914; *The Vatican Cellars*), which Gide very explicitly refused to call novels, reverting to such genres as the *récit* and the archaic *sotie.* Indeed he wrote only one book to which he gave the name novel (and it may perhaps more aptly be called an anti-novel), *Les Faux-monnayeurs* (1926; *The Counterfeiters*).

Swann's Way unquestionably represents the culmination of *belle époque* fiction and constitutes the hinge between the pre- and post–World War I French novel. Oscillating between the omniscient, third-person narrator, who recounts the novel within a novel, *Un Amour de Swann,* and Marcel, the first-person narrator whose *Bildung* is the narrative stuff of Proust's multi-volume magnum opus, *À la recherche du temps perdu* (1913–27; translated as *Remembrance of Things Past* and also as *In Search of Lost Time*), *Swann's Way* is a transitional novel that carries the fusion of fiction and auto-fiction to its logical extreme.

Nineteenth-century French fiction, with some memorable exceptions—the final paragraph of Flaubert's *A Sentimental Education,* for example—had been relentlessly forward driven, little given to retrospection. Memory, longing for the past and the lost, nostalgia, and an endless if intermittent mourning are the new affects that inhabit the Proustian narrator. Neither the grail nor fame and fortune are his objects of desire; anamnesis is, rather, the object of his quest. An inveterate reader of the 19th-century French fiction he so deftly parodies in *Pastiches et Mélanges* (1919), Proust, no less than Flaubert and Zola, wrote in the shadow of Balzac to whom he devotes two essays in *Contre Sainte-Beuve* (written 1908–10, published 1954; *Against Sainte-Beuve*), even as he inaugurates the modern novel.

To speak in terms of realism, naturalism, and even symbolism in the case of Proust is strangely beside the point. A contemporary of Freud and Bergson, Proust was the prototypical modernist, participating in an epoch-making shift from a fiction ruled by space to a fiction informed by time and its vagaries. Although leading critics of modernism have argued the opposite, the equation of modernism with space seems counterintuitive, for Proust unquestionably belongs to "the culture of time" that took hold at the turn of the century.

NAOMI SCHOR

See also Against Nature; Critics and Criticism (19th Century); Decadent Novel; Gustave Flaubert; André Gide; Victor Hugo; Ideology and the Novel; Naturalism; Marcel Proust; Rougon-Macquart; George Sand

Further Reading

Barbéris, Pierre, *Balzac: Une mythologie réaliste,* Paris: Larousse, 1971
Cohen, Margaret, and Christopher Prendergast, editors, *Spectacles of Realism: Body, Gender, Genre,* Minneapolis: University of Minnesota Press, 1995
Compagnon, Antoine, *Proust entre deux siècles,* Paris: Seuil, 1989; as *Proust: Between Two Centuries,* New York: Columbia University Press, 1992

Culler, Jonathan, *Flaubert: The Uses of Uncertainty,* Ithaca, New York: Cornell University Press, and London: Elek, 1974; revised edition, Ithaca, New York: Cornell University Press 1985

Hamon, Philippe, *Expositions: Littérature et architecture au XIXe siècle,* Paris: Corti, 1989; as *Expositions: Literature and Architecture in Nineteenth-Century France,* Berkeley: University of California Press, 1992

Kleeblatt, Norman, editor, *The Dreyfus Affair: Art, Truth, and Justice,* Berkeley: University of California Press, 1987

Schor, Naomi, *Zola's Crowds,* Baltimore: Johns Hopkins University Press, 1978

Shattuck, Roger, *The Banquet Years: The Origins of the Avant-Garde in France, 1885 to World War I,* New York: Harcourt Brace, and London: Faber, 1958; revised edition, New York: Random House, 1968; London: Cape, 1969

Suleiman, Susan Rubin, *Authoritarian Fictions: The Ideological Novel as a Literary Genre,* New York: Columbia University Press, 1983

French Novel

1914–1945

The period from 1914 through 1945 was one of broad cultural changes, including radical changes in the arts. The novel both reflected and contributed to these changes. Characterized by a great deal of vitality and originality, the first half of the 20th century must be viewed as one of the major periods of French fiction. Despite unfavorable conditions for creative work and the wartime death of numerous established and aspiring writers, an impressive number of novelists were active. Before 1914, André Gide, Marcel Proust, Roger Martin du Gard, Jules Romains, and others had introduced fictional innovations in form and content, and the new departures corresponded to changes in their understanding of what literature could and should do and how it related to reality, both outer and inner. After 1918, certain of these innovations were further developed, and additional fictional experiments were undertaken by the surrealists and others.

Among the departures illustrated before 1914 and developed subsequently were the emphasis on crowd as agent in Romains' work, Proust's interior monologue (devised independently of Anglophone stream-of-consciousness writing), and Gide's multi-layered fiction and *composition en abyme* (internal reproduction of the narrative). But some fictional developments seem to have been spawned by World War I itself and its cataclysmic effect on France and the minds of those who reached adulthood then, many of them in the trenches. Before 1914, Jacques Rivière, in a suggestive article, had called for a "novel of adventure"—a rejection of fixed modes. The war provoked a more radical break with the past than he could have imagined, and in its aftermath widespread revulsion against the Western values and nationalist system that had not prevented the bloodbath led to denunciation of inherited cultural products, including the novel, and frenzied attempts to create new ones. The understanding of what comprised suitable form and appropriate subject matter broadened, and numerous authors devised imaginative ways to render what they saw as a vastly altered reality.

The most famous French novel of World War I, Henri Barbusse's *Le Feu: Journal d'une escouade* (1916; *Under Fire: The Story of a Squad*), based partly on his battlefield diary, is illustrative. The episodic construction, collective action, slang, and violence—all uncharacteristic of most prewar French fiction—reflect the conditions of battle, including the tendency toward loss of individuality and the horror and formlessness of events, which at their worst defy linear narration. The book sold widely and was translated into German and other languages.

To be sure, after 1914 some inherited types and modes continued to flourish. Foremost among them is realism, as established by 19th-century novelists, from romantic realists—Stendhal, Prosper Mérimée, and Honoré de Balzac—through Gustave Flaubert and the naturalists, chiefly Émile Zola, Guy de Maupassant, and Jules and Edmond de Goncourt. Such writers as Maurice Barrès, Paul Bourget, and the ironist Anatole France, who all lived past 1920 and were highly regarded by middle-class readers, continued the tradition. One must distinguish here between mimetic realism, which attempts to depict accurately the material world, and the formulaic, often reductive realist fiction that is characterized by edifying themes and positivistic social ideas, including the assumption that social mechanisms are knowable. Whereas mimetic fiction remained dominant from 1914 through 1945 and did not disappear wholly even among the experimental novelists of the 1950s, characteristic 19th-century ways of handling plot and character fell from favor. Many authors, turned cynical, were loath to impose order on a disordered reality, instead allowing events and impressions to dictate the shape of their work.

Novelists practicing mimetic realism displayed a tendency toward fictional expansiveness, reflecting the desire to render accurately and broadly a complex society. Authors who produced lengthy novels include Roger Martin du Gard, who, after *Jean Barois* (1913; *Jean Barois*), a dialogue-novel, returned to third-person narration and authorial omniscience in *Les Thibaults* (1922–40; *The Thibaults*), a roman-fleuve or novel cycle that mirrors with great intelligence segments of 20th-century French society and characters' individual dramas. Another practitioner of the roman-fleuve, Georges Duhamel, undertook to portray multiple families and lives. Similarly, in his 27-volume *Les Hommes de bonne volonté* (1932–46; *Men of Good Will*), Romains dealt with numerous representative characters and groups and attempted to depict the mass experience of war. Even Proust, whose seven-part masterpiece *À la recherche du temps perdu* (1913–27; translated as *Remembrance of Things Past* and also as *In Search of Lost Time*) is highly subjective and poetic in vision and style, is a realist, whose accounts of parties and receptions extend to hundreds of pages. Not only can Balzacian mannerisms be found readily in Proust's chef d'oeuvre, along with a pastiche of the Goncourts, but his probing analysis of appearances, social mechanisms, and behavior as well as his descriptions, precise even when lyrical, make him Balzac's closest 20th-century emulator. These panoramic works testify to the invasion of historical concerns into literature, even as some writers (including Proust himself) were practicing artistic escapism.

Other writers eschewed the series novel but still cultivated the mimetic vein. Gide experimented with form and rejected mechanistic psychology and the "slice-of-life" realistic formula, which his 1914 burlesque *Les Caves du Vatican* (*The Vatican Cellars*) mocks explicitly. Yet he remained concerned with rendering reality, both psychological, as in *La Symphonie pastorale* (1919; *The Pastoral Symphony*), and social, as in *Les Faux-monnayeurs* (1926; *The Counterfeiters*). The professed Catholic François Mauriac, who, before 1914, had published fiction of psychological analysis dealing with tortured, and torturing, human beings, wrote dozens of additional novels marked by stylistic mastery, perceptive depictions of geographic and social milieux, and keen psychological insight. Among those most admired are *Le Baiser au lépreux* (1922; *The Kiss to the Leper*), *Thérèse Desqueyroux* (1927; *Thérèse*), and *Le Noeud de vipères* (1932; *Vipers' Tangle*).

Numerous novelists who came to maturity slightly later have been classified as neorealists, even neonaturalists, since they deal in direct, nonallegorical terms with such topics as the relationships between groups and individuals, the workings of the mind, the behavior of crowds, and social and political issues. The controversial *Voyage au bout de la nuit* (1932; *Journey to the End of the Night*) by Louis-Ferdinand Céline, an embittered war survivor, depicted sordid human experience in powerful images and an idiosyncratic style based on colloquial speech. The work showed how thoroughly former aesthetic standards had been undermined: the idols of style, taste, consistency, rationality, and verisimilitude still had adherents but had been successfully challenged, along with illusions about the perfectibility of society. Jean Giono, known as a pastoralist and displaying a strong tendency toward the mythopoetic, still depicted country life with fidelity, and published a graphic World War I novel, *Le Grand Troupeau* (1931; *To the Slaughterhouse*). Although Georges Bernanos, perhaps the most powerful of French Catholic novelists, abhorred 19th-century scientism and eschewed all models, he nonetheless is a realistic novelist. His studies of perverted or saintly souls in *Sous le Soleil de Satan* (1926; *The Star of Satan*), *La Joie* (1929; *Joy*), and his 1936 masterpiece *Journal d'un curé de campagne* (*The Diary of a Country Priest*) are diagnostics of the exterior world and of tormented individuals whose souls serve as spiritual battlefields. The novels of Julien Green, a Catholic convert, are brooding, melodramatic tales of passion in a world possessed by evil.

There is also a persistent classical vein in the fiction of the period. This term may cause confusion, since 17th-century French classicism was illustrated most brilliantly in the theatre, not the novel. But classical standards of taste, style, and composition, valuing concision, density, and control, were applied likewise in fiction, which centered on psychological analysis and social dynamics. The same themes of manners, behavior, and motivation, rendered in dense yet balanced and polished style, characterize many pages by Proust, Gide, Mauriac, Jean Cocteau, and others. Except for Proust, these authors tended to prefer shorter works—sometimes called *récit* (narrative) rather than *roman* (novel)—with spare plots and few characters.

A brilliant novel, *Le Diable au corps* (1923; *The Devil in the Flesh*) by the prodigy Raymond Radiguet, is in this classical vein, although the youth it portrays display a modern rootlessness and amorality. Similarly, although her subject matter and sensibility are strikingly modern, Colette, who began publishing in 1900 and wrote for the next half-century, is known for her subtle psychological analysis and concise, sensitive prose, which recalls classical styles. Her treatment of women in love and, more generally, the feminine condition is, however, that of an emancipated woman of the 20th century, a feminist in her own mode, even as she acknowledges fealty to the male principle. *Chéri* (1920) and *La Maison de Claudine* (1922; *My Mother's House*) are among her most admired works of the interwar period. With *Alexis; ou, Le Traité du vain combat* (1929; *Alexis*), another woman writer, Marguerite Yourcenar, showed her mastery of the *récit* form and of classical psychological analysis, although in numerous subsequent works she used more complex plots and turned to historical and mythical topics. Another classical-style novelist is Henry de Montherlant, who published novels of psychological analysis and social observation, such as his eccentric war book *Le Songe* (1922; *The Dream*) and *Les Bestiaires* (1926; *The Bullfighters*), in both of which his aristocratic bent is seen in the concise, penetrating style and in his indifference to any values besides those of the inner man, self-controlled and self-sufficient.

Despite mimetic undertakings and an enduring classicism, the 1920s, a period of great vigor in the arts, were marked by new departures, a proclamation of artistic freedom, and some erosion of the very idea of the novel, which had in any case always been the most malleable of genres. Some fictional forms approached the amorphous, while others displayed an increased complexity with multiple levels of narration and points of view, circularity or fragmentation of plot, unstable characterization, fictional self-referentiality and self-consciousness, and open endings. The idea of the unconscious, foreshadowed in Racine's drama and other works, was slow to reach France in Freudian form but ultimately did penetrate French thought and was reflected in French fiction. Additional foreign influences cannot be overlooked: Fedor Dostoevskii and Franz Kafka were particularly influential, as William Faulkner and John Dos Passos would be later. Certain philosophers exercised a decisive influence on novelists: Karl Marx and Friedrich Nietzsche are the foremost, but one should also mention Edmund Husserl and Henri Bergson. The tendency to replace absolutes and objectivity (in form and content, particularly ethics) with relatives and subjectivity has occasionally led commentators to speak of Einsteinian relativity in fiction, but this dubious analogy serves only to draw attention to generalized changes in modern vision.

Innovations in other arts may have played a role in encouraging fiction writers to abandon fixed forms. Cubism, with its multiple perspectives and nonrepresentational approach, was probably influential. Nevertheless, even at its most radical, fiction retained throughout the period strong mimetic elements as well as the referential power of words themselves, not yet called into question. One observes certainly a mixing of genres, analogous to developments in poetry (free verse, prose poems, mixed genres) and other artistic experiments. Many of Proust's pages would not be out of place in an anthology of aesthetic criticism. Gide compared an ideal novel to Bach's *Art of the Fugue,* and critics have sometimes spoken of his "Cubist" art. The extended monologue of André Breton's *Nadja* (1928) is a psychic experiment. Other fiction is heavily philosophical.

Proust's immense work, the first part of which had startled prewar readers, illustrates fictional change. By its subjectivity, expansion, and apparent aimlessness it seemed to subvert traditional understandings of plot, characterization, and structure, despite the mimetic and classical elements noted above. For his part, Gide developed in *The Counterfeiters* techniques he had introduced earlier in a multilayered, self-conscious fiction involving by turns social and psychological realism, aesthetic theory, and challenges to received notions of morals and the self. Even as he denounced the novel as a genre, André Breton, the principal proponent and leader of surrealism, created in *Nadja* a poetic fiction that rejected traditional narrative (with its presentation of "pseudo-facts") and aimed to recreate psychic reality. Louis Aragon's surrealistic collage narrative, *Le Paysan de Paris* (1926; *Nightwalker*), may be considered an essay on poetic urbanism. Jean Giraudoux, admired for his drama, illustrated in novels such as *Suzanne et le Pacifique* (1921; *Suzanne and the Pacific*) an idiosyncratic poetic style that eschewed mimetic realism in favor of fantasy and psychological games.

Broadly speaking, by 1930 fiction had become less innovative. Proust was dead, and his monumental enterprise found no emulators. Gide's short feminist novel *Geneviève* (1936), a sequel to *L'École des femmes* (1929; *The School for Wives*), was inferior in insight and originality to his previous fiction. Surrealist prose did not disappear, but with the loss of several members (to death and communism) the movement was less productive. Fiction afforded ample evidence, whether direct or indirect, of the pressing social and political dilemmas of the decade, starting with the economic crisis and rearmament of Germany, then the fall of the Weimar Republic and rise of Hitler, followed by the Popular Front government in France, the Spanish Civil War, and the approach of World War II. The euphoria of the rebellious and vigorous 1920s was gone; a powerful, destructive history, which had already terrorized Europe in the form of generalized war once before, seemed again to overwhelm human beings and destroy their freedom to act. What Aragon termed "the real world" increasingly replaced, in fiction, the world of subjectivity, the imagination, and literary experiment. Authors turned away from fanciful and subtle forms in favor of straightforward prose narrative with recognizable situations and characters and social and political themes.

The tendency throughout the decade toward political polarization—the left extreme occupied by doctrinaire and militant communism, the right by monarchism, anti-Semitism, even fascism—is reflected in fiction. Having embraced communism, Aragon undertook realist fiction intended to portray the flawed French class structure and the heroism of the proletariat. *Les Beaux Quartiers* (1936; *Residential Quarter*) is one such work. Paul Nizan, a gifted communist writer, published fictional critiques of capitalism and the bourgeoisie. Eugène Dabit wrote of the extremely modest circumstances he had known. Louis Guilloux similarly depicted, with powerful imagination, what he saw

as modern psychosis and the sufferings of the oppressed. Pierre Drieu La Rochelle, a former surrealist, published a handful of brilliant, idiosyncratic anatomies of contemporary life, including *La Comédie de Charleroi* (1934; *The Comedy of Charleroi and Other Stories*) and *Gilles* (1939), which shed light on his embrace of fascist ideology in 1934. Céline produced another masterpiece, *Mort à crédit* (1936; *Death on the Installment Plan*), before turning to right-wing political polemic.

Three other authors of the late 1920s and 1930s stand out. In masterly, searching prose, André Malraux succeeded in combining metaphysical brooding with political and historical themes. *Les Conquérants* (1928; *The Conquerors*) and *La Voie royale* (1930; *The Royal Way*) are highly original fictions of politics and adventure whose singular style and structure (sometimes considered cinematic), emphasis on acts rather than sentiments, and metaphysical sensibility constitute a radical departure from conventional novels of psychology and manners. Malraux rendered powerfully the Chinese revolution in his 1933 masterpiece *La Condition humaine* (*Man's Fate*) and the Spanish Civil War in *L'Espoir* (1937; *Man's Hope*). Antoine de Saint-Exupéry, another master stylist, pursued the theme of aviation, which he had introduced in *Courrier-sud* (1929; *Southern Mail*), in his narrative about South American mail routes, *Vol de nuit* (1931; *Night Flight*), and in his semifictional *Terre des hommes* (1939; *Wind, Sand and Stars*). Jean-Paul Sartre published *La Nausée* (1938; *Nausea*), his brilliant novel of anti-essentialism and phenomenological adventure, which reveals the influence of both naturalism and surrealism and shows, like Proust's work, that fiction consisting mostly in mental action, or (inaction) can still be dynamic. *Le Mur* (1939; *The Wall and Other Stories*), which has a title story dealing with the Spanish conflict, also contains a superb novella attacking the right-wing bourgeoisie. Two other widely admired existentialist novelists published their first fiction shortly after 1940. Albert Camus' *L'Étranger* (1942; *The Stranger*) conveyed the disengagement and alienation of a generation and became a postwar best-seller. Simone de Beauvoir's first novel, *L'Invité* (*She Came to Stay*), a psychological study in the existentialist mode, appeared in 1943.

Despite these outstanding works by highly talented writers, the last years before World War II, the war years themselves, and the immediate postwar period constitute in some ways the conclusion of a literary period. Rarely have the pressures of history on literature been so great, as social strife increased and the precarious interwar peace was replaced by armed conflict, leading to the fall of France. Under the German occupation, fiction, like poetry, often served as an instrument of protest. Since all works published openly were subject to censorship, anything critical of the German presence could appear only clandestinely. Some resistance novels were brought out by Les Editions de Minuit, a clandestine press, including *Le Silence de la mer* (1941; *The Silence of the Sea*) by Vercors (pseudonym of Jean Bruller), an indictment of the occupation. Others were published in England and parachuted into France. After the war, many works appeared dealing with the war, the occupation, and especially the Resistance.

By 1945, however, some established novelists (Nizan, Saint-Exupéry, Drieu La Rochelle, Robert Brasillach, executed for collaboration) were dead. Malraux turned his attention chiefly to art criticism. Céline, condemned to exile for purported collaboration (his political positions were highly unpopular), subsequently published brilliant books that found few readers. Older authors, such as Colette, Gide, Martin du Gard, and Mauriac, published little or no fiction, although Martin du Gard left a vast posthumous novel. Some outstanding novelists of the 1950s and thereafter, such as Nathalie Sarraute, Samuel Beckett, Claude Simon, and Marguerite Duras, had begun their careers, but either their fiction attracted little notice when it first appeared in the prewar or war years—Sarraute's 1939 *Tropismes* (*Tropisms*) is an example—or was published only after 1945.

The situation of Sartre, whose existentialism became the reigning outlook of the postwar period, is pertinent. In 1945 he brought out two volumes in his series *Les Chemins de la liberté* (*Roads to Freedom*), a third in 1949. Composed before the war's end, they treat the prelude to the conflict and the war itself. The middle volume, *Le Sursis* (*The Reprieve*), shows Sartre at his most innovative, depicting, by means of psychological impressionism, multiple plots and characters, crowd scenes, the Munich crisis, and France's failures. These novels were, however, his last. Liquidating the disengaged man of the prewar, he preferred henceforth political militancy and "committed literature" in the form of drama, journalism, and philosophical essays. While numerous other writers either followed him further into the political arena or continued publishing social or historical novels—Aragon did both—some writers tired of literature's immersion in history: amid the immense social and political problems plaguing France after 1945, including the Cold War, younger authors began to eschew fiction as a social document and to develop a radical subjectivism in startling forms, called, variously, "aliterature," "literature of the absurd," or the nouveau roman.

Catharine Savage Brosman

See also Louis-Ferdinand Céline; André Gide; Man's Fate; Nausea; Politics and the Novel; Marcel Proust; Roman-Fleuve; Stranger; Surrealist Novel; War and the Novel

Further Reading

Becker, Lucille Frackman, *Twentieth-Century French Women Novelists,* Boston: Twayne, 1989

Bersani, Leo, *Balzac to Beckett: Center and Circumference in French Fiction,* New York: Oxford University Press, 1970

Brée, Germaine, *Twentieth-Century French Literature,* Chicago: University of Chicago Press, 1983

Brée, Germaine, and Margaret Guiton, *An Age of Fiction: The French Novel from Gide to Camus,* New Brunswick, New Jersey: Rutgers University Press, 1957; London: Chatto and Windus, 1958; revised as *The French Novel from Gide to Camus,* New York: Harcourt Brace, 1962

Brombert, Victor, *The Intellectual Hero: Studies in the French Novel, 1880–1955,* Philadelphia: Lippincott, and London: Faber, 1961

Brosman, Catharine Savage, editor, *French Novelists, 1900–1930* (Dictionary of Literary Biography, 65), Detroit, Michigan: Gale Research, 1988

Brosman, Catharine Savage, editor, *French Novelists, 1930–1960* (Dictionary of Literary Biography, 72), Detroit, Michigan: Gale Research, 1988

Cocking, J.M., and Martin Jarrett-Kerr, *Three Studies in Modern French Literature,* New Haven, Connecticut: Yale University Press, 1960

Cruickshank, John, editor, *French Literature and Its Background,* volume 6, *The Twentieth Century,* London and New York: Oxford University Press, 1970

Frohock, W.M., *Style and Temper: Studies in French Fiction, 1925–1960,* Cambridge, Massachusetts: Harvard University Press, and Oxford: Blackwell, 1967

Frohock, W.M, editor, *Image and Theme: Studies in Modern French Fiction,* Cambridge, Massachusetts: Department of Romance Languages and Literatures, Harvard University, 1969

Green, Mary Jean Matthews, *Fiction in the Historical Present: French Writers and the Thirties,* Hanover, New Hampshire, and London: University Press of New England, 1986

Greene, Robert W., *Just Words: Moralism and Metalanguage in Twentieth-Century French Fiction,* University Park: Pennsylvania State University Press, 1993

King, Adele, *French Woman Novelists: Defining a Female Style,* London: Macmillan, and New York: St. Martin's Press, 1989

Pasco, Allan H., *Novel Configurations: A Study of French Fiction,* Birmingham, Alabama: Summa, 1987; 2nd edition, 1994

Peyre, Henri, *The Contemporary French Novel,* New York: Oxford University Press, 1955; revised as *French Novelists of Today,* New York: Oxford University Press, 1967

Reck, Rima Drell, *Literature and Responsibility: The French Novelist in the Twentieth Century,* Baton Rouge: Louisiana State University Press, 1969

Suleiman, Susan Rubin, *Authoritarian Fictions: The Ideological Novel as a Literary Genre,* New York: Columbia University Press, 1983

French Novel

1945–

Any discussion of the contemporary novel in France must take into account the impact on the genre of two major events: the emergence of existentialism immediately after World War II and of the *nouveau roman* in the 1950s. The intersection of the history of the French nation and the history of French publishing implicit in both these events must also be recognized if the successive renewals (some would say crises) that the novel in France has undergone since 1945 are to be fully understood. It is noteworthy, for example, that after the war the eminent house of Gallimard, which had continued to function under the German

Occupation, published existentialist "committed writers" like Jean-Paul Sartre and Simone de Beauvoir, whereas Les Editions de Minuit, founded as a clandestine press for the Resistance in 1941, became the cradle of the signally formalist, hence ostensibly apolitical, *nouveau roman.*

The key role of three landmark monthlies in the history of the contemporary French novel should also be noted: *La Nouvelle revue française* (1909–43; 1953–) published by Gallimard; *Les Temps modernes* (1945–), introduced by Gallimard but soon relinquished to les Editions Julliard; and *Critique* (1946–), published by Les Editions de Minuit from 1950 onward. *Les Temps modernes,* which came into existence in the vacuum left by *La Nouvelle revue française* after its suppression by the Commission d'épuration de l'édition in 1944, marks the beginning of a new period in French literature and is therefore a useful vantage point from which to view subsequent developments in the novel—a genre on which it exerted considerable influence.

Edited by Sartre, and appearing for the first time on 1 October 1945, just over a year after the Liberation, *Les Temps modernes* introduced the notion of "committed writing," setting out to account for the modern times that were beginning in the wake of World War II and enlisting philosophy, literature, and politics in the service of this endeavour. For Sartre, writers were always "situated" in a society, whether they acknowledged it or not. To declare oneself a committed writer, however, was to recognize the social function of writing and therefore consciously to assume responsibility for the action in and on history that all writing (with the exception of poetry, so Sartre initially claimed) implies.

"What Is Literature?"—a full-blown account of committed writing—was serialized in *Les Temps modernes* from February to July 1947 under the following headings: "What Is Literature?" "What Is Writing?" "Why Write?" "For Whom Does One Write?" "Situation of the Writer in 1947," and "Writing for One's Age." It is these questions, rather than the answers Sartre so confidently provided at the time, that have remained vital throughout the half-century since they were posed. The various positions adopted by successive generations of writers vis-à-vis the issues Sartre articulated in the aftermath of the Occupation have continued to produce new developments in the French novel, regardless of whether Sartre's program was rejected (as it was by the practitioners of the *nouveau roman,* for example) or ignored (as seems to have been the case with their successors).

"What Is Literature" is not Sartre's only influence on the contemporary French novel, however. *La Nausée* (1938; *Nausea*), with its antihero Roquentin, was a key work in the development of the genre. Incorporating a vigorous critique of those mainstays of fiction—memory and narrative—*Nausea,* Janus-like, looks back to Marcel Proust with an irreverently jaundiced eye and forward to the *nouveau roman,* many of whose preoccupations it anticipates. By the end of World War II Sartre himself was nonetheless turning away from novel writing in favor of the theatre. Thus, of the projected four volumes of his *Les Chemins de la liberté* (1945–49; *Roads to Freedom*), only three were completed.

If Sartre had abandoned the novel form by the end of the 1940s, Simone de Beauvoir (his companion and cofounder of *Les Temps modernes*) continued to produce fiction, albeit of a strongly autobiographical bent. Although her ground-breaking study of women's condition *Le Deuxième sexe* (1949; *The Second Sex*) was badly received by contemporary critics, *Les Man-*

darins (1954; *The Mandarins*), a roman à clef depicting her and Sartre's milieu and their preoccupations as left-wing intellectuals, won the Prix Goncourt in 1954. (Literary prizes, of which there are a remarkable number available for award in France and in French-speaking countries, exert a significant influence on the publication and distribution of novels.) After 1964, however, with the single exception of *La Femme rompue* (1968; *The Woman Destroyed*), Beauvoir devoted herself to nonfiction, notably memoirs. These range from *Mémoires d'une jeune fille rangée* (1958; *Memoirs of a Dutiful Daughter*), the first of four volumes that together provide an invaluable description of intellectual life in Paris during and after World War II, through *Une Mort très douce* (1964; *A Very Easy Death*), an extraordinary account of her mother's terminal illness, to her last book, *Journal de guerre* (1990; *War Journal*), the hitherto unpublished diaries she had kept during World War II. Sartre would eventually turn to autobiography as well, if much less exhaustively, in *Les Mots* (1963; *The Words*), an affecting description of his childhood.

Immediately after the war, Albert Camus (whose novel *L'É-tranger* [1942; *The Stranger*] would later be invoked as a forerunner of the *nouveau roman* and who had refused to join the board of *Les Temps modernes*) published *La Peste* (1947; *The Plague*), in which the plague in Oran is an allegory for the Occupation and for the human condition in general. This was followed by *La Chute* (1956; *The Fall*) and eventually by the publication in draft form of *Le Premier homme* (1994; *The First Man*), the autobiographical novel he had been writing at the time of his premature death in 1961. In the intense discussion provoked by *The First Man* on both sides of the Atlantic, the issues of committed writing, of Camus' position vis-à-vis his native Algeria, and of his political differences with Sartre were again raised after more than a 30-year interval—an indication of their continued pertinence no less than of the powerful place Camus occupies in post–World War II French writing.

The oeuvre of Marguerite Yourcenar represents an interesting variant on the interplay between fiction and memoir that has become progressively more overt in the French novel since 1945. Thus it was the fictitious memoirs of a Roman emperor, *Mémoires d'Hadrien* (1951; *Memoirs of Hadrian*), brilliantly conceived and executed, that initially brought her fame as a novelist, and the three-volume autobiography *Le Labyrinthe du monde* (1974–88; The Labyrinth of the World) that brought her career to a close. Yourcenar, the first woman to be elected (in 1981) to the Académie Française, had joined Gallimard in 1964, well after the success of *Memoirs of Hadrien*, which had been published by Plon. Her complete works were later collected in Gallimard's *Bibliothèque de la Pléiade,* a series whose prestige makes it a powerful lure in the wooing of established writers.

Attracting already well known writers was not on the agenda of Les Editions de Minuit, the "midnight" publishers, when they emerged from secrecy at the end of the war. Minuit had been founded as a clandestine press under the Occupation by Pierre de Lescure and the novelist Vercors (Jean Bruller), whose *Le Silence de la mer* (1941; *The Silence of the Sea*), which depicted the dilemma of a sympathetic German officer, caused a sensation at the time. In 1948 Jérome Lindon, then in his early 20s, assumed the directorship and in 1951 (the year *Memoirs of Hadrien* appeared) he published *Molloy* (1951; *Molloy*), the first of a suite of three novels by a relatively obscure Irishman writing in French—Samuel Beckett. Lindon has repeatedly claimed that it was *Molloy*, which had been turned down by six publishers (including Gallimard, on the advice of Camus) that "made him an editor," and it was indeed the publication of *Molloy* that launched Les Editions de Minuit as the publisher of the avant-garde at the same time that it inaugurated Beckett's fame. "If Les Editions de Minuit exist, it is to Samuel Beckett that they owe their existence," according to Lindon, for whom the reading of *Molloy* in manuscript, toward the end of 1950, was a watershed. If, as he claimed, "Nothing much had happened" during his previous two years as director, "everything that happened thereafter was the direct result [of that reading]," Lindon has said.

With the publication of *Molloy*, followed in rapid succession by *Malone meurt* (1951; *Malone Dies*), the now world-famous play *En attendant Godot* (1952; *Waiting for Godot*), and *L'Innommable* (1953; *The Unnamable*), Beckett's reputation was made (he would be awarded the Nobel prize for literature in 1969), and the course of Les Editions de Minuit as the publishers of as yet undiscovered, challenging, and boldly innovative writers was set. The monthly *Critique*, published by Minuit, played a crucial role in both these developments, since Lindon was able to obtain timely and serious reviews (in Beckett's case by such eminent figures as Georges Bataille and Maurice Blanchot) in *Critique* for the unknown novelists he was promoting. It is an irony of post–World War II publishing in France that *Les Temps modernes*, which had published Beckett in the 1940s, should see him appropriated by Minuit within the decade. *Critique*, whose circulation fell far short of that of *Les Temps modernes* (in 1950, *Critique* circulated 2,700 as compared to *Les Temps modernes*' estimated 10,000), provided a forum not only for the establishment of Minuit's literary image but for the elaboration of a literary theory that was opposed to Sartre's. It was thus in *Critique* that the premonitory signs of what was subsequently called the *nouveau roman* were first to be discerned.

In addition to being influential critics, Georges Bataille (editor of *Critique*) and Maurice Blanchot, a regular contributor to both *Critique* and *La Nouvelle revue française*, were themselves novelists (like many other French critics, then and now) and their novels—Bataille's singular, erotic *Madame Edwarda* (1941/1956; *Madame Edwarda*) and *Le Bleu du ciel* (written in 1935, published 1957; *Blue of Noon*), and Blanchot's obscure and compelling *Thomas l'Obscur* (1941; *Thomas the Obscure*), *Aminadab* (1942), and *Le Très-haut* (1948; *The Most High*)—appear, with hindsight, to announce the advent of the *nouveau roman*.

The term *nouveau roman* was coined by the critic and novelist Émile Henriot, who had no other term for the works—by writers as diverse as Samuel Beckett, Michel Butor, Claude Ollier, Robert Pinget, Alain Robbe-Grillet, Nathalie Sarraute, and Claude Simon—that Les Editions de Minuit began to publish in the 1950s. The label *nouveau roman* was quickly adopted by Lindon and Robbe-Grillet, who immediately saw its utility as a peg on which to hang the uniformly disturbing yet highly disparate novels the press was attracting. The publication of critical essays such as those collected in Nathalie Sarraute's *L'Ère du soupçon* (1956; *The Age of Suspicion*), in Robbe-Grillet's *Pour un nouveau roman* (1963; *For a New Novel*), and in Michel Butor's *Répertoires I–V* (1960–82; *Inventory*) lent further credence to the advent of a *nouveau roman* even as these writers rejected the notion of a school to which they, or anyone else, might be said to belong. It should be noted, in this regard, that Samuel

Beckett, despite his association with it in time, can hardly be described as a practitioner of the *nouveau roman*, and that all of Sarraute's books have been brought out by Gallimard, with the single exception of her first, *Tropismes* (1939; *Tropisms*), the second edition of which was published by Minuit in 1957.

Broadly speaking, the *nouveau roman* marked a rejection at once of certain established conventions of the French novel (plot and character as they had been traditionally conceived, the notion of psychological types, the analysis of feelings) and of Sartre's recent "committed writing"; the new novelists did not share Sartre's views on the social function of literature. The *nouveau roman* set out to question and challenge the novel in its traditional, realist form (a form often too quickly and reductively attributed to Honoré de Balzac). By constantly drawing attention to the novel's fictional status, the *nouveaux romanciers* (new novelists) set out to frustrate their readers' inclination to identify with characters, seeking instead to elicit an identification with the writer (actual or virtual) to whose words alone these characters owed their existence—an existence, moreover, that was rigorously limited to the page. It was argued, notably by Nathalie Sarraute, that the lack of incident and the inconclusiveness of the *nouveau roman*, together with the opacity of the characters and the discontinuity of their conversation, made it in fact more true to life, hence more realistic, than traditional fiction, whose eventful, coherent world peopled by purposeful, relatively transparent individuals is a novelistic convention rather than a representation of reality as most people experience it.

Insisting that it be regarded as a literary genre and not merely as a diversion, the *nouveau roman*, by refusing to sustain the illusions on which the pleasure of readers of novels traditionally depends, made stringent demands on its public, which tended therefore to consist largely of writers and intellectuals. Nonetheless, the *nouveau roman* was well known outside of France, and the work of many of its practitioners (notably Robbe-Grillet, Sarraute, Butor, and Simon) quickly became available in translation.

Representative examples of the *nouveau roman* are Robbe-Grillet's *Les Gommes* (1953; *The Erasers*)—a variant on the detective (gumshoe) novel, described by one critic as "halfway between Simenon and Joyce"—*Le Voyeur* (1955; *The Voyeur*), *La Jalousie* (1957; *Jealousy*), and *Dans le labyrinthe* (1959; *In the Labyrinth*); Sarraute's *Portrait d'un inconnu* (1948; *Portrait of a Man Unknown*), *Martereau* (1953; *Martereau*), *Le Planétarium* (1959; *The Planetarium*)—a brilliantly innovative treatment of a a highly Balzacian theme: the elaborate efforts of a socially ambitious young man to acquire his aging aunt's desirable Paris apartment—and *Les Fruits d'or* (1963; *The Golden Fruits*); Butor's *Passage de Milan* (1954), *L'Emploi du temps* (1956; *Passing Time*), *La Modification* (1957; *A Change of Heart*) written in the second-person plural, and *Degrés* (1960; *Degrees*)—an attempt at a phenomenological description of a high school class on Columbus' discovery of America; Simon's *Le Vent* (1957; *The Wind*), *L'Herbe* (1958; *The Grass*), *La Route des Flandres* (1960; *The Flanders Road*), which hauntingly evokes the disastrous defeat of the French in 1940 via a soldier's quest for the truth about his captain's (and cousin's) death, and *Le Palace* (1962; *The Palace*). Simon was awarded the Nobel prize for literature in 1985. Pinget's *Graal Flibuste* (1956), a voyage journal in the first person describing an explorer's travels in the realm ruled over by the deity named in the title, and *Passacaille* (1969; *Passacaglia*), as well as Claude Ollier's *Eté Indien*

(1963; Indian Summer), should also be noted. The interaction of fiction and theory has been the major preoccupation of Jean Ricardou in his three published novels: *L'Observatoire de Cannes* (1961; The Cannes Observatory), *La Prise de Constantinople* (1965; The Taking of Constantinople), and *Les Lieux-dits* (1969; Localities). Ricardou has also made important contributions to the theory of the *nouveau roman* with *Pour une théorie du nouveau roman* (1971; Towards a Theory of the New Novel) and *Le nouveau roman* (1973; The New Novel).

Of the original *nouveaux romanciers* who survive, Nathalie Sarraute, Claude Simon, Claude Ollier, and Robert Pinget continue to produce fiction. *Ouvrez* (Open Up) by Sarraute (now in her 90s) and *Le Jardin des plantes* (The Botanical Gardens), Simon's first novel since 1989, appeared in the fall of 1997.

Two highly innovative women writers whose fiction was only fugitively associated with the *nouveau roman* were Marguerite Duras and Monique Wittig. Duras, whose *Moderato Cantabile* (1958; Moderato Cantabile) was published by Minuit, remained prolific throughout her long life and earned considerable fame outside France with such novels as *Le Ravissement de Lol V. Stein* (1964; The Ravishing of Lol V. Stein), *Le Vice-Consul* (1966; The Vice-Consul), and especially the autobiographical *L'Amant* (1984; The Lover), winner of the Prix Goncourt and also published by Minuit. Wittig, a Minuit writer whose *L'Opoponax* (1964; The Opoponax) is at once a remarkable evocation of childhood and adolescence and a stylistic tour de force, appears to have abandoned the novel.

The experimental novels written by the members of the group Oulipo (Ouvroir de Littérature Potentielle), created in 1960 and dedicated, in the words of one of its founders, Raymond Queneau, to "the search for new forms and structures that may be used by writers in any way they see fit," should also be mentioned. Oulipo novels, while they play with language, depend on and exploit a chosen linguistic constraint, as in Georges Perec's *La Disparition* (1969; A Void), a 300-page novel written without the letter *e*. Prominent among them are Queneau's *Zazie dans le métro* (1959; Zazie), in which hilarious language play is combined with sharp social comment; Perec's *La Vie mode d'emploi* (1978; Life, A User's Manual), an exhaustive account of all the objects and events in a ten-story Paris apartment building just before 8 P.M. on 23 June 1975; and Jacques Roubaud's *La Belle Hortense* (1985; Our Beautiful Heroine), *L'Enlèvement d'Hortense* (1987; Hortense Is Abducted), in which the author appropriates the history and theory of the novel to comic effect, and *Le Grand Incendie de Londres* (1989; The Great Fire of London), in which Roubaud conducts formal experiments with traditional autobiography.

With the exception of Queneau's *Une Trouille verte* (1947; A Blue Funk), Minuit did not publish the Oulipians, and the "writing adventure" of Philippe Sollers has likewise been pursued outside their purview. The author of a widely acclaimed and quite traditional first novel, *Une Curieuse Solitude* (1958; A Strange Solitude), Sollers, after founding the influential review *Tel Quel* in 1961, went on to produce novels such as *Drame* (1965; Event), *Nombres* (1968; Numbers), and *Lois* (1972; Laws), whose density, length, and idiosyncratic punctuation test the limits of writing (and reading). His fiction took a new turn in 1983 with *Femmes* (Women), the first in a series of romans à clef that includes *Portrait du joueur* (1984; Portrait of a Player) and *Le Coeur absolu* (1987; The Absolute Heart).

Hélène Cixous' quite different, though equally experimental, fiction has never carried the Minuit imprint, despite the fact that her first novel, *Dedans* (1969; Inside), was awarded the Prix Médicis by a jury of Minuit writers. Closely associated with the feminist press *des femmes*, founded in 1973, her verbally playful and highly poetic novels, such as *Tombe* (1973; Tomb), are characterized by an apparently uninhibited flow of language—for her, the mark of a feminine sensibility regardless of the writer's gender. Significantly, Cixous has not used the descriptor *novel* for her fiction since 1973, although she remains a notably prolific writer.

In addition to experimental fiction, more or less traditional novels continued to appear during the 1960s and 1970s, just as works by important writers such as Julien Gracq (*Le Rivage des Syrtes* [1951; The Opposing Shore]) and Julien Green (*Chaque Homme dans sa nuit* [1960; Each Man in His Darkness]) were published alongside the *nouveau roman*. Michel Tournier's mythical novels, *Le Roi des Aulnes* (1970; The Ogre) and *Vendredi; ou, La Vie sauvage* (1971; Friday and Robinson: Life on Eperanza Island), all from Gallimard, have appealed to a popular and literary audience on both sides of the Atlantic as have the novels of Patrick Modiano. Modiano's work focuses on memory, with specific reference to the period of the Occupation, the setting for *La Place de l'étoile* (1968), *La Ronde de nuit* (1969; Night Rounds), and *Les Boulevards de la ceinture* (1972; Ring Roads).

For Jérome Lindon, nonetheless, the period from 1957 (the year of Claude Simon's first novel, *The Wind*) to 1979 (when he published Jean Echenoz's *Le Méridien de Greenwich* [The Greenwich Meridian]) was, he has said, a "slack" one. Monique Wittig and Tony Duvert (*Paysage de fantaisie* [1973; Strange Landscape]) were the only "real writers," by his standard, that Minuit published during the 1960s and 1970s, and both have since given up writing fiction.

Evidently the *nouveau roman* had set a challenging precedent; its practitioners had not only called the novel form into question but had left a body of theory that was bound to make the next generation of novelists self-conscious. In its wake young writers seemed only to have two choices, neither of them interesting: to imitate the *nouveau roman* or to react against it, and it began to look as if the "literary adventure" of Minuit (to use Lindon's phrase) would be limited to the *nouveau roman*.

In fact it took some 20 years for the impact of the *nouveau roman* to be absorbed, but at the end of this interval Les Editions de Minuit again emerged as the publisher of a group of experimental writers, dubbed this time *impassibles* (impassive) or, alternatively, *minimalistes,* an appropriate term to the extent that, with the exception of Jean Echenoz, they tend to produce novels of fewer than 200 pages. The common thread between these writers, however, is their publisher, Minuit. In addition to Echenoz, whose novels—which include *Cherokee* (1983; Cherokee), *L'Equipée malaise* (1986; Double Jeopardy), *Lac* (1989; Lac), and *Nous trois* (1992; We Three)—parody the detective novel and the spy story, other minimalist writers include Jean-Philippe Toussaint (*La Salle de bain* [1985; The Bathroom]), Patrick Deville (*Longue vue* [1988; Long View]), Marie Redonnet (*Splendid Hotel* [1986; Hotel Splendid]), Eric Chevillard (*Le Caoutchouc décidément* [1992; Undoubtedly Rubber]), François Bon (*Limite,* 1985), Christian Gailly (*Dring,* 1991), and Christian Oster (*L'Aventure* [1993; The Adventure]).

Unlike the *nouveaux romanciers,* these writers do not develop theories about the novel alongside and independent from their fiction, which nonetheless includes reflection on itself. Their work tends to be "readable," in contrast to the popular conception of the *nouveau roman* (*The Bathroom* sold 50,000 copies), although several of the new writers have adopted the practice of *mise-en-abyme* so dear to their predecessors. Intertextuality (oblique reference to a wide range of literature) is also characteristic of these novelists and is frequently, in its slyness, a source of the humor that was generally lacking in the *nouveau roman.* At the same time, references to science (the epigraph of *The Bathroom* is Pythagoras' theorem) and popular culture (American B movies and jazz in Echenoz's case) have broadened the focus of the contemporary novel.

Although the work of these writers is generally taken to mark a return to narrative, this does not mean a return to the conventions of the traditional novel. Thus the characters are often caricatures, the narrative thread frequently leads only to digression, and the most important event turns out to be writing itself. On the other hand, in the novels of Jean Rouaud, Marie Ndiaye, and Hervé Guibert, three other Minuit writers of the same generation, it is possible to identify and follow a consistent narrative voice. Thus in Rouaud's *Les Champs d'honneur* (1990; *Fields of Glory*), an autobiographical novel, scenes from the middle-aged narrator's past progressively reveal the series of deaths that have punctuated his family history since World War I. Hervé Guibert's autobiographical fiction (*Des Aveugles* [1995; *Blindsight*]), in which the writer's homosexuality is a major theme, becomes focused toward the end of his short life on his fatal infection with the AIDS virus, while Ndiaye's *Comédie classique* (1987; *Classic Comedy*) is composed of a single sentence recounting the events of a single day in the narrator's life.

In France, as in the United States, autobiography continues to make inroads on fiction. In addition to writers like Annie Ernaux, whose declared aim in *Une femme* (1987; *A Woman's Story*), an account of her mother's life, is to remain "a cut below literature," Nathalie Sarraute (*Enfance* [1983; *Childhood*]), Marguerite Duras (*The Lover*), and, most surprisingly perhaps, Alain Robbe-Grillet—*Le Miroir qui revient* (1984; *Ghosts in the Mirror*), *Angélique; ou, l'Enchantement* (1987; *Angélique; or, The Enchantment*), and *Les derniers jours de Corinthe* (1994; *The Last Days of Corinth*)—have overtly used their own lives as material. Serge Doubrovsky has coined the term *autofictions* for this new genre, which he has himself practiced in *Le Livre brisé* (1989; *The Broken Book*), a journal harrowingly interrupted by the death of his young wife, and *L'Après-vivre* (1994; *Living-After*).

Unlike the *nouveaux romanciers,* the work of the new Minuit novelists is not widely known outside France. Thus the editor of *Granta, 59, France, the Outsider* (Autumn 1997), claiming that "outside France and small pockets of Francophilia, hardly anyone knows" where French writing stands today, challenges his readers to "name six living French novelists [or] six contemporary novels" and presents short texts by five novelists writing in French in an effort to close this information gap. These are René Belletto, Patrick Chamoiseau, Assia Djebar, Michel Houllebecq, and Caroline Lamarche. That these names are additional to those listed above is an indication that whatever crises it has endured or is enduring, the French novel (the novel in *French* as well as the novel in *France*) is very much alive at the end of the 20th century.

MARY LYDON

See also African Novel: Northern Africa; Samuel Beckett; Canadian Novel (Francophone); Caribbean Novel (Francophone); Marguerite Duras; Irish Novel (on Beckett); Nausea; Nouveau Roman; Georges Perec; Politics and the Novel; Alain Robbe-Grillet; Claude Simon; Stranger; Michel Tournier

Further Reading

Atack, Margaret, and Phil Powrie, editors, *Contemporary French Fiction by Women: Feminist Perspectives,* Manchester: Manchester University Press, and New York: St. Martin's Press, 1990

Britton, Celia, *The nouveau roman: Fiction, Theory, and Practice,* New York: St. Martin's Press, 1992

Cook, Martin, editor, *French Culture since 1945,* London and New York: Longman, 1993

Dembo, L.S., editor, *Interviews with Contemporary Writers: Second Series, 1972–1982,* Madison: University of Wisconsin Press, 1983

O'Flaherty, Kathleen Mary Josephine, *The Novel in France, 1945–1965: A General Survey,* Cork: Cork University Press, 1973

Oppenheim, Lois, editor, *Three Decades of the French New Novel,* Urbana: University of Illinois Press, 1986

Porter, Charles A., editor, *After the Age of Suspicion: The French Novel Today* (special issue of Yale French Studies), New Haven, Connecticut: Yale University Press, 1988

Prince, Gerald, *Narrative as Theme: Studies in French Fiction,* Lincoln: University of Nebraska Press, 1992

Rigby, Brian, *Popular Culture in Modern France: A Study of Cultural Discourse,* London and New York: Routledge, 1991

Roudiez, Leon, *French Fiction Revisited,* Elmwood Park, Illinois: Dalkey Archive Press, 1991

Thompson, William, editor, *The Contemporary Novel in France,* Gainesville: University Press of Florida, 1995

Tilby, Michael, editor, *Beyond the Nouveau Roman: Essays on the Contemporary French Novel,* New York: Berg, 1990

Carlos Fuentes 1928–

Mexican

Carlos Fuentes is a leading writer of the internationally recognized boom of Latin American literature that began during the 1960s. Fuentes is best known for his 20 books of fiction, but he has also published essays and plays. An avid reader of Jorge Luis Borges and Miguel de Cervantes, Fuentes has written often about his debts to these two writers. When Fuentes began writing in the 1950s, one of his interests was to universalize Mexican literature, at that time dominated by nationalist intellectuals. To explain his more universal outlook, Fuentes has written that the most important lesson he learned from his mentor Alfonso Reyes was that "Mexican literature is good not because it is Mexican, but because it is literature."

His first novel, *La región más transparente* (1958; *Where the Air Is Clear*), is a technically daring work that offers a panoramic view of Mexican society. This lengthy and fragmented novel shifted Mexican literature from its focus on predominantly rural settings to urban spaces. It is also the first of Fuentes' historical approaches to Latin American society. *Where the Air Is Clear* is a highly polemical work, and upon its publication in Mexico it received widespread praise, as well as criticism from some sectors of the nation's literary elite.

With *La muerte de Artemio Gruz* (1962; *The Death of Artemio Cruz*), Fuentes helped launch the boom. Using an innovative point of view and structure, he employs three voices narrating in first, second, and third person. The novel tells the story of Artemio Cruz, a symbol of the new order that took power in Mexico during the 1920s, after the Mexican Revolution. *Artemio Cruz* was acclaimed throughout the Hispanic world, as Fuentes, Gabriel García Márquez, Mario Vargas Llosa, and Julio Cortázar rose as major international writers, in addition to functioning as public voices for political and social change in Latin America. Fuentes took the lead in supporting the Cuban Revolution and in insisting upon a revolutionary role for the Latin American writer.

Throughout the 1960s, Fuentes wrote prolifically, publishing numerous essays, the short novel *Aura* (1962), the lengthy and complex *Cambio de piel* (1967; *A Change of Skin*), and the experimental novels *Zona sagrada* (1967; *Holy Place*) and *Cumpleaños* (1969; Birthday). In these works, Fuentes moved away from the intense social critique of his earlier fiction and engaged in a more self-reflective exploration of Mexican identity. He also began to undermine traditional concepts of time and space. *Aura* deals with a young Mexican historian's experience of finding himself as a double—caught up as a character in the history he is writing. *A Change of Skin* tells the story of four characters on a car trip to Cholula, Mexico, slipping into different historical times to illustrate the complex context of relationships as well as individual identity. *Holy Place* is a kind of Bildungsroman, its protagonist the 29-year-old son of a celebrity actress. *Cumpleaños* is set in London and deals with a multiple set of identities.

The political, aesthetic, and personal alliances among the writers of the boom began to disintegrate in the early 1970s. During this period, Fuentes was deeply immersed in the research and writing of the massive novel *Terra Nostra* (1975; *Terra Nostra*), his major work on the history and identity of Latin American culture. (Preferring to avoid the term Latin America, as it was coined by the French in the 19th century, Fuentes has proposed the alternate term Indo-Afro-Ibero-America.) In *Terra Nostra*, Fuentes returns to the origins of Hispanic culture in 16th-century Spain, one of the novel's main settings. (More specifically, it is set in El Escorial, the palace built by Phillip II.) This novel also represents Fuentes' most ambitious and exhaustive subversion of conventional ideas of time and space. Multiple characters (and their doubles) appear on different continents and in different centuries, as Fuentes ignores any unity of time and space. With *Terra Nostra*, Fuentes explores numerous motifs and techniques of postmodern fiction, some of which he inherited from Borges. *Terra Nostra* is also a rewriting of the medieval, Renaissance, and neoclassical architecture of El Escorial. Several critics have emphasized the unresolved contradictions of postmodern culture, and Fuentes' palace in *Terra Nostra* contains a number of such contradictions. The novel also offers the double coding typical of postmodern fiction, portraying characters, for example, who are and are not historical characters.

After the publication of *Terra Nostra*, Fuentes wrote a series of accomplished but less ambitious, less totalizing works. However, he continued working along postmodern lines with *La cabeza de la hidra* (1978; *The Hydra Head*), *Una familia lejana* (1980; *Distant Relations*), *Gringo viejo* (1985; *The Old Gringo*), and *Cristóbal nonato* (1987; *Christopher Unborn*). *The Hydra Head* is Fuentes' one foray into the genre of the spy thriller. In *Distant Relations*, Fuentes takes a new look at the issue of cultural identity, in this case the relationship between French culture and Mexican identity, creating an alter ego for himself as well as a set of historical alternative identities. *The Old Gringo* takes place during the Mexican Revolution and deals with the relationship between Mexico and the United States. The point of departure for the plot is the disappearance of the American writer Ambrose Bierce in Mexico. One of Fuentes' most experimental texts, *Christopher Unborn* takes place on 6 January 1992 and is narrated by the title character from the womb of his mother. Looking to the future, Fuentes imagines a Mexico that has trivialized not only its national myths and its institutions but its very identity.

Fuentes' fiction of the 1990s includes *La campaña* (1990; *The Campaign*), *El Naranjo o los círculos del tiempo* (1993; *The Orange Tree*), and *Diana, o la cazadora solitario* (1994; *Diana, the Goddess Who Hunts Alone*). *The Campaign* relates the story of Balthasar Bustos, a Latin American child of the Enlightenment who is obsessed with a woman and joins the revolutionary forces that forged the independence of Latin American nations in the early 19th century. *The Orange Tree* can be read as a five-chapter novel or as a volume of five short stories. The image of the orange tree and the consistency of historical themes, however, invite the reader to consider it a novel. *Diana, the Goddess Who Hunts Alone* is the most autobiographical of Fuentes' novels and deals with his brief (real-life) relationship with an American actress. This novel also reveals Fuentes' ideas about the United States, American culture, and his personal relationships with women and with writing.

In his fiction, Fuentes expresses his belief in the liberating power of the imagination. After imagination, Fuentes tends to believe in the power of ideas over other forces, such as the economic or the sexual. Most of Fuentes' fiction explores spaces and times of change. He often fictionalizes those forces that transform individuals, cultures, and societies.

RAYMOND LESLIE WILLIAMS

See also Death of Artemio Cruz; Terra Nostra

Biography

Born in Panama City, 11 November 1928. As a child lived in the United States, Chile, and Argentina; returned to Mexico at age 16. Attended Colegio Francisco Morelos; Universidad Nacional Autónoma de México (UNAM), Mexico City, LL.B. 1948; Institut des Hautes Études Internationales, Geneva. Member, then Secretary, Mexican delegation, International Labor Organization, Geneva, 1950–52; assistant chief of press section, Ministry of Foreign Affairs, Mexico City, 1954; press secretary, United Nations Information Center, Mexico City, 1954; secretary, then assistant director of cultural department, UNAM, 1955–56; Head of Department of Cultural Relations, Ministry of Foreign Affairs, 1957–59; editor, *Revista mexicana de Literatura*, 1954–58, *El Espectador*, 1959–61, *Siempre* and *Politico* from 1960; lived primarily in Europe during the 1960s; Mexican Ambassador to France, 1974–77. Fellow, Woodrow Wilson International Center for Scholars, 1974; Virginia Gildersleeve Visiting Professor, Barnard College, New York, 1977; Norman Maccoll Lecturer, 1977, and Henry L. Tinker Lecturer, Columbia University, New York, 1978; professor of English, University of Pennsylvania, Philadelphia, 1978–83; Fellow of the Humanities, Princeton University, New Jersey; professor of comparative literature, 1984–86; Bolívar Professor, Cambridge University, 1986–87; Robert F. Kennedy Professor of Latin American Studies, since 1987, Harvard University, Cambridge, Massachusetts.

Novels by Fuentes

La región más transparente, 1958; as *Where the Air Is Clear*, translated by Sam Hileman, 1960

Las buenas conciencias, 1959; as *The Good Conscience*, translated by Sam Hileman, 1961

La muerte de Artemio Cruz, 1962; as *The Death of Artemio Cruz*, translated by Sam Hileman, 1964; also translated by Alfred MacAdam, 1991

Aura, 1962; as *Aura*, translated by Lysander Kemp, 1965

Zona sagrada, 1967; as *Holy Place*, translated by Suzanne Jill Levine in *Triple Cross*, 1972

Cambio de piel, 1967; as *A Change of Skin*, translated by Sam Hileman, 1968

Cumpleaños [Birthday], 1969

Terra Nostra, 1975; as *Terra Nostra*, translated by Margaret Sayers Peden, 1976

La cabeza de la hidra, 1978; as *The Hydra Head*, translated by Margaret Sayers Peden, 1978

Una familia lejana, 1980; as *Distant Relations*, translated by Margaret Sayers Peden, 1982

Gringo viejo, 1985; as *The Old Gringo*, translated by Margaret Sayers Peden, 1985

Cristóbal nonato, 1987; as *Christopher Unborn*, translated by Fuentes and Alfred MacAdam, 1989

La campaña, 1990; as *The Campaign*, translated by Alfred MacAdam, 1991

Diana, o la cazadora solitaria, 1994; as *Diana, the Goddess Who Hunts Alone*, translated by Alfred MacAdam, 1995

La frontera de cristal, 1995; as *The Crystal Frontier*, translated by Alfred MacAdam, 1997

Other Writings: short stories, plays, a collection of poems, and essays (including *La nueva novela hispanoamericana* [1969; The New Spanish American Novel] and *Geografía de la novela* [1993; Geography of the Novel]).

Further Reading

Befumo Boschi, Liliana, and Elisa Calabrese, *Nostalgia del futuro en la obra de Carlos Fuentes*, Buenos Aires: Fernando García Cambeiro, 1974

Brody, Robert, and Charles Rossman, editors, *Carlos Fuentes: A Critical View*, Austin: University of Texas Press, 1982

Durán, Gloria, *The Archetypes of Carlos Fuentes: From Witch to Androgine*, Hamden, Connecticut: Archon, 1980

Faris, Wendy, *Carlos Fuentes*, New York: Ungar, 1983

Giacoman, Helmy, editor, *Homenaje a Carlos Fuentes*, New York: Las Américas, 1971

Hernández de López, Ana María, editor, *La obra de Carlos Fuentes: Una visión múltiple*, Madrid: Pliegos, 1988

Simson, Ingrid, *Realidid y ficción en "Terra Nostra" de Carlos Fuentes*, Frankfurt: Vervuert, 1989

Williams, Raymond Leslie, *The Writings of Carlos Fuentes*, Austin: University of Texas Press, 1996

G

Carlo Emilio Gadda 1893–1973

Italian

The Italian writer Carlo Emilio Gadda gained an international reputation as a novelist in the mid–20th century, primarily on the basis of his exuberant stylistic invention. His style has provoked numerous comparisons with James Joyce, although his characteristic linguistic pastiche owes perhaps more to François Rabelais. Italo Calvino called Gadda the last of the great Italian narrative modernists, who uses his fiction to probe the nature of reality. He is also notable for his passionate opposition to fascism, expressed in irrepressible satire, parody, and invective.

Gadda's World War I diary, *Giornale di un guerra a di prigionia* (1955; Journal of War and Imprisonment), already shows an early version of his distinctive macaronic style. A foundation of highly literary, hypotactic Italian supports a wealth of scientific and technical vocabulary (Gadda was an electrical engineer) and foreign words and phrases, as well as a range of Lombard dialects, Neapolitan, Venetian, and Roman. As Gadda described his writing, "I want the doublet-doubloons ('i doppioni'), all of them, for the sake of my mania of possession and greed, and I also want the triploons, and the quadriploons, even if the Catholic King has not yet coined them." Reference to Gadda's Baroque style has become a critical commonplace, but he himself insisted that it only represents the multiplicity and complexity of reality. For the same reasons, he denied the propriety of the term *grotesque,* which critics commonly apply to his fiction.

Gadda's early work, consisting mostly of essays, poems in prose, and short stories, was eventually collected in *I sogni e la folgore* (1955; Dreams and Lightning). The stories evince a talent for incisive psychological and sociological analysis, which is underscored by parodies of contemporary public language in all its manifestations—"bureaucratese" and propaganda, the latter comprising both a typical Latinate magniloquence and Mussolini's highly individual and inspirational "plain-speaking" rhetoric, which was very influential at the time.

A master of invective, Gadda condemned empty oratory (*vaniloquio*) as morally or even spiritually pernicious: "ingenera la non-vita, in che vi si presta, cioè l'errore e la tenbra" (it engenders non-life, that is, error and darkness, in its user). Gadda's stylistic play tries to thwart the misuse and degradation of language by fascism. With his penchant for elaboration, Gadda combines an insistence upon clarity and concreteness, which are particularly apparent in his delineation of objects in space. Gadda's descriptive precision and the solidity of his settings derive directly from the work of Honoré de Balzac, who generally served as a model for Gadda. Paradoxically, the realistic settings and the meticulously described objects and people have a grotesque effect.

Gadda's talent for satire and parody animate *La cognizione del dolore* (1963; *Acquainted with Grief*), a political satire on fascist Italy set in an imaginary Latin American comic-opera dictatorship. Serialized between 1938 and 1941, the novel muted its invective to some extent to appease the fascist government. Its political concerns are balanced by a strong autobiographical element. The central character is a self-portrait, shown particularly in his relationships with his much-beloved brother and his mother. Critics argue whether the novel's misogyny is to be ascribed to the author or to the age he portrays.

Gadda's next major work, *Quer pasticciaccio brutto de via Merulana (That Awful Mess on Via Merulana)* was serialized in 1946 and published as a volume in 1957 in a new, enlarged version. The novel is a murder mystery that does not focus on the identity of the murderer so much as on the nature of evidence and the multiple possible causes. At the same time, *That Awful Mess* is a novel of a city—Rome—and another satire of fascism, even more outspoken than *Acquainted with Grief*. Gadda enriches his macaronic style with a wealth of classical allusions, which stand in sharp contrast to the different Roman and other Italian dialects that Gadda exploits in the dialogue. The novel established Gadda's international reputation.

Gadda constantly revised and reordered his work. Strictly speaking, *Acquainted with Grief* and *That Awful Mess*, published in different versions during Gadda's lifetime, were still unfinished at his death—perhaps the most eloquent testimony to Gadda's understanding of universal complexity.

SUZANNE KIERNAN

See also That Awful Mess on Via Merulana

Biography

Born 14 November 1893 in Milan. Studied electrical engineering, volunteering during World War I and working as

461

electrical engineer abroad during the 1920s. Began writing in the 1930s. Died 21 May 1973.

Novels by Gadda

Quer pasticciaccio brutto de via Merulana, 1957; as *That Awful Mess on Via Merulana,* translated by William Weaver, 1965

La cognizione del dolore, 1963; enlarged edition, 1970; as *Acquainted with Grief,* translated by William Weaver, 1969

Other Writings: short stories and essays, some collected in *I sogni e la folgore* (1955; Dreams and Lightning).

Further Reading

Adams, Robert Martin, *After Joyce: Studies in Fiction after "Ulysses,"* New York: Oxford University Press, 1977

Calvino, Italo, introduction to *That Awful Mess on Via Merulana,* by C.E. Gadda, translated by William Weaver, New York: Braziller, 1984

Cattaneo, Giulio, *Bisbetici e bizzarri nella letteratura italiana,* Milan: Fabbri, 1957

De Benedictis, Maurizio, *La piega nera: Groviglio stilistica ed enigma della femminilita in C.E. Gadda,* Anzio: De Rubeis, 1991

Dombroski, Robert S., *Properties of Writing: Ideological Discourse in Modern Italian Fiction,* Baltimore: Johns Hopkins University Press, 1994 (see chapter 6, "Carlo Emilio Gadda: Travesties")

Galdós, Benito Pérez. *See* Pérez Galdós, Benito

Gabriel García Márquez 1927–

Colombian

Gabriel García Márquez is the best-known 20th-century novelist from the Hispanic world and one of the most popular Nobel prize winners of all time. One of the few writers who has become a household name in his own and other countries, García Márquez's celebrity status has been important in maintaining the prestige and practice of reading literature throughout Latin America. At the heart of his success is his ability to draw on the experiences and belief systems of the inhabitants of his own home region—the tropical coastlands of northern Colombia—while writing works of universal significance. His earliest influence was Franz Kafka, who was soon superseded by William Faulkner and Ernest Hemingway; but García Márquez's own characteristic style is unique and usually recognizable in the first phrase of any given novel.

La hojarasca (1955; *Leaf Storm*), his first novel, draws directly on recollections of his childhood in the small plantation town of Aracataca—transformed in the novel into Macondo, García Márquez's equivalent of Faulkner's Yoknapatawpha. As in almost all his work, its point of departure is a death, a funeral attended by three different generations of a rural family, each with its own perspective on the life of the deceased. The novel's orientation is realist but tinged with a popular mythical consciousness, a mix that would mark all his later work to various degrees. *Leaf Storm* also set the style and tone for García

Márquez's best stories, especially those in the collection *Los Funerales de la Mamá Grande* (1962; *Big Mama's Funeral*).

El coronel no tiene quien le escriba (1957; *No One Writes to the Colonel*) remains for many critics García Márquez's most perfectly executed work, reminiscent of Hemingway's *The Old Man and the Sea* (1952) despite the very different subject matter. A short novel set in 1956 at the height of Colombia's undeclared civil war, in which perhaps 250,000 people died, it tells the story of an ex-colonel who fought in the earlier War of the Thousand Days (1898–1901) and is still waiting for his pension in a stifling atmosphere dominated by curfews, censorship, corruption, and military authoritarianism. Slightly less successful is *La mala hora* (1962; *In Evil Hour*), on a similar theme but lacking the intensity, balance, and cohesion of *No One Writes to the Colonel.*

The truth is that García Márquez was searching for some other literary mode that could allow him to encompass the whole of the worldview he had absorbed as a permanently astonished and apprehensive child in his native Aracataca of the 1930s: a world at once modern and underdeveloped, a world in which the Spanish conquest was still a recent event and where Africa and Europe continually confronted one another and produced new fusions and new confusions. The moment of inspiration came in 1965 and the result was published in 1967 as *Cien años de soledad* (*One Hundred Years of Solitude*), a novel of extraordinary and fantastical events narrated in a tone of almost biblical imperturbability that radically changed the way in which educated Latin Americans viewed their own historical identity.

El otoño del patriarca (1975; *The Autumn of the Patriarch*), García Márquez's next novel, was short on punctuation and long on hyperbole. Curiously poetic, the novel evokes the barbaric life of a Latin American dictator by recounting his last, "autumnal" days. It partially achieves one of its main purposes, which was to liberate the novelist from his overwhelming and inhibiting identification with the magic realist discourse of *One Hundred Years of Solitude*. Indeed, his next novel, *Crónica de una muerte anunciada* (1981; *Chronicle of a Death Foretold*), marks a return to the earlier, realist perspective of his first three novels. However, where those works appear to aspire to some "classical" status, *Chronicle* seems aware that its narrator has achieved it. The novel gives a surprisingly baleful reading of the "honor and shame" syndrome that has marked Mediterranean societies and their Latin American extensions for half a millennium. The author gives a self-confident rhetorical flourish by announcing in the first line (as well as the title) that its protagonist is doomed to die and defies his readers to put the novel down.

With *El amor en los tiempos del cólera* (1985; *Love in the Time of Cholera*) García Márquez, who had won the Nobel prize in 1982, set himself another challenge: to write a successful novel about love at an age when "serious" writers have found this almost impossible. He succeeds triumphantly, inscribing his postmodern narrative on the border between the sentimental, the satirical, and the parodic, yet finding enough space there to allow his characters to breathe—and even to love.

As if this were not audacious enough, García Márquez then embarked on a work about the last days of Simón Bolívar, the most revered figure in the history of Latin America: *El general en su laberinto* (1989; *The General in His Labyrinth*). It is no small tribute to the writer's sureness of touch that Bolívar somehow maintains his mythical status despite becoming a familiar García Márquez character: a man who, mightily fallen, retains his courage and greatness of spirit in even the most desperate and humiliating circumstances, at the end of his "mad chase between his woes and his dreams." It is a conclusion through which the novelist speaks, once again, for a region in which dreams of beauty and justice never die, despite the most desperate disillusionment; and in this García Márquez speaks also for his century.

GERALD MARTIN

See also Love in the Time of Cholera; Magic Realism; One Hundred Years of Solitude

Biography

Born in Aracataca, Colombia, 6 March 1928. Attended Colegio San José, Barranquilla, 1940–42; Colegio Nacional, Zipaquirá, to 1946; studied law and journalism at the National University of Colombia, Bogotá, 1947–48; University of Cartagena, 1948–49. Journalist, 1947–50, 1954; European correspondent in Rome and Paris, for the newspaper *El Espectador*, 1955; lost his post when this newspaper was closed down by the dictator Rojas Pinilla. Traveled to the Soviet Union. Journalist for *El Heraldo*, Barranquilla, 1950–54; founder, Prensa Latina (Cuban press agency), Bogotá: worked in Prensa Latina office, Havana, 1959, and New York, 1961. Lived in Venezuela, Cuba, the United States, Spain, and Mexico; returned to Colombia in 1982. Founder, 1979, and since 1979 president, Fundación Habeas; also founder of film school near Havana. Awarded Nobel prize for literature, 1982.

Novels by García Márquez

La hojarasca, 1955; as *Leaf Storm,* translated by Gregory Rabassa, in *Leaf Storm and Other Stories,* 1972

El coronel no tiene quien le escriba, 1957; as *No One Writes to the Colonel,* translated by J.S. Bernstein, in *No One Writes to the Colonel and Other Stories,* 1968

La mala hora, 1962; as *In Evil Hour,* translated by Gregory Rabassa, 1980

Cien años de soledad, 1967; as *One Hundred Years of Solitude,* translated by Gregory Rabassa, 1970

El otoño del patriarca, 1975; as *The Autumn of the Patriarch,* translated by Gregory Rabassa, 1976

Crónica de una muerte anunciada, 1981; as *Chronicle of a Death Foretold,* translated by Gregory Rabassa, 1982

El amor en los tiempos del cólera, 1985; as *Love in the Time of Cholera,* translated by Edith Grossman, 1988

El general en su laberinto, 1989; as *The General in His Labyrinth,* translated by Edith Grossman, 1990

Del amor y otros demonios, 1994; as *Of Love and Other Demons,* translated by Edith Grossman, 1995

Other Writings: short stories, novellas, plays, journalism, and essays.

Further Reading

Bell, Michael, *Gabriel García Márquez: Solitude and Solidarity,* New York: St. Martin's Press, and London: Macmillan, 1993

Bell-Villada, Gene, *García Márquez: The Man and His Work,* Chapel Hill: University of North Carolina Press, 1990

Bloom, Harold, editor, *Gabriel García Márquez,* New York: Chelsea House, 1989

Fiddian, Robin, editor, *García Márquez,* London and New York: Longman, 1995

Martin, Gerald, *Journeys Through the Labyrinth: Latin American Fiction in the Twentieth Century,* London and New York: Verso, 1989

McGuirk, Bernard, and Richard Andrew Cardwell, *Gabriel García Márquez: New Readings,* Cambridge and New York: Cambridge University Press, 1987

McMurray, George, editor, *Critical Essays on Gabriel García Márquez,* Boston: G.K. Hall, 1987

Minta, Stephen, *García Márquez: Writer of Colombia,* New York: Harper and Row, and London: Cape, 1987

Moretti, Franco, *Modern Epic: The World System from Goethe to García Márquez,* London and New York: Verso, 1996

Williams, Raymond Leslie, *Gabriel García Márquez,* Boston: Twayne, 1984

Elizabeth Gaskell 1810–65

English

Critics commonly measure Elizabeth Gaskell in the early years of her career against Charlotte and Emily Brontë, and in the later years against George Eliot, and grant her an important but secondary place in relation to their achievements. It is worth noting, however, that her reading audience was as wide as theirs, that Patrick Brontë, the father of Charlotte and Emily, selected Gaskell to write Charlotte's life, a biography still regarded as one of the finest Victorian examples of its kind, and that most of her fiction has remained in print throughout the 20th century. While Gaskell lacks the imaginative intensity of the Brontës and the intellectual scope of Eliot, her commitment to fiction is fully as serious as theirs. Her importance as a novelist does not come from formal innovation, although recent criticism suggests strongly that she is a far more self-conscious writer, capable of writing against convention, than earlier critics assumed. Her importance, instead, comes from her willingness to extend the spectrum of realistic fiction into areas unusual for a Victorian woman writer: the complex problems produced by the industrial revolution (*Mary Barton*, 1848; *North and South*, 1855), sexual behavior and illegitimacy (*Ruth*, 1853), the provincial laboring and middle class at the time of the French Revolution (*Sylvia's Lovers*, 1863), and social rank and social Darwinism (*Wives and Daughters*, 1866). If Gaskell did not explore the implications of the issues she engaged to their full depths—and it must be said that, with the exception of Eliot, few novelists did—she did raise them, even if the resolutions of her novels tend to depend on fictional conventions that compromise her strongly realistic impulse.

Gaskell's background and situation uniquely equipped her to address what was called "the Condition of England," the rapid separation within the socioeconomic structure of the wealthy few and the laboring many generated by laissez-faire industrial capitalism. Her Unitarian background forms the basis of her liberal intellectualism, which keeps her from solving complex problems by retreating to the comforting simplifications of ideology. And the fact that her husband, a Unitarian minister, established himself at Manchester, in the heart of the industrialized Midlands, brought her as a minister's wife into direct contact with the laboring class—as she put it in the preface to *Mary Barton*, with "the lives of those who elbowed me daily in the busy streets of the town in which I resided." Thus, her representation of Manchester life bears the authority of direct experience, an authority immediately recognized by her first reviewers.

As a realist, however, Gaskell is more than an accurate and detailed observer. An acute psychologist, she realized that the "laboring poor," often reduced to the term "hands" by their employers, is an abstraction, and that her function as a realistic novelist was to individualize her characters in order to create a sympathetic response from her middle-class readers, a didactic aim for realistic fiction that George Eliot was to make an explicit program for her own fiction. The risks that Gaskell willingly took in this direction are most clear in *Ruth*, in which Ruth, seduced and abandoned in her teens by a man of the upper classes, emerges as the moral touchstone by which the rest of the characters in the novel are judged. Gaskell's husband would not allow the book in the house, and in at least one instance it was burned. Not until Thomas Hardy's *Tess of the D'Urbervilles* (1891) would a novelist of stature attempt to portray an unmarried mother sympathetically as a "pure woman," and the current of negative reaction against Hardy, 40 years later, was as strong as that against Gaskell.

Gaskell's novels that thematize current socioeconomic issues and conditions (*Mary Barton* and *North and South*) and female sexuality and the male double standard (*Ruth*) vividly demonstrate both the power of realistic narrative and its inherent limitations or contradictions. The power lies in her ability to reproduce complex individual responses to the actual conditions of industrialization (as against Charles Dickens' allegorical or type characters in *Hard Times*). At this level, as well as in the representation of family dynamics and social interaction within and between classes, firmly based on her sensitivity to gendered behavior and class conditioning, Gaskell achieves her subtlest and most penetrating effects. Particularly in *North and South*, Margaret Hale and John Thornton's misreading of each other's verbal communication and even body language, primarily the result of the conditioning of their different social classes (Margaret comes from the lower gentry, while Thornton is a rising industrialist of humbler background), is both fundamental to Gaskell's exploration of class issues and fully functional in the complications of the romance plot in which these two characters are the central figures. This psychological acuteness remains constant in novels less overtly focused on large issues of national concern (*Cranford*, 1853; *Sylvia's Lovers*; and the unfinished *Wives and Daughters*), in which Gaskell turns instead to the social anthropology of provincial society, particularly to the effects of the cultural construction of gender and the ways it constrains and silences women.

The demands of plot—the necessity of forming her material into narrative that achieves closure—ultimately compromise the realistic thrust of Gaskell's fiction. The central problem is that fictional closure, whether it takes the form of romantic comedy, as in *North and South*, which ends with the reconciliation and marriage of Margaret Hale and John Thornton, or tragedy, as in *Ruth*, which elevates Ruth, the "fallen woman," to the status of martyr, cannot resolve the social, moral, and economic issues that these novels address. Simply put, the historical realities of these issues continue to exist outside the novels. As Raymond Williams observes in *Culture and Society* (1958), migrating to Canada (*Mary Barton* and *Sylvia's Lovers*) merely allows an escape from acute problems that remain unresolved, even if migration as an escape from intolerable conditions is part of the 19th-century historical record. Yet it must be said in Gaskell's favor that she does not falsify history by projecting utopian solutions for the difficult issues in her novels. While her closures may solve, or at least mitigate, the problems of her characters, they work as solutions for those particular characters; she resists generalizing from the individual to the culture.

JAMES L. HILL

Biography

Born in Chelsea, London, 29 September 1810; raised in Knutsford, Cheshire, by her aunt. Attended Byerley sisters' school, Barford, later Stratford on Avon, 1822–27. Married the Unitarian minister William Gaskell in 1832. Lived in Manchester from 1832; contributor, Dickens' *Household Words*, 1850–58; met and befriended Charlotte Brontë, 1850; visited her at Haworth, 1853; organized sewing-rooms during the cotton famine, 1862–63; contributor, *Cornhill Magazine*, 1860–65. Died 12 November 1865.

Novels by Gaskell

Mary Barton: A Tale of Manchester Life, 1848
The Moorland Cottage, 1850
Ruth, 1853
Cranford, 1853
North and South, 1855
Sylvia's Lovers, 1863
Wives and Daughters, 1866

Other Writings: short stories, letters, a diary, and a biography of Charlotte Brontë (*The Life of Charlotte Brontë*, 1857).

Further Reading

Craik, W.A., *Elizabeth Gaskell and the English Provincial Novel*, London and New York: Methuen, 1975
Easson, Angus, *Elizabeth Gaskell*, London and Boston: Routledge and Kegan Paul, 1979
Gallagher, Catherine, *The Industrial Reformation of English Fiction: Social Discourse and Narrative Form, 1832–1867*, Chicago: University of Chicago Press, 1985
Schor, Hilary, *Scheherezade in the Marketplace: Elizabeth Gaskell and the Victorian Novel*, New York: Oxford University Press, 1992
Spencer, Jane, *Elizabeth Gaskell*, London: Macmillan, and New York: St. Martin's Press, 1993
Uglow, Jenny, *Elizabeth Gaskell: A Habit of Stories*, London and Boston: Faber, 1993

Gattopardo. *See* Leopard

Gender. *See* Feminist Criticism of Narrative; Sex, Gender, and the Novel

---

Genji monogatari. *See* Tale of Genji

Genre Criticism

Problems in Categorizing the Novel as a Genre

The generic approach to literature attempts to formulate terms for categorizing and organizing texts of the same literary kind. This activity has important implications for the evaluation of individual texts by insisting that texts be judged according to the criteria appropriate to the genre to which they belong. Texts are grouped into genres according to a variety of generic principles: formal structure, distinctive subject matter, historical status, shared allusions or motifs, linguistic conventions, and the like. There are particular problems associated with the work of defining or comprehending the novel as a genre. The popularity of the novel, which has caused it to overtake, and in many cases to subsume, other literary forms, has produced a definition of the novel that is so comprehensive as to be useless in a generic sense. The novel is commonly regarded as an extended fictional prose narrative. This definition indicates the extent to which the novel has subsumed other genres of prose fiction, but the result is that such a comprehensive genre has only a weak sense of unity. Malcolm Bradbury, in *Possibilities: Essays on the State of the Novel* (1972), observes that "[t]he novel is not a traditional literary genre, like tragedy or comedy, but a general, varied, categorically distinctive form like poetry and drama. . . . There is no one kind of matter [novels] contain or effect they produce."

In *The Rise of the Novel* (1957), Ian Watt notes that the novel was historically distinguished by its originality and its very freedom from generic constraints:

> Previous literary forms had reflected the general tendency of their cultures to make conformity to traditional practice the major test of truth: the plots of classical and Renaissance epic, for example, were based on past history or fable, and the merits of the author's treatment were judged largely according to a view of literary decorum derived from the literary models in the genre. This literary traditionalism was first and most fully challenged by the novel, whose primary criterion was truth to individual experience—individual experience which is always unique and therefore new. The novel is thus the logical literary vehicle of a culture which, in the last few centuries, has set an unprecedented value on originality, on the novel; and it is therefore well named.

In English, the term *novel* is derived from the Italian *novella* (of which Giovanni Boccaccio's *Decameron* is the best-known collection), which signifies *the new*; in this respect the novel is distinguished by what it is not. And it is here that we have the origin of the novel as a mixed genre, incorporating multiple literary forms, like Henry Fielding's "comic epic in prose."

In most European languages the novel is referred to as the *roman,* indicative of its status as a descendant of the epic and courtly romance. This is only one aspect of the novel's derivation: it is also the descendant of the letter, journal, memoir, or chronicle. In fact, the deflation of idealized fictional forms offered an incentive to early writers of the novel, such as Miguel de Cervantes (in *Don Quixote,* 1605–15) and, in English, Henry Fielding, Samuel Richardson, and Daniel Defoe. Thus, the conflict that marks the novel as a genre between a legendary and imaginary impulse, on the one hand, and a commitment to the realistic and mundane world, on the other, has always been present in the novel. This tension between the epic and the ordinary is reflected in the distinction made repeatedly since the 18th century between the verisimilar novel and the romance. This distinction was formulated perhaps most famously by Nathaniel Hawthorne in his preface to *The House of the Seven Gables* (1851), but it was subsequently given powerful articulation by Henry James.

In his preface to the New York edition of *The American,* James wrote:

> The real represents to my perception the things we cannot possibly *not* know, sooner or later, in one way or another; it being but one of the accidents of our hampered state, and one of the incidents of their quantity and number, that particular instances have not yet come our way. The romantic stands, on the other hand, for the things that, with all the facilities in the world, all the wealth and all the courage and all the wit and all the adventure, we never *can* directly know; the things that can reach us only through the beautiful circuit and subterfuge of our thought and our desire.

The relationship between the romance and the real may be seen to influence all the subgenres of the novel, which are identified according to the way in which they depart from a standard provided by the romance and the verisimilar novel. Most obvious in this connection is the distinction between the novel of incident and novel of character: the former is seen to focus upon what happens and where, with a particular interest in the external details of the fictional world; the latter is seen to focus upon the subjective experiences and imaginings of individuals. Other types of novel are distinguished according to subject matter, formal emphasis, and artistic intention: the Bildungsroman (novel of development), and *Künstlerroman* (development of the artist), and *Erziehungsroman* (novel of education); picaresque novel, epistolary novel, psychological novel, surrealist novel, sociological novel, novel of manners, sentimental novel, historical novel, domestic novel, city novel, regional novel, factory novel, school or university novel, Gothic novel, stream-of-consciousness novel, detective novel, war novel, and adventure novel; and, recently, the *nouveau roman* and antinovel. Complicating the attempt to provide a comprehensive typology for such a diverse form as the novel is the inclusion of another generic type within a novel: some novels include poems (Vladimir Nabokov's *Pale Fire,* 1962), short stories (Fielding's *Tom Jones,* 1749), plays (Thomas Pynchon's *The Crying of Lot 49,* 1966), other art forms (Lily Briscoe's painting in Virginia Woolf's *To the Lighthouse,* 1927; daguerreotyping in *The House of the Seven Gables*). The mixed nature of the novel as a genre, then, is reflected in the multiple generic strands that are found in individual examples of the genre.

Perhaps because of the difficulty of describing such a generically impure form as the novel, definitions of just what belongs to the category of *the novel* have remained generalized and imprecise. Henry James complained that the English novel, in contrast to the European, and especially the French, novel, "had no air of having a theory, a conviction, a consciousness of itself behind it—of being the expression of an artistic faith, the result of choice and comparison." Instead, he went on, it was assumed that "a novel is a novel, as a pudding is a pudding, and that our only business with it could be to swallow it." For James, the novel "is in its broadest definition a personal, a direct expression of life"; an imaginative and unmediated representation of the artist's perception that should be "all one and continuous, like any other organism" (1948). James praises Gustave Flaubert, for example, for his ability to create works of fiction that are thoroughly integrated and unified, in which every element relates to and is a part of every other element of the whole and, crucially, in which the form is inseparable from the subject matter of the novel. From this comes the authenticity of the novel as a work of art since, in James' view, the moral sense of a work of art comes from "the amount of felt life concerned in producing it." He goes on:

Here we get exactly the high price of the novel as a literary form—its power not only, while preserving that form with closeness, to range through all the differences of the individual relation to its general subject-matter, all the varieties of outlook on life, of disposition to reflect and project, created by conditions that are never the same from man to man (or, so far as that goes, from man to woman), but positively to appear more true to its character in proportion as it strains, or tends to burst, with a latent extravagance, its mould.

The conception of the novel as expressing an artistically unified experience of life underpins the novelistic canon formulated by F.R. Leavis in *The Great Tradition* (1948). Leavis argues that "the major novelists [Austen, Eliot, James, and Conrad] . . . are significant in terms of that human awareness they promote; awareness of the possibilities of life." Leavis, fearful of the fate of high culture in what he termed the modern "technologico-Benthamite" society of mass civilization, looked to these novelists to promote proper judgment and a sense of humane values that he felt were otherwise under threat. The novelistic genre proposed by Leavis, then, is much more than a set of formal conventions or criteria for textual evaluation. Invested in the works of the great English novelists was the capacity to prescribe a relation to the world that took its power from the artist's formal novelistic skill. Similarly, D.H. Lawrence described the novel as a way of responding to the world that is uniquely powerful and, indeed, transcendent: "Books are not life. They only make tremulations on the ether. But the novel as a tremulation can make the whole man alive tremble. Which is more than poetry, philosophy, science or any other book-tremulation can do" (*Selected Literary Criticism*, 1956). For Lawrence, the novel was not merely one literary kind among many but the equivalent to the essence of great literature; thus in Lawrence's view, the Bible and Homer and Shakespeare are "the supreme old novels."

In a very different intellectual and theoretical context, Northrop Frye undertakes the description of the novelistic genre precisely in terms of the essence of great literature. Frye's *Anatomy of Criticism* (1957) equates myth with literature, where the former is "a structural organizing principle of literary form"; in *The Stubborn Structure* (1970) he explains further that "mythology as a whole provides a kind of diagram or blueprint of what literature as a whole is all about, an imaginative survey of the human situation from the beginning to the end, from the height to the depth, of what is imaginatively conceivable." Not surprisingly, the novel forms an important vehicle of this "survey." Frye does, however, use the novel as a concept in a very specific way: he treats both fiction and nonfiction as equivalent within the single category of prose. The actual literary genres he discusses in *Anatomy of Criticism* are comedy (the mythos of spring), romance (the mythos of summer), tragedy (the mythos of fall), and irony (the mythos of winter). The novel is carefully set off against concepts of prose fiction, fiction itself, the prose romance, autobiography or confession, and Menippean satire (expressed in the form either of dialogue or anatomy). Frye's four constituent ingredients of literary prose are romance, confession, novel, and anatomy, which are mixed according to the qualities of introversion or extroversion, and intellectual or nonintellectual character: "The novel tends to be extroverted and personal; its chief interest is in human character as it manifests itself in soci-

ety. The romance tends to be introverted and personal: it also deals with characters, but in a subjective way. . . . The confession is also introverted, but intellectualized in content. Our next step is evidently to discover a fourth form of fiction which is extroverted and intellectual." Frye identifies that form as Menippean satire. This complex typology of fictional forms offers, on the one hand, a terminology with which to analyze the component formal features of prose narratives. On the other hand, this typology serves to reduce the importance of the novel as the genre that, Frye admits, subsumes the other components of literary form that he wants to link with mythic archetypes. The very diversity and heterogeneity of the novel enables the genre to incorporate the mythic forms of comedy and romance and tragedy and irony, as well as the fictional forms of romance, confession, and irony.

It was the heterogeneous nature of the novel that motivated one of the 20th century's most powerful theories of literary genre. Mikhail Bakhtin, Pavel Medvedev, and Valentin Voloshinov (the so-called Bakhtin circle) worked within a Marxist framework to formulate a linguistic-based theory of ideology in the novel. For the Bakhtin School, utterances (*slovo*) always occur within the material reality of language, which, as a system of dynamic social signs, carries different meanings and associations for different social classes and different historical situations (see Voloshinov, *Marksizm i filosofiia iazyka* [1929; *Marxism and the Philosophy of Language*]). Verbal context is intimately bound up with social and economic context and ideology in the formation and expression of consciousness. Language is made up of multiple social discourses representing multiple ideological belief systems or worldviews, which Bakhtin termed *heteroglossia* (see "Discourse in the Novel" in Bakhtin's *The Dialogic Imagination*, 1981). Language, therefore, is not a passive medium but a dynamic system of exchange in which all expressions are addressed to a listener or reader and an isolated monologic expression is not possible. Bakhtin was responsible for applying this theory of the imbeddedness of language in the arena of class struggle to the novel genre.

In *Problemy poetiki Dostoevskogo* (originally published in 1929; *Problems of Dostoevsky's Poetics*) Bakhtin contrasts the works of Lev Tolstoi with those of Fedor Dostoevskii to demonstrate the ways in which Tolstoi subordinates the multi-accentuality of the fictive voices to the author's intellectual control. The conditions of fictive truth are defined by Tolstoi in monologic terms—there is only one truth—at the expense of alternative value systems. Dostoevskii's achievement, Bakhtin claims, was to liberate alternative voices from the authority of the authorial voice. Dostoevskii's novels are "polyphonic" or "dialogic" while Tolstoi's are "monologic." Tolstoi's characters are permitted to express various points of view, but these are rigorously controlled by the writer, who draws them into a condition of unity that reflects the single version of truth available within the fictive world. Bakhtin's concept of the liberating and subversive power of dialogic novelistic form constitutes an important challenge to the value placed on organic unity by generations of novelists, theorists, and critics. Even before the romantic privileging of organic form, concepts of literary decorum in the 18th century controlled the ways in which unity or coherence was achieved in literary expression. Bakhtin draws attention to the fact that in many novels the consciousness of the characters is made to coincide with that of the author and the ideological values of the author's class, place, and time. In the dialogic novel, however, characters remain independent and autonomous subjects; the class interests they articulate as part of their discrete value systems remain in tension or dialogue and the *heteroglossia* (the open and indeterminate utterance) that is their expression is not shaped to a false unity imposed by the single (authoritative) voice of the author. It is the diversity of voices or heteroglossia that Bakhtin isolates as characteristic of the novel: "The novel can be defined as a diversity of social speech types (sometimes even diversity of languages) and a diversity of individual voices, artistically organized." He concludes that, as a consequence, every novel is a "hybrid," an utterance in which distinct linguistic consciousnesses coexist: "What is realized in the novel is the process of coming to know one's own language as it is perceived in someone else's language, coming to know one's own belief system in someone else's system. There takes place within the novel an ideological translation of another's language, and an overcoming of its otherness—an otherness that is only contingent, external, illusory" ("Discourse in the Novel"). This overcoming of otherness is often a violent struggle among opposed ideological positions in which one must triumph over the others. Bakhtin offers his interpretation of the realism-versus-romance debate in precisely these terms. He identifies a line of development within the novel genre that originates in the "Sophistic novels" of ancient Greece characterized by a monologic control of meaning in language and an attempt to destroy heteroglossia entirely. In contrast, the novelistic form that develops from medieval chivalric romances is characterized by the absence of a centralized linguistic consciousness and corresponding free expression of a range of social languages and class consciousness. It should be noted that Bakhtin treats the novel less as a formal category of literary form and more as a force or principle of disruption and instability at work in the production of literary meaning; consequently, it is ever changing, "ever-questing, ever examining itself and subjecting its established forms to review," for the novel has its identity in its resistance to closure and the canonical limitation of meaning.

Another major 20th-century Marxist critic of the novel is Georg Lukács. Where Bakhtin emphasizes the complex role of language in the construction and articulation of ideology, Lukács developed what he termed a "reflection" model to describe the relationship between (literary) art and reality. The reality reflected in the novel is not simply the superficial details of everyday life, reflected in a quasi-photographic image, but the consciousness every person ordinarily has of human nature and interpersonal relationships as well as of objects. The underlying conflicts and contradictions of the social order, the class conflict, is the real subject of novelistic art. The embeddedness of human existence within a material environment and, more important, a dynamic historical development is what the novelist struggles to represent (see *A történelmi regény* [1937; *The Historical Novel*]; *Essays über Realismus* [1948; *Studies in European Realism*]). For Lukács, the dynamic view of history arises from his commitment to a Marxist/Hegelian view of history as a dialectical progression. Internal contradictions are generated as aspects of the class struggle within every mode of production, and these contradictions can only be resolved dialectically. The resolution of such contradictions within the formal unity of the novel is the achievement Lukács privileges. His attack on modernism (in *Wider der missverstandenen Realismus* [1958; *The Meaning of Contemporary Realism*]), with its emphasis on subjective experience within the context of individualism and radical formal experimentation, is motivated by his insistence that the representation of individual experience must take place within social and historical contexts if the novel is to exercise its artistic power to articulate a totalized view of reality.

Fredric Jameson also draws upon Hegel, rather than Marx, in his discussions of the political embeddedness of the novel as a genre. In *Marxism and Form* (1971) and *The Political Unconscious* (1981) Jameson proposes a dialectical criticism that focuses simultaneously on the inward-looking and outward-looking aspects of the individual novel and of the genre as a whole. This means that the critic should strive to connect the deep linkages between the text, its own "inner form," and the concrete reality of its production and reception. In this way, what will emerge are the "strategies of containment" or ideologies by which all societies seek to repress knowledge of history or necessity and the strategies of repression by which individual texts seek to forget their history.

For Jameson, narrative is an "epistemological category" or form of knowledge that functions like the Freudian unconscious as the medium for the irruption of repressed memories or experience into knowledge. The experience of reality is always present to human knowledge in the form of story or narrative. So the irruption of painful experience into knowledge always occurs within narrative, the formal medium for this conversion. The novel, the genre of extended fictional narrative, is therefore of particular importance to the ongoing social dynamic of the class struggle. Jameson offers an interpretation of the novel and a critical methodology that seeks significant absences indicating the presence of repressed knowledge. The identification of these absences and the interpretation of their significance requires three levels of analytical intervention: immanent analysis, social or discursive analysis, and, lastly, historical analysis. This method allows attention to be paid to the heterogeneity of the novel genre and individual genres within the context of social and cultural diversity, making the novel distinctive for its peculiar engagement with history. In this respect, Jameson's work is placed clearly within modern approaches to the novel as a genre, which have sought to clarify precisely the terms with which the novel engages with history, culture, personal and social values, the literary past, and the future.

Margaret Anne Doody's monumental study *The True Story of the Novel* (1996) is one of the most powerful attacks on the coherence of the English novelistic tradition to appear in recent years. Doody argues that the novel is not, as Ian Watt and others have suggested, a form that suddenly appeared fully formed in British culture of the 18th century. Rather, the novel had existed in Greek and Roman antiquity, novel writing happened during the Middle Ages, and novels mark the European Renaissance's rediscovery of the cultures of the Orient and the East. This persuasive contextualization of the novelistic genre does more than enrich our understanding of the tropes and structures that characterize subsequent fiction; Doody's perception that the novel is a much more generous and flexible form than heretofore allowed actually carries with it a deeply subversive threat to the generic autonomy claimed for the novel by critics like Watt. Her "secret history" of the novel is of course no secret at all, as she admits in the opening pages. But Doody resists the accepted practice of consigning ancient novels to the margins of scholarly study of the European novel and insists that the novels of the ancient world and the non-Christian world be placed firmly at the center of discussions concerning the novel as a literary genre. This means that the Protestant and bourgeois origin posited for the novel by Ian Watt, and assumed by those who followed him, is no longer tenable. We must look for more subtle and more historical forces as responsible for the novel's explosion in 18th-century England, and we must also broaden our conceptions and expectations of the kinds of texts that may go by the generic name of *novel*. In some respects, Doody's work is related to recent postcolonial investigations of the exclusions coded into metropolitan definitions of the novel as a genre. Doody challenges the nationalistic, religious, and political assumptions that underlie received definitions of "the English Novel."

DEBORAH L. MADSEN

See also Canon; Class and the Novel; Critics and Criticism (all sections); Epic and Novel; Dialogism; Formalism; Greek and Roman Narrative; Historical Writing and the Novel; Ideology and the Novel; Mimesis; Myth and Novel; Novel and Romance: Etymologies; Novella; Prose Novelistic Forms; Realism; Romance; Verse Narrative

Further Reading

Bakhtin, M.M., *Problemy tvorchestva Dostoevskogo,* Leningrad: Priboi, 1929; 2nd edition, revised, as *Problemy poetiki Dostoevskogo,* Moscow: Sov. Pisatel, 1963; as *Problems of Dostoevsky's Poetics,* Ann Arbor, Michigan: Ardis, 1973; new edition and translation, Minneapolis: University of Minnesota Press, and Manchester: Manchester University Press, 1984

Bakhtin, M.M., *The Dialogic Imagination: Four Essays,* translated by Caryl Emerson and Michael Holquist, edited by Holquist, Austin: University of Texas Press, 1981

Booth, Wayne, *The Rhetoric of Fiction,* Chicago: University of Chicago Press, 1961; 2nd edition, Chicago: University of Chicago Press, and London: Penguin, 1983

Brooks, Peter, *Body Work: Objects of Desire in Modern Narrative,* Cambridge, Massachusetts: Harvard University Press, 1993

Danahy, Michael, *The Feminization of the Novel,* Gainesville: University of Florida Press, 1991

Doody, Margaret Anne, *The True Story of the Novel,* New Brunswick, New Jersey: Rutgers University Press, 1996; London: HarperCollins, 1997

Fowler, Alastair, *Kinds of Literature: An Introduction to the Theory of Genres and Modes,* Oxford: Clarendon Press, and Cambridge, Massachusetts: Harvard University Press, 1982

Frye, Northrop, *Anatomy of Criticism: Four Essays,* Princeton, New Jersey: Princeton University Press, 1957

Hunter, J. Paul, *Before Novels: The Cultural Contexts of Eighteenth-Century English Fiction,* New York: Norton, 1990

James, Henry, "The Art of Fiction," in *The Art of Fiction and Other Essays,* edited by Morris Roberts, New York: Oxford University Press, 1948

Jameson, Fredric, *The Political Unconscious: Narrative as a Socially Symbolic Act,* Ithaca, New York: Cornell University Press, and London: Methuen, 1981

Leavis, F.R., *The Great Tradition: George Eliot, Henry James, Joseph Conrad,* London: Chatto and Windus, and New York: Stewart, 1948

Lukács, Georg, *A történelmi regény,* Budapest: Hungaria, 1937; as *The Historical Novel,* London: Merlin Press, 1962; New York: Humanities Press, 1965

Lukács, Georg, *Essays über Realismus,* Berlin: Aufbau, 1948; as *Studies in European Realism: A Sociological Survey of the Writings of Balzac, Stendhal, Zola, Tolstoy, Gorki, and Others,* London: Hillway, 1950; New York: Fertig, 1996

Lukács, Georg, *Wider den missverstandenen Realismus,* Hamburg: Claasen, 1958; as *The Meaning of Contemporary Realism,* London: Merlin Press, 1963; as *Realism in Our Time: Literature and the Class Struggle,* New York: Harper, 1964

Scholes, Robert, and Robert Kellogg, *The Nature of Narrative,* New York: Oxford University Press, 1966

Stevick, Philip, editor, *The Theory of the Novel,* New York: Free Press, 1967

Watt, Ian, *The Rise of the Novel: Studies in Defoe, Richardson, and Fielding,* London: Chatto and Windus, and Berkeley: University of California Press, 1957

German Novel

Any approach to the novel in Germany raises questions of definition relating to both the genre and the nation. If the novel is viewed in general terms as a substantial fictional narrative in prose, then it seems reasonable to exclude, despite its status and quality, the shorter *Novelle,* or novella, which derived from the Italian novella and which, from the late 18th century, became an established subgenre north of the Alps thanks to the work of Gottfried Keller, Theodor Storm, Conrad Ferdinand Meyer, and other masters. Furthermore, the frontiers of Germany and of the

German-speaking area do not coincide, and both have fluctuated considerably over time. Although Austria and Switzerland receive attention elsewhere in this volume, limited reference to them here is justified by the close contacts between the German-speaking countries in the field of literature, which have occasionally led Austrian and Swiss novelists to reside in Germany, to have their work published there, and to contribute to movements and trends that have their roots there.

The origins of the German novel may be traced beyond the

16th century to the prose versions of French verse epics such as *Lanzelot*. From the later Middle Ages to the end of the 16th century a series of *Volksbücher* (*Till Eulenspiegel, Faustbuch, Wagnerbuch, Fortunatus*) appeared and continued to reach a large readership well after 1600. The bourgeois novels of Jörg Wickram (*Der jungen Knaben Spiegel* [1554; Mirror for Youth] and *Der Goldfaden* [1557; *The Golden Thread*]) represent another strand of this native German development. However, although the bourgeois novel was popular in both its sensational and didactic form, it did not last and proved less significant than the following series of phases, each defined by a type that owes its general character to foreign models. (Interest in these models grew after Johann Fischart's adaptation of François Rabelais in his *Geschichtklitterung* [1575, 1582; Travesty of History] and the appearance in German of the *Amadís de Gaula*, Heliodorus' *Aethiopica Historia* [*Theagines und Chariklea*], and Miguel de Cervantes' *Don Quixote*.) This series began with the courtly novel (indebted to Florence Barclay and Sir Philip Sidney), and continued with the pastoral novel (Jorge de Montemayor and Honoré d'Urfé), the picaresque novel (Francisco Goméz Quevedo, Mateo Aleman, Richard Head, Juan de Luna, Francisco Lopez de Ubeda, Paul Scarron), the gallant novel (Madame de Lafayette), the political novel of enlightened absolutism (François de Salignac Fénelon), the satirical novel of the Enlightenment (Voltaire), the *Entwicklungsroman* (Henry Fielding), and the novel of sensibility (Samuel Richardson, Laurence Sterne, Jean-Jacques Rousseau).

Throughout this period the dependence of the German novel on foreign influences was so marked that its specifically German character seems hardly worth considering, but one acknowledged masterpiece of the 17th century, Johann Jakob Christoffel von Grimmelshausen's *Der abenteuerliche Simplicissimus Teutsch und Continuatio* (1668; *Simplicius Simplicissimus*), transcends its initial status as the most important German contribution to the picaresque novel. An example of social realism based on the personal experience of an author who had lived through the catastrophe of the Thirty Years War, it also presents in an explicitly didactic spirit a translation of the baroque worldview in terms of that experience. In its combination of a low-life realism and a homiletic appeal to turn away from the temptations of the world, *Simplicius Simplicissimus* had numerous imitators in the immediate aftermath of its publication. Except in occasional novels with a strong picaresque element, such as Johann Carl Wezel's *Belphegor* (1776), which was an attack on Enlightenment optimism plainly modeled on Voltaire's *Candide* (1759), or in other satires closer to the Enlightenment mainstream, such as Christoph Martin Wieland's *Geschichte der Abderiten* (1781; *The Republic of Fools*), these features were not to be revived until the 20th century, when they were given a modern framework in the work of Alfred Döblin and Günter Grass. Only *Simplicius Simplicissimus*' encyclopedic tendency aiming at totality may be said to have been carried over into the novel of personal development (Entwicklungs- and Bildungsroman) and the panoramic social novel of later periods.

For long the novel had to struggle against the low status it was granted in classical aesthetics, which favored the epic and the drama (especially tragedy). In the 18th century, when market demand for escapist entertainment first encouraged the creation of a publishing industry in the modern sense, this view seemed to be confirmed. Other forces, however, combined to challenge this

vulgarization, above all the Enlightenment and the particular public and private habits that it fostered, all of which can be associated with the growth and eventual dominance of middle-class values. Both rationalism and the cult of sensibility, which is often interpreted as a reaction against rationalism, are only fully comprehensible when set against the background of the social processes in which an educated middle class gained confidence and found a voice in those parts of the public sphere open to it—literary magazines with their substantial reviewing sections, public libraries, and, to some extent, educational institutions. While government remained the monopoly of the aristocracy, whose power was perpetuated by its feudal dominance in the extensive rural areas and by its executive role in the vast number of small states created by Germany's fragmentation, the intellectual life of the nation was taken over by a social group, the so-called *Bildungsbürgertum* (educated middle class), which arguably has retained its hegemony to the present and has defined its identity from the outset in opposition to that of its "betters."

The principal social tension evident in the novels of the 18th and 19th centuries lies between the middle class and the nobility, as in both Christian Fürchtegott Gellert's *Leben der schwedischen Gräfin von G . . .* (1747–48; *The Life of the Swedish Countess de G . . .*) and Sophie von La Roche's *Geschichte des Fräuleins von Sternheim* (1771; *The History of Lady Sophia Sternheim*), the latter an epistolary novel in the manner of Samuel Richardson. Here the title characters, although themselves of aristocratic birth, champion bourgeois sensibility and charity over the intrigues and loose morals of the court. Only at a late date did the conflicts characteristic of the novel in France and Britain, within the middle class between businessmen and clerisy and between the middle and working classes, make themselves felt. The occasional forays by novelists into political activity via attempts to influence the ruling class directly (for example, the role of Christoph Martin Wieland, Johann Gottfried von Herder, Johann Wolfgang von Goethe, and Friedrich von Schiller in the formation of a *Musenhof*, or court of the muses, in Weimar) should be understood as signs of self-confidence rather than as acts of craven submission to an alien value system. To a large extent, however, the *Bildungsbürgertum* was content to assert its values within its own section of the public sphere. This section was what we would now call a hyperreality created within the media, and a divorce from the contemporary world of work and government was soon apparent in the novel, encouraged also by the strong utopian strain in German thinking in both its religious/theological and secular forms. Beside the protagonists of Honoré de Balzac's *La Comédie humaine* (1842–48; *The Human Comedy*) and Stendhal's *Le Rouge et le noir* (1830; *The Red and the Black*) and *La Chartreuse de Parme* (1839; *The Charterhouse of Parma*), the protagonists of German novels seem singularly devoid of worldly ambition; German novelists were content to let their characters find (or fail to find) themselves, rather than political influence, worldly goods, or a marriage partner with the social status to which they aspired. The entire tradition of the Bildungsroman concerns average persons in search of a moderate stability. The dangers that threaten this achievement have their origin not in the world of affairs and commodities, which is largely ignored, but in the distortions of inwardness that follow from grandiose artistic ambitions or labyrinthine philosophical speculations. The other feature that distinguished the German novel from its foreign counterparts was its strong utopian strain, evident already in Johann Gottfried Schnabel's *Die Insel Felsenburg* (1731–43; Rock Castle Island) and Wilhelm Heinse's *Ardinghello* (1787), and perpetuated in 20th-century works (which occasionally take dystopian form) by Gerhart Hauptmann, Alfred Döblin, Hermann Hesse, Ernst Jünger, and Arno Schmidt.

It is no accident that *Bildung* constitutes part of terms defining a social group and one kind of novel it favored, for the development of the middle class during the late 18th century coincided with the emergence of a view of education that allowed scope to individual mental and spiritual growth without immediate reference to the demands of the state or the professions. Even the broadest acceptable definition of the Bildungsroman, "A novel which concentrates on the intellectual and social development of a central figure who, after going out into the world and experiencing both defeats and triumphs, comes to a better understanding of self and to a generally affirmative view of the world" (see Hardin, 1991), gives appropriate emphasis to self-understanding and inwardness, and although reflection is always accompanied by action, the latter is in some examples of the genre reduced to a minimum. The first German theoretician of the novel, Friedrich von Blankenburg, defined in *Versuch über den Roman* (1774; Attempt to Define the Novel), the novelist's task: to tell *"die innere Geschichte eines Menschen"* (the inner story of a human being). He could point to the emergence of the epistolary novel (*Briefroman*) as evidence of this tendency.

At the same time, the introduction of letters by various correspondents indicates another feature of the German novel that contrasts with the concentration on the inner life of one figure; even Goethe's *Die Leiden des jungen Werthers* (1774; The Sufferings of Young Werther)—the story of frustrated passion and suicide that encapsulated the mood of a generation, in which only the title figure's letters appear—offers another view in the framing fiction, and with time the novel became the arena in which numerous differing perspectives were presented in juxtaposition. The narrative sophistication usually associated with the rise of modernism (the ironic play with the roles of the narrator and reader, the fiction of a narrator telling his/her own story) was present, thanks to the influence of Miguel de Cervantes and Laurence Sterne, to an increasing degree in the work of Wieland, Goethe, and Jean Paul (Friedrich Richter). Thus, as early as the mid–18th century, partly owing to these parallel but contrasting developments (the reduction of the role of the narrator to allow the inner life of characters to speak for themselves via letters or otherwise, and the elaboration of that role to allow his/her inner life to emerge), the narrative convention of a third-person omniscient distant narrator with an identifiable presence who guarantees the truth of what is narrated ceased to be paramount in Germany. The consequence was a focus on psychology, first in the presentation of "rounded" characters, then in the dissolution of such portraits, which in turn led to a reduction of those elements that are normally considered the essentials of conventional narrative, action and speech. The primary agents in this dissolution were the techniques of *style indirecte libre* (in German *erlebte Rede*), i.e., the presentation of consciousness via third-person narrative and inner monologue or stream of consciousness, often in the form of the minute registration of sensory impressions and their interpretation in intellectual terms. This development went hand in hand with an expansion of the content of the novel as novelists tried to keep abreast of the increasing complexity of modern society in their concern for totality. The consequent accumulation of microscopic and macroscopic detail produced an inflationary spiral that eventually brought about a crisis of the novel demanding new solutions, such as essay-like meditations (as in Robert Musil's *Der Mann ohne Eigenschaften* [1930–43; The Man Without Qualities] and Thomas Mann's later novels) and montage (as in Döblin's *Berlin Alexanderplatz,* 1929).

These general developments were typical of the European and American novel throughout the transition to a modern society in which industrial and technological change together with increasing freedom from dogmatic constraints undermined stratification within national, local, and family structures. However, just as German history took a course untypical of other advanced nations according to the thesis of a German *Sonderweg,* or special course, so the German novel from the mid–18th century onward showed a peculiar amalgam of features characteristic of the European/American novel as a whole and aspects peculiar to itself, especially the preoccupation with *Innerlichkeit* and other-worldliness. Similarly, the German novel continued to absorb more specific impulses from outside while preserving its own distinctive note, which in turn exerted a profound influence outside Germany (exemplified by the reception of *The Sufferings of Young Werther*), thanks in good measure to the intermediary work of Madame de Staël in *De l'Allemagne* (1810; On Germany) and Thomas Carlyle in numerous translations and essays. Indeed, from the middle of the 18th to the middle of the 19th century a complex process of mutual stimulation took place, evident not only in thematically explorative and formally innovative novels but also in the popular subgenres, such as the *Schauerroman,* or tale of terror, which developed to cater to the tastes of a mass readership. Even such a quintessentially German product as Goethe's *Wilhelm Meisters Lehrjahre* (1795–96; Wilhelm Meister's Apprenticeship) brought together a variety of foreign influences that had already left their mark on other German authors. While it recalls *Don Quixote* in its treatment of the relation between art and reality, it also contains features of the picaresque novel, the baroque political novel, the novel of sensibility (especially in the introduction of letters and the *Bekenntnisse einer schönen Seele*), the popular subgenres of the secret society novel (in the *Turmgesellschaft*) and the horror novel (in the figures of Mignon and the harpist). Wieland's *Die Geschichte des Agathon* (1766–67; The History of Agathon) paved the way for the Bildungsroman, but *Wilhelm Meister's Apprenticeship*—together with *Wilhelm Meisters theatralische Sendung* (written 1777–85, published 1911; Wilhelm Meister's Theatrical Mission), the original version of books 1–6, and its sequel *Wilhelm Meisters Wanderjahre* (1821; Wilhelm Meister's Travels)—have been the benchmark against which later examples of the subgenre have been measured.

The romantic novel could not have developed as it did without the foundation provided by *Wilhelm Meister,* although attitudes of individual romantics toward it differed: for Friedrich Schlegel, who took up *Wilhelm Meister* in his essay "Über Goethes Meister," Goethe's novel was an event as significant as the French Revolution and Johann Gottlieb Fichte's philosophy, but for Novalis (Friedrich von Hardenberg) it lacked what he sought to realize in his novel *Heinrich von Ofterdingen* (1802). Building on their view of the novel as *ein romantisches Buch,* which should be poetic through and through (*durch und durch*

Poesie), as well as on their admiration for Cervantes, medieval romances, Sterne, and the Denis Diderot of *Jacques le fataliste* (1796; *Jacques the Fatalist*), the early romantics advocated self-reflexiveness, a mingling of genres, a combination of wit and sentiment, and the introduction of the marvelous. They also drew on the popular literature of the time, with its stock-in-trade of heroes of unknown parentage, visions and dreams, warning figures, initiation rituals, missionary journeys, disguises, mysterious towers, vaults and caverns, and secret societies that often guided (or misled) a developing hero, together with the eccentric but stereotyped figures of the evil monk and the serene hermit, the demonic woman, the impressionable youth and the madman, and such properties and motifs as the mysterious caskets, elixirs, secret writing, magic mirrors, and rings and books (see Blackall, 1983). These features, however, were not introduced merely to thrill, but also to illuminate the inner life of the characters and to provide a concrete ground for the metaphysical view that the artist as the model man must relate to the Absolute and that his work must depict an artist-hero in search of it.

In Part One of *Heinrich von Ofterdingen* (the quintessential German romantic novel), the central symbol of the blue flower activates the protagonist's quest for its meaning in a progressive intensification of experience; between Parts One and Two an allegorical *Märchen* (fairy tale) marks the transition between the real and the symbolic worlds and prefigures in its end the projected Absolute of Part Three; in Part Two the quest has reached fulfillment in the poeticization of the world; Part Three, which was never written, was to be set in Infinity. Here, as in Friedrich Hölderlin's *Hyperion* (1797–99), the quest is viewed as positive, as a search for a repetition on a higher plane of an Edenic state of integration with nature, in which divisions merge in the unity of the transcendental poetic vision resolving whatever tensions have been manifest in the quest.

Problems arose with the definition of the Absolute, of the means by which contact with it could be achieved, and of its effects on those who seek such contact, such as the inflation or dissolution of the personality. (Sigmund Freud's occasional illustration of his theories by reference to figures from these novels is a testimony to the romantics' interest in abnormal psychology and the depth of its portrayal in their work.) In the novels of Jean Paul (*Siebenkäs*, 1796–97, 1818; *Flegeljahre* [1804–05; *Walt and Vult*]; *Hesperus*, 1795, 1798; *Titan*, 1800–03; *Der Komet* [1820–22; The Comet]); Ludwig Tieck (*Franz Sternbalds Wanderungen* [1798; Franz Sternbald's Travels]; *Geschichte des Herrn William Lovell* [1795–96; History of Mr. William Lovell]); and the later romantics—Achim von Arnim (*Gräfin Dolores* [1810; Countess Dolores] and *Die Kronenwächter* [1817; The Guardians of the Crown]); Clemens Brentano (*Godwi*, 1801); E.T.A. Hoffmann (*Die Elixiere des Teufels* [1815–16; *The Devil's Elixirs*] and *Lebens-Ansichten des Katers Murr* [1820–22; The Cat Murr's Views on Life]); Joseph von Eichendorff (*Ahnung und Gegenwart* [1815; Presentiment and Presence]); and Eduard Mörike (*Maler Nolten* [1832; Nolten the Artist])—the quest was rendered problematic by the need to make adjustments to everyday reality and to resist the temptations of titanism and the sinister and diabolic aspects of the Absolute, while in the *Nachtwachen* (1804; Night Vigils) of the pseudonymous Bonaventura, this idealism gave way to a chilling nihilism. Although Goethe was resolutely opposed to what he considered romantic excesses, his late novel of adultery *Die*

Wahlverwandtschaften (1809; *The Elective Affinities*), in its relation of human psychology to natural (chemical attraction) and supernatural (the morally neutral element in personality defined as *das Dämonische*) forces ultimately beyond human control, can be related to these preoccupations. The influence of the German romantic novelists outside Germany (with the exception of Hoffmann) was limited, but their impact within the German-speaking area was to be profound, especially on the fantastic literature of decadence, and even on the prose fiction of the GDR, where authors (Fritz Rudolf Fries, Franz Fühmann, and Christa Wolf) were to find in them a counterweight to the officially prescribed norms. Political, religious, and ethical concerns were strong in Jean Paul, Eichendorff, and Arnim, while in the work of Jean Paul and Hoffmann the reality principle, in its clash with the idealism of protagonists, can extend the variety of moods to include the comic grotesque. Here, the opposition of the finite and the infinite makes up the stuff of life, transcendence of which can be achieved only in the dreams of a select few.

In the case of the historical novel, an already existing subgenre rose in status thanks to the foreign example of Sir Walter Scott, yet his contribution can only be fully understood if his own debt to the German *Sturm und Drang* (Storm and Stress)—especially Goethe's play *Götz von Berlichingen* (produced 1774), which Scott translated—is taken into account. German historical novelists—Wilhelm Hauff (*Lichtenstein*, 1826), Willibald Alexis (*Die Hosen des Herrn von Bredow* [1846; Herr von Bredow's Trousers], *Ruhe ist die erste Bürgerpflicht* [1852; The First Duty of the Citizen Is to Remain Calm]), and Theodor Fontane (*Vor dem Sturm* [1878; *Before the Storm*])—benefited from Scott's concern for historical authenticity (too easily dismissed as mere antiquarianism), and adopted his focus on a fictional hero(ine) of average talents and social status, whom fate brings into contact with real figures of influence. They went beyond Scott, however, in their concern to see in the past an explication or reflection of present political and social problems. With time, however, the historical novel participated in what has been viewed as the central problem of the German novel, its failure to develop a form of social realism that would place its practitioners in the ranks of their European contemporary counterparts, such as Charles Dickens, George Eliot, Lev Tolstoi, Honoré de Balzac, and Gustave Flaubert. This lack has given rise to a continuing debate on the nature of realism in the novel.

In the work of the politically radical *Junges Deutschland* (Young Germany) writers, a strenuous attempt was made to open the novel to contemporary material, but in trying to overcome what they saw as the aestheticism of their predecessors—indicated by their definition of classicism and romanticism as a *Kunstperiode* (aesthetic period)—they sacrificed literary merit to the proclamation of their own ideological agenda (as in Heinrich Laube's *Das junge Europa* [1837; Young Europe]). Meanwhile, the strength of the Bildungsroman tradition is evident in novelists who attempted to reflect contemporary reality (Karl Immermann in *Die Epigonen*, 1836), as much as in those who aimed to escape from it (the Austrian Adalbert Stifter in *Der Nachsommer* (1837; *Indian Summer*), or who accommodated themselves to its provincial form only after a long and tortuous progress along its margins (the Swiss Gottfried Keller, *Der grüne Heinrich* [1853–55, revised 1880; *Green Henry*]). At first sight Karl Gutzkow, whose roots lay in the *Junges Deutschland* group, appears to renounce in the massive *Die Ritter vom Geiste*

(1850–51; The Knights of the Spirit) the tendencies associated with the Bildungsroman in favor of a panoramic *Roman des Nebeneinander* (novel of simultaneity) that looks forward to 20th-century innovations. However, closer examination reveals that his complex multistrand plot is held together by familial links and an idealistic program centered on the quasi-Masonic group named in the title, features characteristic of the earlier novel. These mid-century works indicate how attempts to amalgamate the Bildungsroman in its pristine form with the novel of social realism proved more and more difficult, as it became increasingly clear that the former's ideal of harmonious integration into society through all-round cultivation of the personality could no longer plausibly be realized in a world marked by industrial progress and social upheaval.

Only Theodor Fontane, in showing the relation between private misfortune and public attitudes in a clearly defined locale (usually Berlin or estates of the landed gentry in provincial Prussia), built up an oeuvre comparable in range and depth with the social realism of his European contemporaries, a success achieved, it should be noted, by abandoning any aim to preserve and update the Bildungsroman. Consequently, Fontane's masterpiece *Effi Briest* (1895) can bear comparison as a novel on adultery with Tolstoi's *Anna Karenina* (1875–77) and Flaubert's *Madame Bovary* (1857). However, while in his portrayal of minor characters and social set-pieces Fontane's debt to Charles Dickens and William Makepeace Thackeray (and to his own experience of London) is clear, the formal subtleties of his work, which can be defined by the term *poetic realism* and have ensured it an eminence above the host of other novels on similar themes, owe more to the related genre of the Novelle as practiced by Theodor Storm, Gottfried Keller, and Conrad Ferdinand Meyer than to the novels of Fontane's contemporaries inside or outside Germany.

A note of resignation and an elegiac quality are evident in 19th-century novels that, unlike Gustav Freytag's *Soll und Haben* (1855; *Debit and Credit*), refuse to endorse the contemporary norms of rectitude, conformity, and industry and instead bring to the reader's attention the special qualities of characters who have withdrawn from the pursuit of wealth and recognition. While in the extensive oeuvre of Wilhelm Raabe such figures are legion, their eccentricity is usually the occasion for nothing more than humorous interaction in a provincial setting. By the end of the century, however, the intellectual debate produced by the challenge to accepted ideas in the work of Charles Darwin, Karl Marx, Arthur Schopenhauer, Henrik Ibsen, and Friedrich Nietzsche (to be followed later by Sigmund Freud) prompted writers to probe more deeply into human nature. Friedrich Theodor Vischer's *Auch einer* (1879; *A Rabid Philosopher*) has features of the 19th-century provincial novel centered on a clumsy eccentric and yet points to later novels in which these influences made themselves felt. Although it appeared much later, Gerhart Hauptmann's *Der Narr in Christo Emanuel Quint* (1910; *The Fool in Christ, Emanuel Quint*), the story of a more extreme marginal figure (a wandering preacher), which can be interpreted as both a study in religious mania and a tract for the times, belongs equally to this transitional phase.

All German novelists associated with high modernism came to believe that human beings are subject to conflicting impulses within their own psyche over which they can exert limited rational control, and that the pace of change, especially in certain environments such as the big city, affects the psyche in unprecedented ways. In consequence, whether (s)he is portrayed in terms of Schopenhauer's will and imagination, or Nietzsche's Dionysian and Apollonian, or Freud's ego, id, and super-ego, the character in the novel of modernism is divided within him/herself and from the world.

With *Buddenbrooks* (1901; *Buddenbrooks*), Thomas Mann succeeded in presenting a family saga that combines temporal range and topographical concentration. Its appearance at the turn of the century marks it as both an end and a beginning. The sophistication of its portrayal of character and milieu shows a debt to the Russian and Scandinavian novel of the late 19th century. Its characters are both individuals and typical of their class and of the phases in which that class rose and fell, and every aspect of their ascent and decline can be related to specific social and economic trends that historians have traced. For these qualities alone *Buddenbrooks* was bound to gain the admiration of the Marxist critic Georg Lukács. Yet the philosophical basis of this development, derived from Schopenhauer and Nietzsche, according to whom bourgeois success and artistic talent are mutually exclusive or exist in inverse relation to one another, is of greater significance than historical accuracy and introduces a new dimension to the portrayal of psychological processes at critical moments (as in *Der Tod in Venedig* [1912; *Death in Venice*]), and over a long period (as in *Tonio Kröger*, 1903). It also signals the final dissolution of the original Bildungsroman ideal, so that the subgenre could be kept alive only by artificial respiration in a hermetically sealed environment (*Der Zauberberg* [1924; *The Magic Mountain*]), by parody (*Bekenntnisse des Hochstaplers Felix Krull* [1954; *Confessions of Felix Krull, Confidence Man*]), or by deconstruction (Günter Grass' *Die Blechtrommel* [1959; *The Tin Drum*]).

German modernism, thanks to its radical approach to encompassing these tumultuous changes in man's view of the world, could afford to largely ignore the innovations present in its counterparts in other European countries: the activation of fine sensibility in the cultivation of memory in Marcel Proust's *À la recherche du temps perdu* (1913–27; translated as *Remembrance of Things Past* and also as *In Search of Lost Time*) and the reflexivity of André Gide's *Les Faux-monnayeurs* (1926; *The Counterfeiters*) were acknowledged but failed to exert influence; even the impact of James Joyce's *Ulysses* (1922), apparent in the work of Döblin, Hans Henny Jahnn, and the Austrian Hermann Broch, consisted largely of encouragement to follow to the end a course already started rather than the delivery of new impulses. Thomas Mann's *The Magic Mountain,* marked by the gradual transition from a position of unpolitical conservatism defined as *machtgeschützte Innerlichkeit* (inwardness protected by power) to a view that humanism is compatible with progress via democracy, is a characteristic compromise between German and non-German traditions on the level of ideas; its formal features, on the other hand, owe nothing to high modernism in other countries.

The midcareer novels of Hermann Hesse (*Demian* [1919; *Demian*]; *Siddhartha* [1922; *Siddhartha*]; *Der Steppenwolf* [1927; *Steppenwolf*]; and *Narziss und Goldmund* [1930; *Narcissus and Goldmund*]) owe their posthumous fame (which reached its climax during the 1960s student movement) to their combination of romantic aspirations towards the Absolute (here given an oriental coloring) and the Bildungsroman centered on the eccentric and contemporary psychology; of these only the latter can be associated with modernism. Franz Kafka's originality in *Der Prozess* (1925; *The Trial*) and *Das Schloss* (1926; *The Castle*) lies mainly in the exclusiveness with which the author's inner world is explored and revealed; his work proved influential (especially in recent Austrian literature), but ultimately inimitable. The path taken by German and Austrian modernism therefore represents a *Sonderweg* as significant and distinctive as that noted through the 19th century.

In one respect, however, the progress of the German novel coincided with developments in the other arts and in the new media inside and outside Germany in that authors resorted to a technique comparable to collage in the visual arts and montage in film, the juxtaposition of material from disparate sources, in order to render the reality of metropolitan life or to convey or imply social criticism. Alfred Döblin, in his "Berliner Programm" of 1913, in which he took issue with the futurist manifestoes of Emilio Marinetti, called for a return to the epic naïveté of Homer and the development of a cinematic style, with the aim of reversing the inflation of psychology that arises from the focus on a central protagonist and giving quantity and variety of material priority over formal integration. In realizing this program (elaborated in "Der Bau des epischen Werks" and other theoretical writings), Döblin was able to renew the historical novel in *Wallenstein* (1920) and *Die drei Sprünge des Wang-lun* (1915; *The Three Leaps of Wang-lun*) and then create in *Berlin Alexanderplatz* (1929) a metropolitan novel for which, despite the efforts of Karl Gutzkow and Theodor Fontane, there had been no German precedent. An episodic plot of sordid simplicity set in the criminal underworld, involving the failed attempts of a convict discharged from prison to go straight, is summarized at the beginning of each of the nine books by a narrator whose naive didacticism recalls the fairground ballad-monger. However, plot and narrative persona form merely a skeleton fleshed out by the montage elements drawn from numerous extraneous sources and assembled in an apparently haphazard manner that occupy most of the latter sections of each book. The narrative persona is clearly a relic from a bygone age, as if Döblin had accidentally devised Mikhail Bakhtin's polyphonic (or dialogic) novel after deciding to retain the privileged narrator of tradition.

Montage can be defined as the main artistic innovation associated with the artistic trend known as *Neue Sachlichkeit* (new objectivity) and is evident also in other genres and media, above all the cinema. Its critical potential varies from work to work, but in all its manifestations montage counters the focus on psychology that had remained strong in the Bildungsroman tradition. It undoubtedly represented the greatest challenge to the tradition of *Innerlichkeit* (inwardness) in the German novel and influenced the experimental novel of the postwar period when it underwent further transformations. Montage can be related to the general tendency to return to first principles by devising building blocks that form largely independent units, as in Joyce's *Ulysses*. The unified plot conveyed by an identifiable or conspicuous narrator was abandoned, either in favor of discrete stories told by personal narrators within a frame (a technique that goes back to Giovanni Boccaccio and had been cultivated by the masters of the 19th-century Novelle) as in Döblin's *Hamlet; oder, Die lange Nacht nimmt ein Ende* (1956; *Hamlet; or, The End of the Long Night*), or in favor of the "polyhistorical," multistrand novel such as Broch's trilogy *Die Schlafwandler* (1931–32; *The Sleepwalkers*).

The recognition of the giants of high modernism since 1945

should not blind us to their limited impact during their lifetimes. Broch, Musil, and Kafka, as citizens of the Austro-Hungarian empire and its successor states, had contacts with Germany but did not belong to the mainstream of the novel's development there. Besides, their major works in the genre appeared posthumously (Kafka) or, because of political changes, too late to bring them to prominence before the middle of the century (Musil's *The Man without Qualities* in 1930, 1933, 1943 and Broch's *Sleepwalkers* in 1931–32). Döblin had to wait until 1929 with the publication of *Berlin Alexanderplatz* for the acknowledgement that was his due, while Hans Henny Jahnn, who published little before the appearance of *Perrudja* in the same year, remained an outsider throughout his career. Even Thomas Mann, whose status as a public figure steadily grew, had to compete within the *Bildungsbürgertum* that formed the core of his readership with novelists whose star has since waned (Gerhart Hauptmann, Walter von Molo, Paul Ernst, Bernd von Heiseler, Josef Ponten). After the appearance of *The Magic Mountain*, Mann was occupied mainly with political exhortations and the slow gestation of the massive tetralogy *Joseph und seine Brüder* (*Joseph and His Brothers*), which appeared at intervals between 1933 and 1943, its third and fourth volumes outside Germany. While in *The Magic Mountain*, he rendered palatable the intellectual concerns that formed the background to modernism by means of their ironic reflection in the social comedy created within a "ship of fools" scenario, in the tetralogy Mann explored myth. He did so with a similar modern awareness of the eternal opposition of spirit and flesh in order to reveal the relationship of myth to psychology and sexuality, as well as to the progressive humanization and politicization of mankind, and to dismiss as a proto-fascist delusion the preoccupation of contemporary mystagogues with myth as a path to a prerational state.

The years of the Weimar Republic were a time when less intellectually ambitious or artistically innovative talents had the opportunity, thanks to the removal of a conservative cultural establishment and its royal patrons, to devise a social realism that would reflect contemporary sociopolitical changes. Their limited success had more to do with the political polarization of society than with the inhibiting effect the giants of modernism might have exerted. At the same time the interest of their work for us today lies precisely in its reflection of, and on those problems which resulted from, the battle between ideologies. Heinrich Mann had begun as a novelist alienated like his brother Thomas from the grasping bourgeoisie of Wilhelmine society and equally predisposed by Nietzsche's influence to castigate the escapism and psychological velleities of decadent aestheticism. The attempt in *Die Göttinnen* (1903; *The Goddesses*) to create an artificial *haute volée* environment, in which decadence might be exposed and overcome by Nietzschean aestheticism without concessions to social tendencies represented by the Wilhelmine establishment or the politicized working class, proved to be an artistic cul-de-sac. The social satire present in later works culminated in Mann's masterpiece *Der Untertan* (1918; translated as *The Patrioteer* and also as *Man of Straw*). Two further volumes, *Die Armen* (1917; *The Poor*) and *Der Kopf* (1925; *The Head*), were added to form a *Kaiserreich* (imperial) trilogy, in which the public psyche of the Second Reich is exposed from the standpoint of a republicanism adumbrated in the small-town Italian setting of *Die kleine Stadt* (1909; *The Little Town*). Heinrich's commitment to the view that *Geist* (intellect) must be opposed to *Macht* (power) brought him close to politically active expressionist circles in the transition from the Second Reich to the Weimar Republic and gave him a key role in later ideological debates on the left, especially during the period of exile.

The same view was evident in other novelists (mostly Jewish) active throughout these years, in particular Jakob Wassermann, Lion Feuchtwanger, Arnold Zweig, Döblin, and the Austrian Joseph Roth. Wasserman exhibited a moral and spiritual earnestness owing much to Dostoevskii in plots centered on miscarriages of justice (*Der Fall Maurizius* [1928; *The Maurizius Case*]). Feuchtwanger's success throughout his career as a novelist lay in his ability to combine the tensions of an often sensational plot and a strong sense of the role of mass psychology in historical change with the reflection of his own developing intellectual concerns. These came together most successfully in *Erfolg* (1930; *Success*), which weaves together a campaign for the rehabilitation of an unjustly imprisoned cultural figure and the private and professional options of a writer (an authorial projection) with the political machinations that led to Adolf Hitler's failed Munich putsch of 1923, thus demonstrating the close interaction of political, psychological, and material factors in a short period of rapid change.

Arnold Zweig followed a similar strategy in the volumes that were eventually to form the cycle *Der grosse Krieg der weissen Männer* (1927–58; The Great War of the White Men), which is held together as much by the central figure of a scrupulous intellectual (another authorial projection) as by the events (mainly on the battlefields and behind the front lines during World War I). Much later, in the tetralogy *November 1918* (written 1938–43, published 1939–50), Döblin examined the abortive revolution of 1918–19 as the spiritual odyssey of an intellectual protagonist who, after returning wounded from the front, is purged through suffering and despair; the result is a mixture of historical documentary and *eine Geschichte zwischen Himmel und Hölle* (a story between heaven and hell). *Neue Sachlichkeit,* in part a disillusioned reaction to the idealism of expressionism, in part an acknowledgement of the effect of technological advances on perceptions and attitudes, encouraged a cynicism that was reflected and challenged by some novelists—in particular Hans Fallada, Leonhard Frank, Erich Kästner, Erich Maria Remarque, Hermann Kesten, and Irmgard Keun—in plots that focused on the trials and tribulations of vulnerable working and petty bourgeois figures in the economic crises and political upheavals that marked the Weimar Republic. At the same time, a temporary vogue for novels based on authors' experience of World War I (initiated by Remarque's *Im Westen nichts Neues* [1929; *All Quiet on the Western Front*]) demonstrated more clearly that disillusionment had political implications.

All these initiatives—the major modernist experiments; the social and historical panoramas of Heinrich Mann, Feuchtwanger, and Arnold Zweig; and the social microcosms of the *Neue Sachlichkeit* writers—were to be stifled when the Nazis took power in 1933. With few exceptions these writers went into exile, and Nazi cultural policy concentrated on the encouragement of attitudes that could be harnessed to the realization of the regime's long-term aims. The novel, with its focus on individual difference and its private form of consumption, received less attention from official quarters than the other major genres, which could be more easily adapted to the public creation of the *Volksgemeinschaft* (community of the people), poetry in marching songs, elegies to the martyrs of the movement, and drama in the (re)creation of critical situations from the immediate and distant past that aimed to test the heroic protagonist in such a manner that the live audience would be unable to resist the ideological implications. The conservative writers of the Weimar Republic were allowed to satisfy a largely fellow-traveling middle-class reading public with work that, without explicitly extolling Nazi policies, hypostatized the German "soul," or proclaimed the virtues of self-sacrifice (by men in public and women in private) in the name of a vaguely adumbrated cause. Since Nazi cultural policy challenged modernism in all the arts, writers who had been drawn to it, yet remained in Germany throughout the Third Reich insofar as they had the opportunity to publish, had to make some concessions, at least in formal terms, to imposed norms. In 1945, when the suppression of modernism was reversed, they accepted and appreciated it but did not embrace it wholeheartedly.

Novels produced by writers in exile belong to three groups. The first is comprised of works by major figures who, while they did not engage in the ideological debates prompted by the ease with which the Nazis had taken over the cultural life of Germany, were concerned to maintain a cultural tradition self-evidently opposed to Nazism (Thomas Mann, Broch, and Musil, to whom may be added Hermann Hesse in *Das Glasperlenspiel* [1943; translated as *Magister Ludi* and also as *The Glass Bead Game*], although as a naturalized Swiss he cannot be defined as an exile). The second group of novels reflected the Third Reich, the exile situation, and the sociopolitical crisis that had destroyed the Weimar Republic (Klaus Mann in *Mephisto*, 1936; Feuchtwanger in *Die Geschwister Oppenheim* [1933; *The Oppermanns*] and *Exil* [1940; *Paris Gazette*]; Oskar Maria Graf in *Anton Sittinger*, 1937; Irmgard Keun in *Nach Mitternacht* [1937; *After Midnight*]; Anna Seghers in *Das siebte Kreuz* [1947; *The Seventh Cross*] and *Die Toten bleiben jung* [1949; *The Dead Stay Young*]; Willi Bredel in the trilogy *Verwandte und Bekannte* [1941–53; Relations and Acquaintances]; and Arnold Zweig in *Das Beil von Wandsbek* [1947; *The Axe of Wandsbek*]). The third group consists of historical novels that aim to place contemporary problems in the context of earlier upheavals and their effect on exemplary figures, whether intellectuals in their search for a role or rulers in the fulfillment of their political task (Thomas Mann in the Joseph tetralogy; Heinrich Mann in the two volumes of *Henri Quatre*, 1935, 1938; Bruno Frank in *Cervantes*, 1934; Feuchtwanger in the Josephus trilogy, 1932–45; Stefan Zweig in *Triumph und Tragik des Erasmus von Rotterdam* [1934; *Erasmus of Rotterdam*] and *Castellio gegen Calvin* [1936; *The Right to Heresy*]; Hermann Kesten in the Spanish trilogy, 1936–52; Gustav Regler in *Die Saat* [1936; The Seed]; Alfred Neumann in the Napoleon III trilogy, 1934–40; Döblin in *Amazonas* [1937–38; The Amazon]; and even Brecht in *Die Geschäfte des Herrn Julius Cäsar* [1957; Julius Caesar's Business Career]). In their concern to take issue with the Nazi phenomenon and reach a foreign readership, even noncommunist exiles were forced to retreat from modernism. The sole great modernist to tackle the issue of Germany's drift towards Nazism in a more than episodic manner, Thomas Mann in *Doktor Faustus* (1947; *Doctor Faustus*) adopted a strategy of indirection by choosing as protagonist a composer whose solitary dedication to the advancement of his art is made to reflect the contemporary attempt within the *Bildungsbürgertum* to cope with an essentially spiritual crisis by resorting to extreme political solutions.

Despite the effects of Joseph Stalin's internal and foreign *Realpolitik*, committed communists who had begun their careers during the Weimar Republic played a key role during the exile period in the development of an antifascist agenda and the fiction to support it, before settling in the Soviet zone after Hitler's defeat. Their work before and after 1945 represented a solid base on which later GDR novelists could build. However, in the GDR even the mildest cultivation of modernist technique was branded as "formalism" by the cultural apparatchiks who followed the Moscow line of Andrey Zhdanov, while Georg Lukács consistently rejected modernism in the name of a socialist realism he viewed as the heir to the critical realism of the 19th-century social novel. As GDR writers came to define their position in relation to the crude socialist realism that had become the norm in the Soviet Union during the period of high Stalinism, a threefold division within the cultural life of the GDR gradually but inevitably emerged: the conformists who accepted without question the party line; others who sought a measure of artistic independence within the system; and the "dissidents," initially small in number but rapidly growing in the 1970s and 1980s, most of whom left for the West before the *Wende* (the collapse of the GDR in 1989). The constantly shifting and overlapping composition of these groups was an index of the changing temperature of official cultural policy, yet it is possible to extrapolate from these fluctuations a development (mainly centered on the second group) in which fiction recognized outside the GDR's borders played a prominent part.

While the first native talents (Erik Neutsch, Max Walter Schulz, Dieter Noll, and Erwin Strittmatter) were content for the most part to follow in the footsteps of the former exiles (Johannes R. Becher, Hans Marchwitza, Ludwig Renn, Willi Bredel, Anna Seghers, Stefan Heym, and Stephan Hermlin), the following age groups showed a measure of independence in their artistic approach to approved themes (the conversion to antifascism of the "front generation," the struggle to reconstruct the economy on socialist lines, and the socialist Bildungsroman centered on the professional progress of figures previously denied educational opportunities), particularly Franz Fühmann, Brigitte Reimann, Christa Wolf, and Hermann Kant. In the 1970s and 1980s Günter de Bruyn, Christa Wolf, Jurek Becker, Christoph Hein, Karl-Heinz Jakobs, Volker Braun, and Ulrich Plenzdorf conducted an ever more radical investigation of the dilemmas that had emerged from the clash between collective pressures and the desire for personal fulfillment. Myth and fantasy broke the mold of realism and were adapted to a feminist agenda in the work of Irmtraud Morgner (*Trobadora Beatriz,* 1974, and *Amanda,* 1983) and Christa Wolf (*Kassandra* [1983; *Cassandra*] and *Medea: Stimmen* [1996; Medea: Voices]). The historical novel (especially in the hands of Stefan Heym) was given a function similar to the one it had during the exile period: to reflect in more or less coded form on the relations between *Geist* and *Macht*—a perennial German theme that took on a new relevance as the system became ever more sclerotic.

In the West the transition to democracy after 1945 did not lead immediately to a social realism based on foreign models, but instead led to an airless magic realism imbued with a dour existentialism, as in Hermann Kasack's *Die Stadt hinter dem Strom* (1947; *The City Beyond the River*), Stefan Andres' trilogy *Die Sintflut* (1949, 1951, 1959; The Flood) and Hans Erich Nossack's novels, all of which differed little in style from the more significant works of the "inner emigration," such as Ernst Jünger's *Auf den Marmorklippen* (1939; *On the Marble Cliffs*), the historical novels of Jochen Klepper, Werner Bergengruen, and Reinhold Schneider; Elisabeth Langgässer's *Das unauslöschliche Siegel* (1946; The Ineradicable Seal); and the novels of Ernst Wiechert, all inspired (with the exception of Jünger) by the Christianity of the catacombs. The social realism that emerged in the Federal Republic in its initial phase in the work of Gerd Gaiser, Heinrich Böll, Alfred Andersch, and Wolfgang Koeppen integrated to some degree modernist innovations, but only Arno Schmidt devoted himself singlemindedly to a project that aimed to adapt and develop further a strand of modernism that had received little attention in Germany, the exploration of the interface between linguistic creativity and depth psychology.

The year 1959 marked a turning point with the publication of Heinrich Böll's *Billard um halb zehn* (*Billiards at Half-Past Nine*), Uwe Johnson's *Mutmassungen über Jakob* (*Speculations about Jakob*), and Günter Grass' *The Tin Drum*, followed in 1960 by *Halbzeit* (*Half-Time*), the first part of Martin Walser's trilogy centered on the postwar man-on-the-make Anselm Kristlein. The concessions to modernism in these works were greater than those made in the previous phase, but they varied in degree and type. Böll and Johnson adopted multiple perspectives, Grass the unreliable narrator with some of the features of the picaro, and Walser the ironical stance of an unobtrusive narrator toward an antihero whose consciousness suffuses the novel. At the same time Peter Weiss, who belonged to the younger generation of exiles and had begun as an artist influenced by surrealism, produced a series of short, partly autobiographical prose works in which techniques resembling those of the *nouveau roman* were evident. Each of these five developed his own compromise between social realism and experimentalism in later works. Activated by an unorthodox Catholicism, Böll held up a mirror to his fellow citizens in order to expose postwar complacency and vestiges of a mentality encouraged by Nazism. In the following parts of the Danzig trilogy (*Katz und Maus* [1961; *Cat and Mouse*] and *Hundejahre* [1963; *Dog Years*]) Grass added an ethical dimension to existentialism, but in a style that has nothing in common with Jean-Paul Sartre and Albert Camus, whose stance otherwise resembles his. Johnson cultivated a determined detachment from the opposing ideological restrictions imposed by the Cold War division of Germany, and in the four volumes of *Jahrestage* (1970, 1971, 1973, 1983; *Anniversaries*), expanded his horizons to take in the metropolitan modernity of New York in 1968 and the provincial restrictions of Mecklenburg during the Third Reich. Walser, in concentrating on the crises of his mainly male and middle-class protagonists, has remained closest to the mainstream of sociopsychological realism in the English-speaking countries, as represented by John Updike, Kingsley Amis, and Angus Wilson. Weiss, after achieving prominence as a dramatist, devoted himself in *Die Ästhetik des Widerstandes* (The Aesthetics of Resistance) to an account in three volumes (1975, 1978, and 1981) of the odyssey of a working-class exile who is made a vehicle for a profound and agonized investigation of the tribulations of the homeless left caught between the murderous systems of Hitler and Stalin. *Anniversaries* and *Die Ästhetik des Widerstandes* are two mighty erratic blocks in the postwar German literary landscape; the former in its determination to place the division of Germany in the context of the global confrontation between the systems that marked the Cold War, the latter in its attempt to reintegrate and bring to the notice of a later generation the full spectrum of those artistic, intellectual, and political movements that had been marginalized during the Third Reich and, to a certain extent, the postwar restoration.

The process by which German writers in both states sought to come to terms with the Nazi past had already reached its climax with a series of independently conceived large-scale novels consisting of Siegfried Lenz's *Deutschstunde* (1968; *The German Lesson*), Böll's *Gruppenbild mit Dame* (1971; *Group Portrait with Lady*), Andersch's *Winterspelt* (1974; *Winterspelt*), Christa Wolf's *Kindheitsmuster* (1976; *A Model of Childhood*), and Horst Bienek's Gleiwitz tetralogy (1975–82). With the deaths of Weiss (1982), Johnson (1984), and Böll (1985) this phase may be said to have come to an end, and although Grass and Walser have continued to produce major works, these cannot be viewed as typical of later phases in the post-1945 development of the novel.

This modernistic social realism gave way to a phase of *neue Subjektivität* (new subjectivity) that bore fruit in confessional literature in all genres. Here the French *nouveau roman*, in its focus on the microscopic perceptions and psychological disorientation of the narrator, paved the way, especially through the work of Dieter Wellershoff (*Die Schattengrenze* [1969; The Shadow's Limit]), and a small group originally associated with him whose members later went their separate ways (Gisela Elsner, Rolf Dieter Brinkmann, Nicolas Born, and Günter Herburger). While in the GDR this subjective tendency marked a necessary stage in the growth away from socialist realism and therefore had a liberating effect (as in Christa Wolf's *Nachdenken über Christa T.* [1968; *The Quest for Christa T.*] and *A Model of Childhood*), in the West it was largely a consequence of the frustration felt by those who had been politically active during the student movement and therefore a means to express disillusionment, as in Born's *Die erdabgewandte Seite der Geschichte* (1976; The Far Side of History), and Bernward Vesper's *Die Reise* (1977; The Trip). However, at the same time members of an older generation made their own contributions to the subjective trend in retrospective ruminations on longer life phases, as in Hermann Lenz's seven-part autobiographical cycle (1966–), Wolfgang Hildesheimer's *Tynset* (1965) and *Masante* (1973), Wolfgang Koeppen's *Jugend* (1976; Youth), Stephan Hermlin's *Abendlicht* (1979; *Evening Light*), and Hubert Fichte's early autobiographical works. Grass' *Der Butt* (1977; *The Flounder*), although its author makes no secret of its autobiographical foundation, cannot be bracketed with the subjectivity of either the younger or the older generation. Its historical sweep (4,000 years), its formal sophistication (the parallel plots of the narrator's account of his wife's pregnancy, the adventures of the flounder drawn from one of the Grimms' fairy tales, and the contribution to human progress of 11 female cooks, integrated by the principal theme of the battle of the sexes), and its relevance to contemporary issues place it in a special category along with Stefan Heym's *Ahasver* (1981; *The Wandering Jew*), which similarly combines a multistrand plot, historical range, and a revision of myth and social satire.

Although Grass continued to make his mark with *Kopfgeburten* (1980; *Headbirths*) and *Die Rättin* (1986; *The Rat*), in which an already evident apocalyptic tone became more strident, the 1980s were instead dominated by three talents who are eccentric to the compromise outlined above. Of these Thomas Bernhard and Peter Handke, as Austrians, deserve only passing

mention here, although they, like their compatriot Ingeborg Bachmann, have received far more attention in Germany than normally granted to Austrian literature. Whether the third, Botho Strauss, is Germany's star in the international postmodernist firmament (beside Thomas Pynchon, John Barth, Umberto Eco, Italo Calvino, Milan Kundera, and Salman Rushdie) is still a matter of debate, but there is no doubt that in *Der junge Mann* (1984; The Young Man) and other prose works he is acutely aware of those phenomena that are normally associated with the postmodernist condition.

In the 1990s, despite the transformation of the political scene produced by unification, the cultural scene remained in a state of transition marked by *Unübersichtlichkeit* (impossibility of taking an overview). Initially, Germany maintained economic stability despite the strains that accompanied the need to bring the standard of living of the former GDR to the level of the West, and the tensions that arose from the fear of mass immigration from the East and the Third World were solved thanks to a combination of firm but flexible government policy and grassroots soul-searching. In other words, Germany presented all the conditions for an indigenous form of postmodernism comparable to what had rapidly become an international norm. Yet the three major literary controversies of the 1990s—the *deutsch-deutscher Literaturstreit* centered on Christa Wolf as representative of a GDR literature that had avoided commitments to the systems of East and West during the Cold War; the debate prompted by an essay by Botho Strauss, "Anschwellender Bocksgesang" (The Rising Song of Goats), which had castigated from a "new right" point of view the factitious superficiality of a civilization dominated by the electronic media; and the reception of Grass' monumental novel *Ein weites Feld* (1995; A Big Area), which offered a sceptical view of post-1990 Germany based on an earlier left consensus sensitive to resurgent nationalism—demonstrated the degree to which established writers, however different from one another, were out of sympathy with the national mood. As a consequence the German literary scene, although far from stagnant, appeared marked by stasis and uncertainty about the direction writing would take, while the reading public drew its own conclusions by turning to translations of foreign work. Yet if the German novel stood at a crossroads, it was because German society had largely overcome those sociopolitical upheavals and concomitant intellectual and psychological destabilizations that had challenged earlier generations of novelists to respond, either with the strenuous conceptualizations and artistic démarches of Mann, Musil, Broch, Döblin, and Jahnn, or with the critical neorealism characteristic of such post-1945 figures as Siegfried Lenz, Hans Werner Richter, Andersch, Böll, Walser, Grass, and those GDR writers who had proved acceptable in the West. To some extent a vacuum was created, to be filled by Austrians and Swiss.

Austrian novelists (including Peter Handke, Gerhard Roth, Peter Rosei, and Barbara Frischmuth) who did not espouse the cause of an Austrian cultural autonomy with strong conservative overtones (for a time officially propagated) continued to find favor in Germany. Both the Swiss Max Frisch and his compatriot Friedrich Dürrenmatt, whose reputation outside the German-speaking countries continued to rest on the plays they wrote in the early postwar years, experienced an Indian summer of creativity as novelists—Frisch with *Montauk* (1975; *Montauk*), *Der Mensch erscheint im Holozän* (1979; *Man in the Holocene*), and

Blaubart (1982; *Bluebeard*); Dürrenmatt with *Justiz* (1985; *The Execution of Justice*), *Der Auftrag* (1986; *The Assignment*), and *Durcheinanderthal* (1989). Significantly, Christoph Ransmayr's *Die letzte Welt* (1988; *The Last World*) and Patrick Süskind's *Das Parfum* (1985; *Perfume*), normally adduced in discussions of the German novel's opening to postmodernism, were by an Austrian and a Swiss, evidence that the margins had become more representative than the center, a phenomenon that found a parallel in the English-speaking world. Other writers who have been linked to postmodern trends, Wolfgang Hildesheimer (in *Marbot: Eine Biographie* [1981; *Marbot: A Biography*]), Gert Jonke, Klaus Hoffer, Gerold Späth, and Hermann Burger, also belonged by birth and/or choice to the periphery.

Toward the end of the century German novelists, in the absence of a major new talent, consisted of fabulists with a lightness of touch unusual in German literature (Uwe Timm, Gerhard Köpf, Sten Nadolny, Thorsten Becker, and the independently working brothers Peter and Michael Schneider), women writers whose work was suffused with feminine sensibility yet devoid of strident feminism (Brigitte Kronauer, the Swiss Gertrud Leutenegger), immigrant writers who adapted the narrative traditions of their original homelands to plots that turned on the obstacles to multiculturalism in Germany (for example, Rafik Schami), experienced practitioners of the family saga and the semifictional biography of cultural figures from the past (Dieter Kühn, Pieter Härting, the Swiss Adolf Muschg, and Hanns-Joseph Ortheil), and providers of broad historical panoramas imbued with a strong element of mythical fantasy (Herbert Rosendorfer, Carl Amery, Stefan Schütz, Gerd Heidenreich, and Günter Herburger).

A long tradition in German theory and criticism has seen the development of the novel as a process in which the novelist tries strenuously and with varying degrees of success to yoke together an account of the conflicting perceptions of his/her characters with an objective portrayal of the surrounding world—a task rendered increasingly difficult as the inner life of the characters (especially of the central protagonist) became more psychologically complex and the world, even when socially constricted (as it usually is in the novels of the 18th and 19th centuries), became more socially and politically complex. A further dimension was added by the view that the spiritual sureties that existed throughout the medieval and early modern periods were undermined, especially by the various philosophical movements that contributed to the emergence of a *Weltanschauung* marked by *transzendentale Obdachlosigkeit* (transcendental homelessness), a phrase coined by Georg Lukács in his seminal *Die Theorie des Romans* (1920; *The Theory of the Novel*). The elegiac tone evident in this work can be traced back to German idealist philosophy, especially to the remarks on the novel in G.W.F. Hegel's *Ästhetik* (1835; *Aesthetics*), and is maintained in Broch's scattered theoretical pronouncements on *Zerfall der Werte* (dissolution of values) and their novelistic realization in his trilogy *The Sleepwalkers*, as well as in the aesthetics of Walter Benjamin and Theodor W. Adorno. The innovations of modernism were in this view the results of an artistic impasse or symptoms of spiritual malaise.

However, such a view of aesthetic change failed to take account of the liberating effect of experiment, the momentum of formal innovation, and the urge to go further on the same path or to seek an equally innovative alternative. Significant innovations in the further development of modernism included the extension of montage beyond Döblin's practice through the inclusion of material from the nonliterary media (as in Rolf Dieter Brinkmann's *Rom, Blicke* (1979; *Views of Rome*); the creation of hypothetical situations in which a fluid identity may be realized (as in Musil's *The Man without Qualities* and the novels of Max Frisch, especially *Mein Name sei Gantenbein* (1964; translated as *A Wilderness of Mirrors* and also as *Gantenbein*); the juxtaposition of numerous and conflicting perspectives of which none receives authorial endorsement; the cultivation of fantasy in a spirit of play or in the invention of utopias or dystopias, often accompanied by switches in time levels; the exploration of a single subjectivity; and the accretion of essayistic or discursive material. These techniques all became the stock-in-trade of novelists who no longer associated them with the dissolution of the certainties on which aesthetic norms, up to and including 19th-century realism, had been based.

However, such innovations tended to challenge the norms and expectations created by a realism that aimed to reflect social forces in a historically identifiable situation, and most German novelists since World War I wished not only to reflect but also to challenge these forces, especially as they found expression in the political development of the Weimar Republic, the Third Reich, the initial phase of the Federal Republic (often defined as a "restoration" associated with the paternalism of its first chancellor, Konrad Adenauer), and the final phase of the German Democratic Republic (in which the ideological underpinning provided by antifascism was gradually eroded). Consequently, German novelists throughout this period remained subject to the conflicting impulses generated by these sociopolitical forces and by the innovations of high modernism and thus steered a course between them. Each found a place on a spectrum that extended from realism to experimentalism. Just as in the 19th century their forebears came to a compromise between the foreign stimulus of realism and the native traditions of *Bildung* and romantic inwardness, they achieved in their own way an accommodation of these clashing impulses.

MALCOLM HUMBLE

See also Austrian Novel; Bildungsroman; Heinrich Böll; Alfred Döblin; Theodor Fontane; Johann Wolfgang von Goethe; Günter Grass; Hermann Hesse; Historical Novel; Uwe Johnson; Franz Kafka; Thomas Mann; Notebooks of Malte Laurids Brigge; Novella; Simplicius Simplicissimus; Swiss Novel (German Language); Christa Wolf

Further Reading

Aust, Hugo, *Der historische Roman*, Stuttgart: Metzler, 1994
Bance, Alan, *The German Novel, 1945–1960*, Stuttgart: Akademischer Verlag Hans-Dieter Heinz, 1980
Bauer, Matthias, *Der Schelmenroman*, Stuttgart: Metzler, 1994
Baumgart, Reinhard, *Aussichten des Romans oder Hat Literatur Zukunft?*, Neuwied: Luchterhand, 1968
Beddow, Michael, *The Fiction of Humanity: Studies in the Bildungsroman from Wieland to Thomas Mann*, Cambridge and New York: Cambridge University Press, 1982
Blackall, Eric A., *The Novels of the German Romantics*, Ithaca, New York: Cornell University Press, 1983
Brauneck, Manfred, editor, *Der deutsche Roman im 20.*

Jahrhundert: Analysen und Materialien zur Theorie und Soziologie des Romans, 2 vols., Bamberg: Buchners, 1976

Bullivant, Keith, *Realism Today: Aspects of the Contemporary West German Novel,* Leamington Spa: Oswald Wolff, and New York: St. Martin's Press, 1987

Bullivant, Keith, editor, *The Modern German Novel,* Leamington Spa and New York: Berg, 1987

Durzak, Manfred, *Der deutsche Roman der Gegenwart,* Stuttgart: Kohlhammer, 1971; 3rd edition, 1979

Grimm, Reinhold, editor, *Deutsche Romantheorien. Beiträge zu einer historischen Poetik des Romans in Deutschland,* Frankfurt am Main: Athenäum, 1968

Hardin, James, editor, *Reflection and Action: Essays on the Bildungsroman,* Columbia: University of South Carolina Press, 1991

Hillebrand, Bruno, *Theorie des Romans,* 2 vols., Munich: Winkler, 1972

Hillebrand, Bruno, editor, *Zur Struktur des Romans,* Darmstadt: Wissenschaftliche Buchgesellschaft, 1978

Jacobs, Jürgen, *Wilhelm Meister und seine Brüder: Untersuchungen zum deutschen Bildungsroman,* Munich: Fink, 1972

Kimpel, Dieter, *Der Roman der Aufklärung,* Stuttgart: Metzler, 1967; 2nd edition, 1977

Klotz, Volker, editor, *Zur Poetik des Romans,* Darmstadt: Wissenschaftliche Buchgesellschaft, 1965

Koopmann, Helmut, editor, *Handbuch des deutschen Romans,* Düsseldorf: Bagel, 1983

Lämmert, Eberhard, editor, *Romantheorie: Dokumentation ihrer Geschichte in Deutschland seit 1880,* Cologne: Kiepenheuer and Witsch, 1975

Lukács, Georg, *Die Theorie des Romans,* Berlin: Cassirer, 1920; as *The Theory of the Novel,* Cambridge, Massachusetts: MIT Press, 1971

Lukács, Georg, *A történelmi regény,* Budapest: Hungaria, 1937; German edition, *Der historische Roman,* Berlin: Aufbau, 1955; as *The Historical Novel,* London: Merlin Press, 1962; New York: Humanities Press, 1965

Mayer, Gerhart, *Der deutsche Bildungsroman: Von der Aufklärung bis zur Gegenwart,* Stuttgart: Metzler, 1992

Meid, Werner Volker, *Der deutsche Barockroman,* Stuttgart: Metzler, 1974

Müller, Götz, *Gegenwelten: Die Utopie in der deutschen Literatur,* Stuttgart: Metzler, 1989

Pascal, Roy, *The German Novel,* Manchester: Manchester University Press, and Toronto: University of Toronto Press, 1956

Paulsen, Wolfgang, editor, *Der deutsche Roman und seine historischen und politischen Bedingungen,* Bern: Francke, 1977

Petersen, Jürgen H., *Der deutsche Roman der Moderne. Grundlegung, Typologie, Entwicklung,* Stuttgart: Metzler, 1991

Scheunemann, Dietrich, in *Moderne Literatur in Grundbegriffen,* edited by Dieter Borchmeyer and Viktor Zmegac, Frankfurt am Main: Athenäum, 1987

Selbmann, Rolf, *Der deutsche Bildungsroman,* Stuttgart: Metzler, 1984

Selbmann, Rolf, editor, *Zur Geschichte des deutschen Bildungsromans,* Darmstadt: Wissenschaftliche Buchgesellschaft, 1988

Singer, Herbert, *Der galante Roman,* Stuttgart: Metzler, 1961

Steinecke, Hartmut, editor, *Theorie und Technik des Romans im 20. Jahrhundert,* Tübingen: Max Niemeyer, 1972; 2nd edition, 1979

Swales, Martin, *The German Bildungsroman from Wieland to Hesse,* Princeton, New Jersey: Princeton University Press, 1978

von Wiese, Benno, editor, *Der deutsche Roman vom Barock bis zur Gegenwart,* 2 vols., Düsseldorf: Bagel, 1963

Waidson, H.M., *The Modern German Novel: A Mid-Twentieth Century Survey,* London and New York: Oxford University Press, 1959; 2nd edition as *The Modern German Novel, 1945-1965,* 1971

Welzig, Werner, *Der deutsche Roman im 20. Jahrhundert,* Stuttgart: Kröner, 1967; 2nd edition, 1970

Ziolkowski, Theodore, *Dimensions of the Modern Novel,* Princeton, New Jersey: Princeton University Press, 1969; German edition, as *Strukturen des modernen Romans: Deutsche Beispiele und Europaische Zusammenhange,* Munich: List, 1972

Geroi nashego vremeni. *See* Hero of Our Time

André Gide 1869–1951

French

Perhaps André Gide's greatest achievement was simply being André Gide. His life as a man of letters and ideas counts more than individual achievements and overflows even the sum of his writings. He worked in all major genres, especially fiction, and numerous secondary ones (criticism, letters, treatises, autobiography). His *Journal* remains a monument. He also played with generic boundaries and wrote fiction that contributed to the loosening and reinventing of genres. Marginalized himself (despite his upper-bourgeois origins and independent income) because of his homosexuality, he had a penchant for the socially and aesthetically exceptional. A writer rather than an activist, he nevertheless took a public stand on some controversial issues.

Early in his career, under the influence of symbolism, Gide rejected realist and naturalist fictional models. He even produced works that may be called symbolist fiction, marked by a turning away from external reality, which is characteristic of symbolist drama and poetry. His first book, *Les Cahiers d'André Walter* (1891; *The Notebooks of André Walter*), laden with late-19th-century clichés, concentrated on dramas of the soul couched in ethereal terms. He attempted to express the psychological complexity of his clearly autobiographical hero without acknowledging the true source of his torment. The effort led to a complicated reflexive structure of notebooks, "white" and "black," plus "found pages," all coextensive with the book. The notebooks form a complex arrangement of reflections, reminiscences, questionings, quotations, and notes on the *hero's* book-in-progress, "Allain."

Thus, from his very first work, Gide used the form of notebooks—which recur in or constitute numerous subsequent works—and reflexive, multi-level plots that contain little external action. This mirroring is an expression of the mirror of Gidean narcissism, which appears in *André Walter* and elsewhere, explicitly or implicitly, and is related to the omnipresent theme of sincerity.

Although previous novelists had used the diary form, Gide refined it further, both formally and psychologically. *André Walter* had few contemporary imitators, but it set a model for such later authors as Robbe-Grillet, Butor, and Ollier, who similarly exploited reflexivity. Speaking of his *La Tentative amoureuse* (1893; *The Lovers' Attempt*), another multi-layered narrative, Gide applied the heraldic term *mise en abyme* (the internal mirroring of the work) to fiction, and it is now widely used in French critical vocabulary to refer to specularity.

Gide also wrote several examples of what he would later label the *sotie*. The word derived from medieval theatre terminology, indicating a performance of *sots* (fools), or farce. His *Paludes* (1895; *Marshlands*) is a ludic treatment of some of the themes of *André Walter*: the passive, neurotic writer, the somewhat ethereal female figure (here rather ridiculous, unlike Emmanuèle in *André Walter*), the effort to write a book within a book—in this case, "Paludes." That the hero gives up the project eventually and decides instead to write "Polders" (drained wetlands) merely underlines the themes of stagnation and circularity. Various elements, including paratexts (texts beyond the story proper)—"Table of the Most Remarkable Sentences from Paludes," left mostly blank, is the most striking—reintroduce into French fiction certain liberties taken by Laurence Sterne and Denis Diderot in the 18th century. The preface, which announces that the meaning of the book will be left up to the public, foreshadows indeterminacy of meaning in 20th-century literature and the literary and linguistic theories that have supported it. Gide's following *sotie*, *Le Prométhée mal enchaîné* (1899; *Prometheus Illbound*), introduced other farcical elements that break the realistic illusion, such as Greek characters strolling in Paris. The claim that the book was written with a feather from Prometheus' eagle puts the adventure of plot and the adventure of writing on the same plane.

The work also introduced the notion of the gratuitous act—an act bereft of all motivation and purpose—which amounts to a denial of psychological verisimilitude as demanded in realism. It is illustrated more extensively in the third *sotie*, *Les Caves du Vatican* (1914; *The Vatican Cellars*), in an episode in which Lafcadio, the hero, pushes someone from a train for no reason. This episode—as well as his ridicule of the Church—contributed to Gide's reputation as an immoralist and tended to overshadow other aspects of the book's originality. In *The Vatican Cellars*, Gide expanded his use of multiple plots and themes and, in the burlesque mode, undertook social satire on an extended scale. Undercutting its overt themes of biological and social determinism and simple-minded belief, the work plays with human possibilities. It also deconstructs, explicitly and implicitly, the formulas of realistic fiction, creating in their place an elaborate mock-epic.

Early in his career, Gide also renewed French psychological realism, which went back to the 17th century. Indeed, to many readers he is preeminently a psychological novelist. *L'Immoraliste* (1902; *The Immoralist*) is a masterpiece of psychological analysis that, while highly autobiographical, was more successful than *André Walter* in taking a dispassionate view of Gide's own psychological mechanisms. *The Immoralist* is a frame narrative in which the distance between the obtuse inner narrator and the outer narrator (who sets down the story in epistolary form for an anonymous reader) creates moral and psychological uncertainty. The contradictory impulses in the hero, who wishes both to develop and dissipate his material and intellectual patrimony, seem uncannily modern, paralleling Freud's understanding of destructive human impulses and the drive to surpass the self that Nietzsche had celebrated. (Gide had not yet read Freud but did know Nietzsche somewhat.) The subcurrent of homosexuality, subtle enough, apparently, to have gone unnoticed by many readers, anticipates Gide's later work.

Sometimes labeled *novel, The Immoralist* is a *récit*, or linear narrative marked by psychological analysis. Two subsequent works of this type have appealed to large audiences and contributed to Gide's reputation as a subtle dissector of sentiment and moral dilemmas. *La Porte étroite* (1909; *Strait Is the Gate*) is the critical counterpart of *The Immoralist*, showing not hedonism and self-dissipation but, instead, the ascetic impulse, which proves equally destructive, since the heroine's denial of herself in the name of religion, encouraged by a passive and overly scrupulous suitor, destroys two lives. Narrated by the hero, it also includes portions of the heroine's notebooks, which shed oblique and correcting light on what precedes. The impulses that Gide depicted here were, like those in *The Immoralist,* his own (and his wife's). Both works, he claimed, were not only a critical analysis but a form of self-therapy. His 1919 *récit La Symphonie pastorale (The Pastoral Symphony)* similarly involved self-projection. The story of a Protestant pastor who becomes enamored of his ward, it subtly exposes religious and sentimental deceit. A double notebook structure with complex chronology supports the theme of psychological blindness. While self-expression had been commonplace since romanticism, the Gidean modes are particularly modern, since they involve the repressed self. Unfortunately, Gide's attempts to treat the questions of marriage and feminism through complementary and self-deceiving perspectives in *L'École des femmes* (1929) and its two sequels (all translated in *The School for Wives*) are less subtle and inventive.

In *Les Faux-monnayeurs* (1926; *The Counterfeiters*), the techniques and themes featured elsewhere (notebooks, novel-in-novel, exploration of sincerity and other psychological questions, social criticism, evaluation of homosexuality) are combined in an elaborate structure with multiple plots. (*See separate entry,* The Counterfeiters.) The novel's concern with crime echoes that in *Isabelle* (1911), a *récit,* and *The Vatican Cellars.* Gide also contributed to the renewed use of Greek myth in the 20th century, with works in various genres, including the *récit Thésée* (1946; *Theseus*), a brilliant, idiosyncratic mythological fiction.

As a novelist, and still more as an intellectual figure, Gide has appealed to different audiences: a traditional psychological novelist to some, an innovative modernist to others, to still others a superb stylist, major literary critic, social crusader, or spokesman for homosexual rights. These multiple achievements and the rich variety of his production justify the label applied to him in the 1920s and after: "le contemporain capital" (the great contemporary).

CATHARINE SAVAGE BROSMAN

See also Counterfeiters

Biography

Born 22 November 1869 in Paris, France. Attended École Alsacienne, Paris, 1878–80; Lycée in Montpellier, 1881; boarder at M. Henri Bauer, 1883–85, and at M. Jacob Keller, 1886–87; École Alsacienne, 1887; École Henri IV: baccalauréat 1890. Mayor of a Normandy commune, 1896; juror in Rouen, 1912; special envoy of Colonial Ministry on trip to Africa, 1925–26. A founder of *Nouvelle Revue française,* 1909. Awarded Nobel prize for literature, 1947. Died 19 February 1951.

Novels by Gide

Les Cahiers d'André Walter, 1891; translated in part as *The White Notebook,* by Wade Baskin, 1965; complete translation as *The Notebooks of André Walter,* 1968
La Tentative amoureuse, 1893; as *The Lovers' Attempt,*

translated by Dorothy Bussy, in *The Return of the Prodigal,* 1953
Le Voyage d'Urien, 1893; as *Urien's Voyage,* translated by Wade Baskin, 1964
Paludes, 1895; as *Marshlands,* translated by George D. Painter, with *Prometheus Misbound,* 1953
Le Prométhée mal enchaîné, 1899; as *Prometheus Illbound,* translated by Lilian Rothermere, 1919; as *Prometheus Misbound,* translated by George D. Painter, with *Marshlands,* 1953
L'Immoraliste, 1902; as *The Immoralist,* translated by Dorothy Bussy, 1930
La Porte étroite, 1909; as *Strait Is the Gate,* translated by Dorothy Bussy, 1924
Isabelle, 1911; translated by Dorothy Bussy, in *Two Symphonies,* 1931
Les Caves du Vatican, 1914; as *The Vatican Cellars,* translated by Dorothy Bussy, 1914; as *The Vatican Swindle,* translated by Bussy, 1925; as *Lafcadio's Adventures,* 1927
La Symphonie pastorale, 1919; as *The Pastoral Symphony,* translated by Dorothy Bussy, in *Two Symphonies,* 1931
Les Faux-monnayeurs, 1926; as *The Counterfeiters,* translated by Dorothy Bussy, 1927; as *The Coiners,* translated by Bussy, 1950
L'École des femmes, 1929; as *The School for Wives,* translated by Dorothy Bussy, 1929
Thésée, 1946; as *Theseus,* translated by John Russell, 1948

Other Writings: journals, notebooks, letters, poetry, plays, autobiography, critical essays, treatises.

Further Reading

Apter, Emily S., *André Gide and the Codes of Homotextuality,* Saratoga, California: Anma Libri, 1987
Babcock, Arthur, *Portraits of Artists: Reflexivity in Gidean Fiction, 1902–1946,* Columbia, South Carolina: French Literature Publications, 1982
Bettinson, Christopher D., *Gide—"Les Caves du Vatican,"* London: Arnold, 1972
Bettinson, Christopher D., *Gide: A Study,* Totowa, New Jersey: Rowman and Littlefield, and London: Heinemann, 1977
Cancalon, Elaine Davis, *Techniques et personnages dans les récits d'André Gide,* Paris: Lettres Modernes, 1970
Davies, John Charles, *"L'Immoraliste" and "La Porte étroite,"* London: Arnold, 1968
O'Brien, Justin, *Portrait of André Gide,* New York: Knopf, and London: Secker and Warburg, 1953
O'Neill, Kevin, *André Gide and the Roman d'aventure,* Sydney: Sydney University Press, 1969
Walker, David H., *André Gide,* London: Macmillan, and New York: St. Martin's Press, 1990
Weinberg, Kurt, *On Gide's Prométhée: Private Myth and Public Mystification,* Princeton, New Jersey: Princeton University Press, 1972

The Gift by Vladimir Nabokov

Dar 1937–38/52

Vladimir Nabokov was not alone in considering *The Gift,* the last book he wrote in his native tongue, to be the best of his Russian novels; most critics choose it as the high point of Nabokov's Russian period. Written in Germany, it had as its first audience the Russian émigré community among whom the action of the novel takes place. In fact, sketches of Russian intellectual émigré life in Berlin make up one part of the narrative. Nabokov wrote the novel in Berlin and published it serially in the émigré journal *Sovremennye zapiski* (*Contemporary Annals*) in 1937–38, without the fourth chapter, a biography of the radical Russian critic Nikolai Chernyshevskii. The novel was published in its entirety only in 1952 in New York, and the English translation appeared in 1963.

The title, *Dar,* in Russian has deep connotative meanings, which ultimately summarize various themes and motifs of the novel. As opposed to the word *podarok,* which simply means "present," *dar* can also mean a "talent" or an "offering." Thus, on one level, *dar* refers to the hero Fyodor's developing talent as a writer, his imagination, his ability to see the world around him, and his skill in using words to transform reality into art; on another level, Fyodor (whose own name, notes Sergei Davydov [1985], means "gift of God") gives to his beloved Zina as an offering (*dar*) of his love the novel *Dar,* which she, in essence, "gave" to him as his muse, his inspiration. The novel they "give" to each other represents their union in love.

Interestingly, in his introduction to the novel, Nabokov identifies Russian literature rather than Zina as the heroine of the book. As Davydov has shown, each of the chapters stands for separate decades of 19th-century Russian literature: the Golden Age of the 1820s; the poet Aleksandr Pushkin's turn to prose in the 1830s; Nikolai Gogol's investigation of *poshlost'* (vulgar, crass materialism) in the 1840s; the literary polemics of the 1860s; and the "accursed questions" examined by Lev Tolstoi and Fedor Dostoevskii in the 1870s and 1880s. In *The Gift* Fyodor's youthful poems (chapter one), the incomplete, fantasy biography of his father (chapter two), his daily life among the émigrés (chapter three), his biography of Chernyshevskii (chapter four), and his philosophical and aesthetic musings (chapter five) parallel this literary history. At the end of the book, Fyodor is completing his odyssey from poetry to prose and is preparing to write the novel the reader has just completed. The narration ends with an "Onegin stanza" (the *ababeecciddiff* rhyme scheme of Pushkin's novel in verse, *Eugene Onegin*) set in prose. Other parodies of Russian literature and émigré life appear throughout the novel.

The narration shifts from first to third person as different genres take prominence: poems, biographies, a travelogue of sorts, sketches of émigré life, imagined dialogues, literary criticism, and the novel itself. In a loose sense the novel almost mimics romantic prose with its merging and blurring of genre lines. One could almost say that the first three chapters cast Fyodor in the role of a romantic writer preparing for the polemic in chapter four with the quintessential man of the 1860s, Chernyshevskii, whose view of the relationship of art to reality is anathema to a writer as sensitive to literature as Fyodor.

The fourth chapter of the novel, Chernyshevskii's biography, turned out to be too controversial to publish in the émigré intellectual community, an irony not lost on Nabokov and the critics. The editors of *Contemporary Annals* feared a desecration of the memory of the radical critic, whose ideas were a major source of Lenin's revolutionary theories—in effect, the reason why they had all emigrated from the repressive Soviet government. As it turns out, however, Fyodor's biography of Chernyshevskii may be one of the best accounts of the critic's life, even though it exposes the arid, destructive force of Chernyshevskii's utilitarian aesthetic philosophy, the polar opposite of Fyodor's.

Fyodor becomes Nabokov's spokesman for his theories of art, criticism, and biography. Nabokov's ideas about literature emerge in Fyodor's imagined dialogues with another émigré poet, Koncheev, while his views on science appear in Fyodor's fantasy biography of his father, a naturalist, whom he describes on an expedition to Central Asia. But Fyodor puts into practice Nabokov's method of biographical writing in the life of Chernyshevskii, which he organizes based on recurring themes and motifs—not unlike Nabokov's own study of Nikolai Gogol'.

Fyodor resorts to art to create—or recreate—life, first by trying to recapture his past in his collections of poems about his childhood. He then turns to writing biographies, both real and imagined, in attempts to capture the truth about the lives of his father and Chernyshevskii. In addition, he muses on the life and death of one of his contemporaries, Yasha Chernyshevskii, a distant relation of the critic who ended his life in suicide, and, ultimately, on Zina. Of course, as Fyodor investigates the lives of others, he finds out truths about his own. In the end, he writes his artistic autobiography, the novel *The Gift*.

It is fitting that Nabokov ended his Russian years with a novel whose hero's biography closely resembles his own, especially at a time of transition, a new phase in his creative life. *The Gift* may also be seen as a bridge to Nabokov's first American novel, *The Real Life of Sebastian Knight* (1941), in which the main character sets out to reconstruct his half-brother's life. Nabokov's novels are often mutually self-referential, and *The Gift* proves to be no exception. But *The Gift* not only looks back to Russia's (and the author's) literary past, it also looks ahead to Nabokov's future works.

CHRISTINE A. RYDEL

See also Vladimir Nabokov

Further Reading

Begnal, Michael H., "Fiction, Biography, History: Nabokov's *The Gift,*" *Journal of Narrative Technique* 10 (1980)

Berdjis, Nassim Winnie, *Imagery in Vladimir Nabokov's Last Russian Novel ("Dar"), Its English Translation ("The Gift"), and Other Prose Works of the 1930s,* Frankfurt am Main and New York: Peter Lang, 1995

Boyd, Brian, *Vladimir Nabokov: The Russian Years,* London: Chatto and Windus, and Princeton, New Jersey: Princeton University Press, 1990

Clancy, Laurie, *The Novels of Vladimir Nabokov,* London: Macmillan, and New York: St. Martin's Press, 1984

Davydov, Sergei, "*The Gift*: Nabokov's Aesthetic Exorcism of Chernyshevskii," *Canadian-American Slavic Studies* 19 (1985)

Hyde, G.M., *Vladimir Nabokov: America's Russian Novelist*, London: Boyars, and Atlantic Highlands, New Jersey: Humanities Press, 1977

Johnson, Donald Barton, *Worlds in Regression: Some Novels of Vladimir Nabokov*, Ann Arbor, Michigan: Ardis, 1985

Karlinsky, Simon, "Vladimir Nabokov's Novel *Dar* as a Work of Literary Criticism: A Structural Analysis," *Slavic and East European Journal* 7 (1963)

Rampton, David, *Vladimir Nabokov: A Critical Study of the Novels,* Cambridge and New York: Cambridge University Press, 1984

Rowe, William W., *Nabokov's Spectral Dimension,* Ann Arbor, Michigan: Ardis, 1981

Salehar, Anna Maria, "Nabokov's *Gift*: An Apprenticeship in Creativity," in *A Book of Things About Vladimir Nabokov,* edited by Carl R. Proffer, Ann Arbor, Michigan: Ardis, 1974

Toker, Leona, *Nabokov: The Mystery of Literary Structures,* Ithaca, New York: Cornell University Press, 1989

Johann Wolfgang von Goethe 1749–1832

German

Goethe is, by any standard, Germany's greatest literary figure. His voluminous output included novels, poetry, drama, autobiography, correspondence, as well as a considerable body of scientific writing to which he himself attached particular importance. The range is bewildering, not least when one sets it in the context of a life that takes him from "angry young man" to courtier, writer in residence, theatre director, and administrator in Weimar. Goethe's life and creative output are, to say the least, challenging in their combination of multiplicity and coherence. This protean quality has led some commentators to argue that Goethe both engages with the pluralism of modern culture and integrates that pluralism within a unified sensibility.

Although Goethe wrote prose narratives throughout his life, he is not customarily regarded as a "natural storyteller"; he seems at best to have a tentative interest in sustaining plot, creating setting, or developing vivid characters. Yet his achievement in prose fiction is richly expressive, and his novels demonstrate a modernity that critics are only gradually coming to appreciate. He once—discussing his novel *The Elective Affinities*—cited as his aim "to portray social circumstances and the conflict between them in symbolic concentration." One could apply this remark to his narrative production generally. In the context of the societally-anchored European novel of the late 18th and 19th centuries—particularly as it evolved in England and France—Goethe's narrative output seems bereft of that abundant acknowledgment of social particulars and affairs that we have come to expect from the novel of modern life. Yet the symbolic distillation of social experience Goethe refers to in the remark quoted above is all-important. Goethe is remarkable for his ability to capture the mentality of a particular culture, to anchor the novel in a comprehension of the characters' consciousness *of* the world and of their consciousness *in* the world.

Goethe's first novel, *Die Leiden des jungen Werthers* (first edition 1774, second, revised edition 1787; *The Sufferings of Young Werther*) was an amazing popular success. It belongs in the company of the great epistolary novels of the European 18th century (such as those by Richardson, Rousseau, or Choderlos de Laclos). But what distinguishes *Werther* is its sheer radicalism. Goethe understands that the novel couched in letter form is, by definition, heavily committed to the expression of human subjectivity; but in this novel the letters are a one-way traffic, essentially because (although there is, initially at any rate, a correspondent to whom Werther is writing) all sense of genuine human dialogue fades from the letters as Werther becomes obsessed with writing into existence the scenario of his own selfhood and of an outer world that corroborates that selfhood. The novel was a European best-seller, and in a sense its reception is part of its theme: it became a cult book, and it understood with unique intensity the cultishness and emotionalism of its time.

Throughout Goethe's creative life as a novelist, one project never relinquished its hold on his imagination; it concerns an eager but in many ways unremarkable young man of bourgeois stock named Wilhelm Meister. The first novel of the sequence, *Wilhelm Meisters theatralische Sendung* (written 1777–85, published 1911; *Wilhelm Meister's Theatrical Mission*), concerns the young protagonist's move away from the mercantile world in which he grew up and recounts his attempts to take up a theatrical career. There is great vivacity to this novel; the text highlights both the charms of bohemian existence and the intellectual and emotional demands made by any strenuous attempt to use the theatre as a site of challenging interrogation of (real or potential) human experience.

Goethe returned to the project later in life, taking up and rewriting the "theatre novel" in order to integrate it into a larger structure—*Wilhelm Meisters Lehrjahre* (1795–1821; *Wilhelm Meister's Apprenticeship*). As before, the theatre initially occupies Wilhelm's energies; but in the later phases of the novel we see him turning his back on the theatre in order to associate himself with the Society of the Tower, a group of enterprising young people devoted to the project of self-cultivation in the context (and acknowledgment) of socially fruitful tasks. In generic terms the novel engages with particular forms of bourgeois literacy at the time—the novel of theatrical life, the pietistic autobiography (captured in the interpolated manuscript "The Confessions of a Beautiful Soul"), and the novel of the secret society. In this sense, *Wilhelm Meister's Apprenticeship* explores, in a complexly mediated mode, key issues of bourgeois culture: the aspiration to reconcile individualism with community, private with public imperatives, the claims of socio-economic (and psychological) specialization with a belief in psychological and societal wholeness. Goethe's novel proves to be of immense significance for the subsequent development of the German novel, not least because it inaugurates the tradition of the Bildungsroman, a novelistic form that explores the complex, often diffuse and wayward processes by which a young person comes to question and understand the nature of human identity as such and to discover the particular commitments of which he or she is most appropriately capable. Goethe continues the argument in the late narrative *Wilhelm Meisters Wanderjahre* (first edition 1821, second, revised edition 1829; *Wilhelm Meister's Travels*), in which the novel form opens out into a loose but complexly integrated structure. The main narrative thread accommodates interpolated narratives that frequently explore the revelations and confusions of human passion. Characters move in and out of focus; social concerns, above all the aspiration to emigrate to America, coexist with philosophical maxims and cosmological speculations. The novel is by turns reflective and passionate, both didactic and strangely visionary in its attempt to reconcile prose and poetry, practical endeavor and expansive longing, craftsmanship and creative artistry. Aesthetically, *Wilhelm Meister's Journeymanship* is not so much unified as sustained by shifting, contrapuntal effects.

In 1809 Goethe published a novel entitled *Die Wahlverwandtschaften* (*The Elective Affinities*). It is, by any standards, a remarkable text. At one level, it is a novel of manners, reminiscent of the contemporaneous novels of Jane Austen. Eduard and Charlotte, husband and wife, live peacefully on their modest estate, devoting themselves to the pastimes (particularly landscaping) of the minor landed gentry. They invite two friends to join them, the Hauptmann (Captain) and Ottilie, Charlotte's niece. The advent of the two new figures undermines the harmony of life on the estate. Eduard falls in love with Ottilie, the Hauptmann with Charlotte. While the latter two are more able to contain their passion, Eduard and Ottilie are consumed by theirs. The novel is claustrophobically dominated by a complex texture of symbols. But in spite of—or perhaps more accurately because of—this density of interpretive signs and portents, it is difficult for us to stabilize the meaning of the text. Are we confronted by a social drama, a psychological study, or is the novel ultimately concerned to articulate some mysterious, supernatural destiny? We cannot be sure. All we can know is that the glittering play of meanings is both inviting and bewildering. Perhaps Goethe is primarily asking us to understand the complex and ceaseless processes enshrined in the functioning of human consciousness. In *The Elective Affinities*, as elsewhere in his fiction, Goethe's concern with the consciousness of his characters and with the mentality of their culture expresses itself in a highly sophisticated, self-reflexive, and often quite demanding narrative mode.

MARTIN SWALES

See also Elective Affinities; Sufferings of Young Werther

Biography

Born 28 August 1749 in Frankfurt, Germany. Law student at Leipzig University, 1765–68; studied drawing with Adam Oeser; after a period of illness, resumed his studies in Strasbourg, 1770–71, licentiate in law 1771. Practiced law in Frankfurt, 1771–72, and Wetzlar, 1772; contributor, *Frankfurter Gelehrte Anzeigen*, 1772–73; welcomed by Duke Karl August into the small court of Weimar in 1775: council member, 1776, president, war commission, 1779, director of roads and services, 1779; ennobled 1782, and managed the financial affairs of the court; after visit to Italy, 1786–88, released from day-to-day government duties: general supervisor for arts and sciences, 1788, and director of the court theatres, 1791–1817. Edited a variety of magazines and yearbooks, including, with Schiller, *Xenien*, 1796–97; with J.H. Meyer, *Die Propyläen*, 1798–1800; *Kunst und Altertum*, 1816–32; and *Zur Naturwissenschaft*, 1817–24. Served as chancellor of the University of Jena. Died 22 March 1832.

Novels by Goethe

Die Leiden des jungen Werthers, 1774; revised edition, 1787; as *The Sorrows of Werter*, translated by Richard Graves or Daniel Malthus, 1780; numerous subsequent translations, including as *The Sufferings of Young Werther*, translated by Michael Hulse, 1989

Wilhelm Meisters Lehrjahre [and *Wanderjahre*], 1795–1821; as *Wilhelm Meister's Apprenticeship* [and *Travels*], translated by Thomas Carlyle, 1824–27, revised editions 1842, 1865; several subsequent translations, including by H.M. Waidson, 1977–79

Die Wahlverwandtschaften, 1809; as *Kindred by Choice*, translated by H.M. Waidson, 1960; as *Elective Affinities*, translated by Elizabeth Mayer and Louise Brogan, 1963; also translated by R.J. Hollingdale, 1971; John Winkelman, 1987

Other Writings: poetry, drama (*Götz von Berlichingen*, 1773; *Egmont*, 1788; *Iphigenie auf Tauris*, 1787; *Torquato Tasso*, 1790; *Faust*, 1832), autobiography (*Dichtung und Wahrheit*), scientific work (botany, geology, color theory), and letters.

Further Reading

Barnes, Harry George, *Goethe's "Die Wahlverwandtschaften": A Literary Interpretation*, Oxford: Clarendon Press, 1967

Berghahn, Klaus, and Beate Pinkerneil, *Am Beispiel "Wilhelm Meister,"* Königstein/Ts.: Athenäum, 1980

Blackall, Eric A., *Goethe and the Novel*, Ithaca, New York: Cornell University Press, 1976

Blessin, Stefan, *Die Romane Goethes*, Königstein/Ts.: Athenäum, 1979

Goethe-Bibliographie, Heidelberg: Winter, 1955– (serial)

Hardin, James N., editor, *Reflection and Action: Essays on the Bildungsroman*, Columbia: University of South Carolina Press, 1991

Herrmann, Hans Peter, *Goethes "Werther": Kritik und Forschung*, Darmstadt: Wissenschaftliche Buchgesellschaft, 1994

Herrmann, Helmut G., *Goethe-Bibliographie: Literatur zum dichterischen Werk*, Stuttgart: Reclam, 1991

Reiss, Hans, *Goethe's Novels*, London: Macmillan, and New York: St. Martin's Press, 1969

Roberts, David, *The Indirections of Desire: Hamlet in Goethe's "Wilhelm Meister,"* Heidelberg: Winter, 1980

Rösch, Ewald, editor, *Goethes Roman "Die Wahlverwandtschaften,"* Darmstadt: Wissenschaftliche Buchgesellschaft, 1975

Schlaffer, Hannelore, *Wilhelm Meister: Das Ende der Kunst und die Wiederkehr des Mythos,* Stuttgart: Metzler, 1989

Schlechta, Karl, *Goethes "Wilhelm Meister,"* Frankfurt am Main: Klostermann, 1953

Swales, Martin, *Goethe: "The Sorrows of Young Werther,"* Cambridge and New York: Cambridge University Press, 1987

Nikolai Gogol' 1809–52

Russian

Although Fedor Dostoevskii's statement "We all came out from under Gogol's 'Overcoat'" may be apocryphal, it nevertheless accurately describes the course of much of late 19th- and all of 20th-century Russian literature. It has long been a cliché to group Russian writers into two traditions: Aleksandr Pushkin's and Nikolai Gogol's. To the former belong those writers such as Mikhail Lermontov, Sergei Aksakov, Ivan Turgenev, and Lev Tolstoi, whose prose style generally reflects Pushkinian clarity and translucence; to the latter belong writers whose style more appropriately may be termed ornamental because of its tendency to draw attention to itself, to intrude into the narrative. Dostoevskii, Nikolai Leskov, Mikhail Saltykov-Shchedrin, early Anton Chekhov, Andrei Belyi, Mikhail Zoshchenko, the Serapion Brothers, Mikhail Bulgakov, Iuri Olesha, and Vladimir Nabokov, among others, may be counted among Gogol's literary heirs.

Gogol' is also Russia's greatest comic writer, although this aspect of his art has also spawned a cliché of criticism, namely, that his works evoke "laughter through tears." Even Pushkin, after having heard Gogol' read to him the early pages of *Mertvye dushi* (1842; *Dead Souls*), remarked on the sadness mingled with humor, which, in Gogol', normally derives from linguistic play, especially puns. The sadness arises out of Gogol's satire of Russian society, provincial life, and the generally concupiscent nature of humanity. From his earliest days as a writer, Gogol' saw himself in the role of moral arbiter of society. Although it is difficult to classify his works, he may also be seen as the "father of Russia's Golden Age of prose realism," thanks mainly to his masterpiece, *Dead Souls*. However, before he developed his own brand of realism, one that prominently displays a fantastic world, Gogol' went through various stages of literary development. But even in his earliest works hints of later themes and concerns emerge.

Before he wrote *Dead Souls*, Gogol' gained popular acceptance with his collections of folk-inspired tales of good and evil set in his native Ukraine: *Vechera na khutore bliz Dikan'ki* (1831–32; *Evenings on a Farm Near Dikanka*) and *Mirgorod* (1835). These were followed by essays on various topics, literary and historical, and the first of his famous Petersburg stories in the collection *Arabeski* (1835; *Arabesques*). In addition to his satirical play *Revizor* (1836; *The Inspector-General*), two stories, "Koliaska" ("The Carriage") and "Nos" ("The Nose"), appeared in the same year. "Shinel" (1842; "The Overcoat"), the last of his Petersburg tales, is considered by many to be his best piece of short fiction.

Critical response to these works led to Gogol's being misunderstood in his own time and for many decades to follow. His contemporaries had difficulty trying to figure out exactly what kind of writer Gogol' was. The reactionary critic Faddei Bulgarin used the term "Natural School" to describe Gogol' and several minor writers (Bulgarin used the term disparagingly). Later the civic literary critic, Vissarion Belinskii, employed the term as a synonym for realism. Except for the inclusion of "dirty details," the Natural School had nothing in common with French naturalism. Besides concentrating on insulting details connected to the "voice of nature," writers of this bent compared people to animals and inanimate objects, twisted language into an almost meaningless "crooked-tonguedness," and resorted to stupid, illogical conversations between characters who generally appeared in schematic pairs, often as caricatures but never as dark villainous types. Normally events took place in gray, murky, muddy, snowy locales—especially Petersburg.

Belinskii at first saw in Gogol' a critic of Nicolaevan Russia. He lauded Gogol' mainly for his social concerns about poor, exploited "little men" and saw his works as calls for reform. However, he was completely mistaken, for Gogol' had always been an arch conservative, an adherent of Russian orthodoxy and autocracy and a defender of Russia's national identity and messianic mission. As a result of this misapprehension, a dismayed Belinskii sent his infamous "Letter to Gogol'" to the author after having read Gogol's didactic work *Vybrannye mesta iz perepiski s druz'iami* (1847; *Selected Passages from Correspondence with Friends*), a series of articles on many subjects from the state of Russian literature to Gogol's self-image as the Russian messiah, the leader who issues a call back to orthodoxy. In his letter, banned from circulation by the government, Belinskii accused Gogol' of being a traitor to the common good. However, up to that point Gogol' had probably never had any philanthropic message to impart. Only after *Revizor* was produced and people saw it as an attack on the government did Gogol' justify it. In fact Czar Nicholas I loved the play.

Not really a social critic, Gogol' was rather a satirist of the human condition that allowed people to yield to the temptations of evil. From the earliest times Gogol' concerned himself with problems of good and evil, the paths through which evil enters the world, the boundaries between the real and the fantastic, and the parallel universe one finds in the magical world of dreams. He also gradually developed his view of art and the artist, along the way equating beauty with purity and innocence and equating evil with the devil and "human philistinism." He saw art as a religion and the artist as the savior of the world who would bring together a fragmented humanity in aesthetic unity. Several of his stories show the artist succumbing to evil in the forms of women and/or the devil (he sometimes equated the two). In later stories boredom replaces evil as an indicator of humanity's shallowness and a cause of its spiritual death. The perils of deception and *poshlost'* (crass, vulgar materialism) also gain prominence as themes in *Dead Souls,* Gogol's ultimate statement on spiritual death.

As important as Gogol's themes may be, his real contribution lies in his extraordinary use of language. His unique style, although at times polysyllabically inelegant, employs all levels of language. He combines high-pitched rhetoric with grotesque farce. He resorts to many tropes and figures of speech, especially oxymoron, synesthesia, and comparisons, and he excels in Homeric similes. However, sound and rhythm emerge as the two dominant elements of his poetic style. He enjoys word and sound repetition and creates ordered patterns of alliteration and assonance.

As Gogol' matured as a writer, his narrator distanced himself more and more from the events and the characters of his works. Instead, the narrator tends to become the main character by drawing attention to himself and the devices he uses to tell his story. In effect the language of the stories becomes more important than the stories themselves. In his writing, Gogol' put into practice his own theories of art and the artist by giving the word power over the deed.

CHRISTINE A. RYDEL

See also Dead Souls

Biography
Born 19 March 1809 in Sorochintsy, Poltava, Ukraine. Attended Poltava boarding school, 1819–21, and Nezhin high school, 1821–28. Civil servant, St. Petersburg, 1829–31; history teacher, Patriotic Institute, St. Petersburg, and private tutor, 1831–34; assistant lecturer in history, University of St. Petersburg, 1834–35; traveled to Germany, Switzerland, and France, 1836; lived in Rome, 1837–39; traveled in Western Europe and Russia, 1839–48; visited the Holy Land, 1848; returned to Russia, 1849. Died 21 February 1852.

Fiction by Gogol'
Novel
Mertvye dushi, 1842; as *Home Life in Russia,* 1854; as *Tchitchikoff's Journeys or Dead Souls,* translated by Isabel F. Hapgood, 2 vols., 1886; as *Dead Souls,* translated by S. Graham, 2nd edition, 1915; also translated by C.J. Hogarth, 1916; George Reavey, 1936; Andrew R. MacAndrew, 1961; David Magarshack, 1961; Helen Michailoff, 1964; as *Chichikov's Journeys; or, Home-Life in Old Russia,* translated by Bernard G. Guerney, 1942; Guerney's translation revised and annotated by Susanne Fusso as *Dead Souls,* 1996

Collections
Collected Works (includes *Dead Souls; The Overcoat and Other Stories; Evenings on a Farm near Dikanka; The*

Government Inspector and Other Stories), translated by Constance Garnett, 6 vols., 1922–27
The Complete Tales, edited by Leonard J. Kent, 2 vols., 1985

Other Writings: stories, plays, letters, essays on a variety of topics.

Further Reading
Bernstein, Lina, *Gogol's Last Book: The Architectonics of "Selected Passages from Correspondence With Friends,"* Birmingham: Department of Russian Language and Literature, University of Birmingham, 1994

Debreczeny, Paul, *Nikolay Gogol and His Contemporary Critics,* Philadelphia: American Philosophical Society, 1966

Erlich, Victor, *Gogol,* New Haven, Connecticut: Yale University Press, 1969

Fanger, Donald, *The Creation of Nikolai Gogol,* Cambridge, Massachusetts: Belknap Press of Harvard University Press, 1979

Frantz, Philip E., editor, *Gogol: A Bibliography,* Ann Arbor, Michigan: Ardis, 1983

Fusso, Susanne, *Designing "Dead Souls": An Anatomy of Disorder in Gogol,* Stanford, California: Stanford University Press, 1993

Fusso, Susanne, and Priscilla Meyer, editors, *Essays on Gogol: Logos and the Russian Word,* Evanston, Illinois: Northwestern University Press, 1992

Karlinsky, Simon, *The Sexual Labyrinth of Nikolai Gogol,* Cambridge, Massachusetts: Harvard University Press, 1976

Magarshack, David, *Gogol: A Life,* London: Faber, 1956; New York: Grove Press, 1957

Maguire, Robert A., *Gogol From the Twentieth Century: Eleven Essays,* Princeton, New Jersey: Princeton University Press, 1974

Maguire, Robert A., *Exploring Gogol,* Stanford, California: Stanford University Press, 1994

Nabokov, Vladimir, *Nikolai Gogol,* Norfolk, Connecticut: New Directions, 1944

Peace, Richard A., *The Enigma of Gogol: An Examination of the Writings of N.V. Gogol and Their Place in the Russian Literary Tradition,* Cambridge and New York: Cambridge University Press, 1981

Rancour-Laferriere, Daniel, *Out From Under Gogol's Overcoat: A Psychoanalytical Study,* Ann Arbor, Michigan: Ardis, 1982

Setchkarev, Vsevolod, *N.V. Gogol: Leben und Schaffen,* Berlin: Harrassowitz, 1953; as *Gogol: His Life and Works,* London: Owen, and New York: New York University Press, 1965

Shapiro, Gavriel, *Nikolai Gogol and the Baroque Cultural Heritage,* University Park: Pennsylvania State University Press, 1993

Woodward, James B., *Gogol's "Dead Souls,"* Princeton, New Jersey: Princeton University Press, 1978

Woodward, James B., *The Symbolic Art of Gogol: Essays on His Short Fiction,* Columbus, Ohio: Slavica, 1982

Zeldin, Jesse, *Nikolai Gogol's Quest for Beauty: An Exploration into His Works,* Lawrence: Regents Press of Kansas, 1978

The Golden Bowl by Henry James

1904

Henry James' novels fall into three periods, which have been humorously labeled "James I," "James II," and "James the Old Pretender." *The Golden Bowl*, along with *The Ambassadors* (1903) and *The Wings of the Dove* (1902), belongs to the third of these "Jacobean" periods and is in many ways its prize exhibit. At this stage of his career James had become the éminence grise of American and English novelists and had developed an elaborate prose style in which sentences of extraordinarily complex syntax and delicate refinement were woven with elaborate artifice around love stories of strangely tragic beauty.

The Golden Bowl is an acquired taste—beginners might better enjoy the less convoluted *Washington Square* and *The Portrait of a Lady* (both 1881). It is a final reward for readers steeped in Jamesian subtleties to the point of addiction and accustomed to the tortuous exploration of consciousness that is the cause of, and justification for, his remarkable technique. Through a series of novels from *What Maisie Knew* (1897) to *The Ambassadors*, James had perfected his "point of view" method. He commented extensively on his method in the essay "The Art of Fiction" (1884) and in the prefaces for the New York edition (1907–09) of *The Portrait of a Lady* and *The Ambassadors*. His image for fiction was that of a house with many windows from each of which a watcher is observing the scene, some seeing more, more seeing less, but all seeing with a unique vision, interpretation, and evaluation of events. The emphasis was thus upon psychology and inwardness. There were few things more exciting to him, James wrote, than "a psychological reason." In *The Ambassadors* his peculiar triumph was to present everything as seen and experienced by his unheroic hero, Lambert Strether, with a resultant ambiguity that makes the novel at once eminently true to life and alluringly elusive. In *The Golden Bowl*, point of view is more various, but the novel has an equal verisimilitude and a still greater elusiveness. In *The Wings of the Dove*, which also has multiple viewers, the drama of consciousness reaches its peak in Milly Theale's self-sacrificing recognition of the psychological processes that have come to make her the prey of her friend Kate and her lover Densher. Similarly, *The Golden Bowl* has an inwardly psychological drama of intimate trust betrayed by friend and husband, turning on Maggie Verver's consciousness of what it is that she is involved with. Consciousness is enfolded in a plot hinging on delicacy of perception translated into correspondingly tactful action. Tragedy lies at the heart of this novel, implicit in the title's allusion to Ecclesiastes 12:1, "Or ever the silver cord be loosed, or the golden bowl be broken . . .". Significantly, the heroine does not succumb to her misfortune but transmutes it into a sort of divine comedy.

Critical opinion, however, is not entirely in agreement about the virtuousness of Maggie's achievement. To distinguished readers such as R.P. Blackmur, Dorothea Krook, and John Bailey, she is a saint-like creature whose love expresses itself in the tender artfulness with which she foils the destructiveness of evil and creates instead a harmony that leaves those involved unexposed and forgiven. But F.R. Leavis—although he rates James so highly as to make him one of only three novelists truly exemplary of "the great tradition"—finds the art-collecting complacency of Maggie and her father at best ironical, at worst part of a sterility that comes from an overvaluation of style. Leavis' sympathies lean more toward Charlotte and the Prince: "in a stale, sickly and oppressive atmosphere they represent life." What he considers most damning is the fact that James, in his judgment, is unaware of the distaste the Ververs excite. Walter Wright, on the other hand, sees Maggie as "neither saint nor witch" but an ignorant—perhaps rather than innocent—woman who learns in the end to shift her affections from her false conception of the artistic perfection of the Prince to the Prince as a living and fallible human being: "The man with whom she is in love at the end is the true prince, not her earlier illusion."

The interaction of art and life, however, leads in James' fiction to a verbal experience for the reader that, although it involves the consideration of moral rights and wrongs, becomes virtually an end in itself. This is where modern linguistic criticism finds James' work, and particularly *The Golden Bowl*, a veritable mine, full of the most deviously winding but also richest seams. The most accomplished exponent of this approach is Ruth Bernard Yeazell, whose *Language and Knowledge in the Late Novels of Henry James* (1976) grapples with the central problem in the late James that knowledge is communicated by an elaborate linguistic structure that foregrounds itself, rendering the knowledge subjective, relative, and above all fluid. Yeazell regards the traditional point of view approach to James inadequate. Referring to the passage in which Charlotte Stant waits to be cross-questioned, Yeazell comments, "the dizzying shifts of feeling grant us no fixed sense of a reality against which we are to measure and judge Charlotte's own." Even the drama of consciousness becomes not a matter of one consciousness inwardly realized and pitched against another inwardly realized consciousness, but of linguistic creations that become a substitute for referential knowledge.

In James' own development, *The Golden Bowl* stands at the peak of the point of view method. However, it merges almost imperceptibly with that poetic use of language that, as in the work of the French poet Stéphane Mallarmé and the American poet Wallace Stevens, plays with its own fluctuations and felicities. *The Golden Bowl* grows out of the tradition created by the epistolary novels of Samuel Richardson, which turn inward to the psychological state of characters and their romantic histrionics of feeling rather than outward, as in the case of Henry Fielding, to plot and the mock-heroic rhetoric of 18th-century classical culture. James' work draws also on the bourgeois concerns of the 19th-century novel and its moral dilemmas, especially as they unfold in the novels of Jane Austen, Charlotte Brontë, and George Eliot. But in becoming ever more intricately involved with its own artifice, the novel creates a self-reflexive linguistic construct akin to the interior monologues of Virginia Woolf and James Joyce. Like *The Waves* (1931) and *Ulysses* (1922), *The Golden Bowl* freed the novel from its attachment to realism and made way for the flourishes of language and consciousness that continue to fascinate more recent novelists such as Vladimir Nabokov, Margaret Atwood, and Julian Barnes.

R.P. DRAPER

See also Henry James

Further Reading

Armstrong, Paul B., *The Phenomenology of Henry James*, Chapel Hill: University of North Carolina Press, 1983

Edel, Leon, editor, *Henry James: A Collection of Critical Essays*, Englewood Cliffs, New Jersey: Prentice-Hall, 1963

Fogel, Daniel Mark, *Henry James and the Structure of the Romantic Imagination*, Baton Rouge: Louisiana State University Press, 1981

Leavis, F.R., *The Great Tradition: George Eliot, Henry James, Joseph Conrad*, London: Chatto and Windus, and New York: New York University Press, 1948

McCormic, Peggy, "The Semiotics of Economic Language in James' Fiction," *American Literature* 58:4 (December 1986)

Tanner, Tony, editor, *Henry James*, London: Macmillan, 1968

Wessel, Catherine Cox, "Strategies for Survival in James' *The Golden Bowl*," *American Literature* 55:4 (December 1983)

Wilson, R.B.J., *Henry James' Ultimate Narrative: "The Golden Bowl,"* St. Lucia and New York: University of Queensland Press, 1981

Yeazell, Ruth Bernard, *Language and Knowledge in the Late Novels of Henry James*, Chicago: University of Chicago Press, 1976

Young, Arlene, "Hypothetical Discourse as Ficele in *The Golden Bowl*," *American Literature* 61:3 (October 1989)

Golden Lotus. *See* Six Classic Chinese Novels

The Golden Notebook by Doris Lessing

1962

The full impact of *The Golden Notebook* since its publication in 1962 is not yet clear, because its effects continue to be felt. More recently, for instance, critics have identified its relationship to socialist realism, and it has been included—implicitly in novels by J.M. Coetzee and explicitly by Patrick Colm Hogan (see *Research in African Literatures* 25:2 [1994])—as part of the literature exploring colonial and postcolonial themes of identity. These new readings of her masterpiece might please Doris Lessing more than have earlier ones. She has had, as Coetzee notes, "an uneasy relationship with the women's movement—which claimed the book as a founding document—and a positively hostile relationship with academic commentators, who claimed it as a prototypical postmodern novel" (*New York Review of Books*, 22 December 1994).

Lessing's uneasiness notwithstanding, *The Golden Notebook* deserves its reputation among antirealist and feminist writers. Anna Freeman Wulf is a powerful characterization of a "free" woman in a novel foregrounding women's experience. *The Golden Notebook* was inevitably read as a successor to the work of Simone de Beauvoir and as a contribution to the birth of second-wave feminism. Anna Wulf's response to her existential crisis—that of a woman and an intellectual in London—is to keep separate, color-coded notebooks: black for old memories and business matters, red for her political activities, yellow for sketches of stories and novels, and blue for her emotional diary. This strategy is meant to prevent aspects of her life and mind from collapsing together what was formerly seen as both clearly defined and structurally united. Episodes from Lessing's/Anna's earlier realist stories and memoirs are critically represented in *The Golden Notebook* so that the reality they supposedly reveal is seen to be actively constructed by the telling. Anna's relationships appear to her as creations, either of her notebook writing or of a social ideology.

In the preface to the 1971 edition, Lessing claims *The Golden Notebook*'s formal reflexiveness is not a gesture to recent intellectual fads but a strategy as old as Samuel Richardson's *Clarissa* (1747-48); that its support for women's liberation is secondary to the theme of ideological and personal breakdown. While the novel belongs, she explains, in the context of socialist literature and literary theory, she declares herself as part of the project of committed social critical writing originated by 19th-century Russians, writing that does not "bother about your stupid personal concerns." As a communist in colonial Rhodesia, this view of literature and "subjectivity" came to her "from people doing everything one respected most: like, for instance, trying to fight color prejudice in South Africa."

So it is that in *The Golden Notebook* Anna Wulf says of her fellow ex-communists that "we are people, because of the accident of how we were situated in history, who were so powerfully part—but only in our imaginations, and that's the point—of the great dream, that now we have to admit that the great dream has faded and the truth is something else—that we'll never be any use." Alienation from her party and her former political convictions is indissolubly connected to Anna's inability to write or to replace the marriage she has lost. If years spent in the communist party were wasted, she asks herself, then what is the value of her writing done as a communist? How can she form intimate relationships when these were formerly based on shared communist radical ethics and party goals?

In her subsequent writing a replacement "truth" is identified with mysterious psychological forces, with what might be called historical *mysticism* rather than historical materialism. In *The Golden Notebook* the possibility for a psychic unity—one that can replace the unifying process of socialist revolution—is achieved by Anna Wulf and her lover Saul Green through their radical experience of the artificiality of their "individuality": "They 'break down'," comments Lessing, "into each other, into other people, break through the false patterns and formulas they have made to shore up themselves and each other, dissolve." *The Golden Notebook* treats "the tiny individual," says Lessing, as a "microcosm" in order to "break through the personal, the subjective, making the personal general."

This resolution of the dilemmas posed by *The Golden Notebook* is a contribution to the socialist-realist novel, just as Lessing insists in her preface: it is a solution of the perennial problem of how to include personal and subjective themes within a novelistic tradition that is intolerant of subjectivity. With discussion of *The Golden Notebook*'s formal experiment specifically grounded in this way on socialist realism, more questions can be asked. Other features of the socialist literary tradition, apart from those identified by Lessing, have been useful to 20th-century writers. While *The Golden Notebook* emphasizes the importance of the typical over the merely average character and event, it does not focus on life in moments of class struggle. Other writers have responded differently to the collapse of Stalinism and its literary effects. These considerations would place *The Golden Notebook* next to "ex-centric" or "peripheral" writing, such as that by Australia's Dorothy Hewett or Amanda Lohrey or South Africa's Nadine Gordimer. This is also the context that frees the novel from the academic commodification Lessing fears and allows it to continue its unique intervention in politics.

ALLAN GARDINER

See also Doris Lessing

Further Reading

Lessing, Doris, *Under My Skin*, London and New York: HarperCollins, 1994

Robinson, Sally, *Engendering the Subject: Gender and Self-Representation in Contemporary Women's Fiction*, Albany: State University of New York Press, 1991

Taylor, Jenny, editor, *Notebooks, Memoirs, Archives: Reading and Rereading Doris Lessing*, London and Boston: Routledge and Kegan Paul, 1982

Witold Gombrowicz 1904–69

Polish

Witold Gombrowicz, regarded by Polish critics as the leading novelist of the 20th century, has exerted great influence on contemporary Polish fiction and contributed a great deal to the understanding of modernity in his country of origin. Although the immoderate cult of his works by members of the intellectual elite in Poland occasionally gives reason for concern, many talented scholars still attempt to assess his contribution from various perspectives. Gombrowicz found enthusiasts also outside Poland, particularly in France and Italy, and belongs to the few Polish novelists who are at least mentioned in books on modern fiction.

Gombrowicz's own theoretical declarations are whimsical and self-contradictory, as he continually constructed and deconstructed his artistic image. As a consequence, his theoretical views have to be characterized with great caution. Convinced that the author, rather than invent stories, constitutes the true substance of literary works, Gombrowicz blended fiction with nonfiction, personal content with general message, literary game with professed idea. The highly intellectual substance of his novels is offset, in the first two in particular, by Rabelaisian clowning and the carnivalesque, as the author never questioned the importance of "fun" in his narratives, either in sophisticated or more popular forms. He once said in an interview, "I am a humorist, clown, acrobat, trouble-maker, and my works tend to stand upside down to be admired." In the introduction to *Trans-Atlantyk* (1953; *Trans-Atlantyk*), he maintained that this novel could be of any value only if capable of providing joy and excitement. This strategy of game and entertainment affects the way Gombrowicz delivers his message. As Italo Calvino wrote in *The Literature Machine* (1987), he had "the habit of cultivating the most compromising speculative and erudite passions without taking them entirely seriously." He vacillated between destruction and construction, blasphemy and utopian ideals, and eventually between clown and master. In this manner Gombrowicz anticipated postmodernism.

Gombrowicz's understanding of the human self and the role of language in our perception of reality has close links with major intellectual trends in the 20th century. His presentation of characters is based on the notion of *form*, which one can relate both to Sartre's concept of "being-for-others" and to the structuralist idea of the tyranny of language, which constrains and defines individuals. In the French essay "J'étais structuraliste avant tout le monde" (I was a structuralist before everybody else),

Gombrowicz describes form as follows: "Our form is mainly being created in the interpersonal zone. Thus we come to a certain relativisation of personality. I am honest with somebody, dishonest with somebody else, wise with one and silly with another. . . . It can be said that every moment I am 'created' by others." In another proclamation Gombrowicz wondered "whether the human being was not just a sort of sentence," "a variant of a structure . . . belonging to the self-evolving form." In order to be "for themselves," his protagonists escape into a game of "immaturity," founded on the continual transformation of one form into another consistent with changing roles. These transformations deprive existing stereotypes of any logical coherence.

The narrative art of Gombrowicz's fiction undermines the formal discipline imposed on the novel in the later years of the 19th century and thus emancipates its earlier, digressive structure. The author's interest in popular literature resulted in a fairly successful attempt at writing an ordinary thriller, *Opętani* (published posthumously in 1973; *Possessed*). In a letter to Jerzy Giedroyc, he claimed that "every text must abound in 'enticements,' must be sensational or otherwise compulsive." He had little sympathy for experiments *per se*, was dismissive of the *nouveau roman*, and never questioned the traditional principle of telling stories. His novels parodied long-established subgenres: Voltairean philosophical tales, Polish oral tales, narratives about country life or school years, or detective stories. This parodying is combined with a 20th-century inclination to metafictional commentary, in which the very principle of creating stories comes to the foreground and affects the structure of the novel. Gombrowicz's sympathy for immaturity produces a kind of narrative extravaganza that obscures inner order behind an illogical course of events. The first-person narrator, united with the real author by name and vocation, constitutes an essential part of the game. While his playful attitude toward established conventions approaches romantic irony, it is simultaneously inhibited by a modern awareness that creativity has its limits: there is no escape from the *form* and its stereotypes, and its tyranny can be only temporarily suspended. The laughter and mockery at the end of *Ferdydurke* (1937; *Ferdydurke*) and *Trans-Atlantyk* actually conceal the writer's anxiety behind the outbursts of carnivalesque self-assurance.

The adventures of a 30-year-old who is transformed into a schoolboy by an intimidating teacher in *Ferdydurke* unmask Gombowicz's notion of *form* and disclose the unprotected self "created by others." When an individual finds no escape from one or another role determined by human relations, the exposed "authenticity" emerges in violent brawling. *Trans-Atlantyk*, set in Buenos Aires at the beginning of World War II, questions everything and relativizes any value. The grotesque representation of the Polish community and its pompous patriotic rhetoric about "fatherland" is rendered in the style of the 17th-century memoirist Jan Chryzostom Pasek, one of the best known representatives of the "Sarmatian" culture associated with old Polish nobility. The "sonland," a sensual counterpart to "fatherland," introduces the social circle of an Argentinean homosexual and questions nationalist standards, but offers no other conclusion than all-embracing mockery.

Gombrowicz's last two novels, far less humorous than the others, are more concerned with the organizing proclivity of the human mind. *Pornografia* (1960; *Pornografia*), set in Poland during World War II, not only denounces traditional approaches to love, patriotic conspiracy, and moral values, it also inverts tra-ditional novelistic stereotypes. Its portrayal of the attempts of two elderly gentlemen to transform reality into a palatable story lays bare the futility of any imposed construction. In *Kosmos* (1965; *Cosmos*) the endeavor to force rhythm and structure upon the surrounding reality dominates the story line. The narrator and his friend exert themselves in a frustrating effort to find a pattern in a confusing web of "clues," which they consider suspicious and implicating. Those detective ambitions, supported by artificial "adjustments" of reality to a preconceived model, are eventually deconstructed in an ironic anticlimax: the narrator eventually gives up and dines on chicken fricassee.

Gombrowicz is the leading representative of Polish modernism in fiction, but his works actually heralded postmodern tendencies; he blended popular literature with metafiction, enjoyed various language games and stressed the role of stereotypes in our perception of reality. By staying near the borderline between "writerly " and "readerly" texts, as defined by Roland Barthes, he exposed dilemmas symptomatic of the novel in the later years of the 20th century.

STANISLAW EILE

See also Ferdydurke

Biography

Born 4 August 1904 in Maloszyce, Poland. Educated privately; St. Stanislas Kostka (Catholic high school), 1916–22; Warsaw University, 1922–26, law degree 1926; Institut des Hautes Études Internationales, Paris, 1926–27. Part-time law clerk, Warsaw, 1928–34; reviewer for several newspapers, Warsaw, 1935; traveled to Argentina and unable to return to Poland because of war, 1939; reviewer (under pseudonym) for newspapers in Buenos Aires from 1940; secretary, Polish Bank, Buenos Aires, 1947–55; left Argentina, 1963; lived in Vence, France, from 1964. Died 25 July 1969.

Novels by Gombrowicz

Ferdydurke, 1937; as *Ferdydurke*, translated by Eric Mosbacher, 1961
Trans-Atlantyk, 1953; as *Trans-Atlantyk*, translated by Carolyn French and Nina Karsov, 1994
Pornografia, 1960; as *Pornografia*, translated by Alastair Hamilton, 1966
Kosmos, 1965; as *Cosmos*, translated by Eric Mosbacher, 1966
Opętani, 1973; as *Possessed; or, The Secret of Myslotch*, translated by J.A. Underwood, 1980

Other Writings: short stories, plays, a diary, memoirs, essays, conversations.

Further Reading

Błoński, Jan, *Forma, śmiech i rzeczy ostateczne: Studia o Gombrowiczu*, Krakow: Znak, 1994
Czachowska, Jadwiga, and Alicja Szałagan, editors, *Współcześni polscy pisarze i badacze literatury: Słownik biobibliograficzny*, Warsaw: Wydawnictwa Szkolne i Pedagogiczne, 1994
Eile, Stanislaw, *Modernist Trends in Twentieth-Century Polish Fiction*, London: School of Slavonic and East European Studies, 1996
Jarzębski, Jerzy, *Gra w Gombrowicza*, Warsaw: Panstwowy Instytut Wydawniczy, 1982

Jelenski, Constantin, and Dominique de Roux, editors, *Gombrowicz,* Paris: Editions de l'Herne, 1971

Łapiński, Zdzisław, editor, *Gombrowicz i krytycy,* Krakow: Wydawnictwo Literackie, 1984

Legierski, Michał, *Modernizm Witolda Gombrowicza,* Stockholm: Almqvist and Wiksell, 1996

Thompson, Ewa M., *Witold Gombrowicz,* Boston: Twayne, 1979

van der Meer, Jan I.J., *Form vs. Anti-Form: Das semantische Universum von Witold Gombrowicz,* Amsterdam: Rodopi, 1992

The Good Soldier by Ford Madox Ford

1915

The Good Soldier is by general agreement Ford Madox Ford's finest novel. Of his other novels, only the tetralogy *Parade's End* (1924), *No More Parades* (1925), *A Man Could Stand Up* (1926), and *The Last Post* (1928) even maintains a contemporary reputation. *The Good Soldier* was also Ford's own favorite of his early books, according to the preface he wrote in 1927 for the collected American edition of his works. Before writing *The Good Soldier,* Ford noted that he had "never really tried to put into any novel of mine all that I knew about writing." His emphasis on craft suggests a just pride in technical facility. Although subtitled *A Tale of Passion, The Good Soldier* is noteworthy not only for its ironic portrayal of sexual intrigue but for the sophistication of its narrative techniques. Ford was strongly influenced by the narrative impressionism of his friend Joseph Conrad, with whom he collaborated on several works. Conrad's use of mediating narrators in "Heart of Darkness" (1902) and *Lord Jim* (1900) and the abrupt shifts of chronology in *Nostromo* (1904) and *The Secret Agent* (1907) made a particularly strong impression on Ford. Yet, where Conrad uses his narrator Marlow to emphasize the essential philosophical obscurity of human motivation, and employs abrupt chronological shifts as markers of history's discontinuities, Ford turns these techniques to psychological ends. John Dowell, the narrator of *The Good Soldier,* emerges as a confused and at times contradictory character. His attempts to understand his friend Edward Ashburnham—the "good soldier" of the title—reflect his inability to understand the world around him, as he explores adultery, intrigue, and the conflicts of religious and national character in which he has unwittingly been involved.

Dowell's narrative contains many unusual technical devices. As he reflects upon the nine-year friendship between Leonora and Edward Ashburnham and his wife, Florence, and himself, Dowell demonstrates a distance from his own experience, beginning, "This is the saddest story I have ever heard." (The novel's original title, *The Saddest Story,* was changed for marketing purposes during World War I.) Throughout, Dowell demonstrates the difficulty he has in reconciling his recent knowledge of his wife's adultery and suicide—a knowledge gained shortly before the time of the narration—with his delusional memories of their happy life together. He tells the story out of chronological order, looping backward to a series of important events that take place on August 4th of different years, and at times providing strongly contradictory interpretations of the same events. Dowell's reinterpretations suggest his unwillingness or inability to confront the information about the affair between Edward and Florence. They mirror the reader's necessary reinterpretations as more information becomes available about Dowell's and Ashburnham's past. For instance, in one central scene, the outing to the castle at Marburg, the reader eventually reaches an understanding of the dynamics between the couples, on the basis of information Dowell himself provides about Ashburnham.

Dowell's emotional distance from his own life is matched by his preternatural innocence. He has never consummated his marriage with Florence because he thinks she has a "heart" (the novel's shorthand for "heart disease," but also an ironic emblem for "compassion"). He has been blind to his wife's infidelities for years. Dowell's extreme naïveté is, however, crucial to the novel's themes. The epigram to *The Good Soldier* is *beati immaculati,* a quotation from Psalm 119 meaning "blessed are the undefiled." Dowell emerges from the narrative of madness, lust, and dishonor as perhaps the only undefiled character. Ashburnham, Leonora, and Florence are all guilty of different kinds of deceit, self-delusion, and betrayal. While Ford's moral dissection of their different cases is subtle—his treatment of the degree to which Leonora's family and her Catholicism influence her behavior is particularly acute—Dowell alone appears, however ironically, as morally unbesmirched. Ford leaves Dowell trapped in an asexual menage with the girl Nancy, who has been mentally destroyed by Edward's and Leonora's machinations. The novel's end poses the unanswerable question of whether Dowell's increased knowledge has led to an increased sense of his identity and position in the world, or whether his inability to recognize deception and conflict leaves him at the mercy of the world.

Ford thought of *The Good Soldier* as the last in a line of novels rather than as the start of something new, much as its character Ashburnham is a final doomed example of the feudal way of life, or as the character Christopher Tietjens in *Parade's End* would become known as the "Last Tory." Ford's treatment of marriage, not as a comic resolution but as a tragic beginning, owes something to the Victorian examples of George Eliot and George Gissing. As a dark comedy of cultural difference between Americans and the English in Europe, *The Good Soldier* may also be seen as a sly revision of Henry James.

Although a version of the beginning of the novel appeared in

Wyndham Lewis' radical journal *Blast,* Ford was acutely aware of the "rest of the clamorous young writers who were then knocking at the door" of modernism and that the book was "of a race that will have no successors." Dowell's struggling narrative, however, and the relationship posited by the novel between telling a story and defining one's life are the arguable forerunners of postmodern narratives in English that play upon the untrustworthiness of the first-person narrator and the relationship between self and story, such as Samuel Beckett's *Molloy* (1951) or J.M. Coetzee's *In the Heart of the Country* (1977). The narrative sophistication of *The Good Soldier* and its unblinking treatment of sexual mores mark a crucial point of linkage between the late Victorian and contemporary novel.

SCOTT W. KLEIN

Further Reading

Armstrong, Paul B., *The Challenge of Bewilderment: Understanding and Representation in James, Conrad, and Ford,* Ithaca, New York: Cornell University Press, 1987

Cassell, Richard A., *Ford Madox Ford: A Study of His Novels,* Baltimore: Johns Hopkins University Press, 1961

Green, Robert, *Ford Madox Ford: Prose and Politics,* Cambridge and New York: Cambridge University Press, 1981

Leer, Norman, *The Limited Hero in the Novels of Ford Madox Ford,* East Lansing: Michigan State University Press, 1966

Levenson, Michael, *Modernism and the Fate of Individuality: Character and Novelistic Form from Conrad to Woolf,* Cambridge and New York: Cambridge University Press, 1991

Lid, Richard Wald, *Ford Madox Ford: The Essence of His Art,* Berkeley: University of California Press, 1964

Lynn, David H., *The Hero's Tale: Narrators in the Early Modern Novel,* New York: St. Martin's Press, and London: Macmillan, 1989

Meixner, John A., *Ford Madox Ford's Novels: A Critical Study,* Minneapolis: University of Minnesota Press, 1962

Snitow, Ann Barr, *Ford Madox Ford and the Voice of Uncertainty,* Baton Rouge: Louisiana State University Press, 1984

The Good Soldier Švejk and His Fortunes in the World War by Jaroslav Hašek

Osudy dobrého vojáka Švejka za svetové války 1921–23

The Good Soldier Švejk analyzes the predicament of a human being caught in the wheels of an impersonal, totalitarian bureaucratic system that negates natural reality and destroys individuality. Most Czech critics refused to regard *Švejk* as serious literature until well after World War II. *The Good Soldier Švejk* originally achieved international renown through a German translation.

For Hašek's compatriots, *Švejk* was unacceptably subversive. In 1918, after three centuries of foreign domination, a new, democratic Czechoslovakia was created following the collapse of Austria-Hungary. Offended by Švejk's negative attitude toward officialdom, the founders and supporters of the new Czechoslovak state saw the novel as an assault on the country's newfound independence. Perhaps the most important interwar Czech literary historian, Arne Novák, totally misunderstood Švejk, describing him as a "scoundrel and a pleasure-seeking cynic." Another critic worried that Švejk's resistance to authority and military discipline could paralyze the Czechoslovak army's ability to defend the country. The novel was banned from the Czechoslovak army in 1925, the Polish translation was confiscated in 1928, the Bulgarian translation was suppressed in 1935, and the German translation burned on Nazi bonfires in 1933.

The Good Soldier Švejk is a rambling, picaresque work that follows the aimless wanderings of the antihero through the impersonal, idiotic, and destructive machinery of the Austrian army. There are only two modes in which Švejk is allowed to exist, compulsion and prohibition, in a direct assault on his identity. Švejk is a popular "Everyman," an ordinary person called up at the beginning of World War I (a war that was absurd and alien for the Czechs, who in 1914 were citizens of the Austro-Hungarian empire; they were required to lay down their lives for a foreign power that dominated their nation). He is also an ambiguous character, an "empty shell," a center from which the author develops his extraordinarily dynamic narrative in countless directions. Indestructible and imperturbable, Švejk has mythical dimensions. Calm and indifferent, he typically wears a benign smile and a trusting look in his blue eyes. The character is left deliberately incomplete. A "man without qualities," he prefigures the heroes of Franz Kafka and Robert Musil.

Švejk applies an imaginative method to his predicament. He chooses to play games for his own amusement and the amusement of those around him. The games are primarily verbal, but he also play-acts, especially in the company of superiors. By game-playing, he is able to resist the destructive, bureaucratic machinery, overwhelming it with exuberant and irrepressible vitality. Whatever happens, Švejk dominates the situation with an endless, unstoppable stream of anecdotes. The authorities assume that Švejk is an idiot: on most occasions he fulfills orders to the letter and with exemplary ardor, but mayhem invariably ensues. Pretending to be an idiot proves to be a reliable method of avoiding manipulation and domination by the authorities. Even the reader cannot always tell whether Švejk is pretending or is truly stupid.

Jaroslav Hašek's life is highly relevant to the structure and the thematic content of the novel. Hašek was relatively well regarded in Prague before World War I for his talents as a humorist. He wrote countless humorous stories, which he published in magazines. On a personal level, Hašek had a controversial reputation. It has been suggested that he was a homosexual who found it difficult to come to terms with life in the staid Czech society. At one stage of his life, Hašek sympathized with the anarchists. He frequently wandered through Bohemia as a vagrant, without a permanent job.

Hašek was a master of parody and mystification. As an assistant in the editorial offices of an obscure magazine, *The Life of Animals,* he wrote and published "scholarly" articles about animals that he invented. At another time, he started a fierce polemic between two different periodicals, under two separate pseudonyms, arguing with himself so fiercely that the editors of the two periodicals feared the matter would end up in court. During the 1911 election campaign, Hašek parodied political life by founding his own "Party for Moderate Progress within the Limits of the Law" and later published its "Political and Social History," a satirical account of the times.

After being drafted into an Austrian army, Hašek became a Russian prisoner of war in 1915. He took part in the Russian revolution on the side of the Bolsheviks, but returned to Czechoslovakia in 1921 probably because his life was threatened in Russia on account of his critical attitude toward some Bolshevik practices. Hašek published *The Good Soldier Švejk and His Fortunes in the World War* in installments and sold it in pubs with his friend Franta Sauer.

The basis of Hašek's humor is everyday banality, placed in an ironic and parodic context. In literary texts based on experiences from his early wanderings through the Czech countryside, Hašek created folksy, ordinary characters filled with natural feelings and a naive matter-of-factness. Their simple, straightforward ways contrasted with the hypocrisy of the more sophisticated classes. Similarly, Hašek found a living source of inspiration in the popular art of storytelling as it occurs in pubs.

The Good Soldier Švejk suggests that the horrors of World War I amounted to a total collapse of all values associated with prewar Europe. After experiencing the war, one could only return to elementary self-defense and to the most basic values of life. In Hašek's view, new sources of humanity could only be found in ordinary, plebeian characters who are always naturally indifferent to higher values and therefore uncorrupted by the spiritual crisis of the collapsing era. Simplicity was their saving grace.

The Good Soldier Švejk uses documentary material enlivened by the author's exceptional narrative talent. However, the documentary evidence, in all its vivid detail, is systematically parodied. The essence of Hašek's humor resides in the ambiguity of Švejk's statements. In the most dramatic, existential situations, when all values are being destroyed, the only workable attitude is Švejk's idiotically indifferent smile. The only value Švejk defends is bare human existence. Nevertheless, he seems to retain his personal integrity even under overwhelming impersonal bureaucratic pressure.

JAN ČULÍK

Further Reading

Arie-Haifman, Hana, "Švejk, the homo ludens," in *Language and Literary Theory: In Honor of Ladislav Matějka,* edited by Benjamin A. Stolz, I.R. Titunik, Lubomír Doležel, Ann Arbor: University of Michigan Press, 1984

Bělohradsky, Václav, "The Retreat into the Uniform and the Disintegration of Order: Švejk as an Integral Part of Central-European Literature," *Scottish Slavonic Review* 2 (1983)

Chalupecký, Jindřich, "The Tragic Comedy of Jaroslav Hašek," in *Cross Currents: A Yearbook of Central European Culture,* number 23, Ann Arbor: Department of Slavic Languages and Literatures, University of Michigan, 1983

Doležel, Lubomír, "Circular Patterns: Hasek and *The Good Soldier Švejk,*" in *Poetica Slavica: Studies in Honour of Zbigniew Folejewski,* edited by J. Douglas Clayton and Gunter Schaarschmidt, Ottawa: University of Ottawa Press, 1981

Kosík, Karel, "Hašek and Kafka, 1883–1922/23," in *Cross Currents: A Yearbook of Central European Culture,* number 23, Ann Arbor: Department of Slavic Languages and Literatures, University of Michigan, 1983

Parrott, Cecil, Sir, *The Bad Bohemian: The Life of Jaroslav Hašek, Creator of "The Good Soldier Švejk,"* London: Bodley Head, 1978

Pynsent, R.B., "Jaroslav Hašek (1883–1923)," *European Writers: The Twentieth Century* 9 (1989)

Stern, J.P., "On the Integrity of the Good Soldier Švejk," in *Czechoslovakia Past and Present,* volume 2, *Essays on the Arts and Sciences,* edited by Miloslav Rechcígl, Jr., The Hague: Mouton, 1968

Nadine Gordimer 1923–

South African

Nadine Gordimer, South African novelist, short-story writer, and essayist, gradually rose to international prominence over a period of more than 40 years as her country's foremost interpreter of life under the South African apartheid system of racial discrimination. Together with such writers as Alan Paton, J.M. Coetzee, and André Brink she is now one of the most well-known South African writers of her time, and recognition of her achievements as a writer and political novelist was solidified internationally when she received the Nobel prize for literature in 1991.

Gordimer grew up in Springs, a small mining town on the East Rand outside Johannesburg. Kept out of school by her mother for some years owing to an alleged heart problem, Gordimer educated herself in the literary methods and moral passions of late 19th- and early 20th-century English and European literature, and began to write and publish while still in her teens.

Heavily influenced by her reading, her early work showed a strong Lawrentian sensibility, married to an acutely perceptive social conscience. Her early work was largely dismissed within South Africa for its perceived lack of modernist experimentation and adherence to the techniques of European realism, but her ability to capture the minutiae of daily South African experience with a rare sensitivity and insight was recognized and admired. Confining her focus mostly to the highveld area around Johannesburg where she was born and has lived most of her life, Gordimer has been called a regional writer, and her early strength as a writer was seen to lie in her finely nuanced evocations of the sensory and emotional impact of the South African landscape upon her characters (in her own words, "catching the shimmer of things"), and in her sensitive exploration of their conflicted and anguished sensibilities.

Part Jewish in background, Gordimer was also early sensitized to anti-Semitic strains in small-town South African society, a theme prominent in her first semi-autobiographical novel, *The Lying Days* (1953). More particularly, her desire to write truthfully of a local world often dismissed as unworthy of attention within her parents' Anglo-colonial contexts led her to a growing focus on the crippling effects of the country's policies of racial division and oppression on the individual growth of both black and white South Africans. Concerned from the start with the problem of how to live a morally responsible life in such a society, her subject quickly became the liberal white South African's struggle to construct an acceptable identity and home for himself on a continent in which he was identified chiefly as an oppressor and transient colonizer.

Although never directly politically active herself in the years before 1991, Gordimer soon established herself as an acute observer on the fringes of anti-apartheid activism and became a sharp critic of the ambiguities, moral compromises, and failures of white South African liberalism. Her growing admiration for those activists, both black and white, who succeeded in transcending these limitations expressed itself in an increasing focus in her novels and short stories on the dilemmas and problems that political *engagement* posed for individuals reluctantly drawn into activism by the example of personal heroism in others. In several novels she also incorporated a record of the shifting debates within the liberation movement from decade to decade (such as the putative link between capitalism and apartheid as a subtext in *The Conservationist*, 1974), and sought to publish within a fictional framework some of the major arguments and documents of the anti-apartheid movement that the South African government had banned from circulation (*Burger's Daughter*, 1979). As a result her work several times fell afoul of the South African government's censorship laws, and Gordimer very early in her career decided to publish her work internationally to ensure that it would reach an audience beyond the country's borders. Her sympathy with Black Consciousness politics was expressed in a number of portraits of black activist leaders, and she incorporated some of the major insights of revisionist South African historians as background in a number of later novels. In her writings she sought not only to bring to the attention of her audience the reality, extent, and impact of oppression at home (publishing several "letters from the Front" in such international forums as *The New York Review of Books*; see "Living in the Interregnum," 1982) but also to interpret movements and events elsewhere in Africa (in *A Guest of Honour*, 1970), to offer an imagined account based on the suppressed history of the African National Congress' anti-apartheid activism beyond the country's borders (in *A Sport of Nature*, 1987), and to imagine the shape the country's future might take (apocalyptic in *July's People*, 1981; triumphantly idealized in *A Sport of Nature*). Although some critics have found a didactic thrust in her work, Gordimer consistently has refused to consider herself an exponent of any particular political ideology, and has claimed repeatedly that her only intention in her work has been to depict the complexities of life in South Africa as fully and truthfully as possible. Nevertheless, together with writers around South Africa, she hailed the coming liberation in 1990 as a release from the straitjacket of needing to write "in battle-dress," and looked forward to the pleasures of being able to write about anything she pleased.

Although early in her career Gordimer was known chiefly as a fine short-story writer, she came increasingly to believe that the novel form was better suited to the themes she wished to explore. Describing herself in 1964 in a well-known statement as "a romantic struggling with reality," she has continued to exhibit in her work the influence of the premodernist and modernist writers who shaped her early sensibilities. Never merely modish in her handling of narrative, she has nevertheless incorporated a number of modernist techniques in her work over the years, such as experiments with stream of consciousness, shifting point of view, and multiple narrative voices. In a seminal study of Gordimer's novels, Stephen Clingman (1986) claimed for her work a Lukácsian thrust, showing that one of the defining characteristics of her work has been her ability to transform the individual and the personal into the typical and the definitive. In tandem with this, her overriding concern with social, moral, and political issues also expresses itself in an increasing thematic focus on the need to subordinate the drive for personal fulfillment to the political and public demands of the time. (Indeed, some critics have found the endings of her novels problematic, claiming they are driven not by fidelity to character development but by the need to make a polemical political point.)

Gordimer's works characteristically focus on a single central consciousness and employ a first-person narrative voice that has frequently been male (*A World of Strangers*, 1958; *A Guest of Honour*; *The Conservationist*; *My Son's Story*, 1990). Gordimer responded to feminist criticisms of her privileging of male voices by claiming that the writer is essentially androgynous. Her refusal to label herself a feminist expressed itself in the 1970s and 1980s in her adherence to the position (widely held in the liberation movement at the time) that the liberation of the people as a whole had to take precedence over the claims of women alone. However, with the shift in priorities that accompanied the handing over of political power in the early 1990s, Gordimer in her recent work has increasingly focused on women's issues in the postcolonial/postapartheid world (for example, in her latest novel, *None to Accompany Me*, 1994). Among her most enduring concerns has been to examine the formative relationship between parents and children and to emphasize the universality of traditional humanist values.

Gordimer has stated repeatedly that her writings have comprised her contribution to the liberation struggle in South Africa. Like the character Will in *My Son's Story*, she has concentrated upon representing to the world at large "what it really was like to live a life determined by the struggle to be free." Recent critical responses, however, have focused on the postmodernist aspects of her work and have sought to place it historically within the larger stream of postcolonial writing around the world.

KATHY WAGNER

See also Conservationist

Biography

Born 20 November 1923 in Springs, Transvaal. Educated at a convent school, and the University of the Witwatersrand, Johannesburg. Visiting Lecturer, Institute of Contemporary Arts, Washington, D.C., 1961, Harvard University, Cambridge, Massachusetts, 1969, Princeton University, New Jersey, 1969, Northwestern University, Evanston, Illinois, 1969, and the University of Michigan, Ann Arbor, 1970; Adjunct Professor of Writing, Columbia University, New York, 1971; presenter, *Frontiers* television series, 1990. Awarded Nobel prize for literature, 1991.

Novels by Gordimer

The Lying Days, 1953
A World of Strangers, 1958
Occasion for Loving, 1963
The Late Bourgeois World, 1966
A Guest of Honour, 1970
The Conservationist, 1974
Burger's Daughter, 1979
July's People, 1981
A Sport of Nature, 1987
My Son's Story, 1990
None to Accompany Me, 1994

Other Writings: short-story collections (including *Six Feet of the Country,* 1956, and *Something Out There,* 1984), television plays (including *A Terrible Chemistry,* 1981), and nonfiction (including *Lifetimes Under Apartheid,* 1986, and *Three in a Bed: Fiction, Morals, and Politics,* 1991).

Further Reading

Clingman, Stephen, *History from the Inside: The Novels of Nadine Gordimer,* London and Boston: Allen and Unwin, 1986; 2nd edition, Amherst: University of Massachusetts Press, 1992; London: Bloomsbury, 1993
Cooke, John, *The Novels of Nadine Gordimer: Private Lives/Public Landscapes,* Baton Rouge: Louisiana State University Press, 1985
Driver, Dorothy, editor, *Nadine Gordimer: A Bibliography of Primary and Secondary Sources, 1937–1992,* London: Hans Zell, 1994
Ettin, Andrew Vogel, *Betrayals of the Body Politic: The Literary Commitments of Nadine Gordimer,* Charlottesville: University Press of Virginia, 1993
Haugh, Robert, *Nadine Gordimer,* New York: Twayne, 1974
Head, Dominic, *Nadine Gordimer,* Cambridge and New York: Cambridge University Press, 1994
Heywood, Christopher, *Nadine Gordimer,* Windsor, Berkshire: Profile, 1983
King, Bruce, editor, *The Later Fiction of Nadine Gordimer,* London: Macmillan, and New York: St. Martin's Press, 1993
Newman, Judie, *Nadine Gordimer,* London and New York: Routledge, 1988
Smith, Rowland, editor, *Critical Essays on Nadine Gordimer,* Boston: G.K. Hall, 1990
Wade, Michael, *Nadine Gordimer,* London: Evans, 1978
Wagner, Kathrin, *Rereading Nadine Gordimer,* Bloomington: Indiana University Press, 1994

Maksim Gor'kii 1868–1936

Russian

Acknowledged as the most important prerevolutionary novelist after Lev Tolstoi, Maksim Gor'kii became renowned as the "founder" of socialist realism in the Soviet period. His experience coincided with the late 19th-century "movement of the masses" from the Russian countryside into the cities. This phenomenon was reflected less directly in his novels than in his short stories, his plays, and his autobiographical trilogy, but it was mainly through his novels that he acquired his reputation for political commitment.

Gor'kii never mastered the genre fully. Episodic, often poorly constructed, his novels tend to start well, introducing interesting characters with thumbnail exactitude, and then to rely on a frequently tedious, scene-by-scene format that usually culminates in a somewhat contrived moment of drama. This is not to deny his outstanding descriptive powers, his forceful use of rich verbal coloration allied to a quasi-lyrical prose manner, and his effectiveness in writing expressive naturalistic dialogue.

"I came into the world in order to disagree" was his motto, and in the petit-bourgeois world he depicted he celebrated the maverick, the opponent of property, the antibourgeois element. His first novel, *Foma Gordeev* (1899; *Foma*), portrays the life of Foma, heir to enormous wealth derived from barge traffic on the Volga. Foma eventually makes an ineffectual protest against mercantilism and is rejected as mad by his fellow merchants. Vivid characterizations of his father Ignat and other spokesmen of the merchant class as well as those opposed to it give the novel a vital appeal, but Foma's protest, illustrative of what Gor'kii called "the stupidity of the brave," catches the imagination.

His second novel, *Troe* (1900; *The Three*), was a less successful version of the same theme of protest, in this case Il'ia Luniov's protest against the hypocrisy of local tradespeople. Murder, brutality, and urban squalor form the background to what ultimately is a story flawed by melodrama.

More intense political engagement, even a programmatic tone, came with Gor'kii's third and most famous novel, *Mat'* (1906; *Mother*). The central image of the mother of Pavel Vlasov, the young political activist, establishes a close relationship between this novel and the first part of Gor'kii's autobiographical trilogy *My Childhood* (1913), which contains a portrait of his grandmother. Generally speaking, his female characters are by nature more virtuous than his male figures, and the portrait of his grandmother and the central character of *Mother* fit into that mold. Interestingly, the mother undergoes a conversion of sorts under the influence of her son's socialist ideas. Since the novel is presented from her viewpoint, these ideas are given a deeper personal meaning through her love for her son.

Mother underwent at least four revisions, but the first draft was written largely in America during Gor'kii's visit in 1906. As a consequence, its initial legal status was that of a work of American literature. This was not the only paradox associated with this cornerstone work of socialist realism. Although it was concerned with the industrial proletariat and the politicizing of their anticapitalist protest along Bolshevik lines, Gor'kii did not have first-hand experience of large-scale industrial conditions and depicted the factory workers as reified by their work without so much as indicating what exactly they manufactured. Its political message only emerges explicitly in Pavel's tirade at novel's end. Nevertheless, the deeper commitment to socialism and revolutionary change is clearly implied by the mother's self-sacrifice for the cause.

Although the novel was venerated during the Soviet period after Lenin gave it his approval, Gor'kii himself was dissatisfied with it. He never returned to this theme. All his later novels focused on the peasantry (*narod*), the merchant class, and the petit-bourgeois intelligentsia and avoided the overtly proselytizing class bias of *Mother*. Allegory, never far below the surface in Gor'kii's work, assumes a very important role in *Ispoved'* (1908; *A Confession*). Devoted to the then-popular notion of God-Building (*bogostroitel'stvo*), the idea that the collective will of the people could create its own God, this "confession" by an itinerant narrator tells of his search for an anti-individualistic God capable of working miracles. A tendency to mannered overwriting, always typical of Gor'kii's allegories, mars this otherwise impressive short novel.

Two works joined by the presence of a single hero, *Gorodok Okurov* (1909; Okurov City) and *Zhizn' Matveia Kozhemiakina* (1910–11; *The Life of Matvei Kozhemyakin*), added little to Gor'kii's repertoire as a novelist, but they distill two common elements in his work: the inertia of small-town life and a quasi-biographical type of portraiture that was increasingly designed to relate the past to the present. Nowhere is this latter feature more clearly evident than in what many regard as his best novel, *Delo Artamonovykh* (1925; *The Artamonov Business*). A return to the vivid characterizations of *Foma*, this novel tells the story of three successive generations of linen manufacturers descended from a former peasant. His son, Piotr Artamonov, presides over the successful business with much moral soul-searching, while other relatives are more ruthless in their pursuit of commercial gain and material pleasures. Fate finally overtakes them in 1917. Although a study in degeneration, the novel could not help being in part a valediction to the energy of the merchant class that was swept away by the revolution.

Gor'kii's final, unfinished epic novel, *Zhizn' Klima Samgina* (The Life of Klim Samgin, 1925–36; translated in 4 vols. as *The Bystander, The Magnet, Other Fires*, and *The Spectre*), concentrates on the intelligentsia, its shallow revolutionism, loquacity, and lack of moral fiber. Klim himself, trained as a lawyer, epitomize the scepticism of the pre-1917 intelligentsia, and yet he is too thinly drawn to elicit real sympathy as a character. Encompassing the period from the 1870s to 1917 and packed with dialogue, the novel dissolves at the end into fragments, much, it seems, like Klim himself. Gor'kii disagreed with violent revolution as much as he had disagreed with the life preceding it.

RICHARD FREEBORN

Biography

Born Alexei Maksimovich Peshkov, in Nizhnyi Novgorod, Russia, 16 March 1868. Attended parish school, Nizhnyi Novgorod; Kumavino elementary school, 1877–78. Apprenticed to a shoemaker at age 11; later draughtsman's clerk and cook's boy on a Volga steamer; became active in revolutionary politics beginning in 1888; first arrested in 1889; began publishing in prominent journals around the mid-1890s; member of publishing cooperative Knowledge, and literary editor of *Zhizn'* [Life], St. Petersburg, from 1899; employed at the publishing house Znanie, 1900, rising to become its leading editor; exiled to Arzamas, central Russia, for his part in an underground printing press, 1901; joined the Bolshevik Party, 1905; visited the United States, 1906; lived in Capri, 1906–13; established revolutionary propaganda school, 1909; returned to Russia upon the granting of general amnesty, 1913: founding editor, *Letopis'* [Chronicles] magazine, 1915–17, and newspaper *Novaia Zhizn'* [New Life], 1917–18; set up the publishing house Vsemirnaia Literatura [World Literature]; participated in Petrograd Workers and Soldiers Soviet; left Russia in 1921: editor, *Dialogue*, Berlin, 1923–25, and in Sorrento during most of 1924–32; editor, *Literary Apprenticeship* magazine, 1930; returned to Russia permanently in 1933: helped found the Biblioteka Poeta [Poet's Library] publishing project; traveled widely in the Soviet Union, assumed a leading role at the All-Union Congress of Soviet Writers, 1934, and contributed to the installment of Socialist Realism as the artistic orthodoxy. Died 18 June 1936.

Novels by Gor'kii

Foma Gordeev, 1899; as *Foma Gordeyev*, translated by Herman Bernstein, 1901; also translated by Margaret Wettlin, 1956; as *The Man Who Was Afraid*, translated by Bernstein, 1905; as *Foma*, 1945

Troe, 1900; as *Three of Them*, translated by Alexandra Linden, 1902; as *Three Men*, translated by Charles Horne, 1902; also translated by A. Frumkin, 1919; as *The Three*, translated by Margaret Wettlin, 1958

Mat', 1906; as *Mother*, 1907; revised translation by Isidor Schneider, 1947; as *Comrades*, 1907

Ispoved', 1908; as *A Confession*, translated by Frederick Harvey, 1910; as *The Confession*, translated by Rose Strunsky, n.d.

Gorodok Okurov [Okurov City], 1909

Zhizn' Matveia Kozhemiakina, 1910–11; as *The Life of Matvei Kozhemyakin*, translated by Margaret Wettlin, 1960

Delo Artamonovykh, 1925; as *Decadence*, translated by Veronica Dewey, 1927; as *The Artamonov Business*,

translated by A. Brown, 1948; as *The Artamonovs,* translated by H. Altschuler, 1952
Zhizn' Klima Samgina [The Life of Klim Samgin] (unfinished), 1925–36; as *The Bystander, The Magnet, Other Fires,* and *The Spectre,* translated by Bernard Guilbert Bakshy, 4 vols., 1931–38

Other Writings: stories, plays, autobiographical writings and memoirs, letters, verse, and essays on literature, politics, and culture.

Further Reading

Borras, F.M., *Maxim Gorky the Writer: An Interpretation,* Oxford: Clarendon Press, 1967
Gourfinkel, Nina, editor, *Gorky,* New York: Grove Press, 1960
Hare, Richard, *Maxim Gorky: Romantic Realist and Conservative Revolutionary,* London and New York: Oxford University Press, 1962
Kaun, Alexander Samuel, *Maxim Gorky and His Russia,* New York: Cape and Smith, 1931; London: Cape, 1932
Levin, Dan, *Stormy Petrel: The Life and Work of Maxim Gorky,* New York: Appleton-Century, 1965; London: Muller, 1967
Mikhailovskii, B.V., and Evgenii Borisovich Tager, *Tvorchestvo M. Gor'kogo,* Moscow: Gos. Uchebno-Pedagog. Izd.vo, 1951
Volkov, Anatolii Andreevich, *Put' khudozhnika: M. Gor'kij do Oktiabra,* Moscow: Izdvo. Khudozhestv. Literatura, 1969
Weil, Irwin, *Gorky: His Literary Development and Influence on Soviet Intellectual Life,* New York: Random House, 1966

Gothic Novel

The history of the Gothic novel, or Gothic romance as it was sometimes called, conventionally begins with the publication of Horace Walpole's *The Castle of Otranto,* subtitled *A Gothick Story,* in 1764. Walpole, who was a Whig member of parliament, concealed himself behind two personae, framing the story as a 15th-century manuscript by one "Onuphrio Muralto," translated by "William Marshall, Gent." The first reviewers sensed something fake, but they were unsure about the status of this "manuscript." The public, however, was enthusiastic, and after the first edition sold out in a matter of months, Walpole was prevailed upon to identify himself. Born appropriately illegitimate, the Gothic novel belatedly acquired its father and became a genre whose conventional end point in literary history is usually marked at around 1820 with the publication of Charles Maturin's tremendous anti-Catholic epic, *Melmoth the Wanderer* (although, of course, novels following in the Gothic tradition continue to be written and published today).

The Castle of Otranto anticipates many of the formal and thematic obsessions that would characterize the Gothic novel. It looks back to a feudal world in which the Lord of the Manor, Manfred, the first in a long line of Gothic villain-heroes, exercises seigneurial rights over the minds and bodies of his subjects. His castle, however, according to an ancient prophecy, is haunted by a gigantic ancient suit of armour, which falls on his sickly son, Conrad, and kills him. Manfred's obsession with primogeniture and the inability of his wife, Hippolita, to provide him with a son and heir lead Manfred to offer himself in a vaguely incestuous fashion to his one-time prospective daughter-in-law, Isabella. Isabella refuses him indignantly, and, pursued by the would-be rapist, flees into the subterranean vaults of the castle, taking refuge in the monastery church, sheltered there by a good priest. In the end, Manfred is revealed as the son of a usurper of the true line of Otranto, which is represented by a mysteriously articulate young peasant, Theodore, who saves and marries the harrassed Isabella and takes over his rightful estate.

The Castle of Otranto is permeated with many of the conventions of the Gothic romance that would flourish between 1764 and 1820: the antiquarian pretense that the author is merely the editor of a found manuscript; the setting in medieval, "superstitious" (Catholic) southern Europe, which, for an English Protestant audience, invokes darkness and otherness and the contemporary Jacobite threat; the running allusions to the gloom and tragedy of William Shakespeare's *Hamlet* and *Macbeth* (another play with anti-Jesuit, anti-Jacobite associations) in the plot and setting; the conflation of villain and hero in the brooding figure of Manfred, who is subject to outbursts of rage and violence; a subtextual meditation on the decay of feudal and aristocratic rights in general, and of primogeniture in particular; a fictional acknowledgment of the rise of an ambitious 18th-century bourgeoisie (represented in part by Manfred himself) eager to exercise individual freedom in marriage and inheritance; the focus on victimized but often defiant women threatened with rape and incest; and the use of confined spaces—castles, dungeons, monasteries, and prisons—to symbolize extreme emotional states through labyrinthine images of confinement, burial, and incarceration. All of these Gothic modalities spring into existence, more or less fully formed, in Walpole's tale.

There is an intriguing contradiction between subject matter and language in Walpole's text that does not occur in later Gothic novels. Stylistically *The Castle of Otranto* is terse, dry, and witty, suffused with the rational virtues of 18th-century prose. Romantic expansiveness is entirely foreign to it, despite the melodrama of its events, which gives to the whole an air of genial spoof. Walpole wrote and spoke French extremely well and was personally close to several figures of the Enlightenment in France. He was not uncritical of the movement, however, and his antiquarianism and dilettantism stand in an equivocal relationship to Enlightenment scientific rationalism. On the other hand, beneath a facade of humorous scepticism, Walpole revealed serious interests in medieval art and architecture, neglected areas of historical scholarship, and alternative modes of awareness. In a famous account of the genesis of his novel from a dream, which proved interesting to André Breton and the French surrealists, Walpole shows that he was allowing his unconscious to dominate the writing process (see Breton, 1937).

This rich and somewhat contradictory relationship between the French Enlightenment and the Gothic novel is an enduring theme in the survival of the Gothic beyond its first phase as an 18th-century genre into the 19th and 20th centuries (see Botting, 1993). Ann Radcliffe's novels feature what came to be known as "the explained supernatural," initiating a rhetorical tradition in the later Gothic that deliberately uses "explanation" and the apparatus of reason as a teasing device to provoke doubt and edge the reader toward the inexplicable.

Mid-18th-century aesthetics in England were founded on Pierre Corneille's *Horace*—a polished, witty, decorous, and above all conscious writing that is built on an aesthetics of *product*. But the Longinian tradition of the sublime, revived also in midcentury by Edmund Burke in his *A Philosophical Enquiry into the Origin of Our Ideas of the Sublime and Beautiful* (1757), demands an aesthetics of *process*, foregrounding the affective relationship between reader and text. The birth of sensibility as a value, which derives partly from the Enlightenment, signified a new interest in the emotions. The neo-romanticism of Burke's treatise became a blueprint for the style of the later Gothic novel after Walpole, an aesthetics of terror and horror, which laid down a set of rhetorical conditions and models (including John Milton's Satan in *Paradise Lost*) for the excitement of awe in the reader. The rhetoric of obscurity and the perverse, sadomasochistic seduction of the reader into a gloomy excess of anticipation, so typical of the later Gothic novel, is codified in Burke's treatise and becomes a fashionable mode in the poetry, prose, and the visual arts of the later 18th century (see Fiedler, 1966; Mishra, 1994).

All these features crystallized in the following well-known passage from the most famous Gothic novel of all, Ann Radcliffe's *The Mysteries of Udolpho* (1794), in which the abducted Emily gazes for the first time at the castle in which she is to be imprisoned:

> "There," said Montoni, speaking for the first time in several hours, "is Udolpho."
>
> Emily gazed with melancholy awe upon the castle which she understood to be Montoni's; for, though it was now lighted up by the setting sun, the Gothic greatness of its features, and its mouldering walls of dark grey stone, rendered it a gloomy and sublime object. As she gazed, the light died away on its walls, leaving a melancholy purple tint, which spread deeper and deeper as the thin vapour crept up the mountain, while the battlements above were still tipped with splendour. From those, too, the rays soon faded, and the whole edifice was invested with the solemn duskiness of evening. Silent, lonely, and sublime, it seemed to stand the sovereign of the scene, and to frown defiance on all who dared to invade its solitary reign. As the twilight deepened, its features became more awful in obscurity; and Emily continued to gaze, till its clustering towers were alone seen rising over the tops of the woods, beneath whose thick shade the carriages soon after began to ascend.

Although the setting is the 16th-century Italian Appenines, the feeling is purely contemporary 18th century: the whole passage is a narrative enactment of Burkean aesthetics with its references to sublime Alpine painting (Salvator Rosa is the model) and the Miltonic connection between the apparently Satanic Montoni, Emily's abductor, and the ruined phallic towers of the castle. A liminal moment comparable in foreboding to the entry of Duncan into Macbeth's castle, this description would echo down through the Gothic tradition.

All the descriptive terms of this passage act as emotional triggers, telling the reader what to feel as much as describing an object, and none more so than the term *Gothic* itself. But by the 1790s, the label Gothic had become a complex term, encompassing quite contradictory meanings that polarize roughly between the Tory and Whig elements of the readership, dependent on which historiographical tradition one supposes to be foremost in a reader's mind. To the Tory readership Radcliffe's phrase "Gothic greatness" conjures up patriotic images of the Plantagenets, high Anglo-Catholic ritual, and past victories against the French—"banners," as another Gothic novelist, William Beckford, puts it, "from haughty Gallia torn." Henry VII's chapel in Westminster Abbey was Gothic in this sense. To another sort of reader, "Gothic greatness" would mean "primitive, rugged but barbaric," and this in turn would split into either an honorific or pejorative sense. The honorific sense came from the Whig tradition of historiography, in which the Goths were portrayed as a progressive, democratic, Germanic, freedom-loving people who removed from Europe the yoke of the Holy Roman Empire and laid the foundations of the English Constitution and the Common Law; but equally, if readers were to take their bearings from the Italian Renaissance historiographic tradition, "Gothic greatness" would have a much more oxymoronic flavor and mean "barbarously out of scale, crude, precivilized, preclassical, un-English, and belonging to the Dark Ages," and it could inspire a feeling of threat or opposition rather than a latent or overt patriotism. Equally, it might be possible to feel a confused but still nationalistic mixture of these things, as Samuel Coleridge tended to do (see Sage, 1990; Kliger, 1945; Miles, 1993).

After Walpole, the Gothic retreated to the magazines and miscellanies, but two decades later, in the 1780s, the Minerva Press, backed by the new circulating libraries, began to pour out Gothic three-deckers to a formula that derived from Walpole but that lacked his comic astringency of tone (see Blakey, 1939). By the end of the 1790s the demand for such books had grown into an addiction, a fact reflected by Jane Austen's famous parody of the Gothic novel, *Northanger Abbey*, the satirical parts of which were probably written in 1800 but not published until after the author's death in 1818, when it became one of the texts that helped to mark the death-knell of the genre's first phase. This text is a parody of both the Radcliffean Gothic and of patriarchal attempts in the magazines to control the female addiction to reading, which was commonly likened to gin drinking. It is interesting to note that Isabella Thorpe's list of "Horrid Novels" was thought to have been made up by Jane Austen until the 1920s, when Michael Sadleir demonstrated the existence of all of these once popular, but quickly forgotten, texts (see Sadleir, 1927).

Two years after *The Mysteries of Udolpho*, Matthew Gregory Lewis, another Whig member of parliament, published *The Monk* (1796). Set in 16th-century Spain, *The Monk*'s blend of Catholic superstition, incest, rape, murder, and Faustian metaphysics proved a *succès de scandale*. Lewis was forced to withdraw the book and edit it after a review, often attributed to

Coleridge, accused him of blasphemy, a crime punishable by imprisonment (see Parreaux, 1960). In 1797 Ann Radcliffe replied to Lewis with *The Italian,* half of which is set near Naples and half in the dungeons of the Roman Inquisition. The Gothic genre was now fully established. By 1800 the Marquis de Sade was announcing that these novels were "the necessary fruits of the revolutionary tremors felt by the whole of Europe," a remark that has proven highly influential in later critical debate, initiating a tradition of linking the Gothic novel with the French Revolution (see Paulson, 1983).

Politically the 1790s were a turbulent decade, and Gothic novels were the focus of various crosscurrents in contemporary culture: English antiquarianism, Whig dilettantism, German influences from the Sturm und Drang, homosexuality, anti-Jacobitism; occult and radical secret societies such as the Freemasons and the Illuminati from southern Germany; anti-Catholicism, Godwinianism, conservative English nationalism, French revolutionary propaganda, among many others. In 1798 Richard Sheridan's Drury Lane Theatre performed *The Castle Spectre,* a Gothic drama by M.G. "Monk" Lewis. William Pitt's government, nervous at the possibility of revolutionary subversion and propaganda, financed several magazines and kept a close eye on literary and popular culture.

During this decade many foreign writers visited London, some of them destined to contribute to other streams of the Gothic. Among them was perhaps the most remarkable and obscure, the deeply romantic Polish count, Jan Potocki. He drew inspiration for his extraordinary masterpiece, *The Manuscript Found in Saragossa* (1805), from a stay in London at this time, catching the currency of the Gothic idiom and transporting it to a Spanish and Islamic context, "a la Radcliffe," as he wrote in a letter to a friend. Likewise, the American writer Charles Brockden Brown took his inspiration from the English Gothic novelists, particularly William Godwin, and began, in his extraordinary *Wieland* (1798), a powerful tradition in American Gothic writing that survived throughout the 19th century in Edgar Allan Poe, Herman Melville, and Nathaniel Hawthorne, to say nothing of Henry James. Brockden Brown was very much a mediator between the earlier generation and the young romantics: Thomas Love Peacock said at the time that *Wieland* was one of the deepest influences on Percey Shelley. John Keats, Walter Scott, and William Hazlitt read Brockden Brown, and Mary Shelley was reading him just before embarking on *Frankenstein* (see Punter, 1996).

Thus there are both conservative and radical strains of the Gothic novel. Godwin, for example, in *Caleb Williams* (1794) and *St. Leon* (1799), adapted the Burkean sublime to his own political radicalism, and Mary Wollstonecraft also showed the influence of Gothic novels in *Maria* (1798). But it was their daughter, Mary Shelley, who produced one of the most popular novels of the Gothic tradition: *Frankenstein; or, The Modern Prometheus* (1818) was a book Shelley afterward referred to as her "hideous progeny," a remark sometimes taken as an allusion not simply to the monster but to a number of tragic miscarriages and infant deaths she had to suffer in life. Famously, the book was conceived in 1816 at the Villa Diodati, in the company of her husband, Percey Shelley—who had been discussing the work of Signor Galvani—Lord Byron, and Dr John Polidori, whose contribution to this competition to produce a horror story was one of the early vampire tales.

The plot of *Frankenstein*—the story of a scientist who, having discovered the secret of artificial reproduction from corpses, creates a being, and then, revolted by its apparent monstrosity, morally and physically abandons it—has become nothing less than a modern myth in the postwar period. Given the discovery of the atom bomb, the subsequent Cold War and arms race, developments in genetics and computers, and the ethical issues raised by all these matters, this complex and ambiguously horrifying story codifies in miniature many contemporary concerns. It has acquired a resonance through reproduction in a number of popular cultural forms—Hammer Films, Hollywood versions (a stage play ran continuously until the 1880s), comics, radio plays—and the novel still appears to many to speak to us directly of our own condition in the face of technology.

By 1820 the excesses of the earlier genre began to be thought of as somewhat Grand Guignol. Perhaps this was due to the effect of parodies such as Austen's *Northanger Abbey* and Peacock's *Nightmare Abbey* (1818) or the Enlightenment relativism of Walter Scott and the rise of his new genre, the historical romance, which had begun to seem more modern to a post-Napoleonic, postheroic age. After 1820 the radicalism, confusion, and anarchy of the old Gothic novel, with its deliberately fantastic treatment of history, gave way to the new standards of technical accuracy and historical research of the *Waverly* era (roughly 1820–37). The Minerva Press gave up the Gothic and turned to children's books. The publication of the Dublin Calvinist Pastor Charles Maturin's hyperbolic, Faustian *Melmoth the Wanderer* (1820), which enjoyed particular success in France, conventionally marks the end of the first phase of the Gothic novel.

It is at this historical point that the Gothic novel broke up and became (in today's common parlance) "the Gothic"—a scattered but now permanent and widely influential aspect of literary sensibility rather than a homogenous genre or concerted movement. In the 1830s a polarization occurred between popular forms: the "penny dreadfuls" of writers such as G.W.M. Reynolds and the Newgate novels of Harrison Ainsworth, and the popular stage melodrama, on the one hand; on the other, the literary tradition of historical romance dominated by Scott. Ann Radcliffe survived into the Victorian period as a writer's writer, or a clumsy forerunner of romanticism (the young Wilkie Collins read her as part of a "hash of diablerie"), but Christopher North's *Blackwoods* and Henry Colburn's *New Monthly Magazine* had kept alive the Gothic flame, and by the 1840s both Charles Dickens and the Brontë sisters were showing unmistakable signs of the Gothic influence.

In the *Dublin University Magazine* of the 1830s, the ballads and plays of Friedrich von Schiller and Johann Wolfgang von Goethe and the tales of E.T.A. Hoffmann were systematically translated by James Clarence Mangan. The *Dublin University Magazine* probably is where Charlotte Brontë first became acquainted with the German wildness that formed a model for her own fictional tone. Later, from the 1840s onward, this magazine was edited and owned by Sheridan Le Fanu, one of the great Victorian masters of the Gothic horror tale. In America, Poe, following Radcliffe and Brockden Brown, began to produce his tales in magazines. In Scotland, defiant of the Enlightenment rationalism of Scott, James Hogg, the Ettrick Shepherd, used the Gothic convention of the doppelgänger (or double, probably also derived from Hoffmann) to satirize the growth of evangelical Calvinism in his *The Private Memoirs and Confessions of a Justified Sinner* (1824), a truly schizophrenic text. Eventually

Dickens planned a similar confessional climax for his last, unfinished doppelgänger novel, *The Mystery of Edwin Drood* (1870).

By the mid–19th century the Gothic novel was apparently extinct and the term *Gothic,* if used at all, was predominantly an architectural term. But paradoxically, this diversified underground role, the diffusion of a genre into a popular discourse that had no need to name itself, guaranteed its literary survival. The cultural conditions in which the novels had originally appeared—the unease about Enlightenment modes of thought, empirical science, and the epistemological doubt inherited from Hume and the 18th century; the economic independence of women as readers and writers; Catholic emancipation; the increasingly shrill assertion of Protestant rationality (see Gordon, 1983; Sage, 1988); the taboo on superstition; the sublime; the split self; and the curiosity about the nature of fantasy and sexual excitement—all these conditions, far from passing away, had intensified in the Victorian period.

By midcentury, the advent of Charles Darwin and the fears of social, cultural, and psychological regression that evolutionary thought brought to the Victorian imagination added new layers and contexts to the discourse of the Gothic—new dreams of horror, darkness, and the unspeakable. Dickens' novels from *Bleak House* (1853) on are an excellent index of the diffusion of the Gothic into an insistent strain of obscurity and terror: Dickensian London is a labyrinth of dark courts and filthy alleyways, the Thames is a polluted Styx of floating corpses, and the selves of his characters are frequently distorted or split. Later Victorian Gothic writing developed the Darwinian theme more explicitly. The allegory of Robert Louis Stevenson's *The Strange Case of Dr. Jekyll and Mr. Hyde* (1886) is a meditation on the nature of the psyche, a near-perfect anticipation of Sigmund Freud's early work on the ego and the id. Stevenson heralds a connection between the late Victorian and the modern sense of an irrevocable split in the definition of the self. Drawing on the German Gothic writer Hoffmann, Freud eventually codified his own responses to horror in his essay "Das Unheimliche" (1919; "The 'Uncanny'"), which forms an endpoint of 19th-century tradition and also a starting point for any thoughts about the modernity of the Gothic. From this point a line runs out into the modernist period via imperialism (Castle, in Brown and Nussbaum, 1987). Some Victorian Gothic, though, was recycled into German Expressionism and eventually into the postwar movies of Berlin-trained Alfred Hitchcock (see Castle, 1987).

This process of diffusion meant that the presence of the Gothic in Victorian writing was taken for granted, thanks to the currency of the magazines and the work of romantics such as Shelley, Coleridge, and Keats. Even Scott, by an interesting paradox, contributed to the creation of a Gothic narrative vocabulary through the immense popularity of his early Border ballads. It became *de rigueur* for any Victorian writer worth his or her salt to attempt the macabre or bizarre in a tale. Recent scholarly attention has been directed toward the popular "sensation" novel of the 1860s, a blend of realism, melodrama, and Gothic, whose name refers to its powerful affective designs on the reader's nerves, a feature that replays the connection between the original Gothic novel and the Burkean tradition of affective aesthetics. Le Fanu's masterpiece of the Victorian Gothic, *Uncle Silas* (1864), was marketed in this best-selling genre. Wilkie Collins' *The Woman in White* (1860), another sensation novel,

also has strong Gothic elements, his command of suspense earning him the title of "Mrs. Radcliffe brought down to date."

Medieval fantasy of all kinds became a Victorian obsession in poetry, narrative, architecture, crafts, and the iconography of the visual arts. Some of these elements are clearly visible in the greatest example of the 19th-century Gothic, Bram Stoker's *Dracula* (1897), perhaps the most reproduced and recycled of all the Gothic texts. Stoker's arch-vampire, the undead Count Dracula, like Frankenstein and Jekyll and Hyde, has entered the contemporary popular consciousness of the 20th century, in this case as a modern myth of vampirism, a reference point for nightmares from the 1960s onward—whether they be Cold War fantasies of invasion or infiltration from within, fantasies about sexual diseases, homosexuality, drugs, the transfer of bodily fluids, or new technologies of the body.

The postwar period has seen a remarkable revival of interest in the interpretation and the practice of the Gothic tradition, which is often now seen as a whole. In the last 20 years, serious critical commentary on the Gothic has expanded exponentially. Debate is keen about how "subversive" the Gothic is. Every college has its course on horror and the Gothic. Nowadays, every station concourse, supermarket, bookstore, and airport bookstall carries a category of pulp fiction called "Horror" or "Gothic" that includes an unpredictable mixture of the popular and high literary: Julio Cortázar or Tommaso Landolfi rub shoulders with Ramsay Campbell, William Gibson, and Angela Carter. Indeed, the world's greatest-selling contemporary writers—Anne Rice and Stephen King—are also the most direct descendants of Ann Radcliffe, Mary Shelley, and Bram Stoker, all of whom are integral to the global recycling of traditional myths that is the modern Gothic (see Sage and Lloyd Smith, 1996).

VICTOR SAGE

See also Crime, Detective, and Mystery Novel; Critics and Criticism (18th Century); Dracula; English Novel (18th Century; 1800–40); Frankenstein; Horror Novel; Irish Novel; Melmoth the Wanderer; Mysteries of Udolpho; Romance; Romantic Novel

Further Reading

Baldick, Chris, *In Frankenstein's Shadow: Myth, Monstrosity, and Nineteenth-Century Writing,* Oxford: Clarendon Press, and New York: Oxford University Press, 1987

Blakey, Dorothy, *The Minerva Press, 1790–1820,* London: Bibliographical Society at the University Press, Oxford, 1939

Botting, F., "Power in the Darkness: Heterotopias, Literature and Gothic Labyrinths," *Genre* 26 (Summer/Fall 1993)

Breton, André, "Limites non frontières du Surréalisme," *Nouvelle Revue Française* 48:1 (1937); translated as "Limits Not Frontiers of Surrealism," in *Surrealism,* edited by Herbert Edward Read, London: Faber, and New York: Harcourt, 1936

Castle, T., "The Spectralization of the Other," in *The New Eighteenth Century: Theory, Politics, English Literature,* edited by Laura Brown and Felicity Nussbaum, New York: Methuen, 1987

Dijkstra, Bram, *Idols of Perversity: Fantasies of Feminine Evil in Fin de Siecle Culture,* Oxford and New York: Oxford University Press, 1986

Duncan, Ian, *Modern Romance and Transformations of the Novel: The Gothic, Scott, Dickens,* Cambridge and New York: Cambridge University Press, 1992

Fiedler, Leslie, *Love and Death in the American Novel,* New York: Dell, 1960; revised edition, 1966

Fleenor, Juliann E., editor, *The Female Gothic,* Montreal: Eden Press, 1983

Frank, Frederick S., *Gothic Fiction: A Master List of Twentieth-Century Criticism and Research,* London: Meckler, 1987; Westport, Connecticut: Meckler, 1988

Gordon, Jan B., "Narrative Enclosure as Textual Ruin: An Archaeology of Gothic Consciousness," *Dickens Studies Annual* 11 (1983)

Howard, Jacqueline, *Reading Gothic Fiction: A Bakhtinian Approach,* Oxford: Clarendon Press, and New York: Oxford University Press, 1994

Jackson, Rosemary, *Fantasy: The Literature of Subversion,* London and New York: Methuen, 1981

Kilgour, Maggie, *The Rise of the Gothic Novel,* London and New York: Routledge, 1995

Kliger, S., "The 'Goths' in England: An Introduction to the Gothic Vogue in Eighteenth-Century Aesthetic Discussion," *Modern Philology* (November 1945)

McNutt, Dan J., *The Eighteenth-Century Gothic Novel: An Annotated Bibliography of Criticism and Selected Texts,* Folkestone: Dawson, and New York: Garland, 1975

Miles, Robert, *Gothic Writing, 1750–1820: A Genealogy,* London and New York: Routledge, 1993

Mishra, Vijay, *The Gothic Sublime,* Albany: State University of New York Press, 1994

Parreaux, Andre, *The Publication of "The Monk": A Literary Event, 1796–1798,* Paris: Didier, 1960

Paulson, Ronald, *Representations of Revolution (1789–1820),* New Haven, Connecticut, and London: Yale University Press, 1983

Punter, David, *The Literature of Terror: A History of Gothic Fictions from 1765 to the Present Day,* London and New York: Longman, 1980; 2nd edition, 1996

Sadleir, Michael, *The Northanger Novels: A Footnote to Jane Austen,* Oxford: Oxford University Press, 1927

Sage, Victor, *Horror Fiction in the Protestant Tradition,* London: Macmillan, and New York: St. Martin's Press, 1988

Sage, Victor, editor, *The Gothick Novel: A Casebook,* London: Macmillan, 1990

Sage, Victor, and Allan Lloyd Smith, editors, *Modern Gothic: A Reader,* Manchester: Manchester University Press, and New York: St. Martin's Press, 1996

Sedgwick, Eve Kosofsky, *The Coherence of Gothic Conventions,* New York: Arno, 1980; London: Methuen, 1986

Juan Goytisolo 1931–

Spanish

Juan Goytisolo, a member of the "mid-century generation" of post–Civil War Spain, began writing as a social realist, opposed to the frivolity of "art for art's sake." With the waning of the social novel in the late 1960s, Goytisolo moved to experimentalism, without completely abandoning social criticism. More recently, his novels exhibit increased humor and ludic obfuscation, with protean characters and shifting ontological ground, making them typically postmodern. While social criticism does not vanish entirely in these later works, the target is no longer Spain, but instead more universal aspects of capitalist and Western culture.

Goytisolo's oeuvre may be divided into three distinct periods. First is a youthful, formally and structurally conventional period comprising five novels, wherein young Goytisolo denounces the wrongs of Spanish society. These novels, adhering to many tenets of social realism in the 1950s and early 1960s, are "committed" protest fiction. *Juegos de manos* (1954; *The Young Assassins*) portrays a group of young men opposed to the government and Spanish social values who plan to "make a statement" via a political assassination. The title in Spanish, literally "sleight of hand," refers to the contrived selection of one

character, David, to carry out the murder. *Duelo en el paraíso* (1955; *Children of Chaos*) could be viewed as an earlier stage in the lives of the characters in *The Young Assassins*. Set in a small Spanish town during the Civil War, the story employs as allegorical intertext the biblical tale of Cain and Abel. As the defeated Republican troops leave, orphaned children take advantage of the anarchy before the victors arrive, regressing into a primitive state, recalling William Golding's *Lord of Flies* (1954). Taking possession of the school, the children commit a series of heinous crimes that echo wartime atrocities. The remaining three novels of the first period, *El circo* (1957; The Circus), *Fiestas* (1958; *Fiestas*), and *La resaca* (1958; The Undertow), are termed a trilogy but lack common characters. Thematic unity and common motifs include the poverty of people under a fascist regime, the hypocrisy of the church, Spain's ossified social structure, and the general social malaise of the 1950s.

Novels from Goytisolo's second period contrast with earlier works owing to their reduced combativeness and nearly continuous experimentation. Russian formalism evidently influenced Goytisolo, as evidenced by his statements in essays and interviews. Formal experimentation begins with the first novel in the

Mendiola Trilogy, *Señas de identidad* (1966; *Marks of Identity*), which exhibits progressive complexity and sophistication. This experimentation becomes still more marked in *Reivindicación del Conde don Julián* (1970; *Count Julian*) and culminates with *Juan sin tierra* (1975; *Juan the Landless*). Besides unconventional typographical layout, these novels incorporate formalist devices such as laying bare, literary borrowing, retardation, and defamiliarization. (While the terminology has changed—"intertextuality" for literary borrowing and "self-aware narrator" for laying bare—the function has remained the same.)

Goytisolo had by the 1970s become fully aware of the indivisibility of form and content. His criticism of Spanish society and the Catholic Church is no longer overwhelming, composing instead a more subtle part of the narrative tapestry, one of the myriad elements found in the Mendiola Trilogy. *Marks of Identity*, the story of a Spanish exile seeking his roots, provides an intense psychological study of the protagonist, Alvaro Mendiola, from his birth to the novel's present. *Count Julian*, set in Tangier, continues Alvaro's search for a *raison d'être* and shows clearly for the first time what had been apparent to a lesser degree in earlier works: Goytisolo's great love for Muslim culture. As Alvaro roams around Tangier, the reader is presented with a sort of internal monologue peppered with free associations and flashbacks. Among other things, *Count Julian* constitutes a violent voyage into the mind, history, and myth; a treatise on linguistics, literature, philosophy, psychology, and religion; and a political statement. Thanks to smoking *kif*, Alvaro conjures up the shade of Count Julian, who allowed the Muslims to invade Spain in 711, subjecting his rejected homeland to repeated acts of invasion and destruction. *Juan sin tierra* continues Alvaro's search for identity in the Muslim world.

Goytisolo's third period begins with *Paisajes después de la batalla* (1982; *Landscapes After the Battle*). Bitter attacks against Spain subside in *Landscapes* as the author targets many contemporary ills and foibles. Also notable is the appearance of humor for the first time in Goytisolo's writings, a device which becomes increasingly prevalent in his subsequent work. *Landscapes* is set in the Sentier, a Parisian neighborhood where many Arabs reside. While criticizing discrimination against Arabs in France and the pernicious invasion of United States culture, Goytisolo engages in theoretical musings on the relationship between author and text. At one point the intertextual author is kidnapped and blown to pieces, becoming as fragmented as the text. In *Las virtudes del pájaro solitario* (1988; *The Virtues of the Solitary Bird*), Goytisolo takes a mystical voyage through the past and the future. Employing the mystic writings of Saint John of the Cross and certain Sufi writers, Goytisolo discourses upon ills affecting the planet, from pollution to AIDS. Essentially, the novel constitutes a palimpsest, a tapestry of the writings of the mystics, often becoming more poetry than prose. Goytisolo's most recent novel to date, *El sitio de los sitios* (1995; The Siege of Sieges), set in Sarajevo, unmistakably indicts the United Nations' inability to deal with genocide in the former Yugoslavia, while simultaneously continuing to experiment with the nature of authorship. Thus, the novel comprises many texts in the form of letters, official reports, and poems, all seemingly belonging to different authors.

Goytisolo has also written a good deal of literary criticism and various autobiographical volumes. While decades of expatriation undoubtedly have hampered understanding of Goytisolo by the Spanish public, post-Franco critics increasingly recognize his importance. Translations of most of his works into numerous languages attest to a growing appreciation beyond the Hispanic world.

GENARO J. PÉREZ

Biography

Born in Barcelona, 5 January 1931; brother of the writer Luis Goytisolo. Attended the universities of Madrid and Barcelona, 1948–52. Member of Turia literary group, with Ana María Matute and others, Barcelona, 1951; emigrated to France, 1957; employed at Gallimard publishers, Paris, 1958–68; has traveled to Cuba, Europe, the Middle East, and Africa; visiting professor at universities in the United States.

Novels by Goytisolo

Juegos de manos, 1954; as *The Young Assassins*, translated by John Rust, 1959
Duelo en el paraíso, 1955; as *Children of Chaos*, 1958
El circo [The Circus], 1957
Fiestas, 1958; as *Fiestas*, translated by Herbert Weinstock, 1960
La resaca [The Undertow], 1958
Señas de identidad, 1966; as *Marks of Identity*, translated by Gregory Rabassa, 1969
Reivindicación del Conde don Julián, 1970; as *Count Julian*, translated by Helen R. Lane, 1974
Juan sin tierra, 1975; as *Juan the Landless*, translated by Helen R. Lane, 1977
Makbara, 1980; as *Makbara*, translated by Helen R. Lane, 1981
Paisajes después de la batalla, 1982; as *Landscapes After the Battle*, translated by Helen R. Lane, 1987
Las virtudes del pájaro solitario, 1988; as *The Virtues of the Solitary Bird*, translated by Helen R. Lane, 1991
La cuarentena, 1991; as *Quarantine*, translated by Peter Bush, 1994
El sitio de los sitios [The Siege of Sieges], 1995

Other Writings: short stories, travel books, autobiography, literary theory and criticism, social and political commentary.

Further Reading

Navajas, Gonzalo, *La novela de Juan Goytisolo*, Madrid: Sociedad General Española de Libreria, 1979
Pérez, Genaro J., *Formalist Elements in the Novels of Juan Goytisolo*, Madrid and Potomac, Maryland: Porrúa Turanzas, 1979
Schwartz, Kessel, *Juan Goytisolo*, New York: Twayne, 1970
Six, Abigail Lee, *Juan Goytisolo: The Case for Chaos*, New Haven, Connecticut: Yale University Press, 1990
Spires, Robert C., "Latrines, Whirlpools and Voids: The Metafictional Mode of *Juan sin tierra*," *Hispanic Review* 48 (1980)
Ugarte, Michael, *Trilogy of Treason: An Intertextual Study of Juan Goytisolo*, Columbia: University of Missouri Press, 1982

A Grain of Wheat by Ngugi wa Thiong'o

1967

Ngugi's third novel, *A Grain of Wheat* continues his portrayal of the harsh conditions suffered by the peasant population during the years of the Emergency in Kenya (1952–56). During this period thousands of Kenyans took to the forests to join the "land and freedom" (Mau-Mau) fighters battling against British colonial rule. In common with much of Ngugi's post-independence fiction, *A Grain of Wheat* explores Kenyan hopes and suffering during the years leading up to independence (1963) and also the immediate ramifications for national reconstruction in the post-independence period. Widely acclaimed and considered by many to be Ngugi's first mature work as a novelist, the novel marks a decisive turning point in the style and technique of Ngugi's fiction.

Critics have noted that *A Grain of Wheat*'s carefully planned and constructed narrative represents a departure from the somewhat attenuated characterizations and disjointed scenic structures of Ngugi's previous work. Ngugi has acknowledged that the novel departs from the linear/biographical unfolding of a story in favor of telling "stories within stories in a series of flashbacks," a technique that figured prominently in his masterpiece *Petals of Blood* (1977). In *Decolonising the Mind* (1986) he writes: "The multiple narrative voices, apart from helping me in coping with flexible time and space, also helped me in moving away from a single character novel. In *A Grain of Wheat* all the main characters are of almost equal importance, and the people—the village people—in their motion in history are the real hero of the novel." Ngugi develops a complex narrative structure that moves backward and forward between various time periods. David Cook (1977) regards this "interlocking of different phases of time" as essential to Ngugi's juxtaposition of various aspects of characters' lives, since he is concerned to "move out of a period of simple heroics into the much more baffling and complex realities of our independence."

A Grain of Wheat also indicates Ngugi's growing interest in the psychological profiles of his characters as he traces their moral and emotional responses through a variety of personal struggles deriving from the Mau-Mau Emergency. Constructed as a montage of narrative passages, interior monologues, dialogue, recollections, and anecdotes, the novel attempts to demonstrate how each character's present state of mind is the result of numerous past events and circumstances. Additionally, Ngugi refrains from taking an omniscient narratorial position; in this way the reader becomes aware of the characters' inner lives at the same time that the characters gradually come to know themselves.

Critics have noted that Ngugi's technique of temporal oscillation and of delaying information within the narrative, which breaks decisively with Ngugi's previous unilinear plots, suggests a profound debt to Joseph Conrad's narrative strategies. *A Grain of Wheat* also marks Ngugi's firm commitment to Marxist thought, projecting a socialist vision that meshes with the religious metaphor alluded to in the book's title and epigraph, which is taken from I Corinthians 15:36. Neil Lazarus (1990) considers the novel to be "situated on the border between a messianic and intellectualist field of vision, by the late 1960s representing decolonization as a failure, and a more concretely committed socialism, casting the decolonizing process in similarly radical but more soberly material and historical terms." Unlike Ngugi's previous fiction, which sought out messianic heroes, *A Grain of Wheat* consciously reveals the weaknesses and limitations of its characters to be the result of material and social contexts. Always seeking to derive political lessons from the state's persecution of the people, Ngugi nevertheless has managed to combine a trenchant political critique of the newly emerging "comprador bourgeoisie" in post-independence Kenya with incisive descriptions of the fortitude of the Kenyan peasants. In light of his next novel, *Petals of Blood,* one may retrospectively recognize Ngugi's emergent criticism of the new MPs and their entrepreneurial capitalist activities as they set about instituting a black bourgeoisie that exploited the rural peasant population just as ruthlessly as the ex-colonial white rulers did. In this respect *A Grain of Wheat* marks an increasing politicization in Ngugi's representation of post-independence Kenya, with its far-reaching political corruption and perpetuation of economic inequities.

TIM S. WOODS

See also Ngugi wa Thiong'o

Further Reading

Cook, David, "A New Earth: A Study of Ngugi wa Thiong'o's *A Grain of Wheat,*" in his *African Literature: A Critical View,* London: Longman, 1977

Cook, David, and M. Okenimkpe, *Ngugi wa Thiong'o: An Exploration of His Writings,* London: Heinemann, 1983; 2nd edition, Oxford: James Currey, and Portsmouth, New Hampshire: Heinemann, 1997

Gikandi, Simon, *Ngugi wa Thiong'o: The Ideology of Form,* Cambridge: Cambridge University Press, 1998

Killam, G.D., "*A Grain of Wheat,*" in *An Introduction to the Writings of Ngugi,* London and Exeter, New Hampshire: Heinemann, 1980

Lazarus, Neil, *Resistance in Postcolonial African Fiction,* New Haven, Connecticut: Yale University Press, 1990

Ogundele, Wole, "*Natio,* Nation, and Postcoloniality: The Example of Ngugi," in *Ngugi wa Thiong'o: Texts and Contexts,* edited by Charles Cantalupo, Trenton, New Jersey: Africa World Press, 1995

Palmer, Eustace, "James Ngugi: *A Grain of Wheat,*" in *An Introduction to the African Novel,* by Palmer, London: Heinemann, and New York: Africana, 1972

Robson, C.B., *Ngugi wa Thiong'o,* London: Macmillan, and New York: St. Martin's Press, 1979

Grande sertão: veredas. *See* Devil to Pay in the Backlands

The Grapes of Wrath by John Steinbeck

1939

The Grapes of Wrath is a singular text that draws upon a number of literary traditions while defying simple classification. John Steinbeck's story of economic exploitation in Depression-era California first angered and moved Americans when it appeared in 1939 and has since remained one of the most widely debated novels in American letters. It has been called painstakingly accurate, utterly false, obscene, utopian, apolitical, and profoundly political. It is a biblical narrative with California as the promised land, or an Eden whose promise is lost; it is an ideological novel that transmutes Christian symbols into a secular, even socialistic, sermon. It exhibits elements of naturalism and modernism but perhaps best fits the category of the proletarian novel—a literature that, in the teeth of the Depression, sought answers for the apparent failure of the American Dream.

Commonly termed a product of naturalism, *The Grapes of Wrath* also represents a departure from that literary movement. Steinbeck's novel is concerned with the country rather than the city, and while it does focus on the lower class and, at times, has the feel of environmental determinism, it treats both subjects in new ways. An amateur biologist, Steinbeck saw nothing degrading in a person's status as an animal. The Joads may be animals in the physical sense, earthy and sensual, but they are not brutes à la Frank Norris' *McTeague* (1899): the California border guards who characterize them as "apes," for example, think and sound like bigots. In the midst of systematic attempts to dehumanize them, the Joads maintain their dignity and compassion, symbolized by Rose of Sharon's offering of her mother's milk to a starving man—*agape* in the truest form and a gesture Steinbeck had in mind from the beginning. In this sense, *The Grapes of Wrath* owes less to naturalism than realism. The characters know the difference between right and wrong and act accordingly; as such, they follow in the tradition of Sydney Carton, Christopher Newman, and Lily Bart. Naturalistic novels like Émile Zola's *Germinal* (1885), Theodore Dreiser's *Sister Carrie* (1900), and Norris' *The Octopus* (1901) depict men and women so pushed and pulled by forces beyond their control that individual choice is rendered almost meaningless. The Joads are pushed west ostensibly by a drought and threatened at novel's end by a devastating flood, but they have the will and the means to fight the economic forces that drive them. Even the natural disasters are rendered inseparable from issues such as land management and housing: the "Dust Bowl" effect in Oklahoma was exacerbated, as one intercalary chapter implies, by the willful overplanting of cotton for profit, while the climactic flood punishes the migrant pickers far more than "the comfortable people in tight houses."

The structural experimentation exemplified by the intercalary chapters is a prime characteristic of modernist texts. Steinbeck, drawing possibly upon Dos Passos' *U.S.A.* trilogy (1930–36), alternates his main storyline with commentaries that connect the Joads' private drama to the public condition of an entire dispossessed class. Modernist, too, is Steinbeck's use of symbolism: the famous turtle of the early chapters provides a nice foreshadowing of the Joads' own journey—a slow but inexorable and ultimately indomitable westering. Ma Joad, Tom, and Jim Casey all have a symbolic, even mythic dimension (common to such modernist novels as James Joyce's *Ulysses*, 1922), which Steinbeck himself termed "super-essence." It was meant, like the intercalary chapters, to layer upon these individuals the hopes, dreams, and disappointments of a collective much larger than themselves.

The Grapes of Wrath is perhaps the paradigm of the genre of the proletarian novel. Picking up themes outlined in books such as William Cunningham's *The Green Corn Rebellion* (1935), Steinbeck dramatized the plight of working-class Americans under an economic system that marginalized and exploited them. In the process, he managed to strike a sympathetic chord in a nation still struggling from the Depression; it was as if the novel encapsulated the decade and its problems. Mike Gold, in a March 1940 review for the *Sunday Worker,* wrote that "our American proletarian literature . . . has finally culminated in two sure classics—Steinbeck's *Grapes of Wrath* and Richard Wright's *Native Son.*" Yet the conditions Steinbeck railed against were in the process of change even as the book came out, with President Franklin Roosevelt's social safety net transforming American capitalism and World War II promising to end the Depression even as it presented the very real threat of fascism. It is difficult to trace the influence of Steinbeck's book in postwar American letters, but *The Grapes of Wrath* falls into a select company of novels that have transcended the bounds of literature to influence the national consciousness. Like Harriet Beecher Stowe's *Uncle Tom's Cabin* (1852), it electrified a nation; like Margaret Mitchell's *Gone with the Wind* (1936), it became a major film and a symbol for an entire period of history. During its time, it inspired a ballad by Woody Guthrie. Fifty-odd years later, Bruce Springsteen could find no better figure to represent the common man than Tom Joad.

The novel's critical status has remained uncertain. Uniquely American, it has found its warmest reception overseas—300,000 copies of the novel were printed in Russia during 1941 alone, and the Nobel Committee, in awarding Steinbeck the Nobel prize for literature in 1962, called it a "great work" and an "epic chronicle." To charges that it was a false chronicle, the novel's early defenders pointed to Steinbeck's research as a freelance reporter covering the migrant labor problem. But the success of the novel itself helped push Steinbeck's life in a direction away from the people he once knew so well. In 1960, attempting to refamiliarize himself with America, Steinbeck would embark on a nationwide journey dubbed *Travels with Charley* (1962), secretly calling the project "operation windmills" and his truck Rosinante. Perhaps on some level he felt the project was a quixotic dream: that he could never again place his finger on the pulse of America as he had when writing *The Grapes of Wrath*.

SCOTT EARLE

See also Proletarian Novel

Further Reading

Benson, Jackson J., *The True Adventures of John Steinbeck, Writer*, New York: Viking, and London: Heinemann, 1984
DeMott, Robert, editor, *Working Days: The Journals of "The Grapes of Wrath," 1938–1941*, New York: Viking, 1989

Elliott, Emory, editor, *Columbia Literary History of the United States*, New York: Columbia University Press, 1988
Foley, Barbara, *Radical Representations: Politics and Form in U.S. Proletarian Fiction, 1929–1941*, Durham, North Carolina: Duke University Press, 1993
French, Warren, *A Companion to "The Grapes of Wrath,"* New York: Viking, 1963
French, Warren, *John Steinbeck's Fiction Revisited*, New York: Twayne, 1994
Lisca, Peter, "*The Grapes of Wrath* as Fiction," *PMLA* 72 (1957)
Steinbeck, John, *Steinbeck: A Life in Letters*, New York: Viking, and London: Heinemann, 1975
Timmerman, John H., *John Steinbeck's Fiction: The Aesthetics of the Road Taken*, Norman and London: University of Oklahoma Press, 1986
Wyatt, David, editor, *New Essays on "The Grapes of Wrath,"* Cambridge and New York: Cambridge University Press, 1990

Graphic Novel

In an interview, Will Eisner, a major innovator in comics history, takes credit for coining the term *graphic novel* in a perhaps apocryphal story: "I created the term 'graphic novel' on the spur of the moment. . . . When I got the [book] editor on the phone, I said, 'I have something new for you, something very different.' And he said, 'Yeah, what's that?' I looked down and I suddenly realized: *I could not tell him this was a comic book!!* I wanted desperately to get a meeting, so I said, 'Well, I have a graphic novel here.' And he said, 'Oh, that's interesting—I never heard of that. Bring that up.' So I came to his office a few days later and he looked at *A Contract with God*, and then he looked up at me and said, 'You know, it's still a comic book'."

Eisner went on to use *graphic novel* to market *A Contract with God* (1978), and this semi-autobiographical work, consisting of four stories of 1930s tenement life, is accepted by most as the first graphic novel. The term became widely employed in the American and British comics industries in the early 1980s, reaching the general public via a 1986–87 publicity campaign in particular. *Graphic novel* has come to represent an extended pictorial narrative employing the developed grammar and syntax of comics storytelling, a fusion of text and images most often using dialogue in balloons and a panel-to-panel format. The length of graphic novels allows for complexity and depth characteristic of extended prose fiction, and it is positioned in relation to the short-form comic book as the prose novel is to the short story. The basic types of graphic novels are: (1) a single original narrative longer than a normal comic, and (2) a collection of a serialized work previously published but with a self-contained narrative unity and cohesion. The graphic novel also sometimes encompasses a selection excerpted from a larger comics continuity, collecting several installments into a single volume, although there are some who dislike admitting such works. Some key works accepted as graphic novels are arguably really short-story collections (including *A Contract with God*) and others would more accurately be described as "graphic autobiography," lacking significant fictional dimension. The most highly praised graphic novel, Art Spiegelman's *Maus* (1980–91, collected 1986, 1991), by its unique nature frustrates traditional categorizing of narratives, and thus the liberally inclusive use of the term *graphic novel* tends to prevail. Works called graphic novels are often quite short compared to prose novels: the typical American comic book periodical story is usually 22 pages. Eisner labels his 46-page *The Dreamer* (1986) a graphic novelette, whereas Neil Gaiman and Dave McKean's 44-page *Violent Cases* (1987) is commonly referred to as a graphic novel. Some hold that a graphic novel should have more than 48 pages, which is the typical page length of a European album. Attempts to fix a minimum length criteria seem destined to fail, however, because page counts ignore different narrative strategies or constructions and the demands they place on readers.

There are lingering doubts about the validity of this new category, as contained in Eisner's origin story: many feel the differences between graphic novels and ordinary comic books are not significant enough to warrant the distinction. They believe the new term reflects only marketing considerations, an openly acknowledged attempt to destigmatize the comic book and sell it as literary and adult fare to a new consumer audience. In the United States, while comic strips are read by all ages and classes, appearing as they do in newspapers, comic books have been considered purely a children's medium, a subliterate genre to be abandoned with the onset of maturity. As Eisner has written, historically comics have mostly been confined to (visually oriented) narrations of intense episodes of brief duration. The general tendency has thus been for comics to depict the immediate, with a premium on physical action and dramatic violence rather than introspection or the examination of human experience. In order to counter this perceived bias against book-form comics, the graphic novel category is generally used only for works aimed at mature readers, although that is not part of its definition per se. The view that this vocabulary shift means nothing in terms of actual quality or content has been voiced by many comics industry insiders. Spiegelman is a prominent dissenter, arguing that graphic novels are just "well-dressed comic books." Critic Robert Harvey (1996) is another, stating that *A Contract with God* and Eisner's subsequent graphic works are "still comic books, not graphic novels," because they display no discernible differences or advances in storytelling techniques from traditional comics.

Spiegelman shares the industry's desire for a terminological shift to lift the burden of association with comics (puerile, adolescent), but he favors the word *commix* as a quality designator rather than affixing significance to the length of the narrative, since many graphic novels are extremely mediocre. Eisner himself prefers *sequential art* to comics for similar reasons. One rationale for this alternative is that much of the work by highly regarded comic art practitioners falls outside the graphic novel category: for example, episodic newspaper comic strip art or the bulk of the work by underground comics creators. Significantly, in other cultures in which comics have a tradition of adult readership, there has been no similar perceived need for a shift in terminology between short-form and long-form comics. Franco-Belgians use *bande desinée* (drawn strip), Italians *fumetti* (little puffs of smoke, after their word for speech balloons), Spaniards *tebeos* (after *T.B.O.*, a well-known paper), Germans *Bilderstreifen* or *Bildergeschichte* (picture strip or story). Some European writers use the English *graphic novel* to discuss contemporary American and British longer comics works. The Japanese use *manga* to cover comics, cartoons, and caricature, but since the mid-1960s they have used the term *gekiga* (dramatic picture) to designate works of a serious realistic nature.

The scepticism over the term *graphic novel* is furthered by a tendency of the term's supporters to use evolutionary metaphors, insisting on an identity split between comics and the graphic novel (some going so far as to claim that the graphic novel is a step forward from prose fiction, a revolution in visual literacy, and the literature of the future). In typical fashion, Eric La Brecque (1993) says Lorenzo Mattotti's *Fuochi* (1984; *Fires*) "combined words and pictures the way a comic book did but it wasn't a comic book"; so comic books are held to be a form defined by the archetypes and tropes of their basest number and an artistically worthwhile story in comics format cannot by definition be a comic book. *Fires* is a comic book, however, and the graphic novel is, as Eisner's sceptical editor says, "still a comic book," just a longer one. After all, few today question the validity of attaching the term *novel* to generic, poor-quality, even serial, long prose fiction; they are not "literature," according to many, but novels all the same. Stripped of hyperbole and detached from the burdens of the familiar high/low dynamic as a way of denoting quality, the graphic novel may yet be a valid and useful category because there are differences between the potentials and achievements of long-form and short-form narratives, in graphic form as well as in prose.

It should be noted that since graphic novels by definition utilize comics' signifying practices, the term therefore excludes other forms of conventionally illustrated novels as well as experimental novels with a significantly visual dimension, particularly in the use of typography and images. Historians both supportive and critical of the comics form have long looked for ways to separate comics from related forms to avoid a taxonomic nightmare. A comics narrative of any length is said to need both verbal and visual dimensions for its comprehension. Critics disagree on the primacy of image or text in comics, some arguing that the text serves a metafunction in giving meaning to the images, some arguing that the images dominate and establish reality. Others have argued that the height of comics achievement is a balance between the two components in which neither is dominant. Believing in the necessity of both elements, critics have focused on signifying codes that connect the visual and verbal realms, such as the speech balloon, as being constitutive and essential to comics. This classifying principle has become dogmatized by some critics as to exclude wordless panel to panel narrations (such as Eric Drooker's *Flood! A Novel in Pictures* [1992], which follows the tradition of Lynn Ward's and Franz Masereel's wordless graphic narratives), and to characterize any works that confine dialogue to the captions as illustrated prose or captioned pictures (such as Jim Steranko's *Chandler* [a.k.a. *Red Tide*, 1976]). There are many who disagree with this restriction; it may be argued that the use or non-use of such devices should be seen rather as a choice of effect sought by writers and artists, and not as the defining strategy of the work.

Narrative printed pictorial strips have existed since the 15th century, and David Kunzle (1973), the preeminent historian of the early period, believes the key elements defining the comic strip are present by the 1780s in Europe. For a variety of reasons, economic and technological, most early comic art is of short length. Through the 19th century, the longest comic is held to be the Frenchman Gustave Doré's *Histoire de la Sainte Russie* (1854; *The Rare and Extraordinary History of Holy Russia*), at around 500 illustrations. The most relevant precursors to the graphic novel are the "picture story" albums (collected in *Histoires en Estampes* [1846–47; Stories in Etchings]) of Swiss Rodolphe Töpffer, who was also a novelist in the conventional sense. Töpffer also wrote perceptively about the potentials of the form, envisioning a meeting of words and pictures that clearly anticipates the qualities of the contemporary graphic novel (some have called him the father or inventor of the comics as we now know them). The important pictorial codes and signifying devices taken to define the modern comic strip were established as regular components of the form by the US newspaper comic strip industry during the 1890s, in particular the dialogue balloon, which in subsequent decades became accepted worldwide. These strips were mostly episodic "gag" strips until the 1930s, when a number of important "continuity" strips emerged that continued storylines from week to week, allowing for more complicated plots and greater character development. An example is the adventure strip *Terry and the Pirates* by Milton Caniff (1934–46; continued by others to 1973). Although a case could be made for it, critics do not refer to such continuity strips in collected format as graphic novels.

Just as earlier comic forms paralleled the popular literature of their day, sharing common traits with penny dreadfuls and dime novels, US comic books derived much of their style and content from contemporaneous pulp serials when they first appeared in the 1930s. The specific iconography and patterns of the super-hero genre crystallized in 1938 and have since dominated US comic books. These monthly magazines have maintained a consistently episodic format, following continuing characters but generally confining plots to single issues. Occasionally, however, storylines have run several issues (for example, *The Monster Society of Evil* [1943–45] by Otto Binder and C.C. Beck was published in *Captain Marvel Adventures* in 25 installments, totaling more than 200 pages); such long narratives shared the familiar formal constructions of serials in pacing and "cliffhanger" transitions. For the most part, however, as Umberto Eco (1979) has pointed out, comics shared dynamics of stasis and repetition with serial fiction that work against change and significant narrative events—that is, things must return to normal at the end of the episode (this has become significantly less true in the recent past). Writers and artists had little reason to do otherwise in the assembly line industry: most comics were disposable, only on display for a month, and were targeted at the very young. Comic adaptations of literary and film works of this era (such as the *Classics Illustrated* series) tend to bear the closest physical resemblance to today's self-contained graphic novels, but they were a marginal part of the industry's total output.

Responding to a rise in crime, violence, and horror stories after World War II (raised to artistic heights by EC Comics), the industry passed self-imposed standards, the 1954 Comics Code, which asserted that comics were for children. The code established extremely confining rules, squashing any story containing gore, overt sexuality, moral ambiguity, or bad grammar and ensuring that mainstream comics would stick to uncontroversial fantasy stories. During the late 1960s, underground independent creators began to publish without the approval of the code and repeatedly violated every stricture, their excesses perhaps a necessary counter to the mandated simplicity and pleasantness of code-approved comics. One of their number, Jack Jackson, went on during the 1970s to create influential long-form comics that could be called graphic novels (*Comanche Moon*, 1979; *Los Tejanos*, 1982), based on American-Indian history.

The work of US underground artists reached continental Europe and profoundly changed mainstream comic production there. European comics were typically published in anthology magazine format. The serialized children's comic *Tintin* (1929–76) by Hergé (Georges Rémi) was so popular that the stories were subsequently collected into album format as early as 1930. Although comics had on occasion been repackaged and sold in collections before, this particular album format caught on and by the 1960s was common practice in the dominant Franco-Belgian industry. The continued availability of comics stories had a significant impact on the value perceptions of both producer and consumer and resulted in a different ethic of artistic craftsmanship. Following the lives of the comics creators eventually became as significant to the public as the characters in their stories. Children's literature still dominated, but comics such as the humorous *Astérix* (1959–) by René Goscinny and Albert Uderzo were also made to be appreciated by older read-

ers. During the 1960s, partly owing to the influx of US undergrounds, European creators increased their output of mature audience–oriented material; their works were distinguished by higher production standards compared to the rudimentary self-printed look of US comics, however. European comics have since exhibited a much broader range of subject matter and cultivated stronger traditions of realism, melodrama, and historical fiction than their US counterparts. Continental Europe (and Latin America, as well) also has had, since the late 1940s, a popular tradition of the "photo novel," usually soap-opera style stories told with photographs rather than drawn images in a comic-like format; attempts at such photo novels in the United States have met with little success.

Perhaps the most famous and influential European creator to emerge during this period is French artist Jean Giraud (a.k.a. Moebius), well known for his *Blueberry* western series (1963–), written by Jean-Michel Charlier, and for his science-fiction narratives, such as *The Incal* (1982–88), written by Chilean film-maker Alejandro Jodorowsky. French Jacques Tardi with *Les Aventures extraordinaires d'Adèle Blanc-sec* (1976– ; *Most Extraordinary Adventures of Adele Blanc-sec*) is credited with being one of the first to break with the conventional album format and produce truly novel-length narratives. Other notable creators include French Philippe Druillet (*Lone Sloane*, 1966–); French François Bourgeon (*Les Passagers du Vent* [1979–84; *Passengers of the Wind*]); French Pierre Christin and expatriate Yugoslavian Enki Bilal (*Les Phalanges de l'Ordre Noir* [1979; *The Ranks of the Black Order*] and *Partie de Chasse* [1983; *The Hunting Party*]); Belgian Hermann (*Les Tours de Bois Maury* [1984– ; *Towers of Bois Maury*]); Belgians Benoit Peeters and François Schuiten (*Les cités obscurés* [1982– ; *Cities of the Fantastic*]); Italian Hugo Pratt (*Corto Maltese*, 1967–); Italian Milo Manara (*Viaggio a Tulum* [1991; *Trip to Tulum*], a collaboration with Federico Fellini); Spaniard Daniel Torres (*Rocco Vargas*, 1983–); and German Matthias Schultheiss (*Le Théoreme du Bell* [1985–88; *Bell's Theorem*]). US novelist Jerome Charyn has produced intriguing graphic novels in collaboration with French artist François Boucq (*La Femme du magicien* [1984–85; *The Magician's Wife*] and *Bouche du Diable* [1989; *Billy Budd, K.G.B.*]), and with other artists.

The changes in Europe made an impact in the United States through imports and translations during the 1970s. The dominant mainstream company of the 1960s, Marvel Comics, had already connected with an older audience by adding a dose of real-world problems to their heroes. The undergrounds and the surrounding cultural revolutions of the 1960s further moved several mainstream superhero writers (at DC Comics as well) to inject more gritty realism into their stories. The Comics Code was challenged, modified, and then rendered virtually irrelevant with the emergence of the "direct sales market" during the 1970s, dedicated comics shops that sold non-code-approved work. Alternative small publishers and creators working outside the mainstream now had a distribution outlet outside newsstands and the drug-related stores that sold the undergrounds. Publishers began experimenting with differing formats and higher European-style production standards and sought to place their product in regular bookstores. Eisner, who had contributed much to the birth of the traditional US comic book and strip of the 1940s, was inspired by these changes to create a more personal work aimed at adult book readers, the aforementioned *A*

Contract with God. Publisher and creator Byron Preiss used *visual novel* and *graphic novel,* among other terms, to describe his *Fiction Illustrated* line starting in 1976, predating Eisner. Preiss also brought out Samuel Delany's and Howard Chaykin's *Empire* (1978), to which comics historian Mike Benton (1989) awards the "first graphic novel" honor, and sponsored numerous experiments in the format from the mid-1970s onward. Another historically significant work was Don McGregor and Paul Gulacy's *Sabre* (1978), believed to be the first direct-sales-only graphic novel. In 1978, Marvel published an original 100-page Stan Lee and Jack Kirby *Silver Surfer* (previous collections of Marvel and DC stories that had existed in book market were story reprints). In 1982, Marvel inaugurated a Graphic Novel line with Jim Starlin's *The Death of Captain Marvel* (inexplicably described by writers Greg McCue and Clive Bloom [1993] as the "first graphic novel"), mostly self-contained stories using their regular characters. (The existence of numerous "first graphic novels" confirms the lack of an accepted history and definition of the term; Robert Harvey [1996] believes that Gil Kane's *His Name Is Savage* [1968] qualifies as a graphic novel more than Eisner's *A Contract with God,* and Roger Sabin [1993] also notes the prior existence of various minor paperback comic-style narratives.)

The establishing of the graphic novel in public consciousness was mostly due to the high visibility of two mainstream superhero works and one from outside the mainstream. Frank Miller's revisionist *Batman: The Dark Knight Returns* (1986) has been widely imitated for its hardboiled style and brutal violence, and for its achievements in cinematic visual storytelling, particularly in its awareness of levels of media representation. British Alan Moore's and Dave Gibbons' *Watchmen* (1986–87) is an apocalyptic narrative that dismantles virtually every cliché and buried subtext of the superhero genre. Miller and Moore were allowed significant creative freedom by DC Comics to escape the boundaries set for the monthly continuing comics: although Miller was working with pre-established characters, his story was set in an alternate universe in which he could do whatever he wanted, and Moore adapted his own universe that he could explode with impunity. Both Miller and Moore have continued to produce other influential comics works in different genres. A number of revisionist-minded British writers followed Moore's lead, bringing an outsider perspective to inventive, primarily dark, interpretations of the peculiarly US genre. These writers also brought a more extravagantly literary prose style, Grant Morrison (*Batman: Arkham Asylum,* with Dave McKean, 1989) and Neil Gaiman (*Sandman,* with various artists, 1989–96) being the more notable examples. Revisionism became a subgenre of comics, diluting its initial value as lesser writers began to imitate the operations performed by Moore, Miller, or Gaiman without introducing any new insights or themes; rather than expanding the audience, such works began to accentuate the insularity and failure of the industry to escape the formulas they were examining.

The third key text, Spiegelman's *Maus,* was serialized in the independent *RAW* (1980–), gaining wide attention in the United States when *Maus* was collected in 1986 and 1991. It chronicles the experiences of Spiegelman's father, Vladek, during the Holocaust and traces the troubled relationship between father and son as these stories are passed down. *Maus'* mixing of a simple rudimentary art style and a complex weave of personal and world history confounded expectations. Some critics were uncomfortable with Spiegelman's device of using animals for people (Jews are mice, Nazis are cats, etc.). For many, however, the device, which could only really work in comics format, was crucial to allowing the reader a new way of accessing very difficult material. Spiegelman addresses a subject few would have thought appropriate for comics, and *Maus* is undoubtably the most important text to date in demonstrating the capacities of the medium (Spiegelman was awarded a Pulitzer in recognition).

Making less of an impact outside comics circles but also similarly important were Jamie and Gilbert Hernandez's stories in *Love and Rockets* (1982–), which produced several notable continuing storylines (notably Gilbert's *Poison River*). These stories contain doses of melodrama and a current of magic realism, together with an easy visual style using traditional comics imagery and language to draw readers in. Other noteworthy US comics situated outside the heroic or fantastic genres include surreal works like Daniel Clowes' *Like a Velvet Glove Cast in Iron* (1989–92, 1993) and Charles Burns' *Black Hole* (1995–); autobiographical or fact-based works from Harvey Pekar and Joyce Brabner in *Our Cancer Year* (1994, art by Frank Stack), David Wojnarowicz in *Seven Miles a Second* (1996, art by James Romberger), Howard Cruse in *Stuck Rubber Baby* (1995); Joe Sacco's *Palestine* (1993–96) and Joe Kubert's *Fax from Sarajevo* (1996). In Canada, Chester Brown also produced revealing autobiographical work (*The Playboy,* 1990) and Dave Sim's fantasy *Cerebus* (1977–), which started as an episodic parody, shifted in the 1980s to epic narratives with convoluted plots at lengths beyond the rest of the field. The first of the series, *High Society,* had 512 pages. In England, long narratives of note were produced by Bryan Talbot (*The Adventures of Luther Arkwright,* 1982–88, sometimes called the first British graphic novel, and *The Tale of One Bad Rat,* 1995) and Raymond Briggs (*When the Wind Blows,* 1982). The most high-profile novelist to write a graphic novel to date, Rhodesian/British writer Doris Lessing, had little impact on the field (*Playing the Game,* art by Charlie Adlard, 1995).

The major center of non-Western comics art, Japan, has developed along a considerably different trajectory than the European-US continuum, resulting in a slightly different grammar and set of pictorial codes. Comics in Japan are consumed in great quantities by all ages (representing almost one-quarter of all books published there) and, as in Europe, there has been a greater variety of subject matter to match. After World War II, when the industry grew exponentially, longer narratives began to appear, pioneered by Osamu Tezuka, who looked to film effects and pacing for inspiration. For a variety of reasons, comics in Japan have reached continuity lengths, dwarfing the longer works produced by Europe and the United States. These longer lengths (and perhaps different cultural values) have facilitated leisurely drawn-out exposition rare in typical Western work, both in depicting action and in describing emotional states and behaviors. Japanese artists often produce 30 pages per week, and stories are often 2,000 pages when completed, serialized in weekly magazines, and then collected in book volumes. Two of the most famous are *Hadashi no Gen* (1973– ; *Barefoot Gen*) by Keiji Nakazawa, an account of the Hiroshima atomic bomb and its aftermath, and *Kozure Okami* (1970–76; *Lonewolf and Cub*) by Kazuo Koike and Goseki Kojima, a historical samurai adventure saga that reached an impressive 8,400 pages in 28 volumes. Popular with the world market are Japanese science-fiction comics, such as *Akira* (1984–) by Katsuhiro Otomo, which should run approximately 1,800 pages upon completion. As Japanese comics become more available in the West, their different values and narrative styles may have a significant impact on the ambitions and scale of the Western graphic novel genre. It is noteworthy that the Japanese have taken little interest in mainstream US comics that superficially imitate their specific signifying conventions and stylizations (for example, heavy use of speed lines and exaggerated facial expressions); however, they *have* taken an interest in US independents whose personal work uses visual information and symbolism to address the experiences and interior lives of characters, achieving an effect similar to that of the best manga work, even though the two traditions are removed in the particulars.

JOHN SMYLIE

See also Illustrations and Engravings

Further Reading

Benton, Mike, *The Comic Book in America: An Illustrated History,* Dallas, Texas: Taylor, 1989

Eco, Umberto, "The Myth of Superman," in his *The Role of the Reader: Explorations in the Semiotics of Texts,* Bloomington: Indiana University Press, 1979; London: Hutchinson, 1981

Eisner, Will, *Comics and Sequential Art,* Tamarac, Florida: Poorhouse Press, 1985; expanded edition, 1990

Groth, Gary, and Robert Fiore, editors, *The New Comics,* New York: Berkley, 1988

Harvey, Robert C., *The Art of the Comic Book: An Aesthetic History,* Jackson: University Press of Mississippi, 1996

Horn, Maurice, editor, *The World Encyclopedia of Comics,* New York: Chelsea House, 1976

Inge, M. Thomas, *Comics as Culture,* Jackson: University Press of Mississippi, 1990

Kunzle, David, *The Early Comic Strip: Narrative Strips and Picture Stories in the European Broadsheet from c. 1450 to 1825,* Berkeley: University of California Press, 1973

Kunzle, David, *The History of the Comic Strip: The Nineteenth Century,* Berkeley: University of California Press, 1990

La Brecque, Eric, "In Search of the Graphic Novel," *Print* 47 (January-February 1993)

McCloud, Scott, *Understanding Comics: The Invisible Art,* Northampton, Massachusetts: Tundra, 1993

McCue, Greg S., and Clive Bloom, *Dark Knights: The New Comics in Context,* London and Boulder, Colorado: Pluto Press, 1993

Print 42 (November-December 1988), special comics issue containing Art Spiegelman's "Commix: An Idiosyncratic Historical and Aesthetic Overview"

Sabin, Roger, *Adult Comics: An Introduction,* London and New York: Routledge, 1993

Sabin, Roger, *Comics, Comix, and Graphic Novels,* London: Phaidon, 1996

Schodt, Frederik L., *Manga! Manga! The World of Japanese Comics,* Tokyo and New York: Kodansha, 1983

Silbermann, Alphons, and Hans-Dieter Dyroff, editors, *Comics and Visual Culture: Research Studies from Ten Countries,* Munich and New York: Saur, 1986

Wiater, Stanley, and Stephen R. Bissette, editors, *Comic Book Rebels: Conversations with the Creators of the New Comics,* New York: Fine, 1993 (contains Will Eisner interview source)

Witek, Joseph, *Comic Books as History: The Narrative Art of Jack Jackson, Art Spiegelman, and Harvey Pekar,* Jackson: University Press of Mississippi, 1989

Günter Grass 1927–

German

Since the publication of *Die Blechtrommel (The Tin Drum)* in 1959, Günter Grass has written a series of epic novels, including *Hundejahre* (1963; *Dog Years*), *Der Butt* (1977; *The Flounder*), *Die Rättin* (1986; *The Rat*), and *Ein weites Feld* (1995; An Open Question). In addition, he has published shorter works that are spin-offs from or preparations for the longer texts. These are *Katz und Maus* (1961; *Cat and Mouse*), *Aus dem Tagebuch einer Schnecke* (1972; *From the Diary of a Snail*), *Das Treffen in Telgte* (1979; *The Meeting at Telgte*), *Kopfgeburten; oder, Die Deutschen sterben aus* (1980; *Headbirths; or, The Germans Are Dying Out*) and *Unkenrufe* (1992; *The Call of the Toad*). *Örtlich betäubt* (1969; *Local Anaesthetic*) does not fall cleanly into either category, although in some ways it is a postscript to *The Tin Drum, Cat and Mouse,* and *Dog Years,* which have come to be known as the *Danzig Trilogy.*

Grass' work to date is protean but unified by a continuing interest in the remarkable history of his birthplace—the free port of Danzig, with its richly varied population, which is now the more homogenous Polish city of Gdansk. Himself born of mixed German and Kashubian parentage, Grass has consistently affirmed heterogeneity, repudiating systematic ideologies of whatever stamp. His teenage identification with Nazism forms the background of his later rejection of all forms of mindless uniformity.

In Grass' work Danzig functions as a microcosm of history precisely because the free port has disappeared. As Grass writes in *Dog Years,* "Once there was a city, and it had a suburb called Langfuhr. Langfuhr was so big and so small that everything that happens in this world or could happen in it, happened, or could have happened in Langfuhr." A committed imaginative artist, Grass also has been a committed witness of and participant in the history of his own time. For all the magic realist aspects of his work, with its glass-splitting voices, impossible perspectives, and talking wildlife, the factual and moral reference to historically specific circumstances is always clear.

Grass' first moral preoccupation was with recent German history and contemporary politics. This was succeeded in the 1970s and 1980s by a concern with world issues, feminism, hunger, and ecology. In his two latest works to date, *The Call of the Toad* and *Ein weites Feld,* Grass returns to specific German questions. Both novels address the reunification of Germany, something Grass has opposed consistently as idea and as reality since the 1960s. Grass preferred to maintain the boundaries between the two Germanys, which, he argues, would have related better to each other in their difference than within an enforced homogeneity.

Grass' work frequently crosses the boundaries of genre and medium. The *Danzig Trilogy,* for instance, relied on the dust jackets to clarify the novels' central motifs. From *Dog Years* onward, Grass has created a growing number of distinct yet mutually illuminating fictions within a single work. In *The Flounder,* lyric poetry is an integral and vital part of the composition. From *Headbirths,* the rival medium of film has been reflected in the textual strategies Grass employs. *The Call of the Toad* contains illustrations by the author. *Ein weites Feld,* with its strong intertextual dependence upon the work of other German writers, particularly Theodor Fontane and Hans Joachim Schädlich, returns to a more exclusively literary orientation.

All Grass' texts teem with life, reveling in inventive plots and reappearing characters. Nevertheless, however sprawling they seem at first glance, they are highly wrought and considered artifacts. Grass' use of language, which presents a great challenge for a translator, is famously exuberant, employing redundancies and repetitions. While Grass is a meticulous craftsman of language, he is always a performer. Language for him is not passively referential but always creative, its use a unique act of creation like a drawing or sculpture.

In *The Flounder* and later novels, Grass plays conspicuously with historical and mythological time. In its nine sections, this novel relates fictional autobiography to a series of mythological and historical periods, from a parodistic prehistorical matriarchy to the actuality of the Gdansk shipyards of the 1970s. *Headbirths* initiates an inclusion of the future—which Grass dubs "Vergegenkunft," a coinage from the German words for past, present, future—which anticipates the apocalyptic narrative of *The Rat. The Meeting at Telgte* and *Ein weites Feld* both construct intricate parallels between two historical moments: the German baroque and the period immediately following World War II in the first case, the first and second unifications of Germany in the second.

Grass' untiring experiments with point of view exclude the possibility of an innocent perspective. All perspectives, including those of artists, are subject to the moral determinants that, for Grass, are inseparable from reality. *From the Diary of a Snail* is the turning point in this regard, with Grass speaking in his own voice for the first time. His voice is no more free from guilt, dishonesty, or fear than his notoriously guilty, fearful, and dishonest narrators. This narrative situation expresses Grass' metaphysics more powerfully than before: in a fallen yet still human reality there is no transcendent perspective, but instead a multitude of appetite-driven partial ones that collide but that also cooperate. The art of cooking—material, existential, communal—is often invoked by Grass as the model for the other arts.

Grass' work has always been controversial, and as Germany's foremost living author he can rely upon critical acrimony coupled with healthy sales. It is true that the perils of mannerism, self-repetition, and even self-indulgence are ever-present in his work, especially since *The Flounder,* but they are inseparable from his undeniably extraordinary artistic gifts.

MICHAEL MINDEN

See also Danzig Trilogy

Biography
Born 16 October 1927 in Danzig, Germany (now Gdansk, Poland). Attended Volksschule and Gymnasium in Danzig; apprenticed to stone mason, 1947; studied art at the Academy of Art, Düsseldorf, 1949–52, and State Academy of Fine Arts, Berlin, 1953–56. Served in World War II, 1944–45: taken prisoner, Marienbad, Czechoslovakia. Worked as farmhand, miner, apprentice stonecutter, jazz musician; speech writer for Willy Brandt (mayor of West Berlin); writer-in-residence, Columbia University, New York, 1966; coeditor, *L,* from 1976, and Verlages L'80, publishers, from 1980. Member, Gruppe 47.

Novels by Grass
(all translations are by Ralph Manheim)
Danziger Trilogie, 1980; as *The Danzig Trilogy,* 1987
    Die Blechtrommel, 1959; as *The Tin Drum,* 1962
    Katz und Maus, 1961; as *Cat and Mouse,* 1963
    Hundejahre, 1963; as *Dog Years,* 1965
Örtlich betäubt, 1969; as *Local Anaesthetic,* 1969
Aus dem Tagebuch einer Schnecke, 1972; as *From the Diary of a Snail,* 1973
Der Butt, 1977; as *The Flounder,* 1978
Das Treffen in Telgte, 1979; as *The Meeting at Telgte,* 1981
Kopfgeburten; oder, Die Deutschen sterben aus, 1980; as *Headbirths; or, The Germans Are Dying Out,* 1982
Die Rättin, 1986; as *The Rat,* 1987
Unkenrufe, 1992; as *The Call of the Toad,* 1992
Ein weites Feld [An Open Question], 1995

Other Writings: plays, ballet libretti, lyric poetry, essays, open letters, political speeches; also drawings, engravings, sculptures, and volumes containing poetry, prose, and drawings as an integrated form (*Zunge Zeigen* [1988; *Show Your Tongue*] and *Totes Holz: Ein Nachruf* [1990]).

Further Reading
Brady, Philip, Timothy McFarland, and John J. White, editors, *Günter Grass's "Der Butt": Sexual Politics and the Male Myth of History,* Oxford: Clarendon Press, and New York: Oxford University Press, 1990
Harscheidt, Michael, *Günter Grass: Wort, Zahl, Gott: Der "phantastische Realismus" in den Hundejahren,* Bonn: Bouvier, 1976
Hayman, Ronald, *Günter Grass,* London and New York: Methuen, 1985
Hollington, Michael, *Günter Grass: The Writer in a Pluralist Society,* London and Boston: Marion Boyars, 1980
Keele, Alan Frank, *Understanding Günter Grass,* Columbia: University of South Carolina Press, 1988
Lawson, Richard H., *Günter Grass,* New York: Ungar, 1985
Mason, Ann L., *The Skeptical Muse: A Study of Günter Grass' Conception of the Artist,* Bern: Lang, 1974

Mason, Ann L., "The Artist and Politics in Günter Grass' *Aus dem Tagebuch einer Schnecke*," *Germanic Review* 51 (1976)

Neuhaus, Volker, *Günter Grass*, Stuttgart: Metzler, 1979; 2nd edition, 1993

Osinski, Jutta, "Aspekte der Fontane-Rezeption bei Günter Grass" [on *Ein weites Feld*], *Fontane-Blätter* 62 (1996)

Reddick, John, *The "Danzig Trilogy" of Günter Grass*, London: Secker and Warburg, and New York: Harcourt Brace, 1975

Weber, A., "Johann Matthias Schneuber: Der Ich-Erzähler in Günter Grass' *Das Treffen in Telgte*," *Daphnis* 15 (1986)

Gravity's Rainbow by Thomas Pynchon

1973

Gravity's Rainbow is set in Europe during and immediately after World War II, and it attempts to capture, via a number of complex literary strategies, the confusion and chaos associated with the war and its aftermath. As such, the book participates in the tradition of the historical novel, and it is replete with historical information and commentary. But *Gravity's Rainbow* grows very much out of the cultural and historical context of the 1960s and uses its treatment of World War II largely as a means of tracing the mentality that led to American involvement in Vietnam. Meanwhile, the book's complex self-reflexive textuality, unconventional narrative form, and carnivalesque mood challenge accepted models of history. These challenges mark the text as a key example of what Linda Hutcheon has described as postmodern "historiographic metafiction" (see Hutcheon, 1988). Indeed, the massive *Gravity's Rainbow* is one of the central defining texts of postmodernist fiction, according to some critics playing much the same role for postmodernism that James Joyce's *Ulysses* (1922) plays for modernism. *Gravity's Rainbow* has received more critical attention than any other postmodernist novel and has proved a major influence on other postmodernist writers ever since its publication. It is also a major work of American literature that builds in important ways upon the works of predecessors from Herman Melville and Nathaniel Hawthorne to William Gaddis and William S. Burroughs.

The title of *Gravity's Rainbow* refers primarily to the arc traversed by German V2 rockets as they hurtle toward London, bringing destruction and death. The central plot involves an American serviceman, Lieutenant Tyrone Slothrop, who has (apparently) received some sort of mysterious childhood programming at the hands of the German scientist Lazlo Jamf. This programming may or may not be responsible for the fact that Slothrop seems to be able to predict (on the basis of his erections) the sites on which the rockets will land. But little is known for certain about this plot, and Slothrop himself eventually dissolves out of existence, absorbed into the bizarre landscape of the book. In addition, there are dozens of other complex (and often interrelated) plots and subplots involving hundreds of other characters. Many of these plots involve ominous conspiracies (generally engineered by a ubiquitous but unidentified "Them") that are afoot in the world. It is hinted, for example, that World War II may be an international capitalist conspiracy designed to increase profits for a few large multinational corporations.

At the same time, none of these plots is fully resolved, and many of the conspiracies may be the paranoid imaginings of the characters only. Most of the characters are involved in futile attempts to piece together the bewildering array of information that surrounds them into some sort of meaningful pattern. Pynchon tempts his readers to do the same, and one of the most striking aspects of *Gravity's Rainbow* is its ability to involve readers in interpretive activities that parallel those of his characters. The difficulties experienced by both readers and characters in attempting to force information and experience into preconceived interpretive systems (figured by the book's central metaphor of paranoia) then serve as a powerful statement of scepticism toward such systems. Offering a tantalizing variety of clues to the various mysteries it poses, *Gravity's Rainbow* constantly invites such modes of reading, but refuses finally to reward them.

The encyclopedic scope of historical reference in *Gravity's Rainbow* extends beyond major events to include the trivial and the everyday. Although Pynchon constructs an intricate web of allusions and echoes that recalls (often in parodic and irreverent ways) much of the Western cultural tradition, including not only literature but music and visual art, the book's range of cultural reference extends beyond "high" culture to include the "low" realm of popular culture. Indeed, *Gravity's Rainbow* is the best example in Pynchon's oeuvre of his famed ability to make effective use of images and terminology from sources such as film, television, advertising, comic books, and popular music. Pynchon also extends his range of reference beyond the cultural to include philosophy, psychology, and other discourses. In particular, *Gravity's Rainbow* well illustrates the ability of Pynchon, a former engineering student, to incorporate ideas and images from science and technology into his literary works. Among other things, Pynchon's use of such images has helped to make his book a crucial influence on recent "cyberpunk" science-fiction writers such as William Gibson.

Most important, however, is the way *Gravity's Rainbow* combines presumed polar opposites such as the significant and the banal, the "high" and the "low," and the literary and the nonliterary, not only to deconstruct conventional hierarchical distinctions between the two poles, but to challenge the validity of the distinctions altogether. In its deconstructions of polar oppositions and in its radical refusal of fixed and final interpretations, *Gravity's Rainbow* has a great deal in common with the projects of such poststructuralist philosophers as Jacques Derrida, Gilles Deleuze, and Jean Baudrillard. In its encyclopedic scope and its numerous subversive challenges to conventional authority (literary and otherwise), *Gravity's Rainbow* clearly participates in a long line of novels (one might list François Rabelais' *Gargantua and Pantagruel* [1534], Laurence Sterne's *Tristram Shandy* [1759–67], Herman Melville's *Moby-Dick* [1851], and *Ulysses* as key examples) that draw upon the cultural impulses that Mikhail Bakhtin has associated with Menippean satire. But the particularly parodic and irreverent way in which Pynchon combines materials from disparate sources has an especially postmodernist tone that places it in the company of postmodern Menippean epics such as William Gaddis' *The Recognitions* (1955) and *JR* (1975), John Barth's *Giles Goat-Boy* (1966), Don DeLillo's *Ratner's Star* (1976), and Joseph McElroy's *Women and Men* (1987).

M. KEITH BOOKER

See also Thomas Pynchon

Further Reading

Berressem, Hanjo, *Pynchon's Poetics: Interfacing Theory and Text,* Urbana: University of Illinois Press, 1993

Clerc, Charles, editor, *Approaches to Gravity's Rainbow,* Columbus: Ohio State University Press, 1983

Cowart, David, *Thomas Pynchon: The Art of Allusion,* Carbondale: Southern Illinois University Press, 1980

Hayles, N. Katherine, *The Cosmic Web: Scientific Field Models and Literary Strategies in the Twentieth Century,* Ithaca, New York: Cornell University Press, 1984

Hite, Molly, *Ideas of Order in the Novels of Thomas Pynchon,* Columbus: Ohio State University Press, 1983

Hume, Kathryn, *Pynchon's Mythography: An Approach to "Gravity's Rainbow,"* Carbondale: Southern Illinois University Press, 1987

Hutcheon, Linda, *A Poetics of Postmodernism: History, Theory, Fiction,* New York: Routledge, 1988

McHoul, A.W., and David Wills, *Writing Pynchon: Strategies in Fictional Analysis,* Urbana: University of Illinois Press, and London: Macmillan, 1990

Mendelson, Edward, "Gravity's Encyclopedia," in *Mindful Pleasures: Essays on Thomas Pynchon,* edited by George Levine and David Leverenz, Boston: Little Brown, 1976

Schaub, Thomas H., *Pynchon: The Voice of Ambiguity,* Urbana: University of Illinois Press, 1981

Seed, David, *The Fictional Labyrinths of Thomas Pynchon,* Iowa City: University of Iowa Press, 1988

Weisenburger, Steven, *A "Gravity's Rainbow" Companion: Sources and Context for Pynchon's Novel,* Athens: University of Georgia Press, 1988

Great Expectations by Charles Dickens

1861

The 13th of Dickens' 15 novels, *Great Expectations* provides a striking example of the way in which many of the masterpieces of Victorian fiction were influenced by the circumstances of publication and the dictates of the literary marketplace. Dickens' weekly magazine *All the Year Round,* launched under his editorship in April 1859, was by the fall of the following year in serious difficulties: circulation figures had dropped alarmingly, and financial disaster threatened. The magazine published works of fiction in installments as well as nonfiction articles, and Dickens decided that the only remedy was to come to its rescue by writing a new novel himself and relying on his enormous popularity to boost sales.

Although he had at that time been planning to write a novel suitable for publication in longer, monthly parts, he quickly turned his attention to the problem of writing for weekly installments. He worked rapidly, and the first installment appeared in *All the Year Round* on 1 December. Further installments continued to appear until the conclusion of the story on 3 August 1861. At about the same time, the novel was published in the expensive three-volume format that was widely used throughout the 19th century and was intended primarily for the circulating libraries.

The genesis of the novel helps to explain why *Great Expecta-*

tions is more tightly constructed and economically written than most of Dickens' other novels. It has little of the expansiveness, digressiveness, and multiplication of plots and subplots that are generally regarded as characteristically "Dickensian." The limited space available for each of the weekly portions forced upon Dickens a self-discipline that may have been irksome but was, artistically, to the advantage of his novel. Many critics, indeed, have judged *Great Expectations* the most formally satisfying of all his works. Starting from a single crucial incident, vividly recounted, the story unfolds logically and naturally to its conclusion.

This is one of Dickens' two novels written entirely in the first person (the other is *David Copperfield,* 1850), and this restricted point of view is fully exploited. The reader's knowledge is frequently limited to that possessed by the narrator-hero, and we may actually find ourselves sharing his errors of understanding and judgment. At the same time Dickens introduces a double focus whereby the mature Pip who tells the story—a middle-aged, disillusioned, and somewhat melancholy figure—draws attention to the contrast between later knowledge and the earlier innocence of his younger self. (In chapter 8, for instance, the narrator comments, "I thought it a strange thing then, and I thought it a stranger thing afterwards. . . .")

The tracing of Pip's development from childhood, through the years of young manhood, to the older self who is the mature narrator, makes this novel one of the outstanding examples in English of the Bildungsroman, a genre with Continental prototypes (notably Goethe's *Wilhelm Meisters Lehrjahre* [1795–96; *William Meister's Apprenticeship*]). It thus belongs to, and contributed to, an important tradition of fiction in English that includes such later examples as Samuel Butler's *The Way of All Flesh* (1903) and James Joyce's *A Portrait of the Artist as a Young Man* (1916).

The hero's transition from boyhood to adult life is accompanied by a physical movement from the blacksmith's cottage in a quiet village on the Kentish marshes to fashionable London. Although Pip's early life is far from idyllic, Dickens draws on elements of the pastoral convention, as George Eliot and Thomas Hardy will also do later. The city is identified with temptation and corruption, while village life represents innocence and unworldly values. Revealingly, it is to his first home that Pip returns after the collapse of his ambitions and the loss of his wealth.

As with much of Dickens' fiction, a layer of archetypal motifs derived from folktale and fairy tale may be detected beneath the surface realism. Pip, like the protagonist of many such tales, is an orphan, and Magwitch the convict and Miss Havisham, both of whom have symbolic names, are contrasting versions of the good and wicked fairies who transform the hero/heroine's destiny, as well as (on a more Freudian reading) father and mother substitutes. The villain Orlick has been seen as a double or doppelgänger of Pip himself, acting out his unacknowledged desires.

Dickens wrote two endings for this novel, thus in a sense anticipating the alternative and purposefully ambiguous endings of such later novels as John Fowles' *The French Lieutenant's Woman* (1969). The original ending, which many critics have found superior in honesty and realism, rejects the "happy ending" convention with which Dickens had previously seemed to be content. It foretells an uncompromisingly bleak and lonely future for the hero. A fellow-novelist advised Dickens that the public would not like this, and Dickens thereupon substituted an ending (used in the weekly serial and in most subsequent editions) that hints broadly at the possibility of happiness. This sacrifice to the demands of the reading public is one further instance of the commercial and external pressures exerted on the Victorian novelist, especially one writing for serial publication. In its conception and intention, however, *Great Expectations* is probably the most "modern" of Dickens' novels.

The novel, popular with contemporary readers, revived the flagging circulation of Dickens' magazine. Its reception by the reviewers of the day, however, may surprise readers today. Many insisted on regarding it as primarily a comic novel and compared it with such earlier examples as *Martin Chuzzlewit* (1844)—with which it has relatively little in common—as well as making the more obvious comparison with *David Copperfield*. For modern critics, on the other hand, it is, together with such longer novels as *Little Dorrit* (1857) and *Our Mutual Friend* (1865), unmistakably one of Dickens' "dark" novels, expressive of a deep unease with the growing materialism of Victorian society. Its use of the autobiographical method, meanwhile, represents a significant advance in subtlety and sophistication on that of *David Copperfield*.

NORMAN PAGE

See also Charles Dickens

Further Reading
Andrews, Malcolm, *Dickens and the Grown-up Child*, London: Macmillan, and Iowa City: University of Iowa Press, 1994
Daldry, Graham, *Charles Dickens and the Form of the Novel*, Totowa, New Jersey: Barnes and Noble, 1986; London: Croom Helm, 1987
Leavis, F.R., and Q.D. Leavis, *Dickens the Novelist*, London: Chatto and Windus, 1970; New York: Pantheon, 1971
Lodge, David, "Ambiguously Ever After," *Essays by Divers Hands* 41 (1980)
Morgan, Nicholas H., *Secret Journeys: Theory and Practice in Reading Dickens*, London: Associated University Presses, and Rutherford, New Jersey: Farleigh Dickinson University Press, 1992
Moynahan, Julian, "The Hero's Guilt: The Case of *Great Expectations*," *Essays in Criticism* 10 (1960)
Page, Norman, editor, *Dickens: "Hard Times," "Great Expectations," and "Our Mutual Friend": A Casebook*, London: Macmillan, 1979
Ricks, Christopher, "*Great Expectations*," in *Dickens and the Twentieth Century*, edited by John Gross and Gabriel Pearson, London: Routledge, 1962
Smith, Grahame, *Charles Dickens: A Literary Life*, London: Macmillan, and New York: St. Martin's Press, 1996
Van Ghent, Dorothy, *The English Novel: Form and Function*, New York: Rinehart, 1953

The Great Gatsby by F. Scott Fitzgerald

1925

In retrospect, it is perhaps not surprising that contemporary reviewers mainly missed the mark in their appraisals of F. Scott Fitzgerald's masterpiece, *The Great Gatsby*. His first novel, *This Side of Paradise* (1920), a novel of growth, is a thinly disguised autobiography written in the third person, a viewpoint that numerous reviewers saw as flawed. *The Beautiful and Damned* (1922) is marred by a self-conscious preoccupation with the deterministic philosophy that undergirds American literary naturalism. By 1925, Fitzgerald was known primarily as the historian of the Jazz Age (which he named) and the chronicler in slick American weeklies and monthlies of the American flapper (a type he had invented in fiction). His best artistic efforts had appeared in middlebrow, mass-circulation magazines such as *The Saturday Evening Post* or had been buried in H.L. Mencken's sophisticated but low-circulation *Smart Set* before their appearance in two slightly publicized collections with flashy titles, *Flappers and Philosophers* (1920) and *Tales of the Jazz Age* (1922).

Critics and reviewers were understandably caught off-guard when, at the height of the Roaring Twenties, Fitzgerald published a novel that would later not infrequently be cited as the "Great American Novel." Typical of the early reviews of *The Great Gatsby* was the first, whose spirit is caught in its headline: "F. SCOTT FITZGERALD'S LATEST DUD." Even Mencken, who noted some of the book's redeeming qualities, saw it finally as "a glorified anecdote." In the minority was T.S. Eliot, who was deeply moved by the novel and hailed it as "the first step American fiction has taken since Henry James," an opinion that has now been echoed and elaborated upon in scores of books and more than 100 journal articles dealing with *The Great Gatsby*.

Fitzgerald's ambitious goal as he approached the composition of *The Great Gatsby* was to "write something *new*—something extraordinary and beautiful and simple + intricately patterned." And it is indeed largely because of his concern with matters of form aimed at simplicity and intricacy of pattern that the novel succeeds on so many levels: the simplicity, or apparent simplicity, of Nick Carraway's first-person viewpoint allows the reader, on the one hand, to see how the narrative is being constructed and, on the other, to participate in Nick's sense of discovery as the separate narrative strands take on meaning at various levels of abstraction in such a way that they seem, both to Nick and to the reader, to have been inseparably linked from the beginning. There was, of course, nothing new about first-person narration in the 1920s. It had a long history in the English novel dating back to the mid–18th century. In the United States, two distinguished first-person narratives, Herman Melville's *Moby-Dick* (1851) and Mark Twain's *The Adventures of Huckleberry Finn* (1884), preceded *The Great Gatsby,* as did scores of first-person narratives by Edgar Allan Poe. But Fitzgerald, who was reading and studying Joseph Conrad during the composition of *The Great Gatsby,* was interested in exploring subtle uses of narrative viewpoint. On the novel's first and most superficial level, that of Jay Gatsby's all-consuming love and pursuit of Daisy Buchanan, Nick becomes a logical choice as narrator. His physical proximity to the main characters and his trustworthiness situ-

ate him ideally to serve as a kind of Jamesian confidant on several fronts, one who knows details of the story from many points of view and observes much of the action firsthand.

Obviously, the creation of a reliable narrator of the Gatsby-Daisy story at the heart of *The Great Gatsby* is central in Fitzgerald's achieving verisimilitude. However, the simple love story is merely the foundation for a narrative structure that accommodates Fitzgerald's ideas about irreconcilable contradictions within the American Dream and ultimately about the ideal quest itself. Young Jay Gatsby, through the discipline of Benjamin Franklin-like charts and schedules, has prepared himself to receive all that America has to offer and believes naively that he can have the embodiment of it, the wealthy Louisville debutante Daisy Fay, the only "nice" girl he has ever known, if he can but find the currency to buy his way into her life. It is Nick, the middle-class everyman without particular allegiance to either the privileged or working class, who has enough objectivity to comprehend the awful irony that Gatsby's dream has been futile from the beginning: he will never be accepted into the world of old money that Daisy can never leave. At this level, the love story approaches allegory, and because Nick, like all of the main characters in the novel, is a westerner, he is credible as narrator of the allegory, which he calls "a story of the West, after all." He knows about the infinite hope of the frontier spirit, and he also has witnessed the corruption of the American promise of equality for all.

On the second level, therefore, Fitzgerald transcends the novel of Jazz-Age, bull-market manners that it could have been in the hands of a less ambitious craftsman and ascends to the level of the great 19th-century French novelists, who, in Lionel Trilling's words, "take the given moment as a moral fact." But beyond this, Nick's narrative must carry the burden of the novel's more abstract concern with idealism in the real world. Gatsby "sprang from his Platonic conception of himself." He creates "the Great Gatsby" from the raw material of his early self, James Gatz, and from a boundless imagination, an embodied spirit capable of anything it chooses to do. But when, at last, Gatsby kisses Daisy and "forever wed his unutterable visions to her perishable breath, his mind would never romp again like the mind of God." The ideal world, in Gatsby's case, shatters in the face of the real one. It has, of course, happened before with Dutch sailors who "for a transitory and enchanted moment" contemplated the "fresh green breast of the new world." And, as Nick knows, it will happen as long as there is a human spirit to contemplate mystery.

The intricate weaving of the various stories within *The Great Gatsby* is accomplished through the complex symbolic substructure of the narrative. The green light, which carries meaning at every level of the story—as Gatsby's go-ahead sign, as money, as the "green breast of the new world," and as springtime—is strategically placed in chapters one, five, and nine. The eyes of T.J. Eckleburg "brood on over the solemn dumping ground," which is the wasteland that America has become, and their empty gaze is there at crucial moments such as that of Tom's visit to his mistress in the Valley of Ashes and before and after her death, a reminder that God has been replaced by fading signs of American materialism. The sustained good driver/bad driver metaphor, through which Fitzgerald hints at standards of morality and immorality, is evident at virtually every turn of the novel: Daisy runs over Myrtle with an automobile and will not stop to accept responsibility; Jordan Baker (whose name combines two brands of automobile from the 1920s) wears her careless driving as a badge of honor; and Owl Eyes, the drunken philosopher in Gatsby's library who shows up at his funeral to informally eulogize him as "the poor son of a bitch," is involved in an accident leaving Gatsby's party. With these symbols and motifs, Fitzgerald imparts, in the words of his editor, Maxwell Perkins, "a sort of sense of eternity."

It is difficult to assess the enormous influence of *The Great Gatsby*. John O'Hara and J.D. Salinger are two of many American authors who have proclaimed Fitzgerald's brilliance, and Salinger's first-person narrative *The Catcher in the Rye* (1951), shares thematic and formal concerns with *The Great Gatsby*. However, Fitzgerald's is "a fiction that is difficult to imitate but from which much can be learned." While *The Great Gatsby* undoubtedly advanced the novel form in the tradition of Henry James, as Eliot maintained, its primary legacy is perhaps its affirmation of Fitzgerald's hope that, despite the great experimentation of modernism, the traditional novel could still contain, in his words, "something *new*—something extraordinary and beautiful."

BRYANT MANGUM

See also F. Scott Fitzgerald

Further Reading

Berman, Ronald, *"The Great Gatsby" and Modern Times,* Urbana: University of Illinois Press, 1994
Bruccoli, Matthew J., *Some Sort of Epic Grandeur: The Life of F. Scott Fitzgerald,* London: Hodder and Stoughton, and New York: Harcourt Brace, 1981; revised edition, New York: Carroll and Graf, 1993
Bruccoli, Matthew J., editor, *New Essays on "The Great Gatsby,"* Cambridge and New York: Cambridge University Press, 1985
Donaldson, Scott, editor, *Critical Essays on F. Scott Fitzgerald's "The Great Gatsby,"* Boston: G.K. Hall, 1984
Eble, Kenneth, *F. Scott Fitzgerald,* New York: Twayne, 1963; revised edition, Boston: Twayne, 1977
Lehan, Richard Daniel, *F. Scott Fitzgerald and the Craft of Fiction,* Carbondale: Southern Illinois University Press, 1966; London: Feffer and Simons, 1969
Lehan, Richard Daniel, *The Great Gatsby: The Limits of Wonder,* Boston: Twayne, 1991
Miller, James E., Jr., *F. Scott Fitzgerald: His Art and Technique,* New York: New York University Press, 1964; London: Peter Owen, 1965
Mizener, Arthur, editor, *F. Scott Fitzgerald: A Collection of Critical Essays,* Englewood Cliffs, New Jersey: Prentice-Hall, 1963
Roulston, Robert, and Helen H. Roulston, *The Winding Road to West Egg: The Artistic Development of F. Scott Fitzgerald,* Lewisburg, Pennsylvania: Bucknell University Press, and London: Associated University Presses, 1994
Sklar, Robert, *F. Scott Fitzgerald: The Last Laocoon,* New York: Oxford University Press, 1967; London: Oxford University Press, 1969
Stern, Milton R., *The Golden Moment: The Novels of F. Scott Fitzgerald,* Urbana: University of Illinois Press, 1970

Greek and Roman Narrative

Forms of the Novel in the Ancient World

Extended works of prose fiction in Latin and Greek first appear toward the end of the Hellenistic age (323–31 B.C.). The fragments of *Ninus*, for instance, identified as the first example of the form, belong to the first century B.C. Little is known about most of the authors or dates of the works. The exceptions are Petronius, author of the *Satyrica* (in English versions as *Satyricon*), who can be identified with a courtier of Nero who died in A.D. 66; Apuleius, creator of the *Golden Ass,* whose philosophical and rhetorical works can be placed in North Africa between A.D. 150 and 180; and the fictional *True Story* of Lucian of Samosata (roughly A.D. 120–180). Technical criteria, such as letter forms, make it possible to date fragments of prose fiction that have been preserved on papyrus, mostly to the first three centuries A.D. This is consistent with the evidence that appears in the works themselves. Iamblichus, for example, provides information in the *Babylonian Story* that enables us to date it shortly after A.D. 165. The chief exception to the pattern is Heliodorus,

author of *An Ethiopian Story,* a text that many scholars believe alludes to events dated after A.D. 350 and does not appear on papyrus until A.D. 550.

The principal works of prose fiction preserved complete from antiquity are Achilles Tatius' *Leucipppe and Clitophon* (about A.D. 150), Apuleius' *Golden Ass* or *Metamorphoses,* Chariton's *Chaereas and Callirhoe* (A.D. 50); Longus' *Daphnis and Chloe* (A.D. 200), Heliodorus' *An Ethiopian Story* (A.D. 250–350), and Lucian's *A True Story* (A.D. 170). The anonymous *Alexander-Romance* (fourth century) and *Story of Apollonius, King of Tyre* (fifth or sixth century) appear to be adaptations of earlier works and may not be complete in their present form. Petronius' *Satyrica* is preserved only in excerpts and fragments, except for the narrative of the *Banquet of Trimalchio.* Xenophon of Ephesus' *An Ephesian Tale* and the anonymous *Ass* currently ascribed to Lucian, both apparently from the second century, are presented in the manuscript tradition as complete texts but are probably abbreviations of longer works. Several other works are known to us only from fragments preserved on papyrus in Egypt and rediscovered in the past two centuries, or from summaries and encyclopedia references put together in Constantinople in the ninth and tenth centuries. The most important of these fragmentary works are Antonius Diogenes' *The Wonders Beyond Thule,* Iamblichus' *A Babylonian Story,* Lollianus' *A Phoenician Story,* and the anonymous tales of *Ninus, Metiochius and Parthenope, Iolaus,* and *Sesonchosis.* Complete texts and translations may be found in Stephens and Winkler (1995).

Few titles have firm manuscript authority, but the use of ethnographic terms such as *Phoenician Story* (literally *Phoiniki-ka,* or "*Phoenician Things*") is common. Works may also be referred to by the names of the protagonists, often a couple, as in *Leucipppe and Clitophon.* Significantly, in some cases only the female partner is named: Chariton's work may have been called *Callirhoe;* Heliodorus' *Ethiopian Stories* may also have had the title *Chariclea.*

Several of the narratives (the works of Achilles Tatius, Chariton, Heliodorus, Longus, and Xenophon, for example) are love stories with happy endings in successful marriages; among the fragmentary works, Iamblichus' *A Babylonian Story* as well as the *Metiochius and Parthenope* and *Ninus* appear to have had a similar structure. However, this was not the only form of narrative fiction: the Greek *Ass* and Apuleius' *Golden Ass* focus on magic (the adventures of a young man turned into a donkey by a witch), Antonius Diogenes' *The Wonders Beyond Thule* and Lucian's *True Story* deal with imaginary travel, Petronius' *Satyrica* describes in a comic tone the exploits, sexual and otherwise, of a trio of young Greek men in southern Italy, and the relationships at the core of the *Story of Apollonius, King of Tyre,* on the other hand, are those of parent and child.

The connection of these ancient prose fictions with the modern novel was first suggested by Pierre-Daniel Huet (1678), who was seeking, in the Renaissance manner, a respectable classical forerunner for the form that was developing in France. The oxymoronic term *ancient novel* is typical among classical scholars who claim, for example, that Chariton's *Chaereas and Callirhoe* is the first novel in European history (Blake, 1939). Although some scholars of the modern novel such as Hunter (1990) stress the particularity and novelty of the genre that developed in late 18th-century England, many others who work outside of classical scholarship, such as Bakhtin (1981), Heiserman (1977), and Doody (1996), accept the suitability of the modern term for the ancient form and stress the continuities and similarities between Greek, Roman, and modern European novels. Although extended works of fiction were written in both Greek and Latin during the classical period, with the exception of terms meaning "narrative" (*diegema*) or "composition" (*syntagma*) there was no one consistent term applied to them. The authors themselves described their works as "history" (*historia;* Longus) and "drama" (*dramatikon*). The view that Greek and Roman fiction constituted a defined genre may be no older than Huet (Selden, in Tatum, 1994). The absence of a critical history is partly a result of philosophical concerns about fiction as lying (Gill and Wiseman, 1993) as well as the more rapid development of the form *after* Aristotle's generic classification of literature. Not until the fourth and fifth centuries A.D., in a letter of the Emperor Julian and a *Commentary* by Macrobius on Cicero's *Dream of Scipio,* do we meet a technical vocabulary for prose fiction. Macrobius writes

of "narratives (*argumenta*) full of fictional stories of lovers," while Julian writes of "fictions *(plasmata)* in the form of history" and "love intrigues" (*erotic hypotheses*) (Holzberg, in Schmeling, 1996).

Several stories have a similar plot structure in which teenagers fall in love at first sight, undergo a series of hair-raising adventures that challenge their loyalty to each other, and then are finally united and married. Winkler (in Tatum, 1994) and Konstan (1994) emphasize the degree to which the familiar structure of the romance—of young, heterosexual, reciprocal love leading to marriage—is a construct of the prose fiction of the Hellenistic and Imperial Roman eras. The preferred themes of other Greek and Roman forms of love literature are pursuit, seduction, surrender, and control, not infrequently in homoerotic and pederastic contexts. Documentary and literary evidence makes it clear that in the wealthy classes at least, arranged marriages for property and dynastic reasons were the norm; the growth of a significant literature about love in marriage preceded rather than followed actual social practice.

Many narrative elements, such as falling in love at first sight, love as sickness or fever, capture by pirates (who turn out, like Robin Hood, to be noblemen down on their luck), the paradox of apparent death and its inevitable follow-up, burial alive, and the elaborate strategies whereby virginal heroines avoid rape and seduction by predatory males are repeated in several of the novels (notably those of Chariton, Xenophon, Achilles Tatius, and Heliodorus). There has been a tendency to focus on these similarities and to treat the narratives that include them as examples of a highly conventional and rather fixed formulaic genre, the "Ideal Greek Romance." A careful reading of the texts suggests that a one-size generic garment does not, in fact, fit all bodies. Iamblichus' *A Babylonian Story,* for example, structurally may have been a love story, but the summary of its sensational plot suggests anything but an "Ideal Romance" (see Stephens and Winkler, 1995). Even with a theme so central to the romantic love story as sexual loyalty or chastity, Chariton, Longus, Achilles Tatius, and Heliodorus use sharply differentiated assumptions. The themes of travel to exotic lands and the fascination with astonishing and paradoxical turns of event, crucial to the work of Xenophon, for instance, are entirely missing from that of Longus, whose pastoral novel is restricted to the island of Lesbos and includes very little startling adventure. Achilles Tatius, on the other hand, treats most of the themes in such an over-the-top manner as to suggest parody. The publication of fragments, such as those of Lollianus and Iolaus, which appear to deal with sex and religion in a sensational manner, shows that the range of topics and concerns in Greek prose fiction was far from limited to sentimental romances about adolescents. In addition, the narratives of Antonius Diogenes and of the *Apollonius of Tyre,* both of which do include love affairs, still do not follow a stereotypical formula, and the love affairs are not the sole focus of the narrative. The preservation of several love romances with similar narrative structures may reflect more the taste of some readers in late antiquity than the existence of a single, "typical" form of the genre.

Ben Perry (1967) asserted that the first Greek novel was a conscious literary creation of an individual author rather than a development from previously existing forms. The groundbreaking, deliberately created work he hypothesized has never been identified. Even if one accepts Perry's model, such an author did not work in a vacuum, and it is both possible and useful to establish a literary and social background for the new form (see Ruiz-Montero, in Schmeling, 1996).

Around 360 B.C., the Athenian historian Xenophon undertook a biography of the first ruler of the Persian empire, Cyrus the Great. Drawing on contemporary examples of praise-oratory (*encomia*) and on speculation about the formation of the ideal ruler, his *Cyropedia* (*The Education of Cyrus*), which presents an idealistic account of an exemplary monarch rather than attempting historical accuracy, plays a crucial role in the adaptation to fiction of modes of discourse proper to history. Included in the *Cyropedia* as an example of the King's nobility is his treatment of his captive, Pantheia, and her husband, Abradates, whose loyalty to one another, even unto death, is offered as a striking moral example. Ancient scholarship knew of three Xenophons besides the Athenian historian, from Antioch, Cyprus, and Ephesus, each of whom wrote on erotic themes. Perry suggests that as a result of the *Cyropedia*, "Xenophon" became a suitable pseudonym for the narrator of love stories in prose, a suggestion that is supported by several recollections in the novels of the tale of Pantheia.

Xenophon's biography of Cyrus, like his own career as a Greek soldier in the service of a Persian prince, is linked to another feature of the ancient novels: rarely is their setting limited to the area of original Greek settlement roughly correspondent to the modern Republic of Greece. Most of the narratives in Greek deal with Greeks of the diaspora, in contact with other Mediterranean cultures in Egypt, Babylonia, and Ethiopia. Authors such as Petronius and Apuleius, moreover, were concerned with the interaction of Greek and Latin speakers in both Italy and Greece.

Contacts between Greeks and other cultures intensified after the world conquests of Alexander the Great and the foundation of Alexandria, the polyglot capital of Macedonian Egypt. Although connections have been detected by many scholars between Greek fiction and that of Egypt, Mesopotamia, and India (all cultures with which Greeks had greater contact after Alexander's conquests), no specific non-Greek model has been discovered for any existing text. It is, however, noteworthy that authors of ancient novels presented themselves as belonging to a world of literary and cultural crossovers. Iamblichus, for instance, describes himself as Syrian in culture and Heliodorus as Phoenician, although the literary and rhetorical contexts of their works are entirely Greek.

Traditions surrounding Alexander the Great himself play a large part in the connections between cultures. Although the existing *Alexander-Romance* was put together in Alexandria no earlier than the second century A.D., its sources may be traced to soon after Alexander's death in 323 B.C., and versions in Armenian and Syriac soon gave it an extensive influence outside the Greek and Roman world. This tradition—more interested in Alexander's complex personality, relationships, and emotions than in his military and political achievements—finds a reflection in many of the first Greek fictional works that describe the internal and personal experiences of supposedly historical figures (*Ninus*) or fictional characters (*Chaereas and Callirhoe*) placed in a setting of world politics and conflict. Alexander's epic journeys to distant and exotic lands, such as India and Egypt, develop in the *Alexander-Romance* into experiences with the fantastic and incredible. The theme of extended travel to both known and imaginary worlds, recurrent in many early novels (Heliodorus, Antonius Diogenes, Lucian's *True Story*) reflects this Alexandrian tradition far more than myths of travel and homecoming such as Homer's *Odyssey*.

Winkler (in Tatum, 1994) notes that the tale of Zariadres and Odatis, a story of mutual love leading to marriage set in Iran, was included by Chares of Mytilene in his history of King Alexander. Chares was himself a bridge between cultures. He was a Greek who held a court position that Alexander had adopted from Iranian ceremonial: the "announcer" of those who entered the King's presence. His choice of an Iranian setting for a tale of love at first sight illustrates the Greek association of erotic romance narratives with the non-Greek world opened to them by Alexander's conquests.

After Alexander, the predominant political structure in the region became the Roman Empire: a huge state incorporating several different cultural, political, and religious traditions ruled by a single monarch. By the end of the last century B.C., Rome had conquered the great Hellenistic kingdoms of Syria and Egypt and was itself ruled by an emperor. The intense involvement of male citizens in the political life of their city, typical of fifth-century Athens, changed in the Hellenistic and Roman world to a more passive role as loyal subject to a distant King or Emperor. Reardon (1989, and elsewhere) has emphasized how much this political situation led to an increased focus on the personal, the individual, and the emotional as opposed to the external and political, and how this became an ideal climate for the development of the novel.

Several of the texts in Greek are love narratives with happy endings. On the other hand, the two extended texts in Latin, by Petronius and Apuleius, have a different focus: one comic and satiric, the other dealing with magic and religion. As a result, there has been a tendency to oppose "ideal" Greek "romances" to "comic," or "realistic," Roman novels. However, the distinction is misleading. There are works written in Greek that are as comic and realistic as the two Latin works, both of which, it should be noted, are profoundly Greek in context. Petronius deals with the adventures of Greeks in southern Italy, while Apuleius adapts a preexisting Greek story, known as *The Ass*, that recounts the experiences of a Greek speaker (with a Roman name but a Greek pedigree) from the Roman colony of Corinth in the heart of Greece. In the Roman Empire the choice of linguistic code was not necessarily a mark of ethnicity: the Roman emperor Marcus Aurelius wrote his philosophical *Meditations* in Greek; the Latin epic poet Statius came from a Greek family living in Naples; while Ammianus Marcellinus, historian in Latin of the later Roman Empire, was a Greek from Antioch in Syria.

Who were the readers of the ancient novels? As with modern novels, there has often been an assumption of an uneducated, juvenile, or female audience. This assumption was first stated in its baldest form by Perry (1967), and there are still traces of it in Hägg (1983). There is, in fact, little evidence to support this assumption, and it may be based on no more than scholars' perceptions of the fiction itself. If male, adult, educated critics perceive a work as sentimental or unsophisticated, they look for possible sentimental and unsophisticated readers among those unlike themselves. Classical novels were not popular in the way a contemporary work can be. In the ancient world, books were expensive, and there are no more copies of novels preserved on papyrus than there are of other forms of literature. Literacy was far from universal in the ancient world, though possibly more common than at any time until the 17th century. The bureaucratic and economic structures of the empires after Alexander presupposed the existence of a fairly large administrative class of literate clerks and accountants, but there is little evidence to suggest that the Hellenistic empires brought about a major change in the literacy level such as took place in 17th- and 18th-century Europe. Ancient fiction is quite allusive to other forms of literature, and this suggests a readership moderately familiar with other forms. Even the least sophisticated text, *Xenophon of Ephesus*, suggests an awareness of the dramas of Euripides. For Heliodorus and Longus, the lists of references are much longer, and the method of allusion subtler. The preserved ancient novels do not appear to have been aimed at the semiliterate.

In class terms, the protagonists of the ancient novels are drawn largely from the traditional elite: an urban, slave-owning class that drew its wealth from large agricultural holdings, although the novels show a much greater awareness of other classes than do other forms of literature from antiquity. The reading public in the Hellenistic world certainly included more than this traditional property-owning class: among the newly important groups one should include the professionals, military and civilian, who administered the empires, as well as the educators, particularly the teachers of public speaking, the *sophists* or *rhetors* who provided most of the secondary education. To what extent there was anything resembling a bourgeois (manufacturing and trading) class and how educated its taste was for literature, prose fiction or otherwise, remains problematic. Petronius' portrayal of the semiliterate ex-slave entrepreneur Trimalchio does not mean there were no persons of culture among merchants and traders. However, one cannot claim, as one might for Western Europe at the time of the development of the modern novel, that in the Hellenistic kingdoms and Roman Empire the growth of a new economic and social class led to a new form of literature.

Did the ancient novels have a female readership? The suggestion, seen in George Thornley's description (1657) of *Daphnis and Chloe* as "A most Sweet and Pleasant Pastorall Romance for Young Ladies" (see title page reproduced in Doody, 1996), is more a reflection of 17th- and 18th-century views of both literature and sex roles. The ancient evidence is ambiguous. The characters and personalities of women in the ancient novel, especially the resourceful and resilient protagonists Callirhoe (Chariton) and Chariclea (Heliodorus), find few parallels in other literatures. This may, as Hägg (1983) suggests, point to a female readership. The extreme seclusion of women in fifth-century B.C. Athens should not be taken as a norm for all of classical antiquity. At the time the ancient novels were written, there certainly were women readers in both Greek and Roman contexts with broader experiences than those of the Athenian housewife (see Jahne, in Schmeling, 1996). It is unlikely, on the other hand, that there were enough female readers to constitute a separate market. Indeed, the very concept of a target audience as a market is profoundly anachronistic for Greek and Roman literature.

The most likely audience for ancient novels would appear to be, as argued by Doody (1996), economically prosperous, moderately educated men and women. Some novelists, such as Longus and Apuleius, assumed a higher degree of education in their readers than others. Likewise, some novelists, such as Chariton, show more interest in female perspectives than others.

As in other areas, the tendency to treat "ancient novels" or "Greek romances" as alike in their treatment of, or attractiveness to, women misrepresents the diversity of ancient prose fiction.

Another issue of readership has to do with religion, which plays a large part in the ancient novels. In Chariton, characters view their lives as controlled by the gods of Love, Eros and Aphrodite. In Xenophon of Ephesus, lovers believe they have been saved by the Egyptian goddess Isis. Longus' *Daphnis and Chloe* is described as a dedication to the gods, to Love, Pan, and the Nymphs. Heliodorus describes himself as belonging to the descendants of the sun god, gives the priests of several cults a central part in his narrative, and concludes by making the protagonists priest and priestess of the Ethiopian cults of the Moon and the Sun. Lucius, the narrator and subject of Apuleius' *Golden Ass,* is returned to human form by Isis and becomes an official of her cult.

The novels of Longus, Heliodorus, and Apuleius are profoundly religious works, and it is striking that none is concerned with the traditional Olympian gods of Greek or Roman state religion. The cult of the Egyptian goddess Isis, actively supported by the Ptolemaic rulers of Egypt as a source of unity in their empire, spread well beyond Egyptian spheres of influence. The devotion of several figures in the novels to her cult, and their trust in her as a savior, is an authentic representation of concurrent religious belief. The idea that a savior god intervenes personally in the lives of isolated individuals is seen by many scholars as another aspect of the personal, internal focus of the post-Alexandrian world. The core myth of Isis, which includes her love for her husband, Osiris, their separation, her travels to rediscover him, and their eventual reunion, has obvious parallels to the narrative structure of several of the novels and ultimately places them in a religious context.

Throughout his distinguished career, Reinhold Merkelbach has argued that the ancient novels have a far closer relation to specific "mystery" religions into which the believer was ritually initiated (see Merkelbach, 1995). In this interpretation, events in the narratives have special, secret, coded meanings to the initiate: the "apparent death," for example, of the protagonist recalls, represents, or symbolizes the enactment of death of the old self and the subsequent rebirth into a new life, an apparently common element of initiation rituals. Capture by pirates alludes to tests and trials by fellow initiates and ultimately recalls the capture of the god Dionysus by pirates in the Homeric *Hymn to Dionysus*. Ultimately, as Beck (in Schmeling, 1996) and Doody (1996) suggest, Merkelbach's argument fails to convince because it is unnecessary. The narratives are comprehensible on their own terms: pirates *can* be explained as just pirates; the characters have meaning as characters and are not just figures in a holy drama. It is important to recognize that the novels and "mystery" religions of Greco-Roman antiquity share the same metaphors of journey, loss, rediscovery, alienation, and companionship. It is also important to recognize the degree to which the novels are valuable evidence of the nature of pagan belief shortly before the advent of Christianity. Yet in the final analysis, Greek and Roman narrative fictions are not religious parables or confessions but instead works of the creative imagination set in profoundly religious contexts.

Another important context for the ancient novel was rhetoric. Political life in democratic Athens and republican Rome was intensely oral and oratorical. Rhetoric, the persuasive art of the skilled speaker in the assembly or law courts, was a prerequisite for political and social success. Education beyond simple literacy was largely rhetorical, and the techniques of the debater affected almost all forms of literature. In the Hellenistic kingdoms and the Roman Empire, the political importance of rhetoric declined, but it nevertheless remained the dominant expression of culture and education, and an education in rhetoric was still mandatory for men of the ruling class.

In the rhetorical schools of the first century A.D., students debated imaginary cases on obscure points of law (*controversiae*, "controversies"). In the "Second Sophistic" of the second century A.D., the focus turned to form rather than content, and rhetoric became a performance art practiced before huge audiences who came not to be persuaded by the sophist's argument, but to be overwhelmed by his style and presentation. Among the arts of the sophist were those of description of objects, events, or works of art, as well as the explanation (*exegesis*) of their significance.

The Second Sophistic, which reached its peak in the second century A.D., coincided closely with the most productive period for the ancient novel. There are many connections between the novels and the display oratory of the period, in both Latin and Greek. Achilles Tatius, Apuleius, Heliodorus, and Longus produced the novels most akin to contemporary rhetoric. We know from his other works that Apuleius was a highly skilled virtuoso speaker. The novels of both Achilles Tatius and Longus are formally descriptions of a work of art. Bartsch (1989) provides a sophisticated account of the interpretive skills demanded of the reader both by the descriptive passages in Achilles Tatius and Heliodorus and by the novels themselves. Besides the art of description, the "sophistic" novels of the second century A.D. and later share with contemporary rhetoric a self-conscious style that is sometimes simple (as with Longus) but more often ornate, rhythmical, and bordering on the bizarre (as with Apuleius).

The role of Greek and Latin fiction in the development of the novel in most Western European traditions is considerable, as has been emphasized by Doody (1996). Among the most important early strains are Boccaccio's use of Apuleius; the Catalan *Tirant lo Blanc*, whose setting in Constantinople seems to reflect ultimately on the Greek novels; and Miguel de Cervantes, who drew on both Heliodorus and Apuleius. In France, the adaptation of Greek novels began with Nicolas de Montreux's *Oeuvre de la chasteté* in 1595 (see Sandy, in Schmeling, 1996). Even English works from the late 18th and early 19th centuries to which the term "novel" applies most specifically—Samuel Richardson's *Clarissa* (1747–48) and Frances Burney's *The Wanderer* (1814), for instance—are, as Doody suggests, profoundly Heliodoran (in Tatum, 1994).

Are the ancient prose fictions fairly described as novels? If one uses the term as it was first used—applied to an extended fictional prose narrative that involves characters from normal life in a complex plot—it is difficult to refuse the title to at least some examples of ancient fiction. If one looks for the ten features identified by Hunter (1990) as characteristic of the realistic English novel of the 18th century (contemporaneity, credibility, familiarity, rejection of traditional plots, tradition-free language, individualism, empathy, coherence, digressiveness, and self-consciousness about innovation), most can be discovered in the range of ancient fiction, and some (the degree of self-consciousness in the characters, the freedom to digress and parenthesize) are singularly appropriate. The novels of

Apuleius, Heliodorus, and Petronius in some ways exemplify these tendencies better than English novels. If the definition of novel is not limited to elements present in 18th-century English examples and attempts to include *Tirant lo Blanc*, Cervantes, James Joyce, and Vladimir Nabokov, it is harder still to exclude Greek and Roman examples. The applicability of the term may be seen in what Doody calls the *tropes* of the novel: deep, symbolic themes such as "Breaking," "the Labyrinth," "the Goddess"—themes that characterize a wide range of fictions, both ancient and modern. Another reason to consider these texts *novels* may be extrapolated from the singular success of scholars in applying to Greek and Roman novels a variety of modern critical methods first used for their modern counterparts (see Fusillo, in Schmeling, 1996). Among the most noteworthy examples are the narratologial (Winkler, 1985), reader-response (Bartsch, 1989), and psychoanalytical (Franz, 1970).

HUGH J. MASON

See also Comedy and Humor in the Novel; Epic and Novel; Genre Criticism; Historical Writing and the Novel; Myth and Novel; Novel and Romance: Etymologies; Pastoralism in the Novel; Romance

Further Reading

Bakhtin, M.M., *The Dialogic Imagination: Four Essays*, translated by Caryl Emerson and Michael Holquist, edited by Holquist, Austin: University of Texas Press, 1981

Bartsch, Shadi, *Decoding the Ancient Novel: The Reader and the Role of Description in Heliodorus and Achilles Tatius*, Princeton, New Jersey: Princeton University Press, 1989

Blake, Warren E., editor, *Chariton's "Chaereas and Callirhoe,"* Ann Arbor: University of Michigan Press, 1939

Doody, Margaret Anne, *The True Story of the Novel*, New Brunswick, New Jersey: Rutgers University Press, 1996; London: HarperCollins, 1997

Franz, Marie-Luise von, *A Psychologial Interpretation of the Golden Ass of Apuleius*, New York: Spring Publications, 1970; 2nd edition, Irving, Texas: Spring Publications, 1980

Gill, Christopher, and T.P. Wiseman, editors, *Lies and Fiction in the Ancient World*, Exeter: University of Exeter Press, and Austin: University of Texas Press, 1993

Hägg, Tomas, *The Novel in Antiquity*, Oxford: Blackwell, and Berkeley: University of California Press, 1983

Heiserman, Arthur, *The Novel before the Novel: Essays and Discussions about the Beginnings of Prose Fiction in the West*, Chicago: University of Chicago Press, 1977

Huet, Pierre-Daniel, *Lettre de Monsieur Huet à Monsieur de Segrais de l'origine des romans*, Paris: Mabre-Cramoisy, 1678; tricentenary edition, Paris: A.-G. Nizet, 1971

Hunter, J. Paul, *Before Novels: The Cultural Contexts of Eighteenth-Century English Fiction*, New York: Norton, 1990

Konstan, David, *Sexual Symmetry: Love in the Ancient Novel and Related Genres*, Princeton, New Jersey: Princeton University Press, 1994

Merkelbach, Reinhold, *Isis Regina, Zeus Sarapis: Die griechisch-ägyptische Religion nach den Quellen dargestellt*, Stuttgart: Teubner, 1995

Perry, Ben Edwin, *The Ancient Romances: A Literary-Historical Account of Their Origins,* Berkeley: University of California Press, 1967

Reardon, Bryan P., editor, *Collected Ancient Greek Novels,* Berkeley: University of California Press, 1989

Schmeling, Garth, editor, *The Novel in the Ancient World,* Leiden and New York: Brill, 1996

Stephens, Susan A., and John J. Winkler, editors, *Ancient Greek Novels: The Fragments: Introduction, Text, Translation, and Commentary,* Princeton, New Jersey: Princeton University Press, 1995

Tatum, James, editor, *The Search for the Ancient Novel,* Baltimore: Johns Hopkins University Press, 1994

Winkler, John J., *Auctor & Actor: A Narratological Reading of Apuleius' "Golden Ass,"* Berkeley: University of California Press, 1985

Graham Greene 1904–91

English

Graham Greene's immense and varied oeuvre is informed by a unifying vision of a ravaged world through which God's love moves in terrifying ways. It was, Greene claimed, the sense of hell lying about him in his infancy that brought him to this bleak pessimism. Indeed, the autobiographical *A Sort of Life* (1971) delineates an appallingly unhappy childhood, but the "facts" of these years have recently been questioned. Early Greene may be partly a fictional construct. Nevertheless, *something* happened to the man within to create the belief that his life did not matter and that, therefore, there was nothing to lose. Confirmed in that paradox, Greene risked and gained all.

The profusion of Greene's writing has diminished his reputation, preventing due recognition of his best work and obscuring his mastery of form. The assumption seems to be that one cannot be popular and good at the same time. Greene is popular, *ergo*. . . . In fact, the ease of the early novels is the result of their skillful telling. If much is in the vein of Robert Louis Stevenson, John Buchan, and Rider Haggard, or even Marjorie Bowen's *The Viper of Milan* (1906), the Boys' Own Adventures, and romantic horror fiction, these proclivities were always tempered by an admiration for and emulation of the narrative complexity and control of Henry James, Joseph Conrad, and (especially) Ford Madox Ford.

Yet Greene's first novels were not successes. *The Man Within* (1929) was noted by reviewers, but those following were barely recognized. The exception was *Stamboul Train* (1932), which caught the public imagination. Greene would later distinguish between such "entertainments" (*A Gun for Sale, The Confidential Agent*) and his serious novels, yet the former largely created his reputation and made possible the deserved success of *Brighton Rock* (1938), the first of the great works. Throughout his career, Greene supplemented his income with other writing (at least 500 words daily): short stories, film criticism, articles, and occasional pieces. These exercises comprised both strategies for survival and a shaping of his skills. The masterpieces received their definition from such professionalism.

The relationship of Greene's Catholicism to his writing remains a central mystery, and the definition of his belief is scarcely less elusive. If marriage drew him to the Church, Greene was not an easy convert, preferring to describe himself as a writer who was a Catholic (or not, as the spirit moved), rather than a Catholic writer. Yet a sacramental sense informs the novels that follow his conversion. By 1936 Greene had made his *Journey Without Maps* through Liberia. When his attack in print upon Shirley Temple's "dimpled depravity" obliged him to leave England, he chose Mexico. *The Lawless Roads* (1939) is the remarkable record of his pilgrimage and, despite its prejudices, a valuable depiction of Mexico by an outsider. It led to *The Power and the Glory* (1940), which also assumes Cardinal Newman's sense of humanity's implication in "some terrible aboriginal calamity." Greene combined the moral parable and the saint's life with a realism as gritty and disgusting as anything he observed, and with a cinematic control that explores structural antinomies (Priest versus Lieutenant) without reducing them to a mere schematic. The strength of the novel—the artistry that conceals its art—is often underestimated.

Similar intimations of corrupt power and shabby glory shape *The Heart of the Matter* (1948), often considered Greene's finest novel. Set against the seedy fecundity of Sierra Leone and drawing upon Greene's association with the Secret Service, the novel follows Scobie, caught between his hollow marriage with the pious Louise and an adulterous love for the agnostic Helen, through a crisis of faith that ends in suicide. The novel made the Vatican's *Index* of forbidden books for its provocative suggestion that a God who cares for the heart of the matter will be less concerned with the transgression of dogma.

The End of the Affair (1951), Greene's most complex narrative, similarly subverts the Church's teaching. The changing perspectives suggest Ford's *The Good Soldier* (1915), as the relationship of Maurice Bendix to Sarah Miles moves to her "affair" with God and his perplexed understanding of that affair—and of himself. More than the novels that preceded it, this story exemplifies Greene's most significant contribution to the novel form: blending narrative complexities with the paradoxes of faith, so that the uncertainties and contradictions of the one mirror those of the other. *A Burnt-Out Case* (1961) and *Monsignor Quixote* (1982) achieve the same complex interrelatedness.

Here is no space to do justice to the range and achievement of Greene's other and later writings: the variety of their settings (Haiti, Vietnam, Argentina), acutely observed yet always with the sense of hell that Greene carried about him; the fascination with espionage and intrigue; Greene's dubious involvement with the politically corrupt (*Getting to Know the General*); his quixotic confrontation with the Marseilles mafia (*J'Accuse*). Since Greene's death, several biographical studies have emerged, the most comprehensive being Norman Sherry's authorized version. Others have complicated Sherry's portrayal, including Father Durán, who administered Greene the Last Rites, Anthony Mockler, and Michael Shelden, whose dismissive debunking of Greene as a 20th-century Rochester—morally unscrupulous and making monkeys of us all—for all its absurdities scores some palpable hits. If I have returned to the life from the literature, that is perhaps as it should be, for Greene's stature as a novelist runs parallel to his standing as a complex individual. His achievement is still debated, but in the current climate of literary betrayal and revisionist polemics some certainties remain: his novels will be read because they are well written, and his life will continue to fascinate because (even in its fictionalized form) it is among the fullest on record.

CHRIS ACKERLEY

Biography

Born in Berkhamsted, Hertfordshire, 2 October 1904. Attended Berkhamsted School; Balliol College, Oxford. Served in the Foreign Office, London, 1941–44. Joined Roman Catholic church, 1926; staff member at the London *Times,* 1926–30; film critic, 1937–40, and literary editor, 1940–41, *Spectator,* London; director, Eyre and Spottiswoode (publishers), London, 1944–48, and The Bodley Head (publishers), London, 1958–68. Died 3 April 1991.

Novels by Greene

The Man Within, 1929
The Name of Action, 1930
Rumour at Nightfall, 1931
Stamboul Train: An Entertainment, 1932; as *Orient Express,* 1933
It's a Battlefield, 1934; revised edition, 1948
England Made Me, 1935; as *The Shipwrecked,* 1953
A Gun for Sale, 1936; as *This Gun for Hire,* 1936
Brighton Rock, 1938
The Confidential Agent, 1939
The Power and the Glory, 1940; as *The Labyrinthine Ways,* 1940
The Ministry of Fear, 1943
The Heart of the Matter, 1948
The Third Man, and The Fallen Idol, 1950
The End of the Affair, 1951
Loser Takes All, 1955
The Quiet American, 1955
Our Man in Havana, 1958

A Burnt-Out Case, 1961
The Comedians, 1966
Travels with My Aunt, 1969
The Honorary Consul, 1973
The Human Factor, 1978
Doctor Fischer of Geneva; or, The Bomb Party, 1980
Monsignor Quixote, 1982
The Tenth Man, 1985
The Captain and the Enemy, 1988

Other Writings: short stories, plays, screenplays, verse, essays, travel writings, autobiography, film criticism, children's literature.

Further Reading

Adamson, Judith, *Graham Greene, The Dangerous Edge: Where Art and Politics Meet,* London: Macmillan, and New York: St. Martin's Press, 1990

Allott, Kenneth, and Miriam Farris, *The Art of Graham Greene,* New York: Russell and Russell, and London: Hamilton, 1963

Cassis, A.F., *Graham Greene: An Annotated Bibliography of Criticism,* Metuchen, New Jersey: Scarecrow Press, 1981

Cassis, A.F., *Graham Greene: Man of Paradox,* Chicago: Loyola University Press, 1994

Couto, Maria, *Graham Greene: On the Frontier: Politics and Religion in the Novels,* London: Macmillan, and New York: St. Martin's Press, 1988

De Vitis, A.A., *Graham Greene,* Boston: Twayne, 1986

Diemert, Brian, *Graham Greene's Thrillers and the 1930s,* Montreal and Buffalo, New York: McGill-Queen's University Press, 1996

Greene, Graham, *L'autre et son double: Entretiens avec Marie-Françoise Allain,* Paris: Belfond, 1981; as *The Other Man: Conversations with Graham Greene,* New York: Simon and Schuster, and London: Bodley Head, 1983

Hoskins, Robert, *Graham Greene: A Character Index and Guide,* New York: Garland, 1991

Miller, Robert H., *Graham Greene: A Descriptive Catalog,* Lexington: University Press of Kentucky, 1979

Miller, Robert H., *Understanding Graham Greene,* Columbia: University of South Carolina Press, 1990

O'Prey, Paul, *A Reader's Guide to Graham Greene,* New York and London: Thames and Hudson, 1988

Shelden, Michael, *Graham Greene: The Man Within,* London: Heinemann, 1994

Sherry, Norman, *The Life of Graham Greene,* 2 vols., London: Cape, and New York: Viking, 1989, 1994

Wobbe, R.A., *Graham Greene: A Bibliography and Guide to Research,* New York: Garland, 1979

David Grossman 1954–

Israeli

In the 1980s, David Grossman rose to prominence as one of the most celebrated and influential Israeli writers. His contribution to the Hebrew novel is important because he introduced new themes to the genre, including Arab/Jewish relations in the Occupied Territories, and the effects of the Holocaust on the children of survivors. Grossman also has made pioneering use of fantasy and postmodernist experiment in his narrative technique.

Grossman is best known in English translation for his political reportage, particularly *Hazeman hatsahov* (*The Yellow Wind*), an account of life in the West Bank and Gaza. When published in Israel in 1987, this work shook many of Israel's Jews out of their complacency regarding the post-1967 status quo. Grossman's observations anticipated the explosion of tensions that was soon to follow in the Arab uprising known as the Intifada. Grossman had expressed similar concerns in his first novel, *Chiyuch hagediy* (1983; *The Smile of the Lamb*), which features an Israeli soldier who becomes increasingly uncomfortable with the role of occupier and seeks wisdom in the company of an Arab visionary/storyteller. Even as Grossman addresses urgent contemporary issues in his fiction, he also integrates fictional vignettes and short stories into his reportage. Combining concern for current events with literary interests, Grossman follows in the tradition of his predecessors in Israeli letters, notably A.B. Yehoshua and Amos Oz, both of whom are as well known for their political essays and activist stances as for their narrative art. After *The Yellow Wind* Grossman continued to pursue the topic of Arab/Jewish relations in *Nochechim venifkadim* (1992; *Sleeping on a Wire*), an account of the lives of Palestinian Arabs who are citizens of the State of Israel.

Grossman's greatest artistic achievement, undoubtedly, is his second novel, *Ayen erech: Ahavah* (1986; *See Under: Love*). Each of its four sections attempts, in complex and highly diverse ways, an innovative approach to Holocaust themes. The first part is oriented to the inner life of a nine-year-old boy, Momik, who is determined to decode his parents' secrets. Survivors reluctant to speak of their Holocaust experiences, his parents' traumatic past leaves its imprint on every aspect of the family dynamics. The events take place in Jerusalem in 1959, a time when Israeli culture often resisted identification with Diaspora Jews. Many Israelis saw European Jews as victims, the antithesis of the new, strong, self-reliant natives of the Jewish State. In *See Under: Love* Momik's outlook is informed by an opposition between heroism and victimhood, but his growing awareness of the past unsettles the boundaries between the two. As a result, one may view the novel as a reassessment of Diaspora Jewry, as a meditation on the relationship between strength and brutality, and also as a response to the widespread malaise in 1980s Israeli society over the uses of military force. Grossman's treatment of these issues, along with the focus on second-generation Holocaust society, brought new dimensions to Hebrew fiction.

In the second section of the novel, Momik has grown up and become a writer. Fascinated by the Polish-Jewish writer Bruno Schulz, who was murdered by the Nazis, Momik spins a yarn that transforms Schulz into a fish in the depths of the sea. This rewriting of the past allows Schulz to escape his historical fate

and reflects the artist's wish to discover a world with enough imagination to defy violence and atrocity. Section three, set in a concentration camp, features Momik's granduncle, Anshel Wasserman, who is unable to die and remains impervious to gas and bullets. A writer of juvenile fiction, Wasserman agrees to entertain an SS officer by telling stories, but only on the condition that each day the commandant promises to try again to kill him. In this inversion of the Scheherazade plot, Wasserman's tales finally move the hardened Nazi to a new and humane compassion. The final section is set up as an encyclopedia (with entries such as *conscience, loneliness, fiction,* and *love*) that documents the exploits of a group of characters from Wasserman's stories, the Children of the Heart. Relocated to the Third Reich, these characters try, despite all hardships, to care for an infant whose life is accelerated to undergo growth, maturity, and old age in the space of 24 hours. All four sections of *See Under: Love* revolve around a central set of tensions—innocence versus evil, love versus violence—and so pose the question: can art and the imagination somehow defeat horror or transform it into understanding and compassion?

Grossman's experimentation with fantasy set new standards for the Hebrew novel, which until then had been dominated by realism. Such writers as Gabriel García Márquez, Günter Grass, Bruno Schulz, and Juan Rulfo had considerable impact on the Israeli literary imagination in the 1980s, and *See Under: Love* was one of the first Hebrew texts to explore the possibilities of magic realism. It was followed quickly by the novels of Meir Shalev, Dan Benayah Seri, and Anton Shammas, which likewise infuse familiar social and historical milieus with phantasmagoria. Subsequently, Israeli fiction increasingly embraced experimentation with postmodernist collage and hybrid narrative forms as represented by the works of Yoel Hoffman, Yuval Shimoni, and Orly Castel-Bloom.

In the 1990s a boom of new writing in Israel tended to move away from collective concerns, delving into private worlds and disregarding national ideological struggles. Grossman has contributed to this "post-Zionist" phenomenon by turning toward depictions of personal life. His third novel, *Sefer hadikduk hapenimiy* (1991; *The Book of Intimate Grammar*) focuses on the painful inner life of a boy who, between the ages of 11 and 14, becomes isolated from those around him when he fails to grow physically. His arrested maturation suggests an inability or a refusal to leave behind the innocence of childhood for the corruptions and corporality of adulthood.

Attention to children and their perceptions has in fact proved to be the most abiding of Grossman's themes. It is central not only to *See Under: Love* and *The Book of Intimate Grammar* but also to another novel, *Yesh yeladim zigzag* (1994; *The Zigzag Kid*). This novel offers a juvenile adventure story that turns into a more complex journey of discovery during which the young protagonist discovers his family's secret past as well as hidden aspects of his own personality. Grossman's concern with children struggling to understand the adult world also dominates his play, *Gan Riki* (1988; *Riki's Kindergarten*), in which all the characters are four-year-olds. In addition, like many of the major modern Hebrew authors who have penned books for children as well as adults, Grossman has written a range of picture books for very young children. This practice, which began in the late 19th century, developed from a collective desire to encourage Hebrew literacy and cultural rebirth, which included an extraordinary process of revitalizing the ancient Hebrew language as a modern vernacular. Grossman has made a mark for himself not only for his ability to express and explore the worlds of children, but also through his willingness to incorporate and play with the conventions of juvenile literature as part of his investigation of childhood within adult novels.

NAOMI SOKOLOFF

Biography
Born in Jerusalem in 1954. Studied philosophy and theatre at Hebrew University; graduated 1979. Has served in the military and worked as editor and commentator for Israeli radio.

Novels by Grossman
Chiyuch hagediy, 1983; as *The Smile of the Lamb,* translated by Betsy Rosenberg, 1990
Ayen erech: Ahavah, 1986; as *See Under: Love,* translated by Betsy Rosenberg, 1989

Sefer hadikduk hapenimiy, 1991; as *The Book of Intimate Grammar,* translated by Betsy Rosenberg, 1994
Yesh yeladim zigzag, 1994; as *The Zigzag Kid,* translated by Betsy Rosenberg, 1997

Other Writings: political reportage (including *Hazeman hatsahov* [1987; *The Yellow Wind*]), short stories, a play, and children's books.

Further Reading
Alter, Robert, "Magic Realism in the Israeli Novel," *Prooftexts* 16:2 (May 1996)
Mintz, Alan, "Dark Passages," *Partisan Review* 63:3 (1996)
Morahg, Gilead, "Breaking the Silence: Israel's Fantastic Literature of the Holocaust," in *The Boom in Israeli Fiction,* edited by Alan Mintz, Hanover, New Hampshire: University Press of New England, 1997
Shaked, Gershon, "The Children of the Heart and the Monster: *See Under: Love,*" *Modern Judaism* 9 (October 1989)
Shaked, Gershon, *Sifrut az, kan ve'akhshav* (Literature Then, Here and Now), Tel Aviv: Zemora Bitan, 1993
Sokoloff, Naomi, "Reinventing Bruno Schulz," *AJS Review* 13 (1988)
Sokoloff, Naomi, *Imagining the Child in Modern Jewish Fiction,* Baltimore: Johns Hopkins University Press, 1992

Guerra del fin del mundo. *See* War of the End of the World

Gulliver's Travels by Jonathan Swift

1726

Jonathan Swift's *Gulliver's Travels* was published in 1726 (without the author's name) and was immediately a success. Swift's contemporaries delighted in its creative energy, but they also were sensitive to the work as a topical satire on their society. The text can only loosely be described as a novel: the form itself was an unstable one at the beginning of the 18th century. In their own terms, even critics of the period deemed the book monstrous, absurd, and unjust: Samuel Johnson, in his *Lives of the English Poets* (1781), describes *Gulliver's Travels* as: "a production so new and strange, that it filled the reader with a mingled emotion of merriment and amazement.... Criticism was for a while lost in wonder; no rules of judgment were applied to a book written in open defiance of truth and regularity."

On one level *Gulliver's Travels* works through allusions, allegories, and keys to the true identity of its fictional characters. Accordingly, disputes between Lilliput and Blefescu are a version of conflicts between Protestants and Catholics; the Lilliputians also mirror the Whig party, with Flimnap as Walpole, together with the emergence of a factional party politics that made concerted use of satirical writing. Yet the text may be enjoyed without detailed readings of this sort, and much of the satire is on a general level. For F.P. Lock (1980) the tale is "occasionally disfigured by temporary, topical, allusions and teasingly opaque allegories." Noting the status of the book as a children's classic, John Traugott (1984) marries politics and psychological criticism to show that the text's foregrounding of infantile behavior playfully mirrors the adult games of political power.

Other critics have been more concerned with explaining how the satire operates than with listing its targets. At first the reader is inclined to trust the narrator and to be guided by his common-sense views. Yet narratorial uncertainty emerges metaphorically in the references to the weakness of Gulliver's eyes and his need for spectacles; symptomatically he finds it difficult to adjust when his sense of the customary is disrupted. Gulliver sometimes exhibits the bigoted, proud, narrowminded views of his worst contemporaries. Swift turns him into an unpredictable and unreliable narrator: at times he is the object of the satire as the author ironically undermines his position. Moreover, the notion of the implied author allows the reader to retain a sense of the shifting gap between Gulliver and the reliability or credibility that Swift grants him. The more ironic the narrative becomes, the more it constructs (and undermines) a commonsense reader whose role is continually manipulated.

Another way of understanding and approaching the text's instability is to note its antithesis to the tradition of subsequent 19th-century narrative voices that faithfully guide our ethical interpretation of events. In early prose narrative the reader often lacks an anchor and only with difficulty navigates through the polyphonic discourses that are produced by the text. Often, multiple discourses exist in the text as parody. For example, Swift mocks the discourses and devices of the popular travel genre, poking fun at earlier works such as George Psalmanazar's *An Historical and Geographical Description of Formosa* (1704). Technical details and nautical jargon are used to lend credibility to the writing, but they also unravel themselves so as to undermine any fixed boundary between fact and fiction. Similarly, Gulliver gives us detailed accounts of legal and constitutional issues, but it is ironic that in Lilliput Gulliver is sentenced "without the formal proofs required by the strict letter of the law." Gulliver's behavior is manipulated by means of legal documents and mystifying jargon, but in practice these discourses undo themselves.

Swift's style is most characteristically protean in its movement between the matter of fact and the purely imaginary. The text could be understood simply as a satirical prose narrative rather than a novelistic genre that coherently traces the evolution of its hero. As already observed, Gulliver is as much a satirical "device" as a character. More broadly, the book belongs to a tradition of learned satires that includes Sir Thomas More's *Utopia* (1516), Francis Bacon's *New Atlantis* (1627), and Desiderius Erasmus' *Encomium moriae* (1511; *The Praise of Folly*).

One early critic, James Beattie, noted that *Gulliver's Travels* "is abominable . . . because it abounds in filthy and indecent images." Indeed, Swift's interest in the body and its functions has many thematic links with François Rabelais' *Gargantua* (1534) in which Gargantua, for instance, pisses on the Parisians, killing over 260,000 of them. Many 19th-century critics linked the mind of the author with the work. Another critic, T.B. Macaulay, concluded that Swift's mind was "richly stored with images from the dung-hill and the lazar house." The novelist William Makepeace Thackeray remarked, "As is the case with madmen, certain subjects provoke him, and awaken his fits of wrath." Swift's inclusion of such topics returns his readers forcefully to a recognition of the body and its processes, which the civilized mind tends to repress. These issues have attracted critics such as Phyllis Greenacre (1955) and Norman O. Brown, who worked in the psychological schools of criticism that emerged after Freud. In terms of its unstable narrative voice, its satirical structure, and its interest in representing the body, Swift's text, then, would appear to have provided a model more for 20th-century novelists than for either his contemporaries or the novelists of the 19th century.

IAN MCCORMICK

See also Satirical Novel

Further Reading

Crane, R.S., "The Houyhnhnms, the Yahoos and the History of Ideas," in *Reason and the Imagination: Studies in the History of Ideas, 1600–1800,* edited by Joseph Anthony Mazzeo, New York: Columbia University Press, 1962

Downie, J.A., *Jonathan Swift: Political Writer,* London and Boston: Routledge and Kegan Paul, 1984

Fabricant, Carole, *Swift's Landscape,* Baltimore: Johns Hopkins University Press, 1982; London: University of Notre Dame Press, 1995

Gravil, Richard, editor, *Swift: "Gulliver's Travels,"* London: Macmillan, 1974

Greenacre, Phyllis, *Swift and Carroll: A Psychoanalytic Study of Two Lives,* New York: International Universities Press, 1955

Hammond, Brean S., *Gulliver's Travels,* Milton Keynes and Philadelphia: Open University Press, 1988

Lock, F.P., *The Politics of "Gulliver's Travels,"* Oxford: Clarendon Press, and New York: Oxford University Press, 1980

Nicolson, Marjorie, and Nora M. Mohler, "The Scientific Background of Swift's 'Voyage to Laputa'," in *Fair Liberty Was All His Cry: A Tercentenary Tribute to Jonathan Swift, 1667–1745,* edited by A. Norman Jeffares, London: Macmillan, and New York: St. Martin's Press, 1968

Rawson, Claude J., editor, *The Character of Swift's Satire: A Revised Focus,* Newark: University of Delaware Press, and London: Associated University Presses, 1983

Rogers, Pat, *Eighteenth Century Encounters: Studies in Literature and Society in the Age of Walpole,* Brighton, Sussex: Harvester Press, and Totowa, New Jersey: Barnes and Noble, 1985

Sherbourn, George, "Errors Concerning the Houyhnhnms," *Modern Philology* 56 (1958)

Traugott, John, "The Yahoo in the Doll's House: *Gulliver's Travels* the Children's Classic," in *English Satire and the Satiric Tradition,* edited by Claude Julien Rawson and Jenny Mezciems, Oxford and New York: Blackwell, 1984

H

Hakhnasath kallah. *See* Bridal Canopy

Knut Hamsun 1859–1952

Norwegian

"The whole modern school of fiction in the twentieth century stems from Hamsun," writes Isaac Bashevis Singer in his introduction to Hamsun's first novel *Sult* (1890; *Hunger*). Although Knut Hamsun was also a poet, short-story writer, and dramatist, Singer and other writers and critics think of him first and foremost as the creator of a new type of novel, what Hamsun himself described as "a book without marriages, country picnics or dances up at the big house. A book about the delicate vibrations of a sensitive human soul, the strange and peculiar life of the mind, the mysteries of the nerves in a starving body."

At the same time sad and humorous, *Hunger* is the first-person account of a young writer in Kristiania (now Oslo) whose periodic experiments with hunger act as a mind-expanding drug. In Hamsun's next novel, *Mysterier* (1892; *Mysteries*), the influence of Friedrich Nietzsche and Fedor Dostoevskii is noticeable in the novel's treatment of pride and humility. The hero is involved in a double project of the will—to gain the hand of a beautiful young girl and restore a sense of pride in a local outcast—and he fails on both counts. The long novel, written during short intervals between travels, suffers from a lack of structure, but its intriguing characters, many beautiful passages, and pioneering stream-of-consciousness technique have made it a favorite with Hamsun lovers. The short novel *Pan* (1894), about the tragic love relationship between a proud hero and heroine, is set in the land of the midnight sun and contains nature descriptions of great beauty and a story line that unwinds in short chapters of passionate prose. In *Victoria* (1898) the social difference between the lovers is more clearly marked. He is the son of a poor miller, she the daughter of a great estate owner, and their life story is unusual for Hamsun in that it includes their childhood. Also unusual are the tales and allegories scattered through the text—Hamsun's hero

this time is a professional poet. Less striking than *Pan*, *Victoria* has sweetness and charm, and Arthur Koestler has called it "one of the great love stories in World Literature."

Although it is generally agreed that Hamsun's novels from the 1890s are his greatest, Hamsun wrote 15 more novels during the next 40 years, many of them masterworks. In some, the love story is less important than the social setting. In *Konerne ved vandposten* (1920; *The Women at the Pump*) Hamsun writes with humor and irony about the transformation of country communities into urban areas: "Ah, that little ant hill! Everyone busy with his own affairs, crossing each other's path, elbowing each other aside, sometimes even trampling on each other. That's the way it is, sometimes they even trample on each other . . .". Best known of these novels from the middle period is *Markens grøde* (1917; *The Growth of the Soil*), about an anonymous character, Isak, who wanders into the wilderness to clear new land for himself and his family. H.G. Wells' enthusiasm for the book—"It impresses me as among the very greatest novels I have ever read. It is wholly beautiful; it is saturated with wisdom and humour and tenderness"—may be a reaction against the senselessness of World War I. Hamsun's back-to-nature program also impressed the Swedish Academy, which awarded him the Nobel prize for literature in 1920.

Deeply disillusioned over World War I and its outcome, Hamsun wrote two of his most pessimistic novels in the early 1920s. Then, after undergoing psychoanalytic treatment, he regained his writing ability and some of the humor of his first social novels. The trilogy about the good companions Edevart and August (1927–33) contains many elements of his earlier work—the tragic love story and the back-to-nature message, for example—but it is first and foremost a novel about 20th-century emigration and general rootlessness. The first volume in the trilogy, *Landstrykere* (1927; *Wayfarers*), is Hamsun's longest novel and one of his best. Hamsun's last novel, *Ringen sluttet* (1936; *The Ring Is Closed*), is the first part of a book that was never completed, but even as a torso it is one of his great works. The hero, Abel Brodersen, is a hippie long before the time of hippies. A sailor who has lived in a commune in Kentucky, Brodersen returns to the home of his childhood, disillusioned, but totally without social ambition and, in that limited sense, a free man. A stoic, like many of the author's earlier heroes, Abel Brodersen is more than any other Hamsun protagonist a man of our own time.

During World War II, Hamsun sided with Germany and wrote articles defending its actions in occupied Norway. When the war was over he was arrested and was found by a psychiatrist to suffer from "permanently reduced mental faculties." Hamsun was tried and found guilty and sentenced to surrender everything he owned to the state of Norway. Despite his advanced age, Hamsun was able to include these and many other experiences into a charming and moving memoir, *På gjengrodde stier* (1949; *On Overgrown Paths*), published after his 90th birthday.

Hamsun was above all an aesthete, a stylist, a writer more concerned with his medium than with his message. Typical of his style is a strong reliance on rhythm and repetition, which he employed until the end of his days, even though his lyricism gradually gave way to a more epic manner of presentation. Strangely, Hamsun's lifelong theme of alienation is always accompanied by a message of joy. Henry Miller responded to that message when he wrote, "It was from . . . Knut Hamsun that I derived much of my love of life, love of nature, love of men."

HARALD S. NAESS

See also Hunger

Biography
Born Knut Pedersen in Lom, Norway, 4 August 1859. Apprenticed to a shoemaker in Bodö, then a road worker; lived in the United States, 1882–84, 1886–88; streetcar conductor in Chicago, farm worker in North Dakota, and secretary and lecturer in Minneapolis; lived in Paris for several years, early 1890s; traveled in Finland, Russia, and Denmark during the 1890s and 1900s; writer after 1890, and farmer after 1911. Openly supported Quisling's pro-German party during World War II; arrested, tried and found guilty, and ordered to surrender all his belongings to the state of Norway after the war (also briefly confined to a mental institution). Awarded Nobel prize for literature, 1920. Died 19 February 1952.

Selected Novels by Hamsun
Sult, 1890; as *Hunger*, translated by George Egerton, 1899; also translated by Robert Bly, 1967, and by Sverre Lyngstad, 1996
Mysterier, 1892; as *Mysteries*, translated by Arthur G. Chater, 1927; also translated by Gerry Bothmer, 1971

Pan, 1894; as *Pan*, translated by W.W. Worster, 1920; also translated by James McFarlane, 1955
Victoria, 1898; as *Victoria*, translated by Arthur G. Chater, 1923; as *Victoria: A Love Story*, translated by Oliver Stallybrass, 1969
Under høststjœrnen, 1906; as *Autumn*, translated by W.W. Worster, in *Wanderers*, 1922; as *Under the Autumn Star*, translated by Oliver and Gunnvor Stallybrass, in *The Wanderer*, 1975
En vandrer spiller med sordin, 1909; as *With Muted Strings*, translated by W.W. Worster, in *Wanderers*, 1922; as *A Wanderer Plays on Mute Strings*, translated by Worster, 1922; as *On Muted Strings*, translated by Oliver and Gunnvor Stallybrass, in *The Wanderer*, 1975
Segelfoss by, 1915; as *Segelfoss Town*, translated by J.S. Scott, 1925
Markens grøde, 1917; as *The Growth of the Soil*, translated by W.W. Worster, 1920
Konerne ved vandposten, 1920; as *The Women at the Pump*, translated by Arthur G. Chater, 1928; also translated by Oliver and Gunnvor Stallybrass, 1978
Landstrykere, 1927; as *Vagabonds*, translated by Eugene Gay-Tifft, 1930; as *Wayfarers*, translated by James W. McFarlane, 1980
August, 1930; as *August*, translated by Eugene Gay-Tifft, 1931
Ringen sluttet, 1936; as *The Ring Is Closed*, translated by Eugene Gay-Tifft, 1937

Other Writings: plays, short stories, poetry, travel writing, essays, autobiography, and letters.

Further Reading
Baumgartner, Walter, *Knut Hamsun*, Reinbek bei Hamburg: Rowohlt, 1997
Ferguson, Robert, *Enigma: The Life of Knut Hamsun*, New York: Farrar, Straus and Giroux, and London: Hutchinson, 1987
Hansen, Thorkild, *Prosessen mot Hamsun*, Oslo: Gyldendal, 1978
Kittang, Atle, *Luft, Vind, Ingenting: Hamsuns desillusjonsromanar frå "Sult" til "Ringen sluttet,"* Oslo: Gyldendal, 1984; 2nd edition, 1996
McFarlane, James W., "The Whisper of the Blood: A Study of Knut Hamsun's Early Novels," *PMLA* 71 (1956)
Naess, Harald S., *Knut Hamsun*, Boston: Twayne, 1984
Nettum, Rolf Nyboe, *Konflikt og visjon: Hovedtemaer i Knut Hamsuns forfatterskap 1890–1912*, Oslo: Gyldendal, 1970
Nilson, Sten Sparre, *En ørn i uvær*, Oslo: Gyldendal, 1960
Østby, Arvid, *Knut Hamsun* (bibliography), Oslo: Gyldendal, 1972
Popperwell, Ronald, "Critical Attitudes to Knut Hamsun, 1890–1969" (bibliography), *Scandinavica* 9 (1970)

Han ye. *See* Cold Nights

The Handmaid's Tale by Margaret Atwood

1985

The Handmaid's Tale, a best-seller and Margaret Atwood's most popular work, was short-listed for the Booker Prize, won the Arthur C. Clarke Award for science fiction, and was made into a mainstream film. Drawing on a tradition of dystopias such as Aldous Huxley's *Brave New World* (1932) and George Orwell's *Nineteen Eighty-Four* (1949), the novel is set in Gilead, a near-future right-wing totalitarian regime in which the function of the caste of women called handmaids is reduced to childbearing. The novel also responds to the political climate of the 1980s: Gilead contains elements of the American extreme right, religious fundamentalism, and antifeminist backlash. Not surprisingly, much of the novel's early criticism focused on whether or not this dystopia accurately predicted the future of North American society.

The Handmaid's Tale is characterized by a fragmented narrative and disjointed subjectivity. The handmaid, Offred, is a reluctant narrator, periodically fictionalizing her life story when it becomes too painful for her to relate. The reader is presented with a set of competing narratives, one having no more authority than another. For example, Offred describes her affair with her lover, Nick, as sensual and erotic, only then to confess that their liaison did not actually happen in the way she has suggested. The second version of their meeting is characterized by the distance between them: they quote lines from films because they have no words of their own. Ultimately, Offred admits that neither of these stories is accurate. Not only does this scene exemplify the novel's use of fragmented narration, it demonstrates the way in which Atwood rejects conventional plot structures: there is no romantic "happy ending" to this tale.

Offred's refusal to relate a cohesive narrative creates a complicated relationship between the novel and its readers. For example, Gilead has deprived Offred of her name, supplying her instead with the patronymic Offred, or "of Fred," after the commander for whom she is handmaiden. Although Offred tells Nick what her name is, she does not disclose this information to the reader, denying the reader easy access to her character.

Offred's narrative is presented as a protest against the society and has political ramifications. In a nation where women are not allowed to read or write, a woman's autobiography is a dangerous weapon. Offred's own distrust of political movements ensures that she does not write her narrative *instead* of instigating revolution; rather, she demonstrates that telling women's stories is itself a revolutionary act. At times she breaks off from her autobiography to tell the stories of other women, because she finds their stories to be less painful than her own. In this manner she relates the story of Moira, a woman whom she views as assertive in a way she herself is unable to be, in Moira's voice. By recounting the stories of Moira and other women victimized by Gilead, the novel moves beyond the fictional autobiography of one woman to tell the story of a society of women.

One of the most significant aspects of *The Handmaid's Tale* is its conclusion, which departs from Offred's faltering, emotional narrative. The final section is entitled "Historical Notes on the Handmaid's Tale" and consists of excerpts from an academic conference studying Gilead in the year 2195. In these notes the academics express their regret that Offred chose to describe her emotions rather than political regimes, believing her story to be the "wrong" story. However, the final section also informs the reader that these academics have edited Offred's narrative. The novel therefore plays on the idea of authenticity and truth as the reader discovers that the preceding text was shaped by people who have no interest in Offred as a person.

The location of the academic conference is the University of Denay, Nunavit, a name that implicitly suggests that the reader should "deny none of it," reminding the reader of the importance of Offred's story. After the academics construct their own narrative around Offred's tale, the novel ends with a professor asking if there are any questions. This open-ended conclusion invites the reader to evaluate the conflicting narratives and then to create his or her own. *The Handmaid's Tale* offers a feminist perspective on the utopian novel tradition, serving to alert the reader to the problems of contemporary society. It is a postmodern tale that bridges the gap between science fiction, literature, and popular fiction. Its engagement with feminism makes it an inherently political novel that says as much about the position of women today as in a nightmarish fictional future.

ERIN STRIFF

See also Margaret Atwood

Further Reading

Bouson, J. Brooks, *Brutal Choreographies: Oppositional Strategies and Narrative Design in the Novels of Margaret Atwood,* Amherst: University of Massachusetts Press, 1993

Howells, Coral Ann, *Margaret Atwood,* London: Macmillan, and New York: St. Martin's Press, 1996

McCombs, Judith, editor, *Critical Essays on Margaret Atwood,* Boston: G.K. Hall, 1988

McCombs, Judith, and Carole L. Palmer, editors, *Margaret Atwood: A Reference Guide,* Boston: G.K. Hall, 1991

Nicholson, Colin, editor, *Margaret Atwood: Writing and Subjectivity*, New York: St. Martin's Press, 1994

VanSpanckeren, Kathryn, and Jan Garden Castro, editors, *Margaret Atwood: Vision and Forms*, Carbondale: Southern Illinois University Press, 1988

Wilson, Sharon R., Thomas B. Friedman, and Shannon Hengen, editors, *Approaches to Teaching Atwood's "The Handmaid's Tale" and Other Works*, New York: Modern Language Association of America, 1996

Thomas Hardy 1840–1928

English

Hardy is now generally recognized as the most important English novelist of the last quarter of the 19th century. His career began immediately after the death of Dickens, but he had a much closer affinity with George Eliot. Eliot's depictions of rural life in such works as *Adam Bede* (1859) and *Silas Marner* (1861) created a tradition on which Hardy consciously drew, as his contemporaries were quick to acknowledge. One of the leading English exponents of the regional novel, he set most of his stories in a landscape partly real, partly imaginary, and invoked in loving and deeply informed detail a culture at a particular phase of its history. His admiration for the work of Sir Walter Scott, the founding father of the regional novel in English, is significant in this respect. Some of Hardy's later novels are, among other things, experiments in a tragic mode that owes much to dramatic prototypes, especially Shakespeare and the Greek dramatists. This experimentation with dramatic form is evident as early as *The Return of the Native* (1878), in which the first five books correspond to the five acts of a Shakespearean play, while the final short book serves as an epilogue. In these and other respects, Hardy created a type of fiction that is distinctive and even idiosyncratic, while at the same time working (if sometimes uneasily) within established Victorian publishing conventions.

Hardy turned to the novel in his late 20s, after his initial attempts to publish poetry had met with failure. His first novel, never published and later destroyed, was titled *The Poor Man and the Lady,* which anticipates the recurring theme of social and economic divisions that pose an obstacle to love. This novel, known to have been satirical and "socialistic," was evidently the work of an angry young man. Hardy took the advice of the novelist George Meredith, who was then a publisher's reader, and did not attempt to publish it.

Apparently searching for a marketable variety of fiction, Hardy next turned his attention to the "sensation novel." This genre, popularized by Wilkie Collins and others in the 1860s, had proved immensely popular, but Hardy's *Desperate Remedies* (1871) was not a success. It was followed by *Under the Greenwood Tree* (1872), based on material from his own early life, which revealed a much surer touch. After two false starts, Hardy had come to terms with the fact that his humble rural origins, although a source of social discomfort, were a rich source of novelistic material. His first major success was another, more ambitious portrayal of rural life, *Far from the Madding Crowd* (1874), in which many reviewers detected the influence of George Eliot. Some, indeed, had suspected that the unsigned serial version might have been written by her.

All of Hardy's novels are love stories, and many of the early ones have happy endings, although these conclusions are sometimes reached by way of somber and even tragic events, including madness and murder in *Far from the Madding Crowd,* for instance. In the 1880s, however, Hardy's fiction took on a more serious cast, and *The Mayor of Casterbridge* (1886) inaugurates a series of great tragic novels that often include strong elements of social criticism, especially in relation to questions of love, sex, marriage, and divorce. Some of Hardy's contemporaries regarded his questioning of the institution of marriage as deeply subversive, and his later novels, especially *Tess of the d'Urbervilles* (1891) and *Jude the Obscure* (1895), while winning him a large readership throughout the English-speaking world, were bitterly attacked.

Hardy's diversity of aims and interests resulted in a remarkable formal eclecticism. *Tess,* for instance, is simultaneously a poetic and tragic love story, a depiction of rural life at a particular moment of English agrarian history, and an attack on Victorian sexual conventions. In terms of literary affinities, it may be said to have connections with ballad and folk song, with tragedy and (through its Miltonic allusions) epic, and with the propaganda novel or social-problem novel of the day. Part of the explanation must be that he was always a somewhat unwilling novelist whose deep interest in poetry and tragic drama found expression in fictions that were, outwardly at least, produced in conformity with the demands of the marketplace. As a result, Hardy's novels are difficult to characterize briefly.

In common with the work of earlier Victorian novelists such as Dickens, Thackeray, Trollope, and George Eliot, most of Hardy's novels appeared as serials in newspapers or magazines before achieving publication in volume form, which affected their form and content. Hardy himself readily admitted that serialization generated a superfluity of incident. His increasing frankness in dealing with sexual relationships brought him into conflict with editors and publishers of magazines intended for family reading: nervous of offending their readers, they compelled Hardy to bowdlerize or even "dismember" his own work. The latter word is used by Hardy in connection with *Tess,* which appeared at about the same time that an English publisher was imprisoned for publishing the work of Émile Zola: a reminder that very different standards prevailed in England and France.

Hardy's 14 published novels divide into two roughly equal groups, often designated "major" and "minor" (or "lesser"). In preparing a collected edition (the Wessex Edition) in 1912, he himself divided them into three groups, "Novels of Character and Environment," "Romances and Fantasies," and "Novels of Ingenuity." The first of these is the largest and contains all the novels traditionally regarded as major. Recent critics have recognized that the other groups also contain highly accomplished, if more experimental, work. It is revealing, for instance, that the short, very late novel *The Well-Beloved* (1897) was much admired by Marcel Proust. *The Hand of Ethelberta* (1876) may be regarded as an early example of the feminist novel.

Although Hardy's novels seem superficially to conform to Victorian structural conventions, his narrative technique is in many respects original. To a striking extent, for instance, he renounces the convention of the omniscient narrator in favor of a voyeuristic observer who draws conclusions from close scrutiny of the visible world but has no privileged access to the inner lives of the characters. Moreover, his sensibility, like his unconventional views on sexual morality and family life, is distinctively modern. He was an important influence on D.H. Lawrence, who read his work with close attention and wrote the posthumously published *Study of Thomas Hardy* (1985).

Hardy, who lived well into the modernist period, abandoned the novel more than 30 years before his death and devoted the rest of his life to poetry. The savage attacks of critics on his later work were no doubt partly responsible for this decision, but it is important to stress that poetry had always been his first love and that the financial independence afforded by his success as a novelist enabled him to devote himself to what he regarded as a superior mode of literary expression. He remains unique in English as a major novelist who is also a major poet, and his novels are often, in important ways and on several levels, poetic—not only in conception and form but in language and imagery. They have remained widely popular, not only throughout the English-speaking world but, through numerous translations, beyond it, while countless adaptations for theatre, radio, cinema, television, and opera have made the novels familiar to millions who have never opened Hardy's books.

NORMAN PAGE

See also Jude the Obscure; Tess of the d'Urbervilles

Biography

Born 2 June 1840 in Higher Bockhampton, Dorset. Attended local schools, 1848–56; articled to the ecclesiastical architect John Hicks in Dorchester, 1856–62. Continue his architectural training and worked as an assistant to Arthur Blomfield in London, 1862–67; returned to Dorset and set about writing fiction, 1867, while continuing to work as an architect in Dorset and London, 1867–72; began writing full-time in 1872; lived at Max Gate, Dorchester, from 1885. Justice of the peace for Dorset; member, Council of Justice to Animals. Died 11 January 1928.

Novels by Hardy

Desperate Remedies, 1871
Under the Greenwood Tree, 1872
A Pair of Blue Eyes, 1873
Far from the Madding Crowd, 1874
The Hand of Ethelberta, 1876
The Return of the Native, 1878
The Trumpet-Major, 1880
A Laodicean, 1881
Two on a Tower, 1882
The Mayor of Casterbridge, 1886
The Woodlanders, 1887
Tess of the d'Urbervilles, 1891
Jude the Obscure, 1895
The Well-Beloved, 1897

Other Writings: poetry, plays, short stories, essays; personal, literary, and architectural notebooks, published posthumously.

Further Reading

Boumelha, Penny, *Thomas Hardy and Women: Sexual Ideology and Narrative Form,* Brighton: Harvester, and Totowa, New Jersey: Barnes and Noble, 1982

Bullen, J.B., *The Expressive Eye: Fiction and Perception in the Work of Thomas Hardy,* Oxford: Clarendon Press, 1986

Cox, Reginald Gordon, editor, *Thomas Hardy: The Critical Heritage,* London: Routledge, and New York: Barnes and Noble, 1970

Ebbatson, Roger, *Hardy: The Margin of the Unexpressed,* Sheffield: Sheffield Academic Press, 1993

Garson, Marjorie, *Hardy's Fables of Integrity: Woman, Body, Text,* Oxford: Clarendon Press, and New York: Oxford University Press, 1991

Gatrell, Simon, *Hardy the Creator: A Textual Biography,* Oxford: Clarendon Press, and New York: Oxford University Press, 1988

Hands, Timothy, *Thomas Hardy,* London: Macmillan, and New York: St. Martin's Press, 1995

Higonnet, Margaret R., editor, *The Sense of Sex: Feminist Perspectives on Hardy,* Urbana: University of Illinois Press, 1993

Kramer, Dale, *Thomas Hardy: The Forms of Tragedy,* London and New York: Macmillan, 1975

Langbaum, Robert, *Thomas Hardy in Our Time,* London: Macmillan, and New York: St. Martin's Press, 1995

Meisel, Perry, *Thomas Hardy: The Return of the Repressed,* New Haven, Connecticut: Yale University Press, 1972

Miller, J. Hillis, *Thomas Hardy: Distance and Desire,* Cambridge, Massachusetts: Belknap Press of Harvard University Press, and London: Oxford University Press, 1970

Millgate, Michael, *Thomas Hardy: His Career as a Novelist,* London: Bodley Head, and New York: Random House, 1971

Morgan, Rosemarie, *Cancelled Words: Rediscovering Hardy,* London and New York: Routledge, 1992

Page, Norman, *Thomas Hardy,* London and Boston: Routledge, 1977

Taylor, Richard H., *The Neglected Hardy: Thomas Hardy's Lesser Novels,* London: Macmillan, and New York: St. Martin's Press, 1982

Harlem Renaissance. *See* African-American Novel; United States Novel (1900–1945)

Wilson Harris 1921–

Guyanese

In an early essay, Guyanese novelist Wilson Harris expressed the view that the novel of the West Indies "belongs—in the main—to the conventional mode" ("Tradition and the West Indian Novel," in *Tradition, the Writer, and Society,* 1967). Harris equates the "conventional mode" with realism and an approach that endeavors to persuade readers of the inevitability of given modes of behavior. Against this he posits the possibility of a mode of fiction that rejects "apparent common sense" for a dialectical attempt to achieve both a new aesthetic and a new view of personality. In the aforementioned essay Harris takes the view that most 20th-century novelists continue to write within "the framework of the nineteenth-century novel," and he sees this as inappropriate in the Caribbean and South American contexts, where social, historical, and even personal continuities have been fractured, particularly but not exclusively by the pre-Columbian/post-Columbian divide. In consequence Harris takes issue with writers such as V.S. Naipaul, whose *A House for Mr. Biswas* (1961) Harris views as a realist classic that "restricts the open and original ground of choice."

From the very beginning of his career Harris has committed his craft to open, dialogic structures that interrogate the staples of the classic European novel. He produced three drafts of his first novel, *Palace of the Peacock* (1960), before he eventually arrived at the technique that, with significant variations, has characterized all his subsequent fiction. It is a technique in which a dream-like logic blurs the distinction between actual and imagined events, in which past and present come together, in which the dead can be resurrected, subject can become object and vice versa, and the most fundamental tenets of post-Cartesian Western thought, such as the autonomy of the individual self, are collapsed. In *Palace of the Peacock,* the "I" narrator, who appears to dream most of the novel's events, has an alter ego, Donne, who on one level represents the fossilized condition of the colonial psyche. Donne, named after the 17th-century English poet, is an archetypal imperialist who leads a mixed crew representative of the various ancestral strands of the Guyanese people, or more generally of the crew of mankind, on a mission upriver into the country's heartland. This crew retraces the voyage of an earlier crew that has perished in the rapids, but past blurs with present as the interior journey unfolds in a manner reminiscent of Joseph Conrad's "Heart of Darkness" (1902). Both crews pursue the "folk," the pre-Columbian inhabitants of the region, but the possibility of a different outcome is always possible for the second group of plunderers, who in one sense are the first, just as Donne is the dreaming "I" narrator and vice versa. Harris' concern, one which is also developed in all his subsequent

fiction, is to disturb our habitual ways of perceiving experience and to open up new ways of revisioning events. In *Palace of the Peacock* and the three subsequent novels that make up the *Guyana Quartet—The Far Journey of Oudin* (1961), *The Whole Armour* (1962), and *The Secret Ladder* (1963)—Harris, who was a surveyor before he left Guyana to reside in England during the late 1950s, reinvents the Guyanese terrain as an open field in which alternative versions of human identity can be explored. *Palace of the Peacock,* which remains his best-known novel, culminates in a mystical vision of enlarged human possibilities in which deaths usher in a resurrection and Christian symbolism is fused with Amerindian myth.

Subsequent Harris novels draw extensively on a range of world mythologies. Although at times his influences (which include William Blake, T.S. Eliot, William Butler Yeats, and the writings of the medieval alchemists) may seem distinctively European, he also has made use of numerous elements from Arawak and Carib mythology and on occasion Afro-Caribbean folk forms, such as limbo and vodun. He has frequently noted the commonalities found in the world's various mythologies. This Jungian view is, however, resistant to the Barthean suggestion that such mythopoeia involves a kind of cosmic conservatism, since it precludes the possibility of transformation. Harris' work always insists on the fluidity of archetypes and the possibility of metamorphosing them.

In his more recent fiction Harris has increasingly stressed the cross-cultural nature of all experience, writing novels set in a variety of locations, including England, Scotland, and Mexico. *Jonestown* (1996) takes the People's Temple massacre, which occurred in the Guyanese interior in 1978 when American cult leader Jim Jones persuaded his followers to take their own lives, as its departure point and moves between Guyana and California. Once again the novel occupies characteristic Harris territory, suggesting that psychic regeneration offers the only real hope for human fulfillment. He expresses this via a method rooted in metaphorical transformations that departs sharply from the documentary-like reportage that has characterized other accounts of the Jonestown tragedy.

Harris' fascination with the esoteric side of the alchemical quest, which is concerned with spiritual rather than material values, finds a correlative in the New World myth of El Dorado; from *Palace of the Peacock* (which reaches its culmination in an El Dorado heartland) onward, all of Harris' subsequent fiction aspires toward the creation of a utopian spiritual vision. While the origins of the El Dorado myth may be in the Old World, his emphasis on the possibility of magical transformation has strong affinities with the shamanistic thinking of pre-Columbian American cultures. His fictional technique invites comparison with that of Latin American magic realism, and he has always stressed the continuities between Caribbean and Latin American experience. Yet at the same time his novels demonstrate a highly individual blend of poetry and prose, of religious and political thinking, and of European modernism and postcolonial resistance to categorization. In addition to his fiction, Harris has also published a number of critical books that both explain his own conception of the writer's task and comment on a wide range of other novelists. His numerous essays and talks are brought together in *Tradition, the Writer, and Society, Explorations* (1981), *The Womb of Space* (1983), and *The Radical Imagination* (1992).

JOHN THIEME

Biography
Born 24 March 1921 in New Amsterdam, British Guiana (now Guyana). Attended Queen's College, Georgetown. Worked as government surveyor during the 1940s, and senior surveyor, 1955–58, Government of British Guiana; moved to London in 1959. Since 1970 has taught at colleges and universities in the United States, England, Canada, Australia, India, and Jamaica.

Novels by Harris
The Guyana Quartet, 1985
  Palace of the Peacock, 1960
  The Far Journey of Oudin, 1961
  The Whole Armour, 1962
  The Secret Ladder, 1963
Heartland, 1964
The Eye of the Scarecrow, 1965

The Waiting Room, 1967
Tumatumari, 1968
Ascent to Omai, 1970
Black Marsden: A Tabula Rasa Comedy, 1972
Companions of the Day and Night, 1975
Da Silva da Silva's Cultivated Wilderness, and Genesis of the Clowns, 1977
The Tree of the Sun, 1978
The Angel at the Gate, 1982
Carnival, 1985
The Infinite Rehearsal, 1987
The Four Banks of the River of Space, 1990
Resurrection at Sorrow Hill, 1993
Jonestown, 1996

Other Writings: short stories, poetry, critical essays, lectures, and talks.

Further Reading
Gilkes, Michael, *Wilson Harris and the Caribbean Novel*, Trinidad and Jamaica: Longman Caribbean, 1975
Hearne, John, "The Fugitive in the Forest: Four Novels by Wilson Harris," in *The Islands in Between*, edited by Louis James, London: Oxford University Press, 1968
James, C.L.R., *Wilson Harris: A Philosophical Approach*, Trinidad and Tobago: University of the West Indies, 1965
Maes-Jelinek, Hena, *The Naked Design: A Reading of "Palace of the Peacock,"* Aarhus: Dangaroo Press, 1976
Maes-Jelinek, Hena, *Wilson Harris*, Boston: Twayne, 1982
Riach, Alan, and Mark Williams, editors, *The Radical Imagination: Lectures and Talks by Wilson Harris*, Liege: Liege and Literature, 1992

Nathaniel Hawthorne 1804–64

United States

Although Nathaniel Hawthorne judged his own work as "unsuccessful," he is now firmly established in the canon of American novelists and is a central figure in the American Renaissance. Renaissance writers, in F.O. Matthiessen's view, shared a common vision of the Puritan past and drew inspiration from it to create literature that, for the first time, was as good as anything written in Europe yet was uniquely American in character. Writers like Ralph Waldo Emerson, Henry David Thoreau, Herman Melville, and Hawthorne looked not only to the Puritan origins of American history but also to Puritan styles of rhetoric such as typology, allegory, and symbolism to create a distinctive American literary voice (see Matthiessen, 1941).

Hawthorne himself was acutely aware of his own Puritan roots. He had been born in Salem and was a descendant of a prominent Puritan family, which included the notorious hanging judge, John Hathorne, of the 17th-century witchcraft trials. In his fiction, Hawthorne pursues a fascination with the culture of his ancestors, in his preoccupation with colonial New England, with the dark side of Puritan theology, and with the decline of the theocracy and its complex legacy for Hawthorne's 19th-century America. Three novels from his most inspired period of creativity in the 1850s—*The Scarlet Letter* (1850), *The House of the Seven Gables* (1851), and *The Blithedale Romance* (1852)—share this focus.

Hawthorne's "The Custom-House" sketch, which appears prefatory to *The Scarlet Letter* and is based partly on his experience as surveyor of the Port of Salem, offers his most bitter indictment of the direction in which American history was moving. Hawthorne describes the city of Salem as decrepit and rotting, deserted of trade, human interest, and all its earlier grandeur. Into this setting, he introduces recollections of family stories concerning his earliest American ancestor, William, a persecutor of Quakers, and his son John, the unrepentant persecutor of witches. The decline in family status and prestige—from magistrate and judge to a surveyor in the customhouse—matches the decline of the city.

The ironic subtext of the preface suggests that the centuries have betrayed Hawthorne, depriving him of an environment where his artistic skills would have been properly appreciated. He initiates this subtext with a description of the statue of the federal eagle, that "unhappy fowl," which hovers menacingly at the entrance of the customhouse:

> Nevertheless, vixenly as she looks, many people are seeking, at this very moment, to shelter themselves under the wing of the federal eagle; imagining, I presume, that her bosom has all the softness and snugness of an eider-down pillow. But she has no great tenderness, even in her best of moods, and, sooner or later,—oftener soon than late,—is apt to fling off her nestlings with a scratch of her claw, a dab of her beak, or a rankling wound from her barbed arrows.

The story that follows tells of the earliest American victims—Hester Prynne, Arthur Dimmesdale, and Roger Chillingworth—of Puritan obsession, spiritual ferocity, and all-encompassing self-concern. With the decline of the theocracy, and in the absence of religious fervor, all that remains as the legacy of New England's colonial origins is the darkness and seriousness of the New England temper. Hawthorne interprets the spiritual history of New England for his contemporary world in which the importance of moral concerns has shrunk. His is a pessimistic view of the spiritual health and destiny of the United States. Destiny is more openly at issue in *The House of the Seven Gables*, in which a family legacy, passed down since the 17th century, operates as an inherited curse. The land taken from Matthew Maule by the man who condemned him to death, Judge Pyncheon, works upon generations of the Pyncheon family to emphasize their material and spiritual decline.

American culture, Hawthorne suggests, is too callow, too undeveloped, too lacking in history and sophisticated manners to offer the writer the materials appropriate to the novel form. As a consequence, he preferred to call his narrative fictions "romances" in recognition of the importance of allegory, symbolism, and emblematic expressions, as well as the emphasis on the abstract and spiritual. In the preface to *The House of the Seven Gables*, Hawthorne sets out precisely what he means by the distinction between the romance and the novel:

> [t]he latter form of composition is presumed to aim at a very minute fidelity, not merely to the possible, but to the probable and ordinary course of man's experience. The former—while, as a work of art, it must rigidly subject itself to laws, and while it sins unpardonably, so far as it may swerve aside from the truth of the human heart—has fairly a right to present that truth under circumstances, to a great extent, of the writer's own choosing or creation.

In prefatory essays to *The Scarlet Letter* and *The Blithedale Romance*, Hawthorne repeatedly emphasizes that his fiction should not be interpreted literally—first, because the fantasy will always be found inferior to the reality, and second, because such a reading misses the subtleties of the romancer's craft. Hawthorne

laments that in the Old World the writer is allowed a poetic license denied him in the New.

The Blithedale Romance is a case in point: set in a utopian New England community, the story is, as Hawthorne confesses in his preface, not unrelated to his own experience as a member of the Brook Farm community, which led to speculation about the possibility that the doomed heroine Zenobia is a portrait of the transcendentalist Margaret Fuller. In fact, contemporary reviewers found that such speculation lent the story most of its charm. Yet, for Hawthorne, the power of the romance to mediate between the real and the abstract made available a particular capacity for communication that could not be found in other literary forms. In the preface to *Twice-Told Tales* (1837; enlarged 1842), he insists that every sentence, "so far as it embodies thought or sensibility, may be understood and felt by anybody, who will give himself the trouble to read it, and will take up the book in a proper mood." It is the imagistic logic according to which the narratives operate—like the emblematic sympathy of nature to human feeling and the three contrasting scaffold scenes, which condense so much of the meaning of *The Scarlet Letter*—that conveys sensibility where other fictional forms would communicate mere reason.

Hawthorne wrote his fourth novel, *The Marble Faun* (1860), after his term as consul for the United States in Liverpool, England, and out of his experience touring the great cities of Europe. The Old World, rather than the New, provided inspiration for this novel, which is very different in theme and tone from the New England novels. Hawthorne questions the influence of European culture upon two American artists working in Rome, in a narrative that focuses on the loss of innocence and the birth of knowledge through suffering. In this respect, the novel may be seen as a precursor to the work of Henry James and Edith Wharton, exploring the "international theme" of American letters.

DEBORAH L. MADSEN

See also Scarlet Letter

Biography

Born Nathaniel Hathorne in Salem, Massachusetts, 4 July 1804. Attended Samuel Archer's School, Salem, 1819; Bowdoin College, Brunswick, Maine, 1821–25. Writer and contributor to periodicals, 1825–36; editor, *American Magazine of Useful and Entertaining Knowledge*, Boston, 1836; weigher and gager, Boston Customs House, 1839–41; invested in the Brook Farm Commune, West Roxbury, Massachusetts, and lived there, 1841–42; surveyor, Salem Customs House, 1846–49; US Consul, Liverpool, England, 1853–57; lived in Italy, 1858–59, and London, 1859–60. Died 19 May 1864.

Novels by Hawthorne

Fanshawe, 1828
The Scarlet Letter, 1850
The House of the Seven Gables, 1851
The Blithedale Romance, 1852
Transformation; or, The Romance of Monte Beni, 1860; as *The Marble Faun*, 1860
Septimius Felton, 1872; as *Septimius Felton; or, The Elixir of Life*, 1872
The Dolliver Romance, 1876
Dr. Grimshaw's Secret, 1883

Other Writings: tales and short stories, sketches, literature for children, notebooks, letters.

Further Reading

Baym, Nina, *The Shape of Hawthorne's Career,* Ithaca, New York: Cornell University Press, 1976

Bloom, Harold, editor, *Nathaniel Hawthorne,* New York: Chelsea House, 1986

Colacurcio, Michael J., editor, *New Essays on "The Scarlet Letter,"* Cambridge and New York: Cambridge University Press, 1985

Crews, Frederick C., *The Sins of the Fathers: Hawthorne's Psychological Themes,* New York: Oxford University Press, 1966

Fogle, Richard Harter, *Hawthorne's Fiction: The Light and the Dark,* Norman: University of Oklahoma Press, 1952; revised edition, 1964

Matthiessen, F.O., *American Renaissance: Art and Expression in the Age of Emerson and Whitman,* London and New York: Oxford University Press, 1941

Miller, J. Hillis, *Hawthorne and History: Defacing It,* Oxford and Cambridge, Massachusetts: Blackwell, 1990, 1991

Millington, Richard H., *Practicing Romance: Narrative Form and Cultural Engagement in Hawthorne's Fiction,* Princeton, New Jersey: Princeton University Press, 1992

Swann, Charles, *Nathaniel Hawthorne: Tradition and Revolution,* Cambridge and New York: Cambridge University Press, 1991

Hazarski rečnik. *See* Dictionary of the Khazars

Anne Hébert 1916–

Canadian

Anne Hébert's novels have been published by a major French publisher (Seuil) and a major Quebec publisher (Boréal), and they have won prestigious literary prizes and achieved significant sales figures (several have been widely taught and widely translated). They also play an important role in the intense dialectic of continuity and revolt within the evolution of the novel in Quebec and elsewhere.

The fantastic has had a significant presence in the evolution of the novel in Quebec. Fantastic elements in Hébert's first novel, *Les Chambres de bois* (1958; *The Silent Rooms*) include an isolated manor/château located deep in a dark woods, mysterious, cruel hunter-aristocrats, pent-up women gazing owlishly through flickering windows—an element recognized in the title of Maurice Émond's important book, *La femme à la fenêtre* (1984). Aurélie Caron, a character in Hébert's brilliant second novel, *Kamouraska* (1970; *Kamouraska*), is presented as a witch. The fantastic predominates in Hébert's *Les Enfants du sabbat* (1975; *Children of the Black Sabbath*): joining the witch is a sorcerer who may be Satan himself, and a myriad of horrific events follows. Hébert's title character in *Héloïse* (1980; *Heloise*) belongs to a community of vampires that dwells among abandoned Parisian subway stations.

Alongside the fantastic, rural realism constitutes another important current in the evolution of the Quebec novel. In Hébert's novels, the two elements often complement each other. In *Children of the Black Sabbath* the isolation and poverty of 1930s rural life facilitate the spell the sorcerer and witch are able to cast over the country folk. In so emphasizing rural isolation and unhappiness, Hébert's novel draws surprisingly close to Ringuet's famous debunking of the myth of idyllic peasant life in Quebec, *Trente arpents* (1938; *Thirty Acres*). Hébert's novel *Les Fous de Bassan* (1982; *In the Shadow of the Wind*), which won the Prix Fémina, shows an anglophone Protestant village, Griffin Creek, in which rural life is associated with similar problems as those depicted in *Children of the Black Sabbath*: poverty, family violence, sexual abuse, and incest, with the dominance of the pastor echoing that of the sorcerer/Satan. The semirural environment in which the youthful characters of *L'Enfant chargé de songes* (1992; *Burden of Dreams*) experiment with life and fall under the spell of another sorceress-like character, Lydia, who besots/bewitches both boy and girl and leads the latter to her death, also contributes to this depiction of life in nature as being woeful.

Hébert's most explicit novelistic meditation on the essence of Quebec, *Le Premier Jardin* (1988; *The First Garden*), shares significant elements with that earlier novelistic tradition, the pro-rural, pro-agriculture, pro-church *roman du terroir* (novel of the land) that her other novels reject. Hébert's *The First Garden* from its very title equates the beginnings of French life in the New World with no less idyllic a myth than the Garden of Eden before the Fall. An apple tree and bountiful fields sown by none other than Hébert's ancestor Louis Hébert (the first French farmer in New France) all contribute to a lionizing depiction of the struggle by a tiny, brave people to establish their own garden/space/nation despite the Iroquois, neglect and abandonment by France, and English military harassment, invasion, and conquest. The situation is more complex in Hébert's novella *Aurélien, Clara, Mademoiselle, et le lieutenant anglais* (1995; *Aurélian, Clara, Mademoiselle, and the English Lieutenant*) in which the rural-urban dichotomy is complicated by the foregrounding of a rural-rural dichotomy between agriculture and nature. Nature turns (agri)culture nightmarish with massive rainfalls and flooding that changes fields of crops into puddles of rot; yet nature is beautifully evoked in its richness of dense forest and denser scents, of brilliant sunshine and crystalline colors. Pathetic "adventurer" though he be, the exiled English lieutenant and the novella itself relate Hébert's corpus to yet another Québécois literary tradition, that of the wanderer, the adventurer, the *survenant,* the *coureur des bois,* living life in all its intensity and boredom, suffering and delight among the savage beauty and cruelty of the Canadian wilderness. The lieutenant's status as sexual abuser of children and yet instrument by which Clara attains a new stage in her discovery of life and reality and in her evolution toward adulthood illustrates the sometimes troubling dialectic in Hébert's work between evil and good and their often unexpected intertwining.

The tradition of urban realism is much less present in Hébert's novels. However, the opening lines of *The Silent Rooms,* which portray apocalyptic images of a mining town with its soot-blackened sky and flaming, fuming, sky-clawing smokestacks, are an example. The novel's implicit condemnation of this industrial universe connects Hébert's novels with the ecological current prevalent in so many literatures recently. *The Silent Rooms* also expresses social criticism, as it alludes to the despair of the unemployed. The Hébert corpus again echoes the thematics of urban realism in the seedy hotel where the final narrator concludes *In the Shadow of the Wind.*

Hébert's novels draw on and redirect two dominant novelistic strains in French Canadian writing: the historical novel and the psychological novel. Nineteenth-century French Canada placed enormous emphasis on its history as a way of ensuring identity and fueling the struggle for cultural survival. Important in this connection, *Kamouraska* is based on stories Hébert's mother had told her but also on historical research. Yet Hébert's *The First Garden* is her most reflectively historical novel. Two main characters—actress Flora Fontanges and Raphaël, a history student—devote much time to re-creating the world of New France, denouncing the female condition, and searching for the fundamental significance of the French presence in the New World and the Québécois/French-Canadian struggle to persevere. And while all Hébert's novels foreground the exploration of their characters' psychology and its development, *The Silent Rooms* focuses most closely on the psychological development of a limited number of characters.

Hébert's novels have also assumed a prominent position in more recent novelistic tendencies in French Canada, including the strong feminist current that runs through her writing. *The Silent Rooms,* however traditional its third part may seem (the new man in Catherine's life asks her to leave her present husband for him), in fact ends with Catherine keeping her options open. The novel presents a woman's evolution toward greater autonomy, self-fulfillment and happiness. *Kamouraska* is the moving tale of another woman's attempt, and failure, to so evolve in 19th-century Quebec. *Children of the Black Sabbath* and *The First Garden* denounce the oppression of women. The novel that has most often been viewed by critics as explicitly feminist is also often considered her finest masterpiece, *In the Shadow of the Wind,* although some critics have questioned its feminism. Writing techniques and themes characterizing the French *nouveau roman* and those associated with the postmodern novel are also richly present in Hébert's novels. Paterson (1985) has identified postmodern qualities in various Hébert novels, including intertextuality, textual specularity (references by the text to itself and its writing, to other works of art, and to artistic processes), and the reworking of the tradition of the historical novel.

While Hébert's novels have developed within an intense dialectic of continuity and clash, echo and renewal, that has taken place in the evolution of the Quebec novel, Hébert's originality is impressive and multifaceted. It ranges from her refutation of the traditional French-Canadian myths of woman as being naturally destined exclusively to the wife-mother role, of the church as always good in intent and act, of the agricultural destiny of the French-Canadian people, of men as benevolent protectors of women and children, of intersexual harmony, and of romantic love leading to "happily ever after" marriages to her meditations on the origins and fundamental significance of Quebec's history and existence, the dialogue between Quebec and France, the dialogue between francophone Quebec and native peoples' heritage, and between men and women. That originality is brilliantly demonstrated in her reversal of the French-English minority-majority dynamic, as her *In the Shadow of the Wind* transforms "White Anglo-Saxon Protestant" North America into a failing minority and then uses this inverted microcosm as an instrument to reflect on the reality of francophone Quebec/Canada. Fortunately, whatever the difficulties of francophone Quebec/Canada, its present state and future prospects seem better than those of the tiny, timorous WASP community of Griffin Creek—thanks largely to the sense of national pride and to the international presence that writers such as Anne Hébert have given to French Canada.

NEIL B. BISHOP

Biography
Born 1 August 1916 in Sainte-Catherine-de-Fossambault, Quebec. Attended Collège Saint-Coeur de Marie, Merici, Quebec, and Collège Notre Dame, Bellevue, Quebec. Worked for Radio Canada, 1950–53, and the National Film Board of Canada, 1953–54, 1959–60.

Novels and Novellas by Hébert
Les Chambres de bois, 1958; as *The Silent Rooms,* translated by Kathy Mezei, 1974

Kamouraska, 1970; as *Kamouraska,* translated by Norman Shapiro, 1973

Les Enfants du sabbat, 1975; as *Children of the Black Sabbath,* translated by Carol Duplon-Hébert, 1977

Héloïse, 1980; as *Heloise,* translated by Sheila Fischman, 1982
Les Fous de Bassan, 1982; as *In the Shadow of the Wind,* translated by Sheila Fischman, 1983
Le Premier Jardin, 1988; as *The First Garden,* translated by Sheila Fischman, 1990
L'Enfant chargé de songes, 1992; as *Burden of Dreams,* translated by Sheila Fischman, 1994
Aurélien, Clara, Mademoiselle, et le Lieutenant anglais, 1995; as *Aurélien, Clara, Mademoiselle, and the English Lieutenant,* translated by Sheila Fischman, 1996

Other Writings: short stories, poetry, and plays.

Further Reading

Bishop, Neil B., *Anne Hébert, son oeuvre, leurs exils,* Talence, France: Presses universitaires de Bordeaux, 1993
Émond, Maurice, *La femme à la fenêtre: L'univers symbolique d'Anne Hébert dans "Les chambres de bois,"* *"Kamouraska," et "Les enfants du sabbat,"* Quebec: Presses de l'Université Laval, 1984
Gould, Karen, "Absence and Meaning in Anne Hébert's *Les fous de Bassan,*" *The French Review* 59:6 (May 1986)
Green, Mary Jean, "The Witch and the Princess: The Feminine Fantastic in the Fiction of Anne Hébert," *American Review of Canadian Studies* 15:2 (1985)
Howells, Coral Ann, "Anne Hébert: *Héloïse,*" in *Private and Fictional Words: Canadian Women Novelists of the 1970s and 1980s,* London and New York: Methuen, 1987
Paterson, Janet M., *Anne Hébert: Architexture romanesque,* Ottawa: Presses de l'Université d'Ottawa, 1985
Russell, Delbert W., *Anne Hébert,* Boston: Twayne, 1983
Thériault, Serge A., *La quête d'équilibre dans l'oeuvre romanesque d'Anne Hébert,* Hull, Quebec: Asticou, 1980
Whitfield, Agnès, "*Kamouraska,* ou la Confession occultée," in *Le je(u) illocutoire: Forme et contestation dans le nouveau roman québécois,* Quebec: Presses de l'Université Laval, 1987

Ernest Hemingway 1899–1961

United States

Along with many of his American contemporaries—most notably F. Scott Fitzgerald, John Dos Passos, Sinclair Lewis, and William Faulkner—Ernest Hemingway reacted against the realist fiction of the late 19th and early 20th centuries, represented by the works of Mark Twain, Henry James, and William Dean Howells. Although Hemingway admired Mark Twain, much of the realist writing of the period appeared to him outmoded and quaint when read in the context of the horrors of World War I. In his own writing, Hemingway created a distinctive form of modernist prose that strove to go beyond the realism of American writers in its attempt not merely to describe a scene or record a dialogue for the reader, but to write in such a way that the reader would actually experience the emotion felt by the author.

Because of his commitment to the recreation of emotional experience, Hemingway's fiction is deliberately devoid of allusion. His language is simple and concrete, yet his words are combined in highly original patterns. Because he strove to write only what was true, his work is completely devoted to the artistic recreation of his own experience.

Hemingway insisted that a skillful writer could leave out material that the astute reader would sense and, thereby, give weight and dignity to spare prose. He told an interviewer that he "always wrote on the principle of the iceberg. There is seven eighths of it under water for every part that shows. Anything you know you can eliminate and it only strengthens your iceberg. It is the part that doesn't show. If a writer omits something because he does not know it then there is a hole in the story" (see Baker, 1961). In good modernist fashion, Hemingway's fiction demands that the reader participate in making sense of his words by filling in the gaps or by looking under the surface for meaning implied by the author's artful omissions.

Hemingway's modernist style is linked closely to his thematic concerns. Like his disillusioned contemporaries, he mistrusted the ideas of earlier generations of novelists and therefore refused, in large part, to use their words and prose style. Because abstract words such as *faith, courage, patriotism, sacrifice, nobility,* and *honor* had come to mean something very different to Hemingway and other World War I veterans, he favored simple words grounded in actual experience. His use of simple, concrete prose was not merely a stylistic ideal, but a deliberate attempt to write more truthfully.

Because his work contains elements of determinism and doom, some critics characterize Hemingway as a naturalist or even a nihilist. His view of life was tragic, but not hopeless, and although his characters suffer and most of his novels end in defeat, he insisted that meaning can be found in daily existence. His work is suffused with references to natural beauty, to the satisfaction of hard work, to the pride in doing a task well, to the joy of companionship (mostly male), and to a spirit of endurance in the face of pain and loss. His characters may be destroyed, but they are not defeated; they may eventually die, but they succeed in their struggle to find meaning.

After a sophomoric attempt to satirize the prose of Sherwood Anderson in *The Torrents of Spring* (1926), Hemingway burst onto the literary scene with the publication of *The Sun Also Rises* (1926). The novel is truly modern in style and theme. It tells the story of various victims of World War I who turn to alcohol, violence, and irresponsible sex in an attempt to cope with their despair. Although his language is simple, Hemingway uses understatement and omission to show how the old beliefs that sustained pre–World War I Americans have been destroyed. In their place, Hemingway offers the beauty and permanence of nature (the sun may go down, but it also rises), the commitment of workers to their assigned tasks, and the companionship of men of similar interests. The war has left Hemingway's protagonist Jake Barnes impotent, but he is a survivor, portrayed in stark contrast to his burned-out friends. The reader is left with the characters' sense of futility, but also with a sense that the core values of human experience will endure.

Hemingway's second major novel, *A Farewell to Arms* (1929), documents his generation's loss of faith in traditional mores and ends in tragic loss. Nevertheless, the novel is not without hope. Frederic Henry, the protagonist, comes of age while retreating from the front with the Italian army. In a simple prose style that deliberately contradicts the ornate language of hallow patriotism, Henry recounts his farewell to the slaughter and hypocrisy of the war and retreats to Switzerland with his love Catherine Barkley. In the Swiss Alps they find solace and meaning in each other and in the grandeur of nature. Catherine and their unborn child die at the end of the novel, leaving Henry despondent and alone, but his experience saves him from nihilism.

To Have and Have Not (1937), Hemingway's novel about a Key West rum-runner, lacks the continuity, subtlety, and substance of his other work. Originally conceived as a long short story, its failings may be traced to its being written in fits and starts over a period of several years.

For Whom the Bell Tolls (1940), Hemingway's long novel about the Spanish Civil War, describes the interaction between members of a loyalist guerrilla band and Robert Jordan, an American volunteer sent by loyalist officers to blow up a bridge behind fascist lines. Faulted by American leftist writers for his depiction of loyalist (communist) as well as fascist atrocities in the novel, Hemingway, who supported the loyalists, defended his novel by arguing that he wrote fiction, not propaganda. At the end of the novel, Robert Jordan dies, yet throughout the novel Hemingway celebrates the beauty of nature, self-sacrifice, the sustaining power of love, and the interconnectedness of all human beings.

After coming dangerously close to self-parody in *Across the River and into the Trees* (1950), Hemingway established himself as America's preeminent novelist with the publication of *The Old Man and the Sea* (1952). The story of Santiago, an old Gulf Stream fisherman, depicts a world filled with struggle, pain, and loss but also shows how a human being may find meaning in such a tragic world. In this novel Hemingway uses his protagonist's skill as a fisherman to comment on his own skill as a writer. In describing Santiago's desire to fish far beyond the limits of ordinary fishermen, he describes his own desire to go beyond the ordinary literary practices and conventions practiced by other authors. Hemingway also articulated his intent to transcend the work of others in his acceptance speech for the Nobel prize for literature in 1954: "For a true writer each book should be a new beginning where he tries again for something that is beyond attainment. He should always try for something that has never been done or that others have tried and failed. Then sometimes, with great luck, he will succeed. How simple the writing of literature would be if it were only necessary to write in another way what has been well written. It is because we have had such greater writers in the past that a writer is driven far out past where he can go out to where no one can help him."

Hemingway's unique prose style, which today sounds so familiar because it has been so often imitated, owes its develop-

ment to Hemingway's courage to go "far out past" where other writers had gone, and his reputation as one of the world's major novelists can be traced to his consistent affirmation of the true and beautiful in a world that often seems so trivial and bleak. Hemingway's contributions to the development of the novel, then, are twofold: his courageous, innovative style and his unflinching commitment to the truth. His style—characterized by simple, understated prose, realistic dialogue, concrete nouns, and spare, objective descriptions—is a deliberate attempt to recreate for the reader meaningful experience and is, therefore, inextricably linked to his passion for truth-telling. In his best writing, Hemingway records the truth and in so doing affirms the tragicomic nature of human existence.

KURT J. KRUEGER

See also Farewell to Arms; Sun Also Rises

Biography

Born 21 July 1899 in Oak Park, Illinois. Attended Oak Park High School, graduated 1917. Reporter, Kansas City *Star*, 1917; Red Cross ambulance driver in Italy, 1918; also served on the western front with the Italian Arditi: wounded in action; reporter, then foreign correspondent, Toronto *Star* and *Star Weekly*, 1920–23; moved to Paris, 1921, and became associated with the expatriate community, whose members included Gertrude Stein and Ezra Pound; reported on the Greco-Turkish War, 1922; Paris correspondent for Hearst newspapers, 1924–27; moved to Key West, Florida, 1928, Cuba, 1940, and Idaho, 1958; war correspondent for North American Newspaper Alliance, in Spain, 1937–38, and for *Collier's* in Europe, 1944–45. Awarded Nobel prize for literature, 1954. Died (suicide) 2 July 1961.

Novels by Hemingway

The Torrents of Spring: A Romantic Novel in Honor of the Passing of a Great Race, 1926
The Sun Also Rises, 1926; as *Fiesta*, 1927
A Farewell to Arms, 1929
To Have and Have Not, 1937
For Whom the Bell Tolls, 1940
Across the River and into the Trees, 1950
The Old Man and the Sea, 1952
Islands in the Stream, 1970 (posthumous)
The Garden of Eden, 1986 (posthumous)

Other Writings: journalism, short stories, verse, plays, autobiography.

Further Reading

Baker, Carlos, *Hemingway: The Writer as Artist*, Princeton, New Jersey: Princeton University Press, 1952; 4th edition, 1972
Baker, Carlos, *Hemingway and His Critics: An International Anthology*, New York: Hill and Wang, 1961
Baker, Carlos, *Ernest Hemingway: A Life Story*, New York: Scribner, and London: Collins, 1969
Beegel, Susan F., *Hemingway's Craft of Omission: Four Manuscript Examples*, Ann Arbor, Michigan: UMI Research Press, 1988
Bush, Frederick, "Reading Hemingway without Guilt," *The New York Times Book Review* (12 January 1992)

Griffin, Peter, *Less Than a Treason: Hemingway in Paris,* New York: Oxford University Press, 1990

Gurko, Leo, *Ernest Hemingway and the Pursuit of Heroism,* New York: Crowell, 1958

Lynn, Kenneth S., *Hemingway,* London and New York: Simon and Schuster, 1987

Mellow, James R., *Hemingway: A Life Without Consequences,* Boston: Houghton Mifflin, 1992; London: Hodder and Stoughton, 1993

Reynolds, Michael, *Hemingway: The 1930s,* New York: Norton, 1997

Wagner-Martin, Linda, editor, *Ernest Hemingway: Six Decades of Criticism,* East Lansing: Michigan State University Press, 1987

Young, Philip, *Ernest Hemingway: A Reconsideration,* New York: Harcourt Brace, 1966

Hero. *See* Character

A Hero of Our Time by Mikhail Lermontov

Geroi nashego vremeni 1840

Mikhail Lermontov's *A Hero of Our Time* is the first major Russian novel—that is, the first lengthy, original prose narrative in Russian depicting a recognizable world peopled by realistic characters and wielding an enduring influence on subsequent Russian literature. In the half century prior to *A Hero of Our Time,* when the modern Russian literary tradition was in its formative phase, prose fiction had consisted mainly of short narratives, such as romances, adventure stories, society tales, and travel notes, along with some minor novels weakly imitating Western European sentimental, Gothic, or historical fiction and known today only to specialists. Even the single prose novelistic foray of Russia's great writer Aleksandr Pushkin, *Kapitanskaia dochka* (1836; *The Captain's Daughter*), merits attention primarily because Pushkin wrote it; its simple style, historical subject matter, and conventional characterizations left few lasting reverberations and failed to resolve the debates then flourishing over what would constitute an authentically Russian novel. *A Hero of Our Time* was different. Strikingly innovative and contemporary in language, subject, and characterizations, it charted a new literary course for Russia and at last began laying those debates over the novel to rest.

The short-lived Lermontov (1814–41) was an unlikely pioneer of the novel. While actively pursuing a military career, he gained fame in Russia as a poet and then took up prose on the side, penning a few short stories and two unfinished novels before turning in 1837 to *A Hero of Our Time,* in which he episodically portrays incidents and reflections scattered over five years in the life of the main protagonist, Grigorii Pechorin, a Russian army officer posted to the then-exotic region of the Caucasus. After publishing several sections of the novel in the Russian journal *Otechestvennye zapiski* (*Notes of the Fatherland*) during 1839 and 1840, Lermontov brought out the complete version in 1840, followed by a second edition in 1841 that included an author's introduction responding to hostile criticisms of the work. Those criticisms, voicing a conservative nationalism, condemned the novel as factitious and un-Russian, while reviling Pechorin as vicious and amoral; even Czar Nicholas I worried that the novel would rouse contempt for humanity through its cynical rendering of human relations and behavior. But *A Hero of Our Time* also had its staunch contemporary defenders, including the politically liberal, preeminent literary critic of the day, Vissarion Belinskii, who deemed Pechorin a perfectly valid representative of his country and his time. Belinskii also reproached critics who found the work's structure and style insufficiently coherent to justify the label of a novel, arguing that its extended, persuasive presentation of a psychologically compelling protagonist fully qualified it as an exemplar of this modern genre.

It is true that the structure and style of *A Hero of Our Time* are markedly disjointed. The role of narrator in its five chapters shifts among three different characters: a nameless traveler journeying through the Caucasian mountains, an old army officer traveling with him who had once served with Pechorin, and Pechorin himself through excerpts from his diary, which the nameless traveler has ostensibly obtained and published after Pechorin's death. The novel is further complicated both structurally and stylistically by the nonchronological sequence of the five chapters and by each one's affinities with a different literary genre: the travelogue, the physiological sketch, the adventure story, the society tale, and the philosophical *conte.*

Nonetheless, as Belinskii had observed, despite its structural and stylistic disjunctures, *A Hero of Our Time* gets all the unity a novel needs from its central character, for the progressive disclosure of Pechorin's remarkable nature subtly binds the disparate chapters together. Gradually revealed to be at once arrogant and insecure, callous and sensitive, perceptive and oblivious, Pechorin is the first highly complex personality in Russian prose fiction. He also contributes to the Russian literary tradition as its first prose embodiment of that conspicuously Russian literary character type "the superfluous man," affording a telling counterpart to the kindred eponymous character of Pushkin's famed narrative poem *Evgenii Onegin* (1831; *Eugene Onegin*). Intelligent and willful, yet doomed to social alienation, aimlessness, inactivity, and dissatisfaction, this character type appears prominently in the fiction of virtually every notable Russian author after Lermontov—including Ivan Turgenev (who christened the type in a short story of 1850, "Dnevnik lishnego cheloveka" ["Diary of a Superfluous Man"]), Ivan Goncharov, Fedor Dostoevskii, Lev Tolstoi, and Anton Chekhov—down to the Russian Revolution.

Pechorin is a particularly self-absorbed and self-revealing superfluous man. Hungering for the grandeur and renown of a romantic hero, he lacks the virtues to become one. And he knows it, bluntly confessing to hypocrisy, betrayal, and even murder. This very knowledge makes Pechorin at most a different kind of hero. A failed romantic, he becomes a protorealist, prizing his hideous self-awareness over any ennobling self-affirmation—and rendering *A Hero of Our Time,* according to many critics, the first Russian novel of psychological realism. Pechorin is thus more than simply superfluous; he serves as a forerunner of the full-fledged modern "antihero" created by Dostoevskii in *Zapiski iz podpol'ia* (1864; *Notes from Underground*), the Underground Man, whose chief virtues, like Pechorin's, are keen intelligence and shocking self-knowledge. Ultimately, however, these virtues act upon Pechorin just as they do upon the Underground Man: they expose a character of disturbing psychological depravity.

But Lermontov did not create Pechorin solely to depict a depraved psyche. In the introduction to the novel's second edition, Lermontov faults his own society (including its literary critics) for failing to recognize the irony of the work's title, explaining that he had created the figure of Pechorin to represent "all the vices of our generation." Hence, in an ironic sense, Pechorin does indeed constitute a "hero" of his time, a time Lermontov believed to be as ignoble, alienated, spiritually atrophied, and morally bankrupt as Pechorin himself. And yet Lermontov offers no remedy for this condition. "Suffice it that the disease has been pointed out," he concludes the introduction, "God knows how to cure it." *A Hero of Our Time* is therefore in essence a psychological, social, and ethical diagnosis; it would remain to future generations of Russian writers to find the cure.

ELIZABETH CHERESH ALLEN

Further Reading

Barratt, Andrew, and A.D.P. Briggs, *A Wicked Irony: The Rhetoric of Lermontov's "A Hero of Our Time,"* Bristol: Bristol Classical, 1989

Chances, Ellen, *Conformity's Children: An Approach to the Superfluous Man in Russian Literature,* Columbus, Ohio: Slavica, 1978

Eikhenbaum, Boris, *Lermontov: A Study in Literary-Historical Evaluation,* Ann Arbor, Michigan: Ardis, 1981

Freeborn, Richard, "*A Hero of Our Time,*" in *The Rise of the Russian Novel,* Cambridge: Cambridge University Press, 1973

Garrard, John Gordon, *Mikhail Lermontov,* Boston: Twayne, 1982

Gilroy, Marie, *The Ironic Vision in Lermontov's "A Hero of Our Time,"* Birmingham: University of Birmingham, 1989

Mersereau, John, Jr., "Lermontov's Fiction and Psychological Realism," in *Russian Romantic Fiction,* Ann Arbor, Michigan: Ardis, 1983

Nabokov, Vladimir, "Translator's Foreword," in Mikhail Lermontov's *A Hero of Our Time,* Garden City, New York: Doubleday, 1958

Todd, William Mills, III, "*A Hero of Our Time*: The Caucasus as 'Amphitheater'," in *Fiction and Society in the Age of Pushkin,* Cambridge, Massachusetts: Harvard University Press, 1986

Herzog by Saul Bellow

1964

When *Herzog* first appeared in 1964, it was immediately heralded as a masterpiece. A successful best-seller, it went on to win the National Book Award for fiction in 1965. Readers responded to Saul Bellow's scorching attack on fashionable literary pessimism and his emphasis on the duties and responsibilities—rather than the rights and freedoms—of the human being. When his hero derided the "cheap mental stimulants of Alienation," there were cheers from readers tired of a diet of James Joyce, Gustave Flaubert, George Eliot, and Charles Baudelaire and ready for the more politically-conscious 1960s. There were, nonetheless, some dissenting voices. John W. Aldridge described the novel as "heaving a fatty sigh of middle-class intellectual contentment" (see Wilson, 1990), while Richard Poirier detected sentimentalism and a failure to acknowledge the extent to which Bellow himself peddled the Waste Land outlook (see Rovit, 1975). In general, however, the novel struck a popular chord.

Herzog's wife throws him out in October 1963, a month before the assassination of John F. Kennedy, and Herzog's post-divorce grief focused the grief and betrayal of a nation.

Herzog was a much revised and carefully crafted novel, with 20 different versions surviving in manuscript. In formal terms the novel was remarkable for building its themes into its structure. In rejecting the therapeutic emphasis of American culture, Bellow mounted a thoroughgoing attack on popular Freudianism. The novel begins and ends with Herzog on the couch ("If I am out of my mind, it's all right with me" is his opening statement). Bellow's protagonist goes over the past repetitively and in ever-receding terms, from the recent to the not-so-recent in a fashion that suggests a flight into neurosis and an escape into the deepest recesses of the psyche. Employing an intricately organized time scheme (brilliantly analyzed by Alexandre Maurocordato, 1969), Bellow targets the core idea of psychoanalysis as the attempt to emancipate the patient from the burden of history, underlining the extent to which popular psychoanalysis offers an attractive possibility of avoiding the political context. The novel also contains a series of unsent letters addressed to such public figures as Martin Luther King, Jr., Eisenhower, Hegel, Nietzsche, and Nehru. Through this formal device Bellow offers an image of an alternative flight into history, which is portrayed as massively dwarfing the individual. Both psychoanalysis and history absolve the individual from responsibility for himself and for his own particular history, surrendering to the determinism of psychoanalytic mechanisms or to all-encompassing historical movements. The formal strategies of the novel therefore raise the question of the individual's position in history. Is history essentially neurosis? Or is Herzog's neurosis the product of his involvement, as a scholar and an intellectual, in the history of culture? Each view of the novel has found forceful proponents. John J. Clayton understands *Herzog* as primarily a study in neurosis, specifically in sadomasochism and the Oedipal complex (see Clayton, 1979; also notable for discussing the antifeminism of Bellow's protagonist). In Harold J. Mosher's analysis, however, Herzog's problem is not an ahistorical tendency but an excessive commitment to his historical role: he escapes responsibility for his actions by locating them in world history (see Mosher, 1971). An alternative reading argues that the novel marks a decisive break with victim literature, as opposed to such earlier works as *Dangling Man* (1944), *The Victim* (1947), or *Seize the Day* (1956), and that the action makes Herzog see that history is neither curse nor supreme value but the medium in which both he (and implicitly the reader) must make difficult moral judgments (see Newman, 1984). As Herzog remarks, "You must start with injustices that are obvious to everybody, not with big historical perspectives." A crucial example is offered in the climactic scene of the novel, in which Herzog witnesses a trial. Prophetically, given the late 20th-century furor over the so-called false memory syndrome and the moral panic over the welfare of children, the case concerns child abuse. Herzog's wife Madeleine was abused as a child, as was Herzog himself, but where she allows her victim status to control her life, he refuses to embrace the victim role, insisting upon the need for individual responsibility. Although real suffering is firmly foregrounded, the novel mounts a strenuous resistance to the therapeutic model of the permanently traumatized individual. However, the novel closes on a note of lyricism that seems to undo this conclusion. Finally, the danger remains that Herzog's movement from unanchored ideas to "obvious" moral injustices caters to a dominant strain of American anti-intellectualism.

The problematic relationship of author-narrator-character in *Herzog* anticipates the critical problems posed (and the rewards offered) by Bellow's later novels. Herzog may not be a mere mouthpiece for Bellow, but it remains difficult to locate an external point from which to judge him. All the action is filtered through his mind. As Peter Hyland has noted, the potentially autobiographical elements of the novel fuel the identification of author and character (see Hyland, 1992). Herzog's immigrant background in Montreal is similar to Bellow's, and Bellow's own bitter divorce was a factor in some readers' minds. Later novels—*Mr. Sammler's Planet* (1970), *Humboldt's Gift* (1975), *The Dean's December* (1982), and *More Die of Heartbreak* (1987)—intensified the monologic quality of the fiction and the lack of external action. More positively, however, the engagement with the past launched Bellow on his major theme. If amnesia is, as Gore Vidal reputedly remarked, America's middle name, memory is Bellow's. After *Herzog,* the remembrance of things past becomes the central focus of Bellow's fiction, even in such short stories as "Cousins" and "A Silver Dish" (both 1984) and the novella *The Bellarosa Connection* (1989).

JUDIE NEWMAN

See also Saul Bellow

Further Reading

Clayton, John J., *Saul Bellow: In Defense of Man,* Bloomington: Indiana University Press, 1968; 2nd edition, 1979

Fuchs, Daniel, *Saul Bellow: Vision and Revision,* Durham, North Carolina: Duke University Press, 1984

Hyland, Peter, *Saul Bellow,* London: Macmillan, and New York: St. Martin's Press, 1992

Josipovici, Gabriel, *The World and the Book: A Study of Modern Fiction,* London: Macmillan, and Stanford, California: Stanford University Press, 1971; 3rd edition, London: Macmillan, 1994

Maurocordato, Alexandre, *Les Quatre dimensions du "Herzog" de Saul Bellow,* Paris: Lettres Modernes, 1969

Mosher, Harold J., "The Synthesis of Past and Present in Saul Bellow's *Herzog,*" *Wascana Review* 6:1 (1971)

Newman, Judie, *Saul Bellow and History,* London: Macmillan, and New York: St. Martin's Press, 1984

Rovit, Earl, editor, *Saul Bellow: A Collection of Critical Essays,* Englewood Cliffs, New Jersey: Prentice-Hall, 1975

Wilson, Jonathan, *"Herzog": The Limits of Ideas,* Boston: Twayne, 1990

Hermann Hesse 1877–1962

German

Hesse's literary career is divided by what he wrote before and after 1917. Until that year he had established himself as a talented, entertaining, but superficial storyteller. The major studies devote minimal space to that period. The turning point occurred between 1914 and 1917. The vicious public reaction to his anti-war essays and several personal calamities brought him so near a nervous collapse that his physician recommended psychoanalysis, which he underwent in 1916–17. He emerged rejuvenated, producing vital, energetic, and troubling works on the human condition.

The first product of the new Hesse is the phenomenal best-seller *Demian* (*Demian*), which he wrote in 1917 but published in 1919. Like Hesse's subsequent novels, *Demian* is a Bildungsroman (novel of education, apprentice), a form that most contemporary novelists regarded as obsolete. Typically it depicts the protagonist's often arduous struggle for enlightenment. For Hesse the final stage involved a spiritual rebirth similar to his own. He believed that beyond the everyday world there exists a realm of supreme unity where all polarities are reconciled. This Third Kingdom (*Drittes Reich*), as he called it until 1933, is not unlike the Christian millennium or the Golden Age of the ancient Greeks. It is a spiritual realm of eternal values that exists independently of the phenomenal world. His main concern is now the quester's struggle to attain that realm. This basic pattern prevails with each configuration of characters.

Also characteristic of the Bildungsroman is the spiritual guide who assists the hero in his quest and who initiates him into the principles of the group he represents—usually a secret society. As Sinclair's mentor Max Demian introduces him to the precepts of Christian Gnosticism, according to which self-knowledge is equivalent to knowledge of the godhead and consequently the temporal experience of the Third Kingdom. Each of his following novels features the seeker-mentor relationship; Vasudeva and Kamala to Siddhartha; Pablo and Hermine to Harry Haller; Narcissus to Goldmund; the Music Master to Josef Knecht.

Siddhartha (1922; *Siddhartha*) is structured like *Demian* in that instead of a tightly knit plot there is a series of loosely connected episodes that influence Siddhartha's spiritual and emotional maturation, culminating in his final illumination. Siddhartha's spiritual awakening is informed by his ability to perceive the relationship of all things to one another and experience the world as simultaneity and totality, which is symbolized by the river. Most of Hesse's novels display a symbol for totality: Demian's Abraxas, Harry Haller's Magic Theater, Goldmund's *magna mater,* the glass bead game. Like Hesse's other tortured self-seekers, Siddhartha gains his goal not by following conventional systems but by going his own way. In his essay "My Faith" (1931) Hesse stated "that my *Siddhartha* . . . disdains dogma and makes the experience of unity the central point."

Der Steppenwolf (1927; *Steppenwolf*) is also a quester novel. The difference is that Harry Haller has given up the search. He is forced against his will by Hermine and Pablo to resume the quest. Harry's education culminates in the Magic Theater, where he learns to stop viewing himself and the world as composed of irreconcilable polarities; he learns also that opposites exist only

in the mind and are the chief cause of human misery. Although Harry is denied entrance into the spiritual realm until he has achieved psychic harmony, he is permitted, like Moses, to glimpse the promised land: once when he interviews Goethe in a drunken dream, and again when he meets Mozart in a narcotic fantasy. The novel ends optimistically. Although Harry has not attained his goal, he now knows how.

Hesse's primary innovation in *Steppenwolf* consists in structuring the novel according to the sonata form: exposition, development, recapitulation. The exposition states one major and one minor theme (Wolf-bourgeois). The development explores the possibilities of each one (despair, Hermine and her world). Recapitulation restates the themes in the same key and resolves the conflict (the Magic Theater). Music as a structural principle was also employed by Hesse's contemporaries Hermann Broch and Thomas Mann.

The reconciliation of nature and spirit is also the theme of *Narziss und Goldmund* (1930; *Narcissus and Goldmund*). Hesse wants to show that totality can be apprehended in different ways. Narcissus is the personification of mind, the intellectual who delights in words and abstractions. Goldmund is the extroverted artist, the personification of nature and the flesh who devotes his life to seeking the memory of his mother, and beyond her the primal mother of all humanity. Spirit and nature are reconciled through his art, as he gives form to the spirit and so renders the transitory eternal.

Das Glasperlenspiel (1943; *The Glass Bead Game*) is Hesse's last novel. It depicts the development of Josef Knecht from boyhood to his elevation as *magister ludi* (another title under which this novel has appeared in English), his defection from Castalia, and his death. The action takes place in the utopian setting of Castalia around the year 2400. The inhabitants are an elite group of intellectuals who devote their lives exclusively to playing the glass bead game, an act of synthesis in which all knowledge—scientific, humanistic, cultural, and spiritual—is seen as simultaneously present. The novel also warns of the danger inherent in pure intellectualism. The Castalians have become insensitive to the needs of the outside world. When Knecht awakens to this problem he leaves the order to serve the living world (*Knecht*: "the servant"). Knecht's poetry and the three lives appended to the novel emphasize the relationship between service to the community and spiritual fulfillment.

Critics have sought to classify Hesse variously as a romantic or as an existentialist, since he displays tendencies of each. He is neither one systematically. He is, in fact, a transitional figure. From romanticism he borrows form and style and the belief in a transcendental ideal of unity, which finds expression in *Siddhartha*. At the same time he anticipates such thinkers as Jean-Paul Sartre and Albert Camus and their doctrine of freedom and responsibility in a meaningless world, which is best exemplified in *Demian* and *Steppenwolf*. This ambivalence is also characteristic of many of Hesse's contemporaries.

Hesse's importance to the development of the novel of education resides in his extensive experimentation. While the underlying theme of the novels remains the traditional one of self-realization, he altered the form radically to suit his own needs. He demonstrated how the genre can be employed for autobiography as well as for psychology and social criticism. *Demian* is the first novel to incorporate Carl Jung's speculations about the role of the unconscious in the development of the individual, thus showing that the Bildungsroman can also function as a psychoanalytical novel. *Steppenwolf* represents a further development. In a unique twist, Hesse turns the genre upside down so that it becomes an *Umbildungsroman* (novel of re-education). The cynical, aging Harry learns that he must renounce the values that are the cause of his misery and go backward rather than forward to recapture the innocence and unity of his youth.

Likewise, *The Glass Bead Game,* as an apprentice novel, far exceeds the traditional limits. It is both biographical and autobiographical. It projects our Western cultural traditions far into the future to their logical conclusion, making it a utopian novel. It is also dystopian by virtue of its social and political criticism. Furthermore, it successfully incorporates characteristics of the roman à clef, containing a multitude of thinly veiled references to actual places and people in Hesse's life.

Thus Hesse expanded the Bildungsroman form in new directions by inventing new narrative techniques and by experimenting with new literary structures. He, along with Thomas Mann, is directly responsible for that form's resurgence in modern literature.

JOHN D. SIMONS

See also Steppenwolf

Biography
Born 2 July 1877 in Calw, Württemberg, Germany. Attended Basle Mission; Rector Otto Bauer's Latin school, Göppingen, 1890–91; Protestant Seminary, Maulbronn, 1891–92; Cannstatt Gymnasium, 1892–93. Apprentice, clock factory in Calw, 1894–95; apprentice, Heckenhauer bookshop in Tübingen, 1895–98, then assistant, 1898–99; worked for booksellers in Basle, 1899–1903; freelance writer from 1903; editor, *März,* 1907–15; coeditor, *Vivos Voco,* 1919–20; also editor of publishers' book series in 1910s and 1920s; regular contributor to *Corona* and *Bonniers Litterära Magasin* in 1930s. Lived in Gaienhofen, Germany, 1904–12, near Berne, Switzerland, 1912–19, and in Montagnola, Switzerland, 1919–62. Awarded Nobel prize for literature, 1946. Died 9 August 1962.

Novels by Hesse
Peter Camenzind, 1904; as *Peter Camenzind,* translated by W.J. Strachan, 1961; also translated by Michael Roloff, 1969
Unterm Rad, 1906; as *The Prodigy,* translated by W.J. Strachan, 1957; as *Beneath the Wheel,* translated by Michael Roloff, 1968
Gertrud, 1910; as *Gertrude and I,* translated by Adèle Lewisohn, 1915; as *Gertrude,* translated by Hilda Rosner, 1955
Rosshalde, 1914; as *Rosshalde,* translated by Ralph Manheim, 1970
Demian, 1919; as *Demian,* translated by N.H. Priday, 1923; also translated by Michael Roloff and Michael Lebeck, 1965
Siddhartha, 1922; as *Siddhartha,* translated by Hilda Rosner, 1951
Der Steppenwolf, 1927; as *Steppenwolf,* translated by Basil Creighton, 1929; revised edition by Joseph Mileck, 1963
Narziss und Goldmund, 1930; as *Death and the Lover,* translated by Geoffrey Dunlop, 1932; as *Goldmund,* 1959; as *Narcissus and Goldmund,* translated by Ursule Molinaro, 1968; also translated by Leila Vennewitz, 1993
Das Glasperlenspiel, 1943; as *Magister Ludi,* translated by Mervyn Savill, 1949; as *The Glass Bead Game,* translated by Richard and Clara Winston, 1969

Other Writings: poetry, novellas, short stories, tales, essays, newspaper articles, reviews, open letters, prefaces, and editorial work.

Further Reading
Bauschinger, Sigrid, and Albert Reh, editors, *Hermann Hesse: Politische und wirkungsgeschichtliche Aspekte,* Bern: Francke, 1986
Boulby, Mark, *Hermann Hesse: His Mind and Art,* Ithaca, New York: Cornell University Press, 1967
Field, George Wallis, *Hermann Hesse,* New York: Twayne, 1970
Freedman, Ralph, *Hermann Hesse, Pilgrim of Crisis: A Biography,* New York: Pantheon, 1978; London: Cape, 1979
Hardin, James N., *Reflection and Action: Essays on the Bildungsroman,* Columbia: University of South Carolina Press, 1991
Mileck, Joseph, *Hermann Hesse: Life and Art,* Berkeley: University of California Press, 1978
Pfeifer, Martin, editor, *Internationale Hermann-Hesse Kolloquium in Calw, 1984,* Bad Liebenzell: Gengenbach, 1984
Stelzig, Eugene, *Herman Hesse's Fictions of the Self: Autobiography and the Confessional Imagination,* Princeton, New Jersey: Princeton University Press, 1988
Wilson, Colin, *The Outsider,* London: Gollancz, and Boston: Houghton Mifflin, 1956
Ziolkowski, Theodore, *The Novels of Hermann Hesse: A Study in Theme and Structure,* Princeton, New Jersey: Princeton University Press, 1965

Ḥikāyat Zahrah. *See* Story of Zahra

His Natural Life by Marcus Clarke

1874

In his introduction to the 1970 Penguin edition of *His Natural Life*, Stephen Murray-Smith declares that Marcus Clarke's most famous novel is "unambiguously the greatest novel to emerge from . . . colonial Australia." However, when it was first serialized in the March 1870 edition of the *Australian Journal*, both the literary critics and reading public were far from positive in their response. Clarke's intention had been to complete his tale of convict life in 12 monthly installments; in fact it ran to 27, stretching reader loyalty to the limit and causing sales of the *Journal* to fall. In 1872, when Clarke was free to have it published as a novel, he was advised to revise the text. When it re-emerged in 1874, the novel was substantially shorter and a variety of narrative details had been altered. The first edition retained the serial's title, *His Natural Life*, but in 1885 the new edition was retitled *For the Term of His Natural Life*. It was the abridged version that was published and circulated most widely in Britain, Europe, and the United States, and although the *Australian Journal* did reissue the original version in installments in 1881 and 1886, it was not available as a self-contained novel until 1970. In light of its publication history—almost from its first appearance, the text has existed and been readily available to the reading public in two distinct editions—another dimension is added to any analytical assessment of the novel, both in terms of its individual merit and in reference to its relationship with other texts and a diversity of generic influences.

The mid– and late–19th century saw a growing concern with crime and punishment that spanned national boundaries, a concern articulated in political discussion and made the subject of contemporary fiction. Charles Dickens' *Great Expectations* (1861) and Fedor Dostoevskii's *Prestuplenie i nakazanie* (1867; *Crime and Punishment*) are two examples of texts that articulate this preoccupation with criminality. Not only did these narratives focus on the overt effect of imprisonment upon the individual, but they often attempted an analysis of the social causes and effects of crime and the systems of punishment. The narrator of *His Natural Life* shares in this fascination, often directly addressing the reader in order to highlight and condemn the brutal and dehumanizing effects of transportation upon both the convicts and their warders.

Because of the particular circumstances of its colonization, Australia proved a particularly rich source of convict narratives, and Clarke was able to draw upon a variety of factual and fictional accounts. In 1870 he had been sent by the Melbourne *Argus* to Tasmania to investigate the legacy of its penal system. It was this visit, coupled with the transportation records he uncovered while working in the city library, that provided an underlying historical foundation for Clarke's fictional and often melodramatic novel: the retrospective, omniscient narrative unfolds both as an account of one man's suffering and as an historical and realistic depiction of life during the period of transportation. It is this alliance with fact and social realism that has established *His Natural Life* as the most famous and archetypal "antisystem" novel of Australia.

The earliest literature to emanate from the British colonies included first-hand records of daily colonial life encapsulated in memoirs, journals, and letters and also in an oral culture that borrowed and adapted the traditional ballads of the "old" country. *His Natural Life* taps into these early traditions, incorporating the voyage narrative and emigrant letter within the general framework of the novel. Also, in the characterization of the novel's convict-hero, Clarke reiterates and reinforces a myth already prevalent in the memoirs and ballads, that of the innocent man falsely convicted and transported. However, while Clarke did appropriate some of the subject matter of the oral tradition for *His Natural Life*, there is a significant shift away from the collective voice of the early ballads. (In these early ballads, the experience of the convict functioned as an anchor for a sense of community and social solidarity that sought to counter the alienating effects of transportation and settlement.) Interestingly, the novel's main character, the ill-omened Richard Devine (alias Rufus Dawes), is elevated in symbolic isolation from the other convicts who, in contrast to him, are often depicted as depraved and subhuman. Devine is individualized and given a psychological depth not shared by his forebears in the ballad stories. He may be read in a variety of ways, not only as the symbolic personification of bourgeois moral ideology but also as a Gothic hero ensnared in a web of coincidences and mishaps, an Everyman who battles against a cruel destiny.

The Gothic romance saw a resurgence in popularity in the later decades of the 19th century, a renaissance that also fueled a fierce critical debate as to the relative values of romance and realist texts. While champions of realism claimed it as a true reflection of lived reality and therefore necessarily superior to the sensational fancifulness of the romance, others hailed the Gothic romance as a liberating force for the articulation of society's unconscious desires and repressed terrors. What is evident in Devine's ambiguous heroic status in *His Natural Life* is a process of hybridization: appropriated and reiterated facts of realist journalism and first-hand accounts are melded with the universalizing and psychological imperatives of the Gothic romance.

Clarke's real achievement was to effectively mythologize the history of transportation. For those reading it in the context of late-19th-century Australian society, his narrative established a reassuring distance from which to exorcise the ghosts of past atrocities and simultaneously to endorse the present as an enlightened age. For those writers who followed him, Clarke's hybrid novel represented a prototype for narratives of national identity. Therefore, while *His Natural Life* was influenced by sources both inside and outside the boundaries of colonial experience, the strongest indication of its own influence on subsequent Australian writing rests in the specificity of its reinterpretation and reiteration of historical origin from the colonial periphery. *His Natural Life* was a constitutive force in the colonies' emergent sense of an Australian identity and national literature.

DEBORAH ZERASCHI

Further Reading

Edwards, P.D., "The English Publication of *His Natural Life*," *Australian Literary Studies* 10:4 (October 1982)

Hergenhan, L.T., "The Contemporary Reception of *His Natural Life*," *Southerly: A Review of Australian Literature* 31 (1971)

Hergenhan, L.T., "English Publication of Australian Novels in the Nineteenth Century: The Case of *His Natural Life*," in *Bards, Bohemians and Bookmen: Essays in Australian Literature*, edited by Leon Cantrell, St. Lucia: University of Queensland Press, 1976

Hodge, Bob, and Vijay Mishra, *Dark Side of the Dream: Australian Literature and the Postcolonial Mind*, Sydney: Allen and Unwin, 1990

McDonald, A.G., "Rufus Dawes and Changing Narrative Perspectives in *His Natural Life*," *Australian Literary Studies* 12:3 (May 1986)

Pollard, A., "Three Ways of Treating Convicts: An Examination of Three Australian Novels," in *Australian and New Zealand Studies: Papers Presented at a Colloquium at the British Library, 7–9 February 1984*, edited by Patricia McLaren-Turner, London: British Library Press, 1985

Ramson, William Stanley, "Marcus Clarke: *His Natural Life*," in *The Australian Experience: Critical Essays on Australian Novels*, edited by William Stanley Ramson, Canberra: Australian National University Press, 1974

Stewart, K., "Life and Death of the Bunyip: History and the Great Australian Novel," *Westerly: A Quarterly Review* 28:2 (June 1983)

Wilding, Michael, *Marcus Clarke*, St. Lucia: University of Queensland Press, 1976

Historical Novel

The idea that history can be presented in a pure form, without any fictional admixture, has been widely accepted only for a few centuries. Most pre–18th-century histories contain what would now be regarded as fictional supplements (e.g., the invented speeches in Thucydides' history of the Peloponnesian War). Historical fiction exists as a distinct genre from the late 17th century onward, when attempts to purge history of fiction began in earnest, even as historical novelists did their best to recreate, refine, and occasionally redefine the old mixture. Their attempts have often had a conspicuous theoretical side; over the centuries, historical novels have tended to be accompanied by manifestoes, prefaces, bibliographies, footnotes, and other authenticating or argumentative devices. The historical novelist, in other words, must attempt to justify a combination of modes that once seemed natural—or at least customary—but no longer does. Because of such efforts, historical fiction as a genre often seems to be the product of bad faith or guilty conscience, and the often formidable energies of the genre spring partly from an attempt to rationalize its own apparent sins out of existence. A standing offense against both the autonomy of aesthetic form and the scientific integrity of facts, historical fiction is a perennial embarrassment, liable to generate many forms of critical inquiry. Few or none of these forms should be taken at face value; all of them, nonetheless, have illuminated the problem of how history can be comprehended secondhand—typically by a middle-class reader who is conversant with neither the obscurity of archives nor the ardor of revolutionary crowds.

The first distinctive group of books to identify themselves as historical novels emerged in France, after the Fronde (a series of rebellions against royal authority, 1648–53). Initially, the Fronde stimulated Madeleine de Scudéry and other aristocrats to write long, intricate romans à clef glorifying their own defiance of Mazarin and the young Louis XIV. The *nouvelle historique* both refines this practice and reacts against it. Erica Harth argues that the *nouvelle* craze of the 1660s and after should be considered a corrective to the emerging ideology of absolutism (see Harth,

1983). Both official and unofficial *nouvelles* (those published abroad, because they did not pass the French censors) attempt to provide new forms of secret or particular history that show the human side of the Sun King's court or of other royal milieux. The pattern of such books was partly set by Jean Regnault de Segrais, working under the royal patronage of Mademoiselle de Montpensier—La Grande Mademoiselle, granddaughter of Henry IV, who had been exiled to her estate in Burgundy, to repent her own exploits in the Fronde (among other feats, she had ordered that cannons be fired in the general direction of Louis XIV and his army). An author herself, La Grande Mademoiselle sponsored Segrais' *Nouvelles françaises* (1657), which purport to be a series of stories told by Mademoiselle and her friends, their identities thinly disguised. The *Nouvelles françaises* feature historical settings populated by both actual and imaginary figures; Segrais' storytellers speak of Scotland during the time of William the Conqueror and of Paris during the Fronde, among other periods. Segrais' typical subject is romantic love, complicated by political and psychological dilemmas.

After a conflict with La Grande Mademoiselle, Segrais became close to Madame de Lafayette, who had contributed to Mademoiselle's *Divers Portraits* (1659), and whose first historical novel (perhaps written in collaboration with him) is intriguingly titled *La Princesse de Montpensier* (1662). This work is not about Mademoiselle, however, but a previous Montpensier, who attracts eminent admirers on both sides of the Wars of Religion of the 16th century. Six years later Madame de Lafayette published what is now the best-known *nouvelle historique* of the 17th century, *La Princesse de Clèves* (1678; *The Princess of Cleves*). This novel inspired a sort of critical war, in which the book's disconcerting position between history and fiction and its disconcerting play with issues of probability were intensely debated. The author herself contributed some of the best shots. Out of this controversy (and other, related polemics) emerged a shared sense of the issues stirred up by the *nouvelle historique*. A contemporary critic, Jean-Antoine Charnes, commented that works in this genre are neither pure fictions nor tales taken from history and embellished by the author but rather a third species—copies of true history that concentrate on particular actions of private people. This comment accurately suggests the genre's slipperiness, its desire not so much to scavenge or elaborate upon official history as to replace it with narratives that claim factuality while remaining in significant respects unverifiable. *Nouvelles historiques* are typified by their use of proper names (their aggressive referentiality serves a large audience, eager for inside knowledge and not accustomed to decoding the romans à clef popular a few decades before); by their brevity and their smallness as physical volumes; by their concentration on the emotions of love, jealousy, and ambition, which are effectively held to shape human behavior; by their use of the established historical record to establish an often richly evoked courtly milieu in which largely invented stories of romance can be played out; by their frequent insinuation that romance—a secret matter—shaped many events in the public record (the assassination of the Prince of Condé, the imprisonment of Don Carlos); and by their attempt to humanize the elite of the court and to imagine its members as fallible. This combination of features often produces at least the illusion of a historical moment fully imagined. The Frondeurs had been elated about their ability to *make* history (or at least to stir things up), but the romans à clef of Scudéry do not fully communicate the excitements of the struggles against Mazarin. The *nouvelle*, although it usually concentrates on earlier periods instead of on history in the making, is often extremely effective in presenting historical turning points—e.g., the transition from Henry II to Francis II in *La Princesse de Clèves* (a political turn echoed in the conflicts of the heroine's secret emotional life) or the failed conspiracies so effectively evoked by the Abbé Saint-Réal. *Nouvelles* were written by many different sorts of people: out-of-work historians (like Saint-Réal), court insiders (like Madame de Lafayette), and journalists on the make. The presiding spirit is that of La Grande Mademoiselle, brooding over those exhilarating moments when she had seemed to enter upon the stage of politics and war—a spirit evoked by the work of Segrais and developed further in the *nouvelles* of his many successors.

Throughout the 18th century, many novels in French and English alike identify themselves as *nouvelles historiques,* or historical novels. The earliest English-language example is probably *The Amours of Edward IV* (1700). Sometimes the form swells to roman à clef length, as in La Paix de Lizancourt's murky dynastic fantasy on the Stuarts and the Bourbons, *Perkin Faux Duc D'Yorck sous Henri VII* (1732). But there are relatively faithful revivals of the form as well. After 1760, it is Baculard d'Arnaud, a disciple of Voltaire turned conservative, who writes the best-known volumes adapting the 17th-century style (d'Arnaud is notorious for his Gothic and sentimental transformations of the *nouvelle*). After the French Revolution, Madame de Genlis, governess of the future King Louis-Philippe, turned out a whole series of novels imitating Madame de Lafayette. (She wrote one *nouvelle historique* about Madame de Lafayette, a metacritical divertissement astounding for its lack of insight into the tradition it invokes.) The related tradition of "secret histories" concurrently sustains the techniques and concerns of the *nouvelle historique*. Thus, although this latter form was central for perhaps only a quarter of a century, it remained a point of reference and a revivable genre, capable of producing best-sellers and making reputations until well into the romantic period.

Nonetheless, however much they may borrow from the tradition of the *nouvelle historique*, the historical novels of the 18th century open up fundamentally new questions. The best survey in English is J.M.S. Tompkins' chapter "The Stirring of Romance" from *The Popular Novel in England 1770–1800* (1932). Although she dates the English historical novel as beginning in 1762 with the anonymous *Longsword, Earl of Salisbury: An Historical Romance,* Tompkins clearly acknowledges the French antecedents. *Longsword* narrates the life of a medieval English warrior forced to fight his way home after the French wars, only to find on arrival that his castle and lands have been usurped. His young son, fortunately, reaches sanctuary—that favorite motif of 18th-century Gothicists. *Longsword* raises questions about the forms and narratives of historical fiction explored more fully elsewhere. Two closely connected masterpieces, the Abbé Prévost's *Le Philosophe anglais; ou, Histoire de Monsieur Cleveland* (1731–39; *The Life and Adventures of Mr. Cleveland*) and Sophia Lee's *The Recess* (1783–85), are particularly rich examples of the new historical novel, defining between them several fundamental shifts in the genre. Begun during Prévost's first visit to England, *Cleveland* borrows from Edward Hyde Clarendon's *History of the Rebellion and Civil Wars in England* (1703) and many less reputable sources to tell the tale (in first-person, memoir form) of an illegitimate son of Oliver Cromwell, hunted by his embarrassed father and for many years forced to live in a cave with his mother. After her death, Cleveland gradually reenters society. The book describes first his adventures, then, in a story within the story, those of his half brother (another persecuted bastard fleeing Cromwell). Each sibling pursues power and love, dogged but not defeated by his distinguished, dubious parentage. Cleveland visits North America and rules an Indian tribe; his brother discovers an island inhabited by Huguenots who have fled from the disasters of La Rochelle. The later sections of this huge romance are centered on questions of English court intrigue after the Restoration and on the fate of Cleveland's much-loved daughter. Will she marry the future pretender, Monmouth, and thus attach Cleveland to the royal family? How does her possible marriage reflect back on the doleful narrator's life? *Cleveland* finds its crisis and culmination in this daughter's death.

Sophia Lee works with similar materials. Her two main characters, legitimate daughters of Mary Stuart, reside in the Recess (a hiding place once used by Catholic monks) during the early Reformation. All the same, the narrative disposition of certain crucial materials—two protagonists in hiding, tales within tales encouraging comparison and contrast of these protagonists, international adventures mixing romantic disaster with large-scale power politics, disastrous ends for both second siblings, changes of regime followed by shifts of the spotlight to a new generation in which a return to royal status seems possible, only to prove a chimera—all these parallels announce an intimate connection between the two books. Between them, Prévost and Lee create a kind of novel that at once reverts to the works of Scudéry (especially in intricacy of narrative structure and sheer length) and opens up a new global and political panorama. Each novelist is fascinated by questions of succession, both generational and monarchical. Each displays a governing interest in secret history, now consistently associated with hiding places, sanctuaries, and asylums of various kinds (in the *nouvelle historique*, by comparison, the court is fundamentally inescapable). Prévost and Lee attempt to discover whether history can or indeed should be escaped by its heroes. Each exhibits a sustained interest in pretenders, characters treated by others as fictional or made-up, even when they have certifiable claims to authenticity. Surprisingly—since such figures are apparently nostalgic, harking back to a lost past—each links its pretenders with civil war or revolution. By the time of Lee's novel, of course, this topic is terrifyingly urgent. As revealed in the introduction to her translation of d'Arnaud's *Warbeck* (1774), Lee disapproves of the American Revolution, although *The Recess* describes a New World slave revolt with surprising sympathy. Each, finally, is fascinated by the idea of interlinked historical crises, occurring during the same period but in different parts of the world. The motif of sibling-doubles is especially useful for getting this subject into a usable fictional form. Along with many lesser writers, both Prévost and Lee extend the range of historical fiction drastically, not least by reimagining the space in which history occurs. No longer can a claustrophobic and basically inescapable court contain or represent history. The court must be conceived within a much larger space. From the late 18th century on, the historical novel is also the geographical novel.

Historical fiction is by definition referential, gesturing toward a world commonly understood to have existed. (This may even be true of 20th-century science-fiction alternative histories such as Philip K. Dick's *The Man in the High Castle* [1962].) But the genre has not always promised reliability of detail. It has felt free to tell imaginary stories about persons who actually existed (the real Princess of Clèves' life did not resemble the one that Madame de Lafayette attributes to her) and to insist, even if equivocally, on the importance of the exemplary. (The Princess is famously described by her creator as an "inimitable example.") A feature largely missing from Lee and Prévost but represented *ab ovo* by other fictions of the 18th century is the learned antiquarianism practiced by such historians as Edward Gibbon. As Arnaldo Momigliano has argued, the antiquarian is not just a collector of authentic details but a sociologist in the making (see Momigliano, 1966). To use the language of the time, antiquaries provide not exemplary instances but what the learned writers of the 18th and 19th century call illustrations, scholarly examples that evoke the typical or popular life of an era. Tompkins nominates the anonymous *The Minstrel; or, Anecdotes of Distinguished Personages in the Fifteenth Century* (1793) as a work attempting a real and fundamentally new integration of learning and narrative, less free and more faithful than previous syntheses of history and fiction. Such a book is quintessentially illustrative.

The strengths of antiquarian illustration are perhaps best seen in Sir Walter Scott's Waverley novels, the first of which was published shortly after Napoléon's defeat at Waterloo. In his brilliant but skewed study of *A történelmi regény* (1937; *The Historical Novel*), Georg Lukács argues that, for all practical purposes, Scott invented historical fiction. This is patently not true. Fluent in French and widely read, Scott followed the most conventional path imaginable in choosing a pretender (Charles Edward) as the crucial historical figure in *Waverley* (1814) itself and in using a narrative of travel—the Englishman Waverley explores Scotland—as the framing device for his account of the Jacobite rebellion of 1745. Once again, geography is intimately connected with history, rather as though space were standing in for time. Scott thus builds on work that the 18th century had done superbly well. Nonetheless, Lukács' account of Scott's originality is partly

convincing. If Scott does not invent, then he reinvents the form. Significantly, he does so at a moment immediately after a great historical crisis. As the Fronde is to the *nouvellistes,* so (with qualifications) are the Napoleonic wars to the author of *Waverley.* In both cases, history seems to become a participant rather than a spectator sport, touching individuals and indeed whole classes much more obviously than is the norm. The difference between the two cases is established largely by Scott's antiquarian and sociological mastery for detail. For Scott, although not for the *nouvellistes,* an increase in the apparent velocity of change, signaled by frequent changes in manners, suggests that societies have directions in time, that they develop through specific stages and toward specific ends. Scott's illustrations of the past are thus remarkable both for their relative precision and for their implicit understanding of history's directionality.

Lukács analyzes several further features of the "classical historical novel." Scott first shows the "complex and involved character of popular life itself," as visible through and in the fortunes of a "mediocre" hero, usually from the "petty aristocracy." Only after the genesis and growth of a mass crisis has been fully portrayed is a major historical figure brought upon the scene. Moreover, this figure compositionally plays only a small role; for this reason he or she can be understood as a product of the times, an answer of sorts to the historical dilemma posed at a given moment in a country's history. This apt account gets at the sociological core of Scott's antiquarian imagination. Lukács does not, however, fully realize the importance of the complex interactions between the historical novel and the related genre of the national tale in the early 19th century, nor does he seem to have read either William Godwin's "republican" romances, at once an imitation and a revision of Scott's politically conservative historical narratives, or John Galt's brilliant Tacitean revisions of the Scott formula (see Ferris, 1991, and Trumpener, 1997). To this extent, Lukács may overrate the singularity of the Waverley novels and the possibility of other authors developing alternative mixes of history and fiction. By the same token he may underrate the form's power of survival after Scott. At times Lukács seems to believe that historical fiction is not a genre at all; at other times he seems to suggest that Balzac effectively killed it, using its sociological and antiquarian techniques to describe the present rather than the past and thereby co-opting Scott's innovations.

Among the later 19th-century elaborations of the genre, three may be singled out—both for their influence in their own time and for their shaping effect on subsequent historical fiction. Perhaps the most popular adaptations of the classic historical novel are the tales of adventure, written in successive generations by Alexandre Dumas, Robert Louis Stevenson, and Rafael Sabatini. In Stevenson's *Kidnapped* (1886), the fundamental point of these novels is made clear: adventure—prototypically, the defense of a narrow place against great odds—is the identifying mark of epic. Stevenson's Alan Breck is an epic hero in a mercantile world; his exploits are a dramatized version of uneven development, the clash between cultures that belong to different stages of civilization. To complicate this scheme further, the ideal of epic adventure is often mixed up with what would appear to be a supremely different notion of male heroism; the epic adventurer can be reinterpreted as a blasé urban dandy. The implications of this fascinating but highly anachronistic character are worked out first in fiction, then, from the 1920s onward, in Hollywood adaptations starring such unforgettable icons as Douglas Fairbanks and Errol

Flynn. The historical novel as adventure story offers not only a powerful wish fulfillment (the desire to combine apparently contradictory virtues) but in certain instances a metacommentary on its own impossible nostalgia. The historical novels of John Buchan, a politician of note, an excellent popular historian, and an ardent exponent of Scott, represent one outstanding instance (see the one-volume collection of these books, published in 1939 as *A Five-Fold Salute to Adventure: An Omnibus Volume of the Historical Novels of John Buchan*).

A second variation on Scott is the children's historical novel. From Madame de Lafayette onward, the genre of historical fiction has usually contained an element of popularization; the audience that most urgently requires history to be popularized is an audience of the young, a fact acknowledged by many writers in the Waverley mode including Scott himself, who during his later years devoted much energy to his *Tales of a Grandfather* (3 vols., 1830). Instances of children's historical fiction date back to the 18th and early 19th centuries (see, for instance, Madame Herbster's *The Cavern of Roseville*, which recounts a tale of two aristocratic children hiding out during the French Revolution [translated into English by Alexander Jamieson, 1817]). Later in the 19th century, many of Scott's best-known successors—Mark Twain, Charlotte Yonge, and G.A. Henty—wrote historical novels still well known and specifically directed at children. (Such books, as well, are generally *about* children.) To reconceive historical fiction in terms of this audience is to insist on its function as a means of education, of indoctrination, benign or otherwise, in a carefully fabricated national past. The past is edited for the comprehension of people who have not been alive very long and for whom, therefore, the idea of history is not necessarily intuitive. During the Victorian period, much historical fiction originally written for adults was gradually redirected to a younger readership. Indeed, until perhaps a generation ago, Scott's *Ivanhoe* (1819) was a favored set text in high schools. One need only play a round of that venerable card game Authors to sense the pervasiveness of historical fiction for and about children. This cultural institution retains considerable importance to the present day.

Both the adventure stories and the children's books discussed above tend, like the Waverley novels themselves, to come in series. Following the three musketeers through sequel after sequel or provisionally identifying with an almost endless procession of Henty heroes, we are encouraged to peruse historical fiction en masse and by this means to keep filling in chronological gaps, working toward an inclusive knowledge of the multifarious museum of world history. We learn about history by pretending to be *in* it, even while acknowledging that the immersion is temporary, soon to be replaced by some other provisional time trip. There is, however, a contrasting aesthetic also available to historical novelists after Scott. Books like Alessandro Manzoni's *I promessi sposi* (3 vols., 1827; *The Betrothed*), Gustave Flaubert's *L'Education sentimentale* (1869; *A Sentimental Education*), and most spectacularly Lev Tolstoi's *Voina i mir* (1863–69; *War and Peace*) present themselves as ultimate, singular masterpieces. All three of these novels take a great deal from Scott. This is especially true of *War and Peace*, which turns on Pierre's false identification with Napoléon no less than *Waverley* turns on its eponymous hero's falsely conceived worship of the invading pretender. All three, however, reject the serial aesthetic of the Waverley novels. Perhaps as much as any books written in

their period, those of Manzoni, Flaubert, and Tolstoi attempt to convey ultimate truths about human life in time, and to do so definitively. Scott's metahistorical prefaces, often conceived as satires of antiquarianism, are highly evasive by contrast; always eager to postpone a final reckoning with the meaning of it all, the author of Waverley is less a moralist than he might at first seem. Tolstoi's epilogue is an explicit attempt to formulate a theory of history that will explain the nature of power and the nature of the force that guides the movement of nations. The directness of Tolstoi's attempt to answer these ultimate questions is more interesting than the answers he gives. He apparently feels an absolute faith that fiction is an appropriate medium in which to present the cases that necessarily (for him) precede such an investigation. This is to make a high claim indeed for a genre so frequently connected with idle daydreaming or juvenile entertainment. Manzoni also raises the stakes. *The Betrothed* attempts a theological reading of history, a reading that will superimpose on the idea of cultural and social development a universal, immutable set of moral standards. Although against the grain of the genre, this project is carried out brilliantly. Flaubert's tribute to the Waverley novels takes the form of satire—his hero, Frédéric Moreau, longs in his youth to become the Sir Walter Scott of France. The novel gives what Clifford Geertz might call a "thick description" of the years closely preceding and following the revolution of 1848. This sustained act of evocation eventually suggests that events whose vivid incoherence we have witnessed, as it were, up close, are hollow and meaningless. Time does not so much reveal as devour truth. Whether Flaubert's devastating sentimental history of his own generation manages or even attempts to draw back from its own apparent nihilism remains a matter of debate. Perhaps the book is best understood as a definitive refusal of meaning and directionality in history.

In the 20th century, several revivals of historical fiction have further extended its possibilities. Lion Feuchtwanger's *Jud Süss* (1925) was an important early catalyst; its success in the British Isles made historical fiction by contemporary authors marketable there once again, after a gradual decline in popularity. One line of work after Feuchtwanger is popular and humanist; this mode is represented by Heinrich Mann's *Die Jugend des Königs Henri Quatre* (1935; *Young Henry of Navarre*) and its sequel *Die Vollendung des Königs Henri Quatre* (1938; *Henri Quatre, King of France*), among the few 20th-century works discussed appreciatively by Lukács, and later by Boris Pasternak's *Doktor Zhivago* (1957; *Doctor Zhivago*). The modernist historical novel, which flourished between the two world wars, offers a different aesthetic. In Virginia Woolf's *To the Lighthouse* (1927), Mr. Ramsay reads Scott's *The Antiquary* (1816) obsessively and appreciatively, as though to prepare himself for producing a revival of the form. Woolf subsequently published such works as *Orlando* (1928) and *Between the Acts* (1941), both attempting a distinctively modernist interpretation of classical historical fiction. When modernists like Woolf adapt Scott's inventions, they draw (in the manner of Ezra Pound or James Joyce) on those spatializations of time recently called myth. The modernist historical novel evokes the past as dramatically as possible—calling it up, as does the best of Scott—while standing on the verge of the eternal present inhabited by such works as *The Waste Land* (1922). Woolf's Orlando is the second cousin of T.S. Eliot's Tiresias, an immortal, androgynous witness to the passing of time. Scott's sense of historical directionality is critiqued and sometimes denied altogether by means of such a perspective. Perhaps it is in some cases recuperated. The modernist historical fiction of this era deserves a reappraisal, which for the most part it has not yet had. Representative novelists worth investigation include John Dos Passos (*U.S.A.*, 1930-36, on 20th-century America), Naomi Mitchison (*The Corn King and the Spring Queen*, 1931, on a Spartan revolt), John Cowper Powys (*Owen Glendower*, 1940, on the Welsh nationalist uprising of the 15th century), Marguerite Yourcenar (*Mémoires d'Hadrien*, 1951; *Memoirs of Hadrien*, on the Roman emperor Hadrian), and Sylvia Townsend Warner (*Summer Will Show*, 1936, on the French revolution of 1848). William Faulkner (*Absalom, Absalom!*, 1936) has, of course, received much more attention than these others, although not, perhaps, within a very large frame of reference. Even Faulkner's best readers tend to underrate or ignore his intricate relation to the Scott tradition and its wide range of modernist revisions.

In some quarters modernism survived World War II. Warner and Powys, for instance, wrote their most extraordinary historical novels during the war. Warner's *The Corner That Held Them* (1948), an annalistic account of life in a medieval nunnery, was published in 1948, Powys' *Porius*, a visionary evocation of Arthurian Britain, in 1951. The latter book is one of the latest and, perhaps, the greatest of the modernist historical novels. Along with Warner's *Corner* (remarkable for its dispersion of experience among a stunning variety of characters) and a few other postwar works, including Alejo Carpentier's *Los passos perididos* (1953; *The Lost Steps*), and his *El siglo de las luces* (1962; *Explosion in a Cathedral*), *Porius* sums up an era of intricate and beautiful experiments in narrating, analyzing, and critiquing the life of the past as it impinges on the present. At the same time, these novels could also be read as early experiments in magic realism, the most pervasive innovation in historical fiction during the latter half of the 20th century. The novel most representative of magic realism is Gabriel García Márquez's *Cien años de soledad* (1967; *One Hundred Years of Solitude*), which retells the history of Colombia as though it were a sort of Saussurean folktale. History, as in structuralism, becomes a self-referential and self-generating system, in which actual events—such as a 1928 massacre of banana workers, reimagined by García Márquez—seem to assume a mainly formal reality. Whether this fresh, postwar mythification of history is as interesting as the modernist version between the wars remains unclear. The style has certainly produced many entertaining and shrewdly constructed national chronicles, gradually wandering back from Latin America and India to various European and North American venues in Thomas Pynchon's *Gravity's Rainbow* (1973) and Salman Rushdie's *Midnight's Children* (1981).

Aside from its play with self-referential fantasy, two contributions of magic realism stand out at present. The 19th-century tendency for historical fiction to metamorphose into stories told for, about, and especially from the viewpoint of children or of a childlike observer (including, perhaps, Manzoni's wandering naïfs in *The Betrothed*) is revived and elaborated in work like that of García Márquez. Indeed, there is a subgenre of the magic realist historical novel in which some traumatic event is retold through the estranged and perhaps innocent eyes of a child, Günter Grass' *Die Blechtrommel* (1959; *The Tin Drum*) being one of the most successful instances. Thus, what might once

have been seen as a trivializing feature of the genre turns out to be one of its most formally and ideologically significant features. The success of García Márquez and others of the same school has brought historical fiction of many different kinds back into fashion. Such canny literary politicians as Susan Sontag and Philippe Sollers have tried their hand at the genre. At least one literary scholar of international prominence—Umberto Eco with *Il nome della rose* (1980; *The Name of the Rose*) and other novels—has chosen historical fiction as a way of dramatizing difficult theoretical ideas. Ambitious historians have produced factual books with novelistic aspirations, Natalie Zemon Davis with *The Return of Martin Guerre* (1983) being a prominent example. A group of Italian writers—Leonard Sciascia, Marta Morrazoni, and Roberto Pazzi—have reinvented the historical novel as a compact elegiac meditation, intricate in form and strikingly self-critical in its integration of factual and fictional material. Finally, the most internationally prominent novelists of many different nations—José Saramago of Portugal, Orhan Pamuk of Turkey, and Amin Maalouf of Lebanon—have chosen historical or metahistorical fiction as a favored genre. Throughout the world, as these instances suggest, the historical novel occupies a position of prominence and often of vitality.

RICHARD MAXWELL

See also Adventure Novel and Imperial Romance; Children's Novel; Critics and Criticism (18th- and 19th-century sections); English Novel (19th-century sections); Epic and Novel; French Novel (17th-, 18th-, and 19th-century sections); Historical Writing and the Novel; Magic Realism; Alessandro Manzoni; National Tale; Realism; Roman à Clef; Romance; Romantic Novel; Sir Walter Scott; Scottish Novel; Lev Tolstoi

Further Reading

Allemano, Marina, *Historical Portraits and Visions: From Walter Scott's "Waverley" to Michel Tournier's "Le Roi des Aulnes" and Thomas Pynchon's "Gravity's Rainbow,"* New York: Garland, 1991

Baker, Ernest, *History in Fiction: A Guide to the Best Historical Romances, Sagas, Novels, and Tales,* 2 vols., London: Routledge, and New York: Dutton, 1907

Beasley, Faith, *Revising Memory: Women's Fiction and Memoirs in Seventeenth-Century France,* New Brunswick, New Jersey: Rutgers University Press, 1990

Chandler, James, *England in 1819: The Politics of Literary Culture and the Case of Romantic Historicism,* Chicago: University of Chicago Press, 1998

Duncan, Ian, *Modern Romance and Transformations of the Novel: The Gothic, Scott, Dickens,* Cambridge and New York: Cambridge University Press, 1992

Ferris, Ina, *The Achievement of Literary Authority: Gender, History, and the Waverley Novels,* Ithaca, New York: Cornell University Press, 1991

Fleishman, Avrom, *The English Historical Novel,* Baltimore: Johns Hopkins University Press, 1971

Harth, Erica, *Ideology and Culture in Seventeenth-Century France,* Ithaca, New York: Cornell University Press, 1983

Lukács, Georg, *A történelmi regény,* Budapest: Hungaria, 1937; as *The Historical Novel,* London: Merlin Press, 1962; New York: Humanities Press, 1965

Maigron, Louis, *Le Roman Historique à l'Époque Romantique: Essai sur l'Influence de Walter Scott,* Paris: Hachette, 1898

Manzoni, Alessandro, *On the Historical Novel,* Lincoln: University of Nebraska Press, 1984

Maxwell, Richard, "Porius, Mitchison, and the Period Character of Historical Fiction between the Wars," *The Powys Journal* 6 (1996)

Momigliano, Arnaldo, *Studies in Historiography,* New York: Harper and Row, and London: Weidenfeld and Nicolson, 1966

Sanders, Andrew, *The Victorian Historical Novel, 1840–1880,* London: Macmillan, 1978; New York: St. Martin's Press, 1979

Sheppard, Alfred Tressider, *The Art and Practice of Historical Fiction,* London: Toulmin, 1930

Tompkins, J.M.S., *The Popular Novel in England, 1770–1800,* London: Methuen, 1932; Lincoln: University of Nebraska Press, 1961

Trumpener, Katie, *Bardic Nationalism: The Romantic Novel and the British Empire,* Princeton, New Jersey: Princeton University Press, 1997

Welsh, Alexander, *The Hero of the Waverley Novels,* New Haven, Connecticut: Yale University Press, 1963; expanded edition, Princeton, New Jersey: Princeton University Press, 1992

Wesseling, Elisabeth, *Writing History as a Prophet: Postmodernist Innovations of the Historical Novel,* Amsterdam and Philadelphia: John Benjamins, 1991

Wilt, Judith, *Secret Leaves: The Novels of Walter Scott,* Chicago: University of Chicago Press, 1985

Historical Writing and the Novel

The relationship between the novel and historical narratives is very complex. Because the two kinds of narrative writing change over time, the boundary between them is also subject to change. Rather than positing two distinct, homogeneous modes of narrative, it is important to recognize that "the novel" or "historical writing" are artificial constructs. Since the dialogic relationship between novels and historiography "fluctuate[s] with the way historians and writers perceive themselves and each other at a particular point in time," an exploration of the relations between them has to take into account the fact that neither of the two genres is fixed over time (see Blum, 1985).

The main difference between novels and historical writings lies in their respective epistemological status, their claims to truth. The distinctive feature of a novel is usually seen to be its fictionality, while historians write about real people and events. This standard view that historical narratives deal only with fact whereas fictional narratives refer to fiction goes back to the well-known distinction between history and poetry made by Aristotle in his *Poetics.* According to Aristotle, the historian differs from the poet in that the former speaks of what *has* happened while the latter is concerned with what *might* or *can* happen. "Thus, history is reserved for that species of narrative in which we try to describe something that happened according to the discoverable testimony about it and by means of certifiable techniques for gathering and identifying such testimony" (see Berthoff, 1970). Historical writing since the beginning of the 19th century has thus claimed to be making true statements about the past that can be checked against documentary evidence, whereas novels can lay claim to neither verifiability nor truth: "Ideally, then, history is descriptive, and its problem is verification. Fiction is constitutive or inventive, and its problem is veracity" (see Berthoff, 1970).

Despite the differences that exist between nonfictional and fictional texts, however, historical writings and novels have much in common. The most obvious similarity between them is that as a rule both take the form of narrative: "Since each is realized in and through narrative, the shape of narrative and the view of the world that particular narrative forms convey may well be common to both at any given time" (see Gossman, 1978). As narrative, both prose fiction and historical writing are imaginative constructions endowing facts with meaning by resorting to conventional plot structures.

Focusing mainly on formal features and on the shared aims of prose fiction and historical writing, metahistorians (i.e., theorists of historiography) have recently shown the extent to which the discourse of the historian and that of the novelist resemble each other. As Hayden White has remarked, "Although historians and writers of fiction may be interested in different kinds of events, both the forms of their respective discourses and their aims in writing are often the same. In addition, in my view, the techniques or strategies that they use in the composition of their discourses can be shown to be substantially the same" (see White, 1978). Some observers have argued that historiography and fictional narrative are structurally identical (see White, 1973; Ricoeur, 1984).

The main problem in comparing the novel and historical writing in purely theoretical terms, whether epistemological or formal, is that the issue itself has an important historical dimension. As Lionel Gossman has shown in his *Between History and Literature,* the status of history as a branch of knowledge has not been constant over time, nor have the rules that stand behind historical writing been permanently fixed. They have been, in fact, as much subject to historical change as the conventions of novelistic discourse. Since the conventions of both genres are ever changing, and since the terms *novel* and *history* take on different meanings at different times, one way of determining the relationship between these two kinds of narrative is to look at the ways in which the novel has developed in relation to historical writing (see Heitmann, 1970; Gossmann, 1978, 1990).

From its beginnings as a distinct genre until almost the middle of the 19th century, the novel's relationship to historical writing was influenced by the view that historiography itself was a branch of rhetoric and a genre of literary art. "For a long time," as Gossman writes of pre-1800 practice, "the relation of history to literature was not notably problematic. History was a branch of literature" (see Gossman, 1978). Since there was a widespread belief in the artistic nature and didactic value of history, historians, like novelists, were expected to demonstrate great rhetorical and stylistic skills in order to make their works didactically persuasive. The task of both the historian and the novelist was thought to be the moral improvement of the reader. Reconstructing 18th-century thinking about historiography, metahistorians have demonstrated the extent to which "the priorities of invention of humanist history provided the form and themes of novels" (see Tinkler, 1988; Vera Nünning, 1994). For their part, literary historians have shown that humanist, neoclassical, and rhetorical historiography were among the precursors of the novel (see Davis, 1983; McKeon, 1987) and that the relationship between historical writing and the novel, between story and history, was very close in the 18th century (see Braudy, 1970; Ray, 1990).

Rather than accept a barrier separating fiction from historical narrative, most 18th-century novelists tried to imitate historical writing (see Beck, 1985). Since the novel as a genre was subject to critical condescension and moral disapproval, 18th-century novelists felt obliged to justify their work by emphasizing the moral exemplariness and significance of their invented histories. Defoe, Fielding, and a host of other writers persistently claimed that they were writing history rather than fiction. They strove to align their works with the rhetoric of humanist history, which was considered to be a highly respected genre (see Heitmann, 1970). History was "divided between scholars and rhetorical writers, and, in this division, the novel came to fulfil some of the functions of rhetorical history" (see Tinkler, 1988). "The shift away from [the novel] and towards history," Beck observes, "can be seen most readily on the title pages of works published between 1700 and 1740, as the word novel or roman disappears almost completely and is replaced by histoire and Geschichte" (see Beck, 1985). The narrators in Henry Fielding's novels, for instance, assume the conventional role of historian, and Samuel Richardson refers to himself as the "Author of the History (or rather Dramatic Narrative) of Clarissa" in the postscript to Clarissa (1747–48).

While the boundary separating history and the novel was rather vague during the 18th century, the relationship between literature and historiography underwent significant changes as the century drew to a close: "It was not until the meaning of the word literature, or the institution of literature itself, began to change, toward the end of the 18th century, that history came to appear as something distinct from literature" (see Gossman, 1978). The romantics at the end of the century (and many of their successors) associated literature more closely with poetry, while historical writing came to be regarded as a faithful record of empirical reality.

The advent of the historical novel and the popularity of Sir Walter Scott's works exerted in turn a great influence both on historiographical practice and on the relationship between the novel and historical writing. Being the inventor of a new and lively mode of representing history, based on detailed description, local color, and exciting plots, it was Scott "who was the original catalyst and model for the historians' emphasis on vivid narration" (see Rigney, 1990). Scott inspired a wave of imitators who encroached upon the traditional domain of the historian. Just as 18th-century novelists had taken over the rhetoric and

style of historians, the latter now began to emulate the narrative techniques of historical novelists.

In the wake of Scott's highly successful literary innovations, there was an increasing degree of competition between novelists and historians, each vying for the attention and recognition of the reading public. Nineteenth-century novelists and historians alike modeled their works on Scott, combining novelistic and historical techniques and presenting popular subject matter in a new and vivid manner. While authors of historical novels such as Edward Bulwer-Lytton strove to give fiction the semblance of the scientific, historians turned their attention to material that the historical novel had appropriated and tried to make their works as novelistic as possible. Announcing that he was going to write the "history of the people," Thomas Macaulay, for instance, wished to reclaim from the novelists subjects that 18th-century historians had largely neglected.

In the first part of the 19th century, historical narrative still shared a number of epistemological, ideological, thematic, and structural features with the novel. It is largely owing to the persistent influence of the rhetorical tradition and the great popularity of the conventions of historical narrative that many early 19th-century historians were very much "concerned with the literary work involved in conveying the character and significance of past events to a contemporary reader" (see Rigney, 1990). There were strong textual similarities between the realist Victorian novel and such historiographical works as Macaulay's *The History of England* (1848–61) and J.A. Froude's *History of England* (1856). With regard to such matters as titles, the use of figurative language, narrative devices such as the use of an omniscient narrator, and the striving for objectivity and conventional modes of emplotment in both fictional and nonfictional genres, historical narration "becomes the commanding narrative convention" in the 19th century (see Ermarth, 1997).

Over the course of the 19th century, however, the relationship between historiography and the novel changed in the wake of the rise of positivist historiography, the emergence of history as an academic discipline, and the concomitant increase in professionalization. These factors had far-reaching effects on the practice of historical writing and the definition of historiography, the result being that historical and fictional writing were driven further and further apart. Under the influence of German scholarship, historiography was becoming a scientific discipline that purported to be different in kind, not just in degree, from all branches of literature. Nineteenth-century aspirations toward a scientific form of historiography differ substantially from the claims historians made before or since (see Bann, 1984; Gossman, 1990; Rigney, 1990). Historical writing and fictional narrative came to be regarded as "being apparently of such separate orders, there was no common ground worth making an issue of" (see Rigney, 1990). It is because of these developments that by the end of the 19th century the functional similarity that had come to prevail between the historical novel and historiography gave way to a functional polarity.

During the first half of the 20th century, the narrative experiments of modernist fiction and its concomitant high degree of artistic self-consciousness led to a further divergence between the novel and historical writing. In the three decades after World War I, modernist novelists transformed or supplanted the traditional conventions of Victorian, Edwardian, and earlier fiction, reshaping the form of the novel itself. Novelists such as James Joyce,

Virginia Woolf, and Marcel Proust experimented with point of view and narrative perspective, with style, and with innovative means of structuring fiction and new modes of presenting consciousness in fiction, while historians eschewed comparable departures from established convention. Even after the advent of the "New History," historiography continued to be characterized by its adherence to more conventional forms of writing. The methodologies and writing practices of historians have changed substantially since the 1930s, and even more since the 1960s, but these developments have not substantially reduced the distance that has separated historiography from the novel since the emergence of history as an academic discipline. Practitioners of the "New History" have developed a broad range of textual innovations that have radically altered the conventions of historical writing (see Carrard, 1992), but they have not challenged the basic distinction between fictional and nonfictional narratives.

Since the end of World War II, however, the conventional distinction between historical writing and fictional narrative, like the paradigm and presuppositions of positivist historiography, has been called into question (see Berkhofer, 1995). Nowadays, "the very idea that the historian's activity consists in discovering and reconstituting, by whatever means, a past reality conceived of as something objectively fixed, has begun to be questioned" (see Gossman, 1978). Those who challenge the boundary separating these two kinds of narrative writing share an intense interest in narrativity, a growing scepticism with regard to humanity's ability to acquire objective knowledge of the past, and a new view of the representation of history that is regarded as specifically postmodern: namely, the conviction that historical writing is unavoidably selective, subjective, relative, and constructed. Challenging positivist notions of historiography as an objective and disinterested recording of the past, constructivist and deconstructionist critics have suggested that the real, both past and present, is something we construct. Moreover, the narrativist school of historiography has shown that narrative is not a transparent medium for representing historical reality but inevitably imposes an artificial continuity, shape, and structure on history by situating events in a particular chronological sequence and by endowing them with significance and meaning.

The way postmodernist fiction situates itself vis-à-vis historiography differs substantially, however, from the practices that were prevalent in the 18th and 19th centuries. In contrast to their Victorian predecessors, postmodernist novelists "do not consider it their task to propagate historical knowledge, but to inquire into the very possibility, nature, and use of historical knowledge from an epistemological or a political perspective" (see Wesseling, 1991). This has resulted in a progressive blurring of the different generic conventions that used to distinguish novels from historical writing.

Among the novelistic genres that have been instrumental in crossing the conventional borders between historiography and prose fictional narrative, one deserves to be singled out; namely, the postmodern variant of the historical novel that Linda Hutcheon has christened "historiographic metafiction" (see Hutcheon, 1988). Historiographic metafiction not only experiments with innovative modes of representing the past in fiction but also reflects many of the insights of modern theories of history (see Engler, 1994; Ansgar Nünning, 1995). By undermining the belief that historical processes can ever be objectively known, such novels as John Berger's G. (1972), Salman Rushdie's Mid-

night's Children (1981), Graham Swift's Waterland (1983), Julian Barnes' Flaubert's Parrot (1984), John Fowles' A Maggot (1985), Penelope Lively's Moon Tiger (1987), and A.S. Byatt's Possession: A Romance (1990) call into question key concepts of positivist historiography such as objectivity, unity, continuity, causality, and linear teleology. The structure and metahistoriographic self-consciousness of these novels overtly bring to the fore the creative and interpretive role of the historian, who constructs rather than reconstructs history. By challenging the notion of historical truth, historiographic metafiction questions the ontological boundary between fact and fiction, the real and the imaginary, historical and fictional narrative. Historiographic metafiction has breached the border between fiction and historiography, closing the gap between history and stories.

In addition to historiographic metafiction, the insights of metahistorical and literary studies of historical writing have led to a fundamental reassessment of the relation between the novel and historical writing. By exposing the insurmountable gap between historical events and their written representations, metahistorical studies, like many postmodernist novels, have laid bare what Michel de Certeau regards as the central paradox of historiography: "Historiography (that is, 'history' and 'writing') bears within its own name the paradox—almost an oxymoron—of a relation established between two antinomic terms, between the real and discourse. Its task is one of connecting them and, at the point where this link cannot be imagined, of working as if the two were being joined" (see de Certeau, 1988). Despite the fact, then, that the term historiography suggests that historians create a nexus between history and writing, postmodernist novels and metahistorians remind us that the gulf between the real past and discourse, between history as it is experienced and the history that appears as the product of researchers' investigations, is, in the end, unbridgeable. By crossing borders and blurring genres, postmodernist historical fiction confirms what Hayden White has demonstrated in his enquiries into the epistemological status of history; namely, that historical discourse "constitutes the objects which it pretends only to describe realistically and to analyze objectively" (White, 1978).

The growing scepticism with regard to historiography's claim to truth and objective representation, the insights of contemporary literary theory, especially of structuralism, deconstruction, the New Historicism, and radical constructivism, and the development of "a new poetics and rhetoric of history" (see Berkhofer, 1995) have culminated in a postmodernist identification of historiography and literary fictions. Examining mainly the literary aspects of historical writing in the 19th century and primarily concerned with issues of textualization, such theorists as Hayden White, Dominick LaCapra, and Stephen Bann, to name but a few, have argued that there is a close affiliation of narrative historiography with literature and myth because historical works are themselves textual constructs that are ultimately nothing but "verbal artifacts" (see White, 1978).

Works prominent in this attempt to reconceptualize the received distinction between the novel and historical discourse are Hayden White's influential Metahistory (1973) and Tropics of Discourse (1978). White considers historical writing as "a verbal structure in the form of a narrative prose discourse that purports to be a model, or icon, of past structures and processes in the interest of explaining what they were by representing them" (White, 1973). Examining how historical texts operate rhetorically, White focuses on the "specifically 'literary' aspect of historical narrative" (White, 1984). Emphasizing "the essentially provisional and contingent nature of historical representations" and "the fictive nature of historical narrative" (White, 1978), White shows to what extent historians rely on literary techniques, imposing tropes and modes of emplotment on the facts: "This transition is effected by a displacement of the facts onto the ground of literary fictions, or what amounts to the same thing, the projection onto the facts of the plot-structure of one or another of the genres of literary figuration" (White, 1984). According to White, by drawing on plot structures that endow stories with meaning, "the historian performs an essentially poetic act" (1973). Elsewhere, White writes that "This is essentially a literary, that is to say fiction-making, operation" (1978).

White's identification of historical narrative with literary emplotment challenges the traditional distinction between novels and historical writings. According to White, the latter are nothing but "verbal fictions, the contents of which are as much invented as found and the forms of which have more in common with their counterparts in literature than they have with those in the sciences." Emphasizing the "fictive nature of historical narrative" and the "essentially literary nature of historical classics," White argues that there "are many histories that could pass for novels, and many novels that could pass for histories, considered in purely formal (or, I should say, formalist) terms. Viewed simply as verbal artifacts histories and novels are indistinguishable from one another. . . . History is no less a form of fiction than the novel is a form of historical representation." White's characterization of "historiography as a form of fiction-making" ultimately calls into question the very possibility of distinguishing between literary and nonfictional narratives, "wiping out the boundary between fiction and history" (see Ricoeur, 1988). Michel de Certeau even goes so far as to maintain that "the past is the fiction of the present" (see de Certeau, 1988).

Some theorists, however, have questioned White's thesis that historical writings are nothing but "translations of fact into fictions," pointing out that his case is based solely on such formal features and deep structures of historical works as the different modes of emplotment and basic tropes. Even if one grants that "all historical texts are signifying constructs," Rigney observes, one need not necessarily "follow Hayden White in concluding that they are also 'verbal fictions'" (see Rigney, 1990). The narratologist Dorrit Cohn, for instance, argues that White ignores both the level of discourse and "the referential level of historical narrative" (see Cohn, 1990). It has also been objected that White does not take into consideration the completely different discursive conventions that the social systems known as "Literature" and "Academe" follow, the constraints that historiography adheres to, or the many privileges that historical fiction enjoys with regard to selecting, inserting, and combining reality references (see Ansgar Nünning, 1995).

In order to account for the different orientations of prose fictional narrative and historical narrative to the question of truth, it is not enough to compare their respective modes of emplotment; we must also, in Rigney's words, "bring more clearly into focus the particular constraints involved in historical, as distinct from fictional, narration" (see Rigney, 1990). With regard to their institutional affiliations, novelists and historians each operate in completely different frameworks governed by discursive conventions that are diametrically opposed to each other. Be-

longing to the literary system, novels are written and read according to aesthetic rules such as ambiguity and the fictionality convention. Historical writing, by contrast, follows the conventions of facts, of monovalence, and of reference to some extratextual documentary base. Unlike the writing of novels, the process of historiographic reconstruction is "highly constrained and controlled, subject to the author's justification and the reader's scrutiny, with its obligatory correspondence to the happenings it narrates overtly displayed in the text itself" (see Cohn, 1990). As a result of the "referential constraints on the discursive level of historical narratives" (Cohn, 1990), the historian is not free to invent or rewrite events, while the novelist, not being bound by similar constraints, "is traditionally allowed greater freedom than the historian to speculate in order to create what history has failed to provide" (see Turner, 1979).

Novels may also be distinguished from historical writing on the basis of what Ricoeur describes as "the undeniable asymmetry between the referential modes of historical and fictional narrative" (see Ricoeur, 1984): "Whereas fictional events are brought into being with the discourse which narrates them, historical events have by definition an existence prior to, outside of, the particular discourse in which they are represented" (see Rigney, 1990). As a result, writes Cohn, "the process that transforms archival sources into narrative history is qualitatively different from (and indeed hardly comparable to) the process that transforms a novelist's sources (whether autobiographical, anecdotal, or even historical) into his fictional creation." In contrast to novels, which deal with imaginary events and characters and which can "be said to be plotted but not emplotted," the historian fashions his narrative out of "more or less reliably documented evidence of past events" (see Cohn, 1990). The aim of the historian is thus entirely different from that of the novelist: "Unlike novels, historians' constructions do aim at being reconstructions of the past" (see Ricoeur, 1988). In addition, there is a broad range of textual features that distinguish fictional narratives from historiography and that function as "signposts of fictionality" (see Cohn, 1990). Such paratextual signals as titles, subtitles, author's notes, chapter headings, epigraphs, prologues and epilogues, and footnotes explicitly or implicitly indicate whether material is factual or fictitious. Metanarrative and metafictional commentary by a narrator often serve a similar function of laying bare the fictionality of a novel.

Drawing on the analytical tools and insights of narratology, a number of literary theorists have addressed the question of distinguishing between fictional and nonfictional narratives, arguing that novels are qualitatively different from historical writing: "Marked by their distinctive discursive modes, historical fiction and history are different in kind, not merely in degree" (see Cohn, 1990). Providing a theoretical distinction between historical and fictional narratives, Dorrit Cohn, Gérard Genette, and Ansgar Nünning have shown that there is a broad range of narratological signposts of fictionality. One of them is that "fictional narratives demand, historical narratives preclude, a distinction between the narrator and the implied author" (see Hernadi, 1976). Unlike novels, historical writing is defined by an identification between author and narrator (see Genette, 1990; Cohn, 1990). Moreover, while a novelist may employ any number of different types of narrator, including an omniscient narrator and an unreliable narrator, the historian "seeks to stand aside from his own discourse by systematically omitting any direct allusion to the originator of the text" (see Barthes, 1970). In addition, novelists can employ a broad range of narrative modes for presenting speech and consciousness in fiction (also referred to as discourse representation), including dialogue, free indirect discourse, psycho-narration, and interior monologue. By contrast, historical discourse can conventionally neither reproduce dialogues nor "present past events through the eyes of a historical figure present on the scene, but only through the eyes of the forever backward-looking historian-narrator" (see Cohn, 1990).

That critics should hold conflicting views about the relation between the novel and historical writing shows that their relationship is still an issue. The new emphasis on the poetics of history and the literary dimension of historical writing, the "revival of narrative" (see Stone, 1979) in both fiction and historiography, and the popularity of historiographic metafiction have all led to the current tendency to conflate historical and fictional narrative. "If fiction is now less securely the defining feature of the novel," Tinkler observes, "so fact is now less securely the defining feature of history" (see Tinkler, 1988). Other theorists yet emphasize that there are important textual and contextual differences between fictional and historical narratives. The many unresolved issues surrounding the relation between the novel and historical writing, the current destabilization of generic distinctions, and the blurring of the fact/fiction boundary in postmodernist culture bear out Ricoeur's observation that the "relation between fiction and history is assuredly more complex than we will ever be able to put into words" (see Ricoeur, 1988).

ANSGAR NÜNNING

See also Critics and Criticism (all sections); English Novel (19th-century sections); Genre Criticism; Greek and Roman Narrative; Historical Novel; Journalism and the Novel; Metafiction; Mimesis; Narrative Theory; Narratology; Narrator; Postmodernism; Realism; Romance; Structuralism, Semiotics, and the Novel; Time in the Novel

Further Reading

Bann, Stephen, *The Clothing of Clio: A Study of the Representation of History in Nineteenth-Century Britain and France,* Cambridge and New York: Cambridge University Press, 1984

Barthes, Roland, "Historical Discourse," in *Structuralism: A Reader,* edited by Michael Lane, London: Cape, 1970

Beck, Hamilton, "The Novel Between 1740 and 1780: Parody and Historiography," *Journal of the History of Ideas* 46 (1985)

Berkhofer, Robert F., *Beyond the Great Story: History as Text and Discourse,* Cambridge, Massachusetts: Belknap Press of Harvard University Press, 1995

Berthoff, Warner, "Fiction, History, Myth: Notes toward the Discrimination of Narrative Forms," in *The Interpretation of Narrative: Theory and Practice,* edited by Morton W. Bloomfield, Cambridge, Massachusetts: Harvard University Press, 1970

Blum, Antoinette, "The Uses of Literature in Nineteenth- and Twentieth-Century British Historiography," *Literature and History* 11 (1985)

Braudy, Leo, *Narrative Form in History and Fiction: Hume, Fielding and Gibbon,* Princeton, New Jersey: Princeton University Press, 1970

Carrard, Philippe, *Poetics of the New History: French Historical Discourse from Braudel to Chartier,* Baltimore: Johns Hopkins University Press, 1992

Cohn, Dorrit, "Signposts of Fictionality," *Poetics Today* 11 (1990)

Davis, Lennard J., *Factual Fictions: The Origins of the English Novel,* New York: Columbia University Press, 1983

de Certeau, Michel, *L'Ecriture de l'histoire,* Paris: Gallimard, 1975; as *The Writing of History,* New York: Columbia University Press, 1988

Engler, Bernd, "The Dismemberment of Clio: Fictionality, Narrativity, and the Construction of Historical Reality in Historiographic Metafiction," in *Historiographic Metafiction in Modern American and Canadian Literature,* edited by Bernd Engler and Kurt Müller, Paderborn: Schöningh, 1994

Ermarth, Elizabeth Deeds, *The English Novel in History, 1840–1895,* London and New York: Routledge, 1997

Gearhart, Suzanne, *The Open Boundary of History and Fiction: A Critical Approach to the French Enlightenment,* Princeton, New Jersey: Princeton University Press, 1984

Genette, Gérard, "Fictional Narrative, Factual Narrative," *Poetics Today* 11:4 (1990)

Gossman, Lionel, "History and Literature: Reproduction or Signification," in *The Writing of History: Literary Form and Historical Understanding,* edited by Robert H. Canary and Henry Kozicki, Madison: University of Wisconsin Press, 1978

Gossman, Lionel, *Between History and Literature,* Cambridge, Massachusetts: Harvard University Press, 1990

Heitmann, Klaus, "Das Verhältnis von Dichtung und Geschichtsschreibung in älterer Theorie," *Archiv für Kulturgeschichte* 52 (1970)

Hernadi, Paul, "Clio's Cousins: Historiography as Translation, Fiction, and Criticism," *New Literary History* 7:2 (1976)

Hutcheon, Linda, *A Poetics of Postmodernism: History, Theory, Fiction,* London and New York: Routledge, 1988

LaCapra, Dominick, *History, Politics, and the Novel,* Ithaca, New York: Cornell University Press, 1987

McHale, Brian, *Postmodernist Fiction,* London and New York: Methuen, 1987

McKeon, Michael, *The Origins of the English Novel 1600–1740,* Baltimore: Johns Hopkins University Press, 1987; London: Radius, 1988

Müllenbrock, Heinz-Joachim, "Historischer Roman und Geschichtsschreibung: Ein Abriss ihrer Entwicklung und Wechselbeziehungen im Viktorianischen England," *Literatur in Wissenschaft und Unterricht* 12 (1979)

Nünning, Ansgar, "Mapping the Field of Hybrid New Genres in the Contemporary Novel: A Critique of Lars Ole Sauerberg, *Fact into Fiction,* and a Survey of Other Recent Approaches to the Relationship between 'Fact' and 'Fiction'," *Orbis Litterarum* 48 (1993)

Nünning, Ansgar, *Von historischer Fiktion zu historiographischer Metafiktion: Theorie, Typologie und Poetik des historischen Romans,* Trier: Wissenschaftlicher Verlag Trier, 1995

Nünning, Vera, "'In Speech an Irony, in Fact a Fiction':

Funktionen englischer Historiographie im 18. Jahrhundert im Spannungsfeld zwischen Anspruch und Wirklichkeit," *Zeitschrift für historische Forschung* 21:1 (1994)

Ray, William, *Story and History: Narrative Authority and Social Identity in the Eighteenth-Century French and English Novel*, Oxford: Blackwell, 1990

Ricoeur, Paul, *Temps et récit*, Paris: Editions du Seuil, 1983–85; as *Time and Narrative*, 3 vols., Chicago: University of Chicago Press, 1984–88

Rigney, Ann, *The Rhetoric of Historical Representation: Three Narrative Histories of the French Revolution*, Cambridge and New York: Cambridge University Press, 1990

Seamon, Roger G., "Narrative Practice and the Theoretical Distinction Between History and Fiction," *Genre* 16:3 (1983)

Stone, Lawrence, "The Revival of Narrative: Reflections on a New Old History," *Past & Present* 85 (1979)

Tinkler, John E., "Humanist History and the English Novel in the Eighteenth Century," *Studies in Philology* 85 (1988)

Turner, Joseph W., "The Kinds of Historical Fiction: An Essay in Definition and Methodology," *Genre* 12:3 (1979)

Wesseling, Elisabeth, *Writing History as a Prophet: Postmodernist Innovations of the Historical Novel*, Amsterdam and Philadelphia: John Benjamins, 1991

White, Hayden, *Metahistory: The Historical Imagination in Nineteenth Century Europe*, Baltimore and London: Johns Hopkins University Press, 1973

White, Hayden, *Tropics of Discourse: Essays in Cultural Criticism*, Baltimore: Johns Hopkins University Press, 1978

White, Hayden, "The Question of Narrative in Contemporary Historical Theory," *History and Theory* 23:1 (1984)

Zimmerman, Everett, *The Boundaries of Fiction: History and the Eighteenth-Century British Novel*, Ithaca, New York: Cornell University Press, 1996

The Hive by Camilo José Cela

La colmena 1951

The Hive was presented to dictator Francisco Franco's censors on 7 January 1946 and was not approved. One censor, the poet Leopoldo Panero, accepted it for its literary merits, but another censor, Father Andrés de Luca, said it attacked moral and Catholic dogma. He considered the novel quasi-pornographic and irreverent. *The Hive* was published in Buenos Aires in 1951, its sexual innuendo sanitized to satisfy the Peronist censorship. The first uncut version of the novel was published in Madrid in 1966.

The Hive portrays the events of a few days in December 1943 (or 1942, according to some critics), a few years after the end of the Spanish Civil War, when the brutal repression of Francoism was at its peak. The setting is Madrid, which was then a police city. The scars of the recent conflict are still visible everywhere, forming a distinct presence. The novel has 346 characters, 50 of whom are taken from real life. Most of the characters are poor, either because they were born into the working class or because they fell into poverty in the postwar economic crisis. The hive metaphor, representing the hard work of ordinary people, is used to rather cynical effect, showing the characters in the effort to reconstruct the country and their lives in the wake of war—not out of any patriotic or altruistic motives, but merely out of an innate instinct for survival.

The novel is organized along several story lines, focused on Doña Rosa's coffeehouse, a brothel, and the streets. The different story lines converge on the murder of Doña Margot, which is being investigated by the police. Martín Marco, an unemployed poet, is the central character in that he is a part of all the different story lines and so provides additional cohesion to this tightly structured novel. The action is concentrated into a period of a little more than 24 hours, from one afternoon through the evening of the next day, with an epilogue set a few days later. Using a technique that critics have called cinematographic, the narrative jumps back and forth between the two principal days to create an impression of simultaneity.

The Hive is one of the key novels in the transition from *tremendismo* (a movement characterized by a focus on the trauma of the Spanish Civil War) to "behaviorism," the neorealist literary movement that pursued a scientific objectivity in representations of reality and human behavior. The novel's *tremendismo* characteristics include the frequent references to the scars of the civil war and an indirect indictment of the repressive Franco regime. For instance, *The Hive* attacks the excessive power of the police, which extends into the political realm. It depicts a reality dominated by famine and fear of political persecution, the epithet "red" being a dangerous weapon in the hands of any neighbor who harbors ill feeling. The novel also attacks the Catholic pieties of Francoism, showing it to be a mere facade that covers up such realities as prostitution, even child prostitution, which are simply an economic necessity for the poor. Portraying a network of relationships that have survived the political manipulations of the fascist state, the novel also shows the limits of fascism and its ability to set people against each other: many of the characters are looking for Martín Marco in order to help him in spite of the dictatorship.

The novel is a forerunner of behaviorism in its attention to physical details. For instance, the setting, a few blocks in Madrid that critics have identified with precision, is described with meticulous realism. *The Hive* also presents the intimacy of the middle-class parlor, kitchen, and bedroom in descriptions that are reminiscent of 19th-century realism. The novel's sexual explicitness, however, gives a distinctly 20th-century accent to the form and set an important precedent for behaviorism.

The neorealism of *The Hive,* even though it helped to establish the behaviorist movement, is qualified by the omniscient narrator.

The narrator plays a godlike role in the novel, manipulating events and destroying characters when he sees fit. Anything but impartial, he judges the characters, displays tenderness toward them, and laughs at their expense. This antirealist narrator points to different literary antecedents, one of which in fact predates the modern novel, going as far back as Fernando de Rojas' pseudo-dramatic *La Celestina* (1502). In fact, Cela conceived his novel, with its explicit descriptions of sex, as part of the scatological literary tradition that descends from *La Celestina*. More recent influences include John Dos Passos' *Manhattan Transfer* (1925), André Gide's *Les Faux-monnayeurs* (1926; *The Counterfeiters*), and Aldous Huxley's *Point Counter Point* (1928), modernist novels whose narrators frequently intrude to comment on the nature of fiction. The novel's open ending, which leaves Doña Margot's murder unsolved and refuses to explain Martín Marco's elusiveness, also associates *The Hive* with modernism.

In 1982, the film director Mario Camús made *The Hive* into a movie, casting Cela himself in a cameo role as Matías Martí, inventor of words. Interestingly, the film version closes the novel's open ending, indicating that Martín Marco cannot be found be-cause he is hiding from the police, whose main suspect he is in the case of Doña Margot's murder. In the film, Martín is eventually found and arrested but released again when Doña Margot's death is ruled a suicide instead of a murder.

SALVADOR A. OROPESA

See also Camilo José Cela

Further Reading

Dougherty, Dru, "Form and Structure in *La colmena*: From Alienation to Community," *Anales de la Novela de Posguerra* 1 (1976)

Foster, David W., *Forms of the Novel in the Work of Camilo José Cela*, Columbia: University of Missouri Press, 1967

Insula 45:518–19 (1990), special issue on Cela

McPheeters, D.W., *Camilo José Cela*, New York: Twayne, 1969

Review of Contemporary Fiction 4:3 (Fall 1984), special issue on Cela

Roy, Joaquín, editor, *Camilo José Cela: Homage to a Nobel Prize*, Coral Gables, Florida: University of Miami Press, 1991

Hombres de maíz. *See* Men of Maize

Honglou meng. *See* Six Classic Chinese Novels

Hopscotch by Julio Cortázar

Rayuela 1963

With the international recognition of the Boom of the Latin American novel in the 1960s, Julio Cortázar came to the forefront as a world-class writer. Before that, he had been known primarily in the Spanish-speaking world as a superb author of short fiction. His novel *Hopscotch* gained the immediate respect of writers and intellectuals in Latin America, and soon was considered one of the major works of the Boom. In the 1960s and 1970s, several scholars and critics declared *Hopscotch* to be one of the most innovative and experimental Latin American novels of the century. With the publication of his short fiction and this novel, Cortázar was considered the leading intellectual figure by the writers of the Boom themselves, including Carlos Fuentes, Mario Vargas Llosa, and Gabriel García Márquez.

Until the appearance of *Hopscotch*, formal innovation in the Latin American novel tended to be limited to modernist strategies pioneered originally by such writers as Marcel Proust, John

Dos Passos, and William Faulkner. Faulkner had exercised considerable influence on Latin American writers, including García Márquez, Fuentes, and Vargas Llosa. With *Hopscotch,* however, formal experimentation assumed a radically new meaning. The basic structure of the novel invites the reader to pursue a variety of possible readings. In the first and simplest reading, Cortázar offers the possibility of reading chapters 1–56 in a linear fashion—the conventional mode of reading. In this 56-chapter novel, the protagonist, Horacio Oliveira, is engaged in a spiritual quest and suffers failed relationships in Paris and then later in Buenos Aires. In this reading, the remaining 99 chapters are identified by Cortázar as "expendable." The second reading that Cortázar offers consists of 155 chapters, following a different order of chapters set forth at the outset. This reading is far less linear than the first 56 chapters. These "expendable" chapters not only expand the plot, but also offer a theory of the novel, literature, and the creative process, as set forth by a character named Morelli. This theory is not a consistent and systematically developed aesthetic concept, but a self-consciously diverse and fragmented promotion of ideas associated with innovation and experimentation. With respect to the novel in particular, Morelli's articulation of the innovative and experimental novel is identified as the "anti-novel."

In Paris, Oliveira pursues relationships with a woman named La Maga, and a series of friends and acquaintances involved with jazz, the other arts, and bohemian life in general. Oliveira's spiritual quest—his attempt to find himself—culminates in Paris with his failure and degradation. After barely surviving his crisis in Paris, Oliveira goes to Buenos Aires where he connects with his childhood friend, Traveller. Ironically, Traveller has never traveled anywhere and has no interest in doing so. An opposite of Oliveira, Traveller does not share Oliveira's interest in defining existence, either. As the novel develops, Oliviera and Traveller become double figures that eventually become one. Oliveira tends to associate Traveller's wife, Talita, with La Maga from his days in Paris. The anecdotes in Buenos Aires relate a series of often bizarre and incongruous events, such as a scene in which Talita walks across a board extended between two buildings, with Oliveira and Traveller awaiting her. At the end, Oliveira and his friends are operating an insane asylum, and Oliveira seems to be on the border of insanity himself.

The incongruity of certain anecdotes of the plot of *Hopscotch* has parallel incongruities at other levels of reading. There is a frequently troubled relationship between the book's overall focus and certain minute details that Cortázar offers in some chapters. In fact, some of these minutiae—esoteric bits of knowledge—appear so incongruous that the reader has difficulty finding any association at all with the novel's larger meaning.

Language itself is one of the main subjects of *Hopscotch.* Cortázar experiments with multiple types of language, from the everyday to the literary and esoteric. In one section of the novel, his characters communicate in an entirely invented, nonsensical language. In other sections, his narrator and his characters question the capability of language to communicate authentic ideas and feelings. Morelli and other characters are devastatingly satirical and critical of conventional literary language. They are particularly critical of 19th-century realist conventions, often ridiculing the Spanish writer who best represented everything re-lated to conventional realism, Benito Pérez Galdós. Oliveira and Morelli also ridicule the most trivial use of everyday language, the cliché. *Hopscotch* questions the language of clichés as well as of language that we use thoughtlessly every day—the language expressing our unquestioning acceptance of reality as given, superficial. As Robert Brody has pointed out (1976), Cortázar sometimes achieves his critique of language through mockery. Oliveira emphasizes the difference between him and La Maga by pointing out her uncomplicated view of the world in which fish swim downstream and leaves belong on trees. Oliveira cannot easily tolerate such a common, everyday vision of reality, or that others accept this reality so easily. To interrupt the flow of everyday language (and the everyday reality that accompanies it), Cortázar interrupts serious passages with playful language.

Hopscotch was intended to be a revolutionary novel in both the aesthetic and political spheres. Its revolutionary aesthetics rejected traditional and conventional literary forms; at the same time, it proposed a literary revolution for a new novel in Latin America and the West. Cortázar does not associate himself with any specific revolutionary political agenda or ideology in *Hopscotch.* Rather, he conceives of his revolutionary project as a fiction that proposes to question all conventional modes of thought, thus liberating the mind and opening the imagination to radically new political alternatives. In the search, the streets and other spaces of Paris become the symbolic equivalent of a gigantic game of hopscotch for Oliveira.

Few Latin American novels of this century have had the impact of *Hopscotch,* which has already exercised enormous influence on two generations of Latin American writers. Since the publication of the novel, numerous younger writers have written the "open" novel proposed by Morelli. Cortázar also opened the door to linguistic innovation of the Spanish language, much as James Joyce did for English.

RAYMOND LESLIE WILLIAMS

See also Julio Cortázar

Further Reading

Barrenechea, Ana María, "La estructura de *Rayuela,* de Julio Cortázar," in *Litterae Hispanae et Lusitanae,* edited by Hans Flasche, Munich: Hueber, 1968
Boldori, Rosa, "Sentido y trascendencia de la estructura de *Rayuela,*" *Boletín de Literaturas Hispánicas* (1966)
Boldy, Steven, *The Novels of Julio Cortázar,* Cambridge and New York: Cambridge University Press, 1980
Brody, Robert, *Julio Cortázar: "Rayuela,"* London: Grant and Cutler, 1976
Brushwood, John, *The Spanish American Novel: A Twentieth-Century Survey,* Austin: University of Texas Press, 1975
Loveluck, Juan, "Aproximación a *Rayuela,*" *Revista Iberoamericana* 34 (January-April 1968)
Paley de Francescato, Marta, "Bibliografía de y sobre Julio Cortázar," *Revista Iberoamericana* 39 (July-December 1975)
Sosnowski, Saúl, *Julio Cortázar: Una búsqueda mítica,* Buenos Aires: Noé, 1973
Yovanovich, Gordana, *Julio Cortázar's Character Mosaic: Reading the Longer Fiction,* Toronto: University of Toronto Press, 1991

Horror Novel

The horror novel is a subgenre of Gothic fiction characterized by gruesome effects, uncanny events, monstrous beings, and obsessive introspection. Noel Carroll argues that the evil must appear to the reader to be plausible, physically and morally threatening, and impure or unclean (see Carroll, 1987). Through corruption, decay, or disease, horror attacks the coherence of the body and, by extension, the stability of the mind, threatening physical, psychological, and cosmic disintegration.

Horror results from the startling representation of unsettling metaphysical and psychological concepts in such diverse forms as poems, short stories, and novels, as well as visual genres such as painting and film. Because of their compressed length, poems and short stories are able to sustain intense horror, while painting and film offer explicit and immediate suspense, shock, and gore. By contrast, the horror novel commonly alternates conventional narrative with lurid episodes, since it is difficult to sustain uninterrupted mayhem through a prolonged narrative. Its scope allows for the development of a multilayered theme and the exploration of the intricacies of consciousness and perception. Elements of horror may provide the primary focus of an entire novel, or they may occur as subordinate aspects of more conventional narratives. For example, Stephen King's *Pet Sematary* (1983) includes scenes of ordinary domestic life, but these scenes serve only as contrast for the narrator's growing instability. On the other hand, in William Faulkner's *As I Lay Dying* (1930) the stench given off by the decaying body of Addie Bundren is a horror that only adds to the dominant themes of dissolution and transfiguration.

In *Danse Macabre* (1981), Stephen King identifies the levels of horror chiefly through degrees of revelation: *terror* of an unknown but implied evil; *horror* of the glimpsed evil; and *disgust* for the explicitly displayed evil. Aware of the psychological benefits of fantasy and sublimation, King defines the purposes of horror fiction as aesthetic, offering the rush of extreme fear and, at the end, a sense of order reestablished. Such a restoration is apparent in Clive Barker's *The Damnation Game* (1985), which concludes, "Everything was in its place, despite the insanity that had mauled their lives of late . . . he saw for the first time how fine that was." King declares that it is "this feeling of reintegration from a field specializing in death, fear, and monstrosity that makes the danse macabre so rewarding."

The horror novel may offer simple sensationalism, intellectual complexity, or any degree of sophistication in between. The slimy monsters and screaming blonds of pulp novels are both interchangeable and disposable, offering the sensation and approximate duration of a good roller coaster ride. However, the horrors of the grotesque in Flannery O'Connor's *Wise Blood* (1952), of the demonic in Charles Williams' *All Hallows Eve* (1945), and of the corrupt in H.P. Lovecraft's *The Dunwich Horror* (1945) challenge the reader both in feeling and in thought, causing nightmares long after the books are closed.

The conventions of the horror novel suppose the existence, or at least the appearance, of a natural order that may be violated with disastrous results. Corruption, decay, dismemberment, and psychological dislocation all endanger this order. The characters' initial response to the horror is disbelief. In Bram Stoker's *Dracula* (1897), Jonathan Harker dismisses the alarms of the Transyl-vanian peasants as superstition. His host's habits and isolation suggest eccentricity, perhaps even madness, but Harker scarcely believes in vampires until Dracula is about to bite him. Furthermore, those characters who do know about the monsters find it difficult to convince others. When Dr. von Helsing says that Lucy Westenra is losing blood to a vampire, the other characters are incredulous. The tension between what appears to be happening and what reason and experience allow as possible raises questions regarding evidence and conclusions and ultimately about the validity of reason and perception itself.

Horror characters, from monsters and magicians to heroes and innocents in distress, derive from and reflect the genre's concern with threats to order. Mary Douglas associates horror with defilement, locating its source in things that threaten our understanding of reality—categorical such as the part-human, part-animal werewolf, contradictious such as the living dead, and things lacking physical integrity such as a zombie shedding disintegrating flesh (see Douglas, 1966). The monster itself is an unnatural creature intruding from another dimension or created by the transgressions of a magician or scientist. He (most, although not all, monsters are male) poses a threat to the hero, the woman, and sometimes the child, not only to their lives but to their mental and physical coherence. The genre's monsters range in type from ghosts and spirits to vampires, constructs, shape-changers, and psychotic killers.

In Peter Straub's *Ghost Story* (1979) the old men of the Chowder Club are haunted by an embodiment of their collective guilt, while in Shirley Jackson's *The Haunting of Hill House* (1959), the least stable character, Eleanor, is possessed by the malevolent spirit of the "leprous house." More frequently, however, the monster has a human shape, the better to illustrate the horrors of the collective unconscious. Vampires such as Stoker's Dracula and Anne Rice's Lestat drain the lives of their victims, and worse, turn them into vampires. These creatures reflect a debased sexuality that is an affront to purity. The full decadence of vampirism appears in Rice's *Interview with a Vampire* (1976) when Lestat and Louis turn the child Claudia into a vampire and then play out a parody of family life. A third monster is the construct, the creature devised by magic or by science. Frankenstein's monster from Mary Shelley's *Frankenstein; or, The Modern Prometheus* (1818) is one of the first of this breed, which also includes the "ideal" robotic wives of Ira Levin's *The Stepford Wives* (1972) and the replicant Rachael in Philip K. Dick's *Do Androids Dream of Electric Sheep?* (1968). These beings are all products of technology, but the magical creations such as Lovecraft's mutants from *The Shadow over Innsmouth* (1936) are poured from the same vat. Science and magic are both pursuits that extend the powers of their practitioners to control nature. Shape-changers include such folk figures as the werewolf and the cat woman. In *The Body Snatchers* (1955) by Jack Finney, the "pod" beings overcome and assume the bodies of the humans, and in John Carpenter's film version of *The Thing* (1982) the aliens can take any shape from that of a sled dog to that of a patient undergoing surgery. These creatures' ability to invade and overcome both the bodies and the identities of their victims make it impossible to distinguish friend from foe, or even human from not human.

The king of modern monsters is probably the psychopath represented, for example, by the murderous cannibal, Hannibal Lector, of Thomas Harris' *Silence of the Lambs* (1988). The psychotic killer is the most plausible of all monsters. Insanity is a violation of natural and individual order that can and does occur in the real world and, therefore, its appearance in fiction is both convincing and horrific. No one has ever seen a werewolf but Henry Lee Lucas and Jeffrey Dahmer are well authenticated. Furthermore, the existence of insanity causes the characters in a novel, and by extension the readers, to question their own perceptions. In Robert Bloch's *Psycho* (1959), Norman Bates murders women who appear to him as reflections of his loved and hated mother; according to him, his murders are not only reasonable but necessary.

Monsters exist in the plot to endanger the human characters, the magicians and scientists as well as the heroes and victims. The magician—and his modern incarnation, the scientist—are undone by their *superbia*, their overreaching of the natural order. The hero, on the other hand, confronts and subdues the chaos. The victims, menaced by the monsters and saved by the heroes, are attractive women or, occasionally, children. Clearly, the corrupt depravity of the monster is most shocking in contrast to the beauty of the woman or the purity of the child. The reader is filled with disgust when the rotten flesh of the monster approaches the pure flesh of the victim and is relieved when the hero is able to prevent the desecration.

The beauty and the sexual purity of the victims raise the issue of eroticism in horror fiction. Even the earliest plots usually involved male monsters victimizing women or children. In Western iconography, sex is often the source of corruption, and virginity represents sacred purity. Therefore, an evil invasion implies a sexual invasion. The sexual violence of the horror novel has led some feminist critics to suggest that horror, like pornography, validates violence toward women. In *Men, Women, and Chain Saws,* Carol J. Clover qualifies this judgment. Whereas the promiscuous blond is sure to die—a fate she deserves, since her sexual impurity invites the advances of the monster—the bright and virtuous young woman is often able to unravel the mystery, confront the monster, and survive the disaster (see Clover, 1992).

H.P. Lovecraft's *Supernatural Horror in Literature* (1945) offers one of the most thorough and astute histories of the genre. Although most discussions of horror begin with the Gothic innovations of the mid–18th century, Lovecraft sees the roots of horror fiction in the need for physical and psychological coherence enacted through the darker elements of primitive ritual. He begins his study with the archaic folktales and ballads of demons, ghosts, and the undead. He suggests that horror, while including the devices of the parent Gothic narratives, also has "an atmosphere of breathless and unexplainable dread of outer and unknown forces . . . a malign and particular defeat of those fixed laws of Nature." Thus while he refers to Horace Walpole's *The Castle of Otranto* (1764) and Ann Radcliffe's *The Mysteries of Udolpho* (1794), Lovecraft maintains that horror narrative is of a much older stock, which only came to dominate a subgenre of the novel in such works as Matthew Gregory Lewis' *The Monk* (1796), Mary Shelley's *Frankenstein*, and the horror and detective novels of Edgar Allan Poe. Lewis' novel portrays ghoulish violence and sexual perversity that lead to psychological and metaphysical disintegration, while Shelley's novel employs the quasi-scientific plot of the unnatural monster who longs to be human and thereby questions the meaning of humanity. Poe's chief contribution to the genre is his use of sickness, often hereditary, to represent personal and social decay. Lovecraft says that Poe's "use of disease raised perversity and decay to the level of artistically expressible themes."

In such novels as *The Turn of the Screw* (1898) Henry James expanded the psychological dimension of horror; for him the form had "the immense merit of allowing the imagination absolute freedom of hand." He used a domestic setting for supernatural events rather than the usual ruin or blasted heath. And when the governess sees the ghosts of the evil servants, she sees them outdoors by daylight. James includes what he defines as the characteristic modern horror: insanity, unreliable perception, and an altogether slippery grasp of reality. A central issue in the novel is the governess' own sanity; does she *see* ghosts or *imagine* ghosts? Both of these devices have proved influential for later writers. Shirley Jackson's *We Have Always Lived in the Castle* (1962) deals with murderous obsession in the home and in the confines of a small town, while Charles Williams' *Descent into Hell* (1937) begins with a tea party and mixes scenes of village life with apocalyptic scenes of damnation.

As European horror haunted ruins, moors, and the medieval past, so American horror novels represent regional and antiquary fiction, primarily the New England of Nathaniel Hawthorne and the South of William Faulkner and Flannery O'Connor. In the early decades of the 20th century, the stories of Lovecraft, set almost exclusively in New England, were the strongest representatives of the genre in the United States. Located in isolated backwaters, where villagers are haunted by the curse of an evil and incomprehensible past, the stories of Cthulu and the Old Ones provide a coherence to Lovecraft's work and a foundation for his imitators. His skill is in the implied horror, what he calls "the scratching of outside shapes." In the story "The Call of Cthulu" the narrator says, "The Old Ones are eternal . . . not in the spaces we know, but between them."

In the American South, the secretive landscapes of mountain caves, alluvial swamps, and isolated hamlets have combined with a history of violence and slavery to suggest novels of degenerate families, sexual perversion, and grotesque but prophetic heroes. Lovecraft's "The Call of Cthulu," although set mostly in New England, features a terrifying pursuit of an evil cult through the bayous and swamps of Louisiana on a moonless night. On a more cerebral level, William Faulkner offers Thomas Sutpen, who ripped his plantation from the dark forest with his own cruel violence and the labor of his "foreign" slaves. In *Wise Blood* and *The Violent Bear It Away* (1960), Flannery O'Connor uses motifs of disease and deformity to reveal the cracks in traditional Southern values.

Recent novelists such as Peter Blatty, Stephen King, and Clive Barker combine the Lovecraftian sense for formless dread with the Jamesian fear of mental instability. Blatty's *The Exorcist* (1971) represents the fear of possession and the loathsome corruption of innocence. King's *Carrie* (1974) shows the correspondence between interior and exterior evil and the uneasy reliance on an unreliable narrator. Barker's *The Damnation Game,* loosely based on Charles Robert Maturin's *Melmoth, the Wanderer* (1820), reveals the horror in infinite guilt and irrational retribution. These fictions set the parameters of the contemporary horror novel. However, novels not usually classified as such also make use of horror effects. In *Child of God* (1973) Cormac

McCarthy follows Flannery O'Connor in his images of Southern violence and decadence, while in his two western novels, *All The Pretty Horses* (1992) and *The Crossing* (1994), bizarre encounters and unnatural cruelty reflect a sense of menace from beyond literal and figurative borders. In these and similar novels, writers employ the techniques of horror to explore the darker corners of the id; as Walt Kelly's cartoon character Pogo says, "We have met the enemy, and he is us."

It is nearly impossible to discuss the novel of horror without reference to poetry, painting, and film. Since early in the 19th century, artists of all media have appropriated its devices, often influencing one another in both form and content. Struck by the vivid detail in the writings of Edgar Allan Poe, the French poet Charles Baudelaire began to use elements of horror as symbols in his poetry. In *Les fleurs du mal* (1861; *The Flowers of Evil*), Baudelaire likens a dead dog to a dead whore, describing its putrifaction and maggots with enthusiasm and pointing out to his lover that she too will eventually be, like the dog, "horrible, filthy, undone." Symbolist painters such as Gustave Morreau and surrealists such as Yves Tanguy, Max Ernst, and Salvador Dali also juxtapose unlikely images and depict scenes of sadism and death with graphic detail. The importance of these painters to the development of fiction is clear in, for example, the novels, stories, and film scripts of Alain Robbe-Grillet, who dedicates one of his more lurid tales "The Secret Room" to the painter Morreau.

With the development of film, horror has become immediate, explicit, and abruptly shocking. The script for the German Expressionist film *Nosferatu* (1922), directed by F.W. Murnau, is a version of *Dracula*, pirated to avoid paying royalty to Stoker's heirs. Other horror films drew heavily from novels. *Frankenstein*, *Dracula*, and Robert Louis Stevenson's *The Strange Case of Dr. Jekyll and Mr. Hyde* (1886) have all been filmed frequently, along with sequels, variations, and parodies. The relationship between genres has been circular, however, each form drawing from the devices and themes of the other. Stephen King's *The Shining* (1977) draws motifs from ghost films like *The Haunting* (1963; based on Shirley Jackson's novel, *The Haunting of Hill House*) as well as psychological films like *What Ever Happened to Baby Jane?* (1962); the film *The Shining* has, in turn, influ-enced subsequent films and novels. The developments of horror fiction and horror film have become so intertwined that it is nearly impossible to separate them.

As Noel Carroll has observed, the public acceptance of horror narrative is cyclical and related to social and economic pressures. At present, horror novels and horror films are plentiful, financially rewarding for their creators, and often aesthetically significant as well. Yet even in lean years, an audience survives. Lovecraft said that horror "is a narrow though essential branch of human expression, and will chiefly appeal . . . to a limited audience with keen sensibilities." However, the development of sophisticated technique and complex content renders horror an effective artistic tool for the exploration of the darker corners of consciousness in both genre novels and in more conventional narratives.

Janet P. Sholty

See also Gothic Novel

Further Reading

Carroll, Noel, "The Nature of Horror," *Journal of Aesthetic and Art Criticism* 46 (1987)

Carroll, Noel, *The Philosophy of Horror; or, The Paradoxes of the Heart,* New York: Routledge, 1990

Clover, Carol J., *Men, Women, and Chainsaws: Gender in the Modern Horror Film,* London: BFI, 1992; Princeton, New Jersey: Princeton University Press, 1993

Douglas, Mary, *Purity and Danger: An Analysis of the Concepts of Pollution and Taboo,* London: Routledge and Kegan Paul, and New York: Praeger, 1966

Joshi, S.T., *The Weird Tale: Arthur Machan, Lord Dunsany, Algernon Blackwood, M.R. James, Ambrose Bierce, H.P. Lovecraft,* Austin: University of Texas Press, 1990

Lovecraft, H.P., *Supernatural Horror in Literature,* New York: Abramson, 1945

Summers, Montague, *The Gothic Quest: A History of the Gothic Novel,* London: Fortune Press, 1938

Wuletich-Brinberg, Sybil, *Poe: The Rationale of the Uncanny,* New York: Peter Lang, 1988

The Hound of the Baskervilles by Sir Arthur Conan Doyle

1902

The Hound of the Baskervilles is among the major works in one of the most successful literary series in publishing history: Sir Arthur Conan Doyle's Sherlock Holmes stories, comprising four short novels and five volumes of tales, from *A Study in Scarlet* (1888) to *The Case-Book of Sherlock Holmes* (1927).

Sherlock Holmes, the brilliant criminal investigator, is probably a more famous literary character than Hamlet or Odysseus. Because he invented a fictitious personage so compelling that thousands of readers have actually sent letters to Holmes (rather than for any significant innovations in form or theme), Conan Doyle earns a prominent place in the history of the novel. And yet Holmes often seems not so much a character but a set of fetishized accessories—a pipe, a violin, a syringe—and, before all else, a method.

The case of the Hound is initiated, as in so many of the Sherlock Holmes stories, by the appearance of a client in Holmes' rooms on Baker Street. Dr. Mortimer announces that he has brought an old manuscript; Holmes replies that he knows this already: he has seen the paper protruding from Mortimer's pocket. Moreover: "It would be a poor expert who could not give the date of a document within a decade or so. . . . I put that at 1730." Actually, the date is 1742. Holmes has only just kept within his parameter of "a decade or so." This is the quintessence of Holmes: a brilliant show-off with just enough skill as a sleuth to think that he must appear almost always successful. In this sense, even Holmes himself seems to be in thrall to the fictional ideal of "Sherlock Holmes."

Conan Doyle underscores Holmes' uniqueness by contrasting him with the ordinary Dr. Watson, the ostensible narrator of the stories, "not [himself] luminous, but . . . a conductor of light." It is one of Conan Doyle's main achievements to make this relationship, intellectually so unequal, seem emotionally vital to both parties. Holmes and Watson enact a type of homosociality, not sexual but devoted and exclusive, which seems rare in post-Edwardian literature, and which consequently holds a special fascination for contemporary readers.

Aside from Holmes and Watson, *The Hound of the Baskervilles* contains some memorable characters—notably the butterfly-catching villain, Stapleton. However, these characters are thinly presented: a comparison (given the moorland setting) of Stapleton and his supposed sister with Catherine and Heathcliff from Emily Brontë's *Wuthering Heights* (1847) would make this clear. The select qualities of these characters that Conan Doyle presents, essentially, are what matter to Holmes: the characters are important for the part they play in the specific problem that he travels to Dartmoor to solve. The novel sustains its length, however, through the richness of its physical, historical, and psychosymbolic environment: the moor exhibits more personality than most of the human beings who appear on it. This is not so much a weakness in Conan Doyle's story as a playing out of one of its main concerns: the continuing vulnerability of men and women to the physical dangers of nature and, still more, to the threatening forms that the nonhuman world can assume in the human mind, owing to superstition, stress, or mental illness.

Thus, the mysterious presence in the novel of prehistoric humans (or their relics, upon the moor), of 17th-century England (at the origin of the legend of the Hound), and of atavism (the modern murderer is a throwback to evil ancestors), together with the wildness of the moor itself, the danger of the mire, and the nearby Dartmoor prison, may be linked to a more general concern with psychological vulnerability. Sir Henry Baskerville seems in danger of being driven mad by the case and has to take a cruise to recuperate afterward. Without Holmes, Conan Doyle implies, Baskerville would surely have succumbed mentally, if not physically, to the Hound. Elsewhere in the novel, Conan Doyle's interest in other manifestations of human waywardness and corruption is often obvious: the Stapletons, for example, have a relationship that for a while (before all the facts are established) seems possibly incestuous.

Some readers may question whether the longer Holmes texts are really novels, or merely protracted detective stories. In the history of the detective genre, Conan Doyle was anticipated, in important respects, by Edgar Allan Poe and by Wilkie Collins, whose *Moonstone* (1868), for example, clearly deserves to be classified as a novel for its scale and complexity in a way that the long Holmes stories do not. But *The Hound of the Baskervilles* is not simply a crime puzzle of the Agatha Christie kind: its significance does not evaporate upon the solution of its mystery. In fact, the identity of the villain comes as no great surprise. Yet, as in all the Holmes stories, there is a feeling that, although one particular crime has been solved, the social conditions and human tendencies that produced that crime will continue, and that there will soon be another knock on Holmes' consulting-room door. "I think . . . we may turn our thoughts into more pleasant channels," says Holmes to Watson in the last paragraph of the novel, but only "for one evening."

Conan Doyle famously became disenchanted with Holmes, viewing him as a distraction from his other work—which, indeed, is still neglected—such as the historical novels *The White Company* (1891) and *Sir Nigel* (1906), and pioneering works of science fiction such as *The Lost World* (1912). But Holmes' general popularity shows no sign of diminishing, especially as, through cinema and television (as formerly in the theatre), he is reinvented by successive generations: from the noble, if quirky, gentleman played by Basil Rathbone in films of the 1930s and 1940s, to the vain, obsessive, and quasi-criminal Holmes of the British television series of the 1980s and 1990s. In literary detective fiction, Holmes has spawned a multitudinous progeny of flawed champions of truth and justice. Examples include Dorothy Sayers' Lord Peter Wimsey and, more recently, Colin Dexter's Inspector Morse. But none has proved so memorable as Sherlock Holmes, who remains the model of the criminal investigator par excellence.

DOMINIC RAINSFORD

Further Reading

Green, Richard Lancelyn, editor, *The Uncollected Sherlock Holmes*, London: Penguin, 1983

Lellenberg, Jon L., editor, *The Quest for Sir Arthur Conan Doyle: Thirteen Biographers in Search of a Life*, Carbondale: Southern Illinois University Press, 1987

Orel, Harold, editor, *Critical Essays on Sir Arthur Conan Doyle*, New York: G.K. Hall, and Toronto: Macmillan, 1992

Pound, Reginald, *The Strand Magazine, 1891–1950*, London: Heinemann, 1966

Symons, Julian, *Bloody Murder: From the Detective Story to the Crime Novel*, 4th edition, London: Pan, 1994

Wilson, Edmund, "Mr. Holmes, they were the footprints of a gigantic hound," in *Classics and Commercials: A Literary Chronicle of the Forties*, New York: Farrar Straus, 1950

The House by the Medlar Tree by Giovanni Verga

I Malavoglia 1881

The House by the Medlar Tree, published in 1881, was intended as the first in a five-volume novel cycle, *I vinti* (The Vanquished/Defeated). Of the others, only the second, *Maestro Don Gesualdo* (1889; *Master Don Gesualdo*) was completed; the first chapter only was written of the next, *La Duchessa di Leyra*, and the remaining two exist in title only: *L'onorevole Scipioni* (Scipioni, MP) and *L'uomo di lusso* (The Man of Luxury). The intention of the cycle was to examine a general human impulse to self-betterment interpreted in biological and economic terms, leaving out of the picture any possibility of spiritual transcendence. In the two completed novels, Verga engages with, while not necessarily endorsing, contemporaneous ideas drawn from positivism and social Darwinism; the projected cycle was to illustrate an overarching principle of evolution and progress in human affairs. First translated into English by Mary A. Craig in 1890, *The House by the Medlar Tree* is the work we may confidently consider to be Verga's point of arrival, his most mature and his greatest novel, although it was not a critical success in its time.

The House by the Medlar Tree tells the story of a Sicilian family, fisher folk in the coastal village of Aci Trezza, whose only possessions are their boat, the *Providence,* and the family house by the medlar tree. Verga gives a collective portrait of a community, with its rivalries, resentments, differences, and—almost as an unintended consequence of these—resources for mutual support. He presents his characters as seemingly autochthonous, their culture scarcely distinguishable from nature, like mollusks cleaving to the rocks. Looked at thus, the perdurable conditions of the lives of the rural poor seem to lie outside history. Yet, at the same time, and although they cannot realize it, it is with the coming of the new unified Italy and the modern state after 1861 that the fortunes of the Malavoglia family, and its identity as a small, patriarchal unit of society, begin to decline.

Old Padron ("Boss") 'Ntoni rules over three generations of the family known as the *Malavoglia,* although that is not their real name. Their real surname, Toscano, is as inappropriate to their reality as subsistence fisher folk remote from the developed region it indicates (as the location of the nation's new capital) as is their ironic local nickname—conventionally translated as "ill-will," although "shiftless" is more appropriate in this case. This is an industrious, cooperative, and honest family, hard hit economically when in 1863 the eldest grandson, also called 'Ntoni, is called up under the recent law requiring military service.

Padron 'Ntoni is persuaded by the village usurer to buy a shipment of lupins on credit, to sell in a nearby port town. The *Providence* is shipwrecked, 'Ntoni's son Bastianazzo drowns, the cargo is lost, and Padron 'Ntoni is left with the debt. Against the background of village life, rendered with an experimental realism for which Verga is famous, a succession of misfortunes afflicts the family.

When the second grandson, Luca, leaves to serve in the military, the family has already grown accustomed to it, as if twice were an endless repetition. Hope for the restitution of the family's fortunes perhaps rests with him, his grandfather thinks, "if God grants him long life." But, observes the impersonal narrator, God did not grant him long life—simply because that is the way God is. It is one of a very few instances of Verga's calculated use of narrative anticipation (prolepsis, a technique of epic) and evidence of a pessimistic philosophy based on an assumption of a deterministic universe in which the individual life assumes no importance.

Luca is killed in the naval battle of Lissa (1866) and Padron 'Ntoni's daughter-in-law dies in the cholera epidemic of 1867. The debt for the cargo of lupins prevents the marriage of granddaughter Mena (she has no dowry) and results in the loss of the family house by the medlar tree. Wrecked in the patched-up *Providence*, Padron 'Ntoni is left injured and unfit for work. His eldest grandson, 'Ntoni, dissatisfied with village life after seeing the world in the course of his military service on the mainland, ends up in prison, while Lia, the youngest, ends up a prostitute in another town. None of the old patriarch's folk wisdom (habitually expressed in proverbs) and faith (in a providential God, in the family, in male honor) serves to redeem the fortunes of the Malavoglia. Padron 'Ntoni dies in the poorhouse. Alessi, his youngest grandson, finally resumes possession of the house.

The time span that may be deduced from *The House by the Medlar Tree* is 1863–77. A great deal of social and political history is artfully concealed in Verga's representation of a corner of post–Unification Italy through the fictionalized experience of people without the means of fully understanding it. Verga's particular genius and innovation in this novel consists in his elaboration of a decentered free indirect narrative discourse, with recourse to dialect syntax to give an impression of "artlessness" and "truth" unmediated and uncontaminated by "literature." This verismo, propounded by Verga here and in works such as his equally well-known short story "Cavalleria rusticana," may be more fully understood in a general context of aesthetic realism.

Tragedy and *epic* are terms frequently adduced for the human pessimism transpiring from *The House by the Medlar Tree,* its approach to representing radical historical change in consciousness, and the loss of an apparently ordered world in which "everybody knew everybody . . . and the fish didn't let themselves be caught by just anybody."

SUZANNE KIERNAN

See also Giovanni Verga

Further Reading

Cambon, G., "Verga's Mature Style," *Comparative Literature* 14:2 (1962)

Cecchetti, Giovanni, *Giovanni Verga*, Boston: Twayne, 1978

Ginsburg, Michal Peled, "*I Malavoglia* and Verga's 'Progress'," *Modern Language Notes* 95:1 (January 1980)

Woolf, D., *The Art of Verga: A Study in Objectivity*, Sydney: Sydney University Press, 1977

The House of the Spirits by Isabel Allende

La casa de los espíritus 1982

The success enjoyed by Isabel Allende's first novel, *The House of the Spirits,* ought to come as no surprise, given the topics it addresses and the nature of the novel itself. In relating a family saga in which the fantastic and farfetched exist alongside the grim reality of day-to-day life in a Latin American country not unlike Chile, *The House of the Spirits* appears to tell its story in what has come to be recognized as the magic realism associated with the Latin American "Boom" novel in general and Colombian author Gabriel García Márquez's *Cien años de soledad* (1967; *One Hundred Years of Solitude*) in particular. But Allende shifts attention from the role of men in history to the lives of women, and she does so in an engaging and highly readable manner. Even though the historical dimensions of the narrative, its readability, and the overwhelming presence of the feminine make for a text that corresponds closely to contemporary popular and critical interests, thus ensuring its commercial and academic success, the novel is both more subtle and more poignant than many of its champions and detractors acknowledge.

And *The House of the Spirits* is not without its detractors. Some critics take Allende to task for those things that distinguish the novel as part of the Latin American literary tradition, dismissing *The House of the Spirits* as a faint and flawed imitation of García Márquez's *One Hundred Years of Solitude* by claiming that the fantastic elements intrude on or disrupt the verisimilitude of the narrative. Others reveal a certain chauvinism by stressing that *The House of the Spirits* is but Allende's first novel or by alluding to her background as a journalist who wrote the column "Civilice a su troglodita" ("Civilize Your Troglodyte"), published biweekly in Chile in the bourgeois women's magazine *Paula.* Still others remark negatively on the novel's female protagonists and patently feminist—if bourgeois—slant, while there are those who, acknowledging the popularity of *The House of the Spirits,* lament its stereotypical portraits of women in Latin American culture.

However, it is important to recognize the narrative traditions and genres in *The House of the Spirits* and how they work in concert. With respect to the issue of magic realism, Robert Antoni (1988) and especially Philip Swanson (1994) show how the relationship between Allende and García Márquez, between *The House of the Spirits* and *One Hundred Years of Solitude,* is not merely one of imitation but of a more complex engagement and critique. Although indeed indebted to García Márquez, Allende fashions from her novel a narrative that is post-Boom, moving away from the fantastic toward a more strict notion of history. That is, the progression toward something new—as seen in the chain of similarly named but strikingly different women in the novel: Nívea (snowy), Clara (clear, white), Blanca (white), and Alba (white, dawn, daybreak), in which the final link in the chain is precisely an awakening or new dawn—alerts us to an escape from the circularity of *One Hundred Years of Solitude.* In this respect, *The House of the Spirits* may be understood as a response to and not merely a flawed imitation of García Márquez's novel. *The House of the Spirits* represents what comes after the Boom.

One indication of the degree to which *The House of the Spirits* may be read as a response to *One Hundred Years of Solitude* is in the novel's three narrative voices. Two of these voices belong to Alba. She functions as the omniscient third-person narrator of the bulk of the text, her observations being based on the notebooks of her grandmother, Clara. She is also the first-person narrator of the opening sentences and the epilogue. The third voice belongs to Esteban Trueba, whose brief sections of narration serve as a counterpoint to Alba's narrative voice and as an expression of conservative, capitalistic, and patriarchal ideology. The dialogue between the narratives of Alba and Esteban, between one voice moving toward the future and another caught up in the past, serves as an allegory of some of the differences between Allende and García Márquez.

The House of the Spirits may also be read as a historical novel, particularly given the obvious references to contemporary Chilean politics, and it is perhaps in this regard that the role of women in the novel is best understood. If the traditional historical novel tends to focus on male protagonists and cataclysmic events and upheavals, Allende's revision takes up women's lives and the day-to-day tasks that shape them and those around them. This is not to say that *The House of the Spirits* ignores defining historical moments—elections, revolutions, and the like—but that these moments are presented in relation to the women in the novel, hence the importance of Clara's notebooks for Alba's narrative, as these contain Clara's minute observations of everyday life. In the seemingly mundane lives of women, *The House of the Spirits* reveals another way of looking at history. Although the chain of mothers and daughters in the novel—Nívea, Clara, Blanca, and Alba—could suggest that history indeed repeats itself, at the end of the novel Alba, who bears within her the women who preceded her, also is carrying a child, who portends the possibility of a future. And Alba looks back over the recent past, which includes imprisonment, rape, and torture, without rancor or a desire for vengeance.

Thus, the house of the spirits, which is the house in which Clara lived and continues to live as a spirit even in death, in which she invoked the spirits and held séances, becomes the dwelling place of a nascent visionary spirit, in which history can be reread and rewritten from a new perspective. That Allende appears to veer away from this revisionary historical perspective in her subsequent literary endeavors—among them *De amor y de sombra* (1984; *Of Love and Shadows*), *Eva Luna* (1987; *Eva Luna*), *Los cuentos de Eva Luna* (1990; *The Stories of Eva Luna*), *El plan infinito* (1991; *The Infinite Plan*), and *Paula* (1994; *Paula*)—perhaps lends credence to those critics who view her as a one-book wonder. But the popular and critical achievement of *The House of the Spirits* is undeniable and worthy of comment, irrespective of the merit of Allende's other novels.

JAMES MANDRELL

See also Isabel Allende

Further Reading

Antoni, Robert, "Parody or Piracy: The Relationship of *The House of the Spirits* to *One Hundred Years of Solitude,*" *Latin American Literary Review* 16 (1988)

Cortínez, Verónica, "El pasado deshonroso de Isabel Allende," *Revista Iberoamericana* 60 (1994)

Earle, Peter G., "Literature as Survival: Allende's *The House of the Spirits*," *Contemporary Literature* 28 (1987)

Hart, Patricia, *Narrative Magic in the Fiction of Isabel Allende*, Rutherford, New Jersey: Fairleigh Dickinson University Press, and London: Associated University Presses, 1989

Mandrell, James, "The Prophetic Voice in Garro, Morante, and Allende," *Comparative Literature* 42 (1990)

Martínez, Z. Nelly, "The Politics of the Woman Artist in Isabel Allende's *The House of the Spirits*," in *Writing the Woman Artist: Essays on Poetics, Politics, and Portraiture*, edited by Suzanne W. Jones, Philadelphia: University of Pennsylvania Press, 1991

Mora, Gabriela, "Las novelas de Isabel Allende y el papel de la mujer como ciudadana," *Ideologies and Literature* (new series) 2 (1987)

Swanson, Philip, "Tyrants and Trash: Sex, Class, and Culture in *La casa de los espíritus*," BHS 71 (1994)

Bohumil Hrabal 1914–97

Czech

Bohumil Hrabal is a writer with a highly idiosyncratic, energetic, and entertaining style. He synthesized a number of major 20th-century cultural and artistic influences—psychoanalysis, surrealism, slapstick comedy, pub talk, the language of William Faulkner and Jaroslav Hašek, James Joyce's stream of consciousness, and Jackson Pollock's abstract expressionism. In his literary texts, which range from the highly experimental to the relatively conventional, Hrabal shows ordinary human beings in the context of their everyday existence and looks for the spark of magic in their lives. Hrabal's work has significantly influenced 20th-century Czech fiction, both in style and in subject matter.

Although Hrabal received a legal degree in 1946, he never practiced law, partly because of his temperament and partly as a result of unfavorable political circumstances. He supported himself as a clerk, a railwayman, a steelworker, and a handler of waste paper at a waste-paper collection point. He started writing poetry and experimental prose in the 1940s. For political reasons, his first book of short stories *Perlička na dně* (A Pearl in the Deep) was not published until 1963, when the Czechoslovak communist regime became relatively liberal. Hrabal's scheduled literary debut, *Ztracená ulička* (A Lost Street), originally to have been published in 1948, did not come out until 1991.

Hrabal's creative output ranges over several genres. In his earliest period, he wrote poetry, primarily influenced by Czech interwar poetism and surrealism. The 1950s were a period of "total realism." During this time, he wrote poems in free verse as well as prose texts, ranging from experimental to more conventional work. Gradually his attention shifted from poetry to prose.

Between 1963 and 1970, several volumes of Hrabal's shorter prose texts and novellas came out, increasing his celebrity. Jiří Menzel's film version of Hrabal's short novel *Ostře sledované vlaky* (1965; *Closely Watched Trains*) received an Oscar for the Best Foreign Film in 1967. Following the 1968 Warsaw Pact invasion, Hrabal again suffered a total publication ban in his native country during the first half of the 1970s; between 1976 and 1989 only bowdlerized versions of his texts were published. Yet in the 1970s and 1980s Hrabal produced his most profound and mature works.

Hrabal's creative method was protean. His main inspiration was the colloquial speech of ordinary people, which he stylized during the process of writing. Until around 1970, Hrabal continually reworked his themes, sometimes producing parallel versions of the same work in different genres or in different styles. During his later creative period, he primarily used the technique of "automatic writing" pioneered by the surrealists, typing his texts spontaneously, relying on inspiration from the subconscious. Hrabal's texts matured in his mind until he put them down on paper at incredible speed. The novel *Obsluhoval jsem anglického krále* (1971; *I Served the King of England*) was written at a breakneck speed over three summer weeks on an old typewriter, with Hrabal sitting on the roof of a shed in blinding sunlight. The sun prevented him from seeing what he was actually typing. Hrabal wrote in order to gather energy and to produce moments of ecstasy, madness, and magic, through which he attempted to transcend the ordinary world.

Hrabal's short stories, published in the 1960s, were the reworking of the raw, experimental texts written during the 1950s, partially conventionalized and formalized. Nevertheless, even the revised versions were received very warmly as a major new phenomenon in Czech literature. A group of young Czech film directors made some of Hrabal's stories into a feature film, which launched the "new wave" of Czech cinema in the 1960s.

Most of Hrabal's texts are set in Czech working-class environments, with a focus on dialogue and on the energetic zaniness of Hrabal's "palaverers," the tellers of tall tales. Hrabal's third published volume, *Taneční hodiny pro starší a pokročilé* (1964; *Dancing Lessons for the Advanced in Age*), takes that interest to an extreme level: the work is a single, long sentence spoken by an old man for the amusement of a young girl. This work is also characterized by the techniques of collage, surprising juxtaposition of motifs, and imaginative associations.

Closely Watched Trains is a relatively traditional reworking of two earlier, rawer texts that are recast in the classical form of a short novel. It is the story of a young apprentice station master, Miloš Hrma, who works at a small railway station in German-occupied Bohemia toward the end of World War II. The events of history are racing by, but the employees at the railway station do not participate in the war—as members of an enslaved nation, they have been relegated to the status of children and they concern themselves with juvenile (some might say human) matters. Hrma is preoccupied with his problem of premature ejaculation. When he eventually proves himself as a man, he also carries out an act of sabotage against the Germans. This act of growing up and entering the stage of history costs him his life.

After the Warsaw Pact invasion of 1968, the Russians reinstated a harsh neo-Stalinist regime in Czechoslovakia. Hrabal reacted by returning nostalgically to the world before World War II. In *Postřižiny* (written 1970, published 1976; Haircutting), he drew a picture of life in the small town of Nymburk, as seen through the eyes of his young mother, the wife of the manager of a local brewery. Here he developed a rich, impressionistic style, with a number of multiple adjectives, recurrent motifs, superfluous conjunctions, and a mesmerizing repetition of expressions he liked. Another nostalgic, bravura performance, a dirge for bygone times of old-fashioned, democratic Czechoslovakia, is the novel *Městečko, ve kterém se zastavil čas* (written 1973, published 1978; *The Little Town Where Time Stood Still*). The work is an homage to Hrabal's boisterous, energetic Uncle Pepin, who came to visit for a fortnight and stayed for the rest of his life. The intensely moving scene of Uncle Pepin's deathbed is a convincing metaphor for the demise of the democratic era in Czechoslovakia.

The novel *I Served the King of England* is again a comment on the predicament of an ordinary man, a childlike Everyman (his surname is Dítě, child) who strives for social acceptance. However, the political regimes in Central Europe in the 20th century change too quickly for the hero to keep pace with them.

Possibly the most powerful work by Hrabal is the short novel *Příliš hlučná samota* (1976; *Too Loud a Solitude*). Three variations of this work exist: one written in verse, one in colloquial Czech, and one in literary Czech. The hero, a workman named Hant'a, employed at a waste-paper collecting point, has spent 35 years of his life operating a hydraulic press, making huge cubes of waste paper. Large amounts of precious, often banned books come his way, which he rescues and reads. Thus, he is "educated against his own will." The novel is Hant'a's monologue, written in sonata form. Hant'a bows to the task of destroying old books, that is, destroying European culture with a centuries-long tradition. As is the case with many of Hrabal's plebeian heroes, Hant'a actively participates in the destruction, yet he is horrified by it. Eventually, however, he can no longer reconcile himself with the modern communist world, symbolized by a state-of-the-art paper-processing plant.

In the 1980s, Hrabal wrote a three-volume recapitulation of his life as seen through the eyes of his wife: *Svatby v Domě, Vita nuova,* and *Proluky* (Weddings in the House, Vita nuova, and Vacant Sites). In 1989, shortly before the fall of communism, he returned to the present. Starting with the dramatic text "Kouzelná flétna" (1989; "The Magic Flute"), which relates the events of the first week of large anticommunist demonstrations in January 1989, he recorded the democratic revolution and his experiences from the first few years of life in Czechoslovakia after the fall of communist rule with his own idiosyncratic energy.

JAN ČULÍK

Biography

Born 28 March 1914 near Brno. Attended grammar school and Charles University in Prague, law degree 1946. Employed as lawyer's clerk, railwayman, salesman, steel worker in Kladno foundries, laborer, stage hand, and extra. Died 3 February 1997.

Novels by Hrabal

Ostře sledované vlaky, 1965; as *A Close Watch on the Trains*, translated by Edith Pargeter, 1968; as *Closely Watched Trains*, 1968
Obsluhoval jsem anglického krále, 1971; as *Jak jsem obsluhoval anglického krále*, 1980; as *I Served the King of England*, translated by Paul Wilson, 1989
Příliš hlučná samota, 1976; as *Too Loud a Solitude*, translated by Michael Henry Heim, 1990
Městečko, ve kterém se zastavil čas, 1978; as *The Little Town Where Time Stood Still*, translated by James Naughton, 1993
Svatby v Domě [Weddings in the House], 1984
Proluky [Vacant Sites], 1986
Vita nuova [Vita nouva], 1987

Other Writings: poetry, experimental prose, short stories, and autobiographical semi-journalistic texts.

Further Reading

Čulík, Jan, "Bohumil Hrabal—Looking Back," *Scottish Slavonic Review* 10 (Spring 1988)
Čulík, Jan, "Bohumil Hrabal Interviewed in Scotland," *Scottish Slavonic Review* 16 (Spring 1991)
Gibian, George, "*The Haircutting* and *I Waited on the King of England*: Two Recent Works by Bohumil Hrabal," in *Czech Literature since 1956: A Symposium*, edited by William Edward Harkins and Paul Trensky, New York: Bohemica, 1980
Gibian, George, "Forward Movement through Backward Glances: Soviet Russian and Czech Fiction (Hrabal, Syomin, Granin)," in *Fiction and Drama in Eastern and Southeastern Europe: Evolution and Experiment in the Postwar Period: Proceedings of the 1978 UCLA Conference*, edited by Henrik Birnbaum and Thomas Eekman, Columbus, Ohio: Slavica, 1980
Heim, Michael, "Hrabal's Aesthetic of the Powerful Experience," in *Fiction and Drama in Eastern and Southeastern Europe: Evolution and Experiment in the Postwar Period: Proceedings of the 1978 UCLA Conference*, edited by Henrik Birnbaum and Thomas Eekman, Columbus, Ohio: Slavica, 1980
Roth, Susanna, *Laute Einsamkeit und bitteres Gluck: Zur poetischen Welt von Bohumil Hrabals Prosa*, Bern and New York: Peter Lang, 1986
Roth, Susanna, "The Reception of Bohumil Hrabal in Czechoslovakia and in the 'West'," *Czechoslovak and Central European Journal* 11 (Summer 1992)
Sebrané spisy Bohumila Hrabala (Collected Works of Bohumil Hrabal), volume 19: *Bibliografie, dodatky, rejstříky* (Bibliography, Supplements, Indexes), Prague: Prazská imaginace, 1997
Škvorecký, Josef, "American Motifs in the Work of Bohumil Hrabal," *Cross Currents* 1 (1982)

Huckleberry Finn. *See* Adventures of Huckleberry Finn

Victor-Marie Hugo 1802–85

French

As Victor Hugo set out to pen his first narrative in just two weeks—on a bet—at the age of 16, his destiny as the most renowned French literary figure and political refugee of the century lay well before him. Today he is best known as the author of *Notre-Dame de Paris* (1831; *The Hunchback of Notre-Dame*) and *Les Misérables* (1862), both of which achieved instant, enduring success, and have maintained their status as part of the international consciousness through numerous stage and film renditions. Leading the burgeoning French romantic movement during the 1820s, Hugo established himself early on as a daring innovator in poetry and theatre alike. His first three novels—*Han d'Islande* (1823; *Hans of Iceland*), *Bug-Jargal* (1826; *The Slave-King*), and *Le Dernier Jour d'un condamné* (1829; *The Last Day of a Condemned Man*)—represent equally original experiments in prose fiction. Hugo's prowess in this realm was not recognized, however, until the publication of *The Hunchback of Notre-Dame*, in which his unique ability to amalgamate drama, narrative, and poetry becomes apparent. At the same time, the moral, social, and aesthetic issues addressed in these four texts signal a remarkably consistent imaginative universe, one that points to the prose masterworks of Hugo's maturity.

An avid teenage reader of Sir Walter Scott, Hugo dreamed of renewing French literature by similarly interweaving fact and fiction, history and story. Set in late 17th-century Norway, *Hans of Iceland* was among the first French historical novels, anticipating Alfred de Vigny's *Cinq-Mars* (1825; *The Conspiracy*), Prosper Mérimée's *Chronique du règne de Charles IX* (1829; *A Chronicle from the Reign of Charles IX*), and Honoré de Balzac's *Les Chouans* (1829; *The Chouans*) by several years. Hugo stamps the work with his own originality by incorporating conventions from other popular genres of the time, most notably melodrama and the Gothic novel. As a result, his wild and witty tale of political villainy, omniverous monsters, and generational strife that culminates in a spectacular trial scene already bears the distinct imprint of all Hugolian fiction—an aesthetic of *démesure*, or excessiveness, that defies the conventional bounds of taste and genre.

Pursuing his ambition of forging the modern French novel, Hugo completed three full-length narratives with an array of common threads within the next decade. Like *Hans of Iceland*, both *The Slave-King* and *The Hunchback of Notre-Dame* have historical settings: the former deals with the 1791 slave uprising in the French colony of Santo Domingo, and the latter with cultural, social, and artistic conflicts in late medieval Paris. Although *The Last Day of a Condemned Man* takes place in contemporary France, its indictment of the nation's penal system echoes related themes in the historical novels. In each case, criminal, outlaw, or marginalized characters win the reader's sympathy over the forces of law and order. The condemned murderer of *The Last Day of a Condemned Man* reveals the nightmarish horror of capital punishment through a powerful first-person narrative that stands as a fine example of the French psychological novel. The rebel leader Bug-Jargal—the protagonist of Hugo's adolescent tale, reworked into a longer novel after Haiti's independence in 1825 (and perhaps in response to Claire de Duras' highly successful *Ourika*, published in 1823)—is the first black action hero in French fiction. He also reveals himself, in a brilliant use of framing, to be morally superior to the white colonialist narrator. Similarly, the two central outcasts of *The Hunchback of Notre-Dame*, the gypsy dancer Esmeralda and the hunchbacked bell ringer Quasimodo, model the charity, devotion, and confraternity lacking in the paternalistic rule givers who control their fate.

Hugo's shift during this period from the comic ending of *Hans of Iceland* to tragic denouements was accompanied by the development of a totalizing aesthetic. In his 1827 preface to *Cromwell*, which became the manifesto for the French romantic movement, he articulates his notion of the modern artistic ideal. Like nature itself, it must mingle "l'ombre à la lumière, le grotesque au sublime, le corps à l'âme, la bête à l'esprit" (darkness and light, the grotesque and the sublime, body and soul, the beast and the mind). Rather than holding a dualistic worldview, however, the author insists that "Tout se tient" (Everything holds together). The oxymoronic figure of the sublime outlaw, beginning with Bug-Jargal and Quasimodo and finding its quintessential expression in Jean Valjean, the ex-convict hero of *Les Misérables*, thus serves as an emblem for Hugo's all-encompassing aesthetic enterprise as well as for the all-embracing French Republic. In *The Hunchback of Notre-Dame*, the grotesque and the sublime, Quasimodo and Esmeralda, appear not so much as opposites as reverse images of each other. Akin to the cathedral, which embodies both principles, the misshapen bell ringer achieves moral and spiritual grandeur through love and self-sacrifice. Hugo's consummate orchestration of dramatic confrontations, lyrical passages, satirical humor, Gothic terror, political forecasting, urban mysteries, and historical and theoretical digressions had a profound impact on the reading public and challenged several generations of novelists, including Charles Dickens, Eugène Sue, and Émile Zola.

In the 30 years that separated *The Hunchback of Notre-Dame* and *Les Misérables*, Hugo suffered two immense personal losses. His beloved daughter, Léopoldine, drowned soon after her marriage in 1843, and the fledgling Second Republic—in which he had participated as a legislative representative—collapsed with Louis-Napoléon Bonaparte's 1851 coup d'état. As Hugo sharpened his satirical and visionary gifts during 19 years in exile, he produced a shower of poetic and prose masterpieces. While the romantic movement officially ended during the early 1840s, Hugo stayed true to his concept of the novel as a deeply heterogeneous genre, not just in *Les Misérables* but in *Les Travailleurs de la mer* (1866; *The Toilers of the Sea*), *L'Homme qui rit* (1869; *The Laughing Man*), and *Quatre-Vingt-Treize* (1874; *Ninety-Three*) as well.

All four novels qualify as historical fiction: the first two are set in the relatively recent past; the last two, respectively, in 17th-century England and the post-Revolutionary Reign of Terror. Indeed, all four works constitute shadow histories that both impugn current events, from Napoléon III's Second Empire to the civil strife of the 1871 Commune, and suggest a utopian vision of the future. As in the earlier narratives, the endings remain tragic, but with an important difference. In forging a complex system of repeating patterns and metaphorical analogies, Hugo invests the self-abnegation and death of his four main protagonists—Jean Valjean, Gilliatt, Gwynplaine, and Gauvain, respectively—with a transcendent status that gestures toward individual and collective renewal. In thus marrying realism with idealism, the grotesque with the sublime, and the local color and historical detail of Honoré de Balzac with the spiritual and utopian discourse of George Sand, he unites the two major currents of the 19th-century French novel into a single comprehensive perspective.

Les Misérables is among the most widely read novels of all time. The action-packed plot and indelible cast of social underdogs, with all but the most wretched seeking a higher order of integration and harmony, proved enormously popular. Through the martyrdom and triumph of the saintly outlaw Jean Valjean, Hugo penetrates the secular belief in personal and social progress with the power of universal religious myths of heaven and hell, sin and redemption, and death and resurrection. As a master storyteller, he develops and resolves dramatic tensions at every level of the plot; as a political subversive, he uses the novel's scoundrels—and, in a slightly different manner, its historical digressions—to satirize both the rulers and the bourgeois supporters of the Second Empire; as a poetic genius, he infuses his prose with stunning lyrical and metaphorical resonances. The globalizing aspiration expressed by the narrator—"Faire le poème de la conscience humaine, ne fût-ce qu'à propos d'un seul homme, ne fût-ce qu'à propos du plus infime des hommes, ce serait fondre toutes les épopées dans une épopée supérieure et définitive" (To write the poem of the human conscience, if only about a single man, even the lowliest of men, would be to merge all epics into one superior and final epic)—is echoed in the works of such writers as Fedor Dostoevskii, Lev Tolstoi, Marcel Proust, and James Joyce.

Although less well known, Hugo's last three novels represent further experiments with the genre. In *The Toilers of the Sea*, he explores, sometimes in astonishingly poetic prose, the ways in which science, dreams, meditation, blood-sucking monsters, physical dexterity and valor, selfless devotion, and death serve to expand the boundaries of our inner and outer universe. In so doing, he constructs a romantic megamyth by using one man's epic battles on a reef against the most fearsome forces of nature to al-

legorize his own lonely stand against tyranny. The deformed protagonist of *The Laughing Man*—possibly Hugo's most oneiric text—combines the monster and the hero in a single personage, not unlike Quasimodo. Blurring the distinctions between theatre, politics, and poetic vision, Hugo again creates a unique generic mix that defies categorization. Finally, the interplay of realist and visionary discourse in *Ninety-Three,* in which three generations of the same family clash over the future of the French nation, underscores his lifelong pursuit of higher aesthetic and political harmonies.

Numbering among the great 19th-century masters of the French language (along with Balzac, Gustave Flaubert, and Théophile Gautier), Hugo invented his own version of the historical novel and continued to explore and refine its possibilities for more than 55 years. Few novelists have achieved such mass appeal while spinning verbal patterns of equal substance, unity, and complexity. The quest to transcend limits—to bridge rhetorical, generic, conceptual, and historical discontinuities—marks him as one of the most modern writers of his age.

KATHRYN M. GROSSMAN

See also Les Misérables

Biography

Born 26 February 1802 in Besançon, France. Attended Cordier and Decotte's school, Paris, 1814–18. Editor, with his two brothers, *Le Conservateur littéraire,* 1819–21; founded newspaper *L'Evénement* (later *L'Événement du Peuple*), 1848; elected to assembly, 1849, but exiled in 1851, first in Brussels, then in Jersey and Guernsey to 1870, and intermittently after that; visited France, 1870–71; deputy at Bordeaux Assembly, 1871; defeated as a result of his tolerance of Communards, 1872; elected to Senate, 1876. Chevalier, Légion d'honneur, 1825; Member, Académie française, 1841. Ennobled as Vicomte Hugo, 1845. Died 22 May 1885.

Novels by Hugo

Han d'Islande, 1823; as *Hans of Iceland,* translated anonymously, 1825; also translated by A. Langdon Alger, 1891; John Chesterfield, 1894; Huntington Smith, 1896; as *Hans of Iceland; or, The Demon of the North,* translated by J.T. Hudson, 1843; as *The Demon Dwarf,* 1847; as *The Outlaw of Iceland,* translated by Gilbert Campbell, 1885

Bug-Jargal, 1826; as *The Slave-King,* translated anonymously, 1833; as *Bug-Jargal,* translated anonymously, 1844; also translated by "Eugenia de B," 1894; Arabella Ward, 1896; as *The Noble Rival,* 1845; as *Jargal,* translated by Charles E. Wilbour, 1866; as *Told Under Canvas,* translated by Gilbert Campbell, 1886

Le Dernier Jour d'un condamné, 1829; as *The Last Day of a Condemned Man,* translated by P. Hesketh Fleetwood, 1840; also translated by Arabella Ward, 1896; and Metcalfe Wood, 1931; as *Under Sentence of Death; or, A Criminal's Last Hours,* translated by Gilbert Campbell, 1886; as *The Last Day of a Condemned,* translated by G.W.M. Reynolds, 1840; also translated by "Eugenia de B," 1894; and Lascelles Wraxall, 1909; as *The Last Day of a Condemned Man,* edited and translated by Geoff Woollen, in *The Last Day of a Condemned Man and Other Prison Writings,* 1992

Notre-Dame de Paris, 1831; as *Notre Dame de Paris,* translated by A. Langdon Alger, 1832(?); also translated by

Isabel F. Hapgood, 1888; Jessie Haynes, 1902; M. Dupres, 1949; as *The Hunchback of Notre-Dame,* translated by Frederic Shoberl, 1833; also translated by Henry Llewellyn Williams, 1862; Lowell Bair, 1982; as *La Esmeralda,* 1844; as *Notre Dame of Paris,* translated by J. Carroll Beckwith, 1892; also translated by John Sturrock, 1978

Les Misérables, 1862; as *Les Misérables,* translated by Charles E. Wilbour, 1862; also translated by Lascelles Wraxall, 1862; Isabel F. Hapgood, 1887; William Walton and others, 1892–93; Norman Denny, 1976

Les Travailleurs de la mer, 1866; as *The Toilers of the Sea,* translated by W. Moy Thomas, 1860; also translated by Isabel F. Hapgood, 1888; Mary W. Artois, 1892; as *The Workers of the Sea,* translated by Gilbert Campbell, 1887

L'Homme qui rit, 1869; as *The Man Who Laughs,* translated by William Young, 1869; also translated by Isabel F. Hapgood, 1888; as *By Order of the King,* translated by Mrs. A.C. Steele, 3 vols., 1870; as *The Laughing Man,* 1887; also translated by Bellina Phillips, 1894

Quatre-Vingt-Treize, 1874; as *Ninety-Three,* translated by Frank Lee Benedict and J. Hain Friswell, 1874; Gilbert Campbell, 1886; Alino Delano, 1888; Helen B. Dole, 1888; Jules Gray, 1894; Lowell Bair, 1962; as *'93,* translated by E.B. d'Espinville Picot, 1874

Other Writings: poetry, plays, history, literary manifestoes, critical essays, travel literature, an opera libretto, and political speeches and essays; cofounded several literary reviews and political dailies; produced hundreds of drawings and watercolors, including haunting dreamscapes that have achieved widespread critical acclaim.

Further Reading
Baudouin, Charles, *Psychanalyse de Victor Hugo,* Geneva: Editions du Mont-Blanc, 1943; Paris: Armand Colin, 1972
Brombert, Victor, *Victor Hugo and the Visionary Novel,* Cambridge, Massachusetts: Harvard University Press, 1984
Grant, Richard B., *The Perilous Quest: Image, Myth, and Prophecy in the Narratives of Victor Hugo,* Durham, North Carolina: Duke University Press, 1968
Grossman, Kathryn M., *The Early Novels of Victor Hugo: Towards a Poetics of Harmony,* Geneva: Librairie Droz, 1986
Grossman, Kathryn M., *"Les Misérables": Conversion, Revolution, Redemption,* New York: Twayne, and London: Prentice-Hall International, 1996
James, Tony, *Dream, Creativity, and Madness in Nineteenth-Century France,* Oxford: Clarendon Press, and New York: Oxford University Press, 1995
Maurois, André, *Olympio; ou, La Vie de Victor Hugo,* Paris: Hachette, 1954; as *Victor Hugo,* London: Cape, 1956
Maxwell, Richard, *The Mysteries of Paris and London,* Charlottesville: University Press of Virginia, 1992
Piroué, Georges, *Victor Hugo romancier; ou, Les Dessus de l'inconnu,* Paris: Denoël, 1964
Ubersfeld, Anne, *Paroles de Hugo,* Paris: Messidor, 1985

The Human Comedy by Honoré de Balzac

La Comédie humaine 1842–48; most titles originally published earlier

Balzac's *Human Comedy* (hereafter *Comédie*) was published in 16 volumes by the consortium of Furne, Dubochet, Hetzel, and Paulin between 1842 and 1846, with a foreword by the author—the "Avant-propos"—in which the overall design and purpose of the work are explained in detail. A further volume, containing two masterpieces devoted to the theme of poor relations, *La Cousine Bette* (*Cousin Bette*) and *Le Cousin Pons* (*Cousin Pons*), appeared in 1848. Whether viewed as a single, monumental epic comparable to *The Divine Comedy* or *Paradise Lost,* as Balzac repeatedly urged, or as a series of 90 loosely connected novels and short stories, these 17 volumes contain virtually all the completed works of prose fiction that Balzac wrote after he began to publish under his own name in 1829. Not included in the *Comédie* were some early potboilers published under various pseudonyms between 1821 and 1825, the satirical *Contes drolatiques* (*Droll Stories*) in the style of Rabelais (1832), and a handful of unsuccessful plays, together with a large number of unfinished works and newspaper articles. In the eyes of the general public, therefore, as well as of most specialists, the terms "Balzac" and "the author of the *Comédie humaine*" are virtually synonymous.

While detailed plans to publish the *Comédie* in its eventual form did not begin to take shape until 1841 (the contract was signed in April, while the earliest mention of the title dates from the spring of the previous year), the notion of combining separate works into an organic whole may be traced to the beginning of Balzac's mature career. The titles of his earliest collections, *Scènes de la vie privée* (1830; Scenes of Private Life) and *Romans et contes philosophiques* (1831; later incorporated into the *Études philosophiques*), encouraged readers to see thematic links among the various stories gathered therein. The notion of a much deeper level of artistic unity, a relation of parts to whole that Balzac would often compare to the structure of a cathedral, began to emerge in the autumn of 1834. In a lengthy, much quoted letter to his mistress Madame Hanska (October 26), and again in the introductions to the *Études de Moeurs* (1834) and

Études philosophiques (1835)—introductions signed by his friend Félix Davin, but undoubtedly inspired if not actually written by the novelist himself—Balzac outlined the program for what was to be a kind of updated, Westernized *Arabian Nights*. The basis of the work, the foundation stone on which the entire edifice would rest, was the series of *Études de Moeurs*, studies of contemporary life that would probe into every corner of French society. According to Davin, the purpose of these *études* was to illustrate by dramatic example how social, economic, and political circumstances shaped individual and collective behavior. Since much of this social observation—in which the most prolific side of Balzac's genius found expression—overlaps with what we now refer to as the social sciences, it is difficult for late 20th-century readers to appreciate Balzac's originality, many of his favorite themes having become the stock-in-trade of journalistic and academic social commentary. Take 10,000 veterans of a heroic war, put them out to pasture on half pay with nothing but their memories to sustain them, in a world that is growing rapidly indifferent to their victories: is it any wonder that a whole segment of society is eaten away with boredom and despair? Or again, ask an entire generation of young women with virtually no education to play simultaneously the combined roles of wife, mother, mistress, household manager, hostess, *ingénue,* and *coquette*: most will fail, often with disastrous consequences to themselves and those around them. As for their brothers who crowd the benches of the Law Faculty in the belief that a law degree will quickly lead to fame and fortune—especially in a restored monarchy in which careers were supposed to be open to the talented—they will learn the bitter truth that Vautrin explains to Rastignac in a memorable scene in *Le père goriot* (1835; *Le Père Goriot*): at the top of the legal profession in 1819, there were only 20 positions, while 20,000 energetic and ambitious young men jostled one another for a place in the sun. Situations like these, which lie at the core of Balzac's fiction, have become the commonplaces of sociological and socio-psychological enquiry. To understand Karl Marx's reported comment that he learned more from the *Comédie humaine* than from all the economists and political scientists combined, we need to recall that, in 1840, the attempt to examine the workings of society scientifically was not yet a cliché, and that in the *Études de Moeurs,* as in his work as a whole, Balzac was not so much repeating such commonplaces as inventing them.

After observing the *effects* of social behavior, the author, still according to Davin, would turn his attention to the *causes,* which were to be the subject of the *Études philosophiques*. It was in this section, with remarkable consistency, that Balzac gave fullest expression to his theory of energy and individual will. Most of the heroes of Balzac's philosophical tales live life to the fullest, spending their allotted ration of vital energy by giving themselves over entirely to a passion that eventually consumes them. Between these *viveurs* and the smaller number of "hoarders"—the detached observers who sit out life in the wings, like the moneylender Gobseck or the antiquarian in *La Peau de chagrin* (1831; *The Wild Ass's Skin*)—Balzac's sympathies clearly lay with the former. Indeed, for many critics, Balthasar Claës' frantic search for the mysterious substance underlying all physical matter in *La Recherche de l'Absolu* (1834; *The Search for the Absolute*), Frenhofer's pursuit of an unattainable artistic ideal in *Le Chef d'Oeuvre inconnu* (1831; *The Unknown Masterpiece*), César Birotteau's tireless struggle to clear his name of the infamy

of bankruptcy in *Grandeur et Décadence de César Birotteau* (1837; *Cesar Birotteau*), maybe even Goriot's blind, unswerving love of his daughters—all are variations on the essentially Promethean pattern of their creator's life. After all, despite an exceptionally robust constitution, the novelist did manage to kill himself with overwork just after his 51st birthday.

At the highest level, intended as the crowning achievement of the entire design, there would be the *Études analytiques*. Having demonstrated the effects and causes at work in society, the philosopher-turned-dramatist would then, according to plan, turn his attention to the *principles* that underlie social behavior. As things turned out, so little of this third and final layer of the grand design actually got written that one can only guess at what Balzac meant by principles and how they differed from causes or effects.

In 1845, even before publication of the *Comédie* was complete, Balzac already was planning a new edition in 26 volumes. The outline for this edition survived and was published in 1850; it is reproduced below (see Appendix). This outline gives an accurate picture of the overall structure of Balzac's work and a measure of his successes and failures in realizing an undertaking the ambitiousness of which was without precedent in the history of the novel. With 62 published titles out of 105 projected—a ratio of 59 percent that rises to more than 72 percent if we exclude the repeatedly promised, repeatedly neglected *Scènes de la vie militaire*—it is clear that the *Études de Moeurs* dwarf the other two categories. The *Études analytiques,* with their catchy journalistic titles but only one work completed, must be rated as a total failure. The glaring discrepancy between intention and achievement, together with the somewhat arbitrary nature of the various divisions and subdivisions (Balzac himself had second thoughts about the most appropriate slot for several major novels), has led some critics to take a sceptical view of his claim that his work ought to be judged as an artistic whole. Indeed, for some of his contemporaries, the various *scènes* and *études* were little more than a commercial ploy; the reissue of established, successful works such as *Eugénie Grandet* (1833) alongside a bevy of new titles, or in cheaper or more expensive editions, could be seen as nothing more than a way of attracting new readers and boosting sales. However true at the biographical level (as is well known, Balzac was rarely out of debt, and his need to make money was unquestionably one of the driving forces of his creative life), this view today seems irrelevant. In contrast to later novel cycles that were meticulously planned in advance—Zola's *Les Rougon Macquart* (1871–93) and Roger Martin du Gard's *Les Thibault* (1922–40; *The Thibaults*) come immediately to mind—the unity of the *Comédie* grew naturally over the years out of Balzac's worldview and the subjects he chose to write about. It was enhanced by, although by no means dependent on, the device of reappearing characters that Balzac used systematically from *Le Père Goriot* onward. Rather than viewing the inherent overlap between the different divisions of the *Comédie* as a flaw, modern readers have come to recognize this generic flexibility as a source of aesthetic richness, as the space between different series and categories gives additional resonance to individual novels. *Illusions perdues* (1837–43; *Lost Illusions*), a central and most characteristic masterpiece in its own right, undoubtedly gains if read as a sequel to *Le Père Goriot*; *La Recherche de l'Absolu,* a study of scientific curiosity and the terrible demands it may place on family members and fellow citizens alike, fills out thematic material hinted at but not fully realized in *Louis Lambert* (1835); while *César Birotteau,* which began life as a philosophical study and ended up as a scene of Parisian life, takes on greater significance if we admit that it fits equally well in either category.

However, Balzac's obsession with the principle of unity—a lifelong preoccupation rooted, no doubt, in his own temperament and reinforced by the close study of writers as diverse as Emanuel Swedenborg and the zoologist Geoffroy Saint-Hilaire—had consequences that transcend the aesthetic dimension that is the natural concern of any artist, particularly one whose working schedule was as frantic as Balzac's. Unity lay at the very heart of what he called his system. Everything connects: "tout se tient," as more than one Balzacian narrator remarks. Of the hundreds of aphorisms and maxims offered as signposts to readers throughout the *Comédie,* this one, on the inherent connectedness of things, sums up best, perhaps, the essence of Balzac's work. What fascinated him, whether writing as a historian, a would-be sociologist, a psychologist, or a mere spinner of tales, was the network of relationships that determine how men and women behave, both in the real world and in the fictional world that mirrors it.

Of these systems of relationships, the range and complexity of which are without parallel in the history of Western fiction, the most original, perhaps, certainly the best known, is the connection between people and things. While physical objects (clothes, houses, furniture, and so on) all had a role to play in earlier fiction, in Balzac they take on a totally new dimension, both in terms of the textual space allotted to them and in their symbolic expressiveness. The second-rate furniture and third-rate food described in such exhaustive (and, for some readers, exhausting) detail at the beginning of *Le Père Goriot* are not simply a stage setting for the drama that is about to unfold: they sum up how far Goriot has come down in the world, while at the same time explaining Rastignac's urgent need to move into a more affluent part of Parisian society. By the same token, the detailed description of Balthasar Claës' house at the beginning of *La Recherche de l'Absolu,* with its venerable doorway, contrasting brickwork, and delicately leaded lattice windows—all carefully maintained by generations of family retainers—is a clear indication to the reader that there is a public dimension to the private drama that has already begun to unfold behind this respectable facade. The heroes of the *Comédie*—if we may trust a well-worn cliché of Balzac criticism—were the first characters in fiction, perhaps in all literature, to spend more time worrying about the state of their clothing (were their gloves clean? did their shirt and breeches meet in the approved manner?) than about how their mistress would receive them. Balzac was neither a determinist nor a materialist (although he was familiar with most of the 18th-century thinkers who were). What fascinated him, both as a thinker and as a novelist, was the *terrain vague* where the physical world and mental states impinge on one another. Indeed, much of his best work could be read as an extended, dramatic footnote to Cabanis' *Rapports du physique et du moral de l'homme* (1802; *On the Relations between the Physical and Moral Aspects of Man*). If the boarders whose portraits are sketched in the opening scene of *Le Père Goriot* are so reminiscent of the caricatures of Honoré Daumier, it is because Balzac focuses on their mechanical gestures, their worn-out voices, and their incongruous clothes. In the same novel, it is Rastignac's

girl-like skin that arouses Victorine Taillefer out of her indifference; Vautrin's control over his own physical reactions, as the police try to lure him into resisting arrest, highlights his exceptional strength; while Goriot's protracted deathbed scene, which comes dangerously close to pure melodrama, is made more believable by the series of accurately observed symptoms of serous apoplexy: dryness in the throat, alternating pallor and hot flushes, and delirium. Whether one approves or disapproves of the introduction of such massive doses of physicality into a genre that had hitherto concerned itself primarily with the analysis of mental states, it is beyond question that after Balzac, fiction would never be quite the same.

Many of the relational systems analyzed in the *Comédie* take the form of binary oppositions, such as the daily struggle, particularly fierce during the first years of the Restoration, between older and contemporary value systems: liberals versus royalists (in *La Vieille Fille* [1837; The Old Maid], *Pierrette* [1840], and *Un Épisode sous la Terreur* [1830/44; *An Episode During the Terror*]); aristocrats versus bourgeois, throughout the *Comédie,* but quintessentially in *Le Cabinet des Antiques* (1839; *The Cabinet of Antiquities*); peasants versus landed gentry in *Les Paysans* (completed by Mme Balzac, 1855; *The Peasantry*); and artistic idealism versus the realities of publishing in *Illusions perdues.* Many of these conflicts are not so much ideological as prosaically financial: at least one-quarter of Balzac's stories hinge on inheritances, dowries, compensation given to or withheld from returning *émigré* families, advantageous marriages, and so on. In an imaginary world of such dimensions, with a cast of more than 3,000 characters, it may perhaps be foolhardy to generalize about what constitutes a typically "Balzacian" theme; however, the impecunious student in pursuit of a rich (and usually older) widow, statistically and typologically, lies as close as any other topic to the heart of Balzac's comedy. Other frequently encountered oppositional systems include Parisians learning about provincial customs or, more often, vice versa; apologists of social change trying to outflank defenders of the status quo; and at the level of private passions, especially within families, natural hoarders who come into conflict with incorrigible spendthrifts. Inevitably, individual characters often find themselves at the point where such opposing value systems collide. In his initial clash with his daughter over her inheritance, and in many other dramatic moments in *Eugénie Grandet,* including the deathbed scene, in which he instinctively grabs at the gold crucifix that the priest is using to administer the last rites, Félix Grandet reminds us of the traditional miser of myth and folklore: suspicious of strangers, increasingly alone, happy only when contemplating the tangible signs of his wealth. But at other points in the novel he behaves like a thoroughly modern kind of capitalist, buying and selling, scouring the country to secure better deals or interest rates, moving his capital around at such a pace that even the Parisian brokers are outsmarted.

Above all, the *Comédie humaine* is woven out of a series of relationships between people. To some extent, of course, such interrelationships are endemic to the genre: it is difficult to imagine a novel since Madame de Lafayette's *La Princesse de Clèves* (1678; *The Princess of Cleves*) that does not hinge upon them. Yet one has only to think of the major novels of Richardson or Goethe, Rousseau or Stendhal, Austen or Constant to recognize that the spotlight in these canonical works remains for the most part on a few central figures; most typically, on the thoughts and feelings of one, two, or at most three characters. Balzac invites his readers to look at the world through a much wider-angled lens. The carefully built-up portrait of Goriot illustrates this fundamental point. Long before the reader discovers the full details of his situation, thanks to a series of recapitulative summaries by the Duchesse de Langeais, by a certain Monsieur Muret, and eventually by the narrator himself, the protagonist is brought to life by the social space that Balzac creates around him. In other words, even before we know him, we believe in him, because he seems to exist for everyone else. For Madame Vauquer, he had been a potential suitor, at least until he fell on hard times. For Sylvie and Christophe, the servants, he is someone who clearly has the means to give large tips, but doesn't. For Rastignac, fresh from the provinces, he is a typically Parisian enigma, visited by duchesses during the day and twisting up the family silver by night with the obvious intention of taking it to the nearest pawn shop. For the boarders as a whole, he is an eccentric, possibly with eccentric sexual tastes, a scapegoat at whose expense they can exercise their student wit (and thus forget for a while their own, equally modest situation). Needless to say, Balzac did not invent this kind of social space: it was well established by the English novelists of the previous century. But he placed it at the center of his work; it is the essential dimension of that work, which explains why readers of all persuasions, from professional devotees to casual readers of only one or two novels, habitually refer to the *Comédie humaine* as a world, a society in its own right, functioning mythopoetically and autonomously, while at the same time acting as an incomparably complete representation of French society of the 1820s and 1830s.

At the center of this mythical world and, by implication, of the real world Balzac saw around him were money and passion: "or et plaisir," the twin driving forces of modern society, play a major role in virtually all of his stories. For Henry James, the real hero of Balzac's work, the "great general protagonist" was the 20-franc piece: "other things come and go, but money is always there." In semiotic parlance, it is unquestionably the principal "actant" of the *Comédie,* even in cases when the title or some other indication—a preface or a typically lengthy exposition—seems to promise a quite different emphasis: in *La Femme abandonnée* (1832; *The Abandoned Woman*), the illicit (but nonetheless idyllic) relationship between Madame de Beauséant and Gaston de Nueil is destroyed only when the latter's mother unearths a rich widow, whose fortune will allow him to reenter polite society. As already noted, *La Recherche de l'Absolu* is a story about genius; it becomes a tragedy only when the bills for material and glassware get out of hand. Understandably, such an obsessive concern for the material side of life did not endear Balzac to those who believed that novels should be morally uplifting; in Victorian England, with a few exceptions, the *Comédie humaine* exemplified everything that was sordidly French, while the Catholic Church, which had placed all of Balzac's writings on the Index of Prohibited Books in 1841, never saw reason to modify its position: in the latest (and last) edition of the *Index librorum prohibitorium* (1948), one can still read, "Balzac, Honoré de. *Omnes fabulae amatoriae.*"

While Balzac explored the theme of money—getting it, spending it, dreaming about it—with a single-mindedness worthy of one of his monomaniacal heroes, his treatment of desire (and the play of passions generally) is remarkable for its range and variety. Apart from the many faces of love, from the most spiritual

(*Louis Lambert*) to the most crudely physical (*La Maison Nucingen,* 1838; *The Firm of Nucingen*), together with the broad spectrum of greater or lesser sins that govern the lives of so many of his characters, Balzac went out of his way to illustrate the more positive sides of social behavior, including charity (*l'Envers de l'histoire contemporaine* [1846–48; *The Underside of Contemporary History*]), friendship (*Illusions perdues; Splendeurs et Misères des courtisanes* [1844; *Splendors and Miseries of Courtesans*]; *Le Cousin Pons*), and commitment to social reform (*Le Médecin de campagne,* 1833; *The Country Doctor*). But whether emphasizing virtue (as he often did, partly to answer his critics and, more particularly, to calm the easily ruffled moral sensibilities of Madame Hanska) or the many forms of vice with which he is more often associated, Balzac never lost sight of the essentially tragic theory of desire first developed in *La Peau de chagrin.* The choice confronting most of his heroes is not so much between good and evil as between living and vegetating. Goriot's love for his daughters, Chabert's sense of honor, Louis Lambert's quest for a form of knowledge lying beyond the physical world are all inherently noble urges; carried to excess, like so many other *idées fixes* in the *Comédie humaine,* they are nonetheless fatal.

To translate this wide-ranging albeit unified picture of contemporary society, Balzac drew on a much larger repertoire of technical devices than is generally realized. In the popular mind (and in some academic circles), a typical novel by Balzac opens with a leisurely description of the setting, leading into a review of the principal dramatis personae, in the manner of Walter Scott. After this lengthy exposition, and only then, events move at an accelerating pace to a melodramatic (and often fatal) climax. In reality, only one-third of the stories open with descriptions. (Another one-third begin *in medias res,* while the remainder establish reader complicity by way of a general discussion of the problem that the novel in question will illustrate: how will improved communications between Paris and the provinces affect people's lives? how should the authorities in a restored monarchy treat those who had fought for the Revolution?) Far from following a set formula, Balzac experimented with many different types of narrative: *La Maison Nucingen* consists almost entirely of dialogue, *Mémoires de Deux Jeunes Mariées* (1842; *Memoirs of Two Young Married Women*) takes up the epistolary form that had been dominant in the previous century, while *Le Lys dans la Vallée* (1836; *The Lily of the Valley*) is only one of many framed narratives. In *Madame Firmiani* (1832), the heroine is described in a series of conflicting vignettes by those who believe they know her, a prism-like fragmentation of personality that anticipates Proust. As for the narrators, whose overwhelming presence in the opening pages has attracted so much critical notice, they frequently withdraw and allow the story to tell itself with an objectivity worthy of Flaubert.

Concerning Balzac's status and influence in the history of the novel, only the briefest comments may be offered here. He is universally recognized as a founder of European realism, although the exact nature of that realism has often been questioned; important critics such as Curtius (1933) and Béguin (1946), following up a perceptive comment by Baudelaire, preferred to see him as a visionary. Library surveys confirm that he is the most frequently read of French authors, while a glance at any issue of *Les livres disponibles* (the French equivalent of *Books in Print*) suggests that he also is the most frequently republished. His influence on subsequent fiction has never been adequately surveyed, although writers as diverse as Fedor Dostoevskii, Marcel Proust, and Michel Butor have freely acknowledged the extent of their debt. For more than a century, the *Comédie humaine* has supported an academic industry whose size and international scope far outstrip that devoted to any other novelist. A school of Balzac critics and textual editors thrived at the University of Chicago in the 1920s; since World War II, a series of Russian, Japanese, and Italian scholars have passed on the torch to their students. As befits the study of a writer who idolized Napoléon, this army of *balzaciens* is not only large but exceptionally well organized, in part, no doubt, because of the unusual concentration in one place of his literary remains. For almost half a century, Charles Spoelberch de Lovenjoul gathered together letters, manuscripts, galley proofs, and early editions, which were bequeathed to the French Institute in 1907. Having virtually all the material under one roof (originally in Chantilly, now in Paris) undoubtedly fostered a spirit of collaboration (rather than rivalry) among Balzac scholars. With the bicentennial of his birth in 1999, a plethora of conferences and publications (including a CD-ROM produced by the "Groupe international de recherches balzaciennes") will explore new avenues through the maze of Balzac's writing, while celebrating, for a new generation of readers, the work of a man whom many critics and historians regard as the Shakespeare of the novel form.

If this reputation is deserved—as, in the opinion of many historians of the genre, it undoubtedly is—it has to be said that Balzac did not come by it easily. For George Saintsbury, who translated the *Comédie* in its entirety and whose article in the 11th edition of the *Encyclopædia Britannica* is still worth reading, Balzac achieved greatness despite himself. Throughout the 19th century and well into the 20th, professors of literature found much to criticize in his style, which is indeed often clumsy and inelegant. His legendary feats of composition—major works sometimes completed in under three weeks, short stories expanded into full-length novels, massive corrections and additions at the galley-proof stage, sections removed from an existing book and incorporated into a new one—may have ensured a much-needed, although sporadic, income, but it played havoc with the structural integrity of many stories. While the *Comédie humaine* as a whole provides ample illustration of Mikhail Bakhtin's notion of the novel form as a polyphony of competing voices, it must be admitted that the results are by no means always harmonious: the voice of Balzac's narrators frequently drowns that of the characters, just as elaborate explanations (*Voici pourquoi*—"here is the reason for . . ."—is one of his favorite phrases) tend to dwarf the events being explained. In the introduction to the *Études philosophiques*, Balzac's spokesman promised "typified individuals" and "individualized types," but it is the types that predominate. Even the most memorable characters, such as the convict-turned-policeman Vautrin, lack the depth and complexity of an Anna Karenina or a Julien Sorel. Balzac wrote more than one undisputed masterpiece: *La Cousine Bette*, *La Recherche de l'Absolu*, and, to judge by university syllabuses, *Le Père Goriot* come immediately to mind. But for all their power, even his best novels lack the formal control of Flaubert's *Madame Bovary* (1857), the sustained intensity of Dostoevskii's *Crime and Punishment* (1867), or the verbal inventiveness of Joyce's *Ulysses* (1922). It is something of a para-

dox, then, that the *Comédie,* despite its many flaws, has been judged worthy of standing alongside these other pinnacles of the genre. The concluding remarks of this brief notice will try to address this paradox.

If we look at Balzac's work as a whole and compare it to that of his contemporaries or immediate successors, three qualities in particular stand out: an exceptional understanding of contemporary history and the way the historical process shapes the lives of private individuals; an insatiable, encyclopedic curiosity; and an innate conviction that everybody and everything deserved to find a place in his fictional universe: behind the humblest life or the most prosaic of subjects, there lay a story worth telling.

While Balzac occasionally turned his attention to former times, the evocation of the past had already been mastered by his mentor, Sir Walter Scott; accordingly, the vast majority of his stories deal with strictly contemporary society. To the study of that society he brought a historical understanding at least as acute as Alexis de Tocqueville's. More particularly, the *Comédie humaine* is a major contribution to what the French refer to as *l'histoire des mentalités,* the study of what people in a given period thought and felt. From a novelist's standpoint, it was undoubtedly an advantage to live in an age of uncertainty and rapid change. A satirical scene at the beginning of *La Peau de chagrin* makes the point that, in the aftermath of the July Revolution, ideas, institutions, even the meaning of words were in a state of constant flux. (It should be recalled that when this novel appeared in 1831, everyone over the age of 50 had experienced the Ancien Régime, 10 years of violent revolution, 15 years of Empire during which France was mostly at war with the rest of Europe, and another 15 years of a restored monarchy that could never make up its mind just how far the constitutional clock could be turned back.) Balzac's achievement was not merely to bring these troubled times alive: many minor writers like Eugène Sue, as well as major ones like Charles Dickens, were just as skilled at doing that. Rather, what the *Comédie* explores in depth is the extent to which ordinary men and women are inserted into the historical process itself, whether or not they understand it. Needless to add, it is on this aspect of Balzac, particularly as it relates to the emergence of the bourgeoisie as the dominant class in French life, that Marxist critics such as André Wurmser, Pierre Barbéris and Fredric Jameson have, quite properly, laid special emphasis. Of the many titles listed in the 1845 catalogue, none is more intriguing than No. 71: "L'Histoire et le roman." Whatever Balzac intended to do with such a topic, the work was never finished, probably never even begun. It would have made a fine subtitle to his modern epic, since the work as a whole stands at the point where individual stories, the stuff of fiction, intersect with the larger story of an entire society. Among the major novelists, only Tolstoi can make a similar claim to be taken seriously as a historian.

If Balzac had been able to hear the eulogy delivered by Victor Hugo at his funeral in August 1850, he would have been gratified, for the most part, by his friend's tribute: few writers have written as cogently about a contemporary. One phrase, however, would probably have given him pause. "Whether he knew it or not, whether he intended it or not, whether he consented to it or not, the author of this immense and strange work belongs to the hardy race of revolutionary writers." A thoroughgoing conservative, Balzac would have hesitated before accepting the label of "revolutionary." But Hugo was right. The introduction into the novel of a whole range of nonfictional discourse, together with a parallel expansion of the kind of characters whose stories needed telling, did indeed constitute a revolution in the history of the form.

One of the great puzzles of Balzac studies, only partially solved by his biographers, is how he managed to acquire such intimate knowledge of so many areas of human endeavor. That he should have an understanding of business and the law was hardly surprising: he had been a businessman and a law student. But only a kind of natural sympathy for other people's lives, together with an exceptional ability to absorb information, can explain the range of topics touched upon, not always superficially, in his novels. A lifelong fascination for mysticism and what we would now regard as pseudo-sciences (mesmerism, thought-transfer, phrenology, and the like) should not obscure the fact that he had a real understanding of contemporary science and medicine. Nothing seemed to have bored him; his enthusiastic disquisitions on topics as diverse as paper making (*Illusions perdues*), musical theory (*Gambara*, 1837), and banking (*Gobseck*, 1830/42), while arousing the suspicion of academic purists, may go some way toward explaining his universal appeal to a broad spectrum of "common readers." His careful analyses of how bureaucracies and small businesses work (in *Les Employés* [1838] and *César Birotteau*, respectively) are as relevant today as they were in 1840. One may object that this encyclopedic knowledge is not always tailored to the needs of the plot: lengthy debate on a question of political theory, or speculation about the significance of the latest discoveries in paleontology, can (and does) delay the outcome of the "story proper." On such a basic matter of what belongs in a work of fiction and what doesn't, readers usually make up their own minds. But in terms of the history of the genre, such objections miss a fundamental point. When Balzac began writing in 1821, subscription libraries, then at the height of their popularity in France because of the high cost of books, invariably distinguished between "novels" and "literature." Novels were for entertainment; literature was for self-improvement, increased knowledge, and moral education. If this distinction had begun to break down by the time of Balzac's death in 1850, it was in no small measure because of his efforts to expand the intellectual horizons of the genre to accommodate the discourses of science, architecture, law, and philosophy—and, of course, a nascent sociology—thus paving the way for the modern novel of ideas as it would be developed by George Eliot, the great Russians, and Marcel Proust.

Finally, Balzac's insatiable intellectual curiosity was matched by an equally generous attitude toward people. The exigencies of time and space, together with the imperatives of contemporary taste, imposed limits on the number of characters whose stories could be crowded into a single novel. And as a writer strongly attracted to drama, Balzac naturally focused attention on the major crises in the lives of a few exceptional and/or representative characters. Yet even minor characters are generally individualized by a physical trait, a turn of phrase, an item of clothing, or a quick summary of their past or present situation. The rise and fall of a perfume manufacturer deserved to be taken as seriously as that of Julius Caesar. Small passions, like the abbé Birotteau's desire for a room of his own, if properly observed, are just as interesting as the grand ones that agitated the hearts of Racine's heroines. This side of Balzac's genius (which he evokes in the opening paragraphs of *Facino Cane*, 1837) is neatly summed up by an anecdote reported by Baudelaire in his review of the paintings in the 1855 Universal Exhibition. The novelist is supposed to have stopped in front of a winter scene depicting a peasant's cottage, exclaiming, "How fine! But what are they doing in there? What do they think about, what are their sorrows? Were the crops good this year? No doubt their mortgage payments are overdue?" It is no small irony that a writer who once stood as a Royalist candidate and devoted a major section of the "Avant-propos" to a defense of the Monarchy and the Catholic Church should have played such a crucial role in what one can only call the "democratization" of the novel form.

GRAHAM FALCONER

See also Père Goriot

Further Reading

Barbéris, Pierre, *Balzac et le mal du siècle: Contribution à une physiologie du monde moderne*, 2 vols., Paris: Gallimard, 1970

Bardèche, Maurice, *Balzac, romancier*, Paris: Plon, 1940

Béguin, Albert, *Balzac visionnaire*, Geneva: Skira, 1946

Brooks, Peter, "Balzac: Representation and Signification," in his *The Melodramatic Imagination: Balzac, Henry James, Melodrama, and the Mode of Excess*, New Haven, Connecticut: Yale University Press, 1976

Chollet, Roland, *Balzac journaliste: Le tournant de 1830*, Paris: Klincksieck, 1983

Curtius, E.R., *Balzac*, translated by H. Jourdan, Paris: Grasset, 1933

Dällenbach, Lucien, *La canne de Balzac*, Paris: Corti, 1996

Hemmings, F.W.J., *Balzac: An Interpretation of "La Comédie humaine,"* New York: Random House, 1967

Hunt, H.J., *Balzac's "Comédie humaine,"* London: Athlone Press, 1959

Kanes, Martin, *Balzac's Comedy of Words*, Princeton, New Jersey: Princeton University Press, 1975

Lukács, Georg, *Balzac und der französische Realismus*, Berlin: Aufbau, 1951; as *Balzac et le réalisme français*, Paris: Maspero, 1967

Prendergast, Christopher, *Balzac: Fiction and Melodrama*, London: Arnold, and New York: Holmes and Meier, 1978

Prendergast, Christopher, *The Order of Mimesis: Balzac, Stendhal, Nerval, Flaubert*, Cambridge and New York: Cambridge University Press, 1986

Pugh, Anthony R., *Balzac's Recurring Characters*, Toronto: University of Toronto Press, 1974; London: Duckworth, 1975

Robb, Graham, *Balzac: A Biography*, London: Picador, 1994; New York: Norton, 1995

Vachon, Stéphane, *Les travaux et les jours d'Honoré de Balzac*, Montreal: Les Presses de l'Université de Montréal, 1992

Appendix

In 1845, Balzac compiled a plan for a second edition of the *Comédie humaine*. It was published immediately after his death in August, 1850 by Amédée Achard in *L'Assemblée Nationale* and is reproduced below. A few works, not included in the plan, were published in 1848 in Vol. 17 of the Furne edition: Un homme d'affaires; Gaudissart II; les Parents pauvres (la Cousine Bette; le Cousin Pons); Petites Misères de la vie conjugale.

In this plan, please note the following typographical markers:

1. Titles in **BOLD CAPITALS** refer to the principal divisions and sub-divisions of the *Comédie*, categories that Balzac used consistently from the Werdet editions (1834–35) onward, although individual novels were sometimes moved from one category to another.
2. Titles in CAPITALS refer both to novels grouped together by theme (e.g. Nos. 36–38 deal with celibacy) and to ones that consist of separate episodes (e.g. Nos. 50–52).
3. Titles in *italics* were never published.

* * *

Première Partie: ÉTUDES DE MOEURS.
Deuxième Partie: ÉTUDES PHILOSOPHIQUES.
Troisième Partie: ÉTUDES ANALYTIQUES.

Première Partie: ÉTUDES DE MOEURS

Six livres: 1. Scènes de la vie privée; 2. Scènes de la vie de province; 3. Scènes de la vie parisienne; 4. Scènes de la vie politique; 5. Scènes de la vie militaire; 6. Scènes de la vie de campagne.

SCÈNES DE LA VIE PRIVÉE (4 volumes, tomes I à IV). - 1. *Les Enfants.* - 2. *Un pensionnat de demoiselles.* - 3. *Intérieur de collège.* - 4. La Maison du Chat-qui-pelote. - 5. Le Bal de Sceaux. - 6. Mémoires de deux jeunes mariées. - 7. La Bourse. - 8. Modeste Mignon. - 9. Un début dans la vie. - 10. Albert Savarus. - 11. La Vendetta. - 12. Une double famille. - 13. La Paix du ménage. - 14. Madame Firmiani. - 15. Etude de femme. - 16. La Fausse Maîtresse. - 17. Une fille d'Eve. - 18. Le Colonel Chabert. 19. Le Message. - 20. La Grenadière. - 21. La Femme abandonnée. - 22. Honorine. - 23. Béatrix ou les Amours forcées. - 24. Gobseck. - 25. La Femme de trente ans. - 26. Le Père Goriot. - 27. Pierre Grassou. - 28. La Messe de l'athée. - 29. L'Interdiction. - 30. Le Contrat de mariage. - 31. *Gendres et belles-mères.* - 32. Autre étude de femme.

SCÈNES DE LA VIE DE PROVINCE (4 volumes, tomes V à VIII). - 33. Le Lys dans la vallée. - 34. Ursule Mirouet. - 35. Eugénie Grandet. - LES CÉLIBATAIRES : 36. Pierrette. - 37. Le Curé de Tours. - 38. Un ménage de garçon en province (la Rabouilleuse). - LES PARISIENS EN PROVINCE : 39. L'Illustre Gaudissart. - 40. *Les Gens ridés.* - 41. La Muse du département. - 42. *Une actrice en voyage.* - 43. *La Femme supérieure.* - LES RIVALITÉS : 44. *L'Original.* - 45. *Les Héritiers Boirouge.* - 46. La Vieille Fille. - LES PROVINCIAUX À PARIS : 47. Le Cabinet des antiques. - 48. *Jacques de Metz.* - 49. Illusions perdues, 1re partie : les Deux Poètes; 2e partie : Un grand homme de province à Paris; 3e partie : les Souffrances de l'inventeur.

SCÈNES DE LA VIE PARISIENNE (4 volumes, tomes IX à XII). - HISTOIRE DES TREIZE : 50. Ferragus (1er épisode). - 51. La Duchesse de Langeais (2e épisode). - 52. La Fille aux yeux d'or (3e épisode). - 53. Les Employés. - 54. Sarrasine. - 55. Grandeur et décadence de César Birotteau. - 56. La Maison Nucingen. - 57. Facino Cane. - 58. Les Secrets de la princesse de Cadignan. - 59. Splendeurs et misères des courtisanes. - 60. La Dernière Incarnation de Vautrin. - 61. *Les Grands, l'Hôpital et le Peuple.* - 62. *Un prince de la bohème.* -63. *Les Comiques sérieux (les Comédiens sans le savoir).* - 64. *Echantillons de causeries françaises.* - 65. *Une vue du palais.* - 66. Les Petits Bourgeois. - 67. *Entre savants.* - 68. *Le théâtre comme il est.* - 69. *Les Frères de la Consolation* (l'Envers de l'histoire contemporaine).

SCÈNES DE LA VIE POLITIQUE (3 volumes, tomes XIII à XV). - 70. Un épisode sous la Terreur. - 71. *L'Histoire et le roman.* - 72. Une ténébreuse affaire. - 73. *Les Deux Ambitieux.* - 74. *L'Attaché d'ambassade.* - 75. *Comment on fait un ministère.* 76. Le Député d'Arcis. - 77. Z. Marcas.

SCÈNES DE LA VIE MILITAIRE (4 volumes, tomes XVI à XIX). - 78. *Les Soldats de la République* (3 épisodes). - 79. *L'Entrée en campagne.* - 80. *Les Vendéens.* - 81. Les Chouans. - LES FRANÇAIS EN EGYPTE (1er épisode) : 82. *Le Prophète*; (2e épisode): 83. *Le Pacha* ; (3e épisode): 84. Une Passion dans le désert. - 85. *L'Armée roulante.* - 86. *La Garde consulaire.* - 87. SOUS VIENNE, 1re partie : *Un combat*; 2e partie : *l'Armée assiégée*; 3e partie : *la Plaine de Wagram.* - 88. *L'Aubergiste.* - 89. *Les Anglais en Espagne.* - 90. *Moscou.* - 91. *La Bataille de Dresde.* - 92. *Les Traînards.* - 93. *Les Partisans.* - 94. *Une croisière.* - 95. *Les Pontons.* - 96. *La Campagne de France.* - 97. *Le Dernier Champ de bataille.* - 98. *L'Emir.* - 99. *La Pénissière.* - 100. *Le Corsaire algérien.*

SCÈNES DE LA VIE DE CAMPAGNE (2 volumes, tomes XX à XXI). - 101. Les Paysans. - 102. Le Médecin de campagne. - 103. *Le Juge de paix.* - 104. Le curé de village. - 105. *Les Environs de Paris.*

Deuxième partie : ÉTUDES PHILOSOPHIQUES

(3 volumes, tomes XXII à XXIV). - 106. *Le Phédon d'aujourd'hui.* - 107. La Peau de chagrin. - 108. Jésus-Christ en Flandre. - 109. Melmoth réconcilié. - 110. Massimilla Doni. - 111. Le Chef-d'oeuvre inconnu. - 112. Gambara. - 113. Balthazar Claës ou la Recherche de l'absolu. - 114. *Le Président Fritot.* 115. *Le Philanthrope.* - 116. *L'Enfant maudit.* - 117. Adieu. - 118. Les Marana. - 119. Le Réquisitionnaire. - 120. El Verdugo. - 121. Un drame au bord de la mer. - 122. Maître Cornélius. - 123. L'Auberge rouge. - 124. SUR CATHERINE DE MÉDICIS : I. Le Martyre calviniste. - 125. ID. : II. La Confession des Ruggieri. 126. ID. : III. Les Deux Rêves. - 127. *Le Nouvel Abeilard.* - 128. L'Elixir de longue vie. - 129. *La Vie et les aventures d'une idée.* - 130. Les Proscrits. - 131. Louis Lambert.- 132. Séraphita.

Troisième partie : ÉTUDES ANALYTIQUES

(2 volumes, tomes XXV à XXVI). - 133. *Anatomie des corps enseignants.* - 134. Physiologie du mariage. - 135. *Pathologie de la vie sociale.* - 136. *Monographie de la vertu.* - 137. *Dialogue philosophique et politique sur les perfections du XIXe siècle.*

Humorous Novel. *See* Comedy and Humor in the Novel; Parody and Pastiche

---

Hundejahre. *See* Danzig Trilogy

Hungarian Novel

Whereas poetry and even drama flourished in Hungary as early as the 16th century, the novel was a genre unknown until the 18th century. The era of the Enlightenment favored didactic tales and it was in this vein that György Bessenyei wrote the satirical novel *Tariménes utazása* (1804; The Travels of Tarimenes), which registers the influence of Voltaire. A less critical writer, András Dugonics scored the first popular success with *Etelka* (1788; Etelka). A loosely constructed pseudo-historical romance, the story is set at the time of the 9th-century conquest of Hungary by the ancestors of the Magyars. Its success was due to the emergence of a strong Hungarian national consciousness and to the fact that it satisfied the nobility's nostalgia for a glorious and less complicated past. Paradoxically, *Tariménes utazása* is more readable today than *Etelka,* which is full of dialect words that have disappeared or become obsolete.

If the classicists believed in the power of reason, the sentimentalists, sometimes called pre-romantics, stressed the rights of the heart and favored a melancholic and often mournful manner. The best Hungarian representative of this trend was József Kármán, whose novel of letters *Fanni hagyományai* (1794; The Memoirs of Fanny) is the story of a delicate young girl born into a wealthy landowning family. She falls in love with a young man who is of lower social standing and thus unacceptable to her family. The sad story of frustrated love unfolds in the letters Fanni writes to a certain Baroness L. After Fanni gains the reader's sympathy with her suffering, it is related that she has passed away. The novel has little plot but is rich in psychological detail. Kármán published his novel in the literary quarterly *Uránia,* which targeted women readers. Unfortunately, he could not secure enough support for his magazine, which closed down after three numbers. Kármán's initiative was more or less forgotten, and his work was rediscovered only in the 1840s.

The language reforms of the first two decades of the 19th century gave new impetus to the hitherto neglected genre of the novel. The reformers, mostly writers and linguists, were led by Ferenc Kazinczy, a man of letters passionately in favor of modernization. He and his circle coined numerous words to fit new concepts of urban life and industrial social organization. They also tried to create a unified literary language out of a number of regional languages with different orthographies. Kazinczy himself did not write novels, although he translated a minor sentimental German novel into Hungarian. Having been imprisoned by the Austrian authorities for his participation in the plot of the Hungarian Jacobins, he wrote the memorable autobiography *Fogságom naplója* (The Journal of My Captivity), which was published in book form only in 1931. His greatest contribution to the Hungarian novel was his successful struggle to broaden the scope and register of literary Hungarian.

In the first decades of the 19th century, poetry and drama developed rapidly, and the key figure of Hungarian romanticism, Mihály Vörösmarty was an outstanding poet and playwright. Prose soon followed suit with a novel by András Fáy, *A Bélteky ház* (1832; The House of the Béltekys), a dramatized narrative about a generational conflict in a noble family during the social and economic reforms of the 1820s. The novel, written in the "new style" created by the language reforms, has been criticized for all its social insights as rambling and diffuse. Indeed, it discusses broad social issues as well as art and literature and also contains an account of foreign travels.

A more talented contemporary, Baron Miklós Jósika is often called the father of the Hungarian historical novel. He came from a wealthy noble family and made a career as an army officer before he took up writing in his 40s. His literary model was Sir Walter Scott, and his native Transylvania served as his "Scotland" in his first novel *Abafi* (1836; Abafi). The hero of this Bildungsroman changes his dissolute life through the ennobling effect of love and becomes in the end a self-sacrificing patriot. Although romantic with respect to the adventurous plot, *Abafi* attempts to paint an authentic historical background that underscores the verisimilitude of the narrative.

The reform era that lasted from the mid-1820s to the revolution of 1848 saw the transformation of Pest-Buda into a center of cultural life. The foundation of the Hungarian Academy of Sciences (1825), the opening of the first Hungarian-language theatre in Pest (1837), and the publication of regular literary almanacs and journals such as *Aurora* and *Atheneum* were among the more significant contributions to this transformation. The reading public was large enough by the 1830s to support

Western-style literary magazines, enabling at least some writers to live on their earnings. While the literature of the first two or three decades of the century still reflected the tastes and expectations of the nobility, eventually writers appeared whose creative method was closer to social or psychological realism and whose readership became increasingly more urban, consisting of people in the free professions, young clerks, and students.

The shift from romanticism to realism that affected Western Europe after the 1840s failed to take place in Hungary. Owing to the political debacle of the post-1849 period, there was more critical realism in Hungarian prose before the 1848 revolution than after the War of Independence of 1848 and 1849. The leading Hungarian novelists of the mid–19th century were József Eötvös, Zsigmond Kemény, and Mór (or, as he was known in England, "Maurus") Jókai. Of the three, Jókai made the greatest impact on Hungarian readers; he is also the most romantic of the three.

Baron József Eötvös studied law and philosophy at Pest University and made his literary debut with plays. He also took an active part in politics, being a deputy at the Hungarian Diet and usually championing liberal and humanitarian causes. His first novel, *A karthausi* (1839; The Carthusian), was much influenced by contemporaneous French fiction. Indeed, it is set in France, where the hero, having had a number of dissatisfying or tragic love affairs, enters a Carthusian monastery to serve a community rather than lead a selfish, uncaring life. It has been described as the first genuine and important Hungarian social novel, but it has technical deficiencies that do not commend it to a modern reader. Eötvös' next novel, *A falu jegyzője* (1845; *The Village Notary*), was hailed as perhaps the best social novel written during the reform era. It is fiercely critical of all the abuses of law, the corruption, the arbitrariness, and the bureaucratic injustice of the administration of an imaginary Hungarian county. The novel is in fact closer to a social satire with strong didactic undertones. Its hero is a liberal and compassionate village notary beset by political enemies. He manages to foil their plans to discredit him through the self-sacrifice of an outlaw farmer. Eötvös tried his hand at the historical novel, too, and while *Magyarország 1514-ben* (1847; Hungary in 1514) is less cohesive than *The Village Notary*, he managed to create an impressive picture of a country that had failed to introduce reforms in time and that, because of this omission, was plunged into the Peasant Rebellion of György Dózsa of the early 16th century.

Zsigmond Kemény, another baron born in Transylvania, spent most of his creative life in Vienna and Pest-Buda. Kemény had a particular interest in psychological analysis, and his novels focus on human conflict against a historical backdrop. Most of his novels are set in 16th- or 17th-century Hungary. His view of history is uniformly pessimistic: most of his characters are overcome by the forces of history. Kemény's career may be roughly divided into two periods. Between 1847 and 1855, he wrote novels that could still be described as romantic, but after 1855 a shift can be detected toward the historically defined realism of such writers as Honoré de Balzac or Charles Dickens. Both *Özvegy és leánya* (1855; The Widow and Her Daughter) and *A rajongók* (1859; The Fanatics) deal with tragic conflicts brought about by religious fanaticism and family feuds in which the protagonists become victims of forces and circumstances beyond their control. In *Zord idő* (1862; Stormy Times), Kemény paints a broad historical panorama of Hungary at the time of the Turk-

ish conquest that serves as the setting for a tragic love story. Kemény may have become a realist in his descriptions of society, but in the interpretation of human destiny he remained a romantic pessimist, which may have contributed to his relative unpopularity. Although he is sometimes regarded as a precursor of 20th-century fiction, he nevertheless cannot vie with the fame of Jókai.

Mór Jókai was a most prolific writer, having more time to write than Eötvös, who was minister of education in the first post-1867 Hungarian government, or Kemény, who was forced to support himself with journalism. Born in Komárom to a middle-class family, Jókai began to write when he was still studying law. His first novel, *Hétköznapok* (Weekdays), published in 1846, was much influenced by the French romantics, especially Victor Hugo. Jókai took part in the 1848 revolution and the struggle for independence and was forced into hiding for a while. He reemerged in the 1850s as a very active and influential writer and journalist. Like Kemény, he adopted the only genre that regularly made it past the censors—the historical novel.

In fact, Jókai wrote adventure novels set in the 16th and 17th centuries, when Hungary was fighting the Turks. He moved closer to the present in *Egy magyar nábob* (1854; A Hungarian Nabob) and its sequel, *Kárpáthy Zoltán* (1853–55; Zoltan Kárpáthy). Both deal with the fortunes of the Kárpáthy family in the reform era. Through a contrast between the egoistic rich older Kárpáthy and his noble-minded, patriotic son, Jókai manages to show the clash between the old and new Hungary that led to the revolution of 1848. These novels are still romantic and are composed mainly of anecdotes and incidents. In the long novel *A kőszívű ember fiai* (1859; Sons of the Stone-Hearted Man), Jókai shows, through the saga of the Baradlay family, the developments that made 1848 almost inevitable, and he gives a fair account of the atmosphere of the War of Independence. The construction of the book is melodramatic and the characters are drawn in black and white, but the novel enjoyed immense popularity in Hungary because of its sympathetic depiction of the Hungarian drive for independence.

Taken out of the nationalistic context, Mór Jókai is still significant, particularly for his utopian novels, which are also his most accomplished. Some of his novels have a highly personal quality, such as *Az aranyember* (1873; The Man With the Golden Touch, also translated as *Timár's Two Worlds*), the colorful story of Mihály Timár, a rich merchant of Komárom who is torn between two different and conflicting ways of life, exemplified by two women, and finds happiness eventually in the paradise of a small, secluded island in the lower Danube. This is a highly romantic work abounding in realistic detail and exciting confrontations between complex characters. While it could be labeled an escapist work, it also displays some of Jókai's most notable strengths of style and storytelling.

The novel *Fekete gyémántok* (1870; The Dark Diamonds) deals with problems raised by rapid industrialization and the exploitation of natural resources—coal. The book's hero is an engineer turned entrepreneur, Ivan Berend, a model capitalist, an inventor, a philanthropist, and a patriot. He is the embodiment of Jókai's romantic anticapitalism, which is nevertheless based on strong positivist beliefs in the unlimited technological progress awaiting mankind.

Jókai was also a pioneer of science fiction. In the voluminous novel *A jövő század regénye* (1872–74; Novel of the Next Century), which is set in the mid–20th century, he shows a major clash between a modernized Austro-Hungarian empire and a despotic, quasi-communist Russia. The main scientific discovery of the century is a glass-like material, *ichor,* found and utilized by the Hungarian-Sekler genius Dávid Tatrangi, who uses it to build flying machines. In fact, one of the highlights of the novel is an immense air battle fought over Siberia. Long before Jules Verne, Jókai's imagination anticipated technological progress that would completely change human thinking. In this novel, as indeed in many other works, Jókai dazzles the reader with his encyclopedic erudition and his stylistic pyrotechnics. As one critic put it, he succeeded in "making the novel a Hungarian genre." Whole generations were brought up on his liberal, broad-minded, although often too benign and optimistic, views of Hungary and the world.

The first important Hungarian naturalist was Sándor Bródy, who was influenced by Émile Zola and first broke certain taboos in his short stories, published as early as 1884. Bródy's novels, of which *A nap jegyese* (1902; The Knight of the Sun) is perhaps the best, suffer from a lack of structure. They abound in criticism of urban living conditions and unscrupulous careerism, but his characters are not particularly interesting or memorable.

Kálmán Mikszáth continues the anecdotal, joking style so characteristic of the provincial Hungarian gentry in some of his work. Other novels conform to critical realism, making acute observations about social conflicts. His first short stories were conceived in the traditional spirit, but once his name was established he began to write with an unexpectedly critical edge. *Szent Péter esernyője* (1895; St. Peter's Umbrella), one of Mikszáth's most admired works abroad, is based on a legend from Upper Hungary about a miraculous umbrella. It is notable for its artfully meandering plot, warm humor, and superb irony. *Új Zrínyiász* (1898; New Zrinyiad) impresses with its fierce social criticism and deep insights into the workings of contemporary Hungarian society. Mikszáth was a liberal, a member of parliament for several decades and a critic of the gentry, which had entrenched itself in the state administration of the post-1867 period. He also shared the anticlericalism of the political elite, a fact easily deduced from *Különös házasság* (1900; A Strange Marriage). The novel, based on a true story, is an eventful but realistic account of a young aristocrat's lifelong and unsuccessful struggle to get the Catholic Church to annul a marriage that was forced upon him. In *A Noszty fiú esete Tóth Marival* (1908; The Young Noszty's Affair with Mary Toth), a penniless young peer is after the hand and dowry of a middle-class girl whose father has made a fortune in America. Mikszáth uses many romantic devices, but the general tone of the narrative is ironic and realistic, its social criticism devastating. His third and last novel from this period, *A fekete város* (1911; The Black City) is probably Mikszáth's most realistic work. It is much less popular than his other books, indicating that his readers preferred entertainment to truth.

Géza Gárdonyi wrote three historical novels, each one of them popular. The first, *Egri csillagok* (1901; Eclipse of the Crescent Moon) recalls some of Jókai's best historical novels with its colorful, fast-moving narrative about Gergely Bornemisza, a 16th-century Hungarian captain who took part in the successful defense of Eger Castle against a huge Turkish army. This novel became one of the most popular books for young people. *A láthatatlan ember* (1902; Slave of the Huns), set in the time of

Attila the Hun (not the barbarian of Western myth but a powerful and intelligent proto-Hungarian ruler), is more a psychological novel than a "novel of adventure," its main theme being unrequited love and its fatal influence on human lives. Gárdonyi's third historical novel, *Isten rabjai* (1908; God's Captives), tells the story of Saint Margaret, a 13th-century royal princess who chooses the frugal and self-deprecating existence of a nun. It delves deeply into the complex psychology of the mystics. Gárdonyi influenced Ferenc Móra, who wrote *Ének a búzamezőkről* (1927; Song of the Wheatfields), about the life of country people disrupted by World War I, and the charming *Aranykoporsó* (1930; The Gold Coffin), a love story taking its theme from antiquity.

The modern era of Hungarian literature is usually dated from the publication of Endre Ady's *Új versek* (New Poems) in 1906 and the launching of the periodical *Nyugat* two years later. This review became the rallying point of all writers who opposed provincialism dressed up as patriotism and who wanted to change both the style of Hungarian literature and the tastes of the reading public. Its orientation was middle class, with a strong representation of reformist, left-wing intellectuals. The review's tone became more radical, even pacifist, during World War I. While *Nyugat* published all the eminent poets of the period, before 1918 it was associated with only three important novelists, namely Margit Kaffka, Zsigmond Móricz, and Gyula Krúdy.

Margit Kaffka wrote a number of realist novels dealing mostly with women's position in society. *Színek és évek* (1912; Colors and Years), the story of several generations of women, has the highest reputation for its subtle psychological characterization. *Hangyaboly* (1917; Ant Heap), her last novel, published just before her untimely death, evokes the stifling atmosphere of a provincial school run by nuns. It is well constructed and shows Kaffka's considerable powers of observation. Zsigmond Móricz, although he is considered a realist by most critics, in fact went through various phases. He made a living as a journalist and often toured the country for material. There is a documentary streak in his prose, which often finds its themes in peasant life. His first novel, *Sárarany* (1910; Pure Gold), shows a village rent by social conflicts. Its peasant hero's "biological revolt" against the status quo is described in harsh, naturalistic colors. In *A fáklya* (1917; The Torch), Móricz depicts the backwardness of a typical Hungarian village and the isolation of an idealistic young Protestant minister from his parishioners. Despite his wishes, he cannot be a "torch" for his community, which is symbolically destroyed by a fire at the end of the book. Critics who find a shift toward critical realism in *The Torch* in spite of its obvious symbolism, usually praise *Rokonok* (1930; Relatives), a critique of the former gentry class, which had invaded all positions of the state bureaucracy, and of the corrupt, nepocratic, pseudo-parliamentary system of government between the two world wars. Another novel with accents of social criticism is *Légy jó mindhalálig* (1921; Be Faithful unto Death), the sensitive psychological portrait of a poor schoolboy in Debrecen, based partly on the author's own experiences.

The most important of Móricz's historical novels is the trilogy *Erdély* (1922–35; Transylvania). It is set in the 17th century, at a time when Transylvania enjoyed semi-independence. The two central characters are Prince Gábor Báthori, an impulsive romantic, and his successor, the cautious realist Prince Gábor

Bethlen. Although its construction has been criticized, the narrative is spellbinding and the slightly archaic language powerful.

Another writer associated with *Nyugat* was Gyula Krúdy, who owed a debt to Jókai and Mikszáth but created his own inimitable style, which is often compared to Marcel Proust's. Krúdy is best described as a neoromantic with a penchant for handling time in a peculiarly modern way. Style is more important than plot, and atmosphere is privileged over reality. Krúdy's output was huge and his writing often uneven. His best novels are probably *A vörös postakocsi* (1914; *The Crimson Coach*), the short but enchantingly atmospheric *Az útitárs* (1919; *The Companion*), and, from the later period, *Hét bagoly* (1922; *The Seven Owls*) and *Boldogult úrfikoromban* (1930; In the Happy Days of My Youth).

Expressionism appears in the Hungarian novel at the end of World War I with the publication of Dezső Szabó's *Az elsodort falu* (1919; The Village That Was Swept Away), a rambling novel that became one of the most influential books of the next generation with its rejection of cosmopolitan decadence and the projection of a romantic cult of peasant health. With the collapse of the Austro-Hungarian monarchy in 1919, the now independent Hungary lost two-thirds of its territory and some of its finest intellectuals. Aladár Kuncz published a novelistic account of his internment by French authorities during the war, *Fekete kolostor* (1931; The Black Monastery). The Sekler writer Áron Tamási wrote *Ábel a rengetegben* (1932; *Abel Alone*), the story of a young Sekler lad adapting to difficult circumstances with common sense and mischievous humor. Tamási was an outstanding stylist, and his masterly use of Hungarian won him wide recognition.

Dezső Kosztolányi, the eminent poet of the pre-1919 years, emerged in the 1920s as the best prose writer of the time. He had tried his hand at short stories before the war, but it was only in 1922 that he first proved his skill at writing longer fiction with *Nero, a véres költő* (*The Bloody Poet: A Novel About Nero*). This novel, which appeared with Thomas Mann's approving foreword, is strong on psychological introspection and shows the dangers of mingling art with politics. Psychology again prevails in the short novel *Pacsirta* (1924; *Skylark*), which investigates close human relationships, and in *Édes Anna* (1926; *Wonder Maid*, also translated as *Anna Edes*), the story of a "perfect" servant girl who is driven to murder by repression and repeated humiliation. Kosztolányi's passionate interest in psychoanalysis and psychopathology makes him a forerunner of modernist and, to some extent, of postmodernist prose.

Kosztolányi was followed and emulated by Sándor Márai, who started his career as a journalist and foreign correspondent. He lived in Paris for five years, returning to Budapest in 1928, when his first novel, *Bébi, vagy az első szerelem* (Baby, or First Love) was published. This was followed by a succession of popular novels and the excellent autobiography *Egy polgár vallomásai* (1934–35; Confessions of a Middle-Class Citizen). In Márai's hands, the novel turns into something between fiction and an essay collection. As his career soared, Márai moved back in time. His first "period novel," *Vendégjáték Bolzanóban* (1940; Guest Performance at Bolzano), describes an episode in the life of Casanova in a manner that recalls Thomas Mann's treatment of Goethe in *Lotte in Weimar* (1939; *The Beloved Returns*). Hungarian critics regard this book and *Szindbád hazamegy* (1940; Sindbad Returns Home) as the apogee of Márai's work as a novelist. After World War II he left Hungary, never to return. He produced four more novels, all of them "period pieces" focusing on the problem of faith and freedom of thought, but his best writing went into his *Napló* (Diaries), a part of which was first published as *Föld . . . föld . . .* in 1972 and translated as *Memoir of Hungary, 1944–1948* in 1996.

A leading exponent of populist ideology and an excellent essayist, László Németh continued the Kosztolányi line of the psychological novel. Németh went to medical school before he began writing. Among his numerous novels, *Iszony* (1947; *Revulsion*) stands out as the most accomplished. A "microscopic study of female frigidity" (see Czigány, 1984), the novel is set against a backdrop of village life and customs. In the majority of Németh's novels, the central characters are women rather than men, suggesting that the author was truly interested only in female psychology.

Milán Füst's remarkable *A feleségem története* (1942; *The Story of My Wife*) is a gripping psychological novel on the jealousy of a Dutch sea-captain. Füst, a leading poet and playwright, is an excellent stylist. His novel, full of acute observations, has a brooding, almost Scandinavian, atmosphere, evoked by the protagonist's near-pathological thoughts and fantasies. The still insufficiently appreciated work of Zsigmond Remenyik, who spent many years in South America and also wrote in Spanish, shows similarities to Füst's. Remenyik planned a series of novels under the title of *Apocalypsis Humana*, which was to cover all aspects of human society. The title itself is indicative of Remenyik's dark and pessimistic tone. *Élők és holtak* (1948; The Living and the Dead) and *Por és hamu* (1955; Dust and Ashes) are his most accomplished novels.

The novel-reading public increased rapidly in interwar Hungary but exhibited a marked preference for popular fiction. Lajos Zilahy, who made his name with *Halálos tavasz* (1922; Deadly Spring), a torrid love story, wrote to these preferences in well-constructed novels such as *Két fogoly* (1927; *Two Prisoners*), which focuses on the experiences of World War I. His most lasting work, however, was written after his emigration to the United States in 1947. The Dukay trilogy (*The Dukays*, 1949; *Angry Angel*, 1954; *Century in Scarlet*, 1966), first published in English, is the saga of a Hungarian aristocratic family and its eventual demise during World War II. Apart from Zilahy at least two other Hungarian writers scored popular successes outside Hungary: Ferenc Körmendi with *A budapesti kaland* (1932; *Escape to Life*) and Jolán Földes with *A halászó macska uccája* (1936; *The Street of the Fishing Cat*).

The very opposite of a literature written for entertainment was the elitist fiction of Miklós Szentkuthy, an odd man out in Hungarian literature. His massive novel *Prae* (1934; *Prae*) is essayistic in the extreme, and while it has exceedingly well-written analytical parts, it is almost devoid of narration. After World War II, Szentkuthy wrote a number of historical novels and also novels on composers' lives, the best known of which, *Divertimento* (1957; *Divertimento*), evokes the life of Mozart. They are much more accessible than *Prae* and show enormous erudition. More avant garde but equally distinguished is the expatriate Győző Határ, who has lived in England since 1956. His *Heliane* (1947; Heliane), a satirical utopia, is written in a language and with a narrative structure influenced by François Rabelais and Laurence Sterne. Határ's most ambitious novel is probably *Köpönyeg sors* (1985; A Cloaklike Fate), a novel on the youth of

Julian the Apostate, about dissimulation in a complex political-historical situation. Határ's vocabulary is extremely rich, and his use of the language is ingenious, but the structure of his plots is often weak.

The development of Hungarian fiction after World War II was retarded by political factors such as the communist takeover of 1948–49 and the ensuing period of compulsory socialist realism. The writer who stood up best against the pressures of power was Tibor Déry, a writer from a middle-class Jewish background whose grand novel *A befejezetlen mondat* (The Unfinished Sentence), written before the war, could not be published, for political reasons, until 1947. Déry was a Marxist and a well-traveled writer who was attacked by a communist party spokesman for the "deficiencies" of his book *Felelet* (1950–52; The Answer) but refused to rewrite it. His short novel *Niki* (1956; *Niki, The Story of a Dog*) is an intensely moving work showing human suffering in Stalinist Hungary through the fate of a dog. After the 1956 uprising, Déry was jailed by the communist regime for "anti-State" activities, that is, his critique of the communist monopoly of power. After his release from prison, he wrote several novels including *A kiközösítő* (1966; The Excommunicator) and a fascinating autobiography, *Ítélet nincs* (1969; No Verdict), but critical opinion now regards his short stories as his best achievement.

The 1960s favored a critical realism trained on the recent past, as can be found in the work of Magda Szabó. Her first novels, including *Az őz* (1959; *The Fawn*), focused on the crisis of provincial middle-class society, which had also provided the theme of many of László Németh's books. Among her novels, a special place is occupied by *Régimódi történet* (1977; An Old-Fashioned Story), which traces the story of the author's mother and is a family novel in the best sense of the word. Other prominent examples of critical realism are Endre Fejes' *Rozsdatemető* (1962; *Generation of Rust*) and Ferenc Sánta's *Húsz óra* (1964; Twenty Hours). The mid-1960s also saw the dramatic debut of József Lengyel, an old communist émigré who was arrested and imprisoned in the Soviet Union in the 1930s and returned to Hungary only in 1955. Apart from some heart-rending stories of the Gulag, Lengyel also published the short novel *Elejétől végig* (1963; *From Beginning to End*), which earned him the epithet of the "Hungarian Solzhenitsyn." He also wrote a sequel to his Siberian experiences, a short, outspoken novel, *Szembesítés* (1971; *Confrontation*), about conditions in postwar Russia. It was first published in English in 1973, but not until 1988 in Hungary.

The realistic mainstream was challenged by a number of writers for philosophical or purely aesthetic reasons. Gyula Hernádi produced a remarkable short novel, *A péntek lépcsőin* (1959; On the Steps of Friday), that was hailed by some critics as the first piece of existentialist prose in Hungary. Even more important was the publication of Géza Ottlik's *Iskola a határon* (1959; *School at the Frontier*). Although not particularly innovative in its narrative technique, it is a milestone in modern Hungarian fiction, a modernist novel of education in the manner of Robert Musil. Its sequel *Buda* (1993; Buda), a posthumous publication, does not quite match the quality of the first book, but Ottlik has nevertheless maintained a unique reputation. Among prose writers, the only author sometimes compared to him is Miklós Mészöly, whose first novel, *Az atléta halála* (1966; Death of an Athlete), had to wait long for publication, the French edition preceding the Hungarian original by one year. Mészöly rejects the 19th-century narrative model with its omniscient narrator and vast social canvas. His heroes are usually somewhat mysterious individuals whose lives can be perceived only dimly through the perspectives of different narrators. The short novel *Film* (1976; Film) forms an exception in Mészöly's oeuvre, with its cinematic technique reminiscent of the *nouveau roman* and its diachronic mode of narration. Mészöly's latest work *Családáradás* (1995; Family Flooding) marks a return to the more traditional theme of the family saga, but his technique remains thoroughly modern.

Another writer who cannot be called postmodernist but whose work unites elements of traditional fiction with modern techniques and modes of narration is György Konrád. His first novel, *A látogató* (1969; *The Case Worker*) leads us into a labyrinth of social deprivation and deviancy seen from the point of view of a sensitive social worker. It is a kind of lyrical monologue written with extraordinary linguistic skill. Some critics consider it Konrád's best work, although both *A városalapító* (1977; *The City Builder*) and *A cinkos* (1982; *The Loser*) have merit, the plot of the latter novel featuring a Hungarian communist turned dissident who eventually becomes a recluse. Most of Konrád's work has been translated into English and he is now internationally the most well-known Hungarian novelist.

Several Hungarian novelists have been active outside Hungary's current borders. Istvan Szilágyi, who lives in Romania, writes psychological novels, while the equally talented but more versatile Lajos Grendel, from Bratislava, is more sensitive to social change than the completely introverted Szilágyi. Of the Hungarian writers living in the West, the best novelist, apart from Győző Határ, is probably Tamás Kabdebó, whose still incomplete Danube trilogy depicts the experiences of different generations of Hungarians and anchors the narrative in the timeless flow of the great river.

The historical novel has undergone new developments in György Spiró's *Kerengő* (1974; Cloisters) and *Az ikszek* (1981; Society of the Xs) and Péter Dobai's short, cinematic *Csontmolnárok* (1974; Bone Grinders). They provide a provocative and controversial picture of 19th-century society in Hungary and Poland, laying bare the hidden psychological motivations of their heroes and society's collective myths and complexes. The most dramatic change took place in 1979 with the publication of Péter Esterházy's *Termelési-regény (kisregény)* (Production-Novel [Little Novel]), a complex novel, picaresque and parodistic, that pokes fun at 19th-century Hungarian social conventions and the socialist realism of the 1950s. The Hungarian critic Péter Balassa speaks of a new sensibility emerging from the work of Esterházy and Péter Nádas (see Balassa, 1986). These writers share an emphasis on formal elements. In Esterházy's case that emphasis translates into a constant readiness to pun and to subvert the original meaning of words. Esterházy's *A szív segédigéi* (1985; *Helping Verbs of the Heart*) and *Hrabal könyve* (1990; *The Book of Hrabal*) come closest to the traditional novel with one or more central characters. His writing fits neatly into the postmodernist category on account of its intertextuality and perspectivism.

Péter Nádas made his debut with *Egy családregény vége* (1977; *The End of a Family Novel*), a short novel set in the 1950s, displaying the eternal conflict of generations in a political context and using guilt and betrayal as the unifying factors. His main achievement, however, is the vast *Emlékiratok könyve* (1986; *A Book of Memories*), a novel composed of three different narratives, including descriptive chapters set in a late-19th-century German bourgeois milieu. Nádas' style is reminiscent of Marcel Proust and Thomas Mann, favoring long, undulating, and perfectly turned-out sentences, and the minute analysis of emotional conflicts and of the incessant struggle for sexual domination is often brutally outspoken.

Gábor Karátson's fascinating *Ulrik úr keleti utazása avagy A zsidó menyasszony* (1992; The Eastern Trip of Mr. Ulrik, or, The Jewish Bride) is simultaneously a rich family novel and a parody of the subgenre. It lacks a single plot and contains a disjointed autobiographical narrative interspersed with short essays on art history and meditations on Chinese philosophy, complete with ideograms. It is an example of postmodernism at its best.

The Hungarian novel has struck out in different directions since the early 1970s. Apart from the postmodernists discussed above, at least two prose writers of real stature appeared whose works exhibit existentialist traits but are difficult to classify within any stylistic trend. Imre Kertész wrote only one novel, *Sorstalanság* (1975; *Fateless*), which is remarkable in its detached treatment of the Holocaust as seen and narrated by a Jewish adolescent, the author himself. Ádám Bodor's excellent *Sinistra körzet* (1992; The Sinistra District) is situated somewhere "at the edge of the world" in the Carpathian Mountains and features strange characters communicating in laconic dialogues. Bodor deftly creates an atmosphere with a minimum of words, in contrast to László Krasznahorkai's first two novels, *Sátántangó* (1985; The Devil's Tango) and *Az ellenállás melankóliája* (1989; The Melancholy of Resistance), which are long on relentless gloom and social pessimism. *Az urgai fogoly* (1992; The Prisoner of Urga), his third novel, provides moments of relief. The intensity and, in parts, the beauty of Krasznahorkai's language make this narrative of a visit to China very memorable.

Hungarian fiction traditionally has taken a back seat to poetry. This situation changed in the mid-1970s, and Hungarian prose writers began to command international respect. At present, all kinds of fiction are being produced in Hungary, with a particular emphasis on the realist, the modernist-objective, and the postmodernist trends. The tastes of the reading public are slowly changing, but the first two types of fiction still have a numerically much greater readership than works written in the spirit of postmodernism.

GEORGE GÖMÖRI

See also Péter Esterházy; György Konrád

Further Reading

Balassa, Péter, "On Recent Hungarian Prose: Survey and Introduction," *Formations* 3:1 (Spring 1986)

Birnbaum, Marianna D., "György Konrad's *The Loser*," *Cross Currents* 7 (1988)

Czigány, Lóránt, *The Oxford History of Hungarian Literature from the Earliest Times to the Present*, Oxford: Clarendon Press, and New York: Oxford University Press, 1984

Esterházy, Péter, "On Hungarian Contemporary Literature," *Cross Currents* 9 (1990)

Fuentes, Carlos, introduction to György Konrád's *The City Builder*, New York: Penguin, 1987

Gömöri, George, "József Lengyel: Chronicler of Cruel Years," *Books Abroad* 49:3 (Summer 1975)

Jones, David Mervyn, *Five Hungarian Writers*, Oxford: Clarendon Press, 1966

Reményi, Joseph, *Hungarian Writers and Literature: Modern Novelists, Critics, and Poets*, New Brunswick, New Jersey: Rutgers University Press, 1964

Sanders, Iván, "Péter Nádas: Emlékiratok könyve," *World Literature Today* 61:2 (Spring 1987)

Scheer, Steven C., *Kálmán Mikszáth*, Boston: Twayne, 1977

Tezla, Albert, *Hungarian Authors: A Bibliographical Handbook*, Cambridge, Massachusetts: Belknap Press of Harvard University Press, 1970

Új magyar irodalmi lexikon, 3 vols., edited by Péter László, Budapest: Akademiai Kiado, 1994

Hunger by Knut Hamsun

Sult 1890

In *The Western Canon* (1994), Harold Bloom offers a provoking definition of the great novel as that which bears an uncanny relation to tradition: "When you read a canonical work for a first time you encounter a stranger, an uncanny startlement rather than a fulfillment of expectations." Just such a stranger, Knut Hamsun's first novel is arguably also the first modern novel in the Western canon. *Hunger* is a first-person narrative that recounts the mostly dire experiences of an anonymous young man trying (and just as often not trying) to make a living from writing, while having (or choosing) to go without food or fixed address, in the city of Kristiania. A mixture of ecstatic, traumatic, and delirious events concludes with the narrator leaving town on a ship bound for England. Hamsun's book resembles other 19th-century works of fiction, and yet it startles and eludes every conventional generic classification. One of his more recent biographers, Harald Naess, cites a letter in which Hamsun states simply, "My book is not to be looked upon as a novel" (see Naess, 1984). Perhaps such a claim can be made of any great novel, but *Hunger* is nevertheless a remarkable instance of historical originality and elusiveness.

A reliable English translation has become available only very recently. Sverre Lyngstad's 1996 translation of the original Norwegian is in innumerable respects more accurate and complete than that of either Mary Dunne (alias George Egerton) in 1899 or Robert Bly in 1967. It may be that this new translation will help to bring *Hunger* to a wider audience. In the foreword to Lyngstad's new translation, Duncan McLean likens the novel to Irvine Welsh's *Trainspotting* (1993) and other innovative contemporary fiction, a parallel that is at once insightful and misleading. No doubt the uncanny elusiveness of the novel does reside partly in its peculiar resonances with current writing: it is difficult, for example, to read the work of Paul Auster without a recurrent awareness of the lurking presence of *Hunger,* and indeed Auster's 1970 essay on Hamsun's novel remains one of the best critical accounts in recent years. But *Hunger* is also a text that locates itself very specifically in late 19th-century Oslo (or Kristiania, as it was then called) and that "belongs" to its time both in sociocultural and literary historical terms.

Some of its literary and philosophical precursors can be readily, if inadequately, named: Poe (for perversity), Dostoevskii (for narrative delirium), Twain (for frivolity), Nietzsche and Strindberg (for fragmented and multiple identity). But the originality of Hamsun's work can perhaps best be understood in two ways. First, it is a novel in which narrative time itself disintegrates. As John Vernon puts it: "a pure narrative present, a sense of time continuously billowing and literally getting nowhere, for the first time fully occupies fiction" (see Vernon, 1984). Second, it is a novel explicitly concerned with writing and the desire or need to fail. As Auster points out: "it would be wrong to dismiss the hero of *Hunger* as a fool or a madman. In spite of the evidence, he knows what he is doing. He does not want to succeed. He wants to fail. Something new is happening here, some new thought about the nature of art is being proposed in *Hunger*" (see Auster, 1990). In its elaboration of the links between writing and failure, between writing, hunger (in various forms), and self-annihilation, Hamsun's novel seems uncannily to "project" the writings and voices of Franz Kafka, Maurice Blanchot, Georges Bataille, and Samuel Beckett. One may hear the tragicomic tonalities of Beckett, for example, in "I sat down once more on a bench near the Church of Our Saviour and dozed with my head on my breast, limp after my last excitement, sick and worn-out with hunger. Time passed. . . . I had picked up a little stone, which I brushed off and stuck in my mouth to have something to munch on. Otherwise I didn't stir, didn't even move my eyes. People came and went." Or one may hear the strangeness of the narrative voice of Blanchot's "The Madness of the Day," in such an exchange as the following:

> I began . . . running my head against the lampposts on purpose . . . and biting my tongue in frenzy when it didn't speak clearly, and I laughed madly whenever it fairly hurt.
> "Yes, but what shall I do?" I asked myself at last. I stamp my feet on the pavement several times and repeat, "What shall I do?" A gentleman just walking by remarks with a smile, "You should go and ask to be locked up."

What this last passage also brings out—and the Lyngstad translation does this with a precision and consistency lacking in earlier translations—are the eerie temporal dislocations generated by the novel's delirious shifting between past and present tenses ("I asked," "I stamp," and so on). Such shifts testify to the singular *writtenness* of this text about the aporias and impossibilities of satisfying the intoxicating, deathly hunger of writing itself.

NICHOLAS ROYLE

See also Knut Hamsun

Further Reading

Auster, Paul, "The Art of Hunger," in *Ground Work: Selected Poems and Essays 1970–1979,* London: Faber, 1990

Buttry, Dolores, "The Passive Personality: Hamsun's Hamlets," *Symposium* 36:2 (1982)

Ellmann, Maud, *The Hunger Artists: Starving, Writing and Imprisonment,* London: Virago, and Cambridge, Massachusetts: Harvard University Press, 1993

Ferguson, Robert, *Enigma: The Life of Knut Hamsun,* New York: Farrar, Straus and Giroux, and London: Hutchinson, 1987

McFarlane, James W., "The Whisper of the Blood: A Study of Knut Hamsun's Early Novels," *PMLA* 71 (1956)

Naess, Harald S., *Knut Hamsun,* Boston: Twayne, 1984

Riechel, Donald C., "Knut Hamsun's 'Imp of the Perverse': Calculation and Contradiction in *Sult* and *Mysterier,*" *Scandinavica: International Journal of Scandinavian Studies* 28:1 (1989)

Vernon, John, *Money and Fiction: Literary Realism in the Nineteenth and Early Twentieth Centuries,* Ithaca, New York: Cornell University Press, 1984; London: Cornell University Press, 1985

I

Icelandic Novel. *See* Scandinavian Novel

Ideology and the Novel

The ideological novel, as a genre, would seem at first to have nothing unclear about it: we call novels with clear-cut ideological objectives—that is, novels that leave no doubt that they advocate a particular set of moral, social, political, or religious beliefs and that they aim to impart them to their readers—ideological novels. Unmistakably dogmatic novels from any location on an ideological spectrum would meet the criteria for such a definition. *Germinal* (1885), a novel by Émile Zola that exposed and deplored the subhuman conditions under which miners toiled in 19th-century France, as well as Charles Dickens' *Hard Times* (1854), Victor Hugo's *Les Misérables* (1862), Harriet Beecher Stowe's *Uncle Tom's Cabin* (1852), Chinua Achebe's *No Longer at Ease* (1960), Nadine Gordimer's *July's People* (1981), and George Orwell's *Burmese Days* (1934), vastly different as they are, could all be considered ideological novels in this sense. Of course, in addition to the aforementioned novels, all of which decry the situations they describe from a position sympathetic to the victims of oppression, those supporting a conservative or reactionary ideology, as well as those actively promoting the domination the novels above oppose, would qualify equally as ideological novels. Maurice Barrès' reactionary *Les Déracinés* (1897; *The Rootless*), for instance, sought a return to an ideal of French "purity" not found since, in his view, urban decadence had come to signify the nation's heritage. Rudyard Kipling's *Kim* is an ideological novel that upheld the legitimacy of British imperialist policy in India. We could also include in the category such a novel as Fedor Dostoevskii's *Prestuplenie i nakazanie* (1867; *Crime and Punishment*), a novel of ideas with a highly delineated moral, rather than political, agenda.

Yet the ideological novel is more difficult to characterize than it might appear from our starting position. For although it overlaps considerably with the political novel, the social novel, the philosophical novel or novel of ideas, and the religious novel,

among others, the ideological novel occupies a murky, tenuous, and often shunned terrain that its cousin genres manage largely to avoid.

Several factors account for this difficulty. First, many contemporary literary critics and theorists (primarily those of a Marxist and/or poststructuralist bent) would maintain that *any* novel may be considered ideological, in the sense of reflecting an ideology. And if every novel is inherently ideological, does it make any sense to designate a separate genre for the ideological novel? The whole concept of the ideological novel is founded on what many today would hold to be a naive idea of what ideology is. Furthermore, the notion of ideology itself is vexed. To speak of the ideological novel, one would need to ascribe a definitive and coherent meaning to the concept of ideology—an unlikely prospect, given the range of past and current debates on the subject.

Add to these problems the contempt aroused historically at the mention of the genre: the ideological novel, like the socialist-realist novel with which it bears much in common, has come to be associated with heavy-handed propaganda literature. While many novelists have written novels they are proud to call political, social, moral, or religious, and while any number of authors have sought to influence their readers' beliefs by creating a novelistic universe representing the ultimate consequences of certain sorts of ideas and actions, few writers would gladly accept the designation of their novels as ideological. The genre of the ideological novel has sometimes served as a catch-all category that includes all novels that have met with disdain for the prominence of their political messages. Usually, as Susan Rubin Suleiman points out in *Authoritarian Fictions: The Ideological Novel as Literary Genre* (1983)—probably the most complete treatment of the subject—the term *ideological novel* is used pejoratively. An ideological novel would be one deemed overly determined and thus constricted by the didactic message—political, religious, moral—that it wants to get across. To call a novel ideological has generally been to condemn it for its single-mindedness and, implicitly, for its closed-mindedness; to call attention to a novel's heavily didactic nature has come to suggest that such a novel must hence be limited in its aesthetic appeal, in its quality *tout court*. Yet if we accept this view of the ideological novel, how do we account for novels that both promote a cause and delight us with their style? Do "novels with a purpose" that we happen to enjoy—take Dickens' novels, for example—simply cease to be ideological because we enjoy them?

Another related problem with the designation of a novel as ideological is that such a judgment is directly connected to the (political, social, moral, religious) position of the subject who makes it. It is important to understand that those who call a novel ideological or who object to it because they regard it as being dominated by its own argument are most often doing so because they do not share the point of view the novel seems so persistently to express. Further, by proclaiming a novel's ideological nature, we suggest that other ways of thinking (including those portrayed in other novels) are not ideological, and hence somehow truer, less illusory. If I say your novel is ideological, I am claiming not to be bound by any ideology myself. That is to say, I am maintaining that I am able to be objective, that my experience of the world and interest in it do not have anything to do with the way I see it. Obviously, such a claim to freedom from bias, or illusions, is itself an illusion—the product of another ideology.

To understand the ways in which any or every novel may be considered "ideological," as well as to appreciate the ways in which the ideological novel has defined itself as a genre, we will have to make sense of the term *ideology*. Yet ideology is no simple matter itself, since the word is used in so many and often contradictory ways. In his book *Ideology* (1991), Terry Eagleton submits that no one has ever managed to define *ideology* in a way that accounts for all of its meanings, and he goes on to cite 16 ordinary usages of the term. The philosopher Raymond Geuss, meanwhile, counts as many as 24!

Ideology can be, among other things, a set of ideas you share with others who think as you do; this ideology you share may typify the group you belong to because it reflects your group interests. Your ideology may express your interests in a way that justifies your group's domination of others, or that justifies your oppression by a more powerful group. Ideology here would be a set of ideas that invade and take over—or simply are—your consciousness, determining how you see the world. If you do not recognize that this ideology is responsible for what you think and believe that you are seeing the world for what it is, another definition of *ideology* would make it synonymous with your "false consciousness"—that is, your inability to be fully conscious of the reality of your existence. For some observers, everyone has an ideology—no one is capable of thinking absolutely freely, no one thinks without preconceptions and sets of inherited ideas. For others, it is only those whose beliefs do not question the logic of injustice who are thinking ideologically.

Of course, the reason that the concept of ideology has so many meanings is that everybody wants to be able to explain why it is that people think in certain ways instead of others. Why do humans frequently think, and consequently act, alike? Why do we see the world the way we do, while other people see it en-

tirely differently? From these considerations, another set of urgent questions arises: how do we get the people who do not agree with us to see matters as we do? May we lead them to accept our way of thinking and disregard theirs if we explain to them how they are not seeing clearly? Or are they irredeemably bound to think the way they do by their economic (or ethnic, or political, or racial, or religious, or social, or . . .) position? Naturally, these same questions are asked about us and our way of thinking by the people whom we reproach for seeing things incorrectly.

Investigations of the relations between ways of thinking and seeing have preoccupied thinkers since ancient times, but the term *ideology* and the study of ideology's causes and effects have in recent times most commonly been associated with writers in the Marxist tradition. Karl Marx himself saw ideology as being produced directly by the material and historical conditions under which people live. As opposed to those who understood ideology as an abstract entity, as a set of ideas that existed independently of the material world, Marx and Friedrich Engels assert in *Die deutsche Ideologie* (1846; *The German Ideology*) that ideology is inextricably related to the actions and behaviors of human beings. For Marx and Engels, ideology determines how one sees the world, but this way of seeing the world will be determined by the way one experiences the world—and the world being the unfair, distorted place it is, and one's experience of such a world reproducing all of its contradictions, it is only to be expected that an unfair, distorted ideology will result. In *The German Ideology*, ideology is a set of illusions under which the ruling classes live, illusions created as a direct result of their wealth and social privilege. Defeating ideology entails changing the material conditions that produced it in the first place; this is not to say that Marx and Engels did not hold ideas to be important, but rather, that ideas for them come into being because of the way people live their lives, and not the other way around.

A novel considered ideological according to this definition of *ideology* would be any novel that represented and thus implicitly promoted a ruling class, and hence, a distorted experience of the world. Naturally, this category of ideological novels would include, in an orthodox Marxist view, a good many of the novels written, including those that do not seem to be setting out to demonstrate the virtues of a particular point of view. Not that this sort of ideological novel would necessarily be anathema to Marx or Marxists, of course; Marx was famously devoted to the novels of Honoré de Balzac, whose *La Comédie humaine* (1842–48; *The Human Comedy*) cycle reproduced and diagnosed the behind-the-scenes machinations of class and privilege that enabled the French bourgeoisie to come to power. While Balzac did not specifically endorse the various sorts of excess he describes, neither did he write in a revolutionary mode rejecting bourgeois values. However, his novels are considered invaluable sources of information by those who seek to trace and understand the success of bourgeois ideology.

Another use of the term *ideology* has been, instead of pejorative—as in the case of Marx who sees it as something that would best be escaped—positive. For some proponents of the socialist-realist or proletarian novel, ruling-class ideology may be challenged by working-class (and/or Marxist) ideology. This understanding of ideology allows for a multiplicity of ideologies, some right, some wrong. To *praise* a novel for its ideological character has generally meant congratulating it for promoting a *particular* ideology (as opposed to promoting "ideology," an activity no one would condone), the ideology that expresses the interests of the oppressed, against the dominant ideological current.

The French philosopher Louis Althusser was influential in developing Marx's idea that ideology is inextricably linked to fundamental economic relations and thus impossible to separate from material, lived reality. For Althusser, all of the institutions in our society are not only ideological in the messages they convey, but further, they themselves are constitutive of ideology. Because these institutions that govern our experience of the world are themselves ideological, they may endlessly and effortlessly reproduce the ideology they embody. Thus, for example, ideology is not only what is taught in schools, or printed in a newspaper, but further, it is the educational system itself, and the institution of journalism itself that, along with other aspects of organized cultural life, embody ideology; and because the institution itself is ideological without necessarily appearing so, ideology manages to insinuate itself infinitely. In his important essay "Ideology and Ideological State Apparatuses" (1971), Althusser explains how the state (understood as the class state, i.e., one with a dominant class whose distinct interests are pursued by the state) exercises power over its subjects by means of what he calls Ideological State Apparatuses: religion, the family, the media, the legal and political systems, cultural institutions, and even trade unions function as Ideological State Apparatuses, and serve to legitimate and protect the state's interests. These seemingly benevolent institutions promote the same state interests that the army, police, jails, and other more traditionally coercive institutions do, but they do so with ideology, instead of force.

Althusser's notion of ideology is useful in understanding how novels may be considered ideological. Unlike Marx's understanding of ideology, which in the main locates ideology in the fundamental—and fundamentally distorted—conceptions and actions of the dominant classes, Althusser's account serves to explain how ideology not only permeates but even constitutes all aspects of society. There is no escaping ideology; there is no way to step outside its distortions and take an independent view of the world, because "we" is constituted by ideology. We cannot get rid of ideology, not even by writing (or reading) a novel that does not seem to uphold "bourgeois values." The very institution of the novel, along with other cultural productions, is by nature ideological. This is the position held by such a critic as Lennard J. Davis (1987), who maintains that readers of novels must attempt to come to terms with the inherently and insidiously ideological novelistic enterprise by resisting them—that is, by becoming informed, "defensive" readers. Yet with such pervasive, all-encompassing models for the functioning of ideology, all novels are always already ideological. And if all novels are ideological, does it mean anything to call a particular novel, still less a set (a genre) of novels, ideological? The very proposition of an ideological novel is, in these philosophical frameworks, something of a tautology.

Still another difficulty with which the notion of the ideological novel must contend, in addition to those sketched out above, is that, among many poststructuralist thinkers, the term *ideology* itself has come to be seen as largely devoid of meaning, or simply has no place in their conception of the way humans organize and understand the world. The influential philosopher-historian Michel Foucault (1980) rejects the term ideology for its suggestion that something called "truth" might be its opposite. He finds further difficulty in making use of the term *ideology* in its reliance on a preunderstood concept of a subject. Foucault's project is, at its core, one of exploring how the subject itself is a construct of different kinds of historical and societal practices. To use *ideology* as it has typically been used presumes far too much about the subject. At this level, Foucault has a point of contact with Althusser; yet while Althusser sees ideology everywhere forming subjects, Foucault wonders why we should view this formation in such gross terms. Foucault also finds the concept of ideology problematic because it is held (by such thinkers as Marx) to be subordinate to material and economic conditions—an untenable position, to Foucault's way of thinking, since ideas and economic practices are both determined by complex relations of power.

In view of the difficulties we have only begun to address in attempting to determine the limits of ideology and the ideological, is it possible to go on speaking of the ideological novel as a genre? To a certain degree, the term, along with the novel it used to claim to describe, is a relic of a bygone era. It is a telling sign that ideology persists as a hotly debated subject, generating many interesting new books and articles, while the ideological novel has, for quite some time, been largely neglected or discredited by critics. Yet does this mean that the term ought to be discarded? Perhaps our problems defining the term may be resolved by distinguishing between novels that are ideological—this may mean particular novels or all of them, depending on our understanding of the term ideology—and something called "the ideological novel"—a subcategory of novels that meet certain stylistic or thematic criteria. Such novels would encode their didactic messages, or arguments, in the construction and development of their plots and characters, as well as in other ways, in their structures and linguistic codes. The latter approach to defining the genre is taken by Suleiman, who understands the ideological novel to be synonymous with what the French call a *roman à thèse*, or thesis novel (a term used as early as 1903 by the French critic Louis Cazamian in his pioneering study *Le Roman social en Angleterre 1830–1850* [*The Social Novel in England, 1830–1850*]). While she acknowledges that virtually any novel might be read as a *roman à thèse* (including, as she points out, Marcel Proust's *À la recherche du temps perdu* [1913–27; translated as *Remembrance of Things Past* and also as *In Search of Lost Time*]—which, with its famously lengthy and nuanced treatment of aesthetic and psychological themes, would appear a most unlikely candidate for consideration as an ideological novel), Suleiman restricts her focus to the ideological novel whose thesis recognizably matches up with and seeks to demonstrate the legitimacy of a political, philosophical, or religious doctrine. The *roman à thèse* is, for Suleiman, a quintessentially authoritarian genre. It imposes a singular and unequivocal message on the reader in a way that most novels, Proust's included, do not.

Basing her argument mainly on openly polemical French novels of the 19th and 20th centuries, Suleiman discerns several important textual characteristics that define the *roman à thèse*: a realist aesthetic, a marked redundancy in its rhetoric (i.e, a message that readers cannot escape because they are confronted with it repeatedly), a dualistic system of values (i.e., the novel views its subject matter in terms of good versus evil), and the suggestion or imposition of rules of action for readers. She further explores the structures of apprenticeship and confrontation typically found in the *roman à thèse,* as well as certain self-sub-verting features of the genre.

While Suleiman's work on the ideological novel stands as the most important and coherent contemporary attempt to come to terms with the genre, it is doubtful that *Authoritarian Fictions* will be the last word on the subject. Sooner or later, the debates raging around the meaning and use of the notion of ideology are bound to lead into future reassessments of the ideological novel.

CAROLYN BETENSKY

See also Canon; Censorship and the Novel; Class and the Novel; Critics and Criticism (20th Century); Genre Criticism; Journalism and the Novel; Marxist Criticism of the Novel; Novel of Ideas; Politics and the Novel; Postcolonial Narrative and Criticism of the Novel; Proletarian Novel; Social Criticism; Socialist Realism

Further Reading

Althusser, Louis, "Ideology and Ideological State Apparatuses," in his *Lenin and Philosophy, and Other Essays,* London: New Left Books, 1971; New York: Monthly Review Press, 1972; 2nd edition, London: New Left Books, 1977

Davis, Lennard J., *Resisting Novels: Ideology and Fiction,* London and New York: Methuen, 1987

Eagleton, Terry, *Ideology: An Introduction,* London and New York: Verso, 1991

Foucault, Michel, "Truth and Power," in *Power/Knowledge: Selected Interviews and Other Writings, 1972–1977,* translated by Colin Gordon, New York: Pantheon, and Brighton, Sussex: Harvester Press, 1980

Geuss, Raymond, *The Idea of a Critical Theory: Habermas and the Frankfurt School,* Cambridge and New York: Cambridge University Press, 1981

Hawkes, David, *Ideology,* London and New York: Routledge, 1996

Macdonell, Diane, *Theories of Discourse: An Introduction,* Oxford and New York: Blackwell, 1986

Marx, Karl, and Friedrich Engels, *The German Ideology,* in *The Marx-Engels Reader,* edited by Robert C. Tucker, New York: Norton, 1972; 2nd edition, 1978

Suleiman, Susan Rubin, *Authoritarian Fictions: The Ideological Novel as a Literary Genre,* New York: Columbia University Press, 1983

The Idiot by Fedor Dostoevskii

Idiot 1869

Of Dostoevskii's four great novels of the 1860s and 1870s (*Crime and Punishment, The Idiot, The Devils* [also translated as *The Possessed*] and *The Brothers Karamazov*), *The Idiot* is probably the most experimental in terms of narration, characterization, and structure. It was also Dostoevskii's personal favorite, and he was always flattered to receive letters from admirers who shared his predilection. On the other hand, Dostoevskii was not completely satisfied with the work and wrote his niece that he had succeeded in expressing only one-tenth of what he had envisioned. Since *The Idiot* was serialized, critics and friends began to respond to the work soon after the first part appeared in print. The initial responses, although few in number, were almost all favorable. Critics and readers alike praised the conception of the hero, Prince Myshkin, and expressed great interest in the further direction of the novel. The little negative criticism of part one focused on the "fantastic" nature of the novel's characterization and plot—that is, its lack of verisimilitude. Dostoevskii's close friend Apollon Maykov saw everything and everyone bathed in a supernatural light; it was wonderful but also strange and not completely credible. Dostoevskii later was to defend the fantastic nature of his novels as a higher form of realism. The completed work, which did not receive nearly the acclaim of the first part, was largely passed over in silence. The conservative political and social ideas that undergird the final three parts of the novel, including its direct attacks against the ideology and political activities of Russian radical intelli-gentsia, effectively removed the novel from aesthetic critical discourse. Dostoevskii was sufficiently upset by the reception of *The Idiot* that he put off publication of a separate edition of the novel for six years, until 1874.

Like most of his other large novels, *The Idiot* encompasses a vast world in which politics, economic and social conditions, Russian history, philosophy, and theology all play large roles. It contains brilliant examples of every aspect of Western narrative, all of the forms of fiction Northrop Frye elaborated in his *Anatomy of Criticism* (1957): novel, romance, anatomy, and confession. But in the history of the novel, *The Idiot* is most significant for Dostoevskii's characterological and structural experiments: specifically, his attempt simultaneously to create a positive Christ-like hero (an *obraz*—an icon, the highest religious manifestation of form) and to produce a novel (a structure) that would adequately express chaos (*bezobrazie*—the absence of form). Much of Dostoevskii's contemporaries' dissatisfaction with *The Idiot*'s "fantastic" characterization, enigmatic plotting, and narrative disjunctures stem primarily from the novel's experimental agendas.

After he completed the first part of *The Idiot,* Dostoevskii wrote his niece that there was nothing more difficult on earth to accomplish than to depict

a positively beautiful individual. . . . All writers, not only ours, but even all Europeans who have attempted to depict the positively beautiful have always given up. . . . On earth there is only one positively beautiful person—Christ. . . . I will mention only that of the beautiful figures in Christian literature the most finished is Don Quixote; but he is beautiful solely because he is at the same time comic. . . . I have nothing comparable, absolutely nothing, and therefore I'm terribly afraid that it will be a complete failure.

The Christ-like Prince Myshkin descends from the mountains of Switzerland on a mission to save Russia from an apocalyptic fate, toward which it is rushing at breakneck speed. Not only does Myshkin's mission fail, but Myshkin himself is dragged down into the very abyss from which he had hoped to save Russia. He becomes involved in love intrigues, scandals, and political controversies. He has conflicting thoughts, harbors suspicions, breaks promises to himself and to others. Some critics, especially feminist critics, have argued that, rather than an innocent Christ-like hero, Myshkin is actually the main cause of the novel's catastrophic conclusion: the murder of Nastas'ia Filippovna and the marriage of Aglaia to a Polish Catholic (for this novel, a fate worse than death). Some fault Myshkin for loving too purely (asexually), some for not loving purely enough. Some fault him for being too little of this world, some for being too much of this world. Realistically, Myshkin could hardly escape the inevitable contamination that results when a character originally conceived in terms of a Gospel text or of hagiography enters the ironic world of the novel. But much of Myshkin's tarnished image in recent criticism results from a Western critical bias that judges novelistic characters in terms of the consequences of their actions. Dostoevskii, an obvious intentionalist, seems less concerned in *The Idiot* with the consequences of his hero's action than with the ideal that he represents. How successful Dostoevskii was in realizing his intentions will always be debated, but by attempting to integrate a figure of the Gospel text into the chaotic world of 19th-century Russia, Dostoevskii was able brilliantly to play off the inherent tensions arising not only between hagiography and the novel, but between the clash of form and formlessness—of *obraz* and *bezobrazie*.

But Dostoevskii faced an equally formidable novelistic challenge in attempting to write a novel about chaos: to create a form that would adequately represent or at least convey the idea and feeling of contemporary Russian disorder and dissolution—*bezobrazie*. Russia's rapid transition from an old order to a new order was undermining the moral and cultural foundations of Russian society, but no new foundations were being laid to take their place. Instead of something "built up," there was nothing but "everlasting destruction," "chips flying in all directions, rubbish and disorder." But how does one describe such disorder? One solution, suggested by the hero's tutor in a later novel (*A Raw Youth*, 1875) is to avoid writing about the present altogether: "If I were a Russian novelist and had talent I would certainly choose my heroes from the old Russian nobility, because only in that type of cultivated Russian can one find at least the semblance of beautiful order and sensibility that a novel must have in order to produce an artistic effect on the reader." The problem was that the nobility associated in the above passage with the beautiful, harmonious forms of the old novel had disappeared, and the contemporary novelist who still was tied to these forms, according to Dostoevskii, was no longer writing literature, but history. If moral, social, and political disorder and chaos are the main ideas of *The Idiot*, then this chaos had to be reflected somehow in the form of the novel itself. Yvor Winters, who coined the term imitative, or expressive form, in English, saw this type of representation as a fallacy, employing it pejoratively to describe art, romantic poetry in particular, that, to quote Henry Adams, "had to be confused in order to express confusion." To be sure, the notion of imitative form as an operative method of poetry or criticism can be abused; but Dostoevskii knew that although the absence of aesthetic harmony was hardly a virtue, the old ideals of artistic form were incompatible with the representation of Russian *bezobrazie*. Critics who see formal perfection as a novelistic ideal either bemoan *The Idiot*'s aporias of plot, narration, and style or attempt to see in the novel an underlying order (*obraz*) in what seems to be disorder. But those who reconstruct an underlying order for *The Idiot* succeed only at the expense of undercutting the impression of disorder that Dostoevskii tries to create by a disjointed plot, fantastic characterization, and multiple narrators—including some narrators placed directly in the maelstrom of events.

Although some of Dostoevskii's later novels continue the characterological and narrative experiments of *The Idiot*, they do so in a much less radical way. As far as Dostoevskii's successors are concerned only Andrei Belyi, in *Petersburg* (1916) and several other experimental novels, pushed the novel form further than Dostoevskii. Because of the radical social and political demands placed on literature after the Bolshevik Revolution (1917), especially after the consolidation of power by Stalin, the formal and characterological experiments of *The Idiot* were fated to remain essentially unexplored. Yet given the uniqueness of Dostoevskii's genius and his own doubts about his immense task, both before and after the novel was written, one must always remain sceptical about the possibilities that his experiments in *The Idiot* opened up for his successors in the novel.

GARY ROSENSHIELD

See also Fedor Dostoevskii

Further Reading

Dalton, Elizabeth, *Unconscious Structure in "The Idiot": A Study in Literature and Psychoanalysis*, Princeton, New Jersey: Princeton University Press, 1979

Frank, Joseph, "A Reading of *The Idiot*," *Southern Review* 5 (1969)

Ivanov, Vyacheslav, *Freedom and the Tragic Life: A Study in Dostoevsky*, New York: Noonday, and London: Harvill, 1952

Jones, Malcolm, *Dostoyevsky: The Novel of Discord*, New York: Barnes and Noble, and London: Elek, 1976

Miller, Robin Feuer, *Dostoevsky and "The Idiot": Author, Narrator, and Reader*, Cambridge, Massachusetts: Harvard University Press, 1981

Peace, Richard, *Dostoyevsky: An Examination of the Major Novels*, Cambridge: Cambridge University Press, 1971; New York: Cambridge University Press, 1975

Terras, Victor, *"The Idiot": An Interpretation*, Boston: Twayne, 1990

Illustrations and Engravings

Book illustration, of course, has existed in various forms for centuries. A comprehensive history of book illustration might detail many of its forms, including medieval illuminated manuscripts, Japanese woodblock prints, William Blake's poetic productions, European and American children's literature from the 18th to the 20th century, and late 20th-century graphic novels and coffee table photographic books. By contrast, the history of novel illustration offers a more historically concise field of study—its major developments occurred largely from the mid–18th to the early 20th century. In this essay, I refer to novel illustrations from a number of different illustrative traditions, but I concentrate on the English and French traditions. As David Bland (1958) has argued, these two traditions are especially important because their aesthetic achievements influenced illustration work within a number of other traditions, especially the American and German traditions.

The story of novel illustration begins with the many 18th-century European publishers who produced lavishly illustrated editions of novels (or previously published novels) for the luxury book market. In general, French publishers fashioned the century's most opulent illustrated novels, which featured elegant illustrations in rococo and then neoclassical styles. Jean-Michel Moreau's ("Moreau le Jeune") illustrations for Jean-Jacques Rousseau's works (1774–83) most famously exemplify the richly ornamented neoclassical designs that characterize late 18th-century French book illustration. The large size of most 18th-century books—pages in this particular edition measured nine and one-half by seven and one-quarter inches—helped foreground the detailed artistry of their illustrations. French illustrations also influenced book illustration throughout 18th-century Europe. For example, the work of David Chodowiecki, who illustrated Goethe's *Die Leiden des jungen Werthers* (*The Sufferings of Young Werther*), shows the powerful impact French styles had on 18th-century German artists. When he worked in London designing illustrations for a number of English novels, including editions of Henry Fielding's *Tom Jones* (1750) and the first illustrated edition of Samuel Richardson's *Pamela* (1742), Hubert François-Bourguignon ("Gravelot") helped import French styles to England. Reciprocally, however, Gravelot and other 18th-century French illustrators were themselves influenced by English graphic artists. The foremost artist of the latter group, William Hogarth, also created important book illustrations in the period, such as his illustrations for the famous 1738 Spanish edition of Cervantes' *Don Quixote*. All of these books, however, reached a very small audience of readers. Because they degenerated after a relatively small number of printings, the expensive copper plates that artists used to engrave practically all 18th-century book illustrations reduced the numbers of illustrated books the publishers of the period could produce. The high cost of these plates also helped raise the prices of illustrated books; these prices, in turn, limited sales to only the most affluent bibliophiles. In fact, the prices were often so prohibitive that some booksellers sold prints of novel illustrations separately from the novels themselves.

A series of developments in early 19th-century literary culture helped modify the basic forms and functions of European novel illustrations. Various critics have proposed theories about whether changes in the period's mass-market publishing practices, technological innovations, or shifts in aesthetic paradigms were the primary influence upon the 19th-century illustrated novel. As the mid– to late–19th century comprised perhaps the most important era of novel illustration, I will briefly outline these theories and the developments they describe. Responding to the precipitous rise in literacy rates that began in the early 19th century, publishers in the 1830s and 1840s exploited the growing mass market for literary works. By serializing novels, these publishers created a cheaper literary product that reached less affluent readers; this strategy, in turn, made the serialized illustrated novel into an important mass-market art form. In general, novel serializations tended to print an illustration or two within each monthly number; such numbers usually featured an engraving on their covers, and booksellers placed these covers in their shop windows to entice potential buyers. As Ségolène Le Men (1994) has argued, these illustrations were part of a strategy aimed at attracting readers to the book as object and to a written culture. While some serialized novels were published separately, others ran in monthly illustrated magazines that were also aimed at the mass market.

In addition to these marketing strategies, late 18th and early 19th-century printers and engravers developed important new technologies that made graceful but cheaper book illustrations. Most important, Thomas Bewick's hugely popular *A General History of Quadrupeds* (1790) and *History of British Birds* (2 vols., 1797) showed that woodblock engravings could exhibit a real delicacy of line that rivaled the etched line of copper engravings. Since wood engravings were less expensive and much longer lasting than copper engravings (Bewick estimated that one of his engraved woodblocks endured more than 100,000 printings), this technique helped inaugurate a new era of cheap illustrated publications. The large amount of illustration work these publications generated, in turn, energized the engraving profession. For example, French publishers often contracted with several different artists to draw illustrations for their books; teams of engravers then etched plates or carved woodblocks based on those drawings. This type of production line could quickly manufacture many illustrations: the famous 1835 illustrated edition of Alain LeSage's *Gil Blas* had more than 600 woodcuts after Jean François Gigoux. Throughout much of the century, similar large-scale efforts characterized American book publishing. As Beverly R. David (1986) has detailed, Mark Twain and his publishers maximized their profits by producing copiously illustrated editions of his early travel works and novels such as *The Adventures of Tom Sawyer*. By the second half of the 19th century, illustrators throughout Europe and America used woodblock engravings more than any other method of illustration.

Early 19th-century publishing also popularized the newly invented lithography process, especially in France and Germany. Many of the children's books that deployed cheap forms of lithography in this period enjoyed limited artistic success, but early to midcentury German lithographers such as Adolph Meisel did create some significant illustrations. Invented in early 19th-century North America to print banknotes, steel engraving was used by many illustrators. George Cruikshank and Hablot K. Browne ("Phiz") cut steel as well as woodblock engravings to illustrate novels by Charles Dickens and William Ainsworth, among other authors. The famous illustrated edition of Victor Hugo's *Notre Dame de Paris* (1836) featured many illustrations, including steel engravings by the most prolific 19th-century French illustrator, Tony Johannot. While somewhat more expensive than wood engravings, steel engravings suited 19th-century mass-market publications because they could withstand thousands of printings, and their finely etched line remained clearly defined even within the smaller space the period's less lavishly produced novels accorded to illustrations.

Shifts in 19th-century aesthetic paradigms also informed some of the artistic visions associated with novel illustration in the period. The 19th-century novel illustrations that foreground solitary figures in spare landscapes, for example, certainly reflect the prominence of romanticist aesthetics during this time. J.R. Harvey (1970) and others, however, have also shown how a particular tradition of English graphic satire heavily influenced 19th-century novel illustration. These critics have detailed the way in which graphic artists such as Hogarth, James Gillray, and Thomas Rowlandson produced satiric prints (or series of prints) that combined verbal and visual imagery with emblematic material. This effect forced viewers to "read" the pictures in order to interpret them. According to these critics, the "readable" and literate qualities of illustrations within this tradition made them ideal complements to the highly visual imaginations of many 19th-century novelists. In contrast to the rococo and neoclassical styles of 18th-century French illustrators and to the long-standing English tradition of grotesque satiric prints, the Hogarthian tradition also aided 19th-century illustrators in defining a new style of satiric caricature that more realistically depicted demotic life. This style, which emphasized character over caricature, was easily integrated with the more urban, industrial, and "realistic" settings that attracted many 19th-century novelists.

Recent critical theories have also claimed that the types of artistic visions we connect with 19th-century visual art may have derived less from particular generic traditions than from a profound change in the period's notions of vision. Many critics have pointed to the emergence of romanticism to illuminate this change. Jonathan Crary (1990), however, provides an alternate explanation. According to Crary, the 1830s and 1840s saw the invention of new optical devices such as the stereoscope, which were based on a radical abstraction and reconstruction of optical experience. Crary argues that the advent of such devices combined with certain social and intellectual shifts to produce a new kind of subjective observer and to prioritize a new model of subjective vision. The history Crary charts might help explain why romantic ideas about the artistic imagination influenced so much 19th-century visual art, including Victorian book illustration. However, Crary has more difficulty proving his claim that the particular model of the subjective observer he describes was the predominant model throughout 19th-century Europe.

Whether or not publishing practices, technological innovations, or shifts in aesthetic theories were the primary influence on 19th-century novel illustration, they all certainly contributed to the shape and functions of these illustrations, which in turn aided in creating the imaginative vision we associate with mid-century authors such as Dickens, Hugo, or Twain. A brief analysis of certain aspects of specific Victorian illustrated novels will demonstrate how 19th-century novel illustrations accomplished this. Gerard Curtis (1995) argues that the partnership between the textual and the pictorial line was in fact one of the great cul-

tural achievements of the Victorian period. Achieving this partnership, however, took some time. The first Victorian serial novel, Dickens' *The Pickwick Papers* (1837), was originally contracted as a series of prose sketches to accompany Robert Seymour's satiric prints. After Seymour committed suicide early in the project, Dickens asserted more control over the final product and emphasized the primacy of the text in relation to the illustrations. Some subsequent novels, however, show Dickens in more collaborative enterprises. Documentary evidence indicates that Dickens consulted his then more famous partner Cruikshank both before and during the time in which he wrote *Oliver Twist* (1838). Dickens' letters also indicate that the author considered providing scenes for this novel that he thought Cruikshank could easily illustrate. In his pamphlet "The Artist and the Author" (1872), Cruikshank even argued that he had suggested some of the novel's most important episodes to Dickens. While most scholars have minimized Cruikshank's claims, the record of his collaboration with Dickens in *Oliver Twist* does imply that 19th-century novel illustrators did not always simply supply graphic equivalents of the novelist's textual material; they often actively participated in creating the novel's aesthetic vision.

In part because he drew illustrations for several of his own works, William Makepeace Thackeray's artistic efforts present an especially interesting example of the way in which illustrations helped modify the form of the mid-Victorian novel. As Judith L. Fisher has argued in her essay "Image versus Text in the Illustrated Novels of William Makepeace Thackeray" (1995), much of Thackeray's graphic work for *Vanity Fair* (1848) actually serves as an ironic counterpoint to the text. While the narrator implicitly sympathizes with the socially ambitious heroine Becky Sharp, for example, Thackeray's caricatures of Becky portray a stereotypically conniving and evil female character. In other words, one cannot accurately comprehend Becky's character (and Thackeray's complex satire) without closely attending to the illustrations. In fact, all Victorian illustrators' representative choices reshape the novels they serve. Some illustrators integrate iconographic material that is not contained in the text; others emphasize symbolism that the text downplays. In general, Victorian illustrators' choices about what material should be visually depicted provide an extra layer of interpretation that frames readers' experiences of illustrated novels. Meaning in these novels thus derives in part from a dialogue between the verbal and the visual. This collaboration, in turn, suggests the complex interrelations between two of the period's most important artistic traditions: graphic satire and the novel.

As Thackeray's strategies in *Vanity Fair* imply, illustrations and other types of popular graphic material had an especially powerful impact on novelistic characterization. Obviously, novelists such as Thackeray used illustrations as a type of shorthand with which they could explain their characters or themes to readers. This strategy drew upon a long-standing novelistic tradition. In Henry Fielding's *Joseph Andrews* (1742), for example, the narrator informs readers that if they want to understand specific characters in the novel, they should compare them with some of Hogarth's more famous caricatures. Some novel illustrations, however, tended to stereotype the novel's characters. For instance, the hooked nose and the dirty rags that Cruikshank deploys to depict the Jewish fence Fagin in Dickens' *Oliver Twist* make it difficult to envision the character as anything but an anti-Semitic stereotype—whether or not the author intended to give additional nuances to his portrayal of Fagin. Many popular Victorian novel illustrations exaggerate such stereotypes, because the smaller space these works accorded to illustrators (in comparison to 18th-century works) often forced them to rely heavily on cruder forms of caricature to express their satiric intent more clearly. This type of choice foregrounded characters' faces as the most detailed and expressive part of these drawings, which in turn often made these illustrations look like exercises in physiognomy or phrenology. Such an aesthetic demonstrates that despite the strong influence of the more realistic Hogarthian tradition, the broad satiric genres of caricature and the grotesque still informed Victorian novel illustrations. The prominence of caricature in these illustrations further implies that individual characters in the novels themselves verge on caricature; this association, in turn, explains why some 19th-century authors did not want their realistic fictions illustrated. Not accidentally, the rise of realism as the dominant form of the mid-19th-century British and French novel corresponded with illustrators' declining influence on the novel as a genre.

The fast pace of mid- to late-century serial publication also contributed to this decline. Unlike many 18th-century illustrators whose drawings reinterpreted already published novels, many mid- to late-19th-century illustrators who worked on serial novels, especially weekly serials, did not have the time or the artistic latitude to modify or expand the authors' ideas. Time constraints forced authors such as Dickens to give brief verbal or written descriptions of the type of illustrations they wanted for each number; sometimes illustrators such as "Phiz" did not read the actual text that surrounded their drawings until later in the publication process. Another time-saving practice that became increasingly prominent at midcentury, the technique of facsimile wood engraving, further subordinated illustrators and engravers to the novels to which they contributed. In this process, illustrators drew directly on the woodblocks, and teams of engravers then completed the carving. Combined with the division of labor this effort mandated, the large numbers of 19th-century illustrators and engravers working on book illustration ensured that many of the period's artists in effect became contract artisans for publishers.

At the end of the 19th century, novel illustration took a much less prominent role in book illustration as a whole. Many late-century literary works certainly still sported etchings, watercolors, forms of lithography, or woodcuts. Neither of the two most prominent new styles of late-century European book illustration, however, were often associated with novels. The first deliberately archaic style derived from the wood-engraved page decoration associated with William Morris' Kelmscott press. The second more modern style, art nouveau, was heavily influenced by the Japanese tradition of Ukiyo-e woodblock prints, especially the landscape prints and novel illustrations of Hokusai (1760–1849). So what happened to the European tradition of novel illustration during this period? First and foremost, illustration became increasingly associated with children's literature. John Tenniel's drawings for Lewis Carroll's Alice books, of course, were some of the 19th century's most celebrated illustrations, and the partnership between different forms of the visual and the textual still structures much of children's literature today. The comic book and the recent generic outgrowth of this form, the graphic novel, comprise one logical endpoint of this partnership. As the period's European and American vogue for Japanese prints exemplifies, moreover, late-19th- and early-20th-century book illustrators enjoyed an expanded field of stylistic influences from different cultural traditions. Along with these new influences, the many new photographic and other print technologies available to these illustrators helped initiate an explosion of different types of images within various texts. As many have argued, photographic illustration and the many graphic styles photography inspired signaled the advent of a new age of book illustration in the early 20th century. This new age, however, also consigned the etching and the woodcut (and associated graphic traditions) to technological, economic, and stylistic obsolescence, and the golden age of 19th-century European novel illustration ended without much ceremony.

WILLIAM WEAVER

See also Children's Novel; Graphic Novel; Periodicals and the Serialization of Novels

Further Reading

Bland, David, *A History of Book Illustration: The Illuminated Manuscript and the Printed Book*, Cleveland, Ohio: World Publishing, and London: Faber, 1958

Brenni, Vito, *Book Illustration and Decoration: A Guide to Research*, Westport, Connecticut: Greenwood Press, 1980

Christ, Carol T., and John O. Jordan, editors, *Victorian Literature and the Victorian Visual Imagination*, Berkeley: University of California Press, 1995

Crary, Jonathan, *Techniques of the Observer: On Vision and Modernity in the Nineteenth Century*, Cambridge, Massachusetts: MIT Press, 1990

Curtis, Gerard, "Shared Lines: Pen and Pencil as Trace," in *Victorian Literature and the Victorian Visual Imagination*, edited by Carol T. Christ and John O. Jordan, Berkeley: University of California Press, 1995

David, Beverly R., *Mark Twain and His Illustrators*, Troy, New York: Whitson Publishing, 1986

Fisher, Judith L., "Image versus Text in the Illustrated Novels of William Makepeace Thackeray," in *Victorian Literature and the Victorian Visual Imagination*, edited by Carol T. Christ and John O. Jordan, Berkeley: University of California Press, 1995

Harvey, J.R., *Victorian Novelists and Their Illustrators*, London: Sidgwick and Jackson, 1970; New York: New York University Press, 1971

Kobayashi, Tadashi, *Ukiyo-e: An Introduction to Japanese Woodblock Prints*, New York and London: Kodansha International, 1992

Le Men, Ségolène, "Book Illustration," in *Artistic Relations: Literature and the Visual Arts in Nineteenth-Century France*, edited by Peter Collier and Robert Lethbridge, New Haven, Connecticut: Yale University Press, 1994

Patten, Robert L., editor, *George Cruikshank: A Revaluation*, Princeton, New Jersey: Princeton University Press, 1974

Ray, Gordon Norton, *Art of the French Illustrated Book, 1700–1914*, 2 vols., New York: Pierpont Morgan Library, 1982

Ray, Gordon Norton, *The Illustrator and the Book in England from 1790 to 1914*, new edition, New York and London: Pierpont Morgan Library, 1991

Imperial Romance. *See* Adventure Novel and Imperial Romance

Implied Author

The concept of the implied author was introduced by Wayne C. Booth in his influential book *The Rhetoric of Fiction* (1961), and it soon became one of the standard terms in the critical discourse on fiction. Booth describes the implied author as the real author's "second self," which is "created in the work" as "an implied version of 'himself' that is different from the implied authors we meet in other men's work," as "an ideal, literary, created version of the real man." According to Booth, the implied author embodies the text's norms and values and satisfies "the reader's need to know where, in the world of values, he stands—that is, to know where the author wants him to stand."

The implied author is thus not a specific technical or formal device but the origin of a work's meaning, the embodiment of both its semantic content and its ethics and morality: "Our sense of the implied author," Booth observes, "includes not only the extractable meanings but also the moral and emotional content of each bit of action and suffering of all the characters. It includes, in short, the intuitive apprehension of a completed artistic whole." Through the narrative resources Booth designates as "the rhetoric of fiction," an implied author imposes his or her (or rather its) intention, beliefs, and norms and values on the implied reader, which most theorists assume to be "the mirror image" of the implied author (see Chatman, 1990).

Ever since Booth proposed the implied author as a category for literary studies, it has been the subject of intense debate. While many critics consider it to be among the basic, important, and indispensable categories of textual analysis, others have argued for the abandonment of the concept because they consider the implied author to be a vague and ill-defined notion. Although Seymour Chatman, one of the most prominent narratologists and defenders of the implied author, implicitly admits that Booth's legacy to literary criticism is problematic in that he rejects no fewer than four of the five explanatory concepts provided by Booth, he still considers Booth's notion of the implied author as "the core of norms and choices" to be indispensable—"essential to narratology and to text theory in general" (see Chatman, 1990).

The majority of narratologists have followed Booth and provided almost identical definitions of the implied author. Representative of attempts at definition is the following, where the contradictory features of the concept are unmistakable: "He is 'implied', i.e., he is a construction or reconstruction by the reader, and he is not the narrator, but rather the man who invented the narrator (if there is one), in short, the man who stacked the cards in this particular way, who had these things happen to these people" (see Chatman, 1975). On the one hand, it is emphasized that the implied author is an abstract entity constructed by the reader, but, on the other hand, "he" is taken to be the personalizable inventor of the narrator or even the originator of the fiction. Similarly, Booth observes that the "'implied author' chooses, consciously or unconsciously, what we read," yet refers to him as "the product of a choosing, evaluating person rather than as a self-existing thing," as "the sum of his own choices."

The main objection that critics have raised to the category of the implied author involves the lack of clarity of the concept, something evident from the number of heterogeneous features that Chatman, in *Coming to Terms: The Rhetoric of Narrative in Fiction and Film,* for example, wishes to see subsumed under this rubric. The implied author is not only "the reader's source of instruction about how to read the text and how to account for the selection and ordering of its components" but also figures as "the inventor," "the text itself in its inventional aspect," "the principle which has invented the text," "text implication," "text instance," "text design," and "text intent," manifesting itself finally in the form of "the patterns in the text," "the text itself," and its "codes and conventions" (see Chatman, 1990). Such an almost unlimited expansion of meaning ultimately makes the category useless as a critical tool. Similarly, such definitions of the implied author as Paul Ricoeur's "a disguise of the real author, who disappears by making himself the narrator immanent in the work—the narrative voice" (see Ricoeur, 1988) seem to confirm the suspicion of those theorists who see the implied author as a catch-all for all those features that narrative theory cannot easily integrate into a coherent model: as Mieke Bal has stated, "That reinforces my impression that, in fact, the implied author is a remainder category, a kind of passepartout that serves to clear away all the problematic remainders of a theory" (see Bal, 1981b).

About the only thing that seems uncontroversial is that the implied author is to be distinguished from the narrator. While the characters and the narrator in a narrative text are identifiable as textual speakers with clearly delimited speech segments, the implied author, like the implied reader, is a hypothetical construct that has no verbal instantiation. Even the adherents of the concept of the implied author admit that it is not realized as a speaker: "Unlike the narrator, the implied author can tell us nothing. He, or better, it has no voice, no direct means of communicating. It instructs us silently, through the design of the whole, with all the voices, by all the means it has chosen to let us learn" (see Chatman, 1978). Chatman later argues that "that inventor is no person, no substance, no object: it is, rather, the patterns in the text which the reader negotiates" (see Chatman, 1990).

But if the implied author is indeed voiceless, it would seem to be a "contradiction in terms to cast it in the role of the addresser in a communication situation," as Shlomith Rimmon-Kenan observes, coming to the conclusion "that the implied author cannot literally be a participant in the narrative communication situation" (see Rimmon-Kenan, 1983). Moreover, if it is formal relationships in the work as "a completed artistic whole," as Booth puts it, that are actually being referred to, this fact is disguised by the use of a deceptive term like implied author, which suggests that it is a question of a personalizable voice or an anthropomorphic entity.

There is general agreement by now that "the notion of the implied author must be depersonified, and is best considered as a set of implicit norms rather than as a speaker or a voice (i.e. a subject)" (see Rimmon-Kenan, 1983). Even the French structuralist Gérard Genette accepts such a deanthropomorphized reconceptualization of the implied author: "If one means by it that beyond the narrator (even an extradiegetic one), and by various pinpointed or global signs, the narrative text (like any other text) produces a certain idea . . . of the author, one means something obvious, which I can only acknowledge and even insist on" (see Genette, 1988).

From a theoretical point of view the concept of the implied author is also problematic because it creates the illusion that it is a purely textual phenomenon. But it is obvious from many of the definitions that the implied author is a construct established by the reader on the basis of the whole structure of a text. When Chatman writes that "we might better speak of the 'inferred' than of the 'implied' author" (see Chatman, 1990), he implicitly concedes that we are dealing with something that has to be worked out by the reader. Being a structural phenomenon that is voiceless, the implied author must be seen "as a construct inferred and assembled by the reader from all the components of the text" (see Rimmon-Kenan, 1983). Michael Toolan has made the sensible suggestion that one should look at the implied author not as a speaker but as a component of the reception process, as the reader's idea of the author: "The implied author is a real position in narrative processing, a receptor's construct, but it is not a real role in narrative transmission. It is a projection back from the decoding side, not a real projecting stage on the encoding side" (see Toolan, 1988).

Recently some prominent narratologists have again emphatically come out in favor of the implied author, while others have argued just as strongly against the concept. William Nelles does not even question the concept, arguing that the implied author and the implied reader "each has its distinctive function: . . . the implied author means, the implied reader interprets" (see Nelles, 1993). In order to justify the usefulness of the implied author as an analytic tool, Chatman argues that the concept makes possible "a way of naming and analyzing the textual intent of narrative fictions under a single term but without recourse to biographism. . . . Positing an implied author inhibits the overhasty assumption that the reader has direct access through the fictional text to the real author's intentions and ideology" (see Chatman, 1990). Like Booth, Chatman argues that the notion of the implied author is necessary in order to account for both dramatic irony and the manipulations of an unreliable narrator.

By contrast, others, including Nilli Diengott (1993a) and Ansgar Nünning (1997), are highly suspicious of the concept and try to demonstrate the problems it raises for narrative poetics. Diengott attempts to clear up the confusion in the use of the term implied author, which has traditionally been conceived of as an anthropomorphized fictional entity, by proposing a "depersonified understanding" of it (see Diengott, 1993b). Even Diengott,

however, holds on to the concept and suggests that once it is thus remodified "the term is applicable within the interpretive activity and is extremely useful in discussing literary works." Neither Nelles' attempt to define "the intermediary agent of the implied author" (see Nelles, 1993) nor Diengott's compromise, which hinges upon looking at the implied author as "something depersonified, the image of the real author, a set of attitudes, the whole meaning of a text" (see Diengott, 1993b), has managed to settle the issue.

The most controversial aspect of the concept of the implied author is that it carries far-reaching, although largely unacknowledged theoretical implications. First, the concept of implied author reintroduces the notion of authorial intention, although through the backdoor. As Chatman has pointed out, "the concept of implied authorship arose in the debate about the relevance of authorial intention to interpretation" (see Chatman, 1990). Providing "a new link to the sphere of the actual author and authorial values" (see York, 1987), the implied author turns out to be little more than a terminologically presentable way of making it possible to talk again about the author's intention: as John Ross Baker has written, "The concept of 'the implied author,' with its air of being an inference from the work and thus as it were, like plot, an objective feature of the work, enables Booth to talk about the author under the guise of still appearing to talk about the work" (see Baker, 1972–73; also Juhl, 1980). Second, representing the work's norms and values, the implied author is intended to serve both as a yardstick for a moralistic kind of criticism and as a check on the potentially boundless relativism of interpretation. Third, the use of the definite article and the singular misleadingly suggests that there is only one correct interpretation: "The very fact that Booth and Chatman speak of the implied author already implies, suggests the existence of one ideal interpretation of the narrative text" (see Berendsen, 1984). In short, the concept of the implied author appears to provide the critic again with a basis for judging both the acceptability of an author's "moral position" (about which, according to Booth, a writer "has an obligation to be as clear . . . as he possibly can be") and the correctness of an interpretation.

The lack of terminological clarity and the problematic theoretical implications associated with the notion of the implied author have led some narratologists to argue that the concept should be abandoned (see Bal, 1981b; Jakobsen, 1977; Toolan, 1988; Nünning, 1997). Some theorists have recognized that it has not fulfilled the promise "to account for the ideology of the text" (see Bal, 1981a) and is not capable of doing what it was supposed to do: "It not only adds another narrating subject to the heap but it fails to resolve what it sets out to bridge: the author-narrator relationship" (see Lanser, 1981). In comparison with the multitude of voices that have been raised against the implied author, however, there have as yet been only a modest number of constructive counterproposals (see Reid, 1986; Diengott, 1993b). Nünning (1997) proposes that, instead of setting up an "implied author" and an "implied reader," it would be more sensible to conceptualize a textual level that encompasses the entirety of the structural properties of a work.

ANSGAR NÜNNING

See also Diegesis and Diegetic Levels of Narration; Framing and Embedding; Narratology; Narrator; Unreliable Narrator

Further Reading

Baker, John Ross, "From Imitation to Rhetoric: The Chicago Critics, Wayne C. Booth, and *Tom Jones*," *Novel: A Forum on Fiction* 6 (1972–73)

Bal, Mieke, "Notes on Narrative Embedding," *Poetics Today* 2 (1981a)

Bal, Mieke, "The Laughing Mice or: On Focalization," *Poetics Today* 2 (1981b)

Berendsen, Marjet, "The Teller and the Observer: Narration and Focalization in Narrative Texts," *Style* 18 (1984)

Booth, Wayne, *The Rhetoric of Fiction*, Chicago: University of Chicago Press, 1961; 2nd edition, Chicago: University of Chicago Press, and London: Penguin, 1983

Bronzwaer, W.J.M., "Implied Author, Extradiegetic Narrator and Public Reader: Gérard Genette's Narratological Model and the Reading Version of *Great Expectations*," *Neophilologus* 62 (1978)

Chatman, Seymour, "The Structure of Narrative Transmission," in *Style and Structure in Literature: Essays in the New Stylistics,* edited by Roger Fowler, Oxford: Blackwell, and Ithaca, New York: Cornell University Press, 1975

Chatman, Seymour, *Story and Discourse: Narrative Structure in Fiction and Film,* Ithaca, New York: Cornell University Press, 1978

Chatman, Seymour, *Coming to Terms: The Rhetoric of Narrative in Fiction and Film,* Ithaca, New York: Cornell University Press, 1990

Diengott, Nilli, "Implied Author, Motivation and Theme and Their Problematic Status," *Orbis Litterarum* 48 (1993a)

Diengott, Nilli, "The Implied Author Once Again," *Journal of Literary Semantics* 22 (1993b)

Fludernik, Monika, *Towards a "Natural" Narratology,* London and New York: Routledge, 1996

Genette, Gérard, *Discours du récit*, in *Figures III*, Paris: Seuil, 1972; as *Narrative Discourse*, Ithaca, New York: Cornell University Press, 1980

Genette, Gérard, *Nouveau discours du récit*, Paris: Seuil, 1983; as *Narrative Discourse Revisited,* Ithaca, New York: Cornell University Press, 1988

Jakobsen, Arnt Lykke, "A Critique of Wayne C. Booth's *A Rhetoric of Irony*," *Orbis Litterarum* 32 (1977)

Juhl, P.D., "Life, Literature, and the Implied Author," *Deutsche Vierteljahrsschrift für Literaturwissenschaft und Geistesgeschichte* 54 (1980)

Lanser, Susan Sniader, *The Narrative Act: Point of View in Prose Fiction*, Princeton, New Jersey: Princeton University Press, 1981

Nelles, William, "Historical and Implied Authors and Readers," *Comparative Literature* 45 (1993)

Nünning, Ansgar, "The Resurrection of an Anthropomorphicized Passepartout or the Obituary of a Critical Phantom? Deconstructing and Reconceptualizing the 'Implied Author'," *Anglistik: Organ des Verbandes Deutscher Anglisten* 8 (1997)

Reid, Ian, "The Death of the Implied Author? Voice, Sequence and Control in Flaubert's *Trois Contes*," *Australian Journal of French Studies* 23 (1986)

Ricoeur, Paul, *Temps et récit*, Paris: Editions du Seuil, 1983–85; as *Time and Narrative,* 3 vols., Chicago: University of Chicago Press, 1984–88

Rimmon-Kenan, Shlomith, *Narrative Fiction: Contemporary Poetics*, London and New York: Methuen, 1983

Toolan, Michael J., *Narrative: A Critical Linguistic Introduction*, London and New York: Routledge, 1988

York, Lorraine M., "'The Pen of the Contriver' and the Eye of the Perceiver: *Mansfield Park*, the Implied Author and the Implied Reader," *English Studies in Canada* 13 (1987)

In Search of Lost Time by Marcel Proust

À la recherche du temps perdu 1913–27

Written over a period of 14 years (1908–22) and published during a time span equally long (1913–27), this 3,000-page novel is Marcel Proust's greatest achievement; it is a milestone in French literature—the equivalent in scope, insight, and import of the masterpieces of James Joyce and Fedor Dostoevskii—and a lasting source of pleasure to generations of readers, whether they read it in the original version or in a translation. (As a result of recent important textual discoveries, the novel should not be read in a French edition that predates 1987 or in an English translation published before 1992.) Although the title of the first English-language translation, *Remembrance of Things Past* by C.K. Scott Moncrieff, quotes a Shakespearean sonnet, it gives a false impression of both Proust's intentions and what he managed to produce; a dynamic quest better rendered by the more

literal version now used, *In Search of Lost Time*. Proust loved words and word play, and while the fundamental polysemic nature of *perdu* in French—both "lost" and "wasted"—is evident, even French-speaking readers often fail to note that the title could also be interpreted as "In Search of the Lost Tense" (*temps* referring both to *time* and to *verb tense*), a plausible interpretation, since Proust succeeded in turning upside down almost every novelistic convention of his 19th-century predecessors, such as Balzac, Flaubert, and Zola.

Proust's novel is a challenge to realism and its close cousin naturalism, different as the practioners of those two schools might be, in that he defies the twin tenets of conventional narrative, chronology and causality. It is true that large parts of *In Search of Lost Time* (hereafter *Recherche*) are roughly chronological, but this is undermined by the fact that the very dates of the fiction—roughly from the mid-1870s to the mid-1920s—are impossible to deduce with any certitude because of the fact that internal and external references and allusion contradict each other. Furthermore, in the very first part of the novel, time progresses at three different speeds simultaneously, as many a reader of "Combray" has discovered. As for causality, Proust does not remove it entirely as in more recent literary productions, such as the French New Novel. Rather he tends to provide a multiplicity of causes for any single event, each of which could be equally plausible, although if they were to be taken literally and put together, they would logically exclude one another. In many cases, the reader is left with this open-ended "explanation" of characters' motivations or actions. The universe of the *Recherche* is definitely a subjective one and can be compared to impressionist painting as opposed to the realist tradition of the first half of the 19th century. In the novel, things are often not what they are supposed to be according to both common sense and so-called scientific truth. Proust makes deliberate use of what Russian formalists were to call "defamiliarization" (*ostranenie*). In the many scenes in which painting is thematized, art is valued for its ability to convey a fresh point of view on reality, even if this means that a factual error is involved. For example, in a painting of a seaside town by the fictitious painter named Elstir—after Whistler—the seascape and the landscape overlap, causing a strange, uncanny juxtaposition of maritime and urban images. Rationally, we know this is impossible because there must be a definite line of demarcation, but subjectively this rendering of the scene is *true* because it corresponds to the "naive" impressions of someone who is able to discard or at least put aside the constraints of rational thought and Cartesian logic. This example serves to illustrate just how subversive Proust's novel is of so many literary traditions in the novels of his predecessors. Rather than assigning a single cause to a single result, anchoring his narrative solidly in a chronological sequence, or showing how his characters live and develop "normally," Proust sought to portray his characters in four dimensions, the fourth being time—not the time of clocks and calendars but the personal, human time of our inner lives, the time that plays tricks on our minds and bodies.

"Longtemps je me suis couché de bonne heure" (For a long time I would [used to] go to bed early)—for an author known for his long sentences and labyrinthine syntax, one could hardly imagine a more banal beginning. This simple, almost conversational sentence, complete with its verb in a nonliterary tense—the *passé composé* that Albert Camus was to use to such effect in *L'Étranger* (1942; *The Stranger*)—is a mirror image of the entire work. The first word describes both the length and the subject of the enterprise, and the last word, literally "hour," refers to time, just as *time* will be the last word of the seven-volume novel. In addition, the last two words are homonymous with *bonheur* (happiness). Although we never learn for sure the name of the first-person narrator—there are two instances in the unrevised manuscript that lead one to think that he may have the same first name as the author—the grammatical agreement of the past participle (*couché*) tells us from the outset we are dealing with a masculine subject. Exactly how long is "a long time," or how early is "early," or when this habit began and ended are things that will forever elude us, as will the narrator's reason for going to bed early. It is important to note that the verb *coucher*, along with its sexual connotations, also has another meaning: to inscribe or write down. Hence the self-reflexivity of the sentence is oriented to both the corporeal and the textual. Appropriately enough, Proust's narrator begins by describing those moments of first wakefulness when a person is disoriented, forgetting where, when, and—in this case—even who he is. The first pages of the novel thus describe those most common events: going to bed, sleeping, waking, going back to sleep, dreaming, waking again, daydreaming, and remembering experiences, places, and people from the near and distant past. Although the Proustian narrator will describe his childhood in the first section of the novel, in all likelihood the first sentence does not refer to childhood but rather to a period of depression in the adult narrator's life, presumably that time of sterility before he discovered his vocation as a writer, which will lead to the period of ensuing productivity and happiness when, like the notoriously nocturnal Proust, he will stay up many a night writing his book.

The *Recherche* is an autobiographical novel based loosely on selective elements of Proust's life, although there are significant differences between the author and his narrator. The former, for example, was homosexual whereas the latter is a heterosexual, albeit fascinated by all things "queer." The novel tells the story of one man's life from childhood to middle age. The first volume, *Du côté de chez Swann* (*Swann's Way*), takes its title from one of the Sunday walks that the narrator and his family would go on after Françoise's copious Sunday lunches. The volume is divided into three parts: "Combray," "Un amour de Swann," and "Noms de pays: le nom." Combray is the name of the small town the narrator and his parents would visit during Easter vacation to be with his mother's relatives. One of their neighbors is Charles Swann. Looked down upon by some of his middle-class friends for his marriage to Odette, a former call girl, Swann is in fact on intimate terms with members of the aristocracy and the future king of England! It is his love affair with Odette that forms the subject of the second part of the first book. Unlike the rest of the novel, this flashback is told in the third person. The final part of the volume takes "Marcel" up to young adolescence before a final flash forward to the mature years preceding the discovery of his writerly vocation.

The sequel to *Swann's Way* was not to be published for another six years because of World War I. Proust said that he wrote the first and last parts of his novel at the same time, by which he meant the last part of the last volume, *Le temps retrouvé* (*Time Regained*). Disillusioned with the party life he had led for so long, in ailing health, and disheartened by the deaths of so many of his friends at the front, Proust had little to do but write, and write he did, turning what was originally going to be a much shorter novel into the great masterpiece it was to become. In fact, he was going to write up to the very day he died in 1922. And even then, the novel remains unfinished—some characters die and then reappear; there are inconsistencies with names, although some of these have been tidied up by modern editors. However, whatever time was to be allotted to Proust, he had a kind of textual insurance policy in the form of that last volume. During the war years the *Recherche* more than tripled in length, and it grew inevitably in the middle. What were to have been a couple of volumes became five, including the three published posthumously: *À l'ombre des jeunes filles en fleurs* (1919; *Within a Budding Grove*), *Le Côté de Guermantes* (1920–21; *The*

Guermantes Way), *Sodome et Gomorrhe* (1921–22; *Sodom and Gomorrah*), *La Prisonnière* (1923; *The Captive*), and *Albertine disparue* (1925; *The Fugitive*), nestled between *Swann's Way* (1913) and *Time Regained* (1927).

To understand the novel, one has to read all of it, and one has to read it in the proper order. This is not a roman-fleuve, like Zola's *Les Rougon-Macquart* (1871–93), where one can choose whether to read the whole cycle or any single volume. In order to understand Proust, you have to start with "Combray" and progress through each of the volumes. It will take a long time, and this is as it should be, for our memories of the events and characters will cloud and then be refreshed just as those of the narrator's are. Memory, of course, is one of the principal themes of the novel. Proust's narrator discovers it takes three forms, the first of which is the "memory" of the past that we learn from others, in other words, tales of the historical past, whether oral or written down, whether of the recent or ancient past. This is the type of memory that underpins the section entitled "Un amour de Swann," for it recounts events predating the narrator's birth, presumably sometime around 1880. The second form of remembering is what Proust calls voluntary memory. This is the type of memory described at the beginning of "Combray," when the by now fully wake and insomniac narrator recalls experiences of his childhood. Though vivid, this type of remembering is limited, and in fact the narrator always remembers the same scenes, especially one eventful evening when after being sent to bed early during one of Swann's visits, he refused to go to sleep without his mother's nightly kiss. (In the end, the parents gave in to their headstrong son, and the mother spent the night in his room reading to him.) Voluntary memory takes on an obsessive quality as he relives these primitive—and highly Oedipal—moments of his past. It is like a vicious circle from which there is no release until one day, as a mature and disillusioned adult, he eats a *petite madeleine* and dunks it in a cup of tea. Suddenly he is infused with an intense feeling of joy, even euphoria: this is the all-important experience of involuntary memory. Using sexually charged language, the narrator describes a rush, a "coming" as he searches for—and eventually discovers—the source of his happiness. After an inner struggle, the mystery reveals itself: it is as banal as the process was both delicious and arduous. It turns out that his wacky invalid Aunt Léonie used to give him a bite of her little cake when he went to visit her on Sunday morning before mass. But the importance of involuntary memory is not the content but rather the journey itself, since it allows us to travel back in time—and space—to other parts of our lives. As Proust puts it:

> And as in the game wherein the Japanese amuse themselves by filling a porcelaine bowl with water and steeping in it little pieces of paper which until then are without character or form, but, the moment they become wet, stretch and twist and take on colour and distinctive shape, become flowers or houses or people, solid and recognisable, so in that moment all the flowers in our garden in M. Swann's park, and the water-lilies on the Vivonne and the good folk of the village and their little dwellings and the parish church and the whole of Combray and its surrounding, taking shape and solidity, sprang into being, town and gardens alike, from my cup of tea. [*Swann's Way*]

Such essentially Proustian moments are always triggered by some sensory input: a smell or a taste as here in the first volume, a sound or a touch as in the last volume. Involuntary memory in Proust takes on all the poignancy and uncanniness of soul travel, which is hardly an exaggeration as he believed that we are many selves. A mnemonic flash puts us in touch with a former self, one we had forgotten. This in fact is the key to the whole Proustian enterprise, one that is often neglected: without *forgetting* there can be no involuntary memory, just as the whole search for lost time is intimately linked to the quest for lost spaces and places.

Time, space, and memory—such are the "hyper-" or super-themes of the *Recherche*. In some ways, they are so important, so omnipresent that one might be lured into neglecting other important themes, such as reading (in fact, the novel was originally conceived of as an essay on reading) and writing, or rather the terrible writer's block that the narrator suffers from for most of his life. Here I will concentrate on two equally important themes: error and inversion.

The novel contains a multitude of examples of the characters' misperceptions, such as the narrator's misinterpretation of Swann's social status. Typically this type of error crops up in the sections of the novel devoted to society. One's place in the social hierarchy is neither stable nor single, for everyone is engaged in a kind of minuet in which the places of the dancers are continuously changing. The Dreyfus Affair put Jews such as Swann in disgrace, whereas World War I allows the infamous Mme Verdurin, an art patron of monumental stupidity, to rise to the very top, for she ends up marrying the Prince de Guermantes. The Guermantes represent the aristocratic side of the narrator's social life, just as the original "côté de Guermantes" was the other, longer walk that he and his family sometimes took if the weather was fine. The two directions—Swann and Guermantes—stood in total antithesis in the child's mind, and indeed it is only much, much later in his life that he learns that he was wrong, and that rather than being 180 degrees apart, the two *côtés* or walks form a kind of giant circle. For all his life, the narrator was mistaken about something as simple as the basic geography of the countryside around Combray. In a similar manner, a bourgeois such as Swann has links with the aristocracy, which is made all the more concrete when Swann's daughter marries Robert De Saint-Loup, a member of the Guermantes family, even if Swann does not live to see it. When the narrator meets Mlle de Saint-Loup at the Princess' tea party near the very end of the novel—by now she is 18—she incarnates for him, and for us, not only lost time but also the physical union of what had for so long appeared to be two irreconcilable dimensions of his own life as well as of French society in general.

There are other misperceptions in the novel, and many of them have been programmed into the text so that readers will inevitably make mistakes. For example, the beautiful lady in pink whom the narrator met when a boy at his uncle's one day turns out to be no other than Odette, Swann's wife. Charlus, the man who passes for Odette's lover even after her marriage, is really a homosexual. It is Françoise, the cook who enjoys killing chickens and tormenting her pregnant kitchen aide, who is more sadistic than Mlle Vinteuil. Although the latter allows her lesbian lover to spit on a photograph of her father, in many ways she is in reality a good person so innocent of the world that she cannot imagine sex as an unevil thing, and it is thanks to the efforts of her lover that Vinteuil's illegible manuscripts will be deciphered and transcribed, thereby allowing his music to be played at one of Mme Verdurin's soirees. (Music and sex are intertwined since "Swann in Love," when Swann associates his passion for Odette with a musical phrase, also by Vinteuil.) These are just a few examples of what is in many ways an unreliable narrative. Truth in Proust is never a simple matter: it is constructed, deconstructed, and reconstructed. What was the "truth" turns out to be a gross error, which—after the misperception is eventually understood—is altered in the light of new information, which in the long run turns out itself to be equally false. The novel could well be entitled "In Search of Lost Truth." The example of social status as the paradigm of error is significant. One's status is not writ in stone. Rather it is a perception—and therefore to a large extent a misperception—by X number of people, all of whom are in turn the objects of other misperceptions. Add to this the temporal factor and one realizes that the only way to portray this upstairs-downstairs menagerie of bourgeois upstarts, degenerate aristocrats, and their uppity servants would be with a three-dimensional model that moves, as in a mobile. The other solution to representing what the narrator calls the "social kaleidoscope" is, of course, to write subtle, detailed analytical prose of the kind that only Proust is capable of.

Error is also the source of much humor in the Proustian narrative. The popular image of Proust is that of a difficult author, but in reality he is one of the great comic writers of all time. In fact, it is impossible to read even a few pages of the *Recherche* without laughing. Sometimes the humor is biting, as in the social satire in which Proust depicts the aristocracy as a bunch of ignorant but pretentious buffoons, whereas at other times it is gentle and loving, as in the scene when the grandmother, a great fan of all things natural, walks in the family garden during a rainstorm, never thinking to "save her plum-colored skirt from the mudstains beneath which it would gradually disappear to a height that was the constant bane and despair of her maid" (*Swann's Way*).

Inversion in the *Recherche* refers first of all to the narrator's ideas about homosexuality: supposedly a male homosexual is a woman in a man's body, whereas a lesbian is a man in a woman's body. While today this would correspond more to our ideas about transsexuals, it was not an uncommon view at the end of the 19th century. After discovering that the Baron de Charlus is "really" a woman, the narrator is led to write an essay on inversion at the beginning of *Sodom and Gomorrah*. Named after the "cities of the plain" in Genesis punished by God for the sin of homosexuality—although modern Biblical scholars think it more likely that the sin in question was inhospitality—Sodom and Gormorrah correspond respectively to male and female homosexuality. Thus the second part of the *Recherche* is structured by this binary opposition based on two place names, just as the first half was structured by the Swann/Guermantes opposition. Of course, the former still continues to function in the later parts of the novel, so that there are various combinations that Proust can play with, such as aristocratic Sodomites (Charlus) or middle-class Gomorrheans. The essay on male homosexuality is characterized by a euphoria caused by this whole new set of signs, to use the term of Gilles Deleuze in his book entitled *Proust et les signes* (1964), one of the most important works written on Proust's novel.

Complicated as the Proustian construction of male homosexuality may be, it is simplicity itself in comparison with female ho-

mosexuality, for which the model is distinctly deconstructionist. Whereas the sign of Sodom is marked by an excess of semiotic production—mannerisms, intonations, gestures—that forms a veritable code or cipher, the sign of Gomorrah is a discrete and puzzling absence of obvious signs. There is no essay on lesbianism, although as a textual element of the *Recherche* it takes up more space than the other "side." The narrator's experiences with male homosexuals allow him to remain a detached observer, like a bird watcher. On the other hand, Gomorrah comes to torment him personally since he suspects the young woman with whom he falls in love to be a lesbian. Albertine, the character whose name, like his first love Gilberte, is very close to a common masculine name in French, will be the great love of the narrator's life, but he never understands her or her sexuality. He suspects her of desiring women, and this fuels his jealousy—like Swann's jealousy of Odette—to fever pitch. Things get very complicated in *The Captive*, for if Albertine is really a man in a women's body then surely the narrator has fallen in love with someone who is psychologically a man, and therefore he himself must be an "invert." Albertine will forever remain a "mystery wrapped up in an enigma." Indeed, after she leaves the narrator and then dies (in *The Fugitive*), he continues to torment himself about her sexual orientation even while living through the mourning process. For each clue that she may have had lesbian tendencies, there is a counterproof: the evidence is tainted, the witness unreliable, etc. Albertine remains forever unknowable, a kind of mysterious, unattainable truth. It is no doubt for this reason that the narrator is so fascinated by her, for she represents the ultimate quest, the one whose goal is forever sought after but never reached.

However, inversion is not just a theme in Proust, it is also a trope, a textual paradigm. Nothing is what it appears to be, and, as mentioned, the truth turns out more often than not to be a "falsehood disguised." The whole movement or dynamic of the novel may be considered a never-ending series of inversions, some of which concern sexuality, although many do not. For example, for some time after the death of the narrator's grandmother, he feels nothing. But after returning to Balbec, the seaside resort on the English Channel where he spent a previous summer with her, he suddenly realizes just how profound, how visceral, how heart-wrenching is his grief. This example, taken from *Sodom and Gomorrah*, constitutes what Proust calls "intermittences of the heart," an expression that he thought about using as a title for the whole novel. Whether in the areas of love, sexuality, social hierarchy, or art, everyone and everything are inverted at some time or another. This topsy-turvy world lies at the heart of the Proustian universe; indeed, it is as important as time itself. The novel is driven by inversion as though it were the plot's "motor." This can make for maddening reading at first, but once readers have gotten used to decoding the trope of inversion for the ultimate Proustian "trip," it leads us on a fascinating search for just how many different ways inversion can come into play in a novel that is based on decoding ever reversible signs.

The *Recherche* is a novel of initiation, a series of quests through various domains or fields of enquiry: friendship, which ranks low in the Proustian scale of values, has a part to play; bourgeois and especially high-class (i.e., aristocratic) society provides a fascinating area to explore, although in the end the narrator concludes that it is fundamentally empty of any content;

the signs of nature are much more significant for the pleasure they afford the narrator, whether it be the hawthorns in "Combray" or the play of light on wave in the never-ending spectacle of the seascape at Balbec; love is very important, not for the identity or personality of the beloved but for the introspection it forces on the jealous lover. Indeed, love has the power to turn someone as intellectually lazy as Swann into a kind of literary detective and someone as incurious as the narrator into a monstrous combination of policeman, judge, and chief inquisitor all rolled up in one. Then there are the signs of memory. These furnish the transition between mourning for lost love and its sublimation in the creative act. There are many semifictional artists in the *Recherche*: Bergotte the novelist, La Berma the actress, Elstir the painter, and Vinteuil the composer (whose music is based on that of Camile Saint-Saëns, César Franck, and Gabriel Fauré, to name a few of Proust's favorites). Such artists provide models for the narrator's own writing in the novel within the novel that he embarks on to chronicle all the different ways he wasted his time before discovering his literary vocation. Some of the most beautiful pages of the novel are those in which Proust describes works of art, in particular music. Proust verbalizes and textualizes musical themes and leitmotifs in visual (i.e., metaphorical) terms: "A page of symphonic music by Vinteuil, familiar already on the piano, revealed, when one heard it played by an orchestra—like a ray of summer sunlight which the prism of the window decomposes before it enters a dark dining-room—all the jewels of the *Arabian Nights* in unsuspected, multicolored splendour" (*The Captive*). The quest for signs becomes the sign of the quest, whether pictorial, musical, or textual.

The quest did not end with Proust's death. Editions of the novel and critical texts about it proliferate. Moreover, every serious novelist of the 20th century has written in Proust's shadow. Writers such as Jean-Paul Sartre, Nathalie Sarraute, and Claude Simon, not to mention less obvious examples such as Jean Genet, Samuel Beckett, and William Faulkner, all owe a debt to Proust. Indeed, the importance of this novel is based in large part on its influence on the writing of fiction in the 20th century. If one were to oppose the two traditions represented respectively by the third-person narratives of Flaubert and Proust's innovative use of the first person, it is now clear, near the end of the 20th century, which of these narrative rhetorics won out in the long run. The Proustian model has had an enormous influence, especially on the French novel, so much of which is in the autobiographical mode, whatever the style and content. It should also be added that just as Proust is remarkable for the significance of his narrative innovations, his style—with its long, modulated sentences, some of which extend to several pages in length—broke with conventional French prose, which was more given to short, pithy prose. In this a writer such as Claude Simon is truly Proust's "son."*À la recherche du temps perdu* is in a very real and fundamental sense the most important "intertext" of our century, for readers and writers alike. To read Proust is not just to learn about turn-of-the-century French society or the torments of love and jealousy: reading Proust is an act of learning and empowerment, for it is first and foremost a matter of learning to read and hence to write.

RALPH SARKONAK

See also Marcel Proust

Further Reading

Beckett, Samuel, *Proust,* New York: Grove Press, and London: Chatto and Windus, 1931
Bersani, Leo, *Homos,* Cambridge, Massachusetts: Harvard University Press, 1995
Bowie, Malcolm, *Freud, Proust and Lacan: Theory as Fiction,* Cambridge and New York: Cambridge University Press, 1987
Compagnon, Antoine, *Proust entre deux siècles,* Paris: Seuil, 1989; as *Proust: Between Two Centuries,* New York: Columbia University Press, 1992
Deleuze, Gilles, *Proust et les signes,* Paris: Presses Universitaires de France, 1964; as *Proust and Signs,* London: Lane, and New York: Braziller, 1972
Descombes, Vincent, *Proust: Philosophie du roman,* Paris: Minuit, 1987; as *Proust: Philosophy of the Novel,* Stanford, California: Stanford University Press, 1992
Doubrovsky, Serge, *La Place de la madeleine: Écriture et fantasme chez Proust,* Paris: Mercure de France, 1974
Ellison, David R., *The Reading of Proust,* Baltimore: Johns Hopkins University Press, and Oxford: Blackwell, 1984
Erman, Michel, *L'Oeil de Proust: Écriture et voyeurisme dans "À la recherche du temps perdu,"* Paris: Nizet, 1988
Goodkin, Richard E., *Around Proust,* Princeton, New Jersey: Princeton University Press, 1991
Kristeva, Julia, *Proust and the Sense of Time,* London: Faber, and New York: Columbia University Press, 1993
Kristeva, Julia, *Le Temps sensible: Proust et l'expérience littéraire,* Paris: Gallimard, 1994; as *Time & Sense: Proust and the Experience of Literature,* New York: Columbia University Press, 1996
Poulet, Georges, *L'Espace proustien,* Paris: Gallimard, 1963; as *Proustian Space,* Baltimore: Johns Hopkins University Press, 1977
Richard, Jean-Pierre, *Proust et le monde sensible,* Paris: Seuil, 1974
Rivers, J.E., *Proust and the Art of Love: The Aesthetics of Sexuality in the Life, Times, and Art of Marcel Proust,* New York: Columbia University Press, 1980
Roger, Alain, *Proust: Les plaisirs et les noms,* Paris: Denoël, 1985
Sedgwick, Eve, *The Epistemology of the Closet,* Berkeley: University of California Press, 1990; London: Harvester Wheatsheaf, 1991
Shattuck, Roger, *Proust's Binoculars: A Study of Memory, Time, and Recognition in "À la recherche du temps perdu,"* New York: Random House, and London: Chatto and Windus, 1963
Shattuck, Roger, *Proust,* London: Fontana, 1974
Tadié, Jean-Yves, *Proust et le roman: Essai sur les formes et techniques du roman dans "À la recherche du temps perdu,"* Paris: Gallimard, 1971
Vogely, Maxine Arnold, *A Proust Dictionary,* Troy, New York: Whitston, 1981
Wolitz, Seth L., *The Proustian Community,* New York: New York University Press, 1971

Indian Novel

The story of the Indian novel appears at first sight to be a deceptively simple one, made more so by the unusual—perhaps unique—historical accuracy with which one can date its origins. In 1835, following an intense series of debates between Orientalists such as Sir William Jones and Horace Wilson on one side and Anglicists and India House ideologues such as Thomas Babington (later Baron Macaulay) and Sir William Bentinck on the other, the British Parliament passed the English Education Act mandating the use of English literary texts in the education of Indians. Among those most in favor of introducing English literature in India was Thomas Macaulay, a Scotsman, poet, famed author of the five-volume *History of England* (1849–61), and president of the India Council. A gifted scholar and prodigious author in his own right, Macaulay is legendary for the baldness of his critical positions: in the Minute on Indian Education meant to rouse his supporters and persuade his opponents, Macaulay, ignorant of all Oriental languages, nonetheless declared that "a single shelf of a good European library is worth the entire literature of Asia and Arabia." In an effort, therefore, to rectify matters and to introduce modernity into these "backward races," Macaulay proposed the introduction of English literature as a means to "create a class of persons, Indian in blood and colour, but English in taste, opinions, morals and intellect."

The result was the introduction of English literary texts in the classrooms and curricula of Indian educational institutions and the appearance of the novel into a world of letters where epic, poetry, and drama dominated (in that order) and where prose fiction had a negligible position. While the ancient *Panchatantra Tales* and the 18th-century Urdu *dastan* or episodic romances were indeed examples of prose fiction that were native to India, the novel as such had yet to emerge in the literary horizon until it was ushered in following the mandates of the 1835 Education Act.

From this relatively straightforward origin, the novel took off exuberantly in India. Library holdings from the period record that while fiction initially constituted a third or less of the total holdings in public libraries, it was requested for circulation four times more often by Indian readers than books in other subjects. By mid-century, the Calcutta Public Library (founded 1835) rued the inordinate requests for purchases in fiction. The Bagbazar Library (founded 1883), also in Calcutta, demonstrated a more sanguine attitude toward its membership's requests for fiction, reporting that "the enormous preponderance of fiction and the comparatively small attention paid to more serious literature are no doubt to be regretted, but they indicate the tendency of the age from which Bengali society is by no means free. It is hoped that the progress of education and a due appreciation of the requirements of practical life will lead to a more reasonable distribution of the readers' patronage" (*Report of the Bagbazar Reading Room,* 1903).

Two issues are immediately evident from this report: first, that the history of the novel in India (its origin, emergence, and development) is inextricably linked to the manner in which the newly introduced genre circulated in 19th-century India; and second, that any attempt to understand the forms in which the novel emerged in India must be predicated on the manner in which Indian readers consumed novels—both Indian and British—in the colonial period. Furthermore, notwithstanding the general indifference and highly sporadic control that the British colonial authorities exercised over the circulation of print in the territory, colonial import policies ensured that more than 95 percent of the books that circulated in India were British. American, French, and Russian novels had a small place in the market, induced in some part by the imposition of a 3 percent foreign import tax upon them. Meenakshi Mukherjee (1985) presses the consequences of this point further:

> It is perhaps unfortunate that the nineteenth-century Indian novelist had as his model primarily the British Victorian novel; with hindsight after a century, it seems the British model was perhaps the least suitable for the Indian mind in the nineteenth century. The brooding inwardness and the philosophical quality of the nineteenth-century Russian novel or the intensely moral preoccupation of the nineteenth-century American writer might have demonstrated to early practitioners of Indian fiction alternative modes of writing novels.

In the first half of the 19th century, English novels circulated on two registers, indirect and direct. While the colonial literary curriculum was structured around poetry, not novels, it indirectly—through the emphasis on language and "Englishness"—created an appetite for all things English, in which imaginative prose figured increasingly prominently. More directly, as an English-educated elite began to emerge in the large commercial cities (Calcutta, Bombay, Madras), a number of institutions purveying English books and ideas were established by and for Indians. Public libraries were significant, as were a host of "literary societies" where monthly discussions on extraliterary topics of community edification (such as "Advantages and Disadvantages of Society" or "On Female Education") were scheduled. As interest in Englishness and the novel increased, translations and "adaptations" of fiction were made and another layer of Indian society (one not part of the narrow English-educated strata) encountered the novel, this time through the medium of various regional languages including Bengali, Tamil, Marathi, Urdu, and Malayalam, among others. In this manner, the novel entered the world of Indian letters and spread both among the English-speaking elite and the non-English-educated middle classes. By the early decades of the 20th century, a vigorous circuit of involvement and commentary between an expanding reading public, the press, and regional-language novelists who often also wrote for the press became visible in the public sphere of most of the major languages.

Inasmuch as Indian translation records from the 19th century document novelistic consumption, two major trends are clear: first, the popularity of 18th-century fiction of the broadly didactic model (Samuel Johnson's *Rasselas* [1759], Jonathan Swift's *Gulliver's Travels* [1726], and Oliver Goldsmith's *The Vicar of Wakefield* [1766] were favorites); and, second, a taste for exuberantly imaginative prose (romances, melodrama, sensational novels) from the 1840s on. The emergence of the Indian novel remains consistent, at least to some extent, with this earlier trend: the affection for reading didactic prose initiated a proliferation of reformist themes in early Indian novels (so much so that the designation *novel* in some Indian languages often simply indicated a story or tale with a reformist agenda). Meanwhile, the affection for "exuberantly imaginative prose" had an unexpected effect on the forms in which the Indian novel emerged. The intense debates among colonial authorities surrounding the Education Act continued around the issue of what type of literature was most appropriate for creating the "ideal Indian," and the Department of Public Instruction was entrusted with the role of selecting the best English works for the project. Despite the care that went into the selection of a "good canon," newly literate Indian readers clamored for titles decidedly *not* on the "good" list, to the extent that the Calcutta Public Library went so far as to destroy all copies of G.W.M. Reynolds' *Mysteries of London* (1846–48), "in consequence of the very objectionable nature of its contents" (see under the year 1854 in *Report on the Calcutta Public Library for 1847– 93*, 1893). The library also repeatedly sent reminders to its supplier that "in the supply of the works of fiction, care should be taken in excluding works of demoralizing tendency" (1866).

Despite these benign and sometimes less benign attempts at low-grade censorship, extant holdings and circulation records from public libraries in each of the three main Presidency capitals (Bombay, Madras, and Calcutta) reveal a robust and continuing preference among Indian writers for novelists such as G.W.M. Reynolds, Marie Corelli, H. Rider Haggard, Captain Florence Marryat, William Ainsworth, and Edward Bulwer-Lytton, whose works proliferated among library holdings, in translations, as well as in press reports and literary debates of the period. Indeed, many Indian novelists record their debt to these figures, and it is something of a conundrum to explain what the appeal of these figures was and how it remained so persistent well into the 20th century. "I read several volumes of a novel by George W.M. Reynolds," Mulk Raj Anand confessed to Virginia Woolf in the 1920s; "I am afraid his long sentences may have affected my writing . . . I find the same about Rider Haggard who wrote *She*, and Marie Corelli, and Charles Garvice" (see Anand, 1981).

One common explanation for these low-brow reading tastes has been that the British dumped unsold and unsellable fiction in the colonies, so that Indian consumers had no other choice than to read "bad" British novelists such as Reynolds and Corelli. Yet, if one examines the publishing world of the period, one sees that plenty of "good" books were in fact available in the marketplace, and a well-defined sense of what constituted "good" and "bad" novels pervaded both the Indian and British literary worlds in India. By the second half of the 19th century, numerous British publishers recognized that the lack of circulating libraries in India afforded significant opportunity for commerce, and firms such as Macmillan, Routledge, Longman, Bentley, Cassells, and others began publishing fiction in "colonial" and "foreign" library series meant exclusively for sale in India and the colonies. From examining these lists, it becomes clear that the reading tastes Indian readers had manifested earlier in the century were being satisfied in the various colonial series. The careful selection of novels in these late 19th-century series was in marked contrast to the list put out in the first (and largely failed) series initiated by John Murray in 1843, which contained virtually no fiction and was replete with books of a "moral and edifying tendency." Later in the 19th century, readers' reports from

various London publishing houses provide an important record of prevailing literary trends and judgments, as well as the categories that British publishers used in order to select fiction. This archive demonstrates the care and consideration that was put into the Indian market and helps dismiss the oft-persistent theory of "colonial dumping." Mowbray Morris, the irascible editor of *Macmillan's Magazine* and eventually scabrous chief reader for the firm, routinely rejected manuscripts on the basis of their chances in the firm's Colonial Library. About one submission, he proffered in 1900: "One never hears her name, and the few notices I read of her last story were certainly not enthusiastic. From what I have gathered of the qualifications of your Colonial Library, I do not think that either [this book] or its author possesses them" (*Macmillan Archives*, 1982).

The best model for understanding the conditions under which the Indian novel emerged is neither conquest and dominance nor clash and confrontation, but rather what Harish Trivedi has identified as a series of "colonial transactions": "an interactive, dialogic, two-way process, rather than a simple active-passive one; a process involving complex negotiation and exchange . . . on both sides to facilitate give and take" (see Trivedi, 1993). This model adds nuance and complexity to the deceptively simple story that might otherwise emerge from the disarming clarity of dates. According to it, both India and Britain affected the other, and each was transformed in significant and lasting ways by the contact. Numerous studies have been published on the manner in which the colonies broadly and India specifically have affected the contours of British fiction: adventure romances such as H. Rider Haggard's *King Solomon's Mines* (1885), *She* (1886); detective fiction from its very beginning in Wilkie Collins' *The Moonstone* (1868) to its best-known in Arthur Conan Doyle; and boys' stories from Thomas Hughes' *Tom Brown's School Days* (1857) to G.A. Henty's adventure novels— all have received considerable critical attention as works inspired, shaped, and inflected by Britain's colonial experience and her acquisition of overseas territories (see Green, 1979; McClintock, 1995). More recently, Edward Said's *Culture and Imperialism* (1993) has been part of another trend that has identified not just the new and "minor" forms (adventure romance, boys' stories) produced by the colonial encounter, but also the formative and lasting impact of the "colonial transaction" visible in such canonical and "high" fiction as Jane Austen's (see also Perera, 1991).

In a parallel vein, emerging scholarship on the Indian novel has proposed that rather than scrutinizing British fiction for instances of India in the Western imagination, as has been popular in the past, more productive insights may be gained by examining the circulation of ideas and trends between India and London during the colonial period (see Joshi, 1998). To this end, researching the history of readership from extant colonial archives has begun to animate a provocative new portrait, just barely visible, in which Indian readers' reading tastes and consumption patterns of the 19th-century British novel in turn affected the contours of Britain's most valuable cultural export. According to emerging data in this field, colonial readers placed demands on British publishers, whose willingness to please this new and palpable market force was reflected in the kinds of novels that eventually got published in Britain. While considerable research needs to be completed before this view can become definitive, it is worth mentioning in this context in order to highlight the complexity that Trivedi's transaction model helps uncover. One point that is incontestable, however, is that the manner and kind of novels consumed in the 19th century shaped the forms in which the novel eventually emerged in India. While English education—and, through it, English ideas—were undoubtedly a force in the 19th century, they were in constant play with other, perhaps stronger, influences, such as Indian cultural, religious, and educational practices. Despite the copiousness and range of influence associated with English education, it must be placed in historical perspective: in the words of one critic, like Sanskrit culture and learning in ancient India, English was largely "associated with the ruling power and . . . divorced from the people at large" (see Das, 1991). Thus Indian readers' intentional selection and fashioning of a foreign literary corpus to their own symbolic needs cannot be overemphasized: from reading low- and middle-brow Victorian melodrama in Reynolds and Corelli and historical romances from Ainsworth and Bulwer-Lytton, Indian novelists produced a collective oeuvre of powerful and internationally regarded novels that early and clearly established a separate identity from their 19th-century British inspirations.

Trivedi's transaction model is a relatively recent one that has yet to fully dislodge older literary approaches: historically, when the first Indian novels began to emerge, they were still regarded as imitators and weak offspring of British loins. Bankim Chandra Chatterji (1838–94), one of the most important early novelists of India, was named the "Scott of Bengal," in part because of his experiments with historical fiction, although as recent criticism has pointed out this epithet fails to credit Bankim's originality and complexity (Mukherjee, 1985). His oeuvre spans three of the more turbulent decades of colonial rule, from *Rajmohan's Wife,* his first novel, published in English in 1864, to *Dharmatattva,* a collection of essays, in 1888. *Anandamath* (1882; translated as both *Anandamath* and *The Abbey of Bliss*) is perhaps his best-known work touching on many of the issues that persist even today in the form and content of Indian fiction. The novel is set around a 1773 Sanyasi rebellion in Bengal in which Indian patriots successfully fought against oppressive Muslim and British rulers. In it, Chatterji inaugurated the theme of nation as woman, specifically as Mother India, which was immediately appropriated as a rallying cry throughout Bengal and eventually all of India in the intensifying anticolonial struggle. The Sanskrit song *Bande Mataram* (Hail, Mother) that he wrote for the novel became the first anthem of the anticolonial movement, and, despite appropriations by various communal groups in the post-Independence period, it remains the unofficial anthem of a unified nation. While Bankim (as he is almost uniformly called) had before him two earlier Bengali prose models, Peary Chandra Mitra's *Alaler Gharer Dulal* (1858; The Spoilt Child of a Rich Family) and Bhudev Mukhopadhyay's *Anguriya Vinimay* (1862; The Exchange of Rings), he chose to write not just a work of colloquial prose as the other two had before him, but a novel. His writing presents a world of "great internal variety" (see Kaviraj, 1995) that, for the first time in Indian letters, came close to mapping and defining the social world of his readers.

While Bankim claims in *Rajasingha* (1882) that he had never written a historical novel before, he managed in *Anandamath* to give his readers a usable history—to disengage the past from the status of myth and epic into something appropriate for resisting both empire and a rapidly approaching modernity. Indeed, Bankim's work addresses one of the greatest anxieties among his 19th-century readers: how to fashion from a glorious past a history with which to revise and challenge the dishonor of colonialism. As Sudipta Kaviraj points out, "Bengalis do not lack the events; but they need a narrative to put [these events] into order" (see Kaviraj, 1995). By rewriting the Sanyasi Rebellion in contemporary terms, Bankim provided both a narrative to do this and an alternative to the existing social order. Despite the fact that Bankim wrote exclusively in Bengali (after his first, ill-fated *Rajmohan's Wife*), he was translated almost immediately into all the major Indian languages and is often regarded the father of the Indian novel. His historical method evinced a powerful chord among Indian readers, who began to take a great interest in historical narrative more generally. A British work that is particularly notable in this regard is Lieutenant Colonel James Tod's *Annals and Antiquities of Rajasthan* (1829–32), which was translated into virtually every major Indian language during the 19th century. An 1884 record of a new Bengali translation opines, "it is published in the hope that its perusal will rouse the historical sense of the Hindus, and enable them to understand their position as descendants of the brave, warlike, chivalrous and patriotic people whose achievements it records." What *Anandamath* did, then, was to prime a generation of readers and to provide them with a symbolic language (history) and narrative structure (the novel) in which to articulate their dreams. At the same time, the novel also underscores the tenuousness of this narrative order. Both Salman Rushdie's *Midnight's Children* (1981) and Amitav Ghosh's *The Shadow Lines* (1988) a century later adumbrate in different ways the power of stories and of some, more intoxicating, stories overtaking other, more stable, ones.

However, in numerous pre-Independence novels, Bankim's Mother India trope became central, although, while the mantle of novelty he carried was often enough to mute his critics (many of whom found the intense contradictions in Bankim's work impossible to justify), others had to confront the anti-colonial theme more systematically. In many ways, the novels of Rabindranath Tagore (1861–1941) do just this. Known mostly in the West for his poetry (which won him the Nobel prize in 1913), Tagore was an equally powerful force in the development of the Bengali novel. His *Ghaire Baire* (1915; *The Home and the World*) takes *Anandamath*'s nationalist worship of Mother India to its conclusion, when Bimala, a secluded upper-class zamindar's wife, is made to choose between her liberal, intellectual husband and the fiery Swadeshi revolutionary with whom she becomes infatuated after he anoints her as the face and focus—the Mother India—of his struggle. In enshrining Bimala as Mother India, Tagore highlights the tensions between the home (untouched by empire, therefore the putatively "pure" space from which to mount anticolonial resistance) and the larger social world outside it. Recent critics have challenged whether Bimala ever has any agency beyond that anointed to her by the men in her life (see Chatterjee, 1993), but the more pertinent question is the extent to which the presence of women (as characters, authors, readers, and consumers) and the broader issues of gender together began to shape the form of the Indian novel from the very early years. In numerous novels of this period (Nazir Ahmad's Urdu *Mirat-ul-Arus* [1869; *The Bride's Mirror*], Pandit Gauri Dutt's Hindi *Devarani Jethani ki Kahani* [1870;

The Sister-in-Laws' Story], O. Chandu Menon's Malayalam *Indulekha* [1888; *Crescent Moon*]), women figure as the terrain on which contesting ideologies of home and world, tradition and modernity, and religion and secularism are played out.

Alongside the glorification of women (as mother, inspiration, ideal), an equally urgent theme in early Indian novels was the uplifting of women around a host of social issues such as education, child marriage, widow remarriage, polygamy, social inequality, and so on. Many of the early novels on women were written by men who tended to use indignance over social wrongs affecting women as a means to cloak their frequent moral righteousness and piety toward the status quo. The first figure to challenge the woman-as-always-pure theme is the successful and highly entertaining Urdu novelist Mirza Mohammad Hadi Ruswa (1858–1931). His 1899 novel *Umrao Jan Ada* (*The Courtesan of Lucknow*) is frequently called "the first true novel in Urdu" (see Russell, 1970). It recounts the story of a young girl who is stolen at girlhood and sold into the courtesan's trade in Lucknow, where she becomes a legendary singer and scholar, welcomed into the most aristocratic and Nawabi homes. The frankness with which Ruswa deals with sex in the novel was bad enough for his detractors, but perhaps far worse was his glorification of Umraon Jan and his unwillingness to condemn his protagonist's lifestyle, reserving what blame he had to dispense for the middle classes who masked their complicity in the courtesan's trade (first as purveyors of young girls and later as their customers) by great moral superiority. In Ruswa's novel, the dark, unattractive prostitute is transformed into the scholarly courtesan whose ruminations on poetry, literature, and politics are symbolically pitted against the pieties of the middle-class morality that has sold her into the *kotha*. The novel plays on the irony that courtesans such as Umraon Jan are in fact repositories and preservers of culture at the very highest level: when the harsh British reprisals against the 1857 Mutiny begin, the courtesans lose their patrons but carry Nawabi culture and learning to other places. Its controversial content aside, Ruswa introduced to the Indian novel a kind of conversational realism unmatched in most earlier novels. Furthermore, his novel appropriates the languages of the journalist, ethnographer, and social historian.

Against the two strands already identified in 19th-century Indian novels (nationalist and emerging realist) is a third: the social novel, whose most skilled figure is the Hindi and Urdu writer Premchand (pseudonym of Dhanpat Rai Srivastava, 1881–1936), who wrote in both languages. Premchand is best known for his short stories, among which "Shatranj ke Khilari" (1924; "The Chess Players") and "Kafan" (1936; "The Shroud") are his most famous. His novel *Godaan* (1936; subtitled *A Novel of Peasant Life*) is often described as "the saga of Indian rural life" (see Das, 1995) in which the narrative drama focuses on that exemplar of feudal India, the peasant farmer. While the city and urban forms of capital intrude in the novel at numerous places, Premchand's focus remains the village and its people that Gandhi and the nationalist cause had been promoting as the backbone of India. Among Premchand's contributions to Indian literature was his powerful role in the standardization of Hindi as a modern literary language, which in turn inspired an expansion and greater participation of the Hindi reading public in the development of the novel. Furthermore, his attention to the lives of poor, rural, low-caste figures widened the lit-

erary universe of the Indian novel from the urban and elite and won him the critical acclaim of both literati and nationalists such as Gandhi and Nehru.

In his Hindi and Urdu journal, *Hans*, and in his literary and public work, Premchand advocated a vigorous platform of social reform on numerous levels. He counted Tolstoi as a formative influence and himself became a mentor of sorts in the 1930s to a young generation of Indian writers who named themselves the All-Indian Progressive Writers' Association and undertook in the words of Ahmed Ali, one of its founders, "an intellectual revolt against the outmoded past, the vitiated tendencies in contemporary thought and literature" (see Ali, in *Marxist Influences and South Asian Literature*, edited by Carlo Coppola, 1988). This was an ambitious project, a manifesto both for and against modernity: for the social and political equality of a liberal democratic state (proposing an end to ignorance, piety, exploitation); but against the forms of modernity ushered in by empire (the contaminated, perverted, "vitiated" tendencies in contemporary society). Ali's description is for a Herculean project, one far greater than a writers' movement could accommodate. Novelists from numerous Indian languages joined the association in various publication and translation projects initiated after its first (and only) meeting in 1936, over which Premchand presided. Despite the wide membership of the association, to which virtually every important writer of the 1930s belonged, the two who most defined it were Ahmed Ali (1910–94) and Mulk Raj Anand (b. 1905), both novelists who wrote in English. Ali was the literary guardian and the finer writer, Anand the ideological spearhead, whose socialist-realist novels such as *Untouchable* (1935) and *Two Leaves and a Bud* (1937) lambasted both empire and Indian society almost equally. In the end, most literary historians concur that the movement's "progressive" tendencies capitulated unreservedly to Anand's exuberant communism, and the association lost both its appeal and power when Ali broke with it in 1940.

Ali himself is an important, albeit enigmatic, figure: his first novel, *Twilight in Delhi* (1940), brought to the Indian novel what Bankim's experiments with historical events were unable to do. Ali introduced a historical realism to the form, in an English that so perfectly captured the rhythms of Delhi's elegant Urdu that many readers even today believe the novel was written in Urdu. Linear, chronological time, so much the staple of European realism, was a bane for the Indian novelist writing in a culture where time was epic, cyclical, nonexistent, and nonteleological, often all at the same time. *Twilight in Delhi* found a way to represent the nonsynchronous time in which a family remains trapped in part as a consequence of the events surrounding the 1857 mutiny and the disastrous consequences that occur when "modernity" is allowed to intrude into this hitherto isolated world. Appropriating an 18th-century Urdu poetic form, the *shehrashob* (the lament for a ruined, sacked, or depraved city), Ali makes Delhi the protagonist of his novel, linking as it were the extent to which empire has penetrated both the private and public world of its subjects.

This theme of the public, civic consequences of empire—its scars on the city and the urban landscape—returns again and again in the Indian novel: Amitav Ghosh plays with it compellingly in *The Shadow Lines*, having an English character break down when she sees the monstrous excess of colonial arrogance imprinted forever in the Calcutta landscape in the form of the Victoria Memorial. The opening of Premchand's famous

Hindi short story "The Chess Players" depicts this theme evocatively: "Lucknow was plunged deep in luxurious living," while the East India Company's armies march in and depose its Muslim ruler. None can grieve—or even recognize—the loss of sovereignty except the city itself: "The broken archways of the ruins, the crumbling walls, and dusty minarets looked down on the corpses and mourned," ends the story.

While progressivism as a literary movement may have been short-lived, it inspired the work of numerous women writers, particularly in the regional languages. The decades following the 1870s had seen women figuring as centerpieces in an increasingly vigorous debate on social reform that found comment in numerous 19th-century novels. However, these novels, like the social debate, were conducted largely by male reformists, a condition that changed dramatically by the turn of the century (for example, in Krupa Satthianadhan's *Kamala: A Story of Hindu Life* [1894], on the condition of child marriage and widows). Novels by women authors in the period before Independence were marked by a resilient iconoclasm and stylistic experimentation. Figures such as Ismat Chugtai (*Terhi Lakir* [1943; *The Crooked Line*]) and Rokeya Sakhawat Hossain (*Sultana's Dream*) took daring risks in their fiction, incurring the wrath of family and establishment by writing on serious social issues, including lesbianism, prostitution, and domesticity. The 1970s and 1980s, however, produced what some find to be a bourgeoisification of women's writing around "safer" themes of middle-class ennui and marital despair that were voiced so prominently in *Femina*, the leading English women's magazine of the day. Shashi Deshpande represents this condition in women's writing with great sensitivity in *That Long Silence* (1988), and among Anita Desai's many novels, *Fire on the Mountain* (1977) most falls within this trend.

Another important aspect of modern Indian literature in which the novel plays an increasingly key role is the extent to which it has addressed issues surrounding modernity. Philosophy generally, and social theory more precisely, undertook the task in the post-Enlightenment West but were ill-equipped to do so in India. Increasingly today, political and social philosophers on India turn to literature for evidence in constructing broader theories of modernity (particularly around issues such as citizenship, subjectivity, identity, community, and even nationalism). With the expansion and increased involvement of its reading public from the early decades of the 20th century, the novel participated unreservedly in social and political debates of the period, in which it commented, analyzed, complicated, and developed issues much in the manner that Enlightenment philosophy had done in 18th-century Europe. In some cases, that discourse appears in fiction wrapped around gentle satire, as in the Malgudi series of English novels by R.K. Narayan (b. 1906), a contemporary of Ali's and Anand's who, nevertheless, never joined the Progressive Writers' Movement. In social comedies dissecting the dilemmas of modernization, Narayan explores the conflict between English education and Indian expectations in *The Bachelor of Arts* (1937); between East and West in *The Vendor of Sweets* (1967); and between mysticism and faith in *The Guide* (1958). In other cases, the discourse on modernity is couched in terms drawing on India's Vedic philosophy and mythic history, as Raja Rao's (b. 1908) philosophical novel *The Serpent and the Rope* (1960) or Shashi Tharoor's allegory of the Mahabharata, *The Great Indian Novel* (1989).

Undoubtedly the most penetrating account comes in Salman Rushdie's *Midnight's Children* when the raison d'être of the modern nation state is subjected to relentless critique on a number of registers, from philosophical, political, and historical to satirical, parodic, and mocking. In many ways, Rushdie severed the critical and stifling affiliation between British English and the subcontinent, bringing a historical distance from which to observe and analyze the condition of being once-colonial subjects. *Midnight's Children* inaugurated what seemed like an endless stream of "nationsroman" in the 1980s—novels of the nation, including I. Allan Sealy's Parsi version, *The Trotter-Nama* (1988), Ghosh's *The Shadow Lines*, and Tharoor's *The Great Indian Novel*. The most striking feature of this wave of "nationsroman" is exactly how *un*nationalistic they are. Unlike Bankim's unmistakable, albeit contradictory, nationalism or Tagore's more probing version of almost a century earlier, the novelists of the 1980s seem more elegiac than celebratory of the nation. These are *national* novels, yes, but hardly *nationalist* ones. Each in its own way, and collectively, these works have made the novel into a suitably Indian genre, and yet it is almost as if the nation had to totter before the genre could take off. If the novel was a genre whose ascendance was twinned to the consolidation of the nation-state in Europe (see Anderson, 1983), the story is subtly different in India. In the early years of the 20th century the novel's rise in Indian letters could be understood by its immense explanatory capacities. It was seen as the form most capable of consolidating anticolonial sentiment, of resisting orthodoxy, and of promoting social change. It is fair to expect that the novel might also have been the literary form best equipped for nationalism, but this was not to be. The period 1880–1940 saw the emergence and the development of the novel in just about every language in India, yet the period following Independence (1947) was marked by a complete lull. The novel in India seemed better equipped for liberation than for nationalism, and the boom in novelistic output that has subsequently occurred in the 1980s has taken place at a time when the future of the Indian nation-state is being questioned, when Rushdie's enigmatic ending in *Midnight's Children* of a "broken creature spilling pieces of itself into the street" is echoed in communal unrest and separatist violence. If, in their obsession with the nation-state, these novels of the 1980s formulate—or expose—a collective "myth of the nation," then theirs is a curious obsession: to mythologize the nation not at its moment of·birth when it was the glorious victor of a liberation struggle, but in its unglamorous middle age, riddled by the maladies of modernity and despair, which the novels proceed to catalogue in painstaking detail.

Clearly, not all novels of this period have taken on as their theme the crisis of the Indian nation, nor had all novels of the past ignored the issue. Rather, the boom of Indian writing in the 1980s has given the Indian novel—particularly in English—a form to reflect the reality of the "out there," and this form has captured a wider slice of "out there" than hitherto. The ambitions of the form are voracious, but more than an appetite for stories, the form takes on history, demanding an association with the world in which it is produced. The world has responded in kind: two Booker Prizes (Britain's highest literary award, won by Rushdie in 1981 and by Arundhati Roy for *The God of Small Things* in 1997) and widespread press coverage in the West have made the Indian novel seem global, postmodern, and postcolonial. In this regard, the Indian novel in English has been particularly successful over the equally robust novel in regional languages: unhampered by difficulties of translation or by cultural barriers, the Indian novelist in English since the 1980s has found an almost immediate appeal in the cosmopolitan west. Numerous Indian critics point out that this cosmopolitanization ironically exposes the great isolation in which the anglophone elite in India exist from the "masses," from whom they are increasingly alienated by language and culture. It is a theme that the novels are acutely conscious of and often address: Upamanyu Chatterjee's *English, August* (1988) hilariously reflects upon the angst that a 24-year-old in India's elite civil service suffers when sent on his first posting to the provincial hinterland far from Delhi and his sophisticated, Westernized friends.

Yet the cosmopolitan Indian novel of today has not shirked its wider responsibility. In many ways, the contemporary anglophone novel in India (along with the boom novels of Carlos Fuentes and Gabriel García Márquez from Latin America or Francophone writing from North Africa) can seriously be considered a form of what some social critics call "minority literature" (see Deleuze and Guattari, 1986): namely, a literature constructed by a social or political minority through which it exerts a critical, political force on "great" (or established) literature. Minority literature is an outcome of critique and conscience, and it functions on numerous registers to expose, revise, or otherwise resist the triumphalist narratives of groups in power. In this regard, the postcolonial novel at its best takes on some of the great narratives of modernity and offers powerful alternatives to them. The proliferation of the "nationsroman" noted earlier may now be explained by the impetus to critique the Enlightenment myth of nationalism within the discourse of the novel. The remarkable point of 1980s fiction is its unabashed ambition, as well as the seriousness with which it is taken within public culture in India. However, as in the writings of Franz Kafka from which Gilles Deleuze and Félix Guattari developed their thesis on minority literature, effective critique needs both a voice and an audience. The first political, postmodern, postcolonial anglophone novel of India came well before the 1980s: G.V. Desani's *All about H. Hatterr* appeared in 1948, when the world had little time for Desani's profound wit and bracing parody of imperial mongrelization. The Indian novel took a turn during the 1950s and thereafter into a leaden regionalism and socialist realism, from which *Midnight's Children*, belatedly following *All about H. Hatterr*'s lead, liberated Indian fiction.

Today, the critical identity of a minority literature from India has found a new equilibrium. If national politics and history characterized the novels of the 1980s in the immediate wake of *Midnight's Children*, then the novels of the 1990s verge on public memory and private history. Vikram Seth's sprawling *A Suitable Boy* (1993) and Arundhati Roy's *The God of Small Things* have realigned the critical mode of Indian writing into what might be considered more conventional literary terrain. The tensions between subject and community still prevail (see also Ardashir Vakil's *Beach Boy* [1997] and Rohinton Mistry's *A Fine Balance* [1995]), but they are wrapped in private memories of 1950s Patna (Seth) or 1969 Ayemenem (Roy). The origins in British sensational fiction, melodrama, and romance from which Indian readers and writers first encountered the novel have today found widespread prominence in another prolific form, namely film, or the so-called Bollywood *masala* movies. Mean-

while, the Indian novel has come to inhabit the critical plane occupied in the West by history and philosophy, from which plane it enjoys substantial prestige.

PRIYA JOSHI

See also Mulk Raj Anand; Anita Desai; R.K. Narayan; Postcolonial Narrative and Criticism of the Novel; Salman Rushdie

Further Reading

Anand, Mulk Raj, *Conversations in Bloomsbury*, New Delhi: Arnold-Heinemann, and London: Wildwood House, 1981

Anderson, Benedict, *Imagined Communities: Reflections on the Origin and Spread of Nationalism*, London: Verso, 1983; revised edition, London and New York: Verso, 1991

Chatterjee, Partha, *The Nation and Its Fragments: Colonial and Postcolonial Histories*, Princeton, New Jersey: Princeton University Press, 1993

Clark, T.W., editor, *The Novel in India: Its Birth and Development*, Berkeley: University of California Press, and London: Allen and Unwin, 1970

Das, Sisir Kumar, *A History of Indian Literature, 1800–1910: Western Impact: Indian Response*, volume 8, Delhi: Sahitya Akademi, 1991

Das, Sisir Kumar, *A History of Indian Literature, 1911–1956: Struggle for Freedom: Triumph and Tragedy*, volume 9, New Delhi: Sahitya Akademi, 1995

Deleuze, Gilles, and Félix Guattari, *Kafka: Pour une littérature mineure*, Paris: Editions du Minuit, 1975; as *Kafka: Toward a Minor Literature*, Minneapolis: University of Minnesota Press, 1986

Gaeffke, Peter, *Hindi Literature in the Twentieth Century*, Wiesbaden: Harrassowitz, 1978

Green, Martin, *Dreams of Adventure, Deeds of Empire*, New York: Basic Books, 1979; London: Routledge and Kegan Paul, 1980

Iyengar, K.R. Srinivasa, *Indian Writing in English*, London and New York: Asia Publishing House, 1962; 6th edition, New Delhi: Sterling, 1987

Joshi, Priya, "Culture and Consumption: Fiction, the Reading Public, and the British Novel in Colonial India," *Book History* 1:1 (1998)

Kaviraj, Sudipta, *The Unhappy Consciousness: Bankimchandra Chattopadhyay and the Formation of Nationalist Discourse in India*, Delhi and New York: Oxford University Press, 1995

Macmillan Archives, Cambridge and Teaneck, New Jersey: Chadwyck-Healey, 1982

McClintock, Anne, *Imperial Leather: Race, Gender, and Sexuality in the Colonial Conquest*, New York: Routledge, 1995

Mukherjee, Meenakshi, *The Twice-Born Fiction: Themes and Techniques of the Indian Novel in English*, New Delhi: Heinemann, 1971

Mukherjee, Meenakshi, *Realism and Reality: The Novel and Society in India*, Delhi and New York: Oxford University Press, 1985

Nandy, Ashis, *The Intimate Enemy: Loss and Recovery of Self under Colonialism*, Delhi: Oxford University Press, 1983

Ohdedar, Aditya, *The Growth of the Library in Modern India: 1498–1836*, Calcutta: World Press, 1966

Perera, Suvendrini, *Reaches of Empire: The English Novel from Edgeworth to Dickens,* New York: Columbia University Press, 1991

Report of the Bagbazar Reading Room for the 19th Year Ending in June 1902, Calcutta: Mookerjee, 1903

Report on the Calcutta Public Library for 1847–1893, Calcutta: Sanders, Cones, 1893

Russell, Ralph, "The Development of the Modern Novel in Urdu," in *The Novel in India: Its Birth and Development,* edited by T.W. Clark, Berkeley: University of California Press, and London: Allen and Unwin, 1970

Said, Edward W., *Culture and Imperialism,* New York: Knopf, and London: Chatto and Windus, 1993

Shaw, Graham, *South Asia and Burma Retrospective Bibliography, Stage I: 1556–1800,* London: British Library, 1987

Tharu, Susie, and K. Lalita, editors, *Women Writing in India, 600 B.C. to the Present,* 2 vols., New York: Feminist Press, and London: Pandora, 1991–93

Trivedi, Harish, *Colonial Transactions: English Literature and India,* Calcutta: Papyrus, 1993

Viswanathan, Gauri, *Masks of Conquest: Literary Studies and British Rule in India,* New York: Columbia University Press, 1989; London: Faber, 1990

Zbavitel, Dusan, *Bengali Literature,* Wiesbaden: Harrassowitz, 1976

Indiana by George Sand

1832

When, early in 1831, the 26-year-old woman who was to become George Sand left her provincial home to live in Paris with her 19-year-old lover, she was wreaking havoc with her age's ideas of her duties as wife, mother, and woman. She intimidated her husband into accepting her departure by giving him a stark choice: either he would agree to her alternating three months in Paris with three months at home or she would live in Paris all the time. The French legal code adamantly insisted on the wife's duty to obey her husband, which meant that Sand's stance toward hers broke written as well as unwritten law. Moreover, her move to the capital also overturned standard views of motherhood, for she left her children behind. Her son was six, her daughter two. To confide them to another's care risked impressing some as even more outrageous than taking a lover 16 years her husband's junior, 7 years her own.

Once she reached Paris, Sand made other dramatic assaults on standard ideas of womanly propriety. Distressed to learn that certain Parisian attractions were closed to her because of her sex, she reacted by dressing—and passing—as a man, by choosing frock coats, trousers, and cigars over crinoline, lace, and decorum. Nineteenth-century France had rigid ideas on what women could do and how they should look, none of which had the slightest influence over what Sand did and how she looked in 1831.

One of the things she did was begin to write, on her own and in collaboration with her lover, Jules Sandeau. Late in 1831 she and Sandeau published a jointly authored novel they signed with the pen name "J. Sand." Early in 1832 Sand wrote *Indiana* by herself and signed it "G. Sand," both to avoid family concerns over use of her own name and to capitalize on the modest success J. Sand had acquired. She would remain George Sand from the appearance of *Indiana* in 1832 until her death in 1876, for her friends as well as her readers. In the name she took (as in the clothes she wore and the life she led), Sand mounted an all-fronts insurgency against the imperative that things masculine be reserved for men alone.

Indiana, a major offensive in her struggle, represents gendered traits in such a way that masculinity and femininity both proclaim their contingency; neither is allowed to retain the ideologically molded appearance of an inborn essence. Indiana, the novel's title character, has much of the weakness 19th-century convention ascribed to women. Her husband's brutality appears to have broken her spirit, and her lover's indifference plunges her into suicidal despair. Yet she also commands a towering strength of resistance. To her dictatorial husband, Indiana declares that a wife's soul will always remain hers no matter what the laws require. "I know that I am the slave and you are the lord; the law of this country has made you my master . . . but over my will, sir, you have no rights." To her faithless lover, she declares that the power he feels as a man is an illusion created by social and religious systems instituted for the sole purpose of perpetuating established authority. "All your morality, all your principles are the self-interest of your society, which you have erected into laws that you pretend to have received from God." Sand wrote that her heroine was a "typical woman, strong and weak, bowed down by the weight of the air and strong enough to shoulder the sky." What makes Indiana a "typical woman" is that she can be everything and anything, feminine and masculine, strong and weak, cowardly and heroic, brilliant and stupid, submissive and rebellious. She is a typical woman because she is not a type but a person.

Gendered behavior is a basic organizing principle for the characters of *Indiana,* but the novel excludes every idea of a causal connection between behavior and anatomy, gender and sex. The traits defined as manly or womanly migrate between men and women. A woman too weak to stand can be strong enough to defy the world, a man who is a mighty Don Juan can become a henpecked worm.

Migration of gendered features is particularly important in the novel's narrator, G. Sand, a "young man" who displays many of the prejudices associated with that condition. In blunt terms, G.

Sand can be very piggy indeed. He announces, for instance, that "woman is imbecilic by nature" and then explains why. Other characters demonstrate that nothing is inherent to either men or women, that each can display all the characteristics associated with the other. But the narrator believes that anatomy is destiny. Besides taking a man's name on her title page and a man's body in her narrative, Sand gave herself a man's prejudices, too.

Yet the voice articulating those prejudices comes from a woman. The sex of the author of *Indiana* was broadly known before publication and universally known just afterward, which means that the experience of reading this novel has always included an encounter with a disorienting paradox: the person who defines woman as imbecilic by nature is by nature a woman. Because of his/her double gender, the narrator's patriarchal certainties are so many ways to destabilize patriarchy. Everything s/he defines as a "natural" feature of men or women actually demonstrates that neither is naturally anything at all. Women can be phallic pontificators, men can sound imbecilic by nature.

The narrator is both a sexist man and a feminist woman, the title character too weak to bear the weight of air and strong enough to hold up the sky. Don Juan becomes Walter Mitty—the cumulative effect is to discombobulate the ideology of gender. While she was writing *Indiana,* Sand's daily life was a vigorous assault on the idea that sexual identity is a function of genital anatomy. Her first novel continued the assault by other means.

SANDY PETREY

See also George Sand

Further Reading

Barry, Joseph, *Infamous Woman: The Life of George Sand,* Garden City, New York: Doubleday, 1976
Crecelius, Kathryn J., *Family Romances: George Sand's Early Novels,* Bloomington: Indiana University Press, 1987
Maurois, André, *Lélia: The Life of George Sand,* New York: Harper, and London: Cape, 1953
Moers, Ellen, *Literary Women,* Garden City, New York: Doubleday, 1976; London: Allen, 1977
Naginski, Isabelle Hoog, *George Sand: Writing for Her Life,* New Brunswick, New Jersey: Rutgers University Press, 1991
Petrey, Sandy, "Men in Love, Saint-Simonism, *Indiana,*" *George Sand Studies* 14 (1995)
Sand, George, *Story of My Life: The Autobiography of George Sand,* Albany: State University of New York Press, 1991
Schor, Naomi, *George Sand and Idealism,* New York: Columbia University Press, 1993
Thomson, Patricia, *George Sand and the Victorians: Her Influence and Reputation in Nineteenth-Century England,* London: Macmillan, and New York: Columbia University Press, 1977

Indonesian Novel. *See* Southeast Asian Novel: Indonesia

Inferred Author. *See* Implied Author

Interior Monologue. *See* Stream of Consciousness and Interior Monologue

The Interpreters by Wole Soyinka

1965

Wole Soyinka had already earned a reputation for his early plays and poems, his short stories, his theatrical productions, his journalism, and his critical articles by the time he published *The Interpreters* in 1965. Even though the novel drew a mixed response from critics, it became clear that Soyinka also had to be taken seriously as a writer of extended prose fiction.

Soyinka himself has described *The Interpreters* as "an attempt to capture a particular moment in the lives of a generation which was trying to find its feet after independence." That "particular moment" included artists seeking to come to terms with inherited myths, timeservers emulating alien fashions, and politicians wondering how large a slice of the national cake they could secure for themselves. To capture the moment, Soyinka employed a modernist style, making extensive use of flashbacks, dispensing with straightforward narrative, reveling in the interplay between characters, incorporating a range of references, and indulging in lavish and luxurious descriptions. The immediacy and the abundance of the satire initially confused and bewildered readers, and it still tends to obscure the deeper structure of the work.

The vigor and ambition of the novel certainly astonished critics who recognized the nature of the challenges it posed. One reviewer compared Soyinka to James Joyce, William Faulkner, and Nathalie Sarraute. On the other hand, there are those who deny Soyinka's literary gifts. In the highly politicized African context, where Soyinka is regarded by some as a controversial social critic and an erratic political activist, there are readers who are unwilling to engage with this novel. Some claim to have given up reading after the first line, "Metal on concrete jars my drink lobes." Others base their rejection on the time shifts employed in the opening sequence and on the interwoven themes. Eustace Palmer has not been alone in rejecting the novel for "tedious formlessness" (see Palmer, 1979).

Soyinka is certainly demanding. He has created articulate, experienced, widely traveled, highly educated central characters who know one another well and speak with passion, anger, and wit. They are ready to joke, to tease, to rail, or to wax lyrical, and, in the case of Sagoe, to indulge in fantasies about "drink lobes." In presenting the interaction of past and present, Soyinka had abundant Western models, but he bends his daring experiments with time to the local context: *The Interpreters* hinges on Yoruba views of time and on the numinous state of transition between the past, the present, and the future, the connection between the dead, the living, and the unborn.

The Interpreters remains a difficult book to read because of its open-ended complexities. It is not clear, for example, what options are open to Egbo. Will his work in the Foreign Office ever enable him to bring about change? Could he really have a greater impact by taking up a traditional leadership role in the Niger Delta? And does Sagoe, the investigative journalist, have alternatives? Will his writing raise awareness, or is he destined to see all his exposés spiked by his editor? The problem of judging and assessing is particularly acute because of the authority that gathers around the least sharply realized of the interpreters: the university teacher Bandele and the engineer-turned-artist Sekoni. Although these are shadowy figures, lacking the vivid life imparted to Egbo and Sagoe, they nonetheless raise decisive questions and make major statements. For example, Sekoni's death is central to the novel, and in the final scene it is Bandele who, after various interpreters have been involved in another death, speaks out to condemn the superficial values of the university community.

Those who come to Soyinka's book aware of the satirical tradition of Kingsley Amis' *Lucky Jim* (1954) will readily recognize elements of iconoclasm in the campus scenes. This iconoclasm does not extend to the attitude toward mythology that, manipulated with characteristic independence, links Soyinka with other novelists who have made use of mythological structures. In this respect, *The Interpreters* looks back to James Joyce and forward, in Soyinka's oeuvre, to *Season of Anomy* (1973), a novel set during the Nigerian Civil War (1967–70) that evokes patterns associated with the myth of Orpheus and Eurydice. *The Interpreters* also anticipates the epic and mythic quality of Ben Okri's *The Famished Road* (1991) and Ayi Kwei Armah's *Osiris Rising* (1995). In these texts, transitions from one dimension to another can take place at any time. Soyinka's decision to place the death of Sekoni at the center of his book and to explore its sacrificial dimension links the novel with Judeo-Christian writings, with practices and performances vital to Yoruba life, and with the mythology of the Nile Valley.

A particularly rich, daring, and accomplished novel, *The Interpreters* comes from the time between independence and the declaration of the emergency in the western region of Nigeria, a period when it was still possible to hope and when aesthetic issues were still high on the agenda. In November 1965, a few months after the publication of his first novel and following rigged elections, Soyinka daringly held up a Nigerian radio station in an attempt to rally dissidents. The country had by that time been stripped of its innocence, and the author of *The Interpreters* had felt compelled to take the kind of action that none of the characters in his book had been capable of embarking on. Significantly, his next extended prose work was *The Man Died* (1972), a prison diary.

JAMES GIBBS

Further Reading

Gibbs, James, *Critical Perspectives on Wole Soyinka,* Washington, D.C.: Three Continents Press, 1980; London: Heinemann, 1981

Jones, Eldred D., *The Writing of Wole Soyinka,* London: Heinemann, 1973

Kinkead-Weekes, Mark, "The Interpreters: A Form of Criticism," in *Critical Perspectives on Wole Soyinka,* edited by James Gibbs, Washington, D.C.: Three Continents Press, 1980; London: Heinemann, 1981

Larson, Charles R., *The Emergence of African Fiction,* revised edition, Bloomington: Indiana University Press, 1972; London: Macmillan, 1978

Maduakor, Obi, *Wole Soyinka: An Introduction to His Writings,* New York: Garland Press, 1986

Moore, Gerald, *Wole Soyinka,* London: Evans, and New York: Africana, 1971

Morrison, Kathleen, "The Second Self as Vision of Horror in Wole Soyinka's *The Interpreters,*" *Black American Literature Forum* 22:4 (Winter 1988)

Morrison, Kathleen, "'To Dare Transition': Ogun as Touchstone in Wole Soyinka's *The Interpreters,*" *Research in African Literatures* 20:1 (1989)

Omole, James Olukayode, "A Sociolinguistic Analysis of Wole Soyinka's *The Interpreters,*" *DAI* 46:2283A

Omole, James Olukayode, "Code-Switching in Soyinka's *The Interpreters,*" *Language and Style* 20:4 (Fall 1987)

Omole, Olukayode, "Elegant Variations and Characterization in *The Interpreters,*" *West African Association for Commonwealth Literature and Language Studies Journal* 1 (1989)

Owusu, Kofi, "Interpreting *The Interpreters*: The Fictionality of Wole Soyinka's Critical Fiction," *World Literature Written in English* 27:2 (1987)

Palmer, Eustace, *The Growth of the African Novel,* London: Heinemann, 1979

Wright, Derek, *Wole Soyinka Revisited,* New York: Twayne, 1993

Invisible Cities by Italo Calvino

Le città invisibili 1972

Italo Calvino's *Invisible Cities* is widely recognized as an exemplar of European postmodernism. One of the most interesting aspects of the novel is that, although ostensibly its formal architectural qualities reflect its urban themes, the invisibility invoked by the title problematizes any direct correspondence between form and content. Appropriately, the two foci for most critics are the complex structure of the novel and the nature of its fictionality.

Calvino's literary experiments in the early 1960s in the Oulipo Laboratory (an acronym for Ouvroir de Littérature Potentielle, or Workshop for Potential Literature), in which he worked with the French writer Raymond Queneau and the mathematician François Le Lionnais, furnished him, as Alastair Brotchie notes, with a number of techniques for "incorporating mathematical structures into the process of literary creation."

In many ways, *Invisible Cities* is less a novel than a collection of fragmented narratives structured in a sequence of orderly sections. These sections, outlined on the contents page, divide the novel into nine parts, with each part bound by a pair of framing narratives (italicized in most versions of the text). The first and last parts contain ten framed vignettes, and all the other parts comprise five vignettes between the framing narratives. There is a complex but logical progression at work in the text: the titles of the framed narratives invoke different urban moods, or dimensions: for example, "cities and memory," "cities and desire," "cities and signs," "thin cities," and "trading cities." The sections move through an intertwined sequence of one to five, to be replaced by another emergent sequence. Thus, as the critic Carol James (1982) indicates, parts one and nine are arranged 1, 2–1, 3–2–1, 4–3–2–1, and 5–4–3–2, 5–4–3, 5–4, 5 respectively, and the other parts follow a 5–4–3–2–1 logic: "in so far as possible each city is followed by one from the next set so that the sequencing forms a pattern of simultaneous forward and reverse movement." However, although this mathematical structure suggests a formal whole, the discontinuous narrative actually undermines such a rigid structure, the chief themes being invisibility, undecidability, and ontological uncertainty. Indeed, as

Laurence A. Breiner (1988) discerns, "the elaborated numerical structure seems a red herring, no more meaningful than simple chapter numbers, because nothing is added in the way of significant subordinations." As such, the playful aspects of the novel are highlighted over its tight structure in a manner comparable with two of Calvino's other major books: *Il castello dei destini incrociati* (1973; *The Castle of Crossed Destinies*) and *Palomar* (1983; *Mr. Palomar*).

Invisible Cities is loosely based on the 13th-century Venetian explorer Marco Polo's *Travels.* The opening framing narrative of Calvino's novel introduces it as a collection of traveler's tales to which the emperor Kublai Khan listens even though he "does not necessarily believe" them. Nevertheless, the Khan persistently attempts to trace a "pattern" through Polo's fragmented tales in an attempt to reconstitute an orderly empire from the "endless, formless ruin" of discontinuous cities. The tension between the Khan's imperial instinct and Marco Polo's interest in aesthetic detail is a theme woven throughout the book. As Breiner (1988) has indicated, Kublai Khan and Marco Polo act as focalizers for two possible readings of the novel. First, the emperor tries to reconstruct design and significance from the narrative fragments, mirroring the apparent logic of the novel's numerical structure; on reflecting on the "invisible order that sustains cities," the Khan "thought he was on the verge of discovering a coherent, harmonious system underlying the infinite deformities and discords." By way of contrast, the merchant traveler revels in the quality of his narrative fragments and the memories, desires, and moods that are generated by the retelling of stories. He comments on the instability of perception ("the eye does not see things but images of things that mean other things"), the ambiguity of location ("the city displays one face to the traveler arriving overland and a different one to him who arrives by sea"), and the ultimate futility of mapping the world in order to contain it within the covers of an atlas ("each city takes to resembling all cities, places exchange their form, order, distances, a shapeless dust cloud invades the continents"). The final exchange between the two suggests that the promised land that the Khan seeks is unattainable; Polo states, "If I tell you that the city toward which my journey tends is discontinuous in space and time, now scattered, now more condensed, you must not believe the search for it can stop." Furthermore, the traveler's final comments indicate that the ultimate journey should not be a quantifiable conquest of land but an inward journey into the personal inferno of suffering.

William Franke (1989) comments that some critics have "construed the Polo-Khan relation in dialectical terms" as a model for understanding history as a complex series of continuities and discontinuities. However, Franke goes on to argue that, although the framing narratives are constructed as dialogues, "there is no real dialectic between respective positions; there are only two different positions which unfold themselves each in its difference, beyond every possibility of synthesis or even interaction." Thus, Franke concludes that the novel is less about synthesis and reconciliation than about the affirmation of social difference. In this respect *Invisible Cities* has a political subtext that links it to the concerns of Calvino's early novel of Italian neorealism, *Il sentiero dei nidi di ragno* (1947; *The Path to the Nest of Spiders*) and plugs into some of the ideas presented in his collection of essays, *Una pietra sopra: Discorsi di letteratura e società* (1980; *The Uses of Literature*). On this view, the critics who emphasize Marco Polo's final triumph over the Khan seem vindicated. As Calvino comments in a 1976 essay entitled "Right and Wrong Political Uses of Literature," "This is the only chance we have of becoming different from the way we are—that is, the only way of starting to invent a new way of being."

MARTIN HALLIWELL

See also Italo Calvino

Further Reading

Botta, Anna, "Calvino's *Citta invisibili*: Opening an Atlas of Similitude," *Italian Culture* 10 (1992)

Breiner, Laurence A., "Italo Calvino: The Place of the Emperor in *Invisible Cities*," *Modern Fiction Studies* 34:4 (Winter 1988)

Calvino, Italo, "Right and Wrong Political Uses of Literature," in *The Uses of Literature: Essays*, San Diego, California: Harcourt Brace Jovanovich, 1986

Cannon, JoAnn, *Italo Calvino: Writer and Critic*, Ravenna: Longon, 1981

Christensen, Peter G., "Utopia and Alienation in Calvino's *Invisible Cities*," *Forum-Italicum* 20:1 (Spring 1986)

Franke, William, "The Deconstructive Anti-Logic of *Le città invisibili*," *Italian Quarterly* 30:115–116 (Winter-Spring 1989)

Harris, Paul, "*Invisible Cities*: The Code, the Chinaman and Cities," *Mosaic* 23:4 (Fall 1990)

James, Carol P., "Seriality and Narrativity in Calvino's *Le città invisibili*," *Modern Language Notes* 97:1 (January 1982)

Kirkpatrick, Ken, "The Khan's Chessboard: The Failure of Order in Calvino's *Invisible Cities*," *Texas Review* 10:1–2 (Spring-Summer 1989)

Lucente, G.L., *Beautiful Fables: Self-Consciousness in Italian Narrative from Manzoni to Calvino*, Baltimore: Johns Hopkins University Press, 1986

Palmore, Michael J., "Diagramming Calvino's Architecture," *Forum-Italicum* 24:1 (Spring 1990)

Queneau, Raymond, *Oulipo Laboratory: Texts from the Bibliotheque Oulipienne*, London: Atlas, 1995

Schneider, Marilyn, "Subject or Object? *Mr. Palomar* and *Invisible Cities*," in *Calvino Revisited*, edited by Franco Ricci, Ottawa: Dovehouse, 1989

Springer, Carolyn, "Textual Geography: The Role of the Reader in *Invisible Cities*," *Modern Language Studies* 15:4 (Fall 1985)

Invisible Man by Ralph Ellison

1952

Few American novels of the postwar era have generated the immediate attention and lasting influence of Ralph Ellison's single novel and masterpiece, *Invisible Man*. Written when the author was only 38, the novel became an instantly acclaimed classic, winning for Ellison the National Book Award (1953), the American Academy of Arts and Letters Fellowship to Rome (1955–1957), the Medal of Freedom (1969), and, within his lifetime, more than a dozen honorary degrees.

The novel itself is a Bildungsroman and picaresque tale, following the unnamed narrator from his rural southern college to Harlem, where he undergoes the slow process of change from naive bumpkin and idealist to a sceptical but still determined individual. Framing the narrator's chapters are his prologue and epilogue, both written at the end of the linear narrative from a wiser—if somewhat more cynical—perspective. Throughout the novel, as the narrator recounts his extraordinary mishaps and escapades, the reader benefits from the duality of Invisible Man's initial experience glossed by his ironic interpretation and sarcastic retrospective view. For example, Invisible Man naively views the great southern school where the narrative commences (likely Tuskegee Institute, attended by Ellison) as a place of opportunity. However, the college is presented to the reader through the sarcastic symbolism of the wiser narrator, who recognizes its oppressive racist atmosphere. Likewise, in New York City, a brotherhood (communist) leader whom the protagonist initially admires is described by the seasoned narrator in far less adulatory tones, as are the many individuals and institutions encountered by Invisible Man during his development.

The novel's artistic influences are numerous; Ellison constructs a highly symbolic patchwork of cultural and literary references. Beginning with the narrator literally holed up underground, the work clearly references Fedor Dostoevskii's *Zapiski iz podpol'ia* (1864; *Notes from Underground*), in which the embittered narrator has retreated from society, unwilling to wrestle against its negative influences. Ellison's protagonist, however, is not ready to yield and retire; his hibernation, he tells us, is only temporary, as he prepares in the epilogue to "shake off the old skin and come up for air." As the Dostoevskii reference is inverted to suit the author's theme, so, too, are the works of dozens of other mainstream American and European authors, such as George Eliot, James Joyce, Franz Kafka, André Malraux, Ralph Waldo Emerson, Herman Melville, Mark Twain, and, of course, H.G. Wells. The novel likewise demonstrates a breathtakingly comprehensive compendium of African-American cultural influences seamlessly connected with those mentioned above. References to black oratory, literature, politics, music, folklore, and even cuisine construct the lens through which the narrator projects his tale. Quotations and allusions to Booker T. Washington and Frederick Douglass, respectively, provide a significant counterpoint to represent the narrator's evolution from accepting innocence to awakened interaction.

Importantly, African-American music informs *Invisible Man*'s theme and structure at every turn. Beginning with the prologue's theme song, "What Did I Do to Be So Black and Blue," the novel contains references to black spirituals, folk songs, the blues, swing, and bebop. Even Ellison's overall understanding of American culture and his potential remedy for racial inequality are musically oriented (he was, after all, a trained classical musician). The author suggests that jazz might represent the ideal paradigm for improvising a creative and harmonic blending of influences in American culture, mixing the talents and tensions of its participants like a successful jazz combo in performance. Pursuing this model, the narrator implies at the end of the novel that the culture could become a dynamic and flexible society in which everyone benefits from the strengths and contributions of others.

Ellison's use of a dual-perspective narrative voice owes a great debt to W.E.B. DuBois' concept of double consciousness, as set forth in the latter's *Souls of Black Folk*. In this 1903 memoir and study, DuBois examines the "two-ness" experienced by American blacks who are ever (self-)conscious of belonging to two diametrically opposed social groups, guided by "two warring ideals in one dark body." While DuBois is never named in *Invisible Man*, his theory of double consciousness is present both in Ellison's double-voiced narrative as well as in the narrator's frequent sensations of being pulled in emotionally polar directions and of viewing himself from an onlooker's perspective. Like DuBois, the narrator ultimately attempts to articulate a unified vision of society at the close of his story, aware that contradictions in American culture abound but convinced that unity is achievable and desirable.

Another key theoretical concept of Ellison's novel is the exploration of the theme of invisibility, an idea previously examined in the works of Richard Wright. For the narrator in Ellison's novel, invisibility is doubly experienced: whites and those in power fail to recognize him for his true self, demeaning both his ambition and potential because of his race. Yet the narrator also overlooks his true nature in an effort to please others, to blend in and accommodate expectations. Ellison's figurative use of invisibility throughout the novel has influenced dozens of subsequent creative and political writers who view the experience of invisibility as a consequence of racial, ethnic, or sexual marginalization.

While the reviews of *Invisible Man* were overwhelmingly positive and catapulted Ellison to literary stardom, there were detractors. Not surprisingly, the American Communist Party was incensed with his thinly veiled portrayal of it in the Brotherhood. Black nationalists took exception to Ellison's theme of racial harmony, seeing the narrator's call for inclusion at the end as subservient to the dominant white society. Coming as it did two years before the historic *Brown v. the Board of Education* decision, the novel was viewed by left-wing black intellectuals as overly focused on craft and inadequately concerned with the timely issue of black power. In addition, some white critics, most notably Irving Howe, condemned Ellison for abandoning the naturalism so admired in the works of Richard Wright and also for de-emphasizing the protest tradition of earlier African-American writing. Finally, many artists of the Black Arts movement rejected Ellison for his insistence that America be a land of cultural exchange and synergy.

Ellison's response to such criticisms can be found in his essays and lectures. He produced two influential books of collected essays, *Shadow and Act* (1964) and *Going to the Territory* (1986), numerous scholarly articles, and short stories that resolutely promote the idea of a multicultural America. Defining his purpose as a writer in *Shadow and Act*, Ellison stated that "one of the obligations I took on when I committed myself to the art and form of the novel was that of striving for the broadest range, the discovery and articulation of the most exalted values." Untold numbers of writers and scholars of all races, from the United States and abroad, continue to reap inspiration from Ellison's novel, and reappraisals of its achievements have appeared regularly since its publication. It is, as the writer Jonathan Yardley states, about as close to being "that mythical, unattainable dream of American literature, 'the great American novel'," as any work ever published.

GINA L. TAGLIERI

Further Reading

Benston, Kimberly, editor, *Speaking for You: The Vision of Ralph Ellison*, Washington, D.C.: Howard University Press, 1987

Graham, Maryemma, and Amritjit Singh, editors, *Conversations with Ralph Ellison*, Jackson: University Press of Mississippi, 1995

Hersey, John, editor, *Ralph Ellison: A Collection of Critical Essays*, Englewood Cliffs, New Jersey: Prentice-Hall, 1974

O'Meally, Robert G., *The Craft of Ralph Ellison*, Cambridge, Massachusetts: Harvard University Press, 1980

O'Meally, Robert G., editor, *New Essays on "Invisible Man,"* Cambridge: Cambridge University Press, 1988

Sundquist, Eric J., editor, *Cultural Contexts for Ralph Ellison's "Invisible Man,"* Boston: Bedford, 1995

Iranian Novel

Although storytelling has a long tradition in Iran, prose fiction, and particularly the novel, is a relatively recent phenomenon in the history of Persian literature. Traditionally, verse has always been preferred to prose, and for that reason verse was usually employed for writing long stories. Until the late 19th century, prose literature had consisted mostly of histories, philosophical and scientific treatises, and the like. Exceptions to this rule are a number of popular medieval romances, which can be regarded as precursors to the modern Persian novel. Another pre-20th-century exception is the genre of travel memoirs. The writers of travel memoirs often delved into the realm of imagination and provided fictionalized accounts of the places and people they visited. With regard to narrative style and structure, this genre of writing provided a model for Persian novelists of ensuing generations. In fact, the first modern Persian novel, *Siyahatnameh-ye Ebrahim Beyg* (1895; The Travel Memoirs of Ebrahim Beyg) by Zeynol'abedin Maragheh'i, is a fictional travel account of a young Iranian born and raised in Egypt who journeys to his ancestral homeland. Although Maragheh'i uses the format and style of 19th-century travel memoir genre, his purpose in writing this novel is social and political criticism, an approach favored by an increasing number of reform-minded Iranian intellectuals who had begun to emerge in the last decades of the 19th century and who were at least partly responsible for the uprisings that eventually led to the Constitutional Revolution of 1906–11. Instead of writing a polemical treatise, as was common among his contemporary reformists, Maragheh'i used fiction as a subterfuge for the expression of his views, in part to avoid the consequences of enraging the authorities.

The Constitutional Revolution and the ensuing social, cultural, and political turmoil and developments resulted in the fall of the Qajar dynasty (1779–1925) and the coming to power of Reza Shah Pahlavi, who established a new dynasty. But while many poets depicted the topical issues of the time in their work, Maragheh'i's example of including sociopolitical topics in prose fiction was not immediately duplicated. Instead, the prominent novelists of this period directed their attention to historical subject matter, the result of which was the publication of a series of historical novels and love stories, or often a combination of both. For example, between 1907 and 1910, Mohammad Baqer Khosravi wrote three novels that were set in the 13th century during the rule of the Ilkhanids in Iran, while Musa Nasiri used pre-Islamic Iran as a setting for a series of historical novels, including *Eshq-o Saltanat ya Fotuhat-e Kurosh-e Kabir* (1919; Love and Kingship or the Conquests of Cyrus the Great). This trend continued for more than three decades, particularly during the reign of Reza Shah Pahlavi (1925–41). The titles of novels such as *Dastan-e Bastan* (1921; The Tale of Antiquity) by Hasan Badi', and *Damgostaran ya Enteqamkhahan-e Mazdak* (1921; Trap-Setters or Avengers of Mazdak), *Dastan-e Mani-ye Naqqash* (1927; The Story of Mani the Painter), and *Salahshur* (1933; Warrior) by San'atizadeh-Kermani, which are set during the Sasanian period in Iran, show on the one hand the popularity of historical themes and, on the other—and more important, especially with regard to authors who depicted pre-Islamic settings—the political climate of the country, which was instigated

and supported by the government's advocacy of a strong sense of patriotism and nationalism.

Infatuation with the pre-Islamic history of Iran also implied the rejection of Islam and the Islamic era in Persian history by many Iranians. And while the increasing control and censorship of all published materials, including novels, made the choice of historical settings and characters safe for writers, at the same time writers were able to engage in implicit criticism of the government in the guise of historical subject matter. It should also be added that many of these pre–World War II novelists made a conscientious effort at historical accuracy, sometimes painstakingly supplying scholarly footnotes to their novels to convince their readers that their fictional accounts were based on fact. This indicates that in the early parts of the 20th century, Iranian readers had not yet come to terms with this new genre. Although they were quite familiar with and accepted imaginary tales presented in verse, they were reluctant to embrace novels as the product of imagination. In other words, just as Maragheh'i chose the format of the travel memoir, the writers of historical novels, similarly, tried to convince their readers of the authenticity of the stories they were writing.

A major concern of Reza Shah Pahlavi during his rule was to modernize Iran. To him and many educated Iranians of the time, modernization was synonymous with Westernization. Western-style education, which was regarded to be the source of progress in Western countries, especially European countries, was on the top of his agenda for bringing Iran into the 20th century. An increasing number of young Iranians had, of course, begun to travel to Europe to learn the Western sciences since the early decades of the 19th century, and the first Western-style school was established in Tehran in 1851, during the Qajar period. Reza Shah, however, wanted to bring about more drastic changes—changes viewed as being more in form than in substance. Banning women's veils and men's turbans and replacing traditional Iranian clothes with Western dress were among some of the superficial changes that Reza Shah instigated to modernize Iran. At the same time, the gradual involvement of women in public life opened the way to social problems, which had not existed or at least had not been quite as visible in the traditional Iranian society. Before long, this new social climate, and particularly the more open social interaction between women and men, began to be reflected in the works of novelists who, on the one hand, in keeping with the social trends, advocated women's suffrage and equal rights for women, but, on the other, wrote novels that depicted women, particularly young, educated, middle-class women, who fall victim to the sexual schemes of male predators. Novels such as *Homa, Parichehr,* and *Ziba,* all named after women, by Mohammad Hejazi, as well as *Fetneh, Juda,* and *Hendu,* again, all women's names, by Ali Dashti, are the products of this trend in Persian fiction. But while writers such as Hejazi and Dashti merely used the social themes as a vehicle to write rather titillating stories for middle-class readers, mostly women, there were, of course, writers such as Mohammad Mas'ud, a journalist by profession, whose *Ta-frihat-e Shab* (1970; Night Entertainment) and *Golha'i keh dar Jahanam Miruyad* (1964; Flowers That Grow in Hell) were intended as social, and in the case of the latter, political, criticism.

Although in the history of the development of the modern Persian novel the works of the writers discussed so far deserve mention, the trend in 20th-century Persian fiction that has led to the maturation of this genre began with the works of Mohammad Ali Jamalzadeh in the early 1920s and a decade later by Sadeq Hedayat and Bozorg Alavi. Jamalzadeh, who began his literary career with a pioneering collection of anecdotal short stories called *Yeki Bud, Yeki Nabud* (1921; *Once Upon a Time*), had already been living in Europe for a decade, and with this collection, as he remarked in the preface, called for "literary democracy" in Iran by advocating writing stories in the Western style, by which he meant a literature that would deal with the daily lives of ordinary people, as opposed to Persian classical literature, which by and large deals with mystical and philosophical subject matter and panegyric topics. Jamalzadeh's contribution to the development of modern Persian fiction was also in his advocacy and use of the spoken language of ordinary people, an aspect of his work that facilitated the task of later writers to develop the writing of colloquial Persian for use in novels. Jamalzadeh, who was born in 1895, after a 20-year silence during the Reza Shah period, continued his literary career with other collections of short stories, novels, and essays on literature and other aspects of Persian culture, becoming one of the most prolific Iranian authors in the 20th century. Even though he lived in Europe all of his adult life, except for a few brief visits to Iran, his writing deals almost exclusively with Iran and Iranian culture, albeit somewhat outdated in terms of themes and out-of-touch with the advancements made in later decades in novel writing.

The writer who has had perhaps the greatest impact on modern Persian fiction in general and the modern Persian novel in particular is Sadeq Hedayat (1903–51). By the 1930s, when Hedayat had already made a reputation for himself as an innovator and something of a rebel in fiction writing, an increasing number of Western novels had appeared in Persian translation and an increasing number of students were going to Europe to further their education. These direct contacts with the West and Western culture resulted in great influences on Persian writings, not only in terms of subject matter and theme, but equally important, on form. Hedayat's best-known novel, *Buf-e Kur* (1937; *The Blind Owl*), can certainly be regarded as an outstanding fruit of these influences. Although this relatively short novel is profoundly Persian in terms of subject matter and theme, Hedayat's innovative mode of presentation seemed alien to many Iranian readers. But this Kafkaesque and enigmatic novel, which has intrigued readers and critics for more than half a century and which has been regarded as the first authentic example of the modern Persian novel, may at the same time be considered a legitimate offspring of the Iranian literary tradition, both in terms of philosophical contemplation and symbolic representation of life. Hedayat's later work includes stories in which, with few exceptions, he abandons the enigmatic approach to fiction and engages in more direct satirical social criticism. But his suicide in Paris in 1951 particularly reinforced his image as the mysterious writer of the enigmatic novel and in some ways a representative of an emerging young generation of intellectual outcasts.

The emergence of this young generation that included a larger number of writers had begun a few years prior to Hedayat's death. Political events in the early 1950s created a climate that had a significant psychological effect on the entire nation, particularly on the young people, who, unlike their mostly illiterate parents, had been educated in the new Western-style school system. The prime minister, Dr. Mohammad Mosaddeq, had become a popular national figure, especially through his efforts to nationalize the Iranian oil and stop foreign influence in the internal affairs of the country. His overthrow in 1953, instigated by the British, who had lost control over Iranian oil, and with the help of the CIA, was followed by a decade of martial law, autocratic military rule, and strict censorship, causing despair among the young generation, who had begun to see a ray of hope for the future. Their disappointment in the political developments resulted in two kinds of reaction among this generation of Iranian novelists. On the one hand, some writers turned inward and produced stories with despairing, nihilistic antiheroes about the futility of life. In *Yakoliya va Tanha'i-ye U* (1956; *Yakoliya and Her Loneliness*), for example, Taghi Modarressi (1932–97) escapes into the world of Old Testament mythology in order to cope with the intolerable political and social realities of the time. Another example is *Safar-e Shab* (1967; *The Night's Journey*), which Bahman Sholevar had begun writing a decade earlier. *The Night's Journey* depicts the life of a young man of the same generation struggling to find his identity through drinking, whoring, and art. Another form of escape fiction consisted of sentimental love stories, often initially serialized in one of a growing number of magazines. Novels by such writers as Javad Fazel sold hundreds of thousands of copies, in contrast to the best-selling "serious" novels, of which only a few thousand copies were printed. On the other hand, the second and eventually more dominant trend among the writers of this generation was to react to the social conditions and political oppression in the society by depicting in their work the most negative aspects of life in Iran and choosing their characters mostly from among the poor, the downtrodden, and the disenfranchised. While by the 1960s the government of the Shah, Mohammad Reza Pahlavi, was trying to present to the nation and to the world a picture of a prospering and developing modern Iran through programs involving land reform, women's rights, and education, under the rubric of the White Revolution, with the Shah as the father figure of a large happy family, these efforts were undermined to some extent with the works of writers and artists who focused their attention on the social ills and politically oppressive rule of the regime. Although the security forces, particularly the SAVAK, its secret service, and the censorship apparatus of the regime had tight control over any antigovernment or dissident activity, writers were able to write and publish their work often by resorting to a highly symbolic and encoded approach to fiction-writing in order to escape the scrutiny of the censors and the wrath of the government. In fact, as the censors began to learn the literary codes and symbols employed by fiction writers and the censorship apparatus became more sophisticated, writers developed new ways and devised new codes to express their discontent. At the same time, an important criterion that was predominant among the mainstream writers and their readers, who mostly consisted of educated urban classes, university students, and the like, was what they called *ta'ahhod-e adabi,* or literary commitment, which became a touchstone for judging literary works on the basis of the writer's commitment to social and political causes. In a sense, engagé writing became the norm, and writers who did not conform to the precepts of this literary trend were generally dismissed as pro-regime and shunned by the literary community and their devoted readers.

Among the most prominent novelists who had begun their literary careers by writing short stories in the 1940s but who established themselves as major literary figures in the 1950s and particularly the 1960s are Sadeq Chubak, Ebrahim Golestan, Jalal Al-e Ahmad, and Behazin. Sadeq Chubak published his first novel, *Tangsir* (*Tangsir*), in 1963 and his second novel, *Sang-e Sabur* (*The Patient Stone*), in 1966. In *Tangsir*, Chubak bases his story on an actual incident in the early 20th century in the port city of Bushehr on the Persian Gulf, where a young worker, whose life savings have been embezzled by a prominent local merchant with the help of a cleric, decides to take the law into his own hands and goes on a rampage with a rifle, shooting those he thinks are responsible for his misfortune, and makes a successful escape, with the help of the local people. Chubak set his story during the reign of the previous regime. *Tangsir* passed through the scrutiny of government censorship, but the message of the novel, whether intended or not, did not escape the audiences who viewed the main character as a hero and his actions the call for armed uprising and revenge against the oppressive rulers.

Chubak's second novel, *The Patient Stone,* which was the product of more than two decades of writing and should perhaps, at least thematically, be included in the novels of a decade or so earlier, is by far his most ambitious undertaking as a novelist. Thematically, *The Patient Stone* belongs to the mainstream of engagé fiction in the post–World War II period in Iran, as it depicts its characters from the lowest strata of the society. But its significance in the history of the Persian novel owes to its experimentation with novelistic form and structure as well as its use of various levels of language. This stream-of-consciousness novel is presented through the interior monologues of several characters of different ages and backgrounds and essentially is a contemplation of Iranian identity and human life from the dawn of creation through Iranian history and into the 20th century. Chubak's recording of spoken Persian, in which he pays attention not only to vocabulary and pronunciation but also to the syntax of colloquial Persian, paved the way for later novelists in their experimentation with the language of the novel.

Among Chubak's contemporary writers, Jalal Al-e Ahmad occupies a place of distinction, perhaps not so much for his innovation and mastery as a fiction writer as for his popularity as an engagé artist and an outspoken social critic of his time. Although he died in 1969, a decade prior to the Islamic Revolution in Iran, because of his implicit stance against the regime of the Shah and also seemingly pro-Islamic tendencies (he was the son of a cleric) he is regarded as a revolutionary hero in the eyes of the government of the Islamic Republic, which came to power in Iran in 1979. Al-e Ahmad excels in his use of the Persian language. His prose usually consists of short, precise, scathing sentences, sometimes only one or two words. In his novel *Nun val-Qalam* (1961; *By the Pen*), which he sets in medieval Iran and which embodies his own social and political philosophy, Al-e Ahmad produced perhaps his best work of fiction.

Representative of the next generation of Iranian novelists are Gholamhoseyn Sa'edi, Simin Daneshvar, Hushang Golshiri, and Ahmad Mahmud. By profession a psychiatrist but at the same time one of the most prolific writers in 20th-century Iran, Sa'edi is known not only as a writer of fiction but also as one of the most prominent playwrights in Iran. Like Al-e Ahmad, Sa'edi is also known as one of the most outspoken social critics of the 1960s and 1970s and, as were many other literary artists, was incarcerated for a period of time by the regime. Sa'edi's works are significant in the development of the Persian novel, particularly in terms of psychological insight into his characters and his abundant use of dialogue instead of description in the unfolding of his plots.

With the death of Jalal Al-e Ahmad in 1969, not only did writers such as Sa'edi find prominence among the Iranian dissident novelists, but perhaps more important, with the publication of Simin Daneshvar's *Savushun* (1969; *Savushun*), the road was paved for women novelists to come to the forefront of the Persian literary scene. Daneshvar (who was Al-e Ahmad's wife) had published short stories since the late 1940s, but was established as one of the most prominent Iranian novelists with this novel, which had become the best-selling novel of all time in Iran prior to the revolution in 1979 and had gone through 16 printings and sold more than half a million copies by the late 1980s. Set in the city of Shiraz during World War II, the novel depicts the life of an upper-class family and chronicles the development, search for identity, and maturation of the protagonist from a submissive wife and devoted mother to champion of social causes and self-confident woman.

Another major novelist of the 1960s and 1970s is Hushang Golshiri, who gained prominence with his first novel, *Shazdeh Ehtejab* (*Prince Ehtejab*), in 1969. On the surface, *Prince Ehtejab* is the story of a declining aristocratic family, but in fact it is a psychological study of power and powerful rulers. Given its complex narrative technique, *Prince Ehtejab* was overlooked initially by the censors, but soon it was banned as a political novel criticizing the regime of the Shah, disguised as a story about an old prince from a deposed dynasty. A prolific writer, Golshiri has continued to hold a position of prominence among Persian novelists, particularly because of his mastery of Persian prose and his innovations in narrative technique. He is one of the few established novelists of the pre-Islamic-revolutionary period who has continued his work—albeit under difficult new conditions of censorship—to the present. In Golshiri's work since his first stories, one can see the maturation process of the Persian novel, particularly in terms of depth of thematic insight, development of characters, and novelistic techniques. And although an advocate of social engagement for writers, Golshiri views the responsibility of the writer as commitment to the craft and art of fiction as opposed to merely using the novel as a vehicle for advancing political and social agendas.

Another writer of the previous generation and, in fact, one of the first articulators of the concept of literary commitment is university professor, poet, critic, and novelist Reza Baraheni, who had attempted to publish a novel prior to the Islamic Revolution, but because of his rather outspoken stance against the Shah's regime had not been allowed to do so. In the wake of the revolution, he published several novels, mostly dealing with such subject matter as the activities of political dissidents a decade earlier and their treatment by the Shah's regime or the involvement of the US military and intelligence services in the affairs of Iran. The relative success of Baraheni's novels, especially in the early years of the revolution, were obviously due to the creation of a new climate, the fall of the monarchy, and the worsening of relations between Iran and the West, which allowed open discussion of these subjects and the publication of novels dealing with political issues.

With the outset of the Islamic Revolution in Iran and the inevitable changes that occurred in all aspects of life in that country, a number of younger writers appeared on the scene. At the same time, partly due to the social conditions that were imposed shortly after the revolution, including the ban on Western movies, the absence of entertainment programs on television, and the lack of other forms of recreation, particularly outside the home, the readership for novels increased. A monumental novel of nearly 3,000 pages, *Kelidar* (Kelidar) by Mahmud Dowlatabadi (published between 1978 and 1983), became the best-selling work of fiction of all time in Iran. The phenomenon of *Kelidar*'s popularity had an important implication for novelists in Iran. Prior to *Kelidar,* no writer, including Dowlatabadi himself, who already was a well-known writer in the prerevolutionary period, had been able to make a living through the sale of his or her works, which is to say that all Persian novelists were obliged to have a primary job in order to make a living. With *Kelidar,* Dowlatabadi became the first Iranian novelist who no longer had to make a living through another profession. In some respects, the phenomenon of the financial success of *Kelidar* became an incentive for younger writers to pursue their craft more seriously. Moreover, the readership's reception of longer works of fiction helped establish the novel as the predominant genre in Persian literature for the first time. Besides the events and developments during the revolution, Iranian novelists also witnessed the onset of the Iran-Iraq war soon after in 1980, which in turn provided the subject matter of an increasing number of novels. The revolution and the war became the subject of many novels by both already-established writers, such as Mahshid Amirshahi and Esma'il Fassih, and new novelists. While Amirshahi, for instance, chronicles the day-to-day events of the revolution in her *Dar Hazar* (1987; At Home), Esma'il Fassih addresses the effects of the war on Iranians in large cities, in *Zemestan-e '62* (1987; The Winter of '83/'84), and those living in exile in Europe in *Sorayya dar Eghma'* (1983; *Sorraya in a Coma*).

Perhaps the most significant development with regard to the novel in postrevolutionary Iran is the predominance of women novelists. Prior to the revolution, several women fiction writers, including Simin Daneshvar, Mahshid Amirshahi, and Goli Taraqqi, had found a place of distinction among Iranian writers. After the revolution, however, not only did these writers maintain their prominence, but a larger number of younger women writers gained popularity with important major works. In fact, if one were to name a dozen or so of the best-known and most widely read novelists since the 1980s, the majority would be women, a phenomenon that should seem in contradiction to the increasing restrictions on the dress and social interaction of women with men, among other obstacles.

Major postrevolutionary Iranian women novelists include Shahrnush Parsipur, Moniru Ravanipur, and Ghazaleh Alizadeh. Parsipur's reputation was established with *Tuba va Ma'na-ye Shab* (1988; Tuba and the Meaning of Night), a novel that deals with the subject of mysticism and is reminiscent of the work of Hushang Golshiri in terms of theme and language. What is un-

conventional in this work is that the protagonist of this mystical quest, a role that has been traditionally reserved for men, is a woman. Later, Parsipur published a shorter novel called *Zanan Bedun-e Mardan* (1989; Women Without Men), which, owing most likely to certain sexual scenes, was banned soon after its publication and resulted in her departure from Iran into exile in the United States. Her latest novel is called *Aql-e Abi* (1994; Blue Logus), in which she combines elements of philosophy, mysticism, and magic realism in a setting of war-stricken Iran.

Moniru Ravanipur is one of the younger writers who gained almost overnight success with her novel *Ahl-e Gharq* (1989; The Drowned). Ravanipur focuses in her novels as well as her short stories mostly on the people and their lives, customs, and beliefs in small villages in southern Iran. *Ahl-e Gharq* is, in fact, the story of the village in which she grew up and which was later consumed by the flood of progress and modernization. What distinguishes *Ahl-e Gharq* from other Persian novels is Ravanipur's approach to storytelling, which she insists is based on the oral traditions of her childhood village. In *Ahl-e Gharq*, she narrates actual events involving the imaginary manifestations of the superstitious people living in a small isolated community, and by juxtaposing the real and fantastic she creates a story reminiscent of works of magic realism. Another aspect of Ravanipur's work is her bold experimentation with narrative voice, which, combined with her often satirical treatment of her subject matter and characters, makes her work inaccessible to some audiences. Ghazaleh Alizadeh, with her masterfully crafted *Khaneh-ye Edrisiha* (1992; The House of the Edrisis), is another distinguished woman writer after the revolution, whose recent untimely death deprived Persian fiction of a novelist of great promise.

Among women writers of the previous generation, Simin Daneshvar has remained active—now having acquired the unofficial title of The Grand Lady of Persian Fiction—with the first of a trilogy called *Jazireh-ye Sargardani* (1993; The Island of Bewilderment), an obvious reference to US President Carter's calling Iran an "island of stability," in which she explores the idea of reducing the distance between the author and herself as a fictional character. Goli Taraqqi, known for her prerevolutionary works, such as her novel *Khab-e Zemestani* (1973; *Winter Sleep*), continues writing in exile in Paris and has published several stories, including some chapters of her latest novel, *Adat-e Gharib-e Aqa-ye Alef dar Ghorbat* (The Bizarre Comportment of Mr. A in Exile). Similarly, Mahshid Amirshahi has published the sequel to her *Dar Hazar,* called *Dar Safar* (1995; Away from Home), chronicling life in exile.

Important male novelists of the 1980s and 1990s include Abbas Ma'rufi and Ja'far Modarres-Sadeqi, each with several novels to his credit. Ma'rufi's *Samfoni-ye Mordegan* (1989; The Symphony of the Dead) is regarded as one of the best novels written in Iran in recent years. Also a publisher and editor of a literary magazine, Ma'rufi was forced to leave Iran and lives in Germany because of his widely publicized criticism of censorship in Iran. Modarres-Sadeqi, on the other hand, has become one of the most prolific writers and an outstanding representative of the younger novelists. His novels, including *Gavkhuni* (1996; *The Marsh*) and *Kaleh-ye Asb* (1991; The Horse's Head), exemplify a new trend in Persian fiction, which thematically involves a quest for Iranian individual and collective identity in the late 20th century.

The modern Persian novel in the course of its history of about a century has been, for the most part, a vehicle for the expression of discontent and has dealt, generally, with social and political criticism. Its reception by the general public was initially enthusiastic. The first Persian novel, *Siyahatnameh-ye Ebrahim Beyg*, is reported to have been read in neighborhood gatherings to audiences consisting mostly of illiterate people. Eventually, as writers addressed social ills and blamed them partly on not only the system of government but also the institution of religion, their work caused strong reaction on the part of politicians and clerics alike. Books by such authors as Jamalzadeh were burned in public squares in the early decades of the century, and, in postrevolutionary Iran, bookstores were set on fire by the followers of both groups. There were also moral purists, such as Ahmad Kasravi, a highly visible reformist and at one time minister of justice, who in the 1940s regarded novels as instruments of corruption. Kasravi, in fact, established for his followers a Feast of Book Burning, to which they were asked to contribute their private collection of novels. Despite such impediments, as well as the general resistance of the literati to include the novel in the literary canon, this genre has continued to develop, and by the end of the 20th century has become the main channel for literary expression in Iran. The increasing number of female as well as male novelists in postrevolutionary Iran, along with the attention writers have given in recent years to the art of the novel, promises a bright future for this genre in Iran.

M.R. GHANOONPARVAR

Further Reading

Baraheni, Reza, *The Crowned Cannibals: Writings on Repression in Iran*, New York: Vintage, 1977

Bashiri, Iraj, *Hedayat's Ivory Tower: Structural Analysis of "The Blind Owl,"* Minneapolis, Minnesota: Manor House, 1974

Bashiri, Iraj, *The Fiction of Sadeq Hedayat*, Lexington, Kentucky: Mazda, 1984

Beard, Michael, *Hedayat's "Blind Owl" as a Western Novel*, Princeton, New Jersey: Princeton University Press, 1990

Browne, Edward, *A Literary History of Persia*, New York: Scribner, and London: Unwin, 1902

Ghanoonparvar, M.R., *Prophets of Doom: Literature as a Socio-Political Phenomenon in Modern Iran*, Lanham, Maryland, and London: University Press of America, 1984

Ghanoonparvar, M.R., *In a Persian Mirror: Images of the West and Westerners in Iranian Fiction*, Austin: University of Texas Press, 1993

Javadi, Hasan, *Satire in Persian Literature*, Rutherford, New Jersey: Farleigh Dickinson University Press, 1988

Kamshad, Hassan, *Modern Persian Prose Literature*, Cambridge: Cambridge University Press, 1966; Bethesda, Maryland: Iranbooks, 1996

Milani, Farzaneh, *Veils and Words: The Emerging Voices of Iranian Women Writers*, Syracuse, New York: Syracuse University Press, and London: Tauris, 1992

Rahimieh, Nasrin, *Oriental Responses to the West: Comparative Essays on Select Writers from the Muslim World*, Leiden and New York: Brill, 1990

Ricks, Thomas M., editor, *Critical Perspectives on Modern Persian Literature*, Washington, D.C.: Three Continents Press, 1984

Rypka, Jan, *Dejiny perske a tadzicke literatury*, Prague: Nakl. Ceskoslovenske akademie ved, 1956; as *History of Iranian Literature*, Dordrecht, Holland: Reidel, 1968

Yarshater, Ehsan, editor, *Persian Literature*, Albany, New York: Bibliotheca Persica, 1988

Irish Novel

The novel has been a central genre in Irish literature since the end of the 18th century. Full appreciation and understanding of the Irish novel has for many years been limited by attempts to subsume Irish novels as "British" and by a concentration on major figures such as James Joyce, so that a great many other significant Irish novelists have been neglected. Traditional surveys such as Ernest Baker's *History of the English Novel* (1924–39) and Walter Allen's *The English Novel: A Short Critical History* (1954) absorbed the Irish novel into the English tradition, much as Ireland itself had been annexed by England much earlier. In fact, the Irish novel represents a distinct tradition that should be seen not only on its own terms but also for its role in the development of the novel in other countries.

Classic studies such as Horatio Sheafe Krans' *Irish Life in Irish Fiction* (1903) and Thomas Flanagan's *The Irish Novelists, 1800–1850* (1958) introduced such a consideration of the Irish novel but limited their gaze to the 19th century. More recently, although scholarship on the Irish novel has broadened and deepened, producing several valuable studies of the subject, more articles and books are published each year on James Joyce than on all other Irish novelists combined.

The history of the Irish novel is often presented as beginning in 1800 with the publication of Maria Edgeworth's *Castle Rackrent*—an appealing and convenient demarcation because the Act of Union uniting England and Ireland was passed in the same year, and because it is arguably the first great Irish longer work of fiction. It inaugurated several conventions, such as its bold use of the oral tradition, its unreliable narrator, its close attention to Irish history and class conflict, its pointed sense of humor, and its rambling style confounding traditional classical "unities" of plot and structure. Yet several novels by Irish authors set in Ireland were published earlier, beginning with William Chaigneau's *The History of Jack Connor* (1752), Thomas Amory's *The Life of John Buncle* (1756), Henry Brooke's *The Fool of Quality* (5 vols., 1764–70), and Charles Johnstone's *The History of John Juniper* (1781). These little-known works established a convention that persisted throughout the 19th century: that of the upper-class English or Anglo-Irish protagonist who visits Ireland and gains an understanding of the country's exotic or hidden ways. Such an approach is not surprising given that the readership of Irish novels throughout the 19th century was English or Anglo-Irish rather than native Irish, and that Irish novels were more often published in London than Ireland.

Before the first appearance of Irish novels (defined as those concentrating on Ireland as subject), there was Jonathan Swift. *Gulliver's Travels* (1726), while not focused on Ireland, greatly influenced such later authors of Irish satiric and fabulist fiction as Joyce, Eimar O'Duffy, and Samuel Beckett. This imaginative travel fantasy written in the voice of a commoner looks ahead to such novels as Joyce's *Ulysses* (1922), O'Duffy's *The Spacious Adventures of the Man in the Street* (1928), and Flann O'Brien's *The Third Policeman* (1967). Similarly, the Irish-born Laurence Sterne's absurdist masterpiece, *Tristram Shandy* (1759–67), while not generally considered an Irish novel, yet pervasively influenced and foreshadowed Joyce's *Finnegans Wake* (1939) and O'Brien's *At Swim-Two-Birds* (1939).

In the 18th and 19th centuries, English novelists wrote for a solid and expanding middle-class readership whose sense of national and linguistic identity was strong. In contrast, Irish novelists suffered under the handicaps of far fewer publishers in Ireland, a very small middle class, and little clearly unified linguistic or national identity. These disadvantages were the results of a history in which, since the late Middle Ages, England had enforced Irish religious, political, and socioeconomic inferiority. When Swift was a young man, in 1690, the Protestant King William's forces defeated those of Catholic King James at the Battle of the Boyne, and it was followed by an anti-Catholic Penal Age extending into the 19th century, made even worse by the ruling class' reactions against the uprisings of 1798 and 1803. For example, the lands of a Catholic were required by law to be equally subdivided, following his death, among all of his sons rather than given to his oldest son—thus accelerating the overpopulation of farmers and laborers on increasingly small holdings, which greatly exacerbated the Great Hunger of 1845–51 that contributed to the halving of the population of Ireland (from about 8 million in 1800 to about 4 million in 1900). The gap between a small elite and a large underclass grew larger and larger. A partial "Catholic Emancipation" was enacted in 1828, but the devastating Great Hunger and other crop failures and land struggles throughout the century made the 19th century even more devastating in Ireland than the 18th century had been.

Very little of a middle class developed. Irish novelists had a lot to write about, but they could not depend on enough Irish publishers to publish their novels or readers to read them. More publishers and readers were available to them in England, but there they had to counter such English writers about Ireland as Giraldus de Barris, Edmund Spenser, Fynes Moryson, John Davies, and Barnabe Rych, who had reflected and influenced negative English attitudes since the 12th century. Rych, for example, assured his readers in 1609 that the Irish were "more uncivil, more uncleanly, more barbarous and more brutish in their customs and demeanures, than in any other part of the world that is knowne."

The effects of such patterns of readership and publication were evident in such early 19th-century novelists as Maria Edgeworth, Sydney Owenson (Lady Morgan), John Banim, Gerald Griffin, and William Carleton. These novelists examined Irish society from the differing perspectives of the upper-class Ascendancy (Edgeworth and Owenson), the middle class (Banim and Griffin), and the peasantry (Carleton). The first Irish novelist to make a significant impact on readers in both England and Ireland was Edgeworth. Published by Joseph Johnson in London in 1800 with the full title of *Castle Rackrent, an Hibernian Tale: Taken from Facts, and from the Manners of the Irish Squires, before the Year 1782*, Edgeworth's tale called attention to itself as Irish. King George III reported that after reading this book, "I rubbed my hands and said what what—I know something now of my Irish subjects." By 1800 the attitudes of some of Edgeworth's English readers had been changed by the satiric and polemical prose of Swift, beginning with his first Irish pamphlet, *The Story of the Injured Lady* (1707), and culminating in his famous *A Modest Proposal for Preventing the Children of Poor People from Being a Burthen to Their Parents or the Country* (1729), in which he slyly suggested that both hunger and overpopulation in Ireland could be solved if the babies of poor families were sold as meat to landlords, "who, as they have already devoured most of the parents, seem to have the best title to the children." Also positively influential was the liberal Arthur Young's *A Tour in Ireland* (1780), which Edgeworth described at the end of *Castle Rackrent* as "the first faithful portrait" of Ireland by an Englishman.

Edgeworth combined Swift's satiric vision and Young's liberal humanism in her remarkable book, narrated by Thady Quirk, who was closely modeled on John Langan, a steward on the Edgeworth family estate in County Longford. Replete with asterisked footnotes, Edgeworth's tale is Thady's ostensibly sympathetic account of the decline and fall of several generations of his landlord masters, all told in a style never seen previously: "Now I've come to 'Poor Thady'; for I wear a long great-coat* winter and summer, which is very handy, as I never put my arms into the sleeves." *Castle Rackrent* was the first "Big House" novel set on an Ascendancy estate; the first Irish family chronicle; and the first fictional book to make Irish history and politics central to its story and theme. Its loose, rambling form and colloquial narrator (without which not only *Ulysses*, but also *Huckleberry Finn* [1884], would be hard to imagine) were features central to the Irish novel and influential beyond Ireland. Generally speaking, Irish novels tend to depend more on their narrators and less on their plots, perhaps partly because of the strong oral storytelling tradition in Ireland, often echoed in its novels.

Castle Rackrent has also often been described as the first "regional novel," particularly because of its key influence on Walter Scott, who "felt that something might be attempted for my own country [Scotland], of the same kind with that which Miss Edgeworth so fortunately achieved for Ireland." But to an Irish ear, "regional" sounds untrue, even offensive if suggesting that Ireland is merely a "region" within the development of "British" fiction. The book's setting within Ireland is left deliberately vague; *Ormond* (1817) is Edgeworth's only Irish novel with a more specific setting, and within the contexts of Irish fiction itself, the regional novel began earlier with the works of Sydney Owenson.

Castle Rackrent encouraged other Irish authors because it was a huge financial as well as critical success. Edgeworth's subsequent Irish novels *Ennui* (1809), *The Absentee* (1812), and *Ormond* were worthy but much more conventional works, and she ended her work despairing that "it is impossible to draw Ireland as she now is in the book of fiction—realities are too strong, party passions too violent."

The next significant Irish novelist of the early 19th century was Sydney Owenson, an itinerant actor's daughter who became "Lady Morgan" when she married Sir Charles Morgan in 1812. Commissioned by her London publisher Richard Phillips as a travel book about Ireland, but developed instead as an epistolary account of an Ascendancy protagonist's encounters with a beautiful peasant woman and the west of Ireland, *The Wild Irish Girl* (1806) created a sensation as a best-seller. By 1807 Owenson herself was playing the role of Glorvina, her heroine, in salons and the popular press. She went on to write *O'Donnel: A National Tale* (1814), *Florence Macarthy: An Irish Tale* (1818), and *The O'Briens and the O'Flahertys: A National Tale* (1827), and to support the Catholic Emancipation cause. Ascendancy writer Charles Maturin published *The Wild Irish Boy* (1808), an obvious but less successful sequel to Owenson's novel. His major achievement was *Melmoth the Wanderer* (1820), a huge, rambling, Gothic novel in which a Trinity College, Dublin student endures tales about the shadowy, dangerous ancestor named in the title.

John and Michael Banim and Gerald Griffin were the first successful middle-class Catholic Irish novelists (of a background common among Irish novelists only a century later, with Joyce and his successors). To make their way as writers, John Banim and Griffin journeyed to London, where they became friends in 1823, while Michael Banim remained in the Banims' native Kilkenny, becoming a shopkeeper and postmaster. The Banim brothers' numerous, frequently coauthored novels included Gothicism, realistic portraits of rural Irish life, and historical novels. John Banim's *The Boyne Water* (1826) combined these features in a historical novel in the mode of Scott; as the first successful Irish historical novel, it encouraged dozens of other Irish writers to explore this vein. Along with Owenson and her attention to the west of Ireland, these writers also expanded the role of regionalism within Irish fiction, with the Banims often focusing on the region around Kilkenny in the southeast, and Griffin on the Limerick area in the west. John Banim's *The Nowlans* (1826) is a striking narrative of a young man who leaves the priesthood, goes to Dublin, and lives with a woman; Banim developed gritty Dublin scenes that struck a new note in Irish fiction. The Banims' careers began in 1825 with *Crohoore of the Billhook*, *The Fetches*, and *John Doe*, and their collaborative efforts included the 1828 *Boyne Water* sequels, *The Last Baron of Crana*, *The Conformists*, and *The Anglo-Irish of the 19th Century*.

Griffin's best novel was *The Collegians* (1829), perhaps the most striking novel of this period after *Castle Rackrent*. Based on an actual case in County Clare in 1809, this novel focuses on an Ascendancy man who secretly marries a peasant woman but then has her killed so he can marry a wealthy woman (who is in turn saved and married instead by Griffin's hero, significantly a middle-class Catholic). Characterization is strong here, with compelling secondary characters such as the Ascendancy villain's grasping mother and Myles na Coppaleen (Myles of the little

horses), the Gaelic horseman who later reappeared as a major character in Dion Boucicault's 1860 play *The Colleen Bawn* and as the pseudonym of Flann O'Brien for his amazing mid-20th-century satiric columns in the *Irish Times*. Griffin published a few other, lesser novels, but died at the age of 37.

William Carleton has received more critical attention than any other Irish novelist of this period after Edgeworth. His long, difficult career illustrates the pitfalls that confronted 19th-century Irish novelists. Carleton was a Gaelic-speaking, Catholic peasant from County Tyrone who went to Dublin, converted to Protestantism, and published 1830s stories and novels often seen as attacking the peasantry, followed by 1840s novels perceived as more patriotic, and then spent the rest of his career in decline, dying fairly poor in 1869. He wrote some of the best and some of the worst fiction of the period, and the mix of great talent and opportunism in his career is poignant. While publishers of the most successful English novelists of the period filled shelves with their many handsomely bound volumes, Carleton was always scrambling for publishers in Dublin, writing at one moment for the Ascendancy *Dublin University Magazine*, at the next for the nationalist Thomas Davis' newspaper *The Nation*. *Fardorougha, the Miser* (1839) incorporated vivid dialogue and strong characterizations in a story well focused on the protagonist's conflict between his destructive greed and his love for his son. No one had a better ear for peasant speech; Carleton introduced to the Irish novel a new faithfulness to dialect, so often marred during the 19th century by inaccurate representations. After *Fardorougha*, *Valentine M'Clutchy* (1845), *The Black Prophet* (1847), and *The Emigrants of Ahadarra* (1848) are his more interesting novels. After the Great Hunger the artistic quality of his novels was no better than the depressed socioeconomic state of Ireland at the time. Carleton was in many ways a better short-story writer than a novelist.

The middle part and second half of the 19th century were difficult times for Irish novels, even though more of them than ever before were being published—including not only many forgettable works but also valuable ones, such as the somber analysis of Charles Lever's *The Martins of Gro' Martin* (1847), the Gothic inventiveness of Sheridan LeFanu's *The House by the Churchyard* (1863), the feminism of Emily Lawless' *Grania* (1892), and the best work of this period, *The Real Charlotte* (1894) by Somerville and Ross.

On the surface, the Protestant Charles Lever's career stands in stark contrast to Carleton's. While Carleton had to struggle mightily, Lever succeeded apparently without effort; during his time, he was almost as generously published and well known as his friends Charles Dickens, William Makepeace Thackeray, and Anthony Trollope. He wrote his first novel, *The Confessions of Harry Lorrequer* (1839), serially for the *Dublin University Magazine* and felt that when asked to write another book, "I was ready to reply, *not one, but fifty*"—and managed 37. His second novel, *Charles O'Malley, the Irish Dragoon* (1841), was an episodic series of hilarious incidents set around Trinity College. His books sold extremely well (especially for an Irish novelist), but unfortunately Lever got the undeserved reputation of an anti-Irish novelist and was regularly dismissed by nationalist critics, who alliteratively (but inaccurately) linked him with his fellow Protestant novelist Samuel Lover as "Lover and Lever." Like Carleton this time, Lever tried to overcome this reputation with patriotic novels such as *St. Patrick's Eve* (1845), *The Martins of Gro' Martin,* and *Lord Kilgobbin* (1872), but only recently have critics begun to appreciate his works again.

As editor of the *Dublin University Magazine,* Sheridan Le Fanu published Carleton, Lever, and many others. (It has often been said that in Dublin, a literary movement consists of two or more writers who cordially despise each other.) Like Maturin and Lever, Le Fanu was a Trinity College graduate with diverse activities (Maturin was also an ordained minister, Lever a doctor), and like Carleton, Le Fanu had conflicting political loyalties. In his first two novels, *The Cock and Anchor* (1845) and *The Fortunes of Colonel Torlogh O'Brien* (1847), LeFanu found it safest to avoid the politics of his own day in favor of the remote nationalist periods of the late 17th and earlier 18th centuries. Best known for his Gothic short stories, LeFanu followed Maturin in importing Gothicism into Irish fiction in his best Irish novel, *The House by the Church-yard,* a rambling book of intrigue set in and around a Big House in Chapelizod—also the setting of Joyce's *Finnegans Wake,* on which LeFanu's novel had some influence.

Charles Kickham's *Knocknagow* (1879) was perhaps the most popular of the many nationalist Irish novels published during the second half of the 19th century. (One can find in Father Stephen J.M. Brown's *Ireland in Fiction* [1919] listings and plot summaries of many of these generally very romantic books.) That Kickham had served time in prison after participating in the abortive Young Ireland rebellion of 1848 only solidified his credentials for many Irish readers. By 1879 the number of Irish publishers had increased, despite Carleton's understandable prediction in the wake of the Great Hunger that there would be "a lull, an obscurity of perhaps half a century" in the Irish novel.

1886 was the peak year of the Home Rule campaign, marked also by the publication of Emily Lawless' *Hurrish,* a novel focused on a family feud set amid Land League struggles, a movement for tenants' rights that eventually led to the enactment of a system allowing tenants to buy their own farms through the Wyndham Land Act of 1903. *Hurrish* attracted the sympathetic attention of Prime Minister William Gladstone much as Edgeworth's *Castle Rackrent* had done earlier with King George. A more original and striking novel was *Grania,* preceded only by the likes of *The Wild Irish Girl* as precedent for 20th-century Irish feminist novels. This tragic, naturalistic account of its peasant protagonist's attempt to establish her own identity was set on Inis Meáin, the most isolated of the Aran Islands off Galway; *Grania* was closely identified with this harsh but beautiful island.

A comparable novel, Somerville and Ross' *The Real Charlotte* was perhaps the best novel of the 19th century after *Castle Rackrent*. Along with their wonderfully comic "Irish R.M." stories, this novel was the paramount achievement among the many books coauthored by these two Ascendancy women—cousins who overcame their isolation at separate Big Houses in counties Galway and Cork to form the closest major literary coauthorship in the English language. Unlike Addison and Steele, Edith Somerville and Violet Martin ("Ross" derived from the name of the latter's home in Galway) wrote every sentence together, handing the pen back and forth. After Martin's death in 1915, Somerville published all of her remaining books (such as her 1925 novel *The Big House of Inver*) under both their names, convinced throughout the remaining 32 years of her life that she remained in spiritual contact with her cousin. Women such as

Edgeworth, Lawless, and Somerville and Ross were important inspirations for subsequent 20th-century women as well as for other Irish writers.

Somerville and Ross' *The Real Charlotte* is a tragic novel focused on two women but with a striking cast of other characters. Charlotte Mullen, a middle-aged woman who drives hard bargains collecting rents for a landlord, secretly wants to marry their land agent—who instead marries Francie Fitzgerald, Charlotte's niece from Dublin. Somerville and Ross' portrait of the Dysarts, the paralyzed landlord family, brings to mind D.H. Lawrence's Lord Chatterley, but here there is no hero to rescue either Charlotte or Francie. In an unsettling coincidence, Francie falls from her horse much as Violet Martin did in real life four years after the novel's publication.

Also comparable is George Moore's *A Drama in Muslin* (1886), which examined the expeditions of young, rural Irish Ascendancy women led by their mothers to the "marriage market" centered on the Shelbourne Hotel in Dublin. Moore became the most celebrated Irish novelist of the early 20th century, until eclipsed by his rival, Joyce. *The Lake* (1905) is parallel in many ways to *A Portrait of the Artist as a Young Man* (1916), and Moore's novel did have some influence on Joyce. Moore named his protagonist, a wayward priest, after Joyce's friend Oliver Gogarty, and when Gogarty's mother complained, Moore replied, "Madame, supply me with two such joyous dactyls and I will gladly change the name." (Joyce did so, renaming him "Malachi Mulligan" in *Ulysses*.) Moore's Gogarty eventually abandons the priesthood, fakes a drowning, and swims across his symbolic lake in order to escape anonymously to New York—a scene also parodied at the beginning of *Ulysses* when Buck Mulligan plunges into Dublin Bay. Linking himself to Europe rather than to his Irish rival, Joyce expressed his debt to the French novelist Edouard Dujardin, but in fact Moore had already nearly perfected a method of writing "interior monologue" that Dujardin had merely sketched. *The Lake* is a sharply focused symbolist novel as much concerned with the process of writing itself as with its protagonist's transformation.

Because of the wide-ranging changes in Irish political life during the early 20th century, marked by the formation of several strongly nationalist cultural, political, and military movements, by the Irish Civil War of 1922–23, and by the rise of censorship, studying the development of the Irish novel in the 20th century is like entering a whole new world, and also sometimes literally another language. For example, while other genres of writing in Irish Gaelic date back many centuries, Irish-language novels were new to the 20th century. Writing and publication in Irish had fallen off greatly during the 19th century, especially following the Great Hunger, which killed and forced Irish speakers to emigrate in numbers disproportionately high in the country's population; the percentage of people usually speaking Irish was about 50 percent in 1800 as opposed to perhaps 15 percent in 1900 (and 3 to 5 percent today). Many more people learned Irish in schools as the 20th century proceeded, however, and an increasing number of Irish Gaelic books were published. Pádraig Ó Duinnín's *Cormac Ó Connaill* (1901) was the first Irish Gaelic novel ever published in book form, but the first to make a big impact on readers was Father Peadar Ó Laoghaire's *Séadna* (1898), serialized in the *Gaelic Journal* beginning in 1894. In his Gaelic twist on the Faust theme, Ó Laoghaire (or O'Leary) practiced what he preached about writing the way people talked in Irish. His story of a shoe-maker who sells his soul to the devil before eventually regaining it is narrated by a young girl, as if to even younger listeners beside a fireplace. Generations of students read it in schools.

Séadna was traditional, but throughout the 20th century, Irish Gaelic novels were often at the cutting edge of fictional experimentation and achievement. *Deoraíocht* (1910; *Exile*) was a remarkable novel about expatriate life in London by Pádraic Ó Conaire, a Galwayman who had taken to heart Patrick Pearse's advice that writers in Irish should get in touch with the best fiction being written on the European continent. Ó Conaire's picaresque protagonist encounters grotesque characters that call to mind the American writer Flannery O'Connor. Séamus Ó Grianna wrote compellingly about peasant life in Donegal in such novels as *Mo Dhá Róisín* (1920; My Two Little Roses), *Caisleáin Ó ir* (1924; Castles of Gold), and *Bean Ruadh de Dhálach* (1966; A Red-Haired O'Donnell Woman). And two of the funniest and best novels in any language were written in Irish Gaelic at mid-century: Flann O'Brien's *An Béal Bocht* (1941; *The Poor Mouth*) and Máirtín Ó Cadhain's *Cré na Cille* (1949; *Churchyard Clay*). Published under the pseudonym of Myles n gCopaleen (borrowed from Gerald Griffin), *The Poor Mouth* is a hilarious, laconic, Swiftian account of a nameless young Gael's difficult boyhood, a parody of such classic Kerry autobiographies as Tomás Ó Criomhthain's *An tOileanach* (1929; *The Islandman*), Muiris Ó Súilleabháin's *Fiche Blian ag Fás* (1933; *Twenty Years a-Growing*), and Peg Sayer's *Peig* (1936). *Cré na Cille*, generally considered the *Ulysses* of the Irish language, is the most ambitious and impressive novel in that language. This novel (by a writer whose career also included stints as an Irish Republican Army man and Trinity College professor) presents the obsessive dialogues of the souls of the corpses in a Galway graveyard, especially an old woman and the erstwhile local schoolmaster. The likes of Ó Conaire and Ó Cadhain inspired such contemporary novelists in Irish as Eoghan Ó Tuairisc (*L'Attaque*, 1962), Breandán Ó hEithir (*Lig Sinn i gCathú* [1976; *Lead Us into Temptation*]), and Diarmaid Ó Súilleabháin (*Aistear* [1983; Journey]). The volume of writing in Irish today belies the endangered status of the spoken language.

James Stephens was one of several Irish novelists who, although writing in English, were influenced by the Irish language and by Irish myth and folklore. His gritty yet mythical novella *The Charwoman's Daughter* and his Celtic, Blakean fable *The Crock of Gold*, both published in his *annus mirabile* of 1912, anticipated respectively both the earlier realistic works and the later fabulist fictions of Joyce. In fact, Stephens claimed (perhaps wrongly) that he was born on the same day as Joyce, 2 February 1882, and in 1927 Joyce—who loved Stephens' work and the notion that they could sign a coauthored book "JJ & S," the trademark of John Jameson and Sons, his favorite brand of whiskey—suggested to Stephens that he could finish the "Work in Progress" that became *Finnegans Wake* if Joyce himself were unable to complete it. Similarly, W.B. Yeats remarked in 1914, "When the other day I read *The Demi-Gods* [1914] of Mr. James Stephens, I felt that he alone . . . could take care of the future of Irish literature."

Stephens never lived up to the high hopes of Joyce and Yeats; after he left his position as registrar of the National Gallery of Ireland in 1925, he lived in London and in his later years was best known as a lecturer and BBC broadcaster. However, his early books influenced many later Irish fiction writers. Especially as an alternative to and release from the grimly conservative social world of Ireland, Stephens' books offered a vision of imaginative freedom rooted in a much different, ancient Irish world. His best works also illustrated the potentially rich interactions of realism and fantasy, two modes of writing that dominated Irish fiction during the first half of the 20th century (and are still prevalent today). His Dublin charwoman's daughter is named Mary Makebelieve; she is trapped in the Dublin slums, yet she envisions a brighter, more beautiful world.

Such experimental and playful works as Ó Conaire's *Deoraíocht* and Stephens' *The Crock of Gold* anticipated the innovations of James Joyce. Within the contexts of his country's literature, Joyce's *A Portrait of the Artist as a Young Man*, *Ulysses*, and *Finnegans Wake*—with their use of interwoven tales as a structural device, their encyclopedic devotion to the details of Irish life and the special qualities of the English language in Ireland, and their often humorous celebration of the mythological Irish past—reacted to the tradition of the Irish novel as a whole and played a major role in changing the nature of that tradition for the rest of the century. These three masterly novels moved increasingly from realism to fantasy, profoundly influencing many subsequent Irish novelists, who continued to write in these two modes.

The two novelists most obviously and pervasively influenced by Joyce, and also the two most celebrated 20th-century Irish novelists other than Joyce, were Flann O'Brien and Samuel Beckett. These two writers present sharply different, indeed virtually opposite case studies of the "anxiety" of Joyce's influence. Both began their careers writing more like Joyce and then wrote less like him later in their careers, but for O'Brien Joyce's influence was largely an impediment that often constricted his own development, whereas Beckett was able to clear his own creative space, produce a very different style, and become a writer who was just as important and influential as Joyce. Here I only briefly summarize these patterns in the careers of two important novelists (examined fully in their own entries).

Like Joyce, O'Brien was an Irish Catholic graduate of University College, Dublin, with a brilliant comic vision and a golden ear for Dublin dialogue; his strengths were so close to Joyce's that he found it difficult to escape the older writer's considerable shadow. His brilliant first novel, *At Swim-Two-Birds*, had the misfortune to be published in the same year as *Finnegans Wake* and, during the aftermath of World War II, remained largely forgotten until rediscovered and republished in the early 1960s, when O'Brien's work finally began to attract critical attention. Perhaps even more than *Finnegans Wake*, *At Swim-Two-Birds* "deconstructed" itself, offering three completely different beginnings for the reader to choose from, followed by wildly divergent and hilarious narrative strands involving, among others, the ancient Irish hero Finn MacCool (also key to the *Wake*); the folkloric Pookha and Sweeney, the mythical tree-bound poet; Jem Casey, proletarian poet and author of "A Pint of Plain Is Your Only Man"; John Furriskey, who was born at the age of 25; William Tracy, author of cowboy romances set in Dublin; an unnamed student narrator, suspiciously reminiscent of Joyce's Stephen Dedalus; Dermot Trellis, a pubkeeper who is the subject of a novel that the student is trying to write; and Orlick Trellis, Dermot's son, who revenges himself on his father by writing a novel about him in which he is tortured. A key difference between Joyce and O'Brien is that while Joyce's humor tends to be expansive and all-encompassing, O'Brien's is deflating and explosive: this novel, for example, is abandoned at the end with mention of yet another character who "went home one evening and drank three cups of tea with three lumps of sugar in each cup, cut his jugular with a razor three times and scrawled with a dying hand on a picture of his wife good-bye, good-bye, good-bye."

While Joyce's ubiquitous puns in the *Wake* are parts of a mythologized, universalized world, O'Brien characteristically explodes puns and clichés by taking them literally. Joyce's *Wake* is constructed according to a circle that is inclusive and nearly boundless, like Yeats' gyres, but in O'Brien's *The Third Policeman* (published in 1967 but written more than 30 years earlier), "Hell goes round and round. In shape it is circular and by nature it is interminable, repetitive and very nearly unbearable." O'Brien's unnamed protagonist's punishment for the crime he commits is to relive his life endlessly over and over—albeit in a weirdly phantasmagoric world in which policemen say things that are strange, but perhaps no stranger than the real, civil-service world of Ireland. Another difference between Joyce and O'Brien is that O'Brien mastered Irish Gaelic (a language in which Joyce only dabbled), as evident in his novel *The Poor Mouth,* his translations of Middle Irish verse in *At Swim-Two-Birds,* and his uproariously comic "Myles" articles in Irish and about the Irish language in *The Irish Times.* In those columns he alternately praised Joyce, complaining that he never won the Nobel prize, and sardonically attacked him: "What would you think of a man who entered a restaurant, sat down, suddenly whipped up the tablecloth and blew his nose in it? You would not like it. . . . That is what Joyce did with our beloved tongue that Shakespeare and Milton spoke."

Joyce was Beckett's mentor and friend in Paris and the subject of Beckett's first publication, an essay entitled "Dante . . . Bruno. Vico . . . Joyce," in *Our Exagmination round His Factification for Incamination of Work in Progress* (1929), the collection of essays on the *Wake* that Joyce organized fully a decade before his novel was completed. Beckett's first novel, *Murphy* (1938), was, like *At Swim-Two-Birds,* a Joycean, absurdist novel. *Watt* (1953), however, withdrew into a more detached, isolated universe close to the Protestant Big House world such as the one Beckett grew up in near Foxrock, south of Dublin. And in his great trilogy of novels *Molloy* (1951), *Malone meurt* (1951; *Malone Dies*), and *L'Innomable* (1953; *The Unnamable*), Beckett abandoned English and obviously realistic settings in favor of narratives in French that move increasingly toward solitude—culminating with an unnamed narrator/protagonist/author dragging himself through the mud, finally deciding that "you must go on, I can't go on, I'll go on." As Beckett himself succinctly remarked with his typically self-disparaging wit, "The more Joyce knew the more he could. He's tending toward omniscience and omnipotence as an artist. I'm working with impotence, ignorance." He wrote in French in an attempt to discard the idioms of his native English, then often translating his French "back into English." After *Comment c'est* (1961; *How It Is*), a narrative that further departs from conventional punctuation and syntax, Beckett pretty much abandoned the novel altogether, writing increasingly shorter and shorter prose works. The trilogy and *How It Is* avoid realistic examinations of his native country, yet the novels are filled with references, echoes, and in fact descriptions of places in Ireland. And in his thorough dismantling of traditional narrative form, replacing it with the oral-styled monologues of a series of shifting but persistent versions of an artist as an old man, Beckett was more Irish than the Irish themselves.

When asked why he had returned to Paris in the middle of World War II after a trip to Dublin, Beckett (who was active in the French Resistance) famously quipped, "I prefer France at war to Ireland at peace." Soon thereafter, the censorship and repressive mores of the Irish Free State were memorably satirized in Mervyn Wall's novels *The Unfortunate Fursey* (1946) and *The Return of Fursey* (1948), the latter including a Censor with two independently moving eyes—one to focus only on the "dirty" words and the other to read everything else. (This recalls the parallel obsession of a Dubliner in O'Brien's *The Poor Mouth,* whose every other word is the equivalent of "Gael" or "Gaelic.") By cleverly avoiding any actual mention of sex except when it comes under attack by churchmen, Wall avoided official censorship of these books, even though they represent a thoroughgoing attack on the mores of the Irish church and state. In *The Unfortunate Fursey,* the Devil strikes a deal with the Catholic clergy of Ireland that he will exempt Ireland from temptation to sex if they will stop preaching against "simony, nepotism, drunkenness, perjury and murder," to which they readily agree since these "are but minor offences when compared with the hideous sin of sex." The two novels are set ostensibly in the Middle Ages—perhaps suggesting that in the middle of the 20th century, Ireland was still in the "dark ages"—and the most authoritative figure in both books is an archbishop bearing a striking resemblance to Bishop McQuaid, who ordered Dublin bookstores not to carry these books.

As in the cases of Eimar O'Duffy, Joseph O'Neill, and Flann O'Brien, Wall's writings were partly attempts to escape his depressing career in the Irish civil service. In *King Goshawk and the Birds* (1926), O'Duffy brings the ancient Irish hero Cúchulainn to modern Dublin, much as Joyce had done with Ulysses and Stephens with Angus Ó g and Pan a few years earlier. (In *Wind from the North* [1934] Joseph O'Neill reversed this pattern by giving his 20th-century protagonist a knock on the head that causes him to wake up as an ancient Norse hero.) Jonathan Swift was an even bigger influence on O'Duffy: in *King Goshawk* Cúchulainn is like Gulliver among the Lilliputians, and in the rest of O'Duffy's "Cuanduine trilogy," Aloysius O'Kennedy is transported to the planet Rathé, in *The Spacious Adventures of the Man in the Street,* much as Gulliver is to Brobdingnag and Laputa, and *Asses in Clover* (1933) is as packed with political, economic, social, and religious satire as anything in Swift. On Rathé (an obvious anagram for "Earth"), people are extremely uptight about food and are "monophagous," eating just one fruit all their lives—yet sex is viewed as something to be enjoyed regularly, without guilt, with different people. O'Duffy's protagonist reads a brilliant Rathean novel, reminiscent of Hawthorne, about "a woman who has eaten a wild strawberry in her childhood, and whose whole life is made miserable by the fear of the iniquity becoming known. When finally she is betrayed she goes out into the night to die rather than endure the shame which would have followed."

Better known as a poet, Austin Clarke lost his job teaching literature at University College, Dublin, because his marriage did not take place in a church. Like Wall and O'Duffy, Clarke wrote fantasy novels steeped in Irish mythology and focused on the conflict between Irish puritanism and erotic love: these included *The Bright Temptation* (1932), *The Singing-Men at Cashel*

(1936), and *The Sun Dances at Easter* (1952). In the last-named novel, Orla is advised to make a pilgrimage to a well to find the cure that will enable her to provide her husband with a child. There she finds that the "cure," much to her surprise, is provided by a virile, otherworldly lover. As is so often the case in Irish literature, behind Christianity lurks pagan Eros.

Before the beginning of the Free State and its Censorship of Publications Act, Brinsley MacNamara's first novel, *The Valley of the Squinting Windows* (1918), had been burned "in the best medieval fashion" in Delvin, his hometown in County Westmeath, whose natives surmised that their town was the inspiration for MacNamara's Garradrimna, a town where everyone watches everyone else through "squinting windows." (One critic called MacNamara the originator of the "'squinting windows' school of Irish realistic fiction.") MacNamara was one of several Irish novelists—including also O'Duffy and Joyce—who worked in realism as well as fantasy. MacNamara's *The Various Lives of Marcus Igoe* (1929) is a strikingly experimental novel that asks, What if our lives had taken a different course? What if we had moved elsewhere or married someone else? MacNamara's narrative shifts between contrasting scenarios, ending in a suggestion of eternal recurrence very similar to the conclusion of Flann O'Brien's *The Third Policeman*.

Seán O'Faoláin, who was better known for his short stories and for his influence on younger writers as editor of *The Bell* between 1940 and 1946, published three vividly realistic novels set in his native Cork (and his ancestral Limerick), with three increasingly older protagonists: *A Nest of Simple Folk* (1933), a historical novel and family chronicle in which a young boy eventually inherits his uncle's 19th-century Fenianism; *Bird Alone* (1936), in which a young man experiences the loss of all he loves; and *Come Back to Erin* (1940), in which an older man slowly comes to realize that his rebel stance has become outdated in the Ireland of the 1930s. Much later in his career, O'Faoláin published a fantasy novel entitled *And Again?* (1979) that is comparable to MacNamara's *The Various Lives of Marcus Igoe*. After almost getting hit by a truck that kills a young boy instead, James J. Younger receives an offer in the mail from the gods that he cannot refuse: to relive his life backwards. Beginning at retirement age in 1965, Younger lives with and loves in turn a woman, her daughter, and her granddaughter—each of whom, of course, grows older and further beyond his reach as he himself gets younger. O'Faoláin's fellow Corkman and close friend Frank O'Connor—also better known for his short stories—published two novels, *The Saint and Mary Kate* (1932) and *Dutch Interior* (1940), centered on innocent young protagonists who encounter the bizarre, difficult, adult world. O'Connor returned to the roots of Irish fiction in the oral tradition: he writes for the ear, and his novels consist of episodic vignettes that read like discrete short stories.

Similarly, Liam O'Flaherty was best known as a master of the short story. Like O'Connor and O'Faoláin, his short stories dealt with Cork and the rural west of Ireland as powerfully as Joyce had examined urban Dublin in the short stories making up *Dubliners*. Yet O'Flaherty also published 17 novels, and while his determination to write the great Irish novel led to uneven results, he was perhaps the most influential earlier 20th-century Irish novelist after Joyce. A native Irish speaker from Inis Mór in the Aran Islands, O'Flaherty was forced to exile himself and (except for one volume of stories) to write in English in order to

succeed as a writer. In several ways O'Flaherty's career reads like a somewhat more successful version of William Carleton's a century earlier. Both were Irish speakers whose English prose still contains the sound of native authenticity; both were earmarked for the priesthood early in their lives, but ended up as anti-clerical critics of the Catholic Church instead; both used their fiction partly as polemical vehicles for their pronounced views of Irish society; and both were peasants who were unashamedly self-serving in doing whatever was necessary to launch their careers. A large part of O'Flaherty's influence on other Irish writers stemmed from his radical departure from the novelistic style of Joyce; his style and his naturalistic vision were much closer to Hemingway. *Famine* (1937) is perhaps the best Irish historical novel ever published. Here O'Flaherty, drawing on his own intimate experiences with recurrent famines while growing up on Inis Mór at the turn of the century, powerfully presents the Great Hunger of 1845–51 through the eyes of the Kilmartin family.

O'Flaherty's popularity helped inspire a new group of "peasant novelists," recalling the generation of the Banims, Griffin, and Carleton a century earlier. Among the best of them were Peadar O'Donnell and Michael McLaverty, who also wrote novels set on offshore islands (to the north, in O'Donnell's native County Donegal and McLaverty's County Antrim). O'Donnell, like O'Flaherty, was a socialist, but a much more active one; he was perhaps even better known as an organizer and editor than as a novelist. *Storm* (1926) is an autobiographical novel about a schoolteacher who leaves the island to join the nationalist struggle on the mainland, and *Islanders* (1928) examines the pull of emigration from the island to the Lagan Valley in County Down and then on to Scotland and America. *Adrigoole* (1929) was based on a real incident concerning a mother and her children who were found dead of starvation after the mother was shunned by her Free State neighbors following the imprisonment of her Republican husband during the Civil War. *The Knife* (1930) focuses on the interactions of Catholic and Protestant neighbors in the Lagan Valley.

Michael McLaverty's novels also deal with the movement from the island to the mainland and from the past to the future. In *Call My Brother Back* (1939)—separated into two books, "The Island" and "The City"—the MacNeill family is forced to leave Rathlin Island for the Falls Road in Belfast, and young Colm MacNeill loses his link to the land, his education, and his older brother in the process. *Lost Fields* (1941) tells the story of a Falls Road family that eventually moves back to the countryside, while *In This Thy Day* (1945) shows how rural elderly people can oppress the young, preventing marriage by refusing to let go of their land.

A parallel but more satiric novel is *Tarry Flynn* (1948) by Patrick Kavanagh, who is better known as a poet. Tarry also has to leave the farm because his inner artistic vision is too much at odds with the grotesque social world of a place in which "hating one's next-door neighbour was an essential part of a small farmer's religion." A very different "peasant" writer was Francis MacManus, author of 11 novels set in the Kilkenny area (which also produced the Banims). Several of MacManus' books deal with conflicts between the middle class and the peasantry. In *This House Was Mine* (1937), for example, Martin Hickey is prevented by his prideful father, who approaches marriage like he does land purchase, from marrying their servant, and witnesses the eventual loss of the family home. Alice Lennon in the rivetting *Watergate* (1942) returns from America to find her family home inhabited by her sister and husband but controlled by a grasping peasant woman, whom Alice eventually supplants, but only at the expense of her own freedom and dignity. In *The Fire in the Dust* (1950), a sexually repressed woman tries to marry a widowed man by "playing the wicked stepmother to his mother before she had the ring on her finger," eventually causing indirectly the death of one of his sons.

Increasingly, however, as the 20th century progressed, women spoke for themselves in Irish fiction. Women's novels, impressively diverse in their range, were yet linked by a realistic perspective on Irish society from distinctively female points of view. Elizabeth Bowen and Molly Keane came from Big House backgrounds similar to those of Somerville and Ross. The plot of Bowen's best Irish novel, *The Last September* (1929), is representative enough to appear allegorical: during the Anglo-Irish War, a young Anglo-Irishwoman promises to marry an English soldier, but she is unable to love him and he is not accepted by her domineering mother. Finally he is shot dead in a Republican ambush, and her family's Big House is burned to the ground (in a fictional projection of Bowen's feelings about her own family estate in County Cork). The contemporary novelist Jennifer Johnston has written several Big House novels in much the same vein, similarly and effectively examining the divisions among people of different genders, religions, and nationalities in Ireland, including *The Captains and the Kings* (1972), *The Gates* (1973), *How Many Miles to Babylon?* (1974), *The Old Jest* (1979), *Fool's Sanctuary* (1987), and *The Invisible Worm* (1991). Molly Keane adopted a somewhat more comic attitude to the Big House and also boldly wrote about the sexual problems found within its walls, in such novels as *Devoted Ladies* (1934) and *The Rising Tide* (1937).

Middle-class Ireland was analyzed by such novelists as Kate O'Brien, Maura Laverty, and Mary Lavin. In *Without My Cloak* (1931), *The Anteroom* (1934), *The Land of Spices* (1941), and *The Last of Summer* (1943), O'Brien wrote insightfully of the upper-middle-class Catholic world of her native County Limerick, developing a rich panorama of characters in novels recalling 19th-century works by the likes of Jane Austen more than any of her own Irish contemporaries. *The Land of Spices* is a particularly excellent work, banned in the Free State because of a single sentence in the book that contained an oblique reference to a homosexual liaison. As a "double Bildungsroman" telling the stories of Helen Archer, the head of an Irish convent school, and Anna Murphy, a young student there, and of how these two characters help each other, this novel offered a feminist alternative to Joyce's *A Portrait of the Artist as a Young Man*, which influenced so many other Irish Bildungsromane. Maura Laverty, who (like O'Brien) worked as a governess in Spain, similarly celebrated friendships between young girls and older women, in *Never No More* (1942) and *No More than Human* (1944). Mary Lavin was best known for her short stories, but her novels *The House in Clewe Street* (1945) and *Mary O'Grady* (1950) were effective portraits of the small-town struggles of women as well as men.

Edna O'Brien is the most senior, most popular, most prolific, and perhaps most influential novelist among the current generation of Irish women. With startling new frankness, her first novel, *The Country Girls* (1960), as well as its sequels *The Lonely Girl* (1962) and *Girls in Their Married Bliss* (1964), deal with growing up female in rural County Clare. Like Kate O'Brien's *The Land of Spices*, *The Country Girl Trilogy* (republished in 1986 with a new epilogue) is a "double Bildungsroman," but here Kate and Baba grow increasingly apart as they respond in different ways to the challenges of sex, marriage, divorce, and adult life in Dublin and London. In *The Maiden Dinosaur* (1964), Janet McNeill treats the subject of sexual abuse in the otherwise very different world of upper-class Protestant Belfast.

A series of feminist alternatives to the historical and political novels published by men grappled with the Anglo-Irish and Civil wars and the creation of the Republic of Ireland. Among these were Iris Murdoch's *The Red and the Green* (1965), Eilís Dillon's *Across the Bitter Sea* (1973) and *Blood Relations* (1977), and Julia O'Faoláin's *No Country for Young Men* (1980). Also to be considered in this group is the aforementioned Jennifer Johnston, who has published not only Big House novels but also *Shadows on Our Skin* (1977), set in Derry in the midst of the northern Irish "Troubles." Several other talented women novelists emerged in the 1980s and 1990s, including Clare Boylan (*Holy Pictures*, 1983), Mary Leland (*The Killeen*, 1985), and Maeve Binchy (*Circle of Friends*, 1990).

While the Catholic-Protestant conflict in Northern Ireland has dominated the attention of those outside of Ireland, social and political developments in the Republic of Ireland since the 1950s have been more positive for Irish novelists (both female and male)—helping to explain, for example, how Edna O'Brien's sexually bolder novels could sell so well in the 1960s while Kate O'Brien's much more reserved novel could be banned in 1941. Censorship has eased since the 1950s. People in Ireland became more interested in the rest of the world and in economic development. The conservative Éamon de Valera was replaced as head of state by the progressive Seán Lemass, whose administration during 1958–63 marked a significant turning point. Ireland's economy experienced a comparative boom during the 1960s, and it joined the European Economic Community in 1973. Even though a recession arrived in the late 1970s, and unemployment and emigration remain major problems today, Ireland nonetheless remains in many ways a much more modernized country than it had been before 1960. State patronage of the arts improved the situation of the writer (who enjoys tax-free status in the Republic of Ireland), and publishing grew to the point where a monthly magazine, *Books-Ireland,* was founded to keep readers abreast of developments in the Irish book industry. Irish bookstores today are well stocked with a striking variety of new Irish novels. Although Irish novelists still have to hope their books will sell overseas—especially in England and the United States—if they are to be really successful, they are much more attuned to writing for Irish publishers and readers than their predecessors had been.

Like Edna O'Brien, male novelists such as Benedict Kiely, Brian Moore, and John McGahern were therefore able, with the help of these improved conditions, to build long careers—successfully publishing, over several decades, realistic novels appealing to many readers, yet also experimenting and taking some risks. Kiely's early novels *Land Without Stars* (1946) and *In a Harbour Green* (1949) deal with his upbringing in the North and with the experience of living in neutral Ireland during World War II, whereas *The Cards of the Gambler* (1953) was a new departure imaginatively interweaving folktales and their novelistic reworkings. Author of a 1948 study of his fellow Tyrone native William Carleton as well as a 1950 survey of Irish fiction, Kiely's work was very well rooted in the traditions of the Irish novel. *The Captain with the Whiskers* (1960) and *Dogs Enjoy the*

Morning (1968) also draw on folklore and fantasy, whereas *Proxopera* (1977) and *Nothing Happens in Carmincross* (1985) expose and attack northern IRA violence. Another novelist from the North, Belfast native Brian Moore, has enjoyed an even more prolific and varied career, beginning with his widely praised first novel, *The Lonely Passion of Judith Hearne* (1955), a striking study of the futility of a middle-aged, unmarried woman; interestingly, his later *The Temptation of Eileen Hughes* (1981), as if in counterpoint to *Judith Hearne*, presents a more successful female protagonist from Belfast. *The Feast of Lupercal* (1957) and *The Emperor of Ice-Cream* (1965), the latter Moore's Bildungsroman, deal with young men entrapped in Belfast. *Catholics* (1972) is a futuristic Irish novel whose CBS television adaptation did much to increase's Moore's fame. He emigrated from Belfast to Toronto in 1948, later resettling in the United States, and is perhaps best known internationally for some of his numerous works set outside Ireland.

Like Moore, John McGahern made an auspicious debut with a sympathetic and very well written portrait of a middle-aged Irishwoman (married and dying of cancer), *The Barracks* (1963). *The Dark* (1965) is his sardonic, latter-day, small-town portrait of a young man unable to become an artist, which cost McGahern his teaching job since it introduced the word "fuck" on its first page; it is not coincidental that *The Leavetaking* (1974) concerns a teacher's last day on the job before leaving for England. Also suggestive of McGahern's victimization over *The Dark* is *The Pornographer* (1979), in which a writer of racy potboilers (whose narratives are interwoven intertextually into the novel) is redeemed at the end. The domineering father introduced in *The Barracks* and *The Dark* reappears in *Amongst Women* (1990), a memorable study of the daughters whom he dominates.

Along with Edna O'Brien, McGahern and Brian Moore are the most celebrated, veteran Irish novelists writing today. Others include Aidan Higgins, John Banville, William Trevor, and James Plunkett. Like Jennifer Johnston, Higgins (*Langrishe, Go Down*, 1966), Banville (*Birchwood*, 1973), and Trevor (*Fools of Fortune*, 1983) have experimented with Gothic, postmodernist versions of the Big House novel as emblems of deep historical divisions in Irish society. Plunkett explored societal conflicts in the best contemporary Irish historical novel, *Strumpet City* (1969), a panoramic treatment of the period surrounding the 1913 Dublin lockout—and its sequels ranging from the 1920s to the 1950s, *Farewell Companions* (1977) and *The Circus Animals* (1990). Authors of historical novels also included Walter Macken (*Seek the Fair Land*, 1959; *The Silent People*, 1962; *The Scorching Wind*, 1964) and Michael Farrell (*Thy Tears Might Cease*, 1963), while other types of realistic novels were published by Sam Hanna Bell (*December Bride*, 1951), Anthony C. West (*The Ferret Fancier*, 1963), John Broderick (*The Waking of Willie Ryan*, 1965), Richard Power (*The Hungry Grass*, 1969), Thomas Kilroy (*The Big Chapel*, 1971), and Anthony Cronin (*The Life of Riley*, 1964; *Identity Papers*, 1979).

A number of promising younger novelists emerged in the 1980s and 1990s, including Bernard MacClaverty (*Cal*, 1983), Neil Jordan (*The Past*, 1980), Desmond Hogan (*A Curious Street*, 1984), and Patrick McGinley (*The Lost Soldier's Song*, 1994). On the whole, more good Irish novelists are writing today than ever before in history.

JAMES M. CAHALAN

See also Samuel Beckett; Elizabeth Bowen; Maria Edgeworth; English Novel; French Novel (1945– present; on Beckett); James Joyce; Melmoth the Wanderer; George Moore; Flann O'Brien

Further Reading

Beckett, J.C., *The Making of Modern Ireland, 1603–1923*, London: Faber, and New York: Knopf, 1966

Brown, Malcolm, *The Politics of Irish Literature: From Thomas Davis to W.B. Yeats*, London: Allen and Unwin, and Seattle: University of Washington Press, 1972

Brown, Stephen J.M., *Ireland in Fiction: A Guide to Irish Novels, Tales, Romances, and Folklore*, volume 1, Dublin and London: Maunsel, 1916; new edition, 1919; reprint, Shannon: Irish University Press, and New York: Barnes and Noble, 1969

Brown, Stephen J.M., and Desmond Clarke, *Ireland in Fiction: A Guide to Irish Novels, Tales, Romances, and Folklore*, volume 2, Cork: Royal Carbery, 1985

Cahalan, James M., *Great Hatred, Little Room: The Irish Historical Novel*, Syracuse, New York: Syracuse University Press, and Dublin: Gill and Macmillan, 1983

Cahalan, James M., *The Irish Novel: A Critical History*, Boston: Twayne, and Dublin: Gill and Macmillan, 1988

Cahalan, James M., *Modern Irish Literature and Culture: A Chronology*, New York: Macmillan, 1993

Deane, Seamus, *Short History of Irish Literature*, London: Hutchinson, and Notre Dame, Indiana: University of Notre Dame Press, 1986

Deane, Seamus, et al., editors, *The Field Day Anthology of Irish Writing*, 3 vols., Derry, Northern Ireland: Field Day, and London: Faber, 1991

Finneran, Richard J., editor, *Recent Research on Anglo-Irish Writers*, New York: Modern Language Association, 1983

Flanagan, Thomas, *The Irish Novelists, 1800–1850*, New York: Columbia University Press, 1958

Foster, John Wilson, *Forces and Themes in Ulster Fiction*, Totowa, New Jersey: Rowman and Littlefield, and Dublin: Gill and Macmillan, 1974

Foster, John Wilson, *Fictions of the Irish Literary Revival: A Changeling Art*, Syracuse, New York: Syracuse University Press, and Dublin: Gill and Macmillan, 1987

Foster, R.F., *Modern Ireland, 1600–1972*, London: Allen Lane, 1988; New York: Penguin, 1989

Harmon, Maurice, and Patrick Rafroidi, editors, *The Irish Novel in Our Time*, Villeneuve-d'Ascq: Publications de l'Université de Lille III, 1976

Kiberd, Declan, *Inventing Ireland*, London: Cape, 1995; Cambridge, Massachusetts: Harvard University Press, 1996

Kiely, Benedict, *Modern Irish Fiction: A Critique*, Dublin: Golden Eagle, 1950

Titley, Alan, *An tÚrscéal Gaeilge* (The Gaelic Novel), Dublin: An Clóchomhar, 1991

Weekes, Ann Owens, *Irish Women Writers: An Uncharted Tradition*, Lexington: University Press of Kentucky, 1990

Welch, Robert, editor, *The Oxford Companion to Irish Literature*, Oxford and New York: Clarendon Press, 1996

Israeli Novel

The development of the Israeli novel has been closely linked to Israel's political history, with beginnings even before the creation of the independent state in 1948. And behind those beginnings lies the long tradition of Hebrew narrative, extending over several millennia and to all parts of the world where Jewish communities and culture flourished.

Hebrew narrative is as old as the Bible, which, in its canonical form, opens with stories—creation stories, family sagas, accounts of the ancestors of the human family in general and the Hebrew family in particular. These stories and the self-contained narratives of such later books as *Ruth* and *Esther* have functioned as precursors to the Hebrew novel. Hebrew literature of the Rabbinic period, roughly from the first century B.C. through the early Middle Ages, usually took its starting point in the Bible and included exegesis, homiletics, and storytelling. Secular Hebrew literature emerged in the ninth century in southern Spain, initially in competition with Arabic literary forms but subsequently in a mode that took no account of non-Jewish literary development.

Secular Hebrew literature opened itself up once more to outside influences under the pressure of emancipation and the Enlightenment. Movements originating in 18th-century Germany sought to reintroduce the Jews into the cultural world of Europe and created a literature to promote this cause. However, not until the early 19th century do we have anything that could plausibly be called novels in Hebrew—the epistolary satires of Hasidic life and mores composed in Galicia. Some critics push the origin of the Hebrew novel even further up to mid-19th-century Vilna, with Avraham Mapu's pseudo-biblical romance, which deploys biblical language exclusively. Fighting the constraints of this biblical style, writers toward the end of the century struggled for increased lexical and syntactic scope, using Hebrew from all periods and also imitating Yiddish models, to open up medieval and traditional narrative modes to the forms and techniques of the realistic novel. The Zionist Movement gathered strength at the same time, encouraging the everyday use of the Hebrew language, as well as the propagation of a large-scale secular literature, on the European model, in all genres.

The Israeli novel, following the tradition of the new Hebrew literature, encapsulates two major trends: the secularizing tendency of the Jewish Enlightenment and the nationalistic tendency envisioning a return to the ancient Palestinian homeland where the reborn culture might flourish unhampered. Until World War I, the chief centers of modern Hebrew creativity remained in the Diaspora, particularly in Eastern Europe. The existence of a largely autonomous Jewish society facilitated the production of a specifically Jewish literature, mainly in Hebrew and Yiddish. But the ravages of war, the Bolshevik revolution, and the Russian civil war effectively destroyed the old-style Pale of Settlement and the *shtetl* within. This process of decline was to be completed by the Holocaust. But already, Hebrew writers had established themselves in Palestine, so that by the 1920s a self-conscious Palestinian-Hebrew literature had been created. Avraham Shlonsky, Uri Zvi Greenberg, and Natan Alterman, all poets nourished in Eastern Europe, moved to Palestine during this period. The person who may perhaps be regarded as the greatest of all Hebrew novelists and short-story writers, S.Y.

Agnon, returned to Palestine from Germany in 1924 after an earlier stay there before World War I. The Oriental Hebrew novelist Yehuda Burla was Palestinian-born, as was the poet Esther Raab. In short, by 1939 the Jewish community in Palestine announced itself as the new Hebrew Center as well as an emerging independent political entity.

The new Palestinian-Hebrew literature helped to forge the new Israeli national identity. Native writers emphasized their relationship to the local soil, while some of the immigrant writers sought to assume a Palestinian identity by obliterating traces of the Diaspora. The third wave of immigration (1919–24) brought Jews who saw the creation of a specifically local literature as a major goal.

By 1948, then, a national literature had been established, just as the social and political molds had also settled. The subject matter was, in general, emergent Israel: the absorption of immigrants, the war, the kibbutz, and other issues of the new state. The orientation was practical and ideological, concerned with matters of public polity rather than the individual. Some of the most notable and typical exponents of the Israeli novel already had established a reputation. The Palestinian-born novelist S. Yizhar (Smilansky) wrote novels that are short on plot, seeking to express the consciousness of a central character. His central concerns are the landscape, the difficulties or even the impossibility of moral choice, and the texture of the Hebrew language. The movement of the narrative remains characteristically unresolved, and no change takes place. Between the mid-1960s and throughout the 1970s and 1980s, Yizhar wrote almost no fiction, but he has already published three full-length novels in the 1990s, again focusing on memories of childhood, on the sense of identity of young people under the British Mandate, and the overwhelming power of the landscape. The poetry and prose of Haim Gouri is similarly informed by a typically Israeli range of themes—war, the hero, his beloved, and his bloody memories—a very local subject matter. Many of the heroes in the novels and stories of Moshe Shamir are not only native-born but see themselves as a different species from the Diaspora Jew. The Israeli (the new Hebrew) is characterized as simple, direct, active, healthy, single-minded, and strong, in contrast to the split, urban, tortured Diaspora Jew. Shamir's journal, *Yalkut hareim*, was intended as a mouthpiece for "Palmach literature," named after the striking arm of the Israeli defense force because of its origins in a sense of comradeship and a single, collective purpose.

The 1950s witnessed change on various fronts. Writers became more introspective and sceptical, doubtful of the collective thrust, and began uncertainly to look back to their forebears and to earlier Jewish existence. Yehuda Amichai made much of the contrast between the generations in poetry and in prose. Pinhas Sadeh started to produce a type of confessional prose with an uncharacteristic focus on the self, truth, and God (intense religious experience has not been a prominent theme of Israeli authors). The heroes of Israeli novels of the 1950s and 1960s are seen in flight from their official or their imagined roles. Shamir's work moved in this direction. And the characters of the novelist Aharon Megged are sometimes disillusioned, making their way from the kibbutz to the city, as in *Hedvah vaani* (1953; Hedva and I) or away from the sense of subjugation to the national myth, as in *Hahai al hamet* (1965; *The Living on the Dead*).

Israeli society was, of course, multifaceted. Besides the militant Zionism of public policy, other voices made themselves heard. One alternative ideology was aired in the periodical *Alef*, which was founded in the 1940s to advocate a sort of Hebrew Semitic Union unconnected with Diaspora Jewry and which continued to press for a secular Middle Eastern state. Another, less dogmatic, ideology appeared in a forum entitled *Liqrat*, distributed from 1952. But these alternative voices were often muted as Israeli literature in general became less sure of itself and its direction less certain. And as Israel has become increasingly "normalized," its literature has become less publicly oriented.

More recent years have seen projections to the earlier history that informs the present. Aharon Appelfeld, in fiction such as *Badenheim, ir nofesh* (1979; *Badenheim 1939*), writes mainly of Israel's prehistory, describing a European Jewry in its twilight world, reaching for assimilation on its path to destruction, and of the world of the survivors in Israel who are rooted in that past. By focusing on the world of his childhood, Appelfeld lays bare an often unacknowledged aspect of Israeli identity. The novelist A.B. Yehoshua, author of *Bithilat kayits 1970* (1972; *Early in the Summer of 1970*) and *Hame'ahev* (1977; *The Lover*), among others, has stated that it is his goal to deepen the understanding of the paradoxical dilemmas of Israelis. Amos Oz has sought symbols for the Israeli situation in the images of terror and siege that haunt ordinary people with extraordinary interior lives. He too has attempted to recover his own childhood and the pre-1948 Palestinian world in a collection of novellas entitled *Har ha'etsah hara'ah* (1976; *The Hill of Evil Counsel*). A more recent novel, *Panter ba'martef* (1995; *Panther in the Basement*), returns to the last days of the British Mandate in Palestine as perceived by a child.

Recent Israeli fiction is marked by various departures from realism. Amalia Kahana-Carmon has long been writing intensely rendered stream-of-consciousness fiction, often as though narrated by a child or by an adult with a childlike vision, fixated on another individual. Yaakov Shabtai has produced a series of short narrative extravaganzas, then a long novel consisting of a single paragraph, *Zikhron devarim* (1977; *Past Continuous*), moving from the death of the narrator's father at its opening to the suicide of his son at its close. The novel moves from the banal to the tragic with apparently effortless control. His posthumous novel, *Sof davar* (1984; *Past Perfect*), was issued without the author's final revisions following his untimely death. A generally associative narrative, it experiments with different modes and time scales. Shabtai's contribution in particular has exercised a tremendous influence on subsequent fiction. His two novels, because of their artistic success, have suggested new ways of representing reality in fiction. The earlier novel links together the experiences of different characters through associations and motifs. Externality bears closely on internal awareness and does much to engender it. Nevertheless, the specific shape of the text is created by the individual consciousness, so that there is a constant interplay between different views of reality. Despite the ceaseless shifts in point of view, the novel expresses a unity of vision that derives in part from the way the lives of the three protagonists intertwine. More importantly, the novel is held together by Shabtai's detailed observation, linguistic precision, mental associations, and humor. Shabtai's posthumous novel, in

the main, adopts a different approach, with a single focus of consciousness. Presenting an especially critical phase in the protagonist's life, the narrative brings together reality and fantasy, waking and dream world, present and past. The reader can never be sure whether objective reality is presented or an alternative version of that reality, mixing memory and fancy.

These flexible versions of reality have caused a shift in recent Israeli fiction. One of the leading voices of the 1980s, David Grossman, is much concerned with alternative versions of reality, not just in any one particular novel, but between different works in different genres. We can see *Chiyuch hagediy* (1983; *The Smile of the Lamb*) and *Hazeman hatsahov* (1987; *The Yellow Wind*) as the two sides of a single coin. Both works describe the situation in the Israeli-occupied West Bank and the course of the Intifada. But the earlier work is a novel, with a complex view of character, time, motivation, and development, and the latter is a journalistic and polemical account, a straightforward attempt to persuade the reader of a certain understanding of events. The relationship between these works is complicated by the fact that generic conventions are frequently deliberately jumbled. For example, a story is inserted in *The Yellow Wind*. Grossman's *Ayen erech: Ahavah* (1986; *See Under: Love*) is a very ambitious effort to see the Holocaust afresh, focused on the experience of a child as the primary point of view but supplying a variety of narrative devices, including surrealism, fantasy, and dictionary definition, that deviate from the linear narrative arrangement. In later work, Grossman has pursued these two tracks of probing Jewish-Arab relations, as in *Nochechim venifkadim* (1992; *Sleeping on a Wire*), and of recreating childhood in fictional form, as in *Sefer hadikduk hapenimiy* (1991; *The Book of Intimate Grammar*).

Dan Ben-Amots adopted the confessional autobiography pioneered by Pinhas Sadeh, although without Sadeh's religious mysticism but with a fair admixture of humor. David Schutz's *Haesev vehahol* (1978; The Grass and the Sand) is a striking reconstruction of the European background, transmitted by a Berlin-born narrator. Although the narrator Emmanuel dominates the novel, his narrative incorporates different voices, presenting their account of events and family. Emmanuel returns "home" to attempt a reconciliation with his past, with his family and background, with a history that goes back to Central Europe at the turn of the century. The subsequent novels of this Berlin-born author continue to investigate the complex web of interrelations in Israeli families.

In the 1980s, fiction proved the most adventurous and innovative of the genres in Israeli Hebrew literature. The range and variety of forms indicate some impatience with traditional linear narrative and with the traditional constraints of Hebrew grammar and vocabulary. Modes and forms were mixed, chronological points juxtaposed, voices transposed, points of view shuffled, time sequences broken, narrative segments highlighted or challenged by alternative versions and statements—all in the hope of reaching a deeper truth. Leading experimenters include established authors. Amos Oz has investigated various methods of handling plot development. In *Kufsah shechorah* (1987; *Black Box*), he exploits the epistolary novel form to present a story from different viewpoints. *Lada'at ishah* (1989; *To Know a Woman*) locates the central narrative consciousness in the novel's hero, but the different time scales allow an alternative perspective. A.B. Yehoshua has continued to experiment with narrative technique, particularly in *Mar Mani* (1990; *Mr. Mani*), which gives one side of a dialogue, as if we are present while someone conducts a telephone conversation. It is left to the reader to construct the other side of the dialogue. A further technical surprise in the novel lies in its reversal of conventional expectations, moving backward in time. In a series of five episodes opening with the most recent, set in the 1980s, *Mr. Mani* moves back over two centuries exploring the Mani family's place in history. Playing with fantasy, surprise, reversal, and stream of consciousness, Yehoshua has also written a traditional narrative in *Molcho* (1987; *Five Seasons*), but even there the reader is involved in the creation of the narrative.

Other writers also engage the reader in the construction of the story. Y. Hoffman has his novels printed only on one side of the leaf, so that the reader is confronted by a blank page for every printed page. The reader has no alternative but to create his own story, his own counterpoint. Youval Shimoni, in *Meof hayonah* (1990; The Flight of the Dove), writes two parallel stories on facing pages in different typefaces, and these stories intersect in time and place. One is the story of an American couple visiting Paris as tourists and the other is of a lonely woman living there. In other fictional experiments, plot is abandoned completely, as in Aner Shalev's *Opus 1* (1988), where, as the title implies, narrative aspires to the condition of music, to use Walter Pater's phrase. Instead of the normal components of narrative, such as linear time, logical sequence, and coherent plot, the novel uses a sort of musical notation—staccato, legato, etc. Avraham Heffner's *Sefer hameforash* (1991; Explicated Book) is a work with its own commentary attached to the text. In this particular case, the reader is not left to draw his conclusions but is bombarded with suggestions, options, and interpretations.

One of the most notable features of recent Israeli literature is the growing prominence of women writers, a dynamic presence in the world and on the page. Amalia Kahana-Carmon's work has long given expression to a specifically feminine view of relationships. But now many others are entering a domain hitherto held to be an exclusively male preserve, generally placing women in the forefront of the fiction as narrators and protagonists. Together with a transformed view of the world, women's novels bring a new tone to fiction, humorous, slangy, and irreverent. Of such a character are the surrealistic forays of Orly Castel-Bloom, the slangy and challenging naturalism of Irit Linur, and the demotic humor of Yehudit Katzir. A collection of Katzir's novellas, *Sogrim et hayam* (1990; *Closing the Sea*), presented with deft wit, was immediately successful, as it appealed to a reading public ready for a lowering of the prevailing high literary seriousness. Linur's two novels, *Shirat hasirenah* (1991; The Siren's Song) and *Shete shilgiyot* (1993; Two Snow-Whites), are first-person narratives in which the author dons an effective disguise. She uses a conversational argot, building up a credible, exciting narrative of everyday life in Tel-Aviv. *Shirat hasirenah* is set at the time of the Gulf War, with the threat of Scud missiles hanging over the city. Paradoxically, *Shete shilgiyot*, already far removed from the crisis of the Gulf War, is of a more somber character. Linur's principal innovation is the deployment of an apparently colloquial language to serve as an alternative literary mode. Most recent women's fiction, displaying private passions in the public sphere, relishes the delights of the flesh and expresses the anguish of amorous frustration. Women

tend to take the initiative, and they are interested in men without being subservient. The intervention of women writers in Israeli fiction in the last decade or so has introduced a new dimension. Now the personal theme dominates rather than the social, public, philosophical, or political. And women's fiction supplies the humor that Hebrew literature has traditionally lacked. Linur's heroines, for example, do not take themselves too seriously, and an admirable distance is preserved between the narrative voice and the person of the author. This quality has been notably absent in other sorts of confessional or first-person Hebrew narrative.

A further element of complexity in the Israeli novel derives from the fact that literature in other languages is being produced by, for example, English-speaking expatriates, more recent Soviet immigrants, and Arabs, challenging Hebrew and Jewish hegemony. Moreover, the Hebrew literary tradition itself has been inherited and modified, sometimes by writers with little knowledge of or sympathy for that tradition. Rich in traditional and liturgical associations, Hebrew is young as a vernacular. Its writers belong to several generations and vastly disparate cultural and geographical backgrounds. But they jostle together in the turbulent currents of Hebrew literature: the young and the old, the Israeli-born and the recent immigrant, the Zionist conservative and the radical, the Oriental and the European Jew, the Arab writing in Hebrew, the religious and the secular Jew, the hopeful and the disillusioned.

LEON I. YUDKIN

See also S.Y. Agnon; Aharon Appelfeld; Biblical Narrative and the Novel; David Grossman; Amos Oz; A.B. Yehoshua

Further Reading

Alter, Robert, *After the Tradition: Essays on Modern Jewish Writing,* New York: Dutton, 1969

Epstein, George L., and Max Zeldner, editors, *Modern Hebrew Literature,* New York: Hebrew, 1948

Halkin, Simon, *Modern Hebrew Literature: From the Enlightenment to the Birth of the State of Israel,* New York: Schocken, 1970

Klausner, Joseph, *A History of Modern Hebrew Literature,* London: Cailingold, 1932

Rabinovich, Isaiah, *Major Trends in Modern Hebrew Fiction,* Chicago: University of Chicago Press, 1968

Ribalow, Menachem, *Ketavim u-megilot,* New York: Hotsaat Ogen, 1942; as *Modern Hebrew Literature: A Volume of Literary Evaluation,* London: Vision Press, and New York: Twayne, 1959

Sandbank, S., introduction to *Contemporary Israeli Literature: An Anthology,* edited by Elliott Anderson, Evanston, Illinois: Northwestern University Press, 1977

Yudkin, Leon I., *Escape into Siege: A Survey of Israeli Literature Today,* London and Boston: Routledge and Kegan Paul, 1974

Yudkin, Leon I., *1948 and After: Aspects of Israeli Fiction,* Manchester: Manchester University Press, 1984

Yudkin, Leon I., *Beyond Sequence: Current Israeli Fiction and Its Context,* Northwood: Symposium, 1992

Italian Novel

After the splendid sunset of the Renaissance at the end of the 16th century, Italian literature lost its creative vitality and became highly derivative of external influences for about the next two centuries. The narrative tradition, which had been represented so authoritatively by Boccaccio, turned to French, Spanish, and, somewhat later, English models for inspiration. Translations played a major role in this mediation. Italian writers of the 17th and 18th centuries, following the enthusiasm for classical subjects that first surfaced during the Renaissance, often turned to Hellenistic stories (especially Heliodorus' *An Ethiopian Story*). The works produced in this period make up long lists that are duly recorded in the histories of literature for inventory's sake, but they count for little else.

At the end of the 18th century an important narrative appeared, the *Ultime lettere di Jacopo Ortis* (first version 1798, second version 1802; The Last Letters of Jacopo Ortis). Its author, Ugo Foscolo, was an exquisite neoclassical poet, one of the major figures of Italian romanticism. The novel, in epistolary form, tells of the unhappy love and political disillusionment borne by a Venetian patriot, who eventually commits suicide. Rousseau's *Julie; ou, La Nouvelle Héloïse* (1761; *Julie; or, The New Eloise*) and Goethe's *Die Leiden des Jungen Werthers* (1774; *The Sufferings of Young Werther*) are Foscolo's main avowed models. Other influences, however, may be detected: from classical (Greek and Latin) imagery and phrasing to the subtle irony of Laurence Sterne, whose *A Sentimental Journey* (1768) was, later, partly translated by Foscolo. The deeper source of inspiration, however, lies in the author's own experiences: some striking similarities exist between certain passages of the *Ultime lettere* and the actual letters the author was writing to his lovers and friends during those same years. In spite of the European dimension of Foscolo's adventurous life (several travels and, eventually, a long exile in England), the work did not enjoy its well-deserved renown.

The year 1827 was an *annus mirabilis* for Italian literature. In that year two very different works by two unequal authors were published: Giacomo Leopardi's *Operette morali* (Moral Tales) and Alessandro Manzoni's *I promessi sposi* (The Betrothed). The former, a collection of short prose pieces akin to the *conte philosophique*, echoes in its title Plutarch's *Moralia* and is reminiscent of Lucian's cynicism and Voltaire's keenness; the latter, a large fresco of 17th-century northern Italy painted around the vicissitudes of an engaged couple until their marriage, inaugurates the Italian historical novel in the tradition of Walter Scott's works. The *Moral Tales* is the creation of a classicist whose spirit ripened in the isolation of a small town of the Church State, Recanati, in Central Italy, and with only the support of a large library. While the work seems to seal a bygone era, the radical novelty of its message (rejection of any religious faith or secular illusion of progress) did not find a receptive audience in post-Napoleonic Europe, and its nihilism, overtly celebrated by Schopenhauer and Nietzsche among others, has heavily marked the author's standing, especially in the English-speaking world. *The Betrothed,* on the other hand, with its candid view of human kindness and human wickedness, its idyllic faith in divine providence, and the popular (or rather populistic) angle privileged in the historical representation—a firm Catholic loyalty—

was an immediate success, and is still revered by legions of critics and teachers, with an enthusiasm not shared by many readers. Manzoni's language in *The Betrothed*—a cultivated standard Italian with a simple syntax and an unpersuasive flavor of contemporary spoken Florentine—proves an interesting pendant to his popular program and sets the model for prose writing for subsequent generations. This linguistic form was the result of a thorough reworking of a former version of the novel, entitled *Fermo e Lucia,* from the names of the novel's two protagonists.

The historical scaffolding of *The Betrothed* is a structuring element also found in Ippolito Nievo's *Confessioni d'un italiano* (Confessions of an Italian), first published posthumously in 1867 as *Confessioni d'un ottuagenario* (Confessions of an Octogenarian). Nievo, a Venetian patriot, was a member of Giuseppi Garibaldi's expedition to Sicily in 1860, where he died in a mysterious shipwreck. The novel is a Bildungsroman with a captivating local, mostly rural, color (Friuli, in northeastern Italy), and an unprecedented attention to the ethos of early childhood.

The unification of Italy in 1861, unwelcome by many Italians, did not inspire any relevant patriotic celebration. The most insightful account of this political event is the austere reflection found in *Il Gattopardo* (literally "cheetah," but translated as *The Leopard*) one of the masterpieces of 20th-century Italian narrative. In the book, published posthumously in 1959 (an immediate, although controversial, success), the superior scepticism of the aristocrat author, Giuseppe Tomasi, count of Lampedusa and prince of Salina, provides an incomparable vantage point for the decline of the Sicilian ancien régime after Garibaldi's invasion and the uncontrollable emergence of the bourgeoisie and its vulgarity. The drama of those years, so impeccably depicted with irony and nostalgia by Tomasi, is captured in all its unspeakable tragedy by Giovanni Verga in one of the gems of Italian short fiction, "La libertà" ("Freedom").

Born to an affluent family of Catania (Sicily), Verga is the most significant figure of the veristic writers of southern Italy. Following the lead of French naturalism (Émile Zola, in particular), these authors pursued the impossible goal of representing human events from a totally impersonal point of view, and the hopeless condition of the lower classes in the south often became the object of this literary experiment. In Verga, the Darwinism of the contemporary positivistic sociology coalesced with an archaic fatalistic view, in which society appeared to have the iron necessity of nature. *I Malavoglia* (1881; literally "bad will," the nickname of the Toscano family, the protagonist, but translated as *The House by the Medlar Tree*) is a dark saga of the vain efforts of a poor fisherfolk family to overcome their ancestral condition of poverty. Verga's other novel, *Mastro-don Gesualdo* (1889; *Master Don Gesualdo*), the second in a projected five-novel series entitled *I vinti* (The Vanquished), portrays the inexorable downfall of an industrious master-mason (maestro) who had achieved a factitious nobility (expressed by the title *don*) through an interclass marriage. Qo'eleth's admonition on the vanity of all things seems to be the most suitable epigraph for this ghastly philosophy.

While Verga's activity declined in the early 1890s, the veristic program continued in a manneristic tone with Luigi Capuana's *Il marchese di Roccaverdina* (1901; The Marquis of Roccaverdina). Quite removed from Verga's terseness is the emphatic populism of the Neapolitan Matilde Serao, whose *Il ventre di Napoli* (1884; The Belly of Naples) echoes the title—and the title only—of Zola's *Le Ventre de Paris* (1873; *The Belly of Paris*), which is a crude epic of instincts and interests. In Sardinia, another woman writer, Grazia Deledda (a Nobel prize winner in 1926), sketches a picture, mythical and tender, candid and tragic, of the local society and folklore, from *Marianna Sirca* (1915) to *Elias Portolu* (1903). Incidentally, in all the above veristic authors the realistic and popular subject does not find an adequate match in linguistic choice. The prose remains in standard, literary Italian without any deviation toward dialect or dialectal color: a most relevant element in a tradition like the Italian one, so deeply marked by a dramatic gap between written and spoken language.

To the world of Mediterranean rural mythology still belong the "Novelle dell Pescara" (Novellas of the Pescara, a region in eastern central Italy), the early work of an author, Gabriele D'Annunzio, who was about to grow into a quite different, and greater, writer. His novels, in which the grand style of Italian prose writing is resurrected right from its Renaissance glory, usually portray the downfall of a character, from the painter Andrea Sperelli in *Il piacere* (1889; *The Child of Pleasure*) to the writer Stelio Effrena in *Il fuoco* (1900; *The Flame*), as well as providing a luxuriant picture of the lifestyle of upper classes in the major Italian cities.

The term *decadent,* ambiguous and misleading in its moral and aesthetic ambivalence, is often used for other writers besides D'Annunzio: among them is Antonio Fogazzaro, whose *Malombra* (1886; literally "evil shadow," translated as *The Woman*) is permeated with morbid sensualism and spiritistic apprehensions. A more ambitious design, Manzonian and patriotic, is in his later and most famous novel *Piccolo mondo antico* (1895; *The Little World of the Past*).

To the late 19th century also belong two works of unequal quality and comparable success: Carlo Collodi's *Le avventure di Pinocchio* (1883; *The Adventures of Pinocchio*) and Edmondo De Amicis' *Cuore* (1886; *Heart: A Schoolboy's Journal*). While *Heart* is a cunningly crafted display of unashamed sentimentalism, *Pinocchio,* the world-renowned story of a wood puppet that becomes a man, is remarkable for its well-measured retelling of a millennial topos of initiation, with all the nuances and persuasiveness of reality (including details of local Florentine idioms).

The anti-romantic tradition, which had a foremost representative in the aristocratic ironist Carlo Dossi (*L'altrieri* [1868; The Day Before Yesterday] and *Vita di Alberto Pisani* [1870; Life of Alberto Pisani]), is later resumed in diluted form by Italo Svevo (born Ettore Schmidt, from Trieste). After *Una vita* (1892; *A Life*) and *Senilità* (1898; *As a Man Grows Older*), *La coscienza di Zeno* (1923; *The Confessions of Zeno*), with its unconventional structure and psychologistic introspectiveness, betrays various influences, including James Joyce (his *Ulysses* was known to Svevo long before its publication in 1922) and Sigmund Freud (*Der Witz und seine Beziehung zum Unbewussten* [1905; *Jokes and Their Relation to the Unconscious*]), in particular.

A comparable fragmentation of characters may be found in the work of Luigi Pirandello. The paradoxical philosophy of plural and elusive personalities—and, ultimately, of an undefin-

able reality—is the structuring principle of Pirandello's plays and novels. Among the latter are stories of lost identity, such as *Il fu Mattia Pascal* (1904; *The Late Mattia Pascal*), and of divided selves, such as *Uno, nessuno, e centomila* (1926; *One, None, and a Hundred Thousand*). In *Si gira* (1916; later published as *Quaderni di Serafino Gubbio, operatore* [*Shoot! Si gira . . . The Notebooks of Serafino Gubbio*]), the obstinate silence of the protagonist following a traumatic experience is symbolic of a global rejection: renunciation of languages as a way of abolishing reality.

Different confutations of everyday existence are to be found in the metaphysical fables of Massimo Bontempelli: *La scacchiera davanti allo specchio* (1910; The Chess-Board in Front of the Mirror) and *Eva ultima* (1923; Last Eve). The fairy-tale candor of his prose can be contrasted with the darker enigmas of two other writers who drew directly from the sources of European fantastic narrative: Alberto Savinio and Tommaso Landolfi. Regardless of their individual differences they are presented together here for their intellectual and stylistic finesse, marked in both cases by transalpine experiences and influences (mostly French for the former, French and Russian for the latter). On both the fantastic and the realistic registers is the novelistic production of Dino Buzzati, whose sentimental report *Un amore* (1963; *A Love Affair*) contrasts with the Kafkaesque mythology of *Il deserto dei Tartari* (1941; *The Tartar Steppe*).

Still in the 1920s and 1930s, some authors paid belated homage to the 19th-century tradition: Riccardo Bacchelli's extensive epic *Il mulino del Po* (1937–40; *The Mill on the Po*) reflects the idealistic view of history as the realization of a rational spirit, while Federigo Tozzi constructs his old-fashioned novels, *Tre croci* (1920; *Three Crosses*) and *Il podere* (1821), around a single character, in which a whole regional culture is mirrored (with a touch of Dostoevskiian anxiety).

Like the unification of Italy, the advent of Fascism in 1923 did not prompt any relevant literary flourishing. Indirectly—or, rather, *a contrario*—it inspired the vitriolic satire of Benito Mussolini (and of any dictatorship) in *Eros e Priapo* (1967), by Carlo Emilio Gadda. Within the context of resistance—if not opposition to Fascism—can be viewed the main realistic trend of 20th-century Italian narrative.

The merciless, almost perverse, look at reality, with its biological driving forces of sex and greed—as apparent in the *caposcuola* Alberto Moravia (born Alberto Pincherle)—could be perceived as an underlying critique of the facile optimism heralded by the Fascist regime. Moravia himself lived in voluntary exile for the better part of 20 years, protected from political persecution by his literary renown, already achieved with his first novel *Gli indifferenti* (1929; *The Time of Indifference*), which had been hailed by such an influential critic as Georg Lukács.

A different denunciation of the dictatorship is to be found in the work of Secondo Tranquilli (better known by the pseudonym Ignazio Silone, adopted during his antifascist militancy). His first novel, *Fontamara* (literally "bitter spring," a place name in rural central Italy), was published anonymously in 1933 in Switzerland. The social and political accusation implicit in the realistic portrayal of a small peasant community exploited by landowners with Fascist support in *Una manciata di more* (1952; *A Handful of Blackberries*) developed into an evangelical judgment over the radical injustice of society and history in the later play *L'avventura di un povero cristiano* (1968; *The Story of a Humble Christian*), on the Dantean figure of Pope Celestino V. Another poignant report on the archaic life of rural southern Italy is *Cristo si è fermato a Eboli* (1945; *Christ Stopped at Eboli*) by the physician and painter Carlo Levi, who, born in Turin, was sentenced by the Fascist police to live in forced residence in Lucania.

Centered on the World War II years are two novels, *Kaputt* (1944), on the Nazi invasion of Poland and the Ukraine, and *La pelle* (1949; *The Skin*), on the moral degradation of Naples and Italy under American occupation (a Goyesque picture in which horror exists alongside the grotesque), by one of the eclipsed giants of 20th-century Italian narrative, Curzio Malaparte (born Kurt Suckert, of German father and Tuscan mother). Controversial and unorthodox (from his early exposé of the social injustices perpetrated during World War I in *La guerra dei santi maledetti* [The War of the Forsaken Saints]), regardless of his initial sympathy for the Fascist revolution (which he appreciated for its antibourgeois character), Malaparte kept his integrity throughout the turmoil of the Italian political scene: a virtue rarely forgiven, especially in times of heavy intellectual conformism, and usually punished with the conspiracy of silence. Other uncompromising documents of the horrors of war and persecution are Primo Levi's testimonies of the Holocaust: *Se questo è un uomo* (1947; *If This Is a Man*) and *La tregua* (1963; *The Truce*), in which the author is able to transcend the moral and historical judgment and convey a message of hope and humanism.

In other writers realism takes an interesting turn when it comes into contact with North American literature. Two authors, coming from two different parts of Italy, Cesare Pavese (Piedmont) and Elio Vittorini (Sicily), expanded their home landscapes to the limits of a universal, atemporal symbolism by means of a transfiguration that may be defined as "mythical realism." Pavese, a heedful reader of William Faulkner and a graceful translator of Daniel Defoe (*Moll Flanders*), Herman Melville (*Moby-Dick* and *Benito Cereno*), and James Joyce (*Dedalus*), transforms his homeland into a scene in which primordial, violent acts are iterated: in particular *La bella estate* (1949; *The Beautiful Summer*) and *La luna e i falò* (1950; *The Moon and the Bonfires*). Time, which is suspended in Pavese's stories, unfolds into a promise of utopian future in Elio Vittorini. His *Conversazione in Sicilia* (1938–39; *Conversation in Sicily*) creates a mythical aura within everyday life and present history, in which the protagonist embarks upon a quest for truth and lost humanity.

Writing as a civic and political act has been the lifelong commitment of another Sicilian writer, Leonardo Sciascia. From his early accusation of mafia (*Il giorno della civetta* [1961; *The Day of the Owl*]) to the perceptive probings into the connivance of mafia with the ruling political party, the Christian Democracy (*A ciascuno il suo* [1966; *To Each His Own*]), and down to the exposure of political compromise of any color (*Il contesto* [1971; *Equal Danger*]), Sciascia firmly and courageously pursues his secular and illuministic ideal of democracy.

Difficult to situate, in spite of his anti-romantic wit, is Carlo Emilio Gadda. After *La Madonna dei filosofi* (1931; The Madonna of the Philosophers) and *La cognizione del dolore* (1963; *Acquainted with Grief*), his masterpiece, *Quer pasticciaccio brutto de via Merulana* (*That Awful Mess in Via Meru-*

lana), first serialized in the journal *Letteratura* in 1946 and then published in book form in 1957, is a detective story that provides a subtle psychological study of its characters. The novel's outstanding feature, however, is its language: a concoction of Roman and other southern vernaculars, personal idiolects, and neologisms. The author demiurgically re-creates, with Rabelaisian liberty, a literary jargon whose main aim seems to be the reader's wonder: hence the Baroque element of his style. Although the lexical inventiveness may seem Joycean, Gadda's language has a more corporeal density that is reminiscent of the macaronic poetry of the Renaissance (or the kaleidoscopic exuberance of Francesco Colonna's *Hypnerotomachia Poliphili* [1499], a Grecian mythical flourishing that still enchanted Gerard de Nerval). A less distant paragon of his style is indicated in Vittorio Imbriani, a Neapolitan writer whose expressive vividness and popular jest takes deep roots in the local color and novelistic tradition of his fellow citizen of the 17th century, Giambattista Basile.

A different multilingualism is to be found in *Il Partigiano Johnny* (unfinished and published posthumously in 1968; *Johnny the Partisan*), a crucible of neologisms and American slang by the Piedmontese Beppe Fenoglio, who had already given an incisive account of a World War II episode in *I ventitre giorni della città di Alba* (1952; The Twenty-Three Days of the City of Alba).

War experiences are still central in Elsa Morante's *La storia* (1974; *History: A Novel*), in which the extensive apparatus of historical notes, appended to the already voluminous text, seem to champion the rights of fiction as the ultimate truth. Aside from the polemics it stirred, the novel stands as a powerful document of human drama, in which the redeeming force of compassion seems to be the only justification for the horrors of history. The intention to reach the largest possible audience (the author renounced her copyrights in order to keep the price of the book low) is emblematized in the epigraph "por el analfabeta a quien escribo" (for the illiterate I am writing to), taken from a line of the Peruvian poet César Vallejo.

The endemic realism of the Italian tradition unfolds into magic in Italo Calvino, one of the best established writers of the post–World War II period. Launched by Pavese in 1947 with his *Il sentiero dei nidi di ragno* (*The Path to the Nest of Spiders*), a novel still under the spell of neorealism, Calvino absorbed the tradition of Italian folktales, later explored in *Fiabe italiane* (1956; *Italian Folktales*), as well as the influence of contemporary fantastic short stories, (particularly the surrealism of Henri Michaux, whose *Ailleurs* (1948; Elsewhere) is echoed in *Le città invisibili* (1972; *Invisible Cities*). The author, however, was heedful of the philosophy of science in the collection of stories *Ti con zero* (1967; *T Zero*) and *Palomar* (1983; *Mr. Palomar*), semiotics in *Il castello dei destini incrociati* (1973; *The Castle of Crossed Destinies*), and *rezeptionstheorie* in *Se una notte d'inverno un viaggiatore* (1979; *If on a winter's night a traveler*). With his extensive production, crowned by his superb—and, regrettably, unfinished—*Lezioni americane* (1988; *Six Memos for the Next Millennium*), Calvino remains a central figure in the literary scene of postwar Italy, both as an influential editor in the Einaudi publishing house and as a sharp and unprovincial intellectual.

MASSIMO MANDOLINI PESARESI

See also Adventures of Pinocchio; Italo Calvino; Confessions of Zeno; Carlo Emilio Gadda; Johnny the Partisan; Leopard; Alessandro Manzoni; Alberto Moravia; Giovanni Verga

Further Reading

Agamben, Giorgio, et al., *Per Elsa Morante,* Milan: Linea d'ombra, 1993

Asor Rosa, Alberto, editor, *Letteratura italiana,* volume 3: *Le forme del testo,* part 2, *La Prosa,* Torino: Einaudi, 1984

Baranski, Zygmunt, and Lino Pertile, editors, *The New Italian Novel,* Edinburgh: Edinburgh University Press, 1993

Brand, Peter, and Lino Pertile, editors, *The Cambridge History of Italian Literature,* Cambridge and New York: Cambridge University Press, 1996

Brioschi, Franco, and Costanzo Di Girolamo, *Manuale di letteratura italiana: Storia per generi e problemi,* volume 3: *Dalla metà del Settecento all'Unità d'Italia,* and volume 4: *Dall'Unità d'Italia alla fine del Novecento,* Torino: Bollati-Boringhieri, 1995–96

Caesar, Michael, and Peter Hainsworth, *Writers and Society in Contemporary Italy,* New York: St. Martin's Press, and Leamington Spa: Berg, 1984

Cambon, Glauco, editor, *Pirandello: A Collection of Critical Essays,* Englewood Cliffs, New Jersey: Prentice-Hall, 1967

Contini, Gianfranco, *Quarant'anni d'amicizia: Scritti su Carlo Emilio Gadda,* Torino: Einaudi, 1989

Dombroski, Robert S., *L'apologia del vero: Lettura e interpretazione dei "Promessi sposi,"* Padua: Liviana, 1984

Dombroski, Robert S., *Properties of Writing: Ideological Discourse in Modern Italian Fiction,* Baltimore: Johns Hopkins University Press, 1994

Farrell, Joseph, *Leonardo Sciascia,* Edinburgh: Edinburgh University Press, 1995

Fubini, Mario, *Romanticismo italiano: Saggi di storia della critica e della letteratura,* Bari: Laterza, 1953; 2nd edition, 1971

Gatt-Rutter, John, *Italo Svevo: A Double Life,* Oxford: Clarendon Press, and New York: Oxford University Press, 1988

Gioanola, Elio, *La letteratura italiana,* Milan: LIBREX, 1985

Harris, MacDonald, *Three Italian Novelists: Moravia, Pavese, Vittorini,* Ann Arbor: University of Michigan Press, 1968

Hume, Kathryn, *Calvino's Fictions: Cogito and Cosmos,* Oxford: Clarendon Press, and New York: Oxford University Press, 1992

Lucente, Gregory L., *The Narrative of Realism and Myth: Verga, Lawrence, Faulkner, Pavese,* Baltimore: Johns Hopkins University Press, 1981

Lucente, Gregory L., *Beautiful Fables: Self-Consciousness in Italian Narrative from Manzoni to Calvino,* Baltimore: Johns Hopkins University Press, 1986

Pacifici, Sergio, *The Modern Italian Novel from Capuana to Tozzi,* Carbondale: Southern Illinois University Press, and London: Feffer and Simons, 1973

Raimondi, Ezio, *Il romanzo senza idillio: Saggio sui "Promessi sposi,"* Torino: Einaudi, 1974

Valesio, Paolo, *Gabriele D'Annunzio: The Dark Flame,* New Haven, Connecticut: Yale University Press, 1992

Wlassics, Tibor, *Pavese falso e vero: Vita, poetica, narrativa,* Torino: Centro Studi Piemontesi, 1985

Wood, Sharon, *Italian Women's Writing, 1860–1994,* London and Atlantic Highlands, New Jersey: Athlone Press, 1995

Ivanhoe by Sir Walter Scott

1819

Walter Scott was still "the Great Unknown," the anonymous author of nine popular novels about the Scottish experience of assimilation and modernization within the British Empire, when he published *Ivanhoe: A Romance* in December 1819. This tale of chivalry, derring-do, and the emergence of "England" from Saxon/Norman conflict in the age of Richard the Lion-Hearted sold like hotcakes, made the author's regional fame international, and established a certain kind of "historicism" as foundational for the 19th-century English novel.

The novel was published four months after the Peterloo massacre, a clash between angry workers from Manchester and the local yeomanry. In light of such events, *Ivanhoe* has struck some readers as an exercise in nostalgia, a diversion from the contemporaneous history unfolding at Peterloo, as well as a reproach to the myriad dislocations of the agricultural and industrial revolutions. But *Ivanhoe* is more complex than that. A fiction of origins for the contemporary English reader, its lure resides in the location of its narrative within a history of "progress." This oblique commentary is implied by the plotting, which values people of moderate and tolerant political and psychological cast, no matter how confused and repressed they may be, and leaves behind, with some reluctance, people of intense and brilliant but "antique" politics and feelings.

After *Ivanhoe,* the historical novel blossomed into the huge mass-cultural phenomenon it remains to this day. Moreover, while mainstream novelists like Charles Dickens, William Makepeace Thackeray, and George Eliot would occasionally write a specifically historical novel, they would now always write historicist novels in the realist tradition—stories that live urgently in their own times as "history" but mute the more revolutionary impulses of their times. Locating the present toward the end of a history representing a long climb from barbarism to civilization, the 19th-century novel after Scott disarms the radical implications of its social criticism with the notion of historical progress.

Ivanhoe marked, in some respects, the beginning of Scott's third writing career. He was first drawn to the medieval and the Gothic as a collector of Scottish ballads, translator of European Gothic, popular poet, and dramatist. A lawyer and historian, a Scottish patriot, and a rising member of the Lowlands middle class, Scott moved closer to his own history and began a second career with the novel *Waverley* (1814), set two generations back. He followed it up with eight more tales in which young Scottish people ponder a proud, risk-taking, God-haunted Celtic and Stewart past, eye an ambiguously English-dominated and compromising (but rational and fertile) present, and choose the latter. The novels follow the format of the Bildungsroman through key images and conflicts. *Ivanhoe* then applied that model to medieval English history and, through that, to the whole of Western history.

In the Scottish novels, the "matter of history" is filtered through dramas of exile and compromised inheritance. Ancient Scottish and sometimes English houses seek renewed lives through what Alexander Welsh (1963) called "romances of property," the devious conservation of lands, goods, ideals, and identity itself amid whirlwinds of change in governments, religions, and nations, as well as revolutions in value and character. A sometimes surprising scrutiny of the simultaneous persistence and fragility of standard racial, national, and gender categories is the result.

Ivanhoe reframes this regional drama in the global perspective of the crusades. In the brilliant tournaments and games of the first part of the novel and the Sherwood Forest battles and sieges of the second part, Saxon knights confront their Norman counterparts in a continuation of the 100-year effort to throw off "the Norman yoke." But the novel teaches the reader that, in the necessary cauldron of the Palestinian war, the Norman Richard and the Saxon Wilfrid of Ivanhoe have been remade as "English." The Saxon "resistance" has stalemated between the comically sluggish royal Athelstane ("the Unready") and the comically volatile Cedric of Ivanhoe (compared to Shakespeare's Hotspur). The situation is transformed at the siege of Norman Torquilstone Castle by the presence of the newly Englished Richard and Ivanhoe.

"The English" is a new national mixture, which needs not only components that can be assimilated but also those that resist assimilation, as a foil to define itself against. *Ivanhoe's* special place in the canon of the English novel comes from its evocation of two steadfastly unassimilable figures, Isaac the Jew and his daughter Rebecca. Michael Ragussis (1993) argues that Scott's Isaac restaged for the guilty English conscience of 1819 both the nation's medieval persecution of Jews and its Enlightenment evangelical project of Jewish conversion. The novel critiques the barbarity of persecution and forced conversion in an effort to purify the English democratic virtue of "tolerance," a process at work throughout 19th-century narrative.

Rebecca resembles the Celtic dark ladies of the Scottish novels, the Flora MacIvors and Minna Troils, in being more active than her fair counterpart, more active even than the conflicted and self-repressed male protagonist. She is a proper candidate for the tournament's title "Queen of Love and Beauty." She is a healer and a voice of moderation between Saxon and Norman glory-hounds at the siege of Torquilstone. She is both prey and prize at the novel's final battle between the corrupt religious cosmopolitans of the Order of Templars, who have condemned her to death as a Jew and/or a witch, and the newly constituted and tolerant "English," who arrive to rescue her.

Like the Celtic dark ladies, she attracts the protagonist but is ultimately not for him—because, unlike them, she and her way of life are not dissolving into the new race. Compellingly "other," standing fast (if standing aside), Rebecca is and was from her first appearance the most popular of Scott's characters. Ina Ferris (1991) calls her the reason why *Ivanhoe* is "the canonical moment" in Scott, because for early 19th-century readers she was the rational, fully realized, but rejectable female "other" who guaranteed the "manliness" and "health" of the reading experience; because for late 19th-century readers she was the fantasy female who makes all the novels of Scott enjoyably dismissable as boys' adventure books; because the mixture of antiquarian Tory resistance, decent Christian liberal guilt, and male desire that went into her making render her particularly available to a late 20th-century multi-theoretical analysis.

JUDITH WILT

See also Sir Walter Scott

Further Reading

Duncan, Ian, *Modern Romance and Transformations of the Novel: The Gothic, Scott, and Dickens,* Cambridge and New York: Cambridge University Press, 1992

Ferris, Ina, *The Achievement of Literary Authority: Gender, History, and the Waverley Novels,* Ithaca, New York: Cornell University Press, 1991

Millgate, Jane, *Walter Scott: The Making of a Novelist,* Edinburgh: Edinburgh University Press, and Toronto and Buffalo, New York: University of Toronto Press, 1984

Ragussis, Michael, "Writing Nationalist History: England, the Conversion of the Jews, and *Ivanhoe,*" *English Literary History* 60:1 (Spring 1993)

Vanden Bossche, Chris R., "Culture and Economy in *Ivanhoe,*" *Nineteenth Century Literature* 42:1 (June 1987)

Welsh, Alexander, *The Hero of the Waverley Novels,* New Haven, Connecticut: Yale University Press, 1963; expanded edition, Princeton, New Jersey: Princeton University Press, 1992

Wilt, Judith, *Secret Leaves: The Novels of Walter Scott,* Chicago: University of Chicago Press, 1985

J

Jalousie. *See* Jealousy

Henry James 1843–1916

American/English

Henry James' place in the history of the novel is both central and transitional. Working from the novel of manners of Samuel Richardson and Jane Austen, James mediated between realism and the impressionism and formal experimentation of the modern and postmodern novel. He claimed for the novel the highest aesthetic, philosophical, and ethical importance, and his criticism is foundational for Anglo-American novel theory. A permanent expatriate who died a British subject, James was a cosmopolitan writer influenced by his precursors Ivan Turgenev, Honoré de Balzac, Émile Zola, Charles Dickens, and George Eliot, as well as Nathaniel Hawthorne. James also wrote short fiction, plays, autobiography, biography, travel literature, and literary and cultural criticism.

In their rich social and psychological observation, James' early novels are recognizable descendents of the European realists. Yet they also accommodate elements of romance and melodrama. *Roderick Hudson* (1875), whose plot of American artists in Italy is borrowed from Hawthorne's *The Marble Faun* (1860), overtly rehearses James' anxiety of influence vis-à-vis Hawthorne. The novel inaugurates what James called the reflector or center of consciousness, the third-person narrative that focalizes point of view through one character's mind. In part a reaction to the Victorian omniscient narrator, the reflector courts a deliberate impressionism. As the preface to *The Princess Casamassima* (1886) states, "The figures in any picture, the agents in any drama, are interesting only in proportion as they feel their respective situations. . . . Their being finely aware—as Hamlet and Lear, say, are finely aware—*makes* absolutely the intensity of their adventure, gives the maximum of sense to what befalls them."

The American (1877), like *Roderick Hudson,* uneasily mixes realism and melodrama and introduces central Jamesian themes of collectorship, spectatorship, vicariousness, and objectification. *The Portrait of a Lady* (1881), James' realist masterpiece, is a tragic marriage novel that recalls Eliot's *Middlemarch* (1872) and *Daniel Deronda* (1876). In this work James elevates the central consciousness from a technical device into an aesthetic and phenomenological principle. Isabel Archer is at once the novel's reflector, its formal and conceptual center, and its originating "germ." This formalist conceptualization is typically Jamesian as is his emphasis on the inextricability of character from plot. Thus James notes that Isabel's "vigil of searching criticism, a representation simply of her motionlessly *seeing*" the tragic consequences of her choices "throws the action further forward than twenty 'incidents' might have done."

James' realist novels of the 1880s depict a larger social and political canvas. Hyacinth Robinson, the central reflector of *The Princess Casamassima,* is fatally divided between the imperatives of art and politics. With its indebtedness to Turgenev's *Nov'* (1877; *Virgin Soil*), its Zolaesque and Dickensian prison scenes, and its deterministic overtones, *The Princess Casamassima* is James' most naturalistic novel. *The Bostonians* (1886) playfully satirizes the suffrage and New England reform movements. *The Tragic Muse* (1890) revisits the conflict between aesthetics and politics that had structured *The Princess Casamassima* and, with its actress protagonist, thematically anticipates James' formal interest in drama.

Largely for financial reasons (the reception of *The Princess Casamassima* and *The Bostonians* had been critically and commercially disappointing), James attempted a career as a dramatist during the early 1890s. Doomed to failure by the gap between his belief in the drama's aesthetic potential and the commercial demands of the theatre, which he held in contempt, his theatrical career came to a humiliating end when he was booed off the stage following the opening-night performance of *Guy Domville* in 1895. James was devastated, but he was determined thereafter to apply to the novel the dramatic techniques he had developed, and these innovations shaped his fiction to the end of the century. The resulting "scenic method" aspires to a tight, play-like construction and privileges dialogue over exposition. His major scenic novels are *The Spoils of Poynton* (1897), *What Maisie Knew* (1897), and *The Awkward Age* (1899). Although the scenic method's emphasis on dialogue might seem antithetical to his notion of reflector, its foreshortening effect was suited to James' desire to represent dramas of consciousness. Thus *What Maisie Knew*, James' most rigorous deployment of the reflector, modulates midway into a scenic dialogue novel. In fact, the reflector's restriction of perspective is more an ideal than a consistent practice; even the scenic novels tend to invoke a hypothetical observer much like an omniscient narrator. (And as Julie Rivkin points out [1996], the reflector's claim to ground or center its narratives is contradicted by the substitutive or displaced structure that designates the reflector as authorial delegate.)

The last work of this experimental period is *The Sacred Fount* (1901), often read as a self-parodic allegory of the problematics of Jamesian representation. With its unreliable narrator, its alienated and paranoid feel, and its foregrounded indeterminacy, *The Sacred Fount* forshadows the *nouveau roman* and the modernist and postmodernist novel. Like the novellas *The Aspern Papers* (1888) and *The Turn of the Screw* (1898), *The Sacred Fount* is a rare exception to James' general avoidance of first-person narrative in full-length works. As William R. Goetz has argued (1986), James saw long, first-person narrative as formally and epistemologically unstable, "foredoomed to looseness." In his view, the Victorian narrator's first-person intrusions destroyed the novelist's *locus standi*, the very ground or backbone of representation. James' first-person narratives are self-reflexively preoccupied with the hermeneutic perplexity of their narrators, who are typically mystified or mad.

James' late masterpieces—*The Wings of the Dove* (1902), *The Ambassadors* (1903), and *The Golden Bowl* (1904)—return to his early international theme of Americans in Europe, although the thematic structure contrasting American innocence to European worldliness or corruption is increasingly nuanced. His late work is notable for its formal and linguistic experimentation, which presages Virginia Woolf and James Joyce in its preoccupation with point of view, its modernist attenuation of plot and realistic setting, and its cultivation of ambiguity. In a letter to his brother, the pyschologist and religious philosopher William James voiced a remark that reflects the unappreciative public reception of Henry James' work (which never again saw the popularity of the best-selling novella *Daisy Miller*, 1878): William complained of *The Wings of the Dove* that Henry had "reversed every traditional canon of storytelling (especially the fundamental one of *telling* the story, which you carefully avoid)." As William's complaint registers, James had both redefined the novel's object of representation as internal and developed a radically figurative style that tended to delay or suspend reference. His late style is given to abstraction, complex periodic sentences, proliferating qualification and circumlocution, reworked cliché, elliptical

and stichomythic dialogue, and elaborately developed metaphor. Elements of his work anticipate interior monologue and stream of consciousness (the latter term coined by William James).

Although it was a commercial failure, the magisterial New York edition of James' works published by Scribner (1907–09) is now understood as the capstone of his career. James selected and extensively revised the included works and composed retrospective prefaces to introduce the originally envisioned 18 volumes of novels and tales. Collected in 1934 as *The Art of the Novel*, the prefaces proved seminal to Anglo-American novel theory. Such key Jamesian terms as *picture, scene, dramatic, panoramic, foreshortening*—his conceptual metaphors are drawn equally from theatre and the visual arts—have become staples of formal and rhetorical criticism. (On the diverse legacy of James' critical writings, see the essays by Sarah B. Daugherty, Daniel R. Schwarz, and Thomas M. Leitch in *A Companion to Henry James Studies*, edited by Daniel Mark Fogel.) Ranging from personal anecdote to theoretical speculation, the prefaces are intertextually allusive (both to James' own and to other texts), figuratively dense, and heterogeneous in their implications. For example, their organicist aesthetic likening the artwork to a natural object links James to the New Criticism. Yet their recognition of the inevitable discrepancy between intention and realization and James' assertion in the preface to *The Golden Bowl* that "deviations and differences" were "my very terms of cognition" link James to the linguistic and philosophical insights of Ferdinand de Saussure and Jacques Derrida. Other major essays include the 1879 critical biography *Hawthorne*, "The Art of Fiction" (1884), "The Science of Criticism" (1891), and "The Future of the Novel" (1899). James' letters and notebooks afford fascinating glimpses into his creative process and the evolution of individual works.

In 1864 James lamented "the absence of any critical treatise upon fiction" and called for "some attempt to codify the vague and desultory canons, which cannot, indeed, be said to govern, but which in some measure define" the novel. His critical writings fulfill this aspiration, even as his fiction upholds his claims for the novel's formal and philosophical value. One sees the imprint of this remarkable double achievement in the works of novelists as different as Joseph Conrad, Virginia Woolf, Edith Wharton, James Joyce, and Rebeccca West.

SHEILA TEAHAN

See also Ambassadors; Golden Bowl; Portrait of a Lady

Biography

Born 15 April 1843 in New York City; brother of the philosopher William James. Attended Richard Pulling Jenks School, New York; traveled in Europe with his family from an early age: studied with tutors in Geneva, London, Paris, and Boulogne, 1855–58, Geneva, 1859, and Bonn, 1860; lived with his family in Newport, Rhode Island, 1860–62; attended Harvard Law School, Cambridge, Massachusetts, 1862–63. Lived with his family in Cambridge and wrote for *Nation* and *Atlantic Monthly*, 1866–69; traveled in Europe, 1869–70; returned to Cambridge, 1870–72; art critic, *Atlantic Monthly*, 1871–72; lived in Europe, 1872–74, Cambridge, 1875, and Paris, 1875–76; writer for New York *Tribune*, Paris, 1875–76; moved to London, 1876, and lived in England thereafter;

settled in Rye, Sussex, 1896; toured the United States, 1904–05; became British citizen, 1915. Died 28 February 1916.

Major Novels by James

Roderick Hudson, 1875
The American, 1877
Watch and Ward, 1878
The Europeans: A Sketch, 1878
Daisy Miller: A Study, 1878
Confidence, 1879
Washington Square, 1881
The Portrait of a Lady, 1881
The Bostonians, 1886
The Princess Casamassima, 1886
The Aspern Papers, 1888
The Reverberator, 1888
The Tragic Muse, 1890
The Other House, 1896
The Spoils of Poynton, 1897
What Maisie Knew, 1897
In the Cage, 1898
The Turn of the Screw, 1898
The Awkward Age, 1899
The Sacred Fount, 1901
The Wings of the Dove, 1902
The Ambassadors, 1903
The Golden Bowl, 1904
The Ivory Tower, 1917 (unfinished)
The Sense of the Past, 1917 (unfinished)

Other Writings: short stories, novellas, letters; notebooks, collected in *The Complete Notebooks of Henry James,* edited by Leon Edel and Lyall H. Powers, 1987; literary criticism, gathered in *Henry James, Literary Criticism,* 2 vols., edited by Leon Edel, 1984.

Further Reading

Bell, Millicent, *Meaning in Henry James,* Cambridge, Massachusetts: Harvard University Press, 1991
Brodhead, Richard H., *The School of Hawthorne,* New York and Oxford: Oxford University Press, 1986
Fogel, Daniel Mark, *Covert Relations: James Joyce, Virginia Woolf, and Henry James,* Charlottesville: University Press of Virginia, 1990
Fogel, Daniel Mark, editor, *A Companion to Henry James Studies,* Westport, Connecticut: Greenwood Press, 1993
Goetz, William R., *Henry James and the Darkest Abyss of Romance,* Baton Rouge: Louisiana State University Press, 1986
Grover, Philip, *Henry James and the French Novel: A Study in Inspiration,* London: Elek, and New York: Barnes and Noble, 1973
McWhirter, David, editor, *Henry James's New York Edition: The Construction of Authorship,* Stanford, California: Stanford University Press, 1995
Perosa, Sergio, *Henry James and the Experimental Novel,* Charlottesville: University Press of Virginia, 1978
Powers, Lyall, *Henry James and the Naturalist Movement,* East Lansing: Michigan State University Press, 1971
Rivkin, Julie, *False Positions: The Representational Logics of Henry James' Fictions,* Stanford, California: Stanford University Press, 1996
Rowe, John Carlos, *The Theoretical Dimensions of Henry James,* Madison: University of Wisconsin Press, 1984; London: Methuen, 1985
Stowe, William W., *Balzac, James, and the Realistic Novel,* Princeton, New Jersey: Princeton University Press, 1983

Jane Eyre by Charlotte Brontë

1847

After Charlotte Brontë's failure to secure a publisher for her first novel, *The Professor* (published posthumously in 1857), she took to heart the critical comments on its "want of varied interest" when completing her second and most well-known novel, *Jane Eyre*. Its immediate and continued success, even notoriety, allowed Brontë the freedom to explore her creative impulses in her third and fourth novels, *Shirley* (1849) and *Villette* (1853), which some critics have found more satisfying in terms of their complexity and profundity.

If *Jane Eyre* bears the marks of Brontë's response to commercial pressures, its unique use of the conventions and features of the novel genre is apparent in a number of ways. Most readers find that the sympathetic and gritty depiction of the orphan Jane's violent and abusive childhood may be compared favorably to other portrayals of children in the works of novelists like Charles Dickens. Jane is not merely a vehicle for social commentary, and she does not embody romantic notions of innocence. She is deliberately contrasted with the character Helen Burns, who serves both those purposes and whose passive acceptance of suffering and philosophy of unworldly resignation differ from Jane's healthy self-interest and rebellious questioning of rules and conventions. This contrast creates an ironic commentary on religious hypocrisy at Lowood school; inflexible religious posturing remains a target elsewhere in the novel, for example, in the portrayal of St. John Rivers.

As an adult heroine, Jane is equally unconventional, being plain, poor, and forced to earn her own living as a governess. The novel severely criticizes the limited options open to educated but impoverished women and examines some of the bitter experiences of social exclusion of the governess class. In many other ways, *Jane Eyre* is frank and controversial for the period in its portrayal of femininity. Perhaps the clearest statement of what could be described as a protofeminist position is the comment that "women feel just as men feel," which, in its resistance to an ideology of separate spheres of emotional as well as practical experience, would have been extremely unsettling for the conventional Victorian reader. The novel is also particularly open in its description of Jane's romantic feelings for the gloomy Byronic hero, Mr. Rochester. As her employer, Rochester holds a position of power over Jane, but Brontë's clear emphasis on Jane's sense of self-worth appears in both her teasing banter with Rochester and in her refusal to become his mistress when his first wife's existence is uncovered.

Jane's discovery at the altar that Rochester has an insane wife hidden in the attic is the solution to one of the greatest mysteries of the novel genre and displays Brontë's controlled use of a number of popular techniques, conventions, and genres such as suspense, the Gothic, the supernatural, and the fairy tale. Jane's mysterious dreams and portents before her wedding day, the horrific laughter audible from the dark and oppressive third floor of Thornfield Hall, and Rochester's brooding, guilty silences all serve not merely to maintain the reader's interest in the text but also to create a new and serious exploration of feminine identity. As critics Sandra Gilbert and Susan Gubar (1979) have argued, Bertha Mason, Rochester's Creole wife, who is pictured as the embodiment of madness, demoniacal strength, uncivilized aggression and emotion, and racial impurity, can be seen to represent all the transgressive, subversive impulses in Jane herself. As Jane's double, Bertha suggests both the deliberately fractured portrayal of the feminine self in the text and the existence of a subversive pressure against the realist surface of the novel.

The reader's enjoyment of *Jane Eyre*'s exploration of femininity is assured by the use of first-person retrospective narration. Jane's voice leads the reader through her trials in a way that encourages empathy with her situation. As William Makepeace Thackeray remarked on reading the novel, "We forgot both commendations and criticism, identified ourselves with Jane in all our troubles, and finally married Mr. Rochester about four in the morning." As a mock autobiography, *Jane Eyre* joins a long tradition of memoirs, but its credible and informal tone may obscure its formal and allegorical complexity, as Jane progresses, in the manner of a pilgrim, on her journey from the appropriately named Gateshead to Lowood to Thornfield to Moor House to Ferndean. Her acquisition of relatives and an inheritance before her return to the now-powerless Rochester—maimed and blinded while attempting to save Bertha from a fire—have caused many to remark on the concluding ambivalence behind the apparently confident assertion, "Reader, I married him." Jane returns as Rochester's equal, at least.

The novel was an immediate commercial success, or rather, a *succès de scandale*. Reviewers speculated about the identity, and particularly the gender, of the author, who had hidden behind the ambiguous pseudonym Currer Bell. Some believed that aspects of theme and language clearly suggested a male author. Others guessed that the authors of *Jane Eyre* and *Wuthering Heights* were the same person. With the publication of Elizabeth Gaskell's 1857 biography of Charlotte, the Brontë myth began to develop around the three sisters. This had three important effects on the reception of the novel, which are still influential: the first emphasized the autobiographical aspects of the text at the expense of its innovative complexity; the second harnessed the critical reputations of the Brontë sisters; and the third overemphasized the extent of the Brontës' isolation in the drab and wild northern Yorkshire town of Haworth. As a result, the critical fortunes of *Jane Eyre* have often been linked to *Wuthering Heights*. Initially, the latter had to be explained and defended by Charlotte to secure a readership, but when New Criticism began to dominate literary scholarship during the first half of the 20th century, *Jane Eyre* was perceived as inferior to *Wuthering Heights* in terms of complexity. As F.R. Leavis wrote in *The Great Tradition* (1948), "It is tempting to retort that there is only one Brontë . . . the genius, of course, was Emily." However, since the explosion of interest in feminist criticism of literature, *Jane Eyre* has regained its justified share of critical attention.

The impact of *Jane Eyre* on the novel genre has been immense. One obvious derivative is the popular romantic fiction of the bodice-ripping variety; more interesting parallels are apparent in Daphne du Maurier's *Rebecca* (1938) and Jean Rhys' *Wide Sargasso Sea* (1966), which explore some of the colonialist implications of the novel by telling the story of Rochester's ill-fated Creole wife. Such direct allusions to the novel testify to its lasting power to stir, puzzle, and provoke its readers.

SUSAN WATKINS

See also Charlotte Brontë

Further Reading

Barker, Juliet, *The Brontës*, London: Weidenfeld and Nicolson, 1994; New York: St. Martin's Press, 1995

Boumelha, Penny, *Charlotte Brontë*, London: Harvester Wheatsheaf, and Bloomington: Indiana University Press, 1990

Burkhart, Charles, *Charlotte Brontë: A Psychosexual Study of Her Novels*, London: Gollancz, 1973

Eagleton, Terry, *Myths of Power: A Marxist Study of the Brontës*, London: Macmillan, and New York: Barnes and Noble, 1975; 2nd edition, London: Macmillan, 1988

Ewbank, Inga Stina, *Their Proper Sphere: A Study of the Brontë Sisters as Early Victorian Female Novelists*, London: Arnold, and Cambridge, Massachusetts: Harvard University Press, 1966

Gezari, Janet, *Charlotte Brontë and Defensive Conduct: The Author and the Body at Risk*, Philadelphia: University of Pennsylvania Press, 1992

Gilbert, Sandra, and Susan Gubar, *The Madwoman in the Attic: The Woman Writer and the Nineteenth-Century Literary Imagination*, New Haven, Connecticut, and London: Yale University Press, 1979

Martin, Robert Bernard, *The Accents of Persuasion: Charlotte Brontë's Novels*, London: Faber, and New York: Norton, 1966

Maynard, John, *Charlotte Brontë and Sexuality*, Cambridge and New York: Cambridge University Press, 1984

Shuttleworth, Sally, *Charlotte Brontë and Victorian Psychology*, Cambridge and New York: Cambridge University Press, 1996

Japanese Novel

The critic Miyoshi Masao has warned of the dangers, in considering the literary contribution of countries such as Japan, of exaggerating the familiar aspects of a text and thereby obscuring the ways it stands out against, or even resists, the traditions of first-world literature. On the other hand, lacking a truly epic tradition, Japanese fictional narratives are all too readily dismissed in terms of their "exoticism" or "lyricism" (see Miyoshi, 1974). Unless we seek to understand Japanese texts in terms of their inherent dynamics rather than in comparison with Western literature, the critical shibboleths about the Japanese novel will remain uncontested. However, it is difficult to avoid establishing the Western novel as an initial point of reference. If we accept Ian Watt's conclusion, in *The Rise of the Novel* (1957), that it was "the rise of individual autonomy and serendipitous relationships" that "paved the way for the development of modern fiction in the West," then it is hard to disagree with Edward Fowler's assertion of a central difference between the Western and Japanese traditions, given that the Japanese "have been less convinced of (we might even say they have been uninterested in) the self's tangibility or value, even after their massive exposure to western civilization in the Meiji period" from 1868 to 1912 (see Fowler, 1988).

Moreover, it was only with the arrival of Western fiction, when Japan reopened its doors to outside influence after two and a half centuries of almost total isolation, that full-length novels with a unity and clear structure emerged in Japan. Early Meiji critics coined the term *shōsetsu* to designate this burgeoning form. Literally meaning "telling tales," the term was a Japanese rendering of the Chinese *hsaio-shuo*, referring to the unofficial histories and other popular, loosely historical accounts written in the vernacular. The term thus carried a stigma: here was a branch of "nonserious" literature that, in contrast to poetry and the formal essay, rarely led to fame and social prestige.

The *shōsetsu* is a much broader category than the novel, including narratives that use the techniques of the essay, diary, confession, and other nonfiction forms. Subsequent generations sought to elevate the *shōsetsu* to the realm of "refined," as opposed to "vulgar," literature by downplaying invention and insisting that the narratives are true to the author's life experience. Developing in the opposite direction from the realist novel, in which "a credible fabrication is yet constantly held up as false," the *shōsetsu* represents "an incredible fabrication that is nevertheless constantly held up as truthful" (see Miyoshi, 1974). Here is an art form that discounts its own artfulness and holds up honesty and sincerity for intense scrutiny.

This survey of the novel form in Japan, therefore, will include consideration of texts not readily identifiable as fiction by Western standards, and it must start with the various premodern narrative strands that formed the building blocks of the *shōsetsu*.

The first two examples of written Japanese literature emerged in the eighth century: *Kojiki* (712; A Record of Ancient Matters) and *Nihongi* (720; Chronicles of Ancient Japan). They represent the first authorized accounts of the emergence of the Japanese nation. Important for their historical content, they were equally significant in terms of their linguistic contribution. *Kojiki* uses Chinese characters as phonetic symbols to represent Japanese words, while *Nihongi* makes fuller use of the richness of the Chinese literary tradition.

Compiled shortly after the creation of the first permanent capital in Nara, *Kojiki* and *Nihongi* were followed by the first imperial anthology of poetry, *Man'yōshū* (c. 760; *The Ten Thousand Leaves*), a work of great variety that also made an important contribution to the creation of a linguistic medium appropriate to the prose narrative tradition. *The Ten Thousand Leaves* developed the *man'yōgana*, a more rationalized and systematic use of Chinese characters for their phonetic value, which was subsequently simplified into the *hiragana* and *katakana* syllabaries. Initially used in poetry, *hiragana* was first deployed in extended prose form by Ki no Tsurayuki in the preface to the *Kokinshū* (*A Collection of Poems Ancient and Modern*), an anthology of the early tenth century. However, the tradition of Chinese as the language of learning persisted for several centuries and use of *hiragana* was largely restricted to female writers and male authors writing under a female pseudonym, as in the case of Ki no Tsurayuki's own *Tosa nikki* (935; *The Tosa Diary*).

By this time, the imperial court was firmly established in the new capital of Heian-kyō, and the majority of the prose literature of this period (794–1185) took the form of the *nikki* (literary diary), in which the world of the court assumes center stage. A prime example of this genre is the *Kagerō nikki* (late tenth century; *The Gossamer Years*), a psychologically interesting work often cited as the first text of social realism in Japan. At the same time, the first tentative steps toward fictional narrative were being taken in *Taketori monogatari* (c. 920; *The Tale of the Bamboo Cutter*), a work rich in Chinese influence but Japanese in style, usually cited as pioneer of the *monogatari* (tale) form. Within decades, the *monogatari* was firmly established and achieved an increasingly complex interplay between poetic and prose sections. With *Ise monogatari* (mid–tenth century; *The Tales of Ise*) came the model for the "poetry with prose contexts" genre that was to remain predominant for several centuries. Highly episodic, *Ise* consists of 125 isolated vignettes that suggest aspects of the life of a popular courtier but remain far from a biographical portrait. Each section includes at least one *waka* poem, while the prose passages are often little more than poetic commentary or description of the circumstances of composition. *The Tales of Ise* stimulated the development of the *zuihitsu* (random jottings). Exemplified by Sei Shōnagon's *Makura no sōshi* (c. 1000; *The Pillow Book*), such works tend to focus on four types of content: lists, eyewitness accounts, stories the author wishes to pass on, and short fictional sketches.

More significant for a discussion of the development of the Japanese novel is *Genji monogatari* (early 11th century; *The Tale of Genji*), which is the epitome of the courtly genres of the 10th and 11th centuries. By any measure, *Genji* represents a critical benchmark by which to assess subsequent Japanese fiction. In the insights it offers into Heian society and its use of language—in which the conjunction of Chinese characters with the phonetic *hiragana* is more sophisticated than in earlier texts—the work was highly influential in establishing the domain for the prose narrative in Japanese letters.

One other literary development of the era had far-reaching repercussions on subsequent trends: the *setsuwa*, moralistic tales, usually with Buddhist overtones and culled from the Indian, Chinese, and Japanese oral traditions. Going as far back as the ninth-century *Nihon ryōiki* (822; *Miraculous Stories*), they showed, through purportedly true examples, how good and evil deeds are invariably rewarded and punished in this and future lives. The tradition is epitomized by *Konjaku monogatari* (*Tales of Times Now Past*), an early 12th-century collection of down-to-earth tales ranging from the didactic to the humorous.

The fall of the Heian court and the emergence of the first shogunate located in Kamakura in the late 12th century brought with it a clear division between cultural and military responsibilities. The court remained the arbiter of good taste and form, leaving the emerging warrior class to develop new media to record their own experiences. The resulting *gunki monogatari* (war tales) focus on deeds of valor and military prowess, and the *Heike monogatari* (12th century; *Tales of the Heike*), the epitome of the genre, approximates the Western epic tradition in terms of scope and thematic unity. Nevertheless, the work remains episodic, largely in consequence of decades of oral recitation, traditionally by blind itinerant monks, before they were written down.

In these and the works that continued to emerge from the court, there is an intellectual and spiritual depth that clearly reflects a continued preoccupation with Buddhist concerns. At the same time, a new literary style, the *wakan konkōbun*, came to perfection and spawned a new form of popular fiction, the *otogi zōshi* (companion or entertainment booklets). Born of the oral tradition, they highlight the extent to which dissemination of popular literature had progressed even before the introduction of woodblock printing.

With the exception of the *nikki* form and two oft-cited *zuihitsu*, *Hōjōki* (1212; *An Account of My Hut*) and *Tsurezuregusa* (c. 1330; *Essays in Idleness*), the courtly literary tradition reflected waning imperial fortunes. With the arrival in 1600 of the Tokugawa shogunate in Edo, however, a new urban culture rapidly emerged, and this, combined with the development of woodblock (*hanga*) printing techniques, led to the popularization of literature in the form of *kanazōshi* (*kana* booklets). The genre that most closely captured the psychological temper of the age was the *ukiyo zōshi*, in which the term *ukiyo*, traditionally used to refer to the Buddhist notion of worldly transience, came to mean the "floating world," the pleasure quarters frequented by the burgeoning merchant class.

These developments were rooted in paradox. To the shogunate, which sought to found its polity on neo-Confucian orthodoxy, literature remained official anathema. Rebelliousness ensued, but one author in particular, Ihara Saikaku, challenged the regime's neo-Confucian strictures. Replete with skillful parodies of Heian conventions, Saikaku's narratives exude an immediacy born of his fascination with the world around him and his eye for detail. But his importance lies in his mastery of style, even more than in the content of his stories.

The latter half of the Tokugawa era (until 1868) saw two parallel traditions. Such authors as Ueda Akinari, Santō Kyōden, and Takizawa Bakin tried to remove the stigma of popular literature by pursuing a more serious, intellectual fiction. Their so-called *yomihon* (literally, reading books) tended to reflect Chinese themes recorded in a classical Japanese style. But their overt didacticism, aiming to "encourage virtue and chastise vice," militated against the genre in favor of more popular fiction, or *gesaku*. These texts, in which urban concerns and theatrical influences predominate, remain parodic and episodic, but

they display a tension—born of the need to comply with official strictures even while undermining them—that increased as the shogunate ran its course. The *gesaku* tradition comprises a series of subgenres: *kibyōshi* (in which images predominate over text), *sharebon* (pseudo-Chinese-style stories designed to promote the lifestyle of the connoisseur of the pleasure quarters), *kokkeibon* (picaresque travelogues), and *ninjōbon* (depicting the emotions of those frequenting the pleasure quarters).

As a consequence of this focus, the low reputation of literature as overly "popular" persisted until the Meiji Restoration (1868). All the more remarkable, therefore, was the acceptance of fiction within mainstream society during the subsequent decades. In part, this was a consequence of the deliberate policy of modernization pursued by the new Meiji oligarchy: the 1880s, in particular, saw a deluge of translations of the Bible, William Shakespeare, Jean-Jacques Rousseau, and other Western classics, which in turn led to a trend toward political novels emulating Western "revolutionary" histories. Equally significant as a contributing factor to the reevaluation of fiction, however, was a growing awareness of the suitability of the form for expressing the new self-awareness and individualism, along with the accompanying confusion, of modern Japanese society.

Progress during the first decades of the Meiji era was rapid. The critic Tsubouchi Shōyō, in particular, facilitated the acceptance of the emerging *shōsetsu* as a serious art form. In 1885 Tsubouchi published "Shosetsu shinzui" (The Essence of the Novel), a remarkable treatise arguing for the autonomy and artistic integrity of fiction and calling for greater literary realism. This was no simple attack on the *gesaku* tradition. Tsubouchi argued in favor of a form better suited to the demands of the new Meiji era. Claiming that "the principal aim of the novel is human emotions; society and customs follow next," Tsubouchi recommended a greater emphasis on character, less convoluted plots, and a less classical style of language. Tsubouchi's call for a more natural style was not new: the Ken'yūsha coterie had called for *genbun itchi* (unification of plot and spoken style), by which they meant a flexible, precise, and vigorous style applied to the delineation of contemporary conditions. But where the Ken'yūsha had pleaded in vain, Tsubouchi captured the contemporary literary imagination. It is little exaggeration to claim that the prose narrative form came to rest firmly at the center of 20th-century Japanese literature as a result of Tsubouchi's campaign.

One of Tsubouchi's pupils, Futabatei Shimei, heeded the call of "Shōsetsu shinzui," writing *Ukigumo* (1887; *Ukigumo*), a work in which contemporary issues were discussed with unprecedented realism. Unimpressed with Meiji advances, alienated and introspective, the protagonist, Bunzo, is a "superfluous hero" after the Russian models that had inspired Futabatei. Bunzo is rapidly outstripped, socially, by a more pragmatic colleague. The action is mundane. It is rather the author's mastery in analyzing human emotions, coupled with the freshness of his language, that accounts for *Ukigumo*'s reputation as "Japan's first modern novel."

The gauntlet had been thrown down. But for a decade or so, no writers willing or able to build on these advances appeared. Futabatei himself promptly returned to translating the Russian classics. And the Ken'yūsha, despite experiments with the literary language, continued to produce shallow, *gesaku*-type adventures. (One notable exception was the female writer Higuchi

Ichiyō. She captured the rapidly changing Japanese world through her poignant portrayals of poverty in the pleasure quarters in a series of short stories that express a deep sensitivity to adolescent loneliness and teenage psychology. However, she died at 24, before writing a full-length novel.)

The late 1890s saw the emergence of a series of writers who contributed much to what the critic Karatani Kōjin has described as the formulation of a national literature (see Karatani, 1993). Making a clean break with the literary style of the Tokugawa era, this group of writers was steeped in a combination of English romantic poetry, Christianity, and Western individualism. They built up a sizable body of works promoting a new romantic understanding of the individual and his place in society. Inspired by Kitamura Tōkoku and his concept of the inner life, the group contributed to the inward turn of Japanese literature in the early 20th century. As Edward Fowler notes, however, this interiority represents not so much "an expression of 'self-validation' in 'modern' society but rather a move . . . away from political and social integration promoted by Meiji bureaucratism and toward a quietist and separatist ideal of domestic exile that makes possible a peculiarly Japanese kind of selfhood" (see Fowler, 1988). An implicit attack on the earlier utilitarian view of literature, this vision locates literature's true worth in the support of spiritual growth, the last sphere in which the individual exercised autonomy.

First to recognize the potential of the novel for expressing such concerns was Shimazaki Tōson. He describes the awakening of the outcast hero Ushimatsu, in the ground-breaking *Hakai* (1906; *Broken Commandment*), with unprecedented insight and psychological verisimilitude. The title of the novel suggests that the moral issue at stake is whether Ushimatsu should break his father's commandment never to reveal his ancestry as a member of the despised *eta* community. However, Kenneth Strong, Tōson's translator, points out that "the *eta* hero is primarily an embodiment of Shimazaki's own longing for inner spiritual emancipation." The concern here is with Ushimatsu's progression toward self-definition rather than any notion of the absolute dignity of the individual. In the end, Ushimatsu sets sail for a new life in Texas after he breaks the commandment and falls from grace in society. An unlikely eventuality, Ushimatsu's departure is nevertheless a plausible new beginning for an awakened individual.

As *Broken Commandment* progresses, so the focus on Ushimatsu's inner life as a reflection of the author's own private world becomes more pronounced. This tendency is even more marked in Tayama Katai's *Futon* (1907; *The Quilt*), a contender with *Broken Commandment* for the title of "Japan's first naturalist novel." But in *The Quilt* the outside world does not impinge on the protagonist's movements. Its focus on a single story as seen through a single pair of eyes was the more influential in the establishment of the confession as a literary form in Japan.

Meanwhile, Natsume Sōseki and Mori Ōgai opposed the naturalist, confessional mode. Sōseki rejected the naturalists' tendency to interpret individual unhappiness in terms of environment, heredity, and other uncontrollable factors, seeking to locate the cause within the sufferers themselves. He was deeply concerned with the fate of modern man, especially the idle intelligentsia, rendered vulnerable by the new pragmatism and egoism and destined to suffer, without religion or love to console them. His work features a series of protagonists who suggest that individuals are destroyed not by society but by their own inability to handle newfound freedoms. The issue is central to Sōseki's classic, *Kokoro* (1914; *Kokoro*— the untranslatable title hints at the wide range of spiritual, religious, psychological, and volitional movements of the heart). Its profound psychological insights and lyrical beauty enable the author to penetrate deep into the mind of a man faced with his own egoistic desires.

Some critics accused even Sōseki of pandering to popular tastes. Such critics turned to Ōgai, an Enlightenment scholar who strove to understand the impact of Westernization on the indigenous modernization process and who combined his literary activity with a career as army physician. A protracted period of study in Germany in the 1880s inspired Ōgai to translate prominent European literature, including Henrik Ibsen, August Strindberg, and Gerhart Hauptmann. But he is best remembered as a creative writer. His early novels lack the psychological drama and narrative buildup of Sōseki's work, but his later works, in which he turned increasingly to historical sources, reveal a depth of philosophical insight and a precision of observation that goes far beyond the romantic fantasy that so often passes for historical fiction. Ōgai transformed the *shiden* (historical essays)—a genre with obvious precedents in the medieval *gunki monogatari*—into an intensely personal literary vehicle. His *shiden* describe not only the life of the characters but also the process of writing biography, leading the critic Katō Shūichi to call them "biography in progress" (see Katō, 1979–83).

Both Sōseki and Ōgai attributed their confidence in the prose narrative form (as the ideal vehicle for depicting intellectual angst) to extended periods of study abroad. However, few were so fortunate, and Japanese prose narrative in the early 20th century developed toward the *shishōsetsu,* that peculiarly Japanese variant of the first-person novel (often referred to as the "I-novel"), in which vivid descriptions of the mundane reality of the author's own private world predominate. Much has been made of the autobiographical "purity" of these works. But, as Fowler notes in his seminal study of the genre, the *shishōsetsu* text owes its uniqueness rather to an "ultimate distrust of western-style realistic representation from which it has presumably borrowed so heavily" (see Fowler, 1988). The *shishōsetsu,* then, is fundamentally referential in nature, deriving its meaning from an extraliterary source: the author's private life. In sharp contradistinction to Western equivalents, in which the author creates protagonists possessed of the power to change their own world, the Japanese *shishōsetsu* authors, lacking faith in such authority of representation, resorted to barely mediated transcription of the world as they experienced it. The consequent distinction between private person and narrative persona—indeed that between autobiography and fiction—thus largely dissolves as the author, as diarist/confessor, seeks to transcribe lived experience.

The *shishōsetsu* clearly relies heavily on personal experience. Ultimately, however, the genre is not designed to reveal the individual engaged in psychoanalytical self-scrutiny. The *shishōsetsu* are not expressions of a burgeoning individuality and selfhood. Instead, individualism implies a retreat into the world of nature and private experience. In time, however, this retreat enabled the author to plumb the depths of the self in a way unattainable in the conventional novel with its complex conventions of fictionalization. This trait—the apparent deconstruction of the 19th-century Western novel—has led several critics to describe the form as "postmodern."

Given their subjective tenor, the range of experience depicted in these *shishōsetsu* is hardly surprising. Two contrasting authors, Shiga Naoya and Dazai Osamu, may be cited as typifying the genre. Shiga was a founding member of the *Shirakaba-ha* (White Birch Society), an idealistic circle of authors with aristocratic pretensions. Dubbed the "*shōsetsu no kamisama*" (god of the novel), Shiga's ability to transform the mundane into something worthy of our attention is unrivaled. Remembered largely for his short stories, his one full-length novel, *An'ya kōrō* (1937; *A Dark Night's Passing*), is a masterpiece, an extended and moving portrayal of the protagonist's quest for inner salvation. Given his reputation, Shiga's audience required little assistance in identifying the autobiographical underpinnings of the novel. But the concerted focus on the protagonist's effort to come to terms with an incestuous past succeeds in blurring fantasy and reality in a convincing manner.

Although from a similarly well-to-do background, Dazai rejected the complacency of the *Shirakaba-ha* and came to epitomize the spirit of rebelliousness toward prevailing social and literary trends, which was shared by fellow members of the *Burai-ha* (Decadents). Far from offering mere chronicles of his own life, he used farce to create characters who are weak but by no means evil and who ultimately impress us with their purity. Dazai's most popular novel, *Shayō* (1947; *The Setting Sun*), addresses many social, human, and philosophical issues. But his most incisive is his final novel, *Ningen shikkaku* (1948; *No Longer Human*), which was published weeks before his suicide and represents both an attack on the traditions of Japan and a record of one man's deracination.

Also during this period a group of proletarian writers was determined to use personal and working experience to illustrate socialist principles. Although few of these writers' works achieved real artistic merit, they nevertheless accurately reflect the influx of Marxist and anarchic ideology during the interwar years. By the early 1930s, however, their voices had effectively been suppressed, often through forcible extraction of *tenkō* (conversion) oaths.

In place of literary opposition to the growing militarization of the era, the 1930s—and indeed the war years—saw the emergence of a group of writers who extended Japanese realism to include the more fanciful aspects of storytelling and to touch on a greater range of human experience. For instance, Nagai Kafū in his lyrical evocations of the past invested his characters with an unshakable sense of attachment to the world in spite of alienating circumstances. More enduring was the legacy of Tanizaki Jun'ichirō and Kawabata Yasunari, who succeeded, even during the war years, in suggesting the cultural confusion of modern Japan. Both suffered heavily at the hands of wartime censors: Tanizaki's nostalgic vision of the past in *Sasameyuki* (1948; *The Makioka Sisters*) and Kawabata's lyrical depictions of a world far removed from the war in *Yukiguni* (1937, revised and enlarged 1948; *Snow Country*) were deemed contrary to the national endeavor and were only allowed full circulation after the war.

In 1945, when the need for national reconstruction was paramount, the future of the Japanese novel appeared bleak. Nevertheless, the next few years saw a renaissance every bit as remarkable as that of the first decades of the Meiji era. Censorship restrictions eased sufficiently to permit publication of those works that established the reputations of Dazai, Tanizaki, Kawabata, and others. The *sengoha* (postwar generation), several of whom had personal experience of the prewar proletarian tradition and were still struggling to come to terms with the *tenkō*, also made an important contribution. For these writers, the war inevitably represented the formative experience. Noma Hiroshi and Ōka Shōhei, for instance, had seen active service and sought literary treatments of the meaning of war and of lives placed *in extremis*. Haniya Yutaka, Shiina Rinzō, and others attempted to deal with the ruins, the despair, and the sense of hopelessness of the Occupation years. Their work exudes an intense preoccupation with moral, philosophical, and political issues, coupled with an insistence on the author's own individuality. Reminiscent of the prewar tradition, this combination was highly influential in determining the direction of the *shōsetsu* during the subsequent boom decades.

The latter years of the Occupation saw the emergence of yet another group—the so-called *daisan no shinjin* (third generation of new writers)—who sought to delineate the scope of the postwar *shishōsetsu*. Led by Endō Shūsaku, Shimao Toshio, Yasuoka Shōtarō, and Kojima Nobuo, these authors made few attempts to conceal the extent to which they resorted to personal experience as material for their novels. But, in their increased concern for the social implications of their stories, their works are a far cry from the "unmediated reality" of their *shishōsetsu* predecessors.

Not all writers who emerged during the immediate postwar period are so readily categorized. Mishima Yukio and Abe Kōbō, for instance, are both highly idiosyncratic in their literary approach. Mishima, more than any other author, attempted a synthesis of the Western and Japanese literary traditions. Abe, a symbolist possessed of vivid powers of imagination, was most successful in addressing the rootlessness of the modern individual. His *Suna no onna* (1962; *The Woman in the Dunes*) is a reductionist classic; the ever-shifting sand that threatens to engulf the village where the protagonist finds himself stranded serves as a powerful metaphor of human alienation.

Also prominent on the postwar literary scene was a series of female writers determined to address the role and status of women in a rapidly changing society. Enchi Fumiko, Uno Chiyo, and other pioneers contributed most to breaking the male-dominated mold. They were shortly followed by female writers who explored female sexuality from a variety of perspectives and others who turned their attention to social issues. For instance, Ishimure Michiko portrayed the scandals surrounding a mercury-poisoning incident at Minamata. Ariyoshi Sawako depicted the problems of care for the elderly in Japan.

By the late 1950s, the economic miracle firmly established, the Japanese novel evinced an increased political awareness, particularly the work of such authors as Kaikō Ken and, most notably, Ōe Kenzaburō. Ōe's early protagonists are inspired by the dream of political revolution, but, especially following the birth of his severely handicapped son, his writing evinces a moralism and advocacy of individual responsibility (his receipt of the 1994 Nobel prize for literature was attributed to these very qualities). Another writer to confront the political and social consequences of Japan's development was Ibuse Masuji, best remembered for *Kuroi ame* (1965; *Black Rain*), in which he depicts man's ultimate inhumanity to man—in the form of the nuclear attack on Hiroshima. Ibuse uses contrasts between horror and humor, destruction and beauty, the state and the individual, to transform the horrors of atomic destruction into art.

The collapse of the economic bubble in the 1970s coincided with a return to the *shishōsetsu* tradition, as exemplified in the novels of Dazai's daughter, Tsushima Yūko, and in Shimao Toshio's masterpiece, *Shi no toge* (1977; *The Sting of Death*). By the end of the decade, "a generation of the void" had emerged, comprising those raised during the affluent 1950s and 1960s. These writers' social concerns and awareness differ, not surprisingly, from those of their parents. Influenced to a considerable degree by the powerful consortium that by now existed between writers, critics, and publishers, contemporary writers Murakami Ryū, Tanaka Yasuo, Yamada Eimi, Yoshimoto Banana, Murakami Haruki, and others tend to adopt an ironic and sophisticated tone, but many of their novels ultimately read as crude apologia for affluence. For all this focus on consumer culture and the postmodern tenor of much contemporary fiction, however, the past continues to hold sway. Authors such as Ōe and Nakagami Kenji incorporate Japanese myth and folk traditions into their fictional worlds. Nakagami is notable for his depictions of the marginal worlds of the *roji* (alleyways), reminiscent of those created by William Faulkner and Gabriel García Márquez. However, in spite of significant recent work, the increasing popularity of the *manga* and various hi-tech forms in Japan poses a serious threat to the continued vitality of the Japanese novel.

MARK WILLIAMS

See also Black Rain; Endō Shūsaku; Kawabata Yasunari; Mishima Yukio; Natsume Sōseki; Ōe Kenzaburō; Tale of Genji; Tanizaki Jun'ichirō

Further Reading

Fowler, Edward, *The Rhetoric of Confession: Shishōsetsu in Early Twentieth Century Japanese Fiction*, Berkeley: University of California Press, 1988

Fujii, James A., *Complicit Fictions: The Subject in the Modern Japanese Prose Narrative*, Berkeley: University of California Press, 1993

Hibbett, Howard, *The Floating World in Japanese Fiction*, Oxford and New York: Oxford University Press, 1959

Hijiya-Kirschnereit, Irmela, *Rituals of Self-Revelation: Shishōsetsu as Literary Genre and Socio-Cultural Phenomenon*, Cambridge, Massachusetts: Harvard University Press, 1996

Karatani, Kōjin, *The Origins of Modern Japanese Literature*, Durham, North Carolina: Duke University Press, 1993

Katō, Shūichi, *Nihon bungakushi josetsu*, Tokyo: Chikumashobo, 1975; as *A History of Japanese Literature*, 3 vols., Tokyo and New York: Kodansha International, and London: Macmillan, 1979–83

Keene, Donald, *World Within Walls: Japanese Literature of the Pre-Modern Era, 1600–1867*, New York: Holt, Rinehart, and Winston, and London: Secker and Warburg, 1976

Keene, Donald, *Dawn to the West: Japanese Literature in the Modern Era*, New York: Holt, Rinehart, and Winston, 1984

Keene, Donald, *Seeds in the Heart: Japanese Literature from Earliest Times to the Late Sixteenth Century*, New York: Holt, 1993

Konishi, Jin'ichi, *A History of Japanese Literature*, 3 vols., Princeton, New Jersey: Princeton University Press, 1984–91; previously published as *Nihon bungeishi*

Miner, Earl, Hiroko Odagiri, and Robert Morrell, *The Princeton Companion to Classical Japanese Literature*, Princeton, New Jersey: Princeton University Press, 1985

Miyoshi, Masao, *Accomplices of Silence: The Modern Japanese Novel*, Berkeley: University of California Press, 1974

Miyoshi, Masao, "Against the Native Grain: The Japanese Novel and the Postmodern West," in *Postmodernism and Japan*, Durham, North Carolina: Duke University Press, 1989

Pollock, David, *Reading Against Culture: Ideology and Narrative in the Japanese Novel*, Ithaca, New York: Cornell University Press, 1992

Rimer, J. Thomas, *Modern Japanese Fiction and Its Traditions*, Princeton, New Jersey: Princeton University Press, 1978

Ryan, Marleigh Grayer, *Japan's First Modern Novel: Ukigumo of Futabatei Shimei*, New York: Columbia University Press, 1967

Sakai, Naoki, *Voices of the Past: The Status of Language in Eighteenth-Century Japanese Discourse*, Ithaca, New York: Cornell University Press, 1992

Suzuki, Tomi, *Narrating the Self: Fictions of Japanese Modernity*, Stanford, California: Stanford University Press, 1996

Ueda, Makoto, *Modern Japanese Writers and the Nature of Literature*, Stanford, California: Stanford University Press, 1976

Walker, Janet, *The Japanese Novel in the Meiji Period and the Ideal of Individualism*, Princeton, New Jersey: Princeton University Press, 1979

Washburn, Dennis C., *The Dilemma of the Modern in Japanese Fiction*, New Haven, Connecticut: Yale University Press, 1995

Jealousy by Alain Robbe-Grillet

La Jalousie 1957

Jealousy is the most famous title associated with the so-called *nouveau roman* of the 1950s and 1960s, enjoying a privileged status of the sort conferred earlier on Camus' *L'Étranger* (1942; *The Stranger*). Robbe-Grillet had already published prize-winning works that employed his unusual camera-like and kaleidoscopic narrative point of view, notably *Les Gommes* (1953, *The Erasers*) and *Le Voyeur* (1955; *The Voyeur*), but *Jealousy* became an international success, even as it perplexed and annoyed some readers who could not fathom Robbe-Grillet's disjointed and sometimes contradictory propositions or appreciate his unemotional mathematical style. Robbe-Grillet himself has pointed out in *Pour un nouveau roman* (1963; *For a New Novel*) that his first novels met with critical rejection. He castigated critics for their insistence that the novelist not explain his intentions, an arrogant prejudice that he claims further tainted the reception of *Jealousy*:

> [I]f there is one thing in particular which the critics find hard to endure, it is that the artist should explain himself. I certainly realized as much when, after having expressed these and several other notions quite as obvious, I published my third novel (*Jealousy*). Not only was the book attacked, decried as a kind of preposterous outrage against belles-lettres; it was even proved that such an abomination was only to be expected, for *Jealousy* was a self-acknowledged product of premeditation: its author— O the scandal of it!—permitted himself to have opinions concerning his own profession.

The novel, whose plot is kept deliberately to a minimum, involves the lives of the manager of a banana plantation in the tropics through whose eyes and/or in whose imagination the action is registered, A . . ., whom we take to be his wife, and their neighbor, Franck, who frequently dines with them. Franck's wife, Christiane, does not come to visit during the time frame of the novel owing to the illness of her child and her own despondancy at having to live in this tropical environment, and she is only alluded to in conversation or suggested by the presence at the table of her empty chair and a fourth place setting. There is a supporting cast of servants and plantation workers who function more as automatons or reified shapes than as psychological entities. The novel is mainly descriptive, but one key incident recurs that is either "real" or imagined by the jealous husband: Franck and A . . . have gone or are about to go to the port city with the expectation that they will be back late that day. There is an alleged breakdown of the car and Franck and A . . . must spend the night in the hotel in town. The reader does not learn for certain what occurs, but there are indicators—such as A . . .'s returning from her shopping mission with only one small package, Franck's lack of precision regarding the details of the breakdown, a glimpse of blue letter paper (A . . .'s?) sticking out of Franck's shirt pocket, and the body language on the part of A . . . and Franck (the posture of Franck's back suggesting a kiss as A . . . gets out of Franck's car at the plantation, unnatural gestures, and exchanged glances)—that Franck and A . . . have had an affair. Or, we may ask, is not the whole perception of these "indicators" rather a product of the husband's jealous imagination?

The novel is a tour de force that stimulates the reader to seek an overarching rationale for the narrative. Were such a procedure not manifestly anachronistic, one might suspect that the author used a computer to write and then cut and paste episodes, which he then added to, subtracted from, or altered slightly. The brilliance of the novel lies in its unsettling virtuosity.

The reader is overwhelmed by the recurring descriptions in *Jealousy* of the arrangement of palm trees in quincunxes, and of the trapezoids, rectangles, and ovals by which Robbe-Grillet defines various objects, as well as by the narrator's obsession with visual bisecting—as when the reality of one visual plane overlaps with that of another, for example, the mass of a truck as seen through a window, or the interior of a room as seen through venetian blinds (the word for which, in French, is *jalousies*).

The novel is presented from the point of view of the person presumed to be the husband of A . . ., a person not manifested, except perhaps for a glimpse of his hand holding a glass in a photograph of A . . . . Indeed, the novel's point of view seems almost robotic, like that of a roving camera, and brings to mind the innovative cinematic techniques of about the same period. The notion of the spectator as a "stand-in" for the character is similar to the technique applied by Robbe-Grillet in his early novels, which is not surprising considering Robbe-Grillet's parallel preoccupation with the cinema.

Given that *Jealousy* consists of a limited number of perceptions, images or actions that are juxtaposed without logical transition (e.g., Franck and A . . . drinking and eating on the terrace; A . . . combing her hair or writing a letter; a centipede crushed on the wall and the stain left behind; the geometrical layout of the banana trees; men crouched near a stream and some logs that will be used to rebuild a bridge over the stream, seen over and over again from slightly different angles and/or in a slightly different light; a truck and Franck's car), the serious reader who does not simply reject the novel out of hand as patent gimmickry is tempted to seek elsewhere than in the limited plot action a rationale for the narrative's peculiar style.

It is difficult to distinguish the imaginative eye from the virtual eye in this tale. The reader is tempted to make much of such things as the word *maintenant* (right now) that occurs at critical moments throughout the novel; but the recurrent descriptions, both visual and aural, are implacably measured, be they real or imagined, for imaging, whether retinal or imaginary, ultimately involves the same cerebral reality. The only variation occurs in a few passages, such as the narrator's contradictory grasp of the plot of the novel that Franck and A . . . have been discussing ("This company's business is going badly, rapidly turning shady. This company's business is going extremely well. The chief character—one learns—is dishonest. He is honest . . ."). It is significant that this information is second or third hand and not graphically available to the narrator and perhaps, therefore, either poorly registered or of indifference to the phenomenologically obsessed narrator.

The recording of events is primarily optical, but there are some auditory notations, such as when the narrator's jealous mind turns predatory and surrounding animal cries achieve greater acuity, or when furtive animal noises underline the erotic tension between Franck and A . . ., or when the hissing of the hurricane lamp shuts out the noises of the plantation before it suddenly stops and night sounds impinge, or when the singing of the natives prods the narrator to what amounts to subliminally condescending racist reflections of the sort one might expect of the typical colonizer. Strangely, considering the novel's tropical decor, there is not an abundance of color in the description but for some greens, reds, and browns, but these change according to the lighting, time of day, and perhaps the vantage point of the narrator's spying eye . . . or imagining eye. Disparate images such as darkish spots on the ground, a ruddy streak running down the side of the house from the corner of a windowsill, and the stain from the crushed centipede are all rationally explicable, yet they take on a sinister sense of portent in light of their juxtaposition with other images, such as a knife or fingers clutching a sheet. These seemingly violent images alter the disparate images by virtue of their very proximity to them.

In the early days of film, Lev Kuleshov and Pudovkin made an interesting experiment that underlines the creative potential of transitionless juxtaposition of things and people, a process familiar to moviegoers, but not standard in fiction of the 1950s. Sydney Diamond (1956) has described the experiment:

> Kuleshov took three close-ups of an actor's face, showing no particular expression of any kind, and spliced a totally different shot onto each close-up. The actor's face was followed, first, by a shot of a plate of soup standing on a table; then, by a scene showing the body of a woman lying in a coffin; and finally, by a shot of a little girl playing with a stuffed animal.

Pudovkin, who collaborated with Kuleshov in this experiment, reported that an audience, who had not been let in on the secret that the three pictures of the actor's face were all the same, raved about the actor's ability and "pointed out the heavy pensiveness of his mood over the forgotten soup, were touched and moved by the deep sorrow with which he looked on the dead woman, and admired the light, happy smile with which he surveyed the girl at play."

In much the same manner, readers of Robbe-Grillet's novel will interpret the coldly recorded images of objects and people in light of adjacent images. Despite the seemingly aloof descriptive technique of *Jealousy*, the reader derives from the novel a progressive breakdown in the narrator's ability to distinguish fact from supposition; the various distortions become expressionistic, the objects the instruments of jealousy, paranoia, and psychic degeneration into violence, past or impending.

Robbe-Grillet has, in *For a New Novel*, condemned the use of metaphor and its tendency to anthropomorphize things that should, more properly, be allowed simply to exist in their own dehumanized essence. Indeed, *Jealousy* is practically devoid of simile and metaphor; a rare example is the comparison to a circumflex of the shape of a string by which a calendar hangs from a nail. The very lack of metaphor in *Jealousy* has led some critics to suggest that the entire narrative, dichotomized as it is on racial, gender, colonial, and social levels, is a global metaphor for the state of France immediately following World War II (see Leenhardt, 1973); or to explore the critical split between narrator and author; or to consider the phenomenological import of Robbe-Grillet's novel as antinovel, that is, more as a denial of previous writers' interpretations of things and man's relationship to them (see Stoltzfus, 1964; Robbe-Grillet, 1963); or as an ideological rejection of Jean-Paul Sartre's Zhdanovian stance that literature without political commitment and a utilitarian application is specious "art for art's sake" (see Britton, 1992; Fletcher and Calder, 1986; Robbe-Grillet, 1963); or as a document that assumes new meaning in terms of postmodern theories and new emphases on sado-eroticism and the like (see Ramsay, 1992); or, finally, as a parody of modernism with some possible intertextual winks at a famous voyeur scene in Marcel Proust's *In Search of Lost Time* and Nathaniel Hawthorne's scarlet letter "A" signifying adultery.

If *Jealousy* seems calculated and overly "stylized" (even though its author in principle rejects the notion of style altogether), it remains a fascinating virtuoso exercise that, to be fully appreciated, must be read, as Jacques Leenhardt suggests, with the political and philosophical climate of the years during and immediately following World War II firmly in mind.

ERIC SELLIN

See also Alain Robbe-Grillet

Further Reading

Britton, Celia, *The Nouveau Roman: Fiction, Theory and Politics,* New York: St. Martin's Press, 1992

Diamond, Sydney A., "Creating for the Screen," *New World Writing* 10 (1956)

Fletcher, John, and John Calder, editors, *The Nouveau Roman Reader,* London: Calder, and New York: Riverrun Press, 1986

Leenhardt, Jacques, *Lecture politique du roman: "La jalousie" d'Alain Robbe-Grillet,* Paris: Editions de Minuit, 1973

Leki, Ilona, *Alain Robbe-Grillet,* Boston: Twayne, 1983

Morrissette, Bruce, *Les romans de Robbe-Grillet,* Paris: Editions de Minuit, 1963; as *The Novels of Robbe-Grillet,* Ithaca, New York: Cornell University Press, 1975

Ramsay, Raylene L., *Robbe-Grillet and Modernity: Science, Sexuality, and Subversion,* Gainesville: University Press of Florida, 1992

Robbe-Grillet, Alain, *Pour un nouveau roman,* Paris: Editions de Minuit, 1963; as *For a New Novel: Essays on Fiction,* New York: Grove Press, 1965

Stoltzfus, Ben F., *Alain Robbe-Grillet and the New French Novel,* Carbondale: Southern Illinois University Press, 1964

Jewish-American Novel

The Jewish-American novel has achieved remarkable success, with two authors who may be considered practitioners receiving the Nobel prize for literature: Saul Bellow in 1976 and Isaac Bashevis Singer in 1978. Some of the authors who have been associated with this form by readers and critics have argued that the category is too narrow. Chaim Potok has stated: "I do not care for pigeonholes like 'American Jewish writer' . . . unless one is prepared to call Cheever, say, an 'American Protestant writer.' I find distasteful the essentially reductionist label 'ethnic literature'" ("The First Eighteen Years," *Studies in American Jewish Literature* 4 [1985]). This is an attitude that both Saul Bellow and Bernard Malamud have expressed as well. There are, however, identifiable aspects to Jewish-American writing that serve to identify it when compared to the writing of non-Jewish American authors. Some of these are set out concisely by Bonnie K. Lyons in a useful essay, "American-Jewish Fiction Since 1945" (in Fried, 1988). After discussing the legacy of Yidishkayt, the particularly Jewish way of viewing the world, which developed over the centuries, Lyons notes the following peculiarities of Jewish writing in the United States: the tension between the coming together of the American and the Jewish; the problems of acculturation and assimilation; the questioning of the traditions and values of both cultures; and economic and social change—from ghetto or shtetl (small Jewish village) to city to suburb and from peddler and garment worker to the professions. In terms of psychology, Jewish-American writing is often involved in a search for meaning or authority; it attempts to fill the void that accompanied rapid change and the loss of traditional values and meaning that existed in shtetl life: "The breakup of that world gave rise to doubt, anxiety, questioning, and guilt—emotions and themes which dominate American-Jewish literature and give rise to a tone of complexity, complaint, skepticism, and irony" (Lyons, in Fried, 1988). To this might be added that the works tend toward humanism, are usually set in a city, and the protagonists are schlemiels (a type of antihero)—small men, who are oriented toward introspection rather than action. These elements frequently lead to crises of identity. While the work of non-Jewish novelists may depict some of these elements, the Jewish novels frequently have a preponderance of them.

The first Jewish-American novel having literary merit was *The Rise of David Levinsky* (1917) by Abraham Cahan. Cahan had the support of William Dean Howells, referred to as the Dean of American letters, who thought his earlier work showed him to be an important new realist. The novel chronicles the movement from European poverty to American material success. David Levinsky flees the shtetl of Antomir because of the pogroms of 1881–82 and journeys to the United States and apostasy, becoming a successful clothing manufacturer but never achieving happiness. The novel presents a history of the growth of the garment industry in New York City through the story of the tragedy of a Jewish immigrant who succumbs to the pressures of American success and who, while leaving behind a violently anti-Semitic society (Levinsky's mother was murdered by a mob), also leaves behind his religion, culture, and a way of life that gave his existence meaning. The novel created a format for later Jewish-American novels in that it dealt with the central issues of assimilation and identity. Some Jews found the book anti-Semit-

ic because of its protagonist's growing ruthlessness in climbing the ladder of secular success in a philistine society. Levinsky is affected by Spencer and Darwin but believes that he might just as easily have come under the influence of Marx. The novel thus contains references to a number of the differing influences upon Jewish immigrants and sets the stage for future works that view American success with disillusionment.

Anzia Yezierska's *Bread Givers* (1925) concerns the transition between first- and second-generation Jewish immigrants and is an early autobiographical and "feminist" novel. Like *The Rise of David Levinsky*, it presents vivid descriptions of life on the Lower East Side of New York City, and depicts the rise to success of an ambitious immigrant who is willing to forsake the stringent, and what she sees as Old World, requirements of Jewishness for secular achievement. However, in *Bread Givers* it is a woman who is striving to escape not the anti-Semitism of Europe but the tyranny of an Orthodox father in the United States. The subtitle of the novel is "A struggle between a father of Old World and a daughter of the New," the struggle being that between Jewish customs and acculturation to American ways, the family versus the individual, and the roles of men and women. Judaism is a patriarchal religion, the customs of which were enshrined in everyday life in Eastern Europe. This novel shows the conflict between a very religious man trying to transplant his customs intact to his adopted land, and a daughter who sees the United States as a place where one can break with the past, obtain an education, and be an individual rather than an extension of a religion, a family, and a father's demands. Most immigrant Jewish women fulfilled traditional roles as wives and mothers. However, as in Eastern Europe, many also worked long hours to help support their families financially. *Bread Givers* shows the changes that were to come to the Jewish female offspring of the earlier German immigrants and of Yezierska's from Eastern Europe. Interestingly, at the end of the novel, Sarah takes in her old father to live with her. The tyrannical father will teach Hebrew to her liberal husband. Thus, the traditional ways still have force.

Ludwig Lewisohn's *The Island Within* (1928) depicts the disappointments of attempted assimilation. Second-generation American Jews' desire to reject their Jewish past and disappear into American society became a central theme of novels set in the period of World War I and the 1920s, during which time immigration quota laws were passed and an emphasis placed upon "Americanism." Coming from a well-assimilated German Jewish family, Lewisohn experienced anti-Semitism when he tried to obtain a post in a university English department and was told in no uncertain terms that his Jewishness made success unlikely. This novel is semiautobiographical and views assimilation from the perspective of loss, undermining the simplicity of the American Dream. The protagonist, Arthur Levy, goes through the process of believing in assimilation and even marries a Christian woman, but in the end he commits himself to rediscovering his Jewishness.

The openness of a secular society was something that many Jews had not experienced before. Whereas religious Jews were awaiting the coming of the Messiah, others became secularized and came to view the United States as a place where the messianic age could be ushered into existence by human efforts—secular messianism. To some Jews, socialism and communism took on this role, and Michael Gold (born Irving Granich) published the first important proletarian novel, *Jews without Money* (1930). The strength of this plotless, not very well written novel resides in Gold's descriptions of the seamy aspects of East Side life: its prostitutes and pimps, gamblers and politicians. Especially effective are his descriptions of the difficulties of sheer survival: the poverty, tenement flats, and early deaths. The messianic dreams of communism could, Gold came to believe, transform this slum and raise its people.

Call It Sleep (1934), one of the greatest novels of the 1930s, and one of the best American novels of any period, was not a proletarian novel concerned with social transformation. In it, Henry Roth depicted the attempts of David Schearl, a sensitive six- to eight-year-old boy, to adjust to the Lower East Side and to cope with his violent father. For 60 years, *Call It Sleep* was the only novel Roth produced, part of the reason being, he said, that his membership in the Communist party demanded that he write social realism and keep an eye on the proletariat and class struggle. This he could not do, having a lyrical, not a political, gift. The father/son conflict is common in the writing of American Jewish authors. This harks back to the traditional relationship between Jehovah and Israel, which had been transmuted into the patriarchal relationship that prevailed between fathers and sons in Europe. In the United States this relationship increasingly became confrontational, as the pressures of a new country created conflict between generations. Because of their education in the public schools, children of immigrants often adjusted better to their environment than did their fathers, who tried to retain their stature as heads of families. An added theme for Roth was the Oedipal conflict, with insights gained from Freudian psychology. The novel is a tour de force in its use of dialects and interior monologue. *Call It Sleep* continues to be recognized as a groundbreaking novel and is considered by many the finest of all Jewish-American novels.

While not approaching Roth's novel in artistic skill, Daniel Fuchs' "Williamsburg Trilogy" (*Summer in Williamsburg*, 1934; *Homage to Blenholt*, 1936; and *Low Company*, 1937) provides a graphic depiction of the "in-between" situation of second-generation Jews who live in a cramped Brooklyn neighborhood. Although the novels contain first-generation characters, the stress is upon their children, who want nothing to do with the world of European Jewishness represented by their parents and who do everything they can to act as they think real Americans would. Despite their being aware of events outside its confines, their world is the narrow area of Williamsburg, where they try to acculturate to American life. This theme of tension between generations is a common one in Jewish-American novels, providing a major source of the conflict within them.

Of Meyer Levin's many novels, *The Old Bunch* (1937) is the most accomplished. Set between 1921 and 1934, the novel traces the lives of 20 Jewish teenagers in Chicago who belong to the same club. The decisions they make in their attempts to leave the ghetto and what happens to them as they try to become a part of American life show the effects of their two cultures. Readers see different types of Jewishness set against the demands for full membership in American society. Always present are conflicts with parents and grandparents over the young people's loss of interest in Jewishness and desire for assimilation. As in

the "Williamsburg Trilogy," the second generation strives for entry into American life, the requirement as they understand it being the elimination of their Jewish cultural heritage.

It is in the novels that appeared after World War II that the Jewish-American novel came into its own. Saul Bellow, Bernard Malamud, Philip Roth, Chaim Potok, Bruce Jay Friedman, Edward Lewis Wallant, and Cynthia Ozick are some of the numerous fiction writers who show the range and quality of the Jewish-American novel. The Polish-born author Isaac Bashevis Singer is more difficult to classify, as he wrote all his works in Yiddish (although he was often involved in their translation into English). His best novels are set in his native Eastern Europe and are concerned with somewhat different themes than those of authors born in North America. Although US-born authors may feel the weight of the Yiddish masters (Sholom Aleichem, I.L. Peretz, and Mendele Mocher Sforim), they are more frequently influenced by the American Jewish writers discussed above, who attempted to come to terms with the American experience, and by non-Jewish American authors. Nonetheless, no discussion of the Jewish-American novel would be complete without examining Singer's contribution.

In *Satan in Goray* (1955; dates given here for Singer's novels refer to the published English translations from the Yiddish), *The Magician of Lublin* (1960), and *The Slave* (1962), Singer immerses the reader in the world of Eastern European Judaism and Jewish culture. The United States is not relevant in these novels, which are concerned with matters of religious faith and the social codes within which European Jews lived in a Christian society. In these novels Singer shows readers the world from which emigrated the first-generation American Jews. This is the world from which originated the ancestors of the overwhelming majority of American Jews of the second and later generations. These ancestors of Eastern European and Russian origin arrived in the United States mostly between 1881 and 1924. Singer's works, then, provide a background for Jewish-American literature produced in the United States. *The Manor* (1967) and its sequel *The Estate* (1969) chronicle the transition of the Jews of Poland from a traditional to a modern world during the latter half of the 19th century, a period known as the Jewish Enlightenment, during which ideas that had affected Western Europe some 100 years earlier filtered into Eastern Europe. The various characters each react in his or her own way to rationalism and the new scientific ideas. The new ideas lead to scepticism concerning religion, and a way of life established for centuries comes under attack. Singer shows the price paid for giving up religious belief in the name of scientific truths. He transports some of the characters to the United States, the emblem of secularism, but the focus of the novel remains on Eastern Europe. Singer's knowledge of Judaism and Jewish culture in Eastern Europe has great depth; it is against this background that his characters act and his plots develop.

Jews in the United States never experienced a level of anti-Semitism similar to that which they had faced in Europe. The peak of anti-Jewish feelings in the United States occurred in 1935, at the height of the Depression. However, as Jews began to leave the tenements, seek more prestigious jobs, live in better neighborhoods, vacation at more salubrious resorts, and join formerly all-Christian clubs, social exclusion became more common. In *The Victim* (1947) Saul Bellow presents this phenomenon through a WASP character whose American ancestry dates back to Governor Winthrop and who feels dispossessed by the Jewish presence in New York. The Jewish character, Leventhal, questions his responsibility for Albee's having lost his job, viewing his accusations as nothing more than anti-Semitism. He is forced to consider issues of his own Jewish identity and also must widen his sense of responsibility toward others in order to become a complete human being. This early novel pursues one of Bellow's important themes: namely, how should a good man live?

This question is a central theme in *Herzog* (1964) in which Bellow's protagonist rails against the nihilism of the 20th-century wasteland attitude. Moses Herzog tries to sort out the world by writing letters (which he never sends) to those he sees as having had an influence on the 20th-century ethos, in part because he cannot create order in his personal life. An intellectual historian, he tries to understand his own existence and that of the 20th century through the world of ideas, finally realizing that his efforts are futile and lapsing into silence. A man of heart (*Herz* means "heart" in German) who has been deeply affected by his upbringing by immigrant parents, it is to the heart that he ultimately returns, having no messages for anyone. *Herzog* depicts the problems of the assimilated, successful Jew who is, nonetheless, adrift in what Bellow referred to as the "swamp of prosperity." This theme of worldly success, tinged with a sense of something of great value having been lost, may be seen as far back as Cahan's *The Rise of David Levinsky*. Jewish-American novels often chronicle the price paid for "making it."

In Bernard Malamud's *The Assistant* (1957), the nature of the moral individual is pursued relentlessly. Malamud once said: "Every man is a Jew though he may not know it," thus stressing the metaphorical nature of his use of Jewishness to signify the selfless, responsible, moral individual. It is not material success that is important but ethical behavior, which is seen in the saintly, if schlemiel-like, immigrant grocer Morris Bober, who serves as teacher to an Italian drifter desperate to become a moral man. An impressive work, this morality tale uses the hardships of the Jewish immigrant experience not as something to be escaped at all costs but as a valuable training ground in selflessness. It carries forth the moral concern in these novels, particularly in the prevalence of the Bildungsroman as a common form.

In *The Fixer* (1966), Malamud wrote a historical novel based upon a real case: the blood libel leveled at Menaham Mendel Beilis in Czarist Russia between 1911 and 1913. Awarded both a National Book Award and a Pulitzer Prize, the novel examines the growth in morality that results from suffering. Jewishness is forced upon Yakov Bok, as is his awareness that he suffers for others, suffering being a basis for moral growth not only in Malamud's works but in that of other Jewish-American novelists. The moralistic impetus and importance placed upon acceptance of Jewish identity, here in its broadest humanistic sense, relates this novel to those of other post–World War II Jewish-American authors.

In the 1960s, some Jewish-American authors began writing novels that dealt with aspects of the Holocaust. Most Jewish-American writers have not concentrated upon the Holocaust but upon its survivors and the American experience of adjustment, assimilation, and identity crises. Some of the most accomplished of these are Edward Lewis Wallant's *The Pawnbroker* (1961), Saul Bellow's *Mr. Sammler's Planet* (1970), Isaac Bashevis Singer's *Enemies, a Love Story* (1972), and Philip Roth's *The Ghost Writer* (1979).

The Pawnbroker presents the event through the psychological scars and memories of a survivor-protagonist, a former professor in Europe who has become a New York pawnbroker. The hopeful American present does not exist for Sol Nazerman; his only way of getting through a day is to remain insensitive to all around him in order to avoid any emotion that might bring back his sufferings and loss in the death camps. Although by the end of the novel Sol has developed the capacity to see suffering and beauty in the Harlem faces around him, the American present has become unreal for the reader, given the horrors related. While this is another Bildungsroman, a part of the Jewish-American novelistic type, the orientation is not toward acculturation as such but more toward a character's rejoining humanity.

In Saul Bellow's *Mr. Sammler's Planet*, the protagonist is a survivor who, although presumed dead, has dragged himself out of a mass grave. He is an intellectual Polish immigrant who views the New York of the 1960s with a fearful sense that the decadence he sees about him might be a sign that the world could collapse once more into chaos. Here, the United States is not salvation but a black pickpocket exhibiting himself to an elderly, cultured survivor. The United States is free, but as Bellow wrote in *Herzog*, that freedom is "a howling emptiness." Surrounded by younger members of his family and others, all of whom lack what he understands to be values and morality, he is an arch critic of modern America, viewing it askance through his one good eye. This novel focuses not so much on the Holocaust as on its place in an intellectual's reactions to what the United States had become.

In *Enemies, a Love Story*, Singer describes the effects of the Holocaust on a survivor in the United States. Finding it extremely difficult to discover any basis for living, Herman Broder tries to understand how God could have allowed the Holocaust to happen and is cynical of God's mercy. For Herman, the United States is a place to hide, like the hayloft in which he hid from the Nazis. The United States becomes at times just another Poland, as the protagonist relives his ordeal. Thus, survival and escape have made no real difference to Herman, who sees many other survivors starting their lives over again, something which in his bitterness toward God and humanity he cannot accomplish.

Philip Roth wrote several novels containing an alter ego, Nathan Zuckerman. The best of these is the first, *The Ghost Writer*. Here Roth depicts a young Jewish writer who flees his home turf to seek approbation from a famous Jewish-American writer. When one of his stories is published nationally, rather than bringing forth praise from his parents and the Jewish community, it is seen as a betrayal of both. Depicting one of Roth's themes, that of the misunderstood Jewish writer, the novel criticizes the Jewish community's paranoia and its inability to accept criticism or, as Zuckerman would have it, the truth told to the outside world. Roth is well within the tradition of previous Jewish-American writers who have been critical of the insularity of the Jewish community, although for reasons other than the community's resistance to art. The novel postulates acceptance of the individual if he attaches himself to an icon of the culture who is beyond criticism—in this case, Anne Frank. The Jewish community's response to Roth's work and what he depicts in this novel show the insecurity and sensitivity of an apparently successful and well-integrated ethnic group.

Immersion in the Holocaust's terror occurs in Cynthia Ozick's *The Shawl* (1989), the single volume containing the short story

"The Shawl" (1980) and its sequel, the novella *Rosa* (1983). "The Shawl" treats the world of death marches and concentration camps, but *Rosa* is set in Florida, with the eponymous character remembering the events presented in the earlier story. The novella revolves around memory and the way it can color and prevent life in the present. It is this emphasis upon memory that relates these Holocaust novels to those dealing with cultural adaptation. The end of Ozick's tale implies that adjustment to the new world will eventually occur and that the horrors depicted will be left in Europe to be replaced by problems connected with an unthreatening but alien and shallow culture.

The novelist Bruce Jay Friedman coined the term "black humor" to refer to a way of approaching reality that the author finds too absurd or horrific to describe in any way but through humor. The difficulties of achieving happiness in a disoriented, meaningless, technological, urban society led some writers, mostly of the 1960s, to feel that only an outraged humor could adequately describe modern life. Actions do not yield any recognizable pattern, and events are often inexplicable. In Friedman's novel *Stern* (1962), the protagonist finds his world thrown into chaos when a neighbor pushes his wife and makes an anti-Semitic remark. Stern's attempts at revenge and resolution provide the basis of the humor. In *A Mother's Kisses* (1964), the oppressiveness of a stereotypical Jewish mother in an Oedipal situation is overcome when the protagonist, Joseph, convinces his mother, who had been living with him at college, to go home and allow him to get on with his education. In both novels the small "victories" of the protagonists are presented in a very humorous fashion, with the novels showing the difficulties of schlemiels (and, by implication, of 20th-century people in general) in dealing with a world of unexpected and incomprehensible events.

Chaim Potok is unusual among Jewish-American novelists in that his novels show the relevance of traditional Judaism or of Jewish belief in the 20th century. His characters are not alienated outsiders; some characters question certain aspects of traditional Jewish beliefs and practices, but they see their worth. His first novel, *The Chosen* (1967), compares the pressures toward assimilation and traditional belief of the son of a Hasidic rebbe who is to inherit his father's role and the son of an orthodox Jew who is viewed by the Hasidim as not practicing Judaism in quite the correct manner. Both boys and their fathers must come to grips with what Potok has called the "umbrella civilization," under which they are trying to preserve particular types of Judaism. The novel was a best-seller and was made into a film. Potok wrote a sequel called *The Promise* (1969), which follows the boys into their college years and again shows the importance of traditional beliefs, even in the United States. In *My Name is Asher Lev* (1972), Potok produced his best novel, which concerns the difficulties of a Ladover Hasid who is also a child prodigy as an artist. Both his family and religious group are very critical of anyone spending time painting—an activity viewed with great suspicion because of the second commandment's admonitions concerning "graven images." As in *The Chosen,* the characters are all good people whose disagreements stem from strongly held religious and ethical beliefs. Potok has contributed the "good versus good" theme to the American Jewish novel. He portrays no gratuitous sex or violence, and his characters try to live moral, religious lives attached to Judaism. American society often makes this goal difficult because of the attractiveness of its secular culture. Thus appear again the themes of acculturation and assimilation, although Potok allows his characters to arrive at an acceptable accommodation.

Philip Roth's novel of growing up absurd, *Portnoy's Complaint* (1969), takes as its primary inspirations the stand-up Jewish comedians of the "borscht belt" and the stereotype of the overprotective Jewish mother and the ineffectual father. Underlying the humor, however, is a tale about identity crisis and assimilation, the common currency of the Jewish-American novel. Although Portnoy is well educated and has a prestigious job with the ironic title of "Assistant Commissioner for Human Opportunity," he feels as much an outsider in Protestant America as the characters in the novels from the 1920s and 1930s. He wants to be outside the burden of Jewish history, to be able to create himself anew. In some ways, Portnoy's attempts to re-create himself—through sexual conquest of non-Jewish women—parallels the desires of immigrants in earlier novels who, particularly in the 1920s, wished to become wholly American, giving up all ties to their parents' or grandparents' Jewish history and culture. The novel was viewed by some critics as soft-core pornography, and it does contain numerous passages that may be interpreted in this way. Roth had become accustomed to criticism from the Jewish community, which he felt wanted its writers to function as public-relations men, not as individuals who would tell the truth about American Jews, namely, that they have the same flaws as other members of the human race. In 1975 Roth commented on this phenomenon: "The novelist asks himself, 'What do people think?'; the PR man asks, 'What will people think?'" The Jewish family, Jewish culture, and Judaism are all seen as oppressive to a Jew who wants to "belong" with no strings attached; indeed, Portnoy is presented as relating his story from a psychiatrist's couch, desperate to be cured, and characterized as highly neurotic. Whether, in fact, this has anything to do with his Jewish background, as Portnoy insists, is open to question.

Scholars often regard Cynthia Ozick as the best Jewish-American female writer. Primarily a writer of short stories and essays, her short novel *The Messiah of Stockholm* (1987) takes the reader into Ozick's world of idolatry and Jewishness, a Jewishness not addressed in the works of most Jewish-American authors. She shares with Chaim Potok a belief in the importance of Judaism, the religion, not just Jewishness, the culture. The novel refers to the attempt to rediscover "The Messiah," ostensibly a lost manuscript by the Kafkaesque writer Bruno Schulz who was murdered by the Nazis. Ozick is concerned with Jewish life in the United States and the place of Judaism and of spiritual life in the world. She believes that even she, as an author, is guilty of idolatry in her worship of art and in the fictions she creates. Is the hunt for the missing manuscript idolatrous? As one reviewer put it, the novel is about "faith and authenticity," subjects placed in a much wider context than that usually associated with Jewish-American novels.

The Jewish-American novel has changed as different generations of Jews have reacted to the American experience. Having brought with them from Europe a heritage of religious learning and shared values that saw them through adversity, Jews adapted to the American environment by turning in large numbers from religious to secular pursuits. They achieved great material successes, but there was a price to be paid in surety and cohesiveness. Jewish-American novelists chronicle this change.

EDWARD A. ABRAMSON

See also Saul Bellow; Call It Sleep; Bernard Malamud; Portnoy's Complaint; Isaac Bashevis Singer

Further Reading
Bilik, Dorothy S., *Immigrant Survivors: Post-Holocaust Consciousness in Recent Jewish-American Literature,* New York: Wesleyan University Press, 1980
Burstein, Janet H., *Writing Mothers, Writing Daughters: Tracing the Maternal in Stories by American Jewish Women,* Urbana: University of Illinois Press, 1996
Fried, Lewis, editor, *Handbook of American-Jewish Literature: An Analytical Guide to Topics, Themes, and Sources,* New York: Greenwood Press, 1988
Girgus, Sam, *The New Covenant: Jewish Writers and the American Idea,* Chapel Hill: University of North Carolina Press, 1984
Guttmann, Allen, *The Jewish Writer in America: Assimilation and the Crisis Identity,* New York: Oxford University Press, 1971
Harap, Louis, *The Image of the Jew in American Literature,* Philadelphia: Jewish Publication Society of America, 1974; 2nd edition, 1978

Harap, Louis, *Creative Awakening: The Jewish Presence in Twentieth Century American Literature, 1900–1940s,* New York and London: Greenwood Press, 1987
Harap, Louis, *In the Mainstream: The Jewish Presence in Twentieth Century American Literature, 1950s–1980s,* New York: Greenwood Press, 1987
Knopp, Josephine, *The Trial of Judaism in Contemporary Jewish Writing,* Urbana: University of Illinois Press, 1975
Liptzin, Sol, *The Jew in American Literature,* New York: Bloch, 1966
Pinsker, Sanford, *Jewish-American Fiction, 1917–1987,* New York: Twayne, and Toronto: Macmillan, 1992
Schulz, Max, *Radical Sophistication: Studies in Contemporary Jewish-American Novelists,* Athens: Ohio University Press, 1969
Sherman, Bernard, *The Invention of the Jew: Jewish-American Education Novels, 1916–1964,* New York: Thomas Yoseloff, 1969
Walden, Daniel, editor, *Studies in American Jewish Literature 3* (1983)
Wisse, Ruth, *The Schlemiel as Modern Hero,* Chicago: University of Chicago Press, 1971

Jin Ping Mei. *See* Six Classic Chinese Novels

Johnny the Partisan by Beppe Fenoglio

Il Partigiano Johnny 1968

Published posthumously, *Johnny the Partisan* was greeted immediately as an extraordinary literary achievement. Critics referred to the work as a "modern Odyssey" and as a novel of biblical proportions. It was considered the masterpiece of a writer who, isolated in the provinces and reluctant to conform to the literary establishment, had previously been known only to a restricted literary circle. Although incomplete, *Johnny the Partisan* reflects Beppe Fenoglio's stylistic and linguistic search for a new literary expression within the context of his characteristic epic representation of reality. The result, even in its unfinished state, is one of the most original novels of 20th-century Italian literature. Fenoglio's unique exploration of language, combined with an unrhetorical, antiheroic, and bitterly realistic interpretation of the antifascist armed resistance in Italy, best illustrates the author's nonconformist role in the panorama of contemporary Italian narrative.

The manuscript was first edited and published in 1968 by Lorenzo Mondo, who pieced together two incomplete versions found among the author's unpublished writings. Autobiographical in part, it is the story of Johnny, a young Anglophile with an inherent aversion to fascist pomp, who was also the protagonist of Fenoglio's *Primavera di bellezza* (1959; Springtime of Beauty). In fact, *Primavera di bellezza* is only a small part of a more elaborate project Fenoglio had worked on for several years. This vast project was to appear in two volumes and was to cover the period from 1940 to 1945. Instead, the published work starts late in 1942, when Johnny is called to arms, and ends with his return home from Rome soon after the armistice on 8 September 1943. *Johnny the Partisan* begins where *Primavera di bellezza* leaves off and continues into the early months of 1945, shortly before the war's conclusion. During this period the protagonist evades the fascists' call to arms and joins the partisans. He remains alone in the Piedmontese mountains through the bitter winter of 1944 when the partisans are forced to disband and the resistance becomes a dramatic struggle for survival. He finally rejoins the antifascist troops in the spring of 1945.

In this novel, Fenoglio represents war as a universal human experience. *Johnny the Partisan* is a novel of the existential crisis of identity of an entire generation of young men compelled to enter into the conflict. In this narrative of civil war, Fenoglio does not pass judgment on the sides involved in the struggle. Instead, he transforms the realities of the resistance into a comprehensive symbol of the drama and cruelty of human existence, which he sees as dominated by tragic violence.

The richness and originality of this text lie in its language, a creative and subjective effort that demonstrates an English influence. Fenoglio had translated English and American texts, experimenting with language and style, which had an enormous impact on his creative works. However, it is unclear just how we must construe Fenoglio's linguistic experiments. Shortly after his death, his surviving manuscripts gave rise to a philological debate about compositional chronology that resulted in a highly controversial reconstruction of the genesis of *Johnny the Partisan*. The editors of the 1978 edition of Fenoglio's complete works separated the two drafts of *Johnny the Partisan* and included a third, fragmented English version as the first phase of Fenoglio's partisan war epic. Following the arrangement of the texts, the editors advanced the theory that *Johnny the Partisan* was written in the immediate postwar years. They speculated that the drafts formed a narrative reservoir from which the author drew from the beginning of his career until his death. The stylistic excesses of the first draft, they argued, suggest a period of literary apprenticeship. Moreover, the editors held that the author's later works, beginning with the first draft of *Primavera di bellezza*, clearly distance themselves from the two *Johnny the Partisan* texts and display a stylistic restraint that is the result of a much greater maturity. Critics opposing this theory have argued that the drafts of *Johnny the Partisan* were, instead, written in the mid-to-late 1950s by a more seasoned author, who had left behind his early neorealism and had set his sights on bilingual experimentation.

Distancing himself from Italian traditions—of both postwar neorealism and of the elegant *prosa d'arte*—Fenoglio turned to the Anglo-Saxon world for inspiration. Once free of the stifling and rhetorical tradition of Italian letters, he sought to achieve a concise, lean, and rhythmic prose consonant with his apprecia-

tion of English and American literature. In the final evaluation of the expressive apparatus invented by Fenoglio for the two drafts of *Johnny the Partisan*, the reader must keep in mind the incomplete and therefore provisional nature of the text, which the author most certainly would have subjected to subsequent revisions. As Italo Calvino noted in a 1972 interview, the stylistic richness of *Johnny the Partisan*, which has fascinated readers and critics alike, was not the ultimate aim of its author. Instead, according to Calvino, the semi-elaborated material represents a type of "mental language," an intermediary of the creative act that was destined to "disappear once in print." The many drafts, or rewritings, are a testimony to Fenoglio's labors in fashioning a new and distinctive style.

MARK PIETRALUNGA

Further Reading

Beccaria, Gian Luigi, *La guerra e gli asfodeli: Romanzo e vocazione epica di Beppe Fenoglio*, Milan: Serra e Riva, 1984

Bigazzi, Roberto, *Fenoglio: Personaggi e narratori*, Rome: Salerno, 1983

Corti, Maria, *Storia di un "continuum" narrativo*, Padua: Liviana, 1980

De Nicola, Francesco, *Come leggere "Il partigiano Johnny" di Beppe Fenoglio*, Milan: Mursia, 1985

De Nicola, Francesco, *Introduzione a Fenoglio*, Rome: Laterza, 1989

"Fenoglio: Dieci anni dalla morte," edited by Mario Micinesi, *Uomini e libri* 40 (1972)

Grignani, Maria Antonietta, *Beppe Fenoglio*, Florence: Le Monnier, 1981

Isella, Dante, "La lingua del 'Partigiano Johnny'," in *Beppe Fenoglio Romanzo e racconti*, Turin and Paris: Einaudi-Gallimard, 1992

Lagorio, Gina, *Fenoglio*, Florence: La Nuova Italia, 1970

Meddemmen, John, "Documenting a Mobile Polyglot Idiolect; Beppe Fenoglio's *Partigiano Johnny* and Its Critical Edition," *Modern Language Notes* 97 (1982)

Pietralunga, Mark, *Beppe Fenoglio and English Literature: A Study of the Writer as Translator*, Berkeley: University of California Press, 1987

Soletti, Elisabetta, *Beppe Fenoglio*, Milan: Mursia, 1987

Uwe Johnson 1934–84

German

Uwe Johnson was the youngest of the important triad of novelists after World War II trying to come to terms with Germany's role in the 20th century. A decade younger than Günter Grass and almost two decades younger than Heinrich Böll, Johnson was born in 1934 in Kämmin (then Pomerania, today part of Po-

land) as the son of a minor agrarian technician who was taken into custody by the Russians in 1945 and never heard from again. Johnson's mother had her husband declared legally dead in 1948, and she worked at various jobs to support herself and her two children, Uwe and Elke. The relationship between the author and his mother was a strained one, owing in no small part to the fact that she had been a willing believer and participant in Nazi ideology; she had agreed to have Uwe attend a special Nazi school for precocious children. The end of the war brought an end to this unwelcome experience of half a year, when the Johnson family had to relocate, settling in Mecklenburg, the former grand-duchy on the shores of the Baltic Sea, in the small village of Recknitz, then in Güstrow. Here, Johnson completed his schooling, graduating as "by far the best student in his class." He came to consider Mecklenburg his emotional home and made the region the focal point of all his works.

Johnson's novels frequently portray the situations of average and ordinary people living under totalitarian political systems that claim to contain absolute truth. Having experienced such claims from Germany's various governments, he had come to believe that "one's own experiences are the only thing an author can vouch for," and he based his novels on just that: the facts of his own experience. But he also was concerned with the use of language, both the language used by the author (who does not, according to Johnson, have a "god-like overview like a Balzac") and that used by the characters in his fictions, who are formed by the language they are born into and by the language choices they make. Johnson learned from the writings of William Faulkner—a major literary experience for him—and became the first German author to use multiperspectivism effectively: each of his fictive figures is as important for the story, with his or her own point of view, as the author with his outsider's view. Thus, in *Mutmassungen über Jakob* (1959; *Speculations about Jakob*), the "truth" of the action emerges as all the people who have known the protagonist (the railroad dispatcher Jakob, already dead when the novel begins) relate their personal experiences pertaining to him, which the reader then, as another active ingredient in the novel, must abstract from what the author has put down on paper.

Johnson does not follow the same pattern in all his novels, however. He believed that each theme needs to find its appropriate structure. In *Das dritte Buch über Achim* (1961; *The Third Book about Achim*), Karsch, a West German journalist, while visiting a former girlfriend in East Germany, is persuaded to write the biography of an East German bicycle racer, who has not only become an idol of the masses but is also claimed as a symbol of the "new and vigorous" East German state. To preserve this image, Karsch is only allowed to write about those aspects of the racer's life that keep the idolatry intact. However, he finds himself unable to use the German language for such a purpose or to propagate the ideology of the state.

In *Zwei Ansichten* (1965; *Two Views*), the building of the Berlin Wall causes a love affair to be thwarted, in Romeo and Juliet fashion. The young photographer B. smuggles Nurse D. from East Berlin to West Berlin, only to find that their half-hearted affair had simply been enhanced by the obstacle of the wall. The two do not marry, and Nurse D. begins a new life in a different political system.

Johnson's magnum opus is the novel *Jahrestage* (1970–83; *Anniversaries*). In this work, Gesine Cresspahl, the beloved of Jakob Abs from *Speculations about Jakob* (note the similarities to Faulkner: parts of Johnson's fictive universe are used again, with the same characters, of which now different ones are highlighted), lives in New York City with her daughter Marie, Jakob's child. The novel consists of diary entries (spanning the

year from 21 August 1967 to 20 August 1968) that are purportedly related by Gesine to the person she calls "Genosse Johnson" (Comrade Johnson), a friend who lends his experience as an author to the enterprise. Gesine tells of daily happenings at 96th and Broadway, where she and Marie live on Riverside Drive, along with stories from the *New York Times* that catch her attention during her daily perusal of the paper. At the same time, we hear the Cresspahl family history, as told to Marie, from World War I to the present: Gesine's father Heinrich had been lured back to Mecklenburg by his love for Lisbeth Papenbrock, just as Hitler came to power; Lisbeth committed suicide when Gesine was five years old, in 1938, to atone for the murder of the Jews in her hometown Jerichow. Both parents' family backgrounds are given in great detail, as are the circumstances of life in Mecklenburgian Germany in the 1930s. Of Gesine, we learn that she would rather live in New York than in West Germany because she suffers from feelings of guilt over the deeds perpetrated under Hitler, particularly the systematic killing of Jews (seeing a photo of corpses from Auschwitz traumatizes her). However, New York is not home, and Gesine finally concludes that nowhere is there a "moral Switzerland" into which one can escape. Gesine does, however, encourage her banker employer to aid the newly humanized socialism in Czechoslovakia with bank loans to further the country's emerging "socialism with a human face." The novel ends as Gesine prepares to board her flight to Prague on 20 August 1968—not knowing, as does the reader, that she will be landing there at the same time that Russian tanks are squelching the "Prague Spring."

Johnson gives the technique of stream of consciousness a new twist in this book of almost 2,000 pages. All events, contemporary as well as historical, are held in the one consciousness of the protagonist, Gesine Cresspahl, and through her "reading" of them—including her reading of selections from the *New York Times*—we are given her particular subjective reactions colored by her particular consciousness, a consciousness that was formed and deformed by the country and history into which she happened to be born. "Geschichte ist ein Entwurf," her old teacher says toward the end of the novel, which can mean "History is a plan (or blueprint)" as well as "History is a hasty sketch."

Uwe Johnson's works won many literary prizes: in 1960, the Berlin Fontane prize; in 1962, Prix International de la Littérature; in 1971, the Georg Büchner prize; in 1975, the Braunschweig Wilhelm Raabe prize; and in 1979, the Lübeck Thomas Mann prize. The great body of secondary literature about his works continues to grow steadily, revealing a vast interest in his quite unmistakable voice.

LISELOTTE M. DAVIS

Biography

Born 20 July 1934 in Kämmin, Pomerania (now in Poland). Attended school in Güstrow; University of Rostock, 1952–54; University of Leipzig, 1954–56 (broke off studies without graduating). Freelance writer; lived in Güstrow until 1959, in West Berlin, 1959–74, and in England from 1975; lecturer, Wayne State University, Detroit, and Harvard University, Cambridge, Massachusetts, 1961; editor of German writing, Harcourt Brace, publishers, New York, 1966–67. Died 15 March 1984.

Novels by Johnson

Mutmassungen über Jakob, 1959; as *Speculations about Jakob,* translated by Ursule Molinaro, 1967

Das dritte Buch über Achim, 1961; as *The Third Book about Achim,* translated by Ursule Molinaro, 1967

Zwei Ansichten, 1965; as *Two Views,* translated by Richard and Clara Winston, 1966

Jahrestage: Aus dem Leben von Gesine Cresspahl, 1970–83; as *Anniversaries: From the Life of Gesine Cresspahl,* volumes 1–2 translated by Leila Vennewitz, 1975; volumes 3–4 by Vennewitz and Walter Arndt, 1987

Ingrid Babendererde: Reifeprüfung 1953, 1985

Versuch, einen Vater zu finden: Marthas Ferien, 1988

Heute Neunzig Jahr, 1996

Other Writings: short stories, essays.

Further Reading

Bengel, Michael, editor, *Johnsons "Jahrestage,"* Frankfurt am Main: Suhrkamp, 1985

Boulby, Mark, *Uwe Johnson,* New York: Ungar, 1974

Fahlke, Eberhard, *Die "Wirklichkeit" der Mutmassungen: Eine politische Lesart der "Mutmassungen über Jakob" von Uwe Johnson,* Frankfurt am Main: Lang, 1982

Fickert, Kurt J., *Neither Left nor Right: The Politics of Individualism in Uwe Johnson's Work,* New York: Peter Lang, 1987

Fickert, Kurt J., *Dialogue with the Reader: The Narrative Stance in Uwe Johnson's Fiction,* Columbia, South Carolina: Camden House, 1996

Gansel, Carsten, and Nicolai Riedel, editors, *Uwe Johnson zwischen Vomoderne und Postmoderne,* Berlin and New York: de Gruyter, 1995

Gerlach, Ingeborg, *Auf der Suche nach der verlorenen Identität: Studien zu Uwe Johnsons "Jahrestagen,"* Königstein: Scriptor, 1980

Helbig, Holger, *Beschreibung einer Beschreibung: Untersuchungen zu Uwe Johnsons Roman "Das dritte Buch über Achim,"* Göttingen: Vandenhoeck and Ruprecht, 1996

Neumann, Bernd, *Utopie und Mimesis: Zum Verhältnis von Ästhetik, Gesellschaftsphilosophie und Politik in den Romanen Uwe Johnsons,* Kronberg: Athenäum, 1978

Neumann, Bernd, *Uwe Johnson,* Hamburg: Europäische Verlagsanstalt, 1994

Paulsen, Wolfgang, *Innenansichten: Uwe Johnsons Romanwelt,* Tübingen: Francke, 1997

Riedel, Nicolai, *Uwe Johnson: Bibliographie 1959–1980,* Bonn: Bouvier, 1981

Schmitz, Walter, *Uwe Johnson,* Munich: Beck, 1984

Schwarz, Wilhelm Johannes, *Der Erzähler Uwe Johnson,* Bern: Francke, 1970; 2nd edition, 1973

Journalism and the Novel

It is probably fair to say that the novel as a form would not have happened if there had not been journalism. On the other side, journalism probably required the novel for its existence. This dialectical relation between what is essentially a fictional form and what is essentially a factual one is extremely complex and began in the late 16th and early 17th century in England and Europe with the emergence of the printing press.

The deployment of print during the 16th century virtually created the possibility of novels and news—both of which require the informational dispersal technology that the press provided, and both of which are defined by typography. (One could argue that the novel preceded print, that novels existed in ancient Greece or in medieval Europe, but most readers would probably agree that the production we now call "the novel" could not exist without typography.) Indeed, the word *novel* was used interchangeably with *news* in England before the 18th century to describe printed ballads and tales. The ballad was a hybrid form, written in rhyme and meter, printed and sold on a single sheet of paper, and acting as, in essence, a news report of extraordinary, criminal, amorous, and often supernatural events, presenting them as if they were indeed real events. Likewise, jests, tales, and brief stories were called interchangeably "news" or "novels."

During the 17th century, the poetic ballad was replaced by the prose newsbook or news pamphlet. This period begins to see a consolidation of what is "factual" under the rubric of "news" and what is "fictional" under the rubric of "novel." The prime cause of this separation of fact from fiction is extremely difficult to pinpoint. In England, with the overthrow of the monarchy, and in Europe, with the growth of republican tendencies, news became ideological, and control of the news became part of a political struggle. Thus it was in the interests of the state to distinguish news from other kinds of writing. Further, with the development of rule by ideology and persuasion rather than rule by pure force, the printing press became a central instrument, and symbolic production in culture became an important activity for contending forces. Whether one creates symbols through fiction or journalism, one does so to affect what Jürgen Habermas (1989) has called "the public sphere." Indeed, libel laws controlling the production of printed material, refined in England in the 18th century, sealed these distinctions between fact, which was legally actionable, and fiction, which was not.

All these conditions led to a conjunction of a means of distributing symbolic production and literate segments of society that could readily absorb that production. In other words, print had to become fully accepted as a "neutral" method of distributing symbolized ideas and formations, and society had to conceive of itself as a "public" made up of autonomous units linked by that very process of symbolic production.

Thus, the novel is dependent on print and on a "public" virtually constructed to receive that print, as writers such as Benedict Anderson (rev. ed., 1991) have pointed out. Furthermore, the novel depends on the construction of and division between intellectual spaces we now call "fact" and "fiction." That is, the existence of fiction depends on the category of the factual; fiction is dialectically dependent on journalism and history. In reality, experience is a continuum of events that achieve different degrees of substantiation. The arbitrary cutting of that continuum into "fact" and "fiction" is the product of Enlightenment thought systems as well as laws. The dialectic of Enlightenment, as Theodor Adorno and Max Horkheimer have pointed out (in *The Dialectic of Enlightenment*, 1972), is precisely one that arises from an ideological belief in the power of positivistic thought. Our modern sciences, and our very way of thinking, are dependent on the convenient limiting of experience to the realm of the factual. By creating this positivistic space, it is then possible to posit a purely "fictional" space for symbolic production. That fictional space is called many things in the 18th century—one of them is "the novel." It certainly can be argued that this fictional space is also called "the female," "the irrational," or "the colonial." Similarly, the space of "fact" might also be called "the male," "the rational," "the imperial," and so on.

Therefore, by the 18th century, a clearer distinction emerged between journalism and fiction. Although clearer, the distinction remained somewhat blurred in the sense that fiction often would be used to report on the world in a disguised (and legally protected) manner. Likewise, journalism was a kind of reified category that, like history, proposed itself as objective, while of course being determined by ideological predispositions.

Novelists of the 18th century clearly were well aware of the dialectics of fact and fiction, since almost all the major novelists were in effect journalists as well. Daniel Defoe, author of *Robinson Crusoe* (1719), *Colonel Jack* (1722), *Moll Flanders* (1722), *Roxana* (1724), *Duncan Campbell* (1720), *A Journal of the Plague Year* (1722), and *Jonathan Wild* (1725), among many other works, was also the writer for the newspaper the *Review* along with the *Observator*. Indeed, his novels purported to be factual accounts or reports on famous or infamous people.

Daniel Defoe himself was a bit of an enigma insofar as his own factual status was concerned. He had been jailed for writing a pamphlet entitled *The Shortest Way with the Dissenters* (1702) in which he, himself a dissenter, advocated through a fictionalized voice that all members of his own religious sect be banished from England and their preachers hanged. Defoe did this to make the High Church seem ridiculous, but his intentions were misunderstood. In order to be released from jail, Defoe agreed to edit a newspaper that would appear to oppose the government but would actually write what the government wished. Defoe also acted as a spy and edited many publications under disguised names or pretexts. In other words, Defoe himself was suited to write in a genre that emphasized the dialectic between fact and fiction. His novels all purported to tell the true and remarkable stories of newsworthy criminals, castaways, charlatans, and pirates, and so were not that different from the contemporaneous, and very popular, news accounts of the same.

Henry Fielding, author of *Joseph Andrews* (1742), *Tom Jones* (1749), and *Amelia* (1751), was the editor of the newspaper *The Champion* as well as the author of many news-related pamphlets. Samuel Richardson, author of *Pamela* (1740), *Clarissa* (1747–48), and *Sir Charles Grandison* (1753–54), although not a journalist, was a printer of newspapers, and as such was therefore intricately involved in the technology of journalism. Other 18th-century writers such as Samuel Johnson, Joseph Addison, Richard Steele, and Mary Wollstonecraft saw no discrepancy between writing essays or fiction and being journalists.

Since one of the hallmarks of the novel is "realism," it is also possible to find in both novels and journalism an attempt to portray a real world through words. The novel then is a strangely paradoxical art object that can be thought of as a "factual fiction" (see Davis, 1983). As a public form of symbolic production, the novel must disguise its artifice and even its quite symbolic structure by appearing *as if* it were life or experience. This realism serves the function of justifying the very project of making up images, or inventing lies, of creating simulacra that are passed off as quasi-fact.

In addition to realism, one could argue that reporting on the world and writing fictional accounts of that world are deeply interconnected activities. Many novelists, for example, write their works to report on social injustices. One has only to think of the female writers of the 18th and 19th centuries—Mary Wollstonecraft, Anne Brontë, Elizabeth Gaskell, George Eliot—whose aim in part was to reveal to the public at large the injustices committed against women, to understand the intimate connection between writing novels and exposing abuses. British and European novelists such as Charles Dickens, Émile Zola, Thomas Hardy, and Joseph Conrad made careers of writing novels to expose discriminatory and unfair practices. Dickens' *Hard Times* (1854) revealed the abusive nature of factory work; his *Oliver Twist* (1838) was written to reform the poor laws; and *Bleak House* (1853) contained an exposé of Chancery. Zola's *Germinal* (1885) uncovered the cruelty of the mining industry as effectively as his open letter to the President of France, "J'accuse" (1898), highlighted the injustice of the Dreyfus affair; Conrad's "Heart of Darkness" (1902) was a critique of Belgium's exploitation of the Congo, and his *Nostromo* (1904) critiqued the systematic colonialism of Latin America; Hardy's *Jude the Obscure* (1895) castigated the divorce laws in England.

In the United States, the journalistic and novelistic traditions dovetailed so neatly that, as one critic writes, "the usual view is that realism in fiction, from Twain to Hemingway, developed out of the major realists' experience as journalists, so that the techniques of American realism are those of the newsroom and the reporter." American writers who were also novelists included Mark Twain, Stephen Crane, Theodore Dreiser, Ernest Hemingway, John Steinbeck, John Dos Passos, Frank Norris, Katherine Anne Porter, Richard Wright, Eudora Welty, and Sinclair Lewis.

Notable 20th-century American novelists who wrote muckraking novels with strongly investigatory condemnations of industry include Upton Sinclair, who had investigated the Chicago stockyards and then wrote *The Jungle* (1906). Frank Norris, who reported on the Boer War for *Collier's* and the Spanish-American War for *McClure's Magazine*, wrote *The Octopus* (1901), a novel about the raising of wheat in California and the struggle of ranchers against the railroad. Norris also authored *The Pit* (1903) about speculation in the Chicago wheat exchange. Theodore Dreiser, who had been a reporter in St. Louis, Chicago, Pittsburgh, and New York, wrote, among other works, *An American Tragedy* (1925), which was a fictional version of an actual New York murder case.

One case in particular might show the intersection of journalism and fiction in the 20th century. The great American classic *The Grapes of Wrath* (1939) may be seen as a novel, the epic story of the fictional Joad family in their American tragedy from dustbowl to migrant laborers in California. At the same time, its genesis was clearly deeply related to journalism. Steinbeck himself referred to journalism as "the mother of literature." Contemporary critics of the work noted that the book borrowed its techniques from newsreel and print reportage. Indeed, the final chapters of the book probably represent actual events that Steinbeck witnessed in February 1938 near Visalia, California, where 5,000 migrant families were stranded during flooding, and which he initially reported on in the *Monterey Trader*. He had also written about migrants for *The Nation* and the San Francisco *News*. Steinbeck's information in this novel came from news reports as well as personal observation, so in the end one cannot say whether the novel is an extended piece of journalism or a fictional work with journalistic underpinnings.

Many novelists have enlisted their fiction to argue for political causes or to detail, in fictional form, autobiographical experiences of war or political intrigue. Notable among these is George Orwell, whose first novel, *Burmese Days* (1934), reflects his experiences serving with the Indian Imperial Police in Burma (now Myanmar). His fictional autobiographical attempts neatly slid into memoir in his books *Down and Out in Paris and London* (1933), his record of the Spanish Civil War in *Homage to Catalonia* (1938), and his reports on unemployment in *The Road to Wigan Pier* (1937). Ernest Hemingway, too, who was a reporter in Kansas City, later recorded his experiences of the Spanish Civil War in his novel *For Whom the Bell Tolls* (1940). Especially in colonized countries, novelists were often journalists, and wrote fiction of a journalistic nature. Writers such as Colombia's Gabriel García Márquez, Peru's Mario Vargas Llosa, and Nigeria's Buchi Emecheta come to mind.

In the second half of the 20th century, journalism and fiction came together in what has been called the New Journalism, in which writers such as Norman Mailer, John McPhee, Hunter Thompson, Tom Wolfe, Truman Capote, and Don DeLillo blurred the lines between reportage and fiction making. Contemporary novelists often use factual techniques like reportage and combine them with magical or supernatural elements in the genre of magical realism. Indeed, where the novel may be said to have been inaugurated in the 18th century by the division of fact from fiction, the late 20th century is a time when both novelists and journalists are reexamining those originating divisions. One could say that postmodernism and some of its allied discourses such as deconstruction have led to what the French philosopher Jean François Lyotard (in *The Postmodern Condition: A Report on Knowledge,* 1984) has called the breakdown of "meta-narratives." These meta-narratives—history, science, journalism—provide overarching meanings to individual narratives. Novelists and journalists of the late 20th century, without the discursive structuration of meta-narratives, which had provided clear road signs between fact and fiction, are in some sense left free, or perhaps free-falling, to explore the ways that language itself creates (or destroys) the illusion of factuality. Thus the novel of the present has become not so much a factual fiction as a factless fiction.

LENNARD J. DAVIS

See also Class and the Novel; Critics and Criticism (18th Century); English Novel (18th Century); Genre Criticism; Historical Writing and the Novel; Ideology and the Novel; New Journalism; Novel and Romance: Etymologies; Periodicals and the Serialization of Novels; Prose Novelistic Forms; Realism; Reviewers and the Popular Press; Roman-Feuilleton

Further Reading

Anderson, Benedict, *Imagined Communities: Reflections on the Origin and Spread of Nationalism,* London: Verso, 1983; revised edition, London and New York: Verso, 1991

Davis, Lennard J., *Factual Fictions: The Origins of the English Novel,* New York: Columbia University Press, 1983

Davis, Lennard J., *Resisting Novels: Ideology and Fiction,* London and New York: Methuen, 1987

Fishkin, Shelley Fisher, *From Fact to Fiction: Journalism and Imaginative Writing in America,* Baltimore and London: Johns Hopkins University Press, 1985

Frus, Phyllis, *The Politics and Poetics of Journalistic Narrative: The Timely and the Timeless,* Cambridge and New York: Cambridge University Press, 1994

Habermas, Jürgen, *The Structural Transformation of the Public Sphere: An Inquiry into a Category of Bourgeois Society,* Cambridge, Massachusetts: MIT Press, 1989; originally published as *Strukturwandel der Öffentlichkeit: Untersuchungen zu einer Kategorie der burgerlichen Gesellschaft,* 1962

Hellmann, John, *Fables of Fact: The New Journalism as New Fiction,* Urbana: University of Illinois Press, 1981

Sims, Norman, editor, *Literary Journalism in the Twentieth Century,* New York: Oxford University Press, 1990

The Journey of Little Gandhi by Ilyās Khūrī

Riḥlat Ghāndī al-ṣaghīr 1989

With the publication of *Riḥlat Ghāndī al-ṣaghīr* in 1989, Ilyās Khūrī established himself as an important novelist not only in his native Lebanon but also in the rest of the Arab world. The novel's subsequent translations into English (*The Journey of Little Gandhi,* 1994) and French (*Le petite homme et la guerre,* 1995) attest to its international importance as a prime example of the general development of the Arabic novel. *The Journey of Little Gandhi* departs from the traditional narrative structure of a clear beginning, middle, and end that prevailed in the production of the Arabic novel since its inception at the beginning of the 20th century. It opens with the death of Little Gandhi in the summer of 1982 during the Israeli invasion of Lebanon. This novel's significance is derived not only from the historical moment—the Lebanese civil war (1975–90) and the Israeli invasion—but also from interrogating that historical moment about the meaning of life, death, history, and religion.

A distinctive feature of Khūrī's novel is its method of narration, which defies summary because it is constructed of many embedded stories. The first page of the novel reads, "I'm telling the story and it hasn't even ended yet. And the story is nothing but names. When I found out their names, I found out the story." What proceeds are the stories of the many names enumerated in the first page of the novel; the narrative moves from one story to another, from one incident to another, by the mere mention of a name or an association. The narrator asks and investigates but keeps "finding holes in the story." In the narrator's attempt to relate Little Gandhi's journey, a larger story of life and death is told, a story "about those who couldn't escape" from the atrocities of the civil war and the Israeli invasion. It is the story of Gandhi, Alice, the narrator, and many others who either survive or perish in the midst of war.

Most of the stories in *Little Gandhi* revolve around the relationship between writing and death. As Khūrī notes elsewhere,

"writing is a journey towards the known and the unknown. . . . Writing indicates a way of life and not a lesson filled with ideology." In *Little Gandhi,* writing engages itself with and interrogates various concerns, whether they are ideological, political, social, historical, or religious, and becomes a mirror that does not reflect a single absolute truth or reality. Like the mirror, writing approaches reality from many different angles, as the opening verse by the Sufi Ibn ʿArabī in *The Journey of Little Gandhi* tells us: "A face is only one except when it is reflected by many mirrors then it becomes many."

Ilyās Khūrī does not offer any definitive answers for the dilemmas of life, war, and invasion. With its embedded stories, Khūrī's *Little Gandhi* could even be said to parallel the "Lebanese wars" and their seemingly unresolved events. While the "journey" is tragic for most of the characters in the novel, the narrator, like Scheherazade in *A Thousand and One Nights,* wards off death with his stories. In this context, writing, through the creative act, provides life and continuation in the midst of war and destruction.

SABAH GHANDOUR

See also Ilyās Khūrī

Further Reading

Abū Dīb, Kamāl, "Al-naṣṣ wal-ḥaqīqah," *Mawāqif* 69 (Autumn 1992)

Barādah, Muḥammad, "Al-Taʿaddud al-Lughawī fī al-Riwāyah al-ʿArabiyah," *Mawāqif* 69 (Autumn 1992)

Ghandour, Sabah, "Riḥlat ḥayāt aw mawt? Ḥawla riḥlat Ghāndī al-ṣaghīr," *Mawāqif* 72 (Summer 1993)

Ghandour, Sabah, Foreword to *The Journey of Little Gandhi,* by Ilyās Khūrī, Minneapolis: University of Minnesota Press, 1994

Journey to the End of the Night by Louis-Ferdinand Céline

Voyage au bout de la nuit 1932

Céline claimed in an interview that his intention in writing *Journey to the End of the Night* was purely commercial: he wanted to enjoy the same commercial success that Eugène Dabit had garnered from *Hôtel du Nord* (1931).

Céline chose the picaresque form for his novel. This type of text was initiated in 16th-century Spain by the classic anonymous text *Lazarillo de Tormes,* and it is familiar to most people who have studied in the French education system through Alain René Lesage's multivolume *Histoire de Gil Blas de Santillane* (1715–35; *The Adventures of Gil Blas*). The picaresque novel is

always presented by a first-person narrator who suffers a series of failures and reverses, forcing him or her constantly to change location and social station. This provides the narrator the opportunity to describe constantly changing scenes and to depict a multitude of human weaknesses.

Céline made full use of the potential of the picaresque genre. His narrator, Bardamu, undergoes the horrors of World War I as a cavalryman at the front until he is wounded, and he then witnesses the madness of military hospitals and wartime civilian life in Paris. He escapes to a tropical colony in Africa and then moves on to the United States, where he describes New York and—from the worker's perspective—conditions in a 1920s auto plant in Detroit. After a hiatus in the narrative, Bardamu is a poor doctor eking out a living in a Parisian slum. He visits a research institute that strangely resembles the Institut Pasteur, is employed briefly in a Parisian music hall, and after a side trip to Toulouse ends up as temporary director of a madhouse outside Paris. Throughout the novel, Robinson, a mysterious alter ego to the narrator, appears and disappears. The story ends when Robinson is murdered.

Usually the narrator of the picaresque novel is emotionally detached, making mildly ironic comments on the conditions he observes. Céline's Bardamu is much more involved and insists on his loneliness and his angst at not being able to remedy the ills he witnesses. This emotionally involved narrator struck a chord with French readers of the 1930s and still moves readers today.

Had it been interesting only for its content, *Journey to the End of the Night* would probably be forgotten by now. The novel's greatest influence has been in the freeing and expanding of novelistic style by opening it up to the resources of oral language. Since the earliest examples, French novels have on occasion incorporated conventions of speech into written dialogue; many readers, for example, will recall the broad Alsatian accent of Balzac's Baron de Nucingen. But traditionally novels have respected all the rules of formal written grammar in the narrative parts of their text. The dichotomy between formal artistic language and everyday speech is underlined by the use of a special verb tense—the *passé simple*—which, now as in 1932, appears only in literary prose.

Céline swept away these conventions. In the narrative and expository parts of *Journey to the End of the Night*, he used slang and obscenities—surprisingly few from today's perspective, but quite enough to shock conservative critics at the time. He made very liberal use of syntactic constructions found only in oral language—suppressing *ne* (the formal marker of negation) before *pas* (not), *rien* (nothing), and *jamais* (never), placing a noun at the beginning or end of a clause for emphasis, and using a pronoun to represent it in the same clause. Céline also tried to enliven his text with the cadences of oral language, through a liberal use of exclamation marks, question marks, and ellipses. This effort was only partially successful because the typesetters removed much of this nonstandard punctuation in preparing the text for printing. Disgusted, the author commented that they wanted him to read like François Mauriac, but he had no choice but to accept the modifications. Subsequent texts such as *Mort à crédit* (1936; *Death on the Installment Plan*) are closer to the author's original punctuation.

Even the regularized form of *Journey to the End of the Night* was sufficient to provoke a storm of controversy. Many commentators praised the text as a breath of fresh air; old-line critics condemned it as pessimistic, obscene, and ungrammatical. It was an open secret that Céline was to receive the coveted Goncourt Prize for his novel, but at the last minute the committee gave in to establishment pressure and awarded the prize to someone else.

Céline added to the controversy by taking a public anti-Soviet stand in 1936, although he had been a darling of the left as a result of his social commentary in *Journey to the End of the Night*. He subsequently published three rabidly anti-Semitic pamphlets (1937–41) and took an ambiguous stand during the occupation. Condemned in absentia for treason after the Liberation, he was pardoned in 1951 and returned to France. From that time until his death in 1961, Céline insisted that he was primarily a stylist and not interested in expressing ideas. Obviously this insistence was self-serving, at least in part. Those of his working manuscripts that have survived and are in the public domain demonstrate, however, that Céline carefully crafted his texts, revising again and again until he achieved the desired effect.

Louis Aragon and Raymond Queneau are generally considered to be directly influenced by Céline. In her memoirs, Simone de Beauvoir states that in 1932 Jean-Paul Sartre was dazzled by *Journey to the End of the Night*, and in the light of this novel completely revised the style of the book he was working on. This book would subsequently be published as *La Nausée* (1938; *Nausea*). Henry Miller, who knew Céline in Paris between the wars, has also acknowledged his literary debt to the author.

Just as Marcel Proust liberated the French novel from the restrictions of linear plot and consistent characterization, Céline freed it from the confines of grammatical orthodoxy and opened it up to the stylistic richness of oral structures. This is the lasting contribution of *Journey to the End of the Night* to the novel.

PAUL A. FORTIER

See also Louis-Ferdinand Céline

Further Reading

Baudelle, Yves, "*Voyage au bout de la nuit* de Louis-Ferdinand Céline," *Roman 20–50: Revue d'Étude du Roman du XXe Siècle* 17 (1994)

Buckley, William K., editor, *Critical Essays on Louis-Ferdinand Céline*, Boston: G.K. Hall, 1988

Burns, Wayne, *Enfin Céline vint: A Contextualist Reading of "Journey to the End of the Night" and "Death on the Installment Plan,"* New York: Peter Lang, 1988

Damour, Anne-Claude, and Jean-Pierre Damour, *Louis-Ferdinand Céline: "Voyage au bout de la nuit,"* Paris: Presses Universitaires de France, 1985; 3rd edition, 1994

Flynn, James, and C.K. Mertz, editors, *Understanding Céline*, Seattle, Washington: Genitron Press, 1984

Fortier, Paul A., "*Voyage au bout de la nuit*": *Étude du fonctionnement des structures thématiques: Le "Métro émotif" de L.-F. Céline*, Paris: Minard, 1982

Godard, Henri, "*Voyage au bout de la nuit*" de Louis-Ferdinand Céline, Paris: Gallimard, 1991

Hewitt, Nicholas, *The Golden Age of Louis-Ferdinand Céline*, Leamington Spa: Berg, and New York: St. Martin's Press, 1987

Revue des Lettres Modernes 849–856 (1988), special issue on Céline

Vitoux, Frédéric, *La vie de Céline*, Paris: Grasset, 1988

Journey to the West. *See* Six Classic Chinese Novels

James Joyce 1882–1941

Irish

James Joyce ranks as one of the most influential novelists of the 20th century. As an Irishman, Joyce wrote within a culture that lacked a strong novelistic tradition. He was preceded by Maria Edgeworth, Sheridan LeFanu, Oscar Wilde, George Moore, and legions of ephemeral historical novelists who imitated Sir Walter Scott. The Celtic revival of Joyce's youth favored poetry and plays rather than novels, and Joyce made some early attempts in those genres. Yet, once he settled on fiction, Joyce became a major innovator on a number of thematic and technical fronts. As an heir to French naturalism, his subject matter was unparalleled in its frank portrayal of sexuality and marriage. His Dublin stands with Balzac's Paris, Dostoevskii's St. Petersburg, and Dickens' London as a fully imagined fictive city, holding the form of the novel open also to the fragmentation and ambiguity of the modern metropolis. At the same time, and paradoxically, his elevation of Irish experience to European attention made him the first author of "provincial" British origin to influence the European novel since Scott. His work looks backward to the great 19th-century ideal of the novel, while looking forward to the 20th century's thorough revision of that ideal.

Joyce redefined the novel at every level of narrative. In his early works, the collection of short stories *Dubliners* (1914), and his first novel *A Portrait of the Artist as a Young Man* (1916), Joyce uses a form of *style indirect libre,* or free indirect discourse, of unparalleled subtlety. In *Ulysses* (1922), Joyce continued his investigation of the relationship between the mind and the narrative by using the stream-of-consciousness technique, the supposedly "direct" portrayal of a character's thoughts without authorial mediation. *Ulysses* also broke new ground in its introduction of pervasive mythic structures and multiple epic character analogues to the novel. Its compendious allusiveness make unprecedented intellectual demands upon its readers as does its commingling of realist and antirealist passages and chapters and its introduction of multiple narrators and narrative styles. Joyce's final work, *Finnegans Wake* (1939), rejects the conventions of realist fiction altogether, producing instead a massive archetypal and linguistic fantasia that lacks any of the conventional signposts of novelistic realism—plot, coherent characters, even language recognizable as English.

Joyce's novels have been prized for their avant-garde experimentation and, more recently, for their portrayals of the cultural and political tensions between Ireland and England in the period before Ireland achieved independence in 1921. In addition, their unparalleled psychological insights make them works of rare humanity and sympathetic comedy.

Joyce's first novel, *A Portrait of the Artist as a Young Man*—which appeared in serial form in the periodical *The Egoist* between 1914 and 1915—is arguably his most conventional. Belonging to the Germanic traditions of the Bildungsroman (novel of education) and the *Künstlerroman* (novel of the artist's growth), Joyce's treatment of his nearly autobiographical protagonist, Stephen Dedalus, demonstrates many of Joyce's pervasive thematic concerns: the relationship between the individual and his culture; the struggles of the intellectual against the restraints of late 19th-century Irish nationalism, family, and Catholicism; and the search for identity through language, culture, and art. The novel's greatest narrative innovations derive from its assumption of a flexible style that is closely molded to the maturing consciousness of the protagonist and a selective technique whereby events of the greatest psychological import to the protagonist are presented at greatest length. The opening pages—an apparently disconnected series of sensory impressions and intimations of guilt typical of Stephen's childish consciousness—are balanced at the end by excerpts from the diary of Stephen's early manhood. Lengthily reported scenes with implicitly the greatest formative effect on Stephen's maturing sense of self—most notably, the Christmas dinner argument of chapter I and the hellfire sermon of chapter III—are balanced by the merely fragmentary and impressionistic appearances of members of Stephen's family in much of the narrative. The novel's narrative is entirely inflected by Stephen's values and the growth of his consciousness, even as Joyce allows his readers to register ironic distance from Stephen's adolescent self-absorption.

Stephen reappears in Joyce's masterpiece *Ulysses* as one of two focal characters, the other being the Dublin Everyman, Leopold Bloom. *Ulysses* is, in a limited sense, a sequel to *A Portrait of the Artist as a Young Man,* but it is a great deal more than that: it is at once an idiosyncratic recension of the Victorian multiplot novel of marriage, an interrogation of the relationships between fathers and sons, an attempt to write a modern version of the *Odyssey* set in Dublin, and a philosophical attempt to capture as much of human experience as possible through the lens of a single day (16 June 1904). Its 18 chapters offer an elaborately patterned meditation upon the adventures and moral thematics of Homer's epic, and simultaneously furnish the most thorough documentation ever of a place and time in fiction. In its capacious reflections of the culture of a particular venue and the innermost thoughts of its main characters, *Ulysses* presents a peculiarly modern approach to the phenomena of the world: it is both a defense of realism and a philosophical contemplation of realism's limitations—the contingent relationship between representation and fact. Perhaps the most thoroughly factual and researched novel in the canon, *Ulysses'* consistent experiments with styles simultaneously undermine naturalism's claims to any kind of ultimate truth about the world. Chapters such as "Circe," in which a surrealistic play usurps the nearly documentary realism of the novel's opening, the beginning of "Sirens" or the end of "Oxen of the Sun," in which language itself becomes fragmented, suggest that narrative is always at risk of becoming unhinged from the world. However, the novel's ending—the interior monologue of Molly Bloom—seems to reassert language's ability adequately to reflect human experience.

With *Finnegans Wake*, on which he labored for 17 years, Joyce burst through whatever linguistic and narrative constraints he left unexplored in *Ulysses*. So radical were the drafts of sections that appeared in the journal *transition* in the late 1920s (called at that time *Work in Progress*) that even some of Joyce's greatest admirers (such as the poet Ezra Pound) were unsure of Joyce's artistic intent. Joyce held that *Ulysses* was a book of the day and that *Finnegans Wake* would be a book of the night. To express the dream of a Chapelizod innkeeper, the shifting roles played by his family, and his own inexplicable feelings of guilt, Joyce created a kind of portmanteau language, rich with multilingual puns, filled with carnival-like images of European and Irish political history, and packed with phonetic approximations of Dublin speech.

Registering a debt to the theories of historical recurrence of the 18th-century Italian philosopher Giambattista Vico and to the linguistic playfulness of Lewis Carroll, *Finnegans Wake* consistently eludes any attempts at conventional narrative interpretation: its characters, such as they are, are archetypal. They are embodied frequently as aspects of the Dublin landscape, and often act as structural components within a family rather than as realistic figures. Narrators flicker in and out of focus. Critics disagree whether the book can be understood in novelistic terms or whether its linguistic experimentation and complex family romance produce their own ultimately inexplicable genre, a work of prose *sui generis*.

No novelist has ever charted a greater artistic journey than Joyce. From the Flaubertian precision of his early stories to the incipient postmodernism of *Finnegans Wake*, from the analysis of individual minds to discovering in *Finnegans Wake* all of culture within the universal dreaming mind, his influence has been incalculable. The novels of William Faulkner, John Dos Passos, Thomas Pynchon, Samuel Beckett, Flann O'Brien, Alfred Döblin, Salman Rushdie, Julio Cortázar, and Georges Perec are unthinkable without Joyce's example, as are, less directly, the schools of the French *nouveau roman* and the work of the Latin American magic realists such as Gabriel García Márquez. Joyce's novels provide the definitive bridge between the realist conventions of the 19th century and the most radical experiments of the present day.

SCOTT W. KLEIN

See also Finnegans Wake; Portrait of the Artist as a Young Man; Ulysses

Biography
Born 2 February 1882 in Rathgar, Dublin. Attended Clongowes Wood College, County Kildare, 1888–91; Belvedere College, Dublin, 1893–98; B.A., University College, Dublin, 1902; studied medicine for a short time in Paris, 1902–03. Teacher in Dublin, 1903; English teacher at Berlitz schools in Pola, then in Trieste, 1904–15, Zurich, 1915–18, and again in Trieste, 1918–20; began writing full-time in 1920; lived in Paris, 1920–39, and in Zurich, 1940–41; suffered from glaucoma and nearly blind in his later years. Died 13 January 1941.

Novels by Joyce
A Portrait of the Artist as a Young Man, 1916
Ulysses, 1922
Finnegans Wake, 1939

Other Writings: short stories (*Dubliners*, 1914), a play, verse, letters, book reviews, and critical writings.

Further Reading
Attridge, Derek, editor, *The Cambridge Companion to James Joyce*, Cambridge and New York: Cambridge University Press, 1990

Ellmann, Richard, *Ulysses on the Liffey*, New York: Oxford University Press, 1972

Goldberg, S.L., *The Classical Temper: A Study of James Joyce's "Ulysses,"* London: Chatto and Windus, and New York: Barnes and Noble, 1961

Hart, Clive, and David Hayman, editors, *James Joyce's "Ulysses": Critical Essays*, Berkeley: University of California Press, 1974

Herr, Cheryl, *Joyce's Anatomy of Culture*, Urbana: University of Illinois Press, 1986

Kenner, Hugh, *Dublin's Joyce*, London: Chatto and Windus, 1955; Bloomington: Indiana University Press, 1956

Klein, Scott, *The Fictions of James Joyce and Wyndham Lewis: Monsters of Nature and Design*, Cambridge and New York: Cambridge University Press, 1994

Levin, Harry, *James Joyce: A Critical Introduction*, New York: New Directions, and London: Faber, 1941; revised and augmented edition, 1960

Mahaffey, Vicki, *Reauthorizing Joyce*, Cambridge and New York: Cambridge University Press, 1988

Norris, Margot, *Joyce's Web: The Social Unraveling of Modernism*, Austin: University of Texas Press, 1992

Spoo, Robert E., *James Joyce and the Language of History: Dedalus's Nightmare*, New York: Oxford University Press, 1994

Jude the Obscure by Thomas Hardy

1895

Jude the Obscure was the last novel Hardy wrote, and it is sometimes assumed that because of its unfavorable reception Hardy felt compelled to give up novel writing. But his interest seems to have been shifting back to what he declared was his first love, poetry, which he continued to write prolifically until his death in 1928. Moreover, *Jude the Obscure* was, in fact, well received by more discriminating critics. In *The Life of Thomas Hardy* (nominally a biography written by his second wife, Florence, but now generally recognized as virtually Hardy's own work), Hardy is clearly pleased to quote a letter from the poet Swinburne that praises "the beauty, the terror, and the truth" of *Jude* and dubs Hardy "the most tragic of authors."

The adverse reviews mainly took exception to Hardy's breach of the Victorian taboo on sex. This was true of American reviews, too. For example, Jeannette Gilder, critic for the *New York World,* declared of *Jude* that "Aside from its immorality there is coarseness which is beyond belief." When Gilder asked Hardy for an interview, he replied: "Those readers who, like yourself, could not see that *Jude* (though a book quite without a purpose as it is called) makes for morality more than any other book I have written, are not likely to be made to do so by a newspaper article." However, this statement is slightly disingenuous. The criticism, made by various hostile commentators, that *Jude* was an attack on the very institution of marriage does have relevance. If the novel's theme is not precisely the "holy deadlock" (to use A.P. Herbert's graphic phrase) created by the 19th century's inflexible marriage laws, their devastating psychological effect on Jude Fawley and Sue Bridehead contribute to the novel's searingly emotional power.

The novel is also highly critical of education, institutionalized religion, and the status of women. The class prejudice that prevents Jude from becoming a student at Christminster (the novel's fictionalized version of Oxford University) is feelingly portrayed as a barrier that, if it does not destroy him, contributes substantially to his frustration and ultimate tragedy. The criticism of education is closely related to that of religion, since Christminster is also portrayed as the center of a rigid Christian orthodoxy that sustains the social and political status quo. Besides its role in shoring up the class system, the Church is also faulted for inflicting psychological damage on individual believers, generating, for instance, a masochistic, self-destructive sense of guilt in Sue.

Jude the Obscure has attracted much attention from more recent feminist critics for its treatment of "the woman question." With regard to Jude himself, it might be said that he is a dramatization (although not an unsympathetic one) of the patriarchalism that perceives women as either saints or whores. Jude's sexual life involves an impossibly etherealized relationship with Sue and an equally impossible sensuality with Arabella. But Sue herself is portrayed as a cause as well as a victim of this split, and her intellectual aspirations are seen as being, indeed, at odds with her emotional development. In this respect, Hardy seems to be in tune with the avant-garde thinking of his time. In a postscript added to the 1912 edition of the novel, Hardy refers, approvingly it would seem, to the reaction of a German reviewer who saw in Sue Bridehead "the first delineation in fiction of the

woman who was coming into notice in her thousands every year—the woman of the feminist movement." Hardy was undoubtedly interested in this emergent figure, and he both sympathizes with Sue's liberal, emancipationist aspirations and intuits the emotional strain that defiance of conventional mores, especially for women, brings with it. Modern critical opinion is divided on the question of Sue's nature—whether she is to be regarded as the embodiment of the "new woman," or as a peculiarly neurotic case. But there is general agreement that she is more than a foil to the male hero and that her connection with him raises issues (as D.H. Lawrence, in his unfinished "Study of Thomas Hardy," realized) that reflect a fundamental upheaval in the settled order of relations between the sexes.

Jude the Obscure broke new ground not only thematically; structurally, too, this is an innovative novel. In a group of letters to Edmund Gosse, Hardy refers to the plot as "almost geometrically constructed" and "involving a series of contrasts"—"e.g., Sue and her heathen gods set against Jude's reading the Greek testament; Christminster academical, Christminster in the slums; Jude the saint, Jude the sinner; Sue the pagan, Sue the saint; marriage, no marriage; etc., etc." These balancing antitheses create a pattern that expresses Hardy's sense of the contradictoriness of human life. They give shape and coherence to the novel while emphasizing—ironically, perhaps—the self-division of its characters and the fundamental irrationality of the world they inhabit.

In a number of respects, *Jude* also transcends the realistic criteria that form the aesthetic basis of the 19th-century novel. A character (although "character" in this context is to some extent a misleading term) like Little Time and in episodes such as the boy's journey in the railway train and his bizarre killing of his siblings seem absurd when judged by the usual standards of verisimilitude. And yet they have a strangely haunting, poetic power. Together with Hardy's penchant for extremes of coincidence and chance, also to be found in all his earlier novels, this almost deliberate antirealism gives *Jude the Obscure* unexpected affinities with certain examples of 20th-century modernist and postmodernist fiction. Hardy anticipates not only Lawrence, but also novels such as John Fowles' *The French Lieutenant's Woman* (1969) and Peter Ackroyd's *Chatterton* (1987) and *English Music* (1992). At the same time *Jude* gains some of its "modernity" by deliberate anachronism, adapting, for instance, the satirical humor of the 18th-century novelist Henry Fielding to make of the disastrous illusions of Jude Fawley a kind of "comic tragedy."

Nevertheless, *Jude the Obscure* remains a novel of the 19th century. Its narrative method is comparatively straightforward. It begins at the beginning, follows the normal chronological sequence, and ends at the end. Although it experiments some with point of view techniques, as in the striking scene of the young Jude's acting as bird-scarer for Farmer Troutham, it does not approach Henry James' representations of consciousness. Still less is it experimental in the manner of James Joyce's *Ulysses* (1922) or Virginia Woolf's *To the Lighthouse* (1927) and *The Waves* (1931). Hardy's characteristically latinate vocabulary, often complex sentence structure, and occasionally heavy-handed allusiveness notwithstanding, the novel is never obscure or "difficult" in the modernist manner.

In sum, *Jude*—although the culmination of Hardy's novel-writing career—is a transitional work in the development of fiction. It is a novel in which, to quote Ian Gregor (1974), we can "find displayed the consciousness of self, the innate uncertainties, the psychic disturbance with which fiction of our own day is to make us familiar." In addition, the technique can shift suddenly so that the modern reader feels he is in the fictional world of the 20th century. But the novel's style and narrative method still belong to the 19th century, and its social and intellectual preoccupations are definitely those of its own day. *Jude the Obscure* is a Janus among novels, looking back to the relatively stable world of the 19th century, but also forward to the less certain world and aesthetic of the 20th.

R.P. DRAPER

See also Thomas Hardy

Further Reading

Cox, Reginald Gordon, editor, *Thomas Hardy: The Critical Heritage,* London: Routledge, and New York: Barnes and Noble, 1970

Draper, R.P., "Hardy's Comic Tragedy: *Jude the Obscure,"* in *Thomas Hardy: The Tragic Novels,* edited by Draper, London: Macmillan, 1991

Gregor, Ian, *The Great Web: The Form of Hardy's Major Fiction,* London: Faber and Faber, and Totowa, New Jersey: Rowman and Littlefield, 1974

Ingham, Patricia, *Thomas Hardy,* New York: Harvester Wheatsheaf, 1989

Lodge, David, "*Jude the Obscure*: Pessimism and Fictional Form," in *Critical Approaches to the Fiction of Thomas Hardy,* edited by Dale Kramer, London: Macmillan, and Totowa, New Jersey: Barnes and Noble, 1979

Miller, J. Hillis, *Thomas Hardy: Distance and Desire,* Cambridge, Massachusetts: Belknap Press of Harvard University Press, and London: Oxford University Press, 1970

Millgate, Michael, *Thomas Hardy: His Career as a Novelist,* London: Bodley Head, and New York: Random House, 1971

Morgan, Rosemarie, *Women and Sexuality in the Novels of Thomas Hardy,* London and New York: Routledge, 1988

Sumner, Rosemary, *Thomas Hardy: Psychological Novelist,* London: Macmillan, and New York: St. Martin's Press, 1981

Watts, Cedric, "*Jude the Obscure,"* London and New York: Penguin, 1992

Julie; or, The New Eloise by Jean-Jacques Rousseau

Julie; ou, La Nouvelle Héloïse 1761

Julie; ou, La Nouvelle Héloïse was an 18th-century best-seller that caused several generations of readers, from the date of its publication well into the 19th century, to shed copious tears over the tragic misfortunes of the ill-fated couple of Julie and Saint-Preux. This immensely influential novel was born of the disillusioned, aging, and ailing Rousseau's frustrated dream of finding in his own life sexual fulfillment and perfect love with a kindred soul, as his revealing remarks on the genesis of this work in his autobiography, *Les Confessions* (1782–89; *The Confessions*), make clear. Both love and friendship, the two "idols" of Rousseau's heart, as he dramatically puts it in his autobiography, are pivotal notions in this highly idiosyncratic novel. The autobiographical element in Rousseau's inspiration as a reluctant and quasi-accidental novelist should not be overlooked, and it accounts for much of the novel's unique appeal.

Apart from its popular success, *Julie* is also a seminal work in the evolution of the novel in France. For the first time, passionate love is fully vindicated as a source of the most generous and indeed moral human impulses. Whereas in Madame de Lafayette's famous *Princesse de Clèves*—the 17th-century paradigmatic model for practically all French novels of forbidden and adulterous passion—love served as a perpetual source of misery and anxiety for its hapless heroine, Rousseau's Julie is morally uplifted by her illicit involvement with Saint-Preux. Indeed, the theme of sexual passion is transformed into an appealing account of social utopia in the form of the ideal community of Clarens, established by Julie in her new role as Madame de Wolmar.

That Rousseau decided to write his novel in the epistolary form is hardly surprising; by 1761 the form had become a well-established genre, thanks largely to the success in France of Samuel Richardson's sentimentally edifying novels, notably *Clarissa* (1747–48). Rousseau's powerful rhetorical and argumentative skills, reinforced by intense lyrical fervor, appear throughout this profound and rich work of fiction, which blends a singularly compelling narrative of passionate love between two young people, thwarted by familial and social taboos, with a sharply critical assessment of current philosophical, political, social, psychological, moral, and aesthetic issues. In this respect, *Julie* may also be considered the first *roman à thèse* (novel with a message).

Having denounced both the theatre and the novel as frivolous genres conceived mainly to please and flatter the prejudices and preconceptions of blasé and cynical Parisians, Rousseau doubtless felt compelled to reconcile the contradictory yet coexisting impulses at the core of his inspiration: the subjective, passionate, and autobiographical elements with the ideological and didactic components. No wonder, therefore, that *La Nouvelle Héloïse* should have been characterized as a crossroad between Rousseau's literary expression and his political thought. The tension is also reflected in the two prefaces he wrote for *Julie*. These prefatory essays, with their defiant tone, essentially repeat the main themes of his highly polemical 1758 *Lettre à d'Alembert sur les spectacles* (*Letter to d'Alembert on the Theatre*). Rousseau, the apostle of truth and morality, feels challenged to justify writing a work of fiction, which he himself readily acknowledges as dangerous to public morality and especially to young girls, whom he deems all too impressionable and eager to experience the ecstasies of requited sexual passion. He informs his reader that he has especially added the subtitle *La Nouvelle Héloïse* as an unmistakable indication of its inflammatory contents. The young girl who ignores this clear warning will do so at her own peril, he suggests. As for more mature women experienced in the treacherous ways of what passes for love in a corrupt, urban society but who retain a secret nostalgic regret over their lost innocence, Rousseau concedes that they may indeed profit from reading the tragic yet uplifting story of two unsophisticated provincials who must face the formidable pressures of society. Novels are perhaps the ultimate form of moral instruction available for a public satiated with all other forms of entertainment, he proposes, and he has written *Julie* to perform precisely that function.

Paradoxically, the most remarkable women of the 18th and even 19th centuries turned to Rousseau for spiritual sustenance and encouragement. That Rousseau, who sternly exhorted virtuous women to seek personal fulfillment as chaste and devoted wives and mothers, should have been singled out by women whose own unconventional conduct and political and literary activities would have undoubtedly incurred his strong disapproval constitutes a unique case of influence through subjectively perceived affinities. Madame de Staël, Madame Roland, and George Sand, for example, fervently identified with the heroine of *Julie*. They even dared disagree with their mentor when he warned against the consequences of allowing the novel to fall into the hands of impressionable young girls. So convinced were they that the sublime example of generosity and selflessness of Julie would, on the contrary, help them to achieve both happiness and moral status that they somehow managed to overlook the fact that Rousseau's ideal of feminine fulfillment was strictly limited to the domestic sphere.

With its unique combination of lyricism and didacticism and its overheated and hyperbolic style, *Julie* had an enormous impact on European readers during the final decades of the 18th century and played a key role in shaping the post-Revolutionary romantic sensibility. The novel fired the youthful dreams and aspirations of countless readers, both male and female, and left an indelible mark on the Weltanschauung of Goethe, Stendhal, Wordsworth, and many others, even long after they had repudiated, at least in part, the great idol of their adolescent years.

GITA MAY

Further Reading

Blum, Carol, *Rousseau and the Republic of Virtue: The Language of Politics in the French Revolution*, Ithaca, New York: Cornell University Press, 1986

Coulet, Henri, editor, *Le Roman jusquà la Révolution*, Paris: Colin, and New York: McGraw Hill, 1967; 3rd edition, Paris: Colin, 1968

Crocker, Lester, "Julie ou la nouvelle duplicité," *Annales Jean-Jacques Rousseau* 35 (1959–62)

Darnton, Robert, *The Great Cat Massacre, and Other Episodes in French Cultural History,* New York: Basic Books, and London: Allen Lane, 1984

De Man, Paul, *Allegories of Reading: Figural Language in Rousseau, Nietzsche, Rilke, and Proust,* New Haven, Connecticut: Yale University Press, 1979

Ellis, Madeleine B., *"Julie; or, La Nouvelle Héloïse": A Synthesis of Rousseau's Thought (1749–1759),* Toronto: University of Toronto Press, 1949

Gilson, Etienne, "La Méthode de M. de Wolmar," in *Les Idées et les lettres,* Paris: J. Vrin, 1932; 2nd edition, 1955

Gossman, Lionel, "The Worlds of *La Nouvelle Héloïse,*" *Studies on Voltaire and the Eighteenth Century* 41 (1966)

Jones, James F., Jr. *"La Nouvelle Héloïse": Rousseau and Utopia,* Geneva: Droz, 1978

Kamuf, Peggy, *Fictions of Feminine Desire: Disclosures of Heloise,* Lincoln: University of Nebraska Press, 1982

Lecercle, Jean-Louis, *Rousseau et l'art du roman,* Paris: Colin, 1969

May, Gita, *Madame Roland and the Age of Revolution,* New York: Columbia University Press, 1970

May, Gita, "Rousseau's 'Antifeminism' Reconsidered," in *French Women and the Age of Enlightenment,* edited by Samia I. Spencer, Bloomington: Indiana University Press, 1984

Miller, Nancy K., *The Heroine's Text: Readings in the French and English Novel (1722–1782),* New York: Columbia University Press, 1980

Mostefai, Ourida, editor, *Lectures de "La Nouvelle Héloïse,"* no. 4, *Pensée Libre,* Ottowa: North American Association for the Study of Jean-Jacques Rousseau, 1993

Mylne, Vivienne, *The Eighteenth-Century Novel: Techniques of Illusion,* New York: Barnes and Noble, 1965; 2nd edition, Cambridge and New York: Cambridge University Press, 1981

Showalter, English, Jr., *The Evolution of the French Novel (1641–1782),* Princeton, New Jersey: Princeton University Press, 1972

Stewart, Philip, *Half-Told Tales: Dilemmas of Meaning in Three French Novels,* Chapel Hill: Department of Romance Languages, University of North Carolina, 1987

Tanner, Tony, *Adultery in the Novel: Contract and Transgression,* Baltimore: Johns Hopkins University Press, 1979

Trousson, Raymond, *Rousseau et sa fortune littéraire,* Paris: A.G. Nizet, 1977

Vance, Christie McDonald, "The Extravagant Shepherd: A Study of the Pastoral Vision in Rousseau's *Nouvelle Héloïse,*" *Studies on Voltaire and the Eighteenth Century* 105 (1973)

Wells, Byron R., *"Clarissa" and "La Nouvelle Héloïse": Dialectics of Struggle with Self and Others,* Ravenna: Longo, 1985

Justine; or, The Misfortunes of Virtue by Marquis de Sade

Justine; ou, Les Malheurs de la vertu 1791

On 12 June 1791, Sade wrote to his attorney Reinaud of the impending publication of *Justine,* declaring it a work "capable of corrupting the devil. . . . Burn it and do not read it if by chance it falls into your hands: I renounce it." The novel, which did not carry Sade's name (indeed, in the "Note Concerning My Detention," he vehemently and publicly denied his authorship of this final paroxysm of a diseased imagination), was received with disgusted horror by its reviewers, who admonished the young to shun it altogether and "mature men" to "read it to see how far one can go in derangement of the human imagination." At first glance, this reaction seems excessive—revolutionary France was awash with licentious literature; and for obscenity, the narration of her ordeals offered by the virtuous Justine pales beside the third-person account given six years later in his *La Nouvelle Justine; ou, Les Malheurs de la vertu, suivie de L'Histoire de Juliette, sa soeur* (10 vols., 1797; second part translated as *Juliette*) also published anonymously. To what were these early reviewers reacting? For what reasons is Sade both heralded as the very spirit of leftist revolution and condemned as the father of fascist terrorism?

Justine and her sister Juliette are orphaned, virtually penniless, at the ages of 12 and 15 respectively and cast out of the convent in which they had been brought up. Each pursues her fate according to her nature and ideals: Juliette, whose tale is told in the later novel, gives herself over to vice in the interests of material gratification, while Justine, preferring death to ignominy, trusts that virtue and the observance of religious principles will provide for her needs in this world and be amply rewarded in the next. The two part, but meet again many years later, each unknown to the other, Juliette as the Comtesse de Lorsange and mistress of a wealthy nobleman, Justine as the hapless Thérèse, in custody and en route to her execution for crimes of which she is, needless to say, innocent. Framed within this plot is Justine's pathetic story, as she tells the Comtesse, in a language as chaste as the subject matter allows, of the evils that have befallen her at the hands of various libertines and criminals, inflamed by her adherence to virtue. Not until the very end are the sisters' true identities revealed, at which point Juliette, repenting her life of crime, showers considerations upon Justine, vindicated at last—or so it seems. Hardly has she become accustomed to her good fortune when Providence strikes her one last, fatal blow in the form of a lightning bolt. As if daring the reader to draw the obvious conclusion from this, Sade provides a further frame in the authorial voice, beginning and ending the text with a warning against the dangerous sophistries of vice, and enjoining us to conclude, along with Juliette, "that true happiness is to be found nowhere but in Virtue's womb."

As is clear to anyone, of course, the sophistries in *Justine* belong entirely to virtue, and Sade's melodramatic imprecations to the contrary serve only to emphasize this fact. As she is tossed, seemingly with neither will nor memory, from debauched libertine to hardened criminal, Justine attempts each time to dissuade her malefactors from their vile pleasures by arguing the supremacy of virtue on the grounds of the common good, and where this fails, of the promise of heavenly reward. Everyone, from the murderous thief Coeur-de-fer (Heart-of-Iron) to the lubricious monks of Sainte-Marie-des-Bois (Saint-Mary-of-the-Woods)—an episode that parallels, in many details, *Les 120 Journées du Sodome; ou, L'Ecole du libertinage* (published posthumously, 1904/31–35; *The 120 Days of Sodom*), which Sade believed lost—is more than willing to accommodate Justine's taste for philosophy. It is these monologues, punctuated by the cries of countless victims, upon which Sade's doubled reputation is built.

Sade's villains take the Enlightenment materialism and individualism of Voltaire and the *philosophes* to their most perverted extremes: even La Mettrie, whose 1748 *L'homme machine (Man a Machine)*—a book Sade knew well—proclaim that humanity's total subordination to pleasure insists on the satisfactions of virtue and that criminal conscience is its own punishment. In response, Sade claims that conscience may be overcome through sufficient repetition of criminal acts, so that, in time, material rewards are untempered by remorse, and are even heightened by a kind of spiritual elation at the knowledge that one has furthered one's own ends at the expense of another's. After all, says Sade through his libertine heroes, crime is only a social convention: one society's evil is another's good, and nature cares nothing for society. Justine herself must on occasion commit, or at least accept, the spoils of crime for her own survival. Who, then, is the hypocrite, asks the libertine, the one who abandons her principles when expedient, or the one who adopts this very abandonment as principle, to be upheld and systematized no matter the cost? Sade's scandal is to have done precisely this in his writing, of which *Justine* was the first, if not the most obscene, published example.

In his "Idées sur les romans" (1800; "Reflections on the Novel"), Sade writes that the essence of novelistic representation lies in the writer's incestuous relationship with nature, the universal subject. To be true to this relationship is to eschew all limitations: truth is not attained by reproducing "what everyone already knows," but by the writer's "becom[ing] his mother's lover the moment she gives birth to him," by exceeding the bounds of convention and knowledge, and of the understanding itself. This thinking and writing of excess, which Sade was perhaps the first to raise to the level of a systematic concept, has had a profound and often polarizing influence on the literature and philosophy of France and elsewhere. Maurice Heine (*Le Marquis de Sade,* 1950) notes the correspondences between the publication dates of Sade's works in France and Ann Radcliffe's work in England, and suggests that *Justine* probably directly influenced M.G. Lewis' *The Monk* (1796). The restricted circulation of his works during the 19th century probably limited Sade's potential influence: Flaubert, Baudelaire, and Swinburne are perhaps the most famous exceptions. But in the 20th century his impact has been immense and difficult to calculate. His influence on literature, pornographic and otherwise, spreads from the pseudonymous *Histoire d'O* (1954; *The Story of O*) to Jean Genet, Henry Miller, and Angela Carter, to name a few. Hardly a philosopher or theorist of culture in France since the surrealists has not engaged with Sade in some manner. As Susan Sontag writes in "The Pornographic Imagination" (1967), Sade's "position as an inexhaustible point of departure for radical thinking about the human condition" guarantees that the legacy of sadism is not restricted to the catalog of psychopathologies.

SHANE WILCOX

See also Libertine Novel

Further Reading

Airaksinen, Timo, *The Philosophy of the Marquis de Sade,* London and New York: Routledge, 1995

Barthes, Roland, *Sade, Fourier, Loyola,* Paris: Seuil, 1971; as *Sade, Fourier, Loyola,* New York: Hill and Wang, and London: Cape, 1976

Bataille, Georges, *L'Erotisme,* Paris: Editions de Minuit, 1957; as *Death and Sensuality: A Study of Eroticism and the Taboo,* New York: Walker, 1962; as *Erotism: Death and Sensuality,* San Francisco: City Lights Books, 1986

Bataille, Georges, *La littérature et le mal,* Paris: Gallimard, 1957; as *Literature and Evil,* London: Calder and Boyars, 1973; New York: Boyars, 1985

Carter, Angela, *The Sadeian Woman: An Exercise in Cultural History,* London: Virago Press, 1979

Cryle, Peter, *Geometry in the Boudoir: Configurations of French Erotic Narrative,* Ithaca, New York: Cornell University Press, 1994

Gallop, Jane, *Intersections: A Reading of Sade with Bataille, Blanchot, and Klossowski,* Lincoln: University of Nebraska Press, 1981

Klossowski, Pierre, *Sade mon prochain,* Paris: Seuil, 1947; as *Sade My Neighbor,* Evanston, Illinois: Northwestern University Press, 1991; London: Quartet, 1992

Le Brun, Annie, *Soudain un bloc d'abîme, Sade: Introduction aux oeuvres complètes,* Paris: Jean-Jacques Pauvert, 1986; as *Sade: A Sudden Abyss,* San Francisco: City Lights Books, 1990

Lever, Maurice, *Donatien Alphonse François, Marquis de Sade,* Paris: Fayard, 1991; as *Marquis de Sade: A Biography,* London: HarperCollins, 1993; *Sade: A Biography,* New York: Farrar, 1993

K

Franz Kafka 1883–1924

Czech

The Czech writer Franz Kafka has been acclaimed as a central literary figure in European modernism since his premature death from tuberculosis at the age of 40. His writing combines an intensely personal vision with familiar modernist themes of alienation, displacement, and isolation. The concerns of his fiction derive to a large extent from his status as a German Jew living in Prague, which, along with Vienna, were the two most important cultural centers in the Austro-Hungarian Empire during the first quarter of the 20th century. As with other modernist writers, it is very difficult to demarcate the boundaries between modes of autobiography and fiction in Kafka's work; his literary inquiry into the psychological dynamics of persecution parallels his strained relationship with his father, Hermann Kafka, and his feelings of cultural homelessness as a Jew caught uneasily between Germans and Slavs. The two publications for which Kafka is best known are the short story "Die Verwandlung" (1915; "The Metamorphosis") and the novel *Der Prozess* (1925; *The Trial*). He also wrote two unfinished novels, *Das Schloss* (1926; *The Castle*) and *Amerika* (1927; *America*), numerous short stories, fragments, parables, diaries, and letters, many of which were published posthumously by his close friend and biographer Max Brod, despite Kafka's instruction to destroy most of his manuscripts.

The term *kafkaesque* is used often by critics to describe a narrative mode combining a realistic style with the distortions and absurdities of nightmare scenarios. Kafka's work is characterized by the juxtaposition of an impersonal narrative voice with descriptions of what would otherwise be shocking incidents. In this manner his major fiction displays signs of both realism and expressionism: detailed descriptions of objects and events are sharply contrasted with strange perspectives and perceptual distortions. Most of his protagonists—Karl Rossman in *America*, Gregor Samsa in "The Metamorphosis," Josef K. in *The Trial*, and K. in *The Castle*—bear certain physical and psychological similarities to the diarist and unrequited lover who wrote a mass of letters to his two-time fiancée Felicie Bauer. Kafka's whole oeuvre is characterized by a conflict, and also a confusion, between the demands of the external world and an idiosyncratic interior mindscape. For example, he discloses such feelings of uncertainty in a diary entry in December 1911: "I am divided from all things by a hollow space and I don't even push myself to the limits of it." The permeable boundaries between reality and fantasy and between certainty and delusion often throw the reader of Kafka's novels into a similar kind of confusion to that which he and his protagonists share.

Kafka's ill health is another important biographical factor contributing to the fear of physical and mental collapse dramatized in his novels, diaries, and the short story "Ein Hungerkünstler" (1924; "A Hunger Artist"). His physical frailty and aversion to, but obsession with, food provided him with potent symbols to express a world in which words and stories are, at best, liable to collapse and, at worst, lack all form and meaning. He often links images of the emaciated body to a lack of spirituality: "My body is too long for its weakness, it hasn't the least bit of fat to engender a blessed warmth, to preserve an inner fire, no fat on which the spirit can occasionally nourish itself." Kafka's descriptions of a weakening body indicate the importance of tuberculosis as a uniquely "modern" disease, suffered by other modernist writers like Thomas Mann, André Gide, and Katherine Mansfield. Although both Gide in *L'Immoraliste* (1902; *The Immoralist*) and Mann in *Der Zauberberg* (1924; *The Magic Mountain*) explore the effects of tuberculosis on the physical and psychological complexion of the individual, Kafka's oeuvre forms the most extensive modernist meditation on the fictional possibilities of writing about the wasting body.

Kafka's fiction has been critically interpreted as a reaction to the dominant 19th-century German literary tradition epitomized by the Bildungsroman. The kind of moral ascendancy and self-cultivating ethic displayed by the generic protagonist of the Bildungsroman was opposed by less optimistic narrative forms in the early 20th century. For example, in his first novel, *Buddenbrooks* (1901; *Buddenbrooks*), Mann explores the decline and fragmentation of a once-prosperous merchant family, in direct contrast to the self-education novels written after Johann Wolfgang von Goethe's *Wilhelm Meister* cycle (1795–1821). Kafka develops Mann's theme in "The Metamorphosis," the "exceedingly nauseating tale" in which Gregor Samsa is transformed one morning into a "monstrous insect" (*Ein Ungeziefer*). The short narrative questions the unstable boundaries between self-perception and the intrusive belief systems of others; Gregor's family relies on his income but, ironically, he is the one transformed into a parasite and subsequently persecuted by his family.

The Trial also opposes the structure of the Bildungsroman by charting a journey, or process, which, like the form of *America*, lacks direction and tangible progression. In *The Trial*, Josef K. is placed on trial for an unknown (and unknowable) crime by an unidentifiable government organization. The description of lawgiver as mythical authority who condemns victims and to whom there is no recourse provides an ideal subject to explore ideas of persecution but also serves to critique what the German sociologist Max Weber called the bureaucratic "iron cage" of modernity. Josef K. finds himself trapped in a nightmarish labyrinth with no center and no escape; he encounters the effects of law but no identifiable lawgiver, a theme Kafka further developed in *The Castle*: "The Castle hill was hidden, veiled in mist and darkness, nor was there even a glimmer of light to show that the castle was there." Although Kafka is most frequently positioned as a modernist writer, his description of the solitary individual facing an incomprehensible and potentially malevolent universe foreshadows existentialist literature written during the late 1930s and 1940s, while the paranoia experienced by his protagonists greatly influenced the work of American novelists such as Thomas Pynchon and Paul Auster writing during and in the wake of the Cold War.

MARTIN HALLIWELL

See also Trial

Biography
Born 3 July 1883 in Prague, Austro-Hungarian Empire (now Czech Republic). Attended Staatsgymnasium, Prague, 1893–1902; law student at Karl Ferdinand University, Prague, 1901–06; qualified in law, 1907; unpaid work in law courts, 1906–07. Engaged to Felice Bauer twice but never married. Employed at Assicurazioni Generali insurance company,

1907–08; Workers Accident Insurance Institute, 1908–22; contracted tuberculosis, 1917, and confined to a sanatorium, 1920–21; retired because of ill health. Died 3 June 1924.

Novels by Kafka
Der Prozess, 1925; as *The Trial,* translated by Willa and Edwin Muir, 1935
Das Schloss, 1926; as *The Castle,* translated by Willa and Edwin Muir, 1930
Amerika, 1927; as *America,* translated by Edwin Muir, 1928

Other Writings: short stories, diaries, parables, and letters.

Further Reading
Citati, Pietro, *Kafka,* London: Secker and Warburg, and New York: Knopf, 1990
Gilman, Sander, *Franz Kafka, the Jewish Patient,* New York: Routledge, 1995
Gray, Ronald, *Franz Kafka,* Cambridge: Cambridge University Press, 1973
Heller, Erich, *Kafka,* London: Fontana, 1974; New York: Viking, 1975
Hibberd, John, *Kafka, Die Verwandlung,* London: Grant and Butler, 1985
Karl, Frederick, *Franz Kafka, Representative Man,* New York: Ticknor and Fields, 1991
Pawel, Ernst, *The Nightmare of Reason: A Life of Franz Kafka,* New York: Farrar Straus, and London: Harvill, 1984
Robertson, Ritchie, *Kafka: Judaism, Politics and Literature,* Oxford: Clarendon Press, and New York: Oxford University Press, 1985
Stern, J.P., editor, *The World of Franz Kafka,* London: Weidenfeld and Nicolson, and New York: Holt, Rinehart and Winston, 1980

Ghassān Kanafānī 1936–72

Palestinian

Assassinated at the age of 36 by a car bomb planted by Israeli agents in 1972, Ghassān Kanafānī's short life is, in more than one way, that of his people. His writings, which include novels, short stories, and journalism, were closely connected to his life. In 1948, at the age of 12, he fled with his family from his native Acre in Palestine first to Lebanon and then to Syria, where they settled as Palestinian refugees. After finishing his secondary education he studied Arabic literature at the University of Damascus, an institution from which he was later expelled. From there he moved to Kuwait and Beirut, where his literary, journalistic, and, above all, his political activities increased. A member of the Arab Nationalist Movement, he later became one of the leaders

of the Popular Front for the Liberation of Palestine, its spokesperson, and the editor-in-chief of its weekly *Al-Hadaf*.

Three main themes dominate Kanafānī's writings: the experiences of uprootedness, exile, and struggle. Whereas the first two dominate his earlier works, an emphasis on the third characterizes his later output. This shift represents not only his life experience but also his ideological move from nationalist in his early adult life to a more pronounced Marxist during his later years. His first novel, *Rijāl fī al-shams* (1963; *Men in the Sun*), is the story of three Palestinians representing three different generations who attempt to escape to Kuwait in the tank of a water truck only to fatally succumb to the abysmal conditions inside the tank. A very moving short novel narrated in the motivated third person empathetic to the respective characters and filled with flashbacks, *Men in the Sun* was made into a movie, *al-Makhdūʿūn* (The Duped), by the Egyptian director Tawfīq Ṣāliḥ. This novel betrays the struggle of a young writer with his medium and his search for techniques that fit his purpose.

Both political and literary concerns account for the differences between Kanafānī's first novel and his second, *Mā tabaqqā lakum* (1966; *All That's Left to You*). In the latter the influence of William Faulkner and Lawrence Durrell is clear, especially in the use of multiple narrators. There are five narrators who are not separated by different chapters but rather flow one into the other, with changes in font the only indicator of these shifts. Two of the narrators are inanimate (the clock and the desert). The novel is highly dense and symbolic. Ḥāmid, the protagonist, is a young man who is forced to accept the marriage of his sister Maryam (as a second wife) to a man he hates and who is a traitor to his people. Instead of aspiring to go to Kuwait to find a new life, he still dreams of being reunited with his mother from whom he was separated in 1948 when he, a small child, fled with his sister and aunt to Gaza while his mother left for the West Bank. Not knowing whether his mother is alive or not, Ḥāmid attempts to cross the Israeli territory that separates Gaza from the West Bank in order to find her. He becomes lost in the desert, eventually crossing paths with an Israeli soldier who represents those who have taken his land and separated him from his mother. Although he dies before locating his mother, Ḥāmid is, in death, reunited with his lost land, which represents his true mother. This novel is the most ambitious and experimental of Kanafānī's works.

In his next novel, *Umm Saʿd* (1969; Umm Saʿd), there is a clear shift both in subject matter and in technique and language. This shift reflects the situation of the Palestinians following the defeat of the Arab armies in 1967 and the rise of the Palestinian Resistance Movement. It also reflects Kanafānī's increasingly radical and socially oriented outlook. The narrative is told in the first person, but the novel is not about the narrator as much as it is about a woman, Umm Saʿd, whose son joins the resistance movement. Despite her age, she represents the future of her people, not their past. Her discourse, although not learned, is very wise, her language simple and colloquial but sometimes highly poetic and always very expressive. Kanafānī's last published novel, *ʿĀʾid ilā Ḥayfa* (1970; Returning to Haifa), is also rather direct in its political message and its language, although it does not achieve the same effect as *Umm Saʿd*. In these two works one sees clearly the emphasis of a committed writer representing the revolutionary plight of his people together with an anxiety and an uneasiness about the modes of literary representation then acknowledged to be associated with political commitment, especially socialist realism.

Kanafānī left fragments of three novels that were published posthumously. The tension between directness in his later works and the early experimentation with language and form is manifest in those works. What applies to his novelistic writings is also true in his short stories, of which he published four volumes. The works of Kanafānī (and perhaps those of his compatriot, the poet Maḥmūd Darwīsh) are arguably the best literary expressions of the experience of Palestinians in the 20th century. But his impact on the development of the Arabic novel in general has also been great, especially as one of the earliest novelists to grapple with problems of technique while at the same time being true to the experience and struggle of his people.

WALID HAMARNEH

See also Men in the Sun

Biography

Born in 1936. In 1948 he fled with his family from Acre to Lebanon and then to Syria; studied Arabic literature at the University of Damascus, but expelled before receiving a degree; moved to Kuwait, where he first worked as a journalist, and later to Beirut; member of and spokesperson for Political Bureau of the Popular Front for the Liberation of Palestine; editor of *Al-Hadaf*. Killed by a car bomb on 8 July 1972 in Beirut.

Novels by Kanafānī

Rijāl fī al-shams, 1963; as *Men in the Sun and Other Palestinian Stories*, translated by Hilary Kilpatrick, 1978
Mā tabaqqā lakum, 1966; as *All That's Left to You*, translated by May Jayyusi and Jeremy Reed, 1990
Umm Saʿd [Umm Saʿd], 1969
ʿĀʾid ilā Ḥayfa [Returning to Haifa], 1970

Other Writings: journalism, short stories, and literary criticism.

Further Reading

Allen, Roger, *The Arabic Novel: An Historical and Critical Introduction*, Syracuse, New York: Syracuse University Press, and Manchester: Manchester University Press, 1982; 2nd edition, Syracuse, New York: Syracuse University Press, 1995
ʿĀshūr, Raḍwā, *Al-Ṭarīq ila al-khaymah al-ukhrā: Dirāsah fī Aʿmāl Ghassān Kanafānī*, Beirut: Dar al-Adab, 1977
Kilpatrick, Hilary, "Tradition and Innovation in the Fiction of Ghassān Kanafānī," *Journal of Arabic Literature* 7 (1976)
Siddiq, Muhammad, *Man Is a Cause: Political Consciousness and the Fiction of Ghassān Kanafānī*, Seattle: University of Washington Press, 1984
Wild, Stefan, *Ghassān Kanafānī: The Life of a Palestinian*, Wiesbaden: Harrassowitz, 1975

Katz und Maus. *See* Danzig Trilogy

Kawabata Yasunari 1899–1972

Japanese

Kawabata Yasunari is often described as the most traditionally "Japanese" of 20th-century Japanese authors; however, he first appeared on the Japanese literary scene in the 1920s as the chief theorist for the New Perception school (*Shin-kankaku-ha*), a loosely affiliated group of writers influenced by European modernism whose work is noted for its abrupt transitions and juxtapositions of incongruous images. Kawabata is best known in the West for his novel-length works, including *Yukiguni* (1937, revised 1948; *Snow Country*), *Sembazuru* (1952; *Thousand Cranes*), and *Koto* (1962; *The Old Capital*)—the three cited by the Nobel committee when he became the first Japanese writer to be awarded the Nobel prize for literature in 1968. However, the bulk of Kawabata's work is in the short-story form. Indeed, both *Snow Country* and *Thousand Cranes*, as well as *Yama no oto* (1954; *The Sound of the Mountain*), began as short stories that grew gradually to novel length.

Kawabata's first major literary success came in 1926 with the publication of his short story "Izu no odoriko" ("The Dancing Girl of Izu"), by far his best-known and most widely read work in Japan. Earlier, in 1923, Kawabata had joined the editorial staff of what was to become one of the major literary magazines in the country. The following year he founded the magazine *Bungei Jidai*, which promoted the philosophy that literature should view the world with "new perception." This philosophy was a reaction against the dull realism of Japan's autobiographical literature, which in turn was a response to the work of European naturalists. Kawabata's adherence to the tenets of the New Perception school is evident in the sometimes abstruse or jolting quality of his images. However, in most of his work this imagery is tempered by a reverence for classical Japanese literature that manifests itself in the traditional melancholia of his themes and his abiding quest for beauty. It is notable that not one of Kawabata's longer works was published first in completed form. All of Kawabata's novels either began as short stories that grew to novel length after numerous treatments of the same characters in successive stories or were serialized in newspapers or magazines. Kawabata attributed this tendency to compose shorter works to a need for money (longer works required more time and postponed receipt of payment until completion); however, it is more likely that these shorter works were a result of his artistic temperament.

Early in his career, Kawabata began to write what he called "palm-of-the-hand stories," diminutive works that averaged only two or three pages in length. He wrote more than 140 of these works over the course of his career, his last one being "Gleanings from Snow Country," a miniaturization of the novel that had brought him his greatest fame (*Snow Country*). Of these tiny stories Kawabata wrote, "Many men of literature write poetry when they are young, but, instead of poetry, I wrote these palm-of-the-hand stories." Common characteristics of these disparate stories are their length, their distinctive compression of images, the anxiety caused by the gulf between the sexes, and the yearning for the beauty of a virginal or genderless ideal, sometimes to be found only in death. The palm-of-the-hand story may have been Kawabata's basic unit of composition. Many critics have noted the resemblance between Kawabata's work and *renga,* or traditional linked-verse poetry. In this ancient form, a single poem is created by one or more poets by adding successive verses, with a focus on developing the linearity of the poem and not any overarching constraints. It is possible to view Kawabata's longer works as prose versions of *renga*.

Snow Country was the first of Kawabata's works to reach novel length. It began as a short story in 1934, but Kawabata continued to develop the characters for a number of years in pieces published in various magazines until the separate stories were collected, revised, and published in what was to be regarded as a unified work in 1948. Kawabata continued his piecemeal production method with *Thousand Cranes,* publishing related stories in various magazines over a period of more than two years. The publication of *Thousand Cranes* overlapped with the appearance of the stories that formed the first part of *The Sound of the Mountain,* regarded by some critics as Kawabata's finest long work. In 1952, Kawabata published in a single volume all of the sections of what later was published as the independent novel *Thousand Cranes* and the first sections of *The Sound of the Mountain,* despite the lack of any obvious connection between the two works. The hybrid book was awarded a major prize by the Japanese Art Academy. *The Sound of the Mountain* was made into a movie before Kawabata developed the last half of the novel.

Kawabata had shown little sympathy for Japan's militarists during World War II, but the sense of loss after the Japanese defeat affected him greatly; he stated that he could no longer write anything but elegies. However, his postwar works exhibit little change in tone. His novel *The Old Capital*, first serialized in a newspaper in 1961–62, was cited in Anders Esterling's Nobel prize-presenting speech to Kawabata as an example of Kawabata's desire to preserve in fiction the fading vestiges of traditional Japanese culture. Despite such an evaluation and Kawabata's own pronouncements, *The Old Capital,* like many works by Kawabata, exhibits a sensibility perhaps more ambivalent than elegiac. Kawabata's work is not all lamentation: it acknowledges and explores the necessarily ironic and often seductive relationship between innovation and tradition, depicting the interplay of passivity and vitality in human existence and endeavor. The traditional kimono designer in *The Old Capital* deplores insidious Western influences on aesthetics, yet secludes himself in a convent temple with books of paintings by Paul Klee, Marc Chagall, and Henri Matisse to spark his own creativity. Likewise, Kawabata experimented with form and expression in ways that demonstrated his appreciation of Western literature, even as he sought to root himself in traditional Japanese culture.

More than his writing, Kawabata's greatest influence on the development of the novel in Japan is evident in his labors as a critic, mentor, president for 17 years of the Japan PEN Club, and vice president of the International PEN. Kawabata championed the early work of such writers as Ibuse Masuji (author of *Kuroi ame* [1965; *Black Rain*]) and Mishima Yukio, and served on the editorial boards of more magazines and journals and on the juries of more literary prizes than perhaps any other author in the 20th century. His tireless efforts in the PEN Club brought the international congress of that organization to Japan in 1957, focusing the attention of the literary world for the first time on contemporary Japanese authors and promoting the translation of their works into Western languages.

J. MARTIN HOLMAN

See also Snow Country

Biography

Born 11 June 1899 in Osaka, Japan. Attended Ibaragi Middle School, 1915–17, and First Higher School, 1917–20, Tokyo; Tokyo Imperial University, 1920–24, degree in Japanese literature 1924. Writer and journalist; helped found *Bungei Jidai* magazine, 1924, and Kamakura Bunko, publishers, Kamakura, later in Tokyo, 1945. Served for several years as President of the Japanese PEN. Author-in-residence, University of Hawaii, Honolulu, 1969. Awarded Nobel prize for literature, 1968. Died (suicide) 16 April 1972.

Novels by Kawabata

Yukiguni, 1937; revised and enlarged 1948; as *Snow Country*, translated by Edward Seidensticker, 1957

Sembazuru, 1952; as *Thousand Cranes*, translated by Edward Seidensticker, 1959

Meijin, in *Shincho*, 1951; revised and enlarged as *Meijin*, 1954; shorter version as *The Master of Go*, translated by Edward Seidensticker, 1972

Yama no oto, 1954; as *The Sound of the Mountain*, translated by Edward Seidensticker, 1970

Mizuumi, 1955; as *The Lake*, translated by Reiko Tsukimura, 1974

Onna de aru koto [To Be a Woman], 1956–58

Koto, 1962; as *The Old Capital*, translated by J. Martin Holman, 1987

Utsukushisa to kanashimi, 1965; as *Beauty and Sadness*, translated by Howard Hibbett, 1975

Other Writings: short stories and essays.

Further Reading

Gessel, Van C., *Three Modern Novelists: Sōseki, Tanizaki, Kawabata*, Tokyo and New York: Kodansha International, 1993

Keene, Donald, *Dawn to the West: Japanese Literature of the Modern Era*, New York: Holt, Rinehart, and Winston, 1984

Miyoshi, Masao, *Accomplices of Silence: The Modern Japanese Novel*, Berkeley: University of California Press, 1974

Petersen, Gwenn Boardman, *The Moon in the Water: Understanding Tanizaki, Kawabata, and Mishima*, Honolulu: University Press of Hawaii, 1979

Ueda, Makoto, *Modern Japanese Writers and the Nature of Literature*, Stanford, California: Stanford University Press, 1976

Nikos Kazantzakis 1883–1957

Greek

A philosopher by training, as well as a translator, poet, diplomat, and accomplished essayist, Nikos Kazantzakis is best known outside his native Crete for the novels he published late in life. *Vios kai politeia tou Alexē Zorba* (1946; *Zorba the Greek*) and *Ho teleutaios peirasmos* (1955; *The Last Temptation of Christ*) have been best-sellers and the subjects of Hollywood motion pictures. These and other works such as *Ho Christos xanastaurōnetai* (1954; *Christ Recrucified*) and *Ho kapetan Michalēs* (1953; *Freedom or Death*) have received critical acclaim from a number of distinguished scholars on both sides of the Atlantic. Compared frequently to D.H. Lawrence, Kazantzakis also has been linked with European novelists such as Jean-Paul Sartre and Albert Camus as one of the premier ex-

ponents of existentialism in fiction. Scholars have found significant parallels between his work and that of such modern giants as James Joyce, Marcel Proust, Thomas Mann, Joseph Conrad, and William Faulkner, although Kazantzakis uses few of the experimentalist techniques that are trademarks of their work. Like them, however, he does fuse the language of poetry into the medium of prose.

One of Kazantzakis' most significant accomplishments, however, is hardly appreciated by readers outside his native Crete. Although he wrote a number of his novels in French, his most celebrated works were composed in demotic Greek, the colloquial language of the Cretan working classes. For his efforts in preserving his native tongue, Kazantzakis was reviled by the Greek academic establishment, which has insisted that writers use highly stylized language if they wish to be taken seriously. Despite such criticisms, Kazantzakis has achieved a wide popular following for his novels in his native land.

The official castigation of Kazantzakis' works has not been limited to criticism of language, however. For nearly half a century, he provoked the ire of religious officials for his unorthodox attitude toward religion. A brief review of Kazantzakis' unusual brand of existentialism makes it clear why he incurred the wrath of these patriarchs. Influenced by the writings of Friedrich Nietzsche and Henri Bergson, Kazantzakis uses fiction as a vehicle for exploring philosophical and theological issues. Every work is an attempt to explain what Kazantzakis saw as humankind's effort to make meaning out of what was, in his view, an essentially meaningless life. As his good friend and translator Kimon Friar explains in the introduction to *Sodom and Gomorrah* (in *Two Plays*, 1982), Kazantzakis "saw all of life in terms of protagonist and antagonist. The protagonist was Man, the antagonist was God, and all his books are the battleground of that dramatic conflict to the death." In Kazantzakis' worldview, God is not the omnipotent creator of traditional religion; rather, he is a being created by man as a means of explaining the significance of human existence. People create God as they reject the material aspects of life in favor of spiritual fulfillment.

Virtually every one of Kazantzakis' novels is an exposition of his existential philosophy, and all of his great protagonists are existential heroes. In most works, the hero struggles to free himself from the temptations of the flesh to achieve spiritual self-fulfillment. True freedom comes to those who are able to act as if life has meaning even when they know it does not.

The most radical exposition of that philosophy is evident in the most controversial of Kazantzakis' novels, *The Last Temptation of Christ*. Turning on its head the traditional Christian myth of salvation, Kazantzakis transforms the Jesus of Biblical narrative into an existential hero struggling with the (very real) temptations of the flesh. Loosely following the Gospel narratives, he portrays Christ as a rebel against tradition, seeking to promote a new gospel in which every person recognizes that God needs man as much as man needs God: only through man's search for God—a battle to release the spiritual dimension within one's body—does the deity become real. A similar struggle occurs in the life of the young shepherd Manolios, the hero of *Christ Recrucified*. Selected to play Christ in his village's Easter pageant, Manolios gradually takes on the personality of the god he has been selected to portray, abandoning earthly pleasures and embracing a spiritual vision of life that leads him to a cheerful martyrdom at the end of the novel.

Not all of Kazantzakis' novels are so directly concerned with this overtly religious theme, but all depict the author's concern with the battle between flesh and spirit. In *Freedom or Death*, Captain Mihalis, the hero of Kazantzakis' tale of the Cretan revolt of the 1880s, is torn between his desires to lead a comfortable life and his belief that he must take up arms to defend his country. Similarly, in *Zorba the Greek*, Alexis Zorba finds himself battling the conflicting demands of spirit and flesh; unlike most of Kazantzakis' heroes, though, he favors a life of ease over the struggle to achieve spiritual fulfillment. He is the epitome of Bergson's *élan vital*, a vital spirit energized by life's experiences. In contrast, the character known as the Boss, who falls under Zorba's spell and joins him in an ill-fated business venture, is the consummate ascetic. Paralyzed by everyday contacts (especially with women), the Boss must learn from Zorba how to translate his intellectual acceptance of the spiritual life into meaningful action. Zorba's appeal to the Boss, and to readers, comes from his willingness to face life head-on, undeterred by failure and unafraid of death because he has made his life meaningful by living it fully.

At times, Kazantzakis' emphasis on the philosophical dimensions of his novels leads to faults in plotting and characterization. His stories are often sacrificed for symbolic effect, and much of his dialogue is bombastic. At his worst, he is a preacher using fiction as a thin disguise for a philosophical treatise. At his best, however, he is a master at using fiction to illuminate the conflict modern people face in making sense of a world where religion has lost its power to give meaning to life. His best protagonists—Captain Mihalis, Alexis Zorba, Manolios, Jesus—demonstrate that it is possible to rise above the temptations of the flesh and the despair of everyday living and make one's own life meaningful, even heroic.

LAURENCE W. MAZZENO

See also Last Temptation of Christ

Biography

Born 18 February 1883 in Heraklion, Crete. Attended French School of Holy Cross, Naxos, 1897–99; Gymnasium, Heraklion, 1899–1902; University of Athens, 1902–06, degree in law; continued studies in Paris, Germany, and Italy, 1906–10. Director General of Ministry of Public Welfare, 1919–20; Cabinet Minister Without Portfolio, 1945; served in UNESCO's Department of Translations of the Classics, 1947–48. Died 26 October 1957.

Novels by Kazantzakis

Toda-Raba (written in French), 1933; as *Toda Roba*, translated by Amy Mims, 1964

Vios kai politeia tou Alexē Zorba, 1946; as *Zorba the Greek*, translated by Carl Wildman, 1952

Ho kapetan Michalēs, 1953; as *Freedom or Death*, translated by Jonathan Griffin, 1956; as *Freedom and Death*, translated by Griffin, 1956

Ho Christos xanastaurōnetai, 1954; as *The Greek Passion*, translated by Jonathan Griffin, 1954; as *Christ Recrucified*, translated by Griffin, 1954

Ho teleutaios peirasmos, 1955; as *The Last Temptation*, translated by Peter Bien, 1960; as *The Last Temptation of Christ*, translated by Bien, 1960

Ho phtochoules tou Theou, 1956; as *God's Pauper*, translated by Peter Bien, 1962; as *St. Francis*, translated by Bien, 1962

Le Jardin des Rochers, 1959; as *The Rock Garden*, translated by Richard Howard, 1963

Hoi aderphades, 1963; as *The Fratricides*, translated by Athena Gianakas Dallas, 1964

Other Writings: plays, essays, journals, philosophical treatises and translations of philosophical works, modern translations of

Greek classics, including *Odysseia* (1938; *The Odyssey: A Modern Sequel*), and an autobiographical and philosophical work entitled *Anaphora ston Greko* (1961; *Report to Greco*).

Further Reading

Bien, Peter, *Kazantzakis: Politics of the Spirit,* Princeton, New Jersey: Princeton University Press, 1989

Bien, Peter, *Nikos Kazantzakis, Novelist,* Bristol: Bristol Classical Press, 1989

Friar, Kimon, *The Spiritual Odyssey of Nikos Kazantzakis,* St. Paul, Minnesota: North Central, 1979

Journal of Modern Literature 2:2 (Winter 1971–72), special issue on Kazantzakis

Levitt, Morton P., *The Cretan Glance: The World and Art of Nikos Kazantzakis,* Columbus: Ohio State University Press, 1980

Middleton, Darren, and Peter Bien, editors, *God's Struggler: Religion in the Writings of Nikos Kazantzakis,* Macon, Georgia: Mercer University Press, 1996

Gottfried Keller 1819–90

Swiss

Along with sometimes eloquent poetry on both personal and public themes, and novella cycles widely admired for their ingenuity, social comedy, and psychological insight, Gottfried Keller wrote two novels. One, the socially critical *Martin Salander* (1886), undertaken with diminished powers and broken off near the end of his life, is today known mainly to specialists; but the other, *Der grüne Heinrich* (1853–55, revised edition 1880; *Green Henry*), has been called by some critics the greatest Swiss novel. Like all of Keller's writing, it is pronouncedly Swiss in its spirit of conservative republicanism, but specifically *German* Swiss. One must look far in Keller for any notice of the other nationalities of the Swiss Confederation. He was opposed to the idea of a Swiss national literature, insisting that every writer should remain within his own language community, and emphatically regarded himself as belonging to German literature. Much of the autobiographical *Green Henry* takes place in Germany, where the first version was written.

Green Henry is customarily identified as a Bildungsroman. Like other members of the genre, it is in succession to the seminal work, Johann Wolfgang von Goethe's *Wilhelm Meisters Lehrjahre* (1795–1821; *Wilhelm Meister's Apprenticeship*), a story of the acculturation of a youth to maturity, with guidance from mentors, experiences with appropriate and inappropriate girls and women, and attempted involvement in the arts—in Goethe's case, the theatre; in Keller's, painting. Keller was strongly influenced by Goethe; one of Heinrich's formative experiences is a marathon reading of Goethe's works, 30 days in the first version, 40 in the revised. Although the Bildungsroman tended in time to the *Künstlerroman,* the fictional biography of a fledgling artist, Keller, for whom citizenship was paramount, declared explicitly in the first version that it was not a *Künstlerroman,* since it followed Goethe. But *Green Henry* subverts the model in other ways. The Goethean ideal of equilibrium of a stabilized self with an ultimately harmonious reality is acknowledged but unachievable. *Green Henry* is a chronicle of wasted time and balked hopes. Keller's friend, the literary historian Hermann Hettner, provided the most succinct one-word critique: a *Bildungstragödie.* With its tragic tone of frustration and defeat it has been compared with the novels of George Meredith and Samuel Butler, but the English novel that may come most readily to mind is Thomas Hardy's *Jude the Obscure* (1895).

However, in Keller's version, the protagonist's fate is not society's fault, however obtuse society may be in guiding him. The village Romeo and Juliet of Keller's most famous novella die because they see no way of living their love honorably, that is, within society's norms. Heinrich's flaw is deviance born of the imagination, which nourishes an artistic vocation that is self-aggrandizing and therefore delusory. His pubescent experiences with the ethereal Anna and the voluptuous Judith look like allegorizations, but it is Heinrich who allegorizes and thereby instrumentalizes them, loving the idea of Anna better in her absence, ultimately swearing fidelity to her corpse, and conflating Judith with "nature." The mature Heinrich retrospectively narrates such fictionalizations with implacable reprehension. In both versions young Heinrich is exposed to a "reading family" that goes to perdition as a result of reading novels, the daughters becoming unmarriageable slatterns, the son a gambler and swindler ending up in prison. The placement of such a chapter in a *novel* is evidence of Keller's grimly self-ironic sense of humor; to be sure, the lethal novels are bad romances, not Bildungsromane, and the chapter may also be an oblique satire on the low esteem of the novel genre in 19th-century German aesthetics. Still, in the same chapter Heinrich engages in a gross prevarication that leads to a theft from his mother, thus making quite porous the boundary between fiction and lying.

As for art, a fantasizing and trivializing imagination constantly distracts Heinrich from the level gaze of perfect objective mimesis required by Goethe's canonical aesthetic. Near the bottom of his fortunes, Heinrich daubs an abstract labyrinth of meandering lines. But this anticipation of the modern is no more positively regarded than the deranged abstraction in Honoré de Balzac's *Le Chef-d'œuvre inconnu* (*The Unknown Masterpiece*). A more mature painter berates Heinrich with sarcastic praise of the work as the ultimate result of emancipation from reality before punching his fist through the canvas. The last stage of Heinrich's artistic activity is a sub-artisanal task of painting stripes on flagstaffs for a royal wedding in Munich. In the first version, having impoverished his mother with his "studies," he returns home to find her dead and dies himself of shame; in the revised he lives on in dispiriting bureaucratic service, joined to and separated from the splendid Judith in chaste friendship.

Which of the versions is the better novel has been a matter of dispute for decades. Keller himself seems to have come to hate the first version even during its five-year genesis; overcome by his own pathos, he said that he had "smeared the last chapter, on Palm Sunday, no less, literally in tears." Eventually he acquired the remainder and burned it as winter fuel; to the distress of editors, he cursed the right hand of anyone who were to reprint it. The first version is ungainly because it is a third-person narration with very extensive first-person inlays; Keller improved it structurally in the revised version by going to a consistent first-person form, which logically drove him off the excessively melodramatic death scene. Nevertheless, many critics have felt that some of the original freshness was lost in the revision. Nor is the revised ending as conciliatory as some have claimed; the repudiation of the imagination as the prerequisite for living on is a profounder sacrifice than the renunciation thematic in Goethe's own sequel to the genre, *Wilhelm Meisters Wanderjahre; oder, Die Entsagenden* (*Wilhelm Meister's Journeyman Years; or, The Renunciants*). In any case, rarely in the history of the novel can there have been a work so colorfully imaginative that is so relentlessly suspicious of the imagination, and therefore of itself.

JEFFREY L. SAMMONS

Biography
Born 19 July 1819 in Zurich, Switzerland. Attended Armenschule zum Brunnenturm; Landknabeninstitut, to age 13; Industrieschule, 1832–33; studied painting with Peter Steiger, 1834, and Rudolf Meyer, 1837; Munich Academy, 1840–42. Abandoned art for writing in 1842; received government grant to study at the University of Heidelberg, 1848–50, and the University of Berlin, 1850–55; cantonal secretary (Staatschreiber), 1861–76. Died 15 July 1890.

Novels by Keller
Der grüne Heinrich, 1853–55, revised edition 1880; as *Green Henry*, translated by A.M. Holt, 1960
Martin Salander, 1886; as *Martin Salander*, translated by Kenneth Halwas, 1963

Other Writings: short stories, verse, letters.

Further Reading
Beddow, Michael, "Submissions: *Der Nachsommer* and *Der grüne Heinrich*," in *The Fiction of Humanity: Studies in the Bildungsroman from Wieland to Thomas Mann*, Cambridge and New York: Cambridge University Press, 1982
Hart, Gail K., *Readers and Their Fictions in the Novels and Novellas of Gottfried Keller*, Chapel Hill: University of North Carolina Press, 1989
Kaiser, Gerhard, *Gottfried Keller: Das gedichtete Leben*, Frankfurt am Main: Insel, 1981
Laufhütte, Hartmut, *Wirklichkeit und Kunst in Gottfried Kellers Roman "Der grüne Heinrich,"* Bonn: Bouvier, 1969
Menninghaus, Winfried, *Artistische Schrift: Studien zur Kompositionskunst Gottfried Kellers*, Frankfurt am Main: Suhrkamp, 1982
Muschg, Adolf, *Gottfried Keller*, Munich: Kindler, 1977
Pascal, Roy, "Gottfried Keller—*Green Heinrich*," in *The German Novel: Studies*, Toronto: University of Toronto Press, and Manchester: Manchester University Press, 1956
Preisendanz, Wolfgang, "Gottfried Keller: *Der grüne Heinrich*," in *Der deutsche Roman*, volume 2, edited by Benno von Wiese, Düsseldorf: Bagel, 1965
Romberg, Bertil, "*Der grüne Heinrich*," in *Studies in the Narrative Technique of the First-Person Novel*, Stockholm: Almqvist and Wiksell, 1962
Swales, Martin, "Keller: *Green Henry* (1879–1880)," in *The German Bildungsroman from Wieland to Hesse*, Princeton, New Jersey: Princeton University Press, 1978

Yashar Kemal 1922–

Turkish

Yashar Kemal is the best known and most acclaimed Turkish writer of the 20th century. An outspoken critic of the Turkish government's treatment of the peasantry and minority groups, Kemal has frequently been arrested for the views he has expressed in both his fiction and nonfiction. Most recently, in 1995, Kemal was imprisoned for an article published in *Der Spiegel* that condemned the government's oppression of the Kurdish minority and offered support to the Kurdish Workers' Party. This is but the latest example of Kemal's lifelong commitment to the causes of the destitute and powerless masses who still comprise the majority of the people of his native country and of the world.

Kemal is above all a political writer, using the novel primarily as a means of examining social and political issues. It is a testament to Kemal's literary abilities that his novels are always more than mere political allegories or pedagogic exercises, even though he has been criticized for inadequately developing characters and situations in an effort to make broader political points. The thematic focus of his novels is a detailed, patient rendering of the gritty reality of Turkish peasant life in South Anatolia. Kemal's fiction exposes the harsh and marginal existence of the peasants, the cruelty of local rulers, the social dissonance produced by the intersection of tradition and modernity, and the often savage and brutal struggles waged among the peasants themselves. The overwhelming impression left by Kemal's novels is of a bloody, savagely Darwinian society that has little respect for individual life; although this social struggle is played out against a landscape that is beautifully and lyrically described, Kemal's vision of peasant life is not pastoral in the least. Nevertheless, his novels exhibit a deep respect for human life; if a terrible present is unflinchingly depicted, it is in the hope that a better future is on the way.

Kemal's most famous novel, *Ince Memed* (2 vols., 1955; volume 1 translated as *Memed, My Hawk*, volume 2 as *They Burn the Thistles*), follows the Robin Hood-like struggles of the peasant Memed against the evil *agha*'s (landowner's) tyrannical rule. Memed alone realizes the essential injustice of a system in which the peasants must turn over half their grain to a landowner who abuses and nearly starves them. Since there does not seem to be any possibility of forming class consciousness among the peasants, who curse the rains as the reason for their troubles and find solace in religion, Memed flees the village to find a better life for himself. He is soon found and returned to the village, and he and his family suffer even more greatly as a consequence of his failed attempt at escape. Kemal repeats this pattern in the trilogy *Dagin ote yuzu*—*Ortadirek* (1960; *The Wind from the Plain*), *Yer demir, gök bakir* (1963; *Iron Earth, Copper Sky*), and *Ölmez otu* (1969; *The Undying Grass*)—in which only the lone hero (Long Ali) is able to make the break with tradition and challenge the accepted order of things. As with Memed, Long Ali's attempts to improve his life and to gain some measure of freedom repeatedly fail. Kemal's intention is not to suggest that change is impossible and that his protagonists are thus bound to fail. Instead, he shows that there is no simple solution, whether romantic or revolutionary, to the inexorable poverty and injustice of the rural life presented in these novels. The political force of Kemal's writing derives from his willingness to present the stark reality of the peasants' situation, even if this means that his texts are pessimistic about change in the absence of a profound societal transformation.

In his later fiction, Kemal examines peasant life from new perspectives that complicate, enrich, and extend the narratives found in his earlier works. *Binboğalar efsanesi* (1971; *The Legend of the Thousand Bulls*) shows a 20th-century nomadic tribe struggling to maintain its traditional way of life, even as the people begin to modernize themselves. They attempt to secure some land on which to settle in order to improve their material situation, but the villagers, abused by the *agha*, in turn take advantage of these unfortunate wandering shepherds. *Demirciler çarşisi cinayeti* (1974; *Murder in the Ironsmiths Market*), the first volume of *Akçasazin Ağalari* (The Lords of Akchasaz), depicts the strife between the villagers and the landowners from the perspective of the bloody conflict between two ruling families. In this novel, too, the modern world begins to intrude on a blood feud that makes sense only in the context of a way of life that is slowly fading away.

Al gözüm seyreyle salih (1976; *The Saga of a Seagull*) and *Deniz küstü* (1978; *The Sea-Crossed Fisherman*) mark somewhat of a departure for Kemal, as neither book is set on the Chukurova Plain. In the latter book, set in a fishing village that is slowly being engulfed by a rapidly expanding Istanbul, Kemal once again explores the costs of modernization and development. *The Saga of a Seagull* is also set in a coastal town. Salih, an 11-year-old boy, tries to save a seagull with broken wings that he has found by the seashore. Kemal uses Salih's disappointing journey through the town, attempting to find someone who can help him heal the seagull, to reveal from the limited perspective of a child the same callousness, cruelty, and corruption that he depicts more directly elsewhere. The politics of this novel operate at a symbolic level that is unique in Kemal's fiction. Salih's faith in possibility is contrasted with the scepticism of an adult world that no longer believes that anything can be changed or fixed.

Kemal deliberately eschews elaborate literary stylings. He has said that his aim is to document his native society and its traditions for the rest of the world. The historic, cultural, and geographic detail of his novels, his exploration of Turkish myth, folklore, and custom, and his usage of unusual Turkish words and neologisms drawn from southern Turkey make Kemal's novels appear more exotic and otherworldly than he himself might wish. While numerous writers have attempted in the 20th century to speak for the disenfranchised and dispossessed, Kemal is one of the few who has succeeded in representing the vicissitudes of peasant life in the language of the peasants. He neither presumes to speak for those without a voice nor pretends to dignify them through literary representation. Instead, he attempts as much as possible to record simply and honestly a way of life that has only become more difficult with the waning of tradition.

IMRE SZEMAN

Biography

Born in Adana, Turkey, in 1922. Attended schools in Kadirli. Worked as farmhand, cobbler's apprentice, construction worker, clerk, and petition writer in southern Turkey; reporter for *Cumhuriyet* newspaper, Istanbul, 1951–63; editor of *Ant* Marxist weekly, in 1960s; member of Central Committee of Turkish Labour Party; arrested and tried for communist propaganda, 1950, and imprisoned briefly for political views, 1971. Former president, Turkish Writers Union.

Novels by Kemal

Ince Memed, 2 vols., 1955; volume 1 as *Memed, My Hawk*, translated by Edouard Roditi, 1961; volume 2 as *They Burn the Thistles*, translated by Margaret E. Platon, 1977

Ortadirek, 1960; as *The Wind from the Plain*, translated by Thilda Kemal, 1969

Yer demir, gök bakir, 1963; as *Iron Earth, Copper Sky*, translated by Thilda Kemal, 1979

Bütün hikâyeler, 1967; as *Anatolian Tales*, translated by Thilda Kemal, 1978

Ölmez otu, 1969; as *The Undying Grass*, translated by Thilda Kemal, 1978

Ağridaği efsanesi, 1970; as *The Legend of Ararat*, translated by Thilda Kemal, 1978

Binboğalar efsanesi, 1971; as *The Legend of the Thousand Bulls*, translated by Thilda Kemal, 1976

Akçasazin Ağalari [The Lords of Akchasaz]:
   Demirciler çarşisi cinayeti, 1974; as *Murder in the Ironsmiths Market*, translated by Thilda Kemal, 1980

Yusufçuk Yusuf [Yusuf, Little Yusuf], 1975
Yilani Öldürseler, 1976; as *To Crush the Serpent*, translated by
Thilda Kemal, 1992
Al gözüm seyreyle salih, 1976; as *The Saga of a Seagull*,
translated by Thilda Kemal, 1981
Deniz küstü, 1978; as *The Sea-Crossed Fisherman*, translated
by Thilda Kemal, 1985

Other Writings: several volumes of collected essays, political
writings, and newspaper articles, none of which has been translated into English.

Further Reading
Edebiyat: A Journal of Middle Eastern Literatures 5:1–2
(1980), special issue on Kemal

Thomas Keneally 1935–

Australian

Few Australian novelists have had such long and successful international careers as Thomas Keneally; fewer still have had to
endure such local critical odium, often occasioned by envy, distaste for his republican politics, or allegations of misogyny. Early enjoying honors in his own country, winning consecutive
Miles Franklin Awards for fiction with *Bring Larks and Heroes*
(1967) and *Three Cheers for the Paraclete* (1968) (the former
burdened with the sobriquet "the great Australian novel"), Keneally found that his popularity and prolific output were sometimes enlisted against him. Determinedly, he widened the scope
of subjects for his fiction, treating Joan of Arc in *Blood Red, Sister Rose* (1974) and the World War I Armistice in *Gossip from
the Forest* (1975). In 1982 his "faction" *Schindler's Ark* was
deemed eligible for the Booker Prize, publicly signaling a more
permissive definition of the novel form. This tale of the German
industrialist who saved more than 1,000 Jews from the death
camps cemented Keneally's international reputation. Nor has
any other Booker Prize-winning novel sold so well.

Keneally's is an imagination engrossed and greedy, joyful and
permissive, at times to the detriment of his art. He delights in the
plenitude of material offered by the Australian past and present,
as well as historical conflicts, especially civil wars in Europe and
the United States. His fiction is a history of the forms and themes
that have entranced Australian novelists before Keneally, and of
how he has subsumed and revised them. These include saga,
melodrama, mystery; the peopling of a new continent with alien,
European idioms and ideologies; the resilience of the Aborigines;
and the legacy of the Irish in Australia. Keneally has also been
preternaturally alert to features of Australian psychopathology:
to the compulsiveness of stereotyping, the feelings of insecurity
of lodgment in the continent, and fears of dispossession. These
are some of the lineaments of the national melodrama that he
has so ably and extensively explored.

His career began with a Gothic murder mystery in a seminary,
The Place at Whitton (1964), which drew on Keneally's experiences at St. Patrick's, Manly, for its setting. *The Fear* (1965)—
the first of his novels to examine the impact of World War II on
Australia—was a semi-autobiographical transformation of his
childhood in western Sydney. It was followed by other treatments of World War II in *The Cut-Rate Kingdom* (1980) and
Chief of Staff (1991) (the second novel published pseudony-

mously as "William Coyle"). For Keneally, the events of the
past—especially those that took place during critical periods of
war—are always instinct in the present: "There is a direct fuse
line, a fuse that is still burning between the past and the
present."

Bring Larks and Heroes was his initial engagement with the
European settlement of Australia. Together with the novels of
Patrick White, it was a crucial enticement to other writers to
treat such historical material daringly. This was a tragic novel
that was in some measure revised as a comedy 20 years later in
The Playmaker (1987), which tells of the staging of the first play
in this new world. The pointed revision of previous work is also
apparent in another pair of novels: *The Chant of Jimmie Blacksmith* (1972) and *Flying Hero Class* (1991). The first was an attempt to reexamine the bloody rebellion of the part-Aboriginal
Governor brothers against whites at the turn of the century. In a
racial climate so soon to be politicized in Australia, Keneally
ruefully conceded that he must have been a "madman" to undertake the first task. By contrast, *Flying Hero Class* (in which
Arab terrorists kidnap a plane on which members of an Aboriginal dance troupe are passengers) makes Aborigines agents in
their own stories and gives them back a measure of humanity,
which they have routinely been denied.

Keneally has said that "the Aboriginal issue is Australia's Ulster." The comparison is animated by an acute awareness of the
Irish heritage in Australia, which is for Keneally a family and a
tribal affair. Each of his two outstanding anatomies of contemporary Australian society—*A Family Madness* (1985) and *Woman of the Inner Sea* (1994)—involves the exogamous marriage of
an Irish-Australian and the consequences—tragic and comic, indicative of wider prejudices and of impediments to charity—for
those concerned. He has also written a travel book about Ireland, *Now and In Time to Be* (1991), and is completing the story of Thomas Meagher, Irish political prisoner to Van Diemen's
Land, Civil War general, and governor of Montana.

Keneally's fictional forms have been eclectic and heterogeneous; his novels strain to control the many stories that they
wish to tell. In senses that his expanding oeuvre increasingly justifies, he is the Australian Honoré de Balzac, constructor in the
antipodes of his version of the human comedy. In happy combination, rather than contradiction, Keneally is analyst and cele-

brant of modern and historical Australia, whether as novelist or pundit. His fictional career is strewn with risk taking both thematic (addressing Aboriginal issues, writing two novels set in Antarctica) and formal (for instance, using a fetus-narrator in *Passenger*, 1979). In Keneally's humanist vision all fates are entwined, we are all "confederates" (the title of his 1979 American Civil War novel), and all dramas are essentially of the family. His fiction—wherever it is located in time or place—is committed to revitalization and renewal through the use of metaphor in renaming the parts of the world (particularly Australian), the erosion of stereotypes, and the cleansing of prejudice.

PETER PIERCE

Biography

Born 7 October 1935 in Sydney, New South Wales. Attended St. Patrick's College, Strathfield, New South Wales; studied for the priesthood, 1953–60, and studied law. Served in the Australian Citizens Military Forces. High school teacher in Sydney, 1960–64; lecturer in drama, University of New England, Armidale, New South Wales, 1968–69; has also taught at the University of California, Irvine, and at New York University.

Novels by Keneally

The Place at Whitton, 1964
The Fear, 1965
Bring Larks and Heroes, 1967
Three Cheers for the Paraclete, 1968
The Survivor, 1969
A Dutiful Daughter, 1971
The Chant of Jimmie Blacksmith, 1972
Blood Red, Sister Rose, 1974
Gossip from the Forest, 1975
Moses the Lawgiver (novelization of television play), 1975
Season in Purgatory, 1976
A Victim of the Aurora, 1977
Passenger, 1979

Confederates, 1979
The Cut-Rate Kingdom, 1980
Schindler's Ark, 1982; as *Schindler's List*, 1982
A Family Madness, 1985
The Playmaker, 1987
Towards Asmara, 1989; as *To Asmara*, 1989
Flying Hero Class, 1991
Chief of Staff, 1991
Woman of the Inner Sea, 1994
A River Town, 1995

Other Writings: plays and screenplays, nonfiction, children's fiction.

Further Reading

Frow, John, "The Chant of Thomas Keneally," *Australian Literary Studies* 10 (1983)
Kiernan, Brian, "Thomas Keneally and the Australian Novel: A Study of *Bring Larks and Heroes*," *Southerly* 28:3 (1968)
McInherny, Frances, "Women and Myth in Thomas Keneally's Fiction," *Meanjin* 40:2 (1981)
Mitchell, Adrian, "Thomas Keneally and the Scheme of Things," *Australian Literary Studies* 9 (1979)
Pierce, Peter, *Australian Melodramas: Thomas Keneally's Fiction*, St. Lucia and Portland, Oregon: University of Queensland Press, 1995
Quartermaine, Peter, *Thomas Keneally*, London and New York: Arnold, 1991
Tiffin, Chris, "Victims Black and White: Thomas Keneally's *The Chant of Jimmie Blacksmith*," in *Studies in the Recent Australian Novel*, edited by K.G. Hamilton, St. Lucia: University of Queensland Press, 1978
Walker, Shirley, "Thomas Keneally and 'the special agonies of being a woman'," in *Who Is She?* edited by Shirley Walker, St. Lucia: University of Queensland Press, and New York: St. Martin's Press, 1983

Ilyās Khūrī 1948–

Lebanese

Although best known for his novels, prominent Lebanese literary figure Ilyās Khūrī has also written short stories, literary criticism, social and political essays, and film scripts. He is the editor-in-chief of the literary supplement of *Al-Nahār*, the leading newspaper in Lebanon, in which new and emerging Arab voices are constantly introduced to the literary scene. Khūrī belongs to a group of Arab writers that emerged in the 1960s and established what came to be known as the "new novel" or "new sensibility," a style that tackled the personal and political with fresh insight and introduced new techniques. In a 1993 interview, Khūrī spoke of the inter-relatedness of literature and politics: ". . . in theory, we can separate literature from politics; but if you are in Lebanese or Palestinian society, this is impossible because everything is politicized and everything has to be re-thought; in rethinking society you cannot say 'I am not political'."

Since the beginning of his literary career, Khūrī has interrogated and probed existing models of Arabic literature to create new possibilities that enlighten the world we live in. Khūrī's project may be said to operate on two levels. First, he wants to liberate the Arabic language—traditionally divided into standard (written) and colloquial (spoken)—from its rigid diction and syntax. This does not mean he disregards the classical idiom completely;

instead, Khūrī introduces the spoken idiom into the written one. His interest in modernizing the Arabic language is crucial to the second level of his project: a concern for recording the experiences of daily living. According to Khūrī, daily occurrences are best appreciated when the gap between orality and its written form has been bridged.

Although we cannot separate Khūrī's literary development from the history of the Lebanese civil war (1975–90), it would be extremely unfair to consider his writing important only as it relates to the civil war. While the civil war is a point of departure in many of his works, it typically functions as a vital locus to investigate more general the human conditions with specific questions pertaining to life, death, religion, and history.

Most of Khūrī's novels resist being summarized because they do not tell a single story with a clearly delineated plot. Instead, his novels are comprised of many intertwined events and incidents. His first novel, ʿAn alāqat al-dāʾirah (1975; About the Inter-relatedness of the Circle), tells of the life and experiences of a young boy, Manṣūr, at an orphanage, and his initiation into a world filled with social and religious authorities that eventually leads to his death. Khūrī published this novel at the beginning of 1975, just before the outbreak of the Lebanese civil war. With piercing insight and sensitivity, he was able to foretell of the calamities awaiting his country at the time. Khūrī's preoccupation with death is more poignantly apparent in his second novel, Al-Jabal al-ṣaghīr (1977; Little Mountain), which presents various portraits of the war connected through the themes of death and uncertainty. In this novel, Khūrī problematizes issues of life and death, friend and adversary, truth and falsehood, fiction and reality, while implicating all Lebanese for their country's predicament: "the war refers to us."

Al-Wujūh al-baydāʾ (1981; The White Faces) is a novel primarily about coping with war and its atrocities. It deals with death as a means to explore the vivid reality of everyday life. The plot revolves around an investigation into the death of a man whose body was found in the Unesco, a residential district in Beirut. Khūrī weaves an intricate web in which the murder case is riddled with ambiguity and a lack of resolution. The novel presents a world where certain traditionally held eternal truths no longer exist; we are left only with assumptions and predictions.

Abwāb al-madīnah (1981; Gates of the City) is the most abstract of Khūrī's fictional works, a novel in which the dream verges on the real, while the real becomes slippery and intangible. This atmosphere nearly demands that the novel be read as a poetic text. Issues related to love, security, search, death, authority, narration, memory, and writing are raised only to be interrogated and contested. The plot in Gates of the City revolves around a stranger who keeps looking for his lost suitcase, which contains papers, a pen, and his father's picture. His persistent search for the suitcase signifies his urgent need to write down and register his experiences so that his ordeal will not be lost in time nor fade from memory.

Riḥlat Ghāndī al-ṣaghīr (1989; The Journey of Little Gandhi) is the most acclaimed novel among Khūrī's work to date. The novel opens with the death of its title character, a shoe shiner nicknamed Little Gandhi, then proceeds to explore the world in which Gandhi lived. (See separate entry, Journey of Little Gandhi).

Mamlakat al-ghurabāʾ (1993; The Kingdom of Strangers) won the University of Arkansas Press Award for Arabic Literature in Translation. Like The Journey of Little Gandhi, this novel defies a simple summary because of its embedded stories. The Kingdom of Strangers goes beyond the epistemological questions presented in previous works to explore more ontological ones about the kinds of worlds we are living in, how they are constituted, and how we can improve them so that we do not feel like strangers as Christ did.

Khūrī's latest novel, Majmaʿ al-asrār (1994; Box of Secrets), questions whether it is possible to know the truth of any single story. One among a chain of related stories in the novel is that of Ḥannā al-Salmān who is about to be hanged because he confessed to a crime he did not commit. The sentence "Thus the story began," which is repeated throughout the novel, not only exonerates the narrator from assuming an all-knowing role, it also deludes readers from finding out what really happened. By conjuring up various possibilities from the silences and ruptures of the narrative itself, the real issue in Majmaʿ al-asrār becomes how a story is told.

SABAH GHANDOUR

See also Journey of Little Gandhi

Biography
Born in Beirut in 1948. He is the editor of Al-Nahār's literary supplement, and has taught at the American University of Beirut and at Columbia University, New York.

Novels by Khūrī
ʿAn alāqat al-dāʾirah [About the Inter-relatedness of the Circle], 1975
Al-Jabal al-ṣaghīr, 1977; as Little Mountain, translated by Maia Tabet, 1989
Abwāb al-madīnah, 1981; as Gates of the City, translated by Paula Haydar, 1993
Al-Wujūh al-baydāʾ [The White Faces], 1981
Riḥlat Ghāndī al-ṣaghīr, 1989; as The Journey of Little Gandhi, translated by Paula Haydar, 1994
Mamlakat al-ghurabāʾ, 1993; as The Kingdom of Strangers, translated by Paula Haydar, 1996
Majmaʿ al-asrār [Box of Secrets], 1994

Other Writings: short stories, literary criticism, political essays, and film scripts.

Further Reading
Al-ʿĪd, Yumna, Al-Kitābah: Taḥawwul fī al-taḥawwul, Beirut: Dar al-Adab, 1993
Barādah, Muḥammad, editor, Dirāsāt fī al-qiṣṣah al-ʿArabiyah, Beirut: Muassasat al-Abḥath al-ʿArabiyah, 1986
Ghandour, Sabah, foreword to Gates of the City, by Ilyās Khūrī, Minneapolis: University of Minnesota Press, 1993
Ghandour, Sabah, foreword to The Journey of Little Gandhi, by Ilyās Khūrī, Minneapolis: University of Minnesota Press, 1994
Maḥfūẓ, ʿIṣām, Al-Riwāyah al-ʿArabiyah al-ṭalīʿiyah wa-al-shahidah, Beirut: Dar ibn Khaldun, 1982
Said, Edward, foreword to Little Mountain, by Ilyās Khūrī, Minneapolis: University of Minnesota Press, 1989
Suwaydan, Sāmī, Abḥath fī al-naṣṣ al-riwāʾī al-ʿArabī, Beirut: Muassasat al-Abḥath al-ʿArabiyah, 1986

Kim by Rudyard Kipling

1901

For many years, Rudyard Kipling's reputation as a writer rested mainly on the 300 or so short stories he published during a career that extended from the late 1880s to the early 1930s. In recent years, however, critics have argued that he was also a major poet, and not just (as T.S. Eliot suggested) a writer of sometimes great "verse." Few claims have been made for him as a novelist. When Kipling returned from India in 1889 to build his reputation with English readers at home, his agent A.P. Watt duly advised him to write the big three-volume novel that was still taken as the measure of a writer's worth. Kipling acknowledged both the need to do so and his suspicion that he was unequal to the task. Fortunately for him, and for English literature, in 1894 the circulating libraries finally turned their back on the familiar Victorian "triple-decker," allowing the one-volume novel and the short story to come into their own.

Kipling made two early attempts at the novel form. (*The Naulahka,* written in collaboration with Wolcott Balestier in 1892, may be left out of consideration as a false start.) Neither is wholly successful. *The Light That Failed* (1890) oddly combines sadism and misogyny with elements of autobiography and a plea for the integrity of the artistic imagination: all these in a novel that Kipling opportunistically prepared in two versions, one with a happy ending and the other with a tragic one. This novel lends support to George Orwell's view that, at his worst, Kipling was "morally insensitive and aesthetically disgusting." The theme of *Captains Courageous* (1897) is part *rites de passage* and part documentary about the cod-fishing fleet at the end of the 19th century. The two issues come together in Kipling's admiration for the qualities of honesty, justice, and compassion that he finds embedded in the professional skill of the fishermen. The weakness of *Captains Courageous* is that it is a novel with no interest in the exploration of character. Its documentary focus is carried out at the expense of any treatment of consciousness and motivation.

Kim, however, has long been regarded as a masterpiece. It appeared in 1901, 12 years after Kipling had left India, and was his last sustained account of the country in which he had learned to be a writer. Perhaps for that reason, it is marked by a rare depth of affection and generosity of spirit. These qualities are to be admired, but they have their limitations. The novel's vision of a timeless India, sheltered under the wise guidance of the British, is a denial as well as a celebration of the energy and achievement of Indian culture. Twenty years after the emergence of the Congress Party, Kipling writes as if India had no significant history other than the Mutiny of 1857, which figures in *Kim* only as a tragic error. The novel never doubts that the Russians and the British need to play out in India the "Great Game" of spy and counterspy or that there is an eternal distinction between the sahib and the native Indian. In these respects Kipling writes as a man of, or even behind, his time.

But the novel belongs to the wider traditions of world literature as well as to the history of colonial and postcolonial discourse. Its central concerns can be variously described. Within the encompassing adventure of the Great Game, both Kim and the lama (Tibetan monk) whose disciple he becomes pursue their own quests: Kim to find his identity as a sahib and one of the rulers of this world, the lama to find the sacred river in which he may at last lose his attachment to the world. Kipling's achievement is to acknowledge the full value of both these quests, and there are few more compelling accounts of a holy man in literature. The relationship between the ascetic priest and the streetwise Kim has echoes of other stories of male friendship—Don Quixote and Sancho Panza, Huckleberry Finn and Jim—but, more importantly, Kipling's story is a celebration of love. From a Western viewpoint, the final scene of the novel shows the lama dragged from a stream in which he was about to drown; but Kipling takes seriously the old man's sense that what forced him to return to the life he had hoped to reject was the need to share his moment of illumination with his beloved disciple. In *Kim* there is none of the condescension that one finds in (for example) E.M. Forster's treatment of Professor Godbole in *A Passage to India,* published some 20 years later.

Kim is, then, a story of two opposed quests pursued by an old man and a young boy (Kim is about 13 when the novel begins) who come to love each other. It is also a picaresque work, with a gallery of vividly created characters—Mahbub Ali, Afghan horse-dealer and British secret agent; the Babu, with his admiration for Herbert Spencer; and Lurgan Sahib, the disquieting Healer of Sick Pearls—who appear from time to time during Kim's life. All these characters are connected with the Great Game and all trigger or respond to successive episodes. Kim's chief location, the Grand Trunk Road that runs from Bombay in the south up to the North-West Frontier, suggests that among the novel's antecedents is Geoffrey Chaucer's account of the pilgrims in the *Canterbury Tales;* one of the central characters, the talkative old woman from Kulu, bears at least a passing resemblance to the Wife of Bath. The brilliantly suggested detail of Kipling's descriptions of life along the road—of railway stations, bazaars, meals around village fires, regiments setting up and breaking camp—owes something to his seven years as a journalist and perhaps also to his Pre-Raphaelite connections (Edward Burne-Jones was his uncle). But such detail, like the picaresque frame within which it is so hospitably held, is more than a flourish of late 19th-century exoticism. It is also the sign that Kipling's imagination, and Kim's life, will eventually find their true satisfaction *in* the world and not in rejecting it.

Kim is not a novel to be admired unreservedly. It is characterized by what Edward Said has described as Orientalism, or the Western hegemonic stance toward the East; it considers women only in relation to men; and its vision of goodness is perhaps weakened by the absence of a real sense of evil. But it is in two ways a story of love: the love between the lama and his disciple and Kipling's love for India. The war in South Africa, and then World War I, were soon to darken Kipling's sense of the political world, and it was not until the last decade of his life, when his imagination turned to stories of healing and forgiveness, that he was able to rediscover the generosity of his one successful novel.

PHILLIP MALLETT

Further Reading

Mallett, Phillip, editor, *Kipling Considered*, London: Macmillan, and New York: St. Martin's Press, 1989

Mason, Philip, *Kipling: The Glass, the Shadow and the Fire*, London: Cape, and New York: Harper and Row, 1975

Rutherford, Andrew, editor, *Kipling's Mind and Art*, Edinburgh: Oliver and Boyd, and Stanford, California: Stanford University Press, 1964

Tompkins, J.M.S., *The Art of Rudyard Kipling*, London: Methuen, 1959; 2nd edition, London: Methuen, and Lincoln: University of Nebraska Press, 1965

Wilson, Angus, *The Strange Ride of Rudyard Kipling*, London: Secker and Warburg, and New York: Viking, 1977

György Konrád 1933–

Hungarian

György Konrád is one of the best known Hungarian novelists, although his writing career started relatively late: he was already 36 years old when his first novel was published, a situation deriving from adverse political conditions in post-1956 Hungary. For several years after the suppression of the 1956 revolution, Konrád had no fixed occupation, and between 1959 and 1973 he worked mainly as a social worker and later as an urban sociologist. In the event, his life experiences helped Konrád write about society in a more authentic manner than most of his contemporaries, although this authenticity did not endear him to the communist authorities. From 1977 to 1988 his books were banned in Hungary. The ban on his works was caused in part by the unsympathetic treatment of the party-state in his novels and in part by his thoughtful political essays and the sociological tract *Az értelmiseg útja az osztályhatalomhoz* (1978; *The Intellectuals on the Road to Class Power*) written with his friend Iván Szelényi. His success abroad and various scholarships and invitations from the West kept him going. Since 1989, Konrád has emerged as an important intellectual figure and a frequent visitor at international conferences, serving as president of the International PEN writers organization from 1990 to 1992. In recent years he has been writing more essays and articles than fiction.

His first novel, *A látogató* (1969; *The Case Worker*), considered by some critics his best, is a short narrative about the days of a Budapest social worker who has to deal not only with the usual cases of vagrancy and alcoholism but also with maladjusted children or children abandoned by their parents. Too much empathy might lead to self-destruction, and Konrád's protagonist has to be a pragmatist most of the time, but the book is nevertheless a kind of lyrical monologue about the social worker's everyday experiences and secret fantasies. What makes it remarkable is "the force of Mr. Konrad's language . . . the world he conjures up of a vast junkyard of people reduced to objects and the intimations he evokes that the only escape lies in idiocy and death," according to one reviewer. Konrád's first novel was received well in Hungary itself, although most critics hastened to point out that what he described was not typical of the social situation.

Konrád's next novel, *A városalapító* (1977; *The City Builder*), was completed and circulated in manuscript by the early 1970s, but it could not be published until much later and then only in a censored form. There is a certain continuity here with *The Case Worker* in the sense that this novel, too, is a first-person narrative and has a certain poetic, lyrical quality. It is the monologue of an architect from an unnamed Eastern European city for whom the city becomes a metaphor for society ("I am a city planner in the early phase of socialism. . . . I am not a revolutionary, although I shared others' impatience to leave my mark on the world and participated in speeded-up metamorphoses of roles") with all its complications. Although critical of the society that his endeavors helped to create, the architect carefully separates social criticism from utopian dreams—hence the curious mixture of realism and surrealism that characterizes *The City Builder*. The most outspoken pages of the novel are those where the narrator lists certain characteristics of the kind of city he does *not* want to live in. The list adds up to a summary of the conditions of early socialism of the Soviet type, of a society with monolithic tendencies.

Konrád's third novel, first published in English in 1982 as *The Loser* and in Hungarian (as *A cinkos*) in samizdat in 1983, marks a departure from the first two novels. The narrative time of the previous novels was the continuous present; here it is split between various periods in the past and the present. The plot is built on and around identifiable historical moments, containing the experiences of Konrád's early youth and those of the previous generation. The novel recounts the adventures of the narrator K., a half-Jewish, aging ex-communist and his younger and more temperamental brother, Dani. It is here that Konrád first breaks the principal rule of socialist fiction—nothing but good should be said about the Russians—by describing the narrator's war experiences with brutal frankness. Konrád's narrator decides to come clean in October 1956, when the revolution is suppressed by Soviet tanks. The section on the revolution is extremely evocative and colorful, capturing the festive mood of mass demonstrations: "The police are seduced by the crowd's erotic magic; it does not even occur to them to shoot, and they melt into the throngs. The regime's own slogans turn against the system. During the years of oppression we had to greet our neighbors with the word 'Freedom.' Now we give the word a little meaning."

The Loser does not deal only with the high and low points of Hungarian history or the strange adventures of heroes who do or do not believe in the communist utopia; it also examines the private lives of Budapest intellectuals, their tortuous love affairs and hysterical marriages. In fact, the novel ends with a conversation between K. and Dani, soon after Dani confesses to killing his whorish wife in a rage of excessive jealousy. This act highlights the contradictions of communist Hungary: K., who is quite sane but a political dissident, can be incarcerated in a mental institution while his brother, who is mentally imbalanced but politically not dangerous, is considered harmless and does not receive treatment.

Konrád's next novel, *Kerti mulatság* (1989; *A Feast in the Garden*, subtitled "Novel and Working Diary"), is the first volume of a trilogy entitled *Agenda*. The book has a diffuse quality, presenting a chronicle of a fictional city bearing a strong resemblance to Budapest. It recounts the experiences of five different characters, David Kobra, Janos Dragoman, and their women, Melinda, Klara, and Regina. Of these, Kobra is closest to Konrád's alter ego, and the chapter of his reminiscences of World War II is probably autobiographical. The last chapter is the "working diary," where the author drops his mask and starts writing in the first person about his experiences in Colorado Springs (where he taught for a year) and in Budapest. While it is dramatic and exciting, entertaining and humorous in parts, *A Feast in the Garden* lacks the stylistic unity that characterized Konrád's previous novels. Apart from the plurality of characters, there is a generic diversity, including the forms of the essay and even of the feuilleton. As Konrád himself points out: "This is not a novel-like novel. . . . Our structural model is not the arch but the street-crossing. . . . The novel shapes itself in front of the reader."

Agenda was continued in 1995 when its second volume, *Kőóra* (Stone Sundial), came out. It has the same protagonists as *A Feast in the Garden*, with Janos Dragoman, the internationally renowned scholar temporarily back in his home town, as the focus of the narrative. The city now has a name, Kandor, which is a double pun: it is the anagram of the author's name and alludes to *kandúr* (tomcat). Due to certain political changes, Dragoman, the old dissident, now finds acceptance, even fame. He also discovers that he has an illegitimate daughter and even a grandson. He could find happiness in this new family or in the arms of his lover(s), but for a return of the past in the form of a confrontation with one of his old university colleagues, the conservative "Central European monarchist" Kuno Aba. The con-

frontation leads to a fight and ends in Kuno's accidental death. Dragoman has to leave Kandor once again, but not before he has slept with Sandra, Kuno Aba's widow, a new, determined kind of liberated woman. *Kőóra* is full of autobiographical details and contains references to the year 1956, in many ways a decisive date in Konrád's life. The dominant mood of this novel is one of nostalgia, and the author creates a mosaic of images put together from moments of the past and the present.

Konrád's significance in the development of modern Hungarian prose lies mainly in the innovative style of his first novel, which deals with painful social issues but presents them in a cohesive and impressively homogeneous style. In his later work Konrád strove for a compromise between the objective world of society and history and the subjective world of the narrator-intellectual. While this endeavor did not always produce the best results, Konrád can still be regarded as a pioneer of the modern essayistic novel in Hungary.

GEORGE GÖMÖRI

Biography

Born 2 April 1933 in Debrecen, Hungary. Attended Debrecen Reform College; Madách Gymnasium, Budapest, 1947–51; Lenin Institute, Budapest; Loránd Eötvös University, Budapest, degree in teaching literature 1955. Teacher, general gymnasium, Csepel, 1956; editor, *Életképek* [Life Scenes], 1956, and *Magyar Helikon*, 1960–66; social worker, Budapest, 1959–65; sociologist, City Planning Research Institute, 1965–73; arrested and imprisoned for six days, Budapest, 1974; visiting professor of comparative literature, Colorado Springs College, 1986. Also active at the Institute for Literary Scholarship for several years.

Novels by Konrád

A látogató, 1969; as *The Case Worker,* 1974
A városalapító, 1977; as *The City Builder,* 1977
The Loser, 1982; as *A cinkos,* 1983
Agenda (a planned trilogy)
    Kerti mulatság, 1989; as *A Feast in the Garden,* 1992
    Kőóra [Stone Sundial], 1995

Other Writings: political and sociological essays, including *Az értelmiség útja az osztályhatalomhoz* (1978; *The Intellectuals on the Road to Class Power*).

Further Reading

Birnbaum, Marianna D., "György Konrád's *The Loser,*" *Cross Current* 7 (1988)
Gömöri, George, "George Konrád: *The Loser,*" *World Literature Today* 57:3 (Summer 1983)
Sanders, Ivan, "Freedom's Captives: Notes on George Konrád's Novels," *World Literature Today* 57:2 (Spring 1983)
Sennet, Richard, "A Dark Novel of Eastern Europe," *The New York Times Book Review* (26 September 1982)
Veres, András, entry with bibliography in *Új Magyar Irodalmi Lexikon,* volume 2, Budapest: Akadémiai Kiadó, 1994

Korean Novel

In January 1997 in Seoul, the Samsung Cultural Foundation, together with the literary journal *Munhak sasang,* announced the creation of the Samsung Culture and Arts Awards. The centerpiece award is a cash prize of 50 million *wŏn* (at the time, approximately US$60,000) for the Korean novel judged the year's best. The Korean short story, suggested Kwŏn Yŏng-min, editor-in-chief of *Munhak sasang,* had reached an acceptable level of aesthetic accomplishment. The novel, however, mass produced and responding to the lure of commercialism, had remained stunted. It was to remedy this chronic situation and to help realize the flagship potential of the novel in the nation's literature that the Samsung awards were instituted.

The advent of this award illuminates the problematic position of the novel in Korean literary history, and especially in the 20th century. To many Koreans, the novel smacks of newspaper serialization and popular literature. For serious literature, Korean readers turn to the short story, novella, poetry, or personal essay. The position of the novel in Korea has thus influenced, and been influenced by, the literary quality of the genre, its critical evaluation, and its reception by Korean readers. It is no accident that until the announcement of the Samsung awards the two most prestigious fiction prizes in Korea—the Tongin and Yi Sang awards, established in 1956 and 1977, respectively—were awarded for short fiction or novellas.

Because Korean fiction has been demarcated into the novel, novella, and short story only in the 20th century (and the distinction between the latter two is frequently blurred), it makes sense to examine premodern Korean fiction in general to set the context for the development of the novel proper in Korea. Fiction has a long pedigree in Korea: some scholars trace the origin of the novel as far back as the Tangun foundation myth (earliest written mention in the *Samguk yusa* [1281; Memorabilia of the Three Kingdoms]) and various other foundation myths and legends. A more recognizable forebear is Kim Shi-sŭp's *Kŭmo shinhwa* (15th century; Tales of Kŭmo), often cited as the first instance of Korean fiction. Dating from the Chosŏn kingdom (1392–1910), it consists of five short narratives written in *hanmun,* the classical Chinese writing system widely used by educated Koreans before (and after) the advent in 1446 of *hangŭl,* the admirably precise Korean vernacular script.

Two dissimilar fictional works, reflecting two different literary trends, are frequently honored as the twin pillars of the premodern Korean novel: Hŏ Kyun's *Hong Kil-dong chŏn* (Tale of Hong Kiltong) and Kim Man-jung's *Kuun mong* (A Dream of Nine Clouds). *Hong Kil-dong chŏn,* dating from the end of the 16th century, is widely regarded as the first extant Korean fictional narrative written in *hangŭl.* An example of "heroic fiction," based on the vicissitudes of a hero of aristocratic but modest origins, this short work concerns an outcast nobleman who becomes the leader of a group of bandits dedicated to social and economic justice. Linear in structure, it lacks realistic characterization—the bandit leader Hong Kil-dong, like other protagonists in this genre, has supernatural powers—and includes some improbable plot twists. But at a time when literati were routinely banished to the remote countryside for running afoul of the throne, it is likely that this lack of realism was necessary in order to distance the author from the subversive themes of the work,

such as the empowerment of illegitimate sons and the confiscation of wealth amassed illicitly by local magistrates, landholders, and the Buddhist clergy. In his espousal of the cause of illegitimate sons, Hŏ Kyun was drawing on his own life, for one of his most influential tutors, the accomplished Yi Tal, was, like other illegitimate sons, legally barred from the high government posts to which most literati of premodern Korea aspired. Also, the work shares with contemporary fictional accounts of the chaos wreaked by the Japanese invasions of 1592 and 1597 (and similar accounts resulting from the Manchu invasions of 1627 and 1636) pointed suggestions of Chosŏn officialdom's incompetence during times of acute national need. The bandit motif of *Hong Kil-dong chŏn* may have been inspired by the late 14th-century Chinese work *The Water Margin.*

The 17th-century *Kuun mong,* on the other hand, is a romance, and one of many traditional Korean fictional works that revolve around a dream. Although described by some as the oldest major novel written in *hangŭl,* many scholars now believe it was composed in *hanmun* and that the surviving versions are *hangŭl* translations. The protagonist has two contradictory impulses, or "dreams"—great worldly success and total withdrawal from the world—the resolution of which forms the tension of the work. Author Kim Man-jung, like most of his contemporaries in their works, situated his narrative in early China (ninth-century Tang dynasty). In contrast with the linear *Hong Kil-dong chŏn, Kuun mong* employs a cyclical structure. The work harks back to the familiar romance pattern but also prefigures the Faustian theme of a hero who undergoes a fall to earthly temptations followed by an ascent to enlightenment.

Assisted by developments in commercial publishing, traditional Korean fiction reached its zenith during the reigns of the Chosŏn kings Yŏngjo (1724–76) and Chŏngjo (1776–1800). Well known by this time was *Ch'unhyang chŏn* (Tale of Ch'unhyang), perhaps the most famous premodern Korean fictional narrative and certainly one of the best-loved stories in all of Korea. Concerning a nobleman's son who falls in love with the low-born Ch'unhyang and rescues her from the clutches of a debauched magistrate, the tale celebrates not only such traditional virtues as chastity and the punishment of corrupt officials but also the more revolutionary notion of love marriages that cross class lines. *Ch'unhyang chŏn* reached a wide audience not only by virtue of being written in *hangŭl* but also by being adapted for *p'ansori,* an oral narrative that flourished in the 18th and 19th centuries and that has continued to appeal to a wide spectrum of Korean society. Like many other premodern narratives, *Ch'unhyang chŏn* was originally part of the oral tradition and existed in several versions. Standardized versions appeared after the work entered the *p'ansori* repertoire.

Almost all of the premodern fictional narratives in Korea are anonymous, attesting to both the greater prestige accruing to poetry and the reluctance of Confucian-educated men, traditionally averse to commercial enterprise, to attach their names to any works that might be sold. (On the other hand, the great majority of the premodern *poems* by men, which were circulated by literati among one another, are attributed.) The privileged position of poetry in the Korean literary world, reflected in this proclivity in premodern times toward anonymous fiction and attributed poetry, has to the present day affected the reception of the novel in Korea. (It is claimed, for example, that South Korea today leads the world in per capita production of books of poetry.)

The 18th century also witnessed the heyday of *shirhak,* a movement that emphasized practical learning. *Shirhak* lent increasing realism and satire to Korean fiction. Pak Chi-wǒn, the best-known practitioner of *shirhak* fiction, used satire to expose the need for radical reform of the *yangban,* the traditional Korean elite, who, as we have seen, were often found wanting in times of national catastrophe. In many of Pak's works, exemplary characters are drawn from the lower classes, and unsavory characters from the *yangban.*

In spite of this notable instance of progressivism in premodern Korean history, women continued to occupy a very low profile in Korean literature. Gender role expectations confined Korean women within the domestic sphere, making them subservient in turn to father, husband, and son. Women were discouraged from educating themselves, and those rare women who did write almost never circulated their work outside the household. Nevertheless, the latter half of the 20th century has brought to view an impressive amount of women's writing from traditional times, most of it dating from after the promulgation of the vernacular script in the mid–15th century. Most of this literature took the form of long instructional poems from mother to daughter. Of prose works, palace literature is most prominent. Two of the best-known works of this type, *Hanjungnok* (*Memoirs of Lady Hyegyǒng*) and *Kyech'uk ilgi* (1613; Diary of the Year of the Black Ox) are primarily accounts of actual historical events and are more properly read as memoirs. Both were written in *hangŭl.* Another well-known work of palace literature, *Inhyǒn wanghu chǒn* (Life of Queen Inhyǒn), also composed in the vernacular, is a historical novel.

Another variety of premodern novel, the *kajok sosŏl,* or family saga, dates from the late 18th century and prefigures the *taeha sosŏl,* or *roman fleuve,* of modern times. The family novels enjoyed a readership among the palace women in Seoul, who presumably could afford these lengthy opuses, which routinely approached 30 or 40 volumes. *Cho sshi samdaerok* (Three Generations of the Cho Family), consisting of 40 volumes, is representative. Unlike many other premodern novels, which deal with single protagonists of heroic stature, the family novels develop a variety of realistic characters (usually members of the *yangban* aristocracy) drawn from several generations.

The *shin sosŏl,* appearing at the turn of the 20th century, is a literature of transition between these traditional narratives and the modern novel. Writers of the *shin sosŏl* ("New Novel"—the term was coined by contemporary advertisers attempting to pique reader interest by playing up differences between these works and the "old fiction") sought in their works to close the traditional gap between the spoken and written languages. Many of the works, whose length approaches or equals that of the modern novel, were inspired by two watershed events in modern Korean history. The first of these was the enlightenment movement that swept East Asia at the time. Even more important, perhaps, was nationalism, which developed in the wake of encroachments on Korean soil by the Chinese and Japanese, culminating in Japan placing Korea under protectorate status in 1905 and formally colonizing the nation in 1910.

Many writers of the *shin sosŏl* dealt with the ideology of modernization, as expressed in themes such as friendship toward

Japan (where the enlightenment movement in East Asia first took root) and criticism of China (exemplar of feudalism), love marriages versus arranged marriages, gender equality, and love of learning and teaching. Stylistically, the verse that occasionally appears in premodern fiction is dropped in the *shin sosŏl* in favor of an almost completely prose style that progressed toward *ŏnmun ilch'i,* or the unity of written and spoken language. Expressions derived from Chinese are replaced by native Korean equivalents. Maxims and other authorial admonitions are abandoned, and there is a break from the conventions of overstatement and metaphor. Reflection on the past decreases.

Yi In-jik's *Kwi ŭi sŏng* (Voice of the Devil; serialized in the newspaper *Mansebo* in 1907) comes close to achieving *ŏnmun ilch'i.* It shows a further development of the idiomatic and colloquial potential of vernacular Korean. Its language is terse, lively, and idiomatic. Although melodramatic—the novel deals with the abuse of privilege and domestic intrigue—it breaks new ground in its psychological depth, subtle characterization, and skillful narrative.

Several varieties of *shin sosŏl* are apparent. The *kajŏng sosŏl* (novel of domestic intrigue) has its roots in premodern narratives with themes such as the concubine problem. This issue, which is worked out tragically in *Kwi ŭi sŏng,* harks back to *Sa sshi nam chŏnggi* (Madam Sa's Righteous Journey to the South), a well-known premodern example of the genre.

The *t'oron sosŏl,* or "problem novel," gave fictional expression to (often controversial) issues introduced by the enlightenment movement, usually in the form of a debate among several characters. Yi Hae-jo's *Kumagŏm* (1908; The Demon-Expelling Sword) is an example. Indeed, whereas most premodern novels focus on the life of a single protagonist, most *shin sosŏl* are devoted to the resolution of a particular problem.

As Korean authors came to grips with the imminent loss of their nation's sovereignty they looked both to the Korean past and abroad for examples of successful nation building and national heroes. The result was another variety of *shin sosŏl:* historical romances such as Shin Ch'ae-ho's *Ulchi Mundŏk* (1908), about a famous general of the ancient Korean state of Koguryŏ; an account of the founding of Switzerland; and a fictionalized biography of the Italian nationalist Mazzini.

The advent of the *shin sosŏl* was accompanied by increased commercialization of literary production. The birth of vernacular newspapers in the late 1800s, which serialized novels as well as publishing other forms of literature, resulted in the evolution of a writer class. Some of these writers, such as Yi Hae-jo, had experience writing premodern novels; others were new to writing and chose it as a profession. The latter group especially were influenced by the example of those young Koreans who went to Japan to study and who saw there, in the person of Natsume Sōseki and others, the new phenomenon of the professional writer of creative fiction. The appearance of large-scale publishing companies added an additional link between the new professional writers and the Korean readership. Modern Korea now had a recognized body of writers, large-scale means for book production, media for the dissemination of literature, and, because of the almost universal acceptance of *hangŭl* by the 1920s, a widespread audience.

The trends toward a vernacular writing style, treatment of contemporary issues, and realistic characterization and narrative culminated in Yi Kwang-su's *Mujŏng* (1917; The Heartless), generally considered the first modern Korean novel. Although a milestone work, readers and critics today note the pronounced didacticism in the novel (Yi was an outspoken advocate of enlightenment). More problematic was Yi's record, later in the Japanese occupation period, of writing in Japanese and supporting the Japanese war movement, decisions for which he has been reviled by a large segment of the Korean literary community.

In fact, quite a few Korean authors, some living in Korea and some resident on Japanese soil, published at least once in Japanese. Nationalist readers and critics are reluctant to classify such works as Korean literature, but in recent years scholars in and out of Korea are increasingly researching the neglected area of works written by ethnic Korean writers in languages other than Korean, including Chinese, Russian, English, and German. Two of the best-known examples are Richard Kim's English-language novel *The Martyred* (1964) and Yi Mirok's German-language autobiographical novel *Der Yalu Fliesst* (1946; *The Yalu Flows*).

Many of the writers of the early modern Korean novel received at least some of their higher education in Japan. (The term *early modern* is generally applied to Korean literature written between 1917—the publication date of Yi Kwang-su's *Mujŏng*—and liberation from Japanese colonial rule in 1945; the term *contemporary* is used for literature written thereafter.) There they were exposed not only to modern Japanese literature but also to Western (and also early modern Chinese) literature in Japanese translation. French and Russian realists were especially popular, and their influence is evident in the strong streak of realism in the early modern Korean novel. For example, Yŏm Sang-sŏp was influenced by Ivan Turgenev's *Ottsy i deti* (1862; *Fathers and Sons*).

Given the many upheavals of modern Korean history—the abrupt opening to the West in the late 1800s, the enlightenment movement, colonization by the Japanese, civil war, and headlong industrialization with an accompanying imbalance between economic and political development—it should not be surprising that the modern Korean novel has tended to focus more on the real world of Koreans in the 20th century and less on metaphysical and artistic themes. Readers therefore find a number of early modern Korean novels dealing with the privations of the common people or the frustrated aspirations of an intellectual class that even in the colonial era far outnumbered the economic demand for them. Novels after 1945 deal with the turbulent political situation in a recently liberated nation, and novels written in the 1970s focus on the societal strains attending Korea's rush to industrialization under President Park Chung Hee. Novels written in the 1980s and 1990s tend to reexamine postwar Korean history and society in light of the greater freedom of information resulting from democratization in South Korea in the late 1980s, and to treat the increasing visibility of Korean women outside the home, a noteworthy phenomenon in a traditionally patriarchal society.

Some early modern novels, like the premodern *kajok sosŏl*, are family-centered. Yŏm Sang-sŏp's *Samdae* (1931; Three Generations) is a prominent example. Other novels of the time concern the plight of young intellectuals who had been encouraged to devote themselves to learning but who found no place in colonial Korea to exercise their talents. Yi Ki-yŏng's *Kohyang* (1932–33; Hometown) and other novels by writers who were attracted to socialism critique ongoing class divisions in Korean society and reflect the privations of the large peasant class. Still other novels, such as Ch'ae Man-shik's brilliant satire *T'aep'yŏng ch'ŏnha* (1938; *Peace Under Heaven*), paint unflattering portraits of those who waxed rich at the expense of their fellow Koreans under Japanese colonial rule.

The modern period has witnessed the continuation of the multivolume novel, now known as the *taeha sosŏl*, or *roman fleuve*. Many of these enormous works are family sagas. *T'oji* (1969–94; *Land*) by Pak Kyŏng-ni, weighing in at 16 volumes, is perhaps the best known. These novels are set against the panoramic backdrop of Korean history, and are often, especially in the case of Ch'oe Myŏng-hŭi's *Honpul* (1990– ; Spirit Fire), repositories of traditional Korean culture. In the hands of novelists such as Hwang Sŏk-yŏng and Cho Chŏng-nae, the *taeha sosŏl* has become an historical epic. Fascinated with the murky political history of Korea during the five-year period between liberation from Japanese colonial rule at the end of World War II and the outbreak in 1950 of the civil war, Cho set out in his ten-volume *T'aebaek sanmaek* (1986–89; The T'aebaek Mountains) to describe the divisions in Korean society, exacerbated by the superpower presence on the peninsula, that led to the 1950–53 war. Cho's subsequent *Arirang* (the title of Korea's best-loved folk song), an even longer work, extends throughout the Japanese occupation. In contrast, Hwang Sŏk-yŏng's historical epic *Chang Kil-san* (1984) is set in premodern times.

The division of the Korean peninsula since the civil war (as of this writing the two sides still have not concluded a peace treaty) has led to political repression in both North Korea and South Korea. One of the effects of such limitations in the South was the suppression, until the democratization represented by the first direct presidential election in 1987, of the work of the *wŏlbuk* writers, those authors who chose for ideological reasons to migrate from South Korea to North Korea between 1945 and 1950. This has meant that for well over four decades South Korean readers were denied ready access to such landmark novels as Hong Myŏng-hŭi's ten-volume *Im Kkŏk-jŏng* (1928–39), about a bandit folk hero, and Pak T'ae-wŏn's *Ch'ŏnbyŏn p'unggyŏng* (1936–37; Streamside Sketches). Political restraints have led to the jailing of such prominent fiction writers as Yi Ho-ch'ŏl (as well as the better-known poet Kim Chi'ha). The aforementioned Hwang Sŏk-yŏng, one of South Korea's most important novelists, received a lengthy jail term for an unauthorized visit to North Korea in 1989.

The *yŏnjak sosŏl*, or linked novel, a work consisting of discrete stories connected by theme and/or character, reached a high stage of development during the latter half of the 20th century. One of the best examples, and perhaps the most important Korean novel since 1945, is Cho Se-hŭi's *Nanjangi ka ssoaollin chagŭn kong* (1978; A Little Ball Launched by a Little Man). A veiled exposé of the social ills attending Korean industrialization in the 1970s, it is written in language plain enough to be understood by practically any Korean with a grade school education. The novel is a courageous achievement, considering it was written at the height of the Park Chung Hee dictatorship, when national security laws squelched most open criticism of government policies. Another well-known *yŏnjak* novel is Yi Mun-yŏl's *Kŭdae nŭn tashi kohyang e kajimot'ari* (1980; You Can't Go Home Again). The debut work of one of contemporary Korea's most influential novelists, it struck a chord among a generation of younger readers not only for its account of largely bygone rural Korean customs but also for its incisive treatment of the problem of sons and daughters who are made to suffer for the political wrongdoing of their parents. Yang Kwi-ja's *Wŏnmi-dong saram tŭl* (1987; The

People of Wŏnmi-dong) enjoys enduring popularity for its portrayal of the denizens of one of the many satellite communities that have cropped up around Seoul since the 1970s to accommodate the mass influx of countryside people.

Modern Korean literary criticism has tended to revolve around two axes: aesthetics and social engagement. Early modern writer-critics such as Yi Kwang-su, responding to the formalism and stricture of the neo-Confucian tradition that had influenced so much of premodern Korean society, literary production included, emphasized the importance of giving free rein to the author's intellect, aesthetics, and sensibility. With the advent of socialist realism in literature in the 1920s, however, came a stream of literary criticism that emphasized the illumination of class divisions and the resulting inequities in Korean society. These two streams of criticism, reflecting two distinct trends in modern Korean fiction, have continued to the present day, the social engagement school being particularly strong in the 1970s, when the social problems attending industrialization were increasingly visible in Korea's cities.

Literary criticism thrives in South Korea today, thanks to well-attended departments of Korean literature at local universities and a flourishing literary publication network. Much literary criticism deals directly or indirectly with identifying the defining characteristics of Korean literature. This is no small task considering the long history and large output of premodern Korean literature written in Chinese, and the abrupt opening of Korea to the outside world in the late 1800s, which in terms of literature brought a clash of native traditions with foreign influence. Much contemporary criticism deals with the historical, political, and ideological implications of a literary work, and assesses the relevance of a work to Korea and the Korean people. In recent years, Korean literary scholars and critics have grown increasingly familiar with Western literary theory, and a Marxist tinge can be detected, especially in the writing of some younger critics.

Korean novelists today write for two main audiences: a mass readership on the one hand and the literary establishment on the other, the latter consisting of writers, editors of literary journals, literary critics, and university literature professors. Surveys suggest that women constitute a distinct majority of Korean readers today, whereas the literary establishment is overwhelmingly male. Within that establishment there is considerable overlap among the roles of journal editor, critic, and professor. Few university professors of Korean literature would fail to consider themselves literary critics as well. In the 1920s and 1930s, decades that witnessed the first flowering of modern Korean fiction, many authors wrote both fiction and criticism. This tendency has diminished considerably in contemporary times, yet today's critic-scholars wield significant power over all but the most accomplished authors. Their clout, and the massive presence of the literary establishment in the Korean cultural world, is suggested by the fact that very few writers enter the literary mainstream without debuting either in one of the established literary journals or by capturing one of the various newcomers' awards sponsored by Korean dailies and literary journals. Significantly, a third avenue to recognition—recommendation by an established author—is seldom seen today. Underground literature is little known.

Whatever their audience, Korean novelists can write didactically with relative impunity. To do so is to satisfy the perceived need of a substantial sector of the literary establishment that a work of fiction (and its author) exhibit an awareness of the vagaries of modern Korean history. And as modernization threatens to erase traditional culture from the consciousness of younger readers, instruction in Korean tradition plays a large role in the popularity of such previously mentioned novels as *Im Kkŏk-jŏng, T'oji, Honpul,* and *Kŭdae nŭn tashi kohyang e kajimot'ari.*

Women's literature today offers evidence of the impact on Korean culture of women's increasing public participation in Korean society. That women novelists have made genuine inroads into the patriarchal, conservative literary establishment since the 1980s is a reflection of their writing skills, as evidenced by sales of their works, the literary prizes awarded them, and their increasing visibility abroad in translation. It is also a result of their ability to perform the socializing function expected of Korean writers: to bear witness in their literature to the whirlwind that has been 20th-century Korea.

Comparative analysis of the novel in Korea and Japan would seem to be instructive in the broader context of the development of the novel in East Asia. Apt comparisons between the modern novel in Korea and Japan, however, are actually few. The problematic development of the Korean novel, previously mentioned, is one reason for this. While it is generally agreed that there are relatively few Korean novelists of note, modern Japanese fiction writers have been quite successful with the form. Although young Korean intellectuals who journeyed to Japan in the 1910s, 1920s, and 1930s as part of the modernization movement sweeping East Asia at the turn of the century were influenced by Natsume Sōseki's choice of writing as a full-time profession, they did not by and large share his proclivity for the novel as a means of literary expression. Moreover, the strained relations between Korea and Japan resulting from the latter's colonization of the peninsula have worked against widespread Korean acceptance of contemporary Japanese culture. It is quite likely, indeed, that Korean novelists are better known in Japan, where the works of some better-known Korean writers are available in translation, than Japanese novelists are in Korea. Korean novelists, moreover, have been more interested in realism, eschewing the confessional narratives of their Japanese counterparts. Hwang Sun-wŏn, for example, who graduated from Tokyo's Waseda University in 1939, a well-known novelist (although more accomplished as a writer of short fiction), has professed admiration for the work of Shiga Naoya but exhibits little influence by that important early modern Japanese novelist in his own novels.

The audience for the Korean novel has changed over the centuries. Early *hanmun* novels were read by an exclusive audience consisting mostly of males from families of means, who enjoyed the wherewithal and leisure time to master the system of Chinese ideographs that learned Korean men employed for literature. Premodern novels written in *hangŭl* were read by a broader audience, consisting of commoner men and the children not only of aristocrats but also of the merchant and artisan classes. Women who read *hangŭl* far outnumbered those who could read *hanmun,* but the evolution of a mass female readership had to await the 20th century, when the enlightenment movement brought more widespread literacy for women. Finally, the great majority of Korean men were peasants who likely had neither the education nor the leisure to read novels.

The dissemination of premodern novels was, as elsewhere, a function of both entrepreneurship and technology. Until the early 18th century, copies of novels to be circulated were, like the originals, handwritten. The advent of woodblock printing in the early 18th century brought novels to a wider audience. The first novels to be printed in this fashion were written in *hanmun*, reflecting the lingering preference for this literary language among the elite, who controlled literary production. Novels in *hangŭl* began to appear in woodblock-printed versions perhaps a half century later, responding to the widening demand for literature among the growing number of Koreans literate in the vernacular. This demand was in turn bolstered by the appearance of professional book peddlers and book storytellers. The former went from house to house lending or selling, while the latter, emerging over time from the ranks of the former, held sway in marketplaces, where they read in public. Commercial book production was centered not only in the capital of Seoul but also in provincial cities such as Chŏnju.

In the late 19th century, modern Western printing technology quickly replaced woodblock printing. (It is worth noting, however, that movable metal type was used in Korea as early as the 14th century.) Bookstores, available since the late 18th century, were already in place to handle the rapid increase in book production made possible by the modern technology.

The audience for premodern novels was bolstered by the development of *p'ansori*, the oral narrative partly sung and partly spoken by an itinerant performer (*kwangdae*) accompanied by a lone drummer. The *kwangdae* often performed out of doors and appealed especially to the lower classes, because the texts, such as *Ch'unhyang chŏn*, were well known to Koreans. The works in the *p'ansori* repertoire employed a double narrative, conforming to traditional Confucian virtues on the surface but often implicitly criticizing the application of those virtues. Although *p'ansori* libretti combined prose and verse, the standardization of the story that took place over many decades of performance led to the novel versions of those works.

The enlightenment movement at the turn of the 20th century and the Korean opposition to the Japanese annexation had the effect of further broadening the readership for the novel. The enlightenment movement encouraged literacy, especially among women, who had traditionally been discouraged from learning. It also furthered the development of the Korean vernacular press. This development was significant in that most newspapers serialized novels, hiring writers specifically for that purpose and thereby giving birth to the profession of novelist in Korea. Annexation for its part stimulated patriotic Koreans, and especially the literati, to forswear Chinese as a medium of literary expression in favor of the native script. Moreover, the *shin sosŏl*, as we have seen, served the nationalistic purpose of inculcating Koreans in the historical nation-building experiences of other countries.

Newspapers, and more recently literary journals, have continued to bring the novel to a wide readership, and despite the genre's ongoing reputation among critics and scholars as hackwork, today the novel in Korea enjoys unprecedented popularity. It is no longer surprising to find a South Korean novel selling more than a million copies domestically—quite an achievement in a nation of some 45 million—and those few novelists, such as Pak Kyŏng-ni, Pak Wan-sŏ, Cho Chŏng-nae, Ch'oe In-ho, and Yang Kwi-ja, who have managed to combine great commercial success with critical acceptance have become household names. Anecdotal evidence, moreover, suggests that the readership for

the short story and novella has fallen off in recent years. At the same time, there are those who find that the literary quality of these forms has declined. All of which would seem to augur well for the future of the Korean novel.

Information on the development of the novel in North Korea, as with most aspects of North Korean life, is scarce. Socialist realism in literature, developing among socialist writers in Korea from the mid-1920s and having parallels in China and Japan, has been emphasized by the North Korean leadership. But socialist realism as an ideology has also been used to purge writers who have run afoul of the leadership. A unification of North and South Korea, in addition to shedding light on the literary production and the fate of the *wŏlbuk* novelists, such as Yi Ki-yŏng, Yi T'ae-jun, Pak T'ae-wŏn, and Han Sŏl-ya, would undoubtedly fuel a stream of novels as writers both North and South continue to use the form as a means for bearing witness to the many upheavals of modern Korean history. Already South Korean novelists have begun to write about the lives of Northern defectors in the South.

BRUCE FULTON

Further Reading

Cho, Tong-il, *Hanguk munhak t'ongsa* (A Comprehensive History of Korean Literature), 3rd edition, 5 vols., Seoul: Chishik sanŏp sa, 1995

Kim, Hunggyu, *Understanding Korean Literature,* translated by Robert J. Fouser, Armonk, New York: M.E. Sharpe, 1997

Kim, Kichung, *An Introduction to Classical Korean Literature,* Armonk, New York: M.E. Sharpe, 1996

Kim, Tong-uk, and Yi, Chae-sŏn, editors, *Hanguk sosŏl sa* (A History of Korean Fiction), Seoul: Hyŏndae munhak, 1990

Kim, Yun-shik, and Hyŏn Kim, *Hanguk munhak sa* (A History of Korean Literature), Seoul: Minŭm sa, 1973

Kwŏn, Yŏng-min, *Hanguk hyŏndae munhak sa* (A History of Modern Korean Literature), Seoul: Minŭm sa, 1993

Kwŏn, Yŏng-min, "Enlightenment Period Fiction and the Formation of a Writer Class," translated by Bruce Fulton, *Korean Studies* 18 (1994)

Lee, Ann, "Escape from the Inner Room: The Novel of Domestic Intrigue in Early Modern Korean Fiction," *Korean Culture* (Summer 1991)

Lee, Ann, "Yi Kwangsu and Korean Literature: The Novel *Mujŏng* (1917)," *Journal of Korean Studies* 8 (1992)

Lee, Peter H., editor, *Anthology of Korean Literature: From Early Times to the Nineteenth Century,* Honolulu: University Press of Hawaii, 1981

Myers, Brian, *Han Sŏrya and North Korean Literature: The Failure of Socialist Realism in the DPRK,* Ithaca, New York: East Asia Program, Cornell University, 1994

Rutt, Richard, and Chong-un Kim, translators, *Virtuous Women: Three Classic Korean Novels,* Seoul: Royal Asiatic Society, Korea Branch, 1974

Skillend, W.E., *Kodae Sosŏl: A Survey of Korean Traditional Style Popular Novels,* London: School of Oriental and African Studies, University of London, 1969

Yi, Chae-sŏn, *Hyŏndae Hanguk sosŏl sa* (A History of Modern Korean Fiction), Seoul: Minŭm sa, 1991

Yi, Chae-sŏn, *Hanguk munhak ŭi wŏngŭnbŏp* (Perspectives on Korean Literature), Seoul: Minŭm sa, 1996

Kristin Lavransdatter by Sigrid Undset

1920–22

Kristin Lavransdatter is a cycle of historical novels about a woman's life in Norway in the first half of the 14th century. Its grandeur of conception, indomitable heroine, and vast gallery of fully realized characters have won it the status of a national epic. It was also an immediate and enduring international success (translations appeared in more than 70 languages), earned Undset the 1928 Nobel prize, and remains the basis of her literary reputation.

The Nobel committee described *Kristin Lavransdatter* using the water imagery that frequently appears in the novel. Her "vigorous, sweeping" narrative "rolls on like a river, ceaselessly receiving new tributaries," reads the citation. "Its powerful waves . . . carry along the reader, plunged into a sort of torpor. But the roaring of its waters has the eternal freshness of nature." Highest praise is reserved for the moment "when the river meets the sea"—the dramatic end of the heroine's life, when "no one complains of the length of the course which accumulated so overwhelming a depth. . . . In the poetry of all times, there are few scenes of comparable excellence."

Kristin Lavransdatter was written at the midpoint of a literary career that encompassed novels, essays, poetry, plays, biography, hagiography, and polemics. Undset was determined to write about the Middle Ages while still in her teens, but after her first effort was rejected in 1905 she turned to modern themes, and by 1920 only two signs of this interest had appeared in print: her 1909 novel *Fortoellingen om Viga-Ljot og Vigdis* (*Gunnar's Daughter*), set in the late Viking Age, and her own retelling of stories from Arthurian legend, *Fortoellingen om Kong Artur og ridderne av det runde bord* (1915; Tales of King Arthur and the Knights of the Round Table). Her second medieval cycle, *Olav Audunsson i Hestviken* (1925) and *Olav Audunssøn og hans børn* (1927; entire text as *The Master of Hestviken*), was her last fictional work set in the Middle Ages, although she continued to write about medieval subjects in other formats until the end of her life.

Kristin Lavransdatter comes from a national tradition of historical fiction rooted in the 13th-century Icelandic sagas—a tradition revived during Norway's 19th-century national romantic movement in the interest of reestablishing links to the historical period predating the country's 500 years of Danish and Swedish rule. When Norway finally won independence in 1905, national sentiments were intensified, and during the 1920s many distinguished writers took up historical fiction, partly from newfound national pride and partly to affirm links with customs and ways of life rapidly disappearing.

In its attentive use of regional folk literature and careful attention to historical speech forms, *Kristin Lavransdatter* follows the historical novel prototype established by Walter Scott. It deviates from the model, however, by being set in a time of relative peace and social stability, when no event of political importance takes place. Undset wanted to explore the tensions in the nation's intellectual and cultural life, particularly the continuing strain between Old Norse pagan beliefs, which in the 14th century remained alive in folklore and custom, and the still incompletely absorbed culture of European Christendom, introduced to the North only three centuries before.

To illustrate these tensions she created the "domestic epic"—a story on a monumental scale about normal events in an ordinary woman's life. The female viewpoint and the absence of extrinsic drama shift the novel's focus from politics and military adventure to human relationships, domestic life, and spiritual concerns. The main historical components in *Kristin Lavransdatter* are thus philosophical. One component is the idea of romantic love, introduced to the North together with the new religion. Another is the struggle between the still lively pagan idea of honor, which expected generosity between friends and allies but did not tolerate insult, and the newer Christian ideal of abjuring vengeance and forgiving injuries.

Undset illustrates the tension between these conflicting values through incidents or issues in all of her heroine's relationships: for example, Kristin's struggle with her parents over her right to choose a marriage partner, her resort to witchcraft in retaliation for her brother-in-law's humiliating Christian charity, and, most of all, her bitter resentment toward her husband Erlend Nikulaussøn, a charming, romantic adventurer who stirs her blood but fails at the responsibilities of parenthood and husbandry. Such psychological dramas are played out over the span of Kristin's lifetime in the dramatic setting of Norway's landscape, whose natural details Undset portrays with the fidelity of a botanical artist (which she also was). The story's place-rootedness and massive array of detail about everyday life, together with the blunt, almost scientific realism—an influence of the sagas and the 19th-century realists—Undset employs in describing physical experiences such as labor and childbirth (subjects she introduced to world literature), illness, and death give her fictional world a textured, sensuous immediacy. The effect is not to distance and exoticize the past (as in the historical fiction of symbolists Gustave Flaubert and Joris-Karl Huysmans) but to make it homely and familiar, to collapse time between the two eras.

This illusion of collapsed time opened the novel to a wider national debate about historicism. Undset's research encompassed archaeology, civil and ecclesiastical law, folk legends, and medieval literary sources, such as the Icelandic sagas and Scandinavian ballads. The breadth of her knowledge and her scrupulous accuracy of detail impressed all critics. They were divided, however, over whether her psychological characterizations were medieval or modern, a question that still arouses debate.

The main point at issue is Undset's interpretation of the impact of Christianity on the Norwegian medieval mind. In a 1914 thesis, Edvard Bull claimed that Christianity was a superficial veneer over paganism's superior primitive Norse soul, and that this primal soul deserved to be revived and celebrated. Fredrik Paasche counterargued that conversion had brought Norway fully into the community of medieval European Christendom, which had a positive, meliorating effect on Viking brutality and disregard for human life. Kristin's explicitly Christian reconciliation of the warring urges within her marked Undset as a member of Paasche's camp. Later, her increasingly outspoken position on the importance of the Christian ethic would acquire growing moral force, as many primitivists—including fellow Nobel prize winner Knut Hamsun—took up Hitler's race-supremacist ideas.

Another feature of the historicism debate was Marxist objections to *Kristin Lavransdatter*'s focus on the private life of a woman from the gentry rather than on broader social forces affecting the lower classes. Partly because of this, the same critics argued that the book was not about historical processes at all but only a costume romance. Undset had addressed this question in 1915 in *Fortoellingen om Kong Artur og ridderne av det runde bord,* asserting that historical developments changed some things about human life but not others. Social customs, beliefs, ideas, and technology changed over time, she contended, but nothing ever changed "the human heart." Thus, in her view, the tensions in Kristin's emotional life not only reflected the social forces at work in the 14th century, but also provided a bridge to 20th-century readers, who were dealing with emotional repercussions of social change in their own era.

Kristin Lavransdatter belongs not only to the genre of historical fiction but also to a tradition of Norwegian women's writing, where it fits somewhat differently. The focus on family relations and everyday life that distinguishes it from historical writing by male authors (for example, Olav Duun, Johan Falkberget, and Kristofer Uppdal) is typical of works by Norwegian women of the period (such as Ragnhild Jølsen, Hulda Garborg, and Nini Roll Anker). As Vigdis Ystad notes, also typical in women's historical writing are the themes of a strong, independent woman who takes over major responsibilities for an absent or ineffectual male, and the dangers of eros, generally revealed in women's struggles—largely ending in disaster—to maintain both their erotic relationships with men and their own personal/economic integrity. *Kristin Lavransdatter* is typical of women's fiction in addressing all these concerns; it also conforms to pattern by ending in disrupted lives and the collapse of an old order. It is distinguished, however, by its explicitly Christian perspective on eros and on marriage as definitive, life-enhancing adventures, despite their risks and dangers.

Kristin Lavransdatter has had many admirers but few imitators. Not even Undset's own *Olav Audunssøn* cycle achieved its degree of artistic balance. The novel continues to attract scholarly interest in Europe, especially Russia, France, and the Netherlands. In the United States, interest in the historical novel has greatly declined in the late 20th century as fictional techniques are used increasingly in legitimate historical and biographical writing, blurring the borders between genres. Since Michel Foucault, historians' interest in the private lives of ordinary people has generated much scholarly work on the subjects of Undset's fiction, while docudramas on film and television have exploited public taste for history as entertainment. Despite this, since appearing in its first (unsatisfactory) English translation, *Kristin Lavransdatter* has never gone out of print.

SHERRILL HARBISON

See also Sigrid Undset

Further Reading

Bliksrud, Liv, *Natur og normer hos Sigrid Undset,* Oslo: Aschehoug, 1988

Gustafson, Alrik, "Christian Ethics in a Pagan World: Sigrid Undset," in *Six Scandinavian Novelists,* Princeton, New Jersey: Princeton University Press, 1940

Larsen, Hanna Astrup, "Sigrid Undset: Medieval Works," *The American-Scandinavian Review* 17:7 (July 1929)

Lytle, Andrew, *Kristin: A Reading,* Columbia: University of Missouri Press, 1992

Ruch, Velma Naomi, "Sigrid Undset's *Kristin Lavransdatter*: A Study of Its Literary Art and Its Reception in America, England, and Scandinavia," Ph.D. diss., University of Wisconsin, 1957

Slochower, Harry, "Feudal Socialism: Sigrid Undset's *Kristin Lavransdatter,*" in *Three Ways of Modern Man,* New York: International Publishers, 1937

Solberg, Olav, *Tekst møter tekst: Kristin Lavransdatter og mellomalderen,* Oslo: Aschehoug, 1997

Steen, Ellisiv, *Kristin Lavransdatter, en estetisk studie,* Oslo: Aschehoug, 1969

Undset, Sigrid, *Saga of Saints,* London: Sheed and Ward, and New York: Longmans, Green, 1934

Winsnes, Andreas Hofgaard, *Sigrid Undset: A Study in Christian Realism,* New York: Sheed and Ward, 1953

Miroslav Krleža 1893–1981

Croatian

With his poetry, short stories, plays, essays, political tracts, and four novels, Miroslav Krleža occupies a central position in contemporary Croatian literature. His first novel, *Povratak Filipa Latinovicza (The Return of Philip Latinovicz),* was published in 1932, during the modernist, almost expressionistic phase in his development. In depicting a return of a Croatian artist from Western Europe to his small native town and his difficulties in adjusting to provincial life, Krleža follows his lifelong tendency to dramatize ideas and to focus on social themes fraught with conflicts. Philip, "a godless, westernized, restless bird of passage, nervy and decadent," soon realizes that nothing has changed during his absence: corruption, dishonesty, and lethargy still reign supreme, and even there "somebody is always being hunted." Philip gradually fades into oblivion, underscoring the futility of existence in a bourgeois society. There is an echo of Heidegger and anticipation of existentialist philosophers here, although a direct influence cannot be ascertained.

Krleža exercises sharp social criticism without slipping into preaching. A consummate artist, he is able to imbue this traditional, almost old-fashioned novel with refreshing charm. Seemingly endless descriptions are enlivened by a plethora of detail, masterful character sketches, delicate nuances, and a keen eye for color and shape. Krleža revels in hint and allusion, and he knows how to stay in the background. His pessimism—at times even nihilism—and his irony, often turning to sarcasm, are tempered with humor and compassion.

Similar characteristics are present in his other novels. *Na rubu pameti* (1938; *On the Edge of Reason*) and *Banket u Blitvi* (1938–64; Banquet in Blitva) show Krleža's interest in social and political problems. In *On the Edge of Reason,* the protagonist is jailed for his rebellion against the injustices in his society, which are supported by his privileged family. In jail, he engages with a communist, whose ideas he rejects, and a simple peasant, whom he finds much more human and less hypocritical. Even though he was a Marxist himself, Krleža rejected the exclusivist ideas of the communists. After the communists took power, he often was regarded with suspicion by his fellow Marxists. The events in *Banket u Blitvi* are set in the Baltics, but the novel is a criticism of all tyrannical rulers and regimes, including those at home. The author's disdain for all totalitarian systems, including Stalinism, is again evident. This indicates clearly that a humanist philosophy had overcome Krleža's faith in Marxism. The fact that he was primarily an artist no doubt contributed to this attitude.

Krleža's most ambitious work, although artistically not his best, the six-volume novel *Zastave* (1967; Banners) is a panoramic overview of Central European, Balkan, and Croatian cultural, social, and political life between 1912 and 1922. Mixed with autobiographical reminiscences, the novel combines Krleža's usual concern for ideas and social problems with the personal affairs of the protagonists, the former clearly outweighing the latter. This immense novel shows structural weaknesses, but some segments stand out for their artistic merit.

In addition to their artistic value, Krleža's novels reveal his enormous erudition and lifelong adherence to a Marxist philosophy "with a human face." He searched for answers to social problems besetting modern society and advocated an untiring struggle for justice and a better life. Colorful characters and dramatic plots fit neatly into this framework. Strangely, his novels have found few imitators. Like those of Ivo Andrić, Krleža's novels—especially *The Return of Philip Latinovicz*—stand by themselves, as eminent achievements in Croatian literature.

VASA D. MIHAILOVICH

Biography

Born in Zagreb, Croatia (then in the Austro-Hungarian Empire), 7 July 1893. Attended Lucoviceum military academy, Budapest. Served in the Serbian Army, 1912: expelled from Serbia and arrested by the Austrians after being suspected of spying; served in the Austrian Army during World War I. Member of Communist Party from 1918 until 1939, when he was expelled; rehabilitated by Tito, 1952; founded the periodicals *Plamen* [Flame], 1919, *Književna republika* [Literary Republic], 1923–27, *Danas* [Today], 1934, *Pečat* [Seal], 1939–40, and *Republika,* 1945–46; director, Lexicographic Institute, Zagreb, from 1952; editor, *Pomorska enciklopedija,* 1954–64, *Enciklopedija Jugoslavije,* 1955–71, and *Enciklopedija Leksikograftskog savoda,* 1955–64. Deputy, Yugoslav National Assembly; president, Yugoslav Writers Union; vice president, Yugoslav Academy of Science and Art. Died 29 December 1981.

Novels by Krleža

Povratak Filipa Latinovicza, 1932; as *The Return of Philip Latinovicz,* translated by Zora Depolo, 1959
Na rubu pameti, 1938; as *On the Edge of Reason,* translated by Zora Depolo, 1976
Banket u Blitvi [Banquet in Blitva], 3 vols., 1938, 1939, 1964
Zastave [Banners], 6 vols., 1967

Other Writings: short stories, poetry, plays, essays, journals, diaries, travelogues, and political prose.

Further Reading

Bogert, Ralph, *The Writer as Naysayer: Miroslav Krleža and the Aesthetic of Interwar Central Europe,* Columbus, Ohio: Slavica, 1991
Čengić, Enes, *Krleža,* Zagreb: Mladost, 1982
Donat, Branimir, *O pjesničkom teatru Miroslava Krleže,* Zagreb: Mladost, 1970
Engelsfeld, Mladen, *Interpretacija Krležina romana "Povratak Filipa Latinovicza,"* Zagreb: Liber, 1975
Gašparovic, Darko, *Dramatica krleziana,* Zagreb: Centar za kulturnu djelatnost, 1977; 2nd edition, Zagreb: Cekade, 1989
Kadić, Ante, "Krleža's Tormented Visionaries," *Slavonic and East European Review* 45 (1967)
Kalezić, Vasilije, *U Krležinom sazvježdu,* Zagreb: August Cesarec, 1982
Kapetanić, Davor, "Bibliografija djela Miroslava Krleže," in *Zbornik o Miroslavu Krleži,* edited by Marijan Matković, Zagreb: JAZU, 1963
Matvejević, Predrag, *Razgovori s Miroslavom Krležom,* Zagreb: Naprijed, 1969
Suvin, Darko, "Voyage to the Stars and Pannonian Mire: Miroslav Krleža's Expressionist Vision and the Croatian Plebian Consciousness in the Epoch of World War One," *Mosaic* 6:4 (1973)
Žmegač, Viktor, *Krležini evropski obzori: Djelo u komparativnom kontekstu,* Zagreb: Znanje, 1986

Milan Kundera 1929–

Czech

A Czechoslovak author who lives in France, Milan Kundera has made a significant contribution to literary, cultural, and political developments in Czechoslovakia, as well as internationally. He has created his own concept of "the novel as a debate," using inspiration from the era of classicism and the traditions of the Central European novel. Kundera's work matured as he gradually became disillusioned with communism. This process of disillusionment, typical of many Czech intellectuals of his generation, has produced important insights into Central European society, distilled into a series of innovative novelistic structures. In 1975, Kundera left Czechoslovakia and settled in France. The firsthand experience of life in the West has given him new inspiration and informed his understanding of Central European society.

After writing poetry and drama as well as some theoretical literary texts that he now regards as immature, Kundera "found himself as a writer" while working on his first short story, which was later included in one of the editions of *Směšné lásky* (1963, 1965, 1968, 1970; *Laughable Loves*). Kundera now regards this collection of seven short stories as the first of his novels. Not held together by a single, unifying narrative, his novels consist of variations on a number of abstract concepts, often occurring within several self-contained stories. This approach explains the labeling of *Laughable Loves* as the first novel. The stories are bound together by the unifying theme of sexual manipulation between lovers. Kundera closely examines erotic relationships between individuals because he feels this enables him to analyze human nature in sharp focus.

In his first work as in his subsequent writing, Kundera primarily deals with the problem of cognition, coming to the conclusion that the world is unknowable and that we base our perception of it on misconceptions. These mistakes lead to catastrophic consequences. Kundera's philosophical position has a stylistic analog in a crisis of language: arbitrary linguistic signs emancipate themselves from reality and impose their false values upon it. As a result, people fall victim to stereotyped conventions that negate reality. All concepts are shown to be ambiguous in Kundera's novels.

Kundera's most profound novel is perhaps *Žert* (1967; *The Joke*), which sees life as an enormous jest perpetrated on disoriented human beings. The story is set in communist Czechoslovakia in the bleak 1950s, a period of totalitarian Stalinism during which the authorities insisted that man was the master of his own destiny. *The Joke* is the story of a student who, on an impulse, sends his girlfriend a provocative political postcard. As a result, he is expelled from the university and dispatched to a punitive army unit. Years later, he prepares a sexual revenge for the fellow student who informed on him and caused his downfall, but the scheme backfires because circumstances have imperceptibly changed in the course of time. *The Joke* consists of a series of variations on the theme of human misinterpretation of reality. Like all Kundera's novels, its structure is based on the principles of musical composition and embraces pluralism and polyphony. In its seven sections, four main characters tell their overlapping stories in turn, which allows the reader to note the different perceptions and misconceptions of the same events.

Život je jinde (first published in French in 1973, in Czech in 1979; *Life Is Elsewhere*) deals with the fatal attractions of communist collectivism. The work is an analysis of the fictional character of a talented poet who is dependent on a love-hate relationship with his domineering mother (emotional women are highly destructive characters in Kundera's fiction). The poet wants to become a part of the crowd, places his art in the service of the revolution, and ends his life in a grotesque, meaningless death. The seven parts of the novel are constructed according to the laws of the sonata. Changes in the narrative's tempo and in its angle of vision are of particular importance.

After the suppression of the Prague Spring in 1968, more than 400 authors were banned by the communist authorities. Kundera was among them. *Valčík na rozloučenou* (first published in Czech in 1979, definitive French version in 1986; *The Farewell Party*) was intended as Kundera's last novel, his good-bye to literature. The work is a farce, highlighting misunderstandings between the members of five different couples who meet during a few days at a West Bohemian spa. The author also reexamines the theme of violence perpetrated on innocent individuals by society, with the active approval of its citizens.

The novels Kundera wrote after his move to France are the most well-known part of his literary output. *Kniha smíchu a zapomnění* (first published in French in 1979, in Czech in 1981; *The Book of Laughter and Forgetting*) is a set of variations on the concepts of forgetting, laughter, angels, compassion, and the frontier. Kundera reexamines misunderstandings of reality and again attacks the myths of his youth, which he discovers all around him in the West. Irritated by the superficiality of the Western media, Kundera has deliberately written his Western novels in such a way that their contents cannot be summarized in a brief outline.

Kundera rose to international prominence especially as a result of the appearance of his novel *Nesnesitelná lehkost bytí* (first published in Czech in 1985, definitive French edition in 1987; *The Unbearable Lightness of Being*). Kundera again uses the principles of playfulness and variation to examine a number of general concepts from all sides. The novel highlights the fact that human beings live only once and can never correct their mistakes. Since life is unrepeatable, we experience a total lack of responsibility, a lightness of being. Kundera also analyzes the concept of kitsch, a beautiful lie that hides the negative aspects of life and ignores the existence of death. *The Unbearable Lightness of Being* is a relatively linear narrative telling the life stories of Prague surgeon Tomáš and his wife Tereza, who leave Czechoslovakia after the Soviet invasion of 1968 and then go back, to live and die as individuals out of political favor in the neo-Stalinist regime of the 1970s.

Nesmrtelnost (published in French in 1990, in Czech in 1993; *Immortality*) reflects Kundera's Central European experience indirectly. In the author's view, this is his most accomplished version of the "novel as a debate," with characters who are personified ideas. The novel is a critique of contemporary Western civilization, based on the author's experience of life in France. In a number of historical parallels as well as in a fictional narrative, Kundera primarily examines humanity's desire to enter history and become immortal. The author attacks, among other things, the dangers of "imagology," which stem from the unlimited power of today's media. In *Immortality* more often than in Kundera's other work, the narrator freely interrupts the story, interspersing it with essayistic passages.

Kundera wrote his eighth novel in French. *La Lenteur* (1994; *Slowness*) is a playful postscript to this author's work, a short novel with a complex, ironic, and polyphonic structure. *Slowness* is a wry account of the absurd activities of today's intellectuals, offering an image of our world as a godless labyrinth in which people fumble about, weighed down by the pseudo-values that they have themselves brought into being.

In Kundera's hands, the novel is an independent, open, and autonomous genre, capable of incorporating elements of lyricism and of essayistic writing. New forms of cognition, Kundera argues, presuppose new forms of the novel: for him the novel is always poised at the moment of extinction and rebirth. He does not embrace the eclecticism of postmodernist writing, although some postmodernist influences may be detected in his work; rather, his work is best seen in the context of the European philosophical novel developed by Thomas Mann, Robert Musil, Hermann Broch, and Franz Kafka.

JAN ČULÍK

Biography
Born 1 April 1929 in Brno, Czechoslovakia. Emigrated to France, 1975, and became a French citizen, 1981. Attended Charles University, Prague; Academy of Music and Dramatic Arts Film Faculty, Prague, 1956. Assistant professor of film, Academy of Music and Dramatic Arts, Prague, 1958–70; professor of comparative literature, University of Rennes, France, 1975–80; has also taught at École des Hautes Études, Paris. Member of the editorial board, *Literární noviny* [Literary Journal], 1956–59, 1963–68, and *Literární listy,* 1968–69.

Novels by Kundera
Žert, 1967; as *The Joke,* translated by Michael Henry Heim, 1982, revised edition 1992

La Vie est ailleurs, 1973; as *Life Is Elsewhere,* translated by Peter Kussi, 1974; as *Život je jinde,* 1979
La Valse aux adieux, 1976; as *The Farewell Party,* translated by Peter Kussi, 1976; as *Valčík na rozloučenou,* 1979
Le Livre du rire et de l'oubli, 1979; as *The Book of Laughter and Forgetting,* translated by Michael Henry Heim, 1980; as *Kniha smíchu a zapomnění,* 1981
L'Insoutenable Légéreté de L'être, 1984; as *The Unbearable Lightness of Being,* translated by Michael Henry Heim, 1984; as *Nesnesitelná lehkost bytí,* 1985
L'Immortalité, 1990; as *Immortality,* tranlated by Peter Kussi, 1991; as *Nesmrtelnost,* 1993
La Lenteur, 1994; as *Slowness,* translated by Linda Asher, 1996

Other Writings: poetry, plays, and essays, including *The Art of the Novel* (1988) and *Testaments Betrayed* (1996).

Further Reading
Banerjee, Maria Němcová, *Terminal Paradox: The Novels of Milan Kundera,* New York: Grove Weidenfeld, 1990; London: Faber, 1991
Brand, Glen, *Milan Kundera: An Annotated Bibliography,* New York: Garland, 1988
Chvatík, Květoslav, *Die Fallen der Welt: Der Romancier Milan Kundera,* Munich and Vienna: Carl Hanser, 1994
Doležel, Lubomir, "'Narrative Symposium' in Milan Kundera's *The Joke,*" in his *Narrative Modes in Czech Literature,* Toronto: University of Toronto Press, 1973
French, Alfred, *Czech Writers and Politics: 1945–1969,* Boulder, Colorado: East European Monographs, 1982
Liehm, Antonín J., "Milan Kundera: Czech Writer," in *Czech Literature since 1956: A Symposium,* edited by William E. Harkins and Paul I. Trensky, New York: Bohemica, 1980
Matějka, Ladislav, "Milan Kundera's Central Europe," *Cross Currents* 9 (1990)

Künstlerroman. *See* Bildungsroman

Kuroi ame. *See* Black Rain

L

Alex La Guma 1925–85

South African

Alex La Guma began writing fiction in the 1950s while also working as a staff journalist for the progressive Cape Town newspaper *New Age,* for which he managed to write a weekly column until 1962 despite his persecution by the South African authorities. His first short novel, *A Walk in the Night,* was apparently completed by early 1960 but was published only in 1962, in Nigeria, after considerable difficulty in getting the manuscript out of South Africa. Thus began a career that saw all of La Guma's novels published abroad because they had been banned in South Africa. *And a Threefold Cord* (1964) and *The Stone Country* (1967) were originally published in Berlin, *In the Fog of the Seasons' End* (1972) originally appeared in New York, and *Time of the Butcherbird* (1979) was first published in London.

All of La Guma's fiction shows a deep anti-apartheid commitment, although the different novels employ a variety of strategies in their attempt both to reveal the abusive and dehumanizing effects of apartheid on the lives of the South African people and to suggest possible alternatives for a better future. *A Walk in the Night* is an extremely violent and essentially naturalistic novel that devotes most of its energy to vivid depictions of the degrading poverty of Cape Town's nonwhite slums and the humiliation of the residents of these slums who are forced to suffer mistreatment at the hands of the police and other official authorities. *A Walk in the Night* is an angry and pessimistic novel in which characters respond to brutalization by the system with brutality of their own. As La Guma's career developed, however, his delineation of South African society became more sophisticated and his fiction began to include suggestions of more positive modes of resistance. *And a Threefold Cord* contains many of the same suggestions that characters are at the mercy of large, impersonal forces, but it is less violent and more subdued in tone than its predecessor. The depiction of the lives of the "colored" Pauls family in La Guma's second novel resembles the striking depictions of poverty that characterized his first, although La Guma's technique in *And a Threefold Cord* is somewhat more symbolic and less naturalistic than in *A Walk in the Night.* Moreover, the courage and tenacity of the Pauls family in the face of its difficulties begin to point toward a greater sense of hopefulness, especially through the solidarity of oppressed people working together.

La Guma's third novel, *The Stone Country,* is a highly allegorical account of life in a South African prison that in many ways represents South Africa as a whole. The book focuses on the experiences of George Adams, a political prisoner who has been incarcerated for distributing political pamphlets urging resistance to apartheid. And, if conditions in the prison stand in for the oppressive nature of apartheid society as a whole, Adams' determination to work for better conditions in the prison suggests the need for positive political action throughout South Africa. This aspect of La Guma's career comes to full fruition with *In the Fog of the Seasons' End,* probably his best-known work. Cecil Abrahams (1985) notes that this novel combined with *The Stone Country* to make La Guma a "major literary figure in African literature." *In the Fog of the Seasons' End* focuses on the attempts of an underground revolutionary group to undermine the apartheid system through any means at its disposal. The members of this organization suffer great personal hardship. One of them, Elias Tekwane, is tortured and beaten to death by the South African police. And all of them are forced to forgo the comforts and pleasures of everyday life in the interests of the movement. But the movement itself remains strong despite the authorities' attempts to destroy it, and the participation in this effort gives the rebels genuine hope for a better future. Indeed, the book ends on a highly positive note, which suggests the goals of the movement can be accomplished, however difficult the road.

La Guma's brief final novel, *Time of the Butcherbird,* is by far his most symbolic, employing intensely suggestive images in a further elaboration of his support for armed rebellion against apartheid. Its three major characters—a poor black recently released from prison, a rich Afrikaner farmer/politician, and a struggling white English-speaking salesman—are less individuals than representatives of important groups within South African society. The black, Shilling Murile, has sworn revenge against the Afrikaner, Hannes Meulen, for his involvement ten years earlier in the death of Murile's brother. The English-speaking white, Edward Stopes, has come to town on a selling trip and is something of an "innocent bystander" to the events of the novel, which have clear symbolic implications for the possible future of South African society. Murile kills Meulen but in the process kills Stopes as well, suggesting the ultimate fate of both those who support and enforce apartheid and those who simply stand aside and let it continue.

Banned from publication in apartheid South Africa, La Guma's work was pushed to the margins of the struggle against apartheid that was its major thrust. Meanwhile, La Guma's fiction, perhaps because of its overtly leftist political stance, has been less widely accepted in the West than the work of African writers such as Nadine Gordimer, Chinua Achebe, Wole Soyinka, or Ngugi wa Thiong'o. Nevertheless, he is among the best known and most influential of all African novelists. Indeed, Bernth Lindfors' survey of anglophone African universities showed that, among writers known primarily as novelists, La Guma is surpassed only by Ngugi, Achebe, and Ayi Kwei Armah in terms of his prominence in the curricula of those universities (see Lindfors, 1990). La Guma is also among the most politically committed African novelists, and his writing is inseparable from his political activism and from the persecution he suffered as a nonwhite South African who fought against apartheid throughout his life. He is thus appropriately listed by Udenta Udenta (1993) along with Ousmane Sembène and Ngugi as the writers who "naturally come to mind" in the discussion of the development of revolutionary African aesthetics.

M. KEITH BOOKER

Biography
Born in Cape Town on 20 February 1925, the son of a noted crusader for civil rights of nonwhites in South Africa. In 1946 he organized and led a strike among workers at a metal box factory where he was employed; joined the Young Communist League the following year; in 1948, when the electoral victory of the Boer Nationalist Party led to the beginnings of apartheid as a formal government policy in South Africa, La Guma became a member of the South African Communist Party and remained so until 1950, when the party was officially banned. His political activities eventually led to his 1956 arrest on charges of treason; he was acquitted but was arrested again in 1961. La Guma was the first person placed under house arrest under the Sabotage Act of 1962. In 1966 he and his family were granted permanent exit visas and moved to London. In 1977 La Guma was elected secretary-general of the Afro-Asian Writers' Association, and the following year moved to Cuba, where he took up residence in Havana as the chief representative of the African National Congress (ANC) to the Caribbean and Central and South America. Died 11 October 1985.

Novels by La Guma
A Walk in the Night, 1962
And a Threefold Cord, 1964
The Stone Country, 1967
In the Fog of the Seasons' End, 1972
Time of the Butcherbird, 1979

Other Writings: short stories and political essays.

Further Reading
Abrahams, Cecil, *Alex La Guma,* Boston: Twayne, 1985
Abrahams, Cecil, editor, *Memories of Home: The Writings of Alex La Guma,* Trenton, New Jersey: Africa World Press, 1991
Asein, Samuel Omo, "The Revolutionary Vision in Alex La Guma's Novels," *Phylon* 39 (1978)
Balutansky, Kathleen, *The Novels of Alex La Guma: The Representation of a Political Conflict,* Washington, D.C.: Three Continents Press, 1990
Chandramohan, Balasubramanyam, *A Study in Trans-Ethnicity in Modern South Africa: The Writings of Alex La Guma, 1925–1985,* Lewiston: Mellon Research University Press, 1992
Green, Robert, "Alex La Guma's *In the Fog of the Seasons' End:* The Politics of Subversion," *Umoja* 3:2 (1979)
JanMohamed, Abdul R., *Manichean Aesthetics: The Politics of Literature in Colonial Africa,* Amherst: University of Massachusetts Press, 1983
Lindfors, Bernth, "The Teaching of African Literatures in Anglophone African Universities: An Instructive Canon," *Matatu* 7 (1990)
Ngara, Emmanuel, *Art and Ideology in the African Novel: A Study of the Influence of Marxism on African Writing,* London: Heinemann, 1985
Scanlon, Paul A., "Alex La Guma's Novels of Protest: The Growth of the Revolutionary," *Okike* 16 (1979)
Udenta, Udenta O., *Revolutionary Aesthetics and the African Literary Process,* Enugu, Nigeria: Fourth Dimension, 1993

Pär Lagerkvist 1891–1974

Swedish

Pär Lagerkvist was already a practiced and mature artist by the time he turned his attention to the novel. Lagerkvist began his career writing poetry, plays, and short prose. As a young man of 23, he formulated his artistic program in the essay *Ordkonst och bildkonst* (1913; *Literary Art and Pictorial Art*), where he claimed that realism limited the imagination of the writer. Literature should not dwell on psychological or personal issues but should instead deal in universal issues, such as death, angst, love, and war. Modern writers, Lagerkvist argued, need to create new forms of expression for a new age and should look to modern art forms, such as Cubism and Expressionism, for inspiration, or even to primitive writing like the Bible and the Icelandic sagas. As Lagerkvist honed his skills in poetry and short prose, he developed an economy of language and a system of symbolic expression that remained remarkably consistent throughout his writing.

Arguably, Lagerkvist's first novel is *Bödeln* (1933; *The Executioner*), which was also published as a play the following year. *The Executioner* may indeed be considered a hybrid of Lagerkvist's short prose and drama, as it relies more heavily on dialogue than his subsequent novels. Still, Lagerkvist's use of the past in *The Executioner* explicitly makes a point that is only implied in his later novels. Half of the novel is set in the Middle Ages, the other half in a jazz cafe in Nazi Germany. In pointing to the barbarism of the Middle Ages and juxtaposing it with the brutality of fascism, the story makes human violence a universal issue that has existed throughout time. Mankind has simply refined its methods. All of Lagerkvist's subsequent novels are set in a historical, biblical, or legendary past, and the comparison with the present is left to the reader.

Dvärgen (1944; *The Dwarf*), published 11 years later at the conclusion of World War II, is another meditation on human evil. Lagerkvist uses Renaissance Italy, which produced both Leonardo da Vinci and Machiavelli, to comment upon the dualities of human culture, which is capable of great achievements in art and science and also of great violence and treachery. The choice between the two is presented as an existential choice for mankind. In using the past, Lagerkvist does not try to re-create a past era or to practice literary archaeology. He makes no pretensions to accuracy but employs the past as an imaginative and symbolic space. The use of a first-person narrative in *The Dwarf* is unique in his novels. Usually, first-person narratives create a sense of identification between the reader and the narrator, but Lagerkvist's first-person narrator, the Dwarf, is a highly unreliable and dark figure whose very nature pushes readers to distance themselves from the judgments of the narrative.

Barabbas (1950; *Barabbas*) is perhaps his best-known novel since Lagerkvist received the Nobel prize shortly after its publication. Barabbas' struggles to believe in Christ introduce a question that lies behind each of Lagerkvist's subsequent novels: what is the nature of God and how can modern man believe? Lagerkvist referred to himself as a "religious atheist," and this paradox is also embodied by Barabbas, the biblical figure for whom Christ literally died but who cannot seem to experience faith despite his most urgent wishes.

Barabbas' brief encounter with divinity was of questionable benefit to him, and this theme is reprised in *Sibyllan* (1956; *The Sibyl*), where it is said: "God will never abandon the person in whom he has taken up his abode, even if he only remains as a curse." The legendary figure Ahasuerus, the Wandering Jew, seeks out a sibyl who was cast out of Delphi after she was discovered to be pregnant. Now she barely subsists on the margins of civilization with her idiot son. Both have in essence been cursed by their encounter with the divine, and the mysterious ending of the novel raises profound questions about the nature of the deity.

The following three novels constitute a trilogy: *Ahasverus död* (1960; *The Death of Ahasuerus*), *Pilgrim på havet* (1962; *Pilgrim at Sea*), and *Det heliga landet* (1964; *The Holy Land*). Tobias, a criminal like Barabbas, unites the three novels. He has witnessed an apparent miracle and resolves to make a pilgrimage to the Holy Land. The historical setting of the novels is not specific and locations are imbued with symbolic significance. The pilgrimage is a spiritual voyage as well as a physical one. Ahasuerus reappears in the first novel and is finally able to die when he realizes that there must be a source of holiness but that God's caprices keep us from reaching it. After many vicissitudes, Tobias is stranded on a mysterious coast, never having reached the Holy Land. He and his companion Giovanni, a criminal like himself, take up residence in an abandoned temple. With the assistance of equally mysterious female figures, each is able to make his peace with the divine.

From *The Executioner* to his final novel, *Mariamne* (1967; *Herod and Mariamne*), Lagerkvist made use of symbolic characters. Figures like the Hangman, the Prince, Barabbas, and Tobias all have murdered or committed crimes, yet they still possess considerable goodness. This dual nature, the synthesis of good and evil, represents Lagerkvist's conception of mankind. Often these figures are aided in their struggles with their dark side by a woman, who by inspiring love is able to bring out the best in these troubled persons. This same symbolic constellation appears in *Herod and Mariamne* in the figures of Herod and Mariamne. Herod is a cruel tyrant whose cruelty is tempered for a time by his love for the good Mariamne. Ultimately, overcome by possessiveness and jealousy, Herod has Mariamne murdered. In this novel, evil triumphs, which may be interpreted as a warning about the possible outcome of the Cold War.

Lagerkvist remained true to his artistic vision despite shifting literary tastes. During the early part of his career, modernism was not in fashion, but his election to the Swedish Academy in 1940 coincided with a major change in Swedish attitudes toward modernism. Although Lagerkvist considered himself a modernist, his imaginative use of the past, together with the novels of Eyvind Johnson, opened the gates for a flood of postmodern historiographic metafiction in Sweden from the 1960s onward. A younger generation of novelists, including Torgny Lindgren, Sven Delblanc, and Per Gunnar Evander, has followed in Lagerkvist's footsteps by writing between the lines of the Bible and, in so doing, creating a postmodern dialogue with the dominant literary text of Western civilization.

SUSAN BRANTLY

Biography
Born 23 May 1891 in Växjö, Sweden. Attended the University of Uppsala, 1911–12. Theatre critic, *Svenska Dagbladet*, Stockholm, 1919. Awarded Nobel prize for literature, 1951. Died 11 July 1974.

Selected Novels by Lagerkvist
Bödeln, 1933; as *The Hangman*, in *Guest of Reality*, translated by Denys W. Harding and Erik Mesterton, 1936; as *The Executioner*, translated by David O'Gorman, in *The Eternal Smile and Other Stories*, 1971
Guest of Reality (includes *Guest of Reality*; *The Eternal Smile*; *The Hangman*), translated by Denys W. Harding and Erik Mesterton, 1936
Dvärgen, 1944; as *The Dwarf*, translated by Alexandra Dick, 1945
Barabbas, 1950; as *Barabbas*, translated by Alan Blair, 1951
Sibyllan, 1956; as *The Sybil*, translated by Alexandra Dick, 1953; also translated by Naomi Walford, 1958
Pilgrimen [The Pilgrim] (trilogy), 1966
  Ahasverus död, 1960; as *The Death of Ahasuerus*, translated by Naomi Walford, 1962
  Pilgrim på havet, 1962; as *Pilgrim at Sea*, translated by Naomi Walford, 1964

Det heliga landet, 1964; as *The Holy Land,* translated by
   Naomi Walford, 1966

Mariamne, 1967; as *Herod and Mariamne,* translated by
   Naomi Walford, 1968; as *Mariamne,* translated by Walford,
   1968

Other Writings: verse, plays, and essays, the latter including
Ordkonst och bildkonst (1913; *Literary Art and Pictorial Art:
On the Decadence of Modern Literature—On the Vitality of
Modern Art*).

Further Reading

Jonsson, Willy, *Som är från evighet: Om trygghetsgrunden och
   oroshärden I Pär Lagerkvists liv och diktning,* Växjö:
   Kulturföreningen Memoria, 1991

Karahka, Urpu-Liisa, *Jaget och ismerna: Studier i Pär
   Lagerkvists estetiska teori och lyriska praktik,* Stockholm: Bo
   Cavefors Bokförlag, 1978

Pär Lagerkvist-samfundets skriftserie, Växjö: Pär Lagerkvist-
   samfundets forlag, 1992–present

Sjöberg, Leif, *Pär Lagerkvist,* New York: Columbia University
   Press, 1976

Spector, Robert Donald, *Pär Lagerkvist,* New York: Twayne,
   1973

White, Ray Lewis, *Pär Lagerkvist in America,* Stockholm:
   Almqvist and Wiksell, and Atlantic Highlands, New Jersey:
   Humanities Press, 1979

George Lamming 1927–

Barbadian

When Barbadian-born George Lamming published his first
novel, *In the Castle of My Skin,* in 1953, the anglophone
Caribbean novel was still in the process of finding a distinctive
voice and, along with several of his contemporaries, Lamming
faced the double problem of bringing a hitherto unchronicled
experience into literature and finding an appropriate form in
which to do so. *In the Castle of My Skin* is one of a group of
Caribbean novels of boyhood published during the 1950s and
1960s (others include Michael Anthony's *The Year in San Fernando* [1965], Geoffrey Drayton's *Christopher* [1959], and
Austin Clarke's *Amongst Thistles and Thorns* [1965]) that use a
boy's ingenuous angle of vision as a vehicle for exploring the social and natural world in which he is growing up. It is, however,
by far the most complex of this group of novels, for it is as much
about a community's growth into awareness as it is about the
initiation of the boy narrator, and Lamming's varied technique
insists on the relationship between individual and community.
Although certain passages, particularly toward the end of the
novel, evoke James Joyce's *A Portrait of the Artist as a Young
Man* (1916), Lamming's method accords equal prominence to
his Caribbean artist in the making and the village world in which
he is growing up. To this end he produces a polyphonic novel
that moves between realism and allegory and first- and third-
person narration and that incorporates a range of dramatically
conceived dialogues that express the viewpoints of various members of the community: men and women, old and young. This
plurality of approach, along with a poetic use of imagery, becomes the hallmark of most of his subsequent fiction, which usually spirals around a group of characters and employs a variety
of narrative voices. Within his dialogues Lamming employs a
range of Creole registers, and his fiction is notable for its early
and sensitive attempt to bridge the divide between oral
Caribbean discourse and the scribal traditions associated with
the colonial culture. He was not the first Caribbean novelist to
use Creole extensively—V.S. Reid's *New Day* (1949) is written

entirely in a modified form of Jamaican Creole—but he remains
an important innovator because the variety of registers he employs subtly conveys the open, dialogic nature of the social
world about which he writes.

In the Castle of My Skin was followed by three novels over the
next seven years. *The Emigrants* (1954) is about a group of West
Indian emigrants in Britain but has strong similarities to *In the
Castle of My Skin,* since although the main focus of this novel is
the psychology of exile, such a mentality had already typified the
attitudes of characters in the earlier novel who seem alienated
from their history—and ultimately from themselves—as a result
of their colonial situation. Both novels subtly demonstrate how
political and historical forces have determined individual lives.
Lamming's next two novels are also complex studies of the alienating effects of colonialism and stereotyping. *Of Age and Innocence* (1958), built around a series of powerfully conceived
scenes, employs an elliptical narrative method and an assured
use of symbol and fable. Its crisscrossing narrative threads center
on two characters' desires to escape essentialist definition: Mark,
a black revenant to Lamming's fictional Caribbean island of San
Cristobal, feels he must break away from having existed in the
white man's image of himself for too long; Penelope, a white visitor to the island, is shocked by her growing awareness of her
lesbian attraction to a friend because she feels that if this secret
becomes known her identity will be reduced to this single character attribute in other people's eyes. *Season of Adventure*
(1960) focuses on a middle-class, mixed-race protagonist who
undergoes a self-transformation after participating in an Afro-
Caribbean religious rite, the ceremony of souls, which initiates
her into the life of San Cristobal's peasant community; it also
demonstrates a similar absorption with parallels between race
and gender. Once again the probing poetic style enacts the novel's message of resistance to reductive categorizations.

Lamming's nonfictional study *The Pleasures of Exile* (1960)
provides a coda to the novels he had written thus far, offering a

complex reading of imperialist aspects of Shakespeare's *The Tempest*. In this work Lamming stresses the role played by language in cultural formation and, by focusing in some depth on the figures of Miranda and Ariel, extends such allegorical discussion of Shakespeare's play beyond the Prospero-Caliban (colonizer-colonized) opposition that had already become somewhat commonplace with postcolonial critics.

After the publication of his first four novels, Lamming published no further fiction for a number of years. Then during the early 1970s he published the novels *Water with Berries* (1971) and *Natives of My Person* (1972), which further extended his allegorical range. In one sense *Water with Berries,* a novel about the lives of Caribbean exiles in London, seems to offer a continuation of the themes of *The Emigrants,* but on another level it is an allegory of the difficulties experienced by West Indian artists in Britain that once again draws upon *The Tempest* archetypes. So, too, does *Natives of My Person,* Lamming's finest achievement to date. On the surface, *Natives of My Person* is a narrative of a slave ship crossing the Atlantic during the early colonial period. But Lamming uses this as a vehicle for a complex allegory about the Caribbean historical experience more generally, and the novel's themes have as much resonance for the post-independence period as for the historical period in which it appears to be set. The various crew members all have a guilty past, having mistreated their womenfolk in the Old World kingdom of Lime Stone. They journey toward San Cristobal where the women, mysteriously transported to the New World, await their arrival, offering the promise of a new future, which the men, whose voyage has descended into mutiny and murder, have yet to grasp. The multivalent level of the allegory makes *Natives of My Person* Lamming's richest novel to date; it is also his most satisfying novel structurally, with the pattern of the voyage lending it a unity uncharacteristic of his earlier work.

JOHN THIEME

Biography

Born 8 June 1927 in Carrington Village, Barbados. Attended Roebuck Boys' School; Combermere School. Teacher in Trinidad, 1946–50; moved to England, 1950; hosted book review program, BBC West Indian Service, London, 1951. Writer-in-Residence, University of the West Indies, Kingston, 1967–68. Coeditor of Barbados and Guyana independence issues of *New World Quarterly,* Kingston, 1965 and 1967.

Novels by Lamming

In the Castle of My Skin, 1953
The Emigrants, 1954
Of Age and Innocence, 1958
Season of Adventure, 1960
Water with Berries, 1971
Natives of My Person, 1972

Other Writings: short stories, critical nonfiction (including *The Pleasures of Exile,* 1960).

Further Reading

Gilkes, Michael, *The West Indian Novel,* Boston: Twayne, 1981
Lamming, George, *Conversations: Essays, Addresses and Interviews, 1953–1990,* London: Karia Press, 1992
Morris, Mervyn, "The Poet as Novelist: The Novels of George Lamming," in *The Islands in Between,* edited by Louis James, London: Oxford University Press, 1968
Munro, Ian, "George Lamming," in *West Indian Literature,* edited by Bruce King, London: Macmillan, and Hamden, Connecticut: Archon Books, 1979; 2nd edition, 1995
Paquet, Sandra Pouchet, *The Novels of George Lamming,* London: Heinemann, 1982
Ramchand, Kenneth, *An Introduction to the Study of West Indian Literature,* Sunbury-on-Thames, Middlesex: Nelson, 1976

Lao Can youji. *See* Travels of Lao Can

Lao She 1899–1966

Chinese

In the West, Lao She, pen name of Shu Qingchun, is best known as the realist author of the novel *Luotuo Xiangzi* (1937; *Camel Xiangzi*), which was a featured selection of the Book-of-the-Month Club in 1945. In China, however, Lao She is known as a humorist, a master of the Beijing dialect, an essayist, a poet in both the traditional classical style and modern colloquial idiom, and a playwright. During his literary career of 42 years, Lao She wrote 16 novels, 32 plays, numerous short stories, and hundreds of essays. His novels are noted for their humor, lively prose, and an inimitable sense of place. Beiping, the city of Lao She's birth, is also the setting for many of his novels.

Lao She wrote his first three novels while teaching in England at the London School of Oriental Studies from 1924 to 1929. His first novel, *Lao Zhang de zhexue* (1926; The Philosophy of Lao Zhang), is a comic novel about the adventures of the villainous protagonist Old Zhang, an avaricious village schoolmaster, money lender, and minor official. Lao She's second novel, *Zhao Ziyue* (1928; Zhao Ziyue), is also a comic novel about the good-hearted but wrong-headed student protagonist, Zhao Ziyue, and his fellows who indulge in drinking, partying, playing mahjong, and gossiping when they are not engaged in demonstrations. His third novel, *Er Ma* (1929; The Two Mas), is a much more serious and sophisticated work that compares the national characteristics of the Chinese and English through the depiction of a father-son pair and their interaction with English society. Even though these novels are written in Chinese and bear the vestiges of the Chinese storytellers tradition, they also show the literary influence of such English novelists as Charles Dickens, Jonathan Swift, William Makepeace Thackeray, and Joseph Conrad, whose works Lao She read when he was in England. Although lighthearted in appearance, Lao She's work reflects the quest for a sense of identity and of nationhood during his five years in England.

During the seven years after his return to China, Lao She published five more novels and several collections of short stories. Among his major novels are *Mao chengji* (1932; Cat Country), *Lihun* (1933; The Quest for Love of Lao Lee), and *Camel Xiangzi,* which established Lao She's reputation permanently in the pantheon of China's modern writers. *Cat Country* is an allegorical novel, devoid of Lao She's usual sense of humor. It mercilessly satirizes the Chinese national character by transporting the reader to the planet Mars where a colony of selfish, lazy, and scratchy cat people live out their lives astonishingly like the Chinese on earth. *The Quest for Love of Lao Lee* is a novel about four middle-class couples who find their marriages on the rocks, and it is one of the genuinely modern novels in Chinese literature in that it is not circumscribed by the trope of nationalism or identity. It is concerned with the universality of the relationship between the sexes and of a people living in a society undergoing the trauma of modernization. In a society where marriage remains an imperfect institution, and yet neither men nor women can live without it, the only alternative is to let the principals scheme, daydream, and make compromises.

Lao She's signature work is *Camel Xiangzi,* which depicts the trials and tribulations of a tall, strong, and determined young rickshaw puller, Xiangzi, in Beijing during the 1920s. He tries his best, in the old-fashioned way of individual hard work, to better himself. But Xiangzi's rickshaw is repeatedly taken away from him, he loses all his money, and, finally, death takes away his wife and family. He never succeeds in starting his own rickshaw company. Man-made obstacles and natural disasters overwhelm the hard-working Xiangzi. Lao She presents Xiangzi as a classic example of the futility of the individual's struggle against the forces of an impersonal capitalistic society. Xiangzi begins as a morally upright character but ends up totally depraved, morally corrupt, physically decrepit, and with no hopes or aspirations except to survive as he roams the streets of Beijing like a homeless dog. This story embodies the age-old Chinese storytellers' cyclical view of human fortunes: "The road of life is a tortuous one and the heart of man is hard to fathom. . . . Everyone hustles about for the sake of gain but in his ignorance he often reaps nothing but calamities." This view is contrasted with the modern, linear perception of man's unrelenting quest for material wealth and power. *Camel Xiangzi* also captures the spirit of new China's struggles to modernize against the overwhelming forces of poverty and tradition.

Lao She's magnum opus is his trilogy *Sishi tongtang* (Four Generations Under One Roof; for an abridged translation, see *Yellow Storm*), which consists of *Huanghuo* (1944; Bewilderment), *Tousheng* (1945; An Ignoble Life), and *Jihuang* (1950; Famine). The trilogy, about the lives of the ordinary citizens of Beiping under Japanese occupation from 1937 to 1945, is the supreme test of Lao She's skills as a writer as he attempts to reconcile the double demands of patriotism and artistic integrity. *Sishi tongtang* is set in Lao She's beloved Beiping and depicts a tradition-bound, extended family headed by the patriarch, Great-Grandfather Qi, who is the focal point of the story. His limited experience and his great age give him a totally unrealistic picture of 20th-century warfare. The trilogy's composite portrait of Beiping under Japanese occupation contains a gallery of more than 130 characters from various walks of life, including diplomats, professors, teachers, poets, barbers, rickshaw pullers, street performers, and prostitutes. To survive, the inhabitants face difficult moral choices. Some choose to become traitors and collaborators, others resist and become guerrilla fighters, while still others remain silent, passive sufferers. In this sprawling, panoramic work of almost a million words, Lao She takes every opportunity to voice his unhappiness with the shortcomings of Chinese civilization, but his criticism arises from his deep-seated love of Beiping and the nation.

Lao She's last novel, *Zhenghongzi xia* (1961–62; *Beneath the Red Banner*), was written in the early 1960s and published posthumously. It is an unfinished, autobiographical work that recounts Lao She's childhood days in a Manchu household, a subject that he had shunned for many years because of his ambivalent feelings about his Manchu origins. However, in the last years of his life he was able to reconcile himself to his Manchu background. The unfinished novel of 11 extant chapters covers only a fraction of the planned novel, which was to extend over a period of 30 years. Lao She's family belonged to the Red Banner garrison, one of eight military units of the Manchu fighting force. The Manchus were once a nomadic people known for their formidable martial valor. They conquered China in 1644 and ruled over it until 1911. But during this long period of occupation, the Manchus lost their martial spirit and became "privileged idlers." In *Beneath the Red Banner*, Lao She laments this loss of martial prowess among the Manchus but finds redemption in one of the characters, cousin Fuhai, who is a genuine Manchu Bannerman "in full possession of the riding and shooting skills which had been refined over the course of 200 years." Even at the end of his life, Lao She continued his quest for a workable sense of identity.

PETER LI

See also Camel Xiangzi

Biography

Born 3 February 1899 in Beiping. Served as principal of elementary school at age 17, later rising to district supervisor; traveled to England in 1924, teaching Mandarin Chinese to support himself; returned to China in 1931; during Sino-Japanese War and World War II headed the All-China Anti-

Japanese Writers Federation; traveled to the United States on a cultural grant in 1946, where he gave lectures and supervised the translation of several of his novels; returned to China in 1947 and continued his participation in cultural movements and literary committees; believed to have been killed by the Red Guards at the onset of the Cultural Revolution. Died 24? August 1966.

Novels by Lao She

Lao Zhang de zhexue [The Philosophy of Lao Zhang], 1926
Zhao Ziyue [Zhao Ziyue], 1928
Er Ma, 1929; as *The Two Mas*, translated by Kenny K. Huang and David Finkelstein, 1984
Mao chengji, 1932; as *Cat Country*, translated by William A. Lyell, Jr., 1970
Lihun, 1933; as *The Quest for Love of Lao Lee*, translated by Helena Kuo, 1948
Niu Tianci, 1934; as *Heavensent*, 1951; also translated by Xiong Deni, 1986
Luotuo Xiangzi, 1937; as *Rickshaw Boy*, translated by Evan King, 1945; as *Rickshaw*, translated by Jean M. James, 1979; as *Camel Xiangzi*, 1981

Sishi tongtang (trilogy), 1944–50; abridged translation as *Yellow Storm*, translated by Ida Pruitt, 1951
Huanghuo [Bewilderment], 1944
Tousheng [An Ignoble Life], 1945
Jihuang [Famine], 1950
Gushu yiren, 1948; as *The Drum Singers*, 1952; also translated by Helena Kuo, 1987
Zhenghongzi xia, 1961–62; as *Beneath the Red Banner*, translated by Don J. Cohen, 1982

Other Writings: short stories, plays, poetry, and essays.

Further Reading

Hsia, C.T., *A History of Modern Chinese Fiction*, New Haven, Connecticut: Yale University Press, 1961; 2nd edition, 1971
Jameson, Fredric, "Literary Innovation and Modes of Production: A Commentary," *Modern Chinese Literature* 1:1 (September 1984)
Vohra, Ranbir, *Lao She and the Chinese Revolution*, Cambridge, Massachusetts: East Asian Research Center, Harvard University, 1974
Wang, David Der-wei, *Fictional Realism in Twentieth-Century China: Mao Dun, Lao She, Shen Congwen*, New York: Columbia University Press, 1992

Last Chronicle of Barset. *See* Barsetshire Novels

The Last of the Mohicans by James Fenimore Cooper

1826

The Last of the Mohicans is James Fenimore Cooper's most famous novel, its enduring interest demonstrated by the number of times in the 20th century it has been both republished and filmed. Testifying to its mythic status, films readily rearrange its parts and produce substantial changes in the story, while the dimensions of Cooper's tale remain essentially recognizable.

Second in the order of writing and in the chronology of the life of Nathaniel (Natty) Bumppo, the hero of Cooper's "Leatherstocking Tales" who goes by various names derived from his association with Indians, *The Last of the Mohicans* centers on an actual historical event, the massacre of Fort William Henry in 1757, during Britain's war with France over territory in what are now the borderlands between Canada and the United States. Fort William Henry was the second of two English forts strategically situated to defend the important waterways of this area. As the novel opens, the two daughters of the fort's commander and

their escort have been led into an ambush by their Indian scout (Magua), who develops as the "bad" Indian in the novel. Natty, known in this novel as Hawk-Eye, and two Indians, his friend Chingachgook (his companion in all the Leatherstocking Tales) and Chingachgook's son, Uncas, come to the aid of the party. The plot consists of various captivities, rescues, and relationships involving this varied group, with the massacre of the fort's defeated holders at the center of the story. The novel ends with the funeral rites for Uncas, who has been killed by Magua.

It is not immediately obvious why *The Last of the Mohicans* should be seen as Cooper's greatest work or why it was the most popular of his novels. It is hardly more exciting than *The Deerslayer* (1841) or *The Pathfinder* (1840), the other novels of the series that portray Natty in the vigor of his younger manhood. (In *The Pioneers* [1823] Natty is in his 70s, and in *The Prairie* [1827] in his late 80s.) All involve captivity stories, and while they share such elements as Indian trials of endurance and the rescue of women, *The Deerslayer* contains arguably more exotic elements (an "ark" anchored in a lake is the odd home of its besieged Europeans), and it almost outdoes *The Last of the Mohicans* in the violence of its scalping episode. Nor can the historical aspect of *The Last of the Mohicans* account for the book's outstanding popularity. The historical event portrayed, like the war of which it was part, has not attracted strong emotional investment from succeeding generations. The power of the book most obviously has to do with the fact that its mythic lines are keenly drawn, lines which trace the vexed relationship between nature and culture, presented through the relationship between whites and Indians. *The Last of the Mohicans,* with the figures of Uncas and Chingachgook, has, as its title suggests, the strongest Indian presence of all Cooper's novels. Uncas' death at the hands of the evil Magua, and the funeral oration of the sage Tamenund that ends the book, act as vehicles for the enunciation and the assuaging of European guilt about the treatment of Native Americans. In Leslie Fiedler's words, the book may be seen as a "propitiatory offering" for Western (not simply American) guilt (see Fiedler, 1960). The title is still a powerful, mesmerizing call to ponder, through Cooper's presentation of the Indian, the Western sense of loss at the distance from nature brought about by "progress."

Cooper helped to invent a style of natural description to render in words, as the painters of the Hudson River school were doing in pictures, the astounding landscape that is the setting for this mythology. He helped invent an American literary style. He also made an effort to capture the vernacular speech of the backwoodsman and of the Indians. Cooper's research on the latter may have been limited but he made a genuine attempt to go beyond stereotypes.

Through his powerful mythology and compelling descriptions, Cooper carved out new paths for the novel in America. He clearly had one foot in the 18th century, his faith in reason combined with an enlightened capacity to use the savage as a way to criticize the civilized. The historical romances of Sir Walter Scott inspired Cooper to draw stereotypes of light and dark, good and evil; to dichotomize the female into the fair and pure and the dark and tainted; and to represent what would come to be called "local color." The modernity of Cooper's writing, however, lies in his capacity to transform stereotypes and move beyond enlightened certainties. His dark women are active and interesting, if ultimately obliterated, like Cora in this novel, who, of mixed race herself, is attracted to Uncas. Cooper's new hero is neither the English soldier nor the noble savage but the backwoodsman, a figure that crosses between worlds. Cooper gave American literature a type of the American democrat, not least in that democrat's fraught relationship with society. While firmly speaking against miscegenation, Cooper makes the strongest friendship in the book—that between Hawk-Eye and Chingachgook—cross racial boundaries. Through the book's often Gothic darknesses and through complications even in the portrayal of the "bad" Indian, Cooper produced a sense of ambiguity about his country and about the relationship of Western civilization to the "natural" that foreshadowed the more intense ambiguities of the fiction of Nathaniel Hawthorne and Herman Melville. *The Last of the Mohicans* has a great deal to say to us today. As its popularity attests, it is still giving us forms through which to think about concepts fundamental to Western society.

RUTH M. BLAIR

See also James Fenimore Cooper

Further Reading

Fiedler, Leslie, *Love and Death in the American Novel,* New York: Dell, 1960; revised edition, 1966

Franklin, Wayne, *The New World of James Fenimore Cooper,* Chicago: University of Chicago Press, 1982

Maddox, Lucy, *Removals: Nineteenth-Century American Literature and the Politics of Indian Affairs,* New York: Oxford University Press, 1991

McWilliams, John P., *Political Justice in a Republic: James Fenimore Cooper's America,* Berkeley: University of California Press, 1972

Peck, H. Daniel, editor, *New Essays on "The Last of the Mohicans,"* Cambridge and New York: Cambridge University Press, 1992

Porte, Joel, *The Romance in America: Studies in Cooper, Poe, Hawthorne, Melville, and James,* Middletown, Connecticut: Wesleyan University Press, 1969

Rans, Geoffrey, *Cooper's Leather-stocking Novels: A Secular Reading,* Chapel Hill: University of North Carolina Press, 1991

Ringe, Donald A., *James Fenimore Cooper,* New York: Twayne, 1962; updated edition, Boston: Twayne, 1988

Slotkin, Richard, *Regeneration Through Violence: The Mythology of the American Frontier, 1600–1860,* Middletown, Connecticut: Wesleyan University Press, 1973

Tompkins, Jane, *Sensational Designs: The Cultural Work of American Fiction, 1790–1860,* New York: Oxford University Press, 1985

The Last Temptation of Christ by Nikos Kazantzakis

Ho teleutaios peirasmos 1955

Controversy broke out over Nikos Kazantzakis' *The Last Temptation of Christ* even before its publication. Kazantzakis finished the novel in 1951 but did not immediately find a publisher. By 1953 the Greek Orthodox Church had heard of the manuscript and tried to prosecute the author for sacrilege. The next year, the Roman Catholic Church placed *The Last Temptation* on the index of forbidden books. Given this notoriety, the novel quickly became a best-seller when it finally reached print in 1955. Subsequently, Kazantzakis' work provoked protests from the Catholic Church, the Orthodox Church, and various Protestant denominations in the United States when the book came out in translation, and again when Martin Scorsese adapted it to the screen some four decades later.

Kazantzakis raised the ire of religious authorities by his portrayal of Jesus as fully human and intensely tempted by the comforts and consolations of the flesh. His last temptation, in fact, is the lure of normal married life. Kazantzakis alters the biblical account of Jesus' life in other ways as well. In his vision of the Passion, Mary Magdalene is Jesus' scorned love, Judas is his necessary but reluctant accomplice, Matthew is a spirit-led biographer who bends the facts, and Paul is a scornful prevaricator. Not only does Kazantzakis re-imagine the well-known characters, but he also refashions the parables to be more forgiving and inclusive. For example, the parable of the wise and foolish virgins is given a new ending in which all the maidens are welcomed at the wedding celebration. This insistence on universal welcome finds a parallel in Kazantzakis' use of the demotic. Himself from Crete, he passionately championed the language of the Cretan peasantry over classical Greek and always used the simple cadences and concrete imagery of the living language.

Kazantzakis' treatment of the biblical sources is sometimes compared to the use of myth in such modernist novels as James Joyce's *Ulysses* (1922). This comparison suggests itself because *The Last Temptation*, unlike any of Kazantzakis' other novels, relies on modernist innovations in narrative technique. Morton Levitt observes that *The Last Temptation* embodies "a subjective sense of time and limited, sometimes even ambiguous, point of view" (see Levitt, 1980). However, modernist technique in this novel serves a theological version of modernism's philosophical position that truth is available only through the subjective experience of the individual.

Kazantzakis conflates the Matthew who wrote the scholarly, Greek-language gospel that goes by his name and the Matthew who was one of Jesus' followers, an uneducated man who figures in the scholar's gospel account. Using the disciple Matthew as a narrative filter, Kazantzakis achieves a great sense of immediacy. He also exchanges the objective authority of the historian for a limited, even unreliable, perspective, which offers an appropriate mouthpiece for the intense religious experience that motivated *The Last Temptation*. Much has been written about Kazantzakis' engagement with and contribution to process theology, which is associated principally with Alfred North Whitehead. Process theology sees "Jesus as a metaphor, symbol, or paradigm for divinity and therefore, like all literary metaphors, open to multiple readings and resistant to single interpretation" (see Bak, in Middleton

and Bien, 1996). Matthew's fallibility, as much as Jesus' humanity, lies at the heart of Kazantzakis' argument about the nature and meaning of religious experience in the modern era.

Some critics propose that Kazantzakis' Matthew also delivers an indirect commentary on the nature of writing. Certainly he reflects on his own struggles to decipher ambiguities, unravel hidden meanings, and interpret earlier texts:

> [Matthew] noticed how the teacher's saying and deeds were exactly the same as the prophets, centuries earlier, had proclaimed; and if once in a while the prophecies and Jesus' life did not quite match, it was because the mind of man was not eager to understand the hidden meaning of the sacred text. The word of God had seven levels of meaning, and Matthew struggled to find at which level the incompatible elements could find their mates. Even if he occasionally matched things by force, God forgives! Not only would he forgive, he desired this. Every time Matthew took up his quill, did not an angel come and bend over his ear to intone what he was to write?

Although Kazantzakis does not claim angelic inspiration as Matthew does, he experienced the writing of *The Last Temptation* as a religious rather than an artistic undertaking. As he observed in his autobiography, "The more I wrote the more deeply I felt that in writing I was struggling, not for beauty, but for deliverance." While *The Last Temptation* makes use of the novel form and of the techniques of modernism, the novel stands firmly apart from the modernist tradition and its intense scrutiny of art and aesthetics. In fact, it embraces modes of reflection that are, on the whole, foreign to the novel as it has developed over the past several centuries. It should come as no surprise that *The Last Temptation of Christ* has been widely read but rarely imitated.

MOUMIN QUAZI

See also Nikos Kazantzakis

Further Reading

Bien, Peter A., *Kazantzakis: Politics of the Spirit,* Princeton, New Jersey: Princeton University Press, 1989

Friar, Kimon, introduction to *The Odyssey: A Modern Sequel,* by Nikos Kazantzakis, translated by Kimon Friar, New York: Simon and Schuster, and London: Secker and Warburg, 1958

Kazantzakis, Helen, *Nikos Kazantzakis: A Biography Based on His Letters,* translated by Amy Mims, New York: Simon and Schuster, and Oxford: Bruno Cassirer, 1968

Kazantzakis, Nikos, *Report to Greco,* translated by Peter A. Bien, New York: Simon and Schuster, and Oxford: Bruno Cassirer, 1965

Lea, James F., *Kazantzakis: The Politics of Salvation,* University: University of Alabama Press, 1979

Levitt, Morton P., *The Cretan Glance: The World and Art of Nikos Kazantzakis,* Columbus: Ohio State University Press, 1980

Middleton, Darren J.N., and Peter A. Bien, editors, *God's Struggler: Religion in the Writings of Nikos Kazantzakis,* Macon, Georgia: Mercer University Press, 1996

Latin American Novel

Overview

In the second half of the 20th century, a number of influential Latin American writers have brought the novel to unprecedented levels of popular as well as critical acclaim in their own countries and throughout the world. Since the 1960s, the term *boom* (which is also used in Spanish) has come to refer partly to the mushrooming sales and publicity enjoyed by such novelists as Gabriel García Márquez, Julio Cortázar, José Donoso, Mario Vargas Llosa, and Carlos Fuentes. *Boom* also refers to an approach to the novel taken by the most successful Latin American writers of the period, featuring a complex, often playful narrative construction and, in many cases, magical and fantastic elements occurring against a realistic background. These features captivated an international reading public. For the first time, Latin American novelists were able to exert an influence on their counterparts from Europe and the United States. While the Latin American novel is no longer as heavily publicized as when it burst onto the world scene during the boom years, it continues to exercise an influence internationally; the success of such novelists as Manuel Puig, Isabel Allende, and Laura Esquivel, both through their writings and through the film adaptations of their novels, make felt the impact of innovative Latin American narrative of the late 20th century.

The first Latin American novel generally recognized as such is the 1816 *El Periquillo Sarniento* (*The Itching Parrot*) by José Joaquín Fernández de Lizardi (Mexico, 1776–1827). While a number of earlier works are at times cited as precursors of the Latin American novel, none clearly meets the criteria of the genre. It should be remembered that the Spanish government banned the importation and printing of novels in its New World colonies out of apprehension that they would stir dissent. *The Itching Parrot* is unmistakably an adaptation of the picaresque novel that had enjoyed such popularity in Europe. In Lizardi's 1819 "Apology," he explains his choice and adaptation of the European novel form to promote the reform of Mexican society and education. He reports consciously making modifications to suit a Spanish American public; he was especially concerned with reaching readers who were not very sophisticated or skilled at interpretation. *The Itching Parrot* is narrated by a now-reformed rogue and is full of didactic statements on leadership, education, and the making of good and bad citizens.

Lizardi is closely identified with the Spanish New World colonies' struggle to become nations both politically and culturally independent from Spain. *The Itching Parrot* touches on the great issues of the independence era. It marks the beginning of a close relationship between the novel and Latin American intellectuals' efforts to define and reflect on their nations. Authors turn to the novel to project a vision of what their nations should become; they employ the genre to strengthen national identity or, in later works, to criticize the forms that identity has taken.

Romanticism was an important and enduring force in both Spanish American and Brazilian writing. Latin American romanticism, shaped by the concerns of contemporary literary intellectuals, diverges from its European counterpart in many ways. While Latin American romanticism began relatively late (approximately the 1830s), it took hold vigorously; public enthusiasm for romantic novels ran high throughout the mid– to late 19th century. Latin American romanticism does not stand clearly apart from other literary tendencies, and a single work may combine romanticism, realism, naturalism, and traces of other movements. European romantics often expressed revulsion with industrialized society and idealized peasant simplicity. Spanish America had not yet experienced industrialization, and many writers were eager to see their societies become more technically advanced. The glorification of the common people was not consistently a feature of Latin American romantic fiction, owing no doubt to many 19th-century writers' reluctance to admire a population that was often of Indian, African, or mixed ancestry.

Latin American romanticism is closely tied to the problems of the larger society and especially to the struggle, following political independence, to establish stable nations with strong cultural identities. The most widely read romantic novels, such as *O guarani* (1857; The Guarani) and *Iracema: Lenda do Ceará* (1865; *Iracema, The Honey-Lips, a Legend of Brazil*), by José de Alencar of Brazil, who generated a romantic nationalism around idealized figures of the Brazilian Indian; *Amalia* (1851), by the Argentine José Mármol; and the much reprinted *María* (1867; *Maria, a South American Romance*), by the Colombian Jorge Isaacs, all contributed to an effort to create representative national literatures.

A number of 19th-century Latin American novels are devoted in large measure to exposing social ills. This is the case with Cuban antislavery novels such as Cirilo Villaverde's *Cecilia Valdés, o La Loma del Ángel* (1839/82; *Cecilia Valdés, or Angel's Hill*); Anselmo Suárez y Romero's *Francisco* (written 1839, published 1880); and Gertrudis Gómez de Avellaneda's *Sab* (1841; *Sab*). The 1889 *Aves sin nido* (*Birds without a Nest*) by Clorinda Matto de Turner of Peru was dedicated to exposing corruption in Andean towns and the exploitation of Peru's Indians. Mármol's *Amalia* is primarily a denunciation of a repressive regime; the mid–19th century thus saw the beginning of the Latin American "novel of the dictator."

During the heyday of romantic fiction, the Latin American reading public's interest was often whetted by novels published in installments in newspapers. Readers reportedly became so tantalized by the serialization of Alencar's *O Guarani* that they impatiently awaited the train bearing issues with the latest installment, which they then began reading out in the street.

Realism is a component of many Latin American novels, although it often appears commingled with romanticism. Naturalism, in its French form, faced resistance in Latin America; its deterministic outlook conflicted with the Catholic insistence on free will, and its portrayal of human beings as beasts offended many readers. Still, a relatively few well-known novels, such as *Memórias de um sargento de milícias* (1854–55; *Memoirs of a Militia Sergeant*) by Manuel Antônio de Almeida, *O cortiço* (1890; *A Brazilian Tenement*) by Aluísio Azevedo, both from Brazil, and *Sin rumbo* (1885; Adrift) by the Argentine Eugenio Cambaceres, are considered representative of Latin American naturalism.

Modernismo, a movement that took hold about 1880 and re-mained in force until the 1910s, produced mostly poetry and short prose pieces. However, some distinguished novels were composed in this elegant, rather elevated literary manner, which appealed to a more elite public than did romanticism. *De sobremesa* (written c. 1896, published 1925; *After-dinner Conversation*), by the Colombian José Asunción Silva, exemplifies the *modernista* novel, in which moods, ambiences, and the characters' reflections take precedence over plot or action.

During the late 19th century and the early years of the 20th, Joaquim Maria Machado de Assis of Brazil made his name with novels whose subtlety and sophistication were beyond anything yet seen in Latin American fiction. Like many 19th-century novelists, Machado de Assis began his career under the sway of romanticism, but by the time he reached aesthetic maturity, his concepts and practices as a writer could not be classified under any one tendency. In struggling to render novelistic truth, Machado de Assis avoided complete reliance on any of the prevailing modes of representation, including romanticism, realism, naturalism, and symbolism. Machado de Assis' best-known works, *Memórias póstumas de Brás Cubas* (1881; translated as *Epitaph of a Small Winner* and as *Posthumous Reminiscences of Bras Cubas*) and *Dom Casmurro* (1899; *Dom Casmurro*) are known for their often bitter satire, sardonic, pessimistic narrators, and experiments in narrative form that usher in 20th-century innovation.

During the first half of the 20th century, there was little agreement over the direction the Latin American novel should take. Advocates of realistic representation also tended to favor subject matter distinctive to the Americas, such as Indian communities and life in particular regions, and to consider it the duty of Latin American writers to deal with the area's social problems. Realists disparaged the innovative narrative techniques cultivated by their more avant-garde, aesthetically minded contemporaries, although in their own novels they often also tried the new forms that were changing 20th-century fiction.

These realists were opposed to practitioners of a more stylized, abstract, metaphorical narrative that was not necessarily regionalist in its subject matter. *Modernismo* began to wane early in the century and was replaced by the avant-gardes that developed in the 1920s in many Latin American cities, especially Buenos Aires, Mexico City, and São Paulo. (In Brazil, *modernismo* was the term used to designate avant-garde activity. There had been no exact equivalent of Spanish American *modernismo* in Brazilian literature, although the Parnassian movement coincides in some regards.)

Avant-gardists, while they regarded themselves as more advanced than *modernistas*, shared their predecessors' preoccupation with experiments in narrative form and their disdain for conventional plot. Latin American writers with an avant-garde outlook were influenced by such European avant-garde movements as surrealism and futurism, although they were also concerned with making their own national literatures evolve. They employed typically 20th-century innovations, such as stream-of-consciousness narration and the adaptation of cinematic techniques to print narrative. Some avant-garde novels were too radically strange in form to appeal to many readers, but a few caught the public's imagination. The 1928 *Macunaíma*, by Mário de Andrade, called the Pope of Brazilian *Modernismo*, is an avant-garde novel whose ribald humor and distinctively

Brazilian language earned it a place among Brazil's most noted works of fiction.

A reader of Spanish-American novels from the 1920s and 1930s will immediately notice that, in the actual writing of fiction, few novelists complied strictly with either the avant-garde's postulates or the demands of realism. In many novels, allegorical, symbolic, and metaphorical representation occurs alongside realistic descriptions of specific regions. The freedom that novelists felt to combine styles of depiction is well illustrated by the "novels of the land" that appeared in the 1920s: José Eustasio Rivera's *La vorágine* (1924; *The Vortex*); Ricardo Güiraldes' *Don Segundo Sombra* (1926; *Don Segundo Sombra*); and Rómulo Gallegos' *Doña Bárbara* (1929; *Doña Bárbara*). These novels have in common an effort to convey a distinctive national or regional essence, ascribed to the very land on which the characters dwell.

As the 20th century progressed, some novelists, such as Jorge Icaza (Ecuador), who denounced through his fiction the exploitation of Indians, upheld social realism as the best way for Latin American writers to confront the region's problems. However, it became increasingly common for writers of fiction to employ fantastic, mythic, and magical elements in novels that were also a critique of Latin American societies.

Miguel Ángel Asturias, the first Latin American novelist awarded the Nobel prize, was influential in breaking down the distinction between formally innovative narrative and fiction that served to criticize social ills. In his best-known fiction, Asturias explores novelistic subject matter that had generally been given a fairly realistic literary treatment: dictatorship in the 1946 *El Señor Presidente* (translated first as *The President* and then as *El Señor Presidente*) and the plight of Indian communities in *Hombres de maíz* (1949; *Men of Maize*). These novels delivered their social critique not through straightforward plotlines but via narratives that were typical of 20th-century innovation in their pervasive instability of time, place, and narrative voice. Asturias, a student of Mayan myth, worked elements of traditional indigenous narratives, such as the transformation of human beings into other life forms, into *Men of Maize*.

When Asturias' groundbreaking fiction first appeared, detractors expressed concern that the showiness of his novelistic form and his use of myth would distract readers from the social problems being depicted. This strictly realist viewpoint has steadily lost ground ever since. Asturias' vision of social critique via a highly imaginative, mythic-magic novel is the one that has been dominant. It is the concept behind magic realism, the most internationally renowned tendency developed by Latin American novelists and a vigorous force to the present day.

The 1940s, when Asturias and the Cuban Alejo Carpentier began publishing their highly inventive fiction, is widely regarded as the start of *magic realism*, although the term was not applied until the tendency was well underway. Magic realism has never been defined with precision, but readers have found it easy to recognize. The hallmark of this tendency is the occurrence of realistic descriptions and accounts of events alongside the narration of phenomena that defy rational explanation. Much magic-realist fiction is set in isolated rural areas. A link has often been suggested between magic realism and the repository of mythic and magical beliefs provided by Indian and African-diaspora cultures in Latin America: for example, Asturias relied heavily on Maya myth and Carpentier on both

African-Caribbean and Indian material. Magic realism is often regarded as distinctive to Spanish American literature, but some contemporary Brazilian novels, such as João Guimarães Rosa's *Grande sertão: veredas* (1956; *The Devil to Pay in the Backlands*), are in the same vein. The Brazilian novel was not dominated by magic realism the way Spanish American narrative seemed to be; the most significant Brazilian novelist to emerge during this period, Clarice Lispector, stands out for highly original narrative construction but not for the use of myth, magic, or the supernatural.

Gabriel García Márquez of Colombia, 1982 winner of the Nobel prize, created the single most-cited example of magic realism with his 1967 novel *Cien años de soledad* (*One Hundred Years of Solitude*). This celebrated work is a reflection on slightly more than a century of Colombian history and contains novelized accounts of historical events. At the same time, it entertains readers with such fantastic occurrences as a plague of insomnia, which causes mass amnesia and leads to the invention of a memory machine. The ruling-class family on whom the novel centers struggles under the apprehension, which proves justified, that they are living out a curse and will be destroyed after a child is born with a pig's tail. The novel is in many ways an allegory of Latin American society, although not all its fanciful turns can be definitively interpreted.

The appearance of many strikingly original Latin American novels during the 1940s, 1950s, and 1960s gave rise to the term *new novel*. This designation does not single out a particular well-marked tendency, as does *magic realism*. Rather, it directs attention to Latin American novelists' increased concern with adapting the new techniques that characterized innovative 20th-century fiction worldwide. The Latin American new novel stands out from equivalent renovations, such as the French *nouveau roman*, by virtue of its ability to deal with social problems while offering new forms of novelistic construction. In retrospect, the term *new novel* has been called into question; it exaggerates the radical newness of mid-century fiction and gives insufficient recognition to the inventive originality of earlier novels.

As previously indicated, the English term *boom* began to be used in Spanish during the 1960s to refer to the unprecedented international success enjoyed by innovative Latin American novelists such as García Márquez, the Mexican Carlos Fuentes, and the Argentine Julio Cortázar. While *boom* first referred to booming sales and publicity, over time the term *boom novel* came to be applied to a certain type of fiction that flourished during the 1960s, epitomized by García Márquez's *One Hundred Years of Solitude* and Cortázar's 1963 *Rayuela* (*Hopscotch*). The term *boom novel* calls to mind a lengthy work of fiction with a complex structural design, published during the 1960s or perhaps as late as the early 1970s. The phrase also evokes a sanguine time when writers and readers of the Latin American novel believed that its innovations were of revolutionary and epoch-making significance.

As the 1960s drew to a close, some novelists and their readers began to promote a more playful, less weighty version of the Latin American novel. The term *post boom* is used to designate this shift away from the often massive and intricately constructed novels of the boom. There has been some weakening of the confidence, typical of the boom years, that Latin American novelists are producing landmarks of narrative innovation. The post boom often implies a more modest view of what the novel can accomplish. Allusions to contemporary popular culture characterize many of the newer novels, suggesting that they are not being written for the ages, but for a given period.

The post-boom period began before the boom was over. The first novel by the Argentine Manuel Puig, the post-boom writer who has enjoyed greatest critical and popular success, was published in 1968. In this first work, *La traición de Rita Hayworth* (*Betrayed by Rita Hayworth*), Puig showed the concern with mass culture and its effects that would typify many post-boom novels. Puig had originally set out to work in film, and his vast knowledge of cinema, especially US sound movies from Hollywood's golden age, provided him with a distinctive subject matter. Puig's novels certainly draw attention to narrative technique, of which they offer some bizarrely inventive new varieties. Yet compared with some of the great boom novels, his works are playfully constructed, sometimes mimicking such popular-culture genres as serialized romance novels. With the exception of *Rita Hayworth*, his fiction is relatively easy to read.

Not all the writers who have attained prominence in the 1970s–90s period are post boom in the sense of diverging sharply from the typical boom-novel pattern. Perhaps the Latin American writer who has won greatest international celebrity in recent years is the Chilean Isabel Allende. Her best-known novel, *La casa de los espíritus* (1982; *The House of the Spirits*), is similar to the magic realist novels that flourished during the boom period. Perhaps more typical is the Mexican Laura Esquivel, whose work proclaims its kinship with song lyrics, romance novels, and even cookbooks. With exceptions, the trend has been toward a less imposing, more playful novel. More recent novelists do not hold their work apart from popular cultural forms but seek to link it with the rest of contemporary Latin American culture.

NAOMI LINDSTROM

See also, in addition to entries on writers and texts discussed in this Overview and noted at the end of each portion of the Latin American survey below, the entry on Magic Realism

Further Reading

Brotherston, Gordon, *The Emergence of the Latin American Novel*, Cambridge and New York: Cambridge University Press, 1977

Brushwood, John Stubbs, *The Spanish American Novel: A Twentieth-Century Survey*, Austin: University of Texas Press, 1975

Foster, David William, editor, *Handbook of Latin American Literature*, New York: Garland, 1987; revised edition, 1992

Fuentes, Carlos, *La nueva novela hispanoamericana*, Mexico City: Joaquín Mortiz, 1969; 6th edition, 1980

Goic, Cedomil, *Historia de la novela hispanoamericana*, Santiago, Chile: Universidad Catolica de Valparaíso-Chile, 1972

González Echevarría, Roberto, *Myth and Archive: A Theory of Latin American Narrative*, New York and Cambridge: Cambridge University Press, 1990

Jitrik, Noé, *El no existente caballero: La idea de personaje y su evolución en la narrativa latinoamericana*, Buenos Aires: Magápolis, 1975

Kadir, Djelal, *Questing Fictions: Latin America's Family Romance,* Minneapolis: University of Minnesota Press, 1986

Lindstrom, Naomi, *Twentieth-Century Spanish American Fiction,* Austin: University of Texas Press, 1994

Martin, Gerald, *Journeys through the Labyrinth: Latin American Fiction in the Twentieth Century,* London and New York: Verso, 1989

Smith, Verity, editor, *Encyclopedia of Latin American Literature,* Chicago and London: Fitzroy Dearborn, 1996

Latin American Novel

Mexico

Origins of the Mexican Novel

Despite producing the historical writings of Hernán Cortés (1485–1547) and Bernal Díaz del Castillo (1495–1583), the Golden Age dramas of Juan Ruiz de Alarcón (1581–1639), and the lyric poetry of Sor Juana Inés de la Cruz (1651–95), and despite the rich novelistic tradition of Cervantes' Spain, colonial Mexico produced very few real novels before 1816, when José Joaquín Fernández de Lizardi published *El Periquillo Sarniento* (*The Itching Parrot*). The primary reason for this lack of production was censorship. Since the Spanish Crown was concerned to replace indigenous mythologies with Christian ones, it prohibited all New World subjects from reading or printing "profane and fantastic" works such as chivalric and pastoral novels. Although colonial Mexicans did manage to read many such works in spite of the prohibition, the printing of new novels was almost impossible in the New World. Two 17th-century works, however, did make it past the censors by emphasizing Christian themes. Bernardo de Balbuena's *El Siglo de Oro en las selvas de Erífile* (1608; The Golden Age in the Forests of Erífile) and Francisco Bramón's *Los sirgueros de la Virgen sin original pecado* (1620; Linnets of the Virgin without Original Sin) are mixtures of prose and poetry that attempt to present Christian ideas in the form of a Renaissance pastoral romance, imitating the Italian Jacopo Sannazzaro's *Arcadia* (1504). Not surprisingly, neither Balbuena's nor Bramón's works are of great literary merit; both are filled with artificial theological discussions between classical shepherds and shepherdesses.

In contrast, a third work that slipped by the censors, Carlos de Sigüenza y Góngora's *Infortunios de Alonso Ramírez* (1690; *The Misadventures of Alonso Ramírez*), is the first important Mexican novel. A contemporary of Sor Juana, Sigüenza (1645–1700) was a fascinating polymath: poet, mathematician, astronomer, priest, and novelist. *The Misadventures of Alonso Ramírez* is based on the true story of a shipwrecked Puerto Rican, Alonso Ramírez, who visited the author in Mexico. In order to tell the story, Sigüenza creatively utilizes many aspects of the picaresque form, a form of the novel popularized first in Spain by such works as the anonymous *Lazarillo de Tormes* (1554) and Mateo Alemán's *Guzmán de Alfarache* (1599–1604). Like all *pícaros,* Alonso tells his story as a first-person narrative full of adventures, social criticism, and realistic description. He explains how he traveled from Puerto Rico to Mexico and then on to the Philippines, where he became the prisoner of English pirates and was eventually shipwrecked on the Mexican coast. He criticizes Mexican society for its hypocrisy and lack of charity when the local inhabitants steal his belongings, while only the Indians show compassion, sharing their meager possessions with Alonso. The protagonist also makes apparent the freedom enjoyed by English ships; Spain is no longer the mistress of the seas after the defeat of the Armada in 1588. Because of its clever adaptation of the picaresque form, *The Misadventures of Alonso Ramírez* is an important step in the development of narrative prose in Mexico and in Spanish America.

The Novel of Independence and Post-Independence

Like Sigüenza's *The Misadventures of Alonso Ramírez,* José Joaquín Fernández de Lizardi's first three novels are clever adaptations of the picaresque form. Lizardi published the first of these novels in 1816, five years before Mexican independence was secured. It was a period of transition and confusion. In 1807 Napoléon had placed his brother Joseph on the Spanish throne. The legitimate Spanish Cortes, or parliament, went underground and continued operating in Cádiz. Seizing this moment of imperial weakness, *criollos* (full-blooded Spaniards born in the New World) rose up all over Spanish America in 1810. Intellectual *criollos* such as Lizardi saw the need and the opportunity to spread the liberal ideas of the Enlightenment, the ideas of Diderot, Voltaire, Condorcet, and Rousseau, ideas of freedom and social reform. Despite a vice-regal edict decreeing the death penalty for any author of incendiary pamphlets or other writings, Lizardi convinced a printer to risk publishing *The Itching Parrot,* his first novel, in which he inserted many of the reformist pamphlets that he had not been able to publish in past years. Although the novel contains an inordinate amount of reformist moralizing, its picaresque vision of Mexican society continues to delight readers and is one of the all-time best-sellers in the Spanish language. But Lizardi's novels were not simply didactic essays in disguise. He was aware that his imaginative literary creations could get his reformist message across more effectively than pamphlets. Lizardi hoped that his use of European picaresque models would legitimate his message.

Notwithstanding its European form, *The Itching Parrot* is the first truly Spanish-American novel. It is uniquely New World in two ways. First, in the preface to the 1819 edition of the novel, Lizardi justifies his inclusion of vulgar, incorrect language and scenes from the lives of the lower classes. According to the author, such elements must be included, since they typify Mexico. Second, in the same preface, Lizardi states that he has broken with European artistic precepts in his novel because he rejects the pompous elegance of European literary style. In his novel, he often satirizes the high-flown jargon of doctors, lawyers, and noblemen, teaching his *criollo* readers to criticize empty language, to reject inherited imperial norms, and to create a new, uniquely Spanish-American discourse. Lizardi anticipates the subversive message of the 20th-century works of Spanish-American writers such as Carlos Fuentes, Julio Cortázar, Gabriel Cabrera Infante, and others.

If *The Itching Parrot* is a scathing criticism of imperial pomposity, Lizardi's later novel, *Don Catrín de la Fachenda* (1832), is a more concise, more cynical retelling of the same picaresque story, this time without the redemption of the *pícaro* at the end. Lizardi changed the tone and ending because he was aware that the colonial reader had also changed. This story of an unrepentant *pícaro* who is unable to be reformed expresses the disappointment of post-Independence liberals who had become discouraged in their efforts to reform society.

Lizardi was unusually sensitive to his readership. In the preface to *The Itching Parrot*, he recognized that post-Independence Mexican readers were not necessarily well-educated aristocrats. Lizardi saw himself as a disseminator of liberal wisdom to a new reading public, a heterogeneous assortment of people, including an increasing number of women. He was especially aware of these women readers, as evidenced in his second novel, *La educación de las mujeres o La Quijotita y su prima* (1818; The Education of Women, or Little Miss Quixote and Her Cousin). According to Lizardi, he purportedly wrote *La Quijotita* in response to a request by a woman reader who signed herself "La Curiosa" (the Curious Woman), asking him to avoid highly ideological reformist language in his next novel. Whether true or not, the account shows Lizardi's sensitivity to an evolving readership. Unfortunately, the novel itself breaks very little new ground in its depiction of women, offering only very conservative models of how women should and should not behave. Following the 17th-century notions of Abbé Fénelon's *Traité de l'éducation des filles* (1685; On the Education of Daughters) rather than the more enlightened, 18th-century ideas of Helvetius, Lizardi tells the story of two cousins, Pudenciana, the model of feminine goodness, whose family has prepared her well for the only careers appropriate for good women, marriage and motherhood, and Pomposa, "little Miss Quixote," the model of feminine evil, whose family has taught her to seek her own pleasure in frivolous social activities, fashionable clothes, and fantastic novels. Unsurprisingly, La Quijotita is a *pícara* who is punished for her unwillingness to conform and obey like her virtuous cousin. Pomposa becomes pregnant, gets an abortion, marries badly, and eventually meets her tragic end as a prostitute. Although Lizardi's novels often gave voice to the most enlightened ideas of the day, this particular work served only to condemn women who, like the protagonist, had the audacity to express opinions, read books, and live their own lives.

Between Lizardi's death in 1827 and the publication of the first significant work of the succeeding generation, José Díaz Covarrubias' *Gil Gómez el insurgente* (1858; Gil Gómez the Insurgent), Mexican writers produced very few significant novels. It was a time of political and ideological confusion and uncertainty: colonialism and nascent nationalism, conservativism and liberalism, neoclassical rationalism and romantic revolt, warring factions, corruption, and opportunistic tyrants such as Antonio López de Santa Anna (1794–1876). The novels of this tumultuous period expressed a variety of themes: neoclassical esteem for common sense and didacticism, romantic sentimentality, nationalistic novels describing Mexican customs, nostalgic romanticizing of colonial history, idealization of the Indian as a noble savage, and defense of the *criollo*.

Jicoténcal, an anonymous novel published in Spanish in Philadelphia in 1826, expresses some of these themes. Most scholars agree that the novel was written by a Spanish American. Although it is probably impossible to know whether the author was Mexican, *Jicoténcal* certainly shares characteristics of the Mexican novel of that time. The work combines the noble savage theme and a sentimental love story with a romanticized version of the conquest of Mexico by the Spaniards. Three other novels of the period are representative of other thematic tendencies. Manuel Payno's *El fistol del diablo* (1845–46; The Devil's Scarfpin) is valuable for its portrait of post-Independence Mexico. Payno's serialized novel is a good example of the so-called *costumbrista* novel, that is, a novel presenting detailed descriptions of customs and social behavior. *Costumbrismo* had originated in Spain among such writers as Mesonero Romanos and Estébanez Calderón. Payno's novel is a disturbing series of sketches of a chaotic society, a rudderless nation that has permitted itself to drift to the point of losing more than half of its national territory to a foreign aggressor. Justo Sierra O'Reilly's historical novel, *La hija del judío* (1848–50; The Jew's Daughter) is one of the best novels of the period and rivals the works of Sir Walter Scott in its detailed re-creations of historical places. Sierra skillfully presents the Mexico of the colonial Inquisition, relating the story of a young woman who, aided by the protagonist of the novel, a Jesuit whose complex characterization is a significant step forward in the Mexican novel, fights the Holy Office for her rightful inheritance. He is one of the first characters in Mexican fiction who is neither all good nor all bad. Finally, one of the most popular novels of the day, Fernando Orozco y Berra's *La guerra de los treinta años* (1850; The Thirty Years War), reveals the lingering immaturity of both the reading public and the Mexican novel of this period. Although it lacks literary merit, the work achieved remarkable notoriety by recounting in tedious detail the amorous misfortunes of 30 years of the author's life.

The Romantic Novel of the Reform Period

In 1855 a democratic reform movement led by Benito Juárez overthrew the dictatorship of Antonio López de Santa Anna and drafted a liberal constitution. The country was embroiled in the War of Reform from 1857 to 1860. The war silenced Mexico's novelists, with one notable exception: Juan Díaz Covarrubias, a promising young medical student who died in 1859 at the age of 22 while attending to those wounded in the war. Had he not died, Díaz Covarrubias might have become an even more important romantic novelist, since his best novel, *Gil Gómez el insurgente,* reveals more complexity in characterization than its antecedents and provides a moving portrait of Mexico's fight for independence.

During the French Intervention in Mexico between 1862, when Napoléon III's forces invaded, and 1867, when Maximilian was shot in Querétaro, only one event of literary significance occurred: the publication in 1865 of Luis G. Inclán's *Astucia* (The Astute One). Like *Martín Fierro*, the 19th-century outlaw hero of Argentine literature, the protagonist of Inclán's *Astucia* lives outside the law but follows a rural code of honor. Because of its accurate, colorful portrayal of the customs and speech of rural Mexico, the novel has long been a national favorite. *Astucia* is a transitional novel: its melodramatic elements make it romantic, while its authenticity makes it a precursor of realism.

The restoration of the republic in 1867 also brought about Mexico's first real literary renaissance, the guiding spirit of which was Ignacio Manuel Altamirano, the best Mexican novelist before the 20th century. Altamirano's works are classic romantic novels, all of which are models of good taste, unexaggerated sentimentality, carefully designed plots, and restrained, engaging prose. His first novel, *Julia* (1867), is an unpretentious love story about a jilted suitor whose pride makes him refuse the girl when she has a change of heart. In 1869 Altamirano founded the most distinguished literary review in Mexico up to that time and appropriately named it *El Renacimiento* (The Renaissance). Altamirano was an extremely influential literary critic, and in large measure he shaped what would become Mexico's narrative tradition. According to Altamirano, the novelist's vision should include the whole society and should allow him to re-create the people and the setting of this vision. Altamirano also held that novels should teach their readers about the 19th-century liberal principles of freedom and order.

In 1869 *El Renacimiento* published Altamirano's *Clemencia*, a novel in which the author expresses the romantic patriotic ideal in two contrasting male protagonists, one physically appealing, the other not, who suffer for their beliefs in order to show the importance of convictions and the superficiality of physical appearance. In *La navidad en las montañas* (1870; *Christmas in the Mountains*), Altamirano creates a romantic, nostalgic ambiance in the simplicity of a mountain village where a reformist officer spends Christmas Eve. In *El Zarco* (1870; *El Zarco: The Bandit*), Altamirano again describes in wonderful detail a small town, this time telling the story of a romantic young woman who elopes with a bandit. Unlike Inclán's earlier *Astucia*, Altamirano's novel criticizes the bandit and upholds liberal ideas of social order.

By 1876 these liberal ideas had run their course. In November Juárez's successor, Lerdo de Tejada, was defeated by Porfirio Díaz, who came to power with the slogan "effective suffrage, no re-election" and then proceeded to have himself re-elected every four years (except once when he let one of his followers substitute for him) from that time until 1911, when the Mexican Revolution ousted him from power. The advent of the new regime brought with it the rise of a less idealistic, less sentimental form of literary expression, the realist novel.

Realism, "Modernismo," and Naturalism

The realist novel was not, of course, born *ex nihilo* with the advent of the *porfiriato*. Objective re-creation of visible reality had formed a significant element of many romantic novels, such as the *costumbrista* works of Manuel Payno and José Tomás de Cuéllar. Yet the realist movement in Mexican literature did not become especially dominant until the Díaz regime firmly established itself politically between 1885 and 1891. By this time most writers had lost their romantic idealism. The incorporation

of indigenous groups and other elements of the lower classes had come to be regarded officially as an impossibility.

According to one of the most representative novels of this period, *Nieves* (1887; Snows) by José López-Portillo y Rojas, the Díaz regime and the class divisions that it encouraged were not to blame for the plight of the poor. López-Portillo held the common 19th-century assumption that the individual poor person was to blame, since self-improvement was entirely the individual's responsibility. For López-Portillo, the stability of Porfirio Díaz's authoritarianism provided a means of protecting traditional values. In *Nieves*, the author presents a favorable portrait of the *hacienda* system, a type of slave labor arrangement similar in many ways to the plantation system of the antebellum southern United States. According to López-Portillo, there are good and evil *hacendados* (plantation owners), but the system itself is an inevitable, inextricable part of Mexican life. Like other realist novelists of this period, López-Portillo had traded in the idealism of the Reformation for the glorification of the authoritarian status quo. His general tone of naive sympathy and blatant condescension is also apparent in his later works, *La parcela* (1898; The Plot of Land), *Los precursores* (1909; The Forerunners), and *Fuertes y débiles* (1919; The Strong and the Weak).

The novels of Rafael Delgado have more to do with the middle class than those of López-Portillo, but they are equally traditional and supportive of the Porfirian regime. In *La calandria* (1891; The Lovebird) and *Los parientes ricos* (1903; The Rich Relatives), Delgado staunchly upholds rigid class divisions and portrays the middle class as God-fearing and virtuous.

In contrast to López Portillo and Delgado, Emilio Rabasa harshly criticizes the *porfirista* regime in his tetralogy, *Novelas mexicanas* (1887–88; Mexican Novels): *La bola* (1887; The Uprising), *La gran ciencia* (1887; The Grand Science), *El cuarto poder* (1888; The Fourth Power), and *Moneda falsa* (1888; Counterfeit Money). Rabasa criticizes the arbitrary nature of political power in Mexican society in *La bola*, using the word *bola* to refer to a local political skirmish in which an ambitious politician establishes himself as the local boss. In the novel Rabasa effectively satirizes the meaninglessness of such power struggles. People are killed, property is destroyed, and the only outcome is that one man has increased his power. In *La gran ciencia*, Rabasa portrays politics as the grand science of knowing how to play the Machiavellian game of staying in power. *El cuarto poder* takes aim at the press, showing how much of the news is invented in order to sell papers or in order to satisfy personal vendettas. In the fourth novel of the tetralogy, *Moneda falsa*, the two protagonists of all four novels, Juan Quiñones, the journalist, and Mateo Cabezudo, the politician, return home to their provincial hometowns after their careers have been destroyed.

Rabasa's tetralogy is important not only for its critical stance, but also for its literary sophistication. Rabasa's strategic use of the first-person narrator, Juan Quiñones, allows the author to distance himself from the narrator. The tetralogy represents a definite step forward in the evolution of the Mexican novel because it presents realism with a decidedly modern twist. By removing the third-person, objective, authorial narrator, Rabasa presents reality from the interestingly skewed perspective of a vacillating, doubting, and remorseful Quiñones.

A novel even more critical of the Díaz regime is *Tomochic* (1893), by Heriberto Frías, a federal soldier who recounts his experiences as a participant in the army's extermination of the rebellious Indian village Tomochic in northern Mexico during the final months of 1892. Frías' novel is sharply critical, but it is also quite balanced. He respects the heroism and humanitarianism on both sides. He detests the ineptness and corruption among the federal troops, as well as the religious fanaticism among the *tomochitecos.*

In addition to these realist novels, this period also produced a small number of works of prose fiction whose style and themes derive from a uniquely Hispanic literary movement, *modernismo.* The first literary style to originate in Latin America, *modernismo* was mainly a poetic movement, an elegant, exquisitely crafted triumph of intricate form, a reaction to empty romanticism and harsh realism, an original blending of French symbolist sounds and Parnassian imagery. A truly pan-American phenomenon, almost every Latin American nation, from Nicaragua to Colombia to Argentina, produced important *modernista* poets. Some Mexican *modernistas,* including Rubén M. Campos, Efrén Rebolledo, and Amado Nervo, tried their hand at *modernista* prose fiction. Nervo was, without question, the best novelist of the group, and his three prose works, *El bachiller* (1895; The Schoolboy), *Pascual Aguilera* (1896), and *El donador de almas* (1899; The Donor of Souls), are fascinating mixtures of *modernista* preciousness and linguistic innovation and elegance, romantic melancholy, and naturalistic obsession with abnormal psychology. Nervo's first novelistic effort created quite a stir in 1895 because it deals with a young seminarian's struggle to overcome the temptations of the flesh. Mexico's first successful psychological novelist, Nervo shows how the protagonist's inner tensions mount until he feels that he must castrate himself in order to avoid seduction. Nervo's second *modernista* novel, *Pascual Aguilera,* is an extraordinary accomplishment. Like López Portillo's *Nieves,* it deals with the theme of the "evil *hacendado.*" Unlike López Portillo's novel, however, Nervo's work is a meticulous psychological study rather than a broadly conceived social portrait. Nervo dissects the complex desires of Pascual Aguilera, the son of an *hacendado* whose attempt to rape a peasant bride is frustrated. Out of his mind with rage, Aguilera rapes his own stepmother instead. Nervo provides sexual details, and many conservative Porfirian readers condemned the work as scandalous. The novel ends ironically, since the stepmother admits that she enjoyed her encounter with Aguilera, and Nervo explains why in graphic detail. In his last foray into the world of prose, Nervo is equally innovative, this time creating what might be called metaphysical science fiction. In *El donador de almas,* the protagonist is a physician who, at the beginning of the work, has no soul. He wants one, however, and a poet friend finds one for him. The novelist then describes the relationship between the doctor and his soul. Although science fiction had developed as a genre in Mexico and in Latin America, this kind of metaphysical science fiction had found a number of illustrious practitioners in the realm of short fiction, including Mexican authors Alfonso Reyes and Juan José Arreola, and, of course, the Argentine writer Jorge Luis Borges.

Naturalism, the late 19th-century school of narrative technique founded by French author Émile Zola, made its most important contribution to Mexican literature in the novels of Federico Gamboa (1864–1939), arguably the best novelist to this point in Mexican literary history. Naturalism stressed the importance of heredity and environment in determining events and actions. According to Zola, the novelist should observe and record dispassionately, like a scientist. Gamboa, like Zola, stresses environmental circumstances as determining factors, and, after the manner of the scientist, he records observed details in all their uncensored vividness. Yet Gamboa goes beyond naturalism and creates novels that are nearly perfect blendings of modern literary technique and genuinely Mexican characters and themes.

Unfortunately, Gamboa's works have not received due recognition in Mexico because of his political stance against the Mexican Revolution (Gamboa served as foreign minister for Porfirio Díaz and, between 1913 and 1914, for the counterrevolutionary regime of Victoriano Huerta). Gamboa was in exile until 1919, and upon his return he opposed the anticlerical policies of the postrevolutionary administrations of the 1920s and 1930s. Despite Gamboa's political beliefs, his masterpiece, *Santa* (1903), is one of the best-known novels in all of Latin American literature. In addition to becoming Mexico's first best-seller, *Santa* has been the subject of three films, a popular ballad, and two theatrical productions.

Santa is the culmination of the four strengths present in most of Gamboa's writing: his careful, restrained use of the naturalistic method; his ability to capture Mexican settings, customs, and social problems; his rich, sophisticated writing style; and his honest presentation of an erotic theme. *Santa* is the life story—from birth to autopsy—of Santa, a woman who begins life as a beautiful working-class teenager who falls in love with a handsome soldier, gets pregnant, has a miscarriage, is rejected by her family, and, seeing no other alternative, is forced to move into a luxurious brothel in Mexico City. Santa's life as a prostitute is a slow spiritual and physical deterioration that inevitably leads to her death by cancer. Although Gamboa describes the crude reality of Santa's life in unexpurgated detail, he does not blame her for her plight, and the reader sympathizes with Santa and several other characters in the novel. Gamboa's restrained naturalism creates a uniquely Mexican blending of crude detail and sympathetic characterization.

The Novel of the Mexican Revolution

With the fall of the Díaz regime in 1910, the Mexican Revolution produced military leaders, such as Francisco "Pancho" Villa in the north and Emiliano Zapata in the south, and eventually brought about social reforms and the constitution of 1917. This colorful and violent period also produced new art and literature. Diego Rivera, José Clemente Orozco, and David Álfaro Siqueiros painted world-famous murals. Mariano Azuela (1873–1952), Martín Luis Guzmán (1887–1976), Rafael F. Muñoz (1899–1972), Nellie Campobello (1912–), Gregorio López y Fuentes (1897–1966), and Mauricio Magdaleno (1906–84) created what is now known as the "Novel of the Revolution." Many of these novels manifest the following distinctive narrative elements: 1) they are based on personal, eyewitness experiences of the revolution; 2) their structure is episodic, consisting of a series of powerful vignettes; 3) many times their protagonist is collective (sometimes it is the revolution itself); and 4) they contain vivid, concise language, a language full of stark, raw colors and violence.

Like most novelists of the revolution, Mariano Azuela was an eyewitness to many of the events that he describes in his writings. As a small-town doctor in Jalisco, Azuela was a *maderista;* that is, he supported idealistic Francisco I. Madero, the moderate liberal who ousted Porfirio Díaz from power in 1911. After Madero's assassination at the hands of right-wing general Victoriano Huerta in 1913, Azuela, like many Mexican intellectuals, sided with the forces of the revolution. Azuela became a *villista*, accompanying Villa's armies until they were defeated by a rival revolutionary leader, Álvaro Obregón, in 1915. In the same year, Azuela took refuge in El Paso, Texas, where he published what has become the most famous novel of the revolution, *Los de abajo* (1916; *The Underdogs*).

Certainly one of the best Mexican novels of all time, *The Underdogs* in many ways is a step forward in the novel's development in Mexico. It is perhaps the first Latin American novel whose structure complements its theme. Carefully divided into three parts (of 21, 14, and 7 chapters), the novel takes the shape of a *bola* (ball); in Mexico, an uprising is also called a *bola*. The novel begins in 1913 with a group of *campesinos* led by Demetrio Macías defeating federal troops in the Cañón de Juchipila, and it ends in the same place in 1915 with the defeat of Demetrio's men by rival revolutionaries. For Azuela the revolution had been betrayed. Well before 1915 it had become an opportunity merely for violence and self-aggrandizement. *The Underdogs* expresses in its structure the meaninglessness of the revolution by characterizing it as a *bola*, a swirling maelstrom of events that only lead back to their point of origin: violence.

The Underdogs is also innovative in its style and characterization. Linguistically the novel is a treasure trove of colloquial Mexican Spanish. With an exceptional economy of language and plot, Azuela utilizes precise, cinematic prose to describe how Macías' men daringly stand up to the *federales* but get so caught up in the looting and violence of the *bola* that, by the end of the novel, they no longer know why they are fighting. In addition to its strengths in style and action, *The Underdogs* is also full of complex character studies. Macías, for instance, is a hero who leads his men bravely and who fights for a just cause, at least at first. He evolves, however, into a man obsessed with fighting, a man who abandons his wife and son and loses himself in the violence. According to Carlos Fuentes, *The Underdogs* introduced ambiguous characterization to the Latin American novel. Fuentes (1969) captures the originality of *The Underdogs*: "Heroes can be villains, and villains can be heroes. . . . In the literature of the Mexican Revolution there is this narrative seed: heroic assuredness can turn into critical ambiguity, natural fatality into contradictory action, and romantic idealism into ironic dialectic." Azuela portrays many of the characters of the novel with great care and complexity.

Surprisingly, *The Underdogs* was a novel lost in obscurity for nine years after its initial appearance in 1915. First published serially in the literary pages of the newspaper *El Paso del Norte*, the novel remained unheralded until 1924, when Professor Francisco Monterde discovered it and, in the context of a literary debate in Mexico City, presented it as proof that Mexican writers were producing works of great dramatic strength, with themes that could not be called decadent. After the discovery of *The Underdogs*, Azuela became Mexico's foremost novelist and would remain so until his death in 1952. Today the novel is still a bestseller. Azuela wrote other novels before and after *The Underdogs*, several of very high quality, but none achieved the same recognition. *Las moscas* (1917; *The Flies*) is a bitter portrait of Villa's army and the hangers-on (*moscas*, flies) who squeeze every advantage from being *villista* but join the other side if the opportunity presents itself. *Las tribulaciones de una familia decente* (1918; *The Trials of a Respectable Family*) is an interesting companion piece to *The Underdogs* because it shows how the revolution affected not only *campesinos* but also devastated many traditionalist, upper-class families who, like the Vásquez Prado family in the novel, must leave their provincial *hacienda* and struggle to make ends meet in Mexico City. Other than Azuela's three avant-garde novels of the 1920s and 1930s (which will be discussed in the next section of this article), his most significant work after *The Underdogs* was *Nueva burguesía* (1941; *The New Bourgeoisie*), in which he details the rise of a new social class in postrevolutionary Mexico, a lower middle class composed of opportunistic revolutionaries who have abandoned their principles in order to attain power. With cinematic flashes of vividness, Azuela masterfully describes a multitude of characters, many of whom inhabit a tenement house in the Mexico City neighborhood of Nonoalco, later made famous by Luis Buñuel in his film *Los olvidados* (The Forgotten Ones).

Another writer who accompanied Villa's forces until 1915 was Martín Luis Guzmán, a prodigious journalist, great stylist of the Spanish language, and cofounder of *El Ateneo de la Juventud* (The Atheneum of Youth), an intellectual group whose members included some of the most important thinkers of Guzmán's generation: the philosophers José Vasconcelos and Antonio Caso, the historical essayist Pedro Henríquez Ureña, and the polymath Alfonso Reyes. Guzmán's most famous work about the revolution, *El águila y la serpiente* (1928; *The Eagle and the Serpent*), is, like Azuela's *The Underdogs,* based on personal experiences, but Guzmán's work is not a novel in the traditional sense. Blending biography, autobiography, and novelistic dialogue, description, and narration, Guzmán creates a text that is a series of powerful, tightly constructed vignettes that provide a richly ambiguous portrait of Villa and a careful, honest vision of the revolution, both its glorious heroism and the shameful violence of its arbitrary justice.

After Guzmán encounters Villa for the first time in a dark hovel in Ciudad Juárez, he compares him to a jaguar, a barbarous animal in need of taming. Villa is completely unpredictable, at one moment merciful, the next ruthless. At one moment, Villa listens to Guzmán and rescinds his order to execute 160 prisoners who had surrendered to him. At another moment, he allows one of his lieutenants to execute 300 rival revolutionaries by means of a cruel game of target practice. Guzmán admires Villa's boldness and charisma, but he is eventually disillusioned by his uncontrollable barbarism.

One year later, Guzmán published another work based on his own experiences, *La sombra del caudillo* (1929; The Tyrant's Shadow), a novel that explores the dangerous world of postrevolutionary Mexico during the 1920s. A roman à clef from a period of Mexican politics when former generals shifted allegiances daily in order to position themselves better and protect their interests, *La sombra del caudillo* is a suspenseful spy thriller, political novel, and historical document. The protagonist, Ignacio Aguirre, who seeks power himself, meets his death by means of the shadowy machinations of the Caudillo, who pulls the strings behind the scenes, hidden in the darkness. Guzmán effectively utilizes the motif of shadows throughout his carefully crafted novel in his descriptions of nature, the Caudillo (who casts a great shadow over Mexican society), Ignacio (who is the shadow of the shadow, since he is the Caudillo's right-hand man), and others. This novel ranks among the best fictional accounts of the dark, political forces of Mexican politics.

Four other writers also made a significant impact on the novel of the revolution: Rafael F. Muñoz, Nellie Campobello, Gregorio López y Fuentes, and Mauricio Magdaleno. Although Muñoz's first novel, *Vámonos con Pancho Villa* (1931; Let's Go with Pancho Villa), is an action-packed, highly readable work, his second novel, *Se llevaron el cañón para Bachimba* (1941; They've Carried Off the Cannon to Bachimba), presents a much more mature vision of the revolution, looking back on the event after a number of years. Campobello's *Cartucho* (1931; *Cartucho and My Mother's Hands*) is a fascinating assemblage of vignettes narrated from the perspective of a young girl in northern Mexico during the revolution. Relying on her own childhood experiences, Campobello's child narrator describes the horrific violence of the revolution as if it were something natural and, at times, darkly amusing. The first novel written by a woman in Mexico, the work powerfully juxtaposes the protagonist's world of dolls and children's games with the childish games of revolutionary bloodshed and destruction, providing telling insights into the effects of war on children.

Two of López y Fuentes' works are excellent examples of novels of the revolution. His *Campamento* (1931; Encampment) is a telling portrait of a single night in a revolutionary encampment. López y Fuentes creates a collective protagonist consisting of the entire band of soldiers, and the incidents of a single night are emblematic of the entire revolution. One year later, López y Fuentes produced an even better novel, *Tierra* (1932; Land), in which he portrays how the *zapatista* movement of the revolution affected the *hacienda* system. The *peones* eventually join forces with Emiliano Zapata, and many are killed. Zapata himself is a character in the novel, a novel with a collective protagonist, the revolution. The novel is one of the best representations of *zapatismo*, showing the power of Zapata's mythic stature and the limited nature of the *zapatistas'* victory.

In López y Fuentes' next novel, *El indio* (1935; The Indian), the author turns from the revolution to what has become one of the most important themes in Mexican literature and Spanish-American literature as a whole, the struggles of indigenous cultures in Hispanic society. Resulting from the awakening effects of revolutionary ideas, *El indio* was the first Mexican novel to deal somewhat realistically with the injustices and separation experienced by indigenous people in Mexico. Earlier works either ignored the problem altogether or romantically idealized indigenous people, molding them into noble savages acceptable to genteel readers. The first *indigenista* novel, *El indio* provides a well-intentioned, reformist, wonderfully *costumbrista* yet simplistic view of the injustices perpetrated by the white man against indigenous people. White men look for gold with indigenous help and abuse the village's hospitality. The village fights back, and there is no justice for the Indians. Although the novel does not present complex, three-dimensional indigenous characters (none of them are referred to by individual names, producing a disturbingly anonymous group characterization), *El indio* effectively portrays the reality of the prejudices in Mexican society that result from the otherness of indigenous culture. The novel also influenced several of Mexico's subsequent writers who would develop the theme in greater depth, including Rosario Castellanos, Carlos Fuentes, and others.

An even more perceptive and influential *indigenista* novel appeared two years later with Mauricio Magdaleno's *El resplandor* (1937; Sunburst). Portraying the unjust relationships between the Otomí Indians and the white culture, the novel marks an important advance in the development of the *indigenista* theme because it individualizes indigenous characters, allowing the reader to see indigenous reality from within the culture as well as from outside it. Because of the increased complexity of its characters—indigenous, white, and *mestizo* (mixed)—Sunburst is the best Mexican novel of the 1930s.

Perhaps the most original, irreverent, and entertaining novel of the revolution is José Rubén Romero's *La vida inútil de Pito Pérez* (1938; The Useless Life of Pito Pérez), the life story of a rebellious *pícaro* who criticizes with outrageous wit the foibles of a conservative rural village. Taking place during and after the revolution, the novel may be seen as a humorous critique of the oppressive traditionalism of Mexican rural society, a traditionalism that the revolution in many ways changed very little.

The Vanguard Novel

Reacting to the upheaval and ideology of the revolution, to the technological advances of the industrialized world, and to the European avant-garde ideas in art and literature, two groups of Mexican novelists of the 1920s and 1930s began to experiment with technique and theme in their works, the *estridentistas* (the strident ones) and the *contemporáneos* (the contemporaries).

Active between 1921 and 1927, the *estridentistas*, having witnessed the violence of the revolution, expressed their abhorrence of war as well as their futuristic enthusiasm for modern technology in fragmented, hallucinatory prose full of references to electricity, speed, airplanes, cars, power, metal, skyscrapers, and cinema. In contrast to the novelists of the revolution, the *estridentistas* stressed the cosmopolitan, rather than nationalistic, nature of literature. Incorporating the ideas of Italian futurist Felippo Tommaso Marinetti, the *estridentistas* advocated the destruction of traditional syntax and celebrated technology, dynamism, and power. Two of the most notable *estridentista* novels are Arqueles Vela's *El café de nadie* (1926; Nobody's Cafe) and Xavier Icaza's *Panchito Chapopote, retablo tropical o relación de un extraordinario sucedido de la heróica Veracruz* (1928; Panchito Chapopote, Tropical Altar-Piece or Story of an Extraordinary Happening of Heroic Veracruz). Vela's novel communicates the lack of identity of its characters by blending movie characters with those of the narrative, creating a surreal environment in which real identity is never quite clear. Icaza's novel describes the chaos caused by the revolution and foreign investors by fragmenting time and space.

Unlike the *estridentistas*, the *contemporáneos* generally avoided social issues in their works. Like them, however, the *contemporáneos* fragmented time and space, used cinematic techniques, and sought to enrich Mexican literature by utilizing European literary techniques and ideas. The *contemporáneos* were especially interested in the works of André Gide and Marcel Proust, especially in the complex associations of imagery derived from the unconscious. Utilizing elaborate extended metaphors, the *contemporáneos* created novels of great technical virtuosity, such as Gilberto Owen's *Novela como nube* (1928; Novel Like a Cloud), Xavier Villaurrutia's *Dama de corazones* (1928; Queen of Hearts), and Jaime Torres Bodet's *Estrella de día* (1933; Daystar). Owen's entire novel is a highly complex, extended metaphor for the creative process, blending dream sequences and mythology. Villaurrutia's work utilizes an unreliable narrator to describe two sisters, leaving the reader to decide what is reality and what is not. In *Estrella de día*, Torres Bodet mixes film and novel in his story of a moviegoer who falls in love with the image of a movie star, skillfully interweaving cinematic and everyday reality.

These vanguard novels represent an important step forward in the history of the Mexican novel because many of the innovative techniques of these works—fragmentation, complex metaphors, unreliable narrators, dream sequences, and cinematic techniques—would be developed even further by later generations of Mexican novelists.

The Post-Vanguard Novel

Three of the most important Mexican writers of the 20th century—Agustín Yáñez (1904–80), Juan Rulfo (1918–86), and Juan José Arreola (1918–)—were born only a few years apart in the same state, Jalisco, an austere, arid, starkly beautiful region of conservative ways and repressed passions. Together with José Revueltas (1914–76), Luis Spota (1925–84), Sergio Galindo (1926–), Jorge Ibargüengoitia (1928–83), and culminating with Carlos Fuentes (1928–), these writers formed the first internationally recognized generation of Mexican novelists and brought the Mexican novel to a level of sophistication equal to any in the world.

The three novelists from Jalisco, Yáñez, Rulfo, and Arreola, gave voice to the spirit of their region in strikingly different ways, but the works of all three manifest the influence of a wide variety of vanguard techniques from all over the world. Yáñez's masterpiece, *Al filo del agua* (1947; *The Edge of the Storm*), is a haunting vision of a conservative small town in Jalisco in 1909, just before the revolution. The town is repressed by the church, the class system, prejudice, superstition, and general narrow-mindedness. The inhabitants of this hermetic village have reached the breaking point, the edge of the storm. Some long for change, others fear it, but all eventually realize that it is inevitable.

Like that town, the Mexican novel was itself at a pivotal moment in 1947. *The Edge of the Storm* represents the culmination of many of the best tendencies of the Mexican novels that precede it, incorporating *costumbrismo*, social protest, a revolutionary theme, and, most notably, an abundance of vanguard techniques. Yáñez effectively employs stream of consciousness and the blending of subjective and objective reality (as did James Joyce), time distortions such as simultaneity (as did John Dos Passos), and the expression of universal myths from a remote, repressive small-town world (as did William Faulkner). Even more importantly, *The Edge of the Storm* paved the way for the two most important Mexican novels to date, Rulfo's *Pedro Páramo* (1955) and Fuentes' *La muerte de Artemio Cruz* (1962; *The Death of Artemio Cruz*).

Rulfo wrote only one significant novel, yet this novel, *Pedro Páramo,* is one of the best Mexican novels ever written. Translated into all of the principal languages of the world, it has influenced many subsequent Hispanic authors. Nobel laureate Gabriel García Márquez, for instance, has stated that, before writing his masterpiece *Cien años de soledad* (1967; *One Hundred Years of Solitude*), he had memorized Rulfo's *Pedro Páramo* word for word. According to the Colombian writer, Rulfo's writings have influenced him the most. García Márquez,

Octavio Paz, and Fuentes have all commented on perhaps the most original aspect of Rulfo's novel: his ability to imbue the harsh realities of Mexican *caciquismo* (rule by political boss) with an aura of myth and magic that seems as real as everything else in the novel. As the reader gradually discovers that every character in the novel, including the narrator Juan Preciado, has already died, it seems entirely plausible in Rulfo's world that murmuring ghosts should inhabit the dead town of Comala. Life and death, this world and the next, past and present, and time and eternity become indistinguishable in *Pedro Páramo*. Rulfo creates in this novel an early form of what would later be called *magic realism*, a term used to describe works by García Márquez, Alejo Carpentier, and others whose writings mingle realism with unexpected, mythic, and marvelous events as if they were everyday happenings.

Having read widely among European authors, Rulfo utilizes various vanguard narrative techniques, including multiple narrators and temporal fragmentation. The novel begins with Juan Preciado, the abandoned son of the *cacique* Pedro Páramo, deciding to return to Comala in order to claim his due as Páramo's son. Preciado arrives and eventually discovers (with the reader) that everyone in town, including his father and Preciado himself, has died. The entire town has died because Páramo has punished the townspeople for having a fiesta instead of mourning the death of his true love, Susana San Juan. Whether all of the characters are dead literally or only metaphorically—both interpretations are possible—is a question that provides the text with multiple layers of meaning. *Pedro Páramo*, however, is not only one of the most innovative of all Mexican novels, but also one of the best studies of the psychology of the *cacique*. Obsessive and egomaniacal, Páramo kills an entire town simply because his own wishes regarding Susana San Juan go unfulfilled. *Pedro Páramo* belongs to a distinguished group of Latin American novels that have to do with the theme of dictatorship, including Miguel Ángel Asturias' *El Señor Presidente* (1946; *The President*), Augusto Roa Bastos' *Yo el Supremo* (1974; *I the Supreme*), and García Márquez's *El otoño del patriarca* (1975; *The Autumn of the Patriarch*).

Known more for his short stories, Arreola wrote a daring, entertaining novel, *La feria* (1963; *The Fair*). Interestingly, it can be read as a parody of fellow *jaliscense* Agustín Yáñez's *The Edge of the Storm* since it, too, deals with the guilt, sin, and boredom of a repressed small town, but it does so in a ridiculously fragmented, humorous, and satirical manner typical of Arreola. Although he generally shies away from regional or nationalistic themes, in *The Fair* Arreola captures the entire gamut of Mexican speech, from obscenities and slang, traditional proverbs and the latest jokes, to colonial proclamations.

José Revueltas, Sergio Galindo, Jorge Ibargüengoitia, and Luis Spota each contributed to the development of the Mexican novel during this period as well. A passionate Marxist who always sought to document social injustice in his writings, Revueltas skillfully utilizes interior monologue and flashback in *El luto humano* (1943; *The Stone Knife*) in order to denounce the living conditions experienced by many inhabitants of rural Mexico despite their participation in the revolution, in strikes, and other forms of social protest. Revueltas' later novel, *El apando* (1969; *Solitary Confinement*), is perhaps his best work. Borrowing many of the cinematic techniques that he had learned from his lifelong involvement in the film industry as a screenwriter for 30 films, Revueltas creates powerfully visual descriptions of the desperate lives of three prisoners incarcerated in the deplorable conditions of Mexico's famous Lecumberri Prison.

The personal styles of Galindo and Ibargüengoitia have also added much to the Mexican novelistic tradition. Galindo's *Polvos de arroz* (1958; *Rice Powder*) and his *El bordo* (1960; *The Precipice*) are not showcases of vanguard techniques but rather profoundly perceptive, tragic character studies. In contrast, the distinctive feature of Ibargüengoitia's fiction is its sardonic, biting humor, as in his *Los relámpagos de agosto* (1964; Lightning in August), in which a former revolutionary general's memoirs humorously expose his own foibles and those of the many "heroes" around him.

Although Spota never pretended to belong to the serious tradition of deeply searching, experimental novelists such as Yáñez and Revueltas, he was one of the most prolific and best-selling Mexican novelists of the 20th century, and his inflammatory novels of social injustice, such as *Casi el paraíso* (1956; *Almost Paradise*), show a sincere concern for the welfare of others and helped to popularize the theme of social protest.

Mexico's best novelist to date is, without question, Carlos Fuentes. His prolific output, structural innovation, thematic breadth, visual brilliance, and linguistic diversity and creativity make each of his novels a work of outstanding quality. His novels blend a cosmopolitan universalism with a myriad of quintessentially Mexican themes. Fuentes is Mexico's most famous novelist, and rightly so. Many of his novels have been best-sellers not only in Spanish-speaking countries but also as translations into English and other languages all over the world. His *The Death of Artemio Cruz* is widely considered to be Mexico's finest novel, and his *Terra Nostra* (1975; *Terra Nostra*) also represents a landmark innovation in Latin American fiction.

Fuentes, along with the other major Latin American writers of the same generation—Colombian Gabriel García Márquez, Peruvian Mario Vargas Llosa, Argentine Julio Cortázar, and Chilean José Donoso—has been labeled, misleadingly, as a "boom" writer. The term *boom* implies that worthwhile Latin American literature appeared suddenly, like an explosion, during the 1960s, with the translation into English of a few works by the aforementioned authors. This, of course, is far from the truth. Fuentes' works, as well as those of the other so-called boom writers, are parts of rich novelistic traditions. In Fuentes' case, it is apparent that his best works are ingenious blendings of tendencies already present in the *costumbrista* novels of the 19th century, the novels of the revolution, the vanguard experiments in literary technique, and the post-vanguard works of writers such as Yáñez, Rulfo, Arreola, Revueltas, and others.

Fuentes' first two full-length novels, *La región más transparente* (1958; *Where the Air Is Clear*) and *The Death of Artemio Cruz*, are models of technical and thematic creativity. In his first novel, Fuentes employs the fragmented, kaleidoscopic structure and camera eye of John Dos Passos' *Manhattan Transfer* (1925) and his *U.S.A.* trilogy (1930–36). Fuentes creates a collage of newspaper headlines, newsreel footage, snatches of popular song and everyday conversation, advertisements, and other media in order to portray the snobbery and pretentiousness of middle- and upper-class Mexicans during their economic boom of the 1950s. Mingling pre-Columbian and modern histories, Fuentes allows the Aztec god of war Huitzilopochtli to return to Mexico in the form of the character Ixca Cienfuegos, who attempts to

strip away the hypocrisy of the intelligentsia, the *nuevos ricos*, and the stodgy remnants of the Porfirian elite in order to get back to the origins of Mexican culture. Like Cuban author Alejo Carpentier's *Los pasos perdidos* (1953; *The Lost Steps*) and Mexican essayist and poet Octavio Paz's *El laberinto de la soledad* (1950; *The Labyrinth of Solitude*), *Where the Air Is Clear* is a search for national origins.

The Death of Artemio Cruz is a search for national as well as personal origins and identity. A beautifully structured novel, it recounts the stream-of-consciousness flashbacks of the last 12 hours of the life of Artemio Cruz. During each of these hours, Fuentes presents Artemio's life from three different narrative voices, first, second, and third person, that is, *yo* (I), *tú* (you), and *él* (he). Fuentes' interweaving of the self-exalting *yo*, the second-guessing *tú*, and the objective *él*, is a tour de force of narrative technique. Despite this structural complexity, Fuentes does not allow form to get in the way of his story. In fact, the extremely fragmented temporal and narrative structures of the novel enhance Fuentes' ability to express the protagonist's own physical deterioration and psychological disintegration.

The novel is the story of the life of a man and of a nation. Artemio's path reflects that of the nation after the revolution. Abandoning his revolutionary ideals and his only true love, Artemio pretends to be a war hero, marries well, eventually sells his country's resources to the highest foreign bidder, becomes a rich and powerful manipulator of public opinion and private politics, and in the end dies lonely and embittered after a lifetime of self-aggrandizement. In addition to presenting in microcosm many profound aspects of 20th-century Mexican history, *The Death of Artemio Cruz* is also a brilliant expression of universal themes, such as the betrayal of ideals and the elusiveness of identity and love.

Most of Fuentes' other works are equally inventive and provocative. *Aura* (1962; *Aura*) is a short novel that recounts a chilling tale in which an old woman, representing a woman similar to the empress Carlotta, seeks to seduce a young writer, similar in appearance to the emperor Maximilian, by conjuring up a much younger version of herself. With tight structure, precise diction, and vivid imagery Fuentes creates an allegorical encounter between past and present, beauty and ugliness, and reality and fantasy. *Cambio de piel* (1967; *A Change of Skin*) is one of Fuentes' most experimental novels. Its characters "change skins," that is, they seem to change into other characters throughout the novel. In this way, Fuentes allows his readers to participate in the creation of the text, forcing them to decide what the story is. Many characters are doubled in the novel, and sometimes alternate plot possibilities emerge. In *A Change of Skin* the readers must determine their own narrative paths.

One of the most important works of Latin American fiction, *Terra Nostra* breaks new ground both thematically and technically. Ranging over 2,000 years of civilization, from Tiberius' 1st-century Rome to the oppressively abstemious and orderly confines of Felipe II's 16th-century Escorial, from the Aztec myths of the New World to the apocalyptic atmosphere of the late 20th century, *Terra Nostra* is a profound exploration of the conflict between tyranny and liberty in the Hispanic soul. *Terra Nostra* is a compendium of many of the themes of Fuentes' earlier novels: the doppelgänger, the transmigration of souls; the relationship between individuals and nations, between Spain and the New World, between fate and freedom; and the importance of the indigenous past as a means of understanding the New World present.

Terra Nostra is also a compendium of innovative narrative techniques: neologisms, temporal shifts, multivocal narrative, and fictionalized history. The novel is in many ways the technical and thematic culmination of Fuentes' narrative career. Like *Where the Air Is Clear, Terra Nostra* consists of a series of juxtapositions of the indigenous past with the modern world. Like *The Death of Artemio Cruz, Terra Nostra* is an intricately organized novel constructed of many layers of meaning. Unlike *Artemio Cruz, Terra Nostra* is constructed with layers of history rather than layers of personality. As in *A Change of Skin,* the narrative voices of *Terra Nostra* "change their skin."

Terra Nostra is a totalizing novel, that is, it attempts to include all times, all places, and all narrators. It is similar in certain ways to three other important Latin American novels of the 20th century: Carpentier's *The Lost Steps,* Cortázar's *Rayuela* (1963; *Hopscotch*), and García Márquez's *One Hundred Years of Solitude.* Like these three novels, *Terra Nostra* fuses history and myth, religion and philosophy, and Old World and New World.

Women Novelists

After Nellie Campobello's novel of the revolution, *Cartucho,* the first significant novel by a Mexican woman is Magdalena Mondragón's *Yo, como pobre . . .* (1994; *Someday the Dream*), a work of social protest that re-creates with unflinching detail the dehumanizing conditions of those who work and live in Mexico City's garbage dumps. Mondragón's subsequent novel, *Más allá existe la tierra* (1947; *The Land Still Lives*), in which a schoolteacher remembers the bloody days of the Cristero uprisings (conflicts during the 1920s protesting the postrevolutionary government's anticlerical policies). This novel is even more powerful than her earlier work because it offers more psychological insight into the characters, and readers are able to sympathize more with them.

The five most important Mexican women writers of the 20th century are Rosario Castellanos (1925–74), Elena Garro (1920–), Elena Poniatowska (1933–), Luisa Josefin a Hernández (1928–), and María Luisa Mendoza (1938–). They have more than legitimized women as novelists, since their works are equal to and often surpass those of their male counterparts. Castellanos' two novels, *Balún Canán* (1957; *The Nine Guardians*) and *Oficio de tinieblas* (1962; *A Service of Darkness*), for instance, are major advances in the history of the Mexican novel in two ways. First, they represent a vast improvement on *indigenista* novels, such as López y Fuentes' *El indio* and Magdaleno's *Sunburst.* Castellanos' *neoindigenista* characters, such as Catalina Díaz Puiljlá, the *ilol* (priestess) of her second novel who leads the rebellion of her people, are complex, fully developed *chamula* with defects and strengths. Relying on her personal experiences growing up in Chiapas and later working for the National Indigenous Institute, Castellanos moves far beyond the two-dimensional, stereotypical portraits of indigenous characters found in earlier novels. Second, Castellanos' novels are the first self-consciously feminist novels in Mexican literature. Having written her master's thesis in philosophy, *Sobre la cultura femenina* (1950; *On Feminine Culture*), on the role of women in culture, and having studied and written essays about the ideas of Simone de Beauvoir, Simone Weil, and Virginia Woolf, Castellanos incorporates feminist ideas in her writings, offering a pointed critique of the role of women in rural and urban Mexico.

Elena Garro has written four novels, all of which depict, in a manner that partakes of magic realism, the persecution and exploitation of women or other marginalized characters and the circularity of time and memory. In *Los recuerdos del porvenir* (1963; *Recollections of Things to Come*), one woman, Julia, the mistress of a general during the Cristero revolt, escapes her plight by magically fleeing town with her lover. Another woman, Isabel, becomes the general's mistress, abandons her family, and in the end magically turns to stone. Like other Latin American authors, such as Carpentier and García Márquez, Garro describes magical events in a matter-of-fact manner, as if they were plausible, everyday events, thus creating magic realism. Another feature of Garro's first novel is her use of the entire town as the narrator. The novel also is a profound allegory about time and memory, since it really ends where it begins. The general has lost one woman, but another has taken her place. Isabel has turned to stone at the end, but she is the same stone who speaks to the reader at the beginning of the novel. *Recollections of Things to Come* is now considered a classic of Mexican fiction.

Garro's subsequent novels were all published during the 1980s after her departure from Mexico in 1968 following criticism from the political right and the left for her controversial role in the riots of the same year. All three works develop Garro's favorite themes: *Testimonios sobre Mariana* (1981; *Testimonies about Mariana*) presents the contradictory accounts of three different people about Mariana, who at the end is magically helped by the love of an admirer; *Reencuentro de personajes* (1982; *Reencounter of Characters*) details the memories of a sadomasochistic relationship; and *La casa junto al río* (1983; *The House by the River*) is a detective story in which the protagonist seeks the truth about her vanished relatives, dies, but magically passes on to a happier dimension.

Elena Poniatowska combines in her novels a journalistic genius for interviews and historical research with a writer's inventive imagination and concern for language. All four of her novels combine historical data and interviews with fictional dialogue and imaginative conjecture. One of Latin America's best writers, Poniatowska consistently allows the marginalized elements of Mexican society to speak for themselves, in interviews and in her novels. Like other women novelists before her, such as Campobello, Mondragón, Castellanos, and Garro, Poniatowska is a literary champion for the oppressed, critiquing class structure, power relationships, conventional gender roles, and conventional literature.

Based on actual interviews, *Hasta no verte, Jesús mío* (1969; *Until We Meet Again*) is a first-person account that allows a poor, illiterate woman to tell her story, the story of a strong, resilient, rebellious woman who witnesses the revolution and spends her adult life working in miserable jobs in Mexico City. Despite her difficulties, the protagonist does not allow herself to give in, and in this sense she is a liberated heroine, not a failure and not a victim of society, as some critics have charged. *Querido Diego, te abraza Quiela* (1978; *Dear Diego*) is an innovatively structured novel, consisting of 12 fictional letters to Diego Rivera from Quiela (Angelina Beloff, Rivera's lover in real life for ten years in Paris). By showing Quiela's extreme dependence on and admiration of Rivera, Poniatowska provides a silent yet powerful critique of such conventional gender roles. *La "Flor de*

Lis" (1988; The "Fleur de Lis") is an autobiographical Bildungsroman in which a young French girl must adapt to Mexican culture, while *Tinísima* (1992; *Tinisima*) utilizes fictional supposition as well as numerous interviews and exhaustive research about the life of Tina Modotti—model, photographer, and Communist spy—in order to express the pain of the struggles of a male-dominated woman searching for her identity.

Like Poniatowska, María Luisa Mendoza is a journalist who has written extraordinary novels based on her experiences as a writer and as a woman. Luisa Josefina Hernández is an accomplished playwright who has also written 13 novels dealing with, among other themes, women's search for identity. Mendoza's three novels focus on a variety of provocative themes, from the Tlatelolco massacre of 1968 in *Con él, con migo, con nosotros tres* (1971; With Him, with Me, with the Three of Us), to 19th-century feminine eroticism in *De ausencia* (1974; The Life of Ausencia Bautista Lumbre), to an exploration of her own identity in terms of spatial memory in *El perro de la escribana, o, Las Piedecasas* (1982; The Scribe's Dog). Mendoza's structural ingenuity, neologistic diction, and unconventional ideas place her at the forefront of Mexican novelists. Hernández's novels have not received as much critical attention as Mendoza's, partly as a result of the former's fame as a playwright. Notwithstanding, Hernández's novels are rich in thematic complexity, making bold statements about the nature of feminine sexuality, the transcendence of anger through mysticism, and issues of social justice.

Recent Innovations (1960 to the Present)

With the success of Fuentes and the other members of the so-called boom generation, other writers felt encouraged to indulge in literary experimentation. Radical innovation, linguistic ingenuity, and humor were the hallmarks of the literary movement known as La Onda (The Scene; literally, the Wavelength), led by Gustavo Sainz (1940–) and José Agustín (1944–). Rejecting seriousness and overt intellectuality, and embracing the flippant attitudes and social protest of the rock culture, Sainz and Agustín experimented without restraint. Sainz's *Gazapo* (1965; *Gazapo*) mixes dialogue with tape recordings, telephone conversations, and pop songs. Agustín's *Abolición de la propiedad* (1969; Abolition of Cleanliness) is presented partly as a film being shot and partly as a tape recording heard by a character. In *Inventando que sueño* (1968; Imagining I'm Dreaming), Agustín experiments with multiple narrative viewpoints, presenting four apparently unrelated texts, complete with musical subtitles indicating tempo.

At the other end of the experimental spectrum are Salvador Elizondo and Juan García Ponce. These writers have created intensely introspective, hyperliterary texts. Influenced by the French *nouveau roman*, Elizondo obsessively analyzes objects and the act of writing itself in his novels *Farabeuf, o la crónica de un instante* (1965; *Farabeuf, the Chronicle of an Instant*) and *El grafógrafo* (1972; The Graphman). Also a very visual novelist, García Ponce constructs a visual narrator in, for instance, *El gato* (1974; The Cat), a narrator who is more spectator or voyeur. His images often speak for themselves, and the narrator is a neutral observer.

Two other novelists of the 1960s have also influenced the most recent generation of novelists. Fernando del Paso has created multilayered, historically rich novels, such as *José Trigo* (1966), *Palinuro de México* (1977; *Palinuro of Mexico*), and *Noticias del*

Imperio (1987; News of the Empire), which are ambitious, exhaustive metahistories critiquing Mexican history and imaginatively embellishing it. Vicente Leñero has produced psychological novels that problematize narrative perspective in inventive ways. His first novel, *La voz adolorida* (1961; The Suffering Voice), is unreliably narrated by a patient to a psychiatrist. In *Los albañiles* (1964; The Bricklayers), the narrative viewpoint is questioned so much that the reader never learns the identity of the criminal. *El garabato* (1967; The Scrawl) is Leñero's most ingeniously multi-layered questioning of narrative perspective, presenting a reader's comments about a novel, also called *El garabato*, as well as the text of this novel-within-a-novel. The reader/narrator never finishes reading the novel-within-a-novel, but Leñero's work is not about finding out what happens at the end (which is ironic, since the work is a detective novel). Leñero's purpose is, rather, to explore the ambiguities of the reading/writing process.

Although it is difficult to judge the relative significance of more recent novelists, there are numerous writers of the 1970s, 1980s, and 1990s—as many women as men—who have already made a lasting impact on the history of the Mexican novel. In his *Morirás lejos* (1967; *You Will Die Far Away*), José Emilio Pacheco offers a parody of the obsessively visual techniques of the *nouveau roman*, especially the style of Alain Robbe-Grillet, having characters speculate endlessly about the identity of other characters and minutely describing visual perspectives. Humberto Guzmán has written several highly experimental texts, including *Historia fingida de la disección de un cuerpo* (1981; Made-up Story about the Dissection of a Corpse), an antinovel that lacks real subject matter and action and thereby allows Guzmán's playful language to become the protagonist of the work. Arturo Azuela, grandson of Mariano Azuela, the famous novelist of the revolution, mixes political concerns with experimentation in his first novel, *El tamaño del infierno* (1973; The Size of Hell), constructing a collective narrator who recounts the creation and destruction of Mexico. In his most important novel to date, *Manifestación de silencios* (1979; Shadows of Silence), Azuela constantly changes narrative perspective in order to describe the justifiable fear of intellectuals when participating in radical politics in Mexico. Two of the most daring novels in recent years are *El tañido de una flauta* (1972; The Sound of a Flute) and *Juegos florales* (1982; Floral Games) by Sergio Pitol, who in the first novel blends cinematic and narrative reality, imitating many film techniques in his writing, and who in the second novel creates a character who controls the story himself. Ignacio Solares weaves elements of parapsychology, religion, telepathy, dreams, and metamorphosis, writing outstanding works of fantasy, such as *Anónimo* (1979; Anonymous) and *La fórmula de la inmortalidad* (1982; The Formula of Immortality).

Recently, Mexican women writers have often pushed the limits of the novel farther, and have sold more books, than their male counterparts. María Luisa Puga has written highly original, perceptive novels, such as *Las posibilidades del odio* (1978; The Forms That Hate Can Take), in which she draws on firsthand experience in Kenya and allows African, Mexican, and European characters to voice their views about the conflicts that surround them. Ángeles Mastretta's *Arráncame la vida* (1985; *Mexican Bolero*) is a fascinating best-seller about an unconventional wife of the governor of Puebla during the 1930s and 1940s and about how this woman finds some measure of liberation despite the limitations of Mexican patriarchal society. Laura Esquivel has written *Como agua para chocolate* (1989; *Like Water for Chocolate*), which has become one of the best-selling Mexican novels of all time and which effectively utilizes magic realism to enrich an enchanting love story that takes place around the time of the revolution. One of the most impressive recent Mexican novelists is Carmen Boullosa, whose metahistorical novels, *Son vacas, somos puercos* (1991; *They're Cows, We're Pigs*) and *Duerme* (1994; *Sleep*), employ bodiless and androgynous narrators in order to challenge traditional hierarchies during the conquest and early colonial period in Spanish America.

J. PATRICK DUFFEY

See also Carlos Fuentes; Pedro Páramo

Further Reading

Brushwood, John S., *Mexico in Its Novel: A Nation's Search for Identity,* Austin: University of Texas Press, 1966

Brushwood, John S., *Genteel Barbarism: Experiments in Analysis of Nineteenth-Century Spanish-American Novels,* Lincoln: University of Nebraska Press, 1981

Brushwood, John S., *La novela mexicana, 1967–1982,* Mexico City: Grijalbo, 1985

Brushwood, John S., *Narrative Innovation and Political Change in Mexico,* New York: Peter Lang, 1989

Duncan, J. Ann, *Voices, Visions, and a New Reality: Mexican Fiction since 1970,* Pittsburgh, Pennsylvania: University of Pittsburgh Press, 1986

Faris, Wendy B., *Carlos Fuentes,* New York: Ungar, 1983

Foster, David William, editor, *Mexican Literature: A History,* Austin: University of Texas Press, 1994

Franco, Jean, *Plotting Women: Gender and Representation in Mexico,* New York: Columbia University Press, and London: Verso, 1989

Fuentes, Carlos, *La nueva novela hispanoamericana,* Mexico City: Joaquín Mortiz, 1969; 6th edition, 1980

Lafforgue, Julio, editor, *Nueva narrativa hispanoamericana,* Buenos Aires: Paidós, 1969

Langford, Walter, *The Mexican Novel Comes of Age,* Notre Dame, Indiana: University of Notre Dame Press, 1971

Menton, Seymour, *Latin America's New Historical Novel,* Austin: University of Texas Press, 1993

Navarro, Joaquina, *La novela realista mexicana,* Mexico City: Compañía General de Ediciones, 1955

Ocampo de Gómez, Aurora Maura, editor, *La crítica de la novela mexicana contemporánea: Antología,* Mexico City: Universidad Nacional Autónoma de México, 1981

Patán, Federico, *Contrapuntos,* Mexico City: Universidad Nacional Autónoma de México, 1989

Patán, Federico, *Los nuevos territorios,* Mexico City: Universidad Nacional Autónoma de México, 1992

Sefchovich, Sara, *México: País de ideas, país de novelas,* Mexico City: Grijalbo, 1987

Sommers, Joseph, *After the Storm: Landmarks of the Modern Mexican Novel,* Albuquerque: University of New Mexico Press, 1968

Spell, Jefferson Rea, *The Life and Works of José Joaquín Fernández de Lizardi,* Philadelphia: University of Pennsylvania Press, 1931

Steele, Cynthia, *Politics, Gender, and the Mexican Novel, 1968–1988: Beyond the Pyramid,* Austin: University of Texas Press, 1992

Taylor, Kathy, *The New Narrative of Mexico: Sub-Versions of History in Mexican Fiction,* Lewisburg, Pennsylvania: Bucknell University Press, and London: Associated University Presses, 1994

Trejo Fuentes, Ignacio, *Segunda voz: Ensayos sobre la novela mexicana,* Mexico City: Universidad Nacional Autónoma de México, 1987

Warner, Ralph E., *Historia de la novela mexicana en el siglo XIX,* Mexico City: Antigua Librería Robredo, 1953

Latin American Novel

Argentina

The emergence and development of the Argentine novel during the mid–19th and the 20th centuries parallel the social and political struggles of a young country in a dialectic search of its own national identity. To a greater or lesser extent, most Argentine novels, while attempting to establish a national genre tradition, simultaneously represent a highly critical testimony of the unstable and at times quite violent formation of a country under the constant tension between authoritarianism and democracy.

The Argentine novel was born within the framework of European romanticism on the one hand, brought from Paris by Esteban Echeverría in 1830, and on the other hand the highly authoritative regime of Juan Manuel de Rosas, first the governor of the province of Buenos Aires (1829–32) and then the undisputed political leader of the rest of the Confederation of Argentine Provinces (1835–52). The romantic political and literary ideals of fraternity, equality, freedom, independence, revolution, emancipation, and national liberty inspired the creed of the *Joven Argentina* (Young Argentina), originally a literary group named *Salón literario* (Literary Salon) in 1837 and then a political society founded in Buenos Aires in June 1838 by Echeverría, called *Asociación de Mayo* (May Association). Its members saw themselves as heirs to the May Revolution spirit that, from 25 May 1810 until 9 July 1816, had led to Argentina's independence from Spanish colonialism. They clamored for a democratic organization of the country and against the despotic regime of "Rosas the tyrant," so reminiscent of retrograde Hispanic traditions of absolutism. Soon, fearful for their lives, a considerable number of Young Argentina associates, along with Rosas' opponents, the *unitarios,* had to leave the country and were forced to continue their attack from exile. It was precisely a Unitarian exiled writer, José Mármol, who in 1851 began publishing as a serial in a Montevidean newspaper what is reputed to be the first Argentine novel of recognized literary value: *Amalia,* published as a book in Buenos Aires in 1855. Contrary to what its title may suggest and despite its romantic plot, the novel does not center on a female figure or on her tragic amorous relationship with Eduardo, who is finally killed by Federal militia. The novel's narrative strength comes from the historical depiction of a horrified Buenos Aires under the brutal effects of tyranny in 1840. As with other proscribed writers in Uruguay, Chile, and Bolivia, Mármol's combative intention from his exiled position is a clear denouncement of Rosas' and his Federal comrades' political abuses against the European ideals of freedom and civilization, shared by the refined Unitarian elite. *Amalia,* with its two antagonistic and irreconcilable forces of good Unitarians versus evil Federals, marks the starting point in the Argentine novel of the bipolar dynamics that characterize its development. This distinctive dialectic previously had been penned by Domingo Faustino Sarmiento, while exiled in Chile, as civilization versus barbarism in his essay *Facundo* (1845; *Facundo*), in relation to the hypothetical social and geographical opposing facets of the country.

Unitarians and Federals had been the rival forces fighting for the political unity of the Argentine Confederation since almost immediately after Argentina's independence. The Unitarians wanted a centralized constitutional nation with provinces under the leadership of civilized Buenos Aires and ruled by an enlightened elite following European liberal ideals. The Federals, led by "barbarian" hispanicized caudillos, seen as such from the Unitarian point of view, defended provincial autonomies and the right to their own constitutions. The Unitarian-Federal tension continued after Rosas' fall in 1852, apparently coming to an end with Unitarian Mitre's triumph over Federal Urquiza in 1861, which marked the defeat of provincial autonomies and the onset of a centralized nation whose definite liberal and modern identity the Generation of 1880 masterminded. This generation's national design, modeled according to mainstream European nations and the successfully democratic United States, prevailed until the first decades of the 20th century. Civilization had conquered barbarism, or so it seemed.

The hyperactive elite known as the Generation of 1880 combined prolific social, political, and writing activities, especially prose writing. The Argentine novel saw during these years considerable expansion, at least in quantitative, if not in qualitative, terms. Romanticism, while fading (although not completely), was especially present in the novels written by women, such as Juana Manuela Gorriti, Juana Manso, Eduarda Mansilla, and Rosa Guerra. Realism and naturalism were the key European influences that pervaded the novelistic production of the late 19th century until the first decades of the 20th century. With the exception of the autobiographical *Una excursión a los indios ranqueles* (1870; *A Visit to the Ranquel Indians*) by Lucio V. Mansilla and *Juvenilia* (1884; *Youth*) by Miguel Cané (both well-known novels of this period and still read with interest), the rest of the late 19th-century novelistic production is hardly read today by the general public owing to what literary critic Juan Carlos Ghiano (1956) considers tiresome descriptions and schematic characters tightly enclosed by their role as vehicles of the authors' underlying liberal theses. Indeed, the following novels, among several others,

were written by enlightened liberals for a similarly exclusive liberal audience: *Pot-pourri* (1882), *Música sentimental* (1884; Sentimental Music), *Sin rumbo* (1885; Aimless), and *En la sangre* (1887; In the Blood) by Eugenio Cambaceres; *La gran aldea* (1884; The Big Village) by Lucio Vicente López; *Inocentes o culpables* (1884; Innocent or Guilty) by Antonio Argerich; *La Bolsa* (1891; The Stock Market) by Julián Martel; *Horas de fiebre* (1891; Feverish Hours) by Segundo Villafañe; *León Zaldívar* (1888), *Quilito* (1891), *La Ginesa* (1895; The Ginesa), *Tobi* (1896), and *Promisión* (1897; Promise) by Carlos María Ocantos; *Bianchetto, la patria del trabajo* (1896; Bianchetto, the Working Nation) by Adolfo Saldías; *Irresponsable* (1889; Irresponsible) by Manuel T. Podestá; and *Libro extraño* (1895–1902; Strange Book) by Francisco A. Sicardi.

These technically rudimentary novels offer critical interest, however, because they reveal the political agenda of the Generation of 1880 (conquest of the desert, Indian defeat, European immigrants occupying the empty pampas and the newly conquered lands, social and political peace, liberal education, secularism, modernization, capitalism, and material progress). At the same time, they also reveal the growing preoccupations of an autocratic elite that ended up witnessing, with frustration or scepticism, unforeseen limitations, contradictions, and failures of their Europeanized national plan, a plan that was intended to align Argentina with the major civilized Western nations. Soon the economic and political crises of the 1890s evidenced the instability of the liberal order imposed on the country by politically antidemocratic means and signaled that Argentina was not fulfilling its optimistic destiny of grandeur. As projected, Buenos Aires was expanding socially and economically from a tranquil village to a rich city at a vertiginous speed, a transition portrayed in Lucio V. López's *La gran aldea.* However, most immigrants had not settled on the empty plains to pursue agricultural tasks as expected. They preferred mercantile activities and urban spaces, particularly the rapidly prosperous Buenos Aires. The dream of social and political peace was at odds with numerous labor strikes that claimed better working conditions, to which Sicardi alluded in his novels. There was some appreciation of the immigrants' contribution to national progress, as in Sicardi's *Libro extraño,* Saldías' *Bianchetto, la patria del trabajo,* and Ocantos' *Promisión.* However, for most of the 1880 elite, the increasingly materialistic and corrupted society, especially its dynamic middle class, was sickened by dangerous aspirations of economic and social advancement and by contagious foreigners spreading their viruses of unscrupulous monetary ambitions and anarchic ideals of working and political activism. Writers such as Cambaceres, Martel, Argerich, Villafañe, Ocantos, Sicardi, and Podestá reflected the elite's fear of losing their exclusive social and political power to shape and rule the nation. Their novels diagnosed an epidemic of social disorder in urgent need of a cure by an ideological remedy that implied a restoration of the prevailing liberal order (an essentially antidemocratic order) and a condemnation of social nonconformism and anarchism. The narrative techniques of naturalism nicely suited their medical mission. Most novels of the period offer a detailed analysis of a social malady of moral vices, unscrupulousness, materialism, and sensuality through an almost clinical account of the final decades of the 19th century.

The conflict between liberal ideals and a divergent reality, a conflict that would continue to prevail in the early 20th-century

Argentine novel, had not only an urban scenery but also a rural and provincial one, with the literary quintessence of countrymen: the gaucho. Rooted to the mainly lyrical gauchesque literature that had proliferated from the early 19th century and that had been epitomized in José Hernández's epic poem *Martín Fierro* (1872–79), novelistic gauchos and rural characters were condemned, like Fierro, to corruption and extinction by the enforcement of civilization on the countryside and provincial cities. The extremely popular serial novels, such as *Juan Moreira* by Eduardo Gutiérrez (1879), *Las divertidas aventuras del nieto de Juan Moreira* (1910; The Entertaining Adventures of the Grandson of Juan Moreira) by Roberto J. Payró, and *Los caranchos de la Florida* (1916; Birds of Prey of La Florida), and *El inglés de los güesos* (1924; The Englishman of the Bones) by Benito Lynch, are picaresque, realistic, humorous, and at times moralizing rural novels that, with the exception of Payró's, end with the protagonists' deaths. These novels present the rural struggles to adapt to higher civilization, an opposition that ultimately leads to a double failure: even as gauchos and gauchesque protagonists die or are corrupted by the pressures of civilization or civilized characters, civilization itself fails to domesticate the nonurban areas. The idealized gauchos of *Don Segundo Sombra* (1926; *Don Segundo Sombra*) by Ricardo Güiraldes presents a different and more optimistic destiny. The protagonist, the young illegitimate child Fabio Cáceres, grows up on the pampas as a strong, skilled, and virtuous countryman under the mentorship of gaucho Segundo Sombra, who disciplines his pupil by means of the rigorous ethics of the land. However, although Fabio neither dies nor is corrupted in the process, at the end he has to adapt his gaucho formation to civilized requirements, since his rich father has named him heir to his fortune and lands. He will have to learn how to read and write and behave like a gentleman, a task Fabio, reluctantly at first, finally accepts while waving good-bye to his mentor. Like Gutiérrez's, Payró's, and Lynch's antiheroic and picaresque gauchos, Güiraldes' heroic ones ultimately disappear on the horizon or abandon the nomadic lifestyle of the pampas to settle down in a civilized environment.

In its transition to the 20th century, the Argentine novel continued the realistic and naturalistic path of the previous two decades. There were prolific authors with a vast audience, such as Manuel Gálvez, with his still appreciated *La maestra normal* (1914; The Schoolmarm) and *Nacha Regules* (1919), and Hugo Wast (pseudonym of Gustavo Martínez Zuviría). Gálvez's and Wast's numerous novels continued the condemnation of urban vices and the thematic opposition of city versus countryside and provincial areas. Romanticism was also present, producing in 1905 the first best-seller of the 20th century, *Stella*, by César Duayen, pseudonym of female novelist Emma de la Barra. It is not until 1926, with Roberto Arlt, that the contemporary Argentine novel would take its place within the extraordinary development of the Latin American novel during the 20th century.

Although the early 20th-century novel did not significantly deviate from the general narrative characteristics of the previous two decades, considerable changes in the sociopolitical arena would eventually stimulate its renovation during the late 1920s. The liberal order was doomed to collapse by the immigrants' advancement and their contribution to the middle class and proletarian consolidation, a social movement that would profoundly alter the national identity engineered in 1880 and, consequently, the univocal Argentine novel as well. The immigration process,

which had started in 1869 and was especially noteworthy during the 1880s, registered impressive numbers at the beginning of the 20th century. From an almost empty country of close to 2 million inhabitants in 1869, the population of Argentina was 8 million people by 1914, 30 percent of whom were foreigners living mostly in Buenos Aires and in nearby provinces. By 1916, Buenos Aires, whose residents were 50 percent immigrants, accounted for more than 25 percent of the total Argentine population. The magnitude of these numbers was perceived as an alluvial process by the understandably fearful liberal oligarchy. Fraudulent elections were their only means to retain political power in their privileged hands. However, by 1916, in the first authentically democratic elections of the century, they were defeated by the Radical Party, which was supported by a considerable number of middle-class and proletarian voters. From then on, despite continuous antidemocratic attempts by the oligarchy and military allies to regain power between 1930 and the early 1940s, the middle and lower classes (the latter especially after 1943 and the Peronist movement) became active participants in the social, political, and cultural development of the country.

In a parallel manner, the univocal Argentine novel, with its mostly exclusive circle of high-class readers, was entering an era of popularization that would diversify its themes, structures, and points of view. The combination of immigration and liberal education had developed an increasingly large and educated middle class that would eventually transform Argentina into the most literate Latin American country. Writers such as Payró and Gálvez, who were becoming literary professionals attempting to make a living with their works, along with many new publishers, started targeting the growing middle-class market with mass publications. This process of professionalism and popularization would lead to the proliferation of important publishers (Losada, Sudamericana, Rueda, Atlántida, Kapelusz, Kraft, Peuser, etc.) and to a dynamic book industry that would reach production peaks during the mid-1940s, the 1950s, and the 1960s. Although originally translations accounted for an important percentage in the book industry, the public also showed a considerable interest in national literature, an interest strengthened by multiple film adaptations of literary works, including many novels. Argentine books became a profitable and popular merchandise whose vast audience writers had to take into account while creating their works.

In addition to the national framework previously mentioned, international historical and cultural events also promoted the development of the contemporary Argentine novel. Crucial historical events, such as World War I (1914–18), the Russian Revolution (1917), the emergence of fascism from 1922, the financial crisis of 1929, the Spanish Civil War (1936–39), and World War II (1939–45), confirmed the economic, political, scientific, ideological, and cultural wreckage of optimistic Western liberalism (in which the old conservative Argentine order was immersed), an order centered in the conviction of its own infinite progress. Albert Einstein's and other scientists' revolutionary theories in the field of physics, Sigmund Freud's psychoanalysis, Martin Heidegger's and José Ortega y Gasset's philosophical works, and other anthropological and philosophical studies also signaled the end of positivism and liberal knowledge. As a result, the novelistic genre needed to supersede the outdated realism and naturalism, just as dadaism, surrealism, and the emerging cinema were doing in the visual arts. With novelists such as John Dos

Passos, William Faulkner, Henry James, James Joyce, D.H. Lawrence, Virginia Woolf, and others, the novel renewed its narrative devices with techniques such as the stream of consciousness, discursive interpolations, temporal and spatial superpositions, simultaneity, fragmentation, and free associations. All the thematic and formal renovations practiced in European and North American contemporary novels deeply affected the Argentine novel. The translations and studies in Victoria Ocampos' prestigious cultural magazine and publishing house *Sur* served to introduce into Argentina several 20th-century foreign novelists and thinkers. Another significant repercussion, especially for Argentine novelists preoccupied with social issues, came from early 20th-century Latin American novels such as *Los de abajo* (1916; *The Underdogs*) by Mexican Mariano Azuela, *Raza de bronce* (1919; Bronze Race) by Bolivian Alcides Arguedas, *La vorágine* (1924; *The Vortex*) by Colombian José Eustasio Rivera, *Doña Bárbara* (1929; *Doña Bárbara*) by Venezuelan Rómulo Gallegos, and *Huasipungo* (1934; *The Villagers*) by Ecuadorian Jorge Icaza.

The year 1926 may be considered a turning point in the history of the Argentine novel; *El juguete rabioso* (The Rabid Toy) by Roberto Arlt, the previously mentioned *Don Segundo Sombra* by Ricardo Güiraldes, and *Zogoibi* by Enrique Larreta, were all published that year. Güiraldes' and Larreta's novels closed the rural novel cycle, which had started during the last decades of the 19th century and had culminated in *Don Segundo Sombra*. In Güiraldes' masterpiece, written in beautiful lyrical language, the undisputed high-class order, which held political, economic, and intellectual power, along with the right and obligation to educate the lower classes of peasants and gauchos, still prevailed. *El juguete rabioso*, contrastingly, along with Arlt's *Los siete locos* (1929; *The Seven Madmen*) and *Los lanzallamas* (1931; The Flamethrowers), opened up a new novelistic path presenting fictional worlds in which the conservative order trembles and is shaken by new social actors: the petit bourgeoisie and proletarians, both with a high percentage of immigrants. For the first time, Arlt's novels depicted the lower-middle-class and proletarian conflicts from within and not from the elite's perspective, without didactic or moralizing purposes and without the naturalistic opposition between normal and abnormal. Arlt's mad, unbalanced, humiliated, anguished, and tortured characters fail to make sense of their world while they prophesy difficult national times and the destruction of liberal optimism. They have doubts about themselves and about a transforming environment that is blurring the previously clear margins of good and evil. The new scenery is presented as a monstrous and chaotic city that no longer aspires to conform to the harmonious urban ideals of the Generation of 1880; rather, the city represents an oppressive bourgeois space that annihilates individuals. Arlt's unpolished language also deviated from the narrative canon of his time as consecrated by Güiraldes' preciosity and the refined modernism present in Larreta's *La gloria de Don Ramiro* (1908; *The Glory of Don Ramiro*). The combination of multiple discursive modes taken from picaresque, adventure, murder, and serial novels, along with psychological introspection, clearly differentiated Arlt's novels from the other predominantly univocal ones. Arlt demolished the traditional narrative models, allowing the emergence of the contemporary Argentine novel. The pioneer Arlt would inspire the next generations of writers despite the mostly negative criticism his novels originally provoked.

Several critical studies have indicated the profound thematic and formal renovations of the contemporary Argentine novel from Arlt during the late 1920s until today. This double renovation is inserted within a bipolar vision of its development that distinguishes, on the one hand, a committed or neorealistic tendency of social content and, on the other hand, a tendency toward formal experimentation or vanguardism. These two novelistic tendencies are rooted in the 1920s opposition between Florida and Boedo street writers. Elegant Florida street authors, most of them poets, were regarded as vanguards who attempted to renew their lyrical style in accordance with the several early 20th-century European "isms"; on the other hand, writers associated with the proletarian Boedo street, most of them narrators and followers of the early 20th-century leftist and anarchical literature, were concerned with the denunciation of social problems, especially those of the workers. Against the backdrop of the Boedo-Florida antithesis of social content versus innovative form, two main novelistic tendencies schematize, according to most critics, the evolution of the Argentine novel since the late 1920s. The first adheres to the concept that an authentic national literature closely reflects the conflictive sociopolitical reality of the country. Without disdaining the new narrative techniques, novels belonging to this group emphasize sociohistorical content presented from a highly critical perspective. The second is formed by works with very original plots (not necessarily related to the national reality) and complex formal structures. The Boedo-Florida antithesis would receive until the early 1980s different critical wordings, such as social commitment versus vanguardism, liberty versus dependency (on European and mainstream literary models), Peronists versus anti-Peronists, leftist versus bourgeoisie, popular versus refined culture, proletarians versus aestheticians, etc. However, the maturity and originality the Argentine novel would gradually acquire in the next decades, which was remarkable after the late 1950s, despite years of political and economic instability, does not exclusively proceed from a committed content or from an innovative form but rather from their dual interaction to transmit a sense of pessimism and disappointment that can be traced to the frustrating historical path of Argentina.

During the 1930s until the mid-1950s, a considerable number of novels referred to the urban crisis in Buenos Aires and to the marginalized provinces of the rest of the country. Urban novels such as *Un horizonte de cemento* (1940; A Concrete Horizon) and *Reina del Plata* (1946; Queen of the River Plate) by Bernardo Kordon, *Es difícil empezar a vivir* (1941; It's Difficult to Start Living) by Bernardo Verbitsky, and *Los robinsones* (1946; The Robinsons) by Roger Pla, constitute, like Arlt's *El juguete rabioso*, urban formation novels, or Bildungsromane. By means of their young protagonists' walking through the streets of the city while searching for themselves and reflecting on a problematic reality, they reveal the impact of the economic and sociopolitical crisis that had finally erupted during the late 1920s and early 1930s. The key interpreter of this crisis from an urban perspective was Eduardo Mallea. His extensive novelistic production includes the following: *Fiesta en noviembre* (1938; *Fiesta in November*), *La bahía de silencio* (1940; *The Bay of Silence*), *Todo verdor perecerá* (1941; *All Green Shall Perish*), *Las águilas* (1943; The Eagles), *Los enemigos del alma* (1950; The Enemies of the Soul), *La torre* (1951; The Tower), *Cháves* (1953; *Cháves*), and *Simbad* (1957), along with other novels published after the 1950s. All these novels develop Mallea's metaphysical hypothesis (also present in his essays) about the Argentine crisis as a crisis of essences, opposing the visible or superficial Argentina, generally associated with urban areas, to the invisible or essential Argentina, usually in the rural provinces. His almost always highborn characters, tormented by their deep reflections on appearance versus authenticity, clash with a corrupted urban environment of mercantilism and materialism. Mallea was highly regarded in his time, both in and outside Argentina. He exemplified elegant and well-written prose at its best, exactly as the antipode of Arlt's novels, which, although similarly agonizing, presented with an unpolished linguistic style a totally different lower-class perspective. Nowadays, however, most critics and readers have lost interest in Mallea, giving preference to Arlt's intensely innovative works, especially since his recanonization after the middle 1950s. In the line of Arlt's highly original and irreverent novels, Leopoldo Marechal published the philosophical, parodic and humorous *Adán Buenosayres* (1948), a voluminous novel that was the object of mostly negative criticism. Marechal's first novel received little attention until the mid-1960s, when it was critically appreciated and well received.

Along with the previous urban novels and their focus on the city of Buenos Aires, novels written by provincial authors (a prolific corpus that still needs more serious critical attention) also became substantial contributors to the contemporary Argentine novel. Their importance would keep increasing throughout the rest of the century. *La tierra del agua y del sol* (1926; The Land of Water and Sun) by Mateo Booz (Santa Fe), *La raza sufrida* (1929; The Suffering Race) by Carlos B. Quiroga (Catamarca), *El salar* (1930; The Salt Mine) and *El gringo* (1935; The Gringo) by Fausto Burgos (Tucumán and Mendoza), *La ciudad de barro* (1941; The Mud City) by Alejandro Santa María Conill (Mendoza), *Álamos talados* (1942; Fallen Poplars) by Abelardo Arias (Mendoza), *El río oscuro* (1943; The Dark River) by Alfredo Varela (Misiones), *Shunko* (1949) by Jorge W. Abalos (Santiago del Estero), and a variety of other titles superseded the outdated naturalism, realism, and the archetypal bucolic local-color characteristic of the previous provincial novels. They renovated their narrative devices to present a more critical and dialectic perspective of provincial dilemmas of industrialization, marginalization, or underdevelopment.

Another group of novels, numerically much smaller than the previous ones, emphasized imagination to create fictional worlds that have little or nothing at all to do with Argentine realities and dilemmas (although some critics have pointed out that this void ultimately adheres to the Argentine upper and conservative classes' denial of sociopolitical changes). The pseudoscientific and highly original *La invención de Morel* (1940; *The Invention of Morel*) and *Plan de evasión* (1945; *A Plan for Escape*) by Adolfo Bioy Casares constitute extraordinary examples of autonomous worlds whose verisimilitude does not rely on external mimesis but rather on their own narrative organization. Other novels of this type stressed multiperspectivism and inner psychological depictions, resulting in very ambiguous fictional worlds, as in *Sombras suele vestir* (1941; *Shadow Play*) and *Las ratas* (1943; *The Rats*) by José Bianco, *El muro de mármol* (1954; The Marble Wall) by Estela Canto, and *Personas en la sala* (1950; People in the Living Room), by Norah Lange. Multiperspectivism as a central narrative technique also prevails in *Rosaura a las diez* (1955; *Rosa at Ten O'Clock*), a very original murder novel by Marco Denevi.

The year 1955 constituted a second turning point in the historical and novelistic evolution of Argentina, for it marked the overthrow of President Juan Domingo Perón by a military coup and the resumption of an alternating series of military regimes and semidemocratic governments that would continue until 1983. General Perón had entered the political arena with the military coup that deposed President Ramón S. Castillo in 1943, closing the historical period of 1930–43, known as *Década infame* (Infamous Decade, called such owing to the fraudulent political mechanisms exercised by oligarchic neoliberals to maintain their hegemony). Perón, combining his rapid escalation of political power with his remarkable popular charisma, was elected president of Argentina in 1946, the first authentically democratic president since the election of Yrigoyen in 1928. Perón's two presidencies (he was reelected in 1951) confirmed the entrance of workers as active sociopolitical participants. With the adherence of this labor sector, a loyalty promoted to a large extent by his second wife, Evita, Perón irreversibly dismantled the already shaken conservative and landowner hegemony, starting a new chapter in the political evolution of the country. However, Perón's originally democratic government evolved into an increasingly authoritative one, causing the alienation of important social sectors, such as the middle-class intelligentsia, the Catholic Church, and the armed forces, that had never accepted his populist style. Finally, in 1955, continuing a tradition that started in 1930 with Yrigoyen's overthrow, a military coup imposed another de facto regime.

After Perón's defeat, Argentina entered into its most problematic, and eventually tragic, decades. The country, polarized into two irreconcilable forces, the Peronists and the anti-Peronists, witnessed, until 1983, an uninterrupted succession of de facto regimes overthrowing semiconstitutional presidencies (Frondizi in 1962, Illia in 1966, and Onganía in 1970). The political instability of the country ignited increasing economic crises along with a social turbulence that, by the early 1970s, reached dramatic peaks of violence. The anxiously awaited return of Perón in 1973, who again won the democratic presidential elections in the same year, did not pacify the country as some had expected but rather, especially after his death in 1974, triggered more social violence, economic chaos, and, once again, a military coup that in 1976 deposed President María Estela Martínez, Perón's third wife and his successor.

Peronism generated a major cultural impact that clearly affected the consolidating middle-class intellectuals and, consequently, the evolution of the Argentine novel. Immediately after 1955, novelists, most of them adverse to Perón, felt driven to go back to the past (from Rosas' regime to the early 20th century) in order to find historical clues to explain the problematic present after Perón's presidency. This need for national understanding strengthened a novelistic tendency to represent the past as a revelatory mirror of the country's constant sociopolitical turmoil. Beatriz Guido's *Fin de fiesta* (1958; End of Fiesta) and *El incendio y las vísperas* (1964; End of a Day), and David Viñas' *Cayó sobre su rostro* (1955; It Fell upon His Face), *Los dueños de la tierra* (1958; The Landowners), *Dar la cara* (1962; Facing up), *En la semana trágica* (1966; During the Tragic Week), and *Los hombres de a caballo* (1967; The Horse Riders) offer, from different ideological standpoints, central examples of this novelistic search into Argentina's past to seek answers for the then-current national degradation (a degradation caused, in the case of

Guido, by a decadent bourgeoisie reluctant to give up its privileges and, in the case of Viñas, by the continuous exploitation of the lower classes). Ernesto Sábato's second novel, *Sobre héroes y tumbas* (1961; *On Heroes and Tombs*), constitutes an extraordinary example in this novelistic line. With a dual plot that goes back as far as the unsuccessful General Lavalle's military expedition to northwestern Argentina during the early 1840s and, simultaneously, to a bizarre and frustrating love story that takes place during the last days of Perón's presidency, the novel transmits a pessimistic image of an Argentina pervaded with decay and death. Peronism also originated a novelistic constant, present in numerous works until the 1990s, as a controversial key historical dilemma. This is apparent in late 1950s novels, such as *El precio* (1957; The Price) and *Los que no mueren* (1959; The Ones Who Never Die) by Andrés Rivera; novels from the 1960s, such as *El banquete de Severo Arcángelo* (1965; The Banquet of Severo Arcángelo) by Leopoldo Marechal, and *La señora Ordóñez* (1968; Mrs. Ordóñez) by Marta Lynch; novels from the 1970s, such as *No habrá más penas ni olvidos* (1978; *A Funny Dirty Little War*) by Osvaldo Soriano; novels from the 1980s, such as *Cola de lagartija* (1983; *The Lizard's Tail*) by Luisa Valenzuela, and *La novela de Perón* (1985; *The Peron Novel*) by Tomás Eloy Martínez, among many other examples.

Along with the previous novels inspired by the Perón phenomenon, the early 1960s registered a strong impulse to the development of the self-reflexive or metanarrative novel, preoccupied with the narrative process itself. The pervading influence was European structuralism, and Julio Cortázar was the experimental role model. His well known and influential *Rayuela* (1963; *Hopscotch*) presents a highly fragmentary structure that resembles a puzzle to be rearranged by the reader according to multiple reading options suggested by the author. The resulting nonlinear plot represents a multiple narrative kit, proposed by the author but ultimately subject to readers' creative reorganization. Cortázar's structural conception of the novel as a narrator-reader construction, deconstruction, and reconstruction, along with his inquisitive reflections on the narrative role of language present in *Hopscotch*, greatly influenced a considerable number of 1960s and early 1970s novelists, such as Néstor Sánchez, Eduardo Gudiño Kieffer, and Héctor Libertella. Cortázar's *Hopscotch*, however, reputed to be the experimental antinovel paradigm, does not merely pose a metanarrative dilemma but a cultural Argentine one as well: it interrelates the self-reflexive discourse with the parallel fragmentary narration about the upper-middle-class protagonist's futile attempts to make sense of himself—divided between Paris and Buenos Aires—and of his generation.

After the early 1960s the Argentine novel, led by the paradigmatic *Hopscotch*, registered until the early 1970s an increasing process of domestic expansion and internationalization that rapidly transformed it into one of the richest and most original of contemporary Latin American novels. During these years, mass media promoted a closer relationship than had ever been acquired between Argentine authors and their readers, through television appearances, popular magazine interviews and reviews, book signings, many literary prizes, and cinema adaptations of their works, all of which reinforced the interest of the already large Argentine audience. The publishing industry reached another peak by the mid-1960s, aggressively distributing low-priced books, not only in traditional bookstores but also in supermarkets, subways, bus stops, and through street ven-

dors. Simultaneously, starting with widely renowned Cortázar and poet and short story writer Jorge Luis Borges, Argentine writers gradually attained international recognition, not only becoming domestic literary role models, but also affecting European, North American, and especially Latin American writers as well. With respect to the latter, it was a matter of reciprocal interchange, because the impact of Latin American novelists, such as the Mexican Juan Rulfo, the Paraguayan Augusto Roa Bastos, the Colombian Gabriel García Márquez, the Mexican Carlos Fuentes, the Peruvian Mario Vargas Llosa, the Chilean José Donoso, and the Cubans José Lezama Lima, Guillermo Cabrera Infante, and Severo Sarduy, also nourished the Argentine novel with their prodigious narrative originality. The Argentine provinces were actively participating in this expansive novelistic movement. In addition to recognized novels such as *Zama* (1956) by Mendocinian Antonio Di Benedetto, and *Las tierras blancas* (1956; The White Lands) by Juan José Manauta (Entre Ríos), provincial authors continued providing outstanding works, including María Esther de Miguel (Entre Ríos), Héctor Tizón (Jujuy), Daniel Moyano (born in Buenos Aires, but lived in Santa Fe, Córdoba, and mainly La Rioja), and Juan José Saer (Santa Fe). Literary critic Jorge Lafforgue corroborated the relevance of the Argentine novel, devoting the entire second volume of his compilation *La nueva novela latinoamericana* (1969–72) to studies on Argentine works.

The internationally recognized prestige attained by the Argentine novel for its mastering of the most avant-garde narrative techniques did not essentially alter its characteristic feature of deep national concern. With different grades of allusive force, it kept referring to Argentine dilemmas, illusions, and disenchantments. An accomplished novelist such as Juan José Saer, to mention just one remarkable example, juxtaposed in *El limonero real* (1974; The Royal Lemon Tree) a complex structure of multiple discursive modes, cyclical tempo, and self-reflexive narration to carefully detail one day of the peasant protagonist within the framework of an invariable, marginal, and exploited lower-class society of Santa Fe. The pervading hopelessness shared by so many Argentine novels of these years, only to increase after the 1970s, may well be explained by the general scepticism and the loss of faith in rationalism characteristic of the contemporary Western novel. Certainly these novelistic features were also inspired by, and they accounted for, the history of Argentina as an indecipherable enigma of national failure, as a frustrating process of disenchantment and demoralization, and as a painful cycle of destroyed hopes. Indeed, after the high expectations raised in 1916 by a promising democratic and rich country, Argentines after 1930 uninterruptedly witnessed the wreckage of all their country's myths of grandeur, the tumultuous debilitation of democracy, the increasing toughness of authoritarian military regimes, and the escalation of social violence and economic hyperinflation. Argentines also attested to the failure of their most cherished political leaders, especially Perón and Frondizi, to reorganize the country. On top of it all, Argentines would endure during the following years the harshest armed forces dictatorship of the century (1976–83), the infamous Proceso de Reorganización Nacional (National Reorganization Process), which, paradoxically, concluded with a social, economic, and culturally dismantled country.

The flourishing panorama of the Argentine novel, starting during the late 1950s and intensively developing during the 1960s until the early 1970s, could hardly cope with the economic and political instability of the country. After 1973 and systematically from 1976, harsh, even deadly censorship was imposed on writers, readers, literary professionals, and publishers. At the same time, ubiquitous state manipulation of all mass media and educational curricula, hyperinflation, and economic chaos badly damaged the domestic expansion of the book industry. The Argentine novel, of course, received a profound impact as reflected in the dispersion of its authors and in certain prevailing thematic and narrative strategies. Many established novelists and promising new ones, such as Humberto Constantini, Antonio Di Benedetto, Mempo Giardinelli, Juan Carlos Martini, Daniel Moyano, Manuel Puig, Juan José Saer, Osvaldo Soriano, Héctor Tizón, Marta Traba, Luisa Valenzuela, and David Viñas, left the country during the 1970s and dispersed in diverse Latin American, North American, and European locations. Consequently, a considerable number of novels were produced and published outside Argentina. Most of the novelists who remained in the country also experienced an internal exile under the pressures of censorship and the creative limitations imposed on their works. Nevertheless, novelists, both outside and inside the country, continued writing despite the adverse conditions of publishing and reaching the public, which was also constrained by censorship and the ideological military monopoly, along with severe economic conditions. The novels of these years proliferated and diversified the themes of violence and resistance, as in Puig's *El beso de la mujer araña* (1976; *Kiss of the Spider Woman*), Giardinelli's *Qué solos se quedan los muertos* (1985; How Lonely the Dead Ones Stay), Enrique Medina's *El Duke* (1976; *The Duke*), Constantini's *De dioses, hombrecitos y policías* (1979; *The Gods, the Little Guys, and the Police*), Saer's *Nadie Nada Nunca* (1980; *Nobody Nothing Never*), Martini's *La vida entera* (1981; The Entire Life), Moyano's *El vuelo del tigre* (1981; *The Flight of the Tiger*), and Soriano's *Cuarteles de invierno* (1982; *Winter Quarters*). Exile and writing in exile were also recurring themes, as in Moyano's *Libro de navíos y borrascas* (1983; Book of Ships and Tempests), Martini's *Composición de lugar* (1984; Spatial Composition), Tizón's *La casa y el viento* (1984; The House and the Wind), and Rodolfo Rabanal's *El pasajero* (1984; The Passenger).

The novelistic tendency of historical reconstruction to reflect present dilemmas was significantly reinforced during these years. Going back as far as the times of the New World discovery all the way to Peronism and post-Peronism, the following novels, all of them widely diverse in terms of themes, narrative strategies, and ideological perspectives, share a backward-forward historical impulse that ultimately refers to burning national queries: Tizón's *Sota de espadas caballo de bastos* (1975; Jack of Spades, Horse of Clubs), Viñas' *Cuerpo a cuerpo* (1979; Hand to Hand), Puig's *Pubis angelical* (1979; *Pubis Angelical*), Martha Mercader's *Juanamanuela mucha mujer* (1980; Juanamanuela a Lot of a Woman), Saer's *El entenado* (1983; *The Witness*), Abel Posse's *Los perros del paraíso* (1983; *The Dogs of Paradise*), Andrés Rivera's *En esta dulce tierra* (1984; In This Sweet Land), and Constantini's *La larga noche de Francisco Sanctis* (1984; *The Long Night of Francisco Sanctis*), and others. Another conspicuous novelistic feature promoted by muting censorship and authoritarianism, especially evident in novels written by women, was the use of oblique and ironic narrative devices (ellipsis, allegories, metaphorical figures, and parodies) to indirectly refer to violence, repression, patriarchal authoritarianism, horrid denat-

uralizations, and subversive mechanisms of resistance and survival. Some examples, besides several of the novels previously mentioned, are Luisa Valenzuela's *Como en la guerra* (1977; *He Who Searches*), Marta Traba's *Conversación al sur* (1981; *Mothers and Shadows*), and Sylvia Molloy's *En breve cárcel* (1981; *Certificate of Absence*).

The previous novels attempted, directly or indirectly, to boycott authoritarianism and the official order imposed by the military regime, according to which even the slightest deviation from that order was a national danger that should be exterminated. Their narrative strategies stressed marginality and its effectiveness to challenge the official order. *Respiración artificial* (1980; *Artificial Respiration*) by Ricardo Piglia is an excellent example of the vindication of marginality, in this case the power of language itself to set a multiplicity of alternative unofficial stories/histories against an official one. The very first sentence of the novel, which intertwines fictitious characters who search for past relatives with historical ones (such as Rosas, Perón, and, allegorically, the armed forces of *El Proceso*), poses a question that became the paradigmatic literary dilemma of the period, when for many intellectuals notions such as an Argentine nation and Argentine history were vague concepts or a simple matter of fiction: "¿Hay una historia?" (Is there one story/history?) If on the literary plane this question puts the existence of *a* (fictional) story to the test, setting up a narrative query that the rest of the novel addresses with a multiplicity of stories about the same characters, it simultaneously challenges the legitimacy of *a* (national) history, since, being also a linguistic construct, it is consequently condemned to multiple representations of the same inapprehensible past realities, too richly multifaceted to be constrained under one official vision or dogmatic organization.

The final key political event of the 20th century, the reinstallation of democracy in 1983, has indicated an optimistic precursory sign of institutional stability, so far confirmed by the uninterrupted succession of democratic presidencies: Radical Raúl Alfonsín (1983–88), Peronist Carlos Ménem (1989–94), and again Ménem, reelected in 1995. The publishing industry is once more flourishing, not only in Buenos Aires but also, to a lesser extent, in the provinces as well. Although new books do not represent low-priced merchandise, and the economy, albeit relatively stable, leaves most consumers with little disposable income, big bookstores are sufficiently frequented by interested customers. No major thematic changes are noticeable at the turn of the 20th century in the Argentine novel, except a decrease in the themes of violence. Argentina's present and past, directly alluded to or through oblique narrative devices, still nourish numerous and diverse novels, such as César Aira's *La liebre* (1991; The Hare), Marcos Aguinis' *La gesta del marrano* (1991; The Hog's Heroic Deed), Abelardo Castillo's *Crónica de un iniciado* (1991; The Chronicle of an Initiated One), Giardinelli's *El santo oficio de la memoria* (1991; The Holy Office of Memory), Tomás Eloy Martínez's *La mano del amo* (1991; The Lord's Hand), Belgrano Rawson's *Fuegia* (1991), and Andrés Rivera's *El amigo de Baudelaire* (1991; Baudelaire's Friend). No significant formal innovations are noticeable either, although a preference for nonverisimilar and adventurous plots seems to have emerged.

The transition to democracy has been observed by intellectuals with uncertainty and scepticism, but it has also awakened an optimistic faith in the country's prospects, at least in some novelists who had previously emphasized themes of violence. Osvaldo So-riano's *Una sombra ya pronto serás* (1990; *Shadows*) presents a good example of this rather peculiar faith, given the historical an-tecedents of Argentina. The ramshackle and desolated scenery, a sort of never-ending labyrinth cyclically traveled by disoriented characters along roads that lead to the middle of nowhere, direct-ly refers to Argentina's facing democracy in 1983 after the last military regime. Everything indicates irreversible decay, and the protagonist concludes his misadventures in front of the same mo-tionless train that he had previously abandoned. The destroyed machine, a metaphorical reference to Argentina, still lacks pas-sengers and a conductor. Nevertheless, the protagonist, who has observed a green light and a departure sign, is firmly convinced that the train will soon start running again. So he sits down to await the imminent takeoff.

Very likely, the future Argentine novel will bear witness to whether the country fulfills the expectations awakened in 1983 as a harbinger to a stable democracy.

MARINA GUNTSCHE

See also Julio Cortázar; Manuel Puig

Further Reading

Arrieta, Rafael Alberto, *Historia de la literatura Argentina,* 6 vols., Buenos Aires: Peuser, 1960 (see volumes 2, 3, and 4)

Avellaneda, Andrés, *El habla de la ideología: Modos de réplica literaria en la Argentina contemporánea,* Buenos Aires: Sudamericana, 1983

Balderston, Daniel, David William Foster, et al., *Ficción y política: La narrativa argentina durante el proceso militar,* Buenos Aires: Alianza, and Minneapolis: Institute for the Study of Ideologies and Literature, University of Minnesota, 1987

Borello, Rodolfo A., *El Peronismo (1943–55) en la narrativa argentina,* Ottawa: Dovehouse, 1991

Foster, David William, *Currents in the Contemporary Argentine Novel: Arlt, Mallea, Sabato, and Cortázar,* Columbia: University of Missouri Press, 1975

Foster, David William, *The Argentine Generation of 1880: Ideology and Cultural Texts,* Columbia: University of Missouri Press, 1990

García, Germán, *La novela argentina: Un itinerario,* Buenos Aires: Sudamericana, 1952

Ghiano, Juan Carlos, *Constantes de la literatura Argentina,* Buenos Aires: Raigal, 1953

Ghiano, Juan Carlos, *Testimonio de la novela argentina,* Buenos Aires: Leviatán, 1956

Goldar, Ernesto, *El Peronismo en la literatura argentina,* Buenos Aires: Freeland, 1971

Jitrik, Noé, *El escritor argentino: Dependencia o libertad,* Buenos Aires: Del Candil, 1967

Jitrik, Noé, *Ensayos y estudios de literatura argentina,* Buenos Aires: Galerna, 1970

Kohut, Karl, and Andrea Pagni, editors, *Literatura argentina hoy: De la dictadura a la democracia,* Frankfurt am Main: Vervuert, 1989; 2nd edition, 1993

Lafforgue, Jorge, editor, *Nueva novela latinoamericana,* volume 2: *La narrativa argentina actual,* Buenos Aires: Paidós, 1969

Lichtblau, Myron I., *The Argentine Novel in the Nineteenth Century,* New York: Hispanic Institute in the United States, 1959

Matamoro, Blas, *Oligarquía y literatura,* Buenos Aires: del Sol, 1975

Onega, Gladys S., *La inmigración en la literatura argentina (1880–1910),* Buenos Aires: Centro Editor de América Latina, 1982

Orgambide, Pedro, and Roberto Yahni, *Enciclopedia de la literatura argentina,* Buenos Aires: Sudamericana, 1970

Portantiero, Juan Carlos, *Realismo y realidad en la narrativa argentina,* Buenos Aires: Procyón, 1961

Prieto, Adolfo, *Literatura y subdesarrollo,* Rosario: Biblioteca, 1968

Romero, José Luis, *El desarrollo de las ideas en la sociedad argentina del siglo XX,* Mexico City and Buenos Aires: Fondo de Cultura Económica, 1965

Spiller, Roland, editor, *La novela argentina de los años 80,* Frankfurt am Main: Vervuert, 1991; 2nd edition, 1993

Viñas, David, *Literatura argentina y realidad política: De Sarmiento a Cortázar,* Buenos Aires: Siglo XX, 1971

Zanetti, Susana, editor, *Historia de la literatura argentina,* 5 vols., Buenos Aires: Centro Editor de América Latina, 1980–86

Latin American Novel

Peru

The late, and initially slow, development of the novel as a genre in Spanish America has been a matter of much debate among lit-erary critics and historians alike. As late as 1953, the Peruvian critic and author Luis Alberto Sánchez would lament: "America, a novel without novelists." The commonly accepted reasons for this phenomenon range from the 1532 and 1543 edicts by the Spanish Crown prohibiting the writing and publishing of works of fiction in the colonies, or even their importation, to the lack of an educated public with the buying power to acquire and read books for pleasure. With the advent of independence from Spain, the Mexican José Fernández de Lizardi's *El Periquillo Sarniento* (1816; *The Itching Parrot*), generally considered the first novel in Spanish America, served as a guideline for future attempts throughout the continent to reactivate the models established by Miguel de Cervantes, Francesco Gómez de Quevedo, and the picaresque novel.

There is now a consensus that the Peruvian novel had its first expression in the works of Pablo de Olavide. Forgotten until 1969, when Estuardo Núñez discovered six of his novels in libraries in the United States, Olavide was a Peruvian who, like his predecessor Garcilaso de la Vega Inca, had moved to Spain at an early age and lived most of his life in the Spain of Charles III. A liberal exiled by the Inquisition and known as a repentant revolutionary, he was a representative figure of the Enlightenment. He wrote mostly on philosophical and political matters, following the pattern of the French novels at the end of the 18th century. His best-known work is *El evangelio en triunfo, o, Historia de un filósofo desengañado* (1797; The Gospel Triumphant, or, The Story of a Disillusioned Philosopher). Olavide's emphasis is didactic rather than aesthetic. True to the canon of his time, he discarded realism and viewed art as the means to denounce the vices of urban societies, which tend to corrupt man's natural goodness. A friend and an avid reader of Jean-Jacques Rousseau, Voltaire, and Denis Diderot, Olavide can be considered the first Peruvian romantic and, as such, the creator of the Peruvian novel, which was essentially romantic during the following century.

The continuous development of the Peruvian novel did not start, however, until Narciso Aréstegui published his *El Padre Horán* (Father Horán) in 1848. Although deficient in narrative technique, this novel marks the rupture with the preoccupation with Lima as the power and cultural center of the country and initiates a trend of political and social criticism that characterized the genre for years to come. Aréstegui targets the corrupt practices of the Church, abusive Andean landowners, and government officials, themes that prepared the ground for Clorinda Matto de Turner's *Aves sin nido* (1889; *Birds without a Nest*) and for subsequent *indigenista* fiction. Matto de Turner's work was heavily influenced by the iconoclastic—and eventually anarchic—ideology of essayist Manuel González Prada, who denounced the corruption of Peruvian institutions and leaders, in the wake of the War of the Pacific (1879–83), a catastrophic conflict that culminated in the occupation of Lima by Chilean troops and produced substantial loss of territory to Chile. For the first time in Peruvian fiction, Matto de Turner directly attacks the institutionalized oppression and exploitation of Andean Indians by the oligarchy, the military, and the Church, and he calls for massive education and the appointment of humanitarian officials as the solutions to the problem.

Generally acknowledged as the first indigenist novel, a genre that later reached its maximum expression in the works of José María Arguedas, *Birds without a Nest* shows a lack of understanding of Andean society, as it ignores the economic reality of the area and concentrates almost exclusively on its political structure. Matto de Turner's portrayal of the Andean people is external and stereotypical, and, in spite of the author's apparent sympathy, the Indians are shown as individuals to be pitied and are dispossessed of any vestiges of cultural or ethnic identity. Although technically flawed and limited in its understanding of Andean culture, *Birds without a Nest* is the first significant effort to bring to light the appalling condition of the Indian in Peru. It was up to a later generation of writers who steered away from romantic sentimentalism and modernist cosmopolitanism to

place the plight of the Indian in its proper economic and cultural context. Born in the political and ideological turmoil of the second decade of the 20th century, this current was to be called indigenism, and its literary expression, exemplified in the works of Enrique López Albújar, Ciro Alegría, and Arguedas, had a lasting effect on Peruvian fiction.

The political and intellectual upheaval of the 1920s, marked by the Russian and Mexican revolutions, provided fertile ground for the emergence of left-wing political movements such as Victor Raúl Haya de la Torre's Apra. It was, however, José Carlos Mariátegui, founder of the Socialist Party of Peru, who in his *Siete ensayos de interpretación de la realidad peruana* (1928; *Seven Interpretive Essays of Peruvian Reality*) laid out his vision for the emancipation of Indian communities from the endemic oppression of feudalism. The very same year, two dissimilar works appeared that marked the coming of age of Peru's modern novel: *Matalaché* by Enrique López Albújar and *La casa de cartón* (*The Cardboard House*) by Martín Adán. Set in the latter part of the colonial period, *Matalaché* is an historical novel denouncing the institution of slavery. Expressed in deterministic terms, it is essentially romantic and traditional in content and form, somewhat of an anachronism in light of prevalent avant-garde innovations already in use. López Albújar deliberately uses a traditional narrative form in order to question the concept of modernity in Peru by reexamining its past. By analyzing the tensions in a colonial society in its struggle for independence, the novel is an indictment against the failure of independence in social and human terms.

Adán's *The Cardboard House,* on the other hand, is clearly avant-garde, with no discernible narrative and consisting of a series of disconnected vignettes that evoke the author's adolescence in the fashionable coastal city of Barranco, south of Lima. The novel shows the clear influence of Marcel Proust and James Joyce, and, as such, it is a forerunner of the process of renovation and experimentation of the new narrative fiction in the 1950s and 1960s. In the meantime, however, Peruvian fiction maintained its traditional realist mold, of the kind popularized by López Albújar. Social protest was the mainstay of contemporary fiction, where the harsh conditions of the poor, rural and urban, became the dominant theme of a number of authors who found an avid audience in a small, although literate, middle class.

The political upheavals of the first two decades of the 20th century in Latin America, and particularly in Peru, gave rise to indigenism, an intense campaign on behalf of indigenous populations that sought to vindicate native culture as well as to improve the social lot of the Andean Indian. An intellectual and social movement, indigenism succeeded in producing important fictional works, as well as influential nonfiction. The former, however, were limited to a crude realism denouncing the oppression of the Indian, primarily portrayed as the victim of institutionalized injustice, in contrast to the idealized and exotic image of the "noble savage" projected by European romanticism. Authors such as Luis E. Valcárcel in *Tempestad en los Andes* (1927; Tempest in the Andes), César Falcón in *El pueblo sin Dios* (1923; A Town without God), and César Vallejo in *El tungsteno* (1931; *Tungsten*) all write about the economic exploitation of the Indian, denouncing the dominant society that kept them in servitude and bondage. Considerably more radical than *Birds without a Nest,* these novels still characterize the Indian in a superficial and stereotypical way in order to suit the authors' ideological intentions. Indigenism, it must be noted, is a literary genre in which neither the author nor the reader belongs to the ethnic group portrayed in the novel. This feature of indigenism was at the heart of the controversy surrounding the fiction about the Indian. The literary expression of indigenism attempted to fulfill a direct social purpose by promoting a general awareness of the plight of oppressed members of the population, to vindicate their social and economic interests, and to integrate them into a national community. As Dick Gerdes (1992) has noted, during this initial phase of indigenism, stronger communicative ties were forged between the indigenous world and the rest of the country. Although Mariátegui scorned the idea of the existence of a true indigenist literature unless the Indians themselves wrote it, his Marxist ideology contributed to providing a better understanding of the problems facing the indigenous groups in Peru.

The year 1941 marks a watershed in Peruvian narrative fiction with the publication of Ciro Alegría's *El mundo es ancho y ajeno* (*Broad and Alien Is the World*) and José María Arguedas' *Yawar fiesta* (*Yawar Fiesta*), novels in which literary indigenism comes of age. Both novels are protests against the destruction of Indian societies by a white feudal civilization, but they are also a vindication of Indian culture as a way of life that has survived for centuries after the Spanish Conquest. Alegría's novel succeeds in raising the reader's conscience to the plight of the Indian but tends to paint a negative image of the Indian's ability to rebel against oppression, leaving the impression that there is no solution to the problem. A work comparable in scope to its European models of the past century, *Broad and Alien Is the World,* the first novel to represent the clash of cultures in Peru, ranks as the country's first fictional classic. Following in the steps of Alegría, Arguedas, an anthropologist as well as a writer, continued to work toward perfecting the true representation of the Indian and creating a special literary language that would reflect the oral qualities of Quechua, the native language of the Andes. With the publication of *Los ríos profundos* (*Deep Rivers*) in 1958, Arguedas initiated a new stage of development in indigenist fiction now known as neo-indigenism. Neo-indigenism goes beyond the limited purpose of indigenism as exemplified by Alegría's novels, that is, the depiction of general themes such as Western civilization against indigenous cultures. It proposes an internal vision of indigenous values with the purpose of legitimizing and preserving their intrinsic features. More important, neo-indigenism considers autochthonous cultures and values as qualitatively equal alternatives to their European counterparts. Whereas indigenistic literature was informed by the confrontation of the Indian with a white landowning dominant class, Andean neo-indigenistic fiction has as its distinguishing mark the examination of cultural perspectives that go to the root of the clash of cultures among the many segments of Peruvian society.

By the middle of the 20th century, Peruvian fiction began a process of modernization at the hands of a new generation of writers who, although still devoted to denouncing the socio-economic breakdown of the country, adopted more sophisticated narrative techniques, borrowed from their North American and European counterparts, and a more professional attitude toward their work. Essentially urban, this new fiction documented the effects of the social changes taking place as the result of massive migrations from impoverished rural Andean regions to the coastal cities, especially to Lima. The profound ethnic implications of this demographic phenomenon stimulated the emergence of new cultural expressions, reflecting the marginality of a large segment of the country's population, an alienation that manifested itself not only in social values and mores but in every aspect of creative activity. Writers such as Julio Ramón Ribeyro in *Los geniecillos dominicales* (1965; The Sunday Rascals), Enrique Congrains Martín in *No una, sino muchas muertes* (1957; Not One, but Many Deaths), and Oswaldo Reynoso in *En octubre no hay milagros* (1965; There Are No Miracles in October) produced a notable body of novels that have as their central theme the debunking of the myth of Lima as the ideal place for social and economic upward mobility. Set in the 1950s, these novels examine a decadent middle class in the process of losing its ties with vanishing past social privileges and the emergence of a new economic class represented by agro-industrial exporters supported by the military dictatorship of Manuel Odría, a general who took power in 1948. Racial discrimination, unjust economic conditions, political violence, cultural disintegration, and personal alienation are among the topics that permeate the fiction that informs this decade. Parallel to this group of urban writers, another group, represented by Julián Huanay, Eleodoro Vargas Vicuña, and Carlos E. Zavaleta, continued to develop themes related to Andean social and cultural conflicts. Armed with the latest narrative strategies and techniques, these writers went beyond Arguedas' attempts to vindicate Indian culture: they now dealt with the endemic problems arising from the economic disparity between the city and the countryside, and from the threat of impinging economic forces that would eventually displace Indians from their rural environment. Novels such as Huanay's *El retoño* (1950; The Young Branch) and Zavaleta's *Los Ingar* (1955; The Ingars) are fine examples of a period that saw the modernization of Peruvian fiction without abandoning the traditional themes of social protest and the denunciation of corrupt and abusive political practices.

The process of literary renovation initiated in the 1950s culminated in the publication of *La ciudad y los perros* (1963; *The Time of the Hero*) by Mario Vargas Llosa, a novel that received immediate international recognition and that paved the way for the author's meteoric career. One of the pillars of the so-called *boom* of Latin American fiction, Vargas Llosa now ranks with Julio Cortázar, Gabriel García Márquez, and Carlos Fuentes as one of the leading novelists in the continent. Educated in Europe, where he began his literary career, he abandoned conventional approaches to the writing of fiction and questioned the assumptions on which traditional realism had rested. His vision of the world is not one of order or stability but of haunting complexity, a vision that is manifested in his novels by the fragmentation of conventional time and space, the superposition of dialogues, interior monologues, and stream of consciousness, and the use of intermediaries that create a distancing effect from the narrative. Vargas Llosa has produced a substantial body of work that includes such acclaimed novels as *La casa verde* (1966; *The Green House*), *Conversación en La Catedral* (1969; *Conversation in The Cathedral*), *Pantaleón y las visitadoras* (1973; *Captain Pantoja and the Special Service*), and *La guerra del fin del mundo* (1981; *The War of the End of the World*). These novels and more recent ones, such as *Historia de Mayta* (1984; *The Real Life of Alejandro Mayta*), *El hablador* (1987; *The Storyteller*), and his latest, *Los cuadernos de don Rigoberto*

(1997; *The Notebooks of Don Rigoberto*), are the product of Vargas Llosa's life-long rebellion against convention, and of his systematic exposure of Peru's corrupt moral social values bred in a history of militarism, violence, machismo, racial prejudice, ignorance, religious and political fanaticism, and disregard for the most basic human rights.

Although Vargas Llosa has dominated the literary scene in Peru since the 1970s, another author who was to achieve wide international success was Manuel Scorza. A well-known poet, Scorza wrote a cycle of five novels—*Redoble por Rancas* (1970; *Drums for Rancas*); *Historia de Garabombo, el invisible* (1972; *Garabombo the Invisible*); *Cantar de Agapito Robles* (1977; The Song of Agapito Robles); *El jinete insomne* (1978; *The Sleepless Rider*); *La tumba del relámpago* (1979; The Tomb of the Lightning Bolt)—that, because of their themes, ideology and literary language, may be considered as belonging to the neo-indigenist movement. The novels, which are social realist in character but enriched with a heavy dose of magic realism and Andean folklore and mythology, record the historic events surrounding the struggles of Indian communities in the central Andes to defend their ancestral lands.

Peruvian narrative of the last two decades of the 20th century has developed around different tendencies than those that informed the fiction of the 1960s and 1970s. Perhaps the most representative writer of this time is Alfredo Bryce Echenique. Born into an aristocratic family in Lima, Bryce Echenique gained international fame with his masterpiece *Un mundo para Julius* (1970; *A World for Julius*), a novel that dissects Peru's decadent oligarchy. A recent poll among the top literary critics in the country ranked *A World for Julius* as the best and most important novel in Peru's history. Although contemporary with Vargas Llosa, Bryce Echenique was not considered part of the boom, as he did not indulge in the experimentation with form that marked that period. Moreover, his works were at first dismissed as frivolous and inconsequential because of their light tone, intimate subjective themes, and an apparently apolitical stance, at a time when many Latin American writers wholeheartedly embraced the Cuban Revolution. Bryce Echenique's distinguishing narrative mark is his oral tone, a trait that creates an intimate perspective, which, coupled with a rich sense of humor, gives his work a warm sense of familiarity shared by the reader.

With the end of 12 years of military dictatorship in 1980, Peru embarked on a long and dangerous road toward democratization, a process marred by a wave of violence, economic debacle, and the virtual collapse of its social and political institutions. In spite of such fertile ground for moral indignation, recent Peruvian fiction has not attempted to offer ideological solutions or to reexamine the historical roots of the country's problems. Instead, as Dick Gerdes (1992) has noted, it poses more questions than provides answers to the social ills that afflict Peru. Gerdes has identified four general tendencies in the development of Peruvian narrative during the last two decades of the 20th century, categories that are by no means exclusive. The first, and perhaps the most notable, is an intimist perspective that centers on the development of individual characters and focuses on feelings of negativity and scepticism rather than on the examination of the social and historical contexts leading to alienation and disconformity. The recent works of Bryce Echenique (*Reo de nocturnidad* [1997; Prisoner of Night]), Abelardo Sánchez León (*La soledad del nadador* [1996; The Solitude of the Swimmer]), Carmen Ollé (*Las dos caras del deseo* [1994; The Two Faces of Desire]), Alonso Cueto (*Deseo de noche* [1993; Desire at Night]), and Fernando Ampuero (*Caramelo verde* [1992; Green Candy]) are all representative of this phase. A second group of novels, such as *The War of the End of the World* by Vargas Llosa, *Cuando la gloria agoniza* (1989; When Glory Goes into Agony) by José Antonio Bravo, and *No preguntes quién ha muerto* (1986; Ask Not Who Has Died) by Marcos Yauri Montero, are reconstructions of history through the incorporation of official documents and oral narratives that reinterpret past events in the light of present-day ideologies. A third perspective is the crude and direct representation of Peruvian reality in an attempt to capture urban and rural poverty and the alienation of the individual in an unforgiving society. This is accomplished by capturing in an epic, and often carnivalesque, mode the daily struggles of the lower classes. In a style first found in Ribeyro's novels such as *Los geniecillos dominicales* and *Cambio de guardia* (1976; Change of the Guard), Cronwell Jara's *Montacerdos* (1981; Pigriders) and *Patíbulo para un caballo* (1989; Firing Squad for a Horse) depict the moral and ethical deterioration of individual and collective social order. Lastly, the neo-indigenist movement that Arguedas had initiated has evolved into a highly lyrical form of narrative that portrays a positive view of *mestizaje*, the fusion of native American and European cultures and bloods. Perhaps the most representative of this group is *País de Jauja* (1993; Country of Jauja) by Edgardo Rivera Martínez, a novel that is considered one of the most important in Peruvian fiction of all times. Falling outside of these four categories are important works that deserve special attention, such as Laura Riesco's *Ximena de dos caminos* (1994; Ximena at the Crossroads), a novel that provides a new feminine view of Peru's complex and conflictive society, and *La violencia del tiempo* (1992; The Violence of Time) by Miguel Gutiérrez, a novel in the Bildungsroman tradition that is a critical examination of *mestizaje* and its effect on Peruvian history and social development.

The study of the history of the Peruvian novel must reflect on a phenomenon that has tended to hinder rather than to promote its development: the abysmal state of the country's publishing industry. The huge editorial and commercial success of the boom in Spanish American fiction created the false impression that most writers were enjoying this bonanza. However, only a handful of them—Vargas Llosa, Bryce Echenique, Scorza—got most of the attention. The great majority of Peruvian writers, including such prominent figures as Ribeyro, met with great difficulty in having their works published; when it did happen, they were published in very limited editions of questionable quality. Symptomatic of the socio-economic problems of the country, the publishing industry languished under heavy taxation and lack of credit, raw materials, and professional expertise. This state of affairs resulted in expensive books that only a limited public could afford. It was only at the end of the 20th century that new publishing houses, skillfully managed by dedicated and professional editors, began producing an increasing number of books of excellent quality and working with a new generation of writers who, more aware of international trends, are now experimenting with modern narrative techniques.

ISMAEL P. MÁRQUEZ

See also Mario Vargas Llosa

Further Reading

Bendezú Aibar, Edmundo, *La novela peruana: De Olavide a Bryce*, Lima: Lumen, 1992

Castro Arenas, Mario, *La novela peruana y la evolución social*, Lima: Cultura y Libertad, 1964; 2nd edition, Lima: Godard, 1966

Cornejo Polar, Antonio, *La novela peruana: Siete estudios*, Lima: Horizonte, 1977

Delgado, Washington, *Historia de la literatura republicana: Nuevo carácter de la literatura en el Perú independiente*, Lima: Rikchay, 1980; 2nd edition, 1984

Foster, David William, *Peruvian Literature: A Bibliography of Secondary Sources*, Westport, Connecticut: Greenwood Press, 1981

Gerdes, Dick, "Peru," in *Handbook of Latin American Literature*, edited by David William Foster, New York: Garland, 1987; 2nd edition, 1992

Gutiérrez, Miguel, *La generación del 50: Un mundo dividido*, Lima: Labrusa, 1988

Gutiérrez, Miguel, *Celebración de la novela*, Lima: PEISA, 1996

Higgins, James, *A History of Peruvian Literature*, London and Wolfeboro, New Hampshire: Cairns, 1987

Márquez, Ismael P., *La retórica de la violencia en tres novelas peruanas*, New York: Peter Lang, 1994

Rama, Angel, *La novela en América Latina: Panoramas 1920–1980*, Bogotá: Procultura, 1982

Latin American Novel

Colombia

Although the novel in Colombia was a relatively weak literary form until the 20th century, in the latter half of the century the Colombian novel has been at the forefront of innovation in Latin America. Nobel laureate Gabriel García Márquez has been the central and leading figure of the modern novel in Colombia, and a major writer who has been influential throughout Latin America and the rest of the world. Indeed, his novel *Cien años de soledad* (1967; *One Hundred Years of Solitude*) is widely recognized as one of the seminal works of the Spanish language in the 20th century. In the entire history of the Colombian novel, the three works to receive broad recognition outside of Colombia have been *María* (1867; *Maria, a South American Romance*) by Jorge Isaacs, *La vorágine* (1924; *The Vortex*) by José Eustasio Rivera, and *One Hundred Years of Solitude*.

From the 16th to the 18th centuries, under Spanish rule, the novel was prohibited in the territory currently called Colombia. Nevertheless, narratives were written in this region of New Granada (as it was then called). The most prominent of these narrative works was *El carnero* (The Ram), completed in 1638 by Juan Rodríguez Freyle. *El carnero* is a historical chronicle of life in Bogotá during the 16th and 17th centuries. A picaresque chronicle, it is a synthesis of war news, changes of government, customs, psychological portraits, adventure, scandal, crime, historical fact, and legends.

From the period of independence (early 19th century) to the 1930s, Colombian novels are best understood in the context of the four regional cultures that produced them. The Interior Highland region of Bogotá and the surrounding area has been the historical center of literary culture in Colombia; the most recognized novel from that region was Rivera's *The Vortex*. In the region of Greater Antioquia, the major writer of the century was Tomás Carrasquilla, who published his work in the latter part of the 19th and the early part of the 20th centuries. The region of Greater Cauca, in western Colombia, was the setting of one of Latin America's major Romantic classics, Isaacs' *María*. The northern Caribbean region of the Costa has been the setting for a rich and vital oral culture and is the homeland of Gabriel García Márquez.

The culture of the Highland region has been directly linked historically to the literary traditions of Spain. In the 19th century, highly productive novelists, such as Soledad Acosta de Samper and José María Samper, looked to European models in order to write patently imitative fiction without appreciable aesthetic merit. Author of more than a dozen novels, Clotilde de Samper produced a series of romantic and realist works. She is particularly known in Colombia for her novels *Una holandesa en América* (1888; A Dutch Woman in America) and *Los piratas en Cartagena* (1886; The Pirates in Cartagena). Critical of the new middle class in Bogotá and its values, she never seriously questioned, however, the values of the ruling class to which she belonged. Her husband, José María Samper, in fact, was a leader of the Liberal Party in Colombia. The major turn-of-the-century novelists in the Interior Highland region were José María Vargas Vila, Clímaco Soto Borda, and the poet-novelist José Asunción Silva. Following in the Colombian tradition of the poet-novelist, Rivera published *The Vortex* after having already established an identity in Colombia as a poet. *The Vortex* was the author's homage to literary culture more than to its ostensible theme—a critique of the exploitation of rubber workers in the jungles of Colombia.

Unlike the Highland culture, with a predominant Spanish heritage and its venerable Hispanic literary tradition, the Caribbean culture of the northern coast of Colombia is tri-ethnic in heritage and represents a popular and oral culture. While the Highland has been conservative, closed, and unreceptive to change, the Caribbean coast, with its port cities, has been more receptive to outside influences and innovation. In this region, oral culture has coexisted with writing culture, the former located primarily in the small towns and rural areas and the latter in the cities.

Since the publication of Juan José Nieto's novel *Ingermina* in 1844, the literature of the Caribbean coast has been part of both the writing and the established oral traditions of that region. The novelists Gabriel García Márquez, Álvaro Cepeda Samudio, and Héctor Rojas Herazo are all located within the writing culture, although all three employ some oral effects. García Márquez is a special case for a modern novelist, for he participates fully in both the oral and the writing cultures of the Caribbean region. The major novels of this region, in addition to García Márquez's *One Hundred Years of Solitude,* are Nieto's *Ingermina,* José Félix Fuenmayor's *Cosme* (1927), and two well-constructed Faulknerian novels published in 1962: Álvaro Cepeda Samudio's *La casa grande* (*La casa grande*) and Héctor Rojas Herazo's *Respirando el verano* (Breathing the Summer).

Literary culture began to take form in Antioquia during the 1860s and 1870s. In addition to the publication of popular verse during these decades, Antioquia's first printing presses for literature began operation in 1868. The most important prose writer of the 19th century to precede Carrasquilla was Emiro Kastos (pseudonym for Juan de Dios Restrepo, 1823–94), author of numerous articles of customs.

The first major Antioquian novelist, Tomás Carrasquilla typifies the middle-class Antioquian writer who did not belong to the elite that had formerly dominated Colombian literature, an aristocracy based primarily in the Highland region. Carrasquilla produced realist-regionalist fiction in considerable volume between 1896 and 1935. During the 1890s he began publishing short stories; his three renowned novels were *Frutos de mi tierra* (1896; Fruit of My Land), *Grandeza* (1910; Grandeur), and *La Marquesa de Yolombó* (1928; The Marquis of Yolombó). *Frutos de mi tierra,* which concerns an Antioquian family in late 19th-century Medellín, is one of the most outstanding Colombian novels of the realist tradition. In contrast with the cosmopolitan tastes of turn-of-the-century *modernistas* (mostly elite writers in Bogotá), Carrasquilla defended a realist-naturalist type of fiction that carefully located characters in their regional environment. *Grandeza* depends primarily on quaint character types, although it has a more intricate structure than most of the work of the period. In *La Marquesa de Yolombó,* a historical novel set in the late 18th and early 19th centuries, Carrasquilla creates the impression of oral storytelling by using a loose and casual tone.

One of the Antioquian novel's most salient characteristics is its penchant for nostalgia. From the region's early works by Tomás Carrasquilla to the modern work of Manuel Mejía Vallejo and others, nostalgia permeates Antioquian fiction. The culture of this region has been willfully independent of the remainder of Colombia and quite often in direct opposition to it. Three major elements explain Antioquian culture and its fiction. The first is Antioquia's egalitarian tradition. This tendency has fomented a literature based on popular tradition, regional custom, and oral storytelling rather than on the elitist models of writing culture that were important to the Interior Highland. The second major element was the presence of a strong primary oral culture in rural areas in the 19th century. This oral culture influenced written culture in several ways, including the oral residue and oral effects connnected with the late 19th-century writing of Car-

rasquilla. The third major element is a pervasive reaction during the 20th century against modernity. A nostalgia for a lost oral culture is a manifestation of this reaction.

The Greater Cauca, centered in the Valle del Cauca but including Popayán to the south and Chocó to the north, has developed a tradition of cultural heterogeneity. The northern area of this region, geographically and culturally isolated and sparsely populated, has been a stronghold of oral and African traditions with relatively little production of written culture. Nevertheless, the African-Colombian novelist Arnoldo Palacios is from Chocó. The indigenous and black African populations of the Greater Cauca have lived with the Hispanic inhabitants since the 16th century. The Greater Cauca is renowned for the memory of its slave estates in the 18th and 19th centuries; the genteel life of the estate owner was evoked, in different ways, in the 19th-century novels *María* by Isaacs and *El alférez real* (1886; The Royalty) by Eustaquio Palacios. Compared to countries such as Peru and Ecuador, Colombia has never produced a flourishing movement of indigenous fiction. Nevertheless, a few novelists from the Greater Cauca, notably Diego Castrillón Arboleda, have attempted to fictionalize the Indian situation.

The heterogeneous Greater Cauca offers strong writing and oral traditions. Writing culture produced its most prominent literary monuments in the works of the novelist Jorge Isaacs and Eustaquio Palacios and of the poets Guillermo Valencia (1873–1943) and Rafael Maya (1897–1983). The oral tradition here does not have a representative such as García Márquez. Modern writers such as Arnoldo Palacios and Gustavo Álvarez Gardeazábal, more distant from orality than García Márquez and Carrasquilla but less elitist than Isaacs and Estaquio Palacios, do show some traces of the Greater Cauca's residual orality of the 20th century in their fiction.

The rise of the modern novel in Colombia in the mid-1950s and early 1960s was signaled by the publication of García Márquez's *La hojarasca* (*Leaf Storm*) in 1955, followed by Cepeda Samudio's *La casa grande* and Rojas Herazo's *Respirando el verano.* By the mid-1960s it had become increasingly problematic to read the Colombian novel within a strictly regional or national context. Modern and postmodern novelists in Colombia were fully immersed in the writing of international fiction, not attempting to address traditional, regional, and oral cultures, with the exception of García Márquez and David Sánchez Juliao, novelists whose early lives had been directly touched by the oral culture of the Caribbean coast. By the 1960s influences as diverse as television and the irreverent Nadaísta poets were affecting the still predominently conservative and conventional cultural establishment in Colombia. With the increased production of novels in the 1970s and 1980s and a growing readership, the Colombian novel has become more heterogeneous than ever before.

In the broadest terms, it is possible to identify both an essentially modern novelistic tradition and another fundamentally postmodern tendency since the mid-1960s. The modern novel has been cultivated in Colombia by García Márquez, Cepeda Samudio, Rojas Herazo, Fanny Buitrago, Manuel Zapata Olivella, and Manuel Mejía Vallejo. A more innovative and experimental postmodern fiction, best understood within a context of literary theory and other literary forms, has been developed by R.H. Moreno-Durán, Albalucía Angel, Darío Jaramillo Agudelo, and Alberto Duque López.

Since the publication of *One Hundred Years of Solitude* in 1967, a pinnacle of the modern novel in Colombia and Latin America, García Márquez has published several other books of fiction, including *El otoño del patriarca* (1975; *The Autumn of the Patriarch*), *Crónica de una muerte anunciada* (1981; *Chronicle of a Death Foretold*), *El amor en los tiempos del cólera* (1985; *Love in the Time of Cholera*), *El general en su laberinto* (1989; *The General in His Labyrinth*), *Del amor y otros demonios* (1994; *Of Love and Other Demons*), and *Noticia de un secuestro* (1996; *News of a Kidnapping*)—the latter a work of journalism. In his three novels prior to *One Hundred Years of Solitude*—*Leaf Storm, El coronel no tiene quien le escriba* (1957; *No One Writes to the Colonel*), and *La mala hora* (1962; *In Evil Hour*)—García Márquez began the construction of the fictional world of Macondo, using many of the technical lessons he had learned from William Faulkner. The Faulknerian overtones in *Leaf Storm* are abundant, from its language to its structure: it is clearly modeled after *As I Lay Dying* (1930), with three main narrators who alternate in telling the story, which is preceded by a brief section rich in both historical and mythical overtones, told by an omniscient narrator. *One Hundred Years of Solitude* is the story of a family and the complete story of Macondo. In telling these two stories, García Márquez also relates much of the cultural and political history of both Colombia and Latin America in general. Much of the orality of this novel is comparable to the folktale tradition of the tall tale in the United States. What has often been identified by the term *magic realism* in this novel is more precisely described as a written expression of the shift from orality to various stages of literacy. The effects of the interplay between oral and writing culture are multiple. García Márquez has fictionalized numerous aspects of his youth in the tri-ethnic oral culture of the rural Caribbean coast of Colombia. The unique traditionalism and modernity of this novel are based on the various roles the narrator assumes as oral storyteller in the fashion of the tall tale, as narrator with an illiterate person's mindset, and as the modern narrator of a self-conscious (written) fiction.

In many ways, García Márquez's *The Autumn of the Patriarch, Chronicle of a Death Foretold,* and *Love in the Time of Cholera* represent a rupture from the fiction of Macondo. *The Autumn of the Patriarch* is located in an unidentified region of the Caribbean, and its subject is a dictator. Conceiving this work in an international rather than a regional or national context, García Márquez published this dictator novel in conjunction with an international series of novels of this type. *The Autumn of the Patriarch* functions as a literary synthesis of numerous Latin American historical dictators, above all Juan Vicente Gómez of Venezuela. *The Autumn of the Patriarch* is quite complex in its structure; *Chronicle of a Death Foretold* and *Love in the Time of Cholera* are far less demanding. *Chronicle of a Death Foretold* is comparable in some respects to the detective novel. In this case, the reader knows the outcome from the first line and continues reading, with interests similar to those aroused in the detective novel—to see a death consummated. *Love in the Time of Cholera* is a story of love and aging, set in a society as hierarchical and static as in all of García Márquez's novels. It tells of Florentino Ariza's wait of more than 50 years for his beloved Fermina Daza, to whom he declares his love at the funeral of her husband, Dr. Juvenal Urbino.

Fanny Buitrago, Manuel Zapata Olivella, Héctor Rojas Hera-zo, and Manuel Mejía Vallejo also have assimilated the strategems of modern fiction. Buitrago's several novels have evolved from the complex strategies of high modernism to a more recent use of popular culture. Zapata Olivella has published six novels, several of which represent his efforts to rewrite Afro-Colombian history from the colonial period to modern times. Rojas Herazo has used narrative strategies of a Faulknerian modernity in his trilogy of novels published from the early 1960s to the mid-1980s. Most of the novels of Mejía Vallejo have been written in the tradition of Tomás Carrasquilla, and his complete output is a major contribution to the modern novel in Colombia. He has published *El día señalado* (1964; The Appointed Day), *Aire de tango* (1965; Air of Tango), and over a dozen other novels.

García Márquez's accomplishments with his modern fiction project, his international critical acclaim, and his 1982 Nobel prize for literature gained unprecedented visibility in Colombia in the 1980s and 1990s. On the other hand, R.H. Moreno-Durán's postmodern gesture, his public image as the writer's writer, and his hermetic fictional exercises gained him the attention of a smaller group of readers, writers, and critics interested in innovative fiction. Solipsistic experiments do not usually become best-sellers, either in the original version or in translation. Nevertheless, Moreno-Durán and writers such as Albalucía Ángel, Darío Jaramillo Agudelo, and Alberto Duque López have pursued an innovative, fundamentally postmodern project since the 1970s. Cosmopolitan in their interests, most of them have preferred to write abroad; Moreno-Durán and Angel have lived for most of their writing careers in Europe and have been as intellectually attuned to contemporary European writing and theory as to Colombia. Similarly, Duque López has been influenced by such diverse texts as the Argentine Julio Cortázar's *Rayuela* (1963; *Hopscotch*) and American film. The roots of most of Moreno-Durán's fiction are not found in the empirical reality of Colombia but rather, as in the case of much postmodern fiction, in modernist literature. Poems by T.S. Eliot and Paul Valéry influenced Moreno-Durán's early fiction; his early writing also has obvious connections with *Hopscotch*.

The other postmodern novelists in Colombia are generally as demanding of their readers as Moreno-Durán. Albalucía Ángel's recent fiction is part of a feminist project that emanates directly from feminist theory and fiction. Darío Jaramillo Agudelo's *La muerte de Alec* (1983; The Death of Alec) is a metafiction—in this case, a self-conscious meditation on the function of literature. His more recent *Cartas cruzadas* (1995; Crossed Letters) is a lengthy epistolary novel and a self-conscious meditation on literature and life in contemporary Bogotá.

The modern and postmodern novel published in Colombia over the past three decades is a heterogeneous, multivoiced cultural product that far surpasses the ideological and aesthetic limits previously set for the genre in Colombia. The dominant elite had never been particularly interested in the novel, but until the 1960s it had controlled most aspects of its production. The García Márquez phenomenon in the late 1960s, in addition to factors such as the rise of international Latin Americanism and the expansion of multinational publishing houses, opened the Colombian novel to a heterogeneity of voices heretofore impossible in Colombia's regional, often provincial, and always well-controlled literary scene. Given the writer's new independence and the multiple directions found in the novel by the 1980s, it was no longer necessary or even appropriate to speak of García Márquez's "shadow."

While modern and postmodern writers in Colombia may equally be described as ideological, there are some general differences in these novelists' approach to institutions. The modernists, such as García Márquez, Rojas Herazo, and Cepeda Samudio, tend to be more overtly political in that they fictionalize elements generally associated with Colombian and Latin American empirical reality. They criticize specific institutions and at times specific individuals. The postmodernists, such as Moreno-Durán, Ángel, and Duque López, create novels more mediated by theory and other texts and more specifically directed to issues of language. All conventions, including those of the traditional and modern novel, are potentially questioned by these irreverent postmodern writers.

RAYMOND LESLIE WILLIAMS

See also Gabriel García Márquez

Further Reading

Brushwood, John S., *The Spanish American Novel: A Twentieth-Century Survey,* Austin: University of Texas Press, 1975

Ciplijauskaité, Birutė, "Foreshadowing as a Technique and Theme in *One Hundred Years of Solitude,*" *Books Abroad* 47:3 (1973)

Curcio Altamar, Antonio, *Evolución de la novela en Colombia,* Bogotá: Instituto Colombiano de Cultura, 1975; originally published 1957

Duffey, Frank, *The Early Cuadro de Costumbres in Colombia,* Chapel Hill: University of North Carolina Press, 1956

González Echevarría, Roberto, *The Voice of the Masters: Writing and Authority in Modern Latin American Literature,* Austin: University of Texas Press, 1985

Levy, Kurt, *Tomás Carrasquilla,* Boston: Twayne, 1985

Lewis, Marvin, *Treading the Ebony Path: Ideology and Violence in Afro-Colombian Prose Fiction,* Columbia: University of Missouri Press, 1987

McMurray, George, *Gabriel García Márquez,* New York: Ungar, 1977

Menton, Seymour, *La novela colombiana: Planetas y satélites,* Bogotá: Plaza y Janés, 1978

Williams, Raymond Leslie, *Gabriel García Márquez,* Boston: Twayne, 1984

Williams, Raymond Leslie, *The Colombian Novel, 1844–1987,* Austin: University of Texas Press, 1991

Latin American Novel

Chile

The emergence of the novel in Chile was closely linked to independence, which culminated in the establishment of the republic in 1810, and the need to create a national canon that would be idiosyncratic with Chilean society by departing from the cultural imitation of European models. The Enlightenment had contributed to the legitimization of the genre by expanding on the Cervantine model, which was based on the principles of verisimilitude and moral utility. The "modern novel," defined as an authentic expression of society that exposed its errors, would contribute to social regeneration and to the spreading of virtues that would foster national progress. This vision of literature as a reflection of society was adopted by romanticism, which Andrés Bello and others introduced in Chile through the translation of Walter Scott's and Alexandre Dumas' texts and later through some of the most popular romantic authors in Spain, such as José Zorrilla y Moral and José Espronceda y Delgado. By 1840 economic liberalism and social stability, along with the arrival of Argentine intellectuals escaping from Juan Manuel de Rosas' tyranny, gave birth to the intellectual movement of 1842, which made contributions to law, history, philosophy, and the arts. In 1842 José Victorino Lastarria founded the Literary Society. Lastarria was the first to formulate the need to create a literary tradition that would be inspired by European models without imitating them, that would become an authentic expression of Chilean nationality by reflecting on its autochthonous and distinctive elements: climate, landscape, customs, and government.

The first literary productions were still minor, revolving around the romantic topics of unrequited love, blind fate, and outcasts, and not particularly significant to the development of the genre. It was with the adoption of realist tendencies around 1860, about two decades earlier than in the rest of Latin America, that the novel, with its breadth of thematic scope and linguistic accessibility, was adopted as the most adequate vehicle in the formulation of a national identity. (Poetry was at the time overly sentimental and imitative of European poets and accessible only to a minority.) Joaquín Blest Gana, one of the major figures of the period, declared the necessity of the novel to register the moral and material state of society and to be an instrument of social regeneration, but he also warned against an excessive imitation, an exaggerated ideological angle, or a picturesque, superficial characterization of the national reality. The *costumbrista* novel became the paradigm of how to conduct an artistic investigation of social facts. Lastarria's *Don Guillermo* (1860) and Alberto Blest Gana's *La aritmética del amor* (1860; The Arithmetic of Love) incorporate common characters rather than socially alienated romantic heroes as prototypes of certain social strata and a personal narrator that critiques society from a morally superior stance. Both signal the establishment of a realistic literary tradition rooted in a sociological approach that would characterize the Chilean novel far into the 20th century. Its highest exponent was Alberto Blest Gana's *Martín Rivas* (1862).

By 1880 the influence of Émile Zola's naturalism registered in the works of a number of authors. Vicente Grez's *El ideal de una esposa* (1887; A Wife's Ideal) is considered the first naturalist novel in Chile, in which the social environment and temperament are determining factors in characters' behavior and the narrator retains scientific objectivity. Other novels followed this naturalist-realist tradition with varying degrees of aesthetic success. As in other countries in Latin America, Chilean naturalism often echoed the social transformations taking place at the turn of the century, the clash between the creoles' old values and the new immigrants' morals, and the emergence of an enriched class as a result of the end-of-the-century economic prosperity. Still, some authors denounced naturalism for its excessive crudity and showed a preference for Benito Pérez Galdós' style. Others reacted by developing a modernist aesthetic inspired by Joris-Karl Huysmans, Maurice Barrès, Gabriele D'Annunzio, and Maurice Maeterlink that was oriented toward the intimist exploration of feelings, the subjectivization of descriptions, and themes such as the alienated artist with a noble mission and death as artistic inspiration. The Ateneo, founded in 1891, disseminated Maksim Gor'kii, Fedor Dostoevskii, and Lev Tolstoi and inspired the establishment of the short-lived Tolstoian Colony, where Maeterlink, Edgar Allan Poe, Henrik Ibsen, Stéphane Mallarmé, and others were read. Economic progress stimulated the creation of new literary magazines—*La Revista Cómica* (1895), *La Lira Chilena* (1898), *Instantáneas* (1900), and *Pluma y Lápiz* (1900)—which, in addition to inspiring the formation of a literary community and a shared artistic sensibility, gave Chilean writers access to publication.

Novels written prior to the end of World War I continued the realist-naturalist tradition but modified it by incorporating new aesthetic elements from modernism along with a more accentuated social criticism of the aristocratic, money-driven circles. Among those are Alberto Blest Gana's *Durante la Reconquista* (1897; During the Reconquest) and Luis Orrego Luco's *Un idilio nuevo* (1900; A New Romance), which alludes to the materialism and shallowness of a social milieu best reflected years later in his *Casa Grande* (1908; The Large House). Other novels did not stick so closely to the naturalist canon and incorporated romantic or modernist elements. Augusto D'Halmar's *Juana Lucero* (1902) reduces naturalist scientific objectivity by incorporating the supernatural and a subjective, sympathetic narrator. Eduardo Barrios' *El niño que enloqueció de amor* (1915; The Boy Who Died of Love) emphasizes the exploration of intimate feelings. This last novel became a landmark in the development of the genre by introducing a new treatment of point of view and characters' inner conflicts. Barrios' *Un perdido* (1918; A Lost One) incorporates the modernist poetization of psychological states and chromatic descriptions.

Some novels used realist patterns as an ideological vehicle to promote anticlerical positions, such as Joaquín Edwards Bello's *El inútil* (1910; The Useless One) and *El monstruo* (1910; The Monster). Most novels during the 19th century preferred the representation of the social upper strata. By the turn of the century, however, Chilean writers were depicting middle and working classes, if still in an inauthentic manner (Bello's *El inútil* and D'Halmar's *Juana Lucero* are examples). The first Chilean modernist novel was Francisco Contreras' *Piedad sentimental* (1911; Sentimental Piety). This novel and others give fuller depictions of the characters by exploring their inner lives and by employing a style enriched with poetic images and a new vocabulary. This writerly sensibility was a transitional stage in the genre that opened up the conditions for avant-garde experimentation in the 1920s.

Worsening social and economic conditions during the 1920s and 1930s led to a raising of working-class consciousness. Chilean writers reacted to this political turmoil with a growing awareness of their social role. During the 1920s two literary journals, *Claridad* and *Juventud*, and the Chilean Writers' Society organized a professional guild in which literary issues were discussed. The *mundonovista*, or *criollista*, novel, inserted in the realist tradition, explored the idiosyncrasy of the Chilean landscape, which was to be represented as a telluric force shaping its rites and its inhabitants' instinctive forces. Mariano Latorre's *Zurzulita* (1920) was followed by Marta Brunet's *Montaña adentro* (1923; Into the Mountain), *Bestia dañina* (1962; Evil Beast), and *María Rosa, flor del Quillén* (1927; María Rosa, the Flower of Quillén), Francisco Contreras' *El pueblo maravilloso* (1927; The Marvelous Town), and Lautaro Yankas' *Flor Lumao* (1931), among others. It was Contreras who, in his prologue to *El pueblo maravilloso*, coined the term *mundonovismo* to describe an autonomous, genuine literature that would be inspired by tradition, the land, and race, therefore embodying a people's history and collective memory. Urban spaces were also analyzed from the perspective of a growing proletarian force, as in Joaquín Edwards Bello's *El roto* (1920; The Beggar). Nevertheless, exploring the working class' existential anguish and psychological conflicts did not reach the same level of depth as that of the countryside until ten years later, with Manuel Rojas' *Lanchas en la bahía* (1932; Boats in the Bay), in which the protagonist's subjective descriptions of a proletarian background and the incorporation of avant-garde techniques signal a clear departure from conventional naturalist narration. Other novels in this vein are Carlos Sepúlveda Leyton's *Hijuna* (1934) and Juan Marín's *Paralelo 53 sur* (1936; Parallel 53 South), the latter characterized by its evolution from an objective to a subjective perception of urban reality.

In reaction to the realist-oriented principles of *mundonovismo*, the imaginist movement, which had been anticipated by the modernist subjective poetization of reality, emerged at the end of the 1920s, voicing its position through journals such as *Andamios* (1925) and *Letras* (1928). Inspired by the European avant-garde, it proposed an alternative novel that would transform reality through the writer's creativity. In these journals and *Índice*, of *criollista* orientation, literary critics carried out an intellectual debate between these two writing schools. Among the first imaginist novels are Pedro Prado's *Alsino* (1920) and Eduardo Barrios' *El hermano asno* (1922; Brother Asno). These foreshadowed Pablo Neruda's *El habitante y su esperanza* (1926; The Inhabitant and His Hope), the first avant-garde Chilean novel, an open narration with 15 sections of lyrical monologue in the present and a progressively chaotic presentation of time and space. Juan Emar's *Ayer* (1935; Yesterday) and María Luisa Bombal's two most famous novels, *La última niebla* (1935; The House of Mist) and *La amortajada* (1938; The Shrouded Woman), indicated a change in sensibility amid a *criollista* scene that would last until the second half of the century. Writers of this new sensibility employed interior monologues that diminished the importance of an exterior reality and presented narrators with limited perspectives who did not pretend to be impartial like the positivist observer, nor were they able to fully understand or explain their own experiences. These writers favored lyrical language and subjectivity over the representation of social types and called the reader to a higher level of participation in reordering temporally and spatially chaotic sequences. Eschewing the scientific, objective causality of naturalism, imaginist novels explored beyond sensorial reality into the spaces of human consciousness and the unconscious, where the real motivations for individual behavior could be found. These novels represented a departure from positivism as well, in that characters evolved through experiences rather than through predetermined patterns of environment and heritage.

This movement coincided with the increased role of the writer's social function in line with the rise to power of the left through democratic elections and the spread of social humanism on different cultural and political fronts. Novelists of the Generation of 1938 were mostly affiliated with leftist parties and organizations and viewed the literary artifact as a vehicle for the denouncement of social injustice and a voice for the proletariat's demands. Theoretical reflections on this socialist realism in the novel appeared in literary journals such as *Hoy, Multitud,* and *Aurora de Chile.* Some novels of this period were politically very explicit, although not always aesthetically successful. Among the more artistically developed and innovative works are Eugenio González's *Hombres* (1935; Men), Carlos Sepúlveda Leyton's *Camarada* (1938; Comrade), and Nicomedes Guzmán's *Los hombres obscuros* (1939; The Obscure Men), which focus on the working class' heroic struggle for social justice. From this perspective, *criollismo* was seen as a superficial approach to Chilean reality because it ignored historical and political circumstances as the source of conflict. In contrast, socialist-realist authors defined this reality according to the poor sectors in the urban environment and incorporated Marxist categories for their analysis. For the Generation of 1938, the socially and politically committed narrator saw class struggle as a main contributor to the social problems besetting Chile. These conditions made the novel less aesthetically concerned and emphasized an inflexible dichotomy, as may be seen in Reinaldo Lomboy's *Ranquil* (1942), Andrés Sabella's *Norte Grande* (1944; Big North), Fernando Alegría's *Recabarren* (1938) and *Lautaro, joven libertador de Arauco* (1943; Lautaro, Young Liberator of Arauco), and Luis Durán's *Frontera* (1949; Border). Juan Godoy's *Angurrientos* (1943) was a turning point in its depiction of characters no longer as victims of the bourgeoisie but rather as dominated by sex and alcohol and festering in moral decay; it gave birth to the movement known as *angurrientismo,* which identified the essence of Chilean culture with the strength of the proletariat's struggle. Along with this group, two other groups questioned positivist tendencies: the surrealists, led by Braulio Arenas, who maintained a clear scepticism toward any possibility of social change, and an intimist trend of women novelists whose narratives analyzed interior realities from oneiric or subjective perspectives.

From 1950 to 1960 a new generation of writers presented a third antipositivist position while *criollismo* was still in vogue. Manuel Rojas' *Hijo de ladrón* (1951; Born Guilty) rejects the conventions of the traditional novel, as did this new generation of writers who found the novelistic practices of the day too restricting. Enrique Lafourcade realized the need not only to write "new" novels but also for an active campaign to promote them. He coined the term *Generation of 50,* referring to several names and a set of categories that aligned these writers against tradition. This label afforded the group publicity among some sectors and the consciousness of belonging to a system of preferences. These writers rejected the *criollista* modes of representation because they perceived these modes to be lacking in depth. Although writers of previous generations had taken a similar stance, this group was different because its members truly shared a literary program. Seeing no link between themselves and what they saw as a fundamentally realist tradition, the Generation of 50 declared themselves intellectual "orphans." Between 1950 and 1967, a number of their works achieved degrees of success, including José Manuel Vergara's *Daniel y los leones dorados* (1956; Daniel and the Golden Lions), José Donoso's *Coronación* (1957; Coronation) and *Este domingo* (1966; This Sunday), Margarita Aguirre's *El huésped* (1958; The Guest), María Elena Gertner's *Islas en la ciudad* (1958; Islands in the City), Jaime Lazo's *El cepo* (1958; The Trap), Enrique Lafourcade's *La fiesta del rey Acab* (1959; King Acab's Party), Mercedes Valdivieso's *La brecha* (1961; Breakthrough), and Jorge Guzmán's *Job-Boj* (1967). The Generation of 50's most mature novels would be produced in the 1970s and 1980s, notably Donoso's *El obsceno pájaro de la noche* (1970; The Obscene Bird of Night), *Casa de campo* (1978; A House in the Country), *El jardín de al lado* (1981; The Garden Next Door), and *La desesperanza* (1986; Curfew), and also works by Enrique Lihn, Jorge Edwards, and Patricio Manns, among others.

This generation was characterized by an iconoclastic protest tinted by a radically pessimistic worldview. Rather than search for a transcendental or political meaning, these writers described the social vacuum stemming from the international social and political turmoil following World War II. Their novels often contain a deteriorating family environment or a narrator who projects his own hopeless vision on the surrounding world. The narrator's alienation sometimes allows him to discover social fallacies, but, even so, he never acts on his convictions because of his existential disenchantment.

By the beginning of the 1970s, two different orientations toward the novel genre began to emerge. Cristián Huneeus, Carlos Morand, Juan Agustín Palazuelos, and others supported a more academic novel, detached from human conflict. Other writers showed a more direct commitment to Chile's social and political problems, in solidarity with the leftist government established by the Unidad Popular in 1971. Among the most representative authors of this group are Poli Délano, Antonio Skármeta, Manuel Miranda, and Fernando Jerez. These writers defended a conception of the novel as a way to narrate a faith in individual and collective capacities to build a better society. These projects were interrupted by the dramatic experience of the military coup that brought General Augusto Pinochet to power in 1973. From this point, Chilean writers, many of whom had been committed to social criticism, were forced to redefine their roles as they became suspicious of the official discourse. This led to significantly reduced literary production during the first decade under the new regime. Fear of repression caused some intellectuals to leave the country; those who remained felt the effects of government-imposed or self-imposed censorship. Novel production in Chile was split among the following: those that accommodated the values of the regime and reproduced them using traditional realist modes of narration; evasive, ahistorical, mostly lyrical novels; and nonconformist novels. Among the last two, the pessimistic notes sounded by the previous generation were echoed in the representation of the arbitrary forms of dictatorial government, the search for a lost paradise now identified with a democratic past, and the isolation of the individual.

The Chilean novel during this period grew increasingly testimonial; examples include Francisco Simón's *Todos los días un circo* (1988; Every day, a Circus) and *Martes tristes* (1985; Sad Tuesdays) and Isabel Allende's well-known *La casa de los espíritus* (1982; *The House of the Spirits*), in which the process of writing became a cathartic experience. Some novels dealt with the figure of the tyrant, such as Fernando Jerez's *Un día con su Excelencia* (1986; A Day with His Excellency). Narrators became chroniclers of torture, repression, pain, and antagonizing official discourses that ignored or silenced the truth, as in Antonio Skármeta's *Soñé que la nieve ardía* (1975; *I Dreamt the Snow Was Burning*), *Ardiente paciencia* (1985; *Burning Patience*), and *Match Ball* (in Spanish, 1989), although at times the official discourses were only unmasked at the end of the story, as in Ariel Dorfman's *Viudas* (1981; *Widows*). The many forms adopted in these novels—biography, fantastic story, testimonial literature, report—converged in their attempt to understand the dimensions of an historical event that seemed incomprehensible and in showing a political commitment to ending collective suffering. The Chilean novel became very closely linked to an historical present, even while, in indirect ways, emphasizing the dichotomy between the individual and the system and the fracture of human relations as a consequence of the violence of political repression. The new protagonists included those accused or alienated by the system, such as the elderly, prostitutes, and homosexuals. Chilean writers of this period adapted the testimonial mode of writing to incorporate multiple points of view and nonrealistic forms of expression, for more oblique, ambiguous ways of expression were needed to depict a fractured and painful reality.

OLGA LÓPEZ COTÍN

See also Isabel Allende; Obscene Bird of Night

Further Reading

Alegría, Fernando, *La literatura chilena del siglo XX*, Santiago: Zig-Zag, 1962; 3rd edition, 1970

Castillo, Homero, *El criollismo en la novelística chilena*, Mexico City: Ediciones de Andrea, 1962

Goic, Cedomil, *La novela chilena: Los mitos degradados*, Santiago: Universitaria, 1968

Guerra-Cunningham, Lucía, "Panorama Crítico de la novela chilena (1843–1949)," Ph.D. diss., University of Kansas, 1974

Guerra-Cunningham, Lucía, *Texto e ideología en la narrativa chilena*, Minneapolis, Minnesota: Prisma Institute, 1987

Jofré, Manuel Alcides, *La novela chilena, 1974–1984*, Santiago: CENECA, 1985

Promis Ojeda, José, *La novela chilena del último siglo*, Santiago: La Noria, 1993

Promis Ojeda, José, editor, *Testimonios y documentos de la literatura chilena (1842–1975)*, Santiago: Nascimento, 1977

Silva Castro, Raúl, *Panorama de la novela chilena, 1843–1953*, Mexico City: Fondo de Cultura Economica, 1955

Silva Castro, Raúl, *Historia crítica de la novela chilena, 1843–1956*, Madrid: Cultura Hispánica, 1960

Torres-Ríoseco, Arturo, *Breve historia de la literatura chilena*, Mexico City: Ediciones de Andrea, 1956

Urbistondo, Vicente, *El naturalismo en la novela chilena*, Santiago: Andrés Bello, 1966

Zamudio Zamora, José, *La novela histórica en Chile*, Santiago: Flor Nacional, 1949

Latin American Novel

Brazil

Teresa Margarida da Silva e Orta is generally regarded as Brazil's first novelist, despite the fact that she left her homeland at an early age for Portugal, where she wrote *Aventures de Diófanes* (1752), a didactic work inspired by Fénelon's *Télémaque* (1699). The Portuguese and French influence is important not only to Silva e Orta but also to Brazilian literature in general. From its "discovery" in 1500 until its independence in 1822, Brazil was a colony of Portugal, and its intellectual life was affected by developments in France, which had long been a cultural touchstone for the Portuguese. France became increasingly central to Brazil's cultural life after 1808, when the Portuguese royal family fled to Rio de Janeiro to avoid the Napoleonic invasion. French philosophy, literature, and the arts were especially influential in Brazil following its independence, and they remained so throughout the 19th and 20th centuries.

Thus, Antônio Gonçalves Teixeira e Sousa, who was writing in Rio in the 1830s and 1840s, and whose *O filho do pescador* (1843; Fisherman's Son) was perhaps the first novel to appear in Brazil, was strongly indebted to the French feuilletons, which circulated widely in translation in the capital city. The feuilleton, with its melodrama and spectacular adventures, was the favorite reading material of the semiliterate and nascent petit bourgeois. Although not nearly as popular, the narrative works of Portuguese romantics Alexandre Herculano and Almeida Garrett were other important sources for the emerging novel in Brazil. Garrett and Herculano were attractive models to those writing in the newly independent nation: both fought in Portugal's civil war (1832–34) on behalf of a constitutional monarchy and both wrote highly successful fiction about the nation's glorious past. Somewhat like the feuilleton, their novels and plays were often melodramatic and sentimental—attributes found in abundance in the romantic novels of Joaquim Manuel de Macedo. Macedo's *A moreninha* (1844; The Little Brunette), a story about young love, was an immediate success with readers because of its commentaries on domestic and social life in Rio. Writing at the same time as Macedo, although drawn less to emerging middle-class types than to the poor and working classes, was Manuel Antônio de Almeida, author of *Memórias de um sargento de milícias* (1853; Memoirs of a Militia Sergeant). Set in Rio at the beginning of the century, this novel is a witty picaresque adventure whose central protagonist, Leonardo, is reminiscent of the famous Spanish *pícaro*, Larzarillo de Tormes. In addition to following the exploits of Leonardo, whose adventures include a love affair, confrontations with the police, and a brief imprisonment, the book compellingly portrays the popular customs and language of different social types in a bygone era in Rio.

By mid–19th century, Brazil had passed through a series of boom and bust cycles that have come to characterize the country's roller-coaster economy. In the 18th century, diamonds and gold were discovered in Minas Gerais; revenues from these industries were invested in other areas of the economy, such as agriculture and livestock, as well as the slave trade, which, although officially curtailed in 1850, continued to function quietly and internally until 1888, when Brazil finally abolished slavery. Slaves were a vital labor source for the working of not only gold and diamond mines but also plantations that grew products such as coffee, cacao, cotton, and sugar. Brazilians from around the country and thousands of immigrants from Europe flocked to Amazonas and Pará, which were the major centers of the rubber industry.

Brazil's most important novelist of the period was José de Alencar, who wrote historical novels as well as novels about the urban middle class and the remote countryside. His most popular books were romantic tales about what is nowadays called the "cultural encounter" between indigenous and colonizing peoples. Inspired by authors such as François René de Chateaubriand, Alexandre Dumas, and Victor Hugo, whom he read in his youth, Alencar wrote *O guarani* (1857; The Guarani), a love story about a handsome Indian warrior and a pretty European woman, and *Iracema: Lenda do Ceará* (1865; *Iracema, The Honey-Lips, a Legend of Brazil*), whose central characters, a "honey-lipped" Indian maiden and the first Portuguese explorer, beget the first Brazilian. *Iracema* (the title is an anagram for *America*) was a popular and critical success, having won the praise of distinguished writers such as Joaquim Maria Machado de Assis. Alencar's urban novel *Senhora* (1875; *Senhora*) is a subtle critique of the emerging capitalist enterprise in middle-class Rio; focusing on the ritual of the prearranged marriage and the dowry, the novel describes the tradition in terms of buying and selling prospective spouses. Alencar was also a precursor of the regional novelists in Brazil. A native of the northeastern state of Ceará, one of the poorest areas in the country, he wrote of the heroic plight of the rural worker in *O sertanejo* (1875; The Backlander); and although he was not especially familiar with the extreme southern state of Rio Grande do Sul, he published a novel about the plains entitled *O gaúcho* (1870; The Gaucho).

Both the *gaúcho* and the *sertanejo* figures were variations on the "bon sauvage" of his Indian novels.

Ultimately, the *sertanejo* and the *sertão* (backland) replaced the "noble savage" and the primeval forest settings in Brazilian novels of the 1870s and 1880s, especially in works by authors such as Bernardo Guimarães, the Visconde de Taunay, and Franklin Távora. As critic Nelson Werneck Sodré has noted, the urban coastal centers with their growing immigrant populations and rapid modernization were regarded as less authentically "Brazilian" than the largely untouched interior. Guimarães wrote about the central plains, and although he was a romantic author, his descriptions of rural landscape and customs inspired later generations of authors to explore in more realistic fashion areas little known to the reading public. Guimarães' most important works are *O seminarista* (1872; The Seminarian), about a cleric who violates his promise of celibacy and goes mad, and *A escrava Isaura* (1875; The Slave Isaura), which is regarded, rightly or wrongly, as Brazil's *Uncle Tom's Cabin*. There is no doubt that Harriet Beecher Stowe's novel, which was translated into Portuguese shortly after its original publication in 1852, had an impact on Brazilian authors at the time. The Indian and the backlander, one virtually extinct and the other far removed from the urban reader, had been easier to cast as heroic national symbols; the slave, however, whose misery and presence were everywhere evident, was a different sort of character. *Isaura* was unique in its portrayal of a slave as romantic heroine, although it is important to note that Guimarães describes his virtuous and beautiful Isaura as a mulatta whose skin is neither black nor brown but alabaster white.

The end of the 19th century was a time of significant political and economic change. One year after the abolition of slavery in 1888, the imperial government fell and was replaced by a republic. The rubber industry was at its peak, and an immigrant labor force became more important than the slaves in the fields, especially in the northeast. With the abolition of slavery, the plantation system was forced to undergo change. For those *senhores de engenho*, or plantation owners, with resources and foresight, modernization was quickly adopted in the production of sugarcane. The end of the century saw the gradual demise of a colonial system of agriculture as well as a shift in political power from the rural landowners of the northeast to the growing industrial centers of the south, in particular São Paulo. Foreign investment and technical innovations made Brazil's major cities as progressive and modern as those in Western Europe. France remained the model of intellectual greatness, and Auguste Comte's positivism, whose motto "Order and Progress" was adopted for the Brazilian flag, was embraced by a growing entrepreneurial class for whom the future of the country held nothing but promise.

Machado de Assis, Brazil's most distinguished novelist, was less than enthusiastic and even sceptical about this self-ordained order and progress. His cynicism may have been directed toward French philosophies in vogue at the time, such as positivism and determinism, which viewed individuals of color such as Machado himself, who was a mulatto, in a less than positive light. But Machado never openly denounced slavery or the philosophical pronouncements on racial inferiority; rather, he took as his target a certain sector of society given over to greed and manipulation, and his most memorable characters are the *bacharel* (lawyer or any individual with a college degree) and the *agregado* (social parasite), prime examples of which can be found in his master-piece, *Dom Casmurro* (1899; *Dom Casmurro*). Machado was also an experimental stylist, and his novels are unlike anything produced in Brazil at the time. In his first important novel, *Memórias póstumas de Brás Cubas* (1881; *Epitaph of a Small Winner*), the first-person narrator, Brás, speaks from the grave. Machado was clearly indebted to Laurence Sterne and Gustave Flaubert, the former for his formal experiments and satire, the latter for his critique of the leisure class. And although some critics have lamented the absence of clear nationalist themes or identifiably Brazilian characters in his works, he is, ironically, the author who best captures the customs and mores of Rio's middle class at the turn of the century.

Two other important novelists to appear at the end of the century were Raul Pompéia, whose novel *O ateneu* (1888; *The Athenaeum*) is told from the point of view of a former resident of a boys' school who looks back on his educational experience with biting sarcasm and wit; and Aluísio Azevedo, who wrote about the burgeoning urban proletariat in his novels about Rio boardinghouse and tenement life in *Casa de pensão* (1884; *Boardinghouse*) and *O cortiço* (1890; *A Brazilian Tenement*). Azevedo was one of the only Brazilian writers of the period to make a living from his fiction. His *O mulato* (1881; *Mulatto*), regarded as the first "naturalist" novel in Brazil, was less than complimentary of middle-class society in the country's northern state of Maranhão, which was also the birthplace and home of the author. In fact, the local furor over the racial commentary in the novel (the protagonist is the son of a slave who is murdered because of his love for a white woman) was so strong that Azevedo ultimately left Maranhão for Rio, which became the setting for his subsequent novels.

The establishment of the republic in 1889 was made possible by two powerful groups, the military and the plantation owners, who traditionally supported the emperor, Pedro II. Growing republican sentiment had forced the emancipation of slaves, an act that alienated plantation owners, who blamed the emperor for the loss of their cheap labor force and stood by passively as republican pressures increased. At the same time, high-ranking military officers as well as those at the junior ranks were eager for a change in government. The military takeover began and ended peacefully on 15 November 1889, when army commanders at the fort in Rio removed the emperor from power. Civilians and the military shared power in the new democratic government, and a constitution was promulgated in 1891 amid the general euphoria. But financial hard times befell the administration of Prudente de Morais, the first civilian president; his successor, Campos Salles, ultimately turned for support to the conservative plantation owners and exporters. Foreign investment increased dramatically, and the early years of the 20th century witnessed massive industrialization. By 1910 São Paulo was the industrial center of the nation and the continent, largely owing to its production and exportation of coffee.

Notwithstanding its rapidly expanding economy and industrial base, the social structure of Brazil remained fairly static. Few people attended schools, and there was a certain resistance by political leaders to any changes in an educational system that privileged themselves. The public outcry for better education and working conditions would provoke a major political event in 1930; in the meantime, however, the shift to a war economy in Europe as a result of World War I opened up new markets for Brazilian manufactured goods and agricultural products. By the 1920s, President Washington Luís was announcing the end of the "Old Republic" and making plans to usher in a new one.

Some of Brazil's most revered works of literature appeared in the first two decades of the 20th century, often referred to as the "Belle Époque." Shortly following the appearance of Machado's *Dom Casmurro*, Graça Aranha published *Canaã* (1902; *Canaan*), a novel about German immigrant life in the interior of Brazil. In the novel, Aranha juxtaposes very different views of Brazil as seen by his two principal protagonists: Milkau has a quasi-utopian view of miscegenation, while Lentz is obsessed with the superiority of the German race. The novel provides a fascinating look into the social practices of the German community, and it was not reluctant to critique the Brazilian government's unfair treament of the immigrants. The book was also vivid in its descriptions of the landscape, as well as in its portrayal of social violence.

Landscape and violence were also central to Euclides da Cunha's *Os sertões* (1902; *Rebellion in the Backlands*), which describes the author's 1897 journey into the *sertão* alongside government troops, who had been ordered to destroy the religious community of Canudos led by the messianic leader Antônio Conselheiro. Divided into three parts, "Terra" (Land), "Homem" (Man), and "A Luta" (The Struggle), the book is a tour de force in its geographic and ethnographic descriptions; and the account of the destruction of Canudos and the killing of Conselheiro are spellbinding in their graphic detail. The book was a national best-seller, and a year after its publication, Euclides da Cunha was inducted into the Brazilian Historical and Geographic Institute as well as the Brazilian Academy of Letters. *Rebellion in the Backlands* has also inspired other novels on Canudos, most recently Mario Vargas Llosa's *La guerra del fin del mundo* (1981; *The War of the End of the World*).

Writing at the turn of the century, Júlia Lopes de Almeida was the first modern woman to receive a national reputation as an author in Brazil. Critic Lúcia Miguel-Pereira proclaimed her the most important novelist of her time, while historian José Veríssimo considered her a successor of Machado de Assis. Among her numerous books are *A família medeiros* (1891; *The Medeiros Family*), which takes place against the background of the abolitionist movement, and *A falência* (1901; *The Bankruptcy*), which describes the rise and fall of a contemporaneous bourgeois family. Another writer frequently compared to Machado is Lima Barreto, because of his irony and humor and his running critique of positivism. Unlike Machado, however, Lima Barreto (who was also a mulatto) wrote about race and racial discrimination. All these elements can be found in his first novel, *Recordações do escrivão Isaías Caminha* (1909; *Recollections of the Scribe Isaías Caminha*), which many today regard as his finest work. Yet it was *Triste fim de Policarpo Quaresma* (1915; *The Patriot*) that captured the acclaim of contemporaneous critics, one of whom described it as the Brazilian *Don Quixote*. Set in 1893, this novel focuses on the life of Major Policarpo Quaresma, whose patriotism is extreme. He is passionate about *modinhas* (folksongs or ditties), the Brazilian countryside, and the military, and he believes that Tupi should be the national language. Like Quixote, he is both hero and fool; his disillusionment at the end of the book is complete, and he is tried as a traitor by the very army for which he valiantly fought.

The final years of the Belle Époque saw the emergence of a literary vanguard whose members were greatly influenced by artistic developments in Europe. While living in Paris, Oswald de Andrade learned of Marinetti's futurism and was impressed by the free-verse style of the French poet Paul Fort; Ronald de Carvalho cofounded *Orpheu* (1915), Portugal's first modernist literary review, which featured, among others, the poet Fernando Pessoa. By the onset of World War I, newspapers such as the *Estado de São Paulo* were discussing futurism and innovations in the plastic arts. Not everyone, however, was intrigued by the new developments. In 1917, the artist Anita Malfatti, who had studied in Germany, was attacked in print by the distinguished writer Monteiro Lobato, whose article "Paranóia ou Mistificação?" (Paranoia or Mystification?) dismissed her exhibition of cubist- and expressionist-inspired works. Lobato's violent critique was challenged by Oswald de Andrade, Mário de Andrade, and Menotti del Picchia, who were already experimenting with new forms in literature. These three men were also at the center of the Semana de Arte Moderna (Modern Art Week) held in São Paulo in November 1922, which is recognized as the official beginning of the modernist movement in Brazil.

Poetry was the chief interest and principal genre of the early modernist period, although a few important novels did appear between 1922 and 1930, most prominently Oswald de Andrade's satiric and formally innovative *Memórias sentimentais de João Miramar* (1924; *The Sentimental Memoirs of John Seaborne*) and Mário de Andrade's folkloric and surrealistic "rhapsody," *Macunaíma* (1928; *Macunaíma*), with its "hero without any character." But the book that would ultimately have an even greater impact on the course of the Brazilian novel was *A bagaceira* (1928; *Trash*) by the northeastern politician and writer José Américo de Almeida. Following in the tradition of turn-of-the-century regionalists, such as Afonso Arinos and Valdomiro Silveira, Almeida wrote vividly and compellingly about his home state of Paraíba and was openly critical of the economic conditions in the northeast. This coming together of literature and social protest in *Trash* opened the way for even more critical novelistic treatments of the conditions in the northeast, and these books would dominate the literary period from 1930 to 1945—years that coincided with the administration of one of Brazil's most important political figures, the populist president turned dictator Getúlio Vargas.

The economic upswing of the 1920s brought with it greater civil unrest caused chiefly by the government's failure to develop labor and social reforms. The first serious threat to the administration of President Epitácio Pessoa occurred in January 1922, when a group of young military officers, known as *tenentes* (lieutenants), attempted a revolt from the garrison in Rio. Their dissatisfaction with the lack of economic reform in Brazil prompted them to try again in São Paulo two years later, where they were also unsuccessful. Nonetheless, their protest called widespread national attention to the country's problems and to the rebel military officer Luís Carlos Prestes, who led a guerrilla force throughout the interior, inciting the people of the countryside to take up arms and fight. Although Prestes' campaign did not succeed in fomenting a people's revolt, he became a major national figure and heroic symbol to many. He eluded government forces during his 27-month campaign, and finally escaped into Bolivia, where he remained for several years.

The worldwide depression further fueled political unrest, and the *paulista* President Washington Luís added to the tension by naming another *paulista*, Júlio Prestes, to succeed him, when the office should have gone to a candidate from Minas Gerais. A party of opposition leaders called the Aliança Liberal (Liberal Alliance) formed to protest Luís' action, and the *gaúcho* Getúlio Vargas became its leader and presidential nominee. The assassination of João Pessoa, who was the party's candidate for vice president, brought the general turmoil to a head; with the support of *tenentes* and military leaders, Vargas launched a revolt in October 1930, and on 3 November he was named provisional president. Four years later, he was elected president of the "New Republic." But just three years later, in 1937, he declared a state of emergency and proceeded to ban all political parties under the auspices of the Estado Novo (New State), a dictatorship that lasted until 1945.

Some of Brazil's best-known novels were written during this period, despite the restrictions imposed by the dictatorship, which included the surveillance and even imprisonment of several major authors. Literary histories tend to treat as separate genres those 1930s novels written about the northeast and those written during the same period about Rio and São Paulo. What has become known as "the northeastern novel" is described in mostly political terms as protest literature or social realism, whereas the urban novel is usually called "introspective" or "psychological." To a certain extent these classifications are fluid, and the northeastern writer Graciliano Ramos is one of the most significant cases in point. His novels *São Bernardo* (1934; *São Bernardo*), about a rural worker who becomes a landowner and symbol of capitalism, and *Vidas secas* (1938; *Barren Lives*), about a family of *sertanejos* who are forced to migrate because of the drought, are strongly political in their choice of subject matter; these novels, however, tend to focus on the psychological complexities of their protagonists, whose inner struggles provide most of the drama. Other important northeastern writers of this period include one of Latin America's most widely translated authors, Jorge Amado, who has been writing novels since the 1930s. His early works, in particular *Jubiabá* (1935; *Jubiabá*) and *Capitães da areia* (1937; *Captains of the Sands*), are among his strongest because of their social critique, which is framed by Amado's interest in Afro-Brazilian culture as well as his fascination with folklore and oral storytelling. Among his other important works are *Terras do sem fim* (1943; *The Violent Land*), about the cacao plantation society of 19th-century Ilheus; *Gabriela, cravo e canela* (1959; *Gabriela, Clove and Cinnamon*), a picaresque novel often regarded as a sequel to *The Violent Land*; and *Tenda dos milagres* (1969; *Tent of Miracles*), which brought Amado back, after a period of writing about sensual mulattas, to concerns about race and social class.

Amado's early radicalism stems from his 1932 encounter with Rachel de Queiroz, who also wrote novels in the 1930s. *O quinze* (1930; *The Year Fifteen*), written when she was just 20, is a classic about the legendary drought of 1915 that ravaged her homeland in the northeast. Her 1939 novel *As três Marias* (*The Three Marias*) perhaps best exemplifies her concern with the tradition-bound northeast, where middle-class women struggle to find a life outside the home and church—a theme that can also be found in a more recent novel, *Memorial de Maria Moura* (1992; *Memoir of Maria Moura*). In 1977, Queiroz became the first woman elected to the Brazilian Academy of Letters. Novelist José Lins do Rego is generally regarded alongside Ramos, Amado, and Queiroz as the fourth writer in the northeastern group. His books about Paraíba's plantation society are referred to as the "sugarcane cycle," and *Fogo morto* (1943; *Dead Fire*) is the last and best in this series. The novel describes the demise of a feudal landowning class as well as the madness provoked by the suffocating plantation society, especially in the older, single daughters, who represent in the eyes of the failing patriarchs their own impotency and impending doom.

Because of their politics and their unusual settings, the novels of the northeast became national best-sellers, often overshadowing equally impressive works about urban middle-class life. For example, Cyro dos Anjos' *O amanuense Belmiro* (1937; *Diary of a Civil Servant*) is an ironic portrait of middle-class society told from the point of view of a middle-aged man who, somewhat like Dom Casmurro, looks back over his life in the hope to understand its meaning. The power of the novel comes not from any specific intrigue or plot but rather from the observations of a scribe who, in the tradition of Machado de Assis, subtly reveals the pathos and vacuousness of the urban professional class. An especially prolific urban writer of the 1940s was Maria José Dupré, whose books are concerned primarily with lower middle-class families and whose protagonists tend to be women. Among Dupré's most successful creations is Dona Lola, the narrator of her best-selling *Éramos seis* (1943; *We Were Six*), who was so popular with the reading public that in 1949 Dupré wrote a novel entitled *Dona Lola*. Dupré, like a number of other women writers, was ultimately neglected by critics and forgotten over the years. In 1994, a highly successful *telenovela* (soap opera) based on *Éramos seis* was instrumental in bringing Dupré and Dona Lola back to much greater public attention.

The 1940s in Brazil were economically and politically turbulent times. Brazil remained neutral for most of World War II, but troops were sent to Europe in 1942 to fight on the side of the Allies. With the Allied victory, the public was ready for a democratic government, and Vargas lost power in 1945. Following the election of Eurico Dutra as president, a new constitution was approved and personal liberties were restored. Strangely enough, Vargas was successful in his comeback bid for president in 1950, although his administration was troubled from the beginning. On 22 August 1954, the military demanded his resignation; two days later, Vargas took his own life rather than submit to public humiliation. In 1956, Juscelino Kubitschek and João Goulart took office as president and vice president, and their administration would become known for "developmentalism," a plan for economic expansion—especially in the country's vast and underpopulated interior—that depended heavily on foreign investment. Kubitschek also moved the nation's capital from Rio to the middle of the country, thereby assisting in the development program. Brasília was built from the ground up by architects Lúcio Costa and Oscar Niemeyer; in 1960, it became the center of the nation's government.

Brazilian writers of the "postmodern" generation, or those who were publishing novels after 1945, the year of Mário de Andrade's death, made various experiments with the form of the novel; among the best-known writers of this period are Guimarães Rosa and Clarice Lispector. Guimarães Rosa wrote but one novel during his lifetime, *Grande sertão: veredas* (1956; *The Devil to Pay in the Backlands*), but there is nothing else like it in Brazilian literature. An epic about virtue, truth, and the battle between Good and Evil, it draws on local myth and legend from the *sertão,* and its *sertanejo* protagonists, in the Arthurian tradition of medieval knights, ride through the interior on horseback in search of their own Holy Grail. The book's nearly 600 pages are devoid of chapter breaks or any other division, and the events follow no particular chronology. Rosa's language and syntax are baroque-like in their inventiveness and complexity, and he is frequently compared to James Joyce.

There can be no doubt of Joyce's importance to Clarice Lispector, whose first novel, *Perto do coração selvagem* (1944; *Near to the Wild Heart*), draws its title from a line in *A Portrait of the Artist as a Young Man* (1916). Her work also has much in common with French existentialist writings and the *nouveau roman*. Lispector is unequaled in her troubling portraits of middle-class women trapped in their private worlds. In *A Paixão Segundo G.H.* (1964; *The Passion According to G.H.*), a woman's encounter with a cockroach provokes an epiphany and opens her to what feminist critics have described in Lacanian terms as the "imaginary" or realm of the mother before there was the Word. Not surprisingly, French theorists Hélène Cixous and Julia Kristeva were drawn to Lispector, and it is largely because of Cixous' own works on Lispector that she has become one of Latin America's most widely translated and renowned authors.

Rosa and Lispector have tended to dominate discussions of the contemporary novel in Brazil, yet there are a number of authors who were writing at the same time or even earlier and who deserve special mention. Lúcio Cardoso began writing novels in the 1930s, and his earliest works such as *Maleita* (1933; *Malaria*) and *Salgueiro* (1935; *Salgueiro Slum*) are in the style of the northeastern novel; in the late 1950s, however, he wrote *Crônica da casa assassinada* (1959; *Chronicle of the Assassinated House*), one of the first Gothic novels in Brazil, told in flashback through letters, diary fragments, and indirect reports. Érico Veríssimo's three-volume work about Rio Grande do Sul, entitled *O tempo e o vento* (1949; *Time and the Wind*), is the southern complement to the novel produced in the northeast. Dinah Silveira de Quieroz's first novel, *Floradas na serra* (Blossoms on the Mountain), appeared in 1939; set in a tuberculosis sanatorium, it was a best-seller, providing the basis for a movie as well as a radio and television series. She anticipated magic realism in her second novel, *Margarida La Rocque: A Ilha dos Demônios* (1949; Margarida La Roque: Demons' Isle), in which she blends fantasy and verisimilitude to tell the story of a woman stranded on a desert island. In 1954, she wrote an historical novel about the founding of São Paulo (*A muralha* [*The Women of Brazil*]), and she is frequently credited with having introduced "serious" or literary science fiction into Brazil. In 1981, Quieroz became the second woman to be elected to the Brazilian Academy of Letters. Lygia Fagundes Telles also began her career in the 1930s. Although she is mostly known for her short fiction, her first book to gain widespread attention was the novel *Ciranda de pedra* (1954; *The Marble Dance*), which, like many of her works, focuses on middle-class women and sexuality. Her successful career as a writer soared in 1973 with the publication of *As meninas* (*The Girl in the Photograph*), which is fascinating for its experiments with language and point of view. But it was the novel's portrayal of three young women and their experiences with drugs, sex, and violence during a right-wing military dictatorship that made it a national best-seller.

Although his first work appeared in the late 1940s, Autran Dourado's career is characterized by a string of successful novels, beginning in the 1960s with *A barca dos homens* (1961; The Boat of Men), a parody of *A História Trágico-Marítima* (Tragic Maritime Story)—Portuguese chronicles from the Renaissance period that describe the voyages and shipwrecks that occurred during Portugal's age of discoveries. Many of Dourado's best novels focus on the history of his home state, Minas Gerais. These include *Ópera dos Mortos* (1967; The Voices of the Dead), about an old mansion and its mad inhabitants in the interior of the state, which has been likened to Faulkner's "A Rose for Emily" (1931); and *Os sinos da agonia* (1974; The Bells of Agony), an historical novel about 18th-century Minas, which is imbued with the same atmosphere of mystery and suspense as *The Voices of the Dead*. Antônio Callado wrote about messianism in Bahia (*Assunção de Salviano* [1954; The Assumption of Salviano]); the middle class in Rio (*Bar Don Juan* [1971; Don Juan's Bar]); and political turmoil in Brazil in the 1950s and 1960s in perhaps his best-known novel, *Quarup* (1967). Osman Lins was intrigued with literary experiment, as can be seen in his unusual string of "narratives" in *Nove, novena* (1966; Nine, Novena), which is often compared with the *nouveau roman*, and in his widely translated novel *Avalovara* (1973; Avalovara), a love story replete with geometric graphics. Nélida Piñon became the fourth woman elected to the Brazilian Academy of Letters after Lygia Fagundes Telles; in 1996, she became the first woman to be elected Academy President. Piñon writes disorienting novels that are oneiric. Her best work to date is the historical novel *A república dos sonhos* (1984; The Republic of Dreams), a semi-autobiographical book about the migration of a Galician family to Brazil.

The dictatorship that provided the backdrop for Lygia Fagundes Telles' 1973 best-seller *The Girl in the Photograph* began in 1964, when the military ousted President João Goulart and initiated its 20-year rule of Brazil. The coup was justified by those involved because of the rise of inflation and the precarious nature of the economy, whose instability was blamed on various factors including political corruption, communist intervention, the domination of foreign investment, the ineptness of Goulart, and public loss of faith. The late 1960s and early 1970s were especially difficult and repressive years under the military regime; left-wing students and intellectuals were imprisoned and tortured, and an atmosphere of fear and distrust prevailed. The military's attempt to turn Brazil into the economic "miracle" of South America failed miserably. By the late 1970s, *abertura* or a political "opening" began, which was especially significant for women authors, whose books became commercially successful because of their open treatment of heretofore private or prohibited themes such as erotic love.

In this period, Márcia Denser gained immediate attention for her two collections of women's erotic short fiction. Her novel, *O animal dos motéis* (1981; The Animal of the Motels), like her short stories, is characterized by a hard-boiled realism that disdains the idea of romantic love and portrays sex as a quasi-mechanical act bordering on the grotesque. Lya Luft's novels are also about sex, but they are more like modern-day versions of the Gothic, because sex is omnipresent yet forbidden. *A asa esquerda do anjo* (1981; The Left Wing of the Angel) is semi-autobiographical in its description of a young girl born into a German immigrant family in Rio Grande do Sul. The plot turns on the relationship between the girl, who is Brazilian, and her German grandmother-matriarch, whose dark, repressive home resembles the patriarchal abode of 19th-century Gothic litera-

ture. Edla van Steen also writes about love in *Antes do amanhecer* (1977; Good Mourning), which has the fast-paced quality of a movie script.

Although Brazil has not yet secured the political and socioeconomic stability promised by the 1994 election of President Fernando Henrique Cardoso, the country continues to produce exceptional works of literature. And even though short fiction has tended to dominate the literary scene of late, the novel remains a solid fixture. Among the notable works to appear since 1980 are: João Ubaldo Ribeiro's historical novel *Viva o povo brasileiro* (1984; An Invincible Memory), which takes place in Bahia; Silviano Santiago's *Stella Manhattan* (1985), about Brazilians and homosexuality in New York City; and Sônia Coutinho's *O caso Alice* (1991; Alice's Case), which, along with Rubem Fonseca's *O caso Morel* (1973; Morel's Case), is among the best examples of detective fiction, a genre that is just now becoming popular in Brazil. The remarkable success of singer-songwriter Chico Buarque de Hollanda's *Estorvo* (1991; Turbulence), a dark, quasi-dystopian novel about urban Brazil, and *Benjamin* (1995; Benjamin), a love story set in Rio and replete with irony and angst, is perhaps an indication of a certain tendency in the novel that harks back to Graciliano Ramos' *Angústia* (1936; Anguish) but has new meaning in today's Brazil. The setting is the big city, with its vivid extremes of wealthy and poor who are pushed closer together in the landscape; the alienated, often ironic and neurotic protagonist is not all that dissimilar from the hypothetical readers of the book, who struggle to cope with national growth and social change.

DARLENE SADLIER

See also Jorge Amado; Devil to Pay in the Backlands; Clarice Lispector; Joaquim Maria Machado de Assis

Further Reading

Bosi, Alfredo, *História concisa da literatura brasileira*, São Paulo: Cultrix, 1970; 3rd edition, 1981

Cândido, Antônio, *Formação da literatura brasileira*, São Paulo: Martins, 1959; 2nd edition, 1964

Cândido, Antônio, *On Literature and Society*, translated by Howard S. Becker, Princeton, New Jersey: Princeton University Press, 1995

Castello, José Aderaldo, *Aspectos do romance brasileiro*, Rio de Janeiro: Ministério da Educação e Cultura, 1960

Coutinho, Afrânio, *Introduçao a literatura no brasil*, Rio de Janeiro: Livraria São José, 1959; as *An Introduction to Literature in Brazil*, New York: Columbia University Press, 1969

Coutinho, Afrânio, editor, *A literatura no brasil*, Rio de Janeiro: Sul Americana, 1955; 2nd edition, 1968

DiAntonio, Robert E., *Brazilian Fiction: Aspects and Evolution of the Contemporary Narrative*, Fayetteville: University of Arkansas Press, 1989

Driver, David Miller, *The Indian in Brazilian Literature*, New York: Hispanic Institute in the United States, 1942

Ellison, Fred P., *Brazil's New Novel: Four Northeastern Masters*, Berkeley: University of California Press, 1954

Filho, Adonias, *O romance brasileiro de 30*, Rio de Janeiro: Bloch, 1969

Grieco, Agrippino, *Evolução da prosa brasileira*, 2nd edition, Rio de Janeiro: José Olympio, 1947

Johnson, Randal, editor, *Tropical Paths: Essays on Modern Brazilian Literature*, New York: Garland, 1993

Linhares, Temístocles, *História crítica do romance brasileiro, 1728–1981*, Belo Horizonte: Itatiaia, 1987

Lins, Álvaro, *O romance brasileiro contemporâneo*, Rio de Janeiro: Edições de Ouro, 1967

Loos, Dorothy Scott, *The Naturalistic Novel of Brazil*, New York: Hispanic Institute in the United States, 1963

Lowe, Elizabeth, *The City in Brazilian Literature*, Rutherford, New Jersey: Farleigh Dickinson University Press, and London: Associated University Presses, 1982

Marotti, Giorgio, *Il negro nel romanzo brasiliano*, Rome: Bulzoni, 1982; as *Black Characters in the Brazilian Novel*, Los Angeles: Center for Afro-American Studies, University of California, 1987

Martins, Heitor, editor, *The Brazilian Novel*, Bloomington: Department of Spanish and Portuguese, Indiana University, 1976

Martins, Wilson, *O modernismo, 1916–1945*, 3rd edition, São Paulo: Cultrix, 1969 (originally published in 1965); as *The Modernist Idea: A Critical Survey of Brazilian Writing in the Twentieth Century*, New York: New York University Press, 1970

Miguel Pereira, Lúcia, *Prosa de Ficção: de 1870 a 1920*, São Paulo: José Olympio, 1950; 3rd edition, Rio de Janeiro: José Olympio, 1973

Patai, Daphne, *Myth and Ideology in Contemporary Brazilian Fiction*, Rutherford, New Jersey: Farleigh Dickinson University Press, and London: Associated University Presses, 1983

Payne, Judith A., and Earl E. Fitz, *Ambiguity and Gender in the New Novel of Brazil and Spanish America: A Comparative Assessment*, Iowa City: University of Iowa Press, 1993

Pinto, Cristina Ferreira, *O Bildungsroman feminino*, São Paulo: Perspectiva, 1990

Quinlan, Susan Canty, *The Female Voice in Contemporary Brazilian Narrative*, New York: Peter Lang, 1991

Reis, Roberto, *The Pearl Necklace: Toward an Archaeology of Brazilian Transition Discourse*, Gainesville: University Press of Florida, 1992

Sayers, Raymond, *The Negro in Brazilian Literature*, New York: Hispanic Institute in the United States, 1956

Vieira, Nelson, *Jewish Voices in Brazilian Literature: A Prophetic Discourse of Alterity*, Gainesville: University Press of Florida, 1995

Latin American Novel

Central America

When asked about Central American literature, one may be hard pressed to produce more than a few representative names: the great Nicaraguan poet Rubén Darío, possibly, or the 1967 Nobel-prize-winning novelist from Guatemala, Miguel Ángel Asturias. One may recall testimonial writer Rigoberta Menchú, the Guatemalan indigenous winner of the 1992 Nobel peace prize. Televised images of the pope scolding Sandinista poet, priest, and political activist Ernesto Cardenal in Managua in 1983 perhaps come to mind. Central America bears the dubious distinction of being doubly marginalized, that is, as "third world" Latin America's poor cousin. Years ago Chilean Nobel laureate Gabriela Mistral innocently baptized El Salvador "el pulgarcito de América" (the little thumb of America), metaphorically diminishing its stature, and that of its tiny neighbors, in comparison to the rest of the hemisphere.

Each of the Central American countries has at one time or another been called "una novela sin novelistas" (a novel without novelists). Central American literature has been undeservedly slighted—many gifted writers do indeed live and work there. External factors, rather than a lack of talent or literary value, are to blame for this region's dearth of published literature. Economic underdevelopment together with the absence of major publishing houses, a very limited reading public (much of the population is illiterate, and those who can read often cannot afford books), writers away in exile, political censorship, and the absence of serious criticism—all have adversely affected literary production and dissemination. The novel, which arguably requires greater time, effort, and discipline, has especially suffered.

The novel in Central America has tended to lag behind its South American counterpart in major trends and innovations. Anachronistic genres coexist, and one can still find examples of historical, romantic, naturalist, *modernista*, socialist realist, *criollista*, and *costumbrista* narrative published today. The boom-style novel, or new narrative, which took the rest of Latin America by storm during the 1960s, arrived ten years later in Central America.

However, with this lag in mind, the historical development of the novel in Central America has paralleled that of Latin America as a whole. In Central America as in other Latin countries, three general antecedents to narrative writing and specifically the novel may be identified: 1) indigenous (Mayan Quiché and Cakchiquel) oral traditions and sacred writings, such as the *Popol Vuh*; 2) chronicles, reports, and other narratives of conquest and colonization; and 3) travel writings by foreigners visiting Central America.

As in Europe, the rise of the novel as a literary form accompanied the formation and consolidation of the nation-states in Central America. However, the absence of a consuming middle class impeded its full development. Most Central American countries achieved independence in the early 19th century, and the first novels—romantic, historical, sentimental, and/or socially satirical—emerged in the mid- to latter part of the century. Many were published serially as *folletines* in newspapers. Later in the century, realist currents emerged out of romanticism. The *costumbrista* narrative took shape with its zeal for the description of scenes and characters, local color, sketches of manners and customs, and use of colloquial language. *Costumbrismo* could border on the political or polemical as it censured some of the behaviors it described. *Naturalismo* à la French writer Émile Zola, which was received with such enthusiasm by countries such as Argentina and Mexico—perhaps because they were experiencing massive immigration, urbanization, and a general liberalism—was scarcely noticed in the more underdeveloped Central America. More to its literary taste was *modernismo*, the turn of the century movement identified with Rubén Darío that renovated the aesthetic elements of art. The *modernista* novel was a reaction against capitalism, its materialism, and its commodification of art. The rebellion valued "art for art's sake" and, instead of lashing out in social rebellion, turned inward as each individual artist sought formal beauty, harmonious expression, and stylistic perfection. *Posmodernismo* rejected the excessive ornamentation of *modernismo* while the *vanguardia* imported avant-garde techniques from European surrealism and other experimental schools of the early 20th century.

Most of these currents still had their sources in Europe, however, and 20th-century writers began to long for a more nativist expression. Ramón Luis Acevedo (1982) defines *criollismo* as the literary discovery of the rural world of Spanish America. It reached its height between the two world wars in novels such as Colombian José Eustasio Rivera's *La vorágine* (1924; *The Vortex*), Venezuelan Rómulo Gallegos' *Doña Bárbara* (1929; *Doña Bárbara*), Argentine Ricardo Güiraldes' *Don Segundo Sombra* (1926; *Don Segundo Sombra*), and Mexican Mariano Azuela's *Los de abajo* (1916; *The Underdogs*). *Criollista* novels have taken many forms but, according to Acevedo, a common desire has been to capture and interpret that which is perceived to be typically Spanish American. One problem has been that most *criollista* writers have been city dwellers trying to describe a rural reality. Nevertheless, the old 19th-century Sarmientine dichotomy of civilization and barbarism is reversed in the *criollista* novel, which often depicts a mystical kinship between humans and the land. Nationalism, regionalism, *indigenismo,* and political denunciation are all possible dimensions of the complex *criollista* novel, which can also combine vanguardist, realist, socialist realist, or lyrical modes of expression. In Central America any and all of these modes are still practiced in a less rigid chronology than is found elsewhere in the hemisphere.

As previously mentioned, the literary and publishing boom that hit the rest of Latin America in the 1960s—with familiar names such as Julio Cortázar, Carlos Fuentes, Gabriel García Márquez, and Mario Vargas Llosa—arrived in Central America in the 1970s. The boom writers found formal and thematic inspiration in the *vanguardia* to create *nueva narrativa,* innovative strategies of narrating. The post-boom movement later sought to simplify what it deemed excessive complexity. Simultaneously, Central America was beginning to experience the political cataclysms and wars of national liberation of the 1970s and 1980s. *Testimonio* (which has been called the "post-bourgeois novel")

and the testimonial novel, while not unique to the isthmus, proliferated there as in no other place. Testimonial novels documented the conflicts from below through voices not traditionally heard in literature: peasants, workers, women, indigenous groups, and political prisoners all demanded a space to tell their stories and to influence world opinion in their struggles. A democratic opening was created that continues to mark the postmodern moment in cultural and literary production. For example, more women are writing than ever before.

Many contemporary novels have turned more inward than those of the heady days of revolution. Themes and approaches are diverse: feminism, ecofeminism, sexual politics, rewritings of history, reconsiderations of nationalism, processes of globalization, experiences of migration, and transculturation all characterize recent novels from Central America.

Guatemala

The novel developed earlier and the narrative tradition is stronger in Guatemala than in the rest of Central America. As the seat of government for the isthmus, the Audiencia of Guatemala, so designated in 1542 under the viceroyalty of New Spain (Mexico), enjoyed special status as the political, cultural, and social capital of the area. When the first printing press arrived in 1760, arts and letters began to flourish in Guatemala, while the rest of Central America remained isolated.

Guatemala has a larger indigenous population than any of its Central American neighbors, a presence that has uniquely marked its culture, politics, collective psyche, and literary themes and expression. The Maya-Quiché and Cakchiquel mythic mentality and oral traditions, transcribed after the conquest by the conquistadors and their priests in sacred texts such as the *Popol Vuh* (Book of Council) and *Chilam Balam,* have inspired poets and novelists alike.

The first narratives written in Guatemala were chronicles of conquest and missionary accounts documenting evangelization and the extirpation of idolatry. Mixtures of fantasy and history, they preceded the modern novel, which made its appearance in Guatemala in the mid–19th century. Antonio José de Irisarri published irreverently humorous texts that would set the standard for future writers. His *El Cristiano errante* (1847; The Errant Christian) is an autobiographical, *costumbrista,* and picaresque novel. Seymour Menton (1985) calls José Milla ("Salomé Jil") the "father of the Guatemalan novel." Milla wrote several historical romances, such as *La hija del adelantado* (1866; The Governor's Daughter), *Los nazarenos* (1867; The Nazarenes), and *El visitador* (1867; The Visitor). Milla also experimented with realism and *costumbrismo,* creating a stock Guatemalan character, "Juan Chapín." Guatemala's only naturalist writer, Zola disciple Enrique Martínez Sobral, presents the depravity of the lower classes in his many novels, such as *Alcohol* (1900) and *Humo* (1900; Smoke). Despite the chaos following independence, a Guatemalan conscience and sense of identity, which the novel helped to consolidate, were slowly forming.

A reformist spirit characterizes Guatemala's realist and *modernista* novels at the end of the 19th century. The novel became a political tool. Modernist Máximo Soto-Hall wrote the first anti-imperialist novel, *El problema* (1899; The Problem), placing himself and Central America ahead of the rest of Latin America in the treatment of this theme. Guatemala's best known *modernista* writer, the exuberant Rafael Arévalo Martínez, wrote poetry, short stories, and several innovative novels, such as *El mundo de los maharachías* (1938; The World of the Maharachías), some of which condemned the notorious Estrada Cabrera dictatorship (1898–1920) and US imperialism. His use of animal imagery highlights the dehumanization caused by tyranny. Other *modernistas* include novelists César Brañas (1900–1976) and Carlos Samayoa Chinchilla (1898–1973).

Some *modernista-criollista* writers experimented with form and technique, heavily influenced by trends of the *vanguardia* such as surrealism, Freudianism, cinematography, cubism, the oneiric, ruptures and fragmentation in narrative sequencing, and the deformation of language. Carlos Wyld Ospina tries to capture Indian psychology and spirituality in *Los lares apagados* (written in 1939, published 1958; Extinguished Lares), a successful example of *indigenismo*. The other major *criollista*, Flavio Herrera, turns inward to the individual rather than the collective psyche in his novels, *El tigre* (1929; The Tiger) and *Caos* (1949; Chaos), a tendency that appears later in Guatemalan literature.

The year 1944 marked a pivotal moment in modern Guatemalan history. Supporters of democracy brought down the Ubico dictatorship (1931–1944), installing a reformist government under President Juan José Arévalo. In literature, enthusiasm returned for the novel of the land. Literary societies flourished, including the iconoclast Saker-Ti, which emphasized combining the sociopolitical with the artistic and favored ethics over aesthetics. During the "Guatemalan Spring," as this period is now nostalgically remembered, Manuel Galich wrote the first *proto-testimonio*, *Del pánico al ataque* (1949), narrating episodes of student unrest during the Ubico years.

The two Guatemalan writers of this period who had the most influence over successive generations of writers were Generation of 1920 members Miguel Ángel Asturias and Luis Cardoza y Aragón. Both began as poets, traveling to Paris to steep themselves in the avant-garde. Both became politically committed writers. Asturias studied Guatemala's indigenous peoples and cultures, incorporating their mythic worlds into his stories and novels. His work, which won him the Nobel prize for literature in 1967, spans styles and modes of expression from magic realism, *indigenismo*, surrealism, and lyricism to socialist realism and anti-imperialism. Although Cardoza never published a novel, his brilliant cultural essay, *Guatemala, las líneas de su mano* (1955), influenced future novelists and radical resistance prose writers. While he espoused an openly leftist ideology, he refused to embrace the aesthetics of socialist/communist governments or to advocate for conformity to a leftist, party-line literary agenda. He offered a model for a critique of the left from within the left.

Indigenismo reached its culminating point in Guatemalan literature with Mario Monteforte Toledo. Like other committed writers, Monteforte spent time in exile following the Intervention of 1954 (by the US Central Intelligence Agency and the Guatemalan military), which accused Guatemalan reformers of communism, ended Guatemalan democracy, and reinstalled a military regime. His novel *Anaité* (1938) takes up familiar Latin American themes of the power of nature and civilization versus barbarism, while *Entre la piedra y la cruz* (1948; Between the Rock and the Cross), his most famous work, calls for national unity amid the seemingly irreconcilable differences between Indians and ladinos. He later published *Donde acaban los caminos*

(1953; Where the Roads End) and *Una manera de morir* (1957; A Way of Dying), the latter an ideological novel about the role of the intellectual and the loss of idealism to sordid politics.

The 1960s saw an increase in guerrilla resistance activity to counter the repressive dictatorship that had begun seizing Indian lands. Censorship succeeded in silencing almost all creativity and dissent. By the 1980s, various forces of resistance were converging: religious (liberation theology), labor, indigenous, intellectual, and popular organizations. Out of the turmoil rose voices of testimony in one of the most influential narrative forms to come from Latin America in recent years. These *testimonios*, while generally nonfictional, have had significant impact on the novel in Guatemala. The most important *testimonio* is surely *Me llamo Rigoberta Menchú y así me nació la conciencia* (1983; I, Rigoberta Menchú: An Indian Woman in Guatemala), narrated by Quiché activist Rigoberta Menchú to Venezuelan anthropologist Elizabeth Burgos Debray. In it Menchú claims to speak as a member of a community, describing many customs of her people. She also recounts atrocities she witnessed, such as the torture and death of her mother and other family members. But instead of maintaining her uniqueness, she insists that her story is that of an entire people. Other notable Guatemalan testimonies include Mario Payeras' *Los días de la selva* (1983; Days of the Jungle), a lyrical account of the author's own experience as a guerrilla; Victor Montejo's *Testimony: Death of a Guatemalan Village* (1987), about the slaughter of small-town inhabitants by a military unit; and Miguel Angel Albizures' *Tiempo de sudor y lucha* (1987; Time of Sweat and Struggle), which narrates from a worker's perspective the 1984 Coca-Cola strike in Guatemala City.

Other indigenous novelists have followed Menchú's example. Luis de Lión, a partially ladinized Indian, exemplifies Angel Rama's transculturated writer. Lión's novel *El tiempo principia en Xibalba* (written in 1972, published in 1985; Time Begins in Xibalba) protests the living conditions of indigenous communities and the discrimination they suffer at the hands of ladinos. The novel creates a mood that is poetic, oneiric, and erotic using new narrative techniques. Lión paid the price for his activism and was "disappeared" in the early 1980s. Gaspar Pedro Gonzalez is a more recent indigenous voice. His testimonial novel, *La otra cara* (1992; A Mayan Life), weaves together oral traditions and the fictional story of a Mayan male in a literary complement to the testimony of Rigoberta Menchú.

Novels in the realist mode include Carlos Cojulún Bedoya's *¡Violencia!* (1978; Violence), a romance rather than a resistance text set at the time of the 1976 volcanic eruption. Poet Miguel Angel Vázquez published his first novel, *La semilla del fuego* (1976; Seed of Fire) about the Ubico years and 1944 revolution in a combination of testimonial and poetic style. His later novel, *Operación Iscariote* (1989; Operation Iscariot), refers to the final months of the Arbenz regime before the overthrow in 1954.

The theme of violence saturates most other literature as well. As Marc Zimmerman (1995) has observed, "whether conventional or experimental in form, most Guatemalan fictional prose of the late seventies deals with the subjects of oppression, revolution, and guerrilla warfare." Marco Antonio Flores' novel *Los compañeros* (1976; Comrades) marks the first time the forms and techniques of new narrative combine with testimony in Guatemalan literature. From its innovative language, pop slang, fragmentation of narrative sequence, lack of punctuation and traditional syntactical structure, free association, chaotic alternation of a fragmented narrator, and interior monologue, to its audacious sexual imagery throughout, *Los compañeros* exudes insolence. Edwin Cifuentes' *El pueblo y los atentados* (1979; The People and Terrorism) and *La nueva Esmeralda: la novela de París* (1987; The New Esmeralda: The Novel of Paris) share Flores' irreverence and verbal acrobatics, as do Mario Roberto Morales' *Los demonios salvajes* (1978; Savage Demons) and *El esplendor de la pirámide* (1986; Splendor of the Pyramid), which sometimes erupt in rebellious obscenities. Their irony, sardonic humor, and linguistic play place these novels in the tradition of Irisarri's novels in the 19th century.

Military violence in the countryside is the theme of Morales' more recent narrative, *Los señores bajo los árboles* (1994; Men Under the Trees), a mode the author characterizes as "testi-novela." He has abandoned the ludic tone for a more searing presentation of army atrocities on Indian lands. *Los señores bajo los árboles* condemns the struggle between the traditional left and right that has trapped Indians in the middle. Rural violence also characterizes *El tren no viene* (1984; The Train Does Not Arrive) by José Luis Perdomo and *Vida de un pueblo muerto* (1985; Life in a Dead Town) by William Lemus, while the action moves to an urban setting in Francisco Albizúrez Palma's *Ida y vuelta* (1987; Round Trip) and Fernando González Davison's *En los sueños no todo es reposo* (1988; In Dreams Not All Is Restful).

Violence collides with the carnivalesque in Arturo Arias' first novel, *Después de las bombas* (1979; After the Bombs), whose theme is the 1954 Intervention. His work resembles Cifuentes' in its ironic tone, linguistic experimentation, and use of boom techniques. Similar narrative audacity is found in Arias' *Itzam Na* (1981), a look at the self-destructive hippie drug culture of Guatemala, and *Jaguar en llamas* (1989; Jaguar in Flames), a counterhistory of conquest and colonization. His fourth novel, *Los caminos de Paxil* (1990; The Roads of Paxil), changes direction and, like many recent texts in Guatemala and the rest of Central America, becomes more lyrical, introspective, and subjective. In *Caminos* Arias enters the mythical Mayan world and adopts the perspective of a first-person indigenous narrator.

Novels are being written in the Guatemalan diaspora as well. Both Morales and Arias now work from the United States, as do Guatemalan-American-Jewish novelists Victor Perera and Francisco Goldman, although these latter two write in English. Perera's *Rites: A Guatemalan Boyhood* (1986) and *The Cross and the Pear Tree* (1995) examine, among other issues, being Jewish in a Latin American context. Goldman, much like Arias, experiments with new narrative techniques, superimposed texts, and labyrinthine plots in *The Long Night of White Chickens* (1992). But like Perera, Goldman is far less insolent and humorous than Arias. This novel falls within the Guatemalan tradition of psychological introspection as it reconstructs the life and mind of a Guatemalan woman murdered for alleged complicity in child-kidnapping-for-body-parts schemes. In general, Guatemalan novelists beyond the country's borders subscribe to an artistic freedom and "first world" cosmopolitanism, which are foreign luxuries to writers who have stayed at home through the crises, driving a wedge between the two groups.

El Salvador

A history of military, political, social, and economic repression has stunted the development of the novel in El Salvador, the smallest and most densely populated country of the Central American isthmus. Although Salvadorans are a relatively homogeneous people racially and culturally, they have been subjected to a rigid social and economic hierarchy under a powerful oligarchy backed by military force. For years, literature tended toward escapism, romantic idealization of the miserable *campesino* (farm laborer), and an "art for art's sake" inclination. Occasionally, artists would adopt an aesthetics of political engagement to depict the repressive climate they experienced all too frequently. Those who did, such as writers associated with the Juan Montalvo Society at the turn of the century, could expect to suffer censorship, persecution, exile, and sometimes death.

European-style culture came late to El Salvador. The conquistadors, most notably the Alvarado brothers, wrote several accounts of their exploits. The colonial period produced few narratives, with the exception of moral and ecclesiastical histories, didactic texts, and lives of saints written by clergy.

Citizens began to publish newspapers actively after 1840. The University of El Salvador was founded in 1841, although it could not open its doors for several years for lack of funds. With the 1871 establishment of the National Library, the increased interest in and availability of books led to the formation of the first scientific-literary society, "La Juventud" (youth), dedicated to the renovation of romanticism and to the introduction of *modernismo*. However, *modernismo* had little impact in El Salvador. Rather, romanticism found a home and has marked Salvadoran letters ever since with its sentimentality, lyricism, emotionalism, and subjectivity.

The initiator of the *precriollista* novel in El Salvador was in fact a short-story writer, Arturo Ambrogi, who in 1895 published *Cuentos y fantasías,* a glimpse at the harsh conditions of a peasant's life. Francisco Gavidia, the most prominent of all literary figures in El Salvador at the turn of the century and a friend of Rubén Darío, experimented in both narrative and poetry. Antonio Guevara Valdés and Manuel Delgado were among the first writers to attempt novels; the latter's *Roca-Celis* (1908) merits Acevedo's designation as the first Salvadoran novel, although it resembles more a legal treatise than novelistic discourse.

When the world plunged into the Great Depression in the late 1920s and 1930s, El Salvador saw prices of coffee, its main export crop, tumble. As the labor movement coalesced worldwide, its agitation spread to Central America. Socialist theoretician, essayist, orator, and journalist Alberto Masferrer (1868–1932) took up the cause of the *campesino*, who particularly suffered as a result of the falling coffee prices. Masferrer has left works of prose and poetry that cover many periods and movements, from romanticism and *modernismo* to the *vanguardia*. He was forced into exile when military strongman Maximiliano Hernández Martínez, with the blessings of the US government, overthrew the popularly elected Araujo government in March 1931. In January 1932 the Salvadoran Communist leader Agustín Farabundo Martí called for a peasant-worker rebellion in defiance of the coup. Hernández Martínez crushed the revolt within 48 hours, massacring over 30,000 Indian peasants in the western part of the country near Sonsonate and the Izalco volcano. Official coverup and denial have not expunged the 1932 *Matanza* (massacre) from the popular memory. On the contrary, it has remained the galvanizing moment of the national conscience and a point of departure for current protest literature, especially the novel.

Salarrué, pseudonym of Salvador Salazar Arrué, is the best known narrative writer of this period. He could not broach the subject of the *Matanza* directly, but his short stories and novels are saturated with violence. Best known for his short fiction, *Cuentos de barro* (1927; Stories from Mud) and *Cuentos de cipotes* (1928; Children's Stories), Salarrué bridges the gap between *costumbrista* realism, magic realism, and regionalism. His novels, which include *El Cristo Negro* (1927; The Black Christ) and *El Señor de la Burbuja* (1927; The Bubble Man) among others, do not equal his short stories in critical acclaim; nevertheless, they influenced later novelists. Perhaps Salarrué's most important legacy to Salvadoran literature is the masterful incorporation of indigenous and peasant slang into his texts.

Until 1945, only 11 novels had been published in El Salvador. At that time, the Generation of 1940 inaugurated the *criollista* novel in El Salvador, combining their love of the land and rural life with a social message. The major *criollista* novelist, Ramón González Montalvo, published *Las tinajas* (1935; The Water Jugs) and *Barbasco* (1960), imitating rustic speech patterns as found in Salarrué and denouncing the injustices of the *latifundistas* (large landowners) in the manner of the socialist realist and *indigenista* novels of the 1930s from elsewhere in Latin America. A contemporary of González Montalvo, Napoleón Rodríguez Ruíz, wrote a sentimental *criollista/costumbrista* novel, *Jaraguá*, in 1950; Carlo Antonio Castro published *Los hombres verdaderos* (Real Men) in 1959; and social worker and writer Yolanda C. Martínez examined racial issues in two novels, *Sus fríos ojos azules* (1964; Her Cold Blue Eyes) and *Corazón ladino* (1967; Ladino Heart). Romantic elements persist in all.

In 1956 Salvadoran thinker, writer, and statesman Hugo Lindo published his only novel, *El anzuelo de Dios* (God's Bait). In it are apparent his religious and metaphysical concerns as well as his *costumbrista* tendencies, a marked contrast to the more political agendas in the writings of his activist contemporaries in *Gruposéis* (The Group of Six).

Critic, theorist, and *Gruposéis* member Matilde Elena López signaled the changes about to occur in the Central American novel with her *Interpretación social del arte* (1965; Social Interpretation of Art). She documents the revitalized realism of new narrative with formal resources such as interior monologue and ruptures of time and space. Salvadoran Claribel Alegría and her North American husband, Darwin J. Flakoll, wrote *Cenizas de Izalco* (1966; Ashes of Izalco) about the 1932 Matanza in the new mode described by López. Other writers of the renovated novel are David Escobar Galindo, Miguel Cobos, María Elena Mendoza, and Carlos Lobato.

The iconoclast *Generación Comprometida* (Committed Generation) coalesced in 1956, inspired by Pablo Neruda and committed to exploring the social function of literature. Resistant to foreign models, they preferred to develop their own. All genres awaited their renovation. The best known members of *Generación Comprometida* included poet-novelists Roque Dalton and Manlio Argueta. Dalton concurrently formed the *Círculo Literario Universitario* (University Literary Circle), which exists to this day. Their work coincides with the Cuban revolution of 1959, the rise of popular movements in El Salvador in the 1960s and 1970s, and the wars of national liberation in the 1980s.

Dalton interviewed *Matanza* survivor and Salvadoran Communist Party member Miguel Mármol for a novelized testimony entitled *Matanza,* which was published in 1971. It is especially interesting for the colorful, earthy language that Mármol uses and Dalton captures. For Dalton, writing the testimony was essential to rescuing part of Salvadoran history, informing present-day workers of the sacrifices of earlier revolutionaries, and advocating armed struggle to transform Salvadoran society. Other well-known testimonies, albeit less "sophisticated" and "literary," are *Secuestro y capucha* (1979; Kidnapping and the Hood) by baker and union organizer Salvador Cayetano Carpio and *Las cárceles clandestinas de El Salvador* (1978; Clandestine Prisons of El Salvador) by militant Ana Guadalupe Martínez.

Dalton also wrote *Pobrecito poeta que era yo* (Poor Poet That I Am), a Bildungsroman and boom-style novel that blurs genre lines. The book, which examines a writer's angst over his relationship to the political struggle, was published posthumously in 1976 following Dalton's murder by a dissident faction within his own revolutionary party. Another important literary experiment by Dalton is *Las historias prohibidas del Pulgarcito* (1974; Prohibited Stories From the Little Flea). A chaotic and fragmented collage of poems, prose poems, newspaper clippings, advertisements, obituaries, proverbs, songs, and other selections, it decenters canonical linear histories in an attempt to present a more realistic and inclusive vision of the nation.

The trend from poetry to prose (even the pastiche-novel) typifies the development of other writers in El Salvador, such as Roberto Armijo and Manlio Argueta. Following early publications of poetry, Argueta turned to the novel. His first two are examples of new urban narrative: *El valle de las hamacas* (1970; The Valley of Hammocks) and *Caperucita en la zona roja* (1977; Little Red Riding Hood in the Red Zone). Later, Argueta, Alegría, and others shifted their focus to the *campesino* and to the feminization of the struggle, incorporating women's testimonies into novels such as Argueta's *Un día en la vida* (1980; One Day of Life) and *Cuzcatlán: Donde bate la mar del sur* (1986; Cuzcatlán: Where the Southern Sea Beats). These lyrical testimonial novels correspond to the years of emergency and document the coming-to-consciousness of marginalized Salvadorans. These two novels also incorporate the discourse of liberation theology as faith and politics meet.

Most writing in El Salvador has taken a new direction following the United Nations-brokered peace accords of 1993. Argueta's fifth novel, *Milagro de la paz* (1994; Miracle of Peace), is indicative of the more introspective, psychological qualities of contemporary novels in El Salvador.

Honduras

Although Honduras won its political independence from Spain in 1823, it remained in Guatemala's cultural shadow. Problems common to much of Central America and unfavorable to the development of the novel afflicted Honduras as well: few printing presses or publishing houses, high illiteracy and poverty, isolation, and political and social upheaval. Poet and priest Fray José Trinidad Reyes took the first step toward intellectual independence when he founded the University of Honduras in 1847.

Early novels written in Honduras were romantic. Romanticism coincided with the period of liberal reform, which began in 1876 during the presidency of Marco Aurelio Soto. A woman, Lucila Gamero de Medina (1873–1964), wrote the first novels, *Amalia Montiel* (1893) and *Adriana y Margarita* (1897), both of which are now lost. Carlos Federico Gutiérrez is credited with writing the first surviving novel, *Angelina* (1898), a historical romance based on the 19th-century theme of civilization and barbarism. *Angelina* is an allegory of the nation, a beauty and the beast tale: a jealous lover and madman kidnaps and rapes the woman he loves, who is already married to another man, a kind and reasonable person. She commits suicide. Gutiérrez's style is simple and spontaneous, his subject matter erotic and violent. He situates his action in a rural setting where nature plays an important part, a feature that becomes characteristic of future Honduran novels. Gamero de Medina followed him with what is considered her best novel, *Blanca Olmedo* (1903), which caused a scandal because it criticized Church hypocrisy and the social victimization of women.

Modernismo came to Honduras at the turn of the century. Froylán Turcios, a friend of Rubén Darío, helped renovate Honduran literature in its search for a uniquely American language capable of expressing local concerns. Founder of a variety of cultural journals, *El Pensamiento* (Thought), *La Revista Nueva* (New Review), and *Ariel*, Turcios found time to write poetry, short stories, essays, and several novels, including the unpublished *Annabel Lee* (1906), inspired by Edgar Allan Poe, and *El vampiro* (1910, re-edited in 1930; The Vampire). *Modernismo* continued to flourish even into mid-century and coexisted somewhat anachronistically with other forms. Professor, diplomat, journalist, and writer Rafael Heliodoro Valle published short stories, critical essays, poems, and a biographical novel, *Itúrbide, varón de Dios* (1944; Itúrbide, Man of God).

With the 1930s came the development of the *criollista*, or nativist, novel with its continued search for a Honduran identity and a special interest in social issues. The major *criollista* writer, Marcos Carías Reyes, a typical *pensador* and diplomat, applied Argentine Domingo Faustino Sarmiento's lessons of civilization and barbarism to the Honduran reality. He wrote *La heredad* (1931; The Farm), an ideological novel lacking plot and character development, and the more successful *Trópico* (written in 1948, published in 1971; The Tropics). The latter denounces Honduras' dependency on banana companies and its exploitation by the United States. The *criollista* novel *Bajo el chubasco* (1945; Under the Cloudburst) by Carlos Izaguirre is noteworthy for its length—two volumes of over 600 pages each—its excessive moralizing, and its degrading portrayal of women within the confines of eroticism and violence. The prolific Argentina Díaz Lozano has published nearly a dozen well-regarded novels in her lifetime, most on national themes. Her *Peregrinaje* (1944; Pilgrimage) is a novelized autobiography, direct and clearly written, which has been translated into English. Lozano has lived and worked in Guatemala for several decades. Novelist, editor, and diplomat Arturo Mejía Nieto wrote his three novels, *El tunco* (1932; The Swine), *El prófugo de sí mismo* (1934; The Fugitive from Himself), and *Liberación* (1939; Liberation), on Honduran topics while he was abroad. Some critics find him out of touch with local realities because of his absence.

The rise of the *criollista* novel coincided with, and occurred in spite of, the most vicious dictatorship of the century in Honduras, that of Tiburcio Carías Andino. Even though Carías Andino repressed creativity and independence, writers managed to benefit from improved communications and to exchange ideas with intellectuals and artists elsewhere, keeping abreast of the latest currents. Some novelists preferred to write escapist literature about an idealized countryside, while others, like Ramón Amaya-Amador, Honduras' principal writer of socialist realism,

attacked the evils of the banana companies. Amaya-Amador himself had been a banana worker and novelized many of his experiences in his most famous book, *Prisión verde* (Green Prison). Although he wrote the novel in the 1940s, political conditions did not favor publication until 1974. His focus moved to the city in *Constructores* (1959; Builders). Another novel by Amaya-Amador, *Los brujos de Ilamatepeque* (1958; The Witches of Ilamatepeque), inspired Julio Escoto's *El árbol de los pañuelos* (1972; The Handkerchief Tree). Amaya-Amador paid a price for his activism. A communist, he spent much of his life in exile.

By mid-century, Latin American writers were experimenting with new narrative techniques and turning away from *criollismo* and regionalism to more universal themes. At the forefront of the movement in Honduras, short-story writer Oscar Acosta made a narrative breakthrough with *El arca* (1956; The Ark). Novelists to emerge in the 1960s included Marcos Carías and Julio Escoto. Carías has published short stories and an important historical novel, *La memoria y sus consecuencias* (1973; Memory and Its Consequences); a novel of the city, *Una función con móbiles y tentetiesos* (1980; A Function with Mobiles and Tumbler Toys); and finally an interesting fiction, *Vernon y James: Vidas paralelas* (1992; Vernon and James: Parallel Lives), establishing parallels between two North Americans with ties to Central America, ex-military man and diplomat, Vernon Walters, and Catholic priest, James Carney. Carney, a US Army chaplain in World War II, later worked in Honduras, where he espoused liberation theology and the guerrilla cause. Carney was "disappeared" and presumed killed in 1983.

Escoto is the best known fiction writer outside of his country, having won literary prizes in Spain as well as at home. The problem of national identity has been an ever-present theme in his novels: *El árbol de los pañuelos*, about guerrilla warfare; *Días de ventisca, noches de huracán* (1980; Days of Blizzard, Nights of Hurricane); *Bajo el almendro—junto al volcán* (1988; Under the Almond Tree—Next to the Volcano); and his most recent *Madrugada: Rey del albor* (1993; Madrugada: King of Dawn). *Madrugada* is an epic novel, at once a cyberspace spy thriller, love story, and political and cultural commentary about the processes, dangers, and opportunities in transculturation, globalization, and *mestizaje*. Escoto returns to the *Popol Vuh* and the Mayan ruins of Copán to unlock the secrets of Honduras.

The other direction that Honduran narrative has taken in the last 20 years has been *testimonio*. While Honduras has not experienced the same degree of upheaval as its neighbors Guatemala, El Salvador, and Nicaragua, one cannot deny the presence of alarming social, economic, and political conditions that give rise to *testimonio*. Honduras has at least two well-known examples. A woman peasant organizer, Elvia Alvarado, published her testimony *Don't Be Afraid Gringo: A Honduran Woman Speaks from the Heart* (1987) in English to gain solidarity from North American sympathizers. Victor Virgilio López García wrote *La bahía del Puerto del Sol y la masacre de los Garífunas de San Juan* (1994; The Bay of Puerto del Sol and the Massacre of the Garífunas of San Juan) based on an atrocity perpetrated during the Carías regime against the Black Caribs on the Atlantic Coast during the 1930s. It is most likely the fear of political reprisal that caused López García to delay publication until 1994, the year the prime henchman in the massacre died.

Current trends in Honduras suggest several directions, not necessarily mutually exclusive, for the novel: the recovery of history and much intellectual angst over what the 1980s and 1990s really signified for the country; incursions into grand *fin de siglo* themes; and the search for forms that would permit consolidation of a national narrative. Among other important contemporary novelists we find Horacio Castellanos Moya, Roberto Castillo, Jorge Luis Oviedo, Manuel de Jesús Pineda, Roberto Quesada, Nery Alexis Gaytán, and César Rodríguez Indiano.

Nicaragua

Poetry and the short story, not the novel, have defined Nicaragua's literary history. Mestizo culture has dominated literature, and very little beyond oral folktales remains of the indigenous or Afro-Nicaraguan heritage. The historical and political experience of the caudillo (strongman), internal social divisions, foreign interventions, and religious devotion have all marked Nicaraguan cultural production. Literature also functions as a site of tension between elite and popular cultures. The revolution of 1979 played a crucial role in promoting popular literature. Nevertheless, like that of its Central American neighbors, Nicaraguan literature, especially the novel, has matured slowly.

The chronicles of discovery and conquest, the Latin American forerunner of the novel, are among the best literature from the colonial period in Nicaragua. Chronicler Juan Dávila, whose accounts are more didactic and informative than aesthetically refined, is considered the first Nicaraguan writer. The chaos following independence in the early 19th century was not conducive to writing; neither was the failure of the Central American Federation in 1838, which diverted intellectual energies to power struggles, violence, and the need to work for consolidation of the nation-state.

Toward the end of the 19th century, Nicaraguans formed cultural institutions to promote "belles lettres," literature written in the fashion of European models: the National Library in 1880, the first daily newspapers in the 1880s, the first literary society in 1876. Into this more favorable climate emerged the *modernista* poet of international stature, Rubén Darío (1867–1916). Known for his intense preoccupation with formal perfection and versification, rich lyricism, and intense sensuality and exoticism, the poet attempted three novels, only one of which, *Emelina* (1887), is complete. Ramón Luìs Acevedo describes it as a less than first-rate romantic *folletín*, probably intended to be interpreted as a parody (see Acevedo, 1982). Darío's elegance, sonority, irony, and humor anticipate his first important book of poetry, *Azul* (1888). Acevedo concludes that Darío had the potential to be a fine novelist, but that time, circumstances, and Darío's temperament prevented the realization of such promise.

The first Nicaraguan novel, *Amor y constancia* (1878; Love and Constancy), properly belongs to José Dolores Gámez. Like other attempts at the novel by Carlos J. Valdéz and Gustavo Guzmán, this one is romantic, anachronistic, and out of touch with reality. Early in the 20th century Anselmo Fletes Bolaños, Pedro Joaquín Cuadra Chamorro, and Pedro Joaquín Chamorro Zelaya—names associated with Nicaragua's foremost families of journalism and politics—wrote *costumbrista* and picaresque novels.

Beginning in the 1930s, writers began to search for the "national-popular," a national identity that would include all peoples within its borders. In literature, the period was influenced by a socialist realist and regionalist aesthetic, and by the influence of the vanguardists rebelling against the *modernistas*' elitist

cosmopolitanism. Politically and economically, the role of the United States, the sellout by Somoza to US interests, and the resistance of Augusto Sandino provided writers with plenty of material. Socialist realists found inspiration in the novels of the Mexican Revolution, written between 1925 and 1940. In general, however, the writer was a man of letters looking from the outside with a *criollista*'s interest in the world of the peasant or *peón*. Important novels from this period include Hernán Robleto's *Sangre en el trópico* (1930; Blood in the Tropics) which decries US meddling; José Román's *Maldito país* (Damn Country), written in the 1930s as the author accompanied Sandino on his campaigns, but published after the 1979 Sandinista triumph; proto-testimonies and documentary novels, *Itinerario de Little Corn Island* (1936; Itinerary of Little Corn Island) and *Contra Sandino en la montaña* (1942; Against Sandino in the Mountains) by Manolo Cuadra; and Emilio Quintana's *Bananos: La vida de los peones en la Yunai* (1942; Bananas: The Life of Peasants on the Banana Plantations), a nationalistic denunciation of the exploitative United Fruit Company in Central America.

Key vanguardists, including Pablo Antonio Cuadra, José Coronel Urtecho, and renowned poet and Catholic activist Ernesto Cardenal, later established a cultural journal, *El pez y la serpiente* (1961). They espoused a similar nationalism and anti-capitalism, but also searched for a national literature based on an idealized image of the peasant and highly refined modes of expression.

Meanwhile, other tendencies were at work. In the aftermath of the student massacre at León and the Cuban revolution, both occurring in 1959, many intellectuals turned their attention to urban venues and the struggle for national liberation. *El Frente Ventana*, the literary counterpart of the FSLN (Sandinista National Liberation Front) that formed in 1961, believed that the writer should commit him- or herself to social and political change. The earthquake that devastated Managua in 1972 and the poor response by corrupt authorities added impetus to the forces for change. A number of *testimonios* were written documenting the turbulent years preceding the 1979 revolution: female cadre and FSLN leader Doris Tijerino tells her story to Margaret Randall in *Somos millones . . .* (1977; We Are Millions); Carlos José Guadamuz traces the lives of fallen Sandinistas in "*Y las casas quedaron llenas de humo*" (1982; And the Houses Remained Full of Smoke); Tomás Borge blends Marxist social discourse with Christian imagery in *Carlos, el amanecer ya no es una tentación* (1980; Carlos, the Dawn Is No Longer a Temptation), evidence of the important role liberation theology played in the revolution; and Omar Cabezas' *La montaña es algo más que una inmensa estepa verde* (1982; *Fire from the Mountain: The Making of a Sandinista*) is an account of the making of *el nuevo hombre* (the revolutionary new man).

The testimonial novel, which combined the discourse and function of *testimonio* with an aesthetically more sophisticated presentation, developed simultaneously. The publication of Lisandro Chávez Alfaro's *Trágame tierra* (1969; Swallow Me Earth) marks a turning point in Nicaraguan narrative with its incorporation of boom-style techniques. The story of the friction created by the generation gap in one family mirrors the conflict at the national level. Short-story writer and later to be vice president in the Sandinista government, Sergio Ramírez, published his highly acclaimed novel *¿Te dio miedo la sangre?* (*To Bury Our Fathers: A Novel of Nicaragua*) in 1977. He creates a panorama of the Somoza years in a dictator novel without the dictator. This boom-style narrative re-creates Nicaraguan society, especially its more unsavory and colorful elements, in six interwoven but separate plot threads. The political, social, economic, and cultural context for literature changed dramatically between *To Bury Our Fathers* and Ramírez's postrevolutionary novel, *Castigo divino* (1988; Divine Punishment), which re-creates the hypocritical bourgeois milieu of León in the 1930s. This novel's emphasis on a more distant past results in a loss of immediacy, which creates a less engaged tone.

The 1979 revolution introduced a new cultural ethos and ideology. Believing that artistic creation should serve the revolution and that art should be democratic, the Sandinistas, with Cardenal as minister of culture, instituted a literacy crusade, writing workshops, and inexpensive publishing. In opposition, Pablo Antonio Cuadra accused the Sandinistas of vulgarizing culture by moving it to the lowest common denominator instead of educating the people to understand it at a higher level.

Another important postrevolutionary testimonial novel of the period, *La mujer habitada* (1988; *The Inhabited Woman*), by feminist poet and prose writer Gioconda Belli, creates a dramatic fiction with elements of magical realism surrounding an FSLN commando assault that actually took place at the home of a wealthy Nicaraguan. Belli's second novel, *Sofía de los presagios* (1990; Sofia of the Omens), moves away from the political to the ludic and carnivalesque, pursuing themes of eroticism, magic, illuminism, necromancy, feminism, and contemporary women's issues. Belli's latest novel, *Waslala: Memorial del futuro* (1996; Waslala: Memory of the Future), looks at the "third world" in the third millennium, overrun with problems of violence, drug trafficking, and ecological disasters, to find hope in the vague memory of a utopia, Waslala.

With the UNO (National Opposition Union) electoral victory of 1990, Nicaragua once again changed direction. The novel has turned inward and the writers' workshops have ceased. It remains to be seen whether Nicaraguan literature will continue to be a democratic project.

Costa Rica

As in most of Central America, the novel in Costa Rica did not develop until the 20th century. Unlike its counterpart elsewhere, however, it has been dominated by *costumbrismo,* narrative sketches of local customs with detailed descriptions of scenes and characters and a predilection for colloquialisms in language. A highly cultivated *modernismo* never garnered much popularity, perhaps because writers feel they are cut from the same plain cloth as their readers. Costa Rican novelists have participated in a search for a collective national identity.

Ironically, once the poorest area of Central America, Costa Rica is now arguably its cultural capital. History separates Costa Rica from the rest of the isthmus in that it had a sparse population, no wealth in natural resources, no *encomiendas* (special grants by the Crown of forced indigenous labor), a relatively democratic distribution of land, many small farms, high literacy, and an isolated location. There was practically no Indian lower class because Costa Rica's few indigenous peoples were decimated at conquest.

Independence came peacefully to Costa Rica in 1821, followed by the printing press in 1830, and a law mandating free primary education in 1866. The national university, however,

was not established until the 20th century. Most intellectuals worked to consolidate the nation during the 19th century, and there was little time left over for writing fiction. Thus, creative narrative started slowly. Essays dominated the political/literary landscape.

Manuel Arguello Mora wrote several romantic novels in serial form, the first of which was *Risas y llanto* (1888). His was an isolated endeavor, however, which made little impact. Credit for the first Costa Rican novel usually goes to Joaquín García Monge, the respected editor and director of the journal of history and culture, *Repertorio americano* (1919–1958), and leader of *costumbrista* realism. In *El moto* (1900; The Landmark), *Hijas del campo* (1900; The Country Daughters), and *Abnegación* (1902; Abnegation), García Monge identifies with the poor *campesino* and recognizes the regressive nature of patriarchal society, the small-mindedness of political bosses, and the deteriorating conditions in cities to which many of the poor migrate.

García Monge and other members of the Generation of 1900 preferred a direct, simple style with nativist roots. Few Costa Ricans cared to read or write works of exuberant imagination. This tendency did generate opposition from *modernistas* who preferred to imitate the more elegant French styles and incorporate sophisticated language and imagery. It also marked the beginning of a cultural polemic that lasted for many years, and in which the *costumbristas* always prevailed. The most important contemporaries of García Monge include Manuel González Zeledón ("Magón"), whose short novel *La propia* (1911; One's Own) depicts the bestialization of his characters in a *costumbrista* narrative tending toward naturalism. Others are Jenaro Cardona, author of *El primo* (1905; My Cousin), a look at the frivolous urban bourgeoisie, and *La esfinge del sendero* (1914; The Sphynx of the Path), a harangue against "unnatural" and "irrational" clerical celibacy; and the philosopher and philologist Carlos Gagini, who initiated the anti-imperialist novel in Costa Rica with his *El árbol enfermo* (1918; Redemptions) and *La caída del águila* (1920; The Fall of the Eagle). Gagini is also the most idealistic of his generation. His *La sirena* (1920; The Mermaid) is an example of romantic realism with a Costa Rican setting, but among members of high society.

Costa Rica's first woman novelist was Carmen Lyra, pseudonym for María Isabel Carvajal. A school teacher, Lyra left the classroom for a life of political activism and writing. She is famous in Costa Rica today for a collection of children's stories, *Los cuentos de mi tía Panchita* (1920). Her only novel is an early sentimental narrative, *En una silla de ruedas* (1918; In a Wheel Chair), dealing with the disintegration of family life. In later years she produced short stories of denunciation.

By the 1930s, Costa Rica, along with the rest of the world, was suffering from the Great Depression. The rise of worker militancy and demands for social programs—all with the blessings of many progressive intellectuals—met with harassment from businessmen, politicians, and large landowners, who organized anti-communist campaigns.

At the same time, both the University of Costa Rica and the Editorial Costa Rica were founded, and a major literary prize was established in 1940 by publishers Farrar and Reinhart for the best Latin American novel. These events stimulated literary production and creativity, and the writers of the Generation of 1940 took up the challenge. Adolfo Herrera García, a militant Marxist, had just initiated the social novel with *Vida y dolores de Juan Varela* (1939; The Life and Sorrows of Juan Varela). Others in the socialist-realist vein quickly followed, denouncing imperialism and exploitation in the banana industry by the United Fruit Company and defending the proletariat and the underprivileged: *Mamita Yunai* (1941; Mommy "Uni" [United Fruit]) by Carlos Luis Fallas; *Ese que llaman pueblo* (1942; That Thing They Call the People) and *El sitio de las abras* (1950; Where the Clearings Are) by Fabián Dobles; *Puerto Limón* (1950) by Joaquín Gutiérrez; and many short stories. These linear protest narratives, in which a whole community is the protagonist, parallel similar texts elsewhere.

The other narrative tendency at the time, albeit less strident, was the introspective experimental novel. Yolanda Oreamuno wrote *La ruta de su evasión* (1949; The Route of His Escape), an innovative text that explores existential anxieties in an urban environment. Hers is a denunciatory novel in its own right, expressing frustrations at domestic violence and machismo. But such material was traditionally consigned to the "private," or "feminine," sphere while banana plantations were public, political, and masculine spaces.

A contemporary who combined both tendencies, José Marín Cañas was a *criollista* writer and, according to Margarita Rojas and Flora Ovares, the initiator of the contemporary novel in Costa Rica (see Rojas and Ovares, 1995). His *criollismo* was a natural development of the *costumbrista* realist tradition. Several of his early novels experimented with vanguardist techniques. His two best-known novels are *El infierno verde* (1935; Green Hell) and *Pedro Arnáez* (1942). Critics regard the first as the best book about the Chaco Wars of the 1930s between Paraguay and Bolivia, all the more noteworthy since the author had never set foot in either country! Using stream of consciousness, Marín Cañas depicts the horrors of war. *Pedro Arnáez* is more introspective and deals with political and philosophical problems. Vanguardist Max Jímenez scandalized the reading public with his *El domador de pulgas* (1936; The Flea Tamer), a satirical novel about humanized fleas.

The realist novel stagnated during the 1950s and early 1960s. Costa Rica was sinking into economic crisis as people grew disenchanted with the failing model of import substitution and industrialization. Writers looking for new ways to represent reality took inspiration from trends in new narrative. Art no longer needed to be mimetic but interpretive. Reality had several levels.

The novel began its comeback in 1966 with the publication of Carmen Naranjo's *Los perros no ladraron* (The Dogs Did Not Bark) and then *Memorias de un hombre palabra* (1968; Memories of a Man Word). Narrative syntax became fragmented and harmony in the story line disappeared. Naranjo's characters are faceless bureaucrats who are isolated, lonely, hypocritical, and impotent. Both city and family are spaces of crisis. Oppression migrates from outside to inside in anguished beings. Also a playwright, poet, short-story writer, and essayist, Naranjo has gone on to become one of the major voices of Central American literature.

Other renovators of the Costa Rican novel include Daniel Gallegos, who situates his novel *El pasado es un extraño país* (1993; The Past Is a Foreign Country) in the Tinoco dictatorship of the early 20th century and around a person who cannot get rid of his past; Samuel Rovinski, whose *Ceremonia de casta* (1976, Ceremony of Caste) allegorizes the national crisis as a family crisis in an open-ended, complex narrative; and José León

Sánchez, who combines the grotesque and the lyrical in *La isla de los hombres solos* (1967; The Island of Lonely Men), a denunciation of conditions at the San Lucas prison, and *Tenochtitlán: La última batalla de los aztecas* (1986; Tenochtitlán: The Last Battle of the Aztecs), a historical look at the problem of identity. This period also fostered the emergence of an increasing number of women writers, such as Julieta Pinto, who has published at least six novels, the most recent of which is a new twist on a Bible story, *El despertar de Lázaro* (1994; The Awakening of Lazarus); and Rima de Vallbona, author of *Noche en vela* (1968; Night of Vigil) and *Las sombras que perseguimos* (1983; The Shadows We Pursue), a complex and confusing narrative of violence, dream, and reality.

A group of even younger novelists who began publishing in the 1970s and 1980s continue to ponder Costa Rica's national identity, rewrite official history, and deconstruct truth and power. These include Alfonso Chase, Fernando Durán Ayanegui, Quince Duncan, Rafael Angel Herra, Gerardo César Hurtado, Tatiana Lobo, Rosibel Morera, Hugo Rivas, and Anacristina Rossi. Specifically, Duncan explores the marginality of blacks in connection to the exploitation by the fruit companies, while Rossi highlights the struggle to protect and preserve Costa Rica's biological diversity in *La loca de Gandoca* (1992; The Mad Woman of Gandoca), an eco-feminist novel that is part of a hemispheric trend by some women writers.

Panama

Twentieth-century literature, including the novel, in Panama has been consumed by the reality of the canal. A territory divided, an international crossroads, a commercial rather than a cultural or spiritual center, Panama expresses in its literature the transient quality of life on the isthmus.

The novel developed especially late in Panama. To speak of a national literary tradition is to look back only as far as 1903, when Panama seceded from Colombia. The United States supported the move in order to build the canal and since then has dominated its local politics and culture.

The development of the novel in Panama also has been influenced by pre-20th century culture. At the time of the conquest, many indigenous groups lived in the area that is now Panama, but most of their oral traditions died with them at the hands of the Spanish invaders. Modern intellectual traditions began in colonial times when the Jesuits established the University of San Javier in 1749, only to see it close in 1767 upon their expulsion from the continent. Sporadic attempts at literature produced fine examples of poetry, essays, and intellectual history. However, printing presses, which are needed to support a high level of literary activity, especially the publication and dissemination of forms such as the novel, did not arrive until 1821.

The first Spaniard to write narratives in the territory that is now Panama was Rodrigo Galván de Bastidas in the early 16th century. In writings that are more documentary than aesthetic, he records violent encounters with indigenous tribes and his awe upon seeing the lush tropical vegetation of the area.

Poet and statesman Gil Colunje is credited with the first Panamanian novel, *La verdad triunfante* (1879; The Victorious Truth), although Panama was still technically part of Colombia at the time. Published serially, his novel is a story of the triumph of love over societal prejudices. Two other romantic novels appeared later in the century: *Melida* (1888) by Jeremías Jaén, who was inspired by adventure tales, and Manuel José Pérez's *El último delirio de Lord Byron* (1889; The Last Delirium of Lord Byron), a novelized and lyrical account of the English poet's life. Neither novel has anything to do with Panama.

The genre was slow to develop until the 20th century, when the *modernistas* made efforts to create a truly national literature. *Modernismo* provided writers with the tools, training, and confidence to approach universal themes with aesthetic flair. *Modernista* poet, politician, editor, and critic Guillermo Andreve published the novel *Una punta del velo* (1929; A Corner of the Veil), in which the theme is spiritism.

The historical novel in Panama began with Octavio Méndez Pereira, educator and founder of the University of Panama (1935). He authored *El tesoro del Dabaibe* (1934; Treasure of Dabaibe), a biographical novel about the explorer Balboa, which is considered one of the best historical narratives in Panamanian literature. Another important historical novelist is Julio B. Sosa, who wrote *La india dormida* (1936; The Sleeping Indian Woman), an Indianist novel situated in the years of conquest and colonization; *Tú sola en mi vida* (1943; You Alone in My Life), concerning the 19th-century dictator Juan Eligio Alzuru; and *En la cumbre se pierden los caminos* (1957; On the Summit the Paths Are Lost), a *criollista* novel of social protest set in the coffee-growing region. Sosa represents the transition from romanticism to regionalism and *criollismo* in the 1930s and 1940s, a period in which the Panamanian novel comes of age. Later writers associated with historical and *criollista* novels include Ramón H. Jurado, who wrote *San Cristóbal* (1947; Saint Christopher), a "sugar novel" about exploitation in the cane fields; *¡Desertores!* (1952; Deserters), the story of an indigenous caudillo; and *El desván* (1954; The Attic), an existential treatment of writer Francisco Clark. Luisita Aguilera Patiño based her novel *El secreto de Antatura* (1953; The Secret of Antatura) on Panamanian legends and traditions.

Rogelio Sinán, pseudonym of Bernardo Domínguez Alba, perhaps best exemplifies *modernismo* in Panama. He founded the journal *Antena* in 1930 to promote vanguardist aesthetics. His novel *Plenilunio* (1947; Full Moon) incorporates experimental narrative techniques, stream of consciousness, Freudian concepts, and surrealism in a story of bitterness over the social problems created by the canal. Images of sordid city life, where transients and deviants stream in from all over the world, place this novel fully within the dominant current of *novelas canaleras* (canal novels). *Plenilunio* won the first Concurso Ricardo Miró (Ricard Miró Competition), Panama's most prestigious literary award.

The establishment of literary prizes was key to identifying and stimulating promising writers, especially novelists. The Ricardo Miró Competition and Prize, named after the country's most important *modernista* poet and critic (1883–1940), was established in the mid-1940s. Most of the writers subsequently honored combined aesthetic sensibilities with a concern for social justice.

The canal novel flourished in this environment, although one can find precursors. *Josefina* (1903) by Julio Ardila started the movement and coincided with independence and the signing of the treaty giving the United States rights to the zone. *Josefina* was followed by *Noches de Babel* (1913), a lyrical short novel by Miró himself in which he depicts the changes in society resulting from the US presence. The most famous canal novel is ac-

tually a trilogy by Joaquín Beleño, who had been a worker in the Canal Zone. In *Luna verde* (1951; Green Moon), *Los forzados de Gamboa* (1960; Gamboa Road Gang), and *Curundú* (1963), Beleño exposes the miseries and resentments of the workers and reveals the tensions between Panamanians and North Americans. In 1970 he added a fourth novel, *Flor de banana* (Banana Flower), denouncing the abuses of the banana companies. Other well-known canal novels are Renato Ozores' *Playa honda* (1950; Deep Beach), which exposes the immorality of high society's profiteering from the canal; *Puente del mundo* (1951; World Bridge), an attack against the transitory presence of foreigners and privileges related to the canal, as well as winner of the Concurso Miró; and *La calle oscura* (1955; Dark Street), a look at marginals in the city. Other novelists who have contributed to the canal corpus and to related works of social protest are Gil Blas Tejera, César Candanedo, José Isaac Fábrega, Tristán Solarte (pseudonym for Guillermo Sánchez Borbón), and Yolanda Camarano de Sucre. Writers continue to publish canal novels today.

More recently, novels in Panama have taken various directions, some expressing universal concerns rather than local ones, others touching on themes of feminism or psychological analysis, still others practicing formal experimentation. Enrique Chuez combines regional themes and new narrative techniques in *Las averías* (1972; Breakdowns), a novel about fishermen; Chuez is also the author of *La mecedora* (1976; The Rocking Chair) and *La casa de las sirenas pálidas* (1983; The House of the Pale Mermaids). Guillermo E. Beleño Cedeno describes the apocalypse in *Novela absurda* (1966; Absurd Novel).

One of the most important female voices to emerge in Panama in recent years is Gloria Guardia. In 1977 Guardia won the Central American Novel Prize for *El último juego* (The Last Game), in which she experiments with narrative strategies such as interior monologue as she creates a plot that blends history and fiction. Other novels by Guardia include *Tiniebla blanca* (1961; White Darkness) and *Despertar sin raíces* (1966; Waking Up Without Roots). Rosa María Britton has also joined the growing ranks of women writers in Panama, capturing the Miró Prize in 1982 for her novel *El ataúd de uso* (Coffin in Use). She has since published the novels *El señor de las lluvias y el viento* (1985; Lord of the Rain and Wind) and *Esa esquina del paraíso* (1986, That Corner of Paradise) and continues to publish both novels and short stories prolifically.

Two additional contemporary Panamanian authors who bear mentioning are Carlos Guillermo Wilson ("Cubena") and Enrique Jaramillo Levi. Wilson, an Afro-Panamanian now living and working as a writer and professor in the United States, still writes in Spanish about Panamanian themes. His novels include *Chombo* (1981; Nigger) and *Sodinu*. Jaramillo Levi, director of the journal *Maga* and editor of *Editorial Signos,* is primarily a poet and literary critic who also has experimented with the novel in his *Duplicaciones* (1973; Duplications).

Belize

The cultural history of Belize differs from that of its Central American neighbors because of the dominance of the British in the area. Although Spanish conquistadors arrived in Belize in the 1520s and claimed it as part of Guatemala, they did little to settle the territory. From British mahogany cutters in the 17th century through governors who formally established the Colony of

British Honduras in 1862—in opposition to Guatemala, which wanted it back—Britain gained and maintained control of this Caribbean outpost. Belize finally achieved its independence on 21 September 1981 and remains a member of the British Commonwealth.

While English is Belize's official language, Belizeans also speak Spanish, Carib, Mayan Mopán or Ketchi, and/or Creole. The population is ethnically and culturally diverse: almost half of Belaze's people are Creoles (African, African-British, or West Indian), and the rest are mestizos (European and Indian), Mayans, Garífunas (African and Amerindian), East Indians, Chinese, Middle Easterners, Mennonites, and expatriate Canadians and North Americans. An increasing number of Guatemalan and Salvadoran refugees have arrived in Belize in recent years, escaping political turmoil in their homelands. Popular identification still remains largely with the British.

"Sophisticated" written literature developed in Belize even later than in the rest of Central America. Oral traditions and folktales were handed down in the Mayan communities and among peoples of African descent, but most of these have been ignored and remain uncollected. A Garífuna novel, *Tumba le, la Conga*, was written in 1977 by Don Justo (pseudonym of Justín Mejía) and published privately.

Before the early 1880s, literature in the territory of what is now Belize consisted of a few political pamphlets and church material. After Belize's colonial identity was separated from that of Jamaica in 1882, prose publications of a scientific or sociological nature increased. Belizean writers did not publish literary diaries, journals, or memoirs—predecessors of novels in other Latin American countries. Nor did societies, journals, or universities exist to promote literary efforts until the first newspaper, *The Daily Clarion,* was established in 1943. Creative writing began more earnestly after World War II as the publication of short stories and poetry in English was encouraged. As hopes of independence took hold in the 1960s, a more overtly nationalistic literature was published. Part of the project of nation building was the belief that art should serve the national interest. Didacticism, social realism, historiography, and some satire characterized much of the prose. The speeches and autobiography of Belize's first Prime Minister, George Price, make up an important part of its literature. Evan X. Hyde, a Dartmouth-educated writer, is a gifted social realist short fiction writer and polemicist. Hyde's style and language "flecked with argot" may point in the direction of a future literary language in Belize, especially one that reveals Belize's highly multicultural realities.

Belize's first novel is a recent one, *Beka Lamb* (1982) by Zee Edgell, a former journalist and now professor in a US university. *Beka Lamb* has been called a feminist fiction, as well as an autobiographical and academic novel. Edgell uses the technique of the flashback to reconstruct the 1950s, a period when solidarity and enthusiasm built as Belize neared independence. This novel, which combines the personal with the political, won the British Fawcett Society Book Prize for women's literature. Edgell's second novel, *In Times Like These* (1991), again looks at the transition of national life in the early 1980s while piecing together accounts from newspapers, archives, and her own experiences in much the same fashion as Central American testimonial novels. This text describes the status of women during this period and the government response to them; it also addresses a secondary story involving the dispute between Britain and Guatemala.

Glenn D. Godfrey published the second Belizean novel, *The Sinners' Bossanova* (1987), which is known for its numerous plot lines and depictions of Belizean "low life," rather than for outstanding literary qualities. David Ruiz Puga published *Old Benque: Erase una vez un Benque Viejo* (1990; Once Upon a Time There Was an Old Benque), Mayan legends from the western border in the first collection in Spanish by a Belizean, perhaps signaling new multicultural trends in narrative.

Alan McLeod predicts that Belizean literature will adopt a more lyrical and interpretive mode as it moves away from social realism (see McLeod, 1982). The novel and other forms are searching for expressions that reflect the linguistic and cultural blends characteristic of this nation, which is more Caribbean than Spanish American.

LINDA J. CRAFT

See also Miguel Ángel Asturias

Further Reading

Acevedo, Ramón Luis, *La novela centroamericana* (The Central American Novel), Río Piedras: Editorial Universitaria, Universidad de Puerto Rico, 1982

Albizúrez Palma, Francisco, *Historia de la literatura guatemalteca* (History of Guatemalan Literature), 2 vols., Guatemala City: Editorial Universitaria de Guatemala, 1981

Arellano, Jorge Eduardo, *Panorama de la literatura nicaraguense* (Panorama of Nicaraguan Literature), 4th edition, Managua: Nueva Nicaragua, 1982; originally published in 1966

Beverley, John, and Marc Zimmerman, *Literature and Politics in the Central American Revolutions*, Austin: University of Texas Press, 1990

Craft, Linda J., *Novels of Testimony and Resistance from Central America*, Gainesville: University Press of Florida, 1997

Ergood, Bruce, "Belize as Presented in Her Literature," *Belizean Studies* 21:2 (October 1993)

Escoto, Julio, "Narrativa," in *Literatura hondureña: Selección de estudios críticos sobre su proceso formativo* (Honduran Literature: A Selection of Critical Studies on Its Creative Process), edited by Rigoberto Paredes and Manuel Salinas Paguada, Tegucigalpa: Unidos, 1987

Gallegos Valdés, Luis, *Panorama de la literatura salvadoreña* (Panorama of Salvadoran Literature), 3rd edition, San Salvador: UCA Editores, 1981; originally published in 1958

García S., Ismael, *Historia de la literatura panameña* (History of Panamanian Literature), 2nd edition, Mexico City: Universidad Nacional Autónoma de México, 1972; originally published in 1964

Liano, Dante, editor, *Centroamericana*, Rome: Bulzoni, 1990

Lorand de Olazagasti, Adelaida, *El indio en la narrativa guatemalteca* (The Indian in Guatemalan Narrative), San Juan: Editorial Universitaria, Universidad de Puerto Rico, 1968

Martínez, José Francisco, *Literatura hondureña y su proceso generacional* (Honduran Literature and Its Generational Process), Tegucigalpa: Editorial Universitaria, 1987

McLaurin, Irma, "A Writer's Life, A Country's Transition," *Americas* 46:4 (July-August 1994)

McLeod, Alan L., "The English Literature of Belize," *World Literature Today* 56:3 (Summer 1982)

Menton, Seymour, *Historia crítica de la novela guatemalteca*, Guatemala City: Editorial Universitaria de Guatemala, 1960; 2nd edition, 1985

Osses, Ester María, *La novela del imperialismo en Centroamérica* (The Novel of Imperialism in Central America), Maracaibo: Universidad del Zulia, Vicerrectorado Académico, 1986

Rojas, Margarita, and Flora Ovares, *100 años de literatura costarricense* (One Hundred Years of Costa Rican Literature), La Uruca, Costa Rica: Farben, 1995

Sepúlveda, Melida Ruth, *El tema del canal en la novelística panameña* (The Theme of the Canal in the Panamanian Novel), Caracas: Universidad Católica "Andres Bello," Centro de Investigaciones Literarias, 1975

Toruño, Juan Felipe, *Desarrollo literario de El Salvador* (Literary Development of El Salvador), San Salvador: Ministerio de Cultura, 1958

Umaña, Helen, *Literatura hondureña contemporánea: Ensayos* (Contemporary Honduran Literature: Essays), Tegucigalpa: Guaymuras, 1986

Zimmerman, Marc, *Literature and Resistance in Guatemala*, 2 vols., Athens: Ohio University Press, 1995

Latin American Novel

Hispanic Caribbean

The emergence of the novel in Spanish America is associated with the early 19th-century movements for independence and the need to forge a national identity. This was the case in the Spanish Caribbean, with some variations. The Dominican Republic received its independence from Haiti in 1844; Cuba from Spain in 1902; and Puerto Rico remained a colony and was transferred from Spain to the United States after the Spanish American War of 1898. Despite these distinct political situations, the 19th century was a crucial time for the development of national consciousness in the Spanish Caribbean, and the novel recorded the unique historical circumstances unfolding in each country.

Cuba

The beginning of Cuban literature in general and the novel in particular can be traced to Domingo Delmonte, Cuba's most important literary critic of the 19th century. A member of the influential Sociedad Económica de Amigos del País, he was in charge of the newly constituted literary commission. Delmonte wanted to promote a Cuban literature that reflected the island's culture. Delmonte is better known for his literary salons, which he held in his home in Matanzas and later in Havana. There, he met with writer friends and exposed them to his vast library and the latest European literary currents. He also encouraged his colleagues to abandon romanticism and embrace realism and to incorporate the stories of blacks and slaves into their writings.

Delmonte encouraged the slave Juan Francisco Manzano to write his *Autobiografía* (written 1835, published in Spanish in 1937), arguably the first narrative to document life on the island. From Delmonte's salon surfaced such antislavery works as Anselmo Suárez y Romero's *Francisco* (written 1839, published 1880) and Félix Tanco y Bosmeniel's stories *Escenas de la vida privada en la isla de Cuba* (written 1838; Scenes of the Private Life on the Island of Cuba). Although mild by today's standards, these works presented a counter discourse to the hegemonic Spanish power. They were censored for their content but circu-

lated clandestinely among the members of the Delmonte circle, and were included in an antislavery portfolio, given to Richard Madden, the British Arbiter in Mixed Courts, to be presented before the Antislavery Convention in London. Only Manzano's autobiography was published at the time of writing, not in Cuba but in England. Madden translated it as "Life of a Negro Poet" and, together with some of his and Manzano's poems and an interview with Delmonte, published it as *Poems by a Slave in the Island of Cuba* in 1840.

Cecilia Valdés, o La Loma del Ángel (*Cecilia Valdés, or Angel's Hill*), Cuba's national novel, was also written under Delmonte's tutelage. Cirilo Villaverde, one of the most prolific writers of the century, was a member of the literary circle, and he wrote an early short story entitled "Cecilia Valdés" and a first volume in 1839. But the definitive version was not published until 1882, not in Cuba but in New York, where Villaverde lived after he escaped from jail for conspiring against the Spanish government in 1848. Although the short story was included as an early chapter, the first and last versions of the novel are different. The first version documents the triangular relationship among the characters; the second version does the same but sets the story during General Vives' administration from 1812 to 1832 and records the suffering of blacks. Villaverde's experience living in the United States after the US Civil War apparently influenced him to make *Cecilia Valdés* an antislavery novel.

In Spain, Gertrudis Gómez de Avellaneda wrote *Sab* (1841; *Sab*), about slavery and the sacrifices the slave protagonist makes to help his mistress marry. Gómez de Avellaneda, who was not a member of the Delmonte group, did profit from the liberal reforms associated with the Spanish Constitution of 1812, which called for the elimination of slavery.

Although the emphasis here is on the antislavery novel, other kinds of writing appeared during this period. Ramón de Palma y Romay originated indigenism, or what later became known as *ciboneyismo*, which sought inspiration in the life and customs of the Amerindians. He wrote *Matanza y el Yumurí* (1837), the tragic love story of Ornofay and the princess Guarina. In this tradition, Gómez de Avellaneda wrote *Guatimozín* (1846) and *El cacique de Turmeque* (1860; The Chief of Turmeque), novels about the Amerindian past. But Palma was also interested in *costumbrismo*, or customs; his *El cólera en La Habana* (1838; Cholera in Havana) takes up this infestation in the capital city in 1833, and his controversial *La pascua en San Marcos* (1838; Easter in San Marcos) criticizes gambling and the upper classes.

The early literature had a lasting effect on writers in Cuba, and the antislavery theme continued well into the contemporary period. Antonio Zambrana wrote *El negro Francisco* (1873; The Black Francisco), a rewriting of Suárez y Romero's *Francisco* that was published not in Cuba, where slavery continued to be a viable institution until 1886, but in the United States. The critic Francisco Calcagno, who was critical of certain Spanish administrators and of slavery, wrote *Los crímenes de Concha* (written 1863, published 1887; Concha's Crimes), *Romualdo, uno de tanto* (1881; Romualdo, One Among Many), and *Aponte* (1885), which refers to the leader of the Aponte Conspiracy of 1812 that sought to liberate Cuba and emancipate slaves. The black journalist and politician Martín Morúa Delgado did not consider Villaverde's novel to be credible, and he wrote *Sofía* (1891) as a reworking of *Cecilia Valdés*. His *La familia Unzúazu* (1901) takes up the issues of independence and slavery.

In the 20th century, and after the founding of the Cuban Republic, two themes became popular among novelists: Cuban society's decay and slavery. Writers who developed the first theme reflected the mood of the time. The founding of the republic did not usher in the changes everyone expected; the evils of the past continued into the present. Of this period two writers stand out. Miguel del Carrión combines psychology with naturalism and is critical of false religion in *El milagro* (1903; The Miracle). He explores the feminine psyche, women's rights, and other feminist issues in *Las honradas* (1917; The Dignified), *Las impuras* (1919; The Impure), and the unfinished *La esfinge* (1961; The Sphinx). Carlos Loveira distinguishes himself as a student of societal problems. He attacks marital infidelity in *Los inmorales* (1919; The Immorals) and the corruption that accompanied independence in *Generales y Doctores* (1920; Generals and Doctors). *Juan Criollo* (1927) is his most ambitious work, in which he discusses the negative influences of the period, as Cuban society changed from colony to independent republic.

The antislavery theme was continued by Lino Novás Calvo, who earned his reputation as a short-story writer. Calvo's novel *El negrero* (1933; The Slave Trader), which has not received the attention it merits, documents slavery and the slave trade and the life of Pedro Blanco, one of the most notorious and successful slave traders of the 19th century. Cuban writers of this period addressed the topic of slavery not only to explain the past but also to comment on the present.

Alejo Carpentier, one of the most important Spanish American writers of the 20th century, also wrote about blacks. As is the case with other authors whose careers straddled the Cuban Revolution, Carpentier's novels can be divided into two periods, before and after Castro came to power. His early works reflect an interest in Afro-Cuban culture and religion, as seen in the writings of the anthropologist Fernando Ortiz and of the Afro-Cuban poetic movement. Africa and black culture were dominant elements in European vanguard movements, and Cubans looked to their culture for a more meaningful and au-

thentic expression. Carpentier's *¡Écue-Yamba-Ó!* (1933; Lord Praised Be Thou) describes Afro-Cuban rites, religions, and secret societies. His next novel, *El reino de este mundo* (1949; The Kingdom of This World), about blacks in the neighboring country of Haiti, records transitions in Haitian history, from Mackandal's slave rebellion to the Boyer government. Carpentier's visit to Haiti helped him formulate his ideas about America through the employment of "marvellous reality," later confused with magic realism. His two other novels of the pre-Castro period have little to do with blacks. *El acoso* (1956; The Chase) describes the end of the Machado dictatorship, when the protagonist is hunted for betraying his political allies. *Los pasos perdidos* (1953; The Lost Steps), like *The Kingdom of This World,* reflects upon the origin of America, a theme developed by other major writers of the period. The setting is the South American jungle, where the protagonist, alienated from contemporary society, travels through the past to an origin before time and writing, a place that he visits but later is unable to return to.

Carpentier returned to Cuba from Venezuela shortly after Castro acquired power, and his *El siglo de las luces* (1962; Explosion in a Cathedral) was celebrated as a novel of the revolution. Its major theme was the struggle against tyranny and oppression, as the ideas and practices of the French Revolution were implemented in the Caribbean. However, Roberto González Echevarría (1977) has shown that Carpentier had completed the manuscript prior to the revolution and before his return to Cuba. *El recurso del método* (1974; Reasons of State) presents a composite picture of many ruthless Latin American leaders and describes the similarities and differences between a dictator and a rebel student. *Concierto barroco* (1974; Baroque Concerto) inverts the conquest of America, as a Mexican and his servant travel to Europe. The novel underscores the New World's contribution to Western music. *La consagración de la primavera* (1978; The Rite of Spring) is Carpentier's only novel to describe events of the Cuban Revolution, and here he does so only at the end, as he narrates events related to the Spanish Civil War and the Batista dictatorship. *Spring,* as it is used in the title, implying change and rebirth, also refers to Stravinsky's ballet score. Carpentier's last novel, *El arpa y la sombra* (1979; The Harp and the Shadow), also alludes to music, as well as to Christopher Columbus' less saintly attributes and his proposed canonization. Before the revolution, Carpentier's works, and those of other writers of his generation, had limited circulation as the reading public preferred European and North American works. After the revolution, Carpentier became one of the leading figures of Cuban and Latin American literature, and his works were read by an international audience.

The revolution transformed Cuban society, culture, and literature. For better or worse, it remains the single most important event of this century in the Spanish Caribbean. As a result of the revolution, Cuba would experience its own literary explosion and bring its literature and culture to the attention of a world audience. The events surrounding the Cuban missile crisis (October 1962) transformed Cuba and Latin America into preferred areas of study. Cuban literature was no longer viewed as a national or regional enterprise but one with universal meaning, and an increasing number of Cuban literary works became available to Spanish readers and to readers throughout the world, in translation. In his *Prose Fiction of the Cuban Revolution* (1975), Seymour Menton divides this literature into four stages and periods: the struggle against tyranny (1959–60), exorcism and existentialism (1961–65), epos, experimentation, and escapism (1966–70), and the ideological novel (1971–73). Although some works do not fit into these periods, Menton's study continues to be the most exhaustive on the subject.

The early stages of the revolution were characterized by enthusiasm and support for the government, and members of the July 26 movement, which brought Castro to power, promoted literature and the novel. Carlos Franqui's newspaper *Revolución* and Guillermo Cabrera Infante's literary supplement *Lunes de Revolución* opened their pages to established and young writers alike. When Castro proclaimed the revolution to be communist in April 1961, *Lunes de Revolución* was closed; other literary organizations restrictive in their interpretation of literary production emerged. The Union of Writers and Artists of Cuba (UNEAC) and Casa de las Américas, the latter created to break the literary and cultural blockade imposed by the United States, were the two most influential institutions promoting literature. Culture and literature were interpreted as ideological weapons.

While there was pressure to document the accomplishments of the revolution, the most important Cuban writers living in and outside the island wrote about an earlier and less troublesome time. Most of the internationally acclaimed writers left the island. Severo Sarduy, whose first works appeared in *Ciclón* and *Carteles* in the 1950s, obtained a scholarship to study art criticism in Europe and stayed in Paris, where he joined the Tel Quel group, becoming the Latin American series editor of Editions du Seuil. He incorporated techniques associated with the *nouveau roman* into his works. His first novel, *Gestos* (1963; Gestures), describes life during the Batista dictatorship and captures with imaginative flare the activities of a black woman, who by day washes clothing and by night is a terrorist. In *De dónde son los cantantes* (1967; *From Cuba with a Song*), Sarduy affirms that Cuban culture is Spanish, African, and Chinese, as represented by his characters. With *Cobra* (1972; *Cobra*) Sarduy transcends Cuban culture, as his protagonist, a transvestite, searches for meaning and identity in other parts of the world. *Maitreya* (1978; *Maitreya*) takes the search for enlightenment to Asia, and seeks it in Buddhism, but returns to Cuba and the United States. *Colibrí* (1984; Hummingbird) takes place in a homosexual brothel in the Latin American jungle, where the protagonist works as a dancer and wrestler. He escapes persecution only to return and impose on others the same conditions under which he suffered. Sarduy's last work was *Cocuyo* (1990; Cacoon), which he published before his untimely death in 1993.

Guillermo Cabrera Infante is one of the few writers to equal Carpentier in literary stature. Prior to 1959 he served as editor of the movie section of *Carteles*; however, he is better known as the editor of the controversial literary supplement *Lunes de Revolución*. Cabrera Infante later became dissatisfied with the revolution and moved to London in 1966. With *Tres tristes tigres* (1965; *Three Trapped Tigers*) Cabrera Infante joined Julio Cortázar, Carlos Fuentes, Mario Vargas Llosa, and Gabriel García Márquez as one of the leading influences of the Latin American boom. *Three Trapped Tigers* documents the nightlife of Havana prior to the revolution. Havana, Cuban speech, and puns become characters in the novel. Cabrera Infante's other works include *La Habana para un infante difunto* (1979; *Infante's Inferno*), an autobiographical novel narrating the protagonist's sexual exploits, from his early encounters with Julieta to

his conquest of Margarita, while still married to his wife; and *Holy Smoke* (1985), written in English, about the history of the cigar and popular culture.

José Lezama Lima is another major writer of Spanish American literature. Known as a poet and editor of the famed *Orígenes* during the revolution, he wrote *Paradiso* (1966; *Paradiso*), a Bildungsroman that narrates the life of José Cemi, who is guided by his classmates Ricardo Fronesis and Eugenio Foción, and later by Oppiano Licario. The novel is rich in symbolism from various cultures, including Christian, Oriental, Greek, and Nordic mythologies. *Paradiso* met with resistance from government officials because of explicit homosexual descriptions. However, it was rumored that Castro himself read the novel and ordered its distribution. Lezama published posthumously *Oppiano Licario* (1977), named after a character who appeared in *Paradiso*, but this novel did not have the same impact as the earlier work. Although Lezama died in Cuba, he lived as an internal exile.

Of those writers who became novelists after the revolution, Reinaldo Arenas was the most active and best known. As government officials insisted, he wrote about the events of the revolution. However, he did not glorify them and was even critical of the Castro government. His first novel, *Celestino antes del alba* (1967; *Singing from the Well*) received a first mention in a national competition, yet this was the only work he published in Cuba. *El mundo alucinante* (1969; *Hallucinations*) and *El palacio de las blanquísimas mofetas* (1980; *The Palace of the White Skunks*) were smuggled out of the country and published first in French. Dissatisfied with the Cuban government, which persecuted him for his sexual preferences, Arenas escaped detention and went into hiding, fleeing the island during the Mariel Boat Lift in 1980. In the United States he continued to write and denounce the Castro government until his death in 1990.

Arenas' international standing can be attributed to *Hallucinations,* which was awarded *Le Monde*'s first prize for foreign novels. The novel narrates the life of the 17th-century Fray Servando Teresa de Mier, whose memoirs contribute to the novel's subtext. The memoirs describe de Mier's travels and experiences, including his polemical sermon about the origins of the Virgin of Guadalupe that caused his downfall, and his struggles for Mexican independence both at home and abroad. Arenas' goal was not to reconstruct history but to subvert it and uncover its multiple facets.

Arenas wrote and published most of his works in the United States. They include the novels *Otra vez el mar* (1982; *Farewell to the Sea*), which he had begun in Cuba; *La loma del Ángel* (1987; *Graveyard of the Angels*), another rewriting of *Cecilia Valdés*; and *El portero* (1989; *The Doorman*), about life in New York. But his most important work of his exile period was his autobiography *Antes que anochezca* (1992; *Before Night Falls*), a scathing denunciation of the Castro government, written on his deathbed. Arenas provides the reader with his version of the events surrounding his life, and he uses his own homosexuality as a weapon against Castro's supporters, accusing police and government officials of engaging in similar acts.

Many of the writers who remained in Cuba and wrote about contemporary events in the new society did so from an ideological perspective, which considered the revolutionaries good and the counterrevolutionaries and US officials bad. There are a few novelists who were successful in writing about the revolution.

Edmundo Desnoes' *Memorias del subdesarrollo* (1965; *Inconsolable Memories*) best captures a period of conflict, experienced by a well-do-to businessman who decides to stay in Cuba; it examines how the revolution directly affected him. Unlike Desnoes, who has lived in the United States since 1979, Manuel Cofiño wrote and died on the island. In his *La última mujer y el próximo combate* (The Last Woman and the Next Combat), winner of the 1971 Casa de las Américas Prize, the protagonist sacrifices his marriage for the revolution and succeeds in his attempts to help peasants.

The testimonial novel is a more successful subgenre associated with literature in Cuba. It is based on interviews with an informant, usually someone marginal to society whose story has not been recorded. The writer edits the interviews and writes the book. However, it is difficult for the writer to remain objective, for the editing process coincides with the writer's interpretation of events. Miguel Barnet's *Biografía de un cimarrón* (1966; *The Autobiography of a Runway Slave*) was the first work to publicize the testimonial novel. Through interviews with Esteban Montejo, a 106-year-old Afro-Cuban who lived during slavery, the novel explores different periods in Cuban history: slavery, emancipation, and the formation of the republic. Although the interviews also included discussion of the Cuban Revolution, these segments were edited out of the novel.

Puerto Rico

Unlike Cuban literature, the Puerto Rican novel did not emerge out of a coherent movement, but rather it grew from individuals, and European literary currents played a decisive role in the development of the genre. Compared to Cuba, Puerto Rico played a small role in Spain's economy. The societal contradictions and reform movements were not as well developed as those of its sister island. Early instances of the novel include Puerto Rican patriot Eugenio María de Hostos' *La peregrinación de Bayoán* (1873; *Bayoán's Pilgrimage*), a romantic work that outlines the patriot's travels and draws on the Amerindian past and the Spanish colonization. It calls for a united Cuba, Puerto Rico, and Dominican Republic. Although the novel was first published in Madrid in 1863, it was confiscated and was not available to a larger public until its second printing in Chile.

Other writers who promoted this early genre include Manuel Corchado y Juarbe, who wrote *Historias de ultratumba* (1872; Stories from Beyond the Grave), about the author's spiritualism and contact with the dead, and Salvador Brau, who wrote naturalist novels including *La pecadora* (1887; The Sinner), which takes place in the countryside, and *Lejanías* (1912; Distance), an action novel about maritime activities and flights to nearby islands. But Manuel Alonso's *El gíbaro* (1882; Hillbilly) is generally accepted as the island's first major work. It describes scenes from the lives of the peasants, symbols of Puerto Ricans, especially as they migrate to the United States. He also wrote a sequel to the novel seven years later. More in the romantic tradition is Alejandro Tapia y Rivera, who authored narratives such as *La leyenda del cacique* (1852; The Chief's Tale) and *La leyenda de los veinte años* (1874; The Twenty-Year Tale). He also wrote novels that revealed his interest in Asian culture, such as *Enardo y Rosael* (1880) and *Póstumo el transmigrado* (1882; The Reincarnated Soul).

The Puerto Rican novel came into its own with Manuel Zeno Gandía, who captured island culture with great precision. Zeno Gandía abandoned the romanticism of his earlier works and embraced naturalism in a series of works subtitled *Crónica de un mundo enfermo* (Chronicles of a Sick World). *Garduña* (1896) takes place in a sugar mill and describes the protagonist's destruction of the characters. It marks a transition in society, from those who inherited land to those who will do what is necessary to obtain it. His best-known work, *La charca* (1894; *La charca*), explores the society of coffee farms in Puerto Rico, but it also depicts the deterioration of humanity through rape, robbery, murder, and suicide. *El negocio* (1922; The Business), which takes place in the port city of Ponce, documents political injustices. *Redentores* (1925) foretells the naming of a Puerto Rican governor, Aureo Sol, and his relationship with Madelón, a North American woman. Zeno Gandía also wrote an inconclusive novel, *Nueva York*, which outlines Puerto Rican migration to the mainland.

While some authors made attempts to write modernist novels, focusing on aesthetics, others addressed Puerto Rico's political status. More recent writers have documented the mass displacement of Puerto Ricans to New York. If the Cuban Revolution marked the life of every Cuban writer, US control of Puerto Rico did the same for Puerto Rican authors.

In the 1930s Enrique Laguerre emerged as the next important Puerto Rican novelist. His works spanned many decades and each work reflects the concerns of the moment in which he wrote. He indulged in sociological and psychological descriptions in his best-known novel *La llamarada* (1935; The Flare-Up), about the sugarcane industry. *Solar Montoya* (1941) studies the coffee industry and describes attempts to preserve the plantations. *La resaca* (1949; Undertow) looks at colonial life during the last quarter of the century, a time in which Puerto Ricans were discussing their political status. *Los dedos de la mano* (1951; Fingers on the Hand) is a psychological novel. In his later years, Laguerre became more experimental with form and ideas, as seen in *La ceiba en el tiesto* (1956; The Bombax in the Flowerpot), *El laberinto* (1959; *The Labyrinth*), which touches upon the themes of emigration and New York, and *El fuego y su aire* (1970; The Fire and Its Air). His last novel, *Los amos benévolos* (1977; Benevolent Masters), is a commentary on exploitation and greed on the island.

The large migration of Puerto Ricans to the United States influenced Puerto Rican culture and novel writing. Writers of the Generation of the Forties began to document this unprecedented period, caused, to a large extent, by Operation Bootstrap, the US attempt to industrialize the island in the late 1940s and 1950s, making it a model of development for the rest of Latin America. Unfortunately, it also upset the island's economy, sending large numbers of peasants looking for jobs in the capital city, San Juan, and from there to New York City. José Luis González was among the first to document this pattern in his short stories. He also wrote *Paisa* (1950), about the migratory process and the difficulties Puerto Ricans experienced in the United States.

Pedro Juan Soto, better known for his short stories, wrote *Usmaíl* (1959), about the US presence in Puerto Rico, reflected in the troubled child of a black Puerto Rican and a white US officer. In *Ardiente suelo, fría estación* (1961; *Hot Land, Cold Season*), he explores the problem of New York Puerto Ricans who return to the island and have to contend with being foreigners in their own land. In *El francotirador* (1969; The Sniper), Soto addresses an issue facing Puerto Ricans on the island, namely the presence of exile Cubans. He narrates the lives of a Cuban exile writer and a counterrevolutionary in alternating chapters, the two figures representing aspects of the same person. Of a more experimental nature, and closer to the novel of the boom period, is Emilio Díaz Valcárcel's *Figuraciones en el mes de marzo* (1972; *Schemes in the Month of March*); positing a fragmented view of reality, it follows the protagonist in Spain as he defends himself against remnants of the empire. Díaz Valcárcel also wrote about Puerto Ricans in the United States in *Harlem todos los días* (1978; *Hot Soles in Harlem*), which studies the lives of both oppressor and oppressed. This theme is also explored in *Mi mamá me ama* (1981; My Mother Loves Me), but this time in the domestic context.

The Puerto Rican experience abroad is captured from another perspective by those writers born or raised in the United States. This is the case with Latino works such as Piri Thomas' *Down These Mean Streets* (1967), Nicholasa Mohr's *Going Home* (1986), and Judith Ortiz Cofer's *The Line of the Sun* (1989).

The Puerto Rican novel reached a new level of expression with Luis Rafael Sánchez, whose *La guaracha del Macho Camacho* (1976; *Macho Camacho's Beat*) became an instant success. Sánchez skillfully mixes techniques associated with the boom writers with social commentary on the island's political status. Written in the Puerto Rican spoken language, the novel unfolds during an afternoon rush hour in which all the characters are affected, in one form or another, by the same traffic jam. *La importancia de llamarse Daniel Santos* (1988; The Importance of Being Daniel Santos) demystifies the image of the popular Puerto Rican singer. Although this novel was received with less enthusiasm than Sánchez's others, it demonstrates that Puerto Rico is not insular, that the country's symbols are present throughout Latin America and the United States.

Among Puerto Rican novelists, Edgardo Rodríguez Juliá stands out as the conscience of the Puerto Rican nation. The settings of his fiction range from the 18th century to the present, and his works range from *Renuncia del héroe Baltasar* (1974; *The Renunciation*) to *Una noche con Iris Chacón* (1986; A Night with Iris Chacón). For Rodríguez Juliá, Puerto Rican identity is not a fixed concept but is subject to rigorous analysis. With his impressive research, he dismantles images of Puerto Rican history, politics, society, and popular culture. His writing style also calls into question the boundaries between fiction and essay.

Constituting a significant new group of writers, Puerto Rican women authors interpret Puerto Rican political and cultural events from a feminist perspective. They narrate events from a point of view not previously available to other writers and attempt to correct society's perception of women. Certainly, this group has been influenced by the women's movement in the United States. Of these writers Rosario Ferré has been the most active. *Maldito amor* (1986; *Sweet Diamond Dust*) is divided into four stories, each outlining a historical period and interpreted from a woman's perspective. Although she considers herself a Puerto Rican and Spanish American writer, some critics are now promoting her as a Latina writer as a result of her latest novel, *The House on the Lagoon* (1997), which was written in English.

Dominican Republic

The Dominican Republic obtained its independence in 1844 from Haiti. Although Dominicans are partially of African de-

scent, they initially associated this culture not with their own traditions but with those of their neighbor, preferring instead to embrace an idealized Amerindian past. From the Amerindian culture emerges the country's most important work, Manuel de Jesús Galván's *Enriquillo* (1882). Tracing the nation's identity to the time when the island was a Spanish colony, the novel describes the love between the Amerindian Enriquillo and Mencía, daughter of an Amerindian and a Spanish Conquistador. A Christian, Enriquillo is forced to fight against the Spaniards to stop their abuses of his family. The novel depicts the protagonist as having more Christian-like values than the Spaniards and, like the Cuban antislavery novels, encourages the reader to sympathize with someone of a different race and culture.

Novels of this period were written in a different literary style, without abandoning an interest in history. For example, Francisco G. Billini's *Engracia y Antoñita* (1892) is a novel of customs that describes the triangular relationship between two women and a man. But Billini also incorporated history into his work, as did Tulio Manuel Cestero, one of the more prolific writers of this period. Concerned with nativist and modernist portrayals, he also took up historical themes, as seen in *La sangre* (1914; Blood). Another writer to embrace historical themes was Federico García Godoy, whose *Rufinito* (1908), *Alma dominicana* (1911; Dominican Soul), and *Guanuma* (1914) document and reconsider the past.

The 20th-century Dominican novel reflects the political conditions of the country, spurred mainly by three events: the US occupation from 1916 to 1924, the Trujillo dictatorship from 1930 to 1961, and the US invasion in 1965. Examples of the novel documenting the effects of the US occupation are Rafael Damirón's *La cacica* (1944; The Woman Chief) and Ramón Marrero Aristy's *Over* (1939), which use the *criollista* techniques of the times and describe US companies' exploitation of Dominicans.

Traditions of the countryside are best represented in the works of the nation's best-known short-story writer, Juan Bosch, who lived and wrote most of his works in exile. His novel, *La mañosa* (1936), was the most popular of its time. A blend of *costumbrismo* and modernism, the novel takes place in the rural sector and relates the conflicts among the different classes. The coming together of Haitians and Dominicans is present in Julio González Herrera's *Trementina, clerén y bongó* (1943; Turpentine, Booze, and Drums), one of the few works to recognize the neighboring country and its culture.

Trujillo's fall allowed writers to revisit the period of the dictator's rule; formerly, fear had prevented established and younger writers from questioning the government. Their fear was well-founded: Trujillo's henchmen assassinated Andrés Francisco Requena in New York for having written *Cementerio sin cruces* (1949; Cemetery without Crosses), a denunciation of the Trujillo dictatorship. Freddy Prestol Castillo's *El masacre se pasa a pie* (1973; Stepping Over the Massacre) revisits the 1937 Trujillo massacre of Haitians living on the Dominican border. Critical of the 1965 US invasion is Aída Cartagena Portalatín's *Escalera para Electra* (1970; Ladder for Electra).

In the contemporary period, writers are incorporating the experimental techniques associated with the Latin American novel of the boom period. Marcio Veloz Maggiolo's novels are a notable example. Also known for his short stories, his novels include *El prófugo* (1963; The Fugitive), *De abril en adelante*

(1975; From April Onward), and *La biografía difusa de Sombra Castañeda* (1980; The Defused Biography of Sombra Castañeda), which refer to the Trujillo dictatorship. Virgilio Díaz Grullón's *Los algarrobos también sueñan* (1976; The Carob Trees also Dream) belongs to the same tradition.

Two other novels have been welcomed by a general audience. Pedro Vergés' *Sólo Cenizas hallarás: (bolero)* (1980; You Will Find Only Ashes [Love Songs]) is an experimental novel that describes the aftermath of Trujillo's downfall. Viriato Sención's *Los que falsificaron la firma de Dios* (1992; They Forged the Signature of God), recipient of the National Novel Prize, uncovers the complicity between the Church and the Trujillo dictatorship. Sención lives in the United States.

Of particular interest is the wave of Dominican authors writing in the United States. Dominicans began leaving their country of origin after the US invasion of the island, and in greater numbers during the 1970s and 1980s. Of these, Julia Álvarez is already an internationally acclaimed writer. She writes about Dominicans in New York and in the Dominican Republic. *In the Time of the Butterflies* (1994) is about the Mirabal sisters, who were instrumental in dethroning Trujillo, and whom he had assassinated. Álvarez is a Latina writer and her novels are written in English, thus bringing these political travesties to the attention of English-speaking readers. Her works have met with success both in the United States and in the Dominican Republic, where they are available in Spanish translation.

The novel in the Spanish Caribbean will continue to evolve and reflect the changing political realities of the region. The Spanish Caribbean perspective will also become enriched as writers from this region migrate and assimilate, blending their native cultures with those of other lands.

WILLIAM LUIS

See also Caribbean Novel (Anglophone and Francophone); Alejo Carpentier; Latino-American Novel

Further Reading

Arnold, James, editor, *A History of Literature in the Caribbean*, Amsterdam and Philadelphia: Benjamins, 1994

Balaguer, Joaquín, *Historia de la literatura dominicana*, Ciudad Trujillo: Librería Dominicana, 1956

Benítez Rojo, Antonio, *La isla que se repite: El Caribe y la perspectiva posmoderna*, 1989; as *The Repeating Island: The Caribbean and the Postmodern Perspective*, Durham, North Carolina: Duke University Press, 1992; 2nd edition, 1996

Berroa, Rei, editor, *Revista Iberoamericana* 54:142 (1988), issue entitled *La literatura dominicana siglo veinte*

Bueno, Salvador, *Historia de la literatura cubana*, Havana: Minerva, 1954; 3rd edition, Havana: Editorial Nacional de Cuba, 1963

Cabrera, Francisco Manrique, *Historia de la literatura puertorriqueña*, Río Piedras: Cultural, 1971

Gómez Tejera, Carmen, *La novela en Puerto Rico*, Río Piedras: Universidad de Puerto Rico, 1947

González Echevarría, Roberto, *Alejo Carpentier, The Pilgrim at Home*, Ithaca, New York: Cornell University Press, 1977

González Echevarría, Roberto, *La ruta de Severo Sarduy*, Hanover, New Hampshire: Ediciones del Norte, 1987

González Echevarría, Roberto, and Enrique Pupo-Walker, editors, *The Cambridge History of Latin American Literature*, 3 vols., Cambridge and New York: Cambridge University Press, 1996

Henríquez Ureña, Max, *Panorama histórico de la literatura dominicana*, Rio de Janeiro: Companhia brasileira de artes graficas, 1945; 2nd edition, Santo Domingo: Colección Pensamiento Dominicano, 1965

Luis, William, *Literary Bondage: Slavery in Cuban Narrative*, Austin: University of Texas Press, 1990

Luis, William, editor, *Modern Latin-American Fiction Writers*, first series, Detroit, Michigan: Gale Research, 1992

Luis, William, and Ann González, editors, *Modern Latin American Fiction Writers*, second series, Detroit, Michigan: Gale Research, 1994

Menton, Seymour, *Prose Fiction of the Cuban Revolution*, Austin: University of Texas Press, 1975

Rodríguez Monegal, Emir, *El boom de la novela latinoamericana*, Caracas: Tiempo Nuevo, 1972

Rosario Candelier, Bruno, *Tendencias de la novela dominicana*, Santiago, Dominican Republic: Departamento de Publicaciones de la Pontificia Universidad Católica Madre y Maestra, 1988

Sommer, Doris, *One Master for Another: Populism as Patriarchal Rhetoric in Dominican Novels*, Lanham, Maryland: University Press of America, 1983

Latino-American Novel

In 1997 approximately 25 million Latinos lived in the United States, a population made up of about 80 percent Mexican Americans, or Chicanos, 10 percent Puerto Ricans, 5 percent Cuban Americans, and the remainder from Central and South America. High rates of population growth and cultural diversity continue to complicate the search for a usable definition of the Latino novel.

The origins of US Latino culture lie in the encounter between the European-Iberian Spanish and the indigenous peoples of the Americas. These contacts began with Christopher Columbus' landing on the Caribbean island of Hispaniola. Columbus was an Italian in the service of the Spanish Catholic monarchs Ferdinand of Aragon and Isabel of Castile. The subsequent establishment of a far-flung Spanish empire in the Americas, from Tierra del Fuego in the south to above the 49th parallel in the north, brought Spain into contact with many varieties of American civilization. Spanish colonies in what later became the United States of America were confined to the south and west without benefit of the large urban centers that extended cultural development in Mexico, Peru, and Cuba. Controversy still continues among historians over how strong the cultural bond was between the eastern and western regions. This disagreement is still reflected in a lack of Latino consensus about how connected Chicanos and Nuyoricans (New York Puerto Ricans) really are. By the 18th century US hegemony would set the stage for conflict with the Hispanic populations in Florida, Louisiana, Texas, and New Mexico (and later, Puerto Rico and Cuba) and result in US annexation of the northern frontier of the Spanish empire in the Americas. This, in turn, set the stage for cultural and political conflicts with the appropriated populations of these states.

The prenovelistic literature of this period is marked by political expediency and a search for a geographic homeland. Creative works were often used to achieve social or political goals, including the religious conversion of the native population and the subjugation of their communities. Spanish literary structures, especially of the epic and drama, dominated literary output. Incorporation of native oral traditions later became a significant addition, to the Chicano novel in particular.

Unlike the English colonists, whose descendants later spread across the North American continent and who practiced separatism from the indigenous peoples (although racial hierarchies continued), the Spanish attempted to integrate the local population as much as possible into Hispanic society. Catholic missionaries, especially those from the Franciscan and Jesuit orders, fanned out over the northern Spanish frontier from their bases in New Spain. Marriage among the Spanish men and indigenous women became common (as well as childbirth out of wedlock), which created a race of mixed peoples whose very identity and political place were called into question.

It is likely that most Latino literature in the United States in the 19th century was composed and published in the Spanish language, and much has either been lost or lies buried in both private and public archives in the southwest. Texas and New Mexico, in particular, had thriving newspaper and magazine publishing. Many native sons, in particular, received a high-quality formal education, while young women wrote with intelligence on domestic affairs. Memoir, poetry, drama, and the borderlands oral traditions thrived. Puerto Rican and Cuban literature developed as national, cultural entities, later brought to the United States through migration. Although a US Latino literary tradition did indeed develop, not until the 1970s would novel writing become widespread, and, even then, most novels were read by an educated, cultural elite within the national population group.

In fact, until the 1960s, Latino writers often wrote in literary isolation from one another, separated by regionalism and nationalism. Among Mexican Americans, for example, there exists a 125-year-old novelistic tradition, although whether or not the pre-1960s generations knew of this tradition is an open question. There also exists in the United States a long tradition of the novel of the Latin American in exile and more recent traditions for the Puerto Rican novel on the mainland, the Cuban American novel, and the novel of the Latin American immigrant to the United States. A national tradition, pan-US Latino, has only been suggested since the Latino political and cultural activism of the 1970s, fostered by the establishment of several small publishers devoted to publishing Latino fiction across national lines. Only in the past decade has a critical body of work evolved to discuss and define the commonalities that justify the label "US Latino." The Spanish language, colonial past, and the syncretism of Catholicism and native religions are examples. The focus of Latino literature, however, has often been the uniqueness of cultures formed by geography, indigenous culture, and political circumstances.

The Mexican American Novel

Mexican Americans, called Chicanos in some states, Texas Mexicans in Texas, Mexicans, and Spanish, can variously be described as those whose families have lived in what is now the southwest for generations and may have both Spanish and indigenous ancestry; those whose families emigrated from Mexico in the past one or two generations; and those who have immigrated themselves. Because in the 1960s and 1970s it was fashionable to claim that the United States was an occupying power in the southwest and that Chicanos should have claim to the territory, a culture of *la tierra* (the homeland, often called Aztlán after the mythical home of the Aztecs) is frequently explored in Mexican American fiction. Among more recent immigrants, exploration of personal identity often becomes paramount.

Although almost the whole of the Mexican American novel has been written since 1970—and has developed with astonishing speed during that time—the tradition actually reaches back to the late 19th century. The foremost Mexican American novelist of that period was María Amparo Ruíz de Burton. Ruíz de Burton was born in Loreto, Baja California, to a prominent, landowning Californio family. In 1849, one year after Mexico ceded the territory to the United States through the Treaty of Guadalupe Hidalgo, she married Henry S. Burton, a captain in the US Army. Their marriage—a Californio with an Anglo, a Catholic to a Protestant—flouted the contemporary conventions but would have significant influence on the thematic choices in her writing.

Ruíz de Burton's first book, *Who Would Have Thought It?*, published in 1872, was the story of a young girl, born into a patrician Mexican family, who is captured by Indians along with her mother. Ten years later, as the novel begins, Lola arrives at the house of Dr. Norval, who had rescued her and made a promise to her mother to take care of her. By introducing Lola to a Lutheran, Yankee household, the doctor sparks the racist envy of his wife, who is jealous of Lola's family wealth. Set largely during the American Civil War, the book brings out the many ironies of an American republic whose contradictions are embodied in the varied views of its citizens. Marriage between Lola and the doctor's highly principled son provides the necessary optimism for the postwar era.

Ruíz de Burton's second published novel, *The Squatter and the Don* (1885), again focused on the Californio class struggle to retain property in the United States after the 1848 Treaty of Guadalupe Hidalgo moved the US-Mexican border hundreds of miles to the south. The treaty was meant to protect the property rights of the Mexican landholders, but unscrupulous squatters would move in and take over the land, leaving the newly created "Mexican American" with little hope of assistance from an unsympathetic US Congress. The melodrama of Ruíz de Burton's work often obscures an incisive intelligence, political savvy, and dry humor. In both novels the Mexican or Californio upper classes behave with the utmost dignity, while several members of the Anglo upper class and the working classes in general are portrayed as grasping, unethical, and often racist; Protestant clerics are portrayed as venal and corrupt. As in *Who Would Have Thought It?*, the Anglo son and Mexican daughter marry.

In 1892 *El Boletín Popular* published *El hijo de la tempestad* (Son of the Storm) and *Tras la tormenta la calma* (The Calm After the Storm), two short novels composed in Spanish by Eusebio Chacón, the scion of one of New Mexico's most prominent families. In his writing, Chacón attempted to create a local literary prose form, different from Anglo genres based on European models. Born in Peñasco, New Mexico, and raised in southern Colorado, Chacón received an undergraduate degree from Jesuit Las Vegas College in Las Vegas, New Mexico, in 1887 and a law degree from Notre Dame University in 1889. At Notre Dame, Chacón, one of the only Hispanics to attend this prestigious "eastern" university, was exposed almost exclusively to European literatures. Back in New Mexico, he became a forceful essayist and speaker on behalf of Mexican Americans.

El hijo de la tempestad is generally the more highly regarded of the two works; it is a romantic, deterministic portrait of a man caught between the seen and the unseen and infused with superstitions and motifs derived from a combination of indigenous legends and Christian mythology. Although stylistically it falls short of Chacón's ambitious literary aspirations, it nonetheless succeeds in creating an alternative mode of expression, bearing many similarities to popular novels of the time in Mexico and other Spanish-speaking countries.

Several decades after Chacón came Josephina Niggli, whose work is often omitted from discussions of US Latino literature because of her Swiss, Irish, and Alsatian ancestry. Born near Hidalgo, Nuevo Leon, Mexico, where her Texan father and Virginian mother had been living since 1893, Niggli wrote a book of poems, three experimental novellas, a collection of short fiction, plays, and screenplays, but only one novel, *Step Down, Elder Brother* (1947). The next major presence may be found in the regional writings of Fray Angelico Chávez, a Franciscan friar whose dozens of books shed a great deal of light on the Mexican American experience in New Mexico. Chavez's *New Mexico Triptych* (1940) continued a southwestern tradition, linked to Eusebio Chacón, of trying to develop an essential New Mexican form for the novel.

In 1959 a watershed event occurred in the Mexican American novel. Doubleday, a major New York publisher, brought out the first major work by a US Latino since Ruíz de Burton's *The Squatter and the Don*. *Pocho*, by José Antonio Villarreal, was the first novel to deal directly with working-class migration, a topic with which many readers had become familiar after the airing of Edward R. Murrow's "Harvest of Shame" television news series earlier in the decade.

Pocho is slang—usually used in a derogatory way—for an assimilated Mexican immigrant to the United States. The novel *Pocho* is the story of a veteran of the Mexican Revolution and his relationship with his son, Richard Rubio (Richard Blond), the latter a bookish child out of step with the field culture in which he lives. Although *Pocho* represents a significant step in the history of fiction publishing by Latinos, critics have pointed out that the work is unbalanced because the opening section on the revolution has no follow-up and that its characters are unconvincing. Villarreal has written two other novels, *The Fifth Horseman* (1974) and *Clemente Chacón* (1984), yet neither has made the impact of *Pocho*, which remains a landmark in Latino literature for its modern portrait of the Mexican American.

Another author usually omitted from discussions of the Latino novel is John Francisco Rechy, perhaps because his well-known works focused more on the culture of homosexuality than on Latino life. Rechy's first novel, *City of Night* (1963), was a highly acclaimed and controversial work about a young man from an abusive El Paso home who drifts across the United States engaging in a series of homosexual encounters for pay, as told in discreet episodes. Rechy's work made him a pioneer for later Latino writers who centered their work on homosexual main characters, such as Arturo Islas, Cuban American Elias Miguel Muñoz, and Colombian Jaime Manrique. Rechy has written seven other novels, including *The Miraculous Day of Amalia Gomez* (1991), his first novel to focus on Hispanic themes and situations.

Between 1971 and 1973, four seminal works appeared, each of which would represent a new stream of Mexican American fiction. In 1971 Quinto Sol Publications, the first modern publisher to focus on Chicano literature, published *. . . y no se lo tragó la tierra* (literally, *—And the Earth Did Not Swallow Him*) by Tomás Rivera. Rivera was a short-story writer, literary critic, college administrator, and specialist in education. *—And the Earth Did Not Swallow Him* is the story of a young man's coming of age in the migrant farmworker culture of the United States, told in memoir style in vignettes and stories. To Rivera, memory is a powerful conciliator: it brings together the people and the land in a heroic struggle for selfhood and identity, against formidable odds. The structure of the title itself is intriguing, presented as if the reader has come upon the work in midsentence and is left to decide in which part of the book that sentiment might lie. *—And the Earth Did Not Swallow Him* is a powerful literary work, fragmented but highly structured. In addition to Villarreal and Rivera, the best novels on the migrant life include *Peregrinos en Aztlán* (1974; *Pilgrims in Aztlán*) by Miguel Mendez and *The Plum, Plum Pickers* (1969) by Raymond Barrio.

In 1972 Quinto Sol published Rudolfo Anaya's first novel, *Bless Me, Ultima,* a novel that has since sold over 350,000 copies and has been widely used in college and high school courses in Latino literature. The story focuses on a young boy's spiritual awakening during his first years of public schooling. The various Latino inhabitants of the town, which is predominantly Chicano, move easily in and out of Chicano and Anglo culture. As he grows, the boy is guided through the choices he must make between male and female worlds, the influence of sea and moon, station and movement, by the *curandera* (healing woman) Ultima. The story's message is that writing can be redemptive, as the young storyteller reaches back to the roots of pre-Hispanic imagery, to the Aztlanese world that survives in an oral tradition. In total, Anaya has published eight novels, several collections of short stories, anthologies, poetry, and criticism. His most recent novels are *Zia Summer* (1995) and *Jalamanta* (1996).

In 1973 Rolando Hinojosa-Smith, writing under the name Rolando Hinojosa, published *Estampas del valle y otras obras* (*Sketches of the Valley*), the first installment in what was to become the first sustained series of novels by a US Latino, the Klail City Death Trip series. The series follows the lives of the inhabitants of Belken County as told in their own voices through anecdotes, dialogues, and interviews. Setting his novels in this narrow strip of land along the Rio Grande has led many critics to compare him to William Faulkner and Faulkner's Yoknapatawpha County. Another prominent border writer is Aristeo Brito, whose *El diablo en Texas* (1976; *The Devil in Texas*) explores the irony of towns being divided into English-speaking and Spanish-speaking areas by an arbitrary border.

In 1972 Oscar Zeta Acosta, a larger-than-life, self-promoting character and friend of Hunter S. Thompson (he appears as Dr. Gonzo in Thompson's *Fear and Loathing in Las Vegas*, 1971), gained recognition as one of the great legends of Latino letters with the autobiographical novel *The Autobiography of a Brown Buffalo*, a chaotic coming-of-age story set in California. Acosta's second book, *The Revolt of the Cockroach People* (1973), a New Journalism insertion of self into a historical series of events, is based on his experiences as an attorney with El Movimiento (The Movement), a Chicano activist organization based in southern California. The book begins with the takeover of St. Basil's Roman Catholic Church by Movimiento members, who are out to disrupt political and religious hierarchies. Acosta, still in his guise as the Brown Buffalo and now an attorney, signs on to defend the protesters. But the book becomes less a discussion of the Movement than a disquisition on the life of Acosta himself, an exercise in self-mythmaking.

In the 1960s and 1970s, a wave of semi-autobiographical novels appeared, including Floyd Salas' *Tattoo the Wicked Cross* (1966), Richard Vasquez's *Chicano* (1970), and Richard Fariña's *Been Down So Long It Looks Like Up to Me* (1966). Along with Acosta's work, these novels appear to create a critical mass of autobiographical works that parallel the rite-of-passage era of minority groups in the United States. Novelists of the rural and suburban working class, whose influences include Ernest Hemingway and John Steinbeck, are Lionel Garcia, Max Martínez, Genaro Gonzalez, and Dagoberto Gilb.

A wave of feminist Mexican American novels began in the 1970s with the publication of *Victuum* (1976) by Isabella Ríos (real name Diana López), a female Bildungsroman told mostly in dialogue. *Victuum* is a massive exploration of one person's consciousness, prenatal to posthumous. Among Chicana writers *Victuum* was followed by collections of short stories and novels that played with the traditional narrative form, as Rivera had done in *—And the Earth Did Not Swallow Him* and which Hinojosa continued to do in his Klail City Death Trip series.

In 1981 two politically and socially aware feminists and lesbians, Cherrie Moraga and Gloria Anzaldúa, edited an influential anthology titled *This Bridge Called My Back: Writings by Radical Women of Color* (1981). Moraga followed this with the influential "novel" *Loving in the War Years: Lo que nunca pasó por sus labios* (1983), another example of the writer playing with novelistic form. Anzaldúa has also produced one mixed genre work of fiction. *Borderlands/La frontera: The New Mestiza* (1987) is a true mestizaje that mixes fiction and historiography with poetic verse, reflecting her idea of a hemispheric culture of the Americas.

Although several other highly regarded feminist works were published in the 1970s and 1980s, including Ana Castillo's highly structured *The Mixquiahuala Letters* (1986) and Estela Portillo-Trambley's *Trini* (1986), which is often relegated to the Young Adult shelf, the first Chicana to capture national attention (for her book of short stories, *Woman Hollering Creek*, 1991) was Sandra Cisneros. Her only novel to date is *The House on Mango Street* (1983), a Bildungsroman told in well-crafted vignettes that explore a young girl's personal growth.

The Road to Tamazunchale (1975) by Ron Arias, *The Miraculous Day of Amalia Gomez* by John Rechy, *The Rag Doll Plagues* (1992) by Alejandro Morales, and *The Love Queen of the Amazon* (1992) by Cecile Piñeda are examples of Chicano novels that owe a debt to South American magic realism (although the last of these satirizes Latin American machismo and misogyny in the novel). Along with Rechy, Moraga, and Anzaldúa, Chicano novels by lesbians and gays have also made their mark. In *The Rain God: A Desert Tale* (1984) and *Migrant Souls* (1990), Arturo Islas explores family relationships and the dynamics of individual and cultural memory. Sheila Ortiz Taylor explores family relationships in her novels *Faultline* (1982), *Spring Forward/Fall Back* (1985), and *Southbound* (1990), as does Terri de la Peña in *Margins* (1991). Michael Nava creates gay lawyer Henry Ríos to reveal a rich lode for Chicano mystery writers, whose numbers now include Anaya, Lucha Corpi, and Manuel Ramos. Nava's most recent novel featuring Henry Ríos is *The Burning Plain* (1998).

Puerto Ricans on the Mainland

Puerto Rico's unique relationship with the United States has filled its literature with uneasiness. As a result of the Spanish Cuban American War of 1898, the United States came into possession of the island of Puerto Rico and, in 1917, as a result of the Jones Act, Puerto Ricans became citizens of the United States, although the island remained a protectorate. Because of their political status, Puerto Ricans have been able to move back and forth between the island and the mainland, settling mainly in the New York metropolitan area.

Puerto Ricans' freedom to travel between the US mainland and the island has led to the development of several distinct fictional modes of discourse. In the 1950s, "sojourners," as critic Juan Flores has called them, lived for periods of time in New York City before returning to the island. Their experiences provided them with materials for their work. Whether their novels are considered part of the Puerto Rican tradition or the US Latino tradition is an open question. Pedro Juan Soto, who once described his several-year stay in New York City as the worst period of his life, is the most well known of these writers. His works about Puerto Ricans living in New York include *Usmaíl* (1959) and *Ardiente suelo, fría estación* (1961; *Hot Land, Cold Season*). With some exceptions (the work of Ed Vega and Judith Ortiz Cofer, for example), Puerto Rican fiction and autobiography have been characterized by attempts of the main characters to navigate the vicissitudes of poverty and discrimination in the harsh communities of New York City. This has led to unfortunate stereotyping, and one Puerto Rican author has been quoted as saying that, although he does not want to continue to write about the ghetto, "it sells." The best examples of this generally violent and unsympathetic fictional world may be found in *Carlito's Way* (1975) and *Q & A* (1977) by jurist Edwin Torres and *Spidertown* (1993) by Abraham Rodriguez, Jr. Contrary to the large numbers of novels appearing from Chicanos and the growing number and prestige of Cuban American writers, mainland Puerto Ricans have not yet made their mark in the novel (although Puerto Rican poetry on the mainland has flourished).

Perhaps the first Puerto Rican novel on the mainland was Bernardo Vega's *Memorias de Bernardo Vega* (published posthumously in 1977; *The Memoirs of Bernardo Vega*). Although he wrote the work as an autobiographical novel, a friend turned the work back into memoir after his death, and it has since remained in that category (similarly, Edward Rivera would be forced by his publisher to add the subtitle "Memoirs of Growing Up Hispanic" to his novel *Family Installments*, 1982). Vega was a charter member of the Socialist Party and a *tabaquero* (cigar worker), among the most politically advanced segments of the Puerto Rican working class. His early political involvement carried over to his experiences as an emigrant and community leader in New York City where he arrived in 1916. The *Memoirs of Bernardo Vega*, the author's only work, is an account of the following three decades of his life until the aftermath of World War II, which initiated the huge diaspora of Puerto Rican emigrants to the United States and the ghettoization of that community in US urban barrios.

Piri Thomas was the first US-born Puerto Rican narrator to achieve national, mainstream recognition in the United States for his autobiographical work *Down These Mean Streets* (1967), which chronicles Thomas' difficult life in the streets of Spanish Harlem from the Depression era to the early 1960s. Born in New York City to a light-skinned Puerto Rican mother and a dark-skinned Cuban father, Thomas' experiences as a child in the barrio, and as a teenager in an Italian section of East Harlem and later Babylon, Long Island, forced him to confront issues of racial and ethnic identity. For Thomas, this translated into a decision between considering himself a Puerto Rican based on language and family origin or accepting society's label of Afro-American based on skin color.

Down These Mean Streets traces Thomas' early initiation into gangs, violence, drugs, and sex, as well as the period he spent in prison after being convicted of armed robbery, and ends with his reintegration into the community and ultimate personal redemption after being paroled at age 28. The popularity of the book gained Piri Thomas some notoriety and he became a spokesperson for the Puerto Rican community, making frequent appearances on television and radio. Thomas' self-documentation continued with the publication of *Savior, Savior Hold My Hand* (1972) and *Seven Long Times* (1974).

While Thomas used crude street language and Spanish words that normally would have alienated the average US reader, it should be recalled that *Down These Mean Streets* emerged within a political climate that opened up new avenues for minority authors, creating a growing market for works that could help the larger US readership comprehend the reasons for the social unrest taking place around them. The novel has been compared to other testimonials of its time, such as *Manchild in the Promised Land* (1965) by Claude Brown and *Soul on Ice* (1968) by Eldridge Cleaver.

Nicholasa Mohr was born in New York City and grew up in "El Barrio" in the 1940s. *Nilda* (1973), perhaps her most critically recognized work, is a Bildungsroman, a novel of childhood formation so often associated with the growing up of a young man. Mohr extended the genre to young Latinas, situating the growing up process of a young woman in a specific historical context, the years 1941 to 1945, and in a specific geographic place, New York's oldest and largest Latino neighborhood. Similar to other works of this type, the protagonist confronts problems that are fairly universal: family life, sexuality, relationships with peers, friendships, school, and career goals. In this work, however, as in other US Latino fiction, each of these problems is explored within the social reality of growing up as a member of a "minority" in the larger society; ethnicity and culture play an

important role in how the character deals with conflict. *Nilda* fits squarely into the tradition of US Latino literature; at the same time, however, it makes its own distinctly female statement regarding the quest for individuality and maturity within a specifically New York Puerto Rican context.

Edward Rivera was born in Orocovis, Puerto Rico, and moved to New York at the age of seven. Rivera's comic *Family Installments: Memories of Growing Up Hispanic* is a hilarious satire of growing up in New York City. It is also a thoughtful and literary examination of the culture into which Puerto Ricans were thrown upon their arrival in New York: Irish-dominated Catholicism, multi-ethnic neighborhoods, and cold, working-class urban environments. The main character in *Family Installments*, Santos Malánguez, spends his first few years in Puerto Rico. The abruptness of his transition to New York is conveyed by a "jump-cut," a cinematic device that brings him from a classroom with a beloved teacher to a confusing but similar environment in New York. *Family Installments* represents one of the first instances of a Latino writer playing with literature and literary tradition.

Ed Vega is arguably the most ambitious literary novelist of his generation. Despite having received critical acclaim, his three novels *The Comeback* (1985), *Mendoza's Dreams* (1987), and *Casualty Report* (1991) have received little public attention, and he remains a good writer in search of an appreciative audience.

Judith Ortiz Cofer was born in Hormigueros, Puerto Rico, and spent much of her childhood in Paterson, New Jersey. Ortiz Cofer is a poet (*Terms of Survival*, 1987), fiction writer, and memoirist (*Silent Dancing*, 1990). Her novel *The Line of the Sun* (1989), a lyrical, often bittersweet work, is one of the few novels by a Puerto Rican on the mainland to be set outside the ghetto.

The Cuban American Novel

The Cuban American experience differs greatly from those of the Mexican American and Puerto Rican. The Cuban American community existed mainly as an exile community throughout the 19th century and into the last decades of the 20th century, many of its members having fled the political strife on the island. With the Cuban Revolution of 1959, the number of refugees entering the United States escalated, and a large, settled community developed, augmented by various waves of political migration in the 1970s and 1980s.

The most well-known Cuban American writer, and arguably the most well-known Latino writer in the United States, is Oscar Hijuelos. Born in New York City, his first novel was *Our House in the Last World* (1983), one of the best works about immigration to the urban United States. The work is unique in its portrayal of a family arriving in the United States during the years before the Cuban Revolution. His second, *The Mambo Kings Play Songs of Love* (1989), won the Pulitzer Prize for fiction in 1990, the only Pulitzer Prize for fiction ever awarded to a US Latino, and was made into a film starring Armand Assante. The work reinvents the mambo and cha-cha era in New York and explores frustrated crossover dreams; according to critic Marc Zimmerman, the novel is a "literary transposition of a music culture in a prose that uncovers the love songs all but buried in the blur of sex, drink, and US commodification." *The Fourteen Sisters of Emilio Montez O'Brien* (1993), Hijuelos' third novel, is a beautifully composed pastorale about the family of an Irish photographer and his Cuban wife. His most recent work, *Mr. Ives' Christmas*

(1995), is an acclaimed work that explores the possibility of spiritual life in America. Hijuelos is an ambitious writer, bold in his choice of themes and his approach to language.

The most recent Cuban American writer to achieve fame is Cristina Garcia, whose first novel, *Dreaming in Cuban* (1992), won critical and popular acclaim, including a nomination for a National Book Award. Born in Cuba, García immigrated with her family to the United States in 1960 where she studied at Barnard College and Johns Hopkins University, and later worked as a reporter and correspondent for *Time* magazine. A lyrical work that blends realism and dream, *Dreaming in Cuban* chronicles three generations of women of the Cuban del Pino family from the 1930s to the early 1980s and examines the Cuban Revolution's effect on their lives. Garcia's second novel, *The Aguero Sisters* (1997), focuses on similar themes but is characterized by a greater depth of feeling and stylistic maturity.

Among other Cuban American writers, Virgil Suarez has explored both the Cuban American relationship with the island (*The Cutter*, 1991) and the Cuban American community itself (*Latin Jazz*, 1989). Elias Miguel Muñoz has explored gay themes in *Crazy Love* (1989) and Achy Obejas the culture of lesbianism in her hilarious *We Came All the Way from Cuba So You Could Dress Like This?* (1994).

The Dominican American Novel

Although most Dominicans in the United States come from the ranks of the working class, the writer Julia Álvarez arrived as a political refugee, from a prominent family. She began her writing career as a poet but has made her most indelible mark with three novels about politics, family, and assimilation. In her first novel, *How the Garcia Girls Lost Their Accents* (1991), Álvarez created a family of refugees who attempt to reestablish a comfortable life in the United States after being forced to flee their upper-class existence in the Dominican Republic. It is a hilarious, bittersweet musing on assimilation and acclimatization. In her second novel, *In the Time of the Butterflies* (1994), Álvarez took on the legend of the Mirabal sisters, real-life Dominican national heroes assassinated by henchmen of the dictator Trujillo. In her third and most recent work, *Yo!* (1997), Álvarez resurrected the characters of her first book and allowed her fictional stand-in to meditate on her own life and work.

The least known group of US Latino novels is comprised of Dominican American works of fiction written and published in Spanish. This urban expression continues a New York City tradition of ethnic publishing in the language of the country of origin. Its works generally focus on New York City's urban environment and are read almost exclusively by Dominicans, in a similar fashion to Yiddish-language novels written by Jewish immigrants and Italian-language works by Italian immigrants in the early part of the 20th century.

Latin Americans in the United States

A few South Americans and Central Americans living in the United States also have made their mark on the Latino novel. Jaime Manrique's *Latin Moon in Manhattan* (1992) focuses on the Colombian community of Jackson Heights (Queens). Francisco Goldman, whose mother is Guatemalan, has written two highly acclaimed works. In *The Long Night of White Chickens* (1992), Goldman shuttles between revolutionary Guatemala and suburban Boston, possibly a metaphor for his own divided childhood. His second work, *The Ordinary Seaman* (1997), is set on a derelict cargo ship in New York harbor, inhabited by Central American sailors in limbo.

Among other Latin American novelists living and working in the United States, but not generally considered part of the US Latino tradition because they immigrated as adults with an established body of work in their own countries, are Isaac Goldemberg, a Peruvian Jew who wrote *Play by Play* (1985), and Chileans Ariel Dorfman and Isabel Allende.

HAROLD AUGENBRAUM

See also Latin American Novel: Hispanic Caribbean

Further Reading

Augenbraum, Harold, and Margarite Fernández Olmos, editors, *The Latino Reader: An American Literary Tradition from 1542 to the Present*, Boston: Houghton Mifflin, 1997

Bruce-Novoa, *Chicano Authors: Inquiry by Interview*, Austin: University of Texas Press, 1980

Bruce-Novoa, *Retrospace: Collected Essays on Chicano Literature, Theory, and History*, Houston, Texas: Arte Público Press, 1990

Calderón, Héctor, and José David Saldívar, editors, *Criticism in the Borderlands: Studies in Chicano Literature, Culture, and Ideology*, Durham, North Carolina: Duke University Press, 1991

González-Berry, Erlinda, editor, *Pasó por Aquí: Critical Essays on the New Mexican Literary Tradition 1542–1988*, Albuquerque: University of New Mexico Press, 1989

Gutiérrez, Ramón, and Genaro Padilla, *Recovering the U.S. Hispanic Literary Heritage*, Houston, Texas: Arte Público Press, 1993

Herrera-Sobek, María, *Beyond Stereotypes: The Critical Analysis of Chicana Literature*, Binghamton, New York: Bilingual Press, 1985

Herrera-Sobek, María, and Helena María Viramontes, editors, *Chicana Creativity and Criticism: Charting New Frontiers in American Literature*, Houston, Texas: Arte Público Press, 1987

Horno-Delgado, Asunción, Eliana Ortega, Nina M. Scott, and Nancy Saporta Sternbach, editors, *Breaking Boundaries: Latina Writing and Critical Reading*, Amherst, Massachusetts, and London: University of Massachusetts Press, 1989

Kanellos, Nicolás, *Biographical Dictionary of Hispanic Literature in the United States: The Literature of Puerto Ricans, Cuban Americans, and Other Hispanic Writers*, New York and London: Greenwood Press, 1989

Lattin, Vernon E., editor, *Contemporary Chicano Fiction: A Critical Survey*, Binghamton, New York: Bilingual Press, 1986

Lomelí, Francisco A., and Carl R. Shirley, editors, *Dictionary of Literary Biography*, volume 82, *Chicano Writers*, first series, Detroit, Michigan: Gale Research, 1989

Lomelí, Francisco A., and Carl R. Shirley, editors, *Dictionary of Literary Biography*, volume 122, *Chicano Writers*, second series, Detroit, Michigan: Gale Research, 1992

Luis, William, *Dance between Two Cultures: Latino-Caribbean Literature Written in the United States*, Nashville, Tennessee: Vanderbilt University Press, 1997

Mohr, Eugene, *The Nuyorican Experience: Literature of the Puerto Rican Minority,* Westport, Connecticut: Greenwood Press, 1982

Rodríguez-Seda de Laguna, Asela, editor, *Images and Identities: The Puerto Rican in Two World Contexts,* New Brunswick, New Jersey: Transaction, 1987

Saldívar, José David, *The Dialectics of Our America: Genealogy, Cultural Critique, and Literary History,* Durham, North Carolina, Duke University Press, 1991

Saldívar, Ramón, *Chicano Narrative: The Dialectics of Difference,* Madison: University of Wisconsin Press, 1990

Sommers, Joseph, and Tomás Ybarra-Frausto, editors, *Modern Chicano Writers: A Collection of Critical Essays,* Englewood Cliffs, New Jersey: Prentice-Hall, 1979

Stavans, Ilan, *The Hispanic Condition: Reflections on Culture and Identity in America,* New York: HarperCollins, 1995

Tatum, Charles M., *Chicano Literature,* Boston: Twayne, 1982

Zimmerman, Marc, editor, *U.S. Latino Literature: The Creative Expression of a People: An Essay and Annotated Bibliography,* Chicago: Chicago Public Library, 1989; 2nd edition, Chicago: MARCH/Abrazo Press, 1992

Margaret Laurence 1926–87

Canadian

Margaret Laurence began writing seriously in the 1950s during a seven-year stay in Africa, where her husband was working in Somaliland (now Somalia) and later in the Gold Coast (now Ghana). Her first novel, *This Side Jordan* (1960), chronicles the parallel stories of a white and a black couple in the uneasy months prior to Ghana's independence. A sincere, compassionate, moving novel, it is clearly indebted to E.M. Forster's *A Passage to India* (1924) and takes a comparable view of colonial oppression. During this period Laurence also wrote a number of fine short stories, later collected in *The Tomorrow-Tamer* (1963), which are also set in pre-independence Ghana.

In retrospect, Laurence realized that she needed the experience of a totally different culture in order to understand and come to terms with her own Canadianness, her own "tribalism." "Tribalism," she wrote in "Ten Year's Sentences" (see Woodcock, 1983), is an inheritance of us all," harmless if seen as "the bond which an individual feels with his roots, his ancestors, his background," but dangerous if a tribe sees itself as a privileged in-group and regards other people as subhuman. This, Laurence insisted, "is not Africa's problem alone; it is everyone's."

Her own tribal background includes the Scots Presbyterians. She explored their fortunes and their relation to other tribes in the five Manawaka fictions that made her famous: *The Stone Angel* (1964), *A Jest of God* (1966), *The Fire-Dwellers* (1969), *A Bird in the House* (1970), and *The Diviners* (1974). All but one of these are novels in the strict sense of the term; the exception, *A Bird in the House,* is technically a collection of short stories all focused on the same narrator-protagonist but achieves the effect of a conventional novel.

Manawaka is a small Manitoba prairie town based upon Neepawa, Laurence's birthplace. Here the descendants of the original Scots settlers are socially supreme, although other groups are also conspicuous, including Ukrainians and the native Cree. As a setting for a series of fictions, Manawaka bears certain resemblances to Thomas Hardy's Wessex and William Faulkner's Yoknapatawpha County. A shared history and common physical features bind the books together, while references to a number of families and events recur throughout the series. But Laurence's treatment of Manawaka is less comprehensive. With the partial exception of Morag Gunn, in *The Diviners,* who is orphaned and brought up by the local scavenger, all her Scots protagonists are middle-class women, and their predominant concerns are love, sex, and marriage, although these are invariably complicated by differences of race or nation, religious and political squabbles, and the impact of larger events on the domestic sphere. More significant, perhaps, is the fact that, although Laurence's characters are born in Manawaka and are strongly affected by its influence, not one of them spends her life there. Manawaka is a place that moulds character but represents the past rather than the present. It is not a place in which anyone lives permanently.

Laurence's great strength as a novelist was her command of a variety of voices, and in several interviews she compared this quality to "Method" acting. It is especially evident in *The Stone Angel,* where the 90-year-old Hagar is presented through the convincingly authentic idiom of an earlier generation (*see separate entry,* The Stone Angel), and in *A Jest of God,* where Rachel Cameron's articulate intelligence expresses itself in more contemporary speech habits.

Laurence is somewhat less successful in her control of plot. She was rarely able to reconcile the necessary order of art with what she saw as the disorder of life. The experimental freedom achieved in the presentation of voice did not extend to fictional structure; she was too ready to fall back on artificial plot devices, such as the parallel plotting in *This Side Jordan* and the unlikely "overhearing" scenes in *The Stone Angel* and *A Bird in the House.* Her later work is also weighted down with a need to make a public statement. In *The Fire-Dwellers* the various disasters overtaking Stacy's family and acquaintances seem contrived to justify Laurence's vision of an increasingly violent world. Her determination in *The Diviners* to tie up the strands of the series as well as the individual novel also leads to plot manipulation.

In this respect, her most successful novel may well be *A Jest of God,* a penetrating psychological study of a painfully shy but highly perceptive unmarried schoolteacher desperately seeking (while simultaneously fearing) a physical love relationship before it is too late. The "jest of God" is an internal growth that is diagnosed as a benign tumor rather than the pregnancy she half wants and half dreads. Laurence leaves her readers free to interpret this outcome as either providence or chance.

Margaret Laurence was a much-loved, highly influential figure in mid-20th-century Canadian literature, her dedication to the craft of fiction becoming a model for a generation of aspiring writers. Primarily a realist, she was not remarkable for literary innovation, yet, like Hugh MacLennan, she showed how Canadian protagonists and Canadian settings could be successfully employed in fiction. Moreover, she set an important example in women's writing by finding convincing voices for her female protagonists as they learned to take control of their separate lives. She records the yearnings and anguish of ordinary people with sympathy and dignity. Her novels, sophisticated in their handling of time and memory while remaining accessible to the general reader, catch the humor and absurdity as well as the sadness and tragedy of life.

W.J. KEITH

See also Stone Angel

Biography
Born 18 July 1926 in Neepawa, Manitoba. Attended United College, Winnipeg, 1944–47, B.A. in English 1947. Journalist, *Winnipeg Citizen*, 1947–48; lived in England, 1949, Somaliland (now Somalia), 1950–51, Gold Coast (now Ghana), 1952–57, Vancouver, 1957–62, London and Penn, Buckinghamshire, 1962–72, and Lakefield, Ontario, from 1974; writer-in-residence, University of Toronto, 1969–70, University of Western Ontario, London, 1973, and Trent University, Peterborough, Ontario, 1974; chancellor, Trent University, 1981–83. Died 6 January 1987.

Novels by Laurence
This Side Jordan, 1960
The Stone Angel, 1964
A Jest of God, 1966; as *Rachel, Rachel*, 1968; as *Now I Lay Me Down*, 1968
The Fire-Dwellers, 1969
The Diviners, 1974

Other Writings: short stories, essays, travel writing, and literature for children.

Further Reading
Gunnars, Kristjana, editor, *Crossing the River: Essays in Honor of Margaret Laurence*, Winnipeg: Turnstone Press, 1988
Keith, W.J., "Margaret Laurence," in *A Sense of Style: Studies in the Art of Fiction in English-Speaking Canada*, by Keith, Toronto: ECW Press, 1989
Morley, Patricia, *Margaret Laurence*, Boston: Twayne, 1981
Nicholson, Colin, editor, *Critical Approaches to the Fiction of Margaret Laurence*, Vancouver: University of British Columbia Press, and London: Macmillan, 1990
Sparrow, Fiona, *Into Africa with Margaret Laurence*, Toronto: ECW Press, 1992
Thomas, Clara, *The Manawaka World of Margaret Laurence*, Toronto: McClelland and Stewart, 1975
Verdyn, Christl, editor, *Margaret Laurence: An Appreciation*, Peterborough, Ontario: Broadview Press, 1988
Woodcock, George, editor, *A Place to Stand On: Essays by and about Margaret Laurence*, Edmonton, Alberta: NeWest Press, 1983

D.H. Lawrence 1885–1930

English

D.H. Lawrence has no claim to be considered a systematic thinker. Yet, in spite of inconsistencies in outlook, what emerges from his criticism and novels is a remarkable world vision.

There is every reason to treat Lawrence as a major critic of the novel. His stance could be summed up as recognizing the gap between "mind" and "intuition," the same space he explores in his novels. An impressive series of critical articles has been reprinted as a set in *Study of Thomas Hardy and Other Essays* (1985). In "The Novel and the Feelings," Lawrence sees the reader not as listening to the "didactic statements" of the author but to the "calling cries" of the characters. In "Morality and the Novel," he attests to that genre as "a perfect medium for revealing to us the changing rainbow of our living relationships." These essays are revelatory of Lawrence's own practice.

During the first phase of his career, Lawrence was regarded as a competent regional novelist in the line of Thomas Hardy. But even in Lawrence's first novels we can find intimations of the lat-

er work and their focus on heightened consciousness through an intense scrutiny of subjective experience. *The White Peacock* (1911) conveys a sense of the excitement young people experience in the exploration of ideas. In *The Trespasser* (1912), Lawrence goes below the surface of an adulterous love affair, using for the first time the characteristic psychological notation that he developed further in his mature novels.

These two were followed by Lawrence's greatest popular success, *Sons and Lovers* (1913), a Bildungsroman of a strong autobiographical cast. A virtual case study of the Oedipus complex, the novel bears witness to Lawrence's interest in Freudian theory and its emphasis on subconscious motivation and the role of the subjective and irrational in human experience. The characterization of the protagonist, Paul Morel, is typical of Lawrence's craft, with its minute attention to shades of mood and feeling. But *Sons and Lovers* also has an affinity with naturalism, establishing an intimate connection between social environment (a mining village in the Nottingham coalfield) and character. Paul's father, in particular, is depicted as a product of life in the coal mines. The novel's attention to social influences may explain its popularity, as it avoids the hothouse atmosphere typical of the later novels.

The Rainbow (1915) was published to almost universal abuse and was in fact suppressed. The novel focuses almost exclusively on the states of mind of its various characters. Lawrence had written to his editor, Edward Garnett, on 5 June 1914, "You mustn't look in my novel for the old stable ego of the character . . . don't look for the development of the novel to follow the lines of certain characters." Indeed, the following is a fairly typical passage:

> Suddenly, cresting the heavy, sandy pass, Ursula lifted her head and shrank back, momentarily frightened. There was a great whiteness confronting her, the moon was incandescent as a round furnace door, out of which came the high blast of moonlight, over the sea-ward half of the world, a dazzling, terrifying glare of white light. They shrank back for a moment into shadow, uttering a cry. He felt his chest laid bare, where the secret was heavily hidden. He felt himself fusing down to nothingness, like a bead that rapidly disappears in an incandescent flame.
>
> "How wonderful!" cried Ursula, in low calling tones. "How wonderful!"

On the surface, the narrative tells of two lovers on the sand dunes in the moonlight. But it is a significantly full and bright moon, a symbol of womanhood. In the sphere of Ursula's pervasive femininity, her lover, Skrebensky, feels his manhood threatened. It is the inner being of the characters that is the true subject matter here, and Lawrence uses a special vocabulary to get this across to the reader.

The literary public was fazed by the approach, and there is no doubt that the suppression of The Rainbow was cunningly orchestrated. In particular, passages from an article in a daily newspaper by the journalist James Douglas were read out in court to show that Lawrence had a contempt for war and soldiers. This approach was designed to enrage the judge, Sir John Dickinson, whose only son had been killed in the front line a month previously. Under pressure, the publishers agreed to withdraw the book.

The suppression of The Rainbow made it difficult for Lawrence to publish Women in Love (1920), which is evolved from the same matrix. This sister-book takes the technique manifest in The Rainbow even further. Ursula and Birkin, the lovers in Women in Love, engage in a fearsome quarrel that purges them of their respective guilts and doubts before coming together. Here is Birkin, brooding over their temporary severance, and over his previous love, Hermione:

> Fusion, fusion, this horrible fusion of two beings, which every woman, and most men insisted on, was it not nauseous and horrible anyhow, whether it was a fusion of the spirit or of the emotional body? Hermione saw herself as the perfect Idea, to which all men must come: and Ursula was the perfect Womb, the bath of birth, to which all men must come! And both were horrible. Why could they not remain individuals, limited by their own limits? Why this dreadful all-comprehensiveness, this hateful tyranny?

Why not leave the other being free, why try to absorb, or melt, or merge? One might abandon oneself utterly to the *moment,* but not to any other being.

That diction, distinctive as it may seem, was derived from such sources as the Authorized Version of the Bible. One can hear the symbolic lyricism of Solomon's Song behind such a phrase as "bath of birth," which is in fact used by Walt Whitman in his *Leaves of Grass.* Lawrence quotes it in his essay on Whitman, ultimately published in his *Studies in Classic American Literature* (1923). What Lawrence says of Whitman might be relevantly applied to his own work: "By subjecting the *deepest centres* of the lower self, he attains the maximum consciousness in the higher self." The matter at issue for Lawrence was always the flow of life below the super-ego. Thus, in *Women in Love,* Lawrence surveys society, education, the artistic fringe, the intelligentsia, politics, and industry and finds them all wanting, inadequate to his purpose of enlarging inward experience.

In comparison with *Sons and Lovers, The Rainbow,* and *Women in Love,* the later novels are disappointing. *The Lost Girl* (1920), Lawrence's next novel, was begun about the same time as *Sons and Lovers,* set aside, and taken up again much later. Here the autobiography is transmuted into the life experience of a young girl, but the later part of the novel is couched in a symbolic strain that does not match up with the realistic beginning. The so-called "leadership" novels—*Aaron's Rod* (1922), *Kangaroo* (1923), and *The Plumed Serpent* (1926)—are grounded in a naive view of politics, pointing to the natural ascendancy of certain spiritual aristocrats who, through their supernormal powers, are marked out to govern the ordinary people. What goes along with this is a tendency to perfervid writing that, despite excellent individual scenes, can as a whole weary the reader. The novels create the impression of writing from a program, as is also the case with *Lady Chatterley's Lover* (1928). This program is, however, more satisfactorily applied in the economical form of Lawrence's late tales. In "The Captain's Doll," "St. Mawr," and "The Virgin and the Gipsy," there is a sense of emotional development as surely as in *Lady Chatterley's Lover,* but the structure of the long short story prevents overinsistence. Despite the disappointments of the later novels, in everything Lawrence wrote there is an acute sense of the lives about him. He could be dogmatic, even hysterical, yet he projected in remarkably poetic prose a unique world vision.

PHILIP HOBSBAUM

See also Sons and Lovers; Women in Love

Biography
Born 11 September 1885 in Eastwood, Nottinghamshire. Attended Nottingham High School, 1898–1901; University College, Nottingham (now University of Nottingham), 1906–08, teacher's certificate, 1908. Clerk for a firm of surgical appliance makers, Nottingham, 1901; pupil-teacher in Eastwood and Ilkeston, Nottinghamshire, 1902–06; teacher, Davidson Road School, Croydon, Surrey, 1908–12; began writing full-time in 1912; lived in Germany, Italy, and Switzerland, 1912–14, and in England, 1914–19; prosecuted for obscenity (*The Rainbow*), 1915; founder, with Katherine Mansfield and John Middleton Murry, *Signature* magazine, 1916; lived in Florence, Capri, and Sicily, 1919–22; visited

Ceylon and Australia, 1922; lived in the United States and Mexico, 1922–23, England, France, and Germany, 1924, New Mexico and Mexico, 1924–25, Italy, 1925–28, and France, 1928–30; also a painter: one-man show, London, 1929 (shut down by the police). Died 2 March 1930.

Novels by Lawrence
The White Peacock, 1911
The Trespasser, 1912
Sons and Lovers, 1913
The Rainbow, 1915
Women in Love, 1920
The Lost Girl, 1920
Aaron's Rod, 1922
Kangaroo, 1923
The Plumed Serpent, 1926
Lady Chatterley's Lover, 1928

Other Writings: short stories, plays, verse, travel writings, letters, and essays on a wide variety of topics.

Further Reading
Daleski, H.M., *The Forked Flame: A Study of D.H. Lawrence*, Evanston, Illinois: Northwestern University Press, and London: Faber, 1965

Hobsbaum, Philip, *A Reader's Guide to D.H. Lawrence*, London and New York: Thames and Hudson, 1981

Holderness, Graham, *"Women in Love,"* Milton Keynes: Open University Press, 1986

Lawrence, D.H., *Studies in Classic American Literature*, London and New York: Penguin, 1971; originally published in 1923

Lawrence, D.H., *A Study of Thomas Hardy and Other Essays*, edited by Bruce Steele, Cambridge and New York: Cambridge University Press, 1985

Leavis, F.R., *D.H. Lawrence, Novelist*, London: Chatto and Windus, 1955

Murfin, Ross C., *"Sons and Lovers": A Novel of Division and Desire*, Boston: Twayne, 1987

Nehls, Edward, editor, *D.H. Lawrence: A Composite Biography*, Madison: University of Wisconsin Press, 1957

Ross, Charles L., *The Composition of "The Rainbow" and "Women in Love,"* Charlottesville: University Press of Virginia, 1979

Sagar, Keith, *The Art of D.H. Lawrence*, Cambridge: Cambridge University Press, 1966

Widdowson, Peter, editor, *D.H. Lawrence*, London and New York: Longman, 1992

Lazarillo de Tormes (Anonymous)

1554

Lazarillo de Tormes is often called the first picaresque novel, a narrative genre that flowered in 17th-century Spain and had a significant impact on the realistic novel. *Lazarillo*'s most important contribution to the development of modern fiction is its use of a homodiegetic (or first-person) narrator. In fact, its highly sophisticated manipulation of that narrative device was rarely equaled by its imitators. As the self-portrait of a rogue, *Lazarillo* is marked not only by an unprecedented psychological depth, but also by a boldness that subsequent centuries did not dare match. Lázaro recounts his misdeeds and stratagems with great relish and, unlike later pícaros, remains unrepentant at book's end.

Modern readers tend to read *Lazarillo* as a serious and even tragic work that traces the moral corruption of a child. The author's contemporaries regarded it as a fundamentally comic work. For 16th-century readers, *Lazarillo* was less psychological portrait than a sequence of brief anecdotes linked by the presence of an amusing narrator, as Maxime Chevalier has shown (see Chevalier, 1976). Many of its anecdotes, jokes, and characters were drawn from the lively Spanish tradition of oral storytelling. Stock characters include the thieving miller (Lazarillo's father), the miserly priest, and the penniless *escudero* (squire) who becomes Lazarillo's third master. The tricks played on Lazarillo and those he plays to revenge himself on the

tricksters were staples of comic fiction and drama during the Renaissance. More apt to laugh at humor that involves physical injury, 16th-century readers found a source of comedy in what modern readers experience as painful. *Lazarillo*'s first audience was apparently not troubled by the fact that the blind man smashes a wine jug in Lazarillo's face or that his second master, the priest, gives him a blow on the head that leaves him unconscious for three days.

Lazarillo is a very short book, only about 60 pages in a modern edition. It is a novella, rather than a novel, and like many novellas presents in detail only the formative years of its protagonist. Nearly 90 percent of the book deals with Lazarillo's life between the ages of about 12 and 14. Its seven *tratados* or chapters are of very unequal length. The first, which takes Lazarillo from his birth to the end of his service with his first master, a blind beggar, and the third, which tells of his service with an impoverished nobleman, fill about 15 pages each; the fourth and sixth together add up to only three-quarters of a page. The pace of the narrative is equally uneven, proceeding very slowly, even hour by hour, in the early chapters that deal with Lazarillo's childhood and then skipping over periods of several years in, or rather between, the later ones that bring the adult Lázaro to the circumstances in which he finds himself as narrator. He works as a town crier—a royal office, although one without prestige—and lives comfortably through the favor of an archpriest who sleeps with Lázaro's wife. The book ends with Lázaro's assertion that "at this time I was prosperous and at the summit of every sort of good fortune." Lázaro presents his life as a case study of upward mobility, the only morality he acknowledges.

Lázaro tells his life story to an unnamed correspondent, whom he addresses in the prologue as *Vuestra Merced,* "your grace," and whose precise relationship to him is unclear. *Vuestra Merced,* however, is not the sole narratee. Lázaro declares in the prologue that he considers it appropriate that "such remarkable things, perhaps never seen or heard before" should be brought to the attention of many people. Although he calls the book a trifle and says that it is written in a crude style, he is obviously proud of his work as a writer.

In fact, Lázaro's style is anything but crude. The book's full title, *The Life of Lazarillo de Tormes and His Fortunes and Adversities,* suggests a saint's life, while his name, a reference to his birthplace, a mill overhanging the river Tormes, suggests the birth of the protagonist of a romance of chivalry. The book is full of echoes of biblical language. Lázaro describes the punishment of his father, the miller, for stealing grain in terms that recall the Sermon on the Mount. He is also fond of giving an ironic twist to familiar expressions, like his mother's advice "arrímate a los buenos y serás dellos," roughly "a man is known by the company he keeps," which he recalls in the last chapter to justify his acceptance of the archpriest's attentions toward his wife.

Some readers question whether Lázaro is being ironic when he refers to his good fortune in the last sentence of his book or whether he is simply unaware of its implications. Does he recognize that he has lost the innocence he had as a child and, if so,

does he feel that he has been forced to do so in order to survive in a hypocritical and corrupt society? Finally, to what extent does the book reflect the mature Lázaro's view of his own life rather than a presentation he thinks will gain the approval of his readers? Part of the book's appeal rests on the impossibility of giving clear-cut answers to these and a host of similar questions.

THOMAS R. HART

See also Picaresque

Further Reading

Bataillon, Marcel, *Novedad y fecundidad del "Lazarillo de Tormes,"* Salamanca: Anaya, 1968; 2nd edition, 1973

Chevalier, Maxime, *Lectura y lectores en la Espana de los siglos XVI y XVII,* Madrid: Turner, 1976

Deyermond, A.D., *"Lazarillo de Tormes": A Critical Guide,* London: Grant and Cutler, 1975; 2nd edition, 1993

Dunn, Peter N., *Spanish Picaresque Fiction: A New Literary History,* Ithaca, New York: Cornell University Press, 1993

Guillén, Claudio, *Literature as System: Essays Toward the Theory of Literary History,* Princeton, New Jersey: Princeton University Press, 1971

Lázaro Carreter, Fernando, *"Lazarillo de Tormes" en la picaresca,* Barcelona: Ariel, 1972; 2nd edition, 1983

Rico, Francisco, *The Spanish Picaresque Novel and the Point of View,* Cambridge and New York: Cambridge University Press, 1984

Wardropper, Bruce W., "El trastorno de la moral en el *Lazarillo," Nueva Revista de Filología Hispánica* 15 (1961)

Leiden des jungen Werthers. *See* Sufferings of Young Werther

---

The Leopard by Giuseppe Tomasi di Lampedusa

Il Gattopardo 1959

The Leopard is the most popular 20th-century Italian novel and the source of one of contemporary Italy's most engaging literary events. It is a rich historical novel blended with the author's nostalgic, yet tragic, vision of life. The novel tells of the decline of the Sicilian nobility, which was forced to come to terms with a rising bourgeoisie after the Bourbon Kingdom of the Two Sicilies was replaced by the Piedmontese bureaucracy during the latter part of the 19th century. Giuseppe Tomasi de Lampedusa, a Sicilian prince who had remained outside the literary establishment and had published nothing during his lifetime

except for three articles that appeared in an obscure Genoese periodical in the 1920s, wrote the book during the last two years of his life. First rejected by two major Italian publishers, the novel was finally accepted for publication in 1958, a year after Lampedusa's death, by the firm of Giangiacomo Feltrinelli, which had earlier discovered and published Boris Pasternak's *Doktor Zhivago* (1957; *Doctor Zhivago*).

The Leopard became an instant best-seller in Italy and abroad. It won the prestigious Strega Prize and, just a year after the award, had already been republished in 57 editions, an extraordinary achievement for an Italian novel. *The Leopard* elicited contrasting and polemical responses ranging from praise for its poetic treatment of the human condition to attacks for expressing a reactionary philosophy. Italian Marxist critics and the literary left criticized Lampedusa's narrow historical vision and apparent denial of progress, while Catholic intellectuals rejected its pessimistic outlook and anticlerical views. Intervening in the critical debate, France's major Marxist poet, Louis Aragon, declared the novel to be "one of the great books of this century, one of the great books of all time."

The controversy surrounding the novel was largely a result of its publication during a period of transition. Toward the end of the 1950s, neorealism had entered into a crisis and was being reassessed. Despite declaring neorealism to be substantially outmoded, the emerging experimental literature still placed a strong emphasis on the neorealist credo of political and social involvement. These years also witnessed a rising neo–avant garde that subjected the past to critical reconsideration and found modern narrative to be insufficiently experimental. What most troubled the neo–avant garde critics as well as Italy's leading neorealist writers was that seemingly traditional novels, such as *The Leopard*, were being rewarded by both popular and critical acclaim. *The Leopard*'s return to the 19th-century structure of the novel and its apparent lack of any innovative narrative technique was one of the fundamental reasons for its negative reception by these critics. A 19th-century story, set during the *Risorgimento* and told from the perspective of a Sicilian prince (Don Fabrizio, prince of Salina) who has grown disillusioned with the Unification's effects on the social structure, did not appear to be consonant with an Italy that was experiencing the so-called "economic miracle" and rapidly becoming an advanced industrialized country. Nevertheless, Lampedusa's pessimistic, fatalistic version of the *Risorgimento* in Sicily and his scepticism about new ideas and reforms struck a chord in many intellectuals as well as in the ever-growing reading public associated with Italy's economic boom. *The Leopard* signaled the end of neorealist fiction, replacing a bleak and antiliterary treatment of recently shared experiences such as war, unemployment, and social alienation with a lyrical evocation of a lost world.

Lampedusa's "Lezioni su Stendhal" (Lessons on Stendhal), published in the literary review *Paragone* in 1959, reflects his thorough acquaintance with the European tradition of 20th-century discussions of narrative technique, dating back to Henry James and including E.M. Forster, Thomas Mann, Marcel Proust, and James Joyce. As Olga Ragusa (1973) has pointed out, the "Lezioni su Stendhal" is fundamental for a more insightful reading of *The Leopard*. Lampedusa treats all of Stendhal's works, but he devotes special attention to the French writer's *Le Rouge et le noir* (1830; *The Red and the Black*) and *La Chartreuse de Parme* (1839; *The Charterhouse of Parma*), both of which represent the seemingly contradictory characteristics of *The Leopard*: "that of a historical novel and the 'lyrical' outpouring of their author's sentiments." *The Leopard*'s 50-year chronicle of the Unification's effect in Sicily, dating from Garibaldi's landing on the island in 1860 to the final decline of a once-opulent Sicilian family, is selectively represented by the omniscient narrator who, from a vantage point of temporal distance, imposes his own feelings and impressions upon the flux of existence. Contrary to the classical form of the historical novel, the narrator's subjective voice does not aim at objectivity but instead allows the present to in-

trude upon the past. Moreover, *The Leopard*'s composition in blocks, whose sequence of episodes are relatively independent from one another, distinguishes it from the linear narration of the 19th-century novel. As Cristina Della Colletta (1996) notes, Lampedusa does not "aim at providing a total representation and a complete historical account" but, rather, is intent on revealing a fragmentary and conditional historical picture. By choosing as the novel's protagonist one of the last scions of the Sicilian aristocracy who will have no active role in the making of modern Italy, Lampedusa rejects the traditional representation of the Unification. Don Fabrizio's marginalized perspective enables Lampedusa to divest this historical moment of its heroic rhetoric and instead present it as a period of compromise, deception, and self-interest. The choice of an omniscient narrator allows the author to insert personal comments, ironic asides, and modern references into the text in order to draw parallels with the present. Consequently, Lampedusa's depiction of the *Risorgimento* as a failed revolution mirrors his negative sentiments toward more recent historical and social changes.

The Leopard bears many of the characteristics of the Sicilian and European historical novel. Its insistence on death, the pervading sense of languidness, and the sensuality of decay evoke qualities of the decadent novel. Its metaphorical, rhetorical, and highly literary style, however, are reminiscent of the art prose movement in Italy in the 1930s. All considered, *The Leopard* is a book that transcends its period and classifications, owing in large part to the novel's qualities of *poliedricita'* (many-sidedness), a term that Lampedusa attributed to Stendhal.

MARK PIETRALUNGA

Further Reading

Aragon, Louis, "*Il Gattopardo e La Certosa*," *Rinascita* 30 (1960)

Buzzi, Giancarlo, *Invito alla lettura di Giuseppe Tomasi di Lampedusa*, Milan: Mursia, 1972

Colquhoun, Archibald, "Lampedusa in Sicily: The Lair of the Leopard," *The Atlantic Monthly* 211: 2 (1963)

Della Colletta, Cristina, *Plotting the Past: Metamorphoses of Historical Narrative in Modern Italian Fiction*, West Lafayette, Indiana: Purdue University Press, 1996

Forster, E.M., *Aspects of the Novel, and Related Writings*, London: Arnold, and New York: Holmes and Meier, 1974

Gatt-Rutter, John, *Writers and Politics in Modern Italy*, London: Hodder and Stoughton, and New York: Holmes and Meier, 1978

Gilmour, David, *The Last Leopard: A Life of Giuseppe Tomasi di Lampedusa*, London: Quartet, 1988

Lansing, Richard, "The Structure of Meaning in Lampedusa's *Il Gattopardo*," *PMLA* 93 (1978)

O'Neill, Tom, "Ants and Flags: Tomasi di Lampedusa's *Gattopardo*," *The Italianist* 13 (1993)

Pacifici, Sergio, *The Modern Italian Novel from Pea to Moravia*, Carbondale: Southern Illinois University Press, 1979

Ragusa, Olga, "Stendhal, Tomasi di Lampedusa, and the Novel," *Comparative Literature Studies* 3 (1973)

Salvestroni, Simonetta, *Tomasi di Lampedusa*, Florence: La Nuova Italia, 1973

Samona, Giuseppe Paolo, *Il Gattopardo, i racconti, Lampedusa*, Florence: La Nuova Italia, 1974

Doris Lessing 1919–

English

Any reader of Doris Lessing's novels will experience difficulties categorizing her work. During a writing career that has spanned five decades, Lessing has produced striking, sharply observed realist texts, science-fiction novels, formally exploratory postmodernist works, and modern fables. She also has written comics, short stories, poetry, and plays. One of her novels has been adapted as an opera. The first volume of her autobiography, *Under My Skin,* appeared in 1994.

Although Lessing's early novels may be categorized as realist, her use of realism has, from the beginning, been ironic, provisional, and intercut with other literary forms. *The Grass Is Singing* (1950), Lessing's searing examination of the fascination of a white southern African farmer's wife for her black servant, has an almost poetically overdetermined quality as it moves toward its tragic conclusion, a conclusion of which the reader has already been made fully aware at the novel's opening. Lessing, the daughter of white British settlers, arrived in England from Southern Rhodesia (now Zimbabwe) in 1949 with the manuscript of this novel in her suitcase; the fact that her early experiences were formed by an awareness of racial segregation and ethnic difference is certainly significant, not just in the thematic focus of her work but in the deliberately partial, analytical way in which she has handled different prose forms and genres.

Lessing's powerful five-volume sequence *Children of Violence* (1952–69) traces the growth and development of its aptly named heroine, Martha Quest, and is similarly self-conscious about its relationship with the genre of the Bildungsroman—a class of novel that conventionally takes as its subject the character formation of its protagonist in relation to a sharply observed social context. While the constituent novels of the series certainly fit this definition, they always display an awareness of the different position women characters occupy in a literary form that developed in the 19th century with a central focus on male protagonists. Perhaps the most obvious marks of this awareness in the texts occur in the fourth and fifth volumes, *Landlocked* (1965) and *The Four-Gated City* (1969). The tone and texture of *Landlocked* are affected by the fact that Lessing took a break from the *Children of Violence* series to write what may be her most well-known novel, *The Golden Notebook* (1962). Her experimentation with the novel form in that text rubs off on *Landlocked,* the realist surface of which is fractured by dreams, surreal episodes, and the deliberate withholding of information about key characters and events. In *The Four-Gated City* Lessing takes this experimentation further by concluding Martha's story in an imagined future world where Western capitalism and first-world society have broken down and a select breed of humans are beginning to discover telepathic powers. While some readers have objected to this abrupt switching of genres and have found the failure to conclude Martha's story in a conventional way disappointing, Lessing's aim was certainly to question the boundaries between different prose genres, as well as what is meant by the "sense of an ending."

Lessing's increasing interest in what may be termed "inner space fiction" is developed further in *Briefing for a Descent into Hell* (1971) and *Memoirs of a Survivor* (1974). The former takes on some of the ideas of alternative psychiatry in order to question whether the protagonist is insane; the latter balances another dystopian vision of the collapse of Western society with an alternative world that exists behind the narrator's living room wall, where dreamlike, semi-mythical experiences and women's universal childhood memories are played out. These novels are perhaps more satisfying because of their complex, indeterminate quality than Lessing's later science-fiction series, *Canopus in Argos: Archives* (1979–83). Individual novels in this sequence are striking, particularly *Shikasta* (1979), an intriguing perspective on our own planet's problems, and *The Marriages Between Zones Three, Four and Five* (1980), which uses marriage between the kings and queens of a planet's different cultures as a device to encourage their growth and development. However, the overall design of a galaxy of benevolent providers who observe the struggles of less sophisticated planets and peoples is rather disturbing in its colonialist implications.

In the 1980s and 1990s, Lessing has returned to realism in *The Diaries of Jane Somers* (1984), which she originally published under a pseudonym as two novels, *The Diary of a Good Neighbour* (1983) and *If the Old Could—* (1984). The initial reception of these novels, when assumed to be by an "unknown," reveals more about the publishing industry than about the quality of the novels, which tackle an unpopular subject: a middle-aged woman's relationship with her old and infirm female neighbor. Lessing's most recent novel, *Love, Again* (1996), similarly takes as its protagonist a "woman of a certain age" who finds herself experiencing ferocious and absorbing love when she had thought such emotions long gone. *The Fifth Child* (1988), however, is distinguished by the mixing of genres that may be considered Lessing's particular contribution to the novel. Ostensibly a straightforward account of the birth of a couple's fifth child, who has a number of physical and emotional abnormalities, the tale has an almost fabular quality, which suggests debts to the fairy tale, popular mythology, and texts like Mary Shelley's *Frankenstein* (1818).

Lessing's position as one of the most important novelists of the 20th century relates, in part, to her unusual position as an outsider in both English and southern African culture. Her feelings on returning to Rhodesia after a long, compulsory absence (she was banned for a time from entering the country on the grounds of her communist affiliations) are detailed in a powerful essay, *Going Home* (1957). It is this divided heritage that has created the thematic focus of some of her best-known fiction. Her interest in the intersection between race, class, and gender also marks many of her novels, particularly the *Children of Violence* sequence. Novels such as *A Ripple from the Storm* (1958), *The Golden Notebook,* and *The Good Terrorist* (1985) detail the dreary day-to-day life, coupled with sudden dangers, of those involved in communist and left-wing politics. As someone who describes herself as an "old Red," Lessing's involvement in the Communist Party in Rhodesia and England has clearly influenced her life and work. Her experiences as a woman have done so, too; *A Proper Marriage* (1954), for example, is a thought-provoking account of the emotional and ideological pressures that surround Martha Quest's pregnancy and the birth of her child. Lessing's interest in mental and social breakdown and collapse has also dominated most of her writing.

It is not merely in the themes of Lessing's novels that such concerns are apparent, but also in the formal and generic choices that she has made. She may appear to owe a debt to a very English social realist tradition, yet her stated admiration for the great European realists Lev Tolstoi and Stendhal (acknowledged in the preface to *The Golden Notebook*) suggests a rather different place in the history of the novel. It is also possible, because of her formal experimentalism, to align her with contemporary postmodernist novelists such as Angela Carter; but what distinguishes Lessing as a writer is her commitment to the notion that literature should have some worthwhile connection with the real world, infused with an awareness of the problems involved in making such a statement.

Susan Watkins

See also Golden Notebook

Biography
Born 22 October 1919 in Kermansha, Persia; moved with her family to England, then to Banket, Southern Rhodesia, 1924. Attended Dominican Convent School, Salisbury, Southern Rhodesia, 1926–34. Au pair, Salisbury, 1934–35; telephone operator and clerk, Salisbury, 1937–39; typist, 1946–48; journalist, Cape Town *Guardian,* 1949; moved to London, 1950; secretary, 1950; member of the Editorial Board, *New Reasoner* (later *New Left Review*), 1956.

Novels by Lessing
The Grass Is Singing, 1950
Children of Violence:
   Martha Quest, 1952
   A Proper Marriage, 1954
   A Ripple from the Storm, 1958
   Landlocked, 1965
   The Four-Gated City, 1969
Retreat to Innocence, 1956
The Golden Notebook, 1962
Briefing for a Descent into Hell, 1971

The Summer Before the Dark, 1973
Memoirs of a Survivor, 1974
Canopus in Argos: Archives:
   Shikasta, 1979
   The Marriages Between Zones Three, Four and Five, 1980
   The Sirian Experiments, 1981
   The Making of the Representative for Planet 8, 1982
   The Sentimental Agents, 1983
The Diaries of Jane Somers, 1984
   The Diary of a Good Neighbour, 1983
   If the Old Could—, 1984
The Good Terrorist, 1985
The Fifth Child, 1988
Love, Again, 1996

Other Writings: short stories, plays, autobiography, and other nonfiction.

Further Reading
Draine, Betsy, *Substance Under Pressure: Artistic Coherence and Evolving Form in the Novels of Doris Lessing,* Madison: University of Wisconsin Press, 1983
Greene, Gayle, *Doris Lessing: The Poetics of Change,* Ann Arbor: University of Michigan Press, 1994
Kaplan, Carey, and Ellen Cronan Rose, *Doris Lessing: The Alchemy of Survival,* Athens: Ohio University Press, 1988
King, Jeanette, *Doris Lessing,* London: Edward Arnold, 1989
Rowe, Margaret Roan, *Doris Lessing,* London: Macmillan, and New York: St. Martin's Press, 1994
Sage, Lorna, *Doris Lessing,* London and New York: Methuen, 1983
Sprague, Claire, *In Pursuit of Doris Lessing: Nine Nations Reading,* London: Macmillan, and New York: St. Martin's Press, 1990
Sprague, Claire, and Virginia Tiger, *Critical Essays on Doris Lessing,* Boston: G.K. Hall, 1986
Taylor, Jenny, editor, *Notebooks, Memoirs, Archives: Reading and Rereading Doris Lessing,* London and Boston: Routledge and Kegan Paul, 1982
Whittaker, Ruth, *Doris Lessing,* London: Macmillan, and New York: St. Martin's Press, 1988

Letters. *See* Epistolary Novel; Prose Novelistic Forms

Levantine Arabic Novel

The Levant, or Greater Syria (present-day Syria, Jordan, Palestine, and Israel), is a region that in one sense is unified by language and culture, yet it is also sliced and scarred by political boundaries that reflect both a genuine local diversity as well as an arbitrary and artificial historical determinacy. The very intensity of political conflict and fragmentation that this region has undergone during the second half of the 20th century distinguishes it from other parts of the Arab world. Its unique circumstances are reflected in the region's literature. Literary development in the Levant, as in other parts of the Arab world, also cannot be understood without considering its relationship to the West. Contemporary Arabic literature is the result of a long but often accelerated process that had its basis in the *Nahda,* the movement of cultural revival or renaissance that began in the 19th century. This cultural movement, which formulated a dichotomy between the traditional and the modern based on the Western cultural model, has been inextricably tied with the fate of the Levant, where, in many respects, it has undergone its severest tests.

Up to 1950 the influences that left their mark on Arabic writing were largely French and belonged mostly to the category of mid-19th-century romanticism. Among the earliest Levantine authors, the most important was the renowned Jubrān Khalīl Jubrān (Kahlil Gibran), the leader of the émigré literary community in the United States and a leading representative of the *mahjar,* or émigré school, which was formed as a result of emigration from the region in the 19th century. Jubrān's works of fiction, which belong to the earlier part of his career, are not directly relevant to the development of a novel tradition per se but represented a departure from traditional forms of Arabic prose. In the early decades of the 20th century, the genre of the historical novel was elevated to a new level of sophistication and popularity by Jurjī Zaydān, a Lebanese immigrant to Egypt, and emulated in the Levant by such writers as Maʿrūf al-Arnāʾūṭ and Shakīb al-Jābirī in Syria and Khalīl Baydas in Palestine.

While Arab novelists continued to write historical fiction in the 1930s and 1940s, the mood of suspicion and mistrust toward the colonial powers, as well as the *anciens régimes,* with their entrenched and often corrupt power structures, led writers such as the Syrian Tawfīq Yūsuf ʿAwwād to use the genre as an expression of political and social protest. Paradoxically, as the Arabs became more and more politically alienated from the West with the end of World War II, their thought and literature were subject to mounting impact from the same direction. In less than 20 years, the Arab world went through the rapid chain-explosions of European culture that had marked the period roughly between 1910 and 1935. The Arabic modernist novel grew out of the increase in translation and critical attention devoted to Western literature in the period beginning in the early 1950s. During the period from 1950 to 1960, journals played a key role in publishing critical articles, reviews, and translations of Western writers, particularly the works of the existentialists, such as Jean-Paul Sartre and Albert Camus.

The most important source of this influence was *Majallat al-Ādāb,* a magazine published in Beirut by the Suhayl Idrīs, also a major writer of this period. Idrīs wrote a novel called *Al-Ḥayy al-Lātīnī* (1953; The Latin Quarter), in which issues of sexual freedom and individualism predominate. Mutāʿ Ṣafadī's novels, *Jīl al-Qadar* (1960; Generation of Destiny) and *Thāʾir Muḥtarif* (1961; Professional Rebel) are similarly characterized by an emphasis on the individual, particularly in isolation. *Anā Aḥyā* (1958; I Am Alive), by Laylā Baʿlabakkī, was a significant landmark with respect to the expression of individuality in the Arabic novel. The story of a young girl, written from a first-person perspective, it centers on the defiant mood of its protagonist, which is deeply rooted in her egotistic assertion of her individual freedom. *Al-Ālihah al-Mamsūkhah* (1960; The Disfigured Gods), is a more complex novel with a clearly visible structure, in which Baʿlabakkī uses a variety of literary techniques to present her characters, including conventional omniscient narration, the epistolary method, and stream-of-consciousness technique. The Syrian novelist Kūlīt Khūrī (Colette Khouri) also challenged entrenched values at this time with her provocatively titled *Ayyām Maʿahu* (1959; Days With Him) and *Laylah Wāḥidah* (1961; A Single Night), the former a frank description of a love affair between a young girl and an older man.

Jabrā Ibrāhīm Jabrā is a figure of paramount importance in the late 1950s and early 1960s. A Palestinian who went into exile in Baghdad after 1948, he was a literary critic and translator of English literature whose first two novels, *Passage in the Silent Night* (1946) and *Hunters in a Narrow Street* (1960), were originally written in that language. Jabrā's preoccupation in these works is with characters from the social elite, primarily intellectuals, who live a life of alienation and attempt to escape from the problems of life in contemporary Arab society. In the former work, Jabrā's narrator is a young member of the intelligentsia who elopes with a woman above him in social class. When she deserts him, he is plunged into a deep depression. Set against a bleak urban backdrop reminiscent of the works of Fedor Dostoevskii and Rainer Maria Rilke, the novel, despite its dominant melodramatic tone, contains many elements that are clearly antiromantic. The protagonist's mood fluctuates wildly, and this very instability causes him to interrogate his life and existence, and endows his narrative with an existential quality.

Beginning in the early 1960s, individualistic expression in Arabic novels began to transgress the boundaries of bourgeois concerns and to appear in the context of a heightened consciousness with respect to specific social and political issues, such as the status of women, political repression, and the Israeli-Palestinian conflict. With her second novel, *Al-Ālihah al-Mamsūkhah,* Laylā Baʿlabakkī took a significant step away from a mere concern with the expression of individuality and toward the specific feminist concerns that have come to dominate in the work of contemporary Arab women novelists, and that have effected an increasing separation between masculine and feminine narrative in the Arab world. In this novel, we already find a sharp contrast between male and female subjectivity. The protagonist of the narrative is a lonely and alienated woman whose husband discovered on their wedding night that she was not a virgin and has subsequently punished her by refusing to sleep with her, depriving her of the right to have children—a severe loss, since she has no other responsibilities in life that might be a focus for her energies. In a state of disorientation reminiscent of that of the protagonist in Charlotte Perkins Gilman's *The Yel-*

low *Wallpaper* (1899), she superimposes her own imaginings on the real world.

In the mid-1960s, existentialist influence began to appear in tandem with clearly political themes. One of the most notable examples is Ghassān Kanafānī's *Rijāl fī al-shams* (1963; *Men in the Sun*), in which a journey of three Palestinians across the desert from Iraq to Kuwait is presented as an allegory tinged with an absurdist flavor. Kanafānī's *Mā tabaqqā lakum* (1966; *All That's Left to You*) concerns a brother and sister living in Gaza, separated from their mother in 1948. The sister, Maryam, has lost her virginity, become pregnant, and been forced to marry a man who is already married and has five children. To make her humiliation complete, her husband is a known coward and traitor. Driven to despair by this situation, the brother, Ḥāmid, sets out for Jordan in search of his mother.

Thematically, *All That's Left to You* is linked with William Faulkner's *The Sound and the Fury* (1929) by the centrality of the heroine. In both novels, we find a triangle relationship at the center of the plots, consisting of the heroines, the men who threaten their honor, and the men who wish to to defend that honor. In Kanafānī's novel, Maryam's honor is symbolic of that of the nation, and her husband's threat to that honor represents the corruption at the core of society. This dual structure, in which the issue of honor is reflected in both national and personal terms, is supported by another consisting of two types of time: natural time and subjective time. A dual movement is created in the text, representing Ḥāmid's confrontation with the Israeli enemy on the one hand, and Maryam's confrontation with her husband on the other, which in turn reflects Kanafānī's preoccupations with both political awareness and narrative subjectivity.

The Six-Day War of 1967 was a defining moment in modern Arab history and a devastating blow to the pretensions carefully nurtured during the early years of independence and revolution. It is in light of this event especially that the Levant acquires a profound significance within the Arab consciousness, and its literature becomes distinct from that in other parts of the Arab world. The immediate effect upon the novel in the region was a retreat into a wave of politically and ideologically driven narrative, which reflected the shock of the Arab defeat and a renewed search for national identity. In Jabrā's *Al-Safīnah* (1970; *The Ship*), the actions of the characters are more determined by this highly politicized mood than in his previous works, although their chief response to this political climate remains an escapist one. Writers living in the region rather than in exile, however, were forced to deal with the defeat in more intimate and concrete terms. Ḥalīm Barakāt's *ʿAwdat al-Ṭāʾir ilā al-Baḥr* (1969; *Days of Dust*) is a work by a Lebanese novelist that provides a *cinéma vérité* view of the fighting and the terrible plight of Arab refugees during the six days of the June War. Emile Ḥabībī's *Sudāsiyat al-Ayyām al-Sittah* (1969; *Six Days' Sextet*), the work of a Palestinian living in Israel, concentrates on the bitter ironies of life for the Arab citizens of that country, structured as a set of stories of meetings between them and their exiled relatives.

The 1967 defeat produced a sense of moral crisis in the region, culminating in a period of self-criticism and a reappraisal of Arab culture and political practice that first began to be expressed in the novel in the mid-1970s and early 1980s. The novelists of this period were part of a highly politicized generation, aroused by injustices both on an international scale and within

the Arab world itself. Their work is typified by a strong social and political orientation, although often expressed in opposition to the prevailing political "discourse." Among the works of Palestinian authors, Tawfīq Fayyāḍ's *Majmūʿah 778* (1974; *Group 778*) is a work that applies this critical attitude toward the Arab resistance movement. In Saḥar Khalīfah's *Al-Ṣubbār* (1976; *Wild Thorns*), the main character, returning to Palestine, finds to his horror that his family and friends have adjusted to the practicalities of occupation. Commissioned by the resistance to blow up the buses that take workers to their jobs in Israel, he bungles the job. The workers are killed, he and his resistance colleagues are killed, and his family's home is evacuated and blown up.

Emile Ḥabībī, a founding member of the Israeli Communist Party and a former member of the Knesset, developed a unique style in an effort to represent the situation of Arabs living within Israel. He was one of the first Arab novelists to fully exploit the technique of pastiche, incorporating poetry, the short story, the folk tale, the memoir or autobiography, and other literary forms into the novel. Ḥabībī's best-known work, *Al-Waqāʾiʿ al-gharībah fī ikhtifāʾ Saʿīd Abī al-Naḥs al-Mutashāʾil* (1974; *The Secret Life of Saeed, the Ill-Fated Pessoptimist*), is an ironic masterpiece that reflects a melding of the mythical with irony and black humor. Ḥabībī's protagonist, Saeed, is an informer for the Zionist state who can never do enough to please his Israeli masters. A transformation occurs in Saeed's self-awareness, however, when, during the upheaval of the 1967 war, he makes an idiotic blunder and is put in prison by the authorities, who hope that he will be a spy for the state among the prisoners. There, he is brutally beaten by the Israeli guards and put in a cell with his son and namesake, who mistakes him for a freedom fighter like himself. After this, Saeed finds that he can no longer collaborate with the Israelis.

Saeed's change of heart, however, cannot furnish him with a solution to his misery. While he rejects his former role of informer, he is still crippled by his natural cowardice. In *The Pessoptimist*, Ḥabībī gives us a narrative that functions on two levels, one of bantering humor and one of grim reality, prompting comparison to Voltaire's *Candide* (1759) and Jaroslav Hašek's *The Good Soldier Švejk* (1921–23). Its similarity to the latter work lies not only in the antiheroic nature of its protagonist but also in the use of this antiheroic stance as a means—in fact, a strategy—of resistance. In this respect, it breaks fundamentally with the heroic conventions of Palestinian literature. Ḥabībī's character, however, is less consistent and therefore more complex than Švejk. Saeed is not just a fool; he is also a coward, and his cowardice makes him a conscious victim. His narrative is informed by his own self-awareness, which alternates between denial and acknowledgment of his compromised position.

In Syria, the dominant type of novel has continued to be overwhelmingly realist, with Ḥannā Mīnah, Fāris Zarzūr, and Hānī ar-Rāhib its most prominent practitioners. A specialty of Syrian writers is still the historical novel, the most notable exponents of which include Nabīl Sulaymān, Fawwāz Ḥaddād, Khayrī al-Dhahabī, and Nihād Sirris. Among Syria's dissonant voices, the most prominent is Ḥaydar Ḥaydar, whose celebrated novel of this period, *Walīmah li Aʿshāb al-Baḥr* (1974; *Feast for the Vegetation of the Sea*), is a nearly 400-page work in which the main character first escapes political oppression in the Eastern Arab world only to experience social oppression in the Western Arab world, and finally flees from life completely by drowning himself. His flight may be taken primarily to represent a rejection of the reigning political and social conditions in Syria. Ḥaydar's vision of the Arab world is of a dark, gloomy, repressive place, yet his protagonist's trajectory may be seen as not merely a flight from the "aborted" or "miscarried" Arab revolution, but also as a more general escape from the imposed conditions of society to an ideal of natural freedom.

In Lebanon, the generalized sense of injustice of this period was further aroused by the Lebanese civil war, which commenced in 1975 and lasted for 15 years, until 1990. Tawfīq Yūsuf ʿAwwād's novel *Tawāḥīn Bayrūt* (1972; *Death in Beirut*) is a prescient work that depicts Lebanese society on the verge of disaster. Some of the most potent novels to emerge from the Lebanese civil conflict, however, were produced by women writers. In *Bayrūt 75* (1975; *Beirut '75*), the Syrian-born and Lebanese-educated Ghādah al-Sammān describes the psychological and moral condition that reflects all the elements of the social collapse to come. She weaves a horrific narrative in which the various characters compromise themselves morally, sink to depravity, and are killed, condemned, or go mad. While she depicts each of the characters as in the grip of powerful external forces, she also indicts the characters themselves, in each case illuminating some failure on their part to come to grips with their condition. Sammān also anticipates many of the techniques used in the most innovative novels later to emerge from the war experience, such as the lack of focus on a single protagonist and the use of symbolic imagery. While societal self-criticism is nakedly expressed, the manner of description is far removed from the conventions of realism. What Sammān evokes is not a social or political reality, but an inner truth, the state of the city's "soul."

Sammān followed up her narrative experimentation in *Beirut '75* with her novel *Kawābīs Bayrūt* (1976; Beirut Nightmares), which dispenses with chapters altogether, in favor of a progression of vignettes, both real and surreal. The novel describes the fighting around the hotels of the city in November 1975. The protagonist, trapped along with her cousin and uncle, narrates the tale as a mixture of reality and nightmarish fantasy. Although *Beirut '75* is clearly a novel of social protest and makes connections between war and sexuality, it does not concentrate on the situation of women, but rather sees men and women in the position of common victims. *Sitt Marie Rose* (1978), by Etel ʿAdnān, on the other hand, presents a much more radical differentiation between the situation of men and women, depicting the former as in love with war as a substitute for sexuality, the latter as symbols of peace and national unity. The story focuses on a young Christian Lebanese schoolteacher who has fallen in love with a Palestinian Muslim. Held hostage in her school by four young Christian guerrillas, along with her young pupils, she is eventually executed and made a martyr for her defense of a pluralistic society.

While the 1967 war may have sown seeds of doubt in the minds of writers and intellectuals, it is only beginning in the early 1980s that a recognition of the failure of the nationalist struggle really set in and may be said to have become a dominant mood among writers in the region. This change came about at various times in Syria, Lebanon, Jordan, and Palestine, and was tied to different events, notably the occupation of Beirut by the Israelis in 1982 and the failure of the Syrians to challenge this occupation. In Palestine, Saḥar Khalīfah's *ʿAbbād al-Shams*

(1980; The Sunflower) prefigures this mood in its even-handed portrayal of the interaction between Arabs and Israelis. Most strikingly among Lebanese works at this time, the title character of Ḥanān al-Shaykh's *Ḥikāyat Zahrah* (1980; *The Story of Zahra*) enacts a pattern of passive complicity with the forces of war. The ambivalence of this narrative marks it as a kind of watershed, after which we note a return to a more individualized perspective in the novel, accompanied by a new tone of passivity and despair, rather than protest.

In Jordan, the presence of a large Palestinian population has contributed to national, ethnic, religious, and factional strains. The work of Muʾnis al-Razzāz, perhaps the foremost novelist in the country and also among its most prominent activists, reflects the attempt to merge political commitment with a degree of modernist experimentation. His most well-known work, *Iʿtirāfāt Kātim Ṣawt* (1986; Confessions of a Hit Man), concerns an Arab intellectual under house arrest and a political assassin who poses as his bodyguard. The novel has an Orwellian tone, with the protagonist's house under constant surveillance. Implicit in the novel is a rejection and repudiation of power, and an idealization of the higher intellectual and creative faculties. The most original aspect of the novel, however, is the hit man's "confessional" narrative, in which he stubbornly clings to his philosophy of power, by which people are mere objects to be manipulated. Razzāz is working here along the lines of Italo Svevo's *La coscienza di Zeno* (1923; *Confessions of Zeno*), in which the confessional figure is unable to be completely candid either with himself or the reader.

The shift at this time to a more sceptical world view also was tied to a change in the structure of the novel. Arabic novels up to this point, no matter how radically innovative, still had a certain formal cohesiveness, adhering to the rule of a story or plot. This cannot be said of the "new" novelists, such as Ilyās Khūrī (Elias Khoury). Khūrī's work is characterized by a greater looseness of form, in which he abandons many of the "rules" of writing and composition. He has gone out of his way to differentiate himself from some of his predecessors by disparaging the attempt to create a distinctly Arabic literature. His avowed major preoccupation, rather, is with creating a language of artistic expression that can re-create present reality. Khūrī's writing may be contrasted with that of Ḥabībī, for instance, in terms of its lack of investment in the past as a resource or inspiration, as well as his use of a vocabulary of pessimism, rather than one of irony.

Some of the preoccupations of Khūrī's major works, such as *Al-Jabal al-ṣaghīr* (1977; *Little Mountain*) and *Riḥlat Ghāndī al-ṣaghīr* (1989; *The Journey of Little Gandhi*), include the attempt to free narrative from the hegemony of the hero and to focus the reader's attention on the act of narration, both of which he accomplishes by inserting the narrator into the text as a character and assigning to other characters the roles of narrators. His preferred narrative technique is to build the novel on the basis of a series of short stories that interweave and connect. In *Little Mountain*, for instance, there is no longer a fixed relationship between the narrator and narration or between the characters and the story, because the characters share the act of narration with the narrator, and the narrator takes part as a character in the action along with the characters. Instead of reporting a given event from different perspectives or viewpoints in order to give the reader a more complete or objective view of an event, he takes a central event as a point of departure only. For Khūrī, the idea is not to tell a story by means of different witnesses, but to get away from any central event altogether.

Abwāb al-madīnah (1981; *Gates of the City*) is Khūrī's most experimental work. Once again, the subject is the Lebanese civil war, but this time neither the war nor the city is mentioned in concrete terms. It is arguably Khūrī's most powerful novel because in resorting to the most radical strategy he has found the most appropriate and effective way to express the true horror of the civil war. According to Khūrī, *Gates of the City* is an attempt to express situations related to the war symbolically by putting the reader inside the "interior situations" of men, rather than from the point of view of ideas, ideologies, or political positions. The work clearly owes a great deal to the work of Khalīl Jubrān and his contemporary Mīkhā'īl Nuʿaymah, whether through conscious imitation or merely cultural connection. Other possible influences include the Egyptian novelist Edwār al-Kharrāṭ, who produced a symbolist novel, *Rāmah wa-al-Tinnīn* (1980; *Ramah and the Dragon*), the prominent Syrian short-story writer Jurj Sālim, who also wrote in symbolic prose, and the narrative symbolism of Jorge Luis Borges.

Magic realism is also a novelistic genre that uses symbolic imagery, and its premier practitioner in the Arab world is Salīm Barakāt, a Syrian-born Kurd living and working in Cyprus. Barakāt is one of the master stylists writing in Arabic today. His first work, *Al-Jundub al-Ḥadīdī* (1980; *The Iron Grasshopper*), is a memoir set in a poor Kurdish village near the Syrian-Turkish border. Although not a novel, it is a significant work because in it Barakāt is experimenting with the innovative use of vocabulary, sentence construction, images, and narrative voice. With his first novel, *Fuqahā' al-Ẓalām* (1985; *Sages of Darkness*), Barakāt's experimentalism shifts to the use of imagery. Within the framework of a realist narrative, he produces "mutations" in both time and space that upset the normal reality and play havoc with the characters and their situations. The story of *Fuqahā' al-Ẓalām* is set in a small Kurdish Syrian village on the Turkish-Syrian border and involves a child whose growth, from birth, is accelerated to the point that he reaches the age of marriage by the end of the day. Following this precedent, the rest of the villagers apparently age preternaturally, die, and are transformed into a shadowy, ghostly force, in an apparent allegory of the infusion of political consciousness into a minority cultural community.

The most experimental novel to come out of Jordan is Ibrāhīm Naṣr Allāh's *Barārī al-Ḥummā* (1985; *Prairies of Fever*), in which there is no longer any trace of realism. Naṣr Allāh, primarily a poet, is interested in applying to prose specific symbolist techniques more commonly found in poetry, with surreal effect. The narrator of *Prairies of Fever* is a young teacher hired to teach in a remote part of the Arabian peninsula. As the novel opens, he is confronted by five featureless men who appear late one night at his doorstep and demand that, since he is dead, he pay them the expenses of his own funeral. As in Franz Kafka's *Der Prozess* (1925; *The Trial*), the men are faceless and anonymous, representing a type of undefined yet powerful authority. Desperately, the narrator tries to convince them—and himself—that he is still alive. In a subsequent chapter, written in second person, the "he" addresses his double, who is missing and answers to the same name. Later, the double is found and accused of murdering the narrator.

Naṣr Allāh's theme of the divided self is one that surfaces in the European novel from Dostoevskii and Robert Louis Stevenson to Hermann Hesse, and from Thomas Mann to Jean-Paul Sartre. Along with his application of a dualistic scheme in terms of imagery and narrative voice, Naṣr Allāh uses another symbolist technique: that of describing the world not as a whole but metonymically, in parts. Similarly, in narrating an event, he gives the reader suggestions or pieces of it, but never a complete picture. Another symbolist technique used by Naṣr Allāh is that of equivalency. All of his characters are, in effect, one character, interchangeable with one another. He also makes use of anthropomorphism in order to give the elements of the surrounding environment a life of their own. The application of these transformational processes in prose causes inner and outer worlds to lose their distinction. In this context, Kafka, whose theme of transformation underlies "The Metamorphosis," must once again be clearly seen as an influence.

Since the end of the civil war, the locus of literary innovation in the region has returned decisively to Beirut, a phenomenon that may be tied directly to the war experience. In *Taqniyāt al-Bu's* (1989; The Techniques of Misery), Rashīd al-Daʿīf experiments with a radically "objectified" type of narrative. The action of much of the text focuses on the existence of its antiheroic protagonist within the confines of his apartment. Whole pages are devoted to the way he smokes a cigarette, cooks a meal, flushes the toilet, or reads the paper. The misery alluded to in the title refers not only to the failure of appliances, utilities, vehicles, and other aspects of urban life in the face of the civil war, but also to the human "adaptation" to this condition.

Ḥasan Dā'ūd's *Ayyām Zā'idah* (1990; Excess Days) is a novel that achieves more of a balance between the descriptive and the psychological, between the "objectification" of experience and narrative subjectivity. The main character is an old man who gradually becomes more and more infirm. He has only the house that he lives in, and as his infirmity increases his ambiguous sense of time is replaced by a heightened sense of place. He is attached to everything in the house, and as his claim on and connection with these things is gradually reduced, he continues to hold on to them in obsessive fashion. Treated like an object by the members of his family, he plays down to their expectations, pretending when they are present that he doesn't hear or can't speak. One of the most striking aspects of *Ayyām Zā'idah* is simply its theme of old age, a topic that is very rare in the Arabic novel, which has, by and large, been preoccupied with larger social issues, particularly those of war and occupation. Its theme of isolation combined with old age and illness is powerfully reminiscent of Thomas Mann's *Der Tod in Venedig* (1912; *Death in Venice*). Even more striking, however, is that the old man remains an alert and active narrator, and the text, which begins with a picture of a dehumanized individual, ends with a kind of heroic attempt at self-understanding in the face of death.

In *Ḥajar al-Ḍahk* (1990; *The Stone of Laughter*) Hudā Barakāt also focuses on the illness and isolation of her main character, Khalīl, who, because of his effeminate nature, is alienated from his war-torn society. Khalīl objects to the violence around him and tries to keep the personal and public spheres of his life separate. In the midst of the civil war, he spends his time shopping, cooking, cleaning the house, daydreaming about male loved ones, replacing broken window panes, and reading. He closely resembles the "sensitive soul" of European literature, whose illness involves not only a sense of passivity and retreat from the world but also a deeper awareness of the processes of life and death. After the death of his closest friend, Khalīl's physical symptoms become more prominent. When he finally enters the hospital for an operation, he finds a kind of joy in its neat, antiseptic quality, its removal from the rest of the world, and the kindness of the doctors, nurses, and attendants—a viewpoint reminiscent of that of Hans Castorp, the protagonist of Thomas Mann's *Der Zauberberg* (1924; *The Magic Mountain*). As a result of a near-death experience during the operation, Khalīl undergoes a transformation akin to that of Michel, the main character of André Gide's *L'Immoraliste* (1902; *The Immoralist*). At this point, he becomes susceptible to the advances of a sinister homosexual gangster, called the Brother. By falling prey to the Brother's seduction, he willingly chooses the life of a slave. By the conclusion of the novel, the unthinkable has occurred— Khalīl has assumed a brutal male identity in the service of the Brother, and his humanity has been extinguished.

Ḥadīqat al-Ḥawās (1993; The Garden of the Senses), by ʿAbduh Wāzin, is an experimental work that clearly reflects the influence of the French *nouveau roman*. Subtitled a "text" rather than a novel, it contains no dialogue, is not divided into chapters, and is peopled by no characters except that of an anonymous narrator who sits at his desk, gazes out the window, stares at a blank sheet of paper before him, and remembers his lover who has mysteriously departed. The narrator has no identity other than that of an observer. The text is Proustian in its focus on the retrieval of memory, but it relies purely on description rather than narration. There are no events as such, and no time except the present. The text moves along with the act of writing, which depends simply on the shifts of the narrator's attention. The dimensions of the physical universe have shrunk to those of the room, and the outside world is no longer of importance. In this work, the engagement with the world typical of Arabic literature is abandoned. A new note of contemplativeness, introspection, and withdrawal, in which the writing process overshadows the subject itself, has crept into Arabic prose and brought it to the extreme limits of modernist development.

STEFAN MEYER

See also African Novel: North Africa; Egyptian Novel; Iranian Novel; Ghassān Kanafānī; Ilyās Khūrī; Ḥanān al-Shaykh

Further Reading

Allen, Roger, *The Arabic Novel: An Historical and Critical Introduction*, Syracuse, New York: Syracuse University Press, and Manchester: Manchester University Press, 1982; 2nd edition, Syracuse, New York: Syracuse University Press, 1995

Allen, Roger, editor, *Modern Arabic Literature*, New York: Ungar, 1987

Boullata, Issa J., editor, *Critical Perspectives on Modern Arabic Literature*, Washington, D.C.: Three Continents Press, 1980

Boullata, Issa J., and Roger Allen, editors, *The Arabic Novel Since 1950: Critical Essays, Interviews, and Bibliography*, Cambridge, Massachusetts: Dar Mahjar, 1992

Ghazoul, Ferial J., and Barbara Harlow, editors, *The View from Within: Writers and Critics on Contemporary Arabic Literature*, Cairo: American University in Cairo Press, 1994

Jabrā, Jabrā Ibrāhīm, "Modern Arabic Literature and the West," *Journal of Arabic Literature* 2 (1971); reprinted in *Critical Perspectives on Modern Arabic Literature*, edited by Issa Boullata, Washington, D.C.: Three Continents Press, 1980

Jayyusi, Salma Khadra, editor, *Anthology of Modern Palestinian Literature*, New York: Columbia University Press, 1992

Khūrī, Ilyās, "The Unfolding of Modern Fiction and Arab Memory," *The Journal of the Midwest Modern Language Association* 23:1 (Spring 1990)

Makdisi, Saree, "'Postcolonial' Literature in a Neocolonial World: Modern Arabic Culture and the End of Modernity," *boundary 2* 22:1 (Spring 1995)

Mangonaro, Elise Salem, "Bearing Witness: Recent Literature from Lebanon," *The Literary Review* 37:3 (Spring 1994)

Moosa, Matti, *The Origins of Modern Arabic Fiction*, Washington, D.C.: Three Continents Press, 1983; 2nd edition, Boulder, Colorado: Lynne Rienner, 1997

Said, Edward, Foreword to *Little Mountain*, by Ilyās Khūrī, Manchester: Carcanet Press, and Minneapolis: University of Minnesota Press, 1989

Zeidan, Joseph T., *Arab Women Novelists: The Formative Years and Beyond*, Albany: State University of New York Press, 1995

Wyndham Lewis 1882–1957

Canadian/English

Wyndham Lewis was a novelist, painter, polemicist, editor, and self-conscious artistic revolutionary. His early novels are strongly experimental and philosophically inflected by the aesthetics that he expounded in a series of journals—*Blast* (2 vols., 1914–15), *The Tyro* (2 vols., 1921–22), *The Enemy* (3 vols., 1927–29)—and in book-length treatments of philosophy and politics, such as *The Art of Being Ruled* (1926) and *Time and Western Man* (1927). His later novels, more conventional in style (if not in subject matter and form), investigate political issues with a frankness unusual in the English novel.

Early in his career Lewis was disaffected by the conventionality of pre–World War I English modes of art, so he looked to radical European movements of his day, producing with Ezra Pound the movement Vorticism, England's only contribution to the prewar avant-garde. Fascinated by painterly aesthetics and by the hard-edged classicism of space rather than the fluid romanticism of time, he positioned himself polemically against the leading modernist writers of his day. In the 1930s he embraced satire as a vehicle of social and artistic commentary and became controversial as his support of philosophic individuality lapsed into approval of authoritarian politics (most notably in *Hitler*, 1931), a reputation that haunted him long after his recantation of such views.

His first novel, *Mrs. Dukes' Million* (written c. 1909–10), was written to make money but remained unpublished until after his death: a youthful *jeu d'esprit* of no great literary merit, it nonetheless introduces themes of identity, disguise, and trickery that emerge repeatedly in the later novels. His first published novel, *Tarr* (1918), however, is likely his masterpiece. A scathing portrayal of the self-deluding international artistic community in Paris before World War I, *Tarr* weds an avant-garde Vorticist prose style to a searing psychological portrait of the German Kreisler, perhaps the most Dostoevskiian character in English literature.

After World War I, Lewis spent the 1920s "underground," compiling materials for a massive polystylistic work, never published as a whole, to be called *The Man of the World*. A novel that emerged from this project, *The Childermass* (1928) marks a shift in Lewis' fictional materials. A work of fantasy, it presents a vision of an apocalyptic postwar afterlife, and plot as such gives way to extensive and thinly disguised allegorical debates about communism and fascism, ideas Lewis worked out polemically in *The Art of Being Ruled*.

The Apes of God (1930), Lewis' longest novel, is a massive satire on an intentionally Joycean scale, aimed against Bloomsbury in particular and artistic idiocy in general. Lewis adapts the 18th-century picaresque style in his narrative of the hapless would-be poet Dan Boleyn, who is led through the morass of contemporary inanity by the ultimately suspect "expert" Horace Zagreus. *The Apes of God* significantly extends *Tarr*'s treatment of the self-important and ultimately self-destructive artist. The General Strike of 1926, which provides the novel's deus ex machina, asserts the reality of feared political violence against the triviality of a society composed of mechanical poetasters.

Snooty Baronet (1932) is a slighter satire of literary mores, a black comedy that attacks the doctrine of behaviorism while treating its protagonists, as did *The Apes of God*, as little more than puppets. *The Roaring Queen*, an even slighter satire of book reviewers, was withdrawn for fear of libel charges and was not published until 1973.

With *The Revenge for Love* (1937), Lewis returned to a more humane mode, producing what some critics consider his finest novel. By comparison with *Tarr*, its prose style is less flamboyant and daring, its political concerns more focused, and its treatment of characters (particularly female characters) more sympathetic. Originally entitled *False Bottoms* and set partly in Spain before the Spanish Civil War, the novel juxtaposes the satire of the salon-revolutionary and talentless artists against a serious concern for the relation of illusion to reality. *The Revenge for Love* avoids the abstractions of *The Childermass*, portraying communism and fascism in terms of their effects on believably realistic characters.

The Vulgar Streak (1941), another study of politics and false identities, is less successful, notable mainly for the oddity of its protagonist's suicide note, a rejection of physicality reminiscent of the Cartesian dualities in Lewis' earliest stories collected in *The Wild Body* (1927). *Self Condemned* (1954), on the other hand, is Lewis' finest late work. In this elegiac and self-lacerating novel, Lewis draws on autobiography to portray an English intellectual whose marriage crumbles while he and his wife live in intellectual and spiritual exile in a hotel in Canada during World War II.

With *Monstre Gai* (1955) and *Malign Fiesta* (1955), Lewis continued after many years the project begun in 1928 by *The Childermass*; that series, now given the overarching title *The Human Age*, remained unfinished at the time of Lewis' death. They are less dense in prose style (Fredric Jameson, 1979, has speculated that as Lewis gradually lost his eyesight his prose became less visual) and more overtly, if unconventionally, theological than their predecessor. Taken together, they suggest a more cautiously optimistic conception of the human condition than Lewis offers in his earlier work. On the other hand, his final novel, *The Red Priest* (1956), is notable mainly for the nihilism of its ending.

Lewis was critical of other novelists and their theoretical assumptions throughout his career, most notably in *Time and Western Man* and *Men Without Art* (1934), and as a result he risked erasing himself from the history of the novel through his truculent alienation of peers and reviewers. However, his early work introduced avant-garde European currents of characterization and philosophy into the English novel. *Tarr* in particular contains—along with Joyce's linguistic experimentation in *Ulysses*—the most stylistically original novelistic prose of the early 20th century in English. Although Lewis' painterly aesthetics at times stood in contradiction to the novel's need for narrative progression, his stylistic innovations and his sometimes wrong-headed yet strikingly modern analyses of culture earn him a noteworthy yet often overlooked place among the important modernist novelists.

SCOTT W. KLEIN

Biography

Born on a yacht off the coast of Nova Scotia, 18 November 1882; lived in the United States until 1887. Attended schools in London, 1888–96; Rugby School, Warwickshire, 1897–98; Slade School of Art, London, 1898–1901. Served in the Royal Artillery, 1916–17, and with the Canadian War Artists, 1917–18. Traveled in Europe, and lived mainly in Paris, 1902–08; lived in London from 1909; cofounder, Camden Town group, 1911; member of Roger Fry's Omega Workshops, 1913; a founder of the Vorticist group, 1913, and the Rebel Art Centre, 1914; founder, with Ezra Pound, and editor, *Blast*, London, 1914–15; founder, Group X, 1920; editor, the *Tyro* review, 1921–22, and the *Enemy*, 1927–29; lived in Buffalo, New York, 1939, and Canada, 1940–45; lecturer, Assumption College, Windsor, Ontario, 1943–44; returned to London, 1946; art critic, the *Listener*, 1946–51. Works shown in the Tate Gallery, and Victoria and Albert Museum, London; Museum of Modern Art, New York; Toronto Art Museum; Detroit Art Museum. Died 7 March 1957.

Novels by Lewis

Tarr, 1918
The Childermass, 1928

The Apes of God, 1930
Snooty Baronet, 1932
The Revenge for Love, 1937
The Vulgar Streak, 1941
Self Condemned, 1954
Monstre Gai, 1955
Malign Fiesta, 1955
The Red Priest, 1956
The Roaring Queen, 1973
Mrs. Dukes' Million, 1977

Other Writings: short stories, verse, plays, autobiography, letters, and essays on art, philosophy, and public affairs.

Further Reading

Chapman, Robert T., *Wyndham Lewis: Fictions and Satires*, London: Vision Press, and New York: Barnes and Noble, 1973

Jameson, Fredric, *Fables of Aggression: Wyndham Lewis, the Modernist as Fascist*, Berkeley: University of California Press, 1979

Kenner, Hugh, *Wyndham Lewis*, Norfolk: New Directions Books, and London: Methuen, 1954

Klein, Scott W., *The Fictions of James Joyce and Wyndham Lewis: Monsters of Nature and Design*, Cambridge and New York: Cambridge University Press, 1994

Levenson, Michael H., *Modernism and the Fate of Individuality: Character and Novelistic Form from Conrad to Woolf*, Cambridge and New York: Cambridge University Press, 1991

Materer, Timothy, *Wyndham Lewis, the Novelist*, Detroit, Michigan: Wayne State University Press, 1976

Porteus, Hugh Gordon, *Wyndham Lewis: A Discursive Exposition*, London: Harmsworth, 1932

Wagner, Geoffrey, *Wyndham Lewis: A Portrait of the Artist as the Enemy*, New Haven, Connecticut: Yale University Press, and London: Routledge and Kegan Paul, 1957

Wees, William C., *Vorticism and the English Avant-Garde*, Toronto: University of Toronto Press, and Manchester: Manchester University Press, 1972

Les Liaisons dangereuses by Pierre Choderlos de Laclos

1782

Les Liaisons dangereuses, the only published work of fiction by a career soldier who died a general in Napoléon's army, is an enigma in the history of the French and European novel. Although the novel is easy enough to place in the tradition of 18th-century fiction, the tradition does little to explain its originality and power. It has attracted the attention of brilliant commentators such as Charles Baudelaire, Marcel Proust, and André Malraux, but its specific influence on the subsequent history of the novel is difficult to assess.

Les Liaisons reflects two dominant trends in 18th-century French fiction: the impact of the epistolary novel and the fascination with a corrupted form of libertinism. Samuel Richardson's epistolary novel *Clarissa* (1747–48) had great success and influence in France and found many emulators. Rousseau's *Julie; ou, La Nouvelle Héloïse* (1761; *Julie; or, The New Eloise*) is a signal example of the trend. Laclos brilliantly adapted and developed epistolary technique, orchestrating complicated exchanges of letters among 12 writers, each of whom has a distinct style. He also took great care in arranging the order in which the correspondence appeared in the text. Although *Les Liaisons* fits comfortably into the epistolary framework, the content of the letters that detail the slow, ineluctable deception and destruction of certain characters remains unique in French fiction.

Laclos' text possesses nothing of Richardson's tormented sexuality or Rousseau's relentless pleas for asexual friendship. The novel is erotic without being pornographic. Laclos glories in describing Madame de Merteuil's and Monsieur de Valmont's pursuit of their sexual prey, but he never dwells on their inevitable triumph. Neither of his main characters has much respect for the women they encounter, and Valmont would probably agree with Merteuil's sardonic assessment of women as "pleasure machines."

The libertine tradition, as it existed in 18th-century France, helps explain the cynicism of *Les Liaisons'* protagonists. Libertinism had its origins in the 17th century as a philosophical position that stressed clear thinking and a suspicion of all forms of intellectual and religious cant. By the 18th century, the philosophical underpinnings of libertinism had largely been abandoned. It had become a social pose, primarily for young male aristocrats anxious to proclaim an indifference to conventional morality and a disrespect for others, without in any way compromising the privileges of their class. Such a description may easily be applied to Valmont. But what gives the novel its power, and what may also account in part for its subsequent lack of direct influence on the development of French fiction, is that the true libertine, in both the 17th- and 18th-century senses of the term, is Mme de Merteuil.

Mme de Merteuil has no real equivalent in French literature (Sade's Julie is only a pale comparison). She is a highly intelligent, self-educated woman who understands that success for a woman in 18th-century society involves her becoming more of a man than the males around her. In this respect she succeeds admirably. The imagery associated with her is resolutely military; she perceives society as a battleground where the weapons of choice are words. Like a field general, Mme de Mertueil deploys her various correspondents at will; she chooses the places to attack and the moments to withdraw. In the famous Letter 81, Merteuil reveals that her contempt for women is based on their willingness to be used and abused by men. She claims that she acts "to avenge her sex and dominate yours" (the letter is addressed to Valmont). Certainly Mme de Merteuil manipulates the men she encounters with relative ease, and the women with no effort at all. She succeeds largely because she controls rather than allows herself to be controlled.

An obvious reason for the limited direct influence of *Les Liaisons dangereuses* on the French novel is that literary fashion changed. The epistolary form quickly declined in popularity, and in the 19th century the omniscient third-person narrative assumed the dominant role in fictional discourse. There is, nevertheless, another possible explanation for the novel's marginal position in literary history, which stems from the unease created by the portrayal of a woman as intelligent and unscrupulous as she is beautiful. Literary taste traditionally has favored the pale beauty, the frustrated wife, and the fallen woman, and Mme de Merteuil represents a radical break with these stereotypes. She is strong, clever, and amoral. If she needs men, it is for their use-value, not their intellectual superiority or moral guidance. If she scorns most women, it is because they are too passive and credulous for their own good.

It is perhaps not surprising, given the contemporary reevaluation of male-female and female-female relationships, that the novel has taken on a new life. Various recent dramatizations have enjoyed great popularity. And in 1987 Christiane Baroche published a "sequel" to *Les Liaisons* entitled *L'Hiver de beauté* (*The Winter of Beauty*), which details the further adventures of Mme de Merteuil.

WILLIAM CLOONAN

See also Libertine Novel

Further Reading

Davies, Simon, *Laclos: "Les Liaisons dangereuses,"* Wolfeboro, New Hampshire: Grant and Cutler, 1987
Delmas, Andre Albert, *À la recherche des "Liaisons dangereuses,"* Paris: Mercure de France, 1964
Free, Lloyd, editor, *Laclos: Critical Approaches to "Les Liaisons dangereuses,"* Madrid: Jose Porrua Turanzas, 1978
Mylne, Vivian, *The Eighteenth Century French Novel*, New York: Barnes and Noble, and Manchester: Manchester University Press, 1965; 2nd edition, Cambridge and New York: Cambridge University Press, 1981
Rosbottom, Ronald, *Choderlos de Laclos*, Boston: Twayne, 1978
Thelander, Dorothy, *Laclos and the Epistolary Novel*, Geneva: Librairie Droz, 1963
Versini, Laurent, *Laclos et la tradition*, Paris: Librairie Klincksieck, 1968

Libertine Novel

Historically, the libertine novel is a literary phenomenon of the French 18th century. The earliest examples were inspired by the Regency (1715–23) but written and published under Louis XV, while the last ones were written during the French Revolution, notably by the Marquis de Sade. The end of Louis XIV's reign stood under the influence of the austere and religious Madame de Maintenon, and when the king died the court happily anticipated more joyous times, welcoming the Regency style. Free from Versailles etiquette and the centralized power wielded by the self-proclaimed Sun-King, the aristocracy flocked to Paris in search of renewed pleasures. The libertine novel signals this renewal of exuberant and frivolous attitudes, opposed to the strict morality enforced at Versailles after the Revocation of the Edict of Nantes.

The two main branches of the genre end with the French Revolution. The *mondain* libertine novel, an aristocratic genre *par excellence*, declined when French aristocrats were guillotined or went into exile. At the same time, erotic or obscene libertine novels became political, taking the shape of pro- or antirevolutionary or antiroyalist pamphlets directed against Louis XVI or against the very unpopular Marie-Antoinette.

The English term "libertine" encompasses the French *libertin* (masculine) and *libertine* (feminine). The type and its associated thought and behavior are not an 18th-century invention: there had been libertines in the previous century. However, some contemporary critics insist on a distinction between *libertinage érudit* (erudite libertinism) in the 17th century and *libertinage des mœurs* (libertinism of behavior) in the 18th century. The erudite libertines were more explicitly antireligious and more articulate in their philosophical views, although they were also condemned for their sexuality, most notably the practice of sodomy, and their general turpitude. The second-wave libertines appear less concerned with abstract philosophical systems and more directly interested in sexual freedom, but they did have newer systems of beliefs. Theirs was an age that claimed frivolity as a philosophical tenet: far from being avoided or hidden, frivolity was now claimed as a moral and philosophical principle. It was appreciated not only by novelists and writers of fairy tales but also by philosophers who saw in the frivolous an ideal means to practice one of the fundamental tenets of the Enlightenment—didacticism. Jean-Jacques Rousseau, better known for his sentimental *Julie; ou, La Nouvelle Héloïse* (1761; *Julie; or, The New Eloise*) and his political treatises, such as *Du Contrat social; ou, Principes du droit politique* (1762; *Of the Social Contract; or, Principles of Political Right*) also wrote a fairy tale, *La Reine fantasque* (1758; The Whimsical Queen). Voltaire also wrote dozens of philosophical tales of oriental inspiration, and Denis Diderot, the coeditor of the *Encyclopédie*, wrote a libertine novel in the oriental vein, *Les Bijoux indiscrets* (2 vols., 1748; *The Indiscreet Jewels*). The libertine side of otherwise prestigious Enlightenment philosophers was often erased from official histories of French literature: *The Indiscreet Jewels*, a novel in which a sultan who possesses a magic ring can make women's sex ("the jewels") speak, was ignored for nearly two centuries. Diderot's writing a libertine novel has often been attributed to his dire financial situation, a myth created by the philosopher's daughter and by his friends after his death. It is now universally acknowledged that Diderot's libertine novel in fact makes an important contribution to his political and philosophical program. In his *Histoire de la sexualité* (1976; *History of Sexuality*) Michel Foucault analyzed Diderot as a key witness to the sudden increase in discourses on sexuality in the 18th century, although it has now also been recognized that the sexual discourse provided by the jewels are highly biased, as no male "jewel" ever confessed in 18th-century libertine fiction.

But if libertinism is rife among 18th-century novelists and philosophers, there is no real consensus about what exactly constitutes the "libertine novel." The word *libertine* refers to a whole range of types: on the one hand the free-thinking spirit who claims an individual right to knowledge, advocates free inquiry, and refuses the precepts of the Church, and on the other a person who claims as inalienable the right to individual pleasure and sexual gratification outside the moral norms imposed by society. The expression "libertine novel" is just as problematic: to qualify, does the libertine novel have to be about *libertins* and *libertines,* or should the text itself be libertine? In other words, does its ideological program have to follow the precepts advocated by libertines themselves? Rather than reading this apparent confusion as a restriction, I will concentrate on the variety and richness of a genre that remains one of the most distinguishable features of a century that is mostly remembered as "philosophical" but that proudly claimed to be at once libertine and frivolous.

The libertine novel is polymorphous: it can be an epistolary novel, a memoir-novel, a novel in dialogue form, in the first or third person, and so on. The genre has often been split into two main categories: the *mondain* novel (also sometimes called the *galant*) and the erotic libertine novel. The *mondain* novel is often associated with the aristocracy, and it takes the form of confession-memoirs relating the coming of age of young male aristocrats. Prominent examples are *Confessions du comte de **** (1741; The Confessions of Count ***) by Charles Pinot-Duclos and *Les Égarements du cœur et de l'esprit* (1736–38; *The Wayward Head and Heart*) by Crébillon *fils* (not to be confused with his father, Crébillon, a once-famous playwright now mainly forgotten). Other *mondain* or *galant* libertine novels include such epistolary novels as Dorat's *Les Sacrifices de l'amour* (1771; *The Sacrifices of Love*), *Les Malheurs de l'inconstance* (1772; *The Sorrows of Fickleness*), and the most popular French 18th-century novel, Choderlos de Laclos' *Les Liaisons dangereuses* (1782). The epistolary genre was a favorite form of the libertine *mondain* novel as it allowed greater manipulation of characters, the plot unfolding at the same time as the writing of the letter. Better than any other genre, epistolary novels allow libertines to manipulate their preys by controlling not only what they do but ultimately what they read, write, and think. Writing thus becomes the epistolary libertines' lethal weapon but also the cause of their demise—the Marquise de Merteuil's downfall in *Les Liaisons dangereuses* is brought about by the very same letters that had empowered her.

Erotic libertine novels such as Crébillon *fils' Sopha* (1742; *The Sofa*), Diderot's *Indiscreet Jewels,* and La Morlière's *Angola* (1746; *Angola*) include more or less thinly veiled sexual allusions. Because of Antoine Galland's translation of *Les Mille et une nuits* (*The Arabian Nights*) at the beginning of the 18th century, erotic libertine novels often draw on fashionable orientalist themes. They are often dialogues: a *libertin* reads an oriental and salacious tale to the countess he would like to seduce (as in *Angola*), or, in *The Sofa,* an oriental narrator tells a sultan and his sultana of his adventures when, transformed as a sofa, he was able to witness many libertine adventures. These pseudo-oriental novels are often satirical, and the erotic possibilities of the dialogue are never exploited. In fact, the tone is often amused or sarcastic: in Crébillon's novel, the stupidity of the male omnipotent sultan stands in contrast to the refinement of his sultana. La Morlière prefers not to give any clue as to the success of his libertine and leaves the novel unfinished (a libertine characteristic) by declaring that, unfortunately, the editor has not been given the last part of the manuscript.

Still ignored or rejected by some critics, the obscene libertine novel represents at once the most striking and popular genre of the 18th century. If some recent critics are still reluctant to attribute any value to these texts of the "second shelf" (as some French critics have referred to them), obscene novels better exemplify those definitions of the word libertine that include a philosophical dimension. As Robert Darnton has shown, these texts were "philosophical" at the time, and orders from the clandestine book trade included, side by side on the same list, works by philosophers (Diderot, Rousseau, Voltaire) and obscene texts, all under the same category of "philosophical texts" (see Darnton, 1995). Even so, historians have preferred to ignore the erotic production to concentrate on the philosophical impact of the 18th century on contemporary France. Yet the proliferation of philosophical writings coincides, after 1740, with a sudden increase in obscene texts. The vast production and numerous reprintings of obscene libertine novels throughout the century attest to their undeniable popularity.

While the first obscene novels were usually dialogues—*L'École des filles* (*The School for Girls*) in 1655 and *L'Académie des Dames* (Women's Academy), first in Latin and in French in 1680—the 18th-century libertine obscene novel may also be epistolary, written in the first or third person, a memoir-novel, dialogues, or even very close to drama. The first obscene bestseller of the Enlightenment was *Histoire de D[om Bougre], Portier des Chartreux* (1740; History of Dom Bougre) by Gervaise de Latouche, a book which Adélaïde, daughter of Louis XV, appreciated so much that she wanted to share it with her brother. Their father intervened. *Dom Bougre* even spawned an entire obscene dynasty: later in the century, his sister's raunchy confessions were also published as *Mémoires de Suzon, sœur de Dom Bougre* (1777; Memoirs of Suzon, Sister of Dom Bougre) as were his niece's memoirs, *Histoire de Marguerite, fille de Suzon, nièce de Dom Bougre* (1784; History of Marguerite). The most popular obscene novel throughout the 18th century, published the same year as John Cleland's *Fanny Hill*, was *Thérèse philosophe* (1748; The Philosophical Thérèse), attributed to

Boyer d'Argens. It tackles the philosophical problems of human nature, temperament, and social organization and is written in an anticlerical vein. It was reprinted throughout the century, and Sade even calls it the first truly immoral book in his *Juliette* (1797). Then came Fougeret de Monbron's *Margot la ravaudeuse* (1750; Margot the Darner), Andréa de Nerciat's *Félicia ou mes fredaines* (1775; Félicia, or My mischief) and many other scantily dressed confessions.

Contrary to the first (*mondain* or *galant*) or even the second (erotic) *libertinage,* these obscene novels depict characters who either are not of aristocratic origin or do not function in the aristocratic world. And while *libertinage mondain* is interested in male rites of passage organized by more mature women, the obscene *libertinage* focuses mainly, although not exclusively, on female rites of passage (two exceptions include *Dom Bougre* and *Le Libertin de qualité* [1783; The Noble Libertine], attributed to Honoré Gabriel de Mirabeau, whose young hero becomes a gigolo). In obscene *libertinage,* female protagonists either end up in prison or lead a happy life enlightened by philosophy, as is the case with Thérèse.

Whether the novels belong to what today we would call pornography (a word first used in the 19th century) or to the more prestigious genre of *mondain* boudoir pre-Sadean libertinism, they share with Enlightenment philosophers one common concern—pedagogy. All libertine novels are mainly about the education of young men and women and their entry into the world of conventional aristocracy. Consequently, the moral implications of the erotic component are not only indirect but also sly: working against the grain of morality, the libertine novel deals primarily with the nonoppositional integration of new members into a society whose rules are not to be changed. By its nature and its objective (as a Bildungsroman), the libertine novel is faced with a dilemma: how can novels pretend to be at once libertine (i.e., oppositional) and also portray the efforts of heroes and heroines (aristocrats or future prostitutes, male and female) to fit into that particular society? This contradiction is often reflected in the closure of libertine novels: libertine heroes and heroines either eventually find "true love" and live happily ever after, or else they end up disfigured as Laclos' Marquise de Merteuil. Similarly, the heroes and heroines of the obscene branch end up happily married or diseased, locked up or castrated. In other words, they are either completely rejected or just as completely adopted by a society that remains untainted by unruly, but temporary, sexual prowess and practices.

Undoubtedly the most notorious libertine author from the 18th century remains the Marquis de Sade, nicknamed the Divine Marquis. While locked up in the infamous Bastille (accused, among other things, of incest and numerous murders), Sade wrote among the most philosophical and most cruel of libertine novels. The libertine tradition culminates in Sade, who united in his work the old (and rather artificial) divide between the libertinism of credo and of behavior: his works are at once philosophical (notably atheist) and they list with a sometimes suspicious complacency endless varieties of sexual practices that usually involve cruelty. In addition to being among the most prolific libertine authors, Sade is the 18th-century writer whose work has been the most analyzed by members of the 20th-century French intelligentsia, from Georges Bataille, Maurice Blanchot, and Pierre Klossowski to Jean Paulhan and Roland Barthes. Sade wrote in many genres, from short stories (*Les*

Crimes de l'amour [1800; The Crimes of Love]) to epistolary fiction (*Aline et Valcour; ou, Le Roman philosophique,* 1795). His most famous productions are *Les 120 Journées de Sodome* (written approximately 1785, published 1904/31–35; *The 120 Days of Sodom*), *Justine; ou, Les Malheurs de la vertu* (1791; *Justine; or, The Misfortunes of Virtue*), *Histoire de Juliette; ou, Les Prospérités du vice* (1797; *Juliette*), and *La Philosophie dans le boudoir* (1795; *Philosophy in the Bedroom*). Sade's novels, still banned in the 1950s, are now being edited for the prestigious Bibliothèque de la Pléiade, a literary Pantheon immortalizing the classics of French literature. After editions causing much-publicized lawsuits leading to the condemnation in 1957 of publisher Jean-Jacques Pauvert, this collection, printed on a paper referred to as "Bible paper" because of its thinness, marks an ironically fitting fortune for the "Divine Marquis."

Ultimately, the libertines exemplify the paradoxical relationship between the Enlightenment and new forms of morality and sexual ethics. Both fiercely aristocratic and *mondain,* the libertine novel also found comfort in heroes and heroines who reacted against the strict norms imposed by the Church. Ultimately, however, libertines were not allowed to oppose the state apparatus that had allowed the French aristocracy to survive and dominate for so long. Everyone agreed that changes were necessary, but libertines who did not conform were expelled, imprisoned, or maimed. It is not clear, however, if the reason for such closures was strictly moral or if the power to eliminate opposition so drastically was a case of wishful thinking, the last respite of an arrogant and refined class that felt its power and authority were already undermined, as the 1789 revolution would soon confirm.

JEAN MAINIL

See also French Novel (18th Century); Justine; Liaisons dangereuses; Pornographic Novel; Sex, Gender, and the Novel

Further Reading

Brooks, Peter, *The Novel of Worldliness: Crébillon, Marivaux, Laclos, Stendhal,* Princeton, New Jersey: Princeton University Press, 1969
Cazenobe, Colette, *Le système du libertinage de Crébillon à Laclos,* Oxford: Voltaire Foundation, 1991
Cryle, Peter, *Geometry in the Boudoir: Configurations of French Erotic Narrative,* Ithaca, New York: Cornell University Press, 1994
Darnton, Robert, *The Forbidden Bestsellers of Pre-Revolutionary France,* New York and London: Norton, 1995
DeJean, Joan, *Libertine Strategies: Freedom and the Novel in Seventeenth-Century France,* Columbus: Ohio State University Press, 1981
DeJean, Joan, *Literary Fortifications: Rousseau, Laclos, Sade,* Princeton, New Jersey: Princeton University Press, 1984
Feher, Michel, editor, *The Libertine Reader: Eroticism and Enlightenment in 18th-Century France,* New York: Zone Readers, 1997
Goulemot, Jean-Marie, *Forbidden Texts: Erotic Literature and Its Readers in Eighteenth-Century France,* Cambridge: Polity Press, and Philadelphia: University of Pennsylvania Press, 1994

Hunt, Lynn, *The Family Romance of the French Revolution*, Berkeley: University of California Press, and London: Routledge, 1992

Hunt, Lynn, editor, *The Invention of Pornography*, New York: Zone Books, 1993

Kearney, Patrick, *A History of Erotic Literature*, London: Macmillan, 1982

Laroch, Philippe, *Petits-maîtres et roués: Évolution de la notion de libertinage dans le roman français du XVIIIe siècle*, Québec: Presses de l'Université Laval, 1979

Trousson, Raymond, editor, *Romans libertins du XVIIIe siècle*, Paris: Laffont, 1993

Wagner, Peter, *Eros Revived: Erotica of the Enlightenment in England and America*, London: Secker and Warburg, 1988

Libraries

Circulating and Commercial Libraries and Their Place in Novel Readership

I. England

The rising popularity of the novel in England during the 18th century is traditionally attributed in large part to the expansion of the middle classes. The increasing literacy and leisure of the bourgeoisie created an unprecedented market for literature of all kinds, and the private, commercial circulating library sprang up to meet the demands of those who wished to read, but not necessarily buy, printed books, the price of which remained relatively high throughout the period. Almost from the beginning, the circulating library was associated particularly closely with the contemporary novel, the favored reading matter of many of its patrons, and indeed in time it would virtually control the market for new fiction.

It is not known precisely when the first bookseller decided to open a circulating library as a separate establishment, but the earliest such libraries in England are recorded in the provinces and date from the 1720s and 1730s. Other private collections of printed matter existed: book clubs and literary and philosophical societies flourished in the 18th century, and many schools and coffeehouses offered pupils and customers access to their libraries. The circulating library differed from these, however, in that its membership was restricted only by the ability to pay a subscription fee. Considering the usual estimate of more than 1,000 circulating libraries in existence at the end of the 18th century, few catalogues and very few membership lists survive. Nonetheless, literary references and sources such as advertisements and book labels have enabled historians to understand what circulating libraries stocked, how they operated, and to whom they catered.

Although circulating libraries are known to have existed in most provincial towns and cities by the 1790s, for most of the 18th century they operated principally in London and the fashionable spas and watering places patronized by the leisured classes; their rise, particularly in London, was exponential. The stereotypical circulating-library reader, feared and ridiculed by journalists and reviewers, was epitomized by Richard Brinsley Sheridan's Lydia Languish, the heroine of his play *The Rivals* (1775). When Lydia sends her foolish maid out to fetch her latest novels, their sentimental and sensational titles prompt her uncle to fulminate famously that "a circulating library in a town is as an ever-green tree of diabolical knowledge."

Other literary allusions appear to confirm that circulating libraries were patronized by a predominantly young, female readership interested only in "light" literature, above all in novels. A play by George Colman the Elder, *Polly Honeycombe* (1760), featured a heroine just as frivolous and suggestible as Lydia Languish, and a generation later Jane Austen's Catherine Morland in *Northanger Abbey* (1818) and her friend Isabella Thorpe are insatiable in their hunger for the latest popular fiction to reach Bath from London. Many contemporaries were convinced that the romantic novels available from circulating libraries encouraged young women to indulge in dangerous fantasies that could all too easily lead to real-life sexual misconduct; as one opponent put it, "the general effect of novel-reading on the gentler sex is too obvious to be doubted; it excites and inflames the passion which is the principal subject of the tale, and the susceptibility of the female votary of the circulating library is proverbial" (Henry Pye, quoted in Williams, 1970).

Yet 20th-century scholarship has not tended to bear out 18th-century assumptions about the nature of circulating-library stock or its readers. Hilda Hamlyn (1946–47) reported that, in those catalogues she had examined, 20 percent or less of the titles listed belonged to the category of fiction. Keith Manley (1989) argues that two of the largest library proprietors in London in the 1740s, Francis and John Noble, also bucked the supposed trend: "The breadth and range of the Nobles' stock is impressive and effectively buries the view that circulating libraries were comprised solely of novels of the lowest sort." Although novels appear to have constituted the largest single category in many libraries, they were still quite heavily outnumbered by other kinds of literature; in at least one library, described by John Feather (1985), only five percent of the holdings were novels. The catalogue of Ann Yearsley's very small circulating library in Bristol's Hot Wells is noteworthy: despite the library's transient membership (most of Yearsley's patrons were visitors to the wells rather than local residents), nearly two-thirds of its titles were not novels at all and included poetry, travel books, biographies, memoirs, plays, essays, ancient classics, and histories (see Lamoine, 1981).

Less is known about circulating library users than about their catalogues, but Hamlyn suggests that men outnumbered women two to one in the subscription list she consulted for Marshall's Library in Bath from 1793–99. Partly influenced by Hamlyn, subsequent bibliographers such as Feather have argued that the typical subscriber was male and worked either in trade or the church. It is worth remembering, however, that subscription rates were high—typically a guinea per annum—and that a husband or father may well have paid a membership fee that allowed the rest of his family to borrow books indirectly or in his name.

The influence of the circulating-library novel on young female readers was almost certain to be exaggerated by contemporary commentators, given that young women had relatively few other sources of reading matter and were popularly believed to be ignorant, credulous, and morally frail. Nonetheless, it seems reasonable to suppose that women constituted a significant proportion of circulating-library borrowers, and since the surviving evidence shows that many libraries offered a wide range of modern and classic novels in addition to other kinds of literature, it seems equally reasonable to assume that the circulating library contributed in large part to the publishing boom in fiction during and after the 1740s.

Not until the 19th century, however, did the relationship between the novel and the circulating library become virtually symbiotic. When first Mudie's, and later W.H. Smith and Boots, obtained their stranglehold on the fiction market by forcing the novelists they published to conform to the length requirements of the three-volume ("three-decker") novel, they engineered an artificially high price for new fiction that ensured that almost all readers were obliged to borrow rather than buy. As Guinevere Griest (1970) explains, in the end the relationship between the circulating library and the three-decker became so oppressive to authors and readers alike that the library proprietors were forced to abandon it, but this in turn spelled the ultimate demise of the circulating library itself. In its earliest days the circulating library had recognized and adroitly exploited the growing market for fiction in a way which undoubtedly benefited the genre. By the end of the 19th century, it had fostered a dependency that would not survive changing literary tastes, the institution of public library provision, and the increasing availability of modern novels in inexpensive editions.

KATHERINE A. ARMSTRONG

See also English Novel (18th Century)

Further Reading

Feather, John, *The Provincial Book Trade in Eighteenth-Century England,* Cambridge and New York: Cambridge University Press, 1985
Griest, Guinevere L., *Mudie's Circulating Library and the Victorian Novel,* Bloomington: Indiana University Press, and Newton Abbot: David and Charles, 1970
Hamlyn, Hilda M., "Eighteenth-Century Circulating Libraries in England," *The Library* 5:1 (1946–47)
Lamoine, Georges, *Le Catalogue des Livres de la Bibliothèque Circulante de Ann Yearsley à Bristol en 1793,* Bordeaux: Taffard, 1981
Manley, Keith A., "London Circulating Library Catalogues of the 1740s," *Library History* 8 (1989)
McKillop, A. D., "English Circulating Libraries 1725–50," *The Library* 4:14 (1934)
Varma, Devendra P., *The Evergreen Tree of Diabolical Knowledge,* Washington, D.C.: Consortium Press, 1972
Williams, Ioan, *Novel and Romance 1700–1800: A Documentary Record,* London: Routledge and Kegan Paul, and New York: Barnes and Noble, 1970

II. France: Cabinets de Lecture

According to most authorities, the earliest French subscription library, or *cabinet de lecture,* dates from 1761, although the Benedictine scholar Dom Calmet reported that the *Journal des Savants* was available for rent as early as 1714. The practice of borrowing books for a small daily, monthly, or annual fee began in France during the last third of the 18th century, with a sharp increase in the number of such establishments immediately prior to and following the Revolution of 1789. (Their precise role in disseminating both the ideas of the *philosophes* and the latest political news has yet to be studied in depth: eyewitness evidence suggests that it was considerable.) Despite the strict censorship introduced by Napoléon, many catalogues that survived the empire reveal a wide range of material available for home rental (the normal practice until 1815) or reading on the spot, including travel books, essays, moral treatises, pieces by Voltaire and Rousseau, ancien régime bestsellers such as Louis-Sébastien Mercier's *L'an 2440* (1771; *The Year 2440*), and, in most cases, a generous supply of contemporary and older novels.

The heyday of the *cabinets de lecture,* both as a cultural practice and a key segment of the book trade, lasted from 1815 to 1848. The *cabinets* served as a place to read newspapers; catch the latest novel by Pigault-Lebrun, Paul de Kock, or Sir Walter Scott; or to revisit the classics of the previous century, such as Baron d'Holbach's *Systeme de la nature* (1770; *System of Nature*) or Constantin-François Volney's *Les ruines* (1791; *The Ruins*). The *cabinets* were as much a part of the social scene as the café: in 1830, there were over 500 in Paris alone. The most popular *cabinets* were listed in tourist guides.

The popularity of reading rooms is based on several factors. Restoration and July Monarchy governments held liberal views regarding censorship: owners were not required to have licenses until 1826. Policing efforts were relaxed, which encouraged booksellers to meet the needs of a rapidly growing readership. (It should be recalled that public libraries were virtually nonexistent in France until 1860. The great collections of the Bibliothèque Royale and the Arsenal were open at limited times to a very select minority of users.) The *cabinets* varied in size. Holdings ranged from as few as 500 volumes—typically in a corner store run by a war widow—to 20,000 titles, often with subscriptions to 80 European newspapers, as was the case in Galignani's sumptuous rooms in the rue Vivienne. The *cabinets* appealed to a wide variety of people. Their explosive growth during the Restoration and July Monarchy is attributed to the high cost of books. In 1830, an octavo volume cost 7.50 francs: a two-volume novel therefore represented about one-third of the average worker's monthly income. For as little as 3 francs per month, or 24 francs per year (most customers preferred the monthly rate), users could borrow as many as 100 books at a time. (Special, and usually very advantageous, arrangements were made for clients living in the country.)

The steady decline in the number of active *cabinets* in the second half of the century reflects the gradual introduction of public libraries, the availability of novels in feuilleton (i.e., newspaper supplements), and a sharp decline in prices: by 1870 a novel could be purchased for 1.50 francs. However, because such businesses often were combined with other forms of bookselling as well as printing and publishing, many of them survived well into the 20th century, especially in small provincial towns. A consortium launched in 1870 by Graët-Delalain, justifiably named *Panbiblion: Lecture universelle,* had nine branches across France. Its stock of over 200,000 titles included a range of interests and subjects that would be the envy of Everyman or Penguin; it was still in operation in 1935.

Unlike the feuilleton—which had a definite impact on the style of those novelists like Charles Dickens, Eugène Sue, and Alexandre Dumas *père* who published in serial form—the *cabinets de lecture* do not appear to have made any particular impact on the evolution of the genre. Admittedly, contemporaries as well as later historians associated the *cabinets* with popular fiction read for entertainment, rather than with difficult masterpieces. The fact that the *cabinets* were frequented not only by chambermaids—as ironically inclined commentators such as Stendhal suggest—but also by sophisticated and hard-to-please readers like the young Gustave Flaubert support the theory that the *cabinets'* association with popular literature is only part of a much more complex story. The evidence of catalogue holdings, more than 1000 of which survive, also supports this theory. Many *cabinets* stocked no novels at all: those in the Latin Quarter depended on multiple copies of medical and legal textbooks for most of their business. The Sablé Research Centre at the University of Toronto recently acquired 900 volumes, representing about a quarter of the original stock of a *cabinet* opened in Bordeaux in 1817 by J. Magen. All are 8o (rather than the cheaper 12o) paper-backed volumes often associated with the *cabinets,* and most are uniformly bound in contemporary quarter leather. The real importance of such businesses was their contribution to the history of reading. Despite their inherent conservatism—for every copy of Anne Radcliffe, there would be 15 copies of lesser practioners of the Gothic romance—they nevertheless, for more than 100 years, made newspapers and books of all kinds available to readers who couldn't otherwise afford them.

GRAHAM FALCONER

See also Bibliothèque Bleue; French Novel (18th Century)

Further Reading

Allen, James Smith, *Popular French Romanticism: Authors, Readers, and Books in the 19th Century,* Syracuse, New York: Syracuse University Press, 1981

Catalogues de Cabinet de Lecture, introduction by Catherine Cassan, Sablé-sur-Sarthe: Bibliothèque Nationale, 1989

Martin, Henri Jean, and Roger Chartier, *Histoire de l'Edition Française,* Paris: Promodis, 1983–86

Parent-Lardeur, Françoise, *Lire à Paris au temps de Balzac: Les cabinets de lecture à Paris, 1815–1830,* Paris: Editions de l'Ecole des Hautes Etudes en sciences sociales, 1981

III. United States

When the Boston Public Library, the pioneer tax-supported public library, opened its doors in 1854, it provided for lending books, including novels, for use at home; and the first accurate statistics of home use, for 1866, showed that fiction comprised at least 70 percent of total circulation. Other types of libraries showed a similar demand for fiction. Three-quarters of the purchases of the New York Mercantile Library were fiction; and the elite institutions of the Boston Athenaeum and the Charleston Library Society also began, in various stages between the late 1860s and early 1870s, to acquire popular fiction. Both even bought from Mudie's clearance catalogues.

Despite some continuing opposition to fiction on the part of library trustees and librarians, these events concretely demonstrate significant change since the mid–18th century in attitudes toward fiction and in library stocking and circulation of novels. That change was stimulated by commercial circulating libraries, which were in a good position to determine what books people wanted and to supply them. In fact, their very existence depended on doing so.

Before the first known circulating library, another form of library had begun, and these libraries are variously termed social, proprietary, subscription, or association libraries. They could be used by those who purchased or inherited a share, but many were also accessible to individuals who paid an annual fee; and some even permitted borrowing—and paying—by the book. The crucial distinction between the social and the circulating libraries lies not, therefore, in whether one paid. The vital distinction is that the social library saw itself as a community institution, and the circulating library owner saw it as a business.

Social library organizers saw themselves as serving distinctly public purposes. Fiction did not accomplish those public goals. To be sure, an absolute prohibition against fiction was uncommon, and the Beverly (Massachusetts) Second Social Library was an exception for stating in its 1806 regulations: "The Library shall contain no novels, romances, nor plays; but consist principally of the serious productions of Calvinistic Divines; as Baxter, Flavel, Henry, Watts, Doddridge, Edwards, Bellamy, Hopkins, and the like." But these institutions, like the very first of them, the Library Company of Philadelphia, founded in 1731, whose prime mover was Benjamin Franklin, emphasized that its purpose was to provide opportunities for "important enquiries" to be prosecuted, with the consequence that "the good of society would be increased." The precise nature of the useful purpose changed over time, but utility always obtained in the various forms of the social library. The power of the need to provide useful rather than entertaining reading is demonstrated by the Boston Library Society, which was established in 1795 "to form a collection of books for popular use," but its organizers felt compelled to add that it would admit "none of an injurious moral tendency . . . preferring those of solid and standard value."

Not surprisingly, owners of circulating libraries also felt it desirable to express that they served a useful purpose. William Munday of the Baltimore Circulating Library noted in 1812 that he intended to "render this institution as extensively useful as possible," and by his choice of language echoed the discourse that justified libraries by their role in disseminating "useful knowledge." And in Salem, Massachusetts, John Dabney in

1791 felt a particular need to reassure his compatriots with the following statement:

> Circulating Library, like the volume of Nature, is found to be an interesting Miscellany, but composed of an assemblage of productions extremely opposite in their nature and tendency. Many of those productions are known to be highly beneficial, others very agreeable and engaging; and some, it will be added are injurious to Society. If as many of the latter are excluded as possible, and an arrangement be formed of the most eligible, it may be considered not only as a Repository of Rational Amusement, but as a museum, from whence may be derived materials capable of forming the minds of individuals to solid virtue, true politeness, the noblest actions, and the purest benevolence.

The largest library of its time, that of Hocquet Caritat, actually printed before the section of novels in his 1804 catalogue "A general defence of modern novels."

The names of libraries were sometimes chosen carefully to help in that defense. Thus, in Boston there was a "Shakspeare" circulating library. "Union" and "Washington" circulating libraries existed in several cities, but the most common name of all was that of the father of all libraries, Franklin: Boston, 1820; Camden, New Jersey, 1857; Danvers, Massachusetts, 1834; Pawtucket, Rhode Island, 1847; Providence, Rhode Island, 1852; St. Louis, Missouri, 1833; Warren, Rhode Island, 1831; Washington, Ohio, 1857; and Woodstock, Vermont, 1828.

Despite some defensiveness, some seeking prestige and the aura of utility, most circulating library owners emphasized that they provided novels, as did the earliest recorded circulating library catalogue, that of John Mein of Boston in 1765. (The earliest known colonial American circulating library began in 1762 in Annapolis.) The proprietors also emphasized that they had the latest books ("as soon as they are to be had"; or that the library "daily increased")—and the stock included books from London.

Many of the circulating libraries did in fact frequently add books, and they became larger than social libraries. The median size of those libraries for which catalogues exist during the period from 1765 to 1789 was 1,500 volumes; in the following decade, the median was 3,000 volumes. Most social libraries were much smaller: Charleston, South Carolina, 1772, 408 entries; Haverhill, Massachusetts, 1796, 175 entries; Gloucester, Rhode Island, 1796, 115 entries; Portsmouth, New Hampshire, 1796, 220 entries; Boston Library Society, 1797, 500 entries; Bristol, Rhode Island, 1800, 225 entries. The largest social library around 1800 was the Library Company of Philadelphia, which in 1799 had 6,040 entries in its catalogue and supplements. Since 4,000 of these had been in the library as of 1789, Harwood's Circulating Library in Philadelphia, with its 4,863 volumes as of 1803, was perhaps even larger in recent publications. The New York Society Library, which as of 1793 had 2,100 entries, was dwarfed by Hocquet Caritat, who in 1800 claimed to have 30,000 volumes for lending and for sale.

The circulating libraries also had an increasingly large proportion of fiction. Before the Revolutionary Era fiction constituted about one-fourth of circulating library collections; by 1820 it had risen to more than one-half. Thereafter it held approximately level until after midcentury. Since the number of circulating li-

braries grew (9 formed between 1790 and 1794, 12 between 1795 and 1799, 27 new ones between 1800 and 1804, and even more in successive periods until 1825), there was clearly an ever larger readership for the increasing quantities of fiction in the holdings of the libraries.

Little is known about who those readers were. Some information is available through the library register of Thomas Bradford's small circulating library in Philadelphia, which covers December 1771 to December 1772. Nearly two-thirds of the library's 300 books were novels. An analysis of the borrowing for April 1772 shows that out of 617 books borrowed, 86 percent were fiction, with plays and verse adding another 7 percent. Of the 142 borrowers, 53 percent were men and 47 percent women, with the men borrowing slightly more books—55 percent versus 45 percent. The three most frequent borrowers among men and women read the same books almost one-quarter of the time (25 out of 108 books, all novels). Although men had a slight edge in numbers in Bradford's Library, Loudon in New York in 1774 reported that the "ladies are his best customers."

Such seems to have continued to be the case. In 1822 in Baltimore, Joseph Robinson requested that men not congregate or socialize in the main reception and book delivery-room, because a "great proportion of the patrons of the Library are ladies." Other libraries provided separate entrances and special reading rooms for women; some arranged to deliver books to women at home.

No evidence exists that Bradford actively solicited the patronage of women. Others did, however, including William Rind in 1762 and Wood and Gifford in Charleston, 1763 and 1772. The first Philadelphia circulating library, that of Lewis Nicola, opened in 1767 and shared space with a milliner, who advertised silk stockings, among other goods. Moreover, circulating libraries often advertised in their catalogues goods other than books, especially ones that would have attracted female buyers. For example, Goodrich & Co., New York, 1818, in addition to water colors "of every description," sold "durable ink, for marking linen." Others, for example, Pelham's Circulating Library, Charlestown, Massachusetts, 1801, offered a "selection of publications for the Instruction, and Amusement of Young Minds," along with "literary toys" and other kinds of "pleasing inducements to learning."

Women were also often owners of circulating libraries: Widow Bradish's Circulating Library, New York, 1811; Keziah Butler's Circulating Library, Boston, 1804–25; Mary Carroll's Reading Room, New Orleans, 1830–33; Central Circulating Library, Salem, Massachusetts, early 1820s; Caroline H. Fanning's Circulating Library, Boston, 1816; Lucy L. Hunter's Circulating Library, Baltimore, 1819–later than 1882; Miss Jordan's Circulating Library, Lancaster, Pennsylvania, 1821–c. 1845; Union Circulating Library, Philadelphia, 1814; Foreign Library, Boston, 1840s; Lydia Reed's Circulating Library, Cambridge, Massachusetts, 1825; Minerva Circulating Library, Providence, Rhode Island, 1809; Widow Roche's Circulating Library, New Orleans, after 1811; Ann Shallus' Circulating Library, New Orleans, 1822–23; Ann Peters Shallus' Circulating Library, Philadelphia, 1814–24; Mary Sprague's Circulating Library, Boston, 1802–06. There must have been many more.

Although the patronage of women readers was crucial to the success of circulating libraries, and fiction was an important element in that patronage, young men demanded fiction from the mechanics libraries and from the apprentices' and mercantile libraries that were increasingly widespread after 1820. For example, the General Society of Mechanics and Tradesmen in New York asked its Library Committee in 1828 to "inquire into the expediency of discontinuing hereafter the issuing of Plays, Novels and Romances." The Committee reported that the library had not been founded solely to aid the student of mathematics or mechanics, or to assist the "deep devotee to historical knowledge." On the contrary,

> To a child of ten years—to a youth of fifteen,—whose earlier advantages have not inclined him to seek the knowledge to be acquired from books, and at whose time of life amusement has an absorbing influence, something must be offered to arrest his attention, that may be in a certain degree a substitute for the usual out door amusements of this buoyant time of life . . . an amusement suitable to his age. We should say we pitied; we do say we pity the feelings of that man who can look back without pleasure upon the time he first read Robinson Crusoe; and we think we can say with confidence that this book has made, incidentally, more readers than any history extant, and this is a Romance. What apprentice, after having passed his evening, in his chamber, engaged in reading the "Vicar of Wakefield" is not in a more proper state of mind on his retiring to rest, to repeat the prayers which had been taught him in his infancy, and better prepared for the next day's avocations, than if his evening had been employed in street talk.

The justifications are that reading novels stimulates better reading and that it fosters moral well-being by keeping the young from unwholesome entertainments.

As books became cheaper in the 1830s and 1840s, pressure on the libraries to supply new books for youth, especially fiction, increased. So did the tensions over doing so, and they continued well after publicly financed libraries began forming in the 1850s. But the terms of the debate changed. The issue became the proportion of novels in the library and the quality of those novels, not their very presence. That shift began with the libraries for profit, which helped to pull publishers, booksellers, and libraries toward supplying the books that readers wanted, namely, books for entertainment, above all novels.

See also United States Novel (18th Century)

KENNETH E. CARPENTER

Further Reading

Davidson, Cathy N., *Revolution and the Word: The Rise of the Novel in America,* New York: Oxford University Press, 1986

Kaser, David, *A Book for a Sixpence: The Circulating Library in America,* Pittsburgh, Pennsylvania: Beta Phi Mu, 1980

Winans, Robert B., "The Growth of a Novel-Reading Public in Late-Eighteenth-Century America," *Early American Literature* 9 (1975)

Zboray, Ronald J., *A Fictive People: Antebellum Economic Development and the American Reading Public,* New York: Oxford University Press, 1993

Life, a User's Manual by Georges Perec

La Vie mode d'emploi 1978

Awarded the prestigious Prix Médicis upon its publication in 1978, Georges Perec's *Life, a User's Manual* has in the ensuing years acceded to a place of rare privilege in the canon of the European novel. Maximalist in its conception and its execution, this 700-page book is seen by many critics as the worthiest postmodernist successor to the "well-made" modernist novel, a tradition exemplified by such texts as Marcel Proust's *À la recherche du temps perdu* (1913–27; translated as *Remembrance of Things Past* and also as *In Search of Lost Time*), James Joyce's *Ulysses* (1922), and Thomas Mann's *Der Zauberberg* (1924; *The Magic Mountain*). Yet its roots reach even deeper into the soil of tradition: like Honoré de Balzac's *La Comédie humaine* (1842–48; *The Human Comedy*), like Émile Zola's *Les Rougon-Macquart* (1871–93), Perec intended *Life, a User's Manual* as a panorama of French society, a global, all-embracing vision of contemporary reality.

Subtitled *romans* ("novels"), in the plural rather than the singular, *Life, a User's Manual* is composed of a vast number of interwoven stories (107 of them, by Perec's own count). In one way or another, all of these stories concern the inhabitants of a large Parisian apartment building situated at 11 rue Simon-Crubellier. Among them, one story comes to the fore: the tale of Percival Bartlebooth, a quirky, wealthy dilettante who conceives a massive artistic project as a young man, a project intended to afford him some direction in life and that would take 50 years to execute. For ten years, he would take lessons in watercolor painting. Then, for 20 years, he would travel the world, painting a picture of a different port every two weeks. He would send every painting back to Paris as soon as it was finished, where an artisan in his employ, Gaspard Winckler, would glue it onto a piece of wood and cut it into a jigsaw puzzle. Five hundred puzzles would await Bartlebooth upon his return to Paris, and he would devote the next 20 years to solving them. As each puzzle was solved, he would send it back to the port city where it had been painted, and it would be dipped in the water until nothing remained but the original blank paper.

Clearly, ironic analogies obtain between Bartlebooth's project and Perec's own writerly task. *Life, a User's Manual* questions the artistic gesture closely, and casts the work of art as a game (in the fullest sense of that word) in which puzzle-maker and puzzle-solver, writer and reader, engage in a dynamic interplay through which the work itself assumes meaning. In short, like much of Perec's other writings, *Life, a User's Manual* is a reflection upon art and its conditions of possibility.

Initially, *Life, a User's Manual* was received as a narrative tour de force, and Perec himself encouraged this view of his novel. Interviewed in *Le Figaro* shortly after *Life, a User's Manual* was published, Perec stated that in writing it he had been motivated by the desire to tell "stories which one devours, stretched out on one's bed." Yet soon thereafter Perec began to reveal some of the structural principles in the novel, and gradually a different vision of *Life, a User's Manual* emerged: that of the most highly "constructed" novel in French literature. In a piece entitled "Quatre Figures pour *La Vie mode d'emploi*," which he published a year after his novel appeared, Perec spoke about several of those structural principles. The notion of an apartment building whose facade has been removed, allowing one to chart the lives of the people living in it, was inspired by a Saul Steinberg drawing, according to Perec. The building itself, ten stories high by ten rooms wide, reminded Perec of a chessboard, and he adapted an exercise from chess to organize the chapters in his novel. That exercise, known as the "Knight's Tour," calls for the knight to visit each square of the board once and only once. Perec adjusted it to fit a board of ten squares by ten, rather than eight by eight, devoting in this fashion a chapter to each of the "spaces" in the apartment building.

Another principle Perec invoked was still more arcane, involving an algorithm borrowed from higher mathematics. Brought to Perec's attention by one of his colleagues in the Ouvroir de Littérature Potentielle (Oulipo), the eminent graph theorist Claude Berge, it is known as the "orthogonal Latin bi-square order 10." Briefly described, that algorithm allows the symmetrical distribution and permutation of sets of elements in a grid of 10 squares by 10. In his article, Perec said that he had used that principle to elaborate pre-established lists of the 42 different elements (objects, characters, situations, literary allusions and quotations,

and so forth) that would constitute each chapter of *Life, a User's Manual*. He moreover alluded to the voluminous workbook, or register, in which he kept those lists, and which he called the *cahier des charges*.

When that workbook was finally published in a facsimile edition in 1993, it confirmed the "constructivist" vision of *Life, a User's Manual*. For, apart from the many other stories it tells, that novel plays out upon every page a theory of literature that describes the literary text—and indeed any act of storytelling—as a combinatory system based upon certain rules. In other words, if *Life, a User's Manual* takes as its narrative object a *building* and the life within it, its subject is also *building*: building as a creative activity, as the vital, lively process through which art comes into being. From that perspective, *Life, a User's Manual* may properly be seen as a salient landmark in the history of the novel as literary form.

WARREN MOTTE

See also Georges Perec

Further Reading
Berge, Claude, and Eric Beaumatin, "Georges Perec et la combinatoire," *Cahiers Georges Perec* 4 (1990)
Magné, Bernard, "De l'écart à la trace: Avatars de la contrainte," *Etudes Littéraires* 23:1–2 (1990)
Motte, Warren, *The Poetics of Experiment: A Study of the Work of Georges Perec*, Lexington, Kentucky: French Forum Monographs, 1984
Motte, Warren, "Le Puzzle de/dans *La Vie mode d'emploi* de Georges Perec," *Romance Notes* 24:3 (1984)
Perec, Georges, "Quatre Figures pour *La Vie mode d'emploi*," *L'Arc* 76 (1979)
Perec, Georges, *Cahier des charges de "La Vie mode d'emploi*," edited by Hans Hartje, Bernard Magné, and Jacques Neefs, Paris: CNRS, 1993

Clarice Lispector 1925–77

Brazilian

Novelist and short-story and chronicle writer, Clarice Lispector is Brazil's best-known woman author. She began her literary career in 1944 with the publication of the novel *Perto do coração selvagem* (*Near to the Wild Heart*), which has drawn mixed critical attention. Luís Costa Lima, for instance, analyzes the "deceptive simplicity" of Lispector's style in this novel, emphasizing her singular use of language and praising the uniqueness of her text (see Lima, 1970). Others, like Álvaro Lins, have criticized her fragmented, autobiographical prose, derogating it as "feminine" literature (see Lins, 1963).

Lispector's writing style differs greatly from the overwhelmingly realist and sociorealist trend that dominated the Brazilian novel until the 1960s. Following an intensive experimentation with themes, language, and literary conventions that characterized the initial phase of Brazilian modernism (1922–30), the Brazilian novel focused on themes of social justice and regional issues. Unlike most of her peers who wrote between the 1930s and 1960s, Lispector challenged the rules of the realist novel in Brazil. Although texts such as those by João Guimarães Rosa and Graciliano Ramos also investigate their characters' inner worlds, as Earl E. Fitz has discussed (see Fitz, 1985), their prose remains rural and regionalist, whereas Lispector's prose is more urban and comprehensive in scope.

Lispector is often compared with Machado de Assis (Brazil's leading novelist in the 19th century) for having helped heighten and distinguish the psychological novel in Brazil. Both of them write primarily about the subtleties of the human condition, leading the reader to areas of conflict and emotional states, presenting the characters and their actions through textual ambiguity and the play of irony and parody. Like Machado de Assis' fiction, Lispector's novels do not strictly mirror or reproduce reality but rather point to the lack of solidity of life and art, interweave invention and reality, and question commonly accepted "truths."

Lispector's novels and short stories search for a new and special way of translating the characters' feelings and emotions. Her texts analyze the characters' reflections and epiphanies, focusing on feelings, desires, and passions rather than on facts or the circumstances prompting their actions. Since the majority of her protagonists are women, she often examines the conflicts generated by the female characters' rejection of patriarchal ideology and the mechanisms of power that have inhibited their creativity and intellectual development. To construct such a level of introspection in her texts while simultaneously developing characters who embody strong social awareness, Lispector utilizes several literary techniques but especially interior monologues. She often uses abstract concepts, such as love, God, or passion, inverting the commonly accepted meaning of these words. Lispector's unexpected syntax and precise choice of words alert the reader to the implied meanings of the words, and also indicate her pursuit of stylistic control over her writing.

Language, more than characterization or theme, plays an important role in Lispector's fiction. While she is concerned with language as a means of communication, her texts tend to examine failures of communication. Although the awareness of how language functions as a process and a product characterizes all of Lispector's novels, this feature appears more clearly in her last two novels (*A hora da estrela* [1977; *The Hour of the Star*] and *Um sopro de vida: pulsações* [1978; *A Breath of Life: Pulsations*]), in which the narrators compulsively attempt to understand their personal creative processes. The self-reflective nature of these two works is part of Lispector's project to unlock the complexities of self-definition by investigating the evolution of fiction making. These narratives discuss their own craft, emphasizing the relationship between text, reader, narrator, and author.

In both Lispector's novels and short stories, the protagonists experience moments of awareness when, out of an apparently trivial incident, a revelation occurs and a cathartic process takes place, enabling the characters to analyze the roles they have played. While the majority of her short stories focuses on family life and on female characters who are housewives, most of the female protagonists in her novels are professionals without children. They are single, even solitary people. Vitória, the rancher in *A maçã no escuro* (1961; *The Apple in the Dark*), Lóri, the teacher/student of *Uma aprendizagem; ou, o livro dos prazeres* (1969; *An Apprenticeship; or, The Book of Delights*), and G.H., the affluent sculptor of *A Paixão Segundo G.H.* (1964; *The Passion According to G.H.*), present good examples. Even the poverty-ridden Macabéa of *The Hour of the Star*, a naive and helpless figure, fits the model found in the other novels, as she also has a job and supports herself.

Many of Lispector's texts (especially the novels and chronicles) are autobiographical in the sense that one can identify passages reflecting her life. In *Água viva* (1973; *The Stream of Life*), the views expressed by the narrator/character describe Lispector's own feelings and life experiences, especially those regarding loving and being loved, and present philosophical speculations and metaphysical definitions that reiterate Lispector's own thought processes, as expressed in her media interviews. Her novels, more specifically the ones published since 1961, display a protean quality reflecting the incorporation of several other genres. They present traces of philosophical essays, epistolary narratives, autobiographies, diaries, memoirs, confessions, travel literature, and even drama (see *The Stream of Life, The Passion According to G.H., An Apprenticeship*, and *Um sopro de vida: pulsações*).

Lispector died in 1977, leaving a legacy of 23 books, 9 of which are novels. Since then, her work has received worldwide acclaim. This international recognition owes much to Hélène Cixous, the renowned French feminist critic, who has repeatedly praised Lispector's literary achievements, often writing and lecturing about her texts. In 1974, Lispector ironically predicted this unparalleled praise abroad and the reverence she has received in Brazil as she wrote, "After death I will grow and scatter myself, and someone will say my name with love."

MARIA JOSÉ SOMERLATE BARBOSA

Biography
Born in Tchetchelnik, Ukraine, 10 December 1925. Family moved to Brazil in 1926 (Lispector was 2 months old) and settled in Recife in 1927. Attended the Ginásio Pernambuco from 1935 to 1936; Colégio Sílvio Leite in 1937, and later Colégio Andrews; National Faculty of Law, Rio de Janeiro, from 1941 to 1944, received law degree 1944. Edited and contributed to *Agência Nacional* and *A Noite,* while still a student, 1941–44; left Brazil because of her husband's diplomatic postings and lived in Europe, mainly Naples and Bern, until 1952, and in the United States from 1952 to 1959; after separating from her husband she returned to Rio de Janeiro in 1959. Died 9 December 1977.

Novels by Lispector
Perto do coração selvagem, 1944; as *Near to the Wild Heart,* translated by Giovanni Pontiero, 1990

O lustre [The Chandelier], 1946

A cidade sitiada [The Besieged City], 1948

A maçã no escuro, 1961; as *The Apple in the Dark,* translated by Gregory Rabassa, 1967

A Paixão Segundo G.H., 1964; as *The Passion According to G.H.,* translated by Ronald W. Souza, 1988

Uma aprendizagem; ou, o livro dos prazeres, 1969; as *An Apprenticeship; or, The Book of Delights,* translated by Richard Mazzara and Lorri Parris, 1986

Água viva, 1973; as *The Stream of Life,* translated by Elizabeth Lowe and Earl E. Fitz, 1989

A hora da estrela, 1977; as *The Hour of the Star,* translated by Giovanni Pontiero, 1986

Um sopro de vida: pulsações [A Breath of Life: Pulsations], 1978

Other Writings: short stories, journalistic productions and chronicles, translations, and children's literature.

Further Reading

Barbosa, Maria José Somerlate, *Clarice Lispector: Spinning the Webs of Passion,* New Orleans, Louisiana: University Press of the South, 1997

Borelli, Olga, *Clarice Lispector: Esboco para um possivel retrato,* Rio de Janeiro: Nova Fronteira, 1981

Brasil, Assis, *Clarice Lispector,* Rio de Janeiro: Editora Organização Simões, 1969

Fitz, Earl E., *Clarice Lispector,* Boston: Twayne, 1985

Gotlib, Nádia Batella, *Clarice: Uma vida que se conta,* São Paulo: Ática, 1995

Lima, Luís Costa, "Clarice Lispector," in *A literatura no Brasil: Modernismo,* Rio de Janeiro: Sul Americana, 1970

Lins, Álvaro, "A experiência incompleta," in *Os mortos de sobrecasaca,* Rio de Janeiro: Civilização Brasileira, 1963

Numes, Bendedito, *O mundo de Clarice Lispector,* Manaus: Edições Governo do Estado do Amazonas, 1966

Peixoto, Marta, *Passionate Fictions: Gender, Narrative, and Violence in Clarice Lispector,* Minneapolis: University of Minnesota Press, 1994

Sá, Olga de, *A escrita de Clarice Lispector,* Petrópolis: Vozes, 1979

Little Women by Louisa May Alcott

1868–69

Louisa May Alcott's *Little Women* has a curious international publishing history. In Britain and Canada, the novel has appeared as part of a tetralogy, with *Good Wives* (1871), *Little Men* (1871), and *Jo's Boys* (1886), while American editions of *Little Women* include *Good Wives.* The British version, primarily the story of the rebellious tomboy Jo, is more unified, not being weighed down by the lachrymose death of Beth and the serial matrimony of *Good Wives.*

To some extent, 19th-century readers are implicated in the divergence in tone and preoccupation between the beginning and ending of the American version of *Little Women.* Alcott was besieged by readers pressing her to marry Jo off to Laurie, the young male "lead." To her credit, Alcott refused. Yet the later parts—rather like the adventures of the pettish daughter of Catherine Earnshaw with the sickly son of Heathcliff in the second half of *Wuthering Heights*—mark a retreat from the passion and independence of the novel's beginnings. The contrast between the two volumes does much to explain the warring critical views of the novel, which has been seen variously as accepting a damaging creed of female self-denial, emphasizing independence, modeling a utopian image of sisterhood and female community, dramatizing the tensions between woman and artist, and alternately validating or undercutting conventional domestic virtues.

Although the general public remembers Alcott only for *Little Women* and its sequels, Alcott was a prolific writer (publishing some 270 works in every genre from poetry to tragedy) whose taste ran to the lurid. Thanks to the detective work of Madeleine Stern and Leona Rostenberg in particular, a host of her pseudonymous thrillers have been rediscovered—blood and thunder tales that include accounts of predatory erotic stalking, the joys of hashish, sadistic revenge, and passion, with Gothic and orientalist settings ranging from haunted abbeys to Hindu princedoms, Tartar estates, and Cuban coffee plantations. Alcott supported her improvident parents and three sisters entirely by her pen. She wrote *Little Women,* which she described as "moral pap for the young," to commission and without enthusiasm, only to find it such a success that she was trapped forever in the role of children's writer. The novel sold phenomenally and was repeatedly dramatized, the latest instance being the 1994 film version, directed by Gillian Armstrong. In the novel, Jo writes inflammatory page-turners much like Alcott's (e.g., "The Demon of the Jura" for the *Weekly Volcano*) until her husband-to-be, the decidedly unerotic Professor Bhaer, convinces her to abandon her work. Inevitably, therefore, *Little Women* has been read as a regression for Alcott, both as woman and as artist, subduing her own fires to the dictates of male authority and the demands of the Victorian marketplace. Yet the novel is rather more complex than this argument suggests.

Little Women has distinctive merits as a children's story. Compared to the products of the American Tract Society, for example, it is not overtly moralistic. The children puzzle things out for themselves, drawing their own morals. By the standards of the age, Beth's death scene is restrained. When Jo writes children's books, she rejects the usual model, in which (in her description) all naughty boys are eaten by bears and all good children depart this life lisping psalms and sermons. Jo refuses to marry the handsome prince, is embittered rather than ennobled by Beth's death, and, in her slangy expressions and spontaneity, is a worthy predecessor to Huck Finn. In *Little Women,* nobody goes to church. In a fit of murderous sibling rivalry, Jo almost allows Amy to drown. Despite the Alcotts' fervent abolitionism, there is hardly a hint of propaganda for any progressive cause. Alcott's satiric and comic gifts also give the sentimental-domestic idyll a sharper bite than its generic fellows.

As a woman's novel, *Little Women* is classically double, with a feminist subtext always threatening to overwhelm the conventional overplot. Versions of womanhood are distributed among four sisters (domestic Meg, rebellious Jo, Beth as the angel-in-the-house, and socialite Amy) for comparison and reader identification. Nina Auerbach (1978) mounted a memorable defense of the novel as a dramatization of the plenitude and self-sufficiency of an all-female world situating men on the outside looking in and requiring education in the values of the domestic ideal. Arguably, the whole family restructures itself on a female pattern, with men joining the household democracy on female terms as a blueprint for social reform. On the other hand, throughout the novel, the four sisters are described as enacting a moral allegory based upon John Bunyan's *Pilgrim's Progress,* a drama of trials and tribulations, of temptations conquered, and of Christian renunciation. This subtext firmly subordinates the sisters to established religious-aesthetic norms. Indeed, all the women appear to sacrifice artistic impulses (piano playing, writing, sculpture) to the domestic ideal. Yet, prescient for its time, the novel presents identity and gender as performative rather than essential. As Karen Halttunen (1984) notes, Alcott, herself decidedly stage-struck, opens the novel with parlor theatrical—a performance of "The Witch's Curse," a melodrama that allows Jo (in male dress) to play both hero and villain and alternately to terrorize and court her sisters. Throughout the novel, the characters give free rein to their imaginations in their own distinct voices. The reader shares their journals, letters, fantasies, poems, and even a home-produced newspaper. Rather than renouncing women's art, Alcott argues for a movement away from an individualist to a communal aesthetic, rejecting the cutthroat commercial imperatives of the competitive marketplace in favor of cooperative artistic activity. The family becomes the archetypal small cooperative, for whom Jo eventually writes rather better books. One scene, dramatizing a process of group storytelling by both male and female characters, is something of an aesthetic manifesto. The opening conventional tale of a handsome knight in quest of a lovely lady is transformed by successive narrators into a thriller, a slapstick chase, a Gothic melodrama, a comedy, a pirate adventure, a fairy tale, and a sentimental pastiche, finally yielding to a game of "Truth." When Jo's own work receives mixed reviews, she comments that "Not being a genius, like Keats, won't kill me." Rather than acquiescing in womanly self-

denigration, Alcott mounted a challenge to the model of the inspired individual (male) genius in favor of communally oriented artistic activity and autonomy in association. The novel closes with a musical performance, with words by Jo, music by Laurie, and a choir made up of Jo's boys, before the family audience. Alcott may have satirized her father's unsuccessful attempts at founding a commune in *Transcendental Wild Oats,* but the experience and ideal of the commune formed her own aesthetic.

JUDIE NEWMAN

Further Reading

Alcott, Louisa May, *Transcendental Wild Oats,* in *Bronson Alcott's Fruitlands,* edited by Clara Endicott Sears, Boston: Houghton Mifflin, 1915

Auerbach, Nina, *Communities of Women: An Idea in Fiction,* Cambridge, Massachusetts: Harvard University Press, 1978

Dalke, Anne, "The House-Band: The Education of Men in *Little Women,*" *College English* 47:6 (1985)

Fetterley, Judith, "*Little Women:* Alcott's Civil War," *Feminist Studies* (1979)

Halttunen, Karen, "The Domestic Drama of Louisa May Alcott," *Feminist Studies* 10:2 (1984)

Hollander, Anne, "Reflections on *Little Women,*" *Children's Literature* 9 (1981)

MacDonald, Ruth K., *Louisa May Alcott,* Boston: Twayne, 1983

Saxton, Martha, *Louisa May: A Modern Biography of Louisa May Alcott,* Boston: Houghton Mifflin, 1977; London: Deutsch, 1978

Stern, Madeleine B., *Louisa May Alcott,* Norman: University of Oklahoma Press, 1950

Stern, Madeleine B., editor, *Critical Essays on Louisa May Alcott,* Boston: G.K. Hall, 1984

Lolita by Vladimir Nabokov

1955

The Paris publication of *Lolita,* in the plain green covers the Olympia Press reserved for its pornographic works, created a furor of controversy. The book, about a middle-aged scholar's obsession with a prepubescent girl, was banned in England, France, and Italy (although not in the United States, where it was respectably published in 1958). There were violent outbursts in the press, and one British Member of Parliament lost his seat after defending its publication.

Many of the book's assailants would have been surprised to discover that its author, an eminent scholar and translator, shared most of their conservative moral and social values. In his teaching at Cornell University, Nabokov revealed an old-fashioned moralistic view of literature, and he declared in an inter-

view his distaste for the salacious in fiction and his lack of interest in sexual pathology. He was therefore deeply saddened that his book was regarded as a manual for pedophiles, particularly as the reader is never left in any doubt about the abnormal nature of Humbert Humbert's passions, which are always presented with an elliptical reticence and a fastidious restraint.

Nabokov carries over into *Lolita* his predilection in his early Russian novels—*Zashchita Luzhing* (1930; *The Defense*), *Laughter in the Dark* (1932), *Despair* (1936)—for psychotic murderers and scoundrels, paranoid fetishists and fanatics, each of whom reflects Nabokov's own enthusiasms (for chess, cinema, butterflies) in strangely demented and perverted forms. In all other respects, they are as different from himself as is imaginable. These weird, nefarious narrators have been attributed to Nabokov's uninhibited, encyclopedic curiosity and to the lyric artist's disinterested desire for objectivity, to his need to disengage himself from and reject involvement with his creations so as not to be confused and identified with them.

Upon its publication, *Lolita* was regarded as a sexually avant-garde work, but, as Lionel Trilling was quick to notice in a 1958 essay (republished in Page, 1982, and in Bloom, 1987), it looks back to a clearly identifiable Romantic literary tradition in which erotic passion was often presented as the deranged, agonized pursuit of a forbidden intimacy (adultery, incest) which could not be assimilated into married society. Since tolerance is the death of taboos, the proscribed passion burns briefly in the fragile space between opposition and acceptance, its essence being its transience and unattainability. Pushing the taboo frontiers back further, Nabokov makes the prepubescent girl—or nymphet, in the narrator's words—the supreme epitome of these things. "Nympholepsy" had long been part of the Romantic vocabulary, referring to the frenzied attachment to an unattainable object. Nabokov's own nostalgic longings, described in his autobiographical writings, for his lost aristocratic childhood and his beloved Russian language, have erotic undertones that figuratively "nymphetize" the objects of his desire. In *Lolita* the metaphor is literalized, and a real girl becomes the object of a pathological complex in which a mature man perpetually tries to recapture the magical, rapturous intensity of his first childhood love experience. But Humbert's infatuation, and his strangely confected poetic rhetoric, are still strongly colored by the Romantic artist's dream of perfect, inexpressible beauty. In the Afterword to *Lolita,* Nabokov refers to this dream as one of "aesthetic bliss, that is a sense of being somehow, somewhere, connected with other states of being where art (curiosity, tenderness, kindness, ecstasy) is the norm." These notions—of art as norm and goal, of beauty as a pathway to higher, ecstatic states of being—were the axioms of the late 19th-century Pre-Raphaelite and Aesthetic movements and of their counterparts in Nabokov's own country: the prerevolutionary symbolists and the poets Mayakovsky and Aleksandr Blok, who were the formative influences on his early work.

Lolita is a work walled in by literature, bounded on all sides by parody, pastiche, and allusion. (Humbert's dead childhood sweetheart, for instance, is a version of Poe's girlchild Annabel Lee.) At the lowest level, Humbert's diary is a lecherous parody of an archaic tradition of sonneteering overtures to an unviolated, inviolable loved one, from Petrarch's housewife to Poe's child-bride. In this tradition, the hapless worshiper fetishizes the loved one's clothing and jewelry and keeps her ideal image intact by (as Humbert puts it) "safely solipsizing" her in his imagination and making do with voyeuristic and masturbatory pleasures. The tradition is subverted when Lolita, who is only too readily violable, steps out of the portrait, assumes a character of her own—a brash, vulgar one, all soda and chewing gum—and demonstrates powers of reaction and relation. Humbert then falls in love with the real Lolita, not the one of his literary obsession, and proceeds to conceive their relationship in terms very close to married fidelity. However, married to Lolita's mother, he has forfeited any claim to real affection by his pseudoincestuous violation of the bond between child and stepfather which has deprived Lolita of her childhood.

Some early critics of the novel backed away from its taboo material by translating it into an allegory of America and Europe, an inverted parody of New World innocence corrupted by Old World decadence and neurosis. The extent to which Lolita embodies the commercial vulgarity and sexual precocity of modern America is problematic, however, and Humbert, whose quirks are essentially personal and idiosyncratic, is reticent in his narrative on the subject of who corrupts whom. Later deconstructivist readings, fueled by Nabokov's interview statements about the antirealistic nature of his work, presented the book in reflexive, self-referential terms, as a total fiction preoccupied by its own language and constituted from hermetic literary games and hoaxes. These readings construed Lolita's seduction of Humbert as an internal metaphor for the author's aesthetic tantalization of the reader. Nabokov's metafictional convolutions were to become more pronounced in his next two novels, *Pale Fire* (1962) and *Ada* (1969), which earned him the position of father figure to a generation of American postmodernist novelists. In *Lolita,* however, the text's complex weave of self-conscious literariness and psychology does not transcend traditional realism in any thoroughgoing postmodern manner. Humbert's literary and theatrical extravagances—his clownish revelry in games of coincidence and charades—characterize the narrator rather than the author. For example, he deflates his own mental agony at the final parting from Lolita by a cheap parody of a detective thriller. At the deaths of Lolita's mother and the heroine's abductor Claire Quilty, the narrative slips into the styles of police gazette, postmortem report, and Hollywood Western. Humbert's parodies and burlesques, like his own pale imitations of paternity and incest, are barometers that measure his ineptitudes and failures. Humbert's description of his first attempts to shoot Quilty—pathetic and comical at once—may serve as an example. Far from undermining the illusion of reality, the manner in which the narrator plays with style and genre strengthens that illusion. *Lolita* continues to depend upon this realistic illusion for its power to disorient and disturb.

Lolita cannot, finally, be confined in categories. It is at once a poignantly offbeat love story and best-selling *succès du scandale* that makes a taboo subject both moving and funny; a storehouse of literary parody, encompassing romance quest, courtly love, and detective mystery; and a recondite cryptograph designed to hoodwink academics with an endless trail of hermeneutical hoaxes. Indeed, it was precisely the book's multiple potentiality, its playful, protean capacity to be many kinds of novel operating on many different levels (realist and parody, tragedy and farce, satire and elegy) and to slip unsettlingly between modes, that anticipated and made possible the diverse experimentation of much postwar writing. Nabokov's first completely American novel, although grounded in the tradition of European realism, conferred a provisionality and arbitrariness upon the fictional artifact that opened up both his own text and the modern novel to the realm of postmodern possibility. In a sense, Nabokov's entire fictional oeuvre—*Lolita* as well as *Pale Fire*—has its proper setting not in modern America or any other geographical location but in the land of "Zembla," a place of apparent, beguiling resemblances to "reality" where things are both true and untrue, solid and figmentary, and where a distorted mimesis enjoys a unique coexistence with autonomous fictional constructs. This indeterminate realm, which is not to be mistaken for any other real or fictional world, has also been traversed by generations of American and international postmodern novelists—Thomas Pynchon, Gabriel

García Márquez, Salman Rushdie, Michael Ondaatje—who followed in Nabokov's wake. As a forerunner of this body of fiction, his work is a turning point, and *Lolita* a milestone, in 20th-century literature.

DEREK WRIGHT

See also Vladimir Nabokov

Further Reading

Bloom, Harold, editor, *Vladimir Nabokov's "Lolita,"* New York: Chelsea House, 1987

Boyd, Brian, *Vladimir Nabokov: The Russian Years,* London: Chatto and Windus, and Princeton, New Jersey: Princeton University Press, 1990

Boyd, Brian, *Vladimir Nabokov: The American Years,* London: Chatto and Windus, and Princeton, New Jersey: Princeton University Press, 1991

Field, Andrew, *Nabokov, His Life in Art: A Critical Narrative,* Boston: Little Brown, and London: Hodder and Stoughton, 1967

Newman, Charles, and Alfred Appel, editors, *Nabokov: Criticism, Reminiscences, Translations, and Tributes,* Evanston, Illinois: Northwestern University Press, 1970; London: Weidenfeld and Nicolson, 1971

Page, Norman, editor, *Nabokov: The Critical Heritage,* London and Boston: Routledge and Kegan Paul, 1982

Pifer, Ellen, *Nabokov and the Novel,* Cambridge, Massachusetts: Harvard University Press, 1980

Rampton, David, *Vladimir Nabokov: A Critical Study of the Novels,* Cambridge and New York: Cambridge University Press, 1984

Wood, Michael, *The Magician's Doubts: Nabokov and the Risks of Fiction,* London: Chatto and Windus, 1994; Princeton, New Jersey: Princeton University Press, 1995

Lord Jim by Joseph Conrad

1900

Lord Jim first appeared in serial form in *Blackwood's Magazine* between October 1899 and November 1900 and is Joseph Conrad's first great novel. Although it bears the subtitle *A Tale,* the narrative is deceptively complex. Like most of Conrad's early fiction, *Lord Jim* draws upon the author's experience in the merchant marines and blends a knowing investigation into late 19th-century European colonialism with a sense of individual tragic destiny and moral isolation. The novel's themes of adventure and the sea accounted for much of its popularity in Conrad's lifetime, as did its strikingly ambiguous investigation of heroism and moral regeneration. Many readers of Conrad's time were puzzled by the novel's shifts between two apparently disjunct plots—Jim's jump from his ship (the *Patna*) and subsequent trial and his later adventures among the peoples of Patusan in the South China Sea. Conrad himself referred to the break between the two halves of the novel as its "plague spot," but contemporary readers, with the benefit of hindsight, can see the novel's second half as a link between Conrad's stories of the sea, which he wrote throughout his career, and the political novels that would directly follow—*Nostromo* (1904), *The Secret Agent* (1907), and *Under Western Eyes* (1911). The presence in *Lord Jim* of the mediating narrator Marlow (who also appears in the story "Youth" [1898] and the late novel *Chance* [1913]) and the novel's investigation of moral breakdown under the pressures of isolation and foreign experience connect *Lord Jim* closely to Conrad's novella "Heart of Darkness," which he wrote during a break from the composition of the longer work.

Like Miguel de Cervantes' *Don Quixote* (1605–15) and Gustave Flaubert's *Madame Bovary* (1857), *Lord Jim* deals with an idealistic protagonist whose sense of the world comes from books rather than experience. Its investigation of guilt, shame, and the nature of heroism together with Conrad's consciousness of the vexed relationship between storytelling and truth produced one of the most technically complex novels in English since Emily Brontë's *Wuthering Heights* (1847). *Lord Jim* presents its readers with several interpretive challenges: its mediated narrative; its frequently unchronological plot; its suspension of important information, a technique that Ian Watt (1979) called "delayed decoding"; its apparent digressions from Jim's story to the experiences of subsidiary characters; and its doubled narratives of the *Patna* and Patusan.

All work together to illuminate the novel's central theme: the inability of one human to truly know another. Conrad takes the epigram for *Lord Jim* from the German poet and theorist Novalis, "It is certain my conviction gains infinitely, the moment another soul will believe in it." Throughout *Lord Jim*, Marlow's attempts to understand Jim's actions and Jim's attempts to be understood by Marlow—as well as Marlow's attempts to explain his relationship to Jim to a crowd of unnamed listeners—are reinforced by the many signs of division between event or existence and the range of possible interpretations. In the novel's first half, for instance, Conrad delays the revelation that the *Patna*, the boat from which Jim leapt, was towed safely to shore. Because the narrative jumps from the moment of the *Patna*'s impact with an unknown obstacle to Jim's subsequent trial, the reader may incorrectly interpret the event and perhaps feel empathy with Jim. The delayed information forces a retrospective reevaluation of the moral complexity of the events and of Jim's and Marlow's reactions to them. Similarly, the subsidiary narratives that are apparently centrifugal to Jim's story—the suicide of

Brierly and the alcoholic degeneration of the *Patna*'s chief engineer—achieve retrospective meaning by casting ambiguous moral light upon the events on the *Patna,* showing how characters whose moral claims differ from Jim's have reacted to the events that shook his sense of duty and self.

The novel's second half, which explores Jim's attempt to regain his good name, investigates by juxtaposition Jim's struggle toward fulfilling what he believes European culture expects of him. Jim's entry into an adventure plot—the very kind he had learned about from children's books—allows him an apparently new theatre in which to replay and potentially undo his past cowardly behavior. As the narrative becomes less overtly obtrusive—the final events, for instance, unfold in linear chronology in a letter from Marlow to only one "privileged man"—Jim's ability to recreate himself through heroic repetition grows more ambiguous. His mistaken faith in the pirate Gentleman Brown—a version of the German romantic motif of the doppelgänger, or dark self—leads to his failure and death, a moment scarcely interpretable by Marlow or by his philosophic friend Stein. Is Jim a hero or a self-deluded fool? If Jim is, as Marlow consistently says, "one of us," what might that say about the tragic nature of the self and its ultimate isolation? The novel ends in interpretive silence, with its experimentations of form tapering off into the figurative mists that are pervasively present as symbol in Marlow's narrative.

Conrad's technical innovations and unflinching treatment of moral ambiguity may be seen in *The Good Soldier* (1915) by Ford Madox Ford, Conrad's friend and sometime collaborator. *The Good Soldier*'s chronological dislocations are heavily indebted to *Lord Jim,* as are its narrator, who attempts with limited success to understand another man's motivations, and its crushing ironies. These techniques are also present in William Faulkner's work, particularly *Absalom, Absalom!* (1936). Conrad's fascination with the experience of the European against the moral perspective of exotic locales, on the other hand, exerted a strong influence on Graham Greene's novels. Although cinematic adaptations of Conrad tend to untangle the chronologies of his plots, his sophisticated use of the "flashback" and the "flashforward" in *Lord Jim* and his other novels also may be seen as a precursor of cinematic technique.

SCOTT W. KLEIN

See also Joseph Conrad

Further Reading

Berthoud, Jacques, *Joseph Conrad: The Major Phase,* Cambridge and New York: Cambridge University Press, 1978

Cox, C.B., *Joseph Conrad: The Modern Imagination,* London: Dent, and Totowa, New Jersey: Rowman and Littlefield, 1974

Daleski, H.M., *Joseph Conrad: The Way of Dispossession,* London: Faber, and New York: Holmes and Meier, 1977

Guerard, Albert J., *Conrad the Novelist,* Cambridge, Massachusetts: Harvard University Press, 1958

Jameson, Fredric, *The Political Unconscious: Narrative as a Socially Symbolic Act,* Ithaca, New York: Cornell University Press, and London: Methuen, 1981

Miller, J. Hillis, *Fiction and Repetition: Seven English Novels,* Cambridge, Massachusetts: Harvard University Press, and Oxford: Blackwell, 1982

Moser, Thomas, *Joseph Conrad: Achievement and Decline,* Cambridge, Massachusetts: Harvard University Press, 1957

Van Ghent, Dorothy, *The English Novel: Form and Function,* New York: Rinehart, 1953

Watt, Ian, *Conrad in the Nineteenth Century,* Berkeley: University of California Press, 1979; London: Chatto and Windus, 1980

The Lost Steps by Alejo Carpentier

Los pasos perdidos 1953

The Lost Steps is an important early novel in what would eventually become the "boom" period of the 1960s and 1970s in Latin American fiction. It was also the work that established Alejo Carpentier's international reputation, although several of the concepts it develops had appeared in his earlier writings. By 1953 he had been practicing journalism for more than 20 years, had written a history of music in Cuba, and had completed a number of short literary compositions. Above all, he had published two novels, notably *El reine de este mundo* (1949; *The Kingdom of This World*) and its celebrated prologue, in which he introduced his notion of the marvelous in Latin America ("*lo real maravilloso*") and described the aesthetics underlying his view of the history and natural world of the continent. The aesthetic posture developed in this context is maintained in *The Lost Steps,* but the broader scope of the novel makes it more accessible to a wider readership. Whereas the two earlier novels were informed by the precise history, geography, and cultures of Cuba and Haiti, *The Lost Steps* tells a story of more epic proportions: it represents the vastness, diversity, and power of the South American landscape; it succeeds in conveying a broad historical sweep but does so in ways that subordinate the narration of history to the construction of a fictional world; and, by employing a first-person narrator, it incorporates a perspective on the marvelous, which allows readers to join with the narrator in responding to the experiences and phenomena described in the text.

The Lost Steps is a "quest" novel in several senses. At its most superficial level, the quest is embodied in the expedition to the jungle of South America undertaken by the unnamed narrator, a composer who has reluctantly accepted the commission of the curator of a museum in a North American city to look for primitive musical instruments. It is also a journey in search of Latin America. The narrator not only rediscovers the language (Spanish) and culture he knew as a child and had since lost, but his journey appears to take him backward through time as each city, town, or settlement he travels through seems to lead him further into the past. The capital city has a 19th-century air and, in his travels beyond it, he finds himself in places that evoke successively the time of the colony, the Conquest, and the Middle Ages. The further he ventures into the jungle, the further he recedes in time, until he reaches the equivalent of the dawn of civilization, at the end of the Fourth Day of the Creation.

The narrator's journey gives him the opportunity to describe the natural world and human society in Latin America and to show the sense of the marvelous they evoke. Between the city and the jungle, for example, there is the distance of centuries that juxtaposes the primeval with the present and places different periods of civilization alongside each other, combining the people and the cultural artifacts of different times and spaces in the same context. In this way, Carpentier uses the novel to expose the supposedly exhausted vein of artistic creation in Western culture and to counter it with the fresh and vigorous world of "naturally" occurring phenomena in Latin America, sustaining the Spenglerian view of cultural history adopted in his earlier writings.

In view of the decadence of the West, the narrator's journey is also a search for authenticity, a search symbolized in the novel through his relationship with three principal female characters. The monotony and aridity of North American life are represented in part through his wife and her life as an actress. Like the role she performs nightly on stage, their relationship is a programmed performance, lacking spontaneity and creativity. The artificiality of contemporary culture is also represented through Mouche, the narrator's mistress, an astrologer drawn to existentialism and abstract art. Although it is she who eventually persuades the narrator to accept the curator's commission and accompanies him to South America, she is unable to withstand the rigors of the journey through the jungle. As the narrator detaches himself from Mouche and her ways, he begins a new relationship with Rosario, whom he has met on the journey and who lacks the urban sophistication of his former mistress. When Mouche falls ill with malaria and returns to their point of departure, the narrator continues with Rosario and his other traveling companions and eventually sets up house with her in a newly founded city in the heart of the jungle.

For the narrator, the recovery of a sense of authenticity entails a return to a point of origin, not only to the lost culture of his childhood but to the beginnings of civilization itself. As a composer, it is eventually less significant for him to have discovered the musical instruments that were the reason for his quest than to have heard the threnody sung by a shaman in the jungle, which reawakened his creativity and led him to write music with a sense of inspiration denied him in the city. But even his inspiration needs to be materially recorded, and, when the opportunity arises, he leaves the jungle on the plane sent in search of him, hoping to return with sufficient paper on which to complete his composition. At the end of the novel, however, he finds himself at a crossroads: having failed so far to find the channel in the river that would lead him to the settlement in the jungle, he is caught between the possibility of finding his way back or of finding himself once more entrapped in the routines of civilized society from which he had progressively freed himself during the course of his original journey. Having discovered a more authentic self, it is not certain he can preserve it.

The uncertain future that faces the narrator at the end of *The Lost Steps* may, perhaps, also be read as an indicator of the dilemma facing the Latin American artist. Latin America's natural environment and its cultural contexts and history are there for the artist to discover and describe in much the same way as they are represented in Carpentier's novel. But, just as the narrator finds it difficult to return to the world of the threnody that inspired his music, there are obstacles to finding an "authentic" Latin America unaffected by the patterns of life and cultural forms that have imposed themselves on it through conquest, colonization, and immigration. Latin America is unique, but its uniqueness also consists in how it has assimilated or transformed external traditions. It is Carpentier's particular treatment of this condition that gives his novel an important place among other 20th-century works of prose fiction that have also sought to provide a comprehensive view of Latin America and describe its place in the world.

RICHARD A. YOUNG

See also Alejo Carpentier

Further Reading

González Echevarría, Roberto, *Alejo Carpentier: The Pilgrim at Home,* Ithaca, New York: Cornell University Press, 1977
MacDonald, Ian, "Magical Eclecticism: *Los pasos perdidos* and Jean-Paul Sartre," in *Contemporary Latin American Fiction,* edited by Salvador Bacarisse, Edinburgh: Scottish Academic Press, 1980
Müller-Bergh, Klaus, *Alejo Carpentier: Estudio biográfico crítico,* Long Island City, New York: Las Américas, 1972
Palermo, Zulma, "Aproximación a *Los pasos perdidos*," in *Historia y mito en la obra de Alejo Carpentier,* edited by Nora Mazziotti, Buenos Aires: García Gambeiro, 1972
Peavler, Terry J., "The Source for the Archetype in *Los pasos perdidos*," *Romance Notes* 15 (1974)
Smith, Verity, *Carpentier: "Los pasos perdidos,"* London: Grant and Cutler, 1983

Love in the Time of Cholera by Gabriel García Márquez

El amor en los tiempos de cólera 1985

Love in the Time of Cholera followed the publication of Crónica de una muerte anunciada (1981; Chronicle of a Death Foretold). It was Gabriel García Márquez's first novel since he was awarded the Nobel prize for literature in 1982. Because García Márquez had worked as a journalist and had published novels and short stories prior to winning the Nobel prize, he had a strong national readership. Cien años de soledad (1967; One Hundred Years of Solitude) had brought García Márquez to the attention of an international audience. The success of Love in the Time of Cholera cemented his international reputation as a master of the genre of magic realism.

Magic realism is often associated with writers from non-European cultures. Magic realists blend European literary traditions with the indigenous oral tradition of their culture, which may include fantastic occurrences. The realism is dominant, while magical events happen in a way that makes the reader accept them as part of the realist context. Philip Swanson (1995) reverses this emphasis in his definition of the magic realism employed by García Márquez as "basically a matter of presenting extraordinary events in a natural way, thus allowing the reader to share the perspectives of the characters." In this way García Márquez deliberately includes elements of the Latin American storytelling tradition in his work. His novels contain a deeper meaning than can be superficially seen in the narrative. His use of this layering device makes García Márquez crucial to the development of the novel in the 20th century.

The importance of the Latin American oral tradition manifests itself not only in magic realism but also in the use of an omniscient narrator who has the same unevenness of focus as one would expect from a storyteller. Some events are detailed minutely, others are simply glossed over. The narrative voice moves between characters and scenes as they become important to the central plot. The narrator stresses the fundamental significance of letters to the romance of Florentino Ariza and Fermina Daza, yet their contents are never revealed and apparently do not matter. It is sufficient that the narrator describes the pains with which Florentino Ariza composes his letters and the joys they conjure in Fermina Daza. Through the same device, the narrator omits large portions of dialogue. Arguments are reported but not the actual dialogue. When the novel finally does present dialogue, the reader recognizes the importance of what is being spoken. The one true dialogue takes place in the final scene of the novel between Florentino Ariza and the Captain. This dialogue is the crux of the entire novel, the point toward which the narrative has been moving.

The title Love in the Time of Cholera sums up the three major themes of the novel and points to its fantastic elements. It may be difficult to imagine a romance blooming during an outbreak of cholera, but love, time, and death, represented by cholera, are precisely the main concerns of the novel. Specifically, Florentino Ariza and Fermina Daza recapture their love and decide to spend the rest of their lives celebrating that love on an isolated boat. García Márquez draws the reader's attention to two possibilities: first, that love endures in spite of great obstacles, and second, that elderly people are capable of romantic, physical love. A tour de force consciously written against the grain of traditional representations of romantic love, Love in the Time of Cholera manages to be utterly convincing.

The fantastic component of the novel is not clarified until the denouement. The image of cholera that recurs throughout the text and appears at different stages of Florentino Ariza's love life becomes symbolic of the strength of his love for Fermina Daza. He exhibits symptoms of the disease at crucial points of their courtship. García Márquez thus equates the positive power of love with the destructive power of cholera until cholera, or the outward vestiges of it, permits Florentino Ariza and Fermina Daza to do as they want and remain together potentially forever, as Florentino Ariza says. The ship will sail, and it will be seen as a source of infection for as long as there is someone to sail her. The intensity of Florentino Ariza's love suggests that this could truly be for eternity. In the manner of mythic tales, the aim of the narrator and the meaning of the title are left unexplained until the end.

There are several ways in which Love in the Time of Cholera has influenced the 20th-century novel and readers. García Márquez injected factors from his own cultural oral tradition into the European idea of a realist novel. This marks a turn away from novels about ordinary life and a return to the mythic stories and fairy tales that are the ancestors of the novel. Most importantly, Love in the Time of Cholera demonstrates how a novel can be multilayered while only revealing the deeper meanings at its close. Love in the Time of Cholera revitalizes the genre and demonstrates the unique voice of García Márquez.

SAMANTHA J. BARBER

See also Gabriel García Márquez

Further Reading

Bloom, Harold, editor, Gabriel García Márquez, New York: Chelsea House, 1989

Fuentes, Carlos, Gabriel García Márquez and the Invention of America, Liverpool: Liverpool University Press, 1987

McGuirk, Bernard, and Richard Andrew Cardwell, Gabriel García Márquez: New Readings, Cambridge and New York: Cambridge University Press, 1987

McMurray, George, editor, Critical Essays on Gabriel García Márquez, Boston: G.K. Hall, 1987

McNerney, Kathleen, Understanding Gabriel García Márquez, Columbia: University of South Carolina Press, 1989

Oyarzún, Kemy, and William W. Megenney, Essays on Gabriel García Márquez, Riverside: Latin American Studies Program, University of California, 1984

Penuel, Arnold M., Intertextuality in García Márquez, York, South Carolina: Spanish Literature Publications, 1994

Swanson, Philip, The New Novel in Latin America: Politics and Popular Culture after the Boom, Manchester: Manchester University Press, 1995

Vazquez Amaral, Jose, The Contemporary Latin American Narrative, New York: Las Americas, 1970

Williams, Raymond Leslie, Gabriel García Márquez, Boston: Twayne, 1984

Lu Xun 1881–1936

Chinese

Like the traditional Chinese literatus who was expected to master a wide variety of literary forms, the modern writer Lu Xun wrote in many genres, including the random essay (*suiganlu*), satiric essay (*zawen*), prose poem, classical poem, historical tale, short story, letter, and diary. Although he had plans to write two novels, one a revisionist historical work about the famous Tang dynasty concubine Yang Guifei and another about three generations of modern Chinese intellectuals, these plans never materialized. Whereas some have speculated that Lu Xun's style, characterized by a strong tendency toward brevity of form and concision of language, made him fundamentally averse to the novelistic form, which often favors expansiveness and elaborate description, others suggest that his intellectual interests were simply so multiple as to preclude sustained attention to a single long narrative. Yet the question of why Lu Xun, who is often seen as the seminal figure in modern Chinese literature, never wrote a novel is intertwined with the formation of literary modernity in early 20th-century China. Writers who were claiming for literature a new, modern function, especially during the May Fourth period (1915–25) when Lu Xun wrote the bulk of his fiction, did so first and foremost with the short story, and it was not until the late 1920s and 1930s that the "modern" novel appeared. Whereas Lin Shu's (1852–1924) translations of Western novels (including those of Charles Dickens, H. Rider Haggard, Jules Verne, and Alexandre Dumas) in the late Qing period (1895–1911) were widely read, Lu Xun and his younger brother Zhou Zuoren's translations of short fiction from Europe (including stories by Leonid Andreyev, V.M. Garshin, Guy de Maupassant, and Henryk Sienkiewicz) were received with near silence by the reading public. Just more than a decade later, however, the short story had replaced the novel as the form for expression of the new and modern.

It may be surmised that the short story was central to literary modernity in China because it was perceived as a form relatively more free from traditional values than the novel, which had a long history in the premodern period and which had seen a resurgence in the late Qing. The short story was virgin narrative territory that could function better in the subversion of traditional values. With its rhetorical and moralizing narrators and its stories of ghosts, heroes, and lovers, the premodern vernacular novel was seen to embody the worst of the traditional value system that May Fourth intellectuals were struggling against. In the hands of Lu Xun and others, the modern short story was, of course, highly influenced by foreign models, particularly those of Guy de Maupassant, Nikolai Gogol', Anton Chekov, Leonid Andreyev, and Natsume Sōseki. Yet it has also been suggested that in its economy of style the modern short story had links to the exalted premodern genre of the classical essay. The short story was more in keeping with the classical tendency toward brevity and therefore better able to bear the serious moral-social role the May Fourth progressive writers generally sought for literature. It could thus function as a modern literary space through which traditional propensities for classical economy and generalized message could be expressed, the perfect form through which progressive writers could establish for themselves a position

within the literary field also occupied by those who continued to espouse classicism and the popular "Mandarin Ducks and Butterfly" novelists with whom they were competing for the urban readership.

Not only did Lu Xun never write a novel, his entire fictional output is limited to but one classical language story and three volumes of stories in the modern vernacular, *Nahan* (1923; *Call to Arms*), *Panghuang* (1926; *Wandering*), and *Gushi xinbian* (1935; *Old Tales Retold*), totaling a mere 34 short stories. And yet, small as this body of fiction is, its shaping influence on modern Chinese fiction as a whole has been tremendous. As the novelist Mao Dun first pointed out, "nearly every one of the ten some stories in *Call to Arms* has a unique form, and all of these new forms extensively influenced young writers." And although one should be wary of seeing him as a kind of patriarchal progenitor of modern Chinese literature, it is possible to trace back to Lu Xun a variety of literary types that became standard fare among later writers. He played extensively and imaginatively with form and technique, and each of his stories was in some sense a generic experiment. His fiction includes first-person autobiographical reminiscences, satires of intellectual pretension, allegories about the problem of the cultural tradition and the deficiencies of the Chinese national character, revisionist historical tales, and parodies of classical and popular genres. More than any other writer of the time, he explored the complex ironic possibilities of the first-person narrative mode. Frequently in the form of a reminiscence by a progressive-minded intellectual, these first-person stories often play ironically with that perspective, casting doubt on the moral integrity and enlightenment pretensions of the intelligentsia. His satires of the hypocrisy of high-minded, moralizing conservative scholars were heavily imitated, especially in the 1930s. Some of his stories are in the form of parody of previous classical or popular genres, one of the ways Lu Xun asserted himself against his competitors in the literary field at the time. "A Q zhengzhuan" (1921; "The True Story of Ah Q"), for example, is at once a parody of popular fiction and the classical biographical form.

Thematically, too, Lu Xun's fiction set important precedents that were played upon again and again in the hands of later writers. It is often asserted by critics that in setting most of his stories in his hometown of Shaoxing, Lu Xun was the first in a line of "nativist" (or regional) writers, the most famous of whom was Shen Congwen. Like many in his generation, Lu Xun wrote stories about intellectuals' encounters with the lower class, but he problematized this relationship, avoiding the kind of schematization that pits an immaculate subaltern against a decadent elite, in a way that few of his contemporaries did. Lu Xun's fiction helped to forge a discourse of modernity in China. His radical metaphor of tradition as a cannibalistic feast at which the individual is consumed in his famous story "Kuangren riji" (1918; "Diary of a Madman") became a popular designation for the monolithic and oppressive nature of tradition. His character Ah Q, almost invariably taken as a symbol of the problem with Chinese culture, helped spawn a discourse of "national character": "Ah Qism" and "the spirit of Ah Q," meaning a kind of self-deceit endemic in Chinese culture, are terms that continue to be part of the Chinese cultural consciousness. Apart from these stylistic and thematic influences, Lu Xun was also a central figure in the literary field of the 1920s and 1930s. He participated actively in the literary debates of the time, edited or oversaw the editing of numerous journals and publishing projects, was the titular head of the League of Left-wing Writers (1930–36), and was an untiring patron of younger writers (among whom the most well known are Xiao Jun, Xiao Hong, Duanmu Hongliang, and Rou Shi).

The problem of describing the influence of Lu Xun cannot, however, be reduced to the literary or the thematic, so enmeshed in the complex cultural politics of 20th-century China is his name. Arguably, Lu Xun's influence has been greatly exaggerated by the fact that he was, after his death in 1936, canonized by Mao Zedong and Marxist literary historians. Fashioned into a Chinese Maksim Gor'kii, as one Western critic has put it, Lu Xun was made a symbol of the Communist revolution. While other May Fourth writers of his generation were being attacked during the Cultural Revolution (1966–76) for their Westernized literary style and bourgeois themes, Lu Xun was hailed as an intellectual revolutionary forebear and a literary voice that staunchly refused to compromise with the forces of reaction. Yet even as he was hailed as an anti-authoritarian, his image was made to serve the despotic authority of the Maoist regime. Lu Xun's place in the literary history of modern China is intertwined with this politically motivated representation. Yet even as they reacted against Maoist politics, intellectuals and writers continued in the liberalization period after the death of Mao and the end of the Cultural Revolution to reread Lu Xun, refer to him, allude to his work, and delve into the kinds of moral and cultural issues he did. He has been as such recast in this newly emerging canon as a voice of moral conscience and liberal disaffection. From the ironic realist Gao Xiaosheng to the avant-gardism of Yu Hua, Lu Xun's presence may be seen in the writings of a host of contemporary authors in post-Mao China. The struggle over the "idea" of Lu Xun has been central to the literary history of modern China, and his image, both enlightened individualist and Chinese Gor'kii, encapsulates the cultural problematic of modern China caught between the discourses of enlightenment and national salvation. In the West, Lu Xun has recently been cast in a new mold, perhaps equally problematic. The American Marxist Fredric Jameson has portrayed Lu Xun as the prototypical third world intellectual and his short fiction as "third world national allegories" par excellence. Lu Xun is the third world "cultural revolutionary" whom Jameson asserts as the one who will awaken the soundly sleeping first world intellectual caught in an "iron house" of literary irrelevance.

KIRK A. DENTON

Biography
Pseudonym for Zhou Shuren. Born in Shaoxing, Zhejiang province, in 1881. Attended Jiangnan Naval Academy, Nanjing, 1898–99; School of Railways and Mines, Nanjing, 1899–1902; studied Japanese language in Japan, 1902–04, and medicine at Sendai Provincial Medical School, Japan, 1904–06; studied privately in Japan, 1906–09. Teacher in Shaoxing, 1910–11; served in the Ministry of Education, Beijing, 1912–26; Chinese literature instructor at National Beijing University, 1920–26; also taught at Xiamen (Amoy) University, 1926, and University of Canton, 1927; then lived in international settlement of Shanghai: editor, *Benliu* [The Torrent], 1928, and *Yiwen* [Translation], 1934. Translated many works by Russian, German, and Japanese authors. Also a draughtsman. Died 19 October 1936.

Fiction by Lu Xun
Nahan, 1923; as *Call to Arms*, 1981
Panghuang, 1926; as *Wandering*, 1981
Gushi xinbian, 1935; as *Old Tales Retold*, 1961
Ah Q and Others; Selected Stories, 1941
Selected Stories, 1954
Wild Grass (prose poems), 1974
Diary of a Madman and Other Stories, 1990

Other Writings: essays, prose and verse poetry, diaries, letters, and a book of childhood memories.

Further Reading
Hanan, Patrick, "The Techniques of Lu Hsun's Fiction," *Harvard Journal of Asiatic Studies* 34 (1974)
Lee, Leo Ou-fan, *Voices from the Iron House: A Study of Lu Xun*, Bloomington: Indiana University Press, 1987
Lee, Leo Ou-fan, editor, *Lu Xun and His Legacy*, Berkeley: University of California Press, 1985
Lyell, William A., *Lu Hsun's Vision of Reality*, Berkeley: University of California Press, 1976
Semanov, V.I., *Lu Hsun and His Predecessors*, White Plains, New York: M.E. Sharpe, 1980
Wang, Shiqing, *Lu Xun, a Biography*, Beijing: Foreign Languages Press, 1984

Lucky Jim by Kingsley Amis

1954

The immediate success of his first novel, *Lucky Jim*, established Kingsley Amis' reputation as a funny, satirical, and iconoclastic leader of the "new" English novel in the decade after World War II. Amis was quickly identified as a member of the generation of writers dubbed variously "the Movement" and "Angry Young Men," a group that included the dramatist John Osborne, whose *Look Back in Anger* (produced in 1956) was another landmark work, the poets Philip Larkin (to whom *Lucky Jim* is dedicated), Thom Gunn, and Donald Davie, and novelists John Wain, Iris Murdoch, and John Braine. A prolific writer, Amis went on to write some 20 novels, including the Booker Prize–winning *The Old Devils* (1986), several volumes of poetry and short stories, and studies of James Bond and science fiction. But *Lucky Jim* remains his most popular, trademark novel. As A.C. Ward notes in the *Longman Companion to Twentieth Century Literature* (2nd edition, 1975), it was "immediately adopted by critics and journalists as the type-novel of its generation."

Lucky Jim was one of the first campus novels, a subgenre that became increasingly popular in England and the United States during the postwar decades, as a significantly wider cross-section of the population gained access to universities. These new students were not acculturated to the traditional university and were impatient with teachers who complacently peddled traditional pieties in seeming ignorance of more contemporary concerns. These students and the new staff recruited to teach them did, however, identify readily with the misadventures of Amis' Jim Dixon, an outsider struggling with comic ineptitude and mounting anxiety for acceptance into an academic system that, in its incompetence and self-satisfaction, ignored his real desires and ambitions.

In traditional comedy-of-manners style, Amis compares the red-brick provincial universities of the 1950s to the tradition-steeped Oxford of, for example, Evelyn Waugh's *Brideshead Revisited* (1945), with its privileged generation of between-wars undergraduates and dons. In the opening scene of *Lucky Jim*, Dixon and his professor "Neddy" Welch walk across the lawn of a provincial college, Welch blathering fatuously about a boring local concert, while a passing student mistakenly assumes that they are dons discussing history "in the way history might be talked about in Oxford and Cambridge quadrangles." Dixon, angry and frustrated, asks himself silently: "How had he [Welch] become Professor of History, even at a place like this? By published work? No. By extra good teaching? No in italics. Then how?" His questions remain unanswered.

In keeping with its antagonism toward academic smugness and pretension, *Lucky Jim* itself is straightforward and unpretentious. Events proceed chronologically through a short period at the end of the academic year when Dixon's contract is up for review. The third-person narration is attached to the point of view of the principal character and allows access to Dixon's thoughts, but not those of other characters. This invites the reader to enjoy and identify with the hilarious conflict between Dixon's inner and outer lives, a conflict which finds expression in the comic faces he adopts at moments of particular stress. The well-paced turns of plot generate suspense without stretching credulity, at least until the very end, when Dixon is extricated from his series of catastrophes by the intervention of a deus ex machina in the person of the wealthy Julius Gore-Urquhart, who likes his disrespectful and pretension-puncturing attitude. This decidedly fictional delivery of an ending happier than Dixon could reasonably expect is, however, cheering for the sympathetic reader and endorses Dixon's real values and virtues.

Jim Dixon represents a new breed of comic antihero, one exasperated beyond endurance by the incompetence and pretension of his alleged superiors. Professor Welch, for example, exploits Dixon's anxiety about the renewal of his contract to force him to act as an unpaid research assistant. He is also coerced into attending one of Welch's arty weekends, where his detestation of the proceedings leads him to disgrace himself to great comic effect. Then, in a memorable climax, he is reluctantly persuaded to deliver a public lecture on "Merrie England." Having had too many drinks, the nervous Dixon delivers the lecture in a manner mimicking both Professor Welch and the college principal, to the delight of his students and at least some of his audience. Emboldened by alcohol, Dixon reveals his real contempt for his superiors and their system. They respond by dismissing him.

The special quality of Amis' antihero is that he is at once unsure and angry, put-upon and resentful, anxious to please but too honest to succeed. Coming from the "wrong" class, he lacks the pseudo-genteel accomplishments ostentatiously paraded by his colleagues. He responds to the manipulative expectations of his boss and his self-appointed girlfriend Margaret, expectations entirely at odds with his own no-nonsense tastes and desires, by failing the tests they set for him with increasingly hilarious results. He is thus an inverse picaro, not a clever rogue but an angry victim who nonetheless exposes the banality, pretension, and rottenness of his world. Yet, while he blunders ineptly from one scene of comic mayhem to another, at the end of the book, when his qualities of honesty and concern for others are finally endorsed, he has his revenge on his enemies and wins both the job for which he is actually suited and the girl he really desires.

The influence of *Lucky Jim* on postwar English fiction has been considerable. His most obvious successors in recent decades are the satirical Malcolm Bradbury, whose best-known campus novel is *The History Man* (1975), and the witty and irreverent David Lodge, whose trilogy of campus novels, *Changing Places* (1975), *Small World* (1984), and *Nice Work* (1988), are as funny as *Lucky Jim* and just as serious in exposing social and academic phoniness and pretension.

ANTHONY J. HASSALL

Further Reading

McDermott, John, *Kingsley Amis: An English Moralist,* New York: St. Martin's Press, and London: Macmillan, 1989

Morrison, Blake, *The Movement: English Poetry and Fiction of the 1950s,* Oxford and New York: Oxford University Press, 1980

Luotuo Xiangzi. *See* Camel Xiangzi

Luxembourgeois Novel. *See* Belgian and Luxembourgeois Novel
